International Handbook of Universities 2019

International Association of Universities (IAU)

International Handbook of Universities 2019

Twenty-Ninth Edition

Volume 5

World
Higher Education
Database

INTERNATIONAL
ASSOCIATION OF
UNIVERSITIES
INTERNATIONAL UNIVERSITIES BUREAU

palgrave
macmillan

International Association of Universities (IAU)
Paris, France

IAU ISBN 978-92-9002-207-7 (hardback)
ISBN 978-3-319-76970-7   ISBN 978-3-319-76971-4 (eBook)
ISBN 978-3-319-76972-1 (print and electronic bundle)
https://doi.org/10.1057/978-3-319-76971-4

Library of Congress Control Number: 2018963227

Edited by the IAU/UNESCO Information Centre on Higher Education,
International Association of Universities (IAU)
IAU Executive Director/Secretary General and Director of Publication: Hilligje van't Land

This Palgrave Macmillan imprint is published by the registered company Springer Nature Switzerland AG.
The registered company address is: Gewerbestrasse 11, 6330 Cham, Switzerland

PREFACE

The International Association of Universities (IAU) and its IAU/UNESCO Information Centre on Higher Education are pleased to present the twenty-ninth edition of the *International Handbook of Universities*, which offers updated, comprehensive information on universities and university-level institutions worldwide.

The *Handbook* was first published by the IAU in 1959 in response to the growing demand for authoritative information about higher education institutions worldwide. It has grown considerably over the years in both the quantity and the quality of its entries. Today, it includes more than 18,400 higher education institutions extracted from the lists provided by the competent authorities or academic bodies in 196 countries and territories, their websites or official documents. The *Handbook* also comprises basic information on the education system of all countries, a list of fields of study and an index of all institutions. Only higher education institutions offering at least a four-year degree or a four-year professional diploma are included in the *Handbook*.

The compilation of the *Handbook* involves working on documents in many languages, covering a wide range of continuously evolving systems of higher education. Every effort has been made to ensure that the entries are as comprehensive as possible and that the information is accurate. The IAU/UNESCO Information Centre on Higher Education is indebted to those many higher education institutions, governmental agencies and academic bodies, which have provided material for this edition in order to make it a unique and authoritative source of information. Where information was not available in time for inclusion, entries have remained the same as in the previous edition. The date of the latest update is indicated at the bottom of each entry.

The full wealth of data held by the IAU/UNESCO Information Centre - including the information in the *Handbook*, as well as more comprehensive data on higher education systems and credentials offered for more than 18,400 institutions - is available at www.whed.net, the IAU World Higher Education Database (WHED) Portal.

The production of the *Handbook* and of the WHED Portal is part of the continued drive by the IAU to provide access to information on higher education institutions, systems, and credentials worldwide. For academic research on higher education, please refer to the IAU's quarterly scholarly *Journal Higher Education Policy*[1].

---

[1] Higher Education Policy, Palgrave Macmillan.

GUIDE TO THE ENTRIES

This edition of the *International Handbook of Universities* comprises entries for more than 18,400 universities and university-level institutions in 196 countries and terrritories.

COUNTRY CHAPTERS

A short presentation of the education system based upon the information provided by the appropriate higher education authorities in the countries concerned or found on their official websites or in documentation that is provided for each country.

It comprises:

- a short description of the overall structure of the higher education system;
- the different stages of study;
- the admission requirements (including for foreign students);
- the quality assurance/recognition system;
- and information on national bodies responsible for higher education.

The designations employed for countries and territories are those in use in the United Nations system and do not imply any expression of opinion with regard to their status or the delimitations of their frontiers.

INSTITUTIONAL ENTRIES

Entries are selected on the basis of the information contained in the listings provided by the appropriate higher education authorities in the countries concerned or found on their official websites. The inclusion or omission of an institution, therefore, does not imply any judgement on the part of the IAU/UNESCO Information Centre on Higher Education as to the status or quality of that institution. To obtain more detailed information, questionnaires are then sent to those degree-granting institutions, which:

- offer at least a four-year degree or a four-year professional diploma,
- have graduated at least three cohorts of students.

Membership of a higher education institution in the IAU is indicated by ⏺ preceding its name. Higher education institutions wishing to become members should contact: membership@iau-aiu.net.

The institutional entries within each country are generally listed within Public and Private Sections, where relevant, with their postal address and website information. The name of each institution is given in English, except for those institutions that wish to retain their native language name only. Where available, the names of the Academic Head are given.

The lists of faculties, colleges, departments, schools, institutes, etc., are intended primarily as a general guide to the academic structure of the institution of which they form a part. They normally include the various fields of study offered (standardized list).This information is followed by a brief description of the history and structure of the institution.

Admission requirements are usually listed for courses leading to a first degree or similar qualification. Special requirements for admission to studies leading to higher degrees and specialized diplomas are indicated where appropriate.

The names of degrees, diplomas and professional qualifications are generally given in the language of the country concerned. Fields of study are indicated where available. Student services and facilities available in each university are also indicated if provided. Staff and student statistics are provided when available.

LIST OF FIELDS OF STUDY

The complete list of fields of study used in the *Handbook* is provided for information.

INDEX OF HIGHER EDUCATION INSTITUTIONS

The index lists higher education institutions in English so the page numbers given in the index will thus refer users to the English language version of institutional names.

Please refer to the list of institution names before the index for the native language name of an institution listed in English.

PRESENTATION OF THE IAU
"The Global Voice of Higher Education"

The International Association of Universities (IAU), founded in 1950, is a worldwide organization with Member Institutions and Organizations in more than 120 countries. It cooperates with a vast network of international, regional and national bodies. Its permanent Secretariat, the International Universities Bureau, is located at UNESCO headquarters, Paris, France, and provides a wide variety of services to Member Institutions and Organizations and to the international higher education community at large. Institutions/organizations interested in becoming members should contact membership@iau-aiu.net.

IAU GLOBAL FORUM AND MEETINGS

The IAU provides a forum for higher education leaders to discuss major current trends and issues in higher education and higher education policy. Heads of all Member Institutions and Organizations or their representatives are invited to the IAU quadrennial General Conference as well as to annual international events. These events are organized by the Association, either alone or in cooperation with other academic bodies, and provide unique opportunities for the exchange of experience and ideas on issues of international interest and importance. The 15th General Conference was held in Bangkok, Thailand in November 2016, and discussed the theme "Higher education: a catalyst for innovative and sustainable societies". The IAU 16th General Conference is due to take place in 2020 in Dublin, Ireland.

REFERENCE PUBLICATIONS

Services offered to Member Institutions and Organizations include the right to receive the Association's publications either on a complimentary basis or at considerably reduced rates. As from 2014, these include the *International Handbook of Universities*, the quarterly research journal *Higher Education Policy*, the biannual magazine *IAU Horizons*, the monthly electronic Newsletter and associated *IAU Lynx*.

The IAU WHED Portal provides detailed information on thousands of higher education institutions worldwide as well as comprehensive data on higher education systems and credentials, and offers a number of search options. The WHED is used to publish the *International Handbook of Universities* and provides the information available in the IAU WHED Portal.

Higher Education Policy is an international peer-reviewed journal for advancing scholarly understanding of the policy process applied to higher education through the publication of original analyses, both theoretical and practice-based, the focus of which may range from case studies of developments in individual institutions to policy making at systems and at national level.

INFORMATION SERVICES

Also available to Member Institutions and Organizations is the vast body of information housed in the specialized IAU/UNESCO Information Centre on Higher Education. The Centre, managed by the IAU, contains over 50,000 volumes on higher education worldwide and operates two major databases: WHED, as described above, and HEDBIB, the Higher Education Bibliographical Database (www.hedbib.iau-aiu.net). The Centre can also provide various information services (eg. topical bibliographies, institutional data). The IAU website (www. iau-aiu.net) is another important source of information and links.

COOPERATION

The IAU, through its unique networking capacity, provides an important clearinghouse function to Members for academic exchange and cooperation, implying active involvement and participation of Member institutions in the important mission of bringing a real international perspective to the life of higher education institutions. Among the major areas retained for cooperation are: Leadership, Sustainable Development, Intercultural Dialogue; Internationalization; Doctoral Programmes in Africa; Ethics and Technology in Higher Education.

HEADQUARTERS

International Association of Universities
1, rue Miollis
75732 Paris Cedex 15, France
Telephone: +33 1-45-68-48-00
Fax: +33 1-47-34-76-05
E-Mail: iau@iau-aiu.net
Website: https://www.iau-aiu.net

PRESIDENT

Pam Fredman, Former Rector, University of Gothenburg, Sweden

SECRETARY-GENERAL

Hilligje van't Land, Secretary General and Executive Director, International Association of Universities, International Bureau of Universities
Andreas Corcoran, Deputy Secretary General, International Association of Universities, International Bureau of Universities

LIST OF PUBLICATIONS

For a worldwide Association, sharing information, expertise and experience amongst leaders and decision-makers on the central issues facing higher education is key. The IAU makes a substantial input to informed debate on public policy. It maintains databases and produces reference works on higher education systems, institutions and credentials and brings out state of the art research on vital issues that concern higher education. By doing so, it serves the academic community and its leadership, stimulating discussion and advancing action.

Major publications resulting from this commitment are:

- *International Handbook of Universities* published by Palgrave Macmillan, Houndmills, Basingstoke, Hampshire RG21 6XS and 175 Fifth Avenue, New York, N.Y. 10010. https://www.palgrave.com
- *Higher Education Policy (HEP), The IAU quarterly scholarly journal,* Editor: Professor Jeroen Huisman, Ghent University, Belgium. Subscription at: Palgrave Macmillan, Houndmills, Basingstoke, Hampshire, RG21 6XS and 175, Fifth Avenue, suite 203, New York, N.Y. 10010. https://www.palgrave.com/gp/journal/41307

Other publications

- *Internationalization of Higher Education, IAU 5th Global Survey,* Paris, IAU, 2019
- *Higher Education Paving the Way to Sustainable Development, Report of the 2016 IAU Global Survey on Higher Education and Research for Sustainable Development*, Paris, IAU, 2017
- *IAU Horizons/AIU Horizons* - A biannual magazine.

Available from: International Association of Universities, UNESCO House, 1, rue Miollis, 75732 Paris Cedex 15, France. Tel: +33-1-45 68 48-00 - Fax: +33-1-47-34 76 05 Contact: iau@iau-aiu.net and on IAU website.

- *IAU Lynx* – A monthly electronic publication available on the IAU website.
- IAU Website: https://www.iau-aiu.net
- IAU WHED Portal: https://www.whed.net

LIST OF REGIONAL/INTERNATIONAL ORGANIZATIONS

Academic Cooperation Association - ACA
President: Ulrich Grothus
Director: Bernd Waechter
Egmontstraat 15
Brussel 1000
Belgium
Tel: +32(2) 513-2241
Fax: +32(2) 513-1776
Website: http://www.aca-secretariat.be

African Academy of Sciences - AAS
Executive Director: Nelson Torto
PO Box 24916
Nairobi 00502
Kenya
Tel: +254(20) 8060674
Fax: +254(20) 8060675
Website: http://aasciences.ac.ke
The overall goals are to strengthen science and technology capacity, to mobilize science and technology resources in the continent and among the African diaspora, to stimulate problem-solving research and development in pivotal areas of the continent's development, and to market the Academy's activities widely for greater impact on African social development and economic growth.

African Council for Distance Education - ACDE
President: Abdel Raouf Ahmed Abbas Elbadawi
Executive Director: Rotimi Ogidan
Egerton University - Nairobi Campus Stanbank House, 9th Floor Moi Avenue / Mama Ngina Street Junction, City Centre Po Box 8023
Nairobi 00100
Kenya
Tel: +254(20) 221 8850
Website: http://acde-afri.org
The African Council for Distance Education (ACDE) is a continental educational organization comprising African universities and other higher education institutions, which are committed to expanding access to quality education and training through open and distance learning.

African Network for the Internationalisation of Education - ANIE
Chair: Tolly Salvator Mbwette
Executive Director: Charles Ochieng' Ong'ondo
c/o Margaret Thatcher Library, Moi University PO Box 3900
Eldoret 30100
Kenya
Tel: +254 721 917 461
Fax: +254(53) 43047
Website: http://www.anienetwork.org

ANIE is an independent, non-profit, non-governmental membership organisation whose aim is to develop research capacity and constitute an expert network in advancing the understanding of internationalisation of higher education to meet the professional needs of individuals, institutions and organisations.

African Network of Scientific and Technological Institutions - ANSTI
Chair: George Albert Magoha
PO Box 30592
Nairobi 00100
Kenya
Tel: +254(20) 7622619
Fax: +254(20) 7622538
Website: http://www.ansti.org
The aim of ANSTI is to develop active collaboration among African scientific institutions so as to promote research and development in areas of relevance to the development of the region.

African Quality Assurance Network - AfriQAN
Accra
Ghana
Website: http://afriqan.aau.org
To provide assistance to institutions concerned with quality assurance in higher education in Africa.

Agence universitaire de la Francophonie - AUF
President: Sorin Mihai Cîmpeanu
Executive Director: Jean-Paul de Gaudemar
Case postale du Musée, C.P. 49714
Montréal H3T 2A5, Québec
Canada
Tel: +1(514) 343-6630
Fax: +1(514) 343-2107
Website: http://www.auf.org

ASEAN University Network - AUN
Acting Chairperson: Nantana Gajaseni
Executive Director: Choltis Dhirathiti
17th Floor, Chamchuri 10 Building Chulalongkorn University, Phayathai Road
Bangkok 10330
Thailand
Tel: +66(2) 215-3640
Fax: +66(2) 216-8808
Website: http://www.aunsec.org

Asia-Pacific Association for International Association - APAIE
President: Sarah Todd
Room 312 Lyceum, Korea University, Anam-Dong, Seongbuk-Gu
Seoul 136-701
South Korea
Tel: +82(2) 3290-2935
Fax: +82(2) 921-0684
Website: https://www.apaie2018.org
Non-profit organization whose aims are to achieve greater cooperation among those responsible for international education and internationalization in Asia-Pacific higher education institutions and promote the quality of international programmes, activities, and exchanges.

Asian Association of Open Universities - AAOU
Secretary General: Grace Javier Alfonso
President: Melinda de la Pena Bandalaria
Office of the Chancellor, University of the Philippines Open University, Los Baños
Laguna
Philippines
Tel: +63(49) 536-6001
Website: http://aaou.upou.edu.ph
Non-profit organization of higher learning institutions that are primarily concerned with education at a distance. AAOU was founded in 1987.

Asociación de Universidades de América Latina y el Caribe para la Integración - AUALCPI
President: Marcos Sidnei Bassi
General Secretary: Laura Phillips Sanchez
Calle 222 55 - 30
Bogotá
Colombia
Tel: +57 (1) 668 4700 Ext. 220
Website: http://www.aualcpi.net

Asociación de Universidades Grupo Montevideo
President: Waldo Albarracín Sánchez
Vice President: Gerónimo Laviosa González González
Executive Secretary: Alvaro Maglia
Guayabos 1729 Ap. 502
Montevideo 11200
Uruguay
Tel: +598 2400 5411
Fax: +598 2400 5401
Website: http://www.grupomontevideo.edu.uy

Asociación de Universidades Privadas de Centro América - AUPRICA (Association of Private Universities of Central America)
Calle Florida
San José 11303
Costa Rica
Website: http://www.auprica.com

Asociación Iberoamericana de Educación Superior a Distancia - AIESAD (Ibero-American Association for Open University Education)
President: Carlos Eduardo Bielschowsky
Permanent Secretary: Rosario Domingo Navas
Secretaria-Permanente, Calle Bravo Murillo, 38-6 planta
Madrid 28015
Spain
Tel: +34(91) 398-7430
Fax: +34(91) 398-7497
Website: http://aiesad.cederj.edu.br
The association works to promote distance higher education, especially among the 13 nations that make up the association. The Association seeks to contribute to the academic life of managers, teachers and students of its member universities, through its various projects and quality assurance in distance education.

Association des Universités africaines - AUA (Association of African Universities)

President: Orlando Quilambo
Secretary-General: Etienne E. Ehile
PO Box 5744
Accra
Ghana
Tel: +233(21) 774 495
Fax: +233(21) 774 821
Website: http://www.aau.org
International non-governmental organization founded in Rabat, Morocco in November 1967 having its headquarters in Accra, Ghana.

Association des Universités de l'Atlantique (Association of Atlantic Universities - AAU)

President: Alaa Abd-El-Aziz
Executive Director: Peter Halpin
Suite 403, 5657 Spring Garden Road
Halifax B3J 3R4, Nova Scotia
Canada
Tel: +1(902) 425-4230
Fax: +1(902) 425-4233
Website: http://atlanticuniversities.ca
A voluntary association of the 16 universities in the Atlantic region and in the West Indies which offer programmes leading to a degree or have degree-granting status.

Association for Tertiary Education Management - ATEM

President: Carl Rallings
Executive Director: Paul Abela
Building M, University of Sydney Cumberland College 75 East Street (PO Box 170)
Lidcombe 2141, NSW
Australia
Tel: +61(2) 9351-9456
Fax: +61(2) 6125-5262
Website: http://www.atem.org.au
A professional body for tertiary education administrators and managers in Australasia.

Association internationale des Universités - AIU (International Association of Universities - IAU)

President: Pam Fredman
Secretary-General: Hilligje van't Land
UNESCO House 1, Rue Miollis
Paris 75732
France
Tel: +33(1) 45.68.48.00
Fax: +33(1) 47.34.76.05
Website: http://www.iau-aiu.net

Association of Arab Universities - AArU

Secretary-General: Amr Ezzat Salama
PO Box 401 Jubeyha
Amman
Jordan

Tel: +962(6) 506-2048
Fax: +962(6) 506-2051
Website: http://www.aaru.edu.jo

Association of Christian Universities and Colleges in Asia - ACUCA

President: Rux Prompalit
General Secretary: Esther Wakeman
Payap University Super-highway Chiang Mai – Lumpang Road Amphur Muang
Chiang Mai 50000
Thailand
Website: http://www.acuca.net

Association of Commonwealth Universities - ACU

Chair: Amit Chakma
Secretary-General: Joanna Newman
Woburn House 20-24 Tavistock Square
London WC1H 9HF
UK
Tel: +44(20) 7380 6700
Fax: +44(20) 7387 2655
Website: http://www.acu.ac.uk

Association of International Educators - NAFSA

President: Elaine Meyer-Lee
Executive Director and CEO: Esther Brimmer
1307 New York Avenue NW, 8th floor
Washington 20005-4701, DC
USA
Tel: +1(202) 737-3699
Fax: +1(202) 737-3657
Website: http://www.nafsa.org

Association of Pacific Rim Universities - APRU

Secretary General: Christopher Tremewan
Director: Sherman Cheng Cheng
International Secretariat, IAS Building, 3F, 3016 HKUST, Clear Water Bay
Kowloon
China - Hong Kong SAR
Tel: +852 3469 2056
Fax: +852 2719 5756
Website: http://apru.org
Established in 1997 with universities across the Americas, Asia and Australasia, to contribute to the development of an increasingly integrated Pacific Rim community, and now consists of some 40 plus member universities.

Association of Southeast Asian Institutions of Higher Learning - ASAIHL

President: Hamid Mirzadeh
Secretary General: Ninnat Olanvoravuth
Chulalongkorn University, 16th Floor, Chaloem Rajakumari 60 Building
Bangkok 10330
Thailand
Tel: +66(2) 251 6966
Website: http://asaihl.stou.ac.th/page/Showdata.aspx?idindex=10000
Assisting member institutions in their development through cooperation.

Association of the Carpathian Region Universities - ACRU

President: Paul-Serban Agachi

Secretary-General: Jana Mojžišová

University of Veterinary Medicine and Pharmacy in Košice, Komenského 73

Košice 041 81

Slovakia

Website: http://acru.uvlf.sk

The Association has 24 higher education member institutions from Slovakia, Poland, Ukraine, Romania, Hungary and Serbia.

Association of Universities of Asia and the Pacific - AUAP

President: Sung-hee Nam

Secretary-General: Ricardo Pama

Academic Building 2, Room C2-227 Suranaree University of Technology, 111 University Avenue Suranaree Sub-district

Nakhon Ratchasima 30000

Thailand

Tel: +66(85) 768 7474

Website: http://www.e-auap.org

Association of West African Universities - AWAU

Chair: Abdulganiyu Ambali

Secretary-General: Abdullahi Yusufu Ribadu

245 Samuel Ademulegun Way, Central Business District, Opp Arewa Suites

Abuja

Nigeria

Website: http://www.awau.org

Provides coordination and networking for universities in West Africa.

Associação das Universidades de Língua Portuguesa - AULP (Association of Portuguese Language Universities - APLU)

President: Orlando Manuel José Fernandes da Mata

Avenida Santos Dumont, 67, 2°

Lisboa 1050-203

Portugal

Tel: +351(217) 816 360

Fax: +351(217) 816 369

Website: http://aulp.org

The aim of this international association is the development of cooperation between universities and higher research institutions by means of promoting the interchange of researchers and students and the development of joint projects of scientific and technological research as well as the exchange of information.

Associação de Universidades Amazonicas - UNAMAZ (Association of Amazonian Universities)

A. Tancredo Neves 2501 Barrio Montese Campos da UFRA

Belém 66077-530, Pará

Brazil

Tel: +55(91) 3210-5230

Website: http://www.ufpa.br/unamaz

Network of higher education institutions from Bolivia, Brazil, Colombia, Ecuador, Guyana, Peru, Suriname, and Venezuela created in 1993 to promote higher education cooperation for the sustainable development of the Amazonian region.

Aurora Network

President: David Richardson
Secretary-General: Kees Kouwenaar
De Boelalaan 1105
Amsterdam 1081 HV
The Netherlands
Tel: +31(6) 5111 9635
Website: https://aurora-network.global
Founded in 2016 as a small network of research-intensive universities in Europe, all sharing a common core vision of matching world-class academic excellence with societal relevance in a local and global context.

Bibliotheca Alexandrina

Director: Mostafa El-Feki
Scientific Advisor: Mohammed El-Faham
PO Box 138 - Chatby
Alexandria 21526
Egypt
Tel: +20(3) 483 99 99
Website: http://www.bibalex.org
Bibliotheca Alexandrina aims to be a centre of excellence in the production and dissemination of knowledge and to be a place of dialogue, learning and understanding between cultures and peoples.

Bureau canadien de l'éducation internationale - BCEI (Canadian Bureau for International Education - CBIE)

Interim President and CEO: Larissa Bezo
Vice-President, International Partnerships: Basel Alashi
1550 - 220 Laurier Avenue West
Ottawa K1P 5Z9, ON
Canada
Tel: +1(613) 237-4820
Fax: +1(613) 237-1160
Website: http://cbie.ca

Camões - Instituto da Cooperação e da Língua, I.P. (Camões Institute for Cooperation and Language)

Avenida da Liberdade, 270
Lisboa 1250-149
Portugal
Tel: +351(213) 109 100
Fax: +351(213) 143 987
Website: http://www.instituto-camoes.pt

Caribbean Area Network for Quality Assurance in Tertiary Education – CANQATE

President: Ronald Brunton
The University of Trinidad and Tobago (UTT), O'Meara Estate
Arima
Trinidad and Tobago
Tel: +868 642-8888
Fax: +868 643-0268
Website: http://www.canqate.org

Centro Interuniversitario de Desarrollo - CINDA (Inter-University Development Centre)
President: Josep A. Planell
Executive Director: María José Lemaitre del Campo
Santa Magdalena 75, Piso 11, Providencia
Santiago
Chile
Tel: +56 2 2234 1128
Fax: +56 2 2234 1117
Website: http://www.cinda.cl

Commonwealth of Learning - COL
President and Chief Executive Officer: Asha S. Kanwar
4710 Kingsway, Suite 2500
Burnaby V5H 4M2, BC
Canada
Tel: +1(604) 775-8200
Fax: +1(604) 775-8210
Website: https://www.col.org

Conseil africain et malgache pour l'Enseignement supérieur - CAMES (African and Malagasy Council for Higher Education)
Secretary-General: Bertrand Mbatchi
01 BP 134
Ouagadougou
Burkina Faso
Tel: +226 2536-8146
Fax: +226 2536-8573
Website: http://www.lecames.org
Regional body aiming at research dissemination in Africa and in the long-term at accreditation provision within the region.

Consejo Superior Universitario Centroamericano - CSUCA (Central-American University Higher Council)
Secretary-General: Juan Alfonso Fuentes Soria
Avenida las Américas, 1-03 Zona 14, Interior Club Los Arcos
Guatemala 01014
Guatemala
Tel: +502 2502-7500
Fax: +502 2502-7501
Website: http://www.csuca.org
Regional organization that promotes the integration and strengthening of higher education in Central America.

Consortium for North American Higher Education Collaboration - CONAHEC
President of the Board: David Longanecker
Executive Director: Sean Manley-Casimir
University of Arizona PO Box 210158
Tucson 85721-0300, Arizona
USA
Tel: +1(520) 621-7761
Fax: +1(520) 626-2675
Website: http://www.conahec.org
To foster academic collaboration among higher education institutions, organizations and agencies in North America and with their peers around the world. Principal activities include:

encouraging student exchange within their member institutions; convening the higher education community; providing online information and networking; conducting comparative research on educational policy issues affecting North America; providing professional development opportunities; preparing future leaders by involving students in regional dialogue; honouring social responsibilities.

🔳⊚ COPERNICUS Alliance - European Network on Higher Education for Sustainable Development

President: Clemens Mader
Vice-President: Jana Dlouhá
Network Coordinator, Secretariat: Laura Macháčková Henderson
Charles University Environment Center, José Martího 2/407
Praha 162 00
Czech Republic
Tel: +420(2) 20 199 482
Fax: +420(2) 20 199 462
Website: http://www.copernicus-alliance.org

Donaurektorenkonferenz (Danube Rectors' Conference)

President: Friedrich Faulhammer
Manager of the DRC Secretariat: Sebastian Schäffer
DRC Secretariat Hahngasse 6/24
Wien 1090
Austria
Tel: +43(1) 319 72 58 - 32
Website: http://www.drc-danube.org
A network of almost 70 universities in the Danube Region aiming to improve higher education in teaching and research in theregion, and in particular the advancement of our member universities, by establishing and facilitating bilateral and multilateral contacts between the universities.

European Access Network - EAN

President: Mary Tupan-Wenno
Executive Secretary: Mee Foong Lee
Lawrence Building, University of Roehampton, Roehampton Lane
London SW15 5PJ
UK
Tel: +44(20) 8392 3857
Fax: +44(20) 8392 3148
Website: http://www.ean-edu.org
The European Access Network encourages wider access to higher education for those who are currently under-represented, whether for reasons of gender, ethnic origin, nationality, age, disability, family background, vocational training, geographic location, or earlier educational disadvantage. The EAN is the only European-wide, non-governmental organisation for widening participation in higher education. It is organised for educational purposes and operates under English Law. Membership is open to all those with an interest in widening access.

European Alliance for Subject-Specific and Professional Accreditation and Quality Assurance - EASPA

President: Iring Wasser
c/o ASIIN PO Box 101139
Düsseldorf 40002
Germany

Tel: +49(211) 900977-0
Fax: +49(211) 900977-99
Website: http://www.easpa.eu

European Association for International Education - EAIE

President: Markus Laitinen
Director: Leonard Engel
PO Box 11189
Amsterdam 1001 GD
The Netherlands
Tel: +31(20) 344 5100
Fax: +31(20) 344 5119
Website: http://www.eaie.org

European Association for Quality Assurance in Higher Education - ENQA

President: Christoph Grolimund
Director: Maria Kelo
Avenue de Tervuren, 38 - bte 4
Brussels 1040
Belgium
Tel: +32(2) 735-5659
Fax: +32(2) 736-9850
Website: http://www.enqa.eu

European Association for University Lifelong Learning - EUCEN

Executive Secretary: Carme Royo
Balmes, 132-134
Barcelona 08008
Spain
Tel: +34(93) 542-1825
Fax: +34(93) 542-2975
Website: http://www.eucen.eu
The aim of the association is too contribute to the economic and cultural life of Europe through the promotion and advancement of lifelong learning within higher education institutions in Europe and elsewhere, and to foster universities' influence in the development of lifelong learning knowledge and policies throughout Europe.

European Association of Distance Teaching Universities - EADTU

President: Anja Oskamp
Managing Director: George Ubachs
Parkweg 27
Maastricht 6212 XN
The Netherlands
Tel: +31(43) 311 8712
Website: http://www.eadtu.eu

European Association of Institutions in Higher Education - EURASHE

President: Stéphane Lauwick
Secretary General: Michal Karpíšek
Ravensteingalerij 27/3
Brussels 1000
Belgium

Tel: +32(2) 211-4197
Fax: +32(2) 211-4199
Website: http://www.eurashe.eu
EURASHE is the association of European Higher Education Institutions – Polytechnics, Colleges, University Colleges, etc. – devoted to Professional Higher Education and related research within the Bachelor-Masters structure.

European Consortium of Innovative Universities - ECIU

President: Victor van der Chijs
Secretary-General: Katrin Dircksen
c/o Katrin Dircksen, University of Twente PO Box 217
Enschede 7500 AE
The Netherlands
Tel: +31(53) 489 2684
Website: http://www.eciu.org
Network of universities with its base in Europe, but building on the experience and insights of institutions in other parts of the world.

European Council of Doctoral Candidates and Junior Researchers - EURODOC

President: Gareth O'Neill
Secretary: Antoine Dujardin
Rue d'Egmont 11
Brussels, 1000
Belgium
Website: http://www.eurodoc.net
International federation of 34 national organizations of PhD candidates, and more generally of young researchers from 33 countries of the European Union and the Council of Europe.

European Physics Education Network

Chair: Hendrik Ferdinande
Universiteit Gent Department of Subatomic and Radiation Physics Proeftuinstraat 86
Gent 9000
Belgium
Website: http://www.eupen.ugent.be

European University Association - EUA

President: Rolf Tarrach
Secretary-General: Lesley Wilson
Avenue de l'Yser, 24
Brussels 1040
Belgium
Tel: +32(2) 230-5544
Fax: +32(2) 230-5751
Website: http://www.eua.be

Federation of the Universities of the Islamic World - FIUW

Secretary-General: Abdulaziz Bin Othman Altwaijri
ISESCO, Avenue de F.A.R., Hay Ryad BP 2275
Rabat 10104
Morocco
Tel: +212(537) 56 60 52
Fax: +212(537) 56 60 12
Website: http://www.isesco.org.ma/fuiw.org/en

Foundation for International Cooperation in Higher Education of Taiwan - FICHET
Chief Executive Officer: Jen-Sue Chen
Room 202, No. 5, Lane 199, Kinghua Street
Taipei City 10650
China - Taiwan
Tel: +886 (2) 2322-2280
Fax: +886 (2) 2322-2528
Website: http://www.fichet.org.tw
FICHET facilitates international cooperation between Taiwanese and foreign universities. Its main operations are the planning of international educator assemblies in Europe, America, and Asia, and fostering human resources in the field of international education administration. FICHET currently represents 114 member universities as an umbrella body for 4 national associations: 1. the Association of National Universities of Taiwan (ANUT); 2. the Association of Private Universities and Colleges of Taiwan (APUC); 3. the Association of National Universities and Colleges of Technology of Taiwan (ANUCT); and 4. the Association of Private Universities and Colleges of Technology of Taiwan (APUCT).

Fédération internationale des Universités catholiques - FIUC (International Federation of Catholic Universities - IFCU)
President: Fr Pedro Rubens Ferreira Oliveira
Secretary-General: Pr François Mabille
21 rue d'Assas
Paris 75270
France
Tel: +33(1) 44.39.52.26
Fax: +33(1) 44.39.52.28
Website: http://fiuc.org/en
Created by a Decree of the Holy See in 1948, it was recognized by Pope Pius XII in 1949 and became the International Federation of Catholic Universities (IFCU) in 1965.

Global University Network for Innovation - GUNI
President: Jaume Casals
Director: Josep M. Vilalta
Carrer de la Vila, building F, main floor UAB Campus Bellaterra (Cerdanyola del Vallès)
Barcelona 08193
Spain
Tel: +34(93) 481-7099
Website: http://www.guninetwork.org

Graduate Women International - GWI
President: Geeta Desai
Executive Director: Stacy Dry Lara
Chemin du Grand-Montfleury, 48 Versoix
Geneva 1290
Switzerland
Tel: +41(22) 731 2380
Website: http://www.graduatewomen.org
GWI advocates for women's rights, equality and empowerment through access to quality secondary and tertiary education, and training up to the highest levels. Their vision is 100% of girls and women in the world achieving education beyond primary school. Was known as International Federation of University Women (IFUW) until 2015.

Groupement International des Secrétaires Généraux des Universités Francophones - GISGUF (International Group of Secretary-Generals of Francophone Universities)
President: Stéphane Berthet
Maison des Universités 103 Boulevard Saint Michel
Paris 75006
France
Website: http://www.gisguf.org

Grupo Compostela de Universidades (Compostela Group of Universities)
President: Marek Kreglewski
Executive Secretary: Teresa Carballeira
Casa da Cuncha - rúa da Conga, no. 1
Santiago de Compostela 15782
Spain
Tel: +34(981) 812-931
Fax: +34(981) 812-932
Website: http://www.gcompostela.org
The Compostela Group of Universities is a non-profit association aimed at fostering cooperation and promoting dialogue in all fields related to higher education.

⬛ Institute of International Education - IIE
President and CEO: Allan E. Goodman
Senior Counselor to the President: Peggy Blumenthal
809 United Nations Plaza
New York 10017-3580, NY
USA
Tel: +1(212) 883-8200
Fax: +1(212) 984-5452
Website: http://www.iie.org

Inter-University Council for East Africa - IUCEA
Executive Secretary: Alexandre Lyambabje
Plot 4 Nile Avenue 3rd Floor, EADB Building PO Box 7110
Kampala
Uganda
Tel: +256(41) 425-6251
Fax: +256(41) 434-2007
Website: http://www.iucea.org
The mission of the IUCEA is to encourage and develop mutually beneficial collaboration between its member universities, and between them and governments and other organizations, both public and private. It aims at helping its members to contribute to meeting national and regional development needs, to the resolution of problems in every appropriate sector of activity in the region, and to the development of human resource capacity particularly in the disciplines of Science, Technology and Business Studies.

International Association of University Presidents - IAUP
President: Kakha Shengelia
Secretary-General: Gerald Reisinger
809 United Nations Plaza
New York 10017-3580, NY
USA
Website: http://www.iaup.org

An NGO and association of university chief executives from higher education institutions around the world. Membership is limited to those individuals who serve as Presidents, Rectors or Vice-Chancellors at regionally accredited colleges or universities. Its mission is: to increase the exchange of experiences, levels of collaboration and networking between university leaders; to provide a well informed forum for university leaders throughout the world; to contribute to a worldwide vision of higher education; to strengthen the international mission of institutions throughout the world; to make every effort for the voice of educational leaders to be heard; to support sustainable development in a context of global competency; to promote peace and international understanding through education.

International Council for Open and Distance Education - ICDE

President: Belinda Tynan
Acting Secretary-General: Morten Flate Paulsen
Drammensveien 211
Oslo 0281
Norway
Tel: +47 2206 2632
Website: https://www.icde.org
Global membership organization for open, distance, flexible and online education, including e-learning, that draws its membership from institutions, educational authorities, commercial actors, and individuals. ICDE was founded in 1938 in Canada as the International Council for Correspondence Education

International Education Association - ISANA

President: Bronwyn Gilson
228 Liverpool Street
Hobart 7000, TAS
Australia
Tel: +61(3) 6231-0253
Fax: +61(3) 6231-1522
Website: http://www.isana.org.au
ISANA, a body for international education professionals in Australia and New Zealand, works in student services, advocacy, teaching, and policy development in Australia and New Zealand.

International Education Association of South Africa - IEASA

President: Leolyn Jackson
PO Box 27394, Sunnyside
Pretoria 0132
South Africa
Tel: +27(12) 481 2908
Fax: +27(0)86 649 1247
Website: http://www.ieasa.studysa.org
Non-profit organization created to respond to international educational trends.

International Network for Quality Assurance Agencies in Higher Education - INQAAHE

President: Susanna Karakhanyan
The Catalan University Quality Assurance Agency, AQU Catalunya C. dels Vergós, 36-42
Barcelona 08017
Spain
Tel: +34(93) 268-8950
Website: http://www.inqaahe.org
The International Network for Quality Assurance Agencies in Higher Education (INQAAHE) is a world-wide association of over 200 organisations active in the theory and practice of quality assurance in higher education.

International Student Identity Card Association - ISIC
Secretary-General: Todd Almeida
Keizersgracht 174
Amsterdam 1016 DW
The Netherlands
Tel: +31(20) 520 08 40
Website: http://www.isicnederland.nl

Islamic Educational, Scientific and Cultural Organization - ISESCO
Director General: Abdulaziz Bin Othman Altwaijri
Avenue des F.A.R, Hay Ryad PO Box 2275
Rabat 10104
Morocco
Tel: +212(537) 56 60 52
Fax: +212(537) 56 60 12
Website: http://www.isesco.org.ma

League of European Research Universities - LERU
Chair: Bert van der Zwaan
Secretary-General: Kurt Deketelaere
Minderbroedersstraat 8
Leuven 3000
Belgium
Tel: +32(16) 32-99-71
Website: http://www.leru.org
An association of 21 leading research-intensive universities that share the values of high-quality teaching within an environment of internationally competitive research. LERU advocates for: education through an awareness of the frontiers of human understanding; the creation of new knowledge through basic research, which is the ultimate source of innovation in society; and the promotion of research across a broad front in partnership with industry and society at large.

Magna Charta Observatory
President: Sijbolt Noorda
Secretary-General: David Lock
Via Zamboni, 25
Bologna 40126
Italy
Tel: +39.051 2098709
Fax: +39.051 2098710
Website: http://www.magna-charta.org
The Magna Charta Observatory aims to gather information, express opinions and prepare documents relating to the respect for, and protection of, the fundamental university values and rights laid down in the Magna Charta Universitatum signed in Bologna in 1988 by 388 Rectors of worldwide main universities.

Network of Universities from the Capitals of Europe - UNICA
President: Luciano Saso
Secretary-General: Kris Dejonckheere
C/o University Foundation rue d'Egmont n°11
Brussels 1000
Belgium

Tel: +32(2) 514-7800
Fax: +32(2) 514-7900
Website: http://www.unica-network.eu
UNICA is a network of 40 universities from the capital cities of Europe. Its role is to promote academic excellence, integration and co-operation between member universities throughout Europe.

Observatory on Borderless Higher Education - OBHE
Chair: Drummond Bone
Director: Richard Garrett
Redhill Chambers, 2d High Street
Redhill RH1 1RJ, Surrey
UK
Tel: +44(20) 7222 7890
Fax: +44(20) 7182 7152
Website: http://www.obhe.ac.uk
A higher education think tank with institutional members across 30 countries. They offer analysis on trends, business models and policy frameworks, with the aim of providing strategic intelligence for education leaders and policymakers attempting to navigate the opportunities and threats of borderless higher education.

Organisation universitaire interaméricaine - OUI (Inter-American Organisation for Higher Education - IOHE)
President: Óscar Garrido
Executive Director: David Julien
Université de Montréal, 3744, Jean-Brillant, bureau 592
Montreal H3T 1P1, Québec
Canada
Tel: +1(514) 343-6980
Website: http://www.oui-iohe.org

Red de Macrouniversidades de América Latina y del Caribe (Network of of Macro-universities of Latin America and the Caribbean)
President: Marco Antonio Zago
Regional Coordinator: Alfonso Ayala Rico
Secretary-General: Alberto Barbieri
Universidad Nacional Autónoma de México. Edificio CIPPS-Planta Baja, Unidad Internacional de Sedes Universitarias. Circuito Cultural, sin número (Frente a UNIVERSUM), Ciudad Universitaria, Coyoacán
México 04510
México
Tel: +52 (55) 56-22-66-66
Website: http://www.redmacro.unam.mx

Réseau africain francophone de la Formation supérieure et de l'Enseignement technique - RAFSET (Francophone African Network for Higher Training and Technical Education)
President: Bassabi Kagbara
Route de Kpalimé, à côté de la Poste BP 8619
Lomé
Togo
Tel: +228 22 51 65 81
Fax: +228 22 51 44 21

Contributes to the creation of an African area for the promotion of education by training, institutional capacity building and improving management quality in administrations and enterprises.

Santander Group - European Universities' Network
President: Adam Mickiewicz
Executive Secretary: Wioletta Wegorowska
Square de Meeûs 35
Brussels 1000
Belgium
Tel: +32(2) 511-6620
Fax: +32(2) 502-9611
Website: http://www.sgroup.be
The SGroup European Universities' Network aims to strengthen the institutional capacities of its member universities to reinforce their international visibility, to expand their collaboration opportunities in education and research and to improve the quality of their governance, teaching, research and administrative practices. It seeks to achieve this through the transfer of knowledge, the development of strategic alliances and the improvement of intercultural understanding.

SEAMEO Regional Centre for Higher Education and Development - RIHED
Director: Chantavit Sujatanond
5th Floor, Commission on Higher Education Building, 328 Sri Ayuthaya Road, Rajthewee
Bangkok 10400
Thailand
Tel: +66(2) 644-9856
Fax: +66(2) 644-5421
Website: http://www.rihed.seameo.org

Southern African Regional Universities Association - SARUA
Executive Director: M. J. Oosthuizen
Ground Floor, Chardonnay House, Vineyards Office Estate 99 Jip de Jager Drive
Bellville 7530
South Africa
Tel: +27(21) 0351990
Website: http://www.sarua.org
SARUA is an association for the public universities in the SADC region. SARUA aims to promote, strengthen and increase higher education, training and research through expanded inter-institutional collaboration and capacity building initiatives across the region and promote universities as major contributors towards national and regional socio-economic development.

UNESCO - Instituto Internacional para la Educación Superior en América Latina y el Caribe - IESALC (UNESCO Institute for Higher Education in Latin America and the Caribbean)
Director: Pedro Henríquez Guajardo
Head, University Networks: Débora Ramos
Edificio Asovincar 1052-A Av, Los Chorros c/c Calle Acueducto, Altos de Sebucán Apartado Postal 68.39
Caracas
Venezuela
Tel: +58 (212) 286 0555
Fax: +58 (212) 286 0527
Website: http://www.iesalc.unesco.org.ve

Universitas 21
Chair: David Eastwood
Provost: Bairbre Redmond
Strathcona 109 c/o University of Birmingham Edgbaston
Birmingham B15 2TT
UK
Tel: +44(121) 415 8870
Fax: +44(121) 415 8873
Website: http://www.universitas21.com
A global network of research-intensive universities, working together to foster global citizenship and institutional innovation through research-inspired teaching and learning, student mobility, connecting our students and staff, and wider advocacy for internationalisation.

University Network of the European Capitals of Culture - UNeECC
President: Flora Carrijn
Lucian Blaga University of Sibiu 10 Victoriei Bvd
Sibiu 550024
Romania
Website: http://www.uneecc.org
The aim of UNeECC is to to ensure the recognition of the role and contribution of universities to the success of the cities conferred the title "European Capital of Culture"; to provide the member universities with the possibility of continuous and full participation in the European Capitals of Culture movement enhanced by "Universities of the Year"; and to foster inter-university cooperation to develop and reshape the universities' regional position to create new activities for city and university collaboration.

Unión de Universidades de América Latina - UDUAL (Association of Universities of Latin America and the Caribbean)
President: Henning Jensen
Secretary-General: Roberto Ivan Escalante Semerena
Apartado postal 70232 Cuidad Universitaria
México 04510, D.F.
México
Tel: +52(55) 5616-2383
Fax: +52(55) 5622-0092
Website: http://www.udual.org

Universities Caribbean – UC
President: Hilary Beckles
Secretary-General: Myriam Moïse
The University of the West Indies
Regional Headquarters - Mona
Kingston 7
Jamaica
Tel: +1(876) 927-2406
Fax: +1(876) 927-0253
Created as Association of Caribbean Universities and Research Institutes (UNICA) in 1967, and became Universities Caribbean in 2018 to foster cooperation among higher education institutions and centres in the Caribbean region. Universities Caribbean aims to become the region's voice in areas of quality, globalization, resilience, and financial sustainability. The general mandate given to Universities Caribbean is to integrate the regional university sector and enhance its quality and regional impact.

Vives University Network (Xarxa Vives d'Universitats)
President: Josep Maria Garrell i Guiu
1st Vice President: Francesc Xavier Grau i Vidal
Edifici Àgora Universitat Jaume I Campus del Riu Sec
Castelló de la Plana 12006
Spain
Tel: +34(964) 72 89 93
Website: http://www.vives.org
A non-profit institution that represents and coordinates joint action in higher education, research and culture of a number of universities from 4 different European countries. Since 1994 it has offered a platform leader in services for universities, public and private organizations and society. Its main objective is contributing to the construction process of this cross-border interuniversity region in Mediterranean Europe and its social and economic development.

WC2 University Network
International Development
City University London
Northampton Square
London EC1V 0HB
UK
Tel: +44(20) 7040 0072
Website: http://www.wc2network.org
The WC2 University Network has been developed with the goal of bringing together top universities located in the heart of major world cities in order to address cultural, environmental and political issues of common interest to world cities and their universities.

LIST OF FIELDS OF STUDY

AGRICULTURE
Agricultural Business
Agricultural Economics
Agricultural Equipment
Agricultural Management
    Farm Management
Agronomy
Animal Husbandry
   Apiculture
   Cattle Breeding
   Sericulture
Crop Production
   Harvest Technology
Fishery
   Aquaculture
Food Science
   Brewing
   Dairy
   Meat and Poultry
   Oenology
Forestry
   Forest Biology
   Forest Economics
   Forest Management
   Forest Products
Horticulture
   Floriculture
   Fruit Production
   Vegetable Production
   Viticulture
Soil Science
   Soil Conservation
   Soil Management
Tropical Agriculture
Veterinary Science
Water Science
   Irrigation
   Water Management

ARCHITECTURE AND PLANNING
Architecture
   Architectural and Environmental Design
   Architectural
   Restoration

    Landscape Architecture
    Structural Architecture
Regional Planning
Rural Planning
Town Planning

ARTS AND HUMANITIES
Archaeology
Classical Languages
    Ancient Languages
    Greek (Classical)
    Latin
    Sanskrit
Comparative Literature
History
    Ancient Civilizations
    Contemporary History
    Medieval Studies
    Modern History
    Prehistory
Linguistics
    Applied Linguistics
    Grammar
    Philology
    Phonetics
    Psycholinguistics
    Speech Studies
    Terminology
Literature
Modern languages
    Native Language
    African Languages
    Afrikaans
    Albanian
    Amerindian Languages
    Arabic
    Armenian
    Austronesian and Oceanic Languages
    Baltic Languages
    Bulgarian
    Catalan
    Celtic Languages and Studies
    Chinese
    Czech
    Danish
    Dutch
    English
    Eurasian and North Asian Languages
    European Languages
    Finnish
    French

German
Germanic Languages
Greek
Hebrew
Hindi
Hungarian
Icelandic
Indic Languages
Indonesian
Irish
Italian
Japanese
Korean
Kurdish
Malay
Mongolian
Norwegian
Oriental Languages
Persian
Pilipino
Polish
Portuguese
Romance Languages
Romanian
Russian
Scandinavian Languages
Serbocroatian
Slavic Languages
South and Southeast Asian Languages
Spanish
Swahili
Swedish
Thai Languages
Tibetan
Turkish
Urdu
Vietnamese
Philosophy
Ethics
Logic
Metaphysics
Philosophical Schools
Translation & Interpretation
Writing

BUSINESS ADMINISTRATION

Accountancy
Administration
Institutional Administration
Private Administration
Public Administration

Business and Commerce
    Business Computing
    E-Business
    International Business
    Small Business
Finance
    Banking
    Taxation
Human Resources
Insurance
Labour and Industrial Relations
Management
    Industrial Management
    Leadership
    Management Systems
Marketing
    Advertising & Publicity
    Public Relations
Real Estate
Secretarial Studies

EDUCATION
Educational Sciences
    Curriculum
    Distance Education
    Educational Administration
    Educational and Student Counselling
    Educational Research
    Educational Technology
    Educational Testing and
    Evaluation
    Higher Education
    International and Comparative Education
    Pedagogy
    Philosophy of Education
    Staff Development
Special Education
    Bilingual and Bicultural Education
    Education of the Gifted
    Education of the Handicapped
    Education of the Socially Disadvantaged
    Foreigners Education
    Natives Education
Teacher Training
    Adult Education
    Agricultural Education
    Art Education
    Business Education
    Civics
    Computer Education
    Continuing Education
    Foreign Languages Education
    Health Education

Higher Education
Teacher Training
Home Economics Education
Humanities and Social Science
    Education
Industrial Arts Education
Literacy Education
Mathematics Education
Music Education
Native Language Education
Physical Education
Preschool Education
Primary Education
Science Education
Secondary Education
Teacher Trainers Education
Technology Education
Vocational Education

ENGINEERING
Aeronautical and Aerospace Engineering
Agricultural Engineering
Automation and Control Engineering
    Robotics
Bioengineering
Biomedical Engineering
Chemical Engineering
Civil Engineering
    Bridge Engineering
    Construction Engineering
    Geological Engineering
    Road Engineering
    Transport Engineering
Computer Engineering
    Computer Graphics
    Computer Networks
    Data Processing
    Software Engineering
Electrical and Electronic Engineering
    Electrical Engineering
    Electronic Engineering
    Laser Engineering
    Microelectronics
    Microwaves
    Power Engineering
    Telecommunications Engineering
Energy Engineering
    Thermal Engineering
Engineering Drawing and Design
Engineering Management
Environmental Engineering
    Sanitary Engineering
Industrial Engineering

Marine Engineering
   Naval Architecture
Materials Engineering
   Ceramics and Glass Technology
   Explosive Engineering
   Polymer and Plastics Technology
   Rubber Technology
Measurement and Precision Engineering
Mechanical Engineering
   Automotive Engineering
   Hydraulic Engineering
   Machine Building
   Railway Engineering
   Sound Engineering (Acoustics)
Metallurgical Engineering
Mining Engineering
Nuclear Engineering
Petroleum and Gas Engineering
Physical Engineering
Production Engineering
Safety Engineering
Surveying and Mapping

FINE ARTS
Art Criticism
Art History
   Aesthetics
Art Management Design
   Display and Stage Design
   Fashion Design
   Furniture Design
   Graphic Design
   Industrial Design
   Interior Design
   Textile Design
Handicrafts
   Ceramic Art
   Engraving
   Glass Art
   Jewelry Art
   Weaving
Religious Art
Visual Arts
   Painting and Drawing
   Photography
   Sculpture

HEALTH SCIENCES
Alternative Medicine
   Acupuncture
   Ayurveda
   Chiropractic
   Homeopathy

Osteopathy
Paramedical Sciences
Traditional Eastern Medicine
Biomedicine
Dentistry
Dental Hygiene
Dental Technology
Oral Pathology
Orthodontics
Periodontics
Stomatology
Forensic Medicine and Dentistry
Health Administration
Medicine
Anaesthesiology
Cardiology
Dermatology
Diabetology
Endocrinology
Epidemiology
Gastroenterology
Gerontology
Gynecology and Obstetrics
Haematology
Hepathology
Medical Parasitology
Nephrology
Neurology
Oncology
Ophthalmology
Orthopedics
Otorhinolaryngology
Paediatrics
Pathology
Plastic Surgery
Pneumology
Podiatry
Psychiatry and Mental Health
Rheumatology
Tropical Medicine
Urology
Venereology
Virology
Medical Auxiliaries
Medical Technology
Midwifery
Nursing
Optometry
Pharmacy
Public Health
Community Health
Dietetics
Hygiene

    Occupational Health
    Social and Preventive Medicine
    Sports Medicine
  Rehabilitation Medicine and Therapy
    Art Therapy
    Ergotherapy
    Neurological Therapy
    Occupational Therapy
    Physical Therapy
    Psychotherapy
    Respiratory Therapy
    Speech Therapy and Audiology
  Surgery
  Treatment Techniques
    Radiology

HOME ECONOMICS

Child Care & Development
Clothing and Sewing
Consumer Studies
House Arts & Environment
Household Management
Nutrition

INFORMATION SCIENCES

Information Management
Information Technology
Library Science
  Ancient Books
  Archiving
  Documentation Techniques
Mass Communication
  Communication Arts
  Journalism
  Media Studies
  Multimedia
  Radio and Television Broadcasting
Museum Studies
  Museum Management
  Restoration of Works of Art

LAW

Air and Space Law
Canon Law
Comparative Law
Criminal Law
European Community Law
History of Law
Human Rights
International Law
Islamic Law
Justice Administration
Labour Law

Maritime Law
Notary Studies
Private Law
    Civil Law
    Commercial Law
Public Law
    Administrative Law
    Constitutional Law
    Fiscal Law

MATHEMATICS AND COMPUTER SCIENCE

Actuarial Science
Computer Science
    Artificial Intelligence
    Systems Analysis
Mathematics
    Applied Mathematics
    Operations Research
Statistics

NATURAL SCIENCES

Astronomy and Space Science
Biological and Life Sciences
    Agrobiology
    Anatomy
    Biochemistry
    Biology
    Biophysics
    Biotechnology
    Botany
    Cell Biology
    Embryology and Reproduction
        Biology
    Entomology
    Genetics
    Histology
    Immunology
    Limnology
    Marine Biology
    Microbiology
    Molecular Biology
    Neurosciences
    Parasitology
    Pharmacology
    Physiology
    Plant Pathology
    Toxicology
    Zoology
Chemistry
    Analytical Chemistry
    Applied Chemistry
    Industrial Chemistry
    Inorganic Chemistry

Organic Chemistry
Physical Chemistry
Earth Sciences
Crystallography
Geochemistry
Geography
Geology
Geophysics
Mineralogy
Paleontology
Petrology
Seismology
Marine Science & Oceanography
Coastal Studies
Meteorology
Arctic Studies
Arid Land Studies
Physics
Applied Physics
Astrophysics
Atomic and Molecular Physics
Mathematical Physics
Mechanics
Nuclear Physics
Optics
Radiophysics
Solid State Physics
Thermal Physics

PERFORMING ARTS
Cinema and Television
Film
Video
Dance
Music
Conducting
Jazz and Popular Music
Music Theory and Composition
Musical Instruments
Musicology
Opera
Religious Music
Singing
Theatre
Acting

RELIGION
Comparative Religion
Esoteric Practices
Yoga
History of Religion
Holy Writings
Bible

Koran
New Testament
Missionary Studies
Pastoral Studies
Religious Education
Religious Practice
Religious Studies
   Agnosticism & Atheism
   Ancient Religions
   Asian Religious Studies
   Christian Religious Studies
   Judaic Religious Studies
   Primitive Religions
Theology
   Catholic Theology
   Islamic Theology
   Orthodox Theology
   Protestant Theology

SERVICE TRADES
Cooking and Catering
Cosmetology
Hotel and Restaurant
   Hotel Management
Retailing & Wholesaling
   Sales Techniques
   Store Management
Tourism

SOCIAL SCIENCES
Anthropology
   Ethnology
   Folklore
Behavioural Sciences
Cognitive Sciences
Communication Studies
   Communication Disorders
Cultural Studies
   African American Studies
   African Studies
   American Studies
   Asian Studies
   Canadian Studies
   Caribbean Studies
   Central European Studies
   East Asian Studies
   Eastern European Studies
   English Studies
   European Studies
   French Studies
   Germanic Studies
   Hispanic American Studies
   Indigenous Studies

    Islamic Studies
    Jewish Studies
    Latin American Studies
    Mediterranean Studies
    Middle Eastern Studies
    Native American Studies
    Nordic Studies
    North African Studies
    Oriental Studies
    Pacific Area Studies
    South Asian Studies
    Southeast Asian Studies
    Subsahara African Studies
    Western European Studies
Demography and Population
Development Studies
Economics
    Econometrics
    Economic and Finance Policy
    Economic History
    Industrial and Production Economics
    International Economics
Gender Studies
    Men Studies
    Women's Studies
Geography (Human)
    Island Studies
    Mountain Studies
Heritage Preservation
International Studies
    International Relations
Political Science
    Comparative Politics
    Government
Psychology
    Clinical Psychology
    Developmental Psychology
    Educational Psychology
    Experimental Psychology
    Industrial and Organizational Psychology
    Psychoanalysis
    Psychometrics
    Social Psychology
Regional Studies
Rural Studies
Sociology
    Comparative Sociology
    Family Studies
    Futurology
    History of Societies
    Social Policy

Social Problems
Social Studies
Urban Studies

TECHNOLOGY
Building Technology
Crafts and Trades
Food Technology
Graphic Arts
    Printing and Printmaking
    Publishing and Book Trade
Heating and Refrigeration
Instrument Making
Laboratory Techniques
Leather Techniques
Maintenance Technology
    Electrical and Electronic Equipment & Maintenance
    Industrial Maintenance
    Mechanical equipment and Maintenance
Metal Techniques
Optical Technology
Paper Technology
    Packaging Technology
Textile Technology
Wood Technology

TRANSPORT AND COMMUNICATIONS
Air Transport
Marine Transport
    Nautical Science
Postal Services
Railway Transport
Road Transport
Telecommunications Services
Transport Economics
Transport Management

WELFARE AND PROTECTIVE SERVICES
Environmental Studies
    Ecology
    Environmental Management
    Natural Resources
    Pest Management
    Plant and Crop Protection
    Waste Management
    Wildlife
Leisure Studies
Parks and Recreation
Peace and Disarmament
Protective Services
    Civil Security

CONTENTS

Volume 10

OFFICERS OF THE INTERNATIONAL ASSOCIATION OF UNIVERSITIES

Administrative Board 2016-2020

IAU PRESIDENT

Pam FREDMAN, Former Rector, University of Gothenburg, Gothenburg, Sweden

IMMEDIATE PAST PRESIDENT

Dzulkifli ABDUL RAZAK, Rector, International Islamic University, Kuala Lumpur, Malaysia

FULL BOARD MEMBERS

AFRICA

Abdul Ganiyu AMBALI, Former Vice-Chancellor, (IAU Vice-President), University of Ilorin, Ilorin, Nigeria

Ebenezer Oduro OWUSU, Vice-Chancellor, University of Ghana, Accra, Ghana

Paul ZELEZA, Vice-Chancellor, United States International University-Africa, Nairobi, Kenya

AMERICAS

Marta LOSADA FALK, Former President, Antonio Nariño University, Bogotá, Colombia

Mirta MARTIN, President, Fairmont State University, Fairmont, USA

Pierre-André PIERRE, Former Rector, University Notre Dame d'Haiti, Port-au-Prince, Haiti

ASIA & PACIFIC

Salim DACCACHE S.J., Rector, University of St Joseph Beirut, Beirut, Lebanon

Etsuko KATSU, Former Vice-President International, Meiji University, Tokyo, Japan

Carmen LAMAGNA, Vice-Chancellor, American International University, Dhaka, Bangladesh

Pornchai MONGKHONVANIT, President, (IAU Vice-President), Siam University, Bangkok, Thailand

Mahmoud NILI AHMADABDI, President, University of Tehran, Tehran, Iran

Ranbir SINGH, Vice-Chancellor, National Law University, Delhi, India

EUROPE

Andrew DEEKS, President, University College Dublin, Dublin, Ireland

Maria de Fátima MARINHO, Former Vice-Rector for Cooperation and Culture, University of Porto, Porto, Portugal

Remus PRICOPIE, Rector, (IAU Vice-President), National University of Political and Administrative Studies, Buchaust, Romania

Daniel Hernandez RUIPEREZ, Former Rector, University of Salamanca, Salamanca, Spain

Godehard RUPPERT, President, Otto-Friedrich-Universität Bamberg, Bamberg, Germany

Inga ŽALÈNIENÈ, Rector, Mykolas Romeris University, Vilnius, Lithuania

ORGANIZATIONS

Zoltan DUBÉCZI, Secretary-General, Hungarian Rectors Conference, Debrecen, Hungary

Roberto Escalante SEMERENA, (IAU Vice-President), Secretary-General, Unión de Universidades de América Latina y el Caribe (UDUAL), Mexico City, Mexico

SECRETARY GENERAL

Hilligje VAN'T LAND, Executive Director, International Universities Bureau, Paris, France

Andreas CORCORAN, Deputy Secretary General, International Association of Universities, International Bureau of Universities, Paris, France

DEPUTY MEMBERS

ASIA & PACIFIC

Mosleh DUHOKY, President, University of Duhok, Duhok, Iraq

Mohammad Reza POURMOHAMMADI, Former Chancellor, The University of Tabriz, Tabriz, Iran

EUROPE

Constantinos CHRISTOFIDES, Former Rector, University of Cyprus, Nicosia, Cyprus

Henrik DAM, Rector, University of Southern Denmark, Odense, Denmark

Oleg SMESHKO, Rector, Saint-Petersburg University of Management Technologies and Economics, Saint Petersburg, Russian Federation

ORGANIZATIONS

Amr Ezzat SALAMA, Secretary-General, Association of Arab Universities, Amman, Jordan

HONORARY PRESIDENTS

Guillermo SOBERON, President 1980-1985, Former Rector, National Autonomous University of Mexico, Mexico City, Mexico

Blagovest SENDOV, Acting President 1984, Former Rector, University of Sofia, Sofia, Bulgaria

Justin THORENS, President 1985-1990, Former Rector, University of Geneva, Geneva, Switzerland

Hans VAN GINKEL, President 2000-2004, Former Rector, Utrecht University, Tokyo, Netherlands; **Former Rector**, United Nations University, Tokyo, Japan

Goolam MOHAMEDBHAI, President 2004-2008, Former Secretary-General, Association of African Universities, Accra, Ghana

Juan Ramón DE LA FUENTE, President 2008-2012, Former Rector, National Autonomous University of Mexico, Mexico City, Mexico

Japan

STRUCTURE OF HIGHER EDUCATION SYSTEM

Description

Higher education is provided by universities, junior colleges, colleges of technology, as well as specialized schools. These institutions may be national, public or private. The Ministry of Education, Culture, Sports, Science and Technology (MEXT) must approve the foundation of higher education institutions. Universities include one or more faculties offering 4-year courses in a variety of subjects. Junior colleges and colleges of technology do not grant university-level qualifications, but students holding the title of Associate may pursue their studies at universities.

Stages of studies

University level first stage

The first stage of higher education consists of a 4-year course (six years in Medicine, Veterinary Medicine, Dentistry and Pharmaceutics). A credit system is used, with the minimum requirement for graduation set at 124 credits. The degree awarded at the end of the first stage is the Bachelor's degree (Gakushi).

University level second stage

The second stage of higher education takes place in graduate schools (daigaku-in), which do not exist in every university, and leads after two years to a postgraduate diploma or Master's degree (Shushi). It requires a number of additional credits, a research thesis and a final examination. Postgraduate studies in the field of medical sciences lead directly to a Doctor's degree.

University level third stage

The third stage of higher education leads to the the Doctor's degree (Hakase). Studies last for three or five years following upon the Master's degree (four years in Medicine, Dentistry and Pharmaceutical studies but following upon the Bachelor's degree). PhD candidates must submit a thesis and undergo a final examination. The Katei-Hakase (Doctorate by course work) is conferred on those who graduate from a graduate school programme and the Ronbun-Hakase (Doctorate by dissertation) is conferred on those who successfully submit a dissertation.

ADMISSION TO HIGHER EDUCATION

Admission to university-level studies

Name of Secondary school credential required: Kotogakko Sotsugyo Shomeisho
For entry to: Universities and junior colleges
Admission requirements: Students must take the nation-wide entrance examination ("National Centre Test") administered by the National Centre for University Entrance Examinations. At the undergraduate level, an entrance examination is required at all universities. Examinations usually consist of a written test and an interview.

Foreign students admission

Admission requirements: Admission into Japanese higher educational institutions requires 12 years of elementary and secondary education to be completed. Foreign students must pass the Examination for Japanese University (EJU). EJU is an exam to test international students planning to study in Japan on their Japanese proficiency and basic academic abilities.
Entry regulations: A visa must be acquired in order to study in Japan. The foreign student should file an application for a visa directly to an overseas Japanese embassy or consulate or an employee of the educational institution in which the foreign student is scheduled to enroll makes an application to the relevant immigration office for a Certificate of Eligibility for Residence Status on the foreign student's behalf. Once the Certificate of Eligibility is granted, the foreign student wishing to enter Japan takes his/her Certificate of Eligibility to an overseas Japanese embassy or consulate and files an application for a visa.
Language Proficiency: Foreign students' Japanese language ability is expected to be at a N1 or a N2 of the Japanese Language Proficiency Test. Preparatory Japanese language courses are set up in private universities and junior colleges.

© International Association of Universities 2019
International Handbook of Universities 2019,
https://doi.org/10.1057/978-3-319-76971-4_97

RECOGNITION OF STUDIES

Quality assurance system

The approval by the Minister of Education, Culture, Sports, Science and Technology is required in order to establish universities. Self evaluation is mandatory and checked by certified quality assurance and accreditation associations.

Bodies dealing with recognition

Japan Institution for Higher Education Evaluation - JIHEE
President: Toshiji Kuroda
Daini-Seiko Building 2F 4-2-11 Kudankita, Chiyoda-ku
Tokyo 102-0073
Tel: +81(3) 5211 5131
Fax: +81(3) 5211 5132
Website: http://www.jihee.or.jp/en/index.html

Japan University Accreditation Association - JUAA
President: Kyosuke Nagata
2-7-13, Ichigayasadohara-cho, Shinjuku-ku
Tokyo 162-0842
Tel: +81(3) 5228 2020
Fax: +81(3) 5228 2323
Website: http://www.juaa.or.jp/en

National Institution for Academic Degrees and Quality Enhancement of Higher Education - NIAD-QE
President: Hideki Fukuda
1-29-1 Gakuen-nishimachi, Kodaira-shi
Tokyo 187-8587
Tel: +81(42) 307 1500
Fax: +81(42) 307 1552
Website: http://www.niad.ac.jp

NATIONAL BODIES

Ministry of Education, Culture, Sports, Science and Technology - MEXT

Minister: Hirokazu Matsuno
3-2-2 Kasumigaseki, Chiyoda-ku
Tokyo 100-8959
Tel: +81(3) 5253 4111
Website: http://www.mext.go.jp
Role of national body: The Ministry is responsible for education, culture, sports, science and technology policies.

Dokuritsu gyŏsei hŏjin Daigaku Nyushi Center - DNC (National Centre for University Entrance Examinations)

President: Hiroki Yamamoto
2-19-23 Komaba, Meguro-ku
Tokyo 153-8501
Website: http://www.dnc.ac.jp
Role of national body: The Centre is an independent institution that organises the university entrance tests (in January).

National Institute for Educational Policy Research - NIER

Director-General: Tsuyoshi Sugino
3-2-2 Kasumigaseki, Chiyoda-ku
Tokyo 100-8951
Tel: +81(3) 6733 6833
Website: http://www.nier.go.jp
Role of national body: Research body responsible for collecting and analyzing academic research data.

Kokuritsu Daigaku Kyokai (Japan Association of National Universities)

Director-General: Masato Kitani
National Center of Sciences Bldg. 4F, 2-1-2 Hitotsubashi, Chiyoda-ku
Tokyo 101-0003
Tel: +81(3) 4212 3516
Fax: +81(3) 4212 3519
Website: http://www.janu.jp
Role of national body: JANU's motto is "Action, Leadership, and Cooperation". Its objectives are to further enhance the value provided by national universities and to address the requirements of government and society.

Nihon Shiritsu Daigaku Kyokai (Association of Private Universities of Japan)

Chair: Sunao Onuma
Shigakukaikan Bekkan 9F, 4-2-25, Kudankita, Chiyodaku
Tokyo 102-0073
Tel: +81(3) 3261 7048
Fax: +81(3) 3261 0769

Website: http://www.shidaikyo.or.jp
Role of national body: Established on 7 December 1946 as the National Union of Private Colleges. The present name was adopted on 26 March 1948.

Nihon Shiritsu Daigaku Renmei (The Japan Association of Private Universities and Colleges)

President: Kaoru Kamata
Shigaku-kaikan Bekkan Bldg., 4-2-25 kudan-kita, Chiyoda-ku
Tokyo 102-0073
Tel: +81(3) 3262 2420
Fax: +81(3) 3262 2441
Website: http://www.shidairen.or.jp
Role of national body: The Japan Association of Private Universities and Colleges was established in 1951. It comprises private universities and colleges offering four-year/six-year academic programmes.

Data for academic year: 2013–2014
Source: IAU from MEXT Website, Japan and UNESCO/IBE World Data on Education 2010/2011, 2013. Bodies updated 2017.

Public Institutions

Advanced Institute of Industrial Technology (AIIT)

1-10-40 Higashiooi
Shinagawa-ku 140-0011, Tokyo
Tel: +81(3) 3472-7831
Fax: +81(3) 3472-2790
Website: http://aiit.ac.jp
President: Seiichi Kawata

Graduate School
Industrial Technology (Computer Engineering; Industrial Design; Industrial Engineering; Information Technology)
History: Founded 2006
Admission requirements: Entrance Examination
Main language(s) of instruction: Japanese
Accrediting agency: Ministry of Education, Culture, Sports, Science and Technology (MEXT)

Degrees and diplomas: Shushi (Computer Engineering; Design; Engineering; Information Technology; Software Engineering)
Student Services: Library, IT Centre
Last Update: 16-03-2018

Aichi Prefectural University

1522-3 Ibaragabasama
Nagakute-shi 480-1198, Aichi-ken
Tel: +81(561) 64-111, +81(561) 76-8829
Fax: +81(561) 641-101
Website: http://www.aichi-pu.ac.jp
President: Tadayoshi Takashima

School
Education and Welfare (Development Studies; Education; Educational Sciences; Welfare and Protective Services); **Foreign Studies** (American Studies; Asian Studies; Chinese; Cultural Studies; English; English Studies; European Studies; French; French Studies; German; Germanic Studies; International Studies; Latin American Studies; Modern Languages; Spanish); **Information Science and Technology** (Information Sciences; Information Technology); **Japanese Studies** (Asian Studies; Cultural Studies; History; Japanese; Literature); **Nursing and Health** (Health Sciences; Nursing)

Graduate School
Graduate Studies (Development Studies; Health Sciences; Information Sciences; Information Technology; International Studies; Japanese; Nursing)

Research Division
Cultural Symbiosis (Cultural Studies); **Higher Language Education** (Foreign Languages Education); **Information Science and Technology** (*Collaborative*) (Information Sciences; Information Technology); **Lifelong Education** (Continuing Education); **Writing Culture and Cultural Property** (Cultural Studies; Law; Writing)
Further information: Also Moriyama campus and Satellite Campus
History: Founded 1947 Aichi Prefectural Women's Special College. Reorganised as Aichi Prefectural Women's College 1957. Acquired present status and title 1966
Academic year: April to March
Fees: Registration, 282,000; Tuition, 535,800 per annum (Yen)
Main language(s) of instruction: Japanese
Accrediting agency: Ministry of Education, Culture, Sports, Science and Technology (MEXT)
Degrees and diplomas: Hakase (Cultural Studies; Development Studies; Information Technology; International Studies; Japanese; Nursing)

Student Services: Academic Counselling, Social Counselling, Careers Guidance, Nursery Care, Sports Facilities, Language Laboratory, Facilities for disabled people, Health Services, Canteen

Periodicals: Bulletin of Foreign Studies, Bulletin of Information Science and Technology, Bulletin of Letters

Academic Staff 2013-2014	MALE	FEMALE	TOTAL
FULL-TIME			c. 200
Student Numbers 2013-2014			
All (Foreign Included)			c. 3300
Foreign only			40

Last Update: 01-03-2018

Aichi Prefectural University - School of Nursing & Health, Graduate School of Nursing and Health

Tohgoku, Kamishidami Moriyama-ku
Nagoya-shi 463-8502, Aichi
Tel: +81(52) 736-1401
Fax: +81(52) 736-1415
Website: http://www.aichi-nurs.ac.jp
Dean: Keiko Yamaguchi

Course/Programme
Public Service and Nursing Outreach (*Certified*) (Nursing; Social and Community Services)

School
Nursing and Health Sciences (Child Care and Development; Community Health; Health Administration; Health Sciences; Midwifery; Nursing; Psychiatry and Mental Health)

Graduate School
Nursing and Health (Health Sciences; Midwifery; Nursing; Women's Studies)
Further information: Also Nagakute Campus and Satellite Campus
History: Founded 1968 as Aichi Prefectural Junior College. Became Aichi Prefectural College of Nursing and Health 1995. Acquired present title 2009.
Main language(s) of instruction: Japanese
Accrediting agency: Ministry of Education, Culture, Sports, Science and Technology (MEXT)
Degrees and diplomas: Gakushi (Nursing), Shushi (Nursing), Hakase (Nursing)
Last Update: 27-03-2018

Aichi Prefectural University of Fine Arts and Music

1-1 Sagamine, Yazako Nagakute-cho
Aichi-gun 480-1194, Aichi
Tel: +81(561) 62-1180
Fax: +81(561) 62-0083
Website: http://www.aichi-fam-u.ac.jp
President: Koji Matsumura

Faculty
Art (Art History; Ceramic Art; Design; Fine Arts; Handicrafts; Museum Studies; Painting and Drawing; Sculpture); **Music** (Music; Music Theory and Composition; Musical Instruments; Musicology; Singing); **Music** (Music; Musicology)

Centre
Art Education and Student Support (Art Education); **Art Information** (Fine Arts); **Fine Arts and Music Promotion** (Fine Arts; Music)

Graduate School
Fine Arts (Fine Arts); **Music** (Music)
History: Founded 1966. Acquired independent status 2007 when administration was transferred from Aichi prefecture to the Aichi Public University Corporation
Main language(s) of instruction: Japanese
Accrediting agency: Ministry of Education, Culture, Sports, Science and Technology (MEXT)
Degrees and diplomas: Hakase (Fine Arts; Music)
Student Services: Library
Last Update: 01-03-2018

Aichi University of Education

1 Hirosawa Igaya-cho
Kariya-shi 448-8542, Aichi-ken
Tel: +81(566) 26-2178
Fax: +81(566) 26-2170
Website: http://www.aichi-edu.ac.jp
President: Masahisa Matsuda

Faculty
Education (Art Education; Arts and Humanities; Computer Science; Cultural Studies; Education; Educational Sciences; Fine Arts; Foreign Languages Education; Handicrafts; Health Education; Humanities and Social Science Education; Information Technology; Japanese; Molecular Biology; Natural Sciences; Nursing; Primary Education; Psychology; Science

Education; Secondary Education; Social Studies; Social Welfare; Special Education; Teacher Training)

Course/Programme
Special Support Education (Special Education)

Centre
Campus Health and Environment (Environmental Studies; Health Sciences); **Clinical Practice in Education** (Education); **Community-Based Education and Cooperation** (Education; Social and Community Services); **International Exchange**; **Promoting Higher-Quality Teacher Education** (Teacher Training); **Promotion of Science and Technology Education** (Science Education; Technology Education); **Studies of Higher Education** (Higher Education)

Graduate School
Education (Art Education; Development Studies; Education; Educational Psychology; English; Foreign Languages Education; Health Education; Home Economics Education; Humanities and Social Science Education; Japanese; Mathematics Education; Music Education; Nursing; Physical Education; Science Education; Special Education; Technology Education); **Education Practitioner** (Education)

History: Founded as Aichi Prefectural Academy 1873. Acquired university status and reorganized as Aichi Gakugei University 1949. Acquired present title 1966. Merged with Aichi Second Normal College and moved to present site 1970. Incorporated as the National University Corporation Aichi University of Education 2004.
Academic year: April to March (April-September; October-March)
Admission requirements: Graduation from high school or foreign equivalent, and entrance examination
Main language(s) of instruction: Japanese
Degrees and diplomas: Hakase (Education). Also Professional Graduate Degree Programme of School Practitioner.
Student Services: Academic Counselling, Social Counselling, Careers Guidance, Nursery Care, Cultural Activities, Sports Facilities, Language Laboratory, Facilities for disabled people, Health Services, Canteen
Periodicals: Bulletin

Academic Staff 2012-2013	MALE	FEMALE	TOTAL
FULL-TIME			c. 260
Student Numbers 2012-2013			
All (Foreign Included)	1766	2201	3967
Foreign only			68

Last Update: 23-02-2018

Akita International University

193-2 Okutsubakidai Yuwa-Tsubakigawa
Akita-shi 010-1292, Akita
Tel: +81(18) 886-5900
Fax: +81(18) 886-5910
Website: http://www.aiu.ac.jp
President: Norihiko Suzuki

Faculty
International Liberal Arts (Arts and Humanities; Cultural Studies; Education; English; Foreign Languages Education; History; International Business; International Studies; Japanese; Modern Languages; Teacher Training)

Graduate School
Global Communication and Language (Communication Studies; English; Foreign Languages Education; Japanese; Teacher Training)
History: Founded 2004.
Academic year: April to March (April-August; September-March)
Fees: Tuition, 696,000 (Yen)
Main language(s) of instruction: English, Japanese
Accrediting agency: Ministry of Education, Culture, Sports, Science and Technology (MEXT)
Degrees and diplomas: Shushi (Communication Studies; English; Foreign Languages Education; Japanese; Native Language Education)
Student Services: Sports Facilities
Last Update: 01-03-2018

Akita Prefectural University

241-438 Kaidobata-Nishi
Nakano Shimoshinjo 010-0195, Akita
Tel: +81(18) 872-1500
Fax: +81(18) 872-1670
Website: http://www.akita-pu.ac.jp
President: Junichi Kobayashi

Faculty
Bioresource Sciences (*Akita Campus/Ogata Campus*) (Agricultural Business; Agriculture; Animal Husbandry; Biotechnology; Environmental Management; Environmental Studies; Farm Management; Natural Resources); **Systems Science and Technology** (*Honjo Campus*) (Architectural and Environmental Design; Architecture; Architecture and Planning; Artificial Intelligence; Computer Engineering; Electronic Engineering; Engineering Management;

Information Technology; Machine Building; Management; Robotics; Systems Analysis; Town Planning)

Institute
Wood Technology (Wood Technology)

Centre
Research and Education for Comprehensive Science (Natural Sciences); **Science and Technology Integration** (Natural Sciences; Technology)

Graduate School
Bioresource Sciences (Biological and Life Sciences; Genetics; Natural Resources); **Systems Science and Technology** (Architectural and Environmental Design; Architecture; Artificial Intelligence; Computer Engineering; Design; Electronic Engineering; Engineering; Engineering Management; Environmental Engineering; Information Technology; Machine Building; Management)
Further information: Also Honjo campus, Ogata campus
History: Founded 1999
Fees: Entry fee, 282,000 for students from the province and 423,000 for other students; Tuition, 535,800 per annum (Yen)
Main language(s) of instruction: Japanese
Accrediting agency: Ministry of Education, Culture, Sports, Science and Technology (MEXT)
Degrees and diplomas: Hakase (Biological and Life Sciences; Computer Engineering; Genetics; Natural Resources)

Academic Staff 2012-2013	MALE	FEMALE	TOTAL
FULL-TIME			221
Student Numbers 2012-2013			
All (Foreign Included)			1837

Last Update: 01-03-2018

Akita University

1-1 Tegata Gakuen-machi
Akita-shi 010-8502, Akita
Tel: +81(18) 889-2207
Fax: +81(18) 889-2219
Website: http://www.akita-u.ac.jp
President: Fumio Yamamoto

Faculty
Education and Human Studies (American Studies; Art Education; Communication Studies; Education; Educational Psychology; Engineering; English; Environmental Studies; European Languages; Family Studies; Geography; Health Education; History; Humanities and Social Science Education; Information Sciences; International Studies; Mathematics; Modern Languages; Music Education; Physical Education;

Political Sciences; Primary Education; Regional Studies; Special Education); **Engineering and Resource Science** (Analytical Chemistry; Applied Chemistry; Applied Mathematics; Automation and Control Engineering; Cell Biology; Chemical Engineering; Chemistry; Civil Engineering; Computer Engineering; Computer Science; Earth Sciences; Electrical and Electronic Engineering; Electrical Engineering; Electronic Engineering; Engineering; Environmental Engineering; Geological Engineering; Information Technology; Materials Engineering; Molecular Biology; Organic Chemistry; Telecommunications Engineering); **Medicine** (Health Sciences; Medicine; Nursing; Occupational Therapy; Physical Therapy; Social and Preventive Medicine)

Unit
General Technology (Technology)

Centre
Bioscience Education and Research (*BERC*) (Biological and Life Sciences; Science Education); **Educational Research and Practice** (Educational Research); **Geo-Environmental Science** (Environmental Studies; Geology); **Innovative Engineering Design and Manufacturing** (Design; Engineering; Production Engineering); **Promotion of Educational Research and Affairs** (Educational Research); **Research and Education on Mineral and Energy Resources** (*International*) (Energy Engineering; Mineralogy)

Graduate School
Education (Art Education; Education; Educational Psychology; Foreign Languages Education; Health Education; Home Economics Education; Humanities and Social Science Education; Mathematics Education; Music Education; Native Language Education; Physical Education; Primary Education; Science Education; Technology Education); **Engineering and Resource Science** (Applied Chemistry; Applied Mathematics; Automation and Control Engineering; Chemistry; Civil Engineering; Computer Engineering; Computer Science; Earth Sciences; Electrical and Electronic Engineering; Electrical Engineering; Electronic Engineering; Engineering; Environmental Engineering; Geological Engineering; Information Technology; Materials Engineering; Mechanical Engineering; Production Engineering; Robotics; Systems Analysis; Telecommunications Engineering); **Medicine** (Anaesthesiology; Anatomy; Biochemistry; Biology; Cardiology; Cell Biology; Dentistry; Dermatology; Diabetology; Endocrinology; Environmental Studies; Forensic Medicine and Dentistry; Gastroenterology; Gerontology; Gynaecology and Obstetrics; Haematology; Health Education; Health Sciences; Immunology; Information Sciences; Laboratory Techniques; Medical Technology; Medicine; Molecular Biology; Nephrology; Neurological Therapy; Neurology; Nursing; Occupational Therapy; Oncology; Ophthalmology; Oral Pathology; Orthopaedics;

Otorhinolaryngology; Paediatrics; Pathology; Pharmacy; Physical Therapy; Physiology; Plastic Surgery; Psychiatry and Mental Health; Public Health; Radiology; Respiratory Therapy; Rheumatology; Social and Preventive Medicine; Surgery; Urology)

Research Division

Disaster Prevention in the Local Community (Safety Engineering); **Environment** (Environmental Studies); **Radioisotope** (Chemistry)

Further information: Also University Hospital, Hondo Campus, Hodono Campus

History: Founded 1949, incorporating Akita Shihan Gakko (Normal School), founded 1875, Akita Kozan Senmon Gakko (Mining College) 1910, Akita Seinen Shihan Gakko (Normal School for Youth Education) 1944, and Igakubu (School of Medicine) 1970. Responsible to the Ministry of Education, Science, Sports and Culture.

Academic year: April to March (April-September; October-March)

Admission requirements: Graduation from high school or foreign equivalent and entrance examination

Fees: Entrance Fee, 282,000; Tuition fee, 535,800 per annum (Yen)

Main language(s) of instruction: Japanese

Accrediting agency: Ministry of Education, Culture, Sports, Science and Technology (MEXT)

Degrees and diplomas: Hakase (Engineering; Health Sciences; Medicine; Natural Resources)

Student Services: Academic Counselling, Social Counselling, Careers Guidance, Nursery Care, Cultural Activities, Sports Facilities, Language Laboratory, Health Services, Canteen, Foreign Studies Centre

Periodicals: Akita Igaku, Akita University, Memoirs of the Faculty of Education and Humanities, Reports of Research Institute of Natural Resources, Materials and Global Environments, Scientific and Technical Reports of the Faculty of Engineering and Resource Science

Academic Staff 2013-2014	MALE	FEMALE	TOTAL
FULL-TIME			648
Student Numbers 2013-2014			
All (Foreign Included)			5157
Foreign only			185

Last Update: 23-02-2018

Akita University of Art

12-3 Araya-Okawamachi
Akita 010-1632
Tel: +81(18) 888-8100
Fax: +81(18) 888-8101
Website: http://www.akibi.ac.jp
President: Akinori Shiori

Faculty

Fine Arts (Architecture; Communication Arts; Design; Fine Arts; Graphic Design; Industrial Design; Landscape Architecture; Painting and Drawing; Sculpture; Textile Design; Visual Arts)

Course/Programme

Liberal Arts (Aesthetics; Art History; Arts and Humanities; Design; English; Information Sciences; Modern Languages; Museum Management)

Centre

Core Social Contribution (Social and Community Services)

History: Founded 2013 by upgrading the Akita Municipal Junior College of Arts and Crafts

Main language(s) of instruction: Japanese

Accrediting agency: Ministry of Education, Culture, Sports, Science and Technology (MEXT)

Last Update: 01-03-2018

Aomori Public University

153-4, Aza Yamazaki Oaza Goushizawa
Aomori-shi 030-0196, Aomori
Tel: +81(17) 764-1555
Fax: +81(177) 64-1544
Website: http://www.nebuta.ac.jp
President: Yukio Hadoda

College

Business Administration and Economics (Accountancy; Business Administration; Economics; Environmental Management; Human Resources; International Business; Statistics)

Graduate School

Management and Economics (Business Administration; Economics; Management)

History: Founded 1993, University in 2013

Fees: 267,900 per semester (Yen)

Main language(s) of instruction: Japanese

Accrediting agency: Ministry of Education, Culture, Sports, Science and Technology (MEXT)

Degrees and diplomas: Shushi (Business Administration; Economics), Hakase (Business Administration; Economics)

Student Numbers 2012-2013	MALE	FEMALE	TOTAL
All (Foreign Included)			c. 310

Last Update: 01-03-2018

Aomori University of Health and Welfare (AUHW)

Mase 58-1 Hamadate
Aomori-shi 030-8505, Aomori
Tel: +81(17) 765-2000
Fax: +81(17) 765-2188
Website: http://www.auhw.ac.jp
President: Kazuko Ezumi

Faculty

Health Sciences (Nursing; Nutrition; Physical Therapy; Social Sciences; Social Welfare)

Graduate School

Graduate Studies (Health Sciences)
History: Founded 1999
Fees: Entry fee, 225,600 for students from the prefecture and 338,400 for others; Tuition, 535,800 per annum (Yen)
Main language(s) of instruction: Japanese
Accrediting agency: Ministry of Education, Culture, Sports, Science and Technology (MEXT)
Degrees and diplomas: Shushi (Health Sciences), Hakase (Health Sciences)
Student Services: Health Services

Academic Staff 2012-2013	MALE	FEMALE	TOTAL
FULL-TIME			98
Student Numbers 2012-2013			
All (Foreign Included)	182	775	957

Last Update: 01-03-2018

Asahikawa Medical University

Midorigaoka Higashi 2-1-1-1
Asahikawa-shi 078-8510, Hokkaido
Tel: +81(166) 65-2111
Fax: +81(166) 65-5533
Website: http://www.asahikawa-med.ac.jp
President: Akitoshi Yoshida

Course/Programme

Nursing (Nursing)

School

Medicine (Anaesthesiology; Anatomy; Biochemistry; Cardiology; Cell Biology; Dermatology; Forensic Medicine and Dentistry; Gastroenterology; Gynaecology and Obstetrics; Haematology; Health Sciences; Immunology; Laboratory Techniques; Medicine; Microbiology; Nephrology; Neurological Therapy; Neurosciences; Oncology; Ophthalmology; Oral Pathology; Orthopaedics; Otorhinolaryngology; Paediatrics; Parasitology; Pharmacology; Physiology; Pneumology; Psychiatry and Mental Health; Radiology; Surgery; Urology)

Department/Division

General Education (Biological and Life Sciences; Biology; Chemistry; English; German; History; Information Sciences; Mathematics; Philosophy; Physics; Psychology; Sociology)

Centre

Advanced Research and Education (Biochemistry; Medicine; Neurosciences); **Education** (Medicine; Nursing); **Health Administration** (Health Administration; Health Sciences; Social and Preventive Medicine)

Laboratory

Animal Laboratory for Medical Research (Animal Husbandry); **Radioactive Isotope Research** (Biochemistry; Laboratory Techniques); **Sentral Laboratory for Research and Education** (Biochemistry; Biomedical Engineering; Laboratory Techniques)

Graduate School

Medicine (Cardiology; Endocrinology; Gastroenterology; Gerontology; Haematology; Health Administration; Health Education; Immunology; Medicine; Midwifery; Neurology; Nursing; Oncology; Pharmacology; Physiology; Psychiatry and Mental Health; Social and Preventive Medicine)

Research Division

Brain Function and Medical Engineering (Medical Technology; Medicine; Neurosciences; Sports Management)

Chair

Endowed (Cardiology; Gastroenterology; Immunology; Medical Technology; Medicine)
Further information: Also Graduate School (Master and Doctor courses)
History: Founded 1973. Graduate course established 1979
Academic year: April to March (April-September; October-March)
Admission requirements: Graduation from senior high school or equivalent, and entrance examination
Main language(s) of instruction: Japanese
Accrediting agency: Ministry of Education, Culture, Sports, Science and Technology (MEXT)
Degrees and diplomas: Shushi (Nursing), Hakase (Medicine)
Periodicals: Asahikawa Medical College

Academic Staff 2012-2013	MALE	FEMALE	TOTAL
FULL-TIME			325
Student Numbers 2012-2013			
All (Foreign Included)	645	487	1132
Foreign only			9

Last Update: 23-02-2018

Chiba Prefectural University Of Health Sciences (CPUOHS)

Mihama ku Wakaba 2 - chome n ° 10 n ° 1
Chiba 261-0004
Tel: +81(43) 296-2000
Fax: +81(43) 272-1716
Website: http://www.pref.chiba.lg.jp/hoidai
President: Masahiro Tanabe

School

Health Sciences (*The Rehabilitation Department is located in Nitona Campus*) (Dental Hygiene; Health Sciences; Nursing; Nutrition; Rehabilitation and Therapy)
History: Founded 2009 following reorganization of Chiba College of Health Sciences and Chiba College of Allied Medical Science
Academic year: April to March (April -August; October-March)
Fees: 535,800 per annum (Yen)
Main language(s) of instruction: Japanese
Accrediting agency: Ministry of Education, Culture, Sports, Science and Technology (MEXT)
Student Services: Academic Counselling, Careers Guidance, Sports Facilities, Health Services
Periodicals: Annual Report of Education and Research Chiba prefectural University Of Health Sciences

Academic Staff 2012-2013	MALE	FEMALE	TOTAL
FULL-TIME			101
PART-TIME			21
Student Numbers 2012-2013			
All (Foreign Included)	92	642	734

Total number of part-time students: 4
Last Update: 01-03-2018

Chiba University

1-33, Yayoi-cho Inage-ku
Chiba-shi 263-8522, Chiba
Tel: +81(43) 251-1111
Fax: +81(43) 290-2041
Website: http://www.chiba-u.ac.jp
President: Takeshi Tokugawa
Tel: +81(43) 290-2040

Faculty

Education (Continuing Education; Education; Health Education; Nursing; Preschool Education; Primary Education; Secondary Education; Special Education; Sports); **Engineering** (Applied Chemistry; Architectural Restoration; Architecture; Architecture and Planning; Biotechnology; Computer Science; Design; Electrical and Electronic Engineering; Engineering; Mechanical Engineering; Medical Technology; Nanotechnology; Optical Technology; Town Planning); **Horticulture** (*Matsudo*) (Agricultural Business; Agricultural Economics; Applied Chemistry; Architectural and Environmental Design; Biological and Life Sciences; Crop Production; Environmental Studies; Food Science; Horticulture; Landscape Architecture; Natural Resources); **Law and Economics** (Accountancy; Comparative Politics; Economics; International Economics; International Law; Law; Management; Political Sciences; Private Law; Public Law; Social Policy; Welfare and Protective Services); **Letters** (Anthropology; Applied Linguistics; Arts and Humanities; Behavioural Sciences; Cognitive Sciences; Cultural Studies; Eurasian and North Asian Languages; Heritage Preservation; History; International Studies; Japanese; Linguistics; Literature; Modern Languages; Psychology; Sociology); **Pharmaceutical Sciences** (Biological and Life Sciences; Pharmacology; Pharmacy); **Science** (Biology; Chemistry; Earth Sciences; Mathematics; Mathematics and Computer Science; Natural Sciences; Physics)

Course/Programme

Double Degree (*With partner universities in China, Thailand and Indonesia*) (Engineering; Horticulture); **Excellent International Student**

School

Law (*Graduate*) (Law); **Medicine** (Medicine); **Nursing** (Nursing)

Institute

Media and Information Technology (Computer Science; Data Processing; Information Technology; Media Studies)

Centre

Academic Link; **Chemical Analysis** (Chemistry); **Environment, Health and Field Sciences** (Environmental Studies; Health Sciences); **Environmental Remote Sensing** (Surveying and Mapping; Technology); **Forensic Mental Health** (Forensic Medicine and Dentistry); **Frontier Science**; **General Education** (Education); **Hadron Astrophysics** (*International*) (Astrophysics); **International Research and**

Education (Foreigners Education; Modern Languages); **Language Education** (Chinese; English; Foreign Languages Education; French; German; Modern Languages; Native Language Education; Russian); **Preventive Medical Science** (Social and Preventive Medicine); **Radioisotope Research** (Radiology); **Safety and Health Organization** (Health Sciences; Occupational Health; Safety Engineering); **Sustainable Tourism Creation** (Tourism)

Laboratory

Venture Business (Business Administration; Natural Sciences; Technology)

Graduate School

Advanced Integration Science (Computer Science; Information Sciences; Nanotechnology); **Education** (Curriculum; Education; Educational Administration; Humanities and Social Science Education; Music Education; Physical Education; Science Education; Technology Education); **Engineering** (Applied Chemistry; Architecture; Biotechnology; Design; Electrical and Electronic Engineering; Engineering; Information Sciences; Mechanical Engineering; Medical Technology; Nanotechnology; Urban Studies); **Horticulture** (Applied Chemistry; Architectural and Environmental Design; Biological and Life Sciences; Environmental Studies; Food Science; Horticulture; Landscape Architecture; Natural Resources); **Humanities and Social Sciences** (Anthropology; Archaeology; Arts and Humanities; Cultural Studies; History; Japanese; Linguistics; Literature; Management; Modern Languages; Philosophy; Psychology; Public Administration; Social Sciences; Sociology; Sports); **Medical and Pharmaceutical Sciences** (Biological and Life Sciences; Environmental Studies; Health Sciences; Medicine; Pharmacology); **Medicine** (*Inohana*) (Environmental Studies; Gerontology; Immunology; Laboratory Techniques; Medicine; Molecular Biology; Neurosciences; Oncology; Pathology; Physiology; Rehabilitation and Therapy); **Nursing** (Community Health; Health Administration; Health Sciences; Nursing); **Pharmaceutical Sciences** (Biological and Life Sciences; Environmental Studies; Genetics; Medicine; Molecular Biology; Neurology; Pharmacy); **Science** (Biology; Cell Biology; Chemistry; Earth Sciences; Mathematics; Mathematics and Computer Science; Molecular Biology; Natural Sciences; Physics; Statistics)

Research Division

Biomedical Sciences (*Inohana*) (Genetics); **Frontier Medical Engineering** (Medical Technology; Surgery); **Marine Biosystems Research** (Marine Biology; Marine Science and Oceanography); **Medical Mycology** (Biological and Life Sciences; Botany; Immunology; Molecular Biology); **Shanghai Jiao Tong University and Chiba University**

International Cooperative Research Center (*SJTU-CU ICRC*) (Bioengineering; Mechanical Engineering; Robotics)

Further information: Also University Hospital

History: Founded 1949 as a State University incorporating Chiba Medical College, Chiba Normal School, Chiba Youth Normal School, Tokyo Industrial College, and Chiba Agricultural College. Graduate School established 1955. Acquired present status 2004.

Academic year: April to March (April-September; October-March)

Admission requirements: Graduation from high school or equivalent or foreign equivalent, and entrance examination

Fees: Registration, 282,000; tuition, 535,800 (Undergraduate), 535,800 (Master's programme), 520,800 (Doctoral programme) (Yen)

Main language(s) of instruction: Japanese

Accrediting agency: Ministry of Education, Culture, Sports, Science and Technology (MEXT)

Degrees and diplomas: Hakase (Agriculture; Arts and Humanities; Economics; Engineering; Law; Management; Medicine; Natural Sciences; Nursing; Pharmacology; Pharmacy; Public Administration). Also Juris Doctor

Student Services: Academic Counselling, Social Counselling, Careers Guidance, Nursery Care, Cultural Activities, Sports Facilities, Language Laboratory, Facilities for disabled people, Health Services, Canteen, Foreign Studies Centre

Periodicals: Annual Report of Marine Biosystems Research Centre, Annual Report of Research Centre for Pathogenic Fungi and Microbial Toxicoses, Bulletin of Faculty of Horticulture, Bulletin of the Faculty of Education, Chiba University, Economics Journal of Chiba University, Journal of Humanities, Journal of Law and Politics, Journal of School of Nursing, List of Research Publications, School of Medicine, Record of Research Activities, Faculty of Pharmaceutical Science, Research Activities and Interests of Faculty of Engineering, Technical Bulletin of Faculty of Horticulture, Technical Reports of Mathematical Sciences

Last Update: 23-02-2018

Ehime Prefectural University of Health Sciences (EPU)

543, Takoda Tobe-cho, Iyo-gun
Ehime 791-2101
Tel: +81(89) 958-2111
Fax: +81(89) 958-2177
Website: http://www.epu.ac.jp

Faculty

Health Sciences (Health Sciences; Laboratory Techniques; Medical Technology; Midwifery; Nursing)

History: Founded 2005
Fees: Admission fee, 169,200-423,000; Tuition, 535,800 per annum (Yen)
Main language(s) of instruction: Japanese
Accrediting agency: Ministry of Education, Culture, Sports, Science and Technology (MEXT)
Periodicals: Bulletin of Ehime Prefectural University of Health Sciences
Last Update: 01-03-2018

Ehime University

10-13 Dogo-Himata
Matsuyama-shi 790-8577, Ehime
Tel: +81(89) 927-9000
Fax: +81(89) 927-9025
Website: http://www.ehime-u.ac.jp
President: Yuichi Ohashi

Faculty

Agriculture (Agricultural Engineering; Agricultural Management; Agriculture; Aquaculture; Biological and Life Sciences; Environmental Management; Environmental Studies; Food Science; Forest Products; Forestry; Natural Resources); **Agriculture** (Agricultural Engineering; Agriculture; Biological and Life Sciences; Environmental Management; Environmental Studies; Fishery; Forestry); **Education** (Art Education; Education; Education of the Handicapped; Fine Arts; Foreign Languages Education; Health Education; Home Economics Education; Humanities and Social Science Education; Information Sciences; International Studies; Mathematics Education; Music Education; Native Language Education; Peace and Disarmament; Physical Education; Preschool Education; Primary Education; Regional Studies; Secondary Education; Social Studies; Special Education; Sports; Teacher Training; Technology Education; Welfare and Protective Services); **Engineering** (Applied Chemistry; Civil Engineering; Computer Engineering; Computer Science; Electrical and Electronic Engineering; Engineering; Environmental Engineering; Inorganic Chemistry; Materials Engineering; Mechanical Engineering; Organic Chemistry; Polymer and Plastics Technology; Software Engineering); **Law and Letters** (Economics; International Studies; Law; Political Sciences; Public Administration; Regional Studies); **Science** (Biology; Chemistry; Earth Sciences; Mathematics; Natural Sciences; Physics)

Course/Programme

General Education; Japanese Language (Japanese); **Super Science** (Astronomy and Space Science; Biological and Life Sciences; Biotechnology; Earth Sciences; Environmental Studies; Natural Sciences)

School

Medicine (Biological and Life Sciences; Community Health; Gerontology; Health Education; Medicine; Molecular Biology; Nursing; Pathology; Public Health; Social and Preventive Medicine)

Centre

English Education (*EEC*) (English); **Innovative Education for Science and Technology** (Science Education; Technology Education); **Marine Environmental Studies** (Environmental Studies); **Scientific and Industrial Research** (*Cooperative*) (Natural Sciences; Technology)

Laboratory

Venture Business (Business Administration)

Graduate School

Agricultural Sciences (*United*) (Agriculture; Biological and Life Sciences; Natural Resources); **Education** (Clinical Psychology; Curriculum; Education; Educational Psychology; Pedagogy; Preschool Education; Special Education); **Law and Letters** (Arts and Humanities; Cultural Studies; Economics; Industrial Management; International Studies; Law; Literature; Philosophy; Public Law); **Medicine** (Biology; Community Health; Gerontology; Health Sciences; Information Sciences; Medicine; Nursing; Oncology); **Science and Engineering** (Applied Chemistry; Biology; Biotechnology; Civil Engineering; Computer Science; Earth Sciences; Electrical and Electronic Engineering; Electronic Engineering; Engineering; Environmental Engineering; Environmental Studies; Information Technology; Materials Engineering; Mathematics; Mechanical Engineering; Mineralogy; Molecular Biology; Physics; Safety Engineering)

Research Division

Ancient East Asian Iron Culture (Asian Studies; Cultural Studies); **Cell-free Science and Technology** (Biological and Life Sciences; Biotechnology; Engineering; Molecular Biology; Natural Sciences); **Disaster Management Informatics** (Safety Engineering); **Fisheries** (*South Ehime*) (Fishery); **Geodynamics** (Earth Sciences); **Proteo Medicine** (Medicine); **Regional Community Innovation** (Social and Community Services); **Space and Cosmic Evolution** (Astronomy and Space Science)
History: Founded 1949, incorporating Ehime Normal School, founded 1943, Matsuyama Higher School, 1919, Ehime Youth Normal School, 1944, Niihama Technical College, 1939, and Matsuyama Agricultural College,1949
Academic year: April to February (April-July; September-February)
Admission requirements: Graduation from high school or equivalent and entrance examination

Fees: Entrance Fee, 282,000; Tuition fee, 535,800 per annum (Yen)

Main language(s) of instruction: Japanese

Accrediting agency: Ministry of Education, Culture, Sports, Science and Technology (MEXT)

Degrees and diplomas: Hakase (Agriculture; Engineering; Medicine; Natural Sciences)

Student Services: Sports Facilities, Language Laboratory

Academic Staff 2012-2013	MALE	FEMALE	TOTAL
FULL-TIME			967
Student Numbers 2012-2013			
All (Foreign Included)			c. 10000

Last Update: 23-02-2018

Fukui Prefectural University (FPU)

4-1-1 Kenjojima Matsuoka-cho
Yoshida-gun 910-1195, Fukui
Tel: +81(776) 61-6000
Fax: +81(776) 61-6011
Website: http://www.fpu.ac.jp
President: Isoya Shinji

Faculty

Biotechnology (Bioengineering; Biological and Life Sciences; Biotechnology); **Economics** (Accountancy; Business Administration; Economics); **Marine Bioscience** (*Obama Campus*) (Aquaculture; Biology; Fishery; Marine Biology); **Nursing and Social Welfare** (Community Health; Health Sciences; Nursing; Public Health; Social Psychology; Social Welfare; Social Work)

Centre

Arts and Sciences (Arts and Humanities; Natural Sciences)

Laboratory

Marine Environmental Engineering (*Obama Campus*) (Environmental Engineering; Marine Engineering)

Graduate School

Bioscience and Biotechnology (Aquaculture; Bioengineering; Biological and Life Sciences; Biotechnology; Fishery; Marine Biology); **Economics and Business Administration** (Business Administration; Economic and Finance Policy; Economics; International Economics; Management); **Nursing and Social Welfare** (Community Health; Gerontology; Health Education; Health Sciences; Nursing; Psychiatry and Mental Health; Social Welfare; Welfare and Protective Services)

Research Division

Dinosaurs (Paleontology); **Marine Bioresouces** (*Obama Campus*) (Marine Biology; Natural Resources); **Regional Economics** (Business Administration; Economics; Government; Public Administration)

Further information: Also Obama campus

History: Founded 1992

Main language(s) of instruction: Japanese

Accrediting agency: Ministry of Education, Culture, Sports, Science and Technology (MEXT)

Degrees and diplomas: Hakase (Biological and Life Sciences; Biotechnology; Economics; Marine Biology)

Last Update: 01-03-2018

Fukuoka Prefectural University

4395 Ita
Tagawa-shi 825-8585, Fukuoka
Tel: +81(947) 42-2118, +81(947) 42-1365
Fax: +81(947) 426-171
Website: http://www.fukuoka-pu.ac.jp
President: Shibata Yosaburo

School

Human and Social Sciences (Development Studies; Pedagogy; Psychology; Social Welfare; Social Work; Sociology); **Nursing** (Health Sciences; Midwifery; Nursing; Public Health)

Centre

Health Promotion Education and Research (Health Education; Health Sciences)

Graduate School

Human and Social Sciences (Clinical Psychology; Continuing Education; Social and Community Services; Social Sciences; Welfare and Protective Services); **Nursing** (Nursing)

Research Division

Life-long (Development Studies; Welfare and Protective Services)

History: Founded 1992.

Academic year: April to March(April-July; October-December; January-March)

Main language(s) of instruction: Japanese

Accrediting agency: Ministry of Education, Culture, Sports, Science and Technology (MEXT)

Last Update: 01-03-2018

Fukuoka Women's University (FWU)

1-1-1 Kasumigaoka Higashi-ku
Fukuoka-shi 813-8529, Fukuoka
Tel: +81(92) 661-2411
Fax: +81(92) 661-2415
Website: http://www.fwu.ac.jp
President: Tisato Kajiyama

Faculty

Human Environmental Science (Environmental Studies; Health Sciences; Home Economics; Nutrition); **Literature** (Arts and Humanities; English; Japanese; Literature)

College

Arts and Sciences (*International*) (American Studies; Asian Studies; Biological and Life Sciences; Cultural Studies; East Asian Studies; Environmental Studies; International Business; International Economics; International Relations; Japanese; Western European Studies)

Course/Programme

Teacher Training (Teacher Training)

Centre

Industry-Academia-Government (*Regional Cooperation*); **Women's Lifelong Learning Education**

Graduate School

Human Environmental Science (Environmental Studies; Health Sciences; Home Economics; Nutrition); **Literature** (English; Japanese; Literature)
History: Founded 1950
Academic year: April to March
Admission requirements: Graduation from high school and entrance examination
Main language(s) of instruction: Japanese
Accrediting agency: Ministry of Education, Culture, Sports, Science and Technology (MEXT)
Degrees and diplomas: Hakase (English; Literature)
Student Services: Academic Counselling, Sports Facilities, Health Services
Last Update: 01-03-2018

Fukushima Medical University

1 Hikariga-oka
Fukushima City 960-1295, Fukushima
Tel: +81(24) 547-1111
Fax: +81(24) 547-1991

Website: http://www.fmu.ac.jp/index.html
President: Seiichi Takezushita

School

Medicine (Anaesthesiology; Anatomy; Arts and Humanities; Biochemistry; Biological and Life Sciences; Biology; Cardiology; Cell Biology; Community Health; Dermatology; Diabetology; Embryology and Reproduction Biology; Endocrinology; Forensic Medicine and Dentistry; Gastroenterology; Genetics; Gynaecology and Obstetrics; Haematology; Health Administration; Histology; Hygiene; Immunology; Laboratory Techniques; Mathematics; Medical Technology; Medicine; Microbiology; Modern Languages; Molecular Biology; Natural Sciences; Nephrology; Neurological Therapy; Neurology; Oncology; Ophthalmology; Orthopaedics; Otorhinolaryngology; Paediatrics; Pathology; Pharmacology; Physics; Physiology; Plastic Surgery; Psychiatry and Mental Health; Public Health; Radiology; Rehabilitation and Therapy; Rheumatology; Social and Preventive Medicine; Social Sciences; Statistics; Surgery; Urology); **Nursing** (Anthropology; Arts and Humanities; Community Health; Computer Science; Epidemiology; Gerontology; Health Administration; Health Sciences; Midwifery; Modern Languages; Nursing; Psychology; Public Health; Sociology)

Centre

Science and Humanities (*Integrated*) (Arts and Humanities; Natural Sciences)

Graduate School

Graduate Education (Medicine; Nursing)

Research Division

Advanced Medicine (Medicine)
History: Founded 1952
Academic year: April to March (April-October; October-March)
Admission requirements: Graduation from high school and entrance examination
Main language(s) of instruction: Japanese
Accrediting agency: Ministry of Education, Culture, Sports, Science and Technology (MEXT)
Degrees and diplomas: Hakase (Medicine)
Student Services: Sports Facilities
Periodicals: Fukushima Igaku Zassi, Journal
Last Update: 02-03-2018

Fukushima University

1 Kanayagawa
Fukushima-shi 960-1296, Fukushima
Tel: +81(24) 548-5190, +81(24) 548-8006

Fax: +81(24) 548-3180, +81(24) 548-8551
Website: http://www.fukushima-u.ac.jp
President: Nakai Katsumi

Faculty

Administration and Social Sciences (Administration; Cultural Studies; Law; Political Sciences; Regional Studies; Social and Community Services; Social Sciences; Sociology); **Economics and Business Administration** (Business Administration; Economics; International Economics); **Human Development and Culture** (Cultural Studies; Development Studies; Fine Arts; Social Sciences; Sports); **Symbiotic Systems Science** (Arts and Humanities; Engineering; Environmental Management; Natural Resources; Natural Sciences; Social Sciences)

Course/Programme

General Studies (Chinese; Civil Law; Computer Networks; Computer Science; Cultural Studies; Education; Energy Engineering; English; Environmental Studies; French; Gender Studies; German; Health Sciences; Mechanics; Music; Nuclear Engineering; Philosophy; Psychiatry and Mental Health; Regional Studies; Russian; Social Studies; Software Engineering; Spanish; Sports)

Graduate School

Graduate Studies (Administration; Business Administration; Clinical Psychology; Cultural Studies; Economics; Public Administration; Regional Studies; Teacher Training)
History: Founded 1949.
Academic year: April to March (April-September; October-March)
Admission requirements: Graduation from high school or equivalent or foreign equivalent, and entrance examination
Main language(s) of instruction: Japanese, English (some programmes)
Accrediting agency: Ministry of Education, Culture, Sports, Science and Technology (MEXT)
Student Services: Social Counselling, Sports Facilities, Language Laboratory, Health Services, Canteen
Periodicals: Annual Report of the Research Centre for Lifelong Learning and Education, Bulletin of the Healthcare Centre, Bulletin of the Research and Guidance Centre of Teaching Practice, Faculty Bulletins, Journal of Administrative and Social Sciences, Journal of Commerce, Economics and Economic History, Regional Studies

Academic Staff 2013-2014	MALE	FEMALE	TOTAL
FULL-TIME			239
Student Numbers 2013-2014			
All (Foreign Included)	2647	1873	4520

Last Update: 23-02-2018

Fukuyama City University (FCU)

2-19-1 Minato-Machi
Fukuyama City 721-0964, Hiroshima
Tel: +81(84) 999-1113
Fax: +81(84) 928-1248
Website: http://www.fcu.ac.jp
President: Toshitaka Tamaru

Faculty

Education (Child Care and Development; Clinical Psychology; Developmental Psychology; Education; Pedagogy; Preschool Education; Primary Education; Special Education); **Urban Management** (Construction Engineering; Economics; Management; Sociology; Town Planning; Urban Studies)
Further information: Also Kitahonjo Campus
History: Founded 1963 as Fukuyama Junior College for Women. Acquired present status and title 2011
Main language(s) of instruction: Japanese
Accrediting agency: Ministry of Education, Culture, Sports, Science and Technology (MEXT)
Student Services: Canteen

Academic Staff 2012-2013	MALE	FEMALE	TOTAL
FULL-TIME			27
Student Numbers 2012-2013			
All (Foreign Included)			c. 250

Last Update: 02-03-2018

Future University - Hakodate (FUN)

116-2 Kamedanakano-cho
Hakodate-shi 041-8655, Hokkaido
Tel: +81(138) 34-6444, +81(138) 34-6448
Fax: +81(138) 34-6383
Website: http://www.fun.ac.jp
President: Yasuhiro Katagiri

Course/Programme

Applied Communication (Communication Studies; English)

School

Systems Information Science (Computer Engineering; Information Technology; Media Studies; Software Engineering)

Department/Division

Complex and Intelligent Systems (Artificial Intelligence; Cognitive Sciences; Computer Engineering; Electronic Engineering; Information Sciences; Information Technology;

Mathematics; Software Engineering); **Media Architecture** (Cognitive Sciences; Computer Networks; Data Processing; Information Sciences; Information Technology; Media Studies)

Graduate School

Information Sciences (Artificial Intelligence; Cognitive Sciences; Computer Engineering; Design; Information Sciences; Information Technology; Media Studies)
History: Founded 2000
Main language(s) of instruction: Japanese
Accrediting agency: Ministry of Education, Culture, Sports, Science and Technology (MEXT)
Degrees and diplomas: Shushi (Information Sciences), Hakase (Information Sciences)
Student Services: Sports Facilities
Last Update: 02-03-2018

Gifu College of Nursing

3047-1 Egira-cho
Hashima-shi 501-6295, Gifu
Tel: +81(58) 397-2300
Fax: +81(58) 397-2302
Website: http://www.gifu-cn.ac.jp
President: Kuroe Yuriko

School

Nursing (Arts and Humanities; Child Care and Development; English; Health Sciences; Information Management; Japanese; Midwifery; Natural Sciences; Nursing; Social Welfare)

Graduate School

Nursing (Health Administration; Health Education; Health Sciences; Nursing)

Research Division

Nursing (Nursing)
History: Founded 2000
Academic year: April to March (April-September; October-March)
Admission requirements: Completion of the entire senior-high school course or 12 years of regular school education or equivalent; National Center Test for University Entrance Examination
Fees: Entrance examination fee, 17,000; Admission fee: for Gifu Prefecture residents, 226,000; for others 338,000; Tuition 535,800 (Yen)
Main language(s) of instruction: Japanese
Accrediting agency: Ministry of Education, Culture, Sports, Science and Technology (MEXT)

Degrees and diplomas: Hakase (Nursing)
Student Services: Sports Facilities
Periodicals: Gifu Prefectural College of Nursing
Last Update: 02-03-2018

Gifu Pharmaceutical University (GPU)

1-25-4 Daigaku-nishi
Gifu 501-1196, Gifu
Tel: +81(58) 230-8100, +81(58) 237-3931
Fax: +81(58) 230-8105, +81(58) 237-5979
Website: http://www.gifu-pu.ac.jp
President: Takashi Inagaki

Faculty

Pharmaceutical Sciences (Medicine; Pharmacology; Pharmacy)

Institute

Biological Pharmacy (Biotechnology; Pharmacy)

Graduate School

Pharmaceutical Sciences (Analytical Chemistry; Biochemistry; Biomedicine; Microbiology; Molecular Biology; Organic Chemistry; Pharmacology; Pharmacy; Toxicology)
History: Founded 1932 as Gifu College of Pharmacy at the site of Kokonoecho, Gifu City. Acquired present status and title 1948.
Academic year: April to March (April-September; October-March)
Admission requirements: Graduation from high school or equivalent, and entrance examination
Main language(s) of instruction: Japanese
Accrediting agency: Ministry of Education, Culture, Sports, Science and Technology (MEXT)
Degrees and diplomas: Hakase (Pharmacy)
Periodicals: Annual Proceedings
Last Update: 02-03-2018

Gifu University

1-1 Yanagido
Gifu-shi 501-1193, Gifu
Tel: +81(58) 230-1111, +81(58) 2932146
Fax: +81(58) 230-1410, +81(58) 293-2143
Website: http://www.gifu-u.ac.jp
President: Hisataka Moriwaki

Faculty

Applied Biological Science (Biological and Life Sciences; Botany; Ecology; Environmental Studies; Food Science;

Molecular Biology; Zoology); **Education** (Art Education; Education; Foreign Languages Education; Health Education; Home Economics Education; Humanities and Social Science Education; Mathematics Education; Music Education; Physical Education; Primary Education; Science Education; Secondary Education; Special Education; Teacher Training; Technology Education); **Engineering** (Applied Physics; Chemical Engineering; Chemistry; Electrical and Electronic Engineering; Electronic Engineering; Engineering; Information Technology; Mechanical Engineering; Safety Engineering; Telecommunications Engineering); **Regional Studies** (Cultural Studies; Environmental Studies; Government; Political Sciences; Regional Studies; Social Studies; Urban Studies)

School

Medicine (Anaesthesiology; Anatomy; Behavioural Sciences; Cardiology; Community Health; Dermatology; Development Studies; Endocrinology; Forensic Medicine and Dentistry; Gastroenterology; Genetics; Gynaecology and Obstetrics; Haematology; Immunology; Laboratory Techniques; Medicine; Neurology; Nursing; Pathology; Pharmacology; Pneumology; Psychiatry and Mental Health; Radiology; Toxicology; Urology)

Centre

General Education Promotion (Arts and Humanities; Asian Studies; English; Health Sciences; Japanese; Natural Sciences; Social Sciences; Sports)

Graduate School

Applied Biological Sciences (Biological and Life Sciences; Ecology; Environmental Management; Environmental Studies; Food Science; Molecular Biology; Zoology); **Drug Medical Information Studies** (Biochemistry; Information Technology; Medical Technology; Medicine; Pharmacology); **Education** (Art Education; Clinical Psychology; Curriculum; Education; Educational Psychology; Foreign Languages Education; Physical Education; Science Education; Special Education; Teacher Training); **Engineering** (Applied Chemistry; Bioengineering; Biological and Life Sciences; Civil Engineering; Electrical and Electronic Engineering; Electrical Engineering; Electronic Engineering; Energy Engineering; Environmental Engineering; Environmental Management; Geological Engineering; Information Sciences; Information Technology; Materials Engineering; Mathematics; Mechanical Engineering; Molecular Biology; Natural Resources; Production Engineering; Structural Architecture; Thermal Engineering; Town Planning); **Medicine** (Health Administration; Health Education; Medicine; Molecular Biology; Nursing; Oncology; Pathology); **Regional Studies** (Cultural Studies; Economics;

Environmental Studies; Political Sciences; Regional Studies; Social Sciences); **veterinary Science** (Veterinary Science)

History: Founded 1949, incorporating Gifu Normal College founded 1875, and Gifu College of Agriculture and Forestry founded 1924. Faculty of Engineering of Gifu Prefectural University attached 1952. Gifu Prefectural College of Medicine attached 1964 as Faculty of Medicine.

Academic year: April to March (April-September; October-March)

Admission requirements: Graduation from high school or equivalent or foreign equivalent, and entrance examination

Fees: Undergraduate, 520,800 for tuition, 282,000 for admission, 17,000 for entrance examination. Graduate, 520,800 for tuition, 282,000 for admission, 30,000 for entrance examination. Research Student, 28,900 per month, 84,600 for admission, 9,800 for entrance examination (Yen)

Main language(s) of instruction: Japanese

Accrediting agency: Ministry of Education, Culture, Sports, Science and Technology (MEXT)

Degrees and diplomas: Hakase (Agriculture; Biology; Environmental Studies; Natural Resources; Veterinary Science)

Student Services: Careers Guidance, Health Services, Canteen, Foreign Studies Centre

Periodicals: Faculty Research Report, Agriculture, Faculty Research Report, Education, Faculty Research Report, Engineering, Faculty Research Report, General Education, Faculty Research Report, Medicine

Academic Staff 2012-2013	MALE	FEMALE	TOTAL
FULL-TIME			835
Student Numbers 2012-2013			
All (Foreign Included)	4845	2553	7398

Last Update: 23-02-2018

Gunma Prefectural College of Health Sciences (GCHS)

323-1 Kamiokicho Maebashi-shi
Gunma 371-0052, Gunma
Tel: +81(27) 235-1211
Fax: +81(27) 235-2501
Website: http://www.gchs.ac.jp
President: Kunio Doi

School

Nursing (Medical Technology; Nursing; Radiology)

Graduate School

Nursing (Medical Technology; Nursing; Radiology)
History: Founded 1992.
Main language(s) of instruction: Japanese

Degrees and diplomas: Gakushi, Shushi
Periodicals: Annual Report

Student Numbers 2013-2014	MALE	FEMALE	TOTAL
All (Foreign Included)			499

Last Update: 04-06-2018

Gunma Prefectural Women's University (GPWU)

1395-1 Kaminote Tamamura
Sawa-gun 370-1193, Gunma
Tel: +81(270) 65-8511
Fax: +81(270) 65-9538
Website: http://www.gpwu.ac.jp
President: Yoshie Kobayashi

Faculty

Arts and Humanities (Aesthetics; Art History; Arts and Humanities; Cultural Studies; English; Japanese; Literature); **International Communication** (Accountancy; Communication Studies; English; Environmental Studies; International Business; International Studies; Marketing; Political Sciences); **Liberal Arts Education** (Arts and Humanities; Education; Literature)

Course/Programme

Teacher Training (Educational Psychology; Pedagogy; Teacher Training)

Graduate School

Graduate Studies (Arts and Humanities; Cultural Studies; English; International Business; Japanese; Literature)
History: Founded 1980
Academic year: April to March
Admission requirements: Graduation from high school or 12 yrs education
Fees: 535,800 per annum (Yen)
Main language(s) of instruction: Japanese
Accrediting agency: Ministry of Education, Culture, Sports, Science and Technology (MEXT)
Student Services: Academic Counselling, Social Counselling, Careers Guidance, Nursery Care, Sports Facilities, Facilities for disabled people, Health Services, Canteen
Periodicals: Bulletin of Gunma Prefectural Women's University

Student Numbers 2012-2013	MALE	FEMALE	TOTAL
All (Foreign Included)			c. 930

Last Update: 02-03-2018

Gunma University

4-2 Aramaki
Maebashi-shi 371-8510, Gunma-Ken
Tel: +81(27) 220-7111, +81(27) 220-7627
Fax: +81(27) 220-7630
Website: http://www.gunma-u.ac.jp
President: Hiroshi Hiratsuka
Tel: +81(27) 220-7000

Faculty

Education (Art Education; Education; Education of the Handicapped; Educational Psychology; Foreign Languages Education; Health Education; Home Economics Education; Humanities and Social Science Education; Mathematics Education; Music Education; Native Language Education; Physical Education; Science Education; Technology Education); **Medicine** (Health Sciences; Laboratory Techniques; Medicine; Nursing; Occupational Therapy; Physical Therapy); **Science and Technology** (Bioengineering; Chemical Engineering; Chemistry; Civil Engineering; Computer Science; Electronic Engineering; Engineering; Environmental Engineering; Mechanical Engineering; Production Engineering); **Social and Information Studies** (Economics; Environmental Studies; Information Management; Information Sciences; Information Technology; Law; Management; Media Studies; Modern Languages; Political Sciences; Social Sciences; Social Studies)

Course/Programme

Handicapped Children Education (*Special Course*) (Education of the Handicapped)

Graduate School

Education (Art Education; Education; Education of the Handicapped; Foreign Languages Education; Health Sciences; Native Language Education; Primary Education; Science Education; Teacher Training)
History: Founded 1949, incorporating Gunma Normal School, founded 1876, Kiryu Technical College, 1915, and Maebashi Medical College, 1943. Responsible to the Ministry of Education, Science, Sports and Culture.
Academic year: April to March (April-September; October-March)
Admission requirements: Graduation from high school or equivalent, and entrance examination
Fees: Tuition: 535,800 per annum; Registration: 282,000; 17,000 for application (Yen)
Main language(s) of instruction: Japanese
Accrediting agency: Ministry of Education, Culture, Sports, Science and Technology (MEXT)
Degrees and diplomas: Hakase (Biomedicine; Chemical Engineering; Computer Science; Electronic Engineering;

Environmental Management; Health Sciences; Medicine; Molecular Biology; Production Engineering)
Student Services: Academic Counselling, Social Counselling, Careers Guidance, Sports Facilities, Language Laboratory, Health Services, Canteen, Foreign Studies Centre

Academic Staff 2013-2014	MALE	FEMALE	TOTAL
FULL-TIME			924
Student Numbers 2013-2014			
All (Foreign Included)	4195	2361	6556
Foreign only			252

Last Update: 23-02-2018

Hamamatsu University School of Medicine

1-20-1 Handayama Higashi-ku
Hamamatsu 431-3192, Shizuoka
Tel: +81(53) 4352-111
Fax: +81(53) 433-7290
Website: http://www.hama-med.ac.jp
President: Hiroyuki Konno

Faculty

Medicine (Anaesthesiology; Anatomy; Biochemistry; Biological and Life Sciences; Biology; Cardiology; Cell Biology; Chemistry; Community Health; Computer Science; Dentistry; Dermatology; Endocrinology; English; Ethics; Forensic Medicine and Dentistry; Gastroenterology; Gynaecology and Obstetrics; Haematology; Health Administration; Health Education; Hepatology; Immunology; Japanese; Laboratory Techniques; Law; Mathematics; Medicine; Molecular Biology; Nephrology; Neurological Therapy; Neurology; Neurosciences; Oncology; Ophthalmology; Orthopaedics; Otorhinolaryngology; Paediatrics; Parasitology; Pathology; Pharmacology; Physics; Physiology; Psychiatry and Mental Health; Psychology; Radiology; Respiratory Therapy; Rheumatology; Social and Preventive Medicine; Surgery; Urology; Virology); **Nursing** (Community Health; Gerontology; Health Sciences; Midwifery; Nursing; Psychiatry and Mental Health)
History: Founded 1974
Academic year: April to March (April-September; October-March)
Admission requirements: Graduation from high school or equivalent or foreign equivalent, and entrance examination
Main language(s) of instruction: Japanese, English
Accrediting agency: Ministry of Education, Culture, Sports, Science and Technology (MEXT)
Degrees and diplomas: Hakase (Medicine)

Academic Staff 2012-2013	MALE	FEMALE	TOTAL
FULL-TIME			c. 323
Student Numbers 2012-2013			
All (Foreign Included)	482	452	934

Last Update: 02-03-2018

Hirosaki University

1 Bunkyo
Hirosaki 036-8560, Aomori
Tel: +81(172) 36-2111
Fax: +81(172) 39-3919
Website: http://www.hirosaki-u.ac.jp
President: Kei Sato

Faculty

Agriculture and Life Sciences (Agricultural Engineering; Agriculture; Agronomy; Biological and Life Sciences; Biology; Biotechnology; Ecology; Environmental Engineering; Environmental Studies; Farm Management; Food Science; Horticulture; Molecular Biology; Natural Resources; Rural Studies); **Education** (Art Education; Continuing Education; Education; Education of the Handicapped; Foreign Languages Education; Health Education; Home Economics Education; Humanities and Social Science Education; Mathematics Education; Music Education; Physical Education; Preschool Education; Science Education; Secondary Education; Special Education; Teacher Training); **Humanities** (Arts and Humanities; Business Administration; Cultural Studies; Economic and Finance Policy; Economics; Information Management; Information Sciences; International Studies; Management; Social Sciences; Social Studies); **Science and Engineering** (Chemistry; Computer Engineering; Electronic Engineering; Engineering; Environmental Studies; Information Technology; Mathematics; Mechanical Engineering; Natural Sciences; Physics)

School

Medicine (Health Sciences; Laboratory Techniques; Medical Technology; Medicine; Nursing; Occupational Therapy)

Graduate School

Agricultural and Life Sciences (Agriculture; Bioengineering; Biological and Life Sciences; Environmental Studies); **Community Studies** (Social and Community Services); **Education** (Curriculum; Education; Health Education); **Health Sciences** (Health Sciences); **Humanities and Social Sciences** (Arts and Humanities; Cultural Studies; Social Sciences); **Medicine** (Anatomy; Biochemistry; Cardiology; Dermatology; Endocrinology; Epidemiology; Forensic Medicine and Dentistry; Gastroenterology; Genetics; Gynaecology and

Obstetrics; Haematology; Laboratory Techniques; Medical Technology; Medicine; Molecular Biology; Neurology; Oncology; Ophthalmology; Orthopaedics; Otorhinolaryngology; Paediatrics; Pathology; Pharmacology; Pharmacy; Physiology; Psychiatry and Mental Health; Social and Preventive Medicine; Surgery; Urology); **Science and Engineering** (Engineering; Natural Sciences; Safety Engineering)

History: Founded 1949 as a new system national university incorporating Hirosaki High School, founded 1920, Aomori Normal School 1943, Young Men's Normal School 1944, Hirosaki College of Medicine 1948, and Aomori College of Medicine.

Academic year: April-March (April-September; October-March)

Admission requirements: Graduation from high school or equivalent or foreign equivalent, and entrance examination

Fees: Tuition 535,800 per annum (Yen)

Main language(s) of instruction: Japanese, English

Accrediting agency: Ministry of Education, Culture, Sports, Science and Technology (MEXT)

Degrees and diplomas: Hakase (Biological and Life Sciences; Environmental Studies; Health Sciences; Horticulture; Medicine; Natural Sciences; Safety Engineering; Social and Community Services)

Periodicals: Faculty Bulletins

Last Update: 23-02-2018

Hiroshima City University (HCU)

3-4-1, Ozuka-Higashi Asa-Minami-Ku
Hiroshima 731-3194
Tel: +81(82) 830-1500, +81(82) 830-1666
Fax: +81(82) 830-1656
Website: http://www.hiroshima-cu.ac.jp
President: Nobuyuki Aoki

Faculty

Arts (Communication Arts; Design; Fine Arts; Media Studies; Painting and Drawing; Sculpture; Textile Design; Visual Arts); **Information Sciences** (Artificial Intelligence; Automation and Control Engineering; Biomedical Engineering; Biotechnology; Computer Engineering; Computer Networks; Electronic Engineering; Information Sciences; Optical Technology; Software Engineering); **International Studies** (Communication Studies; Cultural Studies; International Business; International Relations; International Studies; Modern Languages; Peace and Disarmament; Political Sciences)

Graduate School

Arts (Design; Fine Arts; Painting and Drawing; Sculpture); **Information Sciences** (Artificial Intelligence; Biology;

Chemistry; Computer Engineering; Computer Networks; Information Sciences; Neurosciences; Physics; Telecommunications Engineering); **International Studies** (International Studies)

History: Founded 1994

Main language(s) of instruction: Japanese

Accrediting agency: Ministry of Education, Culture, Sports, Science and Technology (MEXT)

Degrees and diplomas: Hakase (Artificial Intelligence; Biology; Chemistry; Computer Engineering; Design; Fine Arts; Information Sciences; International Studies; Neurosciences; Physics)

Student Services: Sports Facilities, Language Laboratory

Academic Staff 2012-2013	MALE	FEMALE	TOTAL
FULL-TIME			196
Student Numbers 2012-2013			
All (Foreign Included)			2114
Foreign only			72

Last Update: 25-05-2018

Hiroshima University (HU)

1-3-2 Kagamiyama
Higashi-Hiroshima 739-8511, Hiroshima
Tel: +81(824) 22-7111
Fax: +81(824) 24-6020
Website: http://www.hiroshima-u.ac.jp
President: Mitsuo Ochi

Faculty

Applied Biological Sciences (Animal Husbandry; Biological and Life Sciences; Cell Biology; Environmental Studies; Fishery; Food Science; Molecular Biology); **Dentistry** (Dentistry; Health Sciences; Oral Pathology); **Economics** (Administration; Business Administration; Econometrics; Economic History; Economics; Finance; Information Sciences; Management; Social Sciences); **Education** (Continuing Education; Education; Educational Sciences; Foreign Languages Education; Humanities and Social Science Education; Native Language Education; Primary Education; Psychology; Science Education; Teacher Training; Technology Education); **Engineering** (Applied Chemistry; Biotechnology; Chemical Engineering; Computer Engineering; Electrical Engineering; Engineering Management; Environmental Engineering; Mechanical Engineering); **Integrated Arts and Science** (Arts and Humanities; Behavioural Sciences; Biochemistry; Biological and Life Sciences; Chemistry; Comparative Literature; Computer Graphics; Computer Science; Cultural Studies; English; Environmental Studies; French; Geology; German; Information Sciences; Japanese; Korean;

Linguistics; Literature; Mathematics; Mathematics and Computer Science; Modern Languages; Molecular Biology; Natural Sciences; Neurosciences; Organic Chemistry; Pharmacology; Philosophy; Physics; Psychology; Regional Studies; Social Psychology; Social Sciences; Social Work; Sociology; Sports); **Law** (Commercial Law; International Relations; Law; Political Sciences; Private Law; Public Law); **Letters** (Archaeology; Arts and Humanities; Chinese; Cultural Studies; English; European Languages; French; Geography; German; Heritage Preservation; History; Japanese; Modern Languages); **Medicine** (Health Sciences; Medicine; Nursing; Occupational Therapy; Pharmacy; Physical Therapy); **Pharmaceutical Sciences** (Pharmacology; Pharmacy); **Science** (Astronomy and Space Science; Biological and Life Sciences; Biology; Chemistry; Earth Sciences; Mathematics; Physics)

Course/Programme

Special Education (*Major*) (Special Education)

Institute

Advanced Materials Research (Materials Engineering); **Foreign Language Research and Education** (Foreign Languages Education; Modern Languages); **Peace Science** (Peace and Disarmament); **Sports Sciences** (Sports); **Sustainable Sciences and Development** (Development Studies; Environmental Studies)

Centre

Astrophysical Science (*Hiroshima*) (Astrophysics); **Beijing Research**; **Collaborative Research and Community Cooperation** (Engineering Management); **Contemporary India Studies** (South Asian Studies); **Environmental Research and Management** (Environmental Management; Environmental Studies); **Information Media** (Information Sciences; Media Studies); **Natural Science** (*for Basic Research and Development*) (Natural Sciences); **Study of International Cooperation in Education** (Education; Educational Testing and Evaluation; International and Comparative Education); **Synchrotron Radiation** (*Hiroshima*) (Microwaves)

Graduate School

Advanced Science of Matter (Applied Physics; Biotechnology; Molecular Biology); **Biomedical and Health Sciences** (Biomedicine; Dentistry; Health Sciences; Medicine; Oral Pathology; Pharmacy; Physics; Radiology); **Biosphere Sciences** (Environmental Management; Environmental Studies; Food Science; Marine Biology; Molecular Biology; Zoology); **Education** (Art Education; Continuing Education; Curriculum; Education; Educational Research; Educational Sciences; Foreign Languages Education; Higher Education; Humanities and Social Science Education; Modern Languages; Psychology; Science Education; Social Studies;

Special Education; Technology Education); **Engineering** (Applied Chemistry; Architecture; Automation and Control Engineering; Chemical Engineering; Civil Engineering; Computer Science; Energy Engineering; Engineering; Environmental Engineering; Information Technology; Mechanical Engineering; Mechanics; Structural Architecture; Transport Engineering); **Integrated Arts and Sciences** (Anthropology; Behavioural Sciences; Comparative Literature; Computer Networks; Computer Science; Cultural Studies; Environmental Studies; French; Gender Studies; Geography; Geology; History; Information Sciences; Italian; Korean; Literature; Media Studies; New Testament; Optics; Physics; Regional Studies; Sociology); **International Development and Cooperation** (Cultural Studies; Development Studies; Peace and Disarmament; Regional Planning; Regional Studies); **Law** (Administrative Law; Civil Law; Commercial Law; Constitutional Law; Criminal Law; Fiscal Law; Law; Public Law); **Letters** (Archaeology; Chinese; Cultural Studies; English; European Languages; French; Geography; German; Heritage Preservation; History; Japanese; Linguistics; Literature; Philosophy); **Science** (Astronomy and Space Science; Biological and Life Sciences; Chemistry; Earth Sciences; Mathematics; Natural Sciences; Physics); **Social Sciences** (Economics; Engineering; Law; Management; Political Sciences; Social Sciences; Social Studies)

Research Division

Archaeology (Archaeology); **Higher Education** (Higher Education); **Hiroshima-University STARC IGFET Model** (*HiSIM*) (Electronic Engineering); **Nano Devices and Bio Systems** (Nanotechnology; Systems Analysis); **Radiation Biology and Medicine** (Biology; Environmental Studies; Molecular Biology; Nuclear Engineering; Social and Preventive Medicine)

Further information: Also Kasumi Campus, Higashi-Senda Campus; Hiroshima University Hospital; 11 attached schools

History: Founded 1949, incorporating an existing University and seven colleges. Hiroshima Higher Normal School founded in 1902 and the former Hiroshima University in 1929. Postgraduate courses and Faculty of Medicine established 1953.

Academic year: April to March (April-September; October-March)

Admission requirements: Graduation from high school or recognized equivalent

Fees: Tuition and fees, 535,800 per annum (Yen)

Main language(s) of instruction: Japanese, English

Accrediting agency: Ministry of Education, Culture, Sports, Science and Technology (MEXT)

Degrees and diplomas: Hakase (Arts and Humanities; Biotechnology; Development Studies; Education; Electronic Engineering; Engineering; Environmental Studies; Management; Social Sciences)

Student Services: Health Services, Canteen

Periodicals: Annual Report of Research Centre for Regional Geography, Bulletin of the Faculty of Education-Hiroshima University, Bulletin of the Faculty of Engineering, Bulletin of the Hiroshima University Faculty of School Education, Bulletin of the Institute for Cultural Studies of the Seto Inland Sea, Hiroshima Economic Review, Hiroshima Economic Studies, Hiroshima Journal of Mathematics Education, Hiroshima Journal of Medical Sciences, Hiroshima Law Journal, Hiroshima Mathematical Journal, Hiroshima Peace Science, Hiroshima University Studies-Faculty of Letters, Journal of International Cooperation in Education, Journal of International Development and Cooperation, Journal of Science of the Hiroshima University, Journal of the Faculty of Applied Biological Science, Proceedings of the Research Institute for Radiation Biology and Medicine, Reports of the Miyajima Natural Botanical Garden (Miyajima Shizen Shokubutsu Jikkensho Ronbunshu, Japanese and English), Science Reports, Studies in Area Culture, Studies in Culture and Humanities, Studies in Language and Culture, Studies in Social Sciences, The Economic Studies, The Journal of Hiroshima University Dental Society

Academic Staff 2012-2013	MALE	FEMALE	TOTAL
FULL-TIME			c. 1770
Student Numbers 2012-2013			
All (Foreign Included)			15261
Foreign only			1006

Last Update: 23-02-2018

Hitotsubashi University

2-1 Naka
Kunitachi 186-8601, Tokyo
Tel: +81(42) 580-8000
Fax: +81(42) 580-8006
Website: http://www.hit-u.ac.jp
President: Koichi Tadenuma
Tel: +81(42) 580-8001

Faculty

Commerce and Management (Business and Commerce; Management); **Economics** (Economics); **Law** (Law); **Social Sciences** (Anthropology; Arts and Humanities; Geography (Human); History; Political Sciences; Social Policy; Social Psychology; Social Sciences; Social Studies; Sociology)

Course/Programme

Executive Studies (Economic and Finance Policy; Economics); **Japanese Language Education** (Japanese)

Institute

Economic Research (Economics; International Economics); **Innovation Research** (Business Administration; Management)

Centre

Research and Development for Higher Education (Higher Education)

Graduate School

Commerce and Management (Business Administration; Business and Commerce; Management); **Economics** (Economics); **International and Public Policy** (Government; International Economics; International Relations; Political Sciences; Public Law); **International Corporate Strategy** (Business Administration; Economics; Finance; International Economics; International Relations; Law; Leadership; Management; Political Sciences; Taxation); **Language and Society** (Arts and Humanities; Asian Studies; Cultural Studies; English; Foreign Languages Education; History; Japanese; Linguistics; Modern Languages; Museum Management; Philosophy; Social Studies); **Law** (Law); **Social Sciences** (Arts and Humanities; Cultural Studies; History; International Studies; Philosophy; Political Sciences; Social Sciences; Social Studies; Sociology)

History: Founded 1875 as a provate Commercial Training School, then converted into Tokyo University of Commerce 1920. Present title acquired 1949 following university reorganization.

Academic year: April to March (April-September; October-March)

Admission requirements: Graduation from high school or equivalent and entrance examination

Fees: Registration fee, 282,000 (in first year only); tuition, 535,800 per annum. For Law Schhool same registration fee, but tuition fee is 804,000 per annum (Yen)

Main language(s) of instruction: Japanese, English

Accrediting agency: Ministry of Education, Culture, Sports, Science and Technology (MEXT)

Degrees and diplomas: Hakase (Business Administration; Commercial Law; Economics; Finance; International Business; Law; Modern Languages; Social Sciences)

Student Services: Academic Counselling, Social Counselling, Careers Guidance, Nursery Care, Cultural Activities, Sports Facilities, Language Laboratory, Facilities for disabled people, Health Services, Canteen, Foreign Studies Centre

Periodicals: Center for Student Exchange Journal/ Hitotsubashi Daigaku Ryugakusei Center Kiyou, Cultura Philologia/Gengo Bunka, Economic Research Series/Oubun Keizai Kenkyu Sousho, Economic Review/Keizai Kenkyu, Gengo Shakai, Hitotsubashi Annual of Sport Studies, Hitotsubashi Bulletin of Social Sciences/Hitotsubashi Shakai Kagaku, Hitotsubashi Business Review, Hitotsubashi Hogaku/The Hitotsubashi Journal of Law and International

Studies, Hitotsubashi Journal of Arts and Sciences, Hitotsubashi Journal of Commerce and Management, Hitotsubashi Journal of Economics, Hitotsubashi Journal of Law and Politics, Hitotsubashi Journal of Social Studies, Hitotsubashi Keizaigaku, Hitotsubashi Review of Commerce and Management/Hitotsubashi Shogaku Ronsou, HQ, IER Discussion Paper Series, Jinbun Shizen Kenkyu, Keizai Kenkyu Sousho, Working Paper of Graduate School of Commerce and Management, Working Paper Series (for finance), Working Paper Series (for studies of Japanese companies)

Academic Staff 2013-2014	MALE	FEMALE	TOTAL
FULL-TIME			794
STAFF WITH DOCTORATE			
FULL-TIME	190	35	225
Student Numbers 2013-2014			
All (Foreign Included)	4512	1880	6392
Foreign only	299	390	689

Last Update: 23-02-2018

Hokkaido University (HOKUDAI)

Nishi 5 Kita 8, Kita-ku
Sapporo-shi 060-0808, Hokkaido
Tel: +81(11) 716-2111, +81(11) 706-8027
Fax: +81(11) 706-8036
Website: http://www.hokudai.ac.jp
President: Toyoharu Nawa

Faculty

Agriculture (Agricultural Economics; Agriculture; Agrobiology; Animal Husbandry; Biological and Life Sciences; Chemistry; Environmental Engineering; Forestry); **Engineering** (Applied Chemistry; Applied Physics; Architecture; Artificial Intelligence; Bioengineering; Civil Engineering; Computer Networks; Computer Science; Electronic Engineering; Engineering; Environmental Engineering; Information Sciences; Information Technology; Materials Engineering; Mechanical Engineering; Natural Resources); **Letters** (Arts and Humanities; Modern Languages)

School

Dental Medicine (Dental Technology; Dentistry; Oral Pathology; Orthodontics; Rehabilitation and Therapy); **Economics and Business Administration** (Accountancy; Business Administration; Economics; Management); **Education** (Education); **Fisheries Sciences** (Fishery); **Law** (Law); **Medicine** (Medicine); **Pharmaceutical Sciences and Pharmacy** (Pharmacology; Pharmacy); **Science** (Astronomy and Space Science; Biological and Life Sciences; Chemistry; Earth Sciences; Mathematics; Mathematics and Computer Science; Natural Sciences; Physics); **Veterinary Medicine** (Veterinary Science)

Institute

Genetic Medicine (Genetics; Medicine); **Isotope Science** (*Central*) (Chemistry); **Low Temperature Science** (Meteorology; Physics)

Centre

Education and Research for Topological Science and Technology (Mathematics and Computer Science; Technology); **Environmental and Health Sciences** (Environmental Studies; Health Sciences); **Field Science Centre for Northern Biosphere** (Environmental Studies); **Information Initiative Centre** (Computer Science; Information Technology; Multimedia); **Translational Research** (Biological and Life Sciences; Genetics; Medicine)

Laboratory

Meme Media Laboratory (Media Studies; Robotics; Software Engineering)

Graduate School

Agriculture (Agricultural Economics; Agriculture; Agronomy; Animal Husbandry; Applied Chemistry; Biological and Life Sciences; Biology; Botany; Ecology; Environmental Studies; Food Science; Forest Products; Forestry; Horticulture; Molecular Biology); **Chemical Sciences and Engineering** (Biochemistry; Bioengineering; Chemical Engineering; Chemistry; Materials Engineering; Molecular Biology); **Dental Medicine** (Anaesthesiology; Anatomy; Dental Technology; Dentistry; Gerontology; Oral Pathology; Orthodontics; Periodontics; Pharmacology; Physiology; Radiology; Rehabilitation and Therapy; Social and Preventive Medicine; Stomatology; Surgery); **Economics and Business Administration** (Accountancy; Business Administration; Economics; Management); **Education** (Clinical Psychology; Continuing Education; Education; Educational Psychology; Educational Sciences; Health Education; Pedagogy; Physical Education; Social Sciences); **Engineering** (Applied Physics; Architectural and Environmental Design; Energy Engineering; Engineering; Environmental Engineering; Environmental Management; Environmental Studies; Materials Engineering; Mechanical Engineering; Natural Resources; Structural Architecture); **Environmental Science** (Earth Sciences; Environmental Management; Environmental Studies); **Fisheries Sciences** (Aquaculture; Biology; Biotechnology; Environmental Management; Environmental Studies; Fishery; Food Science; Food Technology; Genetics; Marine Biology; Microbiology; Natural Resources; Safety Engineering); **Health**

Sciences (Health Sciences); **Information Science and Technology** (Bioengineering; Computer Engineering; Computer Networks; Computer Science; Electronic Engineering; Information Sciences; Information Technology; Systems Analysis); **International Media, Communication and Tourism Studies** (Communication Studies; Media Studies; Tourism); **Law** (Law); **Letters** (Art History; Arts and Humanities; Behavioural Sciences; Cultural Studies; Ethics; History; Linguistics; Literature; Philosophy; Psychology; Regional Studies; Religious Studies; Sociology); **Life Science** (Biological and Life Sciences; Biomedicine; Pharmacology); **Medicine** (Anaesthesiology; Anatomy; Applied Chemistry; Biochemistry; Cardiology; Cell Biology; Dermatology; Embryology and Reproduction Biology; Endocrinology; Epidemiology; Forensic Medicine and Dentistry; Gastroenterology; Gynaecology and Obstetrics; Haematology; Histology; Immunology; Medical Technology; Medicine; Microbiology; Molecular Biology; Nephrology; Neurological Therapy; Neurology; Neurosciences; Oncology; Ophthalmology; Orthopaedics; Otorhinolaryngology; Paediatrics; Pathology; Pharmacology; Physiology; Plastic Surgery; Psychiatry and Mental Health; Public Health; Radiology; Rehabilitation and Therapy; Respiratory Therapy; Rheumatology; Social and Preventive Medicine; Surgery); **Pharmaceutical Sciences and Pharmacy** (Applied Chemistry; Biochemistry; Biophysics; Genetics; Microbiology; Molecular Biology; Organic Chemistry; Pharmacology; Pharmacy; Toxicology); **Public Policy** (International Relations; Political Sciences; Public Administration); **Science** (Astronomy and Space Science; Biological and Life Sciences; Communication Studies; Earth Sciences; Mathematics; Natural Sciences; Physics; Seismology); **Veterinary Medicine** (Veterinary Science)

Research Division

Advanced Tourism Studies (Tourism); **Ainu and Indigenous Studies** (Indigenous Studies); **Catalysis** (Chemistry); **Creative Research Institution 'Sousei'** (*CRIS*) (Natural Sciences; Technology); **Electronic Science** (Electronic Engineering); **Environmental Nano and Bio Engineering** (Bioengineering; Environmental Engineering; Nanotechnology); **Experimental Research in Social Sciences** (Social Sciences); **Hokkaido University Archives**; **Information Law and Policy** (Information Sciences; Law); **Integrated Quantum Electronics** (Electronic Engineering); **Integrative Mathematics** (Mathematics); **Language Learning** (Cultural Studies; Modern Languages); **Research and Education Centre for Brain Science** (Behavioural Sciences; Cognitive Sciences; Neurology); **Slavic Studies** (Slavic Languages); **Sustainability Science** (Environmental Engineering); **Zoonosis Control** (Zoology)

Further information: Also Hakodate Campus; Medical, Dental, Veterinary Hospitals; Training Ships

History: Founded 1876 as school, became Sapporo Agricultural College 1876. Became part of Tohuku Imperial University in Sendai 1907-1918. Renamed Hokkaido University 1947. Acquired present status of National University Corporation Hokkaido University 2004.

Academic year: April to March (April-September; October-March)

Admission requirements: Graduation from high school or recognized equivalent (Daiken), and entrance examination (Center Shiken)

Fees: Tuition, 535,800 per annum, except Law School, 804,000 per annum (Yen)

Main language(s) of instruction: Japanese, English

Accrediting agency: Ministry of Education, Culture, Sports, Science and Technology (MEXT)

Degrees and diplomas: Gakushi (Agriculture; Arts and Humanities; Business and Commerce; Dentistry; Economics; Education; Engineering; Fishery; International Relations; Japanese; Law; Mathematics and Computer Science; Medicine; Natural Sciences; Pharmacology; Pharmacy; Veterinary Science), Shushi (Agriculture; Arts and Humanities; Biological and Life Sciences; Biomedical Engineering; Business Administration; Business and Commerce; Chemical Engineering; Chemistry; Dentistry; Earth Sciences; Economics; Education; Engineering; Environmental Studies; Fishery; Health Sciences; Information Sciences; Law; Mass Communication; Mathematics and Computer Science; Media Studies; Medicine; Natural Sciences; Pharmacy; Public Administration; Technology; Tourism; Veterinary Science), Hakase (Agriculture; Arts and Humanities; Biological and Life Sciences; Biomedical Engineering; Biomedicine; Business Administration; Business and Commerce; Chemical Engineering; Chemistry; Communication Arts; Dentistry; Economics; Education; Engineering; Environmental Engineering; Environmental Studies; Fishery; Food Science; Health Sciences; Information Sciences; Information Technology; Law; Mathematics and Computer Science; Media Studies; Medicine; Natural Sciences; Pharmacology; Pharmacy; Tourism; Veterinary Science)

Student Services: Academic Counselling, Social Counselling, Careers Guidance, Cultural Activities, Sports Facilities, Language Laboratory, Health Services, Canteen, Foreign Studies Centre

Periodicals: A Brief Sketch of Hokkaido University, Hokkaido University Newsletter, Hokudai Jiho, Profile of Hokkaido University

Academic Staff 2017-2018	MALE	FEMALE	TOTAL
FULL-TIME			2070
Student Numbers 2017-2018			
All (Foreign Included)			18273

Last Update: 23-02-2018

Hokkaido University of Education (HUE)

5-3-1 Ainosato, Kita-ku
Sapporo-shi 002-8501, Hokkaido
Tel: +81(11) 778-0265
Fax: +81(11) 778-0634
Website: http://www.hokkyodai.ac.jp
President: Kenji Honma

Faculty

Education (Art Education; Art Management; Art Therapy; Cultural Studies; Curriculum; Design; Development Studies; Education; English; Environmental Studies; Fine Arts; Handicrafts; Health Education; Home Economics Education; Humanities and Social Science Education; Japanese; Mathematics Education; Media Studies; Music Education; Music Theory and Composition; Musical Instruments; Nursing; Painting and Drawing; Physical Education; Science Education; Sculpture; Special Education; Sports; Teacher Training; Technology Education)

Graduate School

Education (Art Education; Clinical Psychology; Curriculum; Education; Foreign Languages Education; Health Education; Humanities and Social Science Education; Mathematics Education; Music Education; Native Language Education; Physical Education; Science Education; Teacher Training; Technology Education; Vocational Education)
Further information: Also campuses in Asahikawa, Kushiro, Hakodate and Iwamizawa
History: Founded 1949.
Academic year: April to March (April-September; October-March)
Admission requirements: Graduation from high school and entrance examination
Main language(s) of instruction: Japanese
Degrees and diplomas: Shushi (Education). Also professional degree programmes in Teacher training.
Periodicals: Bulletin of Rural Education Institute, Reports of the Taisetsusan Institute of Science, Studies of Teaching Methods

Academic Staff 2012-2013	MALE	FEMALE	TOTAL
FULL-TIME			788
Student Numbers 2012-2013			
All (Foreign Included)	2511	3129	5640

Last Update: 23-02-2018

Hyogo University of Teacher Education

942-1 Shimokume, Yashiro-cho
Kato 673-1494, Hyogo
Tel: +81(795) 44-2011

Fax: +81(795) 44-2009
Website: http://www.hyogo-u.ac.jp
President: Fukuda Mitsuhiro

Faculty

School Education (Art Education; Child Care and Development; Education; Educational Psychology; Health Education; Home Economics; Humanities and Social Science Education; Information Sciences; Mathematics Education; Music Education; Native Language Education; Preschool Education; Primary Education; Science Education; Technology Education)

Graduate School

Education (Art Education; Behavioural Sciences; Clinical Psychology; Communication Studies; Cultural Studies; Curriculum; Development Studies; Education; Education of the Handicapped; Educational Administration; Educational and Student Counselling; Educational Psychology; Educational Sciences; English; Foreign Languages Education; Health Education; Home Economics; Humanities and Social Science Education; Information Sciences; Japanese; Leadership; Mathematics Education; Music Education; Primary Education; Science Education; Special Education; Teacher Training; Technology Education)
History: Founded 1978
Academic year: April to March (April-September; October-March)
Main language(s) of instruction: Japanese
Accrediting agency: Ministry of Education, Culture, Sports, Science and Technology (MEXT)
Degrees and diplomas: Shushi (Development Studies; Education; Educational Sciences; Special Education), Hakase (Education; Primary Education)
Student Services: Academic Counselling, Social Counselling, Careers Guidance, Sports Facilities, Language Laboratory, Health Services, Canteen, Foreign Studies Centre

Academic Staff 2012-2013	MALE	FEMALE	TOTAL
FULL-TIME	132	32	164
Student Numbers 2012-2013			
All (Foreign Included)	680	893	1573
Foreign only			50

Last Update: 23-02-2018

Ibaraki Prefectural University of Health Sciences (IPU)

4669-2 Ami Ami-machi Inashiki-gun
Ibaraki 300-0394, Osaka
Tel: +81(298) 88-4000

Fax: +81(298) 40-2301
Website: http://www.ipu.ac.jp
President: Hiroshi Nagata

Department/Division
Nursing (Nursing); **Occupational Therapy** (Occupational Therapy); **Physical Therapy** (Physical Therapy); **Radiological Sciences** (Radiology; Rehabilitation and Therapy)

Centre
Humanities and Sciences (Arts and Humanities; English; Information Sciences; Modern Languages; Natural Sciences; Philosophy of Education; Physical Education; Social Studies); **Medical Sciences** (Anaesthesiology; Anatomy; Biochemistry; Histology; Hygiene; Medicine; Microbiology; Neurology; Orthopaedics; Paediatrics; Pathology; Psychiatry and Mental Health; Public Health; Social and Preventive Medicine)

Graduate School
Health Sciences (Health Sciences; Nursing; Occupational Therapy; Physical Therapy; Radiology)
History: Founded 1995
Main language(s) of instruction: Japanese
Accrediting agency: Ministry of Education, Culture, Sports, Science and Technology (MEXT)
Degrees and diplomas: Shushi (Health Sciences; Nursing; Occupational Therapy; Physical Therapy; Radiology), Hakase (Health Sciences)
Student Services: Sports Facilities
Last Update: 02-03-2018

Ibaraki University

2-1-1 Bunkyo
Mito-shi 310-8512, Ibaraki
Tel: +81(29) 228-8600
Fax: +81(29) 228-8019
Website: http://www.ibaraki.ac.jp
President: Nobuo Mimura
Tel: +81(29) 228-8002
Director and Vice President: Hiroyuki Ohta

College
Agriculture (Agriculture; Animal Husbandry; Biological and Life Sciences; Biotechnology; Crop Production; Environmental Studies; Farm Management; Food Science; Horticulture; Information Technology; Molecular Biology; Natural Resources; Regional Studies; Social Sciences); **Education** (Cultural Studies; Education; Environmental Studies; Information Sciences; Nursing; Physical Education; Primary Education; Secondary Education; Social Studies; Special Education; Teacher Training); **Engineering** (Applied Chemistry; Artificial Intelligence; Biochemistry; Bioengineering; Civil Engineering; Computer Science; Electrical and Electronic Engineering; Electronic Engineering; Energy Engineering; Engineering; Environmental Studies; Information Sciences; Information Technology; Materials Engineering; Mechanical Engineering; Media Studies; Molecular Biology; Nanotechnology; Telecommunications Engineering; Town Planning; Welfare and Protective Services); **Humanities** (Arts and Humanities; Communication Studies; Economics; Government; Management; Political Sciences; Public Administration; Social Sciences; Welfare and Protective Services); **Science** (Biology; Chemistry; Earth Sciences; Environmental Studies; Mathematics; Natural Sciences; Physics)

Course/Programme
Special Support Education (*Advanced*) (Education; Education of the Handicapped; Physiology; Psychology; Special Education)

Institute
Arts and Culture (*Izura*) (Cultural Studies; Fine Arts); **Global Change Adaptation Science** (Environmental Studies)

Centre
Astronomy (Astronomy and Space Science); **Instrumental Analysis** (Measurement and Precision Engineering); **Water Environment Studies** (Environmental Studies; Water Science)

Graduate School
Agricultural Sciences (*United*) (Agricultural Economics; Agricultural Engineering; Agricultural Management; Agriculture; Anatomy; Animal Husbandry; Biochemistry; Biological and Life Sciences; Crop Production; Ecology; Environmental Engineering; Environmental Management; Food Science; Genetics; Geology; Natural Resources; Physiology); **Agriculture** (Agriculture; Animal Husbandry; Biological and Life Sciences; Biotechnology; Chemistry; Ecology; Environmental Management; Environmental Studies; Farm Management; Food Science; Natural Resources; Regional Studies); **Education** (Clinical Psychology; Economics; Education; Education of the Handicapped; Fine Arts; Health Education; Linguistics; Mathematics; Nursing; Physical Education; Physiology; Primary Education; Psychology; Social Sciences; Special Education; Technology; Vocational Education); **Humanities** (Administration; Anthropology; Archaeology; Art History; Arts and Humanities; Chinese; Communication Studies; Cultural Studies; Economics; English; French; Geography; German; Grammar; Heritage Preservation; History; Japanese; Law; Linguistics; Literature; Management; Media Studies; Philosophy; Psychology; Public Administration; Regional Studies; Social

Sciences; Sociology); **Science and Engineering** (Artificial Intelligence; Automation and Control Engineering; Biological and Life Sciences; Biology; Chemistry; Civil Engineering; Computer Science; Earth Sciences; Electrical and Electronic Engineering; Electronic Engineering; Energy Engineering; Engineering; Environmental Studies; Industrial Engineering; Information Sciences; Information Technology; Laser Engineering; Machine Building; Materials Engineering; Mathematics and Computer Science; Measurement and Precision Engineering; Mechanical Engineering; Molecular Biology; Multimedia; Natural Sciences; Nuclear Engineering; Optical Technology; Physics; Power Engineering; Production Engineering; Telecommunications Engineering; Town Planning)

Research Division

Applied Atomic Sciences (*Frontier*) (Atomic and Molecular Physics); **Gene** (Genetics)
Further information: Also Hitachi and Ami campuses
History: Founded 1949
Academic year: April to March (April-September; October-March)
Admission requirements: Graduation from high school or recognized equivalent, and entrance examination
Main language(s) of instruction: Japanese
Accrediting agency: Ministry of Education, Culture, Sports, Science and Technology
Degrees and diplomas: Shushi (Computer Science; Electrical and Electronic Engineering; Information Sciences; Materials Engineering; Mechanical Engineering; Media Studies; Molecular Biology; Natural Sciences; Telecommunications Engineering; Town Planning), Hakase (Agriculture; Environmental Studies; Industrial Engineering; Information Sciences; Information Technology; Laser Engineering; Natural Sciences; Physics)
Student Services: Academic Counselling, Careers Guidance, Nursery Care, Sports Facilities, Health Services, Canteen, Foreign Studies Centre

Academic Staff 2013-2014	MALE	FEMALE	TOTAL
FULL-TIME			603
Student Numbers 2013-2014			
All (Foreign Included)			8249
Foreign only			293

Last Update: 23-02-2018

Institute of Advanced Media Arts and Sciences (IAMAS)

3-95 Ryoke-cho
Ogaki-shi 503-0014, Gifu
Tel: +81(584) 75-6600, +81(584) 75-6641
Fax: +81(584) 75-6637
Website: http://www.iamas.ac.jp
President: Masahiro Miwa

Department/Division

Media Creation (Cultural Studies; Design; Fine Arts; Information Sciences; Information Technology; Media Studies; Multimedia)
History: Founded 2001. Part of IAMAS with the International Academy of Media Arts and Sciences
Fees: Tuition, 535,800 per annum (Yen)
Main language(s) of instruction: Japanese
Accrediting agency: Ministry of Education, Culture, Sports, Science and Technology (MEXT)
Degrees and diplomas: Shushi (Media Studies)

Academic Staff 2012-2013	MALE	FEMALE	TOTAL
FULL-TIME			17
PART-TIME			10

Last Update: 02-03-2018

Ishikawa Prefectural Nursing University (IPNU)

1-1 Gakuendai Kahoku
Ishikawa 929-1210
Tel: +81(76) 281-8300
Fax: +81(76) 281-8319
Website: http://www.ishikawa-nu.ac.jp
President: Kazuko Ishigaki

Faculty

Nursing (Arts and Humanities; Child Care and Development; Community Health; Education; Environmental Studies; Gerontology; Health Sciences; Information Sciences; Information Technology; International Studies; Natural Sciences; Nursing; Psychiatry and Mental Health; Social Sciences)

Graduate School

Nursing (Child Care and Development; Community Health; Gerontology; Health Administration; Health Sciences; Nursing)
History: Founded 2000
Main language(s) of instruction: Japanese
Accrediting agency: Ministry of Education, Culture, Sports, Science and Technology (MEXT)
Degrees and diplomas: Shushi (Nursing), Hakase (Nursing)
Student Services: Sports Facilities, Canteen

Academic Staff 2013-2014	MALE	FEMALE	TOTAL
FULL-TIME	45	36	81
Student Numbers 2013-2014			
All (Foreign Included)	25	366	391

Last Update: 02-03-2018

Ishikawa Prefectural University

1-308, Suematsu
Nonoichi 921-8836, Ishikawa
Tel: +81(76) 227-7220
Fax: +81(76) 227-7410
Website: http://www.ishikawa-pu.ac.jp
President: Hidehiko Kumagai

Faculty

Bioresources and Environmental Sciences (Animal Husbandry; Biochemistry; Biological and Life Sciences; Crop Production; Ecology; Environmental Studies; Food Science; Food Technology; Horticulture; Molecular Biology; Natural Resources; Plant and Crop Protection; Safety Engineering; Soil Management; Soil Science; Water Management)

Centre

Liberal Arts Education (Arts and Humanities; Biology; Chemistry; Computer Science; Constitutional Law; Curriculum; Earth Sciences; Economics; Education; Educational and Student Counselling; Educational Psychology; English; Health Sciences; History; Information Technology; Inorganic Chemistry; Law; Literature; Mathematics; Natural Sciences; Organic Chemistry; Pedagogy; Philosophy; Physics; Psychology; Sociology; Sports; Statistics; Teacher Training)

Graduate School

Bioresources and Environmental Sciences (Agriculture; Biological and Life Sciences; Biotechnology; Environmental Studies; Food Science; Food Technology; Horticulture; Microbiology; Natural Resources; Safety Engineering)

Research Division

Bioresources and Biotechnology (Biological and Life Sciences; Biotechnology; Environmental Studies; Food Science; Genetics; Horticulture; Natural Resources)
History: Founded 1971. Acquired present status and title 2011
Fees: Admission fee, 463,000; Tuition fee, 535,800 per annum
Main language(s) of instruction: Japanese
Accrediting agency: Ministry of Education, Culture, Sports, Science and Technology (MEXT)

Degrees and diplomas: Shushi (Agriculture; Biological and Life Sciences; Biotechnology; Environmental Studies; Food Science; Microbiology), Hakase (Agriculture; Biological and Life Sciences; Biotechnology; Environmental Studies)
Student Services: Sports Facilities, Canteen
Last Update: 02-03-2018

Iwate Prefectural University

152-52 Takizawa-aza-Sugo Takizawa
Iwate-gun 020-0173, Iwate
Tel: +81(019) 694-2000
Fax: +81(019) 694-2001
Website: http://www.iwate-pu.ac.jp
President: Atsuto Suzuki

Faculty

Nursing (Nursing); **Policy Studies** (Political Sciences; Social Studies); **Social Welfare** (Administration; Social and Community Services; Social Psychology; Social Welfare; Social Work); **Software and Information Science** (Information Sciences; Software Engineering)

College

Miyako College (Business Administration; Information Sciences; Management); **Morioka Junior College** (Biological and Life Sciences; Cultural Studies; Food Science; International Studies; Nutrition)

Centre

Liberal Arts Education and Research (Arts and Humanities)

Graduate School

Nursing (Nursing); **Policy Studies** (Political Sciences); **Social Welfare** (Social Welfare); **Software and Information Science** (Information Sciences; Software Engineering)
Further information: Also Miyako Campus, Aiina Campus
History: Founded 1998.
Main language(s) of instruction: Japanese
Accrediting agency: Ministry of Education, Culture, Sports, Science and Technology (MEXT)
Degrees and diplomas: Gakushi (Computer Science; Information Sciences; Nursing; Social Welfare), Shushi (Information Sciences; Nursing; Political Sciences; Social Welfare; Software Engineering), Hakase (Information Sciences; Nursing; Social Welfare; Software Engineering)
Student Services: Sports Facilities

Academic Staff 2012-2013	MALE	FEMALE	TOTAL
FULL-TIME			215

Last Update: 27-03-2018

Iwate University

3-18-8 Ueda
Morioka-shi 020-8550, Iwate
Tel: +81(19) 621-6000
Fax: +81(19) 621-6065
Website: http://www.iwate-u.ac.jp
President: Ikura Iwabuchi

Faculty

Agriculture (Agriculture; Analytical Chemistry; Animal Husbandry; Arts and Humanities; Biochemistry; Biological and Life Sciences; Crop Production; Entomology; Environmental Management; Environmental Studies; Farm Management; Food Science; Forestry; Fruit Production; Harvest Technology; Health Sciences; Horticulture; Laboratory Techniques; Microbiology; Natural Resources; Nutrition; Organic Chemistry; Plant and Crop Protection; Soil Science; Vegetable Production; Water Science; Wildlife; Zoology); **Education** (Art Education; Art History; Conducting; Continuing Education; Design; Education; Education of the Handicapped; Educational Psychology; English; Fine Arts; Foreign Languages Education; Japanese; Music; Music Theory and Composition; Musical Instruments; Performing Arts; Physical Education; Psychology; Singing; Special Education; Sports; Teacher Training; Writing); **Engineering** (Analytical Chemistry; Artificial Intelligence; Bioengineering; Biotechnology; Cell Biology; Chemistry; Civil Engineering; Computer Engineering; Computer Networks; Computer Science; Construction Engineering; Electrical and Electronic Engineering; Electrical Engineering; Electronic Engineering; Energy Engineering; Engineering; Environmental Engineering; Information Sciences; Information Technology; Inorganic Chemistry; Landscape Architecture; Materials Engineering; Mechanical Engineering; Media Studies; Molecular Biology; Organic Chemistry; Physical Chemistry; Robotics; Safety Engineering; Transport and Communications; Welfare and Protective Services); **Humanities and Social Sciences** (Administrative Law; Agricultural Economics; Archaeology; Arts and Humanities; Asian Studies; Behavioural Sciences; Chinese; Civil Law; Clinical Psychology; Cognitive Sciences; Commercial Law; Comparative Literature; Computer Engineering; Computer Networks; Constitutional Law; Criminal Law; Cultural Studies; Ecology; Econometrics; Economics; Environmental Studies; Ethnology; European Languages; Finance; Fiscal Law; French; Gender Studies; German; Information Sciences; Information Technology; International Economics; International Law; Japanese; Labour Law; Law; Linguistics; Literature; Management; Modern Languages; Political Sciences; Psychology; Social Psychology; Social Sciences; Statistics; Translation and Interpretation; Western European Studies)

Graduate School

Agricultural Sciences (*United*) (Agriculture; Bioengineering; Biological and Life Sciences; Biology; Forestry; Natural Resources); **Agriculture** (Agriculture; Animal Husbandry; Biochemistry; Bioengineering; Biological and Life Sciences; Environmental Management; Environmental Studies; Food Science; Forestry; Health Sciences; Natural Resources; Plant and Crop Protection; Regional Planning); **Education** (Education; Educational Sciences; English; Fine Arts; Health Sciences; Mathematics; Modern Languages; Music; Natural Sciences; Physical Education; Social Studies; Special Education); **Engineering** (Aeronautical and Aerospace Engineering; Artificial Intelligence; Biochemistry; Bioengineering; Biological and Life Sciences; Biotechnology; Chemistry; Civil Engineering; Computer Engineering; Computer Science; Construction Engineering; Design; Electrical and Electronic Engineering; Electrical Engineering; Electronic Engineering; Energy Engineering; Engineering; Environmental Engineering; Environmental Management; Information Sciences; Information Technology; Inorganic Chemistry; Materials Engineering; Mechanical Engineering; Media Studies; Metal Techniques; Metallurgical Engineering; Molecular Biology; Organic Chemistry; Physical Chemistry; Robotics; Transport and Communications; Welfare and Protective Services); **Humanities and Social Sciences** (Anthropology; Arts and Humanities; Behavioural Sciences; Clinical Psychology; Cultural Studies; East Asian Studies; Economics; English; Environmental Studies; European Languages; French; German; Information Sciences; Law; Linguistics; Modern Languages; Regional Studies; Russian; Social Sciences; Social Studies; Western European Studies); **Veterinary Sciences** (*United - Gifu University*) (Veterinary Science)

History: Founded 1949

Academic year: April to March

Admission requirements: Graduation from high school and entrance examination

Fees: Tuition, 535,800 per annum (Yen)

Main language(s) of instruction: Japanese

Accrediting agency: Ministry of Education, Culture, Sports, Science and Technology (MEXT)

Degrees and diplomas: Shushi (Education; Primary Education; Special Education; Teacher Training), Hakase (Agriculture; Biological and Life Sciences; Veterinary Science)

Student Services: Academic Counselling, Social Counselling, Careers Guidance, Sports Facilities, Language Laboratory, Health Services, Canteen

Periodicals: Arutesu Liberales, Iwatedaigaku Gijyutsubu Hokoku, Kyoikugakubu Kenkyu Nenpo

Student Numbers 2012-2013	MALE	FEMALE	TOTAL
All (Foreign Included)			c. 6000
Foreign only			200

Last Update: 02-03-2018

Japan Advanced Institute of Science and Technology (JAIST)

1-1 Asahidai
Nomi 923-1292, Ishikawa
Tel: +81(761) 51-1111
Fax: +81(761) 51-1959
Website: http://www.jaist.ac.jp
President: Tetsuo Asano

School

Information Sciences (Artificial Intelligence; Computer Engineering; Computer Networks; Information Sciences; Information Technology; Marketing; Robotics; Software Engineering); **Knowledge Science** (Artificial Intelligence; Biological and Life Sciences; Chemistry; Cognitive Sciences; Computer Science; Data Processing; Genetics; Information Management; Information Technology; Natural Sciences; Social Sciences; Social Studies; Systems Analysis); **Materials Science** (Bioengineering; Biological and Life Sciences; Biology; Chemical Engineering; Chemistry; Electronic Engineering; Materials Engineering; Mechanical Engineering; Molecular Biology; Nanotechnology; Physics)

Institute

General Education (Arts and Humanities; English; Japanese)

Centre

Advanced Education for Working Professionals (Information Sciences; Information Technology); **Dependable Network Innovation** (Computer Networks); **Graduate Education Initiative**; **Highly Dependable Embedded Systems Technology** (Computer Science); **Industrial Collaboration Promotion**; **Intelligent Robotics** (Robotics); **Nano Materials and Technology** (Materials Engineering; Nanotechnology); **Regional Innovation**; **Trustworthy e-Society Education and Research**

Research Division

Advanced Computing Infrastructure (Computer Science); **Bio-Architecture**; **Green Devices** (Energy Engineering; Environmental Engineering); **Innovative Lifestyle Design** (Design); **Integrated Science** (Mathematics and Computer Science); **Simulation Science**; **Software Verification** (Software Engineering)
History: Founded 1990 as School of Information Science; School of Materials Science organized 1991 and School of Knowledge Science organized 1996. A University of graduate education and research in Science and Technology
Academic year: April to March (April-September; October-March)

Admission requirements: University degree at Bachelor level
Main language(s) of instruction: Japanese
Accrediting agency: Ministry of Education, Culture, Sports, Science and Technology (MEXT)
Student Services: Academic Counselling, Careers Guidance, Sports Facilities, Language Laboratory, Health Services, Canteen
Periodicals: JAIST

Student Numbers 2012-2013	MALE	FEMALE	TOTAL
All (Foreign Included)	743	148	891
Foreign only			257

Last Update: 01-03-2018

Joetsu University of Education (JUEN)

1 Yamayashiki-machi
Joetsu-shi 943-8512, Niigata
Tel: +81(25) 521-3214, +81(25) 521-3299
Fax: +81(25) 521-3621
Website: http://www.juen.ac.jp
President: Naoya Kawasaki

College

Education (Art Education; Clinical Psychology; Education; Health Education; Humanities and Social Science Education; Music Education; Native Language Education; Preschool Education; Primary Education; Science Education; Teacher Training)

Graduate School

Clinical Psychology (Clinical Psychology); **Education** (Education; Teacher Training); **Science of School Education** (*Union Graduate School with Hyogo University of Teacher Education*) (Art Education; Art History; Biology; Chemistry; Child Care and Development; Clinical Psychology; Clothing and Sewing; Conducting; Design; Developmental Psychology; Earth Sciences; Economics; Education; Educational Administration; Educational Psychology; Educational Sciences; Electrical Engineering; English; Ethics; Family Studies; Fine Arts; Food Science; Foreign Languages Education; Geography; Health Education; Health Sciences; History; Home Economics; Home Economics Education; Humanities and Social Science Education; Information Technology; Japanese; Linguistics; Literature; Mathematics; Mathematics Education; Mechanical Engineering; Media Studies; Music; Music Education; Music Theory and Composition; Musical Instruments; Musicology; Native Language Education; Natural Sciences; Nutrition; Painting and Drawing; Pedagogy; Philosophy; Physical Education; Physics; Political Sciences;

Preschool Education; Primary Education; Science Education; Sculpture; Social Psychology; Social Studies; Sociology; Special Education; Sports; Technology Education)

History: Founded 1978

Academic year: April to March (April-September; October-March)

Admission requirements: Graduation from high school

Main language(s) of instruction: Japanese

Accrediting agency: Ministry of Education, Culture, Sports, Science and Technology (MEXT)

Degrees and diplomas: Shushi (Art Education; Clinical Psychology; Education; Educational Psychology; Foreign Languages Education; Humanities and Social Science Education; Mathematics Education; Music Education; Native Language Education; Science Education), Hakase (Educational Research; Educational Sciences)

Student Services: Social Counselling, Health Services, Canteen

Last Update: 23-02-2018

Kagawa Prefectural University of Health Sciences

281-1 Hara Mure-cho
Kita-gun 761-0123
Tel: +81(87) 870-1212
Fax: +81(87) 870-1202
Website: http://www.kagawa-puhs.ac.jp
President: Katashi Satoh

Faculty

Health and Medical Sciences (Food Science; Food Technology; Genetics; Health Sciences; Laboratory Techniques; Medical Technology; Nursing; Public Health)

School

Midwifery (Midwifery)

Graduate School

Health and Medical Sciences (Health Sciences; Laboratory Techniques; Medical Technology; Medicine; Nursing; Pathology)

History: Founded 2004

Fees: Tuition, 535,800 per annum (Yen)

Main language(s) of instruction: Japanese

Accrediting agency: Ministry of Education, Culture, Sports, Science and Technology (MEXT)

Degrees and diplomas: Shushi (Health Sciences; Medical Technology; Nursing)

Student Services: Sports Facilities

Student Numbers 2013-2014	MALE	FEMALE	TOTAL
All (Foreign Included)			c. 160

Last Update: 02-03-2018

Kagawa University

1 Sachiboshi
Takamatsu 760-8521, Kagawa
Tel: +81(87) 832-1000
Fax: +81(87) 832-1053
Website: http://www.kagawa-u.ac.jp
Head of International Office: Masaaki Tokuda
President: Yamashita Akira

Faculty

Agriculture (Agriculture; Biological and Life Sciences; Chemistry; Environmental Studies; Food Science); **Economics** (Accountancy; Business Administration; Cultural Studies; Economic and Finance Policy; Economics; Information Sciences; Regional Studies; Social Studies; Statistics; Tourism); **Education** (Curriculum; Education; Environmental Studies; Humanities and Social Science Education; International Studies; Preschool Education; Primary Education; Special Education; Teacher Training); **Engineering** (Construction Engineering; Electronic Engineering; Engineering; Environmental Management; Information Technology; Materials Engineering; Mechanical Engineering; Mechanical Equipment and Maintenance; Natural Resources; Optical Technology; Robotics; Safety Engineering; Telecommunications Engineering); **Law** (Law; Political Sciences) **Medicine** (Anaesthesiology; Biological and Life Sciences; Computer Science; Environmental Studies; Gynaecology and Obstetrics; Health Education; Immunology; Laboratory Techniques; Medicine; Molecular Biology; Neurology; Nursing; Ophthalmology; Otorhinolaryngology; Paediatrics; Pathology; Pharmacology; Psychiatry and Mental Health; Radiology; Social and Preventive Medicine; Surgery)

Graduate School

Agriculture (Agriculture; Biological and Life Sciences; Natural Resources); **Economics** (Economics); **Education** (Clinical Psychology; Curriculum; Education; Primary Education; Special Education); **Engineering** (Construction Engineering; Engineering; Information Technology; Materials Engineering; Mechanical Engineering; Safety Engineering); **Law** (*Kagawa-Ehime Universities'*) (Law); **Law** (Law); **Management** (Management; Regional Studies); **Medicine** (Environmental Studies; Medicine; Molecular Biology; Nursing; Rehabilitation and Therapy); **United Agricultural Sciences**

(*Ehime University*) (Biological and Life Sciences; Environmental Management; Natural Resources)

Further information: University Hospital; Centre for Educational Research and Teacher Development

History: Founded 1949. Merged with Kagawa Medical University 2003. Acquired present status 2004

Academic year: April to March (April-October; October-March)

Admission requirements: Graduation from high school or equivalent, and entrance examination

Fees: Tuition fee for undergraduate and graduate students, 535,800 per annum; for research students, 29,700 per month (Yen)

Main language(s) of instruction: Japanese

Accrediting agency: Ministry of Education, Culture, Sports, Science and Technology (MEXT)

Degrees and diplomas: Shushi (Agriculture; Biochemistry; Biological and Life Sciences; Clinical Psychology; Construction Engineering; Economics; Education; Education of the Handicapped; Environmental Management; Food Science; Horticulture; Information Technology; International Business; Law; Management; Materials Engineering; Mechanical Engineering; Medicine; Natural Resources; Nursing; Pedagogy; Primary Education; Psychology; Regional Studies; Safety Engineering), Hakase (Agriculture; Biological and Life Sciences; Construction Engineering; Environmental Management; Information Technology; Law; Materials Engineering; Mechanical Engineering; Medicine; Natural Resources; Rehabilitation and Therapy; Safety Engineering; Social and Preventive Medicine)

Student Services: Careers Guidance, Nursery Care, Sports Facilities, Language Laboratory, Facilities for disabled people, Health Services, Canteen, Foreign Studies Centre

Periodicals: Memoirs of Faculty of Agriculture, Memoirs of Faculty of Education, Technical Bulletin of Faculty of Agriculture

Academic Staff 2013-2014	MALE	FEMALE	TOTAL
FULL-TIME			672
Student Numbers 2013-2014			
All (Foreign Included)			6539
Foreign only			200

Last Update: 25-05-2018

Kagoshima University

Korimoto 1-21-24
Kagoshima 890-8580, Kagoshima
Tel: +81(99) 285-7111
Fax: +81(99) 285-7325

Website: http://www.kagoshima-u.ac.jp
President: Yoshizane Maeda

Faculty

Agriculture (Agriculture; Biochemistry; Biotechnology; Environmental Engineering; Environmental Studies; Natural Resources; Veterinary Science); **Dentistry** (Dentistry); **Education** (Adult Education; Art Education; Cultural Studies; Education; Foreign Languages Education; Health Education; Humanities and Social Science Education; Mathematics Education; Music Education; Native Language Education; Physical Education; Preschool Education; Primary Education; Psychology; Science Education; Secondary Education; Special Education; Teacher Training; Technology Education); **Engineering** (Applied Chemistry; Architecture; Chemical Engineering; Civil Engineering; Electrical Engineering; Electronic Engineering; Engineering; Marine Engineering; Mechanical Engineering; Structural Architecture); **Fisheries** (Agricultural Economics; Agricultural Engineering; Aquaculture; Biochemistry; Biotechnology; Fishery; Food Science; Marine Biology; Marine Science and Oceanography); **Law, Economics and the Humanities** (American Studies; Arts and Humanities; Asian Studies; Business Administration; Computer Science; Cultural Studies; Economics; English; English Studies; European Studies; French; French Studies; German; Germanic Studies; Information Sciences; Japanese; Law; Media Studies; Political Sciences; Regional Studies; Sociology; Southeast Asian Studies); **Medicine** (Anaesthesiology; Anatomy; Biochemistry; Dermatology; Gynaecology and Obstetrics; Health Sciences; Hygiene; Information Sciences; Laboratory Techniques; Medical Technology; Medicine; Neurological Therapy; Oncology; Ophthalmology; Orthopaedics; Otorhinolaryngology; Paediatrics; Pathology; Pharmacology; Physical Therapy; Physiology; Psychiatry and Mental Health; Public Health; Radiology; Rehabilitation and Therapy; Surgery; Urology; Virology; Welfare and Protective Services; Zoology); **Science** (Biological and Life Sciences; Chemistry; Earth Sciences; Environmental Studies; Geography; Mathematics and Computer Science; Natural Sciences; Physics)

School
Law (*Kagoshima University*) (Law)

Academy
Inamori (Arts and Humanities; Communication Studies; Cultural Studies; Ethics; Leadership; Management; Philosophy)

Centre
Computing and Communications (Computer Engineering; Computer Networks; Computer Science; Information

Technology; Media Studies; Telecommunications Engineering); **Education** (Arts and Humanities; Cultural Studies; Foreign Languages Education; Health Sciences; Information Technology; Japanese; Mathematics; Modern Languages; Physical Education; Physics); **International Education and Research for the Pacific Islands** (Pacific Area Studies); **Kagoshima University Innovation** (*KUIC*) (Business Administration; Technology); **North American** (American Studies); **Research and Education for Lifelong Learning** (Adult Education; Social and Community Services)

Graduate School

Agricultural Sciences (*United*) (Agriculture; Fishery; Philosophy); **Agriculture** (Agriculture; Biochemistry; Biological and Life Sciences; Biotechnology; Environmental Engineering; Environmental Studies; Food Science; Forestry; Natural Resources); **Clinical Psychology** (*Professional*) (Clinical Psychology; Psychology); **Education** (Education; Educational Research; Teacher Training); **Fisheries** (Agricultural Economics; Aquaculture; Biochemistry; Biology; Fishery; Food Science; Marine Biology; Marine Science and Oceanography); **Health Sciences** (Health Sciences); **Humanities and Social Sciences** (Art Criticism; Cultural Studies; Economics; Environmental Studies; International Studies; Law; Social Sciences); **Medical and Dental Sciences** (Agriculture; Chemistry; Economics; Health Sciences; Information Management; Medical Technology; Nursing; Sociology); **Science and Engineering** (Engineering; Natural Sciences); **Veterinary Science** (*United - Headquartered in Yamaguchi University*) (Veterinary Science)

Research Division

Frontier Science (*FSRC*) (Biological and Life Sciences; Biotechnology; Environmental Studies; Genetics; Zoology)
History: Founded 1949, incorporating seven high schools, Kagoshima Normal School, Kagoshima Youth Normal School, Kagoshima College of Agriculture and Forestry, and Kagoshima College of Fishery
Academic year: April to March (April-September; October-March)
Admission requirements: Graduation from high school or equivalent, or foreign equivalent, and entrance examination
Main language(s) of instruction: Japanese
Accrediting agency: Ministry of Education, Culture, Sports, Science and Technology (MEXT)
Degrees and diplomas: Shushi (Agriculture; Arts and Humanities; Cultural Studies; Economics; Education; Fishery; Health Sciences; International Studies; Law; Natural Sciences; Social Sciences), Hakase (Clinical Psychology; Dentistry; Law; Medicine)
Student Services: Academic Counselling, Social Counselling, Careers Guidance, Nursery Care, Sports Facilities,

Language Laboratory, Health Services, Canteen, Foreign Studies Centre

Academic Staff 2012-2013	MALE	FEMALE	TOTAL
FULL-TIME			2492
Student Numbers 2012-2013			
All (Foreign Included)	6611	4050	10661
Foreign only			297

Last Update: 23-02-2018

Kanagawa University of Human Services

1-10-1 Heiseicho Yokosuka
Kanagawa 238-8522
Tel: +82(46) 828-2500
Fax: +82(46) 828-2501
Website: http://www.kuhs.ac.jp
President: Nakamura Koji

Course/Programme

Comprehensive Human and Technical Basis Charge (Anatomy; Arts and Humanities; Chemistry; Chinese; English; Korean; Medical Technology; Medicine; Molecular Biology; Natural Sciences; Pathology; Physics; Physiology; Public Health; Rehabilitation and Therapy; Spanish)

Department/Division

Health and Welfare (Health Sciences; Welfare and Protective Services); **Nursing** (Nursing); **Nutrition** (Nutrition); **Rehabilitation** (Physical Therapy; Rehabilitation and Therapy); **Social Welfare** (Social Welfare)

Graduate School

Health and Welfare (Administration; Health Administration; Health Sciences; Human Resources; Nutrition; Rehabilitation and Therapy; Social Policy; Social Welfare; Welfare and Protective Services)
History: Founded 2003
Main language(s) of instruction: Japanese
Accrediting agency: Ministry of Education, Culture, Sports, Science and Technology (MEXT)
Degrees and diplomas: Shushi (Health Sciences; Social Policy; Welfare and Protective Services)
Last Update: 16-03-2018

Kanazawa College of Art

5-11-1 Kodatsuno
Kanazawa-shi 920-8656, Ishikawa
Tel: +81(76) 262-3531

Fax: +81(76) 262-6594
Website: http://www.kanazawa-bidai.ac.jp
President: Masahiko Maeda

Faculty

Art (Aesthetics; Art History; Arts and Humanities; Ceramic Art; Communication Arts; Crafts and Trades; Design; Fine Arts; Industrial Design; Interior Design; Metal Techniques; Museum Studies; Painting and Drawing; Sculpture; Structural Architecture; Textile Design; Visual Arts)

Graduate School

Art (Aesthetics; Architectural and Environmental Design; Art History; Design; Fashion Design; Fine Arts; Handicrafts; Painting and Drawing; Sculpture)

Research Division

Art (Art History; Fine Arts; Metal Techniques; Painting and Drawing)
History: Founded 1946 as Senmon Gakko, became Junior College 1950, acquired present status 1955
Academic year: April to March (April-September; October-March)
Admission requirements: Graduation from high school or foreign equivalent, and entrance examination
Main language(s) of instruction: Japanese
Accrediting agency: Ministry of Education, Culture, Sports, Science and Technology (MEXT)
Degrees and diplomas: Shushi (Aesthetics; Art History; Design; Fashion Design; Handicrafts; Painting and Drawing; Sculpture), Hakase (Aesthetics; Architectural and Environmental Design; Art History; Fine Arts; Handicrafts)
Student Services: Academic Counselling, Social Counselling, Careers Guidance, Sports Facilities, Health Services
Periodicals: Kanazawa Bijutsu Kogei Daigaku Gakuho (Bulletin)

Academic Staff 2012-2013	MALE	FEMALE	TOTAL
FULL-TIME			c. 56
Student Numbers 2012-2013			
All (Foreign Included)			c. 560

Last Update: 06-03-2018

Kanazawa University

Kakuma-machi
Kanazawa 920-1192, Ishikawa
Tel: +81(76) 264-5111
Fax: +81(76) 234-4010
Website: http://www.kanazawa-u.ac.jp
President: Koetsu Yamazaki
Tel: +81(76) 264-6196

College

Human and Social Sciences (Arts and Humanities; Development Studies; Economics; International Studies; Law; Regional Studies; Social Sciences; Teacher Training); **Medical, Pharmaceutical and Health Sciences** (Health Sciences; Medicine; Pharmacology; Pharmacy); **Science and Engineering** (Architectural and Environmental Design; Chemistry; Computer Engineering; Electrical Engineering; Mathematics; Mechanical Engineering; Natural Sciences; Physics)

Course/Programme

Liberal Arts and Science Organisation (Arts and Humanities; Natural Sciences); **Organisation of Frontier Science and Innovation** (Natural Sciences); **Organization of Global Affairs** (International Studies); **Organization of Global Human Resource Development** (Human Resources)

Institute

Foreign Languages (Modern Languages); **Nature and Environmental Technology** (Environmental Engineering)

Centre

Advanced Science Research (Natural Sciences); **Environment Preservation** (Environmental Management); **Health Service** (Health Sciences); **Higher Education Research** (Higher Education); **Information Media** (Information Sciences; Media Studies); **Regional Collaboration** (Regional Studies)

Laboratory

Career Design for Gender Equality (Gender Studies)

Graduate School

Education (Education; Educational Research); **Human and Socio-Environment Studies** (Arts and Humanities; Development Studies; Economics; International Studies; Law; Political Sciences; Regional Studies; Social Sciences; Social Studies; Sociology); **Law** (Law); **Medical Science** (Cardiology; Environmental Studies; Health Sciences; Medicine; Neurosciences; Oncology; Pharmacy); **Natural Science and Technology** (Architectural and Environmental Design; Biological and Life Sciences; Chemistry; Computer Engineering; Computer Science; Electrical Engineering; Environmental Engineering; Environmental Studies; Materials Engineering; Mathematics; Mechanical Engineering; Mechanics; Natural Sciences; Physics; Technology)

Research Division

Cancer (Cell Biology; Medicine; Molecular Biology; Oncology); **Child Mental Development** (Child Care and Development)

History: Founded 1949

Academic year: April to March (April-October, October-March)

Admission requirements: Graduation from high school or equivalent or foreign equivalent, and entrance examination

Fees: Tuition, 535,800 per annum (Yen)

Main language(s) of instruction: Japanese

Accrediting agency: Ministry of Education, Culture, Sports, Science and Technology (MEXT)

Degrees and diplomas: Hakase (Biological and Life Sciences; Cardiology; Computer Science; Electrical Engineering; Environmental Engineering; Environmental Studies; Law; Materials Engineering; Neurosciences; Oncology; Pharmacy; Sociology; Technology)

Student Services: Academic Counselling, Careers Guidance, Sports Facilities, Language Laboratory, Facilities for disabled people, Health Services, Canteen, Foreign Studies Centre

Academic Staff 2012-2013	MALE	FEMALE	TOTAL
FULL-TIME	925	174	1099
PART-TIME	552	170	722
STAFF WITH DOCTORATE			
FULL-TIME	739	120	859
Student Numbers 2012-2013			
All (Foreign Included)	6684	3748	10432

Last Update: 23-02-2018

Kitakyushu University

4-2-1 Kitagata Kokuraminami
Kitakyushu 802-8577, Fukuoka
Tel: +81(93) 964-4022
Fax: +81(93) 964-4020
Website: http://www.kitakyu-u.ac.jp
President: Takashi Matsuo

Faculty

Economics and Business Administration (*Also graduate school*) (Business Administration; Economics; Information Management); **Environmental Engineering** (*Also graduate school*) (Architectural and Environmental Design; Chemical Engineering; Environmental Engineering; Environmental Management; Information Sciences; Information Technology; Mechanical Engineering; Media Studies; Town Planning); **Foreign Studies** (Chinese; Cultural Studies; English; International Relations; International Studies; Modern Languages); **Humanities** (Arts and Humanities; Cultural Studies; Social Studies); **Law** (*Also graduate school*) (Law; Political Sciences; Social Problems)

School

Regional Development (Regional Studies)

Institute

Urban and Regional Policy Studies (Regional Studies; Urban Studies)

Centre

Cultural and Social Studies of Asia (Asian Studies; Cultural Studies; Social Studies); **Fundamental Education**; **Industrial Support**

Graduate School

Business Administration (Business Administration); **Environmental Engineering** (Biotechnology; Energy Engineering; Environmental Engineering; Environmental Studies; Information Technology; Multimedia; Natural Resources; Natural Sciences; Telecommunications Engineering); **Law** (Law; Management); **Social Systems Studies** (Cultural Studies; East Asian Studies; Economics; International Economics; International Studies; Modern Languages; Regional Studies; Social and Community Services; Social Policy; Social Studies; Southeast Asian Studies)

Further information: Also Hibikino Campus

History: Founded 1946

Academic year: April to March (April-September; October-March)

Admission requirements: Graduation from high school or foreign equivalent, and entrance examination

Main language(s) of instruction: Japanese

Accrediting agency: Ministry of Education, Culture, Sports, Science and Technology (MEXT)

Degrees and diplomas: Shushi (Cultural Studies; East Asian Studies; Economics; International Studies; Law; Modern Languages; Social and Community Services; Social Studies), Hakase (East Asian Studies; Environmental Engineering; Environmental Studies; Social and Community Services; Social Studies; Southeast Asian Studies; Telecommunications Engineering)

Student Services: Sports Facilities, Language Laboratory

Periodicals: Bulletin of the Faculty of Foreign Languages, Journal of the Faculty of Economics, Law and Public Affairs, Letters, Studies in Kitakyushu Society, Trade and Industry

Academic Staff 2013-2014	MALE	FEMALE	TOTAL
FULL-TIME			265
Student Numbers 2013-2014			
All (Foreign Included)			6496

Last Update: 09-03-2018

Kitami Institute of Technology

165 Koen-cho
Kitami-shi 090-8507, Hokkaido
Tel: +81(157) 26-9370
Fax: +81(157) 26-9373
Website: http://www.kitami-it.ac.jp
President: Nobuo Takahashi
Tel: +81(157) 26-9107

Faculty

Engineering (Artificial Intelligence; Biochemistry; Bioengineering; Biotechnology; Civil Engineering; Electrical and Electronic Engineering; Electrical Engineering; Electronic Engineering; Engineering; Engineering Management; Environmental Engineering; Food Technology; Information Sciences; Information Technology; Materials Engineering; Mechanical Engineering; Media Studies; Nanotechnology)

Graduate School

Engineering (Applied Chemistry; Biochemistry; Bioengineering; Biomedical Engineering; Biotechnology; Data Processing; Electrical and Electronic Engineering; Energy Engineering; Engineering; Environmental Engineering; Food Technology; Geological Engineering; Information Technology; Machine Building; Materials Engineering; Mechanical Engineering; Medical Technology; Natural Resources; Optical Technology; Production Engineering; Structural Architecture; Telecommunications Engineering; Thermal Engineering; Transport Engineering)
History: Founded 1960 as Kitami Junior College of Technology, reorganized 1966 as Kitami Institute of Technology. Graduate School established 1984. Graduate school reorganised as Master's Program and Doctoral Program
Academic year: April to March (April-September; October-March)
Admission requirements: Graduation from high school and entrance examination
Fees: Tuition, 535,800 per annum for Undergraduate and Master's degree programmes; 520,800 per annum for doctoral programmes (Yen)
Main language(s) of instruction: Japanese
Accrediting agency: Ministry of Education, Culture, Sports, Science and Technology (MEXT)
Degrees and diplomas: Gakushi, Shushi (Applied Chemistry; Civil Engineering; Computer Science; Electrical and Electronic Engineering; Environmental Studies; Materials Engineering; Mechanical Engineering), Hakase (Energy Engineering; Environmental Engineering; Medical Technology; Production Engineering)
Student Services: Academic Counselling, Social Counselling, Careers Guidance, Sports Facilities, Language

Laboratory, Facilities for disabled people, Health Services, Canteen, Foreign Studies Centre
Periodicals: Research Bulletin

Academic Staff 2013-2014	MALE	FEMALE	TOTAL
FULL-TIME			154
Student Numbers 2013-2014			
All (Foreign Included)			c. 1300

Last Update: 09-02-2018

Kobe City College of Nursing

3-4 Gakuen-nishi-machi Nishi-ku
Kobe-shi 651-2103, Hyogo
Tel: +81(78) 794-8080
Fax: +81(78) 794-8086
Website: http://www.kobe-ccn.ac.jp
President: Shizue Suzuki

Department/Division

Midwifery (Midwifery); **Nursing** (Arts and Humanities; Biological and Life Sciences; Cultural Studies; Health Administration; Health Sciences; Modern Languages; Natural Sciences; Nursing; Social Sciences; Social Welfare)

Graduate School

Nursing (Nursing)
History: Founded 1996
Main language(s) of instruction: Japanese
Accrediting agency: Ministry of Education, Culture, Sports, Science and Technology (MEXT)
Degrees and diplomas: Shushi (Nursing), Hakase (Nursing)

Student Numbers 2013-2014	MALE	FEMALE	TOTAL
All (Foreign Included)			453

Last Update: 06-03-2018

Kobe City University of Foreign Studies

9-1 Gakuen-higashi Nishi
Kobe 651-2187, Hyogo
Tel: +81(78) 794-8121
Fax: +81(78) 792-9020
Website: http://www.kobe-cufs.ac.jp
President: M. Akihiro

Institute

Foreign Studies (Chinese; Cultural Studies; English; International Relations; Linguistics; Literature; Modern Languages; Russian; Social Sciences; Spanish)

Graduate School

Foreign Studies (Asian Studies; Chinese; Cultural Studies; English; Foreign Languages Education; International Relations; Japanese; Linguistics; Modern Languages; Russian; South and Southeast Asian Languages; Spanish)

History: Founded 1946 as school, acquired university status 1949

Academic year: April to March (April-September; October-March)

Admission requirements: Graduation from high school or equivalent or foreign equivalent, and entrance examination

Main language(s) of instruction: Japanese

Accrediting agency: Ministry of Education, Culture, Sports, Science and Technology (MEXT)

Degrees and diplomas: Shushi (Asian Studies; Chinese; English; Foreign Languages Education; International Relations; Japanese; Russian; South and Southeast Asian Languages; Spanish), Hakase (Cultural Studies; Linguistics; Social Studies)

Periodicals: Annual Report of Research Institute for Foreign Studies, Foreign Studies Pamphlet, Kobe Municipal College Journal

Academic Staff 2013-2014	MALE	FEMALE	TOTAL
FULL-TIME			87
Student Numbers 2013-2014			
All (Foreign Included)			2253

Last Update: 06-03-2018

Kobe University

1-1 Rokkodai-cho, Nada-ku
Kobe-shi 657-8501, Hyogo
Tel: +81(78) 881-1212
Fax: +81(78) 803-5049
Website: http://www.kobe-u.ac.jp
President: Hiroshi Takeda
Tel: +81(78) 803-5282

Faculty

Agriculture (Agricultural Economics; Agricultural Engineering; Agriculture; Animal Husbandry; Applied Chemistry; Biological and Life Sciences; Botany; Environmental Studies; Food Science; Natural Resources); **Business Administration** (Accountancy; Banking; Behavioural Sciences; Business Administration; Finance; Government; Human Resources; Industrial and Organizational Psychology; Insurance; International Business; Management; Marketing; Taxation; Transport and Communications; Transport Economics; Transport Management); **Economics** (Econometrics; Economic and Finance Policy; Economics; International Economics; Social Policy); **Engineering** (Applied Chemistry; Architecture; Building Technologies; Chemical Engineering; Chemistry; Civil Engineering; Computer Engineering; Computer Science; Electrical and Electronic Engineering; Electronic Engineering; Engineering; Environmental Engineering; Information Technology; Materials Engineering; Mechanical Engineering; Mechanics; Thermal Engineering); **Human Development** (Behavioural Sciences; Child Care and Development; Cultural Studies; Development Studies; Developmental Psychology; Educational Sciences; Environmental Studies; Health Education; Mathematics and Computer Science; Natural Resources; Primary Education; Social Sciences; Sports); **Intercultural Studies** (Communication Studies; Cultural Studies; Information Sciences; International Studies; Regional Studies; Social Studies); **Law** (Civil Law; Commercial Law; Criminal Law; History of Law; International Law; International Relations; Labour Law; Law; Political Sciences; Public Health; Sociology); **Letters** (American Studies; Art History; Arts and Humanities; Chinese; Cognitive Sciences; English Studies; Fine Arts; French Studies; Geography; History; Japanese; Linguistics; Literature; Philosophy; Psychology; Social Sciences; Sociology); **Maritime Sciences** (Environmental Management; Marine Engineering; Marine Science and Oceanography; Marine Transport; Transport Management); **Medicine** (Health Sciences; Medical Technology; Medicine; Nursing; Occupational Therapy; Physical Therapy); **Science** (Applied Mathematics; Astronomy and Space Science; Biology; Chemistry; Earth Sciences; Inorganic Chemistry; Mathematics; Molecular Biology; Natural Sciences; Organic Chemistry; Physical Chemistry; Physics)

Graduate School

Agricultural Science (Agricultural Economics; Agricultural Engineering; Agriculture; Agrobiology; Applied Chemistry; Biological and Life Sciences; Botany; Environmental Studies; Food Science; Natural Resources; Zoology); **Business Administration** (Accountancy; Banking; Behavioural Sciences; Business Administration; Business and Commerce; Engineering Management; Finance; Government; Human Resources; Insurance; International Business; Management; Marketing; Operations Research; Taxation; Transport and Communications; Transport Economics; Transport Management); **Economics** (Comparative Politics; Econometrics; Economic and Finance Policy; Economic History; Economics; International Economics; Social and Preventive Medicine; Statistics); **Engineering** (Applied Chemistry; Architectural and Environmental Design; Architecture; Architecture and Planning; Building Technologies; Chemical Engineering; Chemistry; Civil Engineering; Computer Engineering; Electrical and Electronic Engineering; Electronic Engineering; Energy Engineering; Engineering; Environmental Engineering; Information Technology; Mechanical

Engineering; Mechanics; Physics; Production Engineering; Safety Engineering; Thermal Engineering); **Health sciences** (Biophysics; Community Health; Health Sciences; Nursing; Rehabilitation and Therapy); **Human Development and Environment** (Behavioural Sciences; Child Care and Development; Cultural Studies; Development Studies; Education; Educational Sciences; Environmental Studies; Health Education; Health Sciences; Mathematics and Computer Science; Natural Sciences; Psychology; Social Studies; Sports); **Humanities** (American Studies; Art History; Arts and Humanities; Chinese; Cognitive Sciences; Cultural Studies; English Studies; Ethics; European Studies; Fine Arts; Geography; History; Japanese; Korean; Linguistics; Literature; Philosophy; Psychology; Social Sciences; Social Studies; Sociology); **Intercultural Studies** (Communication Studies; Cultural Studies; Foreign Languages Education; Information Sciences; International Studies; Regional Studies; Social Studies); **International Cooperation Studies** (*GSICS*) (Comparative Law; Development Studies; Economic and Finance Policy; Economics; Education; Environmental Studies; International Economics; International Law; International Relations; International Studies; Political Sciences; Regional Studies; Social Sciences; Urban Studies); **Law** (Commercial Law; Comparative Literature; History of Law; International Relations; Law; Political Sciences; Public Law); **Maritime Sciences** (Environmental Studies; Marine Engineering; Marine Science and Oceanography; Marine Transport; Transport Management); **Medicine** (Biochemistry; Biomedicine; Cell Biology; Health Sciences; Immunology; Medicine; Microbiology; Molecular Biology; Pathology; Physiology; Social and Preventive Medicine; Surgery); **Science** (Applied Mathematics; Applied Physics; Astronomy and Space Science; Biochemistry; Biological and Life Sciences; Biology; Chemistry; Earth Sciences; Environmental Studies; Inorganic Chemistry; Mathematics; Meteorology; Molecular Biology; Natural Sciences; Organic Chemistry; Pharmacology; Physical Chemistry; Physics); **System Informatics** (Artificial Intelligence; Computer Engineering; Computer Science; Information Sciences)

Research Division

Biosignal (Biological and Life Sciences); **Economics and Business Administration** (Business Administration; Economics); **Environmental Genomics** (Environmental Studies; Genetics); **Inland Seas** (Marine Science and Oceanography); **Molecular Photoscience** (Physics); **Urban Safety and Security** (Protective Services; Urban Studies)

Further information: Also Experimental Farm, Medical Centre for Student Health, University Hospital, Office for the Promotion of International Exchange, EU Institute in Japan, Kansai

History: Founded 1902, integrating Kobe University of Economics, Hyogo Normal and Junior Normal Schools, Kobe College of Technology and Himeji High School. Acquired present status and title 1949. Integrated Kobe University of Mercantile Marine 2003

Academic year: April to March (April-September; October-March)

Admission requirements: Graduation from high school or equivalent or foreign equivalent, and entrance examination

Fees: 535,800 per annum (Yen)

Main language(s) of instruction: Japanese

Accrediting agency: Ministry of Education, Culture, Sports, Science and Technology (MEXT)

Degrees and diplomas: Shushi (Astronomy and Space Science; Biology; Chemistry; Earth Sciences; Mathematics; Physics), Hakase (Astronomy and Space Science; Biology; Chemistry; Earth Sciences; Mathematics; Physics)

Student Services: Academic Counselling, Social Counselling, Careers Guidance, Cultural Activities, Sports Facilities, Language Laboratory, Facilities for disabled people, Health Services, Canteen, Foreign Studies Centre

Periodicals: Bulletin of Health Sciences Kobe, Discussion Papers (Business Administration), Discussion Papers (Economics), GSICS Working Papers Series, Kobe Economic and Business Review, Kobe Journal of Mathematics, Kobe Journal of Medical Sciences, Kobe University Economic Review, Kobe University Law Review, Research Arena

Last Update: 23-02-2018

Kochi University

2-5-1 Akebono-cho
Kochi-shi 780-8520, Kochi
Tel: +81(88) 844-0111, +81(88) 844-8643
Fax: +81(88) 844-8033
Website: http://www.kochi-u.ac.jp
President: Hiroshi Wakiguchi

Faculty

Agriculture (Agriculture); **Education** (Arts and Humanities; Continuing Education; Education; Philosophy; Social Sciences; Teacher Training); **Humanities and Economics** (Arts and Humanities; Cultural Studies; Economics; International Studies; Social Sciences); **Science** (Biological and Life Sciences; Environmental Studies; Information Sciences; Marine Engineering; Materials Engineering; Natural Resources; Natural Sciences)

School

Medicine (Medicine; Nursing)

Graduate School

Humanities and Social Sciences (Arts and Humanities; Social Sciences); **Integrated Arts and Sciences** (Agriculture; Education; Medicine; Nursing)

Further information: University farm. University forest. Centre for Research and Training of Teachers

History: Founded as national university 1949, incorporating Kochi High School founded 1923, Kochi Normal School, 1874, and Kochi Youth Normal School, 1923. Merged with Kochi Ika Daigaku 2003

Academic year: April to March (April-October; October-March)

Admission requirements: Graduation from high school or recognized equivalent, and entrance examination

Main language(s) of instruction: Japanese

Accrediting agency: Ministry of Education, Culture, Sports, Science and Technology (MEXT)

Degrees and diplomas: Gakushi, Shushi (Agriculture; Arts and Humanities; Education; Environmental Studies; Health Sciences; Medicine; Natural Sciences; Nursing; Plant and Crop Protection; Social Sciences), Hakase (Environmental Studies; Health Sciences; Marine Science and Oceanography; Natural Sciences). Also Teaching Qualitication, 4 yrs

Student Services: Language Laboratory

Periodicals: Reports of USA Marine Biological Station, Research Reports of Faculty of Agriculture, Research Reports of Faculty of Education, University Research Reports

Last Update: 09-02-2018

Kochi University of Technology (KUT)

185 Miyanokuchi Tosayamada
Kochi 782-8502
Tel: +81(887) 53-1111
Fax: +81(887) 57-2000
Website: http://www.kochi-tech.ac.jp
President: Masahiko Isobe

School

Environmental Science and Engineering (Biological and Life Sciences; Chemistry; Environmental Engineering; Environmental Studies; Materials Engineering; Nanotechnology); **Information** (Computer Engineering; Computer Science; Information Sciences; Information Technology; Media Studies; Telecommunications Engineering); **Management** (Management); **Systems Engineering** (Aeronautical and Aerospace Engineering; Architecture; Electronic Engineering; Mechanical Engineering; Optical Technology; Robotics; Structural Architecture)

Department/Division
Core Studies (English; Mathematics)

Graduate School
Engineering (Civil Engineering; Electronic Engineering; Engineering; Engineering Management; Environmental Engineering; Information Technology; Mechanical Engineering; Physical Engineering)

History: Founded 1997, Public University 2009

Fees: Tuition 535,800 per annum (Yen)

Main language(s) of instruction: Japanese

Accrediting agency: Ministry of Education, Culture, Sports, Science and Technology (MEXT)

Degrees and diplomas: Shushi (Civil Engineering; Electronic Engineering; Engineering Management; Environmental Engineering; Information Technology; Mechanical Engineering; Physical Engineering), Hakase (Engineering; Engineering Management)

Student Services: Sports Facilities

Academic Staff 2013-2014	MALE	FEMALE	TOTAL
FULL-TIME			327
Student Numbers 2013-2014			
All (Foreign Included)			2074
Foreign only			39

Last Update: 06-03-2018

Kumamoto University

2-40-1 Kurokami Chuo-ku
Kumamoto-shi 860-8555, Kumamoto
Tel: +81(96) 344-2111, +81(96) 342-3117, +81(96) 342-2146
Fax: +81(96) 342-3110
Website: http://www.kumamoto-u.ac.jp
President: Harada Shinji
Tel: +81(96) 342-3113

Faculty

Education (Art Education; Education; Foreign Languages Education; Health Education; Home Economics; Humanities and Social Science Education; Industrial Arts Education; Mathematics Education; Nursing; Physical Education; Primary Education; Psychology; Science Education; Special Education; Sports; Teacher Training; Vocational Education; Welfare and Protective Services); **Engineering** (Applied Chemistry; Architectural Restoration; Biochemistry; Building Technologies; Civil Engineering; Electrical and Electronic Equipment and Maintenance; Electrical Engineering; Engineering; Environmental Engineering; Materials Engineering; Mathematics; Mechanical Engineering); **Law** (Administrative Law; Civil Law; Commercial Law; Constitutional Law; Criminal Law; Economic and Finance Policy; Fiscal Law; International Economics; International Law; Labour Law; Law; Political Sciences; Public Law); **Letters** (Archaeology; Arts and Humanities; Cognitive Sciences; Communication Studies; Cultural Studies; East Asian

Studies; Ethics; Folklore; Geography; Geography (Human); History; Information Sciences; Literature; Philosophy; Psychology; Regional Studies; Social Sciences; Sociology); **Life Sciences** (*Graduate*) (Anatomy; Applied Chemistry; Biological and Life Sciences; Biomedicine; Cell Biology; Dermatology; Environmental Studies; Gastroenterology; Haematology; Hepatology; Histology; Medical Technology; Medicine; Microbiology; Molecular Biology; Nephrology; Neurological Therapy; Neurology; Oncology; Ophthalmology; Organic Chemistry; Orthopaedics; Otorhinolaryngology; Pathology; Pharmacology; Physiology; Plastic Surgery; Radiology; Respiratory Therapy; Social Sciences; Surgery; Urology); **Science** (Biological and Life Sciences; Chemistry; Earth Sciences; Mathematics; Natural Sciences; Physics)

School

Medicine (Health Sciences; Laboratory Techniques; Medicine; Nursing; Radiology; Treatment Techniques); **Pharmacy** (Applied Chemistry; Biological and Life Sciences; Natural Sciences; Pharmacology; Pharmacy)

Institute

E-Learning Development (Educational Technology); **Molecular Embryology and Genetics** (Genetics; Molecular Biology); **Resource Development and Analysis** (Biological and Life Sciences)

Centre

AIDS Research (Medicine); **Environmental Safety** (Environmental Studies; Safety Engineering); **Globalization** (International Studies); **Marine Environment Studies** (Marine Science and Oceanography); **Multimedia and Information Technologies** (Information Technology; Multimedia); **Policy Studies** (Public Administration)

Graduate School

Education (Art Education; Education; Foreign Languages Education; Health Education; Home Economics Education; Humanities and Social Science Education; Mathematics Education; Music Education; Native Language Education; Pedagogy; Physical Education; Psychology; Science Education; Special Education; Technology Education); **Health Sciences** (Health Sciences; Laboratory Techniques; Medical Parasitology; Nursing; Radiology); **Law** (*Professional*) (Law); **Medical Sciences** (Anaesthesiology; Anatomy; Behavioural Sciences; Biochemistry; Biology; Cardiology; Cell Biology; Child Care and Development; Clinical Psychology; Cognitive Sciences; Computer Science; Dermatology; Embryology and Reproduction Biology; Endocrinology; Environmental Studies; Ethics; Forensic Medicine and Dentistry; Gastroenterology; Genetics; Gynaecology and Obstetrics; Haematology; Health Sciences; Hepatology; Histology; Immunology; Information Sciences; Medical Technology; Medicine; Microbiology; Molecular Biology; Nephrology; Neurological Therapy; Neurology; Oncology; Ophthalmology; Orthopaedics; Otorhinolaryngology; Paediatrics; Pathology; Pharmacology; Physiology; Plastic Surgery; Psychiatry and Mental Health; Public Health; Radiology; Respiratory Therapy; Rheumatology; Social and Preventive Medicine; Sociology; Surgery; Urology; Virology); **Pharmaceutical Sciences** (Embryology and Reproduction Biology; Environmental Studies; Genetics; Molecular Biology; Pharmacology; Pharmacy; Treatment Techniques); **Science and Technology** (Applied Chemistry; Architecture; Biochemistry; Civil Engineering; Computer Science; Electrical Engineering; Environmental Engineering; Materials Engineering; Mathematics; Mechanical Engineering; Natural Sciences; Technology); **Social and Cultural Sciences** (Art Management; Business Administration; Communication Studies; Cultural Studies; Foreign Languages Education; Law; Management; Native Language Education; Peace and Disarmament; Public Administration; Social Sciences)

Research Division

Bioelectrics (Biological and Life Sciences; Electrical and Electronic Engineering); **Buried Cultural Properties** (Heritage Preservation); **Higher Education** (Educational Research); **Magnesium** (Biological and Life Sciences); **Shock Wave and Condensed Matter** (Physics)

Further information: Also liaison offices in Tokyo and Nankai; overseas offices in Shanghai and Dalian (China), Daejeon (Republic of Korea), Keputih (Indonesia).

History: Founded 1949 incorporating five high schools, founded 1886, Kumamoto College of Technology (1906), Kumamoto Normal School (1874), Kumamoto Pharmacy College (1885), and Kumamoto Medical College (1896). A national university corporation financed by the Ministry of Education, Culture, Sports, Science, and Technology.

Academic year: April to March (April-September; October-March)

Admission requirements: Graduation from high school or equivalent, and entrance examination

Fees: Admission Fees, 282,000; Tuition, 535,800 per annum (Yen)

Main language(s) of instruction: Japanese

Degrees and diplomas: Shushi (Arts and Humanities; Education; Educational Technology; Law; Philosophy; Public Administration), Hakase (Biological and Life Sciences; Health Sciences; Medicine; Nursing; Pharmacology; Pharmacy)

Student Services: Academic Counselling, Social Counselling, Careers Guidance, Sports Facilities, Language Laboratory, Facilities for disabled people, Health Services, Canteen, Foreign Studies Centre

Periodicals: Bulletin of Centre for Education and Guidance, Calanus, Journal of Culture and Humanities, Journal of

Mathematics, Journal of Science, Kumamoto Hogaku (Journal of Law), Medical Journal, Memoirs of the Faculty of Education, Memoirs of the Faculty of Engineering, Physics Reports, Technical Reports
Last Update: 23-02-2018

Kushiro Public University of Economics (KPU)

4-1-1 Ashino
Kushiro-shi 085-8585, Hokkaido
Tel: +81(154) 37-3211
Fax: +81(154) 37-3287
Website: http://www.kushiro-pu.ac.jp
President: Toshiyuki Takano

Course/Programme
Business Administration (Accountancy; Business Administration; Economics; Information Management; Law; Management; Modern Languages; Sociology); **Economics** (Accountancy; Business Administration; Economics; International Relations; Law; Modern Languages; Public Administration; Sociology)
History: Founded 1987
Fees: Tuition, 535,800 per annum (Yen)
Main language(s) of instruction: Japanese
Accrediting agency: Ministry of Education, Culture, Sports, Science and Technology (MEXT)
Student Services: Sports Facilities, Language Laboratory, Canteen
Periodicals: Discussion Paper, Series A, Discussion Paper, Series B, Memoirs of Kushiro Public University of Economics: Humanities and Natural Sciences, Memoirs of Kushiro Public University of Economics: Social Sciences, Regional Research
Last Update: 06-03-2018

Kyoto City University of Arts

13-6 Kutsukake Oe, Nishikyo
Kyoto 610-1197
Tel: +81(75) 332-0701
Fax: +81(75) 332-0709
Website: http://www.kcua.ac.jp
President: Kiyokazu Washida

Faculty
Fine Arts (Architectural and Environmental Design; Arts and Humanities; Ceramic Art; Design; Fine Arts; Handicrafts; Industrial Design; Media Studies; Natural Sciences; Painting and Drawing; Printing and Printmaking; Sculpture; Textile Design); **Music** (Conducting; Music; Music Theory and Composition; Musical Instruments; Musicology; Singing)

Graduate School
Arts (Architectural and Environmental Design; Arts and Humanities; Ceramic Art; Fine Arts; Graphic Design; Handicrafts; Industrial Design; Media Studies; Natural Sciences; Painting and Drawing; Printing and Printmaking; Restoration of Works of Art; Sculpture); **Music** (Conducting; Music; Music Theory and Composition; Musical Instruments; Musicology; Singing)

Research Division
Japanese Traditional Music (*RCJTM*) (Music)
History: Founded 1880
Academic year: April to March (April-October; October-March)
Admission requirements: Graduation from high school or equivalent, and entrance examination
Main language(s) of instruction: Japanese
Accrediting agency: Ministry of Education, Culture, Sports, Science and Technology (MEXT)
Degrees and diplomas: Shushi (Fine Arts; Music)
Periodicals: Ken-kyu-kiyo
Last Update: 06-03-2018

Kyoto Institute of Technology (KIT)

Matsugasaki, Sakyo-ku
Kyoto-shi 606-8585, Kyoto
Tel: +81(75) 724-7128
Fax: +81(75) 724-7710
Website: http://www.kit.ac.jp
President: Masao Furuyama
Tel: +81(75) 724-7001

School
Science and Technology (Architectural and Environmental Design; Architecture; Bioengineering; Biological and Life Sciences; Biology; Chemistry; Computer Engineering; Design; Electronic Engineering; Engineering; Engineering Management; Information Sciences; Materials Engineering; Mechanical Engineering; Molecular Biology)

Centre
Bioresource Field Science (Entomology; Plant and Crop Protection); **Cooperative Research**; **Drosophila Genetic Resource** (Genetics); **Environmental Science** (Environmental Studies); **Fibre and Textile Science** (Textile Technology); **Health Care Service** (Health Administration); **Information**

Science; **Instrumental Analysis**; **Manufacturing Technology** (Production Engineering); **Radioisotope** (Radiology)

Laboratory
Venture

Graduate School
Science and Technology (Architectural and Environmental Design; Architecture; Bioengineering; Biological and Life Sciences; Biology; Chemistry; Computer Engineering; Design; Electronic Engineering; Engineering; Engineering Management; Information Sciences; Materials Engineering; Mechanical Engineering; Molecular Biology)
History: Founded 1949 incorporating Kyoto College of Industry, founded 1902 and Kyoto College of Textile Fibres, 1899
Academic year: April to March (April-October; October-March)
Admission requirements: Graduation from high school or equivalent and entrance examination
Fees: 535,800 per annum (Yen)
Main language(s) of instruction: Japanese
Accrediting agency: Ministry of Education, Culture, Sports, Science and Technology (MEXT)
Degrees and diplomas: Gakushi, Shushi (Architecture; Bioengineering; Biology; Chemistry; Computer Engineering; Design; Electronic Engineering; Engineering Management; Information Sciences; Materials Engineering; Mechanical Engineering; Molecular Biology), Hakase (Design; Engineering; Materials Engineering)
Student Services: Academic Counselling, Social Counselling, Careers Guidance, Sports Facilities, Language Laboratory, Health Services, Canteen, Foreign Studies Centre
Periodicals: Bulletin of the Faculty of Textile Science, KIT International Journal, Memoirs of the Faculty of Engineering and Design
Last Update: 09-02-2018

Kyoto Prefectural University

1-5 Hangi Shimogamo Sakyo
Kyoto 606-8522
Tel: +81(75) 703-5101, +81(75) 703-5144
Fax: +81(75) 703-5149, +81(75) 703-2474
Website: http://www.kpu.ac.jp
President: Takashi Tsukiyama

Faculty

Letters (American Studies; Chinese; Cultural Studies; English; European Languages; European Studies; History; Japanese; Literature); **Life and Environmental Sciences** (Agriculture; Applied Mathematics; Architectural and Environmental Design; Architecture; Biochemistry; Biological and Life Sciences; Biology; Cell Biology; Chemistry; Computer Science; Dietetics; Environmental Studies; Food Science; Food Technology; Forestry; Health Sciences; Landscape Architecture; Materials Engineering; Molecular Biology; Nutrition); **Public Policy** (Arts and Humanities; Public Administration; Social Welfare; Welfare and Protective Services)

Graduate School

Letters (Arts and Humanities; Chinese; English; French; German; History; Japanese; Linguistics; Literature); **Life and Environmental Sciences** (Animal Husbandry; Biological and Life Sciences; Biotechnology; Environmental Studies; Food Science; Forestry; Safety Engineering); **Public Policy** (Economics; Law; Pedagogy; Political Sciences; Psychology; Public Administration; Social Welfare; Sociology; Welfare and Protective Services)
History: Founded 1895
Academic year: April to March (April-October; October-March)
Admission requirements: Graduation from high school or equivalent, and entrance examination
Main language(s) of instruction: Japanese
Accrediting agency: Ministry of Education, Culture, Sports, Science and Technology (MEXT)
Degrees and diplomas: Shushi (Chinese; English; History; Japanese; Linguistics; Literature), Hakase (Chinese; English; History; Japanese; Linguistics; Literature)
Student Services: Sports Facilities
Periodicals: Agriculture, Humanistic Science, Living Science and Welfare, Natural Science, Scientific Reports

Academic Staff 2012-2013	MALE	FEMALE	TOTAL
FULL-TIME			c. 160
Student Numbers 2012-2013			
All (Foreign Included)			c. 1700

Last Update: 06-03-2018

Kyoto Prefectural University of Medicine (KPUM)

465 Kajii-cho Kawaramachi-dori Hirokoji-agaru Kamigyo
Kyoto 602-0841
Tel: +81(75) 251-5111
Fax: +81(75) 211-7093
Website: http://www.kpu-m.ac.jp
President: Hiroshi Takenaka

School

Medicine (Anaesthesiology; Anatomy; Biochemistry; Cell Biology; Dermatology; Gynaecology and Obstetrics;

Medical Technology; Medicine; Microbiology; Molecular Biology; Neurosciences; Ophthalmology; Orthopaedics; Otorhinolaryngology; Paediatrics; Parasitology; Pathology; Pharmacology; Physiology; Psychiatry and Mental Health; Radiology; Surgery; Urology); **Nursing** (Biological and Life Sciences; Community Health; Health Sciences; Nursing; Social and Preventive Medicine; Welfare and Protective Services)

Graduate School

Medical Science (Biological and Life Sciences; Community Health; Medical Technology; Medicine; Social and Preventive Medicine; Treatment Techniques); **Nursing for Health Care Science** (Health Sciences; Nursing; Welfare and Protective Services)

Further information: also Shimogamo Campus
History: Founded 1872 as hospital, became Medical School 1880, acquired university status 1922. Reorganized 1949 and 1955
Academic year: April to March (April-September; September-January; January-March)
Admission requirements: Graduation from high school and entrance examination
Main language(s) of instruction: Japanese
Accrediting agency: Ministry of Education, Culture, Sports, Science and Technology (MEXT)
Degrees and diplomas: Shushi (Medicine; Nursing), Hakase (Medicine)
Periodicals: Kyoto Furitsu Ikadaigaku Fasshi
Last Update: 06-03-2018

Kyoto University

Yoshida-Honmachi Sakyo-ku
Kyoto-shi 606-8501, Kyoto
Tel: +81(75) 753-7531
Website: http://www.kyoto-u.ac.jp
President: Juichi Yamagiwa

Faculty

Agriculture (Agricultural Economics; Agricultural Engineering; Agriculture; Biological and Life Sciences; Biotechnology; Environmental Engineering; Environmental Studies; Food Science; Forestry; Natural Resources); **Economics** (Business Administration; Economics; Social Sciences); **Education** (Education; Educational Psychology; Educational Sciences); **Engineering** (Architecture; Computer Science; Electrical and Electronic Engineering; Engineering; Industrial Chemistry; Mathematics); **Integrated Human Studies** (Arts and Humanities; Cognitive Sciences; Cultural Studies; Environmental Studies; Information Sciences; Natural Sciences); **Law** (Law); **Letters** (Asian Studies;

Behavioural Sciences; Cultural Studies; History; Philosophy; Social Sciences; Western European Studies); **Medicine** (Health Sciences; Medicine); **Pharmaceutical Sciences** (Pharmacology; Pharmacy); **Science** (Astronomy and Space Science; Biology; Chemistry; Earth Sciences; Mathematics; Natural Sciences; Physics)

Unit

Central Administration (Administration)

Institute

Information Management and Communication (Communication Studies; Information Management); **Promotion of Excellence in Higher Education** (Higher Education)

Centre

African Area Studies (African Studies); **Computing and Media Studies** (*Academic*) (Computer Science; Media Studies); **Counseling** (Psychology); **Cultural Heritage Studies** (Cultural Studies; Heritage Preservation); **Ecological Research** (Ecology); **Field Science Education and Research** (Coastal Studies; Ecology; Forest Biology; Marine Biology); **Fundamental Chemistry** (*Fukui*) (Chemistry); **Hakubi Advanced Research**; **Integrated Area Studies** (Cultural Studies); **Kokoro Research**; **Kyoto University Archives** (Archiving); **Kyoto University Research Administration Office** (Administration); **Low Temperature and Materials Science** (Heating and Refrigeration; Materials Engineering); **Promotion of Excellence in Higher Education** (Curriculum; Educational Research; Higher Education); **Promotion of Interdisciplinary Education and Research** (Education); **Radiation Biology** (Biology); **The Kyoto University Museum** (Museum Studies); **Wildlife Research** (Cognitive Sciences; Wildlife; Zoology); **Women Researchers** (Women's Studies)

Group

Agency for Health, Safety and Environment (Environmental Studies; Health Sciences; Safety Engineering); **Kyoto University Library Network** (Library Science); **Organization for the Promotion of International Relations** (International Relations); **Society-Academia Collaboration for Innovation**

Graduate School

Advanced Integrated Studies in Human Survivability; **Agriculture** (Agricultural Economics; Agriculture; Agronomy; Biological and Life Sciences; Biotechnology; Environmental Engineering; Environmental Studies; Food Science; Forestry; Horticulture; Natural Resources); **Asian and African Area Studies** (African Studies; International Studies; Southeast Asian Studies); **Biostudies** (Biological and Life Sciences); **Economics** (Business Administration;

Economics; Social Sciences); **Education** (Education; Educational Sciences); **Energy Science** (Energy Engineering; Environmental Studies); **Engineering** (Aeronautical and Aerospace Engineering; Applied Chemistry; Architecture; Biochemistry; Chemical Engineering; Civil Engineering; Electrical Engineering; Electronic Engineering; Energy Engineering; Engineering; Environmental Engineering; Materials Engineering; Mechanical Engineering; Molecular Biology; Natural Resources; Nuclear Engineering; Polymer and Plastics Technology; Structural Architecture; Town Planning); **Global Environmental Studies** (Ecology; Environmental Engineering; Natural Resources); **Government** (Government); **Human and Environmental Studies** (Cultural Studies; Environmental Studies); **Informatics** (Applied Mathematics; Applied Physics; Computer Engineering; Computer Science; Information Technology; Systems Analysis; Telecommunications Engineering); **Law** (Law); **Letters** (Asian Studies; Behavioural Sciences; Cultural Studies; History; Philosophy; Western European Studies); **Management** (Management); **Medicine** (Health Sciences; Medicine); **Pharmaceutical Sciences** (Biological and Life Sciences; Biomedicine; Chemistry; Computer Science; Genetics; Pharmacy); **Public Health** (Public Health); **Science** (Astronomy and Space Science; Biological and Life Sciences; Chemistry; Earth Sciences; Mathematics; Physics)

Research Division

Advanced Energy (Energy Engineering); **Chemical Research** (Chemistry); **Disaster Prevention Research** (Safety Engineering); **Economic Research** (*Kyoto*) (Economics); **Frontier Medical Sciences** (Medicine); **Humanities** (Arts and Humanities); **Integrated Cell-Material Sciences** (Cell Biology; Materials Engineering); **iPS Cell Research and Application** (Cell Biology); **Mathematical Sciences** (Mathematics); **Primate Research** (Zoology); **Research Reactor** (Nuclear Engineering; Nuclear Physics; Safety Engineering); **Southeast Asian Studies** (Southeast Asian Studies); **Sustainable Humanosphere** (Natural Sciences); **Theoretical Physics** (*Yukawa*) (Physics); **Virus** (Virology)

Further information: Also Teaching Hospital

History: Founded 1897 as Kyoto Imerial University with Colleges of Law, Science and Engineering, Medicine and Letters. Colleges renamed faculties 1919, and acquired present title 1947

Academic year: April to March (April-September; October-March)

Admission requirements: Graduation from high school or equivalent, entrance examination

Main language(s) of instruction: Japanese, English

Accrediting agency: Ministry of Education, Culture, Sports, Science and Technology (MEXT)

Degrees and diplomas: Gakushi, Shushi, Hakase (African Studies; Agriculture; Arts and Humanities; Asian Studies; Biological and Life Sciences; Computer Science; Economics; Education; Energy Engineering; Engineering; Environmental Studies; Law; Medicine; Pharmacy)

Student Services: Academic Counselling, Social Counselling, Careers Guidance, Nursery Care, Cultural Activities, Sports Facilities, Language Laboratory, Facilities for disabled people, Health Services, Canteen, Foreign Studies Centre

Periodicals: Kyoto University at a Glance, Kyoto University Research Activities, Raku-yu

Academic Staff 2012-2013	MALE	FEMALE	TOTAL
FULL-TIME	4903	2239	7142
PART-TIME	3617	3398	7015
Student Numbers 2012-2013			
All (Foreign Included)	17391	5404	22795
Foreign only	769	621	1390

Total number of part-time students: 219
Last Update: 29-05-2018

Kyoto University of Education

1 Fukakusa-Fujinomori-cho Fushimi-ku
Kyoto-shi 612-8522, Kyoto
Tel: +81(75) 644-8100
Fax: +81(75) 644-8113
Website: http://www.kyokyo-u.ac.jp
President: Tomohiro Hosokawa

Faculty

Education (Education; Educational Sciences; Special Education; Teacher Training)

Course/Programme

Japanese Training; **Teacher Training** (Teacher Training)

Graduate School

Education (Curriculum; Education; Primary Education; Special Education; Teacher Training)

History: Founded 1876 as Kyoto Prefectural Normal School, acquired present title 1949

Academic year: April to March (April-July; October-March)

Admission requirements: Graduation from high school, or foreign equivalent, and entrance examination

Fees: Tuition, 535,800 per annum (Yen)

Main language(s) of instruction: Japanese

Accrediting agency: Ministry of Education, Culture, Sports, Science and Technology (MEXT)

Degrees and diplomas: Gakushi, Shushi (Education). Also Special Postgraduate Course in Special Needs Education

Student Services: Academic Counselling, Social Counselling, Careers Guidance, Sports Facilities, Language Laboratory, Facilities for disabled people, Health Services, Canteen
Periodicals: Bulletin of Kyoto University of Education

Academic Staff 2012-2013	MALE	FEMALE	TOTAL
FULL-TIME			134
Student Numbers 2012-2013			
All (Foreign Included)			1708
Foreign only			56

Last Update: 14-02-2018

Kyushu Dental College

2-6-1, Manazuru Kokura-kita
Kitakyushu 803-8580, Fukuoka
Tel: +81(93) 582-1131
Fax: +81(93) 582-6000
Website: http://www.kyu-dent.ac.jp
President: Tatsuji Nishihara

Faculty
Dentistry (Dentistry; Oral Pathology)

Graduate School
Dentistry (Dental Hygiene; Dental Technology; Dentistry; Oral Pathology; Surgery)
History: Founded 1914. Acquired present status 2006.
Academic year: April to March (April-October; October-March)
Admission requirements: Graduation from high school or foreign equivalent, and entrance examination
Main language(s) of instruction: Japanese
Accrediting agency: Ministry of Education, Culture, Sports, Science and Technology (MEXT)
Degrees and diplomas: Gakushi (Dentistry), Hakase (Dentistry; Oral Pathology; Surgery)
Student Services: Sports Facilities
Periodicals: Journal, Kiyo (Research Papers)
Last Update: 28-03-2018

Kyushu Institute of Technology (KYUTECH)

1-1 Sensui-cho Tobata-ku
Kitakyushu-shi 804-8550, Fukuoka
Tel: +81(94) 884-3051, +81(94) 884-3007
Fax: +81(94) 884-3015
Website: http://www.kyutech.ac.jp

Faculty
Computer Science and Systems Engineering (*Iizuka Campus*) (Artificial Intelligence; Biological and Life Sciences; Computer Engineering; Computer Science; Electronic Engineering; Information Sciences; Information Technology; Mechanical Engineering); **Engineering** (*Tobata Campus*) (Aeronautical and Aerospace Engineering; Applied Chemistry; Architecture; Automation and Control Engineering; Civil Engineering; Computer Engineering; Electrical and Electronic Engineering; Electrical Engineering; Electronic Engineering; Engineering; Environmental Engineering; Materials Engineering; Mechanical Engineering)

Graduate School
Computer Science and Systems Engineering (*Iizuka Campus*) (Computer Engineering; Computer Science; Information Sciences; Information Technology); **Engineering** (*Tobata Campus*) (Architecture; Automation and Control Engineering; Automotive Engineering; Civil Engineering; Computer Engineering; Electrical and Electronic Engineering; Electronic Engineering; Engineering; Materials Engineering; Mechanical Engineering; Robotics; Structural Architecture); **Life Science and Systems Engineering** (*Wakamatsu Campus*) (Bioengineering; Biological and Life Sciences; Cognitive Sciences; Computer Engineering; Nanotechnology; Neurosciences)
Further information: Also IIzuka and Wakamatsu campuses; Satellite Office in Malaysia
History: Founded 1907 as Meiji Senmon Gakko, a private Institution. Became National Institution 1921. Acquired present status and title 1949.
Academic year: April to March (April-October; October-March)
Admission requirements: Graduation from high school or recognized equivalent and entrance examination
Main language(s) of instruction: Japanese
Accrediting agency: Ministry of Education, Culture, Sports, Science and Technology (MEXT)
Degrees and diplomas: Gakushi, Shushi (Automation and Control Engineering; Civil Engineering; Computer Engineering; Electrical Engineering; Electronic Engineering; Information Sciences; Information Technology; Materials Engineering; Mechanical Engineering; Structural Architecture), Hakase (Automation and Control Engineering; Civil Engineering; Computer Engineering; Electrical Engineering; Electronic Engineering; Information Sciences; Information Technology; Materials Engineering; Mechanical Engineering; Structural Architecture). Also Double Degree Programmes with partner institutions in overseas (France, China, Taiwan, Republic of Korea, Malaysia).
Periodicals: Annual Bulletin (Faculty of Engineering; Faculty of Computer Science and System Engineering and Graduate School of Life Science and Systems Engineering)

Academic Staff 2013-2014	MALE	FEMALE	TOTAL
FULL-TIME			365
Student Numbers 2013-2014			
All (Foreign Included)			5876

Last Update: 14-02-2018

Kyushu University

6-10-1 Hakozaki
Higashi-ku 812-8581, Fukuoka
Tel: +81(92) 642-2111
Fax: +81(92) 642-2113
Website: http://www.kyushu-u.ac.jp
President: Chiharu Kubo

Faculty

Agriculture (Agricultural Education; Agriculture; Biological and Life Sciences; Biotechnology); **Arts and Science** (Arts and Humanities; Natural Sciences); **Dental Science** (Dentistry); **Design** (Communication Arts; Design); **Economics** (Business Administration; Economics; Engineering Management; International Economics); **Engineering** (Aeronautical and Aerospace Engineering; Applied Chemistry; Applied Physics; Chemical Engineering; Civil Engineering; Earth Sciences; Environmental Engineering; Marine Engineering; Materials Engineering; Mechanical Engineering; Nuclear Engineering); **Engineering Sciences** (Energy Engineering; Engineering; Materials Engineering); **Human Environmental Studies** (Architecture; Education; Urban Studies); **Humanities** (History; Literature; Modern Languages; Philosophy); **Information Sciences and Electrical Engineering** (Electrical and Electronic Engineering; Information Sciences; Information Technology); **Languages and Cultures** (Cultural Studies; Linguistics); **Law** (Criminal Law; International Law; Justice Administration; Law; Polish; Private Law; Public Law); **Mathematics** (Mathematics); **Medical Sciences** (Health Education; Health Sciences; Medicine; Molecular Biology); **Pharmaceutical Sciences** (Medicine; Pharmacology); **Science** (Astronomy and Space Science; Biology; Chemistry; Earth Sciences; Physics); **Social and Cultural Studies** (Cultural Studies; Environmental Studies; Social Studies)

School

Agriculture (*Undergraduate*) (Agriculture; Natural Resources); **Dentistry** (*Undergraduate*) (Dental Hygiene; Dental Technology; Dentistry); **Design** (*Undergraduate*) (Communication Arts; Design; Environmental Engineering; Industrial Design); **Economics** (*Undergraduate*) (Business and Commerce; Economics); **Education** (*Undergraduate*) (Education); **Engineering** (*Undergraduate*) (Aeronautical and Aerospace Engineering; Architecture; Civil Engineering; Computer Science; Earth Sciences; Electrical Engineering; Energy Engineering; Marine Engineering; Materials Engineering; Mechanical Engineering); **Law** (*Undergraduate*) (Law); **Letters** (*Undergraduate*) (Arts and Humanities); **Medicine** (*Undergraduate*) (Biomedicine; Health Sciences; Medicine); **Pharmaceutical Sciences** (*Undergraduate*) (Pharmacy); **Science** (*Undergraduate*) (Biology; Chemistry; Earth Sciences; Mathematics; Physics)

Institute
Advanced Study

Centre
Accelerator and Beam Applied Science; **Advanced Instrumental Analysis**; **Advanced Medical Innovation** (*CAMI*); **Advanced Research in Drug Creation**; **Art, Science and Technology Center for Cooperative Research** (*KASTEC*); **Asian Conservation Ecology**; **Bio-architecture**; **Biotron Application**; **Environment and Safety**; **Epigenome Network Research Center**; **EU Centre** (*EUIJ-Kyushi*); **Future Chemistry**; **Human Proteome Research Center**; **INAMORI Frontier Research Center**; **Incubation Center for Advanced Medical Science** (*ICAMS*); **Institute of Tropical Agriculture**; **Integrated Kansei Design Center**; **Intellectual Property and Private International Law**; **International Center for Space Weather Science and Education**; **International Education Center**; **International Research Center for Hydrogen Energy**; **International Research Center for Molecular Systems**; **Itoh Research Center for Plasma Turbulence**; **Japan-Egypt Cooperation in Science and Technology**; **Kyushu University Archives**; **Laboratory for Ionized Gas and Laser Research**; **Low Temperature Center**; **Material Management Center**; **Natural Disaster Information Center of Western Japan**; **Next-Generation Fuel Cell Research Center**; **Nucleotide Pool Research Center**; **Organic Photonics and Electronics Research**; **Plasma Nano-interface Engineering**; **Radioisotope Center**; **Research and Education Center of Carbon Resources**; **Research Center for Advanced Biomechanics**; **Research Center for Advanced Immunology**; **Research Center for Cancer Stem Cell**; **Research Center for Education in Health Care Systems**; **Research Center for Environment and Developmental Medical Sciences**; **Research Center for Korean Studies**; **Research Center for Steel**; **Research Center for Synchrotron Light Applications**; **Research Institute of Superconductor Science and Systems** (*RISS*); **Research Laboratory for High Voltage Electron Microscopy**; **Risk Science Research Center**; **Robert T.Huang Entrepreneurship Center** (*QREC*); **Science, Technology and Innovation Policy Studies**; **Synthetic Systems Biology Research Center**; **System LSI Research Center**; **Yunus and Shiiki Social Business Center** (*SBRC*)

Graduate School

Bioresources and Bioenvironmental Sciences (Agricultural Economics; Biotechnology; Environmental Studies; Natural Resources); **Dental Science** (Dental Hygiene; Dental Technology; Dentistry); **Design** (Design); **Economics** (*Kyushu University Business School, QBS*) (Business Administration; Economics; Management); **Engineering** (Aeronautical and Aerospace Engineering; Applied Physics; Biochemistry; Chemistry; Civil Engineering; Earth Sciences; Environmental Engineering; Marine Engineering; Materials Engineering; Mechanical Engineering; Nuclear Engineering); **Engineering Sciences** (Earth Sciences; Electronic Engineering; Energy Engineering; Environmental Engineering); **Human-Environment Studies** (Architecture; Behavioural Sciences; Clinical Psychology; Education; Health Sciences; Urban Studies); **Humanities** (Geography; History; Literature; Modern Languages; Philosophy); **Information Sciences and Electrical Engineering** (Electrical and Electronic Engineering; Information Sciences; Information Technology); **Integrated Frontier Sciences** (Automotive Engineering; Library Science); **Law** (Law; Political Sciences); **Law** (*Professional*) (Law); **Mathematics** (Mathematics); **Medical Sciences** (Health Administration; Health Sciences); **Pharmaceutical Sciences** (Pharmacy); **Sciences** (Chemistry; Earth Sciences; Physics); **Social and Cultural Studies** (International Studies; Japanese); **Systems Life Sciences** (Biological and Life Sciences)

Research Division

Applied Mechanics; **Bioregulation**; **Carbon-Neutral Energy Research** (*International*); **Health Sciences**; **Information Technology**; **Materials Chemistry and Engineering**; **Mathematics for Industry**

History: Founded 1903 as Fukuoka College of Medicine of Kyoto Imperial University. Established 1911 as Kyushu Imperial University. Acquired present status 1947. Integrated Kyushu Geijutsu Koka Daigaku/Kyushu Institute of Design 2003

Academic year: April to March (April-September; October-March)

Admission requirements: Graduation from upper secondary school or foreign equivalent, and entrance examination

Fees: 535,800 per annum (Yen)

Main language(s) of instruction: Japanese

Accrediting agency: Ministry of Education, Culture, Sports, Science and Technology (MEXT)

Degrees and diplomas: Gakushi (Arts and Humanities; Biomedical Engineering; Dentistry; Design; Economics; Education; Engineering; Fine Arts; Health Sciences; Law; Medicine; Nursing; Pharmacology; Pharmacy), Shushi (Automotive Engineering; Behavioural Sciences; Design; Economics; Engineering; Fine Arts; Health Sciences; Information Sciences; Law; Library Science; Mathematics; Medicine; Natural Resources; Nursing; Pharmacy; Philosophy),

Hakase (Agriculture; Automotive Engineering; Behavioural Sciences; Dentistry; Design; Economics; Education; Engineering; Health Sciences; Information Sciences; Law; Literature; Mathematics; Medicine; Pharmacology; Pharmacy; Philosophy; Psychology)

Student Services: Academic Counselling, Careers Guidance, Nursery Care, Sports Facilities, Language Laboratory, Health Services, Canteen, Foreign Studies Centre

Periodicals: Kyudai News

Last Update: 25-05-2018

Maebashi Institute of Technology

460-1 Kamisadori-machi
Maebashi-shi 371-0816, Gunma
Tel: +81(27) 265-0111
Fax: +81(27) 265-3837
Website: http://www.maebashi-it.ac.jp
President: Yukikazu Tsuji
Tel: +86(27) 265-0111

Faculty

Engineering (Architectural Restoration; Bioengineering; Biological and Life Sciences; Biomedical Engineering; Biotechnology; Botany; Civil Engineering; Computer Engineering; Computer Science; Data Processing; Design; Engineering; Environmental Engineering; Food Technology; Hydraulic Engineering; Interior Design; Landscape Architecture; Materials Engineering; Software Engineering; Structural Architecture; Town Planning; Water Science)

Graduate School

Engineering (Architecture; Bioengineering; Biological and Life Sciences; Biotechnology; Civil Engineering; Computer Science; Engineering; Environmental Engineering)

History: Founded 1997.

Main language(s) of instruction: Japanese

Accrediting agency: Ministry of Education, Culture, Sports, Science and Technology (MEXT)

Degrees and diplomas: Shushi (Architecture; Biological and Life Sciences; Biomedical Engineering; Biotechnology; Civil Engineering; Computer Science; Environmental Engineering), Hakase (Biomedical Engineering; Environmental Engineering)

Last Update: 06-03-2018

Meio University

1220-1 Biimata
Nago-shi 905-8585, Okinawa
Tel: +81(980) 51-1100

Fax: +81(980) 52-4640
Website: http://www.meio-u.ac.jp
President: Katsunori Yamazato

Faculty
Human Health Sciences (Health Sciences; Nursing; Sports); **International Studies** (Business and Commerce; Cultural Studies; Education; English; Foreign Languages Education; Information Management; Information Sciences; Information Technology; International Studies; Japanese; Management; Modern Languages; Native Language Education; Primary Education; Tourism)

Graduate School
Graduate Studies (Accountancy; Cultural Studies; Dance; E- Business/Commerce; Economics; English; Environmental Studies; Health Administration; Health Sciences; Human Resources; Industrial and Organizational Psychology; Information Sciences; Information Technology; International Business; International Relations; Latin American Studies; Linguistics; Literature; Management; Marketing; Modern Languages; Nutrition; Pathology; Physiology; Public Health; Social Policy; Social Studies; Southeast Asian Studies; Tourism)
History: Founded 1994 as a private university in 1994. Reorganized as a public university 2010
Main language(s) of instruction: Japanese
Accrediting agency: Ministry of Education, Culture, Sports, Science and Technology (MEXT)
Degrees and diplomas: Shushi (Cultural Studies; International Studies; Nursing)
Student Services: Academic Counselling, Social Counselling, Sports Facilities, Health Services, Canteen, Library
Last Update: 06-03-2018

Mie Prefectural College of Nursing

1-1-1 Yumegaoka
Tsu-shi 514-0116, Mie
Tel: +81(59) 233-5600
Fax: +81(59) 233-5666
Website: http://www.mcn.ac.jp
President: Michiko Hishinuma

Faculty
Nursing (Community Health; Gerontology; Midwifery; Nursing; Psychiatry and Mental Health; Public Health)

Graduate School
Nursing (Gerontology; Nursing; Paediatrics; Psychiatry and Mental Health; Public Health)
History: Founded 1997

Fees: Tuition, 535,800 per annum (Yen)
Main language(s) of instruction: Japanese
Accrediting agency: Ministry of Education, Culture, Sports, Science and Technology (MEXT)
Degrees and diplomas: Shushi (Nursing)
Student Services: Sports Facilities, Canteen, Library
Last Update: 06-03-2018

Mie University

1577 Kurimamachiya-cho
Tsu City 514-8507, Mie
Tel: +81(59) 232-1211, +81(59) 231-9707
Fax: +81(59) 231-9000, +81(59) 231-5692
Website: http://www.mie-u.ac.jp
President: Yoshihiro Komada
Tel: +81(59) 231-9707

Faculty
Bioresources (Biological and Life Sciences; Biotechnology; Environmental Engineering; Environmental Studies; Natural Resources); **Education** (Continuing Education; Education; Humanities and Social Science Education; Information Sciences; Teacher Training); **Engineering** (Applied Physics; Architecture; Chemical Engineering; Electrical and Electronic Engineering; Engineering; Information Technology; Materials Engineering; Mechanical Engineering); **Humanities, Law and Economics** (Arts and Humanities; Economics; Law)

School
Medicine (Medicine; Nursing)

Graduate School
Bioresources (Biological and Life Sciences; Environmental Engineering; Environmental Studies; Natural Resources); **Education** (Education; Educational Sciences); **Engineering** (Applied Chemistry; Applied Physics; Architecture; Electrical and Electronic Engineering; Engineering; Information Technology; Materials Engineering; Mechanical Engineering; Systems Analysis); **Humanities and Social Sciences** (Arts and Humanities; Social Sciences); **Medicine** (Medicine; Nursing); **Regional Innovation Studies** (Biological and Life Sciences; Engineering)
History: Founded 1949, with the Faculty of Liberal Arts and the Faculty of Agriculture on the basis of: Mie Prefectural Normal School Watarai Prefectural Normal School (1874) and Mie Prefectural Yuzo School (1875) that merged in 1943; the Mie Higher Agricultural and Forestry College (1944), founded as the Mie Higher Agricultural and Forestry School (1921); the Mie Normal School for Youth School Teachers (1944), founded as the Mie Prefectural Teacher

Training School for Agricultural Continuation School Teachers (1925)

Academic year: April to March

Admission requirements: High school diploma (prospective graduates are allowed); High School Equivalence Test; National Center Test for University Admissions

Fees: Bachelor and Master's degree programmes, c. 535,800 per annum; Doctoral programmes, 520,800 per annum (Yen)

Main language(s) of instruction: Japanese

Accrediting agency: Ministry of Education, Culture, Sports, Science and Technology (MEXT)

Degrees and diplomas: Gakushi, Shushi, Hakase (Bioengineering; Engineering; Medicine; Natural Resources)

Student Services: Academic Counselling, Social Counselling, Careers Guidance, Nursery Care, Cultural Activities, Sports Facilities, Language Laboratory, Health Services, Canteen, Foreign Studies Centre

Periodicals: Annual Report of the Center for International Education and Research, Bulletin of Center for International Education and Research, Bulletin of the Faculty of Education, Bulletin of the Faculty of Humanities, Law and Economics, Bulletin of the Graduate School of Bioresources, Bulletin of the Mie University Forests, Environmental Management Report, Mie Medical Journal, Mie University X, MIU, Research Reports of the Faculty of Engineering, WAVE MIE UNIV

Academic Staff 2013-2014	MALE	FEMALE	TOTAL
FULL-TIME	1044	755	1799
PART-TIME	327	907	1234
STAFF WITH DOCTORATE			
FULL-TIME	319	41	360
Student Numbers 2013-2014			
All (Foreign Included)	4679	2701	7380
Foreign only	87	88	175

Total number of distance students: 7380

Last Update: 06-03-2018

Miyagi University (MYU)

1 Gakuen Kurokawagun
Taiwa-cho 981-3298, Miyagi
Tel: +81(22) 377-8205, +81(22) 377-8333
Fax: +81(22) 377-8282, +81(22) 245-1534
Website: http://www.myu.ac.jp
President: Nobuaki Kawakami

School

Food, Agricultural and Environmental Sciences (Agricultural Economics; Agriculture; Animal Husbandry; Environmental Studies; Farm Management; Food Science; Food Technology; Horticulture; Marketing); **Nursing** (*Also graduate school*) (Arts and Humanities; Nursing); **Project Design** (*Also graduate school*) (Business Administration; Computer Science; Information Sciences; Information Technology; Rural Planning; Town Planning)

Graduate School

Food Industry (Agricultural Business; Agriculture; Business Administration; Environmental Management; Farm Management; Food Technology; Management); **Nursing** (Health Sciences; Information Technology; Nursing); **Project Design** (Business Administration; Management; Technology)

Further information: Also Taihaku Campus

History: Founded 1997

Main language(s) of instruction: Japanese

Accrediting agency: Ministry of Education, Culture, Sports, Science and Technology (MEXT)

Degrees and diplomas: Shushi (Architectural and Environmental Design; Business Administration; Environmental Management; Farm Management; Food Technology; Information Sciences; Management; Nursing), Hakase (Agriculture; Business Administration; Environmental Studies; Food Technology; Information Sciences; Information Technology; Nursing; Social and Community Services)

Last Update: 06-03-2018

Miyagi University of Education

149, Aramaki-aza-Aoba Aoba Ku
Sendai 980-0845, Miyagi
Tel: +81(22) 214-3305
Fax: +81(22) 214-3935, +81(22) 214-3621
Website: http://www.miyakyo-u.ac.jp
President: Kazuyuki Mikami

Faculty

Education (Art Education; Child Care and Development; Computer Education; Education; Education of the Handicapped; Educational Psychology; Foreign Languages Education; Health Education; Home Economics Education; Humanities and Social Science Education; Mathematics Education; Music Education; Native Language Education; Pedagogy; Physical Education; Preschool Education; Primary Education; Science Education; Secondary Education; Special Education; Teacher Training; Technology Education)

Course/Programme

Special Needs Education (Education of the Handicapped; Primary Education; Special Education; Teacher Training)

Graduate School

Teacher Training (Teacher Training)

Research Division

Advanced Teacher Training (*Graduate*) (Art Education; Education; Health Education; Home Economics Education; Humanities and Social Science Education; Mathematics Education; Music Education; Native Language Education; Physical Education; Science Education; Secondary Education; Special Education; Technology Education)

History: Founded 1965 as National University and providing training courses for teachers previously given at Tohoku Daigaku. Financed by the State

Academic year: April to March (April-September; October-March)

Admission requirements: Graduation from senior high school or foreign equivalent, and entrance examination

Fees: Tuition, 535,800 per annum (Yen)

Main language(s) of instruction: Japanese

Accrediting agency: Ministry of Education, Culture, Sports, Science and Technology (MEXT)

Degrees and diplomas: Gakushi, Shushi (Art Education; Foreign Languages Education; Health Education; Home Economics Education; Mathematics Education; Music Education; Native Language Education; Physical Education; Science Education; Special Education; Teacher Training)

Student Services: Academic Counselling, Social Counselling, Careers Guidance, Cultural Activities, Sports Facilities, Language Laboratory, Facilities for disabled people, Health Services, Canteen, Foreign Studies Centre, Residential Facilities

Periodicals: Annual Reports of Science Education Research Institute, Bulletin of Miyagi University of Education

Last Update: 14-02-2018

Miyazaki Municipal University (MMU)

1-1-2 Funatsuka
Miyazaki-shi 880-8520, Miyazaki
Tel: +81(985) 20-2000
Fax: +81(985) 20-4820
Website: http://www.miyazaki-mu.ac.jp
President: Arima Shinsaku

Faculty

Humanities (Arts and Humanities; Communication Studies; Cultural Studies; English; Information Sciences; Information Technology; International Relations; Mass Communication; Media Studies)

Course/Programme

Teacher Training (Teacher Training)
History: Founded 1993
Fees: Tuition, 535,800 per annum (Yen)

Main language(s) of instruction: Japanese
Accrediting agency: Ministry of Education, Culture, Sports, Science and Technology (MEXT)
Student Services: Health Services, Library, Residential Facilities
Last Update: 06-03-2018

Miyazaki Prefectural Nursing University

3-5-1 Manabino
Miyazaki 880-0929
Tel: +81(985) 59-7700
Fax: +81(985) 59-7771
Website: http://www.mpu.ac.jp
President: Chiho Seguchi

Department/Division

Nursing (Anthropology; Community Health; Health Sciences; Nursing; Public Health)

Graduate School

Nursing (Nursing)
History: Founded 1997
Main language(s) of instruction: Japanese
Accrediting agency: Ministry of Education, Culture, Sports, Science and Technology (MEXT)
Degrees and diplomas: Shushi (Nursing), Hakase (Nursing)
Student Services: Library
Last Update: 06-03-2018

Muroran Institute of Technology (MuroranIT)

27-1 Mizumoto-cho
Muroran-shi 050-8585, Hokkaido
Tel: +81(143) 46-5000, +81(143) 46-5024
Fax: +81(143) 46-5032
Website: http://www.muroran-it.ac.jp
President: Yoshikazu Kuga

College

Design and Manufacturing Technology (Design; Production Engineering); **Environmental Technology** (Environmental Engineering); **Information and Systems** (Information Sciences; Information Technology); **Liberal Arts** (Arts and Humanities)

Department/Division

Applied Sciences (Applied Chemistry; Applied Physics; Biochemistry; Biological and Life Sciences; Biology;

Biotechnology; Chemical Engineering; Chemistry; Genetics; Microbiology; Organic Chemistry; Physical Chemistry; Physics); **Civil Engineering and Architecture** (Architectural and Environmental Design; Architecture; Architecture and Planning; Civil Engineering; Construction Engineering; Environmental Engineering; Regional Planning; Structural Architecture; Town Planning); **Information and Electronic Engineering** (Artificial Intelligence; Computer Engineering; Computer Networks; Computer Science; Electrical Engineering; Electronic Engineering; Information Sciences; Information Technology; Mathematics and Computer Science; Software Engineering; Telecommunications Engineering); **Mechanical, Aerospace and Materials Engineering** (Aeronautical and Aerospace Engineering; Automation and Control Engineering; Materials Engineering; Mechanical Engineering; Production Engineering; Robotics)

Centre

Cooperative Research and Development (Development Studies); **Environmental Science and Disaster Mitigation for Advanced Research** (*CEDAR*) (Environmental Management; Environmental Studies); **General Education** (Arts and Humanities); **Health Administration** (Health Administration); **Instrumental Analysis** (Measurement and Precision Engineering); **Manufacturing and Engineering Design** (Engineering Drawing and Design; Production Engineering); **Multimedia Aided Education** (Educational Technology; Multimedia)

Laboratory

Satellite Venture Business (Business Administration)

Graduate School

Engineering (*Doctor's Course*) (Aeronautical and Aerospace Engineering; Applied Chemistry; Architecture; Automation and Control Engineering; Biochemistry; Biophysics; Cell Biology; Chemical Engineering; Chemistry; Civil Engineering; Computer Engineering; Construction Engineering; Electrical Engineering; Electronic Engineering; Energy Engineering; Engineering; Environmental Engineering; Geological Engineering; Heating and Refrigeration; Information Technology; Instrument Making; Landscape Architecture; Marine Engineering; Materials Engineering; Measurement and Precision Engineering; Molecular Biology; Optical Technology; Optics; Organic Chemistry; Production Engineering; Regional Planning; Solid State Physics; Structural Architecture; Thermal Engineering; Town Planning; Water Science); **Engineering** (*Master's Course*) (Aeronautical and Aerospace Engineering; Applied Chemistry; Applied Physics; Architecture; Artificial Intelligence; Biology; Civil Engineering; Computer Engineering; Electrical and Electronic Engineering; Electrical Engineering; Electronic Engineering; Engineering; Information Technology; Materials

Engineering; Mathematics; Mechanical Engineering; Telecommunications Services)

Research Division

Aerospace Plane (Aeronautical and Aerospace Engineering); **Environmentally Friendly Materials Engineering** (Environmental Engineering; Materials Engineering)

History: Founded 1949, incorporating the Civil Engineering Department of Sapporo Agricultural College, founded 1887, and Muroran Higher Technical School (1939)

Academic year: April to March (April-September; October-March)

Admission requirements: Graduation from high school or equivalent, and entrance examination

Main language(s) of instruction: Japanese

Accrediting agency: Ministry of Education, Culture, Sports, Science and Technology (MEXT)

Degrees and diplomas: Gakushi (Engineering), Shushi (Aeronautical and Aerospace Engineering; Applied Chemistry; Applied Physics; Civil Engineering; Computer Engineering; Construction Engineering; Electronic Engineering; Engineering; Information Technology; Mathematics; Mechanical Engineering), Hakase (Aeronautical and Aerospace Engineering; Automation and Control Engineering; Chemical Engineering; Construction Engineering; Engineering; Information Technology; Materials Engineering; Production Engineering)

Student Services: Academic Counselling, Social Counselling, Careers Guidance, Sports Facilities, Language Laboratory, Health Services, Library

Periodicals: Memoirs

Last Update: 23-02-2018

Nagano College of Nursing (NCN)

1694 Akaho Komagane
Nagano 399-4117
Tel: +81(265) 81-5100
Fax: +81(265) 81-1256
Website: http://www.nagano-nurs.ac.jp
President: Yoshiko Shimizu

School

Nursing (American Studies; Arts and Humanities; Biological and Life Sciences; Chemistry; Economics; English; English Studies; Ethics; Gerontology; Health Sciences; Midwifery; Nursing; Paediatrics; Pathology; Psychiatry and Mental Health; Psychology; Rehabilitation and Therapy; Social Sciences)

Graduate School

Nursing (Gerontology; Health Administration; Health Sciences; Midwifery; Nursing; Pathology; Psychiatry and Mental Health; Psychology; Rehabilitation and Therapy)

History: Founded 1995
Main language(s) of instruction: Japanese
Accrediting agency: Ministry of Education, Culture, Sports, Science and Technology (MEXT)
Degrees and diplomas: Shushi (Nursing), Hakase (Nursing)
Student Services: Health Services, Library
Last Update: 07-03-2018

Nagano University

Shimonogo 658-1
Ueda 386-1298, Nagano
Tel: +81(268) 39-0001
Fax: +81(268) 39-0002
Website: http://www.nagano.ac.jp
President: Eizo Nakamura

Faculty

Business and Information (Accountancy; Anthropology; Business Administration; Chinese; Commercial Law; Computer Engineering; Computer Graphics; Computer Networks; Data Processing; Design; Ecology; English; Environmental Studies; Ethics; French; Geography; German; History; Human Resources; Industrial and Production Economics; Information Management; Information Sciences; International Business; Law; Literature; Management; Marketing; Media Studies; Multimedia; Pedagogy; Philosophy; Physical Education; Psychology); **Social Welfare** (Child Care and Development; Psychiatry and Mental Health; Social Welfare; Social Work); **Tourism** (Business Administration; Computer Science; Development Studies; Ecology; Economics; Environmental Management; Environmental Studies; Finance; Gender Studies; Human Resources; International Business; Law; Marketing; Natural Resources; Parks and Recreation; Political Sciences; Regional Studies; Social Studies; Sociology; Statistics; Tourism; Transport and Communications; Welfare and Protective Services)
History: Founded 1966
Main language(s) of instruction: Japanese
Accrediting agency: Ministry of Education, Culture, Sports, Science and Technology (MEXT)
Student Services: Library
Last Update: 07-03-2018

Nagaoka Institute of Design

197 Miyazeki-machi
Nagaoka-shi 940-2088, Niigata
Tel: +81(258) 21-3311

Fax: +81(258) 21-3312
Website: http://www.nagaoka-id.ac.jp
President: Hiromu Wada

Department/Division

Architecture and Environmental Design (Architectural and Environmental Design; Interior Design; Landscape Architecture); **Arts and Crafts** (Handicrafts; Painting and Drawing; Sculpture); **Product Design** (Handicrafts; Industrial Design; Textile Design); **Visual Communication Design** (Advertising and Publicity; Communication Arts; Design; Packaging Technology; Photography; Visual Arts)

Graduate School

Design (Architectural Restoration; Architecture; Architecture and Planning; Communication Arts; Design; Graphic Design; Handicrafts; Industrial Design; Landscape Architecture; Painting and Drawing; Regional Planning; Safety Engineering; Sculpture; Town Planning; Visual Arts)
History: Founded 1994
Academic year: April to March (April-September; September-March)
Fees: Tuition, 976,000 per annum (Yen)
Main language(s) of instruction: Japanese
Accrediting agency: Ministry of Education, Culture, Sports, Science and Technology (MEXT)
Degrees and diplomas: Shushi (Architectural Restoration; Architecture; Architecture and Planning; Communication Arts; Handicrafts; Industrial Design; Landscape Architecture; Painting and Drawing; Regional Planning; Sculpture; Town Planning; Visual Arts), Hakase (Architecture; Architecture and Planning; Design; Graphic Design; Industrial Design)
Student Services: Canteen, Library, IT Centre, Residential Facilities
Last Update: 07-03-2018

Nagaoka University of Technology

1603-1 Kamitomioka
Nagaoka 940-2188, Niigata
Tel: +81(258) 46-6000
Website: http://www.nagaokaut.ac.jp
President: Nobuhiko Azuma

School

Engineering (*Also Master's programme*) (Bioengineering; Civil Engineering; Electrical and Electronic Engineering; Engineering; Environmental Engineering; Information Management; Information Technology; Materials Engineering; Mechanical Engineering)

Graduate School

Engineering (*Doctoral programme*) (Automation and Control Engineering; Bioengineering; Construction Engineering; Electrical and Electronic Engineering; Energy Engineering; Engineering; Environmental Engineering; Information Management; Information Technology; Materials Engineering; Mechanical Engineering; Nuclear Engineering; Safety Engineering); **Management of Technology** (*Professional Degree Course*) (Safety Engineering)

History: Founded 1976

Academic year: April to March (April-August; September-December; January-March)

Admission requirements: Graduation from high school and entrance examination

Main language(s) of instruction: Japanese

Accrediting agency: Ministry of Education, Culture, Sports, Science and Technology (MEXT)

Degrees and diplomas: Gakushi, Shushi (Bioengineering; Civil Engineering; Electrical Engineering; Electronic Engineering; Environmental Engineering; Information Management; Information Technology; Materials Engineering; Mechanical Engineering; Nuclear Engineering; Safety Engineering), Hakase (Biological and Life Sciences; Biotechnology; Energy Engineering; Environmental Studies; Information Sciences; Information Technology; Materials Engineering)

Student Services: Academic Counselling, Careers Guidance, Sports Facilities, Language Laboratory, Health Services, Library

Last Update: 15-02-2018

Nagasaki University

1-14 Bunkyo
Nagasaki 852-8521, Nagasaki
Tel: +81(95) 847-1111
Fax: +81(95) 844-5491
Website: http://www.nagasaki-u.ac.jp
President: Shigeru Katamine

Faculty

Economics (Accountancy; Business Administration; Economic and Finance Policy; Economics; Finance; Information Management; International Relations; Law); **Education** (Art Education; Cultural Studies; Education; Educational Psychology; Health Education; Humanities and Social Science Education; Preschool Education; Primary Education; Science Education; Secondary Education; Special Education; Teacher Training); **Environmental Studies** (Environmental Management; Environmental Studies; Social Studies); **Fisheries** (Biochemistry; Fishery; Marine Biology; Marine Science and Oceanography; Materials Engineering)

Unit
Research Promotion

School

Dentistry (Biological and Life Sciences; Dentistry; Environmental Studies; Medicine; Oral Pathology); **Engineering** (Chemistry; Civil Engineering; Computer Engineering; Electrical and Electronic Engineering; Engineering; Environmental Engineering; Information Sciences; Information Technology; Materials Engineering; Mechanical Engineering); **Medicine** (Health Sciences; Medicine; Pathology; Physiology; Rehabilitation and Therapy; Social and Preventive Medicine); **Pharmaceutical Sciences** (Pharmacology; Pharmacy)

Institute

Atomic Bomb Disease (Health Sciences); **East China Sea Research** (Marine Science and Oceanography); **Tropical Medicine** (Microbiology; Tropical Medicine)

Centre

Education Research and Training (Educational Research); **Frontier Life Sciences** (Biomedicine; Genetics; Organic Chemistry); **Gender Equality** (Gender Studies); **Health and Community Medicine** (Community Health; Health Sciences); **Industry, University and Government Cooperation**; **International Collaborative Research**; **Medical Innovation** (Health Sciences)

Graduate School

Biomedical Sciences (Biomedicine; Dentistry; Health Sciences; Immunology; Medicine; Pharmacology; Pharmacy; Treatment Techniques; Tropical Medicine); **Economics** (Economic and Finance Policy; Economics; Management); **Education** (Education; Teacher Training); **Engineering** (Engineering; Natural Sciences; Technology); **Fisheries Science and Environmental Studies** (Environmental Management; Environmental Studies; Fishery; Marine Science and Oceanography); **International Health Development** (Development Studies; Health Sciences; International Studies)

Research Division

Higher Education (*Research and Development Centre*) (Educational Research; Higher Education); **Infectuous Disease in Asia and Africa** (Immunology); **Nuclear Weapons Abolition** (Peace and Disarmament); **Tropical Infections** (*Animal Research Centre*) (Tropical Medicine); **Tropical Infectious Diseases** (*Animal*) (Tropical Medicine)

History: Founded 1949 following merger of Nagasaki University with Nagasaki Medical College, the College of Pharmaceutical Science of Nagasaki Medical College, Nagasaki

College of Economics, Nagasaki Normal School, Nagasaki Youth Normal School, and Nagasaki High School. Incorporated as National University Corporation 2004
Academic year: April to March (April-September; October-March)
Admission requirements: Secondary school certificate or equivalent and entrance examination
Fees: 800,000 per annum (Yen)
Main language(s) of instruction: Japanese
Accrediting agency: Ministry of Education, Culture, Sports, Science and Technology (MEXT)
Degrees and diplomas: Gakushi (Dentistry; Economics; Education; Engineering; Environmental Studies; Fishery; Health Sciences; Medicine; Nursing; Pharmacology; Pharmacy; Surgery), Shushi (Biomedicine; Business Administration; Economics; Education; Engineering; Engineering Management; Environmental Studies; Fishery; Nursing; Occupational Therapy; Pharmacy; Philosophy; Physical Therapy; Public Health; Tropical Medicine), Hakase (Biomedicine; Business Administration; Dentistry; Engineering; Environmental Studies; Fishery; Management; Marine Science and Oceanography; Medical Technology; Medicine; Pharmacology; Philosophy; Production Engineering)
Student Services: Academic Counselling, Social Counselling, Careers Guidance, Cultural Activities, Sports Facilities, Language Laboratory, Facilities for disabled people, Health Services, Canteen, Foreign Studies Centre, Library
Periodicals: Acta Medica Nagasakiensia, Annual Journal of Economics, Annual Report of the Institute of Tropical Medicine, Annual Report of the Research Institute of Southeast Asia, Annual Report of the School of Dentistry, Bulletin of the Faculty of Education, Bulletin of the Faculty of Fisheries, Bulletin of the School of Allied Medical Sciences, Journal of Business and Economics, Journal of Environmental Studies, Nagasaki Igakkai Zasshi, Report of the Faculty of Engineering, Study Series on Southeast Asia, Tropical Medicine
Last Update: 14-03-2018

Nagoya City University

1, Kawasumi, Mizuho
Nagoya 467-8601, Aichi
Tel: +81(52) 853-8020
Fax: +81(52) 841-7428
Website: http://www.nagoya-cu.ac.jp
President: Kenjiro Kohri

Faculty

Economics (*Also graduate school*) (Accountancy; Business Administration; Economic and Finance Policy; Economics; Finance; Management); **Pharmaceutical Sciences** (*Also graduate school*) (Pharmacology; Pharmacy)

College

General Education (Arts and Humanities; Education; Health Education; Modern Languages; Natural Sciences; Physical Education; Social Sciences)

School

Design and Architecture (*Also graduate school*) (Architectural and Environmental Design; Architecture; Computer Graphics; Design; Environmental Engineering; Environmental Management; Graphic Design; Industrial Design; Information Technology; Interior Design; Landscape Architecture; Safety Engineering); **Humanities and Social Sciences** (*Also graduate school*) (Arts and Humanities; Cultural Studies; Education; Modern Languages; Psychology; Social Sciences; Social Studies); **Medicine** (*Also graduate school*) (Health Sciences; Medicine); **Nursing** (*Also graduate school*) (Health Sciences; Nursing; Welfare and Protective Services)

Institute

Artifical Enviroment Design (Architectural and Environmental Design); **Molecular Medicine** (Medicine; Molecular Biology); **Natural Sciences** (Health Sciences; Information Sciences; Natural Sciences); **Studies in Humanities and Cultures** (Arts and Humanities; Cultural Studies)

Centre

Experimental Animal Science (Zoology)

Graduate School

Design and Architecture (Architectural and Environmental Design; Architecture; Computer Graphics; Design; Electronic Engineering; Environmental Engineering; Graphic Design; Industrial Design; Information Technology; Mechanical Engineering; Media Studies; Software Engineering; Structural Architecture; Telecommunications Engineering; Town Planning); **Economics** (Accountancy; Arts and Humanities; Business Administration; Cultural Studies; Economics; Education; Finance; Gender Studies; Human Rights; Japanese; Management; Psychology; Social Sciences; Social Studies; Welfare and Protective Services); **Medical Sciences** (Biological and Life Sciences; Biology; Health Sciences; Information Sciences; Medicine; Molecular Biology; Physiology; Social and Preventive Medicine; Treatment Techniques); **Natural Sciences** (Biological and Life Sciences; Biology; Information Sciences; Information Technology; Natural Sciences); **Nursing** (Child Care and Development; Community Health; Gerontology; Health Sciences; Midwifery; Nursing; Psychiatry and Mental Health; Social and Preventive Medicine); **Pharmaceutical Sciences** (Biological and Life Sciences; Molecular Biology; Pharmacology; Pharmacy)

Research Division

Advanced Pharmaceutics (Pharmacology); **Biological Diversity** (Biological and Life Sciences); **Economics** (Economics)

Further information: Also Takiko, Tanabe-dori and Kita Chikusa Campuses

History: Founded 1950, incorporating Nagoya Pharmaceutical School, founded 1931, and Nagoya Women's Medical College, founded 1943

Academic year: April to March (April-October; October-March)

Admission requirements: Graduation from high school or equivalent or foreign equivalent, and entrance examination

Main language(s) of instruction: Japanese

Accrediting agency: Ministry of Education, Culture, Sports, Science and Technology (MEXT)

Degrees and diplomas: Gakushi (Architecture; Arts and Humanities; Design; Economics; Medicine; Nursing; Pharmacy; Social Sciences), Shushi (Architecture; Arts and Humanities; Biology; Computer Science; Design; Economics; Industrial Design; Information Sciences; Information Technology; Management; Media Studies; Medicine; Nursing; Pharmacology; Social Sciences; Town Planning), Hakase (Arts and Humanities; Biological and Life Sciences; Biology; Economics; Information Sciences; Medicine; Nursing; Pharmacology; Pharmacy; Social and Preventive Medicine; Social Sciences)

Student Services: Sports Facilities, Language Laboratory, Library, IT Centre

Periodicals: Bulletin of College of General Education, Natural Sciences Section, Faculty of Pharmacy Annual Report, Nagoya Medical Journal, Oikonomika, Studies in Social Sciences and Humanities

Last Update: 07-03-2018

Nagoya Institute of Technology

Gokiso-cho, Showa-ku
Nagoya-shi 466-8555, Aichi
Tel: +81(52) 735-5606
Fax: +81(52) 735-5621
Website: http://www.nitech.ac.jp
President: Hiroyuki Ukai

Department/Division

Architecture and Design (Architectural and Environmental Design; Architecture; Design; Environmental Engineering); **Civil Engineering and Systems Management** (Civil Engineering; Environmental Engineering; Town Planning; Transport Engineering); **Computer Science** (Computer Networks; Computer Science); **Electrical and Electronic Engineering** (Electrical and Electronic Engineering); **Environmental and Materials Engineering** (Environmental Engineering; Materials Engineering; Nanotechnology); **Life and Materials Engineering** (Applied Chemistry; Biochemistry; Bioengineering; Materials Engineering; Molecular Biology; Polymer and Plastics Technology); **Mechanical Engineering** (Applied Mathematics; Applied Physics; Computer Engineering; Computer Science; Energy Engineering; Measurement and Precision Engineering; Mechanical Engineering)

Graduate School

Engineering (Engineering)

History: Founded 1905 as Nagoya Higher Technical School. Merged with Aichi Prefectural College of Technology. Became national institute 1949

Academic year: April-September; October-March

Admission requirements: Graduation from high school or equivalent, or foreign equivalent, and entrance examination

Fees: 267,900 per annum, evening study; 535,800 per annum, day study (Yen)

Main language(s) of instruction: Japanese

Accrediting agency: Ministry of Education, Culture, Sports, Science and Technology (MEXT)

Degrees and diplomas: Gakushi (Engineering; Philosophy), Shushi (Engineering; Philosophy), Hakase (Engineering; Philosophy)

Academic Staff 2013-2014	MALE	FEMALE	TOTAL
FULL-TIME			582
PART-TIME			412
STAFF WITH DOCTORATE			
FULL-TIME			355
Student Numbers 2013-2014			
All (Foreign Included)			5776
Foreign only			247

Last Update: 15-02-2018

Nagoya University

Furo-cho, Chikusa-ku
Nagoya-shi 464-8601, Aichi
Tel: +81(52) 789-5111
Fax: +81(52) 789-2045
Website: http://www.nagoya-u.ac.jp
President: Seiichi Matsuo
Tel: +81(52) 789-2002

School

Agricultural Science (Agriculture; Biological and Life Sciences; Environmental Studies); **Economics** (Business Administration; Economic and Finance Policy; Economic

History; Economics); **Education** (Cultural Studies; Development Studies; Education; Information Sciences; International Studies; Psychology; Psychotherapy); **Engineering** (Aeronautical and Aerospace Engineering; Applied Chemistry; Applied Physics; Architecture; Bioengineering; Biotechnology; Chemical Engineering; Civil Engineering; Electrical and Electronic Engineering; Energy Engineering; Engineering; Information Technology; Materials Engineering; Mechanical Engineering); **Informatics and Science** (Computer Science; Natural Sciences; Social Sciences); **Law** (Comparative Law; Law; Political Sciences); **Letters** (Aesthetics; Art History; Arts and Humanities; Behavioural Sciences; Cultural Studies; English; French; German; History; Japanese; Linguistics; Literature; Modern Languages; Philosophy; Psychology; Sociology); **Medicine** (Health Sciences; Medicine); **Science** (Biology; Chemistry; Earth Sciences; Mathematics; Natural Sciences; Physics)

Institute

Advanced Research (Arts and Humanities; Natural Sciences); **Eco Topia Science**; **Environmental Medicine** (Neurosciences); **Liberal Arts and Science** (Arts and Humanities; Natural Sciences); **Origin of Particles and the Universe** (*Kobayashi-Maskawa*) (Astrophysics); **Solar-Terrestrial Environment** (Astronomy and Space Science)

Centre

Asian Legal Exchange (Law; Political Sciences); **Bioscience and Biotechnology** (Biochemistry; Biomedicine; Biophysics; Biotechnology); **Chronological Research**; **Developmental Clinical Psychology and Psychiatry** (Child Care and Development; Clinical Psychology); **Education for International Students** (Cultural Studies; Japanese); **Experimental Studies**; **Gene Research** (Genetics); **Health, Physical Fitness and Sports** (Health Education; Health Sciences; Sports); **Hydrospheric Atmospheric** (Biochemistry; Environmental Studies; Geophysics; Marine Biology; Marine Science and Oceanography; Waste Management; Water Science); **Information Technology** (Information Technology); **International Cooperation in Agricultural Education** (Agriculture); **Materials Science** (Materials Engineering); **Radioisotope Research** (Radiology); **Studies of Higher Education** (Higher Education); **Theoretical Studies**

Graduate School

Bioagricultural Sciences (Bioengineering; Biological and Life Sciences); **Economics** (Economics; Industrial Management); **Education and Human Development** (Adult Education; Behavioural Sciences; Clinical Psychology; Development Studies; Education; Educational Administration; Educational Sciences; Higher Education; Information Sciences; Physical Education; Psychology; Sports);

Engineering (Aeronautical and Aerospace Engineering; Applied Chemistry; Applied Physics; Biotechnology; Chemical Engineering; Civil Engineering; Computer Engineering; Computer Science; Electrical Engineering; Electronic Engineering; Energy Engineering; Engineering; Mechanical Engineering; Nanotechnology; Telecommunications Engineering); **Environmental Studies** (Architecture; Earth Sciences; Environmental Engineering; Environmental Studies; Social Studies); **Information Science** (Computer Science); **Information Science and Technology** (Computer Science; Mathematics and Computer Science; Media Studies; Natural Sciences; Social Sciences); **International Development** (Communication Studies; International Studies); **Languages and Cultures** (American Studies; Applied Linguistics; Asian Studies; Cultural Studies; East Asian Studies; English; European Studies; Foreign Languages Education; Gender Studies; Japanese); **Law** (Comparative Law; Law; Political Sciences); **Letters** (Aesthetics; Archaeology; Art History; Arts and Humanities; Classical Languages; Cultural Studies; History; Linguistics; Philosophy); **Mathematics** (Mathematics); **Medicine** (Cell Biology; Community Health; Health Administration; Health Sciences; Laboratory Techniques; Medical Technology; Medicine; Molecular Biology; Nursing; Occupational Therapy; Physical Therapy; Radiology); **Science** (Astrophysics; Biological and Life Sciences; Chemistry; Earth Sciences; Environmental Studies; Materials Engineering; Mathematics; Physics)

Research Division

Disaster Mitigation (Safety Engineering); **Green Mobility Collaborative Studies** (Environmental Studies); **Synchrotron Radiation** (Physics)

History: Founded 1871 as Medical School. Became Nagoya Medical College 1931 and Nagoya Imperial University 1939, renamed Nagoya University 1947 and restarted as a University under the new educational system 1949 and reorganized as a National university Corporation 2004

Academic year: April to March (April-September; October-March)

Admission requirements: Graduation from high school or recognized equivalent, and entrance examination

Fees: Tuition 267,900 per semester (Yen)

Main language(s) of instruction: Japanese, English

Accrediting agency: Ministry of Education, Culture, Sports, Science and Technology (MEXT)

Degrees and diplomas: Gakushi (Arts and Humanities; Computer Science; Continuing Education; Economics; Education; Information Sciences; International Studies; Mathematics; Natural Sciences; Psychology; Psychotherapy), Shushi (Agriculture; Arts and Humanities; Asian Studies; Biological and Life Sciences; Business Administration; Chemical Engineering; Chemistry; Comparative Law; Cultural Studies; Development Studies; Earth Sciences;

Economic and Finance Policy; Economics; Education; Educational Sciences; Environmental Engineering; Environmental Studies; Foreign Languages Education; Government; Health Administration; Human Resources; Japanese; Law; Linguistics; Mathematics; Medical Technology; Medicine; Modern Languages; Nursing; Physics; Psychology; Regional Planning; Rehabilitation and Therapy; Rural Planning), Hakase (Agriculture; Arts and Humanities; Biological and Life Sciences; Chemical Engineering; Chemistry; Civil Engineering; Community Health; Comparative Law; Development Studies; Economics; Educational Sciences; Environmental Studies; Mathematics; Medicine; Physics; Psychology)

Student Services: Academic Counselling, Social Counselling, Careers Guidance, Sports Facilities, Language Laboratory, Facilities for disabled people, Health Services, Canteen, Foreign Studies Centre, Library, Residential Facilities

Periodicals: Bulletin, Journals, Memoirs, Proceedings, Scientific Reports

Publishing house: Nagoya University Press

Last Update: 15-02-2018

Nara Institute of Science and Technology (NAIST)

8916-5 Takayama-cho
Ikoma-shi 630-0192, Nara
Tel: +81(743) 72-5111
Fax: +81(743) 72-5939
Website: http://www.naist.jp
President: Naokazu Yokoya
Tel: +81(743) 72-5000

Centre

Information Technology (Software Engineering; Telecommunications Engineering)

Graduate School

Biological Sciences (Biological and Life Sciences; Botany; English); **Information Science and Technology** (Computer Science; English; Information Sciences; Information Technology); **Materials Science** (Materials Engineering)

Research Division

Advanced Science and Technology (Educational Research; Industrial Engineering; Multimedia; Natural Sciences; Technology); **Genetics Education and Research** (Genetics; Molecular Biology); **Materials Science and Education** (Design; Materials Engineering)

History: Founded 1991
Academic year: April to March

Admission requirements: University Degree
Fees: Registration, 282,000 per annum; Tuition, 520,800 per annum (Yen)
Main language(s) of instruction: Japanese
Accrediting agency: Ministry of Education, Culture, Sports, Science and Technology (MEXT)
Degrees and diplomas: Shushi (Biological and Life Sciences; Computer Science; Information Sciences; Information Technology; Materials Engineering), Hakase (Biological and Life Sciences; Information Sciences; Information Technology; Materials Engineering)
Student Services: Academic Counselling, Social Counselling, Careers Guidance, Nursery Care, Sports Facilities, Language Laboratory, Facilities for disabled people, Health Services, Canteen, Foreign Studies Centre, eLibrary
Last Update: 15-02-2018

Nara Medical University

840 Shijo-cho
Kashihara-city 634-8521, Nara
Tel: +81(744) 22-3051
Fax: +81(744) 29-4746
Website: http://www.naramed-u.ac.jp
President: Hiroshi Hosoi

School

Medicine (*Also graduate school*) (Anaesthesiology; Anatomy; Biochemistry; Biology; Cardiology; Cell Biology; Chemistry; Community Health; Dermatology; English; Epidemiology; Forensic Medicine and Dentistry; German; Gynaecology and Obstetrics; Health Administration; Health Sciences; Information Sciences; Mathematics; Medicine; Microbiology; Neurology; Neurosciences; Oncology; Ophthalmology; Orthopaedics; Otorhinolaryngology; Paediatrics; Parasitology; Pathology; Pharmacology; Philosophy; Physical Education; Physics; Physiology; Psychiatry and Mental Health; Public Health; Radiology; Statistics; Surgery; Treatment Techniques; Urology); **Nursing** (Community Health; English; Gerontology; Health Sciences; Midwifery; Nursing; Paediatrics; Philosophy; Psychiatry and Mental Health)

Centre

Education Development (Health Education; Teacher Training)

Graduate School

Medicine (Biomedicine; Community Health; Health Sciences; Medicine)

Research Division

Advanced Medicine (Cardiology; Computer Science; Genetics; Laboratory Techniques; Medicine; Neurology; Radiology)

History: Founded 1945 by Nara Prefecture

Academic year: April to March (April-July; September-December; January-March)

Admission requirements: Graduation from high school and entrance examination

Fees: Tuition, 535,800 per annum (Yen)

Main language(s) of instruction: Japanese

Accrediting agency: Ministry of Education, Culture, Sports, Science and Technology (MEXT)

Degrees and diplomas: Gakushi (Medicine), Shushi (Medicine), Hakase (Biomedicine; Community Health; Health Sciences; Medicine)

Student Services: Library

Periodicals: Journal of Nara Medical Association

Last Update: 07-03-2018

Nara Prefectural University

10 Funahashi
Nara 630-8258
Tel: +81(742) 22-4978
Fax: +81(742) 22-4991
Website: http://www.narapu.ac.jp
President: Tadamichi Ito

Faculty

Regional Art (Anthropology; Arts and Humanities; Cultural Studies; Economics; Modern Languages; Regional Studies; Tourism)

History: Founded 1990

Main language(s) of instruction: Japanese

Accrediting agency: Ministry of Education, Culture, Sports, Science and Technology (MEXT)

Degrees and diplomas: Gakushi (Regional Studies; Tourism)

Student Services: Sports Facilities

Last Update: 07-03-2018

Nara University of Education

Takabatake-cho
Nara-shi 630-8528, Nara
Tel: +81(742) 27-9105, +81(742) 27-9124
Fax: +81(742) 27-9141, +81(742) 27-9146
Website: http://www.nara-edu.ac.jp
President: Hisao Kato

Faculty

Education (Art Education; Cultural Studies; Curriculum; Education; English; Fine Arts; Foreign Languages Education; Health Education; Health Sciences; Heritage Preservation; Home Economics; Home Economics Education; Humanities and Social Science Education; Japanese; Mathematics; Mathematics Education; Music; Music Education; Native Language Education; Natural Sciences; Pedagogy; Physical Education; Preschool Education; Primary Education; Psychology; Science Education; Social Studies; Special Education; Sports; Teacher Training; Technology; Technology Education; Vocational Education)

Course/Programme

Teacher Training for Special Education (*Special Postgraduate Course*) (Educational Research; Special Education; Teacher Training)

Centre

Education and Research of Sustainable Development and Cultural Properties (Cultural Studies; Heritage Preservation); **Educational Research and Development** (Education; Educational Research); **Educational Research of Science and Mathematics** (Educational Research; Mathematics Education; Science Education); **Library and Educational Research** (Educational Research; Library Science); **Natural Environment Education** (Education); **Special Needs Education** (Special Education; Teacher Training)

Graduate School

Education (Curriculum; Education; Primary Education; Teacher Training)

History: Founded 1949, incorporating Nara Normal School and Nara Youth Normal School, acquired present title 1966

Academic year: April to March (April-September; October-February)

Admission requirements: Graduation from high school or equivalent or foreign equivalent and entrance examination

Fees: Tuition, 535,800 per annum (Yen)

Main language(s) of instruction: Japanese

Accrediting agency: Ministry of Education, Culture, Sports, Science and Technology (MEXT)

Degrees and diplomas: Gakushi (Cultural Studies; Curriculum; Education; Heritage Preservation; Teacher Training), Shushi (Curriculum; Education; Teacher Training)

Student Services: Careers Guidance, Sports Facilities, Language Laboratory, Health Services, Foreign Studies Centre, Residential Facilities

Periodicals: Bulletins

Last Update: 15-02-2018

Nara Women's University (NWU)

Kitawoyahigashi
Nara 630-8506, Nara
Tel: +81(742) 20-3204
Fax: +81(742) 20-3205
Website: http://www.nara-wu.ac.jp
President: Haruki Imaoka
Tel: +81(742) 20-3724

Faculty

Human Life and Environment (Cultural Studies; Environmental Studies; Food Science; Home Economics; Nutrition); **Letters** (Ancient Civilizations; Anthropology; Archaeology; Art History; Arts and Humanities; Asian Studies; Child Care and Development; Clinical Psychology; Comparative Literature; Education; Environmental Studies; European Studies; Gender Studies; Geography (Human); History; Information Sciences; Literature; Mass Communication; Media Studies; Museum Studies; Physical Education; Psychology; Sociology; Sports); **Science** (Biological and Life Sciences; Biology; Cell Biology; Chemistry; Computer Science; Information Sciences; Mathematics; Mathematics and Computer Science; Molecular Biology; Natural Sciences; Physics)

Graduate School

Humanities and Sciences (American Studies; Ancient Civilizations; Anthropology; Architectural and Environmental Design; Architecture; Artificial Intelligence; Arts and Humanities; Asian Studies; Behavioural Sciences; Biochemistry; Biological and Life Sciences; Biotechnology; Cell Biology; Chemistry; Chinese; Clinical Psychology; Cognitive Sciences; Computer Science; Cultural Studies; East Asian Studies; Education; English; English Studies; Environmental Studies; Ethics; European Studies; Family Studies; Food Science; Food Technology; French; Gender Studies; Geography; Geography (Human); German; Germanic Studies; Health Sciences; History; Information Sciences; Information Technology; Inorganic Chemistry; International Studies; Japanese; Landscape Architecture; Law; Linguistics; Literature; Mathematics; Mechanics; Microbiology; Modern Languages; Molecular Biology; Music; Natural Sciences; Nuclear Physics; Nutrition; Organic Chemistry; Paediatrics; Philosophy; Physical Chemistry; Physical Education; Physics; Physiology; Psychology; Regional Studies; Social Studies; Sociology; Sports; Textile Technology; Toxicology; Welfare and Protective Services)

History: Founded 1908 as the Nara Higher Normal College for Women, became National University 1949. Reorganized as National University Corporation 2004
Academic year: April to March (April-September; October-March)

Admission requirements: Graduation from high school or equivalent or foreign equivalent, and entrance examination
Fees: 535,800 per annum (Yen)
Main language(s) of instruction: Japanese
Accrediting agency: Ministry of Education, Culture, Sports, Science and Technology (MEXT)
Degrees and diplomas: Gakushi, Shushi (American Studies; Ancient Civilizations; Architectural and Environmental Design; Arts and Humanities; Asian Studies; Behavioural Sciences; Biological and Life Sciences; Biology; Cell Biology; Chemistry; Computer Science; Cultural Studies; Environmental Studies; European Studies; Food Science; Geography; Health Sciences; Information Sciences; International Studies; Japanese; Landscape Architecture; Literature; Mathematics; Molecular Biology; Natural Sciences; Nutrition; Physics; Regional Studies; Social Studies; Sociology; Sports; Textile Technology), Hakase (American Studies; Architectural and Environmental Design; Asian Studies; Behavioural Sciences; Biological and Life Sciences; Biology; Chemistry; Computer Science; Cultural Studies; Environmental Studies; European Studies; Food Science; Geography (Human); History; Information Sciences; Japanese; Mathematics; Natural Sciences; Nutrition; Physics; Social Studies; Sociology)
Student Services: Academic Counselling, Social Counselling, Careers Guidance, Sports Facilities, Facilities for disabled people, Health Services, Canteen, Foreign Studies Centre, Library, IT Centre, Residential Facilities
Periodicals: Annual Report of the Graduate School of Humanities and Sciences, Annual Report on Research and Education, Research Journal of Living Science
Last Update: 15-02-2018

Naruto University of Education

748, Nakashima, Takashima
Naruto 772-8502, Tokushima
Tel: +81(88) 687-6000
Fax: +81(88) 687-6040
Website: http://www.naruto-u.ac.jp
President: Kazuo Yamashita

Faculty

Education (Art Education; Education; Foreign Languages Education; Health Education; Home Economics Education; Humanities and Social Science Education; Industrial Arts Education; Mathematics Education; Music Education; Physical Education; Preschool Education; Science Education; Special Education; Teacher Training; Vocational Education)

Centre

Cooperation for Education (Education; Information Technology); **Education and Research on the Science of Preventive Education** (Child Care and Development; Health Sciences); **Educational Career Development** (Teacher Training); **English Language Education at Elementary Schools** (*CELEES*) (English; Foreign Languages Education; Primary Education); **Health and Counseling Services** (Psychology; Psychotherapy); **Information Technology Services** (Information Technology); **International Cooperation for the Teacher Education and Trainning** (*INCET*) (Teacher Training)

Graduate School

Education (*Professional*) (Education; Educational Administration; Primary Education; Special Education; Teacher Training); **Education** (Arts and Humanities; Biological and Life Sciences; Child Care and Development; Clinical Psychology; Education; English; Fine Arts; Health Education; Health Sciences; International Studies; Japanese; Literature; Mathematics Education; Music Education; Philosophy; Physical Education; Science Education; Social Sciences; Special Education; Teacher Training)

History: Founded 1981. The University participated as a constituent School in the Joint Graduate School (PhD programme) in Science of School Education 1996, Hyogo University of Education

Academic year: April to March (April-July; August-November; December-March)

Admission requirements: Graduation from high school or recognized equivalent and entrance examination. Japanese Language Proficiency Test for international students

Fees: Tuition, 535,800 per annum (Yen)

Main language(s) of instruction: Japanese

Accrediting agency: Ministry of Education, Culture, Sports, Science and Technology (MEXT)

Degrees and diplomas: Gakushi (Education), Shushi (Education). Also Professional Graduate Programme in Education

Student Services: Academic Counselling, Social Counselling, Careers Guidance, Sports Facilities, Health Services, Canteen, Library, IT Centre, Residential Facilities

Periodicals: Research Bulletins

Last Update: 15-02-2018

National Graduate Institute for Policy Studies (GRIPS)

7-22-1 Roppongi
Minato-ku 106-8677, Tokyo
Tel: +81(3) 6439-6000
Fax: +81(3) 6439-6010, +81(3) 6439-6030

Website: http://www.grips.ac.jp
President: Akihiko Tanaka

Graduate School

Policy Studies (Cultural Studies; Development Studies; Economics; Educational Sciences; Finance; International Studies; Japanese; Leadership; Public Administration; Regional Studies)

History: Founded 1997

Fees: Tuition Fee, 535,800 per annum (Yen)

Main language(s) of instruction: Japanese

Accrediting agency: Ministry of Education, Culture, Sports, Science and Technology (MEXT)

Degrees and diplomas: Hakase (Cultural Studies; Development Studies; Government; International Relations; International Studies; Native Language Education; Political Sciences; Public Administration; Safety Engineering; Social Welfare)

Student Services: Social Counselling, Cultural Activities, Sports Facilities, Health Services

Student Numbers 2012-2013	MALE	FEMALE	TOTAL
All (Foreign Included)			417
Foreign only			277

Last Update: 23-02-2018

National Institute of Fitness and Sports in Kanoya

1 Shiromizu-cho
Kanoya-shi 891-2393, Kagoshima
Tel: +81(994) 46-4865, +81(994) 46-4869
Fax: +81(994) 46-2831
Website: http://www.nifs-k.ac.jp
President: Masashi Matsushita

Faculty

Physical Education (Physical Education; Sports)

Centre

Foreign Languages (Modern Languages); **Marine Sports** (Sports)

Graduate School

Physical Education (Physical Education)

History: Founded 1981.

Academic year: April to March (April-November; December-March)

Admission requirements: Graduation from high school or recognized equivalent, and entrance examination

Fees: Tuition, 267,900 per annum (Yen)

Main language(s) of instruction: Japanese

Accrediting agency: Ministry of Education, Culture, Sports, Science and Technology (MEXT)

Degrees and diplomas: Shushi (Physical Education), Hakase (Physical Education)

Student Services: Social Counselling, Careers Guidance, Sports Facilities, Language Laboratory, Health Services

Academic Staff 2012-2013	MALE	FEMALE	TOTAL
FULL-TIME			128
Student Numbers 2012-2013			
All (Foreign Included)			849

Last Update: 23-02-2018

National University Corporation Shizuoka University

836, Ohya, Suruga-ku
Shizuoka-Shi 422-8529, Shizuoka-Ken
Tel: +81(54) 238-4996
Fax: +81(54) 238-5041
Website: http://www.shizuoka.ac.jp
President: Kiyoshi Ishii

Faculty

Agriculture (Agriculture; Applied Chemistry; Biological and Life Sciences; Ecology; Environmental Studies; Forestry; Natural Resources); **Education** (Continuing Education; Design; Education; Fine Arts; Music; Science Education; Teacher Training; Technology Education); **Engineering** (Applied Chemistry; Biochemistry; Bioengineering; Chemical Engineering; Computer Engineering; Electrical and Electronic Engineering; Electrical Engineering; Electronic Engineering; Engineering; Materials Engineering; Mechanical Engineering; Systems Analysis); **Humanities and Social Sciences** (Anthropology; Archaeology; Arts and Humanities; Asian Studies; Business Administration; Civil Law; Clinical Psychology; Comparative Literature; Criminal Law; Economics; English; French; German; History; History of Law; International Law; International Relations; Japanese; Law; Linguistics; Literature; Philosophy; Political Sciences; Psychiatry and Mental Health; Psychology; Public Law; Social Sciences; Sociology); **Informatics** (Arts and Humanities; Computer Science; Information Sciences; Information Technology; Social Sciences); **Science** (Biological and Life Sciences; Chemistry; Earth Sciences; Mathematics; Mathematics and Computer Science; Natural Sciences; Physics)

Graduate School

Agriculture (Agriculture; Biochemistry; Biological and Life Sciences; Environmental Studies; Forestry); **Education** (Education); **Engineering** (Applied Chemistry; Biochemistry; Bioengineering; Business Administration; Computer Engineering; Electrical and Electronic Engineering; Electrical Engineering; Electronic Engineering; Engineering; Management; Materials Engineering; Mathematics; Mechanical Engineering); **Humanities and Social Sciences** (Arts and Humanities; Asian Studies; Clinical Psychology; Cultural Studies; Economics; Management; Modern Languages; Social Sciences; Sociology); **Informatics** (Computer Science; Information Technology); **Law** (*Shizuoka*) (Law); **Science** (Biological and Life Sciences; Chemistry; Earth Sciences; Mathematics; Natural Sciences; Physics); **Science and Technology** (Biological and Life Sciences; Energy Engineering; Environmental Engineering; Information Sciences; Information Technology; Nanotechnology; Optical Technology; Technology)

Research Division

Electronics (Electronic Engineering); **Green Science and Technology** (Environmental Studies; Technology)

Further information: Also Hamamatsu Campus. Japanese language courses for foreign students

History: Founded 1949.

Academic year: April to March

Admission requirements: For applicants to undergraduate programmes: 12-year education course certificate; Examination for Japanese University Admission for International Students; Sufficient level in Japanese language. For applicants to graduate programmes, conditions are the same except that a 16-year education course is requested (or 15-year education course plus recommandation from the university after evaluation of the academic records).

Main language(s) of instruction: Japanese, English

Accrediting agency: Ministry of Education, Culture, Sports, Science and Technology (MEXT)

Degrees and diplomas: Gakushi (Agriculture; Anthropology; Biological and Life Sciences; Biotechnology; Business Administration; Chemistry; Cultural Studies; Economics; Education; Engineering; History; Japanese; Literature; Mathematics and Computer Science; Modern Languages; Natural Sciences; Philosophy; Physics; Psychology; Sociology), Shushi (Agriculture; Anthropology; Arts and Humanities; Biological and Life Sciences; Biotechnology; Business Administration; Chemistry; Cultural Studies; Economics; Education; Engineering; History; Japanese; Law; Literature; Modern Languages; Natural Sciences; Physics; Political Sciences; Psychology; Sociology), Hakase (Agriculture; Education; Engineering; Information Sciences; Law; Mathematics and Computer Science). Also Double Degree Special Programme with Warsaw University of Technology, Poland.

Student Services: Academic Counselling, Social Counselling, Careers Guidance, Nursery Care, Sports Facilities,

Language Laboratory, Facilities for disabled people, Health Services, Canteen, Foreign Studies Centre
Periodicals: University Summary

Academic Staff 2012-2013	MALE	FEMALE	TOTAL
FULL-TIME	933	219	1152
STAFF WITH DOCTORATE			
FULL-TIME			475
Student Numbers 2012-2013			
All (Foreign Included)			10090
Foreign only			202

Total number of part-time students: 109
Last Update: 28-03-2018

Nayoro City University

8 Chome-1 Nishi 4 Jokita
Nayoro 096-8641, Hokkaido
Tel: +81(1654) 2-4194
Fax: +81(1654) 3-3354
Website: http://www.nayoro.ac.jp
President: Kazuhiro Sako

Faculty
Health and Welfare (Health Sciences; Nursing; Nutrition; Social Welfare; Welfare and Protective Services)

Course/Programme
Teacher Training (Constitutional Law; English; Information Technology; Nursing; Nutrition; Physical Education; Social Welfare; Teacher Training)

Department/Division
Juno College (Child Care and Development); **Liberal Arts Education** (Arts and Humanities; Information Sciences; Modern Languages; Sports)
History: Founded 1960. Acquired present status and title 2006
Fees: Tuition fee, 535,800 per annum (Yen)
Main language(s) of instruction: Japanese
Accrediting agency: Ministry of Education, Culture, Sports, Science and Technology (MEXT)
Degrees and diplomas:

Academic Staff 2012-2013	MALE	FEMALE	TOTAL
FULL-TIME			68
Student Numbers 2012-2013			
All (Foreign Included)	114	579	693

Last Update: 07-03-2018

Niigata College of Nursing

240 Shinnancho Joetsu-shi
Niigata-shi 943-0147, Niigata
Tel: +81-25-526-2811
Fax: +81-25-526-2815
Website: http://www.niigata-cn.ac.jp
President: Misako Koizumi

Course/Programme
Nursing (*Also Graduate Programme*) (Anatomy; Community Health; Gerontology; Information Sciences; Midwifery; Nursing; Physiology; Psychiatry and Mental Health; Public Health; Social Sciences)
History: Founded 2002
Main language(s) of instruction: Japanese
Accrediting agency: Ministry of Education, Culture, Sports, Science and Technology (MEXT)
Degrees and diplomas: Gakushi (Nursing), Shushi (Nursing)
Student Services: Library
Last Update: 07-03-2018

Niigata University

8050, Ikarashi 2-no-cho
Niigata-shi 950-2181, Niigata
Tel: +81(25) 223-6161, +81(25) 262-6246
Fax: +81(25) 262-7519
Website: http://www.niigata-u.ac.jp
President: Sugata Takahashi

Faculty
Agriculture (Agriculture; Agrobiology; Biochemistry; Biological and Life Sciences; Chemistry; Environmental Studies; Production Engineering); **Dentistry** (Dentistry; Health Sciences; Oral Pathology; Surgery; Welfare and Protective Services); **Economics** (Business Administration; Economics); **Education** (Biological and Life Sciences; Education; Fine Arts; Health Sciences; Music; Preschool Education; Primary Education; Secondary Education; Sports; Teacher Training); **Engineering** (Architecture; Chemical Engineering; Chemistry; Civil Engineering; Computer Engineering; Electrical and Electronic Engineering; Engineering; Materials Engineering; Mechanical Engineering; Production Engineering; Robotics); **Humanities** (Anthropology; Archaeology; Arts and Humanities; Cultural Studies; European Languages; Geography (Human); History; Japanese; Linguistics; Performing Arts; Psychology; Sociology; South and Southeast Asian Languages; Western European Studies); **Law** (Law); **Medicine** (Health Sciences;

Medicine); **Science** (Biology; Chemistry; Environmental Studies; Geology; Mathematics; Medicine; Natural Sciences; Physics)

School

Health Sciences (Health Sciences; Nursing)

Institute

Brain Research (Neurosciences); **Faculty Development Research** (Teacher Training); **Transdisciplinary Research** (Natural Sciences)

Centre

Academic Information Service (Computer Science; Information Technology); **Cooperative Research** (Biotechnology; Communication Studies; Computer Education; Electronic Engineering; Mechanics); **Instrumental Analysis** (Laboratory Techniques); **Radioisotope** (Radiophysics); **Teaching Profession** (Teacher Training)

Laboratory

Venture Business (Business Administration)

Graduate School

Education (Education); **Health Sciences** (Health Sciences); **Law** (*Professional*) (Law); **Management of Technology** (*Professional*) (Engineering Management; Technology); **Medical and Dental Sciences** (Biological and Life Sciences; Biology; Biomedicine; Cell Biology; Community Health; Dentistry; Medicine; Molecular Biology; Oral Pathology; Welfare and Protective Services); **Modern Society and Culture** (Cultural Studies; Development Studies; Economics; International Studies; Law; Management; Social Sciences; Sociology); **Science and Technology** (Agriculture; Applied Chemistry; Architecture; Biological and Life Sciences; Chemical Engineering; Chemistry; Civil Engineering; Computer Engineering; Earth Sciences; Electrical and Electronic Engineering; Electronic Engineering; Environmental Engineering; Environmental Studies; Food Science; Forestry; Information Technology; Materials Engineering; Mathematics; Mechanical Engineering; Natural Resources; Natural Sciences; Physics; Safety Engineering)

Research Division

Natural Hazards and Disaster Recovery (Environmental Studies)

Further information: Also Medical Hospital. Dental Hospital

History: Founded 1945 as National University. Became National University Corporation 2004.

Academic year: April to March (April-September; October-March)

Admission requirements: Graduation from high school or equivalent or foreign equivalent, and entrance examination

Fees: National : 520,800 per annum (Yen), International : 535,800 per annum except for programmes offered by the Faculty of Law, 804,000 (Yen)

Main language(s) of instruction: Japanese

Accrediting agency: Ministry of Education, Culture, Sports, Science and Technology (MEXT)

Degrees and diplomas: Gakushi (Agriculture; Arts and Humanities; Biological and Life Sciences; Business Administration; Dentistry; Economics; Education; Engineering; Fine Arts; Health Sciences; Law; Mathematics; Medicine; Music; Natural Sciences; Nursing; Oral Pathology; Sports; Welfare and Protective Services), Shushi (Agriculture; Arts and Humanities; Biological and Life Sciences; Biomedicine; Business Administration; Cultural Studies; Dentistry; Economics; Education; Electrical and Electronic Engineering; Engineering; Food Science; Health Sciences; Information Technology; Law; Management; Materials Engineering; Medicine; Natural Sciences; Oral Pathology; Philosophy; Political Sciences; Primary Education; Public Administration; Social Studies; Welfare and Protective Services), Hakase (Agriculture; Biological and Life Sciences; Cultural Studies; Development Studies; Economics; Education; Electrical and Electronic Engineering; Engineering; Food Science; Health Sciences; Information Technology; Law; Literature; Materials Engineering; Natural Sciences; Oral Pathology; Philosophy; Social Studies; Welfare and Protective Services). Also Postgraduate Professional Degrees in Engineering Management and Law

Student Services: Academic Counselling, Social Counselling, Careers Guidance, Cultural Activities, Sports Facilities, Language Laboratory, Health Services, Canteen, Foreign Studies Centre, Library, IT Centre, Residential Facilities

Periodicals: Acta Medica at Biologica, Agriculture and Forestry Studies, Annual Report of the Brain Research Institute, Annual Report of the Research Institute for Hazards in Snowy Areas, Annual Report of the University Medical Hospital, Bulletin of Centre for Educational Research and Practice, Humanistic Studies, Journal of Commerce, Journal of Economics, Journal of General Education, Journal of Law and Politics, Journal of the Study of Modern Society and Culture, Letters from the University Library, Memoirs of the Faculty of Agriculture, Memoirs of the Faculty of Education, News from the School of Dentistry, Niigata Dental Journal, Niigata Medical Journal, Report of the Sado Marine Biological Station, Research Report of the Faculty of Engineering, Science Reports, Series A-E

Last Update: 23-02-2018

Niimi College

1263-2 Nishigata
Niimi 718-8585, Okayama
Tel: +81(867) 72-0634
Fax: +81(867) 72-1492
Website: http://www.niimi-c.ac.jp
President: Hiroyuki Kouma

School

Nursing (Nursing)
History: Founded 1980 as Niimi Women's College. Acquired present status and title 2010
Fees: Tuition, 486,000 per annum (Yen)
Main language(s) of instruction: Japanese
Accrediting agency: Ministry of Education, Culture, Sports, Science and Technology (MEXT)
Degrees and diplomas:

Academic Staff 2012-2013	MALE	FEMALE	TOTAL
FULL-TIME	5	23	28
Student Numbers 2012-2013			
All (Foreign Included)			255

Last Update: 07-03-2018

Obihiro University of Agriculture and Veterinary Medicine

Nishi 2-11, Inada-cho
Obihiro-shi 080-8555, Hokkaido
Tel: +81(155) 49-5321
Fax: +81(155) 49-5319
Website: http://www.obihiro.ac.jp
President: Kiyoshi Okuda
Tel: +81(155) 49-5210

Unit

Agricultural Economics (Agricultural Economics); **Environment Agriculture** (Agricultural Equipment; Agriculture; Botany; Crop Production; Environmental Engineering; Environmental Studies); **Food Science** (Animal Husbandry; Biology; Food Science; Health Sciences); **Life Sciences** (Biological and Life Sciences; Ecology; Embryology and Reproduction Biology; Environmental Studies; Genetics; Microbiology; Physiology; Wildlife); **Livestock International Cooperation** (Animal Husbandry; English; Modern Languages); **Livestock Production Science** (Animal Husbandry; Biology; Cattle Breeding); **Veterinary** (Animal Husbandry; Biology; Veterinary Science)

Graduate School

Agricultural Sciences (*Doctoral, In Union with Iwate University*) (Agriculture); **Animal Husbandry** (Agriculture; Animal Husbandry; Environmental Studies; Food Science; Hygiene; Natural Resources); **Veterinary Medicine** (*Doctoral, in Union with Gifu University*) (Veterinary Science)
History: Founded 1941 as Technical School of Veterinary Science, became College of Veterinary Science and Animal Production 1944, College of Agricultural Science 1946 and University 1949
Academic year: April to March (April-September; October-March)
Admission requirements: Graduation from high school or equivalent, and entrance examination
Main language(s) of instruction: Japanese
Accrediting agency: Ministry of Education, Culture, Sports, Science and Technology (MEXT)
Degrees and diplomas: Gakushi (Agriculture; Animal Husbandry; Veterinary Science), Shushi (Agriculture; Animal Husbandry; Hygiene), Hakase (Agriculture; Animal Husbandry; Hygiene; Veterinary Science)
Periodicals: Research Bulletin
Last Update: 23-02-2018

Ochanomizu University

2-1-1 Otsuka Bunkyo-ku
Tokyo 112-8610
Tel: +81(3) 5978-5106
Fax: +81(3) 5978-5978
Website: http://www.ocha.ac.jp
President: Kimiko Murofushi
Tel: +81(3) 5978-5113

Faculty

Human Life and Environmental Sciences (Biological and Life Sciences; Clinical Psychology; Cultural Studies; Developmental Psychology; Environmental Studies; Family Studies; Food Science; History; Nutrition; Social Sciences); **Letters and Education** (Art Education; Art History; Arts and Humanities; Asian Studies; Chinese; Cultural Studies; Dance; East Asian Studies; Educational Sciences; English; Ethics; French; French Studies; Geography (Human); History; International Studies; Japanese; Modern Languages; Music; Performing Arts; Philosophy; Psychology; Social Sciences; Sociology); **Science** (Biology; Chemistry; Information Sciences; Mathematics; Natural Sciences; Physics)

Course/Programme

Japanese Basic Education (*Universty-wide*) (Japanese)

Institute

Environmental Science for Human Life (Environmental Studies; Food Science; Health Sciences; Nutrition); **Experimental Animal** (Animal Husbandry); **Gender Studies** (Gender Studies); **Glycoscience** (Natural Sciences)

Centre

Comparative Japanese Studies (East Asian Studies); **Education and Research**; **Informational Biology** (Biology); **Simulation Sciences** (Computer Engineering); **Soft Matter Physics** (Physics)

Graduate School

Humanities and Sciences (*Doctoral Programme*) (Arts and Humanities; Biochemistry; Biological and Life Sciences; Chemistry; Child Care and Development; Clinical Psychology; Computer Science; Cultural Studies; Developmental Psychology; East Asian Studies; Educational Sciences; Environmental Studies; Food Science; Gender Studies; Genetics; Japanese; Literature; Mathematics; Modern Languages; Psychology; Social Policy; Social Sciences; Social Studies; Sociology); **Humanities and Sciences** (*Master's Programme*) (Applied Linguistics; Art History; Asian Studies; Biochemistry; Biological and Life Sciences; Biology; Chemistry; Child Care and Development; Clinical Psychology; Computer Science; Cultural Studies; Dance; Education; English; English Studies; Environmental Studies; Family Studies; Food Science; French; French Studies; Gender Studies; Genetics; Geography (Human); History; Japanese; Literature; Mathematics; Music; Nutrition; Philosophy; Physics; Psychology; Social Policy; Social Sciences; Sociology)

Research Division

Human Development and Education (*ORC*) (Child Care and Development; Development Studies)

History: Founded 1874 as School, became National University 1949

Academic year: April to March (April-July; September-March)

Admission requirements: Graduation from high school or equivalent or foreign equivalent and entrance examination

Fees: 520,800 per annum (Yen)

Main language(s) of instruction: Japanese

Accrediting agency: Ministry of Education, Culture, Sports, Science and Technology (MEXT)

Degrees and diplomas: Gakushi (Arts and Humanities; Biological and Life Sciences; Cultural Studies; Education; Environmental Studies; Mathematics; Modern Languages; Natural Sciences), Shushi (Asian Studies; Biological and Life Sciences; Cultural Studies; Education; English; French; Gender Studies; Mathematics; Modern Languages; Psychology; Social Sciences; Sociology), Hakase (Biological and Life Sciences; Child Care and Development; Cultural

Studies; Food Science; Foreign Languages Education; Gender Studies; Information Sciences; Mathematics; Modern Languages; Natural Sciences; Nutrition; Performing Arts; Psychology; Social Studies; Sociology)

Student Services: Careers Guidance, Cultural Activities, Sports Facilities, Health Services, Canteen, Foreign Studies Centre, Library, IT Centre

Periodicals: Natural Sciences Report, Studies in Arts and Culture

Academic Staff 2012-2013	MALE	FEMALE	TOTAL
FULL-TIME			265
Student Numbers 2012-2013			
All (Foreign Included)			3057

Last Update: 25-05-2018

Oita University

700 Dannoharu
Oita 870-1192
Tel: +81(97) 569-3311, +81(97) 549-4411
Fax: +81(97) 554-6069
Website: http://www.oita-u.ac.jp
President: Seigo Kitano

Faculty

Economics (Administration; Business Administration; Cultural Studies; Economic and Finance Policy; Economics; Finance; Information Sciences; Management; Regional Studies); **Education and Welfare Science** (Art Education; Computer Science; Cultural Studies; Foreign Languages Education; Home Economics Education; Humanities and Social Science Education; Information Sciences; International Studies; Mathematics Education; Music Education; Physical Education; Science Education; Social Studies; Technology Education; Welfare and Protective Services); **Engineering** (Applied Chemistry; Architectural and Environmental Design; Architecture; Biochemistry; Biological and Life Sciences; Chemistry; Computer Science; Electrical and Electronic Engineering; Energy Engineering; Information Sciences; Information Technology; Machine Building; Mechanical Engineering; Structural Architecture; Thermal Engineering); **Medicine** (Anaesthesiology; Anatomy; Applied Linguistics; Arts and Humanities; Biology; Cardiology; Cell Biology; Chemistry; Clinical Psychology; Community Health; Dentistry; Dermatology; Environmental Studies; Ethics; Forensic Medicine and Dentistry; Gerontology; Gynaecology and Obstetrics; Mathematics; Medicine; Microbiology; Molecular Biology; Neurology; Nursing; Ophthalmology; Orthopaedics; Otorhinolaryngology; Paediatrics; Pathology; Pharmacology; Pharmacy; Physics; Physiology; Psychiatry and Mental Health;

Public Health; Radiology; Social Psychology; Statistics; Surgery; Urology)

Course/Programme

Liberal Arts Education (Arts and Humanities; Asian Studies; Chinese; English; French; German; Health Sciences; Japanese; Korean; Natural Sciences; Physical Education; Social Sciences; Spanish)

Centre

Health Science (Health Sciences); **International Education and Research** (International Studies); **Medical Information** (Medicine); **Research and Development of Higher Education** (*Support Center*) (Health Education; Higher Education)

Graduate School

Economics (Business Administration; Economic and Finance Policy; Economics; Government; Management; Social Policy); **Education** (Education; Primary Education; Teacher Training); **Engineering** (Applied Chemistry; Artificial Intelligence; Computer Science; Electrical and Electronic Engineering; Electronic Engineering; Energy Engineering; Environmental Engineering; Materials Engineering; Mechanical Engineering; Production Engineering; Structural Architecture; Welfare and Protective Services); **Medicine** (Medicine; Nursing); **Social Service Administration** (Administration; Administrative Law; Business Administration; Child Care and Development; Economics; Law; Political Sciences; Psychology; Social and Community Services; Social Policy; Social Welfare; Social Work; Sociology)

Further information: also Hasama and Oji campuses

History: Founded 1949 as a National University under the new educational system incorporating the Oita College of Economics, Oita Normal School, and Oita Normal School for Youth Education. Graduate School of Economics founded 1977, Graduate School of Education 1992, Graduate School of Engineering 1995, and Graduate School of Social Service Administration 2002. Merged with Oita Medical University 2003

Academic year: April to March (April-September; October-March)

Admission requirements: Graduation from high school or equivalent or foreign equivalent, and entrance examination

Fees: Registration, 282,000; tuition, 520,800 per annum (Yen)

Main language(s) of instruction: Japanese

Accrediting agency: Ministry of Education, Culture, Sports, Science and Technology (MEXT)

Degrees and diplomas: Shushi (Administration; Applied Chemistry; Artificial Intelligence; Computer Science; Economic and Finance Policy; Education; Electrical and Electronic Engineering; Energy Engineering; Management; Mechanical Engineering; Medicine; Nursing; Social Policy;

Structural Architecture; Teacher Training; Welfare and Protective Services), Hakase (Business Administration; Energy Engineering; Environmental Engineering; International Business; Materials Engineering; Medicine; Production Engineering)

Student Services: Careers Guidance, Sports Facilities, Health Services, Canteen, Foreign Studies Centre, Library, IT Centre

Periodicals: Academic Bulletin, Bulletin of the Research Institute of Economics, Reports of the Faculty of Engineering, Research Bulletin of Faculty of Education

Academic Staff 2013-2014	MALE	FEMALE	TOTAL
FULL-TIME	484	101	585
Student Numbers 2013-2014			
All (Foreign Included)	3594	2161	5755

Last Update: 23-02-2018

Oita University of Nursing and Health Sciences

2944-9 Megusuno
Oita-shi 870-1201, Oita
Tel: +81(97) 586-4300
Fax: +81(97) 586-4370
Website: http://www.oita-nhs.ac.jp
President: Sachiyo Murashima

Department/Division

Basic Nursing (Nursing); **Clinical Nursing** (Gerontology; Health Sciences; Midwifery; Nursing; Paediatrics; Psychiatry and Mental Health); **Community Health Nursing** (Community Health; Health Administration; International Studies; Nursing; Public Health); **Health Sciences** (Biology; Computer Science; Health Sciences; Modern Languages; Pathology; Psychology; Sports; Statistics)

Graduate School

Graduate Studies (Community Health; Gerontology; Health Administration; Health Sciences; Midwifery; Nursing; Paediatrics)

History: Founded 1998

Main language(s) of instruction: Japanese

Accrediting agency: Ministry of Education, Culture, Sports, Science and Technology (MEXT)

Degrees and diplomas: Gakushi (Health Sciences; Nursing), Shushi (Community Health; Gerontology; Health Administration; Health Sciences; Midwifery; Nursing; Paediatrics), Hakase (Health Sciences; Nursing)

Student Services: Sports Facilities, Language Laboratory, Health Services, Canteen, Library

Periodicals: The Japanese Journal of Nursing and Health Sciences

Last Update: 07-03-2018

Okayama Prefectural University

111 Kuboki
Soja-shi 719-1197, Okayama
Tel: +81(866) 94-2111
Fax: +81(866) 94-2196
Website: http://www.oka-pu.ac.jp
President: Hideaki Tsuji

Faculty

Computer Science and Systems Engineering (Computer Engineering; Computer Science; Information Technology; Telecommunications Engineering); **Design** (Aesthetics; Design; Industrial Design); **Health and Welfare Science** (Child Care and Development; Health Sciences; Nursing; Nutrition; Social Welfare)

Graduate School

Design (Aesthetics; Design); **Health and Welfare Science** (Health Sciences; Nursing; Nutrition; Welfare and Protective Services); **Systems Engineering** (Computer Engineering; Electronic Engineering; Information Technology; Mechanical Engineering; Telecommunications Services)
History: Founded 1993
Fees: Entrance fee, 188,000-282,000; Tuition fee, 535,800 per annum (Yen)
Main language(s) of instruction: Japanese
Accrediting agency: Ministry of Education, Culture, Sports, Science and Technology (MEXT)
Degrees and diplomas: Gakushi (Computer Engineering; Computer Science; Design; Health Sciences; Welfare and Protective Services), Shushi (Computer Engineering; Computer Graphics; Design; Health Sciences; Nursing; Nutrition; Welfare and Protective Services), Hakase (Computer Engineering; Health Sciences; Welfare and Protective Services)

Academic Staff 2013-2014	MALE	FEMALE	TOTAL
FULL-TIME			165
Student Numbers 2013-2014			
All (Foreign Included)	892	970	1862

Last Update: 07-03-2018

Okayama University

1-1-1 Tsushima-naka Kita-ku
Okayama-shi 700-8530, Okayama
Tel: +81(86) 252-1111
Fax: +81(86) 254-6104
Website: http://www.okayama-u.ac.jp
President: Hirofumi Makino

Faculty

Agriculture (Agriculture; Applied Chemistry; Biology; Botany; Ecology; Environmental Studies; Zoology); **Economics** (Accountancy; Economics; Management; Social Policy; Statistics); **Education** (Art Education; Education; Educational Psychology; Foreign Languages Education; Health Education; Home Economics Education; Humanities and Social Science Education; Mathematics Education; Music Education; Native Language Education; Physical Education; Primary Education; Science Education; Special Education; Technology Education); **Engineering** (Applied Chemistry; Biotechnology; Computer Engineering; Electrical and Electronic Engineering; Information Technology; Mechanical Engineering; Telecommunications Engineering); **Environmental Science and Technology** (Applied Chemistry; Civil Engineering; Environmental Engineering; Environmental Management; Environmental Studies; Mathematics; Mathematics and Computer Science); **Law** (Civil Law; Comparative Law; International Law; Law; Political Sciences; Public Law); **Letters** (American Studies; Arts and Humanities; Asian Studies; Behavioural Sciences; European Languages; European Studies; History; Philosophy; South and Southeast Asian Languages); **Pharmaceutical Sciences** (Medicine; Pharmacology; Pharmacy); **Science** (Biology; Chemistry; Earth Sciences; Mathematics; Physics)

School

Dentistry (Biology; Dentistry; Medicine; Oral Pathology; Surgery); **Law** (*Professional Graduate*) (Law); **Medicine** (Anaesthesiology; Biology; Cardiology; Child Care and Development; Community Health; Environmental Studies; Epidemiology; Ethics; Forensic Medicine and Dentistry; Health Sciences; Immunology; Laboratory Techniques; Medical Technology; Medicine; Neurosciences; Nursing; Oncology; Paediatrics; Pathology; Physiology; Radiology; Social and Preventive Medicine; Treatment Techniques)

Institute

Study of the Earth's Interior (Earth Sciences)

Graduate School

Education (*Professional*) (Education; Educational Administration; Teacher Training); **Environmental and Life Science** (Agriculture; Biological and Life Sciences; Engineering; Environmental Management; Environmental Studies; Natural Resources; Social Sciences); **Health Sciences** (Health Sciences); **Humanities and Social Sciences** (Arts and Humanities; Cultural Studies; Management; Public Administration; Social Sciences); **Medicine, Dentistry and**

Pharmaceutical Sciences (Biological and Life Sciences; Dentistry; Environmental Studies; Medicine; Pathology; Pharmacy; Physiology; Rehabilitation and Therapy; Social Sciences); **Natural Sciences and Technology** (Bioengineering; Biological and Life Sciences; Biotechnology; Chemical Engineering; Chemistry; Computer Engineering; Earth Sciences; Electronic Engineering; Mathematics; Mechanical Engineering; Molecular Biology; Natural Resources; Natural Sciences; Physics)

Research Division
Institute for Bioresources (Natural Resources)
Further information: Also University Hospitals (Dentistry and Medicine). Shikata, Higashiyama, Hirai, Kurashiki and Misasa campuses; Overseas branches in Vietnam (Hue), China (Changchun, Shenyang) and a Collaboraive Research Centre in India
History: Founded 1949 as National University, incorporating Okayama Medical School, affiliated Medical College, Sixth National Higher School, Okayama Normal School, Okayama Youth Normal School, and Okayama Prefectural College of Agriculture. Agricultural Biological Research Institute added in 1951, and Faculty of Engineering established 1960
Academic year: April to March (April-September; October-March)
Admission requirements: Graduation from high school or recognized equivalent, and entrance examination
Fees: Undergraduate tuition, 535,800 per annum; Postgraduate tuition, 804,000 per annum (Yen)
Main language(s) of instruction: Japanese
Accrediting agency: Ministry of Education, Culture, Sports, Science and Technology (MEXT)
Degrees and diplomas: Gakushi, Shushi (Agriculture; Arts and Humanities; Business Administration; Cultural Studies; Dentistry; Economics; Education; Engineering; Environmental Engineering; Environmental Studies; Health Sciences; Law; Medicine; Natural Sciences; Nursing; Pharmacy; Philosophy; Public Administration), Hakase (Agriculture; Arts and Humanities; Cultural Studies; Dentistry; Economics; Engineering; Environmental Engineering; Environmental Studies; Health Sciences; Law; Medicine; Natural Sciences; Pharmacy; Philosophy). Also Potsgraduate Professional Degrees in Education and Law
Student Services: Academic Counselling, Careers Guidance, Nursery Care, Sports Facilities, Language Laboratory, Health Services, Canteen, Foreign Studies Centre, Library, IT Centre, Residential Facilities
Periodicals: Acta Medica Okayama, Bulletin of School of Education, Contributions from the Ushimado Marine Laboratory, Faculty of Engineering, Okayama University, Journal of Humanities and Social Sciences, Journal of the Faculty of Letters, Mathematical Journal, Nogaku Kenkyu, Okayama Economic Review, Okayama Law Journal, Okayama-

Igakkai-Zasshi, Reports of the Research Laboratory for Surface Science, Scientific Reports of the Faculty of Agriculture, Technical Report of ISEI

Academic Staff 2013-2014	MALE	FEMALE	TOTAL
FULL-TIME			1387
Student Numbers 2013-2014			
All (Foreign Included)			13188
Foreign only			465

Last Update: 16-02-2018

Okinawa Prefectural College of Nursing (OPCN)

1-24-1, Yogi Naha
Okinawa 902-0076
Tel: +82(98) 833-8800
Fax: +82(98) 833-5133
Website: http://www.okinawa-nurs.ac.jp
President: M. Kadekaru

Course/Programme
Nursing (Child Care and Development; Community Health; Gerontology; Health Administration; Health Sciences; Midwifery; Nursing; Public Health)

Graduate School
Health Science and Nursing (Health Sciences; Nursing)
History: Founded 1999
Main language(s) of instruction: Japanese
Accrediting agency: Ministry of Education, Culture, Sports, Science and Technology (MEXT)
Degrees and diplomas: Gakushi (Nursing), Shushi (Nursing), Hakase (Nursing)
Student Services: Library
Periodicals: OPCN Journal, Synthesizer
Last Update: 07-03-2018

Okinawa Prefectural University of Arts

1-4, Shuri Tonokura-cho
Naha 903-8602, Okinawa
Tel: +81(98) 882-5000
Fax: +81(98) 882-5033
Website: http://www.okigei.ac.jp
President: Yasuharu Higa

Faculty
Arts and Crafts (Ceramic Art; Design; Fine Arts; Handicrafts; Painting and Drawing; Sculpture; Weaving);

Music (Dance; Music; Musical Instruments; Musicology; Performing Arts; Singing)

Graduate School

Cultural Arts Studies (*PhD*) (Cultural Studies; Ethnology; Fine Arts; Musicology; Performing Arts); **Formative Arts** (*MA: Daily Life Design; Environmental Design; Comparative Art Studies*) (Architectural and Environmental Design; Ceramic Art; Comparative Literature; Design; Ethnology; Fine Arts; Painting and Drawing; Sculpture; Weaving); **Music Arts** (*MA: Music Performance Arts*) (Dance; Music; Music Theory and Composition; Musical Instruments; Musicology; Performing Arts; Theatre)

Research Division

Arts (Cultural Studies; Fine Arts; Handicrafts; Performing Arts)
Further information: Also Shurikinjo and Shurisakiyama campuses
History: Founded 1986
Academic year: April to March (April-September; October-March)
Admission requirements: Graduation from High School or recognized equivalent, and entrance examination
Main language(s) of instruction: Japanese
Accrediting agency: Ministry of Education, Culture, Sports, Science and Technology (MEXT)
Degrees and diplomas: Gakushi (Design; Fine Arts; Handicrafts; Musical Instruments; Musicology; Painting and Drawing; Performing Arts; Sculpture; Singing), Shushi (Ceramic Art; Dance; Design; Ethnology; Fine Arts; Music; Music Theory and Composition; Musical Instruments; Musicology; Painting and Drawing; Sculpture; Singing; Theatre; Weaving), Hakase (Ethnology; Fine Arts; Musicology; Performing Arts)
Student Services: Social Counselling, Careers Guidance, Cultural Activities, Sports Facilities, Facilities for disabled people, Health Services, Canteen, Library
Periodicals: Bulletin

Academic Staff 2013-2014	MALE	FEMALE	TOTAL
FULL-TIME			78
Student Numbers 2013-2014			
All (Foreign Included)	117	424	541

Last Update: 08-03-2018

Onomichi City University

1600 Hisayamadacho Onomichi-shi
Hiroshima 722-8506
Tel: +81(848) 22-8311

Fax: +81(848) 22-5460
Website: http://www.onomichi-u.ac.jp
President: Takeshi Nakatani

Faculty

Art and Culture (Cinema and Television; Communication Arts; Design; Fine Arts; Handicrafts; Japanese; Literature; Painting and Drawing; Visual Arts; Writing); **Economics, Management and Information Science** (Accountancy; Administration; Administrative Law; Commercial Law; Computer Networks; Computer Science; Data Processing; Economics; English; Finance; Information Sciences; Information Technology; International Economics; Management; Software Engineering; Taxation)

Graduate School

Art and Design (Design; Fine Arts); **Economics, Management and Information Science** (Accountancy; Business Administration; Economics; Information Sciences; Management; Taxation); **Japanese Literature** (Japanese; Literature)
History: Founded 2001 as Onomichi University. Acquired present title 2012
Academic year: April to March (April-September; September-March)
Main language(s) of instruction: Japanese
Accrediting agency: Ministry of Education, Culture, Sports, Science and Technology (MEXT)
Degrees and diplomas: Shushi (Economics; Fine Arts; Information Sciences; Literature)
Student Services: Library
Periodicals: Onomichi University Keizai Jyoho Ronsyu

Student Numbers 2013-2014	MALE	FEMALE	TOTAL
All (Foreign Included)			c. 1330

Last Update: 08-03-2018

Osaka City University

3-3-138 Sugimoto Sumiyoshi
Osaka 558-8585
Tel: +81(6) 6605-3453
Fax: +81(6) 6605-2058
Website: http://www.osaka-cu.ac.jp
President: Tetsuo Arakawa
Tel: +81(6) 6605-2000

Faculty

Business (*Also Graduate School*) (Business Administration; Business and Commerce); **Economics** (*Also Graduate School*) (Economic and Finance Policy; Economics); **Engineering** (*Also Graduate School*) (Applied Chemistry; Applied Physics; Architecture; Artificial Intelligence; Building Technologies;

Civil Engineering; Electrical Engineering; Engineering; Environmental Engineering; Information Technology; Mechanical Engineering); **Human Life Science** (*Also Graduate School*) (Environmental Studies; Home Economics; Nutrition; Social Welfare); **Law** (*Also Graduate School*) (Law; Private Law; Public Law); **Literature and Human Sciences** (*Also Graduate School*) (Asian Studies; Behavioural Sciences; Cultural Studies; Education; Geography; History; Literature; Philosophy; Psychology; Social Sciences; Sociology); **Medicine** (*Also Graduate School*) (Medicine); **Science** (*Also Graduate School*) (Biology; Chemistry; Earth Sciences; Mathematics; Natural Sciences; Physics)

School
Nursing (*Also Graduate School*) (Nursing)

Graduate School
Business Administration; **Creative Cities** (Regional Planning; Town Planning; Urban Studies)

History: Founded 1949, incorporating Osaka University of Commerce, Osaka City Technical College, Institute of Economic Research of Osaka City, and Osaka City Women's College. Osaka City Medical School incorporated 1955

Academic year: April to March (April-September; October-March)

Admission requirements: Graduation from high school or recognized equivalent or foreign equivalent, and entrance examination

Main language(s) of instruction: Japanese

Accrediting agency: Ministry of Education, Culture, Sports, Science and Technology (MEXT)

Degrees and diplomas: Shushi (Arts and Humanities; Business Administration; Clinical Psychology; Economics; Engineering; Environmental Studies; Health Sciences; Law; Literature; Medicine; Natural Sciences; Nursing; Social Welfare; Social Work)

Student Services: Academic Counselling, Careers Guidance, Cultural Activities, Sports Facilities, Language Laboratory, Facilities for disabled people, Health Services, Canteen, Foreign Studies Centre

Periodicals: Business Review, Economy Journal, Journal of Economics, Journal of Geoscience, Journal of Law and Politics, Memoirs of the Faculty of Engineering, Osaka City Medical Journal, Osaka Journal of Mathematics, Quarterly Journal of Economic Studies, Studies in Humanities, University Bulletin

Academic Staff	MALE	FEMALE	TOTAL
FULL-TIME			2054
Student Numbers			
All (Foreign Included)	4093	2452	6545
Foreign only			316

Last Update: 08-03-2018

Osaka Prefecture University

1-1 Gakuen-cho Nakaku
Sakai 599-8531, Osaka
Tel: +81(72) 252-1161
Fax: +81(72) 254-9900
Website: http://www.osakafu-u.ac.jp
President: Hiroshi Tsuji
Tel: +81 (72) 254-9100

College
Engineering (Aeronautical and Aerospace Engineering; Chemical Engineering; Chemistry; Electrical and Electronic Engineering; Engineering; Information Technology; Marine Engineering; Materials Engineering; Mathematics; Mechanical Engineering; Physics); **Health and Human Sciences** (Child Care and Development; Education; Family Studies; Health Sciences; Nursing; Occupational Therapy; Physical Therapy; Rehabilitation and Therapy; Social Welfare; Welfare and Protective Services); **Life, Environment, and Advanced Sciences** (Biological and Life Sciences; Biology; Biotechnology; Chemistry; Ecology; Environmental Studies; Natural Sciences; Physics; Social Sciences; Veterinary Science); **Sustainable System Sciences** (Computer Science; Economics; Education; Environmental Studies; Health Sciences; Information Sciences; Information Technology; Management; Philosophy; Production Engineering; Psychology)

School
Comprehensive Rehabilitation (Nutrition; Occupational Therapy; Physical Therapy; Rehabilitation and Therapy); **Economics** (Accountancy; Business Administration; Economics; Finance; Information Technology; Marketing); **Engineering** (Aeronautical and Aerospace Engineering; Applied Chemistry; Chemical Engineering; Computer Science; Electrical Engineering; Electronic Engineering; Engineering; Information Technology; Marine Engineering; Mathematics; Mechanical Engineering; Physics); **Environmental Sciences** (Biological and Life Sciences; Biology; Biotechnology; Environmental Studies); **Humanities and Social Sciences** (Arts and Humanities; Cultural Studies; Social Sciences; Social Welfare); **Liberal Arts and Sciences** (Arts and Humanities; Natural Sciences); **Nursing** (Nursing); **Science** (Biological and Life Sciences; Chemistry; Information Sciences; Mathematics and Computer Science; Natural Sciences; Physics)

Graduate School
Comprehensive Rehabilitation (Health Sciences; Nutrition; Rehabilitation and Therapy); **Economics** (Business Administration; Economics); **Engineering** (Aeronautical and Aerospace Engineering; Electrical Engineering; Electronic Engineering; Engineering; Information Sciences;

Information Technology; Marine Engineering; Materials Engineering; Mathematics; Mechanical Engineering; Nuclear Engineering; Physics); **Humanities and Social Sciences** (Arts and Humanities; Clinical Psychology; Cultural Studies; Gender Studies; History; Modern Languages; Psychology; Social Policy; Social Sciences; Social Studies; Social Welfare); **Life and Environmental Sciences** (Biochemistry; Biological and Life Sciences; Computer Science; Environmental Studies; Veterinary Science); **Nursing** (Community Health; Gerontology; Health Sciences; Nursing; Oncology; Psychiatry and Mental Health); **Science** (Biological and Life Sciences; Chemistry; Computer Science; Information Sciences; Mathematics; Natural Sciences; Physics; Software Engineering)

History: Founded 1949 as Naniwa University, incorporating Osaka Technical College, Osaka Youth Normal School, Osaka Prefectural College of Chemical Engineering, Osaka College of Veterinary Medicine and Zoology, and Osaka Prefecture College of Agriculture. Present title adopted 1955. Incorporated Osaka Women's University and Osaka Prefectural College of Nursing 2005

Academic year: April to March (April-September; October-March)

Admission requirements: Graduation from high school or recognized equivalent, and entrance examination

Fees: National : Tuition, 564,000-764,000 per annum (Yen), International : Tuition, 535,800 per annum (Yen)

Main language(s) of instruction: Japanese

Accrediting agency: Ministry of Education, Culture, Sports, Science and Technology (MEXT)

Degrees and diplomas: Shushi (Aeronautical and Aerospace Engineering; American Studies; Applied Chemistry; Artificial Intelligence; Arts and Humanities; Asian Studies; Biochemistry; Biological and Life Sciences; Business Administration; Chemical Engineering; Chemistry; Clinical Psychology; Computer Science; Econometrics; Economics; Electrical Engineering; Electronic Engineering; English; English Studies; Environmental Studies; Health Sciences; Information Sciences; Information Technology; Japanese; Law; Marine Engineering; Materials Engineering; Mathematics; Mechanical Engineering; Modern Languages; Nuclear Engineering; Nursing; Nutrition; Physics; Rehabilitation and Therapy; Veterinary Science), Hakase (Aeronautical and Aerospace Engineering; Applied Chemistry; Artificial Intelligence; Arts and Humanities; Biochemistry; Biological and Life Sciences; Business Administration; Chemical Engineering; Chemistry; Clinical Psychology; Computer Science; Cultural Studies; Econometrics; Economics; Electrical Engineering; Electronic Engineering; Environmental Studies; Information Sciences; Information Technology; Law; Marine Engineering; Mathematics; Mechanical Engineering; Modern Languages; Nuclear Engineering; Nursing; Physics; Social Welfare; Veterinary Science)

Student Services: Academic Counselling, Social Counselling, Careers Guidance, Sports Facilities, Health Services, Library

Periodicals: Research Report

Academic Staff 2013-2014	MALE	FEMALE	TOTAL
FULL-TIME			691
Student Numbers 2013-2014			
All (Foreign Included)			8051
Foreign only			187

Last Update: 08-03-2018

Osaka University (OU)

1-1 Yamadaoka
Suita-shi 565-0871, Osaka
Tel: +81(6) 6877-5111
Fax: +81(6) 6879-7106
Website: http://www.osaka-u.ac.jp
President: Shojiro Nishio

Faculty
Medicine (Health Sciences; Medicine)

Course/Programme
Kaitokudo for the 21st Century

School
Dentistry (Dentistry); **Economics** (Business Administration; Economics; Management); **Engineering** (Architecture; Electronic Engineering; Energy Engineering; Engineering; Environmental Engineering; Information Technology; Materials Engineering; Mechanical Engineering; Production Engineering); **Engineering Science** (Chemical Engineering; Chemistry; Computer Science; Electronic Engineering; Engineering; Information Sciences; Materials Engineering); **Foreign Studies** (International Studies); **Human Sciences** (Archaeology; Arts and Humanities; Chinese; Comparative Literature; French; Geography; German; Hindi; History; Japanese; Linguistics; Modern Languages; Musicology; Philosophy; Theatre); **Law** (International Studies; Law; Political Sciences); **Letters** (Arts and Humanities); **Medicine** (*Hamamatsu University - Chiba University and University of Fukui*) (Medicine); **Pharmaceutical Sciences** (Pharmacology; Pharmacy); **Science** (Chemistry; Mathematics; Physics)

Department/Division
Environment and Energy Management (Energy Engineering; Environmental Management); **Safety and Hygiene** (Hygiene; Safety Engineering)

Institute

Academic Initiatives (*IAI*); NanoScience Design (Nanotechnology)

Centre

Advanced Medical Engineering and Informatics (*MEI Centre*) (Computer Science; Medical Technology); Biotechnology (*International Centre*) (Biotechnology); Cybermedia (Media Studies); Education and Research (*Bangkok, Gröningen, San Francisco and Shanghai Overseas Centres*); Education in Liberal Arts and Sciences (Humanities and Social Science Education; Science Education); Environmental Innovation Design for Sustainability (Design; Environmental Studies); Global Collaboration; Health Care (Public Health); Information and Neural Networks (Information Sciences; Neurosciences); Intellectual Property (*Iprism*) (Civil Law); Interdisciplinary Research and Education; International Education and Exchange (International Studies); Japanese Language and Culture (Asian Studies; Japanese); Laser Engineering (Laser Engineering); Low Temperature (Electronic Engineering; Physics); Nakanoshima; Quantum Science and Technology under Extreme Conditions (Physics); Renovation of Instruments for Science and Technology (Instrument Making); Study of Communication-Design (Design; Mass Communication); Study of Finance and Insurance (Finance; Insurance); Tekijuku Commemoration

Bureau

Office for University-Industry Collaboration

Graduate School

Dentistry (Dentistry; Oral Pathology); Economics (Business Administration; Economics; Management; Political Sciences); Engineering (Applied Chemistry; Applied Physics; Architecture; Biotechnology; Electrical Engineering; Electronic Engineering; Energy Engineering; Environmental Engineering; Industrial Management; Information Technology; Machine Building; Materials Engineering; Measurement and Precision Engineering; Mechanical Engineering; Production Engineering); Engineering Science (Bioengineering; Engineering; Materials Engineering; Mechanical Engineering); Frontier Biosciences (Biological and Life Sciences); Human Sciences (Arts and Humanities; Social Sciences); Information Sciences and Technology (Applied Mathematics; Biological and Life Sciences; Computer Engineering; Computer Networks; Computer Science; Information Sciences; Information Technology; Mathematics; Multimedia; Physics); International Public Policy (Comparative Politics; International Studies; Political Sciences); Language and Culture (Asian Studies; Cultural Studies; Japanese; Modern Languages; Social Studies); Law (Law); Law and Politics (Law; Political Sciences); Letters (Arts and Humanities; Cultural Studies); Medicine (Health Sciences; Medicine); Pharmaceutical Sciences (Pharmacology; Pharmacy); Science (Astronomy and Space Science; Biological and Life Sciences; Chemistry; Earth Sciences; Mathematics; Molecular Biology; Physics); United Child Development (*United - Osaka University, Kanazawa University*) (Child Care and Development)

Research Division

Environmental Preservation (Environmental Management); Joining and Welding (Metal Techniques); Microbial Disease (Microbiology); Nuclear Physics (Nuclear Physics); Protein Research (Biochemistry); Radioisotope Research (Nuclear Engineering); Scientific and Industrial Research (Engineering; Information Sciences; Natural Sciences); Social and Economic Research (Economics; Social Sciences); Solar Energy Chemistry (Applied Chemistry); Ultra-High Voltage Electron Microscopy (Electronic Engineering; Metallurgical Engineering); WPI Immunology Frontier (Immunology)

Further information: Also short-term student exchange programme. OUSSEP, OUSSEP-Maple and Frontier-Lab@OsakaU programmes; Osaka University Hospital and Osaka University Dental Hospital.

History: Founded in 1931 as Osaka Imperial University, with Faculties of Medicine and Science. The academic origins of humanities schools trace back to Kaitokudo, a general education school for Osaka citizens, founded in 1724. The Faculty of Medicine traces its origin to the Tekijuku, a private school of Western medicine and sciences, founded in 1838. Osaka Engineering College incorporated as Faculty in 1933. Title changed to Osaka University in 1947. Acquired present status in 1949. From April 2004, all of Japan's national universities have become national university corporations/semi-national universities. Merged with Osaka University of Foreign Studies in October 2007

Academic year: April to March (April-September; October-March)

Admission requirements: Graduation from high school or recognized equivalent, and entrance examination

Fees: Registration, 282,000; tuition, 535,800 per annum (Yen)

Main language(s) of instruction: Japanese

Accrediting agency: Ministry of Education, Culture, Sports, Science and Technology (MEXT)

Degrees and diplomas: Gakushi (Dentistry; Medicine), Hakase (Dentistry; Medicine). Also Homu Hakase (Juris Doctor), 3 yrs

Student Services: Academic Counselling, Social Counselling, Careers Guidance, Nursery Care, Cultural Activities, Sports Facilities, Language Laboratory, Facilities for disabled people, Health Services, Canteen, Foreign Studies Centre

Periodicals: Emergent Robotics / Human Interface / Motor Intelligence Annual Report, Emergent Robotics Adaptive Robotics Annual Report, International Public Policy Studies, Memoirs of Graduate School of Human Sciences, Memoirs of the Graduate School of Letters, Memoirs of the Institute of Scientific and Industrial Research, Osaka Economics Papers, Osaka Journal of Mathematics, Studies in Language and Culture, Transactions of JWRI
Publishing house: N/A

Academic Staff 2012-2013	MALE	FEMALE	TOTAL
FULL-TIME			5988
PART-TIME			3335
Student Numbers 2012-2013			
All (Foreign Included)	16917	7690	24607
Foreign only			1938

Total number of part-time students: 1046
Last Update: 23-02-2018

Osaka University of Education

4-698-1 Asahigaoka
Kashiwara-shi 582-8582, Osaka
Tel: +81(72) 976-3211
Fax: +81(72) 978-3316
Website: http://www.osaka-kyoiku.ac.jp
President: Akio Nagao

Department/Division

Arts and Science (Cultural Studies; Environmental Studies; Fine Arts; Health Sciences; Humanities and Social Science Education; Information Sciences; Mathematics; Mathematics and Computer Science; Music; Natural Sciences; Social Sciences; Sports); **Education** (*Also Graduate School*) (Art Education; Cultural Studies; Education; Engineering; English; European Languages; Health Education; Home Economics Education; Japanese; Mathematics Education; Modern Languages; Music Education; Nursing; Oriental Languages; Physical Education; Preschool Education; Primary Education; Science Education; Secondary Education; Social Sciences; Special Education; Technology Education)
Further information: Also evening courses
History: Founded 1874.
Academic year: April to March (April-September; October-March)
Admission requirements: Secondary school certificate or equivalent, and entrance examination
Main language(s) of instruction: Japanese, English
Accrediting agency: Ministry of Education, Culture, Sports, Science and Technology (MEXT)
Degrees and diplomas: Gakushi (Education), Shushi (Education)

Student Services: Library
Periodicals: Memoirs
Last Update: 28-03-2018

Otaru University of Commerce

3-5-21 Midori
Otaru-shi 047-8501, Hokkaido
Tel: +81(134) 27-5200
Fax: +81(134) 27-5213
Website: http://www.otaru-uc.ac.jp
President: Makio Yamamoto

Department/Division

Commerce (Accountancy; Banking; Business Administration; Business and Commerce; Communication Studies; English; Finance; Human Resources; Insurance; International Business; Management; Marketing); **Economics** (Banking; Econometrics; Economic History; Economics; Finance; International Economics; Statistics); **Information and Management Sciences** (Information Management; Information Sciences; Management; Mathematics and Computer Science; Operations Research; Statistics); **Law** (Administrative Law; Civil Law; Commercial Law; Constitutional Law; Criminal Law; International Law; Labour Law; Law)
History: Founded 1910 as School, acquired present status and title 1949.
Academic year: April to March (April-September; October-March)
Admission requirements: Graduation from high school or recognized equivalent, and entrance examination. Japanese Language Proficiency Test
Fees: Entrance, 282,000; tuition, 520,800 per annum (Yen)
Main language(s) of instruction: Japanese, English
Accrediting agency: Ministry of Education, Culture, Sports, Science and Technology (MEXT)
Degrees and diplomas: Shushi (Business Administration; Business and Commerce), Hakase (Business Administration; Business and Commerce)
Student Services: Academic Counselling, Social Counselling, Careers Guidance, Sports Facilities, Facilities for disabled people, Health Services, Canteen
Periodicals: The Economic Journal, The Journal of Liberal Arts
Last Update: 23-02-2018

Prefectural University of Hiroshima

1-1-71 Ujina-Higashi Minami
Hiroshima 734-8558
Tel: +81(82) 251-5178, +81(82) 251-9727
Fax: +81(82) 251-9405

Website: http://www.pu-hiroshima.ac.jp
President: Ken-ichi Nakamura

Faculty

Health and Welfare (*Mihara Campus*) (Chinese; Communication Disorders; Communication Studies; English; German; Health Sciences; Information Sciences; Natural Sciences; Nursing; Occupational Therapy; Physical Education; Physical Therapy; Social Welfare; Sociology; Welfare and Protective Services); **Human Culture and Science** (American Studies; Asian Studies; Biological and Life Sciences; Communication Studies; Cultural Studies; East Asian Studies; English Studies; Food Science; Health Administration; Health Sciences; Modern Languages; Nutrition; Regional Studies; Social Studies; Sports); **Life and Environmental Science** (*Shobara Campus*) (Biological and Life Sciences; Biotechnology; Environmental Management; Environmental Studies; Food Technology; Natural Resources; Waste Management); **Management and Information Systems** (Accountancy; Business Administration; Finance; Information Sciences; Information Technology; Management; Marketing; Public Administration)

Course/Programme

Midwifery (*Graduate*) (Health Sciences; Midwifery; Women's Studies)

Graduate School

Comprehensive Scientific Research (Accountancy; Biological and Life Sciences; Biotechnology; Business Administration; Cultural Studies; Environmental Management; Environmental Studies; Finance; Health Administration; Health Sciences; Human Resources; Information Sciences; Linguistics; Management; Molecular Biology; Natural Resources; Natural Sciences; Nutrition; Public Administration; Social Problems; Social Studies; Social Welfare; Welfare and Protective Services)

Further information: Also Shobara and Mihara Campuses
History: Founded 2005, incorporating Hiroshima Joshi Daigaku (Hiroshima Women's University)
Fees: Tuition, 535,800 per annum (Yen)
Main language(s) of instruction: Japanese
Accrediting agency: Ministry of Education, Culture, Sports, Science and Technology (MEXT)
Degrees and diplomas: Shushi (Cultural Studies; Health Sciences; Information Sciences; Management; Welfare and Protective Services), Hakase (Biological and Life Sciences)
Student Services: Sports Facilities

Student Numbers 2012-2013	MALE	FEMALE	TOTAL
All (Foreign Included)	862	1789	2651

Last Update: 08-03-2018

Prefectural University of Kumamoto (PUK)

3-1-100 Tsukide
Kumamoto 862-8502
Tel: +81(96) 383-2929
Fax: +81(96) 384-6765
Website: http://www.pu-kumamoto.ac.jp
President: Ichibe Makoto

Faculty

Administration (Accountancy; Administration; Business Administration; Computer Science; Economics; Ethics; Health Administration; Information Management; Information Technology; International Relations; Law; Mathematics; Multimedia; Political Sciences; Public Administration; Social and Community Services; Statistics; Welfare and Protective Services); **Environmental and Symbiotic Sciences** (Environmental Studies; Food Science; Health Sciences; Information Sciences); **Letters** (Arts and Humanities; Cultural Studies; English; Foreign Languages Education; History; Japanese; Linguistics; Literature)

Course/Programme

General Education (Chinese; Cultural Studies; English; Environmental Studies; French; German; Health Sciences; Information Sciences; International Studies; Korean; Modern Languages; Natural Sciences; Regional Studies; Sports; Technology)

Graduate School

Administration (Administration; Business Administration; Health Administration; Information Management; Management; Public Administration); **Environmental and Symbiotic Sciences** (Environmental Studies; Food Science; Health Sciences; Natural Resources; Nutrition; Welfare and Protective Services); **Language and Literature** (English; Japanese; Literature; Modern Languages)
History: Founded 1947, acquired present status 1994
Academic year: April to March (April-September; October-March)
Admission requirements: Graduation from high school or equivalent
Main language(s) of instruction: Japanese
Accrediting agency: Ministry of Education, Culture, Sports, Science and Technology (MEXT)
Degrees and diplomas: Shushi (Administration; English; Environmental Studies; Food Science; Health Sciences; Japanese; Literature; Natural Resources; Nutrition; Welfare and Protective Services), Hakase (Administration; English; Environmental Studies; Japanese; Literature)
Student Services: Academic Counselling, Social Counselling, Careers Guidance, Nursery Care, Sports Facilities, Facilities for disabled people, Health Services, Canteen

Periodicals: Faculty Journal

Academic Staff 2012-2013	MALE	FEMALE	TOTAL
FULL-TIME			134
Student Numbers 2012-2013			
All (Foreign Included)			2121

Last Update: 08-03-2018

Saga University

1 Honjo-machi
Saga-shi 840-8502, Saga
Tel: +81(952) 28-8113
Fax: +81(952) 28-8819
Website: http://www.saga-u.ac.jp
President: Kohji Miyazaki

Faculty

Agriculture (*Also Graduate School*) (Agriculture; Applied Chemistry; Biological and Life Sciences; Coastal Studies; Environmental Studies; Food Science); **Culture and Education** (*Also Graduate School*) (Crafts and Trades; Cultural Studies; Education; Environmental Studies; International Studies); **Economics** (*Also Graduate School*) (Business Administration; Economics; Law); **Medicine** (*Also Graduate School*) (Anatomy; Biological and Life Sciences; Biology; Community Health; Forensic Medicine and Dentistry; Genetics; Immunology; Medicine; Nursing; Oncology; Social and Preventive Medicine; Toxicology); **Science and Engineering** (*Also Graduate School*) (Applied Chemistry; Chemistry; Civil Engineering; Electrical and Electronic Engineering; Engineering; Information Sciences; Mathematics; Mathematics and Computer Science; Mechanical Engineering; Natural Sciences; Physics)
History: Founded 1949 as National University incorporating former Normal Schools. Incorporated Saga Ika Daigaku/Saga Medical School 2003.
Academic year: April to March (April-October; October-March)
Admission requirements: Graduation from high school or equivalent or foreign equivalent, and entrance examination
Main language(s) of instruction: Japanese
Accrediting agency: Ministry of Education, Culture, Sports, Science and Technology (MEXT)
Degrees and diplomas: Gakushi (Agriculture; Education; Engineering; Medicine; Natural Sciences; Nursing; Social Sciences), Shushi (Agriculture; Business Administration; Curriculum; Economics; Education; Finance; Health Sciences; Medicine; Nursing), Hakase (Agriculture; Anatomy; Energy Engineering; Engineering; Materials Engineering; Medicine; Pathology; Technology)

Student Services: Academic Counselling, Careers Guidance, Sports Facilities, Language Laboratory, Health Services, Foreign Studies Centre
Periodicals: Faculty journals
Last Update: 23-02-2018

Saitama Prefectural University

820 San-Nomiya Koshigaya
Saitama 343-8540
Tel: +81(48) 971-0500
Fax: +81(48) 973-4807
Website: http://www.spu.ac.jp
President: Kazunori Kayaba
Chairman: Takeshi Erikawa

Department/Division

Health and Social Services (Behavioural Sciences; Health Sciences; Laboratory Techniques; Nursing); **Nursing** (Nursing); **Occupational Therapy** (Occupational Therapy); **Physical Therapy** (Physical Therapy); **Social Work** (Social Welfare; Social Work)
History: Founded 1999
Main language(s) of instruction: Japanese
Accrediting agency: Ministry of Education, Culture, Sports, Science and Technology (MEXT)
Last Update: 08-03-2018

Saitama University (SU)

255 Shimo-Okubo, Sakura-ku
Saitama 338-8570, Saitama
Tel: +81(48) 858-3908
Fax: +81(48) 858-9675
Website: http://www.saitama-u.ac.jp
President: Hiroki Yamaguch Yamaguch

Faculty

Economics (Business Administration; Economics; Environmental Studies; Management; Social Welfare); **Education** (Health Education; Nursing; Teacher Training); **Engineering** (Applied Chemistry; Civil Engineering; Computer Engineering; Electrical and Electronic Engineering; Environmental Engineering; Environmental Studies; Information Sciences; Materials Engineering; Mechanical Engineering); **Liberal Arts** (American Studies; Asian Studies; European Studies; Government; History; Japanese; Philosophy; Sociology); **Science** (Biochemistry; Biology; Chemistry; Mathematics; Molecular Biology; Physics)

Institute

Ambient Mobility Interfaces; **Brain Science** (Natural Sciences); **Environmental Science and Technology** (Environmental Engineering; Environmental Studies)

Centre

Comprehensive Analysis for Science (Natural Sciences); **Education and Research in Cooperative Human Relations**; **English Education and Development** (English); **Japanese Language Education** (Japanese); **Research and Training on International Development** (Development Studies; International Studies)

Graduate School

Cultural Science (Asian Studies; Cultural Studies; Japanese); **Economic Science** (Finance; Management; Public Administration; Regional Studies); **Education** (*The United Graduate School of Education Tokyo Gakugei University (Doctoral course)*) (Education; Special Education); **Science and Engineering** (Biological and Life Sciences; Chemistry; Civil Engineering; Computer Science; Electronic Engineering; Environmental Engineering; Environmental Studies; Materials Engineering; Mathematics; Mechanical Engineering; Mechanics; Physics)

Research Division

Geosphere (Earth Sciences)
History: Founded 1949, incorporating Urawa High School, Saitama Youth School and Saitama Teachers College. Reorganized 1965
Academic year: April to March (Spring semester: April-September, Fall semester: October-March)
Admission requirements: High school graduation certificate or equivalent academic qualification and entrance examination
Fees: 267,900 per semester (Yen)
Main language(s) of instruction: Japanese
Accrediting agency: Ministry of Education, Culture, Sports, Science and Technology (MEXT)
Degrees and diplomas: Hakase (Cultural Studies; Economics; Engineering; Natural Sciences)
Student Services: Academic Counselling, Social Counselling, Careers Guidance, Nursery Care, Sports Facilities, Language Laboratory, Facilities for disabled people, Health Services, Canteen, Foreign Studies Centre
Periodicals: Asian economy and social environment, Research report of Department of Civil & Environmental Engineering, Faculty of Engineering, Saitama University, Saitama mathematical journal
Publishing house: Keyaki, Saitama University bulletin

Academic Staff 2012-2013	MALE	FEMALE	TOTAL
FULL-TIME	392	73	465
STAFF WITH DOCTORATE			
FULL-TIME	294	50	344
Student Numbers 2012-2013			
All (Foreign Included)	6144	2887	9031
Foreign only	286	217	503

Total number of part-time students: 99
Last Update: 23-02-2018

Sapporo City University (SCU)

Kita 11 Nishi 13 Chuo-ku
Sapporo 060-0011
Tel: +81(11) 726-2500
Website: http://www.scu.ac.jp
President: Takashi Hasumi

School

Design (Design); **Nursing** (Nursing)

Department/Division

Midwifery (Midwifery)
History: Founded 1965 as Sapporo City Kotokangogakuin. Acquired present title and status 2006
Main language(s) of instruction: Japanese
Accrediting agency: Ministry of Education, Culture, Science and Technology (MEXT)
Degrees and diplomas: Shushi (Design; Midwifery; Nursing), Hakase (Nursing)
Student Services: Library
Last Update: 08-03-2018

Sapporo Medical University

South 1 West 17 Chuo-ku
Sapporo 060-8556, Hokkaido
Tel: +81(11) 611-2111
Fax: +81(11) 613-7134
Website: http://web.sapmed.ac.jp
President: Taiji Tsukamoto

School

Health Sciences (Health Sciences; Nursing; Occupational Therapy; Physical Therapy); **Medicine** (Medicine; Oncology)

Centre

Medical Education (Arts and Humanities; English; Law; Natural Sciences; Psychology; Sociology)

Graduate School

Master's Programme / Doctoral Programme (Medicine; Midwifery; Occupational Therapy; Oncology; Physical Therapy)

History: Founded 1950 as Sapporo Medical College. Acquired present title and status 2007

Academic year: April to March (April-October; October-March)

Admission requirements: Graduation from high school or recognized equivalent, and entrance examination

Main language(s) of instruction: Japanese

Accrediting agency: Ministry of Education, Culture, Sports, Science and Technology (MEXT)

Degrees and diplomas: Gakushi (Medicine), Shushi (Medicine; Midwifery; Nursing; Occupational Therapy; Oncology; Physical Therapy), Hakase (Medicine; Midwifery; Nursing; Occupational Therapy; Oncology; Physical Therapy)

Student Services: Sports Facilities, Library

Periodicals: Journal of Liberal Arts and Sciences Sapporo Medical College, Sapporo Medical Journal, Tumour Research

Last Update: 08-03-2018

Shiga University

1-1-1 Banba
Hikone-shi 522-8522, Shiga
Tel: +81(749) 27-1172
Fax: +81(749) 27-1174
Website: http://www.shiga-u.ac.jp
President: Ryuichi Ida

Faculty

Economics (Accountancy; Economics; Finance; Management; Management Systems); **Education** (*Otsu-shi*) (Education; Environmental Studies; Information Sciences; Primary Education; Science Education; Secondary Education; Special Education)

Graduate School

Economics (Business Administration; Economics; Finance; Management); **Education** (*Otsu-shi*) (Education; Special Education)

History: Faculty of Education founded 1874 as Shiga Normal School. Faculty of Economics founded 1922 as Hikone Commercial College. Present status and title acquired 1949.

Academic year: April to March (April-September; October-March)

Admission requirements: Graduation from high school (Koto Gakko)

Main language(s) of instruction: Japanese

Accrediting agency: Ministry of Education, Culture, Sports, Science and Technology (MEXT)

Degrees and diplomas: Gakushi (Economics; Education), Shushi (Economics; Education; Finance; Special Education), Hakase (Economics; Education; Management)

Student Services: Academic Counselling, Social Counselling, Careers Guidance, Cultural Activities, Sports Facilities, Language Laboratory, Facilities for disabled people, Health Services, Canteen, Foreign Studies Centre, Library

Periodicals: Hikone Ronso, Kenkyu-Nenpo, Kyoiku-Gakubu Kiyo, Shiga-Eibun-Gakkai-Ronbunshu

Academic Staff 2013-2014	MALE	FEMALE	TOTAL
FULL-TIME	299	120	419
Student Numbers 2013-2014			
All (Foreign Included)	2433	1546	3979
Foreign only	65	61	126

Last Update: 23-02-2018

Shiga University of Medical Science

Seta Tsukinowa-cho
Otsu-shi 520-2192, Shiga
Tel: +81(77) 548-2111
Fax: +81(77) 543-8659
Website: http://www.shiga-med.ac.jp
President: Kohei Shiota
Tel: +81(77) 548-2000

Faculty

Medicine (*Also Graduate School*) (Anatomy; Anthropology; Behavioural Sciences; Biochemistry; Biology; Cell Biology; Chemistry; English; Forensic Medicine and Dentistry; Genetics; German; Health Sciences; Mathematics; Medicine; Microbiology; Molecular Biology; Neurosciences; Pathology; Pharmacology; Philosophy; Physics; Physiology; Social and Preventive Medicine; Sociology); **Nursing** (Nursing)

History: Founded 1974. Graduate School established 1981.

Academic year: April to March (April-September; October-March)

Admission requirements: Graduation from high school and entrance examination

Fees: 434,800 per annum (Yen)

Main language(s) of instruction: Japanese

Accrediting agency: Ministry of Education, Culture, Sports, Science and Technology (MEXT)

Degrees and diplomas: Gakushi (Medicine; Nursing), Shushi (Nursing), Hakase (Epidemiology; Medicine)

Student Services: Academic Counselling, Social Counselling, Careers Guidance, Sports Facilities, Language

Laboratory, Facilities for disabled people, Health Services, Canteen, Library

Periodicals: Bulletin of Shiga University of Medical Science

Publishing house: Shiga University of Medical Science

Student Numbers 2013	MALE	FEMALE	TOTAL
All (Foreign Included)			1107

Last Update: 16-02-2018

Shimane University

1060 Nishikawatsu

Matsue 690-8504, Shimane

Tel: +81(852) 32-6106

Fax: +81(852) 32-6481

Website: http://www.shimane-u.ac.jp

President: Hattori Yasunori

Faculty

Education (Art Education; Biological and Life Sciences; Cultural Studies; Education; Educational Psychology; Environmental Studies; Health Education; Mathematics Education; Music Education; Native Language Education; Physical Education; Preschool Education; Primary Education; Psychology; Science Education; Secondary Education; Social Studies; Teacher Training); **Law and Literature** (Cultural Studies; Economics; Law; Literature; Native Language; Social Studies); **Life and Environmental Science** (Agriculture; Biological and Life Sciences; Biology; Biotechnology; Development Studies; Ecology; Environmental Studies; Forestry; Marine Biology; Regional Studies); **Medicine** (Medicine; Nursing); **Science and Engineering** (*Interdisciplinary*) (Automation and Control Engineering; Earth Sciences; Electronic Engineering; Engineering; Engineering Management; Materials Engineering; Mathematics and Computer Science; Natural Resources)

Graduate School

Education (Education); **Humanities and Social Sciences** (Arts and Humanities; Cultural Studies; Japanese; Law; Native Language; Social Sciences); **Law** (Law); **Life and Environmental Science** (Environmental Studies); **Medical Research** (Medicine); **Science and Engineering** (Automation and Control Engineering; Earth Sciences; Electronic Engineering; Engineering Management; Materials Engineering; Mathematics and Computer Science; Natural Resources)

History: Founded as National University 1949, incorporating Matsue Higher School, Shimane Teachers' Training School, and Shimane Youth Normal School. Graduate School established 1971. Merged with Shimane Medical University (Shimane Ika Daigaku) 2003

Academic year: April to March (April-September; October-March)

Admission requirements: Graduation from high school or recognized equivalent or foreign equivalent, and entrance examination

Main language(s) of instruction: Japanese

Accrediting agency: Ministry of Education, Culture, Sports, Science and Technology (MEXT)

Degrees and diplomas: Shushi (Biological and Life Sciences; Cultural Studies; Economics; Education; Engineering; Environmental Studies; Law; Medicine; Modern Languages; Nursing; Social Sciences), Hakase (Engineering; Law; Medicine)

Student Services: Academic Counselling, Social Counselling, Careers Guidance, Sports Facilities, Facilities for disabled people, Health Services, Library

Periodicals: Bulletin of the Faculty of Agriculture, English Education and English Studies, Geological Reports of Shimane University, Journal of Early Childhood Education, Journal of Economics, Journal of Social Studies Education, Laguna, Literature, Literature and Social Science, Memoirs of the Faculty of Education (Educational Science), Memoirs of the Faculty of Law and Literature (Shimane Law Review), Memoirs of the Faculty of Science, Natural Sciences, Research for Educational Practice, Studies of the San'in Region

Last Update: 09-03-2018

Shimonoseki City University

2-1-1 Daigaku-cho

Shimonoseki 751-8510, Yamaguchi

Tel: +81(83) 252-0288

Fax: +81(83) 252-8099

Website: http://www.shimonoseki-cu.ac.jp

President: Yoichi Kawanami

Faculty

Economics (Business and Commerce; Economics; International Business; Management)

Graduate School

Economics (Economics; International Business)

History: Founded 1956. Acquired present status 1962

Main language(s) of instruction: Japanese

Accrediting agency: Ministry of Education, Culture, Sports, Science and Technology (MEXT)

Degrees and diplomas: Shushi (Economics; International Business)

Student Services: Foreign Studies Centre, Library

Academic Staff 2013-2014	MALE	FEMALE	TOTAL
FULL-TIME			55
Student Numbers 2013-2014			
All (Foreign Included)			2119
Foreign only			61

Last Update: 08-03-2018

Shinshu University

3-1-1 Asahi
Matsumoto-shi 390-8621, Nagano
Tel: +81(263) 35-4600
Fax: +81(263) 34-6481
Website: http://www.shinshu-u.ac.jp
President: Kunihiro Hamada
Tel: +81(263) 37-2100

Faculty

Agriculture (*Also Graduate School*) (Agriculture; Biological and Life Sciences; Biotechnology; Food Science; Forestry); **Arts** (*Also Graduate School*) (Arts and Humanities; Communication Studies; Cultural Studies; History; Philosophy; Psychology; Social Sciences); **Economics** (Economics; Law; Public Administration); **Education** (*Also Graduate School; Nagano City*) (Education; Educational and Student Counselling; Physical Education; Special Education; Teacher Training); **Engineering** (*Nagano City*) (Architecture; Chemical Engineering; Civil Engineering; Electrical and Electronic Engineering; Engineering; Environmental Studies; Information Technology; Materials Engineering; Mechanical Engineering; Technology); **Science** (Biology; Chemistry; Environmental Studies; Geology; Mathematics; Natural Sciences; Physics); **Textile Science and Technology** (*Also Graduate School; Ueda City*) (Biology; Machine Building; Materials Engineering; Mechanical Engineering; Polymer and Plastics Technology; Technology; Textile Technology)

School

General Education (Arts and Humanities; Education; English; French; German; Health Education; Korean; Russian; Science Education; Social Sciences; Teacher Training); **Health Sciences** (Medical Technology; Nursing; Occupational Therapy; Physical Therapy); **Law** (*Graduate*) (Economics; Law; Public Administration); **Medicine** (*Also Graduate School*) (Medicine)

Institute

Innovation Management (Management)

Graduate School

Science and Technology (*Interdisciplinary*) (Environmental Studies; Materials Engineering; Mathematics and Computer Science; Mountain Studies; Textile Technology)

History: Founded 1949, incorporating previously existing regional Colleges and Institutes
Academic year: April to March (April-September; October-March)
Admission requirements: Graduation from high school or recognized equivalent or foreign equivalent, and entrance examination
Fees: 535,800 per annum (Yen)
Main language(s) of instruction: Japanese
Accrediting agency: Ministry of Education, Culture, Sports, Science and Technology (MEXT)
Degrees and diplomas: Gakushi (Agriculture; Economics; Education; Engineering; History; Literature; Medicine), Shushi (Agriculture; Economics; Education; Engineering; History; Law; Literature; Management; Medicine; Social Sciences), Hakase (Agriculture; Environmental Studies; Materials Engineering; Mathematics and Computer Science; Medicine; Mountain Studies; Philosophy; Social Sciences; Textile Technology)
Student Services: Academic Counselling, Social Counselling, Careers Guidance, Sports Facilities, Language Laboratory, Facilities for disabled people, Health Services, Canteen, Foreign Studies Centre, Library
Last Update: 25-05-2018

Shizuoka University of Arts and Culture (SUAC)

1794-1 Noguchicho
Hamamatsu-shi 430-8533, Shizuoka
Tel: +81(53) 457-6111, +81(53) 457-6113
Fax: +81(53) 457-6123
Website: http://www.suac.ac.jp
Head: Akito Arima
Vice-President: Shigeto Ikegami

Faculty

Cultural Policy (*Also Graduate School*) (Art Management; Cultural Studies; International Studies; Regional Studies)

School

Design (*Also Graduate School*) (Architectural and Environmental Design; Fine Arts; Industrial Design)

Graduate School

Design (Design); **Policy Studies** (Cultural Studies; International Studies)
History: Founded 2000
Fees: 538,800 per annum (Yen)
Main language(s) of instruction: Japanese
Accrediting agency: Ministry of Education, Culture, Sports, Science and Technology (MEXT)

Degrees and diplomas: Shushi (Cultural Studies; Design)
Student Services: Foreign Studies Centre, Library
Last Update: 09-03-2018

Takasaki City University of Economics (TCUE)

1300 Kaminamie
Takasaki 370-0801, Gumma
Tel: +81(27) 344-6265
Fax: +81(27) 343-4830
Website: http://www.tcue.ac.jp
President: Motonobu Murayama

Faculty
Economics (Business Administration; Economics); **Regional Policy** (Regional Planning; Regional Studies; Tourism)

School
Graduate Studies (Business Administration; Economics; Regional Planning)
History: Founded 1957
Admission requirements: Graduation from high school and entrance examination
Main language(s) of instruction: Japanese
Accrediting agency: Ministry of Education, Culture, Sports, Science and Technology (MEXT)
Degrees and diplomas: Hakase (Economics; Management; Regional Planning)
Student Services: Academic Counselling, Social Counselling, Careers Guidance, Nursery Care, Health Services, Canteen, Library
Periodicals: Bulletin of the Institute for Research in Regional Economy, The Economics Journal of Takasaki City University of Economics
Last Update: 09-03-2018

The Graduate University for Advanced Studies (SOKENDAI)

1560-35 Aza-kanmon Kamiyamaguchi, Hayama-cho
Miura-gun 240-0193, Kanagawa
Tel: +81(46) 858-1500
Fax: +81(46) 858-1541
Website: http://www.soken.ac.jp
President: Mariko Hasegawa

School
Advanced Sciences (Biological and Life Sciences); **Cultural and Social Studies** (Cultural Studies; Ethnology; History; Japanese; Modern Languages; Oriental Languages; Oriental Studies; Regional Studies; Social Studies); **High Energy Accelerator Science** (Nuclear Physics); **Life Sciences** (Biological and Life Sciences; Biology; Genetics; Molecular Biology; Physiology); **Multidisciplinary Science** (Computer Science; Statistics); **Physical Sciences** (Astronomy and Space Science; Nuclear Physics; Physics)
History: Founded 1988. A postgraduate institution operating in close collaboration with inter-university research institutes
Academic year: April to February (April-September; October-February)
Admission requirements: Five-year doctor course, university degree; three-year doctor course, Master degree or foreign equivalent
Main language(s) of instruction: Japanese, English
Accrediting agency: Ministry of Education, Culture, Sports, Science and Technology (MEXT)
Degrees and diplomas: Hakase (Asian Studies; Astronomy and Space Science; Biological and Life Sciences; Japanese; Natural Sciences; Nuclear Physics; Oriental Studies)
Student Services: Library
Last Update: 23-02-2018

The University of Electro-Communications (UEC)

1-5-1 Chofugaoka
Chofu 182-8585, Tokyo
Tel: +81(424) 43-5014, +81(424) 43-5115
Fax: +81(424) 43-5108, +81(424) 43-5116
Website: http://www.uec.ac.jp
President: Takashi Fukuda

Faculty
Electro-Communications (Applied Chemistry; Applied Physics; Communication Studies; Computer Science; Electronic Engineering; Information Technology; Mechanical Engineering; Systems Analysis; Telecommunications Engineering); **Informatics and Engineering** (Applied Physics; Automation and Control Engineering; Biological and Life Sciences; Biotechnology; Computer Engineering; Computer Science; Electronic Engineering; Engineering; Information Management; Information Sciences; Information Technology; Management; Mathematics; Mathematics and Computer Science; Mechanical Engineering; Media Studies; Optical Technology; Robotics; Telecommunications Engineering)

Institute
Laser Science (Laser Engineering)

Centre
Developing e-Learning (Educational Technology); **Higher Education Development and Research** (Higher Education);

Industrial and Governmental Relations (*CIGR*) (Business Administration; Technology); **Information Technology** (Information Technology)

Graduate School
Electro-Communications (Applied Chemistry; Applied Physics; Computer Networks; Computer Science; Electronic Engineering; Information Sciences; Information Technology; Mathematics; Mathematics and Computer Science; Mechanical Engineering; Media Studies; Telecommunications Engineering); **Informatics and Engineering** (Applied Chemistry; Automation and Control Engineering; Biological and Life Sciences; Biotechnology; Computer Science; Electronic Engineering; Engineering; Information Management; Information Sciences; Information Technology; Management; Mathematics; Mathematics and Computer Science; Mechanical Engineering; Media Studies; Optical Technology; Robotics; Telecommunications Engineering); **Information Systems** (Computer Engineering; Computer Networks; Information Sciences; Information Technology; Media Studies; Software Engineering)

Research Division
Advanced Wireless Communication (*AWCC*) (Telecommunications Engineering)

History: Founded 1918 by Wireless Association, transferred to Ministry of Communications 1942 and to Ministry of Education 1948. Re-established as University 1949. Junior Technical College established 1953, Graduate School of Electro-Communications 1965, and Graduate School of Information 1992

Academic year: April to March (April-September; October-March)

Admission requirements: Graduation from high school and entrance examination

Main language(s) of instruction: Japanese

Accrediting agency: Ministry of Education, Culture, Sports, Science and Technology (MEXT)

Degrees and diplomas: Hakase (Computer Science; Electronic Engineering; Information Technology; Telecommunications Engineering)

Student Services: Academic Counselling, Social Counselling, Careers Guidance, Cultural Activities, Sports Facilities, Language Laboratory, Health Services, Canteen, Foreign Studies Centre

Periodicals: Annual Report of Research, Report of Annual Research Works, Reports

Academic Staff 2012-2013	MALE	FEMALE	TOTAL
FULL-TIME			302
Student Numbers 2012-2013			
All (Foreign Included)			5329

Last Update: 23-02-2018

The University of Shimane

2433-2 Nobara-cho
Hamada-shi 697-0016, Shimane
Tel: +81(855) 24-2200
Fax: +81(855) 24-2208
Website: http://www.u-shimane.ac.jp
President: Kiyohara Masayoshi

Faculty
Policy Studies (Asian Studies; Cultural Studies; East Asian Studies; Economics; International Relations; Political Sciences; Regional Studies; Social Sciences)

Department/Division
Nursing (Nursing)

Graduate School
Northeast Asia Studies (Asian Studies; International Relations); **Regional Development Policy** (Cultural Studies; Development Studies; Economics; Geography (Human); International Relations; Regional Studies; Social Sciences; Sociology)

History: Founded 2000.
Admission requirements: Entrance examination
Main language(s) of instruction: Japanese
Accrediting agency: Ministry of Education, Culture, Sports, Science and Technology (MEXT)
Degrees and diplomas: Gakushi (Social Sciences), Shushi (Asian Studies; Cultural Studies; East Asian Studies), Hakase (Asian Studies; International Relations; Regional Studies; Social Sciences)
Student Services: Careers Guidance, Health Services, Foreign Studies Centre, Library
Last Update: 27-03-2018

The University of Tokyo

7-3-1 Hongo Bunkyo-ku
Tokyo 113-8654
Tel: +81(3) 5841-0297
Fax: +81(3) 5689-7344
Website: http://www.u-tokyo.ac.jp
President: Makoto Gonokami

Faculty
Agriculture (Agricultural Economics; Agriculture; Applied Chemistry; Aquaculture; Bioengineering; Biological and Life Sciences; Biotechnology; Ecology; Environmental Engineering; Environmental Studies; Forest Biology; Forest Products; Landscape Architecture; Marine Biology; Natural Resources; Veterinary Science; Wood Technology; Zoology);

Economics (Business Administration; Economics; Finance; Management); **Education** (Curriculum; Education; Educational Administration; Educational Psychology; Educational Sciences; Health Education; Humanities and Social Science Education; Physical Education); **Engineering** (Aeronautical and Aerospace Engineering; Applied Chemistry; Applied Physics; Architecture; Biotechnology; Chemical Engineering; Chemistry; Civil Engineering; Electrical and Electronic Engineering; Engineering; Information Technology; Materials Engineering; Mathematics; Measurement and Precision Engineering; Mechanical Engineering; Systems Analysis; Telecommunications Engineering; Urban Studies); **Law** (Law; Political Sciences; Private Law; Public Law); **Letters** (Aesthetics; Archaeology; Art History; Arts and Humanities; Chinese; Cultural Studies; English; Ethics; French; German; Greek (Classical); Hindi; History; Islamic Studies; Italian; Japanese; Latin; Linguistics; Literature; Modern Languages; Philosophy; Psychology; Religion; Religious Studies; Slavic Languages; Social Psychology; Sociology; Spanish); **Medicine** (Anatomy; Biochemistry; Biomedical Engineering; Biomedicine; Cell Biology; Community Health; Economics; Epidemiology; Genetics; Gerontology; Gynaecology and Obstetrics; Health Sciences; Immunology; Medical Technology; Medicine; Microbiology; Midwifery; Molecular Biology; Neurosciences; Nursing; Occupational Health; Paediatrics; Pathology; Pharmacology; Physiology; Psychiatry and Mental Health; Radiology; Social and Preventive Medicine; Speech Studies; Statistics; Surgery); **Pharmaceutical Sciences** (Analytical Chemistry; Applied Chemistry; Biochemistry; Biological and Life Sciences; Biology; Cell Biology; Chemistry; Genetics; Immunology; Microbiology; Molecular Biology; Neurology; Neurosciences; Oncology; Organic Chemistry; Pharmacology; Pharmacy; Physical Chemistry; Physiology); **Science** (Astronomy and Space Science; Biochemistry; Biological and Life Sciences; Biology; Biophysics; Chemistry; Computer Science; Earth Sciences; Environmental Studies; Information Sciences; Mathematics; Physics)

College

Arts and Sciences (*Komaba I Campus*) (Arts and Humanities; Natural Sciences; Social Sciences)

Institute

Advanced Studies on Asia (Archaeology; Asian Studies; Cultural Studies; Fine Arts; History; Literature; Political Sciences); **Atmosphere and Ocean Research** (Marine Science and Oceanography; Meteorology); **Cosmic Ray Research** (*ICRR*) (Astronomy and Space Science; Nuclear Physics; Physics); **Earthquake Research** (Architecture; Civil Engineering; Earth Sciences; Information Sciences; Safety Engineering; Seismology); **Historiographical** (Documentation Techniques; History); **Industrial Science** (Architecture; Biological and Life Sciences; Civil Engineering; Computer

Graphics; Computer Science; Electronic Engineering; Energy Engineering; Engineering; Environmental Studies; Marine Engineering; Materials Engineering; Mathematics; Mechanical Engineering; Nanotechnology; Safety Engineering; Software Engineering; Transport Engineering); **Medical Science** (Biochemistry; Cell Biology; Genetics; Health Sciences; Immunology; Medicine; Oncology); **Molecular and Cellular Biosciences** (Cell Biology; Molecular Biology); **Physics and Mathematics of the Universe** (*Kavli - IPMU*) (Mathematics; Physics); **Social Science** (Economics; Law; Political Sciences; Social Sciences; Sociology); **Solid State Physics** (Applied Physics; Chemistry; Engineering; Materials Engineering; Physics; Solid State Physics)

Centre

Asian Natural Environmental Science (Environmental Studies); **Biotechnology Research** (Biotechnology); **Cryogenic Research** (Applied Physics; Heating and Refrigeration); **Elementary Particle Physics** (*International*) (Nuclear Physics); **Environmental Science** (Environmental Studies); **Information Technology** (Information Technology); **Integrated Research System for Sustainability Science** (*IR3S*) (Natural Sciences); **Radioisotope** (Radiology); **Research and Development of Higher Education** (Higher Education); **Research into Artifacts** (Engineering); **Spatial Information Science** (Astronomy and Space Science; Information Sciences); **University Museum** (Museum Studies); **Very Large Scale Integration (VLSI) Design and Education** (*VDEC*) (Design)

Graduate School

Agricultural and Life Sciences (Agriculture; Animal Husbandry; Applied Chemistry; Aquaculture; Bioengineering; Biological and Life Sciences; Biology; Biotechnology; Ecology; Environmental Engineering; Environmental Studies; Forestry; Veterinary Science); **Arts and Sciences** (American Studies; Anthropology; Asian Studies; Behavioural Sciences; Cognitive Sciences; Comparative Literature; Comparative Politics; Cultural Studies; European Studies; Hispanic American Studies; Information Sciences; International Relations; International Studies; Islamic Studies; Japanese; Korean; Linguistics; Measurement and Precision Engineering; Mediterranean Studies; Modern Languages; Natural Sciences; Pacific Area Studies; Social Sciences); **Economics** (Economics; Finance; Management); **Education** (Education; Educational Sciences); **Engineering** (Aeronautical and Aerospace Engineering; Applied Chemistry; Applied Physics; Architecture; Bioengineering; Biological and Life Sciences; Biotechnology; Chemical Engineering; Chemistry; Civil Engineering; Electrical Engineering; Engineering; Engineering Management; Information Sciences; Law; Materials Engineering; Measurement and Precision Engineering; Mechanical Engineering; Nuclear Engineering; Systems Analysis); **Frontier Sciences** (Biological and Life Sciences;

Biology; Computer Science; Energy Engineering; Engineering; Environmental Engineering; Environmental Studies; International Studies; Marine Science and Oceanography; Materials Engineering; Natural Sciences); **Humanities and Sociology** (American Studies; Arts and Humanities; Asian Studies; Cultural Studies; European Studies; Japanese; Korean; Sociology); **Information Science and Technology** (Computer Science; Information Sciences; Information Technology; Mathematics; Mathematics and Computer Science; Mechanical Engineering; Telecommunications Engineering); **Interdisciplinary Information Studies** (Communication Studies; Computer Science; Cultural Studies; Information Sciences; Social Studies); **Law and Politics** (Law; Political Sciences); **Mathematical Science** (Mathematics); **Medicine** (Biology; Biomedical Engineering; Cell Biology; Embryology and Reproduction Biology; Gerontology; Health Sciences; Immunology; Medicine; Microbiology; Molecular Biology; Neurosciences; Nursing; Pathology; Public Health; Radiology; Social and Preventive Medicine; Surgery); **Pharmaceutical Sciences** (Pharmacy); **Public Policy** (Economic and Finance Policy; Government; Law; Public Administration); **Science** (Astronomy and Space Science; Biochemistry; Biological and Life Sciences; Biophysics; Chemistry; Earth Sciences; Physics)

Research Division

Advanced Science and Technology (Natural Sciences; Technology); **Medical Education** (*International*) (Health Education; Medicine); **Policy Alternatives** (*PARI*)

History: Established 1877, amalgamating several institutions that had existed from the 18th and the early 19th centuries. Renamed Imperial University and then Tokyo Imperial University before becoming Tokyo Daigaku (University of Tokyo) again in 1947. Incorporated as National University Corporation in 2004

Academic year: April to March (April-September; October-March) / October-September (for some programmes)

Admission requirements: High school diploma or equivalent and entrance examination

Fees: Enrolment fee, 282,000; tuition, undergraduate and graduate (Master's programmes and Professional programmes), 535,800, graduate (Doctorate programs) (excluding Law School), 535,800, Law School students, 804,000 per annum (Yen)

Main language(s) of instruction: Japanese / English (for programmes offered in English and some courses)

Accrediting agency: Ministry of Education, Culture, Sports, Science and Technology (MEXT)

Degrees and diplomas: Gakushi (Agriculture; Arts and Humanities; Economics; Education; Engineering; Health Sciences; Law; Literature; Mathematics; Medicine; Pharmacology; Veterinary Science), Shushi (Agriculture; Arts and

Humanities; Communication Studies; Computer Science; Economics; Education; Engineering; Fine Arts; Health Sciences; Information Sciences; Information Technology; Law; Mathematics and Computer Science; Mechanical Engineering; Medical Technology; Medicine; Nuclear Engineering; Pharmacy; Philosophy; Physics; Public Administration), Hakase (Agriculture; Arts and Humanities; Communication Studies; Economics; Education; Engineering; Health Sciences; Law; Literature; Medicine; Nuclear Engineering; Pharmacy; Philosophy; Psychology; Public Administration; Sociology)

Student Services: Academic Counselling, Social Counselling, Careers Guidance, Nursery Care, Sports Facilities, Facilities for disabled people, Health Services, Canteen, Foreign Studies Centre

Periodicals: Outline of The University of Tokyo, The University of Tokyo Magazine "TANSEI"

Publishing house: University of Tokyo Press

Last Update: 23-02-2018

Tohoku University

2-1-1 Katahira Aoba-ku
Sendai-shi 980-8577, Miyagi
Tel: +81(22) 217-4844
Fax: +81(22) 217-4846
Website: http://www.tohoku.ac.jp
President: Susumu Satomi

Faculty

Agriculture (Agriculture; Biological and Life Sciences; Environmental Management; Natural Resources); **Arts and Letters** (Arts and Humanities; Development Studies; History of Societies; Linguistics; Social Sciences); **Dentistry** (Dentistry; Stomatology); **Economics** (Business Administration; Economics; Management); **Education** (Educational Sciences); **Engineering** (Aeronautical and Aerospace Engineering; Applied Chemistry; Applied Physics; Architecture; Artificial Intelligence; Biomedical Engineering; Building Technologies; Chemical Engineering; Civil Engineering; Earth Sciences; Electrical and Electronic Engineering; Energy Engineering; Engineering; Geology; Materials Engineering; Measurement and Precision Engineering; Metallurgical Engineering; Telecommunications Engineering); **Law** (International Law; Law; Political Sciences; Public Law); **Medicine** (Health Sciences; Medicine; Rehabilitation and Therapy); **Pharmaceutical Sciences** (Biological and Life Sciences; Chemistry; Pharmacy); **Science** (Astronomy and Space Science; Biology; Chemistry; Environmental Studies; Geology; Geophysics; Mathematics; Mineralogy; Petroleum and Gas Engineering; Physics)

Institute

Development, Ageing and Cancer (Biology; Genetics; Medicine; Neurology; Oncology; Physiology); **Electrical Communication Research** (Computer Science; Electrical Engineering; Telecommunications Engineering); **Fluid Science** (Mechanics; Physics); **Materials Research**; **Multi-disciplinary Research for Advanced Materials** (Automation and Control Engineering; Engineering; Materials Engineering)

Centre

Cyclotron and Radioisotope; **Gene Research**; **Higher Education Research**; **Information Synergy**; **Interdisciplinary Research**; **International Student** (Educational and Student Counselling; Japanese); **Low Temperature Science**; **New Industry Creation Hatchery**; **Northeast Asian Studies** (*Interdisciplinary*)

Graduate School

Educational Informatics (*Education and Research Divisions*); **Environmental Studies** (Chemistry; Cultural Studies; Earth Sciences; Energy Engineering; Environmental Engineering; Materials Engineering); **Information Sciences** (Information Sciences; Mathematics and Computer Science; Social Sciences); **International Cultural Studies** (Communication Studies; Cultural Studies; Economics; Linguistics; Literature; Modern Languages); **Life Sciences** (Biological and Life Sciences; Environmental Studies; Neurosciences)
History: Founded 1907 as Tohoku Imperial University, incorporating College of Science, Sendai, and branch School of Sapporo Agricultural College, Hokkaido. Reorganized as National University 1949. Reorganized as National University Corporation and incorporated College of Medical Sciences Tohoku University 2004
Academic year: April to March (April-September; October-March)
Admission requirements: Graduation from high school or equivalent or foreign equivalent, and entrance examination
Fees: 520,800 per annum (Yen)
Main language(s) of instruction: Japanese
Accrediting agency: Ministry of Education, Culture, Sports, Science and Technology (MEXT)
Degrees and diplomas: Gakushi (Agriculture; Arts and Humanities; Economics; Education; Engineering; Law; Pharmacology), Shushi (Agriculture; Arts and Humanities; Biological and Life Sciences; Cultural Studies; Economics; Education; Engineering; Information Sciences; Law; Medicine; Pharmacy), Hakase (Agriculture; Arts and Humanities; Biological and Life Sciences; Cultural Studies; Economics; Education; Engineering; Information Sciences; Law; Pharmacy)
Student Services: Academic Counselling, Language Laboratory, Health Services, Canteen, Foreign Studies Centre

Periodicals: Annual Report of the Economic Society, Annual Research Bulletin of the Graduate School of Pharmaceutical Sciences, CYRIC Annual Report, Faculty of Engineering, Interdisciplinary Information Sciences, New Industry Creation Hatchery Centre, Northeast Asian Studies, Research Report of the Laboratory of Nuclear Science, Tohoku Geophysical Journal, Tohoku Journal of Experimental Medicine, Tohoku Mathematical Journal, Tohoku University Bulletin
Last Update: 22-02-2018

Tokyo Gakugei University

4-1-1 Nukui-Kitamachi Koganei-shi
Tokyo 184-8501
Tel: +81(42) 329-7111, +81(42) 329-7763
Fax: +81(42) 329-7114, +81(42) 329-7765
Website: http://www.u-gakugei.ac.jp

Faculty

Education (Education; Educational Sciences; Special Education; Teacher Training)
History: Founded 1949, incorporating Tokyo First, Second, and Third Normal Schools, and Youth Normal School, founded between 1873 and 1937
Academic year: April to March (April-September; October-March)
Admission requirements: Graduation from high school (undergraduate), from university with Bachelor's Degree (Master), with Master's Degree (Doctor) or recognized equivalent or foreign equivalent, and entrance examination
Main language(s) of instruction: Japanese
Accrediting agency: Ministry of Education, Culture, Sports, Science and Technology (MEXT)
Degrees and diplomas: Shushi (Education), Hakase (Education)
Student Services: Academic Counselling, Social Counselling, Careers Guidance, Sports Facilities, Language Laboratory, Facilities for disabled people, Health Services, Canteen, Foreign Studies Centre
Publishing house: University Press
Last Update: 22-02-2018

Tokyo Institute of Technology

2-12-1 E3 Ookayama Meguro-ku
Tokyo 152-8550
Tel: +81(3) 5734-2975
Fax: +81(3) 5734-3661
Website: http://www.titech.ac.jp
President: Yoshinao Mishima

School

Bioscience and Biotechnology (*2 Departments, Yokohama City*) (Bioengineering; Biological and Life Sciences; Biotechnology); **Engineering** (*16 Departments*) (Aeronautical and Aerospace Engineering; Applied Chemistry; Architecture and Planning; Automation and Control Engineering; Chemical Engineering; Civil Engineering; Computer Science; Construction Engineering; Electrical and Electronic Engineering; Environmental Engineering; Industrial Engineering; Inorganic Chemistry; Mechanical Engineering; Metallurgical Engineering; Organic Chemistry; Polymer and Plastics Technology; Structural Architecture; Systems Analysis); **Science** (*5 Departments*) (Chemistry; Earth Sciences; Information Sciences; Mathematics; Physics)

Graduate School

Bioscience and Biotechnology (*5 Departments, Yokohama City*) (Bioengineering; Biological and Life Sciences; Biomedical Engineering; Molecular Biology); **Decision Science and Technology** (*4 Departments*) (Industrial Engineering; Industrial Management; Social Sciences); **Information Science and Engineering** (*3 Departments*) (Computer Science; Environmental Engineering; Information Sciences; Mathematics and Computer Science; Mechanical Engineering); **Innovation Management** (*2 Departments*) (Engineering Management); **Interdisciplinary Science and Engineering** (*11 Departments, Yokohama City*) (Applied Chemistry; Applied Physics; Artificial Intelligence; Chemistry; Computer Engineering; Electronic Engineering; Energy Engineering; Environmental Engineering; Information Technology; Materials Engineering; Mechanical Engineering; Systems Analysis); **Science and Engineering** (*20 Departments*) (Aeronautical and Aerospace Engineering; Applied Chemistry; Automation and Control Engineering; Ceramics and Glass Technology; Chemical Engineering; Chemistry; Civil Engineering; Communication Studies; Construction Engineering; Development Studies; Earth Sciences; Electrical and Electronic Engineering; Electronic Engineering; Materials Engineering; Mathematics; Mechanical Engineering; Metallurgical Engineering; Nuclear Engineering; Nuclear Physics; Physics; Polymer and Plastics Technology; Structural Architecture; Systems Analysis; Telecommunications Engineering)

Research Division

Biological Resources and Informatics; **Carbon Recycling and Energy** (Chemistry); **Chemical Resources** (*Yokohama City*) (Applied Chemistry; Chemistry; Inorganic Chemistry; Laboratory Techniques; Molecular Biology; Natural Resources; Organic Chemistry); **Educational Facilities**; **Foreign Language Research and Teaching** (Foreign Languages Education); **Frontier Research**; **Global Scientific Information and Computing** (Computer Engineering; Information Technology); **Low Temperature Physics** (Physics); **Materials and Structures** (*Yokohama City*) (Building Technologies; Materials Engineering; Nanotechnology; Structural Architecture); **Nuclear Reactors** (Energy Engineering; Nuclear Engineering; Safety Engineering); **Precision and Intelligence** (*Yokohama City*) (Bioengineering; Biomedical Engineering; Information Sciences; Information Technology; Materials Engineering; Mechanical Engineering; Microelectronics); **Quantum Nanoelectronics** (Nanotechnology); **Research and Development of Educational Technology** (Educational Technology); **Research for Educational Facilities**; **Research on Carbon Recycling and Energy**; **Volcanic Fluid Research**

History: Founded 1881 as Tokyo Shokko Gakko (Tokyo Vocational School), acquired present status and title 1929, under direct control of the Ministry of Education, Culture, Sports, Science and Technology

Academic year: April to March (April-September; October-March)

Admission requirements: Graduation from high school or recognized equivalent and entrance examination

Fees: Registration, 282,000; tuition, 535,800 per annum (Yen)

Main language(s) of instruction: Japanese, English

Accrediting agency: Ministry of Education, Culture, Sports, Science and Technology (MEXT)

Degrees and diplomas: Hakase (Philosophy)

Student Services: Academic Counselling, Social Counselling, Careers Guidance, Cultural Activities, Sports Facilities, Language Laboratory, Facilities for disabled people, Health Services, Canteen, Foreign Studies Centre, Library

Periodicals: Annual List of Faculty and Staff Publications

Last Update: 23-02-2018

Tokyo Medical and Dental University

1-5-45 Yushima Bunkyo-ku
Tokyo 113-8510
Tel: +81(3) 3813-6111
Fax: +81(3) 5803-0105
Website: http://www.tmd.ac.jp
President: Yasuyuki Yoshizawa

Faculty

Dentistry (Dentistry); **Medicine** (Health Sciences; Medicine)

College

Liberal Arts and Sciences (Arts and Humanities; Biology; Chemistry; Chinese; English; French; German; Mathematics; Physics; Social Sciences; Spanish)

Graduate School

Biomedical Science (*PhD programme*) (Biomedicine); **Health Sciences** (Biological and Life Sciences; Community Health; Health Education; Health Sciences; Nursing); **Medicine and Dentistry** (Dentistry; Medicine)

History: Founded 1946

Academic year: April to March (April-October; October-March)

Admission requirements: Graduation from high school or recognized equivalent, and entrance examination

Main language(s) of instruction: Japanese

Accrediting agency: Ministry of Education, Culture, Sports, Science and Technology (MEXT) National Institution for Academic Degrees and Quality Enhancement of Higher Education (NIAD-QE)

Degrees and diplomas: Shushi (Dentistry; Medicine; Public Health), Hakase (Biomedicine; Dentistry; Health Sciences; Medicine)

Student Services: Sports Facilities, Language Laboratory, Library

Periodicals: Bulletins, Report of the Institute for Medical and Dental Engineering

Last Update: 16-03-2018

Tokyo Metropolitan University (TMU)

1-1 Minami-Ohsawa Hachioji
Tokyo 192-0397
Tel: +81(426) 77-1111
Fax: +81(426) 77-1221
Website: http://www.tmu.ac.jp
President: Jun Ueno

Faculty

Health Sciences (Nursing; Occupational Therapy; Physical Therapy; Radiology); **System Design** (Aeronautical and Aerospace Engineering; Computer Engineering; Electronic Engineering; Industrial Design; Information Technology; Mechanical Engineering); **Urban Environmental Sciences** (Applied Chemistry; Architectural and Environmental Design; Architecture; Architecture and Planning; Civil Engineering; Environmental Engineering; Geography (Human); Tourism; Town Planning; Urban Studies); **Urban Liberal Arts** (Arts and Humanities; Biological and Life Sciences; Business Administration; Chemistry; Cultural Studies; Economics; Electrical and Electronic Engineering; Engineering; Law; Mathematics; Mechanical Engineering; Natural Sciences; Pedagogy; Physics; Political Sciences; Psychology; Social Sciences; Town Planning; Urban Studies)

School

Business Administration (Accountancy; Business Administration; Economic History; Economics; Industrial Engineering; Management; Marketing); **Humanities and Social Sciences** (American Studies; Anthropology; Archaeology; Arts and Humanities; Asian Studies; Cultural Studies; English Studies; European Studies; French Studies; Germanic Studies; History; Literature; Modern Languages; Pedagogy; Philosophical Schools; Philosophy; Psychology; Social Studies; Social Welfare; Sociology; Visual Arts); **Law and Politics** (Administrative Law; Constitutional Law; International Law; Law; Political Sciences; Public Law); **Science and Engineering** (Biological and Life Sciences; Chemistry; Electrical and Electronic Engineering; Engineering; Mathematics; Mechanical Engineering; Natural Sciences; Physics)

Department/Division

Urban Policy (Town Planning; Urban Studies)

Graduate School

Human Health Sciences (Behavioural Sciences; Biochemistry; Food Science; Health Sciences; Nursing; Nutrition; Occupational Therapy; Physical Therapy; Physiology; Radiology; Sports); **Humanities** (Behavioural Sciences; Cultural Studies; History; Philosophy; Social Sciences); **Science and Engineering** (Biological and Life Sciences; Chemistry; Electrical and Electronic Engineering; Information Sciences; Mathematics; Mechanical Engineering; Physics); **Social Sciences** (Accountancy; Business Administration; Economic History; Law; Leadership; Management; Marketing; Political Sciences); **System Design** (Aeronautical and Aerospace Engineering; Computer Engineering; Electronic Engineering; Industrial Design; Mechanical Engineering); **Urban Environmental Sciences** (Applied Chemistry; Architectural and Environmental Design; Architecture; Civil Engineering; Construction Engineering; Environmental Engineering; Geography; Geography (Human); Geology; Meteorology; Social and Community Services; Structural Architecture; Tourism; Town Planning; Urban Studies)

Further information: Also Lidabashi, Harumi, Hino and Arakawa Campuses, Shinjuku and Akihabara Satellite Campuses

History: Founded 1949, incorporating 6 former Colleges. Graduate Schools established 1953. Known as Tokyo Toritsu Daigaku until 2005. Tokyo Toritsu Kagaku Gijutsu Daigaku (Tokyo Metropolitan Institute of Technology), Tokyo Toritsu Hoken Kagaku Daigaku (Tokyo Metropolitan College of Health Sciences) and Shuto Daigaku Tokyo (Tokyo Metropolitan University) incorporated 2005

Academic year: April to March (April-September; October-March)

Admission requirements: Graduation from high school or equivalent and entrance examination

Fees: 520,800 per annum (Yen)

Main language(s) of instruction: Japanese

Accrediting agency: Ministry of Education, Culture, Sports, Science and Technology (MEXT)

Degrees and diplomas: Gakushi (Arts and Humanities; Economics; Engineering; Law; Social Sciences), Shushi (Aeronautical and Aerospace Engineering; Applied Chemistry; Architectural and Environmental Design; Arts and Humanities; Behavioural Sciences; Biological and Life Sciences; Business Administration; Chemistry; Civil Engineering; Cultural Studies; Economics; Electrical and Electronic Engineering; Engineering; Environmental Studies; History; International Studies; Law; Mathematics; Mechanical Engineering; Nursing; Occupational Therapy; Philosophy; Physical Therapy; Physics; Political Sciences; Social Sciences; Tourism; Urban Studies)

Student Services: Sports Facilities, Health Services, Canteen, Library

Periodicals: Geographical Reports, Hogakkai (Journal of Law and Political Science), Jinbungakuho (Journal of Social Sciences and Humanities), Keizai to Keizaigaku (Journal of Economics), Memoirs of Graduate School of Engineering, Ogasawara Kenkyu (Ogasawara Research), Ogasawara Nenpo, Sogo Toshi Kenkyu (Comprehensive Urban Studies)

Academic Staff 2013-2014	MALE	FEMALE	TOTAL
FULL-TIME			1185
STAFF WITH DOCTORATE			
FULL-TIME			281
Student Numbers 2013-2014			
All (Foreign Included)			10313
Foreign only			383

Last Update: 25-05-2018

Tokyo University of Agriculture and Technology (TUAT)

3-8-1 Harumi-cho
Fuchu-shi 183-8538, Tokyo
Tel: +81(42) 364-5506
Fax: +81(42) 364-5898
Website: http://www.tuat.ac.jp
President: Hiroyuki Ohno

Faculty

Agriculture (Agricultural Economics; Agricultural Engineering; Agriculture; Biochemistry; Ecology; Environmental Engineering; Environmental Studies; Farm Management; Forestry; Molecular Biology; Natural Resources; Natural Sciences; Social Sciences; Veterinary Science; Welfare and Protective Services); **Engineering** (*Koganei-shi, Tokyo*) (Applied Chemistry; Applied Physics; Biological and Life Sciences; Biotechnology; Chemical Engineering;

Communication Studies; Computer Science; Electrical and Electronic Engineering; Engineering; Environmental Engineering; Information Sciences; Mechanical Engineering; Organic Chemistry; Polymer and Plastics Technology; Technology)

Graduate School

Agriculture (Agricultural Engineering; Agriculture; Biochemistry; Environmental Engineering); **Bio-Applications and Systems Engineering** (*Koganei-shi, Tokyo*) (Engineering; Natural Sciences); **Technology** (*Koganei-shi, Tokyo*) (Engineering; Natural Sciences; Technology)

History: Founded 1874, acquired present status 1949

Academic year: April to March (April-October; October-March)

Admission requirements: Graduation from high school or recognized equivalent and entrance examination

Fees: 496,800 per annum (Yen)

Main language(s) of instruction: Japanese

Accrediting agency: Ministry of Education, Culture, Sports, Science and Technology (MEXT)

Degrees and diplomas: Gakushi (Agriculture), Shushi (Agriculture), Hakase (Agriculture; Computer Science; Engineering; Health Sciences)

Student Services: Sports Facilities, Language Laboratory, Health Services, Canteen, Foreign Studies Centre, Library

Last Update: 23-02-2018

Tokyo University of Foreign Studies (TUFS)

3-11-1 Asahi-cho Fuchu-shi
Tokyo 183-8534
Tel: +81(42) 330-5183
Website: http://www.tufs.ac.jp
President: Hirotaka Tateishi

Course/Programme

Global Liberal Arts (*Compulsory for all first and second year students*) (Arts and Humanities; English; International Studies; Modern Languages; Regional Studies)

School

International and Area Studies (International Relations; International Studies; Regional Studies); **Language and Culture Studies** (Communication Studies; Cultural Studies; Information Sciences; Literature; Modern Languages)

Graduate School

Area and Culture Studies (Cultural Studies; International Studies; Linguistics; Modern Languages; Regional Studies)

Research Division

Languages and Cultures of Asia and Africa (African Languages; African Studies; Asian Studies)

History: Founded 1899.

Academic year: April to March (April-October; October-March)

Admission requirements: Graduation from high school or foreign equivalent, and entrance examination

Main language(s) of instruction: Japanese

Accrediting agency: Ministry of Education, Culture, Sports, Science and Technology (MEXT)

Degrees and diplomas: Hakase (Arts and Humanities)

Periodicals: Area and Culture Studies

Academic Staff 2012-2013	MALE	FEMALE	TOTAL
FULL-TIME			c. 220

Last Update: 22-02-2018

Tokyo University of Marine Science and Technology (TUMSAT)

4-5-7 Konan Minato-ku
Tokyo 108-8477
Tel: +81(3) 5463-0436
Fax: +81(3) 5463-0437
Website: http://www.kaiyodai.ac.jp
President: Toshio Takeuchi

Faculty

Marine Science (Aquaculture; Fishery; Marine Biology; Marine Engineering; Marine Science and Oceanography; Maritime Law; Molecular Biology); **Marine Technology** (Marine Engineering; Marine Transport; Mechanical Engineering; Power Engineering; Transport Management)

Graduate School

Marine Science and Technology (Aquaculture; Economics; Information Technology; Marine Biology; Marine Engineering; Transport Management)

History: Founded 2003 following merger of Tokyo Suisan Daigaku (Tokyo University of Fisheries), founded 1888 and Tokyo Shusen Daigaku (Tokyo University of Mercantile Marine), founded 1875

Academic year: April to March (April-October; October-March)

Admission requirements: Graduation from high school or recognized equivalent

Fees: 520,800 per annum; Admission fee, 282,000 (first year only) (Yen)

Main language(s) of instruction: Japanese

Accrediting agency: Ministry of Education, Culture, Sports, Science and Technology (MEXT)

Degrees and diplomas: Gakushi (Engineering), Shushi (Engineering), Hakase (Engineering)

Student Services: Academic Counselling, Social Counselling, Sports Facilities, Language Laboratory, Facilities for disabled people, Health Services, Canteen

Last Update: 22-02-2018

Tokyo University of Science, Yamaguchi

1-1-1 Daigakudori Onoda
Yamaguchi 756-0884
Tel: +81(836) 883-500
Fax: +81(836) 883-400
Website: http://www.yama.tus.ac.jp
President: Sanyo Onoda

Faculty

Engineering (Applied Chemistry; Computer Science; Electrical Engineering; Electronic Engineering; Engineering; Mechanical Engineering)

Graduate School

Engineering (Engineering)

History: Founded 1995

Academic year: April to March (April-September; October-March)

Main language(s) of instruction: Japanese

Accrediting agency: Ministry of Education, Culture, Sports, Science and Technology (MEXT)

Degrees and diplomas: Hakase (Materials Engineering; Mechanical Engineering)

Last Update: 14-03-2018

Tokyo University of the Arts

12-8 Ueno Koen Taito-ku
Tokyo 110-8714
Tel: +81(50) 5525-2013
Fax: +81(50) 5525-2479
Website: http://www.geidai.ac.jp
President: Kazuki Sawa

Faculty

Fine Arts (Aesthetics; Architecture; Art History; Crafts and Trades; Design; Painting and Drawing; Sculpture); **Music** (Conducting; Music Theory and Composition; Musical Instruments; Musicology; Singing)

Graduate School

Film (Film; Fine Arts; Media Studies; Music)
History: Founded 1949, incorporating Tokyo School of Fine Arts and Tokyo School of Music established 1887
Academic year: April to March (April-September; October-March)
Admission requirements: Graduation from high school or foreign equivalent, and entrance examination
Main language(s) of instruction: Japanese
Accrediting agency: Ministry of Education, Culture, Sports, Science and Technology (MEXT)
Degrees and diplomas: Hakase (Film; Fine Arts; Music)
Student Services: Library
Last Update: 22-02-2018

Tottori University

4-101 Minami-koyama
Tottori 680-8550
Tel: +81(857) 31-5007
Website: http://www.tottori-u.ac.jp
President: Ryota Teshima

Faculty

Agriculture (Agricultural Management; Agriculture; Bioengineering; Environmental Engineering; Environmental Studies; Forestry; Information Sciences; Production Engineering; Veterinary Science); **Engineering** (Aeronautical and Aerospace Engineering; Applied Mathematics; Applied Physics; Biotechnology; Chemistry; Civil Engineering; Electrical and Electronic Engineering; Engineering; Engineering Drawing and Design; Information Technology; Materials Engineering; Mechanical Engineering); **Medicine** (Anatomy; Biological and Life Sciences; Cell Biology; Health Sciences; Medicine; Microbiology; Molecular Biology; Neurology; Nursing; Pathology; Pharmacology; Physiology; Social and Preventive Medicine; Surgery); **Regional Sciences** (Japanese; Modern Languages; Oriental Languages; Regional Studies; Social Studies)

Graduate School

Agriculture (*United Graduate School*) (Agriculture; Arid Land Studies; Biological and Life Sciences); **Engineering** (Engineering); **Medical Sciences** (Clinical Psychology; Health Sciences; Medicine; Rehabilitation and Therapy); **Regional Sciences** (Education; Regional Studies)
History: Founded 1949 incorporating College of Agriculture and Forestry, founded 1920, College of Medicine, 1948, and Normal School
Academic year: April to March (April-September; October-March)

Admission requirements: Graduation from high school or equivalent or foreign equivalent, and entrance examination
Main language(s) of instruction: Japanese
Accrediting agency: Ministry of Education, Culture, Sports, Science and Technology (MEXT)
Degrees and diplomas: Shushi (Engineering), Hakase (Medicine)
Student Services: Academic Counselling, Social Counselling, Careers Guidance, Sports Facilities, Language Laboratory, Health Services, Library
Periodicals: Arid Land Research Center, Bulletin of Tottori University Forests, Journal of the Faculty of Agriculture, Journal of the Faculty of Education, Reports of the Faculty of Engineering, Yonago Acta Medica, Yonago Igaku Zasshi
Last Update: 14-03-2018

Tottori University of Environmental Studies

1-1-1 Wakabadai Kita
Tottori-shi 698-1111, Tottori
Tel: +81(857) 38-6700
Fax: +81(857) 38-6709
Website: http://www.kankyo-u.ac.jp
President: Takashi Hajime

Faculty

Business Administration (Business Administration; Information Sciences); **Environmental Studies** (Architecture; Environmental Engineering)

Graduate School

Environment and Information Science (Environmental Engineering)
History: Founded 2001.
Main language(s) of instruction: Japanese
Accrediting agency: Ministry of Education, Culture, Sports, Science and Technology (MEXT)
Degrees and diplomas: Gakushi, Shushi (Business Administration; Environmental Studies; Information Sciences)
Last Update: 06-03-2018

Toyama Prefectural University

5180 Kurokawa Kosugi Imizu
Toyama 939-0398
Tel: +81(766) 56-7500
Fax: +81(766) 56-6182
Website: http://www.pu-toyama.ac.jp
President: Mikio Terai

Faculty

Engineering (*Also Graduate School*) (Arts and Humanities; Automation and Control Engineering; Biotechnology; Computer Science; Electronic Engineering; Health Sciences; Information Technology; Mechanical Engineering; Modern Languages; Natural Sciences; Social Sciences; Telecommunications Engineering)

College

Technology (Environmental Engineering)

Graduate School

Engineering (Biotechnology; Computer Engineering; Materials Engineering; Mechanical Engineering)

History: Founded 1990

Main language(s) of instruction: Japanese

Accrediting agency: Ministry of Education, Culture, Sports, Science and Technology (MEXT)

Degrees and diplomas: Hakase (Biotechnology; Engineering)

Student Services: Sports Facilities, Library

Last Update: 14-03-2018

Toyohashi University of Technology (TUT)

1-1 Hibarigaoka Tempaku-cho
Toyohashi-shi 441-8580, Aichi
Tel: +81(532) 44-6577
Fax: +81(532) 44-6547
Website: http://www.tut.ac.jp
President: Takashi Onishi

Department/Division

Architecture and Civil Engineering (Architecture; Civil Engineering; Environmental Engineering); **Computer Science and Engineering** (Computer Engineering; Computer Science; Information Technology); **Electrical and Electronic Engineering** (Electrical and Electronic Engineering); **Environmental and Life Sciences** (Biochemistry; Biological and Life Sciences; Biotechnology; Microbiology; Molecular Biology); **Mechanical Engineering** (Mechanical Engineering)

Institute

Liberal Arts and Sciences (Arts and Humanities; Management; Natural Sciences)

Centre

Engineering Education Development (*International Cooperation*) (Engineering); **Language** (Linguistics; Modern Languages); **Physical Fitness, Sports and Health** (Health Education; Physical Education; Sports)

Laboratory

Civil and Environmental Engineering (Civil Engineering; Environmental Engineering); **Cryogenic Research**; **Information and Communication** (Information Technology; Telecommunications Engineering); **Natural Energy Research** (Energy Engineering); **Radiation** (Information Technology; Nuclear Engineering); **Venture Business**

Graduate School

Engineering (Engineering)

Research Division

Collaborative Regional Planning and Design (Regional Planning); **Cooperative Research Facility**; **Electron Device**; **Future Technology** (Technology); **Future Vehicle**; **Intelligent Sensing System**; **Interdisciplinary Future Environment Ecological Design** (Ecology; Environmental Studies)

History: Founded 1976. Graduate School established 1980. Doctoral Programme established 1986 and reorganized 1995. Turned into independent administrative entity as a National University Corporation 2004

Academic year: April to March (April-July; August-November; December-March)

Admission requirements: Graduation from high school and entrance examination

Fees: 535,800 per annum (Yen)

Main language(s) of instruction: Japanese

Accrediting agency: Ministry of Education, Culture, Sports, Science and Technology (MEXT)

Degrees and diplomas: Gakushi (Engineering), Shushi (Engineering), Hakase (Engineering)

Student Services: Academic Counselling, Social Counselling, Sports Facilities, Language Laboratory, Health Services, Canteen, Foreign Studies Centre, Library

Last Update: 23-02-2018

Tsukuba University of Technology (NTUT)

Amakubo 4-3-15
Tsukuba 305-8520, Ibaraki
Tel: +81(29) 852-2931
Fax: +81(29) 858-9312
Website: http://www.tsukuba-tech.ac.jp
President: Norio Ohkoshi

Faculty

Health Sciences (Acupuncture; Physical Therapy; Traditional Eastern Medicine); **Industrial Technology** (Architectural and

Environmental Design; Architecture and Planning; Artificial Intelligence; Computer Engineering; Computer Networks; Computer Science; Ecology; Electrical Engineering; Electronic Engineering; Environmental Engineering; Industrial Design; Information Sciences; Information Technology; Interior Design; Mechanical Engineering; Multimedia; Polymer and Plastics Technology; Regional Planning; Robotics; Social Welfare; Telecommunications Engineering; Thermal Engineering; Town Planning)

Graduate School

Technology and Science (Acupuncture; Computer Science; Physical Therapy; Technology)

History: Founded 2005. The National University Corporation of Tsukuba University of Technology (NTUT) provide higher education for people with hearing and/or visual disabilities

Main language(s) of instruction: Japanese

Accrediting agency: Ministry of Education, Culture, Sports, Science and Technology (MEXT)

Student Services: Library

Last Update: 22-02-2018

Tsuru University

3-8-1 Tahara
Tsuru 402-8555, Yamanashi
Tel: +81(554) 43-4341
Fax: +81(554) 43-4347
Website: http://www.tsuru.ac.jp
President: Seiji Fukuta

Faculty

Letters (*Also graduate studies*) (Arts and Humanities; Cultural Studies; English; Japanese; Primary Education; Sociology)

History: Founded 1955

Main language(s) of instruction: Japanese

Accrediting agency: Ministry of Education, Culture, Sports, Science and Technology (MEXT)

Student Services: Social Counselling, Language Laboratory, Health Services

Last Update: 14-03-2018

United Nations University (UNU)

5–53–70 Jingumae, Shibuya-ku
Tokyo 150-8925
Tel: +81(3) 5467-1212
Fax: +81(3) 3499-2828
Website: http://unu.edu
Rector: David Malone

Further information: 15 institutes and programmes in 13 countries (Belgium, Canada, China, Finland, Germany, Ghana, Iceland, Japan, Malaysia, Spain, The Netherlands, United States of America, Venezuela) and administrative and services units in Tokyo (headquarters), Bonn, Kuala Lumpur, New York and Paris.

History: Founded 1973.

Main language(s) of instruction: English

Degrees and diplomas: Shushi (Development Studies; Environmental Studies; Geography (Human); Peace and Disarmament; Safety Engineering), Hakase (Administration; Development Studies; Economics; Environmental Studies; Information Technology)

Last Update: 27-03-2018

University of Aizu

Kamiiawase 90 Ikkimachi-tsuruga
Aizuwakamatsu 965-8580, Fukushima
Tel: +81(242) 37-2500
Fax: +81(242) 37-2528
Website: http://www.u-aizu.ac.jp
President: Ryuichi Oka
Tel: +81(242) 37-2525

School

Computer Science and Engineering (Computer Engineering; Computer Science; English; Information Technology)

Graduate School

Computer Science and Engineering (Computer Engineering; Computer Science; Information Technology; Management)

History: Founded 1993

Academic year: April to March

Admission requirements: Upper secondary school leaving certificate (Kotogakko Sotsugyo Shomeisho)

Fees: Enrollment Fees, 282,000 for Fukushima prefecture residents; 564,000 for non-residents. Tuition fee, 520,800 per annum (Yen)

Main language(s) of instruction: Japanese

Accrediting agency: Ministry of Education, Culture, Sports, Science and Technology (MEXT)

Degrees and diplomas: Hakase (Computer Engineering; Information Technology)

Student Services: Careers Guidance, Sports Facilities, Facilities for disabled people, Health Services, Canteen

Periodicals: Journal of the School of Computer Science and Engineering

Academic Staff 2012-2013	MALE	FEMALE	TOTAL
FULL-TIME			c. 107

Last Update: 09-03-2018

University of Fukui

3-9-1 Bunkyo
Fukui 910-8507, Fukui
Tel: +81(776) 23-0500
Fax: +81(776) 27-8518
Website: http://www.u-fukui.ac.jp
President: Mitsufumi Mayumi

Faculty

Education and Regional Studies (Education; Preschool Education; Primary Education; Regional Studies; Secondary Education; Special Education; Teacher Training); **Engineering** (Applied Chemistry; Applied Physics; Architecture; Artificial Intelligence; Biotechnology; Civil Engineering; Educational Technology; Electrical and Electronic Engineering; Engineering; Information Sciences; Laboratory Techniques; Materials Engineering; Mechanical Engineering; Technology); **Medical Sciences** (Medicine; Nursing)

Unit

Headquarters for Innovative Society-Academia Cooperation (*UF-HISAC*)

Graduate School

Education (Education; Pedagogy; Teacher Training); **Engineering** (Applied Chemistry; Applied Physics; Architecture; Artificial Intelligence; Biotechnology; Civil Engineering; Computer Engineering; Electrical and Electronic Engineering; Energy Engineering; Engineering; Information Sciences; Materials Engineering; Mechanical Engineering; Nuclear Engineering; Optical Technology; Safety Engineering); **Medical Sciences** (Biological and Life Sciences; Biomedicine; Community Health; Medicine; Nursing)

Research Division

Biomedical Imaging (Biomedical Engineering; Medical Technology); **Child Mental Development** (Child Care and Development; Psychology); **Development of Far-Infrared Region** (Radiophysics); **Nuclear Engineering** (Nuclear Engineering)
Further information: Also Matsuoka and Tsuruga Campus
History: Founded 1949 incorporating Fukui Normal School, Fukui Youth Normal School, and Fukui Technical Senmon Gakko. Financed by the State through the Ministry of Education, Culture, Sports, Science and Technology (MEXT). Merged with Fukui Ika Daigaku/ Fukui Medical University 2003
Academic year: April to March (April-September; October-March)
Admission requirements: Graduation from high school or equivalent and entrance examination
Fees: Registration, 282,000; tuition, 535,800 per annum (Yen)

Main language(s) of instruction: Japanese
Accrediting agency: Ministry of Education, Culture, Sports, Science and Technology (MEXT)
Degrees and diplomas: Hakase (Biological and Life Sciences; Biomedicine; Community Health; Computer Engineering; Energy Engineering; Engineering; Nuclear Engineering)
Student Services: Academic Counselling, Social Counselling, Careers Guidance, Nursery Care, Sports Facilities, Language Laboratory, Facilities for disabled people, Health Services, Canteen, Foreign Studies Centre
Periodicals: Basic Material, Fukui Daigaku Gakuho Report

Academic Staff 2012-2013	MALE	FEMALE	TOTAL
FULL-TIME			c. 618
Student Numbers 2012-2013			
All (Foreign Included)			5167
Foreign only	123	74	197

Last Update: 01-03-2018

University of Hyogo

Nishi-ku, 8-2-1 Gakuen'nishi town
Kobe-shi 651-2197, Hyogo
Tel: +81(78) 794-6580, +81(78) 794-6631
Fax: +81(78) 794-5575
Website: http://www.u-hyogo.ac.jp
President: Masayochi Kiyohara

College

Nursing Art and Science (*Also Graduate School*) (Community Health; Health Sciences; Nursing)

School

Business Administration (Accountancy; Business Administration; Information Sciences; Management; Marketing); **Economics** (Economics; International Economics); **Engineering** (Chemical Engineering; Chemistry; Computer Engineering; Computer Science; Electrical Engineering; Engineering; Materials Engineering; Mechanical Engineering); **Human Science and Environment** (Cultural Studies; Development Studies; Ecology; Environmental Management; Environmental Studies; Food Science; Health Sciences; Information Sciences; Modern Languages; Natural Sciences; Nutrition); **Science** (Biological and Life Sciences; Biotechnology; Cell Biology; Chemistry; Materials Engineering; Mechanics; Molecular Biology; Natural Sciences; Physics; Physiology)

Institute

Natural and Environmental Sciences (*INES*) (Astronomy and Space Science; Earth Sciences; Ecology; Environmental

Studies; Horticulture; Landscape Architecture; Natural Resources; Rural Studies; Wildlife)

Laboratory

Laboratory of Advanced Science and Technology for Industry (*LASTI*) (Industrial Engineering; Nanotechnology; Physics; Technology)

Graduate School

Accountancy (*Professional*) (Accountancy); **Applied Informatics** (Business Computing; Computer Science; Data Processing; Health Administration; Information Sciences; Management); **Business** (Business Administration; Health Administration); **Business Administration** (Accountancy; Business Administration; Information Sciences; Management; Marketing); **Economics** (Economics); **Engineering** (Computer Engineering; Computer Science; Electrical Engineering; Engineering; Materials Engineering; Mechanical Engineering); **Human Science and Environment** (Anthropology; Architectural and Environmental Design; Biological and Life Sciences; Ecology; Environmental Management; Environmental Studies; Ethics; Food Science; Health Sciences; Literature; Natural Sciences; Psychology; Religion; Social Studies; Sociology; Sports); **Landscape Design and Management** (Horticulture; Landscape Architecture); **Life Science** (Biological and Life Sciences; Biology; Cell Biology; Molecular Biology); **Material Science** (Chemistry; Materials Engineering; Mathematics; Molecular Biology; Solid State Physics); **Simulation Studies** (Computer Science)

Research Division

Economics and Business Administration (*LASTI*) (Business Administration; Economics); **Nursing Care for People and Community** (Community Health; Nursing)

Further information: Also following campuses: Kobe Gakuentoshi, Himeji Shosha, Harima Kohto, Himeji Shinzaike, Akashi, Awaji

History: Founded 2004 incorporating Kobe University of Commerce (founded 1929), Himeji Institute of Technology (founded 1949), and the College of Nursing Art and Science, Hyogo (founded 1993)

Admission requirements: Graduation from high school or equivalent, and entrance examination

Main language(s) of instruction: Japanese

Accrediting agency: Ministry of Education, Culture, Sports, Science and Technology (MEXT)

Degrees and diplomas: Shushi (Anthropology; Business Administration; Chemistry; Computer Science; Electrical Engineering; Environmental Management; Environmental Studies; Materials Engineering; Mechanical Engineering; Nursing; Sociology), Hakase (Anthropology; Business Administration; Chemistry; Computer Science; Electrical Engineering; Environmental Management; Environmental Studies; Materials Engineering; Mechanical Engineering; Nursing; Sociology)

Student Services: Social Counselling, Careers Guidance, Sports Facilities, Health Services

Academic Staff 2012-2013	MALE	FEMALE	TOTAL
FULL-TIME	446	111	557
Student Numbers 2012-2013			
All (Foreign Included)			6695

Last Update: 16-03-2018

University of Kochi

5-15 Eikokuji-cho
Kochi-shi 781-8515, Kochi
Tel: +81(88) 847-8700
Fax: +81(88) 847-8670
Website: http://www.u-kochi.ac.jp
President: Sayumi Nojima

Faculty

Cultural Studies (Cultural Studies; English; Japanese; Literature); **Human Life and Environmental Science** (Environmental Studies; Health Sciences; Home Economics); **Nursing** (*Ike*) (Nursing); **Nutrition** (Health Sciences; Nutrition); **Social Welfare** (*Ike*) (Child Care and Development; Family Studies; Psychology; Social Psychology; Social Welfare; Social Work)

Course/Programme

Global Leadership Training Program in Disaster Nursing (*Graduate*) (Nursing; Welfare and Protective Services)

Graduate School

Human Health Sciences (*Doctoral*); **Human Life** (Health Sciences); **Nursing** (*Ike*) (Nursing)

Further information: Also Eikokuji Campus

History: Founded 1949. Acquired present title 2011

Academic year: April to March

Main language(s) of instruction: Japanese

Accrediting agency: Ministry of Education, Culture, Sports, Science and Technology (MEXT)

Degrees and diplomas: Shushi (Biological and Life Sciences; Nursing; Social Welfare), Hakase (Biological and Life Sciences; Nursing; Social Welfare)

Last Update: 14-03-2018

University of Miyazaki (UOM)

1-1 Gakuen Kibanadai-nishi Miyazaki-shi
Miyazaki-shi 889-2192, Miyazaki
Tel: +81(985) 58-7104
Fax: +81(985) 58-7782, +81(985) 58-2865
Website: http://www.miyazaki-u.ac.jp
President: Chun Ikenosaku
Tel: +81(985) 58-7100

Faculty

Agriculture (Agriculture; Animal Husbandry; Biochemistry; Biological and Life Sciences; Biology; Biotechnology; Ecology; Environmental Studies; Food Science; Genetics; Marine Biology; Nutrition; Public Health; Soil Science; Veterinary Science); **Education and Culture** (American Studies; Arts and Humanities; Constitutional Law; Cultural Studies; Education; English; English Studies; European Studies; French; Geography; German; History; International Relations; Japanese; Law; Primary Education; Secondary Education; Social Sciences; Social Studies; Special Education; Teacher Training); **Engineering** (Applied Chemistry; Applied Physics; Civil Engineering; Computer Engineering; Computer Science; Electrical and Electronic Engineering; Engineering; Environmental Engineering; Mechanical Engineering; Systems Analysis); **Medicine** (Medicine; Nursing)

Centre

Animal Disease Control (Animal Husbandry; Epidemiology); **Collaborative Research and Community Cooperation**; **Education and Student Support**

Graduate School

Agriculture and Engineering (*Interdisciplinary*) (Agricultural Engineering; Agriculture; Biological and Life Sciences; Biotechnology; Computer Science; Energy Engineering; Engineering; Environmental Studies; Information Technology; Marine Biology; Materials Engineering; Production Engineering); **Education and Culture** (Arts and Humanities; Clinical Psychology; Cultural Studies; Education; Educational Psychology; English; Foreign Languages Education; Japanese; Native Language Education; Teacher Training; Vocational Education); **Engineering** (Applied Chemistry; Applied Physics; Civil Engineering; Computer Engineering; Computer Science; Electrical and Electronic Engineering; Energy Engineering; Engineering; Environmental Engineering; Information Technology; Materials Engineering; Mechanical Engineering; Production Engineering); **Medicine** (*Miyazaki Medical College*) (Cell Biology; Environmental Studies; Health Sciences; Immunology; Medicine; Nursing; Pathology); **Medicine and Veterinary Medicine** (*Interdisciplinary*) (Animal Husbandry; Food Science; Hygiene; Medicine; Veterinary Science)

Research Division

Frontier Science (Biological and Life Sciences; Biotechnology; Environmental Studies; Genetics; Molecular Biology)
History: Founded 1949 incorporating Miyazaki Agricultural College, Miyazaki Normal College, Miyazaki Youth Normal College. New Miyazaki University, "University of Miyazaki" was established following integration of Miyazaki Ika Daigaku/ Miyazaki Medical College October 2003
Academic year: April to March (April-September; October-March)
Admission requirements: Graduation from high school or recognized equivalent, and entrance examination
Fees: Tuition, 535,800 per annum (Yen)
Main language(s) of instruction: Japanese
Accrediting agency: Ministry of Education, Culture, Sports, Science and Technology (MEXT)
Degrees and diplomas: Gakushi (Agriculture; Arts and Humanities; Education; Engineering; Medicine; Nursing; Veterinary Science), Shushi (Agriculture; Applied Chemistry; Applied Physics; Arts and Humanities; Civil Engineering; Clinical Psychology; Computer Engineering; Computer Science; Electrical and Electronic Engineering; Environmental Engineering; Foreign Languages Education; Mechanical Engineering; Medicine; Native Language Education; Nursing; Vocational Education), Hakase (Agricultural Engineering; Agriculture; Cell Biology; Energy Engineering; Engineering; Environmental Engineering; Immunology; Information Technology; Materials Engineering; Medicine; Nursing; Pathology; Production Engineering; Veterinary Science)
Student Services: Academic Counselling, Careers Guidance, Sports Facilities, Language Laboratory, Health Services, Canteen, Residential Facilities
Periodicals: Bulletin of Faculty of Agriculture, Bulletin of Faculty of Education and Culture, Bulletin of Faculty of Engineering
Last Update: 23-02-2018

University of Nagasaki

123 Kawashimo-cho
Sasebo-shi 858-8580, Nagasaki
Tel: +81(956) 47-2191
Fax: +81(956) 47-6941
Website: http://sun.ac.jp
President: Hiromichi Ohta

Faculty

Economics (*Sasebo Campus*) (Business Administration; Economic and Finance Policy; Economics; International Economics); **Global Communication** (*Siebold Campus*) (Information Sciences; Information Technology; International Relations; International Studies; Mass Communication; Media Studies); **Nursing and Nutrition** (*Siebold Campus*) (Health Sciences; Nursing; Nutrition)

Centre

East Asian Studies (Cultural Studies; East Asian Studies; Geography; History); **Education Development** (Education); **International Exchange programmes and Foreign Language Education** (Japanese)

Graduate School

Economics (*Sasebo Campus*) (Economics; Industrial and Production Economics); **Global Communication** (*Siebold Campus*) (Communication Studies; Cultural Studies; Information Sciences; Information Technology; International Relations; Mass Communication; Media Studies); **Human Health Science** (*Siebold Campus*) (Health Sciences; Nursing; Nutrition)

History: Founded 1967. An institution under the juridiction of Nagasaki prefecture. Formerly known as Nagasaki Kenritsu Daigaku (Nagasaki Prefectural University). Acquired present title 2008 following merger with Kenritsu Nagasaki Siboruto Daigaku (Siebold University of Nagasaki)

Academic year: April to March

Admission requirements: Graduation from high school and entrance examinations, one in Japanese

Main language(s) of instruction: Japanese

Accrediting agency: Ministry of Education, Culture, Sports, Science and Technology (MEXT)

Degrees and diplomas: Shushi (Economics; Industrial and Production Economics; Information Sciences; International Relations; Media Studies; Nursing; Nutrition)

Student Services: Academic Counselling, Social Counselling, Careers Guidance, Nursery Care, Cultural Activities, Sports Facilities, Language Laboratory, Facilities for disabled people, Health Services, Canteen, Library

Periodicals: Nagasaki Prefectural University Review

Last Update: 16-03-2018

University of Niigata Prefecture

471 Ebigase
Niigata 950-8680
Tel: +81(25) 270-1300
Fax: +81(25) 270-5173
Website: http://www.unii.ac.jp
President: Ryuhei Wakasugi

Faculty

Human Life Studies (Child Care and Development; Dietetics; Nutrition; Welfare and Protective Services); **International Studies and Regional Development** (Development Studies; International Studies; Regional Studies)

History: Created 2009. First cohort graduated 2013

Academic year: April to March (April-September; October-March)

Admission requirements: High school graduation certificate (Kotogakko Sotsugyo Shomeisho) or equivalent

Main language(s) of instruction: Japanese

Accrediting agency: Ministry of Education, Culture, Sports, Science and Technology (MEXT)

Student Services: Academic Counselling, Social Counselling, Careers Guidance, Nursery Care, Sports Facilities, Language Laboratory, Facilities for disabled people, Health Services, Canteen, Foreign Studies Centre

Periodicals: Journal of International Studies and Regional Development, Ningen Seikatsu gaku kenkyu

Academic Staff 2012-2013	MALE	FEMALE	TOTAL
FULL-TIME	49	32	81
PART-TIME	73	44	117
STAFF WITH DOCTORATE			
FULL-TIME	21	16	37
Student Numbers 2012-2013			
All (Foreign Included)	203	794	997

Last Update: 14-03-2018

University of Shiga Prefecture

25 Hassaka
Hikone 522-8533, Shiga
Tel: +81(749) 28-8200
Fax: +81(749) 28-8470
Website: http://www.usp.ac.jp
President: Keiichi Ohta

School

Engineering (*Also Graduate School*) (Electronic Engineering; Glass Art; Materials Engineering; Mechanical Engineering); **Environmental Sciences** (*Also Graduate School*) (Environmental Management; Environmental Studies); **Human Cultures** (*Also Graduate School*) (Food Technology; Home Economics; International Relations; Nutrition; Regional Studies); **Nursing** (*Also Graduate School*) (Nursing)

History: Founded 1995

Admission requirements: Entrance examination

Fees: 535,800 per annum (Yen)

Main language(s) of instruction: Japanese

Accrediting agency: Ministry of Education, Culture, Sports, Science and Technology (MEXT)

Degrees and diplomas: Shushi (Cultural Studies; Environmental Studies; International Relations; Regional Studies), Hakase (Electronic Engineering; Environmental Studies; Home Economics)

Student Services: Sports Facilities, Foreign Studies Centre, Library

Academic Staff 2013-2014	MALE	FEMALE	TOTAL
FULL-TIME			261
Student Numbers 2013-2014			
All (Foreign Included)			2806

Last Update: 09-03-2018

University of Shizuoka

52-1 Yada
Shizuoka 422-8526
Tel: +81(54) 264-5012
Fax: +81(54) 264-5199
Website: http://www.u-shizuoka-ken.ac.jp
President: Hiroshi Kito

Faculty

International Relations (*Also Graduate School*) (International Relations; International Studies)

School

Food and Nutritional Sciences (*Also Graduate School*) (Environmental Studies; Food Science; Nutrition); **Management and Information Sciences** (*Also Graduate School*) (Business Administration; Computer Science; Information Sciences; Information Technology; Mathematics and Computer Science; Statistics); **Nursing** (*Also Graduate School*) (Nursing); **Pharmaceutical Sciences** (*Also Graduate School*) (Pharmacology; Pharmacy)

Institute

Environmental Sciences (*Also Graduate School*) (Environmental Studies)

Graduate School

Programs (Information Sciences; International Relations; Management; Nursing; Nutrition; Pharmacy)

History: Founded 1987, incorporating the existing three Prefectural Colleges (Shizuoka College of Pharmacy, Shizuoka Women's College, and Shizuoka Women's Junior College).

Academic year: April to March (April-September; October-March)

Admission requirements: Graduation from high school or recognized equivalent or foreign equivalent, and entrance examination

Main language(s) of instruction: Japanese

Accrediting agency: Ministry of Education, Culture, Sports, Science and Technology (MEXT)

Degrees and diplomas: Shushi (Health Sciences; Information Sciences; International Relations; Management; Nursing; Nutrition; Pharmacy), Hakase (Electrical Engineering; Food Science)

Student Services: Careers Guidance, Sports Facilities, Language Laboratory, Health Services, Foreign Studies Centre, Library, IT Centre

Last Update: 14-03-2018

University of Teacher Education Fukuoka

1-1 Akamabunkyo-machi
Munakata 811-4192, Fukuoka
Tel: +81(940) 35-1235
Fax: +81(940) 34-1313
Website: http://www.fukuoka-edu.ac.jp
President: Takatoshi Sakurai

Faculty

Education (Art Education; Cultural Studies; Design; Education; Education of the Handicapped; Educational Psychology; Educational Sciences; English; Environmental Studies; Fine Arts; Foreign Languages Education; Health Education; Health Sciences; Home Economics; Home Economics Education; Humanities and Social Science Education; Information Sciences; Japanese; Mathematics; Mathematics Education; Music; Music Education; Native Language Education; Natural Sciences; Painting and Drawing; Performing Arts; Physical Education; Preschool Education; Primary Education; Science Education; Secondary Education; Social Studies; Special Education; Technology; Technology Education; Welfare and Protective Services)

Course/Programme

Postgraduate Diploma (Special Education)

Graduate School

Education (Art Education; Clinical Psychology; Education; Educational Psychology; Educational Sciences; Foreign Languages Education; Health Education; Home Economics Education; Humanities and Social Science Education; Mathematics Education; Music Education; Native Language Education; Pedagogy; Physical Education; Science Education; Special Education; Technology Education)

History: Founded 1949 as Fukuoka University of Liberal Educatio, following merger of Fukuoka First and Second

Normal Colleges and Fukuoka Normal College for Youth. Acquired present title 1966

Academic year: April to March (April-October; October-March)

Admission requirements: Graduation from high school and entrance examination

Main language(s) of instruction: Japanese

Accrediting agency: Ministry of Education, Culture, Sports, Science and Technology (MEXT)

Degrees and diplomas: Gakushi (Education), Shushi (Education)

Student Services: Social Counselling, Sports Facilities, Health Services

Academic Staff 2013-2014	MALE	FEMALE	TOTAL
FULL-TIME			229
Student Numbers 2013-2014			
All (Foreign Included)			3056
Foreign only			80

Last Update: 27-03-2018

University of the Ryukyus

1 Senbaru
Nishihara 903-0213, Okinawa
Tel: +81(98) 895-8131
Fax: +81(98) 895-8102
Website: http://www.u-ryukyu.ac.jp
President: Oshiro Hajime

Faculty

Agriculture (Agriculture; Biology; Biotechnology; Environmental Engineering; Environmental Studies); **Education** (Education); **Engineering** (Architecture; Civil Engineering; Computer Engineering; Electrical and Electronic Engineering; Energy Engineering; Engineering; Information Technology; Mechanical Engineering); **Law and Letters** (Arts and Humanities; Cultural Studies; Law; Modern Languages; Social Policy); **Medicine** (Anatomy; Health Sciences; Medicine); **Science** (Biology; Chemistry; Earth Sciences; Marine Science and Oceanography; Mathematics; Natural Sciences; Physics); **Tourism Sciences and Industrial Management** (Business Administration; Industrial Management; Tourism)

Graduate School

Agriculture (*United Graduate School, Kagoshima University*) (Biological and Life Sciences; Marine Science and Oceanography; Production Engineering); **Education** (Crafts and Trades; Education; Educational Psychology; English; Fine Arts; Handicrafts; Health Education; Home Economics Education; Japanese; Mathematics; Music Education; Natural Sciences; Pedagogy; Physical Education; Psychology; Social Sciences; Special Education; Technology Education);

Engineering and Science (Artificial Intelligence; Biology; Chemistry; Civil Engineering; Earth Sciences; Electrical and Electronic Engineering; Energy Engineering; Engineering; Environmental Engineering; Information Technology; Marine Science and Oceanography; Materials Engineering; Mathematics; Mechanical Engineering; Physics; Structural Architecture); **Health Sciences** (Health Sciences); **Humanities and Social Sciences** (*Graduate Programme*) (Cultural Studies; Economics; Law; Regional Studies; Social Sciences); **Medicine** (Anaesthesiology; Anatomy; Biochemistry; Environmental Studies; Immunology; Medicine; Oncology; Pathology; Physiology; Social and Preventive Medicine; Tropical Medicine)

History: Founded 1950 under the authority of the United States Civil Administration, authority transferred to a Board of Trustees 1952. Transferred to control of Government of the Ryukyus 1966, and became under the jurisdiction of Japanese Ministry of Education, Science, Sports and Culture a National University 1972. Graduate School of Agriculture established 1977

Academic year: April to March (April-October; October-March)

Admission requirements: Graduation from high school or equivalent, and entrance examination

Main language(s) of instruction: Japanese

Accrediting agency: Ministry of Education, Culture, Sports, Science and Technology (MEXT)

Degrees and diplomas: Gakushi (Agriculture; Biological and Life Sciences; Chemistry; Civil Engineering; Education; English; Fine Arts; Geography; Health Sciences; Japanese; Law; Mathematics; Music Education; Physics; Psychology; Social Policy), Shushi (Business Administration; Education; Engineering; Health Sciences; Law; Medicine; Political Sciences; Social Sciences; Tourism), Hakase (Cultural Studies; Energy Engineering; Engineering; Environmental Engineering; Health Sciences; Marine Engineering; Materials Engineering; Medicine; Social Sciences)

Student Services: Academic Counselling, Social Counselling, Foreign Studies Centre, Library

Last Update: 16-03-2018

University of Tokushima

2-24 Shinkura
Tokushima 770-8501
Tel: +81(88) 656-7021
Fax: +81(88) 656-7012
Website: http://www.tokushima-u.ac.jp
President: Sumihare Noji

Faculty

Dentistry (Dentistry); **Engineering** (Applied Mathematics; Applied Physics; Artificial Intelligence; Bioengineering; Chemical Engineering; Civil Engineering; Electrical and

Electronic Engineering; Engineering; Environmental Engineering; Information Technology; Mechanical Engineering; Optical Technology); **Integrated Arts and Sciences** (Asian Studies; Behavioural Sciences; Biological and Life Sciences; Chemistry; Comparative Sociology; Computer Science; Cultural Studies; Economics; Environmental Studies; European Languages; Fine Arts; Geology; Law; Mathematics; Media Studies; Modern Languages; Natural Sciences; Physics; Regional Studies; Social Sciences); **Medicine** (Health Sciences; Medicine; Nutrition); **Pharmaceutical Sciences** (Pharmacology; Pharmacy)

Institute

Genome Research (*Graduate School*) (Biomedicine; Health Sciences)

Graduate School

Advanced Technology and Science (Biological and Life Sciences; Chemistry; Civil Engineering; Earth Sciences; Electrical and Electronic Engineering; Environmental Engineering; Information Sciences; Mechanical Engineering; Optometry); **Health Sciences** (Health Sciences; Nursing); **Human and Natural Environment Sciences** (Environmental Management; Environmental Studies; Psychology; Social Sciences); **Medical Sciences** (Health Sciences; Medicine); **Nutrition and Bioscience** (Biological and Life Sciences; Nutrition); **Oral Sciences** (Dentistry; Oral Pathology); **Pharmaceutical Sciences** (Chemistry; Pharmacology; Pharmacy)

History: Founded 1874 as Tokushima Kisei Normal School. Acquired present status and title 1949

Academic year: April to March (April-September; October-March)

Admission requirements: Graduation from high school or recognized equivalent, and entrance examination

Main language(s) of instruction: Japanese

Accrediting agency: Ministry of Education, Culture, Sports, Science and Technology (MEXT)

Degrees and diplomas: Shushi (Natural Sciences), Hakase (Biological and Life Sciences; Nutrition)

Student Services: Library

Periodicals: Bulletin of Faculty of Engineering, Study Reports (Integrated Arts and Sciences), The Journal of Medical Investigation

Last Update: 23-02-2018

University of Toyama

3190 Gofuku
Toyama-shi 930-8555, Toyama
Tel: +81(76) 445-6082
Fax: +81(76) 445-6093
Website: http://www.u-toyama.ac.jp
President: Endo Shunro

Faculty

Art and Design (Architectural and Environmental Design; Art Management; Design; Fine Arts; Handicrafts); **Economics** (Business Administration; Commercial Law; Economics); **Engineering** (Biological and Life Sciences; Electrical and Electronic Engineering; Information Technology; Materials Engineering; Mechanical Engineering); **Human Development** (*Sugitani Campus*) (Development Studies; Educational Psychology; Information Sciences; Teacher Training); **Humanities** (Arts and Humanities; Cultural Studies; International Studies; Modern Languages); **Medicine** (Anaesthesiology; Anatomy; Biochemistry; Dermatology; Epidemiology; Forensic Medicine and Dentistry; Gerontology; Gynaecology and Obstetrics; Immunology; Medicine; Neurosciences; Nursing; Ophthalmology; Orthopaedics; Otorhinolaryngology; Paediatrics; Pathology; Pharmacology; Psychiatry and Mental Health; Public Health; Radiology; Surgery; Urology; Virology); **Pharmacy and Pharmaceutical Sciences** (Pharmacy); **Science** (Biology; Chemistry; Earth Sciences; Environmental Studies; Mathematics; Physics)

Institute

Natural Medicine (Biochemistry; Neurosciences; Pathology; Pharmacy)

Graduate School

Art and Design (Design; Fine Arts); **Economics** (Business Administration); **Human Development** (Curriculum; Education); **Humanities** (Anthropology; Geography (Human); International Studies; Linguistics; Literature; Philosophy; Psychology; Sociology); **Innovative Life Science** (Biological and Life Sciences); **Medicine and Pharmaceutical Science for Education** (Medicine; Nursing; Pharmacy); **Science and Engineering for Education** (Biological and Life Sciences; Biology; Chemistry; Computer Engineering; Earth Sciences; Electrical and Electronic Engineering; Energy Engineering; Environmental Studies; Information Technology; Materials Engineering; Mathematics; Mechanical Engineering; Physics)

History: Founded 1949 incorporating Toyama Normal College founded 1943, Toyama High School, 1943, Takaoka Vocational School, 1944, and Toyama Normal School for Youth, 1944. Toyama Ika Yakka Daigaku (Toyama Medical and Pharmaceutical University) and Takaoka National College incorporated 2005

Academic year: April to March (April-September; October-March)

Admission requirements: Graduation from high school or recognized equivalent or foreign equivalent, and entrance examination

Fees: 520,800 per annum (Yen)

Main language(s) of instruction: Japanese

Accrediting agency: Ministry of Education, Culture, Sports, Science and Technology (MEXT)

Degrees and diplomas: Shushi (Education), Hakase (Biological and Life Sciences; Engineering; Medicine; Pharmacy)

Student Services: Academic Counselling, Social Counselling, Careers Guidance, Sports Facilities, Language Laboratory, Health Services, Canteen, Foreign Studies Centre, Library

Periodicals: Bulletin of Faculty of Education Toyama University, Bulletin of the Center for Educational Research and Practice Toyama University, Journal of the Faculty of Humanities Toyama University, Mathematics Journal of Toyama University, Memoirs of the Faculty of Education Toyama University, The Fudai Keizai Ronshu, The Journal of Economic Studies Toyama University

Last Update: 22-02-2018

University of Tsukuba (UT)

1-1-1 Tennodai
Tsukuba 305-8577, Ibaraki
Tel: +81(29) 853-2111
Fax: +83(29) 853-2059
Website: http://www.tsukuba.ac.jp/en
President: Kyosuke Nagata
Head, Office of Global Initiatives: Masatoshi Yokose
Tel: +81(29) 853-2058

College

Agro-biological Resources Sciences (Agrobiology; Applied Chemistry; Economics; Environmental Engineering); **Biological Sciences** (Biochemistry; Biology; Botany; Ecology; Embryology and Reproduction Biology; Genetics; Molecular Biology); **Chemistry** (Biotechnology; Chemistry; Genetics; Inorganic Chemistry; Organic Chemistry; Physical Chemistry); **Comparative Culture** (Cultural Studies; Literature; Regional Studies); **Disability Sciences**; **Education** (Development Studies; Education; Educational Administration; Educational Research; International and Comparative Education; Primary Education; Secondary Education); **Engineering Sciences** (Applied Physics; Electronic Engineering; Materials Engineering); **Engineering Systems** (Electrical Engineering; Engineering Management; Environmental Engineering; Mechanical Engineering); **Geoscience** (Geography (Human); Geology; Meteorology; Mineralogy; Paleontology; Water Science); **Humanities** (Archaeology; Folklore; History; Linguistics; Philosophy); **Information Sciences** (Artificial Intelligence; Computer Engineering; Computer Science; Information Sciences; Information Technology; Media Studies; Software Engineering); **International Studies** (Cultural Studies; Development Studies; Economics; Environmental Studies; Information Sciences; International Law; International Relations; Political Sciences); **Japanese Language and Culture** (Cultural Studies;

Japanese); **Knowledge and Library Sciences** (Information Technology; Library Science); **Mathematics** (Mathematics; Mathematics Education); **Media Arts, Science and Technology** (Actuarial Science; Cognitive Sciences; Communication Arts; Communication Studies; Computer Engineering; Computer Networks; Information Sciences; Information Technology; Media Studies; Operations Research; Statistics); **Physics** (Biology; Biophysics; Earth Sciences; Mechanics; Physical Chemistry; Physics; Statistics; Thermal Physics); **Policy and Planning Sciences** (Economics; Management; Regional Planning; Social Studies; Town Planning); **Psychology** (Clinical Psychology; Educational Psychology; Psychology; Social Psychology); **Social Sciences** (Economics; Law; Political Sciences; Sociology)

School

Arts and Design (Art History; Communication Arts; Design; Fine Arts); **Health and Physical Education** (Anatomy; Health Education; Physical Education; Physiology; Sports; Sports Management); **Human Sciences** (Education; Psychology; Social Sciences); **Humanities and Culture** (Arts and Humanities; Cultural Studies); **Informatics**; **Life and Environmental Sciences** (Biological and Life Sciences; Environmental Studies); **Medical Sciences** (Biochemistry; Health Sciences; Pathology; Pharmacology; Physiology); **Medicine** (Biology; Medicine; Social and Preventive Medicine; Sports; Sports Management; Sports Medicine); **Nursing**; **Science and Engineering** (Engineering; Mathematics; Natural Sciences); **Social and International Studies**

Institute

Agricultural and Forest Engineering (Agricultural Engineering; Agriculture; Forestry); **Applied Biochemistry** (Biochemistry); **Applied Physics**; **Art and Design** (Design; Fine Arts); **Basic Medical Sciences** (Health Sciences); **Biological Sciences** (Biological and Life Sciences); **Chemistry**; **Clinical Medicine**; **Community Medicine** (Community Health; Medicine); **Disability Science** (Rehabilitation and Therapy); **Education** (Education); **Engineering Mechanics and Systems** (Engineering; Mechanical Engineering); **Geoscience**; **Health and Sport Sciences** (Health Sciences; Sports); **History and Anthropology**; **Information Sciences and Electronics** (Information Sciences; Information Technology); **Library and Information Sciences** (Information Sciences; Library Science); **Literature and Lingusitics**; **Materials Science**; **Mathematics**; **Modern Languages and Cultures**; **Nursing Sciences** (Nursing); **Philosophy** (Philosophy); **Physics**; **Policy and Planning Sciences**; **Psychology**; **Social Sciences**

Centre

Academic Computing and Communications; **Admission**; **Agricultural and Forestry Research** (Agriculture; Forestry); **Alliance for Research on North Africa** (North

African Studies); **Computational Sciences** (*TARA*) (Computer Science); **Foreign Languages** (Modern Languages); **Gene Research** (Genetics); **International Student**; **Laboratory Animal Resource**; **Plasma Research Centre** (*TARA*); **Proton Medical Research**; **Radioisotope**; **Research Facility for Science and Technology**; **Research for Knowledge Communities**; **Research for University Studies**; **Research on International Cooperation in Educational Development**; **Shimoda Marine Research** (*Shimoda City*); **Special Support Education Research**; **Sport and Physical Education** (Physical Education; Sports); **Sugadaira Montane Research** (*Ueda City*); **Terrestrial Environment Research** (Environmental Studies); **Tsukuba Advanced Research Alliance** (*TARA*); **Tsukuba Critical Path Research and Education Integrated Leading Centre**; **Tsukuba Industrial Liaison and Cooperative Research**; **Tsukuba Research for Interdisciplinary Materials Science**; **University Health Centre**

Graduate School

Area Studies (*Master's Degree Programme*); **Business Sciences** (*Master's Degree Programme*) (Business Administration; Business and Commerce; Commercial Law; Law); **Business Sciences** (*Doctoral Degree Programme*) (Business Administration; Business and Commerce; Commercial Law; Law); **Comprehensive Human Sciences** (*Master's Degree Programme*); **Comprehensive Human Sciences** (*Doctoral Degree Programme*); **Education** (*Master's Degree Programme*); **Health and Sport Sciences** (*Master's Degree Programme*); **Humanities and Social Sciences** (*Master's Degree Programme*) (Cultural Studies; Economics; International Studies; Law; Modern Languages; Political Sciences); **Humanities and Social Sciences** (*Doctoral Degree Programme*) (Anthropology; Asian Studies; Cultural Studies; East Asian Studies; Economics; History; International Studies; Law; Linguistics; Literature; Modern Languages; Philosophy; Political Sciences; Social Sciences); **Library, Information and Media Studies** (*Doctoral Degree Programme*); **Life and Environmental Sciences** (*Doctoral Degree Programme*); **Life and Environmental Sciences** (*Master's Degree Programme*) (Agriculture; Biological and Life Sciences; Environmental Studies); **Pure and Applied Sciences** (*Doctoral Degree Programme*) (Applied Physics; Chemistry; Materials Engineering; Mathematics; Physics); **Pure and Applied Sciences** (*Master's Degree Programme*) (Applied Physics; Chemistry; Materials Engineering; Mathematics; Physics); **Systems and Information Engineering** (*Master's Degree Programme*)

Further information: Tokyo Campus, Satellite Office at BiVi Tsukuba Building, 13 Overseas Offices in 12 countries

History: Established in 1872 as modern Japan's first national institute of higher education, which started as the Normal School, later renamed Tokyo Higher Normal School, the first Teachers' college in Japan. Became Tokyo University of Education in 1947. Reorganized as a comprehensive research university in Tsukuba Science City in 1973. Merged with University of Library and Information Science in 2002. In 2004, Japanese national universities were transformed into national university corporations (NUCs).

Academic year: April to March (Spring: April-Sep; Fall: Oct-Mar)

Admission requirements: Graduation from high school (or recognized equivalent) and entrance examination

Fees: National : Registration, 282,000; tuition, 535,800 per annum (Yen), International : Same as domestic students

Main language(s) of instruction: Japanese, English

Degrees and diplomas: Gakushi (Agriculture; Biological and Life Sciences; Chemistry; Communication Studies; Cultural Studies; Earth Sciences; Education; Engineering; Environmental Engineering; Fine Arts; Graphic Design; Health Sciences; Information Sciences; International Studies; Japanese; Library Science; Mathematics; Media Studies; Medicine; Nursing; Physical Education; Physics; Psychology; Public Administration; Social Sciences; Technology), Shushi (Agriculture; Applied Physics; Behavioural Sciences; Biological and Life Sciences; Business Administration; Chemistry; Commercial Law; Communication Studies; Computer Science; Cultural Studies; Development Studies; Earth Sciences; Economics; Educational Administration; Educational Sciences; Energy Engineering; Environmental Management; Environmental Studies; Fine Arts; Graphic Design; Health Sciences; Heritage Preservation; Information Management; International Studies; Law; Library Science; Materials Engineering; Mathematics; Mechanical Engineering; Media Studies; Medicine; Modern Languages; Natural Sciences; Nursing; Physics; Psychology; Public Law; Safety Engineering; Secondary Education; Social Welfare; Sports; Technology), Hakase (Agriculture; Anthropology; Applied Physics; Behavioural Sciences; Biochemistry; Bioengineering; Biological and Life Sciences; Biomedical Engineering; Biotechnology; Computer Science; Cultural Studies; Development Studies; Earth Sciences; East Asian Studies; Economics; Education; Energy Engineering; Environmental Studies; Graphic Design; Health Sciences; Heritage Preservation; History; Human Resources; Information Management; Japanese; Law; Library Science; Linguistics; Literature; Materials Engineering; Mathematics; Mechanical Engineering; Media Studies; Medicine; Modern Languages; Natural Sciences; Philosophy; Physical Education; Physics; Psychology; Safety Engineering; Social Sciences; Social Welfare; Sports; Sports Medicine; Technology)

Student Services: Academic Counselling, Social Counselling, Careers Guidance, Nursery Care, Sports Facilities, Language Laboratory, Facilities for disabled people, Health Services, Canteen, Foreign Studies Centre, Library, Residential Facilities

Publishing house: University of Tsukuba Press

Student Numbers 2017-2018	MALE	FEMALE	TOTAL
All (Foreign Included)	10349	6429	16778

Last Update: 07-03-2018

University of Yamanashi

4-4-37 Takeda
Kofu-shi 400-8510, Yamanashi
Tel: +81(55) 220-8004
Fax: +81(55) 220-8799
Website: http://www.yamanashi.ac.jp
President: Heisei Shinji Shimada

Faculty

Education and Human Sciences (Art Management; Cultural Studies; Education; Educational Sciences; Social Studies); **Engineering** (Applied Chemistry; Biotechnology; Civil Engineering; Computer Science; Electrical and Electronic Engineering; Environmental Engineering; Information Sciences; Mechanical Engineering); **Life and Environmental Sciences** (Biotechnology; Environmental Engineering; Food Technology); **Medicine** (Health Administration; Medicine; Nursing; Pharmacy)

Institute

Enology and Viticulture (Oenology)

Centre

Co-operative Research and Development (Development Studies); **Data Processing** (Data Processing); **Health Care** (Health Sciences); **Instrumental Analysis** (Instrument Making); **Life Science Research** (Biological and Life Sciences)

Graduate School

Education (Education); **Medicine and Engineering** (*Interdisciplinary*) (Applied Chemistry; Biotechnology; Civil Engineering; Computer Science; Electrical and Electronic Engineering; Engineering; Environmental Engineering; Materials Engineering; Mechanical Engineering; Medical Technology; Medicine; Nursing)

Research Division

Clean Energy (Energy Engineering)
History: Founded 1949 incorporating Yamanashi Technical College, Yamanashi Normal School, and Yamanashi Normal School for Youth. Merged with Yamanashi Ika Daigaku (Yamanashi Medical University) 2002. Became National university corporation University of Yamanashi 2004

Academic year: April to March (April-September; October-March)
Admission requirements: Graduation from high school or recognized equivalent, and entrance examination
Main language(s) of instruction: Japanese
Accrediting agency: Ministry of Education, Culture, Sports, Science and Technology (MEXT)
Degrees and diplomas: Hakase (Medicine)
Student Services: Careers Guidance, Sports Facilities, Language Laboratory, Health Services, Canteen, Foreign Studies Centre, Library
Periodicals: Bulletin of the Faculty of Education and Humanities, Reports of the Faculty of Engineering Yamanashi University
Last Update: 23-02-2018

Utsunomiya University

350 Mine
Utsunomiya 321-8505, Tochigi
Tel: +81(28) 649-8649
Fax: +81(28) 649-5115
Website: http://www.utsunomiya-u.ac.jp
President: Tomoyasu Ishida

Faculty

Agriculture (Agricultural Economics; Agriculture; Animal Husbandry; Applied Chemistry; Bioengineering; Botany; Crop Production; Environmental Engineering; Forestry; Production Engineering; Zoology); **Education** (Art Education; Ecology; Education; Education of the Handicapped; Environmental Studies; Health Education; Japanese; Mathematics Education; Music Education; Physical Education; Primary Education; Science Education; Secondary Education; Social Studies; Special Education; Sports; Teacher Training; Technology Education); **Engineering** (Applied Chemistry; Architecture; Civil Engineering; Electrical and Electronic Engineering; Energy Engineering; Engineering; Environmental Engineering; Information Sciences; Materials Engineering; Mechanical Engineering; Production Engineering); **International Studies** (Cultural Studies; International Studies; Social Studies)
History: Founded 1949 as a National University, incorporating Utsunomiya Senmon Gakko of Agriculture and Forestry founded 1922, Tochigi Normal School 1943, and Tochigi Youth Normal School 1944
Academic year: April to March (April-September; October-March)
Admission requirements: Graduation from high school or equivalent or foreign equivalent, and entrance examination
Main language(s) of instruction: Japanese

Accrediting agency: Ministry of Education, Culture, Sports, Science and Technology (MEXT)
Degrees and diplomas: Gakushi (Agriculture; Education; Engineering), Shushi (Agriculture; Engineering), Hakase (Engineering; International Studies)
Student Services: Social Counselling, Careers Guidance, Sports Facilities, Language Laboratory, Health Services
Periodicals: Bulletin of Faculty of Agriculture, Bulletin of Faculty of Education
Last Update: 16-03-2018

Wakayama Medical University

811-1 Kimiidera
Wakayama-shi 641-8509, Wakayama
Tel: +81(73) 447-2300
Fax: +81(73) 441-0704
Website: http://www.wakayama-med.ac.jp
President: Yoshitaka Okamura

School
Health and Nursing Science (Arts and Humanities; Health Sciences; Nursing); **Medicine** (Medicine)

Graduate School
Health and Nursing Science (Community Health; Health Sciences; Nursing); **Medicine** (Medicine)
History: Founded 1945 as Medical School, became University 1948
Academic year: April to March (April-July; September-December; January-March)
Admission requirements: Graduation from high school and entrance examination
Main language(s) of instruction: Japanese
Accrediting agency: Ministry of Education, Culture, Sports, Science and Technology (MEXT)
Degrees and diplomas: Gakushi (Medicine), Hakase (Medicine)
Student Services: Sports Facilities
Periodicals: Wakayama Medical Reports
Last Update: 14-03-2018

Wakayama University

930 Sakaedani
Wakayama 640-8510
Tel: +81(73) 457-7007
Fax: +81(73) 457-7520
Website: http://www.wakayama-u.ac.jp
President: Hirokazu Taki

Faculty
Economics (*Also Graduate School*) (Business Administration; Economics; Marketing); **Education** (*Also Graduate School*) (Cultural Studies; Education; English; European Languages; Fine Arts; Health Education; International Studies; Japanese; Mathematics Education; Modern Languages; Music Education; Natural Sciences; Oriental Languages; Physical Education; Social Studies); **Systems Engineering** (*Also Graduate School*) (Chemistry; Computer Science; Information Sciences; Materials Engineering; Systems Analysis); **Tourism** (Regional Planning; Tourism)
History: Founded 1871 as School, became College 1922, and University 1949
Academic year: April to March (April-October; October-March)
Admission requirements: Graduation from high school or equivalent or foreign equivalent, and entrance examination
Main language(s) of instruction: Japanese
Accrediting agency: Ministry of Education, Culture, Sports, Science and Technology (MEXT)
Degrees and diplomas: Hakase (Engineering)
Student Services: Academic Counselling, Sports Facilities, Language Laboratory, Library
Periodicals: Bulletin of the Faculty of Education, The Wakayama Economics Review (Keizai Riron)
Last Update: 22-02-2018

Yamagata Prefectural University of Health Sciences

260 Kamiyanagi
Yamagata 990-2212
Tel: +81(23) 686-6688
Fax: +81(23) 686-6674
Website: http://www.yachts.ac.jp
President: Kunihiko Maeda

Course/Programme
General Education (Biological and Life Sciences; Health Sciences; Natural Sciences; Psychology)

Department/Division
Nursing (Nursing); **Occupational Therapy** (Occupational Therapy); **Physical Therapy** (Physical Therapy)
History: Founded 2000
Main language(s) of instruction: Japanese
Accrediting agency: Ministry of Education, Culture, Sports, Science and Technology (MEXT)
Student Services: Library
Last Update: 16-03-2018

Yamagata University

1-4-12 Kojirakawa-machi
Yamagata-shi 990-8560, Yamagata
Tel: +81(236) 28-4119
Fax: +81(236) 28-4125
Website: http://www.yamagata-u.ac.jp
President: Kiyohito Koyama

Faculty

Agriculture (Biotechnology; Ecology; Environmental Studies; Natural Resources); **Education, Art and Science** (Cultural Studies; Education; Environmental Studies; Fine Arts; Food Science; Information Sciences; Nursing); **Engineering** (*Also Graduate School*) (Bioengineering; Chemical Engineering; Chemistry; Computer Science; Electrical Engineering; Engineering; Mechanical Engineering; Polymer and Plastics Technology; Technology); **Literature and Social Sciences** (Cultural Studies; Literature; Social Sciences; Social Studies); **Medicine** (*Also Graduate School*) (Anaesthesiology; Anatomy; Biology; Cardiology; Cell Biology; Community Health; Dermatology; Endocrinology; Gastroenterology; Gynaecology and Obstetrics; Immunology; Medicine; Nephrology; Neurology; Nursing; Oncology; Ophthalmology; Orthopaedics; Paediatrics; Pathology; Pharmacology; Psychiatry and Mental Health; Public Health; Radiology; Social and Preventive Medicine; Surgery; Urology); **Science** (*Also Graduate School*) (Biochemistry; Biology; Earth Sciences; Environmental Studies; Mathematics; Natural Sciences; Physics)

Graduate School

Education (Education); **Social and Cultural Systems** (Cultural Studies; Social Sciences)
Further information: Also Iida Campus, Yonezawa Campus, Tsuruoka Campus
History: Founded 1949 incorporating Yamagata High School, Yamagata Normal School, Yamagata Youth's Normal School, Yonezawa Engineering College, and Yamagata Prefectural Agriculture and Forestry College
Academic year: April to March (April-September; October-March)
Admission requirements: Graduation from high school or recognized equivalent, and entrance examination
Main language(s) of instruction: Japanese
Accrediting agency: Ministry of Education, Culture, Sports, Science and Technology (MEXT)
Degrees and diplomas: Shushi (Education), Hakase (Engineering)
Student Services: Library
Periodicals: Bulletins
Last Update: 23-02-2018

Yamaguchi Prefectural University

3-2-1 Sakurabatake
Yamaguchi 753-8502
Tel: +81(83) 928-0211
Fax: +81(83) 928-2251
Website: http://www.yamaguchi-pu.ac.jp
President: Yuji Nagasaka

Faculty

Intercultural Studies (Cultural Studies; International Studies); **Nursing and Nutrition** (Nursing; Nutrition); **Social Welfare** (Social Welfare)
History: Founded 1941 as Yamaguchi Women's School, reorganized 1950 as Yamaguchi Women's College, became Yamaguchi Women's University 1975 and acquired present title 1996. Incorporated Yamanashi Kenritsu Kango Daigaku (Yamanashi College of Nursing) 2005
Main language(s) of instruction: Japanese
Accrediting agency: Ministry of Education, Culture, Sports, Science and Technology (MEXT)
Degrees and diplomas: Hakase (Health Sciences; Welfare and Protective Services)
Student Services: Library
Last Update: 16-03-2018

Yamaguchi University

1677-1 Yoshida
Yamaguchi-shi 753-8511, Yamaguchi
Tel: +81(83) 933-5981
Fax: +81(83) 933-5029
Website: http://www.yamaguchi-u.ac.jp
President: Masaaki Oka

Faculty

Agriculture (Agriculture; Biological and Life Sciences; Environmental Studies; Veterinary Science); **Economics** (Business and Commerce; Economics; International Economics; Law; Management; Tourism); **Education** (Child Care and Development; Cultural Studies; Education; Information Sciences; Preschool Education; Primary Education; Secondary Education); **Engineering** (Applied Chemistry; Applied Mathematics; Applied Physics; Chemical Engineering; Civil Engineering; Computer Science; Design; Electrical and Electronic Engineering; Engineering; Environmental Engineering; Materials Engineering; Mechanical Engineering; Systems Analysis); **Humanities** (Arts and Humanities; History; Literature; Modern Languages; Philosophy; Social Sciences); **Medicine and Health Sciences** (Health Sciences; Medicine); **Science** (Biology; Chemistry;

Earth Sciences; Information Sciences; Mathematics; Natural Sciences; Physics)

Institute
Education Research and Training (*Integrated Centre*); **Venture Business Laboratory** (Management)

Centre
Business Incubation Square (Business and Commerce); **Collaborative Research** (Engineering); **Design and Products Innovation**; **Media and Information Technology** (Information Technology)

Graduate School
Agriculture (Agriculture); **East Asian Studies** (East Asian Studies; Economics); **Economics** (Economics); **Education** (Education); **Humanities** (Arts and Humanities); **Innovation and Technology** (Technology); **Medicine** (Medicine); **Science and Engineering** (Engineering; Natural Sciences); **Veterinary Science** (Veterinary Science); **Veterinary Science, Tottori University** (Veterinary Science)

Research Division
Science Research

History: Founded 1949 as a National University at 3 campuses.
Academic year: April to March
Admission requirements: Graduation from high school and entrance examination
Fees: 535,800 per annum (Yen)
Main language(s) of instruction: Japanese
Accrediting agency: Ministry of Education, Culture, Sports, Science and Technology (MEXT)
Degrees and diplomas: Shushi (Economics), Hakase (Medicine)
Student Services: Academic Counselling, Social Counselling, Careers Guidance, Cultural Activities, Sports Facilities, Facilities for disabled people, Health Services, Canteen, Foreign Studies Centre, Library
Last Update: 23-02-2018

Yamanashi Prefectural University

5-11-1 Iida
Kofu-shi 400-0035, Yamanashi
Tel: +81(55) 224-5261
Fax: +81(55) 228-6819
Website: http://www.yamanashi-ken.ac.jp
President: Kazuhiko Shimizu

Faculty
Global Policy Management and Communication (Communication Arts; International Studies; Social Policy);

Human and Social Services (Community Health; Development Studies; Welfare and Protective Services); **Nursing** (Nursing)

Graduate School
Nursing (Nursing)
Further information: Also Ikeda Campus
History: Founded 2005 following merger of Yamanashi Kenritsu Kango Daigaku (Yamanashi College of Nursing) and Yamnashi Women's Junior College
Academic year: April to March (April-September; October-March)
Main language(s) of instruction: Japanese
Accrediting agency: Ministry of Education, Culture, Sports, Science and Technology (MEXT)
Student Services: Academic Counselling, Social Counselling, Careers Guidance, Sports Facilities, Health Services, Library
Periodicals: Bulletin
Last Update: 16-03-2018

Yokohama City University (YCU)

22-2 Seto, Kanazawa-ku
Yokohama 236-0027, Kanagawa
Tel: +81(45) 787-2311
Fax: +81(45) 787-2316
Website: https://www.yokohama-cu.ac.jp
President: Yoshinobu Kubota

College
Arts and Sciences (*International*) (Accountancy; Biological and Life Sciences; Cultural Studies; Economics; Environmental Engineering; Fine Arts; Management; Materials Engineering; Medicine; Regional Planning; Social Studies; Town Planning)

School
Medicine (Medicine; Nursing; Pathology; Physiology; Surgery)

Graduate School
International Management (Management); **Medical Life Science** (Biology); **Medicine** (Immunology; Medicine; Neurosciences; Nursing); **Nanobioscience** (Biological and Life Sciences; Genetics; Materials Engineering; Nanotechnology; Natural Sciences); **Urban Social and Cultural Studies** (Cultural Studies; Urban Studies)
Further information: Also Fukuura Campus; Yokohama City University Hospital; Tsurumi Campus; Maioka Campus
History: Founded 1882 as Yokohama School of Commerce. Acquired University status 1949

Academic year: April to March (April-October; October-March)

Admission requirements: Graduation from high school or equivalent, and entrance examination

Main language(s) of instruction: Japanese

Accrediting agency: Ministry of Education, Culture, Sports, Science and Technology (MEXT)

Degrees and diplomas: Hakase (Cultural Studies; Management; Medicine; Urban Studies)

Student Services: Careers Guidance, Nursery Care, Language Laboratory, Canteen

Periodicals: Bulletin of Yokohama City University Society, The Industry and Trade, The Journal of Yokohama City University, Yokohama Medical Bulletin

Last Update: 25-05-2018

Yokohama National University (YNU)

79-1 Tokiwadai Hodogaya-ku
Yokohama-shi 240-8501, Kanagawa
Tel: +81(45) 339-3036
Fax: +81(45) 339-3039
Website: http://www.ynu.ac.jp
President: Yuichi Hasebe

College

Business Administration (Accountancy; Business Administration; International Business; Management Systems); **Economics** (Commercial Law; Economics; International Economics); **Education and Human Sciences** (Cultural Studies; Education; Social Studies; Special Education); **Engineering** (Architecture; Chemical Engineering; Civil Engineering; Computer Engineering; Engineering; Marine Engineering; Materials Engineering; Mechanical Engineering; Physics)

Laboratory

Ecotechnology System (Environmental Studies)

Graduate School

Education (Art Education; Education; Mathematics Education; Physical Education; Psychology; Science Education; Special Education); **Engineering** (Architecture; Chemical Engineering; Civil Engineering; Computer Engineering; Electrical Engineering; Engineering; Materials Engineering; Systems Analysis); **Environment and Information Sciences** (Environmental Studies; Information Sciences; Media Studies; Natural Sciences; Technology); **International Social Sciences** (*International*) (Accountancy; Business Administration; Commercial Law; Development Studies;

Economics; International Economics; International Law; International Relations; Law; Management Systems); **Urban Innovation** (Architecture; Urban Studies)

History: Founded 1949 incorporating Kanagawa Normal School, founded 1876, Kanagawa Youth Normal School 1920, Yokohama Commercial College 1923, and Yokohama Technical College, 1920

Academic year: April to March (April-October; October-March)

Admission requirements: Graduation from high school or equivalent or foreign equivalent, and entrance examination

Main language(s) of instruction: Japanese

Accrediting agency: Ministry of Education, Culture, Sports, Science and Technology (MEXT)

Degrees and diplomas: Shushi (Business Administration; Economics; Education; Engineering; Environmental Studies; Information Sciences; International Business; International Law; Philosophy)

Student Services: Academic Counselling, Social Counselling, Careers Guidance, Nursery Care, Cultural Activities, Sports Facilities, Language Laboratory, Facilities for disabled people, Health Services, Canteen, Foreign Studies Centre, Library

Last Update: 23-02-2018

Private Institutions

Aichi Bunkyo University (ABU)

5969-3 Nenjo-zaka Okusa
Komaki-shi 485-8565, Aichi-ken
Tel: +81(568) 78-2211
Fax: +81(568) 78-2240
Website: http://www.abu.ac.jp
President: Kenhiro Tomita

Faculty

International Culture (American Studies; Chinese; Cultural Studies; English; Hindi; Literature; South Asian Studies)

College

Humanities (Applied Linguistics; Arts and Humanities; Asian Studies; Chinese; English; History; Japanese; Literature)

History: Founded 1998.

Main language(s) of instruction: Japanese

Accrediting agency: Ministry of Education, Culture, Sports, Science and Technology (MEXT)

Degrees and diplomas: Gakushi, Shushi (Cultural Studies)

Last Update: 22-03-2018

Aichi Gakuin University (AGU)

Araike 12 Iwasaki-cho
Nisshin-shi 470-0195, Aichi
Tel: +81(56) 1731-111
Fax: +81(56) 1735-889
Website: http://www.agu.ac.jp
President: Etsujo Sato

Faculty

Arts and Humanities (Arts and Humanities; Asian Religious Studies; Cultural Studies; English; History; International Studies; Religious Studies); **Business and Commerce** (Business and Commerce; Information Sciences); **Law** (Law; Social Studies); **Management** (Business Administration; Management); **Policy Studies** (Social Policy); **Psychological and Physical Sciences** (Psychology)

College

Junior Studies (Dental Hygiene; English)

Course/Programme

Japanese Language for Foreign Students (Foreign Languages Education; Japanese)

School

Dentistry (Dentistry); **Pharmacy** (Health Sciences; Pharmacy)

Department/Division

General Education (Education)

Institute

Foreign Languages (Modern Languages); **Human Cultural Studies** (Cultural Studies); **Zen Studies** (Asian Religious Studies)

Centre

International Studies (International Studies); **Satellite** (*Sakae*) (Aeronautical and Aerospace Engineering)

Graduate School

Commerce (Business and Commerce); **Dentistry** (Dentistry); **Law** (Law); **Letters** (Arts and Humanities; Asian Religious Studies; Asian Studies; Cultural Studies; English Studies; History; Japanese; Religious Studies); **Management** (Management); **Policy Studies** (Health Administration; Insurance; Psychology; Social Policy); **Psychological and Physical Science** (Behavioural Sciences; Cognitive Sciences; Psychology)

Research Division

Advanced Oral Science (Dentistry); **Business Administration** (Business Administration); **Law and Religion** (Law; Religion); **Marketing and Distribution** (Marketing; Sales Techniques)
History: Founded 1950 as Junior College. Acquired present status 1953.
Academic year: April to March (April-September; September-March)
Admission requirements: Graduation from high school and entrance examination
Main language(s) of instruction: Japanese
Accrediting agency: Japan University Accreditation Association
Degrees and diplomas: Gakushi, Shushi (Asian Religious Studies; Asian Studies; Business and Commerce; English Studies; History; Law; Management; Psychology; Social Policy), Hakase (Asian Religious Studies; Asian Studies; Business and Commerce; Dentistry; English Studies; History; Law; Management; Psychology; Social Policy)
Student Services: Sports Facilities, Language Laboratory
Periodicals: Foreign Languages and Literature, Journal of Aichi Gakuin University Dental Society, Journal of the Zen Research Institute, The Aichi Gakuin Law Review, The Business Review, The Journal of Aichi Gakuin University (Humanities and Sciences), Transactions of the Institute of Cultural Studies
Last Update: 22-03-2018

Aichi Gakusen University

1 Shiotori Oike-cho
Toyota-shi 471-8532, Aichi
Tel: +81(565) 35-1313
Fax: +81(565) 35-1677
Website: http://www.gakusen.ac.jp
President: Akira Terabe

Faculty

Business Administration (*Enrolment frozen*) (Business Administration); **Modern Management** (Business Administration; Management)

School

Policy Studies (*Enrolment frozen*) (Social Policy)

Department/Division

Home Economics (Kaseigakubu) (Child Care and Development; Dietetics; Home Economics)
Further information: Also Okazaki Campus

History: Founded 1966 as Aichi Women's University. Changed name to Anjo Gakuen University in Aichi Women's University 1968. Acquired present title 1982.

Fees: Tuition fee for Management programme, 290,000; for Home Economics programme, 355,000 (Yen)

Main language(s) of instruction: Japanese

Accrediting agency: Japan Institution for Higher Education Evaluation (JIHEE)

Degrees and diplomas: Gakushi (Business Administration; Child Care and Development; Dietetics; Home Economics; Management; Social Policy)

Student Numbers 2013-2014	MALE	FEMALE	TOTAL
All (Foreign Included)			c. 390

Last Update: 28-03-2018

Aichi Institute of Technology (AIT)

1247 Yachigusa Yakusa-cho
Toyota-shi 470-0392, Aichi
Tel: +81(565) 48-8121
Fax: +81(565) 48-0277
Website: http://www.aitech.ac.jp
President: Yasuyuki Goto

Faculty

Business Administration (Business Administration; Information Management; Information Sciences; Management; Sports Management); **Engineering** (Applied Chemistry; Architectural and Environmental Design; Architecture; Civil Engineering; Computer Networks; Design; Electrical and Electronic Engineering; Electrical Engineering; Electronic Engineering; Environmental Engineering; Information Technology; Materials Engineering; Mechanical Engineering; Urban Studies); **Information Science** (*Motoyama Campus*) (Computer Science; Information Sciences; Media Studies)

School

Graduate Studies (Applied Chemistry; Business Administration; Computer Science; Construction Engineering; Electrical and Electronic Engineering; Electrical Engineering; Engineering; Materials Engineering; Mechanical Engineering; Production Engineering)

Centre

General Education (Education; Natural Sciences)
Further information: Also Motoyama Campus and Jiyugaoka Campus
History: Founded 1912 as Nagoya Training School of Electricity. Became Junior College 1954. Transformed into

Nagoya Institute of Electricity. Acquired present status and title 1960.

Main language(s) of instruction: Japanese, English

Accrediting agency: Japan Institution for Higher Education Evaluation (JIHEE)

Degrees and diplomas: Gakushi, Shushi (Business Administration; Construction Engineering; Electrical and Electronic Engineering; Materials Engineering; Mechanical Engineering), Hakase (Business Administration; Computer Science; Construction Engineering; Electrical Engineering; Materials Engineering; Production Engineering)

Student Services: Academic Counselling, Careers Guidance, Sports Facilities, Foreign Studies Centre

Last Update: 22-03-2018

Aichi Medical University

1-1 Yazakokarimata Nagakute
Aichi-gun 480-1195, Aichi
Tel: +81(561) 62-3311
Fax: +81(561) 62-4866
Website: http://www.aichi-med-u.ac.jp/index.html
President: Keiji Sato

School

Medicine (Anaesthesiology; Cell Biology; Dermatology; Diabetology; Gastroenterology; Gynaecology and Obstetrics; Haematology; Health Administration; Information Sciences; Laboratory Techniques; Medicine; Nephrology; Neurological Therapy; Neurology; Nursing; Nutrition; Oncology; Ophthalmology; Oral Pathology; Orthopaedics; Otorhinolaryngology; Pathology; Pharmacy; Plastic Surgery; Pneumology; Psychiatry and Mental Health; Radiology; Rehabilitation and Therapy; Rheumatology; Surgery; Urology); **Nursing** (Nursing)

Institute

Comprehensive Medical Research (Medicine); **Medical Science of Ageing** (Gerontology); **Molecular Science of Medicine** (Medicine; Molecular Biology); **Occupational Health Science** (Occupational Health); **Physical Fitness, Sports Medicine and Rehabilitation** (Medicine; Physical Education; Rehabilitation and Therapy; Sports)

Centre

Medical Education Center (Health Education; Medicine); **Multidisciplinary Pain** (Medicine); **Nursing Practice and Research** (Nursing); **Poison Analysis** (Medicine; Toxicology)

Graduate School

Medicine (Anaesthesiology; Anatomy; Biochemistry; Biology; Chemistry; Dermatology; Forensic Medicine and

Dentistry; Gynaecology and Obstetrics; Health Education; Health Sciences; Immunology; Mathematics; Medicine; Microbiology; Modern Languages; Neurological Therapy; Ophthalmology; Orthopaedics; Otorhinolaryngology; Paediatrics; Parasitology; Pathology; Pharmacology; Philosophy; Physical Education; Physics; Physiology; Psychiatry and Mental Health; Psychology; Public Health; Radiology; Social and Preventive Medicine; Surgery; Urology); **Nursing** (Community Health; Gerontology; Health Administration; Nursing; Psychiatry and Mental Health; Public Health)

Research Division
Medicine (*Advanced*) (Medicine)
Further information: Also University Hospital
History: Founded 1971. A private Institution.
Academic year: April to March (April-October; October-March)
Admission requirements: Graduation from high school or equivalent or foreign equivalent, and entrance examination
Main language(s) of instruction: Japanese
Accrediting agency: Japan University Accreditation Association (JUAA)
Degrees and diplomas: Gakushi (Nursing), Shushi (Nursing), Hakase (Medicine)
Student Services: Sports Facilities, Health Services
Periodicals: Bulletin of Liberal Arts and Science, Journal of the Aichi Medical University Association

Academic Staff 2012-2013	MALE	FEMALE	TOTAL
FULL-TIME			604
Student Numbers 2012-2013			
All (Foreign Included)			1239

Last Update: 28-03-2018

Aichi Mizuho College

86-1 Haiwa Hiratobashi-cho
Toyota-shi 470-0394, Aichi
Tel: +81(52) 882-1123
Fax: +81(52) 882-1124
Website: http://amc.mizuho-c.ac.jp
President: Sato Yuzo

Faculty
Human Sciences (Computer Science; Dietetics; Health Sciences; Information Technology; Nursing; Physical Education; Primary Education; Psychology; Secondary Education; Secretarial Studies; Sports)

Graduate School
Human Sciences (Physical Education; Psychiatry and Mental Health)

Further information: Also Nagoya Campus
History: Founded 1993.
Admission requirements: High school degree; Entrance examination
Fees: Admission fee, 300,000; tuition fee, 2,680,000 for a four year programme (Yen)
Main language(s) of instruction: Japanese
Accrediting agency: Japan Institution for Higher Education Evaluation (JIHEE)
Degrees and diplomas: Gakushi, Shushi (Psychiatry and Mental Health)
Last Update: 22-03-2018

Aichi Sangyo University (ASU)

12-5 Harayama Oka-cho
Okazaki-shi 444-0005, Aichi
Tel: +81(564) 48-4511
Fax: +81(564) 48-7756
Website: http://www.asu.ac.jp
President: Tetsumi Horikoshi

Faculty
Bekka (Asian Studies; Japanese); **Business Administration** (Business Administration; Management); **Fine Arts** (*Art University*) (Architecture; Design; Fine Arts)

Course/Programme
Distance Education (Art Education; Foreign Languages Education)

Graduate School
Graduate Studies (Architecture; Architecture and Planning; Structural Architecture; Town Planning)
Further information: A traditional and distance learning institution.
History: Founded 1948 as Aichi Women's High School. Acquired present status and title 1992.
Admission requirements: Entrance examination
Main language(s) of instruction: Japanese
Accrediting agency: Japan Institution for Higher Education Evaluation (JIHEE)
Degrees and diplomas: Gakushi, Shushi (Architecture; Design)
Student Services: Sports Facilities, Canteen
Last Update: 22-03-2018

Aichi Shukutoku University (ASU)

9 Katahira, Nagakute Nagakute-cho
Aichi-gun 480-1197, Aichi
Tel: +81(561) 62-4111

Fax: +81(561) 63-1977
Website: http://www.aasa.ac.jp
President: Shuzo Shimada

Faculty

Business (Accountancy; Business Administration; Chinese; English; Finance; Hotel and Restaurant; Information Sciences; Information Technology; Korean; Management; Tourism); **Global Culture and Communication** (Business Administration; Chinese; Communication Studies; English; Foreign Languages Education; Hotel and Restaurant; International Business; International Studies; Regional Studies; Social and Community Services; Tourism); **Health and Medical Sciences** (Communication Disorders; Health Sciences; Medicine; Nutrition; Ophthalmology; Psychiatry and Mental Health; Sports); **Human Informatics** (Design; Information Management; Information Sciences; Library Science; Psychology); **Human Services** (Child Care and Development; Social and Community Services; Social Welfare; Social Work); **Letters** (Arts and Humanities; Continuing Education; Education; English; Japanese; Literature; Primary Education; Special Education; Teacher Training); **Media Theories and Production** (Architectural and Environmental Design; Media Studies; Town Planning; Writing); **Psychology** (Clinical Psychology; Cognitive Sciences; Developmental Psychology; Psychology; Social Psychology)

Department/Division

Foreign Language Education (Chinese; English; French; German; Italian; Korean; Portuguese; Russian; Spanish)

Centre

Japanese Language and Culture (Asian Studies; Japanese)

Graduate School

Business (Accountancy; Business Administration; Information Technology; International Business; Management); **Creativity and Culture** (Architectural and Environmental Design; Cultural Studies; Information Sciences; Japanese; Library Science; Literature; Media Studies; Town Planning; Writing); **Education** (Education; Primary Education; Teacher Training); **Global Culture and Communication** (American Studies; Asian Studies; Chinese; Communication Studies; Cultural Studies; English; English Studies; European Studies; International Relations; International Studies; Japanese; Literature; Tourism); **Psychology and Medical Sciences** (Clinical Psychology; Cognitive Sciences; Communication Disorders; Developmental Psychology; Medicine; Ophthalmology; Psychology; Social and Community Services; Social Psychology; Speech Therapy and Audiology)

Further information: Also Center for Education of Health Sciences; Multimedia Resource Centre; Also Hoshigaoka campus

History: Founded 1975. Faculty of Communication and Faculty of Creativity and Culture founded 2000.
Academic year: April to March (April-July; October-March)
Admission requirements: Graduation from high school or equivalent
Main language(s) of instruction: Japanese, English
Accrediting agency: Japan University Accreditation Association
Degrees and diplomas: Gakushi, Shushi (Business Administration; Communication Studies; Education; Japanese; Library Science; Media Studies; Psychology), Hakase (Arts and Humanities; Business Administration; Communication Studies; Health Sciences; Japanese; Literature; Media Studies; Psychology)
Student Services: Academic Counselling, Social Counselling, Careers Guidance, Nursery Care, Sports Facilities, Language Laboratory, Facilities for disabled people, Health Services, Canteen, Foreign Studies Centre
Periodicals: Bulletin of Aichi Shukutoku University, Evergreen, Intercultural Communication Studies, Journal of Library and Information Science, Language and Literature (Japan), Language Communication Studies, Studies in Contemporary Society

Student Numbers 2013-2014	MALE	FEMALE	TOTAL
All (Foreign Included)			c. 9205
Foreign only			60

Last Update: 22-03-2018

Aichi Toho University

3-11 Heiwagaoka
Meito-ku 465-8515, Nagoya
Tel: +81(52) 782-1241
Fax: +81(52) 781-0931
Website: http://www.aichi-toho.ac.jp/english
President: Naoki Sakaki

Faculty

Business Administration (Business Administration; Management; Sports Management; Tourism); **Human Studies** (Child Care and Development; Health Sciences; Physical Education; Psychology; Science Education; Social Welfare)
History: Founded 2001 as Toho Gakuen Daigaku (Toho Gakuen University). Acquired present title 2007.
Admission requirements: 12 years of school education; Entrance examination; International students must demonstrate sufficient Japanese language ability
Main language(s) of instruction: Japanese
Accrediting agency: Japan Institution for Higher Education Evaluation (JIHEE)

Degrees and diplomas: Gakushi (Education; Management)
Student Services: Cultural Activities, Sports Facilities

Academic Staff 2012-2013	MALE	FEMALE	TOTAL
FULL-TIME			48
Student Numbers 2012-2013			
All (Foreign Included)			302

Last Update: 22-03-2018

Aichi University

1-1 Machihata-cho
Toyohashi-shi 441-8522, Aichi
Tel: +81(532) 47-4131
Fax: +81(532) 47-4144
Website: http://www.aichi-u.ac.jp
President: Motohiko Sato

Faculty

Business Administration (*Nagoya Campus*) (Accountancy; Business Administration; Finance; Information Sciences; International Business; Management; Marketing); **Economics** (*Nagoya Campus*) (Economic and Finance Policy; Economics; International Economics); **International Communication** (*Nagoya Campus*) (Cultural Studies; English; Modern Languages); **Law** (*Nagoya Campus*) (Commercial Law; Justice Administration; Law); **Letters** (*Toyohashi*) (Arts and Humanities; Behavioural Sciences; Cultural Studies; East Asian Studies; English; French; Geography; German; History; Information Sciences; Japanese; Library Science; Literature; Media Studies; Philosophy; Psychology; Sociology); **Modern Chinese Studies** (*Nagoya Campus*) (Asian Studies; Business Administration; Chinese; Cultural Studies; International Relations); **Regional Policy** (*Toyohashi*) (Cultural Studies; Health Sciences; Public Administration; Regional Studies; Sports; Town Planning)

Institute

International Affairs (*Nagoya Campus*) (International Business)

Centre

Chinese Studies (*International - Nagoya Campus*) (Asian Studies; Chinese); **Regional Cooperation** (*San-En-Nanshin - Toyohashi Campus*) (International Relations); **Toa Dobunshoin University Memorial** (*Toyohashi Campus*)

Graduate School

Graduate Studies (*Toyohashi Campus*) (Arts and Humanities; Asian Studies; Japanese; Western European Studies); **Graduate Studies** (*Kurumamichi Campus*) (Accountancy; Business Administration; Chinese; English; Law; Private Law; Public Law)

Research Division

Community (*Toyohashi Campus*) (Social and Community Services); **Comprehensive Chinese-Japanese Dictionary Editing** (Chinese; Japanese; Publishing and Book Trade); **Industry in Chubu District** (*Toyohashi Campus*); **Management** (*Nagoya Campus*) (Management)
Further information: Also Nagoya and Kurumamichi campuses. One year Japanese language course for foreign students
History: Founded 1946.
Academic year: April to March (April-September; September-March)
Admission requirements: Graduation from high school and entrance examination
Main language(s) of instruction: Japanese, English
Accrediting agency: Japan University Accreditation Association (JUAA)
Degrees and diplomas: Gakushi, Shushi (Business Administration; Chinese; Communication Studies; Economics; Japanese; Social and Community Services; Western European Studies), Hakase (Arts and Humanities; Business Administration; Chinese; Economics; Japanese; Law; Social and Community Services; Western European Studies). Also Professional (graduate) degree courses in Law and Accountancy
Student Services: Nursery Care
Periodicals: Journal of the Association of Economic Sciences, Journal of the Association of Managerial Sciences, Journal of the Institute of International Affairs, Journal of the Managerial Research Institute, Memoirs of the Community Research Institute, Memoirs of the Institute of International Affairs, Memoirs of the Managerial Research Institute, Memoirs of the Research Institute of Industry in Chubu District

Student Numbers 2013-2014	MALE	FEMALE	TOTAL
All (Foreign Included)			c. 9600

Last Update: 22-03-2018

Aichi University of Technology (AUT)

50-2 Manori Nishihasama-cho
Gamagori-shi 443-0047, Aichi
Tel: +81(533) 68-1135
Fax: +81(533) 68-0352
Website: http://www.aut.ac.jp
President: Takashi Yasuda

Department/Division

Engineering (Automation and Control Engineering; Automotive Engineering; Electronic Engineering; Engineering;

Information Technology; Mechanical Engineering; Media Studies; Robotics)

Graduate School

Graduate Studies (Electrical and Electronic Engineering; Engineering; Environmental Engineering; Information Technology; Mechanical Engineering; Telecommunications Engineering)
History: Founded and accredited 1987 as Aichi College of Technology. Acquired present title 2010.
Main language(s) of instruction: Japanese
Accrediting agency: Japan Institution for Higher Education Evaluation (JIHEE)
Degrees and diplomas: Gakushi, Shushi (Automotive Engineering; Engineering; Information Technology), Hakase (Automotive Engineering; Engineering; Mechanical Engineering)
Student Services: Academic Counselling, Social Counselling, Sports Facilities
Last Update: 22-03-2018

Aikoku Gakuen University

1532 Yotsukaido
Yotsukaido-shi 284-0005, Chiba
Tel: +81(43) 424-4410, +81(43) 424-4433
Fax: +81(43) 424-4322
Website: http://www.aikoku-u.ac.jp
President: Tadami Akatsuka

School

Human Cultures (Asian Studies; Business Administration; Business Computing; Chinese; Computer Science; Cultural Studies; Design; Economics; English; European Languages; European Studies; Fine Arts; French; German; Japanese; Modern Languages; Psychology; Secretarial Studies; Social Sciences; Welfare and Protective Services)
History: Founded 1998.
Main language(s) of instruction: Japanese
Accrediting agency: Ministry of Education, Culture, Sports, Science and Technology (MEXT)
Degrees and diplomas: Gakushi (Arts and Humanities; Social Sciences). Qualifications are certified by the Japanese Psychological Association and the Japan Association of University and College for Business Education
Student Services: Sports Facilities

Academic Staff 2012-2013	MALE	FEMALE	TOTAL
FULL-TIME			17

Last Update: 28-03-2018

Aino University

4-5-4 Higashioda
Ibaraki 567-0012, Osaka
Tel: +81(72) 627-1711
Fax: +81(72) 627-1753
Website: http://univ.aino.ac.jp
President: Masatoshi Takeda

Faculty

Health Sciences (Biomedical Engineering; Health Sciences; Nursing; Occupational Therapy; Physical Therapy)
History: Founded 2004 on the basis of Aino Byoin (Hospital), and previously known as Aino Nursing school (1979) and Aino Gakuin Junior College (1985).
Main language(s) of instruction: Japanese
Accrediting agency: Japan University Accreditation Association (JUAA)
Degrees and diplomas: Gakushi (Occupational Therapy; Physical Therapy), Shushi (Nursing)
Last Update: 22-03-2018

Akita University of Nursing and Welfare

2-3-4 Shimizu
Odate 017-0046, Akita
Tel: +81(186) 45-1717
Fax: +81(186) 43-6711
Website: http://www.well.ac.jp
President: Reiko Tanaka

Faculty

Nursing and Social Welfare (Clinical Psychology; Nursing; Psychiatry and Mental Health; Psychology; Social Welfare; Welfare and Protective Services)
History: Founded 1995 as Akita Katsuragi College. Acquired present status and title 2005.
Main language(s) of instruction: Japanese
Accrediting agency: Japan Institution for Higher Education Evaluation (JIHEE)
Degrees and diplomas: Gakushi (Nursing; Welfare and Protective Services)
Student Services: Health Services
Last Update: 27-03-2018

Aomori Chuo Gakuin University (ACGU)

12 Kanda Yokouchi
Aomori 030-0132, Aomori
Tel: +81(17) 728-0131

Fax: +81(17) 738-8333
Website: http://www.aomoricgu.ac.jp
President: Katsumi Hanada

Faculty

Management and Law (Law; Management); **Nursing** (Nursing)
History: Founded 1946 as Aomori Abacus and Accounting School. Became Aomori Chuo Junior College 1970. Acquired university status 1998.
Academic year: April to March (April-September; October-March)
Admission requirements: 12 years of formal school education completed
Main language(s) of instruction: Japanese
Accrediting agency: Japan Institution for Higher Education Evaluation (JIHEE)
Degrees and diplomas: Gakushi (Law; Management; Nursing), Shushi (Management)
Student Services: Academic Counselling, Social Counselling, Careers Guidance, Nursery Care, Cultural Activities, Sports Facilities, Language Laboratory, Facilities for disabled people, Health Services, Canteen, Foreign Studies Centre
Periodicals: Newsletter, Review of Aomori Chuo Gakuin University, Variety of periodicals relating to disciplines and programmes offered

Academic Staff 2013-2014	MALE	FEMALE	TOTAL
FULL-TIME	26	5	31
PART-TIME	39	6	45
Student Numbers 2013-2014			
All (Foreign Included)	444	121	565
Foreign only	57	39	96

Total number of part-time students: 2
Last Update: 22-03-2018

Aomori University

2-3-1 Kobata
Aomori-shi 030-0943, Aomori
Tel: +81(17) 738-2001
Fax: +81(17) 738-0143
Website: http://www.aomori-u.ac.jp
President: Sakiya Yasufumi

Faculty

Business Administration (Accountancy; Business Administration; Information Management; Management; Sports Management); **Pharmaceutical Sciences** (Medicine; Pharmacy); **Software and Information Science** (Computer Engineering; Computer Graphics; Computer Networks; Information Sciences; Multimedia; Robotics; Software Engineering)

Department/Division

Regional Art (Business Administration; Child Care and Development; Cultural Studies; Health Sciences; History; Information Technology; Library Science; Nursing; Production Engineering; Secretarial Studies; Sports; Sports Management); **Sociology** (Social Welfare; Sociology)

Graduate School

Environmental Sciences (Environmental Studies)
Further information: Also Preparatory Japanese Language Course
History: Founded 1968.
Main language(s) of instruction: Japanese
Accrediting agency: Japan Institution for Higher Education Evaluation (JIHEE)
Degrees and diplomas: Gakushi (Computer Engineering; Information Sciences; Management; Pharmacy; Sociology), Shushi (Environmental Studies)
Student Services: Language Laboratory
Last Update: 22-03-2018

Aoyama Gakuin University (AGU)

4-4-25 Shibuya Shibuya-ku
Tokyo 150-8366
Tel: +81(3) 3409-8156
Fax: +81(3) 3409-7923
Website: http://www.aoyama.ac.jp/en
President: Yoshikazu Miki

College

Economics (Economic History; Economics; Environmental Studies; Industrial and Production Economics; International Economics); **Education, Psychology and Human Studies** (Clinical Psychology; Communication Studies; Development Studies; Developmental Psychology; Education; Educational Sciences; Media Studies; Primary Education; Psychology; Social Psychology; Sociology); **Literature** (American Studies; Archaeology; Art History; Asian Studies; Communication Studies; Cultural Studies; English; English Studies; Fine Arts; Foreign Languages Education; French; French Studies; History; Japanese; Linguistics; Literature; Music; Performing Arts; Visual Arts); **Science and Engineering** (Analytical Chemistry; Applied Physics; Biological and Life Sciences; Business Administration; Chemistry; Electrical and Electronic Engineering; Electronic Engineering; Engineering; Industrial Engineering; Information Technology; Inorganic Chemistry; Management; Mathematics; Mechanical

Engineering; Natural Sciences; Organic Chemistry; Physical Chemistry; Physics; Production Engineering; Safety Engineering; Software Engineering; Statistics)

School

Business (Accountancy; Business Administration; Marketing); **Cultural and Creative Studies** (Art Management; Cultural Studies; Social Sciences); **International Politics, Economics and Communication** (Communication Studies; Government; International Business; International Economics; International Relations; International Studies; Political Sciences; Regional Studies); **Law** (*Professional*) (Law); **Law** (Commercial Law; Criminal Law; European Union Law; Human Rights; International Law; Labour Law; Law); **Social Informatics** (Information Sciences; Information Technology; Mathematics; Social Sciences)

Graduate School

Business (Business Administration); **Cultural and Creative Studies** (Art Management; Cultural Studies; Fine Arts); **Economics** (Economics; International Economics); **Education, Psychology and Human Studies** (Education; Psychology); **International Management** (*Professional*) (Finance; International Business; Management; Marketing; Operations Research); **International Politics, Economics and Communication** (Communication Studies; Cultural Studies; International Economics; International Relations; Linguistics; Political Sciences); **Law** (Commercial Law; Law; Private Law); **Literature** (English; Fine Arts; French; History; Japanese; Literature; Modern Languages; Music; Performing Arts; Visual Arts); **Professional Accountancy** (Accountancy); **Science and Engineering** (Astrophysics; Biological and Life Sciences; Chemistry; Electrical and Electronic Engineering; Engineering; Engineering Management; Information Technology; Management; Materials Engineering; Mechanical Engineering; Natural Resources; Physics); **Social Informatics** (Economics; Information Technology; Psychology; Social Sciences)

Further information: Also campus in Sagamihara

History: Founded 1949. Originally a Girls' Elementary School founded 1874 merged with Kokyo Gakusha Boys' School and Methodist Mission Seminary both founded 1879. The Methodist Mission Seminary and Tokyo English School merged to become the Tokyo Anglo-Japanese College 1883. Later renamed Aoyama Gakuin, it merged with Aoyama Jogakuin 1927. Acquired present status 1949. Graduate School established 1952.

Academic year: April to March (April-July; September-February)

Admission requirements: Graduation from high school (Sotsugyo Shomeisho) or foreign equivalent, and entrance examination

Fees: For undergraduate study programmes, entrance fee, 200,000; tuition fee, 780,000-1,131,000 per annum; For graduate study programmes, entrance fee 290,000; tuition fee, 360,000-1,200,000 per annum (Yen)

Main language(s) of instruction: Japanese

Accrediting agency: Japan University Accreditation Association (JUAA)

Degrees and diplomas: Gakushi, Shushi, Hakase (American Studies; Art Management; Business Administration; Communication Studies; Comparative Literature; Economics; Education; Engineering; English; History; International Economics; International Relations; Japanese; Literature; Management; Natural Sciences; Performing Arts; Private Law; Psychology; Public Law; Visual Arts)

Student Services: Academic Counselling, Social Counselling, Careers Guidance, Sports Facilities, Language Laboratory, Facilities for disabled people, Health Services, Canteen, Foreign Studies Centre

Periodicals: Aoyama Business Journal, Journal of Business Administration, Journal of Culture and Creative Studies, Journal of Economics, Journal of General Education, Journal of History, Journal of International Politics, Economics and Business, Journal of Professional Accountancy, Journal of Social Informatics, Law Journal, Law School Journal, Thought Currents in English Literature

Student Numbers 2012-2013	MALE	FEMALE	TOTAL
All (Foreign Included)			19776
Foreign only			377

Last Update: 27-03-2018

Asahi University

1851 Hozumi, Hozumi-cho
Motosu-gun 501-0296, Gifu
Tel: +81(58) 329-1088
Fax: +81(58) 329-1089
Website: http://www.asahi-u.ac.jp
President: Katsuyuki Ohtomo

School

Business Administration (Business Administration; Information Management; Information Sciences); **Dentistry** (Dentistry); **Law** (Law)

Institute

Industry and Information; **Marketing** (Marketing)

Centre

Japanese Language and Culture (*Bekka*) (Asian Studies; Cultural Studies; Japanese); **Teaching Profession** (Teacher Training)

Graduate School

Business Administration (Business Administration); **Dentistry** (Dentistry); **Law** (Law)

Further information: Also Asahi University Hospital; Murakami Memorial Hospital

History: Founded 1971 as Gifu College of Dentistry. Acquired present status and title 1985.

Academic year: April to March (April-September; September-March)

Admission requirements: Graduation from high school or equivalent, and entrance examination

Main language(s) of instruction: Japanese

Accrediting agency: Japan Institution for Higher Education Evaluation (JIHEE)

Degrees and diplomas: Gakushi, Shushi, Hakase (Business Administration; Dentistry; Law)

Student Services: Academic Counselling, Social Counselling, Careers Guidance, Cultural Activities, Sports Facilities, Language Laboratory, Health Services, Canteen, Foreign Studies Centre

Periodicals: Asahi Business Review, Asahi Law Review, International Trade Law Studies, Journal of Gifu Dental Society

Academic Staff 2012-2013	MALE	FEMALE	TOTAL
FULL-TIME			253
Student Numbers 2012-2013			
All (Foreign Included)	1887	599	2486
Foreign only			159

Last Update: 22-03-2018

Asahikawa University

3-23-113 Nagayama
Asahikawa-shi 079-8501, Hokkaido
Tel: +81(166) 48-3121
Fax: +81(166) 48-8718
Website: http://www.asahikawa-u.ac.jp
President: Ryoji Yamauchi

Department/Division

Economics (Accountancy; Business and Commerce; Economics; Management); **Health and Welfare** (*Graduate*) (Health Sciences; Nursing; Psychiatry and Mental Health; Social and Community Services; Social Psychology; Social Work; Welfare and Protective Services)

Graduate School

Economics (Economics)
History: Founded 1968.
Academic year: April to March
Admission requirements: Graduation from high school or equivalent
Main language(s) of instruction: Japanese
Accrediting agency: Japan Institution for Higher Education Evaluation (JIHEE)

Degrees and diplomas: Gakushi (Economics; Welfare and Protective Services), Shushi (Economics)

Student Services: Academic Counselling, Social Counselling, Careers Guidance, Sports Facilities, Language Laboratory, Health Services, Canteen

Periodicals: The Annual Report of the Regional Research Institute, The Journal of Asahikawa University

Academic Staff 2012-2013	MALE	FEMALE	TOTAL
FULL-TIME			c. 30

Last Update: 22-03-2018

Ashikaga Institute of Technology

268-1 Omae
Ashikaga-shi 326-8558, Tochigi
Tel: +81(284) 62-0605
Fax: +81(284) 62-5009
Website: http://www.ashitech.ac.jp
President: Kazuo Shoji

Department/Division

Architecture and Civil Engineering (Architectural and Environmental Design; Architecture; Civil Engineering; Town Planning); **General Education** (English; Mathematics; Physics); **Information System Design** (Information Technology; Software Engineering); **Life Systemics** (Engineering; Medicine); **Mechanical and Electrical Engineering** (Electrical and Electronic Engineering; Electrical Engineering; Mechanical Engineering); **Renewable Energy and Environment** (Energy Engineering; Environmental Engineering)

Graduate School

Engineering (Architecture; Civil Engineering; Computer Engineering; Construction Engineering; Electrical and Electronic Engineering; Engineering; Environmental Engineering; Information Sciences; Information Technology; Mechanical Engineering; Production Engineering)
History: Founded 1967.
Main language(s) of instruction: Japanese
Accrediting agency: Japan Institution for Higher Education Evaluation (JIHEE)

Degrees and diplomas: Gakushi (Architecture; Electrical and Electronic Engineering; Information Technology; Mechanical Engineering), Shushi (Architectural and Environmental Design; Construction Engineering; Electrical Engineering; Engineering; Environmental Engineering; Mathematics), Hakase (Architectural and Environmental Design; Construction Engineering; Electronic Engineering; Energy Engineering; Environmental Engineering; Information Technology; Production Engineering)

Student Services: Sports Facilities

Academic Staff 2012-2013	MALE	FEMALE	TOTAL
FULL-TIME			94
Student Numbers 2012-2013			
All (Foreign Included)			c. 1268

Last Update: 22-03-2018

Ashiya University

13-22 Rokurokuso-cho
Ashiya-shi 659-8511, Hyogo
Tel: +81(797) 23-0661
Fax: +81(797) 23-1901
Website: http://www.ashiya-u.ac.jp
President: Satoru Higa

Faculty

Education (Child Care and Development; Educational Sciences; Preschool Education; Primary Education; Teacher Training); **Management Education** (Business Education; Management)

Graduate School

Graduate Studies (Continuing Education; Education; Foreign Languages Education; Special Education; Technology Education)

Campus

Osaka (Business Administration; Railway Transport; Sports Management; Transport and Communications)
History: Founded 1964 as private co-educational institution. Graduate studies established 1968.
Academic year: April to March (April-July; Octorber-March)
Admission requirements: Graduation from high school or equivalent, and entrance examination
Main language(s) of instruction: Japanese
Accrediting agency: Japan Institution for Higher Education Evaluation (JIHEE)
Degrees and diplomas: Gakushi (Business Administration; Education), Shushi (Education), Hakase (Education)
Student Services: Academic Counselling, Careers Guidance, Nursery Care, Sports Facilities, Health Services, Canteen
Periodicals: Ashiya Daigaku Ronso, The Report on the International Conference on Vocational Guidance
Publishing house: Ashiya University Press

Academic Staff 2012-2013	MALE	FEMALE	TOTAL
FULL-TIME	49	7	56

(continued)

Academic Staff 2012-2013	MALE	FEMALE	TOTAL
Student Numbers 2012-2013			
All (Foreign Included)			c. 700

Last Update: 27-03-2018

Asia University

5-24-10 Sakai
Musashino-shi 180-8629, Tokyo
Tel: +81(422) 36-3255
Fax: +81(422) 36-4869
Website: http://www.asia-u.ac.jp/english
President: Kurita Michiharu

Faculty

Business Administration (Accountancy; Business Administration; Chinese; English; Hotel and Restaurant; Marketing); **Economics** (Economics); **International Relations** (African Studies; Arabic; Asian Studies; Chinese; Cultural Studies; English; Hindi; Indonesian; International Relations; International Studies; Korean; Latin American Studies; Religion; Spanish; Tourism); **Law** (Law)

Course/Programme

Asia University America (*Study abroad programme in the USA*); **Asia University Exchange** (*Student exchanges or student dispatches with partner universities in Asia and North America*); **Asia University Global** (*Undergraduate and junior college level study abroad programme*); **Career Development China** (*Professionally oriented overseas programme with partner university in China*); **Intensive Japanese** (*Japanese*)

Institute

Asian Studies (Asian Studies)

Centre

English Language Education (*CELE*) (English)

Graduate School

Asian and International Business Strategy (Business Administration; International Business); **Business Administration** (Business Administration); **Economics** (Economics); **Law** (Law)
Further information: Also Hinode Campus
History: Founded 1941 as Koa Senmon Gakko-Koa Professional School. Transformed into Nihon Keizai Senmon Gakko-Professional School of Japanese Economics 1945. Reorganized again as Nihon Junior College of Economics 1950. Acquired present status and title 1955.

Academic year: April to March (April-September; October-March)

Admission requirements: Graduation from high school or equivalent; Entrance examination

Main language(s) of instruction: Japanese

Accrediting agency: Japan University Accreditation Association (JUAA)

Degrees and diplomas: Gakushi (Economics; International Relations; Law; Management; Sociology), Shushi (Economics; International Business; Law; Management), Hakase (Business Administration; Economics; International Business; Law)

Student Services: Sports Facilities, Language Laboratory, Canteen

Periodicals: The Annals of Institute of Asian Studies

Academic Staff 2012-2013	MALE	FEMALE	TOTAL
FULL-TIME	143	28	171
Student Numbers 2012-2013			
All (Foreign Included)			c. 6800
Foreign only	189	243	432

Last Update: 22-03-2018

Atomi University

1-9-6 Nakaro
Niiza-shi 352-8501, Saitama
Tel: +81(48) 478-3333
Fax: +81(48) 478-3339
Website: http://www.atomi.ac.jp/univ/index.html
President: Tetsuo Yamada

Faculty

Management (Environmental Management; Management; Tourism)

Department/Division

Literature (Arts and Humanities; Clinical Psychology; Communication Studies; Cultural Studies; Literature; Psychology)

Graduate School

Humanities (Arts and Humanities; Asian Studies; Clinical Psychology; Cultural Studies; Japanese); **Management** (Management)

Further information: Also Bunkyo Campus

History: Founded 1965.

Admission requirements: Entrance examination

Main language(s) of instruction: Japanese

Accrediting agency: Japan University Accreditation Association (JUAA)

Degrees and diplomas: Gakushi (Communication Studies; Cultural Studies; Home Economics; Literature; Management; Sociology), Shushi (Clinical Psychology; Cultural Studies; Management)

Student Services: Health Services, Canteen

Academic Staff 2012-2013	MALE	FEMALE	TOTAL
FULL-TIME			115
Student Numbers 2012-2013			
All (Foreign Included)			4078

Last Update: 22-03-2018

Azabu University

Chuo Fuchinobe 1-17-71
Sagamihara-shi 252-5201, Kanagawa
Tel: +81(42) 754-7111
Fax: +81(42) 754-7661
Website: http://www.azabu-u.ac.jp
President: Masao Asari

College

Environmental Health (Environmental Management; Environmental Studies)

School

Life and Environmental Sciences (Biological and Life Sciences; Environmental Management; Environmental Studies); **Veterinary Medicine** (*Also Graduate School*) (Animal Husbandry; Applied Chemistry; Veterinary Science; Zoology)

Laboratory

Companion Dog (Animal Husbandry)

Graduate School

Environmental Health (Environmental Studies; Health Sciences)

Research Division

Biological Sciences (Biological and Life Sciences)

Further information: Also Veterinary Teaching Hospital

History: Founded 1894 as Azabu Veterinary School. Changed name to Linen Veterinary Animal Husbandry School 1912, to Azabu Veterinary College 1934. Became College 1950. Acquired present title 1980.

Academic year: April to March (April-October; October-March)

Admission requirements: Graduation from high school or equivalent, and entrance examination

Main language(s) of instruction: Japanese, English

Accrediting agency: Japan University Accreditation Association (JUAA)

Degrees and diplomas: Gakushi, Shushi (Biotechnology; Environmental Studies; Health Sciences; Veterinary Science), Hakase (Environmental Studies; Health Sciences; Veterinary Science). Also Eiseikensagishi, Certificate in Public Hygiene, 2 yrs

Periodicals: Bulletin

Last Update: 25-05-2018

Baika Women's University

2-19-5 Shukunosho
Ibaraki-shi 567-8578, Osaka
Tel: +81(72) 643-6221
Fax: +81(726) 43-6137
Website: http://www.baika.ac.jp
President: Nagasawa Shuichi

Faculty

Contemporary Human Studies (Environmental Studies; Psychology; Social Welfare; Welfare and Protective Services); **Cultural and Expression Studies** (Asian Studies; Cultural Studies; English; Information Sciences; Japanese; Media Studies); **Nursing** (Nursing); **Psychology and Children's Studies** (Child Care and Development; Preschool Education; Psychology)

College

Baika Junior (Cooking and Catering; Design; English; Fine Arts; Handicrafts; Japanese)

Graduate School

Graduate Studies (Arts and Humanities; Clinical Psychology; English; Japanese; Literature; Welfare and Protective Services)

History: Founded 1878 as School, acquired present status and title 1964. A private Christian Liberal Arts College for Women.

Academic year: April to March (April-September; October-March)

Admission requirements: Graduation from high school and entrance examination

Main language(s) of instruction: Japanese, English

Accrediting agency: Japanese University Accreditation Association (JUAA)

Degrees and diplomas: Gakushi (Cultural Studies; English; Home Economics; Performing Arts; Psychology; Visual Arts), Shushi (Clinical Psychology; English; English Studies; Health Sciences; Japanese; Literature; Psychology), Hakase (Literature)

Student Services: Academic Counselling, Social Counselling, Careers Guidance, Sports Facilities, Language Laboratory, Facilities for disabled people, Health Services, Canteen, Foreign Studies Centre

Periodicals: Kami-Hikoki, Puck, Baika Review

Last Update: 26-03-2018

Baiko Gakuin University (BGU)

1-1-1 Kouyoucho
Shimonoseki-shi 750-8511, Yamaguchi
Tel: +81(83) 227-1000
Fax: +81(832) 27-1120
Website: http://www.baiko.ac.jp
President: Noriko Higuchi

Faculty

Literature (Asian Studies; Cultural Studies; Japanese; Literature; Writing)

Course/Programme

Liberal Arts Education (Arts and Humanities; Christian Religious Studies; Education; English; Environmental Studies; German; History; Information Sciences; Modern Languages; Natural Sciences; Philosophy)

Department/Division

Children Education (Child Care and Development; Education; Preschool Education; Teacher Training); **International Languages and Cultures** (Chinese; English; Japanese; Korean; Modern Languages)

Graduate School

Letters (Arts and Humanities; English; Japanese; Literature)

History: Founded in 1872 as a Christian School for Women by American missionaries. Co-educational from 2001.

Academic year: April to March (April-July; September-March)

Admission requirements: Graduation from high school

Fees: Admission fee, 150,000; Tuition, 848,000 per annum (Yen)

Main language(s) of instruction: Japanese

Accrediting agency: Japan Institution for Higher Education Evaluation (JIHEE)

Degrees and diplomas: Gakushi, Shushi (Literature), Hakase (American Studies; English; Japanese; Literature)

Student Services: Academic Counselling, Social Counselling, Careers Guidance, Cultural Activities, Sports Facilities, Language Laboratory, Facilities for disabled people, Health Services, Canteen, Foreign Studies Centre

Periodicals: Journal, Studies in English Literature, Studies in Japanese Literature, Studies in Modern Communication

Last Update: 26-03-2018

Beppu University

82 Kitaishigaki
Beppu-shi 874-8501, Oita
Tel: +81(977) 67-0101
Fax: +81(977) 66-9696
Website: http://www.beppu-u.ac.jp
President: Hidaka Koichiro

College
International Management (Accountancy; Information Technology; International Business; Management; Taxation; Tourism)

Course/Programme
Bekka Japanese (Japanese); **Professional Studies** (Library Science; Teacher Training)

School
Food Science (Food Science; Nutrition)

Department/Division
Literature (Archaeology; Arts and Humanities; Cultural Studies; Design; English; Heritage Preservation; History; Japanese; Literature; Modern Languages; Painting and Drawing; Physical Education; Psychology; Sociology)

Graduate School
Graduate Studies (Clinical Psychology; Cultural Studies; Food Science; History; Japanese; Literature; Nutrition)
History: Founded 1950.
Main language(s) of instruction: English
Accrediting agency: Japan Institution for Higher Education Evaluation (JIHEE)
Degrees and diplomas: Gakushi (Cultural Studies; Geography (Human); History; Literature; Management; Social Welfare), Shushi (Geography (Human); Literature; Psychology), Hakase (Cultural Studies; History)
Student Services: Sports Facilities, Language Laboratory

Academic Staff 2013-2014	MALE	FEMALE	TOTAL
FULL-TIME			255
Student Numbers 2013-2014			
All (Foreign Included)			4540

Last Update: 26-03-2018

Biwako Gakuin University (BGU)

29 Fuse-cho
Higashiomi 527-8533, Shiga
Tel: +81(748) 22-3388
Website: http://www.newton.ac.jp/bgu
Kagawa Masaaki

Department/Division
Education and Child Welfare (Child Care and Development; Education; Physical Education; Preschool Education; Psychology; Special Education; Sports; Welfare and Protective Services)
History: Founded as Shiga Gakuen School 1997. Acquired present status and title 2009.
Main language(s) of instruction: Japanese
Accrediting agency: Japan Institution for Higher Education Evaluation (JIHEE)
Degrees and diplomas: Gakushi (Education)
Student Services: Sports Facilities, Canteen

Academic Staff 2012-2013	MALE	FEMALE	TOTAL
FULL-TIME			18
Student Numbers 2012-2013			
All (Foreign Included)			91

Last Update: 26-03-2018

Biwako Seikei Sport College (BSS)

1204 Bidokoro Kitahira Shiga-cho
Shiga-gun 520-0503, Shiga
Tel: +81(77) 596-8410
Fax: +81(77) 596-8419
Website: http://www.bss.ac.jp

Department/Division
Sports Studies (Nutrition; Physical Education; Rehabilitation and Therapy; Sports; Sports Management; Sports Medicine)

Graduate School
Sports Studies (Sports)
Main language(s) of instruction: Japanese
Accrediting agency: Japan Institution for Higher Education Evaluation (JIHEE)
Degrees and diplomas: Gakushi, Shushi (Sports)
Student Services: Academic Counselling, Sports Facilities, Health Services

Academic Staff 2012-2013	MALE	FEMALE	TOTAL
FULL-TIME	38	10	48

Last Update: 26-03-2018

Bukkyo University

96 Kitahananobo-cho Murasakino, Kita-ku
Kyoto-shi 603-8301, Kyoto
Tel: +81(75) 491-2141

Fax: +81(75) 495-5724
Website: http://www.bukkyo-u.ac.jp
President: Norihiko Tanaka

Course/Programme
Jodo Priesthood (Asian Religious Studies)

School
Buddhism (Asian Religious Studies; Asian Studies); **Education** (Clinical Psychology; Education); **Health Sciences** (Health Sciences; Nursing; Occupational Therapy; Physical Therapy); **History** (Anthropology; Archaeology; Asian Studies; Cultural Studies; Folklore; Geography; History); **Literature** (Chinese; English; Japanese; Literature); **Social Welfare** (Child Care and Development); **Sociology** (Cultural Studies; Environmental Studies; Information Sciences; International Relations; International Studies; Media Studies; Sociology)

Graduate School
Education (Clinical Psychology; Education); **Literature** (Asian Studies; Chinese; English; History; Japanese; Literature; Oriental Studies); **Social Welfare** (Social Welfare); **Sociology** (Sociology)
Further information: Also Japanese language courses for foreign students. Correspondence courses; Bukkyo University Los Angeles Extension. A traditional and distance learning institution.
History: Founded 1887 as Jodo-shugaku Honko, became Special School of Buddhism (Bukkyo Senmon Gakko) 1913. Established as a university 1949.
Academic year: April to March (April-September; October-March)
Admission requirements: Graduation from high school or equivalent
Main language(s) of instruction: Japanese
Accrediting agency: Japan University Accreditation Association (JUAA)
Degrees and diplomas: Gakushi (Education; Geography; History; Literature; Philosophy; Psychology; Social Welfare; Sociology), Shushi (Education; Geography; History; Literature; Philosophy; Psychology; Social Welfare; Sociology), Hakase (Education; Geography; History; Literature; Social Welfare; Sociology)
Student Services: Social Counselling, Sports Facilities, Language Laboratory, Health Services
Periodicals: Journal of Letters, Journal of Sociology, Memoirs of the Postgraduate Research Institution, The Bukkyo Daigaku Kenkyukiyo (Journal)

Academic Staff 2012-2013	MALE	FEMALE	TOTAL
FULL-TIME	172	62	234
Student Numbers 2012-2013			
All (Foreign Included)	3724	3228	6952
Foreign only	22	46	68

Total number of distance students: 13325
Last Update: 26-03-2018

Bunka Fashion Graduate University (BFGU)

3-22-1 Yoyogi
Shibuya-ku 151-8521, Tokyo
Tel: +81(3) 3299-2701
Fax: +81(3) 3299-2714
Website: http://www.bfgu-bunka.ac.jp
President: Sunao Onuma

Department/Division
Fashion Creation (Fashion Design; Textile Design; Textile Technology); **Fashion Management** (Business Administration; Management)
History: Founded 2006.
Academic year: April to February
Admission requirements: Entrance examination
Fees: Admission fee, 300,000; Tuition fee, 375,000 per annum (Yen)
Main language(s) of instruction: Japanese
Accrediting agency: Japan Institution for Higher Education Evaluation (JIHEE)
Degrees and diplomas: Shushi (Business Administration; Fashion Design)
Last Update: 24-05-2018

Bunka Gakuen University (BWU)

3-22-1 3-22-1 Yoyogi Shibuya-ku
Tokyo 151-8523, Kanto
Tel: +81(3) 3299-2310
Fax: +81(3) 3299-2637
Website: http://bwu.bunka.ac.jp
President: Katsuhiro Hamada

Faculty
Art and Design (Architectural and Environmental Design; Design; Fine Arts; Graphic Design; Interior Design; Jewellery Art; Media Studies; Textile Design); **Fashion Science** (Advertising and Publicity; Art History; Business Administration; Clothing and Sewing; Cultural Studies; Design; Fashion Design; Management; Production Engineering;

Sociology; Textile Design; Textile Technology); **Liberal Arts and Sciences** (Arts and Humanities; Cultural Studies; English; Fashion Design; Film; International Studies; Journalism; Natural Sciences; Psychology; Public Relations; Tourism)

College
Junior Studies (Business Administration; Clothing and Sewing; Design; Fashion Design; Graphic Design; Interior Design; Management)

Graduate School
Fashion and Living Environment Studies (Business Administration; Clothing and Sewing; Design; Fashion Design; Management; Sociology); **Humanities and Intercultural Studies** (Arts and Humanities; Cultural Studies; Fashion Design; International Studies; Psychology)
Further information: Also Kodaira Campus; Japanese courses are offered to international students
History: Founded as Bunka Women's Junior College 1950. Acquired present title 2012. Formerly known as Bunka Joshi Daigaku (Bunka Women's University).
Academic year: April to March (April-October; October-March)
Admission requirements: Graduation from high school or equivalent, and entrance examination
Main language(s) of instruction: Japanese
Accrediting agency: Japan Institution for Higher Education Evaluation (JIHEE)
Degrees and diplomas: Gakushi (Clothing and Sewing; Fine Arts; Home Economics; International Relations; International Studies; Performing Arts; Psychology; Sociology; Tourism), Shushi (Arts and Humanities; Clothing and Sewing; International Studies), Hakase (Arts and Humanities; Clothing and Sewing; Cultural Studies; Environmental Studies)
Last Update: 26-03-2018

Bunkyo Gakuin University

1-19-1 Mukogaoka
Bunkyo-ku 113-8668, Tokyo
Tel: +81(3) 3814-1661
Fax: +81(3) 5684-4836
Website: http://www.u-bunkyo.ac.jp
President: Hideki Kudo

Faculty
Business Administration (Accountancy; Business Administration; Communication Studies; Finance; Management; Marketing; Visual Arts); **Foreign Studies** (Cultural Studies; English; International Business; International Studies;

Modern Languages); **Health Science Technology** (*Fujimino Campus*) (Health Sciences; Laboratory Techniques; Medical Technology; Occupational Therapy; Physical Therapy); **Human Studies** (*Fujimino Campus*) (Child Care and Development; Communication Studies; Psychology; Social Welfare; Social Work; Sociology)

Graduate School
Business Administration (Business Administration; Health Administration; Marketing; Taxation); **Foreign Studies** (American Studies; Communication Studies; English; English Studies; Foreign Languages Education; International Studies; Linguistics); **Health Care Science** (Health Sciences; Laboratory Techniques; Occupational Therapy; Physical Therapy); **Human Studies** (*Fujimino Campus*) (Child Care and Development; Clinical Psychology; Education; Psychology; Social Work)
Further information: Also Fujimino Campus
History: Founded Bunkyo Women's College. Upgraded into Bunkyo Women's University 1991. Acquired present title 2002.
Main language(s) of instruction: Japanese
Accrediting agency: Japan University Accreditation Association (JUAA)
Degrees and diplomas: Gakushi (Arts and Humanities; Business Administration; International Studies; Management; Medical Technology; Modern Languages), Shushi (Business Administration; Clinical Psychology; Education; Medical Technology; Psychology; Social Work)
Student Services: Academic Counselling, Health Services

Student Numbers 2012-2013	MALE	FEMALE	TOTAL
All (Foreign Included)			c. 4000

Last Update: 26-03-2018

Bunkyo University

3-2-17 Hatanodai Shinagawa-ku
Tokyo 142-0064
Tel: +81(3) 3783-5511
Fax: +81(3) 3783-8300
Website: http://www.bunkyo.ac.jp
President: Kenji Kondo

Faculty
Education (Chemistry; Education; Educational Psychology; Primary Education; Secondary Education; Special Education; Teacher Training); **Health and Nutrition** (Dietetics; Health Sciences; Nutrition); **Human Sciences** (Anthropology; Continuing Education; Psychology; Social Welfare; Sociology); **Information and Communications** (Business

Administration; Communication Studies; Computer Science; Information Management; Information Sciences; Information Technology; Media Studies; Multimedia; Software Engineering); **International Studies** (Cultural Studies; Food Technology; Hotel and Restaurant; International Studies; Leisure Studies; Tourism); **Language and Literature** (Cultural Studies; English; Japanese; Literature; Modern Languages)

Course/Programme
Advanced Education Specialist (*Special Postgraduate Course*) (Educational Administration; Leadership; Primary Education; Teacher Training)

Department/Division
Foreign Student (Asian Studies; Japanese)

Graduate School
Education (Education; Educational Psychology; Teacher Training); **Human Sciences** (Arts and Humanities); **Information and Communications** (Communication Studies; Information Management; Information Sciences; Information Technology); **International Cooperation** (Development Studies; International Business; International Relations; International Studies; Peace and Disarmament; Tourism); **Language and Culture** (Chinese; Cultural Studies; English; Japanese; Modern Languages)

Research Division
Clinical Counseling (*Graduate School affiliated*) (Clinical Psychology); **Education** (*University affiliated*) (Education); **Language and Culture** (*Graduate School affiliated*) (Cultural Studies; Modern Languages); **Living Science** (*University affiliated*); **Shonan** (*University affiliated*)
Further information: Also Koshigaya and Shonan Campuses.
History: Founded as open Rissho kindergarten and Rissho Women's School for Needlework 1927. Founded as Rissho Women's University 1966. Acquired present title 1976.
Academic year: April to March
Admission requirements: Graduation from high school
Main language(s) of instruction: Japanese
Accrediting agency: Japan University Accreditation Association (JUAA)
Degrees and diplomas: Gakushi (Arts and Humanities; Business Administration; Cultural Studies; Dietetics; Education; Modern Languages; Social Sciences), Shushi (Arts and Humanities; Clinical Psychology; Cultural Studies; Dietetics; Education; Information Sciences; Modern Languages; Social Sciences; Sociology; Tourism), Hakase (Arts and Humanities; Cultural Studies; Modern Languages)
Student Services: Academic Counselling, Social Counselling, Careers Guidance, Cultural Activities, Sports Facilities,

Language Laboratory, Facilities for disabled people, Health Services, Canteen, Foreign Studies Centre
Periodicals: Bulletin of Institute of Educational Research, and others

Academic Staff 2012-2013	MALE	FEMALE	TOTAL
FULL-TIME			240
Student Numbers 2012-2013			
All (Foreign Included)			8727
Foreign only			124

Last Update: 26-03-2018

Bunri University of Hospitality

311-1 Kashiwabara-Shinden Sayama-shi
Saitama-shi 350-1336, Saitama
Tel: +87(42) 954-7575
Fax: +87(42) 954-7511
Website: http://www.bunri-c.ac.jp/univ
President: Koen Tokuda

Faculty
Business Administration (Business Administration)

School
Nursing (Nursing)

Department/Division
Health and Welfare Management (Health Sciences; Psychology; Social Welfare)
History: Founded 1999.
Main language(s) of instruction: Japanese
Accrediting agency: Japan Institution for Higher Education Evaluation (JIHEE)
Degrees and diplomas: Gakushi (Business Administration; Management; Psychology; Social Welfare; Tourism)
Student Services: Careers Guidance, Library, Residential Facilities
Last Update: 26-03-2018

Bunsei University of Art

4-8-15 Kamitomatsuri
Utsunomiya-shi 320-0058, Tochgi
Tel: +81(28) 625-6888
Fax: +81(28) 625-6822
Website: http://www.bunsei.ac.jp
President: Kenji Ueno

Faculty
Fine Arts (Art History; Design; Fine Arts; Handicrafts; Painting and Drawing; Sculpture; Visual Arts)

Graduate School

Arts (Art History; Ceramic Art; Design; Fine Arts; Painting and Drawing; Sculpture; Textile Design; Video)
Further information: Also 2 campuses
History: Founded 1989 as Utsunomiya Bunsei College. Acquired present status ans title 1996..
Main language(s) of instruction: Japanese
Accrediting agency: Japan University Accreditation Association (JUAA)
Degrees and diplomas: Gakushi, Shushi, Hakase (Fine Arts)
Student Services: Health Services
Last Update: 26-03-2018

Butsuryo College of Osaka

3-33 Otorikita-cho Nishi-ku
Sakai 593-8328, Osaka
Tel: +81(72) 260-0095
Fax: +81(72) 260-0011
Website: http://www.butsuryo.ac.jp
President: Hiroshi Tanaka

Faculty

Health and Medical Sciences (Health Sciences; Medical Technology)
History: Founded 1933 as Butsuryo School. Renamed Osaka Butsuryo school 1934. Acquired present status and title 2011.
Fees: Entrance fee, 300,000; Tuition fee, 790,000 per annum (Yen)
Main language(s) of instruction: Japanese
Accrediting agency: Ministry of Education, Culture, Sports, Science and Technology (MEXT)
Degrees and diplomas: Gakushi

Academic Staff 2012-2013	MALE	FEMALE	TOTAL
FULL-TIME			21

Last Update: 26-03-2018

Chiba Institute of Science (CIS)

3 Shimicho
Choshi-shi 288-0025, Chiba
Tel: +81(479) 30-4649
Fax: +81(479) 30-4546
Website: http://www.cis.ac.jp
President: Isao Kiso

Faculty

Crisis Management (Environmental Engineering; Environmental Management; Insurance; Management); **Pharmacy** (Biological and Life Sciences; Medicine; Pharmacy)

Course/Programme

Bekka (Japanese)

Graduate School

Crisis Management Studies (Management; Medical Technology; Safety Engineering); **Pharmaceutical Sciences** (Pharmacology; Pharmacy)
History: Founded 2004.
Main language(s) of instruction: Japanese
Accrediting agency: Japan University Accreditation Association (JUAA)
Degrees and diplomas: Gakushi (Environmental Management; Management; Nursing; Pharmacology; Pharmacy), Shushi (Environmental Management; Management; Pharmacology; Pharmacy), Hakase (Environmental Management; Management; Pharmacology; Pharmacy)
Student Services: Health Services

Academic Staff 2013-2014	MALE	FEMALE	TOTAL
FULL-TIME			c. 100
Student Numbers 2013-2014			
All (Foreign Included)			1738

Last Update: 26-03-2018

Chiba Institute of Technology (CIT)

2-17-1 Tsudanuma
Narashino-shi 275-0016, Chiba
Tel: +81(47) 478-0245
Fax: +81(47) 478-3344
Website: http://www.it-chiba.ac.jp
President: Kazuhito Komiya

Faculty

Engineering (Architecture; Biological and Life Sciences; Civil Engineering; Computer Engineering; Design; Electrical and Electronic Engineering; Electrical Engineering; Electronic Engineering; Engineering; Environmental Studies; Mechanical Engineering; Robotics); **Information and Computer Science** (Computer Networks; Computer Science; Information Sciences; Information Technology; Mechanical Engineering; Telecommunications Engineering); **Social Systems Science** (Environmental Management; Finance; Food Technology; Information Management; Information Sciences; Information Technology; Insurance; Management; Mathematics and Computer Science)

Course/Programme

General Education (Chemistry; English; Mathematics; Physics)

Graduate School

Engineering (Architecture; Biological and Life Sciences; Civil Engineering; Computer Engineering; Design; Electrical Engineering; Electronic Engineering; Engineering; Environmental Studies; Mechanical Engineering; Robotics); **Information and Computer Science** (Artificial Intelligence; Cognitive Sciences; Computer Engineering; Computer Networks; Computer Science; Data Processing; Information Sciences; Information Technology; Robotics; Software Engineering; Sound Engineering (Acoustics); Telecommunications Engineering); **Social Systems Science** (Industrial Management; Information Management; Management)

Further information: Also Shin-Narashino campus

History: Founded 1942 in Machida City, Tokyo, as Koa Engineering College. Moved to Kimitsu-machi, Chiba, 1946, and to Narashino-shi, Chiba 1950, and reorganized as Chiba Institute of Technology.

Academic year: April to February (April-July; September-February)

Admission requirements: Graduation from high school or equivalent, and entrance examination

Main language(s) of instruction: Japanese, English

Accrediting agency: Japan Institution for Higher Education Evaluation (JIHEE)

Degrees and diplomas: Gakushi (Computer Science; Engineering; Finance; Information Technology; Management), Shushi (Architecture; Civil Engineering; Computer Engineering; Computer Science; Design; Electrical and Electronic Engineering; Environmental Studies; Information Technology; Management; Mechanical Engineering; Robotics), Hakase (Engineering; Management)

Student Services: Academic Counselling, Careers Guidance, Nursery Care, Sports Facilities, Canteen

Periodicals: Chiba Kogyo Daigaku Kenkyu Houkoku (Research Reports)

Academic Staff 2012-2013	MALE	FEMALE	TOTAL
FULL-TIME			551
Student Numbers 2012-2013			
All (Foreign Included)			9853

Last Update: 26-03-2018

Chiba Keizai University (CKU)

3-59-5 Todoroki-cho Inage-ku
Chiba-shi 263-0021, Chiba
Tel: +81(43) 253-9111
Fax: +81(43) 254-6600
Website: http://www.cku.ac.jp
President: Katsuhiko Sakuma

Department/Division

Business Administration (Accountancy; Business Administration; Economics; Human Resources; Industrial Management; Management; Marketing; Small Business; Taxation); **Economics** (Economic History; Economics; International Economics; Statistics)

Graduate School

Economics (Accountancy; Economic and Finance Policy; Economics; Management; Social Welfare; Taxation)

History: Founded 1988.

Academic year: April to January

Main language(s) of instruction: Japanese

Accrediting agency: Japan Institution for Higher Education Evaluation (JIHEE)

Degrees and diplomas: Gakushi, Shushi

Student Services: Sports Facilities

Last Update: 26-03-2018

Chiba University of Commerce

1-3-1 Konodai
Ichikawa-shi 272-8512, Chiba
Tel: +81(47) 372-4111
Fax: +81(47) 375-1101
Website: http://www.cuc.ac.jp
President: Sachihiko Harashina

Faculty

Commerce and Economics (Accountancy; Business and Commerce; Economics; Industrial and Production Economics; Information Sciences; Law; Management; Modern Languages); **Policy Informatics** (Arts and Humanities; Computer Science; Cultural Studies; Environmental Studies; Information Technology; Media Studies; Political Sciences); **Service Innovation** (Accountancy; Constitutional Law; Economics; Finance; Information Sciences; Marketing; Psychiatry and Mental Health; Service Trades)

Institute

Economics Research (Economics)

Graduate School

Commerce (Business and Commerce); **Economics** (Economics); **Policy Informatics** (Computer Science); **Policy Studies** (Social Policy); **Service Innovation** (Service Trades)

History: Founded 1928 as Sugamo Higher School of Commerce, became Sugamo College of Economics 1944. Acquired present title 1950.

Academic year: April to March (April-September; October-March)

Admission requirements: Graduation from high school or equivalent or foreign equivalent, and entrance examination
Main language(s) of instruction: Japanese
Accrediting agency: Ministry of Education, Culture, Sports, Science and Technology (MEXT)
Degrees and diplomas: Gakushi (Arts and Humanities; Business Administration; Social Sciences), Shushi (Business and Commerce; Economic and Finance Policy; Economics), Hakase (Economic and Finance Policy). Also MBA Programme
Student Services: Academic Counselling, Nursery Care, Sports Facilities, Facilities for disabled people, Health Services, Canteen
Periodicals: Konodai Bulletin of Economic Studies, The Journal of Chiba University of Commerce, The Review of Chiba University of Commerce
Last Update: 26-03-2018

Chikushi Jogakuen University

2-12-1 Ishizaka
Dazaifu-shi 818-0192, Fukuoka
Tel: +81(92) 925-3511
Fax: +81(92) 925-3573
Website: http://www.chikushi.ac.jp
President: Tsukushi Jogakuen

Faculty
Arts and Humanities (Arts and Humanities; Asian Studies; Clinical Psychology; Developmental Psychology; English; Japanese; Literature; Media Studies; Welfare and Protective Services)

Graduate School
Humanities (Arts and Humanities; Asian Religious Studies; Modern Languages)
History: Founded 1988.
Main language(s) of instruction: Japanese
Accrediting agency: Ministry of Education, Culture, Sports, Science and Technology (MEXT)
Degrees and diplomas: Gakushi (Business Administration; Cultural Studies; Education; Modern Languages; Psychology; Sociology), Shushi (Arts and Humanities)

Academic Staff 2012-2013	MALE	FEMALE	TOTAL
FULL-TIME			454
Student Numbers 2012-2013			
All (Foreign Included)			2620

Last Update: 26-03-2018

Chitose Institute of Science and Technology (CIST)

758-65 Bibi
Chitose 066-8655, Hokkaido
Tel: +81(123) 27-6001
Fax: +81(123) 27-6007
Website: http://www.chitose.ac.jp
President: Masaaki Kawase
Tel: +81(123) 27-6049

Faculty
Photonics Science (Applied Physics; Biology; Chemistry; Computer Science; Design; Electronic Engineering; Engineering; English; Information Sciences; Information Technology; Laser Engineering; Materials Engineering; Mathematics; Natural Sciences; Optical Technology; Physics; Solid State Physics; Technology)

Graduate School
Photonics Science (Electronic Engineering; Information Technology; Optical Technology; Robotics; Telecommunications Engineering)
History: Founded 1998.
Main language(s) of instruction: Japanese
Accrediting agency: Ministry of Education, Culture, Sports, Science and Technology (MEXT)
Degrees and diplomas: Gakushi (Applied Physics; Biotechnology; Chemistry; Computer Science; Electrical and Electronic Engineering; Engineering; Information Technology; Medical Technology), Shushi (Applied Physics; Biotechnology; Chemistry; Computer Science; Electrical and Electronic Engineering; Engineering; Information Technology; Medical Technology), Hakase (Engineering; Physics)
Student Services: Academic Counselling, Social Counselling, Careers Guidance, Sports Facilities, Health Services, Canteen
Last Update: 26-03-2018

Chubu Gakuin University

4909-3 Kurachi
Seki-shi 501-3993, Gifu
Tel: +81(575) 24-2211
Fax: +81(575) 24-0077
Website: http://www.chubu-gu.ac.jp
President: Furuta Yoshinori

Faculty
Business Administration (Accountancy; Business Administration); **Rehabilitation** (Physical Therapy; Rehabilitation and Therapy)

Course/Programme
Bekka (Japanese)

Department/Division
Child Care and Development (Child Care and Development; Educational and Student Counselling; Educational Psychology; Preschool Education; Primary Education; Special Education); **Human Welfare** (Art Therapy; Management; Psychology; Social Work; Sports; Welfare and Protective Services)

Graduate School
Human Welfare Studies (Social Welfare; Welfare and Protective Services)
Further information: Also Kakamigahara campus
History: Founded 1997.
Main language(s) of instruction: Japanese
Accrediting agency: Ministry of Education, Culture, Sports, Science and Technology (MEXT)
Degrees and diplomas: Gakushi (Social Welfare), Shushi (Social Welfare), Hakase (Social Welfare)
Student Services: Academic Counselling, Health Services

Academic Staff 2013-2014	MALE	FEMALE	TOTAL
FULL-TIME			94
Student Numbers 2013-2014			
All (Foreign Included)			1406

Last Update: 26-03-2018

Chubu University

1200 Matsumoto-cho
Kasugai-shi 487-8501, Aichi
Tel: +81(568) 51-1111
Fax: +81(568) 51-1141
Website: http://www.chubu.ac.jp
President: Ishihara Osamu

College
Bioscience and Biotechnology (Biochemistry; Biology; Biotechnology; Environmental Studies; Food Science; Nutrition); **Business Administration and Information Sciences** (Accountancy; Business Administration; Information Sciences; Management); **Contemporary Education** (Child Care and Development; Education; Preschool Education); **Engineering** (Applied Chemistry; Architecture; Civil Engineering; Computer Science; Electrical Engineering; Electronic Engineering; Engineering; Information Technology; Mechanical Engineering); **Humanities** (Asian Studies; Communication Studies; English; English Studies; Geography (Human); History; Japanese; Psychology); **International Studies** (Asian Studies; Cultural Studies; International Relations; International Studies); **Life and Health Sciences** (Biological and Life Sciences; Biomedicine; Engineering; Health Sciences; Medicine; Occupational Therapy; Physical Therapy; Sports)

Centre
Information Systems (Information Sciences; Information Technology); **International Programmes**; **Japanese Studies at Chubu University** (Japanese); **Language** (Linguistics; Modern Languages); **Media Education** (Cinema and Television; Media Studies); **Medical Technology Education and Training** (Medical Technology); **Nursing Practicum** (Nursing); **Physical Education and Cultural Activities** (Physical Education; Sports); **Practice for Registered Dietitian** (Dietetics); **Practice of Medical Techniques** (Medical Technology); **Research Collaboration Support**; **Support for Teacher Education** (Teacher Training); **Teaching Practicum** (Teacher Training); **VMS** (*Japanese*)

Graduate School
Bioscience and Biotechnology (*Master's and Doctoral courses*) (Biological and Life Sciences; Biotechnology); **Business Administration and Information Sciences** (*Master's and Doctoral courses*) (Business Administration; Information Sciences; Management); **Education** (Education); **Engineering** (*Master's and Doctoral courses*) (Applied Chemistry; Computer Science; Construction Engineering; Electrical Engineering; Electronic Engineering; Engineering; Mechanical Engineering); **Global Humanics** (*Master's and Doctoral courses*) (Asian Studies; Cultural Studies; English; Geography (Human); History; International Relations; Japanese; Modern Languages; Psychology); **Life and Health Sciences** (Biological and Life Sciences; Biomedicine; Health Sciences; Nursing)

Research Division
Advanced Studies (*Chubu Institute*); **Applied Superconductivity and Sustainable Energy** (Energy Engineering); **Biological Functions** (Biological and Life Sciences; Biology); **Contemporary Education** (Child Care and Development; Primary Education); **Digital Earth Research Center for Synthesis of Knowledge**; **Education in Laboratory Animal** (Laboratory Techniques); **General Research of Science** (Natural Sciences); **Global Humanics** (International Studies; Regional Studies; Social Sciences); **Industry and Economics** (Business Administration; Economics; Industrial and Production Economics); **Information Science** (Information Sciences); **Life and Health Sciences** (Biological and Life Sciences; Health Sciences); **Molecular**

Catalyst (Molecular Biology); **Nutritional Health Science** (Health Sciences; Nutrition); **Production Engineering** (Production Engineering); **Radioisotope** (Radiology); **Science and Technology Research** (Aeronautical and Aerospace Engineering; Energy Engineering; Engineering; Environmental Management; Materials Engineering; Natural Sciences; Technology); **Studies of University Education** (Educational Testing and Evaluation; Higher Education); **Thin Film** (Applied Physics)

Further information: Also Japanese language and culture programme. Study abroad programme

History: Founded 1938 as Nagoya Daiichi Technical Institute, became Chubu Junior College of Technology 1962, Chubu Institute of Technology 1964, and acquired present status 1984. Graduate School established 1972. A private institution governed by the Chubu University Educational Foundation.

Academic year: April to March (April-September; October-March)

Admission requirements: Graduation from high school or foreign equivalent, and entrance examination

Main language(s) of instruction: Japanese

Accrediting agency: Japan Institution for Higher Education Evaluation (JIHEE)

Degrees and diplomas: Gakushi (Architecture; Biomedicine; Biotechnology; Chemistry; Civil Engineering; Communication Studies; Computer Science; Education; English; Food Science; Forestry; Geography (Human); History; Information Management; International Studies; Literature; Mechanical Engineering; Occupational Therapy; Physical Education; Robotics; Sports), Shushi (Aeronautical and Aerospace Engineering; Architecture; Automation and Control Engineering; Business Administration; Chemistry; Electrical Engineering; Electronic Engineering; Geography (Human); Information Technology; International Studies; Literature; Psychology; Rehabilitation and Therapy), Hakase (Applied Chemistry; Biology; Biotechnology; Business Administration; Computer Science; Construction Engineering; Cultural Studies; Electrical and Electronic Engineering; Geography; History; Information Sciences; International Relations; Mechanical Engineering; Modern Languages; Psychology)

Student Services: Sports Facilities, Language Laboratory, Health Services

Periodicals: International Studies, Journal of Information Sciences, Journal of the College of Humanities, Journal of the College of International Studies, Journal of the Research Institute for Industry and Economics, Journal of the Research Institute for Science and Technology, Memoirs of the College of Engineering, Chubu University, The Journal of the College of Business Administration and Information Science

Last Update: 26-03-2018

Chugoku Gakuen University

83 Niwase
Okayama-shi 701-0197, Okayama
Tel: +81(86) 293-1100
Fax: +81(86) 293-3993
Website: http://www.cjc.ac.jp
President: Matsuhata Kiichi

Faculty

Modern Life Science (Biological and Life Sciences; Dietetics; Food Science; Nutrition; Preschool Education; Primary Education; Social Welfare)

Graduate School

Graduate Studies (Child Care and Development; Nutrition)
History: Founded 2002 China Women's College. Acquired present status and title 2002.
Admission requirements: Entrance examination
Main language(s) of instruction: Japanese
Accrediting agency: Japan Institution for Higher Education Evaluation (JIHEE)
Degrees and diplomas: Gakushi (Education; Home Economics; International Studies), Shushi (Nutrition)
Last Update: 26-03-2018

Chukyo Gakuin University

1-104 Sendanbayashi
Nakatsugawa-shi 509-6192, Gifu
Tel: +81(572) 68-4555
Fax: +81(572) 68-4568
Website: http://www.chukyogakuin-u.ac.jp
President: Tadashi Nagano

Faculty

Business Administration (Business Administration); **Nursing** (Nursing)

College

Junior Studies (Child Care and Development; Health Sciences; Nutrition)
Further information: Also Mizunami Campus.
History: Founded 1993.
Admission requirements: Entrance Examination
Main language(s) of instruction: Japanese
Accrediting agency: Japan Institution for Higher Education Evaluation (JIHEE)
Degrees and diplomas: Gakushi (Management)
Student Services: Sports Facilities, Health Services
Last Update: 26-03-2018

Chukyo University

101-2 Yagoto Honmachi, Showa-ku
Nagoya-shi 466-8666, Aichi
Tel: +81(52) 832-2151
Fax: +81(52) 835-7119
Website: http://www.chukyo-u.ac.jp
President: Hitoshi Yasumura

Course/Programme

Japanese Language and Culture (*For Foreign Students*) (Asian Studies; Japanese)

School

Business and Public Policies (Business Administration; Economics; Law; Political Sciences; Social Sciences; Sociology); **Contemporary Sociology** (Sociology); **Economics** (Economic and Finance Policy; Economics; International Economics); **Engineering** (Automation and Control Engineering; Computer Graphics; Electrical and Electronic Engineering; Electronic Engineering; Engineering; Information Sciences; Information Technology; Mechanical Engineering; Media Studies; Production Engineering; Robotics; Visual Arts); **Health and Sport Sciences** (Health Sciences; Physical Education; Sports); **International Liberal Studies** (Arts and Humanities; Chinese; English; French; German; Modern Languages; Russian; Social Sciences; Spanish); **Law** (Civil Law; Constitutional Law; Criminal Law; Law; Political Sciences); **Letters** (Arts and Humanities; Cultural Studies; Japanese; Linguistics; Literature; Writing); **Management** (Business Administration; Business and Commerce; Management); **Psychology** (Developmental Psychology; Experimental Psychology; Psychology); **World Englishes** (American Studies; Asian Studies; Cultural Studies; English; English Studies; International Studies)

Graduate School

Business Administration (Accountancy; Business Administration; Finance; International Business; Management); **Business Innovation** (*MBA*) (Business Administration; Management); **Computer and Cognitive Sciences** (Cognitive Sciences; Computer Science; Information Technology; Media Studies); **Economics** (Economic and Finance Policy; Economics); **Health and Sport Sciences** (Arts and Humanities; Health Sciences; Physiology; Sports); **Law** (Law); **Law** (*Professional*) (Law); **Letters** (Japanese; Literature); **Psychology** (Clinical Psychology; Developmental Psychology; Psychology); **Sociology** (Anthropology; Clinical Psychology; Media Studies; Social Welfare; Sociology); **World Englishes** (American Studies; English; English Studies)

Further information: Also Toyota Campus
History: Founded 1927 as Chukyo Commercial High School, became Junior College 1954, acquired present status 1956.
Academic year: April to March
Admission requirements: Graduation from high school or recognized equivalent, and entrance examination. Provision is made for the recognition of foreign qualifications
Main language(s) of instruction: Japanese, English
Accrediting agency: Japan University Accreditation Association (JUAA)
Degrees and diplomas: Gakushi (Business Administration; Economics; Engineering; English Studies; Health Sciences; International Studies; Law; Literature; Management; Psychology; Sociology; Sports), Shushi (Economics; Law; Political Sciences; Sociology; Sports; Sports Medicine), Hakase (Business Administration; Computer Science; Economic and Finance Policy; Economics; Health Sciences; Law; Literature; Media Studies; Psychology; Sociology; Sports). Also Professional Graduate Programmes: in Law and Business Administration (MBA).
Student Services: Social Counselling, Sports Facilities, Language Laboratory, Health Services, Foreign Studies Centre
Periodicals: Journals
Last Update: 26-03-2018

Chuo University

742-1 Higashinakano
Hachioji-shi 192-0393, Tokyo
Tel: +81(42) 674-2211
Fax: +81(42) 674-2214
Website: http://www.chuo-u.ac.jp
President: Shozaburo Sakai
Tel: +81(426) 74-2112

Faculty

Commerce (Accountancy; Banking; Business Administration; Business and Commerce; Finance; Marketing); **Economics** (Economics; Environmental Studies; Information Sciences; International Economics; Public Administration); **Law** (International Business; International Law; Law; Political Sciences); **Letters** (African Studies; American Studies; Arts and Humanities; Asian Studies; Chinese; Computer Science; Cultural Studies; Education; English; English Studies; European Studies; History; Japanese; Literature; Native Language; Philosophy; Psychology; Sociology; Western European Studies); **Policy Studies** (Cultural Studies; Political Sciences); **Science and Engineering** (Applied Chemistry; Biological and Life Sciences; Civil Engineering; Electrical and Electronic Engineering; Electrical Engineering; Electronic Engineering; Engineering; Environmental

Engineering; Industrial Engineering; Information Sciences; Information Technology; Mathematics; Measurement and Precision Engineering; Mechanical Engineering; Mechanics; Physics; Telecommunications Engineering)

Graduate School

Commerce (Accountancy; Business Administration; Business and Commerce; Economics; Finance; Marketing); **Economics** (Economic and Finance Policy; Economics; International Economics); **International Accounting** (*Professional*) (Accountancy; Environmental Management; Finance; International Business); **Law** (Commercial Law; Criminal Law; International Law; Law; Private Law; Public Law); **Law** (*Professional*) (Commercial Law; Criminal Law; International Law; Law; Public Law); **Letters** (African Studies; American Studies; Asian Studies; Chinese; Cultural Studies; Education; English; English Studies; French; German; History; Japanese; Literature; Native Language; Philosophy; Psychology; Sociology; Western European Studies); **Policy Studies** (Asian Studies; Business Administration; Development Studies; Economic and Finance Policy; Economics; History; International Relations; Law; Management; Social Studies); **Public Policy** (Political Sciences; Public Administration); **Science and Engineering** (Applied Chemistry; Biological and Life Sciences; Civil Engineering; Computer Engineering; Electrical and Electronic Engineering; Industrial Engineering; Information Technology; Mathematics; Measurement and Precision Engineering; Physics; Telecommunications Engineering); **Strategic Management** (*Professional*) (Business Administration; Commercial Law; Human Resources; Management; Marketing)

Research Division

Accounting Research (Accountancy); **Business Research** (Business and Commerce); **Comparative Law in Japan** (Comparative Law); **Cultural Science** (Cultural Studies); **Economic Research** (Economics); **Health and Sports Science** (Health Sciences; Sports); **Policy and Cultural Studies** (Cultural Studies; Political Sciences); **Science and Engineering** (Engineering; Natural Sciences); **Social Sciences** (Social Sciences)

Further information: Also Korakuen and Ichigaya campuses

History: Founded 1885 as Igirisu Horitsu Gakko (the English Law School), recognized as University 1903. Reorganized 1949.

Academic year: April to February (April-August; September-February)

Admission requirements: Graduation from high school or foreign equivalent, and entrance examination

Main language(s) of instruction: Japanese

Accrediting agency: Japan University Accreditation Association (JUAA)

Degrees and diplomas: Gakushi (Biological and Life Sciences; Business Administration; Civil Engineering; Cultural Studies; Economics; Electrical and Electronic Engineering; Engineering; Geography (Human); History; International Relations; Law; Literature; Mathematics and Computer Science; Mechanical Engineering; Physics; Political Sciences; Psychology; Sociology), Shushi (Biological and Life Sciences; Business Administration; Chemistry; Civil Engineering; Cultural Studies; Economics; Education; Electrical and Electronic Engineering; Engineering; Geography (Human); History; Information Technology; Law; Literature; Mathematics and Computer Science; Mechanical Engineering; Philosophy; Physics; Psychology; Sociology), Hakase (Business and Commerce; Economics; Education; Engineering; Law; Literature; Natural Sciences). Also Professional Graduate Diploma in International Accounting (CGSA), Law, and Business Administration (MBA).

Student Services: Academic Counselling, Social Counselling, Careers Guidance, Sports Facilities, Language Laboratory, Facilities for disabled people, Health Services, Canteen, Foreign Studies Centre

Periodicals: Annual of German Culture, Bulletin of French Studies, Bulletin of Graduate Studies, Bulletin of the Faculty of Science and Engineering, Chuo Review, Comparative Law Review, English Language and Literature, Journal of Commerce, Journal of Economics, Journal of Liberal Arts, Journal of Pedagogics, Journal of Policy and Culture, Journal of the Faculty of Literature, The Chuo Law Review

Publishing house: Shuppan-bu (Publishing Office)

Academic Staff 2012-2013	MALE	FEMALE	TOTAL
FULL-TIME			886
Student Numbers 2012-2013			
All (Foreign Included)			27648

Last Update: 26-03-2018

Chuogakuin University

451 Kujike
Abiko-shi 270-1196, Chiba
Tel: +81(471) 836-501-514
Fax: +81(471) 836-532
Website: http://www.cgu.ac.jp
President: Hideaki Sato

Faculty

Commerce (Accountancy; Business Administration; Business and Commerce; Economics; Information Sciences; International Business; Sports Management); **Law** (Commercial Law; Law; Public Administration)

Graduate School

Commerce (*Graduate*) (Accountancy; Business Administration; Business and Commerce)
History: Founded 1966.
Admission requirements: Entrance Examination
Main language(s) of instruction: Japanese
Accrediting agency: Japan University Accreditation Association (JUAA)
Degrees and diplomas: Gakushi (Business Administration; Law), Shushi (Business Administration)
Last Update: 26-03-2018

College of Healthcare Management

960-4 Takayanagi Setaka-machi
Miyama, Fukuoka
Tel: +81(944) 67-7007
Fax: +81(944) 63-3003
Website: http://www.healthcare-m.ac.jp
President: Yoshio Hirota

Department/Division

Health and Medical Department of Business Administration (Accountancy; Business Administration; Economics; English; Finance; Health Administration; Health Sciences; Information Management; Information Sciences; Management; Small Business; Taxation)
Fees: 840,000 per annum (Yen)
Main language(s) of instruction: Japanese
Accrediting agency: Ministry of Education, Culture, Sports, Science and Technology (MEXT)
Degrees and diplomas: Gakushi (Health Sciences; Management)
Student Services: Sports Facilities, Canteen, Library, IT Centre, Residential Facilities
Last Update: 28-03-2018

Cyber University

Fukuoka Kashii Teriha 3 chome 2-1 Higashi-ku
Fukuoka 813-0017
Tel: +81-(0)3-6895-0103
Fax: +81-(0)3-6895-0442
Website: http://www.cyber-u.ac.jp
President: Hiroshi Kawahara

Faculty

IT (Information Technology)
History: Founded 2007.
Main language(s) of instruction: Japanese

Accrediting agency: Japan Institution for Higher Education Evaluation (JIHEE)
Degrees and diplomas: Gakushi
Last Update: 26-03-2018

Daido University

10-3 Takiharu-cho Minami-ku
Nagoya-shi 457-8530, Aichi
Tel: +81(52) 612-6112
Fax: +81(52) 612-0125
Website: http://www.daido-it.ac.jp
President: Jimbo Mutsuko

Faculty

Engineering (Architectural and Environmental Design; Architecture; Civil Engineering; Electrical and Electronic Engineering; Engineering; Interior Design; Mechanical Engineering; Robotics); **Informatics** (Computer Networks; Computer Science; Design; Industrial Design; Information Management; Information Sciences; Information Technology; Media Studies); **Liberal Arts** (Arts and Humanities; Chemistry; English; Health Sciences; Mathematics; Modern Languages; Physical Education; Physics; Social Sciences)

Graduate School

Engineering (Architecture; Electrical and Electronic Engineering; Environmental Engineering; Materials Engineering; Mechanical Engineering; Town Planning); **Information Sciences** (Information Sciences)
History: Founded 1964 as Daido Institute of Technology (Daido Kogyo Daigaku). Acquired present title 2009.
Academic year: April to March
Admission requirements: Entrance examination
Main language(s) of instruction: Japanese
Accrediting agency: Japan Institution for Higher Education Evaluation (JIHEE)
Degrees and diplomas: Gakushi (Engineering), Shushi (Engineering), Hakase (Environmental Engineering; Materials Engineering)
Student Services: Sports Facilities
Last Update: 26-03-2018

Daiichi Institute of Technology

1-10-2 Chuo
Kokubu-shi 899-4395, Kagoshima
Tel: +81(995) 45-0640
Website: http://www.daiichi-koudai.ac.jp
President: Tsuyoshi Yoshitake

Faculty

Engineering (Aeronautical and Aerospace Engineering; Air Transport; Architectural and Environmental Design; Architecture; Automotive Engineering; Building Technologies; Civil Engineering; Construction Engineering; Electronic Engineering; Engineering; Environmental Engineering; Information Technology; Interior Design; Maintenance Technology; Mechanical Engineering; Medical Technology; Robotics; Telecommunications Engineering; Water Management)

Centre

General Education (Education; Higher Education; Teacher Trainers Education)

Admission requirements: Certificate of high school graduation; Recent Examination for Japanese University Admission for International Students (EJU) or Japanese-Language Proficiency Test (JLPT) results (2 years max); Entrance examination

Fees: Admission fee, 150,000; Tuition, 380,000 per annum (Yen)

Main language(s) of instruction: Japanese

Accrediting agency: Ministry of Education, Culture, Sports, Science and Technology (MEXT)

Degrees and diplomas: Gakushi (Engineering)

Last Update: 13-11-2017

Daiichi University of Pharmacy

2-1 Tamagawa-cho Minami-ku
Fukuoka-shi 815-8511, Fukuoka
Tel: +81(92) 541-0161
Fax: +81(92) 542-7372
Website: http://www.daiichi-cps.ac.jp
President: Tsukasa Sakurada

Course/Programme

Pharmacy (Arts and Humanities; Biological and Life Sciences; Chemistry; Communication Studies; Health Sciences; Hygiene; Medicine; Nursing; Nutrition; Pharmacology; Pharmacy; Social Sciences)

History: Founded as school 1956. Acquired present status and title 2006.

Academic year: April to February (April-July; September-February)

Main language(s) of instruction: Japanese

Accrediting agency: Japan Institution for Higher Education Evaluation (JIHEE)

Degrees and diplomas: Gakushi (Pharmacy), Shushi (Pharmacy)

Student Services: Canteen

Last Update: 26-03-2018

Daito Bunka University

1-9-1 Takashimadaira Itabashi-ku
Tokyo 175-8571
Tel: +81(3) 5399-7800
Fax: +81(3) 5399-7823
Website: http://www.daito.ac.jp
President: Kadowaki Hirofumi

Department/Division

Business Administration (Accountancy; Business Administration; Business Computing; Management); **Economics** (Chinese; Economic History; Economics; English; International Economics; International Studies); **Foreign Languages** (Asian Studies; Chinese; Cultural Studies; English; Japanese; Modern Languages); **International Relations** (Arabic; Chinese; Cultural Studies; English; Hindi; Indonesian; International Relations; Korean; Modern Languages; Persian; Political Sciences; Regional Studies; Social Studies; Urdu; Vietnamese); **Law** (Administration; Commercial Law; International Law; Law; Political Sciences; Public Administration); **Literature** (Asian Studies; Chinese; Education; English; Japanese; Literature; Teacher Training; Writing); **Social-Human Environmentology** (Environmental Management; Environmental Studies; Social Problems; Social Sciences; Urban Studies; Welfare and Protective Services); **Sports and Health Science** (Health Sciences; Sports)

Graduate School

Asian Area Studies (Arts and Humanities; Asian Studies; Cultural Studies; Economics; History; Political Sciences; Regional Studies; Social Studies); **Business Administration** (Accountancy; Business Administration); **Economics** (Economics); **Foreign Languages** (Asian Studies; Chinese; English; Japanese; Linguistics; Modern Languages); **Law** (*Juris Doctor's Programme*) (Law); **Law** (Law; Political Sciences); **Literature** (Chinese; Education; English; Japanese; Literature; Teacher Training; Writing); **Sports and Health Science** (Health Sciences; Sports)

Further information: Also Higashimatsuyama and Shinanomachi Campuses. Japanese language programme for foreign students

History: Founded 1923 as College (Daito Bunka Gakuin), became University and renamed Tokyo Bunsei Daigaku 1949. Acquired present title 1953.

Academic year: April to March (April-September; October-March)

Admission requirements: Graduation from high school or equivalent or foreign equivalent, and entrance examination

Main language(s) of instruction: Japanese

Accrediting agency: Ministry of Education, Culture, Sports, Science and Technology (MEXT)

Degrees and diplomas: Gakushi, Shushi, Hakase (Asian Studies; Business Administration; Chinese; Economics; English; Japanese; Law; Linguistics; Political Sciences; Regional Studies; Writing)
Student Services: Language Laboratory
Publishing house: Daito Bunka University Publishing House
Last Update: 26-03-2018

Den-en Chofu University (DCU)

3-4-1 Higashiryurigaoka Aso-ku
Kawasaki-shi 215-8542, Kanagawa
Tel: +81(44) 966-6800, +81(44) 966-9211
Fax: +81(44) 955-4345
Website: http://www.dcu.ac.jp
President: Kumiko Ikuta

Department/Division

Children's Future (Child Care and Development); **Human Welfare** (Education; Social Psychology; Social Welfare; Social Work; Special Education; Welfare and Protective Services)
History: Founded 2002.
Admission requirements: Entrance examination
Main language(s) of instruction: Japanese
Accrediting agency: Ministry of Education, Culture, Sports, Science and Technology (MEXT)
Degrees and diplomas: Gakushi (Child Care and Development; Social Psychology; Social Welfare)
Last Update: 28-03-2018

Digital Hollywood University (DHU)

3F/4F Ochanomizu Sola City Academia 4-6 Surugadai, Kanda
Chiyoda-ku 192-0354, Tokyo
Tel: +81(120) 823-422
Website: http://www.dhw.ac.jp
President: Tomoyuki Sugiyama

College

Digital Arts (Business Administration; Computer Graphics; Computer Networks; Computer Science; Film; Graphic Design; Information Technology; Software Engineering; Visual Arts)

Course/Programme

Japanese Language and Culture (*For international students*) (Cultural Studies; Japanese)

Graduate School

Digital Content Management (Business Administration; Computer Graphics; Information Technology)
History: Founded 2005.
Admission requirements: 12-year course of school education completed; Entrance examinations; International students must also receive the qualification of "college student" (immigrant status) and prove a sufficient level Japanese level through scores to the Japanese Language Proficiency Test (JLPT) or the Examination for Japanese University Admission for International Students (EJU)
Fees: Enrolment fee, 250,000 (first year only); Tuition, 686,000 per annum (Yen)
Main language(s) of instruction: Japanese
Accrediting agency: Japan Institution for Higher Education Evaluation (JIHEE)
Degrees and diplomas: Gakushi (Business Administration; Computer Graphics; Graphic Design), Shushi (Business Administration; Computer Graphics; Graphic Design; Information Technology)
Last Update: 27-03-2018

Doho University

7-1 Inabaji-cho Nakamura-ku
Nagoya-shi 453-8540, Aichi
Tel: +81(52) 411-1113
Fax: +81(52) 411-0333
Website: http://www.doho.ac.jp
President: Kiyofumi Oda

Faculty

Social Welfare (Child Care and Development; Development Studies; Psychiatry and Mental Health; Psychology; Social Welfare; Welfare and Protective Services)

School

Graduate Studies (Arts and Humanities; Asian Religious Studies; Literature; Welfare and Protective Services)

Department/Division

Literature (Arts and Humanities; Asian Religious Studies; Cultural Studies; Japanese; Linguistics; Literature)
History: Founded 1921. Acquired present status 1950.
Accrediting agency: Japan Institution for Higher Education Evaluation (JIHEE)
Degrees and diplomas: Gakushi, Shushi, Hakase (Asian Religious Studies)

Academic Staff 2012-2013	MALE	FEMALE	TOTAL
FULL-TIME			43
PART-TIME			111

(*continued*)

Academic Staff 2012-2013	MALE	FEMALE	TOTAL
Student Numbers 2012-2013			
All (Foreign Included)			989
Foreign only			35

Last Update: 14-11-2017

Dokkyo Medical University

880 Kitakobayashi Mibu-machi
Shimotsuga-gun 321-0293, Tochigi
Tel: +81(282) 86-2108
Fax: +81(282) 86-5678
Website: http://www.dokkyomed.ac.jp
President: Noriyuki Inaba

School
Nursing (Nursing)

Department/Division
Midwifery (Midwifery); **Preclinical Medicine** (Anatomy; Biochemistry; Biology; Cell Biology; Chemistry; English; Forensic Medicine and Dentistry; German; Histology; Hygiene; Immunology; Mathematics; Microbiology; Molecular Biology; Natural Sciences; Parasitology; Pharmacology; Physical Education; Physics; Physiology; Public Health; Tropical Medicine)

Institute
Medical Science (Medicine)

Centre
Medical Informatics (Computer Science)

Graduate School
Medicine (Anaesthesiology; Biochemistry; Biological and Life Sciences; Cardiology; Cognitive Sciences; Dermatology; Endocrinology; Forensic Medicine and Dentistry; Gastroenterology; Gynaecology and Obstetrics; Haematology; Hygiene; Immunology; Laboratory Techniques; Medicine; Neurology; Oncology; Ophthalmology; Orthopaedics; Otorhinolaryngology; Paediatrics; Pathology; Physiology; Pneumology; Psychiatry and Mental Health; Public Health; Radiology; Social and Preventive Medicine; Surgery; Urology; Zoology); **Nursing** (Nursing)

Research Division
Laboratory Animal (Genetics; Laboratory Techniques)
Further information: 3 hospitals attached: the University Hospital, Koshigaya Hospital, and Nikko Medical Center

History: Founded 1973. Forms part of the Dokkyo Gakuen (Dokkyo Group of Academic Institutions), founded 1883 as School for the Association of German Studies.
Main language(s) of instruction: Japanese
Accrediting agency: Ministry of Education, Culture, Sports, Science and Technology (MEXT)
Degrees and diplomas: Gakushi, Hakase (Medicine; Physiology; Social and Preventive Medicine; Surgery)
Student Services: Sports Facilities, Language Laboratory, Health Services
Last Update: 14-11-2017

Dokkyo University

1-1 Gakuen-cho
Soka-shi 340-0042, Saitama
Tel: +81(48) 946-1635
Fax: +81(48) 943-3160
Website: http://www.dokkyo.ac.jp
President: Tadashi Inui

Faculty
Economics (Economics; Management); **Foreign Languages** (English; French; German; International Studies; Modern Languages; Tourism); **International Liberal Arts** (Arts and Humanities); **Law** (International Law; Law; Political Sciences)
Further information: Also Japanese language courses for foreign students
History: Founded 1964, Forms part of Dokkyo Gakuen (Dokkyo Group of Academic Institution), founded 1883 as School for the Association of German Studies.
Academic year: April to March
Admission requirements: Graduation from senior high school or equivalent and entrance examination
Fees: Undergraduate programmes, 1,052,800 per annum; Graduate programmes, 808,800 per annum; Law School programmes, 1,203,100 per annum; 1 year course for Japanese Language Teachers Programme, 1,000,800 (Yen)
Main language(s) of instruction: Japanese, English
Accrediting agency: Japan University Accreditation Association (JUAA)
Degrees and diplomas: Gakushi, Shushi, Hakase (Law; Modern Languages). Also Houmu Hakase (Juris Doctor), a Professional Degree Programme offered by the Faculty of Law.
Student Services: Academic Counselling, Social Counselling, Careers Guidance, Nursery Care, Cultural Activities, Sports Facilities, Language Laboratory, Facilities for disabled people, Health Services, Canteen, Foreign Studies Centre
Periodicals: Brücke, Bulletin d'Études françaises, Dokkyo - Universitaet germanistische Forschungsbeitraege, Dokkyo

Graduate School of Economics, Dokkyo International Review, Dokkyo Journal of Language Learning and Teaching, Dokkyo Law Journal, Dokkyo Law Review, Dokkyo Studies in Data Processing and Computer Science, Dokkyô Studies in Japanese Language Teaching, Dokkyo University bulletin of General Studies, Dokkyo University Bulletin of Liberal Arts and Education, Dokkyo University Gakuho, Dokkyo University studies in English, Dokkyo University Studies in Foreign Language Teaching, Dokkyo University Studies of Economics, Dokkyo Working Papers in English Culture, Encounters, Études de Langue et Culture françaises, Forshungsbericht Germanistik, Informatics, Journal of Informatics, Mathesis Universalis, Multidisciplinary Research for Regions Bulletin of the Institute of Regional Research

Publishing house: Dokkyo News

Academic Staff 2013-2014	MALE	FEMALE	TOTAL
FULL-TIME	169	52	221
PART-TIME	281	143	424
STAFF WITH DOCTORATE			
FULL-TIME	72	26	98
Student Numbers 2013-2014			
All (Foreign Included)	4598	4077	8675
Foreign only	44	43	87

Total number of part-time students: 72

Last Update: 14-11-2017

Doshisha University (DU)

Imadegawa-dori Kamigyo-ku
Kyoto 602-8580, Kyoto
Tel: +81(75) 251-3260
Fax: +81(75) 251-3057
Website: http://www.doshisha.ac.jp
President: Takashi Matsuoka

Faculty

Commerce (Business and Commerce); **Culture and Information Science** (Cultural Studies; Information Sciences); **Economics** (Economics); **Global and Regional Studies** (International Studies; Regional Studies); **Global Communications** (Communication Studies); **Health and Sports Science** (Health Sciences; Sports); **Law** (Law; Political Sciences); **Letters** (Aesthetics; Art History; Cultural Studies; English; Literature; Philosophy); **Life and Medical Sciences** (Biomedical Engineering; Biomedicine; Information Sciences; Medical Technology); **Policy Studies** (Government); **Psychology** (Psychology); **Science and Engineering** (Biochemistry; Chemical Engineering; Chemistry; Electrical Engineering; Electronic Engineering; Energy Engineering; Engineering; Environmental Studies; Information Sciences;

Information Technology; Materials Engineering; Mathematics; Mechanical Engineering); **Social Studies** (Cultural Studies; Education; Journalism; Labour and Industrial Relations; Mass Communication; Media Studies; Social Studies; Social Welfare; Sociology)

School

Theology (Theology)

Institute

Liberal Arts (Business Administration; Cultural Studies; International Business; International Studies; Political Sciences; Social Studies)

Graduate School

Brain Science (Biological and Life Sciences; Cognitive Sciences; Neurosciences); **Business** (*Professional*) (Business Administration); **Commerce** (Business and Commerce); **Culture and Information Science** (Cultural Studies; Information Sciences); **Economics** (Economics); **Global Studies** (International Studies); **Health and Sports Science** (Health Sciences); **Law** (*Professional*) (Law); **Law** (Law; Political Sciences; Private Law; Public Law); **Letters** (Aesthetics; Art History; Cultural Studies; English; History; Linguistics; Literature; Philosophy); **Life and Medical Sciences** (Biological and Life Sciences; Biomedical Engineering; Biomedicine; Information Sciences; Medical Technology); **Policy and Management** (Engineering Management; Government; Management); **Psychology** (Psychology); **Science and Engineering** (Applied Chemistry; Computer Science; Electrical Engineering; Engineering; Environmental Studies; Mathematics; Mechanical Engineering); **Social Studies** (Cultural Studies; Education; Labour and Industrial Relations; Media Studies; Social Studies; Social Welfare; Sociology); **Theology** (Theology)

Further information: Also summer programmes and study abroad programmes

History: Founded 1875 as a Doshisha English School, became College 1912, reorganized 1920 and acquired present status 1948.

Academic year: April to March (April-September; October-March)

Admission requirements: Graduation from high school or equivalent, or foreign equivalent; entrance examination; English proficiency scores

Fees: Undergraduate programmes tuition fee, 1,112,000-1,581,000 per annum; Graduate programmes tuition fee, 904,000-1,256,000 per annum (Yen)

Main language(s) of instruction: Japanese, English

Accrediting agency: Japan University Accreditation Association

Degrees and diplomas: Gakushi, Shushi, Hakase (American Studies; Arts and Humanities; Asian Studies; Education;

Engineering Management; English; History; Industrial Management; International Studies; Japanese; Linguistics; Literature; Management; Media Studies; Neurosciences; Philosophy; Psychology; Religious Studies; Social Studies; Social Welfare; Sociology; Welfare and Protective Services). Also MBA; Juris Doctor

Student Services: Academic Counselling, Social Counselling, Careers Guidance, Sports Facilities, Language Laboratory, Facilities for disabled people, Health Services, Canteen, Foreign Studies Centre

Periodicals: Annual of Philosophy, Annual report of Cultural Studies, Annual Report of the School of Museology, Bulletin of the Centre for Japanese Language, Doshisha American Studies, Doshisha Danso, Doshisha Journal of Health and Sport Sciences, Doshisha Journal of Library and Information Science, Doshisha Literature, Doshisha Psychological Review, Doshisha Review of Sociology, Doshisha Studies in English, Doshisha Studies in Language and Culture, Journal of Education and Culture, Neesima Studies, Science and Engineering Review of Doshisha, SHURYU, Social Science Review, Studies in Christianity, Studies in Cultural History, Studies in Humanities, Studies in the Christian Religion, The Doshisha Law Review, The Doshisha University Economic Review, The Social Sciences, The Society of Aesthetics and Science of Arts, The Study of Christianity and Social Problems, World Wide Business Review

Academic Staff 2012-2013	MALE	FEMALE	TOTAL
FULL-TIME	639	139	778
PART-TIME	955	415	1370
STAFF WITH DOCTORATE			
FULL-TIME	439	92	531
Student Numbers 2012-2013			
All (Foreign Included)	18044	10598	28642
Foreign only	306	355	661

Total number of part-time students: 136

Last Update: 14-11-2017

Doshisha Women's College of Liberal Arts (DWCLA)

Kyotanabe-shi 610-0395, Kyoto
Tel: +81(774) 65-8811
Fax: +81(774) 65-8460
Website: http://www.dwc.doshisha.ac.jp
President: Hiroo Kaga

Faculty

Contemporary Social Sciences (Business Administration; Child Care and Development; Management; Social Sciences; Tourism); **Culture and Representation** (Cultural Studies; English; Japanese; Literature); **Liberal Arts and Science** (Art Therapy; Arts and Humanities; English; Information Sciences; International Studies; Media Studies; Music; Music Education; Sound Engineering (Acoustics)); **Life Sciences** (Biological and Life Sciences; Cooking and Catering; Dietetics; Food Science; Nutrition); **Pharmaceutical Sciences** (Pharmacology; Pharmacy)

Department/Division

Music Major (Music; Musical Instruments)

Graduate School

Letters (Cultural Studies; English; Japanese; Literature); **Life Sciences** (Biological and Life Sciences; Dietetics; Food Science; Home Economics; Nutrition; Welfare and Protective Services); **Pharmaceutical Sciences** (Pharmacology; Pharmacy); **Social System** (*International*) (International Relations; International Studies)

History: Founded as School 1876, acquired present status 1949.

Academic year: April to March (April-September; October-March)

Admission requirements: Graduation from high school or equivalent, and entrance examination

Fees: Admission fee, 260,000; Tuition, 742,000-1,122,000 per annum (Yen)

Main language(s) of instruction: Japanese

Accrediting agency: Japan University Accreditation Association

Degrees and diplomas: Gakushi, Shushi, Hakase (Cultural Studies; English; Japanese; Literature; Pharmacy)

Student Services: Social Counselling, Careers Guidance, Sports Facilities, Facilities for disabled people, Health Services, Canteen

Periodicals: Asphodel, Bulletin of Institute for Interdisciplinary Studies of Culture, Doshisha Home Economics, Nihongo Nihon Bungaku

Academic Staff 2012-2013	MALE	FEMALE	TOTAL
FULL-TIME			177
Student Numbers 2012-2013			
All (Foreign Included)			6472
Foreign only			10

Last Update: 14-11-2017

Edogawa University

474 Komagi
Nagareyama-shi 270-0198, Chiba
Tel: +81(4) 7152-0661

Fax: +81(4) 7154-2490
Website: http://www.edogawa-u.ac.jp
President: Hikota Koguchi

College

Media and Communication (Business Administration; Communication Studies; Mass Communication; Media Studies); **Sociology** (Anthropology; Arts and Humanities; Business Administration; International Business; Management; Psychology; Sociology; Sports Management)
History: Founded 1990.
Fees: Tuition, 340,000 per annum (Yen)
Main language(s) of instruction: Japanese
Accrediting agency: Japan Institution for Higher Education Evaluation (JIHEE)
Degrees and diplomas: Gakushi (Business Administration; Education; International Business; Management; Media Studies; Psychology; Sociology)
Student Services: Academic Counselling, Sports Facilities, Health Services, Canteen

Academic Staff 2012-2013	MALE	FEMALE	TOTAL
FULL-TIME			75
Student Numbers 2012-2013			
All (Foreign Included)			1944

Last Update: 27-03-2018

Elisabeth University of Music (EUM)

4-15 Nobori-cho
Naka-ku 730-0016, Hiroshima
Tel: +81(82) 221-0918
Fax: +81(82) 221-0947
Website: http://www.eum.ac.jp
President: Yuji Kawano

Faculty

Music (Conducting; Music; Music Education; Music Theory and Composition; Musical Instruments; Musicology; Religious Music; Singing)

Graduate School

Music Studies (Music; Musical Instruments; Religious Music; Singing)
History: Founded 1948 as School, became Junior College 1952, acquired present status 1963. Division of Graduate Studies opened 1991. Recognized by the Ministry of Education, Science and Culture. Affiliated to the Pontificio Istituto di Musica Sacra in Rome. Directed by the Society of Jesus.
Academic year: April to March (April-September; September-March)

Admission requirements: Graduation from high school or equivalent, and entrance examination
Fees: Admission fee, 300,000; Tuition, 850,000-1,300,000 per annum (Yen)
Main language(s) of instruction: Japanese
Accrediting agency: Ministry of Education, Culture, Sports, Science and Technology (MEXT)
Degrees and diplomas: Gakushi, Shushi, Hakase (Music)
Student Services: Academic Counselling, Careers Guidance, Sports Facilities, Facilities for disabled people
Periodicals: Arts et Mystica (Review), Research Bulletin
Last Update: 14-11-2017

Ferris University

37 Yamate-cho Naka-ku
Yokohama-shi 231-8651, Kanagawa
Tel: +81(45) 662-4521
Fax: +81(45) 662-6102
Website: http://www.ferris.ac.jp
President: Yo Akioka

Faculty

Global and Intercultural Studies (Cultural Studies; International Studies); **Letters** (Arts and Humanities; Communication Studies; English; Japanese; Literature)

College

Music (Music; Performing Arts; Religious Music)

Graduate School

Graduate Studies (Communication Studies; English; Japanese; Literature)
Further information: Also summer language programmes with: Towson State University; Bath College; IIK, Jena; Tsinghua University, Beijing
History: Founded 1965. Acquired present status and title 1997.
Academic year: April to January (April-July; October-January)
Admission requirements: Graduation from high school or equivalent, and entrance examination
Main language(s) of instruction: Japanese
Accrediting agency: Japan University Accreditation Association
Degrees and diplomas: Gakushi, Shushi, Hakase (Communication Studies; Literature)
Student Services: Academic Counselling, Social Counselling, Careers Guidance, Nursery Care, Sports Facilities, Language Laboratory, Health Services, Foreign Studies Centre
Periodicals: Ferris Studies (College of Music vol.1-vol.2)

Academic Staff 2012-2013	MALE	FEMALE	TOTAL
FULL-TIME			86
Student Numbers 2012-2013			
All (Foreign Included)			2695

Last Update: 15-11-2017

Fuji University

450-3 Shimoneko
Hanamaki-shi 025-8501, Iwate
Tel: +81(198) 23-6221
Fax: +81(198) 41-1310
Website: http://www.fuji-u.ac.jp
President: Shuji Okada

College
General Education (Arts and Humanities; Chinese; Computer Science; Cultural Studies; English; French; German; Korean; Modern Languages)

Course/Programme
Library Science (Library Science); **Teacher Training** (Teacher Training)

Department/Division
Economics (Economic and Finance Policy; Economic History; Economics; International Economics; Law; Management; Social and Community Services); **Information Management** (Accountancy; Business Administration; Business Computing; Finance; Information Management; Information Sciences; Information Technology; Media Studies); **Law and Management** (Commercial Law; Constitutional Law; Criminal Law; Law; Management; Physical Education; Sports Management)

Graduate School
Economics and Management (Business Administration; Economics; Management)
History: Founded 1965.
Admission requirements: Entrance examination
Main language(s) of instruction: Japanese, English
Accrediting agency: Japan Institution for Higher Education Evaluation (JIHEE)
Degrees and diplomas: Gakushi (Economics; Management), Shushi (Economics)
Student Services: Sports Facilities
Last Update: 27-03-2018

Fuji Women's University

Kitaku Kita 16 Nishi 2
Sapporo 001-0016, Hokkaido
Tel: +81(11) 736-0311
Fax: +81(11) 709-8541
Website: http://www.fujijoshi.ac.jp
President: Isao Kida

Faculty
Human Life Sciences (*Hanakawa Campus*) (Child Care and Development; Dietetics; Education; Food Science; Nutrition; Preschool Education; Social Sciences; Social Welfare); **Humanities** (*Sapporo Campus*) (Arts and Humanities; Asian Studies; Cultural Studies; English; English Studies; European Studies; History; Japanese; Literature)

Course/Programme
Japanese Language and Culture (*Intensive*) (Asian Studies; Japanese)

Institute
Christian Culture (Christian Religious Studies); **Quality of Life** (Welfare and Protective Services)

Graduate School
Human Life Sciences (Biological and Life Sciences; Food Science; Nutrition; Social Welfare; Welfare and Protective Services)
Further information: Also Hanakawa campus
History: Founded 1961.
Main language(s) of instruction: Japanese
Accrediting agency: Japan University Accreditation Association
Degrees and diplomas: Gakushi (English; English Studies; Food Science; Japanese; Literature), Shushi
Last Update: 27-03-2018

Fujita Health University

1-98 Dengakugakubo Kutsukake-cho
Toyoake-shi 470-1192, Aichi
Tel: +81(562) 93-2000
Website: http://www.fujita-hu.ac.jp/en
President: Kiyotaka Hoshinaga

Faculty
Health Sciences (Business Administration; Health Administration; Health Sciences; Medical Technology; Nursing; Occupational Therapy; Physical Therapy; Radiology); **Medicine** (Medicine)

School
Nursing (Nursing)

Graduate School
Graduate Studies (Business Administration; Health Administration; Health Sciences; Medical Technology; Medicine; Nursing; Occupational Therapy; Physical Therapy; Radiology)

Further information: Fujita Health University Hospital

History: Founded 1964 as Fujita Academy. Acquired current status and title 1968

Academic year: April to March (April-July; September-December; January-March)

Admission requirements: Graduation from high school or equivalent and entrance examination

Fees: School of Medicine, 6,596,000 (1st yr); 4,786,000 (2nd-6th yr) per annum; School of Health Sciences, 1,596,000-1,846,000 (1st yr); 1,326,000-1,576,000 (2nd-4th yr) per annum (Yen)

Main language(s) of instruction: Japanese, English

Accrediting agency: Japan University Accreditation Association (JUAA)

Degrees and diplomas: Gakushi (Health Sciences; Medicine), Shushi (Health Sciences), Hakase (Health Sciences; Medicine)

Student Services: Academic Counselling, Social Counselling, Careers Guidance, Nursery Care, Sports Facilities, Language Laboratory, Health Services, Canteen, Library

Periodicals: Fujita Medical Journal

Academic Staff 2017-2018	MALE	FEMALE	TOTAL
FULL-TIME			952
Student Numbers 2017-2018			
All (Foreign Included)	1353	1712	3065

Last Update: 25-05-2018

Fukui University of Technology (FUT)

3-6-1 Gakuen
Fukui-shi 910-8505, Fukui
Tel: +81(776) 29-7864
Fax: +81(776) 29-7891
Website: http://www.fukui-ut.ac.jp
President: Yotaro Morishima

Faculty
Engineering (Applied Chemistry; Architecture; Chemical Engineering; Computer Engineering; Design; Electrical and Electronic Engineering; Electrical Engineering; Electronic Engineering; Engineering; Environmental Engineering; Environmental Management; Industrial Engineering; Information Technology; Mechanical Engineering; Nuclear Engineering; Safety Engineering; Structural Architecture; Town Planning)

Graduate School
Engineering (Applied Chemistry; Architecture; Bioengineering; Civil Engineering; Computer Engineering; Design; Electrical and Electronic Engineering; Electrical Engineering; Electronic Engineering; Engineering; Environmental Engineering; Information Sciences; Information Technology; Mechanical Engineering; Nuclear Engineering)

Further information: Awara Campus

History: Founded 1965.

Academic year: April to March (April-September; September-March)

Admission requirements: Graduation from high school and entrance examination

Main language(s) of instruction: Japanese

Accrediting agency: Japan Institution for Higher Education Evaluation (JIHEE)

Degrees and diplomas: Gakushi, Shushi, Hakase (Applied Chemistry; Architecture; Civil Engineering; Computer Engineering; Design; Electrical and Electronic Engineering; Environmental Engineering; Information Technology; Mechanical Engineering; Nuclear Engineering)

Student Services: Sports Facilities

Last Update: 15-11-2017

Fukuoka Dental College (FDC)

2-15-1 Tamura Sawara-Ku
Fukuoka-shi 814-0193, Fukuoka
Tel: +81(92) 801-0411
Fax: +81(92) 801-3678
Website: http://www.fdcnet.ac.jp
Rector: Ishikawa Hiroyuki

College
Dentistry (Anatomy; Biochemistry; Biological and Life Sciences; Cardiology; Dental Technology; Dentistry; Dermatology; English; Gynaecology and Obstetrics; Haematology; Histology; Microbiology; Nephrology; Nutrition; Oncology; Ophthalmology; Paediatrics; Pathology; Pharmacology; Physiology; Pneumology; Sociology; Stomatology; Urology); **Health Sciences** (Dental Hygiene; Dentistry; Health Sciences; Welfare and Protective Services)

Centre
Regenerative Medicine (Medical Technology; Periodontics)

Graduate School
Dentistry (Dentistry)

Research Division

Advanced Science (Biological and Life Sciences; Cell Biology; Genetics); **Control of Aging** (Genetics)
Further information: Also College Hospital
History: Founded 1972.
Main language(s) of instruction: Japanese
Accrediting agency: Japan University Accreditation Association
Degrees and diplomas: Gakushi, Hakase (Dentistry). Also Special Postgraduate programme in Dental Hygiene, 1 yr.
Student Services: Social Counselling, Sports Facilities
Last Update: 15-11-2017

Fukuoka Institute of Technology (FIT)

3-30-1 Wajirohigashi Higashi-ku
Fukuoka-shi 811-0295, Fukuoka
Tel: +81(92) 606-3131
Fax: +81(92) 606-8923
Website: http://www.fit.ac.jp
President: Teruo Shimomura
Tel: +81(92) 606-2211

Faculty

Engineering (Applied Chemistry; Biological and Life Sciences; Biology; Computer Engineering; Electrical and Electronic Engineering; Electrical Engineering; Energy Engineering; Engineering; Environmental Engineering; Food Technology; Information Technology; Machine Building; Mechanical Engineering; Production Engineering; Software Engineering); **Information Engineering** (Artificial Intelligence; Automation and Control Engineering; Computer Engineering; Computer Networks; Computer Science; Engineering Management; Information Sciences; Information Technology; Management; Mass Communication; Multimedia; Radio and Television Broadcasting; Software Engineering); **Socio-Environmental Studies** (Arts and Humanities; Cultural Studies; Economics; Environmental Studies; Law; Management; Political Sciences; Psychology)

Graduate School

Engineering (Accountancy; Artificial Intelligence; Automation and Control Engineering; Bioengineering; Biological and Life Sciences; Biomedical Engineering; Business Administration; Chemistry; Commercial Law; Computer Engineering; Computer Science; Cultural Studies; Economics; Electrical Engineering; Electronic Engineering; Energy Engineering; Engineering; English; Environmental Engineering; Environmental Studies; Information Sciences; Information Technology; International Law; Japanese; Machine Building; Management; Materials Engineering; Measurement and Precision Engineering; Mechanical Engineering; Media Studies; Multimedia; Organic Chemistry; Power Engineering; Production Engineering; Radio and Television Broadcasting; Software Engineering)
Further information: Also graduate school
History: Founded 1963 as Institute of Electron Technology. Acquired present title 1966.
Academic year: April to March (two semesters)
Admission requirements: Secondary school certificate
Fees: Tuition for undergraduate programmes, 630,000-780,000 per annum; Tuition for graduate programmes, (Yen)
Main language(s) of instruction: Japanese
Accrediting agency: Japan University Accreditation Association
Degrees and diplomas: Gakushi, Shushi, Hakase (Artificial Intelligence; Computer Engineering)
Student Services: Academic Counselling, Social Counselling, Careers Guidance, Nursery Care, Facilities for disabled people, Canteen
Periodicals: Reports of Computer Science Laboratory, Fukuoka Institute of Technology, Reports of the Electronics Research Laboratory, Fukuoka Institute of Technology, Research Bulletin of Fukuoka Institute of Technology

Academic Staff 2013-2014	MALE	FEMALE	TOTAL
FULL-TIME	261	15	276
Student Numbers 2013-2014			
All (Foreign Included)			c. 4460
Foreign only			170

Last Update: 15-11-2017

Fukuoka International University

4-16-1 Gojo
Daizaifu-shi 818-0193, Fukuoka
Tel: +81(92) 922-4034
Fax: +81(92) 922-6453
Website: http://www.fukuoka-int-u.ac.jp
President: Oura Takaharu

Faculty

International Communication (Asian Studies; Business Administration; Business and Commerce; Chinese; Economics; English; International Studies; Japanese; Korean; Teacher Training)
History: Founded 1998.
Admission requirements: Entrance examination
Main language(s) of instruction: Japan
Accrediting agency: Japan Institution for Higher Education Evaluation (JIHEE)
Degrees and diplomas: Gakushi
Last Update: 24-11-2017

Fukuoka Jo Gakuin University

3-42-1 Osa Minami-ku
Fukuoka-shi 811-1313, Fukuoka
Tel: +81(92) 575-2970
Fax: +81(92) 575-4456
Website: http://www2.fukujo.ac.jp/university
President: Kazumichi Takashima

Faculty
Human Relations (Child Care and Development; Primary Education; Psychology; Secondary Education; Secretarial Studies); **Humanities** (Cultural Studies; English; Mass Communication; Media Studies; Radio and Television Broadcasting)

College
Junior Studies (English; Tourism)

Graduate School
Human Sciences (Clinical Psychology; Cultural Studies)
Further information: Also Fukuoka Jogakuin Nursing College (Koga Campus)
History: Founded 1990.
Main language(s) of instruction: Japanese
Accrediting agency: Japan University Accreditation Association (JUAA)
Degrees and diplomas: Gakushi (Communication Arts; Education; Literature; Psychology), Shushi (Literature; Psychology)
Last Update: 26-03-2018

Fukuoka University

8-19-1 Nanakuma Jonan-ku
Fukuoka-shi 814-0180, Fukuoka
Tel: +81(92) 871-6631
Fax: +81(92) 862-4431
Website: http://www.fukuoka-u.ac.jp
President: Masatoshi Yamaguchi

Faculty
Commerce (Accountancy; Business Administration; Business and Commerce; Finance; International Business; Management); **Economics** (Economics; Industrial and Production Economics); **Engineering** (Architecture; Chemical Engineering; Civil Engineering; Computer Science; Electrical Engineering; Electronic Engineering; Engineering; Mechanical Engineering); **Humanities** (Anthropology; Archaeology; Art History; Arts and Humanities; Asian Studies; Clinical Psychology; Cultural Studies; East Asian Studies; Educational Psychology; English; French; Geography; German; History; Japanese; Linguistics; Literature; Philosophy; Psychology; Regional Studies; Religion; Sociology); **Law** (Business Administration; Commercial Law; Economic and Finance Policy; Industrial and Production Economics; International Economics; International Studies; Law); **Medicine** (Medicine; Nursing); **Pharmaceutical Sciences** (Health Sciences; Pharmacy); **Science** (Applied Mathematics; Applied Physics; Chemistry; Earth Sciences; Geology; Nanotechnology); **Sports and Health Science** (Health Sciences; Orthopaedics; Physiology; Psychology; Sports; Sports Medicine)

Course/Programme
Japanese Language (*For International Students*) (Cultural Studies; Japanese)

School
Commerce (*Evening Course*) (Accountancy; Business Administration; Business and Commerce; Finance; International Business; Management)

Institute
Legal Practice (*Law School*) (Civil Law; Constitutional Law; Criminal Law; Law)

Centre
General Education (Arts and Humanities; Modern Languages; Natural Sciences; Physical Education); **Language Education and Research** (Modern Languages; Phonetics); **Teaching Profession Course Education** (Teacher Training)

Graduate School
Commerce (Accountancy; Banking; Business and Commerce; Finance; Human Resources; Insurance; International Business; International Economics; Management; Marketing; Operations Research; Taxation; Transport Economics); **Economics** (Econometrics; Economic and Finance Policy; Economic History; Economics; Industrial and Production Economics; International Economics; Operations Research; Taxation); **Engineering** (Architectural and Environmental Design; Architecture; Automation and Control Engineering; Chemical Engineering; Civil Engineering; Computer Science; Construction Engineering; Data Processing; Ecology; Electrical Engineering; Electronic Engineering; Energy Engineering; Engineering; Environmental Engineering; Environmental Management; Industrial Chemistry; Information Technology; Materials Engineering; Mechanical Engineering; Optical Technology; Power Engineering; Production Engineering; Road Engineering; Robotics; Structural Architecture; Thermal Engineering); **Humanities** (Anthropology; Archaeology; Arts and Humanities; Clinical Psychology; Cultural Studies; Educational Psychology; English; French; German; History; Japanese; Literature; Social Studies); **Law**

(Administrative Law; Civil Law; Constitutional Law; Criminal Law; Fiscal Law; History of Law; International Law; Labour Law; Law; Political Sciences; Public Law); **Medical Sciences** (Biological and Life Sciences; Biology; Epidemiology; Health Sciences; Immunology; Medicine; Microbiology; Nursing; Pathology; Physical Therapy; Psychoanalysis; Radiology; Rehabilitation and Therapy; Respiratory Therapy; Social and Preventive Medicine; Social Welfare; Surgery; Welfare and Protective Services); **Pharmaceutical Sciences** (Applied Chemistry; Biochemistry; Cosmetology; Information Sciences; Pharmacology; Pharmacy); **Science** (Applied Mathematics; Applied Physics; Biochemistry; Biology; Chemistry; Earth Sciences; Nanotechnology; Organic Chemistry; Statistics); **Sports and Health Science** (Health Education; Health Sciences; Physical Education; Sports; Sports Medicine)

Further information: Also Fukuoka University Hospital; Fukuoka University Chikushi Hospital;

History: Founded 1934 as Fukuoka Higher Commercial School, acquired present status 1949. Present title adopted 1956.

Academic year: April to March (April-July; September-March)

Admission requirements: Graduation from high school or foreign equivalent, and entrance examination

Main language(s) of instruction: Japanese

Accrediting agency: Japan University Accreditation Association (JUAA)

Degrees and diplomas: Associate's Degree (Academic), Gakushi (Architecture; Business Administration; Chemical Engineering; Chemistry; Civil Engineering; Economics; Education; Law; Management; Mathematics and Computer Science; Mechanical Engineering; Medicine; Modern Languages; Psychology; Sports Medicine), Shushi (Chemistry; Earth Sciences; Economics; Electrical Engineering; Electronic Engineering; Geography; History; Law; Mathematics and Computer Science; Mechanical Engineering; Modern Languages; Natural Sciences; Sports Medicine), Hakase (Applied Mathematics; Applied Physics; Automation and Control Engineering; Biological and Life Sciences; Biology; Business and Commerce; Chemistry; Civil Law; Criminal Law; Earth Sciences; Economics; Education; Energy Engineering; English; Environmental Engineering; French; German; Information Technology; Japanese; Literature; Medicine; Pathology; Pharmacy; Psychology; Public Health; Public Law; Social and Preventive Medicine; Sports Medicine). Also Juris Doctor (JD) - Graduate Professional Diploma in Legal Practice.

Student Services: Sports Facilities, Language Laboratory, Health Services, Foreign Studies Centre

Periodicals: Journals (Law, Economics, Commercial Sciences, Humanities, Medicine, Physical Education, Technological Sciences, Pharmaceutical Sciences)

Academic Staff 2012-2013	MALE	FEMALE	TOTAL
FULL-TIME			1363
Student Numbers 2012-2013			
All (Foreign Included)			20356

Last Update: 26-03-2018

Fukuyama Heisei University

117-1 Syouto Kamiiwanari Miyuki-cho
Fukuyama-shi 720-0001, Hiroshima
Tel: +81(84) 972-5001
Fax: +81(84) 972-7771
Website: http://www.heisei-u.ac.jp

Faculty

Business Administration (Business Administration); **Nursing** (Nursing); **Welfare and Health Science** (Child Care and Development; Education; Health Sciences; Sports; Welfare and Protective Services)

Graduate School

Business Administration (Business Administration; Information Management; Information Sciences; Information Technology; Management); **Midwifery** (Midwifery); **Nursing** (Nursing); **Sports and Health Science** (Health Sciences; Sports)

History: Founded 1994.
Fees: Tuition, 400,000-700,000 per annum (Yen)
Main language(s) of instruction: Japanese
Accrediting agency: Japan Institution for Higher Education Evaluation (JIHEE)
Degrees and diplomas: Gakushi (Management), Shushi
Student Services: Sports Facilities, Canteen
Last Update: 27-03-2018

Fukuyama University

1 Sanzo Gakuen-cho
Fukuyama-shi 729-0292, Hiroshima
Tel: +81(849) 36-2111
Fax: +81(849) 36-2213
Website: http://www.fukuyama-u.ac.jp
President: Fumiko Matsuda

Faculty

Economics (Accountancy; Economics; International Economics; Taxation); **Engineering** (Architecture; Civil Engineering; Computer Engineering; Design; Electrical and Electronic Engineering; Engineering; Information Technology; Mechanical Engineering; Systems Analysis); **Human Cultures** (Cultural Studies; Environmental Studies; Information Sciences;

Media Studies; Psychology); **Life Science and Biotechnology** (Biological and Life Sciences; Biotechnology; Marine Biology; Marine Science and Oceanography; Nutrition); **Pharmacy** (Biology; Pharmacology; Pharmacy)

Graduate School

Graduate Studies (Architecture; Biological and Life Sciences; Biotechnology; Civil Engineering; Design; Economics; Electrical and Electronic Engineering; Electronic Engineering; Information Technology; Mechanical Engineering; Pharmacology; Pharmacy; Production Engineering; Psychology)

Further information: Also Intensive Japanese Programme (IJP) for students of sister universities, held for one month a year. Intensive English Programme (IEP) at UCR (sister university), for one month a year

History: Founded 1975, consisted of the Faculties of Economics and Engineering. Faculty of Pharmacy and Pharmaceutical Sciences added 1983.

Academic year: April to March (April-September; September-March)

Admission requirements: Graduation from high school or equivalent, or foreign equivalent and entrance examination

Main language(s) of instruction: Japanese

Accrediting agency: Japan University Accreditation Association (JUAA)

Degrees and diplomas: Gakushi (Architecture; Computer Science; Economics; Electrical and Electronic Engineering; Mechanical Engineering; Media Studies; Psychology), Shushi (Psychology), Hakase (Bioengineering; Computer Engineering; Electronic Engineering; Engineering; Pharmacy; Production Engineering)

Student Services: Health Services, Canteen

Periodicals: Annual Report of the Faculty of Pharmacy and Pharmaceutical Sciences, Bulletin of the Research Centre for Human Science, Journal of the Faculty of Liberal Arts, Report of the Research Institute of Marine Bioresources, Scientific Report of the Japan Research Institute of Industrial Science, The Fukuyama Economic Review, The Memoirs of the Faculty of Engineering

Academic Staff 2012-2013	MALE	FEMALE	TOTAL
FULL-TIME			c. 240
Student Numbers 2012-2013			
All (Foreign Included)			c. 5500

Last Update: 26-03-2018

Gakushuin University

1-5-1 Mejiro, Toshima-ku
Tokyo 171-8588
Tel: +81(3) 3986-0221
Fax: +81(3) 5992-1005
Website: http://www.gakushuin.ac.jp/univ
President: Toshizaku Inoue

Faculty

Economics (Business Administration; Economics; Management); **Law** (Law; Political Sciences); **Letters** (Aesthetics; Art History; Arts and Humanities; English; Foreign Languages Education; French; German; History; Japanese; Literature; Philosophy; Psychology); **Science** (Chemistry; Mathematics; Molecular Biology; Natural Sciences; Physics)

Course/Programme

Careers studies (Library Science; Teacher Training)

School

Law (*Professional*) (Law)

Centre

Computer (Computer Science); **Foreign Language Teaching and Research** (Arts and Humanities; Chinese; English; Foreign Languages Education; French; German; Literature); **Sports and Health Sciences** (Health Sciences; Sports)

Graduate School

Economics (Economics); **Humanities** (Arts and Humanities; English; French; German; History; Japanese; Literature; Philosophy; Psychology); **Law** (Law); **Management** (Management); **Political Studies** (Political Sciences); **Science** (Chemistry; Mathematics; Physics)

Research Division

Oriental Cultures (Asian Studies)

History: Founded 1877 as School, financed by the Imperial Ministry of Education. Became University 1949. A private Institution financed by student fees and donations.

Academic year: April to March (April-September; September-March)

Admission requirements: Graduation from high school or equivalent and entrance examination

Fees: Registration, 300,000; tuition, 871,300-1,315,800 per annum (Yen)

Main language(s) of instruction: Japanese

Accrediting agency: Japan University Accreditation Association

Degrees and diplomas: Gakushi, Shushi, Hakase (Economics; German; History; Japanese; Law; Literature; Management; Mathematics; Philosophy; Physics; Political Sciences; Technology)

Student Services: Social Counselling, Careers Guidance, Sports Facilities, Facilities for disabled people, Health Services, Canteen, Foreign Studies Centre

Periodicals: Gakushuin Economic Papers, Gakushuin Review of Law and Politics, Gakushuin University Studies, The Annual Collection of Essays and Studies (Faculty of Letters)

Academic Staff 2013-2014	MALE	FEMALE	TOTAL
FULL-TIME			1538
Student Numbers 2013-2014			
All (Foreign Included)			13835

Last Update: 27-11-2017

Gakushuin Women's College

3-20-1 Toyama Shinjuku-ku
Tokyo 162-8650
Tel: +81(3) 3203-1906
Fax: +81(3) 3203-8873
Website: http://www.gwc.gakushuin.ac.jp/english
President: Norishiro Kanda

Faculty
Intercultural Studies (Asian Studies; Communication Studies; Cultural Studies; Development Studies; Economics; English; Environmental Studies; Foreign Languages Education; International Economics; Japanese; Library Science; Media Studies; Native Language Education; Political Sciences)

Graduate School
International Cultural Relations (Art Management; Cultural Studies; International Relations; International Studies)
History: Founded 1998.
Academic year: April to March (April-August; September-January)
Admission requirements: April to August
Fees: Undergraduate tuition, 840,000 per annum; Graduate tuition, 600,000 per annum (Yen)
Main language(s) of instruction: Japanese
Accrediting agency: Japan University Accreditation Association (JUAA)
Degrees and diplomas: Gakushi (International Studies; Japanese), Shushi
Student Services: Health Services

Academic Staff 2012-2013	MALE	FEMALE	TOTAL
FULL-TIME			40
PART-TIME			c. 100
Student Numbers 2012-2013			
All (Foreign Included)			c. 1440
Foreign only			20

Last Update: 27-03-2018

Gifu Keizai University

5-50 Kitagata-cho
Ogaki-shi 503-8550, Gifu
Tel: +81(584) 77-3511
Fax: +81(584) 81-7807, +81(584) 77-3512
Website: http://www.gifu-keizai.ac.jp
President: Takeshi Yamada

Faculty
Economics (Asian Studies; Development Studies; Economic and Finance Policy; Economics; Environmental Studies; International Studies; Public Administration; Social and Community Services; Social Welfare; Welfare and Protective Services)

School
Business Administration (Business Administration; Information Management; Information Sciences; Information Technology; Multimedia; Physical Education; Radio and Television Broadcasting; Sports; Sports Management; Telecommunications Engineering)

Department/Division
Bekka (*For international students*) (Japanese)

Graduate School
Business Administration (Accountancy; Business Administration; Economic and Finance Policy; Information Management; Management; Marketing; Media Studies; Regional Studies; Taxation; Urban Studies)
History: Founded 1967.
Fees: For Japanese students, undergraduate tuition, 700,000 per annum and graduate tuition fee, 570,000 per annum; For international students, undergraduate tuition, 350,000 per annum and graduate tuition fee, 399,000 per annum (Yen)
Main language(s) of instruction: Japanese
Accrediting agency: Japan Institution for Higher Education Evaluation (JIHEE)
Degrees and diplomas: Gakushi (Business Administration; Economics), Shushi (Business Administration; Economics)
Student Services: Sports Facilities, Canteen
Periodicals: Gifu Keizai Daigaku research Sosho, Journal of "local economy"
Last Update: 27-03-2018

Gifu Shotoku Gakuen University

Takakuwanishi Yanaizu-cho
Hashima-gun 501-6174, Gifu
Tel: +81(58) 279-0804

Fax: +81(58) 279-4171
Website: http://www.shotoku.ac.jp
President: Noriyuki Fujii

Faculty

Education (Clinical Psychology; Curriculum; Education; Educational Psychology; Foreign Languages Education; Health Education; Humanities and Social Science Education; Mathematics Education; Music Education; Native Language Education; Physical Education; Preschool Education; Primary Education; Psychology; Science Education; Secondary Education; Teacher Training)

Department/Division

Economic Information (Behavioural Sciences; Economics; Information Sciences); **Foreign Studies** (Chinese; English)

Graduate School

Economic Information (Economics; Information Sciences); **International Cultural Studies** (Cultural Studies; International Studies; Regional Studies)

Research Division

Buddhist Culture (Asian Religious Studies); **Economic Information** (*International*) (Economics; Information Sciences); **Education** (Education)
Further information: Also Gifu Campus
History: Founded 1963 by Shin Buddhist priests (Nishi Honganji Temple), and named after Prince Shotokum (AD 574-622). Known as Shokotu Gakuen Gifu Kyoiku Daigaku/Gifu University for Education and Languages until 1998.
Fees: 200,000 per annum (Yen)
Accrediting agency: Japan Institution for Higher Education Evaluation (JIHEE)
Degrees and diplomas: Gakushi, Shushi, Hakase (Economics; Information Sciences)
Student Services: Academic Counselling, Sports Facilities, Health Services
Last Update: 02-02-2018

Gifu University of Medical Sciences

Seki-shi, Gifu Ichihiraga character Nagamine 795-1
Gifu 501-3892
Tel: +81(575) 22-9401
Fax: +81(575) 23-0884
Website: http://www.u-gifu-ms.ac.jp

School

Health Sciences (Food Technology; Health Sciences; Laboratory Techniques; Medical Technology; Nursing; Public Health; Radiology); **Midwifery** (Midwifery)

History: Founded 2006.
Admission requirements: Entrance examination
Main language(s) of instruction: Japanese
Accrediting agency: Japan Council for Quality Higher Education (JIHEE)
Degrees and diplomas: Gakushi (Health Sciences)

Academic Staff 2013-2014	MALE	FEMALE	TOTAL
FULL-TIME			63
Student Numbers 2013-2014			
All (Foreign Included)			1481

Last Update: 28-03-2018

Gifu Women's University

80 Taromaru
Gifu-shi 501-2592, Gifu
Tel: +81(58) 229-2211
Fax: +81(58) 229-2222
Website: http://www.gijodai.ac.jp
President: Goto Tadahiko

Department/Division

Cultural Creativity Studies (Archiving; Painting and Drawing; Tourism); **Elementary Education** (Child Care and Development; Primary Education; Teacher Training; Vocational Counselling); **Health and Nutrition** (Food Science; Health Sciences; Nutrition); **Life Science** (Biological and Life Sciences; Child Care and Development; Clothing and Sewing; Dietetics; Educational Psychology; Environmental Studies; Family Studies; Fashion Design; Food Science; Home Economics; Information Sciences; Nutrition)

Graduate School

Graduate Studies (Biological and Life Sciences; Cultural Studies; English; Japanese; Primary Education)
Further information: Also special Japanese curriculum for foreign students
History: Founded 1968.
Main language(s) of instruction: Japanese
Accrediting agency: Japan Institution for Higher Education Evaluation (JIHEE)
Degrees and diplomas: Gakushi (Education; Home Economics; Literature), Shushi (Education; Home Economics; Literature)
Student Services: Sports Facilities

Academic Staff 2013-2014	MALE	FEMALE	TOTAL
FULL-TIME			c. 90
Student Numbers 2013-2014			
All (Foreign Included)			1084

Last Update: 27-03-2018

Graduate Institute for Entrepreneurial Studies

3-1-46 Yoneyama Chuo-ku
Niigata-shi 950-0916, Niigata
Tel: +81(25) 255-1250
Fax: +81(25) 255-1251
Website: http://www.jigyo.ac.jp
President: Sengoku Masakazu

Course/Programme
Entrepreneurial Studies (*Professional Degree Course*) (Business Administration; Finance; Management; Marketing)
Further information: Also Tokyo and Nagaoka campuses
History: Founded 2006.
Fees: Tuition, 250,000-550,000 per semester (Yen)
Main language(s) of instruction: Japanese
Accrediting agency: Japan University Accreditation Association
Degrees and diplomas: Shushi (Business Administration)
Last Update: 28-11-2017

Graduate School of Health Care Sciences, Jikei Institute

Osaka Miyahara, Yodogawa-ku, 1-2-8 (Shin-Osaka Station)
Osaka 532-0003
Tel: +81 6-6150-1336
Fax: +81 6-6150-1337
Website: http://www.ghsj.ac.jp
President: Hishiro Takeda

Graduate School
Medical Management
History: Founded 2011.
Main language(s) of instruction: Japanese
Accrediting agency: Japan Institution for Higher Education Evaluation (JIHEE)
Degrees and diplomas: Shushi (Health Administration)
Last Update: 28-11-2017

Graduate School of Management, GLOBIS University

Sumitomo Fudosan Kojimachi Bldg., 5-1 Niban-cho
Chiyoda-ku 102-0084, Tokyo
Tel: +81(120) 800-751
Fax: +81(06) 6391-0218
Website: http://mba.globis.ac.jp
President: Yoshito Hori

Course/Programme
Business Administration (*MBA*) (Accountancy; Business Administration; Finance; Human Resources; Leadership; Management; Marketing)
Further information: Campuses in Sendai and Fukuoka
History: Founded 2006.
Fees: Tuition, 3,800,000 (full-time); 2,826,000 (part-time) (Yen)
Main language(s) of instruction: Japanese, English
Accrediting agency: Japan University Accreditation Association
Degrees and diplomas: Shushi (Business Administration)
Last Update: 27-03-2018

Gumma Paz College

Takasaki, Gunma wholesaler cho 1-7-1
Gunma 370-0006
Tel: +81 27-365-3366
Fax: +81 27-365-3367
Website: http://www.paz.ac.jp
President: Masahiro Kurita

School
Medical Technology (Medical Technology); **Nursing** (Nursing); **Physical Therapy** (Health Sciences)
History: Founded 1998.
Fees: 1350000-1450000 (Yen)
Main language(s) of instruction: Japanese
Accrediting agency: Japan University Accreditation Association
Degrees and diplomas: Associate's Degree (Professional) (Nursing), High-level Specialist's Degree (Medicine), Shushi (Health Sciences)
Student Services: Careers Guidance, Cultural Activities, Sports Facilities, Health Services, Canteen, Library
Last Update: 28-11-2017

Gunma University of Health and Welfare

191-1 kawamagarimachi
Maebashi-shi 371-0823, Gunma
Tel: +81(27) 253-0294
Fax: +81(27) 254-0294
Website: http://www.shoken-gakuen.ac.jp/en
President: Suzuki Toshisada

Faculty
Rehabilitation (Occupational Therapy; Physical Therapy; Rehabilitation and Therapy)

School

Nursing (Nursing); **Social Welfare** (Child Care and Development; Education; Primary Education; Social Psychology; Social Welfare)

Graduate School

Social Welfare (Social Welfare)
Further information: Also Fujioka campus
History: Founded 2002 as Gunma University of Social Welfare. Acquired present title 2010.
Fees: 400,000-480,000 per annum (Yen)
Main language(s) of instruction: Japanese
Accrediting agency: Japan Institution for Higher Education Evaluation (JIHEE)
Degrees and diplomas: Gakushi (Health Sciences; Social Welfare), Shushi (Health Sciences; Social Welfare)
Last Update: 28-03-2018

Hachinohe Gakuin University

13-98 Mihono
Hachinohe-shi 031-8588, Aomori
Tel: +81(178) 25-2711
Fax: +81(178) 25-2729
Website: http://www.hachinohe-u.ac.jp
President: Otani Masaki

Faculty

Business and Commerce (Business Administration; Business and Commerce; Farm Management; Information Management; Information Technology; Management; Public Administration); **Human Health** (Health Sciences; Nursing; Psychology; Social and Preventive Medicine)
History: Founded 1981 as Hachinohe Daigaku (Hachinohe University). Acquired present title 2013.
Main language(s) of instruction: Japanese
Accrediting agency: Japan Institution for Higher Education Evaluation (JIHEE)
Degrees and diplomas: Gakushi (Nursing)
Last Update: 28-03-2018

Hachinohe Institute of Technology (HIT)

88-1 Obiraki Myo
Hachinohe 031-8501, Aomori
Tel: +81(178) 25-8111
Fax: +81(178) 25-1966
Website: http://www.hi-tech.ac.jp
President: Akira Hasegawa

Faculty

Engineering (Architectural and Environmental Design; Architecture; Automotive Engineering; Biological and Life Sciences; Biotechnology; Civil Engineering; Computer Engineering; Computer Graphics; Computer Networks; Computer Science; Data Processing; Electrical and Electronic Engineering; Engineering; Environmental Engineering; Mechanical Engineering; Robotics; Software Engineering; Structural Architecture); **Kansei Design** (Design; Graphic Design; Visual Arts)

Graduate School

Engineering (Biochemistry; Chemical Engineering; Civil Engineering; Electrical and Electronic Engineering; Electrical Engineering; Electronic Engineering; Engineering; Information Technology; Mechanical Engineering; Safety Engineering; Structural Architecture)
History: Founded 1972.
Main language(s) of instruction: Japanese
Accrediting agency: Japan Institution for Higher Education Evaluation (JIHEE)
Degrees and diplomas: Gakushi, Shushi, Hakase (Civil Engineering; Electrical and Electronic Engineering; Mechanical Engineering; Structural Architecture)
Student Services: Sports Facilities, Language Laboratory, Health Services
Last Update: 25-05-2018

Hagoromo University of International Studies

1-89-1 Hamaderaminamimachi
Sakai-shi 592-8344, Osaka
Tel: +81(72) 265-7000
Fax: +81(72) 265-8202
Website: http://www.hagoromo.ac.jp
President: Kishimoto Yukiomi

Faculty

Contemporary Sociology (Cultural Studies; English; Media Studies; Radio and Television Broadcasting; Sports; Tourism); **Human Life** (Food Science; Management; Nutrition; Welfare and Protective Services)
History: Founded 2002.
Main language(s) of instruction: Japanese
Accrediting agency: Japan Institution for Higher Education Evaluation (JIHEE)
Degrees and diplomas: Gakushi (Economics; Media Studies; Social Sciences)
Last Update: 28-03-2018

Hakodate University

51-1 Takaoka-cho
Hakodate-shi 042-0955, Hokkaido
Tel: +81(138) 57-1181
Fax: +81(138) 57-0298
Website: http://www.hakodate-u.ac.jp

Faculty

Commerce (Business Administration; Business and Commerce; English; International Business; Management; Marketing)

Department/Division

International Studies (Teacher Training)
History: Founded 1965.
Accrediting agency: Japan Institution for Higher Education Evaluation (JIHEE)
Degrees and diplomas: Gakushi

Academic Staff 2013-2014	MALE	FEMALE	TOTAL
FULL-TIME			72
Student Numbers 2013-2014			
All (Foreign Included)			388

Last Update: 29-11-2017

Hakuoh University

1117 Daigyoji
Oyama-shi 323-8585, Tochigi
Tel: +81(285) 22-1111
Fax: +81(285) 22-8989
Website: http://hakuoh.jp/english
President: Takayasu Okushima

Faculty

Business Management (Accountancy; Business Administration; Business and Commerce; Information Management; International Business; Management); **Education** (Child Care and Development; Education; Foreign Languages Education; Health Education; Physical Education; Preschool Education; Primary Education; Psychology); **Law** (International Law; Law; Political Sciences)

School

Graduate Studies (Business Administration; Civil Law; Commercial Law; Criminal Law; Law)
History: Founded 1986.
Main language(s) of instruction: Japanese, English
Accrediting agency: Japan University Accreditation Association (JUAA)

Degrees and diplomas: Gakushi (Business Administration; Law), Shushi (Business Administration; Law)
Student Services: Sports Facilities, Canteen

Student Numbers 2013-2014	MALE	FEMALE	TOTAL
All (Foreign Included)			c. 4000

Last Update: 27-03-2018

Hamamatsu Gakuin University (HGU)

3-2-3 Nunohashi
Hamamatsu-shi 432-8012, Shizuoka
Tel: +81(53) 450-7000
Fax: +81(53) 450-7110
Website: http://www.hgu.ac.jp
President: Katsuyoshi Ishida

Department/Division

Children's Communication (Child Care and Development; Leadership; Preschool Education; Primary Education; Teacher Training); **Regional Co-creation** (Management; Psychology)
History: Founded 2004.
Main language(s) of instruction: Japanese
Accrediting agency: Japan Institution for Higher Education Evaluation (JIHEE)
Degrees and diplomas: Gakushi (Child Care and Development; Education; Sociology)
Student Services: Sports Facilities
Last Update: 27-03-2018

Hanazono University

8-1 Tsubonouchi-cho Nishinokyo, Nakagyo-ku
Kyoto-shi 604-8456, Kyoto
Tel: +81(75) 811-5181
Fax: +81(75) 823-0580
Website: http://www.hanazono.ac.jp
President: Mitsuhiro Tanji

Faculty

Letters (Arts and Humanities; Asian Religious Studies; Cultural Studies; History; Japanese; Literature; Religion; Social Studies; Writing); **Social Welfare** (Child Care and Development; Clinical Psychology; Social Welfare)

Graduate School

Graduate Studies (Asian Religious Studies; History; Literature; Social Welfare)

Further information: Also Graduate School
History: Founded 1872.
Fees: Undergraduate tuition, 796,000-799,000 per annum; Graduate tuition, 620,000-623,000 per annum (Yen)
Main language(s) of instruction: Japanese
Accrediting agency: Japan Institution for Higher Education Evaluation (JIHEE)
Degrees and diplomas: Gakushi (Clinical Psychology; Cultural Studies; History; Japanese; Literature; Psychology; Social Welfare), Shushi (Asian Religious Studies; Cultural Studies; Literature; Social Welfare), Hakase (Asian Religious Studies; Cultural Studies; Literature)
Student Services: Canteen

Academic Staff 2013-2014	MALE	FEMALE	TOTAL
FULL-TIME	58	24	82
PART-TIME	171	105	276
Student Numbers 2013-2014			
All (Foreign Included)			2105

Last Update: 27-03-2018

Hannan University

5-4-33 Amamihigashi Matsubara
Matsubara-shi 580-8502, Osaka
Tel: +81(72) 332-1224
Fax: +81(72) 336-2633
Website: http://www.hannan-u.ac.jp
President: Iromu Inoue

Faculty

Business (Business Administration; Management; Marketing; Sports Management); **Economics** (Economics; Information Sciences; Information Technology; International Economics); **International Communication** (Cultural Studies; History; International Studies; Linguistics; Media Studies; Psychology; Radio and Television Broadcasting; Religion; Social Studies; Tourism); **International Tourism** (Advertising and Publicity; Business Administration; Hotel and Restaurant; Management; Marketing; Tourism); **Management Information** (Accountancy; Business Computing; E- Business/Commerce; Information Sciences; Information Technology; Management; Marketing; Multimedia)

Course/Programme

Overseas Study (*International - 1 year, 6 months or 1 month*)

Graduate School

Corporate Information (Accountancy; Business Administration; Economics; Finance; Information Sciences; Information Technology; International Economics; International Relations; Management; Marketing)
Further information: Also Special courses in Japanese for foreign exchange students.
History: Founded 1965.
Main language(s) of instruction: Japanese
Accrediting agency: Japan University Accreditation Association (JUAA)
Degrees and diplomas: Gakushi (Business Administration; Economics; Information Management; Modern Languages; Tourism), Shushi (Business Administration)

Student Numbers 2013-2014	MALE	FEMALE	TOTAL
All (Foreign Included)	3320	1599	4919

Last Update: 27-03-2018

Health Science University

7187 Kodachi
Fujikawaguchiko 401-0380, Yamanashi
Tel: +81 (555) 83 5200
Fax: +81 (555) 83 5100
Website: http://www.kenkoudai.ac.jp
President: Araki Tsutomu

Department/Division

Common Courses (Health Sciences); **Occupational Therapy** (Rehabilitation and Therapy); **Physical Therapy** (Health Sciences)
History: Founded 2003.
Main language(s) of instruction: Japanese
Accrediting agency: Japan Institution for Higher Education Evaluation (JIHEE)
Degrees and diplomas: Gakushi (Health Sciences; Psychology; Rehabilitation and Therapy)
Student Services: Canteen, Library
Last Update: 29-11-2017

Health Sciences University of Hokkaido (HSUH)

1757 Kanazawa
Tobetsu-cho 061-0293, Ishikari-gun
Tel: +81(133) 23-1211
Fax: +81(133) 23-1669
Website: http://www.hoku-iryo-u.ac.jp
President: Masahiro Asaka

Faculty

Pharmaceutical Sciences (Analytical Chemistry; Applied Chemistry; Biochemistry; Biological and Life Sciences;

Biophysics; Environmental Studies; Health Sciences; Hygiene; Immunology; Law; Microbiology; Molecular Biology; Pathology; Pharmacology; Pharmacy; Physical Chemistry; Physiology; Toxicology)

School

Dentistry (Anaesthesiology; Anatomy; Biochemistry; Bioengineering; Biology; Dental Technology; Dentistry; Epidemiology; Gerontology; Histology; Microbiology; Oral Pathology; Orthodontics; Paediatrics; Periodontics; Pharmacology; Physiology; Radiology; Surgery); **Nursing and Social Services** (Anatomy; Child Care and Development; Community Health; Ethics; Gerontology; Health Sciences; Medicine; Nursing; Oncology; Pathology; Physiology; Psychiatry and Mental Health; Social and Community Services; Social Policy; Social Welfare; Social Work; Surgery); **Psychology** (Anatomy; Art Therapy; Behavioural Sciences; Clinical Psychology; Cognitive Sciences; Communication Disorders; Computer Science; Developmental Psychology; Educational and Student Counselling; Educational Psychology; English; Ethics; French; Genetics; Linguistics; Natural Sciences; Neurosciences; Otorhinolaryngology; Philosophy; Phonetics; Physiology; Psychiatry and Mental Health; Psychology; Psychotherapy; Social Psychology; Speech Therapy and Audiology; Statistics); **Rehabilitation Sciences** (Rehabilitation and Therapy); **Vocational Studies** (Dental Hygiene)

Graduate School

Clinical Psychology (Clinical Psychology; Communication Disorders; Linguistics; Speech Therapy and Audiology); **Dentistry** (Anaesthesiology; Anatomy; Biochemistry; Dental Hygiene; Dental Technology; Dentistry; Health Sciences; Histology; Hygiene; Microbiology; Oral Pathology; Orthodontics; Paediatrics; Periodontics; Pharmacology; Radiology; Surgery); **Nursing and Social Services** (Gerontology; Nursing; Oncology; Paediatrics; Psychiatry and Mental Health; Social Sciences; Social Work); **Pharmaceutical Sciences** (Applied Chemistry; Biochemistry; Biological and Life Sciences; Hygiene; Molecular Biology; Pharmacology; Pharmacy; Physics; Physiology); **Rehabilitation Sciences** (Rehabilitation and Therapy)

Further information: Also Campus in Ainosato districts.
History: Founded 1974.
Academic year: April to March (April-September; October-March)
Admission requirements: Graduation from high school and entrance examination
Main language(s) of instruction: Japanese
Accrediting agency: Japanese University Accreditation Association (JUAA)
Degrees and diplomas: Gakushi, Shushi (Biological and Life Sciences; Clinical Psychology; Linguistics; Nursing;

Pharmacology; Rehabilitation and Therapy; Speech Therapy and Audiology), Hakase (Clinical Psychology; Dentistry; Linguistics; Pharmacology; Speech Therapy and Audiology)

Student Services: Academic Counselling, Social Counselling, Careers Guidance, Sports Facilities, Facilities for disabled people, Health Services, Canteen

Student Numbers 2013-2014	MALE	FEMALE	TOTAL
All (Foreign Included)	1376	1926	3302

Last Update: 29-11-2017

Heian Jogakuin St. Agnes University

5-81-1 Nampeidai
Takatsuki-shi 569-1092, Osaka
Tel: +81(72) 693-2311
Fax: +81(72) 696-4919
Website: http://www.heian.ac.jp
President: Yamaoka Keichiro

Faculty

International Tourism (Tourism)

Department/Division

Children's Education (Child Care and Development; Environmental Studies; Preschool Education; Primary Education)
Further information: Also Takatsuki campus
History: Founded 1950.
Fees: Tuition, 490,000 per annum (Yen)
Main language(s) of instruction: Japanese
Accrediting agency: Japan Institution for Higher Education Evaluation (JIHEE)
Degrees and diplomas: Gakushi (Tourism)
Student Services: Health Services, Canteen

Student Numbers 2013-2014	MALE	FEMALE	TOTAL
All (Foreign Included)			427
Foreign only			27

Last Update: 27-03-2018

Heisei College of Music

1658 Takigawa Mifune-cho
Kamimashiki-gun 861-3295, Kumamoto
Tel: +81(96) 282-0506
Fax: +81(96) 282-7800
Website: http://www.heisei-music.ac.jp
President: Keizo Ideta

Department/Division
Children's Education (Child Care and Development; Food Science; Music; Nutrition; Psychology; Teacher Training; Vegetable Production); **Music** (Music; Music Education; Musical Instruments; Performing Arts; Singing)
History: Founded 2001.
Main language(s) of instruction: Japanese
Accrediting agency: Japan Institution for Higher Education Evaluation (JIHEE)
Degrees and diplomas: Gakushi (Music)
Last Update: 26-03-2018

Heisei International University (HIU)

2000 Otateno Mizubuka
Kazo-shi 347-8504, Saitama
Tel: +81(480) 66-2100, +81(480) 66-2277
Fax: +81(480) 65-2101
Website: http://www.hiu.ac.jp
President: Makoto Donomoto

Faculty

Law (Administration; Cultural Studies; English; Law; Management; Modern Languages; Multimedia; Political Sciences; Sports; Welfare and Protective Services)

Graduate School

Law (Law; Political Sciences; Public Administration)

Research Division

Sports Science (Sports)
History: Founded 1996.
Main language(s) of instruction: Japanese
Accrediting agency: Japan Institution for Higher Education Evaluation (JIHEE)
Degrees and diplomas: Gakushi (Law; Political Sciences), Shushi (Law; Political Sciences)
Student Services: Sports Facilities, Language Laboratory
Periodicals: Heisei Kokusai Daigaku Institute Journal, Heisei Kokusai Daigaku Journal, Heisei Kokusai Daigaku Sports Science Institute of information Journal, Heisei Study Law and Politics Journal

Academic Staff 2013-2014	MALE	FEMALE	TOTAL
FULL-TIME			42
Student Numbers 2013-2014			
All (Foreign Included)			1007
Foreign only			1

Last Update: 27-03-2018

Higashi Nippon International University

37 Suganezawa Taira-Kamata
Iwaki-shi 970-8023, Fukushima
Tel: +81(246) 35-0001, +81(246) 35-0002
Fax: +81(246) 25-9188
Website: http://www.shk-ac.jp
President: Koji Yoshimura

Faculty

Bekka (Cultural Studies; Grammar; Japanese; Social Studies; Writing); **Economic Informatics** (Business Administration; Economics; Information Management; Information Technology; International Economics; Management; Sports Management); **Social and Environmental Services** (Environmental Management; Environmental Studies; Social and Community Services; Social Psychology; Social Welfare; Social Work; Teacher Training)
History: Founded 1995.
Fees: 720,000 per annum (Yen)
Main language(s) of instruction: Japanese
Accrediting agency: Japan Institution for Higher Education Evaluation (JIHEE)
Degrees and diplomas: Gakushi
Last Update: 28-03-2018

Higashi Osaka College

3-1-1 Nishitsutsumi Gakuencho
Higashiosaka-shi 577-8567, Osaka
Tel: +81(6) 6782-2824
Fax: +81(6) 6782-2896
Website: http://www.higashiosaka.ac.jp
President: Marukami Yasuhiro

Faculty

Child Science (Asian Studies; Business Administration; Child Care and Development; Cultural Studies; International Studies; Modern Languages; Preschool Education)

College

Junior Studies (Health Sciences; Nutrition; Preschool Education)
History: Founded 2003.
Main language(s) of instruction: Japanese
Accrediting agency: Japan Institution for Higher Education Evaluation (JIHEE)
Degrees and diplomas: Gakushi (Child Care and Development)
Last Update: 28-03-2018

Hijiyama University

4-1-1 Ushita Shin-machi Higashi-ku
Hiroshima-shi 732-8509, Hiroshima
Tel: +81(82) 229-0121
Fax: +81(82) 229-3033, +81(82) 229-5100
Website: http://www.hijiyama-u.ac.jp
President: Ishii Shinji

Faculty
Contemporary Culture (Administration; Advertising and Publicity; Child Care and Development; Clinical Psychology; Communication Studies; Cultural Studies; English; Japanese; Literature; Mass Communication; Modern Languages; Preschool Education; Regional Studies; Social Psychology; Tourism)

College
Junior Studies (Design; Dietetics; Fine Arts; Information Technology; Interior Design; Preschool Education)

Graduate School
Graduate Studies (American Studies; Clinical Psychology; Cultural Studies; English; Foreign Languages Education; Information Management; Information Sciences; Japanese; Linguistics; Media Studies; Modern Languages; Psychiatry and Mental Health; Psychology; Psychotherapy; Social Psychology)
History: Founded 1994.
Main language(s) of instruction: Japanese
Accrediting agency: Japan Institution for Higher Education Evaluation (JIHEE)
Degrees and diplomas: Gakushi (Child Care and Development; Cultural Studies; Dietetics; Education; Mass Communication; Modern Languages; Psychology), Shushi (Cultural Studies; Literature; Mass Communication; Modern Languages; Psychology)
Last Update: 27-03-2018

Himeji Dokkyo University (Dokkyo Group)

7-2-1 Kami-Ono
Himeji-shi 670-8524, Hyogo
Tel: +81(79) 223-6515, +81(79) 223-9157
Fax: +81(79) 223-6508, +81(79) 223-6612
Website: http://www.himeji-du.ac.jp
President: Yoshiaki Honda

Faculty
Economics and information Sciences (Business Computing; Economics; Information Sciences; Information Technology; Teacher Training); **Foreign Languages** (Chinese; English; German; Japanese; Korean; Modern Languages; Spanish; Teacher Training); **Health and Medical Sciences** (Engineering; Health Sciences; Medical Technology; Occupational Therapy; Physical Therapy; Teacher Training); **Law** (Law; Teacher Training)

Department/Division
Pharmacy (Pharmacy)

Graduate School
Economic Information Studies (Economics); **Language Education** (Chinese; Cultural Studies; English; Foreign Languages Education; German; Japanese; Literature); **Law** (Administrative Law; Civil Law; Commercial Law; Constitutional Law; Criminal Law; English; International Law; International Studies; Law; Political Sciences)
History: Founded 1987. Forms part of the Dokkyo Gakuen (Dokkyo Group of Academic Institution), founded 1883 as School for the Association of German Studies.
Admission requirements: Graduation from high school and entrance examination
Fees: For Japanese students, Entrance fee, 300,000; Tuition fee, 800,000-1,400,000 per annum for undergraduate programmes and 500,000 per annum for graduate programmes; For international students, Entrance fee, 200,000; Tuition, 400,000 per semester for undergraduate programmes and 250,000 per semester for graduate programmes (Yen)
Main language(s) of instruction: Japanese
Accrediting agency: Japan University Accreditation Association (JUAA)
Degrees and diplomas: Gakushi, Shushi
Student Services: Sports Facilities, Language Laboratory, Health Services

Academic Staff 2013-2014	MALE	FEMALE	TOTAL
FULL-TIME			c. 150
Student Numbers 2013-2014			
All (Foreign Included)	1356	784	2140

Last Update: 30-11-2017

Hirosaki Gakuin University

13-1 Minori-cho Hirosaki-shi
Aomori-shi 036-8577, Aomori
Tel: +81(172) 34-5211
Fax: +81(172) 32-8768
Website: http://www.hirogaku-u.ac.jp
President: Yoshioka Toshitada

School

Graduate Studies (Literature; Social Welfare); **Nursing** (Nursing); **Social Welfare** (Social Welfare)

Department/Division

Literature (Arts and Humanities; English; Japanese; Literature)
History: Founded 1886.
Main language(s) of instruction: Japanese
Accrediting agency: Japan University Accreditation Association (JUAA)
Degrees and diplomas: Gakushi, Shushi
Last Update: 28-03-2018

Hirosaki University of Health and Welfare

Ooaza Sanpinai 3-chome 18
Hirosaki 036-8102, Aomori
Tel: +81 172-27-1001
Fax: +81 172-27-1023
Website: http://www.hirosakiuhw.jp
President: Atsuko Shimoda

Faculty

Health (Medical Technology; Nursing; Occupational Therapy; Speech Therapy and Audiology)
History: Founded 2002.
Main language(s) of instruction: Japanese
Accrediting agency: Japan Institution for Higher Education Evaluation (JIHEE)
Degrees and diplomas: Gakushi (Nursing; Occupational Therapy; Speech Therapy and Audiology)
Student Services: Library
Last Update: 01-12-2017

Hiroshima Bunka Gakuen University

1-1-1 Gohara Manabinooka
Kure-shi 737-0182, Hiroshima
Tel: +81(823) 703-300
Fax: +89(823) 703-311
Website: http://www.hbg.ac.jp
President: Koji Tanaka

Faculty

Arts and Science (Child Care and Development; Music);
Social Information Science (Information Sciences; Social Sciences)

School

Nursing (Nursing)

History: Founded 1995. Integrated Risshikan Daigaku/Risshikan University 2003. Formerly known as Kure University until 2009.
Main language(s) of instruction: Japanese
Accrediting agency: Japan Institution for Higher Education Evaluation (JIHEE)
Degrees and diplomas: Gakushi, Shushi (Nursing), Hakase (Nursing)
Last Update: 01-12-2017

Hiroshima Bunkyo Women's University

1-2-1 Kabehigashi, Asakita-ku
Hiroshima-shi 731-0295, Hiroshima
Tel: +81(82) 814-3191
Fax: +81(82) 815-6801
Website: http://www.h-bunkyo.ac.jp/university
President: Yamaguchi Iwakuni

Faculty

Humanities (Arts and Humanities; Clinical Psychology; Communication Studies; Education; English; Japanese; Nutrition; Primary Education; Psychology; Social Psychology; Social Welfare; Social Work; Teacher Training; Welfare and Protective Services)

Graduate School

Education and Social Sciences (Clinical Psychology; Education; English; Japanese; Literature; Social Sciences; Social Studies; Social Welfare)
History: Founded 1966.
Academic year: April to March (April-September; October-March)
Admission requirements: Graduation from high school and entrance examination
Main language(s) of instruction: Japanese
Accrediting agency: Japan Institution for Higher Education Evaluation (JIHEE)
Degrees and diplomas: Gakushi, Shushi. Also Teaching Qualifications
Student Services: Sports Facilities, Health Services
Periodicals: Hiroshima Bunkyo Women's College Bulletin, Lilium Bunkyo Japanese Literature
Last Update: 01-12-2017

Hiroshima Cosmopolitan University

5-13-18 Ujinanishi, Minami-ku
Hiroshima 734-0014, Hiroshima-shi
Tel: +81 82-250-1133
Fax: +81 82-250-1134

Website: http://www.hcu.ac.jp
President: Toshiaki Furusawa

Department/Division

Nursing (Nursing); **Occupational Therapy** (Occupational Therapy); **Physical Therapy** (Physical Therapy)
History: Founded 1974 as Chiyoda Institute of Management.
Main language(s) of instruction: Japanese
Accrediting agency: Japan Institution for Higher Education Evaluation (JIHEE)
Degrees and diplomas: Associate's Degree (Professional) (Nursing)
Student Services: Library
Last Update: 01-12-2017

Hiroshima Institute of Technology (HIT)

2-1-1 Miyake, Saeki-ku
Hiroshima-shi 731-5193, Hiroshima
Tel: +81(82) 921-3121
Fax: +81(82) 921-8934
Website: http://www.it-hiroshima.ac.jp
President: Tsuru Mamoru

Faculty

Applied Information Science (Computer Networks; Computer Science; Data Processing; Information Management; Information Sciences; Information Technology; Multimedia); **Engineering** (Architectural and Environmental Design; Automotive Engineering; Building Technologies; Computer Engineering; Construction Engineering; Electrical Engineering; Electronic Engineering; Energy Engineering; Engineering; Information Technology; Materials Engineering; Mechanical Engineering; Production Engineering; Robotics; Structural Architecture; Telecommunications Engineering; Town Planning); **Environmental Studies** (Architectural and Environmental Design; Earth Sciences; Environmental Studies); **Life Sciences** (Biological and Life Sciences; Biotechnology; Food Science)

Institute

International Education (Cultural Studies; Japanese)

Graduate School

Science and Technology (Architectural and Environmental Design; Architecture and Planning; Artificial Intelligence; Civil Engineering; Computer Engineering; Electrical and Electronic Engineering; Energy Engineering; Environmental Studies; Information Technology; Mechanical Engineering; Natural Sciences; Production Engineering; Software Engineering; Structural Architecture; Technology; Telecommunications Engineering)

Further information: Also Yachiyo and Numata Campuses.
History: Founded 1963.
Academic year: April to March (April-September; October-March)
Admission requirements: Graduation from high school or equivalent, and entrance examination
Main language(s) of instruction: Japanese
Accrediting agency: Japan Institution for Higher Education Evaluation (JIHEE)
Degrees and diplomas: Gakushi, Shushi, Hakase (Artificial Intelligence)
Student Services: Nursery Care, Cultural Activities, Sports Facilities
Periodicals: Research Bulletin
Last Update: 01-12-2017

Hiroshima International University

555-36 Kurosegakuendai Higashihiroshima City
Hiroshima-shi 739-2695, Hiroshima
Tel: +81(823) 70-4543
Website: http://www.hirokoku-u.ac.jp
President: Yakehiro Masuhide

Faculty

Engineering (Architectural and Environmental Design; Architecture; Engineering; Information Technology; Interior Design; Real Estate; Telecommunications Engineering); **Health and Welfare** (Health Sciences; Nursing; Social Psychology; Social Welfare; Social Work; Welfare and Protective Services); **Health Sciences** (Bioengineering; Health Sciences; Laboratory Techniques; Medical Technology; Occupational Therapy; Physical Therapy; Radiology; Rehabilitation and Therapy); **Health Services Management** (Business Administration; Health Administration; Health Sciences; Secretarial Studies); **Nursing** (Health Education; Nursing; Public Health); **Pharmaceutical Sciences** (Pharmacy); **Psychology** (Clinical Psychology; Communication Studies; Psychology)

Graduate School

Engineering (Architecture; Engineering; Environmental Engineering; Information Technology; Telecommunications Engineering); **Medical Technology and Health Welfare Sciences** (Health Administration; Health Sciences; Medical Technology; Social and Community Services; Welfare and Protective Services); **Nurisng** (Nursing); **Pharmaceutical Sciences** (Health Sciences; Pharmacy); **Psychological Sciences** (Clinical Psychology; Communication Studies; English; Psychology)
Further information: Also campuses in Kure and Hiroshima.

History: Founded 1998.
Main language(s) of instruction: Japanese
Accrediting agency: Japan Institution for Higher Education Evaluation (JIHEE)
Degrees and diplomas: Gakushi, Shushi, Hakase (Clinical Psychology; Medical Technology; Nursing; Pharmacy). Also Professional Degree Programme in Clinical Psychology

Student Numbers 2012-2012	MALE	FEMALE	TOTAL
All (Foreign Included)			c. 4500

Last Update: 01-12-2017

Hiroshima Jogakuin University

4-13-1 Ushita-Higashi Higashi-ku
Hiroshima-shi 732-0063, Hiroshima
Tel: +81(82) 228-0386
Fax: +81(82) 227-4502
Website: http://www.hju.ac.jp
President: Akiko Minato

Faculty

Human Life Sciences (Architecture; Clothing and Sewing; Construction Engineering; Design; Fashion Design; Information Management; Interior Design; Nutrition; Preschool Education; Psychology); **International Liberal Studies** (African Studies; American Studies; Art History; Asian Studies; Cultural Studies; English; English Studies; Environmental Studies; Fine Arts; Industrial Design; Information Sciences; Information Technology; International Studies; Japanese; Literature; Peace and Disarmament; Religion; Secretarial Studies; Tourism; Translation and Interpretation; Urban Studies; Women's Studies)

Graduate School

Human life Studies (Anthropology; Architecture; Arts and Humanities; Clothing and Sewing; Communication Studies; Design; Development Studies; Information Sciences; Interior Design; Management); **Language and Culture Studies** (American Studies; Architecture; Asian Studies; Cultural Studies; English; English Studies; Japanese; Library Science; Literature; Modern Languages; Nutrition; Psychology)
History: Founded 1932. Acquired present title 1949.
Fees: Undergraduate tuition, 760,000-810,000 per annum; Graduate tuition, 810,000 per annum (Yen)
Main language(s) of instruction: Japanese
Accrediting agency: Japan Institution for Higher Education Evaluation (JIHEE)
Degrees and diplomas: Gakushi, Shushi, Hakase (Cultural Studies; English; Japanese; Literature)
Last Update: 01-12-2017

Hiroshima Kokusai Gakuin University

6-20-1 Nakano Aki-ku, Hiroshima-shi
Hiroshima-shi 739-0321, Hiroshima
Tel: +81(82) 820-2524
Fax: +81(82) 820-2526
Website: http://www.hkg.ac.jp
President: Tsunetaka Sumomogi

Faculty

Contemporary Sociology (Communication Studies; English; Information Technology; Social Welfare; Sociology); **Engineering** (Agricultural Engineering; Bioengineering; Electrical Engineering; Engineering; Food Technology; Mechanical Engineering; Natural Sciences); **Information Design** (Communication Arts; Computer Engineering; Computer Graphics; Computer Networks; Computer Science; Design; Information Sciences; Information Technology; Media Studies; Sound Engineering (Acoustics); Video)

Graduate School

Contemporary Sociology (International Economics; Social Studies; Sociology; Urban Studies; Welfare and Protective Services); **Engineering** (Automation and Control Engineering; Electrical and Electronic Engineering; Electronic Engineering; Engineering; Information Technology; Instrument Making; Materials Engineering; Mechanical Engineering)
History: Founded 1927 as Hiroshima Technical Preparatory School. Renamed Hiroshima Denki Institute of Technology 1967. Acquired present title 1999.
Main language(s) of instruction: Japanese
Accrediting agency: Japan Institution for Higher Education Evaluation (JIHEE)
Degrees and diplomas: Gakushi, Shushi, Hakase (Materials Engineering; Sociology)
Student Services: Sports Facilities
Last Update: 01-12-2017

Hiroshima Shudo University (HSU)

1-1-1 Ozukahigashi Asaminami-ku
Hiroshima-shi 731-3195, Hiroshima
Tel: +81(82) 830-1103
Fax: +81(82) 830-1303
Website: http://www.shudo-u.ac.jp
President: Taichi Ichikawa

Faculty

Commercial Sciences (Accountancy; Administration; Business Administration; Business and Commerce; Finance; International Business; Management; Marketing; Tourism);

Economic Sciences (Business Computing; Computer Science; Economic and Finance Policy; Economics; Finance; Information Sciences; Information Technology; International Economics); **Human Environmental Studies** (Environmental Management; Environmental Studies); **Humanities and Human Sciences** (American Studies; Arts and Humanities; Constitutional Law; Education; Educational Psychology; English; English Studies; Literature; Natural Sciences; Psychology; Psychotherapy; Social Sciences; Sociology); **Law** (Administration; Administrative Law; Asian Studies; Canadian Studies; Civil Law; Commercial Law; Criminal Law; Criminology; English; Fiscal Law; History of Law; International Law; International Relations; Justice Administration; Law; Peace and Disarmament; Political Sciences; Private Law; Public Law; Regional Studies; Southeast Asian Studies)

Course/Programme
General Education (Arts and Humanities; Chinese; English; French; German; Health Education; Japanese; Korean; Modern Languages; Physical Education; Russian; Spanish); **Japanese Language** (*For International Students*) (Japanese)

Graduate School
Commercial Sciences (Accountancy; Business Administration; Business and Commerce; Finance; Insurance; Management; Marketing; Transport Management); **Economic Sciences** (Business Computing; Economic and Finance Policy; Economics; Information Technology; International Economics); **Humanities and Human Sciences** (Education; English; Linguistics; Literature; Psychology; Sociology); **Law** (Comparative Politics; European Studies; International Relations; Law; Peace and Disarmament; Political Sciences; Regional Studies); **Law** (Environmental Studies; Labour Law; Law; Private Law; Social Welfare; Welfare and Protective Services)

Further information: Also Japanese language and culture courses for foreign students

History: Founded 1952 as Junior College, acquired present status and title 1973.

Academic year: April to March (April-July; October-March)

Admission requirements: Graduation from high school and entrance examination

Fees: Undergraduate: registration fee: 280,000 per annum; tuition: 727,000 per annum; graduate: registration: 280,000 per annum; tuition: 557,000 per annum (Yen)

Main language(s) of instruction: Japanese

Accrediting agency: Japan University Accreditation Association (JUAA)

Degrees and diplomas: Gakushi, Shushi, Hakase (Business Administration; Business and Commerce; Economics; Literature; Psychology)

Student Services: Academic Counselling, Social Counselling, Careers Guidance, Sports Facilities, Facilities for disabled people, Health Services, Canteen, Foreign Studies Centre

Periodicals: Journal of Economic Sciences, Papers of the Research Society of Commerce and Economics, Shudo Law Review, Studies in Humanities and Sciences

Last Update: 01-12-2017

Hiroshima University of Economics

5-37-1 Gion, Asa Minami-ku
Hiroshima-shi 731-0192, Hiroshima
Tel: +81(82) 871-1000
Fax: +81(82) 871-1005
Website: http://www.hue.ac.jp
President: Yukio Odani

Department/Division
Business Administration (Accountancy; Business Administration; Business and Commerce; Management; Marketing); **Economics** (Economics); **Information system in Business** (Business Computing; Information Sciences; Information Technology); **Media Studies** (Advertising and Publicity; Media Studies; Publishing and Book Trade; Radio and Television Broadcasting); **Study of Regional Economies** (Cultural Studies; Economics; International Business; Modern Languages; Regional Studies)

Graduate School
Economics (Economics)

History: Founded 1907 as High School, acquired present status and title 1967.

Academic year: April to March (April-September; October-March)

Admission requirements: Graduation from high school or foreign equivalent and entrance examination

Fees: 900,000 per annum (Yen)

Main language(s) of instruction: Japanese

Accrediting agency: Japan Institution for Higher Education Evaluation (JIHEE)

Degrees and diplomas: Gakushi, Shushi, Hakase (Economics)

Student Services: Academic Counselling, Social Counselling, Careers Guidance, Sports Facilities, Language Laboratory, Health Services, Canteen, Foreign Studies Centre

Periodicals: Journal of Economics and Business, Journal of Humanities, Social and Natural Sciences

Last Update: 01-12-2017

Hokkai School of Commerce

6-6-10 Toyohira Toyohira-Ku
Sapporo-shi 062-8607, Hokkaido
Tel: +81(11) 841-1161

Fax: +81(11) 824-0801
Website: http://www.hokkai.ac.jp
President: Masao Morimoto

School

Commerce (Accountancy; Advertising and Publicity; Business and Commerce; Chinese; Communication Studies; English; Finance; Human Resources; Information Technology; International Business; Korean; Management; Tourism)

Graduate School

Commerce (Business Administration)
History: Founded 1977 as Hokkai Gakuen Kitami Daigaku (Hokkai-Gakuen University of Kitami).
Fees: Admission fee, 200,000; Tuition, 872,000 (Yen)
Main language(s) of instruction: Japanese
Accrediting agency: Japan Institution for Higher Education Evaluation (JIHEE)
Degrees and diplomas: Gakushi, Shushi (Business Administration), Hakase (Business Administration)
Student Services: Health Services

Academic Staff 2013-2014	MALE	FEMALE	TOTAL
FULL-TIME	35	6	41
Student Numbers 2013-2014			
All (Foreign Included)			157

Last Update: 04-12-2017

Hokkai-Gakuen University (HGU)

1-40, 4-chome Asahi-machi, Toyohira-ku
Sapporo-shi 062-8605, Hokkaido
Tel: +81(11) 841-1161
Fax: +81(11) 824-3141
Website: http://hgu.jp
President: Yasukata Toshimada

Faculty

Business (Accountancy; Business Administration; Information Sciences; Management; Marketing; Psychology); **Economics** (Development Studies; East Asian Studies; Economics; International Economics; Regional Studies); **Engineering** (Architecture; Architecture and Planning; Building Technologies; Electronic Engineering; Engineering; Environmental Engineering; Town Planning); **Humanities** (American Studies; Arts and Humanities; Asian Studies; Cultural Studies; English; English Studies; History; Literature; Modern Languages; Philosophy); **Law** (Law; Political Sciences)

School

Law (*Professional Graduate*) (Law)

Graduate School

Business Administration (Business Administration); **Economics** (Economics); **Electronics and Information Engineering** (Architecture; Construction Engineering; Electronic Engineering; Information Technology); **Law** (Law; Political Sciences); **Letters** (American Studies; Cultural Studies; English Studies; History; Japanese; Literature)
History: Founded 1887 as English Language School, became College 1950 and University 1952.
Academic year: April to March (April-September; October-March)
Admission requirements: Graduation from high school or recognized equivalent, and entrance examination
Main language(s) of instruction: Japanese
Accrediting agency: Japan Institution for Higher Education Evaluation (JIHEE)
Degrees and diplomas: Gakushi (Architecture; Biotechnology; Civil Engineering; Cultural Studies; Economics; Information Management; Information Technology; Law; Management; Political Sciences), Shushi (Business Administration; Law; Political Sciences), Hakase (American Studies; Architecture; Business Administration; Economics; English; Law)
Student Services: Careers Guidance, Sports Facilities, Language Laboratory, Health Services, Canteen
Periodicals: Gakuen-Ronshu, Hogaku-Kenkyu, Jinbun-Ronshu, Kaihatsu Ronshu, Keiei-Ronshu, Keizai-Ronshu, Kougakubu-Kenkyu-Houkoku
Last Update: 26-03-2018

Hokkaido Bunkyo University

196-1 Koganemachi
Eniwa 061-1449, Hokkaido
Tel: +81(123) 34-0019
Fax: +81(123) 34-0057
Website: http://www.do-bunkyodai.ac.jp
President: Takeo Suzuki

School

Foreign Studies (Chinese; Communication Studies; English; Japanese; Modern Languages); **Human Sciences** (Arts and Humanities; Child Care and Development; Health Sciences; Nursing; Nutrition; Occupational Therapy; Physical Therapy)

Graduate School

Global Communications (Communication Studies; Cultural Studies; Modern Languages)
History: Founded 1999.
Main language(s) of instruction: Japanese
Accrediting agency: Japan University Accreditation Association (JUAA)
Degrees and diplomas: Gakushi, Shushi

Student Services: Sports Facilities

Academic Staff 2013-2014	MALE	FEMALE	TOTAL
FULL-TIME			126
Student Numbers 2013-2014			
All (Foreign Included)			c. 2450
Foreign only			110

Last Update: 04-12-2017

Hokkaido Information University (HIU)

59-2 Nishi Nopporo
Ebetsu-shi 069-8585, Hokkaido
Tel: +81(11) 385-4411
Fax: +81(11) 384-0134
Website: http://www.do-johodai.ac.jp
President: Suguru Sawai

Faculty

Business Administration and Information Sciences (Business Administration; Business Computing; Computer Engineering; E- Business/Commerce; Finance; Information Sciences; Information Technology; Management; Robotics; Tourism); **Information Media** (Computer Graphics; Computer Science; Graphic Design; Information Sciences; Media Studies; Software Engineering; Video; Visual Arts); **Medical Informatics** (Computer Science; Health Administration; Information Management; Information Technology)

School

Distance Learning (Business Administration; E- Business/Commerce; Information Sciences; Information Technology; Management)

Graduate School

Business Administration and Information Science (Business Administration; Information Sciences)
History: Founded 1989.
Admission requirements: 12-year formal education
Fees: Faculty of Business Administration and Information Sciences, 1.22m.-1.28m. per annum; Faculty of Information Media, 1.26m (Yen)
Main language(s) of instruction: Japanese
Accrediting agency: Japan Institution for Higher Education Evaluation (JIHEE)
Degrees and diplomas: Gakushi, Shushi (Business Administration; Information Sciences)
Student Services: Academic Counselling, Social Counselling, Careers Guidance, Sports Facilities, Facilities for disabled people, Canteen
Periodicals: Memoirs of Hokkaido Information University
Last Update: 04-12-2017

Hokkaido Pharmaceutical University School of Pharmacy

7-1 Katsuraoka-cho
Otaru-shi 047-0264, Hokkaido
Tel: +81 11-676-8700
Fax: +81 11-676-8666
Website: http://www.hokuyakudai.ac.jp
President: Yasuhiro Watanabe

School

Pharmacy (Applied Chemistry; Biological and Life Sciences; Biology; Chemistry; Community Health; English; Health Administration; Health Education; Mathematics; Modern Languages; Pharmacology; Pharmacy; Physical Education; Physics; Physiology; Public Health; Rehabilitation and Therapy; Social and Preventive Medicine; Toxicology)

Graduate School

Pharmacy (Analytical Chemistry; Biochemistry; Biological and Life Sciences; Chemistry; Economics; Genetics; Health Administration; Health Sciences; Information Sciences; Microbiology; Pathology; Pharmacology; Pharmacy; Physiology; Public Health; Toxicology)
History: Founded 1974.
Academic year: April to March (April-September; September-March)
Admission requirements: Graduation from high school and entrance examination
Main language(s) of instruction: Japanese
Accrediting agency: Japan Institution for Higher Education Evaluation (JIHEE)
Degrees and diplomas: Gakushi, Shushi (Pharmacy), Hakase (Pharmacy)
Student Services: Sports Facilities
Last Update: 04-12-2017

Hokkaido University of Science (HIT)

4-1, Maeda 7-jo 15-chome
Sapporo-shi 006-8585, Hokkaido
Tel: +81(11) 681-2161
Fax: +81(11) 681-3622
Website: http://www.hit.ac.jp
President: Tsukasa Tomabechi

Faculty

Advanced Engineering (Electrical Engineering; Information Technology; Mechanical Engineering); **Clinical Engineering** (Engineering; Medical Technology; Rehabilitation and Therapy); **Creative Engineering** (Architecture; Civil

Engineering; Environmental Engineering); **Future Design** (Arts and Humanities; Design; Media Studies; Social Sciences)

School

Graduate Studies (Architecture; Biomedical Engineering; Civil Engineering; Construction Engineering; Electrical and Electronic Engineering; Electrical Engineering; Electronic Engineering; Information Technology; Mechanical Engineering)
Further information: Also 260 laboratories
History: Founded 1967. Named Hokkaido Institute of Technology until 2014.
Main language(s) of instruction: Japanese
Accrediting agency: Japan Institution for Higher Education Evaluation (JIHEE)
Degrees and diplomas: Gakushi, Shushi (Architecture; Biomedical Engineering; Civil Engineering; Electrical and Electronic Engineering; Information Technology; Mechanical Engineering), Hakase (Construction Engineering; Electrical Engineering; Electronic Engineering; Mechanical Engineering)
Student Services: Sports Facilities, Language Laboratory, Canteen
Last Update: 04-12-2017

Hokuriku Gakuin University

1 Mitsukoji-machi, I
Kanazawa 920-1396, Ishikawa
Tel: +81 76-280-3850
Fax: +81 76-280-3859
Website: http://www.hokurikugakuin.ac.jp
President: Shiro Kusumoto

Faculty

Human Arts and Sciences (Preschool Education; Sociology)
History: Founded 1884 as a private school. Acquired present status and title 2008.
Main language(s) of instruction: Japanese
Accrediting agency: Japan Institution for Higher Education Evaluation (JIHEE)
Degrees and diplomas: Gakushi (Preschool Education; Social Welfare)
Student Services: Library, Residential Facilities
Last Update: 04-12-2017

Hokuriku University

1-1 Taiyogaoka
Kanazawa-shi 920-1180, Ishikawa
Tel: +81(76) 229-2626

Fax: +81(76) 229-0021
Website: http://www.hokuriku-u.ac.jp
President: Tsutomu Ogura

Faculty

Pharmaceutical Sciences (Anthropology; Biochemistry; Biological and Life Sciences; Biology; Botany; Chemistry; Computer Science; English; Environmental Studies; Genetics; Haematology; Health Sciences; Inorganic Chemistry; Medicine; Microbiology; Molecular Biology; Nutrition; Organic Chemistry; Pharmacology; Pharmacy; Physical Chemistry; Psychology; Rehabilitation and Therapy; Traditional Eastern Medicine)

Course/Programme

Japanese Language (*For International Student*) (Japanese)

School

Future Creation (Accountancy; Administration; Arts and Humanities; Business Administration; Chinese; Communication Studies; Cultural Studies; Economics; English; Environmental Studies; Finance; History; Information Management; International Business; Japanese; Korean; Law; Management; Marketing; Mathematics; Modern Languages; Philosophy; Physical Education; Political Sciences; Religion; Social Studies; Sports)
Further information: Also Japanese language courses for foreign students
History: Founded 1975.
Academic year: April to March (April-September; October-March)
Admission requirements: Graduation from high school and entrance examination
Fees: Tuition fee for Pharmacy programme, 1,700,000 per annum; For Future Creation programme, 900,000 per annum (Yen)
Main language(s) of instruction: Japanese
Accrediting agency: Japan Institution for Higher Education Evaluation (JIHEE)
Degrees and diplomas: Gakushi, Shushi (Pharmacy), Hakase (Pharmacy)
Student Services: Sports Facilities, Language Laboratory, Health Services, Canteen
Periodicals: Bulletin
Last Update: 04-12-2017

Hokusei Gakuen University

2-3-1, Ohyachi-Nishi Atsubetsu-ku
Sapporo-shi 004-8631, Hokkaido
Tel: +81(11) 891-2731

Fax: +81(11) 892-6097
Website: http://www.hokusei.ac.jp
President: Shin'ichi Tamura

Course/Programme

General Education (Arts and Humanities; Chinese; Cultural Studies; English; Foreign Languages Education; French; German; Information Management; Korean; Modern Languages; Natural Sciences; Religion; Social Studies; Technology); **Teacher Education** (Primary Education; Teacher Training)

School

Economics (Economics; Information Management; Law); **Humanities** (Arts and Humanities; Communication Studies; English; Psychology); **Social Welfare** (Psychology; Social Policy; Social Welfare; Social Work)

Graduate School

Economics (Economics); **Literature** (Communication Studies; Cultural Studies; Literature; Modern Languages); **Social Welfare** (Clinical Psychology; Social Welfare)
History: Founded 1887 as School by an American missionary, acquired present status 1962. Financed by tuition fees, Government grant and donations.
Academic year: April to March (April-September; October-March)
Admission requirements: Graduation from high school or equivalent, and entrance examination
Main language(s) of instruction: Japanese
Accrediting agency: Japan University Accreditation Association (JUAA)
Degrees and diplomas: Associate's Degree (Academic), Gakushi, Shushi (Clinical Psychology; Communication Studies; Cultural Studies; Economics; Modern Languages; Social Welfare), Hakase (Social Welfare)
Student Services: Social Counselling, Careers Guidance, Nursery Care, Sports Facilities, Language Laboratory, Facilities for disabled people, Health Services, Foreign Studies Centre
Periodicals: Hokusei Ronshu
Last Update: 04-12-2017

Hokusho University

23, Bunkyodai Ebetsu
Hokkaido 069-8511
Tel: +81(11) 386-8011
Fax: +81(11) 387-3739, +81(11) 387-8011
Website: http://www.hokusho-u.ac.jp
President: Nishimura Hiroyuki

School

Education and Culture (Cultural Studies; Design; Education; Fashion Design; Fine Arts; Health Education; Interior Design; Media Studies; Music; Nursing; Performing Arts; Preschool Education; Primary Education; Psychology); **Lifelong Sport** (Health Sciences; Physical Education; Sports; Welfare and Protective Services)

Graduate School

Human Services (Child Care and Development; Clinical Psychology; Teacher Training); **Lifelong Learning Support Studies** (Educational Psychology; Educational Sciences); **Lifelong Sport** (Health Sciences; Sports)
History: Founded 1997. Renamed Hokkaido Asai Gakuen University and acquired present status 2000. Formerly known as Asai Gakuen Daigaku (Asai Gakuen University). Acquired present title 2007.
Main language(s) of instruction: Japanese
Accrediting agency: Japan Institution for Higher Education Evaluation (JIHEE)
Degrees and diplomas: Gakushi (Design; Education; Health Sciences; Performing Arts; Physical Education; Psychology; Sports; Welfare and Protective Services), Shushi (Child Care and Development; Clinical Psychology; Education; Educational Psychology; Health Sciences; Physical Education; Psychology; Sports; Welfare and Protective Services)
Student Services: Academic Counselling, Social Counselling, Sports Facilities, Health Services
Last Update: 28-03-2018

Hollywood Graduate School of Beauty Business

Roppongi Hills Hollywood Plaza 6-4-1 Roppongi Minato-ku Tokyo
Tokyo 106-8541
Tel: +81 3-3403-3403
Fax: +81 3-3423-6092
Website: http://www.hollywood.ac.jp/mba/english/index.html
Director: Yoshihiro Yamanaka

School

Beauty Business (Business and Commerce; Cosmetology)
History: Founded 2008.
Main language(s) of instruction: Japanese
Accrediting agency: Japan Institution for Higher Education Evaluation (JIHEE)
Degrees and diplomas: Shushi (Business and Commerce; Cosmetology)
Last Update: 28-03-2018

Hosei University

2-17-1, Fujimi Chiyoda-ku
Tokyo 102-8160
Tel: +81(3) 3264-9315
Fax: +81(3) 3238-9873
Website: http://www.hosei.ac.jp
President: Yuko Tanaka

Faculty

Bioscience and Applied Chemistry (*Koganei Campus*) (Applied Chemistry; Biological and Life Sciences; Chemistry; Plant Pathology; Technology); **Business Administration** (*Ichigaya Campus*) (Business Administration; Management; Marketing); **Computer and Information Sciences** (*Koganei Campus*) (Computer Science; Information Sciences; Multimedia); **Economics** (*Tama Campus*) (Business Administration; Economics; International Economics); **Engineering and Design** (*Ichigaya Campus*) (Architecture; Civil Engineering; Design; Engineering; Environmental Engineering); **Global and Interdisciplinary Studies** (*GIS - Ichigaya Campus*) (Arts and Humanities; Cultural Studies; Economics; English; International Relations; International Studies; Linguistics; Literature; Social Studies); **Humanity and the Environment** (*Ichigaya Campus*) (Environmental Studies); **Intercultural Communications** (*Ichigaya Campus*) (Communication Studies; Cultural Studies); **Law** (*Ichigaya Campus*) (International Relations; Law; Political Sciences); **Letters** (*Ichigaya Campus*) (Arts and Humanities; English; Geography; History; Japanese; Philosophy; Psychology); **Life-long Learning and Career Studies** (*Ichigaya Campus*); **Science and Engineering** (*Koganei Campus*) (Aeronautical and Aerospace Engineering; Artificial Intelligence; Computer Engineering; Computer Science; Electrical and Electronic Engineering; Electrical Engineering; Electronic Engineering; Industrial Engineering; Materials Engineering; Mechanical Engineering; Natural Sciences); **Social Policy and Administration** (*Tama Campus*) (Administration; Clinical Psychology; Social and Community Services; Social Policy); **Social Sciences** (*Tama Campus*) (Communication Studies; Media Studies; Political Sciences; Social Studies; Sociology); **Sports and Health Studies** (*Tama Campus*) (Health Sciences; Sports)

School

Correspondence Education (Arts and Humanities; Business and Commerce; Economics; Geography; History; Law; Literature; Teacher Training)

Institute

International Japanese Studies (Cultural Studies; International Studies)

Graduate School

Accountancy (*Professional*) (Accountancy; Information Technology); **Business Administration** (Business Administration); **Business Innovation Management** (*HBS/IM - Professional*) (Business Administration; Information Management; Information Technology; Management; Marketing); **Computer and Information Sciences** (Computer Science; Information Sciences); **Economics** (Economics); **Engineering** (Architecture; Chemistry; Civil Engineering; Electrical Engineering; Electronic Engineering; Engineering; Information Technology; Materials Engineering; Mechanical Engineering); **Engineering and Design** (Architecture; Civil Engineering; Design; Engineering; Environmental Engineering); **Environmental Management** (Environmental Management); **Humanities** (Arts and Humanities; English; Geography; History; Japanese; Literature; Philosophy; Psychology); **Intercultural Communication** (Communication Studies); **Law** (*Professional*) (Law); **Law** (Law); **Policy Sciences** (Political Sciences); **Politics** (Political Sciences); **Regional Policy Design** (Political Sciences; Regional Studies); **Social Governance** (Environmental Management; Government; International Relations; Public Administration); **Social Well-being Studies** (Clinical Psychology; Social and Community Services); **Sociology** (Economics; International Studies; Mass Communication; Media Studies; Political Sciences; Sociology)

Further information: Ichigaya, Tama and Konagei campuses. Also professional schools (Law; Innovation Management; Accountancy)

History: Founded 1880 as Tokyo Hogakusha (Tokyo School of Law), combined in 1889 with Tokyo French School to become Wafutsu Horitsu Gakko (School of Japanese and French Law). Became College 1903 and acquired present status 1949.

Academic year: April to March (April-July; September-March)

Admission requirements: Graduation from high school or equivalent, or foreign equivalent, and entrance examination

Fees: Undergraduate tuition, 974,000-1,470,000; Graduate tuition, 590,000-990,000; Professional studies, 1,025,000-2,120,000 (Yen)

Main language(s) of instruction: Japanese, English

Accrediting agency: Japan University Accreditation Association (JUAA)

Degrees and diplomas: Gakushi, Shushi (Architecture; Business Administration; Civil Engineering; Clinical Psychology; Communication Studies; Computer Engineering; Computer Science; Cultural Studies; Design; Economics; Electrical Engineering; Electronic Engineering; Engineering; English; Environmental Management; Geography; History; Information Sciences; Information Technology; Japanese; Law; Literature; Materials Engineering; Mechanical Engineering; Philosophy; Political Sciences; Psychology; Regional

Studies; Social and Community Services; Sociology), Hakase (Architecture; Business Administration; Civil Engineering; Clinical Psychology; Communication Studies; Computer Engineering; Computer Science; Cultural Studies; Design; Economics; Electrical Engineering; Electronic Engineering; Engineering; English; Geography; History; Information Sciences; Information Technology; Japanese; Law; Literature; Mechanical Engineering; Philosophy; Psychology; Regional Studies; Social and Community Services; Sociology). Also Professional Diplomas in Management, Accountancy and Law
Student Services: Academic Counselling, Social Counselling, Sports Facilities, Language Laboratory, Health Services, Canteen
Periodicals: Bungakubu-kiyou (Bulletin of Faculty of Letters), Daigakuin-kiyou (Graduate School Bulletin), Hogaku-shirin (Law and Political Sciences Review), Hogakubu kenkyu-shubo (College of Engineering Bulletin), Keiei-shirin (Business Journal), Keizai-shirin (The Hosei University Economic Review), Many research reports published by affiliated institutions, Shakai-rodo-Kendyu (Society and Labour)
Publishing house: Hosei University Press
Last Update: 25-05-2018

Hosen College of Childhood Education

Center 2-33-26
Tokyo 164-8631, Nakano-ku
Tel: +81 3-3365-0267
Fax: +81 3-3365-0269
Website: http://hosen.ac.jp
President: Hideyuki Yamamoto

Faculty
Children's Education (Preschool Education)
History: Founded 1935 as Buddhist Association childcare kindergarten teacher training school. Acquired present status and title 2009.
Main language(s) of instruction: Japanese
Accrediting agency: Japan Institution for Higher Education Evaluation (JIHEE)
Degrees and diplomas: Gakushi (Preschool Education)
Student Services: Library
Last Update: 05-12-2017

Hoshi University

2-4-41 Ebara
Shinagawa-ku 142-8501, Tokyo
Tel: +81(3) 3786-1011

Fax: +81(3) 3787-0036
Website: http://www.hoshi.ac.jp
President: Takaharu Tanaka

Faculty
Pharmacy and Pharmaceutical Sciences (Pharmacology; Pharmacy)

Institute
Medical Chemistry (Applied Chemistry; Medicine)

Graduate School
Pharmaceutical Sciences (Clinical Psychology; Pharmacy)

Research Division
Drug Discovery Science (Pharmacology)
History: Founded 1911.
Academic year: April to March (April-September; October-March)
Admission requirements: Graduation from high school and entrance examination
Main language(s) of instruction: Japanese
Accrediting agency: Japan University Accreditation Association (JUAA)
Degrees and diplomas: Gakushi, Shushi (Medicine), Hakase (Medicine; Pharmacy)
Student Services: Academic Counselling, Social Counselling, Careers Guidance, Nursery Care, Sports Facilities, Facilities for disabled people, Health Services, Canteen
Periodicals: Hoshi Yakka Daigaku Kiyo (Proceedings)

Academic Staff 2012-2013	MALE	FEMALE	TOTAL
FULL-TIME			89
Student Numbers 2012-2013			
All (Foreign Included)			1640

Last Update: 05-12-2017

Hyogo College of Medicine

Hyogo Prefecture Mukogawa-cho, No. 1 No. 1
Nishinomiya 663-8501
Tel: +81 798-45-6111
Website: http://www.hyo-med.ac.jp/
President: Koichi Noguchi

School
Medicine (Medicine)

Institute
Advanced Medical Sciences (Neurology)

Further information: Sasayama, Kobe
History: Founded 1972.
Main language(s) of instruction: Japanese
Accrediting agency: Japan University Accreditation Association (JUAA)
Degrees and diplomas: Gakushi (Medicine)
Student Services: Library
Last Update: 05-12-2017

Hyogo University

2301 Shinzaike Hiraoka
Kakogawa 675-0195, Hyogo
Tel: +81(79) 427-5111
Fax: +81(79) 427-5112
Website: http://www.hyogo-dai.ac.jp
President: Makoto Kono

Faculty

Economics and Information Sciences (Accountancy; Business Administration; Computer Engineering; Computer Networks; Economics; Information Sciences; Information Technology; Management); **Health Sciences** (Health Administration; Health Education; Health Sciences; Nursing; Nutrition); **Welfare and Protective Services** (Child Care and Development; Social Welfare; Welfare and Protective Services)

Graduate School

Economics and Information Sciences (Accountancy; Economics; Finance; Information Sciences; Information Technology; Management)
History: Founded 1995.
Main language(s) of instruction: Japanese, English
Accrediting agency: Japan University Accreditation Association (JUAA)
Degrees and diplomas: Gakushi, Shushi (Economics; Information Sciences)
Last Update: 14-03-2018

Hyogo University of Health Sciences (HUHS)

1-3-6 Minatojima Chuo-ku
Kobe-shi 650-8530, Hyogo
Tel: +81(78) 304-3000
Website: http://www.huhs.ac.jp
President: Baba Akemichi

School

Nursing (Community Health; Family Studies; Health Sciences; Midwifery; Nursing; Psychiatry and Mental Health; Public Health); **Pharmacy** (Alternative Medicine; Applied

Chemistry; Biochemistry; Biological and Life Sciences; Biology; Hygiene; Immunology; Medicine; Microbiology; Organic Chemistry; Pharmacology; Pharmacy; Physical Chemistry; Physiology; Toxicology; Traditional Eastern Medicine); **Rehabilitation** (Community Health; Gerontology; Medical Technology; Neurology; Occupational Therapy; Orthopaedics; Physical Therapy; Psychiatry and Mental Health; Rehabilitation and Therapy; Sports Medicine)

Centre

General Education (Anatomy; Astrophysics; Behavioural Sciences; Biology; Biophysics; Chemistry; English; Haematology; Health Sciences; Information Technology; Literature; Medicine; Philosophy; Physiology; Psychology; Sports; Zoology)
Further information: Also Sasayama campus
History: Founded 2007. A member of the Hyogo College of Medicine Group.
Main language(s) of instruction: Japanese
Accrediting agency: Japan University Accreditation Association (JUAA)
Degrees and diplomas: Gakushi
Periodicals: Acta Medica Hyogoensia
Last Update: 05-12-2017

Ibaraki Christian University (ICC)

6-11-1 Omika-cho
Hitachi-shi 319-1295, Ibaraki
Tel: +81(294) 52-3215
Fax: +81(294) 53-5864
Website: http://www.icc.ac.jp
President: Hiroshi Shoji

College

Business Administration (Business Administration); **Life Sciences** (Biological and Life Sciences; Clinical Psychology; Environmental Studies; Food Science; Nutrition; Psychology; Social Welfare; Welfare and Protective Services); **Literature** (Communication Studies; Cultural Studies; Education; English; Information Sciences; Modern Languages; Primary Education); **Nursing** (Nursing)

Graduate School

Life Sciences (Food Science; Nutrition); **Literature** (American Studies; Education; Educational Sciences; English; English Studies; Linguistics; Literature; Phonetics); **Nursing** (Nursing)
History: Founded 1967.
Main language(s) of instruction: Japanese
Accrediting agency: Japan University Accreditation Association (JUAA)

Degrees and diplomas: Gakushi, Shushi (Education; English; Food Science; Linguistics; Literature; Nursing; Nutrition)
Student Services: Academic Counselling
Last Update: 05-12-2017

Institute of Information Security (IISEC)

2-14-1 Tsuruyacho Kanagawa-ku
Yokohama 221-0835, Kanagawa
Tel: +81(45) 311-7784
Fax: +81(45) 311-6871
Website: http://www.iisec.ac.jp
President: Atsuhiro Goto

Graduate School
Information Security (Behavioural Sciences; Business Administration; Computer Networks; Computer Science; Economics; Ethics; Information Management; Information Sciences; Information Technology; Law; Mass Communication; Mathematics and Computer Science; Operations Research; Software Engineering; Statistics)
History: Founded 2004.
Main language(s) of instruction: Japanese
Accrediting agency: Japan University Accreditation Association (JUAA)
Degrees and diplomas: Gakushi, Shushi (Computer Science), Hakase (Computer Science)
Last Update: 05-12-2017

Institute of Technologists

333 Maeya
Gyoda-shi 361-0038, Saitama
Tel: +81(48) 564-3200, +81(48) 564-3816
Fax: +81(48) 564-3201
Website: http://www.iot.ac.jp
President: Akira Akamatsu

Department/Division
Building Technology (Civil Engineering; Construction Engineering; Structural Architecture; Wood Technology); **Manufacturing Technology** (Automation and Control Engineering; Computer Science; Information Management; Machine Building; Maintenance Technology; Mechanical Engineering; Metal Techniques; Production Engineering; Safety Engineering; Technology)
History: Founded 2001.
Main language(s) of instruction: Japanese
Accrediting agency: Japan Institution for Higher Education Evaluation (JIHEE)
Degrees and diplomas: Gakushi

Student Services: Sports Facilities, Library, IT Centre, Residential Facilities
Last Update: 05-12-2017

International Budo University (IBU)

841 Shinkan
Katsuura-shi 299-5295, Chiba
Tel: +81(470) 73-4111
Fax: +81(470) 73-4148
Website: http://www.budo-u.ac.jp
President: Yoshihide Takami

Faculty
Physical Education (Cultural Studies; Japanese; Physical Education; Sports; Sports Management)

Course/Programme
Martial Arts Language (Japanese)

Graduate School
Martial Arts and Sports Studies (Health Sciences; Japanese; Sports)
History: Founded 1984.
Academic year: April to February (April-July; September-December; January-February)
Fees: Tuition, 715,000 per annum (Yen)
Main language(s) of instruction: Japanese, English
Accrediting agency: Japan University Accreditation Association (JUAA)
Degrees and diplomas: Gakushi, Shushi (Health Sciences; Sports; Sports Management; Sports Medicine)
Student Services: Academic Counselling, Careers Guidance, Nursery Care, Sports Facilities, Language Laboratory, Health Services, Canteen, Foreign Studies Centre

Academic Staff 2013-2014	MALE	FEMALE	TOTAL
FULL-TIME			79
Student Numbers 2013-2014			
All (Foreign Included)			548
Foreign only			23

Last Update: 05-12-2017

International Christian University (ICU)

3-10-2 Osawa
Mitaka-shi 181-8585, Tokyo
Tel: +81(422) 33-3038
Fax: +81(422) 33-3355
Website: http://www.icu.ac.jp
President: Junko Hibiya
Tel: +81(422) 33-3005

College

Liberal Arts (American Studies; Anthropology; Arts and Humanities; Asian Studies; Biology; Business Administration; Chemistry; Chinese; Communication Studies; Cultural Studies; Development Studies; Economics; Education; English; Environmental Studies; French; Gender Studies; German; Health Sciences; Heritage Preservation; History; Information Sciences; International Relations; International Studies; Japanese; Korean; Law; Linguistics; Literature; Mathematics; Media Studies; Modern Languages; Music; Natural Sciences; Peace and Disarmament; Philosophy; Physical Education; Physics; Political Sciences; Psychology; Public Administration; Religious Studies; Russian; Social Sciences; Sociology; Spanish)

Course/Programme

Education (*Postgraduate*) (Education)

Institute

Advanced Studies of Clinical Psychology (Clinical Psychology); **Asian Cultural Studies** (Asian Studies); **Educational Research and Service** (Educational Research); **Japanese Language Education** (Japanese; Native Language Education); **Study of Christianity and Culture** (Christian Religious Studies)

Centre

Gender Studies (Gender Studies); **Religious** (Religious Studies); **Rotary Peace**; **Sacred Music** (Religious Music)

Graduate School

Arts and Sciences (Arts and Humanities; Cultural Studies; Education; Natural Sciences; Political Sciences; Psychology; Public Administration; Social Policy; Social Studies)

Research Division

Peace (Peace and Disarmament); **Social Science** (Social Sciences)

Further information: Also summer courses in Japanese language. Study abroad programme in : USA; Canada; Chile; China; Taiwan; South Korea; Philippines; Thailand; Vietnam; UK; Italy; Spain; Netherlands; Belgium; France; Germany; Austria; Russia; Lithuania; Hungary; Czech Republic; Denmark; Sweden; Finland; Iceland, Ghana, South Africa; New Zealand and Australia

History: Founded 1949.

Academic year: April to March (April-June; September-November; December-March)

Admission requirements: Graduation from high school and entrance examination; admittance in April. Foreign students: graduation from high school (completion of 12 yrs of education) and documentary screening; admittance in September. TOEFL and SAT required.

Fees: Registration, 150,000 (One-Year-Regular), 300,000 (Regular); tuition, 1,359,000 per annum (Yen)

Main language(s) of instruction: Japanese, English

Accrediting agency: Japan University Accreditation Association (JUAA)

Degrees and diplomas: Gakushi, Shushi (Cultural Studies; Education; Natural Sciences; Psychology; Public Administration; Social Policy; Social Studies), Hakase (Arts and Humanities; Natural Sciences). Also 1-year Postgraduate Programme in Education

Student Services: Academic Counselling, Social Counselling, Careers Guidance, Sports Facilities, Language Laboratory, Health Services, Canteen

Periodicals: Asian Cultural Studies, Christianity and Culture, Educational Studies, Journal of Social Science, Language Research Bulletin

Academic Staff 2013-2014	MALE	FEMALE	TOTAL
FULL-TIME	89	57	146
PART-TIME	103	53	156
STAFF WITH DOCTORATE			
FULL-TIME	40	15	55
Student Numbers 2013-2014			
All (Foreign Included)	1136	1998	3134
Foreign only			192

Last Update: 25-05-2018

International College for Postgraduate Buddhist Studies (ICABS)

2-8-9 Kasuga Bunkyo-ku
Minato-ku 112-0003, Tokyo
Tel: +81(3) 5981-5271
Fax: +81(3) 5981-5283
Website: http://www.icabs.ac.jp
President: Kyoko Fujii

Institute

International Institute for Buddhist Studies (*IIBS*) (Asian Religious Studies; Cultural Studies; Philology)

Graduate School

Buddhist Studies (Art History; Asian Religious Studies; Cultural Studies; History; Holy Writings; Philology; Religion)

Research Division

Old Japanese Manuscripts of Buddhist Scriptures (Holy Writings)

History: Founded 1996. Campus relocated from Toranomon, Minato-ku 2010.

Academic year: April to March (April-September; October-March)
Admission requirements: Gakushi (Bachelor's degree)
Fees: Registration, 300,000; tuition 600,000 per annum (Yen)
Main language(s) of instruction: Japanese
Accrediting agency: Japan University Accreditation Association (JUAA)
Degrees and diplomas: Shushi, Hakase (Philosophy; Religion)
Student Services: Health Services
Periodicals: Journal of the ICPBS, Sengokuyama Journal of Buddhist Studies, The Taisho Canon Concordance Series
Last Update: 28-03-2018

International Pacific University

721 Kannonji
Seito 709-0863, Okayama
Tel: +81(86) 958-0200
Fax: +81(86) 958-0282
Website: http://www.ipu-japan.ac.jp
President: Eiichi Kajita

Faculty

Education for Future Generations (Child Care and Development; Cultural Studies; Educational Administration; International and Comparative Education; Japanese; Preschool Education; Primary Education; Secondary Education; Teacher Training); **Physical Education** (Health Sciences; Physical Education; Sports; Sports Medicine; Teacher Training)

Department/Division

Educational Management (*Distance Course*) (Educational Administration)
History: Founded 2007.
Main language(s) of instruction: Japanese
Accrediting agency: Japan Institution for Higher Education Evaluation (JIHEE)
Degrees and diplomas: Gakushi (Business Administration; Child Care and Development; Educational Administration; Management; Physical Education; Preschool Education)
Last Update: 28-03-2018

International University of Health and Welfare (IUHW)

2600-1 Kitakanemaru
Otawara-shi 324-8501, Tochigi
Tel: +81(287) 24-3200
Fax: +81(287) 24-3199
Website: http://www.iuhw.ac.jp
President: Takagi Kunimoto

School

Health and Welfare (*Otawara Campus*) (Health Administration; Health Sciences; Social and Community Services; Welfare and Protective Services); **Health Sciences** (*Okawa Campus*) (Medical Technology; Occupational Therapy; Physical Therapy; Speech Therapy and Audiology); **Health Sciences** (*Otawara Campus*) (Nursing; Occupational Therapy; Ophthalmology; Physical Therapy; Radiology; Speech Therapy and Audiology); **Nursing** (*Fukuoka Campus*) (Nursing); **Nursing and Rehabilitation Sciences** (*Odawara Campus*) (Nursing; Occupational Therapy; Physical Therapy; Rehabilitation and Therapy); **Pharmacy** (*Otawara Campus*) (Pharmacology; Pharmacy)

Graduate School

Health and Welfare (Biological and Life Sciences; Clinical Psychology; Health Administration; Health Sciences; Journalism; Pharmacology; Pharmacy; Welfare and Protective Services)
Further information: Odawara Campus in Kanagawa Prefecture, Tenjin Campus in Fukuoka Prefecture, Okawa Campus in Fukuoka Prefecture
History: Founded 1995.
Main language(s) of instruction: Japanese
Accrediting agency: Japan Institution for Higher Education Evaluation (JIHEE)
Degrees and diplomas: Gakushi, Shushi (Biological and Life Sciences; Clinical Psychology; Health Administration; Health Sciences; Pharmacy; Welfare and Protective Services), Hakase (Health Sciences)

Student Numbers 2013-2014	MALE	FEMALE	TOTAL
All (Foreign Included)			c. 6130
Foreign only			50

Last Update: 05-12-2017

International University of Japan (IUJ)

777 Kokusai-cho
Minami-Uonuma-shi 949-7277, Niigata
Tel: +81(25) 779-1104, +81(25) 779-1105
Fax: +81(25) 779-1188, +81(25) 779-1187
Website: http://www.iuj.ac.jp
President: Hiroyuki Itami

Course/Programme

Language Education (English; Japanese); **Non-Degree Studies** (Economics); **Training for Enterprise** (Business Administration; Leadership)

Graduate School

International Management (*GSIM*) (Business Administration; E- Business/Commerce; International Business; Management); **International Relations** (*GSIR*) (Cultural Studies; Development Studies; Economics; History; International Relations; International Studies; Management; Peace and Disarmament; Political Sciences; Public Administration)

History: Founded 1982 with a mission to provide graduate level education in English for future leaders in the global society. It is supported by the Japanese industrial, financial and educational communities and by local community of Urasa.

Academic year: September to August

Admission requirements: University degree at Bachelor level or equivalent

Main language(s) of instruction: English

Accrediting agency: Japan Institution for Higher Education Evaluation (JIHEE)

Degrees and diplomas: Shushi (Business Administration; Development Studies; Economics; International Business; International Relations; International Studies; Management; Peace and Disarmament; Public Administration)

Student Services: Academic Counselling, Social Counselling, Careers Guidance, Sports Facilities, Language Laboratory, Health Services, Canteen

Last Update: 05-12-2017

International University of Kagoshima (IUK)

Sakanoue 8-34-1
Kagoshima-shi 891-0197, Kagoshima
Tel: +81(99) 261-3211
Fax: +81(99) 261-3299
Website: http://www.iuk.ac.jp
President: Sadatoshi Tsumagari

Faculty

Business Administration (Accountancy; Business Administration; Chinese; Commercial Law; Data Processing; Economics; English; Finance; Government; Information Technology; International Business; Korean; Management; Modern Languages; Tourism); **Intercultural Studies** (Arts and Humanities; Communication Studies; Cultural Studies; International Studies; Modern Languages; Music; Music Theory and Composition; Musical Instruments; Performing Arts; Singing); **Welfare Society** (Child Care and Development; Family Studies; Social and Community Services; Social Problems; Social Studies; Welfare and Protective Services)

College

Junior Studies (Information Sciences; Music; Musical Instruments)

Graduate School

Graduate Studies (Cultural Studies; Economics; International Studies; Welfare and Protective Services)

History: Founded 1932 as Kagoshima Commerce College. Renamed Kagoshima Keizai Daigaku/Kagoshima Keizai University 1960. Moved to Shimofukumoto town 1966. Acquired present title 2000.

Main language(s) of instruction: Japanese

Accrediting agency: Japan University Accreditation Association (JUAA)

Degrees and diplomas: Gakushi, Shushi (Cultural Studies; Economics; International Studies; Sociology; Welfare and Protective Services), Hakase (Cultural Studies; Economics; International Studies; Sociology; Welfare and Protective Services)

Student Services: Sports Facilities

Student Numbers 2012-2013	MALE	FEMALE	TOTAL
All (Foreign Included)			3201

Last Update: 27-02-2018

Ishinomaki Senshu University

1 Shinmito Minamisakai
Ishinomaki-shi 986-8580, Miyagi
Tel: +81(225) 22-7717
Fax: +81(225) 22-7809
Website: https://www.senshu-u.ac.jp/english
President: Shigeto Sasaki

Faculty

Business Administration (Accountancy; Business Administration; English; Information Sciences; International Business; Management; Modern Languages; Teacher Training; Tourism); **Humanities** (Arts and Humanities; Cultural Studies; Education); **Science and Engineering** (Bioengineering; Biological and Life Sciences; Electronic Engineering; Environmental Studies; Food Science; Information Technology; Mechanical Engineering; Production Engineering; Teacher Training)

Graduate School

Business Administration (Accountancy; Business Administration; Information Sciences; Management; Teacher Training); **Science and Engineering** (Biological and Life Sciences; Cell Biology; Ecology; Electronic Engineering; Engineering; Environmental Studies; Information Sciences;

Information Technology; Marine Biology; Materials Engineering; Mechanical Engineering; Molecular Biology; Physiology)
History: Founded 1989.
Fees: Tuition, 673,000-968,000 per annum (Yen)
Main language(s) of instruction: Japanese
Accrediting agency: Japan University Accreditation Association
Degrees and diplomas: Gakushi, Shushi (Biological and Life Sciences; Business Administration; Materials Engineering; Mechanical Engineering), Hakase (Biological and Life Sciences; Business Administration; Electronic Engineering; Environmental Studies; Information Technology; Materials Engineering; Mechanical Engineering)
Student Services: Careers Guidance, Sports Facilities, Health Services, Foreign Studies Centre

Student Numbers 2013-2014	MALE	FEMALE	TOTAL
All (Foreign Included)	1199	197	1396

Last Update: 06-12-2017

Iwaki Meisei University

5-5-1 Chuodai Iino
Iwaki-shi 970-8551, Fukushima
Tel: +81(246) 29-7190
Fax: +81(246) 29-5105
Website: http://www.iwakimu.ac.jp
President: Yoji Yamasaki

Faculty
Pharmacy (Pharmacy)

College
Humanities (American Studies; Arts and Humanities; Clinical Psychology; Cognitive Sciences; Comparative Literature; Cultural Studies; English; Film; Japanese; Linguistics; Literature; Philosophy; Psychology; Psychotherapy; Sociology; Translation and Interpretation; Visual Arts; Welfare and Protective Services; Writing); **Science and Engineering** (Automation and Control Engineering; Biological and Life Sciences; Biology; Biotechnology; Cell Biology; Computer Engineering; Computer Networks; Computer Science; Electronic Engineering; Energy Engineering; Environmental Engineering; Environmental Studies; Information Technology; Machine Building; Mechanical Engineering; Microbiology; Natural Sciences; Power Engineering; Production Engineering)

Graduate School
Humanities (African Studies; American Studies; Anthropology; Arts and Humanities; Asian Studies; Clinical

Psychology; Cultural Studies; English; English Studies; History; Japanese; Law; Linguistics; Literature; Modern Languages; Psychology; Social and Community Services; Social Studies; Sociology; Urban Studies; Welfare and Protective Services); **Science and Engineering** (Biological and Life Sciences; Biotechnology; Electronic Engineering; Energy Engineering; Engineering; Environmental Studies; Information Sciences; Information Technology; Materials Engineering; Mechanical Engineering; Molecular Biology; Nanotechnology; Natural Sciences; Physics)
History: Founded 1987. Acquired present status 2001.
Main language(s) of instruction: Japanese
Accrediting agency: Japan University Accreditation Association (JUAA)
Degrees and diplomas: Gakushi, Shushi (American Studies; Clinical Psychology; Cultural Studies; Engineering; English; English Studies; Japanese; Linguistics; Natural Sciences; Sociology), Hakase (Cultural Studies; Engineering; Japanese; Literature; Natural Sciences)

Academic Staff 2012-2013	MALE	FEMALE	TOTAL
FULL-TIME			207
Student Numbers 2012-2013			
All (Foreign Included)	1268	677	1945

Last Update: 06-12-2017

Iwate Medical University

19-1 Uchimaru
Morioka 020-8505, Iwate
Tel: +81(19) 651-5111
Fax: +81(19) 651-8055
Website: http://www.iwate-med.ac.jp
President: Akira Ogawa

Course/Programme
Basic Medicine (Anatomy; Biochemistry; Biological and Life Sciences; Biomedical Engineering; Cell Biology; Embryology and Reproduction Biology; Epidemiology; Forensic Medicine and Dentistry; Genetics; Hygiene; Immunology; Medicine; Microbiology; Molecular Biology; Pathology; Pharmacology; Physiology; Social and Preventive Medicine)

School
Dentistry (Anaesthesiology; Dental Technology; Dentistry; Health Education; Health Sciences; Oral Pathology; Orthodontics; Paediatrics; Periodontics; Radiology; Surgery); **Medicine** (Anaesthesiology; Cardiology; Community Health; Dermatology; Diabetology; Endocrinology; Gastroenterology; Gerontology; Gynaecology and Obstetrics;

Haematology; Hepatology; Laboratory Techniques; Medicine; Nephrology; Neurological Therapy; Neurology; Nursing; Oncology; Ophthalmology; Orthopaedics; Otorhinolaryngology; Paediatrics; Pathology; Plastic Surgery; Pneumology; Psychiatry and Mental Health; Radiology; Rheumatology; Social and Preventive Medicine; Surgery; Urology); **Pharmacy** (Applied Chemistry; Arts and Humanities; Biochemistry; Biology; Biophysics; Cell Biology; Chemistry; Genetics; Immunology; Molecular Biology; Neurosciences; Organic Chemistry; Pathology; Pharmacology; Pharmacy)

Institute

Biomedical Sciences (Biomedicine)

Centre

Liberal Arts and Sciences (Arts and Humanities; Biology; Chemistry; English; German; Information Sciences; Law; Literature; Mathematics; Medical Technology; Modern Languages; Philosophy; Physical Education; Physics; Psychology)

Graduate School

Dental Science (Dentistry); **Medical Science** (Medicine; Pathology; Physiology; Social and Preventive Medicine; Surgery)
Further information: University Hospital
History: Founded 1928 as Iwate Medical College, acquired University status 1952. Faculty of Dentistry added 1965.
Academic year: April to March (April-September; November-March)
Admission requirements: Graduation from high school or equivalent, and entrance examination
Main language(s) of instruction: Japanese
Accrediting agency: Japan University Accreditation Association (JUAA)
Degrees and diplomas: Gakushi, Shushi (Medicine), Hakase (Dentistry; Medicine)
Student Services: Sports Facilities
Periodicals: Dental Journal of Iwate Medical University, Journal of Iwate Medical Association
Last Update: 06-12-2017

J. F. Oberlin University

3758 Tokiwa-machi
Machida-shi 194-0294, Tokyo
Tel: +81(42) 797-2661, +81(42) 797-1542
Fax: +81(42) 797-0132
Website: http://www.obirin.ac.jp
President: Takayasu Mitani

College

Business Administration (Business Administration; Hotel and Restaurant; Hotel Management; Information Technology; International Business; Leisure Studies; Marketing; Tourism); **Business Management** (Air Transport; Business Administration; Hotel and Restaurant; International Business; Management; Marketing; Service Trades; Tourism); **Health and Welfare**; **Liberal Arts** (Arts and Humanities; Biology; Chemistry; Earth Sciences; Economics; Education; Ethics; Geography; History; Law; Literature; Mathematics; Modern Languages; Natural Sciences; Physics; Political Sciences; Psychology; Religion; Social Sciences; Sociology); **Performing and Visual Arts** (Film; Music; Performing Arts; Theatre; Visual Arts)

Institute

Confucius (Chinese; Modern Languages); **Japanese Languages and Culture**

Graduate School
International Studies
History: Founded 1946 as Obirin Gakuen (Obirin University). Changed english name 2006.
Accrediting agency: Japanese University Accreditation Association
Degrees and diplomas: Gakushi, Shushi, Hakase
Student Services: Academic Counselling, Social Counselling, Careers Guidance, Sports Facilities, Language Laboratory, Health Services, Canteen, Foreign Studies Centre

Student Numbers 2012-2013	MALE	FEMALE	TOTAL
All (Foreign Included)			8595

Last Update: 06-12-2017

Japan College of Social Work

3-1-30 Takeoka Kiyose-shi
Tokyo 204-8555
Tel: +81(42) 496-3000
Fax: +81(42) 496-3001
Website: http://www.jcsw.ac.jp
President: Natori Haniwa

School

Social Welfare (Arts and Humanities; English; Health Sciences; Modern Languages; Psychology; Social and Community Services; Social Sciences; Social Welfare; Social Work; Sports); **Social Work** (*Professional*) (Social Work; Welfare and Protective Services)

Department/Division

Community Education (Psychiatry and Mental Health; Secretarial Studies; Social Work; Welfare and Protective Services)

Graduate School

Social Welfare (Social Welfare)
History: Founded 1946.
Fees: Tuition, 535,800 per annum (Yen)
Main language(s) of instruction: Japanese
Accrediting agency: Ministry of Education, Culture, Sports, Science and Technology (MEXT)
Degrees and diplomas: Gakushi (Social Welfare), Shushi (Social Welfare), Hakase (Social Welfare). Also Professional Master's degree in Welfare Management, 1 yr
Student Services: Sports Facilities, Language Laboratory

Academic Staff	MALE	FEMALE	TOTAL
FULL-TIME			208
Student Numbers			
All (Foreign Included)			967

Last Update: 26-03-2018

Japan Institute of the Moving Image (JIMI)

1-16-30 Manpukuji, Aso-ku
Kanagawa 215-0004, Kawasaki-shi
Tel: +81 44-951-2511
Fax: +81 44-951-2681
Website: http://www.eiga.ac.jp
President: Tengan Daisuke

School

Film Studies (Film)
History: Founded 1975. Acquired present status and title 2011.
Fees: 1880000 (First year) (Yen)
Main language(s) of instruction: Japanese
Accrediting agency: Japan Institution for Higher Education Evaluation (JIHEE)
Degrees and diplomas: Gakushi (Film)
Last Update: 06-12-2017

Japan Lutheran College (JLC)

3-10-20 Osawa
Mitaka-shi 181-0015, Tokyo
Tel: +81(422) 31-4611
Fax: +81(422) 33-6405
Website: http://www.luther.ac.jp
President: Eiji Eto

Department/Division

Christian Studies (Christian Religious Studies); **Clinical Psychology** (Clinical Psychology); **Social Work** (Social Welfare; Social Work)

Graduate School

Integrated Human Studies (Clinical Psychology; Social Work)
History: Founded 1963 as Japan Lutheran Theological College. Acquired present title 1996 and status 2001.
Admission requirements: Entrance examination; Japanese Language Proficiency Test.
Fees: 800,000 per annum (Yen)
Main language(s) of instruction: Japanese
Accrediting agency: Japan University Accreditation Association (JUAA)
Degrees and diplomas: Gakushi, Shushi (Clinical Psychology; Social Work)

Student Numbers	MALE	FEMALE	TOTAL
All (Foreign Included)			482

Last Update: 06-12-2017

Japan University of Economics (JUE)

3-11-25 Gojo Dazaifu-shi
Fukuoka-shi 818-0197, Fukuoka
Tel: +81(92) 922-5131, +81(92) 921-9811
Fax: +81(92) 921-9823
Website: http://www.jue.ac.jp
President: Asuka Tsuzuki

Department/Division

Business Administration (Business Administration; Communication Studies; E- Business/Commerce; Information Management; Management); **Commerce** (Accountancy; Business and Commerce; Finance; International Business; Marketing; Tourism); **Economics** (Economics; International Economics); **Health and Sports Business Administration** (Sports Management); **Management Law** (Civil Law; Commercial Law; Law; Management)
Further information: Also Kobe campus
History: Founded 1968 as Daiichi Keizai Daigaku (Daiichi University, College of Economics). Changed name to Fukuoka University of Economics (Fukuoka Keizai Daigaku) 2007. Acquired present title 2010.
Admission requirements: Entrance examination
Fees: Tuition, 310,000 per annum (Yen)
Main language(s) of instruction: Japanese
Accrediting agency: Japan University Accreditation Association
Degrees and diplomas: Gakushi (Economics)
Last Update: 28-03-2018

Japan University of Health Sciences

Satte Satte 1961-2
Saitama 340-0113
Tel: +81 480-40-4848
Fax: +81 480-40-4860
Website: http://www.jhsu.ac.jp
President: Senjun Taira

School

Health Science (Nursing)
History: Founded 1945.
Main language(s) of instruction: Japanese
Accrediting agency: Japan Institution for Higher Education Evaluation (JIHEE)
Degrees and diplomas: Gakushi (Nursing)
Last Update: 07-12-2017

Japan Women's College of Physical Education (JWCE)

8-19-1, Kitakarasuyama Setagaya-ku
Tokyo 157-8565
Tel: +81(3) 3300-2250, +81(3) 3300-2256
Fax: +81(3) 3308-7244
Website: http://www.jwcpe.ac.jp
President: Ishizaki Yoshiko

Faculty

Sports and Health Sciences (Child Care and Development; Dance; Health Sciences; Sports; Sports Management)

Graduate School

Sports Science (Sports)
History: Founded 1922.
Academic year: April to February
Main language(s) of instruction: Japanese
Accrediting agency: Japan Institution for Higher Education Evaluation (JIHEE)
Degrees and diplomas: Gakushi, Shushi (Sports)
Student Services: Social Counselling, Cultural Activities, Sports Facilities, Health Services, Library, Residential Facilities
Last Update: 07-12-2017

Japan Women's University (JWU)

2-8-1 Mejirodai Bunkyo-ku
Tokyo 112-8681
Tel: +81(3) 3943-3131

Website: http://www.jwu.ac.jp
President: Kazuto Sato

Faculty

Human Sciences and Design (Architecture; Architecture and Planning; Child Care and Development; Clothing and Sewing; Economics; Food Science; House Arts and Environment; Household Management; Marketing; Nutrition; Pedagogy; Psychology; Social Sciences; Sociology; Textile Design; Textile Technology); **Humanities** (Arts and Humanities; Cultural Studies; Education; English; History; Japanese; Psychology; Social Welfare; Sociology); **Integrated Arts and Social Sciences** (*Kawasaki City*) (Arts and Humanities; Cultural Studies; Education; History; Philosophy; Psychology; Social Sciences; Social Studies; Social Welfare; Sociology); **Science** (Biological and Life Sciences; Biology; Chemistry; Mathematics; Physics)

Department/Division

Correspondence Courses (Child Care and Development; Food Science; House Arts and Environment; Nutrition)

Institute

Research (Educational Research; History; Philosophy)

Graduate School

Human Life Science (Development Studies; Home Economics; House Arts and Environment); **Human Sciences and Design** (Child Care and Development; Clothing and Sewing; Economics; Food Science; Home Economics; House Arts and Environment; Nutrition; Welfare and Protective Services); **Humanities** (American Studies; Arts and Humanities; Cultural Studies; East Asian Studies; English; English Studies; History; Japanese; Literature; Modern Languages; Oriental Studies; Western European Studies); **Integrated Arts and Social Sciences** (*Kawasaki City*) (Anthropology; Clinical Psychology; Cognitive Sciences; Cultural Studies; Demography and Population; Economics; Education; Educational Psychology; History; Philosophy; Political Sciences; Psychology; Social Sciences; Social Studies; Social Welfare; Sociology; Sports; Technology); **Science** (Biological and Life Sciences; Biology; Cell Biology; Environmental Studies; Mathematics; Molecular Biology; Physical Chemistry; Physics; Physiology)

Research Division

Women's Career
Further information: Also Nishiikuta campus
History: Founded 1901 as Liberal Arts College, became University 1948. Faculty of Integrated Arts and Social Sciences established 1990. Faculty of Science established 1992. A private institution for women. Mainly financed by tuition fees.

Academic year: April to March (April-September; September-March)

Admission requirements: Graduation from senior high school or foreign equivalent, and entrance examination

Fees: Entrance Fee, 300,000; Tuition fee, 640,000-870,000 per annum (Yen)

Main language(s) of instruction: Japanese

Accrediting agency: Japan University Accreditation Association (JUAA)

Degrees and diplomas: Gakushi, Shushi (Biology; Child Care and Development; Clothing and Sewing; Cultural Studies; Economics; Education; English; Food Science; History; Home Economics; House Arts and Environment; Japanese; Mathematics; Nutrition; Physics; Psychology; Social Studies; Social Welfare; Welfare and Protective Services), Hakase (Biology; Education; English; History; Home Economics; Japanese; Mathematics; Physics; Psychology; Social Studies; Social Welfare)

Student Services: Academic Counselling, Social Counselling, Careers Guidance, Nursery Care, Sports Facilities, Language Laboratory, Facilities for disabled people, Health Services, Canteen, Foreign Studies Centre, Library, Residential Facilities

Periodicals: Journals of the faculties, Journals of the Graduate Schools

Last Update: 07-12-2017

Japanese Red Cross Toyota College of Nursing

12-33 Nanamagari Hakusancho
Toyota-shi 471-8565, Aichi
Tel: +81(565) 36-5111
Fax: +81(565) 37-8558
Website: http://www.rctoyota.ac.jp
President: Yayoi Kamakura

College

Nursing (Nursing)

Graduate School

Nursing (Nursing)

History: Founded 2004.

Main language(s) of instruction: Japanese

Accrediting agency: Japan University Accreditation Association (JUAA)

Degrees and diplomas: Gakushi (Nursing), Shushi (Nursing)

Student Services: Academic Counselling, Social Counselling, Canteen, Library

Last Update: 11-12-2017

Jichi Medical University

3311-1 Yakushiji
Shimotsuke-shi 329-0498, Tochigi-ken
Tel: +81(285) 44-2111
Fax: +81(285) 443-625
Website: http://www.jichi.ac.jp
President: Ryozo Nagai

School

Medicine (Anaesthesiology; Anatomy; Biochemistry; Biophysics; Cardiology; Dentistry; Dermatology; Endocrinology; Forensic Medicine and Dentistry; Gastroenterology; Gynaecology and Obstetrics; Haematology; Histology; Immunology; Laboratory Techniques; Medicine; Nephrology; Neurological Therapy; Neurology; Ophthalmology; Oral Pathology; Orthopaedics; Otorhinolaryngology; Paediatrics; Parasitology; Pathology; Pharmacology; Physiology; Plastic Surgery; Pneumology; Psychiatry and Mental Health; Radiology; Rheumatology; Surgery; Toxicology; Urology; Virology; Zoology); **Nursing** (Anatomy; Anthropology; Community Health; Computer Science; Gerontology; Health Education; Health Sciences; Nursing; Pathology; Physiology; Psychiatry and Mental Health)

Centre

Community Medicine (Community Health; Computer Science; Public Health; Traditional Eastern Medicine); **Development of Advanced Medical Technology** (Medical Technology); **Information**; **Medical Simulation** (Medicine); **Molecular Medicine** (Biology; Cell Biology; Genetics; Medicine; Molecular Biology; Rehabilitation and Therapy); **RI (Radio-Isotope)** (Medical Technology)

Laboratory

Experimental Medicine (Medicine)

Graduate School

Medicine (Biological and Life Sciences; Community Health; Environmental Studies; Medicine); **Nursing** (Community Health; Nursing)

Further information: Jichi Medical University Hospital, Jichi Medical University Saitama Medical Center

History: Founded 1972.

Academic year: April to March

Admission requirements: Graduation from high school and entrance examination

Main language(s) of instruction: Japanese

Accrediting agency: Japan University Accreditation Association

Degrees and diplomas: Gakushi, Shushi (Medicine; Nursing), Hakase (Biology; Community Health; Medicine)

Student Services: Sports Facilities, Health Services, Canteen
Periodicals: Jichi Medical University Annual Report, Jichi Medical University Journal
Last Update: 11-12-2017

Jin-ai University

3-1-1 Ohde-cho
Takefu 915-8586, Fukui
Tel: +81(778) 27-2010
Fax: +81(778) 27-1990
Website: http://www.jindai.ac.jp
President: Kaburo Masanobu

Faculty

Human Life (Analytical Chemistry; Anatomy; Anthropology; Asian Religious Studies; Chemistry; Child Care and Development; Chinese; Cooking and Catering; Education; Educational Administration; Educational Psychology; Environmental Studies; Food Science; Food Technology; Foreign Languages Education; French; German; Health Education; Health Sciences; Home Economics Education; Humanities and Social Science Education; Hygiene; Information Sciences; Literature; Mathematics; Microbiology; Modern Languages; Music; Music Education; Nutrition; Organic Chemistry; Philosophy; Physical Education; Physiology; Preschool Education; Primary Education; Public Health; Special Education; Teacher Training); **Human Sciences** (Anthropology; Asian Religious Studies; Chinese; Communication Studies; Cultural Studies; English; Environmental Studies; French; German; Human Resources; Information Sciences; Linguistics; Literature; Modern Languages; Psychology; Regional Studies; Social Studies)

Graduate School

Human Studies (Clinical Psychology)
History: Founded 2001 with the aim of promoting an education based on Buddhist philosophy.
Fees: Tuition, 325,000-390,000 per annum (Yen)
Main language(s) of instruction: Japanese
Accrediting agency: Japan Institution for Higher Education Evaluation (JIHEE)
Degrees and diplomas: Gakushi, Shushi (Clinical Psychology)

Academic Staff 2012-2013	MALE	FEMALE	TOTAL
FULL-TIME			71
Student Numbers 2012-2013			
All (Foreign Included)	367	899	1266

Last Update: 11-12-2017

Jissen Women's University

4-1-1 Osakaue
Hino-shi 191-8510, Tokyo
Tel: +81(42) 585-8800
Fax: +81(42) 585-8818
Website: http://www.jissen.ac.jp
Chairman of the Board of Trustees: Ihara Toru

Faculty

Human Life Sciences (Environmental Studies; Film; Food Science; Health Sciences; Mass Communication; Media Studies; Psychology; Sociology; Welfare and Protective Services); **Humanities** (Aesthetics; Art History; Arts and Humanities; English; Japanese; Literature); **Humanities and Social Sciences** (Arts and Humanities; Business Administration; Communication Studies; Psychology; Social Sciences; Sociology)

College

Junior Studies (Communication Studies; Ecology; English; Japanese; Nutrition; Welfare and Protective Services)

Institute

Japanese Literary Archives and Research (Literature; Philology)

Centre

Information Systems (Information Sciences)

Graduate School

Human Life Sciences (Environmental Studies; Food Science; Nutrition); **Humanities** (Art History; Arts and Humanities; English; Japanese; Literature); **Humanities and Social Sciences** (Arts and Humanities; Social Sciences)
History: Founded 1899.
Academic year: April to March (April-September; October-March)
Admission requirements: Graduation from high school and entrance examination
Main language(s) of instruction: Japanese
Accrediting agency: Japan University Accreditation Association (JUAA)
Degrees and diplomas: Gakushi, Shushi (Art History; English; Environmental Studies; Food Science; Japanese; Literature; Nutrition), Hakase (Japanese; Literature)
Student Services: Academic Counselling, Social Counselling, Careers Guidance, Health Services
Periodicals: Annual Reports of Studies

Student Numbers 2012-2013	MALE	FEMALE	TOTAL
All (Foreign Included)			3936

Last Update: 11-12-2017

Jobu University

634-1 Toyazuka-machi
Isesaki 372-8588, Gunma
Tel: +81(270) 32-1010
Fax: +81(270) 32-1021
Website: http://www.jobu.ac.jp
President: Masashi Shibuya

Faculty

Business and Information Studies (Accountancy; Business Administration; Finance; Information Sciences; Sports Management); **Informatics and Management** (Computer Science; Information Technology; Management; Media Studies)

School

Nursing

Graduate School

Business Administration (Accountancy; Business Administration; Economics; Health Administration; Information Management; Information Sciences; Marketing; Occupational Health; Taxation)
Further information: Also Takasaki campus
History: Founded 1968.
Fees: Tuition, 330,000-550,000 per annum (Yen)
Main language(s) of instruction: Japanese, English
Accrediting agency: Japan University Accreditation Association (JUAA)
Degrees and diplomas: Gakushi, Shushi (Health Sciences; Management)
Student Services: Careers Guidance, Sports Facilities, Language Laboratory
Last Update: 08-12-2017

Josai International University (JIU)

1 Gumyo
Togane-shi 283-8555, Chiba-ken
Tel: +81(475) 55-8855
Fax: +81(475) 53-2194
Website: http://www.jiu.ac.jp
President: Kenji Sugibayashi

Faculty

International Humanities (Arts and Humanities; Cultural Studies; English; Foreign Languages Education; International Studies); **Management and Information Sciences** (Business Administration; Health Administration; Information Management; Information Sciences; Management; Public Administration; Sports Management); **Media Studies** (Data Processing; Design; Information Sciences; Information Technology; Media Studies; Sound Engineering (Acoustics); Video); **Nursing** (Hygiene; Nursing; Paediatrics; Public Health); **Pharmaceutical Sciences** (Pharmacy); **Social and Environmental Studies** (Environmental Studies; Social Studies); **Social Work Studies** (Child Care and Development; Clinical Psychology; Health Education; Social Psychology; Social Welfare; Social Work); **Tourism** (Accountancy; Business Administration; English; Food Technology; Health Sciences; Hotel and Restaurant; Information Sciences; Insurance; Media Studies; Technology; Tourism)

Course/Programme

Japanese Language (Japanese)

Graduate School

Business Design (Business Administration; Communication Studies; Finance; Information Management; Information Sciences; Management; Marketing); **Humanities** (Arts and Humanities; Communication Studies; Cultural Studies; International Studies; Women's Studies); **Management and Information Sciences** (Information Sciences; Information Technology; Management); **Pharmaceutical Sciences** (Health Sciences; Leadership; Pharmacy; Public Health; Welfare and Protective Services); **Social Work Studies** (Social and Community Services; Social and Preventive Medicine; Social Welfare; Social Work)
Further information: Also Awa, Tokyo Kioicho and Makuhari campuses
History: Founded 1992.
Main language(s) of instruction: Japanese, English
Accrediting agency: Japan University Accreditation Association (JUAA)
Degrees and diplomas: Gakushi, Shushi (Business Administration; Communication Studies; Cultural Studies; International Studies; Management; Social Welfare; Women's Studies), Hakase (Cultural Studies; Management; Pharmacy)
Student Services: Language Laboratory
Last Update: 08-12-2017

Josai University

1-1 Keyakidai
Sakado-shi 350-0295, Saitama
Tel: +81(49) 286-2233
Fax: +81(49) 271-7947
Website: http://www.josai.ac.jp
President: Akira Shirahata

Faculty

Business Administration (Business Administration; Management); **Contemporary Policy Studies** (Business

Administration; Commercial Law; Economics; Law; Political Sciences; Public Administration; Sociology; Welfare and Protective Services); **Economics** (Economics; International Economics); **Pharmaceutical Sciences** (Analytical Chemistry; Applied Chemistry; Community Health; Computer Science; Dietetics; Food Science; Health Sciences; Hygiene; Immunology; Information Technology; Nursing; Nutrition; Organic Chemistry; Pathology; Pharmacology; Pharmacy; Physiology; Public Health; Rehabilitation and Therapy; Social Welfare; Statistics; Toxicology); **Science** (Business Computing; Chemistry; Computer Science; Information Technology; Materials Engineering; Mathematical Physics; Mathematics; Molecular Biology; Nanotechnology; Natural Sciences)

College
Junior Studies (*Josai*) (Business Administration)

Graduate School
Business Research Course (Business Administration; International Business; Management; Marketing); **Economics Research Course** (Economic and Finance Policy; Economics; International Economics); **Pharmaceutical Sciences** (Chemistry; Food Science; Medicine; Nutrition; Organic Chemistry; Pharmacy; Physical Chemistry; Physiology; Toxicology); **Science** (Chemistry; Computer Science; Information Sciences; Information Technology; Materials Engineering; Mathematics; Molecular Biology; Nanotechnology; Organic Chemistry; Physics)

History: Founded 1965.
Academic year: April to March (April-September; October-March)
Admission requirements: Graduation from high school and entrance examination
Main language(s) of instruction: Japanese
Accrediting agency: Japan University Accreditation Association (JUAA)
Degrees and diplomas: Gakushi, Shushi (Business Administration; Chemistry; Computer Science; Economic and Finance Policy; Materials Engineering; Mathematics; Medicine; Nutrition; Pharmacology; Pharmacy), Hakase (Pharmacy)
Last Update: 08-12-2017

Joshibi University of Art and Design

1900 Asamizo-dai Sagamihara-shi
Kanagawa 252-8538
Tel: +81(42) 252-8538
Fax: +81(42) 778-6649
Website: http://www.joshibi.ac.jp
President: Katsuki Yokoyama

College
Art and Design (Architectural and Environmental Design; Art Education; Art Management; Ceramic Art; Communication Arts; Design; Fashion Design; Fine Arts; Glass Art; Industrial Design; Media Studies; Museum Studies; Painting and Drawing; Sculpture; Textile Design; Visual Arts); **Joshibi Arts and Design Junior Studies** (Design; Fine Arts)

Graduate School
Art and Design (Architectural and Environmental Design; Art Education; Art History; Art Therapy; Crafts and Trades; Design; Fashion Design; Fine Arts; Industrial Design; Media Studies; Painting and Drawing; Printing and Printmaking; Sculpture; Visual Arts)
Further information: Also Suginami Campus
History: Founded as Private Women's School of Fine Arts 1900. Renamed Women's Academy of Fine Arts 1929 and Women's College of Fine Arts 1949. Acquired present title 2001.
Fees: Undergraduate programmes, 1,268,000; Graduate programmes, 740,000 per annum (Yen)
Main language(s) of instruction: Japanese
Accrediting agency: Japan University Accreditation Association (JUAA)
Degrees and diplomas: Gakushi, Shushi (Design; Fine Arts), Hakase (Design; Fine Arts)
Last Update: 08-12-2017

Jumonji University

2-1-28 Sugasawa
Niiza-shi 352-8510, Saitama
Tel: +81(48) 477-0555
Fax: +81(48) 478-9367
Website: http://www.jumonji-u.ac.jp
President: Kaoru Yokosuka

Course/Programme
Bekka (Asian Studies; Japanese)

Department/Division
Children's Education (Child Care and Development; Education; Primary Education); **Early Childhood Education** (Preschool Education); **Food and Nutrition** (Dietetics; Food Science; Nutrition); **Human Development Psychology** (Psychology); **Human Welfare** (Social Welfare; Social Work; Welfare and Protective Services); **Living Information** (Business Administration; Business Computing; Computer Engineering; Data Processing; Economics; Information Sciences; Information Technology; International Business; Law; Management; Marketing; Software Engineering); **Media Communication** (Mass Communication; Media Studies)

Graduate School

Food and Nutrition (Food Science; Health Sciences; Nutrition)

History: Founded 1922.

Fees: 300,000-370,000 per annum (Yen)

Main language(s) of instruction: Japanese

Accrediting agency: Japan Institution for Higher Education Evaluation (JIHEE)

Degrees and diplomas: Gakushi, Shushi (Food Science; Health Sciences; Nutrition)

Student Services: Careers Guidance, Health Services

Last Update: 11-12-2017

Junshin Gakuen University

1-1-1 Chikusigaoka - Minami-ku
Fukuoka 815-8510
Tel: +81 92-552-2707
Fax: +81 92-552-2707
Website: http://www.junshin-u.ac.jp
President: Yonosuke Fukuda

Faculty

Inspection Sciences (Laboratory Techniques); **Medical Engineering** (Medical Technology); **Nursing** (Nursing); **Radiation Technology Science** (Radiology)

History: Founded 1956.

Main language(s) of instruction: Japanese

Accrediting agency: Japan Institution for Higher Education Evaluation (JIHEE)

Degrees and diplomas: Gakushi (Laboratory Techniques; Medical Technology; Nursing; Radiology)

Last Update: 08-12-2017

Juntendo University

2-1-1 Hongo
Bunkyo-ku 113-8421, Tokyo
Tel: +81(3) 3813-3111
Fax: +81(3) 3814-9100
Website: http://www.juntendo.ac.jp/english/index.html
President: Arai Hajime

Faculty

Health and Sports Science (Health Sciences; Sports); **Health Care and Nursing** (Health Sciences; Nursing); **Health Sciences and Nursing** (Health Sciences; Nursing); **Medicine** (Medicine)

Graduate School

Health and Sports Science (Health Education; Health Sciences; Social Sciences; Sociology; Sports; Sports Management; Sports Medicine); **Health Care and Nursing** (Gerontology; Health Sciences; Immunology; Nursing; Oncology; Paediatrics; Psychiatry and Mental Health); **Medicine** (Anaesthesiology; Anatomy; Behavioural Sciences; Biochemistry; Cardiology; Cell Biology; Dermatology; Endocrinology; Environmental Studies; Epidemiology; Forensic Medicine and Dentistry; Gastroenterology; Gynaecology and Obstetrics; Haematology; Health Administration; Health Education; Hepatology; Immunology; Laboratory Techniques; Medicine; Microbiology; Molecular Biology; Nephrology; Neurological Therapy; Neurology; Neurosciences; Oncology; Ophthalmology; Otorhinolaryngology; Paediatrics; Parasitology; Pathology; Pharmacology; Physiology; Plastic Surgery; Psychiatry and Mental Health; Public Health; Radiology; Rehabilitation and Therapy; Respiratory Therapy; Rheumatology; Surgery; Treatment Techniques; Urology)

Further information: Also Urayasu, Sakura and Mishima campuses. Six hospitals (Main Hospital, Shizuoka Hospital, Urayasu Hospital, Koshigaya Hospital, Koto Geriatric Medical Center, Nerima Hospital)

History: Founded 1838. Acquired present status 1951.

Academic year: April to March

Admission requirements: Graduation from high school and entrance examination

Fees: Undergraduate Programmes, 4,800,000-6,500,000 per programme (4 yrs), except Medicine 20,800,000 (6-yr programme). Graduate Programmes, 1,300,000-1,400,000 for Master's programmes; 2,400,000-2,600,000 for Doctoral programmes (Yen)

Main language(s) of instruction: Japanese, English

Accrediting agency: Japan University Accreditation Association (JUAA)

Degrees and diplomas: Gakushi, Shushi (Health Sciences; Medicine; Nursing; Sports), Hakase (Health Sciences; Medicine; Sports)

Student Services: Academic Counselling, Social Counselling, Careers Guidance, Nursery Care, Sports Facilities, Language Laboratory, Health Services, Canteen

Periodicals: Journal of Health and Sports Science Juntendo University, Journal of Health Care and Nursing, Juntendo Medical Journal, The journal of Juntendo Medical College of Nursing

Academic Staff 2013-2014	MALE	FEMALE	TOTAL
FULL-TIME			1061
PART-TIME			2980
Student Numbers 2013-2014			
All (Foreign Included)			3802

Last Update: 08-12-2017

Kaetsu University

2-8-4, Hanakoganeiminami-cho Kodaira-shi
Tokyo 187-8578
Tel: +81(42) 466-3711
Fax: +81(42) 463-1778
Website: http://www.kaetsu.ac.jp
President: Momoyo Ishikawa

Department/Division

Business Communication (*Women only*) (Business Administration; Communication Studies); **Management and Economics** (Accountancy; Economics; Law; Management; Public Administration)

Graduate School

Business Innovation (Accountancy; Business Administration; Environmental Studies; Information Sciences; Law; Small Business; Taxation)
History: Founded 2001.
Fees: 984,000-1,288,000 per annum (Yen)
Main language(s) of instruction: Japanese
Accrediting agency: Japan Institution for Higher Education Evaluation (JIHEE)
Degrees and diplomas: Gakushi, Shushi (Management)

Academic Staff 2013-2014	MALE	FEMALE	TOTAL
FULL-TIME			68
Student Numbers 2013-2014			
All (Foreign Included)			1495
Foreign only			73

Total number of part-time students: 1
Last Update: 11-12-2017

Kagawa Nutrition University

3-9-21 Chiyoda
Sakado-shi 350-0288, Saitama
Tel: +81(492) 84-6245
Fax: +81(492) 84-6410
Website: http://www.eiyo.ac.jp/daigaku
President: Yoshiko Kagawa

Department/Division

Applied Nutrition (Arts and Humanities; Biology; Business Administration; Chemistry; Community Health; English; Environmental Studies; Food Science; Health Sciences; Modern Languages; Natural Sciences; Nutrition; Physics; Public Health; Sports; Welfare and Protective Services); **Food Culture and Nutrition** (Arts and Humanities; Business Administration; Cooking and Catering; Cultural Studies; Dietetics; Environmental Studies; Ethnology; Food Science; Food Technology; Modern Languages; Natural Sciences; Nutrition; Social Sciences); **Health and Nutrition** (*Evening*) (Arts and Humanities; Environmental Studies; Food Science; Health Sciences; Nutrition; Social Sciences; Teacher Trainers Education); **Health and Nutrition, Division of Health and School Nursing** (Anatomy; Arts and Humanities; Biology; Chemistry; Child Care and Development; Dietetics; Health Education; Health Sciences; Hygiene; Information Sciences; Medicine; Modern Languages; Natural Sciences; Nursing; Nutrition; Physics; Physiology; Psychiatry and Mental Health; Social and Preventive Medicine; Social Sciences; Special Education; Teacher Training; Welfare and Protective Services); **Health and Nutrition, Division of Nutrition Sciences** (Arts and Humanities; Biological and Life Sciences; Biology; Cell Biology; Chemistry; Dietetics; English; Food Science; Food Technology; Health Administration; Health Education; Health Sciences; Histology; Home Economics; Hygiene; Laboratory Techniques; Modern Languages; Natural Sciences; Nursing; Nutrition; Physics; Physiology; Social Sciences; Sports; Sports Medicine)

Graduate School

Health Sciences and Nutrition (Health Sciences; Nutrition)
History: Founded 1961, incorporating Kagawa Nutrition School founded 1939, and Junior College 1950.
Academic year: April to March (April-July; October-March)
Admission requirements: Graduation from high school or equivalent, and entrance examination. Japanese language proficiency certified at Level 1 of the Japanese Proficiency Test
Main language(s) of instruction: Japanese
Accrediting agency: Japan Institution for Higher Education Evaluation (JIHEE)
Degrees and diplomas: Gakushi, Shushi (Health Sciences; Nutrition), Hakase (Health Sciences; Nutrition)
Student Services: Academic Counselling, Social Counselling, Careers Guidance, Cultural Activities, Sports Facilities, Facilities for disabled people, Health Services, Canteen, Foreign Studies Centre
Periodicals: Joshi Eiyo-Daigaku Kiyo (Scientific Report of the College)
Publishing house: Joshi Eiyo Daigaku Shuppanbu (Women's College, Publishing Division)
Last Update: 08-12-2017

Kagoshima Immaculate Heart University

2365 Amatatsu-cho
Sendai-shi 895-0011, Miyagi
Tel: +81(996) 23-5311

Fax: +81(996) 23-5030
Website: http://www.k-junshin.ac.jp/jundai
President: Matsushita Eiko

Faculty

International Human Studies (Child Care and Development; Cultural Studies; English; International Relations; International Studies; Modern Languages); **Nursing and Nutrition** (Health Sciences; Nursing; Nutrition)

Graduate School

Graduate Studies (Clinical Psychology)
History: Founded 1994.
Fees: Tuition, 600,000-800,000 per annum (Yen)
Main language(s) of instruction: Japanese, English
Accrediting agency: Japan Institution for Higher Education Evaluation (JIHEE)
Degrees and diplomas: Gakushi, Shushi (Clinical Psychology)
Student Services: Social Counselling, Sports Facilities

Student Numbers 2013-2014	MALE	FEMALE	TOTAL
All (Foreign Included)			685

Last Update: 11-12-2017

Kaichi International University (NGU)

1225-6 Kashiwa
Kashiwa-shi 277-0005, Chiba
Tel: +81(4) 7167-8655
Fax: +81(4) 7163-0096
Website: http://www.kaichi.ac.jp
President: Tooru Aoki

Faculty

Liberal Arts (Accountancy; Business Administration; Cultural Studies; East Asian Studies; Fine Arts; History; Information Management; Law; Literature; Management; Music; Political Sciences; Psychology; Regional Studies; Religion; Secretarial Studies; Sports Management)
History: Founded 2000. Former Nihonbashi Gakkan University
Fees: Entrance fee, 350,000; Tuition fee, 690,000 per annum
Main language(s) of instruction: Japanese, English
Accrediting agency: Japan Institution for Higher Education Evaluation (JIHEE)
Degrees and diplomas: Gakushi (Business Administration; Cultural Studies; International Studies; Psychology; Regional Studies)
Last Update: 11-12-2017

Kamakura Women's University

6-1-3 Ofuna
Kamakura-shi 247-8512, Kanagawa
Tel: +81(467) 44-2111
Fax: +81(467) 44-7131
Website: http://www.kamakura-u.ac.jp
President: Fukui Mizumitsu

Faculty

Child Studies (Child Care and Development; Health Sciences; Preschool Education; Primary Education; Psychology; Special Education; Welfare and Protective Services); **Education** (Civics; Education; Geography; History; Japanese; Museum Studies; Primary Education; Secondary Education; Social Studies; Special Education; Teacher Training); **Family and Consumer Sciences** (Dietetics; Earth Sciences; Family Studies; Food Science; Home Economics; Nutrition)

College

Junior Studies (Education; Primary Education)

Graduate School

Graduate Studies (Child Care and Development; Preschool Education; Primary Education; Psychology)
History: Founded 1943. Acquired present title 1959.
Main language(s) of instruction: Japanese
Accrediting agency: Japan Institution for Higher Education Evaluation (JIHEE)
Degrees and diplomas: Associate's Degree (Academic), Gakushi, Shushi (Child Care and Development; Education)

Student Numbers 2012-2013	MALE	FEMALE	TOTAL
All (Foreign Included)			c. 510

Last Update: 11-12-2017

Kameda College of Health Sciences

Chiba Prefecture Yokosuka 462
Kamogawa City 296-0001
Tel: +81 4-7099-1211
Fax: +81 4-7099-1327
Website: http://www.kameda.ac.jp
Chairman of the Board: Takaaki Kameda

Faculty

Nursing (Nursing)
History: Founded 1966 as a nursing school.
Main language(s) of instruction: Japanese
Accrediting agency: Ministry of Education, Culture, Sports, Science and Technology (MEXT)

Degrees and diplomas: Gakushi (Nursing)
Last Update: 26-03-2018

Kanagawa Dental College (KDU)

82 Inaoka-cho
Yokusuka-shi 238-8580, Kanagawa
Tel: +81(46) 822-8803
Fax: +81(46) 822-8801
Website: http://www.kdu.ac.jp
President: Takashi Sakurai

School

Dental Hygiene (Dental Hygiene); **Dentistry** (Aesthetics; Arts and Humanities; Dentistry; English; Information Sciences; Linguistics; Natural Sciences; Ophthalmology; Physical Education; Physics); **Nursing** (Nursing)

Graduate School

Dentistry (Anaesthesiology; Anatomy; Biology; Cell Biology; Community Health; Dental Hygiene; Dentistry; Embryology and Reproduction Biology; Laboratory Techniques; Medical Technology; Molecular Biology; Radiology; Surgery)
History: Founded 1964.
Academic year: April to March (April-July; September-December; January-February)
Admission requirements: Graduation from high school or equivalent, and entrance examination
Fees: Tuition, 2,850,000-3,850,000 per annum (I.e., a total of 22,100,000 over 6 yrs) (Yen)
Main language(s) of instruction: Japanese
Accrediting agency: Japan University Accreditation Association (JUAA)
Degrees and diplomas: Gakushi, Hakase (Dentistry)
Student Services: Sports Facilities
Periodicals: Kanagawa Shigaku

Academic Staff 2013-2014	MALE	FEMALE	TOTAL
FULL-TIME			126
PART-TIME			c. 77

Last Update: 12-12-2017

Kanagawa Institute of Technology (KAIT)

1030 Shimo-ogino
Atsugi-shi 243-0292, Kanagawa
Tel: +81(46) 291-3313
Fax: +81(46) 291-3314
Website: http://www.kait.jp

Faculty

Applied Bioscience (Biological and Life Sciences; Biology; Biotechnology; Chemistry; Nutrition); **Creative Engineering** (Automotive Engineering; Electrical Engineering; Electronic Engineering; Engineering; Mechanical Engineering; Robotics); **Engineering** (Applied Chemistry; Electrical and Electronic Engineering; Engineering; Mechanical Engineering); **Information Technology** (Computer Networks; Computer Science; Information Sciences; Information Technology; Media Studies; Telecommunications Engineering)

Graduate School

Engineering (Applied Chemistry; Automation and Control Engineering; Biochemistry; Chemical Engineering; Computer Engineering; Computer Science; Electrical and Electronic Engineering; Electronic Engineering; Engineering; Environmental Studies; Information Technology; Inorganic Chemistry; Machine Building; Materials Engineering; Mechanical Engineering; Media Studies; Organic Chemistry; Physical Chemistry; Polymer and Plastics Technology; Power Engineering; Production Engineering; Telecommunications Engineering; Thermal Engineering)
History: Founded 1975 as Ikutoku Technical University. Acquired present title 1988.
Academic year: April to March (April-September; October-March)
Admission requirements: Graduation from high school
Fees: Tuition fee, 1,310,000-1,340,000 per annum for undergraduate programmes; 600,000 per annum for graduate programmes (Yen)
Main language(s) of instruction: Japanese
Accrediting agency: Japan University Accreditation Association (JUAA)
Degrees and diplomas: Gakushi, Shushi (Applied Chemistry; Computer Science; Electrical and Electronic Engineering; Information Technology; Mechanical Engineering), Hakase (Applied Chemistry; Computer Science; Electrical and Electronic Engineering; Information Technology; Mechanical Engineering)
Student Services: Social Counselling, Careers Guidance, Sports Facilities, Health Services, Canteen, Foreign Studies Centre
Periodicals: Research Reports

Academic Staff 2012-2013	MALE	FEMALE	TOTAL
FULL-TIME			208
Student Numbers 2012-2013			
All (Foreign Included)	4631	612	5243

Last Update: 12-12-2017

Kanagawa University (KU)

3-27-1, Rokkakubashi Kanagawa-ku
Yokohama-shi 221-8686, Kanagawa
Tel: +81(45) 481-5661
Fax: +81(45) 491-7915
Website: http://www.kanagawa-u.ac.jp
President: Yoshio Kaneko

Faculty

Business Administration (Accountancy; Business Administration; Communication Studies; International Business; Management; Sports Management); **Economics** (Accountancy; Business Administration; Economics; Environmental Studies; International Economics; International Studies; Management; Marketing; Social Policy; Social Welfare); **Engineering** (Architectural and Environmental Design; Architecture; Electrical Engineering; Electronic Engineering; Energy Engineering; Engineering; Environmental Engineering; Industrial Engineering; Industrial Management; Information Technology; Materials Engineering; Mechanical Engineering; Nanotechnology; Structural Architecture); **Foreign Languages** (Chinese; Cultural Studies; English; Modern Languages; Spanish); **Human Sciences** (Arts and Humanities; Health Sciences; Psychology; Social Studies; Sports); **Law** (Commercial Law; Government; Law); **Science** (Biochemistry; Biological and Life Sciences; Cell Biology; Chemistry; Ecology; History; Information Sciences; Mathematics; Molecular Biology; Natural Sciences; Physics; Software Engineering)

School

Law (*Graduate - Professional*) (Law)

Institute

Economics and Foreign Trade (Economics; International Business); **Humanities Research** (Arts and Humanities); **International Business and Management** (International Business; Management); **Legal Studies** (Law); **Study of Japanese Folk Culture** (Cultural Studies; Folklore; History)

Centre

Clinical Psychology (Clinical Psychology); **Language Studies** (Modern Languages)

Graduate School

Economics (Accountancy; Business Administration; Economic and Finance Policy; Economics; International Business; International Economics; Marketing; Transport Management); **Engineering** (Analytical Chemistry; Applied Chemistry; Architectural and Environmental Design; Architecture; Architecture and Planning; Automation and Control Engineering; Construction Engineering; Data Processing; Electrical and Electronic Engineering; Electrical Engineering; Electronic Engineering; Energy Engineering; Engineering; Industrial Engineering; Industrial Management; Information Technology; Inorganic Chemistry; Mechanical Engineering; Organic Chemistry; Polymer and Plastics Technology; Power Engineering; Production Engineering; Safety Engineering; Structural Architecture; Telecommunications Engineering; Town Planning; Urban Studies); **Foreign Languages** (American Studies; Asian Studies; Chinese; Comparative Literature; Cultural Studies; English; European Languages; European Studies; Folklore; History; Linguistics; Literature; Modern Languages; Social Studies; Spanish); **History and Folklore Studies** (Folklore; History); **Human Sciences** (Arts and Humanities; Clinical Psychology; Health Sciences; Psychology; Sociology; Sports; Sports Management); **International Business Administration** (Accountancy; Business Administration; Communication Studies; Information Management; International Business; Management); **Law** (Law); **Science** (Biological and Life Sciences; Biology; Cell Biology; Chemistry; Computer Science; Information Sciences; Mathematics; Mathematics and Computer Science; Molecular Biology; Natural Sciences)

Research Division

Engineering (Engineering); **Integrated Science** (Mathematics; Physics); **Nonwritten Cultural Materials** (Cultural Studies)

Further information: Also Shonan-Hiratsuka Campus
History: Founded 1928. Acquired present status and title 1949.
Academic year: April to March (April-September; October-March)
Admission requirements: Graduation from high school or equivalent, and entrance examination
Main language(s) of instruction: Japanese, English
Accrediting agency: Japan University Accreditation Association (JUAA)
Degrees and diplomas: Gakushi, Shushi (Applied Chemistry; Architecture; Asian Studies; Biological and Life Sciences; Business Administration; Chemistry; Chinese; Economics; Electrical and Electronic Engineering; European Languages; European Studies; Experimental Psychology; Folklore; Health Sciences; History; Industrial Management; Information Sciences; Information Technology; Law; Mechanical Engineering; Sociology; Sports), Hakase (Applied Chemistry; Architecture; Asian Studies; Biological and Life Sciences; Business Administration; Chemistry; Chinese; Economics; Electrical and Electronic Engineering; European Languages; European Studies; Experimental Psychology; Folklore; Health Sciences; History; Industrial Engineering; Industrial Management; Information Sciences;

Information Technology; Law; Mechanical Engineering; Sociology; Sports). Also Professional Postgraduate programmes in Law

Student Services: Academic Counselling, Social Counselling, Careers Guidance, Sports Facilities, Health Services

Periodicals: Jinmon Kenkyu (Studies in Humanities), Kanagawa Daigaku Hyoron (Kanagawa University Review), Kanagawa Daigaku Jomin Bunka Shosho (Study of Japanese Folk Culture Series), Kanagawa Hogaku (Review of Law and Politics), Keizai-Boeki-Kenkyu (Studies in Economics and Trades), Kenkyu Nenpo (Annual Report), Kogaku Kenkyusho Shoho (Science Reports of Research Institute for Engineering, Kokusai Keiei Ronshu (International Business Administration Series), Shokei Ronso (Review of Economics and Commerce)

Academic Staff 2013-2014	MALE	FEMALE	TOTAL
FULL-TIME			461
PART-TIME			964
Student Numbers 2013-2014			
All (Foreign Included)			18693

Last Update: 12-12-2017

Kanazawa Gakuin University

10 Sue-machi
Kanazawa-shi 920-1392, Ishikawa
Tel: +81(762) 229-1181, +81(762) 229-8833
Fax: +81(762) 229-1352
Website: http://www.kanazawa-gu.ac.jp
President: Akiyama Minoru

Faculty
Health and Sports (Health Sciences; Sports)

Department/Division
Art and Culture (Cultural Studies; Design; Fine Arts; Handicrafts; Heritage Preservation; Information Sciences; Information Technology; Media Studies; Multimedia; Visual Arts); **Literature** (Cultural Studies; English; English Studies; History; Japanese; Literature); **Management and Information Sciences** (Accountancy; Business Administration; Computer Science; Economics; Information Sciences; Information Technology; Management; Small Business)

Graduate School
Humanities (Art History; Arts and Humanities; English; Japanese; Literature; Psychology; Regional Studies; Sociology; Town Planning); **Management and Information Sciences** (Accountancy; Business Administration; Information Sciences; International Business; Management; Taxation)

History: Founded 1987.
Main language(s) of instruction: Japanese
Accrediting agency: Japan Institution for Higher Education Evaluation (JIHEE)
Degrees and diplomas: Gakushi, Shushi (Information Sciences; Literature; Management), Hakase (Information Sciences; Management)
Student Services: Sports Facilities, Health Services, Canteen
Last Update: 12-12-2017

Kanazawa Institute of Technology (KIT)

7-1 Ohgigaoka
Nonoichi-machi 921-8501, Ishikawa
Tel: +81(76) 294-6725
Fax: +81(76) 294-6718
Website: http://www.kanazawa-it.ac.jp
President: Satoshi Osawa

College
Bioscience and Chemistry (Applied Chemistry; Biological and Life Sciences; Chemistry; Environmental Studies; Genetics; Molecular Biology; Neurosciences); **Engineering** (Aeronautical and Aerospace Engineering; Computer Science; Electrical and Electronic Engineering; Electronic Engineering; Engineering; Information Sciences; Information Technology; Mechanical Engineering; Robotics; Telecommunications Engineering); **Environmental Engineering and Architecture** (Architectural and Environmental Design; Architecture; Civil Engineering; Environmental Engineering; Structural Architecture); **Information Science and Human Communication** (Computer Engineering; Computer Science; Information Management; Information Sciences; Information Technology; Media Studies; Psychology)

Graduate School
Engineering (Architecture; Biochemistry; Business Administration; Civics; Computer Engineering; Electrical and Electronic Engineering; Engineering; Environmental Engineering; Information Technology; Mechanical Engineering; Production Engineering); **KIT Toranomon Campus Office** (*For Professionals*) (Architecture; Business Administration; Construction Engineering); **Psychology** (Clinical Psychology; Psychology)

Research Division
Advanced Materials Processing (Materials Engineering); **Advanced Materials Science Research and Development** (Materials Engineering); **Affective Design Engineering** (Design; Engineering); **Applied Electronics** (Electronic Engineering); **Applied Ethics Center for Engineering and**

Science (Engineering); **Architectural Archives** (Architecture); **Biomechanical Control Systems** (Biological and Life Sciences); **Center for Electric, Optic and Energy (EOE) Applications** (Electrical Engineering; Energy Engineering; Optics); **Computing and Networking Frontier** (Computer Engineering; Computer Networks; Information Technology); **Contents and Technology Integration** (Technology); **Disaster and Environment Science** (Environmental Management; Environmental Studies); **Environmental Research** (Environmental Studies); **Future Design**; **Future Machine Technology** (Technology); **Genome Biotechnology** (Biotechnology; Genetics); **Human Information Systems** (Information Technology); **Information Technologies** (Information Technology); **Integrated Technological Systems** (Technology); **Intellectual Creation and Management** (Management); **Intellectual Property Science** (Law); **International Studies** (International Studies); **Japan Studies** (Cultural Studies); **KIT-Macquarie Brain** (Neurosciences); **KIT/NYU Abu Dhabi MEG** (*Joint*); **KIT/NYU MEG** (*Joint*); **KIT/UCL/CNRS** (*Joint*); **KIT/UMD MEG** (*Joint*); **Materials Systems** (Materials Engineering); **Optoelectronic Device System** (*R&D Centre*) (Electronic Engineering; Optical Technology); **Psychological Sciences** (Psychology); **Regional Planning** (Regional Planning); **Social and Industrial Management Systems** (Management Systems)

Further information: Also Yatsukaho and Tokyo Toranomon campuses; KIT/MIT, KIT/UMD joint research laboratories and KIT/Macquarie University Brain Science research laboratory

History: Founded 1965. Graduate School established 1978.

Academic year: April to March

Admission requirements: Graduation from high school and entrance examination

Fees: Tuition: c. 1.3-1.5m. per annum (Yen)

Main language(s) of instruction: Japanese

Accrediting agency: Japan University Accreditation Association (JUAA)

Degrees and diplomas: Gakushi, Shushi (Clinical Psychology; Engineering; Information Sciences), Hakase (Engineering; Information Sciences)

Student Services: Academic Counselling, Social Counselling, Careers Guidance, Nursery Care, Cultural Activities, Sports Facilities, Language Laboratory, Facilities for disabled people, Health Services, Canteen

Periodicals: KIT Progress

Publishing house: Kanazawa Institute of Technology Press (KIT Press)

Student Numbers 2012-2013	MALE	FEMALE	TOTAL
All (Foreign Included)			7197

Last Update: 12-12-2017

Kanazawa Medical University (KMU)

1-1 Daigaku Uchinada-machi
Kahoku-gun 920-0293, Ishikawa
Tel: +81(76) 286-2211
Fax: +81(76) 286-2373
Website: http://www.kanazawa-med.ac.jp
President: Tsugiyasu Kanda

School

Medicine (Anaesthesiology; Anatomy; Biochemistry; Cardiology; Community Health; Diabetology; Endocrinology; Epidemiology; Forensic Medicine and Dentistry; Gastroenterology; Gerontology; Gynaecology and Obstetrics; Haematology; Health Education; Immunology; Laboratory Techniques; Medicine; Microbiology; Nephrology; Neurology; Oncology; Ophthalmology; Otorhinolaryngology; Paediatrics; Pathology; Pharmacology; Physiology; Plastic Surgery; Public Health; Radiology; Rehabilitation and Therapy; Respiratory Therapy; Social and Preventive Medicine; Surgery; Urology; Zoology); **Nursing** (Nursing)

Institute

Medical Research (Biological and Life Sciences; Biology; Cell Biology; Dermatology; Environmental Studies; Genetics; Health Sciences; Histology; Medicine; Molecular Biology; Oncology; Rehabilitation and Therapy; Virology; Zoology)

Graduate School

Medical Sciences (Biological and Life Sciences; Ecology; Health Sciences; Medicine; Molecular Biology)

Further information: University Hospital

History: Founded 1972. Graduate School established 1984.

Academic year: April to March

Admission requirements: Graduation from high school and entrance examination

Fees: c. 6,000,000 per annum (Yen)

Main language(s) of instruction: Japanese

Accrediting agency: Japan University Accreditation Association (JUAA)

Degrees and diplomas: Gakushi, Hakase (Biological and Life Sciences; Medicine)

Student Services: Academic Counselling, Social Counselling, Sports Facilities, Health Services, Canteen

Periodicals: Journal of Kanazawa Medical University

Publishing house: Kanazawa Medical University Press

Academic Staff 2012-2013	MALE	FEMALE	TOTAL
FULL-TIME	364	110	474
Student Numbers 2012-2013			
All (Foreign Included)			913

Last Update: 12-12-2017

Kanazawa Seiryo University

10-1 Ushi Gosho-machi
Kanazawa-shi 920-8620, Ishikawa
Tel: +81-76-253-3896
Fax: +81-76-253-3617
Website: http://www.seiryo-u.ac.jp
President: Masafumi Miyasaki

Faculty

Economics (Accountancy; Business Administration; Economics; Finance; Information Technology; International Economics; International Studies; Management; Marketing; Tourism); **Human Sciences** (Child Care and Development; Sports; Sports Management)

Graduate School

Strategic Management (Accountancy; Business Administration; Sports Management; Taxation)
History: Founded 1967 as Kanazawa College of Economics.
Academic year: Japan Institution for Higher Education Evaluation (JIHEE)
Main language(s) of instruction: Japanese
Accrediting agency: Japan Institution for Higher Education Evaluation (JIHEE)
Degrees and diplomas: Gakushi, Shushi (Accountancy; Business Administration; Sports Management)
Student Services: Social Counselling, Sports Facilities, Health Services

Academic Staff 2013-2014	MALE	FEMALE	TOTAL
FULL-TIME			69
PART-TIME			101
Student Numbers 2013-2014			
All (Foreign Included)	1369	873	2242
Foreign only			46

Last Update: 12-12-2017

Kanda University of International Studies (KUIS)

1-4-1 Wakaba Mihama-ku
Chiba-shi 261-0014, Chiba
Tel: +81 43-273-1322
Fax: +81 43-273-2220
Website: http://www.kandagaigo.ac.jp/kuis
President: Kuniya Sakai

Course/Programme

Bekka (*For Foreign Students*) (Cultural Studies; Japanese);
Teacher Training (Chinese; Education; Educational and Student Counselling; Educational Psychology; English; Foreign Languages Education; Korean; Spanish; Teacher Training)

School

Foreign Studies (American Studies; Chinese; Communication Studies; English; English Studies; Indonesian; International Business; Korean; Latin American Studies; Portuguese; South and Southeast Asian Languages; Spanish; Thai Languages; Translation and Interpretation; Vietnamese)

Graduate School

Language Sciences (English; Foreign Languages Education; Japanese; Linguistics; Native Language Education)
History: Founded 1987.
Academic year: April to January (April-July; September-January)
Admission requirements: Graduation from High School
Fees: Registration, 250,000; tuition, 890,000
Main language(s) of instruction: Japanese, English, Chinese, Spanish
Accrediting agency: Japan Institution for Higher Education Evaluation (JIHEE)
Degrees and diplomas: Associate's Degree (Academic), Gakushi, Shushi (English; Foreign Languages Education; Japanese; Native Language Education), Hakase (Modern Languages)
Student Services: Academic Counselling, Social Counselling, Careers Guidance, Cultural Activities, Sports Facilities, Language Laboratory, Health Services, Canteen
Periodicals: Intercultural Communications, Kotoba to Bunka (Language and Culture), Studies in Linguistics and Language Teaching

Student Numbers 2013-2014	MALE	FEMALE	TOTAL
All (Foreign Included)	955	2864	3819

Last Update: 12-12-2017

Kansai Gaidai University

16-1 Nakamiyahigashino-cho
Hirakata-shi 573-1001, Osaka
Tel: +81(72) 805-2831
Fax: +81(72) 805-2871
Website: http://www.kansaigaidai.ac.jp
President: Yoshito Tanimoto

Faculty

Foreign and English International Studies (Chinese; Cultural Studies; English; French; German; History; International Business; International Studies; Literature; Media Studies; Spanish)

College

American and English Studies (American Studies; English; English Studies); **Business Pre-view** (Business Administration; English)

Course/Programme

Bekka (*For Foreign Students*) (Cultural Studies; Japanese); **Japanese Teacher Training** (Japanese; Native Language Education; Teacher Trainers Education)

Graduate School

Graduate (Anthropology; Chinese; Classical Languages; Comparative Literature; Cultural Studies; Danish; English; English Studies; Finnish; German; Germanic Languages; Greek (Classical); Hungarian; Japanese; Latin; Literature; Phonetics; Portuguese; Romance Languages; Spanish; Swedish)

Further information: Also Science City campus; Junior college. Japanese language courses for foreign students
History: Founded 1945.
Academic year: September to June (September-December; January-March; March-June)
Fees: Tuition for undergraduate programmes, 720,000-750,000; For graduate programmes, 500,000-750,000 per annum (Yen)
Main language(s) of instruction: Japanese, English
Accrediting agency: Japan University Accreditation Association (JUAA)
Degrees and diplomas: Gakushi, Shushi (English; International Studies), Hakase (English; International Studies)
Student Services: Academic Counselling, Sports Facilities, Health Services, Foreign Studies Centre

Student Numbers 2013-2014	MALE	FEMALE	TOTAL
All (Foreign Included)	4211	8972	13183
Foreign only			624

Last Update: 12-12-2017

Kansai Medical University (KMU)

2-5-1 Shin-mashi
Hirakata City 573-1010, Osaka
Tel: +81(72) 804-0101
Fax: +81(72) 804-2547
Website: http://www.kmu.ac.jp
President: Tomoda Koichi

Faculty

Medicine (Anaesthesiology; Anatomy; Biology; Cardiology; Chemistry; Community Health; English; Forensic Medicine and Dentistry; Health Sciences; Hygiene; Laboratory Techniques; Mathematics; Medicine; Microbiology; Neurological Therapy; Neurology; Neurosciences; Ophthalmology; Otorhinolaryngology; Paediatrics; Pharmacology; Physics; Physiology; Psychology; Radiology; Urology)

School

Nursing (Nursing)

Institute

Biomedical Science (Biomedicine)

Centre

Clinical Study Training Center (Medicine); **Medical Education** (Health Education); **Medical Safety Management** (Medicine); **Regional Medical** (Medicine)

Graduate School

Medicine (Anaesthesiology; Biochemistry; Biology; Biomedicine; Biophysics; Cardiology; Cell Biology; Cognitive Sciences; Dermatology; Endocrinology; Forensic Medicine and Dentistry; Gastroenterology; Gynaecology and Obstetrics; Health Sciences; Immunology; Laboratory Techniques; Medicine; Molecular Biology; Neurological Therapy; Neurology; Neurosciences; Oncology; Ophthalmology; Otorhinolaryngology; Paediatrics; Pathology; Physiology; Public Health; Radiology; Rehabilitation and Therapy; Statistics; Surgery; Urology)

Further information: Also 4 Teaching Hospitals
History: Founded 1928 as Osaka Women's Medical School, became Osaka Women's Medical College 1947, and Kansai Medical School 1954 (co-educational).
Academic year: April to March (April-August; September-December; January-March)
Admission requirements: Graduation from high school or equivalent, and entrance examination
Main language(s) of instruction: Japanese
Accrediting agency: Japan University Accreditation Association (JUAA)
Degrees and diplomas: Gakushi (Medicine), Hakase (Medicine)
Student Services: Sports Facilities, Health Services, Canteen
Periodicals: Kansai Medical University Journal

Academic Staff 2013-2014	MALE	FEMALE	TOTAL
FULL-TIME			738
PART-TIME			225
Student Numbers 2013-2014			
All (Foreign Included)			782
Foreign only			22

Last Update: 12-12-2017

Kansai University

3-3-35 Yamate-cho
Suita-shi 564-8680, Osaka
Tel: +81(6) 6368-1121
Fax: +81(6) 6330-3027
Website: http://www.kansai-u.ac.jp
President: Keiji Shibai

Faculty

Arts and Humanities (American Studies; Art History; Arts and Humanities; Asian Religious Studies; Chinese; Comparative Religion; Cultural Studies; Education; English; English Studies; Ethics; French Studies; Geochemistry; Germanic Studies; Heritage Preservation; History; Japanese; Literature; Modern Languages; Philosophy; Physical Education; Psychology; Regional Studies; Video; Vocational Education); **Business and Commerce** (Accountancy; Business Administration; Business and Commerce; Finance; International Business; Management); **Chemical Engineering Biological and Life Sciences** (Applied Chemistry; Biochemistry; Bioengineering; Biological and Life Sciences; Chemical Engineering; Materials Engineering); **Economics** (Accountancy; Data Processing; Economics; Finance; Industrial and Production Economics; International Economics; Statistics); **Foreign Language** (Chinese; Communication Studies; Cultural Studies; English; French; German; Korean; Linguistics; Modern Languages; Russian; South and Southeast Asian Languages; Spanish; Translation and Interpretation); **General Information** (Arts and Humanities; Communication Studies; Computer Science; Cultural Studies; Economics; Information Sciences; Information Technology; Natural Sciences; Political Sciences; Social Sciences; Technology); **Human Health** (Health Sciences; Sports; Welfare and Protective Services); **Law** (Civil Law; Constitutional Law; Criminal Law; Law; Political Sciences); **Mathematics** (Applied Physics; Electrical and Electronic Engineering; Information Technology; Mathematics; Mathematics and Computer Science; Mechanical Engineering; Physics; Telecommunications Engineering); **Policy Creation** (Administration; Asian Studies; International Law; International Studies; Management; Political Sciences); **Safety Management** (Business Administration; Civil Security; Economics; Engineering; Information Sciences; Law; Political Sciences; Protective Services; Psychology; Safety Engineering; Social and Preventive Medicine; Sociology; Welfare and Protective Services); **Sociology** (Media Studies; Psychology; Social Sciences; Sociology); **Urban and Environmental Engineering** (Applied Chemistry; Energy Engineering; Environmental Engineering; Information Technology; Town Planning)

School

Clinical Psychology (*Professional Graduate*) (Clinical Psychology); **Law** (*Professional Graduate*) (Law)

Department/Division

Research and Development of Innovative Science and Technology (*ORDIST*) (Natural Sciences; Technology)

Institute

Economic and Political Studies (Economics; Political Sciences); **Human Rights Studies** (Human Rights); **Legal Studies** (Law); **Oriental and Occidental Studies** (Oriental Studies; Western European Studies)

Graduate School

Accounting (*Professional*) (Accountancy); **Arts and Humanities** (American Studies; Arts and Humanities; Asian Studies; Chinese; Cultural Studies; English; English Studies; French; Geography; German; History; Japanese; Literature; Philosophy; Physical Education; Spanish; Video; Vocational Education); **Commerce** (Accountancy; Business and Commerce); **East Asia Arts and Sciences** (Cultural Studies; East Asian Studies; Ethnology; History; Literature; Regional Studies; Religion); **Economics** (Economics); **Education** (Education); **Foreign Languages** (Modern Languages); **Government** (Government; Public Administration); **Informatics** (Information Sciences; Information Technology); **Law** (Commercial Law; Law; Political Sciences; Public Administration); **Psychology** (Clinical Psychology; Cognitive Sciences; Developmental Psychology; Psychology; Social Psychology); **Science and Engineering** (Applied Physics; Architecture; Bioengineering; Biological and Life Sciences; Chemical Engineering; Electrical and Electronic Engineering; Energy Engineering; Engineering; Environmental Engineering; Information Technology; Materials Engineering; Mathematics; Mechanical Engineering; Natural Sciences; Physics; Town Planning); **Social Safety Studies** (Protective Services; Safety Engineering); **Sociology** (Mass Communication; Social Sciences; Social Studies; Sociology)

Research Division

Socionetwork Strategies (*RISS*) (Sociology)
Further information: All Faculties have attached graduate schools
History: Founded 1886 as Kansai Law School, became Kansai University 1905. Acquired present status 1948.
Academic year: April to March (April-September; October-March)
Admission requirements: Graduation from high school or equivalent, and entrance examination
Fees: Registration, 260,000; tuition, 670,000 per annum (Yen)
Main language(s) of instruction: Japanese, English
Accrediting agency: Japan Institution for Higher Education Evaluation (JIHEE)
Degrees and diplomas: Gakushi, Shushi (Arts and Humanities; Business and Commerce; Cognitive Sciences; Computer Engineering; Computer Science; Cultural Studies;

Developmental Psychology; East Asian Studies; Economics; Foreign Languages Education; Government; Information Sciences; Law; Mass Communication; Materials Engineering; Political Sciences; Protective Services; Safety Engineering; Social Psychology; Social Studies; Sociology), Hakase (Accountancy; Arts and Humanities; Business and Commerce; Computer Engineering; Computer Science; Cultural Studies; East Asian Studies; Economics; Foreign Languages Education; Law; Mass Communication; Political Sciences; Protective Services; Psychology; Safety Engineering; Social Studies; Sociology). Also Postgraduate Professional Programmes in Clinical Psychology and Law.

Student Services: Academic Counselling, Social Counselling, Careers Guidance, Nursery Care, Sports Facilities, Language Laboratory, Facilities for disabled people, Health Services, Canteen, Foreign Studies Centre

Periodicals: Bungaku Ronshu, Gien, Hogaku Kenkyusho Kenkyu Shoho, Hogaku Ronshu, Johokenkyu, Keizai Ronshu, Keizai-Seiji Kenkyusho Kenkyu Shoho, Kogaku Kenkyu Hokoku, Kogaku to Gijutsu, Review of Business and Commerce, Review of Economics, Review of Law and Politics, Shakaigaku Kiyo, Shogaku Ronshu, Tozaigakujutsu Kenkyusho Kiyo

Publishing house: University Press, Publishing Division

Academic Staff 2013-2014	MALE	FEMALE	TOTAL
FULL-TIME	642	102	744
Student Numbers 2013-2014			
All (Foreign Included)	18330	11848	30178

Last Update: 12-12-2017

Kansai University of Health Sciences

2-11-1 Wakaba, Kumatori-cho, Sennangun
Osaka 590-0482
Tel: +81 724-53-8251
Fax: +81 724-53-0276
Website: http://www.kansai.ac.jp
President: Sohei Yoshida

Faculty

Health and Medical (Acupuncture); **Health Nursing** (Nursing)
History: Founded 1975 as Kansai Acupuncture YawaraSei College. Acquired present status and title 1985.
Main language(s) of instruction: Japanese
Accrediting agency: Japan Institution for Higher Education Evaluation (JIHEE)
Degrees and diplomas: Gakushi (Acupuncture; Nursing), Shushi (Acupuncture)
Last Update: 12-12-2017

Kansai University of International Studies (KUINS)

1-18 Aoyama Shijimicho
Miki-shi 673-0521, Hyogo
Tel: +81(794) 85-2288
Fax: +81(794) 85-1102
Website: http://www.kuins.ac.jp
President: Atsushi Hamana
Tel: +81(794) 84-3500

Faculty

Education (*Amagasaki campus*) (Behavioural Sciences; Child Care and Development; Education; Foreign Languages Education; Social Welfare; Welfare and Protective Services); **Human Sciences** (Business Administration; Clinical Psychology; Criminology; Food Technology; International Business; Management; Psychology; Social Studies; Sociology; Sports Management; Tourism)

Graduate School

Human Behavior (Behavioural Sciences; Clinical Psychology; Criminology; Education; Psychology; Sociology)
Further information: Also Amagasaki campus
History: Founded 1998.
Academic year: April to January (April-July; September-January)
Fees: Tuition, 720,000-827,000 per annum (Yen)
Main language(s) of instruction: Japanese, English
Accrediting agency: Japan Institution for Higher Education Evaluation (JIHEE)
Degrees and diplomas: Gakushi, Shushi (Behavioural Sciences; Clinical Psychology; Criminology; Education; Psychology)
Periodicals: Newsletter of Kansai University of International Studies
Last Update: 12-12-2017

Kansai University of Nursing and Health Sciences

Awaji Shizuki 1456-4
Hyogo 656-2131
Tel: +81 799-60-1200
Fax: +81 799-60-1201
Website: http://www.kki.ac.jp
President: Takako Egawa

Faculty

Adult Nursing (Nursing); **Basic nursing** (Nursing); **Geriatric Nursing** (Nursing); **Maternity Nursing** (Nursing); **Mental Nursing** (Nursing); **Pediatric nursing** (Nursing);

Professional basic fields (General education) (Health Sciences); **Professional basic fields (Medicine)** (Medicine); **Regional and home nursing** (Nursing)
History: Founded 2006 as Junshin-kai University of Nursing and Health. Acquired present status and title 2008.
Main language(s) of instruction: Japanese
Accrediting agency: Japan University Accreditation Association (JUAA)
Degrees and diplomas: Gakushi (Nursing)
Last Update: 13-12-2017

Kansai University of Social Welfare

380-3 Shinden
Ako-shi 678-0255, Hyogo
Tel: +81(791) 46-2500
Fax: +81(791) 46-2501
Website: http://www.kusw.ac.jp
President: Kato Akira

School
Nursing (Nursing); **Social Welfare** (Social Welfare; Social Work)

Graduate School
Nursing (Nursing); **Social Welfare** (Social Welfare)
History: Founded 1997.
Main language(s) of instruction: Japanese
Accrediting agency: Japan Institution for Higher Education Evaluation (JIHEE)
Degrees and diplomas: Gakushi, Shushi (Nursing; Social Welfare)
Periodicals: Kansai University of Welfare Bulletin, Social Welfare Research Bulletin
Last Update: 13-12-2017

Kansai University of Welfare Sciences

3-chome 11th No. 1
Osaka 582-0026
Tel: +81 72-978-0088
Fax: +81 72-978-0377
Website: http://www.fuksi-kagk-u.ac.jp
President: Takeshi Hatta

Faculty
Health and Welfare (Health Sciences; Nutrition); **Social Welfare** (Clinical Psychology; Social Welfare)

School
Health Science (Occupational Therapy; Physical Therapy; Rehabilitation and Therapy)

History: Founded 1997.
Main language(s) of instruction: Japanese
Accrediting agency: Japan Institution for Higher Education Evaluation (JIHEE)
Degrees and diplomas: Gakushi (Clinical Psychology; Health Sciences; Nutrition; Occupational Therapy; Physical Therapy; Social Welfare; Special Education), Shushi (Clinical Psychology; Welfare and Protective Services), Hakase (Welfare and Protective Services)
Last Update: 13-12-2017

Kanto Gakuen University

200 Fujiagu-cho
Ota-shi 373-8515, Gunma-ken
Tel: +81(276) 32-7800, +81(276) 32-7915
Fax: +81(276) 31-2770
Website: http://www.kanto-gakuen.ac.jp/univer
President: Toru Haneda

Faculty
Economics (Accountancy; Business Administration; Economics; Finance; Health Education; Hotel and Restaurant; International Business; Management; Physical Education; Sports Management; Tourism); **Law** (International Law; International Relations; Law)

Graduate School
Economics (Economics); **Law** (*Hiring Frozen*) (Law)
History: Founded 1976 as Department of Economics, added Graduate School of Business Administration and Economics 1981. Added Department of Law 1990 and Graduate School of Law 1994.
Academic year: April to March (April-September; September-March)
Admission requirements: Graduation from High School or equivalent and entrance examination
Fees: Registration, 614,000; tuition, 665,000 per annum (Yen)
Main language(s) of instruction: Japanese
Accrediting agency: Japan Institution for Higher Education Evaluation (JIHEE)
Degrees and diplomas: Gakushi, Shushi (Economics)
Student Services: Academic Counselling, Careers Guidance, Sports Facilities, Language Laboratory, Health Services, Canteen
Periodicals: Journal of Economics, Journal of Law, Journal of Liberal Arts

Student Numbers 2012-2013	MALE	FEMALE	TOTAL
All (Foreign Included)			c. 190

Last Update: 13-12-2017

Kanto Gakuin University

4834 Mutsuura-cho Kanazawa-ku
Yokohama-shi 236-8501, Kanagawa
Tel: +81(45) 786-7015
Fax: +81(45) 786-7043
Website: http://univ.kanto-gakuin.ac.jp
President: Hiroyoshi Kiku

Faculty

Human Environment (Architectural and Environmental Design; Child Care and Development; Communication Studies; Development Studies; Environmental Studies; Health Sciences; Nutrition); **Law** (Law)

School

Law (*Graduate Professional*) (Accountancy; Administrative Law; Commercial Law; Environmental Studies; Law); **Nursing** (Health Sciences; Nursing; Welfare and Protective Services)

Department/Division

Architecture and Environment (Architectural and Environmental Design; Architecture; Environmental Studies); **Economics** (Business Administration; Economics); **Literature** (American Studies; Comparative Literature; Cultural Studies; English; English Studies; Literature; Social Welfare; Sociology); **Sciences and Engineering** (Applied Chemistry; Automotive Engineering; Biological and Life Sciences; Biotechnology; Civil Engineering; Computer Science; Electrical and Electronic Engineering; Engineering; Health Sciences; Industrial Design; Information Technology; Machine Building; Mathematics; Measurement and Precision Engineering; Mechanical Engineering; Natural Sciences; Physics; Protective Services; Robotics; Safety Engineering; Sports; Video)

Institute

Human Environment (Environmental Studies); **Law** (Law); **Materials and Surface Engineering** (Materials Engineering); **Nursing** (Nursing); **Osawa Memorial Building Facilities Engineering** (Architecture; Building Technologies; Environmental Engineering)

Graduate School

Economics (Business Administration; Economics); **Engineering** (Architecture; Biological and Life Sciences; Civil Engineering; Electrical Engineering; Engineering; Industrial Chemistry; Materials Engineering; Mechanical Engineering; Structural Architecture); **Law** (Law); **Letters** (American Studies; Arts and Humanities; Comparative Literature; Cultural Studies; English; English Studies; Japanese; Literature; Sociology)

Research Division

Christianity and Culture (Christian Religious Studies; Cultural Studies); **Economics and Business** (Business Administration; Economics); **Engineering** (Engineering); **Humanities** (Arts and Humanities)

Further information: Also English language and Cultural programmes

History: Founded 1949 with Colleges of Engineering and Economics, but tracing the origins to Baptist Theological Seminary 1884.

Academic year: April to January (April-July; September-January)

Admission requirements: Graduation from high school and entrance examination

Main language(s) of instruction: Japanese

Accrediting agency: Japan University Accreditation Association (JUAA)

Degrees and diplomas: Gakushi, Shushi (Architecture; Business Administration; Civil Engineering; Economics; Electrical Engineering; Industrial Chemistry; Law; Literature; Mechanical Engineering; Sociology; Structural Architecture), Hakase (Architecture; Business Administration; Civil Engineering; Economics; Electrical Engineering; Industrial Chemistry; Law; Literature; Mechanical Engineering; Sociology; Structural Architecture). Also Professional Graduate Programmes in Law

Student Services: Academic Counselling, Social Counselling, Careers Guidance, Sports Facilities, Language Laboratory, Health Services, Canteen

Periodicals: Bulletin of Kanto Gakuin University, Journal of Science and Humanities, Journal of Technological Research (Engineering), Jurisconsultus, Kamariya Life and Letters, Memoirs of the Economic Postgraduate Course of Kanto Gakuin University, Poetry Kanto, Quarterly Journal of Economics, School of Law, Transactions of the Institute of Humanities

Publishing house: Kanto Gakuin University Publishing Co.

Last Update: 13-12-2017

Kawamura Gakuen Woman's University

1133 Sageto
Abiko-shi 270-1138, Chiba
Tel: +81(4) 7183-0111
Fax: +81(4) 7183-9015
Website: http://www.kgwu.ac.jp
President: Sonoko Kumagai

Faculty

Cultural Studies (Cultural Studies; Dietetics; Food Science; Japanese; Literature; Nutrition); **Education** (Child Care and

Development; Curriculum; Development Studies; Education; Educational Psychology; Family Studies; Fine Arts; Food Science; Health Education; Humanities and Social Science Education; Music; Nutrition; Physical Education; Preschool Education; Social Welfare; Teacher Training); **Liberal Arts** (Arts and Humanities; English; History; Psychology)

Graduate School

Humanities and Sciences (Arts and Humanities; Behavioural Sciences; Clinical Psychology; Communication Studies; Comparative Literature; Continuing Education; Cultural Studies; Foreign Languages Education; Humanities and Social Science Education; Primary Education; Psychology; Secondary Education; Women's Studies)
History: Founded 1988.
Main language(s) of instruction: Japanese
Accrediting agency: Japan Institution for Higher Education Evaluation (JIHEE)
Degrees and diplomas: Gakushi, Shushi (Comparative Literature; Education; Psychology), Hakase (Comparative Literature; Cultural Studies)
Last Update: 13-12-2017

Kawasaki Medical School

577 Matsushima
Kurashiki-shi 701-0192, Okayama
Tel: +81(86) 462-1111
Fax: +81(86) 464-1019
Website: http://www.kawasaki-m.ac.jp/med
President: Masao Fukunaga

Department/Division

Applied Medical Science (Hygiene; Medical Technology; Toxicology); **Basic Medical Science** (Anatomy; Biochemistry; Genetics; Medicine; Microbiology; Molecular Biology; Pharmacology; Physiology); **Clinical Medical Science** (Anaesthesiology; Cardiology; Dermatology; Diabetology; Endocrinology; Gastroenterology; Gynaecology and Obstetrics; Haematology; Health Sciences; Information Management; Laboratory Techniques; Medical Technology; Medicine; Nephrology; Neurological Therapy; Neurology; Oncology; Ophthalmology; Orthopaedics; Paediatrics; Pathology; Plastic Surgery; Psychiatry and Mental Health; Public Health; Radiology; Rehabilitation and Therapy; Respiratory Therapy; Rheumatology; Surgery; Urology); **Liberal Arts and Sciences** (Applied Physics; Arts and Humanities; Biology; Chemistry; Computer Science; English; Information Sciences; Linguistics; Natural Sciences; Physics; Statistics); **Medical Research** (*Postgraduate*) (Medicine)

Further information: Also Kawasaki Medical School Hospital
History: Founded 1970.
Academic year: April to March (April-July; September-December; January-March)
Admission requirements: Graduation from high school and entrance examination
Main language(s) of instruction: Japanese
Accrediting agency: Japan University Accreditation Association
Degrees and diplomas: Gakushi, Hakase (Medicine)
Student Services: Sports Facilities, Language Laboratory, Health Services
Periodicals: Medical Journal
Last Update: 13-12-2017

Kawasaki University of Medical Welfare

288 Matsushima
Kurashiki-shi 701-0193, Okayama
Tel: +81(86) 462-1111
Fax: +81(86) 462-1193
Website: http://www.kawasaki-m.ac.jp/mw
President: Tsubahara Akio

Faculty

Medical and Welfare Management (Business Administration; Computer Science; Health Administration; Information Technology; Medical Auxiliaries; Secretarial Studies; Welfare and Protective Services); **Medical Technology** (Medical Technology; Nutrition; Physical Education; Rehabilitation and Therapy)

Department/Division

Medical and Welfare Studies (Health Sciences; Medicine; Nursing; Psychology; Welfare and Protective Services)
History: Founded 1991.
Fees: Tuition, 600,000-1,050,000 per annum (Yen)
Main language(s) of instruction: Japanese
Accrediting agency: Japan University Accreditation Association (JUAA)
Degrees and diplomas: Gakushi, Shushi (Clinical Psychology; Computer Science; Health Administration; Health Sciences; Medical Auxiliaries; Medical Technology; Medicine; Nursing; Nutrition; Physical Education; Rehabilitation and Therapy; Welfare and Protective Services), Hakase (Clinical Psychology; Computer Science; Education; Health Sciences; Medical Technology; Nursing; Nutrition; Rehabilitation and Therapy; Welfare and Protective Services)
Student Services: Sports Facilities, Health Services

Academic Staff 2013-2014	MALE	FEMALE	TOTAL
FULL-TIME			264

(continued)

Academic Staff 2013-2014	MALE	FEMALE	TOTAL
Student Numbers 2013-2014			
All (Foreign Included)	1410	2400	c. 3810

Last Update: 13-12-2017

Keiai University

1-5-21 Anagawa
Chiba-shi 263-8588, Chiba
Tel: +81(43) 251-6363
Fax: +81(43) 251-6407
Website: http://www.u-keiai.ac.jp
President: Sahei Tosho

Faculty

Economics (Accountancy; Business Administration; Economics; Finance; Information Sciences; International Business; Management; Sports Management); **International Studies** (American Studies; Child Care and Development; Cultural Studies; English; English Studies; History; International Business; International Studies; Literature; Native Language Education; Primary Education; Secondary Education; Social Studies)

History: Founded 1966.
Fees: Tuition, 740,000-980,000 per annum (Yen)
Main language(s) of instruction: Japanese
Accrediting agency: Japan University Accreditation Association (JUAA)
Degrees and diplomas: Gakushi
Last Update: 13-12-2017

Keio University

2-15-45 Mita Minato-ku
Tokyo 108-8345
Tel: +81(35) 453-4511, +81(35) 427-1541
Fax: +81(35) 427-7640
Website: http://www.keio.ac.jp/index-en.html
President: Akira Haseyama

Faculty

Business and Commerce (Business and Commerce); **Economics** (Economics); **Environment and Information Studies** (*Shonan Fujisawa Campus*) (Environmental Studies; Information Sciences); **Law** (Law); **Letters** (Aesthetics; Archaeology; Arts and Humanities; Chinese; Education; English; Ethics; Ethnology; French; German; History; Information Sciences; Japanese; Library Science; Literature; Philosophy; Psychology; Social Sciences; Sociology); **Nursing and Medical Care** (*Shonan Fujisawa Campus*) (Health Sciences; Nursing); **Pharmacy** (Pharmacology; Pharmacy); **Policy Management** (*Shonan Fujisawa Campus*) (Leadership); **Science and Technology** (*Yagami Campus*) (Applied Chemistry; Applied Physics; Biological and Life Sciences; Chemistry; Computer Engineering; Computer Science; Electrical and Electronic Engineering; Engineering; Information Sciences; Information Technology; Mathematics; Mechanical Engineering; Natural Sciences; Physics; Statistics; Technology)

School

Law (*Graduate Professional*) (Law); **Medicine** (*Shinanomachi Campus*) (Medicine)

Institute

Advanced Biosciences (Biological and Life Sciences); **Cultural and Linguistic Studies** (Cultural Studies; Linguistics); **East Asian Studies** (East Asian Studies; Regional Studies); **Economic Observatory** (Economics; Industrial Management); **Law and Politics (KILP)** (Law; Political Sciences); **Media and Communications Research (MediaCom)** (Communication Studies; Media Studies); **Oriental Classics** (Oriental Studies); **Physical Education** (*Hiyoshi Campus*) (Physical Education); **Research Institute at SFC** (*Keio, SFC*) (Government; Regional Studies; Social and Community Services)

Centre

Art Center (KUAC) (Art Management); **Fukuzawa Memorial Centre for Modern Japanese Studies** (*Fukuzawa Memorial*) (Cultural Studies); **Health** (Health Sciences); **Integrated Medical Research** (*Shinanomachi Campus*) (Medicine); **International Studies** (Cultural Studies; Economics; English; History; Political Sciences); **Japanese Studies** (Cultural Studies; Japanese); **Leading-edge Laboratory of Science and Technology (KLL)** (*Yagami Campus*) (Natural Sciences; Technology); **Sports Medicine Research** (Sports Medicine); **Teacher Training** (Teacher Training)

Graduate School

Business Administration (*Hiyoshi Campus*) (Business Administration); **Business and Commerce** (Business and Commerce); **Economics** (Economics); **Health Management** (*Shonan Fujisawa Campus*) (Health Administration; Sports Management); **Human Relations** (Education; Psychology; Sociology); **Law** (Journalism; Law; Political Sciences); **Letters** (Aesthetics; Arts and Humanities; Chinese; English; Ethics; French; German; History; Information Sciences; Japanese; Library Science; Literature; Philosophy); **Media and Governance** (*Shonan Fujisawa Campus*) (Government; Media Studies); **Media Design** (Media Studies); **Medicine** (*Shinanomachi Campus*) (Medicine); **Pharmaceutical Sciences** (Pharmacology; Pharmacy); **Science and Technology**

(*Yagami Campus*) (Design; Engineering; Environmental Engineering; Natural Sciences; Technology); **System Design and Management** (Computer Engineering; Systems Analysis)

Research Division

Advanced Research Centers (KARC); **Digital and Media Content (DMC)** (Media Studies); **Foreign Languages Education** (*Hiyoshi Campus*) (Foreign Languages Education); **Frontier Research and Education Collaborative Square (K-FRECS)** (*Shin-Kawasaki*); **Global Security (G-SEC)** (International Studies; Protective Services; Social Studies); **Liberal Arts** (*Hiyoshi Campus*) (Arts and Humanities; Curriculum); **Research and Education Center for Natural Sciences** (Natural Sciences)

Further information: Also following campuses: Hiyoshi, Yagami, Shinanomachi, Shonan Fujisawa, Shiba-Kyoritsu, Shin-Kawasaki Town, Tsuruoka Town, Urawa-Kyoritsu, Keio Osaka City, Keio Marunouchi City; University Hospital and Rehabilitation Centre

History: Founded 1858 as private School to teach Dutch; became private University 1890. Graduate divisions opened 1906. School of Medicine founded 1917 followed by the opening of University Hospital 1920; Faculty of Engineering (1944); School of Library Science (1951); Business School (1962); Shonan Fujisawa Campus (Faculty of Policy Management and Faculty of Environmental Information opened 1990); Graduate School of Media and Governance (1994); Faculty of Nursing and Medical Care (2001); Law School (2004). Merged with Kyoritsu Yakka Daigaku (Kyoritsu College of Pharmacy) 2008.

Academic year: April to March (April-July; September-February)

Admission requirements: Graduation from high school or recognized equivalent, and entrance examination

Fees: Undergraduate tuition, 810,000-2,970,000 per annum: Graduate tuition, 440,000-1,800,000 per annum (Yen)

Main language(s) of instruction: Japanese, English

Accrediting agency: Japan University Accreditation Association (JUAA)

Degrees and diplomas: Gakushi, Shushi (Aesthetics; Business Administration; Business and Commerce; Computer Engineering; Economics; Education; Engineering; Environmental Studies; Ethics; Government; Health Administration; Health Sciences; History; Journalism; Law; Library Science; Literature; Media Studies; Medicine; Native Language Education; Nursing; Pharmacology; Philosophy; Political Sciences; Psychology; Sociology; Sports Management), Hakase (Aesthetics; Business Administration; Business and Commerce; Computer Engineering; Economics; Education; Engineering; Environmental Engineering; Ethics; Government; Health Administration; Health Sciences; History; Law; Library Science; Literature; Media Studies; Medicine;

Native Language Education; Nursing; Pharmacology; Pharmacy; Philosophy; Psychology; Sociology; Sports Management). Also Professional Graduate Degree Programm in Law (Juris Doctor); Double-degree Master's programmes (offered jointly with institutions based in Germany, France Sweden, Italy, Republic of Korea, China) in various fields: Media Studies Arts and Humanities; Economics; Natural Sciences; Tehnology; Business Administration; Media Studies; Government.

Student Services: Academic Counselling, Social Counselling, Careers Guidance, Cultural Activities, Sports Facilities, Language Laboratory, Facilities for disabled people, Health Services, Canteen, Foreign Studies Centre

Periodicals: "Jyuku" (Japanese Only), "KEIO SPIRIT" (Japanese Only), "Mita-Hyoron" (Japanese Only), Correspondence Courses "Sanshokuki (Blue-Red-Blue Flag) Keio Correspondent Monthly" (Japanese Only), Disaster Prevention Guide 2013, Emerging 2012, Keio Journal of Medicine, KOSMOS

Academic Staff 2013-2014	MALE	FEMALE	TOTAL
FULL-TIME	2259	725	2984
Student Numbers 2013-2014			
All (Foreign Included)	22644	10940	33584
Foreign only			1203

Last Update: 13-12-2017

Keisen University

2-10-1 Minamino Tama-shi
Tokyo 206-8586
Tel: +81(42) 376-8211
Fax: +81(42) 376-8218
Website: http://www.keisen.ac.jp/univ
President: Masami Ohinata

College

Humanities (Arts and Humanities; Communication Studies; Cultural Studies; English; History; Japanese)

Department/Division

Sociology (Environmental Studies; Social and Community Services; Sociology)

Graduate School

Graduate Studies (Arts and Humanities; Peace and Disarmament)
History: Founded 1988.
Main language(s) of instruction: Japanese
Accrediting agency: Japan University Accreditation Association (JUAA)

Degrees and diplomas: Gakushi, Shushi (Arts and Humanities; Peace and Disarmament)

Academic Staff 2013-2014	MALE	FEMALE	TOTAL
FULL-TIME			79
Student Numbers 2013-2014			
All (Foreign Included)			1692

Last Update: 13-12-2017

Keiwa College

1270 Tomizuka
Shibata-shi 957-8585, Niigata
Tel: +81(254) 26-3636
Fax: +81(254) 26-3646
Website: http://www.keiwa-c.ac.jp
President: Kota Yamada

Department/Division

English Culture and Communication (Communication Studies; English; English Studies; Foreign Languages Education; Japanese; Psychology); **International Cultural Department** (Asian Studies; Civics; Cultural Studies; Economics; History; Humanities and Social Science Education; Information Sciences; Law; Management; Media Studies; Political Sciences; Primary Education; Teacher Training); **Symbiosis Sociology** (Information Sciences; Management; Media Studies; Secretarial Studies; Social Welfare; Social Work; Sociology; Welfare and Protective Services)
History: Founded 1991.
Main language(s) of instruction: Japanese
Accrediting agency: Japan University Accreditation Association (JUAA)
Degrees and diplomas: Gakushi (Cultural Studies; English; English Studies; Social Welfare)
Student Services: Social Counselling, Sports Facilities, Language Laboratory, Canteen
Last Update: 28-03-2018

Kenichi Ohmae Graduate School of Business

Fujisoft Building 19F 3 Kanda Neribei-cho
Chiyoda-ku, Tokyo
Tel: +81(3) 5860-5531
Website: http://www.ohmae.ac.jp
Dean: Kenichi Ohmae

Graduate School

Business Administration (Business Administration; International Business; Management)

History: Founded 2005.
Main language(s) of instruction: Japanese
Accrediting agency: Ministry of Education, Culture, Sports, Science and Technology (MEXT)
Degrees and diplomas: Gakushi (Business Administration), Shushi (Business Administration)
Last Update: 26-03-2018

Kibi International University

8 Iga-machi
Takahashi-shi 716, Okayama
Tel: +81(866) 22-9189
Fax: +81(866) 22-8133
Website: http://kiui.jp/pc/english
General President: Miyako Kake

Faculty

Health Science and Social Welfare (Health Sciences; Nursing; Occupational Therapy; Physical Therapy; Social Problems; Social Welfare; Social Work; Welfare and Protective Services); **Social Science** (Business Administration; Communication Studies; Health Sciences; Management; Social Sciences; Sports; Sports Management)

Course/Programme

Intensive Japanese Language (Japanese)

School

Agricultural Regional Vitalization (Agriculture); **Cultural Properties** (Art Management; Cultural Studies; Heritage Preservation; Restoration of Works of Art); **Psychology** (Child Care and Development; Education; Psychology)

Graduate School

Conservation and Restoration for Cultural Properties Studies (Cultural Studies; Heritage Preservation; Restoration of Works of Art); **Environmental Risk Management (Distance)** (*Distance*) (Environmental Management); **Health Science Studies** (Health Sciences); **Health Science Studies (Distance)** (Health Sciences); **Intellectual Property Studies (Distance)** (Private Law); **International Cooperation and Development (Distance)** (Development Studies; International Studies); **Psychology Studies** (Psychology); **Psychology Studies (Distance)** (Psychology); **Social Welfare Studies** (Social Welfare); **Social Welfare Studies (Distance)** (Social Welfare); **Sociological Studies** (Sociology)
History: Founded 1990.
Academic year: April to March (April-September; September-March)
Admission requirements: Graduation from high school or equivalent

Fees: 1,030,000-1,496,000 (Yen)
Main language(s) of instruction: Japanese
Accrediting agency: Japan University Accreditation Association (JUAA)
Degrees and diplomas: Gakushi, Shushi (Development Studies; Environmental Management; Health Sciences; Heritage Preservation; International Studies; Private Law; Psychology; Restoration of Works of Art; Social Welfare; Sociology), Hakase (Health Sciences; Psychology; Sociology)
Student Services: Academic Counselling, Social Counselling, Careers Guidance, Cultural Activities, Sports Facilities, Canteen

Academic Staff 2012-2013	MALE	FEMALE	TOTAL
FULL-TIME	144	12	156
Student Numbers 2012-2013			
All (Foreign Included)	1267	866	2133

Last Update: 13-12-2017

Kindai University

3-4-1 Kowakae
Higashiosaka-shi 577-8502, Osaka
Tel: +81(6) 6721-2332
Fax: +81(6) 6729-2387
Website: https://www.kindai.ac.jp/
President: Yoshihiko Hosoi

Faculty

Agriculture (Agriculture; Applied Chemistry; Biological and Life Sciences; Biology; Environmental Management; Fishery; Food Science; Nutrition); **Applied Sociology** (Sociology); **Architecture** (Architecture); **Biology-Oriented Science and Technology** (Biological and Life Sciences; Biomedical Engineering; Biotechnology; Computer Science; Food Science; Food Technology; Genetics; Mechanics; Safety Engineering); **Business Administration** (Accountancy; Business Administration; Management; Marketing); **Economics** (Economics; International Economics; Public Administration); **Engineering** (Architecture; Biotechnology; Chemistry; Computer Science; Electronic Engineering; Engineering; Information Sciences; Information Technology; Mechanical Engineering); **Humanity-Oriented Science and Engineering** (Applied Chemistry; Architecture; Biological and Life Sciences; Business Administration; Computer Science; Design; Electrical Engineering; Engineering; Environmental Studies; Information Sciences; Management; Telecommunications Engineering); **Law** (Law; Political Sciences); **Literature, Art and Cultural Studies** (Arts and Humanities; Cultural Studies; English; History; Literature);

Medicine (Medicine); **Pharmacy** (Pharmacology; Pharmacy); **Science and Engineering** (Applied Chemistry; Architecture; Biological and Life Sciences; Civil Engineering; Computer Science; Electrical and Electronic Engineering; Electrical Engineering; Electronic Engineering; Environmental Engineering; Mechanical Engineering; Natural Sciences)

School

Law (*Professional*) (Law); **Nursing** (Nursing)

Department/Division

Correspondence Studies (Business Administration; Economics; Law; Library Science; Special Education); **Teacher Education** (Teacher Training)

Institute

Advanced Technology (Technology); **Creative Management and Innovation** (Management); **Immunotherapy and Research for Cancer** (Immunology; Oncology); **Industrial and Law Information** (Information Sciences); **Infant Education** (Child Care and Development; Preschool Education); **Japan Cultural Studies** (Cultural Studies); **Molecular Engineering** (Bioengineering; Molecular Biology); **Pharmaceutical Research and Technology** (Pharmacology; Pharmacy; Technology); **Resource Recycling** (Natural Resources); **World Economy** (International Economics)

Centre

Human Rights (Human Rights); **Human Sciences** (*International*) (Arts and Humanities)

Laboratory

Fisheries (Fishery)

Graduate School

Advanced Technology (Computer Science; Data Processing; Electronic Engineering; Fiscal Law; Information Sciences; Management; Materials Engineering; Mathematics; Multimedia; Safety Engineering; Systems Analysis; Technology); **Agriculture** (Agriculture; Biological and Life Sciences; Environmental Management; Fishery); **Biology-Oriented Science and Technology** (Artificial Intelligence; Biological and Life Sciences; Biotechnology; Electronic Engineering; Information Technology; Mechanics); **Commerce** (Accountancy; Business Administration; Business and Commerce; Information Technology; Management); **Economics** (Economic and Finance Policy; Economic History; Economics; International Economics); **Law** (Civil Law; Commercial Law; Constitutional Law; Criminal Law; International Relations; Law; Political Sciences); **Literature and Cultural Studies** (American Studies; Cultural Studies; English; English Studies; International Studies; Japanese;

Linguistics; Literature); **Medical Sciences** (Medicine); **Pharmacy** (Pharmacy); **Science and Engineering Research** (Biological and Life Sciences; Electronic Engineering; Engineering; Environmental Engineering; Information Sciences; Materials Engineering; Mechanical Engineering; Molecular Biology); **Systems Engineering** (Architecture; Biotechnology; Chemical Engineering; Chemistry; Electronic Engineering; Energy Engineering; Environmental Studies; Information Sciences; International Studies; Materials Engineering; Mathematics; Mechanical Engineering; Town Planning)

Research Division

Atomic Energy (Atomic and Molecular Physics; Energy Engineering); **Ethnology** (Ethnology); **Experimental Farms** (Farm Management); **Fundamental Technology for Next Generation** (Technology); **Life Science** (Biological and Life Sciences); **Oriental Medicine** (Traditional Eastern Medicine); **Science and Technology** (Natural Sciences; Technology)

Further information: Nara, Osaka-Sayama, Wakayama, Hiroshima and Fukuoka

History: Founded 1925 as Osaka College. Acquired present status and title 1949, following merger with Osaka Science and Engineering University. As of April 2016, the official English name of the university was changed from Kinki University to Kindai University.

Academic year: April to March (April-September; October-March)

Admission requirements: Graduation from high school or foreign equivalent, and entrance examination

Main language(s) of instruction: Japanese, English

Accrediting agency: Japan University Accreditation Association (JUAA)

Degrees and diplomas: Gakushi, Shushi (Agriculture; Applied Chemistry; Architecture; Artificial Intelligence; Biological and Life Sciences; Biotechnology; Business and Commerce; Chemical Engineering; Computer Science; Cultural Studies; Economics; Electronic Engineering; English; Environmental Management; Fishery; Information Sciences; Information Technology; International Studies; Japanese; Law; Literature; Management; Materials Engineering; Mechanical Engineering; Mechanics; Pharmacology; Pharmacy; Systems Analysis; Town Planning), Hakase (Agriculture; Applied Chemistry; Architecture; Biological and Life Sciences; Biotechnology; Business and Commerce; Chemical Engineering; Computer Science; Economics; Electronic Engineering; Environmental Management; Environmental Studies; Fishery; Information Sciences; Information Technology; Law; Management; Materials Engineering; Mechanical Engineering; Medicine; Systems Analysis; Town Planning)

Student Services: Sports Facilities, Language Laboratory, Health Services

Periodicals: Acta Medica, Bulletin of Faculty of Pharmacy, Journal of Faculty of Science and Engineering, Jurisprudence, Memoirs of Faculty of Agriculture, Proceedings of Commerce and Economics Faculty, Science and Technology

Academic Staff 2013-2014	MALE	FEMALE	TOTAL
FULL-TIME			2328
PART-TIME			3746
Student Numbers 2013-2014			
All (Foreign Included)			32145
Foreign only			329

Last Update: 23-05-2018

Kinjo Gakuin University

2-1723 Omori Moriyama-ku
Nagoya-shi 463-8521, Aichi
Tel: +81(52) 798-0180
Fax: +81(52) 798-4462
Website: http://www.kinjo-u.ac.jp
President: Ryuhei Okumura

Faculty

Contemporary Society and Culture (Business Administration; Computer Engineering; Cultural Studies; Information Sciences; International Studies; Journalism; Management; Media Studies; Regional Studies; Social Studies; Social Work; Sociology; Software Engineering); **Human Life and Environment** (Architectural and Environmental Design; Family Studies; Food Science; Information Sciences; Information Technology; Nutrition; Psychology; Social Work; Welfare and Protective Services); **Human Sciences** (Art Therapy; Child Care and Development; Clinical Psychology; Cognitive Sciences; Cultural Studies; Education; Fine Arts; Music; Psychology; Psychotherapy; Social Psychology; Social Welfare; Sociology); **Humanities** (Arts and Humanities; Chinese; Cultural Studies; English; French; German; History; Japanese; Literature; Modern Languages); **Pharmacy** (Communication Studies; Health Sciences; Information Management; Pharmacy)

Graduate School

Human Ecology (Child Care and Development; Consumer Studies; Development Studies; Ecology); **Humanities** (Arts and Humanities; English; Japanese; Linguistics; Literature; Sociology)

Further information: Also Centres for Christianity

History: Founded 1889 as Kinjo Girls' School. Acquired present status and title 1948.

Academic year: April to January (April-July; September-January)

Admission requirements: Graduation from high school

Fees: Tuition, 720,000-1,250,000 per annum (Yen)

Main language(s) of instruction: Japanese

Accrediting agency: Japan University Accreditation Association (JUAA)

Degrees and diplomas: Gakushi, Shushi (Consumer Studies; Development Studies; English; Linguistics; Literature; Sociology), Hakase (Ecology; English; Linguistics; Literature; Sociology)

Student Services: Academic Counselling, Social Counselling, Careers Guidance, Nursery Care, Cultural Activities, Sports Facilities, Language Laboratory, Facilities for disabled people, Health Services, Canteen, Foreign Studies Centre

Periodicals: Studies in British and American Literature, Studies in Family and Consumer Sciences, Studies in Human Sciences, Studies in Humanities, Studies in Japanese Literature, Studies in Social Sciences

Academic Staff 2013-2014	MALE	FEMALE	TOTAL
FULL-TIME			120
Student Numbers 2013-2014			
All (Foreign Included)			5521

Last Update: 29-01-2018

Kinjo University (KU)

1200 Kasama-machi

Matto 924-8511, Ishikawa

Tel: +81(76) 276-4400

Fax: +81(76) 275-4316

Website: http://www.kinjo.ac.jp/ku

President: Shinichi Kato

Faculty

Health Sciences (Health Sciences; Occupational Therapy; Physical Therapy); **Social Welfare** (Social Welfare; Social Work)

Graduate School

Social Welfare (*Kodomo*) (Child Care and Development; Family Studies; Paediatrics; Social Welfare)

History: Founded 1904. Acquired present status 2000.

Fees: Tuition, 650,000- 960,000 per annum (Yen)

Main language(s) of instruction: Japanese

Accrediting agency: Japan Institution for Higher Education Evaluation (JIHEE)

Degrees and diplomas: Gakushi (Business Administration; Child Care and Development; Fine Arts; Nursing; Occupational Therapy; Physical Therapy; Preschool Education; Social Welfare; Social Work), Shushi (Rehabilitation and Therapy). Also Postgraduate Diploma in Social Welfare

Student Services: Sports Facilities

Last Update: 28-03-2018

Kio University

4-2-2 Umami-naka Kryo-cho

Kitakatsuragi-gun 635-0832, Nara

Tel: +81(745) 54-1601

Fax: +81(745) 54-1600

Website: http://www.kio.ac.jp

President: Masahiko Fuyuki

Faculty

Health Sciences (Architectural and Environmental Design; Health Sciences; Nursing; Nutrition; Physical Therapy)

Department/Division

Education (Education)

Institute

Education (*Modern*) (Education); **Health Sciences** (Health Sciences)

Graduate School

Education (*Qualification in progress*) (Education); **Health Sciences** (Health Sciences); **Midwifery** (Midwifery)

Research Division

Neuro Rehabilitation (Neurological Therapy)

History: Founded 2003.

Main language(s) of instruction: Japanese

Accrediting agency: Japan Institution for Higher Education Evaluation (JIHEE)

Degrees and diplomas: Gakushi, Shushi (Education; Health Sciences), Hakase (Health Sciences). The Master's degree (Shushi) in Education is in the process of qualification. Also professional postgraduate diploma in Midwifery.

Periodicals: Bulletin of Kio University

Student Numbers 2013-2014	MALE	FEMALE	TOTAL
All (Foreign Included)			469

Last Update: 14-12-2017

Kiryu University

Midori 379-2392, Gunma

Tel: +81 277-76-2400

Fax: +81 277-76-9454

Website: http://www.kiryu-jc.ac.jp

President: Isao Okayasu

Faculty

Medical and Health Care (Nursing; Nutrition)
History: Founded 1901 as Kiryu Girls' Sewing School. Then became Kirigaoka Women's Junior College 1963, Kirigaoka Junior College 1971, Kiryu Junior College 1989. Acquired present status and title 2008.
Main language(s) of instruction: Japanese
Accrediting agency: Japan Institution for Higher Education Evaluation (JIHEE)
Degrees and diplomas: Gakushi (Nursing; Nutrition)
Last Update: 14-12-2017

Kitasato University

5-9-1 Shirokane
Minato-ku 108-8641, Tokyo
Tel: +81(3) 3444-6161
Website: http://www.kitasato-u.ac.jp
President: Tomoo Itoh

School

Allied Health Sciences (Health Sciences; Hygiene; Medical Technology; Paramedical Sciences); **Marine Biosciences** (Biological and Life Sciences; Environmental Management; Marine Biology); **Medicine** (Medical Technology; Medicine); **Nursing** (Nursing); **Pharmacy** (Biological and Life Sciences; Pharmacy); **Science** (Biological and Life Sciences; Chemistry; Natural Sciences; Physics); **Veterinary Medicine** (Biological and Life Sciences; Ecology; Environmental Studies; Veterinary Science; Zoology)

Institute

Kitasato Institute for Life Sciences (Immunology; Toxicology)

Graduate School

Infection Control Sciences (Immunology); **Marine Biosciences** (Aquaculture; Biochemistry; Biological and Life Sciences; Environmental Studies; Fishery; Food Science; Marine Biology); **Medical Sciences** (Health Sciences; Hygiene; Medicine); **Nursing** (Health Administration; Nursing); **Pharmaceutical Sciences** (Oncology; Pharmacology; Pharmacy); **Science** (Biological and Life Sciences; Biology; Molecular Biology; Natural Sciences); **Veterinary Sciences** (Environmental Studies; Veterinary Science; Zoology)

Research Division

Oriental Medicine Research Center (Traditional Eastern Medicine)
Further information: Also 4 university hospitals
History: Founded 1962

Academic year: April to March (April-August; September-March)
Admission requirements: Graduation from high school and entrance examination
Main language(s) of instruction: Japanese
Accrediting agency: Japan University Accreditation Association (JUAA)
Degrees and diplomas: Gakushi (Agriculture; Biological and Life Sciences; Fishery; Health Sciences; Medicine; Natural Sciences; Nursing; Occupational Therapy; Orthopaedics; Pharmacy; Physical Therapy; Radiology; Speech Therapy and Audiology; Veterinary Science), Shushi (Agriculture; Biological and Life Sciences; Fishery; Medicine; Nursing; Pharmacy), Hakase (Agriculture; Biological and Life Sciences; Fishery; Medicine; Nursing; Pharmacy; Veterinary Science)
Student Services: Academic Counselling, Careers Guidance, Sports Facilities, Health Services, Foreign Studies Centre, Library
Periodicals: Kitasato Archives of Experimental Medicine

Academic Staff 2017-2018	MALE	FEMALE	TOTAL
FULL-TIME	1192	470	1662
Student Numbers 2017-2018			
All (Foreign Included)	3991	4585	8576

Last Update: 24-05-2018

Kobe College (KC)

4-1 Okadayama
Nishinomiya-shi 662-8505, Hyogo
Tel: +81(798) 51-8585, +81(798) 51-8579
Fax: +81(798) 51-8535
Website: http://www.kobe-c.ac.jp

Department/Division

Human Sciences (Behavioural Sciences; Biological and Life Sciences; Clinical Psychology; Environmental Studies; Psychology; Social Sciences); **Literature** (Aesthetics; Asian Studies; Child Care and Development; Cultural Studies; Economics; English; Ethics; History; International Relations; Japanese; Law; Literature; Philosophy; Religious Studies; Social Welfare; Sociology); **Music** (Dance; Music; Musical Instruments; Singing)

Graduate School

Human Sciences (Behavioural Sciences; Clinical Psychology; Environmental Studies; Health Sciences); **Letters** (Arts and Humanities; English; International Studies; Literature; Sociology; Translation and Interpretation); **Music** (Music; Music Theory and Composition; Musical Instruments; Singing)

History: Founded 1875 as School, became College 1891, acquired present status and title 1948.

Academic year: April to March (April-September; October-March)

Admission requirements: Graduation from high school or foreign equivalent, and entrance examination

Fees: 861,000-1,371,000 (Yen)

Main language(s) of instruction: Japanese

Accrediting agency: Japan University Accreditation Association (JUAA)

Degrees and diplomas: Gakushi, Shushi (Cultural Studies; English; Literature; Music; Social Sciences; Sociology), Hakase (Cultural Studies; English; Literature; Social Sciences)

Student Services: Academic Counselling, Social Counselling, Careers Guidance, Language Laboratory, Health Services

Periodicals: Joseigaku Hyoran, Ronshu (Studies)

Student Numbers 2013-2014	MALE	FEMALE	TOTAL
All (Foreign Included)			2656

Last Update: 14-12-2017

Kobe Design University (KDU)

8-1-1 Gakuennishi-machi Nishi-ku
Kobe-shi 651-2196, Hyogo
Tel: +81(78) 794-2112
Fax: +81(78) 794-5027
Website: http://www.kobe-du.ac.jp
President: Takahito Saiki

School

Progressive Arts (Fine Arts; Handicrafts; Media Studies; Painting and Drawing); **Visual Design** (Architectural and Environmental Design; Design; Fashion Design; Graphic Design; Industrial Design; Textile Design; Visual Arts)

Centre

Design Studies (Chinese; Computer Science; Design; English; Film; French; Korean; Psychology; Sports)

Graduate School

Arts and Design (Architectural and Environmental Design; Arts and Humanities; Design; Engineering; Fashion Design; Fine Arts; Graphic Design; Industrial Engineering; Information Technology; Literature; Media Studies; Natural Sciences; Textile Design; Visual Arts)

History: Founded 1989.

Academic year: April to March (April-September; October-March)

Admission requirements: Graduation from high school (Kato-gakko) or recognized equivalent and entrance examination

Fees: Registration, 150,000 per annum; tuition, 950,000 per annum (Yen)

Main language(s) of instruction: Japanese, English

Accrediting agency: Japan Institution for Higher Education Evaluation (JIHEE)

Degrees and diplomas: Gakushi, Shushi (Design; Fine Arts), Hakase (Design; Fine Arts)

Student Services: Academic Counselling, Social Counselling, Careers Guidance, Nursery Care, Sports Facilities, Canteen, Foreign Studies Centre

Periodicals: Bulletin, Series of Graduate School Lectures

Academic Staff 2013-2014	MALE	FEMALE	TOTAL
FULL-TIME			105
PART-TIME			190
Student Numbers 2013-2014			
All (Foreign Included)			1759
Foreign only			72

Last Update: 14-12-2017

Kobe Gakuin University

518 Arise, Ikawadani-cho Nishi-ku
Kobe-shi 651-2180, Hyogo-ken
Tel: +81(78) 974-1551
Fax: +81(78) 974-5689
Website: http://www.kobegakuin.ac.jp
President: Masami Sato

Faculty

Business Administration (Business Administration); **Economics** (Economics); **Humanities and Science** (Arts and Humanities; Psychology); **Law** (Law); **Nutrition** (Dietetics; Nutrition); **Pharmaceutical Sciences** (Pharmacology; Pharmacy); **Rehabilitation** (Occupational Therapy; Physical Therapy; Rehabilitation and Therapy; Social Work)

Centre

Area Research and Development (Regional Studies)

Graduate School

Economics and Business Administration (Business Administration; Economics); **Food and Medical Sciences** (Food Science; Medicine); **Humanities and Science** (Arts and Humanities; Behavioural Sciences; Cultural Studies; Psychology); **Law** (International Law; International Relations; Law); **Law Practices** (Law); **Nutrition** (Dietetics; Nutrition); **Pharmaceutical Sciences** (Pharmacology; Pharmacy); **Rehabilitation** (Rehabilitation and Therapy; Social Work)

Research Division

Life Sciences (*Cooperative*) (Biological and Life Sciences)
Further information: Also Port Island and Nagata campuses; exchange student programmes (1 yr)
History: Founded 1966.
Academic year: April to March (April-September; October-March)
Admission requirements: Graduation from high school or equivalent or foreign equivalent, and entrance examination
Fees: 460,000-875,500 per semester (Yen)
Main language(s) of instruction: Japanese
Accrediting agency: Japan University Accreditation Association (JUAA)
Degrees and diplomas: Gakushi, Shushi (Behavioural Sciences; Business Administration; Cultural Studies; Economics; International Law; International Relations; Law; Nutrition; Psychology; Rehabilitation and Therapy; Social Work), Hakase (Behavioural Sciences; Cultural Studies; Economics; Food Science; Law; Medicine; Pharmacology; Pharmacy; Rehabilitation and Therapy). Also Professional Graduate Degree Programme in Law (to be abolished when students enrolled in or before AY2012 have completed their courses)
Student Services: Academic Counselling, Social Counselling, Careers Guidance, Nursery Care, Cultural Activities, Sports Facilities, Language Laboratory, Facilities for disabled people, Health Services, Canteen, Foreign Studies Centre
Periodicals: Bulletin of Humanities and Sciences, Economic Papers, Law and Politics Review, Memoirs of the Faculty of Pharmaceutical Sciences

Academic Staff 2012-2013	MALE	FEMALE	TOTAL
FULL-TIME			310
Student Numbers 2012-2013			
All (Foreign Included)	6348	3829	10177

Last Update: 14-12-2017

Kobe Institute of Computing - Graduate School of Information Technology (KIC)

2-2-7 Kano-cho Chuo-ku
Kobe-shi 650-0001, Hyogo
Tel: +81(78) 262-7715
Fax: +81(78) 262-7737
Website: http://www.kic.ac.jp
President: Toshiki Sumitani

Graduate School

Information Technology (Computer Engineering; Information Technology; Software Engineering)
History: Founded 2005.

Fees: Tuition, 1,000,000 per annum (Yen)
Main language(s) of instruction: Japanese, English
Accrediting agency: Japan Institution for Higher Education Evaluation (JIHEE)
Degrees and diplomas: Shushi (Computer Engineering; Information Technology)
Last Update: 14-12-2017

Kobe International University

9-1-6 Koyocho-naka Higashinada-ku
Kobe-shi 658-0032, Hyogo
Tel: +81(78) 845-3131, +81(78) 842-8855
Fax: +81(78) 842-8877
Website: http://www.kobe-kiu.ac.jp
President: Yuki Shimomura

Faculty

Economics (Air Transport; Business Administration; Economics; English; Finance; Hotel Management; Information Technology; International Business; International Economics; Management; Marketing; Psychology; Tourism); **Rehabilitation** (Physical Therapy; Rehabilitation and Therapy)

Course/Programme

International College (Cultural Studies; Grammar; Japanese)
Further information: Also Foundation Course
History: Founded 1968.
Fees: Tuition, 275,000-539,000 per annum
Main language(s) of instruction: Japanese
Accrediting agency: Japan Institution for Higher Education Evaluation (JIHEE)
Degrees and diplomas: Gakushi
Student Services: Sports Facilities, Health Services, Canteen
Last Update: 14-12-2017

Kobe Kaisei College

2-7-1 Aotani-cho Nada-ku
Kobe-shi 657-0805, Hyogo
Tel: +81(78) 801-2277
Fax: +81(78) 801-5190
Website: http://www.kaisei.ac.jp
President: Reiko Ono

Department/Division

Child Psychology (Child Care and Development; Psychology); **English and Career Studies** (English); **Tourism Hospitality** (Tourism)

Centre
Catholic (Catholic Theology)

Research Division
Languages and Cultures (Cognitive Sciences; Cultural Studies; Information Sciences; Linguistics; Modern Languages)
History: Founded 1965.
Fees: Tuition, 800,000-840,000 per annum (Yen)
Main language(s) of instruction: Japanese
Accrediting agency: Japan University Accreditation Association (JUAA)
Degrees and diplomas: Gakushi
Last Update: 14-12-2017

Kobe Pharmaceutical University

4-19-1 Motoyamakita-machi Higashinada-ku
Kobe-shi 658-8558, Hyogo
Tel: +81(78) 453-0031
Fax: +81(78) 435-2080
Website: http://www.kobepharma-u.ac.jp
President: Shuji Kitagawa

Department/Division
Biopharmaceutical Science (Biological and Life Sciences; Pharmacology)

Centre
Educational Center for Clinical Pharmacy (Pharmacy)

Graduate School
Clinical Pharmacology (Pharmacology); Pharmaceutical Sciences (Pharmacology; Pharmacy)
Further information: Also18 laboratories
History: Founded 1930.
Academic year: April to March (April-July; September-March)
Admission requirements: Graduation from high school or equivalent and entrance examination
Main language(s) of instruction: Japanese
Accrediting agency: Japan University Accreditation Association (JUAA)
Degrees and diplomas: Gakushi, Shushi (Pharmacology; Pharmacy), Hakase (Pharmacology; Pharmacy)
Student Services: Sports Facilities, Canteen

Academic Staff 2013-2014	MALE	FEMALE	TOTAL
FULL-TIME			77
PART-TIME			58
Student Numbers 2013-2014			
All (Foreign Included)			1287

Last Update: 14-12-2017

Kobe Shinwa Women's University

7-13-1 Suzurandai-kitamachi Kita-ku
Kobe-shi 651-1111, Hyogo
Tel: +81(78) 591-1651
Fax: +81(78) 591-3113
Website: http://www.kobe-shinwa.ac.jp
President: Hiroyuki Yamamoto

Faculty
Arts and General Culture (Arts and Humanities; Cultural Studies; English; International Studies; Japanese; Regional Studies); Development and Education (Arts and Humanities; Child Care and Development; Clinical Psychology; Development Studies; Education; English; Health Sciences; Information Sciences; Preschool Education; Primary Education; Psychology; Social Welfare; Sports; Sports Management; Welfare and Protective Services)

Graduate School
Letters (Clinical Psychology; Education)
Main language(s) of instruction: Japanese
Accrediting agency: Japan University Accreditation Association (JUAA)
Degrees and diplomas: Gakushi, Shushi (Clinical Psychology; Educational Psychology; Preschool Education; Primary Education)
Last Update: 14-12-2017

Kobe Shoin Women's University

1-2-1 Shinohara-obanoyama-cho Nada-ku
Kobe-shi 657-0015, Hyogo
Tel: +81(78) 882-6122
Fax: +81(78) 882-5032
Website: http://www.shoin.ac.jp
President: Shoji Machida

Course/Programme
Human Sciences (Child Care and Development; Fashion Design; Food Science; Home Economics; Nutrition; Psychology); Literature (English; Japanese; Literature); University-wide Common Studies (Arts and Humanities; Business Administration; Christian Religious Studies; Communication Studies; English; French; German; Health Sciences; Information Sciences; Korean; Modern Languages; Sports)

Graduate School
Graduate Studies (English; Japanese; Linguistics; Literature; Modern Languages; Psychology)

History: Founded 1966.
Fees: Graduate tuition, 480,000 per annum (Yen)
Main language(s) of instruction: Japanese
Accrediting agency: Japan University Accreditation Association (JUAA)
Degrees and diplomas: Gakushi, Shushi (English; Japanese; Literature; Psychology), Hakase (Linguistics)
Last Update: 14-12-2017

Kobe Tokiwa University

Nagata-cho 2-6-2 Otani
Kobe 653-0838, Kyogo-ku
Tel: +81 78-611-1821
Fax: +81 78-643-4361
Website: http://www.kobe-tokiwa.ac.jp
President: Michio Hamada

Faculty
Education (Preschool Education); **Health Science** (Medical Technology; Nursing)
History: Founded 2008.
Main language(s) of instruction: Japanese
Accrediting agency: Japan Institution for Higher Education Evaluation (JIHEE)
Degrees and diplomas: Gakushi (Medical Technology; Nursing; Preschool Education)
Student Services: Careers Guidance, Library
Last Update: 14-12-2017

Kobe University of Fashion and Design

2-1-50 Meinan-cho
Akashi-shi 673-0001, Hyogo
Tel: +81(78) 795-7447
Fax: +81(78) 796-2559
Website: http://english.kobe-du.ac.jp

Course/Programme
Design (Design; Fashion Design; Interior Design)
History: Stopped enrolling students in 2010. Announced it would close down in March 2013.
Main language(s) of instruction: Japanese, English
Accrediting agency: Japan Institution for Higher Education Evaluation (JIHEE)
Degrees and diplomas: Gakushi (Education; Fine Arts), Shushi (Education; Fine Arts), Hakase (Education; Fine Arts)
Last Update: 27-03-2018

Kobe University of Welfare

Kanzaki-gun, Takaoka-cho 1966-5
Fukusaki 679-2217, Hyogo
Tel: +81 790-22-2620
Fax: +81 790-22-6452
Website: http://www.kinwu.ac.jp
President: Tsuzuki Myoju

School
Social Welfare (Management; Social Welfare; Sports)
History: Founded 1973 as a junior Women's college. Known as Kinki Welfare University (Kinki Fukushi Daigaku) until 2008. Acquired present status and title 2000. Kinki Health Welfare University became
Main language(s) of instruction: Japanese
Accrediting agency: Japan University Accreditation Association (JUAA)
Degrees and diplomas: Gakushi (Management; Social Welfare; Sports)
Last Update: 26-03-2018

Kobe Women's University

2-1 Aoyama, Higashi-suma Suma-ku
Kobe-shi 654-8585, Hyogo
Tel: +81(78) 731-4416
Fax: +81(78) 732-5161
Website: http://www.yg.kobe-wu.ac.jp/wu/index.html
President: Minoru Nakajima

Faculty
Common Education (Arts and Humanities); **Home Economics** (Dietetics; Home Economics); **Literature** (Arts and Humanities; Education; English; History; International Studies; Japanese; Literature)

Department/Division
Health and Welfare (Health Sciences; Nutrition; Social Welfare; Welfare and Protective Services)

Centre
Kobe Women's Education; **Open Research** (Environmental Studies; Food Technology; Geography; Geology; Physiology)

Graduate School
Home Economics (Food Science; Home Economics; Nutrition); **Letters** (Arts and Humanities; Education; English; History; Japanese; Literature); **School Education** (Primary Education)

Research Division

Classic Performing Arts (Performing Arts)

Further information: Also Port Island and Sannomiya campuses

History: Founded 1950, reorganized 1966.

Academic year: April to March (April-September; October-March)

Admission requirements: Graduation from high school or equivalent or foreign equivalent, and entrance examination

Fees: 500,000 per semester (Yen)

Main language(s) of instruction: Japanese

Accrediting agency: Japanese University Accreditation Association

Degrees and diplomas: Gakushi, Shushi (Education; English; Food Science; History; Home Economics; Japanese; Literature; Nutrition), Hakase (Home Economics; Literature)

Student Services: Careers Guidance, Sports Facilities, Health Services

Periodicals: Bulletins

Academic Staff 2013-2014	MALE	FEMALE	TOTAL
FULL-TIME			147
Student Numbers 2013-2014			
All (Foreign Included)			3478

Last Update: 14-12-2017

Kobe Yamate University

6-5-2 Nakayamate-douri Chuou-ku
Kobe-shi 650-0004, Hyogo
Tel: +81(78) 371-8000
Fax: +81(78) 371-4938
Website: http://www.kobe-yamate.ac.jp

Department/Division

Sociology (Accountancy; Architectural and Environmental Design; Architecture; Architecture and Planning; Business Administration; Clinical Psychology; Computer Science; Cultural Studies; Developmental Psychology; Economics; English; Environmental Studies; Finance; Hotel Management; Interior Design; International Business; Japanese; Law; Management; Media Studies; Modern Languages; Psychology; Social Psychology; Sociology; Tourism; Welfare and Protective Services)

History: Founded 1999 as a Women's college. Became a co-educational institution 2002.

Fees: Admission fee, 200,000; Tuition, 375,000 per annum (Yen)

Main language(s) of instruction: Japanese

Accrediting agency: Japan Institution for Higher Education Evaluation (JIHEE)

Degrees and diplomas: Gakushi

Student Services: Cultural Activities, Sports Facilities, Language Laboratory

Academic Staff 2013-2014	MALE	FEMALE	TOTAL
FULL-TIME			73
Student Numbers 2013-2014			
All (Foreign Included)			286

Last Update: 14-12-2017

Kogakkan University

1704 Kodakujimoto-cho
Ise-shi 516-8555, Mie
Tel: +81(596) 22-0201
Fax: +81(596) 27-1704
Website: http://www.kogakkan-u.ac.jp
President: Kiyoshi Shimizu

Department/Division

Education (Education; Health Sciences; Preschool Education; Primary Education; Special Education; Sports); **Literature** (Communication Studies; History; Japanese; Literature); **Sociology** (Cultural Studies; Economics; Political Sciences; Social Studies; Social Welfare; Sociology; Welfare and Protective Services)

Graduate School

Letters (Arts and Humanities; Education; History; Japanese)

History: Founded 1882 by Imperial order, became National College 1903 and University 1940. Re-established 1962.

Academic year: April to March (April-October; October-March)

Admission requirements: Graduation from high school or equivalent, and entrance examination

Main language(s) of instruction: Japanese

Accrediting agency: Japan University Accreditation Association (JUAA)

Degrees and diplomas: Gakushi, Shushi (Asian Religious Studies; Education; History; Japanese; Literature), Hakase (Asian Religious Studies; History; Japanese; Literature)

Periodicals: Bulletin

Student Numbers 2012-2013	MALE	FEMALE	TOTAL
All (Foreign Included)			c. 3000

Last Update: 14-12-2017

Kogakuin University

1-24-2 Nishi-Shinjuku Shinjuku-ku
Tokyo 163-8677
Tel: +81(3) 3340-0130

Fax: +81(3) 3340-2440
Website: http://www.kogakuin.ac.jp
President: Mitsunobu Sato

Faculty

Architecture (Architectural and Environmental Design; Architecture; Architecture and Planning; Town Planning); **Engineering** (Applied Chemistry; Chemical Engineering; Electrical Engineering; Energy Engineering; Environmental Engineering; Information Technology; Mechanical Engineering; Telecommunications Engineering); **Global Engineering** (Mechanical Engineering); **Informatics** (Computer Science; Information Technology)

Centre

Collaborative Open Research (CORC); **Techno Creation (TECC)** (Machine Building)

Graduate School

Engineering (Applied Chemistry; Architecture; Chemical Engineering; Computer Science; Electrical and Electronic Engineering; Engineering; Management; Mechanical Engineering)

Research Division

Biomedical Engineering (BERC) (Biomedical Engineering); **Nano Structured Surface and Interface (NASIC)** (Nanotechnology); **Urban Disaster Mitigation (UDM)** (Safety Engineering)
Further information: Also Hachioji Campus
History: Founded 1887 as Koshu Gakko, reorganized as University 1949.
Academic year: April to March (April-September; October-March)
Admission requirements: Graduation from high school or recognized equivalent, and entrance examination
Fees: Admission fee, 30,000; Tuition fee, 470,000 per annum (Yen)
Main language(s) of instruction: Japanese
Accrediting agency: Japan University Accreditation Association (JUAA)
Degrees and diplomas: Gakushi, Shushi (Applied Chemistry; Architecture; Computer Engineering; Electrical and Electronic Engineering; Engineering; Engineering Management; Telecommunications Engineering), Hakase (Applied Chemistry; Architecture; Computer Engineering; Electrical and Electronic Engineering; Engineering; Engineering Management; Telecommunications Engineering)
Student Services: Academic Counselling, Careers Guidance, Sports Facilities, Health Services, Canteen
Periodicals: Research Report (Part A, Engineering), Research Report (Part B, General Culture)
Last Update: 15-12-2017

Kokugakuin University

4-10-28 Higashi Shibuya-ku
Tokyo 150-8440
Tel: +81(3) 5788-7061
Fax: +81(3) 5778-7062
Website: http://www.kokugakuin.ac.jp
President: Masuhisa Akai

Faculty

Economics (Business Administration; Economics; Management; Social Sciences); **Human Development** (Child Care and Development; Health Education; Physical Education; Primary Education); **Law** (Law); **Letters** (Arts and Humanities; Chinese; Cultural Studies; History; Japanese; Literature; Modern Languages; Philosophy); **Shinto Studies** (Asian Religious Studies)

Course/Programme

Shinto Studies (*Special Programme*) (Asian Religious Studies)

School

Law (*Professional Graduate*) (Law)

Institute

Advancement of Teaching and Learning; **Japanese Culture and Classics** (Cultural Studies; Japanese)

Centre

Common Educational; **Curatorial Research**; **Educational Development**; **Kokugakuin Academic Resource**; **Promotion of Excellence in Research and Education**

Graduate School

Law (Law); **Letters** (Arts and Humanities)
History: Founded 1882 as Institute for Japanese Classics (Koten-Koukyusho), acquired present title 1919. Reorganized 1948. Graduate School established 1951.
Academic year: April to March (April-September; October-March)
Admission requirements: Graduation from high school or recognized equivalent, and entrance examination
Main language(s) of instruction: Japanese
Accrediting agency: Japan University Accreditation Association (JUAA)
Degrees and diplomas: Gakushi, Shushi (Arts and Humanities; Economics; Law), Hakase (Arts and Humanities; Law). Also Teaching Qualifications and Certificate in Librarianship; Postgraduate Professional Degree in Law
Student Services: Social Counselling, Careers Guidance, Sports Facilities, Language Laboratory, Health Services, Canteen

Periodicals: Kokugakuin Daigaku Kiyo (Transactions of Kokugakuin Graduate School), Kokugakuin Hogaku (Journal of Faculty of Law), Kokugakuin Keizaigaku (Journal of Faculty of Economics), Kokugakuin Zasshi (Journal), Nihonbunka-Kenkyusho-Kiyo (Transactions of Institute for Japanese Culture and Classics)

Student Numbers 2012-2013	MALE	FEMALE	TOTAL
All (Foreign Included)			c. 11000

Last Update: 15-12-2017

Kokushikan University

4-28-1 Setagaya Setagaya-ku
Tokyo 154-8515
Tel: +81(3) 5481-3111
Fax: +81(3) 5481-5672
Website: http://www.kokushikan.ac.jp
President: Keichi Sato

Faculty

Business Administration (Accountancy; Business Administration; English); **Law** (Commercial Law; Law); **Letters** (Archaeology; Arts and Humanities; Chinese; Cultural Studies; Education; Environmental Studies; Ethics; Geography; History; Japanese; Literature; Modern Languages; Philosophy; Primary Education; Psychology)

Department/Division

21st century Asia (Asian Studies; Business Administration; Communication Studies); **Physical Education** (Physical Education; Sports; Sports Medicine); **Politics and Economics** (Business Administration; Economics; Management; Political Sciences); **Science and Engineering** (Architecture; Biological and Life Sciences; Earth Sciences; Electronic Engineering; Engineering; Health Sciences; Information Sciences; Information Technology; Landscape Architecture; Mathematics; Mechanical Engineering; Medical Technology; Natural Sciences; Town Planning)

Graduate School

Asia (Asian Studies); **Business Administration** (Business Administration); **Comprehensive Intellectual Property** (Law); **Economics** (Economics); **Emergency System** (Safety Engineering); **Engineering** (Computer Engineering; Construction Engineering; Electrical Engineering; Engineering; Mechanical Engineering); **Humanities** (Arts and Humanities; Education); **Law** (Law); **Political Sciences** (Political Sciences); **Sports Systems** (Engineering; Sports)
History: Founded 1917.

Academic year: April to March (April-July; September-March)
Admission requirements: 12 years of school education completed; Entrance examination; a good command of the Japanese language (Examination for Japanese University Admission for International Students (EJU) conducted by JASSO)
Main language(s) of instruction: Japanese
Accrediting agency: Japan Institution for Higher Education Evaluation (JIHEE)
Degrees and diplomas: Gakushi, Shushi (Arts and Humanities; Asian Studies; Business Administration; Construction Engineering; Economics; Education; Electrical Engineering; Engineering; Law; Mechanical Engineering; Political Sciences; Safety Engineering; Sports), Hakase (Arts and Humanities; Asian Studies; Business Administration; Computer Engineering; Economics; Education; Engineering; Law; Political Sciences; Safety Engineering; Sports)
Periodicals: Al-Rafidan, Annual Reports of Health, Physical Education and Sport Science, Bu-Toku, Bulletin of the Institute of Economic Studies, Bulletin of the Science and Engineering Research Institute, Butoku-Kiyo, Collection of Papers on Elementary Education, Keiei Keiri, Kokushi, Kokushikan Comparative Law Review, Kokushikan Daigaku Chirigaku Hokoku, Kokushikan Hogaku, Kokushikan Law Review, Kokushikan Studies in Japanese Literature, Kokushikan Tetsugaku, Kyoikugaku Ronso, Kyoyo-Ronshu, Memoirs of the Kokushikan University Center for Information Science, Seikei Ronso, Seikei Ronso (Politics and Economics Review), Seikyoken Review, Student Law Journal, Studies on Foreign Languages and Cultures, The Graduate School Law Review, The Kokushikan-Shigaku, Transactions of the Academic Society of the Humanities, Transactions of the Faculty of Engineering

Academic Staff 2013-2014	MALE	FEMALE	TOTAL
FULL-TIME			321
PART-TIME			800
Student Numbers 2013-2014			
All (Foreign Included)			13646
Foreign only			770

Last Update: 15-12-2017

Komazawa University

1-23-1 Komazawa Setagaya-ku
Tokyo 154-8525
Tel: +81(3) 3702-9730
Fax: +81(3) 3702-9721
Website: http://www.komazawa-u.ac.jp
President: Hachiro Hasebe

Faculty

Buddhism (Asian Religious Studies); **Business Administration** (Business Administration; Management; Marketing); **Economics** (Business and Commerce; Economics); **Global Media Studies** (Media Studies); **Health Sciences** (Health Sciences; Radiology); **Law** (Law; Political Sciences); **Letters** (American Studies; Arts and Humanities; English; English Studies; Geography; History; Japanese; Literature; Psychology; Social Work; Sociology)

Graduate School

Arts and Sciences (American Studies; Arts and Humanities; Asian Religious Studies; English Studies; Geography; History; Japanese; Literature; Natural Sciences; Psychology; Sociology); **Business Administration** (Business Administration); **Commerce** (Business and Commerce); **Economics** (Economics); **Health Sciences** (Health Sciences; Radiology); **Law** (Law; Private Law; Public Law); **Legal Research and Training** (Law)

History: Founded 1592 as a seminary, the Sendan-Rin School. Relocated in Azabu and reorganised into a university 1882. Renamed Soto-shu University 1905. Acquired present title 1925.

Academic year: April to March (April-July; September-December; January-March)

Admission requirements: Graduation from high school and entrance examination

Fees: Tuition, 540,000-800,000 per annum (Yen)

Main language(s) of instruction: Japanese, English

Accrediting agency: Japan University Accreditation Association (JUAA)

Degrees and diplomas: Gakushi, Shushi (American Studies; Asian Religious Studies; Business Administration; Business and Commerce; Economics; English Studies; Geography; Health Sciences; History; Japanese; Literature; Private Law; Psychology; Public Law; Sociology), Hakase (American Studies; Asian Religious Studies; Business Administration; Business and Commerce; Economics; English Studies; Geography; Health Sciences; History; Japanese; Law; Literature; Private Law; Psychology; Public Law; Sociology)

Student Services: Academic Counselling, Careers Guidance, Sports Facilities, Language Laboratory, Health Services, Canteen, Foreign Studies Centre

Periodicals: Bunka, Journal of Buddhist Studies, Journal of Department of Radiology, Komazawa Junior College, Journal of English Literature, Komazawa Junior College, Journal of Health Sciences of Komazawa University, Journal of Komazawa Junior College, Journal of Radiological Sciences of Komazawa University, Journal of the Faculty of Buddhism, Journal of the Faculty of Economics, Journal of the Faculty of Foreign Languages, Journal of the Faculty of Law of Komazawa University, Journal of the Faculty of Letters, Komazawa Annual Report of Psychology, Komazawa Business Review, Komazawa Business Studies, Komazawa Educational Review, Komazawa Japanese Literature, Komazawa Journal of Geography, Komazawa Journal of Sociology, Komazawa Junior College Journal of Buddhism, Komazawa Law and Political Science Review, Komazawa Law Journal, Regional Reviews, Studies in British and American Literature, The Economic Review of Komazawa University, The Journal of the Historical Association of Komazawa, The Komazawa Junior College Review of Japanese Literature, The Komazawa University Journal of Health and Physical Education, The Revue of Foreign Languages

Student Numbers 2012-2013	MALE	FEMALE	TOTAL
All (Foreign Included)			c. 16000

Last Update: 15-12-2017

Komazawa Women's University

238 Sakahama Inagi-shi
Tokyo 206-8511
Tel: +81(42) 331-1911
Fax: +81(42) 331-1919
Website: http://www.komajo.ac.jp/uni

College

Human Health (Dietetics; Health Sciences; Nutrition); **Humanities** (Anthropology; Architectural Restoration; Arts and Humanities; Cultural Studies; English; Foreign Languages Education; History; Information Technology; Interior Design; International Studies; Japanese; Library Science; Media Studies; Museum Management; Museum Studies; Native Language Education; Philosophy; Psychology)

School

Nursery (*Junior College*) (Child Care and Development)

Graduate School

Humanities and Sciences (Arts and Humanities; Asian Religious Studies; Clinical Psychology; Natural Sciences)

History: Founded 1993.

Main language(s) of instruction: Japanese

Accrediting agency: Japan University Accreditation Association (JUAA)

Degrees and diplomas: Gakushi, Shushi (Asian Religious Studies; Clinical Psychology). Also special Japanese language and culture classes for foreign students.

Student Services: Sports Facilities

Last Update: 15-12-2017

Konan University

8-9-1 Okamoto, Higashinada-ku
Kobe-shi 658-8501, Hyogo
Tel: +81(78) 431-2305
Fax: +81(78) 435-2548
Website: http://www.konan-u.ac.jp
President: Yoshiyuki Nagasaka

Faculty

Business Administration (Business Administration); **Economics** (Economics); **Law** (Law); **Letters** (Arts and Humanities; Cultural Studies; English; History; Japanese; Literature; Social Sciences; Sociology); **Science and Engineering** (Applied Chemistry; Biology; Chemistry; Computer Engineering; Information Sciences; Molecular Biology; Natural Sciences; Physics)

Department/Division

Frontier Research Organization for New Themes (*FRONT*)

Institute

Business Innovation (Business Administration); **Frontier Institute for Biomolecular Engineering Research** (*FIBER*) (Bioengineering; Chemistry; Molecular Biology); **Human Sciences** (Clinical Psychology); **Language and Culture** (Chinese; Cultural Studies; English; French; German; Korean; Modern Languages); **Research**

Centre

Business Law (*Konan*) (Commercial Law); **Business Law** (Commercial Law); **Education and Research in Information Sciences** (Information Sciences); **Education and Research in Sport and Health Science** (Health Sciences; Physical Education; Sports); **General Studies** (Arts and Humanities; Environmental Studies; Health Sciences; History; Information Sciences; International Relations; Natural Sciences; Social Studies); **Teacher Education** (Teacher Training)

Graduate School

Accountancy (*Professional*) (Accountancy); **Humanities** (Arts and Humanities; English; Japanese; Literature; Sociology); **Law** (*Professional*) (Law); **Natural Sciences** (Biological and Life Sciences; Biology; Chemistry; Computer Engineering; Information Sciences; Natural Sciences; Physics); **Social Sciences** (Business Administration; Economics; Social Sciences)

Further information: Also courses for foreign students. The Year-in-Konan Program. Intensive languages courses. Introductory Japanese studies courses

History: Founded 1919 as College, acquired present status 1951.

Academic year: April to March (April-September; October-March)

Admission requirements: Graduation from high school or equivalent or foreign equivalent, and entrance examination

Fees: 706,000 per annum; Science, 1,037,000 (Yen)

Main language(s) of instruction: Japanese

Accrediting agency: Japan University Accreditation Association (JUAA)

Degrees and diplomas: Gakushi, Shushi (Arts and Humanities; Biology; Business Administration; Chemistry; Computer Engineering; Economics; English; Information Sciences; Japanese; Literature; Physics; Sociology), Hakase (Arts and Humanities; Biological and Life Sciences; Business Administration; Computer Engineering; English; Information Sciences; Japanese; Literature; Materials Engineering; Physics; Sociology). Also Professional Graduate Diplomas in Law and Accountancy

Student Services: Academic Counselling, Social Counselling, Careers Guidance, Nursery Care, Cultural Activities, Sports Facilities, Language Laboratory, Health Services, Canteen, Foreign Studies Centre

Periodicals: "Konan University /Clinical Psychology Report", "Language and Culture", "Mental Crises and Clinical Knowledge", Annual Report, Series of General Institute, Annual Review (Letters), Bulletin of the Research Institute, Business Review, EBA Letter, EBA Report, Economic Papers, Law Review, Memoirs of Konan University Science and Engineering, Zephyr Nishikaze

Last Update: 15-12-2017

Konan Women's University (KWU)

2-23, 6 Morikita-machi, Higashinada-ku
Kobe-shi 658-0001, Hyogo
Tel: +81(78) 431-0391
Fax: +81(78) 431-5888
Website: http://www.konan-wu.ac.jp
President: Katsuaki Morita

Faculty

Human Sciences (Biological and Life Sciences; Child Care and Development; Psychology; Sociology); **Letters** (Arts and Humanities; Cultural Studies; English; English Studies; Foreign Languages Education; Japanese; Media Studies); **Nursing and Rehabilitation** (Nursing; Physical Therapy; Rehabilitation and Therapy)

Department/Division

General Education (Biological and Life Sciences; Computer Science; Fine Arts; Health Sciences; Media Studies; Natural Sciences; Sports)

Graduate School

Humanities and Human Sciences (Anthropology; Clinical Psychology; Cultural Studies; Education; Educational Psychology; English; Environmental Studies; Literature; Modern Languages; Primary Education; Psychology; Regional Studies; Sociology); **Nursing** (Community Health; Gerontology; Health Sciences; Nursing; Oncology)

History: Founded 1955 as Junior College, acquired present status and title 1964.

Academic year: April to March (April-September; October-March)

Admission requirements: Graduation from high school or equivalent, or foreign equivalent and entrance examination

Main language(s) of instruction: Japanese

Accrediting agency: Japan Institution for Higher Education Evaluation (JIHEE)

Degrees and diplomas: Gakushi, Shushi (Clinical Psychology; Education; English; Japanese; Literature; Nursing; Psychology), Hakase (Clinical Psychology; Education)

Student Services: Academic Counselling, Sports Facilities, Health Services

Periodicals: Konan Women's University 'Research'

Last Update: 18-12-2017

Koriyama Women's University

3-25-2 Kasei
Koriyama-shi 963-8503, Fukushima
Tel: +81(24) 932-4848
Fax: +81(24) 932-6748
Website: http://www.koriyama-kgc.ac.jp

Department/Division

Food and Nutrition (Biochemistry; Food Science; Nutrition); **Human Life** (Architecture; Child Care and Development; Clothing and Sewing; Cooking and Catering; Dietetics; Food Science; Home Economics; Hygiene; Interior Design; Nutrition; Philosophy; Primary Education; Religious Studies; Secondary Education; Social Welfare; Social Work; Welfare and Protective Services)

Graduate School

Human Life (Anthropology; Architecture; Biological and Life Sciences; Clothing and Sewing; Family Studies; Food Science; Health Sciences; Home Economics; Nutrition; Pedagogy; Philosophy; Religious Studies; Welfare and Protective Services)

History: Founded 1947.

Main language(s) of instruction: Japanese

Accrediting agency: Japan Institution for Higher Education Evaluation (JIHEE)

Degrees and diplomas: Gakushi, Shushi (Home Economics), Hakase (Home Economics)

Student Services: Social Counselling, Careers Guidance, Sports Facilities, Health Services

Last Update: 18-12-2017

Koshien University

10-1 Momijigaoka
Takarazuka-shi 665-0006, Hyogo
Tel: +81(797) 87-5111
Fax: +81(797) 87-8420
Website: http://www.koshien.ac.jp
President: Hideo Nakamura

College

Business Administration (*Modern*) (Business Administration; Health Administration; Welfare and Protective Services)

Department/Division

Arts and Humanities (Arts and Humanities; Cultural Studies; Psychology; Social Studies); **Nutrition** (Food Science; Nutrition); **Psychology** (Psychology)

Graduate School

Nutrition and Humanities Studies (Arts and Humanities; Clinical Psychology; Food Science; Nutrition; Social Psychology)

History: Founded 1967.

Main language(s) of instruction: Japanese

Accrediting agency: Japan Institution for Higher Education Evaluation (JIHEE)

Degrees and diplomas: Gakushi, Shushi (Arts and Humanities; Food Science; Nutrition; Psychology)

Academic Staff 2012-2013	MALE	FEMALE	TOTAL
FULL-TIME			68

Last Update: 18-12-2017

Koyasan University

Wakayama Prefecture Koya-cho, Ito-gun, 385
Ito-gun 648-0280, Wakayama
Tel: +81(736) 56-2921
Fax: +81(736) 56-2746
Website: http://www.koyasan-u.ac.jp
President: Inoui Tatsuhito

Faculty

Letters (Arts and Humanities; Cultural Studies; Japanese; Literature)

Department/Division

Esoteric Buddhism Culture (Asian Religious Studies; Esoteric Practices)

Graduate School

Graduate Studies (Arts and Humanities; Asian Religious Studies; Cultural Studies; Esoteric Practices; Japanese)

History: Founded 1886 as Kogi Daigakurin for the Shingon Sect of Esoteric Buddhism. Became University 1926.

Academic year: April to March (April-September; September-March)

Admission requirements: Graduation from high school or equivalent, and entrance examination

Fees: Tuition, 270,000-680,000 per annum (Yen)

Main language(s) of instruction: Japanese

Accrediting agency: Japan University Accreditation Association (JUAA)

Degrees and diplomas: Gakushi, Shushi (Arts and Humanities; Asian Religious Studies; Cultural Studies; Esoteric Practices; Japanese), Hakase (Arts and Humanities; Asian Religious Studies; Cultural Studies; Esoteric Practices; Japanese)

Student Services: Sports Facilities

Periodicals: Journal, Mikkyo Bunka (The Culture of Esoteric Buddhism)

Last Update: 18-12-2017

History: Founded 1942 as Institute of Oriental Languages, became University of Commerce 1954. Acquired present status 1990 and present title 1994.

Academic year: April to February (April-July; September-February)

Admission requirements: Graduation from high school

Main language(s) of instruction: Japanese

Accrediting agency: Japan University Accreditation Association (JUAA)

Degrees and diplomas: Gakushi, Shushi (Accountancy; Business and Commerce; Cultural Studies; Economics; Environmental Studies; Management; Social Welfare), Hakase (Business and Commerce; Cultural Studies; Economics; Management; Social Welfare)

Student Services: Social Counselling, Careers Guidance, Sports Facilities, Language Laboratory

Periodicals: Daigaku Yoran, Icho Namiki

Academic Staff 2012-2013	MALE	FEMALE	TOTAL
FULL-TIME			180
PART-TIME			329
Student Numbers 2012-2013			
All (Foreign Included)			c. 6441
Foreign only			70

Last Update: 18-12-2017

Kumamoto Gakuen University

2-5-1 Oe, Chuo-ku
Kumamoto-shi 862-8680, Kumamoto
Tel: +81(96) 364-5161
Fax: +81(96) 363-1289
Website: http://www.kumagaku.ac.jp
President: Ryoichi Koda

Faculty

Commerce (Business and Commerce; Hotel and Restaurant; Management; Tourism); **Economics** (Commercial Law; Economics; International Economics); **Foreign Languages** (East Asian Studies; English; Modern Languages); **Social Welfare** (Child Care and Development; Environmental Studies; Family Studies; Social Welfare; Welfare and Protective Services); **Social Welfare** (*Evening Division*) (Social Welfare)

Graduate School

Accountancy (*Professional*) (Accountancy); **Area-based Cultural Studies** (Cultural Studies); **Business and Commerce** (Business Administration); **Economics** (Economics); **Social Welfare** (Environmental Studies; Social Welfare)

Kumamoto Health Science University

325 Izumimachi
Kumamoto-shi 861-5598, Kumamoto
Tel: +81(96) 275-2111
Fax: +81(96) 245-3126
Website: http://www.kumamoto-hsu.ac.jp

Course/Programme

Midwifery Bekka (Midwifery)

School

Health Sciences (Health Sciences; Physical Therapy; Rehabilitation and Therapy; Speech Therapy and Audiology)

Graduate School

Health Sciences (Biological and Life Sciences; Health Sciences; Microbiology; Pathology; Public Health; Rehabilitation and Therapy)

History: Founded 2002.

Main language(s) of instruction: Japanese

Accrediting agency: Japan Institution for Higher Education Evaluation (JIHEE)

Degrees and diplomas: Gakushi, Shushi (Health Sciences; Rehabilitation and Therapy)
Periodicals: Journal of Health Sciences

Academic Staff 2013-2014	MALE	FEMALE	TOTAL
FULL-TIME			105
Student Numbers 2013-2014			
All (Foreign Included)			1534

Last Update: 18-12-2017

Kunitachi College of Music

Kashiwa-Cho 5-5-1
Tachikawa-shi 190-8520, Tokyo
Tel: +81(42) 535-0321
Fax: +81(42) 535-2313
Website: http://www.kunitachi.ac.jp
President: Tadayoshi Takeda

Faculty
Music Studies (Cultural Studies; Music; Music Education; Musical Instruments; Singing)

College
Modular System (Music; Music Education; Musical Instruments; Performing Arts; Preschool Education)

Course/Programme
Piano Technician's Training (*Special Course*) (Maintenance Technology; Musical Instruments)

Graduate School
Music (Art Therapy; Computer Science; Cultural Studies; Music; Music Education; Music Theory and Composition; Musical Instruments; Musicology; Preschool Education; Singing)
History: Founded 1926 as Tokyo School of Music, acquired present status and title 1950.
Academic year: April to March (April-September; October-March)
Admission requirements: High school degree and entrance examination
Main language(s) of instruction: Japanese
Accrediting agency: Japan University Accreditation Association (JUAA)
Degrees and diplomas: Gakushi, Shushi (Music Education; Music Theory and Composition; Musical Instruments; Musicology; Singing), Hakase (Music)

Student Services: Academic Counselling, Careers Guidance, Nursery Care, Sports Facilities, Language Laboratory, Facilities for disabled people, Canteen
Periodicals: Kunitachi College of Music Journal, Kunitachi College of Music Research Institute Bulletin

Academic Staff 2012-2013	MALE	FEMALE	TOTAL
FULL-TIME			108
PART-TIME			322
Student Numbers 2012-2013			
All (Foreign Included)			1952

Last Update: 18-12-2017

Kurashiki Sakuyo University (KSU)

3515 Tamashima-Nagao
Kurashiki-shi 710-0292, Okayama
Tel: +81(86) 523-0888
Fax: +81(86) 523-0811
Website: http://www.ksu.ac.jp
President: Hideki Matsuda

Department/Division
Children Education (Child Care and Development; Education; Preschool Education; Primary Education; Special Education; Teacher Training); **Music** (*Junior College*) (Art Therapy; Music; Musical Instruments; Singing); **Music** (Art Management; Art Therapy; Conducting; Music; Music Education; Music Theory and Composition; Musical Instruments; Performing Arts; Singing); **Nutrition** (Cooking and Catering; Dietetics; Food Science; Health Sciences; Nutrition)

Graduate School
Music (Music; Music Theory and Composition; Musical Instruments; Musicology; Performing Arts)

Research Division
Children's Education (Child Care and Development; Education); **Higher Education** (Higher Education); **Product Development AC**
History: Founded 1966.
Main language(s) of instruction: Japanese
Accrediting agency: Japan Institution for Higher Education Evaluation (JIHEE)
Degrees and diplomas: Gakushi, Shushi (Music)

Student Numbers 2013-2014	MALE	FEMALE	TOTAL
All (Foreign Included)			c. 1404

Last Update: 29-12-2017

Kurashiki University of Science and the Arts (KUSA)

2640 Nishinoura Tsurajima-cho
Kurashiki-shi 712-8505, Okayama
Tel: +81(86) 440-1111
Fax: +81(86) 440-1126
Website: http://www.kusa.ac.jp
President: Hideaki Karaki

Faculty

Arts (Communication Arts; Design; Fine Arts; Visual Arts); **Life Science** (Acupuncture; Biological and Life Sciences; Health Sciences; Sports; Zoology); **Science and Industrial Technology** (Industrial Engineering; Information Management; Information Sciences; Media Studies; Tourism)

Graduate School

Arts (Ceramic Art; Design; Fine Arts; Glass Art; Handicrafts; Painting and Drawing; Sculpture; Visual Arts); **Human Arts and Sciences** (Arts and Humanities; Earth Sciences; Education; Environmental Management; Environmental Studies; Health Sciences; International Business; International Law; International Relations; Literacy Education; Modern Languages; Political Sciences; Social Sciences); **Industrial Science and Technology** (Chemistry; Computer Science; Information Technology; Materials Engineering; Molecular Biology)
History: Founded 1995.
Main language(s) of instruction: Japanese
Accrediting agency: Japan University Accreditation Association (JUAA)
Degrees and diplomas: Gakushi (Chemistry; Design; Fine Arts; Health Sciences; Management; Performing Arts), Shushi (Arts and Humanities; Chemistry; Computer Science; Environmental Management; Environmental Studies; Fine Arts; Handicrafts; Health Sciences; Social Sciences; Sports), Hakase (Chemistry; Computer Science; Fine Arts)
Last Update: 28-03-2018

Kurume Institute of Technology

2228-66 Kamitsu-machi
Kururume 830-0052, Fukuoka
Tel: +81(942) 22-2345
Fax: +81(942) 21-8770
Website: http://www.kurume-it.ac.jp
President: Tatsuo Ozaki

Course/Programme

Bekka (Automotive Engineering)

Department/Division

Architecture and Building Services Engineering (Architecture; Building Technologies; Design; Interior Design; Town Planning); **Education and Creation Engineering** (Education; Information Sciences; Information Technology; Mathematics; Natural Sciences); **Environmental Symbiosis Engineering** (Biotechnology; Earth Sciences; Environmental Engineering; Information Sciences; Materials Engineering; Social Sciences); **Information and Network Engineering** (Business Computing; Computer Engineering; Computer Networks; Information Sciences; Information Technology); **Mechanical Systems Engineering** (Electronic Engineering; Information Technology; Mechanical Engineering; Robotics); **Transport Mechanical Engineering** (Automotive Engineering; Design; Environmental Engineering; Industrial Design; Information Technology; Mechanical Engineering; Transport Engineering)

Graduate School

Automotive System Engineering (Automation and Control Engineering; Automotive Engineering; Design; Electronic Engineering; Environmental Engineering; Production Engineering; Safety Engineering); **Electronics and Information System Engineering** (Applied Mathematics; Applied Physics; Electronic Engineering; Engineering; English; Information Technology); **Energy System Engineering** (Architecture; Energy Engineering; Environmental Engineering; Structural Architecture; Thermal Engineering)
History: Founded 1958.
Main language(s) of instruction: Japanese
Accrediting agency: Japan Institution for Higher Education Evaluation (JIHEE)
Degrees and diplomas: Gakushi (Architecture; Civil Engineering; Education; Engineering; Information Technology; Mathematics Education; Mechanical Engineering; Pedagogy), Shushi (Automotive Engineering; Electronic Engineering; Energy Engineering; Information Technology)
Last Update: 28-03-2018

Kurume University

67 Asahi-machi
Kurume-shi 830-0011, Fukuoka
Tel: +81(94) 235-3311
Fax: +81(94) 232-5191
Website: http://www.kurume-u.ac.jp
President: Kensei Nagata

Faculty

Commerce (*Mii Campus*) (Business and Commerce); **Economics** (*Mii Campus*) (Economics); **Law** (*Mii Campus*)

(International Law; Law); **Literature** (*Mii Campus*) (Arts and Humanities; Cultural Studies; Information Sciences; Literature; Psychology; Social Welfare; Sociology)

School

Medicine (*Asahi-Machi Campus*) (Medicine; Nursing)

Graduate School

Business Administration (Business Administration); **Comparative Studies of International Cultures and Societies** (Comparative Sociology; Cultural Studies; International Studies); **Law** (*Graduate and Professional School*) (Law); **Medicine** (Medicine); **Psychology** (Behavioural Sciences; Clinical Psychology; Psychology)

Further information: Also Mii Campus; Research institutes
History: Founded 1928 as Kyushi Medical School, reorganized as University 1950 and incorporated the School of Commerce.
Academic year: April to March (April-August; September-December; January-March)
Admission requirements: Graduation from high school and entrance examination
Main language(s) of instruction: Japanese, English
Accrediting agency: Japan University Accreditation Association (JUAA)
Degrees and diplomas: Gakushi (Business Administration; Economics; Health Sciences; Law; Literature; Medicine; Psychology; Social Welfare; Sociology), Shushi (Business Administration; Clinical Psychology; Cultural Studies; International Studies; Law; Medicine; Psychology), Hakase (Cultural Studies; International Studies; Psychology; Social Studies). Also Professional Graduate Diploma in Law
Student Services: Careers Guidance, Sports Facilities, Language Laboratory, Health Services
Periodicals: Industrial and Economic Studies, Journal of Kurume Medical Association, Kurume Medical Journal
Last Update: 28-03-2018

Kwansei Gakuin University

1-155 Uegahara-1bancho
Nishinomiya-shi 662-8501, Hyogo
Tel: +81(798) 54-6017
Fax: +81(798) 51-0912
Website: http://www.kwansei.ac.jp
President: Osama Murata

School

Business Administration (Accountancy; Business Administration; Finance; Information Sciences; International Business; Management; Marketing); **Economics** (Economic and Finance Policy; Economics; Environmental Studies; Finance; International Economics; Natural Resources; Social and Preventive Medicine); **Education** (Education; Primary Education); **Human Welfare Studies** (Social Welfare; Social Work; Welfare and Protective Services); **Humanities** (Aesthetics; Arts and Humanities; Cultural Studies; English; Ethics; French; Geography; German; History; Japanese; Linguistics; Literature; Philosophy; Psychology; Regional Studies); **International Studies** (Cultural Studies; Economics; International Studies; Management; Modern Languages; Political Sciences; Social Studies); **Law** (*Professional Graduate*) (Law); **Law and Politics** (Civil Law; Commercial Law; Criminal Law; International Law; Law; Political Sciences); **Policy Studies** (Computer Science; International Studies; Public Administration; Urban Studies); **Science and Technology** (Biological and Life Sciences; Chemistry; Computer Science; Mathematics; Physics); **Sociology** (Information Sciences; Media Studies; Social Problems; Social Psychology; Social Studies; Sociology); **Theology** (Bible; Christian Religious Studies; History of Religion; Missionary Studies; New Testament; Theology)

Institute

Advanced Social Research (Social Studies); **Business and Accounting** (Accountancy; Business Administration); **Human Rights Research and Education** (Education; Human Rights); **Industrial Research** (Industrial Engineering); **Research of Disaster Area Reconstruction** (Civil Engineering; Protective Services; Safety Engineering)

Centre

Child (Child Care and Development; Special Education); **Christian** (Christian Religious Studies); **Common Educational Programmes**; **Japanese Language Education** (Foreign Languages Education; Japanese); **Language** (Chinese; English; French; German; Korean; Modern Languages; Spanish); **Research into and Promotion of Higher Education** (Higher Education)

Graduate School

Business Administration (Accountancy; Business Administration; Finance; Information Sciences; International Business; Management; Marketing); **Economics** (Accountancy; Economics; Education; Taxation); **Education** (Education); **Human Welfare Studies** (Welfare and Protective Services); **Humanities** (Aesthetics; American Studies; Arts and Humanities; Cultural Studies; English Studies; Ethics; French; Geography; German; History; Linguistics; Literature; Philosophy; Regional Studies); **Language, Communication and Culture** (American Studies; Communication Studies; Cultural Studies; East Asian Studies; English Studies; French; French Studies; German; Germanic Studies; Japanese; Linguistics; Modern Languages); **Law and Politics** (Civil Law; Criminal Law; Law; Political Sciences); **Policy Studies** (Computer Science; Engineering;

Environmental Studies; International Studies; Law; Management; Political Sciences; Psychology; Public Administration; Social Sciences; Urban Studies); **Science** (Mathematics and Computer Science; Natural Sciences); **Sociology** (Sociology)

Research Division

Christianity and Culture (Christian Religious Studies); **Teacher Development** (Library Science; Museum Studies; Teacher Training)

Further information: Also international programmes and courses for foreign students; study abroad programmes in 25 colleges and universities in North America, Europe, Asia, and Australia

History: Founded 1889 by Methodist Episcopal Church, South (USA). Accredited as College 1912, acquired University status 1932. An independent private institution financed mainly by student fees (entrance/tuition) and Government support.

Academic year: April to March (April-September; October-March)

Admission requirements: Graduation from high school or foreign equivalent, and entrance examination

Main language(s) of instruction: Japanese, English

Accrediting agency: Japan University Accreditation Association (JUAA)

Degrees and diplomas: Gakushi (Architecture and Planning; Arts and Humanities; Business Administration; Economics; International Studies; Law; Media Studies; Modern Languages; Natural Sciences; Political Sciences; Social Sciences; Social Welfare; Sociology), Shushi (Accountancy; Aesthetics; American Studies; Arts and Humanities; Business Administration; Computer Science; Cultural Studies; East Asian Studies; Economics; Education; English; English Studies; Ethics; French; French Studies; Geography; German; Germanic Studies; History; Japanese; Law; Linguistics; Literature; Mathematics; Natural Sciences; Philosophy; Political Sciences; Preschool Education; Primary Education; Psychology; Public Administration; Regional Studies; Secondary Education; Sociology; Theology; Welfare and Protective Services), Hakase (Business Administration; Civil Law; Criminal Law; Law; Political Sciences; Primary Education; Sociology; Welfare and Protective Services). Also Professional Graduate Diploma in Law; Double Degree Programmes with foregin universities in International Business and International Studies

Student Services: Careers Guidance, Sports Facilities, Language Laboratory, Facilities for disabled people, Health Services, Foreign Studies Centre

Periodicals: Humanities Review, Journal of Business Administration, Journal of Economic Studies, Journal of Law and Politics, Journal of Policy Studies, Law Review, Social Studies, Studies in English, French, German, Christianity, Physical Education, Theological Studies

Student Numbers 2012-2013	MALE	FEMALE	TOTAL
All (Foreign Included)			c. 15500
Foreign only			600

Last Update: 27-03-2018

Kwassui Women's College

1-50 Higashiyamate-machi
Nagasaki-shi 850-8515, Nagasaki
Tel: +81(95) 822-4107
Fax: +81(95) 828-3702
Website: http://www.kwassui.ac.jp

Faculty

Health Studies (Child Care and Development; Design; Education; Health Sciences; Nutrition); **Humanities** (Arts and Humanities; Cultural Studies; English; Japanese; Modern Languages); **Music** (Education; Music Theory and Composition; Musical Instruments; Performing Arts; Rehabilitation and Therapy; Singing); **Nursing** (Nursing)

Graduate School

English Literature and Language (English; Literature; Modern Languages)

Further information: Also campuses in Shintomachi, Omura

History: Founded 1879. Acquired present status and title 1981.

Academic year: April to March (April-September; October-March)

Admission requirements: Secondary school certificate

Main language(s) of instruction: Japanese, English

Accrediting agency: Japan University Accreditation Association (JUAA)

Degrees and diplomas: Gakushi (Arts and Humanities; Education; English; Japanese; Literature; Modern Languages; Music), Shushi (English; Literature; Modern Languages; Nursing; Nutrition)

Student Services: Academic Counselling, Social Counselling, Careers Guidance, Sports Facilities, Language Laboratory, Canteen, Foreign Studies Centre

Periodicals: Bulletin of Kwassui Women's College/ Junior College

Last Update: 28-03-2018

Kyoei University

4158 Uchimaki
Kasukabe-shi 344-0051, Saitama
Tel: +81(48) 755-2932

Fax: +81(48) 755-3198
Website: http://www.kyoei.ac.jp

Faculty

Education (Education; Foreign Languages Education; Humanities and Social Science Education; Preschool Education; Primary Education; Secondary Education; Teacher Trainers Education)

College

International Management (Accountancy; Business Administration; Finance; International Business; Management; Sports Management; Tourism)
History: Founded 2001.
Main language(s) of instruction: Japanese
Accrediting agency: Japan Institution for Higher Education Evaluation (JIHEE)
Degrees and diplomas: Gakushi (Business Administration)
Periodicals: Journal of Kyoei University
Last Update: 28-03-2018

Kyorin University

6-20-2 Shinkawa
Mitaka-shi 181-8611, Tokyo
Tel: +81(422) 47-5511
Fax: +81(422) 44-0892
Website: http://www.kyorin-u.ac.jp
President: Yutaka Atomi

Faculty

Foreign Studies (Chinese; Communication Studies; English; Hotel and Restaurant; Tourism; Translation and Interpretation); **Health Sciences** (Engineering; Health Sciences; Medical Technology; Nursing; Occupational Therapy; Paramedical Sciences; Physical Therapy; Radiology; Treatment Techniques; Welfare and Protective Services); **Medicine** (Biological and Life Sciences; Biology; Chemical Engineering; English; Medicine; Natural Sciences; Nursing; Physics; Social and Preventive Medicine); **Social Sciences** (Accountancy; Business Administration; Economics; Environmental Studies; Law; Management; Political Sciences; Public Administration; Social Sciences; Social Welfare; Taxation)

Graduate School

Health Sciences (Biological and Life Sciences; Engineering; Health Sciences; Laboratory Techniques; Nursing; Paramedical Sciences; Rehabilitation and Therapy); **International Cooperation Studies** (Chinese; Cultural Studies; Development Studies; Health Sciences; International Business; International Economics; International Relations; International Studies; Japanese; Law; Linguistics; Medicine; Modern

Languages; Taxation; Translation and Interpretation); **Medicine** (Medicine; Pathology; Physiology; Surgery)
Further information: Also Hachioji; University Hospital; Japanese training course
History: Founded 1966 as Kyorin Junior College, became University 1970.
Academic year: April to March (April-September; October-March)
Admission requirements: Graduation from high school or foreign equivalent, and entrance examination
Main language(s) of instruction: Japanese
Accrediting agency: Japan University Accreditation Association (JUAA)
Degrees and diplomas: Gakushi (Business Administration; Chinese; Economics; English; Health Sciences; International Studies; Law; Medicine; Social Sciences; Social Welfare; Tourism), Shushi (Cultural Studies; Development Studies; English; Health Sciences; International Studies; Japanese; Medicine; Nursing), Hakase (Development Studies; Health Sciences; Medicine; Nursing). Also Certification Programme in Nursing and Health Sciences
Student Services: Academic Counselling, Social Counselling, Careers Guidance, Sports Facilities, Language Laboratory, Facilities for disabled people, Health Services, Canteen, Foreign Studies Centre
Periodicals: Journal of Arts and Sciences, Journal of Kyorin Medical Society, Journal of Social Sciences, Kyorin University Review

Academic Staff 2012-2013	MALE	FEMALE	TOTAL
FULL-TIME			c. 1000
Student Numbers 2012-2013			
All (Foreign Included)			c. 4820

Last Update: 28-03-2018

Kyoritsu Women's University

2-2-1, Hitotsubashi
Chiyoda-ku 101-8437, Tokyo
Tel: +81(3) 3237-2789
Fax: +81(3) 3237-2413
Website: http://www.kyoritsu-wu.ac.jp
President: Kazuo Irie

Faculty

Arts and Letters (Arts and Humanities; English; Fine Arts; French; Japanese; Literature; Media Studies; Modern Languages; Theatre); **Home Economics** (Architecture; Child Care and Development; Clothing and Sewing; Design; Food Science; Home Economics; Nutrition; Textile Design; Textile Technology); **International Studies** (American

Studies; Asian Studies; Chinese; Cultural Studies; English Studies; European Studies; French; International Economics; International Law; International Relations; International Studies); **Nursing** (Human Resources; Nursing)

Graduate School
Graduate Studies (American Studies; Architectural and Environmental Design; Arts and Humanities; Biological and Life Sciences; Child Care and Development; Chinese; Clothing and Sewing; English; European Studies; Food Science; Home Economics; Home Economics Education; International Economics; International Studies; Japanese; Literature; Nutrition; Performing Arts; Political Sciences; Textile Design)
History: Founded 1886 as Kyoritsu Women's Occupational Institute, became College 1928, and University 1949.
Academic year: April to March (April-September; October-March)
Admission requirements: Graduation from high school or equivalent, and entrance examination
Main language(s) of instruction: Japanese, English
Accrediting agency: Japan University Accreditation Association (JUAA)
Degrees and diplomas: Gakushi (English; Home Economics; Japanese; Performing Arts), Shushi (American Studies; Asian Studies; Chinese; English; European Studies; Home Economics; International Relations; International Studies; Japanese; Literature; Nursing; Performing Arts), Hakase (Home Economics)
Student Services: Sports Facilities
Periodicals: Bulletin
Last Update: 28-03-2018

Kyoto Bunkyo University

80 Senzoku Makishima-cho
Uji-shi 611-0041, Kyoto
Tel: +81(774) 25-2400
Fax: +81(774) 25-2498
Website: http://www.kbu.ac.jp/kbu
President: Hiraoka Sato

Course/Programme
Common Education (Anthropology; Arts and Humanities; Asian Religious Studies; Chinese; Economics; English; Environmental Studies; Folklore; French; Geography; German; History; Human Rights; Information Sciences; International Law; Japanese; Law; Linguistics; Mathematics; Medicine; Modern Languages; Natural Sciences; Political Sciences; Religion; Social Sciences; Social Welfare; Sociology; Spanish; Statistics)

Department/Division
Clinical Psychology (Child Care and Development; Clinical Psychology; Education; Health Sciences; Primary Education; Psychology; Social Psychology; Social Work; Welfare and Protective Services); **Sociology** (Cultural Studies; Economics; International Law; Japanese; Law; Management; Media Studies; Psychology; Regional Studies; Social Psychology; Social Studies; Sociology; Tourism)

Graduate School
Clinical Psychology (Clinical Psychology); **Cultural Anthropology** (Anthropology; Cultural Studies)
History: Founded 1996.
Main language(s) of instruction: Japanese
Accrediting agency: Japan University Accreditation Association (JUAA)
Degrees and diplomas: Gakushi (Clinical Psychology; Sociology), Shushi (Anthropology; Clinical Psychology), Hakase (Clinical Psychology)

Academic Staff 2012-2013	MALE	FEMALE	TOTAL
FULL-TIME			c. 350
Student Numbers 2012-2013			
All (Foreign Included)			1943

Last Update: 28-03-2018

Kyoto College of Arts and Crafts

Nantan Sonobe Nihonmatsu-cho, 1-1
Kyoto 622-0041
Tel: + 81 75-525-1515
Fax: +81 75-533-6033
Website: http://www.kyobi.ac.jp/

Department/Division
Arts and Crafts (Handicrafts)
History: Founded 2012.
Main language(s) of instruction: Japanese
Accrediting agency: Japan Institution for Higher Education Evaluation (JIHEE)
Degrees and diplomas: Gakushi (Handicrafts)
Student Services: Library, Residential Facilities
Last Update: 29-12-2017

Kyoto College of Graduate Studies for Informatics (KCGI)

7 Tanakamonzen-cho
Sakyo-ku 606-8225, Kyoto
Tel: +81(75) 681-6334

Fax: +81(75) 671-1382
Website: http://www.kcg.edu
President: Toshihide Ibaraki

Course/Programme

Information Technology and Business Administration
(Business Administration; Computer Engineering; Computer
Networks; Computer Science; Data Processing; E- Business/
Commerce; Information Management; Information Technol-
ogy; International Business; Management; Marketing; Soft-
ware Engineering; Statistics)
History: Founded 2004.
Main language(s) of instruction: Japanese, English
Accrediting agency: Japan Institution for Higher Education
Evaluation (JIHEE)
Degrees and diplomas: Shushi (Information Technology)

Academic Staff 2012-2013	MALE	FEMALE	TOTAL
FULL-TIME			31
Student Numbers 2012-2013			
All (Foreign Included)			c. 320

Last Update: 28-02-2018

Kyoto College of Medical Science

1-3 Imakita, Oyama-higashi,Sonobe
Nandan 622-0041, Kyoto
Tel: +81 771-63-0066
Fax: +81 771-63-0189
Website: http://www.kyoto-msc.jp
President: Keigo Endo

Faculty

Medical Sciences (Radiology)
History: Founded 1927 as Shimadzu X-ray Technology
Training Sites. Renamed X-ray Technology Vocational
School 1935, Kyoto Radiation Polytechnic 1970, Kyoto
Shimadzu Medical Technology School 1983, Kyoto Medical
College of Technology 1988, Shimadzu School 1991.
Acquired present status and title 2007.
Main language(s) of instruction: Japanese
Accrediting agency: Japan Institution for Higher Education
Evaluation (JIHEE)
Degrees and diplomas: Gakushi (Radiology)
Last Update: 29-12-2017

Kyoto Gakuen University

1-1 Nanjyo-Otani Sogabe
Kameoka-shi 621-8555, Kyoto
Tel: +81(771) 22-2001

Fax: +81(771) 29-2269
Website: http://www.kyotogakuen.ac.jp
President: Soichi Shinohara

Faculty

Bio-environmental Science (Biological and Life Sciences;
Biotechnology; Environmental Engineering; Environmental
Studies); **Business Administration** (Business Administra-
tion; Health Sciences; Japanese; Library Science; Manage-
ment; Museum Studies; Sports); **Economics** (Economic and
Finance Policy; Economics; Finance; Information Sciences;
Social Policy); **Human and Cultural Studies** (Behavioural
Sciences; Clinical Psychology; Communication Studies; Cul-
tural Studies; Ecology; English; Folklore; History; Interna-
tional Studies; Japanese; Media Studies; Psychology; Radio
and Television Broadcasting; Sociology); **Law** (Commercial
Law; Fire Science; Law; Police Studies)

Course/Programme

CFP Certification Education (*Postgraduate*) (Business
Administration; Finance; Insurance; Real Estate; Taxation);
Tax Training (*Postgraduate*) (Taxation)

Graduate School

Bio-Environmental Studies (Biochemistry; Biological and
Life Sciences; Biotechnology; Earth Sciences; Ecology;
Environmental Studies; Food Science; Microbiology; Molec-
ular Biology; Natural Resources; Organic Chemistry; Plant
Pathology); **Business Administration** (Accountancy; Busi-
ness Administration; Finance; Human Resources; Information
Management; Information Sciences; International Business;
Management; Marketing; Small Business); **Economics**
(Accountancy; Econometrics; Economic History; Economics;
Finance; Information Sciences; International Economics; Soci-
ology; Statistics; Taxation); **Human Arts and Sciences**
(Advertising and Publicity; Anthropology; Arts and Humani-
ties; Clinical Psychology; Cognitive Sciences; Cultural Stud-
ies; Educational and Student Counselling; Educational
Psychology; Experimental Psychology; Folklore; Gender
Studies; Geography; History; Information Sciences; Japanese;
Journalism; Library Science; Literature; Multimedia; Natural
Sciences; Political Sciences; Psychiatry and Mental Health;
Psychology; Psychotherapy; Public Relations; Social Psychol-
ogy; Sociology; Video); **Law** (Commercial Law; Law)
History: Founded 1969.
Main language(s) of instruction: Japanese
Accrediting agency: Japan University Accreditation Asso-
ciation (JUAA)
Degrees and diplomas: Gakushi, Shushi (Business Admin-
istration; Cultural Studies; Economics; Information Sciences;
Law; Psychology), Hakase (Environmental Engineering;
Environmental Studies; Law). Also Professional Post-
rgraduate Certifications in Taxation and Finance

Student Services: Sports Facilities, Language Laboratory, Foreign Studies Centre

Academic Staff 2012-2013	MALE	FEMALE	TOTAL
FULL-TIME			c. 200
Student Numbers 2012-2013			
All (Foreign Included)			c. 3000
Foreign only			190

Last Update: 29-12-2017

Kyoto Kacho University

Higashiyama-ku, linker-cho, 3-456
Kyoto 605-0062, Kyoto
Tel: +81 75-551-1211
Fax: +81 75-551-1530
Website: http://www.kyotokacho-u.ac.jp
President: Masaaki Nakano

Faculty
Modern Home Economics (Home Economics)
History: Founded 1911 as Hanaitadaki Girls High School. Acquired present status and title 2011.
Main language(s) of instruction: Japanese
Accrediting agency: Japan Institution for Higher Education Evaluation (JIHEE)
Degrees and diplomas: Gakushi (Home Economics)
Last Update: 28-03-2018

Kyoto Koka Women's University

38 Kadono-cho Nishikyogoku Ukyo-ku
Kyoto-shi 615-0882, Kyoto
Tel: +81(75) 325-5304
Fax: +81(75) 325-5307
Website: http://www.koka.ac.jp
President: Masamichi Ichigo

Faculty
Career Development (Child Care and Development; Information Management; Library Science; Social Welfare; Social Work; Teacher Training); **Health Science** (Dietetics; Health Sciences; Nursing; Nutrition; Sports); **Humanities** (Arts and Humanities; English; Japanese; Library Science; Literature; Museum Studies; Psychology)

Graduate School
Human Relations (Clinical Psychology; Psychology)
History: Founded 1944 as Koka Women's University. Acquired present status 1964.

Main language(s) of instruction: Japanese
Accrediting agency: Japan University Accreditation Association (JUAA)
Degrees and diplomas: Gakushi, Shushi (Psychology)

Student Numbers 2012-2013	MALE	FEMALE	TOTAL
All (Foreign Included)			528

Last Update: 29-12-2017

Kyoto Notre Dame University

1 Minami-Nonogami-cho Shimogamo Sakyo-ku
Kyoto-shi 606-0847, Kyoto
Tel: +81(75) 781-1173
Fax: +81(75) 706-3707
Website: http://www.notredame.ac.jp
President: Masako Sanado

Department/Division
Cross-Cultural Studies (Arts and Humanities; Cultural Studies; Information Sciences; Japanese); **English Language and Literature** (Communication Studies; Cultural Studies; English; Linguistics; Literature); **Home Science and Welfare** (Design; Home Economics; Social Work; Welfare and Protective Services); **Psychology** (Clinical Psychology; Developmental Psychology; Psychology)

Graduate School
Humanities and Social Sciences (Applied Linguistics; Arts and Humanities; Cultural Studies; Home Economics; Social Sciences; Welfare and Protective Services); **Psychology** (Clinical Psychology; Developmental Psychology; Educational Psychology; Psychology)
History: Founded 1961. Acquired present title 2002.
Main language(s) of instruction: Japanese
Accrediting agency: Japan University Accreditation Association (JUAA)
Degrees and diplomas: Gakushi, Shushi (Clinical Psychology; Cultural Studies; Developmental Psychology; Educational Psychology; English; Home Economics; Welfare and Protective Services), Hakase (Psychology)
Student Services: Academic Counselling, Social Counselling, Language Laboratory, Health Services
Last Update: 29-12-2017

Kyoto Pharmaceutical University (KPU)

Misasagi-Nakauchicho 5 Yamashinaku
Kyoto-shi 607-8414, Kyoto
Tel: +81(75) 595-4600

Fax: +81(75) 595-4750
Website: http://www.kyoto-phu.ac.jp
President: Naomasa Gotoh

Faculty

Pharmaceutical Sciences (Medicine; Pharmacology; Pharmacy)

Graduate School

Pharmaceutical Studies (Pharmacology; Pharmacy)
Further information: Also South Campus (Kyoto)
History: Founded 1884 as a private German School, became College 1919. Reorganized and acquired present title 1949.
Academic year: April to March (April-October;October-February)
Admission requirements: Graduation from high school or equivalent or foreign equivalent, and entrance examination
Main language(s) of instruction: Japanese
Accrediting agency: Japan University Accreditation Association (JUAA)
Degrees and diplomas: Gakushi, Shushi (Pharmacology), Hakase (Pharmacology; Pharmacy)
Student Services: Sports Facilities

Academic Staff 2013-2014	MALE	FEMALE	TOTAL
FULL-TIME			111
Student Numbers 2013-2014			
All (Foreign Included)	788	1513	2301

Last Update: 29-12-2017

Kyoto Saga University of Arts

1, Gotoh-cho Saga
Ukyo-kyu 616-8362, Kyoto
Tel: +81(75) 864-7858
Fax: +81(75) 881-7133
Website: http://www.kyoto-saga.ac.jp
President: Takeshi Morimoto

Faculty

Arts (Communication Arts; Design; Fine Arts; Graphic Arts; Graphic Design; Handicrafts; Painting and Drawing; Sculpture; Visual Arts)

Graduate School

Art and Design (Communication Arts; Design; Fine Arts)
History: Founded 2001.
Main language(s) of instruction: Japanese
Accrediting agency: Japan Institution for Higher Education Evaluation (JIHEE)
Degrees and diplomas: Gakushi, Shushi (Design; Fine Arts)
Last Update: 29-12-2017

Kyoto Sangyo University

Motoyama, Kamigamo Kita-ku
Kyoto-shi 603-8555, Kyoto
Tel: +81(75) 705-1455
Fax: +81(75) 705-1456
Website: http://www.kyoto-su.ac.jp
President: Terumasa Oshiro

Faculty

Business Administration (Accountancy; Business Administration; Finance; Management); **Computer Science and Engineering** (Artificial Intelligence; Computer Engineering; Computer Networks; Computer Science); **Cultural Studies** (Cultural Studies; International Studies); **Economics** (Economics); **Engineering** (Biotechnology; Engineering; Information Technology; Telecommunications Engineering); **Foreign Languages** (Chinese; English; French; German; International Relations; Linguistics); **Law** (Law; Political Sciences); **Life Sciences** (Biological and Life Sciences; Environmental Studies; Molecular Biology; Natural Resources; Natural Sciences; Veterinary Science; Zoology); **Science** (Computer Science; Mathematics; Physics)

Course/Programme

General Education (Arts and Humanities; Natural Sciences; Physical Education)

Graduate School

Graduate Studies (Biotechnology; Chinese; Computer Science; Economics; Engineering; English; Information Technology; Law; Linguistics; Management; Mathematics; Modern Languages; Natural Sciences; Physics; Telecommunications Engineering)
History: Founded 1965.
Academic year: Autumn semester: (October-March); Spring semester: (April-September)
Admission requirements: Graduation from high school or equivalent, and entrance examination
Fees: 889,000-1,323,000 per annum (Yen)
Main language(s) of instruction: Japanese
Accrediting agency: Japan University Accreditation Association (JUAA)
Degrees and diplomas: Gakushi, Shushi (Biotechnology; Chinese; Economics; English; Information Technology; Law; Linguistics; Management; Mathematics; Physics; Telecommunications Engineering), Hakase (Biotechnology; Economics; Information Technology; Law; Management; Mathematics; Physics; Telecommunications Engineering). Also Professional Postgraduate Degree in Law and Distance Postgraduate Degree in Economics.
Student Services: Academic Counselling, Social Counselling, Careers Guidance, Cultural Activities, Sports Facilities,

Language Laboratory, Facilities for disabled people, Health Services, Canteen, Foreign Studies Centre
Periodicals: Institute Bulletins, Institute Bulletins

Academic Staff 2012-2013	MALE	FEMALE	TOTAL
FULL-TIME			297
PART-TIME			285
Student Numbers 2012-2013			
All (Foreign Included)	9335	3872	13207
Foreign only	102	96	198

Last Update: 29-12-2017

Kyoto Seika University (KSU)

137 Kino-cho Iwakura
Sakyo-ku 606-8588, Kyoto
Tel: +81(75) 702-5199
Fax: +81(75) 702-5390
Website: http://www.kyoto-seika.ac.jp/eng
President: Keiko Takemiya

Faculty

Art (Ceramic Art; Communication Arts; Fine Arts; Handicrafts; Painting and Drawing; Printing and Printmaking; Sculpture; Textile Design; Video); **Design** (Architecture; Communication Arts; Design; Graphic Arts; Industrial Design; Interior Design; Visual Arts); **Humanities** (Arts and Humanities; Asian Studies; Communication Studies; Cultural Studies; Environmental Studies; Social Studies); **Manga** (Painting and Drawing; Visual Arts); **Popular Culture** (Fashion Design; Music)

Graduate School

Arts (Fine Arts); **Design** (Design); **Humanities** (Arts and Humanities); **Manga** (Painting and Drawing)
History: Founded 1968 as a private two-year College with Departments of Arts and English. In 1979 introduced fully accredited and distinctive 4-yr undergraduate courses in the Faculty of Arts. Faculty of Humanities enrolled its first students 1989. Masters programmes introduced 1991. Doctorate programmes introduced 2003.
Academic year: April to March
Fees: Humanities, undergraduate, 567,600 per annum, 2nd year, 572,600; Art, undergraduate, 812,200; 2nd year, 807,200 (Yen)
Main language(s) of instruction: Japanese
Accrediting agency: Japan University Accreditation Association (JUAA)
Degrees and diplomas: Gakushi, Shushi (Architecture; Arts and Humanities; Design; Fine Arts; Painting and Drawing), Hakase (Fine Arts; Painting and Drawing)
Student Services: Academic Counselling, Social Counselling, Careers Guidance, Cultural Activities, Sports Facilities,

Language Laboratory, Facilities for disabled people, Health Services, Canteen, Foreign Studies Centre
Periodicals: Kinohyoron, Kyoto Seika Daigaku Kiyou

Academic Staff 2013-2014	MALE	FEMALE	TOTAL
FULL-TIME			264
Student Numbers 2013-2014			
All (Foreign Included)			4549

Last Update: 29-12-2017

Kyoto Tachibana University

34 Yamada-cho Oyake Yamashina-ku
Kyoto-shi 607-8175, Kyoto
Tel: +81(75) 574-4121
Fax: +81(75) 571-4122
Website: http://www.tachibana-u.ac.jp
President: Ryouichi Hosokawa

Faculty

Contemporary Business (Architecture; Business Administration; Cultural Studies; Interior Design; Management; Tourism; Town Planning); **Health Sciences** (Clinical Psychology; Developmental Psychology; Educational Psychology; Health Sciences; Industrial and Organizational Psychology; Orthopaedics; Physical Therapy; Social Psychology; Sports); **Human Development and Communication** (Communication Studies; English; Foreign Languages Education; Preschool Education; Primary Education); **Humanities** (Archaeology; Art History; Arts and Humanities; Contemporary History; Fine Arts; Heritage Preservation; History; Japanese; Literature); **Nursing** (Midwifery; Nursing)

Graduate School

Cultural Policy (Cultural Studies); **Humanities** (Arts and Humanities; Cultural Studies; Heritage Preservation; History; Linguistics); **Nursing** (Nursing)
History: Founded 1967 as Tachibana Women's University. Renamed Kyoto Tachibana Women's University 1988. Acquired present title 2005.
Main language(s) of instruction: Japanese
Accrediting agency: Japan University Accreditation Association (JUAA)
Degrees and diplomas: Gakushi, Shushi (Cultural Studies; Heritage Preservation; History; Linguistics; Nursing), Hakase (Cultural Studies; Heritage Preservation; History)
Student Services: Language Laboratory

Student Numbers 2012-2013	MALE	FEMALE	TOTAL
All (Foreign Included)			c. 3450
Foreign only			20

Last Update: 29-12-2017

Kyoto University of Art and Design

2-116 Uryuyama Kita-shikarawa Sakyo-ku
Kyoto-shi 606-8271, Kyoto
Tel: +81(75) 791-9122
Fax: +81(75) 791-9127
Website: http://www.kyoto-art.ac.jp
President: Kazuo Oike

Faculty

Art and Design (Acting; Architectural and Environmental Design; Child Care and Development; Computer Graphics; Cultural Studies; Design; Film; Fine Arts; Heritage Preservation; Industrial Design; Media Studies; Painting and Drawing; Performing Arts; Photography; Textile Design; Writing); **Art and Design (Correspondence Education)** (Architectural and Environmental Design; Architecture; Ceramic Art; Design; Fine Arts; Heritage Preservation; Landscape Architecture; Painting and Drawing; Photography; Textile Design; Writing)

Graduate School

Art and Design (Design; Film; Fine Arts; Handicrafts; Theatre)
Further information: Also Gaien Campus and Osaka Satellite Campus.
History: Founded 1991.
Main language(s) of instruction: Japanese
Accrediting agency: Japan Institution for Higher Education Evaluation (JIHEE)
Degrees and diplomas: Gakushi, Shushi (Design; Fine Arts), Hakase (Fine Arts; Philosophy)

Academic Staff 2012-2013	MALE	FEMALE	TOTAL
FULL-TIME			218
Student Numbers 2012-2013			
All (Foreign Included)			9280
Foreign only			214

Total number of distance students: 5912
Last Update: 29-12-2017

Kyoto University of Foreign Studies (KUFS)

6 Kasame-cho, Saiin Ukyo-ku
Kyoto-shi 615-8558, Kyoto
Tel: +81(75) 322-6043
Fax: +81(75) 322-6243
Website: http://www.kufs.ac.jp
President: Takeshi Matsuda
Tel: +81(75) 322-6710

Faculty

Foreign Studies (American Studies; Arabic; Chinese; Dutch; English; French; French Studies; German; Germanic Studies; Greek (Classical); Hispanic American Studies; Indonesian; International Studies; Italian; Japanese; Korean; Latin; Portuguese; Russian; Spanish)

School

Graduate Studies (Cultural Studies; Modern Languages)

Institute

Language and Peace Research (*International*) (Linguistics; Peace and Disarmament); **Latin-American Studies** (*Kyoto*) (History; Latin American Studies; Linguistics)
Further information: Also Japanese course for overseas students. Study Abroad programmes in USA, UK, Australia, Canada, Argentina, France, Switzerland, Brazil, China, Mexico, Spain, Belgium, Germany, Portugal
History: Founded 1947 as College, acquired present status and title 1959.
Academic year: April to March (April-September; September-March)
Admission requirements: Graduation from high school or equivalent and entrance examination
Fees: Undergraduate programmes tuition fee, 835,000 (Spring)- 585,000 (Autumn) per semester; For graduate programmes tuition fee, 530,000-615,000 (Spring)- 350,000-360,000 (Autumn) per semester (Yen)
Main language(s) of instruction: Japanese
Accrediting agency: Japan University Accreditation Association (JUAA)
Degrees and diplomas: Gakushi (International Studies; Japanese), Shushi (Cultural Studies; Foreign Languages Education; Modern Languages), Hakase (Cultural Studies; Foreign Languages Education; Modern Languages)
Student Services: Academic Counselling, Social Counselling, Sports Facilities, Facilities for disabled people, Health Services, Canteen, Foreign Studies Centre
Periodicals: Academic Bulletin, Cosmica, SELL

Student Numbers 2012-2013	MALE	FEMALE	TOTAL
All (Foreign Included)			4541

Last Update: 27-03-2018

Kyoto Women's University (KWU)

35 Kitahiyoshi-cho Imakumano, Higashiyama-ku
Kyoto-shi 605-8501, Kyoto
Tel: +81(75) 531-7054
Fax: +81(75) 531-7222
Website: http://www.kyoto-wu.ac.jp
President: Tadayuki Hayashi

Faculty

Arts (American Studies; Applied Linguistics; English; English Studies; History; Japanese; Linguistics; Literature); **Home Economics** (Architecture; Development Studies; Dietetics; Fashion Design; Food Science; Health Education; Health Sciences; Interior Design; Nursing; Nutrition; Social Welfare; Textile Design; Welfare and Protective Services); **Human Development and Education** (Child Care and Development; Clinical Psychology; Cognitive Sciences; Developmental Psychology; Education; Educational Psychology; Music; Music Education; Performing Arts; Preschool Education; Primary Education; Psychology; Social Psychology); **Law** (Law); **Study of Contemporary Society** (Information Sciences; International Studies; Public Administration; Social Studies)

Graduate School

Contemporary Society (Social Studies); **Home Economics** (Architecture; Cooking and Catering; Environmental Studies; Food Science; Health Sciences; Home Economics; Interior Design; Nursing; Nutrition; Textile Design; Welfare and Protective Services); **Human Development and Education** (Behavioural Sciences; Child Care and Development; Clinical Psychology; Continuing Education; Education; Education of the Handicapped; Home Economics; Music Education; Pedagogy; Primary Education; Psychology); **Literature** (Asian Religious Studies; English; History; Japanese; Linguistics; Literature)

History: Founded 1920 as Women's Institute of Kyoto, as Women's College, acquired present status 1949.

Academic year: April to March (April-September; October-March)

Admission requirements: High school certificate or foreign equivalent, and entrance examination

Fees: 1,046,000 per annum (Yen)

Main language(s) of instruction: Japanese

Accrediting agency: Japan University Accreditation Association (JUAA)

Degrees and diplomas: Gakushi, Shushi (Behavioural Sciences; Child Care and Development; Cooking and Catering; Development Studies; Education; English; Food Science; History; Interior Design; Japanese; Literature; Nutrition; Psychology; Social Studies; Textile Design; Welfare and Protective Services), Hakase (Education; English; History; Home Economics; Japanese; Literature; Social Studies)

Student Services: Academic Counselling, Social Counselling, Careers Guidance, Sports Facilities, Language Laboratory, Facilities for disabled people, Health Services, Canteen

Periodicals: Bulletin of the Faculty of Human Development and Education, English Literature Review, Gendai Shakai Kenkyu: Contemporary Society, Joshidai Kokubun, Journal of Apparel and Space Design, Journal of Food Science, Journal of Humanities, Journal of Living and Welfare, Shiso, The Shizen Kagaku Ronso

Last Update: 02-01-2018

Kyushu Institute of Information Sciences

6-3-1 Saifu Dazaifu
Dazaifu-shi 818-0117, Fukuoka
Tel: +81(92) 928-4000
Fax: +81(92) 928-3200
Website: http://www.kiis.ac.jp
President: Takashi Aso

Department/Division

Information and Network Science (Computer Networks; Computer Science; Information Sciences; Information Technology); **Information Management** (Accountancy; Business Administration; E- Business/Commerce; Information Technology; International Business; Management; Marketing)

Graduate School

Graduate Studies (Accountancy; Business Administration; Information Management; Information Sciences; Information Technology; Management; Marketing; Taxation)

Further information: Also Office in Seoul (Repubic of Korea)

History: Founded 1998.

Main language(s) of instruction: Japanese

Accrediting agency: Japan Institution for Higher Education Evaluation (JIHEE)

Degrees and diplomas: Gakushi, Shushi (Information Management), Hakase (Information Management)

Student Services: Health Services

Last Update: 29-01-2018

Kyushu International University (KIU)

1-6-1 Hirano Yahatahigashi-ku
Kitakyushu-shi 805-8512, Fukuoka
Tel: +81(93) 671-8910
Fax: +81(93) 671-9035
Website: http://www.kiu.ac.jp
President: Kyoko Nishikawa

Faculty

Law (Law)

School

International Relations (Business Administration; English; International Relations; Korean; Tourism)

Department/Division

Economics (Economics; Management)

Graduate School

Company Policy (Accountancy; Business Administration; Commercial Law; Economics; Finance; Information Management; Insurance; International Business; International Economics; Labour Law; Management; Marketing; Taxation; Transport Management); **Law** (Law)

History: Founded 1947. Acquired present status 1950.

Academic year: April to March (April-September; October-March)

Admission requirements: Graduation from high school and entrance examination

Fees: 820,000 per annum; foreign students, 520,000 (Yen)

Main language(s) of instruction: Japanese

Accrediting agency: Japan University Accreditation Association (JUAA)

Degrees and diplomas: Gakushi, Shushi (Business Administration; Law)

Student Services: Academic Counselling, Social Counselling, Careers Guidance, Cultural Activities, Sports Facilities, Language Laboratory, Facilities for disabled people, Health Services, Canteen, Foreign Studies Centre

Periodicals: KIU Journal of Economics and Business, Kokusai Shogakubu Bulletin, Kyushu International University Law Journal, Kyushu International University Studies of Liberal Arts

Academic Staff 2013-2014	MALE	FEMALE	TOTAL
FULL-TIME	58	16	74
PART-TIME			162
Student Numbers 2013-2014			
All (Foreign Included)			2079

Last Update: 02-01-2018

Kyushu Kyoritsu University

1-8, Jiyugaoka Yahatanishi-ku
Kitakyushu-shi 807-8585, Fukuoka
Tel: +81(93) 693-3305
Fax: +81(93) 603-8186
Website: http://www.kyukyo-u.ac.jp
President: Toshihiro Okuda

Faculty

Economics (Accountancy; Business Administration; Communication Studies; Economics; Environmental Management; Finance; Industrial Management; Information Sciences; International Economics; Management; Sports); **Sports Science** (Physical Education; Sports)

History: Founded 1965.

Fees: Tuition, 834,300 per annum (Yen)

Main language(s) of instruction: Japanese

Accrediting agency: Japan Institution for Higher Education Evaluation (JIHEE)

Degrees and diplomas: Gakushi

Academic Staff 2013-2014	MALE	FEMALE	TOTAL
FULL-TIME			83
Student Numbers 2013-2014			
All (Foreign Included)			2208

Last Update: 02-01-2018

Kyushu Lutheran College (KLC)

3-12-16 Kurokami
Kumamoto-shi 860-8520, Kumamoto
Tel: +81(96) 343-1600
Fax: +81(96) 343-0354
Website: http://www.klc.ac.jp
President: Junko Hirowatari

Faculty

Humanities (Arts and Humanities; Child Care and Development; Clinical Psychology; English; Foreign Languages Education; International Business; Psychiatry and Mental Health; Welfare and Protective Services)

Graduate School

Humanities (Arts and Humanities; Behavioural Sciences; Clinical Psychology; Cognitive Sciences; Communication Disorders; Developmental Psychology; Psychology; Social Welfare; Social Work)

History: Founded 1997.

Main language(s) of instruction: Japanese, English

Accrediting agency: Japan University Accreditation Association (JUAA)

Degrees and diplomas: Gakushi, Shushi (Psychology)

Last Update: 02-01-2018

Kyushu Nutrition Welfare University

5-1-1 Shimoitozu Kokurakita-ku
Kitakyushu-shi 803-8511, Fukuoka
Tel: +81(93) 561-2136
Fax: +81(93) 562-5161
Website: http://www.knwu.ac.jp

Faculty

Food and Nutrition (Food Science; Health Sciences; Nutrition; Social Welfare; Welfare and Protective Services);

Rehabilitation (Cardiology; Child Care and Development; Gerontology; Nursing; Occupational Therapy; Physical Therapy; Plastic Surgery; Psychiatry and Mental Health; Rehabilitation and Therapy; Respiratory Therapy; Sports; Welfare and Protective Services)

Graduate School

Health Sciences (Dietetics; Food Science; Health Sciences; Nutrition; Occupational Health; Physical Therapy)
History: Founded 2001.
Main language(s) of instruction: Japanese
Accrediting agency: Japan Institution for Higher Education Evaluation (JIHEE)
Degrees and diplomas: Gakushi, Shushi (Health Sciences)
Last Update: 02-01-2018

Kyushu Sangyo University (KSU)

2-3-1 Matsukadai
Higashi-ku 813-8503, Fukuoka
Tel: +81(92) 673-5050
Fax: +81(92) 673-5988
Website: http://www.ip.kyusan-u.ac.jp
President: Iwao Yamamoto

Faculty

Business and Commerce (Business and Commerce; Tourism); **Economics** (Economics); **Engineering** (Applied Chemistry; Architecture; Biochemistry; Civil Engineering; Electrical Engineering; Engineering; Information Technology; Interior Design; Mechanical Engineering; Robotics; Town Planning); **Fine Arts** (Design; Fine Arts; Handicrafts; Photography; Visual Arts); **Information Science** (Computer Science; Information Sciences); **International Studies of Culture** (Clinical Psychology; Cultural Studies; International Studies; Japanese; Regional Studies); **Management** (Industrial Management; International Business; Management)

School

Commerce (*Evening*) (Business and Commerce)

Graduate School

Economics and Commerce (Business and Commerce; Economics); **Engineering** (Engineering; Industrial Design; Industrial Engineering); **Fine Arts** (Fine Arts); **Information Science** (Information Sciences); **International Studies of Culture** (Cultural Studies; International Studies)
Further information: Also Special English and Japanese programmes for foreign students. Study Abroad programmes
History: Founded 1960, acquired present status 1963.
Academic year: April to March (April-August; September-March)

Admission requirements: Graduation from high school or equivalent or foreign equivalent, and entrance examination
Fees: 743,000-1,256,000 (Yen)
Main language(s) of instruction: Japanese
Accrediting agency: Japan University Accreditation Association (JUAA)
Degrees and diplomas: Gakushi, Shushi (Business Administration; Business and Commerce; Cultural Studies; Economics; Fine Arts; Industrial Design; Industrial Engineering; Information Sciences; International Studies; Management), Hakase (Business Administration; Business and Commerce; Cultural Studies; Economics; Environmental Engineering; Fine Arts; Industrial Design; Industrial Engineering; Information Sciences; International Studies; Management; Production Engineering)
Student Services: Academic Counselling, Social Counselling, Careers Guidance, Sports Facilities, Language Laboratory, Facilities for disabled people, Health Services, Canteen, Foreign Studies Centre
Periodicals: Kogakukai-Shi, Kokusai Bunka Gakubu-kiyo, Shokei-Ronso

Student Numbers 2013-2014	MALE	FEMALE	TOTAL
All (Foreign Included)	8422	2409	10831

Last Update: 02-01-2018

Kyushu University of Health and Welfare

Yoshino-cho 1714-1
Nobeoka-shi 882-8508, Miyazaki
Tel: +81(982) 23-5555
Fax: +81(982) 23-5530
Website: http://www.phoenix.ac.jp
President: Miyako Kake

Faculty

Health Sciences (Health Sciences; Medical Technology; Occupational Therapy; Ophthalmology; Speech Therapy and Audiology); **Pharmaceutical Sciences** (Animal Husbandry; Pharmacology; Pharmacy); **Social Welfare** (*Also Distance Programmes*) (Business Administration; Child Care and Development; Clinical Psychology; Health Sciences; Social Welfare; Welfare and Protective Services)

Graduate School

Medical Pharmaceutical Sciences (Health Sciences; Medicine; Pharmacy); **Social Welfare Studies** (*Distance Programmes*) (Health Sciences; Social Welfare)
History: Founded 1999.
Fees: Tuition, 1,203,000-2,016,000 per annum (Yen)
Main language(s) of instruction: Japanese

Accrediting agency: Japan University Accreditation Association (JUAA)
Degrees and diplomas: Gakushi, Shushi (Health Sciences; Social Welfare), Hakase (Health Sciences; Pharmacy; Social Welfare)
Student Services: Sports Facilities, Canteen
Periodicals: Journal of Kyushu University of Health and Welfare

Academic Staff 2012-2013	MALE	FEMALE	TOTAL
FULL-TIME			241
Student Numbers 2012-2013			
All (Foreign Included)			2731

Last Update: 03-01-2018

Kyushu University of Nursing and Social Welfare

Tomio 888
Tamana-shi 865-0062, Kumamoto
Tel: +81(968) 75-1800
Fax: +81(968) 75-1811
Website: http://www.kyushu-ns.ac.jp
President: Kiyoshi Shiga

Department/Division
Nursing (Biological and Life Sciences; Clinical Psychology; Gerontology; Health Administration; Nursing; Paediatrics; Psychiatry and Mental Health; Public Health); **Oral Health Sciences** (Community Health; Dental Hygiene; Dental Technology; Dentistry; Health Sciences; Oral Pathology; Periodontics); **Rehabilitation** (Physical Therapy; Rehabilitation and Therapy); **Social Welfare** (Social and Community Services; Social Welfare; Social Work; Welfare and Protective Services); **Sports Acupuncture and Moxibustion** (Acupuncture; Alternative Medicine; Sports; Sports Medicine; Traditional Eastern Medicine)

Graduate School
Nursing and Social Welfare Studies (Nursing; Psychiatry and Mental Health; Social Welfare)
History: Founded 1998.
Main language(s) of instruction: Japanese
Accrediting agency: Japan Institution for Higher Education Evaluation (JIHEE)
Degrees and diplomas: Gakushi, Shushi (Nursing; Psychiatry and Mental Health)
Student Services: Sports Facilities, Canteen
Periodicals: Memoirs of Kyushu University of Nursing and Social Welfare

Academic Staff 2013-2014	MALE	FEMALE	TOTAL
FULL-TIME			106
Student Numbers 2013-2014			
All (Foreign Included)			1653

Last Update: 03-01-2018

Kyushu Women's University

1-1 Jiyagaoka Yahatanishi-ku
Kitakyushu-shi 807-8586, Fukuoka
Tel: +81(93) 693-3087
Fax: +81(93) 92-3245
Website: http://www.kwuc.ac.jp
President: Hiroyuki Fukuhara

Faculty
Home Economics (Clothing and Sewing; Cooking and Catering; Dietetics; Family Studies; Food Science; Home Economics; Nutrition; Welfare and Protective Services); **Humanities** (Arts and Humanities; Child Care and Development; Cultural Studies; Education; Information Sciences; Japanese; Library Science; Nursing; Preschool Education; Primary Education; Psychology; Special Education; Writing)
History: Founded 1962.
Fees: Tuition, 267,000-340,000 per annum (Yen)
Main language(s) of instruction: Japanese
Accrediting agency: Japan University Accreditation Association (JUAA)
Degrees and diplomas: Gakushi

Academic Staff 2013-2014	MALE	FEMALE	TOTAL
FULL-TIME			93
Student Numbers 2013-2014			
All (Foreign Included)			1425

Last Update: 03-01-2018

LEC Graduate University, School of Accounting

Misaki-cho 2-2-15 Misaki-cho Building 7th floor
Chiyoda-ku 101-0061, Tokyo
Tel: +82(3) 3222-5184
Fax: +82(3) 3222-5188
Website: http://www.lec.ac.jp
President: Katsuo Sorimachi

Course/Programme
Accountancy (*Professional*) (Accountancy)
Further information: Also campuses in Osaka.

History: Founded 1979 as Tokyo Legal Mind. Acquired present status. Transformed into LEC Graduate School of Accounting 2005. Formerly known as Tokyo University of Career Development.
Fees: Admission fee, 300,000; Tuition fee, 1,000,000 per annum (Yen)
Main language(s) of instruction: Japanese
Accrediting agency: Japan University Accreditation Association (JUAA)
Degrees and diplomas: Shushi (Accountancy)
Last Update: 03-01-2018

Maebashi Kyoai Gakuen College

1154-4 Koyaharamachi
Maebashi-shi 379-2192, Gunma
Tel: +81(27) 266-7575
Fax: +81(27) 266-7576
Website: http://www.kyoai.ac.jp
President: Akio Omori

Faculty

International Social Studies (Arts and Humanities; Business Administration; Child Care and Development; Cultural Studies; English; Information Technology; International Studies; Management; Primary Education; Psychology; Teacher Trainers Education)
History: Founded 1999.
Fees: Tuition, 153,000 per annum (Yen)
Main language(s) of instruction: Japanese
Accrediting agency: Japan University Accreditation Association (JUAA)
Degrees and diplomas: Gakushi
Student Services: Academic Counselling, Social Counselling, Sports Facilities, Foreign Studies Centre
Last Update: 25-05-2018

Matsumoto Dental University

1780 Gobara-Hirooka
Shiojiri-shi 399-0781, Nagano
Tel: +81(263) 51-2161
Fax: +81(263) 5803-1007
Website: http://www.mdu.ac.jp
President: Ichisuke Kawahara

School

Dental Hygiene (Dental Hygiene; Dental Technology; Dentistry)

Graduate School

Dental Medicine (Dentistry)
Further information: Matsumoto Dental University Hospital
History: Founded 1972.
Main language(s) of instruction: Japanese
Accrediting agency: Japan Institution for Higher Education Evaluation (JIHEE)
Degrees and diplomas: Gakushi, Hakase (Dentistry)
Student Services: Sports Facilities
Last Update: 03-01-2018

Matsumoto University

2095-1, Niimura
Matsumoto-shi 390-1295, Nagano
Tel: +81(263) 48-7211
Fax: +81(263) 48-7290
Website: http://www.matsumoto-u.ac.jp
President: Hiroyuki Sumiyoshi

Faculty

Human Health Sciences (Health Sciences; Nutrition)

Department/Division

Business Administration (Business Administration; Hotel and Restaurant; Tourism)

Graduate School

Health Sciences (Health Sciences)
History: Founded 2002.
Fees: Tuition fee, 700,000-800,000 per annum (Yen)
Main language(s) of instruction: Japanese, English
Accrediting agency: Japan Institution for Higher Education Evaluation (JIHEE)
Degrees and diplomas: Gakushi, Shushi (Health Sciences)
Periodicals: Matsumoto University Kenkyukiyou, The Journal of Matsumoto University

Student Numbers 2012-2013	MALE	FEMALE	TOTAL
All (Foreign Included)			1936

Last Update: 03-01-2018

Matsuyama Shinonome College

3-2-1 Kuwabara Matsuyama-shi
Ehime 790-8531
Tel: +81(89) 931-6211
Fax: +81(89) 933-5559
Website: http://www.shinonome.ac.jp
President: Yasuhiro Konishi

College

Humanities (Arts and Humanities; Child Care and Development; Psychology; Social Psychology; Welfare and Protective Services)
History: Founded 1992.
Main language(s) of instruction: Japanese
Accrediting agency: Japan Institution for Higher Education Evaluation (JIHEE)
Degrees and diplomas: Gakushi
Student Services: Sports Facilities
Last Update: 03-01-2018

Matsuyama University

4-2 Bunkyo-cho
Matsuyama-shi 790-8578, Ehime
Tel: +81(89) 926-7148
Fax: +81(89) 926-7151
Website: http://www.matsuyama-u.ac.jp
President: Tatsuya Mizogami

Faculty

Business Administration (Accountancy; Business Administration; Business and Commerce; International Business; Management); **Economics** (Economic and Finance Policy; Economics; International Economics); **Humanities** (Arts and Humanities; Communication Studies; Education; English; Environmental Studies; European Languages; International Studies; Linguistics; Literature; Media Studies; Modern Languages; Social Studies; Social Welfare; Sociology); **Law** (Civil Law; Commercial Law; Law; Political Sciences; Public Law); **Pharmaceutical Sciences** (Cosmetology; Economics; Information Technology; Law; Marketing; Pharmacy)

Graduate School

Graduate Studies (Business Administration; Communication Studies; Economics; Modern Languages; Sociology)
History: Founded 1923 as Matsuyama Higher Commercial School. Renamed Matsuyama Keizai Senmon Gakko (Matsuyama College of Economics) 1944. Acquired present status and renamed Matsuyama Shouka Daigaku (Matsuyama University of Commerce 1949. Acquired present title 1989.
Academic year: April to March (April-September; October-March)
Admission requirements: Graduation from high school and entrance examination
Main language(s) of instruction: Japanese
Accrediting agency: Japan University Accreditation Association (JUAA)
Degrees and diplomas: Gakushi, Shushi (Business Administration; Communication Studies; Economics; Modern

Languages; Sociology), Hakase (Business Administration; Economics; Sociology)
Student Services: Sports Facilities
Periodicals: Journal of Language and Culture
Last Update: 03-01-2018

Meiji Gakuin University

1-2-37 Shirokanedai Minato-ku
Tokyo 108-8636
Tel: +81(3) 5421-5151
Fax: +81(3) 5421-5458
Website: http://www.meijigakuin.ac.jp
President: Udono Hiroki

Faculty

Economics (Business Administration; Economics; International Business); **International Studies** (Cultural Studies; International Studies); **Law** (Law; Political Sciences); **Letters** (Arts and Humanities; English; Fine Arts; French; Literature; Music; Teacher Training); **Psychology** (Child Care and Development; Education; Psychology); **Sociology and Social Work** (Social Work; Sociology)

Centre

Liberal Arts (Arabic; Arts and Humanities; English; Italian; Modern Languages; Thai Languages)

Graduate School

Arts and Letters (Arts and Humanities; English; Fine Arts; French; Literature; Music); **Economics** (Business Administration; Economics); **International Studies** (International Studies); **Law** (*Professional*) (Law); **Law** (Law); **Law** (Law); **Psychology** (Psychology); **Sociology** (Social Work; Sociology)
Further information: Also Yokohama Campus; Semester and academic year curriculum in Japan and Asian studies for short-term exchange Institutions
History: Founded 1877 as private Protestant College. Reorganized as University 1949. Also Campus in Yokohama 1986.
Academic year: April to March (April-September; October-March)
Admission requirements: Graduation from high school and entrance examination
Fees: Enrolment Fee, 200,000; Tuition fee, 475,550-951,000 per annum for undergraduate programmes; 510,000 per annum for graduate programmes (Yen)
Main language(s) of instruction: Japanese, English
Accrediting agency: Japan University Accreditation Association (JUAA)

Degrees and diplomas: Gakushi, Shushi (Art History; Business Administration; Economics; English; Fine Arts; French; International Studies; Literature; Musicology; Psychology; Social Work; Sociology), Hakase (Art History; Business Administration; Economics; English; French; International Studies; Law; Literature; Musicology; Psychology; Social Work; Sociology; Video). Also Postgraduate Professional Programme in Law.

Student Services: Careers Guidance, Health Services, Foreign Studies Centre

Periodicals: Bulletin of Faculties

Student Numbers 2013-2014	MALE	FEMALE	TOTAL
All (Foreign Included)			12214

Last Update: 03-01-2018

Meiji Pharmaceutical University

2-522-1 Noshio
Kiyose 204-8588, Tokyo
Tel: +81(424) 95-8611
Fax: +81(424) 95-8612
Website: http://www.my-pharm.ac.jp
President: Keitaro Ishii

Faculty

Pharmaceutical Sciences (Biological and Life Sciences; Health Sciences; Pharmacology; Pharmacy)

Graduate School

Pharmaceutical Sciences (Biological and Life Sciences; Health Sciences; Pharmacology; Pharmacy)

Research Division

Asia/Africa Centre for Drug Discovery (Pharmacy); **High-Tech Research Center; Open Research Center** (Pharmacy)
History: Founded 1902 as Tokyo Pharmaceutical School. Acquired present title 1998.
Main language(s) of instruction: Japanese
Accrediting agency: Japan University Accreditation Association (JUAA)
Degrees and diplomas: Gakushi, Shushi (Biological and Life Sciences; Health Sciences; Pharmacology; Pharmacy), Hakase (Biological and Life Sciences; Health Sciences; Pharmacology; Pharmacy)
Student Services: Sports Facilities

Academic Staff 2013-2014	MALE	FEMALE	TOTAL
FULL-TIME			99
Student Numbers 2013-2014			
All (Foreign Included)	980	1310	2290

Last Update: 03-01-2018

▌✓⏣ Meiji University

1-1 Kanda Surugadai Chiyoda-ku
Tokyo 101-8301
Tel: +81(3) 3296-4545
Fax: +81(3) 3296-4360
Website: http://www.meiji.ac.jp
President: Keiichiro Tsuchiya
Tel: +81(3) 3296-4013

School

Agriculture (Agriculture; Applied Chemistry; Biological and Life Sciences; Biotechnology; Environmental Studies; Food Science); **Arts and Letters** (Arts and Humanities; Geography; History; Literature; Psychology; Social Studies); **Business Administration** (Accountancy; Business Administration; Management; Public Administration); **Commerce** (Business and Commerce); **Global Japanese Studies** (International Studies; Japanese); **Information and Communication** (Communication Studies; Computer Networks; Information Sciences; Mathematics; Media Studies; Systems Analysis); **Law** (Law); **Political Science and Economics** (Economics; Government; Political Sciences); **Science and Technology** (Applied Chemistry; Architecture; Biological and Life Sciences; Computer Science; Electronic Engineering; Mathematics; Mechanical Engineering; Natural Sciences; Physics)

Institute

Advanced Study of Mathematical Sciences (*Meiji*) (Mathematics); **Bio-Resource Research** (*Meiji*) (Biological and Life Sciences; Natural Resources)

Centre

Advanced Plant Factory Research Center (Agricultural Equipment; Harvest Technology); **Obsidian and Lithic Studies** (Geology)

Graduate School

Advanced Mathematical Sciences (Mathematics); **Agriculture** (Agriculture); **Arts and Letters** (Arts and Humanities; Literature); **Business Administration** (Business Administration); **Commerce** (Business and Commerce); **Global Business** (International Business); **Global Japanese Studies** (Japanese); **Governance Studies** (Government); **Humanities** (Arts and Humanities); **Information and Communication** (Communication Studies; Information Sciences); **Law** (Law); **Political Science and Economics** (Economics; Political Sciences); **Professional**; **Professional Accountancy** (Accountancy); **Science and Technology** (Natural Sciences; Technology)

History: Meiji University was founded as Meiji Law School in 1881, then acquired university status in 1920.
Academic year: April-March (April-September; October-March)

Admission requirements: Graduation from high school or equivalent, and entrance examination

Main language(s) of instruction: Japanese, English

Accrediting agency: Japan University Accreditation Association (JUAA)

Degrees and diplomas: Gakushi, Shushi (Agricultural Economics; Agriculture; Applied Chemistry; Applied Mathematics; Architecture; Biological and Life Sciences; Business Administration; Business and Commerce; Civil Law; Computer Science; Cultural Studies; Development Studies; Economics; Electrical Engineering; English; Environmental Studies; Ethics; Geography; Government; History; Information Sciences; International Relations; Literature; Mass Communication; Mathematics; Mechanical Engineering; Peace and Disarmament; Philosophy; Physics; Political Sciences; Public Administration; Public Law; Religion; Safety Engineering; Social Studies; Sociology; Teacher Training; Theatre), Hakase (Agriculture; Architecture; Business Administration; Business and Commerce; Cultural Studies; Economics; English; Environmental Studies; Ethics; Foreign Languages Education; History; Information Sciences; Literature; Mathematics; Peace and Disarmament; Philosophy; Public Law; Religion; Theatre). Also Professional Postgraduate Degree Programmes in Law and Accountancy

Student Services: Academic Counselling, Social Counselling, Careers Guidance, Nursery Care, Cultural Activities, Sports Facilities, Language Laboratory, Facilities for disabled people, Health Services, Canteen, Foreign Studies Centre, Library, Residential Facilities

Periodicals: Journal of the Historical Association of Meiji University, Law Review, Meiji Business Review, Research Reports of the School of Science and Technology, Studies in arts and letters

Academic Staff 2016-2017	MALE	FEMALE	TOTAL
FULL-TIME	899	210	1109
PART-TIME	1393	422	c. 1815
Student Numbers 2016-2017			
All (Foreign Included)			c. 31339
Foreign only			1159

Last Update: 25-05-2018

Meiji University of Integrative Medicine

Hiyoshi-cho
Funai-gun 629-0392, Kyoto
Tel: +81(771) 72-1181
Fax: +81(771) 72-0326
Website: http://www.meiji-u.ac.jp

School

Acupuncture and Moxibustion (Acupuncture; Alternative Medicine); **Judo Seifuku Therapy** (Physical Therapy); **Nursing Science** (Nursing)

Centre

Medical Education and Research (Medicine)

Graduate School

Acupuncture and Moxibustion (Acupuncture; Alternative Medicine)

Further information: Also University Hospital, Medical MR Centre, 2 Clinics of Oriental Medicine;

History: Founded 1983 as Meiji Shinkyu Daigaku (Meiji University of Oriental Medicine). Renamed Meiji School of Oriental Medicine 1992. Acquired present title 2008.

Main language(s) of instruction: Japanese

Accrediting agency: Japan Institution for Higher Education Evaluation (JIHEE)

Degrees and diplomas: Gakushi, Shushi (Acupuncture; Alternative Medicine), Hakase (Acupuncture; Alternative Medicine)

Student Services: Sports Facilities

Last Update: 04-01-2018

Meijo University

1-501 Shiogamaguchi Tempaku
Nagoya-shi 468-8502, Aichi
Tel: +81(52) 832-1151
Fax: +81(52) 833-1753
Website: http://www.meijo-u.ac.jp
President: Koichi Yoshihisa

Faculty

Agriculture (Agriculture; Agrobiology; Applied Chemistry; Biochemistry; Biological and Life Sciences; Environmental Studies); **Business Management** (Accountancy; Business Administration; Business and Commerce; Finance; International Business; Management; Marketing); **Economics** (Economics; Industrial and Production Economics); **Human Studies** (Arts and Humanities; Psychology); **Law** (Cultural Studies; International Law; International Relations; Law; Political Sciences); **Pharmacy** (Health Sciences; Pharmacology; Pharmacy); **Science and Technology** (Architecture; Biomedical Engineering; Chemistry; Civil Engineering; Computer Science; Construction Engineering; Electrical and Electronic Engineering; Electrical Engineering; Electronic Engineering; Environmental Engineering; Environmental Studies; Information Sciences; Information Technology; Materials Engineering; Mathematics and Computer Science; Mechanical Engineering; Natural Sciences; Technology; Transport Engineering); **Urban Science** (Urban Studies)

School

Law (*Professional*) (Civil Law; Criminal Law; Public Law)

Graduate School

Agriculture (Agriculture; Biochemistry; Biological and Life Sciences; Crop Production; Environmental Studies; Food Science; Genetics; Horticulture; Landscape Architecture; Natural Resources; Organic Chemistry); **Business Administration** (Accountancy; Business Administration; Finance); **Economics** (Economic and Finance Policy; Economic History; Economics; Industrial and Production Economics); **Environmental and Human Sciences** (Biological and Life Sciences; Environmental Studies; Psychology; Social Sciences; Sociology); **Human Studies** (Anthropology; Communication Studies; Education; Psychology; Social Psychology; Social Studies; Urban Studies); **Informatics** (*Urban*) (Administration; Environmental Studies; Finance; Information Sciences; Information Technology; Regional Planning; Town Planning; Welfare and Protective Services); **Law** (Administrative Law; Civil Law; Commercial Law; Constitutional Law; Criminal Law; Fiscal Law; History of Law; International Law; Labour Law; Law; Political Sciences; Private Law); **Pharmacy** (Pharmacy); **Professional Development for Educational Design and Management** (Education; Higher Education; Primary Education; Secondary Education); **Science and Technology** (Architectural and Environmental Design; Architecture; Automation and Control Engineering; Construction Engineering; Electrical and Electronic Engineering; Electrical Engineering; Energy Engineering; Environmental Studies; Information Technology; Materials Engineering; Mathematics; Mechanical Engineering; Media Studies; Nanotechnology; Production Engineering; Structural Architecture; Telecommunications Engineering; Thermal Engineering; Town Planning; Transport Engineering)

History: Founded 1926 as Nagoya School of Science and Engineering. Acquired present status and title 1949.

Academic year: April to March

Fees: 325,000-685,000 per annum (Yen)

Main language(s) of instruction: Japanese

Accrediting agency: Japan University Accreditation Association (JUAA)

Degrees and diplomas: Gakushi, Shushi (Accountancy; Administrative Law; Agriculture; Anthropology; Architecture; Biochemistry; Biological and Life Sciences; Business Administration; Civil Law; Commercial Law; Communication Studies; Constitutional Law; Construction Engineering; Criminal Law; Economic and Finance Policy; Economic History; Economics; Electrical and Electronic Engineering; Environmental Studies; Finance; History of Law; Horticulture; Industrial and Production Economics; Information Sciences; Information Technology; International Law; Labour Law; Management; Materials Engineering; Mathematics; Mechanical Engineering; Natural Sciences; Political Sciences; Private Law; Psychology; Social Sciences; Social Studies; Town Planning; Transport Engineering), Hakase (Accountancy; Administrative Law; Architectural and

Environmental Design; Architecture; Biological and Life Sciences; Biology; Business Administration; Civil Law; Commercial Law; Constitutional Law; Criminal Law; Crop Production; Electrical and Electronic Engineering; Environmental Engineering; Environmental Studies; Food Science; Genetics; History of Law; Horticulture; Information Sciences; Information Technology; International Law; Labour Law; Landscape Architecture; Management; Materials Engineering; Mathematics; Mechanical Engineering; Organic Chemistry; Pharmacology; Pharmacy; Political Sciences; Private Law; Social Sciences; Town Planning). Also Porfessional Postgraduate Degree in Law

Student Services: Language Laboratory

Academic Staff 2013-2014	MALE	FEMALE	TOTAL
FULL-TIME	.		504
Student Numbers 2013-2014			
All (Foreign Included)			3835
Foreign only			310

Last Update: 04-01-2018

Meikai University

1-2-1 Akemi
Urayasu 279-8850, Chiba
Tel: +81(47) 355-5111
Fax: +81(49) 279-2852
Website: http://www.meikai.ac.jp
President: Yasui Toshikazu

Faculty

Economics (*Urayasu-shi*) (Economics; International Economics; Management); **Languages and Cultures** (*Urayasu-shi*) (American Studies; Business Administration; Chinese; Cultural Studies; East Asian Studies; Economics; English; Japanese); **Real Estate Science** (*Urayasu-shi*) (Business Administration; Finance; Law; Real Estate)

Course/Programme

Bekka Japanese Language (English; Grammar; Japanese; Mathematics)

School

Dentistry (Dental Hygiene; Dental Technology; Dentistry; Oral Pathology; Periodontics; Pharmacy; Surgery); **Hospitality and Tourism Management** (English; Tourism)

Graduate School

Applied Linguistics (Applied Linguistics); **Dentistry** (*Sakado Campus*) (Dentistry); **Economics** (Economics); **Real Estate Science** (Real Estate)

Further information: Also Sakado Campus; Meikai University Hospital; Post-Doctoral Institutes of Clinical Dentistry in Saitama, Tokyo, Urayasu

History: Founded 1970 as Josai Dental University, acquired present title 1988.

Academic year: April to March (April-September; October-March)

Admission requirements: Graduation from high school and entrance examination

Fees: Registration, 140,000-230,000; tuition, 504,000-938,000; Dentistry, registration, 500,000, tuition, 3.9m. per annum (Yen)

Main language(s) of instruction: Japanese, English

Accrediting agency: Japan Institution for Higher Education Evaluation (JIHEE)

Degrees and diplomas: Gakushi, Shushi (Applied Linguistics; Economics; Real Estate), Hakase (Applied Linguistics; Dentistry; Real Estate)

Student Services: Academic Counselling, Social Counselling, Careers Guidance, Cultural Activities, Sports Facilities, Health Services, Canteen

Periodicals: Meikai Economic Review, Meikai Japanese Language Journal, Meikai Journal, Meikai Roundtable in Applied Linguistics, Meikai Studies in Real Estate Sciences, Meikai University Dental Journal, The Journal of Arts and Sciences

Last Update: 04-01-2018

Meisei University

2-1-1 Hodokubo
Hino-shi 191-8506, Tokyo
Tel: +81(42) 591-5793
Fax: +81(42) 591-9973
Website: http://www.meisei-u.ac.jp
President: Tomohiro Ohashi

School

Business Administration (Accountancy; Business Administration; Management; Marketing); **Design** (*Formerly Faculty of Art and Design. Reorganised April 2014.*) (Ceramic Art; Design; Fashion Design; Fine Arts; Glass Art; Industrial Design; Landscape Architecture; Painting and Drawing; Printing and Printmaking; Sculpture; Textile Design; Visual Arts); **Economics** (Economics; English); **Education** (Education; Preschool Education; Primary Education; Secondary Education; Teacher Training); **Humanities** (*Hino*) (Anthropology; Arts and Humanities; Chinese; Clinical Psychology; Cultural Studies; English; International Relations; International Studies; Japanese; Linguistics; Literature; Psychology; Social Work; Sociology; Welfare and Protective Services); **Information Science** (Computer Engineering; Computer Graphics; Computer Science; Information Sciences; Information Technology; Software Engineering); **Science and Engineering** (*Hino*) (Architecture; Biological and Life Sciences; Chemistry; Ecology; Electrical Engineering; Engineering; Environmental Studies; Mechanical Engineering; Natural Sciences; Physics)

Graduate School

Graduate Studies (Artificial Intelligence; Arts and Humanities; Chemistry; Computer Engineering; Computer Graphics; Construction Engineering; Distance Education; Economics; Education; Electrical Engineering; Engineering; Environmental Engineering; Information Sciences; Literature; Mechanical Engineering; Physics; Psychology; Sociology; Software Engineering; Structural Architecture)

Further information: Also Ome Campus

History: Founded 1964.

Fees: Tuition fee, 700,000-940,000 per annum (Yen)

Main language(s) of instruction: Japanese

Accrediting agency: Japan University Accreditation Association (JUAA)

Degrees and diplomas: Gakushi, Shushi (Chemistry; Construction Engineering; Economics; Education; Electrical Engineering; Environmental Engineering; Information Sciences; Literature; Mechanical Engineering; Physics; Psychology; Sociology; Structural Architecture), Hakase (Chemistry; Construction Engineering; Education; Electrical Engineering; Environmental Engineering; Information Sciences; Literature; Mechanical Engineering; Physics; Psychology; Sociology)

Student Services: Social Counselling, Cultural Activities, Sports Facilities, Health Services, Library, IT Centre

Last Update: 04-01-2018

Mejiro University

4-31-1 Nakaochiai
Shinjuku-ku 161-8539, Tokyo
Tel: +81(3) 5996-3117
Fax: +81(3) 5996-3247
Website: http://www.mejiro.ac.jp
President: Gunei Sato

Faculty

Business Administration (Accountancy; Business Administration; Hotel and Restaurant; Marketing; Parks and Recreation); **Foreign Language Studies** (Business Administration; Chinese; Communication Studies; Cultural Studies; English; Japanese; Korean; Native Language Education; Translation and Interpretation; Writing); **Health Sciences** (Health Sciences; Occupational Therapy; Physical Therapy; Rehabilitation and Therapy; Speech Therapy and Audiology); **Human Sciences** (Child Care and Development; Clinical

Psychology; Developmental Psychology; Educational Psychology; Experimental Psychology; Psychology; Social Psychology; Social Welfare); **Nursing** (Community Health; Nursing; Psychiatry and Mental Health); **Studies on Contemporary Society** (Communication Arts; Design; Environmental Management; Fine Arts; Food Technology; Health Administration; Marketing; Mass Communication; Media Studies; Multimedia; Social and Community Services; Social Psychology; Social Studies; Textile Design)

College

College Studies (Biological and Life Sciences; Business Administration; Cooking and Catering; Finance; Hotel and Restaurant; Nursing; Secretarial Studies; Tourism; Welfare and Protective Services)

Course/Programme

Japanese Language (JALP) for Foreign Students (Japanese)

Graduate School

Business Administration (Accountancy; Business Administration; Finance; Management); **International Studies** (International Studies); **Language and Culture Studies** (Chinese; Cultural Studies; East Asian Studies; English; Foreign Languages Education; Japanese; Korean; Modern Languages; Native Language Education); **Nursing** (Community Health; Health Administration; Health Sciences; Nursing); **Psychology** (Clinical Psychology; Developmental Psychology; Psychology; Social Psychology); **Rehabilitation** (Occupational Therapy; Physical Therapy; Rehabilitation and Therapy; Speech Therapy and Audiology); **Social Welfare Services** (Child Care and Development; Social Welfare)
Further information: Also Iwatsuki Campus and Saitama Hospital Campus
History: Founded 1994.
Main language(s) of instruction: Japanese
Accrediting agency: Japan Institution for Higher Education Evaluation (JIHEE)
Degrees and diplomas: Gakushi, Shushi (Business Administration; Chinese; Clinical Psychology; Cultural Studies; East Asian Studies; English; Foreign Languages Education; International Studies; Japanese; Korean; Native Language Education; Nursing; Psychology; Rehabilitation and Therapy; Social Work), Hakase (Business Administration; Psychology)
Last Update: 04-01-2018

Mimasaka University

32 Kamigawara
Tsuyama-shi 708-8511, Okayama
Tel: +81(868) 22-7718
Fax: +81(868) 23-6936
Website: http://www.mimasaka.ac.jp
President: Uzaki Minoru

College

Junior Studies (Child Care and Development; Food Science; Nutrition; Preschool Education; Social Welfare)

Course/Programme

Teacher's Licence Renewal (Teacher Training)

Department/Division

Child Care and Education (Child Care and Development; Parks and Recreation; Preschool Education; Primary Education); **Food Science** (Dietetics; Food Science; Nutrition; Parks and Recreation; Secondary Education); **Town Planning and Welfare** (Architecture and Planning; Secondary Education; Social Welfare; Social Work; Town Planning; Welfare and Protective Services)

Graduate School

Human Development Studies (Curriculum; Development Studies); **Life Sciences** (Biological and Life Sciences; Food Science; Health Sciences; Nutrition)
History: Founded 1967 as Mimasaka Women's College.
Fees: Graduate Tuition, 350,000 per annum (Yen)
Main language(s) of instruction: Japanese
Accrediting agency: Japan Institution for Higher Education Evaluation (JIHEE)
Degrees and diplomas: Gakushi, Shushi (Biological and Life Sciences; Curriculum; Development Studies; Food Science; Health Sciences; Nutrition), Hakase (Biological and Life Sciences; Dietetics; Food Science; Psychology)
Student Services: Library
Last Update: 04-01-2018

Minami Kyushu University

5 Chome-1-2 Kirishima
Miyazaki 880-0032, Miyazaki
Tel: +81(985) 83-2111
Fax: +81(985) 83-3383
Website: http://www.nankyudai.ac.jp

Faculty

Health and Nutrition (Biochemistry; Dietetics; Health Sciences; Hygiene; Nutrition; Public Health); **Human Development** (Archaeology; Biological and Life Sciences; Chemistry; Child Care and Development; Earth Sciences; Economics; Education; Educational Psychology; English; Environmental Studies; Ethics; Health Sciences; History;

Information Sciences; International Relations; Law; Mathematics; Philosophy; Physics; Psychology; Sociology; Sports; Statistics)

College
Liberal Arts (Arts and Humanities)

Department/Division
Environmental Horticulture (Agricultural Business; Biotechnology; Environmental Management; Environmental Studies; Horticulture; Landscape Architecture)

Graduate School
Horticulture and Food Science (Agricultural Economics; Biochemistry; Environmental Management; Food Science; Food Technology; Horticulture; Landscape Architecture; Microbiology)
Further information: Also Miyakonojo and Takanabe Campuses
History: Founded 1967.
Fees: Tuition, 330,000 per annum (Yen)
Main language(s) of instruction: Japanese
Accrediting agency: Japan Institution for Higher Education Evaluation (JIHEE)
Degrees and diplomas: Gakushi, Shushi (Agriculture)
Student Services: Social Counselling, Health Services, Library, Residential Facilities
Last Update: 04-01-2018

Minobusan University

3567 Minobu-cho
Yamanashi-shi 409-2597, Yamanashi
Tel: +81(556) 62-3700
Fax: +81(556) 62-0727
Website: http://www.min.ac.jp
President: Hamajima Norihiko

Department/Division
Buddhism (Asian Religious Studies); **Welfare** (Child Care and Development; Social Work; Welfare and Protective Services)
History: Founded 1995.
Fees: Tuition, 630,000 per annum (Yen)
Main language(s) of instruction: Japanese
Accrediting agency: Japan Institution for Higher Education Evaluation (JIHEE)
Degrees and diplomas: Gakushi
Student Services: Library
Last Update: 04-01-2018

Miyagi Gakuin Women's University (MGU)

9-1-1 Sakuragaoka Aoba-ku
Sendai-shi 981-0961, Miyagi
Tel: +81(22) 279-5837
Fax: +81(22) 279-5978
Website: http://www.mgu.ac.jp
President: Hirakawa Arata

Department/Division
Clinical Development (Child Care and Development; Clinical Psychology; Developmental Psychology; Preschool Education; Psychology; Welfare and Protective Services); **Contemporary Business** (Administration; Business Administration; Business and Commerce; Management; Marketing); **English** (Arts and Humanities; Cultural Studies; English; English Studies; History; Japanese; Linguistics; Literature; Modern Languages); **Food and Nutritional Science** (Dietetics; Food Science; Health Education; Health Sciences; Home Economics; Nursing; Nutrition); **General Education** (Chinese; French; German; Italian; Korean); **Humanities** (Art History; Arts and Humanities; Cultural Studies; Economics; Geography; History; Linguistics; Philosophy; Sociology); **International Studies** (Arabic; Chinese; Cultural Studies; English; Filipino; French; German; Hindi; Italian; Korean; Swahili; Thai Languages; Vietnamese); **Japanese Literature** (Cultural Studies; Japanese; Literature; Modern Languages; Native Language Education; Oriental Languages); **Living and Cultural Science** (Architectural and Environmental Design; Architecture; Environmental Studies; Fashion Design; Home Economics; Home Economics Education; Interior Design; Marketing); **Music** (Music; Musical Instruments; Singing); **Psychology and Behavioral Sciences** (Behavioural Sciences; Psychology)

Graduate School
Graduate Studies (Architectural and Environmental Design; Architecture and Planning; Arts and Humanities; Cultural Studies; English; Environmental Studies; Health Sciences; History; Japanese; Linguistics; Literature; Nutrition; Philosophy; Psychology; Religion; Sociology)
History: Founded 1886. Acquired present status 1949.
Academic year: April to March
Admission requirements: Graduation from senior high school or foreign equivalent, and entrance examination
Fees: National : Tuition, 1,171,800-1,978,400 per annum (Yen), International : Tuition, 1,171,800-1,978,400 per annum
Main language(s) of instruction: Japanese
Accrediting agency: Japan University Accreditation Association (JUAA)

Degrees and diplomas: Gakushi (Architecture and Planning; Arts and Humanities; Business Administration; Education; Health Sciences; Music), Shushi (Architectural and Environmental Design; Arts and Humanities; Cultural Studies; English; Japanese; Literature)
Student Services: Academic Counselling, Social Counselling, Careers Guidance, Nursery Care, Sports Facilities, Language Laboratory, Facilities for disabled people, Health Services, Canteen, Foreign Studies Centre, Library, Residential Facilities
Periodicals: Journal of Miyagi Gakuin Women's University

Academic Staff 2017-2018	MALE	FEMALE	TOTAL
FULL-TIME	71	39	110
Student Numbers 2017-2018			
All (Foreign Included)		2940	2940

Last Update: 25-05-2018

Miyazaki International College (MIC)

1405 Kano, Kiyotake
Miyazaki-shi 889-1605, Miyazaki
Tel: +81(985) 85-5931
Fax: +81(985) 84-3396
Website: http://www.miyazaki-mic.ac.jp
President: Keiko Yamashita

School

International Liberal Studies (American Studies; Anthropology; Art History; Arts and Humanities; Asian Religious Studies; Asian Studies; Canadian Studies; Comparative Politics; Cultural Studies; Economics; English; English Studies; Environmental Studies; Fine Arts; Folklore; History; Information Technology; Japanese; Literature; Natural Sciences; Pacific Area Studies; Philosophy; Political Sciences; Psychology; Religion; Social Sciences; Social Studies; Sociology)

Department/Division

Education (Education; Foreign Languages Education; Music Education; Teacher Training)
History: Founded 1994.
Main language(s) of instruction: English
Accrediting agency: Japan Institution for Higher Education Evaluation (JIHEE)
Degrees and diplomas: Gakushi
Student Services: Sports Facilities, Library, Residential Facilities
Last Update: 04-01-2018

Miyazaki Sangyo-Keiei University

100 Maruo Furujo-cho
Miyazaki-shi 880-0931, Miyazaki
Tel: +81(985) 52-3111
Fax: +81(985) 51-0859
Website: http://www.miyasankei-u.ac.jp
President: Omura Masahiro

Course/Programme

Business Administration (Accountancy; Business Administration; Finance; Information Technology; Management; Taxation); **General Education** (Arts and Humanities); **Law** (Administrative Law; Civil Law; Commercial Law; Constitutional Law; Criminal Law; Law); **Sports** (Sports; Sports Management); **Teacher-training** (Business Administration; Educational Administration; Educational Psychology; Geography (Human); History; Humanities and Social Science Education; Information Sciences; Teacher Training)
History: Founded 1987. Former English name: Miyazaki Industrial Administrative University
Fees: Tuition fee, 600,000 per annum (Yen)
Main language(s) of instruction: Japanese, English
Accrediting agency: Japan Institution for Higher Education Evaluation (JIHEE)
Degrees and diplomas: Gakushi
Student Services: Sports Facilities, Canteen, Library, IT Centre
Last Update: 04-01-2018

Momoyama Gakuin University

1-1 Manabino
Izumi 594-1198, Osaka
Tel: +81(725) 54-3131
Fax: +81(725) 54-3215
Website: http://www.andrew.ac.jp
President: Ninako Makino

Faculty

Business Administration (Accountancy; Business Administration; Information Management; Management); **Economics** (Economics; Industrial and Production Economics; Information Sciences; International Economics; Management); **International Studies and Liberal Arts** (American Studies; Applied Linguistics; Arts and Humanities; Asian Studies; Communication Studies; Cultural Studies; English; European Studies; Japanese; Media Studies); **Law** (Civil Law; Commercial Law; Criminal Law; Law); **Sociology** (Cultural Studies; Social Policy; Social Studies; Social Welfare; Sociology; Welfare and Protective Services)

History: Founded 1959.
Admission requirements: Secondary school certificate
Fees: Undergraduate tuition, 729,000 per annum; Graduate tuition, 525,000 per annum (Yen)
Main language(s) of instruction: Japanese
Accrediting agency: Japan University Accreditation Association (JUAA)
Degrees and diplomas: Gakushi, Shushi (American Studies; Applied Linguistics; Business Administration; Cultural Studies; Economics; Sociology), Hakase (Business Administration; Cultural Studies; Economics; Sociology)
Student Services: Academic Counselling, Social Counselling, Careers Guidance, Cultural Activities, Sports Facilities, Language Laboratory, Facilities for disabled people, Health Services, Canteen, Foreign Studies Centre
Periodicals: Bulletin, St Andrew's Cross
Last Update: 04-01-2018

Morinomiya University of Medical Sciences

Nankokita 1-26-16
Osaka 559-8611, Suminoe-ku
Tel: +81 6-6616-6911
Fax: +81 6-6616-6912
Website: http://www.morinomiya-u.ac.jp
President: Toshio Ogihara

School

Health Science (Acupuncture; Nursing; Physical Therapy)
History: Founded 1973 as Acupuncture College. Acquired present status and title 2007.
Main language(s) of instruction: Japanese
Accrediting agency: Japan Institution for Higher Education Evaluation (JIHEE)
Degrees and diplomas: Gakushi (Acupuncture; Nursing; Physical Therapy)
Last Update: 04-01-2018

Morioka University

808 Sunagome Takizawa
Iwate-gun 020-0183, Iwate
Tel: +81(19) 688-5555
Fax: +81(19) 688-5577
Website: http://www.morioka-u.ac.jp
President: Tokuda Hajime

Faculty

Humanities (Cultural Studies; Education; English; History; International Studies; Japanese; Linguistics; Literature; Primary Education; Social Studies); **Nutritional Sciences** (Cooking and Catering; Food Science; Health Sciences; Nutrition)

Course/Programme

Curator (Museum Studies); **Japanese Teacher Capacity Building** (Foreign Languages Education; Japanese; Teacher Training); **Librarians** (Library Science); **Teacher-training** (Teacher Training)
History: Founded 1981.
Main language(s) of instruction: Japanese
Accrediting agency: Japan Institution for Higher Education Evaluation (JIHEE)
Degrees and diplomas: Gakushi
Student Services: Library
Last Update: 28-02-2018

Mukogawa Women's University (MWU)

6-46 Ikebiraki-cho
Nishinomiya-shi 663-8558, Hyogo
Tel: +81(798) 45-3523
Fax: +81(798) 45-3560
Website: http://www.mukogawa-u.ac.jp
President: Naosuke Itoigawa

Course/Programme

Music (*1 yr, Graduate*) (Music; Musical Instruments; Singing)

School

General Education (Arts and Humanities); **Health and Sports Sciences** (Health Sciences; Sports); **Human Environmental Sciences** (Architecture; Dietetics; Environmental Studies; Food Science; Information Sciences; Media Studies; Nutrition); **Letters** (Arts and Humanities; Child Care and Development; Cultural Studies; Education; English; Japanese; Literature; Preschool Education; Primary Education; Psychology; Secondary Education; Social Welfare; Special Education; Teacher Training); **Music** (Art Management; Art Therapy; Music; Musical Instruments; Performing Arts; Singing); **Pharmaceutical Sciences** (Biological and Life Sciences; Health Sciences; Pharmacology)

Institute

Aesthetics in Everyday Life (Aesthetics); **Biosciences** (Biochemistry; Biological and Life Sciences; Food Technology; Molecular Biology; Nutrition; Organic Chemistry; Pharmacology; Physiology); **Developmental and Clinical Psychology** (Clinical Psychology; Developmental Psychology; Psychology); **Education** (Education; Educational Sciences); **Educational Computing Research** (Computer Education; Information Technology); **Health and Exercise Science**

(Health Sciences); **Linguistic Cultural Studies** (Cultural Studies; Linguistics); **Turkish Culture Studies** (Cultural Studies); **World Health Development** (Health Sciences)

Graduate School

Arts and Humanities (American Studies; Arts and Humanities; Child Care and Development; Clinical Psychology; Curriculum; Education; Educational Administration; Educational Sciences; English; English Studies; Japanese; Linguistics; Literature; Modern Languages; Primary Education); **Clinical Education** (Clinical Psychology; Educational Psychology; Psychology; Social Psychology; Social Welfare); **Health and Sports Sciences** (Health Sciences; Rehabilitation and Therapy; Sports); **Human Environmental Sciences** (Architecture; Dietetics; Food Science; Health Sciences; Information Sciences; Media Studies; Nutrition); **Pharmaceutical Sciences** (Pharmacology; Pharmacy)

Research Division

Nutritional Sciences (Nutrition)
Further information: Also Study Abroad Programme with Mukogawa Fort Wright Institute, Spokane, WA
History: Founded 1949
Academic year: April to March (April-July; September-December). Also Special Winter Session, January-March
Admission requirements: Graduation from senior high school or foreign equivalent, and entrance examination
Main language(s) of instruction: Japanese
Accrediting agency: Japanese University Accreditation Association (JUAA)
Degrees and diplomas: Gakushi, Shushi (Architecture; Clinical Psychology; Education; English; Environmental Studies; Food Science; Health Sciences; Information Sciences; Japanese; Literature; Nutrition; Pharmacology; Pharmacy; Sports), Hakase (Architecture; Education; Environmental Studies; Food Science; Health Sciences; Information Sciences; Japanese; Literature; Nutrition; Pharmacology; Pharmacy; Psychology; Social Welfare; Sports)
Student Services: Academic Counselling, Careers Guidance, Cultural Activities, Sports Facilities, Facilities for disabled people, Health Services, Canteen, Library, IT Centre
Periodicals: Bulletins, Research Reports
Last Update: 05-01-2018

Faculty

Economics (Accountancy; Business Administration; Economics; Finance; International Economics; Management); **Humanities** (American Studies; Asian Studies; Cultural Studies; East Asian Studies; English; English Studies; European Studies; French Studies; Germanic Studies); **Sociology** (Communication Studies; Mass Communication; Media Studies; Social Psychology; Social Sciences; Social Studies; Sociology)

Course/Programme

Curator (Museum Studies); **Teacher-training** (Teacher Training)

Centre

Foreign Language Education (English)

Graduate School

Economics (Economics; Finance; Management); **Humanities** (American Studies; Arts and Humanities; East Asian Studies; European Studies; Sociology)
History: Founded 1921 as Musashi High School. Acquired present status 1949.
Academic year: April to February (April-August; September-February)
Admission requirements: Graduation from high school or equivalent, and entrance examination
Fees: 680,000 per annum (Yen)
Main language(s) of instruction: Japanese
Accrediting agency: Japan University Accreditation Association (JUAA)
Degrees and diplomas: Gakushi, Shushi (American Studies; Arts and Humanities; East Asian Studies; Economics; European Studies; Sociology), Hakase (American Studies; Arts and Humanities; East Asian Studies; Economics; European Studies; Sociology)
Student Services: Academic Counselling, Careers Guidance, Sports Facilities, Canteen, Residential Facilities
Periodicals: Journal (Economics), Journal (Human and Cultural Sciences)
Last Update: 05-01-2018

Musashi University

1-26-1 Toyotama-kami
Nerima-ku 176-8534, Tokyo
Tel: +81(3) 5984-3886
Fax: +81(3) 5984-4065
Website: http://www.musashi.ac.jp
President: Tetsuya Yamasaki

Musashino Academia Musicae

1-13-1 Hazawa, Nerima-ku
Tokyo 176-8521
Tel: +81(3) 3992-1121
Fax: +81(3) 3991-7599
Website: http://www.musashino-music.ac.jp
President: Fukui Naotaka

Faculty

Music (Music; Music Education; Music Theory and Composition; Musical Instruments; Musicology; Singing)

History: Founded 1929 as Musashino School of Music. Officially recognized by the Government 1932. Acquired present status 1949. Financially self-supporting.

Academic year: April to March (April-September; October-March)

Admission requirements: Graduation from high school and entrance examination

Fees: Tuition, 1,220,000 per annum (Yen)

Main language(s) of instruction: Japanese

Accrediting agency: Japan Institution for Higher Education Evaluation (JIHEE)

Degrees and diplomas: Gakushi (Music), Shushi (Music; Musical Instruments), Hakase (Music; Musical Instruments). Also Teaching Qualifications

Student Services: Academic Counselling, Social Counselling, Careers Guidance, Sports Facilities, Language Laboratory, Health Services, Canteen, Library, Residential Facilities

Periodicals: Gakusei no rombun (Collection of theses), Kenkyu Kiyo (Research Bulletin)

Last Update: 05-01-2018

Musashino Art University (MAU)

1-736 Ogawa-cho
Kodaira-shi 187-8505, Tokyo
Tel: +81(42) 342-6021
Fax: +81(42) 342-5193
Website: http://www.musabi.ac.jp
President: Tadanori Nagasawa

College

Art and Design (*Also Correspondence Courses*) (Architecture; Art Management; Communication Arts; Computer Graphics; Design; Display and Stage Design; Fashion Design; Fine Arts; Graphic Design; Handicrafts; Industrial Design; Interior Design; Painting and Drawing; Sculpture; Visual Arts)

Graduate School

Art and Design (Architecture; Art History; Art Management; Communication Arts; Computer Graphics; Design; Display and Stage Design; Fashion Design; Fine Arts; Graphic Design; Handicrafts; Industrial Design; Interior Design; Painting and Drawing; Photography; Printing and Printmaking; Sculpture; Visual Arts)

History: Founded 1929 as Teikoku Art School. Changed name to Musashino Art School 1948. Aacquired University status and title 1962.

Academic year: April to March (April-July; September-March)

Admission requirements: Graduation from high school or equivalent, and entrance examination. Provision is made for the recognition of foreign qualifications

Fees: Registration, 360,000; Tuition, c. 1.2m. per annum

Main language(s) of instruction: Japanese

Accrediting agency: Japan University Accreditation Association (JUAA)

Degrees and diplomas: Gakushi, Shushi (Architecture; Art Management; Computer Graphics; Design; Display and Stage Design; Fashion Design; Fine Arts; Industrial Design; Interior Design; Painting and Drawing; Photography; Printing and Printmaking; Sculpture; Visual Arts), Hakase (Art History; Design; Fine Arts; Industrial Design; Interior Design)

Student Services: Library

Periodicals: Bulletin of Museum Library

Publishing house: University Press

Last Update: 05-01-2018

Musashino Gakuin University

Hirosedai 3-26-1
Sayama-shi 350-1321, Saitama
Tel: +81(4) 2954-6131
Fax: +81(4) 2954-6134
Website: http://www.musashino.ac.jp
President: Takahashi Nobuo

Graduate School

International Communication (Business Administration; Communication Studies; East Asian Studies; Economics; Educational Technology; English; History; International Business; International Studies; Japanese; Linguistics; Political Sciences; Psychology; Social Psychology); **International Communication** (Communication Studies; Computer Science; Cultural Studies; East Asian Studies; History; History of Law; Information Sciences; International Business; International Studies; Japanese; Law; Linguistics; Political Sciences; Psychology; Social Psychology; Sports)

History: Founded 2004.

Fees: Undergraduate tuition, 350,000 per semester; Master's degree, 630,000 per annum; Doctor's degree, 530,000 per annum (Yen)

Main language(s) of instruction: Japanese

Accrediting agency: Japan Institution for Higher Education Evaluation (JIHEE)

Degrees and diplomas: Gakushi, Shushi (Communication Studies; Cultural Studies; East Asian Studies; Economics; English; International Business; International Studies; Japanese; Political Sciences; Psychology; Western European

Studies), Hakase (Communication Studies; Cultural Studies; East Asian Studies; International Business; International Studies; Japanese)

Student Services: Sports Facilities, Canteen, Library

Periodicals: The Bulletin of Musashino Gakuin University

Last Update: 25-05-2018

Musashino University

1-1-20 Shin-machi
Nishi-Tokyo 35-8181, Tokyo
Tel: +81(3) 5530-3818
Fax: +81(3) 5530-7403
Website: http://www.musashino-u.ac.jp
President: Teruma Nishimoto

Faculty

Education (Education; Preschool Education; Primary Education; Secondary Education); **Environmental Science** (Architectural and Environmental Design; Environmental Management; Environmental Studies; Interior Design; Science Education); **Global Communication** (Chinese; Communication Studies; English; Foreign Languages Education; Japanese; Library Science; Teacher Training); **Human Sciences** (Clinical Psychology; Educational and Student Counselling; Environmental Studies; Foreign Languages Education; Library Science; Psychiatry and Mental Health; Psychology; Religion; Social Welfare; Sports); **Literature** (Cultural Studies; Japanese; Library Science; Literature; Native Language Education; Teacher Training); **Nursing** (Health Education; Health Sciences; Nursing; Psychology); **Pharmacy** (Pharmacology; Pharmacy); **Political Science and Economics** (Accountancy; Business Administration; Economics; Foreign Languages Education; Library Science; Political Sciences; Taxation)

Department/Division

Distance Learning (Asian Religious Studies; Child Care and Development; Educational and Student Counselling; Psychology; Social Welfare)

Graduate School

Environmental Science (Architecture; Environmental Management; Environmental Studies); **Human and Social Sciences** (Anthropology; Clinical Psychology; Developmental Psychology; Social Sciences; Social Work); **Human Studies in the Distance Learning Division** (Asian Studies; Social Sciences); **Language and Culture** (American Studies; Cultural Studies; English Studies; Japanese; Literature; Teacher Training); **Nursing** (Health Sciences; Nursing; Oncology; Psychiatry and Mental Health); **Pharmaceutical Sciences** (Pharmacology; Pharmacy); **Political Science and Economics** (Accountancy; Economics; Political Sciences; Taxation)

Further information: Also Ariake Campus

History: Founded 1950 as Musashino Women's Junior College. Upgraded into Musashino Joshi Daigaku/Musashino Women's University 1965. Acquired present title 2003.

Academic year: April to March

Fees: Tuition, 700,000; other expenses, 230,000 (Yen)

Main language(s) of instruction: Japanese, English

Accrediting agency: Japan University Accreditation Association (JUAA)

Degrees and diplomas: Gakushi, Shushi (Anthropology; Asian Religious Studies; Clinical Psychology; Cultural Studies; Economics; English; Environmental Management; Japanese; Literature; Nursing; Pharmacology; Political Sciences; Social Sciences; Social Work), Hakase (Anthropology; Pharmacology)

Student Services: Academic Counselling, Careers Guidance, Sports Facilities, Language Laboratory, Canteen, Foreign Studies Centre, Residential Facilities

Last Update: 05-01-2018

Nagahama Institute of Bio-Science and Technology

1266 Tamura-Cho
Nagahama 526-0829, Shiga
Tel: +81(749) 64-8100
Fax: +81(749) 64-8140
Website: http://www.nagahama-i-bio.ac.jp
President: Masanao Miwa

Department/Division

Animal Bioscience (Animal Husbandry; Biological and Life Sciences; Cell Biology; Molecular Biology; Natural Sciences; Zoology); **Bioscience** (Biological and Life Sciences; Cell Biology; Environmental Studies; Genetics); **Computer Bioscience** (Biological and Life Sciences; Computer Graphics; Computer Science; Data Processing)

Graduate School

Biosciences (Biological and Life Sciences; Biotechnology; Cell Biology; Environmental Studies; Genetics; Molecular Biology)

History: Founded 2003.

Main language(s) of instruction: Japanese

Accrediting agency: Japan University Accreditation Association (JUAA)

Degrees and diplomas: Gakushi, Shushi (Biological and Life Sciences; Biotechnology; Molecular Biology), Hakase (Biological and Life Sciences; Biotechnology)

Last Update: 05-01-2018

Nagaoka University

Goyama cho 80-8
Nagaoka 940-0828, Niigata
Tel: +81 258-39-1600
Fax: +81 258-33-8792
Website: http://www.nagaokauniv.ac.jp
President: Murayama Mitsuhiro

Faculty

Economics and Business Management (Business Administration; Environmental Management)
History: Founded 1905. Acquired present status and title 2001.
Main language(s) of instruction: Japanese
Accrediting agency: Japan Institution for Higher Education Evaluation (JIHEE)
Degrees and diplomas: Gakushi (Business Administration; Environmental Management)
Last Update: 05-01-2018

Engineering; Materials Engineering; Mechanical Engineering; Production Engineering; Structural Architecture)
History: Founded 1942, became College of Shipbuilding 1965 and recently acquired new title.
Academic year: April to March (April-October; October-March)
Admission requirements: Graduation from high school and entrance examination
Main language(s) of instruction: Japanese
Accrediting agency: Japan Institution for Higher Education Evaluation (JIHEE)
Degrees and diplomas: Gakushi (Engineering), Shushi (Electronic Engineering; Environmental Engineering; Information Technology; Production Engineering), Hakase (Environmental Engineering; Information Technology; Production Engineering). Also Teacher Training Certificate
Student Services: Cultural Activities, Sports Facilities, Language Laboratory, Health Services, Library, Residential Facilities
Periodicals: Bulletin, Studies of Peace Culture
Last Update: 05-01-2018

Nagasaki Institute of Applied Sciences

536 Aba-machi
Nagasaki-shi 851-0193, Nagasaki
Tel: +81(95) 839-3111
Fax: +81(95) 839-0584
Website: http://www.nias.ac.jp
President: Takeshi Kinoshita

Faculty

Architecture (Architecture; Civil Engineering; Environmental Studies; Structural Architecture); **Engineering** (Computer Engineering; Electrical Engineering; Electronic Engineering; Engineering; Engineering Drawing and Design; Marine Engineering; Mechanical Engineering; Naval Architecture); **Information Technology** (Information Management; Information Sciences; Information Technology)

Course/Programme

Bekka Japanese Language (Japanese); **Teacher-Training** (Teacher Training)

Centre
General Education

Graduate School

Engineering (Electronic Engineering; Engineering; Environmental Engineering; Information Technology; Marine

Nagasaki International University

Huis Ten Bosch Cho 2825-7 Sasebo
Nagasaki-shi 859-3298, Nagasaki
Tel: +81(956) 39-2020
Fax: +81(956) 39-3111
Website: http://www.niu.ac.jp
President: Kenichiro Nakashima

Faculty

Health Management (Health Sciences; Nutrition); **Human and Social Studies** (Business Administration; Cultural Studies; Modern Languages; Regional Studies; Social Work; Sociology; Sports; Tourism); **Pharmaceutical Science** (Pharmacy)

Graduate School
Human and Social Studies
History: Founded 2000.
Admission requirements: Applicants must be 18 year old as of March 31 in the year of entry and must possess Grade 2 (or equivalent) or above of the Japanese Language Ability Test (JLAT); also entrance examination.
Fees: Entrance examination fee, 10,000; first year, 795,000 per annum for overseas students (Yen)
Main language(s) of instruction: Japanese, English
Accrediting agency: Japan Institution for Higher Education Evaluation (JIHEE)

Degrees and diplomas: Gakushi, Shushi (Health Sciences; International Business; Nutrition; Social Work; Tourism), Hakase (Management; Regional Studies)
Last Update: 05-01-2018

Nagasaki Junshin Catholic University (NJCU)

253 Mitsuyama-machi
Nagasaki-shi 852-8558, Nagasaki
Tel: +81(95) 846-0084
Fax: +81(95) 846-0737
Website: http://www.n-junshin.ac.jp
President: Kataoka Chizuko

Faculty

Humanities (Arts and Humanities; Child Care and Development; Computer Science; Cultural Studies; English; Psychology; Welfare and Protective Services)

Graduate School

Human Arts and Sciences (Anthropology; Arts and Humanities; Child Care and Development; Clinical Psychology; Cultural Studies; Educational and Student Counselling; Psychology; Welfare and Protective Services)
History: Founded 1994.
Admission requirements: Graduation from high school and entrance examination
Main language(s) of instruction: Japanese
Accrediting agency: Japan University Accreditation Association (JUAA)
Degrees and diplomas: Gakushi (Arts and Humanities), Shushi (Child Care and Development; Clinical Psychology; Cultural Studies; Welfare and Protective Services), Hakase (Cultural Studies; Welfare and Protective Services)
Student Services: Academic Counselling, Social Counselling, Careers Guidance, Nursery Care, Cultural Activities, Sports Facilities, Language Laboratory, Facilities for disabled people, Health Services, Canteen, Foreign Studies Centre, Library
Periodicals: Academic Research Series, Collection of Academic Studies on the History of Nagasaki, Junshin Journal of Human Studies, Series of Humanistic Culture Studies, Series of Nagasaki Junshin Lectures
Last Update: 05-01-2018

Nagasaki University of Foreign Studies

3-15-1 Yokoo
Nagasaki-shi 851-2196, Nagasaki
Tel: +81(95) 840-2000

Fax: +81(95) 840-2001
Website: http://www.nagasaki-gaigo.ac.jp
President: Akihito Ishikawa

Course/Programme

Professional Education (Air Transport; Asian Studies; Cultural Studies; East Asian Studies; English; European Studies; International Business; Social Studies; Tourism; Translation and Interpretation)

Department/Division

International Communication (Chinese; Communication Studies; French; German; International Studies; Japanese; Korean; Modern Languages); **Modern English** (English; Modern Languages)
History: Founded 2000.
Fees: Tuition, 590,000-610,000 per annum (Yen)
Main language(s) of instruction: Japanese, English
Accrediting agency: Japan University Accreditation Association (JUAA)
Degrees and diplomas: Gakushi
Student Services: Cultural Activities, Sports Facilities, Library, Residential Facilities
Periodicals: The Journal of Nagasaki University of Foreign Studies

Academic Staff	MALE	FEMALE	TOTAL
FULL-TIME			39
Student Numbers			
All (Foreign Included)			653
Foreign only			83

Last Update: 05-01-2018

Nagasaki Wesleyan University

1057 Eida Isahaya
Nagasaki-shi 854-0082, Nagasaki
Tel: +81(957) 26-1234
Fax: +81(957) 26-2063
Website: http://www.wesleyan.ac.jp
President: Kaishin Sato

Faculty

Contemporary Social Studies (Chinese; Communication Studies; Development Studies; Economics; English; International Business; International Studies; Japanese; Management; Political Sciences; Psychiatry and Mental Health; Social Studies; Social Welfare; Sociology; Welfare and Protective Services)

Course/Programme

Japanese Education (Japanese)

History: Founded 2002.
Fees: 650,000 per annnum (Yen)
Main language(s) of instruction: Japanese, English
Accrediting agency: Japan Institution for Higher Education Evaluation (JIHEE)
Degrees and diplomas: Gakushi (Economics; International Studies; Political Sciences; Social Welfare)
Last Update: 08-01-2018

Nagoya Bunri University

365 Maeda Inazawa-cho
Inazawa 492-8520, Aichi
Tel: +81(587) 23-2400
Fax: +81(587) 21-2844
Website: http://www.nagoya-bunri.ac.jp
President: Kageyama Takashi

Faculty
Health and Human Life (Business Administration; Food Science; Health Sciences; Nutrition); **Information and Media Studies** (Information Sciences; Information Technology; Mass Communication; Media Studies)

College
Food and Nutrition (*Nagoya Bunri*) (Cooking and Catering; Dietetics; Food Science; Food Technology; Nutrition)
Further information: Also campus in Nagoya
History: Founded 1999.
Fees: Tuition fee, 720,000 per annum (Yen)
Main language(s) of instruction: Japanese
Accrediting agency: Japan Institution for Higher Education Evaluation (JIHEE)
Degrees and diplomas: Gakushi
Student Services: Sports Facilities, Residential Facilities
Last Update: 08-01-2018

Nagoya College of Music

7-1 Inabaji cho Nakamura-ku
Nagoya-shi 453-8540, Aichi
Tel: +81(52) 411-1115
Fax: +81(52) 413-2300
Website: http://www.meion.ac.jp
President: Keiko Sato

Faculty
Music (Art Therapy; Business Administration; Computer Science; Dance; Jazz and Popular Music; Music; Music Education; Music Theory and Composition; Musical Instruments; Opera; Singing; Theatre)

Graduate School
Music (Art Therapy; Jazz and Popular Music; Music; Music Education; Music Theory and Composition; Musical Instruments; Musicology; Singing)
History: Founded 1976.
Academic year: April to March (April-August; September-March)
Fees: Tuition, 850,000-1m. per annum (Yen)
Main language(s) of instruction: Japanese
Accrediting agency: Japan Institution for Higher Education Evaluation (JIHEE)
Degrees and diplomas: Gakushi, Shushi (Art Therapy; Music; Music Education; Music Theory and Composition; Musical Instruments; Musicology; Singing)
Student Services: Library
Last Update: 08-01-2018

Nagoya Gakuin University

1350 Kamishinano-cho
Seto-shi 480-1298, Aichi
Tel: +81(561) 42-0350
Fax: +81(561) 42-1147
Website: http://www.ngu.jp
President: Kobayashi Kouichi

Faculty
Commerce (Accountancy; Business Administration; Business and Commerce; Finance; Information Management; Information Technology; International Business; Management; Sports Management); **Economics** (Economic and Finance Policy; Economics; Finance; International Economics); **Foreign Studies** (Business Administration; Chinese; English; Foreign Languages Education; Tourism); **Health and Sports** (Biochemistry; Child Care and Development; Dance; Health Administration; Health Sciences; Parks and Recreation; Pharmacology; Physical Education; Physiology; Psychology; Public Health; Social Work; Sports; Statistics; Welfare and Protective Services); **Law** (Administrative Law; Civil Law; Commercial Law; Constitutional Law; Law; Political Sciences; Public Law); **Rehabilitation Science** (Physical Therapy; Rehabilitation and Therapy; Social and Preventive Medicine)

Institute
Japanese Studies (*Bekka*) (Japanese)

Graduate School
Economics and Business Administration (Accountancy; Agricultural Business; Business Administration; Economics; Finance; International Business; Management; Marketing);

Foreign Languages (Applied Linguistics; Chinese; English; Foreign Languages Education; Linguistics; Literature)
History: Founded 1964.
Academic year: April to March
Admission requirements: Graduation from high school
Fees: Undergraduate tuition, 660,000-790,000 per annum; Graduate tuition, 540,000-740,000 per annum; Institute for Japanese Studies, 620,000 per annum (Yen)
Main language(s) of instruction: Japanese, English
Accrediting agency: Japanese University Accreditation Association (JUAA)
Degrees and diplomas: Gakushi, Shushi (Business Administration; Economics; English; International Studies), Hakase (Business Administration; English; Management)
Student Services: Academic Counselling, Social Counselling, Careers Guidance, Nursery Care, Sports Facilities, Language Laboratory, Facilities for disabled people, Health Services, Canteen, Residential Facilities
Periodicals: Journal of Nagoya Gakuin University
Publishing house: Cosmorama
Last Update: 08-01-2018

Nagoya Sangyo University

3255-5 Araicho
Owariasashi-shi 488-8711, Aichi
Tel: +81(561) 55-5101
Fax: +81(561) 55-0515
Website: http://www.nagoya-su.ac.jp
President: Takagi Hiroe

Faculty

Economics (Economics); **Environment and Information Management** (Environmental Management; Environmental Studies; Information Management)

Graduate School

Environmental Management Studies (Environmental Management; Environmental Studies)
History: Founded 2000.
Fees: Tuition, 650,000 per annum (Yen)
Main language(s) of instruction: Japanese
Accrediting agency: Japan Institution for Higher Education Evaluation (JIHEE)
Degrees and diplomas: Gakushi (Environmental Management; Information Management), Shushi (Environmental Management), Hakase (Environmental Management)
Student Services: Cultural Activities, Sports Facilities, Library, Residential Facilities
Last Update: 08-01-2018

Nagoya University of Arts (NUA)

280 Kumanosho Shikatsu-cho
Nishikasugai-gun 481-8503, Aichi
Tel: +81(568) 240-315
Fax: +81(568) 240-317
Website: http://www.nua.ac.jp
President: Yoshiaki Takemoto

School

Design (*Also postgraduate and research programme*) (Architectural and Environmental Design; Art Management; Ceramic Art; Communication Arts; Design; Industrial Design; Jewellery Art; Media Studies; Painting and Drawing; Textile Design; Visual Arts); **Fine Arts** (*Also postgraduate and research programme*) (Art History; Art Management; Ceramic Art; Communication Arts; Fine Arts; Glass Art; Handicrafts; Painting and Drawing; Printing and Printmaking; Sculpture); **Human Development** (*Also postgraduate and research programme*) (Arts and Humanities; Child Care and Development; Development Studies; Developmental Psychology; Educational and Student Counselling; Literature; Physical Education; Welfare and Protective Services); **Music** (*Also postgraduate and research programme*) (Art Management; Art Therapy; Business Administration; Jazz and Popular Music; Management; Music; Music Education; Music Theory and Composition; Musical Instruments; Musicology; Opera; Performing Arts; Singing)
Main language(s) of instruction: Japanese
Accrediting agency: Japan University Accreditation Association (JUAA)
Degrees and diplomas: Gakushi, Shushi (Child Care and Development; Design; Fine Arts; Music; Musical Instruments; Singing)
Last Update: 08-01-2018

Nagoya University of Arts and Sciences (NUAS)

57 Takenoyama Iwasakicho
Nisshin-shi 470-0196, Aichi
Tel: +81(561) 75-7111
Fax: +81(561) 73-8539
Website: http://www.nuas.ac.jp
Akihiro Igata

College

Junior College (Business Administration; Design; Health Sciences)

School

Human Care Studies (Child Care and Development); **Media and Design** (Design; Fashion Design; Graphic Design; Media Studies; Video; Visual Arts); **Nutritional Sciences** (Food Science; Nutrition)

Institute

Comes (Child Care and Development; Health Sciences; Nutrition)

Graduate School

Child Care (Child Care and Development); **Media and Design** (Design; Media Studies); **Nutritional Sciences** (Management; Nutrition)

History: Founded 2002.

Fees: Tuition, 700,000-985,000 per annum (Yen)

Main language(s) of instruction: Japanese

Accrediting agency: Japan Institution for Higher Education Evaluation (JIHEE)

Degrees and diplomas: Associate's Degree (Academic) (Business Administration; Design; Health Sciences), Gakushi (Child Care and Development; Design; Fashion Design; Media Studies; Nutrition), Shushi (Child Care and Development; Design; Media Studies; Nutrition), Hakase (Nutrition)

Student Services: Sports Facilities, Health Services, Library

Last Update: 08-01-2018

Nagoya University of Commerce and Business (NUCB)

4-4 Sagamine Komenoki-cho
Nisshin-shi 470-0193, Aichi
Tel: +81(52) 203-8111
Fax: +81(561) 73-1202
Website: http://www.nucba.ac.jp
President: Hiroshi Kurimoto

Faculty

Commerce (Accountancy; Business Administration; Finance; Law; Management; Marketing); **Communication** (Communication Studies; Cultural Studies; English; International Studies; Modern Languages; Political Sciences; Social Studies); **Economics** (Economic and Finance Policy; Economics; Finance; International Economics; International Law; Marketing); **Management** (Business Administration; Economics; Information Management; Information Sciences; Law; Management; Marketing)

Course/Programme

Executive MBA (*Graduate*) (Accountancy; Business Administration; Human Resources; Law; Leadership; Management; Marketing); **Global MBA** (*Graduate*) (Accountancy; Business Administration; Economics; Finance; International Business; Leadership; Management; Marketing); **Management** (*Graduate*) (Management); **Taxation** (*Graduate*) (Accountancy; Business Administration; Finance; Taxation)

History: Founded 1935, acquired present status 1953. International College founded 1982. Faculty of Foreign Languages and Asian Studies founded 1998.

Academic year: April to February (April-July; September-February)

Admission requirements: Graduation from high school and entrance examination

Fees: Faculty of Foreign Language and Faculty of Accounting and Finance: 1,432,000 per annum; Faculty of Management and Information Science: 1,392,000 per annum; Faculty of Business Administration: 1,342,00 per annum (Yen)

Main language(s) of instruction: Japanese, English

Accrediting agency: Japan Institution for Higher Education Evaluation (JIHEE)

Degrees and diplomas: Gakushi (Accountancy; Asian Studies; Business Administration; Business and Commerce; Cultural Studies; English; Finance; International Studies), Shushi (Accountancy; Business Administration; Finance; International Business; Management; Taxation). Also Diploma in Cross Cultural Studies, and Teaching Qualifications, 2 yrs

Student Services: Academic Counselling, Careers Guidance, Sports Facilities, Language Laboratory, Health Services, Canteen, Residential Facilities

Periodicals: NUCB Journal of Economics and Management, NUCB Journal of Language, Culture and Communication

Last Update: 08-01-2018

Nagoya University of Economics

61-1 Uchikubo
Inuyama-shi 484-8504, Aichi
Tel: +81(568) 67-0624
Website: http://www.nagoya-ku.ac.jp
President: Haruo Satoshi

Faculty

Business Administration (Accountancy; Business Administration; English; Finance; Health Sciences; History; Human Resources; Information Technology; Japanese; Law; Marketing; Modern Languages; Natural Sciences; Social Studies; Sports); **Economics** (Accountancy; Business Administration;

Commercial Law; Criminal Law; Cultural Studies; Economics; English; Finance; Health Sciences; History; Information Technology; Japanese; Law; Marketing; Modern Languages; Natural Sciences; Small Business; Social Studies; Sports); **Human Life Sciences** (Anatomy; Biochemistry; Biology; Chemistry; Child Care and Development; Cultural Studies; Curriculum; Developmental Psychology; Education; Educational and Student Counselling; Educational Psychology; English; Food Science; Foreign Languages Education; Health Sciences; History; Management; Modern Languages; Natural Sciences; Nutrition; Pathology; Physiology; Preschool Education; Primary Education; Public Health; Social Studies; Social Welfare; Special Education; Sports; Teacher Training); **Law** (Accountancy; Administrative Law; Business Administration; Civil Law; Commercial Law; Constitutional Law; Criminal Law; Cultural Studies; English; Health Sciences; History; Information Sciences; Information Technology; International Law; Japanese; Labour Law; Law; Modern Languages; Natural Sciences; Public Law; Social Studies; Taxation)

Graduate School

Accountancy (Accountancy; Business Administration; Finance; International Business; International Economics; Management; Taxation); **Human Life Sciences** (Child Care and Development; Cooking and Catering; Food Science; Nutrition; Public Health); **Law** (Civil Law; Commercial Law; Criminal Law; International Economics; International Law; Law; Taxation)

Further information: Also Meieki Satelite Campus
History: Founded 1999. Former English name was Nagoya Keizai University
Main language(s) of instruction: Japanese
Accrediting agency: Japan Institution for Higher Education Evaluation (JIHEE)
Degrees and diplomas: Gakushi, Shushi (Child Care and Development; Law; Nutrition), Hakase (Commercial Law)
Student Services: Sports Facilities, Library
Last Update: 08-01-2018

Nagoya University of Foreign Studies (NUFS)

57 Takenoyama Iwasaki-cho
Nisshin-shi 470-0197, Aichi
Tel: +81(561) 74-1111
Fax: +81(5617) 51-723
Website: http://www-e.nufs.ac.jp
President: Ikuo Kameyama

School

Contemporary International Studies (Accountancy; Data Processing; English; Finance; International Business; Journalism; Management; Marketing; Mass Communication; Tourism; Translation and Interpretation); **Foreign Languages** (American Studies; Asian Studies; Chinese; Data Processing; East Asian Studies; English; English Studies; Foreign Languages Education; French; French Studies; Japanese)

Institute
Japanese Language (East Asian Studies; Japanese)

Centre
Japanese Education (*Bekka*) (Japanese); **Teacher Training** (Teacher Training)

Graduate School
International Studies (Chinese; Cultural Studies; Foreign Languages Education; French; International Business; International Relations; Japanese; Linguistics; Management; Native Language Education; Pedagogy)
History: Founded 1988.
Admission requirements: Japanese Language Proficiency Test or Japanese as a Foreign Language (score: 210 and higher) + Japan and the World (score: 4 and higher); Graduation from high school or equivalent for undergraduates, graduation from university for postgraduates.
Fees: Tuition, 765,000-775,000 per annum (Yen)
Main language(s) of instruction: Japanese, English
Accrediting agency: Japan University Accreditation Association (JUAA)
Degrees and diplomas: Gakushi (Business Administration; Chinese; English; Foreign Languages Education; French; International Studies; Japanese), Shushi (Business Administration; Distance Education; English; Foreign Languages Education; French; International Business; International Relations; Japanese; Linguistics; Modern Languages; Native Language Education), Hakase (Cultural Studies; English; English Studies; Foreign Languages Education; International Studies; Japanese; Native Language Education)
Student Services: Academic Counselling, Social Counselling, Careers Guidance, Sports Facilities, Language Laboratory, Health Services, Canteen, Foreign Studies Centre, Library
Periodicals: Journal of School of Foreign Languages, Journal of School of Global Business and Economics
Publishing house: Nogoya University of Foreign Studies Press

Academic Staff	MALE	FEMALE	TOTAL
FULL-TIME			c. 120
Student Numbers			
All (Foreign Included)			c. 3600

Last Update: 08-01-2018

Nagoya Women's University (NWU)

3-40 Shioji-cho Mizuho-ku
Nagoya-shi 467-8610, Aichi
Tel: +81(52) 852-1111
Fax: +81(52) 852-7470
Website: http://www.nagoya-wu.ac.jp
Chacellor: Koshibara Moyuru

Faculty

Human Life and Environmental Sciences (Biological and Life Sciences; Business Administration; Environmental Studies; Food Science; Home Economics; Nutrition); **Literature** (Child Care and Development; English; Literature; Modern Languages; Preschool Education; Primary Education)

College

College of Nagoya Women's University (Business Administration; Clothing and Sewing; Computer Science; Dietetics; Information Technology; Preschool Education)

Institute

Science and Humanities (Arts and Humanities; Natural Sciences)

Graduate School

Human Life Science (Biological and Life Sciences; Environmental Studies; Food Science; Nutrition)
Further information: Also Tempaku Campus
History: Founded 1964.
Fees: Tuition, 560,000-760,000 per annum (Yen)
Main language(s) of instruction: Japanese
Accrediting agency: Japan Institution for Higher Education Evaluation (JIHEE)
Degrees and diplomas: Gakushi, Shushi (Environmental Studies; Food Science; Nutrition), Hakase (Food Science; Nutrition)
Student Services: Sports Facilities
Last Update: 09-01-2018

Nagoya Zokei University of Art and Design

6004 Nenjozaka
Komaki-shi 485-8563, Aichi
Tel: +81(568) 79-1111
Fax: +81(568) 79-1070
Website: http://www.nzu.ac.jp
President: Ryosuke Kobayashi

School

Art and Design (Architecture; Art Management; Ceramic Art; Cinema and Television; Communication Arts; Design; Fine Arts; Graphic Design; Industrial Design; Interior Design; Jewellery Art; Painting and Drawing; Sculpture; Visual Arts)

Graduate School

Art and Design (Architecture; Cinema and Television; Communication Arts; Cultural Studies; Design; Fine Arts; Graphic Design; Industrial Design; Landscape Architecture; Media Studies; Painting and Drawing; Sculpture; Visual Arts)
History: Founded 1989 as Nagoya Zokei Geijutu Daigaku. Acquired present title 2008.
Fees: Tuition, 850,000 per annum for undergraduate programmes; 650,000 per annum for graduate programmes (Yen)
Main language(s) of instruction: Japanese
Accrediting agency: Japan Institution for Higher Education Evaluation (JIHEE)
Degrees and diplomas: Gakushi (Design; Fine Arts), Shushi (Design; Fine Arts)
Student Services: Health Services, Residential Facilities
Last Update: 09-01-2018

Nakamura Gakuen University (NGU)

5-7-1 Befu Jonan-ku
Fukuoka-shi 814-0198, Fukuoka
Tel: +81(92) 851-2531
Fax: +81(92) 841-7762
Website: http://www.nakamura-u.ac.jp
President: Kai Satoshi

Faculty

Business, Marketing and Distribution (*Also graduate school*) (Business Administration; Business and Commerce; Cultural Studies; Information Technology; International Business; International Economics; Marketing; Modern Languages; Transport Management); **Human Development** (*Also graduate school*) (Child Care and Development; Education; Preschool Education; Primary Education; Special Education; Teacher Training); **Nutritional Sciences** (Cooking and Catering; Dietetics; Food Science; Health Sciences; Nutrition; Public Health)

Graduate School

Business, Marketing and Distribution (Business Administration; Information Sciences; International Business; International Economics; Management); **Health and Nutrition** (Dietetics; Health Sciences; Nutrition); **Human Development** (Child Care and Development; Curriculum; Education; Educational Technology; Pedagogy; Social Problems; Special Education; Teacher Training; Welfare and Protective Services)

History: Founded 1965.

Academic year: April to March (April-July; September-March)

Admission requirements: Graduation from high school and entrance examination

Main language(s) of instruction: Japanese

Accrediting agency: Japan University Accreditation Association (JUAA)

Degrees and diplomas: Gakushi, Shushi (Business Administration; Child Care and Development; Dietetics; Education; Nutrition), Hakase (Nutrition)

Student Services: Academic Counselling, Social Counselling, Careers Guidance, Cultural Activities, Sports Facilities, Health Services, Canteen, Library

Last Update: 09-01-2018

Nanzan University

18 Yamazato-cho Showa-ku
Nagoya-shi 466-8673, Aichi
Tel: +81(52) 832-3112
Fax: +81(52) 833-6985
Website: http://www.nanzan-u.ac.jp
President: Yoshifumi Torisu
Tel: +81(52) 832-3113

Faculty

Business Administration (Accountancy; Business Administration; Finance; Marketing); **Economics** (Economics); **Foreign Studies** (American Studies; Anthropology; Arts and Humanities; Asian Studies; Chinese; Cultural Studies; Economics; English; English Studies; French; French Studies; German; Germanic Studies; History; Japanese; Latin American Studies; Linguistics; Literature; Modern Languages; Philosophy; Political Sciences; Social Sciences; Sociology; Spanish); **Humanities** (Anthropology; Archaeology; Arts and Humanities; Asian Studies; Bible; Christian Religious Studies; Japanese; Native Language Education; Philosophy; Psychology); **Information Sciences and Engineering** (*Seto Campus*) (Computer Engineering; Computer Science; Information Technology; Mathematics and Computer Science; Operations Research; Software Engineering; Statistics); **Law** (Law), **Policy Studies** (*Seto Campus*) (Administration; English; French; German; History; International Studies; Korean; Political Sciences; Social Policy; Sociology; Spanish)

College
Junior Studies (English)

Institute
Anthropology (Anthropology; Cultural Studies; Ethnology; Folklore); **Religion and Culture** (Cultural Studies; Philosophy; Religion); **Social Ethics** (Arts and Humanities; Ethics; Human Rights; Law; Social Problems; Sociology)

Centre

American Studies (American Studies); **Asia-Pacific Studies** (Asian Studies; Pacific Area Studies); **English Education** (*Nanzan*) (English); **European Studies** (European Studies); **Japanese Studies** (*for Foreign students*) (Asian Studies; Japanese); **Latin-American Studies** (Latin American Studies); **Teacher Education** (Teacher Training)

Graduate School

Business Administration (Business Administration; Management); **Economics** (Economics); **Humanities** (Anthropology; Arts and Humanities; Christian Religious Studies; Education; Linguistics; Modern Languages; Religious Studies); **International Area Studies** (International Studies); **Law** (Law); **Mathematical Sciences and Information Engineering** (*Seto Campus*) (Information Technology; Mathematics and Computer Science); **Policy Studies** (*Seto Campus*) (Public Administration); **Sciences and Engineering** (*Seto Campus*) (Automation and Control Engineering; Mathematics and Computer Science; Software Engineering)

Research Division

Legal Practice Education and Research (Law); **Linguistics** (Linguistics); **Management Studies** (Accountancy; Business and Commerce; Finance; Human Resources; Management); **Mathematical Sciences and Information Engineering** (Computer Engineering; Computer Networks; Operations Research; Statistics; Telecommunications Engineering); **Study of Human Relations** (Social Sciences)

History: Founded 1932 as Nanzan Middle School for Boys by the Society of the Divine Word, acquired present status 1949.

Academic year: April to March (April-July; September-February)

Admission requirements: Graduation from high school or foreign equivalent, and entrance examination

Fees: First year, 1,265,200; subsequent years, 953,000 (Yen)

Main language(s) of instruction: Japanese

Accrediting agency: Japan University Accreditation Association (JUAA)

Degrees and diplomas: Gakushi (Arts and Humanities; Business Administration; Computer Engineering; Cultural Studies; Economics; Information Technology; Law; Modern Languages; Public Administration; Social Sciences), Shushi (Administration; Anthropology; Automation and Control Engineering; Business Administration; Christian Religious Studies; Cultural Studies; Economics; Education; Electronic Engineering; Information Technology; International Studies; Management; Mathematics; Mathematics and Computer

Science; Modern Languages; Public Administration; Software Engineering), Hakase (Anthropology; Economics; Information Technology; International Studies; Management; Mathematics; Modern Languages; Public Administration; Religious Studies). Also Professional Postgraduate Programmes in Law and Business Administration

Student Services: Academic Counselling, Careers Guidance, Sports Facilities, Language Laboratory, Facilities for disabled people, Health Services, Canteen, Foreign Studies Centre, Library, eLibrary, IT Centre

Periodicals: Academia-Humanities and Social Sciences, Academia-Literature and Language, Academia-Mathematical Sciences and Information Engineering, Academia-Natural Science, Health and Physical Education, Asian Folklore Studies, Bulletin of the Center for International Education, Nanzan University, Bulletin of the Nanzan Centre for Asia-Pacific Studies, Bulletin of the Nanzan Centre for European Studies, Bulletin of the Nanzan Institute for Religion and Culture (in English), Bulletin of the Nanzan Institute for Religion and Culture (in Japanese), Human Relations, Japanese Journal of Religious Studies, Nanzan Journal of American Studies, Nanzan Journal of Economic Studies, Nanzan Law Review, Nanzan Linguistics, Nanzan Management Review, Nanzan Review of Theological Studies, Nanzan Studies on Japanese Language and Culture, Perspectivas Latinoamericanas, Society and Ethics

Last Update: 26-03-2018

Nara University

1500 Misasagi-cho
Nara-shi 631-8502, Nara
Tel: +81(742) 44-1251
Fax: +81(742) 41-0650
Website: http://www.nara-u.ac.jp
President: Tetsuro Shimizu

Faculty

Letters (*Also graduate school*) (Archaeology; Art History; Arts and Humanities; Cultural Studies; Geography; Geography (Human); History; Japanese; Literature; Modern Languages); **Sociology** (*Also graduate school*) (Clinical Psychology; Psychology; Sociology)

College

Liberal Arts (Arts and Humanities; Health Sciences; Modern Languages; Sports)

Department/Division

Distance Education (Cultural Studies; Heritage Preservation; History)

Graduate School

Graduate Studies (Archiving; Geography; Heritage Preservation; Literature; Sociology)

History: Founded 1969 as a college of four Departments (Literature, Japanese Literature, History and Geography). Acquired present status 1988.

Academic year: April to March

Admission requirements: High school graduation or equivalent diploma and entrance examination

Fees: 980,000 per annum (Yen)

Main language(s) of instruction: Japanese

Accrediting agency: Japan Institution for Higher Education Evaluation (JIHEE)

Degrees and diplomas: Gakushi, Shushi (Archiving; Cultural Studies; Geography; Heritage Preservation; Literature; Sociology)

Student Services: Academic Counselling, Social Counselling, Nursery Care, Facilities for disabled people, Canteen, Library, IT Centre

Periodicals: Graduate School Research Annual Report, Memoirs of Nara University

Last Update: 09-01-2018

Naragakuen University (NSU)

3-12-1 Tatsunokita Sango-cho
Ikomo-gun 636-8503, Nara
Tel: +81(745) 73-7800
Fax: +81(745) 72-0822
Website: http://www.naragakuen-u.jp
President: Tsuji Kiichiro

Faculty

Buiness (Accountancy; Business Administration; Finance; Management; Marketing; Public Administration; Sports Management; Taxation; Tourism); **Informatics** (Computer Engineering; Computer Networks; Computer Science; Data Processing; Information Technology; Software Engineering)

History: Founded 1984. Former Nara Sangyo University

Main language(s) of instruction: Japanese

Accrediting agency: Japan Institution for Higher Education Evaluation (JIHEE)

Degrees and diplomas: Gakushi

Student Services: Academic Counselling, Library

Last Update: 09-01-2018

Nihon Bunka University

977 Katakura-cho
Hachioji-shi 192-0986, Tokyo
Tel: +81(42) 636-5211

Website: http://www.nihonbunka-u.ac.jp
President: Endo Toyotaga

Course/Programme
Business Administration (Business Administration);
Psychology (Psychiatry and Mental Health; Psychology);
Public Administration (Administrative Law; Public Administration)
History: Founded 1978.
Main language(s) of instruction: Japanese
Accrediting agency: Japan Institution for Higher Education Evaluation (JIHEE)
Degrees and diplomas: Gakushi
Last Update: 09-01-2018

Nihon Fukushi University

Okuda,Mihama-cho Chita-gun, Aichi-ken
Mihama-shi 470-3295, Chiba
Tel: +81(569) 87-2212
Fax: +81(569) 87-2314
Website: http://www.n-fukushi.ac.jp
President: Yushiro Kodama

Faculty
Child Development (Child Care and Development; Clinical Psychology; Primary Education; Psychology; Vocational Education); **Economics** (Business Administration; Economics; Finance; Health Administration; International Economics); **Health Sciences** (Health Sciences; Information Sciences; Nursing; Occupational Therapy; Physical Therapy; Rehabilitation and Therapy); **International Welfare Development** (English; Information Technology; International Business; Transport and Communications; Welfare and Protective Services); **Social Welfare** (Health Sciences; Psychiatry and Mental Health; Social Welfare; Social Work; Welfare and Protective Services); **Welfare and Business Administration** (*Distance Learning*) (Business Administration; Health Administration; Psychiatry and Mental Health; Social Work; Welfare and Protective Services)

Institute
Health Sciences (Health Sciences); **Social Development Studies** (Development Studies; Social Welfare)

Centre
Health and Social Research (Epidemiology; Health Sciences; Social Studies); **Welfare Policy Evaluation** (Social Policy; Welfare and Protective Services); **Welfare Technology** (Information Technology)

Graduate School
Health and Social Services Management (Health Administration; Social Welfare; Welfare and Protective Services); **International Social Development** (Development Studies; Social and Community Services; Welfare and Protective Services); **Social Welfare Studies** (Clinical Psychology; Social Welfare); **Social Well-Being and Development** (Development Studies; Health Administration; Social Welfare)

Research Division
Asia Welfare and Social Development (Development Studies; Social Welfare; Welfare and Protective Services); **Chita Peninsula** (Cultural Studies; History); **Clinical Psychology** (Clinical Psychology); **Community Care** (Social and Community Services)
History: Founded 1953, acquired present status and title 1957.
Academic year: April to March (April-September; October-March)
Admission requirements: Graduation from high school and entrance examination (in Japanese Language)
Main language(s) of instruction: Japanese
Accrediting agency: Japan University Accreditation Association (JUAA)
Degrees and diplomas: Gakushi (Business Administration; Child Care and Development; Economics; Health Sciences; Social Welfare; Welfare and Protective Services), Shushi (Clinical Psychology; Development Studies; Health Administration; Social Welfare), Hakase (Development Studies; Health Administration; Social Welfare)
Student Services: Academic Counselling, Social Counselling, Careers Guidance, Sports Facilities, Facilities for disabled people, Health Services, Canteen, Foreign Studies Centre
Periodicals: Annual Bulletin of Institute of Alternative Systems of Social Welfare Sciences and Development, Bulletin of Nihon Fukushi University, Chiiki to Rinsho, Chita Hanto no Rekishi to Genzai, Fukushi Kenkyu, Journal of Economic Studies
Last Update: 09-01-2018

Nihon Institute of Medical Science (NIMS)

Shitagawara 1276, Iruma-gun
Moroyama 350-0435, Saitama
Tel: +81 49-294-9000
Website: http://www.nims.ac.jp
President: Hiroaki Shindo

School
Health Science (Biomedical Engineering; Nursing; Radiology; Rehabilitation and Therapy)

History: Founded 1960 as Josai X-ray technology vocational school. Acquired present status and title 2007.
Main language(s) of instruction: Japanese
Accrediting agency: Japan Institution for Higher Education Evaluation (JIHEE)
Degrees and diplomas: Gakushi (Biomedical Engineering; Nursing; Occupational Therapy; Physical Therapy; Radiology)
Last Update: 09-01-2018

Nihon Pharmaceutical University (NPU)

10281 Korumo Inamachi Kita-adachi-gun
Saitama-shi 362-0806, Saitama
Tel: +81(48) 721-1155
Fax: +81(48) 721-6718
Website: http://www.nihonyakka.jp/english/index.html

School
Pharmaceutical Medical Business Sciences (Business Administration; Health Administration; Health Sciences; Pharmacy); **Pharmaceutical Sciences** (Health Sciences; Medicine; Pharmacology; Pharmacy; Traditional Eastern Medicine)
Further information: Also Ochanomizu Campus
History: Founded 2004.
Main language(s) of instruction: Japanese
Accrediting agency: Japan Institution for Higher Education Evaluation (JIHEE)
Degrees and diplomas: Gakushi (Pharmacy)
Last Update: 09-01-2018

Nihon University (NU)

4-8-24 Kudan-Minami Chiyoda-ku
Tokyo 102-8275
Tel: +81(3) 5275-8116
Fax: +81(3) 5275-8315
Website: http://www.nihon-u.ac.jp
President: Kichibee Otsuka

College
Art (Cinema and Television; Design; Film; Fine Arts; Literature; Music; Photography; Radio and Television Broadcasting; Theatre); **Bioresource Sciences** (Agricultural Business; Animal Husbandry; Biological and Life Sciences; Chemistry; Development Studies; Environmental Engineering; Environmental Studies; Food Science; Forest Products; Forestry; Marine Science and Oceanography; Plant and Crop Protection; Veterinary Science); **Commerce** (Accountancy; Business Administration; Business and Commerce); **Economics** (Economic and Finance Policy; Economics; Finance; Industrial Management); **Engineering** (Applied Chemistry; Architecture; Biology; Chemistry; Civil Engineering; Computer Science; Electrical and Electronic Engineering; Mechanical Engineering); **Humanities and Sciences** (Asian Studies; Biology; Chemistry; Chinese; Computer Science; Cultural Studies; Earth Sciences; Education; English; Geography; German; History; Information Technology; Japanese; Literature; Mathematics; Philosophy; Physical Education; Physics; Psychology; Social Welfare; Sociology; Systems Analysis); **Industrial Technology** (Applied Chemistry; Architecture; Bridge Engineering; Civil Engineering; Computer Engineering; Computer Science; Construction Engineering; Electrical and Electronic Engineering; Engineering Drawing and Design; Industrial Engineering; Industrial Management; Management; Mechanical Engineering; Road Engineering; Structural Architecture); **International Relations** (Arts and Humanities; International Relations; International Studies); **Law** (Commercial Law; Economics; Journalism; Law; Media Studies; Political Sciences; Private Law; Public Administration; Public Law); **Science and Technology** (Aeronautical and Aerospace Engineering; Applied Chemistry; Architecture; Civil Engineering; Computer Engineering; Electrical Engineering; Electronic Engineering; Marine Engineering; Materials Engineering; Mathematics; Measurement and Precision Engineering; Mechanical Engineering; Naval Architecture; Physics; Town Planning; Transport Engineering)

School
Dentistry (Dentistry); **Dentistry (Matsudo)** (Dentistry); **Law** (*Professional Graduate Course*) (Civil Law; Criminal Law; Fiscal Law; International Law; Labour Law; Law; Private Law; Public Law); **Medicine** (Medicine); **Pharmacy** (Pharmacy)

Department/Division
Distance Learning (Business and Commerce; Economics; English; History; Japanese; Law; Literature; Political Sciences)

Graduate School
Art (Design; Fine Arts; Literature; Music; Performing Arts; Visual Arts); **Bioresource Sciences** (Biological and Life Sciences; Environmental Engineering; Environmental Management; Natural Resources); **Business** (*Master's Programme only*) (Health Administration; International Business; Management; Small Business); **Business Administration** (*Master's Programme Only*) (Accountancy; Business Administration; Business and Commerce); **Dentistry** (*Doctor's programme only*) (Dentistry); **Dentistry (Matsudo)** (*Doctor's programme only*) (Dentistry); **Economics** (Accountancy; Economic and Finance Policy;

Economics; Finance; Fiscal Law; Small Business); **Engineering** (Architecture; Chemical Engineering; Civil Engineering; Computer Engineering; Computer Science; Electrical and Electronic Engineering; Materials Engineering; Mechanical Engineering); **Industrial Technology** (Applied Chemistry; Architecture; Civil Engineering; Computer Engineering; Electrical and Electronic Engineering; Industrial Engineering; Industrial Management; Information Technology; Mechanical Engineering; Structural Architecture); **Integrated Basic Sciences** (Chemistry; Mathematics; Mathematics and Computer Science; Physics); **Intellectual Property** (*Professional Course*) (Civil Law); **International Relations** (International Relations); **Journalism and Media** (Journalism; Media Studies); **Law** (Political Sciences; Private Law; Public Law); **Literature and Social Sciences** (Chinese; Education; English; German; History; Japanese; Literature; Philosophy; Psychology; Sociology); **Medicine** (*Doctor's programme only*) (Medicine; Social and Preventive Medicine); **Pharmacy** (Pharmacy); **Science and Technology** (Aeronautical and Aerospace Engineering; Applied Chemistry; Architecture; Civil Engineering; Electrical Engineering; Electronic Engineering; Geography; Information Sciences; Marine Engineering; Mathematics; Measurement and Precision Engineering; Mechanical Engineering; Medical Technology; Naval Architecture; Physics; Real Estate; Structural Architecture; Transport Engineering); **Social and Cultural Studies** (*Graduate Programme in Distance Learning*) (Cultural Studies; Economics; Education; Foreign Languages Education; International Business; International Economics; International Relations; Management; Political Sciences; Psychology; Statistics); **Veterinary Medicine** (*Doctor's Program Only*) (Veterinary Science)

History: Founded 1889 as Nihon Horitsu Gakko (Nihon Law School). Title changed to Nihon Daigaku 1903, acquired present status 1949.

Academic year: April to March (April-September; October-March)

Admission requirements: Graduation from high school or equivalent or foreign equivalent, and entrance examination

Fees: Undergraduate tuition, 760,000-1,220,000 per annum; Master's degree tuition, 710,000-1,110,000 per annum; Doctorate's degree tuition, 680,000-1,080,000 per annum (Yen)

Main language(s) of instruction: Japanese

Accrediting agency: Japan University Accreditation Association (JUAA)

Degrees and diplomas: Gakushi (Animal Husbandry; Arts and Humanities; Biological and Life Sciences; Business and Commerce; Dentistry; Economics; Education; Engineering; Fine Arts; Geography; International Relations; Journalism; Law; Mathematics; Medicine; Modern Languages; Natural Resources; Natural Sciences; Nursing; Pharmacy; Physical Education; Political Sciences; Psychology; Sociology; Veterinary Science), Shushi (Architecture; Biological and Life Sciences; Business Administration; Business and Commerce; Chemistry; Chinese; Civil Law; Design; Earth Sciences; Economics; Education; Engineering; English; Fine Arts; German; History; Information Sciences; Information Technology; International Relations; Japanese; Journalism; Literature; Mathematics; Media Studies; Music; Natural Resources; Performing Arts; Pharmacy; Philosophy; Physics; Political Sciences; Private Law; Psychology; Public Law; Real Estate; Sociology; Visual Arts), Hakase (Aeronautical and Aerospace Engineering; Animal Husbandry; Applied Chemistry; Architecture; Biological and Life Sciences; Business and Commerce; Chemistry; Chinese; Civil Engineering; Computer Engineering; Dentistry; Earth Sciences; Economics; Education; Electrical and Electronic Engineering; Electrical Engineering; Electronic Engineering; Engineering; English; Geography; Geography (Human); German; History; Industrial Engineering; Industrial Management; Information Sciences; Information Technology; International Relations; Japanese; Journalism; Literature; Mathematics; Measurement and Precision Engineering; Mechanical Engineering; Media Studies; Medical Technology; Medicine; Natural Resources; Naval Architecture; Pharmacy; Philosophy; Physics; Political Sciences; Private Law; Psychology; Public Law; Real Estate; Sociology; Structural Architecture; Transport Engineering; Veterinary Science). Also Postgraduate Professional Degree in Law

Student Services: Library, Residential Facilities

Periodicals: Annual Reports of The Institute of Information Sciences, Artistic Works, College of Art, Nihon University, Bulletin of Liberal Arts and Sciences, Nihon University School of Medicine, Comparative Law, Hogaku Kenkyu Nenpo, Hogaku Kiyo, Information Science Studies, International Journal of Oral-Medical Sciences, Journal of College of Industrial Technology, Nihon University, Journal of Intellectual Property, Journal of Oral Science, Journal of the College of Engineering, Nihon University, Journal of The College of International Relations, Nihon University, Journal of the Research Institute of Science and Technology, College of Science and Technology, Nihon University, Journalism and Media, Keikaken Reports, Keizai Shushi, Kiyo, Nihon Daigaku Seibutsushigenkagakubu ei Kenkyu, Nihon Daigaku Seibutsushigenkagakubu Sogokenkyujyo Kenkyugyosekishu, Nihon Daigaku Tushinkyouikubu Kenkyu Kiyou, Nihon Hogaku, Nihon University Business Research, Nihon University GSSC Journal, Nihon University Law Review, Nihon University of Journal of Business, Nihon University of Journal of Humanities and Sciences, Omon Ronso, Proceedings of The Institute of Natural Sciences Nihon University, Report of The Research Institute of Industrial Technology, Nihon University, Report of The Research Institute of Sciences for Living, College of International Relations, Nihon University, Research Bulletin in Liberal Arts, Research in Arts, College of Art, Nihon University,

Sangyo Keiei Kenkyu, Seikei Kenkyu, Shoho, Studies in Humanities and Social Sciences, Studies in International Relations, College of International Relations, Nihon University, Survey Report on Business Administration Trends, The Nihon University Journal of Medicine, The Study of Accounting, The Study of Business and Industry, Transactions of Nihon University School of Dentistry, Yakugakubu Kenkyu Kiyou

Academic Staff 2013-2014	MALE	FEMALE	TOTAL
FULL-TIME			2887
PART-TIME	3078	762	c. 3840
Student Numbers 2013-2014			
All (Foreign Included)	53507	24144	77651
Foreign only			1200

Last Update: 09-01-2018

Nihon Wellness Sports University

Oaza Fukawa
Tone 300-1622, Ibaraki
Tel: +81 297-68-6787
Website: http://www.nihonwellness.jp
President: Michio Shibaoka

Faculty
Sports Promotion (Sports Management)
History: Founded 2012.
Main language(s) of instruction: Japanese
Accrediting agency: Ministry of Education, Culture, Sports, Science and Technology (MEXT)
Degrees and diplomas: Gakushi (Sports Management)
Last Update: 09-01-2018

Niigata Institute of Technology

1719 Fujihashi Kashiwazaki
Niigata-shi 945-1195, Niigata
Tel: +81(257) 22-8111
Fax: +81(257) 22-8112
Website: http://www.niit.ac.jp

Course/Programme
General Education (Arts and Humanities; Chinese; English; Korean; Mathematics; Physics; Russian)

Department/Division
Architecture and Building Engineering (Architecture; Construction Engineering; Environmental Engineering; Materials Engineering; Structural Architecture; Town Planning); **Environmental Science** (Bioengineering; Biotechnology; Chemistry; Environmental Engineering; Environmental Studies); **Information and Electronics Engineering** (Automation and Control Engineering; Computer Engineering; Computer Science; Electronic Engineering; Energy Engineering; Information Sciences; Information Technology; Mathematics and Computer Science; Measurement and Precision Engineering; Software Engineering; Telecommunications Services); **Mechanical and Control Engineering** (Automation and Control Engineering; Electronic Engineering; Industrial Engineering; Mechanical Engineering; Robotics)
History: Founded 1995.
Academic year: April to March (April-September; October-March)
Main language(s) of instruction: Japanese, English
Accrediting agency: Japan University Accreditation Association (JUAA)
Degrees and diplomas: Gakushi, Shushi (Artificial Intelligence; Bioengineering; Energy Engineering; Information Technology; Materials Engineering; Mechanical Engineering; Production Engineering; Structural Architecture; Telecommunications Engineering), Hakase (Artificial Intelligence; Bioengineering; Production Engineering; Structural Architecture)
Student Services: Academic Counselling, Careers Guidance, Sports Facilities, Library, Residential Facilities

Academic Staff 2013-2014	MALE	FEMALE	TOTAL
FULL-TIME			48
Student Numbers 2013-2014			
All (Foreign Included)			664

Last Update: 29-03-2018

Niigata Sangyo University (NSU)

4730 Karuigawa
Kashiwazaki-shi 945-1393, Niigata
Tel: +81(257) 24-6655
Fax: +81(257) 22-1300
Website: http://www.nsu.ac.jp
President: Kitahara Yasuo

Faculty
Economics (Accountancy; Agricultural Business; Business Administration; Development Studies; Economics; Management; Social and Community Services; Tourism)

Course/Programme
Museum Curator (Museum Management); **Teacher Training** (Teacher Training)

Institute
East Asia Economic and Cultural Studies (East Asian Studies; Economics)

Graduate School
Economics (Economics; Management)
History: Founded 1988.
Fees: Tuition, 660,000 per annum (Yen)
Main language(s) of instruction: Japanese
Accrediting agency: Japan University Accreditation Association (JUAA)
Degrees and diplomas: Gakushi, Shushi (Economics)
Student Services: Sports Facilities, Library
Last Update: 09-01-2018

Niigata Seiryo University (NSU)

1-5939, suido-cho Chuo-ku
Niigata-shi 951-8121, Niigata
Tel: +81(25) 266-0127
Fax: +81(25) 267-0053
Website: http://www.n-seiryo.ac.jp
Tadashi Isayama

Department/Division
Nursing (Nursing); **Social Welfare and Psychology** (Child Care and Development; Psychology; Social Welfare; Social Work; Welfare and Protective Services)

Graduate School
Clinical Psychology
Main language(s) of instruction: Japanese
Accrediting agency: Japan University Accreditation Association (JUAA)
Degrees and diplomas: Gakushi, Shushi (Clinical Psychology)
Student Services: Cultural Activities, Sports Facilities, Library, IT Centre
Last Update: 09-01-2018

Niigata University of Health and Welfare (NUHW)

1398 Shimamicho Kita-ku
Niigata-shi 950-3198, Niigata
Tel: +81(25) 257-4455
Fax: +81(25) 257-4456
Website: http://www.nuhw.ac.jp
President: Masaharu Yamamoto

Faculty
Health Sciences (Health Sciences; Nursing; Nutrition; Sports); **Healthcare Management** (Computer Science; Health Administration; Information Management); **Medical Technology** (Medical Technology; Occupational Therapy; Physical Therapy; Speech Therapy and Audiology); **Social Welfare** (Social Welfare)

Graduate School
Health and Welfare (Health Sciences; Medical Technology; Nutrition; Occupational Therapy; Physical Therapy; Rehabilitation and Therapy; Social Policy; Social Welfare; Speech Therapy and Audiology; Sports; Welfare and Protective Services)
Further information: Niigata Rehabilitation Hospital and Toyoura hospital
History: Founded 2001.
Fees: Entrance fee, 250,000-350,000; Tuition fee, 400,000-550,000 per annum (Yen)
Main language(s) of instruction: Japanese
Accrediting agency: Japan Institution for Higher Education Evaluation (JIHEE)
Degrees and diplomas: Gakushi (Health Administration; Health Sciences; Medical Technology; Social Welfare), Shushi (Health Administration; Health Sciences; Information Management; Rehabilitation and Therapy; Social Welfare), Hakase (Health Sciences; Welfare and Protective Services)
Student Services: Library
Periodicals: Niigata Journal of Health and Welfare

Academic Staff 2013-2014	MALE	FEMALE	TOTAL
FULL-TIME			207
Student Numbers 2013-2014			
All (Foreign Included)			3439
Foreign only			4

Last Update: 10-01-2018

Niigata University of International and Information Studies

3-1-1 Mizukino Niigata-shi
Niigata-shi 950-2292, Niigata
Tel: +81(25) 239-3111
Fax: +81(25) 239-3690
Website: http://www.nuis.ac.jp
President: Ikuo Hirayama

Faculty
Information and Culture (American Studies; Asian Studies; Chinese; Computer Engineering; Computer Networks;

Cultural Studies; English; Information Management; Information Sciences; Information Technology; Korean; Management; Modern Languages; Russian; Software Engineering; Telecommunications Engineering)

History: Founded 1994.

Fees: Tuition, 675,000 per annum (Yen)

Main language(s) of instruction: Japanese

Accrediting agency: Japan Institution for Higher Education Evaluation (JIHEE)

Degrees and diplomas: Gakushi (Information Sciences)

Student Services: Sports Facilities, Language Laboratory, Canteen, Library

Last Update: 10-01-2018

Niigata University of Management

2909-2 Kibo-ga-oka

Kamo-shi 959-1321, Niigata

Tel: +81(256) 53-3000

Fax: +81(256) 53-4544

Website: http://www.niigataum.ac.jp

President: Tomatsu Watanabe

Department/Division

Management and Information Science (Accountancy; Business Administration; Commercial Law; Information Management; Information Sciences; Information Technology; Management; Marketing; Small Business; Taxation); **Sports Management** (Business Administration; Business and Commerce; Law; Management; Marketing; Sociology; Sports; Sports Management; Statistics)

History: Founded 1994.

Main language(s) of instruction: Japanese

Accrediting agency: Japan Institution for Higher Education Evaluation (JIHEE)

Degrees and diplomas: Gakushi (Information Sciences; Management; Sports Management)

Student Services: Sports Facilities, Library

Last Update: 10-01-2018

Niigata University of Pharmacy and Applied Life Sciences (NUPALS)

Higashijima 265-1 Akiha-ku

Niigata-shi 956-8603, Niigata

Tel: +81(250) 25-5000

Fax: +81(250) 25-5021

Website: http://www.nupals.ac.jp

President: Hiroshi Terada

Department/Division

Applied Life Sciences (Bioengineering; Biological and Life Sciences; Environmental Studies; Food Science; Health Sciences; Science Education); **Pharmacy** (Biology; Chemistry; Community Health; Health Sciences; Medicine; Pharmacy; Physics)

Graduate School

Applied Life Sciences (Analytical Chemistry; Applied Chemistry; Biochemistry; Biological and Life Sciences; Cell Biology; Chemistry; Environmental Engineering; Food Science; Food Technology; Hygiene; Medicine; Microbiology; Pharmacology; Public Health); **Pharmaceutical Sciences** (Analytical Chemistry; Applied Chemistry; Biochemistry; Chemistry; Community Health; Hygiene; Microbiology; Pathology; Pharmacology; Pharmacy; Physics)

History: Founded 1977 as Niigata College of Pharmacy. Acquired present title and status 2002.

Academic year: April to March

Admission requirements: Graduation from high school or equivalent

Main language(s) of instruction: Japanese

Accrediting agency: Ministry of Education, Culture, Sports, Science and Technology (MEXT)

Degrees and diplomas: Gakushi, Shushi (Biological and Life Sciences), Hakase (Biological and Life Sciences; Pharmacy)

Student Services: Social Counselling, Careers Guidance, Sports Facilities, Health Services, Canteen

Periodicals: Bulletin

Last Update: 26-03-2018

Niigata University of Rehabilitation (NUR)

2-16 Kaminoyama

Murakami 958-0053, Niigata

Tel: +81(254) 56-8292

Fax: +81(254) 56-8291

Website: http://nur.ac.jp

President: Chie Yamamura

Department/Division

Occupational Therapy (Occupational Therapy); **Physical Therapy** (Physical Therapy); **Speech and Hearing** (Speech Therapy and Audiology)

Graduate School

Rehabilitation (Occupational Therapy; Rehabilitation and Therapy; Speech Therapy and Audiology)

History: Founded 2007.

Fees: Undergraduate Admission Fee, 350,000; Tuition fee, 500,000 per annum. Graduate entrance fee, 30,000; Tuition fee, 1,100,000 per annum (Yen)
Main language(s) of instruction: Japanese
Accrediting agency: Japan University Accreditation Association (JUAA)
Degrees and diplomas: Gakushi (Rehabilitation and Therapy), Shushi (Rehabilitation and Therapy)
Student Services: Library, Residential Facilities
Last Update: 10-01-2018

Nippon Bunri University (NBU)

1727 Ichigi
Oita-shi 870-0397, Oita
Tel: +81(97) 592-1600
Fax: +81(97) 593-2071
Website: http://www.nbu.ac.jp
President: Sadayoshi Suga

Faculty

Economics (Accountancy; Business Administration; Communication Studies; Economics; Finance; Information Technology; Management; Psychology; Sports Management; Welfare and Protective Services); **Engineering** (Aeronautical and Aerospace Engineering; Architecture; Electrical Engineering; Information Technology; Mechanical Engineering; Media Studies)

Course/Programme

Japanese (*Bekka*) (Japanese)

Graduate School

Engineering (Aeronautical and Aerospace Engineering; Biotechnology; Electronic Engineering; Environmental Studies; Industrial Engineering; Information Sciences; Mechanical Engineering; Physical Engineering; Robotics; Town Planning)
History: Founded 1967. Acquired present status 1982.
Main language(s) of instruction: Japanese
Accrediting agency: Japan Institution for Higher Education Evaluation (JIHEE)
Degrees and diplomas: Gakushi (Business Administration; Economics; Engineering), Shushi (Engineering)
Last Update: 10-01-2018

Nippon Dental University

1-9-20 Fujimi Chiyoda-ku
Tokyo 102-8159
Tel: +81(3) 3261-8311

Fax: +81(3) 3261-8086
Website: http://www.ndu.ac.jp
President: Izumi Nakahara

School

Life Dentistry (Dental Hygiene; Dental Technology; Dentistry; Medicine)

Graduate School

Life Dentistry (Anaesthesiology; Anatomy; Biochemistry; Dental Technology; Dentistry; Histology; Microbiology; Oral Pathology; Orthodontics; Paediatrics; Pathology; Periodontics; Pharmacology; Physiology; Radiology)

Research Division

Advanced Research (Biological and Life Sciences; Dental Technology; Oral Pathology); **Odontology** (Dentistry)
Further information: Also campus in Niigata; 3 affiliated hospitals (Nippon Dental University Affiliated Hospital, Nippon Dental University Niigata Dental Hospital, and Nippon Dental University Medical Hospital)
History: Founded 1907 as Private Kyoritsu Dental School. Reorganized and acquired present name 1949. Graduate School added 1960.
Academic year: April to March (April-September; October-March)
Admission requirements: Graduation from high school or equivalent, and entrance examination
Main language(s) of instruction: Japanese
Accrediting agency: Japan Institution for Higher Education Evaluation (JIHEE)
Degrees and diplomas: Gakushi (Dentistry), Hakase (Dentistry)
Student Services: Sports Facilities
Periodicals: Bulletin, Odontology

Academic Staff 2013-2014	MALE	FEMALE	TOTAL
FULL-TIME			c. 1000
Student Numbers 2013-2014			
All (Foreign Included)			c. 2000

Last Update: 28-02-2018

Nippon Institute of Technology

4-1 Gakuendai Miyashiro-machi
Minamisaitama-gun 345-8501, Saitama
Tel: +81(480) 34-4111
Fax: +81(480) 34-7527
Website: http://www.nit.ac.jp
President: Ken-ichi Narita

Faculty

Engineering (Architectural and Environmental Design; Architecture; Arts and Humanities; Computer Engineering; Electrical and Electronic Engineering; Engineering; English; Environmental Management; Environmental Studies; Information Technology; Mathematics; Mechanical Engineering; Modern Languages; Nanotechnology; Natural Sciences; Physical Education; Physics; Production Engineering; Robotics; Sociology)

Course/Programme

Japanese Language for Overseas Students (Chemistry; Computer Science; English; Japanese; Mathematics; Physics)

Graduate School

Engineering (Architecture; Automation and Control Engineering; Computer Engineering; Electrical Engineering; Information Sciences; Information Technology; Mechanical Engineering; Power Engineering; Software Engineering); **Management of Technology** (Business Administration; Engineering Management; Management; Small Business)
History: Founded 1967. Graduate School established 1982.
Academic year: April to March (April-September; October-March)
Admission requirements: Graduation from high school or technical high school, and entrance examination
Main language(s) of instruction: Japanese, English
Accrediting agency: Japan University Accreditation Association (JUAA)
Degrees and diplomas: Gakushi (Engineering), Shushi (Architecture; Artificial Intelligence; Computer Engineering; Computer Graphics; Electrical Engineering; Engineering; Information Technology; Mechanical Engineering; Production Engineering; Software Engineering; Telecommunications Engineering), Hakase (Architecture and Planning; Automation and Control Engineering; Computer Engineering; Electrical Engineering; Electronic Engineering; Energy Engineering; Engineering; Information Technology; Measurement and Precision Engineering; Mechanical Engineering; Power Engineering; Production Engineering; Robotics; Structural Architecture)
Student Services: Library
Periodicals: Research Reports
Last Update: 10-01-2018

Nippon Medical School

1-1-5, Sendagi Bunkyo-ku
Tokyo 113-8602
Tel: +81(3) 3822-2131
Fax: +81(3) 5802-1947

Website: http://www.nms.ac.jp
President: Akihiro Chori

School

Medicine (Anatomy; Biochemistry; Biology; English; Gastroenterology; Immunology; Medicine; Microbiology; Modern Languages; Pathology; Pharmacology; Physiology; Public Health; Respiratory Therapy; Sociology; Statistics)

Graduate School

Medicine (Anaesthesiology; Anatomy; Biochemistry; Biological and Life Sciences; Biology; Cardiology; Cell Biology; Diabetology; Embryology and Reproduction Biology; Endocrinology; Gastroenterology; Genetics; Gerontology; Gynaecology and Obstetrics; Haematology; Health Administration; Hepatology; Hygiene; Immunology; Information Sciences; Medicine; Microbiology; Molecular Biology; Nephrology; Neurology; Nutrition; Oncology; Ophthalmology; Orthopaedics; Paediatrics; Pathology; Pharmacology; Physiology; Plastic Surgery; Psychiatry and Mental Health; Public Health; Radiology; Social and Preventive Medicine; Surgery; Urology)
Further information: Also Shinmaruko Campus; Four Affiliated Hospitals
History: Founded 1904 as School, became College 1912, acquired present status 1925.
Academic year: April to March (April-July; September-December; January-March)
Admission requirements: Graduation from high school and entrance examination
Main language(s) of instruction: Japanese, English
Accrediting agency: Japan Institution for Higher Education Evaluation (JIHEE)
Degrees and diplomas: Gakushi (Medicine), Hakase (Medicine)
Student Services: Foreign Studies Centre, Library
Periodicals: Journal
Last Update: 10-01-2018

Nippon Sport Science University (NSSU)

7-1-1 Fukasawa Setagaya-ku
Tokyo 158-8508, Kanto
Tel: +81(3) 5706-0900
Fax: +81(3) 5706-0912
Website: http://www.nittai.ac.jp
President: Koji Gushiken

Faculty

Sport Science (Dance; Health Education; Health Sciences; Parks and Recreation; Performing Arts; Physical Education;

Rehabilitation and Therapy; Social Welfare; Sports; Sports Management; Teacher Training)

Course/Programme
Teaching Credential in Physical Education (Physical Education; Teacher Training)

Department/Division
Physical Education and Early Childhood Education (*Women's Junior College of NSSU*) (Health Sciences; Physical Education; Preschool Education; Sports)

Graduate School
Health and Sport Science (Health Education; Health Sciences; Physical Education; Social Sciences; Sports; Sports Medicine)
Further information: Also Yokohama Kenshidai Campus
History: Founded 1891 as School, became university 1949.
Academic year: April to March (April-September; October-March)
Admission requirements: Graduation from high school or equivalent, and entrance examination
Fees: Tuition, 700,000-900,000 per annum (Yen)
Main language(s) of instruction: Japanese
Accrediting agency: Japan Institution for Higher Education Evaluation (JIHEE)
Degrees and diplomas: Gakushi (Dance; Health Education; Health Sciences; Parks and Recreation; Performing Arts; Physical Education; Social Welfare; Sports; Sports Management), Shushi (Health Education; Health Sciences; Physical Education; Social Sciences; Sports; Sports Medicine), Hakase (Health Sciences; Social Sciences; Sports; Sports Medicine)
Student Services: Academic Counselling, Social Counselling, Careers Guidance, Nursery Care, Sports Facilities, Language Laboratory, Health Services, Canteen, Library, Residential Facilities
Periodicals: Bulletin of Nippon Sports Sciences University

Academic Staff 2013-2014	MALE	FEMALE	TOTAL
FULL-TIME			174
Student Numbers 2013-2014			
All (Foreign Included)			5848

Last Update: 10-01-2018

Nippon Veterinary and Life Science University

1-7-1 Kyonancho
Musashino-shi 180-8602, Tokyo
Tel: +81(422) 31-4151
Fax: +81(422) 33-2094
Website: http://www.nvlu.ac.jp
President: Ryozo Akuzawa

Faculty
Applied Life Sciences (Animal Husbandry; Biochemistry; Biological and Life Sciences; Biotechnology; Economics; Embryology and Reproduction Biology; English; Food Science; Food Technology; Genetics; Management; Nutrition; Physiology; Zoology); **Veterinary Medicine** (Veterinary Science)

Graduate School
Veterinary Medicine and Life Science (Anatomy; Biological and Life Sciences; Environmental Studies; Epidemiology; Nursing; Public Health; Veterinary Science)

Research Division
Life Science (Biological and Life Sciences); **Molecular Oncology** (Molecular Biology; Oncology)
Further information: Also Veterinary Medical Teaching Hospital; Fuji Animal Research Farm
History: Founded 1881. Formerly known as Nippon Veterinary and Animal Sciences University.
Academic year: April to March
Admission requirements: Graduation from high school
Main language(s) of instruction: Japanese, English
Accrediting agency: Japan University Accreditation Association (JUAA)
Degrees and diplomas: Gakushi, Shushi (Biological and Life Sciences; Veterinary Science), Hakase (Biological and Life Sciences; Veterinary Science)
Student Services: Sports Facilities, Library
Last Update: 10-01-2018

Nishikyushu University

4490-9 Ozaki Kanzaki-machi
Kanzaki 842-8585, Saga
Tel: +81(952) 52-4191
Fax: +81(952) 524-4194
Website: http://www.nisikyu-u.ac.jp
President: Yuji Fukumoto

Faculty
Children's Studies (Child Care and Development; Preschool Education; Primary Education); **Health and Social Welfare Sciences** (Clinical Psychology; Health Sciences; Nutrition; Psychiatry and Mental Health; Social Welfare; Social Work; Special Education); **Rehabilitation Science** (Occupational Therapy; Physical Therapy; Rehabilitation and Therapy)

Graduate School

Graduate Studies (Clinical Psychology; Dietetics; Health Sciences; Nutrition; Psychology; Rehabilitation and Therapy; Social Welfare; Social Work; Sociology)
Further information: Also Kamizono Campus
History: Founded 1968.
Main language(s) of instruction: Japanese, English
Accrediting agency: Japan University Accreditation Association (JUAA)
Degrees and diplomas: Gakushi (Child Care and Development; Education; Nutrition; Preschool Education; Social Welfare), Shushi (Clinical Psychology; Health Sciences; Nutrition; Rehabilitation and Therapy; Social and Community Services; Social Welfare), Hakase (Social and Community Services; Social Welfare)
Student Services: Sports Facilities, Canteen, Library, IT Centre
Last Update: 28-03-2018

Nishinippon Institute of Technology

1-11 Aratsu Kanda-machi
Miyako-gun 800-0394, Fukuoka
Tel: +81(930) 23-1591
Fax: +81(930) 24-7900
Website: http://www.nishitech.ac.jp
President: Nishio Kazumasa

Faculty

Engineering (Computer Engineering; Electrical and Electronic Engineering; Engineering; Environmental Engineering; Mechanical Engineering; Multimedia; Software Engineering)

School

Design (Architectural and Environmental Design; Architecture; Art Management; Communication Arts; Construction Engineering; Design; House Arts and Environment; Industrial Design; Interior Design; Media Studies)

Graduate School

Production Engineering (Environmental Engineering; Industrial Engineering; Production Engineering)
History: Founded 1967.
Fees: Tuition, 840,000 per annum (Yen)
Main language(s) of instruction: Japanese
Accrediting agency: Japan University Accreditation Association (JUAA)
Degrees and diplomas: Gakushi (Engineering), Shushi (Environmental Engineering; Industrial Engineering)

Student Services: Sports Facilities, Canteen, Library, IT Centre, Residential Facilities

Academic Staff 2013-2014	MALE	FEMALE	TOTAL
FULL-TIME			133
Student Numbers 2013-2014			
All (Foreign Included)			1534

Last Update: 10-01-2018

Nishogakusha University

6-16, Sanbancho
Chiyoda-ku 102-8336, Tokyo
Tel: +81(3) 3261-7423
Fax: +81(3) 3261-8904
Website: http://www.nishogakusha-u.ac.jp
President: Junko Sugahara

Faculty

International Politics and Economics (Administration; East Asian Studies; International Business; International Economics; International Relations; Law; Political Sciences; Social Studies); **Literature** (Arts and Humanities; Asian Studies; Chinese; Comparative Literature; Cultural Studies; East Asian Studies; Fine Arts; Japanese; Korean; Literature; Media Studies; Modern Languages; Theatre)

Graduate School

International Politics and Economics (Business Administration; International Business; International Economics; International Studies; Political Sciences); **Literature** (Chinese; Cultural Studies; East Asian Studies; History; Japanese; Literature; Native Language Education; Oriental Studies)
Further information: Also Kashiwa campus
History: Founded 1877.
Main language(s) of instruction: Japanese
Accrediting agency: Japan University Accreditation Association (JUAA)
Degrees and diplomas: Gakushi (Economics; International Studies; Literature), Shushi (Chinese; International Economics; International Studies; Japanese; Literature; Native Language Education), Hakase (Chinese; Japanese; Literature)
Student Services: Library, IT Centre

Student Numbers 2013-2014	MALE	FEMALE	TOTAL
All (Foreign Included)	1578	1411	2989
Foreign only	10	18	28

Last Update: 10-01-2018

North Asia University (NAU)

46-1 Mamorisawa Shimokitate-sakura
Akita-shi 010-8515, Akita
Fax: +81(18) 836-3321
Website: http://www.nau.ac.jp/eng
President: Ken Koizumi

Faculty

Economics (Accountancy; Business Administration; Economics; Finance; Information Technology; Management; Marketing; Transport Management); **Law** (Business Administration; Civil Law; International Business; Journalism; Law; Management; Political Sciences; Tourism)

Course/Programme

Japanese Language and Culture for Foreign Students (East Asian Studies; Japanese)
History: Founded 1953. Formerly known as Akita Keizai Hoka Daigaku (Akita University of Economics and Law). Acquired present title 2007.
Main language(s) of instruction: Japanese
Accrediting agency: Japan Institution for Higher Education Evaluation (JIHEE)
Degrees and diplomas: Gakushi (Economics; Law)
Student Services: Library, IT Centre
Last Update: 11-01-2018

Notre Dame Seishin University (NDSU)

9-16-2 Ifuku-cho
Okayama-shi 700-8516, Okayama
Tel: +81(86) 255-5585
Fax: +81(86) 255-4117
Website: http://www.ndsu.ac.jp
President: Takako Frances Takagi

Faculty

Human Life Sciences (Arts and Humanities; Child Care and Development; Cultural Studies; Dietetics; Education; Food Science; Medicine; Nutrition; Psychology; Welfare and Protective Services); **Literature** (American Studies; East Asian Studies; English; English Studies; Foreign Languages Education; Japanese; Linguistics; Literature; Social Studies; Sociology)

Centre

Language Education (*LEC*) (Foreign Languages Education; Native Language Education)

Graduate School

Letters (American Studies; Arts and Humanities; Business Administration; Clinical Psychology; Cultural Studies; Development Studies; East Asian Studies; English; English Studies; Environmental Studies; Family Studies; Folklore; Food Science; Japanese; Nutrition; Social Sciences; Social Studies; Social Welfare; Sociology; Women's Studies)

Research Division

Christian Culture (*IRCC*) (Christian Religious Studies)
History: Founded 1949 by the Sisters of Notre Dame de Namur.
Academic year: April to March
Admission requirements: Graduation from high school or recognized foreign equivalent and entrance examination for foreign students
Fees: Tuition, 560,000 per annum (Yen)
Main language(s) of instruction: Japanese, English
Accrediting agency: Japan University Accreditation Association (JUAA)
Degrees and diplomas: Associate's Degree (Academic), Gakushi, Shushi (Clinical Psychology; Cultural Studies; Development Studies; Education; English; Environmental Studies; Food Science; Health Sciences; Japanese; Literature; Nutrition; Social Studies; Sociology; Welfare and Protective Services), Hakase (Cultural Studies; Health Sciences; Japanese; Literature; Nutrition; Psychology; Welfare and Protective Services)
Student Services: Academic Counselling, Social Counselling, Careers Guidance, Sports Facilities, Language Laboratory, Facilities for disabled people, Health Services, Canteen, Foreign Studies Centre, Library

Academic Staff 2013-2014	MALE	FEMALE	TOTAL
FULL-TIME			101
Student Numbers 2013-2014			
All (Foreign Included)			2320

Last Update: 11-01-2018

Ohara Graduate School of Accounting (OCB)

1-2-10 Nishikanda Chiyoda-ku
Tokyo 101-0065
Tel: +81(3) 3237-8760
Fax: +81(3) 3234-6361
Website: http://www.o-hara.ac.jp/grad
President: Kohei Yamada

Course/Programme

Accountancy (*Graduate*) (Accountancy; Civil Law; Economics; Finance; Fiscal Law; Information Sciences; Management; Statistics; Taxation)

History: Founded 1957as O-Hara Boki School specialising in accountancy; Fully accredited in 2006

Academic year: April to March

Admission requirements: (Undergraduate): Secondary School Certificate (Sotsugyo-shosho) and entrance examination; (Graduate School): BA and entrance examination

Fees: Entrance fee, 200,000; Tuition fee, 1.1m. per annum (Yen)

Main language(s) of instruction: Japanese

Accrediting agency: Japan University Accreditation Association (JUAA)

Degrees and diplomas: Shushi (Accountancy). The Shushi/ Master's degree offered is a Professional Degree

Student Services: Academic Counselling, Careers Guidance, Sports Facilities, Language Laboratory, Facilities for disabled people, Health Services, Canteen, Library

Publishing house: O-Hara Press

Last Update: 11-01-2018

Ohkagakuen University

Takeji-48 Sakaecho
Toyoake 470-1193, Aichi
Tel: +81(562)97-6311
Fax: +81(562)97-6959
Website: http://www.ohkagakuen-u.ac.jp
President: Takeshi Ooya

Faculty

Early Childhood Care and Education (Child Care and Development; Preschool Education; Primary Education); **Liberal Arts and Science** (Arts and Humanities; Cultural Studies; English; Tourism)

School

Graduate Studies (Arts and Humanities; Cultural Studies; Social Sciences)

Further information: Also a Campus in Toyota

History: Founded 1998.

Admission requirements: Entrance examination

Main language(s) of instruction: Japanese

Accrediting agency: Japan Institution for Higher Education Evaluation (JIHEE)

Degrees and diplomas: Gakushi, Shushi

Student Services: Library

Periodicals: Bulletin of Ohkagakuen University, Cosmos

Academic Staff	MALE	FEMALE	TOTAL
PART-TIME			94
Student Numbers			
All (Foreign Included)			992

Last Update: 11-01-2018

Ohu University

31-1 Misumido Tomita-machi
Koriyama-shi 963-8611, Fukushima
Tel: +81(24) 932-9013
Fax: +81(24) 933-7372
Website: http://www.ohu-u.ac.jp
President: Kazuo Kiyono

Faculty

Dentistry (Dental Technology; Dentistry; Histology; Oral Pathology; Orthodontics; Pharmacology; Radiology; Surgery); **Pharmacy** (Analytical Chemistry; Applied Chemistry; Botany; Microbiology; Organic Chemistry; Pharmacology; Pharmacy)

Graduate School

Dentistry (Biochemistry; Biology; Dental Technology; Dentistry; Health Sciences; Immunology; Medical Technology; Microbiology; Oral Pathology; Orthodontics; Paediatrics; Periodontics; Pharmacology; Radiology; Surgery)

Further information: Also University Hospital

History: Founded 1972.

Fees: Tuition, 3,500,000 per annum for Dentistry programme; 1,500,000 per annum for Pharmaceutical Sciences programme (Yen)

Main language(s) of instruction: Japanese

Accrediting agency: Japan University Accreditation Association (JUAA)

Degrees and diplomas: Gakushi (Dentistry; Pharmacy), Hakase (Dentistry)

Academic Staff 2013-2014	MALE	FEMALE	TOTAL
FULL-TIME	135	23	158
Student Numbers 2013-2014			
All (Foreign Included)			967

Total number of part-time students: 13

Last Update: 11-01-2018

Okayama Gakuin University

787 Akuri Kurashiki-shi
Okayama-shi 710-8511, Okayama
Tel: +81(86) 428-2651
Fax: +81(86) 429-0323
Website: http://www.owc.ac.jp
President: Hiroshi Harada

Faculty

Human Life, Food and Nutrition (Dietetics; Food Science; Home Economics; Nutrition)
Main language(s) of instruction: Japanese
Accrediting agency: Japan Institution for Higher Education Evaluation (JIHEE)
Degrees and diplomas: Gakushi (Nutrition)
Student Services: Sports Facilities, Canteen, Library, IT Centre, Residential Facilities

Student Numbers 2013-2014	MALE	FEMALE	TOTAL
All (Foreign Included)			157

Last Update: 11-01-2018

Okayama Shoka University

2-10-1 Tsushima-Kyo-machi
Okayama-shi 700-8601, Okayama
Tel: +81(86) 252-0642
Fax: +81(86) 255-6947
Website: http://www.osu.ac.jp
President: Akiko Ijiri

Faculty

Business Administration (Accountancy; Business Administration; Business and Commerce; Design; Finance; Human Resources; Information Sciences; Information Technology; Management; Marketing; Tourism); **Economics** (Data Processing; Economic and Finance Policy; Economics); **Law** (Administration; Business Education; Commercial Law; Economics; Finance; Fire Science; Fiscal Law; Labour Law; Law; Management; Police Studies)

Course/Programme

Liberal Arts (Arts and Humanities; Chinese; English; Literature); **Special Tax Acountant** (*Graduate*) (Accountancy; Fiscal Law; Taxation)

Graduate School

Commerce (Accountancy; Business Administration; Business and Commerce; Finance; Industrial Management; Information Technology; Insurance; Marketing); **Economics** (Economic and Finance Policy; Economics; International Economics; Social Policy; Statistics); **Law** (Administrative Law; Constitutional Law; Fiscal Law; Labour Law; Law)
History: Founded 1965.
Academic year: April to March
Fees: Entrance fee, 220,000; Tuition fee, 660,000 per annum (except for Special Tax Accountant Course, 150,000) (Yen)
Main language(s) of instruction: Japanese
Accrediting agency: Japan Institution for Higher Education Evaluation (JIHEE)
Degrees and diplomas: Gakushi (Business Administration; Economics; Law), Shushi (Business and Commerce; Economic and Finance Policy; Economics; International Economics; Law)
Student Services: Academic Counselling, Social Counselling, Careers Guidance, Nursery Care, Sports Facilities, Language Laboratory, Health Services, Canteen

Academic Staff 2013-2014	MALE	FEMALE	TOTAL
FULL-TIME			78
Student Numbers 2013-2014			
All (Foreign Included)			c. 670

Last Update: 11-01-2018

Okayama University of Science (OUS)

1-1 Ridai-cho
Okayama-shi 700-0005, Okayama
Tel: +81(86)256-8412
Fax: +81(86)256-8452
Website: http://www.ous.ac.jp
President: Yasunobu Yanagisawa

Faculty

Biosphere-Geosphere Science (Anthropology; Archaeology; Astronomy and Space Science; Biological and Life Sciences; Earth Sciences; Ecology; Entomology; Geochemistry; Geology; Geophysics; Meteorology); **Engineering** (Applied Chemistry; Architectural and Environmental Design; Architecture; Architecture and Planning; Automotive Engineering; Biomedical Engineering; Biotechnology; Computer Engineering; Computer Networks; Cosmetology; Electrical and Electronic Engineering; Electrical Engineering; Electronic Engineering; Engineering; Information Technology; Mechanical Engineering; Mechanics); **Informatics** (Asian Studies; Computer Engineering; Computer Science; Cultural Studies; Data Processing; Earth Sciences; Economics; History; Information Sciences; Management; Mathematics; Political Sciences; Social Sciences; Software Engineering); **Science** (Applied Chemistry; Applied Mathematics; Applied Physics; Biochemistry; Biological and Life Sciences; Chemistry; Natural Sciences; Zoology)

Graduate School

Engineering (Applied Chemistry; Architecture; Automation and Control Engineering; Biomedical Engineering; Computer Engineering; Electronic Engineering; Engineering; Information Technology; Mechanical Engineering; Structural Architecture; Systems Analysis); **Informatics** (Biological and Life Sciences; Earth Sciences; Environmental Engineering; Information Sciences; Information Technology; Mathematics; Social Sciences); **Science** (Applied Mathematics; Applied Physics; Biology; Chemistry; Food Science; Natural Sciences; Zoology)

History: Founded 1962, acquired present status 1964.

Academic year: April to March (April to October; October-March)

Admission requirements: Graduation from high school or equivalent, entrance examination (OUS's test) and test of proficiency in Japanese.

Fees: 1,440,000 per annum; 220,000 for 1st entrance fee (Yen)

Main language(s) of instruction: Japanese, English

Accrediting agency: Japan University Accreditation Association (JUAA)

Degrees and diplomas: Gakushi, Shushi (Applied Chemistry; Applied Mathematics; Applied Physics; Architecture; Biological and Life Sciences; Biology; Biomedical Engineering; Chemistry; Computer Engineering; Earth Sciences; Electronic Engineering; Information Sciences; Information Technology; Mechanical Engineering; Social Sciences; Zoology), Hakase (Applied Mathematics; Computer Engineering; Environmental Engineering; Materials Engineering; Mathematics). Also Teaching credentials, Certification for Curatorship, Certification as a Technician for Sanitary Control, Certification for Food Sanitation.

Student Services: Academic Counselling, Social Counselling, Careers Guidance, Sports Facilities, Language Laboratory, Health Services, Canteen, Foreign Studies Centre, Library, IT Centre

Periodicals: Ridai-tsushin

Academic Staff 2013-2014	MALE	FEMALE	TOTAL
FULL-TIME			269
Student Numbers 2013-2014			
All (Foreign Included)			6050
Foreign only			131

Last Update: 11-01-2018

Okazaki Women's University

1-8-4 Nakamachi
Okazaki 444-0015, Aichi
Tel: +81(120) 351018
Website: http://www.okazaki-c.ac.jp
President: Hayashi Yoko

Faculty

Children Education

History: Founded 1965.

Main language(s) of instruction: Japanese

Accrediting agency: Ministry of Education, Culture, Sports, Science and Technology (MEXT)

Degrees and diplomas: Gakushi (Preschool Education)

Last Update: 11-01-2018

Okinawa Christian University

777 Onaga Nishihara-cho
Nakagami-gun 903-0207, Okinawa
Tel: +81(98) 946-1231
Fax: +81(98) 946-1241
Website: http://www.ocjc.ac.jp
President: Tomori Hiroshi

Faculty

Humanities (Arts and Humanities; Japanese)

Department/Division

English Communication (Communication Studies; English; International Business; International Studies)

Graduate School

Intercultural Communication Studies (Communication Studies; Cultural Studies; International Studies)

History: Founded 2004.

Fees: Tuition, 330,000 per annum (Yen)

Main language(s) of instruction: Japanese, English

Accrediting agency: Japan Institution for Higher Education Evaluation (JIHEE)

Degrees and diplomas: Gakushi, Shushi (Communication Studies; International Studies)

Student Services: Library

Periodicals: Journal of Okinawa Christian University

Student Numbers 2013-2014	MALE	FEMALE	TOTAL
All (Foreign Included)	131	344	475

Last Update: 11-01-2018

Okinawa Institute of Science and Technology Graduate University (OIST)

1919-1 Tancha, Onna-son
Okinawa 904-0495, Kunigami-gun
Tel: +81(98)-966-1512
Website: http://www.oist.jp
President/CEO: Peter Gruss

School

Graduate (Natural Sciences)

History: Founded 2005. Acquired present status and title 2012.

Main language(s) of instruction: English

Accrediting agency: Ministry of Education, Culture, Sports, Science and Technology (MEXT)

Degrees and diplomas: Hakase (Biological and Life Sciences; Chemistry; Marine Science and Oceanography; Mathematics; Neurosciences; Physics)

Student Services: Canteen, Library

Academic Staff 2013-2014	MALE	FEMALE	TOTAL
FULL-TIME			48
Student Numbers 2013-2014			
All (Foreign Included)			53

Last Update: 26-03-2018

Okinawa International University (OIU)

2-6-1 Ginowan
Ginowan 901-2701, Okinawa
Tel: +81(98) 892-1111
Fax: +81(98) 893-3273
Website: http://www.okiu.ac.jp
President: Eiken Maetsu

College

Economics and Environmental Policy (Economics; Environmental Management; Environmental Studies; Regional Studies); **Global and Regional Culture** (American Studies; Cultural Studies; East Asian Studies; English; English Studies; Japanese; Psychiatry and Mental Health; Psychology; Regional Studies; Social Studies; Social Welfare; Social Work; Welfare and Protective Services); **Industry and Information Sciences** (Business Administration; Business Computing; E- Business/Commerce; Information Sciences); **Law** (Administration; Law; Political Sciences)

Course/Programme

Foreign Language Education (Chinese; English; French; German; Korean; Spanish); **Information Technology Education** (Information Technology)

Institute

Economics and Environmental Studies (Economics; Environmental Studies); **General Industrial Research** (Industrial and Production Economics); **Law and Politics** (*Okinawa*) (Law; Political Sciences); **Ryukyuan Culture** (Cultural Studies)

Graduate School

Law (Administrative Law; Civil Law; Commercial Law; Constitutional Law; Criminal Law; History of Law; International Law; Law; Public Law); **Regional Business and Economics** (Accountancy; Business and Commerce; Development Studies; Economics; Environmental Studies; Industrial and Production Economics; Management; Marketing; Regional Studies; Social and Community Services; Taxation); **Regional Culture** (American Studies; Clinical Psychology; Contemporary History; Cultural Studies; East Asian Studies; English; English Studies; Folklore; Foreign Languages Education; History; Modern History; Modern Languages; Prehistory; Regional Studies; Social Studies; Social Welfare; Sociology; Southeast Asian Studies)

History: Founded 1972.

Academic year: April to March (April-September; October-March)

Admission requirements: Graduation from high school

Fees: Entrance fee, 120,000; Undergraduate tuition, 610,000 per annum; Graduate tuition, 370,000 per annum (Yen)

Main language(s) of instruction: Japanese

Accrediting agency: Japan University Accreditation Association (JUAA)

Degrees and diplomas: Gakushi (American Studies; Cultural Studies; Economics; English Studies; Industrial and Production Economics; Information Sciences; Japanese; Law; Political Sciences; Psychology; Social Studies; Social Welfare), Shushi (American Studies; Clinical Psychology; Cultural Studies; English Studies; Industrial and Production Economics; Law; Social Welfare)

Student Services: Academic Counselling, Social Counselling, Careers Guidance, Nursery Care, Sports Facilities, Language Laboratory, Facilities for disabled people, Health Services, Canteen, Foreign Studies Centre, Library

Academic Staff 2013-2014	MALE	FEMALE	TOTAL
FULL-TIME			432
PART-TIME			287
Student Numbers 2013-2014			
All (Foreign Included)			5804

Last Update: 25-05-2018

Okinawa University

555 Kokuba
Naha-shi 902-8521, Okinawa
Tel: +81(98) 832-3216
Fax: +81(98) 832-0083
Website: http://www.okinawa-u.ac.jp
President: Masahiro Nagahama

Course/Programme

Japanese Language for International Students (Japanese)

Department/Division

International Communication (American Studies; Asian Studies; Chinese; Communication Studies; English; History); **Law and Economics** (Economics; Law; Management); **Welfare and Culture** (Cultural Studies; Health Sciences; Human Resources; Psychiatry and Mental Health; Social Welfare; Sports)

Graduate School

Contemporary Okinawan Studies (Administration; Anthropology; Business Administration; Economics; Folklore; Government; History; Linguistics; Political Sciences; Regional Studies; Social Studies; Sociology)
History: Founded 1961.
Fees: Entrance fee, 120,000; Tuition, 740,000 (Yen)
Main language(s) of instruction: Japanese
Accrediting agency: Japan University Accreditation Association (JUAA)
Degrees and diplomas: Gakushi (Communication Studies; Cultural Studies; Economics; Law; Modern Languages; Social Welfare), Shushi (Administration; Regional Studies)
Student Services: Library
Last Update: 23-01-2018

Osaka Aoyama University

Shinine 2-11-1
Minoh 562-8580, Osaka
Tel: +81 72-722-4165
Fax: +81 72-722-5190
Website: http://www1.osaka-aoyama.ac.jp
President: Kazuko Shiokawa

Unit

Health Sciences (Health Sciences; Nutrition; Preschool Education)
History: Founded 1967. as Osaka Aoyama Women's Junior College. Acquired present status and title 2005.
Main language(s) of instruction: Japanese
Accrediting agency: Japan Institution for Higher Education Evaluation (JIHEE)
Degrees and diplomas: Gakushi (Health Sciences; Nutrition), Hakase (Preschool Education)
Last Update: 23-01-2018

Osaka College of Music

1-1-8 Shonai-Saiwai-machi
Toyonaka-shi 561-8555, Osaka
Tel: +81(6) 6334-2131
Fax: +81(6) 6333-0286
Website: http://www.daion.ac.jp

Department/Division

Composition (Music Theory and Composition; Musicology); **Instrumental Music** (Musical Instruments); **Vocal Music** (Singing)

Graduate School

Composition (Music; Music Theory and Composition; Musicology); **Instrumental Music** (Music; Musical Instruments); **Vocal Music** (Opera; Singing)
History: Founded 1915 as Osaka School of Music, became High School 1948, Junior College 1951. Acquired present status 1958.
Academic year: April to March (April-September; October-March)
Admission requirements: Graduation from high school or foreign equivalent, and entrance examination
Fees: 1,630,000 per annum (Yen)
Main language(s) of instruction: Japanese
Accrediting agency: Japan Institution for Higher Education Evaluation (JIHEE)
Degrees and diplomas: Gakushi (Fine Arts; Music), Shushi (Conducting; Music; Music Theory and Composition; Musical Instruments; Opera; Singing)
Student Services: Academic Counselling, Social Counselling, Careers Guidance, Nursery Care, Health Services, Canteen
Periodicals: Muse, Music Research
Last Update: 20-02-2018

Osaka Dental University (ODU)

8-1 Kuzuhahanazozno-cho, Hirakata-shi
Osaka-shi 573-1121, Osaka
Tel: +81(72) 864-3111
Fax: +81(72) 864-3000
Website: http://www.osaka-dent.ac.jp
President: Takayoshi Kawazoe

Department/Division

Basic Science (Anatomy; Biochemistry; Dentistry; Oral Pathology; Pharmacology; Physiology; Social and Preventive Medicine); **Clinics** (Dental Technology; Dentistry; Oral Pathology; Orthodontics; Otorhinolaryngology; Periodontics; Stomatology); **General Education** (Biological and Life Sciences; Chemistry; Ethics; Mathematics; Natural Sciences; Physics)
History: Founded 1911, acquired present status 1952. Has three campuses: Kuzuha Campus, Makino Campus, Temmabashi Campus (The University Hospital),

Academic year: April to March (April-June; September-December; January-March)

Admission requirements: Graduation from high school and entrance examination

Main language(s) of instruction: Japanese

Accrediting agency: Japan University Accreditation Association (JUAA)

Degrees and diplomas: Gakushi (Dentistry), Hakase (Dentistry)

Student Services: Academic Counselling, Social Counselling, Careers Guidance, Nursery Care, Sports Facilities, Language Laboratory, Facilities for disabled people, Health Services, Canteen, Library

Last Update: 23-01-2018

Osaka Electro-Communications University (OECU)

18-8 Hatsu-cho
Neyagawa-shi 572-8530, Osaka
Tel: +81(72) 824-1131
Fax: +81(72) 824-0014
Website: http://www.osakac.ac.jp
President: Oishi Toshimitsu

Faculty

Biomedical Engineering (Biomedical Engineering; Health Sciences; Medical Technology; Physical Education; Physical Therapy; Sports); **Engineering** (Automation and Control Engineering; Chemistry; Computer Science; Electrical and Electronic Engineering; Electrical Engineering; Electronic Engineering; Engineering; Environmental Studies; Information Technology; Machine Building; Mathematics; Measurement and Precision Engineering; Mechanical Engineering; Optical Technology; Physics); **Financial Economy** (Accountancy; Business Administration; Economics; Finance; Information Technology; Management); **Information and Communication Engineering** (Artificial Intelligence; Computer Engineering; Computer Networks; Multimedia; Safety Engineering; Software Engineering; Telecommunications Engineering); **Information Science and Arts** (Computer Engineering; Computer Graphics; Computer Networks; Computer Science; Fine Arts; Management; Music; Robotics; Software Engineering; Visual Arts)

Graduate School

Biomedical Engineering (Biomedical Engineering; Biomedicine; Medicine; Safety Engineering; Welfare and Protective Services); **Engineering** (Applied Physics; Artificial Intelligence; Automation and Control Engineering; Computer Graphics; Computer Networks; Computer Science;

Educational Technology; Electronic Engineering; Industrial Engineering; Information Sciences; Information Technology; Materials Engineering; Mathematics; Mechanical Engineering; Microwaves; Natural Sciences; Optical Technology; Robotics; Software Engineering; Telecommunications Engineering); **Information Science and Arts** (Computer Science; Fine Arts; Information Sciences; Information Technology; Mass Communication; Multimedia; Visual Arts)

Further information: Also Shijonawate Campus

History: Founded 1961.

Main language(s) of instruction: Japanese

Accrediting agency: Japan Institution for Higher Education Evaluation (JIHEE)

Degrees and diplomas: Gakushi (Computer Science; Engineering; Finance; Health Sciences; Information Sciences; Information Technology; Technology; Telecommunications Services; Welfare and Protective Services), Shushi (Engineering; Health Sciences; Information Sciences; Welfare and Protective Services), Hakase (Engineering; Health Sciences; Information Sciences; Welfare and Protective Services)

Student Services: Cultural Activities, Sports Facilities, Canteen, Library, IT Centre

Periodicals: Osaka Electro-Communication University Research Journal of Human Sciences, Osaka Electro-Communication University Research Journal of Natural Science

Academic Staff 2013-2014	MALE	FEMALE	TOTAL
FULL-TIME			176
Student Numbers 2013-2014			
All (Foreign Included)			5403

Last Update: 24-01-2018

Osaka Gakuin University

2-36-1 Kishibe-Minami
Suita-shi 564-8511, Osaka
Tel: +81(6) 6381-8434
Fax: +81(6) 6382-4363
Website: http://www.osaka-gu.ac.jp
President: Yoshiyasu Shirai

Faculty

Business Administration (Business Administration); **Corporate Intelligence** (Finance; Health Administration; Information Technology; Social Welfare); **Distribution and Communication Sciences** (Business Administration; Communication Studies; Marketing; Sales Techniques; Service Trades); **Economics** (Business Administration; Economics); **Foreign Languages** (English; French; German; Literature;

Modern Languages); **Hospitality Business Administration** (Administration; Business Administration; Communication Studies; Management; Tourism); **Informatics** (Computer Science; Information Technology); **International Studies** (Cultural Studies; International Studies); **Law** (Law)

Department/Division
Correspondence Studies (Accountancy; Business Administration; Management; Marketing; Sales Techniques)

Graduate School
Commerce (Accountancy; Business Administration; Business and Commerce); **Computer Science** (Computer Engineering; Computer Networks; Computer Science; Data Processing; Information Technology; Multimedia; Software Engineering); **Economics** (Accountancy; Economics; Taxation); **International Studies** (Cultural Studies; International Relations; International Studies); **Law** (Commercial Law; Law; Private Law; Public Law); **Legal Profession** (Commercial Law; Law)

History: Founded 1962 as Junior College, acquired present status 1963. Postgraduate studies introduced 1967.

Academic year: April to March (April-September: October-March)

Admission requirements: Graduation from secondary school and entrance examination

Fees: Tuition, 1.71m.-1.84m. per annum (Yen)

Main language(s) of instruction: Japanese

Accrediting agency: Japan University Accreditation Association (JUAA)

Degrees and diplomas: Gakushi (Business Administration; Communication Studies; Computer Science; Economics; English; Information Technology; International Studies; Law), Shushi (Business and Commerce; Economics; International Studies; Law), Hakase (Business and Commerce; Economics; International Studies; Law)

Student Services: Academic Counselling, Social Counselling, Careers Guidance, Sports Facilities, Language Laboratory, Facilities for disabled people, Health Services, Canteen, Library

Periodicals: Foreign Linguistic and Literary Studies, International Studies, Journal of Distribution, Communication and Administration, Osaka Gakuin Corporate Intelligence Journal, Osaka Gakuin Law Journal, The Bulletin of the Cultural and Natural Sciences in Osaka Gakuin University, The Osaka Gakuin Journal of Economics

Academic Staff 2013-2014	MALE	FEMALE	TOTAL
FULL-TIME			212
Student Numbers 2013-2014			
All (Foreign Included)	4699	1156	5855

Last Update: 25-05-2018

Osaka Health Science University (OSHU)

Tenma 1-chome, No. 9 No. 27
Osaka 530-0043, Kita-ku
Tel: +81 6-6354-0091
Website: http://www.ohsu.ac.jp
President: Masukazu Fukuda

School
Graduate

Department/Division
Occupational Therapy (Occupational Therapy); **Physical Therapy** (Physical Therapy); **Speech and Hearing** (Speech Studies)

History: Founded 2009.

Main language(s) of instruction: Japanese

Accrediting agency: Japan University Accreditation Association (JUAA)

Degrees and diplomas: Gakushi, Shushi (Health Sciences)

Last Update: 24-01-2018

Osaka Institute of Technology (OIT)

5-16-1 Omiya, Asahi-ku
Osaka-shi 535-8585, Osaka
Tel: +81(6) 6954-4097
Fax: +81(6) 6953-9496
Website: http://www.oit.ac.jp
President: Yasushi Nishimura

Faculty
Engineering (*Also Graduate School*) (Applied Chemistry; Architecture; Bioengineering; Civil Engineering; Design; Electrical and Electronic Engineering; Engineering; Environmental Engineering; Information Technology; Landscape Architecture; Mechanical Engineering; Robotics; Structural Architecture; Technology; Telecommunications Engineering; Town Planning); **Information Science and Technology** (*Also Graduate School*) (Computer Networks; Computer Science; Information Sciences; Information Technology; Media Studies); **Intellectual Property** (*Also Graduate School*)

Further information: Also Hirakata Campus: 1-79-1 Kitayama, Hirakata City, Osaka, 573-0196 Japan

History: Founded 1922 as Kansai College of Engineering, acquired present status 1949.

Academic year: April to March (April-September; October-March)

Admission requirements: Graduation from high school or equivalent, and entrance examination

Fees: Registration, 150,000-250,000; tuition, 1.28m. per annum; graduate, 1.11m.-1.21m. per annum (Yen)

Main language(s) of instruction: Japanese, English

Accrediting agency: Japan University Accreditation Association (JUAA)

Degrees and diplomas: Gakushi, Shushi (Engineering; Information Sciences; Law), Hakase (Architecture; Design; Engineering; Information Sciences)

Student Services: Academic Counselling, Social Counselling, Careers Guidance, Sports Facilities, Health Services, Canteen

Periodicals: Series for Liberal Arts (Memoirs), Series for Science and Technology (Memoirs)

Publishing house: Oyodo

Last Update: 24-01-2018

Osaka International University

3-50-1 Sugi
Hirakata 573-0192, Osaka
Tel: +81(06) 6907-4306
Website: http://www.oiu.ac.jp

Faculty

Business (Design; Economics; Finance; Law); **Global Business** (Business Administration; Commercial Law; Economics; Marketing); **Human Sciences** (Curriculum; Education; Psychology; Sports); **International Communication** (Chinese; Communication Studies; English)

Department/Division

Information Design (Design); **Law Policy** (Law)

Graduate School

Management and Information Science (Information Sciences; Management)

Further information: Also School of Japanese studies for foreign students, and a campus in Moriguchi

History: Founded 1929. Acquired present status 1988. Incorporated Osaka International University for Women 2002.

Academic year: April to March

Admission requirements: Graduation from high school or equivalent, or foreign equivalent, with a minimum of 12 yrs of schooling, and entrance examination

Main language(s) of instruction: Japanese

Accrediting agency: Japan Institution for Higher Education Evaluation (JIHEE)

Degrees and diplomas: Gakushi, Shushi (Information Sciences; Information Technology; Management), Hakase (Information Technology; Management)

Student Services: Academic Counselling, Social Counselling, Careers Guidance, Nursery Care, Cultural Activities, Sports Facilities, Language Laboratory, Health Services, Canteen

Academic Staff	MALE	FEMALE	TOTAL
PART-TIME			268

Last Update: 24-01-2018

Osaka Jogakuin University

2-26-54 Tamatsukuri
Chuo-ku 540-0004, Osaka
Tel: +81(6) 6761-9371
Website: http://www.wilmina.ac.jp/ojc
President: Hidekazu Sekine

Course/Programme

English (*Intensive*) (English); **International Collaboration, International Management, or International Communication** (*Four-Year*) (Communication Studies; Eastern European Studies; English; Human Rights; International Business; Management; Natural Sciences; Peace and Disarmament; Religion); **Religious Studies** (*Two-Year*) (Religious Studies)

History: Founded 1968. Acquired present status 2004.

Fees: Tuition, 550,000 per annum (Yen)

Main language(s) of instruction: Japanese, English

Accrediting agency: Ministry of Education, Culture, Sports, Science and Technology (MEXT)

Degrees and diplomas: Gakushi (Modern Languages), Shushi (Human Rights; International Studies; Peace and Disarmament), Hakase (Human Rights; International Studies; Peace and Disarmament)

Last Update: 26-03-2018

Osaka Kawasaki Rehabilitation University

Mizuma 158
Kaizuka 597-0104, Osaka
Tel: +81 72-446-6700
Fax: +81 72-446-6767
Website: http://www.kawasakigakuen.ac.jp

Faculty

Rehabilitation (Occupational Therapy; Physical Therapy; Speech Therapy and Audiology)

History: Founded 1997 as Yamazaki River Medical College. Acquired present status and title 2006.
Main language(s) of instruction: Japanese
Accrediting agency: Japan Institution for Higher Education Evaluation (JIHEE)
Degrees and diplomas: Gakushi (Occupational Therapy; Physical Therapy; Speech Therapy and Audiology)
Student Services: Academic Counselling, Sports Facilities, Library, IT Centre

Academic Staff 2013-2014	MALE	FEMALE	TOTAL
FULL-TIME			38
Student Numbers 2013-2014			
All (Foreign Included)	334	202	536

Last Update: 24-01-2018

Osaka Medical College

2-7 Daigaku-machi
Takatsuki-shi 569-8686, Osaka
Tel: +81(72) 683-1221
Fax: +81(72) 681-3723
Website: http://www.osaka-med.ac.jp
President: Yoshinuri Otsuki

Faculty

Medicine (*Also Graduate School*) (Anaesthesiology; Anatomy; Applied Chemistry; Biology; Chemistry; Dermatology; Forensic Medicine and Dentistry; Gynaecology and Obstetrics; Hygiene; Mathematics; Medicine; Microbiology; Modern Languages; Neurosciences; Ophthalmology; Orthopaedics; Otorhinolaryngology; Paediatrics; Pathology; Pharmacology; Philosophy; Physics; Physiology; Psychology; Public Health; Radiology; Surgery; Urology); **Nursing** (Nursing)

Graduate School

Medicine (Anaesthesiology; Anatomy; Biochemistry; Biological and Life Sciences; Forensic Medicine and Dentistry; Gynaecology and Obstetrics; Hygiene; Laboratory Techniques; Medical Technology; Medicine; Microbiology; Molecular Biology; Neurological Therapy; Ophthalmology; Orthopaedics; Otorhinolaryngology; Paediatrics; Pathology; Pharmacology; Physiology; Psychiatry and Mental Health; Public Health; Radiology; Rehabilitation and Therapy; Social and Preventive Medicine; Surgery; Treatment Techniques; Urology)
History: Founded 1927 as Osaka Professional High School of Medicine. Acquired present status and title 1952.

Academic year: April to March (April-August; September-December; January-March)
Admission requirements: Graduation from high school or equivalent, and entrance examination
Main language(s) of instruction: Japanese
Accrediting agency: Japan University Accreditation Association (JUAA)
Degrees and diplomas: Gakushi (Medicine; Nursing), Hakase (Medicine)
Student Services: Cultural Activities, Sports Facilities, Library
Periodicals: Bulletin, Journal

Student Numbers 2013-2013	MALE	FEMALE	TOTAL
All (Foreign Included)	637	558	1195

Last Update: 24-01-2018

Osaka Ohtani University

3-11-1 Nishikiorikita
Tondabayashi 584-8540, Osaka
Tel: +81(721) 24-1031
Fax: +81(721) 24-5120
Website: http://www.osaka-ohtani.ac.jp
President: Hiroyoshi Asao

Faculty

Education (Education; Preschool Education; Special Education); **Literature** (Archaeology; Art History; Cultural Studies; English; Folklore; History; Japanese; Native Language; Native Language Education); **Pharmacy** (Pharmacy); **Sociology** (Business and Commerce; Community Health; Information Sciences; Social Psychology; Social Sciences; Sports)

School

Graduate Studies (American Studies; Education; English; Japanese; Literature; Social Welfare)
History: Founded 1966. Known as Ohtani Women's University/Otani Joshi Daigaku until 2006.
Academic year: April to March (April-July; October-March)
Admission requirements: Japanese Language Proficiency Test, Level 1 or 2
Fees: Registration, 320,000-400,000 (Pharmacy); tuition, 1.08m.-1.78m. (Pharmacy) per annum (Yen)
Main language(s) of instruction: Japanese
Accrediting agency: Japan Institution for Higher Education Evaluation (JIHEE)
Degrees and diplomas: Gakushi (Education; Literature; Pharmacy; Social Sciences; Social Welfare), Shushi (American Studies; English; Heritage Preservation; Japanese; Literature), Hakase

Student Services: Academic Counselling, Social Counselling, Careers Guidance, Nursery Care, Cultural Activities, Sports Facilities, Facilities for disabled people, Health Services, Canteen, Foreign Studies Centre, Library
Periodicals: Bulletin
Last Update: 24-01-2018

Osaka Sangyo University (OSU)

3-1-1 Nakagaito
Daito-shi 574-8530, Osaka
Tel: +81(72) 875-3001
Fax: +81(72) 871-9765
Website: http://www.osaka-sandai.ac.jp
President: Yasunori Nakamura

Faculty

Business Administration (Accountancy; Business Administration; Management); **Design Engineering** (Architecture and Planning); **Economics** (Economics; International Economics); **Engineering** (Civil Engineering; Electrical and Electronic Engineering; Engineering; Environmental Engineering; Information Technology; Mechanical Engineering; Telecommunications Engineering; Transport Engineering); **Human Environment** (Communication Studies; Cultural Studies; Environmental Management; Health Sciences; Sports; Town Planning; Urban Studies)

Graduate School

Business Administration (Management); **Economics** (Economics; International Economics); **Engineering** (Architectural and Environmental Design; Civil Engineering; Electronic Engineering; Engineering; Environmental Engineering; Information Technology; Mechanical Engineering; Production Engineering; Telecommunications Engineering); **Human Environment** (Environmental Studies)
History: Founded 1928.
Fees: 802,500 - 993,500 per annum depending on programs (Yen)
Main language(s) of instruction: Japanese
Accrediting agency: Japan University Accreditation Association (JUAA)
Degrees and diplomas: Gakushi, Shushi (Computer Engineering; Economics; Electronic Engineering; Environmental Studies; Information Technology; Management; Mechanical Engineering), Hakase (Environmental Engineering; Management; Production Engineering)
Student Services: Sports Facilities, Language Laboratory, Library
Last Update: 24-01-2018

Osaka Seikei University

3-10-62 Aikawa
Higashi-Yodogawa-ku 533-0007, Osaka
Tel: +81(6) 6829-2554
Fax: +81(6) 6829-2509
Website: http://www.osaka-seikei.ac.jp

Faculty

Art and Design (Design; Environmental Studies; Fine Arts); **Education** (Education; Preschool Education); **Management** (Business Administration; Information Technology; Management)
History: Founded 1933 as Seikei Senior Girls' School. Became coeducational in 2003.
Fees: 850,000 per annum (Yen)
Main language(s) of instruction: Japanese
Accrediting agency: Japan Institution for Higher Education Evaluation (JIHEE)
Degrees and diplomas: Gakushi
Student Services: Academic Counselling, Sports Facilities, Canteen, Library
Last Update: 24-01-2018

Osaka Shoin Women's University

4-2-26 Hishiya-nishi
Higashiosaka 577-8550, Osaka
Tel: +81(6) 6723-8183
Fax: +81(6) 6723-8348
Website: http://www.osaka-shoin.ac.jp
President: Shintaro Mori

Faculty

Child Sciences (Preschool Education; Primary Education); **Liberal Arts** (Cosmetology; English; Environmental Studies; Fashion Design; Interior Design; Japanese; Nutrition; Textile Design); **Psychology** (Clinical Psychology; Educational Psychology; Psychology)

Course/Programme

Graduate (Clinical Psychology; Fashion Design; Food Science; Nutrition)
History: Founded 1917. Acquired present status 1949.
Main language(s) of instruction: Japanese
Accrediting agency: Japan Institution for Higher Education Evaluation (JIHEE)
Degrees and diplomas: Gakushi, Shushi
Student Services: Foreign Studies Centre
Last Update: 24-01-2018

Osaka University of Arts

469 Higashiyama Kanan-cho
Minamikawachi-gun 585-8555, Osaka
Tel: +81(721) 93-3781
Fax: +81(721) 93-5360
Website: http://www.osaka-geidai.ac.jp
President: Tsukamoto Kunihiko

Department/Division

Architecture (Architectural and Environmental Design; Architecture); **Art and Primary Education** (Art Education; Art Therapy; Primary Education); **Art Planning** (Art Management; Museum Management); **Broadcasting** (Acting; Advertising and Publicity; Radio and Television Broadcasting); **Character Creative Arts** (Marketing; Painting and Drawing; Software Engineering; Visual Arts); **Crafts** (Ceramic Art; Glass Art; Handicrafts; Metal Techniques; Weaving); **Design** (Architectural and Environmental Design; Computer Graphics; Design; Graphic Design; Industrial Design; Multimedia; Visual Arts); **Fine Arts** (Fine Arts; Painting and Drawing; Printing and Printmaking; Sculpture); **Literary Arts** (Art Criticism; Grammar; Literature; Publishing and Book Trade; Translation and Interpretation; Writing); **Music Performance** (Music; Musical Instruments; Opera); **Musicology** (Music Education; Music Theory and Composition; Musicology; Sound Engineering (Acoustics)); **Photography** (Fine Arts; Photography; Video); **Theatre** (Acting; Dance; Display and Stage Design; Musical Instruments; Performing Arts; Singing; Theatre); **Visual Concept Planning** (Film; Media Studies)

Graduate School

Arts and Culture (Aesthetics; Architectural and Environmental Design; Art History; Cultural Studies; Design; Film; Fine Arts; Handicrafts; Musical Instruments; Musicology; Painting and Drawing; Photography; Sculpture; Singing; Theatre; Video; Visual Arts; Writing)
History: Founded 1964.
Academic year: April to March; April to September; October to March
Admission requirements: Graduation from high school and entrance examination
Fees: Entrance fee, 280,000-330,000; Tuition fee, 830,000-1m. per annum (Yen)
Main language(s) of instruction: Japanese
Accrediting agency: Japan Institution for Higher Education Evaluation (JIHEE)
Degrees and diplomas: Gakushi (Fine Arts), Shushi (Art Management; Cultural Studies; Fine Arts), Hakase (Cultural Studies; Fine Arts). Also Diplomas

Student Services: Sports Facilities, Health Services, Library

Student Numbers 2013-2014	MALE	FEMALE	TOTAL
All (Foreign Included)	623	886	1509

Last Update: 25-01-2018

Osaka University of Commerce (OUC)

4-1-10 Mikuriya Sakae-machi
Higashiosaka-shi 577-8505, Osaka
Tel: +81(6) 6781-0381
Fax: +81(6) 6781-8438
Website: http://ouc.daishodai.ac.jp
President: Ichiro Tanioka

Faculty

Business Administration (Business Administration; Business and Commerce; Management; Public Administration); **Economics** (Economics; Finance; International Economics)

Institute

Regional Studies (Regional Planning)
History: Founded 1928, acquired present status 1949.
Academic year: April-March (April-September; September-March)
Admission requirements: Graduation from high school or equivalent, and entrance examination
Fees: 1m. per annum (Yen)
Main language(s) of instruction: Japanese
Accrediting agency: Japan Institution for Higher Education Evaluation (JIHEE)
Degrees and diplomas: Gakushi (Business Administration; Economics), Shushi, Hakase. Also Graduate Programme, 1 yr
Student Services: Academic Counselling, Social Counselling, Careers Guidance, Nursery Care, Cultural Activities, Sports Facilities, Language Laboratory, Health Services, Canteen
Periodicals: Shodai Ronshu
Last Update: 25-01-2018

Osaka University of Comprehensive Children Education

Higashi Sumiyoshi-ku, 6-4-26 Yusato
Osaka 546-0013, Osaka
Tel: +81 6-6702-7603
Website: http://jonan.jp/soho
President: Yamazaki Takaya

Faculty

Childcare (Preschool Education)
History: Founded 1935 as Seongnam Joshi commercial vocational school. Acquired present status and title 2006.
Main language(s) of instruction: Japanese
Accrediting agency: Japan Institution for Higher Education Evaluation (JIHEE)
Degrees and diplomas: Gakushi (Preschool Education)
Last Update: 25-01-2018

Osaka University of Economics

2-2-8 Osumi Higashiyodogawa-ku
Osaka-shi 533-8533, Osaka
Tel: +81(6) 6328-2431
Fax: +81(6) 6328-2655
Website: http://www.osaka-ue.ac.jp
President: Mitsutoshi Tokunaga

Faculty

Business Administration (*Also Graduate School*) (Business Administration; Commercial Law); **Economics** (*Also Graduate School*) (Economics; Regional Planning); **Human Sciences** (*Also Graduate School*) (Arts and Humanities); **Information Technology and Social Sciences** (*Also Graduate School*) (Finance; Information Management)

School

Graduate Studies (Arts and Humanities; Business Administration; Economics; Information Management)

Institute

Research in Economic History of Japan (Economics; History); **Small Business Research and Business Administration** (Business Administration; Small Business)

Centre

Clinical Psychology (Clinical Psychology)
History: Founded 1932 as Naniwa College of Commerce. Became Showa College of Commerce 1935. Acquired present status 1949. Graduate School added 1966.
Academic year: April to March (April-September; October-March)
Admission requirements: Graduation from high school or foreign equivalent, and entrance examination
Main language(s) of instruction: Japanese
Accrediting agency: Japan University Accreditation Association (JUAA)
Degrees and diplomas: Gakushi, Shushi (Arts and Humanities; Business Administration; Business Computing; Economics), Hakase (Economics)

Student Services: Social Counselling, Careers Guidance, Sports Facilities, Language Laboratory, Health Services
Periodicals: Chushokigyo Kiho, Keiei-Keizai, Kyoyobu Kiho, Osaka Keidai Ronshu
Last Update: 25-01-2018

Osaka University of Economics and Law (OUEL)

6-10 Gakuoniji
Yao-shi 581-8511, Osaka
Tel: +81(72) 943-7760
Fax: +81(72) 943-7035
Website: http://www.keiho-u.ac.jp
President: Riichi Tabata

Faculty

Economics (Business Administration; Business and Commerce; Economics; Management); **Law** (Administration; Consumer Studies; Environmental Studies; Law; Management; Social Welfare)
Further information: YAO Campus
History: Founded 1971.
Main language(s) of instruction: Japanese, English
Accrediting agency: Japan Institution for Higher Education Evaluation (JIHEE)
Degrees and diplomas: Gakushi
Last Update: 25-01-2018

Osaka University of Health and Sport Sciences

1-1 Asashirodai Kumatori-cho
Sennan-gun 590-0496, Osaka
Tel: +81(724) 53-7070
Fax: +81(724) 53-8970
Website: http://www.ouhs.ac.jp
President: Iwakami Yasutaka

School

Health and Sports Sciences (*Also Graduate School*) (Educational and Student Counselling; Educational Psychology; Health Sciences; Physical Education; Sports; Sports Management); **Health and Welfare Sciences** (*Also Graduate School*) (Public Health; Social Welfare; Social Work)
History: Founded 1965.
Academic year: April to March (April-September; September-March)
Admission requirements: Graduation from high school and entrance examination

Main language(s) of instruction: Japanese
Accrediting agency: Japan University Accreditation Association (JUAA)
Degrees and diplomas: Gakushi, Shushi (Sports; Sports Management), Hakase (Sports; Sports Management). Also Graduate Programme, 1 yr
Student Services: Sports Facilities
Last Update: 25-01-2018

Osaka University of Human Sciences

1-4-1 Shojaku
Settsu 566-8501, Osaka
Tel: +81(6) 6381-3000
Fax: +81(6) 6381-3502
Website: http://www.ohs.ac.jp
President: Yasukazu Tanaka

Faculty
Human Sciences (Child Care and Development; Clinical Psychology; Health Sciences; Psychology; Social Sciences; Social Welfare; Speech Therapy and Audiology; Welfare and Protective Services)
History: Founded 2001.
Main language(s) of instruction: Japanese
Accrediting agency: Japan Institution for Higher Education Evaluation (JIHEE)
Degrees and diplomas: Gakushi
Last Update: 25-01-2018

Osaka University of Pharmaceutical Sciences

4-20-1 Nasahara
Takatsuki-shi 569-1094, Osaka
Tel: +81(72) 690-1000
Fax: +81(72) 690-1005
Website: http://www.oups.ac.jp
President: Mikio Masada

Department/Division
Pharmaceutical Sciences (*4-year Programme; also Graduate School*) (Pharmacy); **Pharmacy** (*6-year Programme*) (Pharmacy)
History: Founded 1904.
Fees: 900,000 per annum (Yen)
Main language(s) of instruction: Japanese, English
Accrediting agency: Japan University Accreditation Association (JUAA)

Degrees and diplomas: Gakushi, Shushi (Pharmacy), Hakase
Student Services: Sports Facilities
Last Update: 25-01-2018

Osaka University of Tourism

5-3-1, Okubominami Kumatori-cho Sennan-gun
Osaka-shi 590-0493, Osaka
Tel: +81(724) 53-8222
Fax: +81(724) 53-1451
Website: http://www.tourism.ac.jp

Course/Programme
Foreign Language (English; Modern Languages); **Hotel Industry Management** (Hotel Management; Tourism); **International Tourism** (Tourism); **Leisure** (Leisure Studies; Tourism); **Tourism Culture** (Cultural Studies; Geography; Media Studies; Museum Studies; Tourism); **Travel Industry Management** (Business Administration; Tourism; Transport and Communications)
History: Founded 2000. Formerly known as Osaka Meijo Daigaku (Osaka Meijo University).
Fees: National : Tuition, 650,000 per annum (Yen), International : Tuition, 390,000 per annum (Yen)
Main language(s) of instruction: Japanese
Accrediting agency: Japan Institution for Higher Education Evaluation (JIHEE)
Degrees and diplomas: Gakushi (Tourism)
Student Services: Sports Facilities, Canteen, Library, IT Centre
Last Update: 25-01-2018

Otani University

Kamifusa-cho, Koyama, Kita-ku
Kyoto-shi 603-8143, Kyoto
Tel: +81(75) 411-8114
Fax: +81(75) 411-8149
Website: http://www.otani.ac.jp
President: Kigoshi Yasushi

Faculty
Letters (Anthropology; Asian Religious Studies; Chinese; Clinical Psychology; Cultural Studies; East Asian Studies; Education; English; Ethics; German; History; History of Religion; Japanese; Literature; Philosophical Schools; Philosophy; Religious Studies; Social Welfare; Sociology)

Graduate School

Letters (Asian Religious Studies; Asian Studies; Cultural Studies; Education; Philosophy; Sociology)
Further information: Also Junior College
History: Founded as College 1665, became University 1904. Reorganized and present title adopted 1949.
Academic year: April to March (April-September; October-March)
Admission requirements: Graduation from high school or equivalent or foreign equivalent, and entrance examination
Main language(s) of instruction: Japanese
Accrediting agency: Japan University Accreditation Association (JUAA)
Degrees and diplomas: Gakushi (Arts and Humanities), Shushi (Asian Religious Studies; Philosophy; Sociology), Hakase (Asian Religious Studies; Philosophy; Sociology)
Student Services: Social Counselling, Careers Guidance, Cultural Activities, Sports Facilities, Health Services, Canteen, Foreign Studies Centre
Periodicals: Annual Memoirs of the Otani University Shin Buddhist Comprehensive Research Institute, Annual Report of Research at Otani University, The Otani Gakuho
Last Update: 25-01-2018

Otemae University

6-42 Ochayasho-cho
Nishinomiya-shi 662-8552, Hyogo
Tel: +81(798) 34-6331
Fax: +81(798) 32-5040
Website: http://www.otemae.ac.jp
President: Torigoe Hiroyuki

Faculty

Cultural and Historical Studies (Arts and Humanities; Comparative Literature; Cultural Studies; English; European Languages; History; Japanese; Literature; Media Studies; Modern Languages; Oriental Studies); **Media and Arts** (Advertising and Publicity; Archaeology; Architecture; Design; Geography; Handicrafts; Interior Design; Tourism; Visual Arts); **Modern Social Studies** (Architectural and Environmental Design; Business and Commerce; Cultural Studies; Environmental Studies; Health Sciences; Information Sciences; Information Technology; Media Studies; Psychology; Social Welfare)

Graduate School

Comparative Culture (Cultural Studies)
Further information: Also Distance Education courses (Modern Social Studies)
History: Founded 1966 as Otemae University for Women. Acquired present title 2000.

Academic year: April to March
Admission requirements: Graduation from High School or equivalent
Main language(s) of instruction: Japanese
Accrediting agency: Japan Institution for Higher Education Evaluation (JIHEE)
Degrees and diplomas: Gakushi (Arts and Humanities; Business Administration; Fine Arts; Geography; History; Information Sciences; Multimedia; Nutrition; Performing Arts; Psychology; Tourism), Shushi (Arts and Humanities; Cultural Studies), Hakase (Arts and Humanities; Cultural Studies)
Student Services: Sports Facilities, Library, Residential Facilities
Periodicals: Otemae Winds
Last Update: 27-03-2018

Otemon Gakuin University

2-1-15 Nishiai
Ibaraki-shi 567-8502, Osaka
Tel: +81(72) 641-9631
Fax: +81(72) 643-5651
Website: http://www.otemon.ac.jp
President: Toshiaki Kawahara

Faculty

Economics (*Also Graduate School*) (Economics; International Economics); **International Liberal Arts** (Arts and Humanities; Asian Studies; Chinese; English; European Languages; Literature; Oriental Studies); **Management** (*Also Graduate School*) (Management; Marketing); **Psychology** (Psychology); **Sociology** (Sociology)

Institute

Educational Research (Educational Research)

Centre

Australian Studies (Pacific Area Studies)

Graduate School

Business (Business Administration); **Economics** (Economics); **Letters** (Chinese; English; Sociology); **Psychology** (Psychology)
History: Founded 1966.
Academic year: April to March (April-September; October-March)
Admission requirements: Graduation from high school or equivalent, or foreign equivalent, and entrance examination
Main language(s) of instruction: Japanese
Accrediting agency: Japan University Accreditation Association (JUAA)

Degrees and diplomas: Gakushi (Business Administration; Development Studies; Economics; Japanese; Modern Languages; Psychology; Sociology), Shushi (Business Administration; Chinese; Economics; English; Management; Psychology; Sociology), Hakase (Economics; Management)

Student Services: Social Counselling, Careers Guidance, Sports Facilities, Language Laboratory, Health Services, Canteen, Foreign Studies Centre, Library, IT Centre

Periodicals: Faculty of Letters Journal, Otemon Economic Journal, Otemon Economic Studies, The Otemon Journal of Australian Studies

Last Update: 27-03-2018

Otsuma Women's University

12 Sanban-cho Chiyoda-ku
Tokyo 102-8357
Tel: +81(3) 5275-6011
Fax: +81(3) 3261-8119
Website: http://www.otsuma.ac.jp
President: Masanao Itoh

Faculty

Comparative Culture (*Tama Campus, Tama-shi, Tokyo*) (American Studies; Asian Studies; European Studies); **Home Economics** (*Sayama Campus, Iruma-shi, Saitama-ken*) (Child Care and Development; Clothing and Sewing; Food Science; Home Economics); **Human Relations** (*Tama Campus, Tama-shi, Tokyo*) (Clinical Psychology; Social Psychology; Social Welfare; Social Work; Sociology); **Language and Literature** (*Sayama campus, Iruma-shi, Saitama-ken*) (Communication Studies; Cultural Studies; English; Japanese; Literature; Modern Languages); **Social Information Studies** (*Tama Campus, Tama-shi, Tokyo*) (Information Management; Information Sciences; Information Technology)

Graduate School

Human Culture (Clinical Psychology; Cultural Studies; Modern Languages; Sociology)

Further information: Sayama Campus (Iruma-shi, Saitama-ken); Tama Campus (Tama-shi, Tokyo)

History: Founded 1908 as School for Needlework and Handicrafts, became Junior College 1942, and acquired present status 1992.

Academic year: April to March (April-September; September-March)

Admission requirements: Graduation from high school and entrance examination

Main language(s) of instruction: Japanese

Accrediting agency: Ministry of Education, Culture, Sports, Science and Technology (MEXT)

Degrees and diplomas: Gakushi, Shushi (Clinical Psychology; Sociology), Hakase (Anthropology; Cultural Studies; Home Economics; Modern Languages). Also Teaching Graduation

Student Services: Academic Counselling, Social Counselling, Careers Guidance, Sports Facilities, Health Services, Canteen, Foreign Studies Centre, Library

Periodicals: Ostuma Journal, Ostuma Kokubun, Seien

Last Update: 26-03-2018

Poole Gakuin University

4-5-1 Makizukadai Sakai-shi
Osaka-shi 590-0114, Osaka
Tel: +81(72) 292-7201
Fax: +81(72) 293-5525
Website: http://www.poole.ac.jp

Department/Division

Early Childhood Care and Education (Child Care and Development; Preschool Education); **Education** (Child Care and Development; Education; Health Education; Primary Education; Secondary Education; Special Education); **Intercultural Studies** (Arts and Humanities; Chinese; Cultural Studies; French; German; Italian; Japanese; Korean; Regional Studies); **Liberal Studies** (International Studies; Public Administration; Tourism); **Secretarial Studies** (Finance; Health Administration; Hotel and Restaurant; Information Sciences; Marketing; Media Studies; Tourism)

Graduate School

Intercultural Studies (American Studies; Asian Studies; Cultural Studies; East Asian Studies; English Studies; International Studies; Japanese; South Asian Studies)

History: Founded 1879. Added a Women's junior college with a programme in English and literature 1950. Moved to Saikai 1982. Acquired present status 1995.

Academic year: April to March (April-September; October-March)

Fees: Undergraduate Programme: 1,123,660 per annum. Intercultural Studies, Graduate Programme: 569,430 (Yen)

Main language(s) of instruction: Japanese

Accrediting agency: Japan Institution for Higher Education Evaluation (JIHEE)

Degrees and diplomas: Gakushi, Shushi (International Studies)

Student Services: Sports Facilities, Canteen, Library

Last Update: 29-01-2018

Rakuno Gakuen University (RGU)

582 Bunkyodai-midorimachi
Ebetsu-shi 069-8501, Hokkaido
Tel: +81(11) 386-1111
Fax: +81(11) 388-4129
Website: http://www.rakuno.ac.jp
President: Kazushige Takehana

College

Agriculture, Food and Environment Sciences (Agriculture; Environmental Studies; Food Science)

School

Veterinary Medicine (Veterinary Science)

Graduate School

Dairy Science (Dairy); **Veterinary Medicine** (Veterinary Science)
History: Founded 1933 as Hokkaido Dairy Farming School. Acquired present status 1960.
Academic year: April to March (April-September; October-March)
Admission requirements: Graduation from high school or equivalent or foreign equivalent and entrance examination
Fees: Admission fee, c. 200,000; Tuition fee, c. 940,000 (Yen)
Main language(s) of instruction: Japanese
Accrediting agency: Japan Institution for Higher Education Evaluation (JIHEE)
Degrees and diplomas: Gakushi, Shushi (Agriculture; Dairy; Food Science; Nutrition), Hakase (Agriculture; Dairy; Food Science; Nutrition; Veterinary Science)
Student Services: Academic Counselling, Social Counselling, Careers Guidance, Nursery Care, Sports Facilities, Health Services, Canteen, Foreign Studies Centre
Periodicals: Rakuno Gakuen Dayori, Rakuno Journal

Academic Staff 2013-2014	MALE	FEMALE	TOTAL
FULL-TIME	207	115	322
PART-TIME	36	65	101
STAFF WITH DOCTORATE			
FULL-TIME	129	6	135
Student Numbers 2013-2014			
All (Foreign Included)	2096	1456	3552
Foreign only	9	8	17

Last Update: 29-01-2018

Reitaku University

2-1-1 Hikarigaoka
Kashiwa-shi 277-8686, Chiba
Tel: +81(4) 7173-3500
Fax: +81(4) 7173-3585
Website: http://www.reitaku-u.ac.jp
President: Osamu Nakayama

Faculty

Economics and Business Administration (Administration; Business Administration; Economics; Information Technology; International Business; International Economics; Management; Public Administration); **Foreign Studies** (Chinese; English; European Languages; German; Japanese; Modern Languages; Oriental Languages)

Graduate School

Economics and Business Administration (Business Administration; Economics); **Japanese and Oriental Languages** (*Graduate Programme*) (Japanese; Linguistics; Modern Languages; Oriental Languages)
History: Founded 1935.
Main language(s) of instruction: Japanese, English
Accrediting agency: Japan Institution for Higher Education Evaluation (JIHEE)
Degrees and diplomas: Gakushi, Shushi (Business Administration; Chinese; Economics; English; German; Japanese; Modern Languages), Hakase (Business Administration; Economics)
Student Services: Sports Facilities, Language Laboratory, Library
Last Update: 29-01-2018

Rikkyo University

3-34-1 Nishi Ikebukuro Toshima-ku
Tokyo 171-8501
Tel: +81(3) 3985-2447
Fax: +81(3) 3985-2944
Website: http://www.rikkyo.ac.jp
President: Tomoya Yoshioka
Tel: +81(3) 3985-2201

College

Arts (*Also Graduate School*) (American Studies; Arts and Humanities; Christian Religious Studies; Cultural Studies; Education; Educational Psychology; Educational Research; English; French; German; History; Japanese; Literature; Primary Education; Psychology; Special Education; Theology; Writing); **Business** (*Also Graduate School*) (Business Administration; Business and Commerce; International Business); **Community and Human Services** (*Also Graduate School*) (Social and Community Services; Social Work; Sports); **Contemporary Psychology** (*Also Graduate School*) (Psychology); **Economics** (*Also Graduate School*) (Accountancy; Economic and Finance Policy; Economics;

Finance); **Intercultural Communication** (Chinese; Communication Studies; Cultural Studies; English; French; German; Koran; Spanish); **Law and Politics** (*Also Graduate School*) (Commercial Law; International Law; Law; Political Sciences; Private Law; Public Law); **Science** (*Also Graduate School*) (Biological and Life Sciences; Chemistry; Mathematics; Natural Sciences; Physics); **Sociology** (*Also Graduate School*) (Communication Studies; Cultural Studies; Media Studies; Sociology); **Tourism** (*Also Graduate School*) (Communication Studies; Cultural Studies; Tourism)

Institute

Atomic Energy (Atomic and Molecular Physics); **Business Law Studies** (*Rikkyo Institute*) (Commercial Law); **Christian Education** (*JICE*) (Christian Religious Studies); **Church Music** (*Rikkyo Institute*) (Religious Music); **English Language Education** (*St. Paul's Institute*) (English); **Global Urban Studies** (*Rikkyo Institute*) (Urban Studies); **Japanese Studies** (Asian Studies; East Asian Studies; Japanese); **Latin American Studies** (Latin American Studies); **Leadership Studies** (Leadership); **Legal Practice Studies** (*Rikkyo Institute*) (Law); **Peace and Community Studies** (*Rikkyo Institute*) (Peace and Disarmament; Urban Studies); **Social Welfare** (Social Welfare); **Tourism** (Tourism)

Graduate School

Social Design (Arts and Humanities; Business Administration; Christian Religious Studies; Economics; English; Law; Management; Modern Languages; Political Sciences; Psychology; Social Work; Sociology; Tourism; Translation and Interpretation)

Further information: Also Rikkyo Gender Forum

History: Founded 1874 by Bishop Channing Moore Williams of the Episcopal Church of the USA. Acquired University status 1883. Administration taken over by the Japanese 1920. Reorganized and became co-educational 1949. Graduate School established 1951.

Academic year: April to March (April-September; October-January)

Admission requirements: Graduation from high school or equivalent, and entrance examination

Main language(s) of instruction: Japanese, English

Accrediting agency: Japan University Accreditation Association (JUAA)

Degrees and diplomas: Gakushi (Arts and Humanities; Law; Natural Sciences; Political Sciences), Shushi (Arts and Humanities; Christian Religious Studies; Economics; Law; Natural Sciences; Political Sciences; Sociology; Theology), Hakase (Arts and Humanities; Asian Religious Studies; Business Administration; Economics; Law; Natural Sciences; Political Sciences; Psychology; Sociology; Theology; Tourism; Welfare and Protective Services)

Student Services: Academic Counselling, Sports Facilities, Language Laboratory

Periodicals: Arts and Letters (Eibei-Bungaku), Christian Studies (Kirisutokyo Gaku), Journal of Applied Sociology, Journal of Historical Studies, Journal of Japanese Literature, Rikkyo Quarterly, St Paul's Journal of Law and Politics (Rikkyo Hogaku), St. Paul's Economic Journal

Last Update: 29-01-2018

Rissho University

4-2-16 Osaki Shinagawa-ku
Tokyo 141-8602
Tel: +81(3) 3492-0377
Fax: +81(3) 5487-3346
Website: http://www.ris.ac.jp
President: Noboru Saito

Faculty

Buddhist Studies (*Research*) (Asian Religious Studies); **Business Administration** (Business Administration); **Economics** (Economics); **Geo-Environmental Science** (Environmental Management; Geography); **Law** (Law); **Letters** (History; Literature; Philosophy; Sociology); **Psychology** (Clinical Psychology; Psychology); **Social Welfare** (Social Welfare; Welfare and Protective Services)

Department/Division

Nichiren Buddhist Studies (Asian Religious Studies)

Graduate School

Business Administration (Business Administration); **Economic** (Economics); **Geo-Environmental Science** (Environmental Studies); **Humanities and Sociology** (Literature; Sociology); **Law** (Law); **Psychology** (Psychology); **Social Welfare** (Social Welfare)

Further information: Also Kumagaya Campus and Research Institutes

History: Founded 1904 as Buddhist College, became University 1924, incorporating the College. Acquired present status 1949. Financed by the Nichiren Sect.

Academic year: April to January (April-July; September-January)

Admission requirements: Graduation from high school or equivalent or foreign equivalent, and entrance examination

Main language(s) of instruction: Japanese

Accrediting agency: Japan University Accreditation Association (JUAA)

Degrees and diplomas: Gakushi (Arts and Humanities; Economics; Environmental Management; Environmental Studies; Law; Psychology; Social Welfare), Shushi (Arts and Humanities; Business Administration; Economics;

Education; Environmental Management; Environmental Studies; Geography; History; Law; Social Welfare; Sociology), Hakase (Economics; Environmental Management; Environmental Studies; Geography; History; Psychology; Social Welfare)

Student Services: Social Counselling, Sports Facilities, Health Services, Canteen, Library

Periodicals: Bungakuburonso (Journal of Faculty of Letters), Eibungakuronko (Critical Studies in English Literature), Keizaigakukiho (Quarterly Report of Economics), Kokugokokubungaku (Journal of Japanese Philology and Literature), Osakigakuho (Journal of Nichiren and Buddhist Studies), Risshochiri (Geographical Journal), Risshoshigaku (Historical Research Report), Shakaigakuronso (Critical Studies in Sociology), Tetsugakuronso (Critical Studies in Philosophy)

Last Update: 27-03-2018

Ritsumeikan Asia Pacific University (APU)

Academic Outreach Office 1-1 Jumonjibaru
Beppu-shi 874-8577, Oita
Tel: +81(977) 78-1119
Fax: +81(977) 78-1121
Website: http://www.apu.ac.jp
President: Aruaki Deguchi

College

Asia Pacific Studies (Comparative Sociology; Cultural Studies; Development Studies; Environmental Management; International Studies); **International Management** (Accountancy; Finance; International Business; Management; Marketing)

Graduate School

Asia Pacific Studies (Asian Studies; Economics; Environmental Management; International Relations; Pacific Area Studies; Tourism); **Management** (Asian Studies; Finance; International Business; Management; Marketing; Pacific Area Studies)

History: Founded 2000, part of Ritsumeikan Trust.

Academic year: Spring semester, April-July; Fall semester, October-January

Admission requirements: Has completed a standard 12-years of education outside Japan or be at least 18 years of age and hold an International Baccalaureate Diploma or other qualification (course completion certificate) recognized by APU. Japanese basis applicants: A score of 240 points or more for level 1, or 280 points or more for level 2 on the Japanese Language Proficiency Test (JLPT). English basis applicants: A score of 500 points or more of the paper-based TOEFL (or 173 and 61 for computer-based and internet-

based respectively), or a score of 5.5 or higher on the IELTS (Academic).

Fees: First year Undergraduate : 1,299,000; second year: 1,422,000; third year: 1,422,000; fourth year: 1,135,000. Asia Pacific Studies (Master's Program): 2,800,000 (for 4 semester); Asia Pacific Studies (Doctoral Program): 4,200,000 (for 6 semester); Management (Master's Program): 3,600,000 (for 4 semester) (Yen)

Main language(s) of instruction: English, Japanese

Accrediting agency: Japan University Accreditation Association (JUAA) AACSB TedQual

Degrees and diplomas: Gakushi (Business Administration; Social Sciences), Shushi (Asian Studies; Business Administration; International Relations; Management; Pacific Area Studies), Hakase (Asian Studies; Pacific Area Studies)

Student Services: Academic Counselling, Social Counselling, Careers Guidance, Cultural Activities, Sports Facilities, Language Laboratory, Facilities for disabled people, Health Services, Canteen, Foreign Studies Centre, Library

Periodicals: Crossroads, Polyglossia, Ritsumeikan Journal of Asia Pacific Studies

Last Update: 25-05-2018

Ritsumeikan University

56-1 Toji-in, Kita-machi Kita-ku
Kyoto-shi 603-8577, Kyoto
Tel: +81(75) 813-8137
Website: http://www.ritsumei.ac.jp
President: Mikio Yoshida

Faculty

International Studies (International Relations)

College

Arts and Humanities (Arts and Humanities; Geography; History; Literature; Philosophy); **Business Administration** (Business Administration); **Economics** (Economics); **Image Arts and Sciences** (Media Studies; Visual Arts); **Information Science and Engineering** (Engineering; Information Sciences; Mathematics and Computer Science); **International Relations** (*Graduate Programme*) (International Relations); **Law** (Law); **Life Sciences** (*Graduate Programme*) (Biological and Life Sciences; Natural Sciences); **Pharmaceutical Sciences** (Pharmacy); **Political Science** (Political Sciences); **Science and Engineering** (Biological and Life Sciences; Biotechnology; Chemistry; Civil Engineering; Computer Science; Electrical and Electronic Engineering; Engineering; Environmental Engineering; Mathematics; Mechanical Engineering; Natural Sciences; Physics; Robotics); **Social Sciences** (Social Sciences); **Sports and Health Science** (Health Sciences; Sports)

Institute

Arts and Sciences (Design; Environmental Studies; Finance; Health Administration; Health Sciences; Hotel and Restaurant; Information Technology; Leisure Studies; Physical Therapy; Public Health; Tourism)
Further information: Suzaku, Kinugasa and Biwako-Kusatsu campuses
History: Founded1869 as a College of Law and Politics, renamed Ritsumeikan College 1913. Given the status of a university in 1922.
Academic year: April to March (April-September; October-March)
Admission requirements: Graduation from high school and entrance examination
Main language(s) of instruction: Japanese, English
Accrediting agency: Japan University Accreditation Association (JUAA)
Degrees and diplomas: Gakushi (Engineering; Fine Arts; Law; Natural Sciences; Social Sciences), Shushi (Economics; Engineering; Fine Arts; Information Sciences; International Studies; Law; Natural Sciences; Regional Planning), Hakase (Economics; Engineering; Fine Arts; Information Sciences; International Relations; Law; Management; Natural Sciences)
Student Services: Academic Counselling, Sports Facilities, Language Laboratory
Periodicals: Journals of the Faculties and Research Institutes
Last Update: 29-01-2018

Ryotokuji University

40 Gaiku Akemi
Urayasu-shi, Chiba
Tel: +81(47) 382-2111
Fax: +81(47) 382-2017
Website: http://www.ryotokuji-u.ac.jp
President: Kazuo Mayumi

Faculty

Arts (Cultural Studies; Fine Arts; Painting and Drawing)

Department/Division

Health Sciences (Health Sciences; Medical Auxiliaries; Medicine; Rehabilitation and Therapy; Treatment Techniques); **Nursing** (Nursing); **Physical Therapy** (Physical Therapy)
History: Founded 2006.
Admission requirements: Entrance examination
Main language(s) of instruction: Japanese
Accrediting agency: Japan Institution for Higher Education Evaluation (JIHEE)

Degrees and diplomas: Gakushi
Last Update: 29-01-2018

Ryukoku University

67 Tsukamoto-cho Fukakusa
Fushimi-ku 612-8577, Kyoto
Tel: +81(75) 642-1111
Fax: +81(75) 642-8867
Website: http://www.ryukoku.ac.jp
President: Takashi Irisawa

Faculty

Business Administration (*Also Graduate School*) (Business Administration); **Economics** (*Also Graduate School*) (Economics); **Intercultural Communication** (*Seta Campus; Also Graduate School*) (Communication Studies; Cultural Studies; English; French; International Studies; Korean); **Law** (*Also Graduate School*) (Law); **Letters** (*Omiya Campus; Also Graduate School*) (Arts and Humanities; Asian Religious Studies; Cultural Studies; Education; English; History; Japanese; Literature; Philosophy); **Political Sciences** (Political Sciences); **Science and Technology** (*Seta Campus; Also Graduate School*) (Applied Mathematics; Computer Science; Electronic Engineering; Information Sciences; Materials Engineering; Mechanical Engineering; Natural Sciences; Systems Analysis; Technology); **Sociology** (*Seta Campus; Also Graduate School*) (Sociology)

Graduate School

Master's and Doctor's Degree Program (*Omiya Campus*) (African Studies; Arts and Humanities; Asian Religious Studies; Asian Studies; Cultural Studies; Engineering; International Studies; Law; Oriental Studies; Political Sciences; Technology)
Further information: Also special courses for foreign students: Japanese Culture and Language Program (JCLP) and Janapese and Asian Studies Program (JAS)
History: Founded 1639 as Buddhist Seminary, became College 1900 and University 1922. The University is supported by the Honpa Hongawanji denomination and has 3 campuses: Fukakusa and Omya in Kyoto, and Seta in Shiga Prefecture.
Academic year: April to March (April-September; October-March)
Admission requirements: Graduation from high school or recognized foreign equivalent, and entrance examination
Main language(s) of instruction: Japanese, English
Accrediting agency: Japan University Accreditation Association (JUAA)
Degrees and diplomas: Gakushi, Shushi (African Studies; Arts and Humanities; Asian Religious Studies; Asian Studies; Business Administration; Economics; Engineering;

International Studies; Journalism; Law; Political Sciences; Social Welfare; Sociology; Technology), Hakase (African Studies; Arts and Humanities; Asian Religious Studies; Asian Studies; Business Administration; Cultural Studies; Economics; Education; Engineering; International Studies; Law; Philosophy; Political Sciences; Social Welfare; Sociology; Technology)

Student Services: Academic Counselling, Social Counselling, Careers Guidance, Sports Facilities, Language Laboratory, Facilities for disabled people, Health Services, Library

Periodicals: Bulletin of Institute of Buddhist Cultural Studies, Bulletin of the Research Institute for Social Sciences, Journal of Business Studies, Journal of Economic Studies, Journal of Education, Journal of English Language and English Literature., Journal of Humanities and Sciences, Journal of Japanese History, Journal of Religious Law, Journal of Ryukoku University, Journal of Studies in Shin Buddhism, Law Review, Philosophical Review

Last Update: 29-01-2018

Ryutsu Keizai University (RKU)

120 Hirahata
Ryugasaki-shi 301-8555, Ibaraki
Tel: +81(297) 64-0001
Fax: +81(297) 64-0011
Website: http://www.rku.ac.jp
President: Toshiaki Nojiri

Faculty
Law (Commercial Law; Law)

Department/Division
Economics (Business Administration; Economics); **Health and Sports Science** (Health Sciences; Sports); **Information Studies** (Information Sciences); **Japanese Language** (Japanese); **Sociology** (Sociology; Tourism)

Graduate School
Economics (Economics); **Law** (Law); **Logistics and Information Science** (Transport Management)
Further information: Also Matsudo campus
History: Founded 1965 under the auspices of Nippon Express, an International transportation and distribution Company.
Academic year: April to March (April-September; October-March)
Admission requirements: Graduation from high school and entrance examination
Main language(s) of instruction: Japanese
Accrediting agency: Japan University Accreditation Association (JUAA)

Degrees and diplomas: Gakushi (Economics; Law; Management; Sociology; Transport Management), Shushi (Economics; Health Sciences; Law; Social Sciences; Sports; Transport Management), Hakase (Economics; Law; Social Sciences; Transport Management). Also Graduate Course in: Economics, Sociology, 5 yrs; Distribution and Logistics Systems, 2 yrs
Student Services: Sports Facilities, Health Services, Library
Periodicals: RKU Hougaku, RKU Logistics Journal, RKU Ronshu, RKU Ryutsu Johogakubu Kiyo, RKU Shakaigakubu Ronso
Publishing house: Ryutsu Keizai University Press
Last Update: 29-01-2018

Sagami Women's University

2-1-1 Buhkyo
Sagamihara-shi 252-0307, Kanagawa
Tel: +81(42) 749-5533
Fax: +81(42) 742-1732
Website: http://www.sagami-wu.ac.jp
President: Seishi Kazama

Faculty
Liberal Arts and Science (Arts and Humanities; Child Care and Development; Design; Education; English; Information Sciences; Japanese; Media Studies)

Department/Division
Nutrition (Nutrition); **Sociology** (Sociology)

Graduate School
Nutrition (Nutrition)
History: Founded 1900. Acquired present status 1949.
Main language(s) of instruction: Japanese
Accrediting agency: Japan University Accreditation Association (JUAA)
Degrees and diplomas: Gakushi, Hakase (Nutrition)
Student Services: Academic Counselling, Health Services, Foreign Studies Centre, Library
Last Update: 29-01-2018

Saitama Gakuen University

1510 Kizoro
Kawaguchi-shi 333-0831, Saitama
Tel: +81(48) 294-1110
Fax: +81(48) 294-0294
Website: http://www.saigaku.ac.jp
President: Susumu Minegishi

Faculty

Business Administration (Accountancy; Business Administration; Management); **Economics and Business Administration** (Economics); **Humanities and Child Development** (Child Care and Development); **Humanities and Cultural Studies** (Communication Studies; Cultural Studies; History; Psychology)

Graduate School

Business Administration (Business Administration); **Psychology** (Psychology)
History: Founded 2001.
Admission requirements: Entrance examination
Main language(s) of instruction: Japanese
Accrediting agency: Japan Institution for Higher Education Evaluation (JIHEE)
Degrees and diplomas: Gakushi, Hakase (Business Administration; Psychology)
Student Services: Sports Facilities
Last Update: 30-01-2018

Saitama Institute of Technology (SIT)

1690 Fusaiji
Fukaya 369-0293, Saitama
Tel: +81(120) 604-606
Fax: +81-48) 585-6903
Website: http://www.sit.ac.jp
President: Uchiyama Shunichi

Faculty

Engineering (Applied Chemistry; Computer Science; Electronic Engineering; Mechanical Engineering); **Human and Social Studies** (Information Sciences; Psychology; Social Studies)

Graduate School

Engineering (Applied Chemistry; Computer Science; Electronic Engineering; Materials Engineering; Mechanical Engineering); **Human and Social Studies** (Information Sciences; Psychology)
History: Founded 1976.
Academic year: April to March (April-September; October-March)
Main language(s) of instruction: Japanese
Accrediting agency: Japan University Accreditation Association (JUAA)
Degrees and diplomas: Gakushi (Engineering; Social Studies), Shushi (Applied Chemistry; Computer Engineering; Electronic Engineering; Engineering; Information Sciences; Psychology; Social Studies), Hakase (Applied Chemistry; Computer Engineering; Electronic Engineering; Engineering)
Student Services: Academic Counselling, Social Counselling, Careers Guidance, Sports Facilities, Language Laboratory, Facilities for disabled people, Health Services, Canteen, Library, IT Centre
Periodicals: Bulletin of the Faculty of Human and Social Studies, SIT, Journal of the Faculty of Engineering, SIT
Last Update: 30-01-2018

Saitama Medical University

38 Morohongo Morayama-machi, Iruma-gun
Saitama-shi 350-0495, Saitama
Tel: +81(49) 276-2029
Fax: +81(49) 276-2029
Website: http://www.saitama-med.ac.jp
President: Masayoshi Bessho.

Faculty

Health and Medical Care (Biomedical Engineering; Health Sciences; Medical Technology; Nursing); **Medicine** (Medicine)

Graduate School

Medicine (Biomedicine; Medicine; Social and Preventive Medicine)
Further information: Also University Hospital; Kawagoe Campus; Kawakado Campus; Hidaka Campus and Kawagoe Building
History: Founded 1972.
Academic year: April to March (April-July; September-December; January-March)
Admission requirements: Graduation from high school and entrance examination
Main language(s) of instruction: Japanese, English
Accrediting agency: Japan Institution for Higher Education Evaluation (JIHEE)
Degrees and diplomas: Gakushi (Medicine), Hakase (Medicine)
Student Services: Academic Counselling, Nursery Care, Health Services, Canteen
Periodicals: Saitama Igaku Zasshi (Journal)
Last Update: 30-01-2018

Saku University

2384 Iwamurada,
Saku 385-0022, Nagano
Tel: +81 267-68-6680

Fax: +81 267-68-6687
Website: http://www.saku.ac.jp
President: Masahiro Morioka

School

Nursing (Nursing)
History: Founded 1988 as Shinshu Junior College. Acquired present status and title 2008.
Main language(s) of instruction: Japanese, English
Accrediting agency: Japan Institution for Higher Education Evaluation (JIHEE)
Degrees and diplomas: Gakushi (Nursing), Shushi (Nursing)
Student Services: Library, eLibrary

Academic Staff 2012-2013	MALE	FEMALE	TOTAL
FULL-TIME			47
Student Numbers 2012-2013			
All (Foreign Included)	63	306	369

Last Update: 30-01-2018

Sakushin Gakuin University

908 Takeshita-machi
Utsunomiya-shi 321-3295, Tochigi
Tel: +81(28) 667-7111
Fax: +81(28) 667-7110
Website: http://www.sakushin-u.ac.jp
President: Hiroshi Watanabe

Faculty

Business Administration (Accountancy; Business Administration; Finance; Information Technology; Management; Political Sciences; Public Administration; Sports Management; Tourism; Town Planning); **Human and Cultural Studies** (Cultural Studies; Education; English; Japanese; Psychology)

School

Graduate Studies (Business Administration; Psychology)

Department/Division

Early Childhood Education (Child Care and Development; Preschool Education)
History: Founded 1989.
Academic year: April to March
Admission requirements: Graduation from high school and entrance examination
Main language(s) of instruction: Japanese
Accrediting agency: Japan Institution for Higher Education Evaluation (JIHEE)

Degrees and diplomas: Gakushi, Shushi (Business Administration; Clinical Psychology; Psychology), Hakase (Business Administration)
Student Services: Academic Counselling, Social Counselling, Careers Guidance, Sports Facilities, Language Laboratory, Canteen, Library
Last Update: 30-01-2018

Sanno Institute of Management - Sanno University

Shonan Campus, 1573 Kamikasuya
Isehara-shi 259-1197, Kanagawa
Tel: +81(463) 92-2211
Fax: +81(463) 93-0554
Website: http://www.sanno.ac.jp/english/index.html
President: Shunichi Ueno

School

Information Oriented Management (Information Sciences; Management); **Management** (Information Sciences; Management)

Graduate School

Sanno (Business Administration; Information Management; Information Sciences; Management)
Further information: Also Jiyugaoka and Daikanyama campuses
History: Founded 1979.
Academic year: April to March
Admission requirements: Graduation from high school
Main language(s) of instruction: Japanese
Accrediting agency: Japan Institution for Higher Education Evaluation (JIHEE)
Degrees and diplomas: Gakushi, Shushi (Management)
Student Services: Academic Counselling, Social Counselling, Careers Guidance, Nursery Care, Sports Facilities, Language Laboratory, Facilities for disabled people, Health Services, Canteen, Foreign Studies Centre, Library
Last Update: 30-01-2018

Sanyo Gakuen University

1-14-1 Hirai
Okayama-shi 703-8501, Okayama
Tel: +81(83) 272-6254
Fax: +81(83) 273-3226
Website: http://www.sguc.ac.jp
President: Saito Itoku

Faculty

Human Science (Cultural Studies; Modern Languages; Psychology); **Nursing** (Nursing)

History: Founded as Sanyo Eiwa Women's School, 1886. Acquired present status 1994.

Main language(s) of instruction: Japanese

Accrediting agency: Japan Institution for Higher Education Evaluation (JIHEE)

Degrees and diplomas: Gakushi

Student Services: Library

Last Update: 30-01-2018

Sapporo Gakuin University

11 Bunkyodai
Ebetsu-shi 069-8555, Hokkaido
Tel: +81(11) 386-8111
Fax: +81(11) 386-8115
Website: http://www.sgu.ac.jp
President: Tsurumaru Toshiaki

Faculty

Business Administration (Accountancy; Business Administration; Finance); **Commerce** (Business and Commerce); **Economics** (Economics); **Humanities** (Clinical Psychology; English; European Languages; Literature; Modern Languages; Social Sciences); **Law** (Law); **Social and Information Studies** (Information Sciences; Information Technology; Media Studies; Social Studies)

School

Graduate Studies (Clinical Psychology; Law; Management; Psychology)

History: Founded 1946.

Main language(s) of instruction: Japanese

Accrediting agency: Japan University Accreditation Association (JUAA)

Degrees and diplomas: Gakushi, Shushi (Clinical Psychology; Law; Management)

Student Services: Social Counselling, Sports Facilities, Language Laboratory, Health Services, Library

Last Update: 30-01-2018

Sapporo International University

4-1-4-1 Kiyota
Sapporo-shi 004-8602, Hokkaido
Tel: +81(11) 881-8844
Fax: +81(11) 885-3370
Website: http://www.siu.ac.jp

Faculty

Humanities (Clinical Psychology; Cultural Studies; Media Studies; Psychology; Sociology); **Sport** (Sports; Sports Management)

Department/Division

International Tourism (Tourism)

Graduate School

Clinical Psychology (Clinical Psychology; Psychology); **Tourism** (Tourism)

History: Founded as Sapporo Seishutankidaigaku 1969. Became Seishu Joshi Daigaku (Seishu Women's University) 1993. Acquired present title 1997.

Main language(s) of instruction: Japanese

Accrediting agency: Japan Institution for Higher Education Evaluation (JIHEE)

Degrees and diplomas: Gakushi (Health Sciences; Literature; Sports; Tourism), Shushi (Tourism)

Student Services: Social Counselling, Careers Guidance, Sports Facilities, Language Laboratory, Library

Last Update: 28-03-2018

Sapporo Otani University

Kita 16 Johigashi 9-chome, Higashi-ku
Sapporo 065-8567, Hokkaido
Tel: +81 11-742-1651
Website: http://www.sapporo-otani.ac.jp

Faculty

Social Sciences (Social and Community Services)

School

Art (Conducting; Design; Music Theory and Composition; Musical Instruments; Painting and Drawing; Singing)

History: Founded 1906 as North Sea Girls' School. Acquired present status and title 2006.

Main language(s) of instruction: Japanese

Accrediting agency: Japan Institution for Higher Education Evaluation (JIHEE)

Degrees and diplomas: Gakushi (Fine Arts; Music; Social Sciences)

Last Update: 30-01-2018

Sapporo University

3-1-3-7 Nishioka Toyohira-ku
Sapporo-shi 062-8520, Hokkaido
Tel: +81(11) 852-9138

Fax: +81(11) 856-8268
Website: http://www.sapporo-u.ac.jp
President: Junichi Suzuki

Faculty

Business Administration (*Also Graduate School*) (Accountancy; Business Administration; Industrial Management; Information Management); **Cultural Studies** (*Also Graduate School*) (Cultural Studies; History; Japanese; Regional Studies); **Economics** (*Also Graduate School*) (Economics); **Foreign Languages** (*Also Graduate School*) (Chinese; English; European Languages; Modern Languages; Russian); **Law** (*Also Graduate School*) (Law)
History: Founded 1967.
Admission requirements: Entrance examination
Fees: 770,000 per annum (Yen)
Main language(s) of instruction: Japanese
Accrediting agency: Japan University Accreditation Association (JUAA)
Degrees and diplomas: Gakushi, Shushi (Business Administration; Cultural Studies; Economics; English; Law; Russian)
Student Services: Sports Facilities, Health Services, Library
Last Update: 30-01-2018

Sapporo University of Health Sciences

2 Chome-1-15 Nakanuma Nishi 4 Jo, Higashi Ward
Sapporo 007-0894, Higashi-ku
Tel: +81 11-792-3350
Fax: +81 11-792-3358
Website: http://www.sapporo-hokeniryou-u.ac.jp
President: Yoshie Inaba

Faculty

Nursing (Nursing)
History: Founded 2013.
Main language(s) of instruction: Japanese
Accrediting agency: Ministry of Education, Culture, Sports, Science and Technology (MEXT)
Degrees and diplomas: Gakushi (Nursing)
Student Services: Academic Counselling, Sports Facilities, Canteen, Library, IT Centre
Last Update: 31-01-2018

SBI Graduate School

Yokohama Ota-cho 2-23, Media Business Center, 6th floor
Yokohama 231-0011, Kanagawa
Tel: +81(3) 5293-4100
Fax: +81(3) 5293-4102

Website: http://www.sbi-u.ac.jp
President: Yoshitaka Kitao

School

Management Graduate Entrepreneur (Business Administration; Management)
History: Founded 2008. Distance learning university.
Main language(s) of instruction: Japanese
Accrediting agency: Japan Institution for Higher Education Evaluation (JIHEE)
Degrees and diplomas: Shushi (Business Administration)
Last Update: 31-01-2018

Seian University of Art and Design

4-3-1 Ohginosato-higashi
Otsu-shi 520-0248, Shiga
Tel: +81(77) 574-2111
Fax: +81(77) 574-2120
Website: http://www.seian.ac.jp
President: Okada Shuji

Faculty

Art (Cinema and Television; Design; Fine Arts; Graphic Design; Painting and Drawing; Photography)
History: Founded 1993.
Admission requirements: Entrance examination
Fees: 900,000 per annum (Yen)
Main language(s) of instruction: Japanese
Accrediting agency: Japan Institution for Higher Education Evaluation (JIHEE)
Degrees and diplomas: Gakushi
Student Services: Canteen, Library
Last Update: 31-01-2018

Seibi University

3370 Nishi Kotanigaoka
Fukuchiyama-shi 620-0886, Kyoto
Tel: +81(773) 22-5852
Fax: +81(773) 22-2388
Website: http://uv.seibi-gakuen.ac.jp
President: Akira Uchiyama

Department/Division

Business Design (Business Administration); **Food and Nutrition** (*Junior College*) (Food Technology; Nutrition); **Health and Welfare Management** (Health Administration; Welfare and Protective Services)
History: Founded as Kyoto Sosei Daigaku. Acquired present title 2010.

Admission requirements: Entrance examination
Fees: 700.000 per annum (Yen)
Main language(s) of instruction: Japanese
Accrediting agency: Ministry of Education, Culture, Sports, Science and Technology (MEXT)
Degrees and diplomas: Gakushi
Last Update: 31-01-2018

Seigakuin University (SEIG)

1-1 Tosaki
Ageo-shi 362-8585, Saitama
Tel: +81(48) 781-0925
Fax: +81(48) 762-2962
Website: http://www.seig.ac.jp
President: Masayuki Shimizu

Faculty

Human Welfare (Child Care and Development; Clinical Psychology; Educational Sciences; Environmental Studies; Psychology; Social Welfare; Sociology); **Humanities** (Cultural Studies; English; Japanese; Western European Studies); **Political Sciences and Economics** (Economics; Political Sciences; Social and Community Services)

Graduate School

American-European Cultural Studies (American Studies; Christian Religious Studies; Cultural Studies; English; Ethics; European Studies; History); **Politics and Policy Studies** (Government; Political Sciences; Social Policy; Taxation)
History: Founded 1988.
Academic year: April to March (April-July; September-March)
Admission requirements: Graduation from high school and entrance examination
Main language(s) of instruction: Japanese, English
Accrediting agency: Japan University Accreditation Association (JUAA)
Degrees and diplomas: Gakushi (Cultural Studies; Education; Political Sciences; Psychology; Social Welfare), Shushi (Cultural Studies; Political Sciences; Social Welfare), Hakase (Cultural Studies). Kyoin Menkyo (Teaching Certificate) for Kindergarten, Middle School and High School; Toshokan Shisho (Librarian Certificate)
Student Services: Academic Counselling, Social Counselling, Careers Guidance, Sports Facilities, Language Laboratory, Facilities for disabled people, Health Services, Canteen, Library, IT Centre
Periodicals: Seigakuin Journal
Publishing house: Seigakuin University Press
Last Update: 27-03-2018

Seijo University

6-1-20 Seijo Setagaya-ku
Tokyo 157-8511
Tel: +81(3) 3482-6020
Fax: +81(3) 3482-9049
Website: http://www.seijo.ac.jp
President: Junichi Tobe

Faculty

Arts and Literature (*Also Graduate School*) (Aesthetics; Art History; Cultural Studies; English; European Studies; Film; Fine Arts; Japanese; Mass Communication; Musicology; Theatre); **Economics** (*Also Graduate School*) (Business Administration; Economics); **Law** (*Also Graduate School*) (Law); **Social Innovation** (Psychology; Sociology)
Further information: Also research centers and institutes
History: Founded 1917 as Elementary School, became High School 1926, acquired University status 1950.
Academic year: April to March (April-September; September-March)
Admission requirements: Graduation from high school or foreign equivalent, and entrance examination
Main language(s) of instruction: Japanese
Accrediting agency: Japan University Accreditation Association (JUAA)
Degrees and diplomas: Gakushi (Economics; Fine Arts; Law), Shushi (Business Administration; Economics; English; Fine Arts; Japanese; Law; Literature), Hakase (Economics; Law; Literature; Social Sciences)
Student Services: Academic Counselling, Social Counselling, Careers Guidance, Sports Facilities, Language Laboratory, Health Services, Canteen, Library
Periodicals: English Monographs, Kokubungaku Ronshu (Monographs on Japanese Literature and Language, annually), Minzokugaku Kenkyujo Kiyo (Folklore Studies), Seijo Bungei (Arts and Literature), Seijo Daigaku Keizai Kenkyu (Economic Studies), Seijo Law Journal
Last Update: 31-01-2018

Seijoh University

2-172 Fukinodai Tokai-Shi
Aichi-gun 476-8588, Aichi
Tel: +81(52) 601-6000
Fax: +81(52) 601-6010
Website: http://www.seijoh-u.ac.jp
President: Isao Akaoka

Faculty

Business Administration (Accountancy; Business Administration; Finance; Health Administration; Management;

Marketing; Sports Management; Tourism); **Rehabilitation and Care** (Occupational Therapy; Physical Therapy)
History: Founded 2002.
Admission requirements: Entrance examination
Fees: 600,000 - 800,000 depending on programmes (Yen)
Main language(s) of instruction: Japanese
Accrediting agency: Japan Institution for Higher Education Evaluation (JIHEE)
Degrees and diplomas: Gakushi, Shushi (Health Sciences; Occupational Therapy; Physical Therapy; Rehabilitation and Therapy)
Student Services: Academic Counselling, Foreign Studies Centre, Library, Residential Facilities
Last Update: 31-01-2018

Seikei University

3-3-1 Kichijoji-Kitamachi
Musashino-shi 180-8633, Tokyo
Tel: +81(422) 37-3517
Fax: +81(422) 37-3864
Website: http://www.seikei.ac.jp/university
President: Hiroshi Kitagawa

Faculty

Economics (Economics; Management); **Humanities** (Arts and Humanities; Cultural Studies; English; European Languages; Japanese; Literature; Modern Languages; Oriental Languages; Social Sciences); **Law** (Law; Political Sciences); **Science and Technology** (Computer Engineering; Computer Networks; Energy Engineering; Engineering; Environmental Engineering; Industrial Chemistry; Industrial Engineering; Information Sciences; Materials Engineering; Mechanical Engineering)

Centre

Asian and Pacific Studies (Asian Studies; Pacific Area Studies)

Graduate School

Business (Business and Commerce); **Economics and Management** (Economics); **Humanities** (Arts and Humanities; Cultural Studies; English; European Languages; Japanese; Literature; Modern Languages; Oriental Languages; Social Sciences); **Law** (Law; Political Sciences); **Science and Technology** (Applied Physics; Electrical and Electronic Engineering; Engineering; Industrial Chemistry; Information Sciences; Mechanical Engineering)
Further information: Also Centre for International Exchange
History: Founded 1912. Acquired present title 1949.

Academic year: April to March (April-September; October-March)
Admission requirements: Graduation from high school, and entrance examination
Main language(s) of instruction: Japanese
Accrediting agency: Japan University Accreditation Association (JUAA)
Degrees and diplomas: Gakushi (Economics; Engineering; Fine Arts; Law), Shushi (Computer Engineering; Cultural Studies; Economics; Engineering; English; Japanese; Law; Literature; Management; Materials Engineering; Political Sciences), Hakase (Computer Engineering; Cultural Studies; Economics; English; Japanese; Law; Literature; Management; Materials Engineering; Political Sciences)
Student Services: Academic Counselling, Social Counselling, Careers Guidance, Cultural Activities, Sports Facilities, Language Laboratory, Health Services, Canteen, Foreign Studies Centre, Library, IT Centre
Periodicals: Bulletin of Seikei University, Journal of the Faculty of Economics, Proceedings of the Faculty of Engineering, Proceedings of the Faculty of Letters, The Seikei Japanese Literature, The Seikei Legal Sciences
Last Update: 31-01-2018

Seinan Gakuin University

6-2-92, Nishijin Sawara-ku
Fukuoka-shi 814-8511, Fukuoka
Tel: +81(92) 823-3346
Fax: +81(92) 823-3334
Website: http://www.seinan-gu.ac.jp
President: K. J. Schaffner

School

Graduate (Business Administration; Cultural Studies; Economics; English; French; International Studies; Law; Literature)

Department/Division

Commerce (Business Administration; Business and Commerce); **Economics** (Economics; International Economics); **Human Sciences** (Child Care and Development; Education; Preschool Education; Social Welfare); **Intercultural Studies** (Cultural Studies); **Law** (International Law; International Relations; Law; Political Sciences); **Literature** (Cultural Studies; English; French; Literature; Modern Languages); **Theology** (Christian Religious Studies; Theology)
Further information: Also International Division (courses in English); Junior Year Study Abroad Programme
History: Founded 1916 by the Southern Baptist Missionaries as School, acquired present status 1949.

Academic year: April to March (April-September; October-March)

Admission requirements: Graduation from high school or equivalent, and entrance examination

Fees: National : 720,000 per annum (Yen), International : 740,000 (Yen)

Main language(s) of instruction: Japanese, English

Accrediting agency: Japan University Accreditation Association (JUAA)

Degrees and diplomas: Gakushi (Fine Arts), Shushi (Business Administration; Economics; Law; Modern Languages), Hakase

Student Services: Academic Counselling, Social Counselling, Careers Guidance, Nursery Care, Cultural Activities, Sports Facilities, Health Services, Canteen, Library, Residential Facilities

Periodicals: Academic Research Bulletin, Commercial Journal, Economic Journal, English Language and Literature, French Language and Literature, International Cultures, Law Journal, Studies in Theology, Study in Education and Welfare

Last Update: 31-01-2018

Seinan Jo Gakuin University

1-3-5 Ibori Kokura-kita-ku
Kitakyushu-shi 803-0835, Fukuoka
Tel: +81(93) 583-5123
Fax: +81(93) 583-5614
Website: http://www.seinan-jo.ac.jp

Faculty

Health and Welfare (Midwifery; Nursing; Nutrition; Social Welfare); **Humanities** (Cultural Studies; English; Tourism)

History: Founded 1922 as girl's High School. Acquired present titile and status 1994.

Admission requirements: Entrance Examination

Main language(s) of instruction: Japanese

Accrediting agency: Japan Institution for Higher Education Evaluation (JIHEE)

Degrees and diplomas: Gakushi

Student Services: Academic Counselling, Careers Guidance, Health Services, Foreign Studies Centre, Residential Facilities

Last Update: 31-01-2018

Seirei Christopher University

3543 Mikatahara-cho, Kita-ku
Hamamatsu-shi 433-8558, Shizuoka
Tel: +81(53) 439-1400
Fax: +81(53) 439-1430
Website: http://www.seirei.ac.jp
President: Oshiro Shohei

School

Nursing (*Undergraduate and graduate programmes*) (Midwifery; Nursing); **Rehabilitation Sciences** (*Undergraduate and graduate programmes*) (Occupational Therapy; Physical Therapy; Speech Therapy and Audiology); **Social Work** (*Undergraduate and graduate programmes*) (Child Care and Development; Preschool Education; Social Welfare; Social Work)

History: Founded 1949 as Enshu Christian School, became Seirei Kurisutofa Kango Daigaku (Seirei Christopher College of Nursing) 1992. Acquired present title 2006.

Main language(s) of instruction: Japanese

Accrediting agency: Japan University Accreditation Association (JUAA)

Degrees and diplomas: Gakushi, Shushi (Nursing; Occupational Therapy; Physical Therapy; Rehabilitation and Therapy; Social Welfare), Hakase (Health Sciences)

Student Services: Careers Guidance, Sports Facilities, Health Services, Foreign Studies Centre

Last Update: 31-01-2018

SEISA Dohto University

7-1 Ochiishi-cho
Mombetsu-shi 094-8582, Hokkaido
Tel: +81(11) 372-3111
Fax: +81(11) 372-2580
Website: http://www.dohto.ac.jp

Faculty

Business Administration (Accountancy; Business Administration; Information Technology; Management; Sports Management; Tourism); **Fine Arts** (Architectural and Environmental Design; Architecture; Communication Arts; Design; Fine Arts; Graphic Design; Handicrafts; Interior Design; Painting and Drawing; Sculpture); **Social Welfare** (Child Care and Development; Education; Psychology; Social Psychology; Social Welfare; Social Work; Special Education)

Research Division

International Architecture (Architecture); **International Design** (Design); **International Management and Cultures** (Cultural Studies; Management); **International Welfare** (Welfare and Protective Services)

Further information: Also Sapporo and Mombetsu campuses

History: Founded 1978 as Dohto University. Acquired present name in 2017

Admission requirements: High school level; Entrance examination

Fees: Registration fee, 200,000; Tuition, 720,000-920,000 per annum (Yen)

Main language(s) of instruction: Japanese

Accrediting agency: Japan Institution for Higher Education Evaluation (JIHEE)

Degrees and diplomas: Gakushi

Student Services: Academic Counselling, Health Services, Canteen, Foreign Studies Centre

Academic Staff 2012-2013	MALE	FEMALE	TOTAL
FULL-TIME			118
Student Numbers 2012-2013			
All (Foreign Included)	517	245	762

Last Update: 01-02-2018

Seisa University

5-14 Ryokusen-cho
Ashibetsu-shi 075-0163, Hokkaido
Tel: +81(120) 82-2686
Website: http://www.seisa.ac.jp

Faculty

Symbiosis Sciences (*Basic Introductory Courses*) (Primary Education; Social Welfare; Sports)

History: Founded 1985. Acquired present title 2004.

Main language(s) of instruction: Japanese

Accrediting agency: Japan Institution for Higher Education Evaluation (JIHEE)

Degrees and diplomas: Gakushi

Last Update: 01-02-2018

Seisen Jogakuin University

2-120-8 Uwano
Nagano-shi 381-0085, Nagano
Tel: +81(26) 295-5665
Fax: +81(26) 295-6420
Website: http://www.seisen-jc.ac.jp
President: Yutaka Shibayama

Department/Division

English; **Modern Communication** (Communication Studies; Information Sciences); **Psychology** (Psychology)

History: Founded 1961 as Nagano Seisen Jogakuin high school. Acquired present title 2003.

Main language(s) of instruction: Japanese

Accrediting agency: Japan University Accreditation Association (JUAA)

Degrees and diplomas: Gakushi

Student Services: Academic Counselling, Careers Guidance, Sports Facilities, Canteen, Foreign Studies Centre

Last Update: 01-02-2018

Seisen University

720 Hidachō
Hikone 5521-1123, Shiga
Tel: +85(749) 43-7511
Fax: +85(749) 43-5201
Website: http://www.seisen.ac.jp
President and Chairman: Yuko Tsutsui

Faculty

Faculty of Human Studies (Psychology)

School

Graduate School of Nursing (Nursing); **School of Nursing** (Nursing)

History: Founded 1985. Acquired present status in 2003

Main language(s) of instruction: Japanese

Accrediting agency: Japan Institution for Higher Education Evaluation (JIHEE)

Degrees and diplomas: Gakushi (Psychology)

Last Update: 26-03-2018

Seisen University

3-16-21 Higashi Gotanda Shinagawa-ku
Tokyo 141-8642
Tel: +81(3) 3447-5551
Fax: +81(3) 3447-8642
Website: http://www.seisen-u.ac.jp
President: Akira Sugiyama

Department/Division

Cultural History (Cultural Studies; History); **English Language and Literature** (English); **Global Citizenship Studies**; **Japanese Language and Literature** (Japanese); **Spanish Language and Literature** (Spanish)

Further information: Also Research Institutes

History: Founded 1950. A Catholic Liberal Arts Women's University.

Academic year: April to March (April-September; October-March)

Admission requirements: Graduation from high school and entrance examination

Main language(s) of instruction: Japanese, English
Accrediting agency: Japan University Accreditation Association (JUAA)
Degrees and diplomas: Gakushi, Shushi (Cultural Studies; Modern Languages), Hakase (Cultural Studies; Modern Languages)
Student Services: Sports Facilities, Foreign Studies Centre, Library
Periodicals: Bulletin of Seisen University, Bulletin of Seisen University Research Institute for Cultural Science, Journal of the Institute of Christian Culture Seisen University, Papers in Language, Thought and Culture Seisen University Graduate School, Sesen Bun-en
Last Update: 01-02-2018

Seitoku University

550 Iwase
Matsudo-shi 271-8555, Chiba
Tel: +81(47) 365-1111
Fax: +81(47) 363-1401
Website: http://www.seitoku.jp/univ
President: Hirozumi Kawanami

Faculty
Child Studies (Child Care and Development; Preschool Education; Primary Education); **Human Nutrition** (Nutrition); **Literature** (Communication Studies; English; Japanese; Library Science); **Music** (Music; Music Theory and Composition; Musical Instruments; Musicology; Opera; Performing Arts; Singing); **Psychology and Welfare** (Clinical Psychology; Psychology; Social Psychology; Social Welfare)

Graduate School
Graduate Studies (American Studies; Child Care and Development; Cultural Studies; European Studies; Music; Music Theory and Composition; Nutrition; Psychology)
Further information: Also Research Institutes
History: Founded 1990
Academic year: April to March
Admission requirements: Secondary school certificate and entrance examination
Main language(s) of instruction: Japanese
Accrediting agency: Japan University Accreditation Association (JUAA)
Degrees and diplomas: Gakushi (Business and Commerce; Child Care and Development; Education; English; Linguistics; Management; Music; Nutrition; Psychology; Social Welfare), Shushi (American Studies; Art Therapy; Child Care and Development; English Studies; Japanese; Music; Nutrition; Psychology), Hakase (American Studies; Child Care and Development; English Studies; Japanese; Music; Nutrition; Psychology). Also Associate Degree (2 yrs)
Student Services: Careers Guidance, Cultural Activities, Sports Facilities, Language Laboratory, Health Services, Canteen, Foreign Studies Centre, Residential Facilities
Periodicals: Bulletin of Seitoku University, Bulletin of the Junior College Seitoku University
Last Update: 01-02-2018

Seiwa University

3-4-5 Higashiota
Kisarazu-shi 292-8555, Chiba
Tel: +81(438) 30-5555
Fax: +81(438) 30-5550
Website: http://www.seiwa-univ.ac.jp
President: Kyoichi Oda

Faculty
Law (Commercial Law; Law)
History: Founded 1994.
Main language(s) of instruction: Japanese
Accrediting agency: Japan Institution for Higher Education Evaluation (JIHEE)
Degrees and diplomas: Gakushi
Student Services: Sports Facilities, Library
Periodicals: Seiwa Bulletin, Seiwa Law Study
Last Update: 01-02-2018

Sendai Shirayuri Women's College

6-1 Honda-cho Izumi-ku
Sendai-shi 981-3107, Miyagi
Tel: +81(22) 374-5014
Fax: +81(22) 374-5019
Website: http://www.sendai-shirayuri.ac.jp
President: Nadao Yaguchi

Faculty
Human Sciences (Child Care and Development; Cultural Studies; Development Studies; Food Science; Health Sciences; International Studies; Nutrition; Social Sciences; Social Welfare)
History: Founded 1996.
Main language(s) of instruction: Japanese
Accrediting agency: Japan University Accreditation Association (JUAA)
Degrees and diplomas: Gakushi
Student Services: Academic Counselling, Careers Guidance, Foreign Studies Centre, Library
Last Update: 01-02-2018

Sendai University

2-2-18 Funaoka-Minami
Shibata-gun 989-1693, Miyagi-Ken
Tel: +81(224) 55-1121
Fax: +81(224) 57-2769
Website: http://www.sendaidaigaku.jp
President: Yoshikichi Abe

Faculty

Sports Science (Health Sciences; Nutrition; Physical Education; Sports; Welfare and Protective Services)
History: Founded 1967.
Main language(s) of instruction: Japanese
Accrediting agency: Japan Institution for Higher Education Evaluation (JIHEE)
Degrees and diplomas: Gakushi, Shushi (Sports)
Student Services: Sports Facilities, Library
Last Update: 01-02-2018

Senri Kinran University

5-25-1 Fujisirodai
Suita-shi 565-0873, Osaka
Tel: +81(6) 6872-0721
Fax: +81(6) 6872-7724
Website: http://www.kinran.ac.jp

School

Nursing (Nursing)

Department/Division

Children (Child Care and Development); **Nutrition and Food Science** (Food Technology; Nutrition)
History: Founded 2003.
Admission requirements: Entrance examination
Main language(s) of instruction: Japanese
Accrediting agency: Japan Institution for Higher Education Evaluation (JIHEE)
Degrees and diplomas: Gakushi
Last Update: 02-02-2018

Senshu University

3-8-1 Kandajimbo-cho Chiyoda-ku
Tokyo 101-8425
Tel: +81(3) 3265-6821
Fax: +81(3) 3265-3649
Website: http://www.senshu-u.ac.jp
President: Shigeto Sasaki
Tel: +81(44) 911-1252

School

Business Administration (Business Administration); **Commerce** (Accountancy; Business and Commerce; Finance; Labour and Industrial Relations; Marketing); **Economics** (Economics; International Economics); **Law** (Law); **Legal Affairs** (*Professional*) (Law); **Literature** (English; Geography; Histology; Japanese; Literature; Philosophy; Psychology; Sociology); **Network and Information**

Graduate School

Business Administration (Business Administration; Information Management); **Commerce** (Accountancy; Business and Commerce); **Economics** (Economics); **Humanities** (English; Geography; History; Japanese; Literature; Philosophy; Psychology; Sociology); **Law**
Further information: Also 12 Research Institutes. Also Ikuta Campus. Affiliated institutions: Ishinomaki Senshu University and Hokkaido College, Senshu University.
History: Founded 1880 as School, became Senshu Daigaku 1913, recognized as private University 1922. Reorganized 1949.
Academic year: April to March (April-July; September-March)
Admission requirements: Graduation from high school or foreign equivalent, and entrance examination
Main language(s) of instruction: Japanese
Accrediting agency: Japan University Accreditation Association (JUAA)
Degrees and diplomas: Gakushi (Arts and Humanities; Business Administration; Business and Commerce; Economics; Law), Shushi (Accountancy; Business Administration; Business and Commerce; Economics; English; Geography (Human); History; Japanese; Law; Philosophy; Psychology; Sociology), Hakase (Accountancy; Business Administration; Business and Commerce; Civil Law; Economics; English; Geography (Human); History; Japanese; Law; Philosophy; Psychology; Public Law; Sociology)
Student Services: Academic Counselling, Social Counselling, Careers Guidance, Nursery Care, Sports Facilities, Language Laboratory, Facilities for disabled people, Health Services, Canteen, Foreign Studies Centre, Library
Periodicals: Annual Bulletin of Accounting Studies, Annual Bulletin of Social Science, Annual Bulletin of the Association of Natural Sciences, Annual Bulletin of the Humanities, Annual Bulletin of the Institute of Sports, Physical Education and Recreation, Business Review, Economics Bulletin, Journal of Law and Political Science, Studies in Humanities

Academic Staff 2013-2014	MALE	FEMALE	TOTAL
FULL-TIME			426
PART-TIME			738

(continued)

Academic Staff 2013-2014	MALE	FEMALE	TOTAL
Student Numbers 2013-2014			
All (Foreign Included)	12603	6766	19369
Foreign only			283

Last Update: 27-03-2018

Senzoku Gakuen College of Music

2-3-1 Hisamoto Takatsu-ku
Kawasaki-shi 213-8580, Kanagawa
Tel: +81(44) 856-2727
Fax: +81(44) 856-2710
Website: http://www.senzoku.ac.jp/music/en
President: Shinya Bandai

Department/Division

Composition, Musicology, Music Design (Jazz and Popular Music; Music; Music Theory and Composition; Musicology; Sound Engineering (Acoustics)); **Instrumental Music** (Musical Instruments); **Music Pedagogy and Music Therapy** (Music Education); **Vocal Music** (Opera; Singing)

Graduate School

Music (Music; Music Theory and Composition; Musical Instruments; Opera; Singing)
History: Founded as Senzoku Gakuen Ongaku Daigaku, 1967.
Academic year: April to March (April-September; October-March)
Admission requirements: Graduation from high school or foreign equivalent and entrance examination
Main language(s) of instruction: Japanese
Accrediting agency: Japan Institution for Higher Education Evaluation (JIHEE)
Degrees and diplomas: Gakushi, Shushi (Music; Music Theory and Composition; Musical Instruments; Singing)
Periodicals: Senzoku ronso (Memoirs)
Last Update: 02-02-2018

Setsunan University

17-8 Ikedanaka-machi
Neyagawa-shi 572-8508, Osaka
Tel: +81(72) 839-9104
Fax: +81(72) 826-5100
Website: http://www.setsunan.ac.jp
President: Yagi Kiichiro
Tel: +81(72) 839-9100

Faculty

Business Administration and Information (*Also Graduate School*) (Business Administration; Information Sciences); **Economics** (Economics); **Foreign Studies** (*Also Graduate School*) (Chinese; Cultural Studies; English; French; German; Indonesian; Modern Languages; Spanish); **Law** (*Also Graduate School*) (Law; Political Sciences); **Nursing** (Nursing); **Pharmaceutical Sciences** (*Also Graduate School*) (Environmental Studies; Health Sciences; Pharmacy); **Science and Engineering** (*Also Graduate School*) (Architecture; Civil Engineering; Electrical Engineering; Electronic Engineering; Engineering; Engineering Management; Environmental Engineering; Industrial Engineering; Mechanical Engineering; Structural Architecture; Systems Analysis)
Further information: Also American, Mexican, Indonesian, Chinese studies
History: Founded 1922 as Kansai Technical Institution, acquired present status and title 1975.
Academic year: April to March (April-September; October-March)
Admission requirements: Graduation from high school or equivalent, and entrance examination
Main language(s) of instruction: Japanese
Accrediting agency: Japan Institution for Higher Education Evaluation (JIHEE)
Degrees and diplomas: Gakushi, Shushi (Accountancy; Business Administration; Electrical and Electronic Engineering; Engineering; Information Technology; Law; Management; Mechanical Engineering), Hakase (Business Administration; Information Sciences; Management; Pharmacy)
Student Services: Social Counselling, Careers Guidance, Sports Facilities, Language Laboratory, Health Services, Canteen
Periodicals: Journal of Business Administration and Information, Setsunan Journal of Humanities and Social Sciences, Setsunan Law Journal
Last Update: 02-02-2018

Shibaura Institute of Technology (SIT)

3-7-5 Toyosu, Koto-ku
Tokyo 135-8548
Tel: +81(3) 5859-7140
Fax: +81(3) 5859-7141
Website: http://www.shibaura-it.ac.jp
President: Masato Murakami
Tel: +81(3) 5476-3137

College

Engineering (Architecture; Arts and Humanities; Building Technologies; Civil Engineering; Electrical Engineering; Electronic Engineering; Engineering; Materials Engineering; Mechanical Engineering; Telecommunications Engineering); **Engineering and Design** (Design; Engineering); **Systems**

Engineering and Science (Architecture; Automation and Control Engineering; Computer Engineering; Electronic Engineering; Environmental Engineering; Mathematics)

Graduate School

Engineering and Science (Engineering); **Engineering Management** (Engineering Management)
Further information: Also Toyosu; Omiya and Shibawa campus
History: Founded 1927. Acquired present status 1949.
Academic year: April to January (April-July; September-January)
Admission requirements: Graduation from high school and entrance examination
Main language(s) of instruction: Japanese
Accrediting agency: Japan University Accreditation Association (JUAA)
Degrees and diplomas: Gakushi (Engineering), Shushi (Engineering; Engineering Management), Hakase (Engineering)
Student Services: Academic Counselling, Social Counselling, Careers Guidance, Nursery Care, Sports Facilities, Facilities for disabled people, Health Services, Canteen, Foreign Studies Centre
Periodicals: Human Technology
Last Update: 02-02-2018

Shigakkan University (SGK)

55 Nakouyama, Yokone-machi
Obu-shi 474-8651, Aichi
Tel: +81(562) 46-1291
Fax: +81(562) 44-1313
Website: http://www.sgk.ac.jp
President: Kuniko Tanioka
Tel: +81(562) 46-1293

Faculty

Helath Sciences (Child Care and Development; Health Education; Health Sciences; Nutrition; Sports)

Institute

Health Sciences (Health Sciences)

Graduate School

Health Sciences (Health Sciences)

Research Division

Children's Culture (Child Care and Development)
History: Founded 1905 as Sewing School, known as Chukyo Joshi Daigaku (Chukyo Women's University) in 1963. Acquired current title and became co-educational 1 April 2010.
Academic year: April to March

Main language(s) of instruction: Japanese
Accrediting agency: Japan University Accreditation Association (JUAA)
Degrees and diplomas: Gakushi, Shushi (Health Sciences; Physical Education)
Student Services: Academic Counselling, Social Counselling, Careers Guidance, Nursery Care, Sports Facilities, Language Laboratory, Health Services, Canteen, Library

Academic Staff 2012-2013	MALE	FEMALE	TOTAL
FULL-TIME			56
PART-TIME			97
STAFF WITH DOCTORATE			
FULL-TIME	477	778	1255

Last Update: 02-02-2018

Shigakukan University

1-59-1 Murasakibaru
Kagoshima 899-5194, Kagoshima
Tel: +81(99) 812-8501
Fax: +81(99) 257-0308
Website: http://www.shigakukan.ac.jp
President: Tatsuo Mtasuoka

Faculty

Humanities (Arts and Humanities; Clinical Psychology; Cultural Studies; English; Geography; History; Japanese);
Law (Law)
History: Founded 1907.
Admission requirements: Entrance Examination
Main language(s) of instruction: Japanese
Accrediting agency: Japan Institution for Higher Education Evaluation (JIHEE)
Degrees and diplomas: Gakushi, Hakase (Clinical Psychology)
Student Services: Library

Student Numbers 2013	MALE	FEMALE	TOTAL
All (Foreign Included)			c. 1200

Last Update: 02-02-2018

Shijonawate Gakuen University

No. 11 No. 10, Hojo 5-chome
Daito 574-0011, Osaka
Tel: +81 72 -863 -5043
Website: http://un.shijonawate-gakuen.ac.jp
President: Kazuo Hiroshima

Faculty

Rehabilitation (Occupational Therapy; Physical Therapy)

History: Founded 1926 as Shijonawate Higher Girls' School. Acquired present status and title 2004.
Main language(s) of instruction: Japanese
Accrediting agency: Japan Institution for Higher Education Evaluation (JIHEE)
Degrees and diplomas: Gakushi (Occupational Therapy; Physical Therapy)
Last Update: 05-02-2018

Shikoku Gakuin University

3-2-1 Bunkyo-cho
Zentsuji-shi 765-8505, Kagawa
Tel: +81(877) 62-2111
Fax: +81(877) 62-2225
Website: http://www.sg-u.ac.jp
President: Takaaki Sueyoshi

Faculty
Letters (Arts and Humanities; Cultural Studies; Education; English; European Languages; Literature; Modern Languages)

School
Social Welfare (Child Care and Development; Social Welfare)

Department/Division
Sociology (Sociology)
History: Founded 1949 on the initiative of American Presbyterian missionaries as School, became Junior College 1959, acquired present status 1962.
Academic year: April to March (April-September; October-February)
Admission requirements: Graduation from high school and entrance examination
Main language(s) of instruction: Japanese
Accrediting agency: Japan Institution for Higher Education Evaluation (JIHEE)
Degrees and diplomas: Associate's Degree (Academic), Gakushi (Fine Arts), Shushi (Social Welfare)
Student Services: Social Counselling, Sports Facilities, Facilities for disabled people, Foreign Studies Centre, Library
Periodicals: Karashidane, Ronshu (Studies)
Last Update: 05-02-2018

Shikoku University

123-1 Ebisuno, Furukawa, Ojin-cho
Tokushima-shi 771-1192, Tokushima
Tel: +81(886) 665-1300
Fax: +81(886) 665-8037

Website: http://www.shikoku-u.ac.jp
President: Kazumi Matsushige

Faculty
Human Life Sciences (Child Care and Development; Design; Preschool Education; Primary Education; Psychology; Public Health); **Literature** (Arts and Humanities; Cultural Studies; English; Japanese; Modern Languages); **Management and Information Science** (Information Sciences; Management; Media Studies); **Nursing** (Nursing)

Graduate School
Literature; Nursing; Management and Information Science; Human Life Science (Information Sciences; Literature; Management; Nursing; Public Health)
History: Founded 1925 as Tokusima School of Sewing. Became Shikoku Women's University 1966. Acquired present title 1992.
Admission requirements: High School diploma or equivalent; Japanese Language proficiency
Main language(s) of instruction: Japanese
Accrediting agency: Japan University Accreditation Association (JUAA)
Degrees and diplomas: Gakushi (Biology; Information Sciences; Literature; Management), Shushi (English; Information Sciences; Japanese; Literature; Management; Public Health), Hakase (Information Sciences; Management)
Student Services: Academic Counselling, Social Counselling, Careers Guidance, Nursery Care, Sports Facilities, Facilities for disabled people, Health Services, Canteen, Library
Periodicals: Bulletin of Shikoku University
Last Update: 05-02-2018

Shiraume Gakuen University

Ogawa 1-830
Kodaira 187-8570, Tokyo
Tel: +81 42-346-5618
Fax: +81 42-346-5652
Website: http://daigaku.shiraume.ac.jp
President: Shiomi Toshiyuki

Faculty
Child Education (Child Care and Development; Preschool Education; Social and Community Services)
History: Founded 1942. Acquired present status and title 2005.
Main language(s) of instruction: Japanese
Accrediting agency: Japan Institution for Higher Education Evaluation (JIHEE)
Degrees and diplomas: Gakushi (Child Care and Development; Preschool Education; Social and Community Services), Shushi (Child Care and Development)
Student Services: Library
Last Update: 05-02-2018

Shirayuri University

1-25 Midorigaoka Chofu-shi
Tokyo 182-8525
Tel: +81(3) 3326-5050
Fax: +81(3) 3326-4550
Website: http://www.shirayuri.ac.jp
President: Kuniharu Tabata

Department/Division

Child Studies (*Also Graduate School*) (Arts and Humanities; Child Care and Development; Clinical Psychology; Developmental Psychology; Literature; Social Sciences); **English Language and Literature** (*Also Graduate School*) (English; Literature); **French Language and Literature** (*Also Graduate School*) (French; Literature); **Japanese Language and Literature** (*Also Graduate School*) (Japanese; Literature); **Religion** (Religion)

Graduate School

Language and Literature (English; French; Japanese; Literature)
Further information: Also Special Unit, Developmental Psychology Clinical Centre
History: Founded 1898 as School, acquired present status and title 1965.
Academic year: April to March (April-September; October-March)
Admission requirements: Graduation from senior high school, or recognized foreign equivalent, and entrance examination
Main language(s) of instruction: Japanese, English
Accrediting agency: Japanese University Accreditation Association (JUAA)
Degrees and diplomas: Gakushi, Shushi (English; French; Japanese; Literature; Psychology), Hakase (Literature; Modern Languages; Psychology)
Student Services: Academic Counselling, Social Counselling, Careers Guidance, Cultural Activities, Sports Facilities, Health Services, Canteen, Library
Periodicals: Kannazuki (Japanese Language and Literature), Korobokkuru (Child Development and Juvenile Culture), Lilia Candia (French Language and Literature), Sella (English Language and Literature), Shirayuri Jido Bunka (Juvenile Culture and Literature)
Last Update: 05-02-2018

Shiseikan University

5000 Urata Chinto
Hagi-shi 758-8585, Yamaguchi
Tel: +81(838) 24-4012
Fax: +81(838) 24-4090
Website: http://www.shiseikan.ac.jp
President: Kenichi Harada

Department/Division

Architectural Engineering (Architecture); **Business Culture** (Business and Commerce); **Child Life Study** (Child Care and Development); **Sports Health and Welfare** (Health Sciences; Physical Education; Sports; Welfare and Protective Services)
History: Founded 1999 as Hagi Kokusai Daigaku (Hagi International University). Acquired present title 2007. Formerly Yamaguchi University of Human Welfare and Culture.
Main language(s) of instruction: Japanese
Accrediting agency: Japan Institution for Higher Education Evaluation (JIHEE)
Degrees and diplomas: Gakushi
Student Services: Sports Facilities
Last Update: 05-02-2018

Shitennoji University

3-2-1 Gakuenmae Habikino-shi
Osaka-shi 583-8501, Osaka
Tel: +81(72) 956-3181
Fax: +81(72) 956-6011
Website: http://www.shitennoji.ac.jp/ibu/index.html
President: Hiroshi Iwao

Faculty

Business Administration (Business Administration); **Education** (Child Care and Development; Education; Health Education; Preschool Education)

Department/Division

Humanities and Social Sciences (Arabic; Arts and Humanities; Asian Religious Studies; Education; English; Health Sciences; Home Economics; International Studies; Japanese; Social Welfare; Sociology)

Graduate School

Sociology and Humanities (Arts and Humanities; Social Sciences; Social Welfare)
History: Founded 1967 as Shitennoji Joshi Daigaku/Shitennoji Women's University. Renamed Shitennoji Kokusai Bukkyo Daigaku/International Buddhist University 1981. Acquired present title 2008.
Academic year: Two semesters from April to March or September to August.
Main language(s) of instruction: Japanese
Accrediting agency: Japan Institution for HIgher Education Evaluation (JIHEE)

Degrees and diplomas: Gakushi, Shushi (Arts and Humanities; Home Economics; Social Sciences), Hakase
Student Services: Sports Facilities, Library
Last Update: 05-02-2018

Shizuoka Eiwa Gakuin University

1769 Ikeda
Shizuoka-shi 422-8545, Shizuoka
Tel: +81(54) 261-9201
Fax: +81(54) 263-4763
Website: http://www.shizuoka-eiwa.ac.jp
President: Shibata Satoshi

Department/Division

Community and Social Welfare (Child Care and Development; Family Studies; Social and Community Services; Social Welfare); **Contemporary Communications and Food Science** (Communication Studies; Food Technology); **Humanities and Social Sciences** (Arts and Humanities; Cultural Studies; Finance; Law; Literature; Management; Psychology; Social Sciences; Tourism)
History: Founded 2002.
Fees: 600,000 per annum (Yen)
Main language(s) of instruction: Japanese
Accrediting agency: Japan Institution for Higher Education Evaluation (JIHEE)
Degrees and diplomas: Gakushi
Student Services: Careers Guidance, Language Laboratory, Library, IT Centre

Student Numbers 2013	MALE	FEMALE	TOTAL
All (Foreign Included)			1400

Last Update: 05-02-2018

Shizuoka Institute of Science and Technology (SIST)

2200-2 Toyosawa
Fukuroi-shi 437-8555, Shizuoka
Tel: +81(538) 45-0111
Fax: +81(538) 45-0110
Website: http://www.sist.ac.jp
President: Noguchi Hiroshi

Faculty

Comprehensive Informatics (Artificial Intelligence; Computer Engineering; Computer Graphics; Computer Networks; Information Technology; Software Engineering)

Department/Division

Electrical and Electronical Engineering (Electrical and Electronic Engineering); **Materials and Life Sciences** (Biochemistry; Biological and Life Sciences; Biology; Biotechnology; Food Technology; Microbiology; Molecular Biology; Natural Sciences); **Science and Engineering** (Aeronautical and Aerospace Engineering; Automotive Engineering; Engineering; Information Technology; Materials Engineering; Mechanical Engineering)

Graduate School

Graduate Studies (Computer Engineering; Engineering; Materials Engineering)
History: Founded 1991.
Main language(s) of instruction: Japanese
Accrediting agency: Japan Institution for Higher Education Evaluation (JIHEE)
Degrees and diplomas: Gakushi, Shushi (Computer Engineering; Materials Engineering)
Student Services: Library
Last Update: 05-02-2018

Shizuoka Sangyo University

1572-1 Owara-machi
Iwata-shi 438-0043, Shizuoka
Tel: +81(54) 646-5469
Fax: +81(54) 645-0195
Website: http://www.ssu.ac.jp
President: Hayao Washizaki

School

Information Sciences (Communication Studies; Design; Graphic Design; Industrial Design; Information Sciences; Information Technology; International Relations; Management; Tourism); **Management** (Accountancy; Business Administration; Marketing; Psychology; Sports Management)
Further information: Also campuses in Iwata and Fujieda City
History: Founded 1994.
Academic year: April to March (from April to September - October to March)
Main language(s) of instruction: Japanese
Accrediting agency: Japan Institution for Higher Education Evaluation (JIHEE)
Degrees and diplomas: Gakushi

Student Numbers 2013	MALE	FEMALE	TOTAL
All (Foreign Included)			2200
Foreign only			160

Last Update: 05-02-2018

Shizuoka University of Welfare

549-1 Honnakane
Yaizu-shi 425-8611, Shizuoka
Tel: +81(54) 623-7000
Fax: +81(54) 623-7453
Website: http://www.suw.ac.jp
President: Haruyasu Ota

Department/Division

Health Sciences (Child Care and Development; Health Sciences; Nursing; Nutrition; Sports); **Health Sciences and Social Welfare** (Child Care and Development; Computer Science; Health Sciences; Information Sciences; Social Welfare; Social Work; Statistics); **Psychology** (Psychology)
History: Founded 1992.
Admission requirements: Entrance examination
Main language(s) of instruction: Japanese
Accrediting agency: Japan Institution for Higher Education Evaluation (JIHEE)
Degrees and diplomas: Gakushi
Student Services: Cultural Activities, Sports Facilities, Library
Last Update: 06-02-2018

Shobi University

1373 Toyodahon Kawagoe
Saitama-shi 350-1118, Saitama
Tel: +81(49) 246-3709
Fax: +81(49) 246-3709
Website: http://www.shobi-u.ac.jp
President: Kimito Kubo

Department/Division

Information (Film; Information Sciences; Video); **Life Management** (Cultural Studies; Health Sciences; Sports); **Music** (Music; Musical Instruments); **Policy Management** (Business Administration; Tourism)
Further information: Also campuses in Kawagoe and Saitama.
History: Founded 2000.
Main language(s) of instruction: Japanese
Accrediting agency: Japan Institution for Higher Education Evaluation (JIHEE)
Degrees and diplomas: Gakushi (Music; Public Administration; Social Sciences), Shushi (Music; Public Administration; Social Sciences)
Student Services: Cultural Activities, Sports Facilities, Library
Last Update: 06-02-2018

Shoin University

9-1 Morinosatowakamiya
Atsugi-shi 243-0124, Kanagawa
Tel: +81(46) 247-1511
Fax: +81(46) 247-4234
Website: http://www.shoin-u.ac.jp

Faculty

Communication and Cultural Studies (Communication Studies; Cultural Studies; Japanese; Psychology); **Management** (Business Administration; Commercial Law; Economics; Finance; Management); **Tourism and Media Studies** (Cultural Studies; Information Sciences; Media Studies; Tourism)
History: Founded 2000 as Shoin Joshi Daigaku (Shoin Women's University). Acquired present title 2004.
Main language(s) of instruction: Japanese
Accrediting agency: Japan Institution for Higher Education Evaluation (JIHEE)
Degrees and diplomas: Gakushi, Shushi (Business Administration)
Last Update: 06-02-2018

Shokei Gakuin University

4-10-1 Yurigaoka Natori-shi
Miyagi 981-1295
Tel: +81(22) 381-3300
Fax: +81(22) 381-3325
Website: http://www.shokei.jp
President: Goda Takashi

Faculty

Comprehensive Human Sciences (Child Care and Development; Communication Studies; Cultural Studies; Economics; Health Sciences; Law; Nutrition; Political Sciences; Psychology; Sociology; Welfare and Protective Services)

Graduate School

Comprehensive Human Sciences. (Health Sciences; Nutrition; Psychology)
History: Founded 2003.
Admission requirements: Entrance Examination
Main language(s) of instruction: Japanese
Accrediting agency: Japan Institution for Higher Education Evaluation (JIHEE)
Degrees and diplomas: Gakushi, Shushi (Health Sciences; Nutrition; Psychology)
Student Services: Library

Student Numbers 2013	MALE	FEMALE	TOTAL
All (Foreign Included)			c. 2000

Last Update: 06-02-2018

Shokei University

2155-7 Nirenoki Shimizu-machi
Kumamoto-shi 861-8538, Kumamoto
Tel: +81(96) 362-2011
Fax: +81(96) 363-2975
Website: http://www.shokei-gakuen.ac.jp
President: Masato Mori

Faculty
Arts and Humanities (Arts and Humanities; English; Japanese)

Department/Division
Nutritional Science (Nutrition); **Social Welfare** (Social Welfare)
Further information: Also Tamanoki Campus
History: Founded 1975.
Admission requirements: Entrance examination
Main language(s) of instruction: Japanese
Accrediting agency: Japan Institution for Higher Education Evaluation (JIHEE)
Degrees and diplomas: Gakushi
Student Services: Careers Guidance, Library, Residential Facilities
Last Update: 06-02-2018

Shonan Institute of Technology

1-1-25 Tsujidonishikaigan
Fujisawa-shi 251-8511, Kanagawa
Tel: +81(466) 30-0200
Fax: +81(466) 34-4022
Website: http://www.shonan-it.ac.jp
President: Nobuo Matsumoto

Faculty
Engineering (Computer Science; Electrical Engineering; Engineering; Industrial Design; Information Sciences; Materials Engineering; Mechanical Engineering)

School
Graduate Studies (Electrical Engineering; Information Technology; Materials Engineering; Mechanical Engineering)
History: Founded 1963.
Fees: 1,030,000 per annum (Yen)

Main language(s) of instruction: Japanese
Accrediting agency: Japan University Accreditation Association (JUAA)
Degrees and diplomas: Gakushi, Shushi (Electrical Engineering; Information Technology; Materials Engineering; Mechanical Engineering), Hakase (Electrical Engineering; Information Technology)
Student Services: Social Counselling, Careers Guidance, Sports Facilities, Health Services, Library
Last Update: 06-02-2018

Showa Pharmaceutical University (SPU)

3-3165 Higashitamagawagakuen
Machida-shi 194-8543, Tokyo
Tel: +81(42) 721-1511
Fax: +81(42) 721-1588
Website: http://www.shoyaku.ac.jp
President: Masahiro Nishima

Faculty
Pharmaceutical Sciences (*Also Graduate School*) (Organic Chemistry; Pharmacology; Pharmacy)
History: Founded 1930 as Showa Women's Senmon Gakko of Pharmacy, acquired present status 1950.
Main language(s) of instruction: Japanese
Accrediting agency: Japan University Accreditation Association (JUAA)
Degrees and diplomas: Gakushi, Shushi (Pharmacy), Hakase (Organic Chemistry; Pharmacy)
Student Services: Sports Facilities, Library
Last Update: 06-02-2018

Showa University

1-5-8 Hatanodai Shinagawa-ku
Tokyo 142-8555
Tel: +81(3) 3784-8000
Fax: +81(3) 3784-8012
Website: http://www.showa-u.ac.jp

School
Dentistry (Dentistry); **Medicine** (Medicine; Oncology; Pathology; Physiology; Social and Preventive Medicine; Surgery); **Nursing and Rehabilitation Sciences** (Nursing; Occupational Therapy; Physical Therapy; Rehabilitation and Therapy); **Pharmaceutical Sciences** (Pharmacy)

Graduate School
Graduate Studies (Dentistry; Medicine; Pharmacy)

Research Division

Oncology (Oncology)

Further information: Also Research Centres

History: Founded 1928 as Medical College, became full Medical School 1952 and acquired present status 1964.

Academic year: April to March (April-October; October-March)

Admission requirements: Graduation from high school and entrance examination

Main language(s) of instruction: Japanese

Accrediting agency: Japan Institution for Higher Education Evaluation (JIHEE)

Degrees and diplomas: Gakushi (Medicine; Pharmacy), Hakase (Medicine)

Student Services: Sports Facilities, Library

Periodicals: Journal of the Showa Medical Association

Last Update: 06-02-2018

Showa University of Music

1-11-1 Kamiasao Asao-ku
Kawasaki-shi 215-8558, Kanagawa
Tel: +81(44) 953-1121
Fax: +81(44) 953-1311
Website: http://www.tosei-showa-music.ac.jp
President: Susumu Yanase

Faculty

Music (Art Management; Art Therapy; Music; Music Theory and Composition; Musical Instruments; Singing)

History: Founded 1984. Former name was Showa Academia Musicae

Main language(s) of instruction: Japanese

Accrediting agency: Japan Institution for Higher Education Evaluation (JIHEE)

Degrees and diplomas: Gakushi, Shushi (Conducting; Music; Music Theory and Composition; Musical Instruments; Opera)

Student Services: Library, Residential Facilities

Last Update: 29-03-2018

Showa Women's University (SWU)

1-7 Taishido Setagaya-ku
Tokyo 154-8533
Tel: +81(3) 3411-5249
Fax: +81(3) 3411-6973
Website: http://www.swu.ac.jp
President: Kaneko Tomoko

Faculty

Global Business (Business Administration)

Department/Division

Human Culture (Communication Studies; Cultural Studies; English; History; International Studies; Japanese; Literature); **Sociology** (Architectural and Environmental Design; Arts and Humanities; Clinical Psychology; Economics; Education; Educational Psychology; Environmental Studies; Food Science; Health Sciences; Industrial and Organizational Psychology; Literature; Media Studies; Nutrition; Political Sciences; Primary Education; Psychology; Social Psychology; Social Welfare; Social Work; Sociology)

Graduate School

Letters (American Studies; English; European Languages; Japanese; Linguistics; Literature; Modern Languages; Oriental Languages); **Life Mechanism** (Architectural and Environmental Design; Cultural Studies; Design; Education; Psychology; Social Sciences; Social Welfare)

Further information: Also Showa Boston Study Abroad programmes and Showa Boston Summer Session programmes

History: Founded 1920 as College, acquired present status 1949.

Academic year: April to March (April-July; October-March)

Admission requirements: Graduation from high school and entrance examination

Main language(s) of instruction: Japanese

Accrediting agency: Japan University Accreditation Association (JUAA)

Degrees and diplomas: Gakushi, Shushi (Architectural and Environmental Design; Education; English; Japanese; Linguistics; Psychology; Social Welfare), Hakase (Architectural and Environmental Design)

Student Services: Academic Counselling, Careers Guidance, Sports Facilities, Health Services, Canteen, Library

Periodicals: Gakuen, Josei Bunka Kenkyujo Kiyo, Kokusai Bunka Kenkyujo Kiyo, Seikatsu Shinri Kenkyujo Kiyo

Last Update: 07-02-2018

Shubun University

Nikko-cho, 6
Ichinomiya 491-0938, Aichi
Tel: +81(586) 45-2101
Fax: +81(586) 45-4410
Website: http://www.shubun.ac.jp
President: Toshimitsu Niwa

Faculty

Health and Nutrition (Nutrition)

History: Founded 1941 as Ichinomiya Women's Commercial School. Acquired present status and title 2008.
Main language(s) of instruction: Japanese
Accrediting agency: Japan Institution for Higher Education Evaluation (JIHEE)
Degrees and diplomas: Gakushi (Nutrition)
Student Services: Sports Facilities, Library, IT Centre
Last Update: 07-02-2018

Shuchiin University

70 Nishi-jouuke Mukaijima
Fushimi-ku 612-8156, Kyoto
Tel: +81(75) 604-5600
Fax: +81(75) 604-5610
Website: http://www.shuchiin.ac.jp
President: Suguri Kozui

Faculty
Humanities (Asian Religious Studies); **Social Sciences** (Social Welfare)
Admission requirements: Entrance examination
Main language(s) of instruction: Japanese
Accrediting agency: Japan Institution for Higher Education Evaluation (JIHEE)
Degrees and diplomas: Gakushi
Student Services: Library

Academic Staff 2013-2014	MALE	FEMALE	TOTAL
FULL-TIME			19
Student Numbers 2013-2014			
All (Foreign Included)	116	36	152

Last Update: 07-02-2018

Shujitsu University

1-6-1 Nishigawara, Naka-ku
Okayama-shi 703-8516, Okayama
Tel: +81(86) 271-8111
Fax: +81(86) 271-8222
Website: http://www.shujitsu.ac.jp
President: Hiroyuki Kataoka

Faculty
Education (Education; Educational Psychology; Primary Education); **Human Studies** (Arts and Humanities; English; History; Japanese; Linguistics; Literature)

School
Pharmacy (Pharmacy)

History: Founded 1979 as Shujitsu Joshi Daigaku (Shujitsu Women's University). Acquired present title 2003.
Main language(s) of instruction: Japanese
Accrediting agency: Japan University Accreditation Association (JUAA)
Degrees and diplomas: Gakushi, Shushi (Cultural Studies; English; Japanese; Linguistics)
Student Services: Library
Last Update: 07-02-2018

Shukutoku University

200 Daiganji-cho Chuo-ku
Chiba-shi 260-8701, Chiba
Tel: +81(43) 265-7331
Fax: +81(43) 265-8310
Website: http://www.shukutoku.ac.jp
President: Isooka Tetsuya

Faculty
Business Administration (Business Administration); **Cross-Cultural Communication** (Communication Studies; Cultural Studies); **Humanities** (Arts and Humanities; Communication Studies; History); **Nursing and Nutrition** (Nursing; Nutrition)

School
Policy Studies (*Community*) (Economics; Law; Sociology)

Department/Division
Education (Education)

Graduate School
Social Welfare (Social Welfare)
Further information: Also Study Abroad programmes. Intensive Language Training and Intensive English Training programmes
History: Founded 1965 by Rev. Yoshinobo Hasegawa. A second campus in Saitama added 1996.
Academic year: April to February (April-July; September-February)
Main language(s) of instruction: Japanese
Accrediting agency: Japan University Accreditation Association (JUAA)
Degrees and diplomas: Gakushi (Arts and Humanities; Business Administration; Communication Studies; Education; Social Welfare), Shushi (Psychology; Social Welfare), Hakase
Student Services: Academic Counselling, Social Counselling, Careers Guidance, Cultural Activities, Sports Facilities, Facilities for disabled people, Health Services, Canteen, Library

Periodicals: Annual Research Report, Bulletin, Clinical Studies, Cross-Cultural Business and Cultural Studies, Graduate School Bulletin
Last Update: 27-03-2018

Shumei University

1-1 Daigaku-cho
Yachiyo-shi 276, Chiba
Tel: +81(47) 488-2111
Fax: +81(47) 488-8290
Website: http://www.shumei-u.ac.jp

Faculty
English and Information Technology Management (English; Information Technology); **Management and Administration** (Accountancy; Administration; Business Administration; International Economics; Management); **Teacher Training** (Education; Teacher Training); **Tourism Studies** (Tourism)
History: Founded 1988 as Yachiyo Kokusai Daigaku (Yachiyo International University).
Main language(s) of instruction: Japanese
Accrediting agency: Japan Institution for Higher Education Evaluation (JIHEE)
Degrees and diplomas: Gakushi
Student Services: Library
Last Update: 08-02-2018

Soai University (SOAI)

4-4-1 Nanko-Naka Suminoe-ku
Osaka-shi 559-0033, Osaka
Tel: +81(6) 6612-5905
Fax: +81(6) 6612-2993
Website: http://www.soai.ac.jp
President: Satoru Kaneko

Faculty
Human Development (Child Care and Development; Development Studies; Health Sciences; Nutrition); **Humanities** (Asian Religious Studies; Asian Studies; Cultural Studies; Japanese); **Music** (Music)
History: Founded 1888 as Soai Women's School.
Main language(s) of instruction: Japanese
Accrediting agency: Japan University Accreditation Association (JUAA)
Degrees and diplomas: Gakushi. Also one year postgraduate programme in Music

Student Services: Academic Counselling, Careers Guidance, Sports Facilities, Foreign Studies Centre, Library, Residential Facilities
Last Update: 08-02-2018

Sojo University

4-22-1 Ikeda
Kumamoto-shi 860-0082, Kumamoto
Tel: +81(96) 326-6810
Fax: +81(96) 326-6801
Website: http://www.sojo-u.ac.jp
President: Mineo Nakayama

Faculty
Art (Design; Fine Arts); **Biological and Life Sciences** (Biological and Life Sciences; Biotechnology; Microbiology); **Computer and Information Technology** (Computer Engineering; Information Technology); **Engineering** (Aeronautical and Aerospace Engineering; Architecture; Civil Engineering; Construction Engineering; Design; Mechanical Engineering; Nanotechnology); **Pharmaceutical Sciences** (Applied Chemistry; Biochemistry; Biophysics; Medicine; Microbiology; Oncology; Organic Chemistry; Pharmacology; Pharmacy)

Course/Programme
Japanese (*Bekka*) (Japanese)

Graduate School
Programmes (Biological and Life Sciences; Design; Engineering; Fine Arts; Pharmacy)
History: Founded 1965 as Junior College, became Kumamoto Institute of Technology recognized by the Government 1967. Graduate School established 1982. Acquired present title 2000.
Academic year: April to March (April-September; October-March)
Admission requirements: Graduation from high school and entrance examination
Main language(s) of instruction: Japanese
Accrediting agency: Japan Institution for Higher Education Evaluation (JIHEE)
Degrees and diplomas: Gakushi, Shushi (Aeronautical and Aerospace Engineering; Applied Chemistry; Biological and Life Sciences; Civil Engineering; Computer Engineering; Construction Engineering; Information Technology; Microbiology), Hakase (Applied Chemistry; Biological and Life Sciences; Computer Engineering; Design; Environmental Management; Information Technology; Mechanical Engineering; Microbiology; Pharmacy). Also Teaching Diplomas
Student Services: Library

Periodicals: Bulletin
Last Update: 08-02-2018

Soka University

1-236 Tangi-cho Hachioji
Tokyo 192-0003
Tel: +81(42) 691-8200
Fax: +81(42) 691-2039
Website: http://www.soka.ac.jp
President: Yoshihisa Baba
Tel: +81(42) 691-9481

Faculty

Business Administration (Business Administration); **Engineering** (Bioengineering; Engineering; Environmental Engineering; Information Sciences); **International Liberal Arts** (Business Administration; Cultural Studies; Economics; English; History; International Studies; Political Sciences); **Law** (Law); **Letters** (Arts and Humanities; English)

Course/Programme

Intensive Japanese Studies (Japanese)

School

Nursing (Nursing)

Department/Division

Economics (Economics); **Education** (Education; Primary Education)

Graduate School

Economics (Business Administration; Economics); **Engineering** (Bioengineering; Engineering; Environmental Engineering); **Law** (Law); **Liberal Arts** (Arts and Humanities; Education; English; Sociology)
History: Founded 1971. Graduate Schools established 1975.
Academic year: April to March (April-July; September-March)
Admission requirements: Graduation from high school or equivalent or foreign equivalent, and entrance examination
Main language(s) of instruction: Japanese, English
Accrediting agency: Japan University Accreditation Association (JUAA)
Degrees and diplomas: Associate's Degree (Academic), Gakushi (Arts and Humanities; Business Administration; Economics; Education; Engineering; Law), Shushi (Arts and Humanities; Economics; Education; Engineering; English; Law; Sociology), Hakase (Arts and Humanities; Economics; Education; Engineering; English; Law; Sociology)
Student Services: Library

Periodicals: Bulletin of the Educational Society, Journal of Business Administration, Sociologica, Soka Economic Studies, Soka Law Journal, Studies in English Language and Literature

Academic Staff 2013-2014	MALE	FEMALE	TOTAL
FULL-TIME			315
Student Numbers 2013-2014			
All (Foreign Included)			8143

Last Update: 08-02-2018

Sonoda Women's University

7-29-1 Minami-Tsukaguchi-cho
Amagasaki-shi 661-8521, Hyogo
Tel: +81(06) 6429-1201
Fax: +81(06) 6422-8523
Website: http://www.sonoda-u.ac.jp
President: Akiko Kawashima

Faculty

Education (Preschool Education; Primary Education); **Future Planning** (Computer Engineering; Cultural Studies; English; Japanese); **Health Sciences** (Food Science; Health Sciences; Nursing; Nutrition)
History: Founded 1966.
Main language(s) of instruction: Japanese
Accrediting agency: Japan University Accreditation Association (JUAA)
Degrees and diplomas: Gakushi (Education; Health Sciences; Nursing)
Student Services: Sports Facilities, Foreign Studies Centre, Library, Residential Facilities
Last Update: 27-03-2018

Sophia University

7-1 Kioicho, Chiyoda-ku
Tokyo 102-8554
Tel: +81(3) 3238-4018, +81(3) 3238-3517
Fax: +81(3) 3238-3885
Website: http://www.sophia.ac.jp
President: Yoshiaki Terumichi
Tel: +81(3) 3238-3131

Faculty

Economics (Business Administration; Economics); **Foreign Studies** (Asian Studies; Cultural Studies; English; French; German; International Relations; Linguistics; Modern Languages; Portuguese; Spanish); **Human Sciences** (Education;

Nursing; Psychology; Social and Community Services; Sociology); **Humanities** (Arts and Humanities; English; French; German; History; Japanese; Journalism; Literature); **Law** (Environmental Studies; International Law; Law); **Liberal Arts** (Arts and Humanities; Business Administration; Cultural Studies; International Business; International Economics; Social Studies); **Science and Technology** (Biological and Life Sciences; Communication Studies; Engineering; Information Sciences; Materials Engineering; Natural Sciences); **Theology** (Theology)

Institute

American and Canadian Studies (American Studies; Canadian Studies; History; Political Sciences; Social Studies); **Asian Cultures** (Asian Studies; Cultural Studies; Middle Eastern Studies; South Asian Studies; Southeast Asian Studies); **Bioethics** (Arts and Humanities; Ethics; Natural Sciences; Social Sciences); **Christian Culture** (Christian Religious Studies; Cultural Studies); **Comparative Culture** (Cultural Studies); **European Cultural Studies** (European Languages; European Studies; History; Social Studies); **Global Concern** (International Studies); **Global Environmental Studies** (Environmental Studies); **Grief Care**; **Ibero-American Studies** (Latin American Studies); **Linguistic Institute for International Communication** (Communication Studies; International Studies; Linguistics); **Medieval Thought** (Medieval Studies; Philosophy; Theology)

Centre

Research and Human Development (*Sophia Asia*) (Human Resources)

Graduate School

Economics (Economics; Management); **Foreign Studies** (Linguistics); **Global Environmental Studies** (Environmental Studies; International Studies); **Global Studies** (International Relations; International Studies; Regional Studies); **Human Sciences** (Education; Nursing; Psychology; Social Sciences; Sociology); **Humanities** (Cultural Studies; English; French; German; History; Japanese; Journalism; Literature); **Law** (Law); **Philosophy** (Philosophy); **Science and Technology** (Applied Chemistry; Biological and Life Sciences; Chemistry; Electrical and Electronic Engineering; Information Sciences; Mathematics; Mechanical Engineering; Physics; Theology)

Research Division

Kirishitan Bunko Library (Christian Religious Studies; International Relations)

History: Founded 1913 as College, recognized as University 1928. Graduate School added 1951. The University is a private Institution directed by the Society of Jesus. Financed from tuition and service fees, grants from public and private bodies, and donations.

Academic year: April to March (April-September; Mid-September-March)

Admission requirements: Graduation from high school or foreign equivalent, and entrance examinations conducted by the University

Main language(s) of instruction: Japanese, English

Accrediting agency: Japan University Accreditation Association (JUAA)

Degrees and diplomas: Gakushi (Biological and Life Sciences; Biology; Chemistry; Cultural Studies; Economics; Education; Electrical and Electronic Engineering; Engineering; English; European Languages; European Studies; French; German; History; Information Sciences; International Studies; Japanese; Journalism; Law; Literature; Management; Mathematics and Computer Science; Mechanical Engineering; Modern Languages; Natural Sciences; Nursing; Philosophy; Physics; Portuguese; Psychology; Russian; Social Welfare; Sociology; Spanish; Theology), Shushi (American Studies; Applied Chemistry; Biological and Life Sciences; Biology; Chemistry; Development Studies; Economics; Education; Electrical and Electronic Engineering; English Studies; Environmental Studies; French Studies; German; Germanic Studies; History; Information Sciences; International Business; International Relations; International Studies; Japanese; Journalism; Law; Linguistics; Management; Mathematics and Computer Science; Mechanical Engineering; Nursing; Philosophy; Physics; Psychology; Religion; Social and Community Services; Sociology; Theology), Hakase (American Studies; Applied Chemistry; Biological and Life Sciences; Biology; Chemistry; Development Studies; Economics; Education; Electrical and Electronic Engineering; English Studies; Environmental Studies; French Studies; Germanic Studies; History; International Studies; Japanese; Journalism; Law; Linguistics; Management; Mathematics and Computer Science; Mechanical Engineering; Philosophy; Physics; Psychology; Social and Community Services; Sociology; Theology)

Student Services: Academic Counselling, Social Counselling, Careers Guidance, Nursery Care, Cultural Activities, Sports Facilities, Facilities for disabled people, Health Services, Canteen

Periodicals: AGLOS: Journal of Area-Based Global Studies, Bulletin of the Faculty of Foreign Studies, Sophia University, Catholic Studies, Communications Research, Cosmopolis, Encontros Lusófonos, English Literature and Language, Global Environmental Studies, Grief Care, Historical Studies, Iberoamericana, Institute of Christian Culture bulletin, Japanese Literature Journal, Journal of Global Environmental Studies, Journal of Theological Studies (Shingaku Digest), Les Lettres françaises, Lingua, Monumenta Nipponica, Philosophy Journal, Revue d'Etudes françaises, Sociological studies, Sophia, Sophia Economics Review, Sophia English studies, Sophia Historical studies, Sophia International Review, Sophia journal of European studies, Sophia journalism studies, Sophia Law Review, Sophia linguistica, Sophia Philosophica, Sophia Sci-Tech, SOPHIA TESOL FORUM, Sophia University Graduate Research in Education, Sophia University Studies in Education, Sophia University Studies in physical education, Sophia University Studies in Social Services, Sophia-Universität Beiträge zur deutschen Literatur, Studien des Instituts für die Kultur der deutschsprachigen Länder, Studies in Philosophical Anthropology, Stufe, The Journal of American and Canadian studies, The Journal of Sophia Asian studies, The Psychological report of Sophia University, The Renaissance Bulletin

Academic Staff 2012-2013	MALE	FEMALE	TOTAL
FULL-TIME	377	150	527
PART-TIME	449	283	732
Student Numbers 2012-2013			
All (Foreign Included)	5659	6647	12306
Foreign only			967

Last Update: 25-05-2018

St. Catherine University

660 Hojo
Hojo-shi 799-2496, Ehime
Tel: +81(89) 993-0702
Fax: +81(89) 993-0900
Website: http://www.catherine.ac.jp
President: Jovino San Miguel

Faculty
Health Sciences and Welfare Services (Health Sciences; Social Sciences; Social Welfare; Social Work; Sports; Sports Management)
History: Founded 1988.
Main language(s) of instruction: Japanese
Accrediting agency: Japan University Accreditation Association (JUAA)
Degrees and diplomas: Gakushi
Student Services: Library, Residential Facilities
Last Update: 08-02-2018

St. Luke's International University

10-1 Akashi-cho Chuo-ku
Tokyo 104-0044
Tel: +81(3) 3543-6391
Fax: +81(3) 6226-6376

Website: http://www.slcn.ac.jp
President: Tsuguya Fukui

College
Nursing (Child Care and Development; Community Health; English; Gerontology; Health Education; Information Sciences; Midwifery; Nursing; Psychiatry and Mental Health; Psychology; Sociology)

Graduate School
Nursing Science (Midwifery; Nursing); **Public Health** (Public Health)
Further information: Also St Luke's International Hospital, Summer English Programme at McGill University
History: Founded 1920 as School, became College 1964. Financially supported by tuition fees and Government subsidies.
Academic year: April to March (April-September; October-March)
Admission requirements: Graduation from high school or equivalent, and entrance examination
Main language(s) of instruction: Japanese, English
Accrediting agency: Japan University Accreditation Association (JUAA)
Degrees and diplomas: Gakushi (Nursing), Shushi (Nursing; Public Health), Hakase (Nursing)
Periodicals: Kiyo (Treatise)
Last Update: 08-02-2018

St. Marianna University School of Medicine

2-16-1, Sugao Miyamae-ku
Kawasaki-shi 216-8511, Kanagawa
Tel: +81(44) 977-8111
Fax: +81(44) 977-5542
Website: http://www.marianna-u.ac.jp
President: Akashi Katsuya

School
Medicine (Medicine; Social and Preventive Medicine)

Graduate School
Medicine (Biomedicine; Medicine; Molecular Biology; Oncology)

Research Division
Intractable Diseases (Radiology)
Further information: Also 3 Hospitals
History: Founded 1971 by the St. Marianna Foundation.
Academic year: April to March

Admission requirements: Graduation from high school or foreign equivalent, and entrance examination
Main language(s) of instruction: Japanese
Accrediting agency: Japan University Accreditation Association (JUAA)
Degrees and diplomas: Gakushi (Medicine), Hakase (Medicine)
Student Services: Academic Counselling, Social Counselling, Sports Facilities, Health Services, Canteen, Library
Periodicals: The St. Marianna Medical Journal
Last Update: 08-02-2018

St. Mary's College

Tsubuku-honmachi 422
Kurume 830-8558, Fukuoka
Tel: +81 942-35-7271
Fax: +81 942-34-9125
Website: http://www.st-mary.ac.jp
President: Saburo Ide

Faculty
Nursing
History: Founded 1953. Acquired present status and title 2006.
Main language(s) of instruction: Japanese
Accrediting agency: Japan Institution for Higher Education Evaluation (JIHEE)
Degrees and diplomas: Gakushi (Nursing)
Student Services: Sports Facilities, Canteen, Library
Last Update: 08-02-2018

Sugino Fashion College

4-6-19 Kamiosaki Shinagawa-ku
Tokyo 141-8651
Tel: +81(3) 3491-8152
Fax: +81(3) 3491-8136
Website: http://www.sugino-fc.ac.jp

Course/Programme
Fashion (Fashion Design)

Graduate School
Graduate School (Fashion Design)
History: Founded 1926 as girl's dressmaker School. Became Sugino Gakuen Women's Junior School ,1950. Acquired present status 1964. Known as Sugino Joshi Daigaku (Sugino Women's College) until 2002.
Main language(s) of instruction: Japanese
Accrediting agency: Japan Institution for Higher Education Evaluation (JIHEE)

Degrees and diplomas: Gakushi, Shushi (Fashion Design)
Student Services: Library
Last Update: 08-02-2018

Sugiyama Jogakuen University

17-3 Hoshigaoka-motomachi Chikusa-ku
Nagoya-shi 464-8662, Aichi
Tel: +81(52) 781-1186, +81(52) 781-5674
Fax: +81(52) 781-4466, +81(52) 781-2038
Website: http://www.sugiyama-u.ac.jp
President: Kimio Morimune

School
Cross-Cultural Studies (English; European Languages; European Studies; French; German; Japanese; Literature; Modern Languages; Oriental Languages; Oriental Studies); **Culture-Information Studies** (Behavioural Sciences; Communication Studies; Cultural Studies; Information Sciences; Media Studies; Social Studies; Tourism); **Education** (Child Care and Development; Preschool Education; Primary Education); **Human Relations** (Psychology; Social Sciences); **Life Studies** (Environmental Studies; Food Science; Nutrition); **Modern Management** (Business and Commerce; International Business; Management); **Nursing** (Nursing)

Graduate School
Human Sciences (Clinical Psychology; Education; Sociology); **Life Studies** (Food Science; Home Economics; Nutrition; Social Sciences)
History: Founded 1905.
Academic year: April to March (April-October; October-March)
Admission requirements: Graduation from high school and entrance examination
Main language(s) of instruction: Japanese
Accrediting agency: Japan University Accreditation Association (JUAA)
Degrees and diplomas: Gakushi (Fine Arts), Shushi (Architecture; Clinical Psychology; Education; Food Science; House Arts and Environment; Nutrition; Psychology; Sociology), Hakase (Home Economics)
Student Services: Academic Counselling, Language Laboratory, Foreign Studies Centre, Residential Facilities
Periodicals: Journal

Academic Staff 2013-2014	MALE	FEMALE	TOTAL
FULL-TIME			229
Student Numbers 2013-2014			
All (Foreign Included)			5833

Last Update: 08-02-2018

Surugadai University

698 Azu
Hanno-shi 357-8555, Saitama
Tel: +81(42) 972-1111
Website: http://www.surugadai.ac.jp
President: Tsuneo Yoshida

Faculty
Contemporary Cultures (Cultural Studies); **Economics and Management** (Business Administration; Economics; Information Sciences; Management); **Law** (Law); **Media and Information Resources** (Cultural Studies; Information Management; Library Science; Media Studies); **Psychology** (Psychology)

Graduate School
Contemporary Information Cultural Resources (Information Management); **Economics** (Business Administration; Economics; Information Sciences; Management); **Law** (Law); **Psychology** (Psychology)
History: Founded 1987.
Academic year: April to March
Admission requirements: Graduation from high school, or equivalent
Main language(s) of instruction: Japanese
Accrediting agency: Japan University Accreditation Association (JUAA)
Degrees and diplomas: Gakushi, Shushi (Economics; Information Management; Law; Psychology)
Student Services: Academic Counselling, Social Counselling, Careers Guidance, Sports Facilities, Health Services, Canteen
Periodicals: Bulletin of the Faculty of Cultural Information Resources, Surugadai University, Bulletin of the Institute for Economic Research, Comparative Law and Culture, Surugadai Economic Studies, Surugadai Journal of Law and Politics, Surugadai University Studies
Last Update: 09-02-2018

Suzuka International University

663-222 Koriyama-cho
Suzuka-shi 510-0298, Mie
Tel: +81(120) 919-593
Fax: +81(593) 72-2827
Website: http://www.suzuka-iu.ac.jp
President: Ichino Kiyoharu

Department/Division
International Studies (*Also Graduate Programme*) (English; International Business; International Relations; International Studies); **Tourism and Hospitality** (Hotel and Restaurant; Tourism)
History: Founded 1994.
Main language(s) of instruction: Japanese
Accrediting agency: Japan Institution for Higher Education Evaluation (JIHEE)
Degrees and diplomas: Gakushi, Shushi
Student Services: Academic Counselling, Social Counselling, Careers Guidance, Sports Facilities, Language Laboratory, Library
Last Update: 09-02-2018

Suzuka University of Medical Science (SUMS)

1001-1 Kishioka-cho
Suzuka-shi 510-0293, Mie
Tel: +81(59) 383-9591
Fax: +81(59) 383-9669
Website: http://www.suzuka-u.ac.jp
President: Nagayasu Toyoda

Faculty
Acupuncture and Moxibustion (Acupuncture); **Health Sciences** (Health Sciences; Nutrition; Radiology); **Medical Engineering** (Engineering; Medical Technology); **Pharmaceutical Sciences** (Pharmacy)

Institute
Traditional Chinese Medicine (Traditional Eastern Medicine)

Centre
Medical Imaging (Medical Technology; Radiology)

Graduate School
Health Sciences (Health Sciences)
History: Founded 1991.
Main language(s) of instruction: Japanese
Accrediting agency: Japan Institution for Higher Education Evaluation (JIHEE)
Degrees and diplomas: Gakushi, Hakase (Health Sciences; Medicine; Pharmacy)
Student Services: Library
Last Update: 09-02-2018

Taisei Gakuin University (TGU)

1060-1 Hirao
Mihara-cho 587-8555, Minamikawachi-gun
Tel: +81(72) 362-3731

Fax: +81(72) 362-0598
Website: http://www.tgu.ac.jp

Faculty

Business Administration (Business Administration; Information Management); **Human Studies** (Social Sciences); **Nursing** (Nursing)
History: Founded 1998. Known as Minami Osaka Daigaku (Southern Osaka University) until 2003.
Main language(s) of instruction: Japanese
Accrediting agency: Japan Institution for Higher Education Evaluation (JIHEE)
Degrees and diplomas: Gakushi
Periodicals: Bulletin of Taisei Gakuin University
Last Update: 09-02-2018

Taisho University

3-20-1 Nishisugamo Toshima-ku
Tokyo 170-8470
Tel: +81(3) 3918-7311
Fax: +81(3) 5394-3037
Website: http://www.tais.ac.jp
President: Nobuo Ostuka

Faculty

Buddhist Studies (Asian Religious Studies); **Human Studies** (Arts and Humanities; Asian Religious Studies; Clinical Psychology; Social Welfare); **Literature** (History; International Studies; Japanese; Literature)

School

Graduate Studies
Further information: Japanese Language Programme for foreign students
History: Founded 1926, reorganized 1949.
Academic year: April to March (April-September; October-March)
Admission requirements: Graduation from high school or equivalent, and entrance examination
Main language(s) of instruction: Japanese
Accrediting agency: Japan University Accreditation Association (JUAA)
Degrees and diplomas: Gakushi, Shushi, Hakase
Periodicals: Taisho Daigaku Daigakuin Kenkyuronshu (Journal of the Graduate School of Taisho University), Taisho Daigaku Kenkyu Kiyo (Memoirs of Taisho University)
Publishing house: Taisho University Press
Last Update: 09-02-2018

Takachiho University

2-19-1 Omiya Suginami-ku
Tokyo 168-8508
Tel: +81(3) 3313-0148
Fax: +81(3) 3313-9034
Website: http://www.takachiho.ac.jp

Faculty

Business Administration (Business Administration); **Commerce** (Business and Commerce); **Human Sciences** (Education; Social Sciences)
History: Founded 1903. Formerly known as Takashiho Shoka Daigaku (Takachiho College of Commerce). Acquired present status and title 2001.
Main language(s) of instruction: Japanese
Accrediting agency: Japan University Accreditation Association (JUAA)
Degrees and diplomas: Gakushi, Shushi, Hakase (Business Administration)
Student Services: Social Counselling, Careers Guidance, Sports Facilities, Language Laboratory, Health Services
Last Update: 09-02-2018

Takamatsu University

960 Kasuga-cho
Takamatsu-shi 761-0194, Kagawa
Tel: +81(87) 841-3255
Fax: +81(87) 841-3064
Website: http://www.takamatsu-u.ac.jp
President: Masamichi Tsukuda

Course/Programme

Business Administration (Business Administration; Industrial Management; Management Systems)
History: Founded 1995.
Main language(s) of instruction: Japanese
Accrediting agency: Japan Institution for Higher Education Evaluation (JIHEE)
Degrees and diplomas: Gakushi, Shushi
Last Update: 09-02-2018

Takaoka University of Law

307-3 Toidekokudai
Takaoka-shi 939-1193, Toyama
Tel: +81(766) 63-3388

Fax: +81(766) 636-410
Website: http://www.takaoka.ac.jp

Faculty

Law (Law)
History: Founded 1989.
Main language(s) of instruction: Japanese
Accrediting agency: Japan Institution for Higher Education Evaluation (JIHEE)
Degrees and diplomas: Gakushi
Last Update: 09-02-2018

Takarazuka University

7-27 Tsutsujigaoka Hanayashiki
Takarazuka-shi 665-0803, Hyogo
Tel: +81(727) 56-1231
Fax: +81(727) 58-7869
Website: http://www.takara-univ.ac.jp
President: Masanobu Yamakawa

School

Art and Design (Design; Fine Arts); **Media Content** (*Tokyo campus*) (Media Studies); **Media Design** (Media Studies); **Nursing** (*Umeda Campus*) (Nursing)
History: Founded 1986 as Takarazuka University of Art and Design. Graduate courses started 1993. Acquired present title 2010
Academic year: April to March
Admission requirements: Graduation from high school
Main language(s) of instruction: Japanese
Accrediting agency: Japan Institution for Higher Education Evaluation (JIHEE)
Degrees and diplomas: Gakushi (Design; Fine Arts), Shushi (Design; Fine Arts), Hakase (Design; Fine Arts)
Student Services: Academic Counselling, Social Counselling, Careers Guidance, Nursery Care, Sports Facilities, Health Services, Canteen
Periodicals: Artes
Last Update: 09-02-2018

Takarazuka University of Medical and Health Care

Hanayashiki Midorigaoka 1
Takarazuka 666-0162, Hyogo
Tel: +81 72-736-8600
Fax: +81 72-736-8659

Website: http://www.tumh.ac.jp
President: Iseo Takeda

Faculty

Health Science (Acupuncture; Physical Therapy; Sports)
History: Founded 2000 as Heisei Medical Academy. Acquired present status and title 2011.
Main language(s) of instruction: Japanese
Accrediting agency: Ministry of Education, Culture, Sports, Science and Technology (MEXT)
Degrees and diplomas: Gakushi (Acupuncture; Physical Therapy; Sports)
Student Services: Sports Facilities, Health Services, Canteen, Library, IT Centre
Last Update: 09-02-2018

Takasaki University of Commerce

Negoyamachi 741
Takasaki 370-1214, Gunma
Tel: +81 27-347-3399
Fax: +81 27-347-3389
Website: http://www.tuc.ac.jp
President: Fuchigami Yujiro

Faculty

Commerce (Accountancy; E- Business/Commerce; Finance; Leadership; Management; Marketing; Tourism)
History: Founded 1906 as Sato sewing Girls' school. Acquired present status and title 2001.
Main language(s) of instruction: Japanese
Accrediting agency: Japan Institution for Higher Education Evaluation (JIHEE)
Degrees and diplomas: Gakushi (E- Business/Commerce; Finance; Human Resources; Management; Marketing; Tourism)
Student Services: Academic Counselling, Canteen, Library, IT Centre
Last Update: 09-02-2018

Takasaki University of Health and Welfare

37-1 Nakaorui-machi
Takasaki-shi 370-0033, Gunma
Tel: +81(27) 352-1290
Fax: +81(27) 353-2055
Website: http://www.takasaki-u.ac.jp
President: Kenishi Sudo

Faculty

Health and Welfare (Nutrition; Social Policy); **Health Care** (Nursing; Physical Therapy); **Human Development** (Preschool Education; Primary Education; Secondary Education; Special Education); **Pharmacy** (Pharmacy)

School

Graduate (Health Sciences; Nutrition)
History: Founded 2001.
Main language(s) of instruction: Japanese, English
Accrediting agency: Japan University Accreditation Association (JUAA)
Degrees and diplomas: Gakushi, Shushi, Hakase (Health Sciences; Nutrition)
Last Update: 09-02-2018

Takushoku University

3-4-14 Kohinata Bunkyo-ku
Tokyo 112-8585
Tel: +81(3) 3947-7160
Fax: +81(3) 3947-7812
Website: http://www.takushoku-u.ac.jp
President: Akio Kawana

Faculty

Commerce (Business Administration; Business and Commerce); **Engineering** (Computer Science; Electronic Engineering; Engineering; Industrial Design; Information Sciences; Mechanical Engineering); **Foreign Studies** (Chinese; English; European Languages; Modern Languages; Oriental Languages; Spanish); **International Studies** (International Studies); **Political Science and Economics** (Economics; Political Sciences)

Institute

International Cooperation Studies (*Also Graduate School*) (International Studies)

Graduate School

Commerce (Business and Commerce); **Economics** (Economics); **Engineering**; **Language Education** (English; Japanese)
Further information: Also 13 Research Institutes
History: Founded 1900.
Academic year: April to March
Admission requirements: Graduation from high school and entrance examination
Main language(s) of instruction: Japanese

Accrediting agency: Japan University Accreditation Association (JUAA)
Degrees and diplomas: Gakushi, Shushi, Hakase (Business Administration; Economics; Engineering; Modern Languages)
Student Services: Academic Counselling, Social Counselling, Careers Guidance, Nursery Care, Sports Facilities, Language Laboratory, Health Services, Canteen, Foreign Studies Centre
Periodicals: Kaigai Jijo, Takushoku Daigaku Ronshu
Last Update: 20-02-2018

Tama Art University (TAU)

2-1723 Yarimizu Hachioji-shi
Tokyo 192-0394
Tel: +81(42) 679-5605
Website: http://www.tamabi.ac.jp
President: Akira Tatehata

Faculty

Art and Design (Acting; Architectural and Environmental Design; Art Criticism; Ceramic Art; Dance; Design; Fine Arts; Glass Art; Graphic Design; Industrial Design; Painting and Drawing; Printing and Printmaking; Sculpture; Textile Design)
History: Founded as a private School 1935, became College 1947 and acquired University status 1953.
Academic year: April to March (April-August; September-March)
Admission requirements: Graduation from high school and entrance examination
Fees: National : 1,187,000 (Yen), International : 1,187,000 (Yen)
Main language(s) of instruction: Japanese
Accrediting agency: Japan University Accreditation Association (JUAA)
Degrees and diplomas: Gakushi, Shushi, Hakase
Student Services: Academic Counselling, Social Counselling, Careers Guidance, Cultural Activities, Sports Facilities, Language Laboratory, Facilities for disabled people, Health Services, Canteen, Foreign Studies Centre, Library
Periodicals: Tama Art University Bulletin

Academic Staff 2017-2018	MALE	FEMALE	TOTAL
FULL-TIME	130	53	183
Student Numbers 2017-2018			
All (Foreign Included)	1160	3206	4366

Last Update: 24-05-2018

Tama University

4-1-1 Hijirigaoka
Tama-shi 206-0022, Tokyo
Tel: +81(42) 337-7114
Fax: +81(42) 337-7100
Website: http://www.tama.ac.jp
President: Jitsuro Terashima

School

Global Studies (Computer Networks; English; International Relations; Japanese; Leadership); **Management and Information Sciences** (*Also Graduate School*) (Information Sciences; Management)
Further information: Also Shinagawa and Meguro campuses
History: Founded 1989.
Academic year: April to March
Admission requirements: Graduation from high school and entrance examination
Main language(s) of instruction: Japanese, English
Accrediting agency: Japan Institution for Higher Education Evaluation (JIHEE)
Degrees and diplomas: Gakushi, Shushi, Hakase
Last Update: 21-02-2018

Tamagawa University

6-1-1 Tamagawa Gakuen
Machida-shi 194-8610, Tokyo
Tel: +81(42) 739-8111
Fax: +81(42) 739-8795
Website: http://www.tamagawa.ac.jp
President: Yoshiaki Obara

College

Agriculture (Agriculture; Biological and Life Sciences; Environmental Studies; Natural Resources); **Arts** (Media Studies; Performing Arts; Visual Arts); **Arts and Sciences** (Arts and Humanities; Natural Sciences; Social Sciences); **Business Administration**; **Education** (Child Care and Development; Education); **Engineering** (Engineering; Management Systems; Mechanical Engineering; Software Engineering; Technology); **Humanities** (Arts and Humanities; Cultural Studies; International Studies; Social Sciences)

Department/Division
Correspondence Courses

Research Division
Education (Educational Research)
History: Founded 1929 as Tamagawa Academy, became University 1949.
Academic year: April to March (April-July; September-March)
Admission requirements: Graduation from senior high school or equivalent or foreign equivalent, and entrance examination
Main language(s) of instruction: Japanese
Accrediting agency: Japan University Accreditation Association (JUAA)
Degrees and diplomas: Gakushi, Shushi, Hakase
Periodicals: Mitsubachi Kagaku (Honeybee Science Report), Shohou, Zenjin

Student Numbers 2012-2013	MALE	FEMALE	TOTAL
All (Foreign Included)			7658

Last Update: 21-02-2018

Teikyo Heisei University

4-1 Uruidominami
Ichihara 290-0193, Chiba
Tel: +81(3) 5843-3200
Website: http://www.thu.ac.jp
President: Hiroko Okinaga

Faculty

Community Medicine (Occupational Therapy; Physical Therapy; Speech Therapy and Audiology); **Health and Medical Sciences** (Health Sciences; Medicine); **Human Care** (Acupuncture; Nursing; Sports Medicine); **Modern Life** (Business Administration; Cultural Studies; Media Studies; Sports Medicine; Tourism); **Pharmaceutical Sciences** (Pharmacology)
History: Founded 1987 as Teikyo University of Technology. Forms part of Teikyo University Group.
Academic year: April to January (April-July; September-January)
Admission requirements: Graduation from high school and entrance examination
Main language(s) of instruction: Japanese, English
Accrediting agency: Japan Institution for Higher Education Evaluation (JIHEE)
Degrees and diplomas: Gakushi, Shushi
Student Services: Academic Counselling, Careers Guidance, Nursery Care, Sports Facilities
Last Update: 21-02-2018

Teikyo University

2-11-1 Kaga Itabashi-ku
Tokyo 173-8605
Tel: +81(42) 678-323
Fax: +81(42) 678-3544
Website: http://www.teikyo-u.ac.jp
President: Yoshihito Okinaga

Faculty

Economics (*Hachioji City, Tokyo; Also Graduate School*) (Economics); **Language Studies** (*For foreign students, Hachioji City, Tokyo*) (Japanese); **Law** (*Hachioji City, Tokyo; Also Graduate School*) (Law); **Liberal Arts** (*Hachioji City, Tokyo; Also Graduate School*) (Arts and Humanities; Education; English; History; Psychology; Sociology); **Medical Technology** (*Also Faculty of Fukuoka Medical Technology and Graduate School*) (Medical Technology; Optical Technology; Optics); **Medicine** (*Also Graduate School*) (Medicine); **Pharmaceutical Sciences** (*Sagamiko City, Kanagawa; Also Graduate School*) (Biochemistry; Biophysics; Chemistry; Pharmacy; Physics); **Science and Engineering** (*Utsunomiya City, Tochigi; Also Graduate School*) (Biochemistry; Biomedicine; Biophysics; Engineering; Information Sciences; Materials Engineering; Natural Sciences)
Further information: Also 3 Teaching Hospitals
History: Founded 1966.
Academic year: April to January (April-July; September-January)
Admission requirements: Graduation from high school and entrance examination
Main language(s) of instruction: Japanese, English
Accrediting agency: Japan University Accreditation Association (JUAA)
Degrees and diplomas: Gakushi (Arts and Humanities; Economics; Engineering; Law; Medicine; Ophthalmology; Pharmacy), Shushi, Hakase (Medicine)
Student Services: Academic Counselling, Careers Guidance, Nursery Care, Sports Facilities, Language Laboratory, Facilities for disabled people, Health Services, Canteen, Foreign Studies Centre
Last Update: 21-02-2018

Teikyo University of Science

2525 Yatsusawa Uenohara-cho
Kitatsuru-gun 409-0193, Yamanashi
Tel: +81(120)248-089
Website: http://www.ntu.ac.jp

Faculty

Child Science and Education (Developmental Psychology; Education; Preschool Education); **Life and Environmental Sciences** (Animal Husbandry; Biological and Life Sciences); **Medical Sciences** (Medicine; Nursing; Occupational Therapy; Physical Therapy; Sports Medicine)

Graduate School

Science and Engineering (Animal Husbandry; Biological and Life Sciences; Computer Engineering; Engineering)
History: Founded 1989.
Academic year: April to March (April-September; October-March)
Admission requirements: Graduation from high school and entrance examination
Main language(s) of instruction: Japanese, English
Accrediting agency: Japan Institution for Higher Education Evaluation (JIHEE)
Degrees and diplomas: Gakushi (Engineering), Shushi
Last Update: 21-02-2018

Tenri Health Care University

Bessho-cho, 80-1
Tenri 632-0018, Nara
Tel: +81 743-63-7811
Fax: +81 743-63-6211
Website: http://www.tenriyorozu-u.ac.jp
President: Osamu Yoshida

Faculty

Medical Care (Laboratory Techniques; Nursing)
History: Founded 1967 as Tenri health laboratory technician school. Acquired present status and title 2012.
Main language(s) of instruction: Japanese
Accrediting agency: Ministry of Education, Culture, Sports, Science and Technology (MEXT)
Degrees and diplomas: Gakushi (Laboratory Techniques; Nursing)
Student Services: Canteen, Library
Last Update: 27-02-2018

Tenri University

1050 Somanouchi
Tenri-shi 632-8510, Nara
Tel: +81(743) 63-9005
Fax: +81(743) 63-7388
Website: http://www.tenri-u.ac.jp
President: Nagao Noriaki

Faculty

Health, Budo and Sports Studies (Sports Medicine); **Human Studies** (Clinical Psychology; Comparative Religion; Psychology; Religious Studies; Welfare and Protective

Services); **International Studies** (American Studies; Asian Studies; Chinese; Cultural Studies; English; European Studies; French; German; Indonesian; Japanese; Korean; Russian; Spanish; Thai Languages); **Letters** (Arts and Humanities; Cultural Studies; History; Japanese; Literature)

Graduate School
Clinical Human Studies (Clinical Psychology)
History: Founded 1925. Acquired present status 1949.
Main language(s) of instruction: Japanese
Accrediting agency: Japan University Accreditation Association (JUAA)
Degrees and diplomas: Gakushi, Shushi. Also graduate programme in Clinical Human Studies
Student Services: Library
Last Update: 27-02-2018

Tenshi College

1-30 Higashi 3 Kita 13-jo, Higashi-ku
Sapporo-shi 065-0013, Hokkaido
Tel: +81(11) 741-1051
Fax: +81(11) 741-1077
Website: http://www.tenshi.ac.jp

School
Graduate Studies; **Midwifery** (Midwifery); **Nursing and Nutrition** (Nursing; Nutrition)
History: Founded 2000.
Main language(s) of instruction: Japanese
Accrediting agency: Japan University Accreditation Association (JUAA)
Degrees and diplomas: Gakushi, Shushi
Last Update: 27-02-2018

Tezukayama Gakuin University

2-1823 Imakuma
Osakasaya-mashi 589-8585, Osaka
Tel: +81(72) 368-3108
Fax: +81(72) 368-3112
Website: http://www.tezuka-gu.ac.jp

Faculty
Economics (Business Administration; Economics); **Humanities** (Food Technology; Law; Media Studies; Nutrition; Psychology); **Liberal Arts** (Art History; Chinese; English; Fine Arts; Japanese; Korean; Literature)
History: Founded 1966.
Main language(s) of instruction: Japanese
Accrediting agency: Japan Institution for Higher Education Evaluation (JIHEE)

Degrees and diplomas: Gakushi, Shushi, Hakase (Economics; Law; Psychology)
Student Services: eLibrary
Last Update: 27-02-2018

Tezukayama University

7-1-1 Tezukayama
Nara-shi 631-8501, Nara
Tel: +81(742) 41-4303
Fax: +81(742) 88-6031
Website: http://www.tezukayama-u.ac.jp
President: Iroshi Iwai

Faculty
Business Administration (Business Administration); **Contemporary Human Life Science** (Architectural and Environmental Design; Child Care and Development; Food Technology; Nutrition); **Economics** (Economics); **Humanities** (Asian Studies; English); **Law and Policy** (Law; Political Sciences); **Psychology** (Psychology)

Graduate School
Economics (Economics); **Humanities** (Asian Studies); **Law and Policy** (Law; Political Sciences); **Psychology** (Clinical Psychology; Psychology)
History: Founded 1964.
Main language(s) of instruction: Japanese
Accrediting agency: Japan University Accreditation Association (JUAA)
Degrees and diplomas: Gakushi, Shushi, Hakase (Asian Studies; Clinical Psychology; Cultural Studies; Economics; Psychology)
Student Services: Careers Guidance, Sports Facilities, Language Laboratory, Foreign Studies Centre, Library
Last Update: 27-02-2018

The Graduate School for the Creation of New Photonics Industries (GPI)

1955-1 Kurematsu-cho,Nishiku
Hamamatsu 431-1202, Shizuoka
Tel: +81 53-484-2501
Fax: +81 53-487-3012
Website: http://www.gpi.ac.jp
President: Kato Yohiaki

Research Division
Light Industry Biology (Laser Engineering; Optical Technology)
History: Founded 2004.

Fees: 1,500,000 (per year) (Yen)
Main language(s) of instruction: Japanese
Accrediting agency: Ministry of Education, Culture, Sports, Science and Technology (MEXT)
Degrees and diplomas: Shushi (Laser Engineering; Optical Technology)
Student Services: Library
Last Update: 27-03-2018

The Graduate School of Project Design

Minami-Aoyama, 3-13-16
Tokyo 107-8411, Minato-ku
Tel: +81 3-3478-8411
Website: http://www.mpd.ac.jp
President: Risa Tanaka

Graduate School
Project Design
History: Founded 2012.
Main language(s) of instruction: Japanese
Accrediting agency: Japan University Accreditation Association (JUAA)
Degrees and diplomas: Shushi (Management)
Student Services: Library
Last Update: 27-02-2018

The Japanese Red Cross Akita College of Nursing

Nawashirosawa-17-3 Kamikitatesaruta
Akita 010-1493, Akita
Tel: +81(18) 829-4000
Fax: +81(18)829-3030
Website: http://www.rcakita.ac.jp
President: Hiroko Ando

Faculty
Nursing (Nursing)
History: Founded 2009.
Main language(s) of instruction: Japanese
Accrediting agency: Japan University Accreditation Association (JUAA)
Degrees and diplomas: Gakushi (Nursing), Shushi (Nursing)
Student Services: Library

Academic Staff 2012-2013	MALE	FEMALE	TOTAL
FULL-TIME			47
Student Numbers 2012-2013			
All (Foreign Included)	88	482	570

Last Update: 28-02-2018

The Japanese Red Cross College of Nursing

4-1-3 Hiroo Shibuya-ku
Tokyo 150-0012
Tel: +81(3) 3409-0875
Fax: +81(3) 3409-0589
Website: http://www.redcross.ac.jp
President: Sanae Takada

Faculty
Nursing (Community Health; Health Sciences; International Studies; Midwifery; Modern Languages; Natural Sciences; Nursing; Psychiatry and Mental Health; Public Health)

Graduate School
Nursing (Child Care and Development; Community Health; Gerontology; Health Education; International Studies; Midwifery; Nursing; Psychiatry and Mental Health; Statistics)
Further information: Also Musashino Campus
History: Founded 1986.
Main language(s) of instruction: Japanese
Accrediting agency: Japan University Accreditation Association (JUAA)
Degrees and diplomas: Gakushi (Nursing), Shushi (Health Sciences; Midwifery; Nursing), Hakase (Nursing)
Student Services: Library
Last Update: 28-02-2018

The Japanese Red Cross Hiroshima College of Nursing (JRCHCN)

1-2 Ajinadai-Higashi
Hatsukaichi-shi 738-0052, Hiroshima
Tel: +81(829) 20-2800
Fax: +81(829) 20-2801
Website: http://www.jrchcn.ac.jp
President: Mariko Koyama

Course/Programme
Nursing (*Also Graduate School*) (Community Health; English; Gerontology; Health Sciences; International Studies; Midwifery; Modern Languages; Nursing; Paediatrics; Psychiatry and Mental Health)

Graduate School
Nurse Educators (Community Health; Gerontology; Health Administration; Health Education; Health Sciences; Nursing; Oncology; Paediatrics; Psychiatry and Mental Health)
History: Founded 2000.
Main language(s) of instruction: Japanese

Accrediting agency: Japan University Accreditation Association (JUAA)
Degrees and diplomas: Gakushi (Nursing), Shushi (Health Education; Nursing)
Student Services: Sports Facilities, Canteen, Library
Periodicals: Bulletin of the Japanese Red Cross Hiroshima College of Nursing, Report of the Japanese Red Cross Hiroshima College of Nursing "Futaba", Voluntary Evaluation and Assessment Report
Last Update: 11-12-2017

The Japanese Red Cross Hokkaido College of Nursing

664-1 Akebonocho
Kitami 090-0011, Hokkaido
Tel: +81 157-66-3311
Fax: +81 157-61-3125
Website: http://www.rchokkaido-cn.ac.jp
President: Teruko Hiroshi

Faculty
Nursing
History: Founded 1999.
Main language(s) of instruction: Japanese
Accrediting agency: Japan University Accreditation Association (JUAA)
Degrees and diplomas: Gakushi (Nursing), Shushi (Nursing)
Student Services: Library
Last Update: 28-02-2018

The Japanese Red Cross Kyushu International College of Nursing

1-1 Asty
Munakata-shi 811-4157, Fukuoka
Tel: +81(940) 35-7001
Fax: +81(940) 35-7021
Website: http://www.jrckicn.ac.jp
President: Yayoi Tamura

Department/Division
Nursing (Health Sciences; Nursing)
History: Founded 2001.
Main language(s) of instruction: Japanese
Accrediting agency: Japan University Accreditation Association (JUAA)
Degrees and diplomas: Gakushi, Shushi (Health Sciences; Nursing)
Last Update: 28-02-2018

The Jikei University School of Medicine

3-25-8 Nishi-shinbashi Minato-ku
Tokyo 105-8461
Tel: +81(33) 433-1111
Fax: +81(33) 435-6128
Website: http://www.jikei.ac.jp
President: Senya Matsufuji

School
Medicine (Genetics; Medicine); **Nursing** (Nursing)

Institute
Medical Sciences (Health Sciences)

Centre
Continuing Medical Education; **Medical Information**

Laboratory
Space Medicine
History: Founded 1881 as School of Medicine, became College 1921. Acquired University status 1952.
Academic year: April to March (April-July; September-December; January-March)
Admission requirements: Graduation from high school or equivalent, and entrance examination
Main language(s) of instruction: Japanese
Accrediting agency: Japan University Accreditation Association (JUAA)
Degrees and diplomas: Gakushi (Medicine), Hakase (Medicine)
Periodicals: Jikeikai Medical Journal (in English), Kyoiku Kenkyu Nenpo (Annual Report of Education and Research, in Japanese), Research Activities (in English), Tokyo Jikeikai Ika Daigaku Zasshi (in Japanese)
Last Update: 28-02-2018

The Open University of Japan (OUJ)

2-11 Wakaba, Mihama-ku
Chiba-shi 261-8586, Chiba
Tel: +81(43) 276-5111
Fax: +81(43) 297-2781
Website: http://www.ouj.ac.jp
President: Shin Kisugi

Faculty
Liberal Arts (Arts and Humanities; Computer Science; Cultural Studies; Education; Environmental Studies; Industrial and Production Economics; Natural Resources; Psychology; Social Studies)

Course/Programme

Non-degree Studies (Asian Studies; Biological and Life Sciences; Clinical Psychology; Cultural Studies; Earth Sciences; Energy Engineering; Engineering; Environmental Studies; Food Science; Health Sciences; Japanese; Management; Mathematics and Computer Science; Museum Studies; Psychology; Social Sciences; Social Studies; Social Work; Sports; Welfare and Protective Services)

Graduate School

Graduate Studies (Arts and Humanities; Biological and Life Sciences; Clinical Psychology; Computer Science; Development Studies; Education; Environmental Studies; Government; Natural Resources; Natural Sciences; Social and Community Services)

Further information: Also 49 Study centres throughout Japan

History: Founded 1983 as Open and Distance Institution with own broadcasting station to provide the general public with an opportunity for College-level education. Digital broadcast via telecommunication satellite, supplementing the ground transmission using radio and TV, covering only the Kanto area, began 1998. Now programmes are accessible from every part of Japan. Formerly known as the University of the Air, acquired present title 2007.

Academic year: April to March (April-September; October-March)

Admission requirements: Graduation from high school or foreign equivalent (no entrance examination)

Main language(s) of instruction: Japanese

Accrediting agency: Ministry of Education, Culture, Sports, Science and Technology (MEXT)

Degrees and diplomas: Gakushi, Shushi (Arts and Humanities; Biological and Life Sciences; Clinical Psychology; Computer Science; Development Studies; Education; Environmental Studies; Government; Health Sciences; Natural Resources; Social and Community Services), Hakase. Also Non-Degree Expert Courses

Student Services: Health Services

Periodicals: On Air

Publishing house: The Society for the Promotion of the University of the Air (Hoso Daigaku Kyoiku Shinkokai)

Academic Staff 2012-2013	MALE	FEMALE	TOTAL
FULL-TIME			87
Student Numbers 2012-2013			
All (Foreign Included)			88901

Last Update: 28-02-2018

The University of Human Environments (UHE)

6-2, Kamisanbonmatsu, Motojukucho
Okazaki 444-3505, Aichi
Tel: +81(564) 48-7811
Fax: +81(564) 48-7814
Website: http://www.uhe.ac.jp

Faculty

Human Environments (Agricultural Management; Agriculture; Arts and Humanities; Asian Studies; Business Administration; Clinical Psychology; Educational Psychology; Environmental Studies; History; Humanities and Social Science Education; Industrial and Organizational Psychology; International Studies; Japanese; Literature; Management; Natural Resources; Psychology; Psychotherapy; Social Studies)

Graduate School

Human Environments (Accountancy; Art Therapy; Asian Studies; Clinical Psychology; Economics; Environmental Management; Environmental Studies; Finance; Foreign Languages Education; Japanese; Psychiatry and Mental Health; Psychology; Psychotherapy)

History: Founded 2000.

Main language(s) of instruction: Japanese

Accrediting agency: Japan Institution for Higher Education Evaluation (JIHEE)

Degrees and diplomas: Gakushi (Asian Studies; Business Administration; Environmental Studies; Japanese; Management; Psychology), Shushi (Asian Studies; Clinical Psychology; Environmental Studies; Japanese; Nursing), Hakase (Nursing)

Student Services: Sports Facilities, Canteen, Library

Academic Staff 2013-2014	MALE	FEMALE	TOTAL
FULL-TIME	36	13	49
PART-TIME			47
Student Numbers 2013-2014			
All (Foreign Included)	341	188	529

Last Update: 07-03-2018

Toho College of Music

Imaizumi 84
Kawagoe-shi 350-0015, Saitama
Tel: +81(3) 3946-9667
Website: http://www.toho-music.ac.jp
President: Harumitsu Mimurodo

Faculty

Music (Music; Musical Instruments)
History: Founded 1965.
Academic year: April to March (April-September; October-March)
Admission requirements: Graduation from high school or equivalent or foreign equivalent
Main language(s) of instruction: Japanese
Accrediting agency: Japan Institution for Higher Education Evaluation (JIHEE)
Degrees and diplomas: Gakushi (Music). Also Graduate Course, 1 yr
Last Update: 28-02-2018

Toho Gakuen School of Music

1-41-1 Wakaba-cho
Chofu-shi 182-8510, Tokyo
Tel: +81(03) 3307-4101
Fax: +81(03) 3307-4354
Website: http://www.tohomusic.ac.jp
President: Tokihiko Umezu

School

Music (Conducting; Music; Music Theory and Composition; Musical Instruments; Musicology; Singing)

Graduate School

Music (Conducting; Musical Instruments)
History: Founded 1955. Acquired present status 1961.
Main language(s) of instruction: Japanese
Accrediting agency: Japan Institution for Higher Education Evaluation (JIHEE)
Degrees and diplomas: Gakushi
Last Update: 28-02-2018

Toho University

5-21-16 Omori-nishi
Ota-ku 143-8540, Tokyo
Tel: +81(3) 3762-4151
Fax: +81(3) 3768-0660
Website: http://www.toho-u.ac.jp
President: Junichi Yamazaki

Faculty

Medicine (*Also Graduate School*) (Anatomy; Medicine; Social and Preventive Medicine; Surgery); **Nursing** (Nursing); **Pharmaceutical Sciences** (*Also Graduate School*) (Pharmacology; Pharmacy); **Science** (*Also Graduate School*) (Biology; Chemistry; Information Sciences; Natural Sciences; Physics)
History: Founded 1925 as Imperial Women's Medical College, became private University 1947.
Academic year: April to March (April-July; September-December; January-March)
Main language(s) of instruction: Japanese, English
Accrediting agency: Japan University Accreditation Association (JUAA)
Degrees and diplomas: Gakushi, Shushi, Hakase (Biological and Life Sciences; Chemistry; Environmental Engineering; Information Sciences; Medicine; Pharmacy; Physics)
Student Services: Sports Facilities
Periodicals: Toho Medical Journal (Toho Igakukai Zasshi)

Academic Staff	MALE	FEMALE	TOTAL
PART-TIME			333

Last Update: 01-03-2018

Tohoku Bunka Gakuen University

6-45-16 Kunimi Aoba-ku
Sendai-shi 981-8551, Miyagi
Tel: +81(120) 556-923
Fax: +81(22) 233-8409
Website: http://www.tbgu.ac.jp
President: Shigeru Tsuchiya

Faculty

Medical Science and Welfare (Medicine; Occupational Therapy; Physical Therapy; Social Work; Welfare and Protective Services); **Policy Management** (Economics; Management); **Science and Technology** (Environmental Engineering; Environmental Management; Information Technology)
History: Founded 1999.
Main language(s) of instruction: Japanese
Accrediting agency: Japan Institution for Higher Education Evaluation (JIHEE)
Degrees and diplomas: Gakushi, Shushi
Student Services: Cultural Activities, Sports Facilities
Last Update: 01-03-2018

Tohoku Bunkyo College

Katayachi 515
Yamagata 990-2316, Yamagata
Tel: +81 23-688-2298

Fax: +81 23-688-6438
Website: http://www.t-bunkyo.jp
President: Kazuo Onitake

Faculty

Children's Education (Preschool Education)
History: Founded 1926 as Tomizawa money Yamagata sewing Girls' school. Acquired present status and title 2010.
Main language(s) of instruction: Japanese
Accrediting agency: Japan Institution for Higher Education Evaluation (JIHEE)
Degrees and diplomas: Gakushi (Preschool Education)
Student Services: Careers Guidance, Sports Facilities, Canteen, Library

Academic Staff 2012-2013	MALE	FEMALE	TOTAL
FULL-TIME			40
PART-TIME			74
Student Numbers 2012-2013			
All (Foreign Included)			300

Last Update: 01-03-2018

Tohoku Fukushi University

1-8-1 Kunimi Aoba-ku
Sendai-shi 981-8522, Miyagi
Tel: +81(22) 717-3312
Fax: +81(22) 717-3332
Website: http://www.tfu.ac.jp
President: Otani Testuo

Faculty

Child Development (Preschool Education; Primary Education); **General Management** (*Research*) (Industrial Management; Information Management; Public Administration); **General Welfare** (Education; Psychology; Social Welfare); **Medicine and Health Sciences** (Administration; Nursing; Rehabilitation and Therapy)
History: Founded 1958. Acquired present status 1962.
Academic year: April to March (April-September; October-March)
Admission requirements: Graduation from high school or equivalent or foreign equivalent, and entrance examination
Main language(s) of instruction: Japanese
Accrediting agency: Japan University Accreditation Association (JUAA)
Degrees and diplomas: Gakushi (Sociology), Shushi (Sociology). Also Professional Qualifications
Student Services: Sports Facilities, Library
Periodicals: Bulletin
Last Update: 01-03-2018

Tohoku Gakuin University

1-3-1 Tsuchitoi Aoba-ku
Sendai-shi 980-8511, Miyagi
Tel: +81(22) 264-6425
Fax: +81(22) 264-6515
Website: http://www.tohoku-gakuin.ac.jp
President: Norio Matsumoto

Faculty

Business Administration (Business Administration); **Economics** (Economics); **Engineering** (*Tagajo City*) (Civil Engineering; Electrical and Electronic Engineering; Engineering; Environmental Engineering; Information Technology; Metallurgical Engineering); **Law** (Law); **Letters** (Arts and Humanities; English; History); **Liberal Arts** (Arts and Humanities; Cultural Studies; Education; Information Sciences; Modern Languages; Psychology; Regional Planning; Sociology)

Institute

Accountancy Research (Accountancy); **Business and Management** (Business and Commerce; Management); **Christianity and Culture** (Christian Religious Studies; Cultural Studies); **Computer Science** (Computer Science); **Education** (Education); **English Language and Literature** (English; Literature); **Environmental Protection Engineering** (Environmental Engineering); **European Culture** (Cultural Studies; European Studies); **Law and Political Science** (Law; Political Sciences); **North Japan Culture** (Cultural Studies); **Religious Music** (Religious Music); **Social Welfare Research** (Social Welfare)

Centre

Audio-Visual (Cinema and Television); **Counselling**

Graduate School

Economics (Business Administration; Economics); **Engineering Engineering** (*Tagajo City*) (Applied Physics; Civil Engineering; Electrical Engineering; Mechanical Engineering; Technology); **Graduate School** (Business Administration; Computer Science; Cultural Studies; Economics; Engineering; English; Law)
Further information: Tsuchitoi, Tagajo and Izumi campuses
History: Founded 1886 as Sendai Theological Seminary, acquired present title 1949.
Academic year: April to March (April-September; October-March)
Admission requirements: Graduation from high school and entrance examination
Main language(s) of instruction: Japanese, English

Accrediting agency: Japan University Accreditation Association (JUAA)
Degrees and diplomas: Gakushi, Shushi, Hakase (Arts and Humanities; Economics; Engineering; Law)
Student Services: Academic Counselling, Social Counselling, Careers Guidance, Nursery Care, Cultural Activities, Sports Facilities, Language Laboratory, Facilities for disabled people, Health Services, Canteen, Foreign Studies Centre
Periodicals: Journals
Last Update: 01-03-2018

Tohoku Institute of Technology (TIT)

35-1 Kasumi-cho, Yagiyama Taihaku-ku
Sendai-shi 982-8577, Miyagi
Tel: +81(22) 305-3311
Fax: +81(22) 305-3313
Website: http://www.tohtech.ac.jp
President: Hiroshi Konno

Faculty

Engineering (Civil Engineering; Energy Engineering; Environmental Engineering; Information Technology); **Life Design** (Design; Environmental Engineering; Interior Design; Management)

Centre

General Education (Teacher Training)

Graduate School

Engineering (Architecture; Civil Engineering; Electronic Engineering; Engineering; Environmental Engineering; Industrial Engineering; Structural Architecture; Telecommunications Engineering)
History: Founded 1964.
Academic year: April to March
Admission requirements: Graduation from high school and entrance examination
Main language(s) of instruction: Japanese, English
Accrediting agency: Japan University Accreditation Association (JUAA)
Degrees and diplomas: Gakushi (Engineering), Shushi (Architecture; Civil Engineering; Electronic Engineering; Engineering; Environmental Engineering; Industrial Design), Hakase (Architecture; Civil Engineering; Electronic Engineering; Engineering; Environmental Engineering; Industrial Design)
Student Services: Social Counselling, Careers Guidance, Nursery Care, Sports Facilities, Language Laboratory, Health Services, Canteen, Library
Periodicals: Memoirs of the Tohoku Institute of Technology
Last Update: 01-03-2018

Tohoku Medical and Pharmaceutical University

4-4-1 Komatsushima Aoba-ku
Sendai-shi 981-8558, Miyagi
Tel: +81(22) 234-4181
Fax: +81(22) 275-2013
Website: http://www.tohoku-mpu.ac.jp/english
President: Motoaki Takayanagi

Course/Programme

Cancer Research (Oncology); **Pharmaceutical Sciences** (Chemical Engineering; Hygiene; Pharmacology; Pharmacy)
History: Founded 1939 as School, became College 1949. In 2016 Tohoku Pharmaceutical University changed its name to Tohoku Medical and Pharmaceutical University
Academic year: April to March (April-September; October-March)
Admission requirements: Graduation from high school or equivalent or foreign equivalent, and entrance examination
Main language(s) of instruction: Japanese
Accrediting agency: Japan Institution for Higher Education Evaluation (JIHEE)
Degrees and diplomas: Gakushi (Pharmacy), Shushi (Pharmacy), Hakase (Pharmacy)
Student Services: Sports Facilities
Last Update: 01-03-2018

Tohoku Seikatsu Bunka University

1-18 Nijinooka Izumi-ku
Sendai-shi 981-8585, Miyagi
Tel: +81(22) 272-7513
Fax: +81(22) 301-5602
Website: http://www.mishima.ac.jp
President: Muneyoshi Yamada

Faculty

Home Economics (Handicrafts; Home Economics)
History: Founded 1958. Formerly known as Mishima Gakuen Joshi Daigaku.
Main language(s) of instruction: Japanese
Accrediting agency: Japan Institution for Higher Education Evaluation (JIHEE)
Degrees and diplomas: Gakushi
Last Update: 01-03-2018

Tohoku University of Art and Design

200 Kamisakurada
Yamagata-shi 990-9530, Yamagata
Tel: +81(236) 27-8160

Fax: +81(120) 57-2154
Website: http://www.tuad.ac.jp
President: Kichitaro Negishi

School

Art (Design; Handicrafts; Painting and Drawing; Sculpture);
Design (Architectural and Environmental Design; Architecture; Film; Graphic Design; Media Studies; Textile Design)

Graduate School

Art and Design (Architectural and Environmental Design; Art History; Cultural Studies; Design; Handicrafts; Heritage Preservation; Literature; Painting and Drawing; Sculpture)
History: Founded 1992.
Main language(s) of instruction: Japanese
Accrediting agency: Japan Institution for Higher Education Evaluation (JIHEE)
Degrees and diplomas: Gakushi, Shushi, Hakase (Design; Fine Arts)
Last Update: 01-03-2018

Tohoku University of Community Service and Science

3-5-1 Iimoriyama Sakata
Yamagata-shi 998-8580, Yamagata
Tel: +81(234)41-1284
Fax: +81(234) 41-1133
Website: http://www.koeki-u.ac.jp
President: Nobori Yoshimura

School

Community Services and Science (Business Administration; Computer Science; English; Environmental Studies; Social Sciences)
History: Founded 2001.
Main language(s) of instruction: Japanese, English
Accrediting agency: Japan Institution for Higher Education Evaluation (JIHEE)
Degrees and diplomas: Gakushi, Shushi, Hakase
Student Services: Cultural Activities, Sports Facilities

Academic Staff	MALE	FEMALE	TOTAL
PART-TIME			80

Last Update: 01-03-2018

Tohoku Women's University

1-2-1 Toyohara
Hirosaki-shi 036-8154, Aomori
Tel: +81(172) 33-2289

Fax: +81(172) 33-2486
Website: http://www.tojo.ac.jp

Department/Division

Children's Studies (Preschool Education; Primary Education; Teacher Training); **Home Economics** (Home Economics; Nutrition)
History: Founded 1969.
Main language(s) of instruction: Japanese
Accrediting agency: Japan Institution for Higher Education Evaluation (JIHEE)
Degrees and diplomas: Gakushi
Last Update: 01-03-2018

Tohto College of Health Sciences

Kamishibachonishi 4-2-11
Fukaya 366-0052, Saitama
Tel: +81 48-574-2500
Website: http://www.tohto.ac.jp
President: Toshio Nakajo

Faculty

Human Care (Nursing)
History: Founded 2009.
Main language(s) of instruction: Japanese
Accrediting agency: Japan Institution for Higher Education Evaluation (JIHEE)
Degrees and diplomas: Gakushi (Nursing)
Student Services: Canteen, Library
Last Update: 01-03-2018

Toin University of Yokohama

1614 Kurogane-cho Aoba-ku
Yokohama-shi 225-8502, Kanagawa
Tel: +81(45) 972-5881
Fax: +81(45) 972-5972
Website: http://www.toin.ac.jp

Faculty

Biomedical Engineering (Biological and Life Sciences; Biomedical Engineering); **Culture and Sport Policy** (Cultural Studies; Sports Medicine); **Engineering** (*Also Graduate School*) (Electronic Engineering; Engineering; Information Technology; Materials Engineering; Mechanical Engineering; Robotics); **Law** (*Also Graduate School*) (Law)
History: Founded 1988.
Main language(s) of instruction: Japanese
Accrediting agency: Japan University Accreditation Association (JUAA)

Degrees and diplomas: Gakushi, Shushi (Engineering; Law; Sports Medicine), Hakase (Engineering; Law; Sports Medicine)

Student Services: Academic Counselling, Social Counselling, Library

Last Update: 01-03-2018

Tokai Gakuin University

Kirino-cho Naka
Kakamigahara-shi 504-8511, Gifu-Ken
Tel: +81(58) 389-2200
Fax: +81(58) 389-2205
Website: http://www.tokaigakuin-u.ac.jp

Faculty

Health and Welfare (Social and Community Services; Social Welfare); **Human Relation** (Psychology)

History: Founded 1981. Known as Tokai Joshi Daigaku (Tokai Women's University) until 2007.

Academic year: April to March

Main language(s) of instruction: Japanese

Accrediting agency: Japan Institution for Higher Education Evaluation (JIHEE)

Degrees and diplomas: Gakushi, Shushi

Student Services: Academic Counselling, Social Counselling, Careers Guidance, Sports Facilities, Language Laboratory, Canteen

Last Update: 02-03-2018

Tokai University

4-1-1 Kitakaname
Hiratsuka-shi 259-1292
Tel: +81(463) 50-2086
Fax: +81(463) 50-2457
Website: http://www.u-tokai.ac.jp
President: Tatsuro Matsumae

Course/Programme

Japanese Language for International Students (Japanese); **Shipboard Training** (Marine Engineering; Marine Transport)

School

Agriculture (Agriculture; Biological and Life Sciences; Botany; Zoology); **Art and Technology** (Architectural and Environmental Design; Architecture; Design; Fine Arts); **Biological Science and Engineering** (Artificial Intelligence; Biological and Life Sciences; Computer Science; Genetics; Marine Biology; Marine Science and Oceanography; Technology); **Biological Sciences** (Biological and Life Sciences; Biology; Marine Biology; Marine Science and Oceanography); **Business Administration** (Business Administration; Tourism); **Business Studies** (Business Administration; Management); **Engineering** (Aeronautical and Aerospace Engineering; Applied Chemistry; Architecture; Biochemistry; Biomedical Engineering; Civil Engineering; Electrical and Electronic Engineering; Energy Engineering; Engineering; Materials Engineering; Measurement and Precision Engineering; Mechanical Engineering; Nuclear Engineering; Optical Technology); **Health Sciences** (Nursing; Social Work); **Humanities and Culture** (Arts and Humanities; Cultural Studies; Design; Environmental Studies; Fine Arts; International Studies; Music; Natural Resources); **Industrial and Welfare Engineering** (Computer Science; Electrical Engineering; Health Sciences; Industrial Engineering; Welfare and Protective Services); **Industrial Engineering** (Architecture; Artificial Intelligence; Electronic Engineering; Environmental Management; Industrial Engineering; Mechanical Engineering); **Information and Telecommunication Engineering** (Computer Engineering; Computer Networks; Information Technology; Management; Media Studies; Technology; Telecommunications Engineering); **Information Science and Technology** (Computer Engineering; Information Sciences; Information Technology); **International Cultural Relations** (Communication Studies; Cultural Studies; Design; Development Studies; International Relations); **Letters** (American Studies; Archaeology; Asian Studies; Cultural Studies; English; European Studies; History; Literature; Media Studies; Nordic Studies; Psychology; Sociology; Writing); **Marine Science and Technology** (Biological and Life Sciences; Earth Sciences; Environmental Studies; Fishery; Food Science; Marine Biology; Marine Engineering; Marine Science and Oceanography; Marine Transport; Mineralogy; Natural Resources; Naval Architecture; Transport Management); **Medicine** (Medicine); **Physical Education** (Leisure Studies; Parks and Recreation; Physical Education; Sports; Sports Management); **Political Science and Economics** (Business Administration; Economics; Political Sciences); **Science** (Chemistry; Mathematics; Physics); **Tourism** (Tourism)

Graduate School

Agriculture (Agriculture); **Arts** (Design; Fine Arts; Music); **Biosciences** (Biological and Life Sciences; Natural Resources); **Design** (Design); **Earth and Environmental Sciences** (Astronomy and Space Science; Earth Sciences; Engineering; Environmental Studies); **Economics** (Economics); **Engineering** (Aeronautical and Aerospace Engineering; Architecture; Building Technologies; Civil Engineering; Electrical and Electronic Engineering; Electronic Engineering; Engineering; Industrial Chemistry; Information Sciences; Information Technology; Mechanical Engineering;

Metallurgical Engineering; Natural Sciences; Optics); **Health Sciences** (Health Sciences; Social Work); **High-Technology for Human Welfare** (Bioengineering; Biological and Life Sciences; Biomedical Engineering; Information Technology; Materials Engineering; Telecommunications Engineering); **Human Environmental Studies** (Environmental Studies); **Industrial Engineering** (Architecture; Civil Engineering; Industrial Engineering; Information Technology; Production Engineering); **Information and Telecommunication Engineering** (Information Technology; Telecommunications Engineering); **Integrated Design Studies** (Design); **Law** (Law); **Law** (*Professional*) (Law); **Letters** (Communication Studies; Cultural Studies; English; History; Japanese; Literature); **Marine Science and Technology** (Fishery; Marine Biology; Marine Engineering; Marine Science and Oceanography); **Medicine** (Medicine); **Physical Education** (Physical Education); **Political Science** (Political Sciences); **Regional Development Studies** (Development Studies; Regional Studies); **Sccience and Technology** (Aeronautical and Aerospace Engineering; Architecture; Biological and Life Sciences; Biotechnology; Chemistry; Civil Engineering; Electrical and Electronic Engineering; Information Sciences; Information Technology; Marine Engineering; Marine Science and Oceanography; Materials Engineering; Mathematics; Mechanical Engineering; Physics); **Science** (Chemistry; Mathematics; Physics); **Science and Engineering** (Biological and Life Sciences; Electronic Engineering; Environmental Studies; Information Technology)

Further information: 10 campuses: Sapporo, Asahikawa, Takanawa, Yoyogi, Shonan, Isehara, Shimizu, Numazu, Kumamoto, and Aso

History: Founded 1942 as Aerial Science College, recognized 1946 as Tokai University, and officially authorized by the Ministry of Education. From 2008, Tokai Daigaku (Tokai University) Kyushu Tokai Daigaku (Kyushu Tokai University) and Hokkaido Tokai Daigaku (Hokkaido Tokai University) were integrated under one banner as Tokai University.

Academic year: April to March (April-September; October-March)

Admission requirements: Graduation from high school (upon completion of 16 years of formal education)

Main language(s) of instruction: Japanese, English

Accrediting agency: Japan University Accreditation Association (JUAA)

Degrees and diplomas: Gakushi, Shushi (Agriculture; Architecture; Biomedical Engineering; Chemistry; Civil Engineering; Communication Studies; Cultural Studies; Design; Economics; Electrical and Electronic Engineering; English; Environmental Studies; Fine Arts; History; Information Technology; Law; Marine Science and Oceanography; Mathematics; Mechanical Engineering; Medicine; Music; Nursing; Physical Education; Physics; Political Sciences; Telecommunications Engineering; Tourism), Hakase

(Communication Studies; Cultural Studies; Economics; Engineering; English; Environmental Engineering; Fine Arts; History; Law; Medicine; Nursing; Political Sciences; Technology). Also Postgraduate Diploma in Law (Juris doctor)

Student Services: Academic Counselling, Social Counselling, Careers Guidance, Cultural Activities, Sports Facilities, Language Laboratory, Facilities for disabled people, Health Services, Canteen, Foreign Studies Centre

Academic Staff 2012-2013	MALE	FEMALE	TOTAL
FULL-TIME	1421	312	1733
Student Numbers 2012-2013			
All (Foreign Included)	20826	7772	28598
Foreign only	298	131	429

Last Update: 02-03-2018

Tokaigakuen University

2-901 Nakahira Tenpaku-ku
Nagoya-shi 468-8514, Aichi
Tel: +81(52) 801-1201
Fax: +81(52) 804-1044
Website: http://www.tokaigakuen-u.ac.jp
President: Matsubara Takehisa

School

Graduate; **Human Wellness** (Nursing); **Humanities** (Arts and Humanities; Behavioural Sciences; Film; Journalism; Literature; Psychology; Radio and Television Broadcasting; Video; Writing); **Management** (Business Administration; Management)

Further information: Also Miyoshi Campus

History: Founded 1995.

Main language(s) of instruction: Japanese

Accrediting agency: Japan Institution for Higher Education Evaluation (JIHEE)

Degrees and diplomas: Gakushi (Business Administration), Shushi (Business Administration)

Last Update: 02-03-2018

Tokiwa University (TU)

1-430-1 Miwa
Mito-shi 310-8585, Ibaraki
Tel: +81(29) 232-2511
Fax: +81(29) 231-6078
Website: http://www.tokiwa.ac.jp
President: Tomita Nobutaka

College

Applied International Studies (American Studies; Business and Commerce; English Studies; International Business; International Relations); **Community Development** (Development Studies; Regional Studies; Social and Community Services); **Human Sciences** (Communication Studies; Education; Health Sciences; Nutrition; Psychology; Sociology)

School

Graduate Studies (Development Studies; Psychology; Social Psychology; Social Sciences; Urban Studies)
History: Founded 1983.
Academic year: April to January (April-July; September-January)
Admission requirements: High school diploma or equivalent
Main language(s) of instruction: Japanese
Accrediting agency: Japan University Accreditation Association (JUAA)
Degrees and diplomas: Gakushi, Shushi (Social and Community Services), Hakase (Psychology; Social Studies)
Student Services: Academic Counselling, Social Counselling, Careers Guidance, Sports Facilities, Language Laboratory, Facilities for disabled people, Health Services, Canteen, Foreign Studies Centre, Library
Periodicals: Community Development Studies, Human Science, Tokiwa International Studies Journal
Last Update: 02-03-2018

Tokiwakaigakuen University

1-4-12 Kirehigashi
Hirano-ku 547-0021, Osaka
Tel: +81(6) 4302-8880
Fax: +81(6) 4302-8884
Website: http://www.sftokiwakai.ac.jp

Faculty

Education (Teacher Training)

Course/Programme

International Communication (Communication Studies; International Relations)
History: Founded 1999.
Main language(s) of instruction: Japanese
Accrediting agency: Japan Institution for Higher Education Evaluation (JIHEE)
Degrees and diplomas: Gakushi
Student Services: Cultural Activities, Sports Facilities
Last Update: 02-03-2018

Tokoha University

1-22-1 Sena
Shizuoka-shi 420-0911, Shizuoka
Tel: +81(54) 261-4705
Fax: +81(54) 263-2750
Website: http://www.tokoha-u.ac.jp
President: Eto Hideichi

Faculty

Education (Education; Primary Education); **Foreign Studies** (Communication Studies; Cultural Studies; English; International Business; International Studies; Modern Languages; Spanish)

School

Graduate Studies
History: Founded 1980 as Tokoha Gakuen Daigaku.
Main language(s) of instruction: Japanese
Accrediting agency: Japan University Accreditation Association (JUAA)
Degrees and diplomas: Gakushi (Management), Shushi
Last Update: 27-03-2018

Tokushima Bunri University

Nishihama, Yamashiro-cho
Tokushima 770-8514, Tokushima
Tel: +81(88) 622-9611
Website: http://www.bunri-u.ac.jp
President: Kirino Yutaka

Faculty

Engineering (*Also Graduate School*) (Artificial Intelligence; Bioengineering; Computer Engineering; Electronic Engineering; Engineering; Environmental Engineering; Information Sciences; Mechanical Engineering; Nanotechnology; Robotics); **Health and Welfare** (Medical Technology; Nursing; Radiology; Rehabilitation and Therapy); **Human Life Sciences** (Architectural and Environmental Design; Food Science; Home Economics; Information Technology; Media Studies; Nutrition; Psychology; Social Sciences; Social Welfare; Welfare and Protective Services); **Literature** (*Also Graduate School*) (American Studies; Communication Studies; Cultural Studies; English; European Languages; International Relations; Japanese; Literature; Modern Languages; Oriental Languages); **Music** (*Also Postgraduate one-year courses*) (Music; Musical Instruments; Singing); **Pharmaceutical Sciences** (*Also Graduate School*) (Pharmacology; Pharmacy); **Pharmaceutical Sciences** (*Kagawa Campus; Also Graduate School*) (Pharmacology; Pharmacy); **Policy Studies** (*Also Graduate School*) (Political Sciences)

Graduate School

Home Economics (Environmental Studies; Food Science; Home Economics; Social Sciences; Social Studies)
History: Founded 1895, acquired present status 1966.
Academic year: April to March
Admission requirements: Graduation from high school and entrance examination
Main language(s) of instruction: Japanese
Accrediting agency: Japan Institution for Higher Education Evaluation (JIHEE)
Degrees and diplomas: Gakushi, Shushi, Hakase (Engineering; Literature; Pharmacy)
Student Services: Sports Facilities, Foreign Studies Centre, Library
Last Update: 02-03-2018

Tokuyama University

843-4-2 Kume-Kurigasako
Tokuyama-shi 745-8566, Yamaguchi
Tel: +81(834) 28-0411
Fax: +81(834) 282-088
Website: http://www.tokuyama-u.ac.jp

Faculty

Economics (Economics); **Welfare and Information** (Social Welfare)
History: Founded 1971.
Main language(s) of instruction: Japanese
Accrediting agency: Japan Institution for Higher Education Evaluation (JIHEE)
Degrees and diplomas: Gakushi
Last Update: 02-03-2018

Tokyo Ariake University of Medical and Health Sciences

2-9-1 Ariake Koto-ku
Tokyo 135-0063
Tel: +81(3) 6703-7000
Fax: +81(3) 6703-7100
Website: http://www.tau.ac.jp
President: Ikuo Homma

Faculty

Health Science (Acupuncture; Traditional Eastern Medicine); **Nursing** (Nursing)
History: Founded 1956 as Tokyo High Judo school. Acquired present status and title 2013.
Main language(s) of instruction: Japanese

Accrediting agency: Japan Institution for Higher Education Evaluation (JIHEE)
Degrees and diplomas: Gakushi (Acupuncture; Nursing; Traditional Eastern Medicine), Shushi (Acupuncture; Nursing; Traditional Eastern Medicine)
Student Services: Careers Guidance, Sports Facilities, Canteen, Library, IT Centre
Last Update: 02-03-2018

Tokyo Christian University

3-301-5-1 Uchino
Inzai-shi 270-1347, Chiba
Tel: +81(476) 46-1131
Fax: +81(476) 46-1405
Website: http://www.tci.ac.jp
President: Yoichi Yamaguchi

Course/Programme

Bible (Bible); **Church History**; **Japanese Studies** (Communication Studies; Cultural Studies; East Asian Studies; History; Religion; South Asian Studies; Southeast Asian Studies); **Languages**; **Liberal Arts**; **Missiology**; **Practical Theology** (Theology); **Systematic Theology** (Theology)
History: Founded 1990.
Main language(s) of instruction: Japanese, English
Accrediting agency: Japan University Accreditation Association (JUAA)
Degrees and diplomas: Gakushi (Theology), Hakase (Theology)
Last Update: 02-03-2018

Tokyo City University

1-28-1 Tamazutsumi
Setagaya-ku 158-8557, Tokyo
Tel: +81(3) 5707-2211
Fax: +81(3) 5707-2222
Website: http://www.tcu.ac.jp/english/index.html
President: Miki Chitoshi

Faculty

Engineering (Architecture; Chemical Engineering; Electrical and Electronic Engineering; Energy Engineering; Mechanical Engineering; Safety Engineering; Town Planning); **Environmental Studies**; **Human Life Sciences** (Child Care and Development); **Informatics** (Information Sciences; Media Studies; Sociology); **Knowledge Engineering** (Computer Science; Industrial Management; Information Sciences; Natural Sciences); **Urban Life Studies** (Urban Studies)

Graduate School

Engineering (Architecture; Biomedical Engineering; Chemical Engineering; Civil Engineering; Electrical and Electronic Engineering; Energy Engineering; Mechanical Engineering); **Environmental and Information Studies** (Urban Studies)

History: Founded 1929 as Technical School, became Institute 1949. Known as Musashi Kogyo Daigaku (Musashi Institute of Technology) until April 2009.

Academic year: April to March (April-October; October-March)

Admission requirements: Graduation from high school or recognized equivalent or foreign equivalent, and entrance examination

Main language(s) of instruction: Japanese

Accrediting agency: Japan University Accreditation Association (JUAA)

Degrees and diplomas: Gakushi (Architecture; Civil Engineering; Communication Arts; Computer Science; Electrical and Electronic Engineering; Electronic Engineering; Energy Engineering; Environmental Studies; Information Sciences; Mechanical Engineering), Shushi (Architecture; Biomedical Engineering; Chemical Engineering; Civil Engineering; Electrical and Electronic Engineering; Energy Engineering; Environmental Studies; Industrial Management; Information Sciences; Mechanical Engineering; Nuclear Engineering; Polymer and Plastics Technology), Hakase (Architecture; Biomedical Engineering; Chemical Engineering; Civil Engineering; Electrical and Electronic Engineering; Energy Engineering; Environmental Studies; Industrial Management; Information Sciences; Mechanical Engineering; Nuclear Engineering; Polymer and Plastics Technology)

Student Services: Academic Counselling, Social Counselling, Careers Guidance, Sports Facilities, Facilities for disabled people, Health Services, Canteen, Library

Periodicals: MI-TECH Quarterly

Last Update: 02-03-2018

Tokyo College of Music

3-4-5 Minami-Ikebukuro Toshima-ku
Tokyo 171-8540
Tel: +81(3) 3982-2717
Fax: +81(3) 3986-3317
Website: http://www.tokyo-ondai.ac.jp
President: Minoru Nojima

Course/Programme

Music (Conducting; Music; Music Theory and Composition; Musical Instruments; Opera; Singing)

Institute

Ethno-musicology (Musicology)

Graduate School

Music (Conducting; Music Theory and Composition; Musical Instruments; Musicology; Opera; Singing)

History: Founded 1907.

Main language(s) of instruction: Japanese

Accrediting agency: Japan Institution for Higher Education Evaluation (JIHEE)

Degrees and diplomas: Gakushi, Shushi (Conducting; Music; Music Education; Music Theory and Composition; Musical Instruments; Musicology; Opera; Singing), Hakase (Music; Music Education; Musicology)

Last Update: 02-03-2018

Tokyo Denki University

5 Senju Asahi-cho Adachi-ku
Tokyo 101-8457
Tel: +81(3) 5284-5208
Fax: +81(3) 5280-3599
Website: http://www.dendai.ac.jp
President: Hiroshi Yasuda

School

Engineering (Applied Chemistry; Electrical and Electronic Engineering; Engineering; Information Technology; Mechanical Engineering); **Information Environment** (Architectural and Environmental Design; Communication Studies; Computer Engineering; Computer Networks; Information Management; Information Sciences; Information Technology; Media Studies); **Science and Engineering** (Biological and Life Sciences; Civil Engineering; Engineering; Environmental Engineering; Information Technology; Mechanical Engineering; Natural Sciences); **Science and Technology for the Future Life** (Architecture; Multimedia)

Institute

Construction Technology Research (Construction Engineering); **Technology Research** (Technology)

Centre

Multimedia Resource and Library Science (Library Science; Multimedia)

Laboratory

Applied Superconductivity Research

Graduate School

Advanced Science and Technology (*Doctoral programme*); **Engineering** (*Master's programme*) (Engineering); **Information Environment** (*Master's programme*) (Information Sciences); **Science and Engineering** (*Master's programme*) (Engineering)

Further information: Also Courses for foreign students. Study Abroad programmes in USA
History: Founded 1907 as evening Institute of Electrical and Mechanical Technology. Became Higher Technical School 1939 and College 1949. Two Campuses: Hatoyama (Saitama), and Chiba.
Academic year: April to March (April-September; October-March)
Admission requirements: Graduation from high school or equivalent, and entrance examination
Main language(s) of instruction: Japanese
Accrediting agency: Japan University Accreditation Association (JUAA)
Degrees and diplomas: Gakushi (Engineering), Shushi (Architecture; Bioengineering; Biological and Life Sciences; Civil Engineering; Electrical and Electronic Engineering; Environmental Engineering; Information Sciences; Materials Engineering; Multimedia; Robotics), Hakase (Biological and Life Sciences; Engineering; Mathematics and Computer Science)
Student Services: Academic Counselling, Careers Guidance, Sports Facilities, Health Services, Canteen
Periodicals: Library Reports, Research Reports
Publishing house: The University Press
Last Update: 02-03-2018

Tokyo Dental College

2-9-18 Misakicho Chiyoda-ku,
Tokyo 101-0061
Tel: +81(03) 6380-9001
Website: http://www.tdc.ac.jp
President: Yoshinobu Ide

College
Dentistry (Dentistry)

Graduate School
Dentistry (Dental Hygiene; Dental Technology; Dentistry; Forensic Medicine and Dentistry; Oral Pathology; Orthodontics; Periodontics)
History: Founded 1890 as Takayama Dental School, acquired present title and status 1907. Reorganized 1950.
Academic year: April to March (April-September; October-March)
Admission requirements: Graduation from high school and entrance examination
Main language(s) of instruction: Japanese
Accrediting agency: Japan University Accreditation Association (JUAA)
Degrees and diplomas: Gakushi (Dentistry), Hakase (Dentistry)

Student Services: Academic Counselling, Social Counselling, Careers Guidance, Sports Facilities, Health Services, Canteen, Library
Periodicals: Bulletin of Tokyo Dental College, Shikwa Gakuho
Last Update: 02-03-2018

Tokyo Fuji University (TFU)

3 Chome-8-1 Takadanobaba, Shinjuku,
Tokyo 169-0075
Tel: +81(3) 3362-7297
Website: http://www.fuji.ac.jp

School
Business (Business Administration; Psychology)
History: Founded 1943 as East Asia Institute. Acquired present status and title 2008.
Main language(s) of instruction: Japanese
Accrediting agency: Japan Institution for Higher Education Evaluation (JIHEE)
Degrees and diplomas: Gakushi (Business Administration; Psychology)
Student Services: Foreign Studies Centre, Library
Last Update: 02-03-2018

Tokyo Future University

34-12 Senju, Akebono-cho Adachi-ku
Tokyo 120-0023
Tel: +81(3) 5813-2525
Fax: +81(3) 5813-2529
Website: http://www.tokyomirai.ac.jp

Department/Division
Child Psychology (Child Care and Development; Psychology); **Motivation and Behavioural Science** (Behavioural Sciences)
History: Founded 2007.
Main language(s) of instruction: Japanese
Accrediting agency: Japan Institution for Higher Education Evaluation (JIHEE)
Degrees and diplomas: Gakushi
Last Update: 02-03-2018

Tokyo Healthcare University

2-5-1 Higashigaoka, Meguro-ku
Tokyo 152-8558
Tel: +81(3) 5779-5031

Fax: +81(3) 5421-2081
Website: http://www.thcu.ac.jp
President: Kimura Satoshi

Faculty

Medical and Health Care (Health Administration; Nursing; Nutrition); **Nursing Higashigaoka** (Nursing)
History: Founded 1996. Acquired present status and title 2005.
Main language(s) of instruction: Japanese
Accrediting agency: Japan University Accreditation Association (JUAA)
Degrees and diplomas: Gakushi (Health Administration; Nursing; Nutrition)
Student Services: Library, Residential Facilities
Last Update: 02-03-2018

Tokyo International University (TIU)

4-23-23 Takadanobaba, Shinjuku
Tokyo 169-0075
Tel: +81(3)3362-9644
Fax: +81(3)3362-9643
Website: http://www.tiu.ac.jp

School

Business and Commerce (Business Administration; Business and Commerce); **Economics** (Economics; International Economics); **Human and Social Sciences** (Development Studies; Psychology; Social Sciences; Social Welfare; Sports); **International Relations** (Communication Studies; International Relations; Media Studies); **Language Communication** (Asian Studies; Chinese; English)

Graduate School

Applied Sociology (*Master's course*) (Sociology); **Business and Commerce** (*Master's and Doctoral courses*) (Business and Commerce); **Economics** (*Master's and Doctoral courses*) (Economics); **International Relations** (*Master's Course*) (International Relations)
Further information: Also affiliated Japanese Language School
History: Founded 1965 as the International College of Commerce and Economics. A private institution emphasizing international Education.
Academic year: April to March
Admission requirements: Secondary school certificate or equivalent and entrance examination
Main language(s) of instruction: Japanese, English
Accrediting agency: Japan University Accreditation Association (JUAA)

Degrees and diplomas: Gakushi, Shushi (Business Administration; Economics; International Relations; Marketing; Psychology), Hakase (Economics)
Student Services: Academic Counselling, Social Counselling, Careers Guidance, Nursery Care, Cultural Activities, Sports Facilities, Language Laboratory, Facilities for disabled people, Health Services, Canteen, Foreign Studies Centre

STAFF WITH DOCTORATE	MALE	FEMALE	TOTAL
FULL-TIME			180
Student Numbers 2012-2013			
All (Foreign Included)			6200
Foreign only			769

Last Update: 02-03-2018

Tokyo Junshin University

2-600 Takiyama-cho
Hachioji-shi 192-0011, Tokyo
Tel: +81(426) 92-0326
Fax: +81(426) 92-5551
Website: http://www.t-junshin.ac.jp

Department/Division

Child Care and Culture (Preschool Education; Primary Education; Teacher Training); **International Culture** (Design; English; Music; Painting and Drawing)
History: Founded 1996. Former Tokyo Junshin Women's College
Main language(s) of instruction: Japanese
Accrediting agency: Japan Institution for Higher Education Evaluation (JIHEE)
Degrees and diplomas: Gakushi
Last Update: 05-03-2018

Tokyo Kasei Gakuin University

2600 Aihara-machi
Machida-shi 194-0292, Tokyo
Tel: +81(42) 782-9811
Fax: +81(42) 782-9880
Website: http://www.kasei-gakuin.ac.jp

Faculty

Contemporary Human Life Sciences (Home Economics; Nutrition; Psychology; Social Studies)
History: Founded 1963.
Main language(s) of instruction: Japanese
Accrediting agency: Japan Institution for Higher Education Evaluation (JIHEE)

Degrees and diplomas: Gakushi, Shushi
Student Services: Academic Counselling, Social Counselling, Sports Facilities, Health Services
Last Update: 05-03-2018

Tokyo Kasei University (TKU)

1-18-1 Kaga Itabashi-ku
Tokyo 173-8602
Tel: +81(3) 3961-5226
Fax: +81(3) 3961-1736
Website: http://www.tokyo-kasei.ac.jp
President: Kazuhito Yamamoto

Faculty

Home Economics (Child Care and Development; Clothing and Sewing; Environmental Studies; Home Economics; Nutrition); **Humanities** (*Sayama City*) (Arts and Humanities; Education; English; Psychology)
History: Founded 1881.
Academic year: April to March
Admission requirements: Graduation from high school or equivalent
Main language(s) of instruction: Japanese
Accrediting agency: Japan University Accreditation Association (JUAA)
Degrees and diplomas: Gakushi, Shushi (Arts and Humanities; Child Care and Development; Clinical Psychology; Clothing and Sewing; Education; English; Home Economics; Nutrition; Social Welfare), Hakase (Arts and Humanities; Social Sciences)
Student Services: Academic Counselling, Social Counselling, Careers Guidance, Sports Facilities, Facilities for disabled people, Health Services, Canteen, Foreign Studies Centre
Periodicals: Bulletin of Research, Institution of Domestic Science, Bulletin of Tokyo Kasei University
Last Update: 05-03-2018

Tokyo Keizai University

1-7-34, Minami-cho Kokubunji-shi
Tokyo 185-8502
Tel: +81(42) 328-7711
Fax: +81(42) 328-7770
Website: http://www.tku.ac.jp
President: Kenichi Sakai

Faculty

Business Administration (Business Administration; Marketing); **Communication Studies** (Communication Studies; Social Sciences); **Contemporary Law** (Law); **Economics** (Economics; International Economics)
Further information: Also Graduate Schools in fields of study offered in Faculties
History: Founded 1900 as Okura Commerce School, became University 1949. Graduate School established 1970. Japan's first Faculty of Communication Studies 1995. Formerly known as Tokyo College of Economics.
Academic year: April to March (April-July; October-March)
Admission requirements: Graduation from high school or equivalent, and entrance examination
Main language(s) of instruction: Japanese
Accrediting agency: Japan University Accreditation Association (JUAA)
Degrees and diplomas: Gakushi (Business Administration; Communication Studies; Economics; Law), Shushi (Business Administration; Communication Studies; Economics; Law; Marketing), Hakase (Business Administration; Communication Studies; Economics)
Student Services: Academic Counselling, Social Counselling, Careers Guidance, Cultural Activities, Sports Facilities, Language Laboratory, Facilities for disabled people, Health Services, Canteen
Periodicals: Journal of Communication Studies, Journal of Humanities and Natural Sciences, Journal of Tokyo Keizai University, Tokyo Keizai Law Review
Publishing house: Tokyo Keizai Daigaku-hó
Last Update: 27-03-2018

Tokyo Medical University (TMU)

6-1-1 Shinjuku Shinjuku-ku
Tokyo 160-8402
Tel: +81(3) 3351-6141
Website: http://www.tokyo-med.ac.jp
President: Masahiko Usui

School

Medicine (Anatomy; Medicine; Social and Preventive Medicine; Surgery); **Nursing**

Graduate School

Medicine (Medicine; Surgery)
History: Founded 1916.
Academic year: April to March (April-August; September-December; January-March)
Admission requirements: Graduation from high school and entrance examination
Fees: 3,471,000 per annum (Yen)
Main language(s) of instruction: Japanese
Accrediting agency: Ministry of Education, Culture, Sports, Science and Technology

Degrees and diplomas: Gakushi (Medicine), Hakase (Medicine)
Student Services: Academic Counselling, Nursery Care, Health Services, Canteen, Library
Periodicals: Journal of Tokyo Medical University
Last Update: 23-02-2018

Tokyo Polytechnic University

9-5 Honcho 2-chome Nakano-ku
Tokyo 164
Tel: +81(3) 3372-1321
Fax: +81(3) 3372-1330
Website: http://www.t-kougei.ac.jp
President: Ryuichiro Yoshie

Faculty

Arts (*Also Graduate School*) (Arts and Humanities; Communication Studies; Design; Media Studies; Photography; Social Sciences; Sports; Visual Arts); **Engineering** (*Also Graduate School*) (Computer Graphics; Computer Science; Electronic Engineering; Information Technology; Media Studies)
History: Founded 1923 as Konishi Professional School of Photography. Acquired present title 1977.
Academic year: April to March (April-September; September-March)
Admission requirements: Graduation from high school and entrance examination
Main language(s) of instruction: Japanese
Accrediting agency: Japan University Accreditation Association (JUAA)
Degrees and diplomas: Gakushi (Engineering), Shushi (Engineering), Hakase (Architecture; Electronic Engineering; Energy Engineering; Engineering; Industrial Chemistry; Information Technology)
Student Services: Library
Periodicals: Bulletin
Last Update: 05-03-2018

Tokyo Seiei College

Nishishinkoiwa 1-4-6
Tokyo 124-8530, Katsushika-ku
Tel: +81 3-3692-0211
Fax: +81 3-3692-0213
Website: http://www.tsc-05.ac.jp
President: Tadahiko Tadokoro

Faculty

Health and Nutrition (Food Science; Health Sciences; Nutrition)

History: Founded 1947 as Orimupia dressmaking School. Acquired present status and title 2005.
Main language(s) of instruction: Japanese
Accrediting agency: Japan Institution for Higher Education Evaluation (JIHEE)
Degrees and diplomas: Gakushi (Food Science; Nutrition)
Student Services: Careers Guidance, Library
Last Update: 05-03-2018

Tokyo Seitoku University

2014 Nakadaiyatsu Hoshina
Yachiyo-shi 276-0013, Chiba
Tel: +81(47) 488-1000
Fax: +81(47) 480-5160
Website: http://www.tsu.ac.jp

Faculty

Business Administration (Business Administration); **Humanities** (Cultural Studies; Japanese; Modern Languages; Psychology; Tourism)

Graduate School

Clinical Psychology (Clinical Psychology)
History: Founded 1993.
Main language(s) of instruction: Japanese
Accrediting agency: Japan Institution for Higher Education Evaluation (JIHEE)
Degrees and diplomas: Gakushi, Shushi (Psychology), Hakase (Psychology)
Last Update: 05-03-2018

Tokyo University of Agriculture

1-1-1 Sakuragaoka
Setagaya-ku 156-8502, Tokyo
Tel: +81(3) 5477-2560
Fax: +81(3) 5477-2635
Website: http://www.nodai.ac.jp
President: Katsumi Takano

Faculty

Agriculture (Agriculture; Zoology); **Applied Bio-Science** (Applied Chemistry; Biology; Biotechnology; Food Science; Nutrition); **Bio-industry** (Aquaculture; Food Science; Food Technology); **International Agriculture and Food Studies** (Agriculture; Food Science); **Regional Environmental Science** (Environmental Engineering; Forestry; Landscape Architecture; Production Engineering)

Graduate School

Agriculture (Agricultural Economics; Agricultural Engineering; Agriculture; Animal Husbandry; Chemistry; Food Technology; Forestry; Landscape Architecture; Nutrition); **Bioindustry** (Biology; Business and Commerce; Food Science; Food Technology)

Further information: Also campuses in Hokkaido and Atsugi

History: Founded 1891 as College, became University 1925.

Academic year: April to March (April-September; October-March)

Admission requirements: Competitive entrance examination following graduation from high school. Proficiency in Japanese

Main language(s) of instruction: Japanese, English

Accrediting agency: Japan University Accreditation Association (JUAA)

Degrees and diplomas: Shushi (Agricultural Business; Agricultural Economics; Agricultural Engineering; Agriculture; Animal Husbandry; Biological and Life Sciences; Food Science; Forestry; Landscape Architecture), Hakase (Agricultural Business; Agricultural Engineering; Agricultural Management; Agriculture; Animal Husbandry; Biological and Life Sciences; Food Science; Forestry; Landscape Architecture)

Student Services: Academic Counselling, Social Counselling, Careers Guidance, Sports Facilities, Health Services, Canteen, Library

Periodicals: General Education Journal, Memoirs, Nogaku Shuho (Agricultural Journal)

Publishing house: Tokyo University of Agriculture Press

Last Update: 05-03-2018

Tokyo University of Information Sciences

4-1 Onaridai Wakaba-ku
Chiba-shi 265-8501, Chiba
Tel: +81(43) 236-4603
Fax: +81(43) 236-2215
Website: http://www.tuis.ac.jp
President: Masaharu Sazuki

Faculty

Informatics (*Also Graduate School*) (Business Administration; Business and Commerce; Computer Networks; Cultural Studies; Information Sciences; Information Technology; Media Studies; Social Studies; Software Engineering)

History: Founded 1988.

Academic year: April to March (April-September; October-March)

Admission requirements: Graduation from high school or recognized equivalent, and entrance examination

Main language(s) of instruction: Japanese

Accrediting agency: Japan University Accreditation Association (JUAA)

Degrees and diplomas: Gakushi, Shushi (Information Sciences), Hakase (Information Sciences)

Student Services: Careers Guidance, Sports Facilities, Language Laboratory, Library

Periodicals: Keiei Johoi Kagaku (Management Information Science)

Last Update: 05-03-2018

Tokyo University of Pharmacy and Life Sciences

1432-1 Horinouchi
Hachioji-shi 192-0392, Tokyo
Tel: +81(426) 76-5111
Fax: +81(426) 75-3095
Website: http://www.toyaku.ac.jp

School

Life Sciences (Biological and Life Sciences; Medicine); **Pharmacy** (Pharmacy)

Graduate School

Life Sciences (Biological and Life Sciences); **Pharmacy** (Pharmacy)

History: Founded 1880 as School, acquired present status and title 1949.

Academic year: April to March (April-September; October-March)

Admission requirements: Graduation from high school and entrance examination. Special provisions for foreign students with similar qualifications

Main language(s) of instruction: Japanese

Accrediting agency: Japan University Accreditation Association (JUAA)

Degrees and diplomas: Gakushi (Biological and Life Sciences; Pharmacy), Shushi (Biological and Life Sciences; Pharmacy), Hakase (Biological and Life Sciences; Pharmacy)

Student Services: Library

Periodicals: Annual Report of School of Pharmacy and TUPLS, School of Life Sciences, Tokyo University of Pharmacy and Life Sciences (Annual Report), The Journal of Tokyo University of Pharmacy and Lifes Sciences

Last Update: 05-03-2018

🔳🔳 Tokyo University of Science (TUS)

1-3 Kagurazaka, Shinjuku-ku
Tokyo 162-8601
Tel: +81(3) 3260-8726
Fax: +81(3) 3260-4370
Website: http://www.tus.ac.jp
President: Akira Fujishima

Faculty

Engineering I (Architecture; Electrical Engineering; Engineering; Industrial Chemistry; Management; Mechanical Engineering); **Engineering II** (Architecture; Electrical Engineering; Engineering; Management); **Industrial Science and Technology** (*Noda Campus, Chiba*) (Biological and Life Sciences; Electronic Engineering; Materials Engineering); **Pharmaceutical Sciences** (*Noda Campus, Chiba*) (Pharmacology; Pharmacy); **Science and Technology** (*Noda Campus, Chiba*) (Administration; Architecture; Biology; Chemistry; Civil Engineering; Electrical Engineering; Industrial Engineering; Information Sciences; Mathematics; Mechanical Engineering; Physics); **Science I** (Applied Chemistry; Applied Mathematics; Applied Physics; Chemistry; Information Sciences; Mathematics; Physics); **Science II** (Chemistry; Mathematics; Natural Sciences; Physics)

Course/Programme

Liberal Arts (Arts and Humanities; Social Sciences)

School

Management (*Kuki Campus, Saitama*) (Management)

Graduate School

Biological Science (Biological and Life Sciences); **Chemical Sciences and Technology** (Chemistry); **Engineering** (Architecture; Electrical Engineering; Engineering; Mechanical Engineering); **Global Fire Science and Technology** (Fire Science); **Industrial Science and Technology** (Biological and Life Sciences; Biotechnology; Electronic Engineering; Materials Engineering); **Innovation Studies** (Management); **Management** (Management); **Mathematics and Science Education** (Mathematics; Natural Sciences); **Pharmaceutical Sciences** (Pharmacy); **Science** (Applied Physics; Mathematics; Mathematics and Computer Science; Physics); **Science and Technology** (Applied Chemistry; Architecture; Biology; Chemistry; Civil Engineering; Electrical Engineering; Industrial Management; Information Sciences; Mathematics; Mechanical Engineering; Physics)

Research Division

Biomedical Sciences (Biological and Life Sciences; Gerontology; Molecular Biology; Pathology); **Science and Technology** (*Noda Campus, Chiba*) (Heating and Refrigeration; Natural Sciences; Oncology; Pharmacy; Technology; Thermal Physics)
Further information: Kagurazaka Campus, Tokyo; Noda Campus, Chiba; Oshamambe Campus, Hokkaido; Kuki Campus, Saitama. Also Sister Universities in Yamaguchi and Suwa
History: Founded 1881 as College, reorganized and became University 1949.
Academic year: April to March (April-September; September-March)
Admission requirements: Graduation from high school or recognized equivalent, and entrance examination
Main language(s) of instruction: Japanese, English
Accrediting agency: Japan University Accreditation Association (JUAA)
Degrees and diplomas: Gakushi (Engineering; Management; Pharmacy), Shushi (Applied Mathematics; Applied Physics; Architecture; Biological and Life Sciences; Chemistry; Civil Engineering; Electrical Engineering; Management; Mathematics; Mechanical Engineering; Pharmacy; Physics), Hakase (Biological and Life Sciences; Chemistry; Engineering; Natural Sciences; Technology)
Student Services: Academic Counselling, Careers Guidance, Sports Facilities, Health Services, Canteen, Library
Periodicals: Ridai Science Forum
Last Update: 25-05-2018

Tokyo University of Science, Suwa

Toyohira 5000-1
Nagano 391-0292, Chino
Tel: +81(266) 73-1201
Fax: +81(266) 73-1230
Website: http://www.suwa.tus.ac.jp

Faculty

Engineering (Computer Science; Electrical and Electronic Engineering; Mechanical Engineering)

School

Information Management (Information Management)
History: Founded 1881 as Tokyo physics training office. Acquired present status and title 2002.
Main language(s) of instruction: Japanese
Accrediting agency: Japan Institution for Higher Education Evaluation (JIHEE)
Degrees and diplomas: Gakushi (Engineering; Information Management), Shushi (Engineering), Hakase (Engineering)
Student Services: Canteen, Library, IT Centre
Last Update: 05-03-2018

Tokyo University of Social Welfare (TUSW)

4-23-1 Higashi-Ikebukuro Toshima-ku
Tokyo 170-8426
Tel: +81(3) 5960-7426
Fax: +81(3) 3981-2533
Website: http://www.tokyo-fukushi.ac.jp
President: Tatsuya Matsubara

Course/Programme
Social Welfare (Clinical Psychology; International Studies; Social Welfare; Social Work)

School
Education (Education); **Graduate** (Clinical Psychology; Education; Welfare and Protective Services); **Psychology** (Child Care and Development; Psychology); **Social Welfare** (*Also Graduate School*) (Child Care and Development; Clinical Psychology; Gerontology; Preschool Education; Psychiatry and Mental Health; Social Welfare; Social Work)

Institute
Japanese (Japanese)
Further information: Also Summer Study Programme in USA
History: Founded 2000.
Main language(s) of instruction: Japanese
Accrediting agency: Japan Institution for Higher Education Evaluation (JIHEE)
Degrees and diplomas: Gakushi, Shushi (Child Care and Development; Clinical Psychology; Education; Social Welfare), Hakase (Clinical Psychology; Welfare and Protective Services)
Student Services: Sports Facilities, Library
Last Update: 05-03-2018

Tokyo University of Technology

1404-1 Katakuramachi
Hachioji-shi 192-0982, Tokyo
Tel: +81(42) 637-2111
Fax: +81(42) 637-2112
Website: http://www.teu.ac.jp
President: Isao Karube

School
Bioscience and Biotechnology (Biological and Life Sciences; Biotechnology; Cosmetology; Environmental Studies; Food Science; Medical Technology); **Computer Science** (Computer Engineering; Computer Networks; Computer Science; Robotics; Software Engineering); **Design** (Design); **Health Sciences** (Medical Technology; Nursing; Occupational Therapy; Physical Therapy); **Media Sciences** (Electronic Engineering; Information Technology; Sociology)

Graduate School
Bionics, Computer and Media Sciences (Computer Science; Management; Media Studies)
History: Founded 1986. Formerly known as Tokyo Engineering University.
Academic year: April to March
Admission requirements: Graduation from high school and entrance examination
Main language(s) of instruction: Japanese, English
Accrediting agency: Japan Institution for Higher Education Evaluation (JIHEE)
Degrees and diplomas: Gakushi, Shushi (Business Administration; Computer Science; Media Studies), Hakase (Computer Science; Media Studies)
Student Services: Academic Counselling, Social Counselling, Careers Guidance, Sports Facilities, Facilities for disabled people, Health Services, Library
Periodicals: Sciences and Culture: The Journal of Tokyo Engineering University
Last Update: 06-03-2018

Tokyo Woman's Christian University

2-6-1 Zempukuji Suginami-ku
Tokyo 167-8585
Tel: +81(3) 5382 6340
Fax: +81(3) 5382-6531
Website: http://www.twcu.ac.jp
President: Shoko Ono

School
Arts and Science (Arts and Humanities; Economics; English; History; Japanese; Literature; Mathematics; Philosophy; Psychology; Sociology)

Institute
Comparative Cultural Studies (Cultural Studies); **Women's Studies** (Women's Studies)

Graduate School
Humanities and Sciences (Arts and Humanities; Cultural Studies; Social Sciences); **Science** (Mathematics)
History: Founded 1918 as College, became University 1948. Graduate School established 1971.
Academic year: April to March (April-September; September-March)

Admission requirements: Graduation from high school or equivalent, and entrance examination
Main language(s) of instruction: Japanese, English
Accrediting agency: Japan Institution for Higher Education Evaluation (JIHEE)
Degrees and diplomas: Shushi (Arts and Humanities; Cultural Studies; English Studies; History; Japanese; Literature; Mathematics), Hakase (Arts and Humanities; Mathematics; Social Sciences)
Student Services: Academic Counselling, Social Counselling, Careers Guidance, Health Services, Canteen, Foreign Studies Centre
Periodicals: Annals of Institute for Comparative Studies of Culture, Essays and Studies, Essays and Studies in British and American Literature, Historica, Japanese Literature, Science Reports, Sociology and Economics, Studies in Language and Culture, University Bulletin
Last Update: 06-03-2018

Tokyo Women's College of Physical Education

4 Chome-30-1 Fujimidai, Kunitachi
Tokyo 186-0003, Tokyo
Tel: +81(42) 572-4131
Fax: +81(42) 576-2397
Website: http://www.twcpe.ac.jp

Faculty
Sports and Health Sciences (Dance; Physical Education; Sports)
History: Founded 1926
Main language(s) of instruction: Japanese
Accrediting agency: Japan Institution for Higher Education Evaluation (JIHEE)
Degrees and diplomas: Gakushi, Shushi
Last Update: 06-03-2018

Tokyo Women's Medical University (TWMU)

8-1 Kawada-cho Shinjuku-ku
Tokyo 162-8666
Tel: +81(3) 3353-8111
Fax: +81(3) 3353-6793
Website: http://www.twmu.ac.jp
Chancellor and President: Toshimasa Yoshioka

School
Medicine (Medicine); **Nursing** (Nursing)

Graduate School
Medicine (Medicine); **Nursing** (Nursing)

Research Division
Advanced Biomedical Engineering and Science (Biomedicine; Medicine; Surgery); **Medical** (Medicine)
Further information: Also 3 Research Institutes and Centres, and 2 Hospitals
History: Founded in 1900 by Dr. Yayoi Yoshioka as a Medical School, became College in 1951 and University in 1998.
Academic year: April to March (April-July; September-December; January-March)
Admission requirements: Graduation from high school or foreign equivalent, and entrance examination
Main language(s) of instruction: Japanese
Accrediting agency: Japan University Accreditation Association (JUAA)
Degrees and diplomas: Gakushi (Medicine; Nursing), Shushi (Nursing), Hakase (Medicine)
Student Services: Academic Counselling, Social Counselling, Nursery Care, Sports Facilities, Language Laboratory, Health Services, Foreign Studies Centre, Library
Periodicals: Bulletin of Medical Research Institute, Bulletin of Tokyo Women's Medical University School of Nursing, Journal of Tokyo Women's Medical University
Last Update: 06-03-2018

Tokyo Zokei University

1556 Utsunuki-machi
Hachioji-shi 192-0992, Tokyo
Tel: +81(42) 637-8716
Fax: +81(42) 637-8731
Website: http://www.zokei.ac.jp

School
Graduate Studies (Design; Fine Arts)

Department/Division
Arts (Painting and Drawing; Sculpture); **Design** (Fashion Design; Film; Graphic Design; Industrial Design; Interior Design; Media Studies; Photography; Sculpture; Textile Design)
History: Founded 1966.
Main language(s) of instruction: Japanese
Accrediting agency: Japan Institution for Higher Education Evaluation (JIHEE)
Degrees and diplomas: Gakushi, Shushi (Design; Fine Arts), Hakase (Design; Fine Arts)
Student Services: Library
Last Update: 06-03-2018

Japan

Tomakomai Komazawa University

521-293 Nishikioka Tomakomai-shi
Hokkaido 059-1292
Tel: +81(144) 61-3111
Fax: +81(144) 61-3333
Website: http://www.t-komazawa.ac.jp
President: Kenyu Sakuma

Faculty

Intercultural Studies (Asian Religious Studies; Asian Studies; Business and Commerce; English Studies)
History: Founded 1998.
Main language(s) of instruction: Japanese
Accrediting agency: Japan Institution for Higher Education Evaluation (JIHEE)
Degrees and diplomas: Gakushi, Shushi
Last Update: 06-03-2018

Toyama University of International Studies

65-1 Higashi-kuromaki
Toyama 930-1292
Tel: +81(76) 483-8000
Fax: +81(76) 483-8008
Website: http://www.tuins.ac.jp

Faculty

Contemporary Sociology (Business Administration; Business and Commerce; Environmental Studies; Information Technology; Tourism)
History: Founded 1990.
Main language(s) of instruction: Japanese
Accrediting agency: Japan Institution for Higher Education Evaluation (JIHEE)
Degrees and diplomas: Gakushi
Last Update: 06-03-2018

Toyo Eiwa University

5-14-40 Roppongi, Minato-ku
Tokyo 106-8507
Tel: +81(3) 3583-3325
Fax: +81(3) 3408-3338
Website: http://www.toyoeiwa.ac.jp
Chancellor: Tomoaki Fukai

Faculty

Human Sciences (Child Care and Development; Clinical Psychology; Family Studies; Health Sciences; Psychology; Social Psychology; Social Sciences); **Social Sciences** (Media Studies; Social Sciences)

Graduate School

Graduate Studies (Child Care and Development; Clinical Psychology; International Relations; Preschool Education; Social Sciences)
History: Founded 1989. Graduate School added 1993.
Academic year: April to January (April-July; September-January)
Admission requirements: Graduation from high school, or equivalent
Main language(s) of instruction: Japanese, English
Accrediting agency: Japan University Accreditation Association (JUAA)
Degrees and diplomas: Gakushi (Arts and Humanities; Social Sciences), Shushi (Arts and Humanities; Social Sciences), Hakase (Arts and Humanities)
Student Services: Academic Counselling, Social Counselling, Sports Facilities, Language Laboratory, Health Services, Library
Last Update: 06-03-2018

Toyo Gakuen University

1-26-3, Hongo, Bunkyo-ku
Tokyo 113-0033
Tel: +81(3) 3811-1696
Fax: +81(3) 3811-1964
Website: http://www.toyogakuen-u.ac.jp
President: Kisako Harada

Faculty

Business Administration (Business Administration); **Global Communications** (Asian Studies; Communication Studies; Environmental Studies; Information Technology; International Studies; Urban Studies); **Human Sciences** (Community Health; Psychology; Sociology)

Graduate School

Business Administration (Business Administration)
History: Founded 1992.
Main language(s) of instruction: Japanese, English
Accrediting agency: Japan University Accreditation Association (JUAA)

Degrees and diplomas: Gakushi, Shushi (Business Administration)
Student Services: Library
Last Update: 06-03-2018

Toyo University

5-28-20 Hakusan Bunkyo-ku
Tokyo 112-8606
Tel: +81(3) 3945-8593
Fax: +81(3) 3942-2489
Website: http://www.toyo.ac.jp
President: Makio Takemura

Faculty

Business Administration (Accountancy; Business Administration; Finance; Marketing); **Economics** (Economics; International Economics); **Food Life Science** (Food Technology; Nutrition); **Human Life Design** (Social Problems; Social Studies; Welfare and Protective Services); **Information Sciences and Arts** (Information Sciences; Media Studies); **Law** (*Asaka-shi*) (Commercial Law; Law); **Life Sciences** (Biological and Life Sciences); **Literature** (*Asaka-shi*) (Chinese; Education; English; History; Japanese; Literature; Modern Languages; Pedagogy; Philosophical Schools; Philosophy); **Regional Development Studies** (*Itakura*) (Development Studies; Regional Studies; Tourism); **Science and Engineering** (*Kawagoe-shi*) (Applied Chemistry; Architecture; Civil Engineering; Computer Engineering; Computer Science; Electronic Engineering; Engineering; Environmental Engineering; Information Technology; Mechanical Engineering; Robotics; Telecommunications Engineering); **Sociology** (*Asaka-shi*) (Communication Studies; Media Studies; Social Psychology; Social Welfare; Sociology)

Graduate School

Business Administration (Accountancy; Business Administration; Finance; Marketing); **Economics** (Economics); **Engineering** (Applied Chemistry; Electronic Engineering; Engineering; Environmental Engineering; Environmental Management; Information Management); **Interdisciplinary New Sciences** (*Interdisciplinary*) (Nanotechnology); **Law** (Law; Private Law; Public Law); **Law** (*Professional*) (Law); **Life Sciences** (Biological and Life Sciences); **Literature** (Asian Religious Studies; Education; English; History; Japanese; Literature; Philosophical Schools; Philosophy); **Regional Development Studies** (Development Studies; Regional Studies; Tourism); **Sociology** (Social Psychology; Sociology); **Welfare Society Design** (Social Welfare)

Research Division

Asian Cultures (Asian Studies); **Human Sciences** (Social Sciences); **Industrial Technology** (Technology); **Oriental Studies** (Oriental Studies); **Regional Vitalization Studies** (Development Studies; Regional Studies); **Social Sciences**
Further information: Also academic programmes for foreign students
History: Founded 1887 as 'Tetsugaku-kan' (Academy of Philosophy). Became University and acquired present title 1906. Campuses are located in downtown Tokyo (main campus) and its vicinity (3 other campuses). It is a comprehensive university, consisting of 11 faculties and 44 departments, with a total of approximately 30,000 students.
Academic year: April to March (early April-early August; Late September-early February)
Admission requirements: Graduation from high school or equivalent and entrance examination
Fees: National : 915,000-1,315,000 (depending on the department) (Yen), International : Same as above. However, students with a student visa will receive a scholarship equivalent to 30% of tuition (Yen)
Main language(s) of instruction: Japanese, English
Accrediting agency: Ministry of Education, Culture, Sports, Science and Technology (MEXT); Japan University Accreditation Association
Degrees and diplomas: Gakushi (Architecture; Biological and Life Sciences; Biomedical Engineering; Chemistry; Child Care and Development; Civil Engineering; Development Studies; Economics; Education; Electrical and Electronic Engineering; Engineering; Environmental Engineering; Food Science; History; Information Sciences; International Economics; Law; Literature; Marketing; Mechanical Engineering; Media Studies; Nutrition; Philosophy; Psychology; Regional Planning; Social Work; Sociology; Sports; Tourism), Shushi (Applied Chemistry; Biological and Life Sciences; Biomedical Engineering; Biotechnology; Business Administration; Civil Engineering; Economics; Education; Electrical and Electronic Engineering; Environmental Engineering; Finance; History; Literature; Marketing; Philosophy; Private Law; Psychology; Public Law; Social Welfare; Sociology; Tourism), Hakase (Accountancy; Applied Chemistry; Architecture; Business Administration; Development Studies; Economics; Education; Finance; History; International Economics; Marketing; Mechanical Engineering; Nanotechnology; Philosophy; Private Law; Psychology; Public Law; Regional Planning; Social Welfare; Sociology)

Academic Staff 2013-2014	MALE	FEMALE	TOTAL
FULL-TIME	770	350	1120
Student Numbers 2013-2014			
All (Foreign Included)	17500	11800	c. 29300

Total number of distance students: 1000
Last Update: 25-05-2018

Toyohashi Sozo University

20-1 Matsushita Ushikawa-cho
Toyohashi-shi 440-8511, Aichi
Tel: +81(50) 2017-2100
Fax: +81(50) 2017-2113
Website: http://www.sozo.ac.jp

Faculty

Management and Information Sciences (Accountancy; Computer Networks; Information Sciences; Management; Media Studies; Software Engineering)

Graduate School

Business (Business and Commerce); **Health Sciences** (Health Sciences)
History: Founded 1983 as Junior College. Acquired present status and title 1996.
Main language(s) of instruction: Japanese
Accrediting agency: Japan Institution for Higher Education Evaluation (JIHEE)
Degrees and diplomas: Gakushi, Shushi (Information Management)
Student Services: Cultural Activities, Sports Facilities
Last Update: 06-03-2018

Toyota Technological Institute (TTI)

2-12 Hisakata Tempaku-ku
Nagoya-shi 468-8511, Aichi
Tel: +81(52) 809-1741
Fax: +81(52) 809-1721
Website: http://www.toyota-ti.ac.jp
President: Hiroyuki Sakaki

Faculty

Engineering (Electronic Engineering; Engineering; Materials Engineering; Mechanical Engineering; Systems Analysis)

Graduate School

Engineering (Engineering)
History: Founded 1981.

Academic year: April to March (April-September; October-March)
Admission requirements: Graduation from high school or equivalent, and entrance examination
Fees: Tuition, 496,800; Graduate School of Engineering, 792,180 per annum (Yen)
Main language(s) of instruction: Japanese
Accrediting agency: Japan University Accreditation Association (JUAA)
Degrees and diplomas: Gakushi (Engineering), Shushi (Engineering; Technology), Hakase (Engineering; Technology)
Student Services: Academic Counselling, Social Counselling, Careers Guidance, Sports Facilities, Health Services, Canteen, Library
Periodicals: ADVANCE, Nenpou Kenkyukatsudou
Last Update: 06-03-2018

Tsuda College

2-1-1 Tsuda-machi
Kodaira-shi 187-8577, Tokyo
Tel: +81(42) 342-5113
Fax: +81(42) 341-2444
Website: http://www.tsuda.ac.jp
President: Yuko Takahashi

Department/Division

Computer Science (Computer Science); **English** (American Studies; Communication Studies; English; English Studies; Linguistics; Literature); **International and Cultural Studies** (Comparative Sociology; Cultural Studies; International Economics; International Law; International Studies; Political Sciences; Social Studies); **Mathematics** (Mathematics; Mathematics and Computer Science)

Institute

International and Cultural Studies (Cultural Studies; International Studies); **Mathematics and Computer Science** (Mathematics and Computer Science); **Research in Language and Culture** (Cultural Studies; Modern Languages)

Graduate School

English Language and Literature (English; Literature); **International and Cultural Studies** (Cultural Studies; International Studies); **Mathematics and Computer Science** (Mathematics and Computer Science)
History: Founded 1900 as Joshi Eigaku Juku. Successively transformed into Tsuda Eigaku Juku and Tsuda Juku Senmon Gakko. Acquired present title 1948.
Academic year: April to March (April-September; October-March)

Admission requirements: Graduation from high school or equivalent, and entrance examination
Main language(s) of instruction: Japanese, English
Accrediting agency: Japan University Accreditation Association (JUAA)
Degrees and diplomas: Gakushi, Shushi (Cultural Studies; English; English Studies; International Studies; Mathematics and Computer Science), Hakase (Cultural Studies; English; English Studies; International Studies; Mathematics and Computer Science)
Student Services: Academic Counselling, Social Counselling, Careers Guidance, Nursery Care, Sports Facilities, Health Services, Canteen, Foreign Studies Centre
Periodicals: Study of International Relations, The Jounal of Tsuda College, The Tsuda Review

Academic Staff 2012-2013	MALE	FEMALE	TOTAL
FULL-TIME	73	83	156
PART-TIME	133	209	342
Student Numbers 2012-2013			
All (Foreign Included)	0	2840	2840
Foreign only	0	13	13

Total number of part-time students: 22
Total number of distance students: 2875
Last Update: 06-03-2018

Tsukuba Gakuin University

3-1 Azuma Tsukuba-shi
Ibaraki-shi 305-0031, Osaka
Tel: +81(29) 858-4811
Fax: +81(29) 858-7388
Website: http://www.tsukuba-g.ac.jp

Faculty

Business and Informatics (Business Administration; Computer Science)
History: Founded 1996 as Tokyo Kasei Gakuin Tsukuba Joshi Daigaku (Tokyo Kasei Gakuin Tsukuba Women's University). Acquired present title 2005.
Main language(s) of instruction: Japanese
Accrediting agency: Japan Institution for Higher Education Evaluation (JIHEE)
Degrees and diplomas: Gakushi
Last Update: 06-03-2018

Tsukuba International University

6-20-1 Manabe Tsuchiura-shi
Ibaraki-shi 300-0051, Osaka
Tel: +81(29) 826-6000

Fax: +81(29) 826-6937
Website: http://www.ktt.ac.jp/tiu/
President: Takatsuka Kazufumi

Faculty

Medicine (Nursing; Nutrition; Physical Therapy; Radiology)

Department/Division

Industrial Research (Industrial Engineering; Sociology); **Media and Communication Sciences** (Communication Studies; Media Studies); **Social Welfare** (Social and Community Services)
History: Founded 1994.
Main language(s) of instruction: Japanese
Accrediting agency: Japan University Accreditation Association (JUAA)
Degrees and diplomas: Gakushi
Student Services: Sports Facilities
Last Update: 06-03-2018

Tsurumi University

2-1-3 Tsurumi Tsurumi-ku
Yokohama-shi 230-8501, Kanagawa
Tel: +81(45) 580-8377
Fax: +81(45) 584-4588
Website: http://www.tsurumi-u.ac.jp

School

Dental Medicine (*Also Graduate School*) (Dentistry); **Literature** (*Also Graduate School*) (American Studies; Archiving; Comparative Literature; Cultural Studies; English; Information Sciences; Japanese; Library Science; Literature)

Institute

Buddhist Culture (Asian Religious Studies)
History: Founded 1924 as School, became Junior College 1953, acquired present status and title 1963.
Academic year: April to March (April to September; October to March)
Admission requirements: Graduation from high school or recognized equivalent, and entrance examination
Main language(s) of instruction: Japanese
Accrediting agency: Japan University Accreditation Association (JUAA)
Degrees and diplomas: Gakushi (Dentistry; Literature)
Student Services: Careers Guidance, Sports Facilities, Health Services
Periodicals: Bulletin of the Institute of Buddhist Culture, Bulletin of Tsurumi University
Last Update: 06-03-2018

Ube Frontier Unversity

2-1-1 Bunkyo-dai
Ube-shi 755-0805, Yamaguchi
Tel: +81(836) 38-0500
Fax: +81(836) 38-0600
Website: http://www.frontier-u.jp/index.php/english
President: Tsugio Ahihara

Faculty
Humanities and Social Sciences (Environmental Studies; Psychiatry and Mental Health; Psychology; Social Studies; Social Welfare; Social Work)
History: Founded 2001.
Main language(s) of instruction: Japanese
Accrediting agency: Japan Institution for Higher Education Evaluation (JIHEE)
Degrees and diplomas: Gakushi, Shushi
Last Update: 07-03-2018

Uekusa Gakuen University

1639-3 Oguracho, Wakaba Ward
Chiba 264-0007, Chiba
Tel: +81 43-233-9031
Fax: +81 43-233-9088
Website: http://www.uekusa.ac.jp

Faculty
Human Development and Education (Education)

School
Physical Therapy (Physical Therapy)
History: Founded 1999. Acquired present status and title 2008.
Main language(s) of instruction: Japanese
Accrediting agency: Japan Institution for Higher Education Evaluation (JIHEE)
Degrees and diplomas: Gakushi (Education; Physical Therapy)
Student Services: Careers Guidance, Library
Last Update: 07-03-2018

Ueno Gakuen University

4-24-12 Higashiueno Taito-ku
Tokyo 110-8642
Tel: +81(3) 3842-1021
Fax: +81(3) 3843-7548
Website: http://www.uenogakuen.ac.jp

Faculty
Music and Cultural Studies (Cultural Studies; Music; Music Education; Musical Instruments; Musicology; Singing)
History: Founded 1952. Acquired present status 1958.
Main language(s) of instruction: Japanese
Accrediting agency: Japan Institution for Higher Education Evaluation (JIHEE)
Degrees and diplomas: Gakushi (Music). Also 1-year Postgraduate Diploma programmes
Last Update: 07-03-2018

University of East Asia

2-1 Ichinomiya gakuen-cho
Shimonoseki-shi 751-8503, Yamaguchi
Tel: +81(832) 56-1111
Fax: +81(832) 56-9577
Website: http://www.toua-u.ac.jp
President: Hiji Kushida

Faculty
Allied Health Sciences (Dietetics; Health Sciences); **Design** (Cosmetology; Design; Industrial Design); **Human Sciences** (Cultural Studies; Primary Education; Psychology; Social Studies; Sports Medicine; Tourism)

Graduate School
Integrated Science and Art
History: Founded 1974.
Main language(s) of instruction: Japanese, English
Accrediting agency: Japan Institution for Higher Education Evaluation (JIHEE)
Degrees and diplomas: Gakushi, Shushi, Hakase (Arts and Humanities; Fine Arts; Health Sciences)
Student Services: Academic Counselling, Social Counselling, Sports Facilities, Language Laboratory, Health Services
Last Update: 28-02-2018

University of Human Arts and Sciences

1288 Magome Iwatsuki-ku
Saitama-shi 339-8539, Saitama
Tel: +81(48) 749-6111
Fax: +81(48) 749-6110
Website: http://www.human.ac.jp
President: Mari Kusumi

Faculty
Health Sciences (Dietetics; Health Sciences; Medical Technology; Nursing; Physical Therapy; Psychology; Public

Health; Rehabilitation and Therapy; Sociology); **Human Sciences** (Arts and Humanities; Behavioural Sciences; Biochemistry; Cultural Studies; Developmental Psychology; Food Science; Health Education; Health Sciences; Immunology; Nutrition; Psychiatry and Mental Health; Psychoanalysis; Psychology; Religion)

Graduate School

Comprehensive Human Sciences, Mental and Physical Health Science (Health Sciences; Nutrition; Physical Therapy; Psychiatry and Mental Health)
Further information: Also Iwatsuki Campus
History: Founded 2000.
Main language(s) of instruction: Japanese
Accrediting agency: Japan Institution for Higher Education Evaluation (JIHEE)
Degrees and diplomas: Gakushi (Arts and Humanities; Cultural Studies; Health Sciences; Medical Technology; Nursing; Nutrition; Physical Therapy; Psychology), Shushi (Health Sciences; Nutrition; Physical Therapy; Psychiatry and Mental Health), Hakase (Physical Therapy; Psychiatry and Mental Health). Shushi and Hakase in Physical Therapy and Psychiatry and Mental Health are offered through distance Learning
Last Update: 07-03-2018

University of KinDAI Himeji

Oshio-cho 2042-2
Himeji 671-0101, Hyogo
Tel: +81 79-247-7306
Fax: +81 79-247-7739
Website: http://himeji.koutoku.ac.jp
President: Soichi Ueda

Faculty

Education (Preschool Education); **Nursing** (Nursing)
History: Founded 1951.
Main language(s) of instruction: Japanese
Accrediting agency: Japan University Accreditation Association (JUAA)
Degrees and diplomas: Gakushi (Nursing; Preschool Education)
Student Services: Academic Counselling, Health Services, Canteen, Library

Academic Staff 2012-2013	MALE	FEMALE	TOTAL
FULL-TIME	43	42	85

Last Update: 26-03-2018

University of Marketing and Distribution Sciences (UDMS)

3-1 Gakuen-Nishimachi Nishi-ku
Kobe 651-2188, Hyogo
Tel: +81(78) 794-3095
Fax: +81(78) 794-3094
Website: http://www.umds.ac.jp
President: Jun Nakauchi

Faculty

Commerce (Business Administration; Business and Commerce; Finance; Management; Marketing); **Information Science and Technology** (Economics; Information Sciences; Information Technology; Management); **Policy Studies** (Finance; Information Sciences; Marketing; Regional Studies); **Services Industries** (Public Health; Social and Community Services; Tourism)

Graduate School

Marketing and Distribution Sciences (Business and Commerce; Marketing)
History: Founded 1988.
Admission requirements: 12 years education and/or graduate of (senior) high school or equivalent
Main language(s) of instruction: Japanese, English
Accrediting agency: Japan University Accreditation Association (JUAA)
Degrees and diplomas: Gakushi, Shushi (Business Administration; Finance; Management; Marketing), Hakase (Finance; Management; Marketing)
Student Services: Sports Facilities, Foreign Studies Centre

Student Numbers	MALE	FEMALE	TOTAL
All (Foreign Included)			c. 4000

Last Update: 07-03-2018

University of Occupational and Environmental Health

1-1, Iseigaoka, Yahatanishi-ku
Kitakyushu-shi 807-0804, Fukuoka
Tel: +81(93) 603-1611
Fax: +81(93) 601-3446
Website: http://www.uoeh-u.ac.jp
President: Higashi Toshiaki

School

Health Sciences (Nursing; Social and Preventive Medicine); **Medicine** (Medicine)

Institute
Industrial Ecological Sciences (Ecology; Occupational Health)

Graduate School
Medical Sciences (Medicine; Occupational Health)
Further information: Also University Hospital
History: Founded 1978. Graduate School established 1984.
Academic year: April to March (April-September; October-March)
Admission requirements: Graduation from high school and entrance examination
Main language(s) of instruction: Japanese
Accrediting agency: Japan University Accreditation Association (JUAA)
Degrees and diplomas: Gakushi (Environmental Studies; Medicine; Nursing), Shushi (Medicine), Hakase (Medicine; Occupational Therapy). Also Diplomas and Certificates
Student Services: Academic Counselling, Social Counselling, Careers Guidance, Cultural Activities, Sports Facilities, Health Services, Canteen
Periodicals: Journal of UOEH
Last Update: 07-03-2018

University of the Sacred Heart (USH)

4-3-1 Hiroo Shibuya-ku
Tokyo 150-8938
Tel: +81(33) 407-5811
Fax: +81(35) 485-3884
Website: http://www.u-sacred-heart.ac.jp
President: Yoshiko Okazaki
Tel: +81(33) 407-5037

Faculty
Liberal Arts (Education; English; History; International Relations; International Studies; Japanese; Literature; Philosophy; Primary Education; Psychology; Social Sciences)

Graduate School
Arts (Arts and Humanities; Cultural Studies; Education; English; History; Japanese; Literature; Philosophy; Social Studies)
History: Founded 1910 as Primary and High School. Raised to College status 1948 and University status 1950. Teachers' Training School added 1951. Given the right to grant Sho-gakko (State primary school Teachers' Certificate) 1957.
Academic year: April to March (April-July; October-March)
Admission requirements: Graduation from high school (Koto Gakko) or recognized foreign equivalent, and entrance examination

Fees: 1,035,000 per annum (Yen)
Main language(s) of instruction: Japanese, English
Accrediting agency: Japan University Accreditation Association (JUAA)
Degrees and diplomas: Gakushi, Shushi (Arts and Humanities; Cultural Studies; English; English Studies; History; Japanese; Philosophy), Hakase (Arts and Humanities; Cultural Studies; Education; Psychology; Social Sciences; Social Studies)
Student Services: Academic Counselling, Social Counselling, Careers Guidance, Nursery Care, Cultural Activities, Language Laboratory, Facilities for disabled people, Health Services, Canteen, Foreign Studies Centre
Periodicals: Christian Cultural Institute Publications, Seishin Campus, Seishin Studies

Academic Staff 2013-2014	MALE	FEMALE	TOTAL
FULL-TIME	16	45	61
PART-TIME	15	131	146
STAFF WITH DOCTORATE			
FULL-TIME	35	33	68
Student Numbers 2013-2014			
All (Foreign Included)	0	2251	2251
Foreign only	0	4	4

Last Update: 07-03-2018

University of Tokyo Health Sciences

4-11 Ochiai
Tokyo 206-0033, Tama-shi
Tel: +81(42) 373-8118
Fax: +81(42) 373-8111
Website: http://www.u-ths.ac.jp
President: Yasuo Sakuma

Faculty
Rehabilitation (Occupational Therapy; Physical Therapy)
History: Founded 1950.
Main language(s) of instruction: Japanese
Accrediting agency: Ministry of Education, Culture, Sports, Science and Technology (MEXT)
Degrees and diplomas: Gakushi (Occupational Therapy; Physical Therapy)
Last Update: 07-03-2018

Urawa University

3551 Osaki Midori-ku
Saitama-shi 336-0974, Saitama
Tel: +81(48) 878-3741

Fax: +81(48) 878-3620
Website: http://www.urawa.ac.jp
President: Hideko Hokubo

Faculty

Care Welfare (Social Welfare; Welfare and Protective Services); **English Communication**; **General Welfare** (Social Welfare; Welfare and Protective Services); **Management and Information** (Information Sciences; Management)
History: Founded 2003.
Main language(s) of instruction: Japanese
Accrediting agency: Japan Institution for Higher Education Evaluation (JIHEE)
Degrees and diplomas: Gakushi
Last Update: 07-03-2018

Utsunomiya Kyowa University

131 Kanosaki
Nasushiobara 329-3121, Tochigi
Tel: +81(287) 67-3111
Fax: +81(287) 67-3112
Website: http://www.kyowa-u.ac.jp

Course/Programme

Urban Economics (Economics; English; Information Management; Information Technology; Urban Studies)
History: Founded 1999. Formerly known as Nasu Daigaku (Nasu University).
Main language(s) of instruction: Japanese
Accrediting agency: Japan University Accreditation Association (JUAA)
Degrees and diplomas: Gakushi
Student Services: Sports Facilities
Last Update: 07-03-2018

Wakkanai Hokusei Gakuen University (WAKHOK)

Wakabadai 1-2290-28
Wakkanai 097-0013, Hokkaido
Tel: +81(162) 32-7511
Fax: +81(162) 32 7500
Website: http://www.wakhok.ac.jp
President: Saito Yoshihiro

Faculty

Integrated Media (*Wakhok Main Campus*) (Computer Networks; Computer Science; Information Technology; Mathematics; Media Studies; Multimedia; Software Engineering; Telecommunications Engineering)

Further information: Also Branch, the Tokyo Satellite at Akihabara, Chiyoda Ward, Tokyo
History: Founded 1987. Acquired present status and title 2000.
Admission requirements: Secondary school certificate or equivalent.
Main language(s) of instruction: Japanese
Accrediting agency: Japan Institution for Higher Education Evaluation (JIHEE)
Degrees and diplomas: Gakushi. Bachelor's degree, 4 yrs.
Student Services: Academic Counselling, Social Counselling, Careers Guidance, Cultural Activities, Sports Facilities, Facilities for disabled people, Health Services, Canteen, Foreign Studies Centre
Periodicals: Wakhok Bulletin
Last Update: 07-03-2018

Wako University

2160 Kanai-cho
Machida-shi 195-8585, Tokyo
Tel: +81(44) 988-1431
Fax: +81(44) 989-2241
Website: http://www.wako.ac.jp

Faculty

Economics and Business Management (Business Administration; Computer Science; Economics; Media Studies); **Human Sciences** (Education; Psychology; Sociology; Welfare and Protective Services); **Representational Studies** (Cultural Studies; Fine Arts)

School

Graduate Studies (Cultural Studies; Social Studies)
History: Founded 1966.
Academic year: April to March (April-September; October-March)
Admission requirements: Graduation from high school and entrance examination
Main language(s) of instruction: Japanese
Accrediting agency: Japan University Accreditation Association (JUAA)
Degrees and diplomas: Gakushi, Shushi (Computer Science; Cultural Studies; Economics; Education; Social Studies)
Last Update: 07-03-2018

Waseda University

1-104 Totsuka-machi Shinjuku-ku
Tokyo 169-8050
Tel: +81(3) 3202-7747

Fax: +81(3) 3202-8583
Website: http://www.waseda.jp
President: Kaoru Kamata

Faculty

Commerce (*Undergraduate*) (Business and Commerce); **Education** (*Undergraduate*) (Cultural Studies; Education; English; Japanese; Mathematics; Natural Sciences; Social Sciences; Social Studies); **Letters, Arts and Sciences II** (*Evening Divison, Undergraduate*) (Arts and Humanities; Folklore; History; Linguistics; Literature; Performing Arts; Philosophy; Religion; Social Sciences); **Political Science and Economics** (*Undergraduate*) (Economics; International Economics; Political Sciences)

School

Advanced Science and Engineering; **Creative Science and Engineering**; **Culture, Media and Society**; **Fundamental Science and Engineering**; **Human Sciences** (Behavioural Sciences; Cognitive Sciences; Environmental Studies; Health Sciences; Social Sciences; Social Welfare); **Humanities and Social Sciences** (*Undergraduate*) (Archaeology; Art History; Chinese; Education; English; Environmental Studies; Film; French; German; Health Sciences; History; Japanese; Philosophical Schools; Philosophy; Psychology; Russian; Social Sciences; Social Welfare; Sociology; Theatre); **International Liberal Studies** (Arts and Humanities; International Studies); **Law** (*Undergraduate*) (Administrative Law; Constitutional Law; International Law; Law; Mass Communication; Public Administration; Public Law; Taxation); **Letters, Arts and Sciences I** (*Undergraduate*) (Archaeology; Art History; Arts and Humanities; Chinese; English; Film; French; German; History; Japanese; Mathematics and Computer Science; Natural Sciences; Philosophical Schools; Philosophy; Psychology; Russian; Sociology; Theatre; Writing); **Science and Engineering** (*Undergraduate*) (Applied Chemistry; Applied Physics; Architecture; Biological and Life Sciences; Biomedical Engineering; Chemistry; Civil Engineering; Computer Science; Electrical Engineering; Environmental Engineering; Information Management; Management Systems; Materials Engineering; Mathematics; Mechanical Engineering; Nanotechnology; Natural Resources; Physics); **Social Sciences**; **Sport Sciences** (Sports)

Graduate School

Accountancy (Accountancy; Business Administration); **Advanced Science and Engineering** (Applied Chemistry; Applied Physics; Biochemistry; Biological and Life Sciences; Chemistry; Electrical Engineering; Physics); **Asia-Pacific Studies**; **Commerce**; **Creative Science and Engineering** (Architecture; Civil Engineering; Environmental Engineering; Industrial Engineering; Management Systems; Mechanical Engineering; Natural Resources); **Economics** (Economics); **Education** (Curriculum; Education; Educational Sciences; English; Humanities and Social Science Education; Japanese; Mathematics Education); **Environment and Energy Engineering**; **Finance, Accounting and Law**; **Fundamental Science and Engineering** (Aeronautical and Aerospace Engineering; Applied Mathematics; Computer Engineering; Computer Science; Electronic Engineering; Mathematics; Mechanical Engineering; Multimedia); **Global Information and Telecommunication Studies**; **Human Sciences**; **Information, Production and Systems** (Computer Engineering; Information Sciences; Information Technology); **Japanese Applied Linguistics** (Applied Linguistics; Japanese); **Law** (Civil Law; Law; Public Law); **Letters, Arts and Sciences** (Arts and Humanities; Chinese; Cultural Studies; Education; English; Fine Arts; French; German; History; Japanese; Literature; Natural Sciences; Philosophical Schools; Philosophy; Psychology; Russian; Sociology); **Political Science** (Political Sciences); **Public Management** (*Okuma School*); **Science and Engineering** (Engineering; Mathematics and Computer Science; Natural Sciences); **Social Sciences** (International Studies; Management; Political Sciences; Regional Studies; Social Sciences); **Sport Sciences** (Sports); **Teacher Education** (Education; Teacher Training)

Research Division

Asia-Pacific Studies (Asian Studies; Pacific Area Studies); **Business Administration**; **Comparative Law**; **Comprehensive Research Organisation**; **Contemporary Political and Economic Affairs**; **Education** (*Advanced Studies*); **Environment** (Environmental Studies); **Environmental Safety**; **Global Information and Telecommunications**; **Human Sciences** (*Advanced*) (Social Sciences); **Human Services**; **International Education**; **Japanese Language**; **Materials Science and Technology** (*Kagami Memorial*); **Media Network**; **Open Education**; **Science and Engineering** (*Advanced*) (Engineering; Mathematics and Computer Science; Natural Sciences); **Waseda University Archives**

History: Founded 1882 as Tokyo Senmon Gakko (College). Acquired present title 1902. Reorganized 1949. Graduate School established 1951.

Academic year: April to March (April-July; September-March)

Admission requirements: Graduation from high school or equivalent or foreign equivalent, and entrance examination

Main language(s) of instruction: Japanese, English

Accrediting agency: Japan University Accreditation Association (JUAA)

Degrees and diplomas: Gakushi, Shushi (Arts and Humanities; Business and Commerce; Computer Science; Economics; Education; Engineering; Environmental Engineering; Information Sciences; International Relations; Japanese; Law; Political Sciences; Sociology; Sports Medicine), Hakase (Arts and Humanities; Business and Commerce;

Cognitive Sciences; Economics; Education; Engineering; Environmental Engineering; Information Sciences; International Relations; Japanese; Law; Political Sciences; Sociology; Sports Medicine)
Periodicals: Human Science Research, Waseda Bulletin of Comparative Law, Waseda Business and Economic Studies, Waseda Commercial Journal, Waseda Economic Papers, Waseda Journal of Socio-science, Waseda Law Journal, Waseda Political Studies
Publishing house: Waseda University Press

Student Numbers 2012-2013	MALE	FEMALE	TOTAL
All (Foreign Included)			54113

Last Update: 08-03-2018

Wayo Women's University

2-3-1 Konodai
Ichikawa-shi 272-8533, Chiba
Tel: +81(47)371-3462
Fax: +81(47)371-2532
Website: http://www.wayo.ac.jp
President: Kouji Kishida

School
Human Ecology (Clothing and Sewing; Design; Nutrition; Welfare and Protective Services); **Humanities** (Cultural Studies; English; Japanese; Literature; Psychology; Social Studies)

Graduate School
Human Ecology; **Humanities** (English; Japanese; Literature; Modern Languages)

Research Division
Foreign Language Education (Foreign Languages Education)
History: Founded 1928. Acquired present title 1949.
Main language(s) of instruction: Japanese, English
Accrediting agency: Japan University Accreditation Association (JUAA)
Degrees and diplomas: Gakushi, Shushi (Ecology; Literature), Hakase (Ecology; Literature)
Student Services: Library
Last Update: 08-03-2018

Yamaguchi Gakugei University

Ogōrimiraimachi, 1 Chome 7-7-1
Yamaguchi 754-0001, Yamaguchi
Tel: +81(83) 972-3288

Fax: +81(83) 972-4145
Website: http://www.y-gakugei.ac.jp
President: Miike Hidetoshi

Faculty
Education (Preschool Education)
History: Founded 2007.
Main language(s) of instruction: Japanese
Accrediting agency: Japan University Accreditation Association (JUAA)
Degrees and diplomas: Gakushi (Preschool Education)
Last Update: 08-03-2018

Yamanashi Eiwa College

888 Yokonemachi
Kofu-shi 400-8555, Yamanashi
Tel: +81(55) 223-6020
Fax: +81(55) 223-6025
Website: http://www.yamanashi-eiwa.ac.jp
President: Kazuo Kikuni

School
Humanities (Arts and Humanities; Cultural Studies; English; Information Sciences; Library Science; Media Studies; Museum Studies; Psychology)

Graduate School
Humanities and Clinical Psychology
History: Founded 2002.
Main language(s) of instruction: Japanese, English
Accrediting agency: Japan University Accreditation Association (JUAA)
Degrees and diplomas: Gakushi, Shushi
Last Update: 08-03-2018

Yamanashi Gakuin University

2 Chome-4-5 Sakaori
Kofu-shi 400-8575, Yamanashi
Tel: +81(55) 224-1230
Fax: +81(55) 224-1498
Website: http://www.ygu.ac.jp

Faculty
Business Administration (Business Administration); **Information Management** (Information Management); **Law** (Administrative Law; Commercial Law; Comparative Law; Criminal Law; Fiscal Law; History of Law; Human Rights; International Law; Labour Law; Law; Maritime Law; Private Law; Public Law)

Further information: Also Graduate School
History: Founded 1946, acquired present status and title 1962.
Academic year: April to March
Admission requirements: Graduation from high school
Main language(s) of instruction: Japanese, English
Accrediting agency: Japan Institution for Higher Education Evaluation (JIHEE)
Degrees and diplomas: Gakushi, Shushi (Public Administration)
Student Services: Academic Counselling, Careers Guidance, Nursery Care, Sports Facilities, Language Laboratory, Facilities for disabled people, Canteen, Foreign Studies Centre
Periodicals: Altair
Last Update: 09-03-2018

Yamazaki Gakuen University

Shoto 2-3-10
Tokyo 150-0046, Shibuya-ku
Tel: +81 3-3468-1101
Website: http://univ.yamazaki.ac.jp

Faculty
Animal Nursing (Veterinary Science)
History: Founded 1967. Acquired present status and title 2010.
Main language(s) of instruction: Japanese
Accrediting agency: Japan Institution for Higher Education Evaluation (JIHEE)
Degrees and diplomas: Gakushi (Veterinary Science)
Student Services: Residential Facilities
Last Update: 09-03-2018

Yashima Gakuen University

7-42 Sakuragi-cho Nishi-ward
Yokohama-shi 220-0021, Kanagawa
Tel: +81(45) 410-0515
Fax: +81(45) 323-6961
Website: http://www.yashima.ac.jp
President: Wada Hirohito

Faculty
Lifelong Learning (Archiving; Continuing Education; Library Science)
History: Founded 2004.
Main language(s) of instruction: Japanese
Accrediting agency: Japan Institution for Higher Education Evaluation (JIHEE)

Degrees and diplomas: Gakushi
Student Services: Library
Last Update: 09-03-2018

Yasuda Women's University

6-13-1 Yasuhigashi Asaminami-ku
Hiroshima-shi 731-0153, Hiroshima
Tel: +81(82) 878-8557
Fax: +81(82) 872-2896
Website: http://www.yasuda-u.ac.jp
President: Toshio Seyama

Faculty
Current Business (Business and Commerce); **Education** (*Graduate Programme*) (Education; Primary Education); **Human Ecology** (Nutrition); **Letters** (English; Japanese; Literature; Painting and Drawing); **Nursing** (Nursing); **Pharmacy** (Pharmacy); **Psychology** (Psychology)

Graduate School
Letters (Clinical Psychology; Education; English; Japanese; Psychology)
History: Founded 1966.
Main language(s) of instruction: Japanese
Accrediting agency: Japan Institution for Higher Education Evaluation (JIHEE)
Degrees and diplomas: Gakushi, Shushi (Clinical Psychology; Education; English; Japanese; Nursing; Pharmacy; Psychology), Hakase (Clinical Psychology; Education; English; Japanese; Nursing; Pharmacy; Psychology)
Student Services: Sports Facilities, Library
Last Update: 09-03-2018

Yokkaichi Nursing and Medical Care University

Kayo-cho 1200
Yokkaichi 512-8045, Mie
Tel: +81(59) 340-0700
Fax: +81(59) 361-1401
Website: http://www.y-nm.ac.jp
President: Yasuhito Maruyama

Faculty
Nursing (Nursing)
History: Founded 2007.
Main language(s) of instruction: Japanese
Accrediting agency: Japan Institution for Higher Education Evaluation (JIHEE)

Degrees and diplomas: Gakushi (Nursing), Shushi (Nursing)
Student Services: Academic Counselling, Library, IT Centre

Student Numbers 2012-2013	MALE	FEMALE	TOTAL
All (Foreign Included)	50	422	472

Last Update: 09-03-2018

Yokkaichi University

200 Kayo-cho
Yokkaichi-shi 512-8512, Mie
Tel: +81(59) 365-6588
Fax: +81(59) 365-6630
Website: http://www.yokkaichi-u.ac.jp

Faculty

Economics (Business Administration; Economics); **Environmental and Information Sciences** (Environmental Engineering; Information Sciences); **Policy Management** (Management; Social Policy)
History: Founded 1988.
Academic year: April to March (April-September; October-March)
Main language(s) of instruction: Japanese
Accrediting agency: Japan Institution for Higher Education Evaluation (JIHEE)
Degrees and diplomas: Gakushi
Student Services: Library
Last Update: 09-03-2018

Yokohama College of Art & Design

1204, Kamoshida-cho, Aoba-ku
Yokohama 227-0033, Kanagawa
Tel: +81 45-962-2221
Fax: +81 45-961-7371
Website: http://www.yokohama-art.ac.jp
President: Nobuaki Okamoto

Faculty

Fine Arts (Graphic Design; Handicrafts; Visual Arts)
History: Founded 1966. Acquired present status and title 2001.
Main language(s) of instruction: Japanese
Accrediting agency: Japan University Accreditation Association (JUAA)
Degrees and diplomas: Gakushi (Graphic Design; Handicrafts; Textile Design; Visual Arts)
Student Services: Library
Last Update: 09-03-2018

Yokohama College of Commerce

4-11-1 Higashi-Terao Tsurumiku
Yokohama-shi 230-8577, Kanagawa
Tel: +81(45) 571-3901
Fax: +81(45) 571-4125
Website: http://www.shodai.ac.jp
President: Masato Kobayashi

Faculty

Commerce (Accountancy; Business and Commerce; Crafts and Trades; Economic History; Economics; Finance; International Economics; Law; Management; Small Business; Taxation; Tourism)
History: Founded 1966, acquired present status 1968.
Main language(s) of instruction: Japanese
Accrediting agency: Japan Institution for Higher Education Evaluation (JIHEE)
Degrees and diplomas: Gakushi
Last Update: 09-03-2018

Yokohama Soei University

1 Mihocho, Midori Ward
Yokohama 226-0015, Kanagawa
Tel: +81 45-922-5641
Website: http://www.soei.ac.jp/univ
President: Kenichi Kojima

Faculty

Early Childhood Education (Preschool Education); **Nursing** (Nursing)
History: Founded 1940. Acquired present status and title 2012.
Main language(s) of instruction: Japanese
Accrediting agency: Ministry of Education, Culture, Sports, Science and Technology (MEXT)
Degrees and diplomas: Gakushi (Nursing; Preschool Education)
Student Services: Sports Facilities, Canteen, Library, IT Centre
Last Update: 09-03-2018

Yokohama University of Pharmacy

601 Matano-cho Totuka-ku
Yokohama-shi 245-0066, Kanagawa
Tel: +81(45) 859-1300
Fax: +80(45) 859-1301

Website: http://hamayaku.jp/index.html
President: Leo Esaki

Department/Division

Health Pharmacy (Pharmacology; Pharmacy; Traditional Eastern Medicine)
History: Founded 2006. Formerly Yokohama College of Pharmacy
Main language(s) of instruction: Japanese
Accrediting agency: Japan University Accreditation Association (JUAA)
Degrees and diplomas: Gakushi (Pharmacology; Pharmacy; Traditional Eastern Medicine)
Last Update: 28-03-2018

Jordan

STRUCTURE OF HIGHER EDUCATION SYSTEM

Description

Higher education in Jordan emerged with the creation of two-year teacher training colleges in the 1950s. As for university education, it commenced by the establishment of the University of Jordan in 1962, followed by the establishment of Al-Ahliyya Amman University in 1989 as the first private university. The Ministry of Higher Education was created in 1985 to regulate and coordinate the work of the higher education sector. It is the home of the Council of Higher Education, which is in charge of establishing the higher education policy in the Kingdom. The Accreditation Commission, an independent body, accredits both private and public universities. Each university is managed by an independent board of trustees, which chooses the university president.

Stages of studies

University level first stage

Undergraduate level
Bachelor's degrees normally take four years. The Bachelor's degree normally requires between 130-160 credit hours, depending on the field of study.

University level second stage

Postgraduate level
A Master's degree is awarded after a further two years' study following upon the Bachelor's degree. It can be obtained either by course work and a thesis (c. 24 credit hours of courses and nine credit hours of research), or by course work (c. 33 credit hours) and a comprehensive examination. Candidates should hold the Bachelor's degree with "good" as a minimum rating.

University level third stage

Doctorate
A Doctorate is awarded after three to five years of further study and the submission of an original dissertation. It requires, depending on the subject, 24 credit hours of course work and 24 credit hours of research. Candidates should hold a Master's degree with "very good" as a minimum rating.

ADMISSION TO HIGHER EDUCATION

Admission to university-level studies

Name of Secondary school credential required: Tawjihi
For entry to: Public universities
Minimum score/requirement: Minimum 85% for Medicine and Dentistry, 80% for Pharmacy and Engineering, 75% for allied health sciences, and 65% in the scientific or arts streams according to the nature of the discipline.
Name of Secondary school credential required: Tawjihi
For entry to: Private universities
Minimum score/requirement: 80% for Pharmacy and Engineering in the scientific stream, 75% for allied health sciences specializations, and 55% for all other disciplines.
Other requirements: State Matura Exams (2+2). There are 2 compulsory exams marking the completion of the secondary education and 2 elective exams (out of a 10-subject list – kind of A-levels) for entrance at public HE Institutions. It is at national level. There is an entrance exam at HE Institutions only for study programmes requiring special skills like Sports, Arts, Architecture, some foreign languages, which is provided in the Government Act for admission to public HE Institutions. Admission at public HE Institutions is based on the total score obtained at High School GPA + the 4 grades of the State Matura Exams.

Foreign students admission

Quotas: Foreign students can apply to Jordanian public universities through the Jordanian embassy in their countries. If there is no Jordanian embassy in their countries, they can apply directly to public or private universities.
Admission requirements: For entry to public universities, students should apply through their embassies to the Ministry of Higher Education and Scientific Research if their entry is through cultural exchange. If not, they can apply directly to public or private universities.

© International Association of Universities 2019
International Handbook of Universities 2019,
https://doi.org/10.1057/978-3-319-76971-4_98

RECOGNITION OF STUDIES

Quality assurance system

The Higher Education Council approves the establishment of higher education institutions. The Ministry of Higher Education and Scientific Research recognizes the non-Jordanian higher education institutions and is responsible for issuing equivalencies of certificates. The Accreditation Council defines the regulations, supervises the performance of higher education institutions and ensures that they reach their goals through continuous evaluation of their programmes.

NATIONAL BODIES

Ministry of Higher Education and Scientific Research

Minister: Adel Tweissi
Secretary General: Ahed Al Wahadni
PO Box 138
Aljbaha 11941
Tel: +962(6) 534-7671
Fax: +962(6) 534-9079
Website: http://www.mohe.gov.jo

Association of Arab Universities - AArU

Secretary-General: Amr Ezzat Salama
PO Box 401 Jubeyha
Amman
Tel: +962(6) 506-2048
Fax: +962(6) 506-2051
Website: http://www.aaru.edu.jo

Data for academic year: 2010–2011
Source: IAU from Ministry of Higher Education and Scientific Research, Jordan, August 2010. Bodies updated 2018.

Public Institutions

Al Al-Bayt University

PO Box 130040 Al Jubaiha Al Albayt
Mafraq 25113
Tel: +962(2) 629-7000
Website: http://www.aabu.edu.jo
President: Nabil Shawaqfeh
Tel: +962(2) 629-7000, Ext. 2000

Faculty

Arts and Humanities (Arabic; English; French; German; History; Italian; Literature; Spanish); **Educational Sciences** (Curriculum; Education; Educational Administration; Primary Education; Teacher Training); **Engineering** (Architecture; Civil Engineering; Surveying and Mapping); **Finance and Business Administration** (Accountancy; Banking; Economics; Finance; Public Administration); **Information Technology** (*Prince Hussein bin Abdullah*) (Computer Science; Information Technology); **Law** (Law); **Nursing** (*Princess Salma*) (Child Care and Development; Nursing); **Science** (Biological and Life Sciences; Biology; Chemistry; Computer Science; Mathematics; Physics); **Sharia** (Islamic Law; Islamic Studies)

Institute

Astronomy and Space Sciences (Astronomy and Space Science); **Bayt al-Hikmah** (*House of Wisdom*) (Human Rights; International Law; International Studies; Islamic Studies; Political Sciences); **Earth and Environmental Sciences** (Earth Sciences; Environmental Studies); **Islamic Studies** (Islamic Studies)
History: Founded 1993.
Academic year: October to June (October-January; February-June)
Admission requirements: Secondary school certificate (Tawjihi), with an average of not less than 65% and a good command of Arabic
Main language(s) of instruction: Arabic for Humanities, English for Science
Accrediting agency: Ministry of Higher Education and Scientific Research
Degrees and diplomas: Bachelor's Degree, Master's Degree
Student Services: Academic Counselling, Sports Facilities, Language Laboratory, Health Services, Canteen
Periodicals: Jordan Journal of Islamic Studies
Last Update: 22-11-2011

Al-Balqa' Applied University (BAU)

PO Box 19117
Al-Salt
Tel: +962(5) 349-1111
Fax: +962(5) 353-2743, +962(5) 353-0462
Website: http://www.bau.edu.jo
President: Nabil Shawagfeh
Tel: +962(5) 338-231

Faculty

Agricultural Technology (Agricultural Engineering; Biotechnology; Environmental Management; Food Science;

Food Technology; Natural Resources; Nutrition; Plant and Crop Protection; Water Management); **Engineering** (Civil Engineering; Electrical Engineering; Electronic Engineering; Materials Engineering; Mechanical Engineering; Metallurgical Engineering; Mining Engineering; Software Engineering; Surveying and Mapping); **Graduate Studies** (Biotechnology; Business Administration; Chemistry; Computer Science; Education; Islamic Theology; Law; Metallurgical Engineering; Mining Engineering; Regional Planning; Special Education); **Planning and Management** (Accountancy; Banking; Business Computing; Economics; Finance; Information Management; Library Science; Management; Management Systems; Regional Planning); **Science and Information Technology** (*Prince Abdullah Bin Ghazi*) (Arabic; Chemistry; English; Information Technology; Islamic Law; Islamic Theology; Mathematics; Natural Sciences; Nuclear Physics; Physical Education; Physics)

Deanery
Scientific Research

Institute
Traditional Islamic Arts (Fine Arts; Islamic Studies)
History: Founded 1996, incorporating Amman University College for Applied Engineering 1997, and all State Community Colleges. BAU has seventeen affiliated colleges.
Admission requirements: Secondary School Leaving Certificate (Tawjeehy)
Fees: (Jordanian Dinars): Engineering, 800 per semester; Humanities, 600 per semester (300 for Intermediate Diploma, 2 yrs)
Main language(s) of instruction: Arabic, English
Degrees and diplomas: Bachelor's Degree (Engineering), Master's Degree (Administration; Agriculture; Chemistry; Engineering; Physics), Doctorate
Student Services: Academic Counselling, Social Counselling, Careers Guidance, Nursery Care, Sports Facilities, Language Laboratory, Facilities for disabled people, Health Services, Canteen
Last Update: 20-09-2013

Al-Hussein Bin Talal University (AHU)

PO Box 20
Ma'an
Tel: +962(3) 217-9000
Fax: +962(3) 217-9050
Website: http://www.ahu.edu.jo
President: Taha Al-Khamis

Faculty
Nursing (*Princess Aysha Bint Al-Hussein*) (Nursing)

College
Archaeology, Tourism and Hotel Management (Archaeology; Hotel and Restaurant; Hotel Management; Tourism); **Arts** (Arabic; English; Library Science; Linguistics; Literature; Media Studies); **Business Administration and Economics** (Accountancy; Business Administration; Economics); **Education** (Curriculum; Education; Pedagogy; Special Education); **Engineering** (Chemical Engineering; Civil Engineering; Computer Engineering; Environmental Engineering; Mining Engineering; Telecommunications Engineering); **Information Technology** (Computer Science; Information Technology; Software Engineering); **Science** (Biology; Chemistry; Mathematics; Physics; Statistics)
History: Founded 1999.
Admission requirements: General Secondary Certificate (Tawjeehi) minimum grade 65% for Humanities and Science and 80% for Engineering
Fees: (Jordanian Dinars): 12-40 per programme
Main language(s) of instruction: Arabic, English
Accrediting agency: Ministry of Higher Education and Scientific Research
Degrees and diplomas: Bachelor's Degree, Master's Degree, Doctorate
Student Services: Academic Counselling, Careers Guidance, Nursery Care, Cultural Activities, Sports Facilities, Language Laboratory, Health Services, Canteen, Foreign Studies Centre
Periodicals: AHU Journal for Research and Studies, Al-Haq Ya'lu
Last Update: 21-11-2011

German-Jordanian University (GJU)

PO Box 35247
Amman 11180
Tel: +962(6) 530-0666
Fax: +962(6) 534-1573
Website: http://www.gju.edu.jo
President: Labeeb Khadra

College
Business (*Talal Abu- Ghazaleh*) (Accountancy; Management; Transport Management)

School
Applied Medical Sciences (Biomedical Engineering; Chemical Engineering; Pharmacy); **Applied Natural Sciences** (Energy Engineering; Environmental Engineering; Water Management); **Architecture and Built Environment** (Architecture; Design; Interior Design; Visual Arts); **Informatics and Computing** (Computer Engineering; Computer

Science); **Languages** (English; German; Translation and Interpretation); **Technical Sciences** (Industrial Engineering; Maintenance Technology; Mechanical Engineering)

History: Created in 2005 by a Royal Decree, in accordance with a Memorandum of Understanding between the Ministry of Higher Education and Scientific Research and the German Federal Ministry of Education and Research.

Degrees and diplomas: Bachelor's Degree, Master's Degree
Last Update: 16-09-2010

Jordan University of Science and Technology (JUST)

PO Box 3030
Irbid 22110
Tel: +962(2) 720-1000
Fax: +962(2) 709-5148
Website: http://www.just.edu.jo
President: Mahmoud Y. Al Sheyyab

Faculty

Agriculture (Agronomy; Animal Husbandry; Crop Production; Food Technology; Horticulture; Natural Resources; Nutrition; Plant and Crop Protection; Soil Science); **Applied Medical Sciences** (Chemistry; Dental Technology; Genetics; Haematology; Immunology; Laboratory Techniques; Microbiology; Molecular Biology; Optometry; Paramedical Sciences; Physical Therapy; Radiology; Speech Therapy and Audiology); **Architecture and Design** (Architecture; Town Planning; Urban Studies); **Computer and Information Technology** (Computer Engineering; Computer Networks; Computer Science; Information Technology; Software Engineering); **Dentistry** (Dentistry; Oral Pathology; Periodontics; Surgery); **Engineering** (Architecture; Architecture and Planning; Biomedical Engineering; Chemical Engineering; Civil Engineering; Electrical Engineering; Electronic Engineering; Industrial Engineering; Irrigation; Mechanical Engineering; Nuclear Engineering; Power Engineering; Structural Architecture; Transport and Communications; Urban Studies); **Graduate Studies** (Agriculture; Applied Chemistry; Applied Linguistics; Applied Physics; Architecture; Biology; Computer Science; Dentistry; Design; Engineering; Information Technology; Mathematics; Medicine; Nursing; Pharmacy; Veterinary Science); **Nursing** (Community Health; Midwifery; Nursing); **Pharmacy** (Medical Technology; Pharmacology; Pharmacy); **Science and Arts** (Applied Chemistry; Applied Linguistics; Applied Physics; Biological and Life Sciences; English; Genetics; Immunology; Mathematics; Microbiology; Molecular Biology; Statistics); **Veterinary Medicine** (Anatomy; Animal Husbandry; Embryology and Reproduction Biology; Histology; Hygiene; Microbiology; Pathology; Pharmacology; Physiology; Surgery; Veterinary Science)

Centre

Biotechnology (*Princess Haya*) (Bioengineering; Biotechnology); **Energy** (Energy Engineering); **Nanotechnology** (Nanotechnology); **Science and Technology** (*Consultative*) (Natural Sciences; Technology); **Veterinary Medicine** (Veterinary Science)

Research Division

Environmental Science and Technology (*Queen Rania Al-Abdullah*) (Environmental Studies); **Pharmaceutical Studies** (Pharmacology; Pharmacy)

History: Founded 1986 to train students in the fields of applied sciences.

Academic year: September to June (September-January; January-June). Also summer Semester (June-August)

Admission requirements: Secondary school certificate (Al Tawjihi) or equivalent with different minimum requirements for each Faculty

Fees: 60-215 per credit hour according to Faculty (US Dollar)

Main language(s) of instruction: English
Accrediting agency: Ministry of Higher Education
Degrees and diplomas: Bachelor's Degree (Aeronautical and Aerospace Engineering; Agricultural Engineering; Agricultural Equipment; Animal Husbandry; Applied Chemistry; Applied Mathematics; Applied Physics; Biomedical Engineering; Biotechnology; Chemical Engineering; Communication Arts; Computer Science; Dental Technology; Dentistry; Electrical Engineering; English; Environmental Studies; Food Technology; Genetics; Health Administration; Horticulture; Irrigation; Mechanical Engineering; Medical Technology; Medicine; Natural Resources; Nutrition; Occupational Therapy; Optometry; Pharmacy; Physical Therapy; Power Engineering; Surgery; Transport Engineering; Veterinary Science), Medical Doctor (Dentistry; Medicine; Surgery), Master's Degree (Animal Husbandry; Applied Chemistry; Behavioural Sciences; Biology; Chemical Engineering; Communication Arts; Crop Production; Dentistry; Design; Electronic Engineering; Environmental Studies; Heritage Preservation; Mechanical Engineering; Natural Resources; Nursing; Pharmacology; Pharmacy; Psychiatry and Mental Health; Public Health; Regional Planning; Town Planning; Transport Engineering; Urban Studies; Veterinary Science). Also Diplomas in Public Health, Poultry Diseases, Veterinary Pathology, Artificial Insemination and Embryo Transplant, Therionology, Veterinary Surgery, Veterinary Medicine, and Higher Speciality in General Surgery, Internal Medicine, Obstetrics and Gynaecology, Paediatrics, Family Medicine, Community Medicine, Pathology, Clinical Microbiology and Immunology, Clinical Chemistry, Molecular Biology and Human Genetics, Hematology and Blood Banking

Student Services: Academic Counselling, Social Counselling, Careers Guidance, Cultural Activities, Sports Facilities, Language Laboratory, Facilities for disabled people, Health Services, Canteen, Foreign Studies Centre

Academic Staff 2012-2013	MALE	FEMALE	TOTAL
FULL-TIME			895
PART-TIME			253
Student Numbers 2012-2013			
All (Foreign Included)			3058

Last Update: 22-11-2011

Mu'tah University

PO Box 7 Karak
Mu'tah 61710, Al-Karak
Tel: +962(3) 237-2380
Fax: +962(3) 237-5540
Website: http://www.mutah.edu.jo
President: Thafer Yusif Assaraira

Faculty

Agriculture (Agriculture; Animal Husbandry; Food Technology; Plant and Crop Protection); **Arts** (Arabic; English; European Languages; Literature); **Business Administration** (Accountancy; Banking; Business Administration; Economics; Finance; Management Systems; Marketing; Public Administration); **Educational Sciences** (Curriculum; Education; Educational Administration; Educational and Student Counselling; Educational Sciences; Pedagogy; Psychology; Special Education); **Engineering** (Chemical Engineering; Civil Engineering; Computer Engineering; Electrical Engineering; Engineering; Environmental Engineering; Mechanical Engineering); **Law** (Law; Private Law; Public Law); **Medicine** (Anatomy; Biochemistry; Forensic Medicine and Dentistry; Gynaecology and Obstetrics; Histology; Medicine; Microbiology; Paediatrics; Pharmacology; Physiology; Public Health; Surgery); **Nursing** (Community Health; Nursing); **Science** (Biology; Chemistry; Information Technology; Mathematics; Natural Sciences; Physics; Statistics); **Shari'ah** (Islamic Law); **Social Sciences** (Archaeology; Geography; History; Political Sciences; Psychology; Sociology; Tourism); **Sports Sciences** (Physical Education; Rehabilitation and Therapy; Sports)
History: Founded 1981. A State Institution enjoying academic and administrative autonomy. Acquired present status and title 1986.
Academic year: September to June (September-January; February to June). Also Summer Term (June-August)
Admission requirements: Jordanian General Secondary Certificate (Tawjihi) or equivalent

Main language(s) of instruction: Arabic, English
Degrees and diplomas: Bachelor's Degree (Accountancy; Agricultural Economics; Animal Husbandry; Arabic; Archaeology; Automation and Control Engineering; Banking; Biology; Business Administration; Chemical Engineering; Chemistry; Civil Engineering; Computer Engineering; Computer Science; Economics; Electrical Engineering; Electronic Engineering; Energy Engineering; English; Environmental Studies; Finance; Food Technology; Foreign Languages Education; French; Geography; History; Horticulture; Information Sciences; Islamic Law; Islamic Studies; Law; Literature; Management; Marketing; Mathematics; Mathematics Education; Mechanical Engineering; Nursing; Nutrition; Physical Education; Preschool Education; Public Administration; Science Education; Sociology; Special Education; Thermal Engineering; Tourism; Water Science), Medical Doctor (Medicine), Master's Degree (Applied Linguistics; Arabic; Archaeology; Biology; Business Administration; Business and Commerce; Chemistry; Communication Arts; Criminology; Curriculum; Economics; Educational Administration; Educational Psychology; Engineering Management; English; Environmental Engineering; Finance; Geography; History; Horticulture; International Relations; Islamic Theology; Law; Mathematics; Physics; Police Studies; Public Administration; Social Studies; Sociology; Water Science), Doctorate (Arabic; Criminology; Islamic Studies; Linguistics; Literature; Modern History)
Student Services: Academic Counselling, Social Counselling, Careers Guidance, Nursery Care, Cultural Activities, Sports Facilities, Language Laboratory, Facilities for disabled people, Health Services, Canteen, Foreign Studies Centre
Periodicals: Mu'tah LiL-Buhuth Wad-Dirasat (Humanities and Social Sciences, Natural and Applied Sciences Series), The Jordanian Journal of Arabic Language and Literature
Last Update: 04-08-2015

Tafila Technical University (TTU)

PO Box 179
Tafila 66110
Tel: +962(3) 225-0326
Fax: +962(3) 225-0002
Website: http://www.ttu.edu.jo/
President: Yaqoub Al-Masa'feh

College

Administrative & Financial Sciences (Accountancy; Banking; Business Administration; Business and Commerce; Economics; Finance); **Arts** (Arabic; Arts and Humanities; English; Social Sciences); **Educational Sciences** (Preschool Education; Primary Education; Special Education; Teacher Training); **Engineering** (Chemical Engineering; Civil Engineering; Electrical Engineering; Engineering; Geological Engineering; Mechanical

Engineering; Mining Engineering); **Science** (Applied Physics; Chemistry; Information Technology; Mathematics)
History: Created 1986 as Tafila Applied University College. Acquired current status 2005.
Degrees and diplomas: Bachelor's Degree. Also: Postgraduate Diploma in Education
Last Update: 22-11-2011

The Hashemite University (HU)

PO Box 330127
Zarqa 13115
Tel: +962(5) 390-3333
Fax: +962(5) 382-6613
Website: http://www.hu.edu.jo
President: Kamal Bani-Hani

Faculty

Allied Health Sciences (Dietetics; Medical Auxiliaries; Medical Technology; Nutrition; Occupational Therapy; Physical Therapy; Radiology); **Arts** (Arabic; Arts and Humanities; English; Literature; Social Sciences); **Childhood** (*Queen Rania*) (Child Care and Development; Preschool Education); **Economics and Administrative Sciences** (Accountancy; Banking; Economics; Finance; Management); **Educational Sciences** (Curriculum; Educational Administration; Educational Psychology; Educational Sciences); **Engineering** (Biomedical Engineering; Civil Engineering; Computer Engineering; Electrical Engineering; Engineering; Industrial Engineering; Mechanical Engineering); **Information Technology** (*Prince Al Hussein Bin Abdullah II*) (Computer Science; Information Technology; Software Engineering); **Medicine** (Medicine); **Natural Resources and Environment** (Earth Sciences; Environmental Studies; Rural Planning; Water Management); **Nursing** (Community Health; Midwifery; Nursing); **Physical Education and Sports Sciences** (Physical Education; Rehabilitation and Therapy; Sports; Sports Management); **Sciences** (Biology; Biotechnology; Chemistry; Mathematics; Physics)

Institute

Tourism and Heritage (*Queen Rania*) (Archaeology; Cultural Studies; Heritage Preservation; Management; Museum Studies; Tourism)
History: Founded 1992.
Academic year: September to August (September-January; February-June; June-August)
Admission requirements: Secondary school certificate (Al-Tawjihi) or equivalent
Fees: National : 8-45 per credit hour (Jordanian Dinar), International : 60-75 Normal Programme; 90-115 International Programme (US Dollar)
Main language(s) of instruction: Arabic, English

Degrees and diplomas: Bachelor's Degree, Master's Degree, Doctorate
Student Services: Academic Counselling, Social Counselling, Careers Guidance, Cultural Activities, Sports Facilities, Facilities for disabled people, Health Services, Canteen

Student Numbers 2013-2014	MALE	FEMALE	TOTAL
All (Foreign Included)			28000

Last Update: 04-04-2017

The World Islamic Science and Education University (WISE)

PO Box 1101
Amman 11947
Tel: +962(6) 5062895
Fax: +962(6) 5063042
Website: http://www.wise.edu.jo
Acting President: Salah Jarrar

Faculty

Arts, Humanities and Education Sciences (Arts and Humanities; Educational Sciences); **Basic Sciences** (Administration; Arabic; Art History; Design; Educational Sciences; English; Information Technology; Islamic Studies); **Business and Finance** (Business and Commerce; Finance); **Call and Foudations of Islamic Religion** (Islamic Theology); **Higher Institute for Recitations**; **Higher Studies**; **Information Technology** (Information Technology); **Sheik N. Al-Quda for Sharia and Law** (Islamic Theology); **Traditional Islamic Art and Architecture** (Architecture; Islamic Studies)
History: Founded 2008.
Main language(s) of instruction: Arabic
Accrediting agency: Jordanian Higher Education Accreditation Council
Degrees and diplomas: Bachelor's Degree, Master's Degree, Doctorate
Student Services: Academic Counselling, Language Laboratory
Last Update: 05-09-2012

University of Jordan

Jubaiha Queen Rania Al Abdullah Street
Amman 11942
Tel: +962(6) 535-5000
Fax: +962(6) 535-5511
Website: http://www.ju.edu.jo
President: Azmi Mahafzah
Tel: +962(6) 530-0431

Faculty

Agriculture (Agricultural Economics; Agricultural Equipment; Agriculture; Animal Husbandry; Environmental Studies; Food Technology; Horticulture; Irrigation; Nutrition; Plant and Crop Protection; Soil Science); **Art and Design** (Music; Theatre; Visual Arts); **Arts** (Arabic; Geography; History; Philosophy; Political Sciences; Psychology; Sociology); **Business** (Accountancy; Business Administration; Economics; Finance; Marketing; Public Administration); **Dentistry** (Dental Technology; Dentistry; Oral Pathology; Orthodontics; Periodontics); **Educational Sciences** (Curriculum; Educational Administration; Educational Psychology; Educational Sciences; Special Education); **Engineering and Technology** (Architecture; Chemical Engineering; Civil Engineering; Computer Engineering; Electrical Engineering; Engineering; Industrial Engineering; Mechanical Engineering; Technology); **Foreign Languages** (English; French; German; Italian; Korean; Linguistics; Literature; Modern Languages; Phonetics; Spanish); **Graduate Studies** (Agriculture; Art Education; Humanities and Social Science Education; Information Technology; International Economics; International Relations; Medical Auxiliaries; Science Education; Women's Studies); **International Studies** (*Master Program*) (International Relations; Political Sciences); **Islamic Studies (Shari'a)** (Islamic Law; Islamic Studies; Islamic Theology); **Law** (Law; Private Law; Public Law); **Medicine** (Anaesthesiology; Anatomy; Biochemistry; Community Health; Forensic Medicine and Dentistry; Gynaecology and Obstetrics; Histology; Medicine; Microbiology; Paediatrics; Pathology; Pharmacology; Physiology; Surgery); **Nursing** (Community Health; Nursing); **Pharmacy** (Pharmacology; Pharmacy); **Physical Education** (Health Education; Health Sciences; Physical Education; Sports Management); **Rehabilitation Sciences** (Occupational Therapy; Physical Therapy; Respiratory Therapy; Speech Therapy and Audiology); **Science** (Actuarial Science; Biological and Life Sciences; Chemistry; Geology; Mathematics; Physics)

School

Information Technology (*King Abdullah II*) (Information Technology)

Institute

Arabic Teaching to Speakers of Other Languages (*International Institute (II-TASOL)*) (Arabic); **Archaeology** (Archaeology)

Centre

Computer Science; **Documents and Manuscripts**; **Educational Development**; **Global Development Learning Network**; **Islamic Cultural Studies**; **Languages**; **Strategic Studies**; **Women's Studies**

Further information: Also University of Jordan Hospital; University farm. 6 programmes in Arabic for non-native speakers

History: Founded 1962 as an independent national higher education institution.

Academic year: October to June (October-February; February-June). Also summer session (June-August)

Admission requirements: Secondary school certificate or recognized equivalent with a GPA of not less than 65%

Fees: c. 70-250 per credit hour (Parallel Programmes) (US Dollar)

Main language(s) of instruction: Arabic, English

Degrees and diplomas: Bachelor's Degree (Arts and Humanities; Dentistry; Engineering; Natural Sciences; Pharmacy), Medical Doctor (Medicine), Master's Degree (Accountancy; American Studies; Arabic; Archaeology; Arts and Humanities; Business Administration; Curriculum; Economics; Educational Administration; Educational and Student Counselling; Educational Testing and Evaluation; Finance; Geography; History; International Business; International Studies; Islamic Law; Islamic Studies; Law; Library Science; Linguistics; Management; Marketing; Middle Eastern Studies; Music; Natural Sciences; Peace and Disarmament; Philosophy; Physical Education; Political Sciences; Psychology; Public Administration; Social Work; Sociology; Spanish; Special Education; Translation and Interpretation; Women's Studies), Doctorate (Animal Husbandry; Arabic; Biological and Life Sciences; Chemistry; Civil Engineering; Computer Science; Curriculum; Economics; Educational Administration; Educational and Student Counselling; Educational Psychology; Educational Testing and Evaluation; Electrical Engineering; English; Food Science; Food Technology; Geography; Geology; History; Horticulture; Islamic Law; Linguistics; Mathematics; Nursing; Nutrition; Pharmacy; Philosophy; Physical Education; Physics; Plant and Crop Protection; Political Sciences; Public Law; Sociology; Special Education; Water Management)

Student Services: Academic Counselling, Nursery Care, Sports Facilities, Language Laboratory, Health Services, Canteen

Periodicals: Cultural Journal 'Al-Majallah al-Thaqafiyyahq', Dirasat (Refeered Journal), Profile (English)

Publishing house: University Publishing House

Last Update: 04-04-2017

Yarmouk University (YU)

Shafiq Irshidat Street
Irbid 21163
Tel: +962(2) 721-1111
Fax: +962(2) 721-1133
Website: http://www.yu.edu.jo
President: Zeidan Kafafi

Faculty

Archaeology and Anthropology (Anthropology; Archaeology; Heritage Preservation; Tourism); **Arts** (Arabic; English; Geography; History; Journalism; Literature; Mass Communication; Modern Languages; Oriental Languages; Political Sciences; Sociology); **Economics and Administration** (Accountancy; Banking; Business Administration; Economics; Finance; Marketing; Public Administration); **Education** (Curriculum; Education; Educational Administration; Educational and Student Counselling; Educational Psychology; Teacher Training); **Engineering Technology** (*Hijjawi*) (Computer Engineering; Electrical Engineering; Electronic Engineering; Power Engineering); **Fine Arts** (Aesthetics; Art History; Ceramic Art; Fine Arts; Graphic Design; Music; Painting and Drawing); **Information Technology and Computer Science** (Computer Science; Information Technology); **Law** (Law); **Mass Communication** (Advertising and Publicity; Journalism; Mass Communication; Public Relations; Radio and Television Broadcasting); **Physical Education** (Physical Education; Sports); **Science** (Biology; Chemistry; Earth Sciences; Environmental Studies; Mathematics; Physics; Statistics); **Shari'a and Islamic Studies** (Islamic Law; Islamic Studies); **Tourism and Hotel Management** (Hotel Management; Tourism)

Unit

Marine Sciences Station (Marine Science and Oceanography)

Centre

Computer and Information Technology (Computer Science; Information Sciences); **Consultation and Community Services** (Social and Community Services); **Faculty Members Development** (Development Studies; Educational Research); **Jordanian Studies** (Cultural Studies); **Language** (Linguistics; Modern Languages); **Refugees and Displaced Persons** (Demography and Population); **Speech and Hearing** (Speech Studies; Speech Therapy and Audiology); **Theorical and Applied Physics** (Physics)

Further information: The Language Centre offers a series of integrated programmes of Arabic as a Foreign Language (AFL)

History: Founded 1976 by Royal Decree with Faculty of Arts and Science. A State Institution enjoying academic and administrative autonomy. Largely financed by the State.

Academic year: September to August (September-January; February-June; June-August)

Admission requirements: Secondary school certificate or recognized equivalent

Main language(s) of instruction: Arabic, English

Accrediting agency: Council of Higher Education

Degrees and diplomas: Bachelor's Degree, Master's Degree, Doctorate

Student Services: Academic Counselling, Social Counselling, Sports Facilities, Language Laboratory, Facilities for disabled people, Health Services, Canteen

Periodicals: Abhath al-Yarmouk, Majallat al-Yarmouk, Yarmouk Numismatics

Publishing house: Yarmouk University Press

Student Numbers 2017-2018	MALE	FEMALE	TOTAL
All (Foreign Included)			c. 32000

Last Update: 27-09-2018

Private Institutions

Ajloun National Private University

Ajloun
Website: http://www.anpu.edu.jo
President: Mahmoud Dwairi

College

Arts and Educational Sciences (Arabic; Educational and Student Counselling; Educational Psychology; Educational Sciences; Special Education); **Business Management** (Business Administration; Management); **Information Technology** (Computer Science; Information Technology); **Law** (Private Law; Public Law)

History: Created 2008. First intake 2009.

Degrees and diplomas: Bachelor's Degree

Last Update: 17-09-2010

Al-Ahliyya Amman University

PO Box 183 Al Salt Road
Amman 19328
Tel: +962(5) 350-0211
Fax: +962(6) 535-9472
Website: http://www.ammanu.edu.jo
President: Sari Hamdan

Faculty

Architecture and Design (Architecture; Graphic Design; Interior Design); **Arts and Sciences** (English; Literature; Natural Sciences; Psychology; Special Education; Translation and Interpretation); **Engineering** (Architecture; Biomedical Engineering; Civil Engineering; Computer Engineering; Electronic Engineering); **Information Technology** (Computer Science; Information Technology; Software Engineering); **Law** (Law); **Nursing** (Nursing); **Pharmaceutical and**

Medical Sciences (Medical Technology; Pharmacy; Speech Therapy and Audiology)

School

Business (Accountancy; Business Administration; Business Computing; E- Business/Commerce; Finance; Hotel Management; Marketing; Tourism)

Further information: Also Foundation Year Programme, in co-operation with British universities

History: Founded 1990.

Academic year: September to June (September-January; February-June). Also summer session (June-August)

Admission requirements: Secondary school certificate (Tawijihi) or equivalent

Fees: 2,175-2,550 per semester (US Dollar)

Main language(s) of instruction: English, Arabic

Degrees and diplomas: Bachelor's Degree (Administration; Business Administration; Computer Science; Economics; Engineering; English; Finance; Fine Arts; Hotel Management; Interior Design; Law; Literature; Medicine; Nursing; Pharmacy; Speech Therapy and Audiology; Translation and Interpretation), Master's Degree (Law)

Student Services: Academic Counselling, Social Counselling, Careers Guidance, Nursery Care, Cultural Activities, Sports Facilities, Language Laboratory, Health Services, Canteen, Foreign Studies Centre

Periodicals: Al-Balqu'a (Journal for Research Studies)

Student Numbers 2016-2017	MALE	FEMALE	TOTAL
All (Foreign Included)			6400

Last Update: 30-03-2017

Al-Isra University

PO Box 621286
Amman 11622, Greater Amman
Tel: +962(6) 471-1710
Fax: +962(6) 471-1505
Website: http://www.isra.edu.jo
President: Nu'man Al-Khateeb

Faculty

Administration and Finance (Accountancy; Administration; Banking; Business Administration; Finance; Information Management; Marketing); **Arts and Humanities** (Arabic; Arts and Humanities; Education; English; Literature; Modern Languages; Translation and Interpretation); **Engineering** (Architecture; Civil Engineering; Computer Engineering; Electrical Engineering; Electronic Engineering; Engineering; Telecommunications Engineering); **Law** (Law); **Science and Information**

Technology (Computer Science; Information Technology; Natural Sciences; Software Engineering)

College

Medical Sciences (Medicine; Pharmacy)

Department/Division

Cultural and Public Relations, Continuing Education and Community Services (Continuing Education; Management; Public Relations; Secretarial Studies; Social and Community Services)

Centre

Computer (Administration; Computer Science; Finance)

Further information: Also Engineering Workshop

History: Founded 1991. Acquired present status 1995.

Academic year: September to June (September-January; February-June). Also Summer Course, July-August

Admission requirements: High school certificate or equivalent

Fees: (Jordanian Dinars): 35-75 per credit hour

Main language(s) of instruction: Arabic, English

Accrediting agency: Council for Higher Education - Ministry of Higher Education and Scientific Research

Degrees and diplomas: Bachelor's Degree

Student Services: Academic Counselling, Social Counselling, Sports Facilities, Health Services, Canteen

Periodicals: Al-Ma'rifah (Knowledge), Pharmacare, Translation Bulletin

Last Update: 22-11-2011

Al-Zaytoonah University of Jordan

PO Box 130 Airport Road
Amman 11733
Tel: +962(6) 429-1511
Fax: +962(6) 429-1432
Website: http://www.zuj.edu.jo
President: Turki I. Obaidat
Tel: +962(6) 429-1511 Ext 502

Faculty

Arts (Arabic; English; French; Graphic Design; Teacher Training); **Economics and Administrative Sciences** (Accountancy; Banking; Business Administration; Finance; Information Management; Marketing; Tourism); **Engineering and Technology** (Civil Engineering; Computer Engineering; Electrical Engineering; Energy Engineering; Mechanical Engineering; Power Engineering; Telecommunications Engineering); **Law** (Law); **Nursing** (Nursing); **Pharmacy** (Pharmacy);

Science and Information Technology (Computer Networks; Computer Science; Mathematics; Multimedia; Software Engineering)

History: Founded 1993.

Academic year: October to August (October-February; February-June; June-August)

Admission requirements: Secondary school certificate (Al Tawjihi) or equivalent

Fees: 1,000-1,200 per semester (Jordanian Dinar)

Main language(s) of instruction: Arabic, English

Degrees and diplomas: Bachelor's Degree (Accountancy; Arabic; Banking; Business Administration; Business Computing; Civil Engineering; Computer Engineering; Computer Networks; Computer Science; Electrical Engineering; Energy Engineering; English; Finance; French; Graphic Design; Law; Marketing; Mathematics; Mechanical Engineering; Multimedia; Nursing; Pharmacy; Power Engineering; Software Engineering; Teacher Training; Telecommunications Engineering; Tourism; Translation and Interpretation), Master's Degree (Accountancy; Business Administration; Computer Science; English; Law; Marketing; Nursing; Pharmacy)

Student Services: Academic Counselling, Social Counselling, Cultural Activities, Sports Facilities, Health Services, Canteen

Academic Staff 2016-2017	MALE	FEMALE	TOTAL
FULL-TIME			309
PART-TIME			23
STAFF WITH DOCTORATE			
FULL-TIME			237
Student Numbers 2016-2017			
All (Foreign Included)			7763

Last Update: 04-04-2017

American University of Madaba

PO Box 2882
Amman 11821
Tel: +962(5) 3294444
Fax: +962(5) 3294440
Website: http://www.aum.edu.jo
President: Nabil Ayoub

Faculty

Architecture and Design (Architecture; Graphic Design; Interior Design); **Business and Finance** (Accountancy; Banking; Business Administration; Finance; Marketing); **Engineering** (Civil Engineering; Electrical Engineering; Mechanical Engineering); **Health Science** (Dietetics; Laboratory Techniques; Medical Auxiliaries; Nutrition; Pharmacy); **Information Technology** (Computer Science); **Languages and**

Communication (English; Literature; Translation and Interpretation); **Science** (Biology; Biotechnology; Natural Sciences)

History: Created 2005, first students admitted 2011.

Accrediting agency: Higher Education Accreditation Commission (HEAC), Ministry of Higher Education and Scientific Research

Degrees and diplomas: Bachelor's Degree (Architecture; Biology; Business Administration; Civil Engineering; Computer Science; Dietetics; Electrical Engineering; English; Graphic Design; Interior Design; Mechanical Engineering; Pharmacy; Translation and Interpretation)

Academic Staff 2016-2017	MALE	FEMALE	TOTAL
FULL-TIME			107
PART-TIME			12
STAFF WITH DOCTORATE			
FULL-TIME			86
Student Numbers 2016-2017			
All (Foreign Included)			1652

Last Update: 26-10-2017

Amman Arab University

PO Box 2234
Amman 11953
Tel: +962(6) 479-1400
Fax: +962(78) 777-3102
Website: http://www.aau.edu.jo
President: Maher Saleem

Faculty

Arts and Sciences (English; Mathematics; Translation and Interpretation); **Business** (Accountancy; Business Computing; Finance; Management; Marketing); **Computer Science and Informatics** (Computer Science; Software Engineering); **Educational and Psychological Sciences** (Curriculum; Education; Educational Administration; Educational and Student Counselling; Educational Psychology; Special Education); **Engineering** (Architecture; Civil Engineering); **Law** (Law; Private Law; Public Law); **Pharmacy** (Pharmacy)

History: Founded 2000.

Academic year: October to June

Fees: MA, 120-140 per credit hour depending on field of study; PhD, 180-200 per credit hour (Jordanian Dinar)

Main language(s) of instruction: Arabic, English

Accrediting agency: Ministry of Higher Education, Council of Higher Education

Degrees and diplomas: Bachelor's Degree (Accountancy; Applied Linguistics; Architecture; Business Administration; Business Computing; Civil Engineering; Commercial Law; Computer Science; English; Finance; Law; Marketing;

Mathematics; Pharmacy; Software Engineering; Special Education; Translation and Interpretation), Master's Degree (Accountancy; Architecture; Business Administration; Business Computing; Civil Engineering; Computer Science; Curriculum; Education; Educational and Student Counselling; Educational Psychology; Finance; Management; Marketing; Pharmacy; Private Law; Public Law; Special Education)

Academic Staff 2014-2015	MALE	FEMALE	TOTAL
FULL-TIME			87
PART-TIME			19
Student Numbers 2014-2015			
All (Foreign Included)			1015

Last Update: 01-09-2015

Applied Science Private University (ASU)

Shafa Badran
Amman 11931
Tel: +962(6) 560-9999
Fax: +962(6) 523-2899
Website: http://www.asu.edu.jo
President: Mahfuz Judeh

Faculty

Allied Medical Sciences (Food Science; Natural Sciences; Nutrition); **Art and Design** (Graphic Design; Interior Design); **Arts and Humanities** (Arabic; Education; English; Fine Arts; Islamic Law; Islamic Studies; Literature; Political Sciences; Social Sciences); **Economics and Administrative Sciences** (Accountancy; Administration; Banking; Business Administration; Economics; Finance; Health Administration; Hotel Management; International Relations; Marketing; Political Sciences); **Engineering** (Architecture; Civil Engineering; Computer Engineering; Electrical Engineering; Engineering; Industrial Engineering; Mechanical Engineering; Telecommunications Engineering); **Information Technology** (Computer Networks; Computer Science; Information Technology; Software Engineering); **Law** (Law; Private Law; Public Law); **Nursing** (Community Health; Nursing); **Pharmacy** (Pharmacology; Pharmacy)
History: Founded 1991, the largest private University in Jordan.
Academic year: October to June (October-January; February-June). Also Summer Session (July to September)
Admission requirements: Secondary school certificate (Shahadit Al-Thanaweyya Al Ama) or equivalent
Fees: (Jordanian Dinars): 45-75 per credit hour
Degrees and diplomas: Bachelor's Degree, Master's Degree

Student Services: Academic Counselling, Social Counselling, Careers Guidance, Cultural Activities, Sports Facilities, Facilities for disabled people, Health Services, Canteen
Periodicals: Jordan Journal of Applied Sciences (Humanities), Jordan Journal of Applied Sciences (Natural Sciences)

Student Numbers 2012-2013	MALE	FEMALE	TOTAL
All (Foreign Included)			c. 8000

Last Update: 21-10-2013

Aqaba University of Technology

South Aqaba, Back Ports road, opposite Aqaba Development Company warehouses
Aqaba
Tel: +962(6) 554 8970
Fax: +962(6) 554 8971
Website: http://www.aut.edu.jo
President: Solhe Faisal Alshahateet

Faculty

Business Administration and Finance (Accountancy; Business Administration); **Engineering** (Architecture; Civil Engineering); **Information Technology** (Computer Science; Software Engineering); **Pharmacy** (Pharmacy)
History: Created 2014
Academic year: October to May (Oct to Feb; Feb to May)
Degrees and diplomas: Bachelor's Degree (Accountancy; Architecture; Business Administration; Civil Engineering; Computer Science; Pharmacy; Software Engineering)

Academic Staff 2017-2018	MALE	FEMALE	TOTAL
FULL-TIME			29
STAFF WITH DOCTORATE			
FULL-TIME			29
Student Numbers 2017-2018			
All (Foreign Included)			189

Last Update: 06-08-2018

Arab Open University - Jordan Branch (AOU/Jordan)

PO Box 1339
Amman 11953
Tel: +962(6) 551-4851
Fax: +962(6) 553-0813
Website: http://www.aou.edu.jo
Director: Mohammad Abu Qudais

Faculty

Business Studies (Business Administration; Business and Commerce; Management Systems); **Computer Studies** (Computer Science; Information Technology); **Educational Studies** (Education; Primary Education); **Language Studies** (English; Literature)

History: Founded 2001.

Academic year: October to August (October-January; February-June; July-August)

Admission requirements: Secondary School Certificate (Tawjihi) or equivalent.

Fees: 45-60 per credit hour, other expenses, 170 per credit hour (US Dollar)

Main language(s) of instruction: English, Arabic

Accrediting agency: Local accreditation: Jordanian Ministry of Higher Education and Scientific Research; international accreditation: Open University Validation Service

Degrees and diplomas: Bachelor's Degree (Business Administration; Computer Engineering; English; Information Technology; Literature; Primary Education)

Student Services: Social Counselling, Language Laboratory, Facilities for disabled people, Canteen

Periodicals: The International Arab Journal of e-Technology

Last Update: 21-11-2011

College of Educational Sciences

PO Box 270 Na'ur
Amman
Tel: +962(6) 420-2161
Fax: +962(6) 420-5502
President: Ahmad Subhi Ayyadi

Course/Programme

Education (Educational Sciences; Teacher Training)

History: Founded 1993. Under UNRWA Institute of Education, provides upgrading in teaching qualifications to a first university degree.

Degrees and diplomas: Bachelor's Degree (Education)

Last Update: 16-09-2010

Irbid National University

PO Box 2600
Irbid 21110
Tel: +962(2) 705-6682, +962(2) 705-6686
Fax: +962(2) 705-6681
Website: http://www.inu.edu.jo
President: Mohammed Sabarini

Faculty

Administration and Finance (Accountancy; Banking; Business Administration; Economics; Finance; Hotel Management; Marketing; Tourism); **Arts** (Arabic; Arts and Humanities; English; Graphic Design; Literature; Translation and Interpretation); **Educational Sciences** (Educational and Student Counselling; Educational Psychology; Educational Sciences; Special Education); **Law** (Law); **Nursing** (Nursing); **Science and Information Technology** (Computer Science; Mathematics)

History: Founded 1992.

Main language(s) of instruction: Arabic

Degrees and diplomas: Bachelor's Degree

Student Services: Academic Counselling, Social Counselling, Careers Guidance, Nursery Care, Sports Facilities, Language Laboratory, Health Services, Canteen, Foreign Studies Centre

Periodicals: Irbid Journal for Research and Studies

Last Update: 22-11-2011

Jadara University

PO Box 733
Irbid 21110
Tel: +962(2) 720 1222
Fax: +962(2) 720 1210
Website: http://www.jadara.edu.jo
President: Saleh Oqeili

Faculty

Arts and Languages (Arabic; English; Graphic Design; Information Technology; Literature; Translation and Interpretation); **Economics and Business** (Accountancy; Banking; Business Administration; Business Computing; E-Business/Commerce; Finance; Human Resources; Marketing); **Education Sciences** (Educational Administration; Educational and Student Counselling; Educational Technology; Educational Testing and Evaluation; Special Education); **Engineering** (Civil Engineering; Computer Engineering; Telecommunications Engineering); **Law** (Law); **Pharmacy** (Laboratory Techniques; Pharmacy); **Science and Information Technology** (Computer Networks; Computer Science; Mathematics; Software Engineering)

History: Created 2005.

Academic year: October to June

Main language(s) of instruction: Arabic

Degrees and diplomas: Bachelor's Degree (Accountancy; Arabic; Business Computing; Civil Engineering; Computer Engineering; Computer Science; Educational and Student Counselling; Educational Technology; English; Finance; Graphic Design; Human Resources; Law;

Management; Marketing; Mathematics; Media Studies; Pharmacy; Software Engineering; Special Education; Translation and Interpretation), Master's Degree (Accountancy; Educational Administration; English; Human Resources; Law; Management)

Academic Staff 2017-2018	MALE	FEMALE	TOTAL
FULL-TIME			150
PART-TIME			50
STAFF WITH DOCTORATE			
FULL-TIME			157
Student Numbers 2017-2018			
All (Foreign Included)			3800

Last Update: 06-08-2018

Jerash University

PO Box 311
Jerash 26150
Tel: +962(2) 635-0521
Fax: +962(2) 635-0520
Website: http://www.jpu.edu.jo/
President: Abd El-Rasak Bani Hani

Faculty

Arts (Arabic; English; Literature; Translation and Interpretation); **Economics and Administrative Sciences** (Accountancy; Administration; Banking; Economics; Finance); **Education** (Educational Administration; Foreign Languages Education; Teacher Training); **Law** (Law; Private Law; Public Law); **Nursing** (Nursing); **Science** (Biology; Chemistry; Computer Science; Mathematics); **Shari'a** (Islamic Law; Islamic Studies)

College

Agriculture (Agricultural Economics; Agriculture; Animal Husbandry; Crop Production; Food Science; Nutrition; Plant and Crop Protection; Veterinary Science); **Engineering** (Civil Engineering; Electronic Engineering; Engineering; Telecommunications Engineering)

History: Founded 1992.
Academic year: October to August (October-January; February-May; June-August)
Admission requirements: Secondary school certificate or equivalent
Fees: (Jordanian Dinars): 30-55 per credit hour
Main language(s) of instruction: Arabic, English
Degrees and diplomas: Bachelor's Degree, Master's Degree
Student Services: Academic Counselling, Social Counselling, Nursery Care, Cultural Activities, Sports Facilities, Language Laboratory, Health Services, Canteen, Foreign Studies Centre
Periodicals: Jerash for Research and Studies

Student Numbers 2012-2013	MALE	FEMALE	TOTAL
All (Foreign Included)			c. 5000

Last Update: 05-03-2013

Jordan Academy of Music

PO Box 962127 24 Sayed Qutub Street Shamasani
Amman 11196
Tel: +962(6) 560-4172
Fax: +962(6) 560-6234
Website: http://www.jam.edu.jo
Dean: Iyad Abdel Hafeez Hafez Moh'd

Department/Division

Music (Music; Music Theory and Composition; Musical Instruments)
History: Founded 1989.
Degrees and diplomas: Bachelor's Degree
Last Update: 21-11-2011

Middle East University (MEU)

Airport Road
Amman 11831
Tel: +962(6) 479-0222
Fax: +962(6) 412-9613
Website: http://www.meu.edu.jo
President: Maher Salim
Tel: +962(6) 4790222 ext 338

Faculty

Architecture and Design (Architecture; Graphic Design; Performing Arts); **Arts and Sciences** (Arabic; English; Literature; Political Sciences); **Business** (Accountancy; Business Administration; E- Business/Commerce; Finance; Marketing; Tourism); **Educational Sciences** (Curriculum; Education; Educational Administration; Educational Technology; Special Education); **Engineering** (Civil Engineering; Electrical and Electronic Engineering; Engineering; Environmental Engineering); **Information Technology** (Computer Science; Information Technology); **Law** (Law; Private Law; Public Law); **Media** (Journalism; Media Studies; Radio and Television Broadcasting); **Pharmacy** (Pharmacy)

History: Created in 2005 with Master's programs. At the beginning of the academic year 2008/2009, the university started its second phase, at undergraduate level.
Admission requirements: Bachelor's Criteria: 1. Jordanian secondary school certificate or its equivalent. 2. Meet the minimum required grade average. 3. Jordanian students who wish to transfer from community colleges are admitted provided their score average in the comprehensive

examination is 68% or above and their major is congruent with the field of study they wish to be admitted to. This should be in line with the compatible majors list prepared and approved by the Examination and Measurement Authority. 4. Special needs students with community college degrees who have scored 65% are accepted provided they present a medical report from the Ministry of Health. 5. Jordanian students with community college degrees obtained abroad, provided that their diplomas are accredited and they pass the comprehensive exam prepared and approved by the Authority. 6. Students who wish to transfer from other universities which do not follow distance learning systems, In this case, the student is credited for no more than 50% of his / her overall study. 1. General Secondary Education Certificate holders: • General Secondary Education transcript in Arabic and English or, a certified copy. Photocopy of identity card. • Military Service Record. • Two photos. 2. Community college diploma holders: • All documents required for General Secondary Education Certificate holders. • Community college diploma certified by the Ministry of Higher Educationand Research. 3. Students transferring from other universities. In addition to A & B above, the following are required: • Good conduct certificate issued by the student's ex-university. • Course description. • Transcripts certified by the Ministry of Higher Education and Research. 4. Foreign students and holders of Laissez Passez: • All of the documents submitted by Jordanian nationals, excluding the military service record. • Photocopy of passport. 5. Foreign Secondary School Certificate Holders: • The equivalency of the Certificate certified by the Jordanian Ministry of Higher Education and Research. • An official Transcript or a certified copy. Master's Program Consists of Two Tracks: 1. Comprehensive Exam Track: The student is expected to pass 33 credit hours of which 24 are required and 9 are electives. 2. Thesis Track: The student must successfully pass 33 credit hours, consisting of 9 hours for the thesis in addition to 15 required hours and 9 credit hours of elective courses. C. Admission Terms For Master's Candidates: 1. The required grade rating of "good" or above, in the event a BA program Students with GPA's rating less than good they will be accepted in a Masters program, provided that they meet the rules and conditions given by the Ministry of Higher Education and Research's committee in their meeting (no. 2) on 6/1/2010. 2. Students should be enrolled in regular not distance learning Institutions. 3. English Language Certification: There are different options students can obtain the certification with; either the National Examination (Refer to our registrar for more info about certified centers), or a score of 70 in the iBT TOEFL, score 6.5 or above in IELTS exam. Students must submit their required examination scores prior to admission and enrollment. D. Documents for Admission to the Masters Program: The application should be accompanied by the following

documents: 1. Copy of the Bachelor's degree certified by the Ministry of Higher Education and Research. 2.Transcript certified by the Ministry of Higher Education and Research. 3. Photocopy of identity card. 4.Photocopy of the applicant's passport. 5.Bachelor's equivalent certified by the Ministry of Higher Education and Research. 6.Two photos. 7.Mentioned above English Language certification Passing results.

Fees: National : Bachelors: Average of 14 000 in 4 years (132 credit hours program) Masters : Average of 10 000 in 2 years (33 credit hours program) (Jordanian Dinar), International : Bachelors : Average of 20 000 in 4 years (132 credit hours program) Masters : Average of 14 000 in 2 years (33 credit hours program) (US Dollar)

Main language(s) of instruction: Arabic, English

Accrediting agency: Jordan Ministry of Higher Education and Scientific Research

Degrees and diplomas: Bachelor's Degree (Arabic; Architecture; Arts and Humanities; Business Administration; Civil Engineering; Educational Technology; Electrical and Electronic Engineering; Energy Engineering; English; Finance; Graphic Design; Journalism; Law; Literature; Marketing; Mass Communication; Media Studies; Pharmacy; Radio and Television Broadcasting; Special Education; Tourism; Visual Arts), Master's Degree (Arabic; Arts and Humanities; Business Administration; E- Business/Commerce; Educational Sciences; English; Finance; Information Technology; Journalism; Linguistics; Literature; Marketing; Mass Communication; Political Sciences; Private Law; Public Law; Radio and Television Broadcasting; Teacher Training; Technology Education; Translation and Interpretation)

Student Services: Academic Counselling, Social Counselling, Careers Guidance, Cultural Activities, Sports Facilities, Language Laboratory, Facilities for disabled people, Health Services, Canteen, Library, eLibrary, IT Centre

Academic Staff 2014-2015	MALE	FEMALE	TOTAL
FULL-TIME	64	86	150
PART-TIME	3		3
STAFF WITH DOCTORATE			
FULL-TIME	138	45	183
Student Numbers 2014-2015			
All (Foreign Included)	2113	1075	3188
Foreign only	422	129	551

Last Update: 17-06-2015

Philadelphia University (PU)

PO Box 1101
Amman 19392
Tel: +962(6) 479-9000

Fax: +962(6) 479-9033
Website: http://www.philadelphia.edu.jo
President: Mutaz Sheikh Salem

Faculty

Administrative and Financial Sciences (Accountancy; Banking; Business Administration; Finance; Hotel Management; Marketing; Tourism); **Arts** (Arabic; Development Studies; English; Graphic Design; Interior Design; Psychology); **Engineering** (Architecture; Civil Engineering; Computer Engineering; Electrical Engineering; Electronic Engineering; Engineering; Mechanical Engineering; Telecommunications Engineering); **Information Technology** (Business Computing; Computer Science; Software Engineering); **Law** (Law); **Nursing** (Nursing); **Pharmacy** (Pharmacy); **Science** (Biotechnology; Genetics; Mathematics; Natural Sciences)
History: Founded 1989, acquired present status 1991.
Academic year: October to June (October-January; February-June). Also Summer Courses (July-August)
Admission requirements: Secondary school certificate
Fees: 50-75 per credit hour (Jordanian Dinar)
Main language(s) of instruction: Arabic, English
Degrees and diplomas: Bachelor's Degree (Accountancy; Arabic; Architecture; Banking; Biotechnology; Business Administration; Business Computing; Civil Engineering; Computer Engineering; Computer Science; Development Studies; Electrical Engineering; Electronic Engineering; English; Finance; Genetics; Graphic Design; Hotel Management; Interior Design; Law; Marketing; Mathematics; Mechanical Engineering; Nursing; Pharmacy; Psychology; Software Engineering; Telecommunications Engineering; Tourism), Master's Degree (Arabic; Computer Science; English; Literature; Mechanical Engineering)
Student Services: Academic Counselling, Social Counselling, Nursery Care, Cultural Activities, Sports Facilities, Language Laboratory, Health Services, Canteen, Foreign Studies Centre
Periodicals: Almasira Aljamiyah, Philadelphia Cultural Magazine
Last Update: 04-04-2017

Princess Sumaya University for Technology (PSUT)

PO Box 1438
Amman 11941
Tel: +962(6) 535-9949

Fax: +962(6) 534-7295
Website: http://www.psut.edu.jo
President: Abdullah Al-Refai

Faculty

Business Technology (*King Talal*) (Accountancy; Business Administration; Business Computing; Environmental Management; Marketing); **Computer Sciences** (*King Hussein*) (Computer Graphics; Computer Science; Software Engineering); **Graduate Studies and Scientific Research** (*King Abdullah I*)

School

Engineering (*King Abdullah II*) (Computer Engineering; Electrical Engineering; Electronic Engineering; Energy Engineering; Power Engineering; Telecommunications Engineering)
History: Founded 1991.
Admission requirements: High School Tawjihi Certificate / the Science Stream, or a recognized equivalent certificate (such as the GCE). The minimum Tawjihi average is 60% for IT School applicants, and 80% for Engineering School applicants.
Main language(s) of instruction: Arabic
Accrediting agency: Jordanian Council for Higher Education
Degrees and diplomas: Bachelor's Degree (Accountancy; Business Administration; Business Computing; Computer Engineering; Computer Graphics; Computer Science; Electronic Engineering; Energy Engineering; Marketing; Software Engineering; Telecommunications Engineering), Master's Degree (Business Administration; Computer Engineering; Computer Networks; Computer Science; Electrical Engineering; Environmental Management), Doctorate (Computer Science)

Academic Staff 2015-2016	MALE	FEMALE	TOTAL
FULL-TIME			121
PART-TIME			36
STAFF WITH DOCTORATE			
FULL-TIME			107
Student Numbers 2015-2016			
All (Foreign Included)			3015

Last Update: 25-04-2016

Red Sea Institute of Cinematic Arts

PO Box 1484
Aqaba
Website: http://www.rsica.edu.jo

Course/Programme
Cinematic Arts (Cinema and Television; Film)

History: Founded 2008.
Accrediting agency: Ministry of Higher Education and Scientific Research
Degrees and diplomas: Master's Degree
Last Update: 22-11-2011

The Arab Academy for Banking and Financial Sciences

PO Box 13190
Amman 11942
Tel: +962(6) 550-2900, +962(6) 550-3838
Fax: +962(6) 523-7834
Website: http://www.aabfs.org
President: Isam Zabalawi
Tel: +962(6) 550-2900 Ext. 115

Faculty

Banking and Financial Sciences (*Amman, Jordan*) (Accountancy; Banking; Finance; Management; Marketing); **Information Systems and Technology** (*Amman, Jordan*) (Computer Science; E- Business/Commerce; Information Management; Information Technology)

Deanery

Scientific Research; **Students' Affairs**

College

Banking and Financial Sciences (*Karak, Jordan Branch*) (Accountancy; Banking; Business Administration; Finance; Information Management; Information Sciences; Information Technology; Management; Marketing); **Banking and Financial Sciences** (*Sana'a, Yemen Branch*) (Accountancy; Banking; Business Administration; Finance; Information Sciences; Information Technology; Management); **Post-graduate Studies** (*Damascus, Syria Branch*) (Banking; Computer Networks; Computer Science; Finance; Information Technology); **Post-graduate Studies** (*Cairo, Egypt Branch*) (Accountancy; Banking; Business Administration; Finance; Information Management; Insurance; Marketing)

Course/Programme

Bachelor (*Muscat, Oman Branch*)

Department/Division

Accountancy (Accountancy); **Banking** (Banking); **Banking** (*Islamic*) (Banking); **Business Administration** (Business Administration); **Computer Information Systems** (Information Technology); **Financial Management** (Finance); **Financial Markets** (Finance); **Management Information Systems** (Information Management; Information Technology); **Marketing** (Marketing)

Institute

Banking and Financial Training (*Amman*) (Accountancy; Banking; Finance; Human Resources; Information Technology; Insurance; Management; Small Business); **Banking and Financial Training** (*Cairo*) (Accountancy; Banking; Finance; Human Resources; Information Technology; Insurance; Management; Small Business)

Centre

Banking and Financial Consultancy (Accountancy; Banking; Finance; Information Technology); **Banking and Financial Research** (Accountancy; Arabic; Banking; Insurance; Translation and Interpretation); **Certified Financiers and Bankers** (Banking; Finance); **Design and Printing** (Design; Printing and Printmaking)
Further information: Also representative offices in Beirut, Tripoli, in Saudi Arabia and Tunis.
History: Founded 1988 as Arab Institute. A non-profit, pan-Arab regional Institution for the development of human resources operating at various levels in banks, financial Institutions, companies and Government departments. Emphasis on postgraduate and professional studies.
Academic year: September to June (September-January; February-June). Summer Session (July-September)
Degrees and diplomas: Bachelor's Degree (Accountancy; Banking; Business Administration; Computer Science; Finance; Information Management; Information Sciences; Information Technology; Management; Marketing), Master's Degree (Accountancy; Banking; Business Administration; Computer Science; Finance; Information Management; Information Sciences; Information Technology; Management; Marketing), Doctorate (Accountancy; Banking; Computer Science; Finance; Information Sciences; Islamic Studies; Management)
Periodicals: Academy Bulletin, Journal of Banking and Financial Studies
Last Update: 16-09-2010

University of Petra

PO Box 961343
Amman 11196
Tel: +962(6) 579-9555
Fax: +962(6) 571-5570
Website: http://www.uop.edu.jo
President: Marwan El-Muwalla

Faculty

Administrative and Financial Sciences (Accountancy; Banking; Business Administration; Business Computing; E-Business/Commerce; Finance; Marketing); **Architecture and Design** (Architecture; Computer Graphics; Graphic Design; Interior Design; Multimedia); **Arts and Science** (Arabic; Chemistry; Educational Sciences; English; Literature; Media Studies); **Engineering** (Civil Engineering); **Information Technology** (Computer Networks; Computer Science; Information Technology; Software Engineering); **Law** (Administrative Law; Civil Law; Commercial Law; Constitutional Law; Criminal Law; History of Law; International Law; Labour Law; Law; Private Law; Public Law); **Mass Communication** (Journalism; Radio and Television Broadcasting); **Pharmacy and Medical Sciences** (Biomedicine; Nutrition; Pharmacology; Pharmacy)

History: Founded 1991 as Jordan University for Women. Acquired present status 2000.

Academic year: October to June

Admission requirements: Secondary school certificate with pass grade of at least 60%; Pharmacy and Architecture 80%

Main language(s) of instruction: Arabic, English

Degrees and diplomas: Bachelor's Degree (Accountancy; Arabic; Architecture; Business Administration; Business Computing; Chemistry; Civil Engineering; Computer Graphics; Computer Networks; Computer Science; E- Business/Commerce; Education; English; Finance; Graphic Design; Interior Design; Journalism; Marketing; Mathematics; Nutrition; Pharmacy; Radio and Television Broadcasting; Software Engineering; Translation and Interpretation), Master's Degree (Arabic; Business Administration; Journalism; Marketing; Pharmacy; Translation and Interpretation)

Student Services: Academic Counselling, Social Counselling, Careers Guidance, Nursery Care, Cultural Activities, Sports Facilities, Language Laboratory, Health Services, Canteen, Foreign Studies Centre

Periodicals: Al-Basair, Awraq Jamie'ya

Academic Staff 2016-2017	MALE	FEMALE	TOTAL
FULL-TIME			295
PART-TIME			27
STAFF WITH DOCTORATE			
FULL-TIME			215
Student Numbers 2016-2017			
All (Foreign Included)			6987

Last Update: 27-04-2017

Zarqa University

PO Box 2000
Zarqa 13110
Tel: +962(5) 382-1100
Fax: +962(5) 382-1120
Website: http://www.zpu.edu.jo
President: Yousef Abu Addous

Faculty

Allied Medical Science (Anatomy; Biochemistry; Biological and Life Sciences; Endocrinology; Haematology; Medical Technology; Molecular Biology; Parasitology; Pathology); **Art and Design** (Graphic Design; Interior Design); **Arts** (Arabic; English; History; Journalism; Literature; Translation and Interpretation); **Economics and Administrative Sciences** (Accountancy; Banking; Business Administration; Business Computing; Economics; Finance; Information Management; Management Systems; Marketing); **Educational Sciences** (Education; Educational Sciences; Information Sciences; Library Science; Preschool Education; Primary Education); **Law** (Law); **Nursing** (Nursing); **Science and Information Technology** (Computer Science; Mathematics; Software Engineering; Systems Analysis); **Shari'a** (Islamic Law; Islamic Studies); **Technical Engineering** (Architecture; Civil Engineering; Electrical Engineering; Surveying and Mapping)

History: Founded 1994. Acquired present status 1999.

Admission requirements: Secondary school certificate or equivalent. Minimum marks of 50% for all majors except Allied Medical Sciences

Fees: (Jordanian Dinars): Registration, 20; tuition, 30 - 60 per credit hour

Main language(s) of instruction: Arabic, English

Accrediting agency: Ministry of Higher Education

Degrees and diplomas: Bachelor's Degree

Student Services: Academic Counselling, Social Counselling, Nursery Care, Sports Facilities, Health Services, Canteen

Periodicals: Al A' Afaq (The Horizon), IAJIT, Zarqa Journal for Research and Studies

Last Update: 22-11-2011

Kazakhstan

STRUCTURE OF HIGHER EDUCATION SYSTEM

Description

The education system is regulated by the Government. The Government is responsible for the development and implementation of the education policy. The rectors of national HEIs are nominated by the President of the Republic. Higher education is open to citizens who have completed general secondary, technical and vocational education or further education. Higher education institutions in Kazakhstan are national research universities, national higher education institutions, research universities, universities, academies or institutes. Conservatories, higher schools and higher colleges have a similar status. Since 1993, the number of higher education institutions has increased due to the setting up of non-state (private) universities.

Stages of studies

University level first stage

Undergraduate level
Bachelor's degrees are conferred after four years of studies.

University level second stage

Graduate level
Master's degrees are conferred after a further two years' study after the Bachelor's degree.

University level third stage

Postgraduate level
A PhD usually lasts for minimum three years and is conferred after completion of a thesis based on original research.

ADMISSION TO HIGHER EDUCATION

Admission to university-level studies

Name of Secondary school credential required: Certificate of General Secondary Education

Admission requirements: School graduates are admitted to higher education based on the results of the Unified National Test. Quotas for disadvantaged groups have been established.

RECOGNITION OF STUDIES

Quality assurance system

The procedures for completing institutional accreditation include the following steps: 1st step – self-assessment (internal evaluation) by the higher education institution; 2nd step – external evaluation by the commission of experts of an accreditation agency; 3rd step – making the decision and, if positive, the granting of the certificate of accreditation which is valid for a period of 5 years.

Bodies dealing with recognition

Independent Kazakhstan Quality Assurance Agency in Education - IQAA
President: Sholpan M. Kalanova
20 Dostyk Street, office 801
Astana 010000
Tel: +7(7172) 27-38-20
Fax: +7(7172) 27-38-20
Website: http://www.iqaa.kz

Independent Agency for Accreditation and Rating
Director: Alina Zhumagulova
Kabanbay batyr avenue 42-VP-17
Astana 010000
Tel: +7(7172) 45-24-02
Fax: +7(7172) 45-22-02
Website: http://www.iaar.kz

NATIONAL BODIES

Ministry of Education and Science

Minister: Erlan Sagadiev
8 Orynbor Street
Astana 010000

© International Association of Universities 2019
International Handbook of Universities 2019,
https://doi.org/10.1057/978-3-319-76971-4_99

Tel: +7(7172) 742-425
Website: http://www.edu.gov.kz
Role of national body: The main aims of the Ministry of Education and Science are the implementation of the State policy in the field of education and science, and scientific and methodological guidance of educational and scientific institutions.

Association of Higher Education Institutions of the Republic of Kazakhstan

President: Rahman Alshanovich Alshanov
Executive Director: Bekbolat Shakirbekovich Aytishev
Satpaeva 16-18, 18a, office 712-714
Almaty 050013
Tel: +8(727) 262-1428
Fax: +8(727) 262-1428
Website: http://edurk.kz
Role of national body: Non-profit organization of accredited higher education institutions created in 2002.

Data for academic year: 2013–2014
Source: IAU from the Ministry of Education and Science and IQAA Websites, World Data on Education 2010/2011, UNESCO-IBE and Higher Education in Kazakhstan, EACEA, 2014. Bodies updated 2018.

Public Institutions

Academician E.A. Buketov Karaganda State University (KSU)

ul. Universitetskaja 28
Karaganda 100028
Tel: +7(3212) 77-03-89
Fax: +7(3212) 77-03-84
Website: http://www.ksu.kz
Rector: Erkin Kinayatovich Kubeev

Faculty
Biology and Geography (Biology; Ecology; Geography; Zoology); **Chemistry** (Chemistry); **Economics** (Accountancy; Economics; Finance; Management; Marketing; Public Administration; Service Trades; Tourism); **Foreign Languages** (English; French; German; Modern Languages; Philology; Translation and Interpretation); **History** (Archaeology; Ethnology; Heritage Preservation; History; International Relations; Museum Studies); **Law** (International Law; Law); **Mathematics and Information Technology** (Applied Mathematics; Mathematics; Mathematics and Computer Science; Mathematics Education; Mechanics); **Pedagogy and Social Work** (Pedagogy; Preschool Education; Primary Education; Psychology; Social Work); **Philology** (Foreign Languages Education; Journalism; Literature; Native Language; Philology; Russian); **Philosophy and Psychology** (Cultural Studies; Philosophy; Political Sciences; Psychology; Religious Studies; Social Sciences); **Physical Training and Sports** (Physical Education; Sports); **Physics** (Applied Physics; Electronic Engineering; Environmental Studies; Instrument Making; Materials Engineering; Physics; Power Engineering; Radiophysics; Social Welfare; Telecommunications Engineering); **Professional Arts** (Design; Fine Arts; Library Science; Painting and Drawing; Publishing and Book Trade; Transport and Communications; Vocational Education)
History: Founded 1972 as Karaganda Pedagogical Institute. Acquired present status and title 1997.
Academic year: September to July
Admission requirements: Competitive entrance examination following general or special secondary school certificate
Main language(s) of instruction: Kazakh, Russian
Accrediting agency: Ministry of Education and Science
Degrees and diplomas: Bakalavriat (Architecture and Planning; Arts and Humanities; Education; Engineering; Fine Arts; Law; Mathematics and Computer Science; Natural Sciences; Religion; Social Sciences), Magistratura (Arts and Humanities; Business Administration; Education; Information Sciences; Mathematics and Computer Science; Natural Sciences; Social Work; Tourism), Doctorantura (Biology; Chemistry; Economics; History; Law; Mathematics; Pedagogy; Philosophy; Physics; Primary Education)
Student Services: Academic Counselling, Social Counselling, Careers Guidance, Cultural Activities, Sports Facilities, Language Laboratory, Health Services, Canteen
Last Update: 02-03-2015

Academy of Civil Aviation

ul. Zakarpatskaja 44
Almaty 050039
Tel: +7(727) 383-89-79
Fax: +7(727) 383-89-69
Website: http://www.agakaz.kz
Rector: Mukhtar Kazbekovich Baijumanov

Course/Programme
Aviation Engineering and Technology (Aeronautical and Aerospace Engineering; Air Transport; Technology); **Transport Management** (Air Transport; Transport and Communications; Transport Management)
History: Created 2000. A postgraduate institution.
Admission requirements: Bakalvr or Diplom Spetsialista
Accrediting agency: Ministry of Education and Science

Degrees and diplomas: Bakalavriat (Air Transport; Transport Economics; Transport Management), Magistratura (Aeronautical and Aerospace Engineering; Air Transport; Transport Management)
Last Update: 02-03-2015

Academy of Public Administration under the President of Kazakhstan

prosp. Abaja 33a
Astana 010000
Tel: +7(7172) 75-34-77, +7(7172) 75-33-44
Fax: +7(7172) 75-32-68
Website: http://pa-academy.kz
Rector: Bolatbek S. Abdrassilov

School
Public Policy (*National - NSPP*) (Political Sciences)

Institute
Civil Servants's Retraining and Skills-upgrading (Economics; Finance; Law; Leadership; Political Sciences; Social Sciences); **Diplomacy** (International Relations); **Justice** (Civil Law; Criminal Law); **Public Administration Modernization** (Public Administration); **Public and Local Administration** (Administration; Economics; Finance; Human Resources; Information Technology; Management; Native Language; Public Administration)
History: Founded 1994 as National Higher School of public administration under the President of the Republic of Kazakhstan (NHSPA) on the basis of the Party School at the Central Committee of the Kazakh Soviet Socialist Republic. Became the Academy of public service under the President the Republic of Kazakhstan 1998 after merging with Institute of civil servants' retraining and skill-upgrading under the Government of the Republic of Kazakhstan. Relocated in Astana 2000. Became Academy of public administration under the President the Republic of Kazakhstan 2005 through merger of the reorganized state institutions "The Academy of public service under the President of the Republic of Kazakhstan", "The Academy of Justice at the Supreme court of the Republic of Kazakhstan" and transfer of functions of Diplomatic Academy of the republican state enterprise "Eurasian national university named after L.N. Gumilev" to newly created state body.
Accrediting agency: Ministry of Education and Science
Degrees and diplomas: Magistratura (Administration; Economics; International Economics; International Law; International Relations; Law; Management; Political Sciences; Statistics; Translation and Interpretation), Doctorantura (Administration; Economics; International Relations; Philosophy; Social Work)
Last Update: 12-03-2015

Al-Farabi Kazakh National University (KazNU)

prosp. Al Farabi 71
Almaty 050040
Tel: +7(7273) 77-33-30
Website: http://www.kaznu.kz
Rector: Galimkair Mutanovich Mutanov

Faculty
Biology and Biotechnology (Biology; Biomedicine; Biophysics; Biotechnology; Genetics; Molecular Biology); **Chemistry and Chemical Technology** (Analytical Chemistry; Chemistry; Inorganic Chemistry; Organic Chemistry; Physical Chemistry); **Geography and Environmental Management** (Ecology; Geography; Geography (Human); Meteorology; Surveying and Mapping; Tourism; Water Science); **History, Archaeology, and Ethnology** (Ancient Civilizations; Archaeology; Contemporary History; Ethnology; History; Medieval Studies; Modern History; Museum Studies); **International Relations** (International Law; International Relations; Regional Studies); **Journalism** (Journalism); **Law** (Civil Law; Criminal Law; Fiscal Law; Law; Public Law); **Mechanical Mathematics** (Computer Science; Information Technology; Mathematics; Mathematics and Computer Science; Mechanics); **Oriental Studies** (Arabic; Chinese; East Asian Studies; Hindi; Japanese; Korean; Modern Languages; Persian; Philology; Regional Studies; Translation and Interpretation; Turkish; Urdu); **Philology, Literature, and World Languages** (Linguistics; Literature; Native Language; Philology; Russian; Translation and Interpretation); **Philosophy and Political Science** (Anthropology; Educational Administration; Pedagogy; Philosophy; Political Sciences; Psychology; Religion; Social Work; Sociology); **Physics** (Applied Physics; Astronomy and Space Science; Materials Engineering; Measurement and Precision Engineering; Nuclear Physics; Physics; Thermal Physics)

School
Economics and Business (Accountancy; Business Administration; Economics; Finance; Law; Management; Marketing)
Further information: Also Scientific Technology Park
History: Founded 1934, became autonomous State Institution 1993, acquired present status and title 2001.
Academic year: September to July (September-January; February-July)
Admission requirements: Competitive entrance examination following general or special secondary school certificate
Main language(s) of instruction: Kazakh, Russian
Accrediting agency: Ministry of Education and Science
Degrees and diplomas: Bakalavriat (Agriculture; Arts and Humanities; Business Administration; Computer Science; Earth Sciences; Ecology; Environmental Management;

Environmental Studies; Mass Communication; Mathematics; Natural Sciences; Oriental Studies; Pedagogy; Social Sciences; Sports), Magistratura (Arts and Humanities; Business Administration; Computer Science; Economics; Environmental Studies; Law; Library Science; Linguistics; Mathematics; Modern Languages; Museum Management; Museum Studies; Natural Sciences; Political Sciences; Psychology; Sociology), Doctorantura (Arts and Humanities; Business Administration; Environmental Studies; Information Sciences; Law; Mathematics and Computer Science; Natural Sciences; Social Sciences)
Student Services: Academic Counselling, Social Counselling, Cultural Activities, Sports Facilities, Health Services
Last Update: 08-09-2014

Almaty Technological University (Almaty Tehnologiyalik Universitety)

ul. Tole bi 100
Almaty 050012
Tel: +7(727) 293-52-89
Fax: +7(727) 293-52-92
Website: http://www.atu.kz
Rector: Kuralbek Sadibayevich Kulazhanov

Faculty

Economics and Business (Accountancy; Economics; Finance; Management; Marketing; Service Trades; Tourism); **Engineering and Information Technology** (Computer Science; Engineering; Information Sciences; Information Technology; Physical Education); **Food Production** (Biotechnology; Chemistry; Ecology; Food Science; Food Technology; Organic Chemistry); **Light Industry and Design** (Design; Mathematics; Modern Languages; Physics; Technology; Textile Design)
History: Founded 1952 as Almaty Training-Consulting Branch of All-Union Extra-Mural Institute of Food Industry. Renamed Almaty Technological Institute 1996. Acquired present status and title 2001.
Main language(s) of instruction: Kazakh, Russian
Accrediting agency: Ministry of Education and Science
Degrees and diplomas: Bakalavriat (Business Administration; Computer Science; Economics; Engineering; Fine Arts; Hotel and Restaurant; Natural Sciences; Tourism), Magistratura (Biotechnology; Chemical Engineering; Economics; Finance; Hotel and Restaurant; Industrial Management; Information Technology; Management; Materials Engineering; Mechanical Engineering; Tourism), Doctorantura (Biotechnology; Economics; Engineering; Hotel Management; Management)
Last Update: 05-03-2015

Almaty University of Power Engineering and Telecommunications (AIPET)

ul. Baytursynova 126
Almaty 050013
Tel: +7(727) 292-07-72
Website: http://www.aipet.kz
Rector: Kairat Bakenov

Faculty

Aerospace and Information Technology (Aeronautical and Aerospace Engineering; Computer Science; Electronic Engineering; Information Technology); **Electrical Engineering** (Automation and Control Engineering; Ecology; Electrical Engineering; Power Engineering); **Heat Power Engineering** (Automation and Control Engineering; Industrial Engineering; Physics; Power Engineering; Thermal Engineering); **Radio Engineering and Communication** (Computer Engineering; Electronic Engineering; Engineering; Mathematics; Mechanics; Telecommunications Engineering)
History: Founded 1966 as Almaty Technological Institute, reorganized as Almaty Institute of Power Engineering 1975, became Almaty Institute of Power Engineering and Telecommunications in 1997. Acquired current title 2010.
Academic year: September to July
Admission requirements: Competitive entrance examination following general or special secondary school certificate
Main language(s) of instruction: Kazakh, Russian
Accrediting agency: Ministry of Education and Science
Degrees and diplomas: Bakalavriat (Aeronautical and Aerospace Engineering; Automation and Control Engineering; Computer Science; Electrical and Electronic Engineering; Energy Engineering; Library Science; Safety Engineering), Magistratura (Computer Science; Electrical and Electronic Engineering; Energy Engineering; Safety Engineering; Telecommunications Engineering), Doctorantura (Energy Engineering; Telecommunications Engineering; Thermal Engineering)
Last Update: 23-01-2015

Astana Medical University (AMU)

ul. Beibitshilika 49A
Astana 010000
Tel: +7(7172) 53-94-24
Fax: +7(7172) 53-94-53
Website: http://www.amu.kz
Rector: Mazhit Zeynullovych Shaydarov

Course/Programme

Medicine (Medicine; Stomatology); **Nursing** (Nursing); **Pharmacy** (Pharmacy); **Public Health** (Public Health)

History: Founded 1964.

Accrediting agency: Ministry of Education and Science

Degrees and diplomas: Bakalavriat (Medicine; Nursing; Pharmacy; Public Health; Stomatology), Magistratura (Anaesthesiology; Anatomy; Biology; Cardiology; Forensic Medicine and Dentistry; Gastroenterology; Medicine; Nephrology; Neurology; Nursing; Oncology; Otorhinolaryngology; Paediatrics; Public Health; Rehabilitation and Therapy; Rheumatology; Stomatology; Surgery; Urology), Doctorantura (Biology; Medicine; Public Health)

Last Update: 13-03-2015

Atyrau Institute of Oil and Gas

prosp. Azattyk, 1

Atyrau 060002

Tel: +7(7122) 35-46-54

Fax: +7(7122) 32-95-57

Website: http://www.ainig.kz

Rector: Dyussembek Uringalievich Kulzhanov

Faculty

Automation, Management and Economics (Accountancy; Economics; Information Technology; Management; Marketing); **Engineering** (Chemical Engineering; Chemistry; Energy Engineering; Environmental Engineering); **Mechanics** (Computer Science; Construction Engineering; Machine Building; Materials Engineering; Mathematics; Mechanics; Transport and Communications; Transport Management); **Oil and Petroleum** (Geology; Geophysics; Petroleum and Gas Engineering)

History: Created 1984.

Accrediting agency: Ministry of Education and Science

Degrees and diplomas: Bakalavriat (Accountancy; Building Technologies; Chemistry; Computer Science; Energy Engineering; Fishery; Geology; Information Technology; Management; Marine Engineering; Marketing; Petroleum and Gas Engineering; Surveying and Mapping; Transport Management)

Last Update: 13-01-2015

Caspian State University of Technologies and Engineering named after Sh. Yesenov

14-mikro-rajon 50

Aktau 130000

Tel: +7(7292) 31-42-21

Fax: +7(7292) 31-42-21

Website: http://www.kguti.kz/

Institute

Arts and Humanities and Natural Sciences (Arabic; Biology; Chemistry; Chinese; Foreign Languages Education; French; Geography; German; History; Information Sciences; Literature; Mathematics; Pedagogy; Philosophy; Physical Education; Physics; Psychology; Russian); **Economics and Law** (Accountancy; Economics; Finance; International Relations; Management); **Technology and Engineering** (Building Technologies; Chemical Engineering; Computer Engineering; Ecology; Geology; Marine Engineering; Mechanical Engineering; Mining Engineering; Power Engineering; Transport Engineering)

History: Founded as Aktauskij Universitet im. Š. Yesenova (Sh. Yesenov Aktau State University), acquired present title 2008.

Accrediting agency: Ministry of Education and Science

Degrees and diplomas: Bakalavriat (Architecture and Planning; Arts and Humanities; Business Administration; Education; Engineering; Law; Mathematics and Computer Science; Natural Sciences; Social Sciences), Magistratura (Chemical Engineering; Ecology; Energy Engineering; Geological Engineering; Information Technology; Management; Marine Engineering; Mathematics; Mechanical Engineering; Pedagogy; Petroleum and Gas Engineering; Physics; Primary Education), Doctorantura (Ecology; Geological Engineering; Geology; Pedagogy; Petroleum and Gas Engineering; Philology)

Last Update: 02-03-2015

D. Serikbayev East Kazakhstan State Technical University (EKSTU)

ul. Serikbayeva 19

Ust-Kamenogorsk 070004

Tel: +7(723) 226-25-33

Fax: +7(723) 226-25-33

Website: http://www.ektu.kz

Rector: Zhassulan Shaimardanov

Faculty

Architectural and Civil Engineering (Architecture; Building Technologies; Civil Engineering; Construction Engineering; Design; Forestry; Measurement and Precision Engineering; Transport and Communications; Water Management; Wood Technology); **Economics and Management** (Accountancy; Economics; Finance; History; Law; Management; Native Language; Russian; Taxation); **Information Technology and Power Engineering** (Automation and Control Engineering; Industrial Engineering; Information Technology; Mathematics; Mathematics and Computer Science; Modern Languages; Power Engineering); **Mechanical Engineering and Transport** (Materials Engineering; Mechanical Engineering; Philosophy; Physics; Transport and Communications; Transport Management); **Mining and Metallurgy** (Chemistry; Ecology;

Environmental Management; Environmental Studies; Geology; Metallurgical Engineering; Mining Engineering; Sports; Surveying and Mapping)

Further information: Centres also in Zyryanovsk, Ridder, Semipalatinsk, Kurchatov, Almaty

History: Founded 1958, acquired present status 1996 and title 1997, named after D. Serikbaev.

Academic year: September to June (September-January; February-June)

Admission requirements: Competitive entrance examinations following secondary school certificate (Atestat o srednem obrazovanii) or recognized foreign equivalent

Main language(s) of instruction: Russian, Kazakh

Accrediting agency: Ministry of Education and Science

Degrees and diplomas: Bakalavriat (Accountancy; Business Administration; Computer Science; Design; Economics; Energy Engineering; Environmental Engineering; Finance; Forestry; Geology; Information Technology; Machine Building; Management; Marketing; Mathematics; Metallurgical Engineering; Mining Engineering; Physics; Transport Management; Water Management), Magistratura (Accountancy; Architecture; Computer Science; Design; Economics; Energy Engineering; Forestry; Geology; Information Technology; Machine Building; Management; Marketing; Mathematics; Metallurgical Engineering; Mining Engineering; Philology; Philosophy; Physics; Transport Management), Doctorantura (Computer Science; Machine Building; Mathematics; Metallurgical Engineering; Physics)

Student Services: Academic Counselling, Careers Guidance, Nursery Care, Cultural Activities, Sports Facilities, Language Laboratory, Health Services, Canteen

Academic Staff 2015-2016	MALE	FEMALE	TOTAL
FULL-TIME			321
PART-TIME			145
STAFF WITH DOCTORATE			
FULL-TIME			48
Student Numbers 2015-2016			
All (Foreign Included)			4412

Last Update: 25-07-2016

Hoja Akhmet Yassawi International Kazakh-Turkish University (IKTU)

prosp. B.Sattarkhanov 29
Turkistan 161200
Tel: +7(7253) 36-36-36
Website: http://iktu.kz/
Rector: Ualihan Abdibekov

Faculty

Art (Design; Fine Arts; Painting and Drawing); **Ecology** (Agriculture; Ecology; Environmental Studies; Farm Management; Welfare and Protective Services); **Economics** (Economics; International Economics; Management; Marketing; Tourism); **History** (History; History of Societies; Political Sciences; Religious Studies; Sociology); **Law** (International Law; International Relations; Law); **Medicine** (Medicine; Traditional Eastern Medicine); **Natural Sciences** (Biology; Chemistry; Mathematics; Mechanics; Natural Sciences; Physics); **Philology** (Journalism; Linguistics; Literature; Modern Languages; Philology; Translation and Interpretation)

Department/Division

Economics and Law (Economics; History; Law; Native Language)

Further information: Also Branches in Kentau, Almaty, Taraz and Šymkent. Polyclinic for Medical Studies, Šymkent; Kazakh and Russian courses for foreign students

History: Founded 1991, acquired present status and title 1993 by special agreement between Governments of the Republic of Kazakhstan and the Republic of Turkey.

Academic year: September to July (September-January; February-July)

Admission requirements: Secondary school certificate (Atestat srednem obrazovanii)

Fees: c. 28,800-94,600 per annum (Tenge)

Main language(s) of instruction: Kazakh, Russian, Turkish, English

Accrediting agency: Ministry of Education and Science

Degrees and diplomas: Bakalavriat (Arts and Humanities; Education; Engineering; Information Sciences; Mass Communication; Mathematics and Computer Science; Natural Sciences; Performing Arts; Social Sciences), Magistratura (Art Education; Biology; Chemistry; Computer Science; Ecology; Economics; Energy Engineering; History; Law; Management; Mathematics; Medicine; Modern Languages; Pedagogy; Philology; Philosophy; Physical Education; Physics; Political Sciences; Preschool Education; Primary Education; Religious Studies; Sociology), Doctorantura (Computer Science; Economics; History; Law; Management; Mathematics; Medicine; Native Language; Pedagogy; Physics; Public Health)

Student Services: Academic Counselling, Social Counselling, Careers Guidance, Nursery Care, Cultural Activities, Sports Facilities, Language Laboratory, Facilities for disabled people, Health Services, Canteen, Foreign Studies Centre

Last Update: 02-03-2015

I. Altynsarin Arkalyk State Pedagogical Institute

ul. Auelbekova 17
Arkalyk 110300
Tel: +7(71430) 7-01-87
Website: http://www.api.kz
Rector: Seitbek Kuanyshbayev

Faculty

History and Art (Fine Arts; History; Music; Music Education; Physical Education); **Natural Science and Information Technology** (Biology; Chemistry; Computer Science; Geography; Mathematics; Physics); **Pedagogy and Philology** (Foreign Languages Education; Native Language Education; Pedagogy; Preschool Education; Primary Education)

History: Founded 1972. Acquired current name 1977.

Academic year: September to July

Admission requirements: Competitive entrance examination following general or special Secondary School Certificate

Accrediting agency: Ministry of Education and Science

Degrees and diplomas: Bakalavriat (Economics; Fine Arts; Literature; Music Education; Native Language; Natural Sciences; Pedagogy; Physical Education; Preschool Education; Primary Education; Russian)

Student Services: Sports Facilities, Health Services

Last Update: 23-01-2015

I. Zhansugurov Zhetysu State University (ZHGU)

ul. I. Žansugurova 187a
Taldykorgan 040009
Tel: +7(7282) 22-00-20
Fax: +7(7282) 22-21-94
Website: http://zhgu.edu.kz/
Rector: Abdimanap Bekturganov

Faculty

Art and Culture (Design; Fine Arts; Music Education; Physical Education; Sports); **Finance and Economics** (Accountancy; Economics; Finance; Management); **Humanities** (English; History; Native Language; Philology; Russian); **Law** (Law); **Mathematics and Natural Science** (Biology; Chemistry; Computer Science; Ecology; Geography; Information Sciences; Information Technology; Mathematics; Mathematics Education; Physics; Science Education); **Pedagogy and Psychology** (Education; Pedagogy; Psychology; Teacher Training)

History: Founded 1972 as Taldykorgan University. Acquired present status 1994.

Academic year: September to June

Admission requirements: General or special secondary school certificate (Attestat o Srednem Obrazovanii or Diplom o Srednem Spetsialnom Obrazovanii)

Main language(s) of instruction: Kazakh, Russian

Accrediting agency: Ministry of Education and Science

Degrees and diplomas: Bakalavriat (Accountancy; Administration; Biology; Chemistry; Computer Science; Design; Ecology; Economics; Education; Environmental Management;

Finance; Geography; History; Journalism; Law; Literature; Management; Marketing; Mathematics; Native Language; Physics; Russian; Special Education; Tourism; Translation and Interpretation), Magistratura (Accountancy; Administration; Economics; Finance; History; Law; Literature; Management; Mathematics and Computer Science; Music Education; Native Language; Pedagogy; Physical Education; Preschool Education; Primary Education; Special Education), Doctorantura (Economics; Law; Native Language; Pedagogy)

Last Update: 13-01-2015

International University of Information Technologies

ul. Manass / Zhandosova, 34
Almaty 050040
Tel: +7(727) 320-00-01
Website: http://www.iitu.kz/
Rector: Damir Abdukhaliyevich Shynybekov

Department/Division

Basic Sciences (Computer Science; Natural Sciences); **Economics and Management** (Economics; Finance; Management); **Information Systems, Mathematical Modeling and Computer Science** (Computer Science; Information Sciences; Telecommunications Engineering); **Media** (Journalism; Media Studies)

History: Created 2009.

Accrediting agency: Ministry of Education and Science

Degrees and diplomas: Bakalavriat (Computer Science; Electronic Engineering; Finance; Information Sciences; Journalism; Management; Mathematics; Telecommunications Engineering), Magistratura (Information Sciences; Management; Mathematics), Doctorantura (Computer Science; Information Sciences)

Last Update: 23-01-2015

K. Zhubanov Aktobe Regional State University

ul. A. Moldagulova 34
Aktobe 030000
Tel: +7(7132) 54-06-19
Website: http://arsu.kz
Rector: Kenžegali Kenžebaiev
Tel: +7(3132) 567-843

Faculty

Economics (Accountancy; Banking; Business Administration; Economics; Finance; International Economics; Management;

Marketing; Mathematics); **Foreign Languages** (German; Translation and Interpretation); **Law** (Law); **Natural Science** (Biology; Chemistry; Ecology; Psychology); **Philology** (Literature; Native Language; Native Language Education; Russian); **Physics and Mathematics** (Applied Mathematics; Computer Science; Information Sciences; Mathematics; Mathematics Education; Physics); **Technology** (Chemical Engineering; Design; Metal Techniques; Petroleum and Gas Engineering; Transport and Communications; Transport Management)

History: Created 1966. Acquired current title 2013. Previously known as K. Zhubanov Aktobe State University (Aktiubinskij Gosudarstvennyj Universitet im. K. Žubanova) and merged with Aktiubinskij Gosudarstvennyj Pedagogičeskij Institut (Aktobe State Pedagogical Institute) in 2013.

Accrediting agency: Ministry of Education and Science

Degrees and diplomas: Bakalavriat (Accountancy; Administration; Biology; Building Technologies; Chemistry; Computer Science; Dance; Design; Economics; Finance; Fine Arts; Geography; History; Law; Literature; Management; Mathematics; Metallurgical Engineering; Mining Engineering; Music Education; Native Language; Philology; Physical Education; Physics; Preschool Education; Primary Education; Psychology; Regional Studies; Russian; Special Education; Sports; Tourism; Translation and Interpretation; Transport Management), Magistratura (Biology; Computer Science; Ecology; Economics; History; Marketing; Mathematics; Pedagogy; Philology; Physics; Psychology), Doctorantura (Mathematics)

Last Update: 13-01-2015

Karaganda State Industrial University (KMI)

prosp. Respubliki 30
Temirtau 101400
Tel: +7(7213) 91-56-26
Fax: +7(7213) 91-62-80
Website: http://www.kgiu.kz/
Rector: Marat Kenesovich Ibatov

Faculty

Economics (Accountancy; Economics; Management); **Engineering Technology and Automation** (Automation and Control Engineering; Chemical Engineering; Computer Engineering; Electrical Engineering; Environmental Engineering; Health Sciences; Materials Engineering; Measurement and Precision Engineering; Mechanical Engineering; Organic Chemistry; Safety Engineering; Software Engineering; Transport Engineering); **Metallurgical and Construction Engineering** (Construction Engineering; Metallurgical Engineering; Thermal Engineering)

History: Founded 1963 as Karaganda Polytechnical Institute, acquired present status and title 2006.

Academic year: September to July

Admission requirements: Competitive entrance examination following general or special secondary school certificate

Main language(s) of instruction: Kazakh, Russian

Accrediting agency: Ministry of Education and Science

Degrees and diplomas: Bakalavriat (Business Administration; Economics; Engineering), Magistratura (Economics; Engineering), Doctorantura (Metallurgical Engineering; Nanotechnology; Nuclear Engineering)

Student Services: Careers Guidance, Cultural Activities, Sports Facilities, Language Laboratory, Facilities for disabled people, Health Services, Canteen

Last Update: 02-03-2015

Karaganda State Medical University (KGMU)

ul. Gogolja 40
Karaganda 100008
Tel: +7(7212) 51-38-97
Fax: +7(7212) 51-89-31
Website: http://www.kgmu.kz
Rector: Raushan Sultanovna Dosmagambetova

Course/Programme

Biology (Biology); **Medicine** (Medicine; Rehabilitation and Therapy; Surgery); **Nursing** (Nursing); **Pharmacy** (Pharmacology; Pharmacy); **Public Health** (Public Health)

History: Founded 1950 as Karaganda State Medical Institute. Acquired present status and title 2009. Formerly know as Karagandy Memlekettik Medicina Akademijasy (Karaganda State Medical Academy).

Academic year: September to July

Admission requirements: Secondary Education Certificate (Attestat o Srednem Obrazovanii) and Common National Test (Kazakh, Russian, Languages, History of Kazakhstan, Biology, Mathematics)

Main language(s) of instruction: Kazakh, Russian, English

Accrediting agency: Ministry of Education and Science; Ministry of Health

Degrees and diplomas: Bakalavriat (Biology; Medicine; Nursing; Pharmacology; Pharmacy; Public Health; Stomatology), Magistratura (Cardiology; Endocrinology; Epidemiology; Gynaecology and Obstetrics; Haematology; Medicine; Nephrology; Neurology; Nursing; Oncology; Ophthalmology; Otorhinolaryngology; Paediatrics; Pharmacology; Pharmacy; Pneumology; Psychiatry and Mental Health; Public Health; Rehabilitation and Therapy; Rheumatology; Surgery; Urology), Doctorantura (Medicine; Pharmacology; Pharmacy; Public Health)

Student Services: Academic Counselling, Social Counselling, Careers Guidance, Nursery Care, Cultural Activities,

Sports Facilities, Language Laboratory, Facilities for disabled people, Health Services, Canteen, Foreign Studies Centre
Last Update: 13-03-2015

Karaganda State Technical University (KGTU)

bulvar Mira 56
Karaganda 100027
Tel: +7(7212) 56-44-22
Fax: +7(7212) 56-03-28
Website: http://www.kstu.kz
Rector: Arstan Gazaliev

Faculty

Architecture and Building (Architecture; Building Technologies; Design); **Economics and Management** (Accountancy; Economics; Management; Marketing; Service Trades); **Information Technology** (Computer Engineering; Computer Science; Information Technology; Instrument Making; Software Engineering); **Machine Building** (Materials Engineering; Mechanical Engineering; Metallurgical Engineering); **Military Engineering** (Military Science); **Mining** (Biotechnology; Chemical Engineering; Geology; Mining Engineering; Organic Chemistry; Safety Engineering; Surveying and Mapping); **Power Engineering, Communication and Automation** (Automation and Control Engineering; Electronic Engineering; Heating and Refrigeration; Power Engineering; Telecommunications Engineering); **Road Transport** (Transport and Communications; Transport Management)
Further information: Also Technological College and Technical Lyceum.
History: Founded 1953 as Karaganda Mining Institute. Reorganized 1958 and acquired present status and title 1996.
Academic year: September to June
Admission requirements: Competitive entrance examination of National Centre of State Education Standards following general or special secondary school certificate
Main language(s) of instruction: Kazakh, Russian
Accrediting agency: Ministry of Education and Science
Degrees and diplomas: Bakalavriat (Architecture and Planning; Business Administration; Economics; Engineering; Fine Arts; Transport Management), Magistratura (Economics; Engineering; Management; Surveying and Mapping; Transport Management), Doctorantura (Energy Engineering; Geological Engineering; Machine Building; Metallurgical Engineering; Mining Engineering; Transport Engineering)
Student Services: Academic Counselling, Social Counselling, Careers Guidance, Cultural Activities, Sports Facilities, Language Laboratory, Health Services, Canteen
Last Update: 02-03-2015

Kazakh Abylai Khan University of International Relations and World Languages

ul. Muratbayev 200
Almaty 050022
Tel: +7(727) 292-23-63
Fax: +7(727) 292-44-73
Website: http://www.ablaikhan.kz
Rector: Salima Sagievna Kunanbayeva

Faculty

Foreign Language Teaching (English; Foreign Languages Education; Linguistics; Modern Languages); **International Relations** (Economics; English; International Law; International Relations; Management; Regional Studies); **Management and International Communication** (International Relations; Management; Marketing; Tourism); **Oriental Studies** (Chinese; Cultural Studies; Linguistics; Oriental Languages; Oriental Studies; Philology); **Translation and Philology** (Arts and Humanities; English; French; German; Translation and Interpretation)
History: Founded 1941 as Teacher Training Institute of Foreign Languages. Acquired present status 1998.
Academic year: September to July
Admission requirements: Secondary school certificate (Atestat o srednem obrazovanii)
Fees: National : Undergraduate Studies, 180,000-450,000 per annum; Graduate Studies, 400,000-500,000 per annum; Doctoral Studies, 850,000-1,200,000 per annum (Tenge), International : 30,000 per annum
Main language(s) of instruction: Russian, Kazakh, English, French, German
Accrediting agency: Ministry of Education and Science
Degrees and diplomas: Bakalavriat (Economics; International Law; International Relations; Journalism; Literature; Management; Marketing; Oriental Studies; Pedagogy; Philology; Regional Studies; Russian; Tourism; Translation and Interpretation), Magistratura (Cultural Studies; International Relations; Journalism; Modern Languages; Oriental Studies; Pedagogy; Philology; Regional Studies; Tourism; Translation and Interpretation), Doctorantura (International Relations; Modern Languages; Philology; Translation and Interpretation)
Student Services: Academic Counselling, Social Counselling, Careers Guidance, Nursery Care, Cultural Activities, Sports Facilities, Language Laboratory, Health Services, Canteen, Foreign Studies Centre
Last Update: 13-01-2015

Kazakh Academy of Sport and Tourism

prosp. Abaia 83/85
Almaty 050022

Tel: +7(727) 292-24-21
Website: http://www.kazacademsport.kz/
President: Kairat Zakiryanov

Faculty

Olympic Sports (Physical Education; Sports); **Professional Sports and Martial Arts** (Physical Education; Physical Therapy; Psychology; Sports; Sports Management); **Tourism** (Tourism)
History: Created 1944 as Kazakh Institute of Physical Culture. Acquired current title and status 1998.
Accrediting agency: Ministry of Education and Science
Degrees and diplomas: Bakalavriat (Hotel and Restaurant; Physical Education; Sports; Tourism), Magistratura (Physical Education; Sports; Tourism), Doctorantura (Physical Education; Sports; Tourism)
Last Update: 13-01-2015

Kazakh Humanitarian Law University (KazGJuU)

shosse Korgalzhyn 8
Astana 010000
Tel: +7(7272) 70-30-03
Website: http://kazguu.kz/
Rector: Talgat Maksutovich Narikbayev

School

Economics (Accountancy; Economics; Finance; Management; Natural Sciences; Social Sciences; Tourism); **Law** (Commercial Law; International Law; Law)
History: Founded 1994 as Kazakh State Law Institute. Acquired present title and status 2002.
Academic year: September to June
Admission requirements: Competitive entrance examination following general or special secondary school certificate (Attestat o Srednem Obrazovanii or Diplom o Srednem Spetsialnom Obrazovanii)
Main language(s) of instruction: Kazakh, Russian
Accrediting agency: Ministry of Education and Science
Degrees and diplomas: Bakalavriat (Accountancy; Economics; Finance; Law; Management; Psychology; Social Work; Sociology; Taxation; Tourism; Translation and Interpretation), Magistratura (Business Administration; Economics; Finance; Law; Sociology; Translation and Interpretation), Doctorantura (International Law; Law)
Student Services: Academic Counselling, Social Counselling, Careers Guidance, Cultural Activities, Sports Facilities, Language Laboratory, Health Services, Canteen, Foreign Studies Centre
Last Update: 02-03-2015

Kazakh Kurmangazy National Conservatory

prosp. Abylaj-khana 86
Almaty 050000
Tel: +7(7272) 61-76-40
Fax: +7(7272) 72-63-48
Website: http://conservatoire.kz/
Rector: Zhanija Yakhiyevna Aubakirova

Faculty

Instrumental Performance (Musical Instruments); **Folk Music** (Jazz and Popular Music; Musical Instruments; Singing); **Musicology and Management** (Art Management; Educational Psychology; Music Education; Musicology); **Singing and Conducting** (Conducting; Singing)
History: Created 1944.
Admission requirements: Diplom o Srednem Spetsialnom Obrazovanii (Secondary School Certificate) or equivalent.
Accrediting agency: Ministry of Education and Science
Degrees and diplomas: Bakalavriat (Art Management; Conducting; Music; Music Theory and Composition; Pedagogy; Singing), Magistratura (Conducting; Music; Music Theory and Composition; Musical Instruments; Musicology; Pedagogy; Singing), Doctorantura (Art Management; Conducting; Music; Music Theory and Composition; Musical Instruments; Singing)
Last Update: 13-01-2015

Kazakh National Pedagogical University named after Abai (AASU)

prosp. Dostyk 13
Almaty 050010
Tel: +7(2729) 91-63-39
Website: http://www.kaznpu.kz
Rector: Takir Ospanovich Balykbaev

Faculty

History (Arabic; Chinese; History; Japanese; Persian; Regional Studies)

Institute

Arts, Culture and Sports (Art Education; Design; Fine Arts; Music; Music Education; Sports; Visual Arts); **Law and Economics** (Accountancy; Economics; Finance; Law; Management; Marketing; Political Sciences); **Mathematics, Physics and Informatics** (Applied Mathematics; Applied

Physics; Computer Science; Mathematics; Physics); **Natural Sciences and Geography** (Anatomy; Biochemistry; Botany; Chemistry; Geography; Physiology; Plant Pathology; Science Education; Tourism; Zoology); **Pedagogy and Psychology** (Educational Psychology; Pedagogy; Preschool Education; Primary Education; Special Education); **Philology and Multilingual Education** (English; Foreign Languages Education; International Law; International Relations; Native Language; Native Language Education; Oriental Languages; Russian)

Further information: Also preparatory courses for foreign students in Kazakh and Russian languages

History: Founded 1928 as Kazakh State University. Renamed Kazakh State Pedagogical Institute 1930, and Almaty State University named after Abai 1991. Acquired present status and title 2003.

Academic year: September to June (September-December; January-June)

Admission requirements: Competitive entrance examination following secondary school certificate

Main language(s) of instruction: Kazakh, Russian

Accrediting agency: Ministry of Education and Science

Degrees and diplomas: Bakalavriat (Accountancy; Art Education; Biology; Chemistry; Computer Science; Design; Economics; Finance; Fine Arts; Geography; Graphic Arts; History; International Law; International Relations; Law; Literature; Management; Marketing; Mathematics; Music Education; Native Language; Philology; Physical Education; Physics; Preschool Education; Primary Education; Psychology; Regional Studies; Russian; Special Education; Sports; Tourism; Translation and Interpretation), Magistratura (Accountancy; Art Education; Biology; Chemistry; Computer Science; Economics; Educational Psychology; Finance; Fine Arts; Geography; History; Law; Linguistics; Management; Mathematics; Native Language; Painting and Drawing; Pedagogy; Philology; Physical Education; Physics; Political Sciences; Preschool Education; Primary Education; Psychology; Russian; Sociology; Special Education; Sports; Tourism; Translation and Interpretation), Doctorantura (Art Education; Biology; Chemistry; Computer Science; Economics; Geography; History; Linguistics; Literature; Mathematics; Native Language; Pedagogy; Philology; Philosophy; Physics; Political Sciences; Preschool Education; Primary Education; Russian; Sociology; Special Education)

Student Services: Academic Counselling, Social Counselling, Sports Facilities, Health Services, Canteen

Periodicals: Functioning Languages in the Republic of Kazakhstan, International Relations Problems, Principles of Training Teachers at the University, Problems of Ethnopolicy in Kazakhstan, Problems of Geoecology in Kazakhstan, Problems of Sociology

Publishing house: University Publishing Centre

Last Update: 13-01-2015

Kazakh National University of Agriculture (KGAU)

ul. Abaia 8
Almaty 050010
Tel: +7(7272) 62-19-48
Fax: +7(7272) 62-11-08
Website: http://www.kaznau.kz/
Rector: Tlektes Espolov

Faculty

Agronomy, Agricultural Chemistry and Plant Protection (Agronomy; Biology; Chemistry; Ecology; Horticulture; Plant and Crop Protection; Soil Science); **Animal Health and Zootechnology** (Animal Husbandry; Biochemistry; Fishery; Food Technology; Physiology; Veterinary Science; Zoology); **Economics and Finance** (Accountancy; Agricultural Business; Banking; Economics; Finance; Law; Management; Marketing); **Energy and Information Systems** (Automation and Control Engineering; Computer Science; Electrical and Electronic Equipment and Maintenance; Energy Engineering; Information Sciences; Mathematics; Measurement and Precision Engineering; Physics; Software Engineering); **Engineering and Technology** (Agricultural Engineering; Machine Building; Maintenance Technology; Technology; Transport and Communications; Transport Management; Vocational Education); **Forestry, Land and Water Resources** (Forest Management; Forest Products; Forestry; Hydraulic Engineering; Irrigation; Natural Resources; Surveying and Mapping; Water Management); **Veterinary Medicine and Biotechnology** (Biotechnology; Gynaecology and Obstetrics; Immunology; Microbiology; Parasitology; Pharmacology; Surgery; Veterinary Science; Virology)

Department/Division

Foreign Languages (English; French; German; Modern Languages); **History and Political Science** (History; Political Sciences); **Kazakh Language** (Native Language); **Philosophy and Sociology** (Philosophy; Sociology); **Physical Education and Sport** (Physical Education; Sports); **Russian Language** (Russian)

History: Founded 1929 as Kazakh State Institute of Agriculture. Became Kazakh State University of Agriculture (Kazahskij Gosudarstvennyj Agrarnij Universitet) in 1996. Acquired current title and status in 2001.

Academic year: September to July

Admission requirements: Competitive entrance examination following general or special secondary school certificate

Main language(s) of instruction: Kazakh, Russian

Accrediting agency: Ministry of Education and Science

Degrees and diplomas: Bakalavriat (Agricultural Business; Agricultural Economics; Agricultural Equipment; Agricultural Management; Agronomy; Biotechnology; Computer Science;

Ecology; Forestry; Plant and Crop Protection; Soil Science; Transport Management; Veterinary Science; Zoology), Magistratura (Agricultural Business; Agricultural Economics; Agricultural Equipment; Agricultural Management; Agriculture; Agronomy; Biotechnology; Business Administration; Computer Science; Crop Production; Ecology; Forestry; Information Sciences; Law; Natural Resources; Plant and Crop Protection), Doctorantura (Agricultural Equipment; Agronomy; Ecology; Economics; Food Science; Forestry; Natural Resources; Plant and Crop Protection; Soil Science; Veterinary Science; Water Science)
Last Update: 13-01-2015

Kazakh National University of Arts (KazNUA)

prosp. Tauyelsyzdyk, 50
Astana 010000
Website: http://kazuniart.kz/ru/
Rector: Aiman Musakhodzhayeva

Faculty

Arts (Display and Stage Design; Painting and Drawing; Sculpture); **Dance** (Dance); **Music** (Music; Music Education; Musical Instruments; Musicology; Singing); **Theatre, Cinema and Television** (Acting; Art Criticism; Cinema and Television; Theatre); **Traditional Arts** (Singing)
History: Founded 1998.
Accrediting agency: Ministry of Education and Science
Degrees and diplomas: Bakalavriat (Art Management; Conducting; Cultural Studies; Dance; Music Education; Musical Instruments; Musicology; Painting and Drawing; Sculpture), Magistratura (Acting; Conducting; Cultural Studies; Dance; Music Education; Musical Instruments; Musicology; Painting and Drawing; Sculpture; Singing), Doctorantura (Music; Music Education; Musical Instruments; Musicology)
Last Update: 08-09-2014

Kazakh State Women's Teacher Training University

ul. Aiteke-bi 99
Almaty 050000
Tel: +7(7272) 33-86-16
Website: http://www.kazmkpu.kz
Rector: Gaukhar Aldambergenova Toremuratkyzy

Faculty

Culture and Arts (Art Education; Cultural Studies; Dance; Fine Arts; Library Science; Music; Music Education; Singing); **Education and Psychology** (Education; Educational Psychology; Pedagogy; Physical Education; Preschool Education; Primary Education; Psychology; Special Education); **Humanities and Social Sciences** (Accountancy; Administration; Economics; History; Law; Tourism); **Kazakh Philology and World Languages** (Foreign Languages Education; Literature; Native Language Education; Russian); **Mathematics and Physics** (Applied Mathematics; Computer Science; Mathematics; Mathematics Education; Physics; Science Education; Technology Education); **Natural Sciences** (Biology; Chemistry; Ecology; Geography)
History: Founded 1944. Acquired current status 2008.
Academic year: January to May; September to December
Admission requirements: Competitive entrance examination following general or special secondary school certificate
Fees: 312,000 to 350,00 per annum (Tenge)
Main language(s) of instruction: Kazakh
Accrediting agency: Ministry of Education and Science
Degrees and diplomas: Bakalavriat (Accountancy; Biology; Chemistry; Computer Science; Dance; Ecology; Economics; Education; Fine Arts; Geography; History; Law; Library Science; Linguistics; Management; Mathematics; Music; Native Language; Physics; Psychology; Russian; Social Work; Sociology; Tourism; Translation and Interpretation), Magistratura (Biology; Chemistry; Computer Science; Education; Geography; History; Linguistics; Mathematics; Native Language; Physics; Psychology; Russian; Social Work; Translation and Interpretation), Doctorantura (Biology; Chemistry; Native Language; Philology)
Last Update: 09-09-2014

Kazakh T. Zhurgenov National Academy of Art

ul. Panfilova 127
Almaty 050000
Tel: +7(7272) 61-76-40
Website: http://kaznai.kz/

Faculty

Choreography (Dance); **Design and Decorative Arts** (Computer Graphics; Fashion Design; Graphic Design; Handicrafts; Interior Design); **Film and Television** (Cinema and Television; Radio and Television Broadcasting); **History of Art** (Art History; Cinema and Television; Theatre); **Musical Arts** (Dance; Music; Performing Arts; Singing); **Painting and Sculpture** (Painting and Drawing; Sculpture); **Theatre Arts** (Acting; Display and Stage Design; Singing; Theatre)
History: Founded in 1977 as Almaty State Institute of Art and Performing Arts. Acquired current title and status 2001.
Accrediting agency: Ministry of Education and Science

Degrees and diplomas: Bakalavriat (Acting; Art Management; Conducting; Dance; Design; Display and Stage Design; Graphic Arts; Music; Painting and Drawing; Sculpture; Theatre), Magistratura (Acting; Conducting; Dance; Design; Display and Stage Design; Graphic Arts; Music; Painting and Drawing; Sculpture; Theatre), Doctorantura (Acting; Conducting; Display and Stage Design; Painting and Drawing; Sculpture)
Last Update: 13-01-2015

Kazakh Transport and Communications Academy M. Tynyshpaeva

ul. Shevchenko 97 (ug. ul. Masanchi)
Almaty 050012
Tel: +7(727) 292-09-86
Fax: +7(727) 292-57-21
Website: http://www.kazatk.kz/
President and Rector: Bakytzshan Mukhanbetovich Kuanyshev

Faculty

Automation and Telecommunications (Automation and Control Engineering; Computer Engineering; Computer Networks; Data Processing; Electrical Engineering; Electronic Engineering; Information Technology; Software Engineering; Telecommunications Engineering); **Construction and Economics** (Accountancy; Civil Engineering; Construction Engineering; Economics; Finance; Road Engineering; Transport Engineering); **Transport Engineering** (Measurement and Precision Engineering; Transport Engineering); **Transport Management** (Transport and Communications; Transport Management)
History: Founded 1976.
Accrediting agency: Ministry of Education and Science
Degrees and diplomas: Bakalavriat (Business Administration; Economics; Engineering; Transport and Communications), Magistratura (Economics; Energy Engineering; Marketing; Mechanical Engineering; Telecommunications Engineering; Transport Economics; Transport Management), Doctorantura (Engineering Management; Management; Telecommunications Engineering; Transport Economics; Transport Management)
Last Update: 02-03-2015

Kh. Dosmuhamedov Atyrau State University

prosp. Studencheskij 212
Atyrau 060011
Tel: +7(7122) 27-63-05

Website: http://www.atgu.kz
Rector: Beybit Baymagambetuly Mamrayev

Faculty

Economics and Law (Accountancy; Administration; Economics; Finance; Law; Management; Taxation; Tourism); **Foreign Languages** (Chinese; English; Foreign Languages Education; French; German; Modern Languages; Translation and Interpretation); **History and Philology** (History; Journalism; Literature; Native Language; Philology; Russian); **Natural Science** (Agronomy; Biology; Chemistry; Ecology; Fishery; Food Science; Geography; Water Management; Water Science); **Pedagogy, Psychology and Art** (Acting; Education of the Handicapped; Educational Psychology; Fashion Design; Fine Arts; Graphic Design; Music Education; Pedagogy; Performing Arts; Preschool Education; Primary Education; Psychology); **Physics and Mathematics** (Computer Science; Mathematics; Mathematics Education; Physics)
History: Created 1950.
Accrediting agency: Ministry of Education and Science
Degrees and diplomas: Bakalavriat (Agriculture; Arts and Humanities; Business Administration; Economics; Education; Education of the Handicapped; Fine Arts; Information Sciences; Journalism; Mathematics and Computer Science; Natural Sciences; Tourism; Translation and Interpretation; Water Management), Magistratura (Biology; Chemistry; Computer Science; Ecology; Economics; Education; History; Mathematics; Native Language; Philology; Physics)
Last Update: 13-01-2015

Korkyt Ata Kyzylorda State University (KSU)

ul. Ajteke-bi 29a
Kyzylorda 120014
Tel: +7(7242) 26-17-16
Fax: +7(7242) 26-27-14
Website: http://www.korkyt.kz
Rector: Kylyshbaj Aldabergenovich Bisenov

Faculty

History, Law and Economics (Business Administration; Economics; History; Law); **Humanities and Education** (*Distance Education*) (Archaeology; Biology; Business Administration; Chemistry; Design; Ecology; Economics; Ethnology; Fine Arts; Geography; History; Information Sciences; Journalism; Law; Literature; Mathematics; Modern Languages; Music Education; Native Language; Pedagogy; Physical Education; Physics; Primary Education; Psychology; Russian; Sports; Translation and Interpretation; Vocational Education);

Natural Sciences and Agricultural Technology (Agricultural Engineering; Agricultural Equipment; Agronomy; Mechanical Engineering; Natural Sciences; Transport Management)

Further information: Also Postgraduate studies

History: Founded 1937 as Kyzylorda Pedagogical Institute. Acquired present status and title 1998 following merger with 'I. Žahajev' Kyzylorda Polytechnic Institute (founded 1976), named after Korkyt Ata.

Academic year: September to June (September-January; February-June)

Admission requirements: Competitive entrance examination following secondary school certificate or special vocational school diploma, or special technical professional college diploma

Main language(s) of instruction: Kazakh, Russian

Accrediting agency: Ministry of Education and Science

Degrees and diplomas: Bakalavriat (Arts and Humanities; Business Administration; Education; Engineering; Fine Arts; Journalism; Law; Natural Sciences; Social Work; Transport Management), Magistratura (Agronomy; Biology; Chemical Engineering; Chemistry; Civil Engineering; Computer Science; Ecology; Economics; Education; Environmental Management; Information Sciences; Literature; Management; Mathematics; Modern Languages; Native Language; Pedagogy; Philology; Physics; Primary Education; Safety Engineering; Translation and Interpretation; Water Science)

Student Services: Academic Counselling, Social Counselling, Nursery Care, Cultural Activities, Sports Facilities, Language Laboratory, Health Services, Canteen

Last Update: 02-03-2015

Kostanay State Pedagogical Institute

ul. Tarana 118
Kostanay 110000
Tel: +7(7142) 53-04-55
Fax: +7(7142) 53-04-55
Website: http://www.kspi.kz
Rector: Kuat Maratuly Bajmyrzaev

Faculty

Distance Learning (Biology; Chemistry; Computer Science; Economics; Geography; History; Law; Literature; Mathematics; Modern Languages; Music Education; Native Language; Pedagogy; Physical Education; Physics; Preschool Education; Psychology; Russian; Sports; Tourism; Visual Arts; Vocational Education); **Foreign Languages** (Modern Languages); **History and Art** (Art History; Economics; History; Law; Music Education; Musical Instruments; Visual Arts); **Kazakh and Russian Philology** (Native Language; Philology; Russian); **Natural Science and Mathematics** (Biology; Chemistry; Computer Science; Geography; Mathematics; Physics); **Physical Education and Sports** (Physical Education; Sports; Tourism); **Psychology and Pedagogy** (Preschool Education; Primary Education; Psychology; Special Education)

History: Created 1939 as Kostanaj Pedagogical Institute. Acquired current status and title 2004.

Accrediting agency: Ministry of Education and Science

Degrees and diplomas: Bakalavriat (Arts and Humanities; Computer Science; Education; Fine Arts; Mathematics; Natural Sciences; Psychology; Sports; Tourism), Magistratura (Biology; Chemistry; Geography; History; Literature; Native Language; Pedagogy; Physics; Psychology; Russian)

Last Update: 02-03-2015

Kostanay State University named after Akhmet Baitursynov

prosp. Abaja 28
Kostanay 110000
Tel: +7(7142) 55-84-55
Website: http://ksu.edu.kz/
Rector: Askar Nametov Myrzakhmetovich

Faculty

Agro-Biology (Agronomy; Biology; Chemistry; Ecology); **Economics** (Accountancy; Banking; Economics; Finance; Management; Marketing); **Engineering** (Agricultural Engineering; Energy Engineering; Engineering; Machine Building; Physics; Transport Engineering); **History and Law** (History; Law); **Humanities and Social Sciences** (English; German; History; Journalism; Native Language; Philology; Psychology; Russian; Translation and Interpretation); **Information Technology** (Information Technology); **Veterinary and Food Technology** (Biotechnology; Food Technology; Veterinary Science; Zoology)

History: Founded 1939, acquired present status and title 1992.

Academic year: September to July

Admission requirements: Competitive entrance examination following general or special secondary school certificate

Main language(s) of instruction: Kazakh, Russian, English

Accrediting agency: Ministry of Education and Science

Degrees and diplomas: Bakalavriat (Agricultural Equipment; Arts and Humanities; Business Administration; Law; Mass Communication; Mathematics and Computer Science; Natural Sciences; Social Sciences; Veterinary Science), Magistratura (Agronomy; Biology; Chemistry; Computer Science; Economics; History; Journalism; Law; Management; Pedagogy; Philology; Physics; Veterinary Science), Doctorantura (Agricultural Engineering; Food Science; Veterinary Science)

Last Update: 02-03-2015

L.N. Gumilyov Eurasian National University (ENU)

ul. Mirzoyana 2
Astana 010001
Tel: +7(7172) 70-95-00
Fax: +7(7172) 70-94-57
Website: http://www.enu.kz/
Rector: Yerlan B. Sydykov

Faculty

Architecture and Construction (Architecture; Design; Fine Arts); **Economics** (Accountancy; Economics; Finance; Management; Tourism); **History** (Archaeology; Ethnology; History); **Information Technology** (Computer Science; Information Technology); **International Relations** (International Relations; Modern Languages; Oriental Studies; Political Sciences; Regional Studies); **Journalism and Political Science** (Political Sciences; Printing and Printmaking; Public Relations; Radio and Television Broadcasting); **Law** (Civil Law; Constitutional Law; Criminal Law; International Law; Labour Law; Law); **Mechanics and Mathematics** (Applied Mathematics; Mathematics; Mechanics); **Natural Sciences** (Biology; Biotechnology; Chemical Engineering; Engineering Management; Environmental Engineering; Geography; Natural Sciences); **Philology** (English; French; German; Linguistics; Literature; Modern Languages; Native Language; Philology; Russian; Translation and Interpretation); **Physics and Technical Sciences** (Electronic Engineering; Nuclear Physics; Physics; Radiophysics; Systems Analysis; Telecommunications Engineering); **Social Sciences** (Archaeology; Cultural Studies; Ethnology; History; Pedagogy; Physical Education; Psychology; Religious Studies; Social Sciences; Social Work; Sociology; Sports); **Transport and Energy** (Energy Engineering; Transport Engineering; Transport Management)
History: Founded 1996, acquired present title 2000.
Academic year: September to June (September-January; February-June)
Admission requirements: Competitive entrance examination following general or special secondary school certificate
Main language(s) of instruction: Kazakh, Russian
Accrediting agency: Ministry of Education and Science
Degrees and diplomas: Bakalavriat (Accountancy; Archaeology; Architecture; Computer Science; Cultural Studies; Design; Economics; Finance; History; Industrial Design; International Relations; Journalism; Law; Marketing; Mathematics; Native Language; Painting and Drawing; Philology; Philosophy; Physics; Political Sciences; Psychology; Public Relations; Religious Studies; Russian; Sociology; Sports; Translation and Interpretation), Magistratura (Accountancy; Archaeology; Architecture; Biology; Business Administration; Chemistry; Computer Science; Cultural Studies; Design; Economics; Finance; History; Industrial Design; International Relations; Law; Management; Mathematics; Native Language; Pedagogy; Philology; Philosophy; Physics; Political Sciences; Psychology; Religious Studies; Russian; Social Work; Sociology; Thermal Engineering; Tourism; Transport Management), Doctorantura (Archaeology; Biology; Chemistry; Computer Science; Economics; Finance; International Relations; Journalism; Law; Management; Pedagogy; Philology; Philosophy; Physics)
Student Services: Academic Counselling, Social Counselling, Cultural Activities, Sports Facilities, Health Services, Canteen
Publishing house: 'Eurasia'
Last Update: 08-09-2014

M.H. Dulaty Taraz State University

ul. Tole bi 60
Taraz 080012
Tel: +7(7262) 45-36-64
Website: http://www.tarsu.kz
Rector: Mahmetgali Nurgalievich Sarybekov

Institute

Distance Learning (Arts and Humanities; Economics; Technology); **Economics and Business** (Accountancy; Economics; Finance; Management; Marketing; Service Trades; Tourism); **Humanities and Social Sciences** (History; Journalism; Literature; Modern Languages; Native Language; Philology; Physical Education; Psychology; Russian; Sociology; Sports; Translation and Interpretation); **Law** (Civil Law; Criminology; Law; Philosophy); **Oil and Gas Mechanics** (Engineering; Mechanics; Petroleum and Gas Engineering; Power Engineering; Transport and Communications; Transport Engineering); **Postgraduate Education and Training**; **Technology and Information Systems** (Applied Mathematics; Automation and Control Engineering; Biology; Biotechnology; Chemistry; Computer Science; Design; Food Technology; Information Technology; Inorganic Chemistry; Materials Engineering; Mathematics; Measurement and Precision Engineering; Physics; Software Engineering; Textile Design); **Water Resources, Environment and Construction** (Agronomy; Architecture; Biology; Building Technologies; Construction Engineering; Environmental Engineering; Environmental Studies; Geography; Safety Engineering; Water Management)
Further information: Also Branch in Karatau
History: Founded 1998 by the merging of Zhambyl University, Zhambyl Institute of Irrigation, Land Reclamation and Construction and Zhambyl Technological Institute of Light and Food Industry.
Academic year: September to July

Admission requirements: Secondary school certificate (Atestat o srednem obrazovanii) and Certificate of United National Test

Main language(s) of instruction: Kazakh, Russian

Accrediting agency: Ministry of Education and Science

Degrees and diplomas: Bakalavriat (Agriculture; Arts and Humanities; Business Administration; Education; Engineering; Hotel and Restaurant; Natural Sciences; Tourism; Transport Management), Magistratura (Agriculture; Arts and Humanities; Business Administration; Law; Natural Sciences; Social Sciences; Transport Management), Doctorantura (Chemistry; Environmental Studies; Hydraulic Engineering)

Student Services: Cultural Activities, Sports Facilities, Language Laboratory, Health Services, Canteen

Last Update: 02-03-2015

M. Uezov Southern Kazakhstan State University (M. Auesov SKSU)

prosp. Tauke Khan 5
Shymkent 160012
Tel: +7(7252) 53-50-48
Website: http://www.ukgu.kz/
Rector: Zhumakhan Myrkhalykov

Faculty

Agro-Industry (Biotechnology; Veterinary Science; Water Management; Zoology); **Chemical Engineering** (Chemical Engineering; Chemistry; Ecology; Electronic Engineering; Environmental Management; Petroleum and Gas Engineering); **Economy and Finance** (Accountancy; Business Administration; Economics; Finance; Management; Marketing); **Information Technology, Telecommunication and Automatic System** (Electrical Engineering; Information Technology; Mathematics and Computer Science; Power Engineering; Telecommunications Engineering); **Law and International Relations** (International Relations; Law; Political Sciences); **Mechanics and Civil Engineering** (Architecture; Civil Engineering; Design; Engineering; Industrial Engineering; Mechanics; Road Engineering; Technology; Transport Management); **Philology** (Linguistics; Literature; Modern Languages); **Sports and Tourism** (Psychology; Sports; Tourism)

History: Created in 1998 by the merger of Southern Kazakhstan Technical University (Iužno-Kazahstanskij Tehnieeskij Universitet) (1943) and Southern Kazakhstan Humanities University named after M.Auezov (Iužno-Kazahstanskij Gumanitarnij Universitet im. Auezova)(1968).

Academic year: September to July

Admission requirements: Secondary school certificate

Main language(s) of instruction: Kazakh, Russian

Accrediting agency: Ministry of Education and Science

Degrees and diplomas: Bakalavriat (Agriculture; Arts and Humanities; Business Administration; Education; Engineering; Fine Arts; Food Science; Food Technology; Information Sciences; Mathematics and Computer Science; Natural Sciences; Social Sciences; Sports; Tourism; Transport and Communications; Veterinary Science; Welfare and Protective Services), Magistratura (Accountancy; Archaeology; Architecture; Biology; Biotechnology; Business Administration; Chemical Engineering; Chemistry; Computer Science; Design; Ecology; Economics; Electronic Engineering; Ethnology; Finance; Fine Arts; Geography; History; Information Sciences; Information Technology; Law; Library Science; Machine Building; Management; Marketing; Mathematics; Pedagogy; Petroleum and Gas Engineering; Philology; Philosophy; Physics; Political Sciences; Preschool Education; Primary Education; Psychology; Social Work; Transport Engineering), Doctorantura (Biotechnology; Chemical Engineering; Computer Science; Economics; Environmental Management; Materials Engineering; Mathematics; Mechanical Engineering; Philology)

Student Services: Academic Counselling, Social Counselling, Careers Guidance, Cultural Activities, Sports Facilities, Language Laboratory, Health Services, Canteen, Foreign Studies Centre

Last Update: 13-03-2015

Makhambet Utemissov West Kazakhstan State University (WKSU)

prosp. Dostyk 162
Uralsk 090000
Tel: +7(3112) 51-26-32
Fax: +7(3112) 51-26-32
Website: http://www.wksu.kz
Rector: Imangaliev Askhat Salimovich

Faculty

Education (Computer Science; Education; Pedagogy; Physical Education; Psychology); **History and Law** (History; International Relations; Law; Sociology); **Natural Sciences and Mathematics** (Biology; Chemistry; Computer Science; Ecology; Geography; Inorganic Chemistry; Mathematics; Natural Sciences; Organic Chemistry; Physics); **Philology** (English; Literature; Modern Languages; Native Language; Philology; Russian; Translation and Interpretation)

Institute

Culture and Art (Dance; Library Science; Music Education; Musical Instruments; Painting and Drawing; Singing; Theatre; Visual Arts); **Economics and Management** (Accountancy; Economics; Finance; Information Sciences; Management; Marketing; Public Administration; Tourism)

History: Founded 1932. Acquired present status 2000 by merger of Western Kazakhstan Agrarian University, Western Kazakhstan Humanitarian University and Western Kazakhstan 'Dauletkerey' Institute of Arts. Acquired present title 2003, and is the oldest University in Kazakhstan

Academic year: September to July

Admission requirements: Competitive entrance examination following secondary school certificate (Ammecmam) or equivalent

Main language(s) of instruction: Kazakh, Russian

Accrediting agency: Ministry of Education and Science

Degrees and diplomas: Bakalavriat (Arts and Humanities; Business Administration; Education; Fine Arts; Mathematics and Computer Science; Natural Sciences; Performing Arts; Social Sciences; Tourism), Magistratura (Administration; Biology; Chemistry; Design; Ecology; Economics; Geography; History; Literature; Management; Mathematics; Music Education; Native Language; Philology; Physical Education; Physics; Primary Education; Psychology; Russian)

Student Services: Academic Counselling, Social Counselling, Careers Guidance, Nursery Care, Cultural Activities, Sports Facilities, Language Laboratory, Health Services, Canteen, Foreign Studies Centre

Last Update: 02-03-2015

Marat Ospanov Western Kazakhstan State Medical University

ul. Maresyeva 68
Aktobe 030019
Tel: +7(7132) 54-48-15
Fax: +7(7132) 56-32-01
Website: http://www.zkgma.kz/
Rector: Yerbol Bekmukhambetov

Course/Programme

Medicine (Dentistry; Medicine); **Nursing** (Midwifery; Nursing); **Pharmacy** (Pharmacy); **Public Health** (Public Health)

History: Founded 1957 as Aktobe State Medical Institute. Renamed Aktobe State Medical Academy 1997. Acquired present status and title 2000.

Academic year: September to June

Admission requirements: Secondary school certificate and Common National Test with a minimum passing score of 60

Main language(s) of instruction: Kazakh, Russian, English

Accrediting agency: Ministry of Education and Science

Degrees and diplomas: Bakalavriat (Dentistry; Medicine; Nursing; Pharmacy; Public Health), Magistratura (Anaesthesiology; Anatomy; Cardiology; Gynaecology and Obstetrics; Medicine; Midwifery; Nephrology; Neurology; Nursing; Oncology; Otorhinolaryngology; Paediatrics; Pathology; Pharmacology; Public Health; Surgery; Urology), Doctorantura (Medicine; Public Health)

Student Services: Academic Counselling, Social Counselling, Cultural Activities, Sports Facilities, Language Laboratory, Health Services, Canteen, Foreign Studies Centre

Last Update: 13-03-2015

Nazarbayev University (NU)

prosp. Kabanbay Batyr 53
Astana 010000
Tel: +7(7172) 70-66-88
Website: http://nu.edu.kz/
President: Shigeo Katsu

School

Engineering (Biomedical Engineering; Chemical Engineering; Civil Engineering; Electrical and Electronic Engineering; Energy Engineering; Engineering Management; Materials Engineering; Mechanical Engineering; Robotics); **Humanities and Social Sciences** (Anthropology; Asian Studies; Economics; History; International Relations; Literature; Modern Languages; Political Sciences; Sociology); **Medicine** (Medicine); **Science and Technology** (Biology; Chemistry; Computer Science; Mathematics; Physics; Robotics)

Graduate School

Business (Business Administration); **Education** (Bilingual and Bicultural Education; Educational Administration); **Public Policy** (Political Sciences)

History: Created 2010

Academic year: Fall, Spring

Admission requirements: A pass at all stages of entrance examinations; complete secondary or vocational and technical education with average score not less than 4.5 (out of 5.0) or its equivalent

Main language(s) of instruction: English, Russian, Kazakh

Accrediting agency: Ministry of Education and Science of RK Important. Nazarbayev University is an autonomous oragnization of education that does not require the University to obtain national accreditation

Degrees and diplomas: Bakalavriat (Anthropology; Biology; Chemical Engineering; Chemistry; Civil Engineering; Computer Science; Economics; Electrical and Electronic Engineering; History; International Relations; Literature; Mathematics; Mechanical Engineering; Medicine; Modern Languages; Physics; Political Sciences; Robotics; Sociology), Magistratura (Asian Studies; Bilingual and Bicultural Education; Biological and Life Sciences; Business Administration; Educational Administration; Engineering Management;

International Relations; Political Sciences), Doctorantura (Bilingual and Bicultural Education; Biomedical Engineering; Energy Engineering; Materials Engineering; Robotics)
Last Update: 09-12-2014

Northern Kazakhstan University named after M. Kazybaev (NKSU)

ul. Puškina 86
Petropavlosk 150000
Tel: +7(7152) 49-33-52
Website: http://www.nkzu.kz/
Rector: Undassyn Ašimov

Faculty

Economics (Accountancy; Economics; Finance; Management); **Energy and Mechanical Engineering** (Electronic Engineering; Energy Engineering; Instrument Making; Mechanical Engineering; Telecommunications Engineering); **History and Law** (History; Law); **Information Technologies** (Computer Science; Information Technology; Mathematics; Physics); **Music and Pedagogics** (Design; Music; Pedagogy; Primary Education; Psychology; Singing; Speech Therapy and Audiology); **Natural Sciences and Geography** (Agriculture; Biology; Chemistry; Ecology; Geography; Natural Sciences; Organic Chemistry); **Physical Education** (Military Science; Physical Education; Sports; Tourism); **Transport and Construction Engineering** (Construction Engineering; Engineering; Transport Engineering)

Institute

Language and Literature (English; French; German; Literature; Native Language; Philology; Russian); **Retraining and Raising the Level of Professional Skills** (Administration; Computer Science; Distance Education; English; Ethics; Higher Education; Marketing; Pedagogy; Psychology; Sports; Technology)
History: Founded 1937 as Pedagogical Institute, and acquired present status 1994. Incorporated Petropavlovsk Polytechnical Institute 1996.
Academic year: September to July (September-January; February-July)
Admission requirements: Secondary school certificate (Atestat o srednem obrazovanii)
Main language(s) of instruction: Kazakh, Russian
Accrediting agency: Ministry of Education and Science
Degrees and diplomas: Bakalavriat (Arts and Humanities; Business Administration; Education; Engineering; Law; Mathematics and Computer Science; Natural Sciences; Tourism), Magistratura (Astronomy and Space Science; Economics; Education; Engineering; Journalism; Management; Modern Languages; Natural Sciences; Pedagogy; Philology), Doctorantura (Computer Science; Electrical

and Electronic Engineering; Mechanical Engineering; Telecommunications Engineering)
Student Services: Academic Counselling, Social Counselling, Careers Guidance, Cultural Activities, Sports Facilities, Language Laboratory, Health Services, Canteen, Foreign Studies Centre
Last Update: 02-03-2015

O.A. Baikonurov Zhezkazgan University

prosp. Alashakhana 16
Zhezkazgan 100600
Tel: +7(7102) 73-63-24
Fax: +7(7102) 73-60-15
Website: http://www.zhezu.kz/
Rector: Abdilmalik Argynovich Takishov

Institute

Humanities and Pedagogy (Design; Education; Fine Arts; History; Natural Sciences; Philology); **Mining Engineering** (Electrical Engineering; International Economics; Machine Building; Metallurgical Engineering; Mining Engineering)
History: Founded 1961 as Technical Faculty of Karaganda Polytechnic Institute. Became Zhezkazgan Pedagogic Institute 1975 and acquired present status and title 1996.
Admission requirements: Secondary school certificate (Atestat o srednem obrazovanii)
Main language(s) of instruction: Kazakh, Russian
Accrediting agency: Ministry of Education and Science
Degrees and diplomas: Bakalavriat (Arts and Humanities; Business Administration; Economics; Education; Engineering; Fine Arts; Mathematics and Computer Science; Natural Sciences; Pedagogy; Physical Education; Preschool Education; Primary Education; Sports; Tourism; Transport Management), Magistratura (Biology; Economics; Geography; Mathematics; Pedagogy; Philology)
Student Services: Academic Counselling, Social Counselling, Cultural Activities, Sports Facilities, Language Laboratory, Health Services, Canteen, Foreign Studies Centre
Last Update: 02-03-2015

Pavlodar State Pedagogical Institut

ul. Mira, 60
Pavlodar 140000
Tel: +7(7182) 32-47-96
Website: http://www.ppi.kz/
Rector: Nurgali Rahimgalievich Arshabekov

Faculty

Natural Sciences (Biology; Chemistry; Earth Sciences; Ecology; Geography; Mathematics and Computer Science;

Science Education); **Pedagogy and Sport** (Music Education; Pedagogy; Physical Education; Preschool Education; Primary Education; Sports); **Philology** (Economics; Law; Modern Languages; Native Language; Philology; Philosophy; Russian)
History: Created 1962.
Accrediting agency: Ministry of Education and Science
Degrees and diplomas: Bakalavriat (Educational Sciences; Natural Sciences; Preschool Education; Primary Education; Special Education)
Last Update: 02-03-2015

Rudnyi Industrial Institute

ul. 50-let. Oktjabrja 38
Rudnyi 111500
Tel: +7(71431) 50-70-3
Website: http://www.rii.kz
Rector: Abdrakhman Naizabekov

Faculty

Distance Education (Construction Engineering; Design; Economics; Information Technology; Management; Marketing; Metallurgical Engineering; Mining Engineering; Technology); **Economics and Building** (Construction Engineering; Economics; Management; Marketing); **Metallurgy and Mining** (Industrial Maintenance; Mechanical Equipment and Maintenance; Metallurgical Engineering; Mining Engineering); **Transport and Engineering Machinery** (Mining Engineering; Road Transport; Transport Management)
History: Founded 1959 as branch of Kazakh Polytechnical Institute. Acquired present status and title 1977.
Academic year: September to July.
Admission requirements: Competitive entrance examination following general Secondary School Certificate
Main language(s) of instruction: Kazakh, Russian
Accrediting agency: Ministry of Education and Science
Degrees and diplomas: Bakalavriat (Construction Engineering; Design; Economics; Energy Engineering; Environmental Management; Information Technology; Management; Marketing; Mechanical Equipment and Maintenance; Metallurgical Engineering; Mining Engineering; Road Transport; Transport Management)
Last Update: 23-01-2015

S. Amanzholov East Kazakhstan State University (VKGU)

ul. 30-Gvardeyskoy divizii, 34
Ust-Kamenogorsk 070020
Tel: +7(7232) 54-14-11

Fax: +7(7232) 54-04-07
Website: http://www.vkgu.kz
Rector: Alibec Userbayevich Kuvandykov

Faculty

Culture and Sport (Music Education; Physical Education; Sports); **Distance Education** (Biology; Chemistry; Computer Science; Ecology; Economics; English; Finance; Geography; Government; History; Information Technology; International Relations; Journalism; Law; Literature; Mathematics; Military Science; Native Language; Pedagogy; Physical Education; Physics; Political Sciences; Preschool Education; Psychology; Russian; Sports; Vocational Education); **Economics and Business** (Accountancy; Business Administration; Economics; Finance; Government; Management; Marketing; Tourism); **Environmental and Natural Sciences** (Biology; Chemistry; Ecology; Environmental Studies; Geography); **History, International Relations and Law** (History; International Relations; Law; Philosophy; Political Sciences); **Mathematics, Physics and Technology** (Agricultural Engineering; Computer Science; Materials Engineering; Mathematics; Physics; Vocational Education); **Philology** (English; German; Journalism; Literature; Native Language; Philology; Russian; Translation and Interpretation); **Psychology and Pedagogy** (Educational Psychology; Pedagogy; Preschool Education; Psychology; Social Work)
History: Founded 1952.
Accrediting agency: Ministry of Education and Science
Degrees and diplomas: Bakalavriat (Accountancy; Agricultural Equipment; Biology; Chemistry; Ecology; Economics; Education; Education of the Handicapped; Environmental Studies; Finance; Geography; Information Sciences; International Relations; Journalism; Law; Management; Marketing; Music Education; Native Language; Physics; Political Sciences; Psychology; Russian; Social Work; Tourism; Translation and Interpretation), Magistratura (Biology; Chemistry; Computer Science; Cultural Studies; Ecology; Economics; Education; Education of the Handicapped; Finance; Geography; History; Law; Mathematics; Music Education; Native Language; Philology; Physics; Tourism), Doctorantura (History; Philosophy; Physics)
Last Update: 13-01-2015

S. Seifullin Kazakh Agro-Technical University (KazATU)

prosp. Pobedy 62
Astana 010011
Tel: +7(7172) 317-547
Fax: +7(7172) 316-072
Website: http://www.agun.kz
President: Akhylbek Kazhigulovich Kurishbaev

Faculty

Agronomy (Agronomy; Ecology; Farm Management; Forest Management; Plant and Crop Protection); **Architecture** (Architecture; Design); **Computer Systems and Vocational Training** (Computer Networks; Data Processing; Software Engineering); **Economics** (Accountancy; Business and Commerce; Economics; Finance; Industrial Management; Marketing); **Energy** (Electrical Engineering; Heating and Refrigeration; Power Engineering; Telecommunications Engineering); **Humanities** (Cultural Studies; English; French; German; History; Native Language; Philosophy; Political Sciences; Russian; Sociology); **Land Planning** (Real Estate; Soil Conservation; Soil Management); **Technology** (Farm Management; Mechanical Engineering; Road Engineering; Transport Engineering); **Veterinary Science and Animal Breeding** (Animal Husbandry; Biotechnology; Fishery; Food Science; Veterinary Science)

History: Founded 1957.

Academic year: September to July

Admission requirements: Competitive entrance examination following general or special secondary school certificate

Main language(s) of instruction: Kazakh, Russian

Accrediting agency: Ministry of Education and Science

Degrees and diplomas: Bakalavriat (Agriculture; Architecture and Planning; Business Administration; Natural Sciences; Transport Management), Magistratura (Accountancy; Agricultural Equipment; Agronomy; Architecture; Biotechnology; Computer Science; Economics; Finance; Fishery; Food Science; Forestry; Information Technology; Management; Marketing; Plant and Crop Protection; Soil Science; Telecommunications Engineering; Town Planning; Transport Management; Veterinary Science), Doctorantura (Agricultural Engineering; Agronomy; Architecture; Economics; Food Science; Forestry; Management; Soil Science; Veterinary Science)

Student Services: Sports Facilities, Language Laboratory, Health Services, Canteen

Last Update: 05-03-2015

S. Toraigirov Pavlodar State University (PGU)

ul. Lomova 64
Pavlodar 140008
Tel: +7(3182) 67-36-76
Fax: +7(3182) 67-37-02
Website: http://www.psu.kz
Rector: Serik Maulenovich Omirbaev

Faculty

Agro-Technology (Agronomy; Biotechnology; Forestry; Zoology); **Architecture and Construction** (Architecture; Construction Engineering; Design; Engineering; Environmental Studies; Food Technology); **Business and Law** (Accountancy; Economics; Finance; Management); **Chemical Engineering and Natural Sciences** (Biology; Chemical Engineering; Chemistry; Ecology; Geography; Natural Sciences; Physical Education; Sports; Tourism); **Energy Engineering** (Automation and Control Engineering; Electrical Engineering; Energy Engineering; Engineering; Power Engineering; Telecommunications Engineering); **Engineering, Machine Building and Transport** (Engineering; Machine Building; Metallurgical Engineering; Petroleum and Gas Engineering; Transport and Communications; Transport Engineering); **Humanities and Education** (Archaeology; Arts and Humanities; Education; Ethnology; Journalism; Modern Languages; Philology); **Physics, Mathematics and Information Technologies** (Computer Engineering; Information Technology; Mathematics; Physics)

History: Founded 1960 as Pavlodar Industrial Institute. Acquired present status and title 1996.

Academic year: September to June (September-January; February-June)

Admission requirements: Common National Examination following secondary school certificate (Atestat o srednem obrazovanii)

Main language(s) of instruction: Russian, Kazakh

Accrediting agency: Ministry of Education and Science

Degrees and diplomas: Bakalavriat (Arts and Humanities; Education; Engineering; Information Sciences; Mathematics and Computer Science; Natural Sciences; Social Work; Tourism; Transport Management), Magistratura (Archaeology; Economics; Education; Engineering; Finance; History; Information Sciences; Library Science; Management; Mathematics and Computer Science; Natural Sciences; Philology; Philosophy; Political Sciences; Sociology; Tourism), Doctorantura (Biology; Economics; Energy Engineering; Pedagogy)

Student Services: Academic Counselling, Social Counselling, Careers Guidance, Cultural Activities, Sports Facilities, Language Laboratory, Health Services, Canteen, Foreign Studies Centre

Last Update: 02-03-2015

S.D. Asfendiyarov Kazakh National Medical University (KazNMU)

ul. Tole bi 94
Almaty 050012
Tel: +7(727) 292-70-15, +7(727) 292-78-85, +7(727) 292-79-37
Fax: +7(727) 292-70-15
Website: http://www.kaznmu.kz
Acting Rector: Nurgul K. Khamzina

Faculty

Dentistry (Anatomy; Dentistry; Forensic Medicine and Dentistry; Orthodontics; Stomatology; Surgery); **General Medicine** (Anatomy; Biophysics; Clinical Psychology; Forensic Medicine and Dentistry; Genetics; Histology; Medicine; Molecular Biology; Native Language; Pathology; Pharmacology; Physiology; Psychology; Russian; Statistics; Surgery); **Management** (Health Administration; Management); **Medical Studies** (Anatomy; Biochemistry; Forensic Medicine and Dentistry; Gynaecology and Obstetrics; Medicine; Ophthalmology; Physiology; Surgery); **Medical-prophylactic Studies** (Epidemiology; Hygiene; Nutrition; Occupational Health; Public Health); **Paediatrics** (Paediatrics); **Pharmacy** (Pharmacy)

History: Founded as Kazakh Medical Institute 1931. Renamed Almaty State Medical Institute 1961. Became Kazakh State Medical University 1996. Acquired present status and title 2001.

Academic year: September to July

Admission requirements: Secondary school certificate and entrance examination

Fees: 305,000 (Tenge)

Main language(s) of instruction: Kazakh, Russian, English

Accrediting agency: Ministry of Education and Science; Ministry of Health

Degrees and diplomas: Bakalavriat (Dentistry; Health Administration; Management; Medicine; Nursing; Pharmacy; Public Health), Magistratura (Anatomy; Cardiology; Dentistry; Dermatology; Endocrinology; Gynaecology and Obstetrics; Immunology; Management; Medicine; Nephrology; Nursing; Oncology; Ophthalmology; Otorhinolaryngology; Paediatrics; Pathology; Pharmacy; Physical Therapy; Psychiatry and Mental Health; Public Health; Rheumatology; Stomatology; Surgery; Urology), Doctorantura (Medicine; Pharmacy; Public Health). Also 30 Clinical residencies

Student Services: Academic Counselling, Social Counselling, Careers Guidance, Cultural Activities, Sports Facilities, Language Laboratory, Health Services, Canteen, Foreign Studies Centre

Periodicals: Herald of Kazakh National Medical University

Last Update: 12-03-2015

Satbayev University

ul. Satpaeva 22
Almaty 050013
Tel: +7(727) 292-60-25
Website: http://satbayev.university
Rector: Iskander Beisembetov

Institute

Information Technology (Computer Science; Electrical Engineering; Information Technology; Software Engineering); **Architecture and Civil Engineering** (Architecture; Biotechnology; Civil Engineering; Construction Engineering; Design; Ecology; Environmental Studies; Safety Engineering); **Automation and Telecommunication** (Automation and Control Engineering; Electronic Engineering; Telecommunications Engineering); **Economy and Business** (Accountancy; Economics; Finance; Management; Marketing; Public Administration); **Geological Prospecting** (Earth Sciences; Geological Engineering; Geophysics; Mineralogy); **High Technologies and Sustainable Development** (Chemistry; Ecology; Physics); **Machine Building** (Engineering; Machine Building; Materials Engineering; Mechanics); **Metallurgical Engineering and Polygraphy** (Metal Techniques; Metallurgical Engineering); **Oil and Gas** (Geology; Geophysics; Organic Chemistry; Petroleum and Gas Engineering)

History: Founded 1933 as Semipalatinsk Geological Survey Institute. Transferred to Almaty, became Kazakh Mining and Smelting Institute 1934. Became Kazakh Polytechnical Institute 1960. Tranformed into Kazakh National Technical University 1994. Became K.I. Satbayev Kazakh National Technical University (Kazakhskij Natsionalnyj Tekhničeskij Universitet imeni K.I. Satpaeva) in 1999. Became a National Research University in 2014 and acquired current title in 2017

Academic year: September to July

Admission requirements: Secondary school certificate (attestat zrelosty) and national entrance examination; national test

Fees: (Tenge): 250,000 per annum

Main language(s) of instruction: Kazakh, Russian

Accrediting agency: National Accreditation Centre of the Republic of Kazakhstan (NAC); Accreditation Agency ABET (USA); Association of Engineering Education of Russia; American University Accreditation Council (AUAC).

Degrees and diplomas: Bakalavriat (Accountancy; Administration; Architecture; Biotechnology; Chemistry; Computer Science; Design; Ecology; Economics; Energy Engineering; Finance; Geology; Information Sciences; Machine Building; Management; Marketing; Materials Engineering; Mathematics; Metallurgical Engineering; Mining Engineering; Petroleum and Gas Engineering; Physics), Magistratura (Architecture; Biotechnology; Chemistry; Economics; Finance; Information Sciences; Management; Marketing; Materials Engineering; Metallurgical Engineering; Mining Engineering; Physics; Telecommunications Engineering), Doctorantura (Automation and Control Engineering; Computer Engineering; Geological Engineering; Geology; Industrial Management; Information Technology; Materials Engineering; Mechanical Engineering; Metallurgical Engineering; Mineralogy; Mining Engineering; Organic Chemistry; Petroleum and Gas Engineering; Petrology; Physics; Power Engineering; Production Engineering; Surveying and Mapping; Telecommunications Engineering; Water Science)

Student Services: Academic Counselling, Social Counselling, Careers Guidance, Nursery Care, Cultural Activities, Sports Facilities, Language Laboratory, Health Services, Canteen, Foreign Studies Centre
Last Update: 13-01-2015

Semey State Medical University

ul. Abaja Kunanbaeva 103
Semey 071400
Tel: +7(7222) 52-22-51
Website: http://www.sgma.kz/
Rector: Tolebay Rakhypbekov

Course/Programme

Medicine (Biological and Life Sciences; Medicine; Surgery); **Nursing** (Nursing); **Pharmacy** (Pharmacy); **Public Health** (Public Health); **Stomatology** (Dentistry; Stomatology)
History: Founded 1953. Acquired present status and title 2009.
Academic year: September to July
Admission requirements: Competitive entrance examination following general or special secondary school certificate; personal certificate
Main language(s) of instruction: Kazakh, Russian, English
Accrediting agency: Ministry of Education and Science
Degrees and diplomas: Bakalavriat (Medicine; Nursing; Pharmacy; Public Health; Stomatology), Magistratura (Anaesthesiology; Cardiology; Dermatology; Endocrinology; Epidemiology; Forensic Medicine and Dentistry; Gynaecology and Obstetrics; Immunology; Medicine; Midwifery; Neurology; Oncology; Paediatrics; Pathology; Pharmacology; Psychiatry and Mental Health; Public Health; Rehabilitation and Therapy; Rheumatology; Stomatology; Surgery), Doctorantura (Medicine; Public Health)
Student Services: Academic Counselling, Social Counselling, Nursery Care, Cultural Activities, Sports Facilities, Language Laboratory, Health Services, Canteen, Foreign Studies Centre
Last Update: 13-03-2015

Sh. Ualikhanov Kokshetau State University (KokGU)

ul. Abaja 76
Kokshetau 020000
Tel: +7(7162) 72-19-56
Fax: +7(7162) 25-55-83
Website: http://kgu.kz
Rector: Abdumutalip Abzhapparovich Abzhapparov

Faculty

Economics and Information Technology (Accountancy; Economics; Finance; Information Sciences; Information Technology); **History and Law** (History; Law); **Philology** (Foreign Languages Education; German; Library Science; Literature; Native Language; Philology; Russian; Translation and Interpretation); **Physics and Mathematics** (Computer Engineering; Computer Science; Information Technology; Mathematics; Physics; Software Engineering); **Science Education** (Biotechnology; Education; Geography; Preschool Education; Primary Education; Science Education; Social Work); **Tourism, Sport and Design** (Design; Fine Arts; Hotel Management; Social Work; Sports; Tourism)

Institute

Agro-engineering (Agricultural Engineering; Agronomy; Crop Production; Forestry; Mining Engineering; Soil Science)
History: Founded 1962. Acquired present status and title 1996.
Academic year: September to July (September-January; February-July)
Admission requirements: Competitive entrance examination following general or special secondary school certificate (Attestat o srednem obrazovanii)
Main language(s) of instruction: Kazakh, Russian
Accrediting agency: Ministry of Education and Science
Degrees and diplomas: Bakalavriat (Education; Environmental Studies; Fine Arts; Hotel and Restaurant; Information Sciences; Law; Mathematics and Computer Science; Natural Sciences; Tourism), Magistratura (Agricultural Equipment; Agronomy; Biology; Chemistry; Computer Science; Ecology; Economics; Environmental Studies; Geography; History; Information Sciences; Law; Management; Marketing; Mathematics; Philology; Physics; Preschool Education; Primary Education; Russian; Social Work; Soil Science; Tourism)
Last Update: 13-01-2015

Shakarim State University Semey (SSU)

ul. Glinki 20A
Semey 490035
Tel: +7(7222) 35-83-33
Website: http://www.semgu.kz
Rector: Amirbekov Ahabaevich Sharipbek

Faculty

Agronomy (Agricultural Equipment; Animal Husbandry; Ecology; Environmental Studies; Forestry; Veterinary Science); **Economics and Finance** (Accountancy; Business and Commerce; Economics; Finance; Management; Marketing); **Engineering and Technology** (Building Technologies;

Chemistry; Dairy; Food Technology; Heating and Refrigeration; Machine Building; Meat and Poultry; Mechanics); **Humanities and Law** (History; Journalism; Law; Modern Languages; Native Language; Philology; Philosophy; Psychology; Translation and Interpretation); **Information and Communication Technology** (Geography; Geology; Information Sciences; Information Technology; Surveying and Mapping); **Natural Sciences** (Biology; Chemistry; Geography); **Philology** (Literature; Modern Languages; Native Language; Philology); **Physics and Mathematics** (Computer Science; Mathematics; Mathematics Education; Physics); **Teaching** (Education; Fine Arts; Music Education; Pedagogy)

School

Education (Educational Sciences)
History: Semey State University founded 1995. Acquired present status 2000. Previously known as Semipalatinskij Gosudarstvennyj Universitet imeni Šakarima
Academic year: September to June
Admission requirements: Secondary school certificate (Attestat o Srednem Obrazovanii or Diplom o Srednem Spetsialnom Obrazovanii)
Main language(s) of instruction: Kazakh, Russian
Accrediting agency: Ministry of Education and Science
Degrees and diplomas: Bakalavriat (Accountancy; Agronomy; Biology; Biotechnology; Chemistry; Computer Science; Design; Ecology; Economics; Finance; Fine Arts; Forestry; Geography; History; Journalism; Law; Machine Building; Management; Marketing; Mathematics; Modern Languages; Music Education; Native Language; Philology; Physics; Political Sciences; Preschool Education; Primary Education; Psychology; Russian; Social Work; Sports; Surveying and Mapping; Translation and Interpretation; Transport Management; Veterinary Science), Magistratura (Accountancy; Administration; Agronomy; Biology; Biotechnology; Chemistry; Computer Science; Ecology; Economics; Energy Engineering; Finance; Food Science; Geography; History; Law; Machine Building; Management; Mathematics; Native Language; Pedagogy; Philology; Physics; Psychology; Veterinary Science), Doctorantura (Engineering; Food Science; Physics; Veterinary Science)
Last Update: 13-01-2015

South-Kazakhstan Pedagogical Institute

ul. Dzhangildina 13
Shymkent 160000
Website: http://okmpi.kz/
Rector: Onalbai Ayashyev

School

Humanities and Social Sciences (History; Pedagogy; Psychology; Social Work); **Mathematics and Science** (Biology;

Chemistry; Computer Science; Geography; Mathematics; Physics); **New Technologies** (Art Education; Music Education; Primary Education); **Philology** (Foreign Languages Education; Literature; Modern Languages; Native Language; Native Language Education; Russian)
History: Founded 1992.
Accrediting agency: Ministry of Education and Science
Degrees and diplomas: Bakalavriat (Education; Mathematics and Computer Science; Natural Sciences)
Last Update: 02-03-2015

South-Kazakhstan State Pharmaceutical Academy

pl. Al-Farabi 1
Shymkent 160019
Tel: +7(3252) 40-82-08, +7(3252) 40-82-17
Fax: +7(3252) 40-82-22
Website: http://www.ukgma.kz/
Rector: Bakhytzhan Deribsalyevich Seksenbaev

Faculty

Medicine (Medicine; Midwifery; Nursing; Public Health); **Pharmacy** (Pharmacy)
History: Founded 1979 as Šymkent State Medical Institute, acquired present status and title 1997. Previously known as Iužno-Kazakhstanskaja Gosudarstvennaja Medicinskaja Akademija (South-Kazakhstan State Medical Academy). Acquired current title 2009.
Main language(s) of instruction: Kazakh, Russian
Accrediting agency: Ministry of Education and Science
Degrees and diplomas: Bakalavriat (Medicine; Nursing; Pharmacy; Public Health), Magistratura (Medicine; Neurology; Nursing; Paediatrics; Pathology; Pharmacy; Public Health; Surgery)
Last Update: 13-03-2015

T. Ryskulov Kazakh Economics University

ul. Zhandosova 55
Almaty 050035
Tel: +7(727) 377-11-19
Website: http://www.kazeu.kz/
Rector: Kshishtov Rybinski

School

Applied Science (Computer Science; Economics; Law; Political Sciences; Tourism); **Finance and Accounting** (Accountancy; Banking; Finance; Management)
History: Founded 1963.

Accrediting agency: Ministry of Education and Science
Degrees and diplomas: Bakalavriat (Business Administration; Law; Social Work; Tourism), Magistratura (Accountancy; Business Administration; Computer Science; Ecology; Economics; Finance; Information Technology; International Relations; Management; Marketing; Social Work; Taxation; Tourism), Doctorantura (Accountancy; Business Administration; Economics; Finance; Management; Marketing)
Last Update: 05-03-2015

Taraz State Pedagogical Institute

ul. Tole Bi 62
Taraz 080000
Tel: +7(7262) 43-58-06
Website: http://tarmpi.kz/
Rector: Dariya Perneshovna Kozhamzharova

Faculty

Creative Specialty (Dance; Military Science; Music Education; Painting and Drawing; Physical Education; Vocational Education); **Education** (Pedagogy; Psychology); **History and Geography** (Ecology; Economics; Geography; History; Law; Philosophy; Political Sciences); **Natural Sciences** (Biology; Chemistry; Computer Science; Information Technology; Mathematics; Physics); **Philology** (German; Germanic Languages; Literature; Modern Languages; Native Language; Philology; Russian)
History: Created 1968.
Accrediting agency: Ministry of Education and Science
Degrees and diplomas: Bakalavriat (Economics; Education; Fine Arts; Law; Mathematics and Computer Science; Natural Sciences)
Last Update: 02-03-2015

Zhangir Khan West Kazakhstan Agro-Technical University

ul. Zhangir Khana, 51
Uralsk 090009
Tel: +7(7112) 50-10-00
Fax: +7(7112) 50-13-74
Website: http://www.wkau.kz/
Rector: Nurlan Khabibullovich Sergaliev

Faculty

Agronomy (Agriculture; Agronomy; Biology; Ecology; Environmental Studies; Food Technology; History; Natural Resources; Philosophy; Plant and Crop Protection); **Correspondence and Distance Learning** (Accountancy; Agronomy;

Animal Husbandry; Business Administration; Construction Engineering; Ecology; Electrical Engineering; Environmental Studies; Finance; Food Technology; Forestry; Information Sciences; Instrument Making; Management; Measurement and Precision Engineering; Organic Chemistry; Petroleum and Gas Engineering; Safety Engineering; Vocational Education); **Economics and Business** (Accountancy; Business Administration; Economics; Finance; Management; Marketing); **Mechanical Engineering** (Building Technologies; Chemistry; Construction Engineering; English; German; Mechanical Engineering; Modern Languages; Petroleum and Gas Engineering); **Veterinary Medicine and Biotechnology** (Animal Husbandry; Biological and Life Sciences; Biotechnology; Fishery; Native Language; Physiology; Russian; Veterinary Science; Zoology)

School
Polytechnic (Agricultural Equipment; Energy Engineering; Information Sciences; Mathematics; Physics)
History: Created 1963. Reorganized into West-Kazakhstan Agrarian University 1996. Became part of West Kazakhstan State University 2000. Reorganized into the West-Kazakhstan Agrarian-Technical University 2002. Acquired present title 2003.
Accrediting agency: Ministry of Education and Science
Degrees and diplomas: Bakalavriat (Agriculture; Business Administration; Education; Engineering; Natural Sciences; Transport Management), Magistratura (Agriculture; Economics; Engineering; Natural Sciences; Transport Management), Doctorantura (Agricultural Engineering; Agronomy; Construction Engineering; Food Science; Soil Science; Veterinary Science)
Last Update: 02-03-2015

Private Institutions

A. Myrzakhmetova Kokshetau University (KUAM)

ul. Auezova 189A
Kokshetau 020000
Tel: +7(7162) 23-02-78
Fax: +7(3162) 25-42-59
Website: http://www.kuam.kz/
Rector: Madi Yelubayev

Faculty

Economics (Accountancy; Economics; Finance; Government; Management; Tourism); **Engineering and Environment** (Advertising and Publicity; Architectural and Environmental Design; Art History; Computer Science; Design; Ecology;

Engineering; Environmental Engineering; Fashion Design; Graphic Design; Industrial Design; Information Technology; Interior Design; Transport and Communications); **Humanities and Education** (History; International Relations; Pedagogy; Psychology; Social Work; Translation and Interpretation); **Law** (Law)
History: Founded 2000.
Accrediting agency: Ministry of Education and Science
Degrees and diplomas: Bakalavriat (Arts and Humanities; Business Administration; Design; Education; Environmental Studies; Law; Social Sciences; Social Work; Tourism), Magistratura (Accountancy; Ecology; Finance; Information Technology; Law; Management; Pedagogy), Doctorantura (Finance; Pedagogy)
Last Update: 09-03-2015

Academician K.I. Satpayev Ekibastuz Engineering and Technical Institute

ul. Energetikov 54A
Ekibastuz 141200
Tel: +7(7187) 33-35-03
Website: http://www.eitiedu.kz/
Rector: Bulat Unaibaev

Faculty

Engineering and Economics (Economics; Engineering; Technology; Transport and Communications)
History: Founded 1994.
Accrediting agency: Ministry of Education and Science
Degrees and diplomas: Bakalavriat (Building Technologies; Computer Science; Economics; Electrical and Electronic Engineering; Energy Engineering; Information Sciences; Management; Mechanical Equipment and Maintenance; Metallurgical Engineering; Mining Engineering; Transport Management)
Last Update: 27-01-2015

Academy of Economics and Law

ul. Egizbayeva 13
Almaty 050060
Tel: +7(727) 394-06-11
Website: http://www.aep.kz
Rector: Serikzhan Dzhakupovich Ospanov

Faculty

Economics (Accountancy; Banking; Economics; Finance); **Law** (Law)
History: Founded 1998.

Accrediting agency: Ministry of Education and Science
Degrees and diplomas: Bakalavriat (Accountancy; Economics; Finance; Law; Management), Magistratura (Economics; Law)
Last Update: 27-01-2015

Academy of Humanities and Technology

ul. Žambyla 35
Kokshetau 020000
Tel: +7(7162) 26-49-49
Fax: +7(7162) 26-48-28
Website: http://www.gta.kz/
Rector: Abilmazhin Ayulov

Department/Division

Economics and Management (Economics; Government; Management; Marketing; Service Trades); **Financial Management and Accounting** (Accountancy; Finance; Management); **Information Systems and Computer Engineering** (Computer Engineering; Information Technology); **Socio-Humanities** (Arts and Humanities; English; Philosophy)
History: Founded 1992. Former Kokšetau Higher College of Management and Business. A private, non-profit institution. Previously knonw as Kokšetauskij Institut Ekonomiki i Managementa (Kokshetau Institute of Economics and Management). Acquired current title 2011
Academic year: September to July
Admission requirements: Competitive entrance examinations following secondary school certificate (Atestat srednem obrazovanii)
Main language(s) of instruction: Kazakh, Russian
Accrediting agency: Ministry of Education and Science
Degrees and diplomas: Bakalavriat (Accountancy; Computer Science; Economics; Finance; Information Technology; Management; Marketing), Magistratura (Economics)
Student Services: Careers Guidance, Cultural Activities, Sports Facilities, Language Laboratory, Health Services, Canteen
Last Update: 09-03-2015

Akmeshit Institute for the Humanities and Technology

ul. G. Muratbaeva 43
Kyzylorda 120014
Fax: +7(7242)24-60-47

Course/Programme

Undergraduate (Business Administration; Engineering; Fine Arts; Social Sciences; Social Work; Transport Management)

History: Created 2009
Accrediting agency: Ministry of Education and Science
Degrees and diplomas: Bakalavriat (Business Administration; Computer Science; Construction Engineering; Economics; Energy Engineering; Fine Arts; Law; Library Science; Petroleum and Gas Engineering; Social Work; Transport Management)
Last Update: 09-03-2015

Almaty Academy of Economics and Statistics

ul. Zhandosova 59
Almaty 050035
Tel: +7(727) 309-58-15
Fax: +7(727) 309-30-00
Website: http://www.aesa.kz
Rector: Valerij Korvyakov

Faculty

Accounting (Accountancy); **Economics and Management** (Economics; Management; Marketing); **Evaluation and Statistics** (Statistics); **Finance** (Finance); **Informatics** (Computer Science); **Social Sciences and Humanities** (Commercial Law; Cultural Studies; History; Law; Modern Languages; Native Language; Pedagogy; Philosophy; Political Sciences; Psychology; Russian; Sociology)
History: Founded 1997.
Accrediting agency: Ministry of Education and Science
Degrees and diplomas: Bakalavriat (Accountancy; Computer Science; Economics; Finance; Information Technology; Management; Marketing; Mathematics), Magistratura (Computer Science; Economics; Finance; Marketing)
Last Update: 06-03-2015

Almaty Humanitarian Technical University (AGTU)

ul. Tole 109
Almaty 050012
Tel: +7(727) 292-59-00
Fax: +7(727) 292-24-43
Website: http://www.agtu.kz

Course/Programme

Graduate Studies (Economics; Information Technology; Law; Machine Building; Management; Power Engineering; Transport Management; Vocational Education); **Undergraduate Studies** (Accountancy; Computer Engineering; Design; Ecology; Economics; Engineering; Finance; Law; Management;

Measurement and Precision Engineering; Pedagogy; Power Engineering; Primary Education; Software Engineering; Taxation; Tourism; Transport and Communications; Transport Management; Vocational Education; Wood Technology)
History: Founded 1997.
Admission requirements: Certificate or diploma of basic vocational or secondary vocational school
Main language(s) of instruction: Kazakh, Russian
Accrediting agency: Ministry of Education and Science
Degrees and diplomas: Bakalavriat (Business Administration; Design; Economics; Education; Engineering; Law; Tourism), Magistratura (Computer Science; Economics; Information Technology; Law; Management; Mathematics; Mechanical Engineering; Power Engineering; Transport Engineering; Transport Management), Doctorantura (Economics)
Last Update: 06-03-2015

Astana University

ul. M. Auezova 46/1
Astana 010000
Tel: +7(717) 239-70-19
Website: http://www.astanauniver.kz
Rector: Yerzhan Ertaevich Karsibaev

Faculty

Economics (Business Administration; Economics); **Engineering** (Engineering; Transport and Communications); **Foreign Languages** (International Relations; Modern Languages; Translation and Interpretation); **Humanities** (Ecology; Preschool Education; Primary Education); **Law** (Law)
History: Created 2010.
Accrediting agency: Ministry of Education and Science
Degrees and diplomas: Bakalavriat (Business Administration; Education; Engineering; Information Technology; Law; Social Sciences; Technology), Magistratura (Computer Science; Ecology; Economics; Information Technology; International Law; Law; Machine Building; Marine Engineering; Modern Languages; Petroleum and Gas Engineering; Transport Engineering; Transport Management)
Last Update: 05-03-2015

Atyrau Engineering-Humanitarian Institute

ul. Khudina 5a
Atyrau 060011
Tel: +7(7122) 20-51-08

Website: http://www.aigi.kz
Rector: Ersain Ikhsanov

Course/Programme

Arts and Humanities (Arts and Humanities); **Engineering** (Engineering)
History: Founded 2001.
Accrediting agency: Ministry of Education and Science
Degrees and diplomas: Bakalavriat (Building Technologies; Computer Science; Economics; Finance; Modern Languages; Petroleum and Gas Engineering; Taxation; Telecommunications Engineering)
Last Update: 13-01-2015

Bolashak Karaganda University

ul. Yerubayeva 16
Karaganda 100008
Tel: +7(7212) 42-04-25
Fax: +7(7212) 42-04-21
Website: http://www.kubolashak.kz/
Rector: Kuralbay Nesipbekovich Menlibaev

Faculty

Economics and Informatics (Computer Science; Economics; Finance; Information Technology; Management); **Humanities and Education** (Cultural Studies; Modern Languages; Native Language; Pedagogy; Political Sciences; Preschool Education; Psychology; Translation and Interpretation); **Law** (Civil Law; Criminal Law; Law); **Pharmacy** (Chemistry; Organic Chemistry; Pharmacy)
History: Founded 1995.
Accrediting agency: Ministry of Education and Science
Degrees and diplomas: Bakalavriat (Business Administration; Computer Science; Cultural Studies; Economics; Law; Modern Languages; Pharmacy; Political Sciences; Translation and Interpretation), Magistratura (Economics; Information Technology; Native Language)
Last Update: 09-03-2015

Bolashak University

prosp. Abaja 31A
Kyzylorda 123000
Tel: +7(72422) 20-22-72
Fax: +7(72422) 20-22-80

Course/Programme

Postgraduate (Ecology; Economics; Education; History; Native Language; Pedagogy); **Undergraduate** (Arts and Humanities; Business Administration; Computer Science;

Ecology; Economics; Education; Engineering; Natural Sciences; Transport Management)
History: Founded 1995 as branch of Moscow International University of Business and Information Technologies. Became Kyzylorda University of Economics, Statistics and Informatics 2000. Acquired present title 2002.
Accrediting agency: Ministry of Education and Science
Degrees and diplomas: Bakalavriat (Arts and Humanities; Business Administration; Computer Science; Ecology; Education; Engineering; Law; Library Science; Natural Sciences; Transport Management), Magistratura (Ecology; Economics; History; Native Language; Pedagogy; Primary Education)
Last Update: 09-03-2015

Caspian University

prosp. Seifullina 521
Almaty 050000
Tel: +7(727) 250-69-34
Website: http://www.cu.edu.kz/
Rector: Zholdasbek Nusenov

Course/Programme

Economics and Management (Accountancy; Economics; Finance; Management; Marketing; Psychology); **Engineering** (Architecture; Automation and Control Engineering; Computer Engineering; Computer Science; Design; Engineering Management; Environmental Engineering; Geological Engineering; Petroleum and Gas Engineering); **Humanities** (Literature; Native Language; Nursing; Translation and Interpretation); **Law** (Law)
History: Founded 1992.
Accrediting agency: Ministry of Education and Science
Degrees and diplomas: Bakalavriat (Arts and Humanities; Business Administration; Engineering; Nursing; Social Sciences), Magistratura (Economics; Finance; Geological Engineering; Law; Management; Petroleum and Gas Engineering), Doctorantura (Finance; Law)
Last Update: 06-03-2015

Central Kazakhstan Academy

ul. Pushkina 259
Karaganda 100012
Tel: +7(7212) 47-50-69
Website: http://c-k-a.kz/
Rector: Bakhtybai Zhunusov

Faculty

Economics (Accountancy; Economics; Finance; Management; Marketing; Public Administration); **Education and**

Social Work (Education; Social Work); **Foreign Languages** (Modern Languages; Translation and Interpretation); **Law** (Law)
History: Founded 1996. Previously known as Tsentralno-Kazahstanskij Universitet MGTI-Lingva (Central Kazakhstan University MGTI-Lingua).
Accrediting agency: Ministry of Education and Science
Degrees and diplomas: Bakalavriat (Arts and Humanities; Business Administration; Computer Science; Design; Economics; Education; Psychology; Social Work), Magistratura (Economics; Law; Philology)
Last Update: 09-03-2015

Central-Asian University (CAU)

ul. Dzhandosova 60
Almaty 050060
Tel: +7(727) 274-74-54, +7(727) 274-74-24
Fax: +7(727) 274-78-40
Website: http://www.cau.kz/
Rector: Sailow Kasabekob

Faculty

Automation and Information Technology (Computer Science; Electrical Engineering; Electronic Engineering; Information Technology; Mathematics; Telecommunications Engineering); **Economics and Business** (Accountancy; Economics; Finance; Management; Marketing; Public Administration; Service Trades; Tourism); **Foreign Languages and Translation** (Arabic; Chinese; English; French; German; Regional Studies; Translation and Interpretation; Turkish); **International Relations and Humanities** (Arts and Humanities; Education; International Relations; Natural Sciences); **Law** (International Law; Justice Administration; Law); **Oil and Gas Industry** (Architecture and Planning; Geological Engineering; Mining Engineering; Petroleum and Gas Engineering)

Institute

Mechanical Engineering and Transport (Mechanical Engineering; Transport Management)
History: Founded 1997.
Accrediting agency: Ministry of Education and Science
Degrees and diplomas: Bakalavriat (Arts and Humanities; Education; Engineering; Fine Arts; Information Sciences; Law; Mathematics and Computer Science; Natural Sciences; Transport and Communications), Magistratura (Accountancy; Biotechnology; Computer Science; Ecology; Economics; Finance; Information Technology; Law; Management; Marketing; Materials Engineering; Mathematics; Mechanical Equipment and Maintenance; Native Language; Pedagogy; Petroleum and Gas Engineering; Preschool Education; Psychology; Road Transport; Telecommunications Engineering; Thermal Engineering; Translation and Interpretation; Transport Management), Doctorantura (Computer Science; Economics; Finance; Law; Management; Translation and Interpretation; Transport Management)
Last Update: 13-01-2015

D.A. Kunaev University of Humanities, Law, and Transport

ul. Kurmangazy 107
Almaty 050022
Tel: +7(727) 292-98-87
Fax: +7(727) 292-98-77
Website: http://www.vuzkunaeva.kz/

Faculty

Humanities and Economics (Accountancy; Business Administration; Economics; Finance; Government; History; Modern Languages; Regional Studies; Social Sciences; Translation and Interpretation); **Law** (Civil Law; Constitutional Law; Criminal Law; Criminology; International Law; Law; Police Studies)
History: Founded 1944. Previously known as D.A. Kunaev University (Universitet imeni D.A. Kunaeva). Acquired current title and status 2013.
Accrediting agency: Ministry of Education and Science
Degrees and diplomas: Bakalavriat (Business Administration; Design; Economics; History; Law; Translation and Interpretation; Transport and Communications), Magistratura (Economics; Finance; History; Industrial Management; Law; Road Transport; Transport Engineering; Transport Management), Doctorantura (Industrial Management; Law; Road Transport; Transport Engineering; Transport Management)
Last Update: 05-03-2015

Eurasian Humanitarian Institute

prosp. Zhumabayeva 4
Astana 010009
Tel: +7(717) 256-19-33
Fax: +7(717) 256-19-33
Website: http://www.egi.kz/
Rector: Amangeldi Kusainovich Kusainov

Faculty

Economics and Mathematics (Economics; Finance; Mathematics); **Education** (Education); **Foreign Languages** (Modern Languages); **Kazakh and Russian Philology** (Literature; Native Language); **Law** (Law)

History: Created and acquired status 1995.
Admission requirements: Secondary School Certificate, National Test
Main language(s) of instruction: Kazakh, Russian
Accrediting agency: Ministry of Education and Science
Degrees and diplomas: Bakalavriat (Business Administration; Economics; Education; Law; Modern Languages), Magistratura (Economics; History; Primary Education)
Student Services: Academic Counselling, Social Counselling, Careers Guidance, Cultural Activities, Sports Facilities, Language Laboratory, Health Services, Canteen
Last Update: 05-03-2015

Finance Academy

ul. Sh. Ualikhanova 11
Astana
Website: http://fin-academy.kz/index.php/kz/
Rector: Olga Janovskaja

Department/Division

Accounting (Accountancy); **Economics and Management** (Economics; Management); **Finance** (Finance)
History: Created 2009.
Accrediting agency: Ministry of Education and Science
Degrees and diplomas: Bakalavriat (Accountancy; Computer Science; Economics; Finance; Management; Taxation), Magistratura (Accountancy; Economics; Finance; Management)
Last Update: 23-01-2015

Innovative University of Eurasia (InEU)

ul. Lomova 45
Pavlodar 140003
Tel: +7(7182) 34-47-50
Fax: +7(7182) 34-47-50
Website: http://www.ineu.edu.kz/
Rector: Askar Yusopovich Kamerbayev

College

Economics (Finance; Management); **Information Technology** (Automation and Control Engineering; Electrical and Electronic Engineering; Heating and Refrigeration; Maintenance Technology; Power Engineering; Software Engineering); **Polytechnic** (Construction Engineering; Food Technology; Maintenance Technology; Metal Techniques)

Course/Programme

Aspirantura (*Postgraduate*) (Economics; Electrical and Electronic Engineering; Energy Engineering; Food Science; Food Technology; Mathematics; Metallurgical Engineering; Pedagogy; Psychology; Russian); **Master** (Automation and Control Engineering; Biology; Biotechnology; Computer Science; Economics; Educational Psychology; Heating and Refrigeration; Information Management; Management; Measurement and Precision Engineering; Pedagogy; Philology; Power Engineering; Psychology; Safety Engineering; Sociology; Software Engineering)

Academy

Agricultural Science (*Engineering Academy*) (Animal Husbandry); **Arts** (*Engineering Academy*) (Architecture; Design); **Business and Law** (Accountancy; Economics; Finance; Government; Journalism; Law; Management; Psychology; Taxation); **Education** (*Pedagogical Academy*) (Biotechnology; Chemistry; Economic History; Educational Psychology; English; Geography; German; History of Law; Literature; Mathematics; Native Language; Physical Education; Primary Education; Russian; Sports); **Humanities** (*Pedagogical Academy*) (Chinese; English; German; History; Native Language; Philology; Russian; Translation and Interpretation); **Natural Sciences** (*Pedagogical Academy*) (Biology; Chemistry; Computer Science; Ecology; Geography; Mathematics; Physics); **Service** (*Engineering Academy*) (Maintenance Technology; Transport and Communications; Transport Management); **Technical Science** (*Engineering Academy*) (Biotechnology; Construction Engineering; Food Technology; Heating and Refrigeration; Information Technology; Inorganic Chemistry; Machine Building; Measurement and Precision Engineering; Metallurgical Engineering; Mining Engineering; Organic Chemistry; Power Engineering; Safety Engineering; Transport Engineering)

Research Division

Energy Saving Technologies (Energy Engineering; Metallurgical Engineering; Thermal Engineering); **Social Problems** (Sociology); **Sustainable Regional Development**
History: Founded 1991, acquired present status and title 2006. Previously known as Pavlodarskij Universitet.
Academic year: September to June (September-January; February-June)
Admission requirements: Competitive entrance examination following secondary school certificate (Atestat o srednem obrazovanii)
Main language(s) of instruction: Kazakh, Russian
Accrediting agency: Ministry of Education and Science
Degrees and diplomas: Bakalavriat (Agriculture; Arts and Humanities; Business Administration; Education; Engineering; Environmental Studies; Law; Mathematics and Computer Science; Natural Sciences; Social Sciences; Veterinary Science), Magistratura (Biology; Biotechnology; Chemical Engineering; Computer Science; Economics; Education; Electronic Engineering; Engineering Management;

Environmental Engineering; Information Technology; Management; Mathematics; Metallurgical Engineering; Philology; Psychology; Sociology; Thermal Engineering), Doctorantura (Biotechnology; Economics)

Student Services: Academic Counselling, Social Counselling, Careers Guidance, Cultural Activities, Sports Facilities, Language Laboratory, Health Services, Canteen, Foreign Studies Centre

Last Update: 10-03-2015

International Academy of Business

ul. Rozybakieva 227
Almaty 050060
Tel: +7(727) 302-22-22
Website: http://www.iab.kz/
President-Rector: Asylbek Kozhakhmetov

Course/Programme

Postgraduate (Business Administration; Transport Management); **Undergraduate** (Advertising and Publicity; Business Administration; Economics; Hotel and Restaurant; Information Technology; Law; Regional Studies; Transport Management)

History: Created 1988 as Almaty School of Management (Almatynskaja Škola Menedžmenta). Acquired current title and status 2002.

Accrediting agency: Ministry of Education and Science

Degrees and diplomas: Bakalavriat (Business Administration; Hotel and Restaurant; Law; Social Sciences; Transport Management), Magistratura (Business Administration; Economics; Finance; Marketing; Transport Management), Doctorantura (Business Administration)

Last Update: 05-03-2015

International Educational Corporation

ul. Ryskulbekova 28 Street
Almaty 050043
Tel: +7(727) 309-61-47
Website: http://www.mok.kz/
Rector: Serik Djoldasbekovich Sikhimbayev

Faculty

Applied Sciences (Information Technology; Mathematics; Mathematics and Computer Science; Physics; Telecommunications Engineering); **Architecture** (Architecture; Town Planning); **Building Technologies, Infrastructure and Management** (Building Technologies; Engineering Management; Heating and Refrigeration; Management; Materials Engineering; Safety Engineering; Surveying and Mapping;

Wood Technology); **Construction** (Building Technologies; Civil Engineering; Construction Engineering; Industrial Engineering); **Design** (Design; Fashion Design; Graphic Design; Industrial Design); **Humanities** (Journalism; Law; Political Sciences; Regional Studies; Social Studies; Translation and Interpretation)

History: Created 2007 after merger between Kazakh Leading Academy of Architecture and Civil Engineering (Kazahskaja Golovnaja Arhitekturno-Stroitelnaja Akademija) and Kazakh-American University (Kazahsko-Amerikanskij Universitet).

Accrediting agency: Ministry of Education and Science

Degrees and diplomas: Bakalavriat (Accountancy; Architecture; Computer Science; Design; Earth Sciences; Economics; Finance; International Relations; Journalism; Law; Telecommunications Engineering; Tourism; Translation and Interpretation; Wood Technology), Magistratura (Architecture; Construction Engineering; Design; Earth Sciences; Economics; Environmental Engineering; Environmental Management; Management; Wood Technology), Doctorantura (Architecture; Construction Engineering; Design; Wood Technology)

Last Update: 13-03-2015

International Humanitarian-Technical University

ul. Baitursynova 80
Shymkent 160021
Website: http://hgtu.kz/

Faculty

Economics and Law (Accountancy; Economics); **Fine Arts and Sport** (Fine Arts; Sports); **Pedagogy** (Geography; History; Pedagogy; Philology; Psychology); **Sciences and Technology** (Biology; Chemistry; Ecology; Mathematics and Computer Science; Measurement and Precision Engineering)

History: Created 2010

Accrediting agency: Ministry of Education and Science

Degrees and diplomas: Bakalavriat (Arts and Humanities; Business Administration; Education; Fine Arts; Information Technology; Law; Natural Sciences; Social Sciences), Magistratura (Economics)

Last Update: 12-03-2015

Kainar University

ul. Satpajeva 7a
Almaty 480013
Tel: +7(727) 255-84-58
Website: http://kainar-edu.kz/
Rector: Yerengaip Salipovič Omarov

Course/Programme

Arts (Design; Journalism); **Economics** (Accountancy; Economics; Finance; Management; Tourism); **Humanities** (International Relations; Law; Literature; Modern Languages; Native Language; Translation and Interpretation); **Social Science** (Pedagogy; Psychology); **Technology** (Computer Science; Information Technology)

History: Founded 1991, acquired present status 1992.

Academic year: September to June

Admission requirements: Competitive entrance examinations following secondary school leaving certificate (Atestat o srednem obrazovanii), health certificate, military card (only for males)

Main language(s) of instruction: Kazakh, Russian

Accrediting agency: Ministry of Education and Science

Degrees and diplomas: Bakalavriat (Business Administration; Design; Information Sciences; Modern Languages; Pedagogy; Tourism; Translation and Interpretation), Magistratura (Economics; Finance; History; Information Technology; Law; Management; Native Language; Psychology)

Student Services: Academic Counselling, Social Counselling, Careers Guidance, Nursery Care, Cultural Activities, Sports Facilities, Language Laboratory, Health Services, Foreign Studies Centre

Last Update: 06-03-2015

Karaganda Economics University of Kazpotrebsoyuz (KEUK)

ul. Akademičeskaja 9
Karaganda 100009
Tel: +7(7212) 44-16-12
Website: http://www.keu.kz
Rector: Yerkara Aimagambetov Balkaraevich

Faculty

Accountancy and Finance (Accountancy; Banking; Computer Science; Economics; Finance; Insurance; Physical Education; Taxation); **Business and Law** (Law; Marketing; Social Work; Taxation; Tourism); **Economics and Management** (Economics; International Economics; Management; Mathematics; Modern Languages; Native Language; Public Administration; Russian)

Further information: Branches in Astana, Pavlodar, Kostanai, Shymkent and Kyzylorda

History: Founded 1966, acquired present status and title 1997.

Academic year: September to June

Admission requirements: Secondary school certificate (Gosudarstvennyj obrazovatelnyj sertifikat)

Main language(s) of instruction: Kazakh, Russian

Accrediting agency: Ministry of Education and Science

Degrees and diplomas: Bakalavriat (Business Administration; Ecology; Economics; Hotel and Restaurant; Law; Social Work; Transport Management), Magistratura (Accountancy; Economics; Finance; Information Technology; Law; Management; Marketing; Taxation; Tourism), Doctorantura (Economics; Management)

Student Services: Academic Counselling, Social Counselling, Cultural Activities, Sports Facilities, Health Services, Canteen

Last Update: 09-03-2015

Kazakh Academy of Engineering, Finance and Banking

prosp. Zhibek zholy 184/15-17
Almaty 050000
Tel: +7(727) 253-74-12
Website: http://kifba.kz/

Course/Programme

Postgraduate (Finance; Transport Engineering; Transport Management); **Undergraduate** (Business Administration; Design; Economics; Engineering; Technology; Tourism; Transport Management)

History: Created 2012.

Accrediting agency: Ministry of Education and Science

Degrees and diplomas: Bakalavriat (Business Administration; Engineering; Transport Management), Magistratura (Finance; Transport Engineering), Doctorantura (Transport Engineering)

Last Update: 05-03-2015

Kazakh Academy of Labour and Social Relations

ul. Nauryzbai batyra 9
Almaty 050004
Tel: +7(727) 279-95-70
Fax: +7(727) 279-95-70
Website: http://www.atso.kz/
Rector: Bayan Besbayeva

Faculty

Economics (Accountancy; Computer Science; Economics; Finance; Management; Marketing; Software Engineering); **Humanities** (International Relations; Political Sciences; Psychology; Regional Studies; Social Work)

School

Law (Law)

Department/Division

Oriental and Western Languages (*Interfaculty*) (Chinese; English; French; German; Japanese; Korean; Native Language; Turkish)
History: Founded 1996.
Accrediting agency: Ministry of Education and Science
Degrees and diplomas: Bakalavriat (Accountancy; Computer Science; Economics; Finance; International Relations; Law; Management; Marketing; Psychology; Regional Studies), Magistratura (Economics; Law)
Last Update: 06-03-2015

Kazakh Engineering and Pedagogical University of Friendship of Nations

ul. Tole bi 32
Shymkent 160020
Tel: +7(7252) 53-01-59
Fax: +7(7252) 55-81-63
Website: http://ukpu.kz/
President: Madijar Yunusov

Faculty

Pedagogy (Biology; Chemistry; Fine Arts; Mathematics and Computer Science; Pedagogy); **Philology** (Economics; Geography; Law; Literature; Native Language; Philology)
Accrediting agency: Ministry of Education and Science
Degrees and diplomas: Bakalavriat (Arts and Humanities; Education; Fine Arts; Law; Mathematics and Computer Science; Natural Sciences), Magistratura (Biology; Chemical Engineering; Chemistry; Economics; Education; History; Native Language; Philology; Translation and Interpretation)
Last Update: 12-03-2015

Kazakh Engineering-Technical Academy (CITA)

ul. Zheltoksan 22A
Astana 010000
Tel: +7(7172) 32-07-94
Website: http://www.kazita.kz/
Rector: Kanat Tulenbayev

Course/Programme

Engineering and Technology (Accountancy; Economics; Engineering; Information Technology; Technology)
History: Founded 1997.
Accrediting agency: Ministry of Education and Science

Degrees and diplomas: Bakalavriat (Accountancy; Economics; Finance; Information Technology; Management; Surveying and Mapping), Magistratura (Economics)
Last Update: 05-03-2015

Kazakh Humanitarian Juridical Innovative University

ul. Abaya 94
Semey 0714000
Tel: +7(7222) 52-52-26
Website: http://www.semuniver.kz/
Rector: Kurmanbayeva Shyryn

Faculty

Finance and Economics (Accountancy; Economics; Finance; Management); **Humanities** (Arts and Humanities; Geography; History; Philology); **Information Technology** (Accountancy; Biology; Computer Science; Mathematics)

School

Law (Civil Law; Criminal Law; Law; Public Law)
History: Founded 1997.
Accrediting agency: Ministry of Education and Science
Degrees and diplomas: Bakalavriat (Arts and Humanities; Business Administration; Education; Law; Mathematics and Computer Science; Natural Sciences; Service Trades), Magistratura (Computer Science; Economics; History; Law; Philology)
Last Update: 09-03-2015

Kazakh University of Economy, Finance and International Trade (KazUEFiMT)

ul. Zhubanova 7
Astana 010005
Tel: +7(7172) 27-85-71
Website: http://www.kuef.kz/
Rector: Sarsengali Abdymanapov

School

Applied Science (Computer Science; Design; Marketing; Social Work; Tourism); **Economics** (Accountancy; Economics; Finance; International Economics; Management; Marketing; Statistics)
History: Founded 1999.
Accrediting agency: Ministry of Education and Science
Degrees and diplomas: Bakalavriat (Business Administration; Mathematics and Computer Science; Social Work; Statistics; Tourism), Magistratura (Accountancy; Finance; Management; Mathematics and Computer Science; Social Work; Statistics)
Last Update: 05-03-2015

Kazakh University of Technology and Business

prosp. Respublika 54/2, rajon Sary-Arka
Astana 010000
Website: http://www.kazutb.kz/
Rector: Yesenbai A. Alpeisov

Faculty

Business and Information Technology (Accountancy; Economics; Finance; Information Technology; Management; Tourism); **Technology** (Biotechnology; Building Technologies; Chemical Engineering; Design; Ecology; Environmental Management; Technology)
History: Founded 2004.
Accrediting agency: Ministry of Education and Science
Degrees and diplomas: Bakalavriat (Biotechnology; Business Administration; Ecology; Economics; Information Technology; Tourism), Magistratura (Chemical Engineering; Economics; Information Technology; Management)
Last Update: 05-03-2015

Kazakh-American Free University (KAFU)

prosp. Nezavisimosti 86
Ust-Kamenogorsk 070000
Tel: +7(7232) 52-30-70
Website: http://www.kafu.kz/
President: Yerezhep Mambetkaziyev

Deanery

Pedagogy and Psychology (Pedagogy; Psychology)

School

Business, Law, and Education (Business Administration; Education; Law)

Department/Division

Foreign Languages (Modern Languages; Translation and Interpretation); **Law and International Relations** (International Relations; Law)
History: Founded 1994.
Accrediting agency: Ministry of Education and Science
Degrees and diplomas: Bakalavriat (Business Administration; Economics; Education; Law; Modern Languages; Psychology; Tourism; Translation and Interpretation), Magistratura (Finance; Information Technology; International Relations; Law; Management; Modern Languages; Psychology; Translation and Interpretation), Doctorantura (Law; Management)
Last Update: 09-03-2015

Kazakh-British Technical University (KBTU)

ul. Tole Bi, 59
Almaty 050000
Tel: +7(327) 250-46-58
Fax: +7(327) 272-46-37
Website: http://www.kbtu.kz
Rector: Iskander Kalybekovich Byeisembetov

Faculty

Information Technology (Automation and Control Engineering; Computer Science; Information Technology); **Petroleum and Gas Engineering** (Geological Engineering; Mining Engineering; Petroleum and Gas Engineering)

School

Business (Banking; Economics; Finance; Management); **Chemical Engineering** (Chemical Engineering); **Economics** (Economics)
History: Created in 2001 in conjunction with the British government as a joint venture between the Ministry of Education and Science and the British Council.
Main language(s) of instruction: Russian, English
Accrediting agency: Ministry of Education and Science
Degrees and diplomas: Bakalavriat, Magistratura (Chemical Engineering; Economics; Finance; Information Technology; Management; Petroleum and Gas Engineering), Doctorantura (Chemical Engineering; Management; Materials Engineering; Mathematics and Computer Science; Metallurgical Engineering; Nanotechnology; Petroleum and Gas Engineering)
Student Services: Academic Counselling, Cultural Activities, Sports Facilities, Language Laboratory, Health Services, Canteen
Last Update: 05-03-2015

Kazakh-China Institute

ul. Michurina 1A
Kyzylorda 120000
Tel: +7(7242) 23-02-51
Website: http://www.kazki.kz/
Rector: Kazhdenbek Nuraliyev

Course/Programme

Computer Hardware and Software (Computer Engineering; Software Engineering); **Ecology** (Ecology); **Economics** (Economics); **Finance** (Finance); **Foreign Languages** (Chinese); **History** (History); **Kazakh Language and Literature** (Literature; Native Language); **Music Education** (Music Education); **Oil and Gas Business** (Business Administration;

Petroleum and Gas Engineering); **Pedagogy and Methodology of Elementary Education** (Pedagogy; Primary Education); **Principles of Law and Economics** (Economics; Law)
History: Founded 1993.
Accrediting agency: Ministry of Education and Science
Degrees and diplomas: Bakalavriat (Computer Science; Ecology; Economics; Education; Modern Languages; Music Education; Petroleum and Gas Engineering), Magistratura (Economics; Pedagogy)
Last Update: 09-03-2015

Kazakh-German University (KNU)

ul. Pushkina 111
Almaty 050010
Tel: +7(727) 355-05-51
Fax: +7(727) 355-05-52
Website: http://www.dku.kz/
Rector: Olga D. Moskovchenko

Faculty

Economics (Finance; Management; Marketing); **Engineering and Economics** (Business Computing; Thermal Engineering; Transport Management); **Social and Political Sciences** (International Relations; Political Sciences; Regional Studies)
History: Founded 1999.
Accrediting agency: Ministry of Education and Science
Degrees and diplomas: Bakalavriat (Accountancy; Finance; Information Technology; International Relations; Management; Marketing; Political Sciences; Thermal Engineering; Transport Management), Magistratura (Finance; Management; Regional Studies; Transport Management)
Last Update: 06-03-2015

Kazakh-Russian International University (KRMU)

ul. Aiteke bi 52
Aktobe 030006
Tel: +7(7132) 21-06-64
Fax: +7(7132) 21-06-08
Website: http://www.krmu.kz/
Rector: Altyn Myrzashova

Department/Division

Economics (Business Administration); **Kazakh History** (History); **Law** (Law); **Psychology, Philology and Translation** (Philology; Psychology; Translation and Interpretation); **Technical and Natural Science** (Natural Sciences; Technology)

History: Founded 1994.
Accrediting agency: Ministry of Education and Science
Degrees and diplomas: Bakalavriat (Accountancy; Building Technologies; Chemistry; Computer Science; Design; Environmental Studies; Finance; Information Technology; Law; Management; Marketing; Philology; Psychology; Tourism; Translation and Interpretation), Magistratura (Design; Environmental Management; Finance; Law; Management)
Last Update: 09-03-2015

Kazakhstan Engineering-Technological University (KAZETU)

prosp. Al Farabi 93A
Almaty 050060
Tel: +7(727) 3-000-777
Website: http://www.kazetu.kz/
Rector: Nailya Djerembayeva

Faculty

Computer Science, Automation and Telecommunications (Automation and Control Engineering; Computer Science; Electronic Engineering; Software Engineering; Telecommunications Engineering); **Economics and Finance** (Accountancy; Economics; Finance; Marketing; Service Trades; Tourism); **Natural Sciences** (Biotechnology; Organic Chemistry); **Social Sciences and Humanities** (Economics); **Technology, Standardization and Certification** (Horticulture; Measurement and Precision Engineering; Soil Science)
History: Founded 2001.
Accrediting agency: Ministry of Education and Science
Degrees and diplomas: Bakalavriat (Agriculture; Business Administration; Engineering; Mathematics and Computer Science; Natural Sciences; Tourism), Magistratura (Biotechnology; Food Technology; Horticulture; Maintenance Technology; Mechanical Engineering)
Last Update: 06-03-2015

Kazakhstan Innovative University

ul. Bayseitova 5
Semey 071400
Tel: +7(722) 256-22-53
Website: http://www.kiu.kz/
Rector: Erzhan Zainullinovich Adil'gazinov

Faculty

Economics and Information Systems (Accountancy; Computer Science; Economics; Finance; Information Technology; Management; Tourism); **Law, Education, and Humanities**

(Law; Modern Languages; Native Language; Pedagogy; Psychology)

History: Created 1992 as Agro-technical Institute. Became Kazakh Finance-Economic Academy (Kazahskaja Finansovo-Ekonomičeskaja Akademija) in 2008, and acquired current title and status in 2013.

Accrediting agency: Ministry of Education and Science

Degrees and diplomas: Bakalavriat (Accountancy; Computer Science; Economics; Finance; Fine Arts; Information Technology; Law; Literature; Management; Modern Languages; Pedagogy; Tourism; Translation and Interpretation), Magistratura (Accountancy; Economics; Finance; Information Technology; Law; Literature; Management; Modern Languages; Pedagogy)

Last Update: 13-01-2015

Kazakhstan-Russian Medical University

ul. Torekulova 71
Almaty 050004
Tel: +7(727) 250-83-72
Website: http://www.k-rmu.kz/
Rector: Aliyev Mukhtar

Course/Programme

Medicine (Dentistry; Medicine; Nursing; Pharmacy; Public Health)

History: Founded 1992.

Accrediting agency: Ministry of Education and Science

Degrees and diplomas: Bakalavriat (Dentistry; Medicine; Nursing; Pharmacy; Public Health), Magistratura (Anaesthesiology; Cardiology; Gynaecology and Obstetrics; Immunology; Medicine; Oncology; Ophthalmology; Otorhinolaryngology; Paediatrics; Pharmacology; Psychiatry and Mental Health; Rehabilitation and Therapy; Surgery; Urology)

Last Update: 13-03-2015

KIMEP University

ul. Abay 4
Almaty 050010
Tel: +7(727) 270-42-00
Fax: +7(727) 237-48-02
Website: http://www.kimep.kz
President: Chan Young Bang

College

Business Administration (*Bang*) (Accountancy; Business Administration; Finance; Management; Marketing); **Social Sciences** (Economics; International Relations; Journalism; Mass Communication; Political Sciences; Public Administration; Regional Studies)

School

Law (International Law; Law)

Centre

Language (Chinese; English; French; German; Italian; Japanese; Korean; Native Language; Russian; Spanish)

History: Founded 1992 as Kazahstanskij Institut Menedžmenta, Ekonomiki i Prognozirovanija (Kazakhstan Institute of Management, Economics and Strategic Research) by the Decree of the President of the Republic of Kazakhstan. In 2004 the Institute was reorganized into a non-profit Joint Stock Company, and acquired current title 2012.

Academic year: August to May.

Admission requirements: High school Diploma and English proficiency

Fees: 39,750 per credit (Tenge)

Main language(s) of instruction: English

Accrediting agency: National Accreditation Center under the Ministry of Education and Science

Degrees and diplomas: Bakalavriat (Accountancy; Economics; Finance; International Relations; Journalism; Law; Management; Marketing), Magistratura (Accountancy; Economics; Finance; International Law; International Relations; Journalism; Management; Marketing; Modern Languages), Doctorantura (Business Administration)

Student Services: Academic Counselling, Careers Guidance, Cultural Activities, Sports Facilities, Language Laboratory, Health Services, Canteen, Foreign Studies Centre

Last Update: 23-01-2015

Kokshe Academy (KU)

ul. Esenberlina, 38
Kokshetau 020000
Tel: +7(7162) 33-36-25
Website: http://www.koksheacademy.kz
Rector: Kassym Shokan Zhanatuly

Course/Programme

Postgraduate (Ecology; Economics); **Undergraduate** (Arts and Humanities; Business Administration; Education; Fine Arts; Law; Sports; Tourism)

History: Created in 1993. Previously known as Kokshetau University.

Admission requirements: Unified National Exam or equivalent secondary school certificate

Main language(s) of instruction: Kazakh, Russian

Accrediting agency: Ministry of Education and Science

Degrees and diplomas: Bakalavriat (Accountancy; Design; Finance; History; Law; Native Language; Primary Education; Sports; Tourism), Magistratura (Ecology; Economics)
Last Update: 13-01-2015

Kostanay Social Technical University named after the Academician Z. Aldamzhar (KOSSTU)

ul. Gertsena 27
Kostanay 110000
Tel: +7(7142) 55-40-09
Fax: +7(7142) 55-41-42
Website: http://www.kosstu.kz/
Rector: Kadyrgali Dzhamanbalin

Faculty

Economics, Law and Management (Banking; Economics; Finance; Law; Management; Taxation); **Education** (Economics; Education; Environmental Studies; Geography; History; Law; Literature; Modern Languages; Music Education; Pedagogy; Physical Education; Psychology; Sports; Translation and Interpretation); **Engineering** (Computer Engineering; Computer Science; Electrical Engineering; Information Technology; Physics; Power Engineering; Software Engineering; Transport Engineering; Transport Management; Vocational Education)
History: Founded 1998.
Accrediting agency: Ministry of Education and Science
Degrees and diplomas: Bakalavriat (Business Administration; Education; Geography; History; Law; Modern Languages; Physics; Tourism; Translation and Interpretation; Transport Management), Magistratura (Computer Science; Law; Physics)
Last Update: 09-03-2015

L.B. Goncharov Kazakh Automobile and Road Academy

prosp. Rajymbeka 417a
Almaty 050061
Tel: +7(727) 387-14-22
Website: http://www.kazadi.kz/
Rector: Rakhimzhan Kabashev

Faculty

Automobile and Road (Building Technologies; Business Administration; Economics; Finance; Information Technology; Marketing; Road Engineering; Translation and Interpretation; Transport Engineering)

History: Founded 1944.
Accrediting agency: Ministry of Education and Science
Degrees and diplomas: Bakalavriat (Accountancy; Economics; Finance; Information Technology; Management; Marketing; Transport Engineering; Transport Management), Magistratura (Building Technologies; Transport Engineering; Transport Management)
Last Update: 06-03-2015

M. Dulatova Kostanay University of Engineering and Economics

ul. Chernyshevskogo 59
Kostanay 110007
Tel: +7(7142) 28-07-27
Website: http://kineu.kz/
Rector: Sabit Ismuratov

Faculty

Economics (Accountancy; Economics; Management); **Engineering** (Energy Engineering; Engineering; Food Technology; Information Technology; Measurement and Precision Engineering; Mechanical Engineering; Transport Engineering; Transport Management)
History: Founded 1996 as Institute of Business and Management. Acquired current title 2011.
Accrediting agency: Ministry of Education and Science
Degrees and diplomas: Bakalavriat (Agricultural Equipment; Agronomy; Business Administration; Engineering; Transport Management), Magistratura (Economics; Management)
Last Update: 09-03-2015

M. Saparbayev South Kazakhstan Humanitarian Institute

ul. Madeli Kozha137
Shymkent 160013
Tel: +7(7252) 43-32-03
Fax: +7(7252) 53-56-95
Website: http://www.ukgi.kz/

Course/Programme

Undergraduate (Arts and Humanities; Business Administration; Computer Science; Education; Tourism)
History: Founded 1994.
Accrediting agency: Ministry of Education and Science
Degrees and diplomas: Bakalavriat (Accountancy; Computer Science; Design; Education; Finance; Modern Languages; Native Language; Primary Education; Sports; Taxation; Tourism; Translation and Interpretation)
Last Update: 10-03-2015

Mangistau University of Humanities and Technology

mikrorajon 3B
Aktau 130000
Tel: +7(7292) 50-50-20
Website: http://www.mgtu-aktau.kz/
Rector: Onerbek Kramysov

Course/Programme
Postgraduate (Accountancy; Finance; Law; Petroleum and Gas Engineering); **Undergraduate** (Business Administration; Education; Geological Engineering; International Relations; Law; Modern Languages; Native Language; Petroleum and Gas Engineering; Translation and Interpretation)
History: Previously known as Mangystauskij Institut 'Bolashak' (Bolashak Mangistau Institute).
Accrediting agency: Ministry of Education and Science
Degrees and diplomas: Bakalavriat (Arts and Humanities; Business Administration; Education; Engineering; International Relations; Law; Modern Languages; Translation and Interpretation), Magistratura (Accountancy; Finance; Law; Petroleum and Gas Engineering)
Last Update: 09-03-2015

Miras University

ul. Sapa Datka 2
Shymkent 160012
Tel: +7(7252) 35-72-79
Website: http://www.miras.edu.kz/
Rector: Bolat Myrzaliyev

Faculty
Economics, Law, and Information Technology (Economics; Information Technology; Law); **Education** (Pedagogy; Primary Education)
History: Founded 1997.
Accrediting agency: Ministry of Education and Science
Degrees and diplomas: Bakalavriat (Business Administration; Education; Engineering; History; Mathematics and Computer Science; Natural Sciences; Translation and Interpretation), Magistratura (Biology; Education; Finance; Information Technology; Management)
Last Update: 12-03-2015

Nur-Mubarak Egyptian University of Islam Culture

prosp. Al-Farabi 73
Almaty 050040
Tel: +7(727) 302-09-43
Fax: +7(727) 302-09-30
Website: http://www.nmu.kz/
Rector: Zhuda Abdulgani BASYUNI Basyuni

Course/Programme
Islamic Culture (Comparative Religion; English; Islamic Studies; Literature; Teacher Training)
History: Founded 2001.
Accrediting agency: Ministry of Education and Science
Degrees and diplomas: Bakalavriat (Islamic Studies; Modern Languages; Religious Studies), Magistratura (Islamic Studies; Philology; Religious Studies), Doctorantura (Islamic Studies; Philology; Religious Studies)
Last Update: 06-03-2015

O.A. Dzholdasbekov Academy of Economics and Law

ul. Tauelsizdika 77
Taldykorgan 040000
Tel: +7(7282) 21-01-01
Fax: +7(7282) 21-01-01
Website: http://vuz.ucoz.kz
Rector: Dosbol Suleymenovich Bajgunakov

Faculty
Business and Law (Business Administration; Economics; Law)
History: Founded 2003.
Accrediting agency: Ministry of Education and Science
Degrees and diplomas: Bakalavriat (Business Administration; Economics; Information Technology; Law), Magistratura (Finance; Law)
Last Update: 06-03-2015

Regional Social Innovative University

ul. D. Kurmanbekova b/n
Shymkent 160005
Tel: +7(7252) 35-94-46
Website: http://www.rsiu.kz/index.php/ru/homepage-ru
Rector: Kanat Narbekovich Daurenbekova

Faculty
Business and Technology (Business Administration; Information Technology); **Fine Arts and Sport** (Fine Arts; Sports); **Humanities and Education** (Education; Literature; Native Language); **Natural Sciences** (Biology; Chemistry; Ecology); **Philology and Law** (Law; Modern Languages;

Music); **Physics and Mathematics** (Computer Science; Fine Arts; Mathematics; Physics)

History: Created 2012 out of merger between Shymkent Social-Pedagogical University (Šymkentskij Socialno-Pedagogičeskij Universitet) and Academic Innovation University (Akademicheskij Innovatsionnyj Universitet).

Accrediting agency: Ministry of Education and Science

Degrees and diplomas: Bakalavriat (Arts and Humanities; Business Administration; Dance; Economics; Education; Fine Arts; Law; Mathematics and Computer Science; Music; Natural Sciences; Political Sciences), Magistratura (Accountancy; Biology; Chemistry; Design; Ecology; Economics; History; Law; Mathematics; Native Language; Pedagogy; Philology; Physical Education; Physics; Political Sciences; Primary Education; Sports)

Last Update: 12-03-2015

S. Baishev Aktobe University

ul Br. Zhubanova, 302A
Aktobe 030000
Tel: +7(7132) 97-40-00
Website: http://www.vuzbaishev.kz
Rector: Aliya B. Agzamova

Faculty

Economics (Accountancy; Economics; Finance; Management; Tourism); **Education** (Ecology; Education; Philology; Social Sciences; Translation and Interpretation); **Technology** (Applied Mathematics; Computer Science; Construction Engineering; Design; Petroleum and Gas Engineering; Transport Management)

History: Founded 1996.

Accrediting agency: Ministry of Education and Science

Degrees and diplomas: Bakalavriat (Arts and Humanities; Design; Economics; Education; Engineering; Mathematics and Computer Science; Veterinary Science), Magistratura (Economics; Finance; Management; Native Language; Philology; Philosophy; Russian)

Last Update: 09-03-2015

Shymkent University

ul. Zhibek Zholy 131
Shymkent 160000
Tel: +7(7252) 50-02-20
Website: http://univershu.kz/
Rector: Bakytzhan M. Shyngysbaev

Faculty

Economics (Economics); **Education** (Education); **Humanities** (Arts and Humanities; Mathematics and Computer Science; Natural Sciences)

Accrediting agency: Ministry of Education and Science

Degrees and diplomas: Bakalavriat (Accountancy; Art Education; Biology; Economics; Education; Finance; Geography; History; Law; Mathematics and Computer Science; Modern Languages; Music Education; Primary Education; Sociology), Magistratura (Accountancy; Information Technology; Literature; Mathematics; Native Language; Pedagogy)

Last Update: 12-03-2015

Süleyman Demirel University (SDU)

ul. Ablayhan 1/1
Almaty 040900
Tel: +8(727) 307-95-65
Fax: +8(727) 307-95-58
Website: http://www.sdu.edu.kz/
Rector: Mesut Akgul

Faculty

Economics (Economics; Finance; International Relations; Management; Marketing); **Engineering** (Computer Engineering; Computer Science; Information Technology; Mathematics; Software Engineering); **Philology** (Chinese; English; French; Journalism; Literature; Native Language; Philology; Russian; Translation and Interpretation; Turkish)

History: Created 1996.

Accrediting agency: Ministry of Education and Science

Degrees and diplomas: Bakalavriat (Arts and Humanities; Business Administration; Computer Science; Economics; Information Technology; Journalism; Law; Mathematics), Magistratura (Computer Science; Economics; Management; Mathematics; Modern Languages), Doctorantura (Computer Science; Management; Mathematics; Modern Languages)

Last Update: 05-03-2015

Syrdariya University

ul. Auezova 11
Zhetysai 160500
Tel: +7(32534) 6-30-00
Fax: +7(32534) 6-34-03
Website: http://www.sirdariya.ru.gg/
Rector: Serik Dairbekov

School

Art and Technology (Design; Fine Arts; Music Education); **Humanities and Business** (Education; History; Modern Languages); **Natural Science and Mathematics** (Computer Science; Economics; Law; Mathematics; Natural Sciences; Physics)

History: Founded 1998.
Accrediting agency: Ministry of Education and Science
Degrees and diplomas: Bakalavriat (Arts and Humanities; Business Administration; Design; Education; Fine Arts; Law; Mathematics and Computer Science; Natural Sciences), Magistratura (Biology; Chemistry; Computer Science; Economics; Education; History; Information Technology; Literature; Native Language; Primary Education)
Last Update: 12-03-2015

Taraz Innovative-Humanitarian University (TIGU)

ul. Dekabrya 69B
Taraz 080000
Tel: +7(7262) 50-13-55
Fax: +7(7262) 51-83-12
Website: http://www.tigu.kz/
Rector: Erbolat Saurykov

Faculty
Economics and Philology (Accountancy; Economics; Finance; Modern Languages; Philology); **Education and Law** (Education; Geography; Law; Social Studies); **Science and Humanities** (Biology; Chemistry; Computer Science; Mathematics; Physics; Sports)
History: Founded 2008.
Accrediting agency: Ministry of Education and Science
Degrees and diplomas: Bakalavriat (Arts and Humanities; Business Administration; Education; Fine Arts; Mathematics and Computer Science; Natural Sciences; Pedagogy; Primary Education; Social Sciences), Magistratura (Economics; Education; Finance; History; Law; Mathematics; Native Language; Physics)
Student Services: Sports Facilities, Language Laboratory
Last Update: 12-03-2015

Taraz Technical Institute

ul. Suleimenova 6
Taraz 080012
Tel: +7(7262) 45-42-99
Website: http://tarti.kz/
Rector: Sagat Zhunisbekov

Faculty
Economics and Information Technology (Economics; Information Technology); **Technology** (Engineering; Technology)

History: Created 2008 as an affiliated college of Kainar University. Acquired current status 2011.
Accrediting agency: Ministry of Education and Science
Degrees and diplomas: Bakalavriat (Construction Engineering; Economics; Electronic Engineering; Maintenance Technology; Mining Engineering)
Last Update: 12-03-2015

Turan University

ul. Satpaeva 16-18-18a
Almaty 050013
Tel: +7(727) 260-40-00
Website: http://www.turan-edu.kz/
Rector: Rakhman Alshanov

Faculty
Economics (Accountancy; Economics; Finance; Information Sciences; Management; Marketing; Service Trades); **Humanities and Law** (International Law; International Relations; Journalism; Law; Psychology; Regional Studies; Tourism; Translation and Interpretation)

Academy
Cinema and Television (Cinema and Television)
History: Created 1992.
Accrediting agency: Ministry of Education and Science
Degrees and diplomas: Bakalavriat (Business Administration; Cinema and Television; Law; Service Trades; Social Sciences; Transport and Communications), Magistratura (Accountancy; Computer Science; Economics; Film; Finance; Information Technology; International Relations; Journalism; Law; Management; Marketing; Tourism), Doctorantura (Economics; Management; Psychology)
Last Update: 05-03-2015

Turan-Astana University

ul. Druzhba 29
Astana 010000
Tel: +7(7172) 39-52-10
Fax: +7(7172) 39-81-18
Website: http://www.turan-astana.kz/
Rector: Gulzhamal Dzhaparova

Faculty
Engineering and Economics (Accountancy; Computer Engineering; Design; Economics; Engineering; Finance; Government; Information Sciences; Information Technology; Management; Marketing; Service Trades; Software Engineering; Tourism); **Humanities and Law** (International

Law; Law; Literature; Native Language; Psychology; Russian; Translation and Interpretation)
History: Founded 1998.
Accrediting agency: Ministry of Education and Science
Degrees and diplomas: Bakalavriat (Arts and Humanities; Business Administration; Law; Social Sciences), Magistratura (Accountancy; Economics; Finance; Information Technology; Law; Management; Native Language; Pedagogy; Tourism)
Last Update: 05-03-2015

University of Foreign Languages and Business Careers

ul. Kazybek bi 168
Almaty 050026
Tel: +7 (727) 379-78-94
Website: http://www.ydu.kz/
Rector: Khizmetli Sabri

Faculty

Economics and Management (Accountancy; Computer Science; Economics; Finance; Management; Marketing); **Foreign Languages** (Arabic; Chinese; English; French; Japanese; Korean; Modern Languages; Translation and Interpretation; Turkish); **History and Religious Studies** (History; Religious Studies); **Kazakh Language, Literature and Journalism** (Journalism; Literature; Native Language); **Tourism and Communications** (Journalism; Tourism)
History: Founded 2001.
Accrediting agency: Ministry of Education and Science
Degrees and diplomas: Bakalavriat (Business Administration; Economics; Information Technology; International Relations; Journalism; Modern Languages; Tourism; Translation and Interpretation), Magistratura (History; Modern Languages; Religious Studies; Translation and Interpretation)
Last Update: 06-03-2015

University of International Business (UIB)

ul. Abaja 8a
Almaty 050010
Tel: +7(727) 250-05-05
Fax: +7(727) 267-12-45
Website: http://www.uib.kz/

Department/Division

Accounting and Audit (Accountancy); **Economics and Marketing** (Economics; Household Management; Marketing);

Finance and Credit (Banking; Finance); **Information Systems** (Computer Engineering; Computer Science; Information Sciences; Software Engineering); **Languages** (English; French; German; Native Language; Russian; Spanish); **Management** (Management); **Social Arts** (Journalism; Social Welfare; Sociology)
History: Created 1993 as International Business School. Acquired current title 2001. Acquired status 2002.
Accrediting agency: Ministry of Education and Science
Degrees and diplomas: Bakalavriat (Business Administration; Ecology; Social Sciences; Social Work; Tourism), Magistratura (Accountancy; Economics; Finance; Information Technology; Management; Marketing; Tourism), Doctorantura (Economics; Finance; Management)
Last Update: 05-03-2015

West Kazakhstan Engineering-Humanitarian University (WKEHU)

ul. Ikhsanova 44/1
Uralsk 090006
Tel: +7(7112) 50-90-67
Fax: +7(7112) 51-18-38
Website: http://www.wkehu.kz/
Rector: Nurbulat Kadyrgaliyev

Department/Division

Business and Law (Accountancy; Business Administration; Finance; Government; Law; Management; Taxation); **Computer Science and Information Systems** (Computer Science; Information Technology); **Ecology and Biotechnology** (Animal Husbandry; Biotechnology; Ecology; Environmental Studies; Fishery; Organic Chemistry; Veterinary Science); **Petroleum Engineering and Industrial Technologies** (Industrial Engineering; Petroleum and Gas Engineering); **Social Sciences and Humanities** (History; Modern Languages; Native Language; Philosophy; Physical Education; Religious Studies; Russian; Social Sciences)
History: Founded 2008.
Accrediting agency: Ministry of Education and Science
Degrees and diplomas: Bakalavriat (Arts and Humanities; Business Administration; Ecology; Education; Engineering; Information Technology; Mathematics and Computer Science; Social Sciences; Tourism; Veterinary Science), Magistratura (Economics; Finance; History; Information Technology; Modern Languages; Native Language; Pedagogy; Psychology; Sports)
Last Update: 09-03-2015

Zhambyl Humanitarian-Technical University

ul. Kolbasshy Koigeldi 171
Taraz 080000
Tel: +7(7262) 43-38-61
Website: http://www.zhgtu.kz/
History: Founded 2007.
Accrediting agency: Ministry of Education and Science
Degrees and diplomas: Bakalavriat (Arts and Humanities; Business Administration; Economics; Education; Information Sciences; Law; Library Science; Mathematics and Computer Science; Modern Languages; Natural Sciences; Tourism; Translation and Interpretation), Magistratura (Accountancy; Economics; Finance; History; Information Technology; Law; Literature; Management; Mathematics; Native Language; Pedagogy; Preschool Education; Primary Education)
Last Update: 12-03-2015

Kenya

STRUCTURE OF HIGHER EDUCATION SYSTEM

Description

Higher education is offered in post-secondary school institutions / tertiary institutions. University education is offered in public universities and private universities (some of them with constituent colleges). Universities are autonomous. All administrative functions are independently managed by University Councils and University Management Boards. Academic matters are managed by University Senates. Post-secondary institutions offer training at diploma and certificate levels. Technical and Vocational Education is offered at polytechnics, institutes of technology and technical training institutes.

Stages of studies

University level first stage

Bachelor's degree
Bachelor's degree programmes are offered in all the UNESCO Degree Classifications, including law and engineering, generally obtained after four years of study; veterinary medicine takes five years, and architecture and medicine six years.

University level second stage

Master's degree
Master's degrees in architecture, humanities, law, commerce, science, engineering, medicine and education take between one and a half and three years' further study after the Bachelor's degree.

University level third stage

Doctorate
Holders of a Master's degree need a minimum of three years of course work and research to obtain a PhD.

ADMISSION TO HIGHER EDUCATION

Admission to university-level studies

Name of Secondary school credential required: Kenyan Certificate of Secondary Education
For entry to: University
Minimum score/requirement: C
Alternatives to credentials: Graduates of post-secondary institutions may be admitted to universities as provided for under the Education and Training System alternative pathways. Please consult the MOEST alternative pathways to degree education.

Foreign students admission

Quotas: Admission depends on availability of places and ability to pay.
Admission requirements: Foreign students should have qualifications recognized by the Kenya National Examinations Council.
Entry regulations: Visas are required from countries that require visas for Kenyans.
Language Proficiency: Good knowledge of English is essential.

RECOGNITION OF STUDIES

Quality assurance system

Commission for University Education carries out accreditation of universities, their constituent colleges and campuses; it also deals with the recognition and equivalence of qualifications from overseas universities (within the framework of UNESCO Regional Conventions).

Bodies dealing with recognition

Commission for University Education - CUE
PO Box 54999
Nairobi 00200

© International Association of Universities 2019
International Handbook of Universities 2019,
https://doi.org/10.1057/978-3-319-76971-4_100

Tel: +254(20) 7205000
Fax: +254(20) 2021172
Website: http://www.cue.or.ke

Kenya National Examinations Council - KNEC
PO Box 73598
Nairobi 00200
Tel: +254(20) 317412
Fax: +254(20) 2226032
Website: http://knec.ac.ke

Special provisions for recognition

Recognition for University level studies

University attended must be accredited and recognized in own country.

For Access to Advanced studies and research

University attended must be accredited and recognized in own country.

For the exercise of a profession

University attended must be accredited and recognized in own country. Various professional bodies established under Acts of Parliament may require professionals to meet additional requirements.

NATIONAL BODIES

Ministry of Education, Science and Technology

Cabinet Secretary: Amina Chawahir Mohamed
Principal Secretary, State Department of Education: Richard Belio Kipsang
8th to 10th floor, Jogoo House 'B' P.o Box 9583
Nairobi 00200
Tel: +254(20) 318581
Fax: +254(20) 251991
Website: http://www.education.go.ke
Role of national body: The Ministry is in charge of all education including basic education under the Basic Education Act, 2013; technical and vocational education and training under the TVET Act, 2013; and university education under the Universities Act, 2012.

Commission for University Education - CUE

Chief Executive Officer/Commission Secretary: Mwenda Ntarangwi
Chairman: Chacha Nyaigotti-Chacha

PO Box 54999
Nairobi 00200
Tel: +254(20) 7205000
Fax: +254(20) 2021172
Website: http://www.cue.or.ke
Role of national body: Accreditation and quality assurance of private and public universities; standardization, equivalance and recognition of qualifications; licensing of student recruitment agencies; and granting foreign universities the authority to collaborate with local tertiary institutions under university regulations, standards and guidelines; advises and makes recommendations to the government on matters relating to university education. Was previously called the Commission for Higher Education, and was reorganised in 2012.

African Academy of Sciences - AAS

Executive Director: Nelson Torto
PO Box 24916
Nairobi 00502
Tel: +254(20) 8060674
Fax: +254(20) 8060675
Website: http://aasciences.ac.ke
Role of national body: The overall goals are to strengthen science and technology capacity, to mobilize science and technology resources in the continent and among the African diaspora, to stimulate problem-solving research and development in pivotal areas of the continent's development, and to market the Academy's activities widely for greater impact on African social development and economic growth.

African Council for Distance Education - ACDE

President: Abdel Raouf Ahmed Abbas Elbadawi
Executive Director: Rotimi Ogidan
Egerton University - Nairobi Campus Stanbank House, 9th Floor Moi Avenue / Mama Ngina Street Junction, City Centre
Po Box 8023
Nairobi 00100
Tel: +254(20) 221 8850
Website: http://acde-afri.org
Role of national body: The African Council for Distance Education (ACDE) is a continental educational organization comprising African universities and other higher education institutions, which are committed to expanding access to quality education and training through open and distance learning.

African Network for the Internationalisation of Education - ANIE

Chair: Tolly Salvator Mbwette
Executive Director: Charles Ochieng' Ong'ondo
c/o Margaret Thatcher Library, Moi University PO Box 3900
Eldoret 30100
Tel: +254 721 917 461
Fax: +254(53) 43047
Website: http://www.anienetwork.org
Role of national body: ANIE is an independent, non-profit, non-governmental membership organisation whose aim is to develop research capacity and constitute an expert network in advancing the understanding of internationalisation of higher education to meet the professional needs of individuals, institutions and organisations.

African Network of Scientific and Technological Institutions - ANSTI

Chair: George Albert Magoha
PO Box 30592
Nairobi 00100
Tel: +254(20) 7622619
Fax: +254(20) 7622538
Website: http://www.ansti.org
Role of national body: The aim of ANSTI is to develop active collaboration among African scientific institutions so as to promote research and development in areas of relevance to the development of the region.

Data for academic year: 2016–2017
Source: IAU from the Commission for University Education 2016. Bodies updated 2018

Public Institutions

Chuka University

P.O. Box 109
Chuka 60400
Tel: +254(20) 231-0512/18, +25(715) 50-58-58, +254(731) 62-02-66
Website: http://chuka.ac.ke
Vice Chancellor: Erastus N. Njoka

Faculty
Agriculture and Environmental Studies (FAES) (Animal Husbandry; Environmental Studies; Horticulture; Natural Resources); **Arts and Humanities** (Arts and Humanities); **Business Studies** (Business Administration); **Education and Resources Development** (Education); **Science, Engineering and Technology** (Biological and Life Sciences; Computer Science; Information Technology; Nursing; Physics)
Further information: Also Tharaka Campus
History: Founded 2007 through transformation of the former Egerton University Eastern Campus, a constituent College of Egerton University founded 2004. Acquired current status 2013.
Main language(s) of instruction: English
Accrediting agency: Commission for University Education
Degrees and diplomas: Certificate / Diploma, Bachelor's Degree, Postgraduate Diploma (Education), Master's Degree (Agriculture; Agronomy; Animal Husbandry; Biotechnology; Business Administration; Chemistry; Curriculum; Development Studies; Economics; Educational Administration; Educational and Student Counselling; English; Environmental Studies; Finance; Geography (Human); History; Horticulture; Linguistics; Literature; Management; Mass Communication; Mathematics; Media Studies; Philosophy; Physics; Plant and Crop Protection; Religious Studies; Science Education; Social and Community Services; Sociology; Soil Science; Swahili; Teacher Training; Tourism; Transport Management), Doctor's Degree (Agriculture; Animal Husbandry; Biochemistry; Biomedicine; Biotechnology; Business Administration; Chemistry; Crop Production; Curriculum; Economics; Educational Administration; Educational and Student Counselling; Educational Sciences; English; Environmental Studies; Food Science; History; Literature; Management; Mass Communication; Mathematics; Media Studies; Political Sciences; Religion; Science Education; Sociology; Soil Science; Statistics; Swahili; Teacher Training)
Student Services: Social Counselling, Sports Facilities, Canteen, Library, Residential Facilities
Last Update: 28-06-2016

Dedan Kimathi University of Technology

PO Box 657
Nyeri 10100
Website: http://www.dkut.ac.ke
Vice-Chancellor: P. Ndirangu Kioni

School
Business, Management and Economics (Business Administration; Business and Commerce; Management; Sales Techniques); **Computer Science and Information Technology** (Business Computing; Computer Science;

Information Technology); **Engineering** (Civil Engineering; Electrical and Electronic Engineering; Electronic Engineering; Mechanical Engineering); **Graduate Studies** (Applied Mathematics; Automation and Control Engineering; Business Administration; Economics; Industrial Engineering; Industrial Management; Leather Techniques; Management; Production Engineering; Surveying and Mapping; Thermal Engineering); **Health Sciences** (Nursing); **Science** (Actuarial Science; Chemistry; Mathematics; Physics; Statistics)

Institute

Food Bioresources Technology (Food Science; Food Technology); **Geomatics, GIS and Remote Sensing (IGGReS)** (Geological Engineering; Surveying and Mapping); **Geothermal Energy Training and Research (GETRI)** (Thermal Engineering); **Technical and Professional Studies** (Accountancy; Building Technologies; Computer Networks; Fashion Design; Furniture Design; Information Technology; Interior Design; Metal Techniques; Sales Techniques; Technology); **Tourism and Hospitality Management** (Hotel Management; Tourism)

History: Created 1972 as Kimathi Institute of Technology (KIT), with first students admitted in 1978. Upgraded to University status in 2007, and renamed Kimathi University College of Technology (KUCT), a constituent college of Jomo Kenyatta University of Agriculture and Technology. Acquired full university status and current name after being granted its charter in 2012.

Main language(s) of instruction: English

Accrediting agency: Commission for University Education (CUE)

Degrees and diplomas: Certificate / Diploma, Bachelor's Degree (Actuarial Science; Business Administration; Business and Commerce; Business Computing; Civil Engineering; Civil Security; Computer Science; Criminology; Electrical Engineering; Electronic Engineering; Food Science; Food Technology; Hotel and Restaurant; Industrial Chemistry; Information Technology; Leather Techniques; Management; Mechanical Engineering; Nursing; Surveying and Mapping; Tourism; Transport Management), Master's Degree (Applied Mathematics; Automation and Control Engineering; Business Administration; Economics; Food Science; Food Technology; Industrial Engineering; Industrial Management; Leather Techniques; Management; Production Engineering), Doctor's Degree (Business Administration; Mechanical Engineering)

Student Services: Social Counselling, Sports Facilities, Library, Residential Facilities

Last Update: 21-06-2016

Egerton University (EU)

PO Box 536
Njoro 254(51) 221-78-91/2 221-77-81
Tel: +254(37) 62282, +254(37) 62278
Fax: +254(37) 62527
Website: http://www.egerton.ac.ke
Vice-Chancellor: Rose A. Mwonya
Tel: +254(51) 221-78-06

Faculty

Agriculture (Agricultural Business; Agricultural Economics; Animal Husbandry; Crop Production; Dairy; Food Science; Food Technology; Horticulture; Soil Science); **Arts and Social Sciences** (Civil Security; Economics; History; Linguistics; Literature; Modern Languages; Peace and Disarmament; Philosophy; Religion; Social Studies); **Commerce** (Accountancy; Business Administration; Finance; Management); **Education and Community Studies** (Agricultural Education; Curriculum; Development Studies; Education; Educational Administration; Educational and Student Counselling; Educational Sciences; Psychology); **Engineering and Technology** (Agricultural Engineering; Automation and Control Engineering; Civil Engineering; Electrical Engineering; Energy Engineering; Environmental Engineering; Industrial Engineering); **Environment and Resource Development** (Environmental Studies; Geography; Natural Resources); **Health Sciences** (Anatomy; Community Health; Health Sciences; Medicine; Nursing; Nutrition; Paediatrics; Pathology; Physiology; Surgery); **Law** (Law); **Science** (Biochemistry; Biological and Life Sciences; Chemistry; Computer Science; Mathematics; Molecular Biology; Physics); **Veterinary Medicine and Surgery** (Surgery; Veterinary Science)

School

Open and Distance Learning (Educational Sciences; Media Studies; Military Science; Teacher Training)

Institute

Women, Gender and Development Studies (Development Studies; Gender Studies; Women's Studies)

Campus

Baringo Campus (Business and Commerce; Education; Information Sciences; Library Science); **Nakuru Town Campus College** (Business and Commerce; Health Sciences)

History: Founded 1939 as a Farm School. Upgraded to Egerton Agricultural College 1950, became a University

College of University of Nairobi 1986, and acquired present status and title 1987.

Academic year: September to May

Admission requirements: Kenya Certificate of Secondary Education (KCSE) or equivalent

Main language(s) of instruction: English

Accrediting agency: Commission for University Education

Degrees and diplomas: Certificate / Diploma, Bachelor's Degree, Master's Degree (Agricultural Economics; Agricultural Education; Agricultural Engineering; Agriculture; Agronomy; Animal Husbandry; Applied Mathematics; Biochemistry; Biological and Life Sciences; Biotechnology; Business Administration; Chemistry; Civil Security; Criminal Law; Criminology; Curriculum; Development Studies; Dietetics; Economics; Education; Educational Administration; Educational and Student Counselling; Engineering; English; Environmental Management; Environmental Studies; Floriculture; Food Science; Fruit Production; Gender Studies; Genetics; Geography; Health Administration; History; Horticulture; Human Resources; Journalism; Linguistics; Literature; Mass Communication; Mathematics; Medical Parasitology; Natural Resources; Nutrition; Pest Management; Philosophy; Physics; Plant Pathology; Public Health; Religion; Science Education; Social Work; Sociology; Soil Science; Statistics; Swahili; Water Science; Women's Studies; Zoology), Doctor's Degree (Agricultural Economics; Agricultural Education; Agriculture; Animal Husbandry; Crop Production; Curriculum; Educational Administration; Educational Psychology; Environmental Management; Environmental Studies; Food Science; Geography; Horticulture; Natural Resources; Science Education)

Student Services: Academic Counselling, Social Counselling, Careers Guidance, Nursery Care, Sports Facilities, Language Laboratory, Health Services, Canteen

Periodicals: Egerton Journal

Publishing house: Education Media Centre (EMC)

Last Update: 21-06-2016

Garissa University College (GUC)

P.O Box 1801 - 70100
Garissa
Tel: +254(727) 628-729
Website: http://www.guc.ac.ke
Principal: Ahmed Warfa

School

Arts and Social Sciences (Arts and Humanities; Social Sciences); **Education** (Education); **Information Science** (Information Sciences)

History: Founded 2011 as a constituent college of Moi University. Acquired University Charter 2017

Main language(s) of instruction: English
Accrediting agency: Commission for University Education
Degrees and diplomas: Bachelor's Degree
Student Services: Library
Last Update: 30-10-2017

Jaramogi Oginga Odinga University of Science and Technology (JOOUST)

P.O. Box 210
Bondo 40601
Tel: +254(57) 205-8000
Fax: +254(57) 252-3851
Website: http://www.jooust.ac.ke
Vice-Chancellor: Stephen G. Agong'

School

Agricultural and Food Sciences (Agricultural Business; Agricultural Education; Agricultural Management; Animal Husbandry; Biotechnology; Food Science; Horticulture; Soil Science); **Biological and Physical Sciences** (Biological and Life Sciences); **Built Environment** (Architectural and Environmental Design; Architecture and Planning; Environmental Management; Regional Planning; Town Planning); **Business and Economics** (Business Administration; Management; Tourism; Transport Management); **Education** (Art Education; Curriculum; Education; Educational Administration; Educational and Student Counselling; Educational Technology; Information Technology; Pedagogy; Preschool Education; Science Education; Special Education); **Engineering and Technology** (Building Technologies; Civil Engineering; Construction Engineering; Energy Engineering); **Environment and Natural Resources Management** (Environmental Management; Town Planning; Water Management); **Health Sciences** (Biological and Life Sciences; Community Health; Epidemiology; Public Health; Statistics); **Humanities and Social Sciences** (Development Studies; Geography (Human); History; Linguistics; Literature; Religious Studies); **Informatics and Innovative Systems** (Business Computing; Computer Engineering; Computer Science; Information Management; Information Technology; Library Science); **Mathematics and Actuarial Sciences** (Actuarial Science; Applied Mathematics; Mathematics; Statistics); **Tourism and Hospitality Management** (Tourism)

Further information: Also Kisii and Busia Learning Centres

History: Founded 2009 as Bondo University College (BUC), a constituent college of Maseno University. Acquired current status 2013.

Main language(s) of instruction: English
Accrediting agency: Commission for University Education
Degrees and diplomas: Certificate / Diploma, Bachelor's Degree, Postgraduate Diploma (Computer Science; Information Technology; Management), Master's Degree (Actuarial Science; Applied Mathematics; Biological and Life Sciences; Business Administration; Community Health; Computer Science; Curriculum; Economics; Education; Educational Administration; Educational and Student Counselling; Educational Technology; Epidemiology; Geography (Human); Health Sciences; History; Information Technology; Linguistics; Literature; Management; Mathematics; Pedagogy; Preschool Education; Public Health; Special Education; Statistics; Town Planning; Transport Management), Doctor's Degree (Architectural and Environmental Design; Architecture and Planning; Business Computing; Environmental Management; Information Technology; Regional Planning; Town Planning; Water Management). Also Executive MBA
Student Services: Library, IT Centre
Last Update: 30-06-2016

Jomo Kenyatta University of Agriculture and Technology (JKUAT)

PO Box 62000
Nairobi 00200
Tel: +254(67) 587-00-01/2/3/4/5
Fax: +254(20) 1515-2164
Website: http://www.jkuat.ac.ke
Vice-Chancellor: Victoria Wambui Ngumi

Faculty

Agriculture (Agriculture; Food Science; Food Technology; Horticulture; Rural Planning)

College

Co-operative University College of Kenya (*Constituent College*) (Business and Commerce; Development Studies); **Engineering and Technology** (Bioengineering; Civil Engineering; Computer Engineering; Construction Engineering; Electrical and Electronic Engineering; Electronic Engineering; Environmental Engineering; Geological Engineering; Marine Engineering; Materials Engineering; Mechanical Engineering; Mining Engineering; Petroleum and Gas Engineering; Surveying and Mapping; Telecommunications Engineering); **Kirinyaga University College** (*Constituent College*) (Business Administration; Computer Science; Construction Engineering; Economics; Health Sciences; Hotel and Restaurant; Information Technology; Textile Technology); **Murang'a University College** (*Constituent College*) (Arts and

Humanities; Biological and Life Sciences; Business Administration; Civil Engineering; Computer Science; Construction Engineering; Economics; Electrical and Electronic Engineering; Human Resources; Information Technology; Mathematics; Mechanical Engineering; Physics); **Taita Taveta University College (TTUC)** (*Constituent College*) (Agriculture; Business Administration; Computer Science; Earth Sciences; Economics; Environmental Studies; Mathematics; Mining Engineering; Social Sciences)

School

Architecture and Building Sciences (*SABS*) (Architecture; Construction Engineering; Landscape Architecture); **Biosystems and Environmental Engineering (SOBEE)** (Agricultural Engineering; Bioengineering; Environmental Engineering; Environmental Management; Mechanical Engineering; Soil Management; Water Management); **Business** (Business Administration); **Civil Engineering and Geomatic Engineering (SCEGE)** (Civil Engineering; Construction Engineering; Environmental Engineering; Geological Engineering; Surveying and Mapping); **Communications and Development Studies (SCDS)** (Development Studies; Linguistics; Mass Communication; Media Studies; Modern Languages); **Computing and Information Technology (SCIT)** (Computer Science; Information Technology); **Electrical, Electronic & Information Engineering (SEEIE)** (Computer Engineering; Electrical Engineering; Electronic Engineering; Telecommunications Engineering); **Entrepreneurship, Procurement and Management** (Management); **Law** (Law; Natural Sciences; Private Law; Public Law; Technology); **Mathematical Sciences (SMS)** (Actuarial Science; Applied Mathematics; Mathematics; Statistics); **Mechanical, Manufacturing and Materials Engineering (SoMMME)** (Electronic Engineering; Marine Engineering; Materials Engineering; Mechanical Engineering; Mining Engineering; Petroleum and Gas Engineering); **Open, Distance and eLearning (SODeL)** (Business Administration; Business Computing; Computer Science; Information Technology; Leadership; Management; Mass Communication); **Physical Sciences (SPS)** (Chemistry; Physics)

Institute

Biotechnology Research (IBR) (Biotechnology); **Energy and Environmental Technology** (Energy Engineering; Environmental Engineering; Environmental Management; Occupational Health; Safety Engineering)

Centre

Arusha Centre (Business Administration; Business and Commerce; Human Resources; Information Technology; Leadership; Management); **Kisii Central Business District (CBD)** (Health Sciences; Information Technology; Mathematics; Social Sciences); **Kitale Central Business District**

(CBD) (Agricultural Business; Agricultural Economics; Agriculture; Business Administration; Computer Science; Development Studies; Food Science; Food Technology; Health Sciences; Human Resources; Information Technology; Management; Mathematics; Public Health; Statistics); **KQ Pride Centre** (Business Administration; Computer Engineering; Development Studies; Finance; Human Resources; Information Management; Information Technology; International Business; Leadership; Management; Mass Communication; Software Engineering; Transport Management); **Nairobi Central Business District (CBD)** (Business Administration; Computer Science; Development Studies; Government; Information Technology); **Sino-Africa Joint Research Education Centre (SAJOREC)**; **Sustainable Materials Research and Technology Centre (SMARTEC)** (Construction Engineering); **Urban Studies** (Urban Studies)

Campus

Karen Campus (Actuarial Science; Business Administration; Computer Science; Information Technology; Law; Microbiology; Social Sciences); **Kigali Campus** (Business Administration; Computer Science; Development Studies; Economics; Energy Engineering; Finance; Human Resources; Information Technology; Leadership; Management; Mass Communication; Public Health; Software Engineering; Transport Management)

History: Founded 1981 as the Jomo Kenyatta College of Agriculture and Technology (JKCAT), by the government of Kenya with assistance of the Japanese government. Formally opened 1982. Became Constituent College of Kenyatta University and acquired present title 1988. Acquired present status 1994.

Academic year: March to April (March-August; September-December; January-April)

Admission requirements: Kenya Certificate of Secondary Education (KSCE)

Fees: (Kenyan Shillings): Engineering: Undergraduate programmes, 230,096 per annum (plus an additional 9,000 for books, 18,000 for food and 40,518 for attachment), Postgraduate programmes 282,210 over two years (plus an additional 75,000 per annum for research/field work/computer lab). Architecture and Building Sciences: Undergraduate programmes, 242,720 per annum (plus an additional 9,000 for books, 18,000 for food and 6,948 for attachment), Postgraduate programmes 282,210 over two years (plus an additional 100,000 per annum for research/field work/computer lab); Computer Science and Information Technology, Undergraduate programmes, 190,695 per annum (plus an additional 9,000 for books, 18,000 for food and 40,518 for attachment), Postgraduate programmes 503,710 over two years (plus an additional 15,000 per annum for research/field work/computer lab); Agriculture: Undergraduate programmes, 209,055 per annum (plus an additional 9,000 for books, 18,000 for food and 32,877 for attachment), Postgraduate programmes 161,500 over two years (plus an additional 150,000 per annum for research/field work/computer lab). Science: Undergraduate programmes, 178,730 per annum (plus an additional 9,000 for books, 18,000 for food and 15,000 for attachment), Postgraduate programmes 242,210 over two years (plus an additional 50,000 per annum for research/field work/computer lab). Energy and Environmental Technologies: Postgraduate programmes, 395,710 over two years (plus an additional 150,000 per annum for research/field work/computer lab). Biotechnology: Postgraduate programmes, 456,200 over two years (plus an additional 200,000 per annum for research/field work/computer lab). Human Resource Development: Undergraduate programmes, 159,190 per annum (plus an additional 9,000 for books, 18,000 for food and 6,948 for attachment), Postgraduate programmes 263,233 over two years. Tropical Medicine and Infectious Diseases: Undergraduate programmes, 163,100 per annum (plus an additional 9,000 for books, 18,000 for food and 23,154 for attachment), Postgraduate programmes 491,200 over two years (plus an additional 200,000 per annum for research/field work/computer lab)

Main language(s) of instruction: English

Accrediting agency: Commission for Higher Education; Council for Legal Studies

Degrees and diplomas: Certificate / Diploma, Bachelor's Degree (Actuarial Science; Agricultural Business; Agricultural Economics; Agricultural Management; Agriculture; Analytical Chemistry; Animal Husbandry; Architecture; Automation and Control Engineering; Biochemistry; Bioengineering; Biotechnology; Botany; Business and Commerce; Business Computing; Chemistry; Civil Engineering; Computer Engineering; Computer Science; Construction Engineering; Dietetics; Electrical and Electronic Engineering; Electronic Engineering; Engineering; Environmental Engineering; Finance; Food Science; Harvest Technology; Horticulture; Industrial Chemistry; Information Technology; Laboratory Techniques; Landscape Architecture; Management; Mechanical Engineering; Microbiology; Molecular Biology; Nutrition; Physics; Plant and Crop Protection; Production Engineering; Radiology; Rural Planning; Soil Science; Surveying and Mapping; Telecommunications Engineering; Water Science), Postgraduate Diploma (Laboratory Techniques; Occupational Health; Statistics), Master's Degree (Agricultural Engineering; Applied Mathematics; Architectural Restoration; Biochemistry; Bioengineering; Biotechnology; Business Administration; Chemistry; Construction Engineering; Energy Engineering; Entomology; Environmental Engineering; Environmental Management; Epidemiology; Food Science; Harvest Technology; Health Sciences; Horticulture; Human Resources; Information Technology; Laboratory Techniques; Landscape Architecture; Management; Mechanical Engineering; Medicine;

Microbiology; Molecular Biology; Nutrition; Occupational Health; Parasitology; Physics; Plant Pathology; Public Health; Software Engineering; Soil Science; Statistics; Telecommunications Engineering; Town Planning; Transport Management; Tropical Medicine; Virology; Water Science), Doctor's Degree (Applied Mathematics; Architectural Restoration; Architecture; Architecture and Planning; Biochemistry; Bioengineering; Biotechnology; Botany; Environmental Engineering; Food Science; Geology; Horticulture; Human Resources; Inorganic Chemistry; Landscape Architecture; Management; Mathematics; Mechanical Engineering; Organic Chemistry; Physical Chemistry; Physics; Soil Science; Surveying and Mapping; Telecommunications Engineering; Water Science)

Student Services: Academic Counselling, Social Counselling, Nursery Care, Sports Facilities, Health Services, Canteen, Library, IT Centre

Periodicals: Journal of Agriculture, Science and Technology (JAGST)

Publishing house: University Press

Last Update: 23-06-2016

Karatina University (KARU)

P.O. Box 1957
Karatina 10101
Tel: +254(20) 2176-713
Website: https://www.karu.ac.ke
Vice-Chancellor: Mucai Muchiri

School

Agriculture and Biotechnology (Agricultural Economics; Agriculture; Crop Production; Food Science; Nutrition); **Business** (Business Administration; Economics; Hotel and Restaurant; Human Resources; Management; Tourism); **Education and Social Sciences** (Arts and Humanities; Communication Studies; Curriculum; Education; Educational Administration; Modern Languages; Psychology; Social Sciences); **Natural Resouces and Environmental Studies** (Aquaculture; Computer Science; Earth Sciences; Environmental Studies; Fishery; Geology; Natural Resources); **Pure and Applied Sciences** (Actuarial Science; Biological and Life Sciences; Computer Science; Mathematics; Physics; Statistics)

History: Founded 2007 as Mount Kenya Campus of Moi University. Became Karatina University College, a constituent college of Moi University 2010. Acquired current title and status 2013.

Main language(s) of instruction: English

Accrediting agency: Commission for University Education

Degrees and diplomas: Certificate / Diploma, Bachelor's Degree, Postgraduate Diploma (Food Science), Master's Degree (Aquaculture; Biological and Life Sciences;

Botany; Business Administration; Communication Studies; Ecology; Education; Educational Administration; Entomology; Environmental Studies; Fishery; Geography (Human); History; Horticulture; Hotel and Restaurant; Information Sciences; Linguistics; Literature; Management; Modern Languages; Parasitology; Physiology; Plant Pathology; Preschool Education; Primary Education; Public Administration; Public Relations; Religious Studies; Statistics; Swahili; Tourism; Wildlife; Zoology), Doctor's Degree (Educational Administration; Geography (Human); Plant and Crop Protection). Also Executive MBA; Executive Master of Education

Student Services: Social Counselling, Sports Facilities, Library, IT Centre, Residential Facilities

Last Update: 01-07-2016

Kenyatta University (KU)

PO Box 43844
Nairobi 00100
Tel: +254(20) 810-901
Fax: +254(20) 811-575
Website: http://www.ku.ac.ke
Vice-Chancellor: Paul Kuria Wainaina
Tel: +254(20) 870 Ext.3050/3051

School

Agriculture and Enterprise Development (Agricultural Business; Agricultural Management; Agriculture); **Applied Human Sciences** (Design; Dietetics; Fashion Design; Food Science; Health Education; Marketing; Nutrition; Parks and Recreation; Physical Education; Social and Community Services; Sports); **Architecture and the Built Environment** (Architecture; Architecture and Planning; Construction Engineering; Interior Design; Real Estate; Town Planning); **Business** (Accountancy; Business Administration; Finance; Management); **Creative Arts, Film and Media Studies** (Film; Mass Communication; Media Studies; Theatre); **Digital School of Virtual and Open Learning** (Agricultural Business; Agriculture; Arts and Humanities; Business Administration; Computer Engineering; Educational Sciences; Food Science; Health Education; Hotel and Restaurant; Information Technology; Mathematics; Natural Sciences; Nutrition; Parks and Recreation; Physical Education; Social and Community Services; Social Sciences; Special Education; Sports; Teacher Training; Tourism); **Economics** (Econometrics; Economics; Statistics); **Education** (Curriculum; Education; Educational Administration; Educational Psychology; Educational Sciences; Educational Technology; Information Sciences; Library Science; Preschool Education; Special Education); **Engineering and Technology** (Civil Engineering; Computer Science;

Electrical Engineering; Electronic Engineering; Energy Engineering; Information Technology; Mechanical Engineering; Production Engineering); **Environmental Studies** (Development Studies; Education; Environmental Management; Environmental Studies); **Graduate** (Arts and Humanities; Business Administration; Education; Environmental Studies; Health Sciences; Mathematics; Natural Sciences; Social Sciences); **Hospitality and Tourism** (Hotel Management; Tourism); **Humanities and Social Sciences** (African Languages; Archaeology; Development Studies; English; Fine Arts; Foreign Languages Education; French; Gender Studies; Geography; German; History; Japanese; Korean; Literature; Modern Languages; Philosophy; Political Sciences; Psychology; Public Administration; Religious Studies; Sociology); **Law** (Private Law; Public Law); **Medicine** (Alternative Medicine; Anatomy; Dermatology; Gynaecology and Obstetrics; Laboratory Techniques; Medicine; Nursing; Orthopaedics; Paediatrics; Pathology; Pharmacy; Physiology; Psychiatry and Mental Health; Surgery); **Public Health** (Community Health; Health Administration; Health Sciences; Public Health); **Pure and Applied Sciences** (Actuarial Science; Biochemistry; Biotechnology; Botany; Chemistry; Mathematics; Microbiology; Physics; Statistics; Zoology); **Security, Diplomacy and Peace Studies** (International Relations; Peace and Disarmament; Protective Services); **Visual and Performing Arts** (Dance; Design; Film; Fine Arts; Music; Theatre)

Further information: Also Campuses in Ruiru, Parklands, Mombasa, Kericho, Nairobi City Centre, Nyeri, Nakuru, Dadaab, Arusha

History: Founded 1965 as Kenyatta University College, acquired present status and title 1985.

Academic year: September to June

Admission requirements: Kenya Certificate of Secondary Education (KCSE)

Fees: Undergraduate, 72,000-450,400 per annum for East African students, 125,000-712,220 per annum for Non-East African Students; Postgraduate, 120,000-400,000 per annum for East African students, 150,000-450,000 per annum for Non-East African Students; Summer term, c. 8,000 (Kenyan Shilling)

Main language(s) of instruction: English

Accrediting agency: Commission of University Education; Inter-university Council for East Africa; Africa Association of Universities; International Association of Universities; Commonwealth Universities

Degrees and diplomas: Certificate / Diploma, Bachelor's Degree, Postgraduate Diploma (Educational Administration; Sports Management), Master's Degree (Agricultural Economics; Animal Husbandry; Applied Linguistics; Applied Physics; Biochemistry; Biological and Life Sciences; Biology; Biotechnology; Botany; Business Administration; Chemistry; Curriculum; Design; Development Studies; Dietetics; Ecology; Econometrics; Economic and Finance Policy; Economics; Education; Educational Administration; Educational and Student Counselling; Educational Psychology; Educational Research; Educational Testing and Evaluation; English; Entomology; Environmental Management; Environmental Studies; Ethnology; Fashion Design; Finance; Fishery; Food Science; Forestry; French; Gender Studies; Genetics; Geography (Human); Health Sciences; Hotel and Restaurant; Human Resources; Immunology; Information Sciences; International Business; International Relations; Laboratory Techniques; Library Science; Linguistics; Literature; Management; Marketing; Mathematics; Microbiology; Music; Music Theory and Composition; Musicology; Nutrition; Parasitology; Parks and Recreation; Peace and Disarmament; Pest Management; Philosophy; Physical Education; Plant Pathology; Preschool Education; Public Health; Rural Studies; Social and Community Services; Sociology; Special Education; Sports; Sports Management; Swahili; Tourism), Doctor's Degree (Agricultural Economics; Agricultural Management; Business Administration; Cinema and Television; Demography and Population; Design; Dietetics; Economics; Education; Educational Administration; Educational Sciences; Energy Engineering; Environmental Studies; Fashion Design; Fine Arts; Food Science; Geography (Human); Hotel Management; Leisure Studies; Literature; Marketing; Nutrition; Parks and Recreation; Philosophy of Education; Physical Education; Preschool Education; Public Health; Regional Planning; Social and Community Services; Sociology; Soil Science; Sports; Theatre; Tourism; Town Planning; Water Science)

Student Services: Academic Counselling, Social Counselling, Careers Guidance, Nursery Care, Cultural Activities, Sports Facilities, Facilities for disabled people, Health Services, Canteen, Library, IT Centre, Residential Facilities

Last Update: 16-02-2017

MACHAKOS UNIVERSITY COLLEGE

P.O. Box 136
Machakos 90100
Website: http://www.machakosuniversity.ac.ke
Principal: Francis M. Mathooko

School

Agriculture and Natural Resources (Agriculture; Natural Resources); **Business and Economics** (Business Administration; Economics); **Engineering and Technology** (Engineering; Technology); **Hospitalityand Tourism Management** (Hotel and Restaurant; Tourism); **Humanities and Social Sciences** (Arts and Humanities; Social Sciences); **Pure and Applied Sciences** (Mathematics and Computer Science; Natural Sciences)

History: Founded 2011. A constituent college of Kenyatta University

Main language(s) of instruction: English

Accrediting agency: Commission for University Education
Degrees and diplomas: Certificate / Diploma, Bachelor's Degree, Postgraduate Diploma (Education; Human Resources), Master's Degree (Business Administration; Curriculum; Economics; Educational Administration; Educational Sciences; Educational Technology; Human Resources), Doctor's Degree (Business Administration)
Student Services: Library, eLibrary
Last Update: 04-07-2016

Kibabii University (KIBU)

P.O. Box 169
Bungoma 50200
Tel: +254(20) 202-8660, +254(70) 808-5934
Website: http://www.kibabiiuniversity.ac.ke
Acting Vice-Chancellor: Isaac Ipara Odeo

School

Business and Economics (Accountancy; Business Administration; Economics; Finance; Management); **Computing and Informatics (SCAI)** (Computer Science; Information Technology); **Education and Social Science (FESS)** (African Languages; Criminology; Curriculum; Educational Sciences; Educational Technology; English; Journalism; Literature; Mass Communication; Mathematics Education; Preschool Education; Psychology; Science Education; Social Sciences; Social Work; Swahili; Teacher Training); **Graduate Studies** (Biological and Life Sciences; Business Administration; Chemistry; Education; Educational Sciences; History; Human Resources; Information Technology; Literature; Mathematics; Physics; Religion; Statistics; Teacher Training); **Science** (Agriculture; Biological and Life Sciences; Engineering; Environmental Studies; Mathematics; Natural Sciences; Technology; Veterinary Science)
History: Founded 2007 as Kibabii Teachers Training College. Transformed into Kibabii University College, a constituent college of Masinde Muliro University of Science and Technology, 2011. acquired current status and title 2015.
Fees: Undergraduate, 60,000 per annum; Postgraduate Diploma, 80,000 per annum; Master, 60,000-62,000 per annum; Ph.D., 60,000-72,000 per annum (Kenyan Shilling)
Main language(s) of instruction: English
Accrediting agency: Commission for University Education
Degrees and diplomas: Certificate / Diploma, Bachelor's Degree, Postgraduate Diploma (Education; Information Technology), Master's Degree (Applied Mathematics; Botany; Business Administration; Chemistry; Comparative Literature; Curriculum; Education; Educational Administration; Educational and Student Counselling; History; Human Resources; Information Technology; Mathematics; Native

Language Education; Physics; Religion; Statistics; Teacher Training; Zoology), Doctor's Degree (Chemistry; Curriculum; Educational Administration; Information Technology; Mathematics; Physics; Religion; Teacher Training)
Student Services: Sports Facilities, Library, IT Centre
Last Update: 01-07-2016

Kisii University

P.O. Box 408
Kisii 40200
Tel: +254(720) 127-094, +254(727) 238-343, +254(724) 554-469
Website: http://www.kisiiuniversity.ac.ke
ohn SoranaAkama: John Sorana Akama

Faculty

Agriculture and Natural Resource Management (Agricultural Business; Agricultural Economics; Agricultural Education; Agriculture; Animal Husbandry; Aquaculture; Environmental Studies; Fishery; Natural Resources); **Arts and Social Sciences** (Anthropology; Criminology; Development Studies; Ethics; History; Industrial and Organizational Psychology; International Relations; Linguistics; Peace and Disarmament; Philosophy; Political Sciences; Protective Services; Psychology; Public Administration; Religion; Social Sciences; Social Work; Sociology; Swahili); **Business and Economics** (Accountancy; Administration; Business Administration; Economics; Hotel and Restaurant; Human Resources; Management; Sales Techniques; Secretarial Studies; Statistics; Taxation); **Education and Human Resources Development** (Education; Educational Sciences; Special Education; Teacher Training); **Information Science and Technology** (Computer Science; Information Management; Information Sciences; Information Technology; Library Science; Mass Communication; Media Studies; Software Engineering); **Pure and Applied Sciences** (Actuarial Science; Analytical Chemistry; Applied Mathematics; Biochemistry; Biological and Life Sciences; Biotechnology; Botany; Chemistry; Geophysics; Industrial Chemistry; Laboratory Techniques; Mathematics; Microbiology; Mineralogy; Molecular Biology; Natural Sciences; Parasitology; Pathology; Physics; Physiology; Statistics; Waste Management; Zoology)

School

Health Sciences (Community Health; Dietetics; Haematology; Health Sciences; Medicine; Nursing; Nutrition; Public Health; Surgery); **Law** (Law)

Institute

Gender and Development Studies (Development Studies; Gender Studies; Public Administration)

Campus

Kisii Down Town Campus (Ouru Towers); **Kisii Town Campus** (Agriculture; Animal Husbandry; Business Administration; Computer Science; Information Technology; Law; Library Science; Protective Services; Welfare and Protective Services)

Further information: Also Kisii Down Town (Ouru Towers), Twin Towers, Nyakongo Tower Campuses

History: Founded 1965 as a Primary Teachers' Training College. Established as Kisii University College a constituent college of Egerton University 2007. Acquired current status and title 2013.

Fees: 54,000-160,000 per annum (Kenyan Shilling)

Main language(s) of instruction: English

Accrediting agency: Commission for University Education

Degrees and diplomas: Certificate / Diploma, Bachelor's Degree, Master's Degree (Accountancy; Agricultural Business; Agricultural Economics; Agriculture; Agronomy; Analytical Chemistry; Animal Husbandry; Applied Mathematics; Aquaculture; Business Administration; Chemistry; Curriculum; Development Studies; Economics; Education; Educational Administration; Educational and Student Counselling; Environmental Studies; Fishery; Haematology; Human Resources; Immunology; Information Management; Information Sciences; Information Technology; Inorganic Chemistry; International Relations; Journalism; Management; Mass Communication; Mathematics; Medical Parasitology; Microbiology; Natural Resources; Nutrition; Organic Chemistry; Parasitology; Peace and Disarmament; Philosophy; Physics; Physiology; Plant Pathology; Political Sciences; Public Administration; Public Health; Sales Techniques; Sociology; Statistics; Swahili; Taxation; Teacher Training; Tourism; Water Science), Doctor's Degree (Agricultural Business; Agricultural Economics; Agricultural Education; Agriculture; Analytical Chemistry; Animal Husbandry; Applied Mathematics; Aquaculture; Business Administration; Chemistry; Curriculum; Development Studies; Education; Educational Administration; Educational and Student Counselling; Educational Sciences; Educational Technology; Environmental Studies; Fishery; Gender Studies; Government; Information Sciences; Information Technology; Inorganic Chemistry; Leadership; Management; Mass Communication; Mathematics; Media Studies; Natural Resources; Organic Chemistry; Parasitology; Peace and Disarmament; Philosophy; Physical Chemistry; Physics; Plant Pathology; Political Sciences; Protective Services; Public Administration; Special Education; Statistics; Teacher Training)

Student Services: Library

Student Numbers 2015-2016	MALE	FEMALE	TOTAL
All (Foreign Included)			c. 10000

Last Update: 29-06-2016

Laikipia University

P.O. Box 1100
Nyahururu 20300
Tel: +254(713) 552-761, +254(20) 233-1509, +254(20) 267-1779
Website: http://www.laikipia.ac.ke
Vice-Chancellor: Francis K. Lelo

School

Business (Business and Commerce; Economics); **Education** (Curriculum; Educational Administration; Educational and Student Counselling; Educational Psychology; Educational Sciences); **Humanities and Development Studies** (Communication Studies; Environmental Studies; Literature; Public Administration; Public Relations; Sports); **Science and Applied Technology** (Arid Land Studies; Biochemistry; Biological and Life Sciences; Biomedicine; Biotechnology; Chemistry; Computer Science; Mathematics; Physics; Soil Management)

Further information: Also Upper Hill Campus

History: Founded as a primary school 1929. Served as a Large–scale Farmers training (LSFTC) college betwee 1965 and 1970. Converted into a Animal Husbandry and Industry Training Institute (AHITI) 1979. Taken over as a campus by Egerton University 1990. Became a constituent University College of Egerton University 2011. Acquired current status and title 2013.

Fees: 70,000-140,000 per annum (Kenyan Shilling)

Main language(s) of instruction: English

Accrediting agency: Commission for University Education

Degrees and diplomas: Certificate / Diploma, Bachelor's Degree, Postgraduate Diploma (Child Care and Development; Education; Leadership; Management; Sports; Sports Management), Master's Degree (Applied Linguistics; Business Administration; Communication Studies; Education; Educational Administration; Educational and Student Counselling; Educational Sciences; History; Journalism; Literature; Mass Communication; Religious Studies; Swahili), Doctor's Degree (Applied Linguistics; Communication Studies; Educational Administration; Educational and Student Counselling; Educational Psychology; Educational Testing and Evaluation; History; Swahili). Also Executive MBA

Student Services: Canteen, Library, IT Centre

Last Update: 30-06-2016

Maasai Mara University (MMARAU)

P.O. Box 861
Narok 20500
Tel: +254(20) 513-1400, +254(729) 470-525

Website: http://www.mmarau.ac.ke
Vice-Chancellor: Mary Walingo

School

Arts and Social Sciences (Cultural Studies; Development Studies; Film; Literature; Mass Communication; Media Studies; Modern Languages; Religion; Social Studies); **Business and Economics** (Business Administration; Economics; Management); **Education** (Curriculum; Education; Educational Administration; Educational Sciences; Teacher Training); **Science and Information Sciences** (Biological and Life Sciences; Computer Science; Information Sciences; Information Technology; Mathematics; Physics); **Tourism and Natural Resources Management** (Environmental Studies; Forestry; Tourism; Wildlife)
History: Created 2013.
Fees: Undergraduate, 103,600-125,750 per annum; Postgraduate, 55,875-57,625 per annum; PhD, 195,000-375,000 per annum (Kenyan Shilling)
Main language(s) of instruction: English
Accrediting agency: Commission for University Education (CUE)
Degrees and diplomas: Certificate / Diploma, Bachelor's Degree (Adult Education; Agricultural Economics; Agricultural Management; Art Education; Botany; Business Administration; Chemistry; Computer Science; Criminology; Development Studies; Economics; Educational and Student Counselling; Environmental Management; Forestry; History; Hotel and Restaurant; Human Resources; Information Sciences; Journalism; Linguistics; Literature; Mass Communication; Mathematics; Modern Languages; Physics; Political Sciences; Preschool Education; Primary Education; Public Administration; Public Relations; Religious Studies; Science Education; Social Work; Sociology; Special Education; Statistics; Swahili; Tourism; Wildlife; Zoology), Master's Degree (Adult Education; Business Administration; Civil Security; Criminology; Educational Administration; Educational and Student Counselling; Educational Psychology; Educational Sciences; Educational Testing and Evaluation; Environmental Studies; Geography (Human); History; Human Resources; International and Comparative Education; Linguistics; Philosophy of Education; Political Sciences; Preschool Education; Primary Education; Public Administration; Religious Studies; Sociology; Special Education; Swahili; Tourism; Wildlife), Doctor's Degree (Environmental Studies; Literature)
Student Services: Sports Facilities, Health Services, Library
Last Update: 28-06-2016

Maseno University (MSU)

Private Bag Maseno/Busia Rd
Maseno

Tel: +254(57) 351-008, +254(57) 351-011
Fax: +254(57) 351-153
Website: http://www.maseno.ac.ke
Vice-Chancellor: Julius Omondi Nyabundi
Tel: +254(57) 351-620/22

Faculty

Arts and Social Sciences (African Languages; Anthropology; Archaeology; Design; Fine Arts; French; History; Linguistics; Literature; Media Studies; Modern Languages; Music; Performing Arts; Philosophy; Psychology; Religion; Sociology; Swahili; Theatre; Theology); **Education** (Communication Studies; Curriculum; Education; Educational Administration; Educational Sciences; Educational Technology; Preschool Education; Rehabilitation and Therapy; Special Education); **Medicine** (Anaesthesiology; Anatomy; Biochemistry; Medicine; Microbiology; Paediatrics; Physiology; Surgery)

College

Tom Mboya University College (*Constituent College*) (Agriculture; Business Administration; Economics; Education; Food Science; Public Health; Social and Community Services)

School

Agriculture and Food Security (Agricultural Economics; Agriculture; Rural Planning; Soil Science); **Biological and Physical Science** (Botany; Chemistry; Physics; Zoology); **Business and Economics** (Accountancy; Business Administration; Economics; Finance; Human Resources; Management; Marketing); **Computing** (Business Computing; Computer Science; Information Sciences; Information Technology); **Development and Strategic Studies** (Development Studies; International Relations; Peace and Disarmament; Political Sciences; Protective Services); **Ecotourism, Hotel and Institution Management** (Hotel and Restaurant; Leisure Studies; Management; Parks and Recreation; Sports; Tourism; Wildlife); **Environment and Earth Sciences** (Economics; Environmental Studies; Geography; Meteorology; Mining Engineering; Natural Resources; Water Management; Water Science); **Mathematics, Statistics and Actuarial Science** (Actuarial Science; Applied Mathematics; Mathematics; Statistics); **Planning and Architecture** (Architectural and Environmental Design; Regional Planning; Town Planning); **Public Health and Community Development** (Biomedicine; Health Sciences; Nutrition; Public Health)

Institute

Gender Studies (Development Studies; Gender Studies)

Campus

Kisumu City Campus College (Actuarial Science; Architecture and Planning; Arts and Humanities; Business

Administration; Development Studies; Earth Sciences; Economics; Education; Environmental Studies; Mathematics; Natural Sciences; Public Health; Social Sciences; Statistics)

Further information: Also Town Campus

History: Founded 1991 as a Constituent College of Moi University. Acquired present status 2001.

Academic year: September to May (September-December; January-May)

Admission requirements: Kenya Certificate of Secondary Education (KCSE), level C+ or higher grades

Main language(s) of instruction: English

Accrediting agency: Commission for University Education

Degrees and diplomas: Certificate / Diploma, Bachelor's Degree, Postgraduate Diploma (Education; Educational Technology; Educational Testing and Evaluation; Pedagogy), Master's Degree (Analytical Chemistry; Anthropology; Applied Mathematics; Architecture; Architecture and Planning; Art Education; Biochemistry; Biology; Biomedicine; Biotechnology; Botany; Business Administration; Cell Biology; Chemistry; Crop Production; Curriculum; Ecology; Economics; Educational Administration; Educational and Student Counselling; Educational Psychology; Educational Technology; Entomology; Environmental Management; Environmental Studies; Family Studies; Floriculture; Forestry; French; Fruit Production; Genetics; Geography; History; Horticulture; Hotel and Restaurant; Humanities and Social Science Education; Inorganic Chemistry; Interior Design; International Relations; Irrigation; Linguistics; Literature; Marine Biology; Marketing; Mass Communication; Mathematics; Media Studies; Meteorology; Microbiology; Molecular Biology; Music; Music Theory and Composition; Musicology; Native Language Education; Nutrition; Organic Chemistry; Parasitology; Pedagogy; Philosophy; Physical Chemistry; Physics; Physiology; Plant Pathology; Political Sciences; Public Health; Religion; Social Work; Soil Management; Special Education; Statistics; Swahili; Textile Design; Town Planning; Vegetable Production), Doctor's Degree (Anthropology; Applied Mathematics; Biology; Biomedicine; Botany; Business Administration; Cell Biology; Chemistry; Crop Production; Curriculum; Development Studies; Economics; Educational Administration; Educational Psychology; Educational Technology; Educational Testing and Evaluation; Entomology; Environmental Studies; Film; Floriculture; French; Fruit Production; Geography; History; Horticulture; Hotel and Restaurant; Interior Design; International Relations; Irrigation; Linguistics; Literature; Marine Biology; Mass Communication; Mathematics; Media Studies; Molecular Biology; Music; Music Education; Music Theory and Composition; Musicology; Nutrition; Parasitology; Pedagogy; Philosophy; Physics; Political Sciences; Public Health; Religion; Social and Community Services; Sociology; Soil Management; Special Education; Statistics;

Swahili; Theatre; Vegetable Production). Also Sandwich Courses

Student Services: Academic Counselling, Social Counselling, Careers Guidance, Cultural Activities, Sports Facilities, Health Services, Canteen, Library

Periodicals: Maseno Journal of Education, Arts and Science

Publishing house: Maseno University Desktop Publishing Unit

Last Update: 24-06-2016

Masinde Muliro University of Science and Technology (MMUST)

P. O. Box 190
Kakamega 50100
Tel: +254(56) 31375
Fax: +254(56) 30153
Website: http://www.mmust.ac.ke
Vice-Chancellor: Frederick A. Ochieng' Otieno

Faculty

Agriculture, Veterinary Science and Technology (Agriculture; Veterinary Science); **Business and Economics** (Business Administration; Economics); **Education and Social Sciences** (Criminology; Educational Administration; Educational Psychology; Educational Sciences; Foreign Languages Education; Humanities and Social Science Education; Journalism; Mass Communication; Mathematics Education; Science Education; Social Work); **Engineering** (Civil Engineering; Electrical Engineering; Industrial Engineering; Mechanical Engineering; Structural Architecture; Telecommunications Engineering); **Science** (Applied Chemistry; Biological and Life Sciences; Chemistry; Computer Science; Mathematics; Physics)

School

Graduate Studies (Agriculture; Arts and Humanities; Business Administration; Economics; Education; Mathematics; Natural Sciences; Social Sciences; Teacher Training; Veterinary Science); **Medicine** (Medicine; Surgery); **Nursing and Midwifery** (Midwifery; Nursing); **Open and Distance E-Learning** (Agriculture; Applied Linguistics; Applied Mathematics; Aquaculture; Biological and Life Sciences; Business Administration; Chemistry; Communication Studies; Comparative Literature; Criminology; Curriculum; Educational Administration; Educational and Student Counselling; English; Entomology; Environmental Studies; History; Human Resources; Immunology; Information Technology; Linguistics; Management; Marine Biology; Marketing; Mass Communication; Mathematics; Microbiology; Molecular Biology; Natural Resources; Nursing; Parasitology; Peace and

Disarmament; Physics; Plant and Crop Protection; Protective Services; Religion; Swahili); **Open Learning and Continuing Education** (Adult Education; Advertising and Publicity; Agricultural Engineering; Biology; Business Administration; Chemistry; Civil Engineering; Electrical Engineering; English; Ethics; Food Technology; Information Technology; Mathematics; Mechanical Engineering; Physics; Public Relations; Structural Architecture); **Public Health, Biomedical Science and Technology** (Health Sciences; Laboratory Techniques; Nursing; Nutrition; Optometry; Public Health; Sports)

Centre

Disaster Management and Humanitarian Assistance (Development Studies; Engineering Management; Environmental Management; Environmental Studies; Peace and Disarmament; Protective Services; Safety Engineering)
Further information: Kisumu-Webuye Road
History: Founded 1972 as Western College of Arts and Applied Sciences (WECO). Upgraded to a constituent college of Moi University in 2002. Acquired present status and title in 2007.
Academic year: September to April (September-December; January-April)
Admission requirements: Kenya Certificate of Secondary Education (KCSE) - C+ (Plus)
Fees: 100,000 per semester (Kenyan Shilling)
Main language(s) of instruction: English
Accrediting agency: Commission for University Education
Degrees and diplomas: Certificate / Diploma, Bachelor's Degree (Agricultural Economics; Agricultural Education; Agricultural Management; Agriculture; Art Education; Biology; Biotechnology; Business and Commerce; Chemistry; Civil Engineering; Computer Science; Criminology; Dietetics; Education; Electrical Engineering; Energy Engineering; Environmental Management; Food Science; Food Technology; Foreign Languages Education; Health Education; Health Sciences; Industrial Engineering; Information Technology; Journalism; Laboratory Techniques; Mass Communication; Mathematics; Mechanical Engineering; Medicine; Natural Resources; Nursing; Nutrition; Optometry; Physics; Preschool Education; Science Education; Social Work; Sports; Structural Architecture; Surgery; Telecommunications Engineering), Postgraduate Diploma (Agronomy; Food Technology; Health Sciences; Laboratory Techniques; Sports), Master's Degree (Agriculture; Animal Husbandry; Applied Linguistics; Applied Mathematics; Biochemistry; Biology; Biomedicine; Biotechnology; Business Administration; Cell Biology; Chemistry; Civil Engineering; Communication Studies; Community Health; Comparative Literature; Curriculum; Dietetics; Economics; Education; Educational Administration; Educational and Student Counselling; Educational Sciences; Environmental Studies; Food Science; Genetics; Haematology; Health Education; Health Sciences;

Histology; History; Human Resources; Immunology; Information Management; Information Sciences; Laboratory Techniques; Mathematics; Mathematics Education; Medical Parasitology; Medicine; Microbiology; Nutrition; Optometry; Parasitology; Pedagogy; Pharmacology; Plant and Crop Protection; Public Health; Religion; Science Education; Sports; Statistics; Swahili), Doctor's Degree (Applied Mathematics; Aquaculture; Biochemistry; Biomedicine; Biotechnology; Business Administration; Cell Biology; Chemistry; Communication Studies; Community Health; Curriculum; Dietetics; Economics; Educational Administration; Educational Sciences; Engineering Management; English; Entomology; Environmental Studies; Forensic Medicine and Dentistry; Haematology; Health Sciences; Histology; History; Immunology; Information Technology; International Relations; Linguistics; Marine Biology; Mathematics; Mathematics Education; Medical Parasitology; Medicine; Microbiology; Molecular Biology; Natural Resources; Nutrition; Parasitology; Peace and Disarmament; Pedagogy; Pharmacology; Plant and Crop Protection; Protective Services; Public Health; Religion; Sports; Statistics; Swahili)
Student Services: Academic Counselling, Social Counselling, Careers Guidance, Sports Facilities, Health Services, Canteen, Library, IT Centre
Periodicals: J-Stem Journal
Last Update: 15-02-2017

Meru University of Science and Technology (MUST)

P.O. Box 972
Meru 60200
Tel: +254(712) 524-293
Website: http://www.must.ac.ke
Vice-Chancellor: Romanus Odhiambo Otieno

School

Agriculture and Food Science (Agricultural Business; Agriculture; Animal Husbandry; Dietetics; Food Science; Food Technology; Horticulture; Nutrition); **Business and Economics (SBE)** (Business Administration; Economics; Management; Sales Techniques); **Education** (Education); **Health Sciences** (Health Sciences; Laboratory Techniques; Public Health); **Information Technology and Engineering** (Civil Engineering; Computer Science; Electrical Engineering; Electronic Engineering; Information Sciences; Information Technology; Mechanical Engineering; Software Engineering); **Pure and Applied Sciences** (Actuarial Science; Applied Mathematics; Biochemistry; Biological and Life Sciences; Biotechnology; Entomology; Environmental Management; Environmental Studies; Mathematics and Computer Science; Parasitology; Physics; Statistics)

Further information: Also Meru Town Campus
History: Founded 2008 as a constituent college of Jomo Kenyatta University of Agriculture and Technology. Acquired current status and title 2013.
Main language(s) of instruction: English
Accrediting agency: Commission for University Education
Degrees and diplomas: Certificate / Diploma, Bachelor's Degree, Postgraduate Diploma (Applied Mathematics; Statistics), Master's Degree (Applied Mathematics; Business Administration; Computer Science; Management; Software Engineering; Statistics), Doctor's Degree (Agriculture; Applied Mathematics; Computer Science; Information Technology)
Student Services: Health Services, Library, IT Centre, Residential Facilities
Last Update: 29-06-2016

▮▰▣ Moi University (MU)

P.O Box 3900
Eldoret 30100, Rift Valley
Tel: +254(790) 940-508, +254(736) 138-770, +254(771) 336-911
Fax: +254(53) 43047
Website: http://www.mu.ac.ke
Vice-Chancellor: Isaac S. Kosgey

School

Aerospace Sciences (Aeronautical and Aerospace Engineering); **Agriculture** (Agricultural Education; Agriculture; Animal Husbandry; Biotechnology; Environmental Studies); **Arts and Social Sciences** (Arts and Humanities; Civil Security; Criminology; Development Studies; Education; French; Geography; German; Mass Communication; Media Studies; Modern Languages; Music; Psychology; Social and Community Services; Social Work; Swahili); **Biological and Physical Sciences** (Actuarial Science; Computer Science; Education; Microbiology; Natural Sciences; Statistics); **Business and Economics** (Agricultural Business; Agricultural Economics; Agricultural Management; Business Administration; Economics; Hotel Management; Management; Sports Management); **Dentistry** (Dentistry; Surgery); **Education** (Business Education; Education; Educational Sciences; Preschool Education; Primary Education; Secondary Education; Special Education; Technology Education); **Engineering** (Chemical Engineering; Civil Engineering; Electrical Engineering; Electronic Engineering; Industrial Engineering; Mechanical Engineering; Production Engineering; Structural Architecture; Telecommunications Engineering; Textile Technology); **Human Resource Development** (Advertising and Publicity; Communication Arts; Communication Studies; Graphic Design; Human Resources; Journalism; Management; Mass Communication; Public Relations); **Information Sciences** (Computer Science; Information Sciences; Media Studies); **Law** (*Annex Campus*) (Law); **Medicine** (Medicine; Physical Therapy; Psychology); **Nursing** (Nursing); **Public Health** (Health Sciences; Public Health); **Tourism, Hospitality and Event Management** (Hotel and Restaurant; Management; Tourism)

Campus

Alupe Campus (Art Education; Preschool Education; Primary Education; Special Education)
Further information: Also Town Campus, Eldoret West Campus, Nairobi Campus, Coast Campus (Mombasa), Kitale Campus, Odera Akang'o College Campus
History: Founded 1984.
Academic year: Undergraduate, August to April (August-December; January-April). Postgraduate, September to May (September-January; February-May). Schools of Medicine, Dentistry and Nursing (October to September)
Admission requirements: Minimum of C+ in Kenya Certificate of Secondary Education (KCSE) or equivalent
Fees: National : c.120,000-400,000 per annum (Kenyan Shilling), International : c.1,700-4,800 per annum (US Dollar)
Main language(s) of instruction: English
Accrediting agency: Commission for Higher Education
Degrees and diplomas: Certificate / Diploma, Bachelor's Degree (Aeronautical and Aerospace Engineering; Agriculture; Art Education; Arts and Humanities; Biological and Life Sciences; Business Administration; Chemistry; Dentistry; Economics; Education; Engineering; Hotel and Restaurant; Human Resources; Information Sciences; Law; Medicine; Natural Resources; Nursing; Physics; Preschool Education; Primary Education; Public Health; Social Sciences; Special Education; Tourism), Postgraduate Diploma (Demography and Population; Human Resources; International Relations; Management; Public Relations; Religious Studies), Master's Degree (Agricultural Education; Agricultural Management; Analytical Chemistry; Animal Husbandry; Anthropology; Applied Mathematics; Archiving; Banking; Biological and Life Sciences; Biology; Biotechnology; Business Administration; Child Care and Development; Civil Engineering; Communication Studies; Computer Science; Crop Production; Dairy; Development Studies; Ecology; Economics; Embryology and Reproduction Biology; Entomology; Environmental Engineering; Environmental Studies; Epidemiology; Film; Finance; Fishery; Food Science; Forestry; French; Gender Studies; Genetics; Geography (Human); Gynaecology and Obstetrics; Health Administration; Health Education; Health Sciences; History; Horticulture; Hotel and Restaurant; Human Resources; Hydraulic Engineering; Hygiene; Immunology; Industrial Engineering; Information Sciences; Information Technology; Inorganic Chemistry; International Relations; Journalism; Law; Library Science; Linguistics; Literature; Management;

Mass Communication; Mathematics; Media Studies; Medicine; Meteorology; Microbiology; Nursing; Nutrition; Occupational Health; Oncology; Organic Chemistry; Orthopaedics; Paediatrics; Parasitology; Peace and Disarmament; Philosophy; Physical Chemistry; Physiology; Plant and Crop Protection; Plant Pathology; Private Law; Psychiatry and Mental Health; Psychology; Public Administration; Public Health; Publishing and Book Trade; Radiology; Religious Studies; Sociology; Soil Science; Speech Therapy and Audiology; Statistics; Surgery; Swahili; Textile Technology; Theatre; Tourism; Translation and Interpretation), Doctor's Degree (Agricultural Management; Animal Husbandry; Anthropology; Biological and Life Sciences; Biology; Biotechnology; Business Administration; Communication Studies; Crop Production; Dairy; Development Studies; Ecology; Energy Engineering; Entomology; Environmental Engineering; Environmental Studies; Epidemiology; Fishery; Forestry; Genetics; Geography (Human); Health Education; History; Horticulture; Hotel and Restaurant; Human Resources; Information Sciences; Library Science; Linguistics; Literature; Machine Building; Management; Materials Engineering; Mechanics; Natural Resources; Nutrition; Parasitology; Philosophy; Plant Pathology; Political Sciences; Production Engineering; Public Health; Religion; Sociology; Soil Science; Statistics; Swahili; Tourism; Zoology)

Student Services: Academic Counselling, Social Counselling, Careers Guidance, Nursery Care, Cultural Activities, Sports Facilities, Language Laboratory, Facilities for disabled people, Health Services, Canteen, Foreign Studies Centre, Library, Residential Facilities

Periodicals: Maarifa, The Educator

Publishing house: Moi University Press

Last Update: 16-02-2017

RONGO UNIVERSITY COLLEGE (RUC)

P.O. Box 103
Rongo 40404
Tel: +254(770) 308-253
Website: http://ruc.ac.ke
Principal: Samuel Gudu

School

Agriculture, Natural Resources and Environmental Studies (Agricultural Business; Agricultural Economics; Agronomy; Animal Husbandry; Environmental Studies; Natural Resources); **Business and Human Resource Development** (Business Administration; Hotel and Restaurant; Human Resources; Management; Tourism); **Education** (Art Education; Education; Preschool Education; Science Education; Secondary Education; Special Education); **Information and Communication Studies** (Advertising and Publicity; Communication Studies; Graphic Design; Information

Technology; Journalism; Library Science; Linguistics; Mass Communication; Media Studies; Public Relations); **Science, Technology and Engineering** (Botany; Chemistry; Computer Science; Mathematics; Microbiology; Physics; Statistics; Zoology)

History: Founded 2011. A constituent college of Moi University.

Main language(s) of instruction: English

Accrediting agency: Commission for University Education

Degrees and diplomas: Certificate / Diploma, Bachelor's Degree, Master's Degree (Advertising and Publicity; Business Administration; Communication Studies; Graphic Design; Information Sciences; Information Technology; Journalism; Linguistics; Mass Communication; Public Relations; Soil Science), Doctor's Degree (Communication Studies; Public Relations; Soil Science). Also Executive MBA, Executive Masters in Educational Administration

Student Services: Library

Last Update: 04-07-2016

Multimedia University of Kenya (MMU)

P.O. Box 15653
Nairobi 00503
Tel: +254(20) 207-1391/2
Website: http://www.mmu.ac.ke
Vice-Chancellor: Festus Kaberia
Tel: +254(20) 207-1248

Faculty

Business and Law (Actuarial Science; Business Administration; Human Resources; Law); **Computing and Information Technology** (Business Computing; Computer Engineering; Computer Science; Information Technology; Software Engineering); **Engineering** (Electrical Engineering; Engineering; Telecommunications Engineering); **Media and Communication** (Film; Journalism; Mass Communication; Public Relations; Visual Arts); **Science and Technology** (Analytical Chemistry; Applied Physics; Computer Science; Industrial Chemistry; Mathematics)

Further information: Magadi Road, Rongai

History: Founded as Central Training School (CTS) 1948. Upgraded into Kenya College of Communications Technology (KCCT) 1992 and then into Multimedia University College of Kenya, constituent college of Jomo Kenyatta University of Agriculture and Technology 2008. Acquired current status and title 2013.

Main language(s) of instruction: English

Accrediting agency: Commission for University Education

Degrees and diplomas: Certificate / Diploma, Bachelor's Degree

Student Services: Health Services, Library, Residential Facilities
Last Update: 23-01-2017

Pwani University (PU)

P.O. Box 195
Kilifi 80108
Tel: +254(41) 7525-105
Fax: +254(41) 7522-128
Website: http://www.pu.ac.ke
Vice-Chancellor: Mohammed S. Rajab
Tel: +254(41) 752-5102/3/4/6

School

Agricultural Sciences and Agribusiness (SASA) (Agricultural Business; Agriculture; Animal Husbandry; Crop Production); **Education** (Curriculum; Educational Administration; Educational Psychology; Educational Sciences; Educational Technology; Special Education); **Health and Human Sciences (SHHS)** (Anatomy; Dietetics; Food Science; Nursing; Nutrition; Physiology; Public Health); **Humanities and Social Sciences** (Arts and Humanities; Business Administration; Economics; Hotel and Restaurant; Linguistics; Literature; Management; Modern Languages; Philosophy; Religious Studies; Social Sciences; Tourism); **Pure and Applied Sciences** (Biochemistry; Biological and Life Sciences; Biotechnology; Chemistry; Mathematics; Physics)
History: Founded 1984 as Kilifi Institute of Agriculture. Became a a constituent college of Kenyatta University 2007, formerly known as the Kilifi Institute of Agriculture. Acquired current status and title 2013.
Fees: Phd, 200,000 per annum for East African students; 250,000 per annum for non-East African students (Kenyan Shilling)
Main language(s) of instruction: English
Accrediting agency: Commission for University Education
Degrees and diplomas: Bachelor's Degree, Postgraduate Diploma (Curriculum; Education; Educational and Student Counselling; Social Sciences), Master's Degree (Agriculture; Agronomy; Animal Husbandry; Applied Physics; Archiving; Biochemistry; Biotechnology; Business Administration; Chemistry; Christian Religious Studies; Comparative Politics; Curriculum; Educational Administration; Educational and Student Counselling; Educational Psychology; Educational Sciences; Environmental Studies; Geography; Higher Education; Information Sciences; International Studies; Islamic Theology; Library Science; Linguistics; Literature; Mathematics Education; Philosophy; Philosophy of Education; Physics; Preschool Education; Public Health; Religious Studies; Science Education; Sociology; Soil Management; Special Education; Statistics; Swahili), Doctor's Degree (Animal Husbandry; Botany; Chemistry; Christian Religious Studies; Comparative Politics; Crop Production; Curriculum; Economics; Educational Administration; Educational and Student Counselling; Educational Psychology; Educational Sciences; Educational Technology; Environmental Studies; Fishery; Higher Education; International Studies; Islamic Theology; Mathematics Education; Nutrition; Philosophy; Physics; Preschool Education; Public Health; Religious Studies; Science Education; Statistics; Zoology)
Student Services: Library, IT Centre
Last Update: 29-06-2016

South Eastern Kenya University (SEKU)

P.O. Box 170
Kitui 90200
Website: http://www.seku.ac.ke
Vice-Chancellor: Geoffrey Muluvi
Tel: +254(716) 962-771

School

Agriculture and Veterinary Sciences (Agricultural Business; Agricultural Economics; Agriculture; Food Science; Food Technology; Veterinary Science; Wildlife); **Business and Economics** (Business Administration; Economics; Management); **Education** (Educational Administration; Educational Psychology; Educational Sciences; Educational Technology); **Engineering and Technology** (Agricultural Engineering; Building Technologies; Construction Engineering; Energy Engineering; Industrial Engineering; Production Engineering); **Environment and Natural Resources Management** (Environmental Engineering; Environmental Studies; Forestry; Natural Resources; Soil Management); **Health Sciences** (Nursing; Public Health); **Humanities and Social Sciences** (Anthropology; Communication Studies; Development Studies; Gender Studies; Linguistics; Sociology); **Information and Communication Technology** (Computer Science; Information Technology; Software Engineering; Telecommunications Engineering); **Pure and Applied Sciences** (Actuarial Science; Biochemistry; Biology; Chemistry; Electronic Engineering; Mathematics; Physics); **Water Resources Science and Technology** (Aquaculture; Fishery; Marine Science and Oceanography; Water Management; Water Science)

Institute

Mining and Mineral Processing (Geology; Meteorology)
Further information: Also Machakos, Mtito Andei, Wote Campuses

History: Founded as South Eastern University College, a constituent college of University of Nairobi, 2008. Acquired current status and title 2013.

Fees: Undergraduate, 36,000-84,000 per annum; Master, 120,000 per annum; Ph.D., 150,000 per annum (Kenyan Shilling)

Main language(s) of instruction: English

Accrediting agency: Commission for University Education

Degrees and diplomas: Certificate / Diploma, Bachelor's Degree, Master's Degree (Agricultural Management; Agronomy; Animal Husbandry; Business Administration; Curriculum; Education; Educational Administration; Environmental Management; Forestry; Information Technology; International and Comparative Education; Meteorology; Philosophy of Education; Water Management), Doctor's Degree (Environmental Management; Forestry; Meteorology; Water Management)

Student Services: Library, IT Centre

Student Numbers 2015-2016	MALE	FEMALE	TOTAL
All (Foreign Included)			c. 6000

Last Update: 29-06-2016

Technical University of Mombasa (TUM)

Tom Mboya Street, Tudor
Mombasa 90420
Tel: +254(41) 249-2222/3
Fax: +254(41) 249-0571
Website: http://www.tum.ac.ke
Acting Vice-Chancellor: Laila Abubakar

Faculty

Applied and Health Sciences (Biotechnology; Chemistry; Computer Science; Environmental Studies; Food Technology; Health Sciences; Mathematics; Medicine; Microbiology; Physics; Statistics); **Engineering and Technology** (Automotive Engineering; Building Technologies; Civil Engineering; Electrical and Electronic Engineering; Mechanical Engineering; Medical Technology)

School

Business (Accountancy; Business Administration; Finance; Management); **Humanities and Social Studies** (Communication Studies; Hotel and Restaurant; Social Sciences; Tourism); **Medicine** (Medicine; Surgery)

Institute

Computing and Informatics (Computer Science; Information Technology); **Research, Innovation and Extension (IRIE)**

History: Founded 2007 as Mombasa Polytechnic University College (MPUC). Acquired current status and title 2013.

Main language(s) of instruction: English

Accrediting agency: Commission for University Education

Degrees and diplomas: Certificate / Diploma, Bachelor's Degree, Master's Degree (Public Health)

Student Services: Social Counselling, Health Services, Canteen, Library, Residential Facilities

Last Update: 29-06-2016

The Technical University of Kenya (TU-K)

P.O. Box 52428
Nairobi 00200
Tel: +254(20) 221-9929, +254(20) 334-1639, +254 (20) 334-3672
Website: http://tukenya.ac.ke
Vice-Chancellor: F.W.O. Aduol

Faculty

Applied Sciences and Technology (Biological and Life Sciences; Computer Science; Health Sciences; Information Technology; Mathematics; Natural Sciences; Physics; Statistics; Technology); **Engineering Sciences and Technology** (Architecture; Bioengineering; Civil Engineering; Electrical and Electronic Engineering; Engineering; Engineering Management; Environmental Engineering; Geological Engineering; Mechanical Engineering; Mining Engineering; Production Engineering; Surveying and Mapping); **Social Sciences and Technology** (Business Administration; Cultural Studies; Design; Development Studies; Fashion Design; Fine Arts; Hotel and Restaurant; Information Technology; Management; Mass Communication; Media Studies; Music; Performing Arts; Social Studies; Tourism)

History: Founded 2007 as the Kenya Polytechnic University College, a constituent college of the University of Nairobi. Acquired current status and title 2013.

Main language(s) of instruction: English

Accrediting agency: Commission for University Education

Degrees and diplomas: Certificate / Diploma, Bachelor's Degree, Postgraduate Diploma (Production Engineering), Master's Degree (Applied Linguistics; Applied Mathematics; Biochemistry; Business Administration; Dietetics; Environmental Management; Information Management; International Relations; Management; Mathematics; Mechanical Engineering; Music; Music Education; Music Theory and Composition; Musical Instruments; Nutrition; Parasitology; Statistics), Doctor's Degree (Chemistry; Mathematics; Statistics). Also Advance Diploma in Safety Engineering

Student Services: Social Counselling, Sports Facilities, Health Services, Canteen, Library, IT Centre, Residential Facilities

Last Update: 28-06-2016

University of Eldoret (UOELD)

P.O. Box 1125
Eldoret 30100
Tel: +254(788) 232-004
Website: http://www.uoeld.ac.ke
Vice-Chancellor: Teresa A. O. Akenga

School

Agriculture and Biotechnology (Agricultural Economics; Agricultural Education; Agriculture; Animal Husbandry; Biotechnology; Crop Production; Fashion Design; Food Science; Horticulture; Nutrition; Soil Science); **Business and Management Sciences** (Business Administration; Hotel and Restaurant; Management; Tourism); **Economics** (Economics); **Education** (Agricultural Education; Education; Higher Education Teacher Training; Physical Education; Preschool Education; Primary Education; Special Education; Teacher Training; Technology Education); **Engineering** (Agricultural Engineering; Bioengineering; Civil Engineering; Mechanical Engineering; Production Engineering); **Environmental Studies** (Ecology; Environmental Management; Environmental Studies; Social Sciences); **Natural Resource Management** (Aquaculture; Development Studies; Environmental Studies; Fishery; Forest Products; Forestry; Meteorology; Natural Resources; Water Science; Wildlife; Wood Technology); **Science** (Actuarial Science; Analytical Chemistry; Biochemistry; Biological and Life Sciences; Biotechnology; Botany; Chemistry; Computer Education; Computer Science; Entomology; Information Technology; Laboratory Techniques; Mathematics; Mathematics Education; Microbiology; Parasitology; Physics; Science Education; Statistics; Zoology)
History: Founded as a Large Scale Farmers Training Centre 1946.Converted to a teachers' training college and renamed Moi Teachers' Training College 1984. Taken over by Moi University as a Campus in 1990 and renamed Chepkoilel Campus. Upgraded into a university college and renamed Chepkoilel University College, a constituent college of Moi University 2010. Acquired current status and title 2013.
Main language(s) of instruction: English
Accrediting agency: Commission for University Education
Degrees and diplomas: Certificate / Diploma, Bachelor's Degree, Postgraduate Diploma (Crop Production; Education; Harvest Technology), Master's Degree (Agricultural Economics; Agricultural Education; Agronomy; Animal Husbandry; Aquaculture; Biochemistry; Biological and Life Sciences; Biotechnology; Botany; Business Administration; Chemistry; Crop Production; Dairy; Earth Sciences; Ecology; Economics; Educational Administration; Educational and Student Counselling; Educational Psychology; Educational Sciences; Educational Technology; Environmental Management; Environmental Studies; Fishery; Forest Biology; Forest Economics; Forest Management; Forestry; Harvest Technology; Home Economics Education; Horticulture; Hotel and Restaurant; Information Technology; Law; Mathematics; Mathematics Education; Meat and Poultry; Microbiology; Natural Resources; Nutrition; Paper Technology; Physics; Plant and Crop Protection; Primary Education; Science Education; Soil Science; Technology Education; Textile Technology; Tourism; Tropical Agriculture; Water Science; Wildlife; Wood Technology; Zoology), Doctor's Degree (Agricultural Economics; Agriculture; Analytical Chemistry; Applied Mathematics; Aquaculture; Botany; Chemistry; Crop Production; Ecology; Economics; Educational Administration; Educational and Student Counselling; Educational Psychology; Educational Technology; Entomology; Environmental Management; Environmental Studies; Fishery; Foreign Languages Education; Forestry; Genetics; Health Sciences; Horticulture; Inorganic Chemistry; International Law; Mathematics; Nuclear Physics; Organic Chemistry; Parasitology; Physical Chemistry; Physics; Physiology; Plant Pathology; Preschool Education; Primary Education; Science Education; Soil Science; Statistics; Technology Education; Zoology)
Student Services: Library

Student Numbers 2015-2016	MALE	FEMALE	TOTAL
All (Foreign Included)			c. 33000

Last Update: 30-06-2016

University of Kabianga (UoK)

P.O. Box 2030
Kericho 20200
Tel: +254(700) 000-299, +254(775) 553-311, +254 (20) 217-2665
Website: http://kabianga.ac.ke
Deputy Vice-Chancellor Administration and Finance: Eric K. Prof Koech
Vice-Chancellor: Wilson K. Prof Kipngeno
Deputy vice chancellor Planning Research and Development: Marion Prof Mutugi
Deputy Vice Chanellor Academic and student affairs: Elijah Prof Omwenga

School

Agriculture and Biotechnology (Agricultural Economics; Agricultural Management; Agriculture; Horticulture); **Arts and Social Sciences** (Communication Studies; French; Literature; Public Administration; Public Relations; Swahili); **Business and Economics** (Business Administration; Economics; Hotel and Restaurant; Human Resources; Management; Tourism);

Education (Education; Educational Administration; Educational and Student Counselling; Educational Psychology; Preschool Education; Primary Education; Science Education); **Information Science and Knowledge Management** (Information Management; Information Sciences); **Natural Resource and Environmental Management** (Environmental Management; Environmental Studies; Forest Biology; Forestry; Tropical Agriculture); **Science and Technology** (Actuarial Science; Applied Mathematics; Biochemistry; Biological and Life Sciences; Botany; Chemistry; Computer Science; Environmental Studies; Health Sciences; Information Technology; Mathematics; Medicine; Microbiology; Nursing; Physics; Statistics; Zoology)

Further information: Premier/Taplotin road off Kericho-Sotik Road

History: 1959-founded as Kabianga Farmers Training Centre . 2007- became Kabianga Campus of Moi University. 2009-upgraded into Kabianga University College constituent college of Moi University. 2013-chartered as the University of Kabianga.

Academic year: September to June

Fees: varies according to course with a minimum of 110,000 per year (Kenyan Shilling)

Main language(s) of instruction: English

Accrediting agency: Chartered University by Commission for University

Degrees and diplomas: Certificate / Diploma (Health Sciences; Technology), Bachelor's Degree (Agriculture; Applied Mathematics; Biochemistry; Biological and Life Sciences; Business Administration; Education; Environmental Management; Environmental Studies; Forestry; Health Sciences; Information Management; Linguistics; Literature; Mathematics and Computer Science; Microbiology; Natural Sciences; Nursing; Philosophy; Public Administration; Religion; Social Sciences; Statistics; Technology; Tourism), Master's Degree (Agricultural Economics; Agricultural Management; Agriculture; Applied Mathematics; Business Administration; Chemistry; Educational Administration; Educational and Student Counselling; Educational Psychology; Educational Sciences; Educational Technology; Environmental Management; Environmental Studies; Forestry; Literature; Management; Mathematics; Microbiology; Preschool Education; Primary Education; Statistics; Swahili), Doctor's Degree (Business Administration; Literature; Swahili). Also Executive MBA

Student Services: Academic Counselling, Careers Guidance, Sports Facilities, Facilities for disabled people, Health Services, Library, IT Centre, Residential Facilities

Academic Staff 2016	MALE	FEMALE	TOTAL
FULL-TIME	129	66	195
Student Numbers 2016			
All (Foreign Included)	4768	4089	8857

Last Update: 30-06-2016

🏛 University of Nairobi (UoN)

PO Box 30197
Nairobi 00100
Tel: +254(20) 318-262
Fax: +254(20) 245-566
Website: http://www.uonbi.ac.ke
Vice-Chancellor: Peter M.F. Mbithi
Tel: +254(02) 331-8262

College

Agriculture and Veterinary Sciences (Agricultural Economics; Agriculture; Animal Husbandry; Arid Land Studies; Environmental Studies; Farm Management; Food Science; Food Technology; Nutrition; Pathology; Peace and Disarmament; Pharmacology; Physiology; Plant and Crop Protection; Public Health; Soil Science; Technology; Toxicology; Veterinary Science); **Architecture and Engineering** (Aeronautical and Aerospace Engineering; Architecture; Bioengineering; Building Technologies; Civil Engineering; Construction Engineering; Design; Electrical Engineering; Engineering; Environmental Engineering; Fine Arts; Mechanical Engineering; Nuclear Engineering; Production Engineering; Real Estate; Regional Planning; Surveying and Mapping; Telecommunications Engineering; Town Planning); **Biological and Physical Sciences** (Biological and Life Sciences; Biotechnology; Chemistry; Computer Science; Geology; Mathematics; Meteorology; Physics); **Education And External Studies** (Communication Studies; Education; Educational Administration; Educational Sciences; Educational Technology; Physical Education; Sports); **Health Sciences** (Anaesthesiology; Anatomy; Biochemistry; Dental Technology; Dentistry; Epidemiology; Gynaecology and Obstetrics; Medicine; Microbiology; Nursing; Ophthalmology; Oral Pathology; Orthodontics; Orthopaedics; Paediatrics; Pathology; Periodontics; Pharmacology; Pharmacy; Physiology; Psychiatry and Mental Health; Public Health; Radiology; Rehabilitation and Therapy; Surgery; Tropical Medicine); **Humanities and Social Sciences** (Accountancy; African Studies; Arabic; Archaeology; Arts and Humanities; Asian Studies; Business Administration; Commercial Law; Communication Studies; Demography and Population; Development Studies; Economics; Environmental Studies; Finance; French; Geography; Germanic Studies; History; Human Rights; Information Sciences; International Relations; International Studies; Journalism; Korean; Law; Library Science; Linguistics; Literature; Management; Peace and Disarmament; Philosophy; Political Sciences; Private Law; Psychology; Public Administration; Public Law; Religious Studies; Social Work; Sociology; Swahili; Translation and Interpretation; Women's Studies)

Further information: Parklands, Kenya Science, Kikuyu, Lower Kabete, Upper Kabete Campuses

History: Founded 1956 as Royal Technical College of East Africa, became University College Nairobi 1963 and acquired present status and title 1970.

Academic year: October to July

Admission requirements: Kenya Certificate of Secondary Education (KCSE), prior to Higher School Certificate (HSC) of GCE Advanced ('A') level examinations.

Fees: 80,000-450,000 per annum (Kenyan Shilling)

Main language(s) of instruction: English

Accrediting agency: Commission for University Education

Degrees and diplomas: Certificate / Diploma, Bachelor's Degree, Postgraduate Diploma (Actuarial Science; Adult Education; Agriculture; Communication Studies; Continuing Education; Criminology; Development Studies; Education; Energy Engineering; Environmental Management; Food Science; Gender Studies; Health Sciences; Heritage Preservation; Horticulture; Human Resources; Information Management; International Relations; Labour and Industrial Relations; Management; Meteorology; Nuclear Engineering; Pharmacy; Protective Services; Psychiatry and Mental Health; Psychology; Public Health; Rural Studies; Social and Community Services; Social Work; Sociology; Speech Therapy and Audiology; Water Science), Master's Degree (Actuarial Science; Adult Education; Agricultural Economics; Agricultural Management; Agronomy; Alternative Medicine; Anaesthesiology; Analytical Chemistry; Anatomy; Animal Husbandry; Anthropology; Applied Mathematics; Arabic; Architecture; Architecture and Planning; Arts and Humanities; Biochemistry; Bioengineering; Biological and Life Sciences; Biotechnology; Botany; Business Administration; Business Education; Cardiology; Cell Biology; Chemistry; Christian Religious Studies; Civil Engineering; Clinical Psychology; Communication Studies; Computer Science; Construction Engineering; Continuing Education; Criminology; Curriculum; Demography and Population; Dental Technology; Dentistry; Design; Development Studies; Distance Education; Ecology; Economic and Finance Policy; Economics; Education; Educational Administration; Educational Sciences; Educational Technology; Educational Testing and Evaluation; Electrical and Electronic Engineering; Electrical Engineering; Embryology and Reproduction Biology; Energy Engineering; Engineering; Entomology; Environmental Engineering; Environmental Management; Environmental Studies; Epidemiology; Film; Finance; Food Science; Food Technology; Foreign Languages Education; Forestry; Genetics; Geological Engineering; Geology; Government; Gynaecology and Obstetrics; Health Administration; Higher Education; Horticulture; Human Resources; Industrial Chemistry; Information Management; Information Sciences; Information Technology; Inorganic Chemistry; International and Comparative Education; International Economics; International Relations; International Studies; Laboratory Techniques; Labour and Industrial Relations; Law; Leadership; Leather Techniques; Library Science; Linguistics; Literature; Management; Marketing; Mathematics; Meat and Poultry; Mechanical Engineering; Medicine; Meteorology; Microbiology; Natural Resources; Neurology; Nuclear Engineering; Nursing; Nutrition; Ophthalmology; Organic Chemistry; Orthopaedics; Otorhinolaryngology; Paediatrics; Parasitology; Pathology; Peace and Disarmament; Pedagogy; Periodontics; Pharmacology; Pharmacy; Philosophy of Education; Physical Education; Physics; Physiology; Plant and Crop Protection; Plant Pathology; Plastic Surgery; Political Sciences; Preschool Education; Protective Services; Psychiatry and Mental Health; Psychology; Public Administration; Public Health; Radiology; Real Estate; Religious Education; Rural Studies; Sociology; Soil Management; Soil Science; Sports; Statistics; Surgery; Surveying and Mapping; Swahili; Telecommunications Engineering; Theatre; Town Planning; Toxicology; Translation and Interpretation; Tropical Medicine; Veterinary Science; Water Management; Water Science; Wildlife; Women's Studies; Zoology), Doctor's Degree (Accountancy; Agricultural Business; Agricultural Economics; Agricultural Education; Agricultural Management; Agriculture; Alternative Medicine; Anatomy; Anthropology; Archaeology; Arid Land Studies; Biochemistry; Bioengineering; Biological and Life Sciences; Biotechnology; Business Administration; Chemistry; Civil Engineering; Clinical Psychology; Communication Studies; Computer Science; Cultural Studies; Curriculum; Demography and Population; Dentistry; Development Studies; Distance Education; Economics; Education; Educational Administration; Educational Sciences; Environmental Management; Environmental Studies; Finance; Food Science; Food Technology; Forestry; Geology; History; Information Management; Information Sciences; International Studies; Law; Linguistics; Literature; Management; Mathematics; Medicine; Meteorology; Natural Resources; Nuclear Engineering; Nutrition; Peace and Disarmament; Periodontics; Pharmacy; Philosophy; Physics; Physiology; Political Sciences; Preschool Education; Psychology; Public Administration; Regional Planning; Sociology; Soil Management; Soil Science; Surgery; Town Planning; Veterinary Science; Women's Studies)

Student Services: Academic Counselling, Social Counselling, Careers Guidance, Cultural Activities, Sports Facilities, Language Laboratory, Facilities for disabled people, Health Services, Canteen, Library, Residential Facilities

Publishing house: University of Nairobi Press

Last Update: 28-06-2016

EMBU UNIVERSITY COLLEGE (EUC)

P.O. Box 6
Embu 60100
Tel: +254(20) 244-4136
Website: http://www.embuni.ac.ke
Vice Chancellor: Daniel Mugendi Njiru

School

Agriculture (Agricultural Economics; Agricultural Management; Agriculture; Soil Management; Water Management); **Business and Economics** (Business Administration; Economics); **Education and Social Sciences** (Education; Social Sciences); **Pure and Applied Sciences** (Biological and Life Sciences; Physics)

History: Founded 2011. A constituent college of University of Nairobi.

Main language(s) of instruction: English

Accrediting agency: Commission for University Education

Degrees and diplomas: Bachelor's Degree, Master's Degree (Agricultural Management; Agriculture; Agronomy; Biotechnology; Business Administration; Chemistry; Curriculum; Ecology; Educational Administration; Educational Sciences; Forestry; Genetics; Horticulture; Linguistics; Microbiology; Plant and Crop Protection; Preschool Education; Soil Management; Soil Science; Water Science), Doctor's Degree (Agricultural Management; Business Administration; Ecology; Educational Administration; Entomology; Fishery; Genetics; Horticulture; Microbiology; Parasitology; Plant and Crop Protection)

Student Services: Sports Facilities, Library

Last Update: 04-07-2016

Private Institutions

Adventist University of Africa (AUA)

Private Bag Mbagathi
Nairobi 00503
Tel: +254(733) 333-451/452
Website: http://www.aua.ac.ke
Vice-Chancellor: Delbert W. Baker

School

Postgraduate Studies (Business Administration; Leadership; Public Health)

Department/Division

Theological Seminary (Bible; Missionary Studies; Pastoral Studies; Religion; Theology)

Further information: Also Advent Hill, Magadi Road and Ongata Rongai Campuses

History: Founded 2005. Acquired current status 2013.

Main language(s) of instruction: English

Accrediting agency: Commission for University Education

Degrees and diplomas: Master's Degree (Bible; Business Administration; Leadership; Missionary Studies; Pastoral Studies; Public Health; Theology), Doctor's Degree (Religion)

Student Services: Library, IT Centre, Residential Facilities

Last Update: 16-02-2017

Africa International University (AIU)

P.O. Box 24686 Karen-Dagoretti Road
Nairobi 00502
Tel: +254(20) 260-3663, +254(20) 260-3664
Website: http://www.aiu.ac.ke
Vice-Chancellor: Dankit Nassiuma

School

Business and Economics (SBE) (Accountancy; Business Administration; Human Resources; Information Technology; Leadership; Management; Sales Techniques); **Education, Arts and Social Sciences (SEAS)** (Applied Linguistics; Communication Studies; Development Studies; Education; Linguistics; Psychology; Translation and Interpretation)

Institute

Study of African Realities (ISAR) (Cultural Studies; Social Studies)

Graduate School

Nairobi Evangelical Graduate School of Theology (NEGST) (Bible; Christian Religious Studies; Missionary Studies; Theology)

History: Founded 1983 as Nairobi Evangelical Graduate School of Theology (NEGST). Acquired present status and title 2011.

Fees: Undergraduate, 18,000-54,000 per annum; Postgraduate, 75,000-90,000 per annum (Kenyan Shilling)

Main language(s) of instruction: English

Accrediting agency: Commission for University Accreditation; ACTEA

Degrees and diplomas: Certificate / Diploma, Bachelor's Degree, Postgraduate Diploma (Education; Theology), Master's Degree (Bible; Child Care and Development; Curriculum; Educational Administration; Family Studies; History of Religion; Leadership; Missionary Studies; Pastoral Studies; Religion; Religious Education; Theology; Translation and Interpretation), Doctor's Degree (Bible; Child Care and Development; Christian Religious Studies; Cultural Studies; Curriculum; Development Studies; Education; Educational Administration; Family Studies; Missionary Studies; Religion; Religious Education; Religious Studies; Theology; Translation and Interpretation)

Student Services: Academic Counselling, Sports Facilities, Health Services, Foreign Studies Centre, Library, IT Centre, Residential Facilities

Last Update: 16-02-2017

Africa Nazarene University (ANU)

PO Box 53067 Ongata Rongal Area of Kajiado District
Nairobi 00200, +254(703) 970 520/5

Tel: +254(703) 970-520/5
Fax: +254(20) 252-7170-5
Website: http://www.anu.ac.ke
Vice-Chancellor: Leah Marangu

Course/Programme
Counselling Psychology (Psychology)

School
Business (Business Administration; Business and Commerce; International Business; Management; Sales Techniques); **Governance, Peace and Security** (Civil Security; Criminal Law; Criminology; Parks and Recreation; Peace and Disarmament; Social and Community Services); **Law** (Law)

Department/Division
Computer Science and Information Technology (Business Computing; Computer Networks; Computer Science; Information Technology); **Education** (Education); **Environment and Natural Resource Management** (Environmental Management; Environmental Studies; Natural Resources); **Mass Communication** (Mass Communication; Public Relations); **Pre-University Programme (PUP)** (Business Administration; Christian Religious Studies; Communication Studies; English; Literature; Mathematics); **Religion** (Christian Religious Studies; Religion; Theology)

Institute
Research, Development, and Policy (IRDP)
History: Founded 1993. Acquired present status 2002.
Main language(s) of instruction: English
Accrediting agency: Commission of University Education; International Board of Education
Degrees and diplomas: Certificate / Diploma, Bachelor's Degree, Postgraduate Diploma (Management; Peace and Disarmament), Master's Degree (Business Administration; Civil Security; Education; Environmental Management; Government; Information Technology; Natural Resources; Peace and Disarmament; Psychology; Religion), Doctor's Degree (Religion)
Student Services: Social Counselling, Careers Guidance, Sports Facilities, Health Services, Library, Residential Facilities
Last Update: 21-06-2016

Daystar University

PO Box 44400
Nairobi
Tel: +254(20) 732-002
Fax: +254(20) 728-338

Website: http://www.daystar.ac.ke
Vice-Chancellor: Timothy Wachira
Tel: +254(20) 720-650

Faculty
Arts and Humanities (Bible; Education; International Relations; Peace and Disarmament; Theology); **Science, Engineering and Health** (Actuarial Science; Applied Mathematics; Biomedicine; Computer Science; Environmental Studies; Health Sciences; Mathematics; Nursing; Physics; Statistics)

School
Business and Economics (Accountancy; Business Administration; Business Computing; Economics; Finance; Human Resources; Management; Marketing; Sales Techniques; Transport Management); **Communication, Language and Performing Arts** (Advertising and Publicity; Communication Studies; English; French; Literature; Media Studies; Music; Public Relations; Swahili); **Human and Social Sciences** (Child Care and Development; Clinical Psychology; Development Studies; Family Studies; Psychology; Rehabilitation and Therapy; Social Work)
Further information: Also Athi River Campus
History: Founded 1974, previously Daystar Communications, Daystar University College. Acquired present status and title 1992.
Academic year: August to May
Admission requirements: Kenya Certificate of Secondary Education grade C+, or equivalent
Fees: 5,650.00 per credit hour per semester (Kenyan Shilling)
Main language(s) of instruction: English
Accrediting agency: Commission for Higher Education
Degrees and diplomas: Certificate / Diploma, Bachelor's Degree (Accountancy; Advertising and Publicity; Bible; Business and Commerce; Business Computing; Business Education; Communication Studies; Computer Education; Computer Science; Economics; English; Environmental Studies; Foreign Languages Education; French; Health Sciences; Literature; Marketing; Mathematics; Mathematics Education; Media Studies; Music; Music Education; Nursing; Peace and Disarmament; Physics; Preschool Education; Public Relations; Religious Education; Religious Studies; Sales Techniques; Social and Community Services; Social Work; Swahili; Theology; Transport Management), Postgraduate Diploma (Child Care and Development; Education), Master's Degree (Business Administration; Child Care and Development; Christian Religious Studies; Communication Studies; Finance; Human Resources; Management; Marketing; Media Studies; Psychology; Theology), Doctor's Degree (Communication Studies)
Student Services: Academic Counselling, Social Counselling, Careers Guidance, Sports Facilities, Language Laboratory, Health Services, Canteen

Periodicals: Interdisciplinary Perspectives

Student Numbers 2015-2016	MALE	FEMALE	TOTAL
All (Foreign Included)			c. 1500

Last Update: 21-06-2016

Great Lakes University of Kisumu (GLUK)

P.O. Box 2224
Kisumu 40100, Nyanza
Tel: +254(736) 550-505
Website: http://www.gluk.ac.ke
Vice-Chancellor: Atieno Anne Ndede Amadi

Faculty

Art and Sciences (Agricultural Business; Business Administration; Education; Hotel and Restaurant; Theology; Tourism); **Health Sciences** (Community Health; Medicine; Physical Therapy; Surgery)

School

Nursing and Midwifery (Midwifery; Nursing)

Institute

Tropical Institute of Community Health and Development (TICH) in Africa (Community Health; Development Studies; Health Administration; Nutrition)

Centre

Postgraduate Studies and Research
Further information: Also Kisumu Town, Nairobi and Milimani Campuses
History: Founded 2006 from Tropical Institute of Community Health and Development, founded 1998.
Academic year: 2016/2017
Fees: National : Varies according to programme; Most expensive programme, 222,000 per annum (Kenyan Shilling), International : Varies according to programme; Most expensive programme, 3,525 per annum (US Dollar)
Main language(s) of instruction: English
Accrediting agency: Commission For University Education (CUE)
Degrees and diplomas: Certificate / Diploma, Bachelor's Degree, Postgraduate Diploma (Nutrition), Master's Degree (Business Administration; Community Health; Development Studies; Health Administration; Nursing; Nutrition), Doctor's Degree (Community Health; Development Studies)
Student Services: Library, IT Centre
Last Update: 16-02-2017

Kabarak University

PO Private Bag 20157, Nakuru-Eldama Ravine Highway
Kabarak
Tel: +254(51) 343-234/5
Fax: +254(51) 343-012
Website: http://www.kabarak.ac.ke
Vice-Chancellor: Jones Kaleli
Tel: +254(51) 343028

School

Biological and Physical Sciences (Biology; Chemistry; Physics); **Business and Economics** (Business Administration; Business and Commerce; Business Computing; Economics; Mathematics; Statistics; Transport Management); **Computer Science and Bioinformatics** (Actuarial Science; Computer Science; Information Technology; Statistics; Telecommunications Engineering); **Education** (Art Education; Education; Science Education); **Environmental Studies and Energy Technology** (Environmental Studies); **Law** (Law); **Medicine and Health Sciences** (Dietetics; Environmental Studies; Health Sciences; Medicine; Nursing; Nutrition); **Music and Performing Arts** (Mass Communication; Music; Music Theory and Composition; Religious Music; Theology); **Theology and Biblical Studies** (Theology)
History: Founded 2002. Charter awarded 2008.
Academic year: September to August
Admission requirements: Kenyan Certificate of Secondary Education(KCSE) C+, Diploma
Fees: 40,000 (Kenyan Shilling)
Main language(s) of instruction: English/Kiswahili
Accrediting agency: Commission for Higher Education
Degrees and diplomas: Certificate / Diploma, Bachelor's Degree, Master's Degree (Business Administration; Community Health; Curriculum; Education; Educational Administration; Educational and Student Counselling; Information Technology; Music Education; Music Theory and Composition; Musicology; Religious Music), Doctor's Degree (Information Technology)
Student Services: Academic Counselling, Social Counselling, Careers Guidance, Nursery Care, Sports Facilities, Facilities for disabled people, Health Services, Canteen
Last Update: 22-06-2016

KCA University (KCA)

Main Campus - Thika Road, Ruaraka P.O Box 56808
Nairobi 00200
Tel: +254(208) 070-408/9, +254(203) 537-842
Website: http://www.kca.ac.ke

Vice-Chancellor: Noah Midamba
Tel: +254(20) 856-1803

Faculty

Business and Public Management (Business Administration; Business and Commerce; International Business; Leadership; Management; Marketing; Transport Management); **Computing and Information Management** (Computer Engineering; Computer Networks; Computer Science; Information Management; Information Technology; Software Engineering); **Education and Arts** (Art Education; Curriculum; Education; Educational Administration; Educational Sciences; Preschool Education; Psychology)

School

Graduate Studies and Research; **Professional Programmes** (Accountancy; Administration; Banking; Computer Networks; Computer Science; English; French; German; Management; Real Estate; Secretarial Studies)
Further information: Also Town and ICAD Campus, Kisumu Campus, Western Campus, Monrovia Plaza Campus
History: Founded 1989 as Kenya College of Accountancy. Acquired current title 2007 and received charter 2013.
Main language(s) of instruction: English
Accrediting agency: Commission for University Education
Degrees and diplomas: Certificate / Diploma, Bachelor's Degree, Postgraduate Diploma (Business Administration; Education), Master's Degree (Business Administration; Business and Commerce; Curriculum; Data Processing; Educational Administration; Educational Sciences; Human Resources; Information Management; Information Technology; Management; Marketing; Teacher Training), Doctor's Degree (Information Technology)
Student Services: Library

Student Numbers 2015-2016	MALE	FEMALE	TOTAL
All (Foreign Included)			c. 15000

Last Update: 01-07-2016

Kenya Highland Evangelical University (KHEU)

P.O. Box 123-20200 Off Kisumu Road near Kericho High School
Kericho 20200
Tel: +254(52) 30201, +254(716) 150-220
Website: http://www.kheu.ac.ke
Vice-Chancellor: Robert Lang'at

Course/Programme

Business Management (Business Administration); **Christian Education** (Christian Religious Studies); **Computer Science** (Computer Science); **Counselling** (Psychology); **Education (Arts)** (Art Education); **Education (Early Childhood)** (Preschool Education); **Library and Information Science** (Information Sciences; Library Science); **Theology** (Theology)
History: Founded as Sotik Bible School 1944. Relocated from Sotik to Cheptenye in Belgut area 1950. Transformed into Kenya Highlands Bible School 1955, renamed Kenya Highlands Bible College 1962 and the Bible College Council 1970. Registered by the Commission for Higher Education 1989. Acquired current status and title 2011.
Main language(s) of instruction: English
Accrediting agency: Commission for Higher Education
Degrees and diplomas: Certificate / Diploma, Bachelor's Degree
Student Services: Library, Residential Facilities
Last Update: 01-07-2016

Kenya Methodist University

P.O. Box 267
Meru 60200
Tel: +254(64) 313-12-79, +254(64) 313-10-97
Fax: +254(64) 301-62
Website: http://www.kemu.ac.ke
Vice-Chancellor: Henry K. Kiriamiti

Faculty

Education and Social Sciences (Communication Studies; Education; Educational and Student Counselling; Journalism; Religious Studies; Theology); **Science and Technology** (Agriculture; Biochemistry; Biology; Chemistry; Computer Science; Environmental Studies; Information Sciences; Mathematics; Physics)

School

Business and Economics (Accountancy; Business Administration; Economics; Finance; Hotel and Restaurant; Statistics; Tourism); **Medicine and Health Sciences** (Anatomy; Biochemistry; Community Health; Dietetics; Health Administration; Health Education; Laboratory Techniques; Medical Parasitology; Medicine; Microbiology; Nursing; Nutrition; Pathology; Pharmacy; Physiology; Public Health; Surgery)
Further information: Also Nairobi, Mombasa, Nakuru, Nyeri Campuses
History: Founded 1997. Charter awarded 2006.
Fees: Undergraduate, 10,500-59,800; Postgraduate, 42,000-85,000 (Kenyan Shilling)

Main language(s) of instruction: English
Accrediting agency: Commission for University Education
Degrees and diplomas: Certificate / Diploma, Bachelor's Degree, Postgraduate Diploma (Education), Master's Degree (Agriculture; Business Administration; Computer Engineering; Development Studies; Dietetics; Educational Administration; Educational and Student Counselling; Finance; Health Administration; Information Management; Missionary Studies; Nutrition; Public Health; Religious Studies), Doctor's Degree (Agriculture; Business Administration; Development Studies; Educational Administration; Health Administration; Management). Also Professional and Pre-University Programmes
Student Services: Sports Facilities, Library, IT Centre, Residential Facilities
Last Update: 22-06-2016

Mount Kenya University

P.O.Box 342 General Kago Road
Thika 01000
Tel: +254(672) 820-000
Fax: +254(20) 205-0315
Website: http://www.mku.ac.ke
Vice-Chancellor: Stanley Waudo

School

Business and Economics (Accountancy; Economics; Finance; Hotel Management; Management; Tourism); **Computing and Informatics (SCI)** (Business Computing; Information Management; Information Sciences; Information Technology); **Education** (Curriculum; Educational Administration; Educational Psychology; Educational Sciences; Educational Technology; Preschool Education; Special Education); **Engineering, Energy and the Built Environment** (Electrical Engineering; Electronic Engineering; Energy Engineering; Environmental Engineering); **Health Sciences** (Health Sciences; Medicine; Nursing; Pharmacy; Public Health); **Hospitality, Travel and Tourism Management** (Hotel and Restaurant; Tourism); **Law** (Law); **Postgraduate Studies** (Business Administration; Economics; Education; Health Sciences; Information Technology; Natural Sciences; Nursing; Pharmacy; Social Sciences); **Pure and Applied Sciences** (Actuarial Science; Animal Husbandry; Biological and Life Sciences; Chemistry; Engineering; Information Technology; Mathematics; Physics; Statistics); **Social Sciences** (African Languages; Arts and Humanities; Civil Security; Development Studies; English; Ethics; Government; Journalism; Mass Communication; Modern Languages; Psychology; Social Sciences; Swahili)

Institute

Film, Creative and Performing Arts (Dance; Film; Music; Theatre)

Further information: Also following campuses: Parklands, Towers, Moi Avenue, Union Towers, Mombasa, Nairobi, Virtual Varsity, Nakuru, Kitale, Eldoret, Nkubu (Meru), Kisii, Kisunu Lodwar, Kigali, Kabarnet, Hargeisa, Garissa, Kampala, Bujumbura, Kericho and Malindi.
History: Founded 1996 as Thika Institute of Technology. Acquired present status and title 2011.
Admission requirements: At least KCSE mean grade C Plus
Fees: Undergraduate, 1,000 per annum; Postgraduate, 2,000 per annum (Kenyan Shilling)
Main language(s) of instruction: English
Accrediting agency: Commission for Higher Education
Degrees and diplomas: Certificate / Diploma, Bachelor's Degree, Postgraduate Diploma (Education; Industrial Management; Management; Marketing; Sales Techniques), Master's Degree (Accountancy; Biotechnology; Business Administration; Chemistry; Civil Security; Criminology; Development Studies; Ecology; Economics; Education; English; Entomology; Environmental Management; Environmental Studies; Ethics; Finance; Geography; History; Hotel and Restaurant; Human Resources; Information Sciences; Information Technology; International Relations; Journalism; Justice Administration; Laboratory Techniques; Law; Linguistics; Literature; Management; Marketing; Media Studies; Medicine; Nursing; Police Studies; Preschool Education; Psychology; Public Administration; Public Health; Religious Studies; Special Education; Statistics; Swahili), Doctor's Degree (Business Administration; Education; English; Linguistics; Literature; Management; Preschool Education; Psychology; Religious Studies). Also Executive MBA and International Executive MBA.
Last Update: 27-06-2016

Presbyterian University of East Africa

P.O. Box 387
Kikuyu 00902
Tel: +254(723) 799-904, +254(723) 799-978
Website: http://puea.ac.ke
Vice-Chancellor: Peter B. Kibas

School

Business (Accountancy; Business Administration; Finance; Human Resources; Management; Marketing); **Computer Science** (Business Computing; Computer Science); **Education** (Education; Educational and Student Counselling; Preschool Education); **Health Sciences** (Community Health; Medicine; Nursing; Occupational Therapy; Oral Pathology; Surgery); **Theology** (Pastoral Studies; Theology)
Further information: Also Nairobi campus, St Andrews Campus and Githunguri Campus

History: Founded 1994 as the Presbyterian College. Acquired present status and title 2007.

Admission requirements: A minimum of Grade C+ at the Kenya Certificate of Secondary Examination (KCSE) or equivalent.

Main language(s) of instruction: English

Accrediting agency: Commission for University Education

Degrees and diplomas: Certificate / Diploma, Bachelor's Degree, Postgraduate Diploma (Public Relations), Master's Degree (Business Administration)

Student Services: Library, IT Centre

Last Update: 24-06-2016

Scott Theological College (STC)

P.O. Box 49
Machakos 90100
Tel: +254(713) 745-404, +254(734) 833-832
Fax: +254(44) 21336
Website: http://www.scott.ac.ke
Principal: Mumo Kisau

School

Education (Education; Preschool Education; Secondary Education); **Professional Studies** (Agricultural Business; Business Administration; Business Computing; Computer Science; Development Studies; Hotel and Restaurant; Information Technology; Leadership; Management; Psychology); **Theology** (Bible; Christian Religious Studies; Theology)

Institute

Church Renewal

History: Founded 1962 as College of the Africa Inland Church, Kenya, acquired present status and title 1997.

Academic year: September to July

Admission requirements: Kenya Certificate of Secondary Education (KCSE), C+ or above

Fees: Undergraduate, 38,400-59,925 per annum; Postgraduate, 32,000-64,800 per annum (Kenyan Shilling)

Main language(s) of instruction: English

Accrediting agency: Accreditation Council for Theological Education in Africa (ACETEA); Commission for Higher Education (CHE)

Degrees and diplomas: Certificate / Diploma, Bachelor's Degree, Postgraduate Diploma (Education), Master's Degree (Bible; Business Administration; Education; Leadership; Management; Theology)

Student Services: Academic Counselling, Social Counselling, Sports Facilities, Health Services, Library, Residential Facilities

Periodicals: African Journal of Evangelical Theology

Last Update: 23-06-2016

St Paul's University (SPU)

PO Private Bag
Limuru 00217
Tel: +254(20) 2020505
Fax: +254(66) 73033
Website: http://www.spu.ac.ke
Vice-Chancellor: Joseph D. Galgalo

Faculty

Business and Communication (Art Education; Banking; Business Administration; Business Computing; Child Care and Development; Communication Studies; Computer Science; Education; Film; Information Technology; Journalism; Leadership; Management; Marketing; Preschool Education; Public Relations; Special Education; Translation and Interpretation); **Social Sciences** (Criminology; Development Studies; Leadership; Management; Peace and Disarmament; Protective Services; Psychology; Social and Community Services; Social Work); **Theology** (Christian Religious Studies; Islamic Theology; Religion; Theology)

Further information: Also Nakuru Campus

History: Founded 1903 as St. Paul's Divinity School. Acquired present status and title 2007.

Main language(s) of instruction: English

Accrediting agency: Commission for University Education

Degrees and diplomas: Certificate / Diploma, Bachelor's Degree (Business Administration; Business Computing; Communication Studies; Computer Science; Development Studies; Information Technology; Leadership; Management; Peace and Disarmament; Religion; Translation and Interpretation), Master's Degree (Business Administration; Christian Religious Studies; Development Studies; Islamic Theology; Leadership; Pastoral Studies; Theology), Doctor's Degree (Development Studies; Theology)

Student Services: Library, Residential Facilities

Last Update: 22-06-2016

Strathmore University

Madaraka Estate Ole Sangale Road PO Box 59857 City Square
Nairobi 00200, Nairobi
Tel: +254(703) 034-000, +254(703) 034-200, +254(703) 034-300
Fax: +254(20) 600-7498
Website: http://www.strathmore.edu
Vice-Chancellor: John Odhiambo
Tel: +254(20) 606-268

Faculty

Information Technology (*Faculty Vision Our vision is to be a world-class ICT trainer, promoting integration between*

academia, research and industry in order to promote assimilation and use of technology in business environments.) (Business Computing; Computer Science; Information Technology; Telecommunications Engineering)

School

Accountancy (*Vision To become a leading out-come driven entrepreneurial research University by translating our excellence into major contribution to culture, economic well-being and quality of life.*) (Accountancy); **Business** (*Mission Our mission is "service to society through developing virtuous leaders by providing world-class executive management education in a local setting".*) (Business Administration; Development Studies; Health Administration; Leadership; Management); **Finance and Applied Economics** (*Vision SFAE Aspires to be the top choice for research and higher education in Quantitative analysis and risk management.*) (Actuarial Science; Economics; Finance); **Graduate Studies** (*Vision To create a platform for Strathmore to become a leading outcome-driven university providing high quality graduate education and research.*) (Applied Mathematics; Business Administration; Business and Commerce; Educational Administration; Ethics; Information Technology; Mathematics; Philosophy; Public Administration; Statistics; Telecommunications Engineering); **Humanities and Social Sciences** (*Vision The Vision of the School of Humanities is to enhance the general vision of the university through the teaching of the humanities.*) (Arts and Humanities; Communication Studies; Development Studies; Educational Administration; Ethics; International Studies; Philosophy); **Law** (*Vision Strathmore Law School's vision is to be a centre renowned for excellence in legal education and research, guided by a commitment to pursue justice, to cultivate lawyers of professional and moral competence.*) (Administrative Law; Constitutional Law; International Law; Labour Law; Law); **Management and Commerce** (*Vision We aspire to promote integration between academic research and industry in order to promote business growth in an atmosphere of high ethical and professional performance.*) (Accountancy; Business Administration; Business and Commerce; Finance; International Business; Management; Marketing)

Institute

Mathematical Sciences (*Vision To be a centre of excellence in applied research and innovation in mathematics and mathematical sciences and to highly contribute to the quality of teaching of mathematics.*) (Applied Mathematics; Mathematics; Statistics)

Centre

Strathmore Research and Consultancy (*Strathmore Research and Consultancy Center, SRCC, is the consulting arm of Strathmore University. It coordinates the consultancy work of the university to ensure that clients receive high quality advisory work.*); **Tourism and Hospitality** (*Vision To exert a positive transformational change in the hospitality and tourism education, as well as in industry practice, standards and growth, in order to achieve world class excellence in service.*) (Cooking and Catering; Hotel Management; Tourism)

Research Division

@iLabAfrica (*Vision To be a leading Centre of Excellence in the uses of ICT for development.*) (Information Technology; Management); **Energy** (*Vision To become a leading outcome driven entrepreneurial research centre by translating our excellence into major contribution to greater adaptation and penetration of renewable energy and energy efficiency.*) (Energy Engineering); **Governance (SGC)** (*Vision SGC seeks to promote good governance in the public, private and civic sectors of the Eastern African region by carrying out research and analysis on governance issues.*) (Ethics; Government; Leadership); **Therapeutic Sciences (CREATES)** (*Vision A leader in innovative health research for development.*) (Genetics; Rehabilitation and Therapy)

History: Founded 1961. Acquired present status 2002 and awarded charter 2008.

Academic year: July to June

Admission requirements: Mean Grade C+ at National Secondary School Examinations

Fees: National : 200,000 per annum (Kenyan Shilling), International : 1,900 per annum (US Dollar)

Main language(s) of instruction: English

Accrediting agency: Commission for University Education

Degrees and diplomas: Bachelor's Degree (Accountancy; Actuarial Science; Business and Commerce; Computer Engineering; Finance; Fine Arts; International Studies; Law; Linguistics; Management; Marketing; Mathematics and Computer Science; Modern Languages; Philosophy; Psychology), Master's Degree (Business Administration; Business and Commerce; Computer Science; Educational Administration; Ethics; Information Technology; Philosophy), Doctor's Degree (Accountancy; Computer Science; Management; Psychology; Statistics)

Student Services: Academic Counselling, Social Counselling, Careers Guidance, Sports Facilities, Language Laboratory, Facilities for disabled people, Health Services, Canteen, Library

Periodicals: Strathmore-law-journal

Publishing house: Strathmore University Press

Academic Staff 2016-2017	MALE	FEMALE	TOTAL
FULL-TIME	95	90	185
Student Numbers 2016-2017			
All (Foreign Included)	2568	2479	5047
Foreign only			173

Last Update: 16-02-2017

⧉⊕ The Catholic University of Eastern Africa (CUEA)

PO Box 62157
Nairobi 00200
Tel: +254(20) 891-601
Fax: +254(20) 891-261
Website: http://www.cuea.edu
Vice-Chancellor: Justus Mbae
Tel: +254(20) 890-095

Faculty

Arts and Social Sciences (Development Studies; English; Environmental Studies; Geography; History; Modern Languages; Philosophy; Religious Studies; Social Sciences; Swahili); **Commerce** (Accountancy; Banking; Finance; Human Resources; Management; Marketing); **Education** (Curriculum; Education; Educational Administration; Educational and Student Counselling; Educational Psychology; Educational Research; Educational Testing and Evaluation; Teacher Training); **Law** (International Law; Private Law; Public Law); **Science** (Biology; Chemistry; Computer Science; Mathematics; Physics); **Theology** (Bible; Pastoral Studies; Theology)

School

Graduate Studies (Arts and Humanities; Business and Commerce; Canon Law; Computer Science; Development Studies; Education; Ethics; Mathematics; Regional Studies; Social Sciences; Theology)

Department/Division

Library and information Science (Archiving; Information Sciences; Information Technology; Library Science)

Institute

Canon Law (Canon Law); **Regional Integration and Development** (Development Studies; Economics; Government; International Relations; Law; Political Sciences; Regional Studies)

Centre

Social Justice and Ethics (Administration; Leadership; Peace and Disarmament)

Campus

Gaba Campus (Arts and Humanities; Business Administration; Business and Commerce; Computer Science; Education; Mathematics; Pastoral Studies; Social Sciences); **Kisumu Campus** (Arts and Humanities; Business Administration; Education; Mathematics; Social Sciences)

Further information: Also Kisumu and Campuses
History: Founded 1984 as the Catholic Higher Institute of Eastern Africa. Acquired present status and title 1992.
Academic year: August to April (August-December; January-April)
Admission requirements: Kenya Certificate of Secondary Education (KCSE); Kenya Advanced Certificate of Education or equivalent
Fees: Undergraduate, 190,000 per annum; Postgraduate, 160,000 (Kenyan Shilling)
Main language(s) of instruction: English
Accrediting agency: Commission for Higher Education
Degrees and diplomas: Certificate / Diploma, Bachelor's Degree (Accountancy; Anthropology; Banking; Biology; Business Administration; Business and Commerce; Business Education; Chemistry; Christian Religious Studies; Computer Science; Development Studies; E- Business/Commerce; Economics; English; Ethics; Finance; Geography (Human); History; Human Resources; Humanities and Social Science Education; Leadership; Literature; Management; Marketing; Mathematics; Mathematics Education; Pastoral Studies; Peace and Disarmament; Philosophy; Physics; Political Sciences; Religious Studies; Science Education; Social Work; Sociology; Swahili; Theology), Postgraduate Diploma (Development Studies; Education; Management), Master's Degree (Applied Mathematics; Bible; Business Administration; Canon Law; Curriculum; E- Business/Commerce; Educational Administration; Educational Research; Educational Testing and Evaluation; Finance; Human Resources; Management; Marketing; Mathematics; Pastoral Studies; Philosophy; Religious Studies; Statistics; Theology), Doctor's Degree (Applied Mathematics; Bible; Canon Law; Curriculum; Educational Administration; Educational Research; Educational Testing and Evaluation; Mathematics; Pastoral Studies; Philosophy; Religious Studies; Statistics; Theology). Also Licenciate in Theology
Student Services: Academic Counselling, Social Counselling, Careers Guidance, Cultural Activities, Sports Facilities, Language Laboratory, Health Services, Canteen, Library, IT Centre
Periodicals: African Christian Studies, C.U.E.A.
Publishing house: Catholic University of Eastern Africa Publications
Last Update: 27-06-2016

HEKIMA UNIVERSITY COLLEGE

Joseph Kangethe Road Ngong Rd P.O. Box 21215
Nairobi 00505
Tel: +254(20) 387-6608/9, +254(20) 399-9000
Fax: +254(20) 399-9831
Website: http://www.hekima.ac.ke
Principal: Agbonkhianmeghe Orobator

Course/Programme

Pastoral Theology (Pastoral Studies; Theology); **Peace Studies and International Relations** (International Relations; Peace and Disarmament); **Theology** (Theology)
History: Founded 1993. A constituent college of the Catholoic University of Eastern Africa.
Main language(s) of instruction: English
Accrediting agency: Commission for University Education
Degrees and diplomas: Certificate / Diploma, Bachelor's Degree, Postgraduate Diploma (Pastoral Studies; Theology), Master's Degree (International Relations; Peace and Disarmament)
Student Services: Sports Facilities, Library, IT Centre
Last Update: 04-07-2016

MARIST INTERNATIONAL UNIVERSITY COLLEGE (MIUC)

P.O. Box 24450
Karen 00502
Tel: +254(202) 012-787
Fax: +254(202) 389-939
Website: http://miuc.ac.ke
Principal: Joseph Udeajah

Course/Programme

Arts and Social Sciences (Arts and Humanities; Social Sciences); **Business** (Business Administration); **Education** (Education); **Information Technology** (Information Technology); **Mathematics** (Mathematics); **Religious Studies** (Religious Studies)
History: Founded 2002, a constituent college of the Catholic University of Eastern Africa.
Fees: 63,000 per semester (Kenyan Shilling)
Main language(s) of instruction: English
Accrediting agency: Commission for University Education
Degrees and diplomas: Certificate / Diploma, Bachelor's Degree
Student Services: Sports Facilities, Library
Last Update: 04-07-2016

REGINA PACIS UNIVERSITY COLLEGE (RPUC)

P.O BOX 188
Langata 00517
Tel: +254(20) 240-1816, +254(716) 936-991
Website: http://rpuc.ac.ke

Department/Division

Community Health Development (Community Health); **Medical Education** (Health Education); **Nursing** (Nursing)
History: Founded 2010, a constituent college of the Catholic University of Eastern Africa.
Main language(s) of instruction: English
Accrediting agency: Commission for University Education

Degrees and diplomas: Certificate / Diploma, Bachelor's Degree
Student Services: Social Counselling, Library, Residential Facilities
Last Update: 04-07-2016

TANGAZA UNIVERSITY COLLEGE (TUC)

Langata South Road P.O Box 15055
Nairobi 00509
Tel: +254(20) 806-7667, +254(722) 204-724
Website: http://tangaza.org
Principal: Steven Payne

School

Theology (Bible; Islamic Theology; Missionary Studies; Pastoral Studies; Philosophy; Theology)

Institute

African Studies (*Maryknoll*) (African Studies); **Education** (*Christ the Teacher*) (Art Education; Business Computing; Education; Educational Administration; Preschool Education; Science Education); **Social Communication** (Mass Communication; Media Studies); **Social Ministry** (Development Studies; Management; Sociology); **Spiritaulity and Religious Formation** (Leadership; Religion; Religious Studies; Theology); **Youth Studies** (Child Care and Development; Music; Psychology; Religion)

Centre

Leadership and Management (Leadership; Management)
History: Founded 1997. A constituent college of the Catholic University of Eastern Africa.
Main language(s) of instruction: English
Accrediting agency: Commission for University Education
Degrees and diplomas: Certificate / Diploma, Bachelor's Degree, Master's Degree (African Studies; Educational Administration; Educational Psychology; Management; Marketing; Pastoral Studies; Religion; Religious Studies; Sociology), Doctor's Degree (Development Studies; Management; Sociology)
Student Services: Social Counselling, Sports Facilities, Library
Last Update: 04-07-2016

UZIMA UNIVERSITY COLLEGE

P.O. Box 2502
Kisumu 40100
Tel: +254(703) 727-660, +254(733) 608-574, +254(739) 387-903
Website: http://www.uzimauniversity.ac.ke

School

Informatics (Computer Science; Information Technology); **Medicine** (Child Care and Development; Community Health; Dietetics; Health Sciences; Medicine; Microbiology; Nutrition; Pharmacy; Psychology; Surgery); **Nursing** (Nursing)
History: Founded 2012. A constituent college of The Catholic University of Eastern Africa (CUEA).
Main language(s) of instruction: English
Accrediting agency: Commission for University Education
Degrees and diplomas: Certificate / Diploma, Bachelor's Degree
Last Update: 16-08-2016

The Pan Africa Christian University (PACU)

P.O. Box 56875
Nairobi 00200
Tel: +254(721) 932-050, +254(734) 400-694
Website: http://www.pacuniversity.ac.ke
Vice-Chancellor: Margaret J. Muthwii

Department/Division

Business (Business Administration); **Communications, Languages and Linguistics** (Communication Studies; Linguistics; Modern Languages); **Community Development** (Social and Community Services); **Computing and Information Technology** (Business Computing; Information Technology); **Leadership** (Leadership); **Psychology** (Psychology; Rehabilitation and Therapy); **Theology** (Bible; Theology)
Further information: Also Valley Road Campus
History: Founded 1978 as a Bible College. Acquired present status 2006.
Admission requirements: A minimum of a mean grade C in the Kenya Certificate of Secondary Education (KCSE), or its equivalent.
Fees: 44,100 per term (Kenyan Shilling)
Main language(s) of instruction: English
Accrediting agency: Commission for University Education
Degrees and diplomas: Certificate / Diploma, Bachelor's Degree, Postgraduate Diploma (Leadership; Psychology), Master's Degree (Bible; Business Administration; Leadership; Rehabilitation and Therapy; Religion), Doctor's Degree (Leadership; Rehabilitation and Therapy)
Student Services: Social Counselling, Sports Facilities, Library, Residential Facilities
Publishing house: Evangel Publishing House
Last Update: 22-06-2016

United States International University (USIU)

P. O. Box 14634
Nairobi 00800
Tel: +254(20) 360-6100
Fax: +254(20) 360-6100
Website: http://www.usiu.ac.ke
Vice-Chancellor: Paul Tiyambe Zeleza
Tel: +254(20) 360-6411

School

Business (*Chandaria*) (Accountancy; Business Administration; Business and Commerce; Finance; Hotel and Restaurant; Human Resources; International Business; Management; Marketing; Tourism); **Humanities and Social Sciences** (Clinical Psychology; Criminal Law; International Relations; Psychology); **Pharmacy and Health Sciences** (Health Sciences; Pharmacy); **Science and Technology** (Communication Studies; Computer Science; Information Technology; Journalism)
History: Founded 1969. Acquired status 1999. Merged with the California School of Professional Psychology (CSPP) forming the Alliant International University. USIU-Africa separated itself from the new entity, becoming an independent institution 2005, and receiving its own accreditation as United States International University, from the Western Association of Schools and Colleges (WASC) 2008. Acquired current title 2014.
Academic year: September to August (September-December; January-April; May-August)
Admission requirements: Kenya Certificate of Secondary Education (KCSE), C+ and above.TOEFL score of 550 (213 computer based) Bachelor's Degree and either GRE (Arts) or GMAT (Business) for Graduate Programmes
Fees: 94,800 per semester (Kenyan Shilling)
Main language(s) of instruction: English
Accrediting agency: Commission for University Education (CUE), Kenya; Western Association of Schools and Colleges (WASC) Senior Colleges and University Commission (WSCUC), USA
Degrees and diplomas: Bachelor's Degree (Accountancy; Administration; Computer Science; Criminal Law; Finance; Hotel and Restaurant; Information Technology; International Business; International Relations; Journalism; Pharmacy; Psychology; Tourism), Master's Degree (Business Administration; Clinical Psychology; Communication Studies; Information Technology; International Relations; Psychology), Doctor's Degree (Business Administration; Clinical Psychology; International Relations; Psychology). Also Executive MBA
Student Services: Academic Counselling, Social Counselling, Careers Guidance, Sports Facilities, Language Laboratory,

Facilities for disabled people, Health Services, Canteen, Foreign Studies Centre, Library, IT Centre, Residential Facilities

Academic Staff 2016-2017	MALE	FEMALE	TOTAL
FULL-TIME			100
PART-TIME			178
STAFF WITH DOCTORATE			
FULL-TIME			107
Student Numbers 2016-2017			
All (Foreign Included)			6152

Last Update: 16-08-2016

University of Eastern Africa, Baraton (UEAB)

P.O. Box 2500
Eldoret 30100, Rift Valley
Tel: +254(721) 423-592, +254(731) 793-934
Website: http://www.ueab.ac.ke
Vice-Chancellor: Philip Maiyo

School

Business (Accountancy; Business Administration; Business Computing; Computer Engineering; Finance; Human Resources; Information Technology; Management); **Education** (Agricultural Education; Curriculum; Education; Educational Administration; Educational Psychology; Humanities and Social Science Education; Mathematics Education; Music Education; Psychology; Science Education; Teacher Training); **Health Sciences** (Health Sciences; Laboratory Techniques; Nursing; Public Health); **Humanities and Social Sciences** (Development Studies; English; French; Geography; History; Linguistics; Literature; Music; Music Education; Religion; Swahili; Theology); **Science and Technology** (Agriculture; Automotive Engineering; Biological and Life Sciences; Biology; Biomedicine; Chemistry; Consumer Studies; Electrical and Electronic Equipment and Maintenance; Family Studies; Mathematics; Physics; Technology)

Centre

Kisumu Extension (Nursing; Public Health); **Nairobi Extension** (Accountancy; Business Computing; Chemistry; Development Studies; Dietetics; Finance; Food Science; Food Technology; Management; Music; Nursing; Nutrition; Psychology; Public Health; Religious Studies; Software Engineering; Theology)
History: Founded 1980. Chartered by the Government 1991.
Academic year: September to September (September-December; January-March; April-June; July-September)

Admission requirements: Kenya Certificate of Secondary Education (KCSE), with C+ average grade in 8 subjects
Fees: 90,140.00 per semester (Kenyan Shilling)
Main language(s) of instruction: English
Accrediting agency: Commission for University Education
Degrees and diplomas: Certificate / Diploma, Bachelor's Degree, Postgraduate Diploma (Psychology; Secondary Education), Master's Degree (Biology; Biomedicine; Business Administration; Educational Administration; Educational and Student Counselling; Finance; Health Sciences; Human Resources; Information Management; Management; Marketing; Nursing; Public Health; Teacher Training), Doctor's Degree (Education; Educational Administration; Educational and Student Counselling)
Student Services: Academic Counselling, Social Counselling, Careers Guidance, Sports Facilities, Language Laboratory, Health Services, Canteen, IT Centre
Last Update: 22-06-2016

Korea (Democratic People's Republic of)

STRUCTURE OF HIGHER EDUCATION SYSTEM

Description

Higher education is provided by universities and other institutions of higher education.

Stages of studies

University level first stage
The first stage of higher education includes four to six-year courses leading to a Bachelor's degree.

University level second stage
The second stage leads to a Master's degree.

University level third stage
The title of Doctor is granted, after study and research pursued over several years, to scholars who have performed scientific work of the highest value.

ADMISSION TO HIGHER EDUCATION

Admission to university-level studies

Name of Secondary school credential required: Secondary School Leaving Certificate

NATIONAL BODIES

Ministry of Higher Education

Minister: Thae Hyong Chol
Pyongyang

Data for academic year: 2014–2015
Source: IAU, 2014. Bodies 2016. Bodies 2017.

Institutions

Cha Gwan Su University

Faculty
Biology and Chemistry (Biology; Chemistry); **Foreign Studies** (International Studies); **History and Geography** (Geography; History); **Korean Language and Literature** (Korean); **Mathematics** (Mathematics); **Physical Education** (Physical Education); **Physics** (Physics)
History: Founded 1961.

Chagang University

Kanggye City, Chagang Province

Faculty
Agriculture (Agriculture); **Forestry** (Forestry); **Forestry Engineering** (Forestry); **Forestry Machinery** (Agricultural Equipment); **Horticulture** (Horticulture); **Sericulture** (Sericulture); **Veterinary Medicine and Animal Husbandry** (Animal Husbandry; Veterinary Science); **Wood Processing** (Wood Technology)
History: Founded 1970.
Academic year: September to August (September-February; February-August)
Admission requirements: Graduation from senior middle school
Main language(s) of instruction: Korean
Degrees and diplomas: Bachelor's Degree (Engineering), Master's Degree
Periodicals: Gazette, Newspaper
Publishing house: University Publishing House

Chang Chol Gu University

Pyongchon District
Pyongsong City

© International Association of Universities 2019
International Handbook of Universities 2019,
https://doi.org/10.1057/978-3-319-76971-4_101

Faculty

Cookery (Cooking and Catering); **Management** (Management); **Tailoring** (Clothing and Sewing)

Institute

Commercial Management (Business Administration); **Organizational Techniques** (Management); **Supply Service**
History: Founded 1970. A State institution responsible to the National Education Commission.
Admission requirements: Graduation from senior middle school
Main language(s) of instruction: Korean
Degrees and diplomas: Bachelor's Degree (Engineering), Master's Degree
Periodicals: Gazette, Newspaper
Publishing house: University Publishing House

Changjasan University

Faculty

Biochemistry (Biochemistry); **Foreign Studies** (International Studies); **Home Economics** (Home Economics); **Korean Language and Literature** (Korean; Literature); **Mathematics** (Mathematics); **Pedagogical Psychology** (Pedagogy; Psychology); **Physics** (Physics)
History: Founded 1967.

Changsusan University

Haeju City, South Hwanghae Province

Faculty

Dentistry (Dentistry); **Koryo Medicine and Pharmacy** (Traditional Eastern Medicine); **Pharmacy** (Pharmacy)
History: Founded 1959. A State institution responsible to the National Education Commission.
Academic year: September to August (September-February; February-August)
Admission requirements: Graduation from senior middle school
Main language(s) of instruction: Korean
Degrees and diplomas: Bachelor's Degree, Master's Degree, Doctorate
Periodicals: Gazette, Newspaper
Publishing house: University Publishing House

Chinmyong University

Faculty

Biology and Chemistry (Biology; Chemistry); **History and Geography** (Geography; History); **Korean Language and**

Literature (Korean; Literature); **Mathematics** (Mathematics); **Music and Fine Arts** (Fine Arts; Music); **Physics** (Physics)
History: Founded 1948.

Chong Jun Taek University of Economics

Wonsan City, Kangwon Province

Faculty

Commercial Management (Business Administration); **Finance; Economics** (Economics; Finance); **Materials Supply and Labour Administration** (Administration); **Planning Economics** (Economics)
History: Founded 1960. A State institution responsible to the National Education Commission.
Academic year: September to August (September-February; February-August)
Admission requirements: Graduation from senior middle school
Main language(s) of instruction: Korean
Degrees and diplomas: Bachelor's Degree, Master's Degree, Doctorate
Periodicals: Gazette, Newspaper
Publishing house: University Publishing House

Chongsong University

Hamhung City, South Hamgyong Province

Faculty

Hygiene (Hygiene); **Koryo Medicine** (Traditional Eastern Medicine); **Medicine** (Medicine); **Stomatology** (Stomatology); **Surgery** (Surgery)
History: Founded 1946. A State institution responsible to the National Education Commission.
Academic year: September to August (September-February; February-August)
Admission requirements: Graduation from senior middle school
Main language(s) of instruction: Korean
Degrees and diplomas: Bachelor's Degree, Master's Degree, Doctorate
Periodicals: Gazette, Newspaper
Publishing house: University Publishing House

Chonrigil University

Faculty

Biology and Chemistry (Biology; Chemistry); **History and Geography** (Geography; History); **Korean Language and**

Literature (Korean; Literature); **Mathematics** (Mathematics); **Music and Fine Arts** (Fine Arts; Music); **Physics** (Physics)
History: Founded 1953.

Choson University of Physical Education

Tongdaewon District
Pyongyang

Course/Programme
Physical Education (Physical Education); **Sports** (Sports)
History: Founded 1958. A State institution responsible to the National Education Commission.
Academic year: September to August (September-February; February-August)
Admission requirements: Graduation from senior middle school
Main language(s) of instruction: Korean
Degrees and diplomas: Bachelor's Degree, Master's Degree, Doctorate
Periodicals: Gazette, Newspaper
Publishing house: University Publishing House

Hambuk University

Ranam District
Chongjin City, North Hamgyong Province

Faculty
Agriculture (Agriculture); **Farm Machinery** (Agricultural Equipment); **Pomiculture** (Crop Production); **Veterinary Medicine and Animal Husbandry** (Animal Husbandry; Veterinary Science)
History: Founded 1970. A State institution responsible to the National Education Commission.
Academic year: September to August (September-February; February-August)
Admission requirements: Graduation from senior middle school
Main language(s) of instruction: Korean
Degrees and diplomas: Bachelor's Degree (Engineering), Master's Degree
Periodicals: Gazette, Newspaper
Publishing house: University Publishing House

Huichon University of Technology

Huichon City, Chagang Province

Faculty
Automation Engineering (Automation and Control Engineering); **Electro-Apparatus Engineering** (Electronic Engineering); **Mechanical Engineering** (Mechanical Engineering); **Radio Engineering** (Telecommunications Engineering); **Wire Communication Engineering** (Telecommunications Engineering)
History: Founded 1959. A State institution responsible to the National Education Commission.
Academic year: September to August (September-February; February-August)
Admission requirements: Graduation from senior middle school
Main language(s) of instruction: Korean
Degrees and diplomas: Bachelor's Degree (Engineering), Master's Degree, Doctorate
Periodicals: Gazette, Newspaper
Publishing house: University Publishing House

Inpung University

Kanggye City, Chagang Province

Faculty
Koryo Medicine (Traditional Eastern Medicine); **Medicine** (Medicine); **Surgery** (Surgery)
History: Founded 1969. A State institution responsible to the National Education Commission.
Academic year: September to August (September-February; February-August)
Admission requirements: Graduation from senior middle school
Main language(s) of instruction: Korean
Degrees and diplomas: Bachelor's Degree, Master's Degree
Periodicals: Gazette, Newspaper
Publishing house: University Publishing House

Jangsun University of Pharmacy

Faculty
Herbal Studies (Alternative Medicine); **Koryo Pharmacy** (Traditional Eastern Medicine); **Medical Zoology** (Veterinary Science)
History: Founded 1984.

Kang Gon University

Sariwon City, North Hwanghae Province

Course/Programme

Medicine (Medicine); **Pharmacy** (Pharmacy); **Surgery** (Surgery); **Traditional Eastern Medicine** (Traditional Eastern Medicine)

History: Founded 1971. A State institution responsible to the National Education Commission.

Academic year: September to August (September-February; February-August)

Admission requirements: Graduation from senior middle school

Main language(s) of instruction: Korean

Degrees and diplomas: Bachelor's Degree, Master's Degree

Periodicals: Gazette, Newspaper

Publishing house: University Publishing House

Karimchon University

Hyesan City, Ryangang Province

Course/Programme

Medicine (Medicine); **Traditional Eastern Medicine** (Traditional Eastern Medicine)

History: Founded 1971. A State institution responsible to the National Education Commission.

Academic year: September to August (September-February; February-August)

Admission requirements: Graduation from senior middle school

Main language(s) of instruction: Korean

Degrees and diplomas: Bachelor's Degree, Master's Degree

Periodicals: Gazette, Newspaper

Publishing house: University Publishing House

Kim Chaek University of Technology

Central District
Pyongyang

Faculty

Automatic Engineering (Engineering); **Communication** (Communication Studies); **Computer Engineering** (Computer Engineering); **Electrical Engineering** (Electrical Engineering); **Electronic Engineering** (Electronic Engineering); **Geological Prospecting** (Geological Engineering); **Heating Engineering** (Heating and Refrigeration); **Industrial Management** (Industrial Management); **Machine Building** (Machine Building); **Materials Engineering** (Materials Engineering); **Mechanical Engineering** (Mechanical Engineering); **Metallurgy** (Metallurgical Engineering); **Mining Engineering** (Mining Engineering); **Physical Engineering** (Physical Engineering); **Power-Driven Machine Engineering** (Power Engineering); **Shipbuilding** (Marine Engineering)

History: Founded 1948. A State institution responsible to the National Education Commission.

Academic year: September to August (September-February; February-August)

Admission requirements: Graduation from senior middle school

Main language(s) of instruction: Korean

Degrees and diplomas: Bachelor's Degree (Engineering), Master's Degree, Doctorate

Periodicals: Gazette, Newspaper

Publishing house: University Publishing House

Kim Chol Ju University of Education

Pyongyang

Faculty

Arts (Fine Arts); **Biology and Chemistry** (Biology; Chemistry); **Foreign Studies** (International Studies); **History and Geography** (Geography; History); **Korean Language and Literature** (Korean; Literature); **Mathematics** (Mathematics); **Physical Education** (Physical Education); **Physics** (Physics)

History: Founded 1946.

Kim Hyong Gwon University of Education

Faculty

Biochemistry (Biochemistry); **Foreign Studies** (International Studies); **Korean Language and Literature** (Korean); **Mathematics** (Mathematics); **Physical Education** (Physical Education); **Physics** (Physics)

History: Founded 1961.

Kim Hyong Jik University of Education

Pyongyang

Faculty

Arts (Fine Arts); **Biology** (Biology); **Chemistry** (Chemistry); **Education** (Education); **Geography** (Geography); **History** (History); **Korean Language and Literature** (Korean; Literature); **Mathematics** (Mathematics); **Philosophy** (Philosophy); **Physical Education** (Physical Education); **Physics** (Physics)

History: Founded 1946.

Kim Il Sung University

Taesong District
Pyongyang

Faculty

Automation (Automation and Control Engineering); **Biology** (Biology); **Chemistry** (Chemistry); **Economics** (Economics); **Foreign Languages and Literature** (Modern Languages); **Geography** (Geography); **Geology** (Geology); **History** (History); **Korean Language and Literature** (Korean); **Law** (Law); **Mathematics** (Mathematics); **Philosophy** (Philosophy); **Physics** (Physics)

Institute

Juche Philosophy (Ethics); **Social Sciences** (Social Sciences)

History: Founded 1946, reorganized 1953. A State institution responsible to the National Education Commission.

Academic year: September to August (September-February; February-August)

Admission requirements: Graduation from senior middle school

Main language(s) of instruction: Korean

Degrees and diplomas: Bachelor's Degree, Master's Degree, Doctorate

Periodicals: Gazette, Newspaper

Publishing house: University Publishing House

Kim Je Won University

Haeju City, South Hwanghae Province

Faculty

Agriculture (Agriculture); **Agronomics** (Agronomy); **Farm Machinery** (Agricultural Equipment); **Pomiculture** (Crop Production)

Institute

Agricultural Sciences Research; **Forest and River Protection** (Forestry); **Veterinary Medicine and Animal Husbandry** (Animal Husbandry; Veterinary Science)

History: Founded 1960. A State institution responsible to the National Education Commission.

Academic year: September to August (September-February; February-August)

Admission requirements: Graduation from senior middle school

Main language(s) of instruction: Korean

Degrees and diplomas: Bachelor's Degree (Engineering), Master's Degree, Doctorate

Periodicals: Gazette, Newspaper

Publishing house: University Publishing House

Kim Jong Suk University of Education

Faculty

Arts (Fine Arts); **Biochemistry** (Biochemistry); **Foreign Studies** (International Studies); **History and Geography** (Geography; History); **Korean Language and Literature** (Korean); **Mathematics** (Mathematics); **Physical Education** (Physical Education); **Physics** (Physics)

History: Founded 1967.

Kim Jong Tae University

Faculty

Biochemistry (Biochemistry); **Foreign Studies** (International Studies); **History and Geography** (Geography; History); **Korean Language and Literature** (Korean; Literature); **Mathematics** (Mathematics); **Physical Education** (Physical Education); **Physics** (Physics)

History: Founded 1957.

Koryo University of Pharmacy

Hamhung City, South Hamgyong Province

Course/Programme

Pharmacy (Pharmacy)

History: Founded 1968. A State institution responsible to the National Education Commission.

Academic year: September to August (September-February; February-August)

Admission requirements: Graduation from senior middle school

Main language(s) of instruction: Korean

Degrees and diplomas: Bachelor's Degree (Engineering)

Periodicals: Gazette, Newspaper

Publishing house: University Publishing House

Kumgang University

Faculty

Arts (Arts and Humanities); **Biochemistry** (Biochemistry); **Foreign Studies** (International Studies); **History and Geography** (Geography; History); **Korean Language and Literature** (Korean; Literature); **Mathematics** (Mathematics); **Physical Education** (Physical Education); **Physics** (Physics)

History: Founded 1949.

Kumya University

Sapo District
Hamhung City, South Hamgyong Province

Faculty
Agriculture (Agriculture); **Farm Machinery** (Agricultural Equipment); **Pomiculture** (Crop Production)

Institute
Agricultural Scientific Research (Agriculture); **Veterinary Medicine and Animal Husbandry** (Animal Husbandry; Veterinary Science)
History: Founded 1958. A State institution responsible to the National Education Commission.
Academic year: September to August (September-February; February-August)
Admission requirements: Graduation from senior middle school
Main language(s) of instruction: Korean
Degrees and diplomas: Bachelor's Degree (Engineering), Master's Degree, Doctorate
Periodicals: Gazette, Newspaper
Publishing house: University Publishing House

Kwanje University

Pyonghawa-Dong
Sinuiju City, Pyongan Province

Faculty
Hygiene (Hygiene); **Koryo Medicine** (Traditional Eastern Medicine); **Medicine** (Medicine); **Pharmacy** (Pharmacy); **Stomatology** (Stomatology); **Surgery** (Surgery)
History: Founded 1969. A State institution responsible to the National Education Commission.
Academic year: September to August (September-February; February-August)
Admission requirements: Graduation from senior middle school
Main language(s) of instruction: Korean
Degrees and diplomas: Bachelor's Degree, Master's Degree
Periodicals: Gazette, Newspaper
Publishing house: University Publishing House

Kwanso University

Faculty
Biochemistry (Biochemistry); **History and Geography** (Geography; History); **Korean Language and Literature** (Korean; Literature); **Mathematics** (Mathematics); **Music and Fine Arts** (Fine Arts; Music); **Physical Education** (Physical Education); **Physics** (Physics)
History: Founded 1947.

Kye Ung San University

Sariwon City, North Hwanghae Province

Faculty
Agriculture (Agriculture); **Agrochemistry** (Chemistry); **Agronomy** (Agronomy); **Biology** (Biology); **Economic Plant** (Plant and Crop Protection); **Farm Machinery** (Agricultural Equipment); **Forest and River Protection** (Environmental Studies); **Land Development** (Environmental Studies); **Pomiculture** (Crop Production); **Sericulture** (Sericulture); **Veterinary Medicine and Animal Husbandry** (Animal Husbandry; Veterinary Science)
Academic year: September to August (September-February; February-August)
Admission requirements: Graduation from senior middle school
Main language(s) of instruction: Korean
Degrees and diplomas: Bachelor's Degree (Engineering), Master's Degree, Doctorate
Periodicals: Gazette, Newspaper
Publishing house: University Publishing House

Kyongsong University

Pohang District
Chongjin City, North Hamgyong Province

Faculty
Hygiene (Hygiene); **Koryo Medicine** (Traditional Eastern Medicine); **Medicine** (Medicine); **Pharmacy** (Pharmacy); **Stomatology** (Stomatology); **Surgery** (Surgery)
Further information: Also Research Institute
History: Founded 1948. A State institution responsible to the National Education Commission.
Academic year: September to August (September-February; February-August)
Admission requirements: Graduation from senior middle school
Main language(s) of instruction: Korean
Degrees and diplomas: Bachelor's Degree, Master's Degree, Doctorate
Periodicals: Gazette, Newspaper
Publishing house: University Publishing House

Manpung University

Sinuiju City, North Pyongyang Province

Faculty
Agriculture (Agriculture); **Farm Machinery** (Agricultural Equipment); **Pomiculture** (Crop Production); **Stockraising** (Animal Husbandry)
History: Founded 1969. A State institution responsible to the National Education Commission.
Academic year: September to August (September-February; February-August)
Admission requirements: Graduation from senior middle school
Main language(s) of instruction: Korean
Degrees and diplomas: Bachelor's Degree (Engineering), Master's Degree
Periodicals: Gazette, Newspaper
Publishing house: University Publishing House

Myongsin University

Faculty
Arts (Arts and Humanities); **Biochemistry** (Biochemistry); **Foreign Studies** (International Studies); **History and Geography** (Geography; History); **Korean Language and Literature** (Korean; Literature); **Mathematics** (Mathematics); **Physical Education** (Physical Education); **Physics** (Physics)
History: Founded 1961.

Nampo University

Waudo District
Nampo City

Faculty
Agriculture (Agriculture); **Farm Machinery** (Agricultural Equipment); **Horticulture** (Horticulture); **Pomiculture** (Crop Production)
History: Founded 1967. A State institution responsible to the National Education Commission.
Academic year: September to August (September-February; February-August)
Admission requirements: Graduation from senior middle school
Main language(s) of instruction: Korean
Degrees and diplomas: Bachelor's Degree (Engineering), Master's Degree
Periodicals: Gazette, Newspaper
Publishing house: University Publishing House

Nampo University of Medicine

Nampo City, South Pyongan Province

Faculty
Dentistry (Dentistry); **Medicine** (Medicine); **Pharmacy** (Pharmacy)
History: Founded 1985.
Last Update: 03-05-2011

O Jung Hup University

Faculty
Biochemistry (Biochemistry); **Foreign Studies** (International Studies); **History and Geography** (Geography; History); **Korean Language and Literature** (Korean; Literature); **Mathematics** (Mathematics); **Musics and Fine Arts** (Fine Arts; Music); **Physics** (Physics)
History: Founded 1961.

Ponghwa University

Pyongsong City, South Pyongan Province

Faculty
Koryo Medicine (Traditional Eastern Medicine); **Medicine** (Medicine); **Pharmacy** (Pharmacy); **Stomatology** (Stomatology); **Surgery** (Surgery)
History: Founded 1972. A State institution responsible to the National Education Commission.
Academic year: September to August (September-February; February-August)
Admission requirements: Graduation from senior middle school
Main language(s) of instruction: Korean
Degrees and diplomas: Bachelor's Degree, Master's Degree
Periodicals: Gazette, Newspaper
Publishing house: University Publishing House

Pyongyang Nongop University of Agriculture

Ryongsong District
Pyongyang

Faculty
Agriculture (Agriculture); **Agrobiology** (Agrobiology); **Farm Machinery** (Agricultural Equipment); **Veterinary Medicine and Animal Husbandry** (Animal Husbandry; Veterinary Science)

History: Founded 1981. A State institution responsible to the National Education Commission.
Academic year: September to August (September-February; February-August)
Admission requirements: Graduation from senior middle school
Main language(s) of instruction: Korean
Degrees and diplomas: Bachelor's Degree (Engineering)
Periodicals: Gazette, Newspaper
Publishing house: University Publishing House

Pyongyang University of Cinematics

Tongdaewon District
Pyongyang

Faculty

Acting (Acting); **Cinema** (Cinema and Television); **Cinematography** (Cinema and Television); **Creation** (Fine Arts); **Direction**; **Social Sciences** (Social Sciences); **Technology** (Technology)
History: Founded 1953. A State institution responsible to the National Education Commission.
Academic year: September to August (September-February; February-August)
Admission requirements: Graduation from senior middle school
Main language(s) of instruction: Korean
Degrees and diplomas: Bachelor's Degree, Doctorate
Periodicals: Gazette, Newspaper
Publishing house: University Publishing House

Pyongyang University of Fine Arts

Tongdaewon District
Pyongyang

Faculty

Crafts (Crafts and Trades); **Graphic Art** (Graphic Arts); **Industrial Art** (Industrial Arts Education); **Korean Painting** (Painting and Drawing); **Painting** (Painting and Drawing); **Sculpture** (Sculpture)

Institute

Fine Arts Research (Fine Arts)
History: Founded 1947. A State institution responsible to the National Education Commission.
Academic year: September to August (September-February; February-August)
Admission requirements: Graduation from senior middle school

Main language(s) of instruction: Korean
Degrees and diplomas: Bachelor's Degree, Master's Degree, Doctorate
Periodicals: Gazette, Newspaper
Publishing house: University Publishing House

Pyongyang University of Foreign Studies

Taesong District
Pyongyang

Faculty

Education (Education); **English** (English); **French and Spanish** (French; Spanish); **Russian; Chinese; Arabic; Japanese** (Arabic; Chinese; Japanese; Russian)

Institute

Education Theory (Education); **Simultaneous Interpretation** (Translation and Interpretation); **Training** (Teacher Training)
History: Founded 1949. A State institution responsible to the National Education Commission.
Academic year: September to August (September-February; February-August)
Admission requirements: Graduation from senior middle school
Main language(s) of instruction: Korean
Degrees and diplomas: Bachelor's Degree, Master's Degree, Doctorate
Periodicals: Gazette, Newspaper
Publishing house: University Publishing House

Pyongyang University of Light Industry

Songyo District
Pyongyang

Faculty

Chemical Engineering (Chemical Engineering); **Food Engineering** (Food Technology); **Machine Engineering** (Machine Building); **Management** (Management); **Textile Engineering** (Textile Technology)

Institute

Food Research (Food Science); **Light Industry** (Electrical Engineering); **Paper Technology** (Paper Technology)
History: Founded 1959. A State institution responsible to the National Education Commission.

Academic year: September to August (September-February; February-August)
Admission requirements: Graduation from senior middle school
Main language(s) of instruction: Korean
Degrees and diplomas: Bachelor's Degree, Master's Degree, Doctorate
Periodicals: Gazette, Newspaper
Publishing house: University Publishing House

Pyongyang University of Mechanical Engineering

Taedonggang District
Pyongyang

Faculty
Automation (Automation and Control Engineering); **Construction Machinery** (Machine Building); **Design** (Design); **Mechanical Engineering** (Mechanical Engineering)
History: A State institution responsible to the National Education Comission.
Academic year: September to August (September-February; February-August)
Admission requirements: Graduation from senior middle school
Main language(s) of instruction: Korean
Degrees and diplomas: Bachelor's Degree (Engineering), Master's Degree, Doctorate
Periodicals: Gazette, Newspaper
Publishing house: University Publishing House

Pyongyang University of Medicine

Central District
Pyongyang

Faculty
Basic Medicine (Medicine); **Clinical Medicine** (Medicine); **Hygiene** (Hygiene); **Koryo Medicine**; **Pharmacy** (Pharmacy); **Stomatology** (Stomatology)
History: Founded 1948. A State institution responsible to the National Education Commission.
Academic year: September to August (September-February; February-August)
Admission requirements: Graduation from senior middle school
Main language(s) of instruction: Korean
Degrees and diplomas: Bachelor's Degree, Master's Degree, Doctorate

Periodicals: Gazette, Newspaper
Publishing house: University Publishing House

Pyongyang University of Music and Dance

Taedonggang District
Pyongyang

Faculty
Composition (Music Theory and Composition); **Dance** (Dance); **National Instruments** (Musical Instruments); **Preparatory**; **Vocal Technique** (Singing); **Western Instruments** (Musical Instruments)

Institute
Music and Dance (Dance; Music)
History: Founded 1948. A State institution responsible to the National Education Commission.
Academic year: September to August (September-February; February-August)
Admission requirements: Graduation from senior middle school
Main language(s) of instruction: Korean
Degrees and diplomas: Bachelor's Degree, Master's Degree
Periodicals: Gazette, Newspaper
Publishing house: University Publishing House

Pyongyang University of Railways

Hyongjesan District
Pyongyang

Course/Programme
Railway Engineering (Railway Engineering)
History: Founded 1959. A State institution responsible to the National Education Commission.
Academic year: September to August (September-February; February-August)
Admission requirements: Graduation from senior middle school
Main language(s) of instruction: Korean
Degrees and diplomas: Bachelor's Degree (Engineering), Master's Degree, Doctorate
Periodicals: Gazette, Newspaper
Publishing house: University Publishing House

Pyongyang University of Surgery

Pyongyang

Faculty

Dentistry (Dentistry); **Koryo Medicine** (Traditional Eastern Medicine); **Medical Sciences** (Health Sciences); **Pharmacy** (Pharmacy)
History: Founded 1985.

Ri Kye Sun University

Faculty

Biochemistry (Biochemistry); **Foreign Studies** (International Studies); **Korean Language and Literature** (Korean; Literature); **Mathematics** (Mathematics); **Physical Education** (Physical Education); **Physics** (Physics)
History: Founded 1953.

Ri Su Bok University

Faculty

Antibiotics Pharmacy (Pharmacy); **Chemical Machine Building** (Machine Building); **High Polymer Chemistry** (Chemistry); **Inorganic Synthetic Techniques** (Inorganic Chemistry); **Organic Synthetic Techniques** (Organic Chemistry)
History: Founded 1984.

Ryanggang University

Hyesan City, Ryangang Province

Faculty

Agriculture (Agriculture); **Forestry Engineering** (Forestry); **Wood Processing** (Forest Products)

Institute

Agricultural and Forestry Scientific Research (Agriculture; Forestry); **Stockraising** (Cattle Breeding)
History: Founded 1955. A State institution responsible to the National Education Commission.
Academic year: September to August (September-February; February-August)
Admission requirements: Graduation from senior middle school
Main language(s) of instruction: Korean
Degrees and diplomas: Bachelor's Degree (Engineering), Master's Degree, Doctorate
Periodicals: Gazette, Newspaper
Publishing house: University Publishing House

Ryomyong University

Faculty

History and Geography (Geography; History); **Korean Language and Literature** (Korean; Literature); **Mathematics** (Mathematics); **Music and Fine Arts** (Fine Arts; Music); **Physics** (Physics)
History: Founded 1946.

Saenal University

Faculty

Biochemistry (Biochemistry); **History and Geography** (Geography; History); **Korean Language and Literature** (Korean; Literature); **Mathematics** (Mathematics); **Music and Fine Arts** (Fine Arts; Music); **Physics** (Physics)
History: Founded 1961.

Sanmgwang University

Nampo, South Pyongan Province

Faculty

Arts (Arts and Humanities); **Biochemistry** (Biochemistry); **Foreign Studies** (International Studies); **History and Geography** (Geography; History); **Korean Language and Literature** (Korean; Literature); **Mathematics** (Mathematics); **Physical Education** (Physical Education); **Physics** (Physics); **Technical Education** (Technology Education)
History: Founded 1963.

Sariwon University

Faculty

History and Geography (Geography; History); **Korean Language and Literature** (Korean; Literature); **Mathematics** (Mathematics); **Music and Fine Arts** (Fine Arts; Music); **Physics** (Physics)
History: Founded 1963.

Sinuiju University of Light Industry

Sinuiju City, North Pyongyang Province

Faculty

Chemical Engineering (Chemical Engineering); **Food Technology** (Food Technology); **Machine Engineering** (Machine Building); **Textile Engineering** (Textile Technology)

History: Founded 1982. A State institution responsible to the National Education Commission.
Academic year: September to August (September-February; February-August)
Admission requirements: Graduation from senior middle school
Main language(s) of instruction: Korean
Degrees and diplomas: Bachelor's Degree (Engineering)
Periodicals: Gazette, Newspaper
Publishing house: University Publishing House

Sohae University

Waudo District
Nampo City

Faculty
Fish Farming and Cultivation (Aquaculture); **Fisheries** (Fishery); **Mechanical Engineering** (Mechanical Engineering)
History: Founded 1977. A State institution responsible to the National Education Commission.
Academic year: September to August (September-February; February-August)
Admission requirements: Graduation from senior middle school
Main language(s) of instruction: Korean
Degrees and diplomas: Bachelor's Degree (Engineering)
Periodicals: Gazette, Newspaper
Publishing house: University Publishing House

Songdo University

Kaesong

Faculty
Arts (Arts and Humanities); **Biochemistry** (Biochemistry); **Foreign Studies** (International Studies); **History and Geography** (Geography; History); **Korean Language and Literature** (Korean; Literature); **Mathematics** (Mathematics); **Physical Training** (Physical Education); **Physics** (Physics)
History: Founded 1961.

Songdowon University

Wonsan City, Kangwon Province

Faculty
Koryo Medicine (Traditional Eastern Medicine); **Koryo Pharmacy** (Traditional Eastern Medicine); **Medicine** (Medicine)

History: Founded 1971. A State institution responsible to the National Education Commission.
Academic year: September to August (September-February; February-August)
Admission requirements: Graduation from senior middle school
Main language(s) of instruction: Korean
Degrees and diplomas: Master's Degree, Doctorate
Periodicals: Gazette, Newspaper
Publishing house: University Publishing House

Tonghae University

Wonsan City, Kangwon Province

Faculty
Fish Farming and Cultivation (Aquaculture); **Fisheries** (Fishery); **Marine Products Processing** (Marine Biology); **Mechanical Engineering** (Mechanical Engineering)
History: Founded 1959. A State institution responsible to the National Education Commission.
Academic year: September to August (September-February; February-August)
Admission requirements: Graduation from senior middle school
Main language(s) of instruction: Korean
Degrees and diplomas: Bachelor's Degree (Engineering), Master's Degree, Doctorate
Periodicals: Gazette, Newspaper
Publishing house: University Publishing House

University of Chemical Industry

Hoesang District
Hamhung City, South Hamgyong Province

Faculty
High Polymers Chemical Engineering (Chemical Engineering); **Inorganic Chemical Engineering** (Inorganic Chemistry); **Machine Engineering** (Machine Building); **Organic Chemical Engineering** (Organic Chemistry); **Silicate Engineering** (Mining Engineering)
History: Founded 1947. A State institution responsible to the National Education Commission.
Academic year: September to August (September-February; February-August)
Admission requirements: Graduation from senior middle school
Main language(s) of instruction: Korean

Degrees and diplomas: Bachelor's Degree (Engineering), Master's Degree, Doctorate
Periodicals: Gazette, Newspaper
Publishing house: University Publishing House

University of Coal Mining

Pyongsong City, South Pyongan Province

Faculty

Anthracite Engineering (Mining Engineering); **Automation** (Automation and Control Engineering); **Coal Mine Machine Engineering** (Mechanical Engineering); **Coal Mining** (Mining Engineering)
History: Founded 1968. A State institution responsible to the National Education Commission.
Academic year: September to August (September-February; February-August)
Admission requirements: Graduation from senior middle school
Main language(s) of instruction: Korean
Degrees and diplomas: Bachelor's Degree (Engineering), Master's Degree
Periodicals: Gazette, Newspaper
Publishing house: University Publishing House

University of Construction and Building Materials

Taedonggang District
Pyongyang

Faculty

Architectural Engineering (Architecture); **Architecture** (Architecture); **Building Machines** (Machine Building); **Building Materials** (Materials Engineering); **City Management** (Town Planning); **Civil Engineering** (Construction Engineering); **Construction** (Construction Engineering)
History: Founded 1959. A State institution responsible to the National Education Commission.
Academic year: September to August (September-February; February-August)
Admission requirements: Graduation from senior middle school
Main language(s) of instruction: Korean
Degrees and diplomas: Bachelor's Degree
Periodicals: Gazette, Newspaper
Publishing house: University Publishing House

University of Geology

Sariwon City, North Hwanghae Province

Faculty

Geological Engineering (Geological Engineering); **Geology** (Geology); **Machine Engineering** (Machine Building); **Physical Prospecting**
History: Founded 1970. A State institution responsible to the National Education Commission.
Academic year: September to August (September-February; February-August)
Admission requirements: Graduation from senior middle school
Main language(s) of instruction: Korean
Degrees and diplomas: Bachelor's Degree (Engineering), Master's Degree, Doctorate
Periodicals: Gazette, Newspaper
Publishing house: University Publishing House

University of Hydraulics and Dynamics

Tonghungsan District
Hamhung City, South Hamgyong Province

Faculty

Electrical Engineering (Electrical Engineering); **Hydraulic and Port Construction Engineering** (Construction Engineering; Hydraulic Engineering); **Hydraulic Engineering** (Hydraulic Engineering); **Irrigation** (Irrigation); **Mechanical Engineering** (Mechanical Engineering)
History: Founded 1959. A State institution responsible to the National Education Commission.
Academic year: September to August (September-February; February-August)
Admission requirements: Graduation from senior middle school
Main language(s) of instruction: Korean
Degrees and diplomas: Bachelor's Degree (Engineering), Master's Degree, Doctorate
Periodicals: Gazette, Newspaper
Publishing house: University Publishing House

University of Light Industry

Kaesong

Course/Programme

Textile Technology (Textile Technology)
History: Founded 1992.

University of Mining and Metallurgical Engineering

Pohang District
Chongjin City, North Hamgyong Province

Faculty

Automation (Automation and Control Engineering); **Coal Engineering** (Mining Engineering); **Geotechnology** (Geological Engineering); **Metallurgy** (Metallurgical Engineering); **Mineral Analysis** (Mineralogy); **Mining** (Mining Engineering); **Mining Machine Engineering** (Mechanical Engineering)

History: Founded 1959. A State institution responsible to the National Education Commission.

Academic year: September to August (September-February; February-August)

Admission requirements: Graduation from senior middle school

Main language(s) of instruction: Korean

Degrees and diplomas: Bachelor's Degree (Engineering), Master's Degree, Doctorate

Periodicals: Gazette, Newspaper

Publishing house: University Publishing House

University of National Economics

Pyongyang

Faculty

Agricultural Management (Agricultural Management); **Finance and Banking** (Banking; Finance); **Government** (Government); **Industrial Management** (Industrial Management); **Planning**; **Statistics** (Statistics); **Trade** (Business and Commerce)

History: Founded 1946. A State institution responsible to the National Education Commission.

Academic year: September to August (September-February; February-August)

Admission requirements: Graduation from senior middle school

University of Printing Technology

Pyongyang

Course/Programme

Engineering and Technology (Engineering; Technology); **Printing and Printmaking** (Printing and Printmaking)

History: Founded 1984. A State institution responsible to the Provincial Committee for Administration and Economic Guidance.

Academic year: September to August (September-February; February-August)

Admission requirements: Graduation from senior middle school

Main language(s) of instruction: Korean

Degrees and diplomas: Bachelor's Degree

Last Update: 31-03-2014

University of Science

Pyongsong City, South Pyongan Province

Faculty

Automation (Automation and Control Engineering); **Biology** (Biology); **Chemistry** (Chemistry); **Computer Sciences** (Computer Science); **Electrical Engineering** (Electrical Engineering); **Mathematics** (Mathematics); **Mechanical Engineering** (Mechanical Engineering); **Physics** (Physics)

Further information: Also Research Institute

History: Founded 1967. A State institution responsible to the National Education Commission.

Academic year: September to August (September-February; February-August)

Admission requirements: Graduation from senior middle school

Main language(s) of instruction: Korean

Degrees and diplomas: Bachelor's Degree, Master's Degree, Doctorate

Periodicals: Gazette, Newspaper

Publishing house: University Publishing House

University of Sea Transport

Rajin City, North Hamgyong Province

Course/Programme

Electrical Engineering (Electrical Engineering); **Marine Engineering** (Marine Engineering); **Marine Transport** (Marine Transport); **Nautical Science** (Nautical Science)

History: Founded 1968. A State institution responsible to the National Education Commission.

Academic year: September to August (September-February; February-August)

Admission requirements: Graduation from senior middle school

Main language(s) of instruction: Korean

Degrees and diplomas: Bachelor's Degree (Engineering), Master's Degree, Doctorate

Periodicals: Gazette, Newspaper

Publishing house: University Publishing House

University of Veterinary Medicine and Animal Husbandry

Pyongsong City, South Pyongan Province

Faculty

Animal Husbandry (Animal Husbandry); **Veterinary Science** (Veterinary Science)

History: Founded 1955. A State institution responsible to the National Education Commission.

Academic year: September to August (September-February; February-August)

Admission requirements: Graduation from senior middle school

Main language(s) of instruction: Korean

Degrees and diplomas: Bachelor's Degree (Engineering), Master's Degree, Doctorate

Periodicals: Gazette, Newspaper

Publishing house: University Publishing House

Last Update: 20-05-2016

Wonsan University of Agriculture

Wonsan City, Kwangwon Province

Faculty

Agricultural Machines (Agricultural Equipment); **Agriculture** (Agriculture); **Agrobiology** (Agrobiology); **Agrochemistry** (Agronomy; Chemistry); **Agronomy** (Agronomy); **Botany** (Botany); **Irrigation Engineering** (Irrigation); **Pomiculture** (Crop Production); **Sericulture** (Sericulture)

Further information: Also 3 Research Institutes

History: Founded 1948. A State institution responsible to the National Education Commission.

Academic year: September to August (September-February; February-August)

Admission requirements: Graduation from senior middle school

Main language(s) of instruction: Korean

Degrees and diplomas: Bachelor's Degree (Engineering), Master's Degree, Doctorate

Periodicals: Gazette, Newspaper

Publishing house: University Publishing House

Korea (Republic of)

STRUCTURE OF HIGHER EDUCATION SYSTEM

Description

The South Korean higher education system includes national, public and private institutions. There are several types of institution: universities, colleges and technical institutes, industrial universities, education universities, and technological institutes. There are also online universities. If any person other than the State wants to establish a higher education institution, he/she needs to obtain approval from the Minister of Education. The academic year runs from 1 March to the the end of February of the following year.

Stages of studies

University level first stage

Bachelor's degree
Bachelor's degrees are awarded after four years' study. In medical fields it takes 5 to 6 years.

University level second stage

Master's degrees
Master's degrees are usually awarded after two years' study. Students must submit a thesis and/or pass licensing examinations in addition to completing regular coursework.

University level third stage

Doctoral degrees
Conferred after 3 years of training and research beyond a Master's degree are needed to obtain a Doctoral degree. Students must submit a doctoral dissertation and pass an oral or equivalent examination in addition to required coursework. There are also a certain number of integrated programmes where students enter with a Bachelor's degree and are awarded a Master's degree along the way; these kinds of programmes take up to 6 years.

ADMISSION TO HIGHER EDUCATION

Admission to university-level studies

Name of Secondary school credential required: Jolupjang (High School Diploma)
Admission requirements: Korean scholastic achievement test (CSAT) and/or individual university test
Other requirements: Access to higher education is often based on the composite score of the CSAT and a variety of other demands including high-school academic records, recommendation letters, interview, etc.

Foreign students admission

Definition of foreign student: Students from foreign countries or overseas Koreans with foreign nationality taking up courses, doing research or language studies in an accredited institution. However, students enrolled in distance education or evening schools are not included.
Quotas: No
Admission requirements: Foreign students must hold qualifications equivalent to the high school diploma. Requirements include the following: application form, certificate of graduation, grade points average (records), two references, proof of Korean language proficiency, study plan, curriculum vitae and portfolio (for applicants in arts/physical education).
Entry regulations: Foreign students must secure standard admission issued by the President or the Dean of the university where they intend to study and submit the documents to the Ministry of Justice or to an overseas Korean diplomatic mission. Applicants should secure a D2 visa for degree programmes and D4 visa for language studies.
Health requirements: No
Language Proficiency: Although an increasing number of universities teach classes in English, students are advised to have a good knowledge of Korean.

© International Association of Universities 2019
International Handbook of Universities 2019,
https://doi.org/10.1057/978-3-319-76971-4_102

RECOGNITION OF STUDIES

Quality assurance system

The Ministry of Education is directly responsible for approving a university and indirectly accredits institutions through evaluations of individual universities' compliance with government regulations and policies and provides funding accordingly. Institutional accreditation is carried out by the KUAI, and programme accreditation may be carried out by various professional bodies. Results from accreditation excercises are used by the Ministry for its administrative and financial policies.

Other info sources

http://www.studyinkorea.go.kr

Special provisions for recognition

For the exercise of a profession

A system of licensing exists parallel to college and university degrees in many fields of study leading to professional practices. In colleges such fields include electrical engineering, cosmetology, and auto mechanics, and in universities such fields include government civil service, law, medicine, elementary and secondary teaching, engineering, and architecture. In most cases students must pass a rigorous licensing examination after completing a degree programme.

NATIONAL BODIES

Ministry of Education - MOE

Deputy Prime Minister, Minister of Education: Eun-He Ryu
Government Complex-Sejong, 408 Galmae-ro
Sejong 30119
Tel: +82(2) 6222 6060
Fax: +82(2) 2100 6133
Website: http://www.moe.go.kr
Role of national body: To oversee all educational levels.

Hanguk Daehak Gyoyuk Heopuihoe (Korean Council for University Education - KCUE)

President: Chang Hosung
22-23F, Daesug DPOLIS-A 606 Seobusaet-gil Geumcheon-gu

Seoul 153-803
Tel: +82(2) 6919-3913
Fax: +82(2) 6919-3910
Website: http://www.kcue.or.kr/index.htm
Role of national body: KCUE is the representative association of four-year universities - both public and private - in the Republic of Korea. It works to increase autonomy and innovation, strengthen accountability, and improve education in universities.

Korean University Accreditation Institute - KUAI

President: Jong-Bo Yim
22~23F, Daesung DPOLIS-A 606 Seobusaet-gil Geumcheon-gu
Seoul 08504
Website: https://aims.kcue.or.kr
Role of national body: Affliated with the Korean Council of University Education, the KUAI is responsible for institutional accreditation

National Research Foundation of Korea - NRF

President: Jung-Hye Roe
201 Gaejong-ro, Yuseong-gu
Daejeon 34113
Tel: +82(42) 869-6114
Fax: +82(42) 869-6777
Website: http://www.nrf.re.kr
Role of national body: Research funding agency founded in 2009 through the merger of the Korea Science and Engineering Foundation (KOSEF), the Korea Research Foundation (KRF), and the Korea Foundation for International Cooperation of Science and Technology (KICOS).

Gungnip Gukje Gyoyukwon (National Institute for International Education - NIIED)

President: Kidong Song
191, Jeongjail-ro, Bundang-gu
Seongnam 13557, Gyeonggi
Tel: +82(2) 3668-1300
Fax: +82(2) 742-1064
Website: http://www.niied.go.kr
Role of national body: Executive agency under the Ministry of Education, NIIED administers the Korean government's

scholarship programme, leads and supports the education for overseas Koreans, reinforce the usage of the Korean language, carries out the exchange of international students, supports overseas students, and administers the National English Ability Test (NEAT).

Asia-Pacific Association for International Association - APAIE

President: Sarah Todd
Room 312 Lyceum, Korea University, Anam-Dong, Seongbuk-Gu
Seoul 136-701
Tel: +82(2) 3290-2935
Fax: +82(2) 921-0684
Website: https://www.apaie2018.org
Role of national body: Non-profit organization whose aims are to achieve greater cooperation among those responsible for international education and internationalization in Asia-Pacific higher education institutions and promote the quality of international programmes, activities, and exchanges.

Data for academic year: 2017–2018
Source: IAU from Ministry website, KCUE and KUAI websites and Study in Korea website, 2018.

Public Institutions

Academy of Korean Studies (AKS)

323 Haogae-ro, Bundang-gu
Seongnam-si 13455, Gyeonggi-do
Tel: +82(31) 709-8111
Fax: +82(31) 709-1531
Website: http://intl.aks.ac.kr/english/portal.php
Dean: Gilsang Lee

Department/Division
Culture and Arts (Anthropology; Art History; Computer Science; Folklore; Musicology; Religious Studies); **Global Korean Studies** (Communication Studies; East Asian Studies); **Humanities** (Arts and Humanities; History; Linguistics; Literature); **Social Sciences** (Economics; Education; Ethics; Political Sciences; Sociology)
History: Founded 1980 as Graduate School of Korean Studies. Acquired current title 2005.
Main language(s) of instruction: Korean
Accrediting agency: Ministry of Education
Degrees and diplomas: Master's Degree (Anthropology; Art History; Arts and Humanities; Communication Studies;

Computer Science; East Asian Studies; Economics; Education; Ethics; Folklore; History; Linguistics; Literature; Musicology; Political Sciences; Religious Studies; Sociology), Doctor's Degree (Anthropology; Art History; Arts and Humanities; Communication Studies; Computer Science; Economics; Education; Ethics; Folklore; History; Linguistics; Literature; Musicology; Political Sciences; Religious Studies; Sociology)
Last Update: 30-03-2018

Andong National University (ANU)

1375 Gyeongdong-ro
Andong-si 760-749, Gyeongsangbuk-do
Tel: +82(54) 820-5114, +82(54) 820-7101
Fax: +82(54) 820-7115, +82(54) 820-7108
Website: http://www.andong.ac.kr
President: Tai-hoan Kwon
Tel: +82(54) 820-7000

College
Art and Physical Education (Fine Arts; Music; Physical Education); **Education** (Education; Educational Technology; Ethics; Foreign Languages Education; Information Sciences; Information Technology; Mathematics Education; Mechanical Engineering; Teacher Trainers Education); **Engineering** (Automotive Engineering; Civil Engineering; Computer Engineering; Electronic Engineering; Engineering; Engineering Drawing and Design; Environmental Engineering; Materials Engineering; Mechanical Engineering; Metallurgical Engineering; Multimedia; Structural Architecture; Telecommunications Engineering); **Human Ecology** (Clothing and Sewing; Family Studies; Fashion Design; Food Science; Home Economics; Nutrition; Textile Design; Welfare and Protective Services); **Humanities** (Arts and Humanities; Asian Studies; Chinese; East Asian Studies; English; European Studies; Folklore; History; Korean; Literature; Philosophy; Tourism); **Natural Sciences** (Applied Chemistry; Biological and Life Sciences; Biology; Biotechnology; Botany; Chemistry; Earth Sciences; Environmental Studies; Food Science; Horticulture; Information Sciences; Natural Resources; Natural Sciences; Physics; Plant Pathology; Statistics); **Social Sciences** (Accountancy; Business Administration; Economics; International Business; Law; Public Administration; Social Sciences)

Graduate School
Administration and Management (Administration; Business Administration; Cultural Studies; Economics; Law; Management; Public Administration; Social Policy; Tourism; Welfare and Protective Services); **Education** (Art Education; Computer Education; Education; Educational Technology;

Foreign Languages Education; Home Economics Education; Humanities and Social Science Education; Mathematics Education; Native Language Education; Physical Education; Science Education; Technology Education); **General Graduate Studies** (Bioengineering; Biological and Life Sciences; Biology; Biotechnology; Business Administration; Chemistry; Chinese; Civil Engineering; Clothing and Sewing; Computer Engineering; Earth Sciences; Economics; Educational Technology; Electronic Engineering; Engineering Drawing and Design; English; Environmental Engineering; Environmental Studies; Ethics; Fine Arts; Folklore; Food Science; History; Horticulture; Industrial Engineering; Information Technology; Korean; Law; Literature; Materials Engineering; Mathematics; Measurement and Precision Engineering; Mechanical Engineering; Multimedia; Music; Natural Resources; Nutrition; Philosophy; Physical Education; Physics; Public Administration; Structural Architecture; Telecommunications Engineering; Textile Design)

History: Founded 1947 as Andong Normal School. Closed 1962 and opened as Junior Teachers' College 1965. Acquired present status and title 1979. A State Institution financed by the central Government.

Academic year: March to December (March-June; September-December)

Admission requirements: Graduation from high school or equivalent, and entrance examination

Main language(s) of instruction: Korean

Accrediting agency: Korean Council for University Education (KCUE)

Degrees and diplomas: Bachelor's Degree, Master's Degree (Bioengineering; Biological and Life Sciences; Biology; Biotechnology; Business Administration; Chemistry; Chinese; Civil Engineering; Clothing and Sewing; Computer Engineering; Earth Sciences; Economics; Educational Technology; Electronic Engineering; Engineering Drawing and Design; English; Environmental Engineering; Environmental Studies; Ethics; Fine Arts; Folklore; Food Science; History; Horticulture; Industrial Engineering; Information Technology; Korean; Law; Literature; Materials Engineering; Mathematics; Measurement and Precision Engineering; Mechanical Engineering; Multimedia; Music; Natural Resources; Nutrition; Philosophy; Physical Education; Physics; Public Administration; Structural Architecture; Telecommunications Engineering; Textile Design), Doctor's Degree (Bioengineering; Biological and Life Sciences; Biology; Biotechnology; Business Administration; Chemistry; Chinese; Civil Engineering; Computer Engineering; Earth Sciences; Economics; Educational Technology; Electronic Engineering; Engineering Drawing and Design; English; Environmental Engineering; Environmental Studies; Folklore; Food Science; History; Horticulture; Information Technology; Korean; Law; Literature; Materials Engineering; Mathematics; Mechanical Engineering; Natural Resources; Nutrition;

Physical Education; Physics; Public Administration; Telecommunications Engineering)

Student Services: Library, IT Centre, Residential Facilities

Periodicals: Andong Culture, Bulletin of Basic Science Research Institute, Research Review, Social Science Review, The Andong Moon Wha

Publishing house: Andong National University Press

Academic Staff 2013-2014	MALE	FEMALE	TOTAL
FULL-TIME			c. 720
Student Numbers 2013-2014			
All (Foreign Included)			c. 11600
Foreign only			210

Last Update: 08-03-2018

Busan National University of Education (BNUE)

24, Gyodae-ro, Yeonje-gu
Busan 611-736
Tel: +82(51) 500-7118
Fax: +82(51) 505-7584
Website: http://www.bnue.ac.kr
President: Se-Bok Oh

School

Education (Art Education; Computer Education; Education; English; Ethics; Foreign Languages Education; Home Economics Education; Korean; Mathematics Education; Music Education; Native Language Education; Physical Education; Preschool Education; Science Education; Social Studies)

Graduate School

Education (Art Education; Education of the Gifted; Educational Administration; Educational and Student Counselling; Foreign Languages Education; Home Economics Education; Humanities and Social Science Education; Information Sciences; Mathematics Education; Media Studies; Music Education; Native Language Education; Physical Education; Preschool Education; Primary Education; Science Education)

History: Founded 1946

Main language(s) of instruction: Korean

Accrediting agency: Ministry of Education

Degrees and diplomas: Bachelor's Degree (Primary Education), Master's Degree (Art Education; Educational and Student Counselling; Foreign Languages Education; Humanities and Social Science Education; Mathematics Education; Music Education; Native Language Education; Physical Education; Preschool Education; Primary Education; Science Education)

Student Services: Sports Facilities, Library, IT Centre, Residential Facilities

Academic Staff 2017-2018	MALE	FEMALE	TOTAL
FULL-TIME			140
Student Numbers 2017-2018			
All (Foreign Included)			1424

Last Update: 24-05-2018

Changwon National University

20 Changwondaehak-ro Uichang-gu
Changwon-si 641-773, Gyeongsangnam-do
Tel: +82(55) 213-3000, +82(55) 213-2114
Fax: +82(55) 283-2970
Website: http://www.changwon.ac.kr
President: Chan-Gyu Lee

College

Arts (Dance; Fine Arts; Industrial Design; Music); **Economics and Business** (Accountancy; Business Administration; Economics; Finance; Insurance; International Business; Management; Taxation); **Engineering** (Architecture; Automation and Control Engineering; Ceramics and Glass Technology; Chemical Engineering; Civil Engineering; Computer Engineering; Electrical Engineering; Electronic Engineering; Engineering; Environmental Engineering; Industrial Engineering; Instrument Making; Marine Engineering; Materials Engineering; Mechanical Engineering; Metallurgical Engineering; Naval Architecture; Production Engineering; Structural Architecture; Telecommunications Engineering); **Humanities** (Arts and Humanities; English; French; German; History; Japanese; Korean; Literature; Philosophy; Special Education); **Natural Sciences** (Biochemistry; Biology; Chemistry; Child Care and Development; Clothing and Sewing; Family Studies; Food Science; Health Sciences; Mathematics; Microbiology; Natural Sciences; Nursing; Nutrition; Physical Education; Physics; Statistics; Textile Technology); **Social Sciences** (Asian Studies; Chinese; International Relations; Journalism; Law; Mass Communication; Public Administration; Social Sciences; Sociology)

School
Korean Language (East Asian Studies; Korean)

Institute
Industrial Technology (Industrial Engineering)

Graduate School
Business Administration (*Special Graduate School*) (Accountancy; Business Administration; Economics; Finance; Insurance; International Business; Taxation; Transport Management); **Education** (*Special Graduate School*) (Art Education; Business Education; Education; Educational Administration; Educational and Student Counselling; Educational Psychology; Foreign Languages Education; Home Economics Education; Humanities and Social Science Education; Mathematics Education; Music Education; Native Language Education; Pedagogy; Physical Education; Science Education; Special Education; Technology Education); **Engineering and Information** (*Special Graduate School*) (Automation and Control Engineering; Chemical Engineering; Civil Engineering; Computer Science; Electrical Engineering; Electronic Engineering; Environmental Engineering; Industrial Design; Industrial Engineering; Materials Engineering; Mechanical Engineering; Structural Architecture; Telecommunications Engineering); **Graduate Studies** (Accountancy; Arts and Humanities; Asian Studies; Automation and Control Engineering; Biochemistry; Biology; Business Administration; Chemical Engineering; Chemistry; Chinese; Clothing and Sewing; Computer Engineering; Dance; Economics; Electronic Engineering; Engineering; English; Environmental Engineering; Finance; Fine Arts; Food Science; French; German; Health Sciences; History; Industrial Design; Industrial Engineering; Instrument Making; Insurance; International Business; International Relations; Japanese; Journalism; Korean; Law; Literature; Mass Communication; Materials Engineering; Mathematics; Mechanical Engineering; Music; Nanotechnology; Natural Sciences; Nutrition; Philosophy; Physical Education; Physics; Preschool Education; Production Engineering; Public Administration; Social Sciences; Sociology; Special Education; Statistics; Structural Architecture; Taxation; Telecommunications Engineering; Textile Technology); **Highest Institution of Learning** (*Special Graduate School*) (Business and Commerce; Leadership; Management; Small Business); **Labor** (*Special Graduate School*) (Labour and Industrial Relations; Labour Law; Welfare and Protective Services); **Public Administration** (*Special Graduate School*) (International Studies; Justice Administration; Public Administration)

Research Division
Basic Sciences; **Business and Economic Research**; **Design**; **Genetic Engineering**; **Human Ecology**; **Human Sciences**; **Social Sciences**; **Sport sciences**
History: Founded 1969 as a National Teachers College, acquired present title 1982.
Academic year: March to December (March-June; August-December)
Admission requirements: Graduation from high school and entrance examination
Fees: Undergraduate, 376,500-412,000; Graduate, 399,500-437,000 (Won)

Main language(s) of instruction: Korean
Accrediting agency: Korean Council for University Education (KCUE)
Degrees and diplomas: Bachelor's Degree, Master's Degree (Accountancy; Asian Studies; Automation and Control Engineering; Biochemistry; Biology; Business Administration; Chemical Engineering; Chemistry; Clothing and Sewing; Computer Engineering; Dance; Economics; Education; Electronic Engineering; Engineering; English; Environmental Engineering; Finance; Fine Arts; Food Science; French; German; Health Sciences; History; Industrial Design; Industrial Engineering; Information Technology; Insurance; International Business; International Relations; Korean; Labour and Industrial Relations; Law; Literature; Materials Engineering; Mathematics; Mechanical Engineering; Microbiology; Music; Nanotechnology; Nutrition; Philosophy; Physical Education; Physics; Preschool Education; Production Engineering; Public Administration; Special Education; Statistics; Structural Architecture; Taxation; Telecommunications Engineering), Doctor's Degree (Automation and Control Engineering; Business Administration; Chemical Engineering; Chemistry; Clothing and Sewing; Computer Engineering; Electronic Engineering; English; Environmental Engineering; Industrial Engineering; Instrument Making; International Business; Korean; Law; Literature; Materials Engineering; Mathematics; Mechanical Engineering; Nanotechnology; Philosophy; Physical Education; Physics; Production Engineering; Public Administration; Special Education; Statistics; Structural Architecture; Textile Technology)
Student Services: Careers Guidance, Library, IT Centre, Residential Facilities
Periodicals: Bulletins (in Korean and English), Publications of the Institutes

Academic Staff 2013-2014	MALE	FEMALE	TOTAL
FULL-TIME			406
PART-TIME			c. 551
Student Numbers 2013-2014			
All (Foreign Included)			c. 9320

Last Update: 09-02-2018

Cheongju National University of Education

2065, Cheongnam-ro Heungdeok-gu
Cheongju-si 361-712, Chungcheongbuk-do
Tel: +82(43) 299-0800, +82(43) 299-0613
Fax: +82(43) 299-0616
President: Su-Hwan Kim

Faculty
Education (Art Education; Computer Education; Education; Ethics; Foreign Languages Education; Humanities and Social Science Education; Mathematics Education; Music Education; Native Language Education; Physical Education; Preschool Education; Science Education)

Graduate School
Education (Education)
History: Founded 1941.
Main language(s) of instruction: Korean
Accrediting agency: Korean Council for University Education (KCUE)
Degrees and diplomas: Bachelor's Degree, Master's Degree (Education)

Academic Staff 2013-2014	MALE	FEMALE	TOTAL
FULL-TIME			60
PART-TIME			c. 130
Student Numbers 2013-2014			
All (Foreign Included)			c. 2140

Last Update: 09-02-2018

Chinju National University of Education (CUE)

369 Jinnyangho-ro beon-gil
Jinju-si 660-756, Gyeongsangnam-do
Tel: +82(55) 740-1114
Fax: +82(55) 740-1349
Website: http://www.cue.ac.kr
President: Moon-Seong Choi

School
Undergraduate Studies (Art Education; Computer Education; Education; Ethics; Foreign Languages Education; Humanities and Social Science Education; Mathematics Education; Music Education; Native Language Education; Physical Education; Primary Education; Science Education)

Graduate School
Graduate Studies (Art Education; Computer Education; Curriculum; Education; Educational Administration; Educational and Student Counselling; Foreign Languages Education; Humanities and Social Science Education; Information Sciences; Mathematics Education; Music Education; Native Language Education; Physical Education; Primary Education; Special Education; Technology Education)
History: Founded 1940 as Chinju National Normal School. Acquired present title 1993.

Main language(s) of instruction: Korean
Accrediting agency: Ministry of Education
Degrees and diplomas: Bachelor's Degree, Master's Degree (Art Education; Computer Education; Curriculum; Educational Administration; Foreign Languages Education; Humanities and Social Science Education; Mathematics Education; Music Education; Native Language Education; Physical Education; Primary Education; Special Education; Technology Education)
Student Services: Sports Facilities, Library, IT Centre, Residential Facilities
Last Update: 09-02-2018

Chonbuk National University (CBNU)

567 Baekje-daero Deokjin-gu
Jeonju-si 54896, Jeollabuk-do
Tel: +82(63) 270-2114
Fax: +82(63) 270-2099
Website: http://www.chonbuk.ac.kr
President: Nam-ho Lee

College

Agriculture and Life Science (Agricultural Economics; Agriculture; Applied Chemistry; Biochemistry; Bioengineering; Biological and Life Sciences; Biology; Construction Engineering; Crop Production; Environmental Studies; Food Science; Food Technology; Forest Products; Forestry; Horticulture; Industrial Engineering; Landscape Architecture; Wood Technology; Zoology); **Art** (Dance; Fine Arts; Industrial Design; Music); **Commerce** (Business Administration; Business and Commerce; Economics); **Education** (Education; Ethics; Foreign Languages Education; Humanities and Social Science Education; Mathematics Education; Native Language Education; Physical Education; Science Education; Social Studies); **Engineering** (Aeronautical and Aerospace Engineering; Bioengineering; Biomedical Engineering; Chemical Engineering; Civil Engineering; Computer Engineering; Computer Science; Electrical Engineering; Electronic Engineering; Energy Engineering; Engineering; Environmental Engineering; Industrial Engineering; Information Technology; Materials Engineering; Mechanical Engineering; Metallurgical Engineering; Nanotechnology; Polymer and Plastics Technology; Software Engineering; Structural Architecture; Textile Technology; Town Planning); **Environmental and Bioresource Sciences** (Alternative Medicine; Biotechnology; Environmental Studies; Food Science; Natural Resources); **Human Ecology** (Child Care and Development; Clothing and Sewing; Food Science; Home Economics; Nutrition; Textile Technology); **Liberal Arts** (Anthropology; Archaeology; Arts and Humanities; Chinese; Cultural Studies; English; French; German; History; Information Sciences; Japanese; Korean; Library Science; Literature; Philosophy; Spanish); **Natural Sciences** (Biological and Life Sciences; Chemistry; Computer Science; Earth Sciences; Electronic Engineering; Environmental Studies; Mathematics; Molecular Biology; Natural Sciences; Physics; Sports; Statistics); **Nursing** (Nursing); **Public Service** (Public Administration); **Social Sciences** (International Relations; Mass Communication; Political Sciences; Psychology; Public Administration; Social Sciences; Social Welfare; Sociology); **Veterinary Medicine** (Veterinary Science)

School

Law (*Professional Graduate School*) (Law); **Medicine** (*Professional Graduate School*) (Medicine)

Graduate School

Academia Joint Courses (Agricultural Economics; Agricultural Engineering; Agriculture; Applied Chemistry; Bioengineering; Biology; Chemical Engineering; Computer Engineering; Electrical Engineering; Electronic Engineering; Energy Engineering; Food Science; Food Technology; Forestry; Horticulture; Industrial Engineering; Landscape Architecture; Materials Engineering; Mechanical Engineering; Metallurgical Engineering; Nanotechnology; Polymer and Plastics Technology; Telecommunications Engineering; Zoology); **Arts and Physical Education** (Dance; Fine Arts; Industrial Design; Music; Physical Education); **Dentistry** (*Professional Graduate School*) (Dentistry); **Engineering** (Aeronautical and Aerospace Engineering; Chemical Engineering; Civil Engineering; Computer Engineering; Electrical Engineering; Electronic Engineering; Energy Engineering; Engineering; Environmental Engineering; Industrial Design; Industrial Engineering; Information Technology; Materials Engineering; Mechanical Engineering; Metallurgical Engineering; Nanotechnology; Polymer and Plastics Technology; Software Engineering; Structural Architecture; Textile Technology; Town Planning); **Flexible Pinted Electronics** (*Professional Graduate School*) (Electronic Engineering); **Humanities and Social Sciences** (Accountancy; Anthropology; Archaeology; Arts and Humanities; Business Administration; Business and Commerce; Chinese; Cultural Studies; East Asian Studies; Economics; Education; English; Ethics; French; German; History; Humanities and Social Science Education; Information Sciences; Japanese; Korean; Law; Library Science; Literature; Mass Communication; Modern Languages; Philosophy; Political Sciences; Psychology; Public Administration; Social Sciences; Social Welfare; Spanish); **Interdepartmental Joint Courses** (Archiving; Automotive Engineering; Bioengineering; Biotechnology; Cognitive Sciences; Cultural Studies; Design; E- Business/Commerce;

Ecology; Electronic Engineering; Energy Engineering; Engineering; Foreign Languages Education; Health Sciences; Industrial Engineering; Information Management; Information Sciences; Information Technology; International Business; Landscape Architecture; Mass Communication; Materials Engineering; Measurement and Precision Engineering; Mechanical Engineering; Music; Nanotechnology; Nutrition; Physical Engineering; Production Engineering; Public Administration; Radiology; Rehabilitation and Therapy; Speech Therapy and Audiology; Sports; Technology); **Medicine** (Dentistry; Medicine; Veterinary Science); **Natural Sciences** (Agricultural Economics; Agricultural Engineering; Agriculture; Applied Chemistry; Biological and Life Sciences; Biology; Chemistry; Earth Sciences; Ecology; Environmental Studies; Food Science; Food Technology; Forestry; Home Economics; Horticulture; Landscape Architecture; Mathematics; Mechanical Engineering; Natural Resources; Natural Sciences; Nursing; Physics; Science Education; Statistics; Zoology); **Special Graduate School** (Biological and Life Sciences; Business Administration; Education; Environmental Studies; Industrial Engineering; Information Sciences; Law; Natural Resources; Natural Sciences; Public Administration; Public Health)

Further information: Also University Hospital and 27 Research Institutes and Centres; Also Iksan Campus

History: Founded 1947 under the programme for the decentralization of higher education.

Academic year: March to February (March-August; September-February)

Admission requirements: Graduation from high school or foreign equivalent, and entrance examination

Main language(s) of instruction: Korean

Accrediting agency: Korean Council for University Education (KCUE)

Degrees and diplomas: Bachelor's Degree, Master's Degree (Accountancy; Aeronautical and Aerospace Engineering; Agricultural Economics; Agricultural Engineering; Agricultural Equipment; Agronomy; Anthropology; Archaeology; Architecture; Archiving; Automotive Engineering; Biology; Biotechnology; Business Administration; Chemical Engineering; Chemistry; Chinese; Civil Engineering; Cognitive Sciences; Computer Education; Computer Engineering; Computer Science; Dentistry; Earth Sciences; Ecology; Economics; Education; Electrical Engineering; Electronic Engineering; Energy Engineering; Engineering; English; Environmental Engineering; Environmental Studies; Ethics; Fine Arts; Food Science; Food Technology; Foreign Languages Education; Forestry; French Studies; German; History; Horticulture; Humanities and Social Science Education; Industrial Design; Information Management; Information Sciences; Information Technology; International Business; Japanese; Journalism; Korean; Landscape Architecture; Law; Library Science; Literature; Mass Communication;

Materials Engineering; Mathematics; Mechanical Engineering; Medical Technology; Medicine; Metallurgical Engineering; Mining Engineering; Music; Nanotechnology; Native Language Education; Natural Sciences; Nursing; Nutrition; Philosophy; Physical Education; Physical Engineering; Physics; Political Sciences; Polymer and Plastics Technology; Production Engineering; Psychology; Public Administration; Radiology; Science Education; Social Welfare; Sociology; Software Engineering; Speech Therapy and Audiology; Sports; Statistics; Town Planning; Veterinary Science; Zoology), Doctor's Degree (Accountancy; Aeronautical and Aerospace Engineering; Agricultural Economics; Agricultural Engineering; Agronomy; Anthropology; Applied Chemistry; Archaeology; Architectural and Environmental Design; Architecture; Archiving; Automotive Engineering; Biological and Life Sciences; Biology; Biotechnology; Business Administration; Chemical Engineering; Chemistry; Chinese; Civil Engineering; Cognitive Sciences; Computer Engineering; Computer Science; Dentistry; Earth Sciences; Ecology; Economics; Education; Electrical Engineering; Electronic Engineering; Energy Engineering; Engineering Drawing and Design; English; Environmental Engineering; Environmental Studies; Ethics; Fine Arts; Food Science; Food Technology; Foreign Languages Education; Forestry; French Studies; German; Health Sciences; History; Horticulture; Humanities and Social Science Education; Industrial Design; Industrial Engineering; Information Management; Information Sciences; Information Technology; International Business; Japanese; Journalism; Korean; Landscape Architecture; Law; Library Science; Literature; Mass Communication; Materials Engineering; Mathematics; Mechanical Engineering; Medical Technology; Medicine; Metallurgical Engineering; Music; Nanotechnology; Native Language Education; Natural Sciences; Nursing; Nutrition; Philosophy; Physical Education; Physical Engineering; Physics; Political Sciences; Polymer and Plastics Technology; Production Engineering; Psychology; Public Administration; Radiology; Science Education; Social Welfare; Sociology; Software Engineering; Speech Therapy and Audiology; Sports; Statistics; Town Planning; Veterinary Science; Zoology)

Student Services: Academic Counselling, Social Counselling, Careers Guidance, Cultural Activities, Sports Facilities, Language Laboratory, Health Services, Canteen, Library, IT Centre, Residential Facilities

Periodicals: Annual Bulletins of Research Institutes

Academic Staff 2013-2014	MALE	FEMALE	TOTAL
FULL-TIME			1318
PART-TIME			570
Student Numbers 2013-2014			
All (Foreign Included)			32300
Foreign only			1300

Last Update: 24-05-2018

Chonnam National University (CNU)

77 Yongbong-ro Buk-gu
Gwangju 61186
Tel: +82(62) 530-5114
Fax: +82(62) 530-1189
Website: http://www.jnu.ac.kr
President: Byungseok Jeong

Faculty

Interdisciplinary Studies (Arts and Humanities; Biochemistry; Biology; Chemistry; Civil Law; Communication Studies; Computer Science; Cultural Studies; Economics; English; Environmental Engineering; Finance; History; Information Technology; Law; Literature; Management; Materials Engineering; Mathematics; Natural Sciences; Organic Chemistry; Philosophy; Physics; Political Sciences; Public Health; Social Psychology; Social Sciences; Statistics; Writing)

College

Agriculture and Life Sciences (Agricultural Economics; Agricultural Engineering; Agriculture; Bioengineering; Biological and Life Sciences; Biotechnology; Botany; Environmental Engineering; Food Science; Food Technology; Forest Products; Forestry; Horticulture; Landscape Architecture; Molecular Biology; Wood Technology); **Arts** (Art History; Communication Arts; Design; Fine Arts; Handicrafts; Music; Music Theory and Composition; Musical Instruments; Painting and Drawing; Performing Arts; Singing; Visual Arts); **Business Administration** (Business Administration; Development Studies; Economics; Regional Studies); **Culture and Social Sciences** (Asian Studies; Business Administration; Business and Commerce; Chinese; Communication Arts; Cultural Studies; E- Business/Commerce; East Asian Studies; English; International Business; International Studies; Japanese; Multimedia; Social Sciences; Transport and Communications; Transport Management); **Education** (Art Education; Education; Ethics; Foreign Languages Education; Home Economics Education; Humanities and Social Science Education; Mathematics Education; Music Education; Native Language Education; Physical Education; Preschool Education; Science Education; Special Education); **Engineering** (Architecture; Automotive Engineering; Bioengineering; Biotechnology; Ceramics and Glass Technology; Chemical Engineering; Civil Engineering; Computer Engineering; Electrical Engineering; Electronic Engineering; Energy Engineering; Engineering; Environmental Engineering; Industrial Engineering; Materials Engineering; Mechanical Engineering; Metallurgical Engineering; Natural Resources; Polymer and Plastics Technology; Software Engineering; Structural Architecture); **Engineering Science** (Applied Mathematics; Architecture; Automotive Engineering; Biotechnology; Chemical Engineering; Civil Engineering; Computer Engineering; Electrical and Electronic Engineering; Electrical Engineering; Electronic Engineering; Engineering; Environmental Engineering; Heating and Refrigeration; Marine Engineering; Mechanical Engineering; Nursing; Telecommunications Engineering); **Fisheries and Ocean Sciences** (Aquaculture; Electrical Engineering; Environmental Studies; Fishery; Marine Engineering; Marine Science and Oceanography; Mechanical Engineering; Naval Architecture); **Human Ecology** (Clothing and Sewing; Family Studies; Food Science; Nutrition; Textile Design; Welfare and Protective Services); **Humanities** (Arts and Humanities; Chinese; English; French; German; History; Japanese; Korean; Literature; Philosophy); **Law** (Law); **Medicine** (Anaesthesiology; Anatomy; Biochemistry; Biomedical Engineering; Biomedicine; Cardiology; Dermatology; Forensic Medicine and Dentistry; Gynaecology and Obstetrics; Health Education; Immunology; Laboratory Techniques; Medical Technology; Medicine; Microbiology; Neurological Therapy; Neurology; Occupational Health; Oncology; Ophthalmology; Orthopaedics; Otorhinolaryngology; Paediatrics; Pathology; Pharmacology; Physical Therapy; Physiology; Plastic Surgery; Pneumology; Psychiatry and Mental Health; Radiology; Rehabilitation and Therapy; Social and Preventive Medicine; Surgery; Urology); **Natural Sciences** (Biological and Life Sciences; Chemistry; Earth Sciences; Environmental Studies; Geology; Marine Science and Oceanography; Mathematics; Natural Sciences; Physics; Statistics); **Nursing** (Nursing); **Pharmacy** (Pharmacology; Pharmacy); **Social Sciences** (Anthropology; Communication Studies; Geography (Human); Information Sciences; International Relations; Library Science; Political Sciences; Psychology; Public Administration; Social Sciences; Sociology); **Veterinary Medicine** (Veterinary Science)

School

Biological Sciences and Technology (Bioengineering; Biological and Life Sciences; Biology; Biotechnology); **Law** (*Professional Graduate School*) (Civil Law; Commercial Law; Criminal Law; Criminology; Forensic Medicine and Dentistry; Human Rights; International Law; Law; Private Law; Public Law); **Medical Science** (*Professional Graduate School*) (Anaesthesiology; Anatomy; Biochemistry; Biomedical Engineering; Biomedicine; Cardiology; Dermatology; Forensic Medicine and Dentistry; Gynaecology and Obstetrics; Health Education; Immunology; Laboratory Techniques; Medical Technology; Medicine; Microbiology; Neurological Therapy; Neurology; Occupational Health; Oncology; Ophthalmology; Orthopaedics; Otorhinolaryngology; Paediatrics; Pathology; Pharmacology; Physical Therapy; Physiology; Plastic Surgery; Psychiatry and Mental Health; Public Health; Radiology; Rehabilitation and Therapy; Social and Preventive Medicine; Surgery; Urology)

Graduate School

Business (*Professional Graduate School*) (Accountancy; Business Administration; Finance; Human Resources; Information Management; Information Technology; International Business; Management; Marketing); **Culture** (*Professional Graduate School*) (Communication Arts; Cultural Studies; Media Studies; Tourism); **Dentistry** (*Professional Graduate School*) (Dentistry); **Education** (*Special Graduate School*) (Agricultural Education; Art Education; Business Education; Computer Education; Continuing Education; Education; Educational Administration; Educational and Student Counselling; Ethics; Foreign Languages Education; Home Economics Education; Humanities and Social Science Education; Mathematics Education; Music Education; Native Language Education; Physical Education; Preschool Education; Special Education; Technology Education); **Fisheries and Ocean Sciences** (*Special Graduate School*) (Aquaculture; Environmental Studies; Fishery; Food Science; Food Technology; Marine Engineering; Marine Science and Oceanography; Nutrition; Power Engineering); **Graduate Studies** (Agricultural Business; Agricultural Economics; Agricultural Engineering; Agricultural Equipment; Animal Husbandry; Anthropology; Applied Chemistry; Aquaculture; Architecture; Bioengineering; Biological and Life Sciences; Biology; Biotechnology; Botany; Business Administration; Business and Commerce; Chemical Engineering; Chemistry; Chinese; Civil Engineering; Clothing and Sewing; Computer Engineering; Computer Science; Crop Production; Cultural Studies; Demography and Population; Earth Sciences; East Asian Studies; Ecology; Education; Electrical Engineering; Electronic Engineering; Energy Engineering; English; Environmental Engineering; Environmental Studies; Ethics; Fine Arts; Fishery; Food Science; Food Technology; Foreign Languages Education; Forestry; French; Geography (Human); Geological Engineering; Geology; German; Heating and Refrigeration; History; Horticulture; Humanities and Social Science Education; Industrial Engineering; Information Sciences; Information Technology; International Business; Japanese; Journalism; Korean; Landscape Architecture; Library Science; Literature; Marine Engineering; Marine Science and Oceanography; Mass Communication; Materials Engineering; Mathematics; Mathematics and Computer Science; Mathematics Education; Mechanical Engineering; Music; Native Language Education; Natural Resources; Naval Architecture; Nursing; Nutrition; Pharmacy; Philosophy; Physical Education; Physics; Political Sciences; Polymer and Plastics Technology; Preschool Education; Production Engineering; Psychology; Public Administration; Science Education; Sociology; Special Education; Statistics; Structural Architecture; Surveying and Mapping; Telecommunications Engineering; Textile Design; Translation and Interpretation; Transport and Communications; Transport Management; Veterinary Science; Wood Technology; Zoology); **Industry and Technology** (*Special Graduate School*) (Agricultural Economics; Agriculture; Animal Husbandry; Bioengineering; Chemical Engineering; Civil Engineering; Clothing and Sewing; Computer Engineering; Crop Production; Electrical Engineering; Electronic Engineering; Energy Engineering; Environmental Engineering; Environmental Studies; Food Science; Food Technology; Forestry; Industrial Engineering; Materials Engineering; Mechanical Engineering; Mining Engineering; Polymer and Plastics Technology; Rural Studies; Structural Architecture; Textile Technology; Tourism); **Industry-University Cooperation** (*Special Graduate School*) (Architectural and Environmental Design; Art Management; Automotive Engineering; Bioengineering; Biotechnology; Chemical Engineering; Civil Engineering; Communication Arts; Computer Engineering; Electrical Engineering; Environmental Engineering; Heating and Refrigeration; International Business; Management; Mechanical Engineering; Multimedia; Software Engineering; Telecommunications Engineering; Transport and Communications; Transport Management); **Public Administration** (*Special Graduate School*) (Public Administration)

Further information: Also 39 Research Institutes. Also Yosu campus (former Yosu National University)

History: Founded 1909, acquired present status and title 1952. Merged with Yosu National University 2006.

Academic year: March to February (March-June; September-February)

Admission requirements: Graduation from high school or foreign equivalent, and entrance examination (for Korean citizens)

Fees: Undergraduate tuition, 335-368 per unit; Graduate tuition, 354-463 per unit (US Dollar)

Main language(s) of instruction: Korean, English

Accrediting agency: Korean Council for University Education (KCUE)

Degrees and diplomas: Bachelor's Degree, Master's Degree (Accountancy; Agricultural Business; Agricultural Economics; Agricultural Education; Agriculture; Animal Husbandry; Anthropology; Applied Chemistry; Aquaculture; Architectural and Environmental Design; Architecture; Archiving; Art Education; Automotive Engineering; Bioengineering; Biological and Life Sciences; Biology; Biomedical Engineering; Biomedicine; Biotechnology; Botany; Business Administration; Business Education; Chemical Engineering; Chemistry; Chinese; Civil Engineering; Clothing and Sewing; Communication Arts; Communication Studies; Computer Education; Computer Engineering; Continuing Education; Demography and Population; Dentistry; Development Studies; E- Business/Commerce; Earth Sciences; Economics; Education; Educational Administration; Educational and Student Counselling; Educational Technology; Electrical Engineering; Electronic Engineering; Energy Engineering; Engineering Drawing and Design; English;

Environmental Engineering; Environmental Studies; Ethics; Family Studies; Fine Arts; Fishery; Food Science; Food Technology; Foreign Languages Education; Forest Products; Forestry; French; Geography; German; Health Education; Heating and Refrigeration; History; Home Economics Education; Horticulture; Humanities and Social Science Education; Industrial Engineering; Information Sciences; Information Technology; International Business; Japanese; Korean; Landscape Architecture; Law; Library Science; Literature; Management; Marine Biology; Marine Engineering; Marine Science and Oceanography; Materials Engineering; Mathematics; Mathematics Education; Mechanical Engineering; Medicine; Molecular Biology; Multimedia; Music; Music Education; Nanotechnology; Native Language Education; Natural Resources; Naval Architecture; Neurosciences; Nutrition; Pharmacy; Philosophy; Physical Education; Physics; Police Studies; Political Sciences; Preschool Education; Psychology; Public Administration; Regional Studies; Science Education; Sociology; Software Engineering; Special Education; Statistics; Structural Architecture; Technology Education; Telecommunications Engineering; Textile Design; Transport and Communications; Transport Management; Veterinary Science; Welfare and Protective Services; Wood Technology; Zoology), Doctor's Degree (Accountancy; Agricultural Economics; Agriculture; Animal Husbandry; Anthropology; Applied Chemistry; Architecture; Archiving; Automotive Engineering; Bioengineering; Biological and Life Sciences; Biology; Biomedical Engineering; Biotechnology; Botany; Business Administration; Chemical Engineering; Chemistry; Chinese; Civil Engineering; Clothing and Sewing; Communication Studies; Computer Engineering; Demography and Population; Dentistry; Development Studies; E- Business/Commerce; Earth Sciences; Economics; Education; Electrical Engineering; Electronic Engineering; Energy Engineering; Engineering Drawing and Design; English; Environmental Engineering; Environmental Studies; Family Studies; Fine Arts; Fishery; Food Science; Food Technology; Foreign Languages Education; Forestry; French; Geography; German; Heating and Refrigeration; History; Horticulture; Humanities and Social Science Education; Industrial Engineering; Information Sciences; Information Technology; International Business; Japanese; Korean; Landscape Architecture; Law; Library Science; Literature; Marine Science and Oceanography; Materials Engineering; Mathematics; Mechanical Engineering; Medicine; Molecular Biology; Music; Native Language Education; Natural Resources; Neurosciences; Nutrition; Pharmacy; Philosophy; Physics; Political Sciences; Psychology; Public Administration; Regional Studies; Sociology; Special Education; Statistics; Structural Architecture; Textile Design; Veterinary Science; Welfare and Protective Services; Wood Technology; Zoology)

Student Services: Academic Counselling, Social Counselling, Careers Guidance, Cultural Activities, Sports Facilities, Language Laboratory, Health Services, Library, IT Centre, Residential Facilities

Periodicals: Chonnam National Journal, Journal of Agricultural Science and Technology, Journal of Drug Development, Journal of Natural Science, Journal of Research Institute for Catalysis, Journal of Sciences for Better Living, Journal of Unification Studies, Review of American Studies, Rural Development Review

Publishing house: The University Press

Academic Staff 2013-2014	MALE	FEMALE	TOTAL
FULL-TIME			1168
Student Numbers 2013-2014			
All (Foreign Included)			33195
Foreign only			1128

Last Update: 09-02-2018

Chuncheon National University of Education (CNUE)

Gongji Ro 126 Chuncheon
Gangwon-do 24328
Tel: +82(33) 260-6000, +82(33) 260-6163
Fax: +82(33) 261-4328, +82(33) 260-6162
Website: http://www.cnue.ac.kr/eng/main/main.jsp
President: Hwanki Lee

Department/Division
Art Education (Art Education; Teacher Training); **Computer Education** (Computer Education; Computer Engineering; Computer Science); **Education** (Curriculum; Education; Educational Administration; Educational Psychology; Educational Sciences; Sociology; Teacher Training); **English Education** (English; Foreign Languages Education; Teacher Training); **Ethics Education** (Ethics; Philosophy); **Korean Education** (Grammar; Korean; Literature; Native Language Education; Teacher Training; Writing); **Mathematics Education** (Arts and Humanities; Mathematics Education; Statistics); **Music Education** (Music; Music Education; Teacher Training); **Physical Education** (Physical Education); **Practical Arts Education** (Agricultural Education; Agriculture; Biological and Life Sciences; Clothing and Sewing; Dietetics; Home Economics Education; Robotics; Technology; Technology Education); **Science Education** (Primary Education; Science Education; Teacher Training); **Social Studies Education** (Cultural Studies; Economics; Geography (Human); History; Humanities and Social Science Education; Political Sciences; Primary Education; Social Sciences; Social Studies; Teacher Training)

Graduate School

Graduate Studies (Art Education; Computer Education; Education; Educational Administration; Educational and Student Counselling; Educational Psychology; Foreign Languages Education; Humanities and Social Science Education; Mathematics Education; Music Education; Native Language Education; Physical Education; Primary Education; Science Education; Special Education)

Further information: Also Graduate School

History: Founded 1939 as Chuncheon Normal School. Upgraded into Chuncheon Teachers College 1962. Acquired present status and title 1993.

Main language(s) of instruction: Korean

Accrediting agency: Ministry of Education

Degrees and diplomas: Bachelor's Degree, Master's Degree (Art Education; Bilingual and Bicultural Education; Computer Education; Educational Administration; Educational and Student Counselling; Educational Psychology; Foreign Languages Education; Mathematics Education; Music Education; Native Language Education; Physical Education; Preschool Education; Primary Education; Science Education; Secondary Education; Special Education)

Student Services: Sports Facilities, Canteen, Library, IT Centre, Residential Facilities

Academic Staff 2017-2018	MALE	FEMALE	TOTAL
FULL-TIME			87
Student Numbers 2017-2018			
All (Foreign Included)			1924

Last Update: 08-03-2018

Chungbuk National University (CBNU)

Chungdae-ro 1, Seowon-Gu
Cheongju-si 28644, Chungbuk-do
Tel: +82(43) 261-2114, +82(43) 261-3172
Fax: +82(43) 268-2068, +82(43) 261-3184
Website: http://www.chungbuk.ac.kr
President: Yeo-pyo Yun

College

Agriculture, Life, and Environmental Sciences (*CALES*) (Agricultural Business; Agricultural Economics; Agricultural Engineering; Agriculture; Animal Husbandry; Applied Chemistry; Bioengineering; Biology; Botany; Crop Production; Food Science; Food Technology; Forest Products; Forestry; Horticulture; Industrial Engineering; Paper Technology; Plant Pathology); **Commerce and Business Administration** (Business Administration; Business and Commerce; Information Management; Information Sciences; International Business); **Education** (Computer Education; Education; Ethics; Foreign Languages Education; Humanities and Social Science Education; Mathematics Education; Native Language Education; Science Education); **Electrical and Computer Engineering** (Computer Engineering; Electrical Engineering; Electronic Engineering; Information Technology; Software Engineering; Telecommunications Engineering); **Engineering** (Architecture; Chemical Engineering; Civil Engineering; Engineering; Environmental Engineering; Industrial Chemistry; Industrial Engineering; Materials Engineering; Mechanical Engineering; Safety Engineering; Structural Architecture; Town Planning); **Human Ecology** (*CHE*) (Child Care and Development; Consumer Studies; Fashion Design; Food Science; Home Economics; House Arts and Environment; Information Sciences; Interior Design; Nutrition); **Humanities** (Archaeology; Art History; Arts and Humanities; Chinese; English; French; German; History; Korean; Literature; Philosophy; Russian); **Law** (Law; Private Law; Public Law); **Medicine** (Medicine; Natural Sciences; Nursing); **Natural Sciences** (Astronomy and Space Science; Biochemistry; Biology; Chemistry; Computer Science; Earth Sciences; Environmental Studies; Geology; Information Sciences; Mathematics; Microbiology; Natural Sciences; Physics; Statistics); **Pharmacy** (Pharmacy; Public Health; Social and Preventive Medicine); **Social Sciences** (Economics; International Relations; Political Sciences; Psychology; Public Administration; Social Sciences; Sociology); **Veterinary Science** (Veterinary Science)

Course/Programme

Inter-College Studies (Art Education; Arts and Humanities; Computer Science; Design; Information Technology; Painting and Drawing; Sculpture; Visual Arts)

School

Law (*Graduate*) (Law; Public Law)

Graduate School

Business Administration (Accountancy; Business Administration; Finance; Human Resources; Information Management; International Business; Management; Marketing); **Education** (Education; Teacher Training); **Graduate Studies** (Arts and Humanities; Design; Engineering; Fine Arts; Medicine; Natural Sciences; Physical Education; Social Studies); **Industry** (Computer Engineering; Construction Engineering; Electrical Engineering; Engineering Management; Production Engineering); **Legal Affairs** (Civil Law; Commercial Law; Criminal Law; Law; Public Law); **Medicine** (Medicine); **Public Administration** (Public Administration)

Research Division

Agricultural Science and Biotechnology (Agriculture; Animal Husbandry; Biotechnology; Horticulture); **Construction**

and Industrial Science Technology (Construction Engineering; Industrial Engineering); **Health Medical Treatment Science** (Biological and Life Sciences; Information Sciences; Medicine; Natural Resources; Oncology; Pharmacy; Physical Education; Sports; Veterinary Science); **Humanities** (Arts and Humanities; Asian Studies; Cultural Studies; Eastern European Studies; Russian); **Information Technology and Consulting** (Computer Science; Industrial Management; Information Technology; Telecommunications Engineering); **Natural Sciences** (Astrophysics; Biotechnology; Finance; Mathematics; Nanotechnology; Natural Sciences; Science Education); **Social Science** (Education; Educational Administration; Home Economics; Law; Social Sciences)

History: Founded 1951 as Junior Agricultural College. Merged with Chungnam University and changed name to Chungcheong National University 1962. Reorganized as Chungbuk National College (separated from Chungnam University) 1963. Acquired present title 1983.

Academic year: March to December (March-June; September-December)

Admission requirements: Graduation from high school and entrance examination

Main language(s) of instruction: Korean

Accrediting agency: Korean Council for University Education (KCUE)

Degrees and diplomas: Bachelor's Degree, Master's Degree (Accountancy; Agricultural Economics; Agricultural Education; Agriculture; Animal Husbandry; Archaeology; Architecture; Art Education; Art History; Astronomy and Space Science; Bioengineering; Biological and Life Sciences; Biomedical Engineering; Biotechnology; Botany; Business Administration; Business Education; Chemistry; Child Care and Development; Chinese; Civil Engineering; Civil Law; Commercial Law; Computer Education; Computer Engineering; Computer Science; Construction Engineering; Criminal Law; Design; Earth Sciences; Economics; Education; Educational Administration; Educational and Student Counselling; Electrical Engineering; Electronic Engineering; Engineering Management; English; Environmental Engineering; Environmental Studies; Ethics; Fashion Design; Finance; Fine Arts; Food Science; Foreign Languages Education; Forest Products; Forestry; French; Health Sciences; Home Economics Education; Horticulture; House Arts and Environment; Human Resources; Humanities and Social Science Education; Industrial Arts Education; Industrial Chemistry; Industrial Engineering; Information Management; Information Sciences; Information Technology; International Business; Korean; Law; Literature; Management; Marketing; Materials Engineering; Mathematics; Mathematics Education; Measurement and Precision Engineering; Mechanical Engineering; Medicine; Native Language Education; Nutrition; Pharmacy; Philosophy; Physical Education; Physics; Political Sciences; Primary Education; Production Engineering; Public Administration; Science Education; Statistics; Town Planning; Water Science), Doctor's Degree (Accountancy; Agricultural Economics; Agriculture; Animal Husbandry; Archaeology; Architecture; Art History; Astronomy and Space Science; Bioengineering; Biological and Life Sciences; Biomedical Engineering; Biotechnology; Botany; Chemistry; Child Care and Development; Civil Engineering; Computer Engineering; Computer Science; Construction Engineering; Consumer Studies; Earth Sciences; Economics; Education; Electrical Engineering; Electronic Engineering; English; Environmental Engineering; Environmental Studies; Fashion Design; Food Science; Food Technology; Foreign Languages Education; Forestry; Health Sciences; Heritage Preservation; Horticulture; House Arts and Environment; Humanities and Social Science Education; Industrial Chemistry; Industrial Engineering; Information Management; Information Sciences; Information Technology; International Business; Korean; Literature; Machine Building; Management; Materials Engineering; Mathematics and Computer Science; Mathematics Education; Measurement and Precision Engineering; Mechanical Engineering; Medicine; Nutrition; Pharmacy; Philosophy; Physical Education; Physics; Political Sciences; Statistics; Town Planning; Water Science)

Student Services: Academic Counselling, Careers Guidance, Cultural Activities, Sports Facilities, Health Services, Canteen, Library, Residential Facilities

Periodicals: Chungbuk Times, Gaeshin Four Seasons

Publishing house: University Press

Academic Staff 2015-2016	MALE	FEMALE	TOTAL
FULL-TIME			1288
Student Numbers 2015-2016			
All (Foreign Included)			24300

Last Update: 12-02-2018

Chungnam National University (CNU)

99 Daehak-ro Yuseong-gu
Daejeon 305-764, Chungnam-do
Tel: +82(42) 821-5114
Fax: +82(42) 823-8589
Website: http://www.chungnam.ac.kr
President: Sang-Chul Jung

College

Agriculture and Life Sciences (Agricultural Economics; Agricultural Engineering; Agriculture; Animal Husbandry; Biochemistry; Bioengineering; Biological and Life Sciences;

Biology; Biotechnology; Crop Production; Environmental Studies; Food Science; Food Technology; Forest Biology; Forestry; Horticulture); **Biological Sciences and Biotechnology** (Biological and Life Sciences; Biotechnology; Microbiology; Molecular Biology); **Economics** (Business Administration; Economics; International Business); **Education** (Chemical Engineering; Construction Engineering; Education; Electrical Engineering; Electronic Engineering; Foreign Languages Education; Machine Building; Mathematics Education; Mechanical Engineering; Metallurgical Engineering; Native Language Education; Physical Education; Technology Education; Telecommunications Engineering); **Engineering** (Aeronautical and Aerospace Engineering; Applied Chemistry; Architecture; Chemical Engineering; Civil Engineering; Computer Engineering; Electrical Engineering; Electronic Engineering; Engineering; Engineering Drawing and Design; Environmental Engineering; Information Technology; Marine Engineering; Materials Engineering; Mechanical Engineering; Nanotechnology; Naval Architecture; Polymer and Plastics Technology; Radiophysics; Structural Architecture; Telecommunications Engineering; Textile Technology); **Fine Arts and Music** (Design; Fine Arts; Handicrafts; Music; Music Theory and Composition; Musical Instruments; Painting and Drawing; Sculpture; Singing; Visual Arts); **Human Ecology** (Clothing and Sewing; Consumer Studies; Food Science; Home Economics; Nutrition; Textile Design); **Humanities** (Archaeology; Arts and Humanities; Chinese; English; French; German; Japanese; Korean; Linguistics; Literature; Philosophy); **Law** (Law); **Liberal Arts** (Arts and Humanities; Leadership; Marine Science and Oceanography; Protective Services); **Medicine** (Medicine); **Natural Sciences** (Astronomy and Space Science; Biochemistry; Chemistry; Dance; Earth Sciences; Environmental Studies; Geology; Information Sciences; Marine Science and Oceanography; Mathematics; Natural Sciences; Physics; Sports; Statistics); **Nursing** (Nursing); **Pharmacy** (Pharmacology; Pharmacy); **Social Sciences** (Administration; Communication Studies; Information Sciences; International Relations; Library Science; Political Sciences; Psychology; Public Administration; Social Sciences; Social Welfare; Sociology); **Veterinary Medicine** (Veterinary Science)

School

Law (*Specialized Graduate School*) (Commercial Law; Criminal Law; Law; Private Law; Public Law); **Medicine** (*Specialized Graduate School*) (Anatomy; Biochemistry; Biological and Life Sciences; Biology; Forensic Medicine and Dentistry; Health Education; Medicine; Microbiology; Pathology; Pharmacology; Physiology; Social and Preventive Medicine)

Graduate School

Analytical Science and Technology (*Specialized Graduate School*) (Biological and Life Sciences; Biotechnology; Environmental Engineering; Environmental Studies; Nanotechnology); **Business** (*Professional Graduate School*) (Business Administration); **Drug Development and Discovery** (*Specialized Graduate School*) (Pharmacology); **Education** (*Professional Graduate School*) (Education; Secondary Education; Teacher Training); **Graduate Studies** (Agriculture; Archiving; Arts and Humanities; Biological and Life Sciences; Biomedical Engineering; Business Administration; Criminology; Economics; Electronic Engineering; Engineering; Fine Arts; Health Administration; Home Economics; International Studies; Law; Management; Medicine; Military Science; Music; Natural Sciences; Pharmacy; Public Health; Regional Studies; Social Sciences; Speech Therapy and Audiology; Veterinary Science); **Green Energy Technology** (*Specialized Graduate School*) (Energy Engineering; Materials Engineering); **Industry** (*Professional Graduate School*) (Chemical Engineering; Civil Engineering; Electrical Engineering; Electronic Engineering; Food Technology; Geological Engineering; Industrial Engineering; Information Technology; Marine Engineering; Mechanical Engineering; Metallurgical Engineering; Naval Architecture; Structural Architecture; Textile Technology); **Intellectual Property Law** (*Professional Graduate School*) (Commercial Law; Law; Private Law); **Peace and Security** (*Professional Graduate School*) (Arts and Humanities; Economics; Management; Military Science; Peace and Disarmament; Political Sciences; Protective Services; Social Sciences); **Public Administration** (*Professional Graduate School*) (Management; Public Administration; Social Policy; Social Welfare); **Public Health** (*Professional Graduate School*) (Public Health)

Further information: Also Bowun Campus; University Hospital; c. 107 Research Centres and Institutes

History: Founded 1952 as Chungnam Provincial University. Became Chungcheong National University 1962 after merging with Chungbuk Provincial University. Acquired present title 1963. A State Institution financed by the Government.

Academic year: March to December (March-June; August-December)

Admission requirements: Graduation from high school and entrance examination

Main language(s) of instruction: Korean

Accrediting agency: Korean Council for University Education (KCUE)

Degrees and diplomas: Bachelor's Degree, Master's Degree (Accountancy; Administration; Aeronautical and Aerospace Engineering; Agricultural Economics; Agricultural Engineering;

Agrobiology; Agronomy; Animal Husbandry; Applied Chemistry; Archaeology; Architecture; Archiving; Astronomy and Space Science; Automotive Engineering; Biochemistry; Bioengineering; Biological and Life Sciences; Biomedical Engineering; Biotechnology; Business Administration; Business and Commerce; Chemical Engineering; Chemistry; Chinese; Civil Engineering; Clothing and Sewing; Communication Studies; Computer Engineering; Consumer Studies; Dairy; Dance; Earth Sciences; Economics; Education; Electrical Engineering; Electronic Engineering; Energy Engineering; Engineering Drawing and Design; English; Environmental Engineering; Fine Arts; Food Science; Food Technology; Forestry; French; Geological Engineering; Geology; German; Handicrafts; Health Administration; History; Horticulture; Industrial Engineering; Information Sciences; Information Technology; International Relations; Japanese; Korean; Library Science; Linguistics; Literature; Machine Building; Marine Engineering; Marine Science and Oceanography; Materials Engineering; Mathematics; Mechanical Engineering; Medicine; Metallurgical Engineering; Military Science; Mineralogy; Music; Musical Instruments; Naval Architecture; Nuclear Engineering; Nursing; Nutrition; Peace and Disarmament; Petroleum and Gas Engineering; Pharmacy; Philosophy; Physical Education; Physics; Political Sciences; Private Law; Psychology; Public Administration; Public Health; Radiophysics; Rural Planning; Safety Engineering; Social Welfare; Sociology; Speech Therapy and Audiology; Sports; Statistics; Structural Architecture; Technology Education; Telecommunications Engineering; Textile Design; Textile Technology; Veterinary Science; Water Science), Doctor's Degree (Accountancy; Administration; Aeronautical and Aerospace Engineering; Agricultural Economics; Agricultural Engineering; Agricultural Equipment; Agriculture; Agronomy; Animal Husbandry; Applied Chemistry; Archaeology; Archiving; Astronomy and Space Science; Automotive Engineering; Biochemistry; Bioengineering; Biological and Life Sciences; Biology; Biomedical Engineering; Biophysics; Biotechnology; Business Administration; Chemical Engineering; Chemistry; Chinese; Civil Engineering; Clothing and Sewing; Communication Studies; Computer Engineering; Criminology; Dairy; Dance; Earth Sciences; Economics; Education; Electrical Engineering; Electronic Engineering; Energy Engineering; Engineering Drawing and Design; English; Environmental Engineering; Food Science; Food Technology; Forestry; French; Geology; German; Handicrafts; Health Administration; History; Horticulture; Information Sciences; Information Technology; International Relations; International Studies; Japanese; Korean; Law; Library Science; Linguistics; Literature; Machine Building; Marine Engineering; Marine Science and Oceanography; Materials Engineering; Mathematics; Mechanical Engineering; Medicine; Military Science; Mineralogy; Natural Sciences; Naval Architecture; Nuclear Engineering; Nursing; Nutrition;

Petroleum and Gas Engineering; Pharmacy; Philosophy; Physical Education; Political Sciences; Psychology; Public Administration; Public Health; Radiophysics; Regional Studies; Safety Engineering; Social Welfare; Sociology; Speech Therapy and Audiology; Sports; Statistics; Structural Architecture; Technology Education; Telecommunications Engineering; Textile Design; Textile Technology; Veterinary Science; Water Science)

Student Services: Library, IT Centre, Residential Facilities
Periodicals: Papers of the Faculties
Publishing house: The University Press

Academic Staff 2015-2016	MALE	FEMALE	TOTAL
FULL-TIME			2300
Student Numbers 2015-2016			
All (Foreign Included)			c. 30000
Foreign only			1300

Last Update: 12-02-2018

Daegu Gyeongbuk Institute of Science and Technology (DGIST)

333 Techno Jungang-daero Hyeonpung-myeon Dalseong-gun
Daegu 42988
Tel: +82(53) 785-5147
Fax: +82(53) 785-1139
Website: http://en.dgist.ac.kr
President: Sang Hyuk Son
Tel: +82(53) 785-1000

College

Transdisciplinary Studies (Automation and Control Engineering; Biology; Chemistry; Engineering; Mathematics; Natural Sciences; Physics; Statistics)

Graduate School

Brain and Cognitive Sciences (Cognitive Sciences; Neurosciences); **Emerging Materials Science** (Materials Engineering; Nanotechnology); **Energy Science and Engineering** (Energy Engineering; Environmental Engineering); **Information and Communication Engineering** (Computer Engineering; Information Sciences); **New Biology** (Biochemistry; Biological and Life Sciences; Biophysics); **Robotics Engineering** (Automation and Control Engineering; Robotics)

History: Founded as a research institute 2004, redefined its roles and responsibilities as a research-oriented university by opening graduate programmes 2011. In 2014, DGIST added its undergraduate programme with transdisciplinary curriculum within a single unified school for the first time in Korea, thereby expanding the organization wherein a university and a research institute co-exist.

Academic year: March to December (March-June; September-December)

Admission requirements: Graduation from high school or equivalent (bachelor's); Bachelor's degree or equivalent (master's); Master's degree or equivalent (PhD)

Fees: National : None (Full scholarship from the government for all admitted students), International : None (Full scholarship from the government for all admitted students)

Main language(s) of instruction: English, Korean

Accrediting agency: Ministry of Science and ICT

Degrees and diplomas: Bachelor's Degree (Engineering; Natural Sciences), Master's Degree (Biological and Life Sciences; Energy Engineering; Information Sciences; Materials Engineering; Neurosciences; Robotics), Doctor's Degree (Biological and Life Sciences; Energy Engineering; Information Sciences; Materials Engineering; Neurosciences; Robotics)

Student Services: Academic Counselling, Careers Guidance, Sports Facilities, Facilities for disabled people, Library, Residential Facilities

Academic Staff 2017-2018	MALE	FEMALE	TOTAL
FULL-TIME	445	196	641
STAFF WITH DOCTORATE			
FULL-TIME	245	46	291
Student Numbers 2017-2018			
All (Foreign Included)	1050	409	1459

Last Update: 26-04-2018

Daegu National University of Education (DNUE)

219 Jungang-daero, Nam-gu
Daegu 42411
Tel: +82(53) 620-1114
Fax: +82(53) 651-5369
Website: http://www.dnue.ac.kr
President: Cheong-hwan Lim

Department/Division

Computer Education (Computer Education); **Education** (Education; Primary Education); **English Education** (Foreign Languages Education); **Ethics Education** (Ethics; Humanities and Social Science Education); **Korean Language Education** (Native Language Education); **Mathematics Education** (Mathematics Education); **Music Education** (Music Education); **Physical Education** (Physical Education); **Practical Arts Education** (Agricultural Education; Computer Education; Home Economics Education; Technology Education); **Science Education** (Science Education); **Social Studies Education** (Humanities and Social Science Education); **Special and Compositive Education** (Special Education)

Graduate School

Elementary Teacher Training (Agricultural Education; Art Education; Computer Education; Curriculum; Education; Education of the Gifted; Education of the Handicapped; Educational Administration; Educational and Student Counselling; Educational Psychology; Educational Technology; Ethics; Foreign Languages Education; Home Economics Education; Humanities and Social Science Education; Mathematics Education; Music Education; Native Language Education; Pedagogy; Physical Education; Preschool Education; Primary Education; Science Education; Special Education; Teacher Training; Technology Education)

History: Founded 1950, acquired present status and title 1993.

Admission requirements: Graduation from high school or equivalent, and entrance examination

Main language(s) of instruction: Korean

Accrediting agency: Ministry of Education

Degrees and diplomas: Bachelor's Degree, Master's Degree (Agricultural Education; Art Education; Computer Education; Curriculum; Education of the Gifted; Educational Administration; Educational and Student Counselling; Educational Psychology; Foreign Languages Education; Home Economics Education; Humanities and Social Science Education; Mathematics Education; Music Education; Native Language Education; Pedagogy; Physical Education; Preschool Education; Primary Education; Science Education; Special Education; Technology Education)

Student Services: Academic Counselling, Nursery Care, Sports Facilities, Language Laboratory, Canteen, Library, Residential Facilities

Academic Staff 2016-2017	MALE	FEMALE	TOTAL
FULL-TIME			108
PART-TIME			149
Student Numbers 2016-2017			
All (Foreign Included)			1696

Last Update: 12-02-2018

Gangneung–Wonju National University (GWNU)

7, Jukheon-gil
Gangneung-si 25457, Gangwon-Do

Tel: +82(33) 642-7001
Fax: +82(33) 643-7110
Website: http://www.gwnu.ac.kr
President: Seon-seop Ban

College

Arts and Physical Education (Design; Fashion Design; Fine Arts; Handicrafts; Music; Physical Education); **Culture** (Fashion Design; Music; Women's Studies); **Dentistry** (Dental Technology; Dentistry); **Engineering** (Bioengineering; Ceramics and Glass Technology; Chemical Engineering; Civil Engineering; Electronic Engineering; Engineering; Engineering Management; Industrial Engineering; Information Technology; Materials Engineering; Metallurgical Engineering); **Health and Welfare** (Cultural Studies; Health Sciences; Nursing; Preschool Education; Welfare and Protective Services); **Humanities** (Chinese; East Asian Studies; English; German; History; Japanese; Korean; Literature; Philosophy; Preschool Education; Teacher Training); **Life Sciences** (Biological and Life Sciences; Biotechnology; Botany; Food Science; Food Technology; Landscape Architecture; Marine Biology; Marine Science and Oceanography; Natural Resources; Nutrition); **Natural Sciences** (Biology; Chemistry; Environmental Studies; Materials Engineering; Mathematics; Meteorology; Natural Sciences; Physics; Statistics); **Science and Technology** (Automotive Engineering; Biomedical Engineering; Computer Engineering; Computer Science; Electrical Engineering; Engineering Management; Industrial Engineering; Information Technology; Measurement and Precision Engineering; Mechanical Engineering; Multimedia; Telecommunications Engineering); **Social Sciences** (Accountancy; Business Administration; Business and Commerce; Development Studies; Economics; Government; International Business; Law; Management; Public Administration; Regional Studies; Tourism)

Graduate School

Education (Art Education; Computer Education; Education; Educational Administration; Educational and Student Counselling; Foreign Languages Education; Home Economics Education; Humanities and Social Science Education; Mathematics Education; Native Language Education; Pedagogy; Physical Education; Preschool Education; Science Education); **Graduate Studies** (Arts and Humanities; Engineering; Fine Arts; Medicine; Natural Sciences; Physical Education; Social Sciences); **Industrial Technology** (Automotive Engineering; Bioengineering; Biomedical Engineering; Chemical Engineering; Civil Engineering; Computer Engineering; Computer Science; Electrical Engineering; Electronic Engineering; Energy Engineering; Engineering Management; Environmental Engineering; Food Science; Horticulture; Industrial Arts Education; Industrial Engineering; Information Technology; Landscape Architecture;

Marine Biology; Marine Engineering; Materials Engineering; Measurement and Precision Engineering; Mechanical Engineering; Multimedia; Telecommunications Engineering); **Management and Policy Science** (Accountancy; Business Administration; Business and Commerce; Development Studies; E- Business/Commerce; Industrial and Production Economics; International Business; Law; Management; Military Science; Protective Services; Public Administration; Regional Studies; Tourism)

Research Division

Arts and Physical Education (Fine Arts; Physical Education); **Culture Industry** (Art Management); **Disaster Prevention** (Welfare and Protective Services); **East Sea Life Sciences** (Marine Science and Oceanography); **Engineering** (Engineering); **Governmental Studies** (Government); **Humanities** (Arts and Humanities); **Industrial Technology** (Industrial Engineering); **Natural Sciences** (Natural Sciences); **Social Sciences** (Social Sciences); **Stomatology** (Stomatology); **Student Life** (Sociology)

Further information: Also Wonju Campus

History: Founded 1946 as Kangnung Teacher School. Became Kangnung National University 1991. Acquird present title 2007 following merger with Wonju College.

Academic year: March to February (March-August; September-February)

Admission requirements: Graduation from high school or equivalent, and entrance examination

Fees: According to programme

Main language(s) of instruction: Korean

Accrediting agency: Korean Council for University Education (KCUE)

Degrees and diplomas: Bachelor's Degree, Master's Degree (Accountancy; Art Education; Automotive Engineering; Bioengineering; Biology; Biomedical Engineering; Biotechnology; Business Administration; Business and Commerce; Chemical Engineering; Chemistry; Chinese; Civil Engineering; Computer Education; Computer Engineering; Computer Science; Dentistry; Development Studies; E- Business/Commerce; Economics; Education; Educational Administration; Educational and Student Counselling; Electrical Engineering; Electronic Engineering; Engineering Management; English; Environmental Engineering; Environmental Studies; Fashion Design; Fine Arts; Food Science; Foreign Languages Education; History; Home Economics Education; Horticulture; Humanities and Social Science Education; Industrial and Production Economics; Industrial Arts Education; Industrial Engineering; Information Technology; International Business; Korean; Landscape Architecture; Law; Literature; Marine Biology; Marine Engineering; Materials Engineering; Mathematics; Mathematics Education; Measurement and Precision Engineering; Mechanical Engineering; Meteorology; Military Science; Multimedia; Music; Music Education; Native

Language Education; Nursing; Nutrition; Pedagogy; Philosophy; Physical Education; Physics; Preschool Education; Protective Services; Public Administration; Science Education; Social and Community Services; Statistics; Telecommunications Engineering; Tourism), Doctor's Degree (Bioengineering; Biology; Biotechnology; Business Administration; Chemical Engineering; Chemistry; Civil Engineering; Computer Engineering; Dentistry; Economics; Education; Electrical Engineering; English; Environmental Engineering; Environmental Studies; Food Science; Horticulture; Industrial Engineering; International Business; Korean; Law; Literature; Marine Biology; Materials Engineering; Mathematics; Measurement and Precision Engineering; Mechanical Engineering; Meteorology; Physical Education; Physics; Preschool Education; Public Administration; Social and Community Services; Tourism)

Student Services: Academic Counselling, Careers Guidance, Nursery Care, Cultural Activities, Sports Facilities, Language Laboratory, Facilities for disabled people, Health Services, Canteen, Foreign Studies Centre, Library, Residential Facilities

Publishing house: Kangnung National University Press

Academic Staff 2012-2013	MALE	FEMALE	TOTAL
FULL-TIME			400
PART-TIME			c. 435
Student Numbers 2012-2013			
All (Foreign Included)			c. 8700

Last Update: 20-02-2018

Gongju National University of Education (GJUE)

27 Ungjin-ro Bonghwang-dong
Gongju-si 32553, Chungcheongnam-do
Tel: +82(41) 850-1114
Fax: +82(41) 854-1578
Website: http://www.gjue.ac.kr
President: Byoung-geun Ahn

Department/Division

Computer Education (Computer Education; Multimedia; Primary Education); **Elementary Education** (Pedagogy; Primary Education; Teacher Training); **English Language Education** (English; Foreign Languages Education); **Ethics Education** (Ethics; Primary Education); **Fine Arts Education** (Art Education; Primary Education); **Korean Language Education** (Native Language Education); **Mathematics Education** (Mathematics Education); **Music Education** (Music; Music Education; Musical Instruments); **Physical Education** (Physical Education); **Practical Arts Education** (Child Care and Development; Home Economics Education; Primary Education); **Science Education** (Biology; Chemistry; Earth Sciences; Physics; Primary Education; Science Education); **Social Studies Education** (Home Economics Education; Primary Education)

Graduate School

Education (Art Education; Computer Education; Education; Education of the Handicapped; Educational Administration; Educational and Student Counselling; Educational Psychology; Ethics; Foreign Languages Education; Home Economics Education; Humanities and Social Science Education; Mathematics Education; Music Education; Native Language Education; Physical Education; Primary Education; Science Education; Teacher Training)

History: Founded 1938 as Gongju Teachers' Schoool for Women. Reorganization as Gongju Univeristy of Education 1962. Acquired present status 1982 and present title 1993.

Main language(s) of instruction: Korean

Accrediting agency: Korean Council for University Education (KCUE)

Degrees and diplomas: Bachelor's Degree, Master's Degree (Art Education; Computer Education; Education of the Handicapped; Educational Administration; Educational and Student Counselling; Educational Psychology; Ethics; Foreign Languages Education; Home Economics Education; Humanities and Social Science Education; Native Language Education; Pedagogy; Physical Education; Primary Education; Science Education)

Student Services: Sports Facilities, Library, Residential Facilities

Academic Staff 2013-2014	MALE	FEMALE	TOTAL
FULL-TIME			115
PART-TIME			87
Student Numbers 2013-2014			
All (Foreign Included)			2657

Last Update: 21-02-2018

Gwangju Institute of Science and Technology (GIST)

123 Cheomdangwagi-ro, Buk-gu
Gwangju 61005
Tel: +82(62) 715-2114
Fax: +82(62) 715-2300
Website: http://www.gist.ac.kr
President: Seung-Hyeon Moon

College

GIST College (Biological and Life Sciences; Chemistry; Computer Science; Earth Sciences; Electrical Engineering;

Environmental Engineering; Materials Engineering; Mechanical Engineering; Physics)

School

Earth Science and Environmental Engineering (*Graduate*) (Environmental Engineering; Environmental Studies; Water Science); **Electrical Engineering and Computer Science** (*Graduate*) (Computer Networks; Computer Science; Electronic Engineering; Information Sciences; Information Technology; Microwaves; Optics; Telecommunications Engineering); **Life Sciences** (*Graduate*) (Biochemistry; Biological and Life Sciences; Biophysics; Cell Biology; Molecular Biology; Neurosciences); **Materials Science and Engineering** (*Graduate*) (Chemistry; Electronic Engineering; Materials Engineering; Physics; Polymer and Plastics Technology); **Mechanical Engineering** (*Graduate*) (Automation and Control Engineering; Computer Science; Electrical Engineering; Electronic Engineering; Industrial Engineering; Mechanical Engineering); **Physics and Chemistry** (*Graduate*) (Chemistry; Physics)

Institute

Integrated Technology (*Graduate*) (Artificial Intelligence; Biomedical Engineering; Energy Engineering; Medical Technology; Robotics)
History: A research-oriented institute founded 1993
Academic year: March to February (March-June; September-February)
Admission requirements: Baccalaureate for admission to MS programmes and Master's Degree for PhD programmes
Fees: National : None (Full Scholarship), International : None (Full Scholarship)
Main language(s) of instruction: English, Korean
Accrediting agency: Ministry of Science and ICT
Degrees and diplomas: Bachelor's Degree (Biological and Life Sciences; Chemistry; Earth Sciences; Electrical Engineering; Materials Engineering; Mechanical Engineering; Physics), Master's Degree (Biological and Life Sciences; Biomedical Engineering; Earth Sciences; Electrical and Electronic Engineering; Materials Engineering; Mechanical Engineering; Physics), Doctor's Degree (Biological and Life Sciences; Biomedical Engineering; Earth Sciences; Electrical and Electronic Engineering; Materials Engineering; Mechanical Engineering; Physics)
Student Services: Academic Counselling, Careers Guidance, Nursery Care, Sports Facilities, Language Laboratory, Facilities for disabled people, Health Services, Canteen, Foreign Studies Centre, Library, Residential Facilities

Academic Staff 2017-2018	MALE	FEMALE	TOTAL
FULL-TIME	166	9	175
Student Numbers 2017-2018			
All (Foreign Included)	1446	476	1922

Last Update: 01-06-2018

Gwangju National University of Education (GNUE)

55 Pilmundaero, Buk-gu
Gwangju-si 61204, Gyeonggi-do
Tel: +82(62) 520-4114, +82(62) 520-4058, +82(62) 520-4332
Fax: +82(62) 524-6022
Website: http://www.gnue.ac.kr
President: Jeong Seon Lee

Course/Programme

Computer Science (Computer Education; Computer Science); **English Education** (English; Foreign Languages Education); **Ethics** (Ethics; Humanities and Social Science Education; Teacher Training); **Fine Arts** (Art Education; Fine Arts); **Korean Language** (Korean; Literature; Native Language Education); **Mathematics** (Mathematics; Mathematics Education); **Music Education** (Music Education); **Pedagogy** (Education; Educational Sciences; Pedagogy); **Physical Education** (Physical Education); **Practical Arts Education** (Agricultural Education; Computer Education; Home Economics Education; Industrial Arts Education); **Science Education** (Biology; Chemistry; Earth Sciences; Physics; Science Education); **Social Studies Education** (Humanities and Social Science Education; Social Studies); **Special and Inclusive Education** (Special Education; Teacher Training)

Graduate School

Education (Art Education; Computer Education; Curriculum; Education; Educational Administration; Educational and Student Counselling; Environmental Studies; Ethics; Foreign Languages Education; Humanities and Social Science Education; Mathematics Education; Native Language Education; Pedagogy; Physical Education; Primary Education; Science Education; Special Education; Teacher Training)
History: Founded 1938 as School, became College of Teachers 1961, attached to Chonnam National University 1962 and acquired present status and title 1993. Graduate School established 1996.
Academic year: March to December (March-July; September-December)
Admission requirements: Graduation from high school and entrance examination
Main language(s) of instruction: Korean
Accrediting agency: Ministry of Education
Degrees and diplomas: Bachelor's Degree (Teacher Training), Master's Degree (Art Education; Computer Education; Curriculum; Educational Administration; Educational and Student Counselling; Ethics; Foreign Languages Education; Humanities and Social Science Education; Mathematics Education;

Music Education; Native Language Education; Pedagogy; Physical Education; Preschool Education; Science Education)
Student Services: Academic Counselling, Social Counselling, Careers Guidance, Language Laboratory, Foreign Studies Centre

Academic Staff 2012-2013	MALE	FEMALE	TOTAL
FULL-TIME			96
PART-TIME			92
Student Numbers 2012-2013			
All (Foreign Included)			2204

Last Update: 21-02-2018

Gyeongin National University of Education (GINUE)

62, Gyesan-ro, Gyeyang-gu
Incheon-si 21044
Tel: +82(32) 540-1114
Fax: +82(32) 541-0580
Website: http://www.ginue.ac.kr
President: Dae Hyuk Ko
Tel: +82(32) 540-1100

Department/Division

Art Education (Art Education; Art History; Fine Arts); **Computer Education** (Computer Education; Computer Engineering; Computer Networks; Computer Science; Software Engineering; Statistics); **Early Childhood Education** (Preschool Education); **Education** (Curriculum; Education; Educational Administration; Educational and Student Counselling; Educational Psychology; Educational Sciences; Pedagogy; Special Education); **English Education** (English; Foreign Languages Education); **Ethics Education** (Education; Ethics); **Korean Education** (Korean; Native Language Education); **Mathematics Education** (Mathematics; Mathematics Education); **Music Education** (Music; Music Education; Music Theory and Composition; Musical Instruments; Singing); **Physical Training Education** (Physical Education; Primary Education); **Practical Arts Education** (Agriculture; Clothing and Sewing; Cooking and Catering; Home Economics; Home Economics Education; Information Technology; Primary Education; Technology Education); **Science** (Primary Education; Science Education); **Social Studies Education** (Geography (Human); History; Humanities and Social Science Education; Social Sciences; Social Studies)

Graduate School

Education (Education; Educational Sciences; Primary Education; Special Education; Teacher Training)
Further information: Also Gyeonggi Campus

History: Founded 1946 as a normal school, acquired present status 1993 and name 2003.
Academic year: March to December (March-June; August-December)
Admission requirements: Graduation from high school or equivalent, and entrance examination
Fees: 1,000 per semester (US Dollar)
Main language(s) of instruction: Korean
Accrediting agency: Ministry of Education
Degrees and diplomas: Bachelor's Degree, Master's Degree (Art Education; Computer Education; Education of the Gifted; Educational Administration; Educational and Student Counselling; Foreign Languages Education; Home Economics Education; Human Resources; Humanities and Social Science Education; Mathematics Education; Museum Studies; Music Education; Native Language Education; Pedagogy; Physical Education; Preschool Education; Primary Education; Science Education; Special Education)
Student Services: Academic Counselling, Social Counselling, Careers Guidance, Sports Facilities, Library, Residential Facilities
Periodicals: GINUE Culture Review of Kyouggi and Inchon Area, GINUE Education Research, GINUE Science Education Review

Academic Staff 2013-2014	MALE	FEMALE	TOTAL
FULL-TIME			130
PART-TIME			c. 325
Student Numbers 2013-2014			
All (Foreign Included)			c. 4220

Last Update: 21-02-2018

Gyeongnam National University of Science and Technology (GNTECH)

33 Dongjin-ro Chiram-Dong
Jinju-si 660-758, Gyeonsangnam-do
Tel: +82(55) 751-3124, +82(55) 751-3114
Fax: +82(55) 752-3554, +82(55) 752-9554
Website: http://www.gntech.ac.kr
President: Namkyung Kim

College

Bio-science (Biomedical Engineering; Biotechnology; Food Science; Food Technology; Nutrition); **Business And Economics** (Accountancy; Business Administration; Business and Commerce; E- Business/Commerce; Economics; Industrial and Production Economics; Information Sciences); **Construction and Environmental Engineering** (Civil Engineering; Construction Engineering; Environmental Engineering; Interior Design; Landscape Architecture;

Materials Engineering; Structural Architecture); **Design** (Architecture; Design; Textile Design); **Humanities and Social Science** (Child Care and Development; English; Family Studies; Linguistics; Welfare and Protective Services); **Integral Technology Engineering** (Automotive Engineering; Computer Engineering; Electronic Engineering; Mechanical Engineering); **Lifelong Education** (Arts and Humanities); **Science and Natural Resources** (Agriculture; Animal Husbandry; Forestry; Horticulture; Veterinary Science; Zoology)

School

Graduate Studies (Accountancy; Automotive Engineering; Business Administration; Civil Engineering; Computer Engineering; Construction Engineering; E- Business/Commerce; Electrical and Electronic Engineering; English; Environmental Engineering; Food Technology; Forestry; Horticulture; Industrial and Production Economics; Information Sciences; Landscape Architecture; Management; Materials Engineering; Mechanical Engineering; Microbiology; Natural Resources; Plant and Crop Protection; Social Welfare; Zoology)

Graduate School

Business and Entrepreneurship (Business Administration; Management); **Industry** (Construction Engineering; Engineering; Environmental Engineering; Landscape Architecture); **Social Welfare** (Social Welfare)

History: Founded 1910. Previously known as Jinju National University, Acquired current title 2011.

Main language(s) of instruction: Korean

Accrediting agency: Korean Council for University Education (KCUE)

Degrees and diplomas: Bachelor's Degree, Master's Degree (Accountancy; Animal Husbandry; Automotive Engineering; Business Administration; Business and Commerce; Civil Engineering; Computer Engineering; Construction Engineering; E- Business/Commerce; Electrical and Electronic Engineering; English; Environmental Engineering; Food Technology; Forestry; Horticulture; Industrial and Production Economics; Information Sciences; Landscape Architecture; Mechanical Engineering; Microbiology; Plant and Crop Protection; Social Welfare; Zoology)

Student Services: Library, Residential Facilities

Last Update: 07-03-2018

Gyeongsang National University (GNU)

501 Jinju-daero
Gyeongnam 52828, Gyeongnam-do
Tel: +82(55) 772-0114, +82(55) 772-0272
Fax: +82(55) 751-6134, +82(55) 772-0269
Website: http://www.gsnu.ac.kr/english
President: Sang-gyeong Lee

College

Agriculture and Life Sciences (Agricultural Economics; Agricultural Engineering; Agriculture; Agronomy; Animal Husbandry; Applied Chemistry; Bioengineering; Biological and Life Sciences; Biotechnology; Environmental Studies; Food Science; Food Technology; Forest Products; Forestry; Horticulture; Industrial Engineering; Machine Building; Natural Resources); **Business Administration** (Accountancy; Business Administration; E- Business/Commerce; Information Management; Information Sciences; Information Technology; International Business); **Education** (Art Education; Computer Education; Education; Ethics; Foreign Languages Education; Home Economics Education; Humanities and Social Science Education; Mathematics Education; Music Education; Native Language Education; Physical Education; Science Education; Social Studies); **Engineering** (Aeronautical and Aerospace Engineering; Architecture; Automation and Control Engineering; Bioengineering; Chemical Engineering; Civil Engineering; Computer Engineering; Electrical and Electronic Engineering; Engineering; Industrial Engineering; Information Technology; Mechanical Engineering; Metallurgical Engineering; Nanotechnology; Structural Architecture; Town Planning); **Humanities** (Arts and Humanities; Chinese; Dance; English; French; German; History; Korean; Literature; Modern Languages; Philosophy; Russian); **Law** (Law); **Marine Sciences** (Bioengineering; Biological and Life Sciences; Business Administration; Civil Engineering; Computer Engineering; Electronic Engineering; Environmental Engineering; Fishery; Food Science; Marine Engineering; Marine Science and Oceanography; Marine Transport; Mechanical Engineering; Natural Sciences; Police Studies; Production Engineering); **Natural Science** (Biochemistry; Biology; Chemistry; Clothing and Sewing; Computer Engineering; Computer Science; Earth Sciences; Environmental Studies; Fashion Design; Food Science; Geology; Information Sciences; Mathematics; Microbiology; Natural Sciences; Nutrition; Physics; Software Engineering; Statistics; Textile Technology); **Nursing** (Community Health; Nursing); **Social Sciences** (Economics; Political Sciences; Psychology; Public Administration; Social Sciences; Social Welfare; Sociology); **Veterinary Medicine** (Veterinary Science)

Course/Programme

Korean Language (Korean)

Graduate School

Academics (Agriculture; Arts and Humanities; Engineering; Fine Arts; Information Sciences; Medicine; Music; Natural

Sciences; Social Sciences; Sports); **Aerospace Engineering** (*Specialized Graduate School*) (Aeronautical and Aerospace Engineering); **Business** (Business Administration; Management); **Education** (Education; Educational Sciences; Special Education; Teacher Training); **Industry** (Biological and Life Sciences; Computer Science; Construction Engineering; Economics; Electrical and Electronic Engineering; Environmental Studies; Natural Resources; Production Engineering); **Medicine** (Medicine); **Public Administration** (Administration; Government; Industrial and Organizational Psychology; Justice Administration; Labour and Industrial Relations; Protective Services; Public Administration); **Public Health** (Public Health)

Research Division

Agriculture and Life Sciences (Agriculture; Biological and Life Sciences); **Aircraft Parts Technology** (Aeronautical and Aerospace Engineering); **Computer and Information Communication** (*RICIC*) (Computer Science; Information Sciences); **Culture** (*Gyeong-Nam*) (Cultural Studies); **Education** (*ERI*) (Education); **Engineering** (Engineering); **Environmental and Regional Development** (Development Studies; Environmental Studies); **Environmental Bio-Technology National Core** (Biotechnology; Environmental Engineering); **EU** (European Studies); **Global and Area Studies** (International Studies; Regional Studies); **Health Sciences** (Health Sciences); **Humanities** (Arts and Humanities); **Law** (Law); **Life Sciences** (*RILS*) (Biotechnology; Social Sciences); **Marine Industry** (Marine Engineering; Marine Science and Oceanography); **Natural Sciences** (*RINS*) (Biology; Chemistry; Earth Sciences; Mathematics; Natural Sciences; Physics); **Plant Molecular Biology and Biotechnology** (Biotechnology; Molecular Biology; Plant and Crop Protection); **Social Sciences** (Social Sciences); **Veterinary Medicine** (Veterinary Science); **Women's Studies** (Women's Studies)

Further information: Also Chilam and Tongyeong Campuses
History: Founded 1948 as Junior Agricultural College. Became Provincial College 1953 and National Institution 1968. Graduate courses introduced 1975. Acquired present status and title 1980. Financially supported by the Government.
Academic year: March to February (March-August; September-February)
Admission requirements: Graduation from high school or equivalent and entrance examination
Fees: c. 1.3-2.3 m. per semester (Won)
Main language(s) of instruction: Korean
Accrediting agency: Ministry of Education; Korean Council for University Education (KCUE)
Degrees and diplomas: Bachelor's Degree, Master's Degree (Accountancy; Administration; Aeronautical and Aerospace Engineering; Agricultural Economics; Agricultural Engineering; Agricultural Equipment; Agriculture;

Animal Husbandry; Asian Studies; Automation and Control Engineering; Bioengineering; Biological and Life Sciences; Biology; Biotechnology; Business Administration; Business and Commerce; Chemical Engineering; Chemistry; Chinese; Civil Engineering; Clothing and Sewing; Computer Engineering; Computer Science; Dairy; Dance; Development Studies; Earth Sciences; Ecology; Economics; Education; Electrical and Electronic Engineering; Electrical Engineering; Electronic Engineering; Engineering; English; Environmental Engineering; Environmental Management; Environmental Studies; Ethics; Fine Arts; Fishery; Food Science; Food Technology; Forest Products; Forestry; French; German; Horticulture; Industrial Engineering; Information Management; Information Sciences; Information Technology; International Business; Japanese; Korean; Law; Literature; Management; Marine Engineering; Marine Science and Oceanography; Mass Communication; Materials Engineering; Mathematics; Measurement and Precision Engineering; Mechanical Engineering; Media Studies; Medicine; Microbiology; Multimedia; Music; Nanotechnology; Natural Resources; Natural Sciences; Neurosciences; Nursing; Nutrition; Philosophy; Physics; Political Sciences; Production Engineering; Psychology; Public Administration; Russian; Software Engineering; Sports; Statistics; Structural Architecture; Telecommunications Engineering; Textile Technology; Town Planning; Veterinary Science), Doctor's Degree (Accountancy; Aeronautical and Aerospace Engineering; Agricultural Economics; Agricultural Engineering; Agriculture; Animal Husbandry; Arts and Humanities; Asian Studies; Automation and Control Engineering; Bioengineering; Biological and Life Sciences; Biology; Biotechnology; Business Administration; Business and Commerce; Chemical Engineering; Chemistry; Chinese; Civil Engineering; Clothing and Sewing; Computer Engineering; Computer Science; Dance; Earth Sciences; Economics; Education; Electrical and Electronic Engineering; Electrical Engineering; Electronic Engineering; Engineering; English; Environmental Engineering; Environmental Management; Environmental Studies; Ethics; Fishery; Food Science; Foreign Languages Education; Forest Products; Forestry; French; German; History; Humanities and Social Science Education; Industrial Engineering; Information Management; Information Sciences; Information Technology; International Business; International Relations; Japanese; Korean; Law; Literature; Marine Engineering; Marine Science and Oceanography; Materials Engineering; Mathematics; Mathematics Education; Measurement and Precision Engineering; Mechanical Engineering; Medicine; Microbiology; Nanotechnology; Native Language Education; Neurosciences; Nursing; Nutrition; Philosophy; Physics; Political Sciences; Psychology; Public Administration; Science Education; Social Sciences; Social Welfare; Sociology; Sports; Statistics; Structural Architecture; Telecommunications Engineering; Textile Technology;

Town Planning; Veterinary Science). Also Teaching Certficate

Student Services: Academic Counselling, Social Counselling, Careers Guidance, Nursery Care, Cultural Activities, Sports Facilities, Language Laboratory, Health Services, Canteen, Foreign Studies Centre, Library, IT Centre, Residential Facilities

Publishing house: GSNU University Press

Academic Staff 2015-2016	MALE	FEMALE	TOTAL
FULL-TIME			c. 691
Student Numbers 2015-2016			
All (Foreign Included)			c. 24410

Last Update: 21-02-2018

Hanbat National University

125 Dongseodaero, Yuseong-gu
Daejeon 305-719, Chungnam-do
Tel: +82(42) 821-1114
Fax: +82(42) 825-5395
Website: http://www.hanbat.ac.kr
President: Ha-young Song

Faculty

Global Convergence Sudies (International Studies; Leadership); **Liberal Arts Education** (Arts and Humanities)

College

Construction, Environment and Design (Architectural and Environmental Design; Civil Engineering; Communication Arts; Environmental Engineering; Graphic Design; Industrial Design; Structural Architecture; Town Planning); **Economics and Business Administration** (Accountancy; Business Administration; Economics); **Engineering** (Bioengineering; Building Technologies; Chemical Engineering; Engineering; Industrial Engineering; Industrial Management; Materials Engineering; Mechanical Engineering); **Humanities** (Arts and Humanities; Chinese; English; Japanese); **Information Technology** (Automation and Control Engineering; Computer Engineering; Electrical Engineering; Electronic Engineering; Information Technology; Telecommunications Engineering)

Graduate School

Enterpreneurial Managenment (Business Administration; Economics; Management); **Graduate Studies** (Arts and Humanities; Business Administration; Engineering; Fine Arts); **Industry** (Arts and Humanities; Engineering; Fine Arts; Fire Science; Safety Engineering); **Information and Communication** (Computer Engineering; Information Sciences; Information Technology; Telecommunications Engineering)

History: Founded 1927. Acquired present title 2001.
Main language(s) of instruction: Korean
Accrediting agency: Korean Council for University Education (KCUE)
Degrees and diplomas: Bachelor's Degree, Master's Degree (Accountancy; Applied Chemistry; Automation and Control Engineering; Biotechnology; Building Technologies; Business Administration; Chemical Engineering; Chinese; Civil Engineering; Communication Arts; Computer Engineering; Economics; Electrical Engineering; Electronic Engineering; Engineering Drawing and Design; Engineering Management; English; Environmental Engineering; Finance; Fire Science; Graphic Design; Industrial Design; Industrial Engineering; Information Technology; Japanese; Management; Materials Engineering; Mechanical Engineering; Metal Techniques; Multimedia; Production Engineering; Real Estate; Safety Engineering; Structural Architecture; Telecommunications Engineering; Town Planning), Doctor's Degree (Administration; Chemical Engineering; Civil Engineering; Electrical Engineering; Electronic Engineering; English; Industrial Engineering; Materials Engineering; Mechanical Engineering; Structural Architecture)
Student Services: Sports Facilities, Library

Academic Staff 2012-2013	MALE	FEMALE	TOTAL
FULL-TIME			460
PART-TIME			c. 360
Student Numbers 2012-2013			
All (Foreign Included)			c. 14290

Last Update: 21-02-2018

Hankyong National University (HNU)

67 Sokjong-dong
Anseong-si 456-749, Gyeonggi-do
Tel: +82(31) 670-5114
Fax: +82(31) 670-5469, +82(31) 672-2704
Website: http://www.hankyong.ac.kr
President: Tae-Hee Lim

College

Agriculture and Life Sciences (Agricultural Engineering; Agriculture; Animal Husbandry; Biological and Life Sciences; Biotechnology; Environmental Studies; Horticulture; Natural Resources; Plant and Crop Protection); **Engineering** (Architecture; Automation and Control Engineering; Biotechnology; Chemical Engineering; Civil Engineering; Computer Engineering; Computer Science; Design; Electrical Engineering; Electronic Engineering; Engineering;

Environmental Engineering; Food Science; Information Technology; Mechanical Engineering); **Humanities and Social Sciences** (Arts and Humanities; Business Administration; English; Law; Literature; Natural Sciences; Public Administration; Social Sciences; Writing); **Natural Science** (Applied Mathematics; Child Care and Development; Clothing and Sewing; Cooking and Catering; Landscape Architecture; Natural Sciences; Nutrition; Sports; Welfare and Protective Services)

Graduate School

Bio and Information Technology (Animal Husbandry; Biotechnology; Chemical Engineering; Computer Engineering; Computer Science; Food Science; Genetics; Information Technology; Molecular Biology; Plant and Crop Protection; Telecommunications Engineering); **Electronic Government** (Administration; Educational Administration; Labour and Industrial Relations; Law; Transport Management); **Graduate Studies** (Agricultural Engineering; Animal Husbandry; Applied Mathematics; Architecture; Arts and Humanities; Automation and Control Engineering; Biological and Life Sciences; Biotechnology; Chemical Engineering; Civil Engineering; Communication Arts; Computer Engineering; Computer Science; Ecology; Electrical Engineering; Electronic Engineering; Environmental Engineering; Environmental Studies; Food Science; Graphic Design; Horticulture; Landscape Architecture; Literature; Management; Mechanical Engineering; Modern Languages; Natural Resources; Plant and Crop Protection; Public Administration; Safety Engineering; Structural Architecture); **International Development and Cooperation** (Development Studies; International Studies); **Technology** (Bioengineering; Child Care and Development; Environmental Engineering; Family Studies; Industrial Engineering; Sports; Technology; Welfare and Protective Services)

History: Founded 1939 as Ansung National University of Technology, Graduate School of Industry 1996, acquired present status 1993 and title 1999.

Academic year: March to February (March-August; September-February)

Admission requirements: Graduation from high school

Fees: 1,6m. per annum (Won)

Main language(s) of instruction: Korean

Accrediting agency: Korean Council for University Education (KCUE)

Degrees and diplomas: Bachelor's Degree, Master's Degree (Agricultural Business; Animal Husbandry; Bioengineering; Botany; Business Administration; Chemical Engineering; Child Care and Development; Civil Engineering; Clothing and Sewing; Communication Arts; Computer Engineering; Dairy; Educational Administration; Electrical Engineering; Electronic Engineering; English; Environmental Engineering; Family Studies; Food Science; Food Technology;

Genetics; Horticulture; Information Technology; Labour and Industrial Relations; Landscape Architecture; Law; Mechanical Engineering; Media Studies; Nutrition; Plant and Crop Protection; Public Administration; Safety Engineering; Social Work; Sports; Structural Architecture; Transport Management; Welfare and Protective Services), Doctor's Degree (Animal Husbandry; Bioengineering; Biological and Life Sciences; Biology; Computer Engineering; Dairy; Food Technology; Genetics; Information Technology)

Student Services: Academic Counselling, Social Counselling, Careers Guidance, Sports Facilities, Language Laboratory, Facilities for disabled people, Health Services, Canteen, Library, Residential Facilities

Academic Staff 2012-2013	MALE	FEMALE	TOTAL
FULL-TIME			155
PART-TIME			c. 470
Student Numbers 2012-2013			
All (Foreign Included)			c. 6830

Last Update: 21-02-2018

Incheon National University (INU)

(Songdo-dong) 119 Academy-ro Yeonsu-gu
Incheon-si 406-772
Tel: +82(32) 835-8114, +82(32) 835-9571, +82(32) 835-9575
Fax: +82(32) 835-0715, +82(32) 835-0736
Website: http://www.incheon.ac.kr
President: Dong-Sung Cho
Tel: +82(32) 835-8003

College

Art and Physical Education (Design; Fine Arts; Health Sciences; Painting and Drawing; Performing Arts; Physical Education; Sports); **Business Administration** (Accountancy; Business Administration; Taxation); **Education** (Education; Foreign Languages Education; Humanities and Social Science Education; Mathematics Education; Native Language Education; Physical Education; Preschool Education); **Engineering** (Automotive Engineering; Chemical Engineering; Electrical Engineering; Electronic Engineering; Energy Engineering; Engineering; Industrial Engineering; Materials Engineering; Mechanical Engineering; Robotics; Safety Engineering); **Humanities** (Arts and Humanities; Asian Studies; Chinese; English; French; German; Japanese; Korean; Literature; Modern Languages); **Information Technology** (Computer Engineering; Computer Science; Information Technology; Telecommunications Engineering); **Law** (Law) **Life and Sciences and Bioengineering** (Bioengineering; Biological and Life Sciences; Biology; Medicine;

Molecular Biology; Nanotechnology); **Natural Sciences** (Chemistry; Child Care and Development; Consumer Studies; Fashion Design; Marine Science and Oceanography; Mathematics; Natural Sciences; Physics; Textile Technology); **Northeast Asian Economics and Commerce** (Business and Commerce; Chinese; Economics; English; International Business; Japanese; Russian); **Social Sciences** (Human Resources; Information Sciences; International Relations; Library Science; Mass Communication; Political Sciences; Public Administration; Social Sciences; Social Welfare); **Urban Sciences** (Architecture; Civil Engineering; Construction Engineering; Environmental Engineering; Town Planning; Urban Studies)

Laboratory

Basic Science (Natural Sciences); **Engineering Electronic Technology** (Engineering); **Sport Science** (Sports)

Graduate School

Business Administration (Business Administration; Real Estate); **Cultural Industry** (Art History; Art Management; Arts and Humanities; Cultural Studies); **Education** (Art Education; Education; Educational Sciences; Humanities and Social Science Education; Mathematics Education; Physical Education; Science Education; Teacher Training); **Engineering** (Architectural and Environmental Design; Civil Engineering; Electrical Engineering; Electronic Engineering; Engineering; Environmental Engineering; Fashion Design; Industrial Design; Industrial Engineering; Materials Engineering; Mechanical Engineering; Safety Engineering; Structural Architecture; Textile Technology); **Graduate Studies** (Architectural and Environmental Design; Asian Studies; Biological and Life Sciences; Business Administration; Business and Commerce; Chemistry; Child Care and Development; Chinese; Civil Engineering; Clothing and Sewing; Computer Engineering; Consumer Studies; Cosmetology; Economics; Education; Electrical Engineering; Electronic Engineering; English; Environmental Engineering; Ethics; Fine Arts; French; German; Industrial Engineering; Information Technology; International Business; International Studies; Japanese; Korean; Law; Literature; Mass Communication; Materials Engineering; Mathematics; Mechanical Engineering; Native Language Education; Physics; Political Sciences; Public Administration; Safety Engineering; Sports; Structural Architecture; Telecommunications Engineering; Textile Technology); **Information and Telecommunications** (Computer Engineering; Computer Science; Electronic Engineering; Information Technology; Telecommunications Engineering); **Logistics** (Transport Engineering; Transport Management); **Public Administration** (Justice Administration; Law; Protective Services; Public Administration; Social Welfare)

History: Founded 1979 as Incheon Technical College, a private Institution supervised by Sunin Academic Foundation and renamed as Incheon College same year. Acquired university status and renamed University of Incheon 1988. Merged with Incheon Technical University 2010. Nationalised and acquired present title 2013.

Academic year: March to December (March-June; September-December)

Admission requirements: Graduation from high school or equivalent, and entrance examination

Main language(s) of instruction: Korean, English

Accrediting agency: Korean Council for University Education (KCUE)

Degrees and diplomas: Bachelor's Degree, Master's Degree (Architectural and Environmental Design; Art Education; Art Management; Asian Studies; Biological and Life Sciences; Business Administration; Business and Commerce; Chemistry; Child Care and Development; Chinese; Civil Engineering; Clothing and Sewing; Computer Education; Computer Engineering; Computer Science; Consumer Studies; Cosmetology; Cultural Studies; Curriculum; Economics; Education of the Gifted; Educational Administration; Educational and Student Counselling; Educational Psychology; Educational Sciences; Educational Technology; Electrical Engineering; Electronic Engineering; English; Environmental Engineering; Ethics; Fashion Design; Fine Arts; Foreign Languages Education; French; German; Home Economics; Home Economics Education; Humanities and Social Science Education; Industrial Design; Industrial Engineering; Information Technology; International Business; International Studies; Japanese; Justice Administration; Korean; Law; Literature; Management; Mass Communication; Materials Engineering; Mathematics; Mathematics Education; Mechanical Engineering; Native Language Education; Physical Education; Physics; Political Sciences; Preschool Education; Protective Services; Public Administration; Real Estate; Safety Engineering; Science Education; Social Welfare; Sports; Structural Architecture; Technology Education; Telecommunications Engineering; Textile Technology; Transport Engineering; Transport Management), Doctor's Degree (Architectural and Environmental Design; Art Management; Biological and Life Sciences; Business Administration; Chemistry; Civil Engineering; Clothing and Sewing; Computer Engineering; Computer Science; Cosmetology; Cultural Studies; Economics; Education; Electrical Engineering; Electronic Engineering; Engineering; English; Environmental Engineering; Foreign Languages Education; Industrial Engineering; Information Technology; International Business; International Studies; Japanese; Korean; Law; Literature; Mass Communication; Materials Engineering; Mathematics; Mechanical Engineering; Physics; Political Sciences; Public Administration; Safety Engineering; Sports; Structural Architecture;

Telecommunications Engineering; Textile Technology; Transport Engineering; Transport Management). Also Ms/Ph.D Joint Programmes

Student Services: Academic Counselling, Social Counselling, Sports Facilities, Library, IT Centre, Residential Facilities

Periodicals: Collection of Papers

Publishing house: University Publishing Centre

Academic Staff 2016-2017	MALE	FEMALE	TOTAL
FULL-TIME			c. 471
Student Numbers 2016-2017			
All (Foreign Included)			c. 13822
Foreign only			300

Last Update: 23-02-2018

Jeju National University (JNU)

102 Jejudaehak-ro
Jeju-si 63243, Jeju
Tel: +82(64) 754-2114, +82(64) 754-3114
Fax: +82(64) 755-6130
Website: http://www.jejunu.ac.kr
President: Seok-Eon Song
Tel: +82(64) 754-2002

College

Applied Life Sciences (Agricultural Economics; Agriculture; Animal Husbandry; Biological and Life Sciences; Biotechnology; Botany; Horticulture; Natural Resources); **Arts and Design** (Art Education; Computer Graphics; Conducting; Design; Fine Arts; Industrial Design; Multimedia; Music; Music Education; Music Theory and Composition; Musical Instruments; Painting and Drawing; Singing); **Economics and Commerce** (Accountancy; Business Administration; Business and Commerce; Economics; Information Management; International Business; Management; Tourism); **Education** (Biology; Business Education; Computer Education; Education; English; Ethics; Foreign Languages Education; Geography; Humanities and Social Science Education; Mathematics Education; Native Language Education; Physics; Science Education; Sociology); **Engineering** (Bioengineering; Chemical Engineering; Computer Engineering; Electrical and Electronic Engineering; Energy Engineering; Engineering; Food Technology; Industrial Design; Mechanical Engineering; Nuclear Engineering; Production Engineering; Structural Architecture; Telecommunications Engineering); **Humanities** (Chinese; English; Fine Arts; German; History; Japanese; Korean; Literature; Philosophy; Sociology); **Natural Sciences** (Biology; Chemistry; Clothing and Sewing;

Computer Science; Cosmetology; Food Science; Home Economics; Mathematics; Natural Sciences; Nutrition; Physics; Sports; Statistics; Textile Technology; Welfare and Protective Services); **Nursing** (Nursing); **Ocean Sciences** (Biomedicine; Civil Engineering; Earth Sciences; Environmental Engineering; Marine Biology; Marine Engineering; Marine Science and Oceanography; Police Studies); **Social Science** (Advertising and Publicity; International Relations; Journalism; Law; Political Sciences; Public Administration; Public Relations); **Teachers** (Art Education; Computer Education; Education; Foreign Languages Education; Humanities and Social Science Education; Mathematics Education; Music Education; Native Language Education; Physical Education; Science Education; Teacher Training); **Veterinary Medicine** (Veterinary Science)

Course/Programme

Improvement of Administrators' and Regional Specialists' Ability (*Special Graduate*) (Law; Political Sciences); **Improvement of Creativity and Leadership for Management of Society** (*Special Graduate*) (Administration; Cultural Studies; Economics; Government; Political Sciences; Social Sciences); **Improvement of Managing Ability and Quality** (*Special Graduate*) (Farm Management; Fishery; Industrial Management); **Improvement of the Quality of Agricultural Manager by Offering the Opportunity of Study of Theory and Practice** (*Special Graduate*) (Agriculture; Animal Husbandry; Fruit Production; Horticulture); **Nurturing Environmental Experts to Take Part in Preservation of the Jeju Environment** (*Special Graduate*) (Environmental Management); **Practical Science Leaders Program** (*Special Graduate*) (Leadership); **Taxation College Program** (*Special Graduate*) (Accountancy; Cultural Studies; Economics; Management; Taxation); **Transmission of Theory of Organization and New Management Technique** (*Special Graduate*) (Accountancy; Business Administration; Cultural Studies; Economics; Finance; Management; Tourism)

School

Medicine (*Professional Graduate*) (Medicine)

Graduate School

Business Administration (Accountancy; Business Administration; Information Management; International Business; Management; Tourism); **Education** (Education; Primary Education; Teacher Training); **Humanities and Social Sciences** (Arts and Humanities; Engineering; Fine Arts; Medicine; Natural Sciences; Performing Arts; Physical Education; Social Sciences); **Industry** (Agriculture; Arts and Humanities; Design; Engineering; Fine Arts; Natural Sciences);

Interpretation and Translation (*Professional Graduate*) (Chinese; English; German; Japanese; Korean); **Law** (*Graduate Professional*) (Law); **Public Administration** (Administration; Advertising and Publicity; Government; Journalism; Law; Political Sciences; Public Administration); **Social Education** (Film; Heritage Preservation; Psychotherapy; Social Sciences; Writing)

Further information: 38 Research Institutes (Research Institutes 18, Research Centers 20)

History: Founded 1952 as Cheju Provincial Junior College. Became Cheju National College 1962 and acquired present status and renamed Cheju National University 1982. Merged with Cheju National University of Education and acquired present title 2008

Academic year: March to February

Admission requirements: Graduation from High School

Fees: Undergraduate, 373,000-488,000; Postgraduate, 408,000-534,000 (Won)

Main language(s) of instruction: Korean

Accrediting agency: Korean Council for University Education (KCUE); Ministry of Education

Degrees and diplomas: Bachelor's Degree, Master's Degree (Accountancy; Administration; Agricultural Economics; Agriculture; Animal Husbandry; Aquaculture; Art Education; Atomic and Molecular Physics; Biological and Life Sciences; Biology; Biomedical Engineering; Biotechnology; Business Administration; Business Education; Chemical Engineering; Chemistry; Chinese; Civil Engineering; Clothing and Sewing; Computer Education; Computer Engineering; Computer Science; Construction Engineering; Earth Sciences; East Asian Studies; Economics; Educational Administration; Educational Psychology; Electrical Engineering; Electronic Engineering; Energy Engineering; Engineering Drawing and Design; English; Environmental Engineering; Environmental Studies; Finance; Fine Arts; Fishery; Food Science; Food Technology; Foreign Languages Education; German; Government; Graphic Design; Heritage Preservation; History; Home Economics; Home Economics Education; Horticulture; Humanities and Social Science Education; Industrial Design; Information Management; Information Sciences; Information Technology; International Business; International Relations; Japanese; Journalism; Justice Administration; Korean; Literature; Marine Biology; Marine Engineering; Marine Science and Oceanography; Materials Engineering; Mathematics; Mathematics Education; Mechanical Engineering; Medicine; Meteorology; Music; Music Education; Native Language Education; Nursing; Nutrition; Philosophy; Physical Education; Physics; Political Sciences; Primary Education; Psychotherapy; Public Administration; Public Relations; Real Estate; Rural Studies; Science Education; Sociology; Statistics; Structural Architecture; Telecommunications Engineering; Textile Technology; Tourism; Translation and Interpretation; Veterinary Science; Writing), Doctor's Degree (Accountancy; Agricultural Economics; Agriculture; Art Education; Atomic and Molecular Physics; Biological and Life Sciences; Biology; Biomedical Engineering; Biotechnology; Business Administration; Chemical Engineering; Chemistry; Chinese; Civil Engineering; Clothing and Sewing; Computer Education; Computer Engineering; Computer Science; Development Studies; East Asian Studies; Electrical Engineering; Electronic Engineering; Energy Engineering; English; Environmental Engineering; Ethics; Fishery; Food Science; Food Technology; Foreign Languages Education; History; Horticulture; Humanities and Social Science Education; Information Technology; International Business; Japanese; Journalism; Korean; Literature; Marine Biology; Marine Engineering; Marine Science and Oceanography; Materials Engineering; Mathematics; Mechanical Engineering; Medicine; Meteorology; Native Language Education; Nutrition; Physical Education; Physics; Political Sciences; Primary Education; Public Administration; Public Relations; Rural Studies; Science Education; Sociology; Statistics; Telecommunications Engineering; Textile Technology; Tourism; Veterinary Science)

Student Services: Academic Counselling, Social Counselling, Careers Guidance, Nursery Care, Sports Facilities, Language Laboratory, Facilities for disabled people, Health Services, Canteen, Library, IT Centre, Residential Facilities

Periodicals: Islander

Publishing house: CNU Press Center

Academic Staff 2013-2014	MALE	FEMALE	TOTAL
FULL-TIME			c. 690
Student Numbers 2013-2014			
All (Foreign Included)			c. 12200

Last Update: 23-02-2018

Jeonju National University of Education (JNUE)

50 Seohak-ro Wansan-gu
Jeonju-si 560-757, Jeollabuk-do
Tel: +82(63) 281-7114, +82(63) 281-7441
Fax: +82(63) 281-0102, +82(63) 281-0102
Website: http://www.jnue.ac.kr
President: Gwang-chan Yu

Department/Division

Computer Education (Computer Education; Computer Engineering; Computer Science; Primary Education); **Elementary Education** (Primary Education); **English Language** (English; Foreign Languages Education; Primary Education); **Ethics** (Ethics; Teacher Training); **Fine Arts**

(Art Education; Fine Arts; Primary Education); **Korean Language Education** (Home Economics Education; Korean; Primary Education); **Mathematics Education** (Mathematics; Mathematics Education; Primary Education); **Music Education** (Music; Music Education; Primary Education); **Physical Education** (Physical Education; Primary Education); **Practical Arts Education** (Agriculture; Home Economics Education; Technology); **Science Education** (Biology; Chemistry; Geology; Physics; Science Education); **Social Studies Education** (Humanities and Social Science Education; Primary Education; Social Studies)

Institute

Gifted Children (Education of the Gifted; English; Korean; Mathematics; Natural Sciences)

Centre

Lifelong Education (Continuing Education); **Retraining Center for Teachers** (Teacher Training)

Graduate School

Graduate Studies (*Night School*) (Art Education; Educational Administration; Educational and Student Counselling; Music Education; Primary Education; Special Education); **Graduate Studies** (*Season School*) (Art Education; Computer Education; Education of the Gifted; Educational Sciences; Home Economics Education; Humanities and Social Science Education; Mathematics Education; Music Education; Native Language Education; Primary Education; Science Education)

Research Division

Elementary Education (Educational Research; Primary Education)
Further information: 2 Attached Elementary Schools
History: Founded 1923 as Normal School, acquired present status and title 1983. Moved ot O.I. 2013, Not on list.
Academic year: March to December (March-June; August-December)
Admission requirements: Graduation from high school, Government qualifying examination and university entrance examination
Main language(s) of instruction: Korean
Accrediting agency: Ministry of Education
Degrees and diplomas: Bachelor's Degree (Primary Education; Teacher Training), Master's Degree (Art Education; Computer Education; Education of the Gifted; Educational Administration; Educational and Student Counselling; Educational Sciences; Humanities and Social Science Education; Mathematics Education; Music Education; Native Language Education; Physical Education; Primary Education; Special Education)

Student Services: Academic Counselling, Cultural Activities, Sports Facilities, Health Services, Canteen, Library, IT Centre, Residential Facilities

Academic Staff 2013-2014	MALE	FEMALE	TOTAL
FULL-TIME			c. 70
Student Numbers 2013-2014			
All (Foreign Included)			c. 2400

Last Update: 23-02-2018

Kangwon National University (KNU)

1 Kangwondaehak-gil
Chuncheon-si 200-701, Gangwon-do
Tel: +82(33) 250-6114
Fax: +82(33) 251-9556
Website: http://www.kangwon.ac.kr
President: Seung-Ho Shin

College

Agriculture and Life Sciences (Agricultural Economics; Agricultural Engineering; Agriculture; Bioengineering; Biological and Life Sciences; Biology; Botany; Environmental Studies; Food Science; Food Technology; Horticulture); **Animal Life Sciences** (Animal Husbandry; Biological and Life Sciences; Biotechnology; Food Science); **Art and Culture** (Cultural Studies; Dance; Design; Fine Arts; Music; Visual Arts; Writing); **Biomedical Sciences** (Bioengineering; Biological and Life Sciences; Biomedicine; Biotechnology; Health Sciences; Immunology; Medical Technology; Molecular Biology); **Business Administration** (Accountancy; Business Administration; Economics; International Business; Tourism); **Education** (Education; Foreign Languages Education; Home Economics Education; Humanities and Social Science Education; Mathematics Education; Native Language Education; Science Education); **Engineering** (Architecture; Bioengineering; Biomedical Engineering; Biotechnology; Chemical Engineering; Civil Engineering; Electronic Engineering; Energy Engineering; Engineering; Environmental Engineering; Industrial Engineering; Materials Engineering; Mechanical Engineering; Structural Architecture); **Forest and Environmental Sciences** (Bioengineering; Environmental Management; Environmental Studies; Forest Management; Forest Products; Forestry; Landscape Architecture; Paper Technology); **Humanities** (Arts and Humanities; Chinese; French; German; History; Japanese; Korean; Linguistics; Literature); **Information Technology** (Computer Engineering; Computer Science; Electrical and Electronic Engineering; Electrical Engineering; Electronic Engineering; Information Technology; Telecommunications Engineering); **Law** (Administration; Law); **Medicine** (Medicine; Nursing); **Natural Sciences** (Biochemistry;

Biological and Life Sciences; Chemistry; Environmental Studies; Geology; Geophysics; Mathematics; Natural Sciences; Pharmacy; Physics; Statistics); **Pharmacy** (Pharmacology; Pharmacy); **Social Sciences** (Anthropology; Journalism; Mass Communication; Political Sciences; Psychology; Public Administration; Real Estate; Social Sciences; Sociology); **Veterinary Medicine** (Veterinary Science)

School

Law (*Special Graduate*) (Law)

Graduate School

Business and Public Administration (*Special Graduate*) (Business Administration; Business and Commerce; Public Administration); **Education** (*Special Graduate*) (Education); **Graduate Studies** (Arts and Humanities; Engineering; Fine Arts; Medicine; Natural Sciences; Sports); **Industrial Technology** (*Special Graduate*) (Industrial Engineering); **Information Science** (*Special Graduate*) (Information Sciences); **Medicine** (*Special Graduate*) (Medicine)

History: Founded 1947 as Kangwon Provincial Chuncheon Agricultural College, became university 1978. Merged with Samcheok National University 2006. A State institution under the jurisdiction of the Ministry of Education.

Academic year: March to December (March-June; September-December)

Admission requirements: Graduation from high school or foreign equivalent, and entrance examination

Fees: Undergraduate,1,877,000-2,383,000; Graduate, 2,199,000-4,267,000 (Won)

Main language(s) of instruction: Korean

Accrediting agency: Korean Council for University Education (KCUE)

Degrees and diplomas: Bachelor's Degree, Master's Degree (Agricultural Economics; Agricultural Engineering; Animal Husbandry; Anthropology; Architecture; Biochemistry; Bioengineering; Biological and Life Sciences; Biology; Biomedical Engineering; Biomedicine; Biotechnology; Botany; Business Administration; Chemical Engineering; Chemistry; Chinese; Civil Engineering; Computer Engineering; Computer Science; Cultural Studies; Dance; Design; Economics; Education; Electrical Engineering; Electronic Engineering; Energy Engineering; English; Environmental Management; Environmental Studies; Fine Arts; Food Science; Food Technology; Forest Management; Forest Products; Forestry; French; Geology; Geophysics; German; History; Home Economics Education; Horticulture; Humanities and Social Science Education; Immunology; Industrial Engineering; Information Technology; International Business; Japanese; Journalism; Korean; Landscape Architecture; Law; Literature; Mass Communication; Materials Engineering; Mathematics; Mechanical Engineering; Medical Technology; Medicine; Molecular Biology; Music; Nursing; Paper Technology; Pharmacy; Philosophy; Physics; Political Sciences; Psychology; Public Administration; Real Estate; Regional Studies; Science Education; Sociology; Sports; Statistics; Structural Architecture; Surveying and Mapping; Telecommunications Engineering; Tourism; Veterinary Science), Doctor's Degree (Accountancy; Agricultural Economics; Agricultural Engineering; Agriculture; Animal Husbandry; Anthropology; Architecture; Biochemistry; Bioengineering; Biological and Life Sciences; Biology; Biomedical Engineering; Biotechnology; Botany; Business Administration; Chemical Engineering; Chemistry; Civil Engineering; Computer Engineering; Computer Science; Cultural Studies; Economics; Education; Electrical and Electronic Engineering; Electronic Engineering; Energy Engineering; English; Environmental Engineering; Environmental Management; Environmental Studies; Fine Arts; Food Science; Foreign Languages Education; Forest Management; Forest Products; Forestry; Geology; Geophysics; History; Horticulture; Humanities and Social Science Education; Immunology; Industrial Engineering; Information Technology; International Business; Japanese; Journalism; Korean; Landscape Architecture; Law; Literature; Mass Communication; Materials Engineering; Mathematics; Mechanical Engineering; Medical Technology; Medicine; Molecular Biology; Native Language Education; Nursing; Paper Technology; Pharmacy; Philosophy; Physics; Political Sciences; Psychology; Public Administration; Real Estate; Regional Studies; Science Education; Sociology; Sports; Statistics; Structural Architecture; Surveying and Mapping; Telecommunications Engineering; Tourism; Veterinary Science)

Student Services: Careers Guidance, Cultural Activities, Sports Facilities, Language Laboratory, Health Services, Library, Residential Facilities

Periodicals: Journal of Social Sciences, Journal of the Humanities, Research Bulletin (Science and Technology)

Publishing house: University Press

Academic Staff 2013-2014	MALE	FEMALE	TOTAL
FULL-TIME			c. 825
Student Numbers 2013-2014			
All (Foreign Included)			c. 38064
Foreign only			757

Last Update: 23-02-2018

SAMCHEOK CAMPUS (KNU)

Joongang-ro
Samcheok-si 245-711, Gangwon-do
Tel: +82(33) 572-8611, +82(33) 572-8619
Fax: +82(33) 572-8620
Website: http://foreign.kangwon.ac.kr/eng
President: Seung-Ho Shin

College

Design and Sports (Design; Film; Leisure Studies; Multimedia; Sports; Theatre); **Engineering** (Architecture; Automation and Control Engineering; Automotive Engineering; Chemical Engineering; Civil Engineering; Computer Engineering; Construction Engineering; Electronic Engineering; Energy Engineering; Engineering; Environmental Engineering; Fire Science; Industrial Engineering; Instrument Making; Materials Engineering; Mechanical Engineering; Metallurgical Engineering; Mining Engineering; Safety Engineering; Structural Architecture; Telecommunications Engineering); **Health Science** (Alternative Medicine; Dental Hygiene; Food Science; Health Sciences; Media Studies; Medicine; Nursing; Nutrition; Occupational Therapy; Optometry; Physical Therapy; Radio and Television Broadcasting; Radiology); **Humanities and Social Sciences** (Arts and Humanities; Chemistry; Computer Science; English; History; International Economics; Japanese; Mathematics; Philosophy; Physics; Preschool Education; Public Administration; Tourism)

Graduate School

Disaster Prevention (Environmental Management; Environmental Studies; Geology; Mineralogy; Safety Engineering); **Graduate Studies** (Architectural and Environmental Design; Automotive Engineering; Civil Engineering; Electronic Engineering; English; Environmental Engineering; Fire Science; Graphic Design; Leisure Studies; Materials Engineering; Mechanical Engineering; Preschool Education; Public Administration; Safety Engineering; Sports; Telecommunications Engineering); **Industry and Science** (Administration; Alternative Medicine; Architecture; Automation and Control Engineering; Automotive Engineering; Ceramic Art; Chemical Engineering; Civil Engineering; Computer Engineering; Electrical Engineering; Electronic Engineering; Energy Engineering; English; Environmental Engineering; Fire Science; Food Science; Furniture Design; Industrial Design; Industrial Engineering; Information Technology; Instrument Making; International Economics; Leisure Studies; Materials Engineering; Measurement and Precision Engineering; Mechanical Engineering; Metallurgical Engineering; Mining Engineering; Nutrition; Preschool Education; Safety Engineering; Sports; Structural Architecture; Telecommunications Engineering; Tourism; Wood Technology)

History: Founded 1939 as Samcheok Public Vocational School. Reorganized as a four-year Samcheok Public Engineering School 1944. Successively upgraded into Samcheok Polytechnic College 1979, Samcheok Industrial University 1991 and Samcheok National University (SNU) 1998. Acquired present title following merger with Kangwon National University (KNU) at Chuncheon 2006.

Main language(s) of instruction: Korean
Accrediting agency: Korean Council for University Education (KCUE)
Degrees and diplomas: Bachelor's Degree, Master's Degree (Accountancy; Agricultural Economics; Animal Husbandry; Anthropology; Architectural and Environmental Design; Architecture; Asian Studies; Automation and Control Engineering; Automotive Engineering; Biochemistry; Bioengineering; Biological and Life Sciences; Biology; Biomedicine; Biotechnology; Business Administration; Chemical Engineering; Chemistry; Chinese; Civil Engineering; Computer Engineering; Computer Science; Cultural Studies; Dance; Design; East Asian Studies; Economics; Education; Electrical Engineering; Electronic Engineering; Energy Engineering; Engineering; English; English Studies; Environmental Engineering; Environmental Management; Environmental Studies; Fine Arts; Fire Science; Foreign Languages Education; Forest Biology; Forest Management; Forestry; French; French Studies; Geology; Geophysics; German; Germanic Studies; Graphic Design; Health Sciences; History; Home Economics Education; Horticulture; Humanities and Social Science Education; Industrial Engineering; Information Technology; International Business; International Economics; Japanese; Journalism; Korean; Landscape Architecture; Law; Leisure Studies; Literature; Mass Communication; Materials Engineering; Mathematics; Mechanical Engineering; Medicine; Multimedia; Music; Nursing; Paper Technology; Pharmacy; Philosophy; Physics; Political Sciences; Preschool Education; Psychology; Public Administration; Real Estate; Regional Studies; Rehabilitation and Therapy; Safety Engineering; Science Education; Sociology; Sports; Statistics; Structural Architecture; Surveying and Mapping; Telecommunications Engineering; Telecommunications Services; Tourism; Veterinary Science; Writing; Zoology), Doctor's Degree (Accountancy; Agricultural Economics; Agricultural Engineering; Animal Husbandry; Architecture; Biochemistry; Bioengineering; Biological and Life Sciences; Biology; Biomedicine; Biotechnology; Business Administration; Chemistry; Civil Engineering; Computer Engineering; Computer Science; Design; Economics; Education; Electrical Engineering; Electronic Engineering; Energy Engineering; Engineering; English; Environmental Engineering; Environmental Management; Environmental Studies; Foreign Languages Education; Forest Management; Forestry; Geology; Geophysics; Health Sciences; History; Horticulture; Humanities and Social Science Education; Industrial Engineering; Information Technology; International Business; International Economics; Japanese; Journalism; Korean; Landscape Architecture; Law; Literature; Mass Communication; Materials Engineering; Mathematics; Medicine; Nursing; Paper Technology; Pharmacy; Philosophy; Physics; Political Sciences; Preschool Education; Public Administration; Regional Studies; Rehabilitation and

Therapy; Science Education; Sociology; Sports; Statistics; Structural Architecture; Surveying and Mapping; Telecommunications Engineering; Tourism; Veterinary Science; Zoology)

Student Services: Careers Guidance, Sports Facilities, Library, IT Centre, Residential Facilities

Last Update: 08-03-2018

Kongju National University (KNU)

56 Gongjudaehak-ro
Gongju-si 314-701, Chungcheongnam-do
Tel: +82(41) 850-8114
Fax: +82(41) 850-8000
Website: http://www.kongju.ac.kr
Acting President: Hee-soo Kim
Tel: +82(41) 850-8001

College

Art (Ceramic Art; Communication Arts; Computer Graphics; Dance; Design; Fine Arts; Furniture Design; Information Technology; Jewellery Art; Visual Arts); **Education** (Art Education; Business Education; Computer Education; Education; Foreign Languages Education; Home Economics Education; Humanities and Social Science Education; Mathematics Education; Music Education; Native Language Education; Physical Education; Preschool Education; Science Education; Special Education; Technology Education); **Engineering** (Architectural and Environmental Design; Automation and Control Engineering; Automotive Engineering; Chemical Engineering; Civil Engineering; Computer Engineering; Construction Engineering; Electrical Engineering; Electronic Engineering; Engineering; Engineering Drawing and Design; Environmental Engineering; Graphic Design; Industrial Chemistry; Industrial Design; Industrial Engineering; Information Technology; Materials Engineering; Mechanical Engineering; Metal Techniques; Multimedia; Nanotechnology; Optical Technology; Polymer and Plastics Technology; Structural Architecture; Telecommunications Engineering; Town Planning; Transport Engineering; Visual Arts); **Humanities** (Arts and Humanities; Business Administration; Business and Commerce; Chinese; Economics; English; French; Geography; German; History; International Business; Law; Literature; Public Administration; Social Welfare; Tourism; Translation and Interpretation); **Industrial Sciences** (Animal Husbandry; Botany; Construction Engineering; Food Science; Food Technology; Forestry; Horticulture; Industrial Engineering; Industrial Management; Laboratory Techniques; Landscape Architecture; Mechanical Engineering; Natural Resources; Nutrition; Real Estate; Rural Planning; Social and Community Services); **Natural Sciences** (Applied Mathematics; Biological and Life Sciences; Chemistry; Environmental Studies; Fashion Design; Geography; Heritage Preservation; Marketing; Meteorology; Natural Sciences; Physics); **Nursing and Health** (Health Administration; Health Sciences; Information Management; Information Technology; Medicine; Nursing)

Course/Programme

Courses jointly operated by multiple departments (Computer Science; Food Technology; Hotel Management; Japanese; Korean; Military Science; Museum Studies; Native Language; Oriental Studies; Safety Engineering)

Department/Division

International Studies (Business Administration; Economics; Management; Mathematics; Statistics)

Graduate School

Arts and Sports (Design; Fine Arts; Handicrafts; Industrial Design; Music; Physical Education; Sports; Visual Arts); **Engineering** (Agricultural Engineering; Architecture; Automation and Control Engineering; Chemical Engineering; Computer Engineering; Computer Graphics; Construction Engineering; Electrical Engineering; Electronic Engineering; Engineering; Environmental Engineering; Food Science; Food Technology; Industrial Engineering; Information Technology; Materials Engineering; Mechanical Engineering; Multimedia; Optical Technology; Structural Architecture; Telecommunications Engineering; Town Planning; Transport Engineering; Visual Arts); **Human Sciences and Social Studies** (Administration; Business Administration; Business Education; Chinese; E- Business/Commerce; Education; English; Ethics; Finance; Foreign Languages Education; French; Geography; German; History; Humanities and Social Science Education; International Business; Korean; Law; Literature; Native Language Education; Preschool Education; Public Administration; Real Estate; Social and Community Services; Social Welfare; Special Education; Surveying and Mapping); **Natural Sciences** (Animal Husbandry; Biology; Botany; Chemistry; Computer Education; Computer Science; Environmental Studies; Food Science; Forestry; Geography; Health Administration; Heritage Preservation; Home Economics Education; Horticulture; Laboratory Techniques; Landscape Architecture; Mathematics; Mathematics Education; Medicine; Meteorology; Natural Resources; Natural Sciences; Nursing; Nutrition; Physics; Science Education)

Further information: Also Yesan, Cheonan and Okryong Campuses

History: Founded 1948 as Kongju Provincial Teachers' College, acquired present status 1991. Under the jurisdiction of the Ministry of Education.

Academic year: March to February (March-August; September-February)

Admission requirements: Graduation from high school or foreign equivalent, and entrance examination

Main language(s) of instruction: Korean

Accrediting agency: Korean Council for University Education (KCUE)

Degrees and diplomas: Bachelor's Degree, Master's Degree (Agricultural Engineering; Animal Husbandry; Architecture; Automation and Control Engineering; Biology; Botany; Business Administration; Chemical Engineering; Chemistry; Chinese; Computer Engineering; Computer Graphics; Computer Science; Construction Engineering; Design; E- Business/Commerce; East Asian Studies; Education; Electrical Engineering; Electronic Engineering; English; Environmental Engineering; Environmental Studies; Ethics; Finance; Fine Arts; Food Science; Food Technology; Forestry; French; German; Handicrafts; Health Administration; Heritage Preservation; Horticulture; Hotel Management; Industrial Design; Industrial Engineering; Information Technology; International Business; Japanese; Korean; Laboratory Techniques; Landscape Architecture; Law; Literature; Materials Engineering; Mathematics; Mechanical Engineering; Medicine; Meteorology; Multimedia; Museum Studies; Music; Native Language Education; Nursing; Nutrition; Optical Technology; Oriental Studies; Physical Education; Physics; Preschool Education; Public Administration; Real Estate; Safety Engineering; Social and Community Services; Social Welfare; Software Engineering; Special Education; Sports; Structural Architecture; Telecommunications Engineering; Town Planning; Transport Engineering; Visual Arts), Doctor's Degree (Automation and Control Engineering; Chinese; Computer Education; Computer Graphics; Electrical Engineering; Electronic Engineering; English; Foreign Languages Education; German; Home Economics Education; Humanities and Social Science Education; Korean; Literature; Mathematics Education; Military Science; Museum Studies; Native Language Education; Preschool Education; Science Education; Software Engineering; Visual Arts)

Student Services: Academic Counselling, Careers Guidance, Nursery Care, Cultural Activities, Sports Facilities, Language Laboratory, Facilities for disabled people, Health Services, Canteen, Library, Residential Facilities

Periodicals: Paekche Culture, Science Education, Thesis Collection

Publishing house: University Press

Academic Staff 2013-2014	MALE	FEMALE	TOTAL
FULL-TIME			692
Student Numbers 2013-2014			
All (Foreign Included)			c. 22000
Foreign only			600

Last Update: 28-02-2018

Korea Advanced Institute of Science and Technology (KAIST)

291 Daehak-ro, Yuseong-gu
Daejeon 34141, Chungcheongnam-do
Tel: +82(42) 350-2114
Fax: +82(42) 350-2210, +82(42) 869-2220
Website: http://www.kaist.edu
President: Sung-Chul Shin

College

Business Administration (*Also Graduate School*) (Accountancy; Business Administration; Engineering Management; Environmental Studies; Finance; Information Management; Management; Media Studies); **Engineering** (*Also Graduate School*) (Aeronautical and Aerospace Engineering; Agricultural Engineering; Bioengineering; Chemical Engineering; Civil Engineering; Energy Engineering; Engineering; Environmental Engineering; Marine Engineering; Materials Engineering; Mechanical Engineering; Molecular Biology; Nuclear Engineering; Transport Engineering); **Information Science and Technology** (*Also Graduate School*) (Computer Engineering; Computer Science; Electrical Engineering; Industrial Design; Industrial Engineering; Information Management; Information Sciences; Information Technology; Telecommunications Engineering); **Liberal Arts and Convergence Science** (*Also Graduate School*) (Arts and Humanities; Business Administration; Engineering Management; Natural Sciences; Social Sciences; Technology); **Life Science and Bioengineering** (*Also Graduate School*) (Bioengineering; Biological and Life Sciences; Biomedical Engineering; Medicine); **Natural Sciences** (*Also Graduate School*) (Chemistry; Mathematics; Nanotechnology; Natural Sciences; Physics)

Further information: Also Munji and Seoul Campuses

History: Founded in 1971 as nation's first research-oriented science and engineering institution. Campus moved from Seoul to the Daedeok Science Town in Daejeon in 1989

Academic year: February to January (First semester: February-June; Second semester: August-January)

Fees: National : None (Won), International : None (Won)

Main language(s) of instruction: Korean, English

Accrediting agency: Ministry of Science and ICT

Degrees and diplomas: Bachelor's Degree (Aeronautical and Aerospace Engineering; Bioengineering; Biological and Life Sciences; Biomedical Engineering; Business and Commerce; Chemistry; Computer Engineering; Electrical and Electronic Engineering; Engineering; Environmental Engineering; Industrial Engineering; Materials Engineering; Mathematics; Mechanical Engineering; Natural Sciences; Nuclear Engineering; Physics), Master's Degree (Aeronautical and Aerospace Engineering; Agricultural

Engineering; Automotive Engineering; Bioengineering; Biological and Life Sciences; Biomedical Engineering; Chemical Engineering; Chemistry; Civil Engineering; Civil Law; Computer Engineering; Computer Science; Cultural Studies; Electrical Engineering; Electronic Engineering; Energy Engineering; Engineering; Engineering Management; Environmental Engineering; Environmental Management; Finance; Industrial Design; Industrial Engineering; Information Management; Information Technology; International Business; Journalism; Management; Marine Engineering; Materials Engineering; Mathematics; Mechanical Engineering; Medicine; Molecular Biology; Nanotechnology; Natural Sciences; Nuclear Engineering; Physics; Polymer and Plastics Technology; Robotics; Safety Engineering; Software Engineering; Technology; Telecommunications Engineering; Transport Engineering), Doctor's Degree (Aeronautical and Aerospace Engineering; Agricultural Engineering; Automotive Engineering; Bioengineering; Biological and Life Sciences; Biomedical Engineering; Chemical Engineering; Chemistry; Civil Engineering; Computer Science; Cultural Studies; Electrical Engineering; Electronic Engineering; Energy Engineering; Engineering Management; Environmental Engineering; Industrial Design; Industrial Engineering; Information Management; Information Technology; Management; Marine Engineering; Materials Engineering; Mathematics; Mechanical Engineering; Medicine; Molecular Biology; Nanotechnology; Natural Sciences; Nuclear Engineering; Physics; Polymer and Plastics Technology; Robotics; Safety Engineering; Software Engineering; Technology; Telecommunications Engineering; Transport Engineering)

Student Services: Academic Counselling, Careers Guidance, Nursery Care, Sports Facilities, Facilities for disabled people, Health Services, Foreign Studies Centre, Library, Residential Facilities

Academic Staff 2017-2018	MALE	FEMALE	TOTAL
FULL-TIME			c. 1125
Student Numbers 2017-2018			
All (Foreign Included)			11800
Foreign only			700

Last Update: 24-05-2018

Korea Maritime and Ocean University (KMOU)

727 Taejong-ro Yeongdo-Gu
Busan 49112
Tel: +82(51) 410-4114
Fax: +82(51) 405-2475

Website: http://www.kmou.ac.kr
President: Han-il Park
Tel: +82(51) 410-4000

College
Engineering (Automation and Control Engineering; Civil Engineering; Data Processing; Electrical and Electronic Engineering; Environmental Engineering; Marine Transport; Mechanical Engineering; Telecommunications Engineering); **International Studies** (Administration; Business and Commerce; East Asian Studies; English; European Studies; International Business; International Economics; International Studies; Literature; Maritime Law; Teacher Training); **Maritime Sciences** (Coastal Studies; Industrial Management; Information Technology; International Studies; Marine Engineering; Marine Transport; Nautical Science); **Ocean Science and Technology** (Architecture; Biological and Life Sciences; Energy Engineering; Environmental Studies; Marine Biology; Marine Engineering; Naval Architecture; Physical Education)

School
Ocean Science and Technology (OST) (*Graduate*) (Management; Marine Science and Oceanography)

Graduate School
Education (Computer Education; Education; Educational Administration; Foreign Languages Education; Humanities and Social Science Education; Marine Engineering; Mathematics Education; Physical Education; Preschool Education; Primary Education); **Graduate Studies** (Arts and Humanities; Automation and Control Engineering; Civil Engineering; Computer Engineering; Electrical and Electronic Engineering; Electronic Engineering; Energy Engineering; Engineering; Environmental Engineering; Heating and Refrigeration; Information Technology; Marine Engineering; Marine Transport; Materials Engineering; Mechanical Engineering; Microwaves; Natural Sciences; Naval Architecture; Police Studies; Safety Engineering; Social Sciences; Structural Architecture; Telecommunications Engineering; Thermal Engineering; Transport Engineering; Transport Management); **Maritime Industry** (Civil Engineering; Computer Engineering; Economics; Electrical and Electronic Engineering; Energy Engineering; Engineering; Marine Transport; Maritime Law; Mechanical Engineering; Public Administration; Social Sciences; Transport Management); **Shipping Finance and Logistics** (Business Administration; Business and Commerce; Transport Economics; Transport Management)

History: Founded 1945 as Jinhae Merchant Ship Academy. Merged with Tongyeong Merchant Ship Academy and renamed as Jinhae Maritime College 1946. Renamed as National Maritime College and merged with Incheon Maritime College 1947. Renamed Korea Maritime College 1956. Moved to Busan 1953. Acquired present status and title 1991.

Academic year: March to December (March-June; August-December)

Admission requirements: Graduation from high school

Fees: National : 1,700,000-2,200,000 per semester (Won), International : 1,700,000-2,200,000 per semester (Won)

Main language(s) of instruction: Korean

Accrediting agency: Korean Council for University Education (KCUE)

Degrees and diplomas: Bachelor's Degree (Architecture; Automation and Control Engineering; Business Administration; Business and Commerce; Civil Engineering; Coastal Studies; Data Processing; East Asian Studies; Economics; Education; Electrical and Electronic Engineering; Energy Engineering; Environmental Engineering; European Studies; Information Technology; International Business; International Studies; Leisure Studies; Literature; Marine Biology; Marine Engineering; Marine Science and Oceanography; Marine Transport; Maritime Law; Mechanical Engineering; Nautical Science; Naval Architecture; Public Administration; Telecommunications Engineering; Transport Management), Master's Degree (Administration; Applied Mathematics; Arts and Humanities; Automation and Control Engineering; Civil Engineering; Computer Engineering; Cultural Studies; East Asian Studies; Electrical Engineering; Electronic Engineering; Energy Engineering; Engineering; English; Environmental Engineering; Environmental Studies; European Studies; Heating and Refrigeration; Information Sciences; Insurance; International Business; Linguistics; Literature; Marine Biology; Marine Engineering; Marine Science and Oceanography; Marine Transport; Maritime Law; Materials Engineering; Mathematics; Measurement and Precision Engineering; Mechanical Engineering; Nautical Science; Police Studies; Private Law; Public Law; Safety Engineering; Social Sciences; Structural Architecture; Telecommunications Engineering; Transport Engineering; Transport Management), Doctor's Degree (Administration; Applied Mathematics; Arts and Humanities; Automation and Control Engineering; Business and Commerce; Civil Engineering; Civil Law; Computer Engineering; Cultural Studies; East Asian Studies; Economics; Electrical and Electronic Engineering; Electronic Engineering; Energy Engineering; Engineering; English; Environmental Engineering; Environmental Studies; European Studies; Heating and Refrigeration; Insurance; International Business; Linguistics; Literature; Marine Biology; Marine Engineering; Marine Science and Oceanography; Maritime Law; Materials Engineering; Mathematics and Computer Science; Measurement and Precision Engineering; Mechanical Engineering; Mechanics; Natural Sciences; Nautical Science; Naval Architecture; Police Studies; Public Law; Safety Engineering; Social Sciences; Telecommunications Engineering; Telecommunications Services; Transport Management)

Student Services: Academic Counselling, Careers Guidance, Nursery Care, Cultural Activities, Sports Facilities, Facilities for disabled people, Health Services, Canteen, Foreign Studies Centre, Library, IT Centre, Residential Facilities

Periodicals: Journals

Publishing house: Korea Maritime and Ocean University Press

Academic Staff 2016-2017	MALE	FEMALE	TOTAL
FULL-TIME	162	90	252
Student Numbers 2016-2017			
All (Foreign Included)	6905	1926	8831

Last Update: 24-05-2018

Korea National Open University (KNOU)

86 Daehak-ro, Jongro-gu
Seoul 03087
Tel: +82(2) 3668-4301
Fax: +82(2) 747-7100
Website: http://www.knou.ac.kr
President: Su-Noh Ryu

College

Education (Cultural Studies; Education; Film; History; Pre-school Education); **Liberal Arts** (Arts and Humanities; Chinese; English; French; Japanese; Korean; Literature); **Natural Sciences** (Agriculture; Clothing and Sewing; Computer Science; Environmental Studies; Food Science; Health Sciences; Home Economics; Information Sciences; Natural Sciences; Nursing; Nutrition; Statistics; Textile Design); **Prime College** (Electronic Engineering; Engineering; Finance; Industrial Engineering; Service Trades); **Social Sciences** (Communication Arts; Economics; International Business; Law; Management; Media Studies; Public Administration; Social Sciences; Tourism)

Course/Programme

Non-Degree Courses (Arts and Humanities; Business Administration; Continuing Education; Development Studies; Economics; Health Sciences; Leisure Studies; Management; Rural Studies)

Graduate School

Graduate Studies (African Studies; Agriculture; Biological and Life Sciences; Chinese; Communication Arts; Computer Science; Continuing Education; Distance Education; East

Asian Studies; Education; English; Environmental Studies; French; French Studies; Health Sciences; Home Economics; Japanese; Law; Media Studies; Nursing; Preschool Education; Public Administration; Statistics; Writing)

Further information: Also 12 regional Study Centres, and 27 local Study Centres

History: Founded 1972 as junior college of Seoul National University. Reorganized as an independent university 1981. Instruction is given by radio, TV, computer network system, audio cassettes and correspondence, and students have to attend several face-to-face classes per semester. A State institution under the jurisdiction of the Ministry of Education.

Academic year: March to February (March-August; September-February)

Admission requirements: Graduation from high school or equivalent

Main language(s) of instruction: Korean

Accrediting agency: Ministry of Education

Degrees and diplomas: Bachelor's Degree, Master's Degree (African Studies; Agriculture; Biological and Life Sciences; Chinese; Communication Arts; Computer Science; Distance Education; East Asian Studies; Education; English; Environmental Studies; French; French Studies; Health Sciences; Home Economics; Japanese; Law; Media Studies; Nursing; Preschool Education; Public Administration; Statistics; Writing)

Student Services: Academic Counselling, Social Counselling, Sports Facilities, Facilities for disabled people, Canteen, Library, IT Centre

Periodicals: Distance Education, KNOU Journal

Publishing house: KNOU Press

Academic Staff 2013-2014	MALE	FEMALE	TOTAL
FULL-TIME			3184
Student Numbers 2013-2014			
All (Foreign Included)			160303

Total number of part-time students: 395
Last Update: 24-05-2018

Korea National Sport University (KNSU)

1239 Yangjae Songpa-gu
Seoul 138-763
Tel: +82(2) 410-6700
Fax: +82(2) 418-1877
Website: http://www.knsu.ac.kr/web/kor/home
President: Jong-Wook Kim

Course/Programme
Wellness Program for Top Managers (*Graduate*) (Dance; Health Sciences; Sports)

Department/Division
Adapted Physical Education (Physical Education; Special Education); **Community Sports Science** (Sports); **Dance** (Dance); **Health and Exercise Science** (Health Sciences; Nutrition; Physical Therapy; Sports; Sports Medicine); **Leisure Sport** (Leisure Studies; Sports; Sports Management); **Physical Education** (Physical Education); **Sport and Healthy Aging** (Physical Education; Social Welfare; Social Work); **Taekwondo** (Sports); **Youth Guidance and Sport Education** (Educational and Student Counselling; Psychology; Sports; Welfare and Protective Services)

Graduate School
Education (Education; Physical Education); **Graduate** (*Community Sports Science*) (Arts and Humanities; Leisure Studies; Natural Sciences; Physical Education; Social Sciences; Sports); **Sports and Leisure Studies** (Health Administration; Leisure Studies; Sports; Sports Management)

Research Division
Physical Education and Sport Science (Physical Education)
History: Founded 1976. A State institution under the jurisdiction of the Ministry of Education.
Academic year: March to December (March-June; August-December)
Admission requirements: Graduation from high school
Main language(s) of instruction: Korean
Accrediting agency: Korean Council for University Education (KCUE)
Degrees and diplomas: Bachelor's Degree, Master's Degree (Health Administration; Marketing; Mass Communication; Physical Education; Protective Services; Sports; Sports Management), Doctor's Degree (Physical Education)
Student Services: Sports Facilities, Health Services, Library, Residential Facilities
Periodicals: Monographs of the Physical Education Institute, Monographs of the Research Institute of Physical Education and Sports Science
Last Update: 28-02-2018

Korea National University of Arts (K-Arts)

146-37, Hwarang-ro 32-gil, Seongbuk-gu
Seoul 02789
Tel: +82(2) 746-9073, +82(2) 746-9075
Fax: +82(2) 746-9079
Website: http://eng.karts.ac.kr
President: Bongryol Kim

School
Dance (Dance; Theatre); **Drama** (Acting; Art Management; Display and Stage Design; Theatre; Writing); **Korean**

Traditional Arts (Dance; Music; Music Theory and Composition; Musical Instruments; Performing Arts; Singing); **Music** (Conducting; Music; Music Theory and Composition; Musical Instruments; Musicology; Singing); **Visual Arts** (Aesthetics; Architecture; Design; Fine Arts)
Further information: Also Seocho-dong Campus
History: Founded 1993.
Main language(s) of instruction: Korean, English
Accrediting agency: Ministry of Education
Degrees and diplomas: Bachelor's Degree (Acting; Aesthetics; Architecture; Art Management; Conducting; Dance; Design; Display and Stage Design; Fine Arts; Music; Music Theory and Composition; Musical Instruments; Musicology; Performing Arts; Singing; Theatre; Writing), Master's Degree (Acting; Aesthetics; Architecture; Art Management; Cinema and Television; Conducting; Dance; Design; Display and Stage Design; Film; Fine Arts; Multimedia; Music; Music Theory and Composition; Musicology; Performing Arts; Radio and Television Broadcasting; Sound Engineering (Acoustics); Technology; Theatre; Visual Arts; Writing). Also Artist Diploma, 3 yrs
Student Services: Library

Academic Staff 2017-2018	MALE	FEMALE	TOTAL
FULL-TIME			129
Student Numbers 2017-2018			
All (Foreign Included)			5051

Last Update: 23-03-2018

Korea National University of Cultural Heritage (NUCH)

367, Baekjemun-ro, Gyuam-myeon
Buyeo-gun 33115, Chungcheongnam-do
Tel: +82(41) 830-7221
Fax: +82(41) 830-7242
Website: https://www.nuch.ac.kr/english/main.do
Acting President: Jong-Ho Choe

Department/Division

Archaeology (Archaeology); **Conservation Science** (Museum Studies); **Cultural Properties Management** (Art Management); **Intangible Cultural Heritage Studies** (Heritage Preservation); **Traditional Architecture** (Architecture); **Traditional Arts and Crafts** (Fine Arts; Handicrafts); **Traditional Landscape Architecture** (Landscape Architecture)

Graduate School

Graduate Studies (Fine Arts; Handicrafts; Heritage Preservation; Restoration of Works of Art)
History: Founded 2000.

Main language(s) of instruction: Korean
Accrediting agency: Ministry of Education
Degrees and diplomas: Bachelor's Degree (Archaeology; Architecture; Art Management; Fine Arts; Handicrafts; Heritage Preservation; Landscape Architecture; Museum Studies), Master's Degree (Fine Arts; Handicrafts; Heritage Preservation; Restoration of Works of Art)
Last Update: 28-03-2018

Korea National University of Education (KNUE)

250 Taeseongtabyeon-ro Gangnae-myeon Heungdeok-gu
Cheongju-si 28173, Chungbuk
Tel: +82(43) 230-3114
Fax: +82(43) 233-2207
Website: http://www.knue.ac.kr
President: Hee-Chan Lew
Tel: +82(43) 230-3204

College

1st College (Education; Preschool Education; Primary Education; Secondary Education); **2nd College** (English; English Studies; Ethics; Foreign Languages Education; French; French Studies; German; Germanic Studies; Humanities and Social Science Education; Native Language Education); **3rd College** (Chemistry; Computer Education; Environmental Studies; Home Economics Education; Mathematics Education; Physics; Science Education; Technology Education); **4th College** (Art Education; Music Education; Physical Education)

Institute

Educational Institute of Art and Music, Physical Exercise; **Educational Institute of Humanities and Social Science**; **Educational Institute of Natural Science**; **Educational Research**; **Educational Science**

Graduate School

Education (Teacher Training); **Educational Policy and Administration** (Educational Administration); **Graduate Studies** (Education)
History: Founded 1984. Inception of Master's Degree courses, Opening of Center for Educational Research, In-service Center 1986. Inception of Doctoral courses, Opening of Affiliated elementary and middle school 1988. Opening of Affiliated High School 1994. Opening of Educational Graduate School 1997. Opening of Graduate School of Educational Policy and Administration 2001. International Symposium to found the first Asian Teachers Association 2006.
Academic year: March to February (March-August; September-February)

Admission requirements: Graduation from high school

Fees: c. 1,350,000 per semester (Won)

Main language(s) of instruction: Korean

Accrediting agency: Ministry of Education

Degrees and diplomas: Bachelor's Degree (Education), Master's Degree (Art Education; Computer Education; Curriculum; Education; Education of the Gifted; Educational Administration; Educational Psychology; Educational Sciences; Educational Technology; Foreign Languages Education; Home Economics Education; Humanities and Social Science Education; Mathematics Education; Music Education; Native Language Education; Physical Education; Preschool Education; Primary Education; Science Education; Special Education; Teacher Training; Technology Education), Doctor's Degree (Art Education; Computer Education; Curriculum; Education; Education of the Gifted; Educational Administration; Educational and Student Counselling; Educational Psychology; Educational Sciences; Educational Technology; Foreign Languages Education; Home Economics Education; Humanities and Social Science Education; Mathematics Education; Music Education; Native Language Education; Physical Education; Preschool Education; Primary Education; Science Education; Special Education; Teacher Training; Technology Education)

Student Services: Academic Counselling, Social Counselling, Careers Guidance, Nursery Care, Cultural Activities, Sports Facilities, Language Laboratory, Facilities for disabled people, Health Services, Canteen, Library, Residential Facilities

Periodicals: Newsletter of KNUE

Academic Staff 2013-2014	MALE	FEMALE	TOTAL
FULL-TIME			c. 250
Student Numbers 2013-2014			
All (Foreign Included)			c. 6530

Last Update: 28-02-2018

Korea National University of Transportation (KNUT)

50 Daehak-ro Geomdan-ri, Daesowon-myeon
Chungju-si 27469, Chungbuk-do

Tel: +82(43) 841-5114

Fax: +82(43) 841-1236

Website: http://www.ut.ac.kr

President: Yeong-Ho Kim

College

Advanced Science and Technology (Automation and Control Engineering; Computer Engineering; Electrical Engineering; Electronic Engineering; Information Technology; Software Engineering; Telecommunications Engineering); **Construction and Transportation Engineering** (Architecture; Civil Engineering; Communication Arts; Construction Engineering; Ecology; Graphic Design; Industrial Design; Structural Architecture; Town Planning; Transport Engineering); **Engineering** (Aeronautical and Aerospace Engineering; Bioengineering; Chemical Engineering; Energy Engineering; Environmental Engineering; Industrial Engineering; Materials Engineering; Mechanical Engineering; Polymer and Plastics Technology; Safety Engineering); **Health and Life Science** (Biological and Life Sciences; Biotechnology; Food Science; Food Technology; Health Sciences; Medical Technology; Nutrition; Physical Therapy); **Humanities and Arts** (Arts and Humanities; Chinese; Health Sciences; Literature; Music; Sports; Sports Management; Writing); **International and Social Sciences** (Business and Commerce; Computer Engineering; English; International Business; Multimedia; Preschool Education; Special Education); **Railroad Sciences** (Automotive Engineering; Computer Science; Electrical Engineering; Electronic Engineering; Information Technology; Railway Engineering; Railway Transport; Transport Management); **Social Sciences** (Aeronautical and Aerospace Engineering; Air Transport; Information Management; Information Technology; Public Administration; Service Trades; Social Sciences)

School

Liberal Arts and Sciences (Arts and Humanities; Natural Sciences; Social Sciences); **Liberal Studies** (Air Transport; Cultural Studies; Medicine; Music; Nursing; Physical Therapy; Preschool Education; Sports)

Graduate School

Business Administration and Public Administration (*Specialized*) (Business Administration; Information Management; Information Technology; Public Administration); **Education** (*Specialized*) (Continuing Education; Education; Educational Administration; Educational and Student Counselling; Foreign Languages Education; Preschool Education; Science Education); **Graduate Studies** (Architecture and Planning; Engineering; Natural Sciences; Social Sciences); **Humanities** (*Specialized*) (Arts and Humanities; Chinese; English; Korean; Literature; Sports); **Industry** (*Specialized*) (Architecture; Automation and Control Engineering; Computer Engineering; Computer Science; Construction Engineering; Electrical Engineering; Electronic Engineering; Energy Engineering; Engineering; Environmental Engineering; Food Science; Food Technology; Industrial Engineering; Mechanical Engineering; Real Estate; Safety Engineering; Structural Architecture; Telecommunications Engineering; Town Planning)

Further information: Also Jungpyeong and Uiwang Campuses

History: Founded 1962, acquired present status 1993. Chongju National University. Acquired present title 2012 after merging with Korea National Railroad College.

Admission requirements: High school certificate

Fees: 1,792,800-2,086,200 (upon 18 Credits) (Won)

Main language(s) of instruction: Korean

Accrediting agency: Ministry of Education and Human Resources Development; Korean Council for University Education (KCUE)

Degrees and diplomas: Bachelor's Degree, Master's Degree (Aeronautical and Aerospace Engineering; Architecture; Automation and Control Engineering; Bioengineering; Biotechnology; Business Administration; Chemical Engineering; Chinese; Civil Engineering; Computer Engineering; Computer Science; Construction Engineering; Continuing Education; Educational Administration; Electrical Engineering; Electronic Engineering; Energy Engineering; Engineering Management; English; Environmental Engineering; Food Science; Food Technology; Foreign Languages Education; Industrial Design; Industrial Engineering; Information Management; Information Technology; Korean; Literature; Materials Engineering; Mechanical Engineering; Medicine; Multimedia; Nursing; Physical Therapy; Polymer and Plastics Technology; Preschool Education; Psychology; Public Administration; Real Estate; Safety Engineering; Science Education; Special Education; Sports; Structural Architecture; Telecommunications Engineering; Town Planning; Welfare and Protective Services), Doctor's Degree (Bioengineering; Business Administration; Civil Engineering; Computer Engineering; Electrical Engineering; Industrial Engineering; Information Management; Materials Engineering; Mechanical Engineering; Polymer and Plastics Technology; Public Administration; Safety Engineering; Structural Architecture)

Student Services: Academic Counselling, Social Counselling, Careers Guidance, Nursery Care, Cultural Activities, Sports Facilities, Facilities for disabled people, Health Services, Canteen, Library, IT Centre, Residential Facilities

Academic Staff 2013-2014	MALE	FEMALE	TOTAL
FULL-TIME			c. 350
Student Numbers 2013-2014			
All (Foreign Included)			c. 13400

Last Update: 20-03-2018

Kumoh National Institute of Technology (KIT)

61 Daehak-ro (yangho-dong)
Gumi-si 39177, Gyeongbuk-do

Tel: +82(54) 478-7114, +82(54) 478-7220
Fax: +82(54) 478-7100, +82(54) 478-7222
Website: http://www.kumoh.ac.kr
President: Sang Cheol Lee

College

Architecture (Architectural and Environmental Design; Architecture; Construction Engineering; Structural Architecture; Town Planning); **Civil and Environmental Engineering** (Bridge Engineering; Civil Engineering; Environmental Engineering; Road Engineering); **Computer and Software Engineering** (Computer Engineering; Information Technology; Software Engineering); **Electronic Engineering** (Electronic Engineering); **Industrial Management** (Industrial Management); **Materials and Systems Engineering** (Ceramics and Glass Technology; Industrial Engineering; Materials Engineering; Measurement and Precision Engineering; Nanotechnology; Polymer and Plastics Technology); **Mechanical Engineering** (Automotive Engineering; Computer Engineering; Electronic Engineering; Engineering Drawing and Design; Mechanical Engineering)

School

Natural Science (Applied Chemistry; Applied Mathematics; Natural Sciences; Optical Technology; Statistics)

Graduate School

Education (Education); **Graduate Studies** (Applied Chemistry; Applied Mathematics; Automation and Control Engineering; Automotive Engineering; Civil Engineering; Computer Engineering; Electronic Engineering; Engineering; Environmental Engineering; Fashion Design; Industrial Engineering; Industrial Management; Materials Engineering; Mathematics; Mechanical Engineering; Metallurgical Engineering; Physics; Polymer and Plastics Technology; Production Engineering; Software Engineering; Statistics; Structural Architecture; Telecommunications Engineering; Textile Technology); **Industry** (Industrial Engineering)

Further information: Also 12 Research Institutes

History: Founded 1980. A State institution under the jurisdiction of the Ministry of Education. Financially supported by the Government and tuition fees.

Academic year: March to February (March-August; September-February)

Admission requirements: Graduation from high school and entrance examination

Main language(s) of instruction: Korean

Accrediting agency: Korean Council for University Education (KCUE)

Degrees and diplomas: Bachelor's Degree, Master's Degree (Applied Chemistry; Automation and Control Engineering; Automotive Engineering; Business Administration; Civil Engineering; Computer Engineering; Electrical and

Electronic Engineering; Electronic Engineering; Engineering; Environmental Engineering; Fashion Design; Industrial Engineering; Industrial Management; Materials Engineering; Mathematics; Mechanical Engineering; Mechanics; Metallurgical Engineering; Optical Technology; Physics; Polymer and Plastics Technology; Production Engineering; Software Engineering; Structural Architecture; Telecommunications Engineering; Textile Technology), Doctor's Degree (Applied Mathematics; Computer Education; Educational Administration; Electronic Engineering; Foreign Languages Education; Humanities and Social Science Education; Mathematics Education; Mechanical Engineering; Native Language Education; Science Education; Statistics; Technology Education)

Student Services: Library, IT Centre, Residential Facilities

Periodicals: Academic Journal

Academic Staff 2012-2013	MALE	FEMALE	TOTAL
FULL-TIME			230
PART-TIME			c. 110
Student Numbers 2012-2013			
All (Foreign Included)			c. 10463
Foreign only			162

Last Update: 01-03-2018

Kunsan National University (KSNU)

558 Daehak-ro
Gunsan-si 54150, Jeollabuk-do
Tel: +82(63) 469-4113, +82(63) 469-4114
Fax: +82(63) 469-4197
Website: http://www.kunsan.ac.kr
President: Eui gyun Na
Tel: +82(63) 469-4101

College

Arts (Ceramic Art; Design; Fine Arts; Industrial Design; Music); **Engineering** (Architecture; Automation and Control Engineering; Automotive Engineering; Chemical Engineering; Civil Engineering; Computer Engineering; Construction Engineering; Electrical Engineering; Electronic Engineering; Engineering; Environmental Engineering; Information Technology; Materials Engineering; Mechanical Engineering; Media Studies; Nanotechnology; Naval Architecture; Radio and Television Broadcasting; Robotics; Telecommunications Engineering); **Humanities** (Arts and Humanities; Chinese; Cultural Studies; English; History; Japanese; Korean; Literature; Media Studies; Philosophy); **Natural Sciences** (Biology; Chemistry; Child Care and Development; Clothing and Sewing; Computer Science; Family Studies; Food Science; Home Economics; Interior Design; Mathematics; Natural Sciences; Nursing; Nutrition; Physical Education; Physics; Statistics; Textile

Design); **Ocean Science and Technology** (Aquaculture; Biotechnology; Food Science; Marine Biology; Marine Engineering; Marine Science and Oceanography; Police Studies; Power Engineering); **Social Sciences** (Accountancy; Business Administration; Economics; International Business; Law; Public Administration; Social Sciences; Social Welfare; Transport Management)

Centre

Business Incubator; **Marine Biology Research and Education** (Marine Biology); **Small and Medium Enterprise Business-Academic Cooperation**; **Technology Innovation**

Graduate School

Business and Public Administration (Accountancy; Agricultural Business; Business Administration; Economics; Fishery; International Business; Law; Public Administration); **Graduate Studies** (Arts and Humanities; Engineering; Fine Arts; Natural Sciences; Social Sciences); **Industry** (Automation and Control Engineering; Chemical Engineering; Civil Engineering; Computer Engineering; Construction Engineering; Electrical and Electronic Engineering; Environmental Engineering; Fishery; Food Science; Industrial Engineering; Information Technology; Marine Engineering; Mechanical Engineering; Nutrition; Statistics; Telecommunications Engineering); **Industry** (Asian Studies; Computer Education; East Asian Studies; Education; Educational Administration; Foreign Languages Education; Home Economics Education; Humanities and Social Science Education; Korean; Mathematics Education; Native Language Education; Physical Education; Preschool Education; Science Education)

Research Division

Basic Sciences; **Contemporary Arts**; **Culture and Ideology**; **Engineering**; **Engineering**; **Environment and Construction**; **Environmental Research** (*Saemangum*); **Fisheries Science**; **Humanities Studies**; **Information and Telecommunications Technology**; **Legal Studies**; **Marine Development**; **Red Tide Research**; **Regional Development**; **Saemangeum Integrated Development**; **Sports Science**; **Yellow Sea Rim Area**

History: Founded 1979 as college, acquired present status 1991.

Academic year: March to February (March-August; September-February)

Admission requirements: Graduation from high school or equivalent, and entrance examination

Fees: 1,600-1,800 per semester (US Dollar)

Main language(s) of instruction: Korean

Accrediting agency: Ministry of Education and Human Resources Development; Korean Council for University Education (KCUE)

Degrees and diplomas: Bachelor's Degree, Master's Degree (Accountancy; Administration; Agricultural Business; Asian Studies; Automation and Control Engineering; Biology; Business Administration; Business and Commerce; Chemical Engineering; Chemistry; Child Care and Development; Chinese; Civil Engineering; Clothing and Sewing; Computer Education; Computer Engineering; Computer Science; Construction Engineering; Cultural Studies; Design; Eastern European Studies; Economics; Educational Administration; Electrical and Electronic Engineering; Electronic Engineering; English; Environmental Engineering; Family Studies; Fine Arts; Fishery; Food Science; History; Home Economics; Home Economics Education; Humanities and Social Science Education; Industrial Engineering; Information Technology; Interior Design; International Business; Korean; Law; Literature; Marine Engineering; Marine Science and Oceanography; Materials Engineering; Mathematics; Mathematics Education; Mechanical Engineering; Music; Naval Architecture; Nursing; Nutrition; Physical Education; Physics; Public Administration; Science Education; Social Welfare; Sports; Statistics; Telecommunications Engineering), Doctor's Degree (Accountancy; Administration; Biology; Business Administration; Chemical Engineering; Chemistry; Child Care and Development; Chinese; Civil Engineering; Computer Engineering; Construction Engineering; Design; Economics; Electronic Engineering; English; Environmental Engineering; Family Studies; Fine Arts; Fishery; Industrial Engineering; Information Technology; Korean; Literature; Marine Engineering; Marine Science and Oceanography; Materials Engineering; Mechanical Engineering; Physics; Preschool Education; Sports). Honorary Doctor degrees. Certificates for course completion (Continuing Education Centre and Language Training Centre)

Student Services: Academic Counselling, Careers Guidance, Nursery Care, Cultural Activities, Sports Facilities, Language Laboratory, Health Services, Canteen, Library, IT Centre, Residential Facilities

Publishing house: University Press

Academic Staff 2017-2018	MALE	FEMALE	TOTAL
FULL-TIME			391
Student Numbers 2017-2018			
All (Foreign Included)			7715

Last Update: 01-03-2018

Kyungpook National University (KNU)

80 Daehakro, Bukgu
Daegu 41566
Tel: +82(53) 950-2436, +82(53) 950-2434, +82(53) 950-2425
Fax: +82(53) 950-2419
Website: http://www.knu.ac.kr
President: Sang-Dong Kim

College

Agriculture and Life Sciences (Agriculture; Agronomy; Forest Products; Forestry; Horticulture; Landscape Architecture); **Economics and Commerce** (Business and Commerce; Economics); **Education** (Education); **Engineering** (Architecture; Chemical Engineering; Civil Engineering; Computer Engineering; Electrical and Electronic Engineering; Engineering; Environmental Engineering; Industrial Chemistry; Materials Engineering; Mechanical Engineering; Metallurgical Engineering; Organic Chemistry; Polymer and Plastics Technology); **Human Ecology** (Clothing and Sewing; Ecology; Food Science; Home Economics; Nutrition; Textile Technology); **Humanities** (Anthropology; Archaeology; Arts and Humanities; Chinese; English; French; German; History; Japanese; Korean; Modern Languages; Philosophy; Russian); **Law** (Law; Public Administration); **Music and Visual Arts** (Music; Visual Arts); **Natural Sciences** (Astronomy and Space Science; Biochemistry; Biology; Chemistry; Computer Science; Genetics; Geology; Mathematics; Microbiology; Natural Sciences; Physics); **Social Sciences** (Geography; Information Sciences; International Relations; Journalism; Library Science; Political Sciences; Psychology; Social Sciences)

School

Dentistry (Dentistry); **Medicine** (Medicine; Nursing); **Veterinary Science** (Veterinary Science)

Institute

Agricultural Science and Technology (Agricultural Engineering); **Basic Sciences** (Natural Sciences); **Cancer Research** (Oncology); **Economics and Management Research** (Economics; Management); **Electronic Technology** (Electronic Engineering); **Environment and Open Space** (Environmental Studies); **Environmental Science** (Environmental Studies); **Genetic Engineering** (Genetics); **Humanities** (Arts and Humanities); **Industrial Technology Research** (Industrial Engineering); **Medical Research** (Medicine); **Nursing** (Nursing); **Pacific Rim Studies** (Pacific Area Studies); **Peace Research** (Peace and Disarmament); **Philosophy and Korean Studies** (*Toegye*) (Philosophy; Regional Studies); **Physical Education and Sports Science Research** (Physical Education; Sports); **Science Education Research** (Science Education); **Social Sciences Research** (Social Sciences); **Topology and Geometry Research** (Mathematics; Surveying and Mapping); **Veterinary Science** (Veterinary Science)

Graduate School

Agricultural Development (Agriculture); **Business Administration** (Business Administration); **Education** (Education); **Industry** (Industrial Engineering); **International Study** (International Studies); **Public Administration** (Public Administration); **Public Health** (Public Health)

Further information: Also Sangju Campus

History: Founded as University 1946 incorporating 3 existing Institutions (Teachers, 1923; Medicine, 1933; Agriculture, 1944) and 2 newly established Colleges (Liberal Arts and Sciences). Main Campus at Sankyuk-dong and Medical Campus at Tongin-dong. Under the jurisdiction of the Ministry of Education. Merged with Sangju National University 2008.

Academic year: March to February (March-June; September-February)

Admission requirements: Graduation from high school or foreign equivalent, and competitive entrance examination

Main language(s) of instruction: Korean

Accrediting agency: Korean Council for University Education (KCUE)

Degrees and diplomas: Bachelor's Degree, Master's Degree (Actuarial Science; Aeronautical and Aerospace Engineering; Agricultural Business; Agricultural Economics; Animal Husbandry; Anthropology; Archaeology; Architecture; Archiving; Art Therapy; Astronomy and Space Science; Automotive Engineering; Bioengineering; Biological and Life Sciences; Biomedicine; Biotechnology; Business Administration; Chemical Engineering; Chemistry; Child Care and Development; Chinese; Civil Engineering; Classical Languages; Clothing and Sewing; Communication Arts; Computer Engineering; Computer Graphics; Computer Science; Dentistry; Ecology; Economics; Education; Electrical Engineering; Electronic Engineering; Energy Engineering; English; Environmental Engineering; Environmental Studies; Family Studies; Fashion Design; Finance; Fishery; Food Science; Foreign Languages Education; Forestry; French; Geography (Human); Geology; German; Graphic Design; History; Home Economics Education; Horticulture; Humanities and Social Science Education; Industrial Engineering; Information Sciences; Information Technology; International Business; Japanese; Journalism; Korean; Landscape Architecture; Law; Leisure Studies; Library Science; Literature; Mass Communication; Materials Engineering; Mathematics; Mathematics Education; Measurement and Precision Engineering; Mechanical Engineering; Medical Technology; Medicine; Meteorology; Multimedia; Music; Nanotechnology; Native Language Education; Nursing; Nutrition; Paper Technology; Pharmacy; Philosophy; Physical Education; Physics; Political Sciences; Protective Services; Psychology; Public Administration; Robotics; Russian; Science Education; Social Welfare; Sociology; Software Engineering; Statistics; Structural Architecture; Telecommunications Engineering; Textile Design; Textile Technology; Veterinary Science; Wood Technology), Doctor's Degree (Aeronautical and Aerospace Engineering; Agricultural Economics; Animal Husbandry; Anthropology; Archaeology; Architecture; Archiving; Art Therapy; Astronomy and Space Science; Automotive Engineering; Bioengineering; Biological and Life Sciences; Biomedicine; Biotechnology; Business Administration; Chemical Engineering; Chemistry; Child Care and Development; Chinese; Civil Engineering; Classical Languages; Clothing and Sewing; Communication Arts; Computer Engineering; Computer Graphics; Dentistry; Ecology; Economics; Education; Electrical Engineering; Energy Engineering; English; Environmental Engineering; Environmental Studies; Family Studies; Food Science; Foreign Languages Education; Forestry; French; Geography; Geology; German; Graphic Design; History; Home Economics Education; Horticulture; Humanities and Social Science Education; Industrial Engineering; Information Sciences; Information Technology; International Business; Japanese; Journalism; Korean; Landscape Architecture; Law; Leisure Studies; Library Science; Literature; Mass Communication; Mathematics; Mathematics Education; Medical Technology; Medicine; Meteorology; Multimedia; Music; Native Language Education; Nursing; Nutrition; Paper Technology; Pharmacy; Philosophy; Physical Education; Physics; Political Sciences; Psychology; Public Administration; Public Health; Robotics; Russian; Science Education; Social Welfare; Sociology; Software Engineering; Statistics; Structural Architecture; Telecommunications Engineering; Textile Technology; Veterinary Science; Welfare and Protective Services; Wood Technology)

Student Services: Academic Counselling, Social Counselling, Careers Guidance, Sports Facilities, Health Services

Periodicals: Abstracts of Theses, Graduate School, Agricultural Research Bulletin of Kyungpook National University, Bulletin of the Institute for Industrial and Social Development, Electronic Technology Reports, History Education Review, Journal of English Language and Literature, Journal of Graduate School of Education, Journal of Humanities, Journal of Korean Language and Literature, Journal of Kyungpook Engineering, Journal of Language and Literature, Journal of Law and Political Science, Journal of Natural Sciences, Journal of Physical Education, Journal of Science Education, Journal of Social Sciences, Journal of Student Guidance, Kyungpook Education Forum, Kyungpook Historical Review, Kyungpook Mathematical Journal, Kyungpook University Medical Journal, Magazine of Geology, Nak-Dong Geography, Oriental Culture Research, Peace Research, Philosophy of Korea, Research Review of Kyungpook University, Review of Economics and Business, Saemaul Research Review, Thesis Collection of Korean Language and Literature, Zeitschrift für Germanistik

Publishing house: The University Press

Student Numbers 2015-2016	MALE	FEMALE	TOTAL
All (Foreign Included)			38616
Foreign only			1602

Last Update: 01-03-2018

Mokpo National Maritime University

91, Haeyangdaehak-ro
Mokpo-si 58628, Jeollanam-do
Tel: +82(61) 240-7157, +82(61) 240-7114
Fax: +82(61) 240-7286, +82(61) 242-5176
Website: http://www.mmu.ac.kr
President: Byung-Joo Oh
Tel: +82(61) 240-7000

Department/Division

Marine Electronics and Communication Engineering (Computer Engineering; Computer Networks; Computer Science; Data Processing; Electronic Engineering; Telecommunications Engineering); **Marine Engineering** (Automation and Control Engineering; Electrical Engineering; Heating and Refrigeration; Marine Engineering; Mechanical Engineering; Police Studies; Power Engineering); **Maritime Transportation System** (Computer Networks; Information Technology; Marine Engineering; Marine Transport; Police Studies; Safety Engineering; Telecommunications Engineering; Transport Engineering; Transport Management); **Ocean System Engineering** (Civil Engineering; Environmental Engineering; Marine Engineering; Naval Architecture)

Graduate School

Graduate Studies (Mechanical Engineering; Power Engineering)
History: Founded 1950 as Mokpo fisheries and Marine High School. Upgraded into Mokpo Merchant Marine College 1979. Acquired present status and title 1993.
Academic year: March to December (March-June; September-December)
Admission requirements: Graduation from high school and entrance examination
Fees: 2.8m. per annum (Won)
Main language(s) of instruction: Korean
Accrediting agency: Korean Council for University Education (KCUE)
Degrees and diplomas: Bachelor's Degree, Master's Degree (Electronic Engineering; Information Technology; Marine Engineering; Marine Transport; Maritime Law; Police Studies; Safety Engineering; Telecommunications Engineering; Transport Management), Doctor's Degree (Electronic Engineering; Information Technology; Marine Engineering;

Marine Transport; Safety Engineering; Telecommunications Engineering; Transport Management)
Student Services: Language Laboratory, Library, IT Centre, Residential Facilities

Academic Staff 2012-2013	MALE	FEMALE	TOTAL
FULL-TIME			89
PART-TIME			30
Student Numbers 2012-2013			
All (Foreign Included)	631	112	743

Last Update: 02-03-2018

Mokpo National University (MNU)

61 dorim-ri, 1666 Youngsan-ro Cheonggye-myeon
Jeonnam 534-729
Tel: +82(61) 450-2114
Fax: +82(61) 452-4793
Website: http://www.mokpo.ac.kr
President: Il Choi

College

Business Administration (Business Administration; E-Business/Commerce; Economics; Finance; Insurance; International Business; Tourism); **Education** (Education; Environmental Studies; Ethics; Foreign Languages Education; Mathematics Education); **Engineering** (Architecture; Automation and Control Engineering; Civil Engineering; Computer Engineering; Electrical Engineering; Electronic Engineering; Engineering; Environmental Engineering; Food Technology; Information Sciences; Information Technology; Landscape Architecture; Marine Engineering; Materials Engineering; Mechanical Engineering; Multimedia; Naval Architecture; Structural Architecture; Telecommunications Engineering); **Human Ecology, Music and Fine Arts and Physical Education** (Child Care and Development; Clothing and Sewing; Fine Arts; Food Science; Music; Nutrition; Physical Education; Textile Design); **Humanities** (Anthropology; Archaeology; Arts and Humanities; Chinese; English; German; History; Japanese; Korean; Literature); **Natural Sciences** (Biochemistry; Chemistry; Fishery; Horticulture; Marine Science and Oceanography; Natural Resources; Natural Sciences; Nursing; Physics); **Pharmacy** (Microbiology; Organic Chemistry; Pharmacology; Pharmacy; Toxicology); **Social Sciences** (Law; Media Studies; Political Sciences; Public Administration; Regional Planning; Rural Planning; Social Sciences; Social Welfare; Town Planning)

Course/Programme

Korean language (Korean)

Graduate School

Business Administration (Business Administration; Law; Public Administration); **Education** (Education); **Graduate Studies**; **Industrial Technology** (Industrial Engineering)

History: Founded 1946 as normal school. Acquired present status and title 1990.

Academic year: March to February

Admission requirements: Graduation from high school and entrance examination

Main language(s) of instruction: Korean

Accrediting agency: Korean Council for University Education (KCUE)

Degrees and diplomas: Bachelor's Degree, Master's Degree (Administration; Archaeology; Architecture; Archiving; Art Education; Biology; Business Administration; Business and Commerce; Chemistry; Child Care and Development; Chinese; Civil Engineering; Clothing and Sewing; Computer Education; Computer Engineering; Computer Science; Construction Engineering; Continuing Education; Cultural Studies; Development Studies; E- Business/Commerce; Economics; Education; Education of the Gifted; Educational Administration; Educational and Student Counselling; Electrical Engineering; Electronic Engineering; Energy Engineering; English; Environmental Engineering; Environmental Studies; Ethnology; Finance; Fine Arts; Fishery; Food Science; Food Technology; Foreign Languages Education; History; Home Economics Education; Horticulture; Humanities and Social Science Education; Information Management; Information Technology; Insurance; Interior Design; International Business; Japanese; Korean; Landscape Architecture; Law; Leisure Studies; Literature; Marine Engineering; Materials Engineering; Mathematics; Mathematics Education; Mechanical Engineering; Multimedia; Music; Music Education; Native Language Education; Naval Architecture; Nutrition; Physical Education; Physics; Political Sciences; Public Administration; Regional Planning; Science Education; Social Policy; Social Welfare; Sports; Structural Architecture; Telecommunications Engineering; Textile Technology; Tourism; Town Planning; Traditional Eastern Medicine), Doctor's Degree (Archaeology; Architecture; Biological and Life Sciences; Biology; Business Administration; Business and Commerce; Chemistry; Civil Engineering; Computer Education; Computer Engineering; East Asian Studies; Economics; Education; Electrical Engineering; Electronic Engineering; English; Environmental Engineering; Ethnology; Finance; Fishery; Food Technology; History; Home Economics; Information Management; Information Sciences; Insurance; Japanese; Korean; Law; Leisure Studies; Literature; Marine Engineering; Materials Engineering; Mathematics; Mechanical Engineering; Multimedia; Natural Resources; Naval Architecture; Physics; Real Estate; Sports; Structural Architecture; Tourism; Town Planning; Welfare and Protective Services)

Student Services: Sports Facilities, Health Services, Library, Residential Facilities

Periodicals: Journals of Research Institutes

Publishing house: University Press

Academic Staff 2013-2014	MALE	FEMALE	TOTAL
FULL-TIME			797
Student Numbers 2013-2014			
All (Foreign Included)			12942

Last Update: 02-03-2018

Pukyong National University (PKNU)

45, Yongso-ro Nam-Gu
Pusan 48513
Tel: +82(51) 629-4114
Fax: +82(51) 629-5119
Website: http://www.pknu.ac.kr
President: Young-Seup Kim
Tel: +82(51) 620-6000

College

Business Administration (Business Administration; International Business); **Engineering** (Architecture; Automation and Control Engineering; Automotive Engineering; Biomedical Engineering; Chemical Engineering; Civil Engineering; Computer Engineering; Computer Graphics; Electrical Engineering; Electronic Engineering; Engineering; Engineering Management; Fire Science; Graphic Arts; Heating and Refrigeration; Industrial Chemistry; Information Technology; Materials Engineering; Mechanical Engineering; Metallurgical Engineering; Polymer and Plastics Technology; Safety Engineering; Structural Architecture; Telecommunications Engineering); **Environmental and Marine Sciences and Technology** (Aeronautical and Aerospace Engineering; Bioengineering; Ecology; Energy Engineering; Environmental Engineering; Environmental Studies; Marine Engineering; Marine Science and Oceanography; Meteorology; Naval Architecture); **Fisheries Sciences** (Agricultural Business; Agricultural Economics; Agricultural Education; Aquaculture; Biological and Life Sciences; Biotechnology; Fishery; Food Science; Food Technology; Hygiene; Industrial Management; Marine Biology; Nutrition; Public Health); **Humanities and Social Sciences** (Arts and Humanities; Communication Arts; English; Fashion Design; Graphic Design; History; Industrial Design; International Relations; International Studies; Japanese; Korean; Law; Literature; Mass Communication; Political Sciences; Preschool Education; Public Administration; Regional Studies; Social Sciences); **Natural Sciences** (Applied Mathematics; Chemistry; Microbiology; Natural Sciences; Nursing; Physics; Sports; Statistics)

Department/Division

Undeclared and Exploratory Major program (UEM) (Arts and Humanities; Business Administration; Engineering; Environmental Studies; Fishery; Marine Engineering; Marine Science and Oceanography; Natural Sciences; Social Sciences)

Graduate School

Business Administration (Business Administration; Economics; Hotel and Restaurant; International Business; Taxation; Tourism; Transport Management); **Education** (Art Education; Education; Educational Sciences; Humanities and Social Science Education; Physical Education; Science Education; Teacher Training); **Graduate Studies**; **Industry** (Architecture; Design; Engineering; Marine Science and Oceanography; Natural Sciences); **International Studies** (American Studies; Chinese; Communication Arts; Film; Foreign Languages Education; International Studies; Japanese; Journalism; Political Sciences; Visual Arts)

Further information: Also foreign student programme

History: Founded 1996, incorporating Pusan National University of Technology, now Yongdang Campus (founded 1924), and National Fisheries University of Pusan, now Daeyeon Campus (founded 1941).

Academic year: March to December (March-June; August-December)

Admission requirements: Graduation from high school and entrance examination

Fees: 1.2m (Won)

Main language(s) of instruction: Korean, English

Accrediting agency: Korean Council for University Education (KCUE)

Degrees and diplomas: Bachelor's Degree, Master's Degree (American Studies; Aquaculture; Architecture; Art Education; Asian Studies; Business Administration; Chinese; Communication Arts; Design; Economics; Education; Engineering; Environmental Studies; Fishery; Foreign Languages Education; Humanities and Social Science Education; Industrial Design; International Studies; Japanese; Journalism; Law; Literature; Marine Science and Oceanography; Mass Communication; Natural Sciences; Physical Education; Political Sciences; Public Administration; Regional Studies; Science Education), Doctor's Degree (Aeronautical and Aerospace Engineering; Agricultural Business; Agricultural Economics; Applied Mathematics; Automation and Control Engineering; Bioengineering; Biological and Life Sciences; Biomedical Engineering; Biotechnology; Business Administration; Chemical Engineering; Chemistry; Civil Engineering; Computer Engineering; Construction Engineering; Economics; Educational and Student Counselling; Electrical Engineering; Electronic Engineering; Energy Engineering; English; Environmental Engineering; Environmental

Studies; Fashion Design; Fishery; Food Science; Food Technology; Graphic Arts; Heating and Refrigeration; History; Human Resources; Industrial Chemistry; Industrial Design; Industrial Engineering; Information Technology; International Business; International Relations; International Studies; Japanese; Korean; Law; Literature; Marine Biology; Marine Engineering; Marine Science and Oceanography; Mass Communication; Materials Engineering; Mechanical Engineering; Metallurgical Engineering; Meteorology; Microbiology; Naval Architecture; Physics; Political Sciences; Polymer and Plastics Technology; Preschool Education; Public Administration; Regional Studies; Safety Engineering; Sound Engineering (Acoustics); Structural Architecture; Telecommunications Engineering; Transport Management)

Student Services: Academic Counselling, Careers Guidance, Sports Facilities, Language Laboratory, Health Services, Canteen, Library, IT Centre, Residential Facilities

Periodicals: Pukyong Journal

Academic Staff 2013-2014	MALE	FEMALE	TOTAL
FULL-TIME			c. 570
Student Numbers 2013-2014			
All (Foreign Included)			c. 28100
Foreign only			1000

Last Update: 02-03-2018

Pusan National University (PNU)

2, Busandaehak-ro 63beon-gil Geumjeong-gu
Pusan 46241
Tel: +82(51) 512-0311
Fax: +82(51) 582-6980
Website: http://www.pusan.ac.kr
President: Ho-Hwan Chun

College

Arts (Dance; Design; Fine Arts; Music; Visual Arts); **Economics and International Trade** (Economics; International Business); **Education** (Education); **Engineering** (Aeronautical and Aerospace Engineering; Architecture; Automation and Control Engineering; Chemical Engineering; Civil Engineering; Computer Engineering; Electrical and Electronic Engineering; Engineering; Environmental Engineering; Industrial Engineering; Marine Engineering; Materials Engineering; Measurement and Precision Engineering; Mechanical Engineering; Metallurgical Engineering; Polymer and Plastics Technology; Production Engineering; Textile Technology; Town Planning; Urban Studies); **Human Ecology** (Ecology; Environmental Studies; Home Economics); **Humanities** (Archaeology; Arts and Humanities; Chinese;

English; French; German; History; Japanese; Korean; Linguistics; Literature; Philosophy; Russian); **Law** (Law); **Medicine** (Medicine; Nursing); **Nanoscience and Nanotechnology** (Nanotechnology); **Natural Resource and Life Sciences** (Agricultural Economics; Animal Husbandry; Biochemistry; Bioengineering; Biological and Life Sciences; Biomedical Engineering; Environmental Engineering; Environmental Studies; Food Science; Food Technology; Horticulture; Landscape Architecture; Natural Resources); **Natural Sciences** (Biology; Chemistry; Computer Science; Earth Sciences; Geology; Marine Science and Oceanography; Mathematics; Microbiology; Molecular Biology; Natural Sciences; Physics; Statistics); **Nursing** (Nursing); **Pharmacy** (Pharmacy); **Social Sciences** (Archiving; Communication Studies; Information Sciences; International Relations; Library Science; Political Sciences; Psychology; Public Administration; Social Sciences; Social Welfare; Sociology); **Sport Science** (Sports)

School

Business (Accountancy; Business Administration; Business and Commerce; Economics; International Business; International Studies)

Department/Division

Tourism and Convention (Service Trades; Tourism)

Institute

Basic Sciences (Natural Sciences); **Computer and Information Communication** (Computer Science; Telecommunications Services); **Genetic Engineering** (Genetics); **Industrial Technology** (Industrial Engineering); **Mechanical Technology** (Mechanical Engineering); **Oral Biotechnology** (Biotechnology); **Technology and Industry** (Industrial Engineering; Technology)

Centre

Dielectric and Advanced Matter Physics (Electrical Engineering; Physics); **Dye Manufacturing**; **Korean Studies** (Korean)

Graduate School

Graduate Studies (Arts and Humanities; Business Administration; Economics; Education; Engineering; Fine Arts; Home Economics; International Business; Law; Medicine; Nanotechnology; Natural Sciences; Pharmacy; Social Sciences; Sports)
Further information: Also University Hospital
History: Founded 1946 as Pusan National College, acquired present status and title 1953.
Academic year: March to December (March-June; August-December)
Admission requirements: Secondary school certificate and entrance examination

Main language(s) of instruction: Korean
Accrediting agency: Korean Council for University Education (KCUE)
Degrees and diplomas: Bachelor's Degree, Master's Degree (Accountancy; Aeronautical and Aerospace Engineering; Agricultural Economics; Animal Husbandry; Archaeology; Architecture; Archiving; Automation and Control Engineering; Bioengineering; Biological and Life Sciences; Business Administration; Ceramic Art; Chemical Engineering; Chemistry; Child Care and Development; Chinese; Civil Engineering; Clothing and Sewing; Cognitive Sciences; Communication Studies; Computer Engineering; Computer Graphics; Computer Science; Conducting; Dance; Data Processing; Dentistry; Design; Earth Sciences; Economics; Education; Education of the Gifted; Electrical Engineering; Electronic Engineering; Energy Engineering; Engineering Drawing and Design; English; Environmental Engineering; Environmental Studies; Family Studies; Finance; Fine Arts; Food Science; Foreign Languages Education; Geology; German; Graphic Design; Handicrafts; Heritage Preservation; History; Horticulture; Industrial Engineering; Information Management; Information Sciences; Information Technology; Interior Design; International and Comparative Education; International Business; International Relations; Japanese; Korean; Landscape Architecture; Law; Library Science; Literature; Management; Marine Engineering; Marine Science and Oceanography; Marketing; Materials Engineering; Mathematics; Mechanical Engineering; Media Studies; Meteorology; Molecular Biology; Music; Music Theory and Composition; Musical Instruments; Nanotechnology; Naval Architecture; Nuclear Engineering; Nutrition; Painting and Drawing; Pharmacy; Philosophy; Physical Education; Physics; Political Sciences; Polymer and Plastics Technology; Power Engineering; Preschool Education; Psychology; Public Administration; Robotics; Russian; Science Education; Social Welfare; Sociology; Special Education; Sports; Statistics; Structural Architecture; Surveying and Mapping; Textile Design; Thermal Engineering; Town Planning; Transport Engineering; Visual Arts; Weaving; Women's Studies), Doctor's Degree (Accountancy; Aeronautical and Aerospace Engineering; Animal Husbandry; Archaeology; Architecture; Archiving; Automation and Control Engineering; Bioengineering; Biological and Life Sciences; Business Administration; Ceramics and Glass Technology; Chemical Engineering; Chemistry; Child Care and Development; Chinese; Civil Engineering; Clothing and Sewing; Cognitive Sciences; Communication Studies; Computer Engineering; Computer Graphics; Computer Science; Construction Engineering; Continuing Education; Cultural Studies; Curriculum; Data Processing; Dentistry; Design; Earth Sciences; Economics; Education; Education of the Gifted; Educational Administration; Educational and Student Counselling; Educational Sciences; Electrical Engineering; Electronic Engineering; Energy

Engineering; English; Environmental Engineering; Environmental Studies; Family Studies; Finance; Fine Arts; Food Science; Foreign Languages Education; Geology; German; Handicrafts; Heritage Preservation; History; Horticulture; Humanities and Social Science Education; Industrial Engineering; Information Management; Information Sciences; Interior Design; International and Comparative Education; International Business; International Economics; International Relations; Japanese; Korean; Landscape Architecture; Library Science; Linguistics; Literature; Machine Building; Management; Marine Engineering; Marine Science and Oceanography; Marketing; Materials Engineering; Mathematics; Mechanical Engineering; Media Studies; Metallurgical Engineering; Meteorology; Molecular Biology; Music; Musicology; Nanotechnology; Natural Resources; Naval Architecture; Nuclear Engineering; Nutrition; Oral Pathology; Orthodontics; Painting and Drawing; Periodontics; Pharmacy; Philosophy; Philosophy of Education; Physical Education; Physics; Political Sciences; Polymer and Plastics Technology; Power Engineering; Preschool Education; Production Engineering; Psychology; Public Administration; Robotics; Russian; Science Education; Social Welfare; Sociology; Special Education; Sports; Statistics; Structural Architecture; Surveying and Mapping; Taxation; Textile Design; Thermal Engineering; Tourism; Town Planning; Transport Engineering; Visual Arts; Women's Studies). Also integrated Master's-Doctorate Programmes

Student Services: Academic Counselling, Social Counselling, Careers Guidance, Nursery Care, Cultural Activities, Sports Facilities, Language Laboratory, Health Services, Canteen, Foreign Studies Centre, Library, Residential Facilities

Publishing house: PNU Press

Student Numbers 2015-2016	MALE	FEMALE	TOTAL
All (Foreign Included)			27780
Foreign only			1547

Last Update: 02-03-2018

Seoul National University (SNU)

1 Gwanak-ro, Gwanak-gu
Seoul 151-742
Tel: +82(2) 880-5114
Fax: +82(2) 887-8658, +82(2) 885-5272
Website: http://www.useoul.edu
President: Nak-in Sung
Tel: +82(2) 880-5001/2/3

College

Agriculture and Life Sciences (Agricultural Economics; Agricultural Engineering; Agriculture; Applied Chemistry; Bioengineering; Biological and Life Sciences; Biology;

Biotechnology; Botany; Food Science; Forestry; Rural Planning); **Business Administration** (Business Administration); **Education** (Education; Foreign Languages Education; Humanities and Social Science Education; Mathematics Education; Native Language Education; Physical Education; Science Education); **Engineering** (Aeronautical and Aerospace Engineering; Architecture; Bioengineering; Chemical Engineering; Civil Engineering; Computer Engineering; Computer Science; Electrical Engineering; Energy Engineering; Engineering; Environmental Engineering; Industrial Engineering; Marine Engineering; Materials Engineering; Mechanical Engineering; Naval Architecture; Nuclear Engineering; Structural Architecture); **Fine Arts** (Design; Fine Arts; Handicrafts; Painting and Drawing; Sculpture); **Human Ecology** (Child Care and Development; Clothing and Sewing; Consumer Studies; Cooking and Catering; Nutrition); **Humanities** (Aesthetics; Archaeology; Art History; Arts and Humanities; Asian Studies; Chinese; English; French; German; History; Korean; Linguistics; Literature; Philosophy; Religious Studies; Russian; South and Southeast Asian Languages; Spanish); **Law** (Law); **Liberal Studies**; **Medicine** (Medicine); **Music** (Music; Music Theory and Composition; Musical Instruments; Singing); **Natural Sciences** (Astronomy and Space Science; Biological and Life Sciences; Chemistry; Earth Sciences; Environmental Studies; Mathematics; Natural Sciences; Physics; Statistics); **Nursing** (Nursing); **Pharmacy** (Pharmacy); **Social Sciences** (Anthropology; Communication Studies; Economics; Geography (Human); International Relations; Political Sciences; Psychology; Social Sciences; Social Welfare; Sociology); **Veterinary Medicine** (Veterinary Science)

School

Dentistry (*Professional Graduate*) (Dentistry); **Law** (*Professional Graduate*) (Law); **Medicine** (*Professional Graduate*) (Medicine)

Institute

Asian Institute for Energy (Energy Engineering); **Big Data** (Data Processing); **Greenbio Science Technology** (Biological and Life Sciences; Environmental Studies); **Peace and Unification Studies** (International Relations; Peace and Disarmament); **Research in Finance and Economics** (Economics; Finance)

Graduate School

Business (Business Administration); **Convergence Science and Technology** (Artificial Intelligence; Biological and Life Sciences; Biomedicine; Medicine; Molecular Biology; Nanotechnology; Pharmacology); **Environmental Studies** (Environmental Studies); **Graduate Studies** (Arts and Humanities; Engineering; Fine Arts; Medicine; Music; Natural Sciences; Social Sciences); **International Agriculture**

Technology (Agricultural Engineering); **International Studies** (International Studies); **Public Administration** (Public Administration); **Public Health** (Public Health)

Research Division

Bio-MAX/N-Bio (Biological and Life Sciences); **Environment and Sustainability** (Environmental Studies)

Further information: Also 61 Research Institutes of the Colleges. University Hospital

History: Founded 1946 in succession to former Keijo Imperial University. Reorganized 1975. A State Institution under the jurisdiction of the Ministry of Education.

Academic year: March to February (March-June; September-February)

Admission requirements: Graduation from high school or teachers' college, or equivalent qualification recognized by the Ministry of Education in Korea, and entrance examination

Main language(s) of instruction: Korean, English

Accrediting agency: Korean Council for University Education (KCUE)

Degrees and diplomas: Bachelor's Degree, Master's Degree (Aeronautical and Aerospace Engineering; Aesthetics; Agricultural Economics; Agricultural Education; Agricultural Engineering; Agriculture; Animal Husbandry; Anthropology; Applied Chemistry; Archaeology; Architecture; Archiving; Art Education; Art History; Art Management; Astronomy and Space Science; Bioengineering; Biological and Life Sciences; Biology; Biomedicine; Biophysics; Biotechnology; Business Administration; Cell Biology; Chemical Engineering; Chemistry; Child Care and Development; Chinese; Civil Engineering; Classical Languages; Cognitive Sciences; Communication Studies; Comparative Literature; Computer Engineering; Computer Science; Consumer Studies; Crop Production; Dentistry; Design; Earth Sciences; Economic and Finance Policy; Economics; Education; Electrical Engineering; Energy Engineering; Engineering Drawing and Design; Engineering Management; English; Entomology; Environmental Engineering; Environmental Studies; Family Studies; Fashion Design; Food Science; Foreign Languages Education; Forestry; French; Gender Studies; Genetics; Geography (Human); German; Handicrafts; History; Home Economics Education; Horticulture; Humanities and Social Science Education; Industrial Engineering; International Relations; Korean; Law; Linguistics; Literature; Marine Engineering; Marketing; Materials Engineering; Mathematics; Mechanical Engineering; Medical Technology; Medicine; Meteorology; Microbiology; Music; Music Education; Music Theory and Composition; Musical Instruments; Musicology; Native Language Education; Naval Architecture; Neurosciences; Nursing; Nutrition; Oncology; Painting and Drawing; Performing Arts; Petroleum and Gas Engineering; Pharmacology; Pharmacy; Philosophy; Physical Education; Physics; Political Sciences; Preschool Education; Psychology; Religious Studies; Rural Planning; Russian; Science Education; Sculpture; Singing; Social Welfare; Sociology; Spanish; Special Education; Statistics; Teacher Training; Textile Design; Town Planning; Veterinary Science; Vocational Education; Zoology), Doctor's Degree (Aeronautical and Aerospace Engineering; Aesthetics; Agricultural Economics; Agricultural Education; Agricultural Engineering; Agriculture; Animal Husbandry; Anthropology; Applied Chemistry; Archaeology; Architecture; Archiving; Art Education; Art History; Art Management; Astronomy and Space Science; Bioengineering; Biological and Life Sciences; Biology; Biomedicine; Biophysics; Biotechnology; Business Administration; Cell Biology; Chemical Engineering; Chemistry; Child Care and Development; Chinese; Civil Engineering; Classical Languages; Cognitive Sciences; Communication Studies; Comparative Literature; Computer Engineering; Computer Science; Consumer Studies; Crop Production; Dentistry; Design; Earth Sciences; Economic and Finance Policy; Economics; Education; Electrical Engineering; Energy Engineering; Engineering Drawing and Design; Engineering Management; English; Entomology; Environmental Engineering; Environmental Management; Environmental Studies; Family Studies; Fashion Design; Fine Arts; Food Science; Foreign Languages Education; Forestry; French; Gender Studies; Genetics; Geography (Human); German; Handicrafts; History; Home Economics Education; Horticulture; Humanities and Social Science Education; Industrial Engineering; International Relations; Korean; Landscape Architecture; Law; Linguistics; Literature; Marine Engineering; Marketing; Materials Engineering; Mathematics; Mechanical Engineering; Medical Technology; Medicine; Meteorology; Microbiology; Music; Music Education; Music Theory and Composition; Musical Instruments; Musicology; Native Language; Native Language Education; Naval Architecture; Neurosciences; Nursing; Nutrition; Oncology; Performing Arts; Petroleum and Gas Engineering; Pharmacology; Pharmacy; Philosophy; Physical Education; Physics; Political Sciences; Preschool Education; Psychology; Public Administration; Public Health; Religious Studies; Rural Planning; Russian; Science Education; Singing; Social Welfare; Sociology; Spanish; Special Education; Statistics; Teacher Training; Textile Design; Town Planning; Veterinary Science; Vocational Education; Zoology). Also MBA; Executive MBA

Student Services: Health Services, Library, Residential Facilities

Periodicals: Economic Review, Engineering Report, Home Economics Journal, Journal of Environmental Studies, Journal of Humanities, Journal of Pharmaceutical Sciences, Journal of the College of Education, Korean Business Journal, Korean Development Policy Studies, Korean Economic Journal, Korean Journal of Public Administration, Korean Journal of Public Health, Law Journal, Proceedings of the College of Natural Sciences, Publications of the Research Institutes,

Seoul Journal of Medicine, Social Science Review, Social Sciences and Policy Studies
Publishing house: Seoul University Press

Academic Staff 2017-2018	MALE	FEMALE	TOTAL
FULL-TIME			5315
Student Numbers 2017-2018			
All (Foreign Included)			28378
Foreign only			699

Last Update: 05-03-2018

Seoul National University of Education (SNUE)

96 SeochoJoongang-ro Seocho-gu
Seoul 137-742
Tel: +82(2) 3475-2114
Fax: +82(2) 581-7711
Website: http://www.snue.ac.kr
President: Hang-Gyun Sihn

Department/Division
Computer Education (Computer Education; Teacher Training); **Early Childhood and Special Education** (Preschool Education; Special Education); **Elementary Education** (Primary Education); **English Education** (Primary Education); **Ethics Education** (Education; Ethics; Humanities and Social Science Education); **Fine Arts Education** (Art Education); **Korean Language Education** (Native Language Education); **Mathematics Education** (Mathematics Education); **Music Education** (Music Education); **Physical Education** (Physical Education); **Science and Technology Education for Life** (Science Education; Technology Education); **Science Education** (Science Education); **Social Studies Education** (Humanities and Social Science Education)

Graduate School
Education (Art Education; Computer Education; Cultural Studies; Curriculum; Education; Education of the Gifted; Educational Administration; Educational and Student Counselling; Educational Psychology; Environmental Studies; Foreign Languages Education; Humanities and Social Science Education; Mathematics Education; Museum Studies; Music Education; Native Language Education; Physical Education; Preschool Education; Primary Education; Science Education; Special Education; Technology Education)
History: Founded 1946 as Kyunggi Public Teachers School. Renamed Seoul National Teachers School 1949 and Seoul National Education University 1963. Acquired present status 1981 and present title 1990.
Main language(s) of instruction: Korean, English

Accrediting agency: Ministry of Education
Degrees and diplomas: Bachelor's Degree (Teacher Training), Master's Degree (Art Education; Computer Education; Education of the Gifted; Educational Administration; Educational Psychology; Foreign Languages Education; Humanities and Social Science Education; Museum Studies; Music Education; Native Language Education; Physical Education; Preschool Education; Primary Education; Special Education; Teacher Training)
Student Services: Academic Counselling, Social Counselling, Careers Guidance, Cultural Activities, Sports Facilities, Language Laboratory, Health Services, Library, IT Centre, Residential Facilities

Academic Staff 2013-2014	MALE	FEMALE	TOTAL
FULL-TIME			c. 100
Student Numbers 2013-2014			
All (Foreign Included)			c. 3420

Last Update: 05-03-2018

Seoul National University of Science and Technology (SEOULTECH)

172 Gongneung-dong 2 Nowon-gu
Seoul 139-743
Tel: +82(2) 970-6114, +82(2) 970-7114
Fax: +82(2) 970-6088
Website: http://www.seoultech.ac.kr
President: Jong Ho Kim
Tel: +82(2) 970-6000

Faculty
Cultural and Social Sciences (Arts and Humanities; Business Administration; Cultural Studies; English; Korean; Public Administration; Social Sciences; Sports); **Engineering I** (Automotive Engineering; Industrial Engineering; Materials Engineering; Mechanical Engineering; Safety Engineering); **Engineering II** (Architecture; Building Technologies; Civil Engineering; Engineering Drawing and Design; Structural Architecture); **Engineering III** (Automation and Control Engineering; Computer Science; Electrical Engineering; Electronic Engineering); **Engineering IV** (Chemical Engineering; Environmental Engineering; Food Technology); **Plastic Arts** (Painting and Drawing)

Institute
Technical Education Research

Centre
Computer Science (Computer Science)

Graduate School
Industry (Industrial Engineering)

History: Founded 1910 as a technical school, became Open University 1982; acquired present status and renamed Seoul National University of Technology 1988. Acquired present title 2009.

Academic year: March to December (March-June; August-December)

Admission requirements: Graduation from high school and entrance examination

Main language(s) of instruction: Korean, English

Accrediting agency: Korean Council for University Education (KCUE)

Degrees and diplomas: Bachelor's Degree, Master's Degree (Architectural and Environmental Design; Automation and Control Engineering; Automotive Engineering; Biomedical Engineering; Business Administration; Ceramic Art; Chemical Engineering; Chemistry; Civil Engineering; Computer Engineering; Computer Science; Data Processing; Design; Electrical Engineering; Electronic Engineering; Energy Engineering; Engineering Drawing and Design; English; Environmental Engineering; Fine Arts; Fire Science; Food Science; Food Technology; Health Sciences; Industrial Design; Information Technology; Literature; Materials Engineering; Mechanical Engineering; Nanotechnology; Optometry; Production Engineering; Railway Transport; Safety Engineering; Sports; Structural Architecture; Transport Management; Visual Arts; Weaving; Writing), Doctor's Degree (Automation and Control Engineering; Automotive Engineering; Biomedical Engineering; Business Administration; Ceramic Art; Chemical Engineering; Chemistry; Civil Engineering; Computer Engineering; Computer Science; Data Processing; Electrical Engineering; Electronic Engineering; Energy Engineering; Engineering Drawing and Design; English; Environmental Engineering; Fine Arts; Food Science; Food Technology; Industrial Design; Information Technology; Literature; Materials Engineering; Mechanical Engineering; Nanotechnology; Optometry; Production Engineering; Railway Transport; Safety Engineering; Sports; Structural Architecture; Visual Arts; Weaving; Writing)

Student Services: Academic Counselling, Social Counselling, Careers Guidance, Nursery Care, Cultural Activities, Sports Facilities, Language Laboratory, Canteen

Periodicals: Collegian Life Research, English Journal The Vision, Theses Collection, Vocational and Technical Education

Publishing house: SNPU Times Publishing Centre

Last Update: 08-03-2018

Sunchon National University (SCNU)

255 Jungang-ro
Suncheon-si 57922, Jeollanam-do

Tel: +82(61) 750-3114, +82(61) 750-3141
Fax: +82(61) 750-3016, +82(61) 750-3149
Website: http://www.sunchon.ac.kr
President: Yeong Moo Song

College

Education (Agricultural Education; Computer Education; Education; Foreign Languages Education; Humanities and Social Science Education; Mathematics Education; Native Language Education; Science Education; Teacher Training); **Engineering** (Aeronautical and Aerospace Engineering; Architecture; Automation and Control Engineering; Chemical Engineering; Chemistry; Civil Engineering; Computer Engineering; Electrical Engineering; Electronic Engineering; Engineering; Environmental Engineering; Health Sciences; Information Technology; Materials Engineering; Mechanical Engineering; Multimedia; Polymer and Plastics Technology; Telecommunications Engineering); **Humanities and Art** (Arts and Humanities; Chinese; Communication Arts; Fashion Design; Graphic Design; History; Japanese; Leisure Studies; Literature; Media Studies; Musical Instruments; Philosophy; Photography; Sports; Visual Arts; Writing); **Life Science and Natural Resources** (Agricultural Economics; Alternative Medicine; Animal Husbandry; Biological and Life Sciences; Biology; Botany; Cooking and Catering; Environmental Studies; Food Science; Food Technology; Forestry; Horticulture; Industrial Engineering; Landscape Architecture; Natural Resources; Nursing; Nutrition; Traditional Eastern Medicine; Zoology); **Social Sciences** (Accountancy; Business Administration; Consumer Studies; Economics; International Business; Law; Public Administration; Social Sciences; Social Welfare; Transport Management)

Graduate School

Business and Public Administration (Business Administration; Public Administration); **Education** (Education; Educational Sciences; Special Education; Teacher Training); **Graduate Studies** (Arts and Humanities; Business Administration; Computer Science; Engineering; Fine Arts; Natural Sciences; Social Sciences); **Industry** (Business Administration; Engineering; Information Sciences; Service Trades); **Social Culture and Arts** (Cultural Studies; Design; Fine Arts; Home Economics; Law; Social Welfare)

Research Division

Engineering Technology; Environment and Urban Problems; Food Industry; Humanities; Industrial Waste Material; Innovating Public Service; Jeonnam Silver Welfare; Minorenterprise Management; Namdo Culture; Nano Material Evaluation; Nano Technology; Oil Engineering; Polymer Chemistry; Practical Physical Education; Scientific Education; Social Science; Useful Natural Resource

History: Founded 1935 as Agricultural School. Acquired present status and title 1982.

Academic year: March to February (March-August; September-February)

Admission requirements: Graduation from high school and entrance examination

Main language(s) of instruction: Korean

Accrediting agency: Korean Council for University Education (KCUE)

Degrees and diplomas: Bachelor's Degree, Master's Degree (Administration; Aeronautical and Aerospace Engineering; Agricultural Economics; Agricultural Education; Agricultural Engineering; Alternative Medicine; Animal Husbandry; Biological and Life Sciences; Biology; Business Administration; Chemical Engineering; Chemistry; Child Care and Development; Civil Engineering; Clothing and Sewing; Computer Education; Computer Science; Consumer Studies; Economics; Education; Electrical Engineering; Electronic Engineering; English; Environmental Engineering; Environmental Studies; Family Studies; Food Science; Food Technology; Forestry; History; Horticulture; Industrial Chemistry; Information Technology; International Business; Japanese; Korean; Landscape Architecture; Law; Leisure Studies; Literature; Materials Engineering; Mathematics Education; Mechanical Engineering; Metallurgical Engineering; Multimedia; Nutrition; Pharmacy; Physical Education; Physics; Polymer and Plastics Technology; Public Administration; Sports; Structural Architecture; Telecommunications Engineering; Textile Design; Traditional Eastern Medicine; Transport Management; Visual Arts), Doctor's Degree (Accountancy; Administration; Agricultural Economics; Agricultural Education; Alternative Medicine; Animal Husbandry; Architecture; Automotive Engineering; Biological and Life Sciences; Biology; Business Administration; Business and Commerce; Chemical Engineering; Chemistry; Civil Engineering; Computer Engineering; Computer Science; Cooking and Catering; Cosmetology; Economics; Education; Electrical Engineering; Electronic Engineering; Environmental Engineering; Food Science; Food Technology; Foreign Languages Education; Forestry; Horticulture; Humanities and Social Science Education; Industrial Chemistry; Information Sciences; Information Technology; International Business; Korean; Landscape Architecture; Law; Literature; Materials Engineering; Mathematics; Mathematics Education; Mechanical Engineering; Metallurgical Engineering; Multimedia; Native Language Education; Natural Resources; Nutrition; Pharmacy; Polymer and Plastics Technology; Public Administration; Structural Architecture; Telecommunications Engineering; Transport Management)

Student Services: Careers Guidance, Language Laboratory, Health Services, Canteen, Foreign Studies Centre, Library, Residential Facilities

Periodicals: Bulletin of Information of SNU, Statistical Yearbook of SNU, Sunchon National University Bulletin

Publishing house: University Press. English University Press

Academic Staff 2012-2013	MALE	FEMALE	TOTAL
FULL-TIME			382
Student Numbers 2012-2013			
All (Foreign Included)			11282
Foreign only			144

Last Update: 06-03-2018

Ulsan National Institute of Science and Technology (UNIST)

50, UNIST-gil, Ulju-gun
Ulsan 44919
Tel: +82(52) 217-0114, +82(52) 217-1120
Website: http://www.unist.ac.kr
President: Mooyoung Jung

School

Business Administration (Accountancy; Finance; Management); **Design and Human Engineering** (*Also Graduate*) (Automation and Control Engineering; Industrial Design); **Electrical and Computer Engineering** (*Also Graduate*) (Computer Engineering; Computer Science; Electrical Engineering); **Energy and Chemical Engineering** (*Also Graduate*) (Chemical Engineering; Energy Engineering); **Life Sciences** (*Also Graduate*) (Biology; Biomedical Engineering); **Management Engineering** (*Also Graduate*); **Materials Science and Engineering** (*Also Graduate*) (Materials Engineering); **Mechanical, Aerospace and Nuclear Engineering** (*Also Graduate*) (Aeronautical and Aerospace Engineering; Mechanical Engineering; Nuclear Engineering); **Natural Science** (*Also Graduate*) (Chemistry; Mathematics; Physics); **Urban and Environmental Engineering** (*Also Graduate*) (Environmental Engineering)

Graduate School

Creative Design Engineering; **Interdisciplinary Management**; **Technology and Innovation Management**

History: Created 2009. Became a government-funded research institute for science and technology 2015

Academic year: March to February (March-August; September-February)

Admission requirements: High school certificate or equivalent for undergraduate degrees; Bachelor's degree or equivalent for Master's degrees; Master's degree or equivalent for PhD programme. English test score: a) Applicants should submit a test result of one of TOEIC, TOEFL (Code: 8807), IELTS, TEPS, G-TELP or TOEIC S/W, and the test date shall be within 2 years of the online application deadline; b)

Applicants do not need to submit the English test report if they submit one of the following: certificate stating that they have completed all of their Master's course in English; or applicants who are native English speakers

Main language(s) of instruction: English

Accrediting agency: Korean Council for University Education (KCUE)

Degrees and diplomas: Bachelor's Degree (Biological and Life Sciences; Biomedical Engineering; Business Administration; Chemical Engineering; Computer Engineering; Electrical Engineering; Energy Engineering; Engineering Management; Environmental Engineering; Materials Engineering; Mechanical Engineering; Natural Sciences; Nuclear Engineering), Master's Degree (Biology; Biomedical Engineering; Business and Commerce; Chemical Engineering; Chemistry; Computer Engineering; Computer Science; Electrical Engineering; Energy Engineering; Environmental Engineering; Materials Engineering; Mathematics; Mechanical Engineering; Nuclear Engineering; Physics), Doctor's Degree (Biology; Biomedical Engineering; Chemical Engineering; Chemistry; Computer Engineering; Computer Science; Electrical Engineering; Energy Engineering; Environmental Engineering; Materials Engineering; Mathematics; Mechanical Engineering; Nuclear Engineering; Physics)

Student Services: Sports Facilities, Health Services, Foreign Studies Centre, Library

Academic Staff 2017-2018	MALE	FEMALE	TOTAL
FULL-TIME			281
STAFF WITH DOCTORATE			
FULL-TIME			292
Student Numbers 2017-2018			
All (Foreign Included)			4255

Last Update: 24-05-2018

University of Seoul (UOS)

163 Seoulsiripdaero, Dongdaemun-gu
Seoul 02504
Tel: +82(2) 6490-6114, +82(2) 2210-2114
Fax: +82(2) 2243-2572
Website: http://www.uos.ac.kr
President: Yun-hi Won

College

Arts and Physical Education (Graphic Design; Industrial Design; Music; Physical Education); **Business Administration** (Business Administration); **Engineering** (Chemical Engineering; Civil Engineering; Computer Engineering; Computer Science; Electrical Engineering; Information Technology; Mechanical Engineering); **Humanities** (Asian Studies; Chinese; English; History; Korean; Literature; Philosophy); **Natural Science** (Biological and Life Sciences; Environmental Studies; Horticulture; Mathematics; Physics; Statistics); **Public Affairs and Economics** (Economics; International Relations; Law; Public Administration; Social Welfare; Taxation); **Urban Science** (Administration; Architectural and Environmental Design; Architecture; Computer Science; Earth Sciences; Environmental Engineering; Landscape Architecture; Sociology; Structural Architecture; Town Planning; Transport Engineering; Urban Studies)

School

General Education (Arts and Humanities; Biological and Life Sciences; Chemistry; Computer Science; English; Health Sciences; Mathematics; Physics; Sports; Writing)

Graduate School

Business Administration (Business Administration); **Design** (Design); **Education** (Education; Educational and Student Counselling; Foreign Languages Education; Humanities and Social Science Education; Mathematics Education; Native Language Education); **Graduate Studies** (Administration; Architecture; Biological and Life Sciences; Business Administration; Chemical Engineering; Civil Engineering; Computer Engineering; Computer Science; Design; Economics; Electrical Engineering; Energy Engineering; English; Environmental Engineering; Environmental Studies; History; Horticulture; International Relations; Korean; Landscape Architecture; Literature; Materials Engineering; Mathematics; Mechanical Engineering; Music; Music Theory and Composition; Musical Instruments; Nanotechnology; Philosophy; Physics; Protective Services; Public Administration; Singing; Social Welfare; Sociology; Statistics; Structural Architecture; Surveying and Mapping; Town Planning; Transport Engineering; Urban Studies); **Law** (Law); **Science and Technology** (Chemical Engineering; Civil Engineering; Electrical Engineering; Environmental Studies; Horticulture; Materials Engineering; Mechanical Engineering); **Taxation** (Taxation); **Urban Sciences** (*International*) (Administration; Town Planning); **Urban Sciences** (Administration; Architecture; Civil Engineering; Environmental Engineering; Environmental Management; Landscape Architecture; Protective Services; Public Administration; Social Welfare; Surveying and Mapping; Town Planning; Transport Management; Urban Studies)

Research Division

Humanities (Arts and Humanities); **Industrial Management** (Industrial Management); **Industrial Technology** (Industrial Engineering); **Information and Technology** (Information Technology); **Law** (Law); **Natural Science** (Natural Sciences); **Quantum Information Processing and Systems** (Information Sciences; Systems Analysis); **Seoul**

Institute for Transparency; **Seoul Studies** (Regional Studies); **Taxation** (Taxation); **Urban Safety and Security** (Protective Services; Safety Engineering); **Urban Science** (Urban Studies)

History: Founded 1918 as Seoul Public Agricultural College, became Seoul City University 1974, acquired present status 1987, changed name to University of Seoul 1997.

Academic year: March to February (March-August, September- February)

Admission requirements: Graduation from high school and entrance examination

Main language(s) of instruction: Korean

Accrediting agency: Korean Council for University Education (KCUE)

Degrees and diplomas: Bachelor's Degree (Arts and Humanities; Business Administration; Economics; Engineering; Fine Arts; Natural Sciences; Physical Education; Public Administration; Town Planning; Urban Studies), Master's Degree (Administration; Architectural and Environmental Design; Architecture; Biological and Life Sciences; Business Administration; Chemical Engineering; Civil Engineering; Computer Engineering; Computer Science; Design; Economics; Electrical Engineering; Energy Engineering; English; Environmental Engineering; Environmental Management; Environmental Studies; History; Horticulture; Information Technology; International Relations; Korean; Landscape Architecture; Literature; Materials Engineering; Mathematics; Mechanical Engineering; Music; Music Theory and Composition; Musical Instruments; Nanotechnology; Philosophy; Physics; Protective Services; Public Administration; Singing; Social Welfare; Sociology; Statistics; Structural Architecture; Surveying and Mapping; Taxation; Town Planning; Transport Engineering; Transport Management; Urban Studies), Doctor's Degree (Administration; Architecture; Business Administration; Chemical Engineering; Civil Engineering; Computer Engineering; Computer Science; Design; Economics; Electrical Engineering; Energy Engineering; English; Environmental Engineering; Environmental Studies; History; Horticulture; Information Technology; Korean; Landscape Architecture; Literature; Materials Engineering; Mechanical Engineering; Nanotechnology; Philosophy; Physics; Protective Services; Public Administration; Social Welfare; Sociology; Statistics; Structural Architecture; Surveying and Mapping; Taxation; Town Planning; Transport Engineering). Also MBA, Masters' and Doctorate Programmes offered with external Research Institutes

Student Services: Academic Counselling, Social Counselling, Careers Guidance, Nursery Care, Cultural Activities, Sports Facilities, Language Laboratory, Facilities for disabled people, Health Services, Canteen, Foreign Studies Centre, Library, Residential Facilities

Periodicals: International Journal of Urban Sciences

Publishing house: University of Seoul Press

Student Numbers 2015-2016	MALE	FEMALE	TOTAL
All (Foreign Included)			15967
Foreign only			696

Last Update: 07-03-2018

Private Institutions

Ajou University

Worldcup-ro 206, Yeongtong-gu
Suwon 16499, Gyeonggi-do
Tel: +82(31) 2001, +82(31) 219-2925
Fax: +82(31) 213-5158
Website: http://www.ajou.ac.kr
President: Dong-Yeon Kim

College

Business Administration (Business Administration; E-Business/Commerce; Finance); **Engineering** (Applied Chemistry; Architecture; Bioengineering; Chemical Engineering; Civil Engineering; Engineering; Industrial Engineering; Materials Engineering; Mechanical Engineering; Transport Engineering); **Humanities** (Arts and Humanities; Cultural Studies; English; French; History; Korean; Literature; Modern Languages); **Information Technology** (Computer Engineering; Electrical Engineering; Information Technology; Multimedia; Software Engineering); **International Studies** (Asian Studies; Business and Commerce; International Business; International Studies; Regional Studies); **Law** (Law); **Medicine** (Medicine); **Natural Sciences** (Biological and Life Sciences; Chemistry; Mathematics; Natural Sciences; Physics); **Nursing** (Nursing); **Pharmacy** (Pharmacy); **Social Sciences** (Economics; International Relations; Leisure Studies; Mass Communication; Media Studies; Political Sciences; Psychology; Public Administration; Social Sciences; Sociology; Sports); **University College** (Arts and Humanities; English; Mathematics; Natural Sciences; Writing)

Institute
Suwon Development (Development Studies)

Graduate School
Business Education (*Special Graduate School*) (Accountancy; Business Administration; E- Business/Commerce; Finance; Health Administration; Human Resources; Management; Marketing); **Clinical Dentistry** (*Special Graduate School*) (Dental Technology; Dentistry; Orthodontics;

Paediatrics; Surgery); **Education** (*Special Graduate School*) (Computer Education; Continuing Education; Distance Education; Education; Education of the Gifted; Educational Administration; Educational and Student Counselling; Foreign Languages Education; Higher Education; Humanities and Social Science Education; Mathematics Education; Native Language Education; Preschool Education; Primary Education; Psychotherapy; Science Education; Special Education; Teacher Training); **Engineering** (*Special Graduate School*) (Biotechnology; Chemical Engineering; Energy Engineering; Engineering; Environmental Engineering; Industrial Engineering; Mechanical Engineering; Private Law; Town Planning; Transport Engineering; Transport Management); **General Graduate Studies** (Architecture; Arts and Humanities; Atomic and Molecular Physics; Biological and Life Sciences; Biomedical Engineering; Biotechnology; Business Administration; Chemical Engineering; Chemistry; Civil Engineering; Computer Engineering; Economics; Education; Electrical Engineering; Energy Engineering; Engineering; English; Environmental Engineering; Finance; History; Industrial Engineering; Information Management; Information Technology; International Relations; Korean; Law; Literature; Management; Materials Engineering; Mathematics; Mechanical Engineering; Medicine; Multimedia; Natural Sciences; Nursing; Pharmacy; Physics; Political Sciences; Psychology; Public Administration; Social Sciences; Structural Architecture; Town Planning; Transport Engineering); **Information and Communication** (*Professional Graduate School*) (Computer Engineering; Information Sciences; Information Technology; Software Engineering); **Information and Communication Technology** (*Professional Graduate School*) (Information Management; Information Technology; Telecommunications Engineering); **International Studies** (*Special Graduate School*) (Development Studies; International Business; International Studies); **IT Convergence** (*Special Graduate School*) (Information Technology); **Law** (*Professional Graduate School*) (Law); **Medicine** (*Professional Graduate School*) (Medicine); **Public Affairs** (*Special Graduate School*) (Administration; Computer Science; Government; Real Estate; Social Welfare); **Public Health** (*Special Graduate School*) (Dental Hygiene; Epidemiology; Health Administration; Health Sciences; Occupational Health; Public Health)

Research Division

Ajou Transportation (Transport and Communications); **Automotive Parts Technology** (Automotive Engineering); **Basic Science** (Natural Sciences); **Energy and Climate Change** (Energy Engineering; Meteorology); **Engineering** (Engineering); **Environment** (Environmental Studies); **Humanities** (Arts and Humanities); **Industry-Academy-Research Cooperation**; **Information and Communications**

(Information Technology; Telecommunications Engineering); **Information and Electronics Technology** (Electronic Engineering; Information Technology); **Legal** (Law); **Management** (Management); **Nano and Information Technology** (Information Technology; Nanotechnology); **Social Sciences** (Social Sciences); **Ubiquitous Convergence**

Further information: Also university hospital

History: Founded in 1973

Academic year: March to December (March-June; September-December)

Admission requirements: Graduation from high school or foreign equivalent

Main language(s) of instruction: Korean, English

Accrediting agency: Korean Council for University Education (KCUE)

Degrees and diplomas: Bachelor's Degree, Master's Degree (Applied Chemistry; Applied Physics; Architecture; Bioengineering; Biological and Life Sciences; Biomedical Engineering; Biomedicine; Business Administration; Chemical Engineering; Chemistry; Civil Engineering; Computer Engineering; Computer Science; Cosmetology; Economics; Electrical Engineering; Electronic Engineering; Energy Engineering; Environmental Engineering; Finance; Health Administration; Human Resources; Industrial Engineering; Information Management; Information Technology; International Business; International Relations; Korean; Law; Literature; Management; Mass Communication; Materials Engineering; Mathematics; Mechanical Engineering; Media Studies; Medical Technology; Medicine; Multimedia; Neurosciences; Nursing; Oncology; Pharmacology; Pharmacy; Physics; Political Sciences; Psychology; Public Health; Regional Studies; Social Sciences; Structural Architecture; Town Planning), Doctor's Degree (Applied Chemistry; Applied Physics; Architecture; Bioengineering; Biological and Life Sciences; Biomedical Engineering; Biomedicine; Business Administration; Chemical Engineering; Chemistry; Civil Engineering; Computer Engineering; Computer Science; Cosmetology; Development Studies; Electrical Engineering; Electronic Engineering; Energy Engineering; Environmental Engineering; Finance; Health Administration; Human Resources; Industrial Engineering; Information Management; Information Technology; International Business; International Relations; International Studies; Korean; Law; Literature; Management; Materials Engineering; Mathematics; Mechanical Engineering; Media Studies; Medical Technology; Medicine; Multimedia; Neurosciences; Nursing; Oncology; Pharmacology; Pharmacy; Physics; Political Sciences; Psychology; Public Health; Social and Preventive Medicine; Social Sciences; Town Planning)

Student Services: Academic Counselling, Social Counselling, Careers Guidance, Sports Facilities, Health Services, Canteen, IT Centre, Residential Facilities

Academic Staff 2013-2014	MALE	FEMALE	TOTAL
FULL-TIME			645
Student Numbers 2013-2014			
All (Foreign Included)			14328
Foreign only			672

Last Update: 24-05-2018

Anyang University (AYU)

708-113 Anyang 5-dong Manan-gu
Anyang-shi 430-714, Kyonggi-do
Tel: +82(31) 467-0700
Fax: +82(31) 448-3870
Website: http://www.anyang.ac.kr
President: Chang-duk Jung

College

Humanities (Arts and Humanities; Chinese; Cosmetology; English; International Relations; Korean; Linguistics; Literature; Preschool Education; Russian); **Liberal Arts and Sciences** (Administration; Biotechnology; Business Administration; Computer Science; Marine Biology; Tourism); **Music** (Conducting; Music; Music Theory and Composition; Musical Instruments); **Science and Engineering** (Computer Engineering; Computer Graphics; Electrical Engineering; Electronic Engineering; Engineering; Environmental Engineering; Food Science; Information Technology; Multimedia; Nutrition; Statistics; Telecommunications Engineering; Urban Studies); **Social Sciences** (Business Administration; English; Performing Arts; Public Administration; Retailing and Wholesaling; Tourism; Translation and Interpretation); **Theology** (Christian Religious Studies; Cultural Studies; Religious Education; Religious Studies; Theology)

Centre
Korean Education (Korean)

Graduate School
Business and Public Administration (Business Administration; Public Administration); **Education** (Education); **Theology** (Theology)
Further information: Also Ganghwa Campus
History: Founded 1948, acquired present status 1995.
Academic year: March to December (March-June; August-December)
Main language(s) of instruction: Korean
Accrediting agency: Ministry of Education
Degrees and diplomas: Bachelor's Degree, Master's Degree (Business Administration; Communication Studies; Computer Education; Computer Engineering; Computer Science; Educational Administration; Educational and Student

Counselling; Electrical and Electronic Engineering; Engineering; Environmental Engineering; Family Studies; Foreign Languages Education; Information Sciences; Music; Native Language Education; Preschool Education; Psychology; Public Administration; Religion; Social Welfare; Statistics; Theology; Tourism; Urban Studies), Doctor's Degree (Business Administration; Computer Engineering; Computer Science; Education; Environmental Engineering; Information Sciences; Preschool Education; Telecommunications Engineering; Theology; Tourism; Urban Studies)
Student Services: Academic Counselling, Social Counselling, Careers Guidance, Nursery Care, Sports Facilities, Canteen, Library, IT Centre
Publishing house: The University Press

Academic Staff 2013-2014	MALE	FEMALE	TOTAL
FULL-TIME			220
PART-TIME			c. 201
Student Numbers 2013-2014			
All (Foreign Included)			c. 7540

Last Update: 25-01-2018

Asian Center for Theological Studies and Missions (ACTS)

1276, Gyeonggang-ro Okcheon-myeon
Yangpyeong-gun 476-751, Gyeonggi-do
Tel: +82(31) 770-7722, +82(31) 770-7793
Fax: +82(31) 772-5479, +82(31) 770-7774
Website: http://www.acts.ac.kr
President: Young Ook Kim

School
Theology (Chinese; Christian Religious Studies; Cultural Studies; English; Missionary Studies; Religious Education; Theology)

Graduate School
International Graduate Studies (*International - English*) (Bible; Missionary Studies; New Testament; Pastoral Studies; Philosophy; Religion; Theology); **Theology** (*Korean*) (Bible; Christian Religious Studies; Cultural Studies; Curriculum; Education; Educational and Student Counselling; New Testament; Pastoral Studies; Religious Education; Social Welfare; Theology; Welfare and Protective Services)
History: Founded 1968 as Center for Advanced Theological Studies for Asian Countries (CATS). Acquired present title 1973.
Main language(s) of instruction: Korean
Accrediting agency: Ministry of Education

Degrees and diplomas: Bachelor's Degree, Master's Degree (Bible; Christian Religious Studies; Missionary Studies; New Testament; Pastoral Studies; Religion; Theology), Doctor's Degree (Bible; Christian Religious Studies; Cultural Studies; New Testament; Pastoral Studies; Philosophy; Theology; Welfare and Protective Services)
Student Services: Library, Residential Facilities
Last Update: 08-03-2018

Baekseok University (BU)

76 Munam-ro Dongnam-gu
Cheonan-si 330-704, Chungcheongnam-do
Tel: +82(41) 550-9114
Fax: +82(41) 550-9113
Website: http://www.bu.ac.kr
President: Gab-Jong Choi

Course/Programme
Korean Language (*For International Students*) (Korean); **Special customized Cultural Experience Programmes** (East Asian Studies; Korean)

School
Christian Divinity (Pastoral Studies)

Department/Division
Business and Commerce (Business Administration; Business and Commerce; E- Business/Commerce; International Business); **Christian Fine Arts** (Fine Arts; Handicrafts; Interior Design; Painting and Drawing); **Christian Studies** (Administration; Christian Religious Studies; Media Studies; Missionary Studies; Philosophy; Psychology; Religious Education; Religious Music; Theology; Welfare and Protective Services); **Design and Image** (Communication Arts; Design; Industrial Design; Visual Arts); **Education** (Education; Physical Education; Preschool Education; Special Education); **Health Science** (Health Sciences; Medicine; Nursing; Optics; Physical Therapy); **Information and Communication** (Computer Engineering; Computer Science; Information Management; Information Sciences; Information Technology; Multimedia; Software Engineering); **Language and Literature** (Chinese; English; Japanese; Korean; Literature; Modern Languages; Russian); **Law and Public Administration** (Law; Police Studies; Public Administration); **Music** (Computer Science; Music; Music Theory and Composition; Musical Instruments; Singing); **Social Welfare** (Rehabilitation and Therapy; Social Studies; Social Welfare; Welfare and Protective Services); **Tourism** (Hotel Management; Management; Tourism; Translation and Interpretation)

Graduate School
Christian Studies (Administration; Bible; Christian Religious Studies; Fine Arts; Journalism; Literature; Mass Communication; Missionary Studies; New Testament; Philosophy; Psychology; Religious Music; Social Welfare; Theology); **Counselling** (Christian Religious Studies; Psychology); **Education** (Art Education; Computer Education; Continuing Education; Curriculum; Education; Educational Administration; Educational and Student Counselling; Educational Psychology; Educational Testing and Evaluation; Foreign Languages Education; Music Education; Native Language Education; Preschool Education; Primary Education; Special Education); **Music** (Music; Music Education; Music Theory and Composition; Musical Instruments; Religious Music; Singing); **Pastoral Ministry** (Pastoral Studies); **Social Welfare** (Child Care and Development; Education; Psychology; Psychotherapy; Social Welfare; Welfare and Protective Services)
History: Founded 1993 as a theology college. Acquired university status 1995 and renamed Cheonan University 1996. Formerly known as Cheonan University. Acquired present title 2006.
Main language(s) of instruction: Korean
Accrediting agency: Korean Council for University Education (KCUE)
Degrees and diplomas: Bachelor's Degree, Master's Degree (Administration; Child Care and Development; Christian Religious Studies; Computer Education; Continuing Education; Curriculum; Education; Educational and Student Counselling; Educational Psychology; Educational Testing and Evaluation; Fine Arts; Foreign Languages Education; Journalism; Mass Communication; Missionary Studies; Music; Music Education; Music Theory and Composition; Musical Instruments; Native Language Education; Pastoral Studies; Philosophy; Preschool Education; Primary Education; Psychology; Psychotherapy; Religious Music; Singing; Social Welfare; Special Education; Theology; Welfare and Protective Services), Doctor's Degree (Administration; Christian Religious Studies; Fine Arts; Literature; Missionary Studies; Philosophy; Psychology; Religious Music; Social Welfare; Theology)

Student Numbers 2015-2016	MALE	FEMALE	TOTAL
All (Foreign Included)			c. 14000
Foreign only			100

Last Update: 08-02-2018

Busan Arts College

Busan 71, Route 74
Busan 48429, Gyeonggi-do
Tel: +82(51) 628-3990

Fax: +82(51) 628-2719
Website: https://www.pia.ac.kr

Department/Division

Korean Music (Music); **Practical Dance** (Dance); **Practical Music** (Music); **Social Sports** (Sports); **Theatre** (Theatre); **Welfare, Art Therapy and Counseling** (Art Therapy; Psychology; Welfare and Protective Services)
History: Founded 1994.
Main language(s) of instruction: Korean
Accrediting agency: Ministry of Education
Degrees and diplomas: Bachelor's Degree (Art Therapy; Dance; Music; Psychology; Sports; Theatre; Welfare and Protective Services)
Last Update: 27-03-2018

Busan Digital University (BDU)

57 Jurye-ro, Sasang-gu
Busan
Tel: +82(51) 320-2000
Fax: +82(51) 320-2759
Website: http://uni.bdu.ac.kr
President: Sangbaek Yang

Department/Division

Business Administration (Business Administration; Cooking and Catering; Management); **Child Care and Education** (Child Care and Development; Continuing Education; Education); **Computer Engineering** (Computer Engineering); **Counseling and Therapy** (Art Therapy; Psychology); **Counseling Psychology** (Psychology); **Health Administration** (Health Administration); **Social Welfare** (Social Welfare); **Social Welfare Counseling** (Psychology; Social Welfare; Social Work)

Graduate School

Graduate Studies (Psychology; Social Welfare)
History: Founded 2002 as Dongseo Cyber University. Acquired current title 2003.
Main language(s) of instruction: Korean
Accrediting agency: Ministry of Education
Degrees and diplomas: Bachelor's Degree (Art Therapy; Business Administration; Child Care and Development; Computer Engineering; Continuing Education; Cooking and Catering; Education; Health Administration; Management; Psychology; Social Welfare; Social Work). Also Post-Bachelor Graduate Programme in Social Welfare
Last Update: 21-03-2018

Busan Presbyterian University (BPU)

Gusan-dong 764
Gimhae-si, 1894-68, Gyeongnam
Tel: +82(55) 320-2500
Fax: +82(55) 339-1161
Website: http://www.bpu.ac.kr/Default.aspx#
President: Yongkwan Kim

Course/Programme

Liberal Arts (Arts and Humanities)

Department/Division

Social Welfare Counseling (Psychology; Social Welfare); **Special Education** (Special Education); **Theology** (Theology)

Graduate School

Graduate Studies (Bible; Psychology; Psychotherapy; Social Welfare; Theology)
History: Founded 1953.
Main language(s) of instruction: Korean
Accrediting agency: Ministry of Education
Degrees and diplomas: Bachelor's Degree (Psychology; Social Welfare; Special Education; Theology), Master's Degree (Bible; Psychology; Psychotherapy; Theology)
Last Update: 28-03-2018

Busan University of Foreign Studies (BUFS)

69 Geumsaem-ro 485 beon-gil, Geumjeong-gu
Busan 609-815
Tel: +82(51) 509-5000
Fax: +82(51) 509-5005
Website: http://www.pufs.ac.kr
President: Hae-Lin Chung

College

Commerce and Business (Accountancy; Business Administration; Business and Commerce; Data Processing; E- Business/Commerce; Economics; Hindi; International Business; International Studies; Management; Regional Studies; Russian; Secretarial Studies; Taxation; Transport Management); **English, Japanese, Chinese Studies** (American Studies; Asian Studies; Chinese; East Asian Studies; English; English Studies; Hotel Management; Information Technology; Japanese; Literature; Tourism; Translation and Interpretation); **Humanities and Social Sciences** (Arts and Humanities; Foreign Languages Education; History; International Relations; Korean; Law; Literature; Media Studies; Police Studies; Social Welfare; Tourism); **Natural Sciences**

and **Engineering** (Computer Engineering; Information Technology; Leisure Studies; Mathematics; Multimedia; Natural Sciences; Sports; Sports Management); **Occidental Studies** (Business and Commerce; Eastern European Studies; French; French Studies; German; Germanic Studies; International Business; Italian; Latin American Studies; Portuguese; Russian; Spanish; Western European Studies); **Oriental Studies** (Arabic; Asian Studies; Business and Commerce; Eurasian and North Asian Languages; Hindi; Indonesian; Malay; South Asian Studies; Southeast Asian Studies; Thai Languages; Vietnamese)

Course/Programme

International Management Program for CEOs (*Graduate*) (Computer Science; International Business; International Economics; Management; Modern Languages; Regional Studies)

Graduate School

Education (Business Education; Computer Education; Foreign Languages Education; Humanities and Social Science Education; Mathematics Education; Native Language Education; Physical Education); **Graduate Studies** (Asian Studies; Chinese; Computer Engineering; Electrical Engineering; English; Foreign Languages Education; International Studies; Japanese; Korean; Law; Leisure Studies; Literature; Sports); **International Commerce and Area Studies** (Business and Commerce; Regional Studies); **Interpretation and Translation** (Chinese; English; Japanese; Korean; Translation and Interpretation); **TESOL** (English; Foreign Languages Education)

History: Founded 1982.

Main language(s) of instruction: Korean

Accrediting agency: Korean Council for University Education (KCUE)

Degrees and diplomas: Bachelor's Degree, Master's Degree (Asian Studies; Business and Commerce; Chinese; Computer Engineering; Education; Electronic Engineering; English; Foreign Languages Education; International Business; International Studies; Japanese; Korean; Law; Leisure Studies; Literature; Sports; Translation and Interpretation), Doctor's Degree (Asian Studies; Chinese; Computer Engineering; Education; Electronic Engineering; English; International Studies; Japanese; Korean; Law; Leisure Studies; Literature; Sports)

Student Services: Residential Facilities

Academic Staff 2013-2014	MALE	FEMALE	TOTAL
FULL-TIME			c. 325
Student Numbers 2013-2014			
All (Foreign Included)			c. 9500
Foreign only			1000

Last Update: 09-02-2018

Calvin University

142-12 Mabung-ri, Guseong-eup
Yongin-si 446-912, Gyeonggi-do
Tel: +82(31) 284-4752 284-4752
Fax: +82(31) 284-4588
Website: http://www.calvin.ac.kr
President: Jae-Youn Kim

Course/Programme

Child Care and Development (Child Care and Development); **Practical Music** (Jazz and Popular Music; Music; Musical Instruments); **Religious Music** (Religious Music); **Secretarial Studies and Ministry** (Public Administration; Secretarial Studies; Social Welfare); **Theology** (Theology)

Graduate School

Theology (Theology)

History: Founded 1997.

Main language(s) of instruction: Korean

Accrediting agency: Ministry of Education

Degrees and diplomas: Bachelor's Degree (Child Care and Development; Christian Religious Studies; Music; Musical Instruments; Psychology; Religious Music; Singing; Theology; Welfare and Protective Services), Master's Degree (Art Therapy; Child Care and Development; Education; Pastoral Studies; Psychology; Social Welfare; Theology), Doctor's Degree (Theology)

Student Services: Library, Residential Facilities

Student Numbers 2013-2014	MALE	FEMALE	TOTAL
All (Foreign Included)			c. 340

Last Update: 09-02-2018

Catholic Kwandong University (CKU)

24, Beomil-ro 579 beon-gil
Gangneung-si 210-701, Gangwon-do
Tel: +82(33) 649-7114, +82(33) 649-7085
Fax: +82(33) 641-1010, +82(33) 649-7969
Website: http://www.cku.ac.kr
President: Myung-Hun Chun

College

Basic Education (Arts and Humanities); **Education** (Computer Education; Education; Foreign Languages Education; Home Economics; Humanities and Social Science Education; Mathematics Education; Physical Education); **Humanities** (Advertising and Publicity; Arts and Humanities; Business Administration; Chinese; Cultural Studies; Economics; English; Finance; History; Information Management;

Information Technology; Japanese; Literature; Music);
Police and Law (Law; Police Studies; Public Administration; Social Welfare); **Tourism and Sports** (Health Administration; Health Sciences; Hotel Management; Leisure Studies; Parks and Recreation; Sports; Sports Management; Tourism)

School

Medicine (Business Administration; Medicine; Nursing)

Institute

Convergence (Architecture; Energy Engineering; Engineering; Information Technology; Medical Technology; Structural Architecture)

Graduate School

Business Administration (Administration; Advertising and Publicity; Business Administration; Health Administration; International Business; Police Studies; Public Administration; Social Welfare; Tourism); **Education** (Education; Educational Sciences; Teacher Training); **Fusion Energy** (Energy Engineering); **Graduate Studies** (Arts and Humanities; Business Administration; Engineering; Fine Arts; Health Sciences; Home Economics; Law; Physical Education; Welfare and Protective Services); **Missionary Seminary** (Missionary Studies; Theology)

Further information: Also 12 Research Institutes, 11 Research Centers

History: Founded 1954 as Junior College, acquired present status 1959. Formerly known as Kwandong University until acquired present title 2014. A Christian institution.

Academic year: March to February (March-September; September-February)

Admission requirements: Graduation from high school and entrance examination

Fees: 3,2 m.-4 m. per semester. 40% reduction on tuition fee for international students (Won)

Main language(s) of instruction: Korean

Accrediting agency: Korean Council for University Education (KCUE)

Degrees and diplomas: Bachelor's Degree, Master's Degree (Administration; Advertising and Publicity; Art Education; Art Therapy; Business Administration; Business Education; Civil Engineering; Computer Education; Computer Engineering; Continuing Education; Cooking and Catering; Economics; Educational Administration; Educational and Student Counselling; Educational Technology; Electronic Engineering; Energy Engineering; English; Environmental Engineering; Fine Arts; Foreign Languages Education; Health Administration; Health Education; History; Home Economics Education; Hotel Management; Humanities and Social Science Education; Industrial Arts Education; Information Management; Information Sciences; Information

Technology; Interior Design; International Business; International Studies; Korean; Law; Literature; Marine Engineering; Mathematics Education; Medical Technology; Music; Music Education; Native Language Education; Nursing; Physical Education; Police Studies; Public Administration; Religious Education; Social Welfare; Structural Architecture; Telecommunications Engineering; Tourism), Doctor's Degree (Administration; Business Administration; Civil Engineering; Computer Engineering; Cooking and Catering; Economics; Education; Electronic Engineering; Energy Engineering; English; Environmental Engineering; History; Hotel Management; Information Sciences; International Business; International Studies; Korean; Law; Literature; Nursing; Physical Education; Police Studies; Public Administration; Social Welfare; Structural Architecture; Telecommunications Engineering; Tourism)

Student Services: Academic Counselling, Social Counselling, Careers Guidance, Sports Facilities, Language Laboratory, Facilities for disabled people, Health Services, Canteen, Library, Residential Facilities

Periodicals: Journal of Humanities, Journal of Social Sciences, Journal of Student Life Research, Journal of Tourism Development

Academic Staff 2013-2014	MALE	FEMALE	TOTAL
FULL-TIME			525
Student Numbers 2013-2014			
All (Foreign Included)			9993

Last Update: 09-02-2018

Catholic University of Daegu (CU)

13-13 Hayang-ro, Hayang-eup
Gyeongsan-si 38430, Gyeongsangbuk-do
Tel: +82(53) 850-3052, +82(53) 850-3767
Fax: +82(53) 850-3050, +82(53) 359-6188
Website: http://www.cu.ac.kr
President: Jung-Woo Kim

College

CU-Leaders' (Arts and Humanities; Law; Medicine; Pharmacy; Political Sciences); **Design** (Architectural and Environmental Design; Communication Arts; Computer Graphics; Design; Fashion Design; Fine Arts; Industrial Design; Painting and Drawing); **Economics and Commerce** (Accountancy; Business Administration; Business and Commerce; Economics; Finance; Information Management; Information Technology; International Business; Real Estate; Taxation); **Education** (Computer Education; Education; Foreign Languages Education; Geography; History; Humanities and Social Science Education; Physical Education; Preschool Education); **Engineering** (Architecture; Automotive Engineering; Computer Engineering; Electronic Engineering; Engineering; Mechanical Engineering; Production Engineering; Telecommunications Engineering); **Health and Medical Science** (Biomedical Engineering; Health Sciences; Medicine; Optics; Physical Therapy; Radiology; Speech Therapy and Audiology); **Hospitality and Tourism Administration** (Food Science; Food Technology; Hotel Management; Tourism); **Law and Politics** (International Studies; Law; Police Studies; Political Sciences; Public Administration); **Liberal Arts** (Arts and Humanities; Chinese; Communication Studies; Dance; English; Italian; Japanese; Korean; Literature; Russian; Spanish); **Medicine** (Medicine); **Music** (Music; Music Theory and Composition; Musical Instruments; Singing); **Natural Sciences** (Biochemistry; Biological and Life Sciences; Biotechnology; Environmental Studies; Floriculture; Food Science; Home Economics; Landscape Architecture; Mathematics; Natural Sciences; Nutrition; Occupational Health; Paramedical Sciences); **Nursing** (Nursing); **Pharmacy** (Pharmacology; Pharmacy); **Social Sciences** (Advertising and Publicity; Child Care and Development; Journalism; Library Science; Mass Communication; Psychology; Public Relations; Social Sciences; Social Welfare; Sociology); **Theology** (Theology)

Institute
Korean Language (Korean)

Graduate School
Business Administration (Business Administration; Economic and Finance Policy; International Business; Management); **Design** (Design; Fashion Design; Floriculture; Industrial Design; Textile Design); **Education** (Art Education; Computer Education; Education; Educational Administration; Educational and Student Counselling; Educational Psychology; Environmental Studies; Foreign Languages Education; Home Economics Education; Humanities and Social Science Education; Mathematics Education; Music Education; Physical Education; Preschool Education; Science Education); **Health Science** (Food Science; Health Administration; Health Sciences; Hygiene); **International Studies** (Business Administration; International Business; International Studies); **Social Welfare** (Social Welfare); **Theology** (Bible; Catholic Theology; Theology)

Further information: Also University Hospital; St. Justino and St. Luke Campuses

History: Founded 1914 as Hyosung Women's University. Taegu Catholic College founded 1982, and the two Institutions merged 1995 to create present university.

Academic year: March to December (March-June; September-December)

Fees: 3,052,000-5,045,000 (Won)

Main language(s) of instruction: Korean

Accrediting agency: Korean Council for University Education (KCUE)

Degrees and diplomas: Bachelor's Degree, Master's Degree (Accountancy; Advertising and Publicity; Architectural and Environmental Design; Architecture; Arts and Humanities; Automotive Engineering; Biochemistry; Biological and Life Sciences; Biomedical Engineering; Biotechnology; Business Administration; Child Care and Development; Chinese; Communication Arts; Computer Education; Computer Engineering; Dance; Design; Economics; Education; Electrical Engineering; Electronic Engineering; English; Environmental Studies; Fashion Design; Finance; Floriculture; Food Science; Food Technology; Foreign Languages Education; Home Economics; Hotel Management; Humanities and Social Science Education; Industrial Design; Information Management; Information Sciences; International Business; International Studies; Japanese; Journalism; Korean; Landscape Architecture; Law; Library Science; Literature; Mass Communication; Mathematics; Mechanical Engineering; Medicine; Music Theory and Composition; Musical Instruments; Nursing; Nutrition; Occupational Health; Optics; Painting and Drawing; Paramedical Sciences; Pharmacology; Pharmacy; Physical Education; Physical Therapy; Police Studies; Political Sciences; Preschool Education; Production Engineering; Psychology; Public Administration; Public Relations; Radiology; Real Estate; Russian; Singing; Social Welfare; Sociology; Spanish; Speech Therapy and Audiology; Taxation; Telecommunications Engineering; Theology; Tourism; Welfare and Protective Services), Doctor's Degree (Advertising and Publicity; Biochemistry; Biological and Life Sciences; Biotechnology; Business Administration; Child Care and Development; Chinese; Computer Engineering; Economics; English; Environmental Studies; Finance; Floriculture; Food Science; Food Technology; Home Economics; Hotel Management; Humanities and Social Science Education; International Business; Japanese; Journalism; Korean; Landscape Architecture; Law; Literature; Mass Communication; Mathematics; Nutrition; Occupational Health; Paramedical Sciences; Pharmacology; Pharmacy; Public Relations; Real Estate; Russian; Social Welfare; Sociology; Spanish; Theology; Tourism; Welfare and Protective Services)

Student Services: Academic Counselling, Social Counselling, Careers Guidance, Nursery Care, Cultural Activities, Sports Facilities, Facilities for disabled people, Health Services, Library, Residential Facilities

Periodicals: Journal of the Research Center for Korean Women's Problems Institute, Research Bulletin of Catholic University of Taegu-Hyosung, The Research for Traditional Korean Culture

Publishing house: University Press

Student Numbers 2013-2014	MALE	FEMALE	TOTAL
All (Foreign Included)			c. 17000

Last Update: 09-02-2018

Catholic University of Pusan (CUP)

57 Oryundae-ro Geumjeong-gu
Pusan 609-757
Tel: +82(51) 515-5811
Fax: +82(51) 514-1576
Website: http://www.cup.ac.kr
President: Kyoungchul Youn
Tel: +82(51) 510-0500

College

Applied Sciences (Computer Engineering; Environmental Engineering; Environmental Management; Multimedia; Occupational Health); **Health Sciences** (Dental Technology; Health Administration; Laboratory Techniques; Physical Therapy; Radiology; Speech Therapy and Audiology); **Nursing** (Gerontology; Nursing); **Social Sciences** (Business Administration; Information Management; Information Technology; Management; Psychology; Social Sciences; Social Welfare); **Theology** (Theology)

School

Liberal Art and Humanities (Arts and Humanities)

Graduate School

Graduate Studies (Business Administration; Computer Engineering; Dental Technology; Health Administration; Laboratory Techniques; Nursing; Occupational Health; Physical Therapy; Radiology; Social Welfare; Speech Therapy and Audiology; Theology)
Further information: Also 5 Affiliated Research Institutes
History: Founded 1964 as Pusan Catholic College. Merged with Jisan College, acquired present status and title 1999.
Academic year: March to December (March-June; September-December)
Admission requirements: Graduation from high school
Main language(s) of instruction: Korean
Accrediting agency: Korean Council for University Education (KCUE)
Degrees and diplomas: Bachelor's Degree, Master's Degree (Business Administration; Computer Engineering; Dental Technology; Health Administration; Laboratory Techniques; Nursing; Occupational Health; Physical Therapy; Radiology; Social Welfare; Speech Therapy and Audiology; Theology), Doctor's Degree (Business Administration; Dental Technology; Health Administration; Laboratory Techniques; Nursing; Physical Therapy; Radiology)

Student Services: Academic Counselling, Careers Guidance, Nursery Care, Cultural Activities, Sports Facilities, Language Laboratory, Canteen, Library, IT Centre, Residential Facilities
Last Update: 09-02-2018

CHA University

120, Haeryong-ro
Pocheon-si 487-800, Gyeonggi-do
Tel: +82(31) 850-9200
Fax: +82(31) 543-2716
Website: http://en-new.cha.ac.kr
President: Hoon Kyu Lee

College

Biomedical Sciences (Biological and Life Sciences; Biomedicine; Biotechnology; Food Science; Molecular Biology); **Health Sciences** (Health Administration; Health Sciences; Information Management; Social Welfare); **Integrated Social Science** (Business Administration; International Business; Management; Mass Communication; Media Studies; Psychology; Public Relations; Video); **Nursing** (Nursing); **Pharmacy** (Health Sciences; Pharmacology; Pharmacy)

Graduate School

General Studies (Biomedicine; Health Sciences; Medicine; Molecular Biology; Nursing; Pharmacology; Pharmacy); **Medicine** (Health Sciences; Medicine); **Specialized Studies** (Alternative Medicine; Art Therapy; Health Administration; Health Sciences; Pharmacy; Public Health; Social Welfare; Welfare and Protective Services)
History: Founded 1997.
Admission requirements: Bachelor Degree
Main language(s) of instruction: Korean, English
Accrediting agency: Korean Council for University Education (KCUE); Ministry of Education and Human Resources Development
Degrees and diplomas: Bachelor's Degree, Master's Degree (Alternative Medicine; Art Therapy; Biological and Life Sciences; Biotechnology; Food Technology; Medicine; Pharmacology; Pharmacy), Doctor's Degree (Alternative Medicine; Art Therapy; Biological and Life Sciences; Biotechnology; Food Technology; Medicine; Pharmacology; Pharmacy)
Student Services: Academic Counselling, Social Counselling, Careers Guidance, Sports Facilities, Language Laboratory, Facilities for disabled people, Health Services, Library, Residential Facilities
Periodicals: University and Hospital Journal

Academic Staff 2013-2014	MALE	FEMALE	TOTAL
FULL-TIME			280
PART-TIME			c. 25
Student Numbers 2013-2014			
All (Foreign Included)			c. 840

Last Update: 12-02-2018

Changshin University (CSU)

262, Paryong-ro, Masanheowon-gu
Changwon-si 630-764, Gyeongsangnam-do
Tel: +82(55) 250-3001/9, +82(55) 250-1370
Fax: +82(55) 297-5181, +82(55) 250-1371
Website: http://eng.cs.ac.kr
President: Jungmook Kang

Department/Division

Arts and Music (Cosmetology; Design; Fine Arts; Music); **Arts and Social Science** (Accountancy; Business Administration; Police Studies; Preschool Education; Real Estate; Service Trades; Social Welfare); **Engineering** (Aeronautical and Aerospace Engineering; Civil Engineering; Computer Engineering; Fire Science; Mechanical Engineering; Production Engineering; Safety Engineering; Software Engineering); **Natural Science** (Food Science; Nursing; Nutrition)
History: Founded 1991 as Changshin College, acquired current status and title 2012.
Main language(s) of instruction: Korean
Accrediting agency: Ministry of Education
Degrees and diplomas: Bachelor's Degree (Accountancy; Aeronautical and Aerospace Engineering; Business Administration; Civil Engineering; Computer Engineering; Cosmetology; Design; Fine Arts; Fire Science; Food Science; Mechanical Engineering; Music; Nursing; Nutrition; Police Studies; Preschool Education; Production Engineering; Real Estate; Safety Engineering; Service Trades; Social Welfare; Software Engineering)
Student Services: Residential Facilities
Last Update: 22-03-2018

Cheongju University

298 Daeseong-ro Sangdang-gu
Cheongju-si 360-764, Chungcheongbuk-do
Tel: +82(43) 229-8114
Fax: +82(43) 229-8110
Website: http://www.chongju.ac.kr
President: Seong-Bong Jeong

College

Arts (Communication Arts; Design; Fashion Design; Film; Fine Arts; Handicrafts; Industrial Design; Theatre; Visual Arts); **Economics and Business Administration** (Accountancy; Business Administration; Business and Commerce; Economics; Hotel Management; International Business; Tourism); **Education** (Education; Humanities and Social Science Education; Mathematics Education; Music Education; Physical Education); **Health Sciences** (Biomedicine; Dental Hygiene; Health Administration; Health Sciences; Laboratory Techniques; Nursing; Occupational Therapy; Physical Therapy; Radiology; Sports Medicine); **Humanities** (Arts and Humanities; Chinese; Cultural Studies; English; History; Information Sciences; Japanese; Korean; Library Science; Literature); **Military Studies** (Military Science); **Science and Engineering** (Applied Chemistry; Architectural and Environmental Design; Architecture; Biological and Life Sciences; Biomedicine; Biotechnology; Civil Engineering; Computer Engineering; Electronic Engineering; Energy Engineering; Engineering; Environmental Engineering; Industrial Engineering; Information Technology; Landscape Architecture; Laser Engineering; Natural Sciences; Optical Technology; Pharmacology; Statistics; Structural Architecture; Town Planning)

Department/Division

Aeronautics (Aeronautical and Aerospace Engineering; Air Transport; Mechanical Engineering); **Social Sciences** (Advertising and Publicity; Communication Studies; International Relations; Law; Political Sciences; Public Administration; Public Relations; Real Estate; Social Sciences; Social Welfare; Sociology)

Graduate School

Graduate Studies (Arts and Humanities; Engineering; Fine Arts; Natural Sciences; Performing Arts; Social Sciences)
History: Founded 1947.
Academic year: March to February (March-August; September-February)
Admission requirements: Graduation from high school and entrance examination. Provision is made for the recognition of foreign qualifications
Main language(s) of instruction: Korean
Accrediting agency: Korean Council for University Education (KCUE)
Degrees and diplomas: Bachelor's Degree, Master's Degree (Accountancy; Advertising and Publicity; Architectural and Environmental Design; Bioengineering; Biology; Business Administration; Chemistry; Chinese; Civil Engineering; Computer Engineering; Dance; Economics; Electronic Engineering; English; Environmental Engineering; Film; Handicrafts; History; Hotel Management; Industrial Engineering; Information Sciences; Information Technology; International

Business; International Relations; Japanese; Journalism; Korean; Landscape Architecture; Laser Engineering; Law; Library Science; Linguistics; Literature; Mass Communication; Music; Optical Technology; Painting and Drawing; Physical Education; Physics; Political Sciences; Public Administration; Public Relations; Real Estate; Social Welfare; Structural Architecture; Theatre; Tourism; Town Planning; Visual Arts), Doctor's Degree (Architectural and Environmental Design; Business Administration; Chemistry; Computer Engineering; Economics; Electronic Engineering; English; Environmental Engineering; Film; Information Sciences; Information Technology; International Business; Korean; Landscape Architecture; Law; Library Science; Literature; Public Administration; Real Estate; Social Welfare; Structural Architecture; Theatre; Tourism)

Student Services: Sports Facilities, Library, Residential Facilities

Student Numbers 2013-2014	MALE	FEMALE	TOTAL
All (Foreign Included)			c. 13800
Foreign only			1200

Last Update: 09-02-2018

Chodang University

380 Muanro Muaneup
Muangun 534-701, Jeollanamdo
Tel: +82(61) 453-4960
Fax: +82(61) 453-4969
Website: http://www.chodang.ac.kr
President: Jong-Koo Park

School

Arts and Physical Education (Design; Music; Physical Education; Secretarial Studies); **Health and Medicine** (Environmental Studies; Health Administration; Health Sciences; Medicine; Nursing; Ophthalmology; Optics); **Humanities and Social Science** (Arts and Humanities; Business Administration; Child Care and Development; Chinese; E- Business/Commerce; English; Real Estate; Social Sciences; Social Welfare; Welfare and Protective Services); **Natural Sciences and Engineering** (Architecture; Civil Engineering; Computer Science; Cooking and Catering; Cosmetology; Electronic Engineering; Engineering; Health Sciences; Information Technology; Multimedia; Natural Sciences; Telecommunications Engineering); **Public Officials Nurture** (Economics; Fire Science; Law; Military Science; Police Studies; Political Sciences; Social Psychology; Sociology)

Graduate School

Graduate Studies (Business Administration; Computer Engineering; Cooking and Catering; Environmental Engineering; Industrial Design; Information Technology; Nursing; Ophthalmology; Optics; Physical Education; Public Administration; Social Welfare)

History: Founded 1994 as Chodang University of Technology. Acquired present title 1998.

Main language(s) of instruction: Korean

Accrediting agency: Korean Council for University Education (KCUE)

Degrees and diplomas: Bachelor's Degree, Master's Degree (Business Administration; Computer Engineering; Cooking and Catering; Environmental Engineering; Industrial Design; Information Technology; Nursing; Ophthalmology; Optics; Physical Education; Public Administration; Social Welfare)

Student Services: Library, IT Centre

Academic Staff 2013-2014	MALE	FEMALE	TOTAL
FULL-TIME			208
PART-TIME			176
Student Numbers 2013-2014			
All (Foreign Included)			4351

Last Update: 09-02-2018

Chongshin University (CUS)

San 31-3 Sadang-dong Dongjak-gu
Seoul 156-763
Tel: +82(2) 3479-0200
Fax: +82(2) 596-2602
Website: http://www.chongshin.ac.kr
President: Young-woo Kim
Tel: +82(2) 3479-0201

Department/Division

Child Studies (Child Care and Development); **Christian Education** (Christian Religious Studies; Religious Education); **Early Childhood Education** (Preschool Education); **English Education** (Foreign Languages Education); **History Education** (Humanities and Social Science Education); **Music** (Music); **Social Work** (Social Work); **Theology** (Theology)

Graduate School

Biblical Counseling (Bible; Psychology; Theology); **Christianity Social Work** (Administration; Christian Religious Studies; Social Psychology; Social Work); **Education** (Christian Religious Studies; Education; English; Foreign Languages Education; Linguistics; Literature; Preschool Education; Religious Education); **Graduate Studies** (Bible; Christian Religious Studies; History of Religion; Missionary

Studies; Music; New Testament; Preschool Education; Theology); **Intercultural Studies** (Cultural Studies; Theology); **Pastoral Ministry** (Cultural Studies; Pastoral Studies; Religious Practice; Theology)

History: Founded 1901 as as Pyongyang Seminary, acquired present status and title 1967.

Academic year: March to December (March-June; September-December)

Admission requirements: Graduation from High School or equivalent. For Department of Theology recommandation of a Presbytery of Hapdong denomination. Korean examination for foreign students

Fees: University, 2,144,000 per semester; Seminary, 1,760,000 (Won)

Main language(s) of instruction: Korean

Accrediting agency: Korean Council for University Education (KCUE); Ministry of Education and Human Resources Development; Asia Theological Association (ATA); ICHE

Degrees and diplomas: Bachelor's Degree, Master's Degree (Christian Religious Studies; Cultural Studies; Music; Pastoral Studies; Preschool Education; Psychology; Religious Practice; Social Work; Theology), Doctor's Degree (Bible; Christian Religious Studies; Cultural Studies; History of Religion; Missionary Studies; New Testament; Pastoral Studies; Preschool Education; Religious Practice; Theology)

Student Services: Academic Counselling, Careers Guidance, Language Laboratory, Canteen

Periodicals: Chongshin Review, Chongshin Theological Journal

Publishing house: Chongshin University Press; Chongshin Theological Seminary Press

Academic Staff 2013-2014	MALE	FEMALE	TOTAL
FULL-TIME			77
PART-TIME			148
Student Numbers 2013-2014			
All (Foreign Included)			3623

Last Update: 09-02-2018

Chosun University

375 Seosuk-dong Dong-gu
Gwangju-si 501-759, Gyeonggi-do
Tel: +82(62) 230-6486
Fax: +82(62) 232-7355
Website: http://www.chosun.ac.kr/eng
President: Dong-Oan Kang

College

Art and Design (Art History; Communication Arts; Design; Engineering Drawing and Design; Fine Arts; Industrial Design; Interior Design; Painting and Drawing; Sculpture; Visual Arts); **Business** (Accountancy; Business Administration; Business and Commerce; Economics; Finance; International Business; Management; Marketing); **Counselling Psychology** (Psychology); **Dentistry** (Dentistry); **Education** (Education; Foreign Languages Education; Home Economics Education; Humanities and Social Science Education; Mathematics Education; Music Education; Native Language Education; Science Education; Special Education); **Electronics and Information Engineering** (Automation and Control Engineering; Communication Studies; Computer Engineering; Data Processing; Electrical and Electronic Engineering; Electronic Engineering; Information Technology; Microwaves; Multimedia; Robotics; Telecommunications Engineering); **Engineering** (Aeronautical and Aerospace Engineering; Architecture; Bioengineering; Chemical Engineering; Civil Engineering; Electrical and Electronic Engineering; Electrical Engineering; Electronic Engineering; Energy Engineering; Engineering; Engineering Management; Environmental Engineering; Heating and Refrigeration; Industrial Engineering; Machine Building; Marine Engineering; Materials Engineering; Mechanical Engineering; Nanotechnology; Naval Architecture; Nuclear Engineering; Optical Technology; Polymer and Plastics Technology; Social Sciences; Structural Architecture); **Foreign Studies** (Arabic; Asian Studies; Chinese; English; French; German; Islamic Studies; Japanese; Russian; Spanish; Translation and Interpretation); **General Education** (Arts and Humanities; Communication Studies; Linguistics; Modern Languages); **Humanities** (Archaeology; Arts and Humanities; Chinese; English; History; Korean; Literature; Modern Languages; Philosophy; Writing); **Law** (International Law; Law); **Medicine** (Health Sciences; Medicine; Nursing; Paramedical Sciences); **Military Science** (Military Science); **Natural Medical Sciences** (Alternative Medicine; Biotechnology; Dentistry; Medicine; Pharmacy); **Natural Sciences** (Biological and Life Sciences; Biology; Biotechnology; Cell Biology; Chemistry; Computer Science; Food Science; Genetics; Information Technology; Marine Biology; Mathematics; Microbiology; Molecular Biology; Natural Sciences; Nutrition; Physics; Statistics); **Pharmacy** (Pharmacy); **Physical Education** (Dance; Physical Education; Sports); **Social Sciences** (Administration; International Relations; Journalism; Mass Communication; Police Studies; Political Sciences; Social Sciences; Welfare and Protective Services); **Speech-Language Pathology** (Communication Disorders; Speech Therapy and Audiology)

Graduate School

Art and Sports (Aesthetics; Art History; Communication Arts; Dance; Design; Fine Arts; Industrial Design; Interior Design; Leisure Studies; Multimedia; Music; Physical Education; Sports; Visual Arts); **Engineering** (Aeronautical and Aerospace Engineering; Architecture; Automation and

Control Engineering; Chemical Engineering; Civil Engineering; Computer Engineering; Electrical Engineering; Electronic Engineering; Energy Engineering; Engineering; Environmental Engineering; Industrial Engineering; Information Technology; Marine Engineering; Materials Engineering; Measurement and Precision Engineering; Mechanical Engineering; Mining Engineering; Naval Architecture; Nuclear Engineering; Optical Technology; Structural Architecture; Telecommunications Engineering); **Humanities and Social Sciences** (Accountancy; Arabic; Arts and Humanities; Business Administration; Chinese; Economics; Education; English; Foreign Languages Education; French; German; History; International Relations; Islamic Studies; Japanese; Journalism; Korean; Law; Literature; Mass Communication; Native Language Education; Philosophy; Political Sciences; Psychology; Public Administration; Russian; Social Sciences; Social Welfare; Spanish; Special Education; Speech Therapy and Audiology); **Interdisciplinary Cooperation Program** (Aesthetics; Alternative Medicine; Art History; Art Therapy; Biotechnology; Business and Commerce; Cultural Studies; Design; Engineering Drawing and Design; Health Sciences; Industrial Engineering; Information Technology; International Business; International Studies; Marine Engineering; Naval Architecture; Optical Technology; Pharmacology; Psychotherapy; Regional Studies; Safety Engineering; Translation and Interpretation; Transport Engineering); **Medical Science** (Biotechnology; Dental Technology; Dentistry; Medicine); **Natural Sciences** (Biology; Biotechnology; Chemistry; Computer Science; Earth Sciences; Food Science; Home Economics; Marine Biology; Mathematics; Mathematics Education; Natural Sciences; Nursing; Nutrition; Pharmacy; Physics; Science Education; Statistics)

History: Founded 1946.

Academic year: March to February (March to August; September-February)

Admission requirements: Graduation from high school and entrance examination

Main language(s) of instruction: Korean

Accrediting agency: Korean Council for University Education (KCUE)

Degrees and diplomas: Bachelor's Degree, Master's Degree (Accountancy; Aeronautical and Aerospace Engineering; Aesthetics; Alternative Medicine; Architecture; Art History; Art Therapy; Asian Studies; Automation and Control Engineering; Biology; Biotechnology; Business Administration; Business and Commerce; Chemical Engineering; Chemistry; Civil Engineering; Computer Engineering; Computer Science; Cultural Studies; Dental Technology; Dentistry; Design; Earth Sciences; Economics; Electrical Engineering; Electronic Engineering; Energy Engineering; English; Environmental Engineering; Fine Arts; Food Science; Foreign Languages Education; Health Sciences; History; Humanities

and Social Science Education; Industrial Engineering; Information Technology; Instrument Making; International Business; International Relations; International Studies; Japanese; Journalism; Korean; Law; Literature; Marine Biology; Marine Engineering; Mass Communication; Materials Engineering; Mathematics; Mathematics Education; Measurement and Precision Engineering; Mechanical Engineering; Medicine; Native Language Education; Natural Sciences; Naval Architecture; Nuclear Engineering; Nursing; Nutrition; Optical Technology; Pedagogy; Pharmacology; Pharmacy; Physical Education; Physics; Political Sciences; Public Administration; Safety Engineering; Science Education; Social Welfare; Special Education; Statistics; Structural Architecture; Telecommunications Engineering; Translation and Interpretation), Doctor's Degree (Accountancy; Aeronautical and Aerospace Engineering; Aesthetics; Alternative Medicine; Architecture; Art History; Art Therapy; Asian Studies; Automation and Control Engineering; Bioengineering; Biology; Biotechnology; Business Administration; Business and Commerce; Chemical Engineering; Chemistry; Civil Engineering; Computer Engineering; Computer Science; Cultural Studies; Dentistry; Earth Sciences; Economics; Electrical Engineering; Electronic Engineering; Energy Engineering; English; Environmental Engineering; Fine Arts; Food Science; Foreign Languages Education; Health Sciences; History; Humanities and Social Science Education; Industrial Engineering; Information Technology; Instrument Making; International Business; International Relations; International Studies; Japanese; Journalism; Korean; Law; Literature; Marine Biology; Marine Engineering; Mass Communication; Materials Engineering; Mathematics; Mathematics Education; Measurement and Precision Engineering; Mechanical Engineering; Medicine; Native Language Education; Natural Sciences; Naval Architecture; Nuclear Engineering; Nursing; Nutrition; Optical Technology; Pedagogy; Pharmacology; Pharmacy; Physical Education; Political Sciences; Public Administration; Safety Engineering; Science Education; Social Welfare; Special Education; Statistics; Structural Architecture; Telecommunications Engineering; Translation and Interpretation)

Student Services: Library, IT Centre, Residential Facilities

Periodicals: Cho Dae Hag Bo, Cho Dae Shin Moon, Chong-Hap Theses Collection, Chosun World (English), Maek, Ye-dae Shin Moon

Academic Staff 2013-2014	MALE	FEMALE	TOTAL
FULL-TIME			998
PART-TIME			622
Student Numbers 2013-2014			
All (Foreign Included)			23000
Foreign only			350

Last Update: 09-02-2018

Chugye University for the Arts

190-1 Bukahhyeondong Seodaemun-gu
Seoul 03762
Tel: +82(2) 362-5700
Fax: +82(2) 392-1777
Website: http://www.chugye.ac.kr
President: Sang-Hyok Yim

College

Fine Arts (Painting and Drawing; Printing and Printmaking); **Literature and Visual Communications** (Advertising and Publicity; Film; Mass Communication; Multimedia; Radio and Television Broadcasting; Writing); **Music** (Music; Music Theory and Composition; Musical Instruments; Singing)

Graduate School

Culture and Arts Management (Art Management; Business Administration; Cultural Studies; Film; Mass Communication; Writing); **Education** (Music Education); **Graduate Studies** (Art Management; Cultural Studies; Film; Media Studies; Music; Music Theory and Composition; Musical Instruments; Painting and Drawing; Singing; Writing)
History: Founded as a college 1974. Acquired present status and title 1997.
Main language(s) of instruction: Korean
Accrediting agency: Korean Council for University Education (KCUE)
Degrees and diplomas: Bachelor's Degree, Master's Degree (Art Management; Business Administration; Cultural Studies; Film; Mass Communication; Media Studies; Music; Music Education; Music Theory and Composition; Musical Instruments; Painting and Drawing; Singing; Writing), Doctor's Degree (Art Management; Cultural Studies; Writing). Also 1 year Postgraduate Research Programmes in Education of Korean Traditional Music and Education Policy of Korean Traditional Music.

Academic Staff 2013-2014	MALE	FEMALE	TOTAL
FULL-TIME			70
PART-TIME			c. 260
Student Numbers 2013-2014			
All (Foreign Included)			c. 1500

Last Update: 09-02-2018

Chung-Ang University (CAU)

84 Heukseok-ro Dongjak-gu
Seoul 156-756
Tel: +82(2) 820-5114, +82(2) 820-6114, +82(2) 820-6396
Fax: +82(2) 820-6393 813-8158

Website: http://www.cau.ac.kr/english
President: Chang-Soo Kim

College

Art (Dance; Fashion Design; Film; Fine Arts; Graphic Design; Interior Design; Music; Music Theory and Composition; Musical Instruments; Painting and Drawing; Performing Arts; Photography; Singing; Theatre; Writing); **Biotechnology and Natural Resources** (Animal Husbandry; Biological and Life Sciences; Biotechnology; Food Science; Food Technology; Natural Resources; Natural Sciences); **Business and Economics** (Advertising and Publicity; Business Administration; Economics; International Business; Management; Public Relations; Statistics; Transport Management); **Education** (Education; Foreign Languages Education; Physical Education; Preschool Education); **Engineering** (Chemical Engineering; Civil Engineering; Computer Engineering; Computer Science; Construction Engineering; Electrical and Electronic Engineering; Electrical Engineering; Electronic Engineering; Energy Engineering; Engineering; Environmental Engineering; Materials Engineering; Mechanical Engineering; Town Planning; Urban Studies); **General Education**; **Humanities** (American Studies; Chinese; East Asian Studies; English; English Studies; European Languages; European Studies; French; German; History; Japanese; Korean; Literature; Modern Languages; Philosophy; Russian; South and Southeast Asian Languages); **Medicine** (Medicine); **Natural Sciences** (Biological and Life Sciences; Biomedicine; Chemistry; Mathematics; Physics); **Nursing** (Nursing); **Pharmacy** (Pharmacy); **Social Sciences** (Information Sciences; International Relations; Journalism; Library Science; Mass Communication; Political Sciences; Psychology; Public Administration; Real Estate; Social Sciences; Social Welfare; Sociology; Town Planning); **Sport Sciences** (Sports)

Centre

Academy-Industry-Research Consortium; **Business Incubator** (Business Administration); **Digital Contents Resources** (Information Technology; Multimedia); **Industry-Academic Cooperation**; **Technology Transfer** (Law; Technology)

Laboratory

Advertising and Public Relations (Advertising and Publicity; Public Relations)

Graduate School

Advanced Imaging Science, Multimedia and Film (*Professional*) (Computer Graphics; Design; Film; Multimedia; Photography; Software Engineering; Visual Arts); **Arts** (*Special Graduate Programmes*) (Art Management; Design; Fine

Arts; Performing Arts; Visual Arts); **Chung-Ang Business School** (*Professional*) (Business Administration; Finance; Management); **Construction Engineering** (*Special Graduate Programmes*) (Architectural and Environmental Design; Construction Engineering; Geological Engineering; Structural Architecture; Town Planning); **Education** (*Special Graduate Programmes*) (Art Education; Computer Education; Continuing Education; Education; Educational Administration; Educational and Student Counselling; Educational Technology; Foreign Languages Education; Home Economics Education; Humanities and Social Science Education; Mathematics Education; Music Education; Native Language Education; Physical Education; Preschool Education; Science Education); **Food and Drug Administration** (*Special Graduate Programmes*) (Business Administration; Cosmetology; Food Science; Health Sciences; Pharmacy; Safety Engineering; Social and Preventive Medicine); **Global Human Resource Development** (*Special Graduate Programmes*) (Human Resources); **Graduate Studies** (Arts and Humanities; Engineering; Fine Arts; Medicine; Natural Sciences; Performing Arts; Physical Education; Social Sciences); **Industrial and Entrepreneurial Management** (*Special Graduate Programmes*) (Art Management; Business Administration; Economics; International Business; Management; Real Estate; Transport Management); **Information** (*Special Graduate Programmes*) (Computer Engineering; Computer Science; Information Management; Information Sciences; Information Technology; Software Engineering; Telecommunications Engineering); **International Studies** (*Professional*) (Business Administration; Finance; International Business; International Studies; Modern Languages); **Korean Music** (*Special Graduate Programmes*) (Art Therapy; Music); **Law** (*Professional*) (Civil Law; Criminal Law; Law; Public Law); **Mass Communication** (*Special Graduate Programmes*) (Advertising and Publicity; Journalism; Mass Communication; Media Studies; Public Relations; Publishing and Book Trade; Radio and Television Broadcasting); **Medicine** (Medicine); **Nursing and Health** (*Special Graduate Programmes*) (Gerontology; Health Sciences; Nursing; Oncology); **Public Administration** (*Special Graduate Programmes*) (Administration; Civil Security; Economic and Finance Policy; Police Studies; Protective Services; Public Administration; Social Policy; Welfare and Protective Services); **Social Development** (*Special Graduate Programmes*) (Child Care and Development; Community Health; Real Estate; Social Welfare; Welfare and Protective Services)

Research Division

Arts (Arts and Humanities); **Basic Sciences** (Natural Sciences); **Biomedical and Pharmaceutical Sciences** (Biomedicine; Pharmacy); **Construction and Environmental Engineering** (Environmental Studies); **Economic**

(Economics); **Foreign Studies** (Literature; Modern Languages); **Humanities** (Arts and Humanities); **Industrial Design** (Industrial Design); **Information and Communications** (Communication Studies; Information Sciences); **International Studies** (International Studies); **Japanese Studies** (Japanese); **Korean and Japanese Culture** (*Chung-Ang*) (East Asian Studies); **Korean Cultural Heritage** (Cultural Studies; Folklore; Heritage Preservation); **Korean Education** (Native Language Education); **Korean Music** (Music); **Legal Research** (Law); **Molecules-based New Drug Development** (Pharmacology); **Nursing Science** (Nursing); **Public Policy and Administration** (Public Administration); **Social Sciences** (Social Sciences); **Sports Information Technology** (Information Technology)

Campus

Anseong Campus (Business Administration; East Asian Studies; Economics; Fine Arts; Home Economics; Korean; Modern Languages; Natural Sciences; Performing Arts; Social Sciences; Sports; Technology)

Further information: Also 2 Teaching Hospitals; Campus in Anseong; 45 other research institues attached to the various colleges and graduate schools

History: Founded 1918 as Normal College for Women, became Chungoang (Central) Women's College 1945, co-educational 1948. Accredited with University status by Ministry of Education 1953 as private, non-denominational Institution. Financed by tuition fees and donations.

Academic year: March to February (March-June; September-February)

Admission requirements: Graduation from high school or foreign equivalent, and entrance examination

Fees: Tuition fee, 4,465,000-7,111,000 per semester (Won)

Main language(s) of instruction: Korean, English

Accrediting agency: Korean Council for University Education (KCUE)

Degrees and diplomas: Bachelor's Degree, Master's Degree (Accountancy; Advertising and Publicity; Animal Husbandry; Architecture; Archiving; Art Management; Bioengineering; Biological and Life Sciences; Biomedicine; Botany; Business Administration; Chemical Engineering; Chemistry; Child Care and Development; Cinema and Television; Civil Engineering; Computer Engineering; Computer Science; Construction Engineering; Cultural Studies; Dance; Design; Economics; Education; Electrical and Electronic Engineering; Energy Engineering; English; Fashion Design; Film; Finance; Folklore; Food Science; Food Technology; Foreign Languages Education; French; German; Gerontology; Handicrafts; Health Sciences; History; Home Economics; Human Resources; Industrial and Production Economics; Information Sciences; Information Technology; International Business; International Relations; International Studies; Japanese; Korean; Law; Library Science; Literature; Management;

Mass Communication; Materials Engineering; Mathematics; Mechanical Engineering; Medicine; Music; Nanotechnology; Nursing; Nutrition; Oncology; Painting and Drawing; Pharmacology; Pharmacy; Philosophy; Photography; Physical Education; Physics; Political Sciences; Preschool Education; Psychology; Public Administration; Public Relations; Real Estate; Regional Studies; Russian; Sculpture; Social Welfare; Sociology; Statistics; Structural Architecture; Theatre; Town Planning; Transport Management; Visual Arts; Writing; Zoology), **Doctor's Degree** (Accountancy; Advertising and Publicity; Animal Husbandry; Architecture; Archiving; Bioengineering; Biological and Life Sciences; Biomedicine; Botany; Business Administration; Chemical Engineering; Chemistry; Child Care and Development; Civil Engineering; Computer Engineering; Computer Science; Cultural Studies; Design; Economics; Education; Electrical and Electronic Engineering; Energy Engineering; English; Fashion Design; Film; Food Science; Food Technology; Foreign Languages Education; German; History; Home Economics; Industrial and Production Economics; Information Sciences; Information Technology; International Business; International Relations; Japanese; Korean; Law; Library Science; Literature; Management; Mass Communication; Materials Engineering; Mathematics; Mechanical Engineering; Medicine; Music; Nanotechnology; Nursing; Nutrition; Pharmacology; Pharmacy; Philosophy; Photography; Physical Education; Physics; Political Sciences; Preschool Education; Psychology; Public Administration; Public Relations; Real Estate; Regional Studies; Social Welfare; Sociology; Statistics; Structural Architecture; Theatre; Town Planning; Transport Management; Visual Arts; Writing; Zoology)
Student Services: Sports Facilities, Library, IT Centre, Residential Facilities
Periodicals: Journal (Arts), Journal (Humanities), Journal (Legal Studies), Journal (Management Research), Journal (Medical Science), Journal (Technology and Science)
Publishing house: The Publishing Department; Chung-Ang Research Centre

Academic Staff 2013-2014	MALE	FEMALE	TOTAL
FULL-TIME			982
Student Numbers 2013-2014			
All (Foreign Included)			c. 28221
Foreign only			2336

Last Update: 21-03-2018

Chungwoon University

350-701 Daehakgil-25 Hongseong-eup Hongseong-gun Chungnam-do 350-701
Tel: +82(41) 630-3114
Fax: +82(41) 634-8700
Website: http://www.chungwoon.ac.kr
President: Sang-Lyul Lee

College
Broadcasting and Arts (Acting; Art Management; Cinema and Television; Computer Engineering; Computer Graphics; Information Management; Information Sciences; Media Studies; Multimedia; Music; Performing Arts; Radio and Television Broadcasting; Software Engineering); **Engineering and Applied Sciences** (Artificial Intelligence; Building Technologies; Civil Engineering; Computer Science; Cosmetology; Engineering; Environmental Engineering; Fire Science; Mathematics and Computer Science; Multimedia; Natural Sciences; Railway Engineering; Textile Technology); **Hotel and Tourism Management** (Cooking and Catering; Hotel Management; Leisure Studies; Tourism); **Humanities and Social Sciences** (Advertising and Publicity; Arts and Humanities; Business Administration; Chinese; English; International Business; Public Relations; Social Sciences; Vietnamese); **Nursing** (Nursing)

Department/Division
Liberal Arts and Teachung Progession (Arts and Humanities; Cultural Studies; History)

Graduate School
Graduate Studies (Arts and Humanities; Engineering; Fine Arts; Linguistics; Social Studies; Sports)
History: Founded 1994.
Main language(s) of instruction: Korean
Accrediting agency: Korean Council for University Education (KCUE)
Degrees and diplomas: Bachelor's Degree, Master's Degree (Arts and Humanities; Engineering; Fine Arts; Linguistics; Social Studies; Sports)
Student Services: Sports Facilities, Health Services, Library, IT Centre

Academic Staff 2013-2014	MALE	FEMALE	TOTAL
FULL-TIME			200
PART-TIME			c. 170
Student Numbers 2013-2014			
All (Foreign Included)			c. 5800

Last Update: 24-05-2018

Cyber Hankuk University of Foreign Studies (CUFS)

107 Imun-ro, Dongdaemun-gu
Seoul 02450

Tel: +82(2) 2173-2580
Website: http://www.cufs.ac.kr/eng
President: Joong Ryul Kim

Department/Division

Chinese (Chinese); **English** (English); **Finance and Accounting** (Accountancy; Finance); **Japanese** (Japanese); **Korean** (Korean); **Local Government Studies** (Government); **Spanish** (Spanish); **Vietnam and Indonesia** (Indonesian; Vietnamese)
History: Founded 2004.
Main language(s) of instruction: Korean
Accrediting agency: Ministry of Education
Degrees and diplomas: Bachelor's Degree (Accountancy; Chinese; English; Finance; Government; Indonesian; Japanese; Korean; Spanish; Vietnamese)
Student Services: Library
Last Update: 21-03-2018

Daegu Arts University

San 117-6 Dabu-ri Gasan-myeon
Chilgok-gun 718-912, Gyeongsanbuk-do
Tel: +82(54) 973-5311
Fax: +82(54) 973-5319
Website: http://www.dgau.ac.kr
President: Byoungho Kim

Department/Division

Broadcast Arts (Acting; Cinema and Television; Cosmetology; Dance; Radio and Television Broadcasting; Video); **Design** (Architecture; Communication Arts; Design; Fashion Design; Interior Design; Visual Arts); **Fine Arts** (Fine Arts; Painting and Drawing); **Music** (Jazz and Popular Music; Music; Music Education; Music Theory and Composition; Religious Music); **Photography and Art Therapy** (Art Therapy; Film; Photography); **Social Business** (Administration; Japanese; Police Studies; Social Welfare); **Sports** (Physical Education; Sports; Sports Management)
History: Founded 1997. Acquired present status 2006.
Admission requirements: Secondary School Certificate
Fees: 3.5m (Won)
Main language(s) of instruction: Korean
Accrediting agency: Ministry of Education and Human Resources Development
Degrees and diplomas: Bachelor's Degree (Architecture; Art Therapy; Communication Arts; Dance; Fashion Design; Graphic Design; Interior Design; Jazz and Popular Music; Media Studies; Music; Music Education; Painting and Drawing; Performing Arts; Photography; Protective Services; Religious Music; Visual Arts)

Student Services: Academic Counselling, Nursery Care, Sports Facilities, Health Services, Canteen, IT Centre

Academic Staff 2013-2014	MALE	FEMALE	TOTAL
FULL-TIME			84
PART-TIME			c. 234
Student Numbers 2013-2014			
All (Foreign Included)			c. 1800

Last Update: 08-02-2018

Daegu Cyber University (DCU)

201, Daegudae-ro, Jillyang-eup
Gyeongsan-si 38453, Gyeongsangbuk-do
Tel: +82(53) 859-7500
Fax: +82(53) 859-7599
Website: http://english.dcu.ac.kr
President: Duckryul Hong

Department/Division

Art Therapy (Art Therapy); **Behavior Therapy** (Behavioural Sciences; Psychotherapy); **Counseling Psychology** (Psychology); **Electronic and Information-Communication Engineering** (Electronic Engineering; Telecommunications Engineering); **Korean Language Education and Multi-Culture** (Cultural Studies; Foreign Languages Education; Native Language Education); **Play Therapy** (Art Therapy; Psychotherapy); **Public Administration** (Public Administration); **Rehabilitation** (Rehabilitation and Therapy); **Social Welfare** (Social Welfare); **Special Education** (Special Education); **Speech and Language Therapy** (Speech Therapy and Audiology); **Welfare Public Administration** (Public Administration; Welfare and Protective Services)
History: Founded 2001.
Main language(s) of instruction: Korean
Accrediting agency: Ministry of Education
Degrees and diplomas: Bachelor's Degree (Art Therapy; Behavioural Sciences; Cultural Studies; Electronic Engineering; Foreign Languages Education; Native Language Education; Psychology; Psychotherapy; Public Administration; Rehabilitation and Therapy; Social Welfare; Special Education; Speech Therapy and Audiology; Telecommunications Engineering; Welfare and Protective Services)
Student Services: Library
Last Update: 26-03-2018

Daegu Haany University (DHU)

1 Haanydaero
Gyeongsan-si 712-715, Gyeongsangbuk-do
Tel: +82(53) 819-1000

Fax: +82(53) 819-1258
Website: http://www.dhu.ac.kr
President: Chang Hoon Byun

College

Health and Therapy (Art Therapy; Environmental Management; Health Administration; Health Sciences; Laboratory Techniques; Occupational Health; Pathology; Physical Therapy; Psychology; Rehabilitation and Therapy; Safety Engineering; Secondary Education; Special Education; Sports Medicine); **Herbal Bio-industry** (Biomedical Engineering; Biotechnology; Botany; Business Administration; Cooking and Catering; Cosmetology; Food Science; Health Sciences; Nutrition; Pharmacology; Traditional Eastern Medicine); **International College of Culture and Information** (Chinese; Criminal Law; Economics; English; Foreign Languages Education; Information Technology; Japanese; Justice Administration; Korean; Leisure Studies; Literature; Marketing; Medical Technology; Multimedia; Police Studies; Software Engineering; Tourism); **Oriental Medicine** (Nursing; Traditional Eastern Medicine); **Well-being** (Architectural and Environmental Design; Architecture; Business Administration; Child Care and Development; Civil Engineering; Communication Arts; Educational and Student Counselling; Fashion Design; Finance; Gerontology; Graphic Design; Interior Design; Real Estate; Rehabilitation and Therapy; Welfare and Protective Services)

Institute

Korean Language (*For International Students*) (East Asian Studies; Korean)

Graduate School

Education (Education; Educational and Student Counselling; Foreign Languages Education; Home Economics Education; Humanities and Social Science Education; Mathematics Education; Native Language Education); **Graduate Studies** (Architecture; Biotechnology; Child Care and Development; Cosmetology; Environmental Management; Food Science; Philosophy; Safety Engineering; Traditional Eastern Medicine; Welfare and Protective Services); **Herbal Medical Industry** (Business Administration; Traditional Eastern Medicine); **Public Health** (Art Therapy; Health Sciences; Public Health; Speech Therapy and Audiology); **Social Development** (Cooking and Catering; Esoteric Practices; Food Technology; Justice Administration; Social Welfare; Tourism)
Further information: Also Susung Campus
History: Founded 1981 as Daegu Oriental Medical College. Upgraded into Gyeongsan University 1990. Acquired present title 2004.

Fees: 1,900,000 for 20 weeks of regular course; 3,800,000 for 40 weeks of regular course (Won)
Main language(s) of instruction: Korean
Accrediting agency: Korean Council for University Education (KCUE)
Degrees and diplomas: Bachelor's Degree, Master's Degree (Alternative Medicine; Architecture; Art Therapy; Biotechnology; Business Administration; Child Care and Development; Cooking and Catering; Cosmetology; Educational and Student Counselling; Environmental Management; Esoteric Practices; Food Science; Foreign Languages Education; Health Sciences; Home Economics Education; Humanities and Social Science Education; Justice Administration; Mathematics Education; Native Language Education; Philosophy; Safety Engineering; Social Welfare; Speech Therapy and Audiology; Tourism), Doctor's Degree (Alternative Medicine; Biotechnology; Cosmetology; Food Science; Health Sciences; Oriental Studies; Philosophy; Welfare and Protective Services)
Student Services: Sports Facilities, Residential Facilities

Academic Staff 2013-2014	MALE	FEMALE	TOTAL
FULL-TIME			239
PART-TIME			148
Student Numbers 2013-2014			
All (Foreign Included)			c. 7000

Last Update: 12-02-2018

Daegu University

201, Daegudae-ro
Gyeongsan-si 38453, Gyeongsangbuk-do
Tel: +82(53) 850-5000, +82(53) 850-5681
Fax: +82(53) 850-5009, +82(53) 850-5689
Website: http://www.daegu.ac.kr
President: Duckryul Hong

College

Arts and Design (Design; Fashion Design; Fine Arts; Handicrafts; House Arts and Environment; Industrial Design; Interior Design; Painting and Drawing; Visual Arts); **Economics and Business Administration** (Accountancy; Business Administration; Economics; Finance; Hotel Management; Insurance; International Business; Taxation; Tourism); **Education** (Environmental Studies; Foreign Languages Education; Humanities and Social Science Education; Mathematics Education; Native Language Education; Preschool Education; Primary Education; Science Education; Special Education); **Engineering** (Automotive Engineering; Biotechnology; Chemical Engineering; Civil Engineering; Engineering; Environmental Engineering; Food Science;

Food Technology; Industrial Engineering; Landscape Architecture; Mechanical Engineering; Nutrition; Structural Architecture); **Humanities** (Arts and Humanities; Chinese; English; French; German; Health Sciences; Japanese; Korean; Leisure Studies; Literature; Physical Education; Russian; Sports); **Information and Communication Engineering** (Automation and Control Engineering; Computer Engineering; Electronic Engineering; Information Technology; Multimedia; Telecommunications Engineering); **Law** (Law; Private Law; Protective Services; Public Law); **Life and Environmental Science** (Animal Husbandry; Biological and Life Sciences; Environmental Management; Environmental Studies; Food Science; Forest Products; Forestry; Horticulture); **Natural Resources** (Biological and Life Sciences; Chemistry; Computer Science; Mathematics; Molecular Biology; Natural Resources; Physics; Statistics); **Public Administration** (Development Studies; Justice Administration; Police Studies; Public Administration; Real Estate; Regional Planning; Social and Community Services; Town Planning; Urban Studies; Welfare and Protective Services); **Rehabilitation Sciences** (Occupational Therapy; Physical Therapy; Psychology; Rehabilitation and Therapy; Speech Therapy and Audiology); **Social Sciences** (Family Studies; Information Sciences; International Relations; Journalism; Library Science; Mass Communication; Psychology; Social Sciences; Social Welfare; Sociology; Welfare and Protective Services)

Department/Division

International Studies (East Asian Studies; Korean); **Nursing and Public Health** (Health Administration; Nursing; Public Health)

Graduate School

Design (Design); **Education** (Education); **Graduate Studies** (Accountancy; Animal Husbandry; Arts and Humanities; Biology; Biotechnology; Business Administration; Chemistry; Civil Engineering; Computer Engineering; Design; Economics; Electronic Engineering; Engineering; English; Environmental Engineering; Family Studies; Fashion Design; Fine Arts; Food Science; Food Technology; Geography; German; History; Horticulture; House Arts and Environment; Industrial Engineering; Information Sciences; Information Technology; Interior Design; International Business; Journalism; Korean; Landscape Architecture; Law; Library Science; Literature; Mass Communication; Mathematics; Mechanical Engineering; Natural Resources; Natural Sciences; Nutrition; Physical Education; Physics; Preschool Education; Psychology; Public Administration; Rehabilitation and Therapy; Science Education; Social Sciences; Social Welfare; Sociology; Special Education; Statistics; Structural Architecture; Telecommunications Engineering; Tourism; Urban Studies; Welfare and Protective Services); **Industrial Information** (Information Sciences); **International Management** (International Business; Management); **Public**

Administration (Public Administration); **Rehabilitation** (Rehabilitation and Therapy); **Social Welfare** (Social Welfare); **Special Education** (Special Education)

Further information: Also Graduate Schools and Research Institutes

History: Founded as Daegu University 1956. Renamed Korean Social Work University 1961. Acquired present title 1981.

Main language(s) of instruction: Korean

Accrediting agency: Korean Council for University Education (KCUE)

Degrees and diplomas: Bachelor's Degree, Master's Degree (Accountancy; Animal Husbandry; Applied Chemistry; Automotive Engineering; Biology; Biotechnology; Business Administration; Chemistry; Child Care and Development; Civil Engineering; Computer Engineering; Design; Economics; Education; Electrical Engineering; Electronic Engineering; English; Environmental Engineering; Family Studies; Fashion Design; Fine Arts; Food Science; Forestry; Geography; German; Handicrafts; History; Horticulture; House Arts and Environment; Industrial Design; Industrial Engineering; Information Sciences; Information Technology; Interior Design; International Business; International Economics; Journalism; Korean; Landscape Architecture; Law; Library Science; Literature; Mass Communication; Mathematics; Mechanical Engineering; Multimedia; Natural Resources; Nutrition; Occupational Therapy; Physical Education; Physical Therapy; Physics; Psychology; Public Administration; Rehabilitation and Therapy; Science Education; Social Welfare; Sociology; Soil Science; Special Education; Speech Therapy and Audiology; Sports Management; Statistics; Structural Architecture; Telecommunications Engineering; Tourism; Town Planning; Urban Studies; Water Management; Welfare and Protective Services; Wood Technology), Doctor's Degree (Accountancy; Animal Husbandry; Applied Physics; Automation and Control Engineering; Automotive Engineering; Biotechnology; Business Administration; Cell Biology; Chemistry; Civil Engineering; Computer Engineering; Design; Ecology; Economics; Education; Education of the Handicapped; Electronic Engineering; English; Environmental Management; Environmental Studies; Family Studies; Fashion Design; Finance; Fine Arts; Food Science; Food Technology; Forestry; Horticulture; Humanities and Social Science Education; Industrial Design; Industrial Engineering; Information Sciences; Information Technology; Insurance; International Business; Korean; Landscape Architecture; Library Science; Literature; Mathematics; Mechanical Engineering; Molecular Biology; Nutrition; Occupational Health; Occupational Therapy; Painting and Drawing; Physical Education; Physical Therapy; Preschool Education; Psychology; Public Administration; Public Law; Real Estate; Regional Planning; Rehabilitation and Therapy; Science Education; Secondary Education; Social and Community Services; Social Policy; Social Welfare; Social Work; Special

Education; Speech Therapy and Audiology; Statistics; Structural Architecture; Telecommunications Engineering; Tourism; Town Planning; Visual Arts; Welfare and Protective Services)

Student Services: Sports Facilities, Health Services, Library, IT Centre, Residential Facilities

Academic Staff 2013-2014	MALE	FEMALE	TOTAL
FULL-TIME			798
Student Numbers 2013-2014			
All (Foreign Included)			c. 19593
Foreign only			724

Last Update: 12-02-2018

Daehan Theological University (DTU)

30 Gyeongsu-daero 1406beon-gil, Seoksu-dong, Manan-gu
Anyang, Gyeonggi-do
Tel: +82(31) 470-3333, +82(31) 470-3327
Fax: +82(31) 473-5947
Website: http://www.dtu.ac.kr
President: Seon Lee

Department/Division

Divinity (Religion); **Literature** (Literature; Psychology; Social Welfare); **Theology** (Theology)
History: Founded 1996.
Main language(s) of instruction: Korean
Accrediting agency: Ministry of Education
Degrees and diplomas: Master's Degree (Literature; Religion; Theology), Doctor's Degree (Psychology; Psychotherapy; Social Welfare)
Last Update: 27-03-2018

Daejeon University (DJU)

62 Daehak-ro, Dong-gu
Daejeon 300-716, Chungnam-do
Tel: +82(42) 280-2114
Fax: +82(42) 283-8808
Website: http://www.dju.ac.kr
President: Jong Seo Lee

Faculty

Liberal Arts and Global Studies (Arts and Humanities; English; International Studies)

College

Business Administration (Accountancy; Business Administration; Business and Commerce; Economics; Health Administration; Industrial and Organizational Psychology;

Statistics); **Engineering** (Architecture; Biological and Life Sciences; Civil Engineering; Computer Engineering; Electronic Engineering; Environmental Engineering; Fire Science; Geological Engineering; Information Management; Information Technology; Materials Engineering; Protective Services; Safety Engineering; Structural Architecture; Technology Education; Telecommunications Engineering); **Humanities and Art** (Arts and Humanities; Chinese; Communication Arts; Computer Graphics; Cultural Studies; English; History; Japanese; Korean; Literature; Painting and Drawing; Performing Arts; Philosophy; Radio and Television Broadcasting; Russian; Secondary Education; Special Education; Translation and Interpretation; Visual Arts; Writing); **Liberal Arts** (Chinese; Communication Arts; English; Fine Arts; History; Japanese; Korean; Literature; Philosophy; Russian); **Natural Sciences** (Biological and Life Sciences; Biology; Biotechnology; Business Administration; Child Care and Development; Cosmetology; Educational and Student Counselling; Environmental Studies; Fashion Design; Food Science; Health Sciences; Information Technology; Medical Technology; Microbiology; Natural Sciences; Nutrition; Pathology; Physical Therapy; Protective Services; Sports); **Oriental Medicine** (Alternative Medicine; Nursing; Traditional Eastern Medicine); **Social Sciences** (Journalism; Law; Mass Communication; Military Science; Police Studies; Political Sciences; Public Administration; Public Relations; Social Sciences; Social Welfare)

Graduate School

Business Administration and Social Welfare (*Special Graduate School*) (Business Administration; Police Studies; Social Policy; Social Welfare; Social Work); **Education** (*Special Graduate School*) (Education); **Graduate Studies**; **Health and Sports** (*Special Graduate School*) (Health Sciences; Sports); **Military and Industrial Information** (*Special Graduate School*) (Information Sciences; Military Science)
History: Founded 1980 as Daejeon College. Acquired present status and title 1989.
Main language(s) of instruction: Korean
Accrediting agency: Korean Council for University Education (KCUE)
Degrees and diplomas: Bachelor's Degree, Master's Degree (Accountancy; Biology; Business Administration; Business and Commerce; Chemistry; Chinese; Civil Engineering; Computer Engineering; Computer Science; Construction Engineering; Cultural Studies; Education; Educational Administration; Educational and Student Counselling; Electronic Engineering; Energy Engineering; Engineering Management; English; Environmental Engineering; Fashion Design; Food Science; Geological Engineering; Health Administration; History; Industrial and Organizational Psychology; Information Sciences; Korean; Law; Linguistics; Literature; Materials Engineering;

Mathematics and Computer Science; Medicine; Microbiology; Military Science; Nursing; Nutrition; Painting and Drawing; Physical Education; Physical Therapy; Plastic Surgery; Police Studies; Political Sciences; Preschool Education; Public Administration; Social Policy; Social Work; Statistics; Structural Architecture; Telecommunications Engineering; Traditional Eastern Medicine; Transport Management; Writing), Doctor's Degree (Accountancy; Administration; Aesthetics; Architecture; Biology; Botany; Building Technologies; Business Administration; Business and Commerce; Chemistry; Child Care and Development; Computer Engineering; Computer Science; Construction Engineering; Criminal Law; Cultural Studies; Economics; Education of the Gifted; Educational Administration; Electronic Engineering; Engineering Management; Environmental Engineering; Fashion Design; Finance; Food Science; Government; Health Administration; History; Industrial Management; Information Technology; International Business; Justice Administration; Korean; Linguistics; Literature; Management; Marketing; Mathematics; Medicine; Microbiology; Military Science; Nursing; Nutrition; Painting and Drawing; Pathology; Physical Education; Physical Therapy; Plastic Surgery; Police Studies; Psychology; Psychotherapy; Public Administration; Social Welfare; Social Work; Software Engineering; Statistics; Structural Architecture; Taxation; Telecommunications Engineering; Traditional Eastern Medicine; Writing; Zoology)

Student Services: Sports Facilities, Library, IT Centre, Residential Facilities

Student Numbers 2015-2016	MALE	FEMALE	TOTAL
All (Foreign Included)			12000
Foreign only			300

Last Update: 12-02-2018

Daejin University

1007, Hoguk Road
Pocheon-si 487-711, Gyeonggi-do
Tel: +82(31) 539-1114
Fax: +82(31) 539-1115
Website: http://www.daejin.ac.kr
President: Myeonjae Lee

College

Arts (Architectural and Environmental Design; Cinema and Television; Dance; Design; Fine Arts; Music; Painting and Drawing; Performing Arts; Sculpture; Theatre); **Engineering** (Chemical Engineering; Computer Engineering; Construction Engineering; Electrical Engineering; Electronic Engineering; Engineering; Engineering Drawing and Design; Environmental Engineering; Industrial Engineering; Information Technology; Materials Engineering; Mechanical Engineering; Production Engineering; Structural Architecture; Telecommunications Engineering; Town Planning); **Humanities** (Arts and Humanities; Child Care and Development; Cultural Studies; English; History; Information Sciences; Korean; Library Science; Literature; Philosophy; Preschool Education; Religion; Writing); **Natural Sciences** (Biological and Life Sciences; Chemistry; Computer Science; Food Science; Mathematics and Computer Science; Natural Sciences; Nutrition; Physics; Sports); **Social Sciences** (American Studies; Asian Studies; Business Administration; Chinese; East Asian Studies; Economics; International Business; Japanese; Law; Management; Mass Communication; Media Studies; Multimedia; Public Administration; Social Welfare)

Graduate School

Culture and Arts (Cinema and Television; Dance; Design; Fine Arts; Industrial Design; Music; Performing Arts; Visual Arts); **Education** (Education); **Graduate Studies** (Arts and Humanities; Engineering; Fine Arts; Natural Sciences; Religion; Social Sciences); **Law Affairs-Public** (Law; Public Administration); **Management** (Management); **Reunification** (International Relations; Political Sciences)
Further information: Also Graduate Schools and Research Institutes
History: Founded 1992.
Main language(s) of instruction: Korean
Accrediting agency: Korean Council for University Education (KCUE)
Degrees and diplomas: Bachelor's Degree, Master's Degree (Art Criticism; Art Education; Art Management; Asian Religious Studies; Biology; Business Administration; Chemistry; Civil Engineering; Communication Arts; Computer Education; Computer Engineering; Conducting; Continuing Education; Dance; Design; Display and Stage Design; Economics; Education; Educational Administration; Educational and Student Counselling; Electrical Engineering; Electronic Engineering; English; Environmental Engineering; Film; Fine Arts; Food Science; Foreign Languages Education; History; Home Economics Education; Humanities and Social Science Education; Industrial Design; Industrial Engineering; Information Sciences; International Business; International Relations; International Studies; Korean; Law; Library Science; Literature; Materials Engineering; Mathematics; Mathematics Education; Mechanical Engineering; Multimedia; Music; Music Education; Music Theory and Composition; Musical Instruments; Musicology; Native Language Education; Nutrition; Packaging Technology; Painting and Drawing; Philosophy; Physical Education; Physics;

Political Sciences; Preschool Education; Public Administration; Real Estate; Science Education; Special Education; Structural Architecture; Telecommunications Engineering; Theatre; Town Planning; Visual Arts), Doctor's Degree (Asian Religious Studies; Biochemistry; Chemical Engineering; Civil Engineering; Computer Engineering; East Asian Studies; Education; Electrical Engineering; Electronic Engineering; English; Environmental Engineering; Industrial Engineering; International Relations; International Studies; Literature; Materials Engineering; Philosophy; Physics; Political Sciences; Structural Architecture; Telecommunications Engineering)

Student Services: Sports Facilities, Library, IT Centre, Residential Facilities

Student Numbers 2015-2016	MALE	FEMALE	TOTAL
All (Foreign Included)			7832
Foreign only			275

Last Update: 12-02-2018

Daeshin University

222 Street 33 (Baekcheon-dong 137)
Seongcheong-si 38649, Gyeongsangbuk-do
Tel: +82(53) 810-0701/3
Fax: +82(53) 813-0006
Website: http://www.daeshin.ac.kr
President: Sang-su Chang

Department/Division
Counseling English (English); **Music** (Music); **Social Welfare** (Social Welfare); **Theology** (Theology)
History: Founded 1996.
Main language(s) of instruction: Korean
Accrediting agency: Ministry of Education
Degrees and diplomas: Bachelor's Degree (English; Music; Social Welfare; Theology), Master's Degree (English; Music; Social Welfare; Theology)
Student Services: Library, Residential Facilities
Last Update: 28-03-2018

Dankook University

152, Jukjeon-ro, Suji-gu
Yongin-si 16 890, Gyeonggi-do
Tel: +82(2) 1899-3700
Fax: +82(2) 790-2782
Website: http://www.dankook.ac.kr
President: Hosung Chang

College
Architecture (*Jukjeon*) (Architecture; Structural Architecture); **Arts** (*Cheonan*) (Design; Handicrafts; Music; Painting and Drawing; Sculpture; Writing); **Arts and Design** (*Jukjeon*) (Ceramic Art; Communication Arts; Dance; Design; Fashion Design; Film; Fine Arts; Music; Theatre; Visual Arts); **Business and Economics** (*Jukjeon*) (Accountancy; Business Administration; Economics; International Business; Management); **Convergence Technology** (*Cheonan*) (Energy Engineering; Food Technology; Industrial Engineering; Materials Engineering; Optical Technology; Pharmacology); **Dentistry** (*Cheonan*) (Dentistry); **Education** (*Jukjeon*) (Education; Foreign Languages Education; Mathematics Education; Native Language Education; Physical Education; Science Education; Teacher Training); **Engineering** (*Jukjeon*) (Chemical Engineering; Civil Engineering; Computer Engineering; Electrical and Electronic Engineering; Engineering; Environmental Engineering; Mechanical Engineering; Polymer and Plastics Technology; Software Engineering; Textile Technology); **Foreign Languages** (*Cheonan*) (Arabic; Chinese; English; French; German; Japanese; Modern Languages; Mongolian; Portuguese; Russian; Spanish); **General Education** (Arts and Humanities); **Health Sciences** (*Cheonan*) (Biomedicine; Dental Hygiene; Health Administration; Health Sciences; Information Management; Laboratory Techniques; Nursing; Physical Therapy); **Humanities** (*Jukjeon*) (American Studies; Arts and Humanities; English Studies; History; Korean; Literature; Philosophy); **International Studies** (*Jukjeon*) (International Business; International Studies; Telecommunications Engineering); **Law** (*Jukjeon*) (Law); **Liberal Arts and Sciences** (*Jukjeon*) (Arts and Humanities); **Life and Resource Science** (*Cheonan*) (Animal Husbandry; Biotechnology; Crop Production; Environmental Studies; Horticulture; Landscape Architecture); **Medicine** (*Cheonan*) (Anatomy; Arts and Humanities; Biochemistry; Bioengineering; Biomedical Engineering; Medicine; Microbiology; Parasitology; Pathology; Pharmacology; Physiology; Social and Preventive Medicine); **Music** (*Jukjeon*) (Music; Music Theory and Composition; Musical Instruments; Performing Arts; Singing); **Natural Science** (*Cheonan*) (Biological and Life Sciences; Biomedicine; Chemistry; Food Science; Microbiology; Molecular Biology; Nanotechnology; Natural Sciences; Nutrition; Physics); **Pharmacy** (*Cheonan*) (Pharmacy); **Public Service** (*Cheonan*) (Economics; Environmental Management; Industrial Management; Military Science; Natural Resources; Psychology; Public Administration; Social Welfare); **Social Science** (*Jukjeon*) (Advertising and Publicity; Applied Mathematics; International Relations; Journalism; Media Studies; Political Sciences; Psychology; Public Administration; Public Relations; Real Estate; Regional Planning; Social Sciences; Statistics; Town

Planning); **Sports Science** (Leisure Studies; Parks and Recreation; Sports; Sports Management)

Graduate School

Cinematic Content (*Specialized Graduate School*) (Cinema and Television; Film; Writing); **Culture, Arts and Design** (*Specialized Graduate School*) (Art Management; Design; Fashion Design; Graphic Design; Industrial Design; Performing Arts); **Education** (*Specialized Graduate School*) (Art Education; Business Education; Continuing Education; Curriculum; Education; Educational Administration; Educational and Student Counselling; Foreign Languages Education; Home Economics Education; Humanities and Social Science Education; Mathematics Education; Native Language Education; Pedagogy; Physical Education; Science Education; Teacher Training); **Graduate Studies** (Arts and Humanities; Dentistry; Engineering; Fine Arts; Medicine; Natural Sciences; Performing Arts; Physical Education; Social Sciences); **Industry and Business Administration** (*Specialized*) (Accountancy; Administration; Art Management; Business Administration; Finance; International Business; Management; Marketing; Small Business; Taxation; Tourism); **Information and Media Technology** (*Specialized Graduate School*) (Food Science; Information Sciences; Information Technology; Mass Communication; Nutrition; Radio and Television Broadcasting); **Legal Studies and Public Administration** (*Specialized Graduate School*) (Civil Law; Health Administration; Labour Law; Law; Psychology; Public Administration; Real Estate; Social Welfare); **Policy and Business Administration** (*Specialized Graduate School*) (Civil Engineering; Cultural Studies; Environmental Engineering; Fine Arts; Law; Management; Real Estate; Town Planning); **Public Health and Social Welfare** (*Specialized Graduate School*) (Dentistry; Nursing; Public Health; Social Welfare); **Real Estate and Construction** (*Specialized Graduate School*) (Administration; Architecture; Civil Engineering; Environmental Engineering; Landscape Architecture; Real Estate; Structural Architecture); **Special Education** (*Specialized Graduate School*) (Occupational Therapy; Physical Therapy; Preschool Education; Primary Education; Psychotherapy; Secondary Education; Special Education); **Sports Science** (*Specialized Graduate School*) (Leisure Studies; Marketing; Sports; Sports Medicine); **TESOL** (*Specialized Graduate School*) (Foreign Languages Education; Teacher Training)

Campus

Cheonan Campus (Biomedicine; Biotechnology; Chinese; Dental Hygiene; English; French; German; Health Administration; Japanese; Laboratory Techniques; Middle Eastern Studies; Mongolian; Physical Therapy; Portuguese; Russian; Spanish)
Further information: Also Cheonan Campus; Also 20 Research Institutes

History: Founded 1947.
Academic year: March to February (March-August; September-February)
Admission requirements: Graduation from high school and entrance examination
Main language(s) of instruction: Korean
Accrediting agency: Korean Council for University Education (KCUE)
Degrees and diplomas: Bachelor's Degree, Master's Degree (Administration; Agricultural Education; Alternative Medicine; Applied Physics; Architecture; Art Education; Art Management; Biochemistry; Biotechnology; Business Administration; Business and Commerce; Business Education; Ceramic Art; Chemical Engineering; Chinese; Civil Engineering; Clothing and Sewing; Computer Science; Continuing Education; Curriculum; Dance; Dentistry; Economics; Education; Educational Administration; Educational and Student Counselling; Electrical and Electronic Engineering; English; Environmental Engineering; Fashion Design; Film; Finance; Fine Arts; Food Science; Food Technology; Foreign Languages Education; French; German; Graphic Design; Handicrafts; Health Administration; History; Home Economics Education; Horticulture; Hotel Management; Humanities and Social Science Education; Industrial Design; Industrial Engineering; Information Management; Information Sciences; International Business; International Relations; Journalism; Korean; Labour Law; Law; Leisure Studies; Literature; Management; Marketing; Materials Engineering; Mathematics; Mathematics Education; Mechanical Engineering; Medicine; Microbiology; Molecular Biology; Mongolian; Multimedia; Music; Native Language Education; Natural Resources; Nursing; Nutrition; Physical Education; Physics; Political Sciences; Polymer and Plastics Technology; Primary Education; Psychology; Public Administration; Public Health; Real Estate; Russian; Science Education; Small Business; Social Welfare; Spanish; Special Education; Sports; Sports Management; Sports Medicine; Statistics; Structural Architecture; Taxation; Theatre; Tourism; Town Planning; Transport Management; Visual Arts), Doctor's Degree (Applied Physics; Architecture; Biological and Life Sciences; Biomedicine; Ceramics and Glass Technology; Chemical Engineering; Chemistry; Chinese; Civil Engineering; Clothing and Sewing; Communication Arts; Computer Engineering; Computer Science; Dance; Dentistry; Design; Economics; Education; Electrical and Electronic Engineering; English; Environmental Engineering; Environmental Management; Food Science; Food Technology; German; History; Industrial Engineering; International Business; International Relations; Japanese; Korean; Law; Literature; Management; Materials Engineering; Mathematics; Mathematics Education; Mechanical Engineering; Medicine; Microbiology; Molecular Biology; Mongolian; Music; Nanotechnology; Natural Resources; Nursing; Nutrition;

Pharmacy; Physical Education; Physics; Political Sciences; Polymer and Plastics Technology; Public Administration; Public Health; Real Estate; Science Education; Special Education; Statistics; Structural Architecture; Textile Technology; Town Planning; Writing). Also Special Graduate Courses in Finance, Sports Management, Law

Student Services: Library

Periodicals: Business Studies, Commerce and Economics Review, Dongyang Hak, Essays on Korean Language and Literature, Historical Journal, Home Economic Studies, Journal of Industrial Studies, Law Review, The China Quarterly

Publishing house: University Press

Academic Staff 2013-2014	MALE	FEMALE	TOTAL
FULL-TIME			1012
PART-TIME			1556
Student Numbers 2013-2014			
All (Foreign Included)			28654

Last Update: 22-03-2018

Digital Seoul Culture and Arts University (SCAU)

37 Road 60, Unilo Road, Seodaemun-gu
Seoul 03645
Tel: +82(2) 2287-0253
Fax: +82(2) 379-5736
Website: http://www.scau.ac.kr
President: Chang-Sik Park

Department/Division

Culture and Arts (Acting; Architecture; Cosmetology; Fine Arts; Music; Performing Arts; Sports); **Social and Cultural Studies** (Business Administration; Cultural Studies; East Asian Studies; Hotel and Restaurant; Korean; Psychology; Social Sciences; Social Welfare)

History: Founded 1997.

Main language(s) of instruction: Korean

Accrediting agency: Ministry of Education

Degrees and diplomas: Bachelor's Degree (Acting; Architecture; Business Administration; Cosmetology; Cultural Studies; East Asian Studies; Fine Arts; Hotel and Restaurant; Korean; Music; Performing Arts; Psychology; Social Sciences; Social Welfare; Sports)

Last Update: 27-03-2018

Dong-A University (DAU)

Saha-gu Hadan 2-dong 840 Saha-gu
Pusan 604-714

Tel: +82(51) 200-6442
Fax: +82(51) 200-6445
Website: http://www.donga.ac.kr
President: Oh Chang Kwon

College

Architecture, Design, Fashion (Architecture; Design; Fashion Design; Industrial Design); **Arts** (Fine Arts; Handicrafts; Music; Musical Instruments); **Business** (Business Administration; Business and Commerce; Information Management; International Business); **Engineering** (Chemical Engineering; Civil Engineering; Computer Engineering; Computer Science; Electrical Engineering; Electronic Engineering; Energy Engineering; Engineering; Environmental Engineering; Industrial Engineering; Landscape Architecture; Materials Engineering; Mechanical Engineering; Polymer and Plastics Technology; Structural Architecture; Town Planning); **Human Ecology** (Home Economics; Textile Technology); **Humanities** (Archaeology; Art History; Arts and Humanities; Child Care and Development; Chinese; Cultural Studies; Education; English; Ethics; Family Studies; French; French Studies; History; Korean; Literature; Philosophy; Writing); **International Studies** (Chinese; International Studies; Japanese); **Law** (International Law; Law); **Medicine** (Health Sciences; Medicine; Nursing); **Natural Resources and Life Science** (Bioengineering; Biological and Life Sciences; Biology; Biotechnology; Genetics; Molecular Biology; Natural Resources; Pharmacology); **Natural Sciences** (Biological and Life Sciences; Chemistry; Food Science; Mathematical Physics; Mathematics; Natural Sciences; Nutrition); **Social Sciences** (Economics; Finance; Journalism; Political Sciences; Public Administration; Social Sciences; Social Welfare; Sociology); **Sports Science** (Physical Education; Protective Services; Sports)

School

Law (*Graduate*) (Law); **Medicine** (*Graduate*) (Medicine)

Department/Division
Human Resources

Graduate School

Business Administration (Business Administration); **Culture and Arts** (Art Management; Cultural Studies; Fine Arts); **Education** (Education; Teacher Training); **Graduate Studies** (Arts and Humanities; Engineering; Fine Arts; Law; Medicine; Natural Sciences; Social Sciences); **Industry and Information** (Industrial Engineering; Information Sciences); **International Studies** (International Business; International Studies); **Justice** (Law; Police Studies; Private Law; Real Estate); **Northeast Asian Studies** (*Doctoral Programme*) (Asian Studies; East Asian Studies); **Social Welfare** (Social Welfare; Social Work)

Further information: Also University Hospital; 27 Research Institutes

History: Founded as College 1946, acquired university status 1959.

Academic year: March to February (March-August; September-February)

Admission requirements: Graduation from high school or equivalent, and entrance examination

Main language(s) of instruction: Korean

Accrediting agency: Korean Council for University Education (KCUE)

Degrees and diplomas: Bachelor's Degree, Master's Degree (Accountancy; Applied Physics; Archaeology; Architectural and Environmental Design; Architecture and Planning; Art History; Biological and Life Sciences; Biomedicine; Biotechnology; Business Administration; Chemical Engineering; Chemistry; Child Care and Development; Chinese; Civil Engineering; Communication Studies; Computer Engineering; Cultural Studies; Design; East Asian Studies; Economics; Education; Electrical Engineering; Electronic Engineering; Energy Engineering; English; Environmental Engineering; Ethics; Family Studies; Fashion Design; Finance; Fine Arts; Food Science; History; Industrial Engineering; Industrial Management; Information Management; Information Technology; International Law; International Studies; Japanese; Korean; Landscape Architecture; Law; Literature; Marine Transport; Mathematics; Mechanical Engineering; Medicine; Metallurgical Engineering; Mining Engineering; Music; Musicology; Nursing; Nutrition; Philosophy; Physical Education; Physics; Political Sciences; Public Administration; Social Welfare; Sociology; Sports; Structural Architecture; Textile Design; Tourism; Transport Management; Writing), Doctor's Degree (Accountancy; Archaeology; Architectural and Environmental Design; Architecture and Planning; Art History; Asian Studies; Bioengineering; Biology; Biomedicine; Biotechnology; Business Administration; Chemical Engineering; Chemistry; Child Care and Development; Civil Engineering; Communication Studies; Computer Engineering; Design; East Asian Studies; Economics; Education; Electrical Engineering; Energy Engineering; English; Environmental Engineering; Ethics; Fashion Design; Fine Arts; Food Science; Genetics; German; History; Industrial Engineering; Industrial Management; Information Management; International Business; International Law; Korean; Landscape Architecture; Law; Literature; Marine Transport; Materials Engineering; Mathematics; Mechanical Engineering; Medicine; Metallurgical Engineering; Mining Engineering; Musicology; Nanotechnology; Nursing; Nutrition; Philosophy; Physical Education; Physics; Political Sciences; Public Administration; Sociology; Sports; Structural Architecture; Textile Design; Tourism; Transport Management; Writing)

Student Services: Sports Facilities, Health Services, Canteen, Library, Residential Facilities

Periodicals: Journal of Agriculture, Journal of Engineering, Journal of Law and Economics

Publishing house: University Press

Academic Staff 2012-2013	MALE	FEMALE	TOTAL
FULL-TIME			810
PART-TIME			c. 770
Student Numbers 2012-2013			
All (Foreign Included)	11146	10373	21519

Last Update: 04-06-2018

Dong-Eui University

176 Eomgwangno Busan-jin-gu
Pusan 614-714
Tel: +82(51) 890-1114
Fax: +82(51) 890-1234
Website: http://www.deu.ac.kr
President: Sun-Jin Kong

College

Art and Sport Science (Fine Arts; Industrial Design; Leisure Studies; Physical Education; Rehabilitation and Therapy; Sports); **Commerce and Economics** (Accountancy; Banking; Business Administration; Business and Commerce; E- Business/Commerce; Economics; Finance; Food Technology; Hotel and Restaurant; Hotel Management; Information Management; Information Technology; Insurance; International Business; Management; Real Estate; Tourism); **Engineering** (Architecture; Bioengineering; Biotechnology; Building Technologies; Chemical Engineering; Civil Engineering; Engineering; Engineering Management; Environmental Engineering; Industrial Engineering; Marine Engineering; Materials Engineering; Mechanical Engineering; Naval Architecture; Structural Architecture; Town Planning); **Humanities** (Advertising and Publicity; Arts and Humanities; Chinese; Continuing Education; Educational and Student Counselling; English; French; German; History; Information Sciences; Japanese; Korean; Library Science; Literature; Mass Communication; Media Studies; Philosophy; Preschool Education; Psychology; Public Relations; Radio and Television Broadcasting; Writing); **ICT (Information and Communication, Technologies) Engineering** (Computer Engineering; Computer Graphics; Electrical Engineering; Electronic Engineering; Film; Information Technology; Mechanical Engineering; Multimedia; Software Engineering; Telecommunications Engineering); **Law and Government** (Fire Science; Law; Police Studies; Political Sciences; Public

Administration; Social Welfare); **Natural Sciences and Human Ecology** (Biological and Life Sciences; Biotechnology; Chemistry; Child Care and Development; Computer Science; Data Processing; Fashion Design; Food Science; Information Sciences; Mathematics; Molecular Biology; Nutrition; Physics; Psychology); **Nursing and Healthcare Sciences** (Dental Hygiene; Health Administration; Health Sciences; Laboratory Techniques; Nursing; Physical Therapy; Radiology); **Oriental Medicine** (Traditional Eastern Medicine)

Graduate School

Business Administration (*Specialized Graduate School*) (Banking; Business Administration; Business and Commerce; Economics; Finance; Food Science; Hotel and Restaurant; Hotel Management; Insurance; Management; Real Estate; Transport Management); **Education** (*Specialized Graduate School*) (Art Education; Continuing Education; Education; Educational and Student Counselling; Foreign Languages Education; Home Economics Education; Mathematics Education; Native Language Education; Pedagogy; Physical Education; Preschool Education; Primary Education; Science Education); **Graduate Studies** (Advertising and Publicity; Asian Religious Studies; Biological and Life Sciences; Biology; Biomedicine; Biotechnology; Business Administration; Chemical Engineering; Chemistry; Child Care and Development; Chinese; Civil Engineering; Clothing and Sewing; Computer Engineering; Continuing Education; Cultural Studies; E- Business/Commerce; East Asian Studies; Economics; Electrical Engineering; Electronic Engineering; English; Environmental Engineering; Ethics; Finance; Fine Arts; Fire Science; Food Science; Food Technology; Health Sciences; History; Hotel Management; Industrial Design; Industrial Engineering; Industrial Management; Information Management; Information Sciences; Information Technology; Insurance; International Business; Japanese; Korean; Laboratory Techniques; Law; Library Science; Literature; Management; Marine Engineering; Mass Communication; Materials Engineering; Mathematics; Mechanical Engineering; Multimedia; Music; Naval Architecture; Nursing; Nutrition; Philosophy; Physical Education; Physics; Police Studies; Psychology; Public Administration; Real Estate; Social Welfare; Software Engineering; Statistics; Structural Architecture; Telecommunications Engineering; Textile Technology; Tourism; Town Planning; Traditional Eastern Medicine; Translation and Interpretation; Writing); **Industry and Culture** (*Specialized Graduate School*) (Architectural and Environmental Design; Building Technologies; Civil Engineering; Computer Engineering; Electrical and Electronic Engineering; Engineering Management; Industrial Engineering; Information Technology; Mechanical Engineering; Real Estate; Structural Architecture; Telecommunications Engineering; Town Planning); **Public Administration** (*Specialized Graduate School*) (Public Administration; Real Estate; Social Welfare); **Visual Image and Information** (*Specialized Graduate School*) (Film; Media Studies; Multimedia; Music; Visual Arts)

Further information: 34 research institutes; University hospitals

History: Founded 1976 by the Dong Eui Foundation. A private Institution financed by tuition fees (80%) and the Foundation.

Academic year: March to February (March-July; September-December)

Admission requirements: Graduation from high school or foreign equivalent, and entrance examination

Fees: Tuition, 2,700-5,200 per semester

Main language(s) of instruction: Korean

Accrediting agency: Korean Council for University Education (KCUE)

Degrees and diplomas: Bachelor's Degree, Master's Degree (Advertising and Publicity; Architecture and Planning; Asian Religious Studies; Biological and Life Sciences; Biology; Biomedicine; Biotechnology; Business Administration; Chemical Engineering; Chemistry; Child Care and Development; Chinese; Civil Engineering; Clothing and Sewing; Communication Arts; Computer Engineering; Computer Science; Continuing Education; E- Business/Commerce; East Asian Studies; Economics; Education; Electrical Engineering; Electronic Engineering; Engineering; English; Environmental Engineering; Ethics; Finance; Fine Arts; Fire Science; Food Science; Food Technology; Health Sciences; History; Hotel Management; Industrial Design; Industrial Engineering; Industrial Management; Information Management; Information Sciences; Information Technology; Insurance; International Business; Japanese; Korean; Laboratory Techniques; Law; Library Science; Literature; Management; Marine Engineering; Mass Communication; Materials Engineering; Mathematics; Mechanical Engineering; Multimedia; Music; Naval Architecture; Nursing; Nutrition; Philosophy; Physical Education; Physics; Police Studies; Political Sciences; Psychology; Public Administration; Real Estate; Social Welfare; Software Engineering; Statistics; Structural Architecture; Telecommunications Engineering; Textile Technology; Tourism; Town Planning; Traditional Eastern Medicine; Translation and Interpretation; Visual Arts; Writing), Doctor's Degree (Advertising and Publicity; Asian Religious Studies; Biology; Biomedicine; Biotechnology; Business Administration; Chemical Engineering; Chemistry; Civil Engineering; Clothing and Sewing; Computer Engineering; Computer Science; E- Business/Commerce; East Asian Studies; Economics; Electrical Engineering; English; Environmental Engineering; Ethics; Finance; Fire Science; Food Technology; Health Sciences; History; Hotel Management; Industrial Design; Industrial Management; Information Management; Information Sciences; Insurance; International

Business; Japanese; Korean; Laboratory Techniques; Law; Library Science; Literature; Management; Mass Communication; Mathematics; Mechanical Engineering; Multimedia; Music; Nursing; Philosophy; Physical Education; Physics; Psychology; Public Administration; Real Estate; Social Welfare; Software Engineering; Statistics; Structural Architecture; Telecommunications Engineering; Textile Technology; Tourism; Town Planning; Traditional Eastern Medicine; Writing)
Student Services: Social Counselling, Sports Facilities, Health Services, Library, IT Centre, Residential Facilities

Academic Staff 2012-2013	MALE	FEMALE	TOTAL
FULL-TIME			540
PART-TIME			c. 780
Student Numbers 2012-2013			
All (Foreign Included)			c. 24200

Last Update: 20-02-2018

Dongbang Culture University

Seongbuk-ro 28 road 60, Seongbuk-gu
Seoul
Tel: +82(2) 3668-9800
Fax: +82(2) 3668-9899
Website: http://www.dongbang.ac.kr/eng/html/index
Chief Director: Gwang-Yong Ko

Department/Division

Buddhist Culture and Art (Asian Religious Studies; Fine Arts; Literature; Philosophy; Psychology); **Culture and Arts Contents** (Art Management; Art Therapy; Design; Painting and Drawing; Preschool Education; Teacher Training); **Future Forecast Studies** (Anthropology; Esoteric Practices; Philosophy); **Naturopathy** (Alternative Medicine; Cosmetology; Esoteric Practices; Health Sciences; Psychology; Traditional Eastern Medicine; Yoga)
History: Founded 2005 as Dongbang University. Acquired current title 2015.
Main language(s) of instruction: Korean
Accrediting agency: Ministry of Education
Degrees and diplomas: Master's Degree (Alternative Medicine; Anthropology; Art Management; Art Therapy; Asian Religious Studies; Cosmetology; Design; Esoteric Practices; Fine Arts; Health Sciences; Literature; Painting and Drawing; Philosophy; Preschool Education; Psychology; Teacher Training; Traditional Eastern Medicine; Yoga), Doctor's Degree (Alternative Medicine; Anthropology; Art Management; Art Therapy; Asian Religious Studies; Cosmetology; Design; Esoteric Practices; Fine Arts; Health Sciences; Literature; Painting and Drawing; Philosophy; Preschool Education; Psychology; Teacher Training; Traditional Eastern Medicine; Yoga). Also Combined Master and Doctor Degree

Programmes, 8 semesters; Research Course for Foreign Students, 4 sem.
Last Update: 24-05-2018

Dongduk Women's University

23-1 Wolgok-dong Sungbuk-gu
Seoul 136-714
Tel: +82(2) 940-4000
Fax: +82(2) 940-4182
Website: http://www.dongduk.ac.kr
President: Nakhoon Kim

College

Arts (Art Management; Fine Arts; Handicrafts; Music; Musical Instruments; Painting and Drawing; Singing); **Design** (Design); **Humanities** (Arts and Humanities; Chinese; English; French; German; Japanese); **Information Sciences** (Computer Science; Information Sciences; Statistics); **Natural Sciences** (Applied Chemistry; Food Science; Health Sciences; Natural Sciences; Nutrition; Physical Education); **Performing Arts** (Communication Arts; Computer Graphics; Dance; Mass Communication; Music; Performing Arts); **Pharmacy** (Pharmacy); **Social Sciences** (Business Administration; Child Care and Development; Economics; Information Sciences; International Business; Library Science; Social Sciences; Social Welfare)

Graduate School

Design (*Specialized Graduate School*) (Communication Arts; Fashion Design; Industrial Design; Multimedia); **Education** (*Specialized Graduate School*) (Education; Preschool Education); **Fashion Design** (Design; Fashion Design; Marketing; Textile Design); **Graduate Studies** (Applied Chemistry; Business Administration; Child Care and Development; Chinese; Computer Science; Dance; Data Processing; Economics; English; Fashion Design; Fine Arts; Food Science; French; German; Handicrafts; Health Administration; History; Information Sciences; International Business; Japanese; Korean; Library Science; Linguistics; Literature; Museum Studies; Music; Painting and Drawing; Pharmacy; Physical Education; Social Welfare; Textile Design; Women's Studies; Writing); **International Culture** (*Specialized Graduate School*) (Cultural Studies; International Studies; Tourism); **Obesity Science** (*Specialized Graduate School*) (Aesthetics; Cosmetology; Health Sciences); **Performing Arts** (Dance; Mass Communication; Music; Performing Arts; Radio and Television Broadcasting)
History: Founded 1950.
Academic year: March to February (March-August; September-February)
Admission requirements: Graduation from high school and entrance examination

Main language(s) of instruction: Korean

Accrediting agency: Korean Council for University Education (KCUE)

Degrees and diplomas: Bachelor's Degree, Master's Degree (Aesthetics; Applied Chemistry; Business Administration; Child Care and Development; Chinese; Computer Science; Cosmetology; Cultural Studies; Dance; Data Processing; Design; Economics; English; Fashion Design; Fine Arts; Food Science; French; German; Handicrafts; Health Administration; Health Sciences; History; Industrial Design; Information Sciences; International Business; International Studies; Japanese; Korean; Library Science; Literature; Marketing; Mass Communication; Multimedia; Museum Studies; Music; Painting and Drawing; Pharmacy; Physical Education; Preschool Education; Radio and Television Broadcasting; Social Welfare; Textile Design; Tourism; Women's Studies; Writing), Doctor's Degree (Business Administration; Child Care and Development; Computer Science; Dance; English; Fashion Design; Fine Arts; Food Science; Japanese; Korean; Linguistics; Literature; Museum Studies; Music; Pharmacy; Physical Education; Textile Design; Women's Studies)

Student Services: Sports Facilities, Language Laboratory, Health Services, Library, Residential Facilities

Periodicals: Journal of Korean Studies, Treaties

Publishing house: Dongduk Women's University Press

Academic Staff 2013-2014	MALE	FEMALE	TOTAL
FULL-TIME			202
Student Numbers 2013-2014			
All (Foreign Included)			7093

Last Update: 20-02-2018

Dongguk University

30 Pildong-ro 1 gil Jung-gu
Seoul 04620
Tel: +82(2) 2260-3114
Fax: +82(2) 2260-2277
Website: http://www.dongguk.edu
President: Tae-sik Han

College

Arts (Acting; Art History; Cinema and Television; Film; Fine Arts; Media Studies; Performing Arts; Theatre; Visual Arts; Writing); **Buddhist Studies** (Asian Religious Studies; Social Welfare); **Education** (Education; Home Economics Education; Humanities and Social Science Education; Mathematics Education; Native Language Education; Physical Education); **Engineering** (Chemical Engineering; Civil Engineering; Computer Engineering; Computer Science; Electrical and Electronic Engineering; Energy Engineering; Engineering; Environmental Engineering; Industrial Engineering; Information Technology; Materials Engineering; Mechanical Engineering; Multimedia; Robotics; Structural Architecture; Telecommunications Engineering); **Law** (Law; Political Sciences); **Liberal Arts** (Arts and Humanities; Chinese; English; Ethics; History; Japanese; Korean; Literature; Philosophy); **Life Science and Biotechnology** (Biological and Life Sciences; Biology; Biotechnology; Environmental Studies; Food Science; Medical Technology); **Natural Science** (Chemistry; Mathematics; Natural Sciences; Physics; Solid State Physics; Statistics); **Pharmacy** (Pharmacy); **Social Science** (Advertising and Publicity; East Asian Studies; Economics; Food Technology; Industrial Management; International Business; Journalism; Justice Administration; Mass Communication; Public Administration; Public Relations; Social Sciences; Sociology)

School

Business Administration (*Dongguk*) (Business Administration)

Graduate School

Buddhist Studies (Asian Religious Studies; Esoteric Practices; History of Religion; Social Welfare); **Business Administration** (*MBA*) (Business Administration); **Communication and Information** (Advertising and Publicity; Communication Arts; Communication Studies; Computer Networks; Cultural Studies; Design; Economics; Gender Studies; Graphic Arts; Graphic Design; Information Sciences; Information Technology; Journalism; Law; Management; Marketing; Mass Communication; Materials Engineering; Media Studies; Multimedia; Organic Chemistry; Paper Technology; Political Sciences; Polymer and Plastics Technology; Printing and Printmaking; Psychology; Public Relations; Publishing and Book Trade; Radio and Television Broadcasting; Sales Techniques; Social Studies; Sociology; Telecommunications Engineering; Telecommunications Services; Writing); **Culture and Arts** (Art Management; Art Therapy; Asian Religious Studies; Cultural Studies; Heritage Preservation; Literature; Music; Performing Arts; Theatre; Writing); **Digital Image and Contents** (Advertising and Publicity; Art Management; Cinema and Television; Computer Engineering; Computer Graphics; Cultural Studies; Design; Film; Fine Arts; Mass Communication; Media Studies; Multimedia; Performing Arts; Public Relations; Software Engineering; Sound Engineering (Acoustics); Theatre; Visual Arts; Writing); **Education** (Education); **Graduate Studies** (Accountancy; Agricultural Economics; Agriculture; Alternative Medicine; Art History; Asian Religious Studies; Biology; Chemical Engineering; Chemistry; Chinese; Cinema and Television; Civil Engineering; Computer Science; E- Business/Commerce; East Asian Studies; Economics; Education; Electrical Engineering; Electronic Engineering; English; Environmental

Engineering; Esoteric Practices; Ethics; Fine Arts; Food Science; Food Technology; Forestry; Geography; German; History; Home Economics; Hotel Management; Industrial Engineering; Information Management; Information Technology; International Business; Japanese; Journalism; Korean; Landscape Architecture; Law; Literature; Management; Mass Communication; Mathematics; Mechanical Engineering; Medicine; Multimedia; Nursing; Philosophy; Physical Education; Physics; Political Sciences; Public Administration; Safety Engineering; Sociology; Solid State Physics; Statistics; Structural Architecture; Telecommunications Engineering; Theatre; Tourism); **International Affairs and Information** (Computer Engineering; Computer Networks; Data Processing; E- Business/Commerce; Information Management; Information Technology; Safety Engineering; Telecommunications Engineering); **Legal Affairs** (Art Management; Cultural Studies; Law; Private Law); **Public Administration** (Public Administration)

Further information: Also Ilsan Campus

History: Founded 1906 as Myong Zin School, became Choong Ang Buddhist College 1930, Hye Wha College 1940, Dongguk College 1946. Acquired present title and status 1953.

Academic year: March to February (March-July; September-December)

Admission requirements: Graduation from high school or recognized foreign equivalent, and entrance examination

Main language(s) of instruction: Korean

Accrediting agency: Korean Council for University Education (KCUE)

Degrees and diplomas: Bachelor's Degree, Master's Degree (Accountancy; Acting; Agricultural Economics; Agriculture; Alternative Medicine; Art Criticism; Art History; Asian Religious Studies; Biology; Business Administration; Chemical Engineering; Chemistry; Chinese; Cinema and Television; Civil Engineering; Computer Engineering; Computer Graphics; Computer Science; Cultural Studies; E- Business/Commerce; East Asian Studies; Economics; Education; Electrical Engineering; Electronic Engineering; English; Environmental Engineering; Esoteric Practices; Ethics; Film; Fine Arts; Food Science; Food Technology; Forestry; Geography; German; History; Home Economics; Hotel Management; Industrial Engineering; Information Management; Information Technology; Japanese; Journalism; Korean; Landscape Architecture; Law; Literature; Management; Mass Communication; Mathematics; Mechanical Engineering; Medicine; Multimedia; Music; Nursing; Performing Arts; Philosophy; Physical Education; Physics; Political Sciences; Public Administration; Safety Engineering; Sociology; Software Engineering; Solid State Physics; Sound Engineering (Acoustics); Statistics; Structural Architecture; Telecommunications Engineering; Theatre; Tourism; Visual Arts; Writing), Doctor's Degree (Accountancy; Agricultural Economics; Agriculture; Art Criticism; Art History; Asian Religious Studies;

Biology; Chemical Engineering; Chemistry; Cinema and Television; Civil Engineering; Computer Engineering; Computer Graphics; Computer Science; Cultural Studies; East Asian Studies; Economics; Education; Electrical Engineering; Electronic Engineering; English; Environmental Engineering; Esoteric Practices; Ethics; Film; Fine Arts; Food Science; Food Technology; Forestry; Geography; German; History; Home Economics; Industrial Engineering; Information Management; Information Technology; International Business; Japanese; Korean; Law; Literature; Management; Mass Communication; Mathematics; Mechanical Engineering; Medicine; Multimedia; Music; Music Theory and Composition; Performing Arts; Philosophy; Physical Education; Physics; Political Sciences; Public Administration; Safety Engineering; Sociology; Software Engineering; Statistics; Structural Architecture; Telecommunications Engineering; Theatre; Traditional Eastern Medicine; Visual Arts; Writing)

Student Services: Sports Facilities, Library, Residential Facilities

Periodicals: Bulgyo Hakpo (Buddhist Studies), Dongguk Munhak (Korean Literature), Dongguk Sasang (Buddhist Philosophy), Tripitaka Korean

Academic Staff 2013-2014	MALE	FEMALE	TOTAL
FULL-TIME			1151
Student Numbers 2013-2014			
All (Foreign Included)			28204

Last Update: 22-03-2018

DONGGUK UNIVERSITY GYEONGJU

123, Dongdae-ro
Gyeongju-si 780-714, Gyeongsangbuk-do
Tel: +82(54) 770-2114
Fax: +82(54) 770-2001
Website: http://web.dongguk.ac.kr/english/main/main.jsp
President: Dae Won Lee

College

Buddhist Studies and Culture (Asian Religious Studies; Child Care and Development; Music; Religious Education); **Education** (Home Economics Education; Mathematics Education; Preschool Education); **Humanities** (Archaeology; Art History; Arts and Humanities; Chinese; English; Japanese; Korean; Literature; Sports); **Korean Medicine** (Traditional Eastern Medicine); **Management and Economics** (Business Administration; Hotel Management; International Business; International Economics; Tourism); **Medicine** (Medicine); **PARAMITA College** (Arts and Humanities; English; Social Sciences; Sociology); **Science and Technology** (Bioengineering; Biotechnology; Chemistry; Computer Engineering; Data Processing; Electronic Engineering; Energy Engineering; Information Technology; Landscape Architecture;

Mechanical Engineering; Medical Technology; Nuclear Engineering; Pharmacology; Safety Engineering; Statistics; Telecommunications Engineering); **Social Science** (Police Studies; Public Administration; Social Welfare)

Graduate School

Buddhist Studies and Culture (Asian Religious Studies; Fine Arts; Music); **Education** (Education); **Management** (Business Administration); **Medicine** (Medicine); **Social Science** (Social Sciences)

History: Founded 1979.

Main language(s) of instruction: Korean

Accrediting agency: Ministry of Education

Degrees and diplomas: Bachelor's Degree (Archaeology; Art History; Arts and Humanities; Asian Religious Studies; Bioengineering; Biotechnology; Business Administration; Chemistry; Child Care and Development; Chinese; Computer Engineering; Data Processing; Electronic Engineering; Energy Engineering; English; Home Economics Education; Hotel Management; Information Technology; International Business; International Economics; Japanese; Korean; Landscape Architecture; Literature; Mathematics Education; Mechanical Engineering; Medical Technology; Medicine; Music; Nuclear Engineering; Pharmacology; Police Studies; Preschool Education; Public Administration; Religious Education; Safety Engineering; Social Sciences; Social Welfare; Sociology; Sports; Statistics; Telecommunications Engineering; Tourism; Traditional Eastern Medicine), Master's Degree (Asian Religious Studies; Business Administration; Cultural Studies; Fine Arts; Foreign Languages Education; Humanities and Social Science Education; International Relations; Mathematics Education; Music; Native Language Education; Painting and Drawing; Preschool Education; Psychotherapy; Public Administration; Social Sciences; Social Welfare), Doctor's Degree

Student Services: Library, Residential Facilities

Student Numbers 2015-2016	MALE	FEMALE	TOTAL
All (Foreign Included)			8669

Last Update: 22-03-2018

Dongseo University (DSU)

47 Jurye-ro Sasang-gu
Busan 47011
Tel: +82(51) 320-2092, +82(51) 320-2093
Fax: +82(51) 320-2094
Website: http://www.dongseo.ac.kr/en_dsuII
President: Jekuk Chang

College

Film and Performing Arts (*Im Kwon Taek*) (Acting; Dance; Film; Music; Performing Arts; Theatre; Video)

Course/Programme

Korean Language (Arts and Humanities; Korean)

Department/Division

Architecture and Civil Engineering (Architectural and Environmental Design; Architecture; Architecture and Planning; Civil Engineering; Construction Engineering; Interior Design; Structural Architecture); **Business Administration** (Business Administration; Information Management; Information Sciences; Management); **Computer and Information Engineering** (Computer Engineering; Computer Networks; Information Technology; Multimedia; Telecommunications Engineering); **Design** (Architectural and Environmental Design; Design; Fashion Design; Graphic Design; Industrial Design; Media Studies; Multimedia); **Digital Contents** (Computer Engineering; Computer Graphics; Graphic Design; Multimedia; Software Engineering; Visual Arts); **Energy and Bio-Engineering** (Bioengineering; Biotechnology; Energy Engineering; Environmental Engineering; Environmental Management; Environmental Studies; Food Technology; Materials Engineering); **Foreign Languages** (Chinese; English; Japanese; Modern Languages); **Global Studies** (*Courses in English leading to a Bachelor's degree programmes*) (Biotechnology; Computer Engineering; Film; International Studies; Video); **Health Science** (Biological and Life Sciences; Biomedicine; Chemistry; Dental Hygiene; Health Administration; Health Sciences; Laboratory Techniques; Nursing; Radiology); **Information Systems Engineering** (Automation and Control Engineering; Electronic Engineering; Engineering Management; Information Technology; Mechanical Engineering); **International Studies** (International Business; International Relations; International Studies; Transport Management); **Leisure and Sports Science** (Leisure Studies; Protective Services; Sports); **Police Administration** (Justice Administration; Police Studies); **Social Welfare** (Educational and Student Counselling; Educational Psychology; Social Welfare; Social Work); **Tourism** (Hotel Management; Tourism); **Visual Communication** (Advertising and Publicity; Journalism; Mass Communication; Multimedia; Public Relations; Radio and Television Broadcasting; Writing)

Graduate School

Cross-Border Business Administration (*Busan-Fukuoka*) (Business Administration; International Business; International Economics); **Design** (Design; Industrial Engineering; Information Technology; Service Trades); **General Graduate Studies** (Advertising and Publicity; Bioengineering; Biotechnology; Civil Engineering; Communication Arts;

Electronic Engineering; Information Technology; Japanese; Marketing; Mechanical Engineering; Multimedia; Social Welfare; Structural Architecture; Visual Arts); **Mission and Welfare** (Christian Religious Studies; Educational and Student Counselling; Psychology; Religious Music; Social Welfare; Social Work)

History: Founded 1992.

Fees: 2,500 per semester for programmes in the field of Humanities and Social Sciences and International Studies; 3,500 per semester for programmes in the field of Engineering Sciences, Fine Arts, Film, Biotechnology, Computer Engineering (US Dollar)

Main language(s) of instruction: Korean, English

Accrediting agency: Korean Council for University Education (KCUE)

Degrees and diplomas: Bachelor's Degree, Master's Degree (Bioengineering; Business Administration; Chemical Engineering; Civil Engineering; Communication Arts; Design; East Asian Studies; Educational and Student Counselling; Electronic Engineering; Industrial Engineering; Information Technology; International Business; Japanese; Mechanical Engineering; Psychology; Religious Music; Service Trades; Social Welfare; Structural Architecture), Doctor's Degree (Bioengineering; Chemical Engineering; Civil Engineering; Communication Arts; Design; East Asian Studies; Industrial Engineering; Information Technology; Japanese; Service Trades)

Student Services: Canteen, Library, Residential Facilities

Academic Staff 2016-2017	MALE	FEMALE	TOTAL
FULL-TIME			800
Student Numbers 2016-2017			
All (Foreign Included)			c. 11000
Foreign only			1000

Last Update: 20-02-2018

Dongshin University

185 Gunjaero
Naju-si 520-714, Jeollanam-do
Tel: +82(61) 330-3114, +82(61) 330-4011
Fax: +82(61) 330-2909, +82(61) 330-4019
Website: http://www.dsu.ac.kr
President: Kyun-Bum Lee

College

Culture and Tourism (Air Transport; Child Care and Development; Chinese; Education; Foreign Languages Education; Hotel and Restaurant; Music; Performing Arts; Radio and Television Broadcasting; Service Trades; Tourism; Town Planning); **Engineering** (Civil Engineering; Computer Science; Electrical Engineering; Electronic Engineering; Engineering; Information Management; Landscape Architecture; Pharmacy; Structural Architecture; Telecommunications Engineering); **Medicine** (*Korea*) (Medicine; Nursing); **Social Sciences** (Fire Science; Police Studies; Preschool Education; Social Sciences)

Institute

Health and Welfare (Cosmetology; Food Science; Health Administration; Health Sciences; Nutrition; Occupational Therapy; Ophthalmology; Optics; Physical Education; Physical Therapy; Psychology; Radiology; Social Welfare; Speech Therapy and Audiology; Sports; Welfare and Protective Services)

Centre

Korean Language Education (Korean)

Graduate School

Graduate Studies (Arts and Humanities; Engineering; Medicine; Social Sciences; Sports)

History: Founded 1987.

Academic year: March to February (March-August; September-February)

Main language(s) of instruction: Korean

Accrediting agency: Korean Council for University Education (KCUE)

Degrees and diplomas: Bachelor's Degree, Master's Degree (Architectural and Environmental Design; Business Administration; Civil Engineering; Computer Science; Education; Electrical and Electronic Engineering; Energy Engineering; Environmental Engineering; Environmental Studies; Film; Fine Arts; Fire Science; Information Technology; Korean; Medicine; Metallurgical Engineering; Native Language Education; Nursing; Nutrition; Occupational Therapy; Optical Technology; Photography; Physical Education; Physical Therapy; Physics; Psychology; Radiology; Social Welfare; Sports; Structural Architecture; Telecommunications Engineering; Theatre; Tourism; Town Planning; Traditional Eastern Medicine)

Student Services: Sports Facilities, Canteen, Library

Publishing house: Dongshin University Press

Academic Staff 2013-2014	MALE	FEMALE	TOTAL
FULL-TIME			310
PART-TIME			c. 200
Student Numbers 2013-2014			
All (Foreign Included)			c. 7000

Last Update: 20-02-2018

Dongyang University

1 Kyochon-dong Punggi-eup
Yeongju-si 750-711, Gyeongbuk-do
Tel: +82(54) 630-1114, +82(54) 630-1000
Fax: +82(54) 636-8523
Website: http://www.dyu.ac.kr
President: Sung-Hae Choi

School

Management and Tourism (Hotel Management; Management; Tourism); **Public Administration** (Public Administration)

Department/Division

Airline Secretary (Air Transport; Chinese; English; Japanese; Secretarial Studies; Service Trades); **Architectural and Interior Design** (Architectural and Environmental Design; Architecture; Design; Interior Design); **Architecture and Fire Administration** (Architecture; Fire Science); **Chemical and Biomolecular Engineering** (Bioengineering; Biotechnology; Chemical Engineering; Environmental Engineering; Molecular Biology); **Cinema and Theatre** (Cinema and Television; Film; Radio and Television Broadcasting; Theatre); **Computer Information Warfare** (Computer Engineering; Information Management; Information Technology); **Cultural Property** (Archaeology; Heritage Preservation; Museum Studies); **Design Management** (Business Administration; Design; Management; Marketing); **Early Childhood Education** (Preschool Education); **Electro-Magnetic Technology** (Electrical Engineering; Electronic Engineering; Military Science); **Fashion Design and Stylist** (Cosmetology; Fashion Design); **Information and Communication Engineering** (Information Technology; Military Science; Telecommunications Engineering); **International Commerce and English** (Business and Commerce; English; International Business); **Jewelry and Metals** (Jewellery Art; Marketing); **Nursing** (Health Education; Nursing; Paediatrics); **Practical Physical Education** (Physical Education; Sports); **Public Health and Medical Administration** (Health Administration; Nursing; Public Health); **Rail Way Vehicle Engineering** (Automotive Engineering; Railway Engineering; Railway Transport); **Railroad Civil Engineering** (Civil Engineering; Railway Transport); **Railroad Drive and Control** (Automation and Control Engineering; Railway Engineering; Railway Transport; Safety Engineering); **Railroad Electric Communication** (Computer Engineering; Electronic Engineering; Information Technology; Telecommunications Engineering); **Railroad Management Information** (English; Information Technology; Railway Transport); **Social Welfare** (Social Welfare)

Graduate School

Education (Education; Educational Administration; Teacher Training); **Graduate Studies** (Arts and Humanities; Engineering; Fine Arts; Physical Education; Social Sciences); **Information** (Information Management; Information Sciences; Social Welfare)

History: Founded 1994.
Academic year: March to December (March-June; July-December)
Main language(s) of instruction: Korean, English, Japanese
Accrediting agency: Korean Council for University Education (KCUE)
Degrees and diplomas: Bachelor's Degree, Master's Degree (Administration; Art Education; Asian Studies; Bioengineering; Business Administration; Chemical Engineering; Chinese; Civil Engineering; Computer Education; Computer Engineering; Computer Graphics; East Asian Studies; Educational Administration; Electrical and Electronic Engineering; Electrical Engineering; Foreign Languages Education; Graphic Design; Information Management; Information Technology; Korean; Mathematics Education; Military Science; Physical Education; Preschool Education; Railway Engineering; Safety Engineering; Social Welfare; Structural Architecture; Telecommunications Engineering; Transport and Communications), Doctor's Degree (Administration; Automation and Control Engineering; Business Administration; Computer Engineering; Construction Engineering; Electrical and Electronic Engineering; Information Technology; Social Welfare; Telecommunications Engineering)
Student Services: Academic Counselling, Social Counselling, Careers Guidance, Cultural Activities, Sports Facilities, Facilities for disabled people, Health Services, Canteen, Library, Residential Facilities
Periodicals: Dongyang University News
Publishing house: Dongyang University Press

Academic Staff 2013-2014	MALE	FEMALE	TOTAL
FULL-TIME			180
PART-TIME			c. 110
Student Numbers 2013-2014			
All (Foreign Included)			c. 4310

Last Update: 20-02-2018

Duksung Women's University

419, Ssangmun-dong Dobong-gu
Seoul 132-714
Tel: +82(2) 901-8000
Fax: +82(2) 901-8060
Website: http://www.duksung.ac.kr
President: Won-Bok Rhie

College

Art and Design (Design; Fashion Design; Fine Arts; Graphic Design; Interior Design; Painting and Drawing; Textile Design); **Humanities** (Art History; Arts and Humanities; Chinese; English; French; German; History; Japanese; Korean; Literature; Philosophy; Spanish); **Information and Media** (Computer Engineering; Computer Networks; Computer Science; Information Technology; Multimedia; Software Engineering); **Natural Sciences** (Chemistry; Food Technology; Health Sciences; Mathematics; Natural Sciences; Nutrition; Sports; Statistics); **Pharmacy** (Pharmacology; Pharmacy); **Social Sciences** (Accountancy; Anthropology; Business Administration; Child Care and Development; Cultural Studies; Development Studies; Family Studies; Information Sciences; International Business; International Economics; International Studies; Law; Library Science; Political Sciences; Preschool Education; Psychology; Social Sciences; Social Welfare; Sociology)

Course/Programme

Korean Language and Cultural Programs (*For International Students*) (East Asian Studies; Korean)

Graduate School

Culture and Industries (Archiving; Fashion Design; Marketing; Pharmacology; Textile Design); **Education** (Education; Educational Sciences; Teacher Training); **Graduate Studies** (Administration; Business Administration; Chemistry; Computer Education; Computer Graphics; Computer Science; Design; English; Fine Arts; Food Science; French; Information Technology; Korean; Literature; Management; Mathematics; Multimedia; Museum Studies; Nutrition; Pharmacy; Preschool Education; Psychology; Social Welfare; Statistics)

Further information: Also Jongno Campus

History: Founded 1950 as Duksung Woman's Junior College. Acquired present status and title 1987.

Academic year: March to February (March-August; September-February)

Admission requirements: Graduation from high school or foreign equivalent, and entrance examination

Main language(s) of instruction: Korean

Accrediting agency: Korean Council for University Education (KCUE)

Degrees and diplomas: Bachelor's Degree, Master's Degree (Business Administration; Chemistry; Computer Education; Computer Graphics; Computer Science; Continuing Education; Design; Education; Educational Administration; Educational Psychology; English; Fine Arts; Food Science; Foreign Languages Education; French; Humanities and Social Science Education; Information Technology; Korean; Literature; Management; Mathematics; Museum Studies; Native Language Education; Nutrition; Pharmacy; Preschool Education; Primary Education; Psychology; Secondary Education; Social Welfare), Doctor's Degree (Food Science; Nutrition; Pharmacy; Preschool Education; Psychology). Also Teaching Certificate; Postgraduate Professional and Research Porgrammes

Periodicals: Journal of Professors' Research

Academic Staff 2012-2013	MALE	FEMALE	TOTAL
FULL-TIME			250
PART-TIME			c. 330
Student Numbers 2012-2013			
All (Foreign Included)			c. 600
Foreign only			100

Last Update: 20-02-2018

Eulji University

77 Gyeryong-ro, 771 Beon-gil Jung-gu
Daejeon 201-746, 771 Gyeryong-ro
Tel: +82(31) 740-7419, +82(31) 740-7106
Fax: +82(31) 740-7252, +82(31) 740-7376
Website: http://www.eulji.ac.kr
President: Woo-Hyun Cho

College

Health Industry (*Seongnam Campus*) (Child Care and Development; Fire Science; Food Science; Food Technology; Graphic Design; Health Administration; Health Sciences; Hygiene; Information Technology; Leisure Studies; Marketing; Medical Technology; Nutrition; Preschool Education; Public Relations; Rehabilitation and Therapy; Safety Engineering; Social and Preventive Medicine; Social Welfare; Software Engineering; Tourism); **Health Sciences** (*Seongnam Campus*) (Biomedical Engineering; Biomedicine; Dental Hygiene; Dermatology; Health Sciences; Laboratory Techniques; Medicine; Optometry; Physical Therapy; Radiology; Rehabilitation and Therapy); **Nursing** (*Daejeon Campus*) (Nursing); **Nursing** (*Seongnam Campus*) (Nursing)

School

Medicine (*Daejeon Campus*) (Biomedicine; Biotechnology; Health Administration; Laboratory Techniques; Medicine)

Graduate School

Advanced Practice Nursing (Gerontology; Health Education; Health Sciences; Nursing; Psychiatry and Mental Health); **Graduate Studies** (Medicine; Nursing; Public Health); **Public Health Science** (*Special Graduate School*) (Biomedicine; Health Administration; Laboratory Techniques; Optometry; Physical Therapy; Public Health; Radiology; Rehabilitation and Therapy)

Further information: Also Seongnam Campus; 3 university hospitals

History: Founded 1996 as Eulji Medical College. Acquired present status and title 1999.

Main language(s) of instruction: Korean, English

Accrediting agency: Korean Council for University Education (KCUE)

Degrees and diplomas: Bachelor's Degree, Master's Degree (Medicine; Nursing), Doctor's Degree (Health Sciences; Medicine; Nursing)

Student Services: IT Centre, Residential Facilities

Academic Staff 2013-2014	MALE	FEMALE	TOTAL
FULL-TIME			430
PART-TIME			c. 250
Student Numbers 2013-2014			
All (Foreign Included)			c. 5700

Last Update: 21-03-2018

Ewha Women's University

52, Ewhayeodae-gil Seodaemun-gu
Seoul 03760
Tel: +82(2) 3277-2114
Fax: +82(2) 393-5903
Website: http://www.ewha.ac.kr
President: Heisook Kim
Tel: +82(2) 3277-2011

College

Arts and Design (Ceramic Art; Clothing and Sewing; Communication Arts; Design; Fashion Design; Fine Arts; Graphic Design; Industrial Design; Interior Design; Painting and Drawing; Sculpture; Textile Design); **Business Administration** (Business Administration; International Business; Management); **Education** (Education; Educational Technology; Foreign Languages Education; Humanities and Social Science Education; Mathematics Education; Native Language Education; Preschool Education; Primary Education; Science Education; Special Education); **Engineering** (Architecture; Computer Science; Electronic Engineering; Engineering; Environmental Engineering; Environmental Studies; Food Science; Food Technology; Structural Architecture); **Ewha International Summer College** (*International programme*) (Business Administration; Design; East Asian Studies; Economics; Fine Arts; International Studies; Music; Natural Sciences; Social Sciences; Women's Studies; Writing); **Health Sciences** (Food Science; Health Sciences; Nursing; Nutrition; Sports); **Law** (Law); **Liberal Arts** (Arts and Humanities; Chinese; Christian Religious Studies; English; French; German; History; Korean; Literature; Philosophy); **Music** (Dance; Music; Music Theory and Composition; Musical Instruments; Singing); **Natural Sciences** (Biological and Life Sciences; Chemistry; Mathematics; Nanotechnology; Physics; Statistics); **Pharmacy** (Pharmacy); **Scranton** (International Studies); **Social Sciences** (Advertising and Publicity; Cinema and Television; Consumer Studies; Economics; Information Sciences; International Relations; Journalism; Library Science; Political Sciences; Psychology; Public Administration; Public Relations; Social Sciences; Social Welfare; Sociology)

Institute
Leadership Development (*School for Leadership Development*) (Leadership)

Centre
Ewha Language (Korean); **Innovation in Engineering Education** (Engineering)

Graduate School
Business Administration (Business Administration); **Clinical Dentistry** (Dentistry); **Clinical Health Sciences** (Health Sciences; Nursing; Nutrition; Pharmacy); **Design** (Design; Industrial Design); **Education** (Art Education; Art Therapy; Computer Education; Curriculum; Education; Educational Administration; Educational and Student Counselling; Environmental Studies; Ethics; Foreign Languages Education; Health Education; Home Economics Education; Humanities and Social Science Education; Mathematics Education; Music Education; Native Language Education; Physical Education; Preschool Education; Primary Education; Science Education; Special Education); **Graduate studies** (Architecture; Art History; Art Therapy; Biological and Life Sciences; Business Administration; Chemistry; Child Care and Development; Chinese; Christian Religious Studies; Clothing and Sewing; Cognitive Sciences; Communication Disorders; Communication Studies; Computer Engineering; Computer Science; Consumer Studies; Cultural Studies; Dance; Design; East Asian Studies; Ecology; Economics; Education; Education of the Gifted; Educational Technology; Electronic Engineering; English; Environmental Engineering; Environmental Studies; Ethics; Fine Arts; Food Science; Food Technology; Foreign Languages Education; French; German; Health Education; Health Sciences; History; Humanities and Social Science Education; Information Sciences; International Business; International Relations; Korean; Law; Library Science; Literature; Mathematics; Mathematics Education; Medicine; Meteorology; Multimedia; Music; Nanotechnology; Native Language Education; Nursing; Nutrition; Pharmacology; Pharmacy; Philosophy; Physics; Political Sciences; Preschool Education; Primary Education; Psychology; Public

Administration; Science Education; Social Welfare; Sociology; Special Education; Sports; Statistics; Structural Architecture; Textile Design; Women's Studies); **International Studies** (*GSIS*) (International Business; International Economics; International Law; International Relations; Political Sciences); **Law** (Law); **Medicine** (Medicine); **Performing Arts** (Computer Science; Music; Performing Arts); **Policy Sciences** (Archiving; Mass Communication; Public Administration); **Social Welfare** (*GSSW*) (Social Welfare; Welfare and Protective Services); **Teaching Foreign Languages** (Foreign Languages Education); **Theology** (*EGST*) (Catholic Theology; Theology); **Translation and Interpretation** (Chinese; English; French; Japanese; Translation and Interpretation)

Research Division

Basic Science; **Cell Signaling** (*SRC*); **Ceramics**; **Color Design**; **Communication and Media**; **Computer Graphics and Virtual Reality**; **Curriculum Instruction**; **Environmental Studies**; **Ewha Information Telecom** (*EITI*); **Ewha Institute for Humanities**; **Fashion Design**; **Global Food and Nutrition**; **Human Ecology**; **Korean Culture**; **Korean Women's Studies**; **Legal Science** (*ELSI*); **Management**; **Mathematical Science**; **Medical Studies**; **Movement Science**; **Music**; **Nano-Biotechnology**; **Nursing Science**; **Social Sciences**; **Special Education**

Further information: Also International Educational Institute (IEI). University Hospital; Over 40 additional Research Institutes

History: Founded 1886 as School by Mary Scranton (Methodist Missionary), became College 1910 and University 1946. A private Institution financed by tuition fees, Government grant, and donations.

Academic year: March to February (March-August; September-February)

Admission requirements: Graduation from high school or equivalent, and entrance examination

Main language(s) of instruction: Korean, English

Accrediting agency: Korean Council for University Education (KCUE)

Degrees and diplomas: Bachelor's Degree, Master's Degree (Aesthetics; Architecture; Art History; Art Management; Art Therapy; Biological and Life Sciences; Business Administration; Ceramic Art; Chemistry; Child Care and Development; Chinese; Christian Religious Studies; Cognitive Sciences; Communication Disorders; Computer Engineering; Computer Science; Consumer Studies; Data Processing; Design; Developmental Psychology; East Asian Studies; Ecology; Economics; Education; Education of the Gifted; Educational Technology; Electronic Engineering; English; Environmental Engineering; Environmental Studies; Fine Arts; Food Science; Food Technology; Foreign Languages Education; French; German; Handicrafts; Health Education;

Health Sciences; History; Humanities and Social Science Education; Information Sciences; Information Technology; International Economics; International Relations; International Studies; Korean; Law; Library Science; Literature; Mass Communication; Mathematics; Mathematics Education; Media Studies; Medicine; Meteorology; Music; Nanotechnology; Native Language Education; Nursing; Nutrition; Painting and Drawing; Pharmacy; Philosophy; Physics; Political Sciences; Preschool Education; Primary Education; Psychology; Public Administration; Science Education; Sculpture; Social Welfare; Sociology; Special Education; Statistics; Structural Architecture; Translation and Interpretation; Visual Arts; Women's Studies), Doctor's Degree (Architecture; Art History; Art Therapy; Biological and Life Sciences; Business Administration; Ceramic Art; Chemistry; Child Care and Development; Chinese; Christian Religious Studies; Cognitive Sciences; Communication Disorders; Computer Engineering; Computer Science; Consumer Studies; Data Processing; Design; Developmental Psychology; East Asian Studies; Ecology; Economics; Education; Educational Technology; Electronic Engineering; English; Environmental Engineering; Environmental Studies; Fashion Design; Fine Arts; Food Science; Food Technology; Foreign Languages Education; French; German; Graphic Design; Handicrafts; Health Sciences; History; Humanities and Social Science Education; Industrial Design; Information Sciences; Information Technology; Interior Design; International Economics; International Relations; Korean; Law; Library Science; Literature; Mass Communication; Mathematics; Mathematics Education; Media Studies; Medicine; Meteorology; Music; Musicology; Nanotechnology; Nursing; Nutrition; Painting and Drawing; Pharmacy; Philosophy; Physical Education; Physics; Political Sciences; Preschool Education; Primary Education; Psychology; Public Administration; Public Health; Science Education; Sculpture; Social Welfare; Sociology; Special Education; Statistics; Structural Architecture; Translation and Interpretation; Visual Arts; Women's Studies). Also Professional Postgraduate Diploma in Clinical Dentistry, Medicine (Anatomy, Physiology, Biochemistry, Pathology, Microbiology, Pharmacology, Preventive Medicine, Parasitology, Molecular Medicine, Neuroscience, Medical Education, Medical Ethics and Health Science), Pharmacy, Health Education and Administration, Performing Arts (Music), Public Policy (Public Administration, Mass Communications, Archiving), Law.

Student Services: Academic Counselling, Social Counselling, Careers Guidance, Nursery Care, Cultural Activities, Sports Facilities, Language Laboratory, Facilities for disabled people, Health Services, Canteen, Foreign Studies Centre, Library, Residential Facilities

Periodicals: Abstracts of Graduate School Theses, Academic Journal of Graduate School, Edae Hakbo, Ewha Annual Report, Ewha Bulletin, Ewha Graduate School Bulletin,

International Education Institute Bulletin, Journal of Korean Research Institute for Better Life, Review of Women's Studies, University Museum Catalogue

Publishing house: University Press

Academic Staff 2013-2014	MALE	FEMALE	TOTAL
FULL-TIME			c. 1130
Student Numbers 2013-2014			
All (Foreign Included)			22268

Last Update: 20-02-2018

Far East University

San 5 Wangjang-ri, Gamgok
Eumseong 27601, Chungbuk-do
Tel: +82(43) 879-3500, +82(43) 879-3679
Fax: +82(43) 882-3310, +82(43) 882-3680
Website: http://www.kdu.ac.kr
President: Ki-Il Lyu

School

Airline (Aeronautical and Aerospace Engineering; Air Transport; Chinese; Maintenance Technology; Service Trades); **Arts** (Computer Graphics; Mass Communication; Media Studies; Visual Arts); **Business** (Business Administration; Food Technology; Hotel Management; Information Management; Real Estate; Tourism); **Design** (Advertising and Publicity; Aesthetics; Design; Marketing; Packaging Technology); **Education** (Education; Primary Education; Secondary Education; Special Education); **Engineering** (Computer Engineering; Computer Networks; Electronic Engineering; Engineering; Environmental Engineering; Information Sciences; Information Technology; Safety Engineering; Software Engineering; Telecommunications Engineering); **Foreign Language** (Chinese; English; Japanese; Modern Languages); **Natural Science** (Biochemistry; Biology; Biotechnology; Microbiology; Traditional Eastern Medicine); **Public Health** (Biomedicine; Laboratory Techniques; Nursing; Occupational Therapy; Optics; Public Health; Radiology); **Social Sciences** (Journalism; Law; Mass Communication; Police Studies; Social Sciences; Social Welfare); **Sports Science** (Health Sciences; Leisure Studies; Physical Education; Sociology; Sports)

Graduate School

Business and Public Administration (Air Transport; Business Administration; Business and Commerce; Communication Studies; Hotel and Restaurant; Information Sciences; International Business; Psychology; Psychotherapy; Public Administration; Social Welfare; Tourism); **Education** (Computer Education; Continuing Education; Education; Educational Administration; Educational and Student Counselling); **Graduate Studies** (Business Administration; Communication Studies; Design; Electronic Engineering; Energy Engineering; Information Sciences; Media Studies; Performing Arts); **Public Health** (Health Sciences; Occupational Health; Occupational Therapy; Ophthalmology; Optics; Public Health; Radiology; Traditional Eastern Medicine)

History: Founded 1998.
Main language(s) of instruction: Korean
Accrediting agency: Korean Council for University Education (KCUE)
Degrees and diplomas: Bachelor's Degree, Master's Degree (Air Transport; Business Administration; Business and Commerce; Communication Arts; Communication Studies; Computer Education; Continuing Education; Design; Educational Administration; Educational and Student Counselling; Electronic Engineering; Energy Engineering; Hotel Management; Information Sciences; International Business; Performing Arts; Public Administration; Public Health; Social Welfare; Tourism), Doctor's Degree (Air Transport; Business Administration; Communication Studies; Information Sciences)
Student Services: Sports Facilities, Canteen, Library, IT Centre, Residential Facilities

Academic Staff 2013-2014	MALE	FEMALE	TOTAL
FULL-TIME			62
PART-TIME			58
Student Numbers 2013-2014			
All (Foreign Included)			1897

Last Update: 20-02-2018

Gachon University

191 Hambakmoero Yeonsu-gu
Incheon-si 406-799
Tel: +82(32) 820-4000
Fax: +82(32) 820-4059
Website: http://www.gachon.ac.kr
President: Gil-Ya Lee

College

Arts and Design (*Global Campus*) (Computer Graphics; Design; Fine Arts; Industrial Design; Painting and Drawing; Sculpture; Video; Visual Arts); **BioNano Technology** (*Global Campus*) (Biochemistry; Biological and Life Sciences; Biology; Biomedicine; Genetics; Immunology; Microbiology; Molecular Biology; Nanotechnology; Organic Chemistry); **Business and Economics** (*Global Campus*) (Accountancy; Business Administration; Economics; Health Administration; International Business; Mass

Communication; Statistics; Taxation; Tourism); **Dental Hygiene** (*Medical Campus*) (Dental Hygiene); **Engineering** (*Global Campus*) (Architecture; Bioengineering; Biotechnology; Building Technologies; Chemical Engineering; Civil Engineering; Electrical Engineering; Energy Engineering; Engineering; Environmental Engineering; Fire Science; Food Science; Industrial Engineering; Interior Design; Landscape Architecture; Mechanical Engineering; Protective Services; Safety Engineering; Structural Architecture; Town Planning); **Human Ecology** (*Global Campus*) (Acting; Child Care and Development; Clothing and Sewing; Developmental Psychology; Educational and Student Counselling; Food Science; Home Economics; Leisure Studies; Nutrition; Physical Education; Preschool Education; Rehabilitation and Therapy; Social Welfare; Sports; Sports Management); **Information Technology** (*Global Campus*) (Artificial Intelligence; Computer Education; Computer Engineering; Computer Science; Data Processing; Electronic Engineering; Information Technology; Multimedia; Robotics; Software Engineering; Telecommunications Engineering); **Integrative Studies (Humanities)** (*Global Campus*) (Arts and Humanities); **Korean Medicine** (*Global Campus*) (Alternative Medicine; Anatomy; Pathology); **Law** (*Global Campus*) (Development Studies; Law; Political Sciences; Public Administration); **Liberal Arts** (*Global Campus*) (Arts and Humanities; Chinese; English; French; German; Japanese; Korean; Literature); **Music** (*Global Campus*) (Music; Music Theory and Composition; Musical Instruments; Singing); **Natural Sciences** (*Global Campus*) (Analytical Chemistry; Biochemistry; Chemistry; Inorganic Chemistry; Mathematics; Natural Sciences; Organic Chemistry; Physical Chemistry; Physics; Statistics); **Nursing** (*Medical Campus*) (Nursing); **Pharmacy** (*Medical Campus*) (Pharmacology; Pharmacy)

Graduate School

Business Administration (*Global Campus*) (Business Administration; Economics; Industrial and Production Economics; Industrial Management; International Business; Small Business); **Education** (*Global Campus*) (Education; Education of the Gifted; Educational Administration; Educational and Student Counselling; Educational Psychology; Foreign Languages Education; Home Economics Education; Mathematics Education; Music Education; Native Language Education; Physical Education; Teacher Training); **Environment and Design** (*Global Campus*) (Design; Environmental Engineering; Environmental Studies; Fire Science; Safety Engineering); **Graduate Studies** (*Global Campus*) (Accountancy; Alternative Medicine; Architecture; Biological and Life Sciences; Biotechnology; Building Technologies; Business Administration; Chinese; Civil Engineering; Development Studies; Economics; English; Environmental Engineering; Fine Arts; Fire Science; Food Science; French;

German; Health Administration; Industrial Design; Industrial Engineering; Information Sciences; Information Technology; Interior Design; International Business; Korean; Landscape Architecture; Law; Literature; Mass Communication; Mathematics; Mechanical Engineering; Media Studies; Music; Nanotechnology; Nutrition; Physical Education; Police Studies; Preschool Education; Protective Services; Public Administration; Safety Engineering; Sculpture; Social Welfare; Software Engineering; Taxation; Tourism; Town Planning; Visual Arts); **Hospital Management** (*Special Graduate School - Medical Campus*) (Health Administration); **Media-Information** (*Special Graduate School - Medical Campus*) (Information Sciences; Media Studies; Multimedia); **Medicine** (*Medical Campus*) (Medical Technology; Medicine); **Nursing** (*Special Graduate School - Medical Campus*) (Community Health; Nursing; Public Health); **Public Health** (*Special Graduate School - Medical Campus*) (Public Health); **Social Policy** (*Global Campus*) (Public Administration; Real Estate; Social Policy; Social Studies; Social Welfare); **Sports and Leisure Studies** (*Global Campus*) (Business Administration; Health Sciences; Leisure Studies; Social and Preventive Medicine; Sports; Sports Management)

Further information: Also Global Campus in Seongnam

History: Founded 1997 as Gachon Medical School. Merged with Gachon Gil University 2005. Acquired present title 2011 following merger with Kyungwon University.

Main language(s) of instruction: Korean, English

Accrediting agency: Korean Council for University Education (KCUE)

Degrees and diplomas: Bachelor's Degree, Master's Degree (Accountancy; Acupuncture; Administration; Air Transport; Anatomy; Architecture; Architecture and Planning; Art History; Bioengineering; Biological and Life Sciences; Biotechnology; Botany; Business Administration; Chemical Engineering; Child Care and Development; Chinese; Civil Engineering; Civil Law; Clothing and Sewing; Commercial Law; Communication Arts; Computer Engineering; Cosmetology; Criminal Law; Design; Development Studies; Economic and Finance Policy; Economics; Education of the Gifted; Educational Administration; Educational and Student Counselling; Educational Psychology; Electrical Engineering; Electronic Engineering; Energy Engineering; Engineering Management; English; Environmental Engineering; Environmental Management; Environmental Studies; Finance; Fine Arts; Fire Science; Food Science; Food Technology; Foreign Languages Education; French; German; Graphic Design; Gynaecology and Obstetrics; Health Administration; Health Sciences; Home Economics Education; Hotel Management; Industrial Design; Industrial Engineering; Information Management; Information Sciences; Information Technology; Instrument Making; Insurance; Interior Design; International

Business; International Economics; Journalism; Justice Administration; Korean; Landscape Architecture; Leisure Studies; Linguistics; Literature; Management; Marketing; Mass Communication; Materials Engineering; Mathematics; Mathematics Education; Mechanical Engineering; Media Studies; Molecular Biology; Music; Music Education; Music Theory and Composition; Musical Instruments; Nanotechnology; Native Language Education; Nursing; Nutrition; Pathology; Pharmacology; Physical Education; Physiology; Police Studies; Political Sciences; Preschool Education; Private Law; Protective Services; Public Administration; Public Health; Public Law; Real Estate; Rehabilitation and Therapy; Safety Engineering; Sculpture; Singing; Small Business; Social Welfare; Software Engineering; Solid State Physics; Sports; Sports Management; Statistics; Structural Architecture; Taxation; Tourism; Town Planning; Traditional Eastern Medicine; Translation and Interpretation; Urban Studies; Welfare and Protective Services), Doctor's Degree (Accountancy; Acupuncture; Administration; Air Transport; Anatomy; Architecture and Planning; Bioengineering; Biological and Life Sciences; Biomedicine; Biotechnology; Botany; Chemical Engineering; Chemistry; Civil Law; Clothing and Sewing; Commercial Law; Computer Engineering; Cosmetology; Criminal Law; Economic and Finance Policy; Economics; Educational Administration; Educational and Student Counselling; Educational Psychology; Electrical Engineering; Electronic Engineering; Energy Engineering; Engineering Management; English; Finance; Food Science; Gynaecology and Obstetrics; Health Administration; Hotel Management; Industrial Engineering; Information Sciences; Information Technology; Interior Design; International Business; International Economics; Korean; Literature; Management; Marketing; Materials Engineering; Mechanical Engineering; Medicine; Molecular Biology; Nanotechnology; Pathology; Pharmacology; Physical Education; Physics; Physiology; Preschool Education; Private Law; Public Administration; Public Law; Real Estate; Rehabilitation and Therapy; Safety Engineering; Statistics; Structural Architecture; Taxation; Tourism; Town Planning; Traditional Eastern Medicine; Urban Studies; Welfare and Protective Services)

Student Services: Sports Facilities, Health Services, Library, IT Centre, Residential Facilities

Academic Staff 2013-2014	MALE	FEMALE	TOTAL
FULL-TIME			1200
PART-TIME			c. 1880
Student Numbers 2013-2014			
All (Foreign Included)			c. 18995
Foreign only			633

Last Update: 20-02-2018

Geumgang University (GGU)

14-9 Daemyeong-ri, Sangwol-myeon
Nonsan-si 320-931, Chungnam-do
Tel: +82(41) 731-3114
Fax: +82(41) 731-3049
Website: http://www.geumgang.ac.kr
President: Byung-Jo Chung

School

Buddhist Studies and Social Welfare (Asian Religious Studies; Social Welfare); **International Trade and Public Administration** (Chinese; English; International Business; Japanese; Public Administration; Translation and Interpretation)

Centre

Geumgang Language (*For International Students*) (Asian Studies; Chinese; English; Japanese; Korean)

Graduate School

Social Welfare and Information Sciences (Asian Religious Studies; Comparative Religion; Esoteric Practices; Information Sciences; Psychiatry and Mental Health; Social Policy; Social Welfare; Social Work)

Research Division

International Buddhist Studies (Asian Religious Studies); **Interpretation and Translation** (Translation and Interpretation); **Social Welfare** (Social Welfare)

History: Founded 2003.
Main language(s) of instruction: Korean
Accrediting agency: Korean Council for University Education (KCUE)
Degrees and diplomas: Bachelor's Degree, Master's Degree (Administration; Asian Religious Studies; Esoteric Practices; Social Policy; Social Welfare; Social Work), Doctor's Degree (Asian Religious Studies; Comparative Religion; Social Policy; Social Welfare; Social Work)
Student Services: Academic Counselling, Careers Guidance, Sports Facilities, Language Laboratory, Canteen, Library, eLibrary, IT Centre, Residential Facilities

Academic Staff 2013-2014	MALE	FEMALE	TOTAL
FULL-TIME			22
PART-TIME			37
Student Numbers 2013-2014			
All (Foreign Included)			297

Last Update: 20-02-2018

Gimcheon University (GU)

214, Daehak-ro
Gimcheon 39528, Gyeongsangbuk-do
Tel: +82(54) 420-4000
Fax: +82(54) 420-4005
Website: http://www.gimcheon.ac.kr
President: Sung Ae Kang

College

Arts and Sport Science (Music); **Education** (Preschool Education); **Engineering** (Computer Engineering; Electronic Engineering; Information Technology; Mechanical Engineering; Safety Engineering); **Humanities and Social Science** (Air Transport; Business Administration; English; Hotel Management; Management; Police Studies; Psychology; Psychotherapy; Social Welfare; Tourism); **Nursing and Health Science** (Biomedicine; Cooking and Catering; Dental Hygiene; Dental Technology; Food Science; Health Administration; Hotel and Restaurant; Laboratory Techniques; Nursing; Occupational Therapy; Optometry; Physical Therapy; Radiology; Rehabilitation and Therapy; Speech Therapy and Audiology; Sports)
History: Founded 1978
Main language(s) of instruction: Korean
Accrediting agency: Korean Council for University Education (KCUE)
Degrees and diplomas: Bachelor's Degree (Air Transport; Biomedicine; Business Administration; Computer Engineering; Cooking and Catering; Dental Hygiene; Dental Technology; Electronic Engineering; English; Food Science; Health Administration; Hotel and Restaurant; Hotel Management; Information Technology; Laboratory Techniques; Management; Mechanical Engineering; Music; Nursing; Occupational Therapy; Optometry; Physical Therapy; Police Studies; Preschool Education; Psychology; Psychotherapy; Radiology; Rehabilitation and Therapy; Safety Engineering; Social Welfare; Speech Therapy and Audiology; Sports; Tourism)
Student Services: Health Services, Library, Residential Facilities
Last Update: 09-03-2018

Global Cyber University (GCU)

11, Apgujeong-ro 32-gil, Gangnam-gu
Seoul 613-5, Sinsa-dong
Fax: +82(2) 2160-1199
Website: http://eng.global.ac.kr/home/homeIndex.do
President: Seung-Heun Lee

Department/Division

Counseling Psychology (Psychology); **Culture and Arts** (Mass Communication; Radio and Television Broadcasting; Writing); **Global Business Management** (Business Administration; Marketing); **Integrated Brain Education** (Education); **Oriental Studies** (Oriental Studies); **Practical Foreign Language** (English); **Social Welfare** (Social Welfare)
Further information: Also Cheonan Campus
History: Founded 2010.
Main language(s) of instruction: Korean
Accrediting agency: Ministry of Education
Degrees and diplomas: Bachelor's Degree (Business Administration; Education; English; Marketing; Mass Communication; Oriental Studies; Psychology; Radio and Television Broadcasting; Social Welfare; Writing)
Last Update: 27-03-2018

Gwangju University

277 Hyodeok-Ro Nam-Gu
Gwangju-si 61743, Gyeonggi-do
Tel: +82(62) 670-2114
Fax: +82(62) 674-0078
Website: http://www.gwangju.ac.kr
President: Hyuk-Jong Kim

College

Culture and Art (Communication Arts; Design; Fashion Design; Fine Arts; Industrial Design; Interior Design; Jewellery Art; Musical Instruments; Performing Arts; Photography; Singing; Sports; Visual Arts); **Engineering** (Architecture; Civil Engineering; Computer Engineering; Computer Science; Electrical Engineering; Electronic Engineering; Energy Engineering; Engineering; Information Technology; Military Science; Real Estate; Technology; Telecommunications Engineering; Town Planning); **Health, Welfare and Education** (Alternative Medicine; Continuing Education; Cosmetology; Education; Educational and Student Counselling; Food Science; Health Administration; Health Sciences; Leisure Studies; Medical Technology; Nursing; Nutrition; Occupational Therapy; Preschool Education; Psychotherapy; Social Welfare; Speech Therapy and Audiology; Sports; Welfare and Protective Services); **Humanities and Social Sciences** (Chinese; Computer Engineering; English; Fire Science; Information Sciences; Japanese; Journalism; Korean; Law; Library Science; Literature; Mass Communication; Native Language Education; Police Studies; Public Administration; Writing); **Management** (Air Transport; Business Administration; Finance; Food Technology; Hotel and Restaurant; Hotel Management; Management; Real Estate; Service Trades; Taxation; Tourism; Transport Management)

Department/Division
Self-designed and Open Majors

Institute
Educational-Industrial Cooperation (Architecture; Business Administration; Design; Ecology; Health Sciences; International Business; Optical Technology; Technology; Town Planning); **Humanities and Social Sciences** (Administration; Advertising and Publicity; Art Education; Chinese; English; Humanities and Social Science Education; Information Sciences; Japanese; Law; Library Science; Mass Communication; Police Studies; Preschool Education; Public Relations; Teacher Trainers Education); **Industrial Technology** (Architecture; Civil Engineering; Computer Engineering; Electronic Engineering; Engineering; Environmental Engineering; Industrial Engineering; Structural Architecture; Telecommunications Engineering; Town Planning)

Graduate School
General Studies (Accountancy; Administration; Architecture; Business and Commerce; Civil Engineering; Clothing and Sewing; Computer Engineering; Computer Science; Continuing Education; Design; Electronic Engineering; Environmental Engineering; Finance; Hotel Management; Industrial Design; Industrial Engineering; Information Sciences; Information Technology; Journalism; Law; Library Science; Management; Mass Communication; Music; Occupational Therapy; Optical Technology; Photography; Police Studies; Preschool Education; Public Administration; Real Estate; Structural Architecture; Telecommunications Engineering; Tourism; Town Planning; Transport Management; Writing); **Mass Communication and Advertising** (Advertising and Publicity; Mass Communication; Media Studies; Public Relations); **Social Welfare** (Administration; Child Care and Development; Psychiatry and Mental Health; Rehabilitation and Therapy; Social Policy; Social Welfare; Social Work; Sociology)

Further information: Also 17 other attached Centres and Institutes

History: Founded 1981 as Kwangju Kyung-Sang Junior College. Acquired status of four year college in 1983 as Kwangju Open University and acquired present status and title in 1990.

Academic year: March to December (March-June; September-December)

Admission requirements: Graduation from high school or equivalent

Main language(s) of instruction: Korean

Accrediting agency: Korean University Accreditation Institute; Korean Council for University Education (KCUE); Ministry of Education, Science and Technology

Degrees and diplomas: Bachelor's Degree, Master's Degree (Accountancy; Administration; Architecture; Business and Commerce; Civil Engineering; Clothing and Sewing; Computer Engineering; Computer Science; Design; Electronic Engineering; Environmental Engineering; Finance; Hotel and Restaurant; Information Sciences; Information Technology; International Business; Journalism; Law; Library Science; Management; Mass Communication; Music; Occupational Therapy; Optical Technology; Photography; Police Studies; Preschool Education; Public Relations; Real Estate; Social Policy; Social Work; Structural Architecture; Telecommunications Engineering; Tourism; Town Planning; Transport Management; Writing), Doctor's Degree (Administration; Child Care and Development; Continuing Education; Family Studies; Gerontology; Industrial Design; Journalism; Management; Mass Communication; Music; Preschool Education; Psychiatry and Mental Health; Rehabilitation and Therapy; Social Work; Writing)

Student Services: Academic Counselling, Social Counselling, Careers Guidance, Nursery Care, Cultural Activities, Sports Facilities, Language Laboratory, Facilities for disabled people, Health Services, Canteen, Library, IT Centre, Residential Facilities

Periodicals: Collection of Research Papers and Statistics on Campus Life, Collection of Research Papers on Engineering, Collection of Research Papers on Fine & Applied Arts, Collection of Research Papers on Humanities, Collection of Research Papers on Industrial Management, Collection of Research Papers on Industrial Management, Collection of Research Papers on Social Sciences

Publishing house: Kwangju University Press

Academic Staff 2012-2013	MALE	FEMALE	TOTAL
FULL-TIME			364
PART-TIME			227
Student Numbers 2012-2013			
All (Foreign Included)			c. 9930

Last Update: 21-02-2018

Gwangyang Health Sciences University

Gwangyang-eup 85
Gwangyang 57764
Tel: +82(61) 760-1400
Fax: +82(61) 763-9009
Website: http://gy.ac.kr
President: Sung-wung Lee

Department/Division
Health Sciences (Dental Hygiene; Gynaecology and Obstetrics; Health Administration; Health Sciences; Optics;

Pathology; Physical Therapy; Radiology); **Nursing** (Nursing); **Regional Industrial Relations** (Labour and Industrial Relations; Marine Transport; Transport Management); **Social Work** (Preschool Education; Social Work)

History: Founded 1993 as Gwangyang Junior College, renamed Gwangyang University 1998 and Gwangyang Health College 2001. Acquired current title 2012.

Main language(s) of instruction: Korean

Accrediting agency: Ministry of Education

Degrees and diplomas: Bachelor's Degree (Architecture; Art History; Business Administration; Computer Engineering; Cosmetology; Dental Hygiene; Education; Engineering; Health Sciences; Labour and Industrial Relations; Metallurgical Engineering; Nursing; Occupational Therapy; Physical Therapy; Social Welfare; Social Work; Tourism)

Student Services: Health Services, Library, Residential Facilities

Last Update: 20-03-2018

Gyeongan Theological Graduate University (GTGU)

16-29 Mul han gil Buk hu myeon
Andong 36614, Gyeongsangbuk-do
Tel: +82(54) 859-8001/3
Fax: +82(54) 859-8004
Website: http://www.gyeongan.ac.kr
President: Sungwon Park

Department/Division

Music (Music); **Social Welfare** (Social Welfare); **Theology** (Theology)

History: Founded 2005.

Main language(s) of instruction: Korean

Accrediting agency: Ministry of Education

Degrees and diplomas: Master's Degree (Music; Social Welfare; Theology)

Student Services: Library, Residential Facilities

Student Numbers 2017-2018	MALE	FEMALE	TOTAL
All (Foreign Included)			66
Foreign only			1

Last Update: 24-05-2018

Gyeongju University (GJU)

188, Taejong-ro
Gyeongju-si 780-712, Gyeongsangbuk-do
Tel: +82(561) 770-5114
Fax: +82(561) 746-3012

Website: http://www.gu.ac.kr
President: Soon Ja Lee

College

Cultural and Art (Communication Arts; Cultural Studies; Media Studies; Music); **Industry and Technology** (Energy Engineering; Environmental Engineering; Information Sciences; Military Science); **Public Health and Welfare** (Animal Husbandry; Health Sciences; Horticulture; Leisure Studies; Medicine; Nursing; Physical Education; Public Health; Social Welfare; Sports; Welfare and Protective Services); **Tourism** (Air Transport; Cooking and Catering; Hotel Management; Service Trades; Tourism)

Graduate School

Culture, Tourism and Welfare (Art Management; Business Administration; Cooking and Catering; Fine Arts; Social Welfare; Tourism); **Graduate Studies** (Energy Engineering; Social Welfare; Tourism)

History: Founded 1988 as Korea Tourism University. Acquired present status and title 1993.

Main language(s) of instruction: Korean

Accrediting agency: Ministry of Education

Degrees and diplomas: Bachelor's Degree, Master's Degree (Art Management; Business Administration; Cooking and Catering; Energy Engineering; Fine Arts; Heritage Preservation; Social Welfare; Tourism), Doctor's Degree (Energy Engineering; Heritage Preservation; Tourism)

Publishing house: University Press Centre

Academic Staff 2012-2013	MALE	FEMALE	TOTAL
FULL-TIME			162
PART-TIME			135
Student Numbers 2012-2013			
All (Foreign Included)			4333

Last Update: 21-02-2018

Halla University

28 Halla university-gil
Wonju-si 220-712, Gangwon-do
Tel: +82(33) 760-1114
Fax: +82(33) 762-6705
Website: http://www.halla.ac.kr
President: Pyeong-Rak Choi

College

Business Administration and Sociology (Advertising and Publicity; Business Administration; Business and Commerce; Cosmetology; E- Business/Commerce; Leisure

Studies; Mass Communication; Media Studies; Police Studies; Public Relations; Social Welfare; Sociology; Sports; Tourism); **Engineering** (Architecture; Automotive Engineering; Chemical Engineering; Civil Engineering; Computer Engineering; Computer Graphics; Electrical Engineering; Electronic Engineering; Engineering; Engineering Management; Industrial Engineering; Industrial Management; Information Technology; Materials Engineering; Mechanical Engineering; Radio and Television Broadcasting; Telecommunications Engineering)

Department/Division
Liberal Arts and Teaching (Arts and Humanities; Teacher Training)

Graduate School
Industrial Information (Industrial Engineering)
History: Founded 1995.
Main language(s) of instruction: Korean
Accrediting agency: Korean Council for University Education (KCUE)
Degrees and diplomas: Bachelor's Degree, Master's Degree (Industrial Engineering)
Student Services: Health Services, Canteen, Residential Facilities

Academic Staff 2013-2014	MALE	FEMALE	TOTAL
FULL-TIME			130
PART-TIME			c. 70
Student Numbers 2013-2014			
All (Foreign Included)			c. 4830

Last Update: 21-02-2018

Hallym University

1, Hallymdaehak-gil
Chuncheon-si 24252, Gangwon-do
Tel: +82(33) 248-1000, +82(33) 248-1302/15
Fax: +82(33) 248-3333
Website: http://www.hallym.ac.kr
President: Choongsoo Kim

College
Business (Business Administration; Economics; Finance); **Humanities** (Arts and Humanities; Chinese; English; History; Japanese; Korean; Literature; Philosophy; Russian); **Information and Electronic Engineering** (Computer Engineering; Electronic Engineering; Information Technology; Telecommunications Engineering); **International Studies** (Business Administration; Communication Studies; East Asian Studies; Economics; International Studies; Korean;

Marketing); **Medicine** (Medicine; Nursing); **Natural Sciences** (Biological and Life Sciences; Biomedicine; Biotechnology; Chemistry; Environmental Studies; Food Science; Information Sciences; Mathematics; Natural Sciences; Nutrition; Physical Education; Physics; Speech Therapy and Audiology; Statistics); **Social Sciences** (Communication Studies; Law; Political Sciences; Psychology; Public Administration; Social Sciences; Social Welfare; Sociology)

Department/Division
General Education (Arts and Humanities; Chinese; English; Physical Education; Writing)

Graduate School
Graduate Studies (Arts and Humanities; Engineering; Medicine; Natural Sciences; Physical Education; Social Sciences)
Further information: Also 12 Research Centres
History: Founded 1982
Main language(s) of instruction: Korean
Accrediting agency: Korean Council for University Education (KCUE)
Degrees and diplomas: Bachelor's Degree, Master's Degree (Biology; Biomedicine; Biotechnology; Business Administration; Chemistry; Communication Studies; Computer Engineering; Economics; Electronic Engineering; English; Environmental Studies; Finance; Food Science; Gerontology; History; Korean; Law; Literature; Mathematics; Medicine; Molecular Biology; Nursing; Nutrition; Philosophy; Physical Education; Physics; Political Sciences; Psychology; Social Welfare; Sociology; Speech Therapy and Audiology; Statistics), Doctor's Degree (Biomedicine; Biotechnology; Business Administration; Chemistry; Communication Studies; Computer Engineering; Economics; Electronic Engineering; English; Environmental Studies; Finance; Food Science; Gerontology; History; Korean; Law; Literature; Medicine; Molecular Biology; Nutrition; Physical Education; Political Sciences; Psychology; Public Health; Social and Preventive Medicine; Social Welfare; Sociology; Speech Therapy and Audiology; Statistics)
Student Services: Health Services, Library, IT Centre, Residential Facilities
Publishing house: Hallym University Press

Academic Staff 2012-2013	MALE	FEMALE	TOTAL
FULL-TIME			880
PART-TIME			c. 250
Student Numbers 2012-2013			
All (Foreign Included)			c. 8747
Foreign only			382

Last Update: 26-04-2018

Hallym University of Graduate Studies (HUGS)

405, Yeoksam-ro Gangnam-gu
Seoul 135-841
Tel: +82(2) 3453-9333
Fax: +82(2) 3453-6618
Website: http://www.hugs.ac.kr
President: Junghak Lee

Department/Division

American Law (Law); **Audiology** (Speech Therapy and Audiology); **Convention and Events Management** (Business Administration; Leisure Studies; Management; Tourism); **International Radiological Sciences** (Radiology); **International Studies** (Asian Studies; International Relations; International Studies; Political Sciences; Protective Services; Regional Studies)
History: Founded 2005.
Main language(s) of instruction: Korean
Accrediting agency: Ministry of Education
Degrees and diplomas: Master's Degree (Asian Studies; Business Administration; International Relations; International Studies; Law; Leisure Studies; Management; Political Sciences; Protective Services; Regional Studies; Speech Therapy and Audiology; Tourism)

Academic Staff 2013-2014	MALE	FEMALE	TOTAL
FULL-TIME			c. 50
Student Numbers 2013-2014			
All (Foreign Included)			c. 250

Last Update: 08-03-2018

Handong Global University (HGU)

558 Handong-ro Buk-gu
Pohang-si 37554, Gyeongbuk
Tel: +82(54) 260-1111, +82(54) 260-1763
Fax: +82(54) 260-1149, +82(54) 260-1769
Website: http://www.handong.edu
President: Soon-Heung Chang

School

Communication Arts and Science (Advertising and Publicity; Bible; Christian Religious Studies; Communication Arts; Ethics; Film; History of Religion; Journalism; Law; Mass Communication; Media Studies; Multimedia; Public Relations; Theatre; Video; Writing); **Computer Science and Electronic Engineering** (Computer Engineering; Computer Science; Electronic Engineering); **Counselling Psychology and Social Welfare** (Developmental Psychology; Psychology; Social Work); **Global Leadership** (*GLS*) (Applied Mathematics; Bible; Biology; Education; Educational Psychology; English; Environmental Studies; Food Science; Health Sciences; History; Korean; Literature; Mathematics; Natural Sciences; Physics; Psychology; Sociology; Statistics); **Industrial and Information Design** (Advertising and Publicity; Arts and Humanities; Computer Graphics; Design; Graphic Design; Industrial Design; Management; Marketing; Painting and Drawing; Writing); **International Law** (*Graduate*) (International Law; Law); **International Studies, Languages and Literature** (Asian Studies; Cultural Studies; Economics; English; European Studies; International Relations; International Studies; Linguistics; Literature; Middle Eastern Studies; Political Sciences; Regional Studies); **Law** (Administrative Law; Civil Law; Commercial Law; Criminal Law; History of Law; International Law; Labour Law; Private Law; Public Law); **Life Science** (Biochemistry; Biological and Life Sciences; Biomedicine; Cell Biology; Food Science; Food Technology; Genetics; Immunology; Laboratory Techniques; Microbiology; Molecular Biology; Organic Chemistry); **Management and Economics** (Accountancy; Econometrics; Economics; Finance; Industrial and Production Economics; Information Technology; International Business; International Economics; Management; Marketing; Statistics); **Mechanical and Control Systems Engineering** (Automation and Control Engineering; Automotive Engineering; Computer Graphics; Electronic Engineering; Energy Engineering; Engineering Drawing and Design; Heating and Refrigeration; Mechanical Engineering; Production Engineering; Robotics); **Spatial Environmental Systems Engineering** (Analytical Chemistry; Architecture; Architecture and Planning; Building Technologies; Computer Graphics; Construction Engineering; Environmental Engineering; Materials Engineering; Regional Planning; Road Engineering; Surveying and Mapping; Town Planning)

Academy

Global EDISON (Chinese; English; Korean)

Graduate School

Advanced Green Energy and Environment (*HGS-AGE&E*) (Energy Engineering; Environmental Engineering); **General Studies** (Aeronautical and Aerospace Engineering; Automation and Control Engineering; Biotechnology; Information Technology; Mechanical Engineering); **Global Development and Entrepreneurship** (Development Studies; Management; Social Sciences); **Global Management** (Commercial Law; Economics; English; Finance; Information Technology; International Business; International Law; Management); **Interpretation and Translation** (Applied Linguistics; Translation and Interpretation)

History: Founded 1995.
Admission requirements: High school certificate and National Entrance Examination
Fees: 3,064,000 (Won)
Main language(s) of instruction: Korean, English
Accrediting agency: Korean Council for University Education (KCUE); Ministry of Education
Degrees and diplomas: Bachelor's Degree, Master's Degree (Aeronautical and Aerospace Engineering; Applied Linguistics; Automation and Control Engineering; Biological and Life Sciences; Development Studies; Economics; Energy Engineering; Environmental Engineering; Information Technology; International Business; International Law; Law; Management; Mechanical Engineering; Psychology; Social Sciences; Translation and Interpretation), Doctor's Degree (Energy Engineering; Environmental Engineering). Also First Professional Law Degree (J.D. equivalent), 3 yrs
Student Services: Academic Counselling, Social Counselling, Careers Guidance, Cultural Activities, Sports Facilities, Language Laboratory, Health Services, Canteen, Foreign Studies Centre, Library, IT Centre, Residential Facilities
Publishing house: Handong Press

Academic Staff 2013-2014	MALE	FEMALE	TOTAL
FULL-TIME			c. 150
Student Numbers 2013-2014			
All (Foreign Included)			c. 4120

Last Update: 21-02-2018

Hanil University and Presbyterian Theological Seminary

726-15 Waemok-ro Sanggwan-myeon, Wanju-gun
Jeonbuk 55359, Jeollabuk-do
Tel: +82(63) 230-5400
Fax: +82(63) 284-7863
Website: http://www.hanil.ac.kr/eng
President: Choon-Seo Koo

Faculty
Humanities and Social Sciences (Arts and Humanities; Social Sciences); **Music** (Music); **Psychological Counseling** (Psychology); **Social Welfare** (Social Welfare); **Theology** (Theology)

Department/Division
Nursing Science (Nursing); **Theology** (Theology)

Graduate School
Graduate Studies (Music; Social Welfare; Theology); **NGO Policy Studies** (Social Sciences); **Psycho Therapy** (Art Therapy; Psychotherapy); **Social Welfare** (Social Welfare); **Theological Studies** (*Asia Pacific*) (Theology)
History: Founded 1922.
Main language(s) of instruction: Korean
Accrediting agency: Korean Council for University Education (KCUE)
Degrees and diplomas: Bachelor's Degree (Art Therapy; Music; Nursing; Psychology; Religious Music; Social Sciences; Social Welfare; Theology), Master's Degree (Art Therapy; Bible; Cultural Studies; Missionary Studies; Music; Psychiatry and Mental Health; Psychology; Psychotherapy; Religious Education; Religious Practice; Social Sciences; Social Welfare; Theology; Welfare and Protective Services), Doctor's Degree (Art Therapy; Bible; Cultural Studies; Psychotherapy; Religious Education; Social Welfare; Theology)
Last Update: 09-03-2018

Hankuk University of Foreign Studies (HUFS)

107 Imun-ro Dongdaemun-gu
Seoul 02450
Tel: +82(2) 2173-2114, +82(2) 2173-2063
Fax: +82(2) 960-7898, +82(2) 2173-3387
Website: http://www.hufs.ac.kr
President: In-Chul Kim

College
Business and Economics (Economics; International Economics; International Law); **Central and East European Studies** (*Global Campus*) (Czech; Hungarian; Polish; Romanian; Slavic Languages); **Chinese** (Asian Studies; Business and Commerce; Chinese; International Business; Literature); **Economics and Business** (*Global Campus*) (Business Administration; Economics; Finance; Information Management; International Business; Management); **Education** (Education; English; Foreign Languages Education; French; German; Korean; Native Language Education; Teacher Training); **Engineering** (Business Administration; Computer Engineering; Computer Science; Engineering; Industrial Engineering; Industrial Management; Information Technology; Telecommunications Engineering); **English** (English; Linguistics; Literature; Translation and Interpretation); **Global Business Administration** (Business Administration); **Humanities** (*Global campus*) (Arts and Humanities; Cognitive Sciences; History; Linguistics; Philosophy); **International and Area Studies** (*Global Campus*) (African Languages; African Studies; Asian Studies; Central European Studies; East Asian Studies; Eastern European Studies; French Studies; Korean; Latin American

Studies; Leisure Studies; Russian; Sports; Subsahara African Studies); **Interpretation and Translation** (*Global Campus*) (Arabic; Chinese; English; English Studies; German; Indonesian; Italian; Japanese; Linguistics; Literature; Malay; Spanish; Thai Languages; Translation and Interpretation); **Japanese** (Cultural Studies; East Asian Studies; Japanese; Literature); **Law** (Law); **Natural Sciences** (*Global Campus*) (Biological and Life Sciences; Biotechnology; Chemistry; Environmental Studies; Mathematics; Natural Sciences; Physics; Statistics); **Occidental Languages** (Dutch; French; German; Italian; Portuguese; Russian; Scandinavian Languages; Spanish); **Oriental Languages** (Arabic; Hindi; Indonesian; Malay; Mongolian; Persian; Thai Languages; Turkish; Vietnamese); **Social Sciences** (Advertising and Publicity; Cinema and Television; Film; International Relations; Journalism; Mass Communication; Media Studies; Political Sciences; Public Administration; Public Relations; Social Sciences)

School

Law (*Graduate*) (Administrative Law; Civil Law; Commercial Law; Constitutional Law; Criminal Law; Fiscal Law; Labour Law; Law; Private Law)

Department/Division

International Studies (International Business; International Economics; International Studies); **Language and Diplomacy** (International Relations; Modern Languages; Social Sciences)

Academy
Global Leadership

Centre

FLEX (Foreign Language Examination); **Foreign Language Training and Testing** (Chinese; English; French; German; Hindi; Malay; Modern Languages; Russian; Spanish); **HUFS TESOL Professional Education** (Foreign Languages Education; Teacher Training); **Interpreting and Translation**; **Korean Language and Culture** (East Asian Studies; Korean)

Graduate School

Business (Accountancy; Business Administration; Finance; Human Resources; Industrial Management; Information Management; International Business; Management; Marketing); **Education** (Education; Educational Sciences; Teacher Training); **Graduate Studies** (Arts and Humanities; Engineering; Natural Sciences; Social Sciences); **International and Area Studies** (African Studies; American Studies; Canadian Studies; Central European Studies; Cultural Studies; Development Studies; East Asian Studies; Eastern European Studies; Economics; Human Rights; International

Business; International Law; International Relations; International Studies; Korean; Latin American Studies; Media Studies; Peace and Disarmament; Political Sciences; Regional Studies; Social Studies; Western European Studies); **Interpretation and Translation** (Translation and Interpretation); **Politics, Government and Communication** (Government; Information Sciences; International Relations; Mass Communication; Political Sciences; Public Administration); **TESOL** (English; Foreign Languages Education)

Research Division
Foreign Language and Literature; **International Area Studies**; **Specialized Field Studies**

Campus

Global Campus (Arts and Humanities; Business Administration; Central European Studies; Eastern European Studies; Economics; Engineering; International Studies; Natural Sciences; Translation and Interpretation)

Further information: Also Global Campus in Yongin
History: Founded 1954 with the approval of the Ministry of Education. Receives some financial support from the Government.
Academic year: March to December (March-July; September-December)
Admission requirements: Graduation from high school or equivalent, and entrance examination
Main language(s) of instruction: Korean, English, Japanese, Chinese, Russian
Accrediting agency: Korean Council for University Education (KCUE)
Degrees and diplomas: Bachelor's Degree, Master's Degree (Accountancy; Advertising and Publicity; African Languages; African Studies; Air Transport; American Studies; Arabic; Archiving; Asian Studies; Biological and Life Sciences; Biotechnology; Bulgarian; Business Administration; Business Education; Canadian Studies; Central European Studies; Chemistry; Chinese; Cognitive Sciences; Computer Education; Computer Engineering; Cultural Studies; Czech; Development Studies; East Asian Studies; Eastern European Studies; Economics; Education; Educational Administration; Educational and Student Counselling; Electronic Engineering; English; Environmental Engineering; Environmental Studies; European Studies; Finance; Foreign Languages Education; French; German; Hindi; History; Human Resources; Human Rights; Humanities and Social Science Education; Hungarian; Indonesian; Industrial Engineering; Industrial Management; Information Management; Information Sciences; Information Technology; International Business; International Economics; International Law; International Relations; International Studies; Italian; Japanese; Journalism; Korean; Latin American Studies; Law; Linguistics; Literature; Malay; Management; Marketing; Mass Communication; Mathematics; Mathematics Education; Media Studies; Middle

Eastern Studies; Native Language Education; Peace and Disarmament; Persian; Philosophy; Physical Education; Physics; Polish; Political Sciences; Portuguese; Preschool Education; Public Administration; Public Relations; Radio and Television Broadcasting; Romanian; Russian; Scandinavian Languages; Science Education; Slavic Languages; Social Studies; South and Southeast Asian Languages; South Asian Studies; Spanish; Statistics; Telecommunications Engineering; Thai Languages; Translation and Interpretation; Turkish; Vietnamese), Doctor's Degree (African Studies; American Studies; Arabic; Archiving; Asian Studies; Biological and Life Sciences; Biotechnology; Canadian Studies; Central European Studies; Chemistry; Chinese; Cognitive Sciences; Comparative Literature; Computer Engineering; Cultural Studies; Czech; East Asian Studies; Eastern European Studies; Economics; Electronic Engineering; English; Environmental Engineering; Environmental Studies; European Studies; Foreign Languages Education; French; German; History; Hungarian; Industrial Engineering; Industrial Management; Information Sciences; Information Technology; International Business; International Economics; International Law; International Relations; International Studies; Japanese; Korean; Latin American Studies; Law; Linguistics; Literature; Management; Mass Communication; Mathematics; Middle Eastern Studies; Philosophy; Physics; Polish; Political Sciences; Public Administration; Romanian; Russian; Slavic Languages; Social Studies; South Asian Studies; Spanish; Statistics; Telecommunications Engineering; Translation and Interpretation). Dual Master's degree programme with the UN mandated University for Peace (UPEACE)

Student Services: Sports Facilities, Language Laboratory, Health Services, Canteen, Library, IT Centre, Residential Facilities

Periodicals: Collections of articles

Publishing house: University Press

Academic Staff 2013-2014	MALE	FEMALE	TOTAL
FULL-TIME			652
Student Numbers 2013-2014			
All (Foreign Included)			21240
Foreign only			1264

Last Update: 21-03-2018

Hanlyo University

199-4 Duckrey-ri, Gwangyang-eup
Gwangyang-si 545-704, Jeollanam-do
Tel: +82(61) 761-6700, +82(61) 760-1114
Fax: +82(61) 761-6709, +82(61) 761-6703
Website: http://www.hanlyo.ac.kr
President: Tae-ho Kim

Department/Division

Arts and Physical Education (Fine Arts; Physical Education); **Engineering and Health Science** (Engineering; Health Sciences); **Humanities and Social Studies** (Arts and Humanities; Social Sciences); **Natural Environment** (Environmental Studies; Natural Sciences)

Graduate School

Business and Public Administration (Business Administration; Public Administration; Transport Management); **Industry** (Civil Engineering; Industrial Design; Information Sciences; Information Technology; Mass Communication; Materials Engineering; Modern Languages; Multimedia; Parks and Recreation; Sports; Structural Architecture; Telecommunications Engineering); **Social Welfare** (Social Welfare)

History: Founded 1994.
Main language(s) of instruction: Korean
Accrediting agency: Ministry of Education
Degrees and diplomas: Bachelor's Degree, Master's Degree (Business Administration; Civil Engineering; Industrial Design; Information Technology; Materials Engineering; Modern Languages; Multimedia; Parks and Recreation; Public Administration; Social Welfare; Structural Architecture; Transport Management)
Student Services: Sports Facilities, Language Laboratory, Library, Residential Facilities

Academic Staff 2012-2013	MALE	FEMALE	TOTAL
FULL-TIME			50
PART-TIME			c. 30
Student Numbers 2012-2013			
All (Foreign Included)			c. 950

Last Update: 22-02-2018

Hannam University

70 Hannamro, Daedeok-gu
Daejeon 34430, Chungnam-do
Tel: +82(42) 629-7739
Fax: +82(42) 629-7779
Website: http://www.hannam.ac.kr
President: Duk-Hoon Lee
Tel: +82(42) 623-7100

College

Art and Design (Art Criticism; Art Management; Design; Fine Arts; Visual Arts); **Economics and Business Administration** (Accountancy; Business Administration; Chinese; Economics; Information Management; Information Technology; International Business; Management; Statistics); **Education** (Art Education; Education; Foreign Languages Education; Humanities and Social Science Education; Mathematics Education; Native

Language Education); **Engineering** (Architectural and Environmental Design; Architecture; Civil Engineering; Communication Arts; Computer Engineering; Electronic Engineering; Engineering; Environmental Engineering; Industrial Engineering; Industrial Management; Information Technology; Mechanical Engineering; Media Studies; Multimedia; Telecommunications Engineering); **Law** (Law; Private Law); **Liberal Arts** (Arts and Humanities; Christian Religious Studies; English; French; German; History; Information Sciences; Japanese; Korean; Library Science; Literature; Philosophy; Writing); **Life Sciences and Nano-technology** (Biological and Life Sciences; Biotechnology; Chemical Engineering; Chemistry; Food Science; Information Technology; Materials Engineering; Nanotechnology; Nursing; Nutrition); **Linton Global College** (Communication Studies; Cultural Studies; International Business); **Natural Sciences** (Applied Mathematics; Clothing and Sewing; Mathematics; Mathematics Education; Natural Sciences; Optics; Sports; Textile Technology); **Social Sciences** (Child Care and Development; Communication Studies; Educational and Student Counselling; International Studies; Police Studies; Political Sciences; Public Administration; Real Estate; Social Sciences; Social Welfare; Town Planning)

Graduate School

Business Industry (Business Administration; Chemical Engineering; Civil Engineering; Computer Engineering; Environmental Engineering; Industrial Engineering; Industrial Management; Information Management; Information Technology; Paper Technology); **Education** (Art Education; Computer Education; Education; Educational Administration; Educational and Student Counselling; Foreign Languages Education; Home Economics Education; Humanities and Social Science Education; Mathematics Education; Native Language Education; Physical Education; Primary Education; Science Education); **Graduate Studies** (Arts and Humanities; Business Administration; Education; Engineering; Fine Arts; Home Economics; Information Sciences; Law; Natural Sciences; Religion; Social Sciences; Welfare and Protective Services); **National Defense Strategy** (Military Science; Protective Services); **Public Education and Welfare** (Educational Administration; Police Studies; Private Law; Public Administration; Social Welfare; Statistics; Welfare and Protective Services); **Social Culture** (Arts and Humanities; Business Administration; Education; Fine Arts; Performing Arts; Social Sciences); **Theological Interdisciplinary Studies** (Christian Religious Studies; Pastoral Studies; Theology)
Further information: 9 Research Institutes
History: Founded in 1956 by a Presbyterian Missionary Foundation.
Academic year: March to December (March-June; August-December)
Admission requirements: Graduation from high school and entrance examination
Fees: c. 2.5m (Won)

Main language(s) of instruction: Korean, English
Accrediting agency: Korean Council for University Education (KCUE)
Degrees and diplomas: Bachelor's Degree, Master's Degree (Accountancy; Bioengineering; Biological and Life Sciences; Business Administration; Chemical Engineering; Chemistry; Child Care and Development; Christian Religious Studies; Civil Engineering; Communication Studies; Computer Engineering; Design; Economics; Education; Electronic Engineering; Engineering Management; English; Environmental Engineering; Fine Arts; Food Science; French; History; Industrial Engineering; Information Management; Information Sciences; Information Technology; International Business; International Studies; Japanese; Korean; Law; Library Science; Literature; Materials Engineering; Mathematics; Mechanical Engineering; Microbiology; Multimedia; Nutrition; Philosophy; Physics; Political Sciences; Public Administration; Real Estate; Social Welfare; Sports; Statistics; Structural Architecture; Telecommunications Engineering; Town Planning; Writing), Doctor's Degree (Accountancy; Biological and Life Sciences; Business Administration; Chemistry; Child Care and Development; Christian Religious Studies; Civil Engineering; Computer Engineering; Economics; Education; English; Environmental Engineering; Food Science; Foreign Languages Education; Information Technology; International Business; Korean; Law; Literature; Mathematics; Mechanical Engineering; Microbiology; Multimedia; Native Language Education; Nutrition; Physics; Public Administration; Social Welfare; Sports; Structural Architecture; Telecommunications Engineering; Writing)
Student Services: Academic Counselling, Careers Guidance, Nursery Care, Sports Facilities, Language Laboratory, Health Services, Canteen, Foreign Studies Centre, Library, Residential Facilities
Publishing house: Han Nam University Press

Academic Staff 2012-2013	MALE	FEMALE	TOTAL
FULL-TIME			393
PART-TIME			774
Student Numbers 2012-2013			
All (Foreign Included)			17000
Foreign only			450

Last Update: 22-02-2018

Hansei University

30, Hanse-ro
Gunpo-si 435-742, Gyeonggi-do
Tel: +82(31) 450-5114, +82(31) 450-5138
Fax: +82(31) 457-6517

Website: http://www.hansei.ac.kr
President: Sung-hae Kim

Faculty

Business Administration (Business Administration; E-Business/Commerce); **Communication Arts** (Acting; Advertising and Publicity; Communication Arts; Dance; Journalism; Mass Communication; Performing Arts; Public Relations; Singing); **Design** (Architectural and Environmental Design; Design; Fashion Design; Graphic Design; Industrial Design; Textile Design); **Humanities and Social Sciences** (Arts and Humanities; Criminal Law; English; International Business; Police Studies; Social Sciences; Social Welfare; Tourism; Translation and Interpretation); **Information Technology** (Computer Engineering; Computer Graphics; Data Processing; Electronic Engineering; Information Technology; Software Engineering; Telecommunications Engineering); **Music** (Music; Music Theory and Composition; Musical Instruments; Singing); **Theology** (Christian Religious Studies; Cultural Studies; Missionary Studies; Sports; Theology)

Department/Division

Nursing (Health Sciences; Nursing)

Graduate School

Business Administration (*Special Graduate School*) (Business Administration); **Education** (*Special Graduate School*) (Education; Educational Administration; Educational and Student Counselling; Educational Sciences; Educational Technology; Foreign Languages Education; Pedagogy; Special Education; Teacher Training); **Environment-friendly Design** (*Special Graduate School*) (Architectural and Environmental Design; Design; Teacher Training); **Graduate Studies** (Industrial Engineering; Information Technology; Music; Police Studies; Theology); **Piano Pedagogy** (*Special Graduate School*) (Music Education; Teacher Training); **Police and Law** (*Special Graduate School*) (Law; Police Studies); **Social Welfare** (*Special Graduate School*) (Alternative Medicine; Gerontology; Social Welfare; Welfare and Protective Services); **Youngsan Theology** (*Special Graduate School*) (Bible; Continuing Education; Religion; Theology)
History: Founded 1953. Acquired present title 1997.
Main language(s) of instruction: Korean
Accrediting agency: Korean Council for University Education (KCUE)
Degrees and diplomas: Bachelor's Degree, Master's Degree (Alternative Medicine; Art Management; Art Therapy; Bible; Christian Religious Studies; Educational Administration; Educational and Student Counselling; Educational Technology; Foreign Languages Education; Industrial Engineering; Information Technology; Law; Missionary Studies; Music Theory and Composition; Musical Instruments; New Testament; Police Studies; Psychology; Religious Education; Singing; Social Welfare; Special Education; Telecommunications Engineering; Theology; Welfare and Protective Services), Doctor's Degree (Art Management; Art Therapy; Bible; Christian Religious Studies; Industrial Engineering; Information Technology; Missionary Studies; Music Theory and Composition; Musical Instruments; New Testament; Psychology; Religious Education; Singing; Telecommunications Engineering; Theology)
Student Services: Language Laboratory, Canteen, IT Centre

Academic Staff 2012-2013	MALE	FEMALE	TOTAL
FULL-TIME			133
PART-TIME			335
Student Numbers 2012-2013			
All (Foreign Included)			c. 4180

Last Update: 22-02-2018

Hanseo University

46 Hanseo 1-ro Haemi-myeon
Seosan-si 31962, Chungcheongnam-do
Tel: +82(41) 660-1020, +82(41) 660-1704, +82(41) 660-1706
Fax: +82(41) 660-1024, +82(41) 660-1707
Website: http://www.hanseo.ac.kr
President: Kee-Sun Ham
Tel: +82(41) 660-1102

College

Aeronautical Studies (Aeronautical and Aerospace Engineering; Air Transport; Electronic Engineering; Leisure Studies; Software Engineering; Sports; Tourism); **Fine Arts** (Art Education; Fashion Design; Film; Graphic Arts; Graphic Design; Heritage Preservation; Industrial Design; Interior Design; Music; Theatre; Visual Arts); **Health Sciences** (Cosmetology; Dental Hygiene; Health Administration; Health Sciences; Medical Technology; Nursing; Occupational Therapy; Physical Therapy; Radiology; Rehabilitation and Therapy); **Humanities and Social Sciences** (Arts and Humanities; Business Administration; Child Care and Development; Chinese; English; Gerontology; International Business; International Relations; Japanese; Journalism; Mass Communication; Public Administration; Welfare and Protective Services; Writing); **Science and Engineering** (Biological and Life Sciences; Biotechnology; Chemical Engineering; Chemistry; Civil Engineering; Computer Engineering; Electronic Engineering; Engineering; Environmental Engineering; Food Science; Materials Engineering; Mathematics; Structural Architecture; Telecommunications Engineering); **Sports and Security** (Leisure Studies; Protective Services; Secretarial Studies; Sports)

Department/Division

General Studies (Arts and Humanities; Teacher Training)

Institute

Aerospace Medicine and Safety; Aerotechnology; Chironomics and Industrial Health; Development of the Naepo Area; Environment; Gifted Education; Inorganic Materials Processing and Application; International Humanitarianism

Centre

Conservation Science; East Asian Classics; Industry and Academy Cooperation; Product Surface Design Innovation (*PSDIC*)

Graduate School

Aeronautics, Information and Industry (Aeronautical and Aerospace Engineering; Business Administration; Chinese; Cosmetology; Cultural Studies; Electronic Engineering; Korean; Public Administration; Software Engineering; Sports; Welfare and Protective Services); **Art and Design** (*International*) (Fashion Design; Film; Fine Arts; Heritage Preservation; Industrial Design; Interior Design; Music; Structural Architecture; Theatre; Visual Arts); **Education** (Art Therapy; Education; Educational Administration; Educational and Student Counselling; Foreign Languages Education; Health Education; Mathematics Education; Physical Education); **Graduate Studies** (Air Transport; Architecture; Biology; Business Administration; Chemical Engineering; Chemistry; Child Care and Development; Chiropractic; Civil Engineering; Computer Science; Construction Engineering; Continuing Education; Dental Hygiene; East Asian Studies; Electronic Engineering; English; Environmental Engineering; Gerontology; Health Sciences; International Business; International Relations; Literature; Materials Engineering; Occupational Therapy; Optical Technology; Physical Therapy; Public Administration; Radiology; Rehabilitation and Therapy; Software Engineering; Tourism; Transport and Communications; Transport Management; Welfare and Protective Services); **Health Promotion** (Chiropractic; Health Sciences; Physical Therapy; Radiology)

Research Division

Catalyst Technology (*RICT*); **Conservation Science for Cultural Heritage** (Heritage Preservation)
Further information: Also Taean Campus
History: Founded 1992.
Academic year: March to September
Main language(s) of instruction: Korean
Accrediting agency: Korean Council for University Education (KCUE)
Degrees and diplomas: Bachelor's Degree, Master's Degree (Aeronautical and Aerospace Engineering; Air Transport;

Architectural and Environmental Design; Architecture; Biology; Business Administration; Chemical Engineering; Chemistry; Child Care and Development; Chinese; Chiropractic; Civil Engineering; Computer Science; Continuing Education; Cosmetology; Dental Hygiene; East Asian Studies; Educational Administration; Educational and Student Counselling; Electronic Engineering; English; Environmental Engineering; Fashion Design; Film; Fine Arts; Foreign Languages Education; Gerontology; Health Education; Health Sciences; Heritage Preservation; Industrial Design; Interior Design; International Business; International Relations; Korean; Literature; Materials Engineering; Mathematics Education; Music; Occupational Therapy; Optical Technology; Physical Education; Physical Therapy; Physiology; Public Administration; Radiology; Rehabilitation and Therapy; Software Engineering; Sports; Theatre; Tourism; Visual Arts; Welfare and Protective Services), Doctor's Degree (Air Transport; Architecture; Biology; Chemistry; Child Care and Development; Chiropractic; Computer Science; Construction Engineering; Continuing Education; Environmental Engineering; Gerontology; Health Sciences; Materials Engineering; Physical Therapy; Physiology; Public Administration; Software Engineering; Transport Management; Welfare and Protective Services). Teacher's Certificate
Student Services: Academic Counselling, Social Counselling, Careers Guidance, Nursery Care, Sports Facilities, Language Laboratory, Facilities for disabled people, Foreign Studies Centre

Academic Staff 2013-2014	MALE	FEMALE	TOTAL
FULL-TIME			c. 250
Student Numbers 2013-2014			
All (Foreign Included)			c. 8500

Last Update: 22-02-2018

Hanshin University

Hanshin road 137 Yangsandong
Osan-si 447-791, Gyeonggi-do
Tel: +82(339) 370-6524
Fax: +82(339) 370-6525
Website: http://www.hs.ac.kr
President: Gyu-hong Yeon

College

Global Cooperation (Business Administration; Chinese; E- Business/Commerce; International Business; Japanese); **Human Services** (Child Care and Development; Physical Education; Psychology; Rehabilitation and Therapy; Social Welfare; Special Education); **Humanities** (Arts and Humanities; Chinese; Cultural Studies; English; German;

History; Korean; Literature; Mass Communication; Philosophy; Religious Studies; Writing); **IT** (Computer Engineering; Computer Science; Finance; Information Technology; Mathematics; Statistics); **Liberal Arts Bundling** (Arts and Humanities); **Social Sciences** (Advertising and Publicity; Economics; International Economics; International Relations; Social Sciences; Sociology; Video); **Theology** (Christian Religious Studies; Theology)

Graduate School

Creative Writing; **Education** (Education; Educational Administration; Educational and Student Counselling; Ethics; Foreign Languages Education; Humanities and Social Science Education; Mathematics Education; Physical Education); **Graduate Studies** (Archiving; Asian Studies; Christian Religious Studies; Computer Engineering; Computer Science; Information Technology; Mass Communication; Pastoral Studies; Philosophy; Physical Education; Rehabilitation and Therapy; Religious Studies; Social Policy; Special Education; Telecommunications Engineering; Theology); **Psychoanalysis** (Psychoanalysis); **Social Innovation**; **Social Work** (Social Work); **Sports Rehabilitation Science** (Rehabilitation and Therapy; Sports Medicine); **Theology** (Theology)

Further information: Also Seoul Campus
History: Founded 1940.
Main language(s) of instruction: Korean
Accrediting agency: Ministry of Education
Degrees and diplomas: Bachelor's Degree, Master's Degree (Anthropology; Archaeology; Archiving; Chinese; Christian Religious Studies; Computer Education; Computer Engineering; Educational Administration; Educational and Student Counselling; Ethics; History; Humanities and Social Science Education; Information Technology; Mass Communication; Mathematics Education; Native Language Education; Philosophy; Physical Education; Political Sciences; Rehabilitation and Therapy; Religion; Religious Practice; Secondary Education; Social Policy; Social Sciences; Social Welfare; Sports Medicine; Telecommunications Engineering; Theology; Writing), Doctor's Degree (Archiving; Asian Studies; Developmental Psychology; English; Literature; Rehabilitation and Therapy; Theology)
Student Services: Library, Residential Facilities

Academic Staff 2012-2013	MALE	FEMALE	TOTAL
FULL-TIME			210
PART-TIME			c. 270
Student Numbers 2012-2013			
All (Foreign Included)			c. 5900

Last Update: 08-03-2018

Hansung University (HU)

116 Samseongyoro-16-gil Seongbuk-gu
Seoul 136-792
Tel: +82(2) 760-4114
Fax: +82(2) 760-5800, +82(2) 745-8943
Website: http://www.hansung.ac.kr
President: Ju-taek Jung

College

Arts (Business Administration; Clothing and Sewing; Dance; Design; Fashion Design; Fine Arts; Graphic Design; Industrial Design; Interior Design; Media Studies; Painting and Drawing; Visual Arts); **Culture Teaching Profession** (Arts and Humanities; Teacher Training); **Engineering** (Computer Engineering; Engineering; Industrial Engineering; Industrial Management; Information Technology; Management; Mechanical Engineering; Multimedia; Telecommunications Engineering); **Humanities** (Arts and Humanities; Cultural Studies; English; History; Information Sciences; Korean; Library Science; Linguistics; Literature); **Social Sciences** (Business Administration; Economics; International Business; Management; Public Administration; Real Estate; Social Sciences)

Course/Programme

Characterized Programmes (*Graduate*) (Advertising and Publicity; Cultural Studies; Economics; Information Technology; Korean; Literature; Mass Communication; Media Studies; Real Estate; Technology); **Digital Cultural Technology & Contents** (*Graduate Interdisciplinary Programme*) (Cultural Studies; Mass Communication; Technology); **New Media Advertising Promotion** (*Graduate Interdisciplinary Programme*) (Advertising and Publicity; Computer Engineering; Information Technology; Marketing)

Graduate School

Arts (Aesthetics; Design; Fashion Design; Painting and Drawing); **Business Administration** (Business Administration; Hotel and Restaurant; Hotel Management; Tourism); **Education** (Education; Educational Administration; Educational and Student Counselling; Foreign Languages Education; Native Language Education; Preschool Education); **General Education** (Advertising and Publicity; American Studies; Business Administration; Computer Engineering; Computer Science; Dance; Economics; English; English Studies; Fashion Design; History; Hygiene; Industrial Engineering; Information Sciences; Information Technology; International Business; Korean; Library Science; Literature; Mechanical Engineering; Media Studies; Multimedia; Painting and Drawing; Public Administration; Real Estate; Telecommunications

Engineering); **International Studies** (American Studies; East Asian Studies; European Studies; Information Sciences; International Studies); **Knowledge Service and Consulting** (Management; Small Business); **Public Administration** (Police Studies; Public Administration; Social Welfare; Toxicology); **Real Estate** (Real Estate)

History: Founded 1945, acquired present status and title 1972. Acquired ISO 9001 certification in July 2003

Admission requirements: Graduation from High School

Main language(s) of instruction: Korean

Accrediting agency: Korean Council for University Education (KCUE)

Degrees and diplomas: Bachelor's Degree, Master's Degree (Advertising and Publicity; American Studies; Business Administration; Business and Commerce; Computer Engineering; Cultural Studies; Dance; Economics; English Studies; Fashion Design; History; Hotel and Restaurant; Hygiene; Industrial Engineering; Information Sciences; Information Technology; International Business; International Studies; Korean; Library Science; Literature; Management; Mass Communication; Mechanical Engineering; Media Studies; Multimedia; Painting and Drawing; Police Studies; Protective Services; Public Administration; Small Business; Social Welfare; Telecommunications Engineering; Tourism; Toxicology), Doctor's Degree (Business Administration; Computer Engineering; Economics; English; History; Hygiene; Industrial Design; Industrial Engineering; Information Sciences; Information Technology; Interior Design; International Business; Korean; Library Science; Literature; Management; Media Studies; Public Administration; Real Estate)

Student Services: Academic Counselling, Careers Guidance, Sports Facilities, Language Laboratory, Health Services, Canteen, Library, IT Centre, Residential Facilities

Academic Staff 2013-2014	MALE	FEMALE	TOTAL
FULL-TIME			c. 280
Student Numbers 2013-2014			
All (Foreign Included)			6686
Foreign only			250

Last Update: 22-02-2018

Hanyang Cyber University (HYCU)

Wangsimni-ro 220, Seongdong Gu
Seoul 04763
Tel: +82(2) 2290-0114
Fax: +82(2) 2290-0600
Website: http://en.hycu.ac.kr
President: Young-Moo Lee

Department/Division

Design (Design; Graphic Design; Industrial Design; Interior Design); **Economics and Business Administration** (Advertising and Publicity; Business Administration; Economics; Finance; Hotel and Restaurant; Management; Marketing; Media Studies; Real Estate; Tourism); **Engineering** (Automotive Engineering; Civil Engineering; Computer Engineering; Electrical and Electronic Engineering; Information Technology; Mechanical Engineering; Telecommunications Engineering); **Foreign Languages** (English; Japanese); **General Studies** (Arts and Humanities; Leadership); **Law** (Law); **Social Sciences** (Child Care and Development; Education; Educational Technology; Health Administration; Psychology; Social Welfare)

History: Founded 2002.

Main language(s) of instruction: Korean

Accrediting agency: Ministry of Education

Degrees and diplomas: Bachelor's Degree (Advertising and Publicity; Arts and Humanities; Automotive Engineering; Business Administration; Child Care and Development; Civil Engineering; Computer Engineering; Design; Economics; Education; Educational Technology; Electrical and Electronic Engineering; English; Finance; Graphic Design; Health Administration; Hotel and Restaurant; Industrial Design; Information Technology; Interior Design; Japanese; Law; Leadership; Management; Marketing; Mechanical Engineering; Media Studies; Psychology; Real Estate; Social Welfare; Telecommunications Engineering; Tourism)

Last Update: 28-03-2018

Hanyang University

222 Wangsimni-ro Seongdong-gu
Seoul 133-791
Tel: +82(2) 2290-0114
Fax: +82(2) 2294-2442
Website: http://www.hanyang.ac.kr
President: Young-Moo Lee
Tel: +82(2) 2220-0033

College

Communication and Social Sciences (*ERICA Campus*) (Advertising and Publicity; Communication Studies; Information Sciences; Journalism; Mass Communication; Public Relations; Social Sciences; Sociology); **Design** (*ERICA Campus*) (Design; Graphic Design; Handicrafts; Industrial Design; Metal Techniques; Multimedia; Packaging Technology; Textile Design); **Economics and Business Administration** (*ERICA Campus*) (Business Administration; Economics); **Economics and Finance** (Economics; Finance); **Education** (Art Education; Education; Educational Technology; Foreign

Languages Education; Mathematics Education; Native Language Education); **Engineering** (Architecture; Automotive Engineering; Bioengineering; Chemical Engineering; Civil Engineering; Energy Engineering; Engineering; Environmental Engineering; Industrial Engineering; Materials Engineering; Mechanical Engineering; Mining Engineering; Nanotechnology; Petroleum and Gas Engineering; Structural Architecture; Town Planning); **Engineering Sciences** (*ERICA Campus*) (Architecture; Bioengineering; Chemical Engineering; Civil Engineering; Computer Engineering; Computer Science; Electronic Engineering; Environmental Engineering; Industrial Engineering; Information Technology; Materials Engineering; Mechanical Engineering; Nanotechnology; Structural Architecture; Telecommunications Engineering; Transport Engineering); **Human Ecology** (Clothing and Sewing; Food Science; Home Economics; Interior Design; Nutrition; Textile Design); **Humanities** (Arts and Humanities; Chinese; German; History; Korean; Literature); **Languages and Cultures** (*ERICA Campus*) (Anthropology; Asian Studies; Chinese; Cultural Studies; English; French; Japanese; Korean; Literature); **Law** (Law); **Medicine** (Anatomy; Biochemistry; Cell Biology; Genetics; Medicine; Microbiology; Parasitology; Pathology; Pharmacology; Physiology; Social and Preventive Medicine); **Music** (Music; Music Theory and Composition; Musical Instruments; Singing); **Natural Sciences** (Biology; Chemistry; Mathematics; Natural Sciences; Physics); **Performing Arts and Sport** (Cinema and Television; Dance; Physical Education; Sports Management; Theatre); **Pharmacy** (*ERICA Campus*) (Pharmacy); **Policy Sciences** (Arts and Humanities; Communication Studies; Economics; Law; Modern Languages; Philosophy; Political Sciences; Social Sciences); **Science and Technology** (*ERICA Campus*) (Applied Chemistry; Applied Mathematics; Applied Physics; Biological and Life Sciences; Environmental Studies; Marine Science and Oceanography; Molecular Biology; Natural Sciences; Technology); **Social Sciences** (International Relations; Journalism; Mass Communication; Political Sciences; Public Administration; Social Sciences; Sociology); **Sports and Arts** (*ERICA Campus*) (Dance; Music; Performing Arts; Sports; Sports Management)

School

Business (Accountancy; Business Administration; Finance; Human Resources; Information Management; Information Technology; International Business; Management)

Department/Division

International Studies (International Studies); **Nursing** (Health Sciences; Nursing)

Graduate School

Biomedical Science and Engineering (Biomedical Engineering; Biomedicine; Medicine); **Business Management** (Business Administration; Management); **Education** (Art Education; Education; Educational and Student Counselling; Educational Psychology; Educational Technology; Foreign Languages Education; Humanities and Social Science Education; Music Education; Native Language Education; Physical Education; Preschool Education; Science Education; Vocational Education); **Engineering** (Chemical Engineering; Civil Engineering; Electrical and Electronic Engineering; Engineering; Environmental Engineering; Industrial Engineering; Landscape Architecture; Materials Engineering; Mechanical Engineering; Mineralogy; Structural Architecture); **Global Business** (Accountancy; Finance; Health Administration; Human Resources; Information Management; Information Technology; International Business; Management; Marketing; Media Studies; Radio and Television Broadcasting; Telecommunications Services); **Graduate School of Hanyang University** (Advertising and Publicity; Anthropology; Applied Chemistry; Applied Mathematics; Applied Physics; Architecture; Artificial Intelligence; Arts and Humanities; Automotive Engineering; Bioengineering; Biological and Life Sciences; Chemical Engineering; Chemistry; Chinese; Clothing and Sewing; Computer Engineering; Computer Science; Dance; Economics; Education; Educational Technology; Electrical Engineering; Electronic Engineering; Energy Engineering; English; Environmental Engineering; Environmental Studies; Film; Finance; Fine Arts; Food Science; Foreign Languages Education; French; German; Health Administration; History; Industrial Engineering; Information Technology; Insurance; International Relations; Japanese; Journalism; Korean; Law; Literature; Management; Marine Science and Oceanography; Mass Communication; Materials Engineering; Mathematics; Mathematics Education; Mechanical Engineering; Medicine; Molecular Biology; Museum Studies; Music; Nanotechnology; Natural Resources; Nuclear Engineering; Nursing; Nutrition; Petroleum and Gas Engineering; Pharmacology; Philosophy; Physical Education; Physics; Political Sciences; Power Engineering; Preschool Education; Psychotherapy; Public Administration; Public Relations; Regional Studies; Robotics; Sociology; Software Engineering; Sports; Sports Management; Structural Architecture; Textile Design; Theatre; Tourism; Town Planning; Transport Engineering; Urban Studies); **Information and Clinical Nursing** (Gerontology; Health Sciences; Nursing; Welfare and Protective Services); **Innovation** (Architecture; Art Therapy; Construction Engineering; Design; Industrial Engineering; Industrial Management; Mass Communication; Sports Management; Transport Management); **International Studies** (American Studies; Asian Studies; Chinese; Cultural Studies; East Asian Studies; Eastern European Studies; Economics; English; Japanese; Korean; Political Sciences; Russian; Sociology); **International Tourism** (Hotel and Restaurant; Leisure Studies;

Tourism); **Journalism and Mass Communication** (Advertising and Publicity; Communication Arts; Journalism; Mass Communication; Media Studies; Multimedia; Public Relations; Publishing and Book Trade; Radio and Television Broadcasting); **Law** (Law); **Medicine** (Medicine); **Public Policy** (Development Studies; Government; Health Administration; Public Administration; Real Estate; Social Sciences; Social Welfare); **Technology and Innovation Management** (Engineering Management); **Urban Studies** (Landscape Architecture; Structural Architecture; Town Planning; Transport Engineering; Urban Studies)

Campus

ERICA Campus (Business Administration; Communication Studies; Computer Science; Cultural Studies; Design; Economics; Engineering; Fine Arts; Modern Languages; Natural Sciences; Pharmacy; Social Sciences; Sports; Technology)

Further information: Also 2 University Hospitals; 44 Research Institutes; 16 National R&D Centres; 6 National Research Laboratories

History: Founded 1939 as Dong-Ah Polytechnic Academy, reorganized as Kunkuk College 1945 and Hanyang College of Engineering 1948. Acquired present title and status 1956. A private Institution financed by the Hanyang Educational Foundation.

Academic year: March to February (March-June; September-February)

Admission requirements: Graduation from high school and entrance examination

Fees: 3,513,000-5,202,000 per semester for undergraduate programmes; 4,578,000-7,155,000 per semester for graduate programmes; 5,041,000-8,186,000 per semester for professional/specialized graduate programmes

Main language(s) of instruction: Korean

Accrediting agency: Korean Council for University Education (KCUE)

Degrees and diplomas: Bachelor's Degree, Master's Degree (Accountancy; Advertising and Publicity; American Studies; Anaesthesiology; Anatomy; Anthropology; Applied Chemistry; Applied Mathematics; Applied Physics; Architectural and Environmental Design; Architecture; Art Education; Arts and Humanities; Asian Studies; Automotive Engineering; Banking; Biochemistry; Bioengineering; Biology; Biomedical Engineering; Biomedicine; Biotechnology; Business Administration; Cardiology; Cell Biology; Chemical Engineering; Chemistry; Chinese; Civil Engineering; Clothing and Sewing; Computer Engineering; Dance; Dentistry; Dermatology; Design; East Asian Studies; Eastern European Studies; Economics; Education; Educational Technology; Electrical Engineering; Electronic Engineering; Energy Engineering; English; Environmental Engineering; Environmental Studies; Fashion Design; Film; Finance; Food Science; Foreign Languages Education; French; Genetics; German; Graphic Design; Gynaecology and Obstetrics; Handicrafts; Health Administration; Health Sciences; History; Hotel and Restaurant; Human Resources; Industrial Design; Industrial Engineering; Industrial Management; Information Management; Information Technology; Insurance; Interior Design; International Business; International Relations; Japanese; Journalism; Korean; Landscape Architecture; Law; Leisure Studies; Literature; Management; Marine Science and Oceanography; Marketing; Mass Communication; Materials Engineering; Mathematics; Mathematics Education; Mechanical Engineering; Media Studies; Medical Technology; Medicine; Metallurgical Engineering; Microbiology; Molecular Biology; Multimedia; Museum Studies; Music Theory and Composition; Musical Instruments; Nanotechnology; Native Language Education; Natural Resources; Neurology; Nuclear Engineering; Nursing; Nutrition; Occupational Health; Ophthalmology; Orthopaedics; Paediatrics; Parasitology; Pathology; Petroleum and Gas Engineering; Pharmacology; Pharmacy; Philosophy; Physical Education; Physics; Physiology; Plastic Surgery; Political Sciences; Preschool Education; Psychiatry and Mental Health; Psychotherapy; Public Administration; Public Relations; Radiology; Real Estate; Rehabilitation and Therapy; Robotics; Russian; Service Trades; Singing; Social and Preventive Medicine; Sociology; Software Engineering; Sports; Sports Management; Structural Architecture; Surgery; Technology; Telecommunications Engineering; Textile Design; Textile Technology; Theatre; Tourism; Town Planning; Transport Engineering; Urban Studies; Urology), Doctor's Degree (Accountancy; Advertising and Publicity; American Studies; Anaesthesiology; Anatomy; Anthropology; Applied Chemistry; Applied Mathematics; Applied Physics; Architectural and Environmental Design; Architecture; Art Education; Asian Studies; Automotive Engineering; Banking; Biochemistry; Bioengineering; Biology; Biomedical Engineering; Biomedicine; Biotechnology; Business Administration; Cardiology; Cell Biology; Chemical Engineering; Chemistry; Chinese; Civil Engineering; Clothing and Sewing; Computer Engineering; Computer Science; Conducting; Cultural Studies; Dance; Dentistry; Dermatology; Design; East Asian Studies; Eastern European Studies; Economics; Educational Technology; Electrical Engineering; Electronic Engineering; Energy Engineering; Environmental Engineering; Environmental Studies; Film; Finance; Food Science; Foreign Languages Education; Genetics; German; Graphic Design; Gynaecology and Obstetrics; Handicrafts; Health Administration; Health Sciences; History; Human Resources; Industrial Design; Industrial Engineering; Information Management; Information Technology; Insurance; Interior Design; International Business; International Relations; Japanese; Journalism; Korean; Landscape Architecture; Law; Literature; Management; Marine Science and Oceanography; Marketing; Mass Communication; Materials Engineering;

Mathematics; Mechanical Engineering; Media Studies; Medical Technology; Medicine; Metallurgical Engineering; Microbiology; Molecular Biology; Multimedia; Music; Music Theory and Composition; Musical Instruments; Musicology; Nanotechnology; Native Language Education; Natural Resources; Neurological Therapy; Neurology; Nuclear Engineering; Nursing; Nutrition; Occupational Therapy; Ophthalmology; Orthopaedics; Otorhinolaryngology; Paediatrics; Parasitology; Pathology; Petroleum and Gas Engineering; Pharmacology; Pharmacy; Philosophy; Physical Education; Physics; Physiology; Plastic Surgery; Political Sciences; Psychiatry and Mental Health; Psychotherapy; Public Administration; Public Relations; Radiology; Rehabilitation and Therapy; Robotics; Russian; Service Trades; Singing; Social and Preventive Medicine; Social Sciences; Sociology; Sports; Sports Management; Structural Architecture; Surgery; Telecommunications Engineering; Textile Design; Theatre; Tourism; Town Planning; Transport Engineering; Urban Studies; Urology)

Student Services: Sports Facilities, Health Services, Library, Residential Facilities

Periodicals: Institute Research Publication

Publishing house: Hanyang University Press

Student Numbers 2015-2016	MALE	FEMALE	TOTAL
All (Foreign Included)			35000
Foreign only			6500

Last Update: 09-03-2018

Honam Theological University and Seminary (HTUS)

108 Yangrim-dong Nam-gu
Gwangju-si 503-756, Gyeonggi-do
Tel: +82(62) 650-1552, +82(62) 650-1513
Fax: +82(62) 675-1552
Website: http://www.htus.ac.kr
President: Chong-Soon Cha

Department/Division

Music (Music); **Social Welfare and Counselling** (Social Welfare); **Theology** (Theology)

Graduate School

Christian Care and Counseling (Christian Religious Studies; Developmental Psychology; Pastoral Studies; Psychoanalysis; Psychology); **Church Music** (Conducting; Music Theory and Composition; Musical Instruments; Opera; Religious Music; Singing); **Professional Ministry** (Christian Religious Studies; Developmental Psychology; Ethics;

Pastoral Studies; Philosophy; Psychoanalysis; Psychology; Psychotherapy; Religion; Religious Practice; Theology); **Theology** (Bible; Christian Religious Studies; Ethics; History of Religion; Missionary Studies; New Testament; Pastoral Studies; Religious Education; Theology)

History: Founded 1961.

Main language(s) of instruction: Korean

Accrediting agency: Korean Council for University Education (KCUE)

Degrees and diplomas: Bachelor's Degree (Music; Social Welfare; Theology), Master's Degree (Psychology; Religious Music; Theology), Doctor's Degree (Religion; Theology)

Student Services: Library, Residential Facilities

Academic Staff 2012-2013	MALE	FEMALE	TOTAL
FULL-TIME			55
PART-TIME			82
Student Numbers 2012-2013			
All (Foreign Included)			c. 1100

Last Update: 22-02-2018

Honam University

417 Hwangnam-gu, Gwangsan-gu
Gwangju-si 62399, Gyeonggi-do
Tel: +82(62) 940-5114, +82(62) 940-5642
Fax: +82(62) 940-5005
Website: http://www.honam.ac.kr
President: Gang-seok Seo

College

Arts (Cosmetology; Fashion Design; Film; Fine Arts; Industrial Design; Media Studies; Multimedia; Performing Arts; Theatre; Video); **Business Administration** (Air Transport; Art Management; Business Administration; Chinese; Economics; Hotel Management; International Business; International Studies; Korean; Tourism); **Engineering** (Architecture; Civil Engineering; Computer Engineering; Engineering; Environmental Engineering; Information Technology; Landscape Architecture; Telecommunications Engineering); **Health Science** (Biology; Cooking and Catering; Dental Hygiene; Food Science; Health Sciences; Nursing; Nutrition; Pharmacology; Physical Therapy; Rehabilitation and Therapy; Speech Therapy and Audiology; Sports); **Humanities and Social Sciences** (Arts and Humanities; English; Fire Science; Japanese; Journalism; Law; Literature; Modern Languages; Preschool Education; Psychology; Public Administration; Social Welfare); **Natural Sciences** (Biological and Life Sciences; Environmental Studies; Food Science; Horticulture; Household Management; Natural Sciences)

Graduate School

Education (Education; Educational Sciences; Teacher Training); **Graduate Studies** (Architecture and Planning; Arts and Humanities; Business Administration; Design; Engineering; Fine Arts; Modern Languages; Natural Sciences; Physical Education; Social Sciences); **Industry and Business Administration** (Business Administration); **Welfare and Public Administration** (Public Administration; Welfare and Protective Services)

History: Founded 1978 as Junior Commercial College, became 4-year College 1981, and acquired present status and title 1992.

Academic year: March to December (March-June; August-December)

Admission requirements: Graduation from High school and entrance examination

Fees: Humanities and Social Sciences, 1,896,500 per semester; Engineering and Arts, 2,616,100 per semester; Natural Science and Physical Education, 2,332,600 per semester; Mathematics, 1,977,300 per semester (Won)

Main language(s) of instruction: Korean, English

Accrediting agency: Korean Council for University Education (KCUE)

Degrees and diplomas: Bachelor's Degree, Master's Degree (Architecture; Biology; Business Administration; Civil Engineering; Computer Education; Computer Engineering; Educational Administration; Educational and Student Counselling; Electrical Engineering; English; Environmental Engineering; Fine Arts; Foreign Languages Education; Home Economics Education; Horticulture; Hotel Management; Humanities and Social Science Education; Information Technology; Korean; Landscape Architecture; Law; Literature; Mathematics Education; Native Language Education; Nursing; Physical Education; Public Administration; Rehabilitation and Therapy; Science Education; Social Welfare; Software Engineering; Sports; Telecommunications Engineering; Tourism; Town Planning), Doctor's Degree (Business Administration; Civil Engineering; Computer Engineering; Electrical Engineering; Electronic Engineering; English; Environmental Engineering; Hotel Management; Korean; Landscape Architecture; Law; Literature; Public Administration; Social Welfare; Sports; Tourism)

Student Services: Academic Counselling, Social Counselling, Careers Guidance, Nursery Care, Cultural Activities, Sports Facilities, Language Laboratory, Facilities for disabled people, Health Services, Canteen, Foreign Studies Centre

Periodicals: Honam University Bulletin, Journal of Business and Economics, Journal of Computer and Communication Research, Journal of Industrial Technology, Journal of Research in Humanities and Social Sciences, Thesis Collection of Honam University

Publishing house: Honam University Press

Academic Staff 2013-2014	MALE	FEMALE	TOTAL
FULL-TIME			c. 310
Student Numbers 2013-2014			
All (Foreign Included)			c. 8530

Last Update: 22-02-2018

Hongik University

94 Wausan-ro Mapo-gu
Seoul 121-791
Tel: +82(2) 320-1114
Fax: +82(2) 320-1122
Website: http://www.hongik.ac.kr
President: Young Hwan Kim

College

Architecture (Architecture; Interior Design); **Business Administration** (Business Administration; International Business); **Business Management** (*Jochiwon Campus*) (Accountancy; Business Administration; E- Business/Commerce; Finance; Insurance; Management; Marketing); **Design and Arts** (*Jochiwon Campus*) (Communication Arts; Design; Film; Fine Arts; Graphic Design; Industrial Design; Multimedia; Video; Visual Arts); **Economics** (Economics); **Education** (Education; Foreign Languages Education; Humanities and Social Science Education; Mathematics Education; Native Language Education); **Engineering** (Architecture; Chemical Engineering; Civil Engineering; Computer Engineering; Electrical Engineering; Electronic Engineering; Engineering; Information Technology; Materials Engineering; Mechanical Engineering; Town Planning); **Fine Arts** (Ceramic Art; Communication Arts; Design; Fine Arts; Furniture Design; Graphic Design; Handicrafts; Industrial Design; Painting and Drawing; Printing and Printmaking; Sculpture; Textile Design); **Law** (Law; Private Law; Public Law); **Liberal Arts** (Arts and Humanities; English; French; German; Korean; Linguistics; Literature); **Science and Technology** (*Jochiwon Campus*) (Architecture; Automation and Control Engineering; Bioengineering; Ceramics and Glass Technology; Chemical Engineering; Computer Engineering; Electrical and Electronic Engineering; Electrical Engineering; Electronic Engineering; Marine Engineering; Mechanical Engineering; Metallurgical Engineering; Natural Sciences; Naval Architecture; Power Engineering; Structural Architecture; Technology; Telecommunications Engineering)

School

Advertising and Public Relations (*Sejong Campus*) (Advertising and Publicity; Public Relations)

Department/Division
Industrial Sports (*Sejong Campus*) (Sports)

Institute
East Asian Corporate Management (Management); **Film, Video and Animation** (Film; Video)

Centre
Color Design (*Jochiwon Campus*) (Design; Fine Arts); **Venture Incubation**

Graduate School
Advertising and Public Relations (Advertising and Publicity; Management; Media Studies; Public Relations); **Architecture and Urban Design** (Architectural and Environmental Design; Civil Engineering; Interior Design; Landscape Architecture; Real Estate; Town Planning; Transport Engineering); **Business Administration** (Art Management; Business Administration; Taxation); **Education** (Art Education; Business Education; Computer Education; Continuing Education; Curriculum; Education; Educational Administration; Educational and Student Counselling; Educational Psychology; Foreign Languages Education; Humanities and Social Science Education; Mathematics Education; Native Language Education; Pedagogy; Primary Education); **Film and Digital Media** (Design; Film; Media Studies; Visual Arts); **Fine Arts** (Art Management; Fine Arts; Museum Studies; Painting and Drawing; Printing and Printmaking; Sculpture); **Games** (*Jochiwon Campus*) (Computer Graphics; Graphic Design; Software Engineering; Visual Arts); **General Studies** (Arts and Humanities; Design; Engineering; Fine Arts; Natural Sciences); **Industrial Arts** (Handicrafts; Industrial Design); **Industry** (*Jochiwon Campus*) (Advertising and Publicity; Architectural and Environmental Design; Business Administration; Communication Arts; Design; Electronic Engineering; Environmental Engineering; Industrial Design; Information Sciences; Information Technology; Interior Design; Visual Arts); **International Design school for Advanced Studies** (*IDAS*) (Art Management; Design; Graphic Design; Industrial Design; Multimedia); **Performing Art** (Music; Performing Arts); **Smart Urban Science Management** (Architecture; Information Technology; Town Planning; Urban Studies)

Research Division
Art and Design Technology (Design; Fine Arts; Technology); **Business Administration** (Business Administration); **Ceramic Art** (Ceramic Art); **Design Information and Culture** (Design); **Disaster Prevention and Safety Management** (Safety Engineering); **Economics** (Economics); **Education** (Education); **Electric Equipment** (*Jochiwon Campus*) (Electrical Engineering); **Environmental Arts** (Environmental Studies); **Environmental Development**; **Humanities** (Arts and Humanities); **Industrial Technology** (Industrial Engineering); **Information and Telecommunications** (Communication Studies; Information Sciences); **Law** (Law); **Marine Systems** (*Jochiwon Campus*) (Marine Science and Oceanography); **Mechatronics** (*Jochiwon Campus*) (Mechanical Engineering); **Media and Cultural Contents Strategy**; **Organic Materials and Information Devices**; **Railway and Transportation** (Railway Transport); **Science and Technology** (Natural Sciences; Technology); **Software and System**

Campus
Sejong Campus (Advertising and Publicity; Bioengineering; Business Administration; Chemical Engineering; Computer Engineering; Computer Graphics; Design; Electrical Engineering; Electronic Engineering; Engineering Drawing and Design; Graphic Design; Information Technology; Management; Marine Engineering; Materials Engineering; Media Studies; Naval Architecture; Public Relations; Software Engineering; Sports; Structural Architecture; Technology; Telecommunications Engineering)

Further information: Also Sejong Campus

History: Founded 1946 as a College, incorporated Soo-Do Engineering College and acquired University status 1971

Academic year: March to February (March-August; September-February)

Admission requirements: Graduation from high school and entrance examination

Fees: Liberal Arts/Business/Education: 3,3m. per semester; Arts/Engineering: 4,5m (Won)

Main language(s) of instruction: Korean

Accrediting agency: Korean Council for University Education (KCUE)

Degrees and diplomas: Bachelor's Degree, Master's Degree (Advertising and Publicity; Aesthetics; Architectural and Environmental Design; Architecture; Art Education; Art History; Art Management; Automation and Control Engineering; Business Administration; Business Education; Ceramic Art; Ceramics and Glass Technology; Chemical Engineering; Civil Engineering; Communication Arts; Computer Education; Computer Engineering; Computer Science; Continuing Education; Curriculum; Design; Display and Stage Design; Economics; Education; Educational Administration; Educational and Student Counselling; Educational Psychology; Electrical Engineering; Electronic Engineering; English; Environmental Engineering; Fashion Design; Film; Finance; Fine Arts; Foreign Languages Education; French; Furniture Design; German; Graphic Design; Handicrafts; Higher Education; History; Humanities and Social Science Education; Industrial Design; Industrial Engineering; Information

Technology; Insurance; Interior Design; International Business; Jewellery Art; Korean; Landscape Architecture; Law; Literature; Management; Marine Engineering; Materials Engineering; Mathematics; Mathematics Education; Measurement and Precision Engineering; Mechanical Engineering; Media Studies; Metallurgical Engineering; Multimedia; Museum Studies; Music; Native Language Education; Naval Architecture; Packaging Technology; Painting and Drawing; Pedagogy; Performing Arts; Photography; Physics; Primary Education; Printing and Printmaking; Private Law; Psychology; Public Relations; Real Estate; Sculpture; Software Engineering; Structural Architecture; Taxation; Technology Education; Telecommunications Engineering; Textile Design; Town Planning; Transport Engineering; Urban Studies; Video; Visual Arts), Doctor's Degree (Advertising and Publicity; Aesthetics; Architecture; Art History; Art Management; Automation and Control Engineering; Business Administration; Chemical Engineering; Civil Engineering; Computer Engineering; Computer Science; Design; Economics; Education; Electrical Engineering; Electronic Engineering; English; Film; Fine Arts; French; German; Handicrafts; History; Industrial Design; Industrial Engineering; Information Technology; International Business; Korean; Law; Literature; Materials Engineering; Mathematics; Mechanical Engineering; Public Relations; Structural Architecture; Telecommunications Engineering; Town Planning)

Student Services: Academic Counselling, Social Counselling, Careers Guidance, Cultural Activities, Sports Facilities, Language Laboratory, Facilities for disabled people, Health Services, Canteen, Foreign Studies Centre, Library, IT Centre, Residential Facilities

Periodicals: Art and Design Research Review, Bulletin of the Research Institute of Industrial Technology, Bulletin of the Research Institute of Science and Technology, Economic Review, Education Research Review, Environmental Development Institute, Hongik Faculty Journal, Humanities, Management Review, Studies on East-West Cultures

Publishing house: University Press

Academic Staff 2013-2014	MALE	FEMALE	TOTAL
FULL-TIME			c. 650
Student Numbers 2013-2014			
All (Foreign Included)			c. 22000

Last Update: 26-04-2018

Hoseo University

San 29-1 Sechul-ri Baebang-myeon
Asan-si 336-795, Chungnam-do
Tel: +82(41) 540-5114, +82(41) 540-9521
Fax: +82(41) 548-1831, +82(41) 540-9524
Website: http://www.hoseo.ac.kr
President: Dae Chul Shin
Tel: +82(418) 540-5009

College

Art and Sport Sciences (Art Management; Cinema and Television; Communication Arts; Computer Graphics; Design; Fashion Design; Film; Fine Arts; Graphic Design; Interior Design; Leisure Studies; Media Studies; Music; Music Theory and Composition; Musical Instruments; Protective Services; Software Engineering; Sports; Theatre); **Engineering** (Architecture; Automation and Control Engineering; Automotive Engineering; Chemical Engineering; Civil Engineering; Electrical Engineering; Engineering; Environmental Engineering; Fire Science; Graphic Design; Information Technology; Mechanical Engineering; Military Science; Production Engineering; Protective Services; Robotics; Safety Engineering; Software Engineering; Structural Architecture); **Humanities** (Arts and Humanities; Chinese; Christian Religious Studies; East Asian Studies; English; Korean; Literature; Preschool Education; Psychology; Religious Education; Social Welfare; Theology; Writing); **Natural Sciences** (Biological and Life Sciences; Biotechnology; Computer Science; Cosmetology; Data Processing; Food Science; Food Technology; Information Sciences; Mathematics; Natural Sciences; Nursing; Nutrition; Pharmacology; Pharmacy; Statistics); **New IT Engineering** (Computer Engineering; Electronic Engineering; Information Technology; Materials Engineering; Mechanical Engineering; Optical Technology; Software Engineering; Telecommunications Engineering); **Social Sciences** (Accountancy; Air Transport; Business Administration; Business and Commerce; E- Business/Commerce; Economics; Engineering Management; Industrial and Organizational Psychology; International Business; International Law; Law; Management; Public Administration; Service Trades; Social Sciences; Taxation)

Graduate School

Arts and Sport (Design; Fine Arts; Media Studies; Music; Performing Arts; Sports); **Business Administration** (*Specialized Graduate School*) (Business Administration); **Culture, Welfare, and Counseling** (*Professional Graduate School*) (Cultural Studies; Psychology; Welfare and Protective Services); **Education** (*Specialized Graduate School*) (Education); **Engineering** (Automation and Control Engineering; Electrical Engineering; Engineering; Environmental Engineering; Software Engineering); **Global Entrepreneurship** (*Specialized Graduate School*) (International Business; Management); **Hoseo Divinity School** (*Professional Graduate School*) (Bible; Christian Religious Studies; New Testament; Psychology; Religious

Practice; Theology); **Humanities** (Educational and Student Counselling; English; Korean; Literature; Social Welfare); **Natural Sciences** (Cosmetology; Food Science; Mathematics; Natural Sciences; Nutrition; Statistics); **Public Administration** (*Specialized Graduate School*) (Public Administration); **Social Sciences** (Economics; Industrial and Organizational Psychology; Law; Management; Public Administration; Social Sciences); **Sport Science** (*Specialized Graduate School*) (Sports); **Venture Business** (*Professional Graduate School*) (Cosmetology; Environmental Studies; Management; Sports Management)

History: Founded 1978.

Fees: 5,000 per annum

Main language(s) of instruction: Korean

Accrediting agency: Korean Council for University Education (KCUE)

Degrees and diplomas: Bachelor's Degree, Master's Degree (Art Management; Arts and Humanities; Business Administration; Cosmetology; Cultural Studies; Design; Engineering; Engineering Management; Environmental Engineering; Fashion Design; Fine Arts; Information Management; Information Technology; Management; Music; Natural Sciences; Performing Arts; Psychology; Real Estate; Religion; Social Sciences; Social Work; Sports; Theology; Transport Management; Welfare and Protective Services), Doctor's Degree (Administration; Architecture; Art Management; Automation and Control Engineering; Biochemistry; Bioengineering; Business Administration; Chemical Engineering; Civil Engineering; Computer Engineering; Computer Graphics; Computer Science; Cosmetology; Economics; Electrical Engineering; Electronic Engineering; Energy Engineering; Engineering; Engineering Management; English; Environmental Engineering; Food Science; Human Resources; Information Management; Information Technology; Korean; Law; Literature; Management; Materials Engineering; Mathematics; Mechanical Engineering; Meteorology; Nanotechnology; Nutrition; Physical Education; Real Estate; Safety Engineering; Software Engineering; Sports; Statistics; Structural Architecture; Telecommunications Engineering; Theology; Toxicology; Transport Management; Welfare and Protective Services)

Student Services: Academic Counselling, Careers Guidance, Nursery Care, Sports Facilities, Language Laboratory, Health Services, Canteen, Foreign Studies Centre, Library, Residential Facilities

Academic Staff 2012-2013	MALE	FEMALE	TOTAL
FULL-TIME			490
PART-TIME			c. 560
Student Numbers 2012-2013			
All (Foreign Included)			c. 14500
Foreign only			525

Last Update: 08-03-2018

Howon University

64 Howondae 3gil Impi-myeon
Gunsan-si 54058, Jeollabuk-do
Tel: +82(63) 450-7114, +82(63) 450-7834
Fax: +82(63) 450-6171, +82(63) 450-7840
Website: http://www.howon.ac.kr
President: Hee-sung Kang

College

Culture and Arts (Business Administration; Cosmetology; Design; Fine Arts; Media Studies; Music; Performing Arts; Tourism); **Engineering** (Automotive Engineering; Engineering; Fire Science; Protective Services); **Social Welfare** (Dental Hygiene; Law; Medicine; Nursing; Occupational Therapy; Physical Therapy; Police Studies; Preschool Education; Protective Services; Social Welfare; Speech Therapy and Audiology; Sports; Welfare and Protective Services)

Department/Division

Lifelong Learning (Social Welfare; Sports)
History: Founded 1977.
Main language(s) of instruction: Korean
Accrediting agency: Korean Council for University Education (KCUE)
Degrees and diplomas: Bachelor's Degree (Acting; Agricultural Business; Architecture; Business Administration; Business and Commerce; Computer Graphics; Computer Networks; Electronic Engineering; Energy Engineering; Food Science; Foreign Languages Education; Hotel and Restaurant; Interior Design; Korean; Law; Maintenance Technology; Management; Military Science; Music Theory and Composition; Musical Instruments; Performing Arts; Political Sciences; Real Estate; Safety Engineering; Singing; Software Engineering; Sports; Tourism; Transport Management)
Student Services: Sports Facilities, Library

Academic Staff 2017-2018	MALE	FEMALE	TOTAL
FULL-TIME			250
Student Numbers 2017-2018			
All (Foreign Included)			c. 7000

Last Update: 08-03-2018

Hyupsung University

72 Choerubaek Bongdam-eup
Hwaseong-si 18330, Gyeonggi-do
Tel: +82(31) 299-0900
Fax: +82(31) 227-7501
Website: http://www.uhs.ac.kr
President: Dong-Ill Chang

College

Art (Design; Fine Arts; Graphic Design; Industrial Design; Interior Design; Music; Music Theory and Composition; Musical Instruments; Painting and Drawing; Singing); **Business Administration** (Accountancy; Advertising and Publicity; Business Administration; Film; Finance; Information Technology; Insurance; International Business; Management; Public Relations; Taxation; Transport Management); **Humanities and Social Science** (Arts and Humanities; Child Care and Development; Chinese; Development Studies; Education; English; Literature; Regional Studies; Social Sciences; Social Welfare; Town Planning; Writing); **Science and Engineering** (Computer Engineering; Engineering; Health Administration; Natural Sciences; Structural Architecture; Town Planning); **Theology** (Bible; Christian Religious Studies; History; Religious Practice; Theology)

Graduate School

Arts (Conducting; Design; Fine Arts; Graphic Design; Industrial Design; Interior Design; Music; Music Theory and Composition; Musical Instruments; Performing Arts; Singing); **Education** (Computer Education; Education; Educational Administration; Educational and Student Counselling; Foreign Languages Education; Native Language Education); **General Graduate Studies** (Theology; Town Planning); **Social Sciences** (Social Sciences; Social Welfare); **Theology** (Bible; Christian Religious Studies; Ethics; Missionary Studies; New Testament; Pastoral Studies; Religious Education; Religious Practice; Theology)

History: Founded 1977.

Main language(s) of instruction: Korean

Accrediting agency: Korean Council for University Education (KCUE)

Degrees and diplomas: Bachelor's Degree, Master's Degree (Bible; Christian Religious Studies; Computer Education; Design; Educational Administration; Educational and Student Counselling; Ethics; Fine Arts; Foreign Languages Education; Graphic Design; Industrial Design; Interior Design; Missionary Studies; Music Theory and Composition; Musical Instruments; Native Language Education; New Testament; Pastoral Studies; Religious Education; Religious Practice; Singing; Social Welfare; Theology; Town Planning)

Student Services: Health Services, Library, Residential Facilities

Academic Staff 2012-2013	MALE	FEMALE	TOTAL
FULL-TIME			150
PART-TIME			c. 235
Student Numbers 2012-2013			
All (Foreign Included)			c. 5610

Last Update: 22-02-2018

Incheon Catholic University

495 Dojang-ri, Yangdo-myeon Ganghwa-gun
Incheon-si 417-852
Tel: +82(32) 937-8111
Fax: +82(32) 937-8118
Website: http://www.iccu.ac.kr
President: Heung-Ju Kim

Department/Division

Fine Arts (Architectural and Environmental Design; Design; Fine Arts; Graphic Design; Painting and Drawing; Religious Art; Sculpture); **Theology** (Theology)

History: Founded 1996.

Main language(s) of instruction: Korean

Accrediting agency: Korean Council for University Education (KCUE)

Degrees and diplomas: Bachelor's Degree, Master's Degree (Fine Arts; Religious Art; Theology)

Academic Staff 2012-2013	MALE	FEMALE	TOTAL
FULL-TIME			40
PART-TIME			c. 85
Student Numbers 2012-2013			
All (Foreign Included)			c. 840

Last Update: 22-02-2018

Inha University

100 Inharo Nam-gu
Incheon-si 22212
Tel: +82(32) 860-7114, +82(32) 860-7030
Fax: +82(32) 863-1333, +82(32) 867-7222
Website: http://www.inha.ac.kr
President: Soonja Choe
Tel: +82(32) 860-7000

College

Arts and Sports (Film; Fine Arts; Graphic Design; Physical Therapy; Theatre); **Business Administration** (Banking; Business Administration; Finance; Transport Management); **Economics and International Trade** (Economics; International Business); **Education** (Education; Foreign Languages Education; Humanities and Social Science Education; Mathematics Education; Native Language Education; Physical Education); **Engineering** (Aeronautical and Aerospace Engineering; Architecture; Bioengineering; Chemical Engineering; Civil Engineering; Computer Science; Energy Engineering; Engineering; Environmental Engineering; Geological Engineering; Marine Engineering; Materials

Engineering; Mechanical Engineering; Naval Architecture; Polymer and Plastics Technology; Structural Architecture); **Human Ecology** (Child Care and Development; Clothing and Sewing; Consumer Studies; Fashion Design; Food Science; Nutrition; Textile Design); **Humanities** (Art Management; Arts and Humanities; Chinese; Cultural Studies; East Asian Studies; English; French; French Studies; History; Japanese; Korean; Literature; Philosophy); **Information Technology and Engineering** (Computer Science; Electrical Engineering; Electronic Engineering; Information Technology; Telecommunications Engineering); **Law** (Law); **Medicine** (Nursing); **Natural Sciences** (Biological and Life Sciences; Chemistry; Marine Science and Oceanography; Mathematics; Natural Sciences; Physics; Statistics); **Social Sciences** (Information Sciences; International Relations; Mass Communication; Political Sciences; Public Administration; Social Sciences)

School

Law (*Graduate*) (Civil Law; Commercial Law; Law; Private Law; Public Law); **Logistics** (*Asia Pacific*) (Transport Management); **Medicine** (*Graduate*) (Medicine; Nursing)

Graduate School

Business Administration (Business Administration); **Education** (Education; Educational Sciences; Teacher Training); **Engineering** (Engineering); **Graduate Studies** (Accountancy; Aeronautical and Aerospace Engineering; Archaeology; Art Management; Automation and Control Engineering; Bioengineering; Biological and Life Sciences; Business Administration; Chemical Engineering; Chemistry; Child Care and Development; Chinese; Civil Engineering; Clothing and Sewing; Communication Arts; Computer Engineering; Computer Graphics; Computer Science; Consumer Studies; Cultural Studies; East Asian Studies; Economics; Education; Electrical Engineering; Electronic Engineering; Energy Engineering; English; Environmental Engineering; Food Science; Foreign Languages Education; French; Geological Engineering; German; Government; Health Sciences; Humanities and Social Science Education; Industrial Engineering; Information Sciences; Information Technology; International Business; International Relations; Japanese; Korean; Law; Literature; Marine Engineering; Marine Science and Oceanography; Mass Communication; Materials Engineering; Mathematics; Mathematics Education; Mechanical Engineering; Media Studies; Medicine; Nanotechnology; Native Language Education; Naval Architecture; Nursing; Nutrition; Physical Therapy; Physics; Political Sciences; Polymer and Plastics Technology; Private Law; Public Administration; Service Trades; Statistics; Structural Architecture; Textile Design; Textile Technology; Town Planning; Visual Arts); **Information Technology and Telecommunications** (Information Technology; Telecommunications Engineering); **International Trade and Logistics** (International Business; Transport Management); **Policy Science** (Media Studies; Public Administration; Real Estate; Social Welfare)

Further information: Also 31 Government-supported Research Centres and 62 Affiliated Research Centres

History: Founded 1954 as Institute of Technology, acquired present status and title 1972.

Academic year: March to December (March-July; August-December)

Admission requirements: Graduation from high school and entrance examination

Main language(s) of instruction: Korean, English

Accrediting agency: Korean Council for University Education (KCUE)

Degrees and diplomas: Bachelor's Degree, Master's Degree (Accountancy; Aeronautical and Aerospace Engineering; Anaesthesiology; Anatomy; Applied Mathematics; Archaeology; Architectural and Environmental Design; Architecture and Planning; Art Management; Automation and Control Engineering; Biochemistry; Bioengineering; Biological and Life Sciences; Biomedicine; Business Administration; Cardiology; Chemical Engineering; Chemistry; Child Care and Development; Chinese; Civil Engineering; Clothing and Sewing; Community Health; Computer Engineering; Computer Science; Construction Engineering; Consumer Studies; Continuing Education; Criminal Law; Cultural Studies; Dentistry; Dermatology; Economics; Education; Educational Administration; Educational and Student Counselling; Electrical Engineering; Electronic Engineering; Energy Engineering; Engineering; English; Environmental Engineering; Finance; Fishery; Food Science; Foreign Languages Education; French; German; Government; Graphic Design; Gynaecology and Obstetrics; Health Sciences; History; Home Economics Education; Human Resources; Humanities and Social Science Education; Industrial Engineering; Information Management; Information Sciences; Information Technology; International Business; International Relations; Japanese; Korean; Laboratory Techniques; Linguistics; Literature; Management; Marine Engineering; Marine Science and Oceanography; Marketing; Mass Communication; Materials Engineering; Mathematics; Mathematics Education; Mechanical Engineering; Media Studies; Medicine; Microbiology; Molecular Biology; Multimedia; Nanotechnology; Native Language Education; Naval Architecture; Neurology; Nursing; Nutrition; Oncology; Ophthalmology; Optics; Orthopaedics; Otorhinolaryngology; Paediatrics; Parasitology; Pathology; Pharmacology; Philosophy; Physical Education; Physical Therapy; Physics; Physiology; Plastic Surgery; Political Sciences; Polymer and Plastics Technology; Private Law; Production Engineering; Psychiatry and Mental Health; Public

Administration; Public Law; Radiology; Real Estate; Rehabilitation and Therapy; Robotics; Science Education; Social and Preventive Medicine; Social Welfare; Solid State Physics; Statistics; Structural Architecture; Surgery; Surveying and Mapping; Telecommunications Engineering; Textile Design; Textile Technology; Town Planning; Transport Management; Urology; Visual Arts; Water Science), Doctor's Degree (Accountancy; Aeronautical and Aerospace Engineering; Anaesthesiology; Anatomy; Applied Mathematics; Archaeology; Architectural and Environmental Design; Architecture and Planning; Art Management; Biochemistry; Bioengineering; Biological and Life Sciences; Biomedicine; Business Administration; Cardiology; Chemical Engineering; Chemistry; Child Care and Development; Clothing and Sewing; Computer Engineering; Computer Graphics; Construction Engineering; Consumer Studies; Criminal Law; Cultural Studies; Dentistry; Dermatology; East Asian Studies; Economics; Education; Electrical Engineering; Electronic Engineering; Energy Engineering; English; Environmental Engineering; Finance; Fishery; Food Science; Foreign Languages Education; Geological Engineering; Government; Gynaecology and Obstetrics; Health Sciences; History; Human Resources; Humanities and Social Science Education; Industrial Engineering; Information Sciences; Information Technology; International Business; International Relations; Japanese; Korean; Laboratory Techniques; Linguistics; Literature; Management; Marine Engineering; Marine Science and Oceanography; Marketing; Mass Communication; Materials Engineering; Mathematics; Mathematics Education; Mechanical Engineering; Media Studies; Medicine; Microbiology; Nanotechnology; Native Language Education; Naval Architecture; Neurology; Nursing; Nutrition; Oncology; Ophthalmology; Optics; Orthopaedics; Otorhinolaryngology; Paediatrics; Parasitology; Pathology; Pharmacology; Philosophy; Physical Therapy; Physics; Physiology; Plastic Surgery; Political Sciences; Polymer and Plastics Technology; Private Law; Production Engineering; Psychiatry and Mental Health; Public Administration; Public Health; Public Law; Radiology; Rehabilitation and Therapy; Robotics; Social Sciences; Solid State Physics; Statistics; Structural Architecture; Surgery; Surveying and Mapping; Textile Design; Textile Technology; Town Planning; Transport Management; Urology; Water Management). Postgraduate Diploma in Law (Juris Doctor)
Student Services: Academic Counselling, Social Counselling, Careers Guidance, Nursery Care, Cultural Activities, Sports Facilities, Health Services, Canteen, Library, Residential Facilities
Publishing house: Inha University Press

Academic Staff 2012-2013	MALE	FEMALE	TOTAL
FULL-TIME			1080
PART-TIME			c. 650

(continued)

Academic Staff 2012-2013	MALE	FEMALE	TOTAL
Student Numbers 2012-2013			
All (Foreign Included)			c. 20613
Foreign only			1311

Last Update: 23-02-2018

Inje University

197 Inje-ro
Gimhae-si 621-749, Gyeongsangnam-do
Tel: +82(55) 334-7111, +82(55) 334-7118
Fax: +82(55) 334-0712
Website: http://www.inje.ac.kr
President: Won-Ro Lee
Tel: +82(55) 320-3900

College
Biomedical Science and Engineering (Biological and Life Sciences; Biomedical Engineering; Biomedicine; Food Science; Laboratory Techniques; Occupational Health; Occupational Therapy; Physical Therapy; Safety Engineering); **Design** (Design; Film; Graphic Design; Interior Design; Visual Arts); **Engineering** (Architecture; Automotive Engineering; Civil Engineering; Computer Engineering; Electronic Engineering; Engineering; Industrial Engineering; Management; Mechanical Engineering; Nanotechnology; Pharmacology; Telecommunications Engineering; Town Planning); **Humanities and Social Sciences** (Archaeology; Arts and Humanities; Chinese; Economics; English; English Studies; Health Administration; History; International Business; International Relations; Japanese; Korean; Law; Literature; Management; Mass Communication; Political Sciences; Preschool Education; Psychology; Psychotherapy; Public Administration; Social Welfare; Special Education; Tourism; Welfare and Protective Services); **Medicine** (Arts and Humanities; Medicine; Natural Sciences; Nursing; Social Sciences); **Natural Sciences** (Applied Mathematics; Biochemistry; Computer Science; Data Processing; Environmental Engineering; Leisure Studies; Sports); **Pharmacy** (Pharmacology; Pharmacy)

Course/Programme
Korean Language (*For International Students*) (Korean)

Department/Division
Music (Music; Music Theory and Composition; Musical Instruments; Singing)

Graduate School
Business Administration (Business Administration); **Education** (Child Care and Development; Education;

Environmental Studies; Foreign Languages Education; Humanities and Social Science Education; Mathematics Education; Native Language Education; Physical Education; Special Education); **Graduate Studies** (Arts and Humanities; Design; Energy Engineering; Engineering; Environmental Engineering; Fine Arts; Health Sciences; Information Technology; Medicine; Music; Natural Sciences; Performing Arts; Rehabilitation and Therapy; Social Sciences; Telecommunications Engineering); **Public Health** (Health Administration; Physical Therapy; Public Health); **Social Welfare** (Social Welfare; Social Work)

Further information: Also Pusan and Seoul Campuses; Research Institutes, Graduate Schools and 3 attached Hospitals

History: Founded as College 1979. Acquired present status and title 1989.

Academic year: March to February (March-August; September-February)

Admission requirements: Graduation from high school and entrance examination

Main language(s) of instruction: Korean, English

Accrediting agency: Korean Council for University Education (KCUE)

Degrees and diplomas: Bachelor's Degree, Master's Degree (Administration; Archaeology; Architecture; Arts and Humanities; Biomedical Engineering; Biomedicine; Biotechnology; Business Administration; Chemistry; Child Care and Development; Chinese; Civil Engineering; Communication Studies; Computer Engineering; Computer Science; Consumer Studies; Data Processing; Design; Economics; Electronic Engineering; Energy Engineering; English; Environmental Engineering; Environmental Studies; Family Studies; Food Technology; Foreign Languages Education; Health Administration; Health Sciences; History; Humanities and Social Science Education; Industrial Engineering; Information Technology; International Business; International Relations; Korean; Law; Literature; Management; Mathematics Education; Mechanical Engineering; Medical Technology; Medicine; Music; Nanotechnology; Native Language Education; Nursing; Occupational Health; Occupational Therapy; Pharmacy; Physical Education; Physical Therapy; Political Sciences; Public Health; Rehabilitation and Therapy; Safety Engineering; Social Welfare; Special Education; Telecommunications Engineering), Doctor's Degree (Administration; Arts and Humanities; Biomedical Engineering; Biomedicine; Biotechnology; Business Administration; Chemistry; Civil Engineering; Computer Engineering; Computer Science; Design; East Asian Studies; Economics; Education; Energy Engineering; Environmental Engineering; Environmental Management; Environmental Studies; Food Technology; Health Administration; Health Sciences; Information Technology; International Business; Korean; Law; Literature; Mechanical Engineering; Medical

Technology; Medicine; Music; Nanotechnology; Nursing; Pharmacy; Public Health; Rehabilitation and Therapy; Social Welfare; Telecommunications Services)

Student Services: Sports Facilities, Canteen, Library, Residential Facilities

Periodicals: Bulletin, In Je Journal, In Je Medical Journal

Publishing house: University Press

Academic Staff 2013-2014	MALE	FEMALE	TOTAL
FULL-TIME			997
PART-TIME			400
Student Numbers 2013-2014			
All (Foreign Included)			15641

Last Update: 23-02-2018

International Graduate School of English (IGSE)

17, Yangjae-daero 81-gil, Gangdong-gu
Seoul 05408
Tel: +82(2) 6477-5114, +82(80) 804-0505
Website: http://www.igse.ac.kr/en
President: Young-soo Ahn

Department/Division

ELT Materials Development (Foreign Languages Education); **English Language Teaching** (Foreign Languages Education)

History: Founded 2002.

Main language(s) of instruction: Korean

Accrediting agency: Ministry of Education

Degrees and diplomas: Master's Degree (Foreign Languages Education)

Last Update: 22-03-2018

International University of Korea (IUK)

965 Dongburo Munsan
Jinju-si 52833, Gyeongnam-do
Tel: +82(55) 751-8114, +82(55) 751-8092
Fax: +82(55) 761-7407, +82(55) 751-8099
Website: http://www.iuk.ac.kr/main/index.php
President: Kyung-mo Kang

College

Arts and Sports (Cosmetology; Design; Fine Arts; Music; Performing Arts; Sports); **Education and Science** (Education; Physical Education; Preschool Education; Primary Education; Special Education; Teacher Training); **Engineering** (Automotive Engineering; Electrical Engineering; Energy Engineering; Engineering; Fire Science; Interior Design;

Marine Engineering; Mechanical Engineering; Safety Engineering); **Human Ecology** (Cooking and Catering; Food Science; Nutrition); **Medical Health** (Health Administration; Health Sciences; Nursing; Pharmacology; Physical Therapy; Radiology); **Social Science** (Business Administration; Cultural Studies; Korean; Police Studies; Social Sciences; Social Welfare); **Tourism** (Hotel Management; Japanese; Tourism)

Graduate School

General Graduate Studies (Automotive Engineering; Food Science; Preschool Education; Psychology; Rehabilitation and Therapy; Social Welfare; Special Education); **Special Graduate Studies** (Architecture; Business Administration; Cooking and Catering; Cosmetology; Design; Fine Arts; Fire Science; Hotel Management; Interior Design; Labour and Industrial Relations; Physical Therapy; Public Administration; Radiology; Social Welfare; Tourism)

History: Founded 1978 as Jinjun International University, acquired present title 2008.

Main language(s) of instruction: Korean

Accrediting agency: Korean Council for University Education (KCUE)

Degrees and diplomas: Bachelor's Degree, Master's Degree (Architecture; Automotive Engineering; Business Administration; Cooking and Catering; Cosmetology; Design; Food Science; Interior Design; Physical Education; Physical Therapy; Preschool Education; Psychology; Psychotherapy; Public Administration; Radiology; Safety Engineering; Social Work; Special Education; Tourism), Doctor's Degree (Food Science; Safety Engineering; Social Policy; Special Education)

Student Services: Sports Facilities, Health Services, Library, IT Centre, Residential Facilities

Academic Staff 2013-2014	MALE	FEMALE	TOTAL
FULL-TIME			160
PART-TIME			160
Student Numbers 2013-2014			
All (Foreign Included)			c. 5000

Last Update: 08-03-2018

Jeju International University (JIU)

San-70 Hawon-dong
Sogwipo-si 690-714, Cheju-do
Tel: +82(64) 754-0200
Fax: +82(64) 702-8330
Website: http://www.jeju.ac.kr/en/index.htm
President: Choong-sok Koh

Faculty

Arts (Design); **Business Administration** (Accountancy; Air Transport; Business Administration; Taxation); **Engineering** (Automotive Engineering; Civil Engineering; Computer Engineering; Electrical Engineering; Energy Engineering; Engineering; Fire Science; Mechanical Engineering; Safety Engineering; Structural Architecture); **Humanities and Social Sciences** (Administration; Chinese; English; Government; Japanese; Literature; Police Studies; Preschool Education; Psychology; Public Administration; Social Welfare; Speech Therapy and Audiology; Translation and Interpretation); **Sports** (Leisure Studies; Rehabilitation and Therapy; Sports); **Tourism** (Cooking and Catering; Food Science; Hotel Management; Tourism)

Course/Programme

Liberal Arts (Arts and Humanities; Biological and Life Sciences; Chinese; Computer Science; East Asian Studies; English; Fine Arts; International Studies; Japanese; Modern Languages; Natural Sciences; Social Sciences)

Graduate School

Education (Education; Physical Education; Preschool Education); **Industry** (Automotive Engineering; Civil Engineering; Environmental Engineering; Mechanical Engineering); **Management** (Air Transport; Asian Studies; Business Administration; Chinese; Management; Sports Management; Tourism); **Police Law** (Civil Law; Criminal Law; Law; Police Studies); **Social Welfare** (Social Welfare; Social Work)

History: Founded 1997 as Tamna University. Acquired present title after merging with Jeju College of Technology 2012.

Main language(s) of instruction: Korean

Accrediting agency: Ministry of Education

Degrees and diplomas: Bachelor's Degree, Master's Degree (Business Administration; Computer Education; Education; Educational Administration; Physical Education; Preschool Education; Public Administration; Social Welfare; Social Work; Tourism)

Last Update: 24-05-2018

Jeonju University

303 Cheonjam-ro Wansan-gu
Jeonju-si 55069, Jeollabuk-do
Tel: +82(63) 220-3285, +82(63) 1577-7177
Fax: +82(63) 220-2404
Website: http://www.jeonju.ac.kr
President: Ho-in Lee

College

Arts and Athletics (Communication Arts; Design; Graphic Design; Industrial Design; Interior Design; Music; Musical Instruments; Physical Education; Rehabilitation and Therapy; Sports); **Business Administration** (Accountancy;

Advertising and Publicity; Business Administration; Economics; Finance; Insurance; International Business; Management; Public Relations; Real Estate; Taxation; Transport Management); **Culture and Creative Industry** (Cinema and Television; Computer Graphics; Film; Information Technology; Mass Communication; Media Studies; Multimedia; Performing Arts; Software Engineering; Visual Arts); **Culture and Tourism** (Business Administration; Cooking and Catering; Fashion Design; Food Technology; Hotel Management; Tourism); **Education** (Education; Foreign Languages Education; Home Economics Education; Humanities and Social Science Education; Mathematics Education; Native Language Education; Science Education; Secondary Education; Special Education); **Engineering** (Architecture; Automotive Engineering; Civil Engineering; Computer Engineering; Computer Science; Electrical and Electronic Engineering; Engineering; Engineering Drawing and Design; Environmental Engineering; Information Technology; Materials Engineering; Mechanical Engineering; Nanotechnology; Production Engineering; Safety Engineering; Structural Architecture; Telecommunications Engineering); **Humanities** (Arts and Humanities; Asian Studies; Chinese; Christian Religious Studies; Cultural Studies; East Asian Studies; English; English Studies; History; Japanese; Korean; Literature; Religious Studies); **Medical Science** (Alternative Medicine; Environmental Studies; Food Science; Health Sciences; Nursing; Occupational Therapy; Physical Therapy; Radiology; Rehabilitation and Therapy); **Social Science** (Information Sciences; Law; Library Science; Police Studies; Psychology; Public Administration; Social Sciences; Social Welfare)

Graduate School

Alternative Medicine (Alternative Medicine; Health Sciences; Nutrition); **Business Administration** (Business Administration; Cooking and Catering; Hotel Management; Small Business; Tourism); **Counseling** (Family Studies; Psychology; Vocational Counselling); **Cultural and Industrial Engineering** (Cultural Studies; Industrial Design; Industrial Engineering; Performing Arts; Visual Arts); **Education** (Education; Educational Sciences; Foreign Languages Education; Special Education; Teacher Training); **Graduate Studies** (Agriculture; Art Therapy; Biological and Life Sciences; Business Administration; Education; Engineering Drawing and Design; Industrial Engineering; International Business; Production Engineering; Psychotherapy; Rehabilitation and Therapy; Theology); **Mission and Theology** (Missionary Studies; Theology); **Public Administration** (Police Studies; Public Administration; Real Estate)

Research Division

Chongqing (*Specialized*); **Cultural Industry** (*Specialized*); **Culture and Tourism** (*Specialized*); **Educational Sciences** (*Specialized*); **Engineering Technology**; **Food Industry** (*Specialized*); **Health Sciences**; **Humanities**; **Industrial Studies**; **Korea Institute of Numismatics Mastery** (*Specialized*); **National Institute of Art and Culture**; **Nongsaneop Institute for Strategic Studies** (*Specialized*); **Saemangeum Development** (*Specialized*); **Smart Space Culture Technology**; **Social Science**

History: Founded 1964, acquired present status 1978.

Academic year: March to December (March-June; September-December)

Admission requirements: Graduation from high school or equivalent

Main language(s) of instruction: Korean, English

Accrediting agency: Korean Council for University Education (KCUE)

Degrees and diplomas: Bachelor's Degree, Master's Degree (Acting; Agricultural Business; Agriculture; Alternative Medicine; Archiving; Art Education; Art Therapy; Business Administration; Cinema and Television; Civil Engineering; Computer Engineering; Cooking and Catering; Design; Education; Educational Administration; Educational and Student Counselling; Electrical and Electronic Engineering; Engineering Drawing and Design; English; Environmental Engineering; Environmental Studies; Family Studies; Finance; Fine Arts; Foreign Languages Education; Health Sciences; History; Humanities and Social Science Education; Information Sciences; Information Technology; Insurance; Korean; Law; Library Science; Literature; Materials Engineering; Mathematics Education; Mechanical Engineering; Music; Music Education; Nanotechnology; Native Language Education; Natural Resources; Performing Arts; Physical Education; Police Studies; Production Engineering; Psychology; Psychotherapy; Public Administration; Real Estate; Rehabilitation and Therapy; Safety Engineering; Social Welfare; Special Education; Statistics; Structural Architecture; Telecommunications Engineering; Theatre; Tourism; Visual Arts; Vocational Counselling), Doctor's Degree (Agricultural Business; Agriculture; Alternative Medicine; Archiving; Business Administration; Construction Engineering; Education; Electrical and Electronic Engineering; Energy Engineering; English; Environmental Studies; Finance; History; Industrial Engineering; Information Technology; Insurance; International Business; Korean; Law; Literature; Materials Engineering; Mechanical Engineering; Missionary Studies; Natural Resources; New Testament; Pastoral Studies; Physical Education; Police Studies; Public Administration; Real Estate; Safety Engineering; Statistics; Telecommunications Engineering; Theology; Tourism)

Student Services: Academic Counselling, Social Counselling, Careers Guidance, Nursery Care, Cultural Activities, Sports Facilities, Language Laboratory, Facilities for disabled people, Health Services, Canteen, Library, Residential Facilities

Periodicals: Jeonju University Bulletin, Jeonju University Journal
Publishing house: Jeonju University Press

Academic Staff 2013-2014	MALE	FEMALE	TOTAL
FULL-TIME			c. 470
Student Numbers 2013-2014			
All (Foreign Included)			c. 12000
Foreign only			580

Last Update: 23-02-2018

Jesus University

168-1 Junghwasandong 1(il)-ga Wansan-gu
Jeonju-si, Jeollabuk-do
Tel: +82(63) 230-7700
Website: https://www.jesus.ac.kr
President: Kang Mi Ja Kim

School
Nursing (Health Sciences; Microbiology; Nursing; Pharmacology); **Social Welfare** (Family Studies; Social Welfare; Social Work; Welfare and Protective Services)

Department/Division
Teacher Training (Teacher Training)

Graduate School
Graduate Studies (Nursing)
History: Founded 1950 as a Nursing School. Acquired university status 2002. Acquired present title 2008.
Main language(s) of instruction: Korean
Accrediting agency: Korean Council for University Education (KCUE)
Degrees and diplomas: Bachelor's Degree (Nursing; Social Welfare; Teacher Training), Master's Degree (Nursing)
Student Services: Health Services, Canteen, Library, IT Centre, Residential Facilities

Academic Staff 2012-2013	MALE	FEMALE	TOTAL
FULL-TIME			26
PART-TIME			1
Student Numbers 2012-2013			
All (Foreign Included)			c. 660

Last Update: 23-02-2018

Joong-Ang Sangha University

159-1 Pungmu-dong
Gunpo-si 415-768, Gyeonggi-do

Tel: +82(31) 980-7777
Fax: +82(31) 980-7778
Website: http://www.sangha.ac.kr
President: Kyung-Shik Lee

Course/Programme
Buddhism Scripture Translation (History of Religion; Holy Writings; Linguistics; Translation and Interpretation); **Buddhism Studies** (Asian Religious Studies); **Social Welfare** (Asian Religious Studies; Social Welfare); **Sociology of Dissemination** (Asian Religious Studies; Public Relations)

Graduate School
Graduate Studies (Asian Religious Studies; Social Welfare)
History: Founded 1996.
Main language(s) of instruction: Korean
Accrediting agency: Ministry of Education
Degrees and diplomas: Bachelor's Degree, Master's Degree (Asian Religious Studies; Social Work), Doctor's Degree (Asian Religious Studies)
Student Services: Library, IT Centre, Residential Facilities

Academic Staff 2012-2013	MALE	FEMALE	TOTAL
FULL-TIME			20
PART-TIME			c. 16
Student Numbers 2012-2013			
All (Foreign Included)			c. 250

Last Update: 23-02-2018

Joongbu University (JBU)

201 Daehak-ro Chubu-myeon
Geumsan-gun 32713, Chungnam-do
Tel: +82(41) 750-6500, +82(41) 750-6523
Fax: +82(41) 753-8748, +82(41) 750-6060
Website: http://web.joongbu.ac.kr/eng.do
President: Si-ok Ryu

College
Arts and Physical Education (Cosmetology; Fashion Design; Film; Industrial Design; Interior Design; Music; Physical Education; Sports; Theatre; Video; Visual Arts); **Engineering** (Architectural and Environmental Design; Architecture; Automotive Engineering; Civil Engineering; Computer Engineering; Computer Networks; Electronic Engineering; Energy Engineering; Engineering; Information Management; Information Sciences; Landscape Architecture; Software Engineering; Structural Architecture; Telecommunications Engineering); **Liberal Arts** (Arts and Humanities); **Police Constable** (Administrative Law; Civil Law; Constitutional Law; Criminal Law; Police Studies); **Social Sciences**

(Administration; Advertising and Publicity; Business Administration; Chinese; Computer Engineering; English; Health Administration; Information Sciences; International Business; Journalism; Korean; Library Science; Preschool Education; Primary Education; Public Relations; Radio and Television Broadcasting; Secondary Education; Social Sciences; Social Welfare; Special Education; Transport Management; Welfare and Protective Services); **Tourism and Health** (Air Transport; Alternative Medicine; Animal Husbandry; Biological and Life Sciences; Cooking and Catering; Cosmetology; Food Science; Health Sciences; Hotel Management; Nursing; Nutrition; Pharmacy; Physical Therapy; Service Trades; Tourism; Traditional Eastern Medicine)

Graduate School

Cyber Graduate School (*Distant Education*) (Educational Administration; Educational and Student Counselling; Educational Psychology; Social Welfare; Teacher Training); **Education** (Computer Education; Education; Educational Administration; Educational and Student Counselling; Environmental Studies; Home Economics Education; Mathematics Education; Native Language Education; Physical Education; Preschool Education; Special Education); **General Graduate Studies** (*Master*) (Business Administration; Civil Engineering; Electrical and Electronic Engineering; Health Administration; Information Sciences; International Business; Law; Library Science; Music; Performing Arts; Police Studies; Tourism; Traditional Eastern Medicine); **General Graduate Studies** (*Phd*) (Administration; Business Administration; Civil Engineering; Education; Health Sciences; Information Sciences; Information Technology; Korean; Literature; Social Welfare; Town Planning; Traditional Eastern Medicine); **Humanities and Industry** (Alternative Medicine; Archiving; Automotive Engineering; Business Administration; Civil Engineering; Education; Film; Health Administration; Industrial Design; Industrial Engineering; Information Sciences; Korean; Landscape Architecture; Management; Music; Photography; Public Administration; Sports; Sports Management; Theatre; Video)
Further information: Also Goyang Campus
History: Founded 1983.
Fees: Undergraduate, 3,141,000-3,907,000; Graduate, 2,310,000-4,575,000 (Won)
Main language(s) of instruction: Korean
Accrediting agency: Korean Council for University Education (KCUE)
Degrees and diplomas: Bachelor's Degree, Master's Degree (Archiving; Art Management; Business Administration; Civil Engineering; Computer Education; Education; Educational Administration; Educational and Student Counselling; Electrical and Electronic Engineering; Environmental Studies; Film; Foreign Languages Education; Health Administration; Home Economics Education; Industrial Design; Information

Sciences; International Business; Landscape Architecture; Law; Library Science; Mathematics Education; Mechanical Engineering; Music; Musicology; Native Language Education; Nutrition; Pedagogy; Performing Arts; Photography; Physical Education; Police Studies; Preschool Education; Public Administration; Special Education; Sports Management; Theatre; Tourism; Traditional Eastern Medicine; Video), Doctor's Degree (Administration; Business Administration; Civil Engineering; Computer Engineering; Educational Administration; Educational Technology; Information Technology; Korean; Literature; Preschool Education; Public Health; Social Welfare; Town Planning; Traditional Eastern Medicine)
Student Services: Sports Facilities, Health Services, Library, Residential Facilities

Academic Staff 2012-2013	MALE	FEMALE	TOTAL
FULL-TIME			220
PART-TIME			c. 255
Student Numbers 2012-2013			
All (Foreign Included)			c. 6110

Last Update: 23-02-2018

Jungwon University (JWU)

85 Munmu-ro, Goesan-eup
Goesan 28024, Chungcheongbuk-do
Tel: +82(43) 830-8114
Fax: +82(43) 830-8115
Website: http://www.jwu.ac.kr
President: Byung Hwan Ahn

Faculty
Sport (Protective Services; Sports; Sports Medicine)

College
Aviation (Aeronautical and Aerospace Engineering; Air Transport; Maintenance Technology; Materials Engineering); **Creative and Performing Arts** (Film; Industrial Design; Theatre); **Health Science** (Biomedicine; Cosmetology; Health Administration; Health Sciences; Information Sciences; Laboratory Techniques; Nursing; Occupational Therapy); **Humanities and Social Science** (Business Administration; Business and Commerce; Child Care and Development; Chinese; English; International Business; Japanese; Korean; Law; Police Studies; Psychology; Religious Studies; Social Welfare); **Science and Engineering** (Agricultural Business; Applied Chemistry; Biomedicine; Computer Engineering; Electronic Engineering; Energy Engineering; Environmental Engineering; Food Science; Medical Technology; Natural Resources; Protective Services; Safety Engineering)

Graduate School
Graduate Studies
History: Founded 2009.
Main language(s) of instruction: Korean
Accrediting agency: Korean Council for University Education (KCUE)
Degrees and diplomas: Bachelor's Degree (Aeronautical and Aerospace Engineering; Agricultural Business; Air Transport; Applied Chemistry; Biomedicine; Business Administration; Business and Commerce; Child Care and Development; Chinese; Computer Engineering; Cosmetology; Electronic Engineering; Energy Engineering; English; Environmental Engineering; Film; Food Science; Health Administration; Health Sciences; Industrial Design; Information Sciences; International Business; Japanese; Korean; Laboratory Techniques; Law; Maintenance Technology; Materials Engineering; Medical Technology; Natural Resources; Nursing; Occupational Therapy; Police Studies; Protective Services; Psychology; Religious Studies; Safety Engineering; Social Welfare; Sports; Sports Medicine; Theatre), Master's Degree
Last Update: 09-03-2018

Kangnam University

San 6-2 Gugal-ri, Giheung-eup
Yongin-si 446-702, Gyeonggi-do
Tel: +82(31) 280-3114
Fax: +82(31) 281-3604
Website: http://www.kangnam.ac.kr
President: Shin-il Yoon

College
Business Administration (Business Administration; Information Technology; Management); **Chinese** (Chinese; East Asian Studies); **Education** (Education; Preschool Education; Primary Education; Secondary Education; Special Education); **Engineering** (Applied Mathematics; Architecture; Computer Engineering; Electronic Engineering; Engineering; Industrial Engineering; Structural Architecture; Town Planning); **Fine Arts and Physical Education** (Ceramic Art; Handicrafts; Industrial Design; Leisure Studies; Music; Musical Instruments; Painting and Drawing; Physical Education; Singing; Sports; Visual Arts); **Humanities** (Arts and Humanities; English; Information Sciences; Korean; Library Science; Literature; Philosophy; Theology); **International Studies** (American Studies; Asian Studies; Canadian Studies; English; International Business; International Relations; International Studies); **Social Sciences** (Economics; Law; Public Administration; Real Estate; Social Sciences; Taxation); **Social Welfare** (Gerontology; Social Welfare; Social Work)

Graduate School
Education (Education; Educational Sciences; Special Education; Teacher Training); **Graduate Studies** (Business Administration; Business and Commerce; E- Business/Commerce; Economics; Education; Electronic Engineering; Industrial Design; Information Sciences; Korean; Library Science; Literature; Real Estate; Special Education; Taxation; Theology; Town Planning); **Practical Theology** (Missionary Studies; Pastoral Studies; Religion; Theology; Welfare and Protective Services); **Real Estate and Public Administration** (Public Administration; Real Estate); **Social Welfare** (Social Welfare)

Research Division
Humanities (Arts and Humanities); **Industrial Technology** (Industrial Engineering); **Social Science** (Social Sciences); **Woowon**
History: Founded 1946 as Choongang Theology Institute. Acquired present status and title 1992.
Main language(s) of instruction: Korean
Accrediting agency: Korean Council for University Education (KCUE)
Degrees and diplomas: Bachelor's Degree, Master's Degree (Administration; Art Education; Business Administration; Business and Commerce; Computer Education; Continuing Education; Economics; Education; Educational Administration; Educational and Student Counselling; Electronic Engineering; Humanities and Social Science Education; Industrial Design; Information Sciences; Korean; Library Science; Literature; Missionary Studies; Pastoral Studies; Physical Education; Preschool Education; Public Administration; Real Estate; Religion; Special Education; Speech Therapy and Audiology; Taxation; Theology; Town Planning; Welfare and Protective Services), Doctor's Degree (Business Administration; Korean; Literature; Physical Education; Real Estate; Social Welfare; Taxation; Theology)
Student Services: Sports Facilities, Health Services, Library, IT Centre, Residential Facilities

Academic Staff 2012-2013	MALE	FEMALE	TOTAL
FULL-TIME			c. 280
Student Numbers 2012-2013			
All (Foreign Included)			c. 9870

Last Update: 23-02-2018

Kaya University

1103, Daegaya-ro
Goryeong-gun 717-801, Gyeongbuk-do
Tel: +82(54) 956-3100

Fax: +82(54) 954-6094
Website: http://www.kaya.ac.kr
President: Sang-hee Lee

Faculty

Applied Arts (Cooking and Catering; Handicrafts; Hotel Management; Jewellery Art; Nutrition); **Commerce** (Business and Commerce; Marine Transport; Transport Management); **Education** (Education; Physical Education; Preschool Education; Primary Education; Special Education); **Health and Medical Science** (Health Sciences; Nursing; Occupational Therapy; Ophthalmology; Optics; Physical Therapy; Radiology; Speech Therapy and Audiology); **Humanities** (Police Studies; Social Welfare)

Graduate School

Administration (Administration; Social Welfare); **Education** (Special Education); **Graduate Studies** (Jewellery Art); **Health and Medical Science** (Health Sciences; Medicine; Nursing; Occupational Therapy; Radiology; Speech Therapy and Audiology); **International Information on Ceramics** (Ceramic Art; Ceramics and Glass Technology; International Business); **Urban Development** (Civil Engineering)
Further information: Also Gimhae Campus
History: Founded 1992 as Kaya Ceramic College. Acquired present title and status 1995.
Main language(s) of instruction: Korean
Accrediting agency: Korean Council for University Education (KCUE)
Degrees and diplomas: Bachelor's Degree, Master's Degree (Construction Engineering; Jewellery Art; Preschool Education; Public Administration; Social Work; Special Education), Doctor's Degree (Jewellery Art)
Student Services: Academic Counselling, Social Counselling, Library, Residential Facilities
Last Update: 27-02-2018

KDI School of Public Policy and Management (KDI School)

263 Namsejong-ro
Sejong-si 30149
Tel: +82(44) 550-1281
Fax: +82(44) 550-1223
Website: http://www.kdischool.ac.kr
Dean: Hong Tack Chun

Course/Programme

Development Policy (*Master*) (Economic and Finance Policy); **Development Track** (Development Studies); **Public Administration and Leadership** (Public Administration); **Public Management** (*Master*) (Public Administration); **Public Policy** (*Master*) (Development Studies); **Public Policy** (*Ph.D*) (Development Studies; Economic and Finance Policy); **Regional Development and Environment** (Environmental Management)

Area

Finance and Macroeconomic Policy (Economics; Finance); **Global Governance and Political Economy** (Government; Political Sciences); **Strategic Management and Leadership** (Leadership; Management); **Trade and Industry Policy** (Business Administration; Industrial and Production Economics)

Graduate School

Public Finance and Social Policy (Economic and Finance Policy; Social Policy)
History: Founded 1998. The Korean center of the World Bank Global Development Learning Network and an Asia Pacific Economic Ccoperation (APEC) Education Hub
Fees: Ph.D. programmes, 25,000,000 (Won)
Main language(s) of instruction: English
Accrediting agency: Ministry of Education; NASPAA
Degrees and diplomas: Master's Degree (Development Studies; Economic and Finance Policy; Finance; International Relations; Leadership; Management; Political Sciences; Private Administration; Public Administration; Social Policy), Doctor's Degree (Development Studies; Economic and Finance Policy). Also Global Master's Programme (GMP), 1 year at the KDI School followed by 1 year at a partner institution (including Cornell, Duke, Michigan State, Syracuse, Chicago University) to gain two master's degrees
Student Services: Academic Counselling, Careers Guidance, Nursery Care, Sports Facilities, Language Laboratory, Facilities for disabled people, Health Services, Library, Residential Facilities

Student Numbers 2015-2016	MALE	FEMALE	TOTAL
All (Foreign Included)			400
Foreign only			200

Last Update: 24-05-2018

Keimyung University (KMU)

1095 Dalgubeol-daero Dalseo-gu
Daegu 42601
Tel: +82(53) 580-5114
Fax: +82(53) 580-6025
Website: http://www.kmu.ac.kr
President: Synn Ilhi
Tel: +82(53) 580-5000

College

Architectural Studies (Architectural and Environmental Design; Architecture; Interior Design; Landscape Architecture; Structural Architecture; Town Planning); **Business Administration** (Accountancy; Business Administration; Hotel Management; Information Management; Taxation; Tourism); **Education** (Education; Foreign Languages Education; Humanities and Social Science Education; Native Language Education; Preschool Education); **Engineering** (Automotive Engineering; Chemical Engineering; Civil Engineering; Computer Engineering; Computer Graphics; Electronic Engineering; Energy Engineering; Industrial Engineering; Materials Engineering; Mechanical Engineering; Software Engineering; Transport Engineering); **Environmental Studies** (Environmental Engineering; Environmental Management; Environmental Studies); **Evening Programmes** (Accountancy; American Studies; Business Administration; Chinese; East Asian Studies; Economics; Information Management; International Business; Law; Literature; Public Administration; Tourism); **Fashion** (Fashion Design; Marketing; Textile Design); **Fine Arts** (Communication Arts; Fine Arts; Graphic Design; Handicrafts; Industrial Design; Painting and Drawing; Photography; Video; Visual Arts); **Humanities** (Chinese; Christian Religious Studies; English; Ethics; German; History; Japanese; Korean; Literature; Philosophy; Russian; Writing); **International Studies** (American Studies; Asian Studies; European Studies; Latin American Studies); **Keimyung Adams College (KAC)** (Information Technology; International Business; International Relations); **Law and Police Science** (Law; Police Studies); **Liberal Arts** (Arts and Humanities; Biological and Life Sciences; Engineering; Natural Sciences; Social Sciences); **Medicine** (Biomedical Engineering; Medicine); **Music and Performing Arts** (Dance; Music; Music Theory and Composition; Musical Instruments; Performing Arts; Singing; Theatre); **Natural Sciences** (Biology; Chemistry; Food Science; Food Technology; Mathematics; Microbiology; Nutrition; Public Health; Statistics); **Nursing** (Nursing); **Pharmacy** (Pharmacology; Pharmacy); **Physical Education** (Leisure Studies; Marketing; Physical Education; Sports; Sports Management); **Social Science** (Advertising and Publicity; Business and Commerce; Communication Arts; Consumer Studies; E-Business/Commerce; Economics; Finance; Information Sciences; International Business; International Relations; Journalism; Library Science; Political Sciences; Psychology; Public Administration; Public Relations; Social Welfare; Sociology)

Graduate School

Arts (Design; Fine Arts); **Business** (Business Administration; International Business; Management); **Early Childhood Education** (Preschool Education); **Education** (Education); **Graduate Studies** (Art Therapy; Arts and Humanities; Engineering; Fine Arts; Medicine; Natural Sciences; Performing Arts; Physical Education; Social Sciences); **Intelligent Vehicle and Transportation** (Transport Engineering); **Policy Studies** (Political Sciences); **Sports Industry** (Sports); **Theology** (English; Pastoral Studies; Theology)

Further information: Also Dongsan Medical Centre; Student Exchange Programme; 13 General Research Institutes and 18 Special Research Institutes

History: Founded 1954 by the Presbyterian Church in Korea as a small Christian Liberal Arts College. Received charter from the Government 1956 and became University 1978.

Academic year: March to December (March-June; September-December)

Admission requirements: Secondary school certificate or recognized equivalent

Fees: 2.8m. per semester (Won)

Main language(s) of instruction: Korean, English

Accrediting agency: Korean Council for University Education (KCUE)

Degrees and diplomas: Bachelor's Degree, Master's Degree (Accountancy; Archaeology; Art History; Art Therapy; Biology; Business Administration; Chemical Engineering; Chemistry; Chinese; Civil Engineering; Communication Arts; Computer Engineering; Consumer Studies; Design; East Asian Studies; Economics; Education; Electronic Engineering; English; Environmental Studies; Fashion Design; Fine Arts; Food Science; Food Technology; Foreign Languages Education; History; Industrial Engineering; Information Sciences; Information Technology; International Business; Japanese; Korean; Law; Library Science; Literature; Mass Communication; Materials Engineering; Mathematics; Mechanical Engineering; Medicine; Music; Nursing; Nutrition; Pharmacy; Philosophy; Physical Education; Physics; Police Studies; Preschool Education; Psychology; Public Administration; Public Health; Social Welfare; Sociology; Statistics; Structural Architecture; Textile Design; Theology; Tourism; Town Planning; Translation and Interpretation; Transport Engineering; Writing), Doctor's Degree (Accountancy; Administrative Law; Advertising and Publicity; Anaesthesiology; Analytical Chemistry; Anatomy; Archaeology; Art History; Art Therapy; Bible; Biochemistry; Botany; Chemical Engineering; Chinese; Christian Religious Studies; Civil Engineering; Civil Law; Clinical Psychology; Commercial Law; Computer Engineering; Computer Science; Conducting; Constitutional Law; Construction Engineering; Consumer Studies; Criminal Law; Cultural Studies; Dance; Dentistry; Dermatology; Design; East Asian Studies; Economics; Educational Administration; Educational and Student Counselling; Educational Psychology; Educational Sciences; Educational Technology; Educational Testing and Evaluation; English; Environmental Engineering; Environmental Studies; Experimental Psychology; Fashion Design; Fine Arts; Food Science; Food Technology; Foreign Languages Education; Genetics; Gynaecology and Obstetrics; History; History of Religion; Immunology; Industrial and Organizational Psychology; Industrial Chemistry; Industrial Design; Industrial Engineering; Information Sciences; Information Technology; Inorganic Chemistry; International Business; International Law; Japanese; Journalism; Korean; Laboratory Techniques; Labour Law; Library Science; Linguistics; Literature; Management; Marketing; Mass Communication; Materials Engineering; Mathematics; Mechanical Engineering; Media Studies; Medical Parasitology; Medical Technology; Medicine; Microbiology; Molecular Biology; Music; Music Theory and Composition; Musical Instruments; Musicology; Neurology; New Testament; Nursing; Nutrition; Oncology; Ophthalmology; Optics; Organic Chemistry; Orthopaedics; Otorhinolaryngology; Paediatrics; Pathology; Pharmacology; Pharmacy; Philosophy; Photography; Physical Chemistry; Physical Education; Physics; Physiology; Plastic Surgery; Police Studies; Preschool Education; Private Law; Production Engineering; Psychiatry and Mental Health; Psychology; Public Administration; Public Health; Public Law; Public Relations; Radiology; Rehabilitation and Therapy; Religious Education; Singing; Social and Preventive Medicine; Social Welfare; Social Work; Sociology; Software Engineering; Solid State Physics; Statistics; Structural Architecture; Taxation; Theology; Tourism; Town Planning; Translation and Interpretation; Transport Engineering; Urology; Video; Women's Studies; Writing; Zoology)

Student Services: Academic Counselling, Social Counselling, Careers Guidance, Nursery Care, Cultural Activities, Sports Facilities, Language Laboratory, Facilities for disabled people, Health Services, Canteen, Foreign Studies Centre, Library, Residential Facilities

Periodicals: Accounting Information Review, Acta Koreana, Asian Journal of Business and Entrepreneurship, Business Management Review, Journal of Communication Research, Journal of Cross-Cultural Studies, Journal of International Studies, Journal of the Institute for Industrial Science, Keimyung Law Review, Keimyung Theology, Keimyung University Medical Journal, The Journal of Art and Culture, The Journal of Educational Research, The Journal of Social Sciences, The Journal of the Institute for International Studies, The Journal of the Institute of Natural Sciences, The Proceedings of Mathematical Science

Publishing house: The Keimyung University Press

Academic Staff 2016-2017	MALE	FEMALE	TOTAL
FULL-TIME			1223
Student Numbers 2016-2017			
All (Foreign Included)			c. 22700
Foreign only			1111

Last Update: 27-02-2018

KEPCO International Nuclear Graduate School (KINGS)

658-91 Haemaji-ro, Seosaeng-myeon, Ulju-gun
Ulsan 45014
Tel: +82(52) 712-7124
Fax: +82(52) 712-7129
Website: http://www.kings.ac.kr/eng/main.do

Course/Programme
Nuclear Engineering (Nuclear Engineering)
History: Founded 2012.
Main language(s) of instruction: Korean
Accrediting agency: Ministry of Education
Degrees and diplomas: Master's Degree (Nuclear Engineering)

Academic Staff 2016-2017	MALE	FEMALE	TOTAL
FULL-TIME			14
PART-TIME			5
Student Numbers 2016-2017			
All (Foreign Included)			46
Foreign only			59

Last Update: 29-03-2018

Kkottongnae University (KKOT)

133 Sangsam-gil Hyeundo-myeon Seowon-gu
Cheongju-si 28211, Chungcheongbuk-do
Tel: +82(43) 270-0114
Fax: +82(43) 270-0120
Website: http://www.kkot.ac.kr
President: Won-woo Lee

College
Social Work (Administration; Psychology; Social Welfare; Social Work)

Graduate School
Social Welfare (Business Administration; Social Welfare; Social Work; Welfare and Protective Services)

History: Founded 1998 as Kkottongnae Hyundo University of Social Welfare. Acquired present title 2011.
Main language(s) of instruction: Korean
Accrediting agency: Korean Council for University Education (KCUE)
Degrees and diplomas: Bachelor's Degree (Social Welfare), Master's Degree (Business Administration; Social Welfare)
Student Services: Careers Guidance, Sports Facilities, Library, Residential Facilities

Academic Staff 2012-2013	MALE	FEMALE	TOTAL
FULL-TIME			20
PART-TIME			c. 30
Student Numbers 2012-2013			
All (Foreign Included)			c. 570

Last Update: 27-02-2018

Konkuk University

120 Neungdong-ro Gwangjin-gu
Seoul 05029
Tel: +82(2) 450-3114, +82(2) 450-6213
Fax: +82(2) 452-3257
Website: http://www.konkuk.ac.kr
President: Sanggi Min

College

Animal Bioscience and Technology (Animal Husbandry; Biotechnology; Food Science; Industrial Engineering); **Architecture** (Architectural and Environmental Design; Architecture; Real Estate; Structural Architecture); **Arts and Design** (Ceramic Art; Communication Arts; Design; Film; Fine Arts; Graphic Design; Handicrafts; Industrial Design; Textile Design; Visual Arts); **Bioscience and Biotechnology** (Biological and Life Sciences; Biotechnology); **Business Administration** (Business Administration; Information Management; Information Technology; Management); **Commerce and Economics** (Business and Commerce; Economics; Information Sciences; International Business; Statistics); **Education** (Education; Educational Technology; Foreign Languages Education; Mathematics Education; Music Education; Physical Education); **Engineering** (Aeronautical and Aerospace Engineering; Bioengineering; Chemical Engineering; Civil Engineering; Electrical Engineering; Engineering; Environmental Engineering; Industrial Chemistry; Industrial Design; Industrial Engineering; Materials Engineering; Mechanical Engineering; Nanotechnology; Production Engineering); **Global Integrated Studies** (Business and Commerce; Industrial Engineering; International Business; International Studies); **Information and Communications** (Computer Engineering; Computer Science; Electronic Engineering; Information Sciences; Information Technology; Multimedia; Software Engineering; Telecommunications Engineering); **Liberal Arts** (Arts and Humanities; Chinese; English; History; Journalism; Korean; Literature; Mass Communication; Media Studies; Modern Languages; Philosophy); **Life and Environmental Sciences** (Architectural and Environmental Design; Biological and Life Sciences; Civil Engineering; Environmental Engineering; Environmental Studies; Food Science; Health Sciences); **Political Sciences** (Political Sciences; Public Administration; Real Estate); **Sciences** (Chemistry; Geography; Mathematics; Natural Sciences; Physics); **Veterinary Medicine** (Veterinary Science)

School

Law (*Graduate*) (Law)

Graduate School

Agriculture and Animal science (Agricultural Engineering; Agriculture; Alternative Medicine; Animal Husbandry; Biological and Life Sciences; Biotechnology; Computer Science; Food Science; Food Technology; Forestry; Horticulture; Landscape Architecture; Marketing; Meat and Poultry; Natural Resources; Veterinary Science); **Architecture** (Architecture; Interior Design); **Business (MBA)** (Business Administration; Engineering Management); **Business Administration** (Business Administration); **Design** (Art Therapy; Cosmetology; Design; Fashion Design; Graphic Design; Information Sciences; Interior Design; Marketing; Textile Design); **Education** (Education); **Engineering** (Bioengineering; Civil Engineering; Cosmetology; Electrical Engineering; Engineering; Environmental Engineering; Industrial Management; Protective Services; Sports Management; Structural Architecture); **Graduate Studies** (Aeronautical and Aerospace Engineering; Agricultural Economics; Animal Husbandry; Architecture; Arts and Humanities; Bioengineering; Biological and Life Sciences; Biomedical Engineering; Biomedicine; Biotechnology; Business Administration; Chemical Engineering; Chemistry; Chinese; Cinema and Television; Civil Engineering; Clothing and Sewing; Computer Engineering; Computer Science; Design; Economics; Education; Educational Technology; Electrical Engineering; Electronic Engineering; English; Environmental Engineering; Environmental Studies; Film; Fine Arts; Food Science; Geography; Handicrafts; Heritage Preservation; History; Industrial Engineering; Industrial Management; Information Management; Information Sciences; Information Technology; International Business; Japanese; Korean; Law; Literature; Mass Communication; Materials Engineering; Mathematics; Mathematics Education; Mechanical Engineering; Medicine; Multimedia; Music; Nanotechnology; Natural Resources; Philosophy; Physical Education; Physics; Political Sciences; Production

Engineering; Protective Services; Public Administration; Real Estate; Statistics; Telecommunications Engineering; Veterinary Science); **Information and Communications** (Information Management; Information Sciences; Information Technology; Telecommunications Engineering); **Mass Communication** (Advertising and Publicity; Journalism; Mass Communication; Public Relations; Publishing and Book Trade; Radio and Television Broadcasting; Telecommunications Services); **Public Administration** (Law; Political Sciences; Protective Services; Public Administration; Regional Planning; Social Welfare; Taxation; Town Planning); **Real Estate Studies** (Business Administration; Finance; Management; Real Estate)

Research Division

Intelligent Vehicle and System Technology (INVEST) (Aeronautical and Aerospace Engineering; Automotive Engineering; Environmental Engineering); **SMART Institute of Advanced Biomedical Science** (Agriculture; Biomedical Engineering; Biomedicine; Farm Management; Veterinary Science)

Further information: Konkuk University Hospital (Konkuk University Medical Center); Over 50 Affiliated Specialized Research Centres

History: Founded 1946 as Cho-Sun Political Science School, acquired present status and title 1959. A private Institution financed by the Konkuk University Foundation, but supervised by the Ministry of Education.

Academic year: March to December (March-June; September-December)

Admission requirements: Graduation from high school and entrance examination

Main language(s) of instruction: Korean, English

Accrediting agency: Korean Council for University Education (KCUE)

Degrees and diplomas: Bachelor's Degree (Animal Husbandry; Architecture; Arts and Humanities; Biological and Life Sciences; Biotechnology; Business Administration; Business and Commerce; Design; Economics; Education; Engineering; Environmental Studies; Fine Arts; Information Sciences; International Studies; Mass Communication; Natural Sciences; Political Sciences; Veterinary Science), Master's Degree (Accountancy; Actuarial Science; Aeronautical and Aerospace Engineering; Agricultural Economics; Analytical Chemistry; Anatomy; Animal Husbandry; Applied Physics; Architectural and Environmental Design; Architecture; Architecture and Planning; Arts and Humanities; Automation and Control Engineering; Biochemistry; Bioengineering; Biological and Life Sciences; Biomedical Engineering; Biomedicine; Biotechnology; Botany; Business Administration; Business and Commerce; Cell Biology; Ceramic Art; Chemical Engineering; Civil Engineering; Clothing and Sewing; Communication Arts; Comparative

Literature; Comparative Politics; Computer Engineering; Computer Science; Conducting; Cosmetology; Curriculum; East Asian Studies; Economics; Education of the Gifted; Educational Administration; Educational and Student Counselling; Educational Psychology; Educational Technology; Electrical Engineering; Electronic Engineering; Energy Engineering; English; Environmental Engineering; Environmental Studies; Fashion Design; Film; Finance; Fine Arts; Food Science; Food Technology; Foreign Languages Education; Genetics; Geography; Gerontology; Graphic Design; Handicrafts; Heritage Preservation; Histology; History; Human Resources; Immunology; Industrial Design; Industrial Engineering; Information Management; Information Sciences; Information Technology; Inorganic Chemistry; International Business; International Economics; International Relations; Japanese; Korean; Law; Literature; Management; Marketing; Mass Communication; Materials Engineering; Mathematics; Mathematics Education; Medicine; Meteorology; Microbiology; Molecular Biology; Multimedia; Music Theory and Composition; Musical Instruments; Nanotechnology; Natural Resources; Neurosciences; Nuclear Physics; Oncology; Organic Chemistry; Pathology; Pharmacology; Philosophy; Physical Chemistry; Physical Education; Physiology; Political Sciences; Power Engineering; Preschool Education; Production Engineering; Protective Services; Public Administration; Public Health; Real Estate; Singing; Social and Preventive Medicine; Solid State Physics; Statistics; Structural Architecture; Surgery; Telecommunications Engineering; Textile Design; Thermal Engineering; Thermal Physics; Toxicology; Veterinary Science; Zoology), Doctor's Degree (Accountancy; Aeronautical and Aerospace Engineering; Agricultural Economics; Analytical Chemistry; Animal Husbandry; Applied Physics; Architecture and Planning; Arts and Humanities; Atomic and Molecular Physics; Automation and Control Engineering; Biochemistry; Bioengineering; Biological and Life Sciences; Biology; Biomedical Engineering; Biomedicine; Biotechnology; Botany; Business Administration; Business and Commerce; Cell Biology; Chemical Engineering; Chinese; Civil Engineering; Clothing and Sewing; Communication Arts; Comparative Literature; Comparative Politics; Computer Engineering; Computer Science; Cosmetology; Curriculum; Design; East Asian Studies; Ecology; Economics; Education of the Gifted; Educational Administration; Educational and Student Counselling; Educational Psychology; Educational Technology; Electrical Engineering; Electronic Engineering; Energy Engineering; English; Environmental Engineering; Environmental Studies; Fashion Design; Finance; Food Science; Foreign Languages Education; Genetics; Geography; Gerontology; Graphic Design; Heritage Preservation; Histology; History; Human Resources; Immunology; Industrial Design; Industrial Engineering; Industrial Management; Information Management; Information Sciences; Information

Technology; Inorganic Chemistry; International Business; International Economics; International Relations; Japanese; Korean; Law; Literature; Management; Marketing; Mass Communication; Materials Engineering; Mathematics; Mathematics Education; Medicine; Meteorology; Microbiology; Molecular Biology; Multimedia; Nanotechnology; Neurosciences; Nuclear Physics; Oncology; Organic Chemistry; Pathology; Pharmacology; Philosophy; Physical Chemistry; Physical Education; Physiology; Political Sciences; Power Engineering; Preschool Education; Production Engineering; Protective Services; Public Administration; Public Health; Real Estate; Regional Planning; Social and Preventive Medicine; Solid State Physics; Statistics; Structural Architecture; Surgery; Telecommunications Engineering; Textile Design; Thermal Engineering; Thermal Physics; Town Planning; Toxicology; Veterinary Science; Zoology)

Student Services: Sports Facilities, Language Laboratory, Canteen, Library, eLibrary, Residential Facilities

Periodicals: Journals of the Research Institutes

Publishing house: University Press

Academic Staff 2012-2013	MALE	FEMALE	TOTAL
FULL-TIME			629
Student Numbers 2012-2013			
All (Foreign Included)			c. 21620
Foreign only			2470

Last Update: 28-02-2018

CHUNGJU CAMPUS

268 Chungwon-daero
Chungju-si 27478, Chungcheongbuk-do
Tel: +82(43) 840-3114
Website: http://www.kku.ac.kr
President: Sang-gi Min
Tel: +82(43) 840-3100/3101

College

Art and Design (Advertising and Publicity; Ceramic Art; Communication Arts; Cosmetology; Design; Fashion Design; Film; Fine Arts; Graphic Design; Industrial Design; Interior Design; Metal Techniques; Video); **Biomedical and Health Science** (Biochemistry; Biological and Life Sciences; Biomedical Engineering; Biomedicine; Food Science; Nursing); **International Business** (Business Administration; Cultural Studies; Economics; English; International Business; International Studies; Taxation; Transport Management); **Media and Communication** (Cultural Studies; English; Literature; Mass Communication; Media Studies); **Public Service** (Information Sciences; Library Science; Police Studies; Preschool Education; Public Administration; Social Welfare); **Science and Technology** (Computer Engineering; Electronic Engineering;

Environmental Engineering; Leisure Studies; Nanotechnology; Natural Sciences; Sports)

Graduate School

Agriculture and Husbandry (*Special*) (Agriculture; Animal Husbandry); **Architecture** (*Professional*) (Architecture); **Business Administration** (*Special*) (Business Administration); **Design** (*Special*) (Design); **Education** (*Special*) (Education); **Graduate Studies** (Agricultural Economics; American Studies; Applied Chemistry; Biological and Life Sciences; Biomedical Engineering; Business Administration; Computer Engineering; Design; Economics; English; English Studies; Environmental Studies; Fine Arts; International Business; Mass Communication; Mathematics and Computer Science; Media Studies; Nanotechnology; Natural Resources; Nursing; Preschool Education; Public Administration; Social Welfare; Sports; Writing; Zoology); **Industry** (*Special*) (Industrial Engineering); **Information and Communication** (*Special*) (Information Sciences; Mass Communication); **Law** (*Professional*) (Law); **Media and Public Promotion** (*Special*) (Advertising and Publicity; Media Studies); **Medicine** (*Professional*) (Medicine); **Public Administration** (*Special*) (Public Administration); **Real Estate** (*Special*) (Real Estate); **Social Sciences** (*Special*) (Social Sciences)

History: Founded 1980.

Main language(s) of instruction: Korean

Accrediting agency: Korean Council for University Education (KCUE)

Degrees and diplomas: Bachelor's Degree, Master's Degree (Advertising and Publicity; Agricultural Economics; Applied Chemistry; Biochemistry; Bioengineering; Biomedical Engineering; Biotechnology; Business Administration; Communication Arts; Computer Science; Economics; English; Fashion Design; Fine Arts; Forestry; Graphic Design; Horticulture; Industrial Design; Interior Design; International Business; International Economics; Literature; Management; Mass Communication; Mathematics and Computer Science; Media Studies; Museum Studies; Nanotechnology; Nursing; Preschool Education; Public Administration; Social Welfare; Sports; Translation and Interpretation; Writing; Zoology), Doctor's Degree (Advertising and Publicity; Applied Chemistry; Biochemistry; Bioengineering; Biomedical Engineering; Biotechnology; Business Administration; Communication Arts; Computer Engineering; English; Fashion Design; Fine Arts; Forestry; Graphic Design; Horticulture; Industrial Design; Interior Design; International Business; International Economics; Literature; Management; Mass Communication; Media Studies; Museum Studies; Social Welfare; Translation and Interpretation; Writing; Zoology)

Student Services: Sports Facilities, Language Laboratory, Health Services, Canteen, Library, IT Centre, Residential Facilities

Academic Staff 2015-2016	MALE	FEMALE	TOTAL
FULL-TIME			c. 580
Student Numbers 2015-2016			
All (Foreign Included)			c. 8511

Last Update: 12-02-2018

Konyang Cyber University (KYCU)

158, Gwanjeodong-ro, Seo-gu
Daejeon 35365
Tel: +82 1899-3330
Fax: +82(42) 600-6519
Website: https://www.kycu.ac.kr/eng.do
President: Hee-soo Kim

College

Human Studies (Cultural Studies; Korean; Psychology); **Practical Studies** (Business Administration; Cosmetology; Fire Science; Real Estate; Tourism); **Welfare Studies** (Health Sciences; Welfare and Protective Services)

Course/Programme

Liberal Arts
History: Founded 2011.
Main language(s) of instruction: Korean
Accrediting agency: Ministry of Education
Degrees and diplomas: Bachelor's Degree (Business Administration; Cosmetology; Cultural Studies; Fire Science; Health Sciences; Korean; Psychology; Real Estate; Tourism; Welfare and Protective Services)
Last Update: 28-03-2018

Konyang University

121, Deahak-ro
Nonsan-si 32992, Chungnam-do
Tel: +82(41) 730-5114
Fax: +82(41) 733-2070
Website: http://www.konyang.ac.kr
President: Hee-Soo Kim

College

Culture, Science and Technology (Advertising and Publicity; Biochemistry; Chemistry; Civil Engineering; Cosmetology; Environmental Engineering; Fashion Design; Graphic Design; Health Sciences; Information Management; Information Technology; Mechanical Engineering; Nanotechnology; Radio and Television Broadcasting; Sports); **Global Business Administration** (Business Administration; Finance; Hotel Management; International Business; International Studies; Taxation; Tourism); **Interdisciplinary and Creative Studies** (Biology; Design; Information Technology; Pharmacology); **Medical Engineering** (Architectural and Environmental Design; Biomedical Engineering; Biotechnology; Information Technology; Medical Technology; Pharmacology); **Medical Sciences** (*Daejeon Campus*) (Biomedicine; Dental Hygiene; Health Administration; Laboratory Techniques; Medicine; Occupational Therapy; Optometry; Physical Therapy; Radiology); **Medicine** (*Daejeon Campus*) (Medicine; Nursing); **Military Science and Police Adminstration** (Military Science; Police Studies); **Rehabilitation, Social Welfare and Education** (Child Care and Development; Preschool Education; Primary Education; Psychology; Psychotherapy; Rehabilitation and Therapy; Secondary Education; Social Welfare; Special Education; Teacher Training)

Graduate School

Business and Social Welfare (Business Administration; Social Welfare); **Counselling** (Art Therapy; Psychology); **Education** (Educational Administration; Health Education; Humanities and Social Science Education; Mathematics Education; Media Studies; Native Language Education; Preschool Education; Psychology; Psychotherapy; Science Education); **General Graduate Studies** (Business Administration; Chemical Engineering; Chemistry; Cosmetology; Foreign Languages Education; Health Administration; Health Sciences; Mechanical Engineering; Medical Technology; Medicine; Nursing; Pharmacology; Psychology; Psychotherapy; Public Administration; Radiology; Special Education; Structural Architecture; Taxation); **Military Science and Police Administration** (Military Science; Police Studies; Psychology); **Pubic Health and Welfare** (Health Sciences; Occupational Therapy; Optometry; Pathology; Public Health; Welfare and Protective Services)
Further information: Also Daejon Campus; Konyang University Hospital; 10 Research Institutes
History: Founded 1991 as Konyang College and upgraded into Konyang University 1992.
Fees: Undergraduate, c. 2,640-3,400 per semester; Graduate, c. 1,280-2,750 per semester (US Dollar)
Main language(s) of instruction: Korean
Accrediting agency: Korean Council for University Education (KCUE)
Degrees and diplomas: Bachelor's Degree, Master's Degree (Art Therapy; Business Administration; Chemical Engineering; Chemistry; Cosmetology; Educational Administration; Foreign Languages Education; Health Administration; Health Education; Health Sciences; Humanities and Social Science Education; Mathematics Education; Mechanical

Engineering; Medical Technology; Medicine; Military Science; Nursing; Occupational Therapy; Optometry; Pathology; Pharmacology; Police Studies; Preschool Education; Psychology; Psychotherapy; Public Health; Radiology; Science Education; Social Welfare; Special Education; Sports; Structural Architecture; Taxation), Doctor's Degree (Business Administration; Chemistry; Health Administration; Health Sciences; Medicine; Pharmacology; Psychology; Psychotherapy; Public Administration)

Student Services: Sports Facilities, Health Services, Canteen, Library, Residential Facilities

Academic Staff 2013-2014	MALE	FEMALE	TOTAL
FULL-TIME			c. 320
Student Numbers 2013-2014			
All (Foreign Included)			c. 8210
Foreign only			210

Last Update: 28-02-2018

Kookmin University (KMU)

77 Jeongneung-Ro Seongbuk-Gu
Seoul 02707
Tel: +82(2) 910-4114, +82(2) 910-5836
Fax: +82(2) 910-5830
Website: http://www.kookmin.ac.kr
President: Ji-soo Yu

College

Arts (Cinema and Television; Conducting; Dance; Fine Arts; Music; Music Theory and Composition; Musical Instruments; Painting and Drawing; Performing Arts; Sculpture; Singing; Theatre); **Business Administration** (Business Administration; E- Business/Commerce; Information Management; Information Technology; Management; Statistics); **Design** (Ceramic Art; Design; Fashion Design; Film; Graphic Arts; Graphic Design; Handicrafts; Industrial Design; Interior Design; Jewellery Art; Metal Techniques; Video); **Economics and Commerce** (Business and Commerce; Economics; Finance); **Electrical Engineering and Computer Science** (Computer Science; Electrical Engineering; Information Technology); **Engineering** (Automotive Engineering; Civil Engineering; Engineering; Environmental Engineering; Materials Engineering; Mechanical Engineering); **Forest Science** (Biotechnology; Environmental Management; Environmental Studies; Forest Management; Forest Products; Forestry); **Humanities** (Arts and Humanities; Chinese; Education; English; Korean; Literature); **Law** (Administrative Law; Commercial Law; Criminal Law; Fiscal Law; Law; Private Law; Public Law); **Natural Sciences** (Applied Chemistry; Applied Physics; Arts and Humanities;

Biological and Life Sciences; Design; Engineering; Food Science; Mathematics and Computer Science; Nanotechnology; Natural Sciences; Nutrition); **Physical Education** (Physical Education; Sports; Sports Management); **Social Sciences** (Advertising and Publicity; Asian Studies; East Asian Studies; Eastern European Studies; International Relations; Mass Communication; Media Studies; Political Sciences; Public Administration; Public Relations; Social Sciences; Sociology)

Course/Programme
Innovative Nano Fabrications and Equipments

School
Architecture (Architecture; Design)

Department/Division
General Education (Arts and Humanities; Natural Sciences; Physical Education; Technology); **Teaching Profession** (Teacher Training)

Graduate School

Automotive Engineering (*Professional*) (Automotive Engineering); **Business Administration** (*Specialized*) (Business Administration); **Business Information Technology** (*Professional*) (Business Administration; Business Computing; Information Technology); **Creative Writing** (*Specialized*) (Writing); **Design** (*Specialized*) (Ceramic Art; Communication Arts; Design; Display and Stage Design; Environmental Studies; Fashion Design; Film; Furniture Design; Glass Art; Graphic Design; Industrial Design; Interior Design; Jewellery Art; Leisure Studies; Marketing; Photography; Visual Arts); **Education** (*Specialized*) (Education; Leadership; Teacher Training); **Engineering** (*Specialized*) (Automotive Engineering; Civil Engineering; Computer Engineering; Electronic Engineering; Engineering; Environmental Engineering; Materials Engineering; Mechanical Engineering); **Graduate Studies** (Architecture; Biomedical Engineering; Biomedicine; Biotechnology; Business Administration; Chemistry; Chinese; Civil Engineering; Communication Arts; Computer Science; Cultural Studies; Design; E- Business/Commerce; Economics; Education; Electronic Engineering; English; Environmental Engineering; Fine Arts; Food Science; Forest Products; Forestry; Graphic Design; Handicrafts; Heritage Preservation; History; Information Technology; Interior Design; International Business; International Relations; International Studies; Jewellery Art; Korean; Law; Literature; Mass Communication; Materials Engineering; Mathematics; Mechanical Engineering; Mechanics; Multimedia; Music; Nanotechnology; Natural Resources; Nutrition; Performing Arts; Physical Education; Physics; Political Sciences; Public Administration; Sociology); **Information Finance and Legal Affairs** (*Specialized*)

(Finance; International Business; Law); **Politics and Leadership** (*Specialized*) (Leadership; Political Sciences); **Public Administration** (*Specialized*) (Public Administration); **Sports Industry** (*Specialized*) (Marketing; Sports Management); **Techno Design** (*Professional*) (Design; Marketing); **Total Arts** (*Specialized*) (Dance; Film; Multimedia; Music; Theatre; Visual Arts)

Research Division

Biomaterial Technologies; Materials and Processes of Self-Assembly (CMPS); Seawater Desalination Plant; Smart Home Industrialization Support Centre
Further information: Also 39 Research Institutes
History: Founded 1946 as night College, acquired present status and title 1981.
Academic year: March to February (March-August; September-February)
Admission requirements: Graduation from high school, or recognized equivalent, and entrance examination
Main language(s) of instruction: Korean
Accrediting agency: Korean Council for University Education (KCUE)
Degrees and diplomas: Bachelor's Degree, Master's Degree (Accountancy; Advertising and Publicity; Analytical Chemistry; Architectural and Environmental Design; Art Criticism; Art History; Arts and Humanities; Asian Studies; Biochemistry; Biomedical Engineering; Biomedicine; Biotechnology; Business Administration; Business Computing; Ceramic Art; Chinese; Cinema and Television; Civil Engineering; Communication Arts; Comparative Politics; Computer Science; Continuing Education; Cultural Studies; Curriculum; Dance; Data Processing; Design; Display and Stage Design; East Asian Studies; Eastern European Studies; Economics; Educational Administration; Educational and Student Counselling; Educational Psychology; Educational Sciences; Educational Technology; Electronic Engineering; English; Environmental Engineering; Fashion Design; Film; Finance; Food Science; Food Technology; Forest Products; Forestry; Furniture Design; Geological Engineering; Glass Art; Graphic Design; Handicrafts; History; Hydraulic Engineering; Industrial Design; Information Management; Information Technology; Inorganic Chemistry; Insurance; Interior Design; International Business; International Economics; International Relations; Jewellery Art; Korean; Law; Literature; Management; Marketing; Mass Communication; Materials Engineering; Mathematics; Mechanical Engineering; Mechanics; Metal Techniques; Microwaves; Music; Music Theory and Composition; Musical Instruments; Nanotechnology; Natural Sciences; Nutrition; Organic Chemistry; Painting and Drawing; Philosophy of Education; Photography; Physics; Political Sciences; Psychology; Public Administration; Sculpture; Service Trades; Singing; Social Sciences; Sociology; Special Education; Sports; Structural Architecture; Telecommunications Engineering; Theatre; Transport Management; Visual Arts), Doctor's Degree (Accountancy; Advertising and Publicity; Analytical Chemistry; Architecture; Art Criticism; Art History; Arts and Humanities; Asian Studies; Biochemistry; Biomedical Engineering; Biomedicine; Biotechnology; Business Computing; Chinese; Cinema and Television; Civil Engineering; Comparative Politics; Computer Science; Continuing Education; Cultural Studies; Curriculum; Dance; Data Processing; Design; East Asian Studies; Eastern European Studies; Economics; Educational Administration; Educational and Student Counselling; Educational Psychology; Educational Sciences; Educational Technology; Electronic Engineering; English; Environmental Engineering; Finance; Food Technology; Geological Engineering; History; Hydraulic Engineering; Information Management; Information Technology; Inorganic Chemistry; Insurance; International Business; International Economics; International Studies; Korean; Law; Literature; Management; Marketing; Mass Communication; Materials Engineering; Mathematics; Mechanical Engineering; Mechanics; Microwaves; Music Theory and Composition; Musical Instruments; Nanotechnology; Natural Sciences; Nutrition; Organic Chemistry; Painting and Drawing; Philosophy of Education; Physics; Political Sciences; Protective Services; Psychology; Public Administration; Sculpture; Service Trades; Social Sciences; Sociology; Special Education; Sports; Structural Architecture; Telecommunications Engineering; Theatre; Transport Management). Also Combined Master's and Ph.D. Courses; and Joint Graduate Programmes
Student Services: Academic Counselling, Social Counselling, Careers Guidance, Nursery Care, Sports Facilities, Health Services, Canteen, Library, IT Centre, Residential Facilities
Periodicals: Design Review, Economics and Business Review, Journal of Language and Literature, Journal of Scientific Institute, Law and Political Review, Papers in Chinese Studies, Thesis of Engineering, Thesis of Korean Studies
Publishing house: University Press

Academic Staff 2013-2014	MALE	FEMALE	TOTAL
FULL-TIME			c. 700
Student Numbers 2013-2014			
All (Foreign Included)			c. 24000
Foreign only			1998

Last Update: 28-02-2018

Korea Aerospace University (KAU)

76 Hanggongdaehang-ro Deokyang-gu
Goyang-si 412-791, Gyeonggi-do
Tel: +82(2) 300-0114
Fax: +82(2) 3158-5769

Website: http://www.kau.ac.kr
President: Kang-Woong Lee
Tel: +82(2) 300-0001

College

Aviation and Management (Aeronautical and Aerospace Engineering; Air and Space Law; Air Transport; Business Administration; Transport and Communications; Transport Management); **Engineering** (Aeronautical and Aerospace Engineering; Computer Engineering; Electronic Engineering; Engineering; Information Sciences; Materials Engineering; Mechanical Engineering; Telecommunications Engineering); **Liberal Arts and Sciences** (Arts and Humanities; Chinese; English; French; German; Japanese; Korean; Mathematics; Physical Education; Physics)

Graduate School

Aviation and Management (Air and Space Law; Air Transport; Business Administration; Management; Tourism; Transport and Communications; Transport Management); **General Studies** (Aeronautical and Aerospace Engineering; Air and Space Law; Air Transport; Business Administration; Computer Engineering; Electronic Engineering; English; Information Technology; Materials Engineering; Mechanical Engineering; Telecommunications Engineering; Transport and Communications; Transport Management)
Further information: Also Jung-Seok Campus
History: Founded 1952 by the Ministry of Transport. Administrative control transferred to the Ministry of Education 1968. Transferred to Hanjin Group under Government plan for systematizing the aviation-related circles 1978. Acquired present title 2007. Formerly known as Hankuk Aviation University
Academic year: March to February (March-August; September-February)
Admission requirements: Graduation from high school, or foreign equivalent, and entrance examination
Main language(s) of instruction: Korean
Accrediting agency: Ministry of Education and Human Resources Development; Korean Council for University Education (KCUE)
Degrees and diplomas: Bachelor's Degree, Master's Degree (Aeronautical and Aerospace Engineering; Air and Space Law; Air Transport; Business Administration; Computer Engineering; Electrical Engineering; English; Information Technology; Management; Materials Engineering; Mechanical Engineering; Telecommunications Engineering; Tourism; Transport and Communications; Transport Management), Doctor's Degree (Aeronautical and Aerospace Engineering; Air Transport; Business Administration; Computer Engineering; Electronic Engineering; English; Information Technology; Materials Engineering; Mechanical Engineering;

Telecommunications Engineering; Transport and Communications; Transport Management)
Student Services: Academic Counselling, Social Counselling, Careers Guidance, Nursery Care, Sports Facilities, Health Services, Canteen, Library, IT Centre, Residential Facilities
Periodicals: Journals of Aviation Industry, Policy and Law, Journals of Electronics, Information, and Telecommunication Engineering, Journals of Humanities and Natural Sciences
Publishing house: Hankuk Aviation University Press

Academic Staff 2013-2014	MALE	FEMALE	TOTAL
FULL-TIME			156
Student Numbers 2013-2014			
All (Foreign Included)			6465

Last Update: 28-02-2018

Korea Baptist Theological University (KBTUS)

190, Bugyuseong-daero Yuseong-gu
Daejeon 305-358, Chungnam-do
Tel: +82(42) 828-3114
Fax: +82(42) 825-1354
Website: http://www.kbtus.ac.kr
President: Kwuk-Won Bae

Department/Division

Christian Education (Christian Religious Studies); **Church Music/ Piano** (Music; Musical Instruments; Religious Music); **Counseling Psychology** (Psychology); **Early Childhood Education** (Preschool Education); **English** (English); **Social Welfare** (Social Welfare); **Theology** (Theology)

Graduate School

Church Music (Religious Music); **Counseling and Social Welfare** (Psychology; Social Welfare); **Graduate Studies**; **Missiology** (Missionary Studies); **Pastoral Ministry** (Pastoral Studies); **Theology** (Theology)
History: Founded 1953.
Admission requirements: Bachelor of Arts (B.A) for graduate programme (M.Div); Master of Divinity (M.Div) for postgraduate programmes (Th.M and Ph.D)
Fees: 3,000 per semester (US Dollar)
Main language(s) of instruction: Korean, English
Accrediting agency: Ministry of Education
Degrees and diplomas: Bachelor's Degree, Master's Degree (Christian Religious Studies; Missionary Studies; Music; Pastoral Studies; Psychology; Religion; Religious Music; Social Welfare; Theology), Doctor's Degree (Pastoral Studies; Theology)

Student Services: Academic Counselling, Careers Guidance, Sports Facilities, Facilities for disabled people, Library, Residential Facilities
Periodicals: Gospel and Practice
Publishing house: University Publishing House

Academic Staff 2012-2013	MALE	FEMALE	TOTAL
FULL-TIME			70
PART-TIME			c. 200
Student Numbers 2012-2013			
All (Foreign Included)			c. 2440

Last Update: 28-02-2018

Korea Christian College (KCC)

320, Full Gospel General Assembly Theological Seminary
Duksan-myeon
Jecheon, Chungcheongbuk-do
Tel: +82(432) 645-5571/2
Fax: +82(43) 642-4530
Website: http://kcc.ac.kr
President: Sang-chul Lee

Department/Division
Counseling Psychology (Psychology); **Liberal Arts** (Arts and Humanities); **Music** (Music; Musicology); **Social Welfare** (Social Welfare); **Sports Welfare** (Sports); **Theology** (Theology)
History: Founded 1996.
Main language(s) of instruction: Korean
Accrediting agency: Ministry of Education
Degrees and diplomas: Bachelor's Degree (Musicology; Psychology; Social Welfare; Sports; Theology)
Student Services: Library, Residential Facilities
Last Update: 26-03-2018

Korea Christian University (KCU)

47, Kkchisan-ro, 24-gil, Ganseo-gu
Seoul 07661
Tel: +82(2) 2600-2220
Fax: +82(2) 2600-2224
Website: http://eng.kcu.ac.kr/eng/index.php
President: Sung Taek Lim

Department/Division
Foreign Language and Humanities (Arts and Humanities; Modern Languages); **Management Information** (Information Sciences); **Music** (Music); **Social Welfare** (Social Welfare); **Theology** (Theology)

Graduate School
Education (Education); **Social Welfare** (Social Welfare); **Theology** (Theology)
History: Founded 1958.
Main language(s) of instruction: Korean
Accrediting agency: Korean Council for University Education (KCUE)
Degrees and diplomas: Bachelor's Degree (Arts and Humanities; Education; Information Sciences; Modern Languages; Music; Social Welfare; Theology), Master's Degree (Education; Social Welfare; Theology)
Last Update: 09-03-2018

Korea Counseling Graduate University (KCGU)

366, Hyoryeong-ro, Seocho-gu
Seoul 137-865
Tel: +82(2) 584-6851
Fax: +82(2) 584-6857
Website: http://www.kcgu.ac.kr/english/portal.php
President: Hie Sung Lee

Course/Programme
Child and Adolescent Counseling (Educational and Student Counselling; Psychology); **Couple and Family Counseling** (Psychology); **General Counseling** (Psychology); **Gerontological Counseling** (Psychology); **Literary Counseling** (Psychology); **Philosophical Counseling** (Psychology); **Workplace Counseling** (Psychology; Vocational Counselling)
History: Founded 2010.
Main language(s) of instruction: Korean
Accrediting agency: Ministry of Education
Degrees and diplomas: Master's Degree (Educational and Student Counselling; Psychology; Vocational Counselling)
Student Services: Library
Last Update: 05-06-2018

Korea Nazarene University (KNU)

Wolbong Ro 48 Seobuk-gu
Cheonan-si 31172, Chungcheongnam-do
Tel: +82(41) 570-1534, +82(41) 570-1545, +82(41) 570-7853
Fax: +82(41) 570-7725
Website: http://www.kornu.ac.kr
President: Seung-An Im

College
Arts and Physical Fitness (Conducting; Music; Music Theory and Composition; Sports); **Health and Medical**

(Biomedicine; Health Sciences; Laboratory Techniques; Medical Technology; Nursing; Physical Therapy); **Liberal Arts** (Arts and Humanities; Business Administration; Child Care and Development; Chinese; Christian Religious Studies; English; Hotel Management; Information Sciences; International Business; Library Science; Media Studies; Police Studies; Psychology; Psychotherapy; Radio and Television Broadcasting; Real Estate; Rehabilitation and Therapy; Religious Music; Secretarial Studies; Social Sciences; Social Welfare; Speech Therapy and Audiology; Theology; Welfare and Protective Services); **Natural Science** (Design; Information Technology; Landscape Architecture; Mass Communication; Multimedia; Radio and Television Broadcasting; Rehabilitation and Therapy; Telecommunications Services); **Teacher Training** (Preschool Education; Secondary Education; Special Education; Teacher Training)

Graduate School

Education (Education; Foreign Languages Education; Preschool Education; Special Education; Teacher Training); **General Graduate Studies** (Bible; History of Religion; Philosophy; Rehabilitation and Therapy; Theology); **Rehabilitation** (Rehabilitation and Therapy); **Social Welfare** (Social Welfare; Social Work); **Theology** (Christian Religious Studies; Missionary Studies; Pastoral Studies; Psychology; Religion; Theology)

History: Founded 1954 as Bible College. Acquired Theological College status 1982, and present status and title 1994. Korea Nazarene University is one of 52 Nazarene Universities and Colleges around the world.

Academic year: March to December (March-June; September-December)

Admission requirements: Graduation from high school and SAT score

Main language(s) of instruction: English

Accrediting agency: Ministry of Education; Association of Universities in Korea; Korean Council for University Education (KCUE)

Degrees and diplomas: Bachelor's Degree, Master's Degree (Bible; Christian Religious Studies; Foreign Languages Education; Preschool Education; Rehabilitation and Therapy; Religion; Social Welfare; Social Work; Special Education; Theology), Doctor's Degree (Philosophy; Rehabilitation and Therapy; Theology)

Student Services: Academic Counselling, Careers Guidance, Sports Facilities, Language Laboratory, Facilities for disabled people, Health Services, Canteen, Foreign Studies Centre, Library, Residential Facilities

Periodicals: Jisung Kwa Changjo (Intelligence and Creation), Nasaret Nonchong (Nazarene Review)

Publishing house: Nasaret Daehakgyo Chulpansa (Nazarene University Press)

Academic Staff 2013-2014	MALE	FEMALE	TOTAL
FULL-TIME			c. 230
Student Numbers 2013-2014			
All (Foreign Included)			c. 6070

Last Update: 28-02-2018

Korea Polytechnic University (KPU)

237 Sangidaehak-ro
Siheung-si 429-793, Gyeonggi-do
Tel: +82(31) 8041-1000
Fax: +82(31) 496-8179
Website: http://www.kpu.ac.kr
President: Jun Yeong Choi
Tel: +82(31) 8041-0291

Course/Programme

Special Education Programmes (Business Administration; Engineering; Industrial Engineering; Technology Education)

Department/Division

Advanced Materials Engineering (Materials Engineering); **Business Administration** (Business Administration; E-Business/Commerce); **Chemical Engineering and Biotechnology** (Biotechnology; Chemical Engineering); **Computer Engineering** (Computer Engineering); **Design** (Industrial Design; Industrial Engineering); **Electronic Engineering** (Electronic Engineering); **Energy and Electrical Engineering** (Electrical Engineering; Energy Engineering); **Game and Multimedia Engineering** (Computer Graphics; Multimedia; Software Engineering); **Liberal Arts** (Arts and Humanities; Biology; Chemistry; Chinese; Computer Science; Cultural Studies; Engineering; English; Fine Arts; History; Korean; Mathematics; Modern Languages; Music; Physics; Sports); **Mechanical Design Engineering** (Engineering Drawing and Design; Mechanical Engineering); **Mechanical Engineering** (Mechanical Engineering); **Mechatronics Engineering** (Electrical Engineering; Electronic Engineering); **Nano-Optical Engineering** (Nanotechnology; Optical Technology)

Centre

Korean Language (Korean)

Graduate School

Industrial Technology and Management (Chemical Engineering; Computer Engineering; Electronic Engineering; Engineering Drawing and Design; Industrial Design; Industrial Management; Materials Engineering; Mechanical Engineering; Nanotechnology; Optical Technology);

Knowledge-based Technology and Energy (Artificial Intelligence; Automation and Control Engineering; Biotechnology; Chemical Engineering; Computer Engineering; E-Business/Commerce; Economics; Electrical Engineering; Energy Engineering; Information Technology; Machine Building; Management; Materials Engineering; Nanotechnology; Optical Technology; Production Engineering; Robotics; Telecommunications Engineering; Thermal Engineering)
History: Founded 1997.
Fees: Undergraduate, 7,294,000-7,889,000 per annum; Graduate, 3,650,000-4,750,000 per annum (Won)
Main language(s) of instruction: Korean
Accrediting agency: Korean Council for University Education (KCUE)
Degrees and diplomas: Bachelor's Degree, Master's Degree (Automation and Control Engineering; Biotechnology; Chemical Engineering; Computer Engineering; Electrical Engineering; Electronic Engineering; Energy Engineering; Engineering Drawing and Design; Industrial Design; Industrial Engineering; Industrial Management; Information Technology; Materials Engineering; Mechanical Engineering; Nanotechnology; Optical Technology; Production Engineering; Robotics; Telecommunications Engineering), Doctor's Degree (Automation and Control Engineering; Biotechnology; Chemical Engineering; Computer Engineering; Electrical Engineering; Electronic Engineering; Energy Engineering; Engineering Drawing and Design; Industrial Design; Industrial Engineering; Industrial Management; Information Technology; Materials Engineering; Mechanical Engineering; Nanotechnology; Optical Technology; Production Engineering; Robotics; Telecommunications Engineering; Thermal Engineering)
Student Services: Sports Facilities, Canteen, Library, IT Centre, Residential Facilities

Academic Staff 2016-2017	MALE	FEMALE	TOTAL
FULL-TIME			396
Student Numbers 2016-2017			
All (Foreign Included)			c. 7896
Foreign only			175

Last Update: 28-02-2018

Korea Soongsil Cyber University (KCU)

Jongno Biz-Well 23 Samil-daero30-gil, Jongno-gu
Seoul 03132
Tel: +82(2) 708-7700
Fax: +82(2) 708-7749
Website: http://kcu.ac
President: Moo-sung Chung

College
IT Design (Computer Engineering; Computer Science; Design; Information Management; Information Technology; Telecommunications Engineering); **Language and Literature** (Asian Studies; Chinese; English; Radio and Television Broadcasting; Writing); **Management in Real Estate Studies** (Accountancy; Business Administration; Real Estate; Taxation); **Services Studies** (Continuing Education; Preschool Education; Psychology; Social Welfare); **Social Security** (Fire Science; Law; Welfare and Protective Services)
Further information: Also Soongsil Campus
History: Founded as Korea Cyber University 2000. Acquired present title 2012.
Fees: 80,000 per lecture credit (Won)
Main language(s) of instruction: Korean
Accrediting agency: Ministry of Education
Degrees and diplomas: Bachelor's Degree (Accountancy; Asian Studies; Business Administration; Chinese; Computer Engineering; Computer Science; Construction Engineering; Continuing Education; Cosmetology; Design; Education; Electrical Engineering; Fire Science; Information Technology; Law; Literature; Management; Preschool Education; Protective Services; Psychology; Real Estate; Social Welfare; Social Work; Software Engineering; Taxation; Telecommunications Engineering; Welfare and Protective Services; Writing)

Student Numbers 2013-2014	MALE	FEMALE	TOTAL
All (Foreign Included)			c. 4700

Last Update: 26-03-2018

Korea University

145 Anam-dong Seongbuk-gu
Seoul 02841
Tel: +82(2) 3290-2963, +82(2) 3290-2951
Fax: +82(2) 921-5820
Website: http://www.korea.edu
President: Jaeho Yeom
Tel: +82(2) 3290-1001

College
Business Administration (Business Administration); **Education** (Computer Science; Education; English; Geography; History; Home Economics; Korean; Mathematics Education; Physical Education); **Engineering** (Architecture; Chemical Engineering; Civil Engineering; Electrical Engineering; Engineering; Industrial Engineering; Materials Engineering; Mechanical Engineering); **Law** (Law); **Liberal Arts** (Arts and Humanities; Asian Studies; Chinese; English; French;

German; History; Japanese; Korean; Linguistics; Modern Languages; Philosophy; Psychology; Russian; Sociology; Spanish); **Life Sciences and Biotechnology** (Biological and Life Sciences; Biotechnology; Ecology; Environmental Studies; Food Science); **Medicine** (Medicine; Nursing); **Nursing** (Nursing); **Political Science and Economics** (Economics; International Relations; Mass Communication; Political Sciences; Public Administration; Statistics); **Sciences** (Biology; Chemistry; Computer Science; Earth Sciences; Environmental Studies; Mathematics; Natural Sciences; Physics)

Graduate School

Biotechnology (Biotechnology); **Business Administration** (Business Administration); **Computer Science and Technology** (Computer Science; Technology); **Education** (Educational Sciences); **Industrial Information Technology** (Information Technology); **International Studies** (International Studies); **Journalism and Mass Communication** (Journalism; Mass Communication); **Labour Studies** (Labour and Industrial Relations; Labour Law); **Legal Studies** (Law); **Management and Information** (Information Sciences; Management); **Natural Resources** (Natural Resources)

Research Division

Advanced Materials Chemistry (Chemistry); **Anglo-American Studies** (American Studies; English Studies); **Asiatic Studies** (Asian Studies); **Behavioural Science** (Behavioural Sciences); **Disaster Prevention Science and Technology** (Safety Engineering); **Economics Research** (Economics); **Energy Technology** (Energy Engineering); **Environmental Health** (Occupational Health); **Environmental Technology and Sustainable Development** (Development Studies; Environmental Engineering); **European Union** (European Studies); **German Studies** (German; Modern Languages); **High Technology Materials and Devices** (Materials Engineering; Technology); **Industrial Technology** (Industrial Engineering); **Industry Development**; **Information and Communication Technology** (Communication Studies; Information Technology; Technology); **Korean Culture** (Cultural Studies); **Labour Education**; **Language and Information** (Information Sciences); **Life Sciences** (Biological and Life Sciences); **Mass Communication** (Mass Communication); **Mineral Resources** (Mineralogy); **Natural Resources and Environment** (Environmental Studies; Natural Resources); **Natural Sciences** (Natural Sciences); **Nutrition** (Nutrition); **Peace Studies** (Peace and Disarmament); **Philosophy Studies** (Philosophy); **Plastic Reconstructive and Special Surgery** (Plastic Surgery); **Public Administration** (Public Administration); **Russian Studies** (Russian); **Semiconductor Technology** (Information Technology; Technology); **Social Research** (Social Studies); **Tropical Epidemic Diseases** (Tropical Medicine); **Viral Diseases** (Virology)

Further information: Also Teaching Hospitals (Anam, Guro, Yeoju, Ansan). Courses for Foreign Students. Language training programme (English, Japanese, Chinese). Students Exchange Programme

History: Founded 1905 as Posung College, acquired present status and title 1946. A private Institution operated by the Korea-Choongang Educational Foundation but supervised by the Ministry of Education.

Academic year: March to December (March-June; September-December)

Admission requirements: Graduation from high school or equivalent, and entrance examination

Main language(s) of instruction: Korean and English

Accrediting agency: Korean Council for University Education (KCUE)

Degrees and diplomas: Bachelor's Degree (Medicine), Master's Degree (Accountancy; Administrative Law; Adult Education; Advertising and Publicity; Anaesthesiology; Analytical Chemistry; Anatomy; Ancient Civilizations; Applied Linguistics; Applied Mathematics; Applied Physics; Archaeology; Architectural and Environmental Design; Architecture and Planning; Art History; Asian Studies; Automation and Control Engineering; Automotive Engineering; Banking; Behavioural Sciences; Biochemistry; Bioengineering; Biological and Life Sciences; Biology; Biomedical Engineering; Biomedicine; Biophysics; Biotechnology; Business Administration; Cell Biology; Chemical Engineering; Chemistry; Child Care and Development; Chinese; Civil Engineering; Civil Law; Clinical Psychology; Cognitive Sciences; Commercial Law; Community Health; Comparative Literature; Computer Education; Computer Engineering; Computer Networks; Computer Science; Constitutional Law; Construction Engineering; Consumer Studies; Contemporary History; Continuing Education; Criminal Law; Cultural Studies; Curriculum; Dentistry; Dermatology; Development Studies; E-Business/Commerce; East Asian Studies; Eastern European Studies; Ecology; Econometrics; Economic and Finance Policy; Economics; Educational Administration; Educational and Student Counselling; Educational Sciences; Educational Technology; Educational Testing and Evaluation; Electrical Engineering; Electronic Engineering; Energy Engineering; Engineering; Engineering Management; English; Environmental Engineering; Environmental Management; Environmental Studies; Epidemiology; Fashion Design; Finance; Food Science; Foreign Languages Education; Forensic Medicine and Dentistry; French; Geography; Geography (Human); Geology; Geophysics; German; Germanic Studies; Gerontology; Gynaecology and Obstetrics; Health Administration; Health Sciences; Heritage Preservation; Higher Education; History; Home Economics; Horticulture; Humanities and Social Science Education; Industrial and Organizational

Psychology; Industrial and Production Economics; Industrial Design; Industrial Engineering; Industrial Management; Information Management; Information Technology; Inorganic Chemistry; International Business; International Economics; International Law; International Relations; International Studies; Japanese; Journalism; Korean; Laboratory Techniques; Labour and Industrial Relations; Labour Law; Landscape Architecture; Laser Engineering; Latin American Studies; Law; Linguistics; Literature; Management; Marketing; Mass Communication; Materials Engineering; Mathematics; Mathematics Education; Mechanical Engineering; Media Studies; Medical Technology; Medicine; Medieval Studies; Meteorology; Microbiology; Modern History; Molecular Biology; Multimedia; Nanotechnology; Native Language Education; Natural Sciences; Neurology; Neurosciences; Nuclear Physics; Nursing; Nutrition; Occupational Health; Oncology; Ophthalmology; Optics; Organic Chemistry; Orthopaedics; Otorhinolaryngology; Paediatrics; Parasitology; Pathology; Peace and Disarmament; Pharmacology; Pharmacy; Physical Chemistry; Physical Education; Physics; Physiology; Plant Pathology; Plastic Surgery; Political Sciences; Private Law; Psychiatry and Mental Health; Psychology; Public Administration; Public Health; Radio and Television Broadcasting; Radiology; Regional Studies; Rehabilitation and Therapy; Robotics; Russian; Social and Preventive Medicine; Social Policy; Social Psychology; Social Welfare; Sociology; Software Engineering; Soil Science; Solid State Physics; Spanish; Special Education; Sports; Statistics; Structural Architecture; Surgery; Taxation; Technology; Telecommunications Engineering; Telecommunications Services; Town Planning; Translation and Interpretation; Transport Management; Urology; Video; Visual Arts; Water Science; Welfare and Protective Services; Writing), Doctor's Degree (Accountancy; Administrative Law; Anaesthesiology; Analytical Chemistry; Anatomy; Applied Linguistics; Applied Mathematics; Applied Physics; Archaeology; Architectural and Environmental Design; Architecture and Planning; Art History; Asian Studies; Automation and Control Engineering; Automotive Engineering; Banking; Behavioural Sciences; Biochemistry; Bioengineering; Biological and Life Sciences; Biology; Biomedical Engineering; Biomedicine; Biophysics; Biotechnology; Business Administration; Cell Biology; Chemical Engineering; Chemistry; Child Care and Development; Chinese; Civil Engineering; Civil Law; Cognitive Sciences; Commercial Law; Community Health; Comparative Literature; Comparative Politics; Computer Education; Computer Engineering; Computer Graphics; Computer Networks; Computer Science; Constitutional Law; Consumer Studies; Contemporary History; Continuing Education; Criminal Law; Cultural Studies; Curriculum; Data Processing; Dentistry; Dermatology; Design; E- Business/Commerce; Eastern European Studies; Ecology; Econometrics; Economic and Finance Policy;

Economics; Educational Administration; Educational and Student Counselling; Educational Psychology; Educational Sciences; Educational Technology; Educational Testing and Evaluation; Electrical Engineering; Electronic Engineering; Engineering; Engineering Management; English; Environmental Engineering; Environmental Management; Environmental Studies; Epidemiology; Fashion Design; Finance; Food Science; Food Technology; Foreign Languages Education; Forensic Medicine and Dentistry; French; Geography; Geography (Human); Geology; Geophysics; German; Gynaecology and Obstetrics; Health Administration; Health Education; Health Sciences; Heritage Preservation; Higher Education; History; Horticulture; Humanities and Social Science Education; Industrial and Organizational Psychology; Industrial and Production Economics; Industrial Engineering; Industrial Management; Information Management; Information Technology; Inorganic Chemistry; International Business; International Economics; International Relations; International Studies; Japanese; Journalism; Korean; Laboratory Techniques; Labour Law; Landscape Architecture; Laser Engineering; Latin American Studies; Law; Linguistics; Literature; Management; Marketing; Mass Communication; Materials Engineering; Mathematics; Mathematics Education; Media Studies; Medical Parasitology; Medical Technology; Medicine; Medieval Studies; Meteorology; Microbiology; Microelectronics; Microwaves; Modern History; Molecular Biology; Multimedia; Nanotechnology; Native Language Education; Natural Sciences; Neurology; Neurosciences; Nuclear Physics; Nursing; Nutrition; Occupational Health; Oncology; Ophthalmology; Optics; Organic Chemistry; Orthopaedics; Otorhinolaryngology; Paediatrics; Pathology; Pharmacology; Pharmacy; Philosophy; Physical Chemistry; Physical Education; Physics; Physiology; Plant Pathology; Political Sciences; Polymer and Plastics Technology; Protective Services; Psychiatry and Mental Health; Psychology; Public Administration; Public Health; Radio and Television Broadcasting; Radiology; Rehabilitation and Therapy; Robotics; Russian; Social and Preventive Medicine; Social Policy; Social Psychology; Social Welfare; Sociology; Software Engineering; Soil Science; Solid State Physics; Spanish; Special Education; Sports; Statistics; Surgery; Taxation; Technology; Telecommunications Engineering; Telecommunications Services; Town Planning; Translation and Interpretation; Transport Management; Urology; Visual Arts; Water Science; Writing). Also MBA; Executive MBA; Also dual Master/PhD degree programmes; Teaching qualifications and Certificates in Education, Business Administration and Natural Resources

Student Services: Academic Counselling, Social Counselling, Careers Guidance, Cultural Activities, Sports Facilities, Health Services, Residential Facilities

Periodicals: Business Administration Journal, Business Review, Journal of Asiatic Studies, Kodai Munwha

(Culture), Korean Cultural Studies, Sa Chong (Historical Review), The Granite Tower (English Newspaper), The Phoenix (English Department)

Publishing house: Korea University Press

Student Numbers 2015-2016	MALE	FEMALE	TOTAL
All (Foreign Included)			37493
Foreign only			1545

Last Update: 01-03-2018

SEJONG CAMPUS

2511 Sejong-ro
Sejong City 30019, Chungcheongnam-do
Tel: +82(44) 860-1114
Fax: +82(44) 860-1048
Website: https://sejong.korea.ac.kr/mbshome/mbs/eng/index.do
President: Jae-ho Yeom

College

Economics and Commerce (Business and Commerce; Economics); **Liberal Arts** (Archaeology; Art History; Arts and Humanities; Chinese; English; German; Korean; Sociology; Writing); **Pharmacy** (Pharmacy); **Science and Engineering** (Automation and Control Engineering; Biomedical Engineering; Biotechnology; Chemistry; Environmental Engineering; Information Technology; Leisure Studies; Mathematics and Computer Science; Natural Sciences; Physics; Sports; Technology)

School

International Sports Studies (Sports); **Public Administration** (Public Administration)
History: Founded 1980 as Seochang Campus. Acquired present title 2008.
Main language(s) of instruction: Korean
Accrediting agency: Korean Council for University Education (KCUE)
Degrees and diplomas: Bachelor's Degree (Business Administration; Cultural Studies; Economics; Engineering; Literature; Natural Sciences; Physical Education; Public Administration; Statistics), Master's Degree (Arts and Humanities; Cultural Studies; Education; English; Foreign Languages Education; Public Administration; Social Welfare; Translation and Interpretation), Doctor's Degree (Economic and Finance Policy; Public Administration; Social Policy; Social Welfare)
Last Update: 05-03-2018

Korea University of International Studies (KUIS)

5-357 Hyochang-dong, Yongsan-gu
Seoul 140-897
Tel: +82(02) 2077-8700
Fax: +82(02) 6499-3180
Website: http://www.kuis.ac.kr/eng/index.asp
President: Han Woo Choi

Department/Division

International Area Studies (Foreign Languages Education; International Studies; Native Language Education; Translation and Interpretation); **International Cooperation** (Cultural Studies; Leadership; Theology)
History: Founded 2006.
Main language(s) of instruction: Korean
Accrediting agency: Ministry of Education
Degrees and diplomas: Master's Degree (Cultural Studies; Foreign Languages Education; International Studies; Native Language Education; Translation and Interpretation)
Student Services: Library
Last Update: 21-03-2018

Korea University of Technology and Education (KUT)

1600, Chungjeol-ro Byeongcheon-myeon, Dongnam-gu
Cheonan-si 31253, Chungcheongnam-do
Tel: +82(41) 560-1114, +82(41) 560-2503
Fax: +82(41) 560-2529
Website: http://www.kut.ac.kr
President: Ki-Young Kim

School

Architectural Engineering (Structural Architecture); **Computer Science and Engineering** (Computer Engineering; Computer Networks; Computer Science; Data Processing; Software Engineering); **Electrical, Electronics and Communication Engineering** (Electrical Engineering; Electronic Engineering; Information Technology; Telecommunications Engineering); **Energy, Materials and Chemical Engineering** (Chemical Engineering; Energy Engineering; Materials Engineering); **Industrial Design Engineering** (Industrial Design; Industrial Engineering); **Industrial Management** (E- Business/Commerce; Engineering Management; Human Resources; Industrial Management); **Liberal Arts** (Applied Mathematics; Arts and Humanities; Educational Technology; English; History; Human Resources; Korean; Linguistics; Literature; Mathematics; Modern Languages; Physical Education; Physics; Psychology); **Mechanical Engineering**

(Artificial Intelligence; Automotive Engineering; Computer Engineering; Energy Engineering; Environmental Engineering; Information Technology; Mechanical Engineering); **Mechatronics Engineering** (Automation and Control Engineering; Electronic Engineering; Mechanical Engineering; Mechanics; Production Engineering)

Graduate School

Graduate Studies (Arts and Humanities; Automation and Control Engineering; Biotechnology; Business Administration; Chemical Engineering; Chemistry; Computer Engineering; Computer Science; E- Business/Commerce; Electrical Engineering; Electronic Engineering; Energy Engineering; Engineering Drawing and Design; Environmental Engineering; Materials Engineering; Mechanical Engineering; Nanotechnology; Social Sciences; Structural Architecture; Telecommunications Engineering); **Industrial Studies** (Automation and Control Engineering; Business Administration; Chemical Engineering; Computer Engineering; Computer Science; Electrical Engineering; Electronic Engineering; Energy Engineering; Engineering Drawing and Design; Materials Engineering; Mechanical Engineering; Structural Architecture; Telecommunications Engineering); **Techno HRD** (Business Administration; Educational and Student Counselling; Human Resources; Industrial and Organizational Psychology; Management; Psychology; Psychometrics; Psychotherapy; Public Administration; Vocational Counselling)

History: Founded 1997.

Admission requirements: Graduation from high school and entrance examination

Fees: 3,618,000-5,158,000 (Won)

Main language(s) of instruction: Korean

Accrediting agency: Ministry of Education

Degrees and diplomas: Bachelor's Degree, Master's Degree (Business Administration; Chemical Engineering; Computer Engineering; Computer Science; Electrical Engineering; Electronic Engineering; Energy Engineering; Engineering Drawing and Design; Human Resources; Materials Engineering; Mechanical Engineering; Structural Architecture; Telecommunications Engineering), Doctor's Degree (Business Administration; Chemical Engineering; Computer Engineering; Computer Science; Electrical Engineering; Electronic Engineering; Energy Engineering; Engineering Drawing and Design; Materials Engineering; Mechanical Engineering; Telecommunications Engineering)

Student Services: Academic Counselling, Social Counselling, Careers Guidance, Nursery Care, Sports Facilities, Language Laboratory, Health Services, Library, Residential Facilities

Periodicals: Journal of Technology and Education of Korea University

Publishing house: KUT's Press

Academic Staff 2013-2014	MALE	FEMALE	TOTAL
FULL-TIME			c. 155
Student Numbers 2013-2014			
All (Foreign Included)			4828
Foreign only			87

Last Update: 01-03-2018

Korean Bible University

205 Sanggye 7-Dong Nowon-Ku
Seoul 01757
Tel: +82(2) 950-5401
Fax: +82(70) 4275-0167, +82(2) 950-5411
Website: http://www.bible.ac.kr
President: Uoo-Chung Kang
Tel: +82(2) 950-5426

Department/Division

Information Science (Computer Engineering; Information Sciences; Information Technology; Software Engineering); **Nursing** (Health Sciences; Nursing); **Social Sciences** (Child Care and Development; Preschool Education; Social Sciences; Social Welfare); **Theology** (Bible; Theology)

Graduate School

Divinity (Religion); **Early Childhood Education** (Child Care and Development; Preschool Education; Special Education); **Social Welfare** (Social Welfare); **Theology** (Bible; Christian Religious Studies; Missionary Studies; New Testament; Psychology; Theology)

History: Founded 1952.

Admission requirements: High school diploma

Main language(s) of instruction: Korean

Accrediting agency: Korean Council for University Education (KCUE)

Degrees and diplomas: Bachelor's Degree, Master's Degree (Bible; Child Care and Development; Christian Religious Studies; Missionary Studies; New Testament; Religion; Social Welfare; Theology), Doctor's Degree (Theology)

Student Services: Academic Counselling, Social Counselling, Sports Facilities, Language Laboratory, Facilities for disabled people, Canteen, Library, IT Centre, Residential Facilities

Academic Staff 2013-2014	MALE	FEMALE	TOTAL
FULL-TIME			45
PART-TIME			78
Student Numbers 2013-2014			
All (Foreign Included)			1290

Last Update: 01-03-2018

Kosin University

194 Dongsam-dong Yeongdo-gu
Busan 606-701
Tel: +82(51) 990-2114
Fax: +82(51) 911-2504
Website: http://www.kosin.edu
President: Ahn Min

College

Art (Design; Graphic Design; Interior Design; Performing Arts; Religious Music; Visual Arts); **Humanities and Social Sciences** (Advertising and Publicity; Arts and Humanities; Child Care and Development; Chinese; Computer Science; English; Health Administration; Information Sciences; Literature; Mathematics and Computer Science; Media Studies; Public Relations; Rehabilitation and Therapy; Social Welfare); **Medicine** (Medicine); **Natural Sciences** (Applied Chemistry; Biological and Life Sciences; Biology; Biomedicine; Chemistry; Dermatology; Environmental Studies; Food Science; Natural Sciences; Nutrition; Pharmacology; Public Health); **Nursing** (Nursing); **Theology** (Christian Religious Studies; Computer Science; Cultural Studies; Missionary Studies; Sports; Theology)

Graduate School

Christian Counselling (Psychology); **Christian Music** (Conducting; Music; Music Theory and Composition; Musical Instruments; Religious Music; Singing); **Education** (Education); **Graduate Studies** (Biology; Chemistry; Health Sciences; Medicine; Nursing; Religious Music; Theology); **Mission and Ministry** (History of Religion; Missionary Studies; Religion; Theology); **Public Health** (Environmental Management; Health Administration; Nursing; Public Health); **TESOL** (Foreign Languages Education); **Theology** (*Korea Theological Seminary*) (Bible; New Testament; Theology)
Further information: Also Songdo and Cheonan Campuses; Kosin University Hospital; 22 Research Institutes
History: Founded 1946. A private Institution operated by the Presbyterian Church of Korea.
Academic year: March to December (March-July; September-December)
Admission requirements: Graduation from high school and entrance examination
Fees: Undergraduate, 5,704,000-9,782,000 per annum; Graduate, 2,781,000-5,127,000 per annum (Won)
Main language(s) of instruction: Korean, English
Accrediting agency: Korean Council for University Education (KCUE)
Degrees and diplomas: Bachelor's Degree, Master's Degree (Bible; Biology; Chemistry; Christian Religious Studies; Conducting; Education; Environmental Management; Health Administration; Health Sciences; History of Religion;

Medicine; Missionary Studies; Music Theory and Composition; Musical Instruments; New Testament; Nursing; Public Health; Religious Education; Religious Music; Singing; Theology), Doctor's Degree (Anaesthesiology; Anatomy; Bible; Biochemistry; Cardiology; Christian Religious Studies; Community Health; Dermatology; Ethics; Gynaecology and Obstetrics; Health Administration; Health Sciences; History of Religion; Medicine; Microbiology; Missionary Studies; Neurology; New Testament; Nursing; Ophthalmology; Orthopaedics; Paediatrics; Pathology; Pharmacology; Philosophy; Physiology; Plastic Surgery; Psychiatry and Mental Health; Radiology; Rehabilitation and Therapy; Religion; Religious Education; Social and Preventive Medicine; Surgery; Theology; Urology)
Student Services: Academic Counselling, Social Counselling, Careers Guidance, Nursery Care, Sports Facilities, Language Laboratory, Health Services, Library, IT Centre, Residential Facilities
Last Update: 01-03-2018

Kukje Theological University and Seminary

1577-5 Sinwon dong, Gwanak-gu
Seoul
Tel: +82(2) 839-0388
Fax: +82(2) 839-0385
Website: http://eng.ktu.ac.kr
President: Kyu-Seop Kim

Course/Programme

Arts (Christian Religious Studies; Musicology; Psychology; Social Welfare); **Divinity** (Religion); **Ministry** (Bible; Christian Religious Studies; History of Religion; Missionary Studies; New Testament; Theology); **Theology** (Bible; Christian Religious Studies; History of Religion; Missionary Studies; New Testament; Theology)
History: Founded 1999.
Main language(s) of instruction: Korean, English
Accrediting agency: Ministry of Education
Degrees and diplomas: Master's Degree (Bible; Christian Religious Studies; History of Religion; Missionary Studies; Musicology; New Testament; Psychology; Religion; Social Welfare), Doctor's Degree (Bible; Christian Religious Studies; History of Religion; Missionary Studies; New Testament; Theology)
Last Update: 23-03-2018

Kukje University of Arts (KUA)

47, Dosan Road, Gangnam-gu
Seoul 716-800
Tel: +82(2) 543-8196

Fax: +82(2) 517-1392
Website: http://kua.ac.kr

Department/Division

Applied Music (Music); **Beauty Art Design** (Aesthetics; Design; Fine Arts); **Musical Theatre** (Music; Theatre); **Performing Arts Management** (Art Management); **Studio Composition and Production** (Music Theory and Composition; Sound Engineering (Acoustics)); **Theatrical Arts and Stage Director** (Theatre)
History: Founded 2008.
Main language(s) of instruction: Korean
Accrediting agency: Ministry of Education
Degrees and diplomas: Bachelor's Degree (Fine Arts; Performing Arts)
Last Update: 22-03-2018

Kwangju Women's University (KWU)

165 Sanjeong-dong Kwangsan-gu
Gwangju-si 506-713, Gyeonggi-do
Tel: +82(62) 956-2500
Fax: +82(62) 953-2218
Website: http://www.kwu.ac.kr
President: Sun-jae Lee

Department/Division

Airline Service (Air Transport; Service Trades); **Art Therapy** (Art Therapy); **Beauty Science** (Cosmetology); **Call Marketing** (Marketing); **Childhood English Education** (Foreign Languages Education); **Complementary Alternative Therapy** (Alternative Medicine); **Counseling and Psychology** (Educational and Student Counselling; Psychology); **Dancing** (Dance); **Dental Hygiene** (Dental Hygiene); **Early Childhood Education** (Preschool Education); **Elementary Special Education** (Primary Education; Special Education); **Food and Nutrition** (Food Science; Nutrition); **Health Administration** (Health Administration); **Hygienic and Medical Technology** (Hygiene; Medical Technology); **Interior Design** (Interior Design); **Language Therapy** (Speech Therapy and Audiology); **Nursing** (Nursing); **Occupational Therapy** (Occupational Therapy); **Pharmaceutical Cosmetics** (Cosmetology; Information Management); **Physical Therapy** (Physical Therapy); **Police and Law** (Law; Police Studies); **Secondary Special Education** (Secondary Education; Special Education); **Silver Care** (Health Sciences; Psychology; Social Welfare; Social Work); **Social Welfare** (Social Welfare)

Graduate School

Education (Education; Home Economics Education; Preschool Education; Psychology; Special Education); **Graduate Studies** (Cosmetology; Dance; Food Science; Foreign

Languages Education; Nutrition; Occupational Therapy; Physical Therapy; Preschool Education); **Social Development** (Alternative Medicine; Art Therapy; Korean; Law; Literature; Marketing; Nursing; Police Studies; Social Welfare; Social Work; Speech Therapy and Audiology; Welfare and Protective Services)
History: Founded 1997.
Main language(s) of instruction: Korean
Accrediting agency: Korean Council for University Education (KCUE)
Degrees and diplomas: Bachelor's Degree, Master's Degree (Alternative Medicine; Art Therapy; Clinical Psychology; Cosmetology; Dance; Educational and Student Counselling; Food Science; Korean; Law; Literature; Marketing; Nursing; Nutrition; Occupational Therapy; Physical Therapy; Police Studies; Preschool Education; Psychology; Social Welfare; Social Work; Special Education; Speech Therapy and Audiology; Welfare and Protective Services), Doctor's Degree (Cosmetology; Preschool Education)
Student Services: Sports Facilities, Library, IT Centre, Residential Facilities

Academic Staff 2012-2013	MALE	FEMALE	TOTAL
FULL-TIME			193
PART-TIME			c. 195
Student Numbers 2012-2013			
All (Foreign Included)			c. 4650

Last Update: 01-03-2018

Kwangshin University

San-70 Bonchon-dong Buk-gu
Gwangju-si 61027, Gyeonggi-do
Tel: +82(62) 605-1004
Fax: +82(62) 571-7255
Website: http://www.kwangshin.ac.kr
President: Kyu-nam Jung

School

Counseling (*Graduate*) (Christian Religious Studies; Psychology; Psychotherapy)

Department/Division

Arts and Sciences; **Early Childhood Education** (Child Care and Development; Preschool Education; Teacher Training); **International Korean Language Teacher** (Foreign Languages Education); **Music** (Conducting; Music; Music Theory and Composition; Musical Instruments; Opera; Singing); **Practical Music** (Computer Science; Music; Musical Instruments; Singing; Sound Engineering (Acoustics)); **Social Welfare** (Continuing Education; Educational and Student Counselling; Psychology; Social Welfare; Social Work); **Theology** (Theology)

Graduate School

Education (Education; Preschool Education; Primary Education; Special Education; Teacher Training); **Graduate Studies** (Education; Music; Musicology; Preschool Education; Religion; Theology); **International Studies** (Foreign Languages Education; Korean); **Social Work** (Social Work); **Theology** (Religion; Theology)

History: Founded 1954.

Main language(s) of instruction: Korean

Accrediting agency: Korean Council for University Education (KCUE)

Degrees and diplomas: Bachelor's Degree, Master's Degree (Education; Foreign Languages Education; Musicology; Preschool Education; Psychology; Psychotherapy; Religion; Social Work; Theology), Doctor's Degree (Religion; Theology)

Student Services: Library, Residential Facilities

Academic Staff 2012-2013	MALE	FEMALE	TOTAL
FULL-TIME			66
PART-TIME			c. 88
Student Numbers 2012-2013			
All (Foreign Included)			c. 1034

Last Update: 01-03-2018

Kwangwoon University (KWU)

20 Kwangwoon-ro Nowon-gu
Seoul 01897
Tel: +82(2) 940-5114, +82(2) 940-5015, +82(2) 940-5014
Fax: +82(2) 940-5506, +82(2) 940-5016
Website: http://www.kw.ac.kr
President: Ji-Sang Yoo
Tel: +82(2) 940-5000

College

Business Administration (Business Administration); **Electronics and Information Engineering** (Computer Engineering; Electrical Engineering; Electronic Engineering; Information Technology; Materials Engineering; Robotics; Telecommunications Engineering); **Engineering** (Architecture; Chemical Engineering; Engineering; Environmental Engineering; Structural Architecture); **Law** (Law); **Natural Sciences** (Applied Physics; Chemistry; Leisure Studies; Mathematics; Natural Sciences; Sports); **Northeast Asia Studies** (Asian Studies; Business and Commerce; Chinese; Cinema and Television; Cultural Studies; East Asian Studies; Graphic Design; History; International Relations; Japanese; Korean; Literature; Marketing; Performing Arts; Political Sciences; Publishing and Book Trade; Translation and Interpretation); **Social Science** (English; Industrial and Organizational Psychology; Mass Communication; Media Studies; Public Administration; Radio and Television Broadcasting; Social Sciences)

Department/Division

Korean Language and Literature (Korean; Literature)

Graduate School

Business Administration (Business Administration; Management; Real Estate; Service Trades); **Counseling, Welfare and Policy** (Psychotherapy; Public Administration; Social Welfare); **Education** (Education; Educational Sciences; Special Education; Teacher Training); **Environmental Studies** (Environmental Studies); **Graduate Studies** (Applied Physics; Architecture; Business Administration; Chemical Engineering; Chemistry; Computer Science; Criminology; Electrical Engineering; Electronic Engineering; Engineering; English; Environmental Engineering; Industrial and Organizational Psychology; Information Management; Information Technology; International Business; Journalism; Korean; Law; Literature; Mass Communication; Materials Engineering; Mathematics; Military Science; Public Administration; Real Estate; Regional Studies; Robotics; Structural Architecture; Telecommunications Engineering); **Information and Contents** (Distance Education; Information Sciences; Information Technology; Media Studies); **Legal Affairs in Construction** (Civil Engineering; Construction Engineering; Law; Public Law)

History: Founded 1934 as Institute of Technology, acquired present status and title 1988. A private Institution operated by the Kwangwoon Foundation but supervised by the Ministry of Education.

Academic year: March to February (March-August; September-February)

Admission requirements: Graduation from high school (vocational or training schools are not acceptable), language proficiency over TOPIK level 4 or equivalent and entrance examination (both written and spoken)

Fees: Admission fee, c. 950,000; tuition fee, an average 3,871,000 per semester (Won)

Main language(s) of instruction: Korean, English

Accrediting agency: Korean Council for University Education (KCUE)

Degrees and diplomas: Bachelor's Degree, Master's Degree (Architecture; Biological and Life Sciences; Business Administration; Chemical Engineering; Chemistry; Computer Engineering; Computer Science; Criminology; Electrical Engineering; Electronic Engineering; English; Environmental Engineering; Industrial and Organizational Psychology; Information Management; Information Technology; International Business; Journalism; Korean; Law; Literature; Mass Communication; Materials Engineering; Mathematics; Military Science; Physics; Public Administration; Regional Studies; Robotics; Structural Architecture;

Telecommunications Engineering), Doctor's Degree (Architecture; Biological and Life Sciences; Business Administration; Chemical Engineering; Chemistry; Computer Engineering; Computer Science; Construction Engineering; Criminology; Electrical Engineering; Electronic Engineering; English; Environmental Engineering; Industrial and Organizational Psychology; Information Management; Information Technology; International Business; Journalism; Korean; Law; Literature; Mass Communication; Materials Engineering; Mathematics; Military Science; Physics; Public Administration; Real Estate; Regional Studies; Robotics; Structural Architecture; Telecommunications Engineering; Town Planning)

Student Services: Academic Counselling, Social Counselling, Careers Guidance, Nursery Care, Cultural Activities, Sports Facilities, Language Laboratory, Facilities for disabled people, Health Services, Canteen, Foreign Studies Centre

Periodicals: Kwangwoon University Newspaper, NEXT

Publishing house: and The Kwangwoon Annals

Academic Staff 2015-2016	MALE	FEMALE	TOTAL
FULL-TIME			331
PART-TIME			390
Student Numbers 2015-2016			
All (Foreign Included)			9807
Foreign only			294

Last Update: 01-03-2018

Kyonggi University (KGU)

154-42 Gwanggyosan-ro Woncheon-dong, Yeongtong-gu
Suwon-si 16227, Gyeonggi-do
Tel: +82(31) 249-8770, +82(31) 249-8773
Fax: +82(31) 255-5915, 82(31) 249-8668
Website: http://www.kyonggi.ac.kr//KyonggiEng.kgu
President: In-Kyu Kim

College

Arts (Acting; Architectural and Environmental Design; Art Management; Ceramic Art; Communication Arts; Computer Science; Design; Film; Fine Arts; Handicrafts; Industrial Design; Jewellery Art; Mass Communication; Media Studies; Music; Political Sciences; Visual Arts); **Economics and Business Administration** (Accountancy; Business Administration; Business and Commerce; Economics; Information Management; Information Sciences; Information Technology; International Business; Private Law; Statistics); **Engineering** (Architecture; Chemical Engineering; Civil Engineering; Electronic Engineering; Engineering; Environmental Engineering; Industrial Engineering; Materials Engineering; Mechanical Engineering; Structural Architecture; Town Planning; Transport Engineering); **Humanities** (Arts and Humanities; Chinese; English; French; German; History; Information Sciences; Japanese; Korean; Library Science; Literature; Preschool Education; Russian; Teacher Training; Writing); **International Studies** (Information Sciences; International Relations; International Studies); **Laws** (Law); **Natural Sciences** (Biological and Life Sciences; Biotechnology; Chemistry; Computer Science; Food Science; Mathematics; Natural Sciences; Physics); **Pysical Sciences** (Leisure Studies; Physical Education; Protective Services; Sports; Sports Management); **Social Sciences** (Police Studies; Public Administration; Social Sciences; Social Welfare)

Course/Programme

Korean Language (Korean)

Graduate School

Alternative Medicine (Alternative Medicine; Traditional Eastern Medicine); **Architecture** (Architecture); **Arts and Design** (Design; Fine Arts); **Business Administration** (Business Administration); **Education** (Education); **Industrial and Information Technology** (Industrial Engineering; Information Technology); **International Studies and Culture** (International Studies); **Politics and Policy** (Economic and Finance Policy; Economics; Political Sciences); **Public Administration** (Public Administration); **Social Welfare** (Social Welfare); **Sports Science** (Sports); **Tourism and Hospitality** (Hotel and Restaurant; Tourism)

Further information: Also Seoul Campus; 11 research centers

History: Founded 1947 as Teacher Training College, acquired present status and title 1984. A private institution financed by tuition fees and Foundation support.

Academic year: March to February (March-August; September-February)

Admission requirements: Graduation from high school and entrance examination

Main language(s) of instruction: Korean, English

Accrediting agency: Korean Council for University Education (KCUE)

Degrees and diplomas: Bachelor's Degree, Master's Degree (Accountancy; Acting; Architectural and Environmental Design; Architecture; Bioengineering; Biological and Life Sciences; Biotechnology; Business Administration; Business and Commerce; Chemical Engineering; Chemistry; Chinese; Civil Engineering; Computer Science; Criminal Law; Design; E- Business/Commerce; Economics; Educational Administration; Educational Sciences; Electronic Engineering; Energy Engineering; English; Environmental Engineering; Food Science; French; German; Health Sciences; History; Hotel and Restaurant; Industrial Design; Industrial Engineering; Information Management; Information Sciences; Information Technology; International Business;

Japanese; Journalism; Korean; Law; Leisure Studies; Library Science; Literature; Materials Engineering; Mathematics; Mechanical Engineering; Media Studies; Music; Painting and Drawing; Physical Education; Physics; Preschool Education; Private Law; Protective Services; Psychology; Public Administration; Safety Engineering; Social Studies; Social Welfare; Sports; Sports Management; Statistics; Structural Architecture; Taxation; Tourism; Town Planning; Transport Engineering; Visual Arts; Writing), Doctor's Degree (Accountancy; Alternative Medicine; Applied Physics; Architecture; Bioengineering; Biological and Life Sciences; Biotechnology; Business Administration; Business and Commerce; Chemical Engineering; Chemistry; Civil Engineering; Computer Science; Criminal Law; E- Business/Commerce; Economics; Electronic Engineering; Energy Engineering; English; Environmental Engineering; Food Science; Health Sciences; History; Hotel and Restaurant; Industrial Design; Industrial Engineering; Information Sciences; International Business; Japanese; Korean; Law; Leisure Studies; Library Science; Literature; Materials Engineering; Mathematics; Mechanical Engineering; Parks and Recreation; Performing Arts; Physical Education; Physics; Preschool Education; Protective Services; Psychology; Public Administration; Safety Engineering; Social Studies; Social Welfare; Sports; Sports Management; Statistics; Structural Architecture; Taxation; Tourism; Town Planning; Transport Engineering; Visual Arts)

Student Services: Sports Facilities, Library, Residential Facilities

Periodicals: Journal of Industrial Business Problems, Kyonggi Magazine, Research Journals, Study on Tourism

Academic Staff 2012-2013	MALE	FEMALE	TOTAL
FULL-TIME			590
PART-TIME			c. 990
Student Numbers 2012-2013			
All (Foreign Included)			c. 16400

Last Update: 01-03-2018

Kyung Hee Cyber University (KHCU)

26 Kyunghee-daero, Dongdaemun-gu
Seoul 130-739
Tel: +82(2) 968-2233
Fax: +82(2) 3299-8529
Website: http://khcu.ac.kr/en/main.jsp
President: Inwon Choue

Faculty

Business Management (Accountancy; Business Administration; International Business; Management; Real Estate;

Taxation); **Hotel, Tourism and Restaurant** (Agriculture; Fishery; Hotel Management; Leisure Studies; Tourism); **Information, Culture and Arts** (Art Management; Design; Information Technology; Literature; Media Studies; Multimedia; Telecommunications Engineering; Writing); **International and Regional Studies** (American Studies; Asian Studies; Chinese; East Asian Studies; International Studies; Japanese; Korean); **Social Science** (Public Administration; Social Sciences; Social Welfare; Welfare and Protective Services)

Graduate School

Cultural Creation (Art Management; Cultural Studies; East Asian Studies; Government; Korean; Leadership; Literature; Media Studies; Writing); **Hotel Tourism** (Hotel Management; Tourism)

History: Founded 2001.

Main language(s) of instruction: Korean

Accrediting agency: Ministry of Education

Degrees and diplomas: Bachelor's Degree (Accountancy; Agriculture; American Studies; Art Management; Asian Studies; Business Administration; Chinese; Design; East Asian Studies; Fishery; Hotel Management; Information Technology; International Business; International Studies; Japanese; Korean; Leisure Studies; Literature; Management; Media Studies; Multimedia; Public Administration; Real Estate; Social Sciences; Social Welfare; Taxation; Telecommunications Engineering; Tourism; Welfare and Protective Services; Writing), Master's Degree (Art Management; Cultural Studies; East Asian Studies; Government; Korean; Leadership; Literature; Media Studies; Writing). Also MBA in Hotel Management and Tourism

Last Update: 26-03-2018

Kyung Hee University (KHU)

26, Kyungheedae-ro Dongdaemoon-gu
Seoul 02447
Tel: +82(2) 961-0114, +82(2) 961-0031, +82(2) 961-0032
Fax: +82(2) 962-4343
Website: http://www.khu.ac.kr
President: Inwon Choue
Tel: +82(2) 961-0005

College

Applied Sciences (Applied Chemistry; Applied Mathematics; Applied Physics; Astronomy and Space Science); **Arts and Design** (*Global*) (Acting; Cinema and Television; Computer Graphics; Dance; Fashion Design; Film; Graphic Design; Industrial Design; Landscape Architecture; Textile Design); **Dentistry** (Dental Hygiene; Dental Technology; Dentistry; Oral Pathology; Orthodontics; Periodontics);

Electronics and Information (Biomedical Engineering; Computer Engineering; Electronic Engineering; Information Technology; Telecommunications Engineering); **Engineering** (Architecture; Chemical Engineering; Civil Engineering; Electronic Engineering; Environmental Engineering; Environmental Studies; Industrial Engineering; Materials Engineering; Mechanical Engineering; Nuclear Engineering; Structural Architecture); **Fine Arts** (Fine Arts; Painting and Drawing; Sculpture); **Foreign Language and Literature** (Chinese; English; English Studies; French; Japanese; Korean; Literature; Russian; Spanish); **Human Ecology** (Child Care and Development; Clothing and Sewing; Food Science; Home Economics; Interior Design; Nutrition); **Humanities** (Arts and Humanities; English; History; Korean; Linguistics; Literature; Philosophy; Translation and Interpretation); **International Studies** (International Studies); **Korean Medicine** (Traditional Eastern Medicine); **Law** (Administrative Law; Civil Law; Commercial Law; Comparative Law; Constitutional Law; Criminal Law; Fiscal Law; International Law; Labour Law; Law; Maritime Law; Public Administration; Public Law); **Life Sciences** (Biotechnology; Botany; Environmental Studies; Food Science; Genetics; Horticulture; Natural Resources; Traditional Eastern Medicine); **Management** (Accountancy; Management); **Medicine** (Anaesthesiology; Anatomy; Biochemistry; Biology; Biophysics; Cell Biology; Dermatology; Embryology and Reproduction Biology; Endocrinology; Gastroenterology; Genetics; Gynaecology and Obstetrics; Haematology; Health Administration; Histology; Immunology; Medical Parasitology; Medicine; Microbiology; Molecular Biology; Nephrology; Neurology; Nursing; Oncology; Ophthalmology; Otorhinolaryngology; Pathology; Pharmacology; Physiology; Plastic Surgery; Psychiatry and Mental Health; Radiology; Social and Preventive Medicine); **Music** (Music; Music Theory and Composition; Musical Instruments; Singing); **Nursing** (Nursing); **Pharmacy** (Alternative Medicine; Pharmacology; Pharmacy); **Physical Education** (Management; Physical Education; Sports; Sports Management; Sports Medicine); **Political Science and Economics** (Accountancy; Administration; American Studies; Banking; Business Administration; Business and Commerce; Communication Studies; Comparative Politics; Comparative Sociology; East Asian Studies; Econometrics; Economic and Finance Policy; Economic History; European Studies; Finance; Government; Health Administration; History of Societies; Human Resources; Industrial and Production Economics; Industrial Management; International Business; International Economics; International Relations; International Studies; Journalism; Labour and Industrial Relations; Management; Management Systems; Marketing; Political Sciences; Public Administration; Social Policy; Social Studies; Sociology; Taxation); **Science** (Applied Chemistry; Applied Mathematics; Applied Physics; Atomic and Molecular Physics; Biology; Botany; Cell Biology; Chemistry; Geography; Inorganic Chemistry; Mathematics; Microbiology; Molecular Biology; Natural Sciences; Nuclear Physics; Optics; Organic Chemistry; Physical Chemistry; Physics; Solid State Physics; Statistics; Thermal Physics; Virology; Zoology); **Tourism and Hotel Management** (Cooking and Catering; English; Hotel Management; Japanese; Tourism; Translation and Interpretation)

School
Dance (Dance); **East-West Medical Science** (Medicine); **Law** (Law)

Department/Division
Global Eminence (Business Administration; International Business; Management)

Graduate School
Art and Fusion Design (Design; Fine Arts); **Biotechnology** (Biotechnology); **Business** (Accountancy; Business Administration; Finance; Fiscal Law; International Economics; Management; Marketing; Retailing and Wholesaling; Taxation); **Dentistry** (Dentistry); **East-West Medicine** (Acupuncture; Health Administration; Immunology; Neurology; Nutrition; Oncology; Traditional Eastern Medicine); **Education** (Agricultural Education; Art Education; Business Education; Computer Education; Education; Educational Administration; Educational Psychology; Educational Technology; Ethics; Foreign Languages Education; Humanities and Social Science Education; Mathematics Education; Native Language Education; Preschool Education; Primary Education; Science Education); **Graduate Studies** (Accountancy; Agronomy; Architecture; Astronomy and Space Science; Biology; Ceramic Art; Chemical Engineering; Chemistry; Chinese; Civil Engineering; Clothing and Sewing; Computer Engineering; Dance; Economics; Electronic Engineering; English; Environmental Studies; Fine Arts; Food Science; Food Technology; Forestry; French; Genetics; Geography; History; Home Economics; Horticulture; Industrial Engineering; International Business; Japanese; Korean; Landscape Architecture; Law; Literature; Management; Mass Communication; Mathematics; Mechanical Engineering; Medicine; Music; Nuclear Engineering; Nursing; Nutrition; Pharmacy; Philosophy; Physics; Political Sciences; Public Administration; Sociology; Spanish; Textile Technology; Traditional Eastern Medicine); **International Legal Affairs** (Commercial Law; European Union Law; Fiscal Law; Insurance; International Law; Maritime Law); **Journalism and Mass Communication** (Communication Studies; Journalism; Mass Communication; Media Studies); **Medicine** (*Professional*) (Medicine); **Pan-Pacific International Studies** (Government; Information Technology; International Business; International Economics; Latin American

Studies; Marketing); **Peace Studies** (Comparative Politics; East Asian Studies; Peace and Disarmament; Social Welfare); **Physical Education** (Physical Education; Sports); **Public Policy and Civic Engagement** (Government; Health Administration; Public Administration; Social Welfare); **Technology Management** (Engineering Management); **Tourism** (Cooking and Catering; Hotel and Restaurant; Hotel Management; Leisure Studies; Tourism)

Further information: University and Dental Hospitals and Oriental Hospital. Also Global Campus in Yongin and Gwangneung Campus in Namyangju

History: Founded 1949 as Shin Hung College, acquired present status and title 1951. A private institution financially supported by private business interests, and consisting of three campuses: Seoul, Suwon, and Kwangnung.

Academic year: March to December (March-July; August-December)

Admission requirements: Graduation from high school and entrance examination

Main language(s) of instruction: Korean, English

Accrediting agency: Korean Council for University Education (KCUE)

Degrees and diplomas: Bachelor's Degree, Master's Degree (Accountancy; Architecture; Astronomy and Space Science; Biological and Life Sciences; Biology; Biomedical Engineering; Biomedicine; Biotechnology; Business Administration; Ceramic Art; Chemical Engineering; Chemistry; Child Care and Development; Chinese; Civil Engineering; Clothing and Sewing; Computer Engineering; Cooking and Catering; Dance; Dentistry; Economics; Education; Electronic Engineering; English; English Studies; Environmental Engineering; Environmental Studies; Family Studies; Fine Arts; Food Science; Food Technology; French; Geography; Health Administration; History; Horticulture; Hotel and Restaurant; Industrial Design; Industrial Engineering; Information Technology; Interior Design; International Business; Japanese; Journalism; Korean; Landscape Architecture; Law; Literature; Management; Mass Communication; Materials Engineering; Mathematics; Mechanical Engineering; Medicine; Molecular Biology; Music; Musical Instruments; Nanotechnology; Neurosciences; Nuclear Engineering; Nursing; Nutrition; Pharmacology; Pharmacy; Philosophy; Physical Education; Physics; Political Sciences; Polymer and Plastics Technology; Public Administration; Russian; Sociology; Spanish; Sports Management; Structural Architecture; Telecommunications Engineering; Textile Technology; Tourism; Traditional Eastern Medicine), Doctor's Degree (Accountancy; American Studies; Art History; Astronomy and Space Science; Biological and Life Sciences; Biomedical Engineering; Biomedicine; Biotechnology; Chemical Engineering; Chemistry; Child Care and Development; Chinese; Civil Engineering; Clothing and Sewing; Computer Engineering; Cooking and Catering; Dance; Dentistry; East

Asian Studies; Economics; Education; Electronic Engineering; English; English Studies; Environmental Engineering; Environmental Studies; Family Studies; Food Science; Food Technology; Geography; Health Administration; History; Horticulture; Hotel and Restaurant; Industrial Design; Industrial Engineering; Information Technology; Interior Design; International Business; Japanese; Journalism; Korean; Landscape Architecture; Law; Literature; Management; Mass Communication; Materials Engineering; Mathematics; Mechanical Engineering; Medical Technology; Medicine; Molecular Biology; Music; Nanotechnology; Neurosciences; Nuclear Engineering; Nursing; Nutrition; Pharmacology; Pharmacy; Philosophy; Physical Education; Physics; Political Sciences; Polymer and Plastics Technology; Public Administration; Russian; Sociology; Spanish; Structural Architecture; Telecommunications Engineering; Textile Technology; Tourism; Traditional Eastern Medicine). Also MBA; non-degree professional training programmes

Student Services: Academic Counselling, Social Counselling, Careers Guidance, Nursery Care, Cultural Activities, Sports Facilities, Language Laboratory, Health Services, Foreign Studies Centre, Library

Periodicals: College publications, Peace Forum, Research Institutes' magazines

Publishing house: Kyung Hee University Press

Student Numbers 2015-2016	MALE	FEMALE	TOTAL
All (Foreign Included)			35826

Last Update: 23-03-2018

Kyungbuk Foreign Language Techno College (KFLC)

220-1 Hyupsuk-li Namchum-Myun
Kyungsangbuk-do
Tel: +82(53) 810 -0100
Fax: +82(53) 810 -0139
Website: http://www.yflc.ac.kr

Department/Division

Airline Service (Service Trades; Tourism); **Chinese** (Chinese); **Dental Hygiene** (Dental Hygiene); **English** (English); **Hotel Culinary and Bakery** (Cooking and Catering; Hotel Management); **Japanese** (Japanese); **Medical Information System** (Information Technology); **Multi-images** (Advertising and Publicity; Computer Graphics; Graphic Arts; Video; Visual Arts); **Nursing** (Nursing); **Occupational Therapy** (Occupational Therapy); **Oriental Martial Arts** (Philosophy; Physical Education; Sports); **Police and Security** (Civil Security; Police Studies); **Preschool Education** (Preschool Education); **Public Health Administration** (Health

Administration; Public Administration); **Real Estate Finance Technology** (Finance; Real Estate; Technology); **Russian** (Russian); **Social Welfare** (Social Welfare); **Tourism** (Tourism); **Wedding Coordination**

Research Division

Computing Information Centre; **Culture and Tourism Education Centre**; **Inauguration Incubation Centre**; **International Languages**

History: Founded 1988. Acquired present status 2005. Formerly known as Youngnam Foreign Language College.

Main language(s) of instruction: Korean

Accrediting agency: Ministry of Education

Degrees and diplomas: Bachelor's Degree (Child Care and Development; Dental Hygiene; Energy Engineering; Health Administration; Japanese; Nursing; Nutrition; Occupational Therapy; Preschool Education; Real Estate; Russian; Social Welfare; Sports; Tourism; Welfare and Protective Services)

Last Update: 08-03-2018

Kyungdong University (KDUNIV)

46 4-gil, Bongpo
Goseong-si 219-705, 24764
Tel: +82(33) 639-0189
Fax: +82(33) 639-0303
Website: http://www.kyungdong.ac.kr
President: John Lee

Course/Programme

Architectural Engineering (Structural Architecture); **Architecture Design** (*Metropol Campus - Yangju*) (Architectural and Environmental Design; Architecture); **Business Administration** (Business Administration); **Business Administration** (*Taught in English*) (Business Administration); **Civil Engineering** (*Metropol Campus - Yangju*) (Civil Engineering; Construction Engineering); **Deep Ocean Water** (Marine Science and Oceanography); **Dental Hygiene** (*Medical Campus - Munmak*) (Dental Hygiene); **Design** (*Metropol Campus - Yangju*) (Design); **Early Childhood Education** (*Metropol Campus - Yangju*) (Preschool Education); **Emergency Medical Service** (Medicine); **Food Service Management** (Cooking and Catering; Management); **Hotel Cuisine** (Cooking and Catering; Hotel Management); **Hotel Management** (*Taught in English*) (Hotel Management); **Hotel Management** (Hotel Management); **Korean Language** (Korean); **Leisure and Resort** (Leisure Studies); **Medical Technology** (Medical Technology); **Nursing** (*Medical Campus - Munmak*) (Nursing); **Occupational Therapy** (Occupational Therapy); **Physical Education** (Physical Education); **Physical Therapy** (Physical Therapy); **Police Science** (Police Studies); **Public Administration** (Public Administration);

Secondary Special Education (Secondary Education; Special Education); **Smart Computing** (*Taught in English*) (Computer Science); **Social Welfare** (Social Welfare); **Sports Marketing** (*Metropol Campus - Yangju*) (Marketing; Sports Management); **Teaching Korean as a Foreign Language** (Foreign Languages Education); **Tourism Aviation Management** (Air Transport; Tourism); **Visual Optics** (Optics)

Further information: Also Metropol Campus (Yangju) and Medical Campus (WonjuMunmak)

History: Founded 1996.

Main language(s) of instruction: Korean, English

Accrediting agency: Korean Council for University Education (KCUE)

Degrees and diplomas: Bachelor's Degree (Air Transport; Architectural and Environmental Design; Business Administration; Civil Engineering; Computer Science; Cooking and Catering; Dental Hygiene; Design; Foreign Languages Education; Hotel Management; Leisure Studies; Marine Science and Oceanography; Marketing; Medical Technology; Medicine; Nursing; Occupational Therapy; Optics; Parks and Recreation; Physical Education; Physical Therapy; Police Studies; Preschool Education; Public Administration; Social Welfare; Special Education; Sports Management; Structural Architecture; Tourism)

Student Services: Sports Facilities, Residential Facilities

Academic Staff 2012-2013	MALE	FEMALE	TOTAL
FULL-TIME			110
PART-TIME			c. 50
Student Numbers 2012-2013			
All (Foreign Included)			c. 2550

Last Update: 08-03-2018

Kyungil University (KIU)

50, Gamasil-gil Hayang-eup
Gyeongsan-si 38428, Gyeongbuk-do
Tel: +82(53) 600-4000
Fax: +82(53) 600-4020
Website: http://www.kiu.ac.kr
President: Hyun Tae Chung

College

Arts and Sports (Cosmetology; Design; Fashion Design; Fine Arts; Industrial Design; Photography; Rehabilitation and Therapy; Sports; Video); **Engineering** (Architecture; Arts and Humanities; Chemical Engineering; Civil Engineering; Construction Engineering; Electrical Engineering; Engineering; Fire Science; Food Science; Food Technology; Medical Technology; Nutrition; Railway Engineering; Safety

Engineering; Structural Architecture; Surveying and Mapping; Transport Engineering); **Global Business** (Accountancy; Business Administration; English; Finance; International Business; International Economics; Modern Languages; Railway Transport; Taxation; Tourism); **IT Convergence** (Automotive Engineering; Computer Engineering; Electronic Engineering; Energy Engineering; Engineering Drawing and Design; Information Technology; Mechanical Engineering; Robotics; Safety Engineering); **Nursing and Public Health** (Medical Technology; Nursing; Psychotherapy; Public Health); **Social Science** (Arts and Humanities; Information Sciences; Library Science; Police Studies; Public Administration; Real Estate; Social Welfare; Welfare and Protective Services)

Graduate School

Graduate Studies (Arts and Humanities; Engineering; Fine Arts; Health Sciences; Social Sciences; Welfare and Protective Services); **Health Science and Welfare** (*Master only*) (Arts and Humanities; Engineering; Health Sciences; Social Sciences; Welfare and Protective Services); **Industrial Management** (*Master only*) (Arts and Humanities; Engineering; Fine Arts; Industrial Management; Social Sciences)

Further information: 18 Research Centres

History: Founded 1963 as Kyungpook San Up University. Acquired present title 1997.

Academic year: March to December

Admission requirements: SAT, Grade Point average of high school, and entrance examination

Fees: c. 2,500-3,000 (US Dollar)

Main language(s) of instruction: Korean, English, Chinese

Accrediting agency: Ministry of Education, Science and Technology; Korean Council for University Education (KCUE)

Degrees and diplomas: Bachelor's Degree, Master's Degree (Accountancy; Business Administration; Chemical Engineering; Civil Engineering; Computer Engineering; Cosmetology; Design; Economics; Electrical Engineering; Electronic Engineering; Energy Engineering; Fashion Design; Finance; Fire Science; Food Science; Handicrafts; Industrial Design; Mechanical Engineering; Medical Technology; Photography; Police Studies; Protective Services; Psychology; Public Administration; Railway Engineering; Real Estate; Robotics; Safety Engineering; Social Welfare; Sports Management; Structural Architecture; Surveying and Mapping; Taxation; Welfare and Protective Services; Writing), Doctor's Degree (Accountancy; Architecture; Business Administration; Chemical Engineering; Civil Engineering; Computer Engineering; Cosmetology; Design; Economics; Electrical Engineering; Electronic Engineering; Energy Engineering; Fashion Design; Finance; Fire Science; Food Science; Industrial Design; Mechanical Engineering; Photography; Police Studies; Protective Services; Psychology; Public

Administration; Real Estate; Robotics; Social Welfare; Sports Management; Surveying and Mapping; Taxation)

Student Services: Academic Counselling, Careers Guidance, Sports Facilities, Language Laboratory, Facilities for disabled people, Health Services, Canteen, Foreign Studies Centre, Library, Residential Facilities

Academic Staff 2012-2013	MALE	FEMALE	TOTAL
FULL-TIME			140
PART-TIME			c. 80
Student Numbers 2012-2013			
All (Foreign Included)			c. 8700

Last Update: 01-03-2018

Kyungnam University (KU)

7 Kyungnamdaehak-ro Masanhappo-gu
Changwon-si 51767, Gyeongsangnam-do
Tel: +82(55) 245-5000
Fax: +82(55) 246-6184
Website: http://www.kyungnam.ac.kr
President: Jae-Kyu Park

College

Economics and Commerce (Business Administration; Business and Commerce; E- Business/Commerce; Economics; Finance; International Business; Tourism); **Education** (Art Education; Education; Foreign Languages Education; Home Economics Education; Mathematics Education; Music Education; Native Language Education; Physical Education; Preschool Education; Science Education); **Engineering** (Architecture; Civil Engineering; Computer Engineering; Computer Science; Electrical Engineering; Electronic Engineering; Engineering; Environmental Engineering; Fire Science; Information Technology; Marine Engineering; Mechanical Engineering; Nanotechnology; Naval Architecture; Safety Engineering; Telecommunications Engineering); **Law and Political Science** (International Relations; Journalism; Law; Mass Communication; Military Science; Police Studies; Political Sciences; Protective Services; Public Administration; Secretarial Studies); **Liberal Arts** (Arts and Humanities; Chinese; Cultural Studies; English; History; Korean; Literature; Philosophy; Psychology; Social Welfare; Sociology); **Natural Sciences** (Biotechnology; Clothing and Sewing; Fashion Design; Food Science; Industrial Design; Natural Sciences; Nursing; Nutrition; Physical Therapy; Sports)

Graduate School

Business Administration (Business Administration; Finance; Management); **Education** (Education; Secondary Education; Teacher Training); **Engineering** (Engineering); **Graduate**

Studies (Southeast Asian Studies); **North Korean Studies** (East Asian Studies); **Public Administration** (International Relations; Law; Police Studies; Political Sciences; Protective Services; Public Administration; Real Estate; Safety Engineering; Social Welfare; Sports; Welfare and Protective Services)

Campus

Seoul (Cultural Studies; East Asian Studies; Economics; Information Technology; Journalism; Military Science; Political Sciences; Protective Services; Sociology)

History: Founded 1946 as Kookmin College. Successively renamed Haein College 1952, Masan College 1954 and Kyungnam College 1971. Acquired present status and title 1981.

Academic year: March to February (March-August; September-February)

Admission requirements: Graduation from high school and entrance examination

Main language(s) of instruction: Korean

Accrediting agency: Korean Council for University Education (KCUE)

Degrees and diplomas: Bachelor's Degree, Master's Degree (Arts and Humanities; Business Administration; Business Education; Civil Engineering; Computer Engineering; Continuing Education; Cultural Studies; Curriculum; East Asian Studies; Economics; Education; Educational and Student Counselling; Electrical Engineering; Electronic Engineering; Engineering; Ethics; Fine Arts; Food Science; Foreign Languages Education; Health Sciences; Humanities and Social Science Education; Industrial Engineering; Information Technology; International Relations; Journalism; Law; Management; Marine Engineering; Materials Engineering; Mathematics Education; Mechanical Engineering; Military Science; Naval Architecture; Police Studies; Political Sciences; Preschool Education; Protective Services; Public Administration; Real Estate; Robotics; Safety Engineering; Secondary Education; Social Welfare; Sociology; Sports; Structural Architecture; Telecommunications Engineering), Doctor's Degree (Cultural Studies; East Asian Studies; Economics; Information Technology; Journalism; Military Science; Political Sciences; Protective Services; Sociology)

Student Services: Academic Counselling, Social Counselling, Careers Guidance, Sports Facilities, Language Laboratory, Facilities for disabled people, Health Services, Canteen, IT Centre, Residential Facilities

Publishing house: University Printing Department

Academic Staff 2013-2014	MALE	FEMALE	TOTAL
FULL-TIME			c. 470
Student Numbers 2013-2014			
All (Foreign Included)			c. 14000

Last Update: 01-03-2018

Kyungsung University

309, Suyeong-ro Nam-gu
Busan 48434, Daeyeon-dong
Tel: +82(51) 663-4119, +82(21) 532-7971
Fax: +82(51) 663-4089, +82(21) 532-7972
Website: http://ks.ac.kr
President: Soo-Geun Song

College

Arts (Dance; Design; Fine Arts; Health Sciences; Music; Physical Education; Sports; Sports Medicine); **Chinese Studies** (Business and Commerce; Chinese; Literature; Translation and Interpretation); **Commerce and Economics** (Business Administration; Business and Commerce; Economics; Finance; Food Technology; Hotel and Restaurant; Information Management; Information Technology; International Business; Management; Tourism; Transport Management); **Engineering** (Architectural and Environmental Design; Architecture; Biotechnology; Civil Engineering; Computer Engineering; Computer Science; Electrical Engineering; Electronic Engineering; Engineering; Engineering Management; Environmental Engineering; Food Science; Industrial Engineering; Information Technology; Materials Engineering; Telecommunications Engineering; Town Planning); **Law and Political Science** (Law; Political Sciences; Public Administration; Social Welfare); **Liberal Arts** (Arts and Humanities; Chinese; Education; English; Ethics; French; French Studies; German; Germanic Studies; History; Information Sciences; Japanese; Korean; Library Science; Literature; Philosophy; Preschool Education); **Multimedia** (Advertising and Publicity; Communication Arts; Computer Graphics; Design; Film; Graphic Design; Industrial Design; Interior Design; Mass Communication; Media Studies; Multimedia; Photography; Public Relations; Theatre; Visual Arts); **Pharmacy** (Pharmacy); **Science** (Biology; Chemistry; Fashion Design; Health Sciences; Marketing; Mathematics; Natural Sciences; Nutrition; Physical Therapy; Physics; Statistics); **Theology** (Theology)

Graduate School

Clinical Pharmacy (Pharmacology; Pharmacy); **Digital Design** (*Professional*) (Design; Information Technology; Multimedia); **Education** (Education); **Graduate Studies** (Accountancy; Biological and Life Sciences; Biology; Biotechnology; Business Administration; Chemistry; Chinese; Christian Religious Studies; Civil Engineering; Computer Engineering; Computer Science; Cultural Studies; Dance; East Asian Studies; Economics; Education; Electrical Engineering; Electronic Engineering; English; Environmental Engineering; Fashion Design; Film; Fine Arts; Food Science; History; Home Economics; Hotel Management; Industrial Engineering; Information Management;

Information Sciences; Information Technology; International Business; International Relations; Japanese; Korean; Law; Library Science; Literature; Marketing; Mass Communication; Materials Engineering; Mathematics; Mechanical Engineering; Meteorology; Music; Optical Technology; Pharmacy; Philosophy; Physical Education; Physics; Political Sciences; Preschool Education; Public Administration; Religious Music; Social Welfare; Theatre; Theology; Tourism; Town Planning); **International Business** (International Business; Management); **Multimedia** (Multimedia); **Social Welfare** (Social Welfare)

Further information: Also 7 Reseach Institutes

History: Founded 1955 as Kyungnam Teacher's College and established. Reorganized and renamed Pusan Industrial University 1979. Acquired present status 1983 and present title 1988.

Main language(s) of instruction: Korean, English

Accrediting agency: Korean Council for University Education (KCUE)

Degrees and diplomas: Bachelor's Degree, Master's Degree (Accountancy; Advertising and Publicity; Biology; Biotechnology; Business Administration; Chemistry; Chinese; Christian Religious Studies; Civil Engineering; Computer Engineering; Computer Science; Cultural Studies; Dance; East Asian Studies; Economics; Education; Electrical and Electronic Engineering; Electronic Engineering; Engineering Management; English; Environmental Engineering; Fashion Design; Film; Fine Arts; Food Science; Food Technology; History; Home Economics; Hotel Management; Industrial Engineering; Information Management; Information Sciences; Information Technology; International Business; International Relations; Japanese; Journalism; Korean; Law; Library Science; Literature; Management; Marketing; Mass Communication; Materials Engineering; Mathematics; Meteorology; Multimedia; Music; Optical Technology; Pharmacy; Philosophy; Physical Education; Physics; Political Sciences; Preschool Education; Public Administration; Radio and Television Broadcasting; Religious Music; Social Welfare; Telecommunications Engineering; Theatre; Theology; Tourism; Town Planning), Doctor's Degree (Accountancy; Advertising and Publicity; Analytical Chemistry; Biochemistry; Biology; Biotechnology; Business Administration; Child Care and Development; Chinese; Christian Religious Studies; Civil Engineering; Clothing and Sewing; Computer Engineering; Cultural Studies; East Asian Studies; Economics; Education; Electrical and Electronic Engineering; Electronic Engineering; Engineering Management; English; Environmental Engineering; Fashion Design; Finance; Food Science; Food Technology; Home Economics; Hotel Management; Industrial Engineering; Information Sciences; Information Technology; Inorganic Chemistry; International Business; International Economics; Journalism; Korean; Labour and Industrial Relations; Law; Library Science; Linguistics;

Literature; Management; Marketing; Music; Musicology; Optical Technology; Organic Chemistry; Pharmacy; Physical Chemistry; Physical Education; Physics; Preschool Education; Public Administration; Radio and Television Broadcasting; Real Estate; Service Trades; Social Welfare; Textile Design; Theology; Tourism; Town Planning; Welfare and Protective Services)

Student Services: Sports Facilities, Library, IT Centre, Residential Facilities

Academic Staff 2013-2014	MALE	FEMALE	TOTAL
FULL-TIME			c. 560
Student Numbers 2013-2014			
All (Foreign Included)			c. 13000

Last Update: 01-03-2018

Kyungwoon University

730, Gangdong-ro Sandong-myeon
Gumi-si 39160, Gyeongbuk-do
Tel: +82(54) 479-1114
Fax: +82(54) 479-1029
Website: http://www.kyungwoon.ac.kr
President: Hyang-ja Kim

College

Health and Welfare (Alternative Medicine; Child Care and Development; Dental Hygiene; Health Administration; Health Sciences; Nursing; Occupational Therapy; Optics; Pathology; Physical Therapy; Social Welfare; Tourism; Welfare and Protective Services); **IT and Multimedia** (Architecture; Computer Engineering; Electronic Engineering; Energy Engineering; Information Technology; Materials Engineering; Multimedia; Photography; Software Engineering; Structural Architecture; Telecommunications Engineering; Video)

School

Police Administration (Police Studies); **Protection Science** (Protective Services); **Sport for All** (Sports)

Department/Division

Flight Operation (Air Transport); **Military Science** (Military Science)

Graduate School

Graduate Studies (Dental Hygiene; Energy Engineering; Information Technology; Optics; Pathology; Physical Education; Physical Therapy; Police Studies); **Industry and Information** (Business Administration; Construction Engineering; Multimedia; Photography; Tourism; Video); **Social Welfare** (Social Welfare)

Further information: Also 9 Research Institutes
History: Founded 1997.
Main language(s) of instruction: Korean
Accrediting agency: Korean Council for University Education (KCUE)
Degrees and diplomas: Bachelor's Degree, Master's Degree (Dental Hygiene; Energy Engineering; Information Technology; Optics; Physical Education; Physical Therapy; Police Studies)
Student Services: Library, IT Centre, Residential Facilities

Academic Staff 2012-2013	MALE	FEMALE	TOTAL
FULL-TIME			180
PART-TIME			c. 140
Student Numbers 2012-2013			
All (Foreign Included)			c. 3720

Last Update: 02-03-2018

Luther University (LTU)

17 Sanggal-ri, Kiheung-eup
Yongin-si 17072, Gyeonggi-do
Tel: +82(31) 679-230, +82(31) 283-3593
Fax: +82(31) 283-1505
Website: http://www.ltu.ac.kr
President: Dae-Chul Kwon
Tel: +82(31) 679-2409

College
Counselling (Psychology); **Language Therapeutics** (Speech Therapy and Audiology); **Performing Arts** (Performing Arts); **Social Work** (Social Work); **Theology** (Theology)

Department/Division
English (English)

Graduate School
Language Therapeutics (Speech Therapy and Audiology); **Social Work** (Social Work); **Theology** (Theology)
History: Founded 1966. Acquired present status 1997.
Academic year: March to December (March-June; August-December)
Admission requirements: Graduation from high school
Fees: 3,15m. per semester (Won)
Main language(s) of instruction: Korean
Accrediting agency: Ministry of Education; Korean Council for University Education (KCUE)
Degrees and diplomas: Bachelor's Degree (English; Social Work; Speech Therapy and Audiology; Theology), Master's Degree (Social Work; Speech Therapy and Audiology; Theology)

Student Services: Academic Counselling, Social Counselling, Language Laboratory
Periodicals: Lutu Yunku (Luther Study), Shinhak Kwa Shinang (Theology and Faith)

Academic Staff 2012-2013	MALE	FEMALE	TOTAL
FULL-TIME			30
PART-TIME			20
Student Numbers 2012-2013			
All (Foreign Included)			c. 490

Last Update: 04-06-2018

Mokpo Catholic University

697 Youngsan-ro
Mokpo-si 58607, Jeollanam-do
Tel: +82(61) 280-5000
Fax: +82(61) 280-5109, +82(505) 914-3890
Website: http://www.mcu.ac.kr
President: Timothy Kim

College
Early Childhood Education (Preschool Education); **Nursing** (Nursing); **Social Welfare** (Social Welfare)
History: Founded 1966.
Main language(s) of instruction: Korean
Accrediting agency: Korean Council for University Education (KCUE)
Degrees and diplomas: Bachelor's Degree (Nursing; Preschool Education; Social Welfare)

Academic Staff 2012-2013	MALE	FEMALE	TOTAL
FULL-TIME			20
PART-TIME			16
Student Numbers 2012-2013			
All (Foreign Included)			c. 570

Last Update: 08-03-2018

Mokwon University

88 Doanbuk-ro Seo-gu
Daejeon 302-318, Chungnam-do
Tel: +82(42) 829-7114, +82(42) 825-7114
Fax: +82(42) 825-5022, +82(42) 825-8020
Website: http://www.mokwon.ac.kr
President: Nokwon Park

College
Arts and Design (Ceramic Art; Design; Fashion Design; Fine Arts; Graphic Design; Industrial Design; Painting and

Drawing; Religious Art; Sculpture; Textile Design; Visual Arts); **Education** (Art Education; Computer Education; Education; Foreign Languages Education; Mathematics Education; Music Education; Native Language Education; Preschool Education; Teacher Training); **Engineering** (Architecture; Automation and Control Engineering; Computer Engineering; Electronic Engineering; Engineering; Information Technology; Materials Engineering; Robotics; Telecommunications Engineering; Town Planning); **Humanities** (Arts and Humanities; Cultural Studies; French Studies; German; Germanic Studies; History; Korean; Literature; Social Welfare); **Music** (Jazz and Popular Music; Music; Music Theory and Composition; Musical Instruments; Singing); **Social Sciences** (Advertising and Publicity; Business Administration; Chinese; Economics; Finance; Insurance; International Business; Journalism; Law; Police Studies; Public Administration; Public Relations; Real Estate; Service Trades; Social Sciences); **Techno-Sciences** (Biochemistry; Biological and Life Sciences; Biomedicine; Cosmetology; Fire Science; Health Sciences; Marketing; Mathematics; Microbiology; Nanotechnology; Physical Education; Protective Services; Safety Engineering; Sports); **Theology** (Theology)

Department/Division
TV and Film (Cinema and Television; Film)

Graduate School
Graduate Studies (Arts and Humanities; Design; Engineering; Fine Arts; Mathematics and Computer Science; Natural Sciences; Performing Arts; Social Sciences); **Industrial Information, Journalism and Public Relations** (Advertising and Publicity; Business Administration; Computer Engineering; E- Business/Commerce; Electronic Engineering; Fire Science; Industrial Design; Information Sciences; Journalism; Marketing; Public Administration; Public Relations; Real Estate; Social Welfare; Sports; Structural Architecture; Telecommunications Engineering; Town Planning); **Theology** (Bible; Christian Religious Studies; Ethics; History of Religion; New Testament; Religious Education; Theology)

Further information: Also 10 Research Institutes

History: Founded 1954 as Seminary, acquired present status and title 1980.

Academic year: March to February (March-August; September-February)

Admission requirements: Graduation from high school or foreign equivalent, and entrance examination

Main language(s) of instruction: Korean

Accrediting agency: Korean Council for University Education (KCUE)

Degrees and diplomas: Bachelor's Degree, Master's Degree (Architecture; Biology; Business Administration; Chemistry; Computer Engineering; Cosmetology; Design; E- Business/

Commerce; Economics; Electronic Engineering; English; Fine Arts; Fire Science; German; Industrial Design; Information Technology; International Business; Korean; Law; Literature; Mathematics; Music; Public Administration; Real Estate; Religion; Social Welfare; Sports; Structural Architecture; Telecommunications Engineering; Theology; Town Planning), Doctor's Degree (Architecture; Biology; Business Administration; Computer Engineering; Electronic Engineering; English; Fine Arts; Information Technology; International Business; Korean; Literature; Multimedia; Public Administration; Real Estate; Social Welfare; Telecommunications Engineering; Theology)

Student Services: Facilities for disabled people, Library, Residential Facilities

Academic Staff 2012-2013	MALE	FEMALE	TOTAL
FULL-TIME			330
PART-TIME			c. 870
Student Numbers 2012-2013			
All (Foreign Included)			10000
Foreign only			200

Last Update: 02-03-2018

Myongji University

34 Geobukgol-ro Seodaemun-gu
Seoul 03674
Tel: +82(31) 330-6114, +82(2) 300-1511/5
Fax: +82(31) 332-2459
Website: http://www.mju.ac.kr
President: Byong-Jin You

College
Architecture (Architectural and Environmental Design; Architecture); **Arts and Physical Education** (Cultural Studies; Design; Fine Arts; Leisure Studies; Music; Physical Education; Sports); **Business Administration** (Business Administration; Information Sciences; International Business; Management; Real Estate); **Engineering** (Biotechnology; Chemical Engineering; Computer Engineering; Electrical Engineering; Electronic Engineering; Engineering; Environmental Engineering; Industrial Engineering; Materials Engineering; Mechanical Engineering; Telecommunications Engineering; Transport Engineering); **General Education** (*Bangmok*) (Arts and Humanities; Natural Sciences; Social Sciences; Teacher Training); **Humanities** (Arabic; Art History; Arts and Humanities; Chinese; English; History; Information Sciences; Japanese; Korean; Library Science; Literature; Philosophy; Writing); **Law** (Law); **Natural Science** (Biological and Life Sciences; Chemistry; Computer Science; Food Science; Mathematics; Natural

Sciences; Nutrition; Physics); **Social Science** (Child Care and Development; East Asian Studies; Economics; Education; International Relations; Leadership; Media Studies; Political Sciences; Public Administration; Social Sciences; Social Welfare)

Graduate School

Business (Business Administration); **Culture and Arts** (Cultural Studies; Fine Arts); **Distribution Logistics** (Transport Management); **Education** (Education); **Graduate Studies** (Arts and Humanities; Engineering; Fine Arts; Natural Sciences; Physical Education; Social Sciences); **Industry** (Engineering); **Real Estate** (Real Estate); **Records, Archiving and Information Science** (*Professional*) (Archiving; Information Sciences); **Social Studies** (Social Studies); **Social Work** (Social Welfare)

Further information: 21 Research Institutes and 9 Grant-Based Research Centres; Also Yongin Campus

History: Founded 1948 as a private Institution of Higher Education for Women, reorganized 1962 as Seoul Moon-Lee College of Business and Technology, and acquired present status 1983

Admission requirements: Graduation from high school or equivalent and entrance examination

Main language(s) of instruction: Korean

Accrediting agency: Korean Council for University Education (KCUE)

Degrees and diplomas: Bachelor's Degree, Master's Degree (Administration; Arabic; Architecture; Archiving; Art History; Bioengineering; Biological and Life Sciences; Business Administration; Chemical Engineering; Chemistry; Child Care and Development; Chinese; Civil Engineering; Computer Engineering; Cooking and Catering; Dance; Design; East Asian Studies; Economics; Education; Electrical Engineering; Electronic Engineering; Energy Engineering; English; Environmental Engineering; Film; Food Science; History; Industrial Engineering; Information Management; Information Sciences; International Business; International Relations; Japanese; Korean; Law; Leadership; Leisure Studies; Library Science; Literature; Materials Engineering; Mathematics; Mechanical Engineering; Media Studies; Music; Nanotechnology; Nutrition; Philosophy; Physical Education; Physics; Political Sciences; Preschool Education; Public Administration; Real Estate; Singing; Social Sciences; Social Welfare; Sports; Structural Architecture; Telecommunications Engineering; Town Planning; Transport Engineering; Writing), Doctor's Degree (Administration; Arabic; Architecture; Archiving; Art History; Biological and Life Sciences; Biotechnology; Business Administration; Chemical Engineering; Chemistry; Child Care and Development; Chinese; Civil Engineering; Computer Engineering; Design; East Asian Studies; Economics; Electrical Engineering; Electronic Engineering; Energy Engineering; English;

Environmental Engineering; Food Science; History; Industrial Engineering; Information Management; Information Sciences; Information Technology; International Business; International Relations; Japanese; Korean; Law; Leadership; Leisure Studies; Library Science; Literature; Materials Engineering; Mathematics; Mechanical Engineering; Media Studies; Nanotechnology; Nutrition; Philosophy; Physical Education; Physics; Political Sciences; Preschool Education; Public Administration; Sports; Structural Architecture; Telecommunications Engineering; Town Planning; Transport Engineering; Writing)

Student Services: Academic Counselling, Social Counselling, Sports Facilities, Health Services, Library, IT Centre, Residential Facilities

Academic Staff 2012-2013	MALE	FEMALE	TOTAL
FULL-TIME			540
PART-TIME			c. 420
Student Numbers 2012-2013			
All (Foreign Included)			c. 15000
Foreign only			600

Last Update: 24-05-2018

Nambu University

864-1 Wolgye-dong, Gwangsan-gu
Gwangju-si 62271, Gyeonggi-do
Tel: +86(62) 970-0001, +86(62) 970-0391
Fax: +86(62) 972-6200, +86(62) 970-0118, +86(62) 970-0399
Website: http://www.nambu.ac.kr
President: Sung-soo Cho
Tel: +82(62) 970-0011

Department/Division

Arts (Fine Arts; Leisure Studies; Music; Performing Arts; Sports); **Education** (Education; Preschool Education; Primary Education; Special Education); **Engineering** (Automotive Engineering; Engineering; Information Technology; Mechanical Engineering); **Health Sciences** (Alternative Medicine; Health Sciences; Medical Technology; Nursing; Pharmacology; Physical Therapy; Radiology; Speech Therapy and Audiology); **Humanities and Social Sciences** (Police Studies; Social Welfare); **Natural Sciences** (Cooking and Catering; Cosmetology; Food Science; Hotel and Restaurant; Natural Sciences; Nutrition)

Graduate School

Education (Arts and Humanities; Continuing Education; Education; Educational and Student Counselling; Home Economics Education; Natural Sciences; Preschool Education;

Science Education; Social Sciences; Special Education); **Graduate Studies** (Alternative Medicine; Arts and Humanities; Business Administration; Cooking and Catering; Cosmetology; Engineering; Information Sciences; Mechanical Engineering; Music; Natural Sciences; Police Studies; Radiology; Social Sciences; Social Work; Special Education; Sports); **Public Health** (Alternative Medicine; Business Administration; Korean; Management; Natural Sciences; Nursing; Physical Therapy; Public Health; Social Sciences; Speech Therapy and Audiology)

History: Founded 1998.

Fees: c. 4,000 per annum (Won)

Main language(s) of instruction: Korean, English

Accrediting agency: Korean Council for University Education (KCUE)

Degrees and diplomas: Bachelor's Degree, Master's Degree (Alternative Medicine; Continuing Education; Cooking and Catering; Cosmetology; Educational and Student Counselling; Home Economics Education; Hotel and Restaurant; Information Sciences; Korean; Management; Mechanical Engineering; Music; Nursing; Pharmacology; Physical Therapy; Police Studies; Preschool Education; Radiology; Social Work; Special Education; Speech Therapy and Audiology; Sports), Doctor's Degree (Alternative Medicine; Cooking and Catering; Hotel and Restaurant; Social Work; Special Education)

Student Services: Academic Counselling, Social Counselling, Careers Guidance, Sports Facilities, Language Laboratory, Health Services, Foreign Studies Centre

Academic Staff 2012-2013	MALE	FEMALE	TOTAL
FULL-TIME			24
PART-TIME			196
Student Numbers 2012-2013			
All (Foreign Included)			c. 3430

Last Update: 02-03-2018

Namseoul University (NSU)

91 Daehak-ro Seonghwan-eup Sebuk-gu
Cheonan-si 31020, Chungcheongnam-do
Tel: +82(41) 580-2000
Fax: +82(41) 582-2117
Website: http://www.nsu.ac.kr
President: Chung-ja Kong

Course/Programme

Korean Language and Culture (East Asian Studies; Korean)

School

Business and Management (Advertising and Publicity; Business Administration; Business and Commerce; Hotel Management; International Business; Management; Marketing; Public Relations; Real Estate; Taxation; Tourism); **Design and Sports** (Architectural and Environmental Design; Computer Graphics; Design; Graphic Design; Health Sciences; Sports; Sports Management; Visual Arts); **Engineering** (Architecture; Computer Science; Electronic Engineering; Engineering; Engineering Management; Industrial Engineering; Information Technology; Multimedia; Structural Architecture; Surveying and Mapping; Telecommunications Engineering); **Health and Medicine** (Biomedicine; Dental Hygiene; Health Administration; Health Sciences; Laboratory Techniques; Medicine; Nursing; Physical Therapy); **Humanities and Social Sciences** (Arts and Humanities; Child Care and Development; Chinese; English; Japanese; Social Sciences; Social Welfare; Welfare and Protective Services)

Department/Division

General Education (Arts and Humanities; Information Technology)

Graduate School

Graduate Studies (Architecture; Behavioural Sciences; Business Administration; Child Care and Development; Glass Art; Hotel Management; Information Technology; Rehabilitation and Therapy; Sports Management; Tourism)

Further information: Also Seoul Campus

History: Founded 1994.

Academic year: March to December (March-June; August-December)

Admission requirements: Graduation from high school

Main language(s) of instruction: Korean, English, Japanese, Chinese

Accrediting agency: Korean Council for University Education (KCUE)

Degrees and diplomas: Bachelor's Degree, Master's Degree (Architecture; Business Administration; Child Care and Development; Glass Art; Hotel Management; Information Technology; Sports Management; Tourism)

Student Services: Sports Facilities, Health Services, Library, Residential Facilities

Periodicals: Namseoul Journal

Academic Staff 2013-2014	MALE	FEMALE	TOTAL
FULL-TIME			c. 310
Student Numbers 2013-2014			
All (Foreign Included)			c. 13000
Foreign only			419

Last Update: 02-03-2018

Open Cyber University of Korea (OCU)

C-9F, 353, Mangu-ro Jungnang-gu
Seoul 02087
Tel: +82(2) 2197-4200
Fax: +82(2) 2197-4114
Website: http://en.ocu.ac.kr
President: Il-hong Jang

College

Humanities and Social Sciences (Art Therapy; Business Administration; English; Finance; Management; Police Studies; Protective Services; Psychology; Real Estate; Social Welfare); **Natural Sciences and Arts** (Business Administration; Computer Science; Cosmetology; Design; Fire Science; Information Sciences; Jewellery Art; Multimedia)
History: Founded 2001.
Main language(s) of instruction: English
Accrediting agency: Ministry of Education
Degrees and diplomas: Bachelor's Degree (Chinese; Computer Graphics; Design; English; Japanese; Law; Multimedia; Social Welfare; Writing)
Last Update: 12-03-2018

Pai Chai University (PCU)

155-40 Baejae-ro(Doma-Dong), Seo-Gu
Daejeon 35345, Chungnam-do
Tel: +82(42) 520-5243, +82(42) 520-5454
Fax: +82(42) 520-5799
Website: http://www.pcu.ac.kr
President: Young-Ho Kim

College

Appenzeller (Biological and Life Sciences; Biology; Biomedicine; Biotechnology; Civil Engineering; Computer Engineering; Computer Science; Electrical Engineering; Electronic Engineering; Environmental Engineering; Forestry; Horticulture; Information Technology; Materials Engineering; Mathematics; Nanotechnology; Nursing; Pharmacology; Polymer and Plastics Technology; Robotics; Software Engineering; Technology; Telecommunications Engineering; Transport Engineering); **Howard** (Asian Studies; Business Administration; Chinese; English; Gerontology; Home Economics Education; Japanese; Korean; Latin American Studies; Literature; Modern Languages; Preschool Education; Psychology; Spanish; Theology; Welfare and Protective Services); **Ju Si-Gyeong Liberal Education** (Education; Humanities and Social Science Education; International and Comparative Education); **Kim So-wol** (Advertising and Publicity; Air Transport; Architecture; Clothing and Sewing; Design; Film; Fine Arts; Food Science; Hotel Management; Landscape Architecture; Leisure Studies; Media Studies; Music; Musical Instruments; Photography; Textile Technology; Theatre; Tourism; Visual Arts); **Seo Jae-pil** (Business Administration; Business Computing; E-Business/Commerce; International Business; Law; Public Administration; Social Sciences; Transport Management)

Centre

Continuing Education; **Education for Child Care Teachers** (Child Care and Development); **Kindergarten**; **Korean Language** (Korean); **Teacher Training** (Teacher Training)

Graduate School

Graduate Studies (Administration; Art Management; Business and Commerce; Education; Hotel Management; International Business; Law; Tourism)

Research Division

Children's Foodservice Management (Child Care and Development); **Comparative Legal Studies**; **Daejeon Senior**; **Early Childhood Education** (Preschool Education); **Engineering** (Engineering); **Family Support** (Social Problems); **Gyeryong Children's Food Service Management** (Food Science); **Humanities** (Humanities and Social Science Education); **Innopolis Campus Project Organization** (North African Studies); **International Community**; **Ju Si-Gyeong Liberal Education** (Arts and Humanities); **Korean-Siberian** (Cultural Studies); **Life Sciences** (Biological and Life Sciences); **Local Developing Festival** (Development Studies); **Multicultural Education** (Bilingual and Bicultural Education); **Natural Sciences** (Natural Sciences); **Railroad Infrastructure** (Railway Transport); **Regional Technology Innovation for Biomedical Resources** (*Centre*) (Biomedicine); **Seo-bu Youth Sex Culture** (Sociology); **Small and Medium-sized Enterprises Support** (Small Business); **Social Sciences** (Social Sciences); **Unification** (Peace and Disarmament); **Work Study Program Managing System Education and Research**

Campus

Daeduk Valley (Biological and Life Sciences; Biomedicine; Biotechnology; Computer Engineering; Materials Engineering)
History: Founded 1885 as School, became Junior College 1978 and acquired present status and title 1980. A private Institution under the supervision of the Ministry of Education.
Academic year: March to February (March-August; September-February)
Admission requirements: Graduation from high school and entrance examination (KSAT)

Fees: 2.5m. per semester (Won)
Main language(s) of instruction: Korean
Accrediting agency: Korean Council for University Education (KCUE)
Degrees and diplomas: Bachelor's Degree, Master's Degree (Architecture; Art Management; Biochemistry; Bioengineering; Biological and Life Sciences; Biology; Business Administration; Business and Commerce; Chemistry; Civil Engineering; Clothing and Sewing; Computer Engineering; E- Business/Commerce; East Asian Studies; Electronic Engineering; English; Environmental Engineering; Fine Arts; Foreign Languages Education; Heritage Preservation; Horticulture; Humanities and Social Science Education; Information Technology; International Business; Japanese; Justice Administration; Korean; Landscape Architecture; Law; Leisure Studies; Literature; Materials Engineering; Mathematics; Multimedia; Music; Native Language Education; Physics; Preschool Education; Private Law; Public Administration; Sports; Telecommunications Engineering; Textile Technology; Theology; Tourism; Transport Engineering; Welfare and Protective Services), Doctor's Degree (Asian Studies; Biochemistry; Bioengineering; Biology; Business Administration; Business and Commerce; Chemistry; Civil Engineering; Clothing and Sewing; Computer Engineering; E- Business/Commerce; Electronic Engineering; English; Environmental Engineering; Foreign Languages Education; Horticulture; Information Technology; International Business; Japanese; Korean; Landscape Architecture; Law; Leisure Studies; Literature; Materials Engineering; Multimedia; Physics; Preschool Education; Public Administration; Sports; Telecommunications Engineering; Textile Technology; Theology; Tourism; Transport Engineering; Welfare and Protective Services)
Student Services: Academic Counselling, Social Counselling, Careers Guidance, Nursery Care, Cultural Activities, Sports Facilities, Language Laboratory, Facilities for disabled people, Health Services, Canteen, Foreign Studies Centre
Publishing house: Pai Chai University Press

Student Numbers 2015-2016	MALE	FEMALE	TOTAL
All (Foreign Included)			13000
Foreign only			850

Last Update: 02-03-2018

Pohang University of Science and Technology (POSTECH)

77 Cheongam-Ro Nam-Gu
Pohang-si 37673, Gyeongbuk
Tel: +82(54) 279-0114
Fax: +82(54) 279-2099

Website: http://www.postech.ac.kr
President: Doh-Yeon Kim

Department/Division
Chemical Engineering (Chemical Engineering); **Chemistry** (Chemistry); **Computer Science and Engineering** (Computer Science; Engineering); **Creative IT Engineering** (Computer Engineering; Information Technology); **Electrical Engineering** (Electrical Engineering); **Humanities and Social Sciences** (Arts and Humanities; Social Sciences); **Industrial and Mangement Engineering** (Industrial Engineering; Industrial Management); **Life Sciences** (Biological and Life Sciences); **Materials Science and Engineering** (Materials Engineering); **Mathematics** (Mathematics); **Mechanical Engineering** (Mechanical Engineering); **Physics** (Physics)

Graduate School
Advanced Materials Science (AMS) (Materials Engineering); **Advanced Nuclear Engineering** (Nuclear Engineering); **Chemical Engineering** (Chemical Engineering); **Chemistry** (Chemistry); **Computer Science and Engineering** (Computer Engineering; Computer Science); **Creative IT Engineering (CiTE)** (Computer Engineering; Information Technology); **Electrical Engineering** (Electrical Engineering); **Engineering Mastership** (Engineering); **Environmental Science and Engineering** (Environmental Engineering; Environmental Studies); **Ferrous Technology** (Metal Techniques; Metallurgical Engineering); **Industrial and Management Engineering** (Engineering Management; Industrial Engineering); **Information Technology** (Information Sciences; Information Technology); **Integrative Biosciences and Biotechnology (IBB)** (Biological and Life Sciences; Biotechnology); **Interdisciplinary Bioscience and Bioengineering** (Bioengineering; Biological and Life Sciences); **IT Convergence Engineering (ITCE)** (Computer Engineering; Information Technology); **Life Sciences** (Biological and Life Sciences); **Materials Science and Engineering** (Materials Engineering); **Mathematics** (Mathematics); **Mechanical Engineering** (Mechanical Engineering); **Physics** (Physics); **POSTECH Ocean Science and Technology Institute (POSTI)** (Marine Engineering; Marine Science and Oceanography); **Technology Innovation and Management (TIM)** (Engineering Management; Technology); **Wind Energy (GWE)** (Energy Engineering)
Further information: Also 82 Research Centres and 163 Laboratories
History: Founded 1986 by POSCO.
Academic year: March to December (March-June; August-December)
Admission requirements: Graduation from high school or equivalent, and competitive entrance examination
Main language(s) of instruction: Korean, English

Accrediting agency: Ministry of Education
Degrees and diplomas: Bachelor's Degree, Master's Degree (Bioengineering; Biological and Life Sciences; Biotechnology; Chemical Engineering; Chemistry; Computer Engineering; Computer Science; Electrical Engineering; Energy Engineering; Engineering; Engineering Management; Environmental Engineering; Environmental Studies; Industrial Engineering; Information Technology; Marine Engineering; Marine Science and Oceanography; Materials Engineering; Mathematics; Mechanical Engineering; Metallurgical Engineering; Nuclear Engineering; Physics), Doctor's Degree (Bioengineering; Biological and Life Sciences; Biotechnology; Chemical Engineering; Chemistry; Computer Engineering; Computer Science; Electrical Engineering; Energy Engineering; Engineering; Engineering Management; Environmental Engineering; Environmental Studies; Industrial Engineering; Information Technology; Marine Engineering; Marine Science and Oceanography; Materials Engineering; Mathematics; Mechanical Engineering; Metallurgical Engineering; Nuclear Engineering; Physics)
Student Services: Library

Academic Staff 2013-2014	MALE	FEMALE	TOTAL
FULL-TIME			c. 430
Student Numbers 2013-2014			
All (Foreign Included)			c. 3425

Last Update: 02-03-2018

Presbyterian University and Theological Seminary

25-1 Gwangjangro 5-gil Gwangjin-gu
Seoul 04965
Tel: +82(2) 450-0700, +82(2) 450-0895
Fax: +82(2) 452-3460
Website: http://www.puts.ac.kr
President: Sung Bihn Yim

Faculty

Theology (Music; Religious Education; Religious Music; Theology)
History: Created 1993.
Main language(s) of instruction: Korean
Accrediting agency: Korean Council for University Education (KCUE)
Degrees and diplomas: Bachelor's Degree (Music; Religious Education; Theology), Master's Degree (Religious Education; Religious Music; Theology), Doctor's Degree (Theology)

Academic Staff 2012-2013	MALE	FEMALE	TOTAL
FULL-TIME			13
PART-TIME			15
Student Numbers 2012-2013			
All (Foreign Included)			c. 170

Last Update: 02-03-2018

Pyeongtaek University (PTU)

111 Yongyi-dong
Pyongtaek-si 450-701, Gyeonggi-do
Tel: +82(31) 659-8114
Fax: +82(31) 659-8011
Website: http://www.ptuniv.ac.kr
President: Jong-Keun You
Tel: +82(31) 658-3121

Course/Programme

Major in Multicultural Family Welfare (*Interdisciplinary*) (Family Studies; Welfare and Protective Services)

Department/Division

Advertising and Public Relations (Advertising and Publicity; Public Relations); **American Studies** (American Studies); **Broadcasting and Entertainment** (Radio and Television Broadcasting); **Business Administration** (Business Administration); **Child and Youth Welfare** (Child Care and Development; Welfare and Protective Services); **Chinese Studies** (Asian Studies; Chinese); **Computer Science** (Computer Engineering; Computer Science; Software Engineering); **Digital Information and Statistics** (Data Processing; Information Sciences; Statistics); **Digital Media and Motion Design** (Film; Media Studies); **Fashion Design and Branding** (Business Administration; Fashion Design); **General Education** (Computer Science; English; Physical Education; Protective Services); **Information and Communication** (Information Technology; Telecommunications Engineering; Telecommunications Services); **Integrated Environmental Systems** (Environmental Studies; Information Technology); **International Trade and Logistics** (International Business; Transport Management); **Japanese Studies** (East Asian Studies; Japanese); **Korean Language and Literature** (Korean; Literature); **Music** (Music); **Nursing** (Health Sciences; Nursing); **Practical Music** (Music); **Public Administration** (Public Administration); **Rehabilitation Welfare** (Rehabilitation and Therapy); **Social Welfare** (Social Welfare; Social Work); **Theology** (Theology); **Urban and Real Estate Development** (Real Estate; Town Planning); **Visual Design** (Graphic Design)

Graduate School

Counseling (Art Therapy; Educational and Student Counselling; Family Studies; Pastoral Studies; Psychology); **Education** (Education; Educational and Student Counselling; Foreign Languages Education); **Graduate Studies** (Child Care and Development; Social Welfare); **Logistics and Information** (Business Administration; Communication Studies; Computer Science; Information Sciences; Information Technology; International Business; Real Estate; Transport Management); **Pierson School of Theology** (Christian Religious Studies; Theology); **Social Welfare** (Art Therapy; Christian Religious Studies; Leisure Studies; Rehabilitation and Therapy; Social Work; Welfare and Protective Services)

Further information: Also Graduate Schools

History: Founded 1912 as Union Pierson Memorial Bible Institute. Acquired present name and status 1996.

Fees: c. 3,700 per semester (US Dollar)

Main language(s) of instruction: Korean

Accrediting agency: Ministry of Education; Korean Council for University Education (KCUE)

Degrees and diplomas: Bachelor's Degree, Master's Degree (Art Therapy; Arts and Humanities; Bible; Business Administration; Child Care and Development; Christian Religious Studies; Communication Studies; Computer Science; Educational and Student Counselling; Family Studies; Foreign Languages Education; Information Sciences; International Business; Leisure Studies; Pastoral Studies; Real Estate; Rehabilitation and Therapy; Religion; Social Welfare; Social Work; Theology; Transport Management), Doctor's Degree (Philosophy; Theology)

Student Services: Health Services, Library, Residential Facilities

Academic Staff 2012-2013	MALE	FEMALE	TOTAL
FULL-TIME			145
PART-TIME			c. 95
Student Numbers 2012-2013			
All (Foreign Included)			c. 4159
Foreign only			128

Last Update: 02-03-2018

Sahmyook University

815, Hwarang-ro Nowon-gu
Seoul 01795
Tel: +82(2) 3399-3636
Fax: +82(2) 979-5318
Website: http://www.syu.ac.kr
President: Sung Ik Kim

College

Culture and Arts (Architectural and Environmental Design; Art Management; Art Therapy; Communication Arts; Construction Engineering; Design; Fine Arts; Graphic Design; Handicrafts; Music; Music Theory and Composition; Musical Instruments; Singing; Visual Arts); **Health Science and Social Welfare** (Food Science; Health Administration; Health Sciences; Leisure Studies; Nursing; Nutrition; Physical Therapy; Psychology; Social Welfare; Sports); **Humanities and Social Science** (Asian Studies; Business Administration; Chinese; Computer Engineering; Computer Science; English; English Studies; Information Sciences; Information Technology; Japanese; Preschool Education); **Pharmacy** (Chemistry; Dentistry; Medicine; Microbiology; Pathology; Pharmacology; Pharmacy; Physics; Physiology); **Science and Technology** (Animal Husbandry; Automotive Engineering; Biological and Life Sciences; Biotechnology; Chemistry; Computer Engineering; Computer Science; Electronic Engineering; Horticulture; Natural Sciences; Software Engineering; Zoology); **Theology** (Theology)

School

Business (*Graduate*) (Business Administration; Educational Administration; Health Administration; Management; Private Administration; Public Administration; Small Business)

Graduate School

General Graduate Studies (Energy Engineering; Environmental Studies; Health Sciences; Music; Nursing; Pharmacy; Physical Therapy; Preschool Education; Psychology; Social Welfare; Theology); **Health and Welfare** (Health Sciences; Nursing; Social Welfare; Welfare and Protective Services); **Theology** (Religion; Theology)

History: Founded 1906 as Seventh-day Adventist Denominational Training School, became College 1961 and University 1985. Graduate School established 1981, and Theological Seminary 1990.

Academic year: March to February (March-July; August-February)

Admission requirements: Graduation from high school and entrance examination

Fees: Application fee, for overseas and International Students, 120,000 won (North Korean, 70,000) (Won)

Main language(s) of instruction: Korean

Accrediting agency: Korean Council for University Education (KCUE)

Degrees and diplomas: Bachelor's Degree, Master's Degree (Business Administration; Energy Engineering; Environmental Studies; Health Sciences; Music; Nursing; Pharmacology; Pharmacy; Physical Therapy; Psychology; Social Welfare; Theology), Doctor's Degree (Health Sciences; Nursing; Pharmacology; Physical Therapy; Religion; Theology). Also junior college Diplomas, 2-3 yrs

Student Services: Sports Facilities, Health Services, Canteen, IT Centre, Residential Facilities

Periodicals: Korean Sahmyook University Journal, Sahmyook Hag Bo

Academic Staff 2013-2014	MALE	FEMALE	TOTAL
FULL-TIME			c. 190
Student Numbers 2013-2014			
All (Foreign Included)			c. 5900

Last Update: 05-03-2018

Sangji University

83 Sangjidae-gil
Wonju-si 26339, Gangwon-do
Tel: +82(33) 730-0181, +82(33) 730-0114
Fax: +82(33) 730-0128
Website: http://www.sangji.ac.kr
President: Jaecheon Yu

College

Arts and Physical Education (Ceramic Art; Design; Fine Arts; Graphic Design; Industrial Design; Physical Education; Sports; Textile Design); **Economics and Business Administration** (Accountancy; Business Administration; Economics; Information Management; International Business; Tourism); **Health Sciences** (Bioengineering; Food Science; Health Administration; Medical Technology; Nursing; Nutrition; Pharmacy; Traditional Eastern Medicine); **Humanities and Social Sciences** (Administrative Law; Advertising and Publicity; Arts and Humanities; Chinese; English; Korean; Law; Literature; Mass Communication; Media Studies; Public Administration; Social Welfare); **Life Resource Sciences** (Agriculture; Animal Husbandry; Biotechnology; Botany; Ecology; Food Technology; Forestry; Horticulture; Landscape Architecture); **Oriental Medicine** (Traditional Eastern Medicine); **Science and Engineering** (Biotechnology; Chemistry; Computer Engineering; Computer Science; Construction Engineering; Energy Engineering; Engineering Management; Environmental Engineering; Environmental Studies; Information Sciences; Information Technology; Materials Engineering; Physics)

Course/Programme

Cooperation Course between Departments (*Graduate*) (Medical Technology; Traditional Eastern Medicine)

Graduate School

Education (Art Education; Computer Education; Curriculum; Education; Educational Administration; Environmental Studies; Home Economics Education; Mathematics Education; Native Language Education; Physical Education; Science Education); **Graduate Studies** (Accountancy; Animal Husbandry; Biological and Life Sciences; Botany; Business Administration; Civil Engineering; Computer Engineering; Engineering; English; Environmental Engineering; Forestry; Horticulture; Industrial Design; Information Technology; Korean; Landscape Architecture; Law; Literature; Natural Sciences; Physical Education; Public Administration; Social Sciences; Social Welfare; Sports; Statistics; Telecommunications Engineering; Traditional Eastern Medicine); **Management Industry and Administration** (Accountancy; Business Administration; Civil Engineering; Economics; Environmental Engineering; Information Management; Public Administration; Real Estate; Tourism); **Peace and Security** (Protective Services; Psychology); **Social Welfare Policy** (Social Welfare)

History: Founded 1962.
Main language(s) of instruction: Korean
Accrediting agency: Korean Council for University Education (KCUE)
Degrees and diplomas: Bachelor's Degree, Master's Degree (Accountancy; Animal Husbandry; Art Education; Biological and Life Sciences; Botany; Business Administration; Civil Engineering; Computer Education; Computer Engineering; Curriculum; Economics; Educational Administration; English; Environmental Engineering; Foreign Languages Education; Forestry; Home Economics Education; Horticulture; Information Management; Korean; Landscape Architecture; Literature; Mathematics Education; Native Language Education; Physical Education; Protective Services; Psychology; Public Administration; Real Estate; Science Education; Social Welfare; Statistics; Tourism; Traditional Eastern Medicine), Doctor's Degree (Animal Husbandry; Botany; Business Administration; Civil Engineering; Computer Engineering; Forestry; Horticulture; Korean; Landscape Architecture; Law; Literature; Medical Technology; Physical Education; Public Administration; Social Welfare; Traditional Eastern Medicine)
Student Services: Sports Facilities, Canteen, Residential Facilities

Academic Staff 2013-2014	MALE	FEMALE	TOTAL
FULL-TIME			c. 250
Student Numbers 2013-2014			
All (Foreign Included)			c. 8600

Last Update: 05-03-2018

Sangmyung University

20, Hongimun 2-Gil Jongno-gu
Seoul 03016
Tel: +82(2) 2287-5114, +82(2) 396-7465
Fax: +82(2) 3217-4744

Website: http://english.smu.ac.kr
President: Baek Ehung Gi
Tel: +82(41) 550-5100

College

Art and Culture (Dance; Design; Fine Arts; Multimedia; Music; Music Theory and Composition; Musical Instruments; Singing); **Business** (Business Administration; Economics; Finance; International Business); **Education** (Education; Foreign Languages Education; Mathematics Education; Native Language Education); **Graduate Studies** (Business Administration; Cultural Studies; Design; Education; Fine Arts; Psychology; Technology; Welfare and Protective Services); **Humanities and Social Sciences** (East Asian Studies; Geography (Human); History; Information Sciences; Law; Library Science; Public Administration; Social Welfare); **ICT Convergence** (Computer Graphics; Computer Science; Energy Engineering; Private Law; Software Engineering); **Natural Sciences** (Biological and Life Sciences; Chemical Engineering; Clothing and Sewing; Consumer Studies; Cooking and Catering; Health Sciences; House Arts and Environment; Materials Engineering; Nutrition; Sports; Textile Technology); **University-Industry Cooperation** (Cosmetology; Design; Fine Arts; Hotel and Restaurant; Military Science; Service Trades)

Graduate School

General Studies (Arts and Humanities)

Research Division

Advanced Information Technology; **Advancement**; **Basic Sciences** (Natural Sciences); **Computer Networks** (Computer Networks); **Cultural Studies** (Cultural Studies); **Design** (Design); **Economic Policy** (Economic and Finance Policy); **Formative Art and Music** (Art Education; Music Education); **Future Art**; **Industrial Science**; **Language and Literature** (Literature; Modern Languages); **Marketing Information**; **Natural Sciences** (Natural Sciences); **Photojournalism** (Journalism; Photography); **Sino-Korean Culture and Information**; **Social Studies**; **Strategic Knowledge**; **Student Counselling Centre** (Educational and Student Counselling); **Technology** (Technology); **Unification**
Further information: Also Study Abroad Programme
History: Founded 1937 as Sangmyung Academy for Higher Learning for the Young. Became Sangmyung Girl's Handicraft High School 1965, then renamed Sangmyung Women's University 1983, and acquired present title 1996.
Academic year: March to December (March-August; September-December)
Admission requirements: Graduation from high school or recognized equivalent, and entrance examination
Main language(s) of instruction: Korean

Accrediting agency: Korean Council for University Education (KCUE)
Degrees and diplomas: Bachelor's Degree, Master's Degree (Art Education; Art Management; Biological and Life Sciences; Biology; Business Administration; Chemical Engineering; Chemistry; Child Care and Development; Computer Graphics; Computer Science; Cooking and Catering; Dance; Design; East Asian Studies; Ecology; Economics; Education; Energy Engineering; Engineering; Environmental Engineering; Environmental Studies; Film; Fine Arts; Foreign Languages Education; Geography (Human); Health Administration; Home Economics; Home Economics Education; Humanities and Social Science Education; Information Sciences; Information Technology; International Business; Library Science; Materials Engineering; Mathematics Education; Multimedia; Music; Music Education; Native Language Education; Nutrition; Pedagogy; Performing Arts; Physical Education; Private Law; Protective Services; Psychology; Public Administration; Real Estate; Safety Engineering; Science Education; Social Welfare; Social Work; Software Engineering; Sound Engineering (Acoustics); Sports; Teacher Training; Writing), Doctor's Degree (Art Management; Biological and Life Sciences; Biology; Business Administration; Chemical Engineering; Chemistry; Computer Science; Cooking and Catering; Dance; Design; Ecology; Economics; Education; Energy Engineering; Engineering; Environmental Engineering; Environmental Studies; Fine Arts; Geography (Human); Home Economics; Information Sciences; International Business; Library Science; Materials Engineering; Media Studies; Music; Native Language Education; Nutrition; Performing Arts; Physical Education; Private Law; Public Administration; Real Estate; Software Engineering; Technology; Welfare and Protective Services; Writing). Integrated Master and Doctorate Programmes
Student Services: Academic Counselling, Social Counselling, Careers Guidance, Sports Facilities, Language Laboratory, Health Services, Canteen

Student Numbers 2015-2016	MALE	FEMALE	TOTAL
All (Foreign Included)			6604
Foreign only			1133

Last Update: 09-03-2018

SANGMYUNG UNIVERSITY (CHEONAN CAMPUS) (SMUC)

31, Sangmyungdae-gil, Dongnam-gu
Cheonan 31066, Chungcheongnam-do
Tel: +82(41) 550-5114
Website: http://www.smuc.ac.kr/mbs/eng/index.jsp
President: Ehung Gi Baek

College

Arts (Art Management; Communication Arts; Display and Stage Design; Film; Multimedia; Painting and Drawing; Photography; Theatre; Visual Arts); **Design** (Ceramic Art; Fashion Design; Graphic Design; Industrial Design; Interior Design; Textile Design); **Engineering** (Biomedical Engineering; Civil Engineering; Computer Engineering; Engineering Management; Environmental Engineering; Information Technology; Telecommunications Engineering); **Industry** (Botany; Environmental Studies; Finance; Insurance; Landscape Architecture; Nursing; Physical Education; Sports Management; Technology); **Language and Literature** (English; French; German; Japanese; Korean; Literature; Russian)

Graduate School

Graduate Studies (Arts and Humanities; Engineering; Fine Arts; Natural Sciences; Physical Education; Social Sciences)
History: Founded 1965.
Main language(s) of instruction: Korean
Accrediting agency: Korean Council for University Education (KCUE)
Degrees and diplomas: Bachelor's Degree (Art Management; Biomedical Engineering; Botany; Ceramic Art; Civil Engineering; Communication Arts; Computer Engineering; Display and Stage Design; Engineering Management; English; Environmental Engineering; Environmental Studies; Fashion Design; Film; Finance; French; German; Graphic Design; Industrial Design; Information Technology; Insurance; Interior Design; Japanese; Korean; Landscape Architecture; Literature; Multimedia; Nursing; Painting and Drawing; Photography; Physical Education; Russian; Sports Management; Technology; Telecommunications Engineering; Textile Design; Theatre; Visual Arts)

Student Numbers 2015-2016	MALE	FEMALE	TOTAL
All (Foreign Included)			6604
Foreign only			1133

Last Update: 12-03-2018

Sehan University

72 Sanho-ri Samho-eup
Youngam-si 526-702, Chonnam-do
Tel: +82(61) 469-1114
Fax: +82(61) 462-2510
Website: http://www.sehan.ac.kr
President: Seung Hoon Lee

College

Education (Computer Education; Education; Foreign Languages Education; Mathematics Education; Preschool Education; Special Education; Technology Education); **Health Sciences** (Health Sciences; Nursing; Ophthalmology; Physical Therapy; Rehabilitation and Therapy; Speech Therapy and Audiology); **Humanities and Social Sciences** (Administration; Business Administration; Chinese; Fire Science; Police Studies; Psychology; Social Welfare; Tourism; Welfare and Protective Services); **Marine Leisure Studies** (Leisure Studies); **Performing Arts** (Architectural and Environmental Design; Design; Handicrafts; Music; Musical Instruments; Performing Arts; Visual Arts); **Physical Education** (Physical Education; Protective Services; Sports; Sports Management)

Laboratory
Nano Information Materials

Graduate School

Graduate Studies (Arts and Humanities; Fine Arts; Natural Sciences; Performing Arts; Physical Education; Social Sciences)

Research Division

Chinese Language and Culture; **Community Development**; **Marine Leisure Equipment**; **Marine Leisure Policy**; **Marine Leisure Sports**; **Marine Tourism**; **Traditional Yeonhui**
History: Founded 1994 as Daebul University.
Main language(s) of instruction: Korean
Accrediting agency: Korean Council for University Education (KCUE)
Degrees and diplomas: Bachelor's Degree, Master's Degree (Business Administration; Fine Arts; Fire Science; Industrial Design; Korean; Leisure Studies; Music; Musical Instruments; Nursing; Ophthalmology; Physical Therapy; Public Administration; Social Welfare; Speech Therapy and Audiology; Sports)
Last Update: 05-03-2018

Sejong Cyber University (SJCU)

Gunja-dong 111-1 Gwangjin-gu
Seoul 143-150
Tel: +82(2) 2204-8000, +82(2) 2204-8080
Fax: +82(2) 2204-8036
Website: http://portal.sjcu.ac.kr/jsp/english/jsp/introduction/01.jsp?p_showmenu=0
President: Gichul Kim
Tel: +82(10) 6272-4108

Department/Division

Business Administration (Business Administration); **Cartoon and Traditional Animation** (Computer Graphics;

Painting and Drawing; Visual Arts); **Child Welfare** (Child Care and Development; Welfare and Protective Services); **Convergence Management** (Business Administration; Information Technology); **Counseling Psychology** (Psychology); **Culinary and Food Service Management** (Cooking and Catering; Service Trades); **English Language** (English); **Fashion Business** (Business Administration); **Finance and Insurance** (Finance; Insurance); **Food Service Planning and Franchise Management** (Agricultural Business; Cooking and Catering); **Game and Contents in Film, Video and Multimedia** (Computer Graphics; Film; Multimedia; Software Engineering; Video); **Gerontological Welfare** (Welfare and Protective Services); **Hotel and Tourism Management** (Hotel Management; Tourism); **Information and Communication** (Information Technology; Telecommunications Engineering); **Information Security** (Computer Engineering; Information Management); **Lifelong Education** (Continuing Education); **Marketing and Public Relations** (Marketing; Public Relations); **Mobile Industry** (Human Resources; Industrial Management; Software Engineering); **Real Estate Auction and Brokerage** (Real Estate); **Real Estate Business Administration** (Business Administration; Real Estate); **Real Estate Development and Investment** (Real Estate); **Retails and Logistics** (Retailing and Wholesaling; Transport Management); **Social Welfare** (Social Welfare); **Tax and Accountancy** (Accountancy; Taxation)

Graduate School

Business (Business Administration); **Information Security** (Information Management)
History: Founded 2000.
Main language(s) of instruction: Korean
Accrediting agency: Ministry of Education
Degrees and diplomas: Bachelor's Degree (Accountancy; Business Administration; Child Care and Development; Computer Engineering; Computer Graphics; Cooking and Catering; English; Finance; Hotel Management; Information Management; Korean; Management; Marketing; Painting and Drawing; Public Relations; Real Estate; Retailing and Wholesaling; Service Trades; Social Welfare; Social Work; Software Engineering; Taxation; Tourism; Transport Management; Visual Arts), Master's Degree (Information Management). Also MBA
Student Services: Library
Last Update: 26-03-2018

Sejong University

209, Neungdong-ro Gwangjin-gu
Seoul 05006
Tel: +82(2) 3408-3114
Fax: +82(2) 3408-3220
Website: http://www.sejong.ac.kr
President: Shin Koo
Tel: +82(2) 3408-3001

Faculty

Liberal Arts (Arts and Humanities)

College

Arts and Physical Education (Dance; Fashion Design; Film; Industrial Design; Music; Painting and Drawing; Physical Education; Visual Arts); **Business Administration** (Accountancy; Business Administration; Finance; Information Technology; Management; Marketing); **Electronics and Information Engineering** (Computer Engineering; Electronic Engineering; Film; Information Management; Information Technology; Mass Communication; Optical Technology; Telecommunications Engineering; Visual Arts); **Engineering** (Aeronautical and Aerospace Engineering; Architecture; Civil Engineering; Computer Science; Engineering; Environmental Engineering; Information Technology; Materials Engineering; Mechanical Engineering; Military Science; Mining Engineering; Nanotechnology; Nuclear Engineering; Structural Architecture; Surveying and Mapping); **Hospitality and Tourism Management** (Food Science; Food Technology; Hotel Management; Tourism); **Liberal Arts** (Arts and Humanities; Education; English; History; Japanese; Korean; Literature); **Life Sciences** (Bioengineering; Biological and Life Sciences; Biotechnology; Food Technology; Molecular Biology; Natural Resources); **Natural Sciences** (Astronomy and Space Science; Chemistry; Energy Engineering; Environmental Studies; Mathematics; Natural Sciences; Physics; Statistics); **Social Science** (Business Administration; Business and Commerce; Communication Arts; Economics; International Business; Public Administration; Social Sciences)

Department/Division

Interdisciplinary Studies (Administrative Law; Civil Law; Commercial Law; Criminal Law; Fiscal Law; Human Rights; International Law; Labour Law; Law)

Graduate School

Business (Business Administration); **Graduate Studies** (Arts and Humanities; Business Administration; Engineering; Fine Arts; Music; Natural Sciences; Physical Education; Social Sciences; Tourism); **Special Studies**
History: Founded 1940. Acquired present status 1961.
Academic year: March to December (March-August; September-December)
Admission requirements: Graduation from high school and entrance examination
Fees: 6.7m. per annum (Won)

Main language(s) of instruction: Korean, English

Accrediting agency: Korean Council for University Education (KCUE)

Degrees and diplomas: Bachelor's Degree, Master's Degree (Accountancy; Aeronautical and Aerospace Engineering; Architectural and Environmental Design; Astronomy and Space Science; Biological and Life Sciences; Biotechnology; Business Administration; Chemistry; Civil Engineering; Computer Engineering; Computer Science; Cooking and Catering; Dance; Design; Earth Sciences; Economics; Electronic Engineering; Environmental Engineering; Environmental Studies; Fashion Design; Film; Food Science; Food Technology; Hotel Management; Information Technology; Journalism; Mass Communication; Mathematics; Mechanical Engineering; Mining Engineering; Molecular Biology; Music; Nanotechnology; Painting and Drawing; Physical Education; Physics; Public Administration; Service Trades; Statistics; Structural Architecture; Surveying and Mapping; Telecommunications Engineering; Tourism; Town Planning), Doctor's Degree (Accountancy; Aeronautical and Aerospace Engineering; Architectural and Environmental Design; Astronomy and Space Science; Biological and Life Sciences; Biotechnology; Business Administration; Chemistry; Civil Engineering; Computer Engineering; Computer Science; Cooking and Catering; Dance; Design; Earth Sciences; Economics; Environmental Engineering; Environmental Studies; Fashion Design; Film; Food Science; Food Technology; Hotel Management; Information Technology; Journalism; Mass Communication; Mathematics; Mechanical Engineering; Molecular Biology; Music; Nanotechnology; Performing Arts; Physical Education; Physics; Public Administration; Service Trades; Statistics; Structural Architecture; Surveying and Mapping; Telecommunications Engineering; Tourism; Town Planning; Visual Arts)

Student Services: Academic Counselling, Social Counselling, Careers Guidance, Nursery Care, Sports Facilities, Health Services, Canteen

Periodicals: Journal of Aerospace Industry, Journal of Economic Integration

Publishing house: Sejong University Press

Academic Staff 2013-2014	MALE	FEMALE	TOTAL
FULL-TIME			c. 470
Student Numbers 2013-2014			
All (Foreign Included)			c. 13350

Last Update: 05-03-2018

Semyung University (SMU)

65 Semyung-ro
Jecheon-si 27136, Chungcheongbuk-do
Tel: +82(43) 645-1125

Fax: +82(43) 644-2111
Website: http://www.semyung.ac.kr
President: Young Geol Lee

College

Arts and Humanities (Architectural and Environmental Design; Arts and Humanities; Chinese; Cultural Studies; English; Fashion Design; Foreign Languages Education; Graphic Design; Japanese; Korean; Literature; Media Studies; Modern Languages; Performing Arts; Writing); **Engineering and Information Technology** (Arts and Humanities; Bioengineering; Civil Engineering; Communication Studies; Computer Science; E- Business/Commerce; Electrical Engineering; Electronic Engineering; Engineering; Environmental Engineering; Health Sciences; Information Sciences; Natural Sciences; Safety Engineering; Social Sciences); **General Education** (Education); **Healthcare and Technology** (Biological and Life Sciences; Biotechnology; Cosmetology; Food Science; Laboratory Techniques; Leisure Studies; Natural Sciences; Nursing; Nutrition; Occupational Therapy; Pharmacology; Sports); **Korean Medicine** (Traditional Eastern Medicine); **Social Sciences** (Accountancy; Advertising and Publicity; Air Transport; Arts and Humanities; Fire Science; Hotel Management; International Business; Law; Management; Police Studies; Protective Services; Public Administration; Public Relations; Real Estate; Social Sciences; Social Welfare; Tourism)

School

Graduate Studies (Biological and Life Sciences; Business Administration; Communication Studies; Computer Science; Construction Engineering; Cosmetology; Criminal Law; Design; Development Studies; Education; Educational Administration; Electrical Engineering; Electronic Engineering; Environmental Engineering; Fire Science; Food Science; Information Sciences; Journalism; Korean; Law; Leisure Studies; Literature; Medicine; Nutrition; Police Studies; Psychology; Public Administration; Real Estate; Safety Engineering; Social Welfare; Sports; Tourism; Traditional Eastern Medicine)

Institute

Oriental Studies (Oriental Studies)

Research Division

Humanities and Social Sciences (Arts and Humanities; Social Sciences); **Industrial Technology Research** (Industrial Engineering); **Regional Culture** (Cultural Studies; Regional Studies)

Further information: Also Affiliated Jecheon Oriental Hospital, Affiliated Chungju Oriental Hospital

History: Founded 1991.

Academic year: February to December (February-June; August-December)

Admission requirements: Graduation from high school or equivalent

Main language(s) of instruction: Korean

Accrediting agency: Korean Council for University Education (KCUE)

Degrees and diplomas: Bachelor's Degree, Master's Degree (Biological and Life Sciences; Business Administration; Communication Studies; Computer Science; Cosmetology; Design; Development Studies; Educational Administration; Electrical and Electronic Engineering; Environmental Engineering; Fire Science; Food Science; Information Sciences; Journalism; Korean; Law; Literature; Nutrition; Protective Services; Psychology; Public Administration; Real Estate; Regional Studies; Safety Engineering; Social Welfare; Sports; Structural Architecture; Tourism; Traditional Eastern Medicine), Doctor's Degree (Business Administration; Communication Studies; Computer Science; Development Studies; Electrical and Electronic Engineering; Fire Science; Food Science; Information Sciences; Korean; Literature; Nutrition; Real Estate; Regional Studies; Safety Engineering; Structural Architecture; Traditional Eastern Medicine)

Student Services: Sports Facilities, Health Services, Library, Residential Facilities

Periodicals: Senyung Annual Publication

Academic Staff 2016-2017	MALE	FEMALE	TOTAL
FULL-TIME			638
Student Numbers 2016-2017			
All (Foreign Included)			7383
Foreign only			237

Last Update: 05-03-2018

Seokyeong University (SKU)

16-1 Jungneung-Dong Sungbuk-gu
Seoul 136-704
Tel: +82(2) 940-7006, +82(2) 940-7114
Fax: +82(2) 940-7009
Website: http://www.skuniv.ac.kr
President: Chul Choi Young

College

Arts (Arts and Humanities; Industrial Design); **Humanities** (Arts and Humanities; Chinese; English; French; Japanese; Korean; Philosophy; Russian); **Natural Sciences and Engineering** (Applied Mathematics; Bioengineering; Chemistry; Computer Engineering; Computer Science; Industrial Engineering; Statistics); **Social Sciences** (Accountancy; Business Administration; Computer Education; Economics; Information Management; International Business; Law; Public Administration; Social Sciences)

Department/Division
General Education

Institute
Industrial Technology (Biochemistry; Computer Science; Industrial Engineering); **Industry and Business Administration** (Accountancy; Business and Commerce; Economics); **Liberal Arts** (Arts and Humanities; History; Linguistics; Literature; Philosophy); **Military Study** (Military Science); **Social Sciences** (Business Administration; Economics; Law; Social Sciences); **Unification Affairs** (International Relations)

Academy
Quality

Centre
KEN (Korea Environment and Nano) (Environmental Studies; Nanotechnology); **Korean-Japanese Culture** (East Asian Studies); **Philosophical Thought** (Philosophy); **Urban Research** (Urban Studies)

Graduate School
Beauty Arts (Cosmetology); **Business and Public Administration** (Art Management; Arts and Humanities; Business Administration; Transport Management); **Graduate Studies** (Arts and Humanities; Engineering; Fine Arts; Performing Arts)

Further information: Also Social Education Centre

History: Founded 1947.

Academic year: March to February (March-August; September-February)

Main language(s) of instruction: Korean

Accrediting agency: Korean Council for University Education (KCUE)

Degrees and diplomas: Bachelor's Degree, Master's Degree (Art Management; Arts and Humanities; Bioengineering; Business Administration; Civil Engineering; Computer Engineering; Cosmetology; Cultural Studies; Dance; Design; Electronic Engineering; Environmental Engineering; Film; Music; Nanotechnology; Theatre; Transport Management), Doctor's Degree (Arts and Humanities; Bioengineering; Business Administration; Computer Engineering; Cosmetology; Cultural Studies; Electronic Engineering; Nanotechnology; Transport Management)

Student Services: Academic Counselling, Social Counselling, Careers Guidance, Sports Facilities, Health Services, Canteen, Library

Periodicals: Seo Kyeong Dae Hak Bo

Publishing house: Seo Kyeong University Press

Last Update: 05-03-2018

Seoul Bible Graduate School of Theology (SB)

45-1, Sindaebang 14ga-gil, Dongjak-gu
Seoul 07066
Tel: +82(2) 845-7711
Fax: +82(2) 844-7711
Website: http://www.sb.ac.kr/board/main_eng.php
President: Heung Sik Choi

Faculty

Counseling Studies (Psychology); **Historical Theology** (Theology); **Missiology** (Missionary Studies); **New Testament** (New Testament); **Old Testament** (Bible); **Practical Theology** (Theology); **Social Welfare** (Social Welfare); **Systematic Theology** (Theology)
History: Founded 1999.
Main language(s) of instruction: Korean
Accrediting agency: Ministry of Education
Degrees and diplomas: Master's Degree (Bible; Missionary Studies; Pastoral Studies; Psychology; Religion; Social Welfare; Theology), Doctor's Degree (Theology)
Last Update: 28-03-2018

Seoul Christian University

26-2, Galhyeon-ro 4-gil Eunpyeong-gu
Seoul 03422
Tel: +82(2) 380-2500
Fax: +82(2) 380-2535
Website: http://www.scu.ac.kr
President: Kang-Pyung Lee
Tel: +82(2) 380-2501

Department/Division

Dance (Dance); **Global Business and Information** (Business Education; E- Business/Commerce); **Music** (Music; Musical Instruments); **Social Welfare** (Social Policy; Social Welfare; Social Work); **Theology** (New Testament; Theology)

Graduate School

Healing and Counselling (Health Sciences); **Social Welfare** (Social Welfare); **Social Work** (Social Work); **Theology** (Theology)
History: Founded 1937. Acquired present status 1997. Acquired present title 1999.
Academic year: March to December (March-June; September-December)
Admission requirements: Graduation from senior high school

Fees: 2.9m. per semester (Won)
Main language(s) of instruction: Korean
Accrediting agency: Ministry of Education and Human Resources Development; Korean Council for University Education (KCUE)
Degrees and diplomas: Bachelor's Degree (Business Administration; Dance; Fine Arts; Music; Social Welfare; Theology), Master's Degree (Administration; Bible; History of Religion; Missionary Studies; New Testament; Pastoral Studies; Psychology; Psychotherapy; Religious Education; Social Welfare; Social Work; Theology), Doctor's Degree (Administration; Bible; Christian Religious Studies; History of Religion; Missionary Studies; New Testament; Psychology; Social Welfare; Social Work; Theology)
Student Services: Academic Counselling, Sports Facilities, Language Laboratory, Canteen, Library, IT Centre, Residential Facilities

Academic Staff 2013-2014	MALE	FEMALE	TOTAL
FULL-TIME			45
Student Numbers 2013-2014			
All (Foreign Included)			c. 1170
Foreign only			30

Last Update: 05-03-2018

Seoul Cyber University (SCU)

60, Solmae-ro 49-gil, Gangbuk-gu
Seoul 01133
Tel: +82(2) 944-5000
Fax: +82(2) 980-2222
Website: http://www.iscu.ac.kr
President: Eunjoo Lee
Tel: +82(2) 944 5001

Department/Division

Business (Accountancy; Business Administration; Finance; Insurance; International Business; Small Business; Taxation; Transport Management); **Counseling Psychology** (Family Studies; Psychology; Psychotherapy); **Culture and Arts** (Art Management; Jazz and Popular Music; Musical Instruments; Singing); **Design** (Architectural and Environmental Design; Design; Multimedia); **General Education** (Arts and Humanities; Biological and Life Sciences; Communication Studies; Education; Ethics; International Studies); **IT and Engineering** (Computer Engineering; Information Management; Media Studies; Software Engineering); **Liberal Studies** (Arts and Humanities; Cultural Studies; Leadership; Social Sciences); **Social Science** (East Asian Studies; Health Administration; Korean; Law; Public Administration; Real Estate); **Social Welfare** (Child Care and Development; Family Studies; Management Systems; Social Welfare)

Graduate School

Graduate Studies (Psychology; Social Welfare)
History: Founded 2000
Academic year: February to June (Spring Semester); June to July (Summer Intensive Semester); September to December (Fall Semester); December to January (Winter Intensive Semester)
Fees: National : 78,000 per credit (Won), International : 78,000 per credit (Won)
Main language(s) of instruction: Korean
Accrediting agency: Ministry of Education, Republic of Korea
Degrees and diplomas: Bachelor's Degree (Accountancy; Architectural and Environmental Design; Art Management; Business Administration; Business and Commerce; Design; Engineering; Finance; Health Administration; Information Management; Jazz and Popular Music; Korean; Law; Media Studies; Multimedia; Music; Psychology; Psychotherapy; Real Estate; Small Business; Social Welfare; Software Engineering), Master's Degree (Psychology; Social Welfare). For each degree program, vocational counseling or training session is included as a part of curriculum. For some program, university's certificate is issued to students for the completion of specific courses in the program. Furthermore, some courses in certain programs help students prepare to acquire the national certificate for each area of expertise
Student Services: Academic Counselling, Careers Guidance, Sports Facilities, Facilities for disabled people, Health Services, Library

Academic Staff 2018-2019	MALE	FEMALE	TOTAL
FULL-TIME	24	37	61

Total number of distance students: 10000
Last Update: 24-05-2018

Seoul Digital University (SDU)

424, Gonghang-daero, Gangseo-gu
Seoul 07654
Tel: +82 1544-0981, +82(2) 2128-3110
Fax: +82(2) 2128-3006
Website: http://en.sdu.ac.kr
President: Oh-Young Chung

Department/Division

IT and Cultural Arts (Architectural and Environmental Design; Art Management; Communication Arts; Computer Engineering; Fashion Design; Fine Arts; Jazz and Popular Music; Media Studies; Software Engineering; Visual Arts; Writing); **Liberal Arts and Social Science** (Accountancy; Business Administration; Chinese; Continuing Education; English; Finance; International Business; Japanese; Law; Police Studies; Preschool Education; Psychology; Public Administration; Real Estate; Social Welfare; Taxation; Transport Management)
Further information: Also Mapo and Bucheon Campuses
History: Founded 2001.
Main language(s) of instruction: Korean
Accrediting agency: Ministry of Education
Degrees and diplomas: Bachelor's Degree (Accountancy; Architectural and Environmental Design; Art Management; Business Administration; Chinese; Communication Arts; Computer Engineering; Continuing Education; English; Fashion Design; Finance; Fine Arts; International Business; Japanese; Jazz and Popular Music; Law; Media Studies; Police Studies; Preschool Education; Psychology; Public Administration; Real Estate; Social Welfare; Software Engineering; Taxation; Transport Management; Visual Arts; Writing)
Last Update: 22-03-2018

Seoul Hanyoung University (HYTU)

Gyeongin-ro 290-42 Guro-gu
Seoul 08274
Tel: +82(2) 2669-2200
Fax: +82(2) 2669-2209
Website: http://www.hytu.ac.kr
President: Chun-Soo Kim

Department/Division

Theology (English; Psychology; Religious Music; Social Welfare; Theology)

Graduate School

Graduate Studies (English; Psychology; Social Welfare; Theology)
History: Founded 1981.
Main language(s) of instruction: Korean
Accrediting agency: Ministry of Education
Degrees and diplomas: Bachelor's Degree (English; Psychology; Religious Music; Social Welfare; Theology), Master's Degree (English; Psychology; Social Welfare; Theology)
Student Services: Library, Residential Facilities
Last Update: 28-03-2018

Seoul Institute of the Arts

171 Yesuldaehak-ro, Gojan-dong Danwon-ku
Ansan 15263, Gyeonggi-do
Tel: +82(31) 412-7100

Fax: +82(31) 412-7149
Website: https://www.seoularts.ac.kr/mbs/en
President: Duk-Hyung Yoo

Course/Programme
Arts Management (Art Management)

School
Media (Advertising and Publicity; Communication Arts; Computer Graphics; Graphic Design; Interior Design; Media Studies; Photography; Radio and Television Broadcasting; Writing); **Performance** (Acting; Dance; Music; Performing Arts; Theatre; Writing)

Department/Division
Arts Foundation (Fine Arts)
History: Founded 1962. Ansan Campus opened in 2001.
Main language(s) of instruction: Korean
Accrediting agency: Ministry of Education
Degrees and diplomas: Associate Degree, Bachelor's Degree (Fine Arts)
Student Services: Residential Facilities
Last Update: 20-03-2018

Seoul Jangsin University (SJU)

219-1 Gyungan-dong
Gwangju-si 464-742, Gyeonggi-do
Tel: +82(31) 799-9000
Fax: +82(31) 765-1232
Website: http://www.sjs.ac.kr
President: Joo-Hoon Ahn
Tel: +82(31) 799-9001

Course/Programme
Liberal Arts (Arts and Humanities)

School
Divinity (*Graduate*) (Missionary Studies; Pastoral Studies; Religion; Social Welfare)

Department/Division
Church Music (Conducting; Music Theory and Composition; Musical Instruments; Religious Music; Singing); **Social Welfare** (Social Welfare; Social Work); **Theology** (Theology)

Graduate School
Church Music (Conducting; Musical Instruments; Religious Music); **Graduate Studies/Doctoral Course** (Bible; History of Religion; Missionary Studies; Music Theory and Composition; Musical Instruments; New Testament; Pastoral Studies; Religion; Singing; Theology); **Naturopathy in Mission** (Alternative Medicine); **Social Welfare** (Business Administration; Social Welfare; Social Work); **Worship and Praise in Ministry** (Musical Instruments; Religion)
History: Founded 1954. Acquired present status 1998.
Academic year: March to February (March-August; September-February)
Admission requirements: Graduation from high school
Fees: 3,165,000 per semester; church music department, 4,530,000 (Won)
Main language(s) of instruction: Korean
Accrediting agency: Ministry of Education and Human Resources Development
Degrees and diplomas: Bachelor's Degree (Religious Music; Social Welfare; Theology), Master's Degree (Administration; Alternative Medicine; Bible; Conducting; History of Religion; Missionary Studies; Music Theory and Composition; Musical Instruments; New Testament; Pastoral Studies; Psychology; Religion; Religious Music; Religious Studies; Singing; Social Welfare; Social Work; Theology), Doctor's Degree (Bible; Christian Religious Studies; History of Religion; Missionary Studies; New Testament; Religious Music; Religious Practice; Social Welfare; Theology)
Student Services: Academic Counselling, Social Counselling, Careers Guidance, Nursery Care, Sports Facilities, Language Laboratory, Facilities for disabled people, Health Services, Canteen, Library, Residential Facilities
Periodicals: Seoul Jangsin Non Dan

Academic Staff 2013-2014	MALE	FEMALE	TOTAL
FULL-TIME			c. 40
Student Numbers 2013-2014			
All (Foreign Included)			c. 790

Last Update: 05-03-2018

Seoul Media Institute of Technology (SMIT)

Gangseo Education Campus Gangseo-gu Hwagokoro 61 Road 99
Seoul 07590
Tel: +82(2) 6393-3114
Fax: +82(2) 6393-3280
Website: https://www.smit.ac.kr
President: Seung-chul Park

Department/Division
Fusion Media (Media Studies); **Media Business** (Business Administration; Media Studies); **Media Engineering** (Engineering; Media Studies)

History: Founded 2009 as Korean German Institute of Technology (KGIT), acquired current title 2015.
Main language(s) of instruction: Korean
Accrediting agency: Ministry of Education
Degrees and diplomas: Bachelor's Degree (Media Studies), Master's Degree (Business Administration; Engineering; Media Studies)
Last Update: 26-03-2018

Seoul School of Integrated Sciences and Technologies (aSSIST)

46, Ewhayeodae 2-gil Seodaemun-gu
Seoul 03767
Tel: +82(70) 7012-2700, +82(70) 7012-2224
Fax: +82(70) 7016-2700
Website: http://www.assist.ac.kr/English
President: Tae-Hyun Kim

Course/Programme

Alternative Investment (Finance); **Big Data** (Data Processing); **Business Administration** (Business Administration); **Industrial Security** (Information Management; Safety Engineering)
History: Founded 2004.
Main language(s) of instruction: Korean
Accrediting agency: Ministry of Education
Degrees and diplomas: Master's Degree (Data Processing; Finance; Information Management; Safety Engineering), Doctor's Degree (Business Administration). Also Double Degree Programmes with Aalto University (Formerly Helsinki School of Economics), State University of New York at Stony Brook (SUNY SB); aSSIST CKGSB China-Korea EMBA; Executive Programmes
Last Update: 21-03-2018

Seoul Social Welfare Graduate University

134-2 Yongdungpo-dong 4-ga, Yongdungpo-gu
Seoul 150-034
Tel: 82(2) 835-5551
Fax: 82(2) 835-5554
Website: http://www.ssgu.ac.kr
President: Yuksang Kwon

Department/Division

Social Welfare (Social Welfare; Social Work); **Sports Management** (Health Sciences; Sports Management; Sports Medicine)

History: Founded 1999. Formerly known as Seoul Sports Graduate University.
Main language(s) of instruction: Korean
Accrediting agency: Ministry of Education
Degrees and diplomas: Master's Degree (Child Care and Development; Social Welfare; Social Work; Welfare and Protective Services)
Student Services: Library

Academic Staff 2012-2013	MALE	FEMALE	TOTAL
FULL-TIME			10
PART-TIME			c. 10
Student Numbers 2012-2013			
All (Foreign Included)			c. 100

Last Update: 06-03-2018

Seoul Theological University

101 Sosabon3-dong, Sosa-gu
Bucheon-City 14754, Kyonggi-do
Tel: +82(32) 340-9114
Fax: +82(32) 340-9400
Website: https://stueng.stu.ac.kr
President: Seok-seong You

Department/Division

Applied Music (Music); **Child Care and Education** (Child Care and Development); **Chinese Language** (Chinese); **Christian Education** (Religious Education); **Church Music** (Religious Music); **Early Childhood Education** (Preschool Education); **English Language** (English); **General Education** (Education); **Japanese Language** (Japanese); **Social Welfare** (Social Welfare); **Theology** (Theology); **Tourism Management** (Tourism)

Graduate School

Counseling (Psychology); **Graduate Studies** (Child Care and Development; Preschool Education; Religious Education; Religious Music; Social Welfare; Theology); **Preaching** (Religious Practice); **Seoul Theological Seminary** (Theology); **Social Welfare** (Social Welfare); **Theology** (Theology)
History: Founded 1911 as Kyung-Sung Bible School, renamed Kyung-Sung Seminary 1940, Accredited as Seoul Theological College 1959. Acquired current status and title 2012.
Main language(s) of instruction: Korean
Accrediting agency: Korean Council for University Education (KCUE)
Degrees and diplomas: Bachelor's Degree (Child Care and Development; Chinese; Education; English; Japanese; Music; Preschool Education; Religious Education; Religious

Music; Social Welfare; Theology; Tourism), Master's Degree (Child Care and Development; Missionary Studies; Pastoral Studies; Preschool Education; Psychology; Rehabilitation and Therapy; Religious Education; Religious Music; Social Problems; Social Welfare; Theology), Doctor's Degree (Religious Music; Social Welfare; Theology)
Student Services: Library
Last Update: 12-03-2018

Seoul University of Foreign Studies (SUFS)

17-7 Yangjae 1-dong, Seocho-gu
Seoul 06745
Tel: +82(2) 2182-6000
Fax: +82(2) 2182-6090
Website: http://www.sufs.ac.kr/sufseng/info/info_01.asp
President: Hai-su Youn

Course/Programme

Korean-Chinese Interpretation and Translation (Translation and Interpretation); **Korean-English Interpretation and Translation** (Translation and Interpretation); **Korean-Japanese Interpretation and Translation** (Translation and Interpretation)
History: Founded 2003.
Main language(s) of instruction: Korean
Accrediting agency: Ministry of Education
Degrees and diplomas: Master's Degree (Translation and Interpretation)
Last Update: 24-05-2018

Seoul Venture University (SVU)

405 Bongeunsa-ro, Gangnam-gu
Seoul 135-867
Tel: +82(2) 3470-5112/4
Fax: +82(2) 3470-5131
Website: http://www.svu.ac.kr/main/main.php#
President: Young-gu Kang

Course/Programme

Convergence Industry (Accountancy; E- Business/Commerce; Labour and Industrial Relations; Management; Marketing; Military Science; Protective Services; Welfare and Protective Services); **Relea Estate** (Real Estate); **Social Welfare Counseling** (Psychology; Social Welfare; Social Work; Welfare and Protective Services)
History: Founded 2003.
Main language(s) of instruction: Korean

Accrediting agency: Ministry of Education
Degrees and diplomas: Master's Degree (Accountancy; E-Business/Commerce; Labour and Industrial Relations; Management; Marketing; Military Science; Protective Services; Psychology; Real Estate; Social Welfare; Social Work; Welfare and Protective Services), Doctor's Degree (Accountancy; E- Business/Commerce; Labour and Industrial Relations; Management; Marketing; Military Science; Protective Services; Psychology; Real Estate; Social Welfare; Social Work; Welfare and Protective Services)
Last Update: 26-03-2018

Seoul Women's University (SWU)

621 Hwarangro Nowon-gu
Seoul 01797
Tel: +82(2) 970-5114
Fax: +82(2) 978-7931
Website: http://www.swu.ac.kr
President: Hei-Jung Chun

College

Fine Arts (Ceramic Art; Communication Arts; Fine Arts; Graphic Design; Handicrafts; Industrial Design); **Humanities** (Arts and Humanities; Chinese; Christian Religious Studies; English; French; German; History; Japanese; Korean; Literature); **Information and Media** (Computer Engineering; Computer Graphics; Computer Science; Information Management; Information Sciences; Information Technology; Mass Communication; Media Studies; Multimedia; Software Engineering; Visual Arts); **Natural Sciences** (Architectural and Environmental Design; Biology; Biotechnology; Chemistry; Clothing and Sewing; Computer Science; Food Science; Food Technology; Horticulture; Mathematics; Microbiology; Molecular Biology; Natural Sciences; Nutrition; Rehabilitation and Therapy; Sports; Sports Management); **Social Sciences** (Business Administration; Child Care and Development; Economics; Educational Psychology; Information Sciences; Library Science; Mass Communication; Media Studies; Public Administration; Social Sciences; Social Welfare)

Institute

Art and Design; **Korea Ecology Education** (Ecology); **Women's Studies**

Centre

Childcare Education (Child Care and Development); **Continuing Education**; **IT Education** (Computer Science); **Language Education** (Chinese; English; French; German; Japanese)

Graduate School

Education (Education; Educational Sciences; Teacher Training); **Graduate Studies** (Industrial Engineering; Information Technology); **Professional Therapeutic Technology** (Art Therapy; Psychology; Psychotherapy; Rehabilitation and Therapy); **Social Welfare and Christian Studies** (Christian Religious Studies; Social Welfare)

Research Division

Child Studies; **Computer Science**; **Humanities**; **Natural Science**; **Social Science**; **Student Guidance and Counselling**

History: Founded 1961 by Korean Presbyterian Church.

Academic year: March to February (March-August; September-February)

Admission requirements: Graduation from high school and entrance examination

Main language(s) of instruction: Korean

Accrediting agency: Korean Council for University Education (KCUE)

Degrees and diplomas: Bachelor's Degree, Master's Degree (Art Education; Art Therapy; Business Administration; Chemistry; Child Care and Development; Chinese; Christian Religious Studies; Computer Education; Computer Science; Design; Economics; Educational and Student Counselling; Educational Psychology; English; Environmental Studies; Food Science; Food Technology; Foreign Languages Education; French; German; History; Horticulture; Information Sciences; Korean; Library Science; Literature; Mathematics; Mathematics Education; Media Studies; Multimedia; Native Language Education; Nutrition; Physical Education; Preschool Education; Primary Education; Psychology; Psychotherapy; Public Administration; Science Education; Social Welfare; Social Work; Video), Doctor's Degree (Analytical Chemistry; Art Therapy; Biological and Life Sciences; Business Administration; Chemistry; Child Care and Development; Christian Religious Studies; Computer Science; Cooking and Catering; Dietetics; Ecology; Educational Psychology; Educational Testing and Evaluation; Embryology and Reproduction Biology; English; Environmental Studies; Fashion Design; Food Science; Food Technology; Horticulture; Immunology; Information Technology; Inorganic Chemistry; Korean; Landscape Architecture; Linguistics; Literature; Microbiology; Multimedia; Nutrition; Organic Chemistry; Physical Chemistry; Psychology; Psychotherapy; Rehabilitation and Therapy; Social Welfare; Social Work; Textile Design; Theology; Writing). Also one-year professional counselor-training course offered

Student Services: Sports Facilities, Library, IT Centre, Residential Facilities

Periodicals: Seoul Women's University Bulletin

Publishing house: Seoul Women's University Press

Student Numbers 2015-2016	MALE	FEMALE	TOTAL
All (Foreign Included)			c. 8000

Last Update: 06-03-2018

Seowon University

377-3 Musimseoro Heungdeok-gu
Cheongju-si 28674, Chungbuk-do
Tel: +82(43) 299-8114
Fax: +82(43) 283-8822
Website: http://www.seowon.ac.kr
President: Soek-Min Son

Faculty

Business Administration (Accountancy; Air Transport; Business Administration; Business and Commerce; Economics; Finance; Hotel Management; Information Technology; Insurance; International Business; Management; Mass Communication; Media Studies); **Education** (Education; Foreign Languages Education; Humanities and Social Science Education; Mathematics Education; Music Education; Native Language Education; Physical Education; Preschool Education; Science Education)

School

Convergence Bioscience and Technology (Biotechnology; Cooking and Catering; Cosmetology; Food Science; Food Technology; Pharmacology; Pharmacy); **Design and Environmental Science** (Architecture; Clothing and Sewing; Environmental Engineering; Textile Design); **Fusion Arts** (Design; Film; Fine Arts; Music; Performing Arts; Theatre); **Health and Welfare** (Food Science; Health Sciences; Leisure Studies; Nutrition; Physical Therapy; Rehabilitation and Therapy; Social Welfare; Sports; Welfare and Protective Services); **Information Technology** (Communication Arts; Computer Engineering; Computer Science; Information Technology; Media Studies; Telecommunications Engineering); **Law and Police Science** (Law; Police Studies; Political Sciences; Public Administration)

Department/Division

Language and Culture (Chinese; English; Foreign Languages Education; Korean; Literature)

Graduate School

Education (Education; Educational Sciences; Teacher Training); **Industry** (Architecture; Business Administration; Design; Rehabilitation and Therapy; Sports); **Information Technology** (Information Technology; Telecommunications Engineering)

Further information: Also 5 Affiliated Research Institutes

History: Founded 1968 as Cheongju Women's Junior College. Acquired present status 1992.

Main language(s) of instruction: Korean

Accrediting agency: Korean Council for University Education (KCUE)

Degrees and diplomas: Bachelor's Degree, Master's Degree (Accountancy; Architecture; Art Education; Business Administration; Child Care and Development; Cosmetology; E- Business/Commerce; Educational Administration; Educational Psychology; Foreign Languages Education; Graphic Design; Humanities and Social Science Education; Industrial Design; Information Technology; Mathematics Education; Music Education; Native Language Education; Physical Education; Preschool Education; Rehabilitation and Therapy; Science Education; Sports; Sports Management; Technology Education; Telecommunications Engineering)

Student Services: Careers Guidance, Health Services, Library, Residential Facilities

Academic Staff 2013-2014	MALE	FEMALE	TOTAL
FULL-TIME			c. 210
Student Numbers 2013-2014			
All (Foreign Included)			c. 9600

Last Update: 06-03-2018

Shinhan University

95, Hoam-ro
Uijeongbu-si 480-701, Gyeonggi-do
Tel: +82(31) 870-2822/6
Website: http://en.shinhan.ac.kr
President: Byeong-ok Kim

College

Convergence Science and Technology (*Campus 2*) (Computer Engineering; Electronic Engineering; Energy Engineering; Environmental Engineering; Information Technology; Materials Engineering; Textile Technology); **Convergence Science and Technology** (*Campus 1*) (Automotive Engineering); **Design and Art** (*Campus 1*) (Design; Fashion Design; Industrial Design; Interior Design; Performing Arts); **Global Business** (*Campus 1*) (International Business; Management; Tourism); **Global Business** (*Campus 2*) (International Business); **Health Science** (*Campus 1*) (Biomedicine; Cosmetology; Dental Hygiene; Dentistry; Laboratory Techniques; Medical Technology; Ophthalmology; Optics; Radiology); **Liberal Arts** (*Campus 2*) (Arts and Humanities); **Liberal Arts** (*Campus 1*) (Archaeology; Arts and Humanities; Biology; History; Korean; Mathematics; Natural Sciences; Yoga); **Natural Science** (*Campus 1*) (Cooking and Catering; Food Science; Nutrition); **Nursing** (*Campus 2*) (Nursing);

SHINHAN Lifelong College (*Campus 1*); **Social Sciences** (*Campus 1*) (Mass Communication; Preschool Education; Public Administration; Public Law; Social Welfare)

Graduate School

Knowledge and Social Welfare (Psychology; Social Welfare; Welfare and Protective Services); **Living and Culture** (Child Care and Development; Home Economics; Psychotherapy); **Public Health** (Nutrition; Public Health; Sports)

History: Founded 1960 as Shinheung Agricultural High School, successively renamed Shinheung Commercial High School 1963, Shinheung Health College 1979, Shinheung Industrial College 1980, Shinheung Junior College 1988, Shinheung College Shinheung College 2011, Shinheung University 2013. Acquired current title 2014.

Main language(s) of instruction: Korean

Accrediting agency: Ministry of Education

Degrees and diplomas: Bachelor's Degree (Archaeology; Arts and Humanities; Automotive Engineering; Biology; Biomedicine; Computer Engineering; Cooking and Catering; Cosmetology; Dental Hygiene; Dentistry; Design; Electronic Engineering; Energy Engineering; Environmental Engineering; Fashion Design; Food Science; History; Industrial Design; Information Technology; Interior Design; International Business; Korean; Laboratory Techniques; Management; Mass Communication; Materials Engineering; Mathematics; Medical Technology; Natural Sciences; Nursing; Nutrition; Ophthalmology; Optics; Performing Arts; Preschool Education; Public Administration; Public Law; Radiology; Social Welfare; Textile Technology; Tourism; Yoga), Master's Degree (Home Economics; Public Health; Social Welfare)

Last Update: 23-03-2018

Silla University

140 Baegyang-daero(Blvd) 700beon-gil(Rd) Sasang-gu
Pusan 46958
Tel: +82(51) 999-5480, +82(51) 999-5515
Fax: +82(51) 999-5079, +82(51) 999-5519
Website: http://www.silla.ac.kr
President: Tae Hak Park

College

Arts (Dance; Fine Arts; Handicrafts; Music); **Economics and Business Administration** (Accountancy; Advertising and Publicity; Business Administration; E- Business/Commerce; Economics; International Business; Public Relations; Taxation; Tourism); **Education** (Computer Education; Education; Foreign Languages Education; Humanities and Social Science Education; Mathematics Education; Native Language Education; Preschool Education); **Engineering**

(Architecture; Automotive Engineering; Electronic Engineering; Engineering; Environmental Engineering; Materials Engineering; Mechanical Engineering); **Humanities** (Arts and Humanities; Chinese; English; Geography; History; Information Sciences; International Relations; International Studies; Japanese; Korean; Law; Library Science; Literature; Philosophy; Police Studies; Political Sciences; Public Administration; Social Welfare; Social Work); **IT Design** (Computer Engineering; Fashion Design; Industrial Design; Information Technology; Interior Design; Jewellery Art; Telecommunications Engineering); **Medical and Life Sciences** (Biological and Life Sciences; Food Science; Health Sciences; Nursing; Nutrition; Pharmacy; Physical Education; Physical Therapy)

Department/Division
General Education

Graduate School

Business Administration (Business Administration); **Education** (Education); **Graduate Studies** (Arts and Humanities; Engineering; Fine Arts; Natural Sciences; Performing Arts; Physical Education); **Social Welfare** (Social Welfare)

Further information: Also 10 Attached Institutes and 7 Research Institutes

History: Founded 1964 as Women's College, acquired present status and title 1983.

Academic year: March to February

Main language(s) of instruction: Korean

Accrediting agency: Korean Council for University Education (KCUE)

Degrees and diplomas: Bachelor's Degree, Master's Degree (Advertising and Publicity; Architecture; Archiving; Art Criticism; Automotive Engineering; Biological and Life Sciences; Biotechnology; Business Administration; Chemical Engineering; Clothing and Sewing; Computer Engineering; Dance; Design; Economics; Electronic Engineering; Energy Engineering; English; Environmental Engineering; Environmental Studies; Family Studies; Fine Arts; Food Science; Handicrafts; History; Industrial Design; Information Management; Information Technology; International Business; International Studies; Japanese; Korean; Law; Literature; Management; Materials Engineering; Mechanical Engineering; Music; Music Theory and Composition; Musical Instruments; Nutrition; Painting and Drawing; Performing Arts; Physical Education; Physical Therapy; Public Administration; Public Relations; Sculpture; Social Welfare; Textile Technology; Tourism; Visual Arts), Doctor's Degree (Accountancy; Biological and Life Sciences; Biotechnology; Business Administration; Clothing and Sewing; Computer Education; Computer Engineering; Education; Educational Administration; Educational and Student Counselling; Educational Sciences; Educational Technology; Educational

Testing and Evaluation; Engineering; English; Environmental Engineering; Family Studies; Fine Arts; Foreign Languages Education; Humanities and Social Science Education; Information Technology; International Business; International Economics; International Studies; Japanese; Korean; Law; Literature; Management; Marine Biology; Mathematics Education; Native Language Education; Performing Arts; Philosophy of Education; Physical Education; Preschool Education; Public Administration; Social Welfare)

Student Services: Health Services, Library, IT Centre
Periodicals: Journal, Women's Studies
Publishing house: University Press

Academic Staff 2013-2014	MALE	FEMALE	TOTAL
FULL-TIME			c. 360
Student Numbers 2013-2014			
All (Foreign Included)			c. 10543
Foreign only			673

Last Update: 06-03-2018

Sogang University

35 Baekbeom-ro Mapo-gu
Seoul 04107
Tel: +82(2) 705-8114
Fax: +82(2) 705-8119
Website: http://www.sogang.ac.kr
President: Jong Gou Park
Tel: +82(2) 705-8200

School

Business Administration (Business Administration); **Communication** (Mass Communication); **Economics** (Economics); **Engineering** (Bioengineering; Chemical Engineering; Computer Engineering; Computer Science; Electronic Engineering; Mechanical Engineering; Molecular Biology); **Humanities and International Cultures** (American Studies; Asian Studies; Chinese; East Asian Studies; English; English Studies; French Studies; German; Germanic Studies; History; Japanese; Korean; Linguistics; Literature; Philosophy; Religious Studies); **Integrated Knowledge** (East Asian Studies; Fine Arts; International Studies; Technology); **Interdisciplinary Programmes** (Biotechnology; Economics; Educational Sciences; Gender Studies; Leadership; Media Studies; Philosophy; Political Sciences; Religion; Science Education; Theology); **Natural Sciences** (Biological and Life Sciences; Chemistry; Mathematics; Physics); **Social Sciences** (Political Sciences; Psychology; Sociology)

Centre
Entrepreneurship

Graduate School
Business (*Professional*) (Business Administration); **Economics** (*Special*) (Economics); **Education** (*Special*) (Education); **Graduate Studies** (Bioengineering; Biological and Life Sciences; Biotechnology; Chemical Engineering; Chemistry; Chinese; Communication Studies; Computer Engineering; Computer Science; Economics; Electronic Engineering; English; French; Gender Studies; German; History; Korean; Literature; Mass Communication; Mathematics; Mechanical Engineering; Molecular Biology; Philosophy; Physics; Political Sciences; Psychology; Religious Studies; Sociology; Southeast Asian Studies); **Information Technology** (*Special*) (Information Technology); **International Studies** (*Professional*) (East Asian Studies; Finance; International Business; International Relations; International Studies); **Law** (*Professional*) (Law); **Mass Communication** (*Special*) (Mass Communication); **Media Communications** (*Professional*) (Mass Communication; Media Studies); **MOT (Management of Technology)** (*Professional*) (Management; Technology); **Public Policy** (*Special*) (Public Administration); **Theology** (*Professional*) (Theology)

Research Division
Basic Sciences; **Business**; **East Asian Studies**; **Humanities**; **Information and Communication Technologies**; **International and Area Studies**; **Language and Information**; **Legal Science**; **Life and Culture**; **Philosophical Studies**; **Religion**; **Social Sciences**; **Study of Media Culture**; **Technology Management**; **Theology**

Further information: 21 additional Research Institutes

History: Founded 1960 as College by the Society of Jesus, acquired University status 1970. A private institution financed by tuition fees (60%) and grants.

Academic year: March to December (March-July; August-December)

Admission requirements: Graduation from high school or equivalent, and entrance examination

Fees: Undergraduate, 3,629,000-4,742,000 per semester; Graduate, 4,635,000-9,130,000 per semester (Won)

Main language(s) of instruction: Korean

Accrediting agency: Ministry of Education; Korean Council for University Education (KCUE)

Degrees and diplomas: Bachelor's Degree, Master's Degree (Advertising and Publicity; American Studies; Bioengineering; Biological and Life Sciences; Biomedical Engineering; Biotechnology; Business Administration; Chemical Engineering; Chemistry; Chinese; Communication Studies; Computer Engineering; Computer Science; East Asian Studies; Economics; Electronic Engineering; English; Film; French; Gender Studies; German; History; Information Sciences; Information Technology; International Business; International Relations; International Studies; Journalism; Korean; Law; Linguistics; Literature; Mass Communication; Mathematics; Mechanical Engineering; Media Studies; Philosophy; Physics; Political Sciences; Protective Services; Psychology; Public Relations; Religious Studies; Sociology; Southeast Asian Studies; Theatre; Theology), Doctor's Degree (Advertising and Publicity; Bioengineering; Biological and Life Sciences; Biomedical Engineering; Biotechnology; Chemical Engineering; Chemistry; Computer Engineering; Computer Science; East Asian Studies; Economics; Electronic Engineering; English; Film; Finance; Foreign Languages Education; French; German; History; Information Sciences; International Relations; International Studies; Journalism; Korean; Law; Linguistics; Literature; Mass Communication; Mathematics; Mechanical Engineering; Media Studies; Philosophy; Physics; Political Sciences; Protective Services; Psychology; Public Relations; Religious Studies; Sociology; Theatre; Theology)

Student Services: Academic Counselling, Social Counselling, Careers Guidance, Cultural Activities, Sports Facilities, Language Laboratory, Facilities for disabled people, Health Services, Canteen, Library, IT Centre, Residential Facilities

Periodicals: East Asian Studies, Humanistic Studies, Humanities Journal, Social Science Studies, Sogang Economics Papers, Sogang Journal of Business, Sogang Journal of Media and Culture, Sogang University General Bulletin, Understanding People

Publishing house: Sogang University Press

Academic Staff 2017-2018	MALE	FEMALE	TOTAL
FULL-TIME	539	216	755
PART-TIME			800
Student Numbers 2017-2018			
All (Foreign Included)	5140	4087	9227
Foreign only			1083

Last Update: 24-05-2018

Songwon University

73, Songamro, Nam-gu
Gwangju
Tel: +82(62) 360-5700
Fax: +82(62) 360-5756
Website: http://www.songwon.ac.kr/english
President: Su-tae Choi

College
Engineering (Automotive Engineering; Civil Engineering; Computer Engineering; Electrical Engineering; Electronic

Engineering; Information Sciences; Mechanical Engineering; Structural Architecture)

Course/Programme
Korean Language (Korean)

School
Art and Sports (Acting; Dance; Music; Performing Arts; Sports); **Humanities and Social Sciences** (Air Transport; Finance; Military Science; Preschool Education; Psychology; Railway Transport; Social Welfare; Taxation); **Natural Science** (Cosmetology; Dental Hygiene; Food Science; Nursing; Nutrition; Psychology; Rehabilitation and Therapy; Speech Therapy and Audiology)
History: Founded 2001.
Main language(s) of instruction: Korean
Accrediting agency: Ministry of Education
Degrees and diplomas: Bachelor's Degree (Acting; Air Transport; Automotive Engineering; Civil Engineering; Computer Engineering; Cosmetology; Dance; Dental Hygiene; Electrical Engineering; Electronic Engineering; Finance; Food Science; Information Sciences; Korean; Mechanical Engineering; Military Science; Music; Nursing; Nutrition; Performing Arts; Preschool Education; Psychology; Railway Transport; Rehabilitation and Therapy; Social Welfare; Speech Therapy and Audiology; Sports; Structural Architecture; Taxation)
Last Update: 26-03-2018

Sookmyung Women's University

53-12 Chungpa-dong 2 ka Yongsan-gu
Seoul 140-742
Tel: +82(2) 710-9114
Fax: +82(2) 718-2337
Website: http://www.sookmyung.ac.kr
President: Jung Ai Kang

College
Communication and Media (Mass Communication; Media Studies); **Economics and Business Administration** (Business and Commerce; Consumer Studies; Economics); **Engineering** (Engineering); **English** (English); **Fine Arts** (Architectural and Environmental Design; Design; Fine Arts; Graphic Design; Handicrafts; Industrial Design; Interior Design; Painting and Drawing); **General Education** (Education); **Global Service**; **Human Ecology** (Child Care and Development; Clothing and Sewing; Family Studies; Food Science; Home Economics; Nutrition; Textile Design; Textile Technology); **Law** (Law); **Liberal Arts** (Arts and Humanities; Chinese; Cultural Studies; Education; Educational Psychology; English; French; German; History; Information

Sciences; Japanese; Korean; Library Science; Tourism); **Music** (Music; Music Theory and Composition; Musical Instruments; Singing); **Pharmacy** (Pharmacy); **Science** (Biological and Life Sciences; Chemistry; Computer Science; Dance; Information Sciences; Mass Communication; Mathematics; Multimedia; Natural Sciences; Physical Education; Physics; Statistics); **Social Sciences** (Social Sciences)

School
Business (*Sookmyung*) (Business Administration)

Centre
Asia-Pacific Women's Information Network (*APWINC*) (Computer Networks)

Laboratory
Women's Health (Health Sciences)

Graduate School
Clinical Pharmacy (Health Sciences; Pharmacy); **Computer-assisted Language Learning (TESOL)** (English); **Distance Learning** (Business Administration; Child Care and Development; Cosmetology; Education; Preschool Education; Technology); **Education** (Art Education; Education; Home Economics; Modern Languages; Natural Sciences; Physical Education; Social Sciences); **Graduate Studies** (Arts and Humanities; Engineering; Fine Arts; Natural Sciences; Physical Education; Social Sciences); **Human Resources Development for Women** (Human Resources); **International Services** (International Relations; International Studies; Social Studies); **Life Style Design** (Advertising and Publicity; Ceramic Art; Design; Fashion Design; Fine Arts; Industrial Design; Interior Design; Packaging Technology; Textile Design); **Music Therapy** (Art Therapy; Rehabilitation and Therapy); **Public Policy and Industry** (Public Administration; Social Sciences; Social Welfare); **Social Education** (Humanities and Social Science Education); **Traditional Culture and Arts** (Art History; Cultural Studies; Dance; Music)

Research Division
Asian Women (Social Sciences; Women's Studies); **Child Study** (Child Care and Development; Paediatrics); **Design** (*Sookmyung*) (Industrial Design); **Drug Information** (Toxicology); **Economics and Business Administration** (Business Administration; Economics); **English Language and Cultural Studies** (English; English Studies); **General Education** (Education); **Global Environment**; **Humanities** (*Sookmyung*) (Arts and Humanities); **ICT Convergence** (Information Technology); **Korean Language and Culture** (East Asian Studies; Korean); **Law** (Law); **Multicultural Studies** (*Sookmyung*); **Natural Sciences** (Natural Sciences);

Pharmaceutical Sciences (Pharmacy); **Security Studies** (*Sookmyung*) (Protective Services)

History: Founded 1906, became College 1938, acquired University status 1955.

Academic year: March to December (March-July; August-December)

Admission requirements: Graduation from high school and entrance examination

Main language(s) of instruction: Korean

Accrediting agency: Korean Council for University Education (KCUE)

Degrees and diplomas: Bachelor's Degree, Master's Degree (Accountancy; Administration; Advertising and Publicity; Analytical Chemistry; Architectural and Environmental Design; Archiving; Art Education; Art History; Art Management; Art Therapy; Automation and Control Engineering; Biochemistry; Bioengineering; Biological and Life Sciences; Business Administration; Chemical Engineering; Child Care and Development; Chinese; Clothing and Sewing; Computer Science; Consumer Studies; Continuing Education; Cosmetology; Criminology; Dance; Economic History; Economics; Educational Administration; Educational Psychology; Educational Sciences; Electronic Engineering; Engineering; English; Family Studies; Finance; Fine Arts; Food Science; Foreign Languages Education; French; German; Graphic Design; Handicrafts; History; Home Economics Education; Hotel and Restaurant; Human Resources; Humanities and Social Science Education; Industrial and Organizational Psychology; Industrial Design; Industrial Management; Information Sciences; Information Technology; Inorganic Chemistry; Interior Design; International Business; International Economics; International Relations; Japanese; Korean; Landscape Architecture; Law; Library Science; Linguistics; Literature; Management; Marketing; Mass Communication; Mathematics; Mathematics Education; Mechanical Engineering; Media Studies; Music Education; Music Theory and Composition; Musical Instruments; Native Language Education; Nutrition; Organic Chemistry; Pharmacology; Pharmacy; Philosophy of Education; Physical Chemistry; Physical Education; Physics; Political Sciences; Preschool Education; Psychology; Public Relations; Rehabilitation and Therapy; Robotics; Science Education; Singing; Social Psychology; Sports Management; Statistics; Telecommunications Engineering; Textile Design; Tourism; Translation and Interpretation; Visual Arts; Welfare and Protective Services), Doctor's Degree (Accountancy; Administration; Advertising and Publicity; Analytical Chemistry; Architectural and Environmental Design; Archiving; Art Education; Art History; Art Management; Art Therapy; Biochemistry; Bioengineering; Biological and Life Sciences; Business Administration; Chemical Engineering; Child Care and Development; Chinese; Clothing and Sewing; Computer Science; Continuing Education; Cosmetology; Dance; Design; East Asian Studies; Economic History; Economics; Educational Administration; Educational Psychology; Educational Sciences; Engineering; English; Family Studies; Finance; Fine Arts; Food Science; Foreign Languages Education; French; German; Graphic Design; Handicrafts; History; Home Economics Education; Human Resources; Humanities and Social Science Education; Industrial Design; Industrial Management; Information Sciences; Information Technology; Inorganic Chemistry; Interior Design; International Business; International Economics; International Relations; Korean; Landscape Architecture; Law; Library Science; Linguistics; Literature; Management; Marketing; Mass Communication; Mathematics; Mathematics Education; Mechanical Engineering; Media Studies; Music Education; Music Theory and Composition; Musical Instruments; Native Language Education; Nutrition; Organic Chemistry; Pharmacology; Pharmacy; Philosophy of Education; Physical Chemistry; Physical Education; Physics; Political Sciences; Preschool Education; Psychology; Public Relations; Rehabilitation and Therapy; Science Education; Singing; Sports Management; Statistics; Textile Design; Tourism; Translation and Interpretation; Visual Arts; Welfare and Protective Services). Also MBA; Combined Master's and Doctorate Programmes; Global Dual Degree Programmes

Student Services: Academic Counselling, Social Counselling, Careers Guidance, Nursery Care, Cultural Activities, Sports Facilities, Language Laboratory, Facilities for disabled people, Health Services, Canteen, Foreign Studies Centre, Library, Residential Facilities

Periodicals: Asian Women (English), Chung-Pa (Korean), Gentle Power to Change the World (English)

Publishing house: Sookdae Shinbo (Sookmyung Women's University Press)

Academic Staff 2017-2018	MALE	FEMALE	TOTAL
FULL-TIME			459
Student Numbers 2017-2018			
All (Foreign Included)			12869
Foreign only			634

Last Update: 02-02-2018

Soonchunhyang University (SCH)

646 Eupnae-ri Sinchang-myeon
Asan-si 31538, Chungnam-do
Tel: +82(41) 530-1114, +82(41) 530-1693
Fax: +82(41) 542-4615, +82(41) 530-1381
Website: http://www.sch.ac.kr
President: Kyo Il Suh
Tel: +82(41) 530-1001

College

Engineering (Architecture; Chemical Engineering; Computer Engineering; Computer Science; Electrical and Electronic Engineering; Electrical Engineering; Electronic Engineering; Energy Engineering; Engineering; Environmental Engineering; Information Management; Information Technology; Materials Engineering; Mechanical Engineering; Nanotechnology; Software Engineering; Telecommunications Engineering); **Humanities** (Chinese; Cultural Studies; Dance; Educational and Student Counselling; English; Film; International Studies; Korean; Media Studies; Preschool Education; Special Education; Theatre; Visual Arts); **Medical Sciences** (Biomedicine; Biotechnology; Health Administration; Health Sciences; Information Technology; Laboratory Techniques; Management; Medical Auxiliaries; Medical Technology; Medicine; Occupational Therapy); **Medicine** (Medicine; Nursing); **Natural Sciences** (Biology; Biotechnology; Chemistry; Environmental Studies; Food Science; Health Sciences; Leisure Studies; Marine Biology; Mathematics; Natural Sciences; Nutrition; Parks and Recreation; Physics; Sports Medicine); **Social Sciences** (Business Administration; Business and Commerce; Economics; Finance; Insurance; International Business; Journalism; Law; Mass Communication; Police Studies; Public Administration; Social Welfare; Social Work; Tourism)

Graduate School

Education (Education; Secondary Education); **Forensic Science** (Biomedicine; Forensic Medicine and Dentistry; Physics; Social Sciences); **Global Management** (Finance; Insurance; International Business; Management; Tourism); **Graduate Studies** (Arts and Humanities; Engineering; Medicine; Performing Arts; Physical Education; Social Sciences); **Healthcare Science** (Cosmetology; Health Administration; Health Sciences; Nursing; Psychotherapy); **Industrial Information** (Biological and Life Sciences; E- Business/Commerce; Environmental Studies; Film; Finance; Information Management; Insurance; International Business; International Studies; Journalism; Management; Medical Technology; Natural Resources; Occupational Health; Public Relations; Rehabilitation and Therapy; Telecommunications Engineering; Theatre; Tourism; Visual Arts); **Public Administration** (Peace and Disarmament; Police Studies; Public Administration; Social Welfare)

History: Founded 1978 as Medical College, acquired present status and title 1990.

Academic year: March to December (March-June; August-December)

Admission requirements: Graduation from high school and entrance examination

Main language(s) of instruction: Korean

Accrediting agency: Korean Council for University Education (KCUE)

Degrees and diplomas: Bachelor's Degree, Master's Degree (Architecture; Biological and Life Sciences; Biology; Business and Commerce; Business Education; Chemical Engineering; Chemistry; Computer Education; Computer Engineering; Continuing Education; Cosmetology; Curriculum; Dance; E- Business/Commerce; Economics; Education; Education of the Gifted; Educational Administration; Educational and Student Counselling; Educational Sciences; Electrical Engineering; Electronic Engineering; English; Environmental Engineering; Environmental Studies; Film; Finance; Food Science; Foreign Languages Education; Forensic Medicine and Dentistry; Genetics; Government; Health Administration; Health Sciences; Home Economics Education; Humanities and Social Science Education; Information Technology; Insurance; International Business; International Studies; Journalism; Law; Literature; Management; Marine Biology; Materials Engineering; Mathematics; Mathematics Education; Mechanical Engineering; Media Studies; Medical Technology; Medicine; Native Language Education; Natural Resources; Nursing; Nutrition; Occupational Health; Peace and Disarmament; Performing Arts; Physical Education; Physics; Police Studies; Preschool Education; Psychotherapy; Public Administration; Public Relations; Rehabilitation and Therapy; Robotics; Science Education; Secondary Education; Social Welfare; Special Education; Telecommunications Engineering; Theatre; Tourism; Treatment Techniques; Visual Arts; Water Science), Doctor's Degree (Architecture; Biological and Life Sciences; Biology; Business and Commerce; Chemical Engineering; Chemistry; Computer Engineering; Dance; Economics; Educational Sciences; Electrical Engineering; Electronic Engineering; English; Environmental Engineering; Environmental Studies; Film; Finance; Food Science; Genetics; Health Sciences; Information Technology; Insurance; International Business; Literature; Management; Marine Biology; Materials Engineering; Mathematics; Mechanical Engineering; Medicine; Nursing; Nutrition; Physical Education; Physics; Robotics; Telecommunications Engineering; Theatre; Tourism; Water Science). Also industry-collaboration Master's programmes offered with five institutions: Korea Information Security Agency, Korea Information Technology Research Institute, National Institute of Environmental Research, National Youth Policy Institute and Small & Medium Business Corporation.

Student Services: Academic Counselling, Social Counselling, Careers Guidance, Sports Facilities, Language Laboratory, Health Services, Canteen, Library, IT Centre, Residential Facilities

Publishing house: Soonchunhyang University Press

Academic Staff 2013-2014	MALE	FEMALE	TOTAL
FULL-TIME			c. 380
Student Numbers 2013-2014			
All (Foreign Included)			10619
Foreign only			559

Last Update: 06-03-2018

Soongsil University (SSU)

1-1 Sangdo 5-dong Dongjak-ku
Seoul 156-743
Tel: +82(2) 820-0114
Fax: +82(2) 816-1513
Website: http://www.ssu.ac.kr
President: Jun-Seong Hwang

College

Business Administration (Business Administration); **Business and Economics** (Accountancy; Business Administration; Economics; International Business; Small Business); **Engineering** (Architecture; Chemical Engineering; Electrical and Electronic Engineering; Engineering; Industrial Engineering; Mechanical Engineering; Telecommunications Engineering; Textile Technology); **Humanities** (Arts and Humanities; Chinese; English; French; German; History; Korean; Literature; Philosophy); **Information Technology** (Artificial Intelligence; Computer Science; Information Sciences; Software Engineering; Telecommunications Engineering); **Law** (Law); **Natural Sciences** (Chemistry; Mathematics; Natural Sciences; Physics; Statistics); **Social Sciences** (International Relations; Japanese; Political Sciences; Public Administration; Social Sciences; Social Work)

Department/Division

Baird; **Creative Arts** (Film; Writing); **Sport for all Studies** (Sports)

Institute

Business and Economic Strategies (Business Administration; Finance); **Economics and International Commerce** (Economics; International Business); **Future Technology** (Technology); **High-Tech IT Convergence** (Information Technology); **Humanities** (Arts and Humanities); **Korean Christian Culture Research** (Cultural Studies); **Legal Studies** (Law); **Natural Sciences** (Industrial Engineering); **Social Sciences** (Social Studies); **Soongsil Institute of Fusion Technology** (*SIFT*)

Graduate School

Business Administration (Business Administration); **Christian Studies** (Christian Religious Studies); **Education** (Education); **Graduate Studies** (Accountancy; Actuarial Science; Advertising and Publicity; Architecture; Biological and Life Sciences; Chemical Engineering; Chemistry; Chinese; Christian Religious Studies; Computer Engineering; Computer Science; Continuing Education; Economics; Electrical Engineering; Electronic Engineering; English; Environmental Engineering; French; German; History; Industrial Engineering; Information Management; Information Technology; Interior Design; International Business; International Relations; Japanese; Journalism; Korean; Law; Literature; Management; Mass Communication; Materials Engineering; Mathematics; Mechanical Engineering; Multimedia; Philosophy; Physics; Political Sciences; Public Administration; Public Relations; Radio and Television Broadcasting; Social Welfare; Sociology; Sports; Statistics; Telecommunications Engineering; Writing); **Information Sciences** (Information Sciences); **Small Business** (Small Business)

History: Founded 1897 by the Northern Presbyterian Church of the United States and became 4-year College 1905. Merged with Tae Jon College and became Soong Jun University 1971. Tae Jon College separated from the main campus 1983, and the School restored to its original name of Soong Sil 1987. A private institution.

Academic year: March to February (March-June; August-February)

Admission requirements: Graduation from high school or equivalent, and entrance examination

Main language(s) of instruction: Korean

Accrediting agency: Korean Council for University Education (KCUE)

Degrees and diplomas: Bachelor's Degree (Business Administration; Economics; Engineering; Law; Literature; Natural Sciences; Political Sciences; Public Administration), Master's Degree (Accountancy; Actuarial Science; Advertising and Publicity; Architecture; Biological and Life Sciences; Chemical Engineering; Chemistry; Chinese; Christian Religious Studies; Computer Engineering; Computer Science; Continuing Education; Economics; Electrical Engineering; Electronic Engineering; English; Environmental Engineering; French; German; History; Industrial Engineering; Information Management; Information Technology; Interior Design; International Business; International Relations; Japanese; Journalism; Korean; Law; Literature; Management; Mass Communication; Materials Engineering; Mathematics; Mechanical Engineering; Multimedia; Philosophy; Physics; Political Sciences; Public Administration; Public Relations; Radio and Television Broadcasting; Social Welfare; Sociology; Sports; Statistics; Telecommunications Engineering; Writing), Doctor's Degree (Architecture; Biological and

Life Sciences; Business Administration; Computer Science; Continuing Education; Economics; Information Technology; International Business; Mechanical Engineering; Philosophy; Public Administration; Social Welfare; Structural Architecture)

Student Services: Sports Facilities, Library, Residential Facilities

Periodicals: Essays and Papers of the Graduate School, Joong Sil Sahak, Journal of Graduate School of Regional Development, Journal of Social Sciences, Soong Sil Law Review, Soong Sil University Essays and Papers

Publishing house: Soong Sil University Press

Student Numbers 2015-2016	MALE	FEMALE	TOTAL
All (Foreign Included)			16000
Foreign only			1000

Last Update: 06-03-2018

Specialized Korea Polytechnic (Aviation Campus) (KPAC)

Daehakgil 46
Sacheon 52 549, Gyeongsangnam-do
Tel: +82(55) 55-830-3500
Fax: +82(55) 55-830-3515
Website: http://www.kopo.ac.kr/kapc/index.do

Department/Division

Aircraft Maintenance (Maintenance Technology); **Aviation Control Systems** (Automation and Control Engineering); **Aviation Electronics** (Electronic Engineering); **Aviation Machinery** (Mechanical Engineering); **Aviation Mechatronics** (Electronic Engineering)

History: Founded 2000 as Korea Aviation Polytechnic College, acquired current title 2012.

Main language(s) of instruction: Korean

Accrediting agency: Ministry of Education

Degrees and diplomas: Bachelor's Degree (Engineering; Technology)

Last Update: 28-03-2018

Sun Moon University (SMU)

70 221-beongil, Sunmoon-ro Tangjeong-myeon
Asan-si 31460, Chungnam-do
Tel: +82(41) 530-2114
Fax: +82(41) 541-7424
Website: http://www.sunmoon.ac.kr
President: Jo Hwang Sun
Tel: +82(41) 530-2112

College

Engineering (Architecture; Bioengineering; Chemical Engineering; Civil Engineering; Computer Engineering; Computer Science; Electronic Engineering; Engineering; Engineering Management; Environmental Engineering; Industrial Engineering; Information Sciences; Information Technology; Materials Engineering; Mechanical Engineering; Natural Sciences; Telecommunications Engineering); **General Studies** (Arabic; Arts and Humanities; Chinese; Computer Education; Continuing Education; English; French; Information Technology; Japanese; Modern Languages; Teacher Training); **Health Sciences** (Biomedicine; Dental Hygiene; Food Science; Health Sciences; Marine Biology; Medical Technology; Nursing; Pharmacy; Physical Therapy; Protective Services; Sports); **Humanities and Foreign Languages** (Asian Studies; Chinese; Cultural Studies; East Asian Studies; Eastern European Studies; English; Graphic Design; History; Japanese; Korean; Latin American Studies; Literature; Russian; Spanish); **International Peace Studies** (Asian Studies; East Asian Studies; International Business; International Economics; International Relations; Korean; Leisure Studies; Tourism); **Social Sciences** (Advertising and Publicity; Business Administration; Industrial and Organizational Psychology; Information Management; Information Technology; Journalism; Law; Mass Communication; Police Studies; Public Administration; Public Relations; Social Sciences; Social Welfare); **Theology and Pure Love** (Child Care and Development; Theology)

Graduate School

Education (*Special*) (East Asian Studies; Education; Educational Administration; Educational and Student Counselling; Environmental Studies; Foreign Languages Education; Humanities and Social Science Education; Mathematics Education; Native Language Education; Physical Education; Teacher Training); **General Graduate Studies** (Architecture; Arts and Humanities; Bioengineering; Biological and Life Sciences; Biology; Chemical Engineering; Chemistry; Civil Engineering; Computer Engineering; Electrical Engineering; Engineering; English; Environmental Engineering; History; Industrial Engineering; Information Technology; Korean; Law; Literature; Materials Engineering; Mathematics; Mechanical Engineering; Metallurgical Engineering; Nanotechnology; Natural Sciences; Philosophy; Physical Education; Public Administration; Social Sciences; Telecommunications Engineering); **Integrated Medical Sciences** (*Special*) (Alternative Medicine; Cosmetology; Esoteric Practices; Rehabilitation and Therapy); **Interpretation and Translation** (*Special*) (Chinese; English; Japanese; Korean; Russian; Spanish; Translation and Interpretation); **Public Administration** (*Special*) (Administration; Fire Science; Government; Police Studies; Protective Services; Public Administration; Real Estate); **Social Welfare** (*Special*)

(Family Studies; Psychology; Rehabilitation and Therapy; Social Psychology; Social Welfare); **Theology** (*Professional*) (Missionary Studies; Religion; Theology)

History: Founded 1986, acquired present status 1989.

Academic year: March to December (March-June; September- December)

Admission requirements: Graduation from high school

Fees: 3m. per semester (Won)

Main language(s) of instruction: Korean

Accrediting agency: Ministry of Education and Human Resource Development; Korean Council for University Education (KCUE)

Degrees and diplomas: Bachelor's Degree, Master's Degree (Administration; Alternative Medicine; Analytical Chemistry; Applied Mathematics; Applied Physics; Architecture and Planning; Automation and Control Engineering; Biochemistry; Bioengineering; Biological and Life Sciences; Cell Biology; Chemical Engineering; Chemistry; Chinese; Chiropractic; Civil Engineering; Comparative Literature; Computer Engineering; Computer Science; Construction Engineering; Cosmetology; Educational and Student Counselling; Electronic Engineering; English; Environmental Engineering; Food Science; Food Technology; Foreign Languages Education; Geological Engineering; History; Hydraulic Engineering; Industrial Engineering; Information Technology; Inorganic Chemistry; International Economics; Japanese; Korean; Law; Literature; Management; Marine Biology; Materials Engineering; Mathematics; Mechanical Engineering; Metallurgical Engineering; Missionary Studies; Molecular Biology; Natural Resources; Organic Chemistry; Philosophy; Physics; Russian; Social Welfare; Social Work; Solid State Physics; Spanish; Structural Architecture; Telecommunications Engineering; Theology; Translation and Interpretation), Doctor's Degree (Administration; Applied Chemistry; Applied Physics; Architecture and Planning; Automation and Control Engineering; Biochemistry; Bioengineering; Biological and Life Sciences; Cell Biology; Chemical Engineering; Chemistry; Civil Engineering; Computer Engineering; Computer Science; Construction Engineering; Educational and Student Counselling; Electronic Engineering; Environmental Engineering; Food Science; Food Technology; Geological Engineering; Hydraulic Engineering; Industrial Engineering; Information Technology; Inorganic Chemistry; Korean; Law; Literature; Marine Biology; Materials Engineering; Mechanical Engineering; Metallurgical Engineering; Molecular Biology; Natural Resources; Organic Chemistry; Physics; Solid State Physics; Structural Architecture; Telecommunications Engineering; Theology)

Student Services: Academic Counselling, Social Counselling, Careers Guidance, Cultural Activities, Sports Facilities, Language Laboratory, Facilities for disabled people, Health Services, Canteen, Foreign Studies Centre, Library, Residential Facilities

Publishing house: The University Press

Academic Staff 2013-2014	MALE	FEMALE	TOTAL
FULL-TIME			c. 425
Student Numbers 2013-2014			
All (Foreign Included)			c. 10058
Foreign only			1117

Last Update: 06-03-2018

Sungkonghoe University (SKHU)

320, Yeondong-ro, Guro-gu
Seoul 152-716
Tel: +82(2) 2610-4114, +82(2) 2610-4129
Fax: +82(2) 2683-8858
Website: http://www.skhu.ac.kr
President: Jeongku Lee

College

Engineering (Computer Engineering; Engineering; Information Technology; Software Engineering; Telecommunications Engineering); **Humanities** (Chinese; English; History; Japanese; Theology); **Natural Sciences** (Information Technology); **Social Sciences** (Business Administration; Journalism; Social Sciences; Social Welfare)

Graduate School

Cultural Studies (Art Management; Cultural Studies); **Education** (Education; Special Education); **Graduate Studies** (Asian Studies; Business Administration; Cultural Studies; Development Studies; Social Welfare; Sociology); **NGO** (Asian Studies; Development Studies; Economics; Political Sciences; Public Administration; Women's Studies); **Social Welfare** (Social Welfare); **Theology** (Religious Music; Theology)

History: Founded 1914. A university of the Anglican Church of Korea.

Main language(s) of instruction: Korean

Accrediting agency: Korean Council for University Education (KCUE)

Degrees and diplomas: Bachelor's Degree, Master's Degree (Art Management; Cultural Studies; Development Studies; Education; Management; Religion; Social Welfare; Sociology; Theology), Doctor's Degree (Pastoral Studies; Theology)

Student Services: Academic Counselling, Cultural Activities, Sports Facilities, Library, IT Centre, Residential Facilities

Academic Staff 2013-2014	MALE	FEMALE	TOTAL
FULL-TIME			c. 110
Student Numbers 2013-2014			
All (Foreign Included)			c. 2260

Last Update: 06-03-2018

Sungkyul University

147-2 Anyang 8-dong Manan-gu
Anyang-si 430-742, Gyeonggi-do
Tel: +82(31) 467-8114
Fax: +82(31) 467-0529
Website: http://www.sungkyul.ac.kr
President: Dong Cheol Yoon
Tel: +82(31) 467-8001

College

Arts (Acting; Cosmetology; Film; Fine Arts; Music; Music Theory and Composition; Musical Instruments; Performing Arts; Religious Music; Singing; Theatre); **Education** (Education; Physical Education; Preschool Education); **Engineering** (Computer Engineering; Engineering; Industrial Engineering; Industrial Management; Information Technology; Multimedia); **Humanities** (Chinese; English; Japanese; Korean; Literature); **Liberal Arts and Teaching** (Arts and Humanities; Teacher Training); **Social Science** (Business Administration; Public Administration; Real Estate; Social and Community Services; Social Sciences; Social Welfare; Town Planning; Transport Management); **Theology** (Christian Religious Studies; Missionary Studies; Theology)

Graduate School

Culture Arts (Cosmetology; Cultural Studies; Design; Fashion Design; Music; Performing Arts); **Education** (Cosmetology; Education; Educational Administration; Educational and Student Counselling; Film; Physical Education; Preschool Education; Theatre); **Graduate Studies** (Business Administration; Education; Information Technology; Management; Preschool Education; Public Administration; Social Welfare; Telecommunications Engineering); **Management and Public Administration** (Business Administration; Management; Public Administration); **Social Welfare** (Development Studies; Social and Community Services; Social Welfare); **Theology** (*SungKyul*) (Bible; Ethics; History of Religion; Missionary Studies; New Testament; Psychology; Theology); **Theology** (Bible; Christian Religious Studies; Ethics; History of Religion; Missionary Studies; New Testament; Psychology; Religious Education; Theology)
History: Founded 1962 as Seminary, acquired present status 1991.

Academic year: March to December (March-June; September-December)
Admission requirements: Graduation from high school
Fees: 3.9m. per annum (Won)
Main language(s) of instruction: Korean
Accrediting agency: Asia Theological Association (ATA); Ministry of Education; Korean Council for University Education (KCUE)
Degrees and diplomas: Bachelor's Degree, Master's Degree (Administration; Bible; Business Administration; Christian Religious Studies; Cosmetology; Cultural Studies; Education; Educational Administration; Educational and Student Counselling; Ethics; Fashion Design; Film; History of Religion; Information Technology; Management; Missionary Studies; Music; New Testament; Performing Arts; Physical Education; Preschool Education; Psychology; Public Administration; Real Estate; Religious Education; Social and Community Services; Social Welfare; Telecommunications Engineering; Theatre; Theology; Welfare and Protective Services), Doctor's Degree (Accountancy; Administration; Business and Commerce; Education; Finance; Human Resources; International Business; Management; Marketing; Public Administration; Real Estate; Social Welfare; Transport Management)
Student Services: Academic Counselling, Social Counselling, Careers Guidance, Nursery Care, Cultural Activities, Sports Facilities, Language Laboratory, Health Services, Foreign Studies Centre, Residential Facilities
Periodicals: Collection of Dissertations
Publishing house: University Press

Academic Staff 2012-2013	MALE	FEMALE	TOTAL
FULL-TIME			190
PART-TIME			375
Student Numbers 2012-2013			
All (Foreign Included)			5727

Last Update: 06-03-2018

Sungkyunkwan University (SKKU)

53 Myongnyun-dong 3-ga Jongno-gu
Seoul 110-745
Tel: +82(2) 760-1152
Fax: +82(2) 744-1153
Website: http://www.skku.edu
President: Kyu Sang Chun
Tel: +82(2) 760-1012

College

Education (*Humanities and Social Sciences Campus*) (Chinese; Computer Education; Education; Mathematics

Education); **Engineering** (*Natural Sciences Campus*) (Engineering); **Law** (*Humanities and Social Sciences Campus*) (Law); **Liberal Arts** (*Humanities and Social Sciences Campus*) (Chinese; English; French; German; History; Korean; Library Science; Literature; Philosophy; Russian); **Medicine** (*Natural Sciences Campus*) (Medicine)

School

Art (*Humanities and Social Sciences Campus*) (Cinema and Television; Dance; Design; Film; Fine Arts; Multimedia); **Business Administration** (*Humanities and Social Sciences Campus*) (Business Administration); **Confucian and Oriental Studies** (*Humanities and Social Sciences Campus*) (Arts and Humanities; Asian Religious Studies; Oriental Studies; Philosophical Schools; Philosophy); **Economics** (*Humanities and Social Sciences Campus*) (Economics; Statistics); **Human Life Sciences** (*Humanities and Social Sciences Campus*) (Child Care and Development; Consumer Studies; Family Studies; Fashion Design; Home Economics; Household Management; Psychology); **Information and Communication Engineering** (*Natural Sciences Campus*) (Information Technology; Telecommunications Engineering); **Life Sciences and Natural Resources** (*Natural Sciences Campus*) (Biological and Life Sciences; Biotechnology; Genetics); **Natural Sciences** (*Natural Sciences Campus*) (Biological and Life Sciences; Chemistry; Mathematics; Natural Sciences; Physics); **Pharmacy** (*Natural Sciences Campus*) (Pharmacy); **Social Sciences** (*Humanities and Social Sciences Campus*) (International Relations; Journalism; Mass Communication; Political Sciences; Psychology; Public Administration; Social Sciences; Social Welfare; Sociology); **Sport Science** (*Natural Sciences Campus*) (Leadership; Sports); **Systems Management Engineering** (*Suwon*) (Computer Engineering; Engineering; Management Systems)

History: Founded 992 as sole national institute of higher learning in Koryo Dynasty based on Confucian doctrine and principles. Re-established 1398 on present site during Chosun Dynasty. Recognized by Government as College 1946 and private University 1953.

Academic year: March to December (March-June; September-December)

Admission requirements: Graduation from high school or equivalent recognized by the Ministry of Education, and entrance examination

Fees: Undergraduate, c. 3-5m per semester; Graduate, c.3.7-6 m per semester. Foreign students 30% and 50 % discount for undergraduates and graduates respectively (Won)

Main language(s) of instruction: Korean

Accrediting agency: Ministry of Education and Human Resources Development

Degrees and diplomas: Bachelor's Degree, Master's Degree (Acting; Actuarial Science; Architecture; Art Management; Asian Religious Studies; Bioengineering; Biological and Life Sciences; Biomedicine; Biotechnology; Chemical Engineering; Chemistry; Chinese; Cinema and Television; Civil Engineering; Computer Engineering; Construction Engineering; Consumer Studies; Cultural Studies; Dance; Design; Economics; Education; Educational Psychology; Electrical Engineering; Electronic Engineering; Engineering; Engineering Management; English; Environmental Engineering; Family Studies; Fashion Design; Film; Fine Arts; Foreign Languages Education; French; German; Health Administration; History; Human Resources; Industrial Engineering; Information Sciences; Information Technology; International Business; International Relations; Journalism; Korean; Landscape Architecture; Law; Library Science; Literature; Management; Mass Communication; Materials Engineering; Mathematics; Mathematics Education; Mechanical Engineering; Medicine; Multimedia; Native Language Education; Nursing; Performing Arts; Pharmacy; Philosophy; Physics; Political Sciences; Polymer and Plastics Technology; Psychology; Public Administration; Russian; Safety Engineering; Service Trades; Social and Preventive Medicine; Social Welfare; Sociology; Software Engineering; Sports; Statistics; Structural Architecture; Translation and Interpretation; Water Management), Doctor's Degree (Architecture; Asian Religious Studies; Bioengineering; Biological and Life Sciences; Biomedical Engineering; Biomedicine; Biotechnology; Business Administration; Chemical Engineering; Chemistry; Chinese; Cinema and Television; Civil Engineering; Computer Engineering; Consumer Studies; Cultural Studies; Dance; Design; Economics; Education; Educational Psychology; Electrical Engineering; Electronic Engineering; Energy Engineering; Engineering; English; Environmental Engineering; Family Studies; Fashion Design; Film; Fine Arts; French; German; History; Human Resources; Industrial Engineering; Information Sciences; International Business; International Relations; Journalism; Korean; Landscape Architecture; Law; Library Science; Literature; Mass Communication; Materials Engineering; Mathematics; Mechanical Engineering; Medicine; Multimedia; Performing Arts; Pharmacy; Philosophy; Physics; Political Sciences; Polymer and Plastics Technology; Psychology; Public Administration; Russian; Safety Engineering; Service Trades; Social Welfare; Sociology; Software Engineering; Sports; Statistics; Structural Architecture; Water Management). Also Combined Bachelor-Master and Master-Ph.D.; MBA; Executive MBA; Internet-based MBA

Student Services: Academic Counselling, Social Counselling, Careers Guidance, Nursery Care, Cultural Activities, Sports Facilities, Language Laboratory, Facilities for disabled people, Health Services, Canteen

Periodicals: Sungkyunkwan Journal of East Asian Studies

Publishing house: Sungkyunkwan University Press

Last Update: 08-03-2018

Sungsan Hyo University

543, Seokjeong-ro Namdong-gu
Incheon-si 21503
Tel: +82(32) 433-1996
Fax: +82(32) 421-4528 421-4528
Website: http://www.hyo.ac.kr
President: Seung Gyu Choi

Department/Division

Chemistry (Chemistry); **Child Care and Development** (Child Care and Development); **Family Counseling** (Art Therapy; Educational and Student Counselling; Family Studies); **Music** (Music; Music Education; Music Theory and Composition; Musical Instruments; Religious Music; Singing); **Social Welfare** (Social Welfare; Social Work); **Theology** (Bible; Christian Religious Studies; History of Religion; Theology)

History: Founded 1996. Formerly known as Sungsan Hyo Graduate School.
Main language(s) of instruction: Korean
Accrediting agency: Ministry of Education
Degrees and diplomas: Bachelor's Degree, Master's Degree (Art Therapy; Child Care and Development; Educational and Student Counselling; Family Studies; Music; Psychology; Social Welfare; Theology; Welfare and Protective Services), Doctor's Degree (Chemistry; Continuing Education; Family Studies; Music; Musicology; Psychology; Social Work; Theology)

Academic Staff 2013-2014	MALE	FEMALE	TOTAL
FULL-TIME			27
PART-TIME			11
Student Numbers 2013-2014			
All (Foreign Included)			164

Last Update: 07-03-2018

Sungshin University

2 Bomun-ro 34da-gil Donam-dong, Seongbuk-gu
Seoul 02844
Tel: +82(2) 920-7114
Fax: +82(2) 926-3120
Website: http://www.sungshin.ac.kr
President: Hwa-Jin Shim

College

Arts (Fine Arts; Handicrafts; Industrial Design; Painting and Drawing; Sculpture); **Convergence Culture and Arts** (Acting; Art Management; Cosmetology; Dance; Jazz and Popular Music; Music Theory and Composition; Musical Instruments); **Education** (Chinese; Education; Ethics; Humanities and Social Science Education; Preschool Education); **Human Ecology** (Clothing and Sewing; Consumer Studies; Food Science; Home Economics; Leisure Studies; Nutrition; Social Welfare; Sports; Textile Design); **Humanities** (Arts and Humanities; Chinese; English; French; German; History; Japanese; Korean; Literature); **Law** (Law); **Music** (Music; Music Theory and Composition; Musical Instruments; Singing); **Natural Sciences** (Biological and Life Sciences; Chemistry; Information Technology; Mathematics; Natural Sciences; Statistics); **Nursing** (Medicine; Nursing); **Social Sciences** (Business Administration; Economics; Geography; International Relations; Mass Communication; Media Studies; Political Sciences; Psychology; Social Sciences)

Department/Division

Open Major (Arts and Humanities; Natural Sciences; Social Sciences)

Graduate School

Convergence Design and Arts (*Specialized*) (Cosmetology; Design; Fine Arts; Sculpture); **Cultural Industry** (*Specialized*) (Air Transport; Cultural Studies; Health Sciences; Information Technology; Management); **Education** (*Specialized*) (Art Education; Computer Education; Education; Educational and Student Counselling; Foreign Languages Education; Home Economics Education; Humanities and Social Science Education; Mathematics Education; Music Education; Preschool Education; Science Education); **Graduate Studies** (Art History; Art Therapy; Biology; Business Administration; Chemistry; Chinese; Clothing and Sewing; Computer Science; Consumer Studies; Economics; Education; English; Ethics; Food Science; French; Geography (Human); German; Handicrafts; History; Home Economics; Industrial Design; International Relations; Japanese; Korean; Law; Literature; Mass Communication; Mathematics; Media Studies; Music; Nursing; Nutrition; Painting and Drawing; Physical Education; Political Sciences; Preschool Education; Printing and Printmaking; Psychology; Sculpture; Social Welfare; Social Work; Statistics; Women's Studies); **Lifetime Welfare** (*Specialized*) (Child Care and Development; Health Sciences; Welfare and Protective Services)

Further information: Also 12 Research Institutes
History: Founded 1936.
Main language(s) of instruction: Korean
Accrediting agency: Korean Council for University Education (KCUE)
Degrees and diplomas: Bachelor's Degree, Master's Degree (Air Transport; Art Education; Art History; Art Management; Art Therapy; Biology; Business Administration; Chemistry; Child Care and Development; Chinese; Clothing and Sewing; Computer Education; Computer Science; Consumer

Studies; Cosmetology; Cultural Studies; Design; Economics; Education; English; Ethics; Fine Arts; Food Science; Foreign Languages Education; French; Geography (Human); German; Handicrafts; Health Sciences; History; Home Economics Education; Humanities and Social Science Education; Industrial Design; Information Technology; International Relations; Japanese; Korean; Law; Literature; Management; Mass Communication; Mathematics; Mathematics Education; Media Studies; Music; Music Education; Nursing; Nutrition; Painting and Drawing; Physical Education; Political Sciences; Preschool Education; Printing and Printmaking; Psychology; Science Education; Sculpture; Social Welfare; Social Work; Statistics; Women's Studies), Doctor's Degree (Art History; Biology; Business Administration; Chemistry; Chinese; Clothing and Sewing; Computer Science; Consumer Studies; Economics; Education; English; Fine Arts; Food Science; Geography (Human); German; History; Home Economics; International Relations; Korean; Law; Literature; Music; Nutrition; Physical Education; Political Sciences; Psychology; Sociology)

Student Services: Academic Counselling, Social Counselling, Careers Guidance, Language Laboratory, Health Services, Library, Residential Facilities

Academic Staff 2013-2014	MALE	FEMALE	TOTAL
FULL-TIME			c. 680
Student Numbers 2013-2014			
All (Foreign Included)			c. 13000

Last Update: 07-03-2018

Tamna University

San 7 Hawon-dong
Seogwipo 697-703, Jeju-do
Tel: +82(64) 735-2000
Fax: +82(64) 738-4700

Department/Division

Aeronautical Service (Service Trades); **Business Administration** (Business Administration); **Child Care Education** (Home Economics Education); **Computer Education** (Computer Education); **Counseling Psychology** (Psychology); **Design** (Design); **Educational Administration** (Educational Administration); **English Language Teaching as Foreign Language** (Foreign Languages Education); **Golf** (Sports); **Hotel Management** (Hotel Management); **International Studies** (International Studies); **Leisure and Sport Studies** (Leisure Studies; Sports); **Physical Education** (Physical Education); **Police Administration** (Administration; Police Studies); **Social Welfare** (Social Welfare); **Society and environmental Systems** (Environmental Studies; Social Sciences); **Sociology Education** (Humanities and Social

Science Education); **Sports Management** (Sports Management); **Taekwondo** (Sports); **Tourism Management** (Tourism)

History: Founded 1997.
Main language(s) of instruction: Korean
Accrediting agency: Ministry of Education
Degrees and diplomas: Bachelor's Degree (Administration; Business Administration; Computer Education; Design; Educational Administration; Environmental Studies; Foreign Languages Education; Home Economics Education; Hotel Management; Humanities and Social Science Education; International Studies; Leisure Studies; Physical Education; Police Studies; Psychology; Service Trades; Social Sciences; Social Welfare; Sports; Sports Management; Tourism), Master's Degree
Last Update: 28-03-2018

The Catholic University of Korea (CUK)

43 Jibong-ro
Bucheon 14662, Gyeonggi-do
Tel: +82(2) 2164-4114
Fax: +82(2) 2164-4778
Website: http://www.catholic.ac.kr
President: Luke Jongchul Won

College

Engineering (*Songsim*) (Biotechnology; Computer Engineering; Computer Science; Electronic Engineering; Engineering; Environmental Engineering; Information Sciences; Information Technology; Mass Communication; Telecommunications Engineering); **Humanities and Arts** (*Songsim*) (Arts and Humanities; History; Literature; Music; Philosophy; Religious Studies); **International Fields** (*Songsim*) (American Studies; Asian Studies; Chinese; East Asian Studies; English; English Studies; French; French Studies; International Business; International Relations; International Studies; Japanese; Literature); **Medicine and Nursing** (*Songeui*) (Medicine; Nursing); **Natural Sciences and Human Ecology** (*Songsim*) (Biological and Life Sciences; Chemistry; Child Care and Development; Clothing and Sewing; Consumer Studies; Family Studies; Food Science; Home Economics; Mathematics; Natural Sciences; Nutrition; Physics; Textile Design); **Social Sciences** (*Songsim*) (Administration; Business Administration; Economics; Law; Psychology; Public Administration; Social Sciences; Social Welfare; Sociology; Special Education); **Theology** (*Songsin*) (Theology)

Graduate School

Business Administration (*Specialized*) (Accountancy; Business Administration; Finance; Information Technology;

International Business; Marketing); **Church Music** (*Specialized*) (Religious Music); **Clinical Dental Science** (*Specialized*) (Dental Technology; Dentistry; Orthodontics; Surgery); **Clinical Nursing Science** (*Specialized*) (Nursing; Oncology); **Counseling** (*Specialized*) (Psychology); **Culture and Spirituality** (*Specialized*) (Bible; Cultural Studies; Religion); **Education** (*Specialized*) (Foreign Languages Education; Mathematics Education; Native Language Education); **Education, Special Education** (*Specialized*) (Adult Education; Continuing Education; Educational Administration; Educational and Student Counselling; Educational Technology; Home Economics Education; Humanities and Social Science Education; Preschool Education; Special Education; Vocational Education); **Graduate Studies**; **Healthcare and Policy** (*Specialized*) (Computer Science; Health Administration); **Life Studies** (*Specialized*) (Cultural Studies; Ethics); **Public Administration** (*Specialized*) (Administration; Administrative Law; Asian Studies; East Asian Studies; Government; Health Administration; International Relations; International Studies; Public Administration; Real Estate; Regional Planning); **Public Health** (*Specialized*) (Community Health; Epidemiology; Health Administration; Nursing; Occupational Health; Public Health; Rehabilitation and Therapy); **Social Welfare** (*Specialized*) (Social Welfare; Welfare and Protective Services)

Further information: Also Seoul-based Songsin Theological Campus and Songeui Medical Campus; Seoul St. Mary's Hospital (affiliated)

History: Founded 1855 as St. Joseph's Seminary. Merged with Songsim Women's University 1995 and acquired present status and title 1999.

Academic year: March to December (March-July; September-December)

Admission requirements: Graduation from high school and entrance examination

Main language(s) of instruction: Korean

Accrediting agency: Korean Council for University Education (KCUE)

Degrees and diplomas: Bachelor's Degree, Master's Degree (Arts and Humanities; Biological and Life Sciences; Biomedicine; Biotechnology; Business Administration; Chemistry; Child Care and Development; Chinese; Clothing and Sewing; Computer Engineering; Computer Science; Consumer Studies; East Asian Studies; Electronic Engineering; English; Environmental Engineering; Family Studies; Food Science; Foreign Languages Education; French; Health Education; History; Home Economics; Information Sciences; International Studies; Japanese; Korean; Law; Literature; Mathematics; Media Studies; Medicine; Nursing; Nutrition; Philosophy; Physics; Psychology; Public Administration; Religious Studies; Social Welfare; Sociology; Statistics; Telecommunications Engineering; Textile Design; Theology), Doctor's Degree (Biological and Life Sciences;

Biomedicine; Biotechnology; Business Administration; Chemistry; Computer Engineering; Computer Science; Cultural Studies; Electronic Engineering; English; Environmental Engineering; Ethics; Food Science; Foreign Languages Education; History; Information Sciences; Korean; Literature; Mass Communication; Medicine; Nursing; Nutrition; Philosophy; Psychology; Public Administration; Public Health; Religious Studies; Social Welfare; Telecommunications Engineering; Theology)

Student Services: Academic Counselling, Careers Guidance, Sports Facilities, Health Services, Library, IT Centre, Residential Facilities

Periodicals: Bulletin of Clinical Research Institute, Bulletin of the Catholic Medical, Catholic Theology and Thought, Journal of Catholic Research Institute, Korean Journal of Occupational Health

Publishing house: Catholic University Press

Academic Staff 2013-2014	MALE	FEMALE	TOTAL
FULL-TIME			c. 1030
Student Numbers 2013-2014			
All (Foreign Included)			c. 14297
Foreign only			299

Last Update: 24-05-2018

The Cyber University of Korea (CUK)

106 Bukchon-Ro, Jongno-Gu (1-21 Gye-Dong)
Seoul 03051
Tel: +82(2) 6361-1810
Fax: +82(2) 6361-2000
Website: http://eng.cuk.edu
President: Jin-Sung Kim

Department/Division

Business (Art Management; Business Administration; Real Estate); **Creative Engineering** (Automation and Control Engineering; Electrical and Electronic Engineering; Engineering Drawing and Design; Information Management; Mechanical Engineering; Software Engineering); **Future Convergence** (Cultural Studies; Data Processing; Engineering Management; International Studies; Technology); **Human Service** (Child Care and Development; Continuing Education; Health Administration; Psychology; Social Welfare); **Law and Taxation** (Accountancy; Law; Taxation); **Practical Languages** (English; Korean; Modern Languages)

Graduate School

Interdisciplinary Information Studies (Business Computing; Computer Science; Educational Technology; Information Technology)

History: Founded 2001.

Main language(s) of instruction: Korean

Accrediting agency: Ministry of Education

Degrees and diplomas: Bachelor's Degree (Accountancy; Art Management; Automation and Control Engineering; Business Administration; Child Care and Development; Continuing Education; Cultural Studies; Data Processing; Electrical and Electronic Engineering; Engineering Drawing and Design; Engineering Management; English; Health Administration; Information Management; Information Technology; Korean; Law; Mechanical Engineering; Modern Languages; Psychology; Real Estate; Social Welfare; Software Engineering; Taxation; Technology), Master's Degree (Business Computing; Computer Science; Educational Technology; Information Technology)

Last Update: 26-03-2018

The University of Suwon (USW)

San 2-2 Wau-ri, Bongdam-eup
Hwaseong-si 18323, Gyeonggi-do
Tel: +82(31) 220-2114, +82(31) 220-2562
Fax: +82(31) 222-1405
Website: http://www.suwon.ac.kr
President: In-soo Lee

College

Economics and Business Administration (Business and Commerce; Economics); **Engineering** (Architecture; Chemical Engineering; Civil Engineering; Electrical and Electronic Engineering; Engineering; Environmental Engineering; Genetics; Industrial Engineering; Materials Engineering; Mechanical Engineering; Polymer and Plastics Technology; Town Planning); **Fine Arts** (Fine Arts); **Human Ecology** (Ecology); **Humanities** (Arts and Humanities; English; French; History; Japanese; Korean; Literature; Modern Languages); **Information Technology** (Information Technology); **Law and Political Science** (Law; Political Sciences); **Music** (Music); **Natural Sciences** (Natural Sciences); **Physical Education** (Physical Education)

Graduate School

Art (Design; Fine Arts; Graphic Design; Multimedia); **Business Administration** (Business Administration; Economics; Finance; Sports Management); **Education** (Art Education; Computer Education; Education; Educational Administration; Educational and Student Counselling; Foreign Languages Education; Humanities and Social Science Education; Mathematics Education; Music Education; Native Language Education; Pedagogy; Physical Education; Pre-school Education; Primary Education; Science Education); **Engineering** (Chemical Engineering; Civil Engineering; Computer Engineering; Computer Science; Electrical Engineering; Electronic Engineering; Environmental Engineering; Industrial Engineering; Materials Engineering; Mechanical Engineering; Polymer and Plastics Technology; Real Estate; Town Planning); **Financial Engineering** (Engineering; Finance); **Graduate Studies** (Bioengineering; Biological and Life Sciences; Business Administration; Chemical Engineering; Chemistry; Child Care and Development; Civil Engineering; Computer Science; Dance; Electrical Engineering; Electronic Engineering; English; Environmental Engineering; Fine Arts; Food Science; Genetics; History; Industrial Design; Industrial Engineering; Journalism; Korean; Law; Literature; Mass Communication; Materials Engineering; Mechanical Engineering; Music; Nutrition; Physical Education; Physics; Polymer and Plastics Technology; Public Administration; Real Estate; Social Welfare; Statistics; Structural Architecture; Telecommunications Engineering; Town Planning); **Hotel and Tourism** (Hotel Management; Tourism); **Music** (Music; Music Education; Technology); **Music Technology** (Music; Social Welfare); **Public Administration** (Administration; Business Administration; Public Administration; Real Estate); **Social Welfare** (Social Psychology; Social Welfare)

Research Division

Business Administration (Business Administration); **Genetic Engineering** (Genetics); **Industry Administration**; **Kijon Culture** (Cultural Studies); **Local Society Development**; **Natural Sciences** (Natural Sciences); **Philosophy** (Philosophy); **Social Sciences** (Social Sciences)

Further information: Also Suwon Industrial College

History: Founded 1982.

Academic year: March to December (March-June; September-December)

Admission requirements: Graduation from high school and entrance examination

Main language(s) of instruction: Korean, English

Accrediting agency: Korean Council for University Education (KCUE)

Degrees and diplomas: Bachelor's Degree, Master's Degree (Agriculture; Architecture and Planning; Arts and Humanities; Business Administration; Education; Engineering; Finance; Fine Arts; Home Economics; Hotel Management; Information Sciences; Mathematics and Computer Science; Modern Languages; Music; Natural Sciences; Performing Arts; Public Administration; Social Welfare; Tourism; Welfare and Protective Services), Doctor's Degree (Agriculture; Architecture and Planning; Arts and Humanities; Business Administration; Education; Engineering; Fine Arts; Home Economics; Information Sciences; Mathematics and Computer Science; Natural Sciences; Performing Arts; Public Administration; Service Trades; Social Welfare; Welfare and Protective Services)

Student Services: Library, Residential Facilities

Academic Staff 2013-2014	MALE	FEMALE	TOTAL
FULL-TIME			368
PART-TIME			570
Student Numbers 2013-2014			
All (Foreign Included)			12415

Last Update: 07-03-2018

TLBU Graduate School of Law In Seoul (TLBU)

230, Naeyu-gil, Deogyang-gu
Goyang-si 412-751, Gyeonggi-do
Tel: +82(31) 960-1001/4
Fax: +82(31) 964-7196
Website: http://www.tlbu.ac.kr
President: Byung-Hwa Lyou

Course/Programme
Law (Commercial Law; International Law; Law)
History: Founded 2000.
Main language(s) of instruction: Korean
Accrediting agency: Ministry of Education
Degrees and diplomas: Master's Degree (Law), Doctor's Degree (Law)
Last Update: 28-03-2018

Tongmyong University (TU)

428, Sinseon-ro, Nam-gu
Busan 48520
Tel: +82(51) 629-1000
Fax: +82(51) 629-2000
Website: http://www.tu.ac.kr
President: Hong-Sub Jung

Faculty
Digital Entertainment (Advertising and Publicity; Communication Arts; Media Studies; Public Relations; Radio and Television Broadcasting; Software Engineering; Visual Arts);
Free Majors; **Port Logistics** (Marine Transport; Transport Management)

College
Architecture and Design (Architecture; Fashion Design; Graphic Design; Industrial Design; Interior Design; Structural Architecture); **Business Administration** (Accountancy; Business Administration; Finance; Hotel Management; Information Management; Information Technology; International

Business; Management; Tourism); **Engineering** (Automotive Engineering; Computer Engineering; Electrical Engineering; Electronic Engineering; Heating and Refrigeration; Information Management; Information Technology; Marine Engineering; Mechanical Engineering; Media Studies; Naval Architecture; Robotics); **Health, Welfare and Education** (Communication Disorders; Cosmetology; Education; Food Science; Health Sciences; Medical Technology; Nursing; Nutrition; Physical Education; Preschool Education; Social Welfare; Welfare and Protective Services)

School
International Culture Studies (American Studies; Asian Religious Studies; East Asian Studies; English Studies; Japanese)

Department/Division
Contract

Graduate School
Architecture (Architecture; Interior Design; Structural Architecture); **Business and Social Sciences** (Accountancy; Administration; Advertising and Publicity; Business Administration; Finance; Hotel and Restaurant; Information Management; Information Technology; International Business; Management; Mass Communication; Media Studies; Preschool Education; Public Relations; Social Sciences; Social Welfare; Speech Therapy and Audiology; Sports; Tourism); **Design** (Communication Arts; Cosmetology; Design; Fashion Design; Fine Arts; Graphic Design; Industrial Design; Video; Visual Arts); **Engineering** (Automotive Engineering; Biomedical Engineering; Computer Engineering; Electrical and Electronic Engineering; Electrical Engineering; Electronic Engineering; Engineering; Food Science; Food Technology; Heating and Refrigeration; Information Management; Information Technology; Mechanical Engineering; Multimedia; Naval Architecture; Robotics; Software Engineering; Telecommunications Engineering; Visual Arts)
Further information: Also Graduate Schools
History: Founded 1996 as Tongmyong University of Information Technology. Merged with Tongmyong College and acquired present title 2006.
Main language(s) of instruction: Korean
Accrediting agency: Korean Council for University Education (KCUE)
Degrees and diplomas: Bachelor's Degree, Master's Degree (Accountancy; Advertising and Publicity; Architecture; Automotive Engineering; Biomedical Engineering; Business Administration; Computer Engineering; Cosmetology; Electrical and Electronic Engineering; Electrical Engineering; Electronic Engineering; Fashion Design; Finance; Food Science; Food Technology; Graphic Design; Heating and Refrigeration; Hotel Management; Industrial Design;

Information Management; Information Technology; Interior Design; International Business; Mass Communication; Mechanical Engineering; Media Studies; Multimedia; Naval Architecture; Preschool Education; Public Relations; Robotics; Social Welfare; Software Engineering; Speech Therapy and Audiology; Sports; Structural Architecture; Telecommunications Engineering; Tourism; Visual Arts), Doctor's Degree (Architecture; Business Administration; Communication Arts; Computer Engineering; Electronic Engineering; Fashion Design; Graphic Design; Information Management; Information Technology; Mass Communication; Multimedia; Structural Architecture; Telecommunications Engineering; Tourism; Video; Visual Arts)

Student Services: Sports Facilities, Residential Facilities

Academic Staff 2013-2014	MALE	FEMALE	TOTAL
FULL-TIME			c. 340
Student Numbers 2013-2014			
All (Foreign Included)			9000
Foreign only			300

Last Update: 07-03-2018

Torch Trinity Graduate University (TTGU)

70 Baumero 31-gil, Seocho-gu
Seoul 06752
Tel: +82(2) 570-7372
Fax: +82(2) 570-7379
Website: http://www.ttgu.ac.kr/main.do?lang=en
President: Jung-Sook Lee

Course/Programme

Christian Counseling (Psychology); **Christian Education** (Religious Education); **Divinity** (Religion); **Education** (Education); **Theological Studies** (Theology); **Theology** (Theology); **Worship and Church Music** (Religious Music)
History: Founded 1997.
Main language(s) of instruction: Korean, English
Accrediting agency: Ministry of Education
Degrees and diplomas: Master's Degree (Bible; Education; History of Religion; Missionary Studies; New Testament; Pastoral Studies; Religion; Religious Education; Religious Music; Theology), Doctor's Degree (Psychology; Theology)
Last Update: 29-03-2018

U1 University

310, Daehak-ro Yeongdong-eup, Yeongdong-gun
Youngdong-si 29131, Chungbuk-do
Tel: +82(43) 740-1010, +82(43) 740-1114, +82(43) 740-1321

Fax: +82(43) 740-1019
Website: http://ydueng.u1.ac.kr/html/en/index.html
President: Hun-gwan Chae

Faculty
Liberal Arts Convergence (Arts and Humanities)

College
Education (Education; Preschool Education; Primary Education; Secondary Education; Special Education); **Health Disciplines** (Biomedicine; Cooking and Catering; Cosmetology; Dental Hygiene; Food Science; Food Technology; Health Sciences; Nursing; Nutrition; Occupational Therapy; Physical Therapy; Speech Therapy and Audiology); **Humanities and Social Science** (Administration; Arts and Humanities; Business Administration; Chinese; Communication Arts; Design; English; Hotel Management; Japanese; Physical Education; Police Studies; Social Sciences; Social Welfare; Sports; Tourism; Visual Arts); **Science and Technology** (Civil Engineering; Environmental Engineering; Information Management; Information Technology; Private Law; Structural Architecture)

Graduate School
Industrial Information (Design; Engineering; Social Studies; Sports; Transport Engineering)
History: Founded 1992. Formerly known as Youngdong University.
Main language(s) of instruction: Korean
Accrediting agency: Ministry of Education
Degrees and diplomas: Bachelor's Degree, Master's Degree (Administration; Aesthetics; Business Administration; Civil Engineering; Cosmetology; Design; English; Food Technology; Hotel Management; Physical Education; Police Studies; Psychology; Public Administration; Real Estate; Social Welfare; Sports; Tourism; Visual Arts)
Student Services: Sports Facilities, Library, Residential Facilities

Academic Staff 2012-2013	MALE	FEMALE	TOTAL
FULL-TIME			160
PART-TIME			c. 140
Student Numbers 2012-2013			
All (Foreign Included)			c. 5290

Last Update: 07-03-2018

Uiduk University (UU)

261 Donghae-daero Gangdong-myeon
Gyeongju-si 38004, Gyeongsangbuk-do
Tel: +82(54) 760-1114

Fax: +82(54) 760-1170
Website: http://www.uiduk.ac.kr
President: Uk Heon Hong

College

Da Vinci (Asian Religious Studies; Engineering; English; Fire Science; Information Technology; Japanese; Police Studies); **Energy Systems Technology** (Electrical Engineering; Energy Engineering; Information Technology); **Global Services** (Air Transport; Business Administration; Food Technology; Tourism); **Human Services** (Health Sciences; Nursing; Physical Therapy; Preschool Education; Social Welfare; Special Education; Sports)

School

Buddhism (*Graduate*) (Asian Religious Studies)

Graduate School

Business (Business Administration); **Education** (Computer Education; Education; Educational Administration; Foreign Languages Education; Home Economics Education; Native Language Education; Physical Education; Preschool Education; Secondary Education; Special Education); **Graduate Studies** (Business Administration; Cooking and Catering; Education; Educational Administration; Electronic Engineering; Information Technology; Preschool Education; Social Welfare; Special Education); **Social Work** (Social Welfare; Social Work)
History: Founded 1996.
Main language(s) of instruction: Korean
Accrediting agency: Korean Council for University Education (KCUE)
Degrees and diplomas: Bachelor's Degree, Master's Degree (Accountancy; Asian Religious Studies; Automation and Control Engineering; Business Administration; Computer Engineering; Cooking and Catering; Educational Administration; Electrical Engineering; Electronic Engineering; English; Finance; Foreign Languages Education; Hotel and Restaurant; Information Technology; International Business; Korean; Linguistics; Literature; Management; Marketing; Preschool Education; Social Welfare; Social Work; Software Engineering; Special Education; Telecommunications Engineering), Doctor's Degree (Asian Religious Studies; Automation and Control Engineering; Business Administration; Computer Engineering; Cooking and Catering; Educational Administration; Electrical Engineering; Electronic Engineering; Hotel and Restaurant; Information Sciences; Preschool Education; Social Welfare; Software Engineering; Special Education; Telecommunications Engineering)
Student Services: Sports Facilities, Residential Facilities

Academic Staff 2012-2013	MALE	FEMALE	TOTAL
FULL-TIME			132
PART-TIME			71
Student Numbers 2012-2013			
All (Foreign Included)			c. 4360

Last Update: 07-03-2018

University of Brain Education (UBE)

Nam-gu, Mokcheon-eup, Chungcheongnam-do 284-31 [Chungcheongnam-si 31228, Cheonan-dong
Tel: +82 1577-7369
Website: http://www.ube.ac.kr/home/hmpg/biz/kor/main/HmpgMain.do
President: Ilchi Lee

Department/Division

Brain Education (Health Sciences; Psychology); **Convergence Life Sciences**; **Counseling Psychology** (Psychology); **Earth Management** (Cultural Studies; Management; Social Welfare); **Korean Studies** (Esoteric Practices; Health Sciences; Korean; Sports); **Oriental Studies** (Oriental Studies; Vocational Counselling)
History: Founded 2003.
Main language(s) of instruction: Korean
Accrediting agency: Ministry of Education
Degrees and diplomas: Bachelor's Degree (Cultural Studies; Esoteric Practices; Health Sciences; Korean; Management; Oriental Studies; Psychology; Social Welfare; Sports; Vocational Counselling)
Student Services: Library
Last Update: 29-03-2018

University of North Korean Studies (UNKS)

2 (Samcheong-dong) Bukchon-ro 15-gil, Jongno-gu
Seoul 03053
Tel: +82(2) 3700-0800/2
Fax: +82(2) 3700-0748
Website: http://www.nk.ac.kr/ENG/UNKS_main.aspx
Acting President: Jongdae Shin

Course/Programme

Economic and Information Technology (Economics; Information Technology); **Law and Administration** (Administration; Law); **Military and Security** (Military Science; Protective Services); **Politics and Unification** (International Relations; Political Sciences); **Sociology, Culture and**

Media (Cultural Studies; Media Studies; Sociology); **Unification Education** (Education)
History: Founded 1998.
Main language(s) of instruction: Korean
Accrediting agency: Ministry of Education
Degrees and diplomas: Master's Degree (East Asian Studies; International Relations; Political Sciences), Doctor's Degree (East Asian Studies; International Relations; Political Sciences)
Student Services: Library
Last Update: 26-03-2018

University of Science and Technology (UST)

217 Gajeong-ro Yuseong-gu
Daejeon 305-350
Tel: +82(42) 865-5551
Fax: +82(42) 865-5554
Website: http://www.ust.ac.kr
President: Kil-Choo Moon
Tel: +82(42) 864-5550
History: UST aims at nurturing R&D professionals in association with 30 Korea Government-funded Research Institutes (GFRI).
Academic year: Mar-Feb (Mar-June; Sep-Feb)
Admission requirements: Copy of the certificate of (expected) Bachelor's degree, a copy of transcript of undergraduate records, proposal for study, English test score, a copy of employment certificate-if applicable, (for PhD applicants) a copy of certificate of Master's degree (expected), a copy of transcript of master's program, a copy of thesis, a copy of research achievements.
Fees: 2,500,000 per semester (Won)
Main language(s) of instruction: English, Korean
Accrediting agency: Ministry of Education
Degrees and diplomas: Master's Degree (Biotechnology; Engineering; Environmental Studies; Information Technology; Natural Sciences), Doctor's Degree (Astronomy and Space Science; Biotechnology; Environmental Studies; Information Technology; Natural Sciences)
Student Services: Residential Facilities

Academic Staff 2016-2017	MALE	FEMALE	TOTAL
FULL-TIME			91
STAFF WITH DOCTORATE			
FULL-TIME			13
Student Numbers 2016-2017			
All (Foreign Included)			1292
Foreign only			1267

Last Update: 15-06-2018

University of Ulsan (UOU)

93 Daehak-ro Nam-gu
Ulsan 44610
Tel: +82(52) 277-3101, +82(52) 220-5952
Fax: +82(52) 277-3419, +82(52) 224-2061
Website: http://www.ulsan.ac.kr
President: Yeon-Cho Oh
Tel: +82(52) 220-5957

College
Architecture (Architecture; Structural Architecture); **Business Administration** (Accountancy; Business Administration; Information Management; Information Technology; Management); **Design** (Architectural and Environmental Design; Design; Graphic Design; Industrial Design; Interior Design; Mass Communication; Textile Design); **Engineering** (Aeronautical and Aerospace Engineering; Automotive Engineering; Biomedical Engineering; Chemical Engineering; Civil Engineering; Electrical Engineering; Electronic Engineering; Energy Engineering; Engineering; Environmental Engineering; Industrial Engineering; Information Technology; Marine Engineering; Materials Engineering; Mechanical Engineering; Naval Architecture); **Fine Arts** (Fine Arts; Painting and Drawing; Sculpture); **Human Ecology** (Child Care and Development; Clothing and Sewing; Ecology; Food Science; Interior Design; Nutrition; Textile Design); **Humanities** (Arts and Humanities; Asian Studies; Chinese; Cultural Studies; East Asian Studies; English; English Studies; French; French Studies; History; International Studies; Japanese; Korean; Latin American Studies; Literature; Philosophy; Spanish); **Medicine** (Health Sciences; Medicine; Nursing); **Music** (Music; Musical Instruments; Singing); **Natural Sciences** (Biological and Life Sciences; Biomedicine; Chemistry; Health Sciences; Mathematics; Natural Sciences; Physics; Sports); **Social Sciences** (Economics; International Relations; Law; Police Studies; Public Administration; Social Sciences; Social Welfare; Sociology)

Graduate School
Business Administration (*Special*) (Business Administration); **E-Vehicle Technology** (*Special*) (Electronic Engineering; Industrial Design; Materials Engineering; Mechanical Engineering; Production Engineering); **Education** (*Special*) (Art Education; Computer Education; Education; Educational Administration; Educational and Student Counselling; Foreign Languages Education; Home Economics Education; Humanities and Social Science Education; Native Language Education; Physical Education; Preschool Education; Science Education); **Graduate Studies** (Architecture; Biological and Life Sciences; Business Administration; Chemical

Engineering; Chemistry; Child Care and Development; Civil Engineering; Clothing and Sewing; Computer Engineering; Cultural Studies; Design; Economics; Education; Electrical Engineering; Electronic Engineering; Environmental Engineering; Family Studies; Fine Arts; Food Science; Heritage Preservation; History; Human Resources; Industrial Engineering; Korean; Law; Literature; Marine Engineering; Materials Engineering; Mathematics; Mechanical Engineering; Medicine; Music; Naval Architecture; Nutrition; Philosophy; Physics; Police Studies; Public Administration; Social Welfare; Sociology; Sports; Textile Design; Welfare and Protective Services); **Industry** (*Special*) (Architecture; Construction Engineering; Energy Engineering; English; Environmental Engineering; Industrial Engineering; Industrial Management; Information Technology; Nursing; Sports Management; Urban Studies); **Public Policy** (*Special*) (Public Administration; Social Welfare)

History: Founded 1970 with the aid of the Colombo Plan and Ulsan Foundation.

Academic year: March to February (March-July; September-February)

Admission requirements: Graduation from high school and entrance examination

Main language(s) of instruction: Korean, English

Accrediting agency: Korean Council for University Education (KCUE)

Degrees and diplomas: Bachelor's Degree, Master's Degree (Aeronautical and Aerospace Engineering; Architecture; Automotive Engineering; Bioengineering; Biological and Life Sciences; Biomedical Engineering; Business Administration; Chemical Engineering; Chemistry; Child Care and Development; Civil Engineering; Clothing and Sewing; Communication Arts; Computer Engineering; Cultural Studies; Design; Economics; Electrical Engineering; Environmental Engineering; Family Studies; Fashion Design; Food Science; Graphic Design; Heritage Preservation; History; Industrial Design; Industrial Engineering; Industrial Management; Information Technology; Interior Design; Korean; Law; Literature; Marine Engineering; Mass Communication; Materials Engineering; Mathematics; Mechanical Engineering; Medicine; Music Theory and Composition; Musical Instruments; Naval Architecture; Nutrition; Painting and Drawing; Philosophy; Physical Education; Physics; Police Studies; Public Administration; Sculpture; Singing; Social Welfare; Structural Architecture; Textile Design; Town Planning), Doctor's Degree (Aeronautical and Aerospace Engineering; Architecture; Automotive Engineering; Bioengineering; Biological and Life Sciences; Biomedical Engineering; Business Administration; Chemical Engineering; Chemistry; Child Care and Development; Civil Engineering; Clothing and Sewing; Computer Engineering; Cultural Studies; Economics; Electrical Engineering; Environmental Engineering; Family Studies; Food Science;

Heritage Preservation; History; Industrial Chemistry; Industrial Engineering; Industrial Management; Information Technology; Interior Design; Korean; Law; Literature; Marine Engineering; Materials Engineering; Mathematics; Mechanical Engineering; Medicine; Naval Architecture; Nutrition; Philosophy; Physical Education; Physics; Public Administration; Structural Architecture; Textile Design; Town Planning)

Student Services: Academic Counselling, Social Counselling, Careers Guidance, Cultural Activities, Sports Facilities, Language Laboratory, Health Services, Canteen, Foreign Studies Centre, Library, Residential Facilities

Academic Staff 2013-2014	MALE	FEMALE	TOTAL
FULL-TIME			1078
Student Numbers 2013-2014			
All (Foreign Included)			15000
Foreign only			800

Last Update: 07-03-2018

Vision University, College of Jeonju (JVISION)

235 Cheonjam-Ro, Wansan-Gu
Jeonju-si 55069, Jeollabuk-do
Tel: +82(63) 220-4114
Website: http://en.jvision.ac.kr
President: Young-soo Han

Department/Division

Engineering (Architecture; Automation and Control Engineering; Automotive Engineering; Civil Engineering; Computer Engineering; Electrical Engineering; Electronic Engineering; Energy Engineering; Graphic Design; Information Technology; Marine Engineering; Naval Architecture; Radio and Television Broadcasting; Surveying and Mapping; Technology; Telecommunications Engineering); **Health** (Cosmetology; Dental Hygiene; Health Administration; Medicine; Nursing; Physical Therapy; Public Health); **Military Technology** (Military Science; Technology; Transport Management); **Social Science and Practical Study** (Child Care and Development; Physical Education; Preschool Education; Social Welfare; Sports)

History: Founded 1976 as Jeonju College of Technology. Acquired current title 2006.

Main language(s) of instruction: Korean

Accrediting agency: Ministry of Education

Degrees and diplomas: Bachelor's Degree (Architecture; Automation and Control Engineering; Automotive Engineering; Child Care and Development; Civil Engineering; Computer Engineering; Cosmetology; Dental Hygiene; Electrical Engineering; Electronic Engineering; Energy Engineering;

Graphic Design; Health Administration; Information Technology; Marine Engineering; Medicine; Military Science; Naval Architecture; Nursing; Physical Education; Physical Therapy; Preschool Education; Public Health; Radio and Television Broadcasting; Social Welfare; Sports; Surveying and Mapping; Technology; Telecommunications Engineering; Transport Management)
Student Services: Sports Facilities, Residential Facilities
Last Update: 21-03-2018

Wonkwang Digital University (WDU)

437, Dorimcheon-ro, Yeongdeungpo-gu
Seoul 07448
Tel: +82(2) 1588-2854
Website: http://www.wdu.ac.kr/eng/index.do
President: Namgung Moon

Department/Division
Counseling and Psychology (Psychology); **Korean Costume Science** (Theatre); **Korean Language and Culture** (East Asian Studies; Korean); **Oriental Medicinal Cosmetics and Arts** (Cosmetology); **Oriental Medicine and Healthcare** (Health Sciences; Traditional Eastern Medicine); **Oriental Science** (Oriental Studies); **Physiognomy and Management** (Anthropology; Management); **Police Science** (Police Studies); **Real Estate Management** (Real Estate); **Social Welfare** (Social Welfare); **Speech-Language Pathology** (Speech Therapy and Audiology); **Taekwondo and Bodyguarding** (Protective Services; Sports); **Tea Culture Management** (Agricultural Management); **Traditional Performing Arts** (Performing Arts); **Wellness and Cultural Tourism** (Tourism); **Won-Buddhism** (Asian Religious Studies); **Yoga and Meditation** (Esoteric Practices; Yoga)

Graduate School
Graduate Studies (Alternative Medicine; Esoteric Practices; Health Sciences; Rehabilitation and Therapy; Yoga)
Further information: Also Iksan Campus
History: Founded 2002.
Main language(s) of instruction: Korean
Accrediting agency: Ministry of Education
Degrees and diplomas: Bachelor's Degree (Agricultural Management; Alternative Medicine; Anthropology; Asian Religious Studies; Cosmetology; East Asian Studies; Esoteric Practices; Health Sciences; Korean; Management; Oriental Studies; Performing Arts; Police Studies; Protective Services; Psychology; Real Estate; Rehabilitation and Therapy; Social Welfare; Speech Therapy and Audiology; Sports; Theatre; Tourism; Traditional Eastern Medicine; Yoga). Also Certificates
Last Update: 28-03-2018

Wonkwang University

460 Iksandae-ro
Iksan 54538, Jeonbuk
Tel: +82(63) 850-5114
Fax: +82(63) 850-6666
Website: http://www.wonkwang.ac.kr
President: Do Jong Kim

College
Arts and Design (Architectural and Environmental Design; Ceramic Art; Communication Arts; Design; Fine Arts; Graphic Design; Handicrafts; Industrial Design; Jewellery Art; Metal Techniques; Painting and Drawing; Sculpture; Visual Arts); **Business Administration** (E- Business/Commerce; Economics; Information Sciences; International Business); **Business Administration** (Business Administration; Management); **Engineering** (Architecture; Automotive Engineering; Civil Engineering; Computer Engineering; Electrical Engineering; Electronic Engineering; Engineering; Environmental Engineering; Information Technology; Mechanical Engineering; Structural Architecture; Telecommunications Engineering; Town Planning); **Human Environmental Sciences** (Child Care and Development; Cosmetology; Family Studies; Fashion Design; Food Science; Nutrition; Textile Design; Welfare and Protective Services); **Humanities** (Archaeology; Art History; Arts and Humanities; Chinese; English; History; Jazz and Popular Music; Korean; Literature; Music; Music Theory and Composition; Musical Instruments; Philosophy; Singing; Writing); **Life Science and Natural Resources** (Animal Husbandry; Biochemistry; Biological and Life Sciences; Biotechnology; Botany; Environmental Studies; Food Science; Horticulture; Landscape Architecture; Natural Sciences); **Natural Sciences** (Biochemistry; Biological and Life Sciences; Dance; Mathematics; Microelectronics; Nanotechnology; Natural Sciences; Physical Education; Sports; Sports Management; Sports Medicine; Statistics; Welfare and Protective Services); **Public Policy** (Fire Science; Police Studies); **Social Sciences** (Health Administration; Journalism; Public Administration; Public Health; Social Sciences; Social Welfare); **Won Budddhism** (Asian Religious Studies)

Graduate School
Education (Education); **Food Industry Technology** (Food Technology); **Graduate Studies** (Arts and Humanities; Engineering; Fine Arts; Medicine; Natural Sciences; Social Sciences; Sports); **Law** (Law); **Management** (Management); **Oriental Medicine** (Traditional Eastern Medicine); **Public Administration** (Administration; Police Studies; Public Administration)
History: Founded 1946 as College.

Main language(s) of instruction: Korean

Accrediting agency: Korean Council for University Education (KCUE)

Degrees and diplomas: Bachelor's Degree, Master's Degree (Accountancy; Administration; Agriculture; Applied Chemistry; Archaeology; Art History; Asian Religious Studies; Biochemistry; Biology; Business Administration; Business and Commerce; Chemistry; Child Care and Development; Civil Engineering; Computer Engineering; Cosmetology; Dance; Dentistry; Design; East Asian Studies; Economics; Education; Electrical Engineering; Electronic Engineering; English; Environmental Studies; Family Studies; Fashion Design; Fire Science; Food Science; Forestry; French; German; Handicrafts; Health Sciences; History; Horticulture; Information Technology; International Relations; Japanese; Jewellery Art; Journalism; Korean; Law; Literature; Mass Communication; Mathematics; Mechanical Engineering; Medicine; Metal Techniques; Military Science; Music; Nursing; Nutrition; Painting and Drawing; Pharmacy; Philosophy; Physical Education; Police Studies; Political Sciences; Preschool Education; Public Administration; Public Health; Sculpture; Social Welfare; Social Work; Special Education; Statistics; Structural Architecture; Telecommunications Engineering; Town Planning; Traditional Eastern Medicine; Writing), Doctor's Degree (Accountancy; Agriculture; Applied Chemistry; Archaeology; Art History; Asian Religious Studies; Biochemistry; Biology; Business Administration; Business and Commerce; Chemistry; Child Care and Development; Civil Engineering; Computer Engineering; Cosmetology; Dance; Dentistry; East Asian Studies; Economics; Education; Electrical Engineering; Electronic Engineering; English; Environmental Engineering; Family Studies; Fashion Design; Fire Science; Food Science; Forestry; Handicrafts; Health Sciences; History; Horticulture; Information Technology; International Relations; Japanese; Jewellery Art; Korean; Law; Literature; Mathematics; Mechanical Engineering; Medicine; Metal Techniques; Music; Nutrition; Painting and Drawing; Pharmacy; Philosophy; Physical Education; Police Studies; Political Sciences; Preschool Education; Public Administration; Public Health; Social Welfare; Special Education; Statistics; Structural Architecture; Telecommunications Engineering; Town Planning; Traditional Eastern Medicine; Visual Arts; Writing)

Student Services: Sports Facilities, Library, IT Centre, Residential Facilities

Academic Staff 2013-2014	MALE	FEMALE	TOTAL
FULL-TIME			c. 900
Student Numbers 2013-2014			
All (Foreign Included)			c. 25360

Total number of part-time students: 483
Last Update: 07-03-2018

Woosong University

17-2 Jayang-dong Dong-gu
Daejeon 14696, Chungnam-do
Tel: +82(42) 630-9600, +82(42) 630-9348
Fax: +82(42) 629-6609
Website: http://www.wsu.ac.kr
President: John E. Endicott

College

Asia Management (Chinese; Information Management; International Business; Japanese; Leadership; Management); **Health and Welfare** (Cosmetology; Finance; Fire Science; Health Administration; Health Sciences; Medical Technology; Nursing; Occupational Therapy; Physical Therapy; Preschool Education; Protective Services; Safety Engineering; Speech Therapy and Audiology; Sports; Welfare and Protective Services); **Hotel and Culinary Arts** (Cooking and Catering; Food Technology; Hotel Management; Nutrition; Tourism); **Railroad Transportation** (Civil Engineering; Electrical Engineering; Environmental Engineering; Railway Engineering; Railway Transport; Transport Management); **TechnoMedia** (Architectural and Environmental Design; Architecture; Multimedia; Radio and Television Broadcasting; Software Engineering; Structural Architecture; Visual Arts)

School

SolBridge International School of Business (Business Administration)

Graduate School

Health and Welfare (Biotechnology; Food Science; Health Sciences; Rehabilitation and Therapy; Social Welfare; Sports; Welfare and Protective Services); **Industrial and Design** (Architecture; Computer Graphics; Computer Science; Information Sciences; Multimedia; Software Engineering; Visual Arts); **Management** (Cooking and Catering; Management; Tourism); **Railroad Transportation** (Business Administration; Civil Engineering; Electrical Engineering; Information Technology; Management; Railway Engineering; Telecommunications Engineering); **TESOL-MALL** (English; Foreign Languages Education; Teacher Training)

History: Founded 1995, acquired present status 1996.
Admission requirements: Graduation from high school
Main language(s) of instruction: Korean
Accrediting agency: Korean Council for University Education (KCUE)
Degrees and diplomas: Bachelor's Degree, Master's Degree (Architecture; Biotechnology; Business Administration; Civil Engineering; Computer Engineering; Computer Graphics; Computer Science; Electronic Engineering;

Environmental Engineering; Food Technology; Foreign Languages Education; Health Sciences; Information Technology; International Business; Multimedia; Railway Transport; Rehabilitation and Therapy; Social Welfare; Software Engineering; Sports; Structural Architecture; Telecommunications Engineering; Tourism; Transport Management)

Student Services: Sports Facilities, Library, IT Centre, Residential Facilities

Publishing house: Woosong University Press

Academic Staff 2012-2013	MALE	FEMALE	TOTAL
FULL-TIME			417
Student Numbers 2012-2013			
All (Foreign Included)			c. 15000
Foreign only			800

Last Update: 07-03-2018

Woosuk University (WU)

443, Samnye-ro, Samnye-eup
Wangju-si 55338, Jeollabuk-do
Tel: +82(63) 290-1114, +82(63) 290-1078
Fax: +82(63) 291-9312, +82(63) 290-1122
Website: http://www.woosuk.ac.kr
President: Eung-Gweon Kim

College

Culture and Social Sciences (Advertising and Publicity; Business Administration; Business and Commerce; Chinese; English; Fashion Design; Film; Hotel Management; Industrial Design; Japanese; Journalism; Landscape Architecture; Law; Mass Communication; Music; Public Administration; Social Sciences; Theatre; Tourism; Town Planning; Writing); **Education** (Computer Education; Education; Foreign Languages Education; Humanities and Social Science Education; Mathematics Education; Native Language Education; Preschool Education; Special Education); **Food Science** (Animal Husbandry; Biotechnology; Cooking and Catering; Food Science; Nutrition); **Health and Welfare** (Alternative Medicine; Child Care and Development; Cosmetology; Fire Science; Health Administration; Health Sciences; Information Management; Occupational Therapy; Pharmacy; Police Studies; Psychology; Rehabilitation and Therapy; Welfare and Protective Services); **Oriental Medicine** (Nursing; Traditional Eastern Medicine); **Pharmacy** (Pharmacy; Traditional Eastern Medicine); **Science and Technology** (Applied Chemistry; Architecture; Automotive Engineering; Civil Engineering; Computer Science; Electrical and Electronic Engineering; Environmental Engineering; Interior Design; Mechanical Engineering; Multimedia; Software Engineering; Visual Arts); **Sports Science** (Dance; Leisure Studies; Physical Education; Protective Services; Secretarial Studies; Sports; Sports Medicine)

Graduate School

Education (Educational Sciences; Special Education; Teacher Training); **Graduate Studies** (Business Administration; Education; Engineering; Health Sciences; Mathematics and Computer Science; Natural Sciences; Performing Arts; Welfare and Protective Services); **Management, Public Administration and Cultural Studies** (Advertising and Publicity; Art Therapy; Business Administration; Cultural Studies; Fashion Design; Health Sciences; International Business; Journalism; Management; Native Language Education; Police Studies; Public Administration; Tourism; Welfare and Protective Services; Writing)

Further information: Jincheon Campus; Korean Language Education Centre

History: Founded 1979. Acquired present status 1992. Acquired present title 1995

Academic year: March to December (March-June; September-December)

Fees: National : Undergraduate, 3,000-4,000 per semester; Graduate, 3,500-6,200 per semester (US Dollar), International : Undergraduate, 3,000-4,000 per semester; Graduate, 3,500-6,200 per semester. International students can be offered 50% of scholarship on their tuition; Korean Language Education Centre, 1,700 for a 20 weeks course (US Dollar)

Main language(s) of instruction: Korean

Accrediting agency: Korean Council for University Education (KCUE)

Degrees and diplomas: Bachelor's Degree, Master's Degree (Advertising and Publicity; Art Education; Art Therapy; Automotive Engineering; Bioengineering; Biology; Biotechnology; Business Administration; Child Care and Development; Computer Education; Computer Engineering; Construction Engineering; Education; Educational Administration; Educational and Student Counselling; Electrical and Electronic Engineering; Engineering Management; English; Fashion Design; Foreign Languages Education; Health Sciences; Home Economics Education; Information Management; International Business; Journalism; Korean; Landscape Architecture; Literature; Materials Engineering; Mathematics; Mathematics Education; Music; Music Education; Native Language Education; Nursing; Occupational Therapy; Pharmacology; Pharmacy; Physical Education; Police Studies; Preschool Education; Public Administration; Science Education; Special Education; Sports; Sports Medicine; Tourism; Traditional Eastern Medicine; Welfare and Protective Services; Writing), Doctor's Degree (Biotechnology; Civil Engineering; Education; English; Korean; Landscape Architecture; Literature; Mathematics; Pharmacy; Physical Education; Special Education; Traditional Eastern Medicine)

Student Services: Academic Counselling, Social Counselling, Careers Guidance, Nursery Care, Cultural Activities, Sports Facilities, Language Laboratory, Facilities for disabled people, Health Services, Canteen, Foreign Studies Centre, Library, IT Centre, Residential Facilities

Academic Staff 2013-2014	MALE	FEMALE	TOTAL
FULL-TIME			c. 350
Student Numbers 2013-2014			
All (Foreign Included)			c. 11500
Foreign only			1050

Last Update: 26-04-2018

Yeungnam University (YU)

280 Daehak-Ro
Gyeongsan-si 38541, Gyeongbuk-do
Tel: +82(53) 810-2114
Fax: +82(53) 810-2036
Website: http://www.yu.ac.kr
President: Gil-So Sur

College
Basic Studies (Arts and Humanities; Natural Sciences; Social Sciences); **Business and Economics** (Business and Commerce; Economics; Finance; International Business); **Design and Art** (Communication Arts; Design; Fine Arts; Graphic Design; Industrial Design; Visual Arts); **Education** (Education; Foreign Languages Education; Mathematics Education; Native Language Education; Physical Education; Preschool Education; Special Education); **Engineering** (Chemical Engineering; Civil Engineering; Computer Engineering; Electrical Engineering; Electronic Engineering; Engineering; Environmental Engineering; Information Technology; Materials Engineering; Mechanical Engineering; Medical Technology; Nanotechnology; Polymer and Plastics Technology; Telecommunications Engineering; Textile Technology; Town Planning); **Human Ecology and Kinesiology** (Clothing and Sewing; Family Studies; Fashion Design; Food Science; Health Sciences; Home Economics; Nutrition; Physical Education; Sports); **Law** (Law); **Liberal Arts** (Anthropology; Arts and Humanities; Chinese; Cultural Studies; English; French; German; History; Japanese; Literature; Mass Communication; Media Studies; Philosophy; Psychology; Sociology); **Medicine** (Medicine); **Music** (Music); **Natural Resources** (Agricultural Economics; Biological and Life Sciences; Food Science; Food Technology; Forestry; Horticulture; Landscape Architecture; Natural Resources); **Pharmacy** (Pharmacy); **Political Science and Public Administration** (Development Studies; International

Relations; Military Science; Police Studies; Political Sciences; Public Administration; Welfare and Protective Services); **Sciences** (Biological and Life Sciences; Chemistry; Mathematics; Natural Sciences; Physics; Statistics)

Course/Programme
Interdisciplinary Study (Asian Studies; Biological and Life Sciences; Biomedical Engineering; Business and Commerce; Cultural Studies; E- Business/Commerce; Electronic Engineering; Energy Engineering; Ethics; Fine Arts; Heritage Preservation; Home Economics Education; Human Resources; Humanities and Social Science Education; International Business; International Studies; Labour and Industrial Relations; Mass Communication; Medicine; Natural Sciences; Nuclear Engineering; Real Estate; Science Education; Social Welfare; Technology Education)

School
Architecture (Architectural and Environmental Design; Architecture; Structural Architecture); **Biotechnology** (Biological and Life Sciences; Biotechnology; Microbiology; Molecular Biology); **International Studies** (Communication Studies; Comparative Sociology; Government; International Business; International Economics; International Relations; International Studies; Regional Studies); **Law** (*Professional Graduate*) (Law); **Medicine** (*Professional Graduate*) (Medicine)

Graduate School
Arts and Design (*Special*) (Art Management; Communication Arts; Design; Fine Arts; Painting and Drawing; Visual Arts); **Business Administration** (*Special*) (Business Administration; Business and Commerce; International Business); **Clinical Pharmacy** (*Special*) (Pharmacy); **Education** (*Special*) (Education; Educational Sciences; Special Education; Teacher Training); **Engineering** (*Special*) (Civil Engineering; Computer Engineering; Electrical Engineering; Electronic Engineering; Engineering; Fashion Design; Industrial Engineering; Mechanical Engineering; Safety Engineering; Structural Architecture; Telecommunications Engineering; Town Planning); **Environment and Public Health Studies** (*Special*) (Art Therapy; Environmental Engineering; Environmental Management; Environmental Studies; Nutrition; Public Health); **Graduate Studies** (Art Therapy; Arts and Humanities; Biomedical Engineering; Cognitive Sciences; Design; Electronic Engineering; Engineering; Fine Arts; Foreign Languages Education; International Business; Korean; Leadership; Medicine; Multimedia; Music; Nanotechnology; Natural Sciences; Physical Education; Public Health; Robotics; Sociology; Telecommunications Engineering; Women's Studies); **Park Chung Hee School of Policy and Saemaul**

(*Special*) (East Asian Studies; Economics; History; Political Sciences); **Public Administration** (*Special*) (Development Studies; Government; Public Administration; Social Welfare); **Sports Science** (*Special*) (Sports)

Further information: Also Daemyung Campus; 44 Research Institutes

History: Founded 1947, incorporating Taegu College and Chonggu College founded 1947 and 1950 respectively.

Academic year: March to February (March-August; September-February)

Admission requirements: Graduation from high school or equivalent, and entrance examination

Fees: Undergraduate, 5,700-8,500 per annum; Graduate, 6,700-8,600 per annum (US Dollar)

Main language(s) of instruction: Korean

Accrediting agency: Korean Council for University Education (KCUE)

Degrees and diplomas: Bachelor's Degree, Master's Degree (Aesthetics; Agricultural Business; Agricultural Economics; Agronomy; Anaesthesiology; Anatomy; Anthropology; Architecture; Art Education; Art History; Art Management; Biochemistry; Biological and Life Sciences; Biomedical Engineering; Biomedicine; Biotechnology; Business Administration; Chemical Engineering; Chemistry; Chinese; Civil Engineering; Clothing and Sewing; Computer Engineering; Conducting; Cultural Studies; Dance; Dentistry; Dermatology; Design; Development Studies; East Asian Studies; Economic and Finance Policy; Economics; Education; Educational Administration; Educational and Student Counselling; Electrical and Electronic Engineering; Electrical Engineering; Electronic Engineering; Energy Engineering; Engineering; English; Environmental Engineering; Environmental Studies; European Studies; Family Studies; Fashion Design; Food Science; Foreign Languages Education; Forest Products; Forestry; French; German; Government; Graphic Design; Gynaecology and Obstetrics; History; Home Economics; Home Economics Education; Horticulture; Humanities and Social Science Education; Industrial Arts Education; Industrial Design; Industrial Engineering; Information Management; Information Technology; International Business; International Economics; International Relations; Japanese; Korean; Laboratory Techniques; Landscape Architecture; Leadership; Literature; Mass Communication; Materials Engineering; Mathematics; Mathematics Education; Mechanical Engineering; Media Studies; Medical Technology; Medicine; Metallurgical Engineering; Microbiology; Molecular Biology; Music Education; Music Theory and Composition; Musical Instruments; Native Language Education; Neurological Therapy; Neurology; Nutrition; Oncology; Ophthalmology; Orthopaedics; Otorhinolaryngology; Paediatrics; Painting and Drawing; Pathology; Performing Arts; Pharmacology; Pharmacy; Philosophy; Physical Education; Physics; Physiology; Plastic Surgery; Political Sciences; Preschool Education; Primary Education; Private Law; Psychiatry and Mental Health; Psychology; Public Administration; Public Health; Public Law; Radiology; Rehabilitation and Therapy; Robotics; Safety Engineering; Science Education; Sculpture; Singing; Social and Preventive Medicine; Social Welfare; Sociology; Special Education; Sports; Statistics; Structural Architecture; Surgery; Technology Education; Telecommunications Engineering; Textile Technology; Town Planning; Translation and Interpretation; Urology; Visual Arts; Welfare and Protective Services; Women's Studies; Writing), Doctor's Degree (Aesthetics; Agricultural Economics; Anaesthesiology; Anatomy; Anthropology; Architecture; Art History; Art Therapy; Biochemistry; Biological and Life Sciences; Biomedical Engineering; Biomedicine; Biotechnology; Business Administration; Chemical Engineering; Chemistry; Chinese; Civil Engineering; Clothing and Sewing; Computer Engineering; Cultural Studies; Dentistry; Dermatology; Design; Development Studies; East Asian Studies; Economics; Education; Electrical Engineering; Electronic Engineering; Energy Engineering; Engineering; English; English Studies; Environmental Engineering; Family Studies; Fashion Design; Fine Arts; Food Science; Food Technology; Forest Products; Forestry; Gynaecology and Obstetrics; Health Sciences; History; Home Economics; Horticulture; Industrial Engineering; Information Technology; International Business; International Economics; International Relations; Japanese; Korean; Landscape Architecture; Literature; Mass Communication; Materials Engineering; Mathematics; Mathematics Education; Mechanical Engineering; Media Studies; Medical Technology; Microbiology; Molecular Biology; Musical Instruments; Musicology; Native Language Education; Neurology; Nutrition; Oncology; Ophthalmology; Orthopaedics; Otorhinolaryngology; Paediatrics; Pathology; Pharmacy; Philosophy; Physical Education; Physics; Physiology; Plastic Surgery; Political Sciences; Preschool Education; Private Law; Psychiatry and Mental Health; Psychology; Public Administration; Public Health; Public Law; Radiology; Regional Studies; Rehabilitation and Therapy; Robotics; Safety Engineering; Sociology; Sports; Statistics; Surgery; Telecommunications Engineering; Textile Technology; Town Planning; Urology; Welfare and Protective Services). Professional Graduate Programmes in Medicine and Law

Student Services: Health Services, Canteen, Library, IT Centre, Residential Facilities

Periodicals: Business Administration Memoirs, Industrial Economy, Journal of Oriental Culture, Journal of Silla-Kaya Culture, Public Administration Review, Theses Collections (Humanities, Social and Natural Sciences), Yeungdae Shinmum

Publishing house: University Press

Academic Staff 2013-2014	MALE	FEMALE	TOTAL
FULL-TIME			2094
Student Numbers 2013-2014			
All (Foreign Included)			c. 21000
Foreign only			1000

Last Update: 26-04-2018

Yewon Arts University

271 Changin-ri, Sinpyeong-myeon
Imsil-si 566-822, Jeollabuk-do
Tel: +82(63) 640-7114
Fax: +82(63) 640-7773
Website: http://www.yewon.ac.kr
President: Young-duk Chae

College

Undergraduate Studies (Acting; Arts and Humanities; Dance; Design; Film; Fine Arts; Heritage Preservation; Hotel Management; Jewellery Art; Music; Musical Instruments; Performing Arts; Physical Education; Singing; Theatre; Tourism; Visual Arts)

Graduate School

Culture and Arts (Art Therapy; Arts and Humanities; Cinema and Television; Cultural Studies; Fine Arts; Music; Musical Instruments; Physical Education; Video); **Social Work** (Social Welfare; Social Work); **Video Entrepreneurship Culture** (Management; Video)
History: Founded 2000 as Yewon University. Acquired present title 2003.
Main language(s) of instruction: Korean
Accrediting agency: Korean Council for University Education (KCUE)
Degrees and diplomas: Bachelor's Degree, Master's Degree (Art Therapy; Arts and Humanities; Cinema and Television; Fine Arts; Management; Music; Performing Arts; Physical Education; Social Welfare; Video)
Student Services: Residential Facilities

Academic Staff 2013-2014	MALE	FEMALE	TOTAL
FULL-TIME			70
PART-TIME			c. 80
Student Numbers 2013-2014			
All (Foreign Included)			c. 1000
Foreign only			90

Last Update: 07-03-2018

Yonam College

313, Yeonam-ro, Seonghwan-eup, Seobuk-gu
Cheonan-si, Chungcheongnam-do
Tel: +82(41) 580-1114
Fax: +82(41) 581-0401
Website: http://www.yonam.ac.kr/mbshome/mbs/eng/index.do
President: Yeol-Yug Geun
Tel: +82(41) 580-1001

Department/Division

Animal Care (Animal Husbandry); **Animal Husbandry** (Animal Husbandry); **Beauty Arts** (Cosmetology); **Eco-Friendly Horticulture** (Ecology; Horticulture); **Environment and Landscape Architecture** (Architectural and Environmental Design; Landscape Architecture); **Floral and Design** (Design; Floriculture); **Foodservice and Industry** (Cooking and Catering); **Horticulture and Landscape Architecture** (Horticulture; Landscape Architecture)
History: Founded 1974 as Yonam High Technology School of Animal Husbandry, became Yonam College of Agriculture 1998, and acquired current title 2003.
Main language(s) of instruction: Korean
Accrediting agency: Ministry of Education
Degrees and diplomas: Associate Degree (Animal Husbandry; Architectural and Environmental Design; Cooking and Catering; Cosmetology; Design; Ecology; Floriculture; Horticulture; Landscape Architecture), Bachelor's Degree (Animal Husbandry; Horticulture; Landscape Architecture)

Academic Staff 2015-2016	MALE	FEMALE	TOTAL
FULL-TIME			29

Last Update: 26-03-2018

Yong In University

470 Samga-dong
Yongin-si 17092, Gyeonggi-do
Tel: +82(31) 332-6471, +82(31) 332-6476
Fax: +82(31) 332-6479
Website: http://www.yongin.ac.kr
President: Sun-kyoung Park

College

Arts and Culture (Cultural Studies; Dance; Design; Film; Fine Arts; Heritage Preservation; Korean; Media Studies; Music; Painting and Drawing; Singing; Theatre); **Business and Public Administration** (Business Administration;

Chinese; English; Information Management; Information Technology; Management; Police Studies; Tourism); **Environmental Sciences** (Biological and Life Sciences; Computer Science; Environmental Studies; Health Sciences; Information Technology; Occupational Health; Statistics; Transport Management); **Martial Arts** (Military Science; Physical Education; Protective Services; Sports); **Public Health** (Food Science; Home Economics; Nutrition; Physical Therapy; Public Health; Welfare and Protective Services); **Sports Science** (Leisure Studies; Media Studies; Physical Education; Special Education; Sports)

Graduate School

Arts (Art Therapy; Film; Fine Arts; Music; Performing Arts; Theatre); **Business Administration** (Art Management; Business Administration; Police Studies); **Culture Heritage** (Archaeology; Heritage Preservation); **Education** (Art Education; Computer Education; Educational Administration; Educational and Student Counselling; Environmental Studies; Film; Foreign Languages Education; Home Economics Education; Multimedia; Music Education; Native Language Education; Physical Education; Special Education; Theatre); **Graduate Studies** (Biological and Life Sciences; Business Administration; Dance; Environmental Studies; Food Science; Health Sciences; Nutrition; Physical Education; Physical Therapy; Protective Services; Sports); **Rehabilitation and Health Science** (Physical Therapy; Rehabilitation and Therapy); **Sports and Science** (Leisure Studies; Physical Education; Protective Services; Social and Community Services; Special Education; Sports); **Taekwondo** (Sports; Sports Management)

History: Founded 1953.
Main language(s) of instruction: Korean
Accrediting agency: Korean Council for University Education (KCUE)
Degrees and diplomas: Bachelor's Degree, Master's Degree (Art Therapy; Biological and Life Sciences; Business Administration; Dance; Fine Arts; Food Science; Nutrition; Performing Arts; Physical Education; Protective Services; Public Health; Sports), Doctor's Degree (Business Administration; Dance; Physical Education; Physical Therapy; Protective Services; Public Health; Sports)
Student Services: Sports Facilities, Library, Residential Facilities

Academic Staff 2012-2013	MALE	FEMALE	TOTAL
FULL-TIME			220
PART-TIME			c. 360
Student Numbers 2012-2013			
All (Foreign Included)			7160

Last Update: 07-03-2018

Yongmoon Graduate School of Counseling Psychology (YMGS)

Yulgok-ro 154
Seoul 03136
Tel: +82(2) 763-7448
Fax: +82(2) 3672-1012
Website: https://yongmoon.ac.kr

Course/Programme

Children and Youth Counseling (Psychology); **Crisis Management** (Psychology); **Elderly Welfare Counseling** (Psychology); **Family Counseling** (Psychology); **Positive Psychology** (Psychology)
History: Founded 2009.
Main language(s) of instruction: Korean
Accrediting agency: Ministry of Education
Degrees and diplomas: Master's Degree (Psychology), Doctor's Degree (Psychology)
Student Services: Academic Counselling, Careers Guidance, Sports Facilities, Library

Academic Staff 2017-2018	MALE	FEMALE	TOTAL
FULL-TIME	4	3	7
Student Numbers 2017-2018			
All (Foreign Included)	22	93	115

Last Update: 26-04-2018

Yonsei University

50 Yonsei-ro Seodaemun-gu
Seoul 03722
Tel: +82(2) 1599-1885, +82(2) 2123-4131
Fax: +82(2) 392-0618, +82(2) 364-2364
Website: http://yonsei.ac.kr
President: Yong-Hak Kim

College

Business and Economics (Economics; Statistics); **Dentistry** (Dentistry); **Engineering** (Bioengineering; Chemical Engineering; Civil Engineering; Computer Science; Electrical and Electronic Engineering; Energy Engineering; Engineering; Environmental Engineering; Industrial Engineering; Information Management; Materials Engineering; Mechanical Engineering; Structural Architecture; Technology; Town Planning); **Human Ecology** (Architectural and Environmental Design; Child Care and Development; Clothing and Sewing; Cooking and Catering; Family Studies; Home Economics; Interior Design; Nutrition; Textile Technology);

Liberal Arts (Arts and Humanities; Chinese; Cognitive Sciences; Comparative Literature; East Asian Studies; English; French; German; History; Information Sciences; Korean; Library Science; Literature; Modern Languages; Philosophy; Psychology; Russian); **Life Science and Biotechnology** (Biochemistry; Bioengineering; Biological and Life Sciences; Biotechnology); **Medicine** (Medicine); **Music** (Music; Music Theory and Composition; Musical Instruments; Religious Music; Singing); **Nursing** (Nursing); **Pharmacy** (Pharmacy); **Science** (Astronomy and Space Science; Chemistry; Earth Sciences; Mathematics; Medical Technology; Meteorology; Nanotechnology; Physics); **Sciences in Education** (Education; Physical Education; Sports); **Social Sciences** (Anthropology; Communication Studies; Cultural Studies; Gender Studies; International Relations; International Studies; Political Sciences; Public Administration; Regional Studies; Social Sciences; Social Welfare; Sociology); **Theology** (Theology); **Underwood International College (UIC)** (Arts and Humanities; Biological and Life Sciences; Chemistry; Engineering; Social Sciences); **University College** (Biology; Chemistry; Christian Religious Studies; English; Physics; Writing)

Course/Programme

Global Leadership Division (Leadership)

School

Business (Business Administration)

Institute

Communication Research (Communication Studies); **Economic Research** (Economics); **Educational Research** (*Intercollegiate*) (Educational Research); **Engineering Research** (Engineering); **Humanities** (Arts and Humanities); **Information Technology Research** (Information Technology); **Korean Studies** (Korean); **Korean Unification Studies** (Korean); **Legal Research** (Law); **Life Science and Biotechnology** (Biological and Life Sciences; Biotechnology); **Natural Sciences** (Natural Sciences); **Social Development Studies** (Social Policy); **Social Science Research** (Social Sciences)

Centre

Mathematical Analysis and Computation (Mathematics and Computer Science); **Next-Generation Converged Energy Materials Research** (Energy Engineering)

Graduate School

Business (*Professional*) (Business Administration); **Communication and Arts** (*Professional*) (Communication Arts); **Economics** (*Special*) (Economics); **Education** (*Special*) (Education); **Engineering** (*Special*) (Engineering); **Graduate Studies** (Arts and Humanities; Biological and Life Sciences; Biomedicine; Biotechnology; Business Administration; Business and Commerce; Computer Engineering; Computer Science; Dentistry; Economics; Education; Engineering; Home Economics; Law; Mathematics and Computer Science; Medicine; Music; Natural Sciences; Nursing; Social Sciences; Theology); **Human Environmental Sciences** (*Special*) (Home Economics); **Information** (*Professional*) (Information Sciences); **International Studies** (*Professional*) (International Studies); **Journalism and Mass Communication** (*Special*) (Journalism; Mass Communication); **Law** (*Special*) (Public Health); **Law** (*Professional*) (Law); **Nursing** (*Special*) (Nursing); **Public Administration** (*Special*) (Administration); **Public Health** (*Special*) (Public Health); **Social Welfare** (*Professional*) (Social Welfare); **Theology** (*Professional*) (Christian Religious Studies; Theology)

Further information: Also International Songdo Campus; Wonju Campus; Centres and Research Centres

History: Founded 1885 as Severance Union Medical Clinic. Merged with Chosun Christian College, established 1915, to form present University 1957. The University is related to the United Board for Christian Higher Education in Asia

Academic year: March to February (March-August; September-February)

Admission requirements: Graduation from high school, government qualifying examination and university entrance examination

Main language(s) of instruction: Korean, English

Accrediting agency: Korean Council for University Education (KCUE)

Degrees and diplomas: Bachelor's Degree (Arts and Humanities; Business Administration; Dentistry; Economics; Education; Engineering; Home Economics; International Studies; Leadership; Medicine; Music; Natural Sciences; Nursing; Pharmacy; Religion; Social Sciences), Master's Degree (Architectural and Environmental Design; Arts and Humanities; Astronomy and Space Science; Biochemistry; Bioengineering; Biological and Life Sciences; Biology; Biomedicine; Biotechnology; Business Administration; Chemical Engineering; Chemistry; Child Care and Development; Chinese; Civil Engineering; Clothing and Sewing; Cognitive Sciences; Comparative Literature; Computer Engineering; Computer Science; Cultural Studies; Dentistry; Earth Sciences; East Asian Studies; Economics; Education; Electrical and Electronic Engineering; Energy Engineering; Engineering; English; Environmental Engineering; Ethics; Family Studies; French; Gender Studies; Genetics; German; Gerontology; History; Industrial Engineering; Information Management; Information Sciences; Interior Design; International Business; International Economics; International Relations; International Studies; Korean; Law; Leisure

Studies; Library Science; Literature; Materials Engineering; Mathematics; Mechanical Engineering; Medical Technology; Medicine; Meteorology; Modern Languages; Music; Nanotechnology; Nursing; Nutrition; Philosophy; Physical Education; Physics; Political Sciences; Psychology; Public Administration; Public Health; Regional Studies; Religion; Russian; Social Policy; Social Sciences; Social Welfare; Sociology; Speech Therapy and Audiology; Sports; Statistics; Structural Architecture; Technology; Textile Technology; Theology; Town Planning), Doctor's Degree (Astronomy and Space Science; Biomedical Engineering; Biomedicine; Business Administration; Chemistry; Child Care and Development; Chinese; Comparative Literature; Computer Science; Dentistry; Earth Sciences; East Asian Studies; Economics; Electrical and Electronic Engineering; Engineering; English; Ethics; Family Studies; German; History; Home Economics; Information Sciences; International Business; International Economics; International Relations; International Studies; Laboratory Techniques; Law; Library Science; Literature; Mathematics and Computer Science; Medical Technology; Medicine; Natural Sciences; Nursing; Occupational Therapy; Packaging Technology; Pharmacy; Philosophy; Physical Therapy; Political Sciences; Public Administration; Public Health; Russian; Social Sciences; Statistics; Theology). Also MBA and Executive MBA; International Joint and Dual Degree Programmes with Institutions in USA, Canada, UK, Japan, China, Hong Kong, Taiwan, Indonesia, France

Student Services: Academic Counselling, Social Counselling, Careers Guidance, Nursery Care, Cultural Activities, Sports Facilities, Language Laboratory, Facilities for disabled people, Health Services, Canteen, Foreign Studies Centre, Library, Residential Facilities

Periodicals: Etudes Franco-Coréennes, Journal of East and West Studies, Journal of Educational Science, Journal of Humanities, Journal of Regional Studies and Development, Korean Medical Education Review, Korean Unification Studies, Language Facts and Perspectives, Teaching Korean as a Foreign Language, The Dong Bang Hak Chi (Journal of Far Eastern Studies), The Korean Journal of Economics, Theological Forum, Yonsei Business Review, Yonsei Engineering Review, Yonsei Medical Journal, Yonsei Nonchong, Yonsei Social Science Review

Publishing house: University Press

Academic Staff 2017-2018	MALE	FEMALE	TOTAL
FULL-TIME			1138
PART-TIME			1500
Student Numbers 2017-2018			
All (Foreign Included)			29502
Foreign only			4609

Last Update: 24-05-2018

YONSEI UNIVERSITY (WONJU CAMPUS)

1 Yonseidae-gil
Wonju 26493, Gangwon-do
Tel: +82(33) 760-5088/5086
Website: http://www.yonsei.ac.kr/en_wj
President: Yong-Hak Kim

College

EastAsia International College (Humanities and Social Science Education); **Government and Business** (Business Administration; Economics; Industrial Arts Education; International Relations; Law; Public Administration; Social Sciences); **Health Sciences** (Biomedical Engineering; Biomedicine; Environmental Engineering; Health Administration; Health Sciences; Laboratory Techniques; Medical Technology; Occupational Therapy; Physical Therapy; Radiology); **Humanities and Arts** (Art Management; Arts and Humanities; Cultural Studies; Design; English; History; Korean; Literature; Philosophy); **Science and Technology** (Applied Chemistry; Biological and Life Sciences; Biotechnology; Chemistry; Computer Engineering; Information Sciences; Mathematics; Mathematics and Computer Science; Natural Sciences; Packaging Technology; Physics; Statistics; Telecommunications Engineering); **Wonju College of Medicine** (Medicine)

Department/Division

Global Elite

Graduate School

Education (Education); **Government and Business** (Business Administration; Government); **Graduate Studies** (Arts and Humanities; Engineering; Health Sciences; Medicine; Music; Natural Sciences; Social Sciences; Sports); **Health and Environment** (Environmental Studies; Health Sciences)
History: Founded 1976
Academic year: March to February (Spring semester: March-August; Fall semester: September-February)
Fees: National : 3,537,000-5,306,000 (Won), International : 3,714,000-5,571,000 (Won)
Main language(s) of instruction: Korean, English
Accrediting agency: Korean Council for University Education (KCUE)
Degrees and diplomas: Bachelor's Degree (Applied Chemistry; Art Management; Arts and Humanities; Biological and Life Sciences; Biomedical Engineering; Biomedicine; Biotechnology; Business Administration; Chemistry; Computer Engineering; Cultural Studies; Design; Economics; English; Environmental Engineering; Health Administration; Health Sciences; History; Humanities and Social Science Education; Industrial Arts Education; Information Sciences; International Relations; Korean; Laboratory Techniques;

Law; Literature; Mathematics; Mathematics and Computer Science; Medical Technology; Medicine; Natural Sciences; Occupational Therapy; Packaging Technology; Philosophy; Physical Therapy; Physics; Public Administration; Radiology; Social Sciences; Statistics; Telecommunications Engineering), Master's Degree (Administration; Art Management; Bioengineering; Biological and Life Sciences; Biology; Biomedical Engineering; Biotechnology; Business Administration; Chemistry; Computer Science; Dental Hygiene; Design; Economics; English; Environmental Engineering; Graphic Design; Health Administration; History; Industrial Design; Information Management; International Relations; Korean; Law; Literature; Mathematics; Medicine; Nursing; Occupational Therapy; Packaging Technology; Pathology; Philosophy; Physical Therapy; Physics; Public Administration; Radiology; Rehabilitation and Therapy; Statistics), Doctor's Degree (Biological and Life Sciences; Biomedical Engineering; Biomedicine; Biotechnology; Business Administration; Chemistry; Communication Arts; Computer Science; Dental Hygiene; Economics; English; Environmental Engineering; Graphic Design; Health Administration; Health Sciences; History; Industrial Design; Information Management; International Relations; Korean; Literature; Mathematics; Medicine; Nursing; Occupational Therapy; Packaging Technology; Pathology; Philosophy; Physical Therapy; Physics; Public Administration; Radiology; Statistics)

Student Services: Careers Guidance, Sports Facilities, Health Services, Foreign Studies Centre, Library, Residential Facilities

Academic Staff 2017-2018	MALE	FEMALE	TOTAL
FULL-TIME			801
Student Numbers 2017-2018			
All (Foreign Included)			7510
Foreign only			153

Last Update: 26-04-2018

Youngnam Theological University and Seminary (YTUS)

117 Bonghwoe-ri, Jillyang-eup
Gyeongsan, Gyeongsangbuk-do
Tel: +82(53) 850-0500
Fax: +82(53) 852-9815
Website: http://ytus.ac.kr
President: Gyu-hoon Oh

Department/Division
Christian Education (Religious Education); **Counseling Psychology** (Psychology); **General Graduate Studies**

(Literature; Religious Education; Social Welfare; Theology); **Social Welfare** (Social Welfare); **Theology** (Theology)

Graduate School
Counseling (Psychology); **Social Welfare** (Social Welfare); **Theology** (Theology)
History: Founded 1913, acquired current status and title 1994.
Main language(s) of instruction: Korean
Accrediting agency: Korean Council for University Education (KCUE)
Degrees and diplomas: Bachelor's Degree (Psychology; Religious Education; Social Welfare; Theology), Master's Degree (Bible; History of Religion; Literature; Missionary Studies; Psychology; Religious Education; Social Welfare; Social Work; Theology), Doctor's Degree (Bible; Christian Religious Studies; Missionary Studies; New Testament; Religious Education; Social Welfare; Theology)
Last Update: 12-03-2018

Youngsan University (YSU)

288 Junam-ri (Junam-dong)
Yangsan-si 626-790, Kyungnam-do
Tel: +82(55) 380-9114
Fax: +82(55) 366-4374
Website: http://www.ysu.ac.kr
President: Gu-Wuk Bu

School
Culture Industry (*Busan Campus*) (Acting; Advertising and Publicity; Cinema and Television; Cosmetology; Dance; Fashion Design; Film; Fine Arts; Interior Design; Journalism; Performing Arts; Public Relations; Radio and Television Broadcasting; Singing; Software Engineering; Visual Arts); **Engineering** (*Yangsan Campus*) (Architecture; Automotive Engineering; Computer Engineering; Engineering; Environmental Engineering; Police Studies; Transport Engineering); **Foreign Languages** (*Busan Campus*) (Business Administration; Chinese; English; Hindi; Japanese; Korean; Modern Languages; South and Southeast Asian Languages); **Health Science** (*Yangsan Campus*) (Dental Hygiene; Health Administration; Health Sciences; Nursing; Physical Therapy); **Hotel and Tourism Management** (*Busan Campus*) (Air Transport; Cooking and Catering; Food Science; Food Technology; Hotel Management; Service Trades; Tourism); **Law** (*Yangsan Campus*) (Law); **Law and Business** (*Busan Campus*) (Business Administration; Maritime Law; Transport and Communications); **Law and Business** (*Yangsan Campus*) (Business Administration; Finance; International Business; Law; Management; Police Studies; Public Administration; Real Estate); **Physical Education** (*Yangsan Campus*) (Health

Administration; Physical Education; Sports; Sports Management); **Undeclared Majors** (*Yangsan Campus*) (Arts and Humanities; Social Sciences); **Undeclared Majors** (*Busan Campus*) (Arts and Humanities; Social Sciences)

Graduate School

Asian Studies (*Busan Campus*) (Asian Studies); **Beauty Art** (*Busan Campus*) (Aesthetics; Fine Arts); **Engineering** (*Yangsan Campus*) (Engineering; Information Technology; Transport Engineering); **Graduate Studies** (*Busan Campus*) (Aesthetics; Fine Arts; Hotel Management; Real Estate; Tourism); **Legal Affairs and Business Administration** (*Busan Campus*) (Administration; Business Administration; Korean; Law; Police Studies); **Real Estate** (*Busan Campus*) (Real Estate); **Tourism** (*Busan Campus*) (Cooking and Catering; Hotel and Restaurant; Hotel Management; Tourism)

Further information: Also Busan Campus

History: Founded 1997.

Academic year: March to February

Main language(s) of instruction: Korean

Accrediting agency: Korean Council for University Education (KCUE)

Degrees and diplomas: Bachelor's Degree, Master's Degree (Aesthetics; Asian Studies; Business Administration; Fine Arts; Hotel Management; Information Technology; Law; Real Estate; Tourism; Transport Economics), Doctor's Degree (Aesthetics; Fine Arts; Hotel Management; Real Estate; Tourism)

Student Services: Academic Counselling, Social Counselling, Careers Guidance, Sports Facilities, Language Laboratory, Facilities for disabled people, Health Services, Foreign Studies Centre, Library, IT Centre, Residential Facilities

Periodicals: Youngsan Studies

Academic Staff 2012-2013	MALE	FEMALE	TOTAL
FULL-TIME			630
PART-TIME			c. 390
Student Numbers 2012-2013			
All (Foreign Included)			c. 13800

Last Update: 07-03-2018

Kuwait

STRUCTURE OF HIGHER EDUCATION SYSTEM

Description

Higher education is provided by several private and public institutions, and covers university and post-secondary education and training. The Public Authority for Applied Education and Training deals with technical and vocational training which takes place in specialised training centres and technical institutions.

Stages of studies

University level first stage

Undergraduate studies
Bachelor's degrees are issued after four years' study, and in certain fields such as engineering, after five years' study, and after seven years' study in medicine and surgery.

University level second stage

Postgraduate studies
Higher diplomas are offered two to three semesters after the Bachelor's degree at Kuwait University. Master's degrees require one to two years' study beyond the Bachelor's degree.

University level third stage

Doctoral studies
Doctorates are offered after at least three years' study following postgraduate degrees.

ADMISSION TO HIGHER EDUCATION

Admission to university-level studies

Name of Secondary school credential required: Shahadat Al-Thanawiya-Al-A'ama
Alternatives to credentials: Religious Secondary Education Certificate (only to enrol in the College of Arts and Education, the College of Law, or the College of Islamic Law and Islamic Studies). International Certificate of General Secondary Education; the Baccalauréat.

Foreign students admission

Admission requirements: A limited number of foreign students may be admitted, subject to availability of relevant resources and facilities. Selection is based on merit and national interest. Applicants should have a Bachelor's degree with a GPA of at least 2.67 on a scale of 4. For acceptance for scholarships, certificates must be either in Arabic, English or French or translated into one of these languages and authenticated. They must be attested by the Ministry of Education and the Ministry of External Affairs and the Embassy of Kuwait in the student's country. To obtain a scholarship students must be chosen to study in Kuwait by the students' government or by an institution, or a corporation accredited by the Government. The Kuwait National Commission for Education, Science and Culture is the only organ that has the right to consider each application and take a decision.
Entry regulations: Study visas are necessary for foreign students.
Language Proficiency: Students must have a good knowledge of Arabic or English. A minimum language score is necessary for admission to Master's degree programmes. Each applicant must satisfy one of the language proficiency requirements for the programme to which they are seeking application.

NATIONAL BODIES

Ministry of Education and Higher Education

Minister: Badir al-Isa
PO Box 7
Safat 13001
Tel: +965 483-7890
Fax: +965 483-7601
Website: http://www.mohe.edu.kw
Role of national body: Educational planning and policy; adoption of text books, curricula; supply of human/material resources; coordination of education and development policies.

© International Association of Universities 2019
International Handbook of Universities 2019,
https://doi.org/10.1057/978-3-319-76971-4_103

Public Authority for Applied Education and Training

PO Box 23167
Safat 13092
Tel: +965 180-6611
Website: http://www.paaet.edu.kw
Role of national body: Supervises and plans programmes for applied education and training.

Private Universities Council

Sharq-Sanabel Towers,opposite Sharq Mall Next to Amiri Hospital, levels 34/ 35
Tel: +965 224-0591
Fax: +965 245-5326
Website: http://www.puc.edu.kw
Role of national body: Determines accreditation requirements for private educational institutions and accredits private education programmes and review their performance to ensure commitment to the provisions of their founding decree; deals with recognition and equivalence of degrees issued by private institutions.

Data for academic year: 2008–2009
Source: IAU from Kuwait National Commission for UNESCO, 2008. IBE, UNESCO, 2013 (stages and degrees). Bodies updated 2017.

Public Institution

Kuwait University

PO Box 5969
Safat 13060
Tel: +965 481-1188
Fax: +965 484-8648
Website: http://www.kuniv.edu.kw
President: Abdullatif Ahmad Al-Bader
Tel: +965 484-7559

College

Architecture (Architecture; Interior Design; Visual Arts); **Arts** (Arabic; English; Geography; History; Mass Communication; Philosophy; Psychology); **Business Administration** (Accountancy; Administration; Business Administration; Economics; Finance; Information Management; Management; Marketing; Public Administration); **Computer Science and Engineering** (Computer Engineering; Computer Science; Information Sciences); **Education** (Curriculum; Education; Educational Administration; Educational and Student Counselling; Educational Psychology; Preschool Education; Primary Education; Secondary Education); **Engineering and Petroleum** (Chemical Engineering; Civil Engineering; Electrical Engineering; Industrial Engineering; Mechanical Engineering; Petroleum and Gas Engineering); **Graduate Studies**; **Science** (Biochemistry; Biological and Life Sciences; Chemistry; Computer Science; Earth Sciences; Environmental Studies; Geology; Mathematics; Physics; Zoology); **Shari'a and Islamic Studies** (Comparative Law; Islamic Law; Islamic Studies; Koran); **Social Sciences** (Geography; Information Sciences; Library Science; Political Sciences; Psychology; Social Sciences; Social Work; Sociology); **Women's** (Communication Studies; Environmental Management; Family Studies; Food Science; Information Sciences; Nutrition; Speech Studies; Speech Therapy and Audiology; Technology)

School
Law (Criminal Law; International Law; Law; Private Law; Public Law)

Centre
Arabic Regional Center for Environment Law; **Community Services and Continuing Education**; **Distance Learning**; **Gulf and Arabian Peninsula Studies**; **Health Sciences** (Dentistry; Health Administration; Medical Auxiliaries; Medical Technology; Medicine; Occupational Therapy; Pharmacology; Pharmacy; Physical Therapy; Radiology; Speech Therapy and Audiology)
Further information: A major public university with 14 colleges, 122 academic departments and numerous centres located in Khaldiya, Shuwaikh, Adeliya, Kheifan and Jabriya
History: Founded 1966. A State institution under the jurisdiction of the Ministry of Education.
Academic year: September to August (September-January; February-June; July-August)
Admission requirements: Secondary school certificate or equivalent and entrance examination
Main language(s) of instruction: Arabic, English
Degrees and diplomas: Bachelor's Degree (Engineering; Medicine; Pharmacy; Surgery), Higher Diploma, Master's Degree, PhD
Student Services: Academic Counselling, Social Counselling, Careers Guidance, Cultural Activities, Sports Facilities, Health Services, Canteen
Last Update: 25-07-2013

Private Institutions

American University of Kuwait

P.O. Box 3323
Safat 13034
Tel: +965 2224-8399
Website: http://www.auk.edu.kw/index.jsp
President: Earl L. Sullivan

College

Arts and Sciences (Behavioural Sciences; Communication Arts; Computer Engineering; Computer Science; Electrical Engineering; English; Graphic Design; International Relations; Media Studies); **Business and Economics** (Accountancy; Economics; Finance; Management; Marketing)
History: Founded 2003.
Main language(s) of instruction: English
Accrediting agency: Private Universities Council
Degrees and diplomas: Bachelor's Degree
Last Update: 20-04-2017

American University of the Middle East

P.O. Box 220
Dasman 15453
Tel: +965 2225-1400
Fax: +965 2654-8484
Website: http://www.aum.edu.kw
President: Imad Al-Ateeqi

College

Business Administration (Accountancy; Business Administration; Business Computing; Finance; Human Resources; Management; Marketing); **Engineering and Technology** (Computer Engineering; Electrical Engineering; Industrial Engineering; Information Technology; Telecommunications Engineering)
Accrediting agency: Private Universities Council
Degrees and diplomas: Bachelor's Degree, Master's Degree (Business Administration)
Last Update: 23-07-2013

Arab Open University (AOU)

Kuwait Al-Khaitan - Block 2 P.O. Box 32004
Al-Jabria
Tel: +965 247-67291
Fax: +965 247-67286
Website: http://www.aou.edu.kw
Branch Director: Naif Al Mutairi

Faculty

Business Studies (Business Administration; Business and Commerce); **Computer Studies** (Computer Science; Information Technology; Software Engineering); **Education** (Education); **Language Studies** (English)
Degrees and diplomas: Bachelor's Degree, Master's Degree
Last Update: 25-07-2013

Gulf University for Science and Technology

P.O. Box 7207
Hawally 32093
Tel: +965 2530-7000
Fax: +965 2530-7030
Website: http://www.gust.edu.kw
President: Shuaib A. Shuaib

College

Arts and Sciences (Advertising and Publicity; Anthropology; Arabic; Art History; Chinese; Computer Science; English; French; History; Islamic Studies; Journalism; Linguistics; Mathematics; Music; Natural Sciences; Philosophy; Political Sciences; Psychology; Public Relations; Secondary Education; Sociology; Spanish; Theatre; Translation and Interpretation); **Business Administration** (Accountancy; Business Administration; Business Computing; Economics; Finance; International Business; Marketing)
History: Founded 2000 by Private Universities Decree, No. 34, issued by the State of Kuwait.
Degrees and diplomas: Bachelor's Degree
Last Update: 25-07-2013

Kuwait-Maastricht Business School

Block 3, Kazima Street Next to Kuwait Teachers Society
Dasma
Tel: +965 2251-7091
Fax: +965 2254-5791
Website: http://www.kmbs.edu.kw/
Dean: Hernan E. Riquelme

Course/Programme

Business Administration (Business Administration)
History: Created 2003.
Accrediting agency: Private Universities Council
Degrees and diplomas: Master's Degree (Business Administration)
Last Update: 23-07-2013

Kyrgyzstan

STRUCTURE OF HIGHER EDUCATION SYSTEM

Description

Higher education is provided by universities, academies, institutes, and other institutions, most of them are state-run but there are also several private institutions, as well as several branches of overseas insitutitons. The Ministry of Education and Science is responsible for formulating and implementing the national education policy.

Stages of studies

University level first stage

Bakalavr, Specialist
The first stage of university studies leads to a Bachelor's degree after four years' study or to a Specialist degree after five years' study (6 in Medicine).

University level second stage

Magistr
The second stage leads to a Master's degree after two year's further study following upon a Bachelor's degree.

University level third stage

Aspirantura, Doctorontura
Aspirantura (Candidate of Science) is conferred after a further three years' study beyond the Master's degree or the Specialist degree and the Doctorontura (Doctor of Science) after three more years.

ADMISSION TO HIGHER EDUCATION

Admission to university-level studies

Name of Secondary school credential required: Attestat o Srednem Obščem Obrazovanii
Name of Secondary school credential required: Obščerespublikanskoye testirovaniye
Admission requirements: Yes

RECOGNITION OF STUDIES

Quality assurance system

The Ministry of Education and Science is responsible for implementing the State policy concerning the licensing and accreditation of higher education institutions.

NATIONAL BODIES

Ministry of Education and Science

Minister: Goulmira Koudayberdieva
257 Tynystanov Street
Biškek 720040
Tel: +996 (312) 66-24-42
Fax: +996 (312) 66-15-20
Website: http://edu.gov.kg
Role of national body: Responsible for education policy, its implementation, strategy, standards, training of teachers, and international cooperation.

Data for academic year: 2018–2019
Source: IAU from Ministry website, EACEA document "Higher Education in Kyrgyzstan, 2017", 2018

Public Institutions

Academy of Arts of the Kyrgyz Republic named after the Academic T. Sadykov

Ul. Tsiolkovsky 98
Biškek 720027
Tel: +996(312) 48-32-53
Fax: +996(312) 48-32-44
President: Turgunbay Sadykovich Sadykov

Department/Division
Arts and Humanities (Arts and Humanities); **Fine Arts** (Fine Arts)

© International Association of Universities 2019
International Handbook of Universities 2019,
https://doi.org/10.1057/978-3-319-76971-4_104

History: Founded 1991.
Main language(s) of instruction: Kirghiz, Russian
Degrees and diplomas: Bakalavr (Arts and Humanities)
Last Update: 24-09-2014

Academy of Management under the President of the Kyrgyz Republic (AUPKR)

ul. Panfilov 237
Biškek 720040
Tel: +996(312) 62-31-00, +996(312) 66-46-44
Fax: +996(312) 66-36-14
Website: http://www.amp.kg/
Rector: Chyngyz Bolotbekovich Shamshiev

College
Finance and Economics (*Toktonaliev Bishkek Financial and Economic College*) (Accountancy; Banking; Economics; Finance; Insurance; Management; Marketing; Taxation)

Course/Programme
Business and Management (*Master's programme*) (Business Administration; Economics; Finance; Management; Political Sciences)

Department/Division
International Relations and World Economy (Arts and Humanities; Civil Security; International Economics; International Relations; Modern Languages; Natural Sciences; Social Sciences)

Institute
Distance Education (Accountancy; Banking; Business Administration; Finance; International Economics; International Relations; Law; Marketing; Taxation); **Finance and Accountancy** (Accountancy; Banking; Economics; Finance; Taxation); **Public Administration** (Government; Natural Resources; Political Sciences; Public Administration; Water Management); **Public Administration, Law and Business** (Business Administration; Economics; Information Management; Information Technology; Law; Management; Marketing; Mathematics; Native Language; Physical Education; Public Administration; Russian)

Centre
Advanced Training and Retraining of Public and Municipal Servants (Government; Human Resources; Information Technology; Management; Public Administration)
History: Founded 1992 as Biškek International School of Management and Business. In 1997 the Academy of Management was founded to consolidate the International School.

Academic year: September to June
Admission requirements: Secondary school certificate
Fees: Master, 20,000 per annum; Bachelor and Specialist, 16,400 (Som)
Main language(s) of instruction: Russian, English
Accrediting agency: Ministry of Education, Science and Culture
Degrees and diplomas: Bakalavr (Business Administration; Management; Public Administration), Diplom Specialista (Accountancy; Finance), Magistr (Management). Also degree in Economics, 5 yrs full-time
Student Services: Academic Counselling, Sports Facilities, Language Laboratory, Canteen
Periodicals: Vestnik Academii
Last Update: 29-08-2014

Arabaev Kyrgyz State University (KSU)

ul. Razzakova 51
Biškek 720026
Tel: +966(312) 66-03-47
Fax: +966(312) 66-05-88
Website: http://arabaev.kg
Rector: T.A. Abdrahmanov

Faculty
Artistic Culture and Education (Design; Fashion Design; Fine Arts; Music; Music Education; Native Language; Pedagogy); **Chemistry and Biology** (Biology; Chemistry; Ecology; Geography; Natural Resources; Tourism); **Oriental Studies and International Relations** (East Asian Studies; History; Information Sciences; International Relations; Journalism; Linguistics; Oriental Languages; Oriental Studies; Philology; Translation and Interpretation)

Institute
Developing Qualification in Further Training (Arts and Humanities; History; Natural Sciences; Psychology; Social Sciences; Teacher Training); **Economics and Management** (*International*) (Accountancy; Banking; Business Administration; Economics; Finance; Management); **History, Social and Law Education** (History; Social Studies; Social Work); **Human Studies** (Philology; Political Sciences; Psychology; Public Administration; Sociology; Taxation; Theology); **Linguistics** (European Studies; Information Technology; Linguistics; Modern Languages; Philology); **Manas** (Asian Studies); **New Information Technology** (Applied Mathematics; Computer Science; Mathematics; Physics; Software Engineering); **Pedagogy** (Biomedical Engineering; Mathematics Education; Pedagogy; Primary Education; Special Education); **State Language and Culture** (Literature;

Modern Languages; Native Language); **World Languages** (Philology)

Further information: Also branch in Talas.

History: Founded 1945 as Women's Teacher Training College. Became Kyrgyz Women's Teacher Training Institute 1950, Kirghiz Women's Pedagogical Institute 1952, Kyrgyz State Pedagogical Institute 1992 and Kyrgyz State Pedagogical University 1994. Acquired present status and title 2005, named after Išenaly Arabaev.

Admission requirements: Secondary school certificate

Main language(s) of instruction: Kyrgyz, Russian

Accrediting agency: Ministry of Education and Science

Degrees and diplomas: Bakalavr, Magistr. Also postgraduate studies in Higher Education, 5 yrs

Student Services: Academic Counselling, Nursery Care, Cultural Activities, Sports Facilities, Language Laboratory, Health Services, Canteen, Foreign Studies Centre

Last Update: 01-09-2014

Bishkek Humanities University (BGU/BHU)

Prospect Mira 27
Biškek 720044
Tel: +996(312) 21-86-59
Fax: +996(312) 54-32-21
Website: http://www.bhu.kg
Rector: Musaev Abdylda Inayatovich
Tel: +996(312) 42-52-94

Faculty

Economics and Finance (Accountancy; Business Administration; Economics; Finance; Management; Taxation); **European Civilization** (Economics; English; German; Literature; Modern Languages; Translation and Interpretation); **Journalism and Information Technology** (Computer Science; Information Sciences; Library Science; Pedagogy; Psychology; Social Work); **Kyrgyz Chinese** (Chinese; Economics; Literature); **Kyrgyz Philology** (Journalism; Linguistics; Native Language; Philology; Russian; Translation and Interpretation); **Oriental Studies and International Relations** (African Studies; Arabic; Asian Studies; Chinese; International Relations; Korean; Oriental Languages; Oriental Studies; Persian; Philology; Turkish); **Slavic Studies** (Literature; Modern Languages; Native Language; Philology; Turkish); **Social Work and Psychology** (Psychology; Public Administration; Social Work)

Department/Division

Ecology and Management (Advertising and Publicity; Ecology; Foreign Languages Education; Information Management; Management; Tourism; Water Management); **Postgraduate Studies** (Arts and Humanities; Ecology;

Economics; History; Philology; Philosophy; Political Sciences; Psychology; Sociology)

Institute

Confucius (Chinese); **Continuing and Distance Learning** (Economics; Educational Sciences; Environmental Studies; International Economics; Journalism; Library Science; Modern Languages; Native Language; Philology; Political Sciences; Public Administration; Russian; Social Work; Sociology)

Centre

Academic Development; **Culture and Aesthetic Education**; **Information Technology and Telecommunications**; **Sociological and Marketing Research**

History: Founded in 1979 as Pedagogical Institute of Russian Language and Literature. Became State Institute of Languages and Humanities 1992. Acquired present title and status 1994. A State institution.

Admission requirements: Secondary school certificate (Attestat o srednem obrazovanii) and entrance examination

Fees: 800-1000 per annum (US Dollar)

Main language(s) of instruction: Kyrgyz, Russian, English, Chinese, Korean, Turkish, Arabic, Italian

Accrediting agency: Ministry of Education and Science

Degrees and diplomas: Bakalavr, Diplom Specialista (Accountancy; Economics; Finance; Journalism; Library Science; Management; Native Language; Political Sciences; Preschool Education; Primary Education; Psychology; Public Administration; Russian; Social Work; Sociology; Translation and Interpretation), Magistr (African Studies; Asian Studies; Business Administration; Ecology; Economics; Geography; International Relations; Journalism; Linguistics; Management; Pedagogy; Philology; Political Sciences; Psychology; Regional Studies; Social Work; Sociology; Translation and Interpretation), Aspirantura (Ecology; Economics; History; Philology; Philosophy; Political Sciences; Social Sciences)

Student Services: Language Laboratory, Foreign Studies Centre, Library, IT Centre

Last Update: 01-09-2014

I.K. Akhunbaev Kyrgyz State Medical Academy

Ul. Akhunbaev 92
Biškek 720020
Tel: +996(312) 54-58-81
Fax: +996(312) 54-58-59
Website: http://www.kgma.kg/
Rector: Ashirali Zurdinovich Zurdinov

Faculty

Foreign Citizens (*(In English)*) (Medicine); **Higher Nursing Education** (Nursing); **Medicine** (Biological and Life Sciences; Cardiology; Gynaecology and Obstetrics; Medicine; Oncology; Ophthalmology; Paediatrics; Surgery; Venereology); **Paediatrics** (Paediatrics); **Pharmacy** (Pharmacy); **Post-Diploma Medical Education** (Medicine); **Public Health** (Health Administration; Public Health); **Stomatology** (Dentistry; Stomatology)

Further information: Also Faculty of General Medicine for Foreign Citizens

History: Founded 1939. Previously known as Kyrgyz Mamlekettik Medikalyk Akademiyasy (Kyrgyz State Medical Academy).

Academic year: September to July

Admission requirements: Secondary school certificate

Fees: National : 17,000-30,500 per annum (including Kazakhstan, Russia, Belarus,Tajikistan) (Som), International : 78,100-110,200 per annum (Som)

Main language(s) of instruction: Russian, English, Kirghiz

Accrediting agency: Ministry of Health; Ministry of Education and Science

Degrees and diplomas: Bakalavr (Medicine; Paediatrics; Pharmacy; Public Health; Stomatology), Diplom Specialista (Nursing), Magistr (Medicine), Doctorontura (Medicine)

Student Services: Academic Counselling, Social Counselling, Careers Guidance, Nursery Care, Cultural Activities, Sports Facilities, Language Laboratory, Facilities for disabled people, Health Services, Canteen, Foreign Studies Centre, Library

Periodicals: Vestnik KSMA

Publishing house: KSMA Publishing Centre

Last Update: 01-09-2014

International University of Kyrgyzstan (IUK)

prosp. Čui 255
Biškek 720001
Tel: +996(312) 61-36-57
Fax: +996(312) 61-37-18
Website: http://www.iuk.kg
President: Asanaliev Tilek Asanalievich

Faculty

Social, Human and Natural Sciences (Arts and Humanities; Social Sciences)

College

General Education (Education); **Management, Business and Tourism** (Hotel and Restaurant; Hotel Management; Tourism); **Polytechnic** (Administration; Communication Studies; Computer Science; Economics; Engineering Management; Management)

School

Diplomacy and International Law (International Law; International Relations); **Ecology and Biotechnology** (Biotechnology; Ecology; Environmental Management; Environmental Studies); **Economics and Business** (Banking; Business and Commerce; Economics; International Economics; Management); **Magistracy** (Law); **Medicine (International)** (Medicine); **New Information Technologies** (Computer Networks; Computer Science; Information Management; Information Technology; Public Administration)

Institute

Distance Education (Kyrgyz-Indian Institute) (Business Administration; Finance; Information Technology; Management; Marketing; Tourism); **Distance Education (Kyrgyz-Russian Institute)** (Computer Science; Economics; Law; Management); **Foreign Languages** (English; French; Modern Languages; Native Language; Russian); **International Business** (Economics; International Business; Management); **Law, Business and Computer Technology (Djalal-Abad)** (Banking; Business and Commerce; Economics; Finance; Information Technology; International Economics; International Law; International Relations; Law; Management; Management Systems; Public Administration); **Law, Business and Computer Technology (Karakol)** (Banking; Business and Commerce; Finance; Information Technology; International Economics; International Law; International Relations; Law; Management; Management Systems; Public Administration); **Law, Business and Computer Technology (Osh)** (Accountancy; Banking; Economics; Finance; International Law; International Relations; Taxation); **Media** (Media Studies)

Centre
Foreign Students

Research Division

Economics and Science in Mountain Regions (Economics; Natural Sciences); **Ethnology** (Cultural Studies; Ethnology; Political Sciences; Psychology; Sociology; Turkish)

Further information: Also Branches at Osh, Karakol and Djalal-Abad

History: Founded 1993. Acquired present status 1995.

Academic year: September to June

Admission requirements: Secondary school certificate

Fees: 2,000 per annum (US Dollar)

Main language(s) of instruction: Russian

Accrediting agency: Ministry of Education and Science

Degrees and diplomas: Bakalavr (Ecology; Economics; Information Technology; International Relations; Law; Management; Medicine; Modern Languages; Political Sciences; Systems Analysis; Tourism), Magistr (Computer Science; Economics; International Business; Law; Political Sciences; Public Administration)

Student Services: Sports Facilities, Language Laboratory, Health Services, Foreign Studies Centre, Library

Last Update: 03-09-2014

Issyk-Kul State University named after K. Tynystanov

ul. Abdrahmanova 103
Karakol 722360, Issyk-Kul
Tel: +996(3922) 5-01-23
Fax: +996(3922) 5-04-98
Rector: Kurmanbek Kiyanovich Abdyldaev

Faculty

Art and Modelling (Design; Fine Arts; Painting and Drawing; Textile Design); **Chemistry and Biology** (Biology; Chemistry); **Foreign Languages** (Chinese; English; French; German; Modern Languages; Philology); **Mathematics and Computer Science** (Accountancy; Applied Mathematics; Automation and Control Engineering; Management; Mathematics and Computer Science); **Medicine and Technology** (Medicine; Technology); **Natural Resources and Geography** (Geography; Geography (Human); Natural Resources); **Pedagogy and Physical Education** (Education; Pedagogy; Physical Education; Preschool Education; Psychology); **Philology** (Literature; Native Language; Philology; Russian); **Physics and Technology** (Applied Physics; Engineering; Materials Engineering; Mathematics; Optics; Physical Engineering; Physics; Technology)

Institute

Economics, Management and Law (Accountancy; Economics; Engineering; Finance; Law; Management; Marketing; Mathematics; Physics; Public Administration); **Foreign Languages** (Modern Languages); **Tourism and Ecology** (Ecology; Forestry; Social Sciences; Tourism)

Centre

Distance Training (Education)

Further information: Also Branch in Cholpon-Ata

History: Founded 1940 as Teachers' Institute, reorganized 1953 as Prjevalsk Pedagogical Institute. Attached to Kyrgyz State University 1988. Became independent institution 1992 and acquired present status and title, named after Kasym Tynystanov, the creator of the Kyrgyz Philosophy of the Kyrgyz Republic.

Admission requirements: Secondary school certificate (Atestat o srednem obrazovanii)

Fees: National : 130 (US Dollar), International : 600 (US Dollar)

Main language(s) of instruction: Russian

Accrediting agency: Ministry of Education and Science

Degrees and diplomas: Diplom Specialista, Aspirantura, Doctorontura

Student Services: Social Counselling, Cultural Activities, Library

Last Update: 23-09-2014

Jalalabat State University (JASU)

Lenin Street 57
Jalal-Abad 715600
Tel: +996(3722) 20976
Fax: +996(3722) 50333
Website: http://jasu.edu.kg/
Rector: Abdrashev Akunjan Bakazovich

Faculty

Business and Pedagogy (Biology; Business and Commerce; Computer Science; Economics; English; Mathematics; Modern Languages; Native Language; Philosophy; Physical Education; Physics; Russian); **Medicine** (Medicine); **Technology (Jalal-Abad)** (Chemistry; Food Technology; Mechanical Equipment and Maintenance); **Technology (Kara-Kul)** (Electrical Engineering; Hydraulic Engineering; Machine Building; Mathematics; Physics; Social Sciences); **Technology (Tash-Kemur)** (Chemical Engineering; Civil Engineering; Electrical Engineering; Industrial Engineering; Mathematics; Physics; Social Sciences)

College

Electromechanics (Mayluu-Suu) (Electronic Engineering; Energy Engineering; Machine Building); **Electronic Technology (Kochkor-Ata)** (Microelectronics; Petroleum and Gas Engineering)

School

Zoological and Veterinary Technology (Forestry; Veterinary Science; Zoology)

Further information: Also Branches in Kara-Kul, Taš-Kumyr, Mailuu-Suu and Kočkor-Ata

History: Founded 1993 from former Jala-Abad Pedagogical School and Zoological-Veterinary Technical School.

Academic year: September to June/July

Admission requirements: Secondary school certificate

Main language(s) of instruction: Russian, Kyrgyz

Accrediting agency: Ministry of Education and Science
Degrees and diplomas: Bakalavr, Diplom Specialista, Magistr, Doctorontura (Medicine)
Student Services: Academic Counselling, Social Counselling, Careers Guidance, Nursery Care, Cultural Activities, Sports Facilities, Language Laboratory, Facilities for disabled people, Health Services, Canteen, Foreign Studies Centre
Periodicals: Vestnik
Last Update: 03-09-2014

Kyrgyz Economics University (KEU)

Ul. Togolok Moldo 58
Biškek 720033
Tel: +996(312) 32-51-19, +996(312) 32-53-89
Fax: +996(312) 32-55-09
Website: http://www.keu.edu.kg
Rector: Kamchybekov Tolobek Kadyralievich

Faculty
Accountancy and Finance (Accountancy; Finance); **Management and Tourism** (Economics; International Economics; Management; Tourism)

College
Economics and Service (Accountancy; Banking; Cooking and Catering; Economics; Finance; Hotel Management; Law; Taxation; Tourism)

Institute
Business and Service (Service Trades); **Life-long Open Learning** (Accountancy; Finance; Management; Service Trades)
History: Founded 1953 as College of Soviet trade. Became Bishkek Commercial College 1991, Supreme Commercial College 1997, Bishkek State Institute of Economics and Commerce 1999 and Bishkek State University of Economics and Commerce 2003. Acquired current title 2007.
Main language(s) of instruction: Kirghiz, Russian
Accrediting agency: Ministry of Education and Science
Degrees and diplomas: Bakalavr, Diplom Specialista (Economics; Management), Magistr (Economics; Management), Aspirantura
Last Update: 04-09-2014

Kyrgyz National Agrarian University named after K.I. Skriabin (KNAU)

Ul. Mederova 68
Biškek 720005
Tel: +996(312) 545-210
Fax: +996(312) 540-545

Website: http://www.knau.kg/index.php/ru/
Rector: Risbek Zaryldykovich Nurgaziev

Faculty
Agronomy and Forestry (Agronomy; Forestry); **Economics and Business** (Business and Commerce; Economics); **Engineering and Technology** (Engineering; Technology); **Natural Resources Management** (Natural Resources); **Technology of Production and Processing of Agricultural Products** (Agricultural Engineering); **Veterinary Medicine and Biotechnology** (Biotechnology; Veterinary Science)

Department/Division
Eurasian Innovative Technologies (Technology)

Research Division
Kyrgyz Livestock and Grassland (Animal Husbandry); **Kyrgyz Scientific Irrigation** (Irrigation); **Kyrgyz Veterinary Medicine named Arstanbek Duisheeva** (Veterinary Science)
Further information: Also distance education.
History: Founded 1933.
Fees: 800-900 per annum (including Books, Accomodation, Internship) (US Dollar)
Main language(s) of instruction: Kirghiz, Russian
Degrees and diplomas: Bakalavr, Diplom Specialista, Magistr (Agricultural Engineering; Agricultural Management; Agronomy; Animal Husbandry; Ecology; Forestry; Landscape Architecture)
Student Services: Library, eLibrary
Last Update: 24-09-2014

Kyrgyz National University named after Jusup Balasagyn (KSNU)

ul. Frunze 547
Biškek 720033
Tel: +996(312) 32-33-94
Fax: +996(312) 32-32-21
Website: http://www.university.kg/
Rector: Iskender Isamidinov

Faculty
Business Administration (Business Administration); **Chemistry and Technology** (Chemistry; Technology); **Information and Communication Technologies** (Communication Arts; Information Technology); **Journalism** (Journalism); **Kyrgyz Philology** (Philology); **Mathematics, Informatics and Cybernetics** (Applied Mathematics; Mathematics); **Public Management** (Public Administration); **Social Sciences and Humanities** (Arts and Humanities; Social Sciences)

Department/Division

Biology (Biology); **Foreign Languages** (Modern Languages); **Geography and Ecology** (Ecology; Geography); **History** (History); **Physics and Electronics** (Electronic Engineering; Physics); **Russian and Slavic Studies** (Central European Studies; Russian)

Institute

Business and Management; Economics and Finance; Integration of International Educational Programs; Kyrgyz-Chinese; Law; Target Teacher Training

Centre

"Ethno" Sociological Research; Continuing Education and Training; Health and Sport (Fizkultuty)

History: Founded 1932 as Kyrgyz State Pedagogical Institute. Became Kyrgyz State University 1951 and Kyrgyz State National University 1993. Acquired present title 2002.

Academic year: September to July

Admission requirements: Competitive entrance examination following general or special secondary school certificate

Fees: c.1,200 per annum (US Dollar)

Main language(s) of instruction: Kirghiz, Russian

Accrediting agency: Ministry of Education and Science

Degrees and diplomas: Diplom Specialista, Magistr (Applied Mathematics; Biology; Business Administration; Business and Commerce; Chemical Engineering; Chemistry; Chinese; Computer Engineering; Cultural Studies; E- Business/Commerce; Ecology; Economics; Geography; History; Information Technology; International Relations; Journalism; Law; Linguistics; Management; Mathematics; Pedagogy; Philology; Philosophy; Physics; Political Sciences; Psychology; Regional Studies; Russian; Sociology), Aspirantura, Doctorontura (Architecture; Biology; Cultural Studies; Earth Sciences; Economics; History; Law; Mathematics; Medicine; Philosophy; Physics; Political Sciences; Technology)

Student Services: Academic Counselling, Careers Guidance, Cultural Activities, Sports Facilities, Language Laboratory, Health Services, Canteen, Foreign Studies Centre

Last Update: 05-09-2014

Kyrgyz State Academy of Physical Education and Sports

Ul. Ahunbaeva 97
Biškek 720064
Tel: +996(312) 47-04-89
Fax: +996(312) 47-48-81
Rector: Toktobek Tybynovich Imanaliev

Department/Division

Military Science (*Pre-Military*) (Military Science); **Pedagogical Aspects of Physical Education** (Education; Pedagogy; Physical Education); **Pedagogy** (Education; Pedagogy); **Sport** (Education; Physical Education; Sports; Teacher Trainers Education)

History: Founded 1955.

Academic year: September to June

Admission requirements: Secondary school certificate

Main language(s) of instruction: Russian

Degrees and diplomas: Magistr (Sports)

Student Services: Social Counselling, Careers Guidance, Cultural Activities, Sports Facilities, Language Laboratory, Health Services, Canteen

Periodicals: Theory and Practice of Physical Culture

Last Update: 05-09-2014

Kyrgyz State Technical University named after I. Razzakov (KSTU)

prosp. Mira 66
Biškek 720044
Tel: +996(312) 54-51-25
Fax: +996(312) 54-51-62
Website: http://www.kstu.kg
Rector: Murataly Jamanbaev

Faculty

Ecology and Economics (Ecology; Economics); **Geology Prospecting** (Geology); **Information Technology** (Automation and Control Engineering; Electronic Engineering; Software Engineering; Telecommunications Engineering); **Mining and Metallurgy** (Metal Techniques; Mining Engineering); **Power Engineering** (Electrical Engineering; Engineering Management; Power Engineering; Safety Engineering; Thermal Engineering); **Technology** (*Kara-Balta*) (Food Technology; Textile Technology); **Transport and Machine Building** (Automotive Engineering; Machine Building; Road Transport; Robotics; Transport Management)

Institute

Distance Education and Qualification; Electronics and Telecommunications; Kara-Balta Technological; Kara-Kul Technological; Kyrgyr-German Technical; Kyrgyz Mineral Raw Materials; Kyrgyz-Russian Joint Educational Programs; Kyzyl-Kyi Nature Management and Geo-technology; Management and Business; Mining and Mining Techonolgies named after Usengazy Asanaliev; Tokmok Technical

Research Division

Chemical Technological; **Physical Technical**; **Power Engineering**

Further information: Also six-level intensive English programme at Higher College of English. Preliminary Training Centre and Lyceum.

History: Founded 1954 as Frunze Polytechnic Institute. Acquired present title 1995.

Academic year: September to July

Admission requirements: Secondary school certificate and entrance examination

Main language(s) of instruction: Kyrgyz, Russian, English

Accrediting agency: Ministry of Education and Science

Degrees and diplomas: Bakalavr, Diplom Specialista, Magistr (Animal Husbandry; Applied Mathematics; Automation and Control Engineering; Business and Commerce; Computer Engineering; Computer Science; Construction Engineering; Crop Production; Economics; Electrical Engineering; Environmental Studies; Heating and Refrigeration; Information Sciences; Machine Building; Materials Engineering; Measurement and Precision Engineering; Mechanical Engineering; Mechanical Equipment and Maintenance; Nutrition; Packaging Technology; Petroleum and Gas Engineering; Textile Technology; Transport Management; Water Science), Doctorontura (Ecology; Economics; Geology; Information Technology; Machine Building; Metallurgical Engineering; Mining Engineering; Power Engineering; Technology; Transport and Communications)

Student Services: Cultural Activities, Sports Facilities, Language Laboratory, Health Services, Canteen, Library

Periodicals: Polytechnic

Last Update: 23-09-2014

Kyrgyz State University of Construction, Transport and Architecture

ul. Maldybayeva 34
Biškek 720020
Tel: +996(312) 54-35-61
Fax: +996(312) 54-51-36
Website: http://www.ksucta.kg
Rector: Akymbek Abdykalykovich Abdykalykov

Faculty

Applied Computer Science (Computer Science); **Building and Engineering** (Construction Engineering); **Information Technology** (Information Technology); **Kyrgyz-German Informatics** (Computer Science; German); **Kyrgyz-Indian Computer Engineering** (Computer Engineering)

Department/Division

Education (Education); **Military** (Military Science)

Institute

Architecture and Design (Architecture; Design); **Construction, Economics and Management** (Construction Engineering; Economics; Management); **Ecology and Energy Saving** (Ecology); **Economics and Management** (Economics; Management); **Innovative Professions** (Design; Fire Science; Information Technology; Management); **New Information Technology** (Information Technology); **Transport and Communications** (Transport and Communications)

Centre

Distance Education

Further information: Also branches in Balykchy City and Talas City

History: Founded 1992. Formerly known as Kyrgyz Architectural-Construction Institute and Architectural and Construction Faculties of the Frunze Polytechnic Institute.

Main language(s) of instruction: Russian, Kirghiz

Degrees and diplomas: Magistr (Applied Mathematics; Architecture; Business Computing; Computer Engineering; Computer Science; Construction Engineering; Economics; Environmental Studies; Geography; Heritage Preservation; Information Management; Information Technology; Management; Mechanical Equipment and Maintenance; Surveying and Mapping; Telecommunications Engineering; Transport Engineering; Transport Management; Water Management), Doctorontura (Architecture; Art Criticism; Automotive Engineering; Building Technologies; Civil Engineering; Computer Science; Construction Engineering; Economics; Fine Arts; Handicrafts; Heating and Refrigeration; Hydraulic Engineering; Materials Engineering; Mechanical Engineering; Natural Resources; Railway Engineering; Road Transport; Town Planning; Water Management)

Student Services: Cultural Activities, Sports Facilities, Library, eLibrary

Last Update: 11-09-2014

Kyrgyz-Russian Slavic University named after the First President of Russian Federation B.N. Yeltsin (KRSU)

ul. Kievskaja 44
Biškek 720000
Tel: +996(312) 62-25-67
Fax: +996(312) 43-11-69
Website: http://www.krsu.edu.kg
Rector: Vladimir Ivanovich Nifadiev

Faculty

Architecture, Design and Construction (Architecture; Construction Engineering; Design); **Economics** (Economics);

Humanities (Arts and Humanities); **International Relations** (International Relations); **Law** (Law); **Medicine** (Medicine); **Natural and Technical Sciences** (Chemistry; Mathematics and Computer Science; Natural Sciences; Physics; Technology)

History: Founded 1992 by the Treaty of Friendship, Cooperation and Mutual Assistance between the Russian Federation and the Republic of Kyrgyzstan as the Kyrgyz-Russian Slavic University. Acquired present title 2004.

Main language(s) of instruction: Kyrgyz, Russian

Degrees and diplomas: Bakalavr (Advertising and Publicity; Applied Mathematics; Architectural and Environmental Design; Architecture; Automotive Engineering; Computer Science; Construction Engineering; Cultural Studies; Economics; Electrical Engineering; Electronic Engineering; Environmental Engineering; Environmental Studies; History; Information Technology; Instrument Making; International Relations; Journalism; Law; Linguistics; Management; Mechanical Engineering; Meteorology; Philology; Philosophy; Physics; Political Sciences; Psychology; Religious Studies; Software Engineering; Textile Design; Transport Management), Diplom Specialista (Criminology; Dentistry; International Relations; Medicine; Mining Engineering; Paediatrics; Translation and Interpretation), Magistr (Economics; Law; Management; Philology; Physics; Political Sciences; Software Engineering), Doctorontura

Student Services: Cultural Activities, Sports Facilities, Library

Publishing house: Editorial Review Board (ERB)

Last Update: 11-09-2014

Kyrgyz-Uzbek University (KUU)

ul. Aitiev 27
Oš 723500
Tel: +996(3222) 5-70-55
Fax: +996(3222) 2-54-73
Rector: Anvar Ismanjanov

Faculty

Computer and Telecommunications Technologies (Automation and Control Engineering; Data Processing; Electrical and Electronic Engineering; Software Engineering; Telecommunications Engineering); **Energy Engineering and Transport** (Civil Security; Electrical Engineering; Energy Engineering; Engineering Management; Environmental Engineering; Fire Science; Measurement and Precision Engineering; Natural Resources); **Finance and Economics** (Accountancy; Finance; Industrial and Production Economics; Industrial Management; Institutional Administration; International Economics; Taxation); **Garment Design and Service Trades** (Fashion Design; Hotel and Restaurant; Tourism); **History and Philology** (Foreign Languages Education; Humanities and Social Science Education; Journalism; Literature; Modern Languages; Native Language Education); **Law and Customs** (Law; Taxation); **Music and Pedagogy** (Educational Psychology; Music Education; Pedagogy; Preschool Education; Primary Education); **Natural Sciences and Geography** (Physical Education; Science Education); **Physics and Mathematics** (Computer Education; Mathematics Education; Science Education); **World Languages and International Relations** (Foreign Languages Education; International Relations)

College

Medical (Midwifery; Nursing; Pharmacy); **Technological** (Automation and Control Engineering; Clothing and Sewing; Data Processing; Fashion Design)

School

Postgraduate (Accountancy; Ecology; Economics; Educational Research; Energy Engineering; Finance; History; Linguistics; Literature; Management; Mathematics; Mechanical Engineering; Mining Engineering; Modern Languages; Native Language; Organic Chemistry; Philosophy; Statistics; Surveying and Mapping; Teacher Training); **Vocational** (*Kyrgyz-Uzbek*) (Clothing and Sewing; Cosmetology; Service Trades)

Department/Division

Kyrgyz-Russian (*Branch of Kyrgyz-Russian Social University*) (Computer Science; Finance; History; Law; Management; Power Engineering)

Institute

Humanities and Economics (*Kyzylkia*) (Electrical Engineering; Finance; Humanities and Social Science Education; Industrial and Production Economics; Industrial Management; Law; Literature; Mathematics Education; Modern Languages; Physical Education; Preschool Education; Primary Education; Science Education); **Humanities and Teacher Training** (*Alabuka*) (Finance; Foreign Languages Education; Humanities and Social Science Education; Literature; Mathematics Education; Native Language Education; Physical Education; Preschool Education; Primary Education; Science Education; Taxation)

History: Founded 1994. Acquired present status 1997.

Admission requirements: Secondary school certificate (Attestat o Srednem Obrazovanii)

Main language(s) of instruction: Russian, Kyrgyz

Accrediting agency: Ministry of Education and Science

Degrees and diplomas: Diplom Specialista, Aspirantura

Student Services: Cultural Activities, Sports Facilities, Language Laboratory, Health Services, Canteen, Foreign Studies Centre

Periodicals: Nauka, Obrazovanie, Tehnika, Planeta Drujby
Publishing house: Textbook Making Centre for Uzbek Schools
Last Update: 30-09-2014

Kyrgyzstan-Turkey Manas University (KTMU)

Tynchtyk Avenue 56
Biškek 720044
Tel: +996(312) 54-19-42
Fax: +996(312) 54-19-35
Website: http://manas.edu.kg/
President: Sebahattin Balci
Tel: +996(312) 54-19-40
Co-President: Asylbek Kulmyrzaev
Tel: +996(312) 54-20-04

Faculty

Agriculture (Agriculture; Agronomy; Horticulture; Plant and Crop Protection; Zoology); **Communications** (Advertising and Publicity; Cinema and Television; Journalism; Public Relations; Radio and Television Broadcasting); **Economics and Administrative Sciences** (Economics; Finance; International Relations; Management); **Engineering** (Chemical Engineering; Computer Engineering; Ecology; Environmental Engineering; Food Technology); **Fine Arts** (Graphic Arts; Painting and Drawing); **Letters** (Chinese; Educational Sciences; English; Eurasian and North Asian Languages; European Languages; European Studies; History; Literature; Philosophy; Russian; Slavic Languages; Sociology); **Science** (Biology; Mathematics; Natural Sciences); **Theology** (Theology); **Veterinary Medicine** (Veterinary Science)

School

Foreign Languages (Foreign Languages Education; Modern Languages; Translation and Interpretation); **Tourism and Hotel Management** (Cooking and Catering; Hotel and Restaurant; Hotel Management; Tourism); **Vocational Education** (*Community College*) (Administration; Economics; Technology)

Institute

Natural and Applied Sciences (Applied Chemistry; Applied Mathematics; Applied Physics; Chemical Engineering; Computer Engineering; Ecology; Environmental Engineering; Food Technology; Mathematics; Natural Sciences); **Social Sciences** (Communication Studies; Economics; Education; European Studies; Finance; History; Management; Social Sciences)

Conservatory

Music (Music; Performing Arts)

History: Founded 1995.
Academic year: September to June (September-December; April-June)
Admission requirements: Secondary school certificate and entrance examination
Fees: None
Main language(s) of instruction: Turkish, Kyrgyz
Accrediting agency: Kyrgyz Ministry of Education and Science, Turkish Ministry of Education, Higher Education Council of Turkey
Degrees and diplomas: Bakalavr (Communication Arts; Computer Engineering; Ecology; Economics; Finance; History; Management; Modern Languages; Oriental Studies; Turkish), Magistr (Communication Arts; Economics; Finance; History; Management; Oriental Studies; Turkish), Aspirantura (Economics; Finance; History; Management; Oriental Studies; Turkish)
Student Services: Academic Counselling, Careers Guidance, Cultural Activities, Sports Facilities, Language Laboratory, Health Services, Canteen, Foreign Studies Centre, Library
Periodicals: Science Bulletin, Social Science Bulletin
Last Update: 11-09-2014

Naryn State University (NSU)

ul. Sagynbay Orozbak Uulu 47
Naryn 722600
Tel: +996(3522) 5-08-14
Fax: +996(3522) 5-08-14
Website: http://www.nsu.ktnet.kg
Rector: Kaldybaev Salidin

Faculty

Agriculture and Technology (Agriculture; Crop Production; Environmental Management; Environmental Studies; Natural Resources; Technology); **Distance and Continuing Education** (Continuing Education; Distance Education); **Economics, Business and Management** (Computer Science; Economics; Information Technology; Mathematics; Political Sciences); **Pedagogy** (Pedagogy); **Philology** (English; Linguistics; Literature; Philology; Russian)

College

Agricultural Technical (Agriculture)

Centre

American Studies (American Studies); **Arabic Language and Culture** (Arabic; Cultural Studies); **Korean Studies** (Korean); **Turkish Center** (Turkish)
History: Founded 1996.
Admission requirements: Attestat o Srednem Obrazovanii

Fees: 7,500 per annum (Som)
Main language(s) of instruction: Kyrgyz, Russian
Accrediting agency: Ministry of Education and Science
Degrees and diplomas: Bakalavr, Diplom Specialista, Magistr (Agricultural Equipment; Business Administration; Economics; Management; Pedagogy; Philology)
Student Services: Academic Counselling, Social Counselling, Careers Guidance, Cultural Activities, Sports Facilities, Language Laboratory, Health Services, Canteen, Foreign Studies Centre, Library
Last Update: 12-09-2014

Osh State University (OshGu/OSU)

ul. Lenina 331
Oš 723500
Tel: +996(3222) 2-22-73
Fax: +996(3222) 5-75-58
Website: http://www.oshsu.kg/
Rector: Isakov Kanybek Abduvasitovich

Faculty

Business and Management (Business Administration; Business and Commerce; Economics; International Economics; Management; Mathematics; Social Studies); **Foreign Languages** (Chinese; English; French; German; History; Japanese; Korean; Persian; Translation and Interpretation); **History and Law** (Business Administration; Education; History; Law; Oriental Studies; Philosophy; Public Administration; Social Sciences; Social Work); **International Relations** (Cultural Studies; International Relations; International Studies); **Kyrgyz Philology** (Arts and Humanities; Education; Foreign Languages Education; Information Sciences; Journalism; Literacy Education; Modern Languages; Native Language; Philology); **Mathematics and Information Technology** (Applied Mathematics; Computer Science; Education; Information Sciences; Mathematics; Mathematics and Computer Science; Natural Sciences); **Medicine** (Anatomy; Health Sciences; Latin; Medicine); **Natural Sciences** (Agricultural Economics; Agriculture; Agronomy; Biology; Chemistry; Ecology; Education; Geography; Natural Sciences; Welfare and Protective Services; Zoology); **Pedagogical Sciences and Art** (Design; English; Fine Arts; Industrial Arts Education; Industrial Design; Music; Painting and Drawing; Performing Arts); **Pedagogy and Physical Training** (Education; Pedagogy; Physical Education; Preschool Education; Primary Education; Psychology; Social Sciences); **Physics and Technology** (Applied Physics; Computer Science; Education; English; History; Information Sciences; Mathematics; Physics); **Russian Philology** (Arts and Humanities; Education; Foreign Languages Education; Literacy Education; Philology; Russian); **Theology** (Education; Religion; Theology)

College

Fiscal Studies and Law (Education; History; Law; Oriental Studies; Philosophy; Social Sciences); **Medical** (Anatomy; Health Sciences; Latin; Medicine)

Institute

Arashan (*Biškek*) (Education; Religion; Theology)
Further information: Also Distance Education Centres and Regional Distance Education Centres
History: Founded 1951 as Oš State Pedagogical Institute. Acquired present status and title 1992.
Academic year: September to June (September-January; February-June)
Admission requirements: Secondary school certificate (Atestat o srednem obrazovanii) or foreign equivalent
Fees: National : 1,500-3,000 per annum; students of the CIS countries, 30,000-50,000 (Som), International : 1,350 per annum (US Dollar)
Main language(s) of instruction: Kyrgyz, Russian, English, German, French
Accrediting agency: Ministry of Education and Science
Degrees and diplomas: Diplom Specialista, Magistr (Dentistry; Medicine; Surgery), Aspirantura (Dentistry; Medicine; Surgery), Doctorontura (Dentistry; Medicine; Surgery)
Student Services: Academic Counselling, Social Counselling, Cultural Activities, Sports Facilities, Language Laboratory, Health Services, Canteen, Foreign Studies Centre, Library
Periodicals: Trudy OshGu (OSU Works)
Publishing house: Publishing Centre, Bilim
Last Update: 22-09-2014

Osh Technological University named after M.M. Adyshev (OshTU)

ul. Isanova 81
Oš 723503
Tel: +996(3222) 54087
Fax: +996(3222) 54462
Website: http://www.oshtu.kg
Rector: Abdykadyr Omarovich Abidov

Faculty

Civil Engineering (Civil Engineering); **Cybernetics and Information Technology** (Automation and Control Engineering; Information Technology); **Economics and Management** (Economics; Management); **Energy** (Electrical Engineering; Energy Engineering); **Informatics** (Applied

Mathematics; Computer Science); **Road Transport** (Road Transport); **Technology and Nature Maintenance** (Ecology; Food Technology; Geology)

College
Alai Humanities-Technology (Arts and Humanities; Technology); **Jalal-Abad Management and Technology** (Management; Technology); **Technology (OshTU)** (Technology)

Institute
Advanced Studies and Retraining (Vocational Education); **Language Training and International Centres** (Modern Languages); **Usgen Technology and Education** (Education)

Centre
Vocational Orientation and Pre-University Training
History: Founded 1996 on the basis of Osh Higher Technological College (formerly Faculty of Technical Sciences of the Frunze Polytechnic Institute, 1963).
Academic year: September to June
Admission requirements: Secondary school certificate (Attestat o srednem obrazovanii) and entrance examination
Main language(s) of instruction: Russian, Kyrgyz
Accrediting agency: Ministry of Education and Science
Degrees and diplomas: Bakalavr, Diplom Specialista. Also Diploma, 3 yrs
Student Services: Academic Counselling, Careers Guidance, Sports Facilities, Language Laboratory, Facilities for disabled people, Health Services, Canteen, Foreign Studies Centre
Last Update: 23-09-2014

Talas State University (TSU)

ul. Nurzhanova 25
Talas 724200
Tel: +996(3422) 52015, +996(3422) 53649
Fax: +996(3422) 52580
Website: http://www.tsu.kg/
Rector: Askarbek Isaevich Dzhylkichiev
Tel: +996(03422) 52015

Faculty
Humanities (English; History; Literature; Native Language; Russian); **Natural Sciences and Pedagogy** (Agriculture; Biology; Chemistry; Ecology; Science Education)

College
JMPR Thalgo (Secondary Education)

Institute
Technology (Design; Electrical Engineering; Radio and Television Broadcasting; Technology)

History: Founded 1996. Acquired present status 2000.
Academic year: September to June
Admission requirements: Secondary school certificate (Attestat o srednem obrazovanii)
Fees: National : 120-130 per annum (US Dollar), International : 250-300 per annum (US Dollar)
Main language(s) of instruction: Kyrgyz, Russian, English
Accrediting agency: Ministry of Education and Science
Degrees and diplomas: Bakalavr (Agriculture), Diplom Specialista (Accountancy; Applied Mathematics; Biology; Chemistry; Computer Engineering; Computer Science; Ecology; Economics; Electrical Engineering; Finance; Geography; History; Information Technology; Mathematics; Modern Languages; Native Language; Pedagogy; Physics; Private Administration; Public Administration; Russian; Transport Management)
Student Services: Academic Counselling, Social Counselling, Nursery Care, Cultural Activities, Sports Facilities, Language Laboratory, Facilities for disabled people, Canteen, Foreign Studies Centre, Library
Periodicals: Manas Urpagy
Last Update: 23-09-2014

Private Institutions

American University in Central Asia (AUCA)

205 Abdymomunov Street
Biškek 720040
Tel: +996(312) 66-11-19
Fax: +996(312) 66-32-01
Website: http://www.auca.kg
President: Andrew B. Wachtel
Tel: +996 (312) 661-094

Course/Programme
American Studies (American Studies); **Anthropology** (American Studies; Anthropology; Archaeology; Asian Studies; Cultural Studies; East Asian Studies; Environmental Studies; History; Middle Eastern Studies; Modern Languages; Pacific Area Studies; Religion); **Business Administration** (Accountancy; Advertising and Publicity; Banking; Business Administration; Business and Commerce; Economics; Finance; Human Resources; Information Technology; Insurance; International Business; Leadership; Management; Marketing; Public Administration; Real Estate; Taxation); **Economics** (Economic and Finance Policy; Economics; Finance; Geography (Human); International Economics; Management; Statistics); **European Studies** (Economics;

European Studies; European Union Law; French; Geography (Human); German; Government; History; Literature; Western European Studies); **International and Business Law** (Civil Law; Commercial Law; Constitutional Law; Criminal Law; Ethics; International Law; Labour Law; Private Law; Public Law); **International and Comparative Politics** (Comparative Politics; International Relations; Political Sciences); **Journalism and Mass Communications** (Advertising and Publicity; Cinema and Television; Journalism; Mass Communication; Media Studies; Public Relations; Radio and Television Broadcasting; Writing); **Languages** (English; Modern Languages; Native Language; Russian); **Psychology** (Anatomy; Industrial and Organizational Psychology; Pedagogy; Physiology; Psychoanalysis; Psychology; Social Psychology); **Sociology** (Applied Mathematics; Comparative Sociology; Gender Studies; Philosophy; Social Sciences; Sociology; Statistics); **Software Engineering** (Computer Graphics; Computer Networks; Mathematics and Computer Science; Software Engineering)

History: Founded 1997. In 1993, the Kyrgyz National State University Rector signed an order establishing the Kyrgyz-American Faculty (KAF) which was officially inaugurated and opened in December 1993. Acquired present name 1997.

Admission requirements: Secondary school leaving certificate

Fees: 2775 per semester (Undergraduates) (US Dollar)

Main language(s) of instruction: Russian, English

Accrediting agency: Ministry of Education and Science

Degrees and diplomas: Bakalavr, Magistr (Asian Studies; Business Administration; Economics; Environmental Studies). Also dual degrees (Bachelor of Arts) offered with Bard College, NY, USA.

Student Services: Academic Counselling, Careers Guidance, Cultural Activities, Sports Facilities, Language Laboratory, Health Services, Canteen, Library

Periodicals: Business Seminar Bulletin

Last Update: 29-08-2014

New Technologies (Computer Engineering; Electrical and Electronic Engineering; Industrial Engineering; Mathematics and Computer Science); **Social Sciences** (Chinese; English; Translation and Interpretation; Turkish)

College

Professional (Accountancy; Banking; Computer Science; Marketing)

School

Preparatory (Foreign Languages Education; Native Language Education)

History: Founded 1996 under agreement between Governments of Turkey and Kyrgyzstan. A private institution under the Ministry of Education of the Kyrgyz Republic

Academic year: September to June

Admission requirements: High School or Secondary school (11 yrs) certificate and fluency in English; SAT or ACT

Fees: National : 1,400-1,600 (US Dollar), International : 2,700 (US Dollar)

Main language(s) of instruction: English, Russian, Turkish, Kyrgyz

Accrediting agency: Ministry of Education and Science; International University Accrediting Association and Virtual University Accrediting Association; The South East Europe Education Cooperation Network, Education Network

Degrees and diplomas: Bakalavr, Diplom Specialista, Magistr (Accountancy; Business Administration; Computer Science; Engineering Management), Doctorontura. Also Certificates of English, Turkish and Computer Science

Student Services: Academic Counselling, Social Counselling, Careers Guidance, Sports Facilities, Health Services, Canteen, eLibrary

Periodicals: Alatoo Academic Studies, Eurasian Journal of Business and Economics

Last Update: 02-09-2014

International Atatürk Alatoo University (ALATOO)

Ankara Street 1/8, Tunguch
Biškek 720048
Tel: +996(312) 63-14-25
Fax: +996(312) 63-04-09
Website: http://www.iaau.edu.kg
Rector: Osman Gökalp

Faculty

Economics and Administration (Banking; Finance; International Economics; International Relations; Management);

Lao People's Democratic Republic

STRUCTURE OF HIGHER EDUCATION SYSTEM

Description

Higher education is provided by universities, technical and professional institutes, and teacher training colleges. Higher education institutions are managed by the government. They fall under the responsibility of the Ministry of Education and Sports or, in the case of the University of Health Sciences, the Ministry of Health.

Stages of studies

University level first stage

Bachelor's degree
Universities offer a 4-year course leading to a Bachelor's degree.

University level second stage

Master's degree
Universities offer a 2-year course leading to a Master's degree.

University level third stage

Doctorate
The Doctorate is not widely offered in Lao except in collaboration with foreign universities in very specific disciplines.

ADMISSION TO HIGHER EDUCATION

Admission to university-level studies

Name of Secondary school credential required: Upper Secondary School Diploma
For entry to: University
Minimum score/requirement: 5/10 for each subject
Alternatives to credentials: Selection by quota, each region being entitled to a certain number of students being offered access to higher education; or fee-paying entry

Admission requirements: National entrance examination.
Numerus clausus: Yes

Foreign students admission

Definition of foreign student: Students who do not have the Lao nationality.
Quotas: There are quotas at the national level.
Admission requirements: Students must hold a High School certificate or equivalent.
Entry regulations: Entry is subject to bilateral agreements
Health requirements: Medical certificate.
Language Proficiency: French or English and Laotian

RECOGNITION OF STUDIES

Quality assurance system

All programmes offered at universities are officially recognized and accredited by the Ministry of Education. Credit transfers are subject to direct agreement between institutions.

Special provisions for recognition

For the exercise of a profession
Under MOU between institutions and the industrial sector.

NATIONAL BODIES

Ministry of Education and Sports

Minister: Lachanthaboun Sengduan
PO Box 67 Lanexang Vientiane Avenue
Vientiane
Fax: +856(21) 216 006
Website: http://moes.edu.la

Data for academic year: 2014–2015
Source: IAU from French Ministry of Foreign Affairs, Base Curie, Fiche Laos 2012, 2014. Bodies 2017.

Public Institutions

Bankeun Teacher Training College

Road n° 10, Ban Keunua
Thoulakhom District, Vientiane
Tel: +856(23) 271-032
Fax: +856(20) 552-3409
Website: http://www.bankeun-ttc.edu.la
Director: Chanthamala Southammavong

College
Teacher Training (English; Mathematics Education; Preschool Education; Primary Education; Science Education; Social Sciences; Teacher Training)
History: Founded 1968.
Main language(s) of instruction: Lao
Accrediting agency: Ministry of Education and Sports
Degrees and diplomas: Bachelor's Degree (English; Mathematics Education; Preschool Education; Primary Education; Science Education; Social Sciences)

Banking Institute of Laos

Baan Tam Chai, Xaythany District
Vientiane Capital
Tel: +856(21) 770916
Fax: +856(21) 770967
Website: http://www.bibol.edu.la

Course/Programme
Banking (Finance); **Finance** (Banking)
History: Founded 1979.
Accrediting agency: Ministry of Education and Sports
Degrees and diplomas: Bachelor's Degree (Finance)
Last Update: 03-07-2018

Champasack University

P.O. Box 81 Ban Chat Sanh, Pakse distrikt
Champasack
Tel: +856(31) 260158
Fax: +856(31) 260158
Website: http://www.cu.edu.la
President: Bounmy Hponesavanh

Faculty
Agriculture (Agriculture); **Economics and Management** (Business Administration; Economics); **Education** (Education); **Engineering** (Engineering); **Law and Political Sciences** (Law; Political Sciences); **Natural Sciences** (Natural Sciences)
History: Founded 2002.
Accrediting agency: Ministry of Education and Sports
Degrees and diplomas: Bachelor's Degree (Economics; Engineering; Law; Mathematics; Natural Sciences)

Luang Namtha Teacher Training College

Ban Xaysavang
Luangnamtha
Tel: +856(86) 312201
Website: http://luangnamtha-ttc.edu.la

Course/Programme
Teacher Training (Teacher Training)
History: Founded 1968.
Main language(s) of instruction: Lao
Accrediting agency: Ministry of Education and Sports
Degrees and diplomas: Bachelor's Degree (Teacher Training)
Last Update: 24-08-2018

National University of Laos (NUOL)

PO Box 7322
Vientiane
Tel: +856(21) 770-070
Fax: +856(21) 770-070
Website: http://www.nuol.edu.la
President (Acting): Somsy Gnophanxay

Faculty
Agriculture (*Nabong Campus*) (Agriculture; Agronomy; Animal Husbandry); **Architecture** (Architecture); **Economics and Business Administration** (*Dongdok Campus*) (Business Administration; Economics; Management); **Education** (*Dongdok Campus*) (Curriculum; Education; Pedagogy; Psychology); **Engineering** (*Sokpaluang Campus*) (Civil Engineering; Communication Studies; Electrical Engineering; Electronic Engineering; Engineering; Irrigation; Mechanical Engineering); **Environment and Development Studies** (Development Studies; Environmental Engineering); **Forestry** (Forestry); **Letters** (Arts and Humanities; English; French; German; Literature); **Medical Science** (*Phiavat Campus*) (Dentistry; Health Sciences;

Medicine; Pharmacy); **Sciences** (*Dongkok Campus*) (Biology; Chemistry; Mathematics; Natural Sciences; Physics; Science Education); **Social Sciences** (*Dongdok Campus*) (Administration; Development Studies; Geography; History; Hotel Management; Political Sciences; Social Welfare; Tourism); **Sports** (Sports); **Water Resources** (Water Science)

Institute
Confucius (Chinese); **Human Resources Development Laos-Japan**

History: Founded 1995, incorporating ten existing Institutions and a Centre of Agriculture. Has six campuses: Dongdok Main Campus, Sokpaluang Campus, Phiavat Campus, Donenokkhoum Campus, Tatthong Campus, and Kilometre Five Campus.

Academic year: September to June (September-January; February-June)

Admission requirements: Upper secondary school Certificate or equivalent and entrance examination (for non-quota system)

Main language(s) of instruction: Lao

Accrediting agency: Ministry of Education and Sports

Degrees and diplomas: Bachelor's Degree, Master's Degree

Last Update: 30-06-2014

Savannakhet Teacher Training College

P.O. Box 809 Km 9 Street, Odom Vilai Village
Kaysarn Phromavanh, Savannakhet
Tel: +856(41) 212-180
Fax: +856(20) 213-667
Website: http://savannakhet-ttc.edu.la
Director: Somsak Chaisai

Course/Programme
Teacher Training (English; Mathematics; Natural Sciences; Social Sciences; Teacher Training)

History: Founded 1966.

Main language(s) of instruction: Lao

Accrediting agency: Ministry of Education and Sports

Degrees and diplomas: Bachelor's Degree (Biology; Chemistry; English; Mathematics; Political Sciences; Social Sciences), Master's Degree (Social Sciences)

Savannakhet University (SKU)

P.O. Box: 14 Naxeng Campus Naxeng Village
Kaisonephomvihane, Savannakhet
Tel: +856(41) 253286
Website: http://skulao.org
Rector: Bounpong Keorodom

Faculty
Agriculture and Environment (Agriculture; Animal Husbandry; Environmental Studies; Forestry); **Business Administration** (Banking; Business Administration; Business and Commerce; Finance; Hotel Management; Tourism; Transport Management); **Education** (Education); **Food Science** (Agricultural Business; Food Science; Food Technology); **Linguistics** (English; French; Linguistics); **Natural Sciences** (Mathematics; Natural Sciences)

Centre
Information Technology (Information Technology)

History: Founded 2009.

Main language(s) of instruction: Lao

Accrediting agency: Ministry of Education and Sports

Degrees and diplomas: Bachelor's Degree (Banking; Biology; Business and Commerce; Chemistry; Education; English; Food Science; Food Technology; French; Information Technology; Mass Communication; Mathematics; Tourism; Transport Management)

Student Services: Sports Facilities, Library

Last Update: 27-06-2018

Souphanouvong University

Ban Nasangveuy
Luang Prabang
Tel: +856(20) 99-741-040
Website: https://www.su.edu.la
President: Khamphay Sisavanh

Faculty
Agriculture (Agronomy; Animal Husbandry); **Architecture** (Architecture; Interior Design); **Economics** (Economics; International Business; Management; Tourism); **Education** (Education; English; Mathematics); **Engineering** (Civil Engineering; Computer Engineering; Electrical Engineering); **Letters** (English; Native Language)

History: Founded 2003.

Academic year: October to July

Admission requirements: Pakasaniyabath Chob Matthayom Somboun (Certificate of Completion of Complete Secondary Education)

Main language(s) of instruction: Lao

Accrediting agency: Ministry of Education and Sports

Degrees and diplomas: Bachelor's Degree

Last Update: 02-07-2014

University of Health Sciences

P.O. Box 7444 Thung Tam Road, Phom Wat Temple, Sisattanak District
Ventiane Capital 7322
Tel: +856(21) 222-883
Fax: +856(21) 214-055
Website: http://www.uhs.edu.la
Rector: Phouthone Vangkhonevilay

Faculty

Basic Sciences (Biology; Chemistry; Physics); **Dentistry** (Dentistry); **Medical Technology** (Medical Technology); **Medicine** (Medicine); **Nursing** (Nursing); **Pharmacy** (Pharmacy)
History: Founded 2007.
Main language(s) of instruction: Lao
Accrediting agency: Ministry of Education and Sports
Degrees and diplomas: Bachelor's Degree (Health Sciences), Master's Degree (Health Sciences)
Last Update: 03-07-2014

Private Institutions

Combiz College

Paksanh District, Bolykhamxay
Tel: +856(54) 212-895, +856(20) 233-7314

Course/Programme

Agriculture (Agriculture); **Business and Administration** (Administration; Business and Commerce); **Engineering** (Engineering)
Degrees and diplomas: Bachelor's Degree

Comcenter College

P.O. Box 2224 Khouvieng Boulevard, Nongchanh village, Sisattanak district
Vientiane
Tel: +856(21) 216-532
Fax: +856(21) 222-433
Website: http://www.comcenterblog.com
Director: Xaynhonh Khammavong

Course/Programme

Business Administration (Accountancy; Business Administration; Law; Management; Marketing)
History: Founded 1993.
Main language(s) of instruction: Lao

Degrees and diplomas: Bachelor's Degree (Business Administration), Master's Degree (Business Administration)
Last Update: 02-07-2014

Lao-American College (LAC)

P.O. Box 327 Phonekheng Road
Vientiane Capital
Tel: +856(21) 900-454
Fax: +856(21) 900-453
Website: http://www.lac.edu.la
Founder: Virginia Ostrand

Course/Programme

Business Administration (Business Administration); **English Studies** (English; English Studies)
History: Founed 2002
Main language(s) of instruction: English
Accrediting agency: Ministry of Education and Sports
Degrees and diplomas: Bachelor's Degree (Business Administration; English; English Studies)
Last Update: 14-04-2014

Rattana Business Administration College

P.O. Box 977 Saphanthong Neur Village, Sisattanak District
Vientiane Capital
Tel: +856(21) 413-871
Fax: +856(21) 413-820
Website: http://www.rbac.info

Course/Programme

Business Administration (Business Administration)
Further information: Also Campuses in Naxaythong District, Oudomxay and Xainyabouli Provinces
History: Created in 1974 as Rattana Commercial School. Acquired current title 1994, and accredited in 2002.
Main language(s) of instruction: Lao
Accrediting agency: Ministry of Education and Sports
Degrees and diplomas: Bachelor's Degree (Business Administration), Master's Degree (Business Administration)
Last Update: 14-04-2014

Savan Institute of Management (SIM)

Saiyamungkhun Village, Latsavongseuk Road
Khanthaboury District, Savannakhet Province
Tel: +856(20) 5554-1823
Fax: +856(41) 253252
Director: Viraphanh Latsaphon

Course/Programme
Marketing and Management (Advertising and Publicity; Business Administration; Business Computing; Economic History; English; Finance; Human Resources; Labour Law; Leadership; Management; Marketing; Mathematical Physics; Small Business; Statistics)
History: Founded 2003.
Main language(s) of instruction: Lao
Degrees and diplomas: Bachelor's Degree
Last Update: 04-07-2014

Sengsavanh College

P.O. Box 7463 124 Dongmieng Rd Sisavath Village, Chanthabuli District
Vientiane
Tel: +856(21) 223-822
Chairman: Kamsen Sisavong

College
Business Administration (Accountancy; Business Administration)
History: Founded 1998.
Degrees and diplomas: Bachelor's Degree (Business Administration; E- Business/Commerce; Software Engineering)
Last Update: 14-04-2014

Soutsaka College of Management and Technology

P.O. Box 390 Phonetong Road, Phonepanoa, Xaythany District
Vientiane Capital
Tel: +856(21) 900-337
Fax: +856(21) 900-338
Website: http://www.scmt.edu.la
Director: Sousaka Boumanith

Faculty
Business and Economics (Accountancy; Business Administration); **Communication Art and Language Studies** (Chinese; English; Native Language); **Information Technology** (Computer Science; Information Technology); **Sciences** (Environmental Studies; Mathematics; Philosophy; Political Sciences; Psychology; Social Sciences)
History: Founded 2002. Acquired present title 2008.
Main language(s) of instruction: English
Accrediting agency: Ministry of Education and Sports
Degrees and diplomas: Bachelor's Degree (Business Administration; Computer Science; English; Information Technology)
Last Update: 04-07-2014

Latvia

STRUCTURE OF HIGHER EDUCATION SYSTEM

Description

The system of higher education in Latvia is binary since the Law on Education Establishments sets a difference between academic and professional higher education but it is not strictly institutionalised. Universities and other institutions of higher education mostly run both academic and professional programmes. There can be distinguished three groups of programmes: academic programmes leading to academic degrees, professional programmes based upon a standard of the first academic degree thus making graduates eligible for further academic studies and the applied professional programmes oriented towards higher professional qualifications but not providing background for direct admission to further academic studies.

Stages of studies

University level first stage

Bakalaurs
The first cycle leads to the award of a Bakalaurs (Bachelor' degree), which in most cases includes the preparation of a thesis. The duration of studies varies from three to four years. Holders are eligible for further studies towards a Magistrs degree or higher professional education qualifications.

University level second stage

Maģistrs
The second cycle leads to the award of the Magistrs (Master's degree), a terminal higher education qualification awarded one to two years after the Bakalaurs. This degree also includes the presentation of a thesis. In Medicine and Dentistry, studies are not divided into two stages but the degrees Ārsta grāds (degree in Medicine) - six years - and Zobārsta grāds (degree in Dentistry) - five years - are considered equivalent to the Maģistrs.

University level third stage

Doktors
Doctor's degrees are awarded three to four years after completion of the Master degree and following the public defense of a thesis.

ADMISSION TO HIGHER EDUCATION

Admission to university-level studies

Name of Secondary school credential required: Atestāts par vispārējo vidējo izglītību
Name of Secondary school credential required: Diploms par profesionālo vidējo izglītību
Numerus clausus: At the level of the institution

Foreign students admission

Definition of foreign student: A student who is resident of another country and pursues studies in Latvia.
Quotas: No
Admission requirements: Foreign students must present a School-Leaving Certificate (original) with a transcript which can be recognized as being equivalent to the Latvian secondary education certificate.
Entry regulations: Students must hold a residence permit. Latvian diplomatic missions abroad provide all the necessary information to the applicants, make an initial recommendation and issue entry visas to candidates who have been accepted.
Health requirements: A health certificate is required.
Language Proficiency: Students must prove proficiency in Latvian for programmes offered in Latvian.

© International Association of Universities 2019
International Handbook of Universities 2019,
https://doi.org/10.1057/978-3-319-76971-4_106

RECOGNITION OF STUDIES

Quality assurance system

The Ministry of Education and Science is the education policy-making institution that issues the licenses for opening comprehensive education institutions and sets educational standards along with the teacher training content and procedures.

Bodies dealing with recognition

Akadēmiskās informācijas centrs - Latvijas ENIC/ NARIC (Academic Information Centre - Latvian ENIC-NARIC)
Director: Baiba Ramina
Dzirnavu Street 16, 3rd floor
Riga 1050
Tel: +371 6722 5155
Fax: +371 6722 1006
Website: http://www.aic.lv

Special provisions for recognition

Recognition for University level studies
AIC evaluates a credential and issues a statement which serves as a recommendation for universities and other higher education institutions which take the final decision upon recognition for further studies.

For access to advanced studies and research
AIC evaluates a credential and issues a statement which serves as a recommendation for universities and other higher education institutions which take the final decision upon recognition for further studies.

For the exercise of a profession
AIC evaluates a credential and issues a statement which serves as a recommendation for employers (in non-regulated professions) or competent professional bodies (in regulated professions) which take the final decision upon recognition for professional purposes.

NATIONAL BODIES

Izglītības un Zinātnes Ministrija (Ministry of Education and Science)

Minister: Karlis Sadurskis
Vaļņu iela 2
Riga 1050
Tel: +371 6722 6209
Fax: +371 6722 3905
Website: http://www.izm.gov.lv
Role of national body: The Ministry of Education and Science is responsible for education, science, sports, youth and state language policies in Latvia.

Valsts izglītības attīstības aģentūra - VIAA (State Education Development Agency)

Director: Dita Traidās
Vaļņu iela 1
Riga 1050
Tel: +371 6781 4322
Fax: +371 6781 4344
Website: http://www.viaa.gov.lv
Role of national body: The aim of the activities of VIAA is to implement the national policy in the field of higher education and science, lifelong learning system, vocational education system and general education system, and to implement and monitor projects financed by the European Union (EU) Structural Funds, EU programmes, and other financial instruments, programmes, projects and initiatives.

Augstākās Izglītības Padome - AIP (Council of Higher Education)

Chairman: Janis Vetra
Zigfrīda Annas Meierovica bulv. 12
Riga 1050
Tel: +371 6722 3392
Fax: +371 6722 0423
Website: http://www.aip.lv
Role of national body: Independent institution which develops the national strategy for the development of higher education and higher education institutions in both quality and quantity.

Latvijas Rektoru Padome (Latvian Rectors' Council)

Raina bulv. 19
Riga 1586
Tel: +371 6703 4338
Fax: +371 6703 4368
Website: http://www.aic.lv/rp

Data for academic year: 2015–2016
Source: IAU from the Latvian ENIC/NARIC, 2011, updates from the website of the Ministry of Education and Science and www.studyinlatvia.lv, 2015. Bodies, 2017.

Public Institutions

Art Academy of Latvia (LMA)

Kalpaka bulvāris 13
Rīga LV-1867
Tel: +371(67) 332-202
Fax: +371(67) 228-963
Website: http://www.lma.lv
Rector: Aleksejs Naumovs
Tel: +371(67) 326-068

Faculty

Audio-visual Media (Communication Arts; Display and Stage Design); **Design** (Architectural and Environmental Design; Design); **History and Theory of Art** (Art History; Arts and Humanities; Restoration of Works of Art); **Visual Arts (2D)** (Graphic Design; Painting and Drawing; Textile Design; Visual Arts); **Visual Plastic Arts (3D)** (Ceramic Art; Fashion Design; Glass Art; Sculpture; Visual Arts)
History: Founded 1921.
Academic year: October to May (October-January; February-May)
Admission requirements: Secondary school certificate
Main language(s) of instruction: Latvian. Practical courses in Russian, English
Degrees and diplomas: Bakalaurs, Maģistrs, Doktora
Last Update: 15-04-2015

BA School of Business and Finance (BA)

K.Valdemāra 161
Rīga LV-1013
Tel: +371(67) 360-133
Fax: +371(67) 320-620
Website: http://www.ba.lv
Rector: Andris Sarnovičs

Department/Division

Entrepreneurship and IT (Business Administration; Information Technology; Insurance; International Business; Management); **Finance** (Accountancy; Banking; Finance); **Foreign Languages** (English; German; Grammar; Modern Languages); **Information Sciences** (Information Sciences); **International Studies** (International Studies)
History: Founded 1992, acquired present title 1997.
Academic year: September to June
Admission requirements: Secondary school certificate
Fees: (Lats): 685 per annum
Main language(s) of instruction: Latvian, English

Degrees and diplomas: Diploms par pirmā līmena augstāko profesionālo izglītību, Bakalaurs, Maģistrs, Doktora (Business Administration)
Student Services: Careers Guidance, Sports Facilities, Canteen
Last Update: 16-12-2015

Daugavpils University (DU)

Vienības iela 13
Daugavpils LV-5400
Tel: +371(654) 221-80, +371(654) 229-22
Fax: +371(654) 228-90
Website: http://www.du.lv
Rector: Arvīds Barševkis

Faculty

Education and Management (Education; Educational Psychology; Management; Pedagogy; Physical Education; Pre-school Education; Primary Education; Social Work; Vocational Counselling; Vocational Education); **Humanities** (Arts and Humanities; Baltic Languages; Cultural Studies; English; Foreign Languages Education; French; German; History; Humanities and Social Science Education; Linguistics; Literature; Philology; Polish; Russian; Secondary Education; Slavic Languages; Social Sciences; Spanish; Swedish; Translation and Interpretation); **Music and Arts** (Art Education; Art History; Art Management; Computer Graphics; Conducting; Design; Fine Arts; Graphic Arts; Music; Music Education; Musical Instruments; Secondary Education; Visual Arts); **Natural Sciences and Mathematics** (Anatomy; Chemistry; Computer Education; Computer Science; Environmental Studies; Geography; Information Technology; Mathematics; Mathematics Education; Natural Sciences; Physical Therapy; Physics; Physiology; Science Education; Secondary Education; Solid State Physics; Teacher Training); **Social Sciences** (Economics; Law; Psychology; Social Psychology; Social Sciences; Sociology)

Institute

Comparative Studies (Arts and Humanities; Cultural Studies); **Ecology** (Ecology; Environmental Studies; Forest Biology); **Latgale Region Research** (Regional Studies); **Social Investigation** (Social Studies); **Sustainable Education** (Education); **Systematic Biology** (Biology)

Centre

Innovative Microscopy (*G. Liberts'*) (Physics); **Oral History** (History; Regional Studies)
Further information: Also Centre for teaching Russian as a foreign language

History: Founded 1921 as Teachers' Institute, acquired present status and title 2001.

Academic year: September to June (September-January; February-June)

Admission requirements: Secondary school certificate, test in Latvian language, examination in a foreign language for students of foreign languages

Fees: 1450 (Euro)

Main language(s) of instruction: Latvian

Degrees and diplomas: Diploms par pirmā līmena augstāko profesionālo izglītību, Bakalaurs, Maģistrs, Doktora (Biology; Economics; History; Law; Linguistics; Literature; Management; Mathematics; Pedagogy; Psychology; Solid State Physics). Also 2nd level professional higher education programmes; Professional Master's degree.

Student Services: Cultural Activities, Sports Facilities, Health Services, Canteen, Library

Last Update: 14-04-2015

Jāzeps Vītols Latvian Academy of Music (JVLMA)

Kr. Barona 1
Rīga LV-1050
Tel: +371(67) 228-684
Fax: +371(67) 820-271
Website: http://www.jvlma.lv
Rector: Artis Sīmanis

Department/Division

Accompanists (Music; Musical Instruments); **Chamber Ensemble and Piano Accompaniment** (Music; Musical Instruments); **Choir Conducting** (Conducting); **Choreography** (Dance); **Composition** (Music Theory and Composition); **Compulsory Piano** (Musical Instruments); **Early Music** (Music); **Humanities** (Arts and Humanities; English; Modern Languages); **Jazz Music** (Jazz and Popular Music); **Music Education** (Music Education); **Music Technology** (Music; Technology); **Musicology** (Musicology); **Orchestra Conducting** (Conducting); **Piano** (Musical Instruments); **Science and Research** (Musicology); **Strings** (Musical Instruments); **Vocal Music** (Singing); **Wind Instruments** (Musical Instruments)

History: Founded 1919 as Conservatoire, acquired present status and title 1991.

Main language(s) of instruction: Latvian

Degrees and diplomas: Bakalaurs, Maģistrs (Dance; Music), Doktora (Musicology)

Last Update: 14-04-2015

Latvia University of Agriculture (LLU)

Liela ielā 2
Jelgava LV-3001
Tel: +371(630) 225-84
Fax: +371(630) 272-38
Website: http://www.llu.lv
Rector: Irina Pilvere

Faculty

Agriculture (Agricultural Business; Agricultural Management; Agriculture; Agronomy; Animal Husbandry; Crop Production; Horticulture; Plant and Crop Protection; Soil Management; Soil Science); **Economics** (Accountancy; Business Administration; Economics; Finance; Management; Marketing); **Engineering** (Agricultural Engineering; Art Education; Educational Technology; Engineering; Machine Building; Pedagogy; Technology; Vocational Counselling; Vocational Education); **Food Technology** (Cooking and Catering; Food Science; Food Technology; Hotel and Restaurant; Hotel Management; Nutrition); **Forestry** (Agricultural Engineering; Ecology; Forest Biology; Forest Economics; Forest Products; Forestry; Safety Engineering; Wood Technology); **Information Technology** (Automation and Control Engineering; Computer Science; Information Technology; Software Engineering); **Rural Engineering** (Architecture and Planning; Civil Engineering; Environmental Engineering; Environmental Studies; Landscape Architecture; Regional Planning; Surveying and Mapping; Water Management); **Social Sciences** (Management; Public Administration; Public Relations; Social Sciences; Sociology); **Veterinary Medicine** (Food Science; Hygiene; Veterinary Science)

Further information: Also Veterinary Hospital; Branches in Laidze, Kandava, Limbazi, Smiltene and Sigulda; Training and research centers in Vecauce, Ozolnieki, Engure, Vaive and Peterlauki; Scientific institutes in Jelgava, Ulbroka, Sigulda and Skriveri.

History: Founded 1863 as Department of Riga Polytechnical Institute, became the Faculty of Agriculture and Forestry at the Latvia University 1919, Jelgava Agricultural Academy was founded on this basis 1939. Acquired present status and title 1991.

Academic year: September to June (September-January; February-June)

Admission requirements: Secondary school certificate

Main language(s) of instruction: English, German, Latvian

Degrees and diplomas: Bakalaurs, Maģistrs, Doktora (Agriculture; Civil Engineering; Environmental Engineering; Food Science; Landscape Architecture; Pedagogy; Veterinary Science; Water Science; Wood Technology)

Student Services: Nursery Care, Cultural Activities, Sports Facilities, Health Services, Canteen

Periodicals: Proceedings of the Latvia University of Agriculture
Last Update: 16-12-2015

Latvian Academy of Culture (LKA)

24, Ludzas Str.
Rīga LV-1003
Tel: +371(67) 140-175
Fax: +371(67) 141-012
Website: http://www.lka.edu.lv
Rector: Rûta Muktupâvela

Department/Division

Cultural Theory and History (Cultural Studies; Folklore; Management); **Intercultural Communication and Foreign Languages** (Cultural Studies; Danish; English; French; German; History; International Relations; Italian; Literature; Modern Languages; Norwegian; Polish; Spanish; Swedish; Translation and Interpretation); **Sociology and Management of Culture** (Art Management; Cultural Studies; Museum Management; Museum Studies; Sociology); **Theatre and Audiovisual Arts** (Acting; Cinema and Television; Dance; Film; Theatre; Video)
History: Founded 1990. An autonomous Institution financed by the State.
Academic year: September to June
Admission requirements: Secondary education certificate and entrance examination
Fees: (Lats): c. 400 per term
Main language(s) of instruction: Latvian, German (Media and Culture Management programme)
Accrediting agency: Latvian Accreditation Commission; Council of Higher Education of Latvia
Degrees and diplomas: Bakalaurs, Maģistrs, Doktora (Cultural Studies)
Student Services: Cultural Activities
Periodicals: Kulturas telpa un laiks
Last Update: 15-04-2015

Latvian Academy of Sport Education (LSPA)

Brīvības gatve 333
Rīga LV-1006
Tel: +371(67) 543-433
Fax: +371(67) 543-480
Website: http://www.lspa.lv
Rector: Janis Židens

Department/Division

Anatomy (Anatomy; Biochemistry; Physiology); **Gymnastics** (Sports); **Heavy Athletics** (Sports); **Informatics** (Biology; Computer Science; Mechanics; Sports); **Skiing** (Sports); **Sport Management** (Social Sciences; Sports Management); **Sports Games** (Sports); **Sports Medicine** (Medicine; Physical Therapy; Rehabilitation and Therapy; Sports Medicine); **Swimming** (Sports); **Theory** (Pedagogy; Physical Education; Psychology; Sports; Sports Medicine)
History: Founded 1921 as the Latvian Institute of Physical Education. Acquired present title 1991. Acquired present status 1998.
Degrees and diplomas: Augstākās profesionālās izglītības diploms, Bakalaurs, Maģistrs, Doktora (Sports)
Last Update: 17-04-2015

Latvian Maritime Academy (LJA/LMA)

Flotes iela 5B
Rīga LV-1016
Tel: +371(67) 161-125
Fax: +371(67) 830-138
Website: http://www.latja.lv
Rector: Janis Berzins

Course/Programme

Practical Training (Electrical Engineering; Metal Techniques; Transport and Communications)

School

Marine Studies (Marine Engineering; Marine Science and Oceanography; Marine Transport)

Department/Division

Marine Engineering (Marine Engineering; Marine Transport); **Marine Transport** (Marine Transport; Transport and Communications; Transport Management); **Marine Transportation - Marine Electrical Automation** (Automation and Control Engineering; Electrical Engineering; Marine Transport); **Postgraduate Studies** (Human Resources; Marine Transport; Power Engineering; Transport Management)

Centre

LMA Research and Development (Business Administration; Marine Transport; Metal Techniques; Transport and Communications); **LMA Training** (*TC*) (Marine Transport)
History: Founded 1989 as department of Maritime Studies of Kaliningrad Technical Fishery Institute (Riga), acquired present status and title1993.
Academic year: September to September

Admission requirements: Secondary school certificate (Atestats par videjo izgliti bu) and entrance examination
Accrediting agency: Board of Higher Education
Degrees and diplomas: Bakalaurs, Maģistrs. Also 3rd level secondary professional education
Student Services: Academic Counselling, Social Counselling, Sports Facilities, Health Services, Library
Last Update: 14-04-2015

Liepaja University (LPA)

Lielā iela 14
Liepāja LV-3401
Tel: +371(63) 423-560
Fax: +371(63) 424-223
Website: http://www.liepu.lv
Rector (Acting): Ieva OZOLA Ozola

Faculty

Arts and Humanities (Arts and Humanities; Baltic Languages; Communication Studies; Cultural Studies; Design; English; European Languages; European Studies; French; German; Linguistics; Media Studies; Philology; Russian; Translation and Interpretation; Writing); **Management and Social Sciences** (Business Administration; Industrial and Organizational Psychology; Management; Social Sciences); **Pedagogy and Social Work** (Art Therapy; Dance; Education; Musical Instruments; Pedagogy; Rehabilitation and Therapy; Secondary Education; Singing; Social Psychology; Social Welfare; Social Work; Sports; Teacher Training); **Science and Engineering** (Computer Science; Engineering; Mathematics; Software Engineering)

Department/Division

Adult Education (Adult Education; Education; Vocational Education)
History: Founded 1954. Acquired present title and status 2008.
Academic year: September to June (September-December; February-June)
Admission requirements: Secondary school certificate and entrance examination
Main language(s) of instruction: Latvian, English
Degrees and diplomas: Bakalaurs, Maģistrs, Doktora (Linguistics; Management; Media Studies; Pedagogy)
Student Services: Social Counselling, Sports Facilities, Language Laboratory, Health Services, Canteen
Periodicals: LPA Vestis
Last Update: 17-04-2015

National Defence Academy of Latvia (NAA)

Ezermalas iela 6/8
Rīga LV-1014
Tel: +371(67) 076-883
Fax: +371(67) 076-888
Website: http://www.aic.lv/rec/HE_2002/HE_LV/Progr/STATE/naa.htm
Rector: Egils Leščinskis

Course/Programme

Military Science (Military Science)
History: Founded 1992.
Degrees and diplomas: Augstākās profesionālās izglītības diploms, Bakalaurs, Maģistrs
Last Update: 15-04-2015

Rezekne Higher Education Institution (RA)

Atbrīvošanas aleja 90
Rēzekne LV-4601
Tel: +371(64) 623-709
Fax: +371(64) 625-901
Website: http://www.ru.lv
Rector: Edmunds Teirumnieks

Faculty

Economics and Management (Accountancy; Business Administration; Business and Commerce; Commercial Law; Economics; Finance; Hotel Management; Management; Tourism); **Education and Design** (Architectural and Environmental Design; Business Education; Design; Education; Foreign Languages Education; Household Management; Humanities and Social Science Education; Interior Design; Pedagogy; Rehabilitation and Therapy; Science Education; Special Education; Teacher Training; Translation and Interpretation; Vocational Education); **Engineering** (Computer Engineering; Computer Science; Construction Engineering; E- Business/Commerce; Electronic Engineering; Engineering; Environmental Engineering; Environmental Studies; Mathematics; Mechanical Engineering; Natural Sciences); **Humanities and Law** (Archiving; Arts and Humanities; Baltic Languages; Geography; History; Literature; Philology; Religious Education; Social Sciences)
History: Founded 1993 basis of the branches of the University of Latvia and Riga Technical University, founded 1970.
Academic year: September to June
Admission requirements: Secondary school certificate

Fees: Full-time, 600-900 per programme; Part-time, 630-1,350 per programme (Euro)
Main language(s) of instruction: Latvian
Degrees and diplomas: Diploms par pirmā līmena augstāko profesionālo izglītību, Augstākās profesionālās izglītības diploms, Bakalaurs, Maģistrs, Doktora (Education; Environmental Engineering)
Student Services: Cultural Activities, Sports Facilities, Language Laboratory, Canteen, Foreign Studies Centre
Periodicals: Rezeknes Augstskolas Zinnesis
Publishing house: Rezeknes Augstskolas Izdevnieciba
Last Update: 17-04-2015

Riga Stradiņš University (RSU)

Dzirciema iela 16
Rīga LV-1007
Tel: +371(67) 409-105
Fax: +371(67) 471-815
Website: http://www.rsu.lv
Rector: Jānis Gardovskis

Faculty

Communications (Anthropology; Communication Studies; English; French; German; Journalism; Management; Psychology; Public Relations; Sociology; Spanish); **Continuing Education** (Cardiology; Dentistry; Dermatology; Endocrinology; Forensic Medicine and Dentistry; Gastroenterology; Medicine; Ophthalmology; Orthopaedics; Paediatrics; Radiology; Surgery); **Dentistry** (Dental Hygiene; Dental Technology; Dentistry; Oral Pathology; Orthodontics; Surgery); **Doctoral Studies** (Law; Medicine; Pharmacy; Political Sciences; Sociology); **European Studies** (Advertising and Publicity; Business Administration; Communication Studies; Economics; European Studies; European Union Law; Government; International Relations; Management; Marketing; Political Sciences; Public Administration; Small Business); **Law** (European Union Law; International Law; Law); **Medicine** (Medicine); **Nursing** (Midwifery; Nursing); **Pharmacy** (Chemistry; Pharmacy); **Public Health** (Anatomy; Arts and Humanities; Biochemistry; Epidemiology; Ethics; Microbiology; Philosophy; Physiology; Psychology; Public Health); **Rehabilitation** (Art Therapy; Dental Technology; Nutrition; Occupational Therapy; Orthodontics; Physical Therapy; Rehabilitation and Therapy; Social Work; Speech Therapy and Audiology; Sports)

Campus

Liepaja (Medical Auxiliaries; Midwifery; Nursing)
History: Founded 1950 as Riga Medical Institute. Became Latvian Academy of Medicine 1990. Acquired present status and title 2002.

Academic year: September to June (September-January; February-June)
Admission requirements: Secondary education or secondary medical education (Dokuments par vidējo izglitibu)
Fees: Between 3000 and 14000 depending on programme (Euro)
Main language(s) of instruction: Latvian, English
Accrediting agency: Higher Education Quality Evaluation Centre; Ministry of Education and Science
Degrees and diplomas: Bakalaurs, Ārsta grads, Maģistrs, Doktora (Law; Medicine; Pharmacy; Political Sciences)
Student Services: Academic Counselling, Social Counselling, Nursery Care, Cultural Activities, Sports Facilities, Language Laboratory, Facilities for disabled people, Health Services, Canteen, Foreign Studies Centre, Library
Periodicals: Ķirurģija, Zinātniskie raksti
Publishing house: University Publishing House
Last Update: 17-04-2015

Riga Teacher Training and Educational Management Academy (RPIVA)

Imantas 7 līnija 1
Rīga 1038
Tel: +371(67) 808-010
Fax: +371(67) 808-034
Website: http://www.rpiva.lv
Rector: Daina Voita
Tel: +371(67) 860-666

Faculty

Pedagogy (Art Education; Computer Education; Dance; Education; Humanities and Social Science Education; Mathematics Education; Music Education; Native Language Education; Pedagogy; Preschool Education; Primary Education; Science Education; Secondary Education); **Social Sciences** (Business Administration; Business and Commerce; Computer Education; Computer Science; Educational Administration; Educational Psychology; Human Resources; Humanities and Social Science Education; Labour and Industrial Relations; Management; Marketing; Mathematics Education; Native Language Education; Primary Education; Psychology; Public Relations; Science Education; Secondary Education; Social Sciences; Welfare and Protective Services)
History: Founded 1994.
Degrees and diplomas: Bakalaurs, Maģistrs (Educational Administration; Music Education; Pedagogy; Psychology), Doktora (Pedagogy). Also Professional Bachelor's and Master' degrees.

Academic Staff 2016-2017	MALE	FEMALE	TOTAL
FULL-TIME			6
PART-TIME			89
STAFF WITH DOCTORATE			
FULL-TIME			72
Student Numbers 2016-2017			
All (Foreign Included)			673

Last Update: 17-04-2015

Riga Technical University (RTU)

Kaļķu iela 1
Rīga LV-1658
Tel: +371(67) 089-333
Fax: +371(67) 089-302
Website: http://www.rtu.lv
Rector: Leonids Ribickis

Faculty

Architecture and Town Planning (*FAUP*) (Architectural Restoration; Architecture; Electrical Engineering; Electronic Engineering; Energy Engineering; Fine Arts; Interior Design; Landscape Architecture; Textile Design; Town Planning); **Civil Engineering** (*FCE*) (Bridge Engineering; Civil Engineering; Construction Engineering; Geological Engineering; Heating and Refrigeration; Industrial Design; Materials Engineering; Petroleum and Gas Engineering; Road Engineering; Structural Architecture; Surveying and Mapping; Transport Engineering; Water Science); **Computer Science and Information Technology** (*FCSIT*) (Actuarial Science; Automation and Control Engineering; Business Computing; Computer Engineering; Computer Graphics; Computer Science; Information Management; Information Technology; Mathematics; Software Engineering; Statistics); **E-Learning Technologies and Humanities** (Applied Linguistics; Arts and Humanities; Distance Education; Translation and Interpretation); **Electronics and Telecommunications** (*FET*) (Electronic Engineering; Telecommunications Engineering); **Engineering Economics and Management** (*FEEM*) (Banking; Business Administration; Economics; International Business; Management; Marketing; Occupational Health; Real Estate; Transport Management); **Materials Science and Applied Chemistry** (*FMSAC*) (Applied Chemistry; Chemical Engineering; Materials Engineering; Organic Chemistry; Physics; Polymer and Plastics Technology; Textile Design); **Power and Electrical Engineering** (*FPEE*) (Electrical and Electronic Engineering; Electrical Engineering; Energy Engineering; Environmental Engineering; Heating and Refrigeration; Power Engineering); **Transport and Mechanical Engineering** (*FTME*) (Aeronautical and Aerospace Engineering; Biomedical Engineering; Mechanical Engineering; Mechanics; Nanotechnology; Railway Transport; Road Transport; Safety Engineering; Transport Engineering)

School

Business (*Riga - RBS*) (Business Administration)

Institute

Humanities (*IH*) (Arts and Humanities; Pedagogy; Philosophy; Sociology; Sports; Teacher Training; Vocational Education); **Languages** (*IL*) (Baltic Languages; English; German; Modern Languages; Translation and Interpretation)

Centre

BALTECH Study (Natural Sciences; Technology); **Distance Education** (Air Transport; Automation and Control Engineering; Automotive Engineering; Construction Engineering; Electronic Engineering; Heating and Refrigeration; Hydraulic Engineering; Petroleum and Gas Engineering; Railway Engineering; Surveying and Mapping; Transport Engineering)

Campus

Cēsis (Electrical Engineering; Environmental Studies; Heating and Refrigeration; Materials Engineering; Power Engineering; Real Estate); **Daugavpils** (Automation and Control Engineering; Computer Science; Construction Engineering; Economics; Electrical Engineering; Electronic Engineering; Engineering; Heating and Refrigeration; Information Technology; Machine Building; Mechanics; Power Engineering; Railway Transport; Road Transport; Safety Engineering; Transport Economics); **Liepaja** (Computer Engineering; Construction Engineering; Electrical Engineering; Engineering; Heating and Refrigeration; Human Resources; Machine Building; Management; Mechanics; Metallurgical Engineering; Petroleum and Gas Engineering; Power Engineering; Production Engineering; Telecommunications Engineering; Transport Management; Waste Management); **Ventspils** (Automation and Control Engineering; Computer Engineering; Economics; Electrical Engineering; Electronic Engineering; Engineering; Information Sciences; Machine Building; Management; Mechanics; Power Engineering; Safety Engineering; Taxation; Telecommunications Engineering; Transport and Communications)

Further information: A traditional and distance education institution.

History: Founded 1862 as Riga Polytechnical Institute, became part of Latvia University 1919. Renamed Riga Polytechnical Institute 1958. Acquired present status and title 1990.

Academic year: September to June

Admission requirements: Centralized examinations when graduating from secondary education

Fees: 1850 to 2680 (US Dollar)

Main language(s) of instruction: Latvian, Russian, English

Degrees and diplomas: Bakalaurs, Maģistrs, Doktora (Architecture; Automation and Control Engineering; Chemical Engineering; Civil Engineering; Computer Engineering; Electrical Engineering; Electronic Engineering; Environmental Studies; Information Technology; Mechanical Engineering; Power Engineering; Production Engineering; Telecommunications Engineering)

Student Services: Academic Counselling, Social Counselling, Cultural Activities, Sports Facilities, Language Laboratory, Canteen, Foreign Studies Centre

Periodicals: Scientific Proceedings of RTU

Last Update: 17-04-2015

Stockholm School of Economics in Riga (SSE Riga)

Strēlnieku iela 4a
Rīga LV-1010
Tel: +371(67) 015-800
Fax: +371(67) 830-249
Website: http://www.sseriga.edu
Rector: Anders Paalzow

Department/Division

Business and Management (Accountancy; Anthropology; Business Administration; Commercial Law; Development Studies; Ethics; Leadership; Management; Mathematics; Philosophy; Taxation); **Economics** (Accountancy; Business Administration; Econometrics; Economics; Finance; International Economics); **Languages** (Baltic Languages; English; French; German; Russian; Spanish; Swedish)

History: Founded 1993 as a Branch of the Stockholm School of Economics, Stockholm, Sweden.

Academic year: August to June

Admission requirements: Admission tests and interviews

Fees: Undergraduate tuition, 6000; Students from the Baltic countries 3,500 per annum (Euro)

Main language(s) of instruction: Latvian, English

Degrees and diplomas: Bakalaurs, Maģistrs

Student Services: Academic Counselling, Social Counselling, Careers Guidance, Canteen

Periodicals: SSE Riga Working Papers

Last Update: 17-04-2015

University of Latvia (UL)

Raina bulvaris 19
Rīga LV-1586
Tel: +371(67) 034-331
Fax: +371(67) 034-302
Website: http://www.lu.lv
Rector: Indriķis Muižnieks

Faculty

Biology (Biology; Biotechnology; Botany; Ecology; Microbiology; Molecular Biology; Physiology; Zoology); **Chemistry** (Analytical Chemistry; Chemistry; Environmental Studies; Food Technology; Inorganic Chemistry; Organic Chemistry; Physical Chemistry; Science Education); **Computing** (Computer Education; Computer Engineering; Computer Networks; Computer Science; Information Technology; Mathematics and Computer Science; Natural Sciences; Software Engineering); **Economics and Management** (Accountancy; Business Administration; Demography and Population; E- Business/Commerce; Economics; Environmental Management; European Studies; Finance; Insurance; International Business; International Economics; International Law; International Relations; Management; Marketing; Mathematics; Safety Engineering; Statistics; Tourism; Transport Management); **Education, Psychology and Art** (Adult Education; Art Education; Computer Education; Computer Networks; Computer Science; Education; Educational Administration; Educational Sciences; Foreign Languages Education; Handicrafts; Health Education; Home Economics; Humanities and Social Science Education; Literature; Native Language Education; Pedagogy; Preschool Education; Primary Education; Psychology; Special Education; Sports; Teacher Training); **Geography and Earth Sciences** (Earth Sciences; Environmental Studies; Geography; Geography (Human); Geology; Science Education); **History and Philosophy** (Archaeology; Contemporary History; History; Logic; Medieval Studies; Modern History; Philosophy); **Humanities** (Anthropology; Arts and Humanities; Asian Studies; Baltic Languages; Classical Languages; Cultural Studies; English; English Studies; Finnish; French; German; Hungarian; Linguistics; Oriental Languages; Philology; Romance Languages; Russian; Scandinavian Languages; Slavic Languages; Translation and Interpretation); **Law** (Civil Law; Constitutional Law; Criminal Law; European Union Law; History of Law; Human Rights; International Law; Law; Public Law); **Medicine** (Histology; Medicine; Nursing; Paediatrics; Pathology; Pharmacy; Social and Preventive Medicine; Surgery); **Physics and Mathematics** (Applied Mathematics; Astronomy and Space Science; Astrophysics; Atomic and Molecular Physics; Computer Science; Laser Engineering; Mathematics; Mechanics; Optics; Optometry; Physics; Polymer and Plastics Technology; Science Education; Statistics; Thermal Physics); **Social Sciences** (Cognitive Sciences; Communication Studies; Information Sciences; Library Science; Political Sciences; Social Sciences; Social Work; Sociology); **Theology** (Bible; Ethics;

History of Religion; Religion; Religious Education; Religious Studies; Theology)

Centre

Baltic Studies (Baltic Languages); **Environmental Studies and Management** (Environmental Management; Environmental Studies); **European and Transition Studies** (European Studies); **Family Health Education** (Health Education); **Gender Studies** (Gender Studies); **Judaic Studies** (Judaic Religious Studies); **Language** (Baltic Languages; Chinese; English; French; German; Italian; Japanese; Russian; Spanish; Swedish); **Lithuanistics** (Baltic Languages; Cultural Studies); **North American Studies** (American Studies); **Pre-Studies Training**

Research Division

Advanced Social and Political Sciences (Development Studies; Information Sciences; International Relations; Media Studies; Political Sciences; Regional Studies; Social Sciences); **Astronomy** (Astronomy and Space Science); **Atomic Physics and Spectroscopy** (Atomic and Molecular Physics; Optics; Physics); **Biology** (Biology; Botany; Ecology; Environmental Management; Environmental Studies; Natural Resources; Zoology); **Cardiology** (Cardiology; Epidemiology; Medicine); **Education** (Education; Educational Administration; Educational Sciences); **Experimental and Clinical Medicine** (Biology; Cell Biology; Diabetology; Endocrinology; Medicine; Oncology; Physiology); **Geodesy and Geo-informatics** (Computer Science; Earth Sciences; Geophysics); **History of Latvia** (Anthropology; Archaeology; Ethnology; History; Medieval Studies); **Latvian Language** (Grammar; Linguistics; Native Language; Terminology); **Literature, Folklore and Art** (Arts and Humanities; Comparative Literature; Folklore; Literature; Musicology; Theatre); **Mathematics and Computer Science** (Artificial Intelligence; Computer Engineering; Computer Networks; Mathematics and Computer Science; Systems Analysis); **Microbiology and Biotechnology** (Biotechnology; Cell Biology; Food Technology; Microbiology; Physiology); **Pedagogy** (Computer Education; Continuing Education; Distance Education; Pedagogy); **Philosophy and Sociology** (Philosophy; Sociology); **Physics** (Mechanics; Physics); **Polymer Mechanics** (Materials Engineering; Mechanics; Physics); **Solid State Physics** (Materials Engineering; Optometry; Physics; Radiophysics)

History: Founded 1919. Acquired present status 1990.

Academic year: September to June (September-January; February-June)

Admission requirements: Competitive entrance according to the results of the centralized examination following general or special secondary school certificate

Main language(s) of instruction: Latvian

Degrees and diplomas: Diploms par pirmā līmena augstāko profesionālo izglītību, Augstākās profesionālās izglītības diploms, Bakalaurs, Maģistrs, Doktora (Astronomy and Space Science; Biology; Chemistry; Communication Studies; Computer Science; Demography and Population; Economics; Educational Administration; Environmental Studies; Geography; Geology; Law; Linguistics; Management; Mathematics; Mechanical Engineering; Medicine; Pedagogy; Pharmacy; Philology; Philosophy; Physics; Political Sciences; Psychology; Religious Studies; Sociology; Theology)

Student Services: Academic Counselling, Cultural Activities, Sports Facilities, Language Laboratory, Canteen

Periodicals: Acta Universitatis Latviensis, Automatic Control and Computer Science, Journal of Baltic psychology, Journal of the Latvian Institute History, Latvian Human Rights Quarterly, Latvijas Vēsture, Likums un Tiesības, Linguistica Lettica, Magneto-hydro-dynamics, Mechanics of Composite Materials, Terra, Zvaigžņota Debess

Publishing house: University of Latvia Press

Last Update: 17-04-2015

Ventspils University College (VeA)

Inženieru Iela 101a
Ventspils LV-3601
Fax: +371(63) 629-660
Website: http://www.venta.lv
Rector: Gita Revalde

Faculty

Economics and Business Administration (*FEBA*) (Accountancy; Business Administration; Economics; Finance; Management; Marketing; Social Sciences; Transport Management); **Information Technology** (*FIT*) (Computer Engineering; Computer Science; Electronic Engineering; Engineering; Information Technology; Mathematics; Telecommunications Engineering); **Translation Studies** (Baltic Languages; English; German; Linguistics; Russian; Translation and Interpretation)

History: Founded 1997.

Academic year: September to June

Fees: (Euro): 1,400-2,200 per annum

Main language(s) of instruction: Latvian

Accrediting agency: Latvian Board of Higher Education

Degrees and diplomas: Bakalaurs, Maģistrs, Doktora (Business Administration; Linguistics)

Student Services: Academic Counselling, Sports Facilities, Language Laboratory, Facilities for disabled people, Canteen

Last Update: 17-04-2015

Vidzeme University of Applied Sciences (VIA)

Cēsu Iela 4
Valmiera LV-4200
Tel: +371(64) 207-230
Fax: +371(64) 207-229
Website: http://www.va.lv
Rector: Gatis Krūmiņš

Faculty

Engineering (Computer Networks; Data Processing; Electronic Engineering; Engineering; Information Management; Information Technology; Mechanical Engineering); **Society and Science** (Communication Studies; Government; Journalism; Media Studies; Political Sciences; Public Relations; Social Sciences)

Institute

Socio-technical Systems Engineering (Engineering; Social Sciences)

Centre

Language Study and Examination (Baltic Languages; English; French; German; Translation and Interpretation)
History: Founded 1996, acquired present status 2001.
Academic year: September to June
Admission requirements: Secondary school certificate, English examination
Fees: 1924 (Euro)
Main language(s) of instruction: Latvian, English
Accrediting agency: AIKNC (Higher Education Quality Evaluation Centre of Latvia)
Degrees and diplomas: Bakalaurs, Maģistrs, Doktora (Information Technology)
Student Services: Academic Counselling, Careers Guidance, Language Laboratory
Last Update: 17-04-2015

Private Institutions

Baltic International Academy (BSA)

Lomonosova iela 4
Rīga LV-1003
Tel: +371(67) 100-601, +371(67) 100-626
Fax: +371(67) 112-679 +371(67) 241-272
Website: http://bsa.edu.lv
Rector: Arkadijis Voicišs

Course/Programme

Business Management and Administration (*Postgraduate Professional Education*) (Administration; Business Administration; English; Russian); **Computer Design** (Computer Graphics; Computer Science; Graphic Design); **Computer Science** (Computer Science; Microelectronics); **Cultural Management** (Cultural Studies; Management); **Design** (*Postgraduate Professional Education*) (Computer Graphics; Design); **Entrepreneurship** (*Professional Education*) (Business Administration; International Business; Management); **Environmental Design** (*Professional Education*) (Architectural and Environmental Design; Communication Arts; Interior Design; Visual Arts); **European Studies** (Baltic Languages; English; European Studies; International Relations; Political Sciences; Russian); **European Studies** (*Postgraduate*) (English; European Studies; Russian; Social Studies); **Financial Management** (Finance; Management); **Human Resources Management** (*Interuniversity Postgraduate Professional Education*) (Human Resources; Management); **Jurisprudence (Law)** (*Professional Education*) (Law); **Private Law** (*Postgraduate Professional Education*) (Private Law); **Public Relations** (Baltic Languages; Marketing; Public Relations; Russian); **Regional Economics and Economic Policy** (*International Doctoral Studies*) (Economic and Finance Policy; Economics; English; Russian); **Small and Medium Business Management** (*Professional Education*) (Business Administration; Management; Small Business; Tourism); **Tourism and Hospitality Management** (Hotel and Restaurant; Tourism); **Translation and Interpretation** (Baltic Languages; English; Russian; Translation and Interpretation)

Centre

Foreign Language Learning (English; French; German; Russian; Spanish; Swedish)
Further information: Also campuses in Daugavpils, Rezekne, Yekabpils, Yelgava, Liepaya, Ventspils, Smiltene. A traditional and distance education institution.
History: Founded 1992 as Baltijas Krievu Institūts (Baltic Russian Institute). Acquired present status 1999. Acquired present title 2006.
Fees: National : 300-800 per semester (US Dollar), International : For International students, 630-1,350 per semester (Euro)
Main language(s) of instruction: Latvian, English, Russian
Accrediting agency: Ministry of Education and Science
Degrees and diplomas: Diploms par pirmā līmena augstāko profesionālo izglītību, Bakalaurs, Maģistrs, Doktora (Economics). Also Professional Bachelor's degree; 2nd level professional higher education diploma; MBA
Last Update: 14-04-2015

Baltic Psychology and Management University College

Lomonosova iela 4
Rīga LV-1003
Tel: +371(67) 100-608
Fax: +371(67) 100-218
Website: http://www.psy.lv
Rector: Zhanna Caurkubule
Tel: 371(67) 100-628

Course/Programme

European Economy and Business (Accountancy; Baltic Languages; Banking; Business Administration; Economics; English; European Union Law; Finance; International Business; International Economics; International Law; International Relations; Law; Marketing; Taxation); **Human Resources Management** (Human Resources); **Professional Work Psychology** (*Master*) (Industrial and Organizational Psychology; Psychology); **Psychologist Assistant** (Psychology); **Psychology** (Anatomy; Clinical Psychology; Cultural Studies; Educational Psychology; Gerontology; Logic; Modern Languages; Philosophy; Physiology; Psychology; Social Psychology); **Social Assistance Management** (Social Welfare; Social Work); **Social Work** (Social Work)
Further information: Also branches in Liepaja, Daugavpils, Ekabpils, Elgava.
History: Founded 1995. Acquired present status 2004.
Main language(s) of instruction: Latvian
Degrees and diplomas: Diploms par pirmā līmena augstāko profesionālo izglītību, Bakalaurs, Maģistrs (Human Resources; Psychology)
Student Services: Library
Last Update: 14-04-2015

Higher Institute of Social Technologies (STA)

Bezdelīgu iela 12
Rīga LV-1048
Tel: +371(67) 461-001, +371(67) 461-281
Fax: +371(67) 461-281
Website: http://www.sta-edu.lv
Rector: Juris Zaķis

Course/Programme

Entrepreneurial Economics and Administration (Accountancy; Business Administration; Economics; History; Labour and Industrial Relations; Management; Modern Languages; Philosophy; Political Sciences; Transport Management); **Entrepreneurial Management** (*Postgraduate*) (Accountancy;

Business Administration; Economics; Finance; Management; Marketing; Pedagogy; Psychology; Social Work; Statistics); **Law** (Law; Real Estate; Small Business; Transport and Communications); **Translation and Interpretation** (Baltic Languages; Economics; English; German; Latin; Law; Psychology; Russian; Spanish; Translation and Interpretation)
History: Founded 1991, acquired present status 2000.
Degrees and diplomas: Bakalaurs, Maģistrs
Last Update: 17-04-2015

International Higher School of Practical Psychology (SPPA)

Bruninieku 65
Rīga LV-1011
Tel: +371(67) 803-919
Website: http://www.sppa.lv
President: Janis Mihailovs

Department/Division

Psychology (Psychology); **Translation** (Baltic Languages; Chinese; English; French; German; Italian; Japanese; Polish; Russian; Spanish; Translation and Interpretation)
History: Founded 1988.
Main language(s) of instruction: Latvian, Russian
Degrees and diplomas: Bakalaurs, Maģistrs
Last Update: 17-04-2015

ISMA University (ISMA)

Lomonosova 1, korpuss 6
Rīga LV-1019
Tel: +371(67) 100-607
Fax: +371(67) 241-591
Website: http://www.isma.lv
President: Romans Djakons
Tel: +371(67) 241-515

Department/Division

Business Communications Department (Communication Studies; English; German; Grammar; Spanish; Translation and Interpretation; Writing); **Computer Technologies and Natural Sciences** (Artificial Intelligence; Business Administration; Business Computing; Chemistry; Computer Engineering; Computer Graphics; Computer Networks; Computer Science; Data Processing; Design; E- Business/Commerce; Electronic Engineering; Information Management; Information Technology; Mathematics; Natural Sciences; Operations Research; Physics; Software Engineering; Statistics; Telecommunications Engineering; Transport and

Communications; Transport Management); **Cultural Studies** (Architectural and Environmental Design; Art History; Computer Graphics; Cultural Studies; Ethics; Graphic Design; Interior Design; Marketing; Photography; Safety Engineering); **Law** (Administrative Law; Civil Law; Civil Security; Commercial Law; European Union Law; Fiscal Law; Information Technology; Insurance; Labour Law; Law; Marketing; Protective Services; Psychology; Real Estate; Sociology); **Management and Economics** (Accountancy; Banking; Business Administration; Commercial Law; Economics; Environmental Studies; Finance; Information Sciences; Management; Marketing; Transport Management); **Management and Marketing** (Human Resources; Management; Marketing; Safety Engineering; Tourism)

Further information: Also Latgales Branch and Mission in UIkraine. A traditional and distance education institution.

History: Founded 1996.

Main language(s) of instruction: Latvian

Degrees and diplomas: Diploms par pirmā līmena augstāko profesionālo izglītību, Bakalaurs, Maģistrs, Doktora (Business Administration)

Last Update: 14-04-2015

Latvian Christian Academy (LKRA)

5.līnija 3, Bulduri
Jūrmala LV-2010
Tel: +371(67) 753-360, +371 (67) 811-340
Fax: +371(67) 751-919
Website: http://www.kra.lv
Rector: Skaidrīte Gūtmane

Course/Programme

Biblical Arts (Religious Art); **Public Relations** (Public Relations); **Social Work** (Social Work); **Theology** (Theology)

History: Founded 1993, acquired present status 1997.

Fees: 800-1,300 per programme (Euro)

Main language(s) of instruction: Latvian, English

Degrees and diplomas: Bakalaurs, Maģistrs

Last Update: 17-04-2015

Riga Aeronautical Institute (RAI)

Mezkalnu 9
Rīga LV-1058
Tel: +371(67) 767-831
Fax: +371(67) 767-831
Website: http://www.rai.lv
Rector: Olafs Brinkmanis

Course/Programme

Aviation Engineering (Aeronautical and Aerospace Engineering; Air Transport; Computer Engineering; Electronic Engineering; Maintenance Technology; Power Engineering); **Electronics** (Aeronautical and Aerospace Engineering; Electronic Engineering); **Transport Management** (Air Transport; Transport Management)

History: Founded 1942, acquired present status 1992.

Main language(s) of instruction: Latvian

Degrees and diplomas: Augstākās profesionālās izglītibas diploms, Bakalaurs, Maģistrs

Last Update: 17-04-2015

Riga Graduate School of Law (RGSL)

Strēlnieku iela 4k-2
Rīga LV-1010
Tel: +371(67) 039-230
Fax: +371(67) 039-240
Website: http://www.rgsl.edu.lv
Rector: George Ulrich

Course/Programme

EU Law and Policy (*Graduate*) (Environmental Studies; European Studies; European Union Law; International Law; International Relations); **International and EU Law** (*Graduate*) (Commercial Law; European Union Law; Human Rights; International Law; Public Law); **Law and Business** (Administrative Law; Business Administration; Commercial Law; Comparative Law; Constitutional Law; Demography and Population; Economics; English; Ethics; Finance; French; German; Human Rights; Information Management; International Economics; International Law; Law; Marketing); **Law and Diplomacy** (Arts and Humanities; Business Administration; Comparative Politics; Economics; English; French; German; International Business; International Relations; Law; Psychology); **Law and Finance** (*Graduate*) (Accountancy; Commercial Law; Economics; Finance; International Law; Law; Taxation); **Legal Linguistics** (*Graduate*) (Comparative Law; European Union Law; Law; Linguistics; Philology; Terminology; Translation and Interpretation); **Public International Law and Human Rights** (*Graduate*) (Commercial Law; Criminal Law; Human Rights; International Law; Public Law); **Transborder Commercial Law** (*Graduate*) (Business Administration; Commercial Law; International Business; International Law)

History: Founded 1998 on the basis of a Swedish-Latvian agreement.

Academic year: August to June

Admission requirements: Bachelor of Law or equivalent. TOEFL with minimum score of 550 points or 6.5 at IELTS

Fees: 3500 per programme (Euro)
Main language(s) of instruction: English
Accrediting agency: Ministry of Education and Science
Degrees and diplomas: Bakalaurs, Maģistrs
Periodicals: RGSL Working Papers
Last Update: 17-04-2015

Riga International School of Economics and Business Administration (RISEBA)

Meža iela 3
Rīga LV-1048
Tel: +371(67) 500-265
Fax: +371(67) 500-252
Website: http://www.riseba.lv/
Rector: Irina Sennikova

Course/Programme

Architecture (*Undergraduate Studies*) (Architectural and Environmental Design; Architecture; Media Studies; Structural Architecture); **Audiovisual Media Arts** (*Undergraduate Studies*) (Aesthetics; Art History; Art Management; Cinema and Television; Communication Arts; English; Film; Journalism; Law; Philosophy; Psychology; Radio and Television Broadcasting); **Business Management** (*Postgraduate Studies*) (Accountancy; Business Administration; Commercial Law; Economics; Finance; Information Technology; Management; Marketing; Psychology); **Business Management and Administration of Organizations** (*Doctoral programme*) (Administration; Business Administration; Economics; English; Finance; Human Resources; Management; Marketing; Modern Languages; Operations Research; Safety Engineering); **Business Psychology** (*Undergraduate Studies*) (Industrial and Organizational Psychology); **Business Studies** (*Undergraduate Studies*) (Accountancy; Banking; Business Administration; Civil Law; Commercial Law; Data Processing; English; European Union Law; Finance; Human Resources; Information Technology; International Business; International Economics; International Law; Labour Law; Management; Marketing; Social Psychology; Statistics; Transport Management); **E- Business** (*Undergraduate Studies*) (Business Administration; Business Computing; Computer Graphics; E- Business/Commerce; European Union Law; Information Technology; Marketing; Multimedia; Social Psychology; Statistics); **European Business Studies** (*Undergraduate Studies*) (Accountancy; Civil Law; Commercial Law; Communication Studies; Economics; European Studies; Finance; Information Technology; Law; Management; Marketing); **Human Resource Management** (Accountancy; Business Administration; Economics; European Union Law; Human Resources; Labour Law;

Management; Occupational Health; Social Psychology); **Public Relations and Advertising Management** (*Undergraduate Studies*) (Advertising and Publicity; Marketing; Mass Communication; Psychology; Public Relations); **RISEBA MBA** (*Postgraduate Studies*) (Accountancy; Business Administration; Finance; Human Resources; Management; Marketing); **Work Safety** (*Foundation Degree*) (Occupational Health; Safety Engineering)
Further information: Also Daugavpils Campus.
History: Founded 1992, acquired present status 2000.
Academic year: September-mid-January; mid-January-mid-June
Admission requirements: Depends on course
Fees: c. 2000 per annum (Euro)
Main language(s) of instruction: Latvian, Russian, English
Accrediting agency: Ministry of Education and Science
Degrees and diplomas: Diploms par pirmā līmena augstāko profesionālo izglītību, Bakalaurs, Maģistrs, Doktora (Business Administration). Also MBA.
Student Services: Academic Counselling, Careers Guidance, Sports Facilities, Language Laboratory, Facilities for disabled people, Canteen, Foreign Studies Centre
Last Update: 17-04-2015

Transport and Telecommunication Institute (TSI)

Lomonosova Street 1
Rīga LV-1019
Tel: +371(67) 100-661
Fax: +371(67) 100-660
Website: http://www.tsi.lv
Rector: Igor Graurs

Faculty

Computer Science and Telecommunications (Computer Science; Electronic Engineering; Telecommunications Engineering); **Management and Economics** (Economics; Management); **Transport and Logistics** (Air Transport; Maintenance Technology; Transport and Communications; Transport Management)

Academy

TTI IT (Computer Science; Information Technology)

Campus

Latgalian (Computer Science; Economics; Information Management; Information Sciences; Management; Transport Management)
Further information: Also Latgales branch (Daugavpils)
History: Founded 1919. Acquired present status 1999.

Academic year: September to January; February to June

Admission requirements: Secondary or Higher School Certificate

Fees: (Euros): 2,500 per annum

Main language(s) of instruction: Latvian, Russian, English

Accrediting agency: Ministry of Education and Science; International Civil Aviation Organization (ICAO), Erasmus University Charter

Degrees and diplomas: Diploms par pirmā līmena augstāko profesionālo izglītību, Augstākās profesionālās izglītības diploms, Bakalaurs, Maģistrs, Doktora. Also Professional Diploma

Student Services: Academic Counselling, Social Counselling, Cultural Activities, Sports Facilities, Language Laboratory, Health Services, Canteen

Periodicals: Computer Modelling and New Technologies, Transport and Telecommunication

Last Update: 17-04-2015

Turiba University (SBAT)

Graudu Str. 68
Rīga LV-1058
Tel: +371(67) 622-551
Fax: +371(67) 619-152
Website: http://www.turiba.lv
Rector: Jānis Načisčionis

Faculty

Business Administration (Accountancy; Advertising and Publicity; Business Administration; Economics; Finance); **Communication** (Communication Studies; Public Relations); **International Tourism** (*Tourism and Hospitality Management*) (Hotel Management; Leisure Studies; Public Relations; Tourism); **Law** (Law; Public Administration)

History: Founded 1993.

Main language(s) of instruction: Latvian, English

Degrees and diplomas: Diploms par pirmā līmena augstāko profesionālo izglītību, Bakalaurs (Business Administration; Hotel and Restaurant; Law; Tourism), Maģistrs (Business Administration; Law; Management; Public Administration; Public Relations), Doktora (Business Administration; Communication Arts; Law). Also MBA

Last Update: 14-04-2015

University College of Economics and Culture (UCEC)

Lomonosova 1, korp. 5
Rīga LV-1019
Tel: +371 20-00-90-51

Fax: +371(67) 114-111
Website: http://www.eka.edu.lv
Rector: Gunta Veismane

Department/Division

Cultural Management (Cultural Studies; Interior Design; Management; Marketing; Parks and Recreation; Sales Techniques); **Economics** (Accountancy; Administration; Business Administration; Economics; Management); **Foreign Languages** (Modern Languages; Translation and Interpretation)

History: Founded 1998.

Fees: 2000 (Euro)

Accrediting agency: Ministry of Education and Science

Degrees and diplomas: Diploms par pirmā līmena augstāko profesionālo izglītību, Augstākās profesionālās izglītības diploms, Bakalaurs, Maģistrs

Last Update: 14-04-2015

Lebanon

STRUCTURE OF HIGHER EDUCATION SYSTEM

Description

Higher education in Lebanon is provided by Technical and Vocational Institutes, University Colleges, University Institutes and Universities. Only one of them is a public institution: the Lebanese University. Both the private and public sectors are administrated by the Ministry of Education and Higher Education, Technical and Vocational Institutes are under the Directorate General of Technical and Vocational Education. University Colleges, University Institutes and Universities are under the responsibility of the Directorate General of Higher Education. Admission to higher education institutions is based on the Baccalauréat libanais or equivalent diplomas from other countries.

Stages of studies

University level first stage

Some institutions offer short courses (two to three years) leading to professional qualifications. Where longer studies are involved, the first stage leads, after three to five years' study, to the Licence, the Bachelor's degree or a Diploma, depending on the institution attended.

University level second stage

The second stage involves more specialized work and leads, after one or two years' study beyond the first degree, to the Maîtrise in scientific subjects, the Master's degree at the American University, the Magistère, the Diplôme d'Etudes supérieures, and the Diplôme d'Etudes approfondies. In Medicine, the Medical Doctorate (MD) is awarded after seven years' study. It is a professional qualification.

University level third stage

The third stage involves the writing of a thesis and leads to the award of a Doctorate. In French-speaking universities, a Doctorate is awarded after three years of study beyond the Diplôme d'Etudes approfondies which is equivalent to the PhDs awarded in the American system.

ADMISSION TO HIGHER EDUCATION

Admission to university-level studies

Name of Secondary school credential required: Baccalauréat général

Foreign students admission

Admission requirements: Foreign students are admitted to universities under the same conditions as Lebanese students, provided that they hold a qualification equivalent to the Lebanese Baccalauréat. They are not subject to any special quota system. Scholarships are granted within the framework of bilateral agreements concluded with other countries. In certain universities, students must sit for an entrance examination.

Entry regulations: A visa and resident permit are required.

RECOGNITION OF STUDIES

Quality assurance system

Technical committee for licensing, starting up programmes and auditing HEIs; Equivalence committee for the recognition of degrees; Engineering committee for Engineering qualifications; Examinations for all specialties in Health Sciences (MD, Dentistry, Physiotherapy, Nursing, etc)

Bodies dealing with recognition

Direction générale de l'Enseignement supérieur (Directorate General of Higher Education)
Habib Abi Chahla Street UNESCO Palace
Beirut

© International Association of Universities 2019
International Handbook of Universities 2019,
https://doi.org/10.1057/978-3-319-76971-4_107

Tel: +961(1) 789-611
Fax: +961(1) 789-606
Website: http://www.higher-edu.gov.lb

NATIONAL BODIES

Ministry of Education

Minister: Marwan Hamadeh
Habib Abi-chahla Square UNESCO Palace
Beirut
Tel: +961(1) 772-500
Fax: +961(1) 772-529
Website: http://www.higher-edu.gov.lb

Direction générale de l'Enseignement supérieur (Directorate General of Higher Education)

Director-General: Ahmed El Jammal
Habib Abi Chahla Street UNESCO Palace
Beirut
Tel: +961(1) 789-611
Fax: +961(1) 789-606
Website: http://www.higher-edu.gov.lb
Role of national body: To supervise the activities of higher education institutions in Lebanon and coordinate the activities of: - the Council of Higher Education; - the Technical Committee for licensing, starting up and auditing; - the Equivalence Committee for the recognition of degrees; - the Colloquium Exams Committees; - the Engineering Qualification Recognition Committee; - Accrediting Programme Committe for private institutions.

Universities Association Of Lebanon - UAOLB (Universities Association Of Lebanon - UAOLB)

Camelia II Building, Said Freiha Street Mar Takla
Hazmieh
Tel: +961 (5) 950 410
Website: http://www.uaolb.org
Role of national body: The Universities Association Of Lebanon - UAOLB - is the representative body for the leading public and private research universities in Lebanon;

Data for academic year: 2017–2018
Source: IAU from University of St Joseph Beirut, 2018

Public Institution

Lebanese University (UL)

Place du Musée
Beirut 14/6573
Tel: +961(1) 612-830
Fax: +961(1) 612-815
Website: http://www.ul.edu.lb
Rector: Zouheir Ali Chokr
Tel: +961(1) 612-624

Faculty
Agronomy (Agronomy; Animal Husbandry; Food Science; Landscape Architecture; Plant and Crop Protection); **Arts and Humanities** (Ancient Civilizations; Ancient Languages; Applied Linguistics; Arabic; Archaeology; Arts and Humanities; Classical Languages; Comparative Literature; Contemporary History; Dutch; English; Ethics; French; Grammar; Greek; Hebrew; History; Italian; Latin; Logic; Medieval Studies; Metaphysics; Modern History; Modern Languages; Philology; Philosophical Schools; Philosophy; Phonetics; Prehistory; Psycholinguistics; Terminology; Translation and Interpretation; Turkish); **Economics and Business Administration** (Accountancy; Business Administration; Business Computing; Economics; Finance; Marketing); **Education** (Art Education; Education; Foreign Languages Education; Higher Education; Literacy Education; Music Education; Native Language; Pedagogy; Preschool Education; Primary Education; Science Education; Secondary Education; Teacher Trainers Education; Teacher Training); **Engineering** (Automation and Control Engineering; Bridge Engineering; Construction Engineering; Electrical Engineering; Electronic Engineering; Energy Engineering; Engineering; Geological Engineering; Hydraulic Engineering; Industrial Engineering; Laser Engineering; Machine Building; Measurement and Precision Engineering; Mechanical Engineering; Metallurgical Engineering; Microelectronics; Microwaves; Power Engineering; Production Engineering; Road Engineering; Safety Engineering; Telecommunications Engineering; Transport Engineering); **Information and Documentation** (Archiving; Communication Studies; Documentation Techniques; Information Management; Information Technology; Journalism; Library Science; Multimedia; Radio and Television Broadcasting); **Law, Political Science and Management** (Administration; Administrative Law; Air and Space Law; Civil Law; Commercial Law; Comparative Law; Constitutional Law; Criminal Law; Fiscal Law; History of Law; Human Rights; International Law; Islamic Law; Justice Administration; Labour Law; Law; Management; Maritime Law; Political Sciences; Private Law; Public Law); **Medicine**

(Anaesthesiology; Cardiology; Diabetology; Endocrinology; Epidemiology; Gastroenterology; Gynaecology and Obstetrics; Medicine; Nephrology; Neurology; Oncology; Ophthalmology; Orthopaedics; Otorhinolaryngology; Paediatrics; Parasitology; Pathology; Plastic Surgery; Pneumology; Psychiatry and Mental Health; Radiology; Rheumatology; Surgery; Urology); **Pharmacy** (Pharmacy); **Public Health** (Community Health; Ergotherapy; Midwifery; Nursing; Occupational Therapy; Physical Therapy; Public Health; Social and Community Services; Social Welfare; Social Work; Speech Therapy and Audiology); **Science** (Analytical Chemistry; Anatomy; Biochemistry; Biological and Life Sciences; Biology; Botany; Chemistry; Computer Science; Crystallography; Earth Sciences; Embryology and Reproduction Biology; Entomology; Genetics; Geology; Histology; Immunology; Industrial Chemistry; Inorganic Chemistry; Marine Biology; Mathematical Physics; Mathematics; Mechanics; Microbiology; Mineralogy; Natural Sciences; Neurosciences; Optics; Organic Chemistry; Paleontology; Parasitology; Physical Chemistry; Physics; Plant Pathology; Statistics; Zoology); **Tourism and Hospitality Management** (Cooking and Catering; Hotel and Restaurant; Hotel Management; Sales Techniques; Tourism)

School
Dentistry (Dental Hygiene; Dentistry; Oral Pathology; Orthodontics; Periodontics; Stomatology)

Institute
Fine Arts (Acting; Architecture; Fine Arts; Interior Design; Painting and Drawing; Rural Planning; Theatre; Town Planning); **Social Sciences** (Social Sciences); **Technology** (Bridge Engineering; Civil Engineering; Computer Networks; Construction Engineering; Electrical and Electronic Engineering; Geological Engineering; Industrial Engineering; Road Engineering; Technology; Telecommunications Engineering; Transport Engineering)
History: Founded 1951 as teacher training college, reorganized by decree as university 1953. An autonomous State institution under the responsibility of the Minister of Education. Financially supported by the State.
Academic year: September to July
Admission requirements: Secondary school certificate (baccalauréat) or recognized equivalent
Main language(s) of instruction: Arabic, French, English
Degrees and diplomas: Licence, Diplôme d'Etudes supérieures, Diplôme d'Ingénieur, Maîtrise, Diplôme d'Etudes approfondies, Diplôme de Doctorat
Student Services: Social Counselling, Canteen
Last Update: 12-12-2011

Private Institutions

Al Imam Al Ouzai University

PO Box 14-5355 Avenue al-Malaab Al Baladi
Beirut 2802 1105
Tel: +961(1) 704-454
Fax: +961(1) 704-453
Website: http://www.ouzai.org
President and Chairman, Board of Trustees: Toufic Al-Houri
Tel: +961(1) 311-831

Faculty
Islamic Business Administration (Business Administration); **Islamic Studies** (Arabic; Ethics; European Languages; History; Islamic Law; Islamic Studies; Koran)

Institute
Supervision of Food Products (Food Science)
History: Founded 1979 as Al Imam Al Ouzai College for Islamic Studies. Acquired present status and title 1986.
Degrees and diplomas: Bachelor's Degree, Master's Degree, Doctorate

Al-Kafaat University (AKI)

Ain Saade, Mount Lebanon
Tel: +961(1) 872-225
Fax: +961(1) 872-230
Website: http://www.aku.edu.lb
President: Fathi Oueida

Faculty
Education (Community Health; Education; Gerontology; Preschool Education; Primary Education; Special Education); **Fine Arts and Advertising** (Advertising and Publicity; Cinema and Television; Interior Design; Marketing; Radio and Television Broadcasting; Theatre)

Institute
Technology (Accountancy; Electronic Engineering; Food Technology; Hotel Management; Management; Mechanical Engineering)
History: Founded 1999.
Degrees and diplomas: Diplôme universitaire de Technologie, Licence, Maîtrise
Last Update: 13-12-2011

Al-Manar University of Tripoli (MUT)

PO Box 676 Al-Manar Boulevard, Abou Samra
Tripoli, Abou Samra
Tel: +961(6) 426-800, +961(6) 426-801, +961(6) 426-802
Fax: +961(6) 426-803
Website: http://www.mut.edu.lb
President: Sami Menkara

Faculty

Architecture and Design (Architecture; Fine Arts; Furniture Design; Graphic Design; Industrial Design; Interior Design; Photography); **Arts and Human Sciences** (Arabic; English; French; Literature; Philosophy; Primary Education; Psychology; Sociology; Translation and Interpretation); **Business Administration** (Accountancy; Banking; Economics; Finance; Information Management; Management; Marketing; Tourism); **Engineering and Information Technology** (Biomedical Engineering; Computer Engineering; Computer Networks; Computer Science; Electronic Engineering; Industrial Engineering; Information Technology; Telecommunications Engineering); **Public Health** (Nursing; Nutrition; Public Health; Speech Therapy and Audiology); **Science** (Biology; Chemistry; Mathematics; Physics)
Further information: Also special programmes: Freshman programme; Intensive English Programme (IEP)
History: Founded 1990, courses started 2003.
Admission requirements: Secondary school certificate (Lebanese Baccalaureate or equivalent); and TOFEL or SAT or MUT English entrance examination or equivalent; For Engineering Students, Mathematics and Physics entrance exams
Fees: (Lebanese Pounds): 6.6m. per annum (fall and spring semesters only)
Main language(s) of instruction: English
Degrees and diplomas: Bachelor's Degree (Agricultural Engineering; Architecture; Arts and Humanities; Business Administration; Design; Engineering; Information Technology; Public Health), Master's Degree (Business Administration)
Student Services: Academic Counselling, Social Counselling, Careers Guidance, Language Laboratory, Facilities for disabled people
Periodicals: MUT Quarterly

American University of Beirut (AUB)

PO Box 11-0236 Riad El Solh
Beirut 1107 2020
Tel: +961(1) 350-000
Fax: +961(1) 351-706
Website: http://www.aub.edu.lb
President: Fadlo Khoury

Faculty

Agriculture and Food Science (*Beirut, Bekaa'a Valley*) (Agricultural Economics; Agriculture; Dietetics; Food Science; Irrigation; Landscape Architecture; Nutrition; Soil Science; Zoology); **Arts and Science** (Anthropology; Arabic; Archaeology; Art History; Arts and Humanities; Behavioural Sciences; Biology; Chemistry; Computer Science; Economics; Education; English; Fine Arts; Geology; History; Mathematics; Middle Eastern Studies; Philosophy; Physics; Political Sciences; Psychology; Public Administration; Social Sciences; Sociology); **Engineering and Architecture** (Architecture; Civil Engineering; Computer Engineering; Electrical Engineering; Engineering; Environmental Engineering; Graphic Design; Mechanical Engineering); **Health Sciences** (Demography and Population; Environmental Studies; Epidemiology; Health Administration; Health Education; Health Sciences; Laboratory Techniques; Public Health); **Medicine** (Anatomy; Biochemistry; Gynaecology and Obstetrics; Immunology; Medicine; Microbiology; Ophthalmology; Orthodontics; Paediatrics; Pathology; Pharmacology; Physiology; Psychiatry and Mental Health; Surgery)

Unit

Environment and Sustainable Development (*ESDU*) (Environmental Studies)

School

Business (*Suleiman Olayan School*) (Business Administration); **Nursing** (*Rafic Hariri*) (Nursing)

Institute

Financial Economics (*IFE*) (Economics; Finance)

Centre

Advanced Mathematical Sciences (*CAMS*) (Mathematics); **Agricultural Research and Education** (*AREC*) (Agriculture; Landscape Architecture); **Arab and Middle Eastern Studies** (*CAMES*) (Arabic; Middle Eastern Studies); **Behavioural Research** (*CBR*) (Arts and Humanities; Behavioural Sciences; Social Sciences); **Central Research Science Lab** (*Kamal A. Shair*); **Research on Population and Health** (*CRPH*) (Demography and Population; Health Sciences); **Science and Mathematics Education** (*SMEC*) (Mathematics Education; Natural Sciences); **Teaching and Learning** (*CTL*)
History: Founded 1866 as Syrian Protestant College with School of Medicine added 1867 and Pharmacy 1871. Rechartered as American University of Beirut 1920. Institutional Accreditation granted 2004. A private non-denominational institution under charter from the

educational authorities of the State of New York, USA, with a self-perpetuating Board of Trustees. Supported by fees, income from an endowment, and private gifts and donations. No organic relationship with any government, religious body, etc.

Academic year: September to June (September-February; February-June)

Admission requirements: Graduation from high school, or secondary school certificate, recognized by the University, and entrance examination including SAT and English language proficiency test such as TOEFL

Fees: 8,000-20,000 per annum depending on programme (US Dollar)

Main language(s) of instruction: English

Accrediting agency: Middle States Commission on Higher Education.

Degrees and diplomas: Bachelor's Degree, Professional Doctorate (Medicine), Master's Degree (Bioengineering; Health Administration; International Studies; Islamic Studies; Orthodontics), Doctorate (Arabic; Bioengineering; Civil Engineering; History; Immunology; Microbiology; Molecular Biology; Pharmacology; Physics; Toxicology)

Student Services: Academic Counselling, Social Counselling, Careers Guidance, Cultural Activities, Sports Facilities, Language Laboratory, Facilities for disabled people, Health Services, Canteen

Periodicals: Arab Political Documents, Berytus

Publishing house: Office of University Publications

Last Update: 12-12-2011

American University of Culture and Education

Badaro
Beirut
Tel: +961(5) 467-346
Fax: +961(5) 467-348
Website: http://auce.edu.lb
President: Pierre Gedeon

Faculty

Arts and Science (Computer Science; English; Literature; Translation and Interpretation); **Business** (Accountancy; Advertising and Publicity; Banking; Business Administration; Finance; Human Resources; Information Management; Marketing; Tourism; Transport Management); **Fine Arts** (Fine Arts; Graphic Design; Interior Design)

Academy

Hospitality (*International*) (Cooking and Catering; Hotel Management; Human Resources; Tourism); **Information Technology** (Information Technology)

History: Founded 1983 as CandE College. Acquired present status and title 2000.

Degrees and diplomas: Bachelor's Degree, Master's Degree

Last Update: 12-12-2011

American University of Science and Technology (AUST)

Ave. Alfred Naccache Ashrafieh
Beirut
Tel: +961(1) 218-716
Fax: +961(1) 339-302
Website: http://www.aust.edu.lb
President: Hiam Sakr
Tel: +961(1) 666-384

School

Arts and Science (Arts and Humanities; Biomedical Engineering; Communication Arts; Computer Engineering; Computer Science; Fine Arts; Graphic Design; Interior Design; Mathematics; Molecular Biology; Social Sciences; Toxicology; Translation and Interpretation); **Business and Economics** (Accountancy; Advertising and Publicity; Business Administration; Finance; Management; Marketing; Tourism); **Health Sciences** (Medical Technology; Molecular Biology; Optics; Optometry; Toxicology)

Further information: Also Zahle and Sidon campuses

History: Founded 1989 as the American Universal College. Acquired present title and status 2007.

Main language(s) of instruction: English and French

Degrees and diplomas: Bachelor's Degree, Master's Degree

Last Update: 12-12-2011

American University of Technology (AUT)

Halat-Byblos Highway Fidar
Halat, Mount Lebanon
Tel: +961(9) 478-143
Fax: +961(9) 478-146
Website: http://www.aut.edu.lb
President: Ghada Sakr Hinain
Tel: +961(9) 478-144

Faculty

Applied Sciences (Business Computing; Computer Science; Information Technology; Nutrition; Water Management); **Arts and Humanities** (Communication Arts; Graphic Design; Interior Design; Public Relations; Radio and Television Broadcasting); **Business Administration**

(Accountancy; Advertising and Publicity; Banking; Business Administration; Economics; Finance; Hotel Management; Human Resources; Management; Marketing; Tourism)

History: Founded 2000.

Academic year: October to June

Admission requirements: High school (G12) for Freshman; Baccalaureate for Sophomore admission

Fees: (US Dollars): 1,800 per semester

Main language(s) of instruction: English

Accrediting agency: Ministry of Higher Education

Degrees and diplomas: Bachelor's Degree (Business Administration; Communication Arts; Computer Engineering; Computer Science; Graphic Design; Interior Design), Master's Degree (Business Administration; Computer Science; Finance; Marketing)

Student Services: Academic Counselling, Social Counselling, Careers Guidance, Sports Facilities, Language Laboratory, Canteen

Last Update: 30-09-2010

Antonine University (UPA)

B.P. 40016
Hadath - Baabda
Tel: +961(5) 92 70 70
Fax: +961(5) 92 70 71
Website: http://www.ua.edu.lb/french/home
Rector: Michel Jalakh

Faculty

Advertising and Media Studies (*Zahleh - Bekaa*) (Advertising and Publicity; Cinema and Television; Communication Studies; Graphic Design; Photography; Printing and Printmaking; Public Relations; Radio and Television Broadcasting); **Business Administration** (Accountancy; Banking; Finance; Information Management; Insurance; Management; Marketing; Tourism); **Engineering** (*Zahle-Bekaa*) (Computer Engineering; Computer Networks; Engineering; Multimedia; Telecommunications Engineering); **Information and Communication** (Advertising and Publicity; Graphic Arts; Multimedia; Radio and Television Broadcasting); **Music and Musicology** (Music; Music Education; Musicology); **Public Health** (Nursing; Physical Therapy; Public Health); **Theological Science and Pastoral Studies** (*Other section in Zghorta-North*) (Pastoral Studies; Religion; Theology)

Further information: Also Campus in Zahlé-Békaa and Mejdlaya-Zgharta.

History: Founded 1996. A private institution under the supervision of the Antonin Maronite Order.

Admission requirements: Secondary school certificate (baccalauréat); Language Evaluation Test

Fees: (US Dollars): 1,000-5,000 per annum

Main language(s) of instruction: Arabic, French, English

Accrediting agency: Lebanese Government

Degrees and diplomas: Licence (Accountancy; Advertising and Publicity; Business Administration; Dental Technology; Finance; Graphic Arts; Human Resources; Management; Marketing; Multimedia; Music; Music Education; Pastoral Studies; Physical Education; Physical Therapy; Radio and Television Broadcasting; Sports; Theology), Diplôme d'Ingénieur (Telecommunications Engineering), Teaching Diploma (Music; Physical Education; Sports; Theology), Master's Degree (Accountancy; Advertising and Publicity; Bible; Business Administration; Computer Science; Finance; Human Resources; Information Sciences; Management; Marketing; Music; Nursing; Pastoral Studies; Physical Education; Religious Studies; Sports; Sports Management; Telecommunications Engineering; Theology; Transport Management)

Student Services: Academic Counselling, Social Counselling, Careers Guidance, Nursery Care, Cultural Activities, Sports Facilities, Language Laboratory, Facilities for disabled people, Health Services, Canteen, Foreign Studies Centre

Last Update: 08-10-2018

Arab Open University - Lebanon Branch (AOU)

Omar Bayhoum street Park Sector
Beirut
Tel: +961(1) 392-139
Fax: +961(1) 392-146
Website: http://www.aou.edu.lb
Branch Director: Fayrouz Farah Sarkis
Tel: +961(3) 761-461

Faculty

Business Studies (Accountancy; Business Administration; Business Education; Economics; Marketing); **Computer Studies** (Business Computing; Computer Science; Information Technology); **Education** (Education; Primary Education); **English Studies** (English Studies)

History: Founded 2002. A private accredited Institution-subsidiary of Open University in Britain.

Admission requirements: Secondary school certificate or equivalent

Fees: (US Dollars): 1,500

Main language(s) of instruction: English, Arabic

Accrediting agency: Lebanese Government and OUVS (Open University Validating Services)

Degrees and diplomas: Bachelor's Degree (Business Administration; Computer Science; English), Master's

Degree (Business Administration; English; Literature). Also Postgraduate Diploma in Education

Student Services: Academic Counselling, Careers Guidance, Cultural Activities, Sports Facilities, Health Services

Last Update: 12-12-2011

Arts, Science and Technology University Lebanon

University Building, Commodore Street, Hamra
Beirut
Tel: +961(01) 343-222
Fax: +961(01) 340-219
Website: http://www.aul.edu.lb
President: Adnan Hamzeh

Faculty

Arts and Humanities (Anthropology; Communication Studies; Literature; Performing Arts; Religious Studies; Sociology); **Business Administration** (Accountancy; Advertising and Publicity; Banking; Business Administration; Finance; Management; Marketing); **Science and Fine Arts** (Biology; Chemistry; Computer Science; Environmental Studies; Graphic Design; Interior Design; Mathematics; Physics; Statistics)

History: Founded 2000 as Institute of Management and University Computer Science. Acquired present title and status 2007

Main language(s) of instruction: English, French

Degrees and diplomas: Bachelor's Degree, Master's Degree

Last Update: 30-09-2010

Beirut Arab University (BAU)

PO Box 115020 Riad El Solh
Beirut 1107 2809
Tel: +961(1) 300-110
Fax: +961(1) 818-402
Website: http://www.bau.edu.lb
President: Amr Galal El-Adawi
Tel: +961(1) 818-297

Faculty

Architectural Engineering (Structural Architecture); **Arts** (Arabic; English; French; Geography; History; Literature; Mass Communication; Philosophy; Psychology; Sociology); **Commerce and Business Administration** (Accountancy; Banking; Economics; Finance; Management; Taxation); **Dentistry** (Dentistry; Oral Pathology; Orthodontics;

Surgery); **Engineering** (Civil Engineering; Computer Engineering; Electrical Engineering; Electronic Engineering; Engineering; Environmental Engineering; Industrial Engineering; Industrial Management; Mechanical Engineering; Petroleum and Gas Engineering; Power Engineering); **Health Sciences** (Laboratory Techniques; Nursing; Nutrition; Physical Therapy); **Law and Political Sciences** (Law; Political Sciences); **Medicine** (Medicine; Surgery); **Pharmacy** (Pharmacy); **Science** (Biology; Biotechnology; Chemistry; Computer Science; Environmental Studies; Information Technology; Mathematics; Physics)

Further information: Other campuses in Bekaa, Debbieh and Tripoli.

History: Founded 1960 by the Lebanese El-Bir and El-Ihsan Society.

Academic year: Three semesters: Autumn, Spring, Summer

Admission requirements: Secondary school certificate (baccalauréat) and entrance examinations.

Fees: (US Dollars): c. 2,000-13,000 per annum

Main language(s) of instruction: Arabic, English, French

Degrees and diplomas: Bachelor's Degree (Architecture; Business Administration; Business and Commerce; Dentistry; Engineering; Fine Arts; Health Sciences; Law; Medicine; Pharmacy; Political Sciences), Master's Degree, Doctorate

Student Services: Academic Counselling, Social Counselling, Careers Guidance, Sports Facilities, Language Laboratory, Health Services, Canteen

Periodicals: Al Zamil Magazine, Architecture and Planning Journal, Journal of Human Sciences, Revue des Etudes Juridiques

Academic Staff 2012-2013	MALE	FEMALE	TOTAL
FULL-TIME	150	65	215
PART-TIME	389	365	754
STAFF WITH DOCTORATE			
FULL-TIME	145	58	c. 203
Student Numbers 2012-2013			
All (Foreign Included)	6324	4729	c. 11053
Foreign only	1844	1231	3075

Last Update: 10-06-2013

Beirut Islamic University (BIU)

Dar El–Fatwa – Zyadyé
Beirut
Tel: +961(1) 797-602
Fax: +961(1) 790-667
Website: http://www.biu.edu.lb
President: Mohamad Rachid Kabbani

Faculty

Islamic Sharia (Islamic Law; Islamic Studies)
History: Founded 1986 as Faculty of the Islamic Call. Acquired present status and title 1996.
Main language(s) of instruction: Arabic
Degrees and diplomas: Licence, Magistère, Doctorate

Business Higher School (ESA)

Rue Clémenceau
Beirut
Tel: +961(1) 373-373
Fax: +961(1) 383-374
Website: http://www.esa.edu.lb
Directeur général: Stéphane Attali

Course/Programme

Business Studies (Business and Commerce; Finance; Health Administration; Management)

Institute

Financial and Monetary Studies (Banking; Finance)
History: Founded 1996 by the French and Lebanese Governments. Instituted by Decree no 9033.
Main language(s) of instruction: French
Degrees and diplomas: Master's Degree (Business Administration; Finance; Health Administration; Marketing). Also Master and Mastère de spécialisation

Daawa University Institute for Islamic Studies (Daawa CIS)

Beirut
Tel: +961(1) 854-069
Fax: +961(1) 854-072
President: Abdel Naser Jabri

Course/Programme

Arabic (Arabic); **Islamic Studies** (Islamic Studies)
History: Founded 1999. Affiliated to the Centre of Religion Endowment.
Admission requirements: Lebanese Baccalauréat or equivalent
Main language(s) of instruction: Arabic
Accrediting agency: Ministry of Higher Education
Degrees and diplomas: Licence, Magistère
Student Services: Sports Facilities, Canteen

Global University (GU)

Batrakieh Street
Beirut 15-5085
Tel: +961(1) 358-058

Fax: +961(1) 358-059
Website: http://www.gu.edu.lb
President: Adnan Traboulsi
Tel: +961(3) 725-680

Faculty

Administrative Sciences (Accountancy; Business Administration; Computer Science; Finance; Health Administration; Human Resources; Information Management; Information Sciences; Information Technology; Management; Marketing); **Health Sciences** (Dietetics; Health Sciences; Laboratory Techniques; Midwifery; Nursing; Nutrition; Physical Therapy); **Literature and Humanities** (Arabic; Communication Studies; Education; English; French; Geography; History; Islamic Studies; Linguistics; Literature; Media Studies; Political Sciences; Translation and Interpretation)
History: Created 1992. Acquired current status and title 1999.
Academic year: October to September (autumn semester, 4 months, spring semester, 4 months, summer semester, 2 months)
Admission requirements: Baccalauréat libanais (or equivalent secondary school diploma).
Fees: (Lebanese Pounds): 3m. per semester, autumn and spring; 1m. summer semester
Main language(s) of instruction: English, some Arabic
Accrediting agency: Association of Arab Universities (AARU); Ministry of Higher Education of Lebanon
Degrees and diplomas: Bachelor's Degree (Accountancy; Business and Commerce; Computer Science; Education; Health Administration; Human Resources; Information Technology; Linguistics; Management; Marketing; Translation and Interpretation), Master's Degree (Arabic; Business Administration; Islamic Studies; Literature), Doctorate (Arabic; Education; Islamic Studies; Linguistics; Literature; Translation and Interpretation)
Student Services: Academic Counselling, Social Counselling, Careers Guidance, Nursery Care, Cultural Activities, Sports Facilities, Language Laboratory, Facilities for disabled people, Health Services, Canteen, Foreign Studies Centre

Haigazian University (HU)

PO Box 11-1748 Riad el Sohl
Beirut 11072090
Tel: +961(1) 349-230, +961(1) 353-010
Fax: +961(1) 353-012
Website: http://www.haigazian.edu.lb
President: Paul Haidostian
Tel: +961(1) 739-412

Faculty

Business Administration and Economics (Accountancy; Advertising and Publicity; Business Administration;

Economics; Finance; Hotel Management; Law; Management Systems); **Humanities** (Arabic; Armenian; English; History; Literature; Music; Philosophy; Religion); **Science** (Biology; Chemistry; Computer Science; Mathematics; Medical Technology; Physics); **Social and Behavioural Sciences** (Behavioural Sciences; Christian Religious Studies; Education; Political Sciences; Psychology; Social Sciences; Social Work)

History: Founded 1955, acquired present status 1996.

Academic year: October to June (October-February; February-June)

Admission requirements: Secondary school certificate (baccalauréat). TOEFL test for all students

Fees: (Lebanese Pounds): 9,450,000 per annum (US Dollars, 6,300)

Main language(s) of instruction: English

Accrediting agency: Lebanese Government

Degrees and diplomas: Bachelor's Degree (Arabic; Biology; Business Administration; Chemistry; Christian Religious Studies; Computer Science; Cultural Studies; Economics; Education; English; History; Mathematics; Medical Technology; Music; Physics; Psychology; Social Work), Master's Degree (Business Administration; Education; Psychology). Normal Diploma

Student Services: Academic Counselling, Social Counselling, Cultural Activities, Sports Facilities, Health Services

Last Update: 13-12-2011

Holy Family University - Batroon

Batroon 4001, Norht Lebanon
Tel: +961(6) 642-250
Website: http://www.usf.edu.lb
Rector: Sister Marie du Christ
Tel: +961(3) 549-913

Faculty

Business and Management (Accountancy; Banking; Business Computing; Finance; Insurance; Management; Marketing); **Education and Specialized Education** (Education; Educational Administration; Pedagogy; Special Education; Teacher Training); **Health** (Laboratory Techniques; Medical Auxiliaries; Medical Technology; Midwifery; Nursing; Physical Therapy)

History: Founded 2009.

Academic year: October to July

Degrees and diplomas: Licence, Master's Degree

Last Update: 04-11-2013

Holy Family University Institute of Physiotherapy

Batroun, North Lebanon
Tel: +961(6) 642-250

Fax: +961(6) 743-154
President: Hilda Chlala

Course/Programme

Nursing (Nursing); **Physiotherapy** (Physical Therapy)

History: Founded 2000.

Main language(s) of instruction: French

Degrees and diplomas: Licence

Last Update: 30-09-2010

Holy Spirit University of Kaslik (USEK)

PO Box 446
Jounieh
Tel: +961(9) 600-000
Fax: +961(9) 600-100
Website: http://www.usek.edu.lb
Rector: Fr. Georges Hobeika

Faculty

Agricultural Sciences (Agriculture; Dietetics; Food Science; Food Technology; Nutrition); **Business and Commercial Sciences** (Accountancy; Business Computing; Finance; Hotel and Restaurant; Hotel Management; Information Technology; International Business; Management; Marketing; Transport Management); **Engineering** (Chemical Engineering; Computer Engineering; Electrical Engineering; Electronic Engineering; Mechanical Engineering; Telecommunications Engineering); **Fine and Applied Arts** (Architecture; Fine Arts; Graphic Design; Interior Design; Performing Arts; Religious Art; Theatre; Visual Arts); **Law** (Commercial Law; International Law; Law; Private Law; Public Law); **Letters** (Arabic; Business and Commerce; Communication Studies; English; French; Journalism; Literature; Modern Languages; Translation and Interpretation); **Medicine and Medical Sciences** (Medicine); **Music** (Music; Music Education; Music Theory and Composition; Musicology; Religious Music; Singing); **Philosophy and Humanities** (Clinical Psychology; Education; Educational Psychology; Educational Technology; Industrial and Organizational Psychology; Philosophy; Psychology; Social Sciences); **Science** (Biological and Life Sciences; Chemistry; Computer Science; Mathematics; Technology); **Theology** (*Pontifical*) (Family Studies; Pastoral Studies; Religion; Religious Studies; Theology)

College

Doctoral Studies (Arts and Humanities; Business and Commerce; Fine Arts; Music; Philosophy; Theology)

Institute

History (Archaeology; Art History; History); **Liturgy** (Christian Religious Studies; Religion); **Nursing** (Nursing); **Political Science and Administration** (International Relations; Political Sciences; Public Administration)

Centre

Research

History: Founded 1961 and run by the Lebanese Maronite Order.

Academic year: September to July

Admission requirements: Secondary school certificate (baccalauréat Part II) or foreign equivalent

Fees: 4,320-7,920 per annum (US Dollar)

Main language(s) of instruction: French, English, Arabic

Degrees and diplomas: Bachelor's Degree, Master's Degree, Diplôme de Doctorat (Arabic; Archaeology; Art History; Business Administration; Education; English; French; History; Law; Literature; Music; Music Education; Performing Arts; Philosophy; Psychology; Social Sciences; Theology; Translation and Interpretation; Visual Arts)

Student Services: Academic Counselling, Social Counselling, Careers Guidance, Cultural Activities, Sports Facilities, Language Laboratory, Health Services, Canteen

Periodicals: Actes des colloques de l'Université Saint-Esprit de Kaslik, Annales de Philosophie et des Sciences Humaines, Collection de la bibliothèque de l'Université Saint-Esprit de Kalik, Maronite Encyclopaedia, Parole de l'Orient, Revue des Lettres et de Traduction, Revue juridique, Revue Théologique de Kaslik - RThk, Sciences et Technologies

Publishing house: Publications de l'Université Saint-Esprit de Kaslik (PUSEK)

Student Numbers 2012-2013	MALE	FEMALE	TOTAL
All (Foreign Included)			7141

Last Update: 11-03-2013

International School of Management

Aintoura, Mont-Liban
Tel: +96(9) 233-183
Website: http://www.esig.edu.lb

Course/Programme

Management (Business Computing; Finance; Human Resources; Management; Marketing)

History: Founded 2000

Main language(s) of instruction: English, French

Degrees and diplomas: Licence, Magistère

Last Update: 16-12-2011

Jinan University (JU)

PO Box 818
Tripoli, Abou Samra
Tel: +961(6) 447-906
Fax: +961(6) 447-900
Website: http://www.jinan.edu.lb
President: Bassam Barake

Faculty

Business Administration (Accountancy; Advertising and Publicity; Business Administration; Business Computing; Economics; Finance; International Business; Marketing; Taxation); **Information and Communication** (Communication Studies; Journalism; Radio and Television Broadcasting); **Literature and Humanities** (Arts and Humanities; Education; Islamic Studies; Literature; Translation and Interpretation); **Public Health** (Laboratory Techniques; Medical Technology; Nursing; Public Health; Social Work)

History: Founded 1988. Acquired present status 1999.

Academic year: September to June

Admission requirements: Secondary school certificate, entrance exam for Bachelor's Degree

Fees: (US Dollars): 50-160 per credit

Main language(s) of instruction: Arabic, French, English

Accrediting agency: Ministry of Education and Higher Education

Degrees and diplomas: Bachelor's Degree (Arts and Humanities; Business Administration; Communication Arts; Literature; Public Health), Master's Degree (Arts and Humanities; Business Administration; Communication Arts; Literature), Doctorate (Arts and Humanities; Business Administration; Communication Arts; Literature). Also Honour's degree in Business Administration; Communication; Humanities and Literature (1 yr)

Student Services: Academic Counselling, Social Counselling, Careers Guidance, Nursery Care, Cultural Activities, Sports Facilities, Language Laboratory, Facilities for disabled people, Health Services, Canteen, Foreign Studies Centre

Periodicals: Jinan Journal for Scientific Research

Publishing house: Al-hasad

La Sagesse University (ULS)

Furn El-Chebbak
Beirut 501-50
Tel: +961(1) 291-091
Fax: +961(1) 294-442
Website: http://www.uls.edu.lb
Rector: Camille Moubarak

Faculty

Canon Law (Canon Law; Law); **Ecclesiastical Science** (Religion; Theology); **Health Sciences** (Health Administration; Nursing); **Hospitality Management** (Hotel and Restaurant; Hotel Management; Tourism); **Law** (Law); **Management and Finance** (Business Administration; Economics; Finance; Management); **Political Science and International Relations** (International Relations; Political Sciences)

History: Founded 1875, acquired present status 1999.

Admission requirements: Secondary school certificate (baccalauréat) or recognized equivalent

Fees: (US Dollars): 1,000-4,000

Main language(s) of instruction: Arabic, French, English

Degrees and diplomas: Licence, Diplôme d'Etudes supérieures spécialisées, Diplôme d'Etudes approfondies, Master's Degree, Doctorate. Also Master and Mastère

Student Services: Academic Counselling, Social Counselling, Careers Guidance, Sports Facilities, Language Laboratory, Facilities for disabled people, Health Services

Periodicals: Canon Law, L'alliance de la Sagesse, Law and General Culture, Perspectives

Last Update: 12-12-2011

Lebanese American University (LAU)

PO Box 13-5053 Koritem
Beirut
Tel: +961(1) 867-620
Fax: +961(1) 867-098
Website: http://www.lau.edu.lb
President: Joseph G. Jabbra
Tel: +961(1) 867-618

School

Architecture and Design (Architecture; Computer Graphics; Design; Fine Arts; Graphic Design; Interior Design); **Arts and Science** (Arts and Humanities; Chemistry; Computer Science; Education; Mathematics; Molecular Biology; Natural Sciences; Nutrition; Philosophy; Political Sciences; Psychology; Social Work); **Business** (Business Administration; Business and Commerce; Economics; Tourism); **Engineering** (Civil Engineering; Computer Engineering; Electrical Engineering; Environmental Engineering; Industrial Engineering; Mechanical Engineering); **Medicine** (*Gilbert and Rose-Marie Chagoury*) (Medicine); **Pharmacy** (Pharmacy)

Institute

Banking and Finance (*IBAF*) (Banking; Finance); **Diplomacy and Conflict Transformation** (International Relations; Peace and Disarmament); **Family and Enterpreneurial Business** (*IFEB*) (Management); **Hospitality and Tourism Management** (Hotel and Restaurant; Hotel Management; Tourism); **Islamic Art and Architecture** (Architecture; Art Education); **Media Training and Research** (*Beirut*) (Media Studies); **Migration Studies** (Demography and Population); **Peace and Justice Education** (*IPJ*) (Peace and Disarmament); **Software** (*SI*) (Software Engineering); **Teacher Training** (Teacher Training); **Urban Planning** (*UPI*) (Town Planning); **Water Resources and Environmental Technology** (*IWRET*) (Environmental Studies; Water Science); **Women's Studies in the Arab World** (Women's Studies)

History: Founded 1924 by the United Presbyterian Church, USA. Acquired present status 1994. Campuses in Beirut, Byblos, Sidon

Academic year: October to September (October-February; February-June). Also 2 summer sessions (July to September)

Admission requirements: Graduation from high school with a minimum of 12 yrs study and entrance examination

Fees: 385 per credit per annum, depending on majors (US Dollar)

Main language(s) of instruction: English

Accrediting agency: The University of the State of New York-Albany; American Council on Pharmaceutical Education; French Government; Arab Foundation of Engineering Organisations

Degrees and diplomas: Bachelor's Degree (Arabic; Architecture; Biology; Business and Commerce; Chemistry; Cinema and Television; Civil Engineering; Computer Engineering; Computer Science; Economics; Electrical Engineering; Engineering; English; Fashion Design; Fine Arts; Graphic Design; History; Hotel and Restaurant; Industrial Engineering; Interior Design; Journalism; Mass Communication; Mathematics; Mechanical Engineering; Nursing; Nutrition; Performing Arts; Petroleum and Gas Engineering; Pharmacy; Philosophy; Political Sciences; Psychology; Social Work; Tourism; Translation and Interpretation), Master's Degree (Actuarial Science; Applied Mathematics; Business Administration; Civil Engineering; Commercial Law; Computer Engineering; Computer Science; Economics; Education; Engineering Management; Environmental Engineering; Fine Arts; Gender Studies; Industrial Engineering; International Studies; Medicine; Molecular Biology; Pharmacy), Doctorate (Medicine; Pharmacy)

Student Services: Academic Counselling, Social Counselling, Nursery Care, Cultural Activities, Sports Facilities, Language Laboratory, Facilities for disabled people, Health Services, Canteen

Last Update: 12-09-2017

Lebanese Canadian University (LCU)

PO Box 32 Zouk Mikael
Aintoura, Kesrouan
Tel: +961(9) 233-183, +961(9) 232-183, +961(9) 232-185
Fax: +961(9) 233-184
Website: http://www.esig.edu.lb
President: Rony Abi Nakhlé

Faculty

Arts and Humanities; **Arts and Science** (Computer Science; Geography; Graphic Design; Interior Design; Mathematics; Town Planning); **Management** (Accountancy; Business Administration; Business Computing; Economics; Human Resources; Management; Marketing; Tourism)
History: Founded 2000. Acquired present status 2008.
Main language(s) of instruction: English and French
Degrees and diplomas: Bachelor's Degree, Master's Degree, Doctorate

Lebanese International University

Beirut Campus PO Box 146404
Beirut
Tel: +961(1) 706-881
Fax: +961(1) 306-044
Website: http://www.liu.edu.lb
President: Abdel Rahim Mrad

Faculty

Agriculture (Food Science; Nutrition); **Business and Management** (Accountancy; Business Computing; Finance; Hotel and Restaurant; Information Management; International Business; Management; Marketing; Tourism); **Education** (Education; Foreign Languages Education; Technology Education)

College

Arts and Science (Biochemistry; Computer Science; Fine Arts; Health Sciences; Information Technology; Interior Design; Mathematics; Physics); **Engineering** (Computer Engineering; Electrical Engineering; Electronic Engineering; Industrial Engineering; Mechanical Engineering; Surveying and Mapping; Telecommunications Engineering); **Pharmacy** (Pharmacy)
Further information: Also campuses in Bekaa, Tripoli, Nabatieh, Saida, Jdeideh Aden, Sanaa, Taiz, Mukalla, Nowakchott, Dakar, Casablanca
History: Founded 2001 as Jamiat Al Bekaa (Al Bekaa University), acquired present name 2008. Operates six campuses in Lebanon, four campuses in Yemen, one in Senegal and one in Mauritania.
Admission requirements: Graduation from High School or equivalent secondary school certificate; entrance examination in English, Biology, Chemistry, Physics, Mathematics.
Main language(s) of instruction: English
Degrees and diplomas: Bachelor's Degree, Professional Doctorate, Teaching Diploma, Master's Degree
Last Update: 11-05-2017

Lebanese-French University of Technology and Applied Sciences (ULF)

Rue Maamari, à côté de l'hôpital Bekhazi Clemenceau
Beyrouth
Tel: +961(1) 378 795
Website: http://www.ulf.edu.lb
President: Mohamad Salhab

Faculty

Engineering (Civil Engineering; Electrical Engineering; Electronic Engineering; Energy Engineering; Mechanical Engineering); **Fine Art** (Fashion Design; Graphic Design; Interior Design); **Management** (Business Administration; Business Computing; Finance; Hotel Management; International Business; Marketing); **Science and Letters** (Biomedicine; Environmental Studies; Information Sciences; Information Technology; Mechanics; Social Sciences); **Technology** (Banking; Industrial Engineering; Information Technology; Maintenance Technology; Management)
History: Created 1996 as university institute of technology, acquired current title and status 2007.
Admission requirements: Baccalauréat, or other recognized secondary school certificate
Main language(s) of instruction: English, French
Accrediting agency: Ministry of Education and Higher Education (Directorate General of Higher Education)
Degrees and diplomas: Diplôme universitaire de Technologie (Banking; Industrial Engineering; Maintenance Technology; Telecommunications Engineering), Licence (Biomedicine; Business Administration; Environmental Studies; Fashion Design; Graphic Design; Hotel Management; Information Sciences; Information Technology; Interior Design; International Business; Management; Marketing; Social Sciences; Technology), Diplôme d'Ingénieur (Civil Engineering; Electrical Engineering; Electronic Engineering; Energy Engineering; Mechanical Engineering), Maîtrise (Banking; Business Administration; Computer Science; Finance; Information Technology)
Last Update: 22-08-2017

Lebanese-German University (HLIP)

Sahel Alma, Highway P.O.Box 206
Jounieh, Kaserwan
Tel: +961(9) 938-938
Fax: +961(9) 938-933
Website: http://www.lgu.edu.lb
President: Marwan El Rassi

Faculty

Arts and Education (Film; Performing Arts; Preschool Education; Primary Education; Theatre); **Business and Insurance** (Accountancy; Banking; Finance; Hotel Management; Human Resources; Insurance; Management; Marketing); **Public Health** (Biomedical Engineering; Laboratory Techniques; Nursing; Nutrition; Physical Therapy)

Institute

Chartered Insurance (Insurance); **Family Entrepreneurship** (Business Administration; Home Economics); **Healthcare Management and Quality** (Health Administration); **Media Professional Training** (Media Studies); **School Teacher Training** (Teacher Training)

Centre

Business Training & Research (Business Administration); **Global Languages** (Modern Languages)
History: Founded 1999 as Institut d'Enseignement supérieur de Physiothérapie. Acquired present title and status 2007.
Admission requirements: Secondary school leaving certificate and entrance examination
Main language(s) of instruction: English and French
Degrees and diplomas: Licence, Maîtrise
Last Update: 13-12-2011

Makassed University of Beirut (MUB)

Uthman Bin Affan Street, Mseitbeh
Beirut 14-6179
Tel: +961(1) 377-533
Fax: +961(1) 377-285
Website: http://www.makassed.org.lb
President: Hisham Nashabe
Tel: +961(1) 365-394

Faculty

Management and Information Technology (Information Technology; Management); **Nursing and Health Sciences** (Health Sciences; Nursing; Radiology; Respiratory Therapy)
History: Makassed Association established 1878. Founded 1981. Acquired present status and title 1986.

Admission requirements: Secondary school certificate (baccalauréat) or equivalent
Fees: (US Dollars): 2,500 per annum
Main language(s) of instruction: Arabic, English
Accrediting agency: Ministry of Higher Education
Degrees and diplomas: Bachelor's Degree (Islamic Studies; Nursing), Master's Degree (Islamic Studies), Doctorate (Islamic Studies)
Student Services: Academic Counselling, Social Counselling
Periodicals: The Journal of the University

Middle East University (MEU)

PO Box 1170
Beirut
Tel: +961(1) 883-065
Fax: +961(1) 684-800
Website: http://www.meu.edu.lb
President: L. Hongisto

Faculty

Arts and Science (Biology; Business Administration; Computer Science; English; History; Religion; Teacher Training); **Business Administration** (Accountancy; Banking; Business Administration; Computer Science; Finance; Hotel Management; Management; Marketing); **Education** (Education; Primary Education; Secondary Education); **Philosophy and Theology** (Philosophy; Theology)
History: Founded 1939 as The Adventist College of Beirut in Mouseitbeh. Renamed Middle East College 1946. Acquired present status and title 2001.
Accrediting agency: Lebanese Ministry of Education and Higher learning and Accrediting Association of Seventh-day Adventist Schools, Colleges, and Universities (AAA).
Degrees and diplomas: Bachelor's Degree, Master's Degree
Last Update: 13-12-2011

Modern University for Business and Science (MUBS)

Old Saida Road
Damour, Al-Chouf
Tel: +961(5) 601-801
Fax: +961(5) 601-667
Website: http://www.mubs.edu.lb
President: Ali Cheaib
Tel: +961(3) 740-925

Faculty

Business Administration (Accountancy; Banking; Business Administration; Finance; Human Resources; Information Sciences; Management; Marketing); **Computer and Applied Sciences** (Computer Science; Graphic Design; Information Sciences; Information Technology); **Education and Social Work** (Educational Administration; Preschool Education; Social Work; Teacher Training)

History: Founded 2000. Formerly known as MECAT (Al Mahaad Al Jamee Lilidara wal Ouloum). Acquired present status and title 2007.

Degrees and diplomas: Bachelor's Degree (Business Administration; Computer Engineering; Computer Science; Education; Graphic Design; Social Work), Master's Degree (Business Administration; Management)

Last Update: 05-01-2010

Notre Dame University-Louaizé (NDU)

PO Box 72 Zouk Mikael
Zouk Mosbeh, Kaserwan
Tel: +961(9) 218-950
Fax: +961(9) 218-771
Website: http://www.ndu.edu.lb
President: Walid Moussa
Tel: +961(9) 218-772, +961(9) 208-888

Faculty

Architecture, Art and Design (Architecture; Display and Stage Design; Fashion Design; Fine Arts; Graphic Design; Interior Design; Landscape Architecture; Music Education; Musicology); **Business Administration and Economics** (Accountancy; Banking; Business Administration; Economics; Finance; Health Administration; Hotel and Restaurant; Hotel Management; Human Resources; International Business; Management; Marketing; Tourism; Transport Management); **Engineering** (Civil Engineering; Computer Engineering; Electrical Engineering; Engineering; Mechanical Engineering; Telecommunications Engineering); **Humanities** (Advertising and Publicity; Applied Linguistics; Arabic; Arts and Humanities; Clinical Psychology; Communication Arts; Education; Educational Psychology; English; Industrial and Organizational Psychology; Journalism; Marketing; Mass Communication; Media Studies; Radio and Television Broadcasting; Special Education; Translation and Interpretation); **Natural and Applied Sciences** (Actuarial Science; Biology; Biotechnology; Business Computing; Chemistry; Computer Graphics; Dietetics; Environmental Studies; Geography; Industrial Chemistry; Information Sciences; Information Technology; Insurance; Laboratory Techniques; Mathematics; Mathematics and Computer Science; Mathematics Education; Medical Technology; Natural Sciences; Nutrition; Pharmacology; Physics; Statistics); **Nursing and Health Sciences** (Health Sciences; Nursing); **Political Science, Public Administration and Diplomacy** (American Studies; Comparative Law; Criminal Law; European Studies; International Law; International Relations; Mediterranean Studies; Political Sciences; Public Administration)

Department/Division

Continuing Education (Business Administration; Computer Science; English; Hotel Management; Leadership; Management; Modern Languages; Music)

Research Division

Applied Research in Education (*CARE*) (Curriculum; Education; Educational Research); **Digitization and Preservation** (*CDP*) (Heritage Preservation); **Lebanese Emigration Research** (*LERC*) (Demography and Population); **Marian Studies** (*MSC*) (Religious Studies); **Societal Research** (*Lebanese Center for Societal Research (LCSR)*) (Economics; Educational Sciences; Political Sciences; Social Studies); **Water, Energy and Environment Research** (*WEERC*) (Environmental Management; Environmental Studies; Water Management; Water Science)

Further information: Also campuses in North Lebanon and in the Shouf, southeast of Beirut

History: Founded 1978 as Louaizé Centre for Higher Education, affiliated to Beirut University College. Acquired present status and title 1987.

Academic year: October to August (October-February; February-June; July-August)

Admission requirements: Secondary school certificate (baccalauréat) or equivalent

Fees: 4.6m. per semester; Engineering and Architecture, 5.4m.; Graduate studies, 4.8m (Lebanese Pound)

Main language(s) of instruction: English

Degrees and diplomas: Bachelor's Degree, Teaching Diploma, Master's Degree

Student Services: Academic Counselling, Social Counselling, Careers Guidance, Sports Facilities, Language Laboratory, Facilities for disabled people, Health Services

Periodicals: NDU Chronicle (e-bulletin)

Last Update: 30-09-2010

Rafik Hariri University (RHU)

PO Box 10 Damour – Chouf 2010
Al Mishrief 2010
Tel: +961(5) 603-090

Fax: +961(5) 601-380
Website: http://www.rhu.edu.lb
President: Ahmad Smaili

College

Arts (Advertising and Publicity; English; English Studies; Journalism; Literature; Preschool Education; Primary Education; Psychology; Public Relations; Sociology); **Business Administration** (Accountancy; Business Administration; Business Computing; Finance; Hotel Management; Management; Marketing); **Engineering** (Civil Engineering; Computer Engineering; Electrical Engineering; Environmental Engineering; Mechanical Engineering; Telecommunications Engineering); **Sciences and Information Systems** (Biochemistry; Biology; Chemistry; Computer Graphics; Computer Science; Geology; Mathematics; Physics; Software Engineering)
History: Founded 1999. Previously known as Hariri Canadian University (Moujamaa al Hariri al Kanadi). Acquired current title 2011.
Academic year: September- December; January –April; Summer terms: May-June, July-August
Admission requirements: High School certificate; English proficiency required.
Fees: Contact institution for more details
Main language(s) of instruction: English
Accrediting agency: Ministry of Education and Higher Education, Directorate General of Higher Education.
Degrees and diplomas: Bachelor's Degree (Accountancy; Advertising and Publicity; Biomedical Engineering; Business Computing; Civil Engineering; Computer Engineering; Computer Science; Electrical Engineering; English; Finance; Graphic Design; Health Administration; Human Resources; Interior Design; Journalism; Management; Marketing; Mathematics; Mechanical Engineering; Primary Education; Telecommunications Engineering), Teaching Diploma (Primary Education; Secondary Education), Master's Degree (Biomedical Engineering; Business Administration; Civil Engineering; Computer Engineering; Electrical Engineering; Mechanical Engineering; Telecommunications Engineering)
Student Services: Academic Counselling, Careers Guidance, Sports Facilities, Language Laboratory, Health Services, Canteen

Academic Staff 2012-2013	MALE	FEMALE	TOTAL
FULL-TIME	59	38	97
PART-TIME	58	39	97
STAFF WITH DOCTORATE			
FULL-TIME	24	1	25
Student Numbers 2012-2013			
All (Foreign Included)	835	407	1242
Foreign only	45	44	89

Last Update: 12-10-2017

Saint Paul's Institute of Philosophy and Theology

Harissa via Jounieh
Tel: +961(9) 903-920
Fax: +961(9) 903-818
Rector: Georges Khawam
Tel: +961(9) 903-818

Faculty

Philosophy (Philosophy); **Theology** (Theology)

Research Division
Muslim-Christian Dialogue
History: Founded 1939 as St Paul's School, acquired present status and title 1972.
Academic year: October to May (October-January; February-May)
Admission requirements: Secondary school certificate (baccalauréat) or foreign equivalent
Fees: (Lebanese Pounds): Tuition, c. 2.4m. per annum
Main language(s) of instruction: French
Degrees and diplomas: Licence (Philosophy; Theology)
Student Services: Academic Counselling, Sports Facilities

Saint-Joseph University (USJ)

BP 17-5208 Mar Mikhaël, Rue de Damas
Beirut 1104 2020
Tel: +961(1) 421-000
Fax: +961(1) 421-001
Website: http://www.usj.edu.lb
Recteur: Salim Daccache, s.j.
Tel: +961(1) 421-101

Faculty

Arts and Humanities (*French Literature branches in USJ regional centres: North Lebanon and South Lebanon*) (Anthropology; Archaeology; Arts and Humanities; Clinical Psychology; Communication Studies; Contemporary History; Educational Psychology; Environmental Studies; French; Geography; History; Human Resources; Industrial and Organizational Psychology; International Relations; Literature; Philosophy; Psychology; Public Relations; Sociology; Tourism); **Business Administration and Management** (*Branches in USJ regional centres: North Lebanon, South Lebanon and Bekaa*) (Accountancy; Banking; Business Administration; Finance; Health Administration; Management); **Dentistry** (Dentistry; Oral Pathology; Orthodontics); **Economics** (Banking; Economics; Finance); **Education** (Education; Educational Administration; Educational and

Student Counselling; Educational Sciences); **Law and Political Science** (Commercial Law; Law; Political Sciences; Private Law; Public Law); **Medicine** (Biology; Medicine); **Nursing** (*Branches in USJ regional centres: North Lebanon, South Lebanon and Bekaa*) (Nursing); **Pharmacy** (Biology; Dietetics; Nutrition; Pharmacy); **Religious Sciences** (Religion; Religious Studies); **Science** (Biology; Chemistry; Earth Sciences; Mathematics; Natural Sciences; Physics)

Unit

Open University (Architecture; Art History; Economics; History; Hygiene; Law; Literature; Musicology; Painting and Drawing; Philosophy; Political Sciences; Religious Studies)

School

Agro-industry (*Tanael, Bekaa*) (Agricultural Engineering); **Engineering** (Building Technologies; Civil Engineering; Computer Engineering; Construction Engineering; Electrical and Electronic Equipment and Maintenance; Electrical Engineering; Engineering; Environmental Engineering; Mechanical Engineering; Telecommunications Engineering); **Medical Laboratory Techniques** (Laboratory Techniques); **Mediterranean Agronomy** (*Tanael, Bekaa*) (Agronomy); **Midwifery** (Midwifery); **Social Work Training** (*USJ regional centre in North Lebanon*) (Social and Community Services; Social Work; Special Education); **Translation and Interpretation** (Modern Languages; Translation and Interpretation)

Institute

Business Administration (Advertising and Publicity; Business Computing; Hotel Management; Marketing); **Communication and Information** (Information Sciences; Telecommunications Services); **Confucius** (Chinese); **Health and Social Protection** (Health Administration; Public Health; Social Welfare); **Insurance Studies** (Insurance); **Islamic-Christian Studies** (Christian Religious Studies; Comparative Religion; Islamic Studies); **Oriental Literature** (Arabic; Education; History; Islamic Studies; Philosophy); **Physiotherapy** (Neurological Therapy; Osteopathy; Physical Therapy); **Political Science** (Political Sciences); **Psychomotricity** (Psychometrics; Rehabilitation and Therapy); **Religious Sciences** (Religious Studies); **Speech Therapy** (Speech Therapy and Audiology); **Teachers** (*Lebanese*) (Educational Sciences; Preschool Education; Primary Education; Special Education); **Theatre, Audiovisual and Film Studies** (Cinema and Television; Film; Theatre)

Centre

Arabic Research and Studies (Arabic); **Banking** (Banking; Finance); **Euro-Lebanese Intercultural Studies** (Arts and Humanities; Cultural Studies); **Japanese** (Japanese);

Modern Languages (*Branches in USJ regional centres: North Lebanon, South Lebanon, Bekaa*) (Modern Languages)

Laboratory

Biochemistry (Biochemistry); **Biostatical and Medical Epidemiology** (Epidemiology); **Cartography** (Surveying and Mapping); **E-learning Technologies** (Pedagogy); **Experimental Psychology** (Experimental Psychology); **Human Hispathology** (Histology; Pathology); **Medical Computer Science** (Computer Science); **Medical Genetics** (Genetics); **Mineralized Tissues** (Genetics); **Molecular Biology** (Molecular Biology); **Pharmacology** (Pharmacology); **Physiology** (Physiology); **Socio-economical Reality** (Economics); **Teaching Pedagogy** (Pedagogy; Teacher Training); **Teledetection** (Geography); **Tourism** (Tourism); **Toxicology** (Toxicology)

Research Division

Arabic Terminology (Arabic; Terminology); **Archeology** (*Francis Hours*) (Archaeology; Prehistory); **Bioequivalence and Medicament Control** (Pharmacy); **Chemistry and Physics** (Chemistry; Physics); **Christian Arabs** (Religious Studies); **Construction** (Construction Engineering); **Economics** (Economics); **Electrical Industries and Telecommunications** (Telecommunications Engineering); **Ethics** (Ethics); **European Union Studies** (European Union Law; Law; Regional Studies); **Michel Henry** (French); **Middle East Markets** (Business and Commerce; Middle Eastern Studies); **Modelling and Information Technology** (Computer Networks; Data Processing; Information Sciences; Information Technology); **Modern Arab World Studies** (Middle Eastern Studies); **Religious Interpretation** (Religious Studies); **Rights of the Arab World** (Middle Eastern Studies); **Water and Environment** (Environmental Studies; Water Science)

Further information: Also Teaching Hospital; Speech Therapy Centre; Psychomotor Therapy Centre; Family and Community Health Centre; Dental Care Centres; Technological Pole 'Berytech'; Health Pole 'Berytechll'.

History: Founded 1875 by the Society of Jesus. Title of University confirmed by Pope Leo XIII 1881. Faculty of Medicine established 1883 by agreement with French Government. A private institution. Received some financial assistance from the French State until 1975 when the University became an autonomous institution financed by tuition fees and government subsidies. University Regional Centres at: Ras Maska (North Lebanon), Zahlé/Hazerta (Bekaa) and Saïda-Bramieh (South Lebanon). University Foreign Centres in Abudhabi (United Arab Emirates)

Academic year: September to June (September-January; February-June)

Admission requirements: Secondary school certificate (baccalauréat) or foreign equivalent; French language test; Entrance examination

Fees: (US Dollars): average 100 per credit; lowest, 75 per credit; highest, 201 per credit

Main language(s) of instruction: French, English obligatory in all majors, Arabic required in some majors

Degrees and diplomas: Diplôme d'Université (Child Care and Development; Cognitive Sciences; Community Health; Dental Technology; Dentistry; Ethics; Gastroenterology; Gynaecology and Obstetrics; Health Education; Health Sciences; Information Management; Islamic Studies; Nursing; Occupational Health; Oncology; Pathology; Pedagogy; Pharmacology; Religion; Religious Studies; Social Work; Surgery), Licence (Administration; Advertising and Publicity; Anthropology; Archaeology; Biological and Life Sciences; Biology; Business Administration; Business Computing; Chemistry; Clinical Psychology; Contemporary History; Cultural Studies; Economics; Educational Psychology; Environmental Studies; French; Hotel Management; Insurance; International Relations; Laboratory Techniques; Labour and Industrial Relations; Law; Literature; Mathematics; Midwifery; Modern Languages; Nursing; Nutrition; Orthopaedics; Pedagogy; Philosophy; Physics; Preschool Education; Primary Education; Psychology; Radio and Television Broadcasting; Regional Planning; Rehabilitation and Therapy; Religious Studies; Social Work; Sociology; Special Education; Telecommunications Engineering; Theatre; Tourism), Certificat d'Aptitude pédagogique de l'Enseignement secondaire (Pedagogy), Diplôme d'Etudes supérieures (Dental Technology; Dentistry; Oral Pathology; Orthodontics; Paediatrics; Periodontics; Surgery), Diplôme d'Ingénieur (Agricultural Business; Agronomy; Biomedicine; Civil Engineering; Computer Science; Construction Engineering; Electrical Engineering; Engineering; Environmental Studies; Mechanical Engineering; Transport and Communications; Water Science), Professional Doctorate (Dentistry; Pharmacy), Diplôme d'Etudes supérieures spécialisées (Biology; Medicine), Maîtrise (Biological and Life Sciences; Cosmetology; Cultural Studies; Dentistry; Development Studies; Educational and Student Counselling; Educational Psychology; Food Science; Health Administration; Laboratory Techniques; Paediatrics; Pedagogy; Pharmacy; Safety Engineering; Telecommunications Engineering; Theatre; Tourism; Transport Management; Writing), Diplôme d'Etudes approfondies (Banking; Law; Private Law; Public Law), Magistère (Arabic; Education; History; Islamic Studies; Philosophy), Diplôme de Spécialité (Anaesthesiology; Anatomy; Cardiology; Child Care and Development; Dermatology; Endocrinology; Gastroenterology; Genetics; Gynaecology and Obstetrics; Medical Technology; Medicine; Nephrology; Neurological Therapy; Neurology; Oncology; Ophthalmology; Orthopaedics; Otorhinolaryngology; Paediatrics; Pathology; Plastic Surgery; Pneumology; Psychiatry and Mental Health; Radiology; Rheumatology; Surgery; Urology), Master's Degree (Actuarial Science; Advertising and Publicity; Anthropology; Archaeology; Banking; Biochemistry; Bioengineering; Biology; Business Administration; Business Computing; Cinema and Television; Clinical Psychology; Communication Studies; Computer Networks; Contemporary History; Cultural Studies; Dental Technology; Dentistry; Economic and Finance Policy; Economics; Education; Educational Administration; Educational Sciences; Electrical Engineering; Family Studies; Film; Finance; Food Technology; French; Genetics; Gynaecology and Obstetrics; Health Administration; Health Sciences; Hotel Management; Human Resources; Industrial Engineering; Information Sciences; Information Technology; Insurance; International Relations; Labour and Industrial Relations; Literature; Management; Marketing; Mathematics and Computer Science; Measurement and Precision Engineering; Mediterranean Studies; Microbiology; Nursing; Nutrition; Occupational Therapy; Oral Pathology; Orthodontics; Orthopaedics; Paediatrics; Peace and Disarmament; Pedagogy; Pharmacology; Philosophy; Physical Therapy; Physiology; Political Sciences; Preschool Education; Primary Education; Psychology; Regional Planning; Rehabilitation and Therapy; Religious Studies; Social Problems; Sociology; Soil Science; Sound Engineering (Acoustics); Telecommunications Engineering; Theatre; Tourism; Toxicology; Translation and Interpretation; Water Science), Doctorate (Anthropology; Arabic; Archaeology; Biological and Life Sciences; Chemistry; Civil Engineering; Education; Educational Sciences; Electrical Engineering; French; Geography; Health Sciences; History; Islamic Studies; Law; Literature; Mathematics; Medicine; Modern Languages; Philosophy; Physics; Psychology; Sociology; Theatre). Also Licence d'enseignement in Arab Language and Literature, 180 Credits following Licence and in Educational Sciences, 30 Credits following Licence. Also Diplôme d'études supérieures appliquées (DESA) in Private and Public Contentious Law, 12 months. Diplôme d'éudes spécialisées de banques (DESB), 4 sem. following Licence in Business or Economics; Diplôme supérieur de gestion bancaire, 16 months following DESB

Student Services: Academic Counselling, Social Counselling, Nursery Care, Sports Facilities, Language Laboratory, Facilities for disabled people, Health Services, Canteen

Periodicals: ACES - Actualités cliniques et scientifiques, Al-bayanat al-massihyia al-islamyia al mouchtaraka, Annales d'histoire - Tempora, Annales de Géographie - Géosphères, Annales de l'Institut de langues et de traduction - Al-Kimiya, Annales de l'Institut de lettres orientales, Annales de la Faculté de droit, Annales de lettres françaises- Acanthe, Annales de philosophie - Iris, Annales de psychologie et des sciences de l'éducation - Psy-écho, Annales de sociologie et d'anthropologie - Communautés et sociétés, Annuaire de l'Université de St.-Joseph, Attalkih al-istinahi al-moutajanes wa ghair al-moutajanes, Bulletin annuel de la Faculté de médecine, Bulletin intérieur de l'Institut libanais d'éducateurs, CEMAM Reports, Chroniques politiques, Chroniques sociales, Chronologies du CEMAM, Conférences de l'ALDEC, Déclarations communes islamo-chrétiennes, Enseignement continu post-universitaire, Etudes de droit libanais, Fondements théologiques du dialogue islamo-chrétien, Hommes et sociétés du Proche-Orient - Nouvelle série, Journées d'études post-universitaires, L'Orient des dieux, La revue de l'Institut libanais d'éducateurs, Livret Thèses et mémoires soutenus à l'Institut de lettres orientales(1968-2002), Mélanges de l'Université Saint-Joseph, Méthode rhétorique et herméneutique, Proche-Orient chrétien, Proche-Orient Etudes économiques, Proche-Orient Etudes en management, Proche-Orient Etudes juridiques, Publications techniques et scientifiques de l'ESIB, Questions de bioéthique au regard de l'Islam et du Christianisme - Conférence à deux voix, Regards, Rôle culturel des chrétiens dans le monde arabe- Cahiers de l'Orient chrétien, Tahadyiat attafahum lilmoutabadal, Travaux et Jours

Publishing house: Presses de l'Université Saint-Joseph

Student Numbers 2012-2013	MALE	FEMALE	TOTAL
All (Foreign Included)			11216

Last Update: 11-03-2013

The Islamic University of Lebanon (IUL)

PO Box 30014 Khaldeh Highway
Khalde, Choueifat
Tel: +961(5) 807-711-16
Fax: +961(5) 807-719
President: Hassan Chalabi
Tel: +961(5) 807-718

Faculty

Economics and Business Administration (Accountancy; Banking; Business Administration; Business Computing; Economics; Finance; Health Administration; Industrial Management; Management; Marketing); **Engineering** (Biomedical Engineering; Computer Engineering; Engineering; Surveying and Mapping; Telecommunications Engineering); **Islamic Studies** (Islamic Law; Islamic Studies); **Law** (Commercial Law; Law; Private Law; Public Law); **Literature and Humanities** (Arabic; Arts and Humanities; English; French; Geography; History; Literature; Modern Languages; Philosophy; Psychology; Translation and Interpretation);

Nursing (Nursing); **Political, Administrative and Diplomatic Sciences** (Administration; International Relations; Political Sciences); **Science and Arts** (Biochemistry; Biology; Chemistry; Computer Science; Graphic Design; Interior Design; Mathematics; Physics); **Tourism Sciences** (Hotel and Restaurant; Hotel Management; Tourism)

History: Founded 1994, sponsored by the Higher Islamic Shiite Council.
Admission requirements: Secondary school certificate (baccalauréat) and entrance examination
Fees: (Lebanese Pounds): c. 3.8 m. per annum
Main language(s) of instruction: Arabic, English, French
Accrediting agency: Association of Arab Universities (AARU); AUF and Association of Lebanon universities
Degrees and diplomas: Bachelor's Degree, Master's Degree, Doctorate (Islamic Studies)
Student Services: Academic Counselling, Social Counselling, Careers Guidance, Nursery Care, Cultural Activities, Sports Facilities, Language Laboratory, Facilities for disabled people, Health Services, Canteen, Foreign Studies Centre
Periodicals: Islamic History Review, News of the University

University of Balamand (UOB)

PO Box 100
Tripoli, Abou Samra
Tel: +961(6) 93-0250
Fax: +961(6) 93-0278
Website: http://www.balamand.edu.lb
President: Elias Warrak

Faculty

Arts and Social Sciences (Arabic; Cultural Studies; Education; English; English Studies; French; French Studies; History; Mass Communication; Philosophy; Physical Education; Political Sciences; Psychology; Translation and Interpretation); **Business and Management** (Business Administration; Business and Commerce; Economics; Hotel Management; Management; Tourism); **Engineering** (Aeronautical and Aerospace Engineering; Civil Engineering; Computer Engineering; Electrical Engineering; Engineering; Mechanical Engineering); **Health Sciences** (*Ashrafich, Beirut*) (Health Education; Health Sciences; Laboratory Techniques; Nursing; Public Health); **Medicine** (Medicine); **Postgraduate Medical Education** (*Saint George Hospital, Beirut*) (Anaesthesiology; Cardiology; Gastroenterology; Gynaecology and Obstetrics; Medicine; Oncology; Orthopaedics; Paediatrics; Pneumology; Radiology; Surgery; Urology); **Science** (Computer Science; Mathematics; Natural Sciences; Physics)

Institute
History, Archaeology, Near Eastern Heritage (Archaeology; Heritage Preservation; History); **Theology** (*St John of Damascus*) (Theology)

Academy
Fine Arts (*Lebanese*) (Advertising and Publicity; Architecture; Cinema and Television; Fine Arts; Graphic Design; Interior Design; Town Planning)

Centre
Christian and Muslim Studies (Christian Religious Studies; Islamic Studies); **Computer** (Computer Science); **Engineering and Environmental Studies** (Engineering; Environmental Studies)

History: Founded 1936. Acquired present title and status 1988.

Academic year: October to August (October-February; February-June;July-August)

Admission requirements: Secondary school certificate (baccalauréat), or equivalent. Language tests, special tests based on major's needs

Fees: (Lebanese Pounds): Undergraduate, 280,000-370,000 (average 15 credits per semester); Graduate, 460,000-500,000 per credit (average 9 credits per semester)

Main language(s) of instruction: English, French, Arabic, Greek

Degrees and diplomas: Bachelor's Degree (Business and Commerce; Engineering; Fine Arts; Health Sciences; Theology), Licence, Professional Doctorate (Medicine), Diplôme d'Etudes supérieures spécialisées (Fine Arts), Teaching Diploma (Education), Master's Degree (Architecture; Engineering; Fine Arts; Theology), Doctorate (Education)

Student Services: Academic Counselling, Careers Guidance, Cultural Activities, Sports Facilities, Language Laboratory, Facilities for disabled people, Health Services, Canteen

Periodicals: Al-Markab, Annals of the Faculty of Arts and Social Sciences, Chronos

Student Numbers 2012-2013	MALE	FEMALE	TOTAL
All (Foreign Included)			5316

Last Update: 14-02-2013

University of Sciences and Arts in Lebanon

Old Airport Road
Ghobeiry, Mount Lebanon
Tel: +961(3) 060-529
Fax: +961(3) 453-003
Website: http://www.usal.edu.lb
President: Mohammad Reda Fadlallah

Faculty
Arts and Sciences (Computer Networks; Computer Science; Mass Communication; Public Relations; Radio and Television Broadcasting); **Education** (Mathematics Education; Primary Education; Science Education; Special Education); **Management, Finance and Economics** (Accountancy; Business Computing; Finance; Hotel Management; Human Resources; Management; Marketing)

History: Founded 2013.

Academic year: Fall Semester (October – January); Spring Semester (February-May); Summer Semester (June-July)

Admission requirements: Lebanese Official Baccalaureate or its equivalent, and a placement test (English, Arabic, and Mathematics)

Fees: $125 per credit; $1,875 per semester (US Dollar)

Accrediting agency: Ministry of Higher Education

Degrees and diplomas: Bachelor's Degree (Business Administration; Computer Science; Education; Mass Communication), Teaching Diploma (Education)

Academic Staff 2016-2017	MALE	FEMALE	TOTAL
FULL-TIME			50
PART-TIME			40
STAFF WITH DOCTORATE			
FULL-TIME			20
Student Numbers 2016-2017			
All (Foreign Included)			350

University of Tripoli Lebanon (TUIS)

Abou-Samra
Tripoli, Abou Samra
Tel: +961(6) 441-756
Fax: +961(6) 447-202
Website: http://www.ut.edu.lb
President: Abdulsalam Ghaith
Tel: +961(3) 211-742

Faculty
Educational Sciences (Education); **Shari'a and Islamic Studies** (Islamic Law; Islamic Studies); **The Holy Quran, Multi Readings and Science** (Islamic Theology; Koran)

History: Founded 1982 by the Islah Islamic Association as University Institute of Tripoli for Islamic Studies. Acquired present status and title 2009.

Admission requirements: Secondary school certificate (baccalauréat) or equivalent

Main language(s) of instruction: Arabic

Accrediting agency: Ministry of Education and Higher Education

Degrees and diplomas: Licence, Magistère

Student Services: Academic Counselling, Social Counselling, Careers Guidance, Nursery Care, Cultural Activities, Sports Facilities, Language Laboratory, Health Services, Canteen, Foreign Studies Centre

Periodicals: Al-Islah, Al-Islah Islamic Association, Islamic Conference on Shari'a and Law, Islamic Educational Conference

Last Update: 12-12-2011

Lesotho

STRUCTURE OF HIGHER EDUCATION SYSTEM

Description

Higher education in Lesotho, as defined by the Higher Education Act, is a programme of education or training leading to a qualification higher then the Cambridge Overseas School Certificate (COSC) and accredited by the CHE; it is provided by both public and private institutions and denominationally-owned and administered institutions. There are also several private providers providing programmes validated by overseas institutions.

Stages of studies

University level first stage

Diploma/ Certificate, Bachelor's degree
Diplomas/ Certificates are usually conferred after two to three years' study. The Bachelor's degree is conferred after four years.

University level second stage

Master's degree
The Master's degree is conferred in Arts (MA) and Science (MSc) after two years' study beyond the Bachelor's degree.

University level third stage

Doctorate
The Doctorate is conferred after three years' study beyond the Master's degree. Candidates must submit a thesis and sit for an oral examination.

ADMISSION TO HIGHER EDUCATION

Admission to university-level studies

Name of Secondary school credential required: Cambridge Overseas School Certificate
Minimum score/requirement: 1st or 2nd division with credit in English and Mathematics (for science)

Foreign students admission

Admission requirements: Foreign students must hold qualifications equivalent to those required for entry to the university.

RECOGNITION OF STUDIES

Quality assurance system

The CHE's Higher Education Quality Assurance Committee (HEQAC) is responsible for setting minimum standards and for accrediting all higher education programmes before students are allowed to enrol.

Bodies dealing with recognition

Council on Higher Education - CHE
PO Box 14046
Maseru 100
Tel: +266 2231 3503
Fax: +266 2231 0070
Website: http://www.che.ac.ls

NATIONAL BODIES

Ministry of Education and Training

Minister: Ntoi Rapapa
PO Box 47
Maseru 100
Tel: +266 2232 8547
Website: http://education.org.ls
Role of national body: The Ministry of Education and Training is responsible for the management, provision and regulation of education and training in Lesotho.

Council on Higher Education - CHE

Chairperson: Matjato Moteane
PO Box 14046
Maseru 100

© International Association of Universities 2019
International Handbook of Universities 2019,
https://doi.org/10.1057/978-3-319-76971-4_108

Tel: +266 2231 3503
Fax: +266 2231 0070
Website: http://www.che.ac.ls
Role of national body: Statutory corporate body established by Section 4 of the Higher Education Act of 2004. The overall mandate of CHE is to regulate the higher education sector and promote quality assurance in Lesotho.

Data for academic year: 2016–2017
Source: IAU from CHE website, Lesotho, 2018.

Public Institutions

Lesotho Institute of Public Administration and Management (LIPAM)

P.O. Box 1507 Block A (LNDC) Development House
Maseru
Tel: +266(22) 312-801
Fax: +266(22) 314-848
Director General: John Dzimba

Course/Programme
Human Resource Management (Human Resources); **Labour Laws** (Labour Law); **Leadership and Strategy** (Leadership)
Academic year: From August to May
Main language(s) of instruction: English
Accrediting agency: Ministry of the Public Service
Degrees and diplomas: Diploma/ Certificate (Human Resources), Master's Degree (Labour Law; Leadership). Also Post Graduate Diploma in Human Resources Management and Labour Laws
Last Update: 19-12-2016

⚑⊕ National University of Lesotho (NUL)

P.O. 180
Roma 100, Maseru District
Tel: +266(22) 340-601, +266(522) 213-000
Fax: +266(22) 340-000
Website: http://www.nul.ls
Vice-Chancellor: Nqosa Leuta Mahao
Tel: +266(22) 340-269

Faculty
Agriculture (Agricultural Economics; Agriculture; Animal Husbandry; Computer Science; Crop Production; Dairy; Ecology; Farm Management; Food Science; Food Technology; Genetics; Irrigation; Soil Science; Water Science); **Education** (Agricultural Education; Curriculum; Education; Educational Administration; Educational Research; Educational Technology; Environmental Studies; Higher Education; Mathematics Education; Primary Education; Science Education; Secondary Education); **Health Sciences** (Environmental Studies; Health Sciences; Midwifery; Nursing; Nutrition; Pharmacy); **Humanities** (African Languages; Arts and Humanities; Cultural Studies; Development Studies; English; Ethics; French; Heritage Preservation; History; Information Sciences; Library Science; Linguistics; Literature; Pastoral Studies; Philosophy; Psychology; Religious Studies; Theology; Translation and Interpretation); **Law** (Labour Law; Law); **Science and Technology** (Biology; Biotechnology; Chemical Engineering; Chemistry; Computer Engineering; Computer Networks; Computer Science; Electronic Engineering; Environmental Studies; Geography; Information Technology; Mathematics; Physics; Regional Planning; Statistics; Town Planning); **Social Sciences** (Accountancy; Anthropology; Business Administration; Demography and Population; Development Studies; Economics; Geography (Human); Human Resources; Management; Marketing; Mathematics; Political Sciences; Public Administration; Social Work; Sociology; Statistics)

Institute
Education (Curriculum; Education; Educational Research; Educational Testing and Evaluation; Human Resources); **Extra-Mural Studies** (*IEMS*) (Adult Education; Business Administration; Education; Management; Mass Communication); **Southern African Studies** (*ISAS*) (African Studies; Labour and Industrial Relations)
History: Founded 1945 as Pius XII College, became University of Basutoland, Bechuanaland Protectorate and Swaziland 1966; part of the trinational University of Botswana, Lesotho and Swaziland 1966. Acquired present status 1975.
Academic year: July to June (July-December; January-June)
Admission requirements: Cambridge Overseas School Certificate or equivalent, with credit in English
Fees: National: Undergraduate degree programmes, 4,800-19,835 per annum; Postgraduate degree programmes, 13,295-20,215 per annum (Loti), International: Undergraduate degree programmes, 4,800-46,820 per annum; Postgraduate degree programmes, 13,295-20,215 per annum (Loti)
Main language(s) of instruction: English
Accrediting agency: Council on Higher Education

Degrees and diplomas: Bachelor's Degree (Adult Education; Business Administration; Engineering; Management; Natural Sciences; Primary Education), Master's Degree (Adult Education; Agriculture; Animal Husbandry; Chemistry; Crop Production; Economics; Education; Law; Political Sciences; Public Administration; Social Work; Sociology; Soil Science), Doctorate (African Languages; Development Studies; Education; History; Linguistics; Literature; Modern Languages; Philosophy). Also Postgraduate Diploma in Education, Labour Law, Human Resources; Bachelor of Art Honours in English, Development Studies, Linguistics, Philosophy

Student Services: Social Counselling, Careers Guidance, Nursery Care, Sports Facilities, Facilities for disabled people, Health Services, Canteen, Library, Residential Facilities

Periodicals: Lesotho Law Journal, Lesotho Social Science Review, NUL Journal of Research, NUL Student Law Review, Review of Southern African Studies

Publishing house: NUL Publishing House

Last Update: 19-12-2016

Private Institution

Lesotho Boston Health Alliance (LeBoHA)

Nala House Bowker Road P.O. Box 0813
Maseru West 105
Tel: +266(22) 3242-62
Website: http://www.bu.edu/lesotho
Country Director: Elizabeth Limakatso Nkabane-Nkholongo

Course/Programme

Family Medicine Speciality Training (Community Health)

History: Founded 2007 as a local non-profit organization (public trust), a collaboration of Boston University and Boston Medical Center activities in Lesotho.

Main language(s) of instruction: English

Accrediting agency: Ministry of Health and Social Welfare (MOHSW)

Degrees and diplomas: 4 year part-time programme in Community Health

Last Update: 19-12-2016

Liberia

STRUCTURE OF HIGHER EDUCATION SYSTEM

Description

Higher education is provided by a number of public and private universities. The University of Liberia is the country's largest and oldest university.

Stages of studies

University level first stage

Bachelor's degree
The first stage lasts for four years and leads to the award of the Bachelor's degree (3 years in Law; 5 years in Engineering). The curricular structure generally provides for the first two years to include basic and general courses. This is followed by courses in the student's area of specialization.

University level second stage

Master's degree
A second stage leads to the Master's degree after two years' graduate study.

University level third stage

Doctorate in Medicine
In Medicine, the Doctorate is conferred after seven years of study.

ADMISSION TO HIGHER EDUCATION

Admission to university-level studies

Name of Secondary school credential required: Liberia Senior High School Certificate
Admission requirements: Entrance examination.

RECOGNITION OF STUDIES

Quality assurance system

Recognition in Liberia implies obtaining a charter to operate from the National Legislature and to follow the policies as set by the National Commission on Higher Education.

NATIONAL BODIES

Ministry of Education

Minister: Ansu D. Sonii, Sr
PO Box 10-9012
Monrovia 1000
Tel: +231 880 898 684
Website: http://www.moe.gov.lr

National Commission on Higher Education - NCHE

Director-General: Michael P. Slawon
P.O. Box 1234, S. D. Cooper Road Tubman Blvd
Monrovia
Tel: +231 886 660-067
Website: http://ncheliberia.org
Role of national body: Supervises, coordinates, monitors, evaluates and accredits tertiary-level institutions.

Association of Liberian Universities - ALU

Monrovia

Data for academic year: 2016–2017
Source: IAU from Liberia Permanent Delegation to UNESCO, from National Commission on Higher Education, 2016. Bodies updated 2018

© International Association of Universities 2019
International Handbook of Universities 2019,
https://doi.org/10.1057/978-3-319-76971-4_109

Public Institutions

University of Liberia (UL)

PO Box 9020 Capitol Hill
Monrovia, Montserrado County
Tel: +231(88) 6941-294
Website: http://www.ul.edu.lr
President: Ophelia Inez Weeks
Tel: +231(6) 669-855

College
Agriculture and Forestry (*William R. Toblert, Jr.*) (Agriculture; Agronomy; Forestry; Home Economics; Primary Education; Secondary Education; Wood Technology); **Business and Public Administration** (Accountancy; Business and Commerce; Economics; Management; Public Administration); **Science and Technology** (*T. J. R. Faulkner*) (Biology; Botany; Chemistry; Civil Engineering; Electrical Engineering; Geology; Mathematics; Mining Engineering; Physics; Technology; Zoology); **Social Sciences and Humanities** (Anthropology; English; French; Geography; History; Mass Communication; Political Sciences; Sociology); **Teacher Training** (*William V. S. Tubman*) (Primary Education; Secondary Education; Teacher Training)

School
Law (*Louis Arthur-Grimes*) (Law); **Medicine** (*A. M. Dogliotti*) (Medicine; Public Health); **Pharmacy** (Pharmacy)

Institute
Population Studies (Demography and Population)
History: Founded 1851, opened as Liberia College1862. Became university 1951.
Academic year: March to December (March-July; August-December)
Admission requirements: Secondary school certificate and entrance examination
Main language(s) of instruction: English
Accrediting agency: National Commission on Higher Education
Degrees and diplomas: Bachelor's Degree (Agriculture; Anthropology; Business Administration; Education; Engineering; English; Fine Arts; Forestry; French; Geology; History; Law; Mass Communication; Mining Engineering; Political Sciences; Public Administration; Sociology), Master's Degree (Business Administration; Development Studies; Education; International Studies; Peace and Disarmament; Public Administration; Regional Studies), Doctorate in Medicine (Medicine)
Periodicals: Journal, Liberia Law Journal, Science Magazine
Last Update: 17-05-2017

William V.S. Tubman University

PO Box 3570
Harper, Maryland County
Tel: +231(88) 672-0692
Website: http://www.tubmanu.edu.lr
President: Edward Lama Wonkeryor

College
Agriculture and Food Sciences (Agriculture; Food Science; Food Technology; Nutrition); **Arts and Sciences** (Arts and Humanities; Biology; English; Environmental Studies; Natural Sciences; Performing Arts; Psychology; Social Sciences); **Education** (Education; Educational and Student Counselling; Preschool Education; Primary Education; Secondary Education); **Engineering and Technology** (Civil Engineering; Computer Engineering; Computer Networks; Computer Science; Electrical Engineering; Energy Engineering; Mechanical Engineering; Software Engineering); **Health Sciences** (Community Health; Epidemiology; Health Administration; Nursing); **Management and Administration** (Accountancy; Administration; Economics; Finance; Management; Public Administration)
History: Founded 1978 as William V.S Tubman College of Technology. Acquired current title and status 2009.
Accrediting agency: National Commission on Higher Education
Degrees and diplomas: Bachelor's Degree (Agriculture; Business Administration; Civil Engineering; Community Health; Educational and Student Counselling; Electrical Engineering; Epidemiology; Food Science; Food Technology; Health Administration; Mechanical Engineering; Nursing; Nutrition; Preschool Education; Primary Education; Public Administration; Public Health; Secondary Education)
Last Update: 29-11-2016

Private Institutions

African Methodist Episcopal University (AMEU)

34 Camp Johnson Road
Monrovia 231, Montserrado County
Tel: +231(377) 4751-6114
Website: http://www.ame.edu.lr
President: Joseph T. Isaac

College
Biyant Theological Seminary (Pastoral Studies; Religious Education; Theology); **Business and Public Administration**

(Accountancy; Business and Commerce; Economics; Management; Public Administration); **Education** (Education; Preschool Education; Primary Education; Secondary Education); **Liberal Arts and Social Sciences** (Arts and Humanities; English; Mass Communication; Political Sciences; Social Sciences; Sociology)
History: Founded 1995.
Academic year: September to July
Admission requirements: Secondary school certificate, present WAEC certificate and entrance examination
Fees: Tuition, 17 per credit hour (Liberian Dollar)
Main language(s) of instruction: English
Accrediting agency: National Commission on Higher Education
Degrees and diplomas: Bachelor's Degree (Business Administration; Economics; English; Political Sciences; Religious Education; Sociology; Theology)
Student Services: Academic Counselling, Social Counselling, Sports Facilities, Language Laboratory, Health Services, Library
Last Update: 29-11-2016

Cuttington University (CU)

PO Box 10-0277
Suakoko 1000, Bong County
Tel: +231(88) 651-0952
Fax: +231(88) 651-0301
Website: http://cuttingtonuniversity.edu.lr
President: Herman B. Browne

College

Agriculture and Integrated Rural Development (Agriculture; Rural Planning); **Business, Humanities and Social Sciences** (Arts and Humanities; Business Administration; Social Sciences); **Education** (Education; Primary Education; Secondary Education); **Health Sciences** (Nursing); **Natural Sciences** (Biology; Chemistry; Mathematics; Natural Sciences); **Theology** (Theology)
History: Founded 1889 asuttington College and Divinity School.
Academic year: September to July (September-February; March-July)
Admission requirements: Secondary school certificate or recognized equivalent, and entrance examination
Main language(s) of instruction: English
Accrediting agency: National Commission on Higher Education; Association of Episcopal Colleges, USA; Association of African Universities
Degrees and diplomas: Bachelor's Degree (Arts and Humanities; Natural Sciences; Nursing), Master's Degree

(Business Administration; Education; Educational Administration; Nursing; Public Administration; Public Health; Theology)
Student Services: Academic Counselling, Social Counselling, Sports Facilities, Health Services, Canteen
Periodicals: Cuttington Research Journal
Last Update: 29-11-2016

Stella Maris Polytechnic

St. Joseph Main Campus, Capitol Hill
Monrovia
Tel: +231(88) 6521-104
Website: http://www.stellamarispolytechnic.info
President: Mary Laurene Browne

College

Agriculture (Agriculture); **Business** (Accountancy; Economics; Management); **Health Sciences** (Biology; Nursing; Social Work); **Teacher's Training** (Education; Primary Education); **Technical** (Building Technologies; Civil Engineering; Electrical Engineering)
History: Created 1988 as Don Bosco Polytechnic. Acquired current title and status 2005.
Accrediting agency: National Commission on Higher Education
Degrees and diplomas: Bachelor's Degree (Accountancy; Agriculture; Biology; Building Technologies; Civil Engineering; Economics; Electrical Engineering; Management; Nursing; Primary Education; Social Work)
Last Update: 28-03-2017

United Methodist University

508-C-17, Centinnial Area Ashmun Street
Monrovia 10 1000, Montserrado County
Tel: +231(88) 694-6614
Website: http://umu.edu.lr
President: Johnson Gwaikolo

College

Agriculture (*Associate degree only*) (Agriculture); **Education** (Primary Education; Secondary Education); **Health Sciences** (*Associate degree only*) (Nursing); **Liberal Arts** (Criminology; History; Mass Communication; Peace and Disarmament; Political Sciences; Social Work; Sociology); **Management and Administration** (Accountancy;

Economics; Management); **Science and Technology** (Natural Sciences; Technology); **Theology** (Theology)

History: Created 1998. Acquired status 2002.

Accrediting agency: National Commission on Higher Education

Degrees and diplomas: Bachelor's Degree (Accountancy; Criminology; Economics; History; Management; Mass Communication; Peace and Disarmament; Political Sciences; Primary Education; Secondary Education; Social Work; Sociology), Master's Degree (Theology)

Last Update: 29-11-2016

Libya

STRUCTURE OF HIGHER EDUCATION SYSTEM

Description

Higher education is offered in universities, both general and specialized, technical faculties and higher technical and vocational institutions. Within public institutions, students need pay only a registration fee; at private institutions, students are responsible for tuition fees.

Stages of studies

University level first stage

Bachelor's degree
The Bachelor's degree is conferred after four years' study (five years in Architecture, Dentistry, Pharmacy, Veterinary Medicine and Engineering; 6 years in Medicine and Surgery) in universities.

University level second stage

Master's degree
A Master's degree is conferred after two years' study following the Bachelor's degree. Admission criteria are set by the Ministry.

University level third stage

Doctorate
A Doctorate may be awarded after three to four years' research. The award of this degree is conditional upon the submission of a thesis. Admission criteria are set by the Ministry.

ADMISSION TO HIGHER EDUCATION

Admission to university-level studies

Name of Secondary school credential required: Secondary Education Certificate
For entry to: Universities
Minimum score/requirement: A minimum of 65%, 75% for Medicine and Engineering

Foreign students admission

Language Proficiency: Proficiency is required in Arabic.

RECOGNITION OF STUDIES

Bodies dealing with recognition

National Centre for Quality Assurance and Accreditation of Educational and Training Institutes
Street Tamim ibn Aws, off street Abu Bakr - Ben Ashour
PO Box 80 767
Tripoli

NATIONAL BODIES

Ministry of Higher Education and Scientific Research

Al Nasr Street
Tripoli
Website: http://mohe.gov.ly
Role of national body: Responsible for supervision of and coordination among higher education institutions (administration for universities, technical and vocational Education, and administration of private education.

National Centre for Quality Assurance and Accreditation of Educational and Training Institutes

Street Tamim ibn Aws, off street Abu Bakr - Ben Ashour
PO Box 80 767
Tripoli
Role of national body: Responsible for recognition and equivalence issues and accreditation and quality assurance of public and private institutions.

The National Authority for Scientific Research - NASR

Role of national body: Supervises the administration and funding of scientific research.

© International Association of Universities 2019
International Handbook of Universities 2019,
https://doi.org/10.1057/978-3-319-76971-4_110

Data for academic year: 2016–2017
Source: IAU from European Commission-TEMPUS document (2016), 2017.

Public Institutions

Al-Arab Medical University

PO Box 18251 Hawari Road
Benghazi
Tel: +218(61) 225-007
Fax: +218(61) 222-195
President: Amer Kahil

Faculty
Dentistry (Dentistry; Surgery); **Medicine** (Gynaecology and Obstetrics; Medicine; Ophthalmology; Paediatrics; Pharmacology; Surgery); **Pharmacy** (Pharmacy)

Institute
Medical Technology
Further information: Also 8 Teaching Hospitals; 2 Medical Centres
History: Founded 1984.
Academic year: September to May
Admission requirements: Secondary school certificate or equivalent
Main language(s) of instruction: Arabic, English
Degrees and diplomas: Bachelor's Degree (Dentistry; Medicine; Surgery), Master's Degree (Anaesthesiology; Anatomy; Biochemistry; Community Health; Dermatology; Histology; Laboratory Techniques; Paediatrics; Pathology; Pharmacology; Physiology; Public Health), Doctorate
Student Services: Academic Counselling, Cultural Activities, Sports Facilities, Health Services, Canteen
Periodicals: Garyounis Medical Journal
Last Update: 18-10-2017

Al-Jabal Al Gharbi University

PO Box 64101 Zawia
Gharian
Tel: +218(242) 630-263
Fax: +218(242) 635-316
Website: http://jgu.edu.ly
President: Ahmad Alwear
Tel: +218(9) 1320-4412 (mobile)

Faculty
Accountancy (Accountancy; Economics); **Arts and Education** (Arts and Humanities; Education; Modern Languages); **Education** (Education); **Engineering** (Civil Engineering; Computer Engineering; Electrical Engineering; Engineering); **Law** (Law; Political Sciences); **Science** (Biology; Chemistry; Mathematics; Physics)
History: Founded 1991.
Academic year: September to July
Main language(s) of instruction: Arabic, English
Degrees and diplomas: Bachelor's Degree
Last Update: 18-10-2017

Al Zawiya University

PO Box 16418
Al-Zawia
Tel: +218(23) 626-882
Fax: +218(23) 626-882
Website: http://zu.edu.ly
President: Mohammed Al Morabit

Faculty
Arts (Arabic; Arts and Humanities; English Studies; Geography (Human); History; Islamic Studies; Psychology; Social Sciences; Sociology); **Economics and Accountancy** (Accountancy; Economics; Management); **Engineering** (Architecture and Planning; Civil Engineering; Computer Engineering; Electrical and Electronic Engineering; Engineering); **Law** (Islamic Law; Law; Public Law); **Medical Sciences** (Dentistry; Laboratory Techniques; Medical Technology; Medicine; Physical Therapy; Social and Preventive Medicine); **Natural Resources** (Geological Engineering; Petroleum and Gas Engineering); **Pharmacy** (Biochemistry; Microbiology; Pharmacology; Pharmacy); **Physical Education and Sports** (Physical Education; Sports); **Sciences** (Botany; Chemistry; Computer Science; Geology; Mathematics; Natural Sciences; Physics; Science Education; Statistics; Zoology)
History: Founded 1988 as Jamaa't Assaaba Men April (Seventh of April University). Acquired present title and status 2011.
Academic year: September to July
Main language(s) of instruction: Arabic, English
Degrees and diplomas: Bachelor's Degree (Botany; Chemistry; Computer Science; Geology; Pharmacy; Physical Education; Physics; Statistics; Zoology), Master's Degree (Botany; Chemistry; Computer Science; Physical Education; Physics; Zoology), Doctorate
Student Services: Social Counselling, Sports Facilities, Health Services, Canteen, Foreign Studies Centre
Last Update: 18-10-2017

Asmarya University for the Islamic Sciences

PO Box 471 / 495
Zliten, Ashiekh District
Tel: +218(514) 627-039
Fax: +218(514) 620-040
Website: http://www.asmarya.edu.ly
Secretary of the Administration Committee: Mohammed Kondi
Tel: +218(91) 216-6164

Faculty

Arabic and Islamic Studies (Arabic; History; Islamic Studies; Literature); **Preaching** (*Al-Emama Walkhataba*) (Religion; Religious Practice); **Shari'a and Law** (*Zliten*) (Islamic Law); **Theology** (*Asool Aldeen*) (Theology)
History: Founded 1995
Academic year: September to July
Admission requirements: Secondary school certificate (Ashahada Athanawiya); Student should be a Social Science Secondary school graduate (specialization: shari'a or General Secondary); Student must know by heart the Holy Quran
Fees: Regular students: 20 per annum; 10 per semester; Part-time students: 120 per annum; 60 per semester (Libyan Dinar)
Main language(s) of instruction: Arabic
Degrees and diplomas: Bachelor's Degree (Arabic; History; Islamic Law; Religion), Master's Degree (Arabic; Islamic Law), Doctorate (Islamic Studies; Literature; Philosophy; Religion)
Periodicals: Aljamia University Publication
Last Update: 18-10-2017

Higher Institute of Computer Technology (HICT)

PO Box 6289
Tripoli
Tel: +218(21) 480-0413
Fax: +218(21) 480-0199
Website: http://www.cctt.edu.ly
President: Moftah Algurni

Department/Division

Computer Engineering (Computer Engineering; Computer Networks); **Software Engineering** (Software Engineering); **Training** (Computer Education; Computer Networks)
Admission requirements: High school certificate
Fees: None
Main language(s) of instruction: Arabic, English

Degrees and diplomas: Bachelor's Degree
Student Services: Academic Counselling, Social Counselling, Careers Guidance, Sports Facilities, Canteen
Last Update: 18-10-2017

Misurata University

PO Box 2478
Misurata
Tel: +218(512) 627-203
Fax: +218(512) 627-350
Website: http://www.misuratau.edu.ly
President: Altaher M. Alhubge

Faculty

Agriculture (*Ben Walid*) (Agriculture; Animal Husbandry; Horticulture; Plant and Crop Protection; Soil Management; Soil Science; Water Management; Water Science); **Arts** (*Misurata*) (Arabic; Archaeology; Arts and Humanities; Education; English; French; Geography; History; Islamic Studies; Italian; Library Science; Mass Communication; Media Studies; Philosophy; Psychology; Sociology; Tourism); **Arts and Sciences** (*Alkhomus*) (Arabic; Archaeology; English; Geography; History; Islamic Studies; Media Studies; Philosophy; Psychology; Sociology); **Dentistry** (*Zliten*) (Dentistry; Oral Pathology; Orthodontics); **Economics and Political Science** (*Misurata*) (Accountancy; Administration; Banking; Economics; Management; Marketing; Political Sciences); **Education** (*Misurata*) (Arabic; Art Education; Biology; Chemistry; Computer Education; Education; English; Geography; History; Islamic Studies; Mathematics; Music Education; Physical Education; Physics; Preschool Education; Psychology; Special Education); **Engineering** (*Misurata*) (Architecture; Civil Engineering; Electrical Engineering; Engineering; Industrial Engineering; Materials Engineering; Mechanical Engineering; Petroleum and Gas Engineering); **Engineering** (*Alkhomus*) (Architecture; Civil Engineering; Electrical Engineering; Engineering; Industrial Engineering; Materials Engineering; Mechanical Engineering; Petroleum and Gas Engineering); **Information Technology** (*Misurata*) (Communication Studies; Computer Networks; Computer Science; Information Technology; Software Engineering); **Law** (*Ben Walid campus*) (Criminal Law; Law; Private Law; Public Law); **Medical Technology** (*Mslath*) (Dental Technology; Laboratory Techniques; Medical Technology); **Nursing** (*Misurata*) (Anaesthesiology; Gynaecology and Obstetrics; Nursing); **Pharmacy** (*Misurata*) (Pharmacy); **Science** (*Ben Walid*) (Biology; Botany; Chemistry; Computer Science; Mathematics; Microbiology; Physics; Zoology)
History: Founded 1984. Previously known as Seventh of October University. Acquired current status 2010 after

merger with the University of Elmergib (created 1986 as Nasser University).

Academic year: September to July

Admission requirements: Specialized secondary school certificate.

Main language(s) of instruction: Arabic, English

Degrees and diplomas: Bachelor's Degree (Dentistry; Engineering; Islamic Studies; Medicine), Master's Degree (Civil Engineering; Economics; Education; Electrical Engineering; History; Information Technology; Law; Microbiology; Surgery), Doctorate. Also Licence (Lit. B): 4 yrs

Student Services: Academic Counselling, Social Counselling, Careers Guidance, Nursery Care, Cultural Activities, Sports Facilities, Language Laboratory, Facilities for disabled people, Health Services, Canteen, Foreign Studies Centre

Periodicals: Alsatil

Last Update: 18-10-2017

Omar-Al-Mukhtar University (OMU)

PO Box 919
El-Beida
Tel: +218(84) 632-946
Fax: +218(84) 637-052
Website: http://www.omu.edu.ly
President: Abdulmatlub A. Taher

Faculty

Agriculture (Agriculture); **Arts** (Archaeology; Arts and Humanities; Education; Educational Sciences; English; French; Islamic Studies; Library Science; Literature; Philosophy; Psychology; Sociology); **Arts and Science** (*Tobrak, Al-Quba and Derna*) (Arts and Humanities; Natural Sciences); **Economics** (Accountancy; Business Administration; Economics; Finance; Political Sciences); **Engineering** (Engineering); **Law** (Criminal Law; International Law; Islamic Law; Law; Private Law; Public Law); **Medical Technology** (Medical Technology); **Medicine** (Medicine); **Natural Resources and Environmental Science** (Environmental Studies; Forestry; Marine Science and Oceanography; Natural Resources; Wildlife); **Nursing** (Nursing); **Pharmacy** (Pharmacy); **Science** (Chemistry; Geology; Mathematics; Microbiology; Natural Sciences; Physics; Zoology); **Teacher Training** (*Also in Derna, Tobrak and Al-Quba*) (Teacher Training); **Veterinary Medicine** (Veterinary Science)

College

Education (Educational Sciences; Special Education; Teacher Training)

History: Part of Garyounis University until 1984. Founded 1985.

Academic year: October to July

Admission requirements: High school certificate with a certain minimum percentage

Fees: Depends on faculty

Main language(s) of instruction: Arabic and English

Degrees and diplomas: Bachelor's Degree (Law; Pharmacy), Master's Degree

Student Services: Academic Counselling, Social Counselling, Language Laboratory, Health Services, Canteen

Periodicals: Al-Mukhtar Journal of Humanities, Al-Mukhtar Journal of Science

Last Update: 18-10-2017

Sebha University

PO Box 18758
Sebha
Tel: +218(71) 263-22-42
Fax: +218(71) 262-92-01
Website: http://www.sebhau.edu.ly
President: Massoud Al-Ragig

Faculty

Agriculture (Agriculture); **Arts** (Arts and Humanities; English; Linguistics); **Arts and Science** (Arts and Humanities; Mathematics and Computer Science; Natural Sciences); **Economics and Accountancy** (*Merzig*) (Accountancy; Economics); **Engineering** (*Brak*); **Information and Technology** (Information Technology); **Law**; **Physical Education** (Physical Education)

College

Dentistry (Dentistry); **Energy and Mining**; **Medicine** (Medicine); **Nursing** (Nursing; Public Health); **Science** (Mathematics and Computer Science; Natural Sciences)

History: Founded 1983, incorporating the Faculty of Education of the University of Al-Fateh

Academic year: October to August

Admission requirements: Secondary school certificate

Main language(s) of instruction: Arabic, English

Degrees and diplomas: Bachelor's Degree, Master's Degree

Last Update: 18-10-2017

The Higher Institute of Industry (HII)

PO Box 841
Misurata
Tel: +218(51) 261-5312
Fax: +218(51) 261-5314
Website: http://www.hii.edu.ly
Dean: Majdi Ashiban
Tel: +218(51) 261-4109

Department/Division

Electromechanical Engineering (Electronic Engineering; Mechanical Engineering; Power Engineering); **Electronic Engineering** (Computer Engineering; Electronic Engineering; Telecommunications Engineering); **Industrial Engineering** (Industrial Engineering; Industrial Management; Production Engineering; Safety Engineering)

History: Founded 1989.

Academic year: September to June

Admission requirements: Secondary school certificate

Fees: 12 per semester (Libyan Dinar)

Main language(s) of instruction: Arabic

Degrees and diplomas: Higher Vocational / Technical Diploma (Electrical Engineering; Electronic Engineering; Industrial Engineering; Mechanical Engineering), Bachelor's Degree (Engineering), Master's Degree (Technology)

Student Services: Academic Counselling, Social Counselling, Language Laboratory, Canteen

Last Update: 18-10-2017

The Open University

PO Box 13375

Tripoli

Tel: +218(21) 487-4000

Fax: +218(21) 487-4000

Website: http://www.libopenuniv-edu.org

President: Ibrahim Abu-Farwa

Department/Division

Accountancy (Accountancy); **Administration** (Administration); **Arabic** (Arabic); **Economics** (Economics); **Education and Psychology** (Education; Psychology); **Geography** (Geography); **History** (History); **Islamic Studies** (Islamic Studies); **Law** (Law); **Political Science** (Political Sciences); **Sociology and Social Work** (Social Work; Sociology)

History: Founded 1987

Academic year: September to July

Admission requirements: Secondary school certificate

Fees: 100 per annum + 10 per subject (Libyan Dinar)

Main language(s) of instruction: Arabic

Degrees and diplomas: Bachelor's Degree (Accountancy; Administration; Arabic; Economics; Education; History; Islamic Studies; Law; Political Sciences; Social Work; Sociology). Curricula and teaching programmes, both theoretical and applied, are via written and audiovisual material.

Student Services: Academic Counselling, Facilities for disabled people

Last Update: 18-10-2017

University of Benghazi

PO Box 1308

Benghazi

Tel: +218 (92) 238-1756

Fax: +218(61) 223-0315, +218(61) 222-9022

Website: http://uob.edu.ly

President: Mohammed Dghaim

Faculty

Arts (Arabic; Archaeology; Educational Administration; Educational Sciences; English; French; Geography; History; Information Sciences; Islamic Studies; Italian; Library Science; Mass Communication; Media Studies; Philosophy; Physical Education; Religion; Sociology); **Dentistry** (Dentistry; Oral Pathology; Orthodontics; Periodontics; Radiology); **Economics** (Accountancy; Banking; Business Administration; Economics; Finance; Political Sciences; Public Administration); **Education** (*Benghazi*) (Arabic; Art Education; Biology; Chemistry; Computer Science; English; Mathematics; Mathematics Education; Physical Education; Physics; Preschool Education; Teacher Training); **Engineering** (Architecture; Chemical Engineering; Civil Engineering; Electrical and Electronic Engineering; Engineering; Industrial Engineering; Mechanical Engineering; Petroleum and Gas Engineering; Structural Architecture; Town Planning); **Information Technology** (Computer Engineering; Computer Networks; Computer Science; Information Technology; Software Engineering; Telecommunications Engineering); **Law** (Commercial Law; Criminal Law; International Law; Islamic Law; Law; Private Law); **Media** (Journalism; Media Studies; Public Relations; Radio and Television Broadcasting); **Medicine** (Anaesthesiology; Anatomy; Biochemistry; Dermatology; Forensic Medicine and Dentistry; Gynaecology and Obstetrics; Histology; Laboratory Techniques; Medicine; Microbiology; Ophthalmology; Paediatrics; Parasitology; Pathology; Pharmacology; Physiology; Psychiatry and Mental Health; Radiology; Surgery); **Nursing** (Nursing); **Pharmacy** (Pharmacology; Pharmacy; Toxicology); **Public Health** (Environmental Engineering; Epidemiology; Health Administration; Health Education; Nutrition; Occupational Health; Tropical Medicine); **Science** (Botany; Chemistry; Earth Sciences; Geology; Mathematics; Physics; Statistics; Zoology)

College

Agriculture (Agricultural Economics; Aquaculture; Crop Production; Food Science; Horticulture; Soil Science)

Further information: Also branches in Gmens, Solouq, El-Marj, Alabear, Tukheira, Ajdabia, El-Wahat, EL-Kufrah, AL-Agurea

History: Founded 1955 as University of Libya, reorganized as two separate Universities in Benghazi and Tripoli, 1974. Became Garyounis University, 1976. Acquired present title 2011.
Academic year: October to June (October-January; February-June)
Admission requirements: Secondary school certificate or equivalent
Fees: None
Main language(s) of instruction: Arabic, English
Degrees and diplomas: Bachelor's Degree, Master's Degree, Doctorate
Periodicals: Arts, Economics, Law
Last Update: 18-10-2017

University of Sirte

PO Box 674
Sirte
Website: http://su.edu.ly
Chancellor: Mousa Mohammed Musa

Faculty

Arts and Education (Arabic; Arts and Humanities; English; French; Geography; History; Islamic Studies; Media Studies; Translation and Interpretation); **Economics** (Accountancy; Banking; Business Administration; Economics; Finance; Insurance; Statistics); **Education** (*Sirte*) (Arabic; Computer Education; Education; Educational Psychology; English; Koran; Mathematics; Physics); **Medicine** (Medicine; Surgery); **Science** (Botany; Chemistry; Computer Science; Mathematics; Natural Sciences; Physics; Zoology)

College

Agriculture (Agriculture; Animal Husbandry; Plant and Crop Protection; Soil Science; Water Science); **Arts and Sciences** (*Jufrah*) (Arabic; Arts and Humanities; Chemistry; Computer Science; English; Geography; History; Mathematics; Natural Sciences; Physics; Psychology); **Business Administration** (*Jufrah*) (Accountancy; Business Administration); **Engineering** (Chemical Engineering; Civil Engineering; Electrical Engineering; Engineering; Mechanical Engineering; Petroleum and Gas Engineering); **Law** (Law; Public Law); **Medical Technology** (*Jufrah*) (Laboratory Techniques; Medical Technology; Physical Therapy); **Medicine, Oral and Dental Surgery** (Dentistry; Medicine; Oral Pathology; Stomatology); **Nursing** (Nursing)
Further information: Other sites in Jufrah, Zamzam, Ben Jawad.
History: Founded 1989 as University of Qar Younes. Became Al-Tahadi University 1992
Main language(s) of instruction: Arabic

Degrees and diplomas: Bachelor's Degree, Master's Degree (Arabic; Economic and Finance Policy; Electrical Engineering; Public Law), Doctorate
Student Services: Sports Facilities, Canteen
Last Update: 18-10-2017

University of Tripoli

PO Box 13275
Tripoli, Sedi El-Masri
Tel: +218(21) 462-7910, +218(21) 462-7901
Fax: +218(21) 462-8839, +218(21) 462-7902
Website: http://uot.edu.ly
President: Madani A. Dakhil
Tel: +218 (21)4628839

Faculty

Agriculture (Agricultural Economics; Agricultural Engineering; Agriculture; Animal Husbandry; Aquaculture; Crop Production; Food Science; Forestry; Home Economics; Horticulture; Plant and Crop Protection; Soil Science; Water Science); **Arts** (Arabic; Arts and Humanities; Education; Educational Psychology; English; Geography; History; Islamic Studies; Library Science; Philosophy; Psychology; Psychotherapy; Social Sciences; Sociology; Tourism); **Economics and Political Science** (Accountancy; Banking; Economics; Electrical and Electronic Engineering; Finance; Management; Political Sciences; Statistics); **Education** (*Soak Ghoma*) (Arabic; Art Education; Biology; Chemistry; Computer Science; Education; English; Mathematics; Physics; Preschool Education; Primary Education; Special Education); **Education** (*Janzour*) (Arabic; Chemistry; Computer Education; Education; English; Mathematics; Physics; Preschool Education; Primary Education; Sociology; Special Education); **Education** (*Ghaser Ben Ghasir*) (Arabic; Biology; Chemistry; Computer Science; Education; English; Geography; Islamic Studies; Mathematics; Physics; Preschool Education; Primary Education; Social and Community Services); **Engineering** (Aeronautical and Aerospace Engineering; Architecture; Chemical Engineering; Civil Engineering; Computer Engineering; Electrical and Electronic Engineering; Engineering; Engineering Management; Geological Engineering; Materials Engineering; Mechanical Engineering; Mineralogy; Mining Engineering; Petroleum and Gas Engineering; Structural Architecture; Town Planning); **Fine Arts and Media** (Fine Arts; Information Sciences; Journalism; Music; Radio and Television Broadcasting; Theatre; Visual Arts); **Information Technology** (Computer Networks; Computer Science; Information Technology; Software Engineering); **Languages** (African Languages; Arabic; English; French; Italian; Spanish;

Translation and Interpretation); **Law** (Criminal Law; Islamic Law; Law; Private Law; Public Law); **Medical Technology** (Anaesthesiology; Dental Technology; Medical Technology; Pathology; Physical Therapy; Public Health); **Medicine** (Medicine); **Nursing** (Anaesthesiology; Midwifery; Nursing; Surgery); **Oral Surgery and Dentistry** (Dentistry; Oral Pathology; Orthodontics; Stomatology); **Pharmacy** (Biochemistry; Microbiology; Pharmacology; Pharmacy); **Physical Education** (Physical Education; Physical Therapy; Teacher Training); **Science** (Botany; Chemistry; Computer Science; Geology; Geophysics; Mathematics; Meteorology; Natural Sciences; Physics; Statistics; Zoology); **Veterinary Medicine** (Microbiology; Parasitology; Surgery; Veterinary Science)

History: Founded 1957 as University of Libya, reorganized as two separate universities in Tripoli and Benghazi, 1973. Renamed Al Fateh University in 1976. Acquired former name of University of Tripoli in 2011.

Academic year: September to July (September-January; February-July)

Admission requirements: Secondary school certificate or equivalent

Fees: None

Main language(s) of instruction: Arabic, English

Degrees and diplomas: Bachelor's Degree, Master's Degree

Last Update: 18-10-2017

Private Institutions

Academy of Graduate Studies (AGS)

PO Box 79031 Janzour
Tripoli
Tel: +218(21) 487-2796
Fax: +218(21) 487-3075
Website: http://www.alacademia.edu.ly
Director-General: Saleh Ibrahim Almabruk
Tel: +218(21) 487-3076

School

Administration and Finance (Accountancy; Administration; Banking; Business Administration; Economics; Educational Administration; Finance; Marketing); **Art and Media** (Archaeology; Fine Arts; Media Studies; Theatre); **Basic Sciences** (Biological and Life Sciences; Chemistry; Computer Science; Earth Sciences; Environmental Studies; Mathematics; Physics; Statistics); **Engineering Sciences** (Architecture; Biomedical Engineering; Chemical Engineering; Civil Engineering; Computer Engineering; Electrical and Electronic Engineering; Engineering; Environmental

Engineering; Mechanical Engineering; Petroleum and Gas Engineering); **Humanities** (Arabic; Arts and Humanities; Criminal Law; English; French; Geography; History; International Law; Italian; Law; Modern Languages; Philosophy; Political Sciences; Psychology; Social Sciences); **International and Strategic Studies** (Economics; International Relations; Political Sciences); **Languages** (African Languages; Arabic; English; French; German; Spanish; Translation and Interpretation)

History: Founded 1988 as Institute of Graduate Studies and Economic Sciences. Acquired present status and title 1994.

Academic year: September to February; February to June

Admission requirements: First university degree with general average 'good'.

Main language(s) of instruction: Arabic and English

Degrees and diplomas: Master's Degree, Doctorate. Also Postgraduate Diploma

Student Services: Academic Counselling, Social Counselling, Cultural Activities, Sports Facilities, Language Laboratory, Facilities for disabled people, Canteen, Foreign Studies Centre

Periodicals: The Academy Journal of Humanities and Social Sciences, The Academy Journal of Pure and Applied Sciences

Last Update: 18-04-2012

Libyan International Medical University (LIMU)

Kairawan St., Al-Fwaihat
Benghazi
Tel: +218(61) 470-6647
Fax: +218(61) 223-3909
Website: http://limu.edu.ly/ar
President: Mohammed Saad Ambarak

Faculty

Basic Medical Sciences (Biology; Chemistry; Medicine; Microbiology; Parasitology; Physiology); **Dentistry** (Dentistry; Oral Pathology; Orthodontics); **Health Sciences** (Dental Hygiene; Dental Technology; Health Sciences; Medical Technology; Nursing; Physical Therapy; Radiology; Speech Therapy and Audiology); **Information Technology** (Information Technology); **Medicine** (Anaesthesiology; Forensic Medicine and Dentistry; Gynaecology and Obstetrics; Medicine; Ophthalmology; Paediatrics; Public Health; Radiology; Surgery); **Pharmacy** (Pharmacology; Pharmacy)

Degrees and diplomas: Bachelor's Degree (Dentistry; Health Sciences; Information Technology; Medical Technology; Pharmacy)

Last Update: 18-04-2012

Liechtenstein

STRUCTURE OF HIGHER EDUCATION SYSTEM

Description

Since the law governing higher education came into effect in 1992, Liechtenstein has a limited tertiary-education sector. In addition, Liechtenstein has contractual arrangements with Switzerland, Austria and Tübingen (Baden-Württemberg/Germany) allowing students free entry to university in these countries.

Stages of studies

University level first stage

Bachelor
The final examination organized at the end of the first cycle of university studies, which lasts for at least 6 semesters, leads to the following degrees: Bachelor of Science (Bsc) or Bachelor of Arts (BA) + branch of study.

University level second stage

Master
The final examination organized at the end of second cycle university studies, which lasts for at least 4 semesters, leads to the following degrees: Master of Science (Msc) or Master of Arts (MA) + branch of study.

University level third stage

Doctor
On successful completion of doctoral studies (6 semesters) at the International Academy of Philosophy (IAP), students are awarded the following academic title: Doktor der Philosophie (Dr. Phil). On successful completion of doctoral studies (6 semesters) at the Private University of the Principality of Liechtenstein (UFL), students are awarded the following academic title: Doctor of Scientific Medicine (Dr. scient. med) and Doctor of Property Rights (Dr. jur). Since 2008, the University of Liechtenstein offers doctoral programmes in Economics and Architecture leading to a doctoral degree (Dr)

ADMISSION TO HIGHER EDUCATION

Admission to university-level studies

Name of Secondary school credential required: Berufsmaturitätszeugnis
For entry to: All university-level institutions and universities in Liechtenstein and Austria, universities of applied sciences in Switzerland.
Minimum score/requirement: 4
Name of Secondary school credential required: Maturazeugnis
For entry to: All university-level institutions in Liechtenstein, Austria and Switzerland.
Minimum score/requirement: 4

Foreign students admission

Admission requirements: A short-stay permit can be granted for the duration of one semester or one academic year to students wishing to attend a recognized educational institution in Liechtenstein when: a) the educational institution confirms in writing that the student can take up or continue the studes concerned (confirmation of registration); b) the financial means are sufficient; c) proof of the required health insurance protection is provided; d) the student has the linguistic competences for the course concerned. A prolongation is possible according to the length of studies.
Language Proficiency: Good knowledge of German (written, oral).

RECOGNITION OF STUDIES

Quality assurance system

Education is supervised by the State. All higher education institutions need to be authorized by the government on the basis of institutional and programme accreditations. Accreditation is done by a recognized quality assurance agency. There is no national quality assurance agency in Liechtenstein, but instead strong cooperation with foreign quality assurance agencies, especially from the neighboring countries (Switzerland, Austria and Germany) and the European

© International Association of Universities 2019
International Handbook of Universities 2019,
https://doi.org/10.1057/978-3-319-76971-4_111

Quality Assurance Register for Higher Education (EQAR). Liechtenstein is a full member of EQAR.

Bodies dealing with recognition

Schulamt (Office of Education)
Austrasse 79 Postfach 684
Vaduz 9490
Tel: +423 236 6770
Fax: +423 236 6771
Website: http://www.llv.li/#/11631/schulamt

Informationsstelle für Anerkennungsfragen - NARIC Liechtenstein (National Academic Recognition Information Centre)
Head of Upper Secondary and Higher Education Division: Daniel Miescher
Schulamt Austrasse 79, Postfach 684
Vaduz 9490
Tel: +423 236 6758
Fax: +423 236 6771

NATIONAL BODIES

Ministerium für Inneres, Bildung und Umwelt (Ministry for Home Affairs, Education and Environment)

Minister: Dominique Gantenbein
Secretary-General: Martina Tschanz
Regierungsgebäude, Peter-Kaiser-Platz 1 Postfach 684
Vaduz 9490
Tel: +423 236 6111
Website: http://www.regierung.li/ministries/ministry-for-home-affairs-education-and-environment

Schulamt (Office of Education)

Austrasse 79 Postfach 684
Vaduz 9490
Tel: +423 236 6770
Fax: +423 236 6771
Website: http://www.llv.li/#/11631/schulamt
Role of national body: Maintenance and development of the education system from kindergarten to higher education.

Data for academic year: 2018–2019
Source: IAU from the Schulamt / Office of Education, Liechtenstein, 2018

Public Institution

University of Liechtenstein

Fürst-Franz-Josef-Strasse
Vaduz 9490
Tel: +423 265-11-11
Fax: +423 265-11-12
Website: http://www.uni.li
Rektor: Klaus Näscher

School
Graduate School (Architecture; Banking; Economics; Finance; Information Technology; Management; Small Business)

Institute
Architecture and Planning (Architectural and Environmental Design; Landscape Architecture; Regional Planning; Rural Planning; Town Planning); **Business Computing** (Information Management; Information Technology); **Entrepreneurship** (Business and Commerce; Business Computing; Human Resources; International Business; Leadership; Management; Management Systems; Small Business); **Financial Services** (Banking; Taxation)

Research Division
Centre for Small and Medium Enterprises (*KMU*); **Liechtenstein Economic Institute and Research Centre** (*KOFL*)
History: Founded 1961 as Abendtechnikum Vaduz, acquired title of Hochschule Liechtenstein in 1992. Acquired current title and status 2011
Admission requirements: Secondary school certificate (Matura)
Fees: 750 per semester (Swiss Franc)
Main language(s) of instruction: German, English
Degrees and diplomas: Bachelor (Architecture; International Business; Management), Master (Architecture; Computer Science; Finance; Management), Doctorate (Architecture and Planning; Business and Commerce; Economics). Also Professional qualifications: MBA, Executive MBA, Master of Advanced Studies (MAS) in Business Administration, Executive Master of Laws (LL.M)
Student Services: Careers Guidance, Sports Facilities, Canteen, Library, IT Centre, Residential Facilities
Last Update: 17-12-2015

Private Institutions

International Academy of Philosophy in the Principality of Liechtenstein (IAP)

Im Schwibboga 7b
Bendern 9487
Tel: +423 265-43-43
Fax: +423 265-43-41
Website: http://www.iap.li
Direktor: Daniel von Wachter

Course/Programme

One-to-one tutorials (Einzelunterricht) (Philosophy); **Philosophy** (Philosophy); **Visiting Students** (Philosophy)
History: Founded 1986.
Academic year: September to June (September-January; March-June)
Admission requirements: Master degree (or equivalent, e.g. Magister or Diplom); Admissions is possible with a Master in a subject other than Philosophy with extra training programme and also with a lower level degree under certain requirements.
Fees: 3,250 per semester (a total 19,500 per programme) (Swiss Franc)
Main language(s) of instruction: German, English, Spanish
Accrediting agency: Schulamt, Ressort Bildungswesen Fürstentum Liechtenstein (Office of Education, affiliated to Ministry of Education of the Principality of Liechtenstein)
Degrees and diplomas: Doctorate (Philosophy)
Student Services: Academic Counselling, Language Laboratory, Library
Periodicals: Aletheia
Last Update: 16-12-2015

University of Human Sciences (UFL)

Dorfstrasse 24
Triesen FL-9495
Tel: +423 392-40-10
Fax: +423 392-40-11
Website: http://www.ufl.li
Prorektorin, Rektorin a. i.: Barbara Gant

Faculty

Law (Constitutional Law; European Union Law; International Law; Labour Law; Law; Private Law; Taxation); **Medical Science** (Medicine)

History: Founded 2000. Formerly known as Universität für Humanwissenschaften im Fürstentum Liechtenstein (University of Human Sciences).
Fees: 25,500 per programme (Swiss Franc)
Main language(s) of instruction: German
Degrees and diplomas: Master (Sports Management), Doctorate (Law; Medicine). Also Certificate of Advanced Studies in Law (Health Legislation); Executive Master Degree Programmes in International Civil Law, Property Law and Mediation; MD-PhD programme jointly offered with the Medical University of Innsbruck.
Last Update: 17-12-2015

Lithuania

STRUCTURE OF HIGHER EDUCATION SYSTEM

Description

Lithuania has a binary system of higher education consisting of college and university studies. The focus of college level studies is the preparation for professional activity and applied research. The studies require 180–240 ECTS credits to complete and lead to a degree of profesinis bakalauras (Professional Bachelor). Holders of the degree have the right to enter 2nd cycle (Master) studies. University studies are organized in three cycles. The 1st cycle university studies require 180–240 ECTS credits to complete and lead to a degree of bakalauras (Bachelor). The degree gives access to 2nd cycle studies. The 2nd cycle studies require 60–120 ECTS credits to complete and lead to a degree of magistras (Master). The degree gives access to 3rd cycle studies. The 3rd cycle is usually of 4-6 years and leads to a research degree of daktaras (Doctor). There are also vientisosios (integrated long-cycle) university studies (combining studies of the 1st and 2nd cycle), which are usually offered in several fields of medicine, veterinary medicine, law, and religious studies. The studies require 300–360 ECTS credits to complete and lead to a degree of magistras (Master). Higher education institutions can also offer non-degree programmes, which award additional professional qualification and/or prepare for independent practice in several professional activities. Holders of higher education qualifications are eligible to such programmes. The programmes can be provided by colleges and universities and do not lead to a degree. The aim of programmes is to prepare students for independent professional practice or to upgrade professional qualification. To this type of programmes covers: - rezidentūra (residency) programmes in medicine, odontology, veterinary medicine. Duration of residency studies is from 2 to 6 years. Rezidentūros pažymėjimas (Certificate of Residency) is awarded after completion of residency studies; - programmes in pedagogical studies (pedagoginės studijos). Studijų pažymėjimas (Certificate of studies) is issued after completion of other non-degree granting studies.

Stages of studies

University level first stage

University 1st cycle studies (universitetines pirmosios pakopos studijos)

University 1st cycle studies are offered by university-level institutions called universities (universitetas), academies (akademija), or seminaries (seminarija). Studies last from 3 1/2 to 4 years (210 to 240 ECTS). Studies are research-oriented with subjects related to the field of study and to a certain extent a narrower specialization comprising most of the curriculum. The main standards and requirements irrespective of the field of study are nationally set. To complete the programme, students are expected to prepare and defend a final thesis or, in certain cases, to pass final examinations. Successful graduates are awarded a Bachelor's degree (bakalauro laipsnis) in the field of study. The Bachelor's degree (bakalauro laipsnis) gives access to the 2nd cycle (Master) programmes.

University level second stage

University 2nd cycle studies (universitetines antrosios pakopos studijos)

Master studies: University 2nd cycle studies are offered by university-level institutions called universities (universitetas), academies (akademija), or seminaries (seminarija) where research related to the subject area is conducted. The studies last from 1 1/2 to 2 years (90 to 120 ECTS). They prepare for independent research activities and activities which require scientific knowledge and analytical skills. The main standards and requirements irrespective of the field of study are nationally set. To complete the programme, students are expected to prepare and defend a final thesis, which should be analytical and based on independent research. Successful graduates are awarded a Master's degree (magistro laipsnis) in the field of study. Those who majored in Theology may be awarded a Licentiate degree in Theology (teologijos licenciato laipsnis). The

© International Association of Universities 2019
International Handbook of Universities 2019,
https://doi.org/10.1057/978-3-319-76971-4_112

Master's degree (magistro laipsnis) gives access to the 3rd cycle (Doctoral) programmes. Integrated studies: Integrated (vientisosios) studies are long-cycle studies, which combine the 1st and 2nd university cycles. Holders of Maturity Certificate (Brandos atestatas) or a comparable qualification can be admitted. The studies last from 5 to 6 years (300 to 360 ECTS). The first part of the studies (240 ECTS) is considered to be part of the 1st cycle, the rest of the studies belong to the 2nd cycle. The regulations for each of the cycles apply accordingly. Successful graduates are awarded a Master's degree (magistro laipsnis) in the field of study, which gives access to the 3rd cycle (Doctoral) programmes.

University level third stage

University 3rd cycle studies (universitetines treciosios pakopos studijos)

University 3rd cycle studies are offered by university-level institutions called universities (universitetas), academies (akademija), or seminaries (seminarija), which were granted the right to offer Doctoral studies by the Ministry of Education and Science as able to conduct advanced research activities. At times doctoral studies may be jointly offered by university level higher education institutions and research institutes. Doctoral studies may be offered in the fields of science, humanities, and arts aimed at preparing for independent and/or experimental research. Doctoral studies last from 3 to 4 years (6 years part-time). They consist of doctoral courses (at least 30 ECTS), specific research activities, and preparation and public defence of a doctoral dissertation. Successful graduates are awarded a Degree of Doctor of Science (mokslo daktaro laipsnis) or a Degree of Doctor of Arts (meno daktaro laipsnis).

ADMISSION TO HIGHER EDUCATION

Admission to university-level studies

Name of Secondary school credential required: Brandos atestatas

For entry to: Bachelor's programmes and integrated programmes.

Alternatives to credentials: A comparable qualification.

Other requirements: Generally, maturity (school level and state level) examinations serve as graduation and admission requirement. However, for admission to certain programmes, especially in arts, an entrance examination may be held.

Numerus clausus: There is a numerus clausus, which applies to state funded places, set by the Ministry of Education and Science according to the field of study. Institutions may set their own numerus clausus for fee paying students.

Foreign students admission

Definition of foreign student: A foreign student is a person who is not a permanent resident in Lithuania and is enrolled at a Lithuanian institution of higher education.

Quotas: Study grants awarded to EU students with foreign qualifications, irrespective of their nationality (including Lithuanian citizens who have acquired their education abroad) should not exceed 10 percent of all state funded grants.

Admission requirements: Foreign applicants should at least hold a level of education comparable to a Lithuanian qualification required for admission to the particular study programme. Information on the assessment and comparability of qualifications is provided by the Centre for Quality Assessment in Higher Education (Lithuanian ENIC/NARIC) (www. skvc.lt).

Entry regulations: Entry regulations may vary depending on the country of origin of a foreign student. Foreign nationals are encouraged to contact a Lithuanian embassy or check on the websites of the Ministry of Foreign Affairs (www.urm.lt) and Migration Department (www.migracija.lt) whether they need a visa and a temporary residence permit.

Health requirements: Health insurance is obligatory to all foreign students in Lithuania. EU citizens who have health insurance in their home country do not need additional insurance.

Language Proficiency: A student should be proficient in the language of instruction. Usually, the language of instruction is Lithuanian and an applicant has to pass the pass/fail test in Lithuanian language (www.flf.vu.lt/lsk/). In case the language of instruction is other than Lithuanian (English, German, or Russian), applicants must pass a test to demonstrate their proficiency in that language.

RECOGNITION OF STUDIES

Quality assurance system

While higher education institutions are primarily responsible for the quality assurance and are setting up systems of internal quality assurance, the external quality assurance in higher education is carried out by the Centre for Quality Assessment in Higher Education (www.skvc.lt). The Centre is an independent body, which carries out institutional and study programme assessment for the purposes of accreditation. The list of recognized higher education institutions and accredited study programmes is available at: www.aikos.smm.lt.

Bodies dealing with recognition

Studijų kokybės vertinimo centras - SKVC (Centre for Quality Assessment in Higher Education - Lithuanian ENIC/NARIC)
Director: Almantas Šerpatauskas
Deputy Director: Aurelija Valeikiene.
A. Goštauto g. 12
Vilnius 01108
Tel: +370(5) 210-4772
Fax: +370(5) 213-2553
Website: http://www.skvc.lt

Special provisions for recognition

Recognition for University level studies
Information on academic recognition of foreign qualifications for the purposes of study can be provided by the Centre for Quality Assessment in Higher Education (www.skvc.lt).

For access to advanced studies and research
Information on academic recognition of foreign qualifications for the purposes of study can be provided by the Centre for Quality Assessment in Higher Education (www.skvc.lt).

For the exercise of a profession
Information on academic recognition of foreign qualifications for the purposes of work for non-regulated professions can be provided by the Centre for Quality Assessment in Higher Education (www.skvc.lt). Information on the recognition of regulated professions is available at www.profesijos.lt.

NATIONAL BODIES

Švietimo ir mokslo ministerija (Ministry of Education and Science)

Minister: Algirdas Monkevičius
A. Volano g. 2/7
Vilnius 01516
Tel: +370(5) 219-1190
Fax: +370(5) 261-2077
Website: http://www.smm.lt

Lietuvos mokslo taryba - LMT (Research Council of Lithuania)

Chairman: Valdemaras Razumas
Gedimino pr. 3
Vilnius 01103
Tel: +370(5) 212-4933
Fax: +370(5) 261-8535
Website: http://www.lmt.lt
Role of national body: Created in 1991 as an expert institution to look at the challenges of science development on a national level. It also advises the Goverment on science and research issues, evaluates research performance and represents Lithuanian science in European institutions and other international organisations.

Mokslo ir studijų stebesenos ir analizes centras - MOSTA (Research and Higher Education Monitoring and Analysis Centre)

Head of Innovation Policy Analysis Unit, Acting Managing Director: Ramojus Reimeris
Geležinio Vilko g. 12
Vilnius 03163
Tel: +370(5) 212-6898
Fax: +370(5) 243-0402
Website: http://www.mosta.lt
Role of national body: A state analytical and advisory body. MOSTA draws up recommendations on the development of the national research and higher education systems, performs monitoring function, analyses the state of the Lithuanian research and higher education systems, and participates in the development and implementation of research and higher education policies.

Lietuvos kolgiju direktoriu konferencija (Rectors' Conference of Lithuanian University Colleges)

President: Gintautas Bužinskas
Tvirtovės al. 35
Kaunas 50155
Tel: +370(37) 308-620
Fax: +370(37) 333-120
Website: http://www.kolegijos.lt

Lietuvos universitetu rektorių konferencija (Lithuanian University Rectors' Conference)

President: Artūras Žukauskas
Secretary-General: Kestutis Krišciunas
Laisvės al. 13
Kaunas 44238
Tel: +370(37) 300-137
Website: http://www.lurk.lt

Data for academic year: 2018–2019
Source: Centre for Quality Assessment in Higher Education, Vilnius, 2018.

Public Institutions

Aleksandras Stulginskis University

Studentų g. 11, Akademijos mstl.
Kaunas 53361
Tel: +370(37) 75-23-98
Fax: +370(37) 39-75-00
Website: http://www.asu.lt
Rector: Antanas Maziliauskas
Tel: +370(37) 75-22-05

Faculty

Agricultural Engineering (Agricultural Engineering; Agricultural Equipment; Energy Engineering; Mechanical Engineering); **Agronomy** (Agronomy; Animal Husbandry; Biology; Crop Production; Horticulture; Soil Science); **Economics and Management** (Accountancy; Business Administration; Economics; Finance; Management; Rural Planning); **Forestry and Ecology** (Ecology; Forest Management; Forestry); **Water and Land Management** (Agricultural Management; Hydraulic Engineering; Rural Planning; Surveying and Mapping; Water Management)

Institute

Environment (Environmental Studies; Rural Planning); **Information Technology** (Computer Science; Information Technology; Mathematics); **Rural Culture** (Cultural Studies; Modern Languages; Philosophy; Political Sciences; Psychology; Social Sciences)
Further information: Also Training Farm. Experimental Station. Innovation Centre. Careee Centre
History: Founded 1924 in Dotnuva (Kėdainiai district). Relocated to Kaunas, 1964. Under the resolution of Parliament on October 8th, 1996, the name of Lithuanian Academy of Agriculture was changed to Lithuanian University of Agriculture. Following the resolution of the LR Seimas on June 28th, 2011, it was granted the name of Aleksandras Stulginskis University.
Academic year: September to June (September-January; February-June)
Admission requirements: Secondary school certificate (Vidurinės Mokyklos Baigimo Atestatas)
Main language(s) of instruction: Lithuanian, English, Russian
Accrediting agency: Lithuanian Centre for Quality Assessment in Higher Education
Degrees and diplomas: Bakalauro diplomas (Agricultural Engineering; Agronomy; Ecology; Economics; Forestry; Management; Soil Science; Water Management), Magistro diplomas (Agricultural Engineering; Agronomy; Biotechnology; Ecology; Economics; Engineering; Finance; Forestry; Management; Public Administration; Soil Science; Water Management), Daktaro diplomas (Agricultural Engineering; Agronomy; Ecology; Economics; Forestry; Management; Soil Science; Water Management)
Student Services: Academic Counselling, Social Counselling, Nursery Care, Cultural Activities, Sports Facilities, Language Laboratory, Facilities for disabled people, Health Services, Canteen, Library, Residential Facilities
Periodicals: Science Reports
Publishing house: Lietuvos Žemes Ukio Akademijos Leidybinis Centras
Last Update: 17-03-2015

Kaunas University of Technology (KTU)

K. Donelaičio g. 73
Kaunas 44249
Tel: +370(37) 300-000, +370(37) 300- 421
Fax: +370(37) 324-144
Website: http://www.ktu.lt
Rector: Petras Baršauskas
Tel: +370(37) 300-001

Faculty

Chemical Technology (Applied Chemistry; Chemical Engineering; Chemistry; Environmental Engineering; Environmental Management; Food Science; Food Technology); **Civil Engineering and Architecture** (Architecture; Civil Engineering; Real Estate; Regional Planning; Town Planning); **Design and Technology** (Fashion Design; Furniture Design; Multimedia; Polymer and Plastics Technology; Printing and Printmaking; Textile Design; Textile Technology; Wood Technology); **Electrical and Electronics Engineering** (Automation and Control Engineering; Electrical Engineering; Electronic Engineering; Safety Engineering);

Humanities (Cultural Studies; Linguistics; Media Studies; Philosophy; Translation and Interpretation); **Informatics** (Computer Engineering; Computer Science); **Management and Administration** (*Panevezys*) (Business Administration; Management); **Mathematics and Natural Sciences** (Applied Mathematics; Applied Physics; Mathematics Education; Radiophysics); **Mechanical Engineering and Design** (Industrial Engineering; Materials Engineering; Mechanical Engineering; Packaging Technology; Production Engineering; Thermal Engineering; Transport Engineering); **Social Sciences, Arts and Humanities** (Business Administration; Educational Sciences; Educational Technology; Pedagogy; Public Administration; Sociology); **Technologies and Business** (*Panevėžys*) (Automation and Control Engineering; Civil Engineering; Mechanical Engineering; Transport Engineering); **Telecommunications and Electronics** (Biomedical Engineering; Electronic Engineering; Engineering Management; Measurement and Precision Engineering; Telecommunications Engineering)

School

Economics and Business (Accountancy; Economics; Finance; International Business; Management; Marketing)

Institute

Architecture and Construction (Architecture; Construction Engineering); **Biomedical Engineering** (Biomedical Engineering); **Defence Technologies**; **Environmental Engineering** (Environmental Engineering; Environmental Management; Natural Resources; Waste Management); **Food** (Food Technology); **Health Telematics Science**; **Materials Science** (Chemistry; Materials Engineering); **Mechatronics** (Electronic Engineering; Mechanical Engineering); **Metrology** (Measurement and Precision Engineering); **Ultrasound Research** (*Prof. K. Baršauskas*) (Sound Engineering (Acoustics))

Centre

Computational Technologies (Computer Engineering; Mechanical Engineering; Systems Analysis); **International Studies** (Engineering Management; Mechanical Engineering); **Mechatronics Science, Studies and Information**; **Micro-systems and Nanotechnology Research** (Nanotechnology); **Physical Education and Health** (Health Education; Sports)

History: Founded 1922, became University of Lithuania 1922 and University of Kaunas 1940. Technical Department detached and re-organized into Kaunas Polytechnic Institute 1950. Acquired university status 1990.

Academic year: September to June (September-January; February-June)

Admission requirements: Maturity Certificate (Brandos atestatas) or equivalent

Main language(s) of instruction: Lithuanian, English, German, French, Russian

Degrees and diplomas: Bakalauro diplomas (Engineering), Magistro diplomas (Architecture; Arts and Humanities; Business Administration; Chemistry; Civil Engineering; Computer Engineering; Design; Education; Electrical and Electronic Engineering; Engineering; Environmental Studies; Mathematics; Mechanical Engineering; Musicology; Natural Sciences; Social Sciences; Technology), Daktaro diplomas. Also Mokytojo diplomas in Teacher Training (a further 1 yr after BSc)

Student Services: Academic Counselling, Social Counselling, Careers Guidance, Cultural Activities, Sports Facilities, Language Laboratory, Health Services, Canteen, Library

Periodicals: Chemical Technology, Electronics and Electrical Engineering, Engineering Economics, Environmental Research, Engineering and Management, Information Technology and Control, Materials Science, Measurements, Mechanics, Public Politics and Administration, Social Sciences, Ultrasound

Publishing house: Publishing Centre

Student Numbers 2014-2015	MALE	FEMALE	TOTAL
All (Foreign Included)			10895

Last Update: 17-03-2015

Klaipėda University (KU)

Herkaus Manto g. 84
Klaipėda 92294
Tel: +370(46) 39-89-00
Fax: +370(46) 39-89-99
Website: http://www.ku.lt
Rector: Eimutis Juzeliūnas

Faculty

Arts (Fine Arts; Performing Arts); **Health Sciences** (Health Sciences); **Humanities** (Arts and Humanities); **Marine Engineering** (Marine Engineering); **Natural Sciences and Mathematics** (Mathematics; Natural Sciences); **Pedagogy** (Pedagogy); **Social Sciences** (Social Sciences)

Institute

Coastal Research and Planning (Coastal Studies); **Continuing Studies** (Continuing Education); **History and Archaeology of the Baltic Region** (Archaeology; History); **Marine Seascape Science** (Marine Science and Oceanography); **Maritime** (Marine Science and Oceanography); **Mechatronics Science** (Electrical Engineering; Mechanical Engineering); **Regional Policy and Planning** (Regional Planning)

Centre

American Studies (American Studies); **Baltic Studies** (Baltic Languages); **English Language** (English); **Evangelical Theology** (*Study and Research Centre*) (Christian Religious Studies; Theology); **Oriental Studies** (Asian Studies; Middle Eastern Studies; Oriental Languages); **Scandinavian Languages and Cultures** (Scandinavian Languages); **Slavic Studies**

History: Founded 1991.

Academic year: September to June (September-January; February-June)

Admission requirements: Secondary school certificate (Brandos Atestatas)

Main language(s) of instruction: Lithuanian

Degrees and diplomas: Bakalauro diplomas, Magistro diplomas (Arts and Humanities; Business Administration; Communication Studies; Ecology; Engineering; English; Environmental Studies; Fishery; French; German; Health Sciences; Information Sciences; Linguistics; Management; Marine Engineering; Marine Science and Oceanography; Marketing; Media Studies; Music; Nursing; Pedagogy; Psychology; Public Health; Social Work; Surveying and Mapping), Daktaro diplomas (Ecology; Environmental Studies). KU implements doctoral studies in partnership with other national universities: http://www.ku.lt/en/research/doctoral-phd-studies/

Student Services: Academic Counselling, Cultural Activities, Sports Facilities, Facilities for disabled people, Canteen, Library

Periodicals: Acta Historica Universitatis Klaipedensis, Archaeologica Baltica, Jūra ir aplinka (Sea and Environment), Sociologija: mintis ir veiksmas (Sociology: Thought and Action), Tiltai (Bridges)

Publishing house: Klaipeda University Press

Last Update: 18-03-2015

Lithuanian Academy of Music and Theatre (LMTA)

Gedimino pr. 42
Vilnius 01110
Tel: +370(8-5) 261-2691
Fax: +370(8-5) 212-6982
Website: http://www.lmta.lt
Rector: Zbignevas Ibelhauptas

Faculty

Music (Conducting; Music; Music Theory and Composition; Musical Instruments; Opera; Singing); **Theatre and Film** (Acting; Art Criticism; Art History; Art Management; Cinema and Television; Film; Theatre)

History: Founded 1933. Formerly Lietuvos Muzikos Akademija. In 1949 the Conservatoire of Kaunas and the Conservatoire of Vilnius (founded in 1945) were merged into the Lithuanian State Conservatoire. In 1992 the Conservatoire was renamed Lithuanian Academy of Music (LMA), and in 2004 Lithuanian Academy of Music and Theatre (LMTA).

Academic year: September to June (September-January; February-June)

Admission requirements: Certificate of secondary education and secondary musical education or equivalent

Main language(s) of instruction: Lithuanian, English, German, Russian

Accrediting agency: Ministry of Education and Science; Lithuanian Centre for Quality Assessment in Higher Education

Degrees and diplomas: Bakalauro diplomas (Cinema and Television; Music; Music Education; Musicology; Theatre), Magistro diplomas (Cinema and Television; Music; Musicology; Theatre), Daktaro diplomas (Art History; Musicology)

Student Services: Nursery Care, Sports Facilities, Language Laboratory, Health Services, Canteen, Library

Periodicals: Collection of Scientific Articles

Last Update: 19-03-2015

Lithuanian Sports University (LSU)

Sporto g. 6
Kaunas 44221
Tel: +370(37) 302-621
Fax: +370(37) 204-515
Website: http://www.lsu.lt/
President: Albertas Skurvydas
Tel: +370(37) 302-645

Faculty

Sport Biomedicine (Biology; Biomedicine; Physical Therapy; Rehabilitation and Therapy); **Sport Education** (Health Education; Physical Education; Sports; Sports Management)

Institute

National Wellness; **Sport Science and Innovations** (Sports)

History: Founded 1934.

Main language(s) of instruction: Lithuanian

Degrees and diplomas: Bakalauro diplomas, Magistro diplomas (Sports), Daktaro diplomas (Sports)

Student Services: Sports Facilities

Student Numbers 2014-2015	MALE	FEMALE	TOTAL
All (Foreign Included)			c. 2000

Last Update: 19-03-2015

Lithuanian University of Educational Sciences (LUES)

Studentu g. 39
Vilnius 08106
Tel: +370(5) 279-02-81
Fax: +370(5) 279-05-48
Website: http://www.leu.lt/
Rector: Algirdas Gaižutis

Faculty

Education (Art Education; Dance; Education; Educational Psychology; Ethics; Music Education; Preschool Education; Primary Education; Psychology; Social Work; Theatre); **History** (Anthropology; Catholic Theology; History; History of Religion); **Lithuanian Philology** (Baltic Languages; Linguistics; Literature; Philology); **Philology** (Applied Linguistics; Communication Studies; English; French; German; Modern Languages; Philology; Polish; Russian; Slavic Languages); **Science and Technology** (Biology; Chemistry; Computer Engineering; Geography; Information Technology; Mathematics and Computer Science; Natural Sciences; Physics; Technology Education; Tourism); **Social Sciences** (Economics; Philosophy; Social Sciences; Social Work; Sociology); **Sports and Health Education** (Health Sciences; Physical Education; Sports)
History: Founded 1935, acquired present status 1992 and title 2011. Previously known as Vilniaus Pedagoginis Universitetas.
Academic year: September to June
Admission requirements: Secondary school certificate (Brandos Atestatas)
Main language(s) of instruction: Russian, Lithuanian, English
Degrees and diplomas: Bakalauro diplomas, Magistro diplomas (Dance; Educational Administration; English; Ethics; Music Education; Psychology), Daktaro diplomas. Master Programmes in Russian: Geography; Biology; Fine Arts, Preschool Education, Lingusitics, Communication Studies
Student Services: Cultural Activities, Sports Facilities, Language Laboratory, Facilities for disabled people, Canteen, Library

Periodicals: Istorija (History), Pedagogika (Education), Socialinis ugdymas (Social Education), Ugdymo psichologija (Developmental Psychology, Žmogus ir žodis (Man and the Word)
Publishing house: University Publishing House
Last Update: 19-03-2015

Lithuanian University of Health Sciences (LSMU)

A. Mickevičiaus g. 9
Kaunas 44307
Tel: +370(37) 327-200
Fax: +370(37) 220-733
Website: http://www.lsmuni.lt
Dean: Remigijus Žaliūnas
Tel: +370(37) 327-201

Faculty

Medicine (Anatomy; Biology; Education; Genetics; Mathematics; Medicine; Modern Languages; Oncology; Pharmacology; Physics); **Nursing** (Nursing); **Odontology** (Dentistry); **Pharmacy** (Pharmacy); **Public Health** (Public Health)

Institute

Behavioral Medicine (*Palanga*) (Psychology; Rehabilitation and Therapy); **Cardiology** (Cardiology); **Endocrinology** (Endocrinology); **Neuroscience** (Neurosciences)

Academy

Veterinary Science (Veterinary Science)
Further information: Teaching Hospital of Kaunas University of Medicine
History: Founded 1922 as a Faculty of Medicine of Kaunas University. Reorganized into a separate Kaunas Medical Institute 1950. Became Kaunas Medical Academy 1989. Acquired present title 2010 following merge with Lthuanian Veterinary Academy.
Academic year: September to June (September-January; February-June)
Admission requirements: Secondary school certificate (Brandos atestatas), and entrance examination
Main language(s) of instruction: Lithuanian, English
Degrees and diplomas: Bakalauro diplomas (Nursing; Public Health), Magistro diplomas (Dentistry; Medicine; Nursing; Pharmacy; Public Health), Daktaro diplomas. Also Certificate of Professional Qualification in Nursing (2 yrs)

Student Services: Academic Counselling, Cultural Activities, Sports Facilities, Language Laboratory, Health Services, Canteen, Foreign Studies Centre, Library
Periodicals: Lithuanian Journal of Cardiology, Medicina
Publishing house: Publishing Office of Kaunas University of Medicine
Last Update: 19-03-2015

Mykolas Romeris University (MRU)

Ateities g. 20
Vilnius 08303
Tel: +370(5) 271-46-25
Fax: +370(5) 267-60-00
Website: http://www.mruni.eu
Acting Rector: Inga Žalėnienė

Faculty

Economics and Business (Banking; Business Administration; Computer Engineering; Computer Science; Economics; Finance; International Business; International Studies; Management; Software Engineering; Taxation); **Law** (Administrative Law; Civil Law; Commercial Law; Comparative Law; Constitutional Law; Criminal Law; European Union Law; History of Law; International Law; International Studies; Labour Law; Law; Private Law; Public Law); **Public Governance** (Environmental Management; International Studies; Management; Political Sciences; Public Administration); **Public Security** (Arts and Humanities; Criminal Law; Criminology; Law; Physical Education; Police Studies; Protective Services; Public Administration)

Institute

Communication (Communication Studies; Cultural Studies; International Studies); **Educational Sciences and Social Work** (Education; Educational Technology; International Studies; Law; Leisure Studies; Pedagogy; Social and Community Services; Social Policy; Social Work; Sociology); **Humanities** (Baltic Languages; Chinese; Danish; English; Finnish; French; German; Hebrew; Hindi; Italian; Japanese; Modern Languages; Norwegian; Philosophy; Portuguese; Russian; Spanish; Swedish; Turkish); **Psychology** (Psychology)
History: Founded 1990. Renamed Lietuvos Teisės Universitetas (Law University of Lithuania) 2000. Acquired present title and status 2004.
Academic year: September to June (September-January; February-June)
Admission requirements: Certificate of Secondary Education (Brandos Atestatas). Students are admitted according to average marks in selected exams, plus the average of annual marks in relative subjects. Admission requirements for overseas students are to be found on the university website.
Fees: National : National and EU citizens: Undergraduate Programmes,1270-2160 per year. Graduate Programmes, 2120-4480 per year (Euro), International : Non-EU citizens: Undergraduate Programmes, 2160-2460 per year. Graduate Programmes, 2240-6240 per year (Euro)
Main language(s) of instruction: Lithuanian, English, Russian
Accrediting agency: Lithuanian Centre for Quality Assessment in Higher Education
Degrees and diplomas: Bakalauro diplomas (Computer Science; Economics; Law; Psychology; Public Administration; Social Work), Magistro diplomas (Business Administration; Business and Commerce; Economics; Educational Sciences; Finance; Human Resources; Law; Management; Political Sciences; Psychology; Public Administration; Social Work; Sociology), Daktaro diplomas (Law; Psychology)
Student Services: Academic Counselling, Social Counselling, Careers Guidance, Cultural Activities, Sports Facilities, Language Laboratory, Facilities for disabled people, Health Services, Canteen, Foreign Studies Centre, Library, Residential Facilities
Periodicals: Business systems & Economics, Health Policy and Management, Intellectual Economics, Jurisprudence, Public Policy and Administration, Social Inquiry Into Well-Being, Social Technologies, Social Work, Societal Studies

Student Numbers 2017-2018	MALE	FEMALE	TOTAL
All (Foreign Included)			9000

Last Update: 03-01-2018

Siauliai University (ŠU)

Vilniaus g. 88
Šiauliai 76285
Tel: +370(41) 59-58-00
Fax: +370(41) 59-58-09
Website: http://www.su.lt
Rector: Donatas Jurgaitis
Tel: +370(41) 595-803

Faculty

Arts (Design; Fine Arts; Graphic Arts; Interior Design; Music; Painting and Drawing; Technology; Theatre); **Education** (Educational Research; Physical Education; Preschool Education; Primary Education; Sports; Teacher Training); **Humanities** (Arts and Humanities; Classical Languages; Comparative Literature; Heritage Preservation; History;

International and Comparative Education; International Studies; Linguistics; Literature; Mass Communication; Modern Languages; Philosophy; Translation and Interpretation); **Social Sciences** (Business Administration; Economics; Management; Production Engineering; Public Administration; Teacher Training); **Social Welfare and Disability Studies** (Health Education; Physical Education; Physical Therapy; Special Education; Speech Therapy and Audiology); **Technology and Natural Science** (Biomedical Engineering; Civil Engineering; Construction Engineering; Ecology; Electrical and Electronic Engineering; Electrical Engineering; Environmental Studies; Industrial Design; Information Technology; Mechanical Engineering; Power Engineering; Technology)

Institute

Continuing Education (Computer Science; Educational Sciences; Ethics; Management; Modern Languages; Psychology; Public Administration; Social Work; Special Education; Teacher Training); **Informatics, Mathematics and E-Studies** (Computer Science; Mathematics and Computer Science; Statistics)

Further information: Also Research Centres

History: Founded 1948 as Teacher Training Institute. Acquired present status and title 1997 with the merging of Šiauliai Pedagogigal Institute and Šiauliai Polytechnical Faculty of Kaunas Technological University.

Academic year: September to June (September-December; February-June)

Admission requirements: Secondary school certificate (Vidurines Mokyklos Baigimo Atestatas)

Main language(s) of instruction: Lithuanian, English, Russian

Degrees and diplomas: Bakalauro diplomas (Agriculture; Arts and Humanities; Business Administration; Education; Engineering; Fine Arts; Mathematics and Computer Science; Natural Sciences; Performing Arts; Social Sciences; Technology; Welfare and Protective Services), Magistro diplomas (Arts and Humanities; Business Administration; Computer Science; Education; Engineering; Fine Arts; Mathematics; Performing Arts; Social Sciences; Technology), Daktaro diplomas (Education)

Student Services: Academic Counselling, Careers Guidance, Nursery Care, Cultural Activities, Sports Facilities, Language Laboratory, Facilities for disabled people, Canteen, Foreign Studies Centre, Library

Periodicals: Šiaulių Universitetas

Academic Staff 2014-2015	MALE	FEMALE	TOTAL
FULL-TIME			300
Student Numbers 2014-2015			
All (Foreign Included)			4000

Last Update: 19-03-2015

Vilnius Academy of Arts (VDA)

Maironio g. 6
Vilnius 01124
Tel: +370(5) 210-54-30
Fax: +370(5) 210-54-44
Website: http://www.vda.lt
Rector (Acting): Audrius Klimas

Faculty

Applied Arts (Architecture; Ceramic Art; Clothing and Sewing; Design; Fashion Design; Fine Arts; Textile Design); **Architecture and Design** (Architecture; Design); **Arts** (*Telsia*) (Clothing and Sewing; Design; Furniture Design; Jewellery Art; Sculpture); **Arts** (*Kaunas*) (Architecture; Ceramic Art; Glass Art; Graphic Arts; Painting and Drawing; Sculpture; Textile Design); **Humanities and Social Sciences** (Art Education; Art History; Modern Languages); **Visual and Applied Arts** (Art History; Graphic Arts; Heritage Preservation; Painting and Drawing; Philosophy; Photography; Sculpture; Visual Arts)

Chair

Cultural Management and Cultural Policy (*UNESCO Chair*) (Cultural Studies; Heritage Preservation)

Further information: Branches in Telšiai, Kaunas and Klaipėda

History: Founded 1793 as Faculty of Architecture, of Vilnius University, reorganized 1941 and acquired present status and title 1990. A State institution.

Academic year: September to May (September-December; February-May)

Admission requirements: Secondary school certificate (Brandos Atestatas)

Fees: Undergraduate: 1248-3233 depending on programmes. Graduate: 2242 to 4227 depending on programmes (Euro)

Main language(s) of instruction: Lithuanian

Degrees and diplomas: Bakalauro diplomas (Fine Arts), Magistro diplomas (Architecture; Art History; Design; Fine Arts; Graphic Design; Painting and Drawing; Photography; Sculpture), Daktaro diplomas (Art Criticism; Design; Fine Arts)

Student Services: Cultural Activities, Sports Facilities, Facilities for disabled people, Canteen, Library

Student Numbers 2014-2015	MALE	FEMALE	TOTAL
All (Foreign Included)			1800

Last Update: 19-03-2015

Vilnius Gediminas Technical University (VGTU)

Sauletekio al. 11
Vilnius 10223
Tel: +370(5) 274-50-30
Fax: +370(5) 270-01-12
Website: http://www.vgtu.lt
Rector: Alfonsas Daniūnas
Tel: +370(5) 274-50-00

Faculty

Architecture (Architecture; Regional Planning; Structural Architecture; Town Planning); **Business Management** (Business Administration; Business Computing; Economics; Finance; International Business; International Economics; Law; Management); **Civil Engineering** (Bridge Engineering; Building Technologies; Civil Engineering; Construction Engineering; Economics; Fire Science; Geological Engineering; Materials Engineering; Mechanics; Real Estate; Safety Engineering; Structural Architecture); **Creative Industries** (European Languages; Modern Languages; Philosophy; Political Sciences; Sports; Tourism); **Electronics** (Automation and Control Engineering; Computer Engineering; Electrical Engineering; Electronic Engineering; Telecommunications Engineering); **Environmental Engineering** (Civil Engineering; Energy Engineering; Environmental Engineering; Environmental Studies; Hydraulic Engineering; Road Engineering; Surveying and Mapping; Urban Studies; Water Management); **Fundamental Sciences** (Bioengineering; Chemistry; Computer Graphics; Information Sciences; Information Technology; Materials Engineering; Mathematics; Mechanical Engineering; Physics; Statistics); **Mechanics** (Industrial Management; Machine Building; Mechanical Engineering; Mechanics; Metal Techniques; Printing and Printmaking); **Transport Engineering** (Management; Railway Transport; Road Transport; Transport and Communications; Transport Engineering; Transport Management)

Institute

Aviation (*Antanas Gustaitis*) (Aeronautical and Aerospace Engineering; Air Transport; Mechanics); **Humanities** (Baltic Languages; English; Modern Languages; Philosophy; Physical Education; Political Sciences)

Centre

International Studies (International Studies)

Research Division

Architecture (Architecture); **Aviation** (Aeronautical and Aerospace Engineering); **Bioinformatics** (Biological and Life Sciences; Computer Science); **Building Physics** (Building Technologies; Physics); **Buildings** (Building Technologies); **Business Planning and Environment Economics** (Business Administration; Economics; Environmental Studies); **Calibration** (Measurement and Precision Engineering); **Construction Technology and Management** (Construction Engineering); **Constructions and Materials** (Construction Engineering; Materials Engineering); **Environmental Protection** (Environmental Studies); **Environmental Protection and Working Conditions** (Environmental Studies; Safety Engineering); **Geodesy** (Geology); **Geotechnical Engineering** (Geological Engineering); **High Magnetic Fields** (Physics); **Information Systems** (Information Sciences); **Internet and Intelligent Technologies** (Information Technology); **Labour Safety** (Safety Engineering); **Material Physics** (Physics); **Nuclear Hydrophysics** (Nuclear Engineering); **Numerical Modeling** (Computer Graphics); **Open Source** (Information Sciences); **Parallel Computations** (Computer Science); **Property Valuation** (Real Estate); **Roads** (Road Engineering); **Science** (Natural Sciences); **Special Structures** (*Kompozitas*) (Structural Architecture); **Strength Mechanics** (Mechanics); **Telecommunications** (Telecommunications Engineering); **Territorial Planning** (Regional Planning); **Transport** (Transport and Communications); **Urban Analysis** (Urban Studies); **Vibroacoustics and Diagnostics** (Sound Engineering (Acoustics)); **Welding and Material Science** (Materials Engineering; Metal Techniques)

History: Founded 1956 as Vilnius branch of Kaunas Polytechnic Institute, became Vilnius Civil Engineering Institute 1969, and acquired present status 1990 and title 1996.

Academic year: September to June (September-February, February-June)

Admission requirements: General or special secondary school certificate and entrance examination

Main language(s) of instruction: Lithuanian, English

Accrediting agency: Lithuanian Centre for Quality Assesment in Higher Education

Degrees and diplomas: Bakalauro diplomas (Architecture; Physics; Social Sciences), Magistro diplomas (Biomedical Engineering; Fine Arts; Physics; Social Sciences), Daktaro diplomas (Art History; Civil Engineering; Computer Engineering; Economics; Electrical and Electronic Engineering; English; Environmental Studies; Management; Materials Engineering; Mechanical Engineering)

Student Services: Academic Counselling, Careers Guidance, Sports Facilities, Canteen, Foreign Studies Centre

Periodicals: Aviation, Cultural regionalistics, Gedimino universitetas, Geodesy and Carthography, International Journal of Strategic Property Management, Inžinerija, Journal of Business Economics and Management, Journal of Civil Engineering and Management, Journal of Environmental Engineering and Landscape Management, Journal of Environmental Engineering and Landscape Management,

Mathematical Modelling and Analysis, Mokslas - Lietuvos ateitis, Mokslo ir technikos raida, Santalka: Filologija, Edukologija, Santalka: Filosofija, Komunikacija, Statybinės konstrukcijos ir technologijos, Technological and Economic Development of Economy, The Baltic Journal of Road and Bridge Engineering, Transport, Urbanistika ir arhitektūra, Verslas teorija ir praktika, Verslas, vadyba ir studijos

Publishing house: Publishing House 'Technika' and Taylor and Francis

Last Update: 19-03-2015

Vilnius University (VU)

Universiteto g.3
Vilnius 01513
Tel: +370(5) 268-70-01
Fax: +370(5) 268-70-09
Website: http://www.vu.lt
Rector: Artūras Žukauskas
Tel: +370(5) 268-70-10

Faculty

Chemistry (Analytical Chemistry; Chemistry; Inorganic Chemistry; Organic Chemistry; Polymer and Plastics Technology); **Communication** (Archiving; Communication Studies; Information Management; Information Sciences; Journalism; Library Science; Public Relations); **Economics** (Accountancy; Business Administration; Business and Commerce; Business Computing; Economics; Finance; Insurance; International Business; Management); **History** (Archaeology; Contemporary History; History; Medieval Studies; Modern History); **Humanities** (*Kaunas*) (Business Administration; Computer Science; English; German; Management; Native Language; Philology); **Law** (Civil Law; Commercial Law; Criminal Law; International Law; Labour Law; Law; Public Law); **Mathematics and Informatics** (Applied Mathematics; Mathematics; Mathematics and Computer Science; Software Engineering; Statistics); **Medicine** (Dentistry; Ergotherapy; Hygiene; Medicine; Nursing; Occupational Therapy; Paediatrics; Public Health); **Natural Sciences** (Biophysics; Botany; Ecology; Environmental Management; Environmental Studies; Genetics; Geography; Geology; Meteorology; Microbiology; Molecular Biology; Natural Sciences; Zoology); **Philology** (Classical Languages; Dutch; English; Finnish; French; German; Greek; Latin; Native Language; Philology; Polish; Russian; Scandinavian Languages; Slavic Languages; Translation and Interpretation); **Philosophy** (Clinical Psychology; Educational Psychology; Educational Sciences; Industrial and Organizational Psychology; Philosophy; Psychology; Social Work; Sociology; Special Education); **Physics** (Applied Physics; Astrophysics; Biophysics; Physics; Radiophysics; Solid State Physics; Telecommunications Engineering)

School

Business (*International*) (Finance; International Business; International Law; Marketing; Tourism)

Institute

Applied Research (Materials Engineering); **Biochemistry** (Biochemistry); **Biotechnology** (Biotechnology); **Foreign Languages** (English; German; Romance Languages); **International Relations and Political Science** (International Relations; Political Sciences; Public Administration); **Mathematics and Informatics** (Mathematics and Computer Science); **Theoretical Physics and Astronomy** (Astronomy and Space Science; Physics)

Centre

Gender Studies (Gender Studies; Men Studies; Women's Studies); **Oriental Studies** (Arabic; Asian Studies; Chinese; Japanese; Middle Eastern Studies; Oriental Languages; Sanskrit); **Religious Studies and Research** (Religious Studies)

History: Founded 1579 as Academica et Universitas Vilnensis with two Faculties: Philosophy and Theology. Reorganized 1781 and again 1803 as the Imperial University of Vilnius. Closed by Tsarist Government 1832 when Faculties of Medicine and Theology became separate Academies. Reopened 1919. Closed during German occupation 1943.

Academic year: September to July (September-January; February-July)

Admission requirements: Secondary school certificate (Vidurines Mokyklos Baigimo Atestatas)

Fees: National : Bachelor courses - from 19-58 per ECTS credit. Master courses - from 25-54 per ECTS credit (Euro), International : Bachelor Programmes in English, 1300 / 2400 per annum. Master Programmes in English and Russian, 2120 - 6400. Medicine, 8520; Dentistry, 12960 (Euro)

Main language(s) of instruction: Lithuanian

Accrediting agency: Lithuanian Centre for Quality Assessment in Higher Education

Degrees and diplomas: Bakalauro diplomas, Magistro diplomas (Arts and Humanities; Computer Engineering; Eastern European Studies; Econometrics; Economics; English; European Union Law; Finance; International Law; Marketing; Russian; Social Sciences), Daktaro diplomas (Arts and Humanities; Biochemistry; Biology; Biomedical Engineering; Chemical Engineering; Communication Studies; Computer Engineering; Education; Information Sciences; Mathematics; Medicine; Physics; Public Health; Social Sciences)

Student Services: Academic Counselling, Social Counselling, Careers Guidance, Cultural Activities, Sports Facilities, Language Laboratory, Facilities for disabled people, Health Services, Canteen, Foreign Studies Centre, Library

Periodicals: Acta Orientalia Vilnensia, Acta Paedagogica Vilnensia, Archaelogica Lituana, Baltistica, Book Science, Economics, Information Sciences, Journal of Political Science, Law, Linguistics, Literature, Lithuanian Political Science Yearbook, Management, Problems, Psychology, Respectus Philologicus, Social Theory, Empirics, Policy and Practice, Sociology, Thought and Action, Studies of Lithuanian History, Transformation in Business and Economics

Publishing house: Vilnius University Publishing House

Academic Staff 2014-2015	MALE	FEMALE	TOTAL
FULL-TIME			3769
STAFF WITH DOCTORATE			
FULL-TIME			243
Student Numbers 2014-2015			
All (Foreign Included)			20643
Foreign only			886

Last Update: 18-03-2015

Vytautas Magnus University (VMU/VDU)

K. Donelaičio g. 58
Kaunas 44248
Tel: +370(37) 222-739
Fax: +370(37) 203-858
Website: http://www.vdu.lt
Rector: Juozas Augutis
Tel: + 370(37) 327- 964

Faculty

Arts (Art Criticism; Art History; Fine Arts; Theatre); **Catholic Theology** (Canon Law; Christian Religious Studies; Theology); **Economics and Management** (Economics; Finance; Management); **Humanities** (English; Ethnology; Folklore; French; German; History; Literature; Native Language; Philology; Philosophy); **Informatics** (Computer Science; Mathematics; Statistics); **Law** (Administrative Law; Commercial Law; International Law; Law); **Natural Sciences** (Biology; Chemistry; Environmental Studies; Physics); **Political Science and Diplomacy** (International Relations; Political Sciences); **Social Sciences** (Education; Psychology; Social Welfare; Sociology)

Academy

Music (Music)
History: Founded 1922. Renamed Vytautas Magnus University 1930. Closed 1950, reopened 1989. A State Institution.

Academic year: September to June (September-December; February-June)

Admission requirements: Secondary school certificate (Vidurinės Mokyklos Baigimo Atestatas)

Main language(s) of instruction: Lithuanian

Accrediting agency: Lithuanian Centre for Quality Assessment in Higher Education

Degrees and diplomas: Bakalauro diplomas (Art Criticism; Baltic Languages; Biology; Business Administration; Catholic Theology; Computer Science; English; Environmental Studies; Ethnology; French; German; History; Management; Mathematics; Pedagogy; Philology; Philosophy; Physics; Psychology; Public Administration; Social Work; Sociology), Magistro diplomas (Art Criticism; Baltic Languages; Biology; Business Administration; Chemistry; Communication Arts; Computer Science; Economics; English; Environmental Studies; Ethnology; German; History; Information Sciences; Law; Management; Mathematics; Pedagogy; Philology; Philosophy; Psychology; Public Administration; Social Work; Sociology; Theology), Daktaro diplomas (Art Criticism; Arts and Humanities; Biology; Biomedical Engineering; Ecology; Education; Environmental Studies; Ethnology; History; Law; Management; Philology; Philosophy; Physics; Political Sciences; Psychology; Social Sciences; Sociology; Theology)

Student Services: Academic Counselling, Sports Facilities, Language Laboratory, Facilities for disabled people, Health Services, Canteen, Foreign Studies Centre, Library

Periodicals: Acta Baltica, Aplinkos tyriami inginnerija ir vadyba, Darbai ir dienos, Mintis ir veiksmas, Organizaciju Vadyba, Profesinis rengimas: tyrimai ir realijos, Soter, Teisés apzvalga

Academic Staff 2014-2015	MALE	FEMALE	TOTAL
FULL-TIME			550
Student Numbers 2014-2015			
All (Foreign Included)			10000

Last Update: 19-03-2015

Private Institutions

European Humanities University

Tauro street, 12
Vilnius 01114
Tel: +370(5) 263-9650
Fax: +370(5) 263-9651
Website: http://www.ehu.lt
President: Anatoli Mikhailov

Department/Division

Foreign Languages (English; French; German; Italian; Native Language); **History** (Anthropology; Cultural Studies; Heritage Preservation; History; Social Sciences; Tourism); **Law** (European Union Law; International Law; Law); **Media** (Cultural Studies; Design; Information Sciences; Journalism); **Social and Political Science** (European Studies; Philosophy; Political Sciences; Public Administration)

Centre

Business Studies (Business Administration)

History: Founded in 1992 in Minsk, Belarusia. Closed down by authorities in 2004. Relaunched in Lithuania in 2005 and acquired current status 2006.

Academic year: September to June (September-December; January-March; April-June)

Admission requirements: Completed secondary education; required level of Russian and Belarusian language; foreign language at A2 on the scale of European Language Portfolio

Fees: National : Low Residence Undergraduate Programmes, 400-1000 per annum. High Residence Undergraduate Programmes: 600-2500 per annum. Postgraduate programme, 750-1500. MBA: 6750-7500 (Euro), International : Citizens and permanent residents of countries other than the Republic of Belarus, 1700 per annum (Low Residence Undergraduate Programs), 2500 per annum (High Residence Undergraduate Programs). Postgraduate programme: 2500 for non-Belarusian students. MBA, 6750- 7500 (Euro)

Main language(s) of instruction: Russian, Belarusian, English

Accrediting agency: Centre for Quality Assessment in Higher Education (CQAHE)

Degrees and diplomas: Bakalauro diplomas (Communication Arts; Design; Eastern European Studies; Fine Arts; History; Information Sciences; Law; Leisure Studies; Media Studies; Philosophy; Political Sciences; Radio and Television Broadcasting; Tourism), Magistro diplomas (Business Administration; Cultural Studies; History; Law; Philosophy; Sociology), Daktaro diplomas (Philosophy)

Student Services: Academic Counselling, Careers Guidance, Sports Facilities, Language Laboratory, Canteen

Periodicals: Crossroads, Digest, Historical Belarusian Review, Topos

Publishing house: The EHU Press

Last Update: 17-03-2015

ISM University of Management and Economics (ISM)

E.Ožeškienės St. 18
Kaunas 44254
Tel: +370(37) 302-405
Fax: +370(37) 302-368
Website: http://www.ism.lt
President: Alfredas Chmieliauskas

School

Doctoral Studies (Management); **Executive Studies** (*Co-operation with the BI Norwegian Business School*) (Management); **Graduate Studies** (International Business; Management); **Undergraduate Studies** (Business Administration; Business Education; Economics; Finance; International Business; Political Sciences)

Further information: Also Vilnus campus

History: Founded 1999. Formerly International School of Management (ISM), Tarptautinė Auskštoji Mokykla (ISM).

Main language(s) of instruction: Lithuanian, English

Degrees and diplomas: Bakalauro diplomas (Business Administration; Economics; Management), Magistro diplomas (Business Administration; Economics; International Business; Management), Daktaro diplomas (Management; Social Sciences). The graduates of ISM master's studies in management for executives are awarded the diploma of the founder of the university, BI Norwegian Business School.

Last Update: 17-03-2015

Kazimieras Simonavičius University

J. Basanavičiaus g. 29A
Vilnius 03109
Tel: +370 (5) 213 5172
Fax: +370 (5) 213 5172
Website: http://www.ksu.lt/
Rector: Arūnas Augustinaitis

Faculty

Klaipėda (Information Sciences; Law; Marketing); **Law** (Law)

School

Business (Business Administration)

Department/Division

Internet Engineering (Computer Engineering)

Institute

Creative Society and Economy (Economics)

Centre

Competence Development; **Entrepreneurship and Innovation**; **Research and Development**

History: Founded 2003.
Main language(s) of instruction: Lithuanian
Degrees and diplomas: Bakalauro diplomas, Magistro diplomas (Business Administration; Communication Studies; Economics; Information Sciences; Political Sciences; Public Administration)
Last Update: 18-03-2015

LCC International University (LCC)

Kretingos g. 36
Klaipėda 92307
Tel: +370(46) 31-07-45
Fax: +370(46) 31-05-60
Website: http://www.lcc.lt
President: Marlene Wall Wall
Tel: +370(46) 24-14-10

Faculty

English and Literature (English; Literature); **International Business Administration** (Business Administration); **Lithuanian Studies** (Baltic Languages; Cultural Studies); **Social Sciences** (Psychology); **Theology** (Theology)

Course/Programme

Intensive English Studies (English); **Teaching English to Speakers of Other Languages** (*TESOL - Graduate*) (Foreign Languages Education)
History: Founded 1991 as Lietuvos Krikščioniškojo Fondo Aukštoji Mokykla. Relocated to the Baltic port city, Klaipėda 1992, and acquired present status and title 2000.
Academic year: September to May (September-December; January-May) plus June and July summer sessions.
Admission requirements: High School Diploma (Brandos atestatas) or equivalent; English proficiency test
Main language(s) of instruction: English, Lithuanian
Accrediting agency: Ministry of Science and Education
Degrees and diplomas: Bakalauro diplomas, Magistro diplomas (English). M.A. in International Management program and an M.B.A. offered as a dual degree program in cooperation with Taylor University (Indiana, USA).
Student Services: Academic Counselling, Social Counselling, Careers Guidance, Cultural Activities, Sports Facilities, Language Laboratory, Canteen, Foreign Studies Centre, Library
Periodicals: Transformations
Last Update: 19-03-2015

INTERNATIONAL BUSINESS SCHOOL AT VILNIUS UNIVERSITY

Sauletekio av. 22,

Vilnius 10225
Tel: +370 (5) 236 6893
Website: http://www.tvm.vu.lt
Director: Arūnas Šikšta
Tel: +370(5) 236-6889

School

Business (Business Administration)
Main language(s) of instruction: Lithuanian, English
Degrees and diplomas: Bakalauro diplomas, Magistro diplomas (Business Administration; International Business)
Student Services: Canteen, Library, IT Centre
Last Update: 19-03-2015

Luxembourg

STRUCTURE OF HIGHER EDUCATION SYSTEM

Description

Since 2003, higher education has been offered at the University of Luxembourg, a public institution. Technical secondary schools propose short cycle programmes leading to Advanced Technical Diplomas (BTS). Some private and foreign institutions have been accredited.

Stages of studies

University level first stage

Bachelor
The Bachelor's degree is awarded after three years' study.

University level second stage

Master
The Master's degree is awarded after two years' study.

University level third stage

Docteur
The Doctorate is awarded after a minimum of three years' study and research.

ADMISSION TO HIGHER EDUCATION

Admission to university-level studies

Name of Secondary school credential required: Diplôme de Fin d'Etudes secondaires
Alternatives to credentials: Work experience
Admission requirements: Yes, for certain domains of study
Numerus clausus: Yes, for certain domains of study

Foreign students admission

Definition of foreign student: A student with a non-Luxemburgish secondary school leaving diploma

Admission requirements: Foreign students applying for admission to higher education institutions must hold a Secondary School Leaving Certificate recognized by the Ministère de l'Education nationale. Applications should be made to the individual institutions.
Entry regulations: A visa is required for non-European Union students.
Health requirements: A health visa is required.
Language Proficiency: A perfect command of French, German and English is necessary.

RECOGNITION OF STUDIES

Quality assurance system

External and internal evaluations are compulsory (decree) for the University of Luxembourg.

Special provisions for recognition

Recognition for University level studies
In general, Academic Titles, Degrees and Certificates awarded by foreign universities and other higher education Institutions are recognized in Luxembourg by means of an official Certificate (homologation / inscription au registre des titres) or according to the European guidelines.

NATIONAL BODIES

Ministère de l'Enseignement supérieur et de la Recherche (Ministry of Higher Education and Research)

Minister: Claude Meisch
Ministre délégué à l'Enseignement supérieur et à la Recherche: Marc Hansen
20, Montée de la Pétrusse
Luxembourg 2327
Tel: +352 247 86619
Fax: +352 262 96037
Website: http://www.mesr.public.lu

© International Association of Universities 2019
International Handbook of Universities 2019,
https://doi.org/10.1057/978-3-319-76971-4_113

Data for academic year: 2018–2019
Source: IAU from Ministry of Higher Education and Research / ENIC-NARIC Office, 2018.

Institution

University of Luxembourg (UL)

Maison du Savoir 2, Avenue de l'Université
Esch-sur-Alzette 4365
Tel: +352(46) 66-44-6000
Fax: +352(46) 66-44-6567
Website: http://www.uni.lu
President: Ludwig Neyses

Faculty
Faculty of Language and Literature, Humanities, Arts and Education (*Campus Walferdange*) (Arts and Humanities; Education; Educational Sciences; European Studies; Geography; History; Literature; Philosophy; Psychology; Social Sciences); **Faculty of Law, Economics and Finance** (*Luxembourg School of Finance and Luxembourg Business Academy*) (Accountancy; Banking; Economics; European Union Law; Finance); **Science, Technology and Communication** (*Campus Kirchberg*) (Biological and Life Sciences; Civil Engineering; Engineering; Information Technology; Mathematics and Computer Science; Natural Sciences; Technology)
History: Founded 1848 as Cours supérieur. Centre Universitaire established 1968. Acquired present status and title 2003. A public autonomous institution.
Academic year: September to June (September-January; February-June)
Admission requirements: Secondary school certificate or foreign equivalent.
Fees: National : 200 per semester; 400 per semester (Bachelor) (Euro), International : Same as national
Main language(s) of instruction: French, English, German
Degrees and diplomas: Bachelor (Biology; Computer Science; Cultural Studies; Economics; Educational Sciences; Engineering; History; Law; Management; Mathematics; Medicine; Pharmacy; Philosophy; Physics; Psychology; Social Work), Master (Accountancy; Civil Engineering; Computer Science; Environmental Studies; Finance; Geography; Gerontology; Government; History; Law; Mathematics; Modern Languages; Philosophy; Physics; Power Engineering; Psychology; Social Work), Doctorat (Biology; Chemistry; Computer Science; Economics; Educational Sciences; Engineering; Finance; Geography; History; Law; Linguistics; Literature; Management; Mathematics; Philosophy; Physics; Political Sciences; Psychology; Social Sciences)

Student Services: Academic Counselling, Social Counselling, Careers Guidance, Nursery Care, Cultural Activities, Sports Facilities, Language Laboratory, Facilities for disabled people, Health Services, Canteen, Foreign Studies Centre, Library, eLibrary, Residential Facilities

Student Numbers 2014-2015	MALE	FEMALE	TOTAL
All (Foreign Included)			6157

Last Update: 27-04-2015

Macedonia (The Former Yugoslav Republic)

STRUCTURE OF HIGHER EDUCATION SYSTEM

Description

Higher education is provided by universities.

Stages of studies

University level first stage

Diplomiran
The first-level degree is obtained on completion of a three to four-year course in one of the universities.

University level second stage

Magister
The Magister degree (Master of Science/Master of Arts) is awarded after one to two years' study.

University level third stage

Doktor
The title of Doctor is conferred after three years' study.

ADMISSION TO HIGHER EDUCATION

Admission to university-level studies

Name of Secondary school credential required: Svidetelstvo za polo en maturski ispit
Minimum score/requirement: 40 points in secondary school results and 60 points in entrance examination
Alternatives to credentials: International Baccalaureate or special examinations

Foreign students admission

Language Proficiency: A certificate attesting to knowledge of Macedonian is compulsory.

RECOGNITION OF STUDIES

Bodies dealing with recognition

Ministerstvo za Obrazovanie i Nauka (Ministry of Education and Science)
ul. Sv. Kiril i Metodij br. 54
Skopje 1000
Tel: +389(2) 311 7896
Fax: +389(2) 311 8414
Website: http://www.mon.gov.mk

NATIONAL BODIES

Ministerstvo za Obrazovanie i Nauka (Ministry of Education and Science)

Minister: Renata Deskoska
ul. Sv. Kiril i Metodij br. 54
Skopje 1000
Tel: +389(2) 311 7896
Fax: +389(2) 311 8414
Website: http://www.mon.gov.mk

Data for academic year: 2011–2012
Source: IAU from "World Data on Education 2010-2011", IBE and desktop research, 2015. Bodies, 2017.

Public Institutions

Goce Delchev University Stip

Krste Misirkov bb P.O. Box 201
Štip 2000
Tel: +389(32) 550-093
Fax: +389(32) 390-700
Website: http://www.ugd.edu.mk/
Rector: Sasha Mitrev
Tel: +389(32) 550-002

© International Association of Universities 2019
International Handbook of Universities 2019,
https://doi.org/10.1057/978-3-319-76971-4_114

Faculty

Agriculture (Agriculture; Crop Production; Development Studies; Oenology; Viticulture); **Computer Science** (Business Computing; Computer Science); **Economics** (Accountancy; Banking; Economics; Finance; Health Administration; Insurance; International Economics; Management); **Education** (Archiving; Education; Educational Sciences; Library Science; Pedagogy; Philosophy of Education; Preschool Education; Primary Education; Sociology); **Electrical Engineering** (Automation and Control Engineering; Electrical Engineering); **Law** (European Union Law; International Relations; Journalism; Law; Public Administration; Public Relations); **Mechanical Engineering** (Machine Building; Mechanical Engineering; Production Engineering); **Medicine** (Dental Technology; Dentistry; Laboratory Techniques; Medicine; Nursing; Optometry; Pharmacy; Physical Therapy); **Music** (Jazz and Popular Music; Music; Music Education; Musical Instruments; Singing); **Natural and Technical Sciences** (Architecture; Civil Engineering; Computer Graphics; Furniture Design; Geography; Geological Engineering; Mineralogy; Mining Engineering; Petroleum and Gas Engineering; Technology; Textile Technology); **Philology** (Archaeology; English; French; German; History; Italian; Literature; Native Language; Philology; Slavic Languages; Turkish); **Tourism and Business** (Cooking and Catering; Dietetics; Nutrition; Tourism; Transport Management)

Institute

Archaeology and History (Archaeology; History)
History: Founded 2007.
Main language(s) of instruction: Macedonian
Accrediting agency: Ministry of Education and Science
Degrees and diplomas: Diplomiran, Magister (Architecture; Architecture and Planning; Civil Engineering; Geology; Interior Design; Landscape Architecture; Mining Engineering), Doktor (Agriculture; Computer Engineering; Computer Science; Crop Production; Economics; Education; Electrical Engineering; Law; Mechanical Engineering; Medicine; Music; Philology; Soil Science; Technology; Tourism; Transport Management)
Student Services: Library, eLibrary
Last Update: 01-06-2015

St. Kliment Ohridski University, Bitola (UKLO)

Bulevar '1 Maj' bb
Bitola 7000
Tel: +389(47) 223-788
Fax: +389(47) 223-594
Website: http://www.uklo.edu.mk
Rector: Sasho Korunovski

Faculty

Administration and Information Systems Management (*Bitola*) (Administration; Engineering Management; Information Management; Information Sciences; International Business; Public Administration; Software Engineering); **Biotechnical Sciences** (*Bitola*) (Animal Husbandry; Biotechnology; Farm Management); **Economics** (*Prilep*) (Accountancy; Business Administration; Business Computing; E- Business/Commerce; Economics; Finance; International Business; International Economics; Management; Marketing); **Education** (*Bitola*) (Computer Education; Education; English; Foreign Languages Education; French; German; Library Science; Preschool Education; Technology Education); **Law** (*Kichevo*) (Law); **Security** (*Skopje*) (Civil Security; Criminology; Finance; Protective Services); **Technical Sciences** (*Bitola*) (Computer Engineering; Computer Graphics; Environmental Engineering; Industrial Management; Information Technology; Mechanical Engineering; Power Engineering; Road Engineering; Transport Engineering); **Technology and Technical Sciences** (Food Technology; Nutrition); **Tourism and Hospitality** (*Ohrid*) (Cooking and Catering; Dietetics; Hotel and Restaurant; Insurance; Nutrition; Tourism; Transport Management); **Veterinary Science** (*Bitola*) (Veterinary Science)

School

Medicine (*Bitola*) (Health Sciences; Laboratory Techniques; Medicine; Midwifery; Nursing; Physical Therapy; Radiology)

Institute

Tobacco (*Prilep*) (Agronomy; Chemistry; Genetics)
History: Founded 1979, incorporating previously existing institutions in the Southwest Macedonian Region founded between 1924 and 1979.
Academic year: September to May (September-January; February-May)
Admission requirements: Secondary school certificate and pass grades at the maturity exam (Diploma za polozhena matura).
Main language(s) of instruction: Macedonian
Accrediting agency: Accreditation and Evaluation Board
Degrees and diplomas: Diplomiran, Magister (Animal Husbandry; Biotechnology; Business Administration; Computer Science; Criminology; Economics; Education; Engineering; Farm Management; Food Science; Information Technology; Marketing; Protective Services; Software Engineering; Tourism), Doktor
Student Services: Academic Counselling, Sports Facilities, Language Laboratory, Facilities for disabled people, Health Services, Canteen
Periodicals: Horizonti
Last Update: 01-06-2015

State University of Tetova

Rruga e Ilindenit pn
Tetovo 1200, +389 44
Tel: +389(44) 356-500
Fax: +389(44) 334-222
Website: http://www.unite.edu.mk
Rector: Vullnet Ameti

Faculty

Applied Sciences (Architecture; Architecture and Planning; Civil Engineering; Construction Engineering; Electronic Engineering; Mechanical Engineering; Road Engineering; Town Planning; Transport Engineering); **Arts** (Aesthetics; Art History; Fine Arts; Graphic Design; Music; Painting and Drawing; Sculpture; Theatre); **Business Administration** (Business Administration; Public Administration); **Economics** (Albanian; Economics; Finance; Marketing; Modern Languages; Public Administration; Tourism); **Food Technology and Nutrition** (*Gostivar*) (Food Technology; Nutrition); **Law** (Administrative Law; Civil Law; Constitutional Law; Criminal Law; Human Rights; International Relations; Modern Languages); **Mathematics and Natural Sciences** (Biology; Chemistry; Ecology; Geography; Mathematics and Computer Science; Pharmacy; Physics); **Medicine** (Dentistry; Gynaecology and Obstetrics; Nursing; Pharmacy; Physical Therapy; Speech Therapy and Audiology); **Philology** (Albanian; English; French; German; Italian; Literature; Native Language); **Philosophy** (Arabic; History; Pedagogy; Philosophy; Psychology; Sociology; Turkish); **Physical Education** (Physical Education; Sports; Sports Management)

Institute

Technology and Ecology (Ecology; Technology)
History: Founded in 1994. Obtained current status 2007.
Main language(s) of instruction: Albanian, Macedonian
Accrediting agency: Ministry of Education and Science
Degrees and diplomas: Diplomiran (Biology; Chemistry; Computer Science; Design; Ecology; Economics; Electronic Engineering; Fine Arts; Geography; History; Law; Mathematics; Mechanical Engineering; Modern Languages; Music; Pedagogy; Pharmacy; Philosophy; Physical Education; Physics; Psychology; Sociology; Theatre; Tourism), Magister (Albanian; Architecture; Biology; Chemistry; Civil Engineering; Computer Science; Ecology; Economics; Electronic Engineering; Engineering Management; English; French; Geography; German; History; Mathematics; Mechanical Engineering; Pedagogy; Psychology; Slavic Languages; Sociology; Tourism)
Student Services: Academic Counselling, Careers Guidance, IT Centre
Last Update: 28-05-2015

Sts. Cyril and Methodius University, Skopje (UKiM)

Bul Goce Delcev, 9
Skopje 1000
Tel: +389(2) 3293-293
Fax: +389(2) 3293-202
Website: http://www.ukim.edu.mk
Rector: Velimir Stojkovski
Tel: +389(2) 3293-200

Faculty

Agricultural Science and Food (Agricultural Economics; Agricultural Engineering; Agricultural Equipment; Agriculture; Animal Husbandry; Botany; Cattle Breeding; Crop Production; Fruit Production; Genetics; Horticulture; Mechanical Engineering; Microbiology; Plant and Crop Protection; Soil Conservation; Soil Science; Vegetable Production; Viticulture); **Architecture** (Architectural and Environmental Design; Architecture; Building Technologies; Graphic Design; Mathematics; Town Planning); **Civil Engineering** (Building Technologies; Civil Engineering; Construction Engineering; Hydraulic Engineering; Irrigation; Mathematics; Power Engineering; Railway Engineering; Surveying and Mapping; Water Science); **Computer Science and Engineering** (Computer Engineering; Computer Science); **Dentistry** (Dental Technology; Dentistry; Oral Pathology); **Dramatic Arts** (Acting; Cinema and Television; Film; Theatre; Writing); **Economics** (Accountancy; Business Administration; Computer Science; Economics; Finance; International Economics; Management; Marketing; Mathematics and Computer Science; Statistics); **Electrical Engineering and Information Technology** (Automation and Control Engineering; Computer Science; Electrical and Electronic Engineering; Information Technology; Physics; Power Engineering; Telecommunications Engineering); **Fine Arts** (Art Education; Fine Arts; Graphic Arts; Painting and Drawing; Sculpture; Visual Arts); **Forestry** (Botany; Environmental Management; Forest Biology; Forest Economics; Forest Management; Forest Products; Forestry; Wood Technology); **Furniture and Interior Design** (Furniture Design; Interior Design); **Law** (*Iustinianus Primus*) (Civil Law; Criminology; International Law; International Relations; Journalism; Law; Political Sciences); **Mechanical Engineering** (Hydraulic Engineering; Machine Building; Mathematics and Computer Science; Mechanical Engineering; Mechanical Equipment and Maintenance; Metal Techniques; Power Engineering; Production Engineering; Thermal Engineering); **Medicine** (Anaesthesiology; Anatomy; Cardiology; Endocrinology; Epidemiology; Gynaecology and Obstetrics; Haematology; Health Sciences; Medicine; Nephrology; Neurology; Nursing; Ophthalmology; Orthopaedics; Otorhinolaryngology; Physical Therapy; Physiology; Plastic Surgery; Psychology;

Radiology; Rheumatology; Surgery; Toxicology; Urology); **Music** (Conducting; Music; Music Theory and Composition; Musical Instruments; Musicology; Singing); **Natural Sciences and Mathematics** (Biology; Chemistry; Computer Science; Geography; Mathematics; Natural Sciences; Physics); **Pedagogy** (*St. Kliment Ohrid*) (Library Science; Pedagogy; Preschool Education; Primary Education); **Pharmacy** (Analytical Chemistry; Biochemistry; Botany; Computer Science; Immunology; Inorganic Chemistry; Molecular Biology; Organic Chemistry; Pharmacology; Pharmacy; Toxicology); **Philology** (*Blaze Koneski*) (Albanian; Comparative Literature; English; German; Native Language; Philology; Romance Languages; Slavic Languages; Translation and Interpretation; Turkish); **Philosophy** (Archaeology; Art History; Classical Languages; Family Studies; Gender Studies; History; Pedagogy; Philosophy; Protective Services; Psychology; Social Policy; Social Work; Sociology; Special Education); **Physical Education, Sport and Health** (Health Sciences; Physical Education; Sports); **Technology and Metallurgy** (Biotechnology; Industrial Design; Inorganic Chemistry; Metallurgical Engineering; Organic Chemistry; Technology; Textile Technology); **Theology in Skopje** (*St. Clement of Ohrid*) (Theology); **Veterinary Medicine** (Gender Studies; Microbiology; Pathology; Veterinary Science; Zoology)

Institute

Agriculture (*Skopje*) (Agriculture; Chemistry; Fruit Production; Horticulture; Plant and Crop Protection; Viticulture); **Cattle Breeding** (Animal Husbandry; Cattle Breeding; Zoology); **Earthquake Engineering and Seismology** (Building Technologies; Computer Science; Engineering Management; Geology; Geophysics; Safety Engineering; Seismology); **Economics** (Business Administration; Business and Commerce; Development Studies; Economic and Finance Policy; Economics; Finance; International Economics; International Relations; Management; Marketing; Small Business; Taxation); **Folklore** (*Marko Cepenkov*) (Cultural Studies; Dance; Folklore; Music; Sociology); **Macedonian Language** (*Krste Misirkov*) (Cultural Studies; Literature; Native Language; Slavic Languages; Terminology); **Macedonian Literature** (Comparative Literature; Documentation Techniques; Literature; Native Language; Regional Studies); **National History** (Ancient Civilizations; Documentation Techniques; History; Library Science; Medieval Studies; Modern History; Publishing and Book Trade); **Sociology, Political Science and Law** (Communication Studies; Criminology; Cultural Studies; Demography and Population; Ethnology; Human Resources; Human Rights; International Relations; Law; Marketing; Media Studies; Political Sciences; Social Sciences; Sociology)

Further information: Also branches in Štip and Strumica

History: Founded 1949, incorporating faculties of Letters (1946) and Agriculture and Medicine (1947).

Academic year: October to June (October-January; February-June)

Admission requirements: Secondary school leaving certificate (Matura), entrance examinations, depending on the faculty.

Main language(s) of instruction: Macedonian, Turkish, Albanian

Accrediting agency: Ministry of Education and Science

Degrees and diplomas: Diplomiran, Specijalizacija (Cosmetology; Pharmacy), Magister (Agriculture; Architecture; Civil Engineering; Computer Engineering; Computer Science; Dentistry; Economics; Engineering; Fine Arts; Forestry; Mechanical Engineering; Medicine; Music; Natural Sciences; Pharmacy; Philology; Philosophy; Physical Education; Physical Therapy; Sports Management; Veterinary Science), Doktor (Agriculture; Civil Engineering; Computer Engineering; Computer Science; Dentistry; Engineering; Forestry; Pharmacy; Philosophy; Physical Education; Physical Therapy)

Student Services: Careers Guidance, Cultural Activities, Sports Facilities, Health Services, Foreign Studies Centre

Publishing house: University Press

Last Update: 01-06-2015

University of Information Science and Technology 'St. Paul the Apostle'

Partizanska bb.
Ohrid 6000
Tel: +389(46) 511-000
Fax: +389(46) 511-567
Website: http://uist.edu.mk/
Rector: Marina Ninoslav

Faculty

Applied Information Technology, Machine Intelligence and Robotics (Computer Engineering; Robotics); **Communication Networks and Security** (Computer Networks; Computer Science); **Computer Science and Engineering** (Computer Engineering; Computer Science); **Information and Communication Science** (Information Sciences; Information Technology); **Information Systems, Visualization, Multimedia and Animation** (Computer Graphics; Information Sciences; Information Technology; Multimedia)

History: Created 2008.

Accrediting agency: Ministry of Education and Science

Degrees and diplomas: Diplomiran (Computer Engineering; Computer Science; Information Sciences), Magister (Computer Engineering; Computer Science; Information

Sciences), Doktor (Computer Science; Telecommunications Engineering)
Last Update: 28-08-2015

Private Institutions

Business Academy Smilevski (BAS)

bul. Avnoj 74a
Skopje 1000
Tel: +389 2 2455-754
Website: http://www.bas.edu.mk/
Director: Cvetko Smilevski

Course/Programme
Operational Management (Management); **Strategic Management** (*Postgraduate*) (Management)
Further information: Also a campus in Bitola
History: Founded 2007.
Main language(s) of instruction: Macedonian
Accrediting agency: Ministry of Education and Science
Degrees and diplomas: Diplomiran, Magister (Business Administration)
Last Update: 28-05-2015

Euro-Balkan University (EUBA)

ul. Partizanski odredi br. 63
Skopje 1000
Tel: + 389(2) 3090-731
Fax: + 389(2) 3075-570
Website: http://www.euba.edu.mk
Rector: Mitko B. Panov

Faculty
Social Anthropology (Anthropology; Social Sciences)

School
Fashion Design (Fashion Design)

Department/Division
Architecture, Design, Modern Information and Communication Technologies (Architecture; Design; Information Technology); **Byzantine Studies** (Oriental Studies); **Cultural Studies** (*Higher Education Studies of Second and Third cycle - School for Regional Studies; Adult Education Center*) (Ancient Civilizations; Anthropology; Cultural Studies; Philosophy; Sociology); **Gender Studies** (Gender Studies); **Library** (Library Science); **Political Studies of**

South-Eastern Europe (Eastern European Studies; European Studies; Political Sciences)
Further information: Also Adult Education Centre and Summer programmes.
History: Founded as Institute for Social Sciences and Humanities 'Euro-Balkan'. Acquired present status 2012.
Main language(s) of instruction: Macedonian
Accrediting agency: Board for Accreditation of Higher Education
Degrees and diplomas: Magister (Cultural Studies; Gender Studies; Philosophy; Political Sciences; Sociology), Doktor
Student Services: Library
Last Update: 29-05-2015

European University of Macedonia

Kliment Ohridski Blvd 68
Skopje 1000
Tel: +389(2) 320-2020
Fax: +389(2) 320-2030
Website: http://www.eurm.edu.mk
Chancellor: Lidija Naumovska

Faculty
Art and Design (Fashion Design; Graphic Arts; Interior Design); **Computer Science** (Computer Engineering; Computer Networks; Computer Science; Multimedia); **Dentistry** (Dentistry); **Detectives and Criminology** (Criminal Law; Criminology); **Economics** (Finance; Health Administration; Management; Marketing; Taxation); **Law** (Law); **Political Science** (International Relations; Political Sciences)
Further information: Also Branch in Orhid
History: Created in 2001 as Faculty of Social Science. Obtained current status 2005.
Academic year: October to May (October-January; February-May)
Admission requirements: Secondary School Certificate
Main language(s) of instruction: Macedonian, English
Accrediting agency: Ministry of Education and Science
Degrees and diplomas: Diplomiran, Magister, Doktor
Student Services: Academic Counselling, Social Counselling, Sports Facilities, Language Laboratory, Canteen, Foreign Studies Centre
Last Update: 28-05-2015

Faculty of Business Studies in Skopje

Skopje
Director: Antonija Josifovska

Faculty

Business Administration (Banking; Business Administration; Economics; Finance; Labour and Industrial Relations; Management; Marketing)
Main language(s) of instruction: Macedonian
Accrediting agency: Ministry of Education and Science
Degrees and diplomas: Diplomiran, Magister (Business Administration; Economics; Finance; Marketing)
Last Update: 16-12-2015

FON University

Str. Kiro Gligorov b.b
Skopje 10000
Tel: +389(2) 2445-555
Fax: +389(2) 2244-550
Website: http://www.fon.edu.mk
Vice-Chancellor: Sime Arsenovski

Faculty

Architecture (Architecture); **Communication and Information Technology** (Communication Studies; Computer Engineering; Computer Networks; Computer Science; Information Technology; Software Engineering); **Design and Multimedia** (Design; Multimedia); **Economics** (Banking; Economics; Finance; Management; Marketing); **Foreign Languages** (Albanian; European Languages; Foreign Languages Education; Linguistics; Slavic Languages; Translation and Interpretation; Turkish); **Law** (Law); **Political Sciences** (International Relations; Journalism; Political Sciences); **Security and Detective Studies** (Criminology; Law; Police Studies; Protective Services); **Sport and Sport Management** (Sports; Sports Management)
Further information: Branch in Struga, Gostivar, and Strumica.
History: Previously part of European University of Macedonia (Evropskij Univerzitet Respublika Makedonija). Obtained current status 2003.
Academic year: October to May (October-January; February-May)
Admission requirements: Secondary School Leaving Certificate
Main language(s) of instruction: Macedonian, English, Albanian
Accrediting agency: Ministry of Education and Science
Degrees and diplomas: Diplomiran, Magister (Banking; Design; Economics; European Union Law; Finance; Information Technology; International Relations; Law; Multimedia; Political Sciences; Sports)
Student Services: Academic Counselling, Social Counselling, Careers Guidance, Cultural Activities, Sports Facilities, Language Laboratory, Canteen, Library
Last Update: 29-05-2015

Higher Education Professional Institution for Business Studies Euro College Kumanovo

Done Bozinov 41
Kumanovo 1300
Tel: +389(31) 417-202
Fax: +389(31) 418-025
Website: http://www.eurocollege.edu.mk
Dean: Ljubisa Petrusevski

Course/Programme

Business Administration (Accountancy; Behavioural Sciences; Business Administration; Commercial Law; Communication Studies; Computer Engineering; Computer Networks; Ethics; Finance; Human Resources; Industrial and Organizational Psychology; Information Management; Information Technology; Insurance; International Business; Leadership; Management; Marketing; Statistics; Transport Management)
History: Founded 2003.
Main language(s) of instruction: Macedonian
Accrediting agency: Ministry of Education and Science
Degrees and diplomas: Diplomiran, Magister (Business Administration). Also American Bachelor's, Master's and Doctoral degrees. Collaboration with Apollos University.
Last Update: 01-06-2015

Higher School of Journalism and Public Relations, Skopje (VS)

ul. Jurij Gagarin 17/1-1
Skopje 1000
Tel: +389(2) 3090-004
Fax: +389(2) 3090-104
Website: http://vs.edu.mk
Director: Zaneta Trajkoska

Course/Programme

Corporate Communications and Public Relations (Communication Studies; Public Relations); **Journalism and Production** (Journalism; Media Studies); **Media Management and Multimedia** (*Postgraduate*) (Management; Media Studies; Multimedia); **Strategic Communications Management** (Communication Studies; Management; Mass Communication)
History: Founded 2008.
Main language(s) of instruction: Macedonian
Accrediting agency: Ministry of Education and Science
Degrees and diplomas: Diplomiran, Magister (Journalism)
Last Update: 01-06-2015

Integrated Business Faculty (FBE)

ul. '3-ta Makedonska Brigada' no. 66A - Floor 1
Skopje 1000
Tel: +389(2) 402-160, +389(2) 2402-161
Fax: +389(2) 2466-063
Website: http://www.fbe.edu.mk
Director: Antonija Josifovska

Course/Programme

Banking (Banking); **Financial Management** (Finance); **Marketing Management** (Management; Marketing); **Regional and Local Business Development** (Business Administration); **Sustainable Development - Environmental Economy** (Development Studies; Economics; Environmental Studies)
Fees: 500-600 per annum (Euro)
Main language(s) of instruction: Macedonian
Accrediting agency: Ministry of Education and Science
Degrees and diplomas: Diplomiran (Business Administration), Magister (Banking; Business Administration; Economics; Finance; Management; Marketing)
Student Services: Library
Last Update: 28-05-2015

International Balkan University (IBU)

Tashko Karadza 11A
Skopje 1000
Tel: +389(2) 3214-831
Fax: +389(2) 3214-832
Website: http://www.ibu.edu.mk/
Rector: Şinasi Gündüz

Faculty

Art and Design (Design; Fine Arts; Graphic Design; Visual Arts); **Communication** (Communication Studies; Public Relations); **Economics and Administration Sciences** (Administration; Business Administration; Economics; Management; Public Administration); **Education** (Educational and Student Counselling; English; Foreign Languages Education; History; Pedagogy; Turkish); **Engineering** (Architecture; Civil Engineering; Computer Engineering; Electrical and Electronic Engineering; Industrial Engineering; Information Technology); **Humanities and Social Sciences** (*New Balkan Faculty*) (International Economics; Political Sciences; Psychology; Public Administration; Religious Studies); **Languages** (American Studies; English); **Law** (Law)
History: Founded in 2006 by the Foundation of Development for Education and Culture (USKUP), Skopje through integration of the New Balkan Faculty and New Balkan Technical Sciences. Faculties received accreditation 2007.

Admission requirements: Secondary School Leaving Certificate or equivalent.
Main language(s) of instruction: English
Accrediting agency: Ministry of Education and Science
Degrees and diplomas: Diplomiran (Industrial Engineering; International Economics; International Relations), Magister (Business Administration; Graphic Design; International Relations)
Student Services: Library
Last Update: 29-05-2015

International Slavic University G. R. Derzhavin in Sveti Nikole

Maršal Tito 77
Sveti Nikole 2220
Tel: +389(32) 440-330
Fax: +389(32) 440-202
Website: http://msu.edu.mk
Rector: Dusan Nikolovski

Faculty

Economics and Organization of Entrepreneurship (Banking; Economics; Finance; Human Resources; Management; Marketing); **Informatics** (Computer Engineering; Computer Networks; Computer Science; Software Engineering); **Law** (Law); **Psychology** (Clinical Psychology; Psychology; Social Psychology); **Safety Engineering** (Fire Science; Protective Services)

Institute

Art and Culture (Cultural Studies; Fine Arts); **Engineering Economics** (Economics)
History: Founded 2004 as International Slavic Institute Gavril Romanovich Derzhavin, Sveti Nikole. Acquired present name and status 2013.
Main language(s) of instruction: Macedonian, English
Accrediting agency: Ministry of Education and Science
Degrees and diplomas: Diplomiran, Magister (Clinical Psychology; Fire Science; Human Resources; Management; Marketing; Protective Services; Psychology)
Student Services: Library
Last Update: 29-05-2015

International University of Struga (IUST)

Ezerski Lozja N-1
Struga 6330
Tel: +389(46) 786-160

Website: http://www.eust.edu.mk/
Rector: Aleksander Biberaj

Faculty

Economics (Business Administration; Economics; Finance; Management; Marketing); **Information Technology** (Information Technology); **Law** (Criminology; Law); **Political Science** (Political Sciences)
History: Founded 2007.
Main language(s) of instruction: Macedonian
Accrediting agency: Ministry of Education and Science
Degrees and diplomas: Diplomiran, Magister (Business Administration; Criminology; Economics; Information Technology; Law), Doktor (Economics; Law; Political Sciences)
Student Services: Library
Last Update: 29-05-2015

International Vision University

ul. Major C. Filiposki, 1
Gostivar
Tel: +389(42) 222-325
Fax: +389(42) 222-326
Website: http://www.vizyon.edu.mk
Rector: Fadil Hoca

Faculty

Architecture (Architecture; Design); **Economics** (Economics); **Information Sciences** (Information Sciences); **Law** (Law); **Social Sciences** (Psychology)
History: Created 2014.
Accrediting agency: Ministry of Education and Science
Degrees and diplomas: Diplomiran (Architecture; Economics; Information Sciences; Law; Psychology), Magister (Architecture; Business Administration; Economics; Information Sciences; Law; Psychology)

Academic Staff 2015-2016	MALE	FEMALE	TOTAL
FULL-TIME			52
PART-TIME			20
STAFF WITH DOCTORATE			
FULL-TIME			20
Student Numbers 2015-2016			
All (Foreign Included)			420
Foreign only			147

Last Update: 28-08-2015

MIT University, Skopje (MIT)

bul.Treta Makedonska Brigada BB
Skopje 1000
Tel: +389(78) 268-268

Website: http://www.mit.edu.mk
President: Biljana Apostolova

Faculty

Architecture (Architecture; Design; Engineering; Town Planning); **Computer Science and Technology** (Computer Engineering; Computer Science; E- Business/Commerce; Information Management; Information Technology; Software Engineering); **Dental Medicine** (Dentistry); **Economics** (Economics); **Environmental Resources Management** (Agricultural Business; Ecology; Environmental Studies; Natural Resources); **Management** (Business Administration; Economics; Finance; Government; Health Administration; Management; Public Administration); **Political Sciences and Diplomacy** (International Relations; Political Sciences); **Psychology** (Psychology); **Security Science** (Civil Security; Criminology; Protective Services); **Tourism Management** (Cooking and Catering; Tourism)

College

Aviation (Aeronautical and Aerospace Engineering; Air Transport); **Medical Cosmetology and Physiotherapy** (Cosmetology; Physical Therapy)
History: Founded 2007.
Academic year: October to June
Main language(s) of instruction: Macedonian, English
Accrediting agency: Ministry of Education and Science
Degrees and diplomas: Diplomiran (Accountancy; Aeronautical and Aerospace Engineering; Agricultural Business; Architecture; Banking; Business Computing; Civil Security; Computer Science; Cooking and Catering; Cosmetology; Criminology; Dentistry; Environmental Management; Finance; Food Technology; Health Administration; Information Technology; Insurance; International Relations; Management; Marketing; Physical Therapy; Psychology; Public Administration; Tourism), Magister (Accountancy; Agricultural Business; Architecture; Banking; Civil Security; Criminal Law; Criminology; Dentistry; Design; Finance; Food Technology; Health Administration; Insurance; International Relations; Management; Psychology; Public Administration; Town Planning; Waste Management; Water Management). Dental Medicine - 5 years.

Academic Staff 2016-2017	MALE	FEMALE	TOTAL
FULL-TIME			122
PART-TIME			28
STAFF WITH DOCTORATE			
FULL-TIME			14
Student Numbers 2016-2017			
All (Foreign Included)			834

Last Update: 03-10-2016

South East European University

'Illindenska' p.n.
Tetovo 1200
Tel: +389(44) 356-000
Fax: +389(44) 356-001
Website: http://www.seeu.edu.mk
Rector: Zamir Dika
Tel: +389(44) 356-110

Faculty

Business and Economics (Accountancy; Agricultural Business; Business Administration; Economics; Finance; Health Administration; Information Technology; Management; Marketing; Tourism); **Contemporary Sciences and Technologies** (Business Computing; Computer Engineering; Computer Science; Information Technology; Software Engineering); **Languages, Cultures and Communications** (Albanian; Communication Studies; Cultural Studies; English; German; Literature; Media Studies); **Law** (Civil Law; Criminal Law; Criminology; International Law; Law); **Public Administration and Political Science** (Human Resources; International Business; Management; Political Sciences; Public Administration; Statistics)

Institute

Environment and Health (Environmental Studies; Health Sciences); **Languages, Cultures and Communications** (*Max van der Stoel*) (Albanian; Communication Studies; Educational Administration; English; German)
History: Founded 2001.
Academic year: October to June.
Admission requirements: School certificate and entrance examination.
Main language(s) of instruction: Albanian, Macedonian, English
Accrediting agency: Ministry of Education and Science
Degrees and diplomas: Diplomiran, Magister (Computer Engineering; Computer Networks; Environmental Management; European Studies; Information Technology; Political Sciences; Public Administration; Software Engineering), Doktor (Albanian; Business Administration; Civil Law; Computer Engineering; Computer Networks; Criminal Law; Economics; English; Environmental Management; German; International Law; Political Sciences; Public Administration). Diplomiran equivalent to Bachelor
Student Services: Academic Counselling, Careers Guidance, Sports Facilities, Language Laboratory, Canteen, Library

Student Numbers 2014-2015	MALE	FEMALE	TOTAL
All (Foreign Included)			c. 5000

Last Update: 01-06-2015

University American College in Skopje

Bul. Treta makedonska brigada no. 60
Skopje 1000
Tel: +389(2) 2463-156
Fax: +389(2) 2463-159
Website: http://www.uacs.edu.mk
Rector: Marjan Bojadziev

School

Architecture and Design (Architecture; Interior Design); **Business Economics and Management** (Business Administration; Economics; Finance; Management; Marketing); **Computer Science and Information Technology** (Computer Networks; Software Engineering); **Foreign Languages** (Communication Studies; English; Foreign Languages Education; Literature; Translation and Interpretation); **Legal Studies** (Administrative Law; Law; Public Law); **Political Science** (Human Rights; International Relations; Political Sciences)
History: Created 2005. Obtained status 2006.
Academic year: September to June
Admission requirements: Secondary School Leaving Certificate or equivalent; TOEFL score of at least 530 (written form) or 200 (computer form), for studies in English; High School GPA of 3.5 - 5.0
Main language(s) of instruction: English, Macedonian
Accrediting agency: Ministry of Education and Science
Degrees and diplomas: Magister (Architecture; Banking; Business Administration; Design; Economics; English; Finance; Law; Management; Marketing; Political Sciences). Also Bachelor degree in 3 yrs in: Marketing; Finance; Management; International Relations and Diplomacy; Human Rights; English Language Teaching and Literature; Translation and Interpretation; Business Correspondence and Communication (English); Architecture; Interior Design; Computer Networks; Software Engineering.
Student Services: Academic Counselling, Careers Guidance, Cultural Activities, Sports Facilities, Language Laboratory, Foreign Studies Centre, Library
Last Update: 01-06-2015

University of Audiovisual Arts (ESRA)

st. Nicholas Rusinski no. 1
Skopje 1000
Tel: +389(2) 3061-543
Fax: +389(2) 3067-609
Website: http://www.esra.com.mk
Rector: Jordan Plevnesh

Faculty

Film (Cinema and Television; Design; Film; Photography; Radio and Television Broadcasting); **Sound Production and**

Applied Music (Music; Music Theory and Composition; Sound Engineering (Acoustics)); **Theatre** (Acting; Display and Stage Design; Multimedia; Music; Music Theory and Composition; Theatre)
History: Founded 2007 on the model of the French ESRA Film School.
Admission requirements: Entrance examination.
Accrediting agency: Ministry of Education and Science
Degrees and diplomas: Diplomiran, Magister (Film; Sound Engineering (Acoustics); Theatre)
Last Update: 01-06-2015

University of Tourism and Management in Skopje (UTMS)

Partizanski Odredi no. 99
Skopje 1000
Tel: +389(2) 3093-209, +389(2) 3093-215
Fax: +389(2) 3093-213
Website: http://www.utms.edu.mk
Rector: Ace Milenkovski

Faculty

Economics (Economics); **Human Resources** (Human Resources); **International Marketing and Management** (International Business; Management; Marketing; Public Relations); **Management** (Business Administration; Management); **Tourism** (Hotel Management; Tourism)
Admission requirements: High School Certificate.
Main language(s) of instruction: Macedonian
Accrediting agency: Ministry of Education and Science
Degrees and diplomas: Diplomiran, Magister (Hotel Management; Human Resources; Management; Tourism), Doktor
Last Update: 01-06-2015

Madagascar

STRUCTURE OF HIGHER EDUCATION SYSTEM

Description

Higher education is provided by public and private universities and higher technical institutions. Universities are autonomous institutions. Each university is headed by a Rector and administered by a Conseil d'Administration. The three-tier system (Licence-Master-Doctorat) has gradually been implemented in all institutions.

Stages of studies

University level first stage

Licence
The first stage of higher education lasts three years and leads to the Licence. Studies in Medicine last 8 years, and Veterinary Medicine last 6 years.

University level second stage

Master
The Master is conferred after two year's further study beyond the Licence.

University level third stage

Doctorat
The Doctorat is awarded after two years' study following the Master degree.

ADMISSION TO HIGHER EDUCATION

Admission to university-level studies

Name of Secondary school credential required: Baccalauréat de l'Enseignement secondaire
Minimum score/requirement: 10/20
Name of Secondary school credential required: Baccalauréat professionnel et technique
Minimum score/requirement: 10/20
Admission requirements: Entrance examination

Foreign students admission

Admission requirements: Foreign students must hold the Baccalauréat or an equivalent qualification.
Entry regulations: Overseas students must hold a visa.
Language Proficiency: Good knowledge of French.

NATIONAL BODIES

Ministère de l'Enseignement Supérieur et de la Recherche Scientifique - MESUPRES

Minister: Marie Monique Rasoazananera
BP 4163
Antananarivo 101
Tel: +261(20) 22271 85
Fax: +261(20) 22238 97
Website: http://www.mesupres.gov.mg
Role of national body: To oversee national higher education policy.

Conférence des Présidents des Institutions de l'Enseignement supérieur - CoPRIES

Antananarivo

Association des Établissements d'Enseignement supérieur privés homologués de Madagascar - AEESPHM

Antananarivo

Association des Etablissements de Formation professionnelle supérieure agréés - AEFPSA

Antananarivo

© International Association of Universities 2019
International Handbook of Universities 2019,
https://doi.org/10.1057/978-3-319-76971-4_115

Data for academic year: 2017–2018
Source: IAU from Fiche Curie Madagascar, institutional websites and documentation, 2018.

Public Institutions

Higher Institute of Technology of Antsiranana (IST-D)

BP 453
Antsiranana 201
Tel: +261(20) 82-224-31
Fax: +261(20) 82-294-25
Website: http://www.ist-antsiranana.mg
Directeur général: Lova Raharimihaja Zakariasy

Department/Division

Maintenance Technology (Maintenance Technology); **Tertiary Studies**
History: Founded 1989. Acquired present status 2001.
Accrediting agency: Ministère de l'Enseignement supérieur et de la Recherche scientifique
Degrees and diplomas: Licence. Also Engineering degrees (Master Level)
Last Update: 18-10-2017

Higher Institute of Technology, Antananarivo (ISTT)

RN2 - Ampasampito
Antananarivo 101
Tel: +261(20) 22-414-23
Fax: +261(20) 22-405-43
Website: http://www.ist-tana.mg
Directeur général: Jean Lalaina Rakotomalala

Department/Division

Civil Engineering (Civil Engineering; Construction Engineering); **Industrial Engineering** (Industrial Engineering)
History: Founded 1990. Acquired present status 2001.
Main language(s) of instruction: French
Accrediting agency: Ministère de l'Enseignement supérieur et de la Recherche scientifique
Degrees and diplomas: Licence (Civil Engineering; Engineering; Industrial Engineering), Master (Civil Engineering; Engineering Management; Industrial Engineering)

Academic Staff 2015-2016	MALE	FEMALE	TOTAL
FULL-TIME			71
PART-TIME			150

(continued)

Academic Staff 2015-2016	MALE	FEMALE	TOTAL
STAFF WITH DOCTORATE			
FULL-TIME			27
Student Numbers 2015-2016			
All (Foreign Included)			1360

Last Update: 12-04-2017

National Center for Distance Education of Madagascar (CNTEMAD)

BP 78 Ankadifotsy
Antananarivo 101
Tel: +261(20) 22-600-57
Fax: +261(20) 22-360-90
Website: http://www.cntemad.mg
Directeur: Djohary Andrianambinina
Tel: +261(20) 22-603-86

Course/Programme

Engineering (Computer Engineering; Industrial Engineering; Telecommunications Engineering); **Social Sciences** (Business and Commerce; Communication Studies; Economics; Law; Management; Marketing)
History: Founded 1992
Accrediting agency: Ministère de l'Enseignement supérieur et de la Recherche scientifique
Degrees and diplomas: Licence (Computer Engineering; Industrial Engineering; Law; Management; Marketing; Social Sciences), Master (Computer Engineering; Law; Management)
Last Update: 18-10-2017

National Institute of Accountancy and Business Administration (INSCAE)

Maison des Produits 67 ha
Antananarivo 101
Tel: +261(20) 22-660-65
Fax: +261(20) 22-308-95
Website: http://www.inscae.mg
Directrice générale: Harimino Rakoto

Department/Division

Business Administration and Marketing (Business Administration; Marketing); **Finance and Accountancy** (Accountancy; Finance)
History: Founded 1983. Acquired present title 1986.
Academic year: Undergraduate Studies: January to December (January-May: Summer session; August-December:

Spring Session); Master 1: November to September; Master 2: September to October; MBA: January to December

Admission requirements: Undergraduate Studies: High School Diploma; Master : Bachelor; Master 2: Maîtrise/Master 1; MBA: Engineering Degree or equivalent with at least 3 years of professional experience.

Fees: Undergraduate Studies, 550,000-600,000 per annum; Master 1.5.; Master 2, 600,000; MBA, 450,000 per module, Continuing Education: 75,000 per module (Malagasy Ariary)

Main language(s) of instruction: English, French

Accrediting agency: Ministère de l'Enseignement supérieur et de la Recherche scientifique

Degrees and diplomas: Master (Accountancy; Banking; Business Administration; Finance; Human Resources; International Business; Management; Marketing), Doctorat (Business Administration; Finance; Management; Marketing; Public Administration). Bachelor in Business Administration (3 yrs); Bachelor in Finance and Accountancy (3yrs)

Student Services: Careers Guidance, Cultural Activities, Library

Last Update: 02-09-2016

National Institute of Nuclear Sciences and Techniques (Madagascar-INSTN)

BP 4279
Antananarivo 101
Tel: +261(20) 24-714-03, +261(20) 22-355-84
Fax: +261(20) 22-355-83
Website: http://www.instn.mg
Directeur général: Raoelina Andriambololona
Tel: +261(20) 22 356-96, +261 32-04-520-46

Department/Division

Informatics and Communication Technology (Computer Engineering; Information Technology); **Isotope Hydrology** (Hydraulic Engineering); **Maintenance and Nuclear Instrumentation** (Maintenance Technology; Nuclear Engineering); **Nuclear Analysis and Techniques** (Nuclear Engineering); **Radiation Protection and Dosimetry** (Safety Engineering); **Theoretical Physics** (Physics); **X-ray Fluorescence Techniques and Environment** (Environmental Engineering)

History: Founded 1976 as Laboratory for Nuclear and Applied Physics (L.P.N.P.A). Acquired present status and title 1992. A public autonomous institution.

Academic year: January to September

Admission requirements: Baccalauréat scientifique for two-year cycle leading to technician in radiation protection; Maîtrise ès Sciences for postgraduate study

Main language(s) of instruction: French

Accrediting agency: Ministère de l'Enseignement supérieur et de la Recherche scientifique. International Atomic Energy Agency

Degrees and diplomas: Licence, Master (Nuclear Physics), Doctorat (Nuclear Physics)

Student Services: Academic Counselling, Careers Guidance, Sports Facilities

Periodicals: Journal des Sciences et Techniques Nucléaires, Raoelina Andriambololona Interdisciplinary Seminar

Publishing house: Publishing Unit

Last Update: 02-09-2016

National Institute of Public and Community Health (INSPC)

Befelatanana BP 176
Antananarivo 101
Tel: +261(20) 22-257-01
Directeur Général: Jean de Dieu Marie Rakotomanga

Department/Division

Health Sciences (Community Health; Health Sciences; Nursing; Public Health)

History: Founded 2002.

Accrediting agency: Ministry of Public Health

Degrees and diplomas: Licence (Community Health; Health Sciences; Nursing; Public Health), Master (Community Health; Health Sciences; Public Health)

Last Update: 08-09-2016

National School of Administration (ENAM)

BP 1163 - Androhibe
Antananarivo
Tel: +261(20) 22-420-91
Fax: +261(20) 22-318-15
Website: http://www.enam.gov.mg
Directeur Général: Pascal Pierrot Rabetahina
Tel: +261(20) 24-553-79

Department/Division

Administration (Administration; Public Administration)

History: Founded 1960, attached to the university until 1972, no activity 1972-1988, known as ENAM since 1988, acquired present status 1995.

Admission requirements: Maîtrise and entrance examination

Fees: None

Main language(s) of instruction: French

Accrediting agency: Ministère de la Fonction Publique et des Lois Sociales. Ministère des Finances et du Budget.

Degrees and diplomas: . Equivalent of Master's (professional), 2 yrs

Student Services: Sports Facilities, Language Laboratory, Health Services

Last Update: 01-09-2016

University of Antananarivo (UA)

BP 566 Ambohitsaina
Antananarivo 101
Tel: +261(20) 22-326-39, +261(20) 22-241-14
Fax: +261(20) 22-279-26
Website: http://www.univ-antananarivo.mg
President: Panja Ramanoelina

Faculty

Arts and Humanities (Anthropology; Archaeology; Arts and Humanities; Cultural Studies; English; French; Geography; German; History; Literature; Modern Languages; Philosophy); **Law, Economics, Management and Sociology** (*DEGS*) (Administration; Economics; Law; Management; Sociology); **Medicine** (Gynaecology and Obstetrics; Medicine; Paediatrics; Surgery); **Science** (Chemistry; Mathematics; Natural Sciences; Physics)

School

Agronomy (*ESSA*) (Agricultural Engineering; Agricultural Management; Agriculture; Agronomy; Animal Husbandry; Food Technology; Forestry; Water Management); **Education** (*ENS*) (Chemistry; Education; English; French; Geography; History; Modern Languages; Natural Sciences; Physical Education; Physics); **Polytechnics** (*ESPA*) (Engineering)

Institute

Civilisation, Museum Studies and Archeology (Ancient Civilizations; Archaeology; Museum Studies); **Confucius** (Chinese); **Energy** (Energy Engineering); **Geophysical Observatory** (Geophysics)

Centre

Infectiology (*Charles Mérieux*) (Medicine)

Laboratory

Radioisotopes (Meteorology; Soil Science)
Further information: Also a brach in Antsirabe and Soavinandriana
History: Founded 1955 as Institut des Hautes Etudes tracing origins to School of Medicine (1896) and School of Law (1941). Became Université de Madagascar 1960. Reorganized 1973 with six main divisions, and 1976 as a decentralized institution with six Regional Centres. Acquired present status as independent university 1988.

Academic year: March-December

Admission requirements: Secondary school certificate (baccalauréat) or equivalent, and entrance examination

Fees: 12 for local students; 30 for foreign students (Euro)

Main language(s) of instruction: French, Malagasy

Accrediting agency: Ministère de l'Enseignement supérieur et de la Recherche scientifique

Degrees and diplomas: Licence (Administration; African Studies; Agricultural Management; Agriculture; Agronomy; Animal Husbandry; Anthropology; Arts and Humanities; Biology; Chemistry; Communication Studies; Cultural Studies; Development Studies; Economics; Electrical Engineering; English; Food Technology; Forestry; French; Geography; German; History; Industrial Engineering; Law; Literature; Management; Mathematics; Mathematics and Computer Science; Mechanical Engineering; Media Studies; Natural Sciences; Petroleum and Gas Engineering; Philosophy; Physics; Russian; Sociology; Spanish; Telecommunications Engineering; Tourism), Diplôme de Docteur en Médecine (Animal Husbandry; Medicine; Pharmacy; Veterinary Science), Master (Administration; Agricultural Management; Anthropology; Arts and Humanities; Automation and Control Engineering; Biology; Chemical Engineering; Chemistry; Civil Engineering; Communication Studies; Computer Engineering; Economics; Education; Electronic Engineering; English; Environmental Management; French; Geography; German; History; Industrial Engineering; Law; Linguistics; Literature; Management; Mathematics; Mathematics and Computer Science; Mechanical Engineering; Modern Languages; Native Language; Natural Sciences; Pedagogy; Petroleum and Gas Engineering; Philosophy; Physics; Russian; Sociology; Spanish; Telecommunications Engineering; Tourism; Urban Studies), Doctorat (African Languages; African Studies; Agricultural Management; Agriculture; Anthropology; Applied Chemistry; Arts and Humanities; Biology; Chemistry; Communication Studies; Cultural Studies; Development Studies; Earth Sciences; Ecology; Economics; Education; English; Environmental Studies; Epidemiology; Forest Management; Forestry; French; Geography; German; Health Sciences; History; Information Technology; Law; Linguistics; Management; Mathematics; Natural Resources; Natural Sciences; Pedagogy; Pharmacology; Physical Chemistry; Physics; Public Health; Social Sciences; Spanish; Water Science)

Student Services: Academic Counselling, Nursery Care, Sports Facilities, Health Services

Periodicals: Annales de la Faculté des Lettres et Sciences Humaines, Hiratra, Revue de Géographie, Terre Malgache

Academic Staff	MALE	FEMALE	TOTAL
FULL-TIME			697

Last Update: 07-09-2016

GEOPHYSICAL INSTITUTE AND OBSERVATORY OF ANTANANARIVO (IOGA)

BP 3843 Ambohidempona Campus Universitaire
Antananarivo 101
Tel: +261(20) 22-301-82
Fax: +261(20) 22-301-82
Website: http://www.ioga.mg
Directeur: Gérard Ralambomanana

Department/Division

Geophysics (Earth Sciences; Geophysics)
History: Founded 1989.
Accrediting agency: Ministère de l'Enseignement supérieur et de la Recherche scientifique
Degrees and diplomas: Licence (Earth Sciences; Geophysics), Master (Earth Sciences; Geophysics)
Last Update: 05-09-2016

INSTITUTE OF CIVILIZATIONS, MUSEUM OF ART AND ARCHAEOLOGY (IC/MAA)

BP 564 17 rue Docteur Villette, Isoraka
Antananarivo 101
Tel: +261(20) 24-221-65
Website: http://www.univ-antananarivo.mg/Institut-de-Civilisation-Musee-d
Directeur: Lala Modeste Rakotondrasoa

Institute

Civilizations, Museum of Art and Archaeology (*ICMAA*) (Anthropology; Archaeology; Arts and Humanities; Cultural Studies; Ethnology; Folklore; Geography; History; Musicology; Prehistory)
History: Founded 1964.
Accrediting agency: Ministère de l'Enseignement supérieur et de la Recherche scientifique
Degrees and diplomas:
Last Update: 05-09-2016

INSTITUTE OF ENERGY STUDIES (IME)

BP 566 Ambohitsaina
Antananarivo 101
Tel: +261(20) 22-311-91
Fax: +261(20) 22-279-96
Website: http://www.univ-antananarivo.mg/Institut-pour-la-Maitrise-de-l-Energie
Directeur: Andrianelison Rakotomahevitra

Institute

Energy and Thermal Engineering (Energy Engineering; Thermal Engineering)
History: Founded 1977.
Accrediting agency: Ministère de l'Enseignement supérieur et de la Recherche scientifique
Degrees and diplomas: Licence (Energy Engineering), Master (Energy Engineering)
Last Update: 05-09-2016

RADIO-ISOTOPES LABORATORY (LRI)

BP 3383
Antananarivo 101, Antananarivo
Tel: +261(20) 26 396 47
Website: http://www.laboradioisotopes.mg
Directeur: Lilia Rabeharisoa

Laboratory

Nuclear Medicine and Biology (Biology; Medical Technology)
Further information: Route d'Andraisoro, Ambohimirary Antananarivo Madagascar
History: Founded 1965. Replaced by the decree n°71-254 of 27th May 1971 bearing the status of radio-isotopes laboratory.
Academic year: September to July
Main language(s) of instruction: French, English
Accrediting agency: Ministère de l'Enseignement supérieur et de la Recherche scientifique
Degrees and diplomas: Doctorat (Agriculture; Animal Husbandry; Environmental Studies). Also Master
Last Update: 05-09-2016

University of Antsiranana (UNA)

BP 0
Antsiranana 201
Tel: +261(20) 82-925-96
Website: http://www.univ-antsiranana.edu.mg
Présidente: Cécile Marie Ange Manorohanta
Tel: +261-34-07-039-01

Faculty

Arts and Humanities (Arts and Humanities; Communication Studies; Cultural Studies; French; Linguistics; Modern Languages); **Law, Economics, Management, and Political Sciences** (Accountancy; Economics; Finance; Law; Political Sciences; Private Law; Public Law); **Science** (Chemistry; Environmental Studies; Physics)

Institute

Business Administration (*ISAE*) (Business Administration)

Centre

Computer Studies (Computer Engineering; Electrical and Electronic Engineering; Systems Analysis; Telecommunications Engineering)

Further information: Also a branch in Ambanja

History: Founded 1975 as Regional Centre of the Université de Madagascar. Acquired present status as independent university 1992.

Academic year: March to December

Admission requirements: Secondary school certificate (baccalauréat) or equivalent, and entrance examination

Main language(s) of instruction: French

Accrediting agency: Ministry of National Education and Scientific Research

Degrees and diplomas: Licence (Accountancy; Agronomy; Business Administration; Chemistry; Earth Sciences; Engineering; Environmental Studies; Finance; International Business; Law; Management; Modern Languages; Natural Sciences; Physics), Master (Business Administration; Chemistry; Earth Sciences; Environmental Studies; French; Law; Linguistics; Literature; Management; Modern Languages; Natural Sciences; Physics; Political Sciences), Doctorat (Chemistry; Cultural Studies; Engineering; Environmental Studies; Literature; Modern Languages; Physics)

Student Services: Academic Counselling, Sports Facilities, Language Laboratory, Health Services

Last Update: 05-09-2016

HIGHER POLYTECHNIC SCHOOL (ESPA)

BP 0

Antsiranana 201

Tel: +261(20) 82-211-37, Ext. 49, + 261 32-02-510-80

Fax: +261(20) 82-214-93

Website: http://www.univ-antsiranana.edu.mg/polytechnique/lecole-superieure-polytechnique

Directeur: Tefy Raoelivololona

Department/Division

Electronic Engineering (Electronic Engineering); **Hydraulic Engineering** (Hydraulic Engineering); **Industrial Engineering** (Computer Engineering; Industrial Engineering); **Mechanical Engineering** (Mechanical Engineering)

History: Founded 1977. Acquired present status 1994.

Main language(s) of instruction: French

Degrees and diplomas: Licence (Civil Engineering; Construction Engineering; Electrical Engineering; Electronic Engineering; Mechanical Engineering; Telecommunications Engineering), Master (Civil Engineering; Construction Engineering; Electrical Engineering; Hydraulic Engineering; Mathematics; Mechanical Engineering; Telecommunications Engineering), Doctorat (Automation and Control Engineering; Electronic Engineering; Environmental Engineering)

Academic Staff 2015-2016	MALE	FEMALE	TOTAL
FULL-TIME			c. 70
Student Numbers 2015-2016			
All (Foreign Included)			c. 800

Last Update: 05-09-2016

TEACHER TRAINING COLLEGE FOR TECHNICAL STUDIES (ENSET)

BP 0

Antsiranana 201

Tel: +261(20) 82-211-37, Ext. 50

Fax: +261(20) 82-294-09

Website: http://www.univ-antsiranana.edu.mg/enset

Directeur: Honoré Eugène Rakotondrasoa

Tel: +261 32-02-484-28, + 261 34-09-154-51

Department/Division

Energy Engineering (Energy Engineering); **Mathematics and Computer Science** (Computer Science; Mathematics and Computer Science; Mathematics Education); **Mechanical Engineering** (Mechanical Engineering)

History: Founded 1991. Acquired present status 1994.

Admission requirements: Secondary school certificate (Baccalauréat scientific profile)

Main language(s) of instruction: French

Accrediting agency: Ministère de l'Enseignement supérieur et de la Recherche scientifique

Degrees and diplomas: Licence (Computer Science; Energy Engineering; Mathematics; Mathematics and Computer Science; Mechanical Engineering), Master (Computer Science; Energy Engineering; Mathematics; Mathematics and Computer Science; Mechanical Engineering)

Academic Staff 2015-2016	MALE	FEMALE	TOTAL
FULL-TIME			17
Student Numbers 2015-2016			
All (Foreign Included)			300

Last Update: 05-09-2016

University of Fianarantsoa (UF)

BP 1264 Campus Universitaire d'Andrainjato

Fianarantsoa 301

Tel: +261(20) 75-508-02

Fax: +261(20) 75-513-25

Website: http://www.univ-fianar.mg

President: Fontaine Rafamantanantsoa

Faculty

Art and Human Sciences (Anthropology; Cultural Studies; English; French; History; Modern Languages; Spanish); **Law, Economy, Management and Social Sciences** (*DEGS*) (Economics; Law; Management; Private Law; Public Administration; Public Law; Social Sciences); **Medecine** (Health Sciences; Medicine); **Sciences** (Chemistry; Electrical and Electronic Equipment and Maintenance; Energy Engineering; Mathematics; Mathematics and Computer Science; Natural Sciences; Oenology; Physics)

Institute

Confucius (Chinese); **Environment Science and Technology** (*ISTE*) (Agronomy; Environmental Studies; Technology; Tourism; Water Science)

Centre

Professional Studies (*CUFP (Tanambao)*) (Computer Engineering; Economics; Information Technology; Social Sciences; Surveying and Mapping); **University Regional - Farafangana** (Development Studies; Rural Studies; Social Sciences)

History: Founded 1977 as Regional Centre of the Université de Madagascar. Acquired present status as independent University 1988.

Academic year: October to June

Admission requirements: Secondary school certificate (baccalauréat) or equivalent, and entrance examination

Main language(s) of instruction: Malagasy, French

Accrediting agency: Ministère de l'Enseignement supérieur et de la Recherche scientifique

Degrees and diplomas: Licence (Anthropology; Business Administration; Chemistry; Computer Engineering; Development Studies; Economics; History; Law; Management; Mathematics; Mathematics and Computer Science; Physics; Social Sciences), Master (Adult Education; Chemistry; Computer Science; Economics; Environmental Studies; Law; Management; Mathematics; Pedagogy; Physics; Social Sciences), Doctorat (Anthropology; Computer Engineering; Economics; Government; History; Information Technology; Law; Management; Political Sciences; Social Sciences)

Student Services: Cultural Activities, Sports Facilities, Language Laboratory, Health Services

Last Update: 06-09-2016

HIGHER PEDAGOGICAL SCHOOL (ENS)

BP 1264
Fianarantsoa 301
Tel: +261(20) 75-928-9
Fax: +261(20) 75-506-19
Directeur: Faly Tinasoa Andrianandrasanirina

Department/Division

Educational Sciences (Educational Sciences); **Science and Technology** (Biology; Chemistry; Environmental Studies; Mathematics; Natural Resources; Physics)

History: Founded 1981. Acquired present status 1983.

Admission requirements: Entrance examination

Accrediting agency: Ministère de l'Enseignement supérieur et de la Recherche scientifique

Degrees and diplomas: Licence (Chemistry; Educational Sciences; Environmental Studies; Mathematics Education; Physics; Science Education), Master (Biology; Chemistry; Educational Sciences; Environmental Studies; Mathematics; Natural Resources; Physics)

Last Update: 06-09-2016

INSTITUTE OF ENVIRONMENTAL TECHNIQUES AND SCIENCES (ISTE)

BP 1264 Ambalapaiso
Fianarantsoa 301
Tel: +261(20) 75-905-38
Fax: +261(20) 75-519-17
Directeur: Christian Etienne Jean Baptiste Rakotondravelo

Course/Programme

Environmental Studies (Agronomy; Ecology; Economics; Environmental Studies; Forestry; Management; Tourism; Water Management)

History: Founded 1999.

Main language(s) of instruction: French

Accrediting agency: Ministère de l'Enseignement supérieur et de la Recherche scientifique

Degrees and diplomas: Licence (Agronomy; Environmental Studies; Technology; Tourism; Water Science)

Last Update: 06-09-2016

NATIONAL SCHOOL OF COMPUTER SCIENCE (ENI)

BP 1487 Tanambao
Fianarantsoa 301
Tel: +261(20) 75-508-01
Fax: +261(20) 75-506-19
Website: http://www.univ-fianar.mg
Andriantiana Bertin Olivier Ramamonjisoa
Tel: +261 34-84-959-79

Course/Programme

Computer Science (Computer Engineering; Computer Networks; Data Processing; Software Engineering; Systems Analysis)

Department/Division

Doctoral Studies (Artificial Intelligence; Computer Science; Information Technology)

History: Founded 1980. Acquired present status 1983.

Accrediting agency: Ministère de l'Enseignement supérieur et de la Recherche scientifique

Degrees and diplomas: Licence (Computer Engineering; Computer Networks; Data Processing; Software Engineering), Master (Computer Engineering; Computer Networks; Data Processing; Software Engineering)

Last Update: 06-09-2016

University of Mahajanga

BP 652 Immeuble Kakal, 5 rue Georges V
Mahajanga 401
Tel: +261(20) 62-908-34
Fax: +261(20) 62-233-12
Website: http://www.univ-mahajanga.mg
Président: Andrianony Emmanuel Rakotoarivony

Faculty

Medicine (Biology; Medicine; Natural Sciences; Public Health; Surgery); **Science** (Biochemistry; Biology; Botany; Chemistry; Earth Sciences; Environmental Studies; Natural Sciences)

School

Law and Political Sciences (*EDSP*) (Law; Political Sciences); **Tourism** (Tourism)

Institute

Applied Biology (*IBA*) (Biology); **Dental Technology** (Dental Technology); **Langues and Civilizations** (*ELC*) (Ancient Civilizations; History; Modern Languages); **Management and Business Administration** (*IUGM*) (Business Administration; Management); **Science and Technology** (*ISSTM*) (Civil Engineering; Industrial Engineering); **Tropical Dentistry** (Dentistry)

History: Founded 1977 as Regional Centre of the Université de Madagascar. Acquired present status as independent University 1992.

Academic year: November to July

Admission requirements: Secondary school certificate (baccalauréat) or equivalent, and entrance examination

Main language(s) of instruction: French, Malagasy

Degrees and diplomas: Licence (Biology; Cultural Studies; Dental Technology; Geology; Law; Management; Modern Languages; Paleontology; Political Sciences; Tourism), Diplôme de Docteur en Médecine (Medicine), Master (Biochemistry; Earth Sciences; Environmental Studies; Finance; Geology; Law; Natural Sciences; Paleontology), Doctorat (Biotechnology; Ecology; Environmental Studies; Health Sciences; Nutrition; Pharmacology; Public Health). Also teaching qualifications

Last Update: 06-09-2016

INSTITUTE OF TROPICAL DENTISTRY (IOSTM)

BP 98, 7 rue Maréchal Joffre
Mahajanga 401
Tel: +261(20) 62-022-19
Directrice: Jeanne Angelphine Rasoamananjara

Institute

Tropical Dentistry (Dentistry; Stomatology)
History: Founded 1977.
Main language(s) of instruction: French
Accrediting agency: Ministère de l'Enseignement supérieur et de la Recherche scientifique
Degrees and diplomas: Master (Dentistry; Public Health)
Last Update: 06-09-2016

University of Toamasina

BP 591 Barikadimy
Toamasina 501
Tel: +261(20) 53-322-44
Fax: +261(20) 53-335-66
Website: http://www.univ-toamasina.mg
Président: Jérôme Velo
Tel: +261(20) 53-324-54

Faculty

Arts and Humanities (Anthropology; Arts and Humanities; French; Geography; Philosophy; Social Sciences); **Law, Economics and Management and Mathematic and Computer Science and Applications** (Economics; Law; Management; Mathematics and Computer Science; Software Engineering); **Medicine** (Medicine)

School

National Customs (*ENSD*) (Taxation)

Institute

Environmental Science and Sustainable Development (*ISSEDD*) (Environmental Studies); **Technology - Alaotra Mangory** (*Regional (ISTRALMA)*) (Economics; Law; Management; Political Sciences); **Technology- East-Coast Region** (*ISTRCE*) (Business Administration; Management); **Tourism, Heritage Preservation and Territory Planning** (*ITPT*) (Heritage Preservation; Tourism)

History: Founded 1977 as Regional Centre of the Université de Madagascar. Acquired present status as independent University 1992.

Academic year: October to June

Admission requirements: Secondary school certificate (baccalauréat) or equivalent, and entrance examination
Fees: (Ariary): 5,000-6,000 per annum
Main language(s) of instruction: French, Malagasy
Accrediting agency: Ministère de l'Enseignement supérieur et de la Recherche scientifique
Degrees and diplomas: Licence (Agricultural Management; Agronomy; Business Administration; Economics; Environmental Studies; French; Geography; History; Law; Management; Philosophy; Political Sciences; Tourism), Master (Business Administration; Computer Science; Development Studies; Economics; Environmental Studies; Health Sciences; Heritage Preservation; Law; Management; Mathematics; Political Sciences; Social Sciences; Software Engineering), Doctorat (Business Administration; Computer Science; Development Studies; Environmental Studies; Ethics; Health Sciences; Law; Mathematics; Philosophy; Political Sciences; Social Sciences; Software Engineering). Also: Diplome des Hautes Études Spécialisées en Administration des Douanes (DHESAD)
Student Services: Library
Last Update: 06-09-2016

University of Toliara

BP 185 Maninday
Toliara 601
Tel: +261(20) 94-410-33
Fax: +261(20) 94-443-07
Website: http://www.univ-toliara.mg
President: Hugues Lezo
Tel: +261(32) 07-602-54

Faculty
Arts and Humanities (Arts and Humanities; French; Geography; History; Literature; Philosophy); **Law, Economics, Management and Sociology** (*DEGS*) (Economics; Law; Management; Sociology); **Medicine** (Medicine); **Sciences** (Chemistry; Environmental Studies; Mathematics; Medicine; Natural Sciences; Physics)

School
Education (*ENS*) (Philosophy)

Institute
Halieutics and Marine Science (*IHSM*) (Aquaculture; Biotechnology; Marine Science and Oceanography); **Technology - Anosy** (Marine Science and Oceanography); **Technology - Menabe** (Environmental Engineering; Environmental Studies); **Technology - Toliara** (*IST Toliara*) (Agronomy; Water Science)

Centre
University Regional - Androy (Environmental Studies; Modern Languages; Natural Sciences; Social Sciences; Technology)

Research Division
Art and Oral Traditions of Madagascar (*CEDRATOM*) (Arts and Humanities; Cultural Studies; History)
History: Founded 1977 as Regional Centre of the Université de Madagascar. Acquired present status as independent University 1988.
Academic year: November to July
Admission requirements: Secondary school certificate (baccalauréat) or equivalent, and entrance examination
Main language(s) of instruction: French, Malagasy
Accrediting agency: Ministère de l'Enseignement supérieur et de la Recherche scientifique
Degrees and diplomas: Licence (African Languages; Agronomy; Chemistry; Earth Sciences; Educational Psychology; Educational Sciences; Environmental Studies; French; Geography; History; Law; Management; Marine Science and Oceanography; Modern Languages; Philosophy; Physics; Social Sciences; Water Science), Master (Aquaculture; Earth Sciences; Environmental Studies; French; Geography; History; Marine Science and Oceanography; Philosophy; Physics), Doctorat (Aquaculture; Biotechnology; Cultural Studies; Development Studies; Education; Environmental Studies; French; Geography; History; Literature; Marine Science and Oceanography; Philosophy; Social Sciences)
Student Services: Sports Facilities, Health Services
Periodicals: Talily
Last Update: 07-09-2016

INSTITUTE OF MARINE SCIENCE (IHSM)
BP 141 Route du Port, Avenue De France
Toliara 601
Tel: +261(20) 94-941-67
Fax: +261(20) 94-435-52
Website: http://www.ihsm.mg
Directeur: Thierry Lavitra
Tel: +261(20) 94-419-89

Course/Programme
Aquaculture (Aquaculture); **Coastal Studies** (Coastal Studies); **Fishery** (Fishery); **Marine Science** (Marine Science and Oceanography)
History: Founded 1986.
Main language(s) of instruction: French, Malagasy
Accrediting agency: Ministère de l'Enseignement supérieur et de la Recherche scientifique
Degrees and diplomas: Licence (Aquaculture; Coastal Studies; Marine Science and Oceanography), Master

(Aquaculture; Coastal Studies; Marine Science and Oceanography), Doctorat (Aquaculture; Coastal Studies; Marine Science and Oceanography)
Last Update: 07-09-2016

Private Institutions

ACEEM University

Manakambahiny
Antananarivo
Tel: +261(20) 22-295-34
Website: http://universiteaceem.com
President: William Ratrema

Course/Programme

Engineering (Computer Engineering; Electronic Engineering); **Health Science** (Health Sciences; Ophthalmology); **Law** (Law); **Management** (Management; Marketing)
History: Founded 2008.
Main language(s) of instruction: French
Accrediting agency: Ministère de l'Enseignement supérieur et de la Recherche scientifique
Degrees and diplomas: Licence (Communication Studies; Computer Engineering; Electronic Engineering; Law; Management; Medical Technology; Political Sciences), Master (Communication Studies; International Relations; Law; Management)
Last Update: 14-09-2016

Athénée Saint Joseph Antsirabe (ASJA)

BP 287
Antsirabe 110
Tel: +261(20) 44- 483-19
Website: http://www.univ-asja.net/asja
Recteur: Laurence Ralamboranto

Course/Programme

Science and Technology (Agricultural Engineering; Agronomy; Animal Husbandry; Computer Engineering; Earth Sciences; Food Science; Textile Technology); **Social Sciences** (Business and Commerce; Development Studies; Economic History; Law; Marketing)
History: Founded 2000.
Admission requirements: Baccalauréat
Accrediting agency: Ministère de l'Enseignement supérieur et de la Recherche scientifique
Degrees and diplomas: Licence (Agronomy; Business and Commerce; Computer Engineering; Earth Sciences;

Economics; Law), Master (Agronomy; Business and Commerce; Computer Engineering; Earth Sciences; Economics; Law)
Last Update: 12-04-2017

Catholic University of Madagascar (UCM)

BP 6059 Ambatoroka
Antananarivo 101
Tel: +261(20) 22-340-09
Fax: +261(20) 22-340-13
Website: http://www.ucm.mg
Recteur: Marc Ravelonantoandro

Faculty

Social Sciences (Economics; Law; Management; Political Sciences)

School

Management (*ESSVA*) (Communication Studies; Management; Tourism)

Department/Division

Philosophy (Philosophy); **Psychology** (Psychology); **Theology** (Theology)
History: Founded 1960 as Institut Supérieur de Théologie et de Philosophie de Madagascar. Became Institut Supérieur de Théologie, 1973 then Institut Catholique de Madagascar, 1997. Acquired present status and title 2011.
Admission requirements: Secondary school certificate (Baccalauréat) and entrance examination.
Fees: 780,000-1,2 m. per annum depending on degrees (Malagasy Ariary)
Main language(s) of instruction: French
Accrediting agency: Ministère de l'Enseignement supérieur et de la Recherche scientifique
Degrees and diplomas: Licence (Demography and Population; Development Studies; Economics; Law; Management; Philosophy; Political Sciences; Psychology; Social Sciences; Sociology; Theology), Master (Demography and Population; Development Studies; Economics; Law; Management; Philosophy; Political Sciences; Psychology; Sociology; Theology; Tourism), Doctorat (Demography and Population; Development Studies; Economics; Law; Political Sciences; Sociology)
Student Services: Academic Counselling, Sports Facilities, Health Services, Canteen
Periodicals: Aspect du Christianisme à Madagascar, Collection - ISTA - ICM Antananarivo
Last Update: 02-09-2016

SOCIAL SERVICE SCHOOL
BP 7570 133 Avenue Lénine Antanimena
Antananarivo 101

Department/Division

Social Sciences (Social and Community Services; Social Sciences)
History: Founded 1960.
Accrediting agency: Ministère de l'Enseignement supérieur et de la Recherche scientifique
Degrees and diplomas:
Last Update: 07-09-2016

ST FRANÇOIS D'ASSISE SCHOOL OF NURSING

BP 7002
Antananarivo 101
Directrice: Angelina De Nobrega Baptista

Department/Division

Nursing (Nursing)
History: Founded 1993.
Degrees and diplomas: . Diploma of nursing (3 yrs)
Last Update: 07-09-2016

EEFPS Condorcet

BP 7036, Mahavoky Besarety
Antananarivo 101
Tel: +261 33-11-053-17, +216(24) 377-24
Directrice: Bakoliarinosy Rajoelisona

Course/Programme

Civil Engineering (Civil Engineering); **Industrial Engineering** (Industrial Engineering)
Main language(s) of instruction: French
Accrediting agency: Ministère de l'Enseignement supérieur et de la Recherche scientifique
Degrees and diplomas: Licence (Civil Engineering; Industrial Engineering), Master (Civil Engineering; Industrial Engineering)
Last Update: 02-09-2016

Engineering School of Tourism, Informatics, Interpretership and Management (ESTIIM)

B.P. 8181 Immeuble CENAM 67 Ha Sud
Antananarivo 101
Tel: +261 34-01-936-36
Website: http://www.estiim.net
Directeur Général: M ANDRIANADISON

Department/Division

Science and Technology (Computer Engineering); **Social Science** (Environmental Studies; Hotel Management; Law; Political Sciences; Social Sciences; Tourism)

History: Founded 2002.
Accrediting agency: Engineering School of Tourism, Informatics, Interpretership and Management
Degrees and diplomas: Licence (Computer Engineering; Hotel Management; Law; Management; Tourism), Master (Administration; Business and Commerce; Computer Engineering; Law; Management; Marketing; Political Sciences)
Last Update: 08-09-2016

EUROI

LOT II A 78, Soavimbahoaka
Antananarivo, 101
Tel: +261 32-40-371-37
Website: http://euroi.mg
Directeur Général: Henriette Randriamanantena

Course/Programme

Engineering (Electronic Engineering; Telecommunications Engineering)
History: Founded 1989.
Accrediting agency: Ministère de l'Enseignement supérieur et de la Recherche scientifique
Degrees and diplomas: Licence (Computer Engineering; Electronic Engineering; Telecommunications Engineering), Master (Computer Engineering; Electronic Engineering; Telecommunications Engineering)
Student Services: Sports Facilities
Last Update: 08-09-2016

FFFMM IMD Fianarantsoa

BP 1385 IMD ISAHA
Fianarantsoa 301
Tel: +261 34-05-902-06
Website: http://malagasymahomby.org
Secrétaire général: José Rakotozafy Harison

Course/Programme

Development Studies (Development Studies)
Further information: Also a branch in Antananarivo, Tamatave, Majunga
History: Founded 2003.
Academic year: From February to October.
Admission requirements: Secondary school certificate (Baccalauréat)
Accrediting agency: Ministère de l'Enseignement supérieur et de la Recherche scientifique
Degrees and diplomas: Licence (Development Studies), Master (Development Studies)
Last Update: 12-04-2017

Gate University (GUA Ambohidratrimo)

Lot 67 G 24 Ambohitsimiova
Ambohidratrimo
Tel: +261 34-27-758-24
Website: http://www.gateuniversity-madagascar.com
Directeur: Rivoarison Andrianasolo

Department/Division

Agronomy (Agriculture); **Arts and Humanities** (Tourism);
Social Science (Accountancy; Business and Commerce;
Management; Marketing)
Accrediting agency: Ministère de l'Enseignement supérieur
et de la Recherche scientifique
Degrees and diplomas: Licence (Agronomy; Management;
Tourism), Master (Agronomy; Management)
Last Update: 08-09-2016

Hay Soa Private University (UPHS)

Immeuble CNAPS 67 HA
Antananarivo 101
Tel: +261 32-78-665-91
Président fondateur: Aristide Velompanahy

Department/Division

Civil Engineering (Civil Engineering; Construction Engineering); **Communication Studies** (Communication Studies); **Computer Engineering** (Computer Engineering);
Management (Accountancy; Finance; Management)
History: Founded 2011.
Main language(s) of instruction: French
Accrediting agency: Ministère de l'Enseignement supérieur
et de la Recherche scientifique
Degrees and diplomas: Licence (Business Computing; Civil
Engineering; Economics; Management), Master (Civil
Engineering)
Last Update: 14-09-2016

Higher Christian Studies in Management and Applied Mathematics (HECMMA)

BP 7686, Lot II I Alarobia Amboniloha
Antananarivo 101
Tel: +261(20) 26-393-17, +262 32-41-591-56
Fax: +261(20) 22-298-63
Président: Solonjatovo Rakotonirina

Department/Division

Engineering (Civil Engineering; Computer Science; Engineering; Telecommunications Engineering; Town Planning);
Management and Economics (Applied Mathematics; Economics; Management)
History: Founded 1997.
Main language(s) of instruction: French
Accrediting agency: Ministère de l'Enseignement supérieur
et de la Recherche scientifique
Degrees and diplomas: Licence (Civil Engineering; Computer Engineering; Economics; Electronic Engineering; Management; Telecommunications Engineering; Town
Planning), Master (Civil Engineering; Computer Engineering; Electronic Engineering; Telecommunications Engineering; Town Planning). DISMA (Diplôme supérieur en
Management et Mathématiques appliquées); Bachelor
(3 yrs); MMSI (Master en Management et Sciences de
l'Ingénieur - 5 yrs)
Last Update: 01-09-2016

Higher Institute of Communication, Business and Management (ISCAM)

BP 8224, Lot IVN 68 A Ankadifotsy
Antananarivo 101
Tel: +261(20) 22-224-88, +261(20) 22-256-27
Fax: +261(20) 22-255-43
Website: http://www.iscam.mg
Directeur général: Jaona Ranaivoson

Course/Programme

Business Management and Development (Business
Administration; Development Studies; Management);
Human Resource (Human Resources; Tourism); **International Trade** (Business and Commerce; International Business); **Marketing and Communication** (Communication
Studies; Marketing)
History: Founded in 1990.
Main language(s) of instruction: French
Accrediting agency: Ministère de l'Enseignement supérieur
et de la Recherche scientifique
Degrees and diplomas: Licence (Business and Commerce;
Human Resources; International Business; Marketing), Master (Human Resources; International Business; Management;
Marketing)
Last Update: 31-07-2017

Higher Institute of Computer Science IS-INFO (IS INFO)

Lot IBI 22 Ampasamadinika Andranomena
Antananarivo 101

Tel: +216(24) 611-63, +261 33-37-267-93
Website: http://www.is-info.net

Course/Programme
Computer Engineering (Computer Engineering)
History: Founded 2004.
Accrediting agency: Ministère de l'Enseignement supérieur et de la Recherche scientifique
Degrees and diplomas: Licence (Accountancy; Business and Commerce; Computer Engineering; Finance; Marketing), Master (Computer Engineering; Software Engineering)
Last Update: 28-09-2016

Higher Institute of Electronic and Computer Engineering (ISGEI)

Lot II H 28 Ampandrana Ouest
Antananarivo, 101
Tel: +261(20) 22-248-31

Course/Programme
Engineering (Computer Engineering; Electronic Engineering)
History: Founded 2012.
Main language(s) of instruction: French
Accrediting agency: Ministère de l'Enseignement supérieur et de la Recherche scientifique
Degrees and diplomas: Licence (Computer Engineering; Electronic Engineering), Master (Computer Engineering; Electronic Engineering)
Last Update: 14-09-2016\

IMAGE APPLI Institute

Lot II H 34 L Ter A Ankerana Ankadindramamy
Antananarivo 101
Tel: +261(34) 39-129-77; 261(33) 81-344-75

Course/Programme
Health Sciences (Health Sciences); **Management** (Banking; Business and Commerce; Economics; Law; Management)
Accrediting agency: Ministère de l'Enseignement supérieur et de la Recherche scientifique
Degrees and diplomas: Licence (Business and Commerce; Economics; Management), Master (Health Sciences)
Last Update: 28-09-2016

IMGAM

Ambodivoanjo Ivandry
Antananarivo 101

Tel: + 261(20) 22- 649-74
Website: http://imgam.mg
Directeur: Martin Pierre Rakotoson

Course/Programme
Management (Administration; Banking; Business Administration; Finance; Management; Marketing)
History: Founded 1992. Acquired present title and status 2002.
Fees: National : 16 000 per month per field of study (Malagasy Ariary), International : 23 000 per month per field of study (Malagasy Ariary)
Main language(s) of instruction: French, Malagasy
Accrediting agency: Ministère de l'Enseignement supérieur et de la Recherche scientifique
Degrees and diplomas: Licence (Administration; Banking; Biology; Business Administration; Environmental Studies; Management), Master (Banking; Business Administration; Management; Marketing)
Last Update: 12-09-2016

Institute of Computer Engineering and Management (IESTIME)

Lot IVA 25 Antaninandro
Antananarivo
Tel: 261(20) 22-54-07

Course/Programme
Management (Management)
Further information: Also a branch in Antsirabe
History: Founded 1998.
Main language(s) of instruction: French
Accrediting agency: Ministère de l'Enseignement supérieur et de la Recherche scientifique
Degrees and diplomas: Licence (Management), Master (Management)
Last Update: 14-09-2016

Institute of Geology, Engineering and Environment of Madagascar (ISGIE Madagascar)

Lot II L 110 FAC Ankadivato
Antananarivo, 101
Tel: +261(20) 22-383-28, +260 34-76-104-19
Website: http://www.isgie.com

Course/Programme

Engineering (Civil Engineering; Environmental Engineering; Environmental Studies; Geology; Natural Resources)
Main language(s) of instruction: French
Accrediting agency: Ministère de l'Enseignement supérieur et de la Recherche scientifique
Degrees and diplomas: Licence (Environmental Engineering; Geology), Master (Civil Engineering; Environmental Studies; Geology; Natural Resources)
Last Update: 14-09-2016

Institute of Management and Tourism (IMT)

Lot IVS 30 Antanimena
Antananarivo 101, Antananarivo
Tel: 261 33-41-317-59; 261 34-29-373-32
Website: www.institut-imt.com
General Manager: Alphine Raharisoabako
Tel: 261 34 29 373 32

Institute

Building and Public Works (*Fabric Building - Housing and Energy - Civil Engeneering and Architecture*) (Architectural and Environmental Design; Architectural Restoration; Architecture; Architecture and Planning; Automation and Control Engineering; Bridge Engineering; Building Technologies; Ceramics and Glass Technology; Civil Engineering; Construction Engineering; Electrical and Electronic Engineering; Electrical Engineering; Electronic Engineering; Energy Engineering; Engineering; Engineering Drawing and Design; Engineering Management; Environmental Engineering; Geological Engineering; Industrial Engineering; Landscape Architecture; Marine Engineering; Materials Engineering; Naval Architecture; Polymer and Plastics Technology; Power Engineering; Regional Planning; Road Engineering; Rural Planning; Sanitary Engineering; Structural Architecture; Technology; Thermal Engineering; Town Planning; Transport Engineering); **Hotel and Tourism Management** (*Hotel and Front Office Management - Travel and Tourism Management - Cooking and Catering Management*) (Air Transport; Cooking and Catering; Cosmetology; Ecology; Environmental Management; Environmental Studies; Hotel and Restaurant; Hotel Management; Leisure Studies; Natural Resources; Parks and Recreation; Plant and Crop Protection; Railway Transport; Retailing and Wholesaling; Road Transport; Sales Techniques; Service Trades; Store Management; Tourism; Transport and Communications; Transport Management; Waste Management); **Management and Business Studies** (*Management - Marketing - Accounting*) (Accountancy; Administration; Advertising and Publicity; Air Transport; Banking; Business Administration; Business and Commerce; Business Computing; E- Business/Commerce;

Finance; Human Resources; Industrial Management; Institutional Administration; Insurance; International Business; Labour and Industrial Relations; Leadership; Management; Management Systems; Marine Transport; Marketing; Postal Services; Private Administration; Public Administration; Public Relations; Railway Transport; Real Estate; Road Transport; Secretarial Studies; Small Business; Taxation; Transport and Communications; Transport Management)
Further information: Ambatofotsy Antananarivo
History: The Institute of Management and Tourism - Institute of Management and Technology has been founded in 1998. Acquired present status in 2014.
Academic year: Summer session: October to June. Winter Session: April to december
Fees: National : 130 000 (Malagasy Ariary), International : 45 (Euro)
Main language(s) of instruction: French, English
Accrediting agency: Ministère de l'Enseignement supérieur et de la Recherche scientifique
Degrees and diplomas: Licence (Architecture and Planning; Business Administration; Business and Commerce; Engineering; Hotel and Restaurant; Hotel Management; Technology; Tourism), Master (Architecture and Planning; Business and Commerce; Engineering; Hotel and Restaurant; Hotel Management; Management; Technology; Tourism)
Student Services: Academic Counselling, Careers Guidance, Nursery Care, Sports Facilities, Facilities for disabled people, Health Services, Foreign Studies Centre, Library, Residential Facilities
Periodicals: International journals
Last Update: 14-02-2017

Institute of Social Work (ISTS)

BP 9103 Andoharanofotsy Lot IAV 309 B Mandrimena Iavoloha
Antananarivo 102
Tel: +261(20) 22-460-34
Director: Olga Phan Van Hien

Course/Programme

Social Work (Social and Community Services; Social Welfare; Social Work; Special Education)
History: Founded as Ecole de service social, 1960. Acquired present title and status 2009.
Accrediting agency: Ministère de l'Enseignement supérieur et de la Recherche scientifique
Degrees and diplomas: Licence (Social and Community Services; Social Work; Special Education; Welfare and Protective Services), Master (Social and Community Services; Social Work; Special Education; Welfare and Protective Services)
Last Update: 02-09-2016

Institute of Technical Studies (IFT Antananarivo)

Lot SIBE 5 Bis, Rue Andrianampoinimerina, Soarano
Antananarivo 101
Tel: +261(20) 22-64-172
Directeur: Valisaona Andriambolananirina

Course/Programme

Engineering (Building Technologies; Computer Engineering; Construction Engineering); **Health Science** (Health Sciences); **Information, Communication and Journalism** (Communication Studies; Information Sciences; Journalism); **Law** (Law); **Management** (Management; Tourism)
Further information: Also a branch in Ambositra, Antsirabe, Fianarantsoa, Manjunga, and Toliara
Accrediting agency: Ministère de l'Enseignement supérieur et de la Recherche scientifique
Degrees and diplomas: Licence (Civil Engineering; Construction Engineering; Environmental Studies; Health Sciences; Law; Management; Tourism), Master (Civil Engineering; Computer Engineering; Construction Engineering; Environmental Studies; Health Sciences; Law; Management; Tourism)
Last Update: 02-09-2016

Institute of Technical Technology, Living and Interdisciplinary Arts of Madagascar (INTETLIAM)

Lot VS 99Z ter E Andranovory
Antananarivo 101
Tel: +261 32-04-350, +261 34-50-440-40

Course/Programme

Engineering (Architecture; Civil Engineering; Construction Engineering)
Accrediting agency: Ministère de l'Enseignement supérieur et de la Recherche scientifique
Degrees and diplomas: Master (Architecture; Civil Engineering; Construction Engineering)
Last Update: 14-09-2016

ISM ADVANCEA (ISM ADVANCEA)

BP 8174 Lot VE 9 Ambohijatovo
Antananarivo 101
Tel: +261(20) 22-547-80, +261 33-05-547
Directeur: Mamy Rafalinirina

Course/Programme

Hotel Management (Hotel and Restaurant; Hotel Management); **Social Sciences** (Law; Management); **Tourism** (Tourism)

Department/Division

Engineering (Civil Engineering; Computer Engineering)
History: Founded 1998.
Accrediting agency: Ministère de l'Enseignement supérieur et de la Recherche scientifique
Degrees and diplomas: Licence (Computer Engineering; Law; Management; Tourism), Master (Law)
Last Update: 14-09-2016

Madagascar Institute of Political Studies (IEP)

Bâtiment CFD/FJKM Ampandrana
Antananarivo 101
Tel: +261(20) 22-345- 64, +261 33-37-400-41
Website: http://www.iep-madagascar.com
Directeur: Davida Rajaon

Course/Programme

Poltical Sciences (Economics; Ethics; International Relations; Law; Philosophy; Political Sciences; Public Administration; Sociology)
History: Founded 2010.
Main language(s) of instruction: French
Degrees and diplomas: Licence, Master (Communication Studies; Environmental Studies; International Business; International Relations; Journalism; Law; Political Sciences; Public Administration), Doctorat (Economics; Finance; International Relations; Law; Political Sciences; Public Administration; Sociology)
Last Update: 12-09-2016

Polytechnical Institute of Madagascar (ISPM)

Ambatomaro Antsobolo
Antananarivo 101
Tel: +261 33-12-171-60, +261 34-36-406-05
Website: http://ispm-edu.com
Directeur: Julien Amédée Raboanary

Department/Division

Biotechnology and Agronomy (Agriculture; Agronomy; Animal Husbandry; Biotechnology; Pharmacology);

Business Administration (Accountancy; Business Administration; Commercial Law; Economics; Finance; Management); **Civil Engineering and Architecture** (Architecture; Civil Engineering); **Computer and Telecommunication Engineering** (Artificial Intelligence; Computer Engineering; Computer Science; Mathematics and Computer Science; Software Engineering; Telecommunications Engineering); **Industrial Engineering** (Industrial Engineering); **Tourism** (Tourism)
History: Founded 1993.
Accrediting agency: Ministère de l'Enseignement supérieur et de la Recherche scientifique
Degrees and diplomas: Licence (Architecture; Biotechnology; Business Administration; Civil Engineering; Computer Engineering; Environmental Engineering; Industrial Engineering; Law; Telecommunications Engineering; Tourism), Master (Architecture; Biotechnology; Business Administration; Civil Engineering; Computer Science; Environmental Engineering; Industrial Engineering; Telecommunications Engineering; Tourism)
Student Services: Sports Facilities
Last Update: 12-09-2016

School of Accountancy, Administration and Management (ESCAME)

Lot II Y 14 Bis Cité des Postes, Ambaranjana
Antananarivo
Tel: +261 33-05-523-14

Course/Programme
Management
History: Founded 2002.
Main language(s) of instruction: French
Accrediting agency: Ministère de l'Enseignement supérieur et de la Recherche scientifique
Degrees and diplomas: Licence (Management), Master (Management)
Last Update: 01-09-2016

School of Computer Science and Business Administration (ESIGE)

BP 448, Tsararano Ambony
Mahajanga 401
Tel: +261 33-11-215-54
Website: http://www.esige-majunga.org
Directeur: Karim Ikbalhoussen

Course/Programme
Computer Science (Computer Science); **Law** (Law); **Management** (Management); **Tourism and Hotel Management** (Hotel Management; Tourism)
History: Founded 2003.
Main language(s) of instruction: French
Accrediting agency: Ministère de l'Enseignement supérieur et de la Recherche scientifique
Degrees and diplomas: Licence (Computer Science; Hotel Management; Law; Management; Tourism), Master (Computer Science; Hotel Management; Law; Management; Tourism)
Last Update: 01-09-2016

School of Information and Communication Studies - SAMIS-ESIC

Samis-Esic, BP 3832, Saint Michel Amparibe
Antananarivo
Tel: +261(20) 24 24 450
Website: http://www.samis-esic.mg

Course/Programme
Information and Communication Studies (Communication Studies; Information Sciences; Mass Communication)
History: Founded 2001.
Main language(s) of instruction: French, Malagasy
Accrediting agency: Ministère de l'Enseignement supérieur et de la Recherche scientifique
Degrees and diplomas: Licence (Communication Studies; Information Sciences; Mass Communication), Master (Communication Studies; Information Sciences; Mass Communication)
Last Update: 12-09-2016

School of Sacred Heart Antanimena (ESSCA)

BP 7541
Antananarivo
Tel: +261(20) 22-232-70
Website: http://www.essca.mg
Directeur: Frere Raphaël RAKOTOMIANDRISOA

Course/Programme
Accountancy (Accountancy); **Business Administration** (Business Administration); **Commerce** (Business and Commerce); **Finance** (Finance); **Management** (Management); **Marketing** (Marketing)
History: Founded 1992.

Accrediting agency: Ministère de l'Enseignement supérieur et de la Recherche scientifique
Degrees and diplomas: Licence (Business and Commerce; Finance; Management; Marketing), Master (Accountancy; Finance; Management; Marketing)
Last Update: 01-09-2016

School of Technology (EST Tana)

44, Rue Jean Andriamady, Faravohitra
Antananarivo 101
Tel: +261(20) 24-638-84; 261-34-96-540-10

Department/Division
Business Administration (Accountancy; Finance; International Business; Management; Marketing); **Computer Engineering** (Computer Engineering; Computer Networks; Computer Science; Telecommunications Engineering)
History: Founded 1992.
Main language(s) of instruction: French
Accrediting agency: Ministère de l'Enseignement supérieur et de la Recherche scientifique
Degrees and diplomas: Licence (Accountancy; Computer Engineering; Finance; International Business; Management), Master (Accountancy; Computer Engineering; Economics; Human Resources; Insurance; Management; Tourism)
Last Update: 02-09-2016

Vocational Institute of Madagascar (IS2M)

BP 1091 Analakely Ambohimitsimbina, Lot VT 09 bis Ankaditapaka,
Antananarivo 101
Tel: +261(20) 22-636-24
Website: http://is2m-madagascar.com

Department/Division
Science and Technology (Mathematics and Computer Science); **Social Sciences** (Economics; Management)
Main language(s) of instruction: French
Accrediting agency: Ministère de l'Enseignement supérieur et de la Recherche scientifique
Degrees and diplomas: Licence (Economics; Management; Mathematics and Computer Science), Master (Economics; Management)
Last Update: 14-09-2016

Malawi

STRUCTURE OF HIGHER EDUCATION SYSTEM

Description

Higher education is provided by both public and private universities. The public universities are governed by a Council, most of whose members are appointed by the Government. The Senate, composed of academics, is responsible for academic matters. These universities are mainly supported by government grants and miscellaneous income. The private institutions have independant councils and senates appointed by the proprietors of the mission (who are mostly religious bodies).

Stages of studies

University level first stage

Bachelor's degree
The Bachelor's degree is generally conferred after four to five years' study.

University level second stage

Master's degree
A Master's degree is conferred after one to two years' study beyond the Bachelor's degree.

University level third stage

Doctor's degree
The Doctor's degree is conferred after three to five years' study beyond the Master's degree. Candidates must submit a thesis.

ADMISSION TO HIGHER EDUCATION

Admission to university-level studies

Name of Secondary school credential required: Malawi School Certificate of Education
Minimum score/requirement: Excellent results in subjects the candidate wishes to study.
Admission requirements: Entrance examination

Foreign students admission

Admission requirements: Foreign students should hold qualifications equivalent to the Malawi School Certificate of Education with two of the six credits in English and Mathematics.
Entry regulations: Foreign students must be in possession of a visa. Confirmation of admission to the university must be obtained prior to departure as well as an entry permit from the Chief Immigration Officer, Box 331, Blantyre.
Language Proficiency: Good knowledge of English for regular university courses.

NATIONAL BODIES

Ministry of Education, Science and Technology

Minister: Bright Msaka
Director of Higher Education: Jessie Mbewe
Private Bag 328 Capital Hill Circle
Lilongwe 3
Tel: +265(1) 789-422
Fax: +265(1) 788-064
Website: http://www.education.gov.mw
Role of national body: Government body that is responsible for providing policy guidance and direction on all education, science and technology issues.

National Council for Higher Education - NCHE

CEO: Ignasio Malizani Jimu
Private Bag B371
Llongwe
Tel: +256(1) 755 884
Fax: +256(1) 755 884
Website: http://www.nche.ac.mw

Data for academic year: 2016–2017
Source: IAU from NCHE website and World Bank documents, 2017. Bodies updated 2018.

© International Association of Universities 2019
International Handbook of Universities 2019,
https://doi.org/10.1057/978-3-319-76971-4_116

Public Institutions

Lilongwe University of Agriculture and Natural Resources (LUANAR)

P.O. Box 219
Lilongwe
Tel: +265(1) 277-222, +265(1) 277-260
Fax: +265(1) 277-364
Website: http://www.bunda.luanar.mw
Vice-Chancellor: George Y. Kanyama-Phiri

Faculty

Agriculture (Agricultural Engineering; Agriculture; Animal Husbandry; Crop Production; Horticulture; Soil Science; Veterinary Science); **Development Studies** (Agricultural Business; Agricultural Economics; Agricultural Education; Agriculture; Communication Studies; Development Studies); **Food and Human Sciences** (Development Studies; Ecology; Food Science; Food Technology; Gender Studies; Health Sciences; Nutrition); **Natural Resources** (Aquaculture; Environmental Management; Environmental Studies; Fishery; Forestry); **Postgraduate Studies** (Agricultural Business; Agricultural Economics; Agricultural Education; Agricultural Engineering; Animal Husbandry; Aquaculture; Communication Studies; Crop Production; Development Studies; Ecology; Environmental Management; Environmental Studies; Fishery; Food Science; Food Technology; Forestry; Health Sciences; Horticulture; Nutrition; Rural Studies; Soil Science)

Research Division

Agricultural Research Development (CARD) (Agriculture)

Campus

MACOHA and Sogecoa Golden Peacock Satellite Campuses (Agricultural Business; Agricultural Economics; Agriculture; Communication Studies; Development Studies; Economics; Environmental Studies; Food Science; Food Technology; Gender Studies; Meteorology; Nutrition; Rural Studies); **NRC Campus** (Agriculture; Natural Resources)
History: Founded 1964 as Bunda College of Agriculture (a former constituent college of the University of Malawi). Acquired present status from the merging of Bunda College of Agriculture (Bunda), Natural Resources College (NRC) and Agricultural Research and Extension Trust (ARET), 2012.
Main language(s) of instruction: English

Accrediting agency: National Council for Higher Education (NCHE)
Degrees and diplomas: Bachelor's Degree, Master's Degree (Agricultural Business; Agricultural Economics; Agricultural Education; Agricultural Engineering; Agronomy; Animal Husbandry; Aquaculture; Development Studies; Dietetics; Economics; Entomology; Environmental Studies; Fishery; Food Science; Food Technology; Forestry; Gender Studies; Horticulture; Meteorology; Natural Resources; Plant and Crop Protection; Plant Pathology; Rural Studies; Soil Science), Doctor's Degree (Agricultural Economics; Animal Husbandry; Aquaculture; Development Studies; Environmental Management; Fishery; Natural Resources; Rural Studies). Also Postgraduate Diploma in Horticulture, Harvest Technology, Dietetics; Undergraduate Diploma in Agriculture, Natural Resources
Student Services: Sports Facilities, Health Services, Library, Residential Facilities

Student Numbers 2015-2016	MALE	FEMALE	TOTAL
All (Foreign Included)			c. 5500

Last Update: 24-10-2016

Mzuzu University

Private Bag 201
Luwinga 320-722/575, Mzuzu 2
Tel: +265(1) 320-722, +265(1) 320-575
Fax: +265(1) 333-497
Website: http://www.mzuni.ac.mw
Vice-Chancellor: Robert G. Ridley

Faculty

Education (Biology; Chemistry; Earth Sciences; Education; Geography; History; Literature; Mathematics; Modern Languages; Physics; Religious Studies; Teacher Training; Theology); **Environmental Sciences** (Environmental Studies; Fishery; Forestry; Natural Resources; Soil Management; Water Management); **Health Sciences** (Biomedicine; Health Sciences; Midwifery; Nursing; Optometry); **Information Science and Communication** (Information Management; Information Sciences; Information Technology; Library Science; Telecommunications Engineering); **Tourism and Hospitality Management** (Hotel and Restaurant; Tourism)
History: Founded 1997.
Academic year: January to October (January-June; June-October)
Admission requirements: Malawi Certificate of Education or equivalent
Fees: National : Undergraduate, 43,200 per annum (Kwacha), International : 92,500 per annum (Kwacha)

Main language(s) of instruction: English
Accrediting agency: National Council for Higher Education (NCHE)
Degrees and diplomas: Bachelor's Degree (Biomedicine; Civil Security; Environmental Studies; Fishery; Foreign Languages Education; Forestry; Humanities and Social Science Education; Information Sciences; Information Technology; Library Science; Mathematics Education; Midwifery; Nursing; Optometry; Religious Education; Science Education; Soil Management; Tourism; Water Management), Master's Degree (Educational Administration; Fishery; Information Sciences; Social and Community Services; Teacher Training; Theology), Doctor's Degree (Information Sciences; Theology). Also Diploma in Civil Security, Library Science, Information Sciences; Certificate in Civil Security
Student Services: Academic Counselling, Sports Facilities, Health Services, Canteen, Library, Residential Facilities
Last Update: 24-10-2016

⏚⎏ University of Malawi (UNIMA)

P.O. Box 278
Zomba
Tel: +265(1) 526-622, +265(1) 524-282, +265(1) 524-060
Fax: +265(1) 524-760, +265(1) 524-297, +265(1) 524-031
Website: http://www.unima.mw
Vice-Chancellor: John Kalenga Saka
Tel: +265(1) 524-305

Unit
Gender Studies (Gender Studies)

Centre
Educational Research and Training (CERT) (Educational Research); **Language Studies (CLS)** (Linguistics); **Malaria Alert Centre (MAC)** (Public Health); **Reproductive Health (CRH)** (Health Sciences); **Research Support Centre (RSC)**; **Social Research (CSR)** (Social Studies); **Water, Sanitation, Health and Appropriate Technology Development (WASHTED)** (Health Sciences; Water Management; Water Science)
History: Founded 1964, integrating all the country's facilities for further and higher education.
Academic year: August to May (August-December; January-May)
Admission requirements: Malawi School Certificate of Education or equivalent
Fees: Residential students, 25,000 per annum; non-residential students, 100,000-115,000 per annum (Kwacha)
Main language(s) of instruction: English

Accrediting agency: Ministry of Education, Science and Technology; National Council for Higher Education (NCHE)
Degrees and diplomas:
Student Services: Academic Counselling, Social Counselling, Sports Facilities, Language Laboratory, Facilities for disabled people, Health Services, Canteen, Library
Periodicals: Journal of Religious Education, Journal of Social Science, Malawi Journal of Science and Technology, Physical Scientist, Reports on Research Conferences
Publishing house: Fattani Offset Printers
Last Update: 25-10-2016

CHANCELLOR COLLEGE (CHANCO)
P.O. Box 280
Zomba
Tel: +265(1) 524-222
Fax: +265(1) 524-046
Website: http://www.chanco.unima.mw
Principal: Richard Tambulasi
Tel: +265(1) 524-222

Faculty
Education (Curriculum; Demography and Population; Education; Teacher Training); **Law** (Law); **Science** (Biological and Life Sciences; Computer Science; Earth Sciences; Ecology; Geography; Mathematics; Physics); **Social Science** (Administration; Demography and Population; Economics; History; Political Sciences; Psychology; Sociology)

Department/Division
Humanities (African Languages; Classical Languages; Communication Studies; English; Fine Arts; French; Linguistics; Modern Languages; Performing Arts; Philosophy; Religious Studies; Theology)

Centre
Education Training and Research (Educational Research; Teacher Training); **Language Studies** (Modern Languages); **LEAD Southern and Eastern Africa** (African Studies); **Peace and Conflict Management** (Peace and Disarmament); **Social Research** (Social Studies)
History: Founded 1964. Relocated from Blantyre to Zomba 1973. A constituent college of the University of Malawi.
Main language(s) of instruction: English
Accrediting agency: National Council for Higher Education (NCHE)
Degrees and diplomas: Bachelor's Degree (Arts and Humanities; Biology; Chemistry; Communication Studies; Computer Science; Cultural Studies; Demography and Population; Earth Sciences; Ecology; Economics; Education; Gender Studies; Geography; History; Human Resources; Law; Mathematics; Media Studies; Physics; Political Sciences; Primary Education; Psychology; Public

Administration; Secondary Education; Social Sciences; Social Work; Sociology; Statistics; Theology), Master's Degree (African Studies; Applied Chemistry; Applied Linguistics; Biological and Life Sciences; Biology; Chemistry; Commercial Law; Communication Studies; Curriculum; Development Studies; Earth Sciences; Economics; Educational Administration; Educational Psychology; Educational Sciences; Educational Testing and Evaluation; English; Environmental Studies; Foreign Languages Education; Geography; Government; History; Human Resources; Humanities and Social Science Education; Industrial Chemistry; Labour and Industrial Relations; Linguistics; Literature; Management; Mathematics; Mathematics Education; Media Studies; Native Language Education; Philosophy; Political Sciences; Primary Education; Public Administration; Religious Studies; Science Education; Sociology; Statistics; Theatre; Theology; Water Management), Doctor's Degree (Applied Linguistics; Bible; Biological and Life Sciences; Biology; Chemistry; Development Studies; Economics; Foreign Languages Education; Humanities and Social Science Education; Linguistics; Literature; Public Administration; Religious Studies; Science Education; Sociology; Statistics; Theology). Also Diploma in Law, Theology; University Certificate in Education (Language, Science and Social Studies), Computer Science; Post-Graduate Diploma in Computer Science; Bachelor of Arts (Honours) in Philosophy; Collaborative Master of Arts in Economics (CMAP); Masters in Integrated Water Resources Management (IWRM) in collaboration with WaterNet

Student Services: Sports Facilities, Library, Residential Facilities

Last Update: 25-10-2016

COLLEGE OF MEDICINE (CoM)

Private Bag 360
Chichiri 3, Blantyre
Tel: +265(1) 871-911
Website: http://www.medcol.mw
Principal: Mwapatsa Mipando
Tel: +265(1) 674-473

School

Public Health and Family Medicine (Community Health; Health Administration; Public Health)

Department/Division

Anaesthesia (Anaesthesiology); **Basic Medical Sciences** (Medicine); **Family Medicine** (Community Health); **Gynaecology and Obstetrics** (Gynaecology and Obstetrics); **Information Technology** (Information Technology); **Internal Medicine** (Medicine); **Medical Laboratory Sciencies**

(Medical Technology); **Medicine** (Medicine); **Mental Health** (Psychiatry and Mental Health); **Microbiology** (Biological and Life Sciences; Microbiology); **Paediatrics and Child Health** (Paediatrics); **Pharmacy** (Pharmacy); **Physical Therapy** (Physical Therapy); **Physiology** (Physiology); **Surgery** (Surgery)

History: Founded 1991. A constituent college of University of Malawi (UNIMA).

Academic year: January to November

Admission requirements: 'A' level passes in Biology, Chemistry, Mathematics or Physics

Fees: National : c. 350,000-1,500,000 per annum (Kwacha), International : c. 6,000-8,000 per annum (US Dollar)

Main language(s) of instruction: English

Accrediting agency: National Council for Higher Education (NCHE)

Degrees and diplomas: Bachelor's Degree (Health Administration; Laboratory Techniques; Medical Technology; Medicine; Orthopaedics; Paediatrics; Pharmacy; Physical Therapy; Surgery), Master's Degree (Medicine; Public Health), Doctor's Degree (Health Sciences; Medicine). Also Joint College of Medicine-University of Liverpool PhD degree programs

Student Services: Academic Counselling, Social Counselling, Sports Facilities, Library

Last Update: 25-10-2016

KAMUZU COLLEGE OF NURSING (KCN)

Private bag 1
Lilongwe 265
Tel: +265(1) 751-622
Fax: +265(1) 756-424
Website: http://www.kcn.unima.mw
Acting Principal: Ellen Chirwa

Faculty

Midwifery (Midwifery); **Nursing** (Child Care and Development; Community Health; Nursing; Psychiatry and Mental Health; Surgery)

Department/Division

Basic Studies (Nursing; Psychiatry and Mental Health; Surgery); **Clinical (MCH)** (Nursing); **Clinical (Nursing)** (Nursing); **Community and Mental Health** (Community Health; Nursing; Psychiatry and Mental Health); **Maternal and Child Health Nursing** (Child Care and Development; Nursing); **Medical and Surgical Nursing** (Nursing)

History: Founded 1979. A constituent college of University of Malawi (UNiMA).

Main language(s) of instruction: English

Accrediting agency: National Council for Higher Education (NCHE)

Degrees and diplomas: Bachelor's Degree (Midwifery; Nursing), Master's Degree (Health Education; Health Sciences; Midwifery; Nursing), Doctor's Degree (Health Administration; Midwifery; Nursing). Also University Certificate in Midwifery
Student Services: Library
Last Update: 25-10-2016

THE MALAWI POLYTECHNIC (Poly)

Private Bag 303
Chichiri 3, Blantyre
Tel: +265(1) 870-411
Fax: +265(1) 870-578
Website: http://www.poly.ac.mw
Principal: G.K. Kululanga
Tel: +265(1) 871-637

Faculty

Applied Sciences (Biochemistry; Computer Science; Environmental Studies; Health Sciences; Information Technology; Mathematics; Physics; Statistics); **Built Environment** (Architecture; Surveying and Mapping); **Commerce** (Accountancy; Business Administration; Management); **Education and Media Studies** (Journalism; Mass Communication; Media Studies; Modern Languages; Technology Education); **Engineering** (Civil Engineering; Electrical Engineering; Mechanical Engineering); **Postgraduate Studies** (Business Administration; Transport Management)
History: Founded 1964. A constituent college of University of Malawi.
Academic year: February to December
Admission requirements: A minimum of 'O' levels with at least 6 credits including English or the equivalent from a recognized institution
Main language(s) of instruction: English
Accrediting agency: National Council for Higher Education (NCHE)
Degrees and diplomas: Bachelor's Degree (Accountancy; Architecture; Architecture and Planning; Automotive Engineering; Business Administration; Business Education; Civil Engineering; Communication Arts; Computer Engineering; Electrical and Electronic Engineering; Energy Engineering; Environmental Studies; Health Sciences; Hydraulic Engineering; Industrial Engineering; Information Management; Information Technology; Journalism; Mathematics Education; Mechanical Engineering; Real Estate; Surveying and Mapping; Technology Education; Telecommunications Engineering; Transport Engineering), Master's Degree (Behavioural Sciences; Communication Studies; Energy Engineering; Engineering; Engineering Management; Environmental Management; Environmental Studies; Health Sciences; Industrial Engineering; Industrial Management; Machine Building; Power Engineering; Public Health; Technology Education; Telecommunications Engineering; Transport Engineering; Vocational Education), Doctor's Degree (Business and Commerce; Energy Engineering; Finance; Industrial Engineering; Industrial Management; Information Technology; Machine Building; Management; Power Engineering; Public Health; Sanitary Engineering; Telecommunications Engineering; Transport Engineering). Also Advanced Diploma in Transport Management (TOM); Postgraduate Diploma in Management (DMS); MBA
Student Services: Academic Counselling, Social Counselling, Sports Facilities, Language Laboratory, Health Services, Canteen, Library
Last Update: 25-10-2016

Private Institutions

Africa University of Guidance, Counselling and Youth Development (AUGCYD)

M1 Road - Along Airport Road Opposite Total Filling Station Area 43
Lilongwe
Tel: +265(1) 713-181, +265(1) 713-182
Website: http://augcyd.wixsite.com/augcyd-1
Vice Chancellor: Kenneth Hamwaka

Faculty

Guidance and Counselling (Psychiatry and Mental Health; Psychology); **Youth Development** (Development Studies; Leadership; Management)

Course/Programme

Diplomacy and International Relations (International Relations; Peace and Disarmament; Public Administration; Public Relations)
History: Founded 1994.
Fees: Diploma, 200,000 per semester; Bachelor, 250,000 per semester; Master, 400,000 per semester (Kwacha)
Main language(s) of instruction: English
Accrediting agency: National Council for Higher Education (NCHE)
Degrees and diplomas: Bachelor's Degree (Development Studies; International Relations; Psychology), Master's Degree (Development Studies; International Relations; Psychology), Doctor's Degree (International Relations; Leadership; Management; Psychology). Also Diploma in Psychology
Student Services: Library
Last Update: 26-10-2016

Blantyre International University (BIU)

Private Bag 98
Blantyre
Tel: +265(1) 831-516
Fax: +265(1) 831-514
Website: http://www.cybertechmw.com/biu
Chancellor: Charles Lemson Chanthunya

Faculty

Applied Sciences and Arts (Actuarial Science; Development Studies; Information Technology; Journalism; Law; Psychology; Social and Community Services); **Commerce** (Accountancy; Banking; Business Administration; Economics; Finance; Hotel and Restaurant; Management; Tourism)
History: Founded 2008. Acquired current status 2010.
Fees: 300,000 per semester; Distance programmes, 240,000 per semester (Kwacha)
Main language(s) of instruction: English
Accrediting agency: National Council for Higher Education (NCHE)
Degrees and diplomas: Bachelor's Degree (Accountancy; Actuarial Science; Banking; Business Administration; Development Studies; Economics; Finance; Hotel and Restaurant; Information Technology; Journalism; Law; Management; Psychology; Social and Community Services; Tourism)
Student Services: Residential Facilities
Last Update: 26-10-2016

Catholic University of Malawi (CUNIMA)

Montfort Campus, Nguludi 17 km from Limbe off the Robert Mugabe Highway (Midima Road) P.O. Box 5452
Limbe, Southern Region
Tel: +265(111) 625-071, +265(111) 625-070
Fax: +256(1) 916-015
Website: http://www.cunima.ac.mw
Vice-Chancellor: George Buleya
Tel: +265(8) 553-751

Faculty

Commerce (Accountancy; Banking; Business Administration; Business and Commerce; Finance; Marketing); **Education** (Education; Foreign Languages Education; Geography; Humanities and Social Science Education; Mathematics Education; Natural Sciences; Philosophy; Science Education; Special Education); **Law** (Law); **Social Sciences** (Anthropology; Economics; Leadership; Political Sciences; Social

Sciences; Social Work); **Theology** (Missionary Studies; Philosophy; Religious Studies; Theology)
Further information: Campus in Montfort, Chiradzulu District (founded 2006).
History: Founded 2004. Acquired current status 2006.
Academic year: August to June
Fees: National : 400,000 per semester (Kwacha), International : 2,000 per semester (i.e. 4,000 per annum) (US Dollar)
Main language(s) of instruction: English
Accrediting agency: National Council for Higher Education (NCHE)
Degrees and diplomas: Bachelor's Degree (Accountancy; Anthropology; Banking; Business Administration; Development Studies; Economics; Education; Finance; Humanities and Social Science Education; Law; Leadership; Marketing; Mathematics Education; Nursing; Philosophy; Political Sciences; Science Education; Social Work; Special Education; Statistics; Theology). Also Diploma Porgrammes in Monitoring and Evaluation, Education, Statistics
Student Services: Academic Counselling, Social Counselling, Sports Facilities, Language Laboratory, Facilities for disabled people, Health Services, Canteen, Library
Last Update: 24-10-2016

Columbia Commonwealth University Malawi (CCWU)

Blantyre - MPCC Centre Columbia Commonwealth University P.O. Box 30489 Chichiri
Blantyre 3
Tel: +265(111) 577-059
Website: http://www.ccwum.org/index.php
Vice President: James Buliani

Course/Programme

Business Administration (Business Administration)
Further information: Also Lilongwe Campus
History: Founded 2001. Acquired current status 2002.
Main language(s) of instruction: English
Accrediting agency: Government of Malawi; International Professional Managers Association (IPMA -(UK); The Chartered Institute of Administration & Management (CIAM) Consultants-Ghana; International Institute of Marketing Professionals (IIMP), Canada. CCWUM is also designated as a Certified Study Center (CSC) for Executive Level of Marketing Professionals.
Degrees and diplomas: Bachelor's Degree (Business Administration), Doctor's Degree (Business Administration; Management). Also MBA
Last Update: 26-10-2016

Daeyang University

P.O. Box 30330 Kanengo
Lilongwe
Tel: +265(1) 711-361
Website: http://dyuni.ac.mw

College

ICT (Information Technology); **Nursing** (Midwifery; Nursing)

Institute

Pastoral Training (Pastoral Studies)
History: Founded 2010.
Main language(s) of instruction: English
Accrediting agency: National Council for Higher Education (NCHE)
Degrees and diplomas: Bachelor's Degree (Information Technology; Midwifery; Nursing)
Student Services: Library
Last Update: 31-08-2017

DMI St.John the Baptist University (DMISJBU)

Mangochi Campus P.O. Box 406
Mangochi +265(991) 287-235, +265(1) 599-790
Tel: +265(999) 720-271
Website: http://www.dmisjbu.edu.mw

School

Business Administration (Banking; Management; Taxation); **Commerce** (Accountancy; Business and Commerce; Finance); **Education - Arts** (Education; Humanities and Social Science Education); **Education - Science** (Education; Science Education); **Engineering** (Computer Engineering; Engineering; Information Technology); **Information Technology** (Information Technology); **Social Work** (Development Studies; Social Work)
Further information: Also Lilongwe Campus
History: Founded 2010. Accredited 2011. Accredited by NCHE 2016
Fees: 250,000-450,000 according to the courses (Malagasy Ariary)
Main language(s) of instruction: English
Accrediting agency: Ministry of Higher Education, Government of Malawi; National Council for Higher Education of Malawi (NCHE)

Degrees and diplomas: Bachelor's Degree (Business Administration; Business and Commerce; Computer Science; Education; Social Work). Also Diploma
Student Services: Academic Counselling, Careers Guidance, Sports Facilities, Health Services, Library, Residential Facilities

Academic Staff 2016-2017	MALE	FEMALE	TOTAL
FULL-TIME	33	6	39

Last Update: 26-10-2016

Exploits University (EU)

Near Shayona Cement off Paul Kagame (Chilambula) Road
P.O. Box 40187
Lilongwe 4
Tel: +256(1) 752-621, +256(1) 752-846
Website: http://www.exploitsuniversity.com
Chancellor: Kingstone Prince Ngwira

Faculty

Commerce (Accountancy; Administration; Business Administration; Health Administration); **Postgraduate Studies** (Business Administration; Finance; Human Resources; Management)

Department/Division

Finance and Administration (Administration; Finance)
History: Founded 2010.
Fees: Diploma, 180,000 per semester; Bachelor, 200,000-280,000 per semester; Master, 850,000 per semester; Ph.D., 200,000 per semester (Kwacha)
Main language(s) of instruction: English
Accrediting agency: National Council for Higher Education (NCHE)
Degrees and diplomas: Bachelor's Degree (Accountancy; Business Administration; Health Administration; Human Resources; Transport Management), Master's Degree (Finance; Human Resources; Management), Doctor's Degree (Management). Also Diploma in Management; MBA
Last Update: 26-10-2016

Malawi Adventist University (MAU)

P.O. Box 148
Ntcheu

Tel: +265(999) 759-896, +265(888) 927-605
Website: http://mau.ac.mw
Vice Chancellor: Mozecie Spector John Kadyakapita

Department/Division

Agriculture (Agricultural Business; Agriculture); **Business** (Accountancy; Business Administration; Management; Marketing); **Education** (Agricultural Education; Business Education; Education; Foreign Languages Education; Literature; Religion; Theology)
History: Founded 2000 as Malawi Adventist College. Affiliated as a Junior College to the University of Eastern Africa, Baraton (Kenya) 2007 before acquiring affiliated University status.
Main language(s) of instruction: English
Accrediting agency: National Council for Higher Education (NCHE)
Degrees and diplomas: Bachelor's Degree (Accountancy; Agricultural Business; Agricultural Education; Agriculture; Business Administration; Business Education; Education; Foreign Languages Education; Literature; Management; Marketing; Religion; Theology)
Student Services: Library, Residential Facilities
Last Update: 25-10-2016

Malawi College of Accountancy (MCA)

Ginnery Corner P.O. Box 30644 Chichiri
Blantyre 3
Tel: +265(1) 871-411
Fax: +265(1) 871-853
Website: http://www.mca.ac.mw
Principal: Agrippah Phiri

Course/Programme

Applied Accounting: Auditing and Information Systems (Accountancy; Business Computing); **Business Management and Entrepreneurship** (Business Administration; Management); **Commerce Marketing and Public Relations** (Marketing; Public Relations); **Management Information System** (Business Administration; Information Technology; Management)
Further information: Also Lilongwe and Mzuzu Campuses
History: Founded 1980. A professional training institution and statutory body (Government owned organization)
Main language(s) of instruction: English
Accrediting agency: National Council for Higher Education (NCHE)
Degrees and diplomas: Bachelor's Degree. Also Professional Diploma and Certificate
Student Services: Library
Last Update: 27-10-2016

ShareWORLD Open University (SOUMA)

The Learning Centre M1 Road Area 36 Off Katete Farm Road P.O. Box 1446
Lilongwe
Tel: +265(1) 726-911
Website: http://shareworld.edu.mw

Course/Programme

Business Administration (*BBA*) (Business Administration); **Business and Finance** (Business Administration; Finance); **Disaster Management and Sustainable Development** (Environmental Studies; Protective Services); **HIV and AIDS Management** (Epidemiology; Health Sciences); **Human Resource and Management** (Human Resources; Management); **Managing Rural and Community Development** (Development Studies; Rural Studies); **Mass Communication** (Mass Communication); **Permaculture and Community Development** (Agriculture; Development Studies); **Postgraduate Studies** (Business Administration; Development Studies; Environmental Studies; Finance; Government; Health Administration; Health Sciences; International Relations; Public Health; Social and Community Services); **Public Health** (Public Health); **Undergraduate Diploma** (Law)
Further information: Also Blantyre and Mzuzu Campuses
History: Founded as University in Blantyre 1994. Acquired current status and title 2007.
Main language(s) of instruction: English
Accrediting agency: National Council for Higher Education (NCHE)
Degrees and diplomas: Bachelor's Degree, Master's Degree (Development Studies; Government; Health Administration; Health Sciences; International Relations; Mass Communication; Public Health; Social and Community Services). Also MBA
Last Update: 26-10-2016

Skyway University (SU)

Private Bag A155
Lilongwe, Central Region
Tel: +265(999 561-004, +265(999) 561-005
Website: http://www.skywayuniversity.net
Chancellor: Brown Chiphamba

Course/Programme

Accountancy (Accountancy); **Business Administration** (Business Administration); **Community Development** (Development Studies; Social and Community Services); **Education** (Education; Humanities and Social Science

Education); **Human Resources Management** (Human Resources); **International Diploma Studies** (Accountancy; Business Administration; Computer Science; Cooking and Catering; Development Studies; Epidemiology; Journalism; Management; Marketing; Social and Community Services; Transport Management); **Postgraduate Studies** (Development Studies); **Project Management** (Management); **Public Health** (Public Health)

Further information: Also Blantyre and Mzuzu Campuses

History: Formerly known as Skyway Business College, acquired current status and title 2012.

Fees: National : Undergraduate, Mk200,000-Mk350,000 per semester; Masters Degree, 850,000 per semester (except for thesis semester, 425,000); International Diploma Programmes, MK60.000-Mk100.000 per semester (Kwacha), International : It Varies

Main language(s) of instruction: English

Accrediting agency: National Council for Higher Education (NCHE)

Degrees and diplomas: Bachelor's Degree (Accountancy; Business Administration; Development Studies; Human Resources; Humanities and Social Science Education; Management; Public Health; Social and Community Services), Master's Degree (Development Studies). Also Diploma

Academic Staff 2016-2017	MALE	FEMALE	TOTAL
FULL-TIME	25	3	28
Student Numbers 2016-2017			
All (Foreign Included)	555	442	997

Last Update: 26-10-2016

University of Livingstonia (UNILIA)

P.O. Box 37
Livingstonia
Tel: +265(1) 368-234, +265(1) 368-731
Fax: +265(1) 368-731
Website: http://www.ulivingstonia.com
Vice-Chancellor: Henry P. Kirk

College

Commerce (*Ekwendeni Campus*) (Business Administration; Business and Commerce); **Education** (*Livingstonia Campus*) (Education; Teacher Training); **Nursing** (*Ekwendeni Campus*) (Health Sciences; Nursing); **Technical Studies** (*Livingstonia Campus*) (Business Administration; Computer Science; Mechanical Equipment and Maintenance; Secretarial Studies); **Theology** (*Ekwendeni Campus*) (Christian Religious Studies; Theology)

History: Founded 1875 as Livingstonia Mission. Started offering Higher Education programmes 1895, acquired present title 2003.

Admission requirements: Malawi School Certificate of Education (M.S.CE) or equivalent, with an aggregate of not more than 36 points in the best 6 subjects. Applicants must have a credit in English; Admission tests and interview.

Fees: 120,000 per annum. Application fee, 500 (Kwacha)

Main language(s) of instruction: English

Accrediting agency: National Council for Higher Education (NCHE)

Degrees and diplomas: Bachelor's Degree (Education; Theology). Also Certificates and Diplomas

Student Services: Library, Residential Facilities

Last Update: 24-10-2016

Malaysia

STRUCTURE OF HIGHER EDUCATION SYSTEM

Description

There are some 1.4 million students in higher education and training, of which 1.2 million are enrolled in higher learning institutions (HLIs) under the purview of the Ministry of Education. The Ministry oversees 20 public universities, 33 polytechnics, 91 community colleges and 514 private HLIs. The polytechnics consist of three premier, 5 metro and 25 conventional polytechnics while the 514 private HLIs consists of 70 private universities, 34 private university colleges and 410 private colleges.

Stages of studies

University level first stage

University / University College / Foreign Branch Campus level first stage: Bachelor's degree
Courses leading to the award of the Bachelor's degree (MQF level 6) last for three years. In medical fields, the Bachelor's degree is awarded after five years.

University level second stage

University / University College / Foreign Branch Campus level second stage: Master's degree
The Master's degree is conferred after one to two years' further study following the Bachelor's degree. A Postgraduate Certificate (20 credits) is awarded after at least one semester's further study and a Postgraduate Diploma (30 credits) after 1 - 1/2 years' further study. These qualifications are all at MQF level 7.

University level third stage

University / University College / Foreign Branch Campus level third stage: Doctor of Philosophy
The Doctor of Philosophy degree is awarded after a minimum of two years' further study and research. The minimum entry requirements are a Master's degree and the ability to pursue research in the proposed field. In addition, doctoral candidates must pass oral examinations (proposal defense) and, in some cases, written examinations. Students must defend a thesis during a viva.

ADMISSION TO HIGHER EDUCATION

Admission to university-level studies

Name of Secondary school credential required: Sijil Tinggi Pelajaran Malaysia
Alternatives to credentials: Matriculation Certificate
Other requirements: Admission of students into public higher education institutions in Malaysia is managed by the Student Admission Management Division, Department of Higher Education. Applications for admission start January 20 on the following website: http://upu.mohe.gov.my. Admission of students into community colleges is managed by the Student Intake Division, Department of Community Colleges (DCC)

Foreign students admission

Definition of foreign student: Non resident and non citizen
Admission requirements: Foreign students must hold a student pass and a visa. To apply for a student pass and visa, prospective International students must have already been accepted for a full-time course of study (inclusive of English programme) at a public or private higher educational institution; have the financial capability to meet the course fees and living/travel expenses; possess good health; be seeking entry for study purposes only. All applications for student passes are through Malaysian educational institutions. International students are allowed to work part-time (maximum 20 hours per week during semester breaks or holidays of more than 7 days) while studying full-time in Malaysia, subject to immigration requirements.
Entry regulations: Foreign students must hold a student visa and, depending on the country of origin, a student pass
Health requirements: Students must be in good health
Language Proficiency: The language of instruction is Bahasa Malaysia with some courses in English. Students must be proficient in the national language

© International Association of Universities 2019
International Handbook of Universities 2019,
https://doi.org/10.1057/978-3-319-76971-4_117

RECOGNITION OF STUDIES

Quality assurance system

The Malaysian Qualifications Agency (MQA) is responsible for quality assurance of higher education for both the public and the private sectors. MQA assures programmes through two distinct processes: (1) Provisional accreditation: initial process which helps higher education providers to achieve accreditation by enhancing the standard and quality set in the provisional accreditation evaluation; (2) Accreditation: formal recognition that the certificates, diplomas and degrees awarded by higher education institution are in accordance with the set standards.

Bodies dealing with recognition

Malaysian Qualifications Agency - MQA
Chief Executive Officer: Dato' Dr. Rahmah Binti Mohamed
Tingkat 14B, Menara PKNS-PJ 17, Jalan Yong Shook Lin
Petaling Jaya 46050
Tel: +60(3) 7968-7002
Fax: +60(3) 7956-9496
Website: http://www.mqa.gov.my

NATIONAL BODIES

Kementerian Pendidikan Malaysia (Ministry of Education)

Minister: Mazlee Bin Malik
No. 2, Tower 2, Jalan P5/6, Precinct 5
Putrajaya 62200
Tel: +60(3) 8000-8000
Fax: +60(3) 8000-8001
Website: http://www.moe.gov.my

Jabatan Pendidikan Tinggi - JPT (Department of Higher Education)

Director General: YBhg. Datin Paduka Ir. Dr. Siti Hamisah Binti Tapsir
Aras 9, No. 2, Tower 2, Jalan P5/6, Precinct 5
Putrajaya 62200
Tel: +60(3) 8870-6381
Fax: +60(3) 8870-6840
Website: http://jpt.mohe.gov.my
Role of national body: To ensure higher quality education in attaining global excellence

Malaysian Association of Private Colleges and Universities - MAPCU

President: Datuk Parmjit Singh
Secretary-General: Gan Eng Hong
c/o Asia Pacific Institute of Information Technology (APIIT)
Jln. Innovasi 1, Technology Park Malaysia Bukit Jalil
Kuala Lumpur 57000
Tel: +60(3) 8656-9980
Fax: +60(3) 8656-9981
Website: http://www.mapcu.com.my
Role of national body: MAPCU was registered on 18 March 1997. It is a grouping of private higher education institutions whose objectives are to promote and co-ordinate the development of Malaysia's private higher education industry.

National Association of Private Educational Institutions - NAPEI

President: Mohan Elajsolan
Secretary-General: Kevin Felix Pereira
C-M09, Suria Offices Jalan JJU 10/4C Damansara Damai
Petaling Jaya 47830, Selangor
Tel: +60(3) 6141-0113
Fax: +60(3) 6156-7100
Website: http://www.napei.org.my
Role of national body: Established on 15 September 1987, NAPEI represents all levels of private educational institutions in Malaysia. It seeks to further enhance and maintain the quality of education in the private sector.

Data for academic year: 2017–2018
Source: IAU from the Malaysian Department of Higher Education and MQA, 2018.

Public Institutions

International Islamic University Malaysia (IIUM)

P.O. Box 10
Kuala Lumpur 50728
Tel: +60(3) 6196-4000
Fax: +60(3) 6196-4053
Website: http://www.iium.edu.my
Rector: Dzulkifli Abdul Razak

Faculty
Architecture and Environmental Design (Architecture; Building Technologies; Design; Landscape Architecture;

Regional Planning; Surveying and Mapping; Town Planning); **Economics and Management** (Accountancy; Banking; Business Administration; Finance; Management; Marketing); **Engineering** (Aeronautical and Aerospace Engineering; Automotive Engineering; Biotechnology; Computer Engineering; Electrical Engineering; Engineering; Materials Engineering; Mechanical Engineering; Production Engineering); **Information and Communication Technology** (Information Sciences; Information Technology; Library Science; Telecommunications Engineering); **Islamic Revealed Knowledge and Human Sciences** (Anthropology; Arabic; Communication Studies; English; History; Islamic Studies; Koran; Literature; Political Sciences; Psychology; Sociology); **Law** (Islamic Law; Law; Private Law; Public Law); **Medicine and Healthcare** (*Kuantan Campus*) (Anaesthesiology; Anatomy; Biochemistry; Biomedicine; Community Health; Dentistry; Dietetics; Gynaecology and Obstetrics; Medicine; Microbiology; Nursing; Optometry; Orthopaedics; Paediatrics; Parasitology; Pharmacology; Pharmacy; Physical Therapy; Psychiatry and Mental Health; Radiology; Rehabilitation and Therapy; Speech Therapy and Audiology); **Science** (Biotechnology; Botany; Chemistry; Mathematics; Mathematics and Computer Science; Physics)

Institute

Education (Education); **Islamic Thought and Civilization** (*International*) (Ethics; Islamic Studies; Philosophy)
History: Founded 1983 following a treaty between the Government of Malaysia and the Organization of the Islamic Conference for the Governments of Maldives, Bangladesh, Pakistan, Turkey, Libya, Egypt and Saudi Arabia to become co-sponsors
Academic year: September to June (September - January; February - June)
Admission requirements: Malaysian Higher School Certificate (STPM)
Fees: 500-2,200 per semester (Malaysian Ringgit)
Main language(s) of instruction: English
Accrediting agency: Malaysian Qualifications Agency (MQA); Ministry of Higher Education (MOHE)
Degrees and diplomas: Bachelor's Degree (Accountancy; Anthropology; Architecture; Biotechnology; Botany; Business Administration; Chemistry; Communication Studies; Comparative Religion; Computer Science; Dentistry; Design; Dietetics; Economics; Education; Educational and Student Counselling; Engineering; English; Fine Arts; Foreign Languages Education; History; Hotel and Restaurant; Information Technology; Islamic Law; Islamic Studies; Landscape Architecture; Law; Literature; Marine Science and Oceanography; Mathematics; Medicine; Native Language Education; Nursing; Optometry; Pharmacy; Physical Therapy; Physics; Political Sciences; Psychology; Radiology; Regional Planning; Sociology; Speech Therapy and Audiology; Surgery; Surveying and Mapping; Tourism; Town Planning), Master's Degree (Accountancy; Administrative Law; Anatomy; Arabic; Architecture; Arts and Humanities; Banking; Behavioural Sciences; Biochemistry; Building Technologies; Business Administration; Commercial Law; Comparative Law; Comparative Religion; Economics; Education; Finance; Food Science; Foreign Languages Education; Gynaecology and Obstetrics; Health Sciences; Information Sciences; Information Technology; International Law; Islamic Studies; Justice Administration; Library Science; Linguistics; Literature; Marketing; Medicine; Microbiology; Native Language Education; Natural Sciences; Nursing; Orthopaedics; Parasitology; Pharmacology; Pharmacy; Physiology; Protective Services; Regional Planning; Southeast Asian Studies; Surgery; Surveying and Mapping; Town Planning; Urban Studies), Doctor's Degree (Accountancy; Anatomy; Anthropology; Arabic; Banking; Behavioural Sciences; Biochemistry; Biological and Life Sciences; Biotechnology; Building Technologies; Business Administration; Communication Studies; Comparative Religion; Computer Science; Economics; Education; English; Finance; Food Science; Health Sciences; Heritage Preservation; History; Information Sciences; Information Technology; Islamic Law; Islamic Studies; Law; Library Science; Linguistics; Literature; Medicine; Microbiology; Nursing; Parasitology; Pharmacy; Political Sciences; Psychology; Sociology; Southeast Asian Studies)
Student Services: Academic Counselling, Social Counselling, Careers Guidance, Nursery Care, Cultural Activities, Sports Facilities, Health Services, Canteen, Library, IT Centre
Periodicals: IIU Law Journal, Journal of Islamic Economics
Publishing house: IIUM Press
Last Update: 06-06-2018

🏛️ Islamic Science University of Malaysia (USIM)

Strategic Communication Centre (StraComm) Universiti Sains Islam Malaysia Bandar Baru Nilai
Nilai 71800, Negeri Sembilan
Tel: +60(6) 798-8000
Fax: +60(6) 798-8004
Website: http://www.usim.edu.my
Vice-Chancellor: Musa Ahmad Fasc

Faculty

Dentistry (*Kuala Lumpur*) (Dentistry); **Economics and Muamalat** (Accountancy; Administration; Economics; Marketing); **Engineering and Built Environment** (Building Technologies; Engineering); **Leadership and Management** (Communication Studies; Islamic Studies; Leadership; Management); **Major Language Studies** (Arabic; English);

Medicine and Health Sciences (*Kuala Lumpur*) (Health Sciences; Medicine; Surgery); **Quranic and Sunnah Studies** (Information Management; Islamic Theology; Koran; Multimedia); **Science and Technology** (Actuarial Science; Applied Physics; Biotechnology; Computer Science; Finance; Food Science; Industrial Chemistry; Insurance; Mathematics); **Shariah and Law** (Islamic Law; Law)

Centre

Graduate Studies (Arabic; Economics; Education; Engineering; English; Islamic Law; Koran; Law; Management)
History: Founded 1997 as Kolej Universiti Islam Malaysia (KUIM). Started operating 2000. Acquired present title 2007
Main language(s) of instruction: Arabic, English
Accrediting agency: Ministry of Higher Education; Malaysian Qualifications Agency (MQA)
Degrees and diplomas: Bachelor's Degree (Accountancy; Actuarial Science; Administration; Applied Mathematics; Applied Physics; Arabic; Architecture; Banking; Biotechnology; Computer Science; Dentistry; Electronic Engineering; Finance; Food Technology; Industrial Chemistry; Information Management; Insurance; Islamic Law; Islamic Studies; Koran; Law; Management; Marketing; Mass Communication; Media Studies; Medicine; Multimedia; Psychology; Religious Education; Religious Studies; Surgery), Master's Degree (Accountancy; Actuarial Science; Administration; Arabic; Banking; Biotechnology; Comparative Law; Computer Science; Economics; Finance; Food Technology; Insurance; Islamic Law; Islamic Studies; Koran; Law; Leadership; Management; Mass Communication; Psychology; Social Work), Doctor's Degree (Administration; Arabic; Economics; Education; English; Human Resources; Islamic Law; Islamic Studies; Koran; Law; Management; Mass Communication; Natural Sciences; Psychology; Technology)
Student Services: Library, IT Centre
Last Update: 01-06-2018

National Defence University of Malaysia (UPNM)

Kem Sungai Besi
Kuala Lumpur 57000
Tel: +60(3) 9051-3400
Fax: +60(3) 9051-3028
Website: http://www.upnm.edu.my/en/index.php
Vice-Chancellor: Abdul Halim bin Hj Jalal

Faculty

Defence Studies and Management (Management; Military Science); **Defense and Science Technology** (Military Science; Technology); **Engineering** (Engineering); **Medicine and Defence Health** (Medicine)
History: Founded 1995 as Akedemi Tentera Malaysia (ATMA) or the Malaysian Armed Forces Academy. Acquired current status and title 2006. Started enrolling civilian students as of academic year 2007/2008
Main language(s) of instruction: Malay
Accrediting agency: Ministry of Higher Education; Malaysian Qualifications Agency (MQA)
Degrees and diplomas: Bachelor's Degree (Civil Engineering; Communication Studies; Computer Science; Data Processing; Electrical and Electronic Engineering; Marine Engineering; Marine Transport; Mechanical Engineering; Military Science; Operations Research; Social Sciences; Transport Management), Master's Degree (Biology; Business Administration; Chemical Engineering; Chemistry; Civil Engineering; Computer Science; Education; Electrical and Electronic Engineering; Engineering Management; International Relations; Management; Marine Engineering; Mathematics; Mechanical Engineering; Physics; Statistics; Technology), Doctor's Degree (Biology; Chemical Engineering; Chemistry; Civil Engineering; Computer Science; Education; Electrical and Electronic Engineering; International Relations; Management; Marine Engineering; Mathematics; Mechanical Engineering; Physics; Sports; Statistics; Technology). Also Executive Diploma
Last Update: 08-06-2018

National University of Malaysia (UKM)

Bangi 43600, Selangor
Tel: +60(3) 8921-5555
Fax: +60(3) 8921-4097, +60(3) 8925-6484
Website: http://www.ukm.my
Vice-Chancellor: Mohd Hamdi Abd Shukor

Faculty

Dentistry (Dentistry; Oral Pathology; Periodontics); **Economics and Management** (Accountancy; Agricultural Economics; Business Administration; Development Studies; Econometrics; Economic and Finance Policy; Economics; Industrial and Production Economics); **Education** (Education; Educational Sciences; Special Education; Teacher Training); **Engineering and Built Environment** (Architecture; Chemical Engineering; Civil Engineering; Electrical and Electronic Engineering; Engineering; Materials Engineering; Mechanical Engineering); **Health Sciences** (Biomedicine; Dietetics; Nutrition; Optometry; Pharmacy; Speech Therapy and Audiology); **Information Science and Technology** (Computer Science; Information Management; Information Sciences; Information Technology; Multimedia);

Islamic Studies (Arabic; Islamic Law; Islamic Studies; Islamic Theology; Koran; Middle Eastern Studies); **Law** (Civil Law; Islamic Law; Law); **Medicine** (Anaesthesiology; Anatomy; Biochemistry; Cardiology; Community Health; Dermatology; Diabetology; Endocrinology; Entomology; Epidemiology; Gastroenterology; Gynaecology and Obstetrics; Haematology; Health Sciences; Histology; Immunology; Medical Parasitology; Microbiology; Nephrology; Neurology; Nursing; Oncology; Ophthalmology; Orthopaedics; Otorhinolaryngology; Paediatrics; Parasitology; Pathology; Pharmacology; Physiology; Plastic Surgery; Pneumology; Psychiatry and Mental Health; Radiology; Rheumatology; Social and Preventive Medicine; Surgery; Urology; Venereology; Virology); **Science and Technology** (Actuarial Science; Biological and Life Sciences; Chemistry; Earth Sciences; Environmental Studies; Food Science; Food Technology; Marine Science and Oceanography; Physics; Statistics); **Social Sciences and Humanities** (Anthropology; Arts and Humanities; Cultural Studies; Demography and Population; Development Studies; English; Geography; History; International Studies; Linguistics; Literature; Mass Communication; Modern Languages; Political Sciences; Psychology; Social Sciences; Sociology; Translation and Interpretation; Writing)

Institute

Climate Change (IPI) (Meteorology); **Ear, Hearing and Speech (INSTITUTE-HEARS)** (Speech Therapy and Audiology); **Environment and Development (LESTARI)** (Biological and Life Sciences; Environmental Management; Environmental Studies); **Ethnic Studies (KITA)** (Ethnology); **Fuel Cell (SELFUEL)** (Energy Engineering); **Islam Hadhari (HADHARI)** (Island Studies); **Malay World and Civilization (ATMA)** (Cultural Studies; Southeast Asian Studies); **Malaysian and International Studies (IKMAS)** (International Studies; Southeast Asian Studies); **Medical Molecular Biology (UMBI)** (Molecular Biology); **Microengineering and Nanoelectronics (IMEN)** (Engineering; Nanotechnology); **Pusat PERMATApintar Negara**; **Systems Biology (INBIOSIS)** (Biology); **Visual Informatics (IVI)** (Computer Science)

Graduate School

UKM-GBS Graduate School (Business Administration)

Research Division

Solar Energy (SERI) (Energy Engineering)
History: Founded 1970
Academic year: July to March (July-October; December-March)

Admission requirements: Malaysian higher school certificate (STPM); Matriculation; Diploma
Fees: Arts, 1,750; Science, 2,083; Medicine, 2,550 per annum (Malaysian Ringgit)
Main language(s) of instruction: Malay, English
Accrediting agency: Malaysian Qualifications Agency (MQA); Ministry of Higher Education (MOHE)
Degrees and diplomas: Bachelor's Degree (Arts and Humanities; Biological and Life Sciences; Chemistry; Civil Engineering; Dentistry; Earth Sciences; Economics; Education; Engineering; Health Sciences; Information Sciences; Information Technology; Islamic Studies; Law; Management; Marine Science and Oceanography; Mathematics and Computer Science; Medicine; Pharmacy; Physics; Social Sciences; Technology), Postgraduate Diploma (Islamic Law; Justice Administration), Master's Degree (Accountancy; Agricultural Economics; Anaesthesiology; Anatomy; Anthropology; Applied Physics; Architecture; Art Management; Artificial Intelligence; Banking; Biochemistry; Bioengineering; Biology; Biomedicine; Biotechnology; Botany; Business Computing; Business Education; Chemical Engineering; Chemistry; Civil Engineering; Civil Law; Clinical Psychology; Commercial Law; Communication Studies; Community Health; Comparative Law; Computer Education; Computer Engineering; Computer Networks; Computer Science; Constitutional Law; Construction Engineering; Criminal Law; Curriculum; Data Processing; Dentistry; Dermatology; Development Studies; Developmental Psychology; Dietetics; East Asian Studies; Econometrics; Economics; Education; Educational Administration; Educational and Student Counselling; Educational Psychology; Educational Testing and Evaluation; Electrical and Electronic Engineering; Electronic Engineering; Energy Engineering; Engineering; Entomology; Environmental Engineering; Environmental Management; Environmental Studies; Epidemiology; Finance; Food Science; Foreign Languages Education; Genetics; Geography (Human); Geological Engineering; Geology; Geophysics; Gynaecology and Obstetrics; Haematology; Health Administration; Health Education; Health Sciences; History; Human Rights; Humanities and Social Science Education; Industrial and Organizational Psychology; Industrial and Production Economics; Industrial Engineering; Industrial Management; Information Management; Information Sciences; Information Technology; International Economics; International Law; Islamic Law; Islamic Studies; Law; Literature; Malay; Management; Marine Science and Oceanography; Materials Engineering; Mathematics; Mathematics Education; Mechanical Engineering; Medicine; Microbiology; Midwifery; Mineralogy; Molecular Biology; Multimedia; Native Language Education; Nuclear Physics; Nursing; Nutrition; Occupational Health; Ophthalmology; Optometry; Orthodontics; Orthopaedics; Otorhinolaryngology; Paediatrics; Parasitology;

Pathology; Pedagogy; Periodontics; Pharmacology; Pharmacy; Philosophy; Physics; Physiology; Political Sciences; Preschool Education; Private Law; Production Engineering; Protective Services; Psychiatry and Mental Health; Psychology; Public Health; Radiology; Safety Engineering; Science Education; Social Sciences; Social Work; Sociology; Software Engineering; Special Education; Speech Therapy and Audiology; Sports Management; Statistics; Surgery; Taxation; Telecommunications Engineering; Theology; Zoology), Doctor's Degree (Accountancy; Administrative Law; Adult Education; Agricultural Economics; Anatomy; Anthropology; Arabic; Architecture; Art Management; Banking; Biochemistry; Bioengineering; Biology; Biomedicine; Botany; Business Computing; Business Education; Chemical Engineering; Chemistry; Civil Engineering; Civil Law; Commercial Law; Communication Studies; Community Health; Computer Education; Computer Engineering; Computer Science; Constitutional Law; Construction Engineering; Criminal Law; Curriculum; Dentistry; Development Studies; Dietetics; Econometrics; Economics; Education; Educational Administration; Educational and Student Counselling; Educational Sciences; Educational Testing and Evaluation; Electrical and Electronic Engineering; English; Entomology; Environmental Management; Environmental Studies; Epidemiology; Finance; Food Science; Foreign Languages Education; Genetics; Geography (Human); Geology; Gynaecology and Obstetrics; Health Administration; Health Education; History; Human Resources; Humanities and Social Science Education; Immunology; Industrial and Production Economics; Industrial Engineering; Industrial Management; Information Management; Information Sciences; Information Technology; International Business; International Law; Islamic Law; Islamic Studies; Islamic Theology; Labour and Industrial Relations; Labour Law; Law; Leadership; Linguistics; Literature; Malay; Management; Marine Science and Oceanography; Marketing; Materials Engineering; Mathematics; Mathematics Education; Mechanical Engineering; Microbiology; Native Language Education; Natural Resources; Nuclear Physics; Nutrition; Occupational Health; Ophthalmology; Optometry; Otorhinolaryngology; Paediatrics; Parasitology; Pathology; Pedagogy; Pharmacology; Pharmacy; Philosophy; Physics; Physiology; Political Sciences; Preschool Education; Private Law; Production Engineering; Protective Services; Psychology; Public Health; Public Law; Radiology; Religious Education; Retailing and Wholesaling; Safety Engineering; Science Education; Social Work; Sociology; Speech Therapy and Audiology; Sports Management; Statistics; Surgery; Taxation; Technology Education; Transport Management; Vocational Education; Zoology)

Student Services: Academic Counselling, Social Counselling, Careers Guidance, Cultural Activities, Sports Facilities, Language Laboratory, Facilities for disabled people, Health Services, Canteen, Foreign Studies Centre

Last Update: 08-06-2018

Northern University of Malaysia (UUM)

Sintok 06010, Kedah Darul Aman
Tel: +60(4) 928-4000
Fax: +60(4) 928-3053
Website: http://www.uum.edu.my
Vice-Chancellor: Mohamed Mustafa Ishak
Tel: +60(4) 928-3000

College

Arts and Sciences (Arts and Humanities; Natural Sciences); **Business** (Business Administration); **Law, Government and International Studies** (Government; International Studies; Law)

School

Accountancy (Accountancy; Taxation); **Applied Psychology, Social Work and Policy** (Psychology; Social Policy; Social Work); **Business Management** (Administration; Business Administration; Marketing; Transport and Communications); **Computing** (Artificial Intelligence; Computer Networks; Engineering Management; Information Technology; Multimedia); **Creative Industry Management and Performing Arts** (Art Management; Performing Arts); **Economics, Finance and Banking** (Banking; Economics; Environmental Management; Finance; International Business); **Education and Modern Languages** (Curriculum; Linguistics; Modern Languages; Pedagogy); **Government** (Development Studies; Government; Political Sciences; Public Administration); **International Studies** (International Business; International Studies); **Islamic Business** (Business Administration); **Law** (Law); **Multimedia Technology and Communication** (Communication Studies; Media Studies; Multimedia); **Quantitative Sciences** (Statistics); **Technology Management and Logistics** (Technology; Transport Management); **Tourism, Hospitality and Event Management** (Hotel and Restaurant; Public Relations; Tourism)

Graduate School

Arts and Science (*Awang Had Salleh*) (Arts and Humanities; Computer Science; Education; Modern Languages; Natural Sciences; Social Sciences; Statistics); **Business** (*Othman Yeop Abdullah*) (Business Administration); **Government** (*Ghazali Shafie*) (Government; International Business; International Studies; Law; Public Law; Tourism)

History: Founded 1984 by the University Utara Malaysia (Inc) Order

Academic year: May to May (May-October; November-March; April-May)

Admission requirements: Malaysian Higher School Certificate (STPM) or equivalent

Fees: Undergraduate 550-660 per semester; Graduate 1,200-2,000 per semester (Malaysian Ringgit)

Main language(s) of instruction: Malay, English

Accrediting agency: Ministry of Higher Education; Malaysian Qualifications Agency (MQA)

Degrees and diplomas: Bachelor's Degree (Accountancy; Agricultural Business; Banking; Business Administration; Business Education; Civics; Communication Studies; Computer Education; Economics; Education; Engineering Management; Finance; Hotel and Restaurant; Human Resources; Information Technology; Insurance; International Business; Law; Management; Marketing; Mathematics; Media Studies; Multimedia; Psychology; Public Administration; Social Work; Statistics; Technology; Tourism; Transport Management), Master's Degree (Accountancy; Agricultural Business; Applied Linguistics; Banking; Business Administration; Commercial Law; Communication Studies; Computer Engineering; Computer Science; Data Processing; Economics; Education; Finance; Government; History; Hotel and Restaurant; Human Resources; International Business; International Relations; International Studies; Law; Management; Marketing; Mass Communication; Mathematics; Multimedia; Performing Arts; Political Sciences; Psychology; Public Administration; Social Studies; Social Work; Sociology; Statistics; Technology; Tourism), Doctor's Degree (Accountancy; Agricultural Business; Applied Linguistics; Banking; Business Administration; Commercial Law; Communication Studies; Computer Engineering; Computer Science; Consumer Studies; Economics; Education; Finance; Government; Health Administration; History; Hotel and Restaurant; Industrial and Production Economics; Information Technology; Insurance; International Business; International Relations; Islamic Studies; Leadership; Malay; Management; Marketing; Mass Communication; Mathematics; Mathematics and Computer Science; Multimedia; Performing Arts; Political Sciences; Psychology; Social Work; Statistics; Technology; Tourism; Transport Management). Also Executive Programme

Student Services: Academic Counselling, Social Counselling, Careers Guidance, Nursery Care, Cultural Activities, Sports Facilities, Language Laboratory, Facilities for disabled people, Health Services, Canteen, Foreign Studies Centre, Library, Residential Facilities

Periodicals: Malaysian Management Journal

Publishing house: UUM Press

Last Update: 06-06-2018

Sultan Idris University of Education (UPSI)

Bangunan Canselori
Tanjong Malim 35900, Perak
Tel: +60(5) 450-6000, +60(5) 450-6661
Fax: +60(5) 468-2776
Website: http://www.upsi.edu.my
Vice-Chancellor: Mohammad Shatar bin Sabran
Tel: +60(5) 450-6777

Faculty

Art, Computing and Creative Industry (Communication Studies; Fine Arts; Information Technology); **Human Development** (Cognitive Sciences; Curriculum; Development Studies; Educational and Student Counselling; Educational Psychology; Preschool Education; Primary Education; Special Education); **Human Sciences** (Arts and Humanities; Geography; History; Islamic Studies; Social Sciences); **Languages and Communications** (Arabic; English; Literature; Malay; Modern Languages); **Management and Economics** (Accountancy; Business Administration; Economics; Educational Administration); **Music and Performing Arts** (Music; Performing Arts); **Sciences and Mathematics** (Biology; Chemistry; Mathematics; Natural Sciences; Physics; Technology); **Sports Science and Coaching** (Sports; Sports Management); **Technical and Vocational Education** (Technology)

Institute
Graduate Studies

History: Founded 1922 as Sultan Indris Training College. Acquired present status and title 1997

Academic year: May to March

Admission requirements: Malaysian Higher School Certificate or equivalent

Fees: 630 per semester (Malaysian Ringgit)

Main language(s) of instruction: Malay

Accrediting agency: Ministry of Higher Education; Malaysian Qualifications Agency (MQA); Public Service Department

Degrees and diplomas: Bachelor's Degree (Agriculture; Arts and Humanities; Business Administration; Computer Engineering; Computer Science; Cultural Studies; Economics; Education; Educational Sciences; Fine Arts; Geography (Human); History; Information Technology; Malay; Management; Mathematics; Modern Languages; Music; Natural Sciences; Psychology; Sports; Teacher Training), Master's Degree (Accountancy; Advertising and Publicity; Agriculture; Analytical Chemistry; Applied Mathematics; Arabic; Art History; Artificial Intelligence; Biology; Biotechnology; Business Administration; Chemistry; Child Care and

Development; Chinese; Cognitive Sciences; Communication Studies; Computer Engineering; Computer Graphics; Computer Science; Cultural Studies; Dance; Design; Econometrics; Economics; Education; Educational Technology; Engineering; Finance; Fine Arts; Geography (Human); Grammar; Graphic Design; Handicrafts; History; Human Resources; Information Management; Information Technology; Islamic Law; Islamic Studies; Literature; Malay; Management; Marketing; Mathematics; Multimedia; Music; Music Education; Music Theory and Composition; Musical Instruments; Musicology; Native Language; Native Language Education; Natural Sciences; Physics; Preschool Education; Psychology; Religious Education; Science Education; Software Engineering; South and Southeast Asian Languages; Southeast Asian Studies; Sports; Sports Management; Statistics; Technology; Theatre; Vocational Education; Writing), Doctor's Degree (Accountancy; Advertising and Publicity; Agriculture; Applied Mathematics; Arabic; Art Education; Art History; Artificial Intelligence; Biology; Biotechnology; Business Administration; Business Education; Chemistry; Cognitive Sciences; Computer Education; Computer Graphics; Computer Science; Cultural Studies; Curriculum; Dance; Econometrics; Economics; Education; Educational Administration; Educational and Student Counselling; Educational Psychology; Educational Testing and Evaluation; Finance; Fine Arts; Foreign Languages Education; Geography (Human); History; Human Resources; Humanities and Social Science Education; Information Management; Information Sciences; International Business; Islamic Studies; Literature; Malay; Management; Marketing; Mathematics; Mathematics Education; Media Studies; Multimedia; Music; Music Education; Music Theory and Composition; Musical Instruments; Musicology; Native Language Education; Natural Sciences; Pedagogy; Physical Education; Physics; Preschool Education; Primary Education; Psychology; Religious Education; Science Education; Software Engineering; South and Southeast Asian Languages; Southeast Asian Studies; Special Education; Sports; Sports Management; Statistics; Technology; Technology Education; Theatre; Vocational Education; Writing)

Student Services: Academic Counselling, Social Counselling, Nursery Care, Sports Facilities, Health Services, Canteen, Foreign Studies Centre, Library, IT Centre

Last Update: 06-06-2018

Sultan Zainal Abidin University (UniSZA)

Gong Badak Campus
Kuala Terengganu 21300, Terengganu
Tel: +60(9) 6688-888

Fax: +60(9) 6687-869
Website: http://www.unisza.edu.my
Vice-Chancellor: Ahmad Zubaidi bin Abdul Latif

Faculty
Applied Social Sciences (Social Sciences); **Bioresources and Food Industry** (Agriculture; Biotechnology; Food Science); **Economics and Management Sciences** (Economics; Management); **General Studies and Advanced Education** (Islamic Studies; Management; Modern Languages; Social Studies); **Health Sciences** (Health Sciences); **Informatics and Computing** (Computer Science; Information Sciences); **Inovative Design and Technology** (Engineering Drawing and Design; Technology); **Islamic Contemporary Studies** (Islamic Studies); **Language and Communication** (Communication Studies; Modern Languages); **Law and International Relations** (International Relations; Law); **Medicine** (Medicine); **Pharmacy** (Pharmacy)

History: Created 1980 as Sultan Zainal Abidin Islamic College. Acquired current title and status 2010

Admission requirements: For undergraduate programmes, general requirements: Pass General Certificate of Secondary Education (GSCE)/ Ordinary Level or equivalent with credits in English or Pass; General Certificate of Education (GCE) / Advance Level in English; Pass General Certificate Education (GCE)/ A' Level with at least: Grade C (CGPA 2.00) in general paper; Grade C (CGPA 2.00) in two other subjects; Diploma in related field; Language Requirements: Test of English Foreign Language (TOEFL) score of 500 OR International English Language Testing Service (IELTS) Band 5.5, OR English Placement Test (EPT). For Postgraduate Programmes: Masters' Degree - Bachelor's Degree with CGPA 3.00 and above or equivalent or Candidates with CGPA at least 2.50 and 3 years working experience and other qualifications recognized by UniSZA Senate; Doctor of Philosophy: Candidates must posses a Master's degree or a Bachelor' degree with First Class Honours

Fees: National : Within RM2,000 (some course may vary) (Malaysian Ringgit), International : The fees for international students are based on the prevailing exchanged rate between the USD and Ringgit Malaysia (RM), and may vary accordingly. The university reserves the right to review the fees whenever necessary. Within RM1,000-RM2,000 given a discount rate (US Dollar)

Main language(s) of instruction: Malay, English, Arabic
Accrediting agency: JPA - Public Service Department of Malaysia; Ministry of Higher Education; Malaysian Qualifications Agency (MQA)

Degrees and diplomas: Bachelor's Degree (Accountancy; Agriculture; Animal Husbandry; Anthropology; Aquaculture; Arabic; Biomedicine; Biotechnology; Business Administration; Business and Commerce; Computer Science; Dietetics; Engineering; English; Food Technology; Industrial

Design; Information Technology; International Relations; Islamic Studies; Law; Management; Medical Technology; Medicine; Nutrition; Social Sciences; Social Work; Surgery; Veterinary Science), Master's Degree (Accountancy; Agriculture; Animal Husbandry; Anthropology; Arabic; Astronomy and Space Science; Banking; Behavioural Sciences; Biological and Life Sciences; Biomedicine; Biotechnology; Business Administration; Chemistry; Community Health; Computer Science; Crop Production; Design; Development Studies; Economics; Education; English; Environmental Studies; Finance; Food Science; Food Technology; Health Administration; Health Sciences; Hotel and Restaurant; Hygiene; Industrial and Organizational Psychology; Information Technology; Insurance; International Relations; Islamic Law; Islamic Studies; Koran; Law; Management; Marine Science and Oceanography; Marketing; Mathematics; Medicine; Natural Sciences; Occupational Health; Physics; Public Health; Social Policy; Social Sciences; Sociology; Software Engineering; Sports; Technology; Tourism), Doctor's Degree (Accountancy; Agriculture; Alternative Medicine; Anatomy; Animal Husbandry; Anthropology; Arabic; Astronomy and Space Science; Banking; Behavioural Sciences; Biochemistry; Biological and Life Sciences; Biomedicine; Biotechnology; Business Administration; Chemistry; Commercial Law; Community Health; Computer Science; Design; Development Studies; Economics; Education; English; Environmental Studies; Epidemiology; Ethnology; Finance; Food Science; Food Technology; Forensic Medicine and Dentistry; Genetics; Gerontology; Gynaecology and Obstetrics; Haematology; Health Education; Health Sciences; History; Hotel and Restaurant; Hygiene; Industrial and Organizational Psychology; Information Technology; Insurance; International Law; International Relations; Islamic Law; Islamic Studies; Islamic Theology; Koran; Literature; Management; Marine Science and Oceanography; Marketing; Mathematics; Medical Parasitology; Medicine; Microbiology; Natural Sciences; Nephrology; Neurology; Nursing; Occupational Health; Ophthalmology; Orthopaedics; Otorhinolaryngology; Pathology; Pharmacology; Philosophy; Physics; Physiology; Political Sciences; Psychology; Public Health; Radiology; Rehabilitation and Therapy; Religious Education; Safety Engineering; Social Policy; Social Sciences; Sociology; Sports; Statistics; Surgery; Technology; Tourism; Veterinary Science)

Last Update: 04-06-2018

🏛 Technical University Malaysia Melaka (UTeM)

Karung Berkunci 1200, Hang Tuah Jaya
Durian Tunggal 76100, Melaka
Tel: +60(6) 270-1000
Fax: +60(6) 270-1022
Website: http://www.utem.edu.my
Vice-Chancellor: Shahrin Sahib

Faculty

Electrical Engineering (Automation and Control Engineering; Electrical Engineering; Industrial Engineering; Power Engineering); **Electronics and Computer Engineering** (Artificial Intelligence; Computer Engineering; Computer Networks; Electronic Engineering; Telecommunications Engineering); **Engineering Technology** (Electrical Engineering; Electronic Engineering; Engineering; Mechanical Engineering; Production Engineering; Software Engineering); **Information and Communication Technology** (Artificial Intelligence; Engineering Management; Materials Engineering; Robotics); **Manufacturing Engineering** (Production Engineering); **Mechanical Engineering** (Automotive Engineering; Thermal Engineering); **Technology Management and Technopreneurship** (Human Resources; Industrial Management; Management; Technology)

Centre

Graduate Studies (Business Administration; Design; Engineering; Information Technology; Social Sciences); **Languages and Human Development** (Modern Languages)
History: Founded 2000
Admission requirements: Secondary School Certificate 'A' level for degree programmes.
Fees: National : MBA: 14,460.00; PhD: 13,464.00 (Malaysian Ringgit), International : MBA: 21,210.00; PhD: 26,928.00 (Malaysian Ringgit)
Main language(s) of instruction: English
Accrediting agency: Ministry of Higher Education; Malaysian Qualifications Agency (MQA)
Degrees and diplomas: Bachelor's Degree (Artificial Intelligence; Automation and Control Engineering; Computer Engineering; Computer Networks; Computer Science; Data Processing; Electrical Engineering; Electronic Engineering; Heating and Refrigeration; Industrial Design; Maintenance Technology; Management; Mechanical Engineering; Power Engineering; Production Engineering; Robotics; Software Engineering; Telecommunications Engineering), Master's Degree (Automation and Control Engineering; Automotive Engineering; Business Administration; Communication Studies; Computer Engineering; Computer Science; Data Processing; Electrical Engineering; Electronic Engineering; Energy Engineering; Engineering Management; Human Resources; Industrial and Organizational Psychology; Industrial Design; Industrial Engineering; Information Technology; Management; Measurement and Precision Engineering; Mechanical Engineering; Metallurgical Engineering; Multimedia; Power Engineering; Production Engineering; Robotics; Safety Engineering; Software

Engineering; Telecommunications Engineering), Doctor's Degree (Communication Studies; Computer Engineering; Electrical Engineering; Electronic Engineering; Engineering Management; Human Resources; Industrial and Organizational Psychology; Information Technology; Management; Mechanical Engineering; Production Engineering; Technology Education)

Student Services: Academic Counselling, Social Counselling, Careers Guidance, Nursery Care, Cultural Activities, Sports Facilities, Language Laboratory, Facilities for disabled people, Health Services, Canteen, Foreign Studies Centre, Library, Residential Facilities

Periodicals: Journal of Advanced Manufacturing Technology, Journal of Engineering and Technology, Journal of Human Capital Development, Journal of Mechanical Engineering and Technology, Journal of Telecommunication, Electronics and Computer Engineering

Publishing house: NEWS@UTeM

Student Numbers 2012-2013	MALE	FEMALE	TOTAL
All (Foreign Included)			c. 9900
Foreign only			228

Last Update: 04-06-2018

Tun Hussein Onn University of Malaysia (UTHM)

Beg Berkunci 101, Parit Raja
Batu Pahat 86400, Johor Darul Takzim
Tel: +60(7) 453-7000
Fax: +60(7) 453-6337
Website: http://www.uthm.edu.my/v2
Vice-Chancellor: Wahid bin Razzaly

Faculty

Applied Sciences and Technology (Arts and Humanities; Communication Studies; Natural Sciences; Technology); **Civil and Environmental Engineering** (Building Technologies; Civil Engineering; Construction Engineering; Environmental Engineering; Materials Engineering; Transport Engineering); **Computer Science and Information Technology** (Computer Engineering; Information Technology; Multimedia; Software Engineering); **Electrical and Electronic Engineering** (Automation and Control Engineering; Computer Engineering; Electrical Engineering; Electronic Engineering; Industrial Engineering; Robotics); **Engineering Technology** (Chemical Engineering; Civil Engineering; Electrical Engineering; Engineering); **Mechanical and Manufacturing Engineering** (Industrial Design; Materials Engineering; Mechanical Engineering; Production Engineering); **Technical and Vocational Education** (Education;

Technology; Technology Education; Vocational Education); **Technology Management and Business** (Business Administration; Industrial Management; Management; Real Estate; Technology)

Centre

Diploma Studies; **Graduate Studies** (Engineering; Management; Real Estate; Technology)

Further information: Also Continuing Education Centre
History: Founded 1993 as Pusat Latihan Staf Politeknik. Acquired full university status 2000
Main language(s) of instruction: English
Accrediting agency: Ministry of Higher Education; Malaysian Qualifications Agency (MQA)
Degrees and diplomas: Bachelor's Degree (Aeronautical and Aerospace Engineering; Applied Physics; Architecture; Civil Engineering; Computer Science; Electrical Engineering; Electronic Engineering; Engineering Management; Food Technology; Furniture Design; Information Technology; Mechanical Engineering; Multimedia; Real Estate; Software Engineering; Vocational Education), Master's Degree (Applied Mathematics; Business Administration; Civil Engineering; Computer Science; Construction Engineering; Electrical Engineering; Engineering; Engineering Management; Information Technology; Materials Engineering; Mechanical Engineering; Natural Sciences; Production Engineering; Railway Engineering; Real Estate; Software Engineering; Statistics; Technology; Technology Education; Vocational Education), Doctor's Degree (Civil Engineering; Education; Electrical Engineering; Engineering; Engineering Management; Information Technology; Mechanical Engineering; Natural Sciences; Real Estate; Technology; Technology Education; Vocational Education)
Student Services: Sports Facilities, Library, IT Centre
Last Update: 06-06-2018

University Malaysia Terengganu (UMT)

Kuala Terengganu 21030
Tel: +60(9) 668-4100, +60(9) 668-4391
Fax: +60(9) 668-4390
Website: http://www.umt.edu.my
Vice-Chancellor: Nor Aieni Binti Haji Mokhtar

School

Fisheries and Aquaculture Sciences (Aquaculture; Fishery); **Food Science and Technology** (Agriculture; Aquaculture; Fishery; Food Science; Technology); **Fundamental Sciences** (Biology; Chemistry; Natural Sciences; Physics); **Informatics and Applied Mathematics** (Applied Mathematics; Computer Science); **Marine and Environmental Sciences** (Marine Science and Oceanography; Marine

Transport); **Maritime Business and Management** (Business Administration; Management); **Ocean Engineering** (Marine Engineering); **Social and Economic Development** (Communication Studies; Ecology; History; Modern Languages; Psychology; Social Sciences)

Centre
Foundation and Liberal Education; **Knowledge Transfer and Industrial Linkages**; **Research Management**

Research Division
Marine Biotechnology (Biotechnology; Marine Biology); **Oceanography and Environment**; **Oceanography and Environmental Studies** (Environmental Studies; Marine Science and Oceanography); **Tropical Aquaculture** (Aquaculture); **Tropical Biodiversity and Sustainable Development**

History: Founded 1979. Acquired present status and title 2007

Main language(s) of instruction: Malay

Accrediting agency: Ministry of Higher Education; Malaysian Qualifications Agency (MQA)

Degrees and diplomas: Bachelor's Degree (Accountancy; Analytical Chemistry; Aquaculture; Biological and Life Sciences; Chemistry; Computer Networks; Computer Science; Crop Production; Environmental Management; Environmental Studies; Fishery; Food Technology; Harvest Technology; Marine Biology; Marine Engineering; Marine Science and Oceanography; Marine Transport; Marketing; Mathematics; Mathematics and Computer Science; Natural Resources; Nautical Science; Nutrition; Physics; Social Policy; Software Engineering; Tourism), Master's Degree (Accountancy; Ancient Civilizations; Animal Husbandry; Applied Linguistics; Aquaculture; Arabic; Biochemistry; Biotechnology; Botany; Business Administration; Cell Biology; Chemical Engineering; Chemistry; Coastal Studies; Communication Studies; Computer Science; Crop Production; Ecology; Economics; English; Environmental Engineering; Environmental Management; Finance; Fishery; Food Science; Genetics; Harvest Technology; Japanese; Malay; Management; Marine Engineering; Marine Science and Oceanography; Marine Transport; Marketing; Mathematics; Microbiology; Molecular Biology; Philosophy; Physics; Physiology; Psychology; Social Studies; Spanish; Surveying and Mapping; Tourism; Water Science; Zoology), Doctor's Degree (Accountancy; Ancient Civilizations; Animal Husbandry; Applied Linguistics; Aquaculture; Arabic; Biochemistry; Biotechnology; Botany; Cell Biology; Chemical Engineering; Chemistry; Communication Studies; Computer Science; Crop Production; Ecology; Economics; English; Environmental Engineering; Environmental Management; Finance; Fishery; Food Science; Genetics; Harvest Technology; Japanese; Malay; Management; Marine Engineering; Marine Science

and Oceanography; Marine Transport; Marketing; Mathematics; Microbiology; Molecular Biology; Philosophy; Physics; Physiology; Psychology; Social Studies; Spanish; Surveying and Mapping; Tourism; Water Science; Zoology)

Student Services: Academic Counselling, Careers Guidance, Nursery Care, Cultural Activities, Language Laboratory, Facilities for disabled people, Health Services, Canteen, Foreign Studies Centre, Library

Last Update: 06-06-2018

University of Malaya (UM)

Lembah Pantai
Kuala Lumpur 50603
Tel: +60(3) 7967-7022
Fax: +60(3) 7956-0027
Website: http://www.um.edu.my
Vice-Chancellor: Abdul Rahim Hashim

Faculty
Arts and Social Sciences (Anthropology; Arts and Humanities; Chinese; Demography and Population; East Asian Studies; English; Geography; History; International Studies; Media Studies; Social Sciences; Social Studies; Sociology; Southeast Asian Studies); **Built Environment** (Architecture; Real Estate; Surveying and Mapping); **Business and Accountancy** (Accountancy; Banking; Business and Commerce; Finance; International Business; Islamic Studies; Management; Management Systems; Marketing; Operations Research; Taxation); **Computer Science and Information Technology** (Artificial Intelligence; Computer Science; Information Technology; Library Science; Software Engineering; Systems Analysis); **Dentistry** (Dental Hygiene; Dental Technology; Dentistry; Forensic Medicine and Dentistry; Oral Pathology; Orthodontics; Periodontics); **Economics and Administration** (Administration; Development Studies; Economics; Political Sciences; Statistics); **Education** (Curriculum; Education; Educational Administration; Educational and Student Counselling; Foreign Languages Education; Humanities and Social Science Education; Literacy Education; Mathematics Education; Pedagogy); **Engineering** (Biomedical Engineering; Chemical Engineering; Civil Engineering; Electrical and Electronic Engineering; Engineering; Materials Engineering; Mechanical Engineering; Production Engineering); **Languages and Linguistics** (Arabic; European Languages; Foreign Languages Education; Linguistics; Modern Languages; Native Language; South and Southeast Asian Languages; Translation and Interpretation; Writing); **Law** (Law); **Medicine** (Anaesthesiology; Anatomy; Biochemistry; Gynaecology and Obstetrics; Medical Parasitology; Medicine; Microbiology; Nephrology; Neurology; Otorhinolaryngology; Paediatrics; Parasitology;

Pharmacy; Physical Therapy; Physiology; Psychiatry and Mental Health; Social and Preventive Medicine; Surgery); **Science** (Biochemistry; Biological and Life Sciences; Biology; Biophysics; Biotechnology; Botany; Cell Biology; Chemistry; Embryology and Reproduction Biology; Genetics; Geology; Histology; Immunology; Marine Biology; Mathematics; Molecular Biology; Natural Sciences; Physics; Plant Pathology)

Institute

Asia-Europe (Asian Studies; European Studies); **China Studies** (Business Administration; Business and Commerce; Chinese; Cultural Studies; Economics; History; International Relations; Law; Philosophy; Political Sciences); **Graduate Studies** (Biotechnology; Development Studies; Developmental Psychology; Environmental Studies; Health Sciences; Industrial Engineering; Natural Resources; Philosophy; Technology); **Principalship Studies** (Educational Administration; Leadership; Management; Secondary Education; Teacher Training); **Public Policy and Management** (*International*) (Management; Public Administration); **Research Management and Consultancy** (Management; Technology)

Academy

Islamic Studies (Development Studies; Economics; Human Resources; Islamic Law; Islamic Studies; Koran; Management; Philosophy; Political Sciences); **Malay Studies** (Cultural Studies; Fine Arts; Linguistics; Literature; Malay; Publishing and Book Trade)

Centre

Civilization Dialogue (Cultural Studies); **Culture** (Acting; Aesthetics; Art History; Art Management; Conducting; Cultural Studies; Dance; Display and Stage Design; Educational Technology; Ethnology; Human Resources; Marketing; Music; Music Education; Music Theory and Composition; Musicology; Opera; Performing Arts; Textile Design; Theatre; Visual Arts); **Foundation Studies in Science** (Biology; Chemistry; Japanese; Natural Sciences; Physics); **Sports** (Sports; Sports Management)

Further information: University Hospital; Medical Centre
History: Founded 1905 as King Edward VII College of Medicine. Raffles College founded in 1929. Both merged in 1949 to form the University of Malaya. Rapid growth of the University resulted in the setting up of two autonomous Divisions in Singapore and Kuala Lumpur 1956. Acquired present status and title by Legislation 1962. Reorganized 1997 with new governance, administration and financial structures
Academic year: July to July
Admission requirements: Sijil Pelajaran Malaysia (SPM) or Malaysian Certificate of Education (MCE) or recognized equivalent; Sijil Tinggi Persekolahan (STP) or Higher School

Certificate (HSC) or Sijil Tinggi Persekolahan Malaysia (STPM); equivalent recognized qualification
Fees: 740-1,335 per semester; Postgraduate: 1,237-20,567 per semester for Malaysian candidates and 1,911-30,906 per semester for International candidates (Malaysian Ringgit)
Main language(s) of instruction: English, Malay
Accrediting agency: Malaysian Qualifications Agency (MQA); Ministry of Higher Education (MOHE)
Degrees and diplomas: Bachelor's Degree (Accountancy; Arts and Humanities; Business Administration; Computer Science; Construction Engineering; Cultural Studies; Dentistry; Economics; Engineering; Information Technology; Islamic Studies; Law; Linguistics; Malay; Medicine; Modern Languages; Natural Sciences; Social Sciences; Sports), Postgraduate Diploma (Public Administration), Master's Degree (Accountancy; Administration; Arts and Humanities; Business Administration; Computer Science; Construction Engineering; Cultural Studies; Dentistry; Economics; Education; Educational Administration; Engineering; Information Technology; Islamic Studies; Law; Linguistics; Malay; Management; Medicine; Modern Languages; Public Administration; Social Sciences; Sports), Doctor's Degree (Accountancy; Administration; Arts and Humanities; Business Administration; Computer Science; Construction Engineering; Cultural Studies; Dentistry; Economics; Education; Educational Administration; Engineering; English; Islamic Studies; Law; Linguistics; Literature; Malay; Medicine; Natural Sciences; Social Sciences; Sports)
Student Services: Academic Counselling, Social Counselling, Careers Guidance, Nursery Care, Cultural Activities, Sports Facilities, Language Laboratory, Facilities for disabled people, Health Services, Canteen, Foreign Studies Centre, Library, Residential Facilities
Publishing house: Jabatan Penerbitan Universiti Malaya (University of Malaya Press)
Last Update: 08-06-2018

University of Malaysia Kelantan (UMK)

Kampus Kota Karung Berkunci 36, Pengkalan Chepa
Kota Bharu 16100, Kelantan
Tel: +60(9) 771-7000
Fax: +60(9) 771-7006
Website: http://www.umk.edu.my
Vice-Chancellor: Husaini Omar

Faculty

Agro-Based Industry (Agricultural Business; Agricultural Engineering; Agronomy; Animal Husbandry; Natural Resources); **Architecture and Ekistics** (Architecture); **Bioengineering and Technology** (Bioengineering; Biotechnology); **Creative Technology and Heritage** (Communication

Studies; Design; Fashion Design; Heritage Preservation; Multimedia; Textile Design); **Earth Science** (Earth Sciences; Geology; Natural Resources); **Entrepreneurship and Business** (Business Administration); **Hospitality, Tourism and Wellness** (Hotel and Restaurant; Tourism); **Veterinary Medicine** (Veterinary Science)

Centre

External Education; **Language Studies and Generic Development** (Development Studies; English; Modern Languages; Social Sciences); **Postgraduate Studies** (Business Administration)

Graduate School

Entrepreneurship and Business (*Malaysian Malaysian*) (Business Administration; Management)

History: Founded 2006

Admission requirements: Diploma; Matriculation; Malaysian Higher School Certificate (Sijil Tinggi Persekolahan Malaysia; STPM) or Malaysian Higher Religious Certificate (Sijil Tinggi Agama Malaysia; STAM)

Fees: Bachelor's degree, 1,939-2,089; Master's degree, 2,800-3,200; Ph.D, 6,915-7,515 (Malaysian Ringgit)

Main language(s) of instruction: English

Accrediting agency: Malaysian Qualifications Agency (MQA); Ministry of Higher Education (MOHE)

Degrees and diplomas: Bachelor's Degree (Agricultural Engineering; Animal Husbandry; Banking; Business Administration; Business and Commerce; Fashion Design; Finance; Food Science; Graphic Design; Heritage Preservation; Management; Multimedia; Performing Arts; Retailing and Wholesaling; Textile Design; Transport Management; Visual Arts), Master's Degree (Accountancy; Agricultural Business; Animal Husbandry; Aquaculture; Bioengineering; Biotechnology; Business Administration; Business and Commerce; Communication Arts; Communication Studies; Cultural Studies; Development Studies; Earth Sciences; Education; Energy Engineering; Environmental Studies; Fashion Design; Finance; Food Science; Forestry; Graphic Design; Health Administration; Heritage Preservation; History; Hotel and Restaurant; Industrial and Organizational Psychology; Industrial Design; Industrial Engineering; Management; Materials Engineering; Mathematics; Modern Languages; Multimedia; Natural Resources; Production Engineering; Religion; Retailing and Wholesaling; Social Work; Textile Design; Tourism; Veterinary Science), Doctor's Degree (Accountancy; Agricultural Business; Animal Husbandry; Aquaculture; Bioengineering; Biotechnology; Business Administration; Business and Commerce; Communication Arts; Communication Studies; Cultural Studies; Development Studies; Earth Sciences; Education; Energy Engineering; Environmental Studies; Fashion Design; Finance; Food Science; Forestry; Graphic Design; Health Administration; Heritage

Preservation; History; Hotel and Restaurant; Industrial and Organizational Psychology; Industrial Design; Industrial Engineering; Management; Materials Engineering; Mathematics; Modern Languages; Multimedia; Natural Resources; Production Engineering; Religion; Retailing and Wholesaling; Social Work; Textile Design; Tourism; Veterinary Science)

Student Services: Academic Counselling, Social Counselling, Cultural Activities, Sports Facilities, Language Laboratory, Health Services, Canteen, Library

Periodicals: Qoran, Fasa Infolik, Folio FTKW, Semasa, Teraju

Last Update: 31-05-2018

University of Malaysia Pahang (UMP)

Pekan 26600, Pahang
Tel: +60(9) 424-5000
Fax: +60(9) 424-5055
Website: http://www.ump.edu.my
Vice Chancellor: Daing Nasir Ibrahim
Tel: +60(09) 549-2002

Faculty

Chemical and Natural Resources Engineering (Chemical Engineering; Natural Resources); **Civil Engineering and Earth Resources** (Civil Engineering; Earth Sciences; Natural Resources); **Computer Systems and Software Engineering** (Computer Science; Software Engineering); **Electrical and Electronics Engineering** (Electrical and Electronic Engineering); **Engineering Technology** (Engineering Management; Occupational Therapy; Technology); **Industrial Management** (Industrial Management); **Industrial Sciences and Technology** (Biotechnology; Industrial Chemistry; Industrial Engineering); **Manufacturing Engineering** (Production Engineering); **Mechanical Engineering** (Mechanical Engineering)

Institute
Postgraduate Studies

Centre

German Academic and Career; **Mandarin Languages and Culture** (Asian Studies; Chinese); **Modern Languages and Human Sciences** (Arts and Humanities; Modern Languages)

Further information: Also Gambang Campus

History: Founded 2002, as Kolej Universiti Kejuruteraan dan Teknologi Malaysia

Admission requirements: Degree programme, Matriculation (under the Malaysian Ministry of Education) or equivalent (example: PASUM, Asasi UiTM, etc) with application obtaining at least a CGPA of 2.00 and passed with at least Grade C in the subjects of Mathematics, 2 form Chemistry/ Physics/Biology; STPM or its equivalent passed with at least Grade C in the subjects of General Studies, Mathematic T/Advanced Mathematic T and 2 form Chemistry/Physics/ Biology. Diplome programme, Passed in SPM or its equivalent qualification with at least 5 Credits including: Bahasa Melayu, Mathematics, additional Mathematics, Physics/ Chemistry, 1 in Sciences/Technical Subject; English test.

Main language(s) of instruction: English, Malay

Accrediting agency: Engineering Accreditation Council (EAC); Malaysian Qualifications Agency (MQA); Ministry of Higher Education (MOHE)

Degrees and diplomas: Bachelor's Degree (Automotive Engineering; Biotechnology; Chemical Engineering; Civil Engineering; Computer Science; Electrical and Electronic Engineering; Electrical Engineering; Energy Engineering; Industrial Chemistry; Industrial Management; Mechanical Engineering; Occupational Health; Safety Engineering), Master's Degree (Automotive Engineering; Bioengineering; Biotechnology; Chemical Engineering; Chemistry; Civil Engineering; Computer Science; Construction Engineering; Electrical Engineering; Electronic Engineering; English; Environmental Management; Environmental Studies; Food Science; Food Technology; Foreign Languages Education; History; Human Resources; Industrial Chemistry; Industrial Engineering; Instrument Making; Islamic Studies; Management; Mathematics; Mechanical Engineering; Petroleum and Gas Engineering; Physics; Production Engineering; Safety Engineering; Software Engineering; Statistics), Doctor's Degree (Arts and Humanities; Automotive Engineering; Bioengineering; Biotechnology; Chemical Engineering; Chemistry; Civil Engineering; Computer Science; Construction Engineering; Electrical Engineering; Electronic Engineering; Engineering Management; Environmental Management; Environmental Studies; Food Science; Food Technology; Industrial Chemistry; Industrial Engineering; Instrument Making; Mathematics; Mechanical Engineering; Petroleum and Gas Engineering; Physics; Production Engineering; Software Engineering; Statistics)

Student Services: Academic Counselling, Social Counselling, Careers Guidance, Nursery Care, Cultural Activities, Sports Facilities, Language Laboratory, Facilities for disabled people, Health Services, Canteen, Foreign Studies Centre

Last Update: 31-05-2018

University of Malaysia Perlis (UniMAP)

Campus Kubang Gajah
Arau 02600, Perlis
Tel: +60(4) 979-8008
Fax: +60(4) 977-8422

Website: http://www.unimap.edu.my
Vice-Chancellor: Zul Azhar Zahid Jamal

Faculty

Engineering Technology (*Fe-Tech*) (Chemical Engineering; Engineering; Engineering Management)

School

Bioprocess Engineering (Biotechnology); **Business Innovation and Technopreneurship** (Business Administration; Business Computing; International Business); **Computer and Communication Engineering** (Communication Studies; Computer Engineering); **Electrical Systems Engineering** (Electrical Engineering; Industrial Engineering); **Environmental Engineering** (Environmental Engineering); **Human Development and Techno-Communication** (Social Sciences); **Manufacturing Engineering** (Production Engineering); **Materials Engineering** (Materials Engineering; Metallurgical Engineering); **Mechatronic Engineering** (Electronic Engineering; Mechanical Engineering); **Microelectronic Engineering** (Electronic Engineering; Microelectronics)

Centre

Diploma Studies (*CDS or PPD*) (Engineering)

History: Founded 2001 as Northern Malaysia University College of Engineering (KUKUM). Acquired present status and title 2007

Main language(s) of instruction: Malay

Accrediting agency: Ministry of Higher Education; Malaysian Qualifications Agency (MQA)

Degrees and diplomas: Bachelor's Degree (Agricultural Equipment; Automation and Control Engineering; Bioengineering; Chemical Engineering; Civil Engineering; Computer Engineering; Construction Engineering; Electrical Engineering; Electronic Engineering; Environmental Engineering; Industrial Engineering; Information Technology; Machine Building; Materials Engineering; Mechanical Engineering; Media Studies; Power Engineering; Preschool Education; Production Engineering; Robotics; Telecommunications Engineering), Master's Degree (Accountancy; Applied Mathematics; Bioengineering; Biomedical Engineering; Biotechnology; Business Administration; Civil Engineering; Computer Engineering; Construction Engineering; Economics; Education; Electrical Engineering; Electronic Engineering; Engineering; Engineering Drawing and Design; Environmental Engineering; Finance; Industrial Design; Industrial Engineering; Information Technology; Management; Marketing; Materials Engineering; Mathematics; Mechanical Engineering; Microelectronics; Modern Languages; Nanotechnology; Operations Research; Physical Engineering; Physics; Polymer and Plastics Technology; Power Engineering; Production Engineering; Psychology;

Sports; Statistics; Telecommunications Engineering; Translation and Interpretation), Doctor's Degree (Accountancy; Applied Mathematics; Bioengineering; Biomedical Engineering; Biotechnology; Civil Engineering; Computer Engineering; Construction Engineering; Economics; Education; Electrical Engineering; Electronic Engineering; Environmental Engineering; Finance; Industrial Design; Industrial Engineering; Information Technology; Management; Marketing; Materials Engineering; Mathematics; Mechanical Engineering; Microelectronics; Modern Languages; Nanotechnology; Operations Research; Physical Engineering; Physics; Production Engineering; Psychology; Sports; Statistics; Telecommunications Engineering; Translation and Interpretation)
Student Services: Sports Facilities, Language Laboratory, Library
Last Update: 06-06-2018

University of Malaysia Sabah (UMS)

Jalan UMS
Kota Kinabalu 88400, Sabah
Tel: +60(88) 320-000, +60(88) 320-474
Fax: +60(88) 320-223
Website: http://www.ums.edu.my
Vice-Chancellor: Kamarudin Mudin
Tel: +60(88) 320-203

Faculty
Business, Economics and Accountancy (Accountancy; Banking; Business Administration; Economics; Finance; Hotel Management; Human Resources; International Business); **Computing and Informatics** (Computer Engineering; Computer Networks; Computer Science; E-Business/Commerce; Multimedia); **Engineering** (Chemical Engineering; Civil Engineering; Computer Engineering; Electrical and Electronic Engineering; Mechanical Engineering); **Food Science and Nutrition** (Dietetics; Food Science; Food Technology; Nutrition); **Humanities, Arts and Heritage** (Fine Arts; Music; Visual Arts); **International Finance** (*Labuan*) (Banking; Finance; International Business; Marketing); **Medicine and Health Sciences** (Health Sciences; Medicine); **Psychology and Education** (Development Studies; Education; Psychology; Sports); **Science and Natural Resources** (Aquaculture; Biology; Biotechnology; Electronic Engineering; Environmental Studies; Forestry; Geology; Industrial Chemistry; Natural Sciences; Physics; Technology; Tropical Agriculture); **Sustainable Agriculture** (Cattle Breeding; Crop Production; Horticulture; Landscape Architecture)

Centre
Promotion of Knowledge and Language Learning (Modern Languages)

Research Division
Artificial Intelligence; **Biotechnology** (Biotechnology; Environmental Studies; Microbiology; Molecular Biology; Pharmacology); **Borneo Heritage (BOHRu)**; **Borneo Marine Studies** (Aquaculture; Biotechnology; Marine Science and Oceanography); **Borneo Tourism**; **Endangered Marine Species (UEMS)**; **Entrepreneurship Research and Development**; **Ethnography and Development** (Demography and Population; Ethnology); **Food Safety and Quality**; **Harmful Algal Bloom UHABS**; **Mineral And Material**; **Orchid Studies**; **Psychology and Social Health**; **Remote Sensing and GIS**; **Research and Innovation**; **Rural Education Research** (Education); **Sabah Strategic and Security Research**; **Small Island**; **Sustainable Palm Oil**; **The Development and Health Research Unit (DHRU)**; **Tropical Biology and Conservation** (Biology; Ecology; Environmental Studies; Natural Resources; Tourism); **Tuberculosis**; **Water**
Further information: Also Research Centers and Units
History: Founded 1994
Main language(s) of instruction: Malay
Accrediting agency: Ministry of Higher Education; Malaysian Qualifications Agency (MQA)
Degrees and diplomas: Bachelor's Degree (Accountancy; Agriculture; Anthropology; Arts and Humanities; Business Administration; Computer Engineering; Computer Science; Economics; Education; Engineering; Food Science; International Relations; Mathematics and Computer Science; Medicine; Modern Languages; Natural Sciences; Nutrition; Psychology; Sociology), Postgraduate Diploma (Islamic Studies; Social Work), Master's Degree (Accountancy; Anthropology; Banking; Business Administration; Communication Studies; Computer Education; Curriculum; Economics; Educational Administration; Educational Testing and Evaluation; English; Finance; Fine Arts; Foreign Languages Education; Geography (Human); Health Education; History; Hotel Management; Human Resources; International Business; International Relations; Islamic Studies; Labour and Industrial Relations; Linguistics; Management; Marketing; Music; Pedagogy; Physical Education; Psychology; Science Education; Social Work; Sociology; Sports; Tourism; Visual Arts), Doctor's Degree (Accountancy; Anthropology; Banking; Business Administration; Communication Studies; Computer Education; Curriculum; Economics; Educational Administration; Educational Testing and Evaluation; Finance; Fine Arts; Foreign Languages Education; Geography (Human); Health Education; History; Hotel and Restaurant; Human Resources; International Business; International Relations; Labour and Industrial Relations; Marketing; Music; Physical Education; Psychology; Science Education; Social Work; Sociology; Teacher Training; Tourism; Visual Arts)

Student Services: Cultural Activities, Sports Facilities, Language Laboratory, Health Services, Canteen, Library, IT Centre
Last Update: 08-06-2018

University of Malaysia Sarawak (UNIMAS)

Kota Samarahan 94300, Sarawk
Tel: +60(82) 581-000, +60(82) 581-388
Fax: +60(82) 665-088
Website: http://www.unimas.my
Vice-Chancellor: Mohamad Kadim bin Suaidi
Tel: +60(82) 672-501

Faculty

Applied and Creative Arts (Art Management; Design; Film; Fine Arts; Music; Theatre); **Cognitive Sciences and Human Development** (Cognitive Sciences; Education; Educational Sciences; Human Resources); **Computer Science and Information Technology** (Computer Networks; Computer Science; Information Technology; Software Engineering); **Economics and Business** (Business and Commerce; Economics); **Engineering** (Chemical Engineering; Civil Engineering; Electronic Engineering; Engineering; Mechanical Engineering); **Medicine and Health Sciences** (Dentistry; Health Sciences; Medicine; Nursing; Ophthalmology; Paediatrics; Paramedical Sciences; Radiology; Surgery); **Resource Science and Technology** (Biotechnology; Botany; Chemistry; Earth Sciences; Environmental Management; Marine Biology; Molecular Biology; Natural Resources; Wood Technology; Zoology); **Social Sciences** (Communication Studies; Government; Labour and Industrial Relations; Political Sciences; Social Sciences; Social Work)

Institute

Biodiversity and Environmental Conservation (Biological and Life Sciences; Environmental Studies); **Borneo Studies**; **Health and Community Medicine** (Community Health; Health Sciences); **Research and Innovation**; **Social Informatics and Technological Innovations** (Computer Science; Information Technology)

Centre

Language and Communication (*Also Sign Language and TESL*) (Arabic; Chinese; Communication Studies; English; French; Japanese; Malay; South and Southeast Asian Languages); **Technology Transfer and Consultancy** (Technology)
Further information: Also 4 Teaching Hospitals, Institutes and Centre of Excellence
History: Founded 1992

Academic year: July to June (July-October; November-March; April-June)
Admission requirements: Malaysian Certificate of Education (SPM) or equivalent with a good pass in Bahasa Melayu, and a pass in Sijil Tinggi Persekolahan Malaysia (STPM) or equivalent, with passes in 2 subjects with grade E and 2 subjects with grade R or equivalent, or a pass in Matriculation Programme in local Malaysian Universities
Fees: National : Master, 1,050.00-1,650.00 per semester (Malaysian Ringgit), International : 1,450.00-2,350.00, depending on programmes (Malaysian Ringgit)
Main language(s) of instruction: Malay, English
Accrediting agency: Malaysian Qualifications Agency (MQA); Ministry of Higher Education (MOHE)
Degrees and diplomas: Bachelor's Degree (Accountancy; Animal Husbandry; Biotechnology; Business Administration; Chemical Engineering; Cognitive Sciences; Computer Engineering; Computer Science; Economics; Engineering; Finance; Fine Arts; Medicine; Natural Resources; Nursing; Performing Arts; Psychology; Social Sciences), Master's Degree (Anthropology; Business Administration; Civil Engineering; Cognitive Sciences; Community Health; Computer Engineering; Computer Science; Design; Economics; Engineering; Environmental Management; Environmental Studies; Ethnology; Fine Arts; Health Sciences; Human Resources; Indigenous Studies; Information Technology; Medicine; Natural Resources; Orthopaedics; Performing Arts; Political Sciences; Public Health; Social Sciences; Soil Management; Southeast Asian Studies; Surgery; Technology; Telecommunications Engineering; Water Management), Doctor's Degree (Anthropology; Business Administration; Civil Engineering; Cognitive Sciences; Community Health; Computer Engineering; Computer Science; Design; Economics; Engineering; Environmental Management; Environmental Studies; Ethnology; Fine Arts; Health Sciences; Human Resources; Indigenous Studies; Information Technology; Medicine; Natural Resources; Orthopaedics; Performing Arts; Political Sciences; Public Health; Social Sciences; Soil Management; Southeast Asian Studies; Surgery; Technology; Telecommunications Engineering; Water Management). The Bachelor (Honours Degree) is awarded in the same fields of study as the Bachelor's Degree
Student Services: Academic Counselling, Social Counselling, Careers Guidance, Cultural Activities, Sports Facilities, Health Services, Canteen, Library, IT Centre
Last Update: 06-06-2018

University of Technology Malaysia (UTM)

Office of Corporate Affairs Sultan Ibrahim Chancellery Building Universiti Teknologi Malaysia
Johor Bahru 81310, Johor

Tel: +60(7) 553-3333
Fax: +60(7) 556-1722
Website: http://www.utm.my
Vice-Chancellor: Wahid bin Omar
Tel: +60(7) 553-0003 Ex.3000

Faculty

Biosciences and Medical Engineering (Biomedical Engineering; Biomedicine; Biotechnology; Health Sciences); **Built Environment** (Architecture; Landscape Architecture; Regional Planning; Surveying and Mapping; Town Planning); **Chemical and Energy Engineering** (Chemical Engineering; Energy Engineering; Petroleum and Gas Engineering; Polymer and Plastics Technology); **Civil Engineering** (Civil Engineering; Environmental Engineering; Geology; Hydraulic Engineering; Materials Engineering; Structural Architecture; Transport Engineering); **Computer Science** (Computer Science; Information Technology; Software Engineering); **Education** (Education; Educational Sciences; Mathematics; Multimedia; Social Sciences; Technology Education); **Electrical Engineering** (Automation and Control Engineering; Computer Engineering; Electrical Engineering; Electronic Engineering; Mechanical Engineering; Telecommunications Engineering); **Islamic Civilization** (Islamic Studies; Natural Sciences; Technology); **Management** (Accountancy; Business Administration; Finance; Human Resources; Management); **Mechanical Engineering** (Aeronautical and Aerospace Engineering; Automation and Control Engineering; Automotive Engineering; Design; Hydraulic Engineering; Industrial Engineering; Materials Engineering; Mechanical Engineering; Mechanics; Production Engineering; Thermal Engineering); **Science** (Chemistry; Mathematics; Physics)

School

Advanced Informatics (AIS) (Computer Science); **Advanced Informatics Studies (AIS)** (Computer Engineering; Software Engineering); **Azman Hashim International Business School (IBS)** (Business Administration; Economics; Management); **Graduate Studies** (Architecture; Business Administration; Computer Engineering; Construction Engineering; Design; Engineering; Health Administration; Real Estate; Software Engineering); **Perdana School of Science Technology and Innovation Policy**; **Professional and Continuing Education (SPACE)**; **Razak School of Engineering and Advanced Technology** (Engineering; Technology)

Institute

Malaysia-Japan International Institute of Technology (MJIIT) (Technology)

Academy

Language (Modern Languages)
Further information: Also Campus in Kuala Lumpur
History: Founded 1925 as Technical School, became College 1946 and acquired present status and title 1972
Academic year: July to May
Admission requirements: Malaysian Certificate of Education (SPM) or equivalent.
Main language(s) of instruction: English
Accrediting agency: Ministry of Higher Education; Malaysian Qualifications Agency (MQA)
Degrees and diplomas: Bachelor's Degree (Accountancy; Aeronautical and Aerospace Engineering; Agricultural Management; Architecture; Automotive Engineering; Biological and Life Sciences; Biology; Biomedical Engineering; Chemical Engineering; Chemistry; Civil Engineering; Computer Graphics; Computer Networks; Computer Science; Construction Engineering; Data Processing; Education; Electrical and Electronic Engineering; Electrical Engineering; Foreign Languages Education; Industrial Chemistry; Industrial Design; Landscape Architecture; Materials Engineering; Mathematics; Mechanical Engineering; Multimedia; Naval Architecture; Nuclear Engineering; Petroleum and Gas Engineering; Physical Education; Physics; Production Engineering; Real Estate; Regional Planning; Software Engineering; Surveying and Mapping; Technology; Technology Education; Town Planning), Master's Degree (Bioengineering; Biotechnology; Business Administration; Chemistry; Computer Science; Construction Engineering; Electronic Engineering; Engineering Management; Geological Engineering; Human Resources; Industrial Design; Industrial Engineering; Management; Mathematics; Measurement and Precision Engineering; Mechanical Engineering; Physics; Real Estate; Regional Planning; Surveying and Mapping; Technology; Town Planning; Water Science), Doctor's Degree (Chemistry; Computer Science; Education; Engineering; Health Sciences; Management; Mathematics; Physics; Technology; Technology Education). Also Executive MBA
Student Services: Sports Facilities, Library, IT Centre
Last Update: 15-06-2018

University of Technology MARA

Shah Alam
Shah Alam 40450, Selangor
Tel: +60(3) 5544-2000
Fax: +60(3) 5544-2223
Website: http://www.uitm.edu.my
Vice-Chancellor: Hassan Said
Tel: +60(3) 5544-2222

Faculty

Accountancy (Accountancy); **Administration and Policy Studies** (Law; Public Administration); **Applied Sciences** (Applied Chemistry; Environmental Engineering; Food Technology; Furniture Design; Industrial Engineering; Medical Technology; Microbiology; Natural Sciences; Nursing; Occupational Therapy; Physical Therapy; Polymer and Plastics Technology; Textile Technology; Wood Technology); **Architecture, Planning and Surveying** (Architecture; Building Technologies; Interior Design; Landscape Architecture; Real Estate; Regional Planning; Surveying and Mapping; Town Planning); **Art and Design** (Art Education; Ceramic Art; Design; Fashion Design; Fine Arts; Graphic Design; Industrial Design; Photography; Printing and Printmaking; Textile Design); **Business and Management** (Banking; Business and Commerce; Finance; Human Resources; Insurance; International Business; Management; Marketing; Retailing and Wholesaling; Transport Management); **Chemical Engineering** (Chemical Engineering); **Civil Engineering** (Building Technologies; Civil Engineering; Construction Engineering); **Communication and Media Studies** (Advertising and Publicity; Journalism; Mass Communication; Media Studies; Public Relations; Publishing and Book Trade; Radio and Television Broadcasting); **Computer and Mathematical Sciences** (Mathematics and Computer Science); **Dentistry** (Dentistry); **Education** (Art Education; Education; Health Education; Music Education; Physical Education); **Electrical Engineering** (Electrical Engineering; Electronic Engineering; Power Engineering); **Film, Theatre and Animation** (Acting; Art Management; Cinema and Television; Music; Music Theory and Composition; Performing Arts); **Health Sciences** (Health Sciences); **Hotel and Tourism Management** (Cooking and Catering; Hotel Management; Tourism); **Information Management** (Information Management; Library Science); **Law** (Law); **Mechanical Engineering** (Aeronautical and Aerospace Engineering; Automotive Engineering; Mechanical Engineering; Production Engineering); **Medicine** (Medicine); **Music** (Music); **Pharmacy** (Pharmacology; Pharmacy); **Plantation and Agrotechnology** (Agricultural Engineering; Agriculture); **Sports Science and Recreation** (Leisure Studies; Parks and Recreation; Sports; Sports Management)

Institute

Graduate Studies (IPSiS); **NEO Education (iNED)**

Academy

Contemporary Islamic Studies (ACIS) (Music); **Language Studies (APB)** (English; European Languages; Malay; Modern Languages; Oriental Languages); **UiTM-PDRM Academy of Police**

Centre

Foundation Studies (CFS); **Islamic Thought and Understanding** (Islamic Studies)

Graduate School

Arshad Ayub Graduate Business School (AAGBS) (Business Administration)

Campus

Johor (Accountancy; Business Administration; Information Sciences; Management); **Kedah** (Accountancy; Administration; Business Administration; Information Sciences; Law; Management); **Kelantan** (Accountancy; Banking; Business Administration; Design; Finance; Fine Arts; Information Sciences; Management; Marketing); **Melaka** (Accountancy; Administration; Design; Fine Arts; Law; Management); **Negeri Sembilan** (Accountancy; Administration; Design; Fine Arts; Hotel and Restaurant; Law; Management; Tourism); **Pahang** (Accountancy; Business Administration; Civil Engineering; Information Technology; Natural Sciences; Technology); **Perak** (Accountancy; Architecture and Planning; Design; Fine Arts; Information Technology; Management; Management Systems; Surveying and Mapping; Technology); **Perlis** (Accountancy; Administration; Architecture and Planning; Business Administration; Civil Engineering; Electrical Engineering; Information Technology; Law; Management; Management Systems; Natural Sciences; Secretarial Studies; Surveying and Mapping); **Pulau Pinang** (Engineering); **Sabah** (Accountancy; Banking; Business Administration; Civil Engineering; Computer Science; Hotel Management; Management; Marketing; Natural Sciences; Public Administration; Secretarial Studies; Technology; Tourism); **Sarawak** (Accountancy; Administration; Business Administration; Civil Engineering; Computer Science; Electrical Engineering; Finance; Hotel Management; Information Technology; Law; Leisure Studies; Management; Mathematics; Natural Sciences; Secretarial Studies; Sports; Technology; Tourism); **Terengganu** (Accountancy; Business Administration; Education; Electrical Engineering; Food Science; Hotel Management; Management; Public Administration; Secretarial Studies; Tourism)

History: Founded 1957. Acquired present status 1999

Admission requirements: Malaysian Certificate of Education (Sijil Pelajaran Malaysia) or 'O' Level with 5 credits including English and Mathematics

Fees: 241.50-2874.50 (Malaysian Ringgit)

Main language(s) of instruction: Malay, English

Accrediting agency: Ministry of Higher Education; Malaysian Qualifications Agency (MQA); National Accreditation Board SIRIM (Standard Industrial Research Institute of Malaysia)

Degrees and diplomas: Bachelor's Degree (Accountancy; Administration; Agronomy; Architecture and Planning; Business Administration; Chemical Engineering; Civil Engineering; Dentistry; Design; Education; Electrical Engineering; Engineering; Film; Fine Arts; Health Sciences; Hotel and Restaurant; Information Management; Islamic Studies; Law; Management; Mass Communication; Mathematics and Computer Science; Mechanical Engineering; Media Studies; Medicine; Modern Languages; Music; Parks and Recreation; Pharmacy; Sports; Surveying and Mapping; Technology; Theatre; Tourism; Visual Arts), Master's Degree (Accountancy; Applied Mathematics; Architecture; Art Education; Art History; Art Management; Banking; Business Administration; Commercial Law; Communication Arts; Community Health; Computer Networks; Computer Science; Construction Engineering; Cooking and Catering; Criminal Law; Criminology; Dental Technology; Dentistry; Design; Economics; Education; Educational Administration; Engineering Management; Environmental Engineering; Ethics; Finance; Fine Arts; Food Science; Food Technology; Foreign Languages Education; Geological Engineering; Health Sciences; Heritage Preservation; Hotel and Restaurant; Information Management; Information Sciences; Information Technology; International Relations; Law; Library Science; Management; Maritime Law; Mass Communication; Mathematics; Mathematics Education; Measurement and Precision Engineering; Mechanical Engineering; Media Studies; Medicine; Music Education; Nursing; Occupational Therapy; Orthodontics; Pathology; Periodontics; Pharmacy; Physical Therapy; Private Law; Psychiatry and Mental Health; Public Health; Public Law; Radiology; Real Estate; Road Engineering; Sports; Statistics; Structural Architecture; Technology; Telecommunications Engineering; Tourism; Town Planning; Transport and Communications; Transport Management), Doctor's Degree (Accountancy; Business Administration; Criminology; Finance; Hotel Management; Information Management; Management; Tourism; Transport and Communications; Transport Management)

Student Services: Academic Counselling, Social Counselling, Careers Guidance, Nursery Care, Cultural Activities, Sports Facilities, Language Laboratory, Health Services, Canteen, Library, IT Centre

Periodicals: Journal of Administrative Science, Journal of Bureau and Consultancy, Journal of International Business and Entrepreneurship (MEDEC), UiTM Law Review

Last Update: 06-06-2018

University Putra Malaysia (UPM)

Serdang 43400, Selangor
Tel: +60(3) 8946-6000
Fax: +60(3) 8948-7273

Website: http://www.upm.edu.my
Vice-Chancellor: Aini Ideris Ideris
Tel: +60(3) 8946-6001/ 6002

Faculty

Agriculture (Agricultural Business; Agriculture; Agronomy; Aquaculture; Botany; Crop Production; Horticulture; Plant and Crop Protection; Rural Planning; Soil Conservation; Zoology); **Agriculture and Food Sciences (UPMKB)** (*Bintulu Campus, Sarawak*) (Agricultural Business; Agricultural Engineering; Agriculture; Animal Husbandry; Crop Production; Fishery; Food Science; Forestry); **Biotechnology and Biomolecular Sciences** (Biochemistry; Biotechnology; Cell Biology; Microbiology; Molecular Biology); **Computer Science and Information Technology** (Computer Networks; Computer Science; Information Technology; Multimedia; Software Engineering; Telecommunications Engineering); **Design and Architecture** (Architecture; Industrial Design; Landscape Architecture); **Economics and Management** (Accountancy; Economics; Finance; Management; Marketing; Parks and Recreation; Tourism); **Educational Studies** (Arts and Humanities; Continuing Education; Education; Educational and Student Counselling; Educational Research; Educational Sciences; Modern Languages; Physical Education; Science Education); **Engineering** (Aeronautical and Aerospace Engineering; Agricultural Engineering; Bioengineering; Chemical Engineering; Civil Engineering; Computer Engineering; Electrical Engineering; Electronic Engineering; Engineering; Engineering Management; Environmental Engineering; Food Technology; Mechanical Engineering; Production Engineering; Telecommunications Engineering; Water Management); **Environmental Studies** (Environmental Management; Environmental Studies); **Food Science and Technology** (Cooking and Catering; Food Science; Food Technology); **Forestry** (Forest Management; Forest Products; Forestry; Wood Technology); **Human Ecology** (Consumer Studies; Development Studies; Family Studies; Government; Human Resources; Information Technology; Music; Social Sciences); **Medicine and Health Sciences** (Anatomy; Biomedicine; Community Health; Dietetics; Gynaecology and Obstetrics; Health Sciences; Laboratory Techniques; Medicine; Nursing; Nutrition; Occupational Therapy; Orthopaedics; Paediatrics; Pathology; Psychiatry and Mental Health); **Modern Languages and Communication** (Arabic; Chinese; Communication Studies; English; French; German; Malay; Modern Languages); **Science** (Biology; Chemistry; Industrial Chemistry; Mathematics; Microbiology; Natural Sciences; Petroleum and Gas Engineering; Physics; Science Education; Statistics); **Veterinary Medicine** (Microbiology; Pathology; Veterinary Science)

School

Business (*Putra*) (Business Administration); **Graduate Studies** (Agriculture; Applied Linguistics; Computer Science; Curriculum; Economics; Education; Educational Administration; Educational and Student Counselling; Educational Psychology; Educational Technology; Engineering Management; English; Environmental Engineering; Environmental Studies; Foreign Languages Education; Forest Management; Forest Products; Human Resources; Hydraulic Engineering; Landscape Architecture; Literature; Malay; Native Language Education; Natural Resources; Pathology; Pedagogy; Physical Education; Production Engineering; Road Engineering; Safety Engineering; Sports; Statistics; Structural Architecture; Surveying and Mapping; Technology Education; Transport Engineering; Veterinary Science; Water Management; Wood Technology)

Institute

Advanced Technology (*R & D, ITMA*) (Engineering); **Agricultural and Food Policy Studies** (Agriculture; Food Science); **Bioscience** (*IBS*) (Biological and Life Sciences; Biology); **Gerontology** (Gerontology); **Halal Product Research** (Food Science); **Mathematical Research** (Mathematics); **Social Science Studies** (Social Sciences); **Tropical Agriculture** (Tropical Agriculture); **Tropical Forestry and Forest Product** (Forest Products; Forestry; Tropical Agriculture)

Academy

Sports (Sports)

Centre

Foundation Studies for Agricultural Science (Agriculture)
Further information: Also 7 Service Centres (University Business; Research Management; Alumni; Professional Advancement; Knowledge Management; Cultural Studies and Arts; Islamic Studies), University Agriculture Park, and Campus in Bintulu
History: Founded 1971 through merger with Faculty of Agriculture and Agriculture College in Serdang to form Universiti Pertanian Malaysia. Statutory body under the Ministry of Education. Acquired present status and title 1997
Academic year: May to March (May-September; November-March)
Admission requirements: Malaysian Higher School Certificate (STPM). Diploma: Malaysian Certificate of Education (MCE)/Sijil Tinggi Pelajaran Malaysia (SPM). Undergraduate: higher school certificate (HSC)/Sijil Tinggi Persekolahan (STPM)
Main language(s) of instruction: Malay, English

Accrediting agency: Ministry of Higher Education; Malaysian Qualifications Agency (MQA); Public Service Department
Degrees and diplomas: Bachelor's Degree (Accountancy; Agriculture; Arabic; Architecture; Bioengineering; Biological and Life Sciences; Biotechnology; Business Administration; Chinese; Communication Arts; Communication Studies; Computer Science; Design; Development Studies; Economics; Education; Educational Sciences; Engineering; English; Environmental Studies; Food Science; Food Technology; Forestry; French; German; Health Sciences; Information Technology; Landscape Architecture; Malay; Management; Mathematics and Computer Science; Medicine; Modern Languages; Molecular Biology; Music; Music Education; Natural Sciences; Technology; Veterinary Science), Master's Degree (Agricultural Management; Agriculture; Animal Husbandry; Applied Linguistics; Architecture; Arts and Humanities; Biological and Life Sciences; Biotechnology; Business Administration; Chemistry; Communication Studies; Computer Science; Construction Engineering; Curriculum; Design; Economics; Education; Educational Administration; Educational and Student Counselling; Educational Psychology; Educational Sciences; Engineering; Engineering Management; Environmental Studies; Food Science; Food Technology; Foreign Languages Education; Forestry; Gerontology; Health Sciences; Hotel and Restaurant; Human Resources; Information Technology; Landscape Architecture; Literature; Malay; Management; Mass Communication; Mathematics; Medicine; Modern Languages; Molecular Biology; Native Language Education; Natural Sciences; Physical Education; Physics; Road Engineering; Safety Engineering; Social Sciences; Software Engineering; Soil Management; Sports; Statistics; Surveying and Mapping; Technology; Tourism; Transport Engineering; Tropical Agriculture; Veterinary Science; Vocational Education), Doctor's Degree (Aeronautical and Aerospace Engineering; Agricultural Business; Agricultural Economics; Agricultural Engineering; Agricultural Equipment; Agricultural Management; Agriculture; Agronomy; Anaesthesiology; Analytical Chemistry; Anatomy; Animal Husbandry; Applied Mathematics; Applied Physics; Aquaculture; Arabic; Architecture; Automation and Control Engineering; Biochemistry; Bioengineering; Biological and Life Sciences; Biology; Biotechnology; Botany; Business Administration; Cell Biology; Chemical Engineering; Child Care and Development; Chinese; Communication Studies; Computer Engineering; Computer Networks; Computer Science; Cultural Studies; Data Processing; Design; Development Studies; Ecology; Economics; Educational Administration; Educational and Student Counselling; Educational Psychology; Educational Sciences; Educational Technology; Electrical Engineering; Electronic Engineering; Energy Engineering; English;

Entomology; Environmental Engineering; Environmental Management; Environmental Studies; Epidemiology; Farm Management; Fishery; Food Science; Food Technology; Foreign Languages Education; Forensic Medicine and Dentistry; Forest Management; Forest Products; Forestry; Gender Studies; Genetics; Geological Engineering; Gerontology; Government; Haematology; Harvest Technology; Health Administration; Histology; Home Economics; Horticulture; Hotel and Restaurant; Human Resources; Immunology; Industrial Design; Industrial Engineering; Information Technology; Inorganic Chemistry; Islamic Law; Journalism; Landscape Architecture; Leadership; Linguistics; Literature; Malay; Marine Science and Oceanography; Mass Communication; Materials Engineering; Mathematics; Mathematics and Computer Science; Mathematics Education; Mechanical Engineering; Medical Parasitology; Medical Technology; Medicine; Microbiology; Molecular Biology; Multimedia; Music; Nanotechnology; Native Language Education; Natural Resources; Nursing; Nutrition; Occupational Health; Oncology; Organic Chemistry; Packaging Technology; Paper Technology; Parasitology; Pathology; Pest Management; Pharmacology; Philosophy; Physical Chemistry; Physical Education; Physiology; Plant Pathology; Political Sciences; Power Engineering; Psychology; Public Health; Radiology; Rehabilitation and Therapy; Road Engineering; Rural Studies; Safety Engineering; Social and Community Services; Social Psychology; Software Engineering; Soil Management; Soil Science; Sports; Statistics; Surgery; Surveying and Mapping; Telecommunications Engineering; Tourism; Town Planning; Toxicology; Translation and Interpretation; Transport Engineering; Tropical Agriculture; Veterinary Science; Vocational Education; Water Science; Wildlife; Zoology). Also Jointly PhD awarded with universities in UK and Australia; Dual PhD and Master of Degree Programmes; Dual PhD Programmes; Dual Master's Degree Programmes; Double Postgraduate Master's Degree Programmes

Student Services: Academic Counselling, Social Counselling, Careers Guidance, Nursery Care, Cultural Activities, Sports Facilities, Language Laboratory, Facilities for disabled people, Health Services, Canteen, Foreign Studies Centre
Periodicals: Pertanika
Publishing house: Universiti Putra Malaysia Press
Last Update: 15-06-2018

University Sains Malaysia (USM)

Media and Public Relations Centre Level 1 Building E42, Chancellory II Universiti Sains Malaysia
Minden 11800, Penang
Tel: +60(4) 653-3888, +60(4) 653-2770
Fax: +60(4) 653-6484, +60(4) 653-2781
Website: http://www.usm.my
Vice-Chancellor: Asma Ismail
Tel: +60(4) 653-3101

School
Arts (Design; Fine Arts; Music; Performing Arts; Photography; Sculpture; Theatre); **Biological Sciences** (Biotechnology; Botany; Entomology; Microbiology; Parasitology; Plant Pathology; Veterinary Science); **Chemical Sciences** (Analytical Chemistry; Applied Chemistry; Industrial Chemistry; Inorganic Chemistry; Organic Chemistry; Physical Chemistry); **Communication** (Communication Arts; Communication Studies; Film; Journalism; Media Studies; Radio and Television Broadcasting); **Computer Science** (Computer Engineering; Computer Science; Information Technology; Software Engineering); **Distance Education** (Accountancy; Anthropology; Biology; Chemistry; Economics; Finance; Geography; History; Human Resources; Literature; Management; Mathematics; Physics; Political Sciences; Sociology); **Educational Studies** (Curriculum; Educational Administration; Educational Psychology; Educational Sciences; Preschool Education; Special Education); **Housing, Building and Planning** (Architecture; Building Technologies; Interior Design; Landscape Architecture; Regional Planning; Surveying and Mapping; Town Planning); **Humanities** (English; Geography (Human); History; Islamic Studies; Linguistics; Malay; Translation and Interpretation); **Industrial Technology** (Ecology; Food Technology; Paper Technology; Technology); **Languages, Literacies and Translation** (English Studies; Foreign Languages Education; Translation and Interpretation); **Management** (Development Studies; Finance; Industrial Management; International Business; Management; Marketing); **Mathematical Sciences** (Applied Mathematics; Computer Science; Economics; Mathematics; Statistics); **Pharmaceutical Sciences** (Pharmacology; Pharmacy; Physiology); **Physics** (Applied Physics; Geophysics; Physics); **Social Sciences** (Anthropology; Development Studies; Economics; Political Sciences; Social Work; Sociology; Southeast Asian Studies)

Institute
Higher Education Research (Higher Education)

Centre
Archaeological Research (Archaeology); **Drug Research** (Epidemiology; Toxicology); **Information Technology** (Computer Science; Information Technology); **Instructional Technology and Media** (Educational Technology; Media Studies); **Islamic Centre** (Islamic Studies); **Marine and Coastal Studies** (Coastal Studies; Marine Science and Oceanography); **Policy Research and International Studies** (International Studies); **Research in Molecular Medicine**

(Medical Technology); **Women's Studies and Youth Development** (Social Studies; Women's Studies)

Campus

Engineering (*Pulau Pinang*) (Aeronautical and Aerospace Engineering; Bioengineering; Chemical Engineering; Civil Engineering; Electrical Engineering; Electronic Engineering; Engineering; Environmental Engineering; Industrial Engineering; Materials Engineering; Mathematics; Mechanics; Mineralogy; Mining Engineering; Physical Engineering; Polymer and Plastics Technology; Structural Architecture); **Health** (*Kelantan*) (Anaesthesiology; Anatomy; Applied Chemistry; Community Health; Dentistry; Dietetics; Environmental Studies; Forensic Medicine and Dentistry; Gynaecology and Obstetrics; Haematology; Health Education; Health Sciences; Immunology; Medical Technology; Medicine; Microbiology; Modern Languages; Neurological Therapy; Neurosciences; Nursing; Nutrition; Occupational Therapy; Ophthalmology; Orthopaedics; Otorhinolaryngology; Paediatrics; Parasitology; Pathology; Pharmacology; Pharmacy; Physiology; Psychiatry and Mental Health; Social and Preventive Medicine; Speech Therapy and Audiology; Sports Medicine; Translation and Interpretation)

History: Founded 1979 as University of Penang. Acquired present title 1972

Academic year: July to March (July-October; December-March)

Admission requirements: Malaysian Higher School Certificate (STPM) or equivalent

Fees: 725-915 per semester; Graduate, c. 50-135 per unit; Master's, Doctorate, c.2,000-4,000 per session (Malaysian Ringgit)

Main language(s) of instruction: Malay, English

Accrediting agency: Ministry of Higher Education; Malaysian Qualifications Agency (MQA)

Degrees and diplomas: Bachelor's Degree (Arts and Humanities; Dentistry; Economics; Education; Engineering; Health Sciences; Management; Mathematics and Computer Science; Medicine; Modern Languages; Natural Sciences; Nursing; Pharmacy; Technology; Translation and Interpretation), Master's Degree (Accountancy; Aeronautical and Aerospace Engineering; Anaesthesiology; Anatomy; Anthropology; Applied Physics; Architecture; Biochemistry; Biological and Life Sciences; Biomedicine; Biotechnology; Botany; Building Technologies; Business Administration; Chemical Engineering; Chemistry; Civil Engineering; Clinical Psychology; Cognitive Sciences; Communication Studies; Community Health; Computer Engineering; Computer Networks; Computer Science; Cultural Studies; Data Processing; Dental Technology; Dentistry; Development Studies; Economics; Education; Educational Technology; Electrical and Electronic Engineering; Electronic Engineering; English; Entomology; Environmental Engineering; Environmental

Studies; Epidemiology; Fine Arts; Food Technology; Forensic Medicine and Dentistry; Gender Studies; Genetics; Geography (Human); Geophysics; Gynaecology and Obstetrics; Haematology; Health Education; Higher Education; History; Home Economics; Immunology; Industrial Chemistry; Interior Design; Islamic Studies; Linguistics; Literature; Malay; Management; Marine Biology; Marine Science and Oceanography; Marketing; Materials Engineering; Mathematics; Mathematics Education; Mechanical Engineering; Medical Parasitology; Medical Technology; Medicine; Microbiology; Microelectronics; Mining Engineering; Molecular Biology; Music; Neurology; Neurosciences; Nursing; Nutrition; Occupational Health; Orthopaedics; Otorhinolaryngology; Paediatrics; Paper Technology; Parasitology; Pathology; Periodontics; Pharmacology; Pharmacy; Philosophy; Physics; Physiology; Plant Pathology; Plastic Surgery; Political Sciences; Polymer and Plastics Technology; Psychiatry and Mental Health; Psychology; Public Administration; Public Health; Radiology; Radiophysics; Rehabilitation and Therapy; Social and Community Services; Social Sciences; Social Work; Sociology; Solid State Physics; Speech Therapy and Audiology; Sports; Statistics; Surgery; Surveying and Mapping; Theatre; Tourism; Toxicology; Translation and Interpretation; Treatment Techniques; Water Management; Zoology), Doctor's Degree (Accountancy; Aeronautical and Aerospace Engineering; Anatomy; Anthropology; Architecture; Architecture and Planning; Biochemistry; Biology; Biomedicine; Biotechnology; Botany; Building Technologies; Business Administration; Chemical Engineering; Chemistry; Civil Engineering; Clinical Psychology; Communication Studies; Community Health; Computer Networks; Computer Science; Cultural Studies; Curriculum; Dentistry; Development Studies; Economics; Education; Educational Technology; Electrical and Electronic Engineering; Electronic Engineering; Endocrinology; English; Entomology; Environmental Engineering; Environmental Studies; Epidemiology; Finance; Fine Arts; Food Technology; Foreign Languages Education; Forensic Medicine and Dentistry; Gender Studies; Genetics; Geography (Human); Haematology; Health Education; Health Sciences; History; Immunology; Industrial Chemistry; Interior Design; Islamic Studies; Linguistics; Literature; Malay; Management; Marine Biology; Marine Science and Oceanography; Materials Engineering; Mathematics; Mechanical Engineering; Medical Parasitology; Medical Technology; Medicine; Microbiology; Microelectronics; Mining Engineering; Modern Languages; Molecular Biology; Music; Neurosciences; Nursing; Nutrition; Occupational Health; Paper Technology; Parasitology; Pathology; Pharmacology; Pharmacy; Philosophy; Physics; Physiology; Plant Pathology; Political Sciences; Polymer and Plastics Technology; Psychology; Public Health; Radiology; Rehabilitation and Therapy; Science Education; Social Work; Sociology; Speech Therapy and Audiology; Sports;

Statistics; Surveying and Mapping; Theatre; Toxicology; Translation and Interpretation; Water Management; Zoology)

Student Services: Academic Counselling, Social Counselling, Careers Guidance, Nursery Care, Cultural Activities, Sports Facilities, Language Laboratory, Health Services, Canteen

Periodicals: USM Link

Publishing house: University Sains Malaysia Press

Student Numbers 2012-2013	MALE	FEMALE	TOTAL
All (Foreign Included)			29000

Last Update: 01-06-2018

Private Institutions

AIMST University (AIMST)

Jalan Bedong, Semeling
Bedong 08100, Kedah
Tel: +60(4) 429-8000, +60(4) 429-8108
Fax: +60(4) 429-8007, +60(4) 429-8009
Website: http://www.aimst.edu.my
Vice-Chancellor: Ravichandran Manickam

Faculty

Allied Health Professions (Nursing; Physical Therapy); **Applied Sciences** (Biotechnology); **Business and Management** (Business Administration; Business Computing; Finance; Health Administration; Management; Marketing); **Dentistry** (Dental Technology; Dentistry); **Engineering and Computer Technology** (Computer Science; Electrical and Electronic Engineering; Information Technology; Multimedia; Telecommunications Engineering); **Medicine** (Dentistry; Medicine; Pharmacy; Surgery); **Pharmacy** (Pharmacy)

History: Founded 2001

Main language(s) of instruction: Malay

Accrediting agency: Malaysian Qualifications Agency (MQA); Ministry of Higher Education (MOHE)

Degrees and diplomas: Bachelor's Degree (Accountancy; Biological and Life Sciences; Biotechnology; Business Administration; Computer Science; Dental Technology; Dentistry; Electrical and Electronic Engineering; Finance; Information Technology; Management; Marketing; Medicine; Nursing; Pharmacy; Physical Therapy; Surgery), Master's Degree (Anatomy; Biochemistry; Biotechnology; Management; Microbiology; Pharmacy; Physiology), Doctor's Degree (Biotechnology; Management; Microbiology; Pharmacy)

Student Services: Sports Facilities, Health Services, Library, IT Centre

Academic Staff 2016-2017	MALE	FEMALE	TOTAL
FULL-TIME			245
PART-TIME			220
STAFF WITH DOCTORATE			
FULL-TIME			54
Student Numbers 2016-2017			
All (Foreign Included)			2436

Last Update: 31-05-2018

Al-Madinah International University (MEDIU)

Al-Madinah International University 11th Floor Plaza Masalam 2, Jalan Tengku Ampuan Zabedah E/9E
Shah Alam 40100, Selangor
Tel: +60(3) 5511-3939
Fax: +60(3) 5511-3940
Website: http://www.mediu.edu.my
Rector: Mohammad Khalifa Al-Tamimi

Faculty

Computer and Information Technology (Computer Science; Information Technology); **Education** (Education); **Engineering** (Civil Engineering; Electrical and Electronic Engineering; Engineering); **Finance and Administrative Sciences** (Administration; Finance); **Islamic Sciences** (Islamic Studies); **Languages** (Arabic; English)

Centre

Postgraduate Studies (Business Administration; Computer Science; Education; Finance; Information Technology; Islamic Studies; Modern Languages); **Preparatory Studies and Languages** (Modern Languages)

Further information: Also online campus

History: Created 2008

Academic year: From September to September

Main language(s) of instruction: Arabic, English

Accrediting agency: Ministry of Higher Education; Malaysian Qualifications Agency (MQA)

Degrees and diplomas: Bachelor's Degree (Arabic; Business Administration; Civil Engineering; Computer Engineering; Computer Networks; Computer Science; E- Business/Commerce; Electrical and Electronic Engineering; Information Technology; Islamic Studies; Literature; Management; Marketing), Master's Degree (Accountancy; Arabic; Banking; Business Administration; Computer Science; Curriculum; E- Business/Commerce; Economics; Education; Experimental Psychology; Finance; Information Technology; Islamic Studies; Literature; Management; Pedagogy), Doctor's Degree (Accountancy; Arabic; Business

Administration; Computer Science; Curriculum; Economics; Education; Educational Psychology; Finance; Information Technology; Islamic Studies; Pedagogy)
Student Services: Academic Counselling, Social Counselling, Careers Guidance, Nursery Care, Sports Facilities, Language Laboratory, Health Services, Canteen, Foreign Studies Centre
Last Update: 06-06-2018

Asia e University (AeU)

Tingkat Bawah, Blok Utama, Dataran Kewangan Darul Takaful, No.4, Jalan Sultan Sulaiman
Kuala Lumpur 50000
Tel: +60(3) 2785-0000
Fax: +60(3) 2785-0001, +60(3) 2711-0436
Website: http://www.aeu.edu.my
President: Dato Ansary Ahmed

School

Arts, Humanities and Social Sciences (Arts and Humanities; Media Studies; Modern Languages; Political Sciences; Religion; Social Sciences); **Education** (Education; Foreign Languages Education; Higher Education); **Graduate Studies** (Business Administration; Education; Information Technology; Management); **Information and Communication Technology** (Information Management; Information Technology); **Management** (Business Administration; Management)
History: Founded 2007
Main language(s) of instruction: Malay
Accrediting agency: Ministry of Higher Education; Malaysian Qualifications Agency (MQA)
Degrees and diplomas: Bachelor's Degree (Business Administration; Education; Foreign Languages Education; Graphic Design; Information Technology; Multimedia; Preschool Education; Primary Education), Postgraduate Diploma (Higher Education Teacher Training), Master's Degree (Business Administration; Education; Human Resources; Information Management; Information Technology; Management; Natural Sciences; Social Sciences), Doctor's Degree (Arts and Humanities; Business Administration; Education; Finance; Information Technology)
Student Services: Library, IT Centre
Last Update: 08-06-2018

Asia Metropolitan University (AMU)

G-8, Jalan Kemacahaya 11 Taman Kemacahaya Batu 9, Cheras
Kuala Lumpur 43200, Selangor

Tel: +60(3) 9080-5888
Fax: +60(3) 9080-1995
Website: http://www.amu.edu.my
Vice-Chancellor: Mahmood Nazar Mohamed

Faculty

Business and Information Technology (Business Administration; Information Technology); **Medicine** (Medicine); **Nursing** (Nursing); **Pharmacy** (Pharmacy); **Therapeutic Healthcare** (Health Sciences)

Centre

Foundation Studies (Business Administration; Health Sciences); **Postgraduate Studies** (Business Administration; Health Administration)
History: Founded 2004, acquired current status and title 2012. Formely known as Masterskill College of Health Sciences
Main language(s) of instruction: Malay
Accrediting agency: Ministry of Higher Education; Malaysian Qualifications Agency (MQA)
Degrees and diplomas: Bachelor's Degree (Biomedicine; Business Administration; Health Administration; Medical Auxiliaries; Pharmacy; Physical Therapy; Radiology; Surgery), Master's Degree (Business Administration; Health Administration; Pharmacy), Doctor's Degree (Business Administration; Management)
Student Services: Library, Residential Facilities
Last Update: 08-06-2018

Asia Pacific University of Technology and Innovation (APU)

Technology Park Malaysia Bukit Jalil
Kuala Lumpur 57000
Tel: +60(3) 8996-1000
Fax: +60(3) 8996-1001
Website: http://www.apu.edu.my
Vice-Chancellor: Ron Edwards

Course/Programme

Postgraduate Studies (Business Administration; Computer Science; E- Business/Commerce; Information Management; Information Technology; Management; Multimedia; Software Engineering; Technology)

School

Business, Management, Marketing, Tourism and Media (Business Administration; Management; Marketing; Media

Studies; Tourism); **Computing, Technology and Games Development** (Artificial Intelligence; Business Computing; Computer Engineering; Computer Networks; Computer Science; Information Technology; Multimedia; Software Engineering); **Engineering** (Electrical and Electronic Engineering; Electronic Engineering; Mechanical Engineering; Telecommunications Engineering)

Further information: APU has overseas branches in India, Sri Lanka and Pakistan

History: Founded 1993 as Asia Pacific Institute of Information Technolog (APIIT). Became Asia Pacific University College of Technology & Innovation (UCTI) in 2004

Admission requirements: Completion of 'O' or 'A' levels or equivalent

Main language(s) of instruction: English

Accrediting agency: Malaysian Qualifications Agency (MQA); Ministry of Higher Education (MOHE)

Degrees and diplomas: Bachelor's Degree (Accountancy; Actuarial Science; Banking; Business Administration; Computer Engineering; Computer Science; Engineering; Finance; Information Technology; Management; Marketing; Media Studies; Software Engineering; Technology; Tourism), Master's Degree (Business Computing; Computer Engineering; Data Processing; Information Technology; Management), Doctor's Degree (Computer Science; Engineering; Finance; Management; Technology). Also Dual Master's Programmes with Staffordshire University (UK)

Student Services: Academic Counselling, Social Counselling, Careers Guidance, Cultural Activities, Sports Facilities, Language Laboratory, Health Services, Canteen, Foreign Studies Centre, Library, Residential Facilities

Last Update: 06-06-2018

BERJAYA University College

Level 11 West Berjaya Times Square No. 1 Jalan Imbi
Kuala Lumpur 55100
Tel: +60(3) 2687-7000
Fax: +60(3) 2687-7000, +60(3) 2687-7001
Website: http://www.berjaya.edu.my/university
Vice-Chancellor: Walter Wong
Tel: +60(3) 2687-7199

Faculty
Culinary Arts (Cooking and Catering); **Liberal Arts** (Arts and Humanities)

School
Business (Business Administration)

Centre
Professional Development (Cooking and Catering; Tourism)

History: Founded 2009. Formerly know as Berjaya University College of Hospitality

Main language(s) of instruction: English

Accrediting agency: Ministry of Higher Education; Malaysian Qualifications Agency (MQA)

Degrees and diplomas: Bachelor's Degree (Accountancy; Business Administration; Finance; Hotel and Restaurant; Management; Retailing and Wholesaling; Tourism), Master's Degree (Business Administration)

Last Update: 07-06-2018

Binary University of Management and Entrepreneurship (BUME)

No 1, 101 Business Park, Persiaran Puchong Jaya Selatan
Puchong 47100, Selangor
Tel: +60(3) 8070-6590
Fax: +60(3) 8070-6594
Website: http://www.binary.edu.my
Vice-Chancellor and CEO: Joseph Adaikalam
Tel: +60(3) 8070-6595

School
Accountancy and Finance (Accountancy; Finance); **Business Administration** (Business Administration; Business and Commerce; Marketing); **Entrepreneurship Development** (Business Administration); **Postgraduate** (Business Administration; Computer Science; Information Technology); **Technology Management** (Computer Science; Information Technology)

History: Founded 1984 as a learning centre. Became Binary Business School 1989. Became the first private insitution to offer MBA and MSc IT 1994. Became Binary University College of Management and Entrepreneurship in 2004. Acquired current title 2013

Academic year: Starting in March and September

Admission requirements: For undergraduate programmes, completed foundation Studies. For graduate programmes, a recognised Bachelor degree. For Postgraduate programmes, a reconised Master degree and five years experience.

Fees: Foundation Studies, 9,600; Diploma, 6,300 per annum; Bachelor degree, 13,000 per annum; Masters, 13,500 per annum; Doctorate, 12,000 per annum (Malaysian Ringgit)

Main language(s) of instruction: English

Accrediting agency: Malaysian Qualifications Agency (MQA); Ministry of Higher Education

Degrees and diplomas: Foundation / University Preparatory Programme (Accountancy; Business Administration; Information Technology), Bachelor's Degree (Accountancy; Business Administration; Computer Science; Information Technology; Management; Marketing), Master's Degree

(Accountancy; Banking; Business Administration; Computer Science; Educational Administration; Environmental Management; Finance; Human Resources; Industrial Management; Information Technology; Management; Marketing; Public Administration; Real Estate; Tourism), Doctor's Degree (Banking; Business Administration; Finance; Human Resources; Information Technology; Management; Marketing; Transport Management)

Student Services: Academic Counselling, Social Counselling, Careers Guidance, Cultural Activities, Sports Facilities, Language Laboratory, Health Services, Canteen, Foreign Studies Centre, Residential Facilities

Periodicals: International Journal of Management and Entrepreneurship

Last Update: 15-06-2018

City University (City U)

Menara City U No. 8, Jalan 51A/223
Petaling Jaya 46100, Selangor
Tel: +60(3) 7949-1600
Fax: +60(3) 7957-7721
Website: https://www.city.edu.my
Vice-Chancellor: Noridah Ibrahim

Faculty

Allied Health Sciences (Health Sciences); **Architecture and Built Environment** (Architecture); **Art and Design** (Design; Fine Arts); **Business** (Business Administration); **Education and Liberal Studies** (Arts and Humanities; Education); **Engineering** (Engineering); **Hospitality and Tourism** (Hotel and Restaurant; Tourism); **Information Technology** (Information Technology)

Course/Programme

CCSP (City Career Specialist Programme) (Business Administration; Health Sciences; Occupational Health)

Department/Division

Online Distance Learning (ODL)

Centre

Foundation Studies

Graduate School

City Graduate School (Business Administration; Education; Information Technology; Mechanical Engineering)
History: Founded 1984 as Petaling Jaya Community College, renamed Unity College International (UCI) 1998 and then City University College of Science and Technology (CUCST) 2010, acquired current status and title 2016

Main language(s) of instruction: Malay
Accrediting agency: Ministry of Higher Education; Malaysian Qualifications Agency (MQA)
Degrees and diplomas: Bachelor's Degree (Accountancy; Architecture; Biomedicine; Business Administration; Civil Engineering; Communication Studies; Engineering Management; Finance; Foreign Languages Education; Graphic Design; Health Administration; Information Technology; Interior Design; Journalism; Mass Communication; Mechanical Engineering; Multimedia; Occupational Health; Preschool Education; Psychology; Public Health; Software Engineering; Tourism), Master's Degree (Business Administration; Education; Information Technology; Mechanical Engineering), Doctor's Degree (Business Administration)
Student Services: Health Services, Library
Last Update: 08-06-2018

Cyberjaya University College of Medical Sciences (CUCMS)

No. 3410, Jalan Teknokrat 3 Cyber 4
Cyberjaya 63000, Selangor
Tel: +60(3) 8319-1010
Fax: +60(3) 8319-1100
Website: http://www.cybermed.edu.my
President: Mohamad Abdul Razak
Tel: +60(3) 8313-7010

Faculty

Allied Health Sciences (Biomedicine; Health Sciences; Medical Auxiliaries; Psychology); **Medicine** (Medicine; Surgery); **Pharmacy** (Medicine); **Traditional and Complimentary Medicine** (Alternative Medicine; Homeopathy)

School

Business and Management (Business Administration; Management)
History: Founded in 2005
Admission requirements: Sijil Tinggi Pelajaran Malaysia or other secondary school leaving certificate.
Fees: 50,000 per annum (Medicine and Surgery); 25,000 per annum (Pharmacy) (Malaysian Ringgit)
Main language(s) of instruction: English
Accrediting agency: Malaysian Qualifications Agency (MQA); Ministry of Higher Education (MOHE)
Degrees and diplomas: Bachelor's Degree (Biomedical Engineering; Business Administration; Homeopathy; Medicine; Occupational Health; Pharmacy; Physical Therapy; Psychology; Surgery), Postgraduate Diploma (Psychology), Master's Degree (Business Administration; Clinical Psychology; Health Administration; Medicine; Natural Sciences;

Occupational Health; Pharmacy), Doctor's Degree (Alternative Medicine; Biomedical Engineering; Business Administration; Dietetics; Health Sciences; Homeopathy; Medical Auxiliaries; Medicine; Nutrition; Occupational Health; Pharmacy; Physical Therapy; Primary Education; Psychology; Social Work; Sports; Traditional Eastern Medicine)

Student Services: Academic Counselling, Sports Facilities, Library, Residential Facilities

Last Update: 08-06-2018

HELP University (HU)

BZ-2 Pusat Bandar Damansara
Kuala Lumpur 50490
Tel: +60(3) 2094-2000
Fax: +60(3) 2095-7100
Website: http://www.help.edu.my
Vice-Chancellor, President: Paul Tuck Hoong Chan
Tel: +60(3) 2094-2000

Faculty

Applied Sciences and Multimedia (Business Computing; Computer Graphics; Information Technology); **Behavioural Sciences** (Behavioural Sciences; Psychology); **Business, Economics and Accounting** (Accountancy; Administration; Banking; Business Administration; Economics; Finance; Human Resources; International Business; Management; Taxation); **Education** (Continuing Education; English; Literacy Education; Preschool Education; Teacher Training); **Humanities and Social Sciences** (*Also American degree programme in Arts*) (Advertising and Publicity; Journalism; Marketing; Mass Communication; Media Studies; Public Relations); **Law and Government** (Civil Law; Commercial Law; Law)

School

Hospitality and Tourism (Hotel Management; Tourism)

Institute

Crime and Criminology (Criminology)

Centre

Psychology and Counseling (Clinical Psychology)

Graduate School

HELP Graduate School (Accountancy; Administration; Business Administration; Economics; Management)

History: Founded 1988. Previously known as Kolej Universiti HELP (HELP University College). Acquired current title 2010

Academic year: From Jan to Dec depending on programme

Admission requirements: Bachelor programmes, recognized secondary school certificate(s); Postgraduate, an approved undergraduate degree or equivalent qualification.

Fees: 54,000-60,000 per annum (Malaysian Ringgit)

Main language(s) of instruction: English

Accrediting agency: Malaysian Qualifications Agency (MQA); Ministry of Higher Education (MOHE)

Degrees and diplomas: Certificate, Bachelor's Degree (Accountancy; Business Administration; Business and Commerce; Communication Studies; Computer Science; Economics; Education; English; Finance; Hotel and Restaurant; Human Resources; Information Technology; Law; Management; Marketing; Preschool Education; Psychology; Tourism), Postgraduate Certificate (Software Engineering), Master's Degree (Accountancy; Business Administration; Clinical Psychology; Criminology; Economics; Finance; Foreign Languages Education; Government; Human Resources; Industrial and Organizational Psychology; Management; Psychology; Teacher Training), Doctor's Degree (Business Administration). Also American Degree Programmes

Student Services: Academic Counselling, Social Counselling, Careers Guidance, Sports Facilities, Language Laboratory, Health Services, Canteen, Foreign Studies Centre

Last Update: 15-06-2018

Infrastructure University Kuala Lumpur (IKUL)

Unipark Suria, Jalan Ikram-Uniten
Kajang 43000, Selangor
Tel: +60(3) 8738-3339
Fax: +60(3) 8925-9846
Website: http://www.iukl.edu.my
President and Vice-Chancellor: Roslan Zainal Abidin

Faculty

Applied Science and Foundation Studies (Agriculture; Biotechnology; Horticulture; Religion; Sports Management); **Architecture and Built Environment** (Architecture; Building Technologies; Landscape Architecture; Real Estate); **Arts, Communication and Education** (Communication Studies; English; Foreign Languages Education); **Business and Accounting** (Accountancy; Business Administration; E-Business/Commerce); **Creative Media and Innovative Technology** (Computer Networks; Computer Science; Information Technology; Software Engineering); **Engineering and Technology Infrastructure** (Automation and Control Engineering; Civil Engineering; Construction Engineering; Electrical and Electronic Engineering; Mechanical Engineering; Water Management)

Centre

Postgraduate Studies (CPS) (Architecture; Building Technologies; Business Administration; Communication Studies; Education; Information Technology); **Research Management**

History: Founded 1998. Became Kuala Lumpur Infrastructure University College, 2003. Acquired present status and name 2012

Academic year: 3 intakes: March, June, November.

Admission requirements: Diploma, O level or equivalent; Bachelor's Degree, A level or equivalent; Master's degree, Bachelor's or equivalent

Fees: Diploma, 17,000; Bachelor's Degree, 35,000; Master's degree, 22,000 (Malaysian Ringgit)

Main language(s) of instruction: English

Accrediting agency: Malaysian Qualifications Agency (MQA); Ministry of Higher Education (MOHE)

Degrees and diplomas: Certificate (Business Administration; Engineering; English), Bachelor's Degree (Accountancy; Advertising and Publicity; Business Administration; Civil Engineering; Communication Arts; Computer Engineering; Computer Networks; Computer Science; Construction Engineering; E- Business/Commerce; Electronic Engineering; English; Information Technology; Mechanical Engineering; Software Engineering; Statistics), Postgraduate Diploma (Higher Education Teacher Training), Master's Degree (Architecture; Building Technologies; Business Administration; Civil Engineering; Communication Studies; Construction Engineering; Electronic Engineering; English; Foreign Languages Education; Information Technology; Water Management), Doctor's Degree (Architecture; Building Technologies; Business Administration; Civil Engineering; Communication Studies; Education; Information Technology)

Student Services: Academic Counselling, Careers Guidance, Sports Facilities, Language Laboratory, Canteen, Foreign Studies Centre, Library, IT Centre, Residential Facilities

Last Update: 15-06-2018

INSANIAH University College (KUIN)

Lebuhraya Sultanah Bahiyah
Alor Setah 05350, Kedah
Tel: +60(4) 415-5000, +60(4) 732-0163
Fax: +60(4) 415-5050, +60(4) 732-0164
Website: http://www.insaniah.edu.my
Rector: Fakhrudin bin Abdul Mukti

Course/Programme

Arabic (Arabic); **Business Administration** (Accountancy; Banking; Business Administration; Finance); **Engineering and Information Technology** (Computer Engineering; Electronic Engineering; Graphic Design; Information Technology; Multimedia; Telecommunications Engineering; Video); **Hospitality and Halal Services** (Cooking and Catering; Hotel and Restaurant; Hotel Management; Tourism); **Koran** (Koran); **Law and Islamic Law** (Islamic Law; Law); **Medicine and Surgery** (Medicine; Surgery); **Usuluddin** (Islamic Theology)

History: Founded 1994 as Institut Islam Negeri kedah Darul Aman. Acquired present title and status 2006

Main language(s) of instruction: English

Accrediting agency: Malaysian Qualifications Agency (MQA); Ministry of Higher Education (MOHE)

Degrees and diplomas: Bachelor's Degree (Banking; Business Administration; Finance), Master's Degree (Arabic; Banking; Finance; Islamic Law; Islamic Studies; Islamic Theology; Koran; Psychology; Religious Education), Doctor's Degree (Arabic; Banking; Finance; Islamic Law; Islamic Theology)

Student Services: Library

Last Update: 07-06-2018

International Centre for Education in Islamic Finance (INCEIF)

Lorong Universiti A
Kuala Lumpur 59100
Tel: +60(3) 7651-4000
Fax: +60(3) 7651-4071, +60(3) 7651-4094
Website: http://www.inceif.org
Chancellor: Zeti Akhtar Abd Aziz

Course/Programme

Islamic Finance (Banking; Finance; International Economics; Islamic Law)

History: Created in 2005 by Bank Negara Malaysia (Central Bank of Malaysia)

Academic year: Jan - May; Sep - Dec; also short semester course Jun - July/August

Admission requirements: Master's programme, Bachelor (Hons) or an equivalent professional qualification from institution recognized by INCEIF or Malaysian Government. English proficiency: MUET - band 4 or equivalent; or IELTS - band 6; or TOEFL - total of 550 for paper-based or 213 for computer-based examination; PhD programme, Master degree or an equivalent professional qualification from institution recognized by INCEIF or Malaysian Government. English proficiency: IELTS - band 6; or TOEFL - total of 550 for paper-based or 213 for computer-based examination; for PhD by research candidates also need a minimum 5 years work experience in a financial institution, and the submission of a research proposal

Fees: 22,000-32,000 per annum (Malaysian Ringgit)
Main language(s) of instruction: English
Accrediting agency: Malaysian Qualifications Agency (MQA); Ministry of Higher Education (MOHE)
Degrees and diplomas: Master's Degree (Finance; Islamic Studies), Doctor's Degree (Finance; Islamic Studies). Also Chartered Islamic Finance Professional (CIFP)

Academic Staff 2013-2014	MALE	FEMALE	TOTAL
FULL-TIME			180
PART-TIME			6
STAFF WITH DOCTORATE			
FULL-TIME			31
Student Numbers 2013-2014			
All (Foreign Included)			2692
Foreign only			1311

Total number of distance students: 1814
Last Update: 06-06-2018

International Medical University (IMU)

No.126, Jalan Jalil Perkasa 19 Bukit Jalil
Kuala Lumpur 57000
Tel: +60(3) 8656-7228
Fax: +60(3) 8656-7229
Website: http://www.imu.edu.my
President: Abdul Aziz Baba

School

Dentistry (Dentistry); **Health Sciences** (Biomedicine; Biotechnology; Chiropractic; Dietetics; Health Sciences; Nursing; Nutrition; Psychology; Traditional Eastern Medicine); **Medicine** (Community Health; Medicine; Pathology; Psychology); **Pharmacy** (Pharmacology; Pharmacy); **Postgraduate Studies and Research** (Health Sciences; Medicine)

Centre

Pre-University (Health Sciences)
History: Founded 1992 as International Medical College. Acquired present name and status 1999
Admission requirements: School certificate (Sijil Tinggi Pelajaran Malaysia STPM) or equivalent
Fees: National : 6,500-40,000 per semester (Malaysian Ringgit), International : 10,550- 62,000 per semester (Malaysian Ringgit)
Main language(s) of instruction: English
Accrediting agency: Ministry of Higher Education; Malaysian Qualifications Agency (MQA); Malaysian Medical Council; Malaysian Dental Council; Malaysian Pharmacy Board; Royal Pharmaceutical Society of Great Britain (RPSGB); Nursing Board Malaysian

Degrees and diplomas: Bachelor's Degree (Biomedicine; Biotechnology; Chiropractic; Dentistry; Dietetics; Medical Technology; Medicine; Nursing; Nutrition; Pharmacology; Pharmacy; Psychology; Traditional Eastern Medicine), Postgraduate Diploma (Dental Technology), Master's Degree (Analytical Chemistry; Community Health; Health Education; Health Sciences; Medicine; Pharmacy; Public Health), Doctor's Degree (Health Sciences; Medicine)
Student Services: Academic Counselling, Social Counselling, Sports Facilities, Language Laboratory, Canteen, Library
Last Update: 08-06-2018

International University College of Technology Twintech (TWINTECH)

Podium Plaza, Block E Sri Damansara Business Park
Persiaran Industri, Bandar Sri Damansara
Kuala Lumpur 52200
Tel: +60(3) 6272-5506/7, +60(3) 6286-1200
Fax: +60(3) 6274-1500
Website: http://www.twintech.edu.my
Vice-Chancellor: Tengku Abdul Aziz bin Tengku Zainal

Faculty

Architecture and Built Environment (Architecture and Planning; Interior Design; Surveying and Mapping); **Business and Finance** (Accountancy; Banking; Business Administration; Finance; International Business; Management; Marketing); **Hospitality and Applied Management** (Hotel and Restaurant; Hotel Management; Tourism); **Optometry** (Optometry)
Further information: Also Kota Bharu campus
History: Founded in 1994 as Twintech Institute of Technology. Acquired present title and status, 2003
Main language(s) of instruction: English
Accrediting agency: Malaysian Qualifications Agency (MQA); Ministry of Higher Education (MOHE)
Degrees and diplomas: Bachelor's Degree (Accountancy; Architecture; Banking; Engineering Management; Finance; International Business; Marketing; Surveying and Mapping), Master's Degree (Business Administration)
Student Services: Sports Facilities, Library, IT Centre
Last Update: 08-06-2018

International University of Malaya-Wales (IUMW)

Administration Wing, Block A City Campus, Jalan Tun Ismail

Kuala Lumpur 50480
Tel: +60(3) 2617-3131
Fax: +60(3) 2617-3131
Website: http://iumw.edu.my

Faculty

Arts and Humanities (Arts and Humanities; Communication Studies); **Business and Law** (Business Administration; Law); **Health and Social Science** (Psychology); **Science, Technology, Engineering and Mathematics** (Biotechnology; Computer Science; Engineering; Management; Natural Resources)

Centre

Foundation Studies (Arts and Humanities; Natural Sciences); **Language and Malaysia Studies** (English)
History: Founded 2012 on a mutual partnership between the University of Malaya (UM) & the University of Wales, UK
Main language(s) of instruction: English
Accrediting agency: Ministry of Higher Education; Malaysian Qualifications Agency (MQA)
Degrees and diplomas: Bachelor's Degree (Accountancy; Communication Studies; Finance; Human Resources; International Business; Management; Marketing), Master's Degree (Business Administration; Communication Studies; Engineering; Management; Natural Resources), Doctor's Degree (Business Administration; Communication Studies; Computer Science; Management)
Last Update: 25-05-2018

Inti International University

Lot 12295, Jalan BBN 12/1
Nilai 17800, Negeri Sembilan
Tel: +60(6) 798-2000
Fax: +60(6) 799-7531
Website: http://newinti.edu.my
Vice-Chancellor: Allan Fisher

Course/Programme

Art and Design (Design; Fashion Design; Graphic Design; Interior Design); **Biotechnology and Life Sciences** (Biological and Life Sciences; Biotechnology); **Computing and Information Technology** (Computer Engineering; Engineering; Information Technology); **Engineering** (Civil Engineering; Electrical and Electronic Engineering; Mechanical Engineering; Surveying and Mapping); **Health Sciences** (Health Sciences; Physical Therapy; Traditional Eastern Medicine); **Hospitality** (Hotel and Restaurant; Hotel Management); **Law** (Law); **Postgraduate** (Applied Physics; Business Administration; Information Sciences; Information Technology; International Business; Management)

Further information: Campuses in Subang Jaya, Sabah, Sarawak, Penang, Genting and Kuala Lumpur (Malaysia); Beijing (China); Jakarta (Indonesia)
History: Created 1986 as Inti College Malaysia. Became Inti International University College 2006. Acquired current title and status 2010
Main language(s) of instruction: English
Accrediting agency: Malaysian Qualifications Agency (MQA); Ministry of Higher Education (MOHE)
Degrees and diplomas: Foundation / University Preparatory Programme, Bachelor's Degree (Accountancy; Biotechnology; Business Administration; Business Computing; Civil Engineering; Computer Science; Finance; Human Resources; Information Technology; International Business; Marketing; Mechanical Engineering; Physical Therapy; Psychology; Traditional Eastern Medicine), Master's Degree (Business Administration), Doctor's Degree (Applied Physics; Information Technology; Management). Also some degree programmes offered in collaboration with overseas universities. (Sheffield Hallam University, UK; University of Hertfordshire, UK; Coventry University, UK; Southern New Hampshire University, USA; University of Wollongong, Australia); American University Program Degree; Australian Degree Transfer Programme
Student Services: Academic Counselling, Social Counselling, Cultural Activities, Sports Facilities, Health Services, Canteen
Last Update: 15-06-2018

Islamic University of Malaysia (UIM)

Blok I, Bangunan MKN Embassy Techzone, Jalan Teknokrat 2
Cyberjaya 63000, Selangor
Tel: +60(3) 8324-6666
Fax: +60(3) 8324-6600
Website: https://www.uim.edu.my
President: Mohd Yusof Noor

School

Hertigae and Civilization (Ancient Civilizations; Heritage Preservation); **Law and Siaryah** (Islamic Law; Law)

Institute

Well Being

Graduate School

Management and Finance (*Cyberjaya*) (Finance; Management)
History: Founded 1955 as Kolej Islam Malaya (KIM), campus moved to Jalan Universiti, Petaling Jaya 1966. Absorbed into Universiti Kebangsaan Malaysia (UKM) as Faculty of Islamic Studies 1970. Acquired current status and title 2013

Main language(s) of instruction: Malay
Accrediting agency: Ministry of Higher Education; Malaysian Qualifications Agency (MQA)
Degrees and diplomas: Master's Degree (Finance), Doctor's Degree (Finance; Heritage Preservation; Law; Management)
Last Update: 28-05-2018

KDU University College

Utropolis, Glenmarie Jalan Kontraktor U1/14 Seksyen U1
Shah Alam 40150, Selangor
Tel: +60(3) 5565-0538
Fax: +60(3) 5565-0539
Website: http://university.kdu.edu.my
Vice-Chancellor: Pang Leang Hiew
Tel: +60(3) 5565-0601

Course/Programme

Business (Business Administration); **Communication and Creative Arts** (Design; Fine Arts; Mass Communication); **Computing and Creative Media** (Computer Engineering; Computer Science; Information Technology); **Engineering** (Engineering); **English Language** (English); **Hospitality, Tourism and Culinary Arts** (Cooking and Catering; Hotel and Restaurant; Tourism); **Postgraduate Studies** (Arts and Humanities; Business Administration; Design; Engineering; Natural Sciences)
History: Founded 1983 as Kolej Damansara Utama, acquired current status and title 2010
Main language(s) of instruction: English
Accrediting agency: Ministry of Higher Education; Malaysian Qualifications Agency (MQA)
Degrees and diplomas: Certificate, Bachelor's Degree (Accountancy; Banking; Business Administration; Computer Engineering; Computer Graphics; Computer Science; Electrical and Electronic Engineering; Electronic Engineering; Finance; Hotel and Restaurant; Information Technology; Law; Management; Mass Communication; Mechanical Engineering), Master's Degree (Business Administration; Computer Engineering; Computer Graphics; Computer Networks; Design; Economics; Electrical and Electronic Engineering; Finance; Graphic Design; Hotel and Restaurant; Management; Marketing; Mechanical Engineering; Software Engineering; Tourism), Doctor's Degree (Engineering)
Student Services: Library, Residential Facilities
Last Update: 15-06-2018

KPJ Healthcare University College (KPJUC)

Lot PT 17010 Persiaran Seriemas, Kota Seriemas
Nilai 71800, Negeri

Tel: +60(6) 794-2630
Fax: +60(6) 794-2669, +60(6) 794-2662
Website: https://www.kpjuc.edu.my
Vice-Chancellor: Lokman bin Saim
Tel: +60(6) 794-2692

School

Business and Management (Business Administration; Management); **Medicine** (Medicine); **Nursing** (Nursing); **Pharmacy** (Pharmacy)

Centre

Global Professional and Social Development (Natural Sciences)
Further information: Also Johor Bharu and Penang Campuses, Malaysian College of Hospitality & Management, Johor Bharu
History: Founded 1991, formerly known as PNC International College of Nursing and Health Sciences
Main language(s) of instruction: Malay
Accrediting agency: Ministry of Higher Education; Malaysian Qualifications Agency (MQA)
Degrees and diplomas: Advanced Diploma, Certificate, Bachelor's Degree (Business Administration; Communication Studies; Nursing; Pharmacy; Psychology), Master's Degree (Nursing; Orthopaedics; Otorhinolaryngology; Pharmacy; Radiology; Surgery), Doctor's Degree (Nursing). Also Post Basic Certificate; Professional Certificate
Last Update: 15-06-2018

Kuala Lumpur Metropolitan University College (KLMUC)

Level G, 1-3 Wisma Sachdev Jalan Raja Laut
Kuala Lumpur 50350
Tel: +60(3) 2694-2300
Fax: +60(3) 2604-0906, +60(3) 2691-0400
Website: http://www.klmu.edu.my
Vice-Chancellor: Abdul Rahim Abdul Rahman

Faculty

Design and Creativity (Civil Engineering; Computer Graphics; Design; Fashion Design; Interior Design; Landscape Architecture; Multimedia); **Engineering and Applied Technology** (Computer Engineering; Computer Networks; Electrical Engineering; Electronic Engineering; Engineering; Information Technology; Software Engineering; Telecommunications Engineering); **Hospitality, Tourism and Wellness** (Cooking and Catering; Hotel and Restaurant; Hotel Management; Tourism); **Management and Business Technology** (Accountancy; Administration; Business Administration; E- Business/Commerce; Finance; Human Resources;

Management; Marketing); **Media Studies** (Advertising and Publicity; Cinema and Television; Journalism; Public Relations; Radio and Television Broadcasting)

Centre

Languages, Education and General Studies (Education; Preschool Education; Primary Education)
History: Founded 1991 as Cosmopoint International University College. Acquired present title and status 2006
Main language(s) of instruction: English
Accrediting agency: Malaysian Qualifications Agency (MQA); Ministry of Higher Education (MOHE)
Degrees and diplomas: Advanced Diploma, Graduate Diploma, Bachelor's Degree (Administration; Business Administration; E- Business/Commerce; Human Resources; Information Technology; Management), Master's Degree (Business Administration)
Student Services: Academic Counselling, Careers Guidance, Sports Facilities, Library, IT Centre
Last Update: 15-06-2018

Lincoln University College

Wisma Lincoln, No. 12-18, Jalan SS 6/12
Petaling Jaya 47301, Selangor Darul Ehsan
Tel: +60(3) 7806-3478
Fax: +60(3) 7806-3479
Website: http://www.lincoln.edu.my
Pro-Chancellor: Hajjah Bibi Florina Abdullah

Faculty

Allied Health Science (Health Administration; Nursing; Physical Therapy); **Business, Acounting, and Hospitality Management** (Business Administration; Hotel Management; Human Resources; International Business; Marketing); **Information Technology and Enginerring** (Computer Science; Information Technology; Multimedia); **Medicine and Dentistry** (Alternative Medicine; Dentistry; Medicine); **Pharmacy** (Pharmacy); **Postgraduate Studies** (Business Administration; Health Administration; Health Sciences; Hotel Management; Information Technology; International Business; Midwifery; Nursing; Pharmacy; Public Health)
History: Created 2002
Main language(s) of instruction: English
Accrediting agency: Malaysian Qualifications Agency (MQA); Ministry of Higher Education (MOHE)
Degrees and diplomas: Bachelor's Degree (Accountancy; Biomedicine; Biotechnology; Business Administration; Business and Commerce; Chemical Engineering; Civil Engineering; Computer Networks; Computer Science; Dentistry; Education; Electrical and Electronic Engineering; Finance; Health Administration; Health Sciences; Hotel Management;

Human Resources; Information Technology; Islamic Studies; Management; Marketing; Mass Communication; Mechanical Engineering; Medicine; Multimedia; Nursing; Pharmacology; Pharmacy; Physical Therapy; Psychology; Surgery), Master's Degree (Banking; Biotechnology; Business Administration; Business and Commerce; Civil Engineering; Communication Arts; Communication Studies; Computer Science; Dentistry; Economics; Education; Electrical and Electronic Engineering; Energy Engineering; Finance; Foreign Languages Education; Geology; Health Administration; Hotel and Restaurant; Hotel Management; Human Resources; Insurance; Mechanical Engineering; Medicine; Microbiology; Midwifery; Nursing; Pharmacy; Public Administration; Public Health; Social Work; Telecommunications Engineering; Transport Management; Water Management), Doctor's Degree (Accountancy; Business Administration; Engineering; Health Sciences; Information Technology; Management; Pharmacy; Physiology; Psychology; Social Sciences)
Student Services: Library
Last Update: 07-06-2018

Linton University College

Administrative Building Persiaran UTL Bandar Universiti Teknologi Legenda (BUTL) Batu 12
Mantin 71700, Negeri Sembilan
Tel: +60(6) 758-7888, +60(6) 758-1809
Website: http://www.linton.edu.my
Vice-Chancellor: Kamis Awang
Tel: +60(6) 758-7729

Faculty

Built Environment (Architecture; Civil Engineering); **Business and Accounting** (Accountancy; Business Administration); **Engineering and Technology** (Engineering; Technology)

Academy

Applied and Visual Arts (Fine Arts; Visual Arts)
History: Founded 1987, acquired current status 2010
Main language(s) of instruction: English
Accrediting agency: Ministry of Higher Education; Malaysian Qualifications Agency (MQA)
Degrees and diplomas: Bachelor's Degree (Accountancy; Business Administration; Civil Engineering; Finance), Master's Degree (Accountancy; Business Administration; Civil Engineering; Finance)
Last Update: 08-06-2018

MAHSA University

Jalan SP 2 Bandar Saujana Putra
Jenjarum 42610, Selangor

Tel: +60(3) 5102-2200
Fax: +60(3) 7931-7118
Website: https://mahsa.edu.my
Vice-Chancellor: Khairul Anuar bin Abdullah

Faculty

Business, Finance and Hospitality (Business Administration; Finance; Hotel and Restaurant); **Dentistry** (Dentistry); **Engineering and Information Technology** (Engineering; Information Technology); **Health and Sports Sciences** (Health Sciences; Sports); **Medicine and Biomedical Science** (Biomedicine; Medicine); **Nursing and Midwifery** (Midwifery; Nursing); **Pharmacy** (Pharmacy)

Centre

Pre-University Studies (Business Administration; Natural Sciences)
History: Founded 2005
Main language(s) of instruction: English
Accrediting agency: Ministry of Higher Education; Malaysian Qualifications Agency (MQA)
Degrees and diplomas: Advanced Diploma, Certificate, Bachelor's Degree (Accountancy; Biomedicine; Business Administration; Dentistry; Finance; Health Administration; Health Sciences; Industrial Management; Medicine; Nursing; Occupational Therapy; Pharmacy; Physical Therapy; Public Health; Surgery; Treatment Techniques), Master's Degree (Anatomy; Business Administration; Health Administration; Medicine; Nursing; Pharmacy; Physical Therapy; Public Health), Doctor's Degree (Nursing; Pharmacy). Also some Double degree offered with Anglia Ruskin University (UK)
Last Update: 15-06-2018

Malaysia Institute for Supply Chain Innovation (MISI)

No. 2A, Persiaran Tebar Layar Seksyen U8, Bukit Jelutong
Shah Alam 40150, Selangor
Tel: +60(3) 7841 4823, +60(3) 7841-4800
Website: http://www.misi.edu.my
Chief Executive Officer and Rector: David Gonsalvez
Tel: +60(3) 7841-4801

Course/Programme

Supply Chain Management (Transport Management)
History: Founded 2011 as a joint initiative between the Massachusetts Institute of Technology (MIT) and the government of Malaysia
Main language(s) of instruction: English
Accrediting agency: Ministry of Higher Education; Malaysian Qualifications Agency (MQA)

Degrees and diplomas: Master's Degree (Transport Management), Doctor's Degree (Transport Management). Also Executive Education Programme
Last Update: 25-05-2018

Malaysia University of Science and Technology (MUST)

Block B, Encorp Strand Garden Office NO. 12, Jalan PJU 5/1, Kota Damansara
Petaling Jaya 47810, Selangor
Tel: +60(3) 615068177, +60(3) 7880-1777
Fax: +60(3) 7880-1762
Website: http://www.must.edu.my
President: Premkumar Rajagopal

Course/Programme

Business and Management (Business Administration; Management); **Construction Engineering and Management** (Construction Engineering; Transport Management); **Energy and Environment** (Energy Engineering; Environmental Studies); **Information Technology** (Information Technology); **System Engineering and Management** (Computer Engineering; Engineering Management); **Transportation and Logistics** (Transport Management)
History: Founded 2000. A postgraduate institution established with the assistance of the Massachusetts Institute of Technology
Main language(s) of instruction: Malay
Accrediting agency: Ministry of Higher Education; Malaysian Qualifications Agency (MQA)
Degrees and diplomas: Bachelor's Degree (Business Administration; Information Technology; Telecommunications Engineering; Transport and Communications; Transport Management), Master's Degree (Biotechnology; Business Administration; Construction Engineering; Energy Engineering; Engineering; Environmental Engineering; Environmental Studies; Information Technology; Management; Telecommunications Engineering; Transport Engineering; Transport Management), Doctor's Degree (Computer Engineering; Information Technology; Management; Transport and Communications; Transport Management)
Last Update: 01-06-2018

Management and Science University (MSU)

University Drive, Off Persiaran Olahraga Section 13
Shah Alam 40100, Selangor Darul Ehsan
Tel: +60(3) 5521-6868

Fax: +60(3) 5511-2848
Website: http://www.msu.edu.my
President: Mohd Shukri Ab Yajid

Faculty

Business Administration and Professional Studies (Business Administration); **Health and Life Sciences** (Biomedicine; Food Science; Health Sciences; Laboratory Techniques; Nursing; Occupational Therapy; Physical Therapy; Radiology); **Information Sciences and Engineering** (Engineering; Information Sciences)

School

Education and Social Sciences (Education; Social Sciences); **Graduate Studies** (Business Administration; Health Sciences; Information Technology; International Business; Management); **Medicine** (*International*) (Dentistry; Medicine; Neurology; Nursing; Pharmacy; Physical Therapy; Rehabilitation and Therapy); **Pharmacy** (Chemistry; Medical Technology; Pharmacology; Pharmacy)

Centre

Foundation Studies (Accountancy; Business Administration; Computer Science; E- Business/Commerce; Information Technology; Management)

Graduate School

Management (Business Administration; Management)
Further information: Also Professional advancement Centre
History: Founded 2001. Formerly known as (Kolej Universiti Teknologi Dan Pengurusan Malaysia/ University College of Technology and Management of Malaysia).
Main language(s) of instruction: English
Accrediting agency: Ministry of Higher Education; Malaysian Qualifications Agency (MQA)
Degrees and diplomas: Bachelor's Degree (Accountancy; Air Transport; Art Education; Biological and Life Sciences; Biomedicine; Business and Commerce; Business Computing; Communication Arts; Computer Engineering; Computer Graphics; Computer Science; Cooking and Catering; Cosmetology; Design; Education; Educational Technology; Electrical and Electronic Engineering; English; Fashion Design; Finance; Graphic Design; Health Administration; Industrial Design; Industrial Management; Information Management; Information Technology; International Business; Law; Leisure Studies; Literature; Management; Marketing; Mechanical Engineering; Media Studies; Medical Technology; Medicine; Multimedia; Music; Music Theory and Composition; Musical Instruments; Nursing; Nutrition; Optometry; Pharmacy; Philosophy; Photography; Physical Education; Preschool Education; Psychology; Public Relations;

Retailing and Wholesaling; Science Education; Software Engineering; Surgery; Video; Visual Arts), Master's Degree (Accountancy; Biomedicine; Business Administration; Computer Science; Design; Educational Administration; Finance; Food Technology; Health Sciences; Hotel and Restaurant; Information Technology; International Business; Management; Pharmacy; Tourism), Doctor's Degree (Accountancy; Biomedicine; Business Administration; Computer Science; Education; Engineering; Finance; Food Technology; Health Sciences; Hotel and Restaurant; Information Technology; Management; Medicine)
Student Services: Sports Facilities, Library, IT Centre
Last Update: 01-06-2018

Manipal International University (MIU)

No. 1, Persiaran MIU
Putra Nilai 71800, Negeri Sembilan
Tel: +60(6) 798-9200
Fax: +60(6) 798-9300
Website: https://www.miu.edu.my/miu.html
Vice-Chancellor: Franco Gandolfi

School

Management and Business (Accountancy; Business Administration; Finance; International Relations; Management; Mass Communication); **Science and Engineering** (Biotechnology; Chemical Engineering; Civil Engineering; Computer Engineering; Computer Science; Electrical and Electronic Engineering; Mechanical Engineering)

Centre

Foundation and Language Studies (Business Administration; Engineering; English; Natural Sciences)
History: Founded 2010
Main language(s) of instruction: Malay
Accrediting agency: Ministry of Higher Education; Malaysian Qualifications Agency (MQA)
Degrees and diplomas: Bachelor's Degree (Accountancy; Business Administration; Chemical Engineering; Civil Engineering; Computer Engineering; Electrical and Electronic Engineering; International Business; Mass Communication; Mechanical Engineering), Master's Degree (Business Administration)
Last Update: 28-05-2018

Multimedia University (MMU)

Persiaran Multimedia
Cyberjaya 63100, Selangor
Tel: +60(3) 8312-5012, +60(3) 8312-5803/ 5092

Fax: +60(3) 8312-5115, +60(3) 8312-5080
Website: http://www.mmu.edu.my
President: Ahmad Rafi Mohamad Eshaq

Faculty

Applied Communication (Communication Studies); **Business** (*Melaka Campus*) (Accountancy; Banking; Business Administration; Economics; Finance; Human Resources; International Business; Management; Marketing); **Cinematic Arts** (Cinema and Television); **Computing and Informatics** (*Cyberjaya Campus*) (Computer Engineering; Computer Science); **Creative Multimedia** (*Cyberjaya Campus*) (Film; Media Studies; Multimedia); **Engineering** (*Cyberjaya Campus*) (Computer Engineering; Electronic Engineering; Microwaves; Multimedia; Optical Technology; Telecommunications Engineering); **Engineering and Technology** (*Melaka*) (Engineering; Technology); **Information Science and Technology** (*Melaka Campus*) (Artificial Intelligence; Information Technology; Software Engineering; Systems Analysis); **Law** (*Melaka Campus*) (Law); **Management** (*Cyberjaya Campus*) (Management)

School

MMU Business Schhol (B-SCHOOL)

Institute

Engineering (*Graduate*) (Engineering); **Postgraduate Studies**
Further information: Also Melaka and Johor Campuses
History: Founded 1997
Admission requirements: STPM at least 3 principals
Main language(s) of instruction: English
Accrediting agency: Malaysian Qualifications Agency (MQA); Ministry of Higher Education (MOHE)
Degrees and diplomas: Bachelor's Degree (Accountancy; Advertising and Publicity; Artificial Intelligence; Automation and Control Engineering; Banking; Biological and Life Sciences; Business Administration; Cinema and Television; Communication Arts; Computer Networks; Computer Science; Data Processing; Design; Electrical Engineering; Electronic Engineering; Finance; Graphic Design; Human Resources; Information Technology; International Business; Law; Management; Marketing; Mechanical Engineering; Multimedia; Nanotechnology; Optical Technology; Robotics; Safety Engineering; Telecommunications Engineering), Master's Degree (Business Administration; Computer Science; Educational Technology; Engineering; Information Technology; Management; Multimedia; Software Engineering), Doctor's Degree (Business Administration; Engineering; Information Technology; Management; Multimedia)
Student Services: Academic Counselling, Nursery Care, Sports Facilities, Language Laboratory, Facilities for disabled people, Health Services, Canteen, Foreign Studies Centre, Library, IT Centre
Publishing house: MMU Press
Last Update: 30-05-2018

Nilai University

No 1, Persiaran Universiti, Putra Nilai
Nilai 71800, Negeri Sembilan
Tel: +60(6) 850-2338
Fax: +60(6) 850-2339
Website: http://www.nilai.edu.my
Vice-Chancellor: Sothi Rachagan

Faculty

Applied Sciences (Agricultural Management; Biotechnology; Nursing); **Business** (Accountancy; Administration; Biotechnology; Business Administration; Finance; Human Resources; Information Technology; International Business; Management; Marketing); **Engineering and Technology** (Agricultural Management; Biotechnology; Computer Science; Electronic Engineering; Engineering; Mechanical Engineering); **Hospitality and Tourism** (Cooking and Catering; Hotel and Restaurant; Hotel Management; Tourism); **Humanities and Social Sciences** (Arts and Humanities; English; Social Sciences)

Centre

Foundation Studies; **Postgraduate Studies** (Agriculture; Business Administration; Engineering; Health Sciences; Mathematics and Computer Science; Natural Sciences)
History: Founded as Nilai College in 1997, upgraded to a university college in 2007, Aquired present title and Status 2012
Main language(s) of instruction: English
Accrediting agency: Malaysian Qualifications Agency (MQA); Ministry of Higher Education (MOHE)
Degrees and diplomas: Advanced Diploma, Bachelor's Degree (Accountancy; Biotechnology; Business Administration; Computer Engineering; Computer Science; Electrical and Electronic Engineering; Finance; Hotel and Restaurant; Human Resources; Information Technology; International Business; Management; Marketing; Mechanical Engineering; Nursing; Software Engineering), Master's Degree (Agriculture; Alternative Medicine; Anatomy; Banking; Biochemistry; Biology; Biomedicine; Biotechnology; Business Administration; Chemistry; Computer Science; Environmental Studies; Finance; Food Science; Health Sciences; Human Resources; Management; Marketing; Materials Engineering; Mathematics; Microbiology; Natural Resources; Physics), Doctor's Degree (Agriculture; Biochemistry; Biology; Biomedicine; Biotechnology; Business Administration;

Chemistry; Environmental Studies; Food Science; Health Sciences; Materials Engineering; Microbiology)
Student Services: Social Counselling, Sports Facilities, Canteen, Library
Last Update: 15-06-2018

Open University Malaysia (OUM)

Jalan Tun Ismail
Kuala Lumpur 50480
Tel: +60(3) 2773-2002
Fax: +60(3) 2697-8852
Website: http://www.oum.edu.my
President and Vice-Chancellor: Mansor Fadzil

Faculty

Applied Social Sciences (Communication Studies; Islamic Studies; Malay; Political Sciences; Psychology; Social Sciences); **Education and Languages** (Education; Educational Administration; Educational Technology; English Studies; Preschool Education; Primary Education; Special Education); **Information Technology and Multimedia Communication** (Accountancy; Computer Networks; E- Business/Commerce; Information Sciences; Information Technology; Management; Multimedia; Software Engineering); **Science and Technology** (Chemical Engineering; Civil Engineering; Electrical Engineering; Engineering; Environmental Management; Environmental Studies; Industrial Management; Information Technology; Management; Mathematics; Mechanical Engineering; Occupational Health; Production Engineering; Safety Engineering)

School

Business (Accountancy; Business Administration; Human Resources; Management; Marketing; Tourism); **Nursing and Allied Health Sciences** (Health Sciences; Nursing)

Centre

Graduate Studies (Business Administration; Education; Engineering; Information Technology; Islamic Studies; Natural Sciences; Psychology; Social Sciences; Teacher Training)
History: Founded 2000
Main language(s) of instruction: English
Accrediting agency: Malaysian Qualifications Agency (MQA); Ministry of Higher Education (MOHE)
Degrees and diplomas: Bachelor's Degree (Accountancy; Business Administration; Communication Studies; Education; English; Health Administration; Human Resources; Industrial Management; Information Technology; Islamic

Studies; Management; Occupational Health; Preschool Education; Primary Education; Psychology), Postgraduate Diploma (Teacher Training), Master's Degree (Business Administration; Communication Studies; Education; Educational Technology; English; Human Resources; Information Technology; Islamic Studies; Management; Nursing; Occupational Health; Preschool Education; Psychology), Doctor's Degree (Arts and Humanities; Business Administration; Communication Studies; Education; English; History; Information Technology; Islamic Studies; Measurement and Precision Engineering; Political Sciences; Psychology; Rehabilitation and Therapy; Social Work)
Student Services: Sports Facilities, Library, IT Centre
Last Update: 08-06-2018

Perdana University

Block B & D1, Level 1 MAEPS Building, MARDI Complex
Jalan MAEPS Perdana
Serdang 43400, Selangor
Tel: +60(3) 8941-8646
Fax: +60(3) 8941-7661
Website: http://www.perdanauniversity.edu.my
Vice-Chancellor: Zabidi Azhar bin Mohd Hussin

School

Data Sciences (Biological and Life Sciences; Computer Science); **Foundation Studies** (Mathematics and Computer Science; Natural Sciences); **Occupational Therapy** (Occupational Therapy); **Perdana University and Royal College of Surgeons in Ireland (PU-RCSI) School of Medicine** (Medicine)

Graduate School

Medicine (Medicine)
History: Founded 2011
Main language(s) of instruction: Malay
Accrediting agency: Ministry of Higher Education; Malaysian Qualifications Agency (MQA)
Degrees and diplomas: Bachelor's Degree (Medicine; Occupational Therapy), Postgraduate Diploma (Biological and Life Sciences; Computer Science), Master's Degree (Biological and Life Sciences; Computer Science; Public Health), Doctor's Degree (Health Sciences). Also Bachelor of Medicine (MB), Bachelor of Surgery (BCh) and Bachelor of the Art of Obstetrics (BAO) from the National University of Ireland, as well as the Licentiate Diploma of the Royal College of Physicians of Ireland and Royal College of Surgeons in Ireland (LRCP&SI)
Student Services: Library
Last Update: 15-06-2018

Petronas Technological University (UTP)

Seri Iskandar 32610, Perak
Tel: +60(5) 368-8000
Fax: +60(5) 365-4088
Website: http://www.utp.edu.my
Vice-Chancellor: Mohamed Ibrahim bin Abdul Mutalib
Tel: +60(5) 368-8181

Faculty

Engineering (Chemical Engineering; Civil Engineering; Electrical and Electronic Engineering; Mechanical Engineering); **Geosciences and Petroleum Engineering** (Geology; Geophysics; Petroleum and Gas Engineering); **Science and Information Technology** (Information Sciences; Information Technology)

Department/Division

Management and Humanities (Arts and Humanities; Management)

Centre

Foundation Studies (CFS) (Engineering; Natural Sciences; Technology)
History: Founded 1997
Main language(s) of instruction: English
Accrediting agency: Ministry of Higher Education; Malaysian Qualifications Agency (MQA)
Degrees and diplomas: Bachelor's Degree (Applied Chemistry; Applied Physics; Chemical Engineering; Civil Engineering; Computer Science; Earth Sciences; Electrical and Electronic Engineering; Information Technology; Mechanical Engineering; Petroleum and Gas Engineering), Master's Degree (Arts and Humanities; Chemical Engineering; Civil Engineering; Electrical and Electronic Engineering; Engineering; Information Technology; Management; Mechanical Engineering; Natural Sciences; Petroleum and Gas Engineering), Doctor's Degree (Arts and Humanities; Chemical Engineering; Civil Engineering; Electrical and Electronic Engineering; Engineering; Information Technology; Management; Mechanical Engineering; Natural Sciences; Petroleum and Gas Engineering; Social Sciences)
Student Services: Cultural Activities, Sports Facilities, Library, IT Centre
Last Update: 05-06-2018

Putra Business School (PBS)

Serdang 43400, Selangor
Tel: +60(3) 8946-7441, +60(3) 8948-3118, +60(3) 8656-0350
Fax: +60(3) 8942-1584
Website: http://putrabusinessschool.edu.my
President: Zulkornain Yusop

Course/Programme

Business Administration (Accountancy; Business Administration; Finance; Management; Marketing)
History: Founded 1997 as the Graduate School of Management (GSM) of Universiti Putra Malaysia (UPM), acquired current status and title 2011, now an autonomous private business school located in Universiti Putra Malaysia (UPM)
Main language(s) of instruction: Malay
Accrediting agency: Ministry of Higher Education; Malaysian Qualifications Agency (MQA)
Degrees and diplomas: Master's Degree (Accountancy; Business Administration; Finance; Management; Marketing), Doctor's Degree (Accountancy; Finance; Management; Marketing)
Student Services: Academic Counselling, Library, Residential Facilities
Last Update: 08-06-2018

Quest International University Perak (QIUP)

No. 227, Plaza Teh Teng Seng Jalan Raja Permaisuri Bainun
Ipoh 30250, Perak
Tel: +60(5) 2049-0500
Fax: +60(5) 2049-0503
Website: http://www.qiup.edu.my
Vice-Chancellor: Raman Narayanasamy
Tel: +60(5) 249-0500, Ext.206

Faculty

Business and Management (Accountancy; Business Administration; Cooking and Catering; Finance; Hotel and Restaurant; Marketing; Mass Communication; Preschool Education; Special Education; Tourism); **Medicine** (Biomedicine; Medicine); **Pharmacy** (Pharmacy); **Science and Technology** (Actuarial Science; Biotechnology; Chemistry; Computer Science; Electrical Engineering; Information Technology; Mechanical Engineering); **Social Science** (Social Sciences)

Department/Division

English Language (English)

Centre

Research and Innovation

Research Division

Centre for Angiogenesis and Natural Product Research; **Centre for Infectious Diseases and Parasitology Research**; **Centre for Pharmaceutical Research**; **Centre for Professional and Continuing Education**; **Data Ecosystem Research and Development Centre**

History: Founded 2008, a private and comprehensive research-led University established by Blair Education Services Sdn. Bhd (currently known as Global Integrated Training Associates Sdn Bhd) in the State of Perak, Malaysia with equity participation by Perak State Government

Main language(s) of instruction: English

Accrediting agency: Ministry of Higher Education; Malaysian Qualifications Agency (MQA)

Degrees and diplomas: Diploma (Accountancy; Business Administration; Business Computing; Cooking and Catering; Electronic Engineering; Environmental Engineering; Hotel and Restaurant; Information Technology; Mechanical Engineering; Pharmacy; Preschool Education), Bachelor's Degree (Accountancy; Actuarial Science; Advertising and Publicity; Biomedicine; Biotechnology; Business Administration; Business Computing; Communication Studies; Computer Science; Cooking and Catering; Electronic Engineering; Environmental Engineering; Finance; Foreign Languages Education; Hotel and Restaurant; Information Technology; Journalism; Mass Communication; Mechanical Engineering; Medicine; Pharmacy; Preschool Education; Psychology; Special Education; Surgery; Telecommunications Engineering; Tourism), Master's Degree (Business Administration; Mathematics and Computer Science; Natural Sciences), Doctor's Degree (Business Administration; Mathematics and Computer Science; Natural Sciences). The Bachelor of Accountancy (Hons) and MBA are accredited by the Institute of Certified Management Accountants, Australia. Also English Enhancement Programme (Elementary, Intermediate and Advance Levels)

Student Services: Library

Academic Staff 2017-2018	MALE	FEMALE	TOTAL
FULL-TIME			162
PART-TIME			5
STAFF WITH DOCTORATE			
FULL-TIME			31
Student Numbers 2017-2018			
All (Foreign Included)			350

Last Update: 29-06-2018

Raffles University Iskandar (RUI)

Menara Kota Raya, Aras 9 Jalan Trus
Johor Bahru 80000, Johor

Tel: +60(7) 277-8868
Fax: +60(7) 277-8878
Website: http://www.raffles-university.edu.my
President: Graeme Britton

Course/Programme

Accountancy (Accountancy); **Applied Psychology** (Psychology); **Business Administration** (Business Administration); **Fashion Design** (Fashion Design); **Graphic Design** (Graphic Design); **Interior Design** (Interior Design); **Multimedia Design** (Design; Multimedia); **Supply Chain Management** (Transport Management)

History: Founded 2011

Main language(s) of instruction: English, Malay

Accrediting agency: Ministry of Higher Education; Malaysian Qualifications Agency (MQA)

Degrees and diplomas: Bachelor's Degree (Accountancy; Business Administration; Design; Fashion Design; Graphic Design; Interior Design; Multimedia; Psychology; Transport Management), Master's Degree (Business Administration)

Student Services: Library, Residential Facilities

Last Update: 28-05-2018

SEGi University and Colleges (SEGi)

No.9, Jalan Teknologi Taman Sains Selangor Kota Damansara PJU 5
Petaling Jaya 47810, Selangor
Tel: +60(3) 6145-1777, +60(12) 781-8196
Website: https://segi.edu.my
Vice-Chancellor: Patrick Kee Peng Kong

Course/Programme

Allied Health Sciences (Health Sciences); **American Degree Programme** (Business Administration; Communication Arts; Psychology); **Business and Accounting** (Accountancy; Business Administration); **Communication Studies** (Communication Studies); **Creative Arts and Design** (Design; Fine Arts); **Early Childhood Care and Education** (Child Care and Development; Preschool Education); **Engineering and the Built Environment** (Civil Engineering); **English and Public Relations** (English; Public Relations); **Health Sciences** (Health Sciences); **Hospitality and Tourism** (Hotel and Restaurant; Tourism); **Law** (Law); **Postgraduate Studies** (Business Administration; Communication Studies; Education; Engineering; Environmental Studies; Health Sciences; Information Technology); **Pre U / Foundation** (Arts and Humanities; Business Administration); **Professional Studies** (Business Administration); **Psychology** (Psychology); **Technology and Innovation** (Technology)

Further information: Also Colleges in Kuala Lumpur, Subang Jaya, Sarawak, Penang

History: Founded 1977 as SEGi University College, acquired current status and title 2012

Main language(s) of instruction: Malay

Accrediting agency: Ministry of Higher Education; Malaysian Qualifications Agency (MQA)

Degrees and diplomas: Certificate, Bachelor's Degree (Accountancy; Architecture; Automotive Engineering; Business Administration; Chemical Engineering; Civil Engineering; Communication Arts; Communication Studies; Computer Science; Dentistry; Design; Education; Electrical and Electronic Engineering; English; Finance; Graphic Design; Hotel and Restaurant; Information Technology; Interior Design; Law; Mass Communication; Measurement and Precision Engineering; Mechanical Engineering; Medicine; Multimedia; Nursing; Optometry; Pharmacy; Preschool Education; Psychology; Public Relations; Surgery; Tourism), Master's Degree (Accountancy; Business Administration; Communication Studies; Education; Engineering; Engineering Management; Finance; Health Sciences; Human Resources; Information Technology; Management; Marketing; Telecommunications Engineering), Doctor's Degree (Business Administration; Education; Engineering; Environmental Studies; Information Technology; Management). Also Executive Diplomas. Bachelor's Degree offered with Abertay University (UK), University of Greenwich (UK) and University of Sunderland (UK). MBA, Master's Degree in Business Administration and International Business offered by University of Greenwich (UK). American Bachelor of Science Programmes in: Business Administration, Communication Arts, Psychology

Last Update: 15-06-2018

Selangor International Islamic University College (KUIS)

Bandar Seri Putra 1, Bangi
Kajang 43000, Selangor
Tel: +60(3) 8925-4251, +60(3) 8911-7000
Fax: +60(3) 8926-8462
Website: http://www.kuis.edu.my
Rector: Halim Bin Tamuri
Tel: +60(3) 8925-4251, Ext.1306

Faculty

Economics (Administration; Business Administration; E-Business/Commerce; Economics; Finance; Human Resources; Management); **Education** (Arabic; Education; English; Malay); **Islamic Civilisations and Studies** (*FPPI*)

(Arabic; Islamic Studies; Islamic Theology; Koran); **Science and Information Technology** (*FTSI*) (Computer Science; E-Business/Commerce; Information Technology; Software Engineering; Technology)

History: Founded 1995 as Kolej Islam Selangor Darul Ehsan (KISDAR), acquired present tittle and status 2004

Admission requirements: Malaysian Higher School Certificate

Main language(s) of instruction: Malay

Accrediting agency: Malaysian Qualifications Agency (MQA); Ministry of Higher Education (MOHE)

Degrees and diplomas: Bachelor's Degree (Arabic; Banking; Computer Networks; E-Business/Commerce; Economics; Finance; Human Resources; Information Technology; Islamic Law; Islamic Studies; Koran; Multimedia; Native Language Education; Radio and Television Broadcasting; Software Engineering; Translation and Interpretation), Master's Degree (Islamic Law; Management), Doctor's Degree (Islamic Studies)

Student Services: Library

Last Update: 07-06-2018

Southern University College

Jalan Selatan Utama Off Jalan Skudai
Skudai 81300, Johor
Tel: +60(7) 558-6605
Fax: +60(7) 556-3306
Website: http://www.southern.edu.my
President: Kiah Wah Thock
Tel: +60(7) 558-6605, Ext.103

Faculty

Art and Design (Design; Fine Arts); **Business and Management** (Business Administration; Management); **Chinese Medicine** (Traditional Eastern Medicine); **Education and Public Welfare** (Education; Welfare and Protective Services); **Engineering and Information Technology** (Engineering; Information Technology); **Humanities and Social Sciences** (Arts and Humanities; Social Sciences)

School

Foundation Studies; **Professional and Continuing Education (SPACE)**

Department/Division

English Promotion Committee (English)

Institute

Southern Institute of Technical Education

Centre
Excellent Teaching and Learning; **Modern Language** (Modern Languages); **Sim Mow Yu Chinese Education and Teacher Training Centre** (Teacher Training)

Campus Abroad
General Studies
History: Founded 1990 as Southern College, acquired current status and title 2012
Main language(s) of instruction: English
Accrediting agency: Ministry of Higher Education; Malaysian Qualifications Agency (MQA)
Degrees and diplomas: Bachelor's Degree (Accountancy; Business Administration; Computer Graphics; Educational and Student Counselling; Educational Technology; Electronic Engineering; Finance; Foreign Languages Education; Graphic Design; Human Resources; Management; Marketing; Mass Communication; Preschool Education; Psychology; Software Engineering; Tourism; Traditional Eastern Medicine), Master's Degree (Asian Studies; Business Administration; Chinese; Communication Studies; Computer Science; Cultural Studies; Education; Tourism; Translation and Interpretation). Also Executive MBA Programme; Professional Diplomas
Student Services: Library, Residential Facilities
Last Update: 15-06-2018

Sultan Azlan Shah University (USAS)

Bukit Chandan, Bandar DiRaja
Kuala Kangsar 33000, Pera
Tel: +60(5) 773-2323
Fax: +60(5) 773-2333
Website: www.usas.edu.my/index.php/en
Vice-Chancellor: Nordin Kardi

Faculty
Islamic Studies (Islamic Studies); **Management and Information Technology** (Information Technology; Management)

Centre
Languages and Foundation Studies (Arabic; English)
History: Founded 1999 as Kolej Islam Darul Ridzuan (KISDAR). New campus established at Bukit Chandan, Kuala Kangsar the Royal Town of Perak 2006, renamed Kolej Universiti Islam Sultan Azlan Shah (KUISAS) 2013. Acquired current status and title 2016
Main language(s) of instruction: Malay
Accrediting agency: Ministry of Higher Education; Malaysian Qualifications Agency (MQA)

Degrees and diplomas: Bachelor's Degree (Accountancy; Arabic; Business Administration; Computer Science; Development Studies; Islamic Law; Islamic Studies; Management; Marketing; Psychology), Master's Degree (Business Administration; Commercial Law; Development Studies; Information Technology; Islamic Studies; Management), Doctor's Degree (Development Studies; Islamic Law; Islamic Studies; Management; Technology)
Last Update: 08-06-2018

Sunway University

N°5, Jalan Universiti Bandar Sunway
Petaling Jaya 47500, Selangor
Tel: +60(3) 7491-8622
Fax: +60(3) 5635-8630
Website: https://university.sunway.edu.my
Vice-Chancellor: Graeme Wilkinson

School
Arts (Communication Studies; Design; Fine Arts; Performing Arts); **Business** (Accountancy; Business Administration; Finance; Management); **Healthcare and Medical Sciences** (Health Sciences; Medicine); **Hospitality** (Hotel and Restaurant); **Mathematical Sciences** (Mathematics); **Science and Technology** (Biotechnology; Computer Science; Information Sciences; Information Technology; Multimedia)

Centre
American Education (Aeronautical and Aerospace Engineering; Business Administration; Computer Science; Engineering; Natural Sciences; Psychology; Tourism; Welfare and Protective Services); **English Language Studies** (English)
Further information: Also Campuses in Ipoh, Johor Bahru, and Kuala Lumpur
History: Created in 1987 as Sunway College. Became Sunway University College. Acquired current title and status in 2011
Admission requirements: Sijil Tinggi Pelajaran Malaysia or equivalent Secondary School Certificate.
Main language(s) of instruction: English
Accrediting agency: Ministry of Higher Education; Malaysian Qualifications Agency (MQA)
Degrees and diplomas: Bachelor's Degree (Accountancy; Actuarial Science; Architecture; Biology; Biomedicine; Biotechnology; Business Administration; Business and Commerce; Business Computing; Communication Arts; Communication Studies; Computer Engineering; Computer Networks; Computer Science; Cooking and Catering; Economics; Film; Finance; Hotel Management; Information

Technology; International Business; Management; Marketing; Medical Technology; Multimedia; Music; Musical Instruments; Psychology; Software Engineering; Transport Management), Master's Degree (Biological and Life Sciences; Business Administration; Communication Arts; Computer Science; Information Sciences; Media Studies; Psychology), Doctor's Degree (Biology; Business Administration; Computer Science). Some degrees offered jointly with overseas universities

Student Services: Sports Facilities, Library, IT Centre, Residential Facilities

Last Update: 15-06-2018

TATI University College (TATIUC)

Jalan Panchor Telok Kalong
Kemaman 24000, Terengganu
Tel: +60(9) 860-1000
Fax: +60(9) 863-5863
Website: http://www.tatiuc.edu.my
Rector: Mohd Zamri bin Ibrahim

Faculty

Chemical Engineering Technology (Chemical Engineering); **Computer, Media and Technology Management** (Engineering Management; Media Studies); **Electrical and Automation Engineering Technology** (Automation and Control Engineering; Electrical Engineering); **Manufacturing Engineering Technology** (Production Engineering)

History: Founded 1993 as Terengganu Advanced Technical Institute (TATI), acquired current status and title 2007

Main language(s) of instruction: English

Accrediting agency: Ministry of Higher Education; Malaysian Qualifications Agency (MQA)

Degrees and diplomas: Bachelor's Degree (Chemical Engineering; Computer Networks; Computer Science; Electrical Engineering; Electronic Engineering; Industrial Management; Management; Mechanical Engineering; Polymer and Plastics Technology; Production Engineering), Master's Degree (Industrial Engineering; Production Engineering)

Student Services: Library

Last Update: 08-06-2018

Taylor's University

N°1, Jalan Taylor's
Subang Jaya 47500, Selangor
Tel: +60(3) 5629-5000
Fax: +60(3) 5629-5001

Website: https://university.taylors.edu.my/en.html
Vice Chancellor and President: Michael J. Driscoll

School

Architecture, Building and Design (Architecture; Real Estate; Surveying and Mapping); **Bioscience** (Biomedicine; Biotechnology; Food Science; Nutrition); **Business** (Accountancy; Business Administration; Finance; Human Resources; International Business; Management; Marketing); **Communication** (Advertising and Publicity; Communication Studies; Marketing; Mass Communication; Public Relations); **Computing and Information Technology** (Computer Science; Information Technology; Software Engineering); **Design** (Design; Graphic Design; Interior Design; Multimedia); **Education** (Education; Primary Education; Teacher Training); **Engineering** (Chemical Engineering; Electrical and Electronic Engineering; Engineering; Mechanical Engineering); **Hospitality, Tourism and Culinary Arts** (Cooking and Catering; Hotel Management; House Arts and Environment; Tourism); **Law** (Law); **Medicine** (Medicine; Surgery); **Pharmacy** (Pharmacy)

Centre

Continuing Professional Education; **Languages** (English)

History: Created in 1969 as Taylor's College. Became University College in 2006. Acquired current title and status 2010

Admission requirements: Recognised secondary school certificate.

Main language(s) of instruction: English

Accrediting agency: Malaysian Qualifications Agency (MQA); Ministry of Higher Education (MOHE)

Degrees and diplomas: Bachelor's Degree (Accountancy; Actuarial Science; Advertising and Publicity; Architecture; Banking; Biomedicine; Biotechnology; Chemical Engineering; Computer Science; Cooking and Catering; Economics; Electrical and Electronic Engineering; Finance; Food Science; Hotel and Restaurant; International Business; Law; Marketing; Mechanical Engineering; Medicine; Nutrition; Pharmacy; Primary Education; Psychology; Public Relations; Radio and Television Broadcasting; Software Engineering; Surgery; Surveying and Mapping; Tourism), Master's Degree (Architecture; Business Administration; Communication Studies; Engineering; Finance; Higher Education Teacher Training; Hotel and Restaurant; Law; Management; Natural Sciences; Pharmacy; Teacher Training; Tourism), Doctor's Degree (Business Administration; Education; Engineering; Hotel and Restaurant; Natural Sciences; Pharmacy; Tourism). Also joint degree programmes

Student Services: Academic Counselling, Careers Guidance, Sports Facilities, Canteen, Library, IT Centre

Last Update: 15-06-2018

Tenaga National University (UNITEN)

Km7, Jalan Kajang-Puchong
Kajang 43009, Selangor
Tel: +60(3) 8921-2020
Fax: +60(3) 8928-7166
Website: http://www.uniten.edu.my
Vice-Chancellor: Nasharuddin bin Mustapha
Tel: +60(3) 8921-2020, Ext1002

College

Business Administration and Accountancy (Accountancy; Business Administration; Economics; Finance; Human Resources; Management; Marketing); **Computer Science and Information Technology** (Computer Engineering; Computer Graphics; Computer Networks; Computer Science; Information Technology; Multimedia; Software Engineering); **Energy Business and Economics** (Business Administration; Economics); **Engineering** (Civil Engineering; Electrical and Electronic Engineering; Electrical Engineering; Mechanical Engineering; Power Engineering); **Foundation and Diploma Studies** (Accountancy; Arts and Humanities; Business Administration; Communication Studies; Computer Science; Education; Mathematics; Modern Languages; Natural Sciences; Pedagogy; Social Sciences); **Graduate Studies** (Business Administration; Civil Engineering; Electrical Engineering; Engineering Management; Industrial Engineering; Information Technology; Mechanical Engineering; Telecommunications Engineering)

History: Founded 1976 as Institut Latihan Sultan Ahmad Shah (ILSAS). Renamed Institut Kejuruteraan Teknologi Tenaga Nasional (IKATAN) 1994. Acquired present status 1997.

Academic year: July to June (July-November; December-April; April-June)

Admission requirements: Local students: Passed foundation programme/ STPM/ A-level/ Matriculation/ Diploma or equivalent qualification and have been taking the Malaysian University English Test (MUET). International students: Passed 'A-Level' examinations or equivalent with good grades in Mathematics, Physics and Chemistry (depending on programme chosen) ; obtained minimum grade 'C' for English at 'O-level' examination; Applicants with IELTS (5;5-6;0) or TOEFL (550 and above) can be admitted directly in degree programme; otherwise students are required to pursue the Intensive English Programme in UNITEN.

Fees: Bachelor's degree, 32,000-49,680 per programme; Master's degree by research, 1,300-2,600 per semester; Master's degree by coursework and research, 16,000-20,800 per programme; Master's degree by coursework and project, 23,650-30,000 per programme (Malaysian Ringgit)

Main language(s) of instruction: English

Accrediting agency: Ministry of Higher Education; Malaysian Qualifications Agency (MQA); Engineering Accreditation Council (EAC); Board of Engineers Malaysia (BEM); Institute of Engineering Malaysia (IEM)

Degrees and diplomas: Bachelor's Degree (Accountancy; Business Administration; Civil Engineering; Communication Arts; Computer Graphics; Computer Networks; Computer Science; Economics; Electrical and Electronic Engineering; Electrical Engineering; Human Resources; Information Technology; International Business; Marketing; Mechanical Engineering; Media Studies; Multimedia; Power Engineering; Software Engineering), Master's Degree (Accountancy; Business Administration; Civil Engineering; Computer Engineering; Electrical Engineering; Electronic Engineering; Engineering Management; Finance; Industrial Engineering; Industrial Management; Information Technology; Management; Mechanical Engineering; Software Engineering; Telecommunications Engineering), Doctor's Degree (Business Administration; Engineering; Industrial Engineering; Information Technology)

Student Services: Academic Counselling, Careers Guidance, Nursery Care, Cultural Activities, Sports Facilities, Language Laboratory, Health Services, Canteen, Foreign Studies Centre, Library, Residential Facilities

Periodicals: Electronic Journal of Computer Science and Information Technology, Journal of Business and Management, Journal of Energy and Environment

Last Update: 05-06-2018

Tun Abdul Razak University

Capital Square, Block C & D No. 8, Jalan Munshi Abdullah
Kuala Lumpur 50100
Tel: +60(3) 7627-7000
Fax: +60(3) 7627-7070, +60(3) 7627-7177
Website: http://www.unirazak.edu.my
Vice Chancellor (Acting): Samsinar Md. Sidin
Tel: +60(3) 7627-7001

School

Business and Entrepreneurship (*Bank Rakyat*) (Accountancy; Banking; Business Administration; Finance; Insurance; Management; Taxation); **Government** (Economics; Government; Leadership; Political Sciences)

Centre

English Language (English); **Executive Education** (Leadership; Management); **Fondation Studies** (Arts and Humanities; Business Administration; Economics; Mathematics; Social Sciences; Statistics); **Languages and Malaysian Studies** (Communication Studies; English; Malay)

Graduate School

Business Administration (Business Administration)
History: Founded 1997. Acquired present status 2000. First e-learning private university combining face-to-face classes with web-based courseware and online tutorials

Admission requirements: Foundation Programme, SPM/SPMV/'O' Levels with 5 credits including Mathematics or other equivalent qualification; for International students, minimum TOEFL score of 450 or IELTS band of 4. Diploma Programme, A pass in SPM / SPMV / 'O' Level with 3 credits and at least a pass in Mathematics and English Language or other equivalent. Bachelor Degree, A pass STPM with 3 principals and a pass in Mathematics at SPM/SPMV/'O' Level; or 'A' Levels, Matriculation, Foundation, Unified Examination Certificate (UEC) or Pre-university; or Diploma from a Public or Private Higher Education Institution with a minimum standard required by the Malaysian Qualifications Agency (MQA); or Certificate from a Polytechnic under the Ministry of Higher Education, Malaysia. Masters Degree, Bachelor degree (honours) or equivalent; For International Students, minimum TOEFL score of 550 or IELTS band of 6; Doctorate programme, a Masters degree in Management or equivalent.

Fees: Local students: Bachelor degree, 42,000-55,820; Masters Degree, 16,200-60,960; Doctorate degree, 24,240. International Students: Bachelor degree, 46,200-70,080; Masters Degree, 30,000-60,960; Doctorate degree, 48,480 (Malaysian Ringgit)

Main language(s) of instruction: English

Accrediting agency: Ministry of Higher Education; Malaysian Qualifications Agency (MQA)

Degrees and diplomas: Bachelor's Degree (Accountancy; Business Administration; Economics; Education; English; Government; Hotel Management; Information Technology; Insurance; Leadership; Management; Taxation), Master's Degree (Business Administration; Finance; Human Resources; Leadership; Management; Retailing and Wholesaling), Doctor's Degree (Management)

Student Services: Academic Counselling, Careers Guidance, Language Laboratory, Canteen, Foreign Studies Centre, Library

Last Update: 05-06-2018

Tunku Abdul Rahman University (UTAR)

Petaling Jaya Campus N°13, Section 13/6
Petaling Jaya 46200, Selangor
Tel: +60(3) 7958-2628
Fax: +60(3) 7956-1923
Website: http://www.utar.edu.my
President: Chuah Hean Teik

Faculty

Accountancy and Management (Accountancy; Economics; International Business; Management; Real Estate); **Arts and Social Sciences** (Advertising and Publicity; Arts and Humanities; English; Journalism; Psychology; Public Relations; Social Sciences); **Business and Finance** (Business Administration; Finance); **Creative Industries** (Communication Studies; Design; Graphic Design; Journalism; Media Studies; Multimedia; Preschool Education); **Engineering and Green Technology** (Construction Engineering; Engineering; Environmental Engineering; Industrial Engineering; Petroleum and Gas Engineering); **Engineering and Science** (Architecture; Biochemistry; Biomedical Engineering; Biotechnology; Chemical Engineering; Civil Engineering; Computer Networks; Electrical and Electronic Engineering; Electronic Engineering; Materials Engineering; Mathematics and Computer Science; Mechanical Engineering; Physics; Production Engineering; Software Engineering; Surveying and Mapping; Telecommunications Engineering); **Information and Communication Technology** (Actuarial Science; Applied Mathematics; Computer Engineering; Computer Networks; Computer Science); **Medicine and Health Sciences** (Health Sciences; Medicine; Nursing; Physical Therapy; Surgery; Traditional Eastern Medicine); **Science** (Agriculture; Biochemistry; Biotechnology; Chemistry; Food Science; Microbiology; Natural Sciences; Transport Management)

Institute

Chinese Studies (Chinese); **Management and Leadership Development** (Leadership; Management); **Postgraduate Studies and Research** (Accountancy; Business Administration; Chinese; Communication Studies; Computer Science; Engineering; Information Sciences)

Further information: Also campuses in Perak, Kuala Lumpur and Bandar Sungai Long

History: Created in 1964 as Kolej Tunku Abdul Rahman. Acquired current title and status 2002

Academic year: May to April (May-September; October-December; January-April)

Admission requirements: 2 'A' level passes (or equivalent secondary school certificate) in a relevant subject for undergraduate programmes; Honours Bachelor's degree for postgraduate programmes.

Main language(s) of instruction: English

Accrediting agency: Ministry of Higher Education; Malaysian Qualifications Agency (MQA)

Degrees and diplomas: Bachelor's Degree (Accountancy; Actuarial Science; Advertising and Publicity; Agriculture; Applied Mathematics; Architecture; Banking; Biochemistry; Biomedical Engineering; Biomedicine; Biotechnology; Business Administration; Business Computing; Chemical Engineering; Chemistry; Chinese; Civil Engineering; Computer

Engineering; Computer Networks; Computer Science; Construction Engineering; Economics; Educational and Student Counselling; Electrical and Electronic Engineering; Electronic Engineering; English; Environmental Engineering; Finance; Food Science; Foreign Languages Education; Graphic Design; Health Sciences; Industrial Engineering; Information Technology; International Business; International Economics; Journalism; Marketing; Mass Communication; Mathematics; Mathematics and Computer Science; Mechanical Engineering; Media Studies; Medicine; Microbiology; Multimedia; Nursing; Occupational Health; Operations Research; Petroleum and Gas Engineering; Physical Therapy; Physics; Preschool Education; Production Engineering; Psychology; Public Relations; Radio and Television Broadcasting; Real Estate; Retailing and Wholesaling; Software Engineering; Statistics; Surveying and Mapping; Telecommunications Engineering; Traditional Eastern Medicine; Transport Management; Visual Arts), Master's Degree (Accountancy; Architecture; Business Administration; Chinese; Electrical Engineering; Electronic Engineering; Engineering; Environmental Engineering; Finance; Health Sciences; Industrial and Organizational Psychology; Information Technology; Management; Mass Communication; Mathematics; Mechanical Engineering; Medicine; Natural Sciences; Social Sciences), Doctor's Degree (Business Administration; Chinese; Computer Science; Engineering; Finance; Health Sciences; Mass Communication; Medicine; Natural Sciences; Social Sciences; Traditional Eastern Medicine)

Student Services: Sports Facilities, Library, IT Centre

Last Update: 05-06-2018

Tunku Abdul Rahman University College (TAR UC)

Jalan Genting Kelang, Setapak P.O. Box 10979
Kuala Lumpur 50932, Kuala Lumpur
Tel: +60(3) 4145-0123
Fax: +60(3) 4142-3166
Website: http://www.tarc.edu.my
President: Chik Heok Tan
Tel: +60(3) 4145-0200

Faculty

Accountancy, Finance and Business (Accountancy; Business Administration; Finance); **Applied Sciences** (Food Science; Natural Sciences); **Built Environment** (Architecture; Civil Engineering; Real Estate); **Communication and Creative Industries** (Advertising and Publicity; Design; Mass Communication; Public Relations); **Computing and Information Technology** (Computer Science; Information Technology); **Engineering and Technology** (Engineering;

Technology); **Social Science and Humanities** (Arts and Humanities; Social Sciences)

Centre

Business Incubation and Entrepreneurial Ventures; **Continuing and Professional Education**; **Postgraduate Studies and Research** (Business Administration; Natural Sciences); **Pre-University Studies**

Further information: Also Campuses in Penang, Perak, Johor, Pahang and Sabah

History: Founded 1969 as Tunku Abdul Rahman College ("TAR College"), acquired current status and title 2013

Main language(s) of instruction: English

Accrediting agency: Ministry of Higher Education; Malaysian Qualifications Agency (MQA)

Degrees and diplomas: Bachelor's Degree (Accountancy; Advertising and Publicity; Analytical Chemistry; Applied Physics; Architecture; Automation and Control Engineering; Banking; Biological and Life Sciences; Business Administration; Business and Commerce; Business Computing; Chemistry; Civil Engineering; Communication Arts; Communication Studies; Cooking and Catering; Economics; Electrical and Electronic Engineering; Electronic Engineering; English; Fashion Design; Finance; Food Science; Furniture Design; Graphic Design; Hotel and Restaurant; Human Resources; Information Technology; Interior Design; International Business; Journalism; Management; Marketing; Materials Engineering; Mathematics and Computer Science; Mechanical Engineering; Media Studies; Microelectronics; Multimedia; Psychology; Public Relations; Radio and Television Broadcasting; Real Estate; Retailing and Wholesaling; Software Engineering; Sports; Surveying and Mapping; Telecommunications Engineering; Tourism; Transport Management), Master's Degree (Biological and Life Sciences; Business Administration; Finance; Physics). The MBAs are dual degree programmes jointly offered with Edinburgh Napier University, UK

Student Services: Library

Last Update: 15-06-2018

UCSI University (UCSI)

No 1 Jalan Menara Gading, UCSI Heights, Cheras
Kuala Lumpur 56000
Tel: +60(3) 9101-8880
Fax: +60(3) 9102-3606
Website: https://www.ucsiuniversity.edu.my
President and Vice-Chancellor: Khalid Yusoff

Faculty

Applied Sciences (Biotechnology; Food Science; Nutrition); **Business and Information Science** (Accountancy; Business

Administration; Business Computing; Computer Science; Finance; Information Technology; Management; Marketing); **Engineering, Technology and Built Environment** (Architecture; Building Technologies; Chemical Engineering; Civil Engineering; Construction Engineering; Electrical and Electronic Engineering; Interior Design; Mechanical Engineering; Petroleum and Gas Engineering; Surveying and Mapping); **Hospitality and Tourism Management** (Hotel and Restaurant; Hotel Management; Tourism); **Medicine and Health Sciences** (Health Sciences; Medicine; Nursing; Optometry); **Pharmaceutical Sciences** (Pharmacy); **Social Sciences and Liberal Arts** (English; Fashion Design; Mass Communication; Psychology; Social Sciences)

Course/Programme
Pre-U Studies

Institute
Creative Arts and Design (Design; Fine Arts); **Music** (Music)

Centre
Languages (Modern Languages)
Further information: Campuses also in Sarawak and Terengganu
History: Founded 1986 as Canadian Institute of Computer Science. Became Sedaya International College 1990. Acquired present status and title 2003
Main language(s) of instruction: English
Accrediting agency: Malaysian Qualifications Agency (MQA); Ministry of Higher Education (MOHE)
Degrees and diplomas: Bachelor's Degree (Accountancy; Actuarial Science; Advertising and Publicity; Architecture; Biotechnology; Business Administration; Business and Commerce; Business Computing; Chemical Engineering; Civil Engineering; Computer Graphics; Computer Networks; Computer Science; Economics; Education; Electrical and Electronic Engineering; Electronic Engineering; English; Fashion Design; Finance; Food Science; Graphic Design; Health Sciences; Hotel and Restaurant; Industrial Management; Marine Science and Oceanography; Marketing; Mass Communication; Mechanical Engineering; Medicine; Multimedia; Music; Nutrition; Optometry; Petroleum and Gas Engineering; Pharmacy; Psychology; Telecommunications Engineering; Tourism; Transport Management), Master's Degree (Actuarial Science; Applied Chemistry; Architecture; Biotechnology; Business Administration; Design; Engineering; Fine Arts; Food Science; Gerontology; Health Sciences; Industrial Management; Management; Music; Natural Sciences; Nutrition; Pharmacy; Plastic Surgery; Psychology; Transport Management), Doctor's Degree (Architecture; Business Administration; Engineering; Management; Natural Sciences; Pharmacy)

Student Services: Library
Last Update: 08-06-2018

UNITAR International University

3-01A, Level 3, Tierra Crest, Jalan SS6/3, Kelana Jaya
Petaling Jaya 47301, Selangor
Tel: +60(3) 7627-7200
Fax: +60(3) 7627-7447
Website: http://www.unitar.my
Vice-Chancellor (acting): Noor Raihan Ab Hamid
Tel: +60(3) 7627-7292

Faculty
Business Administration and Information Technology (Business Administration; Information Technology); **Early Childhood Studies** (Child Care and Development; Preschool Education); **Education and Social Sciences** (Curriculum; Education; Educational Administration; Educational and Student Counselling; English; Social Sciences); **Hospitality and Tourism Management** (Hotel and Restaurant; Hotel Management; Tourism); **Information Technology** (Information Sciences; Information Technology; Mathematics and Computer Science)

School
Foundation and General Studies (Arts and Humanities; Business Administration; Education; Information Technology; Service Trades)

Graduate School
Graduate Studies (Business Administration; Education; Information Sciences; Mathematics and Computer Science; Social Sciences)
History: Founded 1997 as University of Management and Technology (UMTECH). Acquired current status and name 2012
Academic year: Feb-June; June-Aug; and Sept-Jan
Admission requirements: Secondary school diploma for undergraduate courses; Undergrduate degree for postgraduate courses.
Fees: c. 19,000 to 70,000 per annum (Malaysian Ringgit)
Main language(s) of instruction: English
Accrediting agency: Malaysian Qualifications Agency (MQA); Ministry of Higher Education (MOHE)
Degrees and diplomas: Bachelor's Degree (Accountancy; Business Administration; Communication Studies; Cooking and Catering; Educational and Student Counselling; Finance; Hotel Management; Information Technology; Management; Preschool Education; Tourism), Master's Degree (Business Administration; Educational Administration; Educational and Student Counselling; Foreign Languages Education; Hotel and Restaurant; Information Technology; Leadership;

Preschool Education), Doctor's Degree (Business Administration; Education; Information Technology; Management)
Student Services: Academic Counselling, Social Counselling, Cultural Activities, Language Laboratory, Foreign Studies Centre, Library, IT Centre
Last Update: 06-06-2018

University College Bestari

Putera Jaya Bandar Permaisuri
Setiu 22100, Terengganu
Tel: +60(9) 609-7102
Fax: +60(9) 609-7109/7/6
Website: http://www.ucbestari.edu.my
Vice-Chancellor: Ab Aziz bin Yusof
Tel: +60(9) 609-7102/9

Faculty

Agro Science (Agriculture); **Economics and Management** (Economics; Management); **Information Technology and Computer Science** (Computer Science; Information Technology); **Islamic Studies** (Islamic Studies); **Social Science** (Social Sciences)
History: Founded 1998 as Kolej Teknologi Bestari (KTB), acquired current status and title 2012
Main language(s) of instruction: Malay
Accrediting agency: Ministry of Higher Education; Malaysian Qualifications Agency (MQA)
Degrees and diplomas: Certificate, Bachelor's Degree (Business Administration; Information Technology; Management; Multimedia; Social Sciences), Master's Degree (Business Administration; Psychology)
Last Update: 15-06-2018

University College of Agroscience Malaysia (UCAM)

Lot 2020, Ayer Pa'abas
Alor Gajah 78000, Melaka
Tel: +60(6) 552-9227
Fax: +60(6) 552-9963
Website: http://www.ucam.edu.my
Vice-Chancellor: Faridah Hanam Binti Mohd Rashid
Tel: +60(6) 552-0212

Faculty

Agro Science (Agriculture); **Business Administration** (Business Administration); **Computer Science** (Computer Science); **Social Science** (Social Sciences)

Course/Programme
Malaysian Certificate of Excellence (Agriculture)

History: Founded 1999 as Kolej Risda, acquired status and title 2014
Main language(s) of instruction: Malay
Accrediting agency: Ministry of Higher Education; Malaysian Qualifications Agency (MQA)
Degrees and diplomas: Bachelor's Degree (Accountancy; Agriculture; Business Administration; Landscape Architecture), Master's Degree (Business Administration)
Last Update: 08-06-2018

University College of Islam Melaka (KUIM)

Batu 28, Kuala Sungai Baru
Melaka 78200
Tel: +60(6) 387-8382
Fax: +60(6) 387-8411
Website: https://kuim.edu.my
Vice-Chancellor: Mohd Taib bin Hj. Dora
Tel: +60(6) 387-8409

Faculty

Business Innovation and Accountancy (Accountancy; Business Administration); **Hospitality Management** (Hotel and Restaurant); **Languages □□and Education** (Education; Modern Languages); **Law, Governance and International Relations** (Government; International Relations; Law); **Nursing and Health Sciences** (Health Sciences; Nursing); **Science and Technology** (Natural Sciences; Technology); **Social Sciences** (Social Sciences)

Institute
Postgraduate Studies (Communication Studies; Educational Administration; Islamic Studies; Leadership; Library Science; Management; Psychology)

Academy
Islamic Studies (Islamic Studies)
History: Founded 1996, acquired current status 2009
Main language(s) of instruction: English
Accrediting agency: Ministry of Higher Education; Malaysian Qualifications Agency (MQA)
Degrees and diplomas: Bachelor's Degree (Accountancy; Banking; Business Administration; Development Studies; E-Business/Commerce; Finance; Hotel and Restaurant; Islamic Studies; Management; Marketing; Nursing; Parks and Recreation; Psychology; Tourism), Master's Degree (Communication Studies; Educational Administration; Islamic Studies; Leadership; Library Science; Management; Psychology), Doctor's Degree (Educational Administration; History; Islamic Studies; Leadership)

Student Services: Sports Facilities, Library, Residential Facilities

Academic Staff 2016-2017	MALE	FEMALE	TOTAL
FULL-TIME			c. 350
Student Numbers 2016-2017			
All (Foreign Included)			4634

Last Update: 08-06-2018

University College of Technology Sarawak (UCTS)

Lot 868, Persiaran Brooke
Sibu 96000, Sarawak
Tel: +60(84) 367-300
Fax: +60(84) 367-306
Website: http://www.ucts.edu.my
Vice-Chancellor: Khairuddin bin Ab. Hamid
Tel: +60(84) 367-366

School

Built Environment (Architecture; Surveying and Mapping); **Business and Management** (Business Administration; Management); **Computing** (Computer Engineering; Computer Science); **Engineering and Technology** (Engineering; Technology); **Foundation Studies** (Arts and Humanities; Social Sciences); **Postgraduate Studies** (Business Administration; Engineering; Management)
History: Founded 2013
Main language(s) of instruction: English
Accrediting agency: Ministry of Higher Education; Malaysian Qualifications Agency (MQA)
Degrees and diplomas: Bachelor's Degree (Accountancy; Architecture; Business Administration; Civil Engineering; Computer Networks; Electrical and Electronic Engineering; Electrical Engineering; Food Technology; Marketing; Mechanical Engineering; Software Engineering; Surveying and Mapping; Wood Technology), Master's Degree (Business Administration; Engineering; Management), Doctor's Degree (Business Administration; Engineering)
Student Services: Library, Residential Facilities
Last Update: 08-06-2018

University Malaysia of Computer Science and Engineering (UNIMY)

Menara Z10, Ground Floor & Mezzanine Floor Jalan Alamanda 2, Presint 1
62000 Putrajaya 62000, Wilayah Persekutuan Putrajaya
Tel: +60(3) 8893-4000, +60(3) 8800-5000
Fax: +60(3) 8893-4011/4022, +60(3) 8800-5011
Website: https://www.unimy.edu.my
Acting Vice Chancellor: Ramli Ismail

Course/Programme

Business Administration (Management Information Systems) (Business Administration; Information Technology); **Computer Science** (Computer Science); **Computing Science and Engineering** (Computer Engineering; Computer Science); **Software Engineering** (Software Engineering)
History: Founded 2012
Main language(s) of instruction: Malay
Accrediting agency: Ministry of Higher Education; Malaysian Qualifications Agency (MQA)
Degrees and diplomas: Bachelor's Degree (Business Administration; Computer Engineering; Computer Science; Information Technology; Software Engineering), Master's Degree (Computer Science), Doctor's Degree (Computer Science)
Last Update: 28-05-2018

University of Kuala Lumpur (UNIKL)

1016, Jalan Sultan Ismail
Kuala Lumpur 50250
Tel: +60(3) 2175-4000
Fax: +60(3) 2175-4001
Website: http://www.unikl.edu.my
President and Chief Executive Officer: Mazliham Mohd Su'ud

College

Medicine (*Royal, Perak*) (Anatomy; Biochemistry; Medicine; Pharmacology; Physiology; Public Health); **Preparatory Studies (CPS)** (Business Administration; Engineering; Natural Sciences; Political Sciences; Technology)

School

Business (Accountancy; Business Administration; Finance)

Institute

Aviation Technology (Aeronautical and Aerospace Engineering); **British Malaysian** (*Gombak*) (Electrical Engineering; Electronic Engineering; Telecommunications Engineering); **Chemical and Bioengineering Technology** (*Alor Gajah*) (Bioengineering; Chemical Engineering; Polymer and Plastics Technology); **Industrial Technology** (Industrial Engineering; Safety Engineering); **Information Technology** (*Malaysian*) (Computer Networks; Information Technology; Multimedia); **Malaysia-France** (*Bandar Baru Bangi*) (Automation and Control Engineering; Automotive Engineering; Industrial Engineering; Maintenance Technology; Mechanical Engineering); **Malaysian Spanish** (*Kulim*) (Automation and Control Engineering); **Marine Engineering Technology**

(*Sitiawan*) (Marine Engineering); **Medical Science Technology** (Medical Technology; Medicine); **Postgraduate Studies** (Computer Science; Engineering; Information Technology; Medicine; Pharmacy; Public Health); **Product Design and Manufacturing** (Industrial Design)

History: Founded 2002

Main language(s) of instruction: Malay

Accrediting agency: Malaysian Qualifications Agency (MQA); Ministry of Higher Education (MOHE)

Degrees and diplomas: Bachelor's Degree (Accountancy; Aeronautical and Aerospace Engineering; Air Transport; Automation and Control Engineering; Automotive Engineering; Bioengineering; Biomedicine; Business Administration; Chemical Engineering; Computer Engineering; Computer Graphics; Computer Networks; Design; Electrical Engineering; Electronic Engineering; Environmental Engineering; Finance; Food Technology; Heating and Refrigeration; Industrial Design; Industrial Engineering; Information Technology; International Business; Machine Building; Management; Marketing; Mechanical Engineering; Medical Technology; Metal Techniques; Multimedia; Naval Architecture; Nursing; Pharmacy; Polymer and Plastics Technology; Production Engineering; Public Health; Safety Engineering; Software Engineering; Surgery; Telecommunications Engineering; Transport Management), Master's Degree (Automation and Control Engineering; Business Administration; Chemical Engineering; Computer Science; Electrical and Electronic Engineering; Energy Engineering; Health Sciences; Industrial Engineering; Industrial Management; Information Technology; Management; Mechanical Engineering; Medicine; Pharmacy; Production Engineering; Public Health), Doctor's Degree (Automation and Control Engineering; Chemical Engineering; Electrical and Electronic Engineering; Information Technology; Management; Mechanical Engineering; Medicine; Production Engineering)

Student Services: Sports Facilities, Library, IT Centre, Residential Facilities

Last Update: 31-05-2018

University of Selangor (UNISEL)

Jalan Zirkon A 7/A, Section 7
Shah Alam 40000, Selangor
Tel: +60(3) 5522-3400
Fax: +60(3) 5522-3551
Website: http://www.unisel.edu.my
President and Vice-Chancellor: Mohammad Redzuan Othman
Tel: +60(3) 5522-3405

Faculty

Business and Accountancy (Accountancy; Business Administration; Finance; Industrial Management; Management; Marketing; Sports Management); **Communication, Visual Art and Computing** (*Bestari Jaya Campus*) (Communication Studies; Computer Science; Mass Communication; Media Studies; Visual Arts); **Communication, Visual Art and Computing** (Communication Studies; Computer Science; Media Studies; Visual Arts); **Education and Social Sciences** (*Bestari Jaya Campus*) (Education; Educational Administration; English; Information Technology; Library Science; Management; Natural Sciences; Preschool Education; Primary Education; Social Sciences); **Engineering and Life Sciences** (*Bestari Jaya Campus*) (Biological and Life Sciences; Civil Engineering; Electrical Engineering; Electronic Engineering; Engineering; Mechanical Engineering; Occupational Health); **Engineering and Life Sciences** (Biological and Life Sciences; Civil Engineering; Electrical Engineering; Electronic Engineering; Engineering; Mechanical Engineering; Occupational Health)

Centre

Foundation and General Studies (Information Technology; Management; Natural Sciences); **Graduate Studies** (Biological and Life Sciences; Biotechnology; Business Administration; Computer Science; Education; Engineering; Information Technology; Management; Social Sciences)

Further information: Also a campus in Bestari Jaya

History: Founded 1999 as Industrial University Selangor. Renamed University of Selangor.

Main language(s) of instruction: English

Accrediting agency: Ministry of Higher Education; Malaysian Qualifications Agency (MQA)

Degrees and diplomas: Bachelor's Degree (Accountancy; Biotechnology; Business Administration; Civil Engineering; Computer Engineering; Computer Science; Education; Electrical and Electronic Engineering; Electrical Engineering; Environmental Studies; Finance; Human Resources; Industrial Engineering; Information Technology; Laboratory Techniques; Library Science; Mass Communication; Mechanical Engineering; Occupational Health; Visual Arts), Master's Degree (Biological and Life Sciences; Biotechnology; Business Administration; Computer Science; Curriculum; Education; Educational Administration; Engineering; Information Technology; Management; Software Engineering; Sports Management), Doctor's Degree (Biotechnology; Computer Science; Education; Engineering; Management; Natural Sciences; Social Sciences)

Student Services: Academic Counselling, Sports Facilities, Canteen, Library, IT Centre, Residential Facilities

Academic Staff 2017-2018	MALE	FEMALE	TOTAL
FULL-TIME			453
PART-TIME			16
STAFF WITH DOCTORATE			

(continued)

Academic Staff 2017-2018	MALE	FEMALE	TOTAL
FULL-TIME			79
Student Numbers 2017-2018			
All (Foreign Included)			5312

Last Update: 04-06-2018

Veritas University College

Aras 6, Menara NB 1 Jalan Bagan Luar
Butterworth 12000, Pulau Pinang
Tel: +60(3) 7960-0063
Fax: +60(3) 7931-8227
Website: http://www.veritas.edu.my

Campus

Penang Campus (Business Administration); **Petaling Jaya Campus** (Business Administration; Communication Studies; Education; Hotel Management; Natural Sciences; Preschool Education; Psychology)
History: Founded 2013, formerly known as Vinayaka Mission International University College (VMIUC)
Main language(s) of instruction: English
Accrediting agency: Ministry of Higher Education; Malaysian Qualifications Agency (MQA)
Degrees and diplomas: Bachelor's Degree (Business Administration; Communication Studies; Preschool Education; Psychology), Master's Degree (Business Administration; Education), Doctor's Degree (Business Administration). Also Executive Diploma
Last Update: 08-06-2018

Wawasan Open University (WOU)

54, Jalan Sultan Ahmad Shah
Georgetown 10050, Pulau Pinang
Tel: +60(4) 2180-333
Fax: +60(4) 226-9323
Website: http://www.wou.edu.my
Vice-Chancellor: Zoraini Wati Abas
Tel: +60(4) 229-3268

School

Business and Administration (Accountancy; Administration; Business Administration; Marketing; Store Management); **Education, Languages and Communication** (Communication Studies; Education; English; Modern Languages; Philosophy; Primary Education); **Humanities and Social Sciences** (Arts and Humanities; Social Sciences); **Science and Technology** (Computer Engineering; Computer Networks; Electronic Engineering; Information Technology; Telecommunications Engineering)

Centre

Graduate Studies (Arts and Humanities; Business Administration; Education; Philosophy); **Professional Development and Continuing Education**

Research Division
Institute for Research and Innovation
History: Founded 2006. Malaysia's first private not-for-profit university
Admission requirements: Undergraduate programmes: Regular entry, Minimum of 2 principals in Sijil Tinggi Pelajaran Malaysia (STPM)/HSC/A- levels or equivalent qualifications. For open entry, minimum age 21, minimum of 1 principal in STPM/HSC/A-levels or equivalent qualifications or PMR/SPM/MCE/UEC or equivalent qualifications with assessment of prior learning and work experience. For postgraduate programmes, Bachelor's degree with or without honours, with 2 years working experience at supervisory/managerial level; Minimum of STPM or equivalent qualifications and minimum of 2 years working experience at supervisory/managerial level and Commonwealth Management Aptitude Test (CEMAT)
Fees: Bachelor's degree, 110.00 - 150.00 per credit unit (minimum of 120 credit units). Master's degree, 300.00 - 600.00 per credit unit (minimum of 48 credit units) (Malaysian Ringgit)
Main language(s) of instruction: English
Accrediting agency: Ministry of Higher Education; Malaysian Qualifications Agency (MQA)
Degrees and diplomas: Graduate Certificate, Graduate Diploma, Bachelor's Degree (Accountancy; Administration; Arts and Humanities; Banking; Business Administration; Business Computing; Computer Engineering; Computer Networks; Computer Science; Construction Engineering; Electronic Engineering; English; Finance; Human Resources; Information Technology; Management; Marketing; Mechanical Engineering; Multimedia; Primary Education; Psychology; Retailing and Wholesaling; Sales Techniques; Small Business; Software Engineering; Telecommunications Engineering; Transport Management), Master's Degree (Arts and Humanities; Business Administration; Computer Science; Education; Industrial Management; Management; Philosophy; Psychology; Public Administration; Social Sciences; Technology), Doctor's Degree (Accountancy; Anthropology; Artificial Intelligence; Computer Engineering; Computer Science; Consumer Studies; Curriculum; Data Processing; Education; Educational Administration; Educational and Student Counselling; Educational Research; Educational Sciences; Educational Technology; Educational Testing and Evaluation; Ethnology;

Higher Education; Human Rights; Humanities and Social Science Education; Industrial Management; Information Technology; Management; Marketing; Mass Communication; Mathematics Education; Mechanical Engineering; Media Studies; Nanotechnology; Native Language Education; Optics; Political Sciences; Production Engineering; Small Business; Sociology; Software Engineering; Southeast Asian Studies; Surveying and Mapping; Taxation; Teacher Training; Women's Studies). Also Commonwealth Executive MBA

Student Services: Academic Counselling, Cultural Activities, Facilities for disabled people, Canteen, Library, Residential Facilities

Publishing house: In house publishing Department

Last Update: 15-06-2018

Maldives

STRUCTURE OF HIGHER EDUCATION SYSTEM

Description

Higher education is provided by both public and private institutions, which offer a number of certificates, diplomas and degrees as laid out in the latest Maldives National Qualifications Framework (MNQF), effective from 2017.

Stages of studies

University level first stage

Undergraduate level
The first stage of university-level studies includes the Associate degree, after two years' study, Bachelor's degree, awarded after three years' study, and the Bachelor's (Honours) degree, which may be awarded after a further year's study following the Bachelor's degree

University level second stage

Postgraduate level
After being awarded a Bachelor's degree, students may go on to study for a postgraduate certificate or postgraduate diploma, and the Master's degree

University level third stage

Doctoral studies
The final stage of university is the doctoral degree, awarded after at least three years' study and independant research, adding a substantial and original contribution to knowledge

ADMISSION TO HIGHER EDUCATION

Admission to university-level studies

Name of Secondary school credential required: GCE A level

RECOGNITION OF STUDIES

Quality assurance system

MQA provides a service for checking the recognition status of academic programs and institutes for individuals who have overseas diplomas

Bodies dealing with recognition

Maldives Qualifications Authority
2nd Floor, H. Velaanaage, Ameer Ahmed Magu
Malé 20027
Tel: +960 334-4077
Fax: +960 334-4079
Website: http://www.mqa.gov.mv

NATIONAL BODIES

Ministry of Education

Minister of Education: Aishath Shiham
Malé
Website: https://www.moe.gov.mv

Department of Higher Education

Velaanaage, 2nd Floor, Ameer Ahmed Magu
Malé
Tel: +960 334 1461, +960 3341307
Fax: +960 334 1385
Website: http://www.dhe.gov.mv

Maldives Qualifications Authority

Chief Executive Officer: Mohamed Waheed Hussain
2nd Floor, H. Velaanaage, Ameer Ahmed Magu
Malé 20027
Tel: +960 334-4077

© International Association of Universities 2019
International Handbook of Universities 2019,
https://doi.org/10.1057/978-3-319-76971-4_118

Fax: +960 334-4079

Website: http://www.mqa.gov.mv

Role of national body: Created as Maldives Accreditation Board (MAB) in 2000 and renamed as Maldives Qualifications Authority (MQA) in 2010 to ensure the quality of post-secondary eduction in the Maldives

Data for academic year: 2017–2018

Source: IAU from desk research, UNESCO Institute for Statistics, and the Education Policy and Data Centre, 2017

Public Institutions

Islamic University of Maldives

King Fahd Building Violet Magu
Malé 20037
Tel: +960 3322 718
Website: https://www.ium.edu.mv
Chancellor and Acting Vice-Chancellor: Mohamed Shaheem Ali Saeed

College

Arabic (Arabic); **Education** (Foreign Languages Education; Koran; Preschool Education; Primary Education; Religious Education); **Islamic Revealed Knowledge and Human Sciences** (History; Islamic Studies; Journalism); **Shariah and Law** (Comparative Law; Islamic Law)
History: Created 2004 as the College of Islamic Studies. Acquired current title and status in 2015.
Accrediting agency: Maldives Qualification Authority
Degrees and diplomas: Bachelor's degree (History; Islamic Law; Islamic Studies; Koran; Preschool Education; Primary Education), Bachelor's Honours degree (Foreign Languages Education; Islamic Law; Islamic Studies; Koran; Religious Education), Master's degree (Comparative Law; Educational Administration; Foreign Languages Education; Islamic Law; Islamic Studies; Journalism; Koran), PhD (Islamic Law)
Last Update: 05-06-2018

The Maldives National University (MNU)

Rahdhebai Higun, Machangolhi
Male' 20373
Tel: +960 3345 101
Website: http://mnu.edu.mv
Vice-Chancellor: Ali Fawaz Shareef

Faculty

Arts (English; Journalism; Native Language; Political Sciences; Psychology; Social Policy); **Education** (Education; Educational Administration; Educational Testing and Evaluation; Environmental Management; Foreign Languages Education; Mathematics Education; Native Language Education; Physical Education; Preschool Education; Primary Education; Secondary Education; Special Education; Teacher Training); **Engineering Technology** (Architecture; Civil Engineering); **Health Sciences** (Health Administration; Laboratory Techniques; Nursing; Public Health; Social Work); **Hospitality and Tourism Studies** (Cooking and Catering; Hotel and Restaurant; Hotel Management; Tourism); **Islamic Studies** (Islamic Studies; Islamic Theology; Religious Education); **Science** (Water Science); **Shari'ah and Law** (Islamic Law; Law)

School

Business (*MNU Business School*) (Accountancy; Business Administration; Business and Commerce; Human Resources; Information Technology; Marketing)

Centre

Centre for Open Learning (Distance Education); **Maritimes Studies** (Marine Engineering; Marine Transport; Primary Education)
History: Created 1973 as the Allied Health Services Training Centre. Became the Maldives College of Higher Education in 1998 and acquired current title and status 2011.
Main language(s) of instruction: Dhivehi
Accrediting agency: Maldives Qualification Authority
Degrees and diplomas: Associate Degree (Primary Education), Bachelor's degree (Accountancy; Architecture; Business and Commerce; English; Environmental Management; Foreign Languages Education; Health Administration; Hotel and Restaurant; Hotel Management; Human Resources; Information Technology; Islamic Law; Islamic Studies; Journalism; Laboratory Techniques; Mathematics Education; Native Language; Native Language Education; Nursing; Physical Education; Political Sciences; Primary Education; Psychology; Secondary Education; Social Work; Special Education; Teacher Training; Tourism), Bachelor's Honours degree (Civil Engineering; Education; Foreign Languages Education; Islamic Law; Islamic Theology; Law; Native Language Education; Preschool Education; Religious Education; Special Education), Graduate Diploma / Post Graduate Diploma (Business Administration; Distance Education; Education; Islamic Law; Law; Public Health), Master's degree (Business Administration; Education; Educational Administration;

Educational Testing and Evaluation; Islamic Law; Native Language; Nursing; Public Health; Social Policy)
Last Update: 05-06-2018

Private Institutions

Avid College

G.Jawaahiru Asseyri, Ameeneemagu
Malé
Tel: +960 3006 768
Fax: +960 3006 768
Website: http://www.avidcollege.edu.mv

Faculty
Business Management (Business Administration; Human Resources; Management); **Education Management** (Educational Administration; Preschool Education; Primary Education; Secondary Education); **Human Development** (Occupational Health; Psychology); **Information Technology** (Information Technology)
History: Created 2005.
Accrediting agency: Maldives Qualification Authority
Degrees and diplomas: Associate Degree (Business Administration; Human Resources; Information Technology; Management; Preschool Education; Primary Education; Psychology), Bachelor's degree (Educational Administration; Human Resources; Information Technology; Management; Occupational Health; Preschool Education; Primary Education), Graduate Diploma / Post Graduate Diploma (Management), Master's degree (Educational Administration; Human Resources; Management; Primary Education; Secondary Education)
Last Update: 05-06-2018

Cyryx College

Bodurasgefaanu Magu
Malé
Tel: +960 3314 620
Fax: +960 3316 516
Website: http://cyryxcollege.edu.mv

School
Business (Business Administration; Finance; Human Resources; Marketing; Public Administration); **Humanities and Education** (Education); **Information Technology** (Computer Networks; Information Technology; Software

Engineering); **Multimedia Arts and Design** (Computer Graphics; Multimedia)
History: Created 1993. Acquired current status 2009.
Accrediting agency: Maldives Qualification Authority
Degrees and diplomas: Associate Degree (Business and Commerce; Information Technology), Bachelor's degree (Finance; Human Resources; Information Technology; Marketing), Bachelor's Honours degree (Human Resources; Information Technology), Master's degree (Business Administration; Public Administration)
Last Update: 05-06-2018

Maldives Business School

Ma. Mary, Nikagas Magu
Malé, 20175
Tel: +960 3300 064
Website: https://www.businessschool.mv

Course/Programme
Business Administration (Accountancy; Business Administration; Human Resources; Management; Marketing)
Accrediting agency: Maldives Qualification Authority
Degrees and diplomas: Bachelor's degree (Accountancy; Human Resources; Management; Marketing), Graduate Diploma / Post Graduate Diploma (Management), Master's degree (Business Administration)
Last Update: 05-06-2018

Mandhu College

G. Pentagreen Majeedhee Magu
Malé 20138
Tel: +960 3330 055
Website: http://www.mandhucollege.edu.mv
Chairman of the Council: Ibrahim Ismail

Course/Programme
Business Administration (Business Administration; Business and Commerce); **Education** (Education; Native Language Education; Primary Education; Secondary Education); **Information Technology** (Information Technology); **Law** (Law)
History: Created 1998.
Accrediting agency: Maldives Qualification Authority
Degrees and diplomas: Associate Degree (Business Administration; Information Technology; Primary Education), Bachelor's degree (Business and Commerce; Education; Information Technology; Law; Native Language Education;

Primary Education; Secondary Education), Bachelor's Honours degree (Education), Graduate Diploma / Post Graduate Diploma (Business Administration; Education), Master's degree (Business Administration; Education)
Last Update: 06-06-2018

Mianz International College

Sakeena Manzil, 3rd Floor, Meduziyaraih Magu
Malé
Tel: +960 3341 545
Website: https://micollege.edu.mv
Acting Rector: Lamya Abdul Hadhee

Faculty

Business, Management and Hospitality (Accountancy; Business Administration; Hotel and Restaurant; Human Resources); **Languagen, Education and Arts** (Education; Preschool Education; Primary Education); **Science and Information Technology** (Multimedia; Software Engineering)
History: Created 2006 as the International Institute for Professional Development (IIPD). Acquired current title and status 2014.
Accrediting agency: Maldives Qualifications Authority
Degrees and diplomas: Bachelor's degree (Accountancy; Business Administration; Human Resources; Multimedia; Preschool Education; Primary Education; Software Engineering), Bachelor's Honours degree (Preschool Education), Graduate Diploma / Post Graduate Diploma (Education), Master's degree (Education)
Last Update: 06-06-2018

☒⊕ Villa College

VC QI Campus, RahDhebai Hingun
Malé 20373
Tel: +960 330 3200
Fax: +960 330 3299
Website: http://villacollege.edu.mv
Rector: Ahmed Anwar

Faculty

Business Management (Accountancy; Business Administration; Business and Commerce; Finance; Human Resources; Management; Marketing); **Education** (Education; Teacher Training); **Information and Communications Technology** (Computer Science; Information Technology); **Marine Studies** (Marine Science and Oceanography); **Shariah and Law** (Islamic Law; Law)

History: Created 2007
Accrediting agency: Maldives Qualification Authority
Degrees and diplomas: Bachelor's degree (Foreign Languages Education; Human Resources; Islamic Law; Mathematics Education; Native Language; Preschool Education; Primary Education; Religious Education), Bachelor's Honours degree (Accountancy; Business and Commerce; Computer Science; Finance; Human Resources; Islamic Law; Law; Management; Marketing; Preschool Education; Primary Education), Graduate Diploma / Post Graduate Diploma (Teacher Training), Master's degree (Accountancy; Business Administration; Education; Information Technology; Islamic Law; Public Health)
Last Update: 05-06-2018

Zikura International College

Ghazee Magu
Fuvahmulah, South Province
Tel: +960 6862 562
Website: http://zikura.com

Faculty

Arts and Humanities (Psychology); **Business** (Accountancy; Business Administration; Business and Commerce; Human Resources; Management; Tourism); **Education** (Education; Educational Administration; Primary Education)
Accrediting agency: Maldives Qualifications Authority
Degrees and diplomas: Associate Degree (Human Resources; Management; Primary Education), Bachelor's degree (Human Resources; Management; Primary Education; Psychology), Graduate Diploma / Post Graduate Diploma (Business Administration; Education; Educational Administration; Management), Master's degree (Business Administration; Education)
Last Update: 06-06-2018

Mali

STRUCTURE OF HIGHER EDUCATION SYSTEM

Description

Higher education is provided by public universities and private higher education institutions. The new three-tier LMD system was acted in 2008 and has now become generalised throughout the higher education system.

Stages of studies

University level first stage

Licence
First stage of university studies lasts three years, or six semesters, and students are awarded the Licence under the recently-established LMD system.

University level second stage

Master
The Master is awarded two years, or four semesters, after the Licence.

University level third stage

Doctorat
A Doctorat is offered after a further three years and a thesis, following the Master.

ADMISSION TO HIGHER EDUCATION

Admission to university-level studies

Name of Secondary school credential required: Baccalauréat
Name of Secondary school credential required: Baccalauréat technique

NATIONAL BODIES

Ministère de l'Enseignement supérieur et de la Recherche scientifique

Minister: Assétou Founè Samaké-Migan
BP E 5466
Bamako
Tel: +223(20) 01 59 00
Website: http://enseignementsup.gouv.ml
Role of national body: To manage and administer higher education.

Data for academic year: 2016–2017
Source: IAU from the MESRS and government website, 2017.

Public Institutions

Higher Institute of Training and Applied Research (ISFRA)

BP E 475
Bamako
Tel: +223-20-21-04-66
Gaoussou Kanouté

Course/Programme
Teacher Training (Higher Education; Teacher Training)
Degrees and diplomas: Diplôme d'Etude supérieures spécialisées, Diplôme d'Etudes approfondies, Doctorat
Last Update: 18-10-2017

National School of Engineering (ENI-ABT)

410 avenue Van Vollenhoven BP 242
Bamako

© International Association of Universities 2019
International Handbook of Universities 2019,
https://doi.org/10.1057/978-3-319-76971-4_119

Tel: +223(20) 22 27 36
Fax: +223(20) 21 50 38
Website: https://www.eni-abt.ml
Directeur général: Mamadou Sanata Diarra

Course/Programme
Civil Engineering (Building Technologies; Civil Engineering; Construction Engineering; Hydraulic Engineering); **Geology** (Geology); **Industrial Engineering** (Electrical Engineering; Energy Engineering; Industrial Engineering; Mechanical Engineering); **Surveying and Mapping** (Surveying and Mapping)
Accrediting agency: Ministry of Higher Education and Scientific Research
Degrees and diplomas: Diplôme d'Etudes universitaires générales, Licence, Diplôme d'Ingénieur. Also Master
Last Update: 12-10-2017

Teacher Training School (ENS)

Rue du 22 octobre 1946 BP 241
Bamako
Tel: +223(20) 22-21-89
Fax: +223(20) 23-04-61
Directeur général: Ibrahima Camara

Course/Programme
Teacher Training (Teacher Training)
Admission requirements: Licence
Accrediting agency: Ministry of Higher Education and Scientific Research
Last Update: 12-10-2017

Technical and Professional Teachers Training School (ENETP)

Rue 311, Porte 445/449 Hamdallaye ACI 2000
Bamako
Tel: +223(20) 22 10 45
Website: http://enetp.edu.ml
Directeur Général: Famory Dembele

Department/Division
Civil Engineering (Civil Engineering); **Electrotechnical Engineering** (Electrical and Electronic Engineering)
Accrediting agency: Ministry of Higher Education and Scientific Research
Degrees and diplomas: Master (LMD) (Civil Engineering; Electrical and Electronic Engineering)
Last Update: 12-10-2017

University of Humanities and Social Sciences of Bamako (ULSHB)

Baco Djicoroni ACI, Rue 627 Porte 83, BP E 2528
Bamako
Tel: +223(20) 22-19-33
Fax: +223(20) 28-02-71
Website: http://www.ulshb.edu.ml
Recteur: Macki Samaké

Faculty
Letters, Languages, and Linguistics (*FLLSL*) (Arts and Humanities; English; Linguistics; Modern Languages); **Social Sciences and Education** (*FSHSE*) (Anthropology; Education; Social Sciences)

Institute
Technology (*IUT*) (Communication Studies; Library Science)
History: Founded 1993.
Main language(s) of instruction: French
Accrediting agency: Ministry of Higher Education and Scientific Research
Last Update: 12-10-2017

University of Law and Political Sciences of Bamako (USJPB)

BP E2528 Campus universitaire de Badalabougou
Bamako
Tel: +223(20) 22-19-33
Fax: +223(20) 22-92-52
Recteur: Abdoulaye Diarra

Faculty
Political and Administrative Sciences (Administration; Political Sciences); **Private Law** (Private Law); **Public Law** (Public Law)
Accrediting agency: Ministry of Higher Education and Scientific Research
Last Update: 12-10-2017

University of Segou

Ségou
Recteur: Abdoulayé Traoré

Faculty

Agronomy and Veterinary Science (Agronomy; Animal Husbandry; Environmental Studies; Veterinary Science); **Engineering** (Civil Engineering; Computer Engineering; Earth Sciences; Electrical Engineering; Energy Engineering; Engineering; Mechanical Engineering; Meteorology); **Health Sciences** (Dentistry; Medicine; Pharmacy; Stomatology); **Social Sciences** (Geography; History; Modern Languages; Public Law; Social Sciences)

Institute

Professional Studies (Accountancy; Crafts and Trades; Engineering; Finance; Hotel Management; Modern Languages; Secretarial Studies; Small Business; Technology; Tourism)
History: Founded 2012.
Main language(s) of instruction: French
Accrediting agency: Ministry of Higher Education and Scientific Research
Degrees and diplomas: Licence, Maîtrise
Last Update: 12-10-2017

University of Social Sciences and Management of Bamako (USSGB)

BP E 2575
Bamako
Tel: +223(20) 22-52-57
Fax: +223(20) 22-19-32
Recteur: Samba Diallo

Faculty

Economics (Economics); **Geography** (Geography); **History** (History); **Management** (Management)

Institute

Territorial Development Studies
History: Established in 2011 after University of Bamako split-off
Accrediting agency: Ministry of Higher Education and Scientific Research
Last Update: 12-10-2017

University of the Sciences, Techniques and Technologies of Bamako (USTTB)

BP E 2528
Bamako
Tel: +223(20) 22-19-33
Fax: +223(20) 222-19-32

Website: http://www.usttb.edu.ml
Recteur: Adama Diaman Keita

Faculty

Medicine and Stomatology (Medicine; Stomatology); **Pharmacy** (Pharmacy); **Science and Technology** (*FAST*) (Applied Mathematics; Biochemistry; Biology; Chemistry; Computer Science; Geology; Mathematics; Microbiology; Natural Sciences; Physics)

Institute

Applied Sciences (Applied Chemistry; Bioengineering; Computer Engineering; Electrical Engineering)
History: Founded 1993 as Université du Mali. Renamed Université de Bamako 2002.
Academic year: October to July
Admission requirements: Secondary school certificate (Baccalauréat) or equivalent
Fees: (CFA Francs): 5000-150,000 per annum; foreign students, 250,000-300,000
Main language(s) of instruction: French
Accrediting agency: Ministry of Higher Education and Scientific Research
Degrees and diplomas: Diplôme de Technicien supérieur, Diplôme d'Etudes universitaires générales, Licence, Diplôme d'Ingénieur, Diplôme de Docteur (Medicine; Pharmacy), Maîtrise, Diplôme d'Etudes approfondies, Master (LMD) (Applied Mathematics; Biochemistry; Chemistry; Information Technology; Mathematics; Microbiology; Physics), Doctorat
Last Update: 12-10-2017

Private Institutions

African Institute of Management (IAM)

BP 3737 Hamadallaye ACI 2000, rue 396, Porte 92
Bamako
Tel: +223(20) 29 29 69
Directeur Général: Mbagnick Guissé

Course/Programme

Auditing and Management Control (Accountancy)
History: Branch of AIM Group
Accrediting agency: Ministry of Higher Education and Scientific Research
Degrees and diplomas: Master (LMD) (Accountancy)
Last Update: 12-10-2017

ESC Mali School Of Management

BP 2599 Kalaban-Coura ACI rue 268 - Porte 276
Bamako
Tel: +223(73) 29 02 00
Website: http://esc-mali.com
Directrice Générale: Mariam Diallo Jacquin

Department/Division

Human and Society Sciences; **Languages, Literature and Fine Arts**; **Legal, Political and Administration Sciences**; **Science and Technology**
Accrediting agency: Ministry of Higher Education and Scientific Research
Degrees and diplomas: Master (LMD) (Business Administration; Communication Arts; Finance; Human Resources; Management; Marketing)
Last Update: 12-10-2017

Gemini International Management Group (GGMI)

BP E 2341 Baco-djicoroni Golf ACI Adeken Rue 882, Port N°7
Bamako
Tel: +223 78 24 37 66; +223 66 03 69 84
Website: http://www.universitegeminimanagement.sitew.com
Président: Ahmed Touré

Course/Programme

Business Administration (Business Administration); **Computer System Management and Telecommunication Networks** (Computer Engineering; Information Technology); **Food Industry Management** (Agriculture; Business Administration); **Hospitality Management** (Hotel Management; Tourism); **Logistics and Transports** (Transport Management); **Management Science** (Business Administration); **Mining and Petroleum Industry Management** (Mining Engineering; Petroleum and Gas Engineering); **Show Business and Broadcast Media Management** (Mass Communication); **Solar Energy and Sustainable Development** (Energy Engineering; Environmental Management)
Accrediting agency: Ministry of Higher Education and Scientific Research
Degrees and diplomas: Master (LMD) (Agriculture; Business Administration; Computer Engineering; Energy Engineering; Environmental Management; Hotel Management; Information Technology; Mass Communication; Mining Engineering; Petroleum and Gas Engineering; Tourism; Transport Management), Doctorat (LMD) (Business Administration)
Last Update: 12-10-2017

Higher Institute of Applied Technologies

BP E 3123 ACI 2000 Hamdallaye 1
Bamako
Tel: +223(20) 29 01 54
Directeur Général: Daouda Diakité

Area

Technical Fields (Computer Engineering; Electrical and Electronic Engineering; Energy Engineering; Software Engineering); **Tertiary Sector** (Accountancy; Banking; Business Administration; Finance; Human Resources; Management; Marketing; Public Relations)
Accrediting agency: Ministry of Higher Education and Scientific Research
Degrees and diplomas: Master (LMD) (Accountancy; Advertising and Publicity; Banking; Business Administration; Computer Engineering; Electrical and Electronic Engineering; Energy Engineering; Finance; Human Resources; Management; Marketing; Public Relations; Software Engineering)
Last Update: 12-10-2017

Institute of Economics, Accountancy and Commerce (INTEC-SUP)

BP E 5671 Hamdallaye ACI 2000
Bamako
Tel: +223(20) 79 20 30; +223(20) 44 27 46 34
Website: http://www.intec-sup.com
Directeur Général: Boubacar Kanté

Department/Division

Business Administration (Business Administration); **Legal and Politcal Sciences** (International Relations; Law; Political Sciences)
Accrediting agency: Ministry of Higher Education and Scientific Research
Degrees and diplomas: Master (LMD) (Human Resources; Management)
Last Update: 12-10-2017

Institute of Political Science, International Relations and Communication (ISPRIC)

BP 763
Bamako
Tel: +223(20) 23 44 43
Website: http://www.ispric.com

Directeur général: Mohamed Gakou
Tel: +223 674-05-74

Department/Division

Business Administration (Accountancy; Economics; Finance; Human Resources; Management; Marketing); **Communication** (Communication Studies; Journalism; Marketing); **Law** (Criminology; International Relations; Law; Political Sciences; Private Law; Public Law)
History: Founded 1999.
Admission requirements: Secondary school certificate (baccalauréat) or Brevet de Technicien
Fees: (CFA Francs): 500,000-700,000
Main language(s) of instruction: French
Accrediting agency: Ministry of Higher Education and Scientific Research
Degrees and diplomas: Diplôme d'Etudes universitaires générales (Communication Studies; Economics; International Relations; Journalism; Law), Licence, Maîtrise, Master (LMD) (Communication Studies; Journalism). Also Master 2 in cooperation with l'Université Cheick Anta Diop (Senegal)
Last Update: 12-10-2017

International Institute of Management of Bamako (I.I.M.-BKO)

03 BP 121
Bamako 03
Tel: +223 279 73 23
Website: http://www.groupbk.org
President: Bassabi Kagbara

Course/Programme

Audit and Business Finance (Business and Commerce; Finance); **Business Law and Management** (Law; Management); **Business Management** (Business and Commerce; Management); **Communication in Politics** (Communication Studies; Political Sciences); **Human Resources Management** (Human Resources); **Marketing and Communication** (Communication Studies; Marketing); **Project Management** (Management)
History: Founded 2008.
Main language(s) of instruction: French
Accrediting agency: Ministry of Higher Education and Scientific Research
Degrees and diplomas: Diplôme de Technicien supérieur, Licence, Maîtrise, Master (LMD) (Finance)
Last Update: 12-10-2017

Private University Ahmed Baba

Sotuba ACI
Bamako
Tel: +223(20) 79 59 52
Website: http://www.universiteahmedbaba.com
Recteur: Famagan-Oulé Konaté

School

Journalism and Communication (Communication Arts; Journalism; Mass Communication; Radio and Television Broadcasting); **Mining and Petroleum** (Environmental Studies; Geology; Geophysics; Industrial and Production Economics; Mining Engineering; Petroleum and Gas Engineering; Petrology); **Polytechnic** (Civil Engineering; Computer Science; Electrical and Electronic Engineering; Environmental Engineering; Industrial Engineering; Mechanical Engineering; Sanitary Engineering; Telecommunications Engineering; Water Science)

Institute

Economics and Business Sciences (Accountancy; Economics; Finance; Human Resources; Management; Marketing; Transport Economics; Transport Management); **Legal and Political Sciences** (Commercial Law; Human Rights; International Relations; Political Sciences; Private Law; Public Law)
Accrediting agency: Ministry of Higher Education and Scientific Research
Degrees and diplomas: Master (LMD) (Accountancy; Civil Engineering; Commercial Law; Communication Arts; Computer Science; Economics; Electrical and Electronic Engineering; Environmental Engineering; Environmental Studies; Finance; Geology; Geophysics; Human Resources; Human Rights; Industrial and Production Economics; Industrial Engineering; International Relations; Journalism; Management; Marketing; Mass Communication; Mechanical Engineering; Mining Engineering; Petroleum and Gas Engineering; Petrology; Political Sciences; Private Law; Public Law; Radio and Television Broadcasting; Sanitary Engineering; Telecommunications Engineering; Transport Economics; Transport Management; Water Science)
Last Update: 12-10-2017

School of Advanced Technological and Commercial Studies (HETEC)

Bamako

Course/Programme

Accounting and Finance (Accountancy; Finance); **Communication and Human Resources Management**

(Communication Arts; Human Resources); **Information System Network and Telecommunication** (Computer Networks; Information Technology); **Marketing and Sales** (Marketing)

Further information: Also Burkina Faso (Bouaké, Ouagadougou) and Ivory Coast (Abidjan)

Accrediting agency: Ministry of Higher Education and Scientific Research

Degrees and diplomas: Master (LMD) (Accountancy; Communication Arts; Computer Networks; Finance; Human Resources; Information Technology; Marketing)

Last Update: 12-10-2017

School of Engineering, Urban Planning and Architecture (ESIAU)

Rue 466 Porte 28 Badialan I
Bamako
Tel: +223(20) 22 74 05
Website: http://esiau-mali.com
Directeur: Abdoulaye Deyoko

Department/Division
Architecture (Architecture); **Civil Engineering** (Civil Engineering); **Urban Planning** (Regional Planning; Rural Planning; Town Planning)

Accrediting agency: Ministry of Higher Education and Scientific Research

Degrees and diplomas: Master (LMD) (Architecture; Civil Engineering; Regional Planning; Rural Planning; Town Planning)

Last Update: 12-10-2017

Schoof of Management (ESG)

BP E 3529 Immeuble EX-Cinéma ABC - Badalian II Rue Soundata Keita
Bamako
Tel: +223(20) 29 68 32

Course/Programme
Accountancy, Management Control, Audit (Accountancy)
Accrediting agency: Ministry of Higher Education and Scientific Research

Degrees and diplomas: Master (LMD) (Accountancy)
Last Update: 12-10-2017

School of Management, Computer Science and Accountancy (ESGIC)

BP E 4895 Badalabougou
Bamako
Tel: +223(20) 23 01 37

Course/Programme
Finance (Finance)
Accrediting agency: Ministry of Higher Education and Scientific Research

Degrees and diplomas: Master (LMD) (Finance)
Last Update: 12-10-2017

Sup' Management Mali

Quartier Hippodrome Rue 214 Porte 297 BP E 5533
Bamako
Tel: +223(20) 21-34-04
Website: https://www.supmanagement.ml
Director: Mahamane Habib Diallo

School
Business Administration (Business and Commerce; Finance; Human Resources; Management; Transport Management); **Diplomacy** (International Relations; Political Sciences); **Engineering** (Information Technology; Telecommunications Engineering); **Tourism** (Communication Arts; Hotel Management; Tourism)

Further information: Spain, Morocco, Côte d'Ivoire, Mauritania, Sénégal, Comoros, Burkina Faso, Niger, RD Congo, Tchad, Guinée, Gabon

Accrediting agency: Ministry of Higher Education and Scientific Research

Degrees and diplomas: Licence (LMD) (Business and Commerce; Communication Arts; Finance; Hotel Management; Human Resources; Information Technology; International Relations; Management; Political Sciences; Telecommunications Engineering; Tourism; Transport Management), Master (LMD) (Business and Commerce; Communication Arts; Finance; Hotel Management; Human Resources; Information Technology; International Relations; Management; Political Sciences; Telecommunications Engineering; Tourism; Transport Management)

Last Update: 12-10-2017

Training and Consulting Centre for Local Development

BP E 4850 Rue 252, Porte 163, Douadabougou
Bamako

Tel: +223(20) 20 36 99
Fax: +223(20) 20 37 01

Course/Programme

Citizenship, Governance and Human Right (Law); **Project Evaluation, Polititc and Development Program** (Development Studies)
Accrediting agency: Ministry of Higher Education and Scientific Research
Degrees and diplomas: Master (LMD) (Development Studies; Law)
Last Update: 12-10-2017

Malta

STRUCTURE OF HIGHER EDUCATION SYSTEM

Description

Public higher and further education in Malta consists of one University (the University of Malta) and several colleges, post-secondary schools and institutes. Education at tertiary level is publicly funded and is free, and sudents receive a stipend as well as an allowance for academic-related expenditure. In addition to public institutions, there exist private higher and further education institutions.

Stages of studies

University level first stage

Bachelor's degree
The Bachelor's degree is obtained in three to four years (180-240 ECTS credits), depending on the field of study.

University level second stage

Master's degree/ Postgraduate diploma
The second stage leads to the award of a Master's degree after 1 to 2 years' study (90-120 ECTS credits) or a Postgraduate diploma after a period of one year of study (60 ECTS credits).

University level third stage

Doctorate
The third stage leads, after at least three years of study following the award of a Master's degree, to the Doctorate. Candidates are required to submit a thesis after a period of research on an approved topic.

ADMISSION TO HIGHER EDUCATION

Admission to university-level studies

Name of Secondary school credential required: MATSEC
For entry to: All programmes except Medicine and Surgery
Minimum score/requirement: C

Alternatives to credentials: Alternative qualifications are considered if comparable. In the case of students over 23, applicants are interviewed and assessed by the Faculty concerned.

Foreign students admission

Definition of foreign student: A foreign student is a student who does not hold Maltese citizenship.
Quotas: In the case of Medical courses, thirty places are reserved for foreign applicants.
Admission requirements: Foreign students must have qualifications equivalent to the Matriculation Certificate, such as the General Certificate of Education at Advanced (A) levels, the International Baccalaureate and the American Advanced Placement System.
Entry regulations: Foreign students must have an entry permit and financial guarantees if they are staying for more than three months.
Language Proficiency: A good knowledge of English is essential. The University provides a Foundation Studies course and a Pre-Sessional Language course prior to entry to a regular course of study.

RECOGNITION OF STUDIES

Quality assurance system

By virtue of Legal Notice 296 issued on the 24th of September 2014, the National Commission for Further and Higher Education (NCFHE) is responsible for licensing, accreditation and quality assurance for further and higher education institutions in Malta. The University of Malta, the Malta College for Arts, Science and Technology and the Institute of Tourism Studies are self-accrediting providers. MQRIC deals with the recognition of foreign qualifications.

Bodies dealing with recognition

Malta Qualifications Recognition Information Centre - MQRIC
Head, Malta Qualifications Recognition Information Centre: Stefan Sant
c/o NCFHE Sir Temi Zammit Buildings, Malta Life Sciences Centre Ltd Malta Life Sciences Park

© International Association of Universities 2019
International Handbook of Universities 2019,
https://doi.org/10.1057/978-3-319-76971-4_120

San Gwann SGN 3000
Tel: +356 2381 0000
Website: http://ncfhe.gov.mt/en/services/Pages/All%20Ser
vices/mqric.aspx

Special provisions for recognition

Recognition for University level studies
Nationals and foreigners are given the same treatment.

NATIONAL BODIES

Ministry for Education and Employment

Minister: Evarist Bartolo
Great Siege Road
Floriana VLT 2000
Tel: +356 2598 0000
Website: http://education.gov.mt

National Commission for Further and Higher Education - NCFHE

Chairman: Godfrey Vella
Sir Temi Zammit Buildings, Malta Life Sciences Centre Ltd
Malta Life Sciences Park
San Gwann SGN 3000
Tel: +356 2381 0000
Website: http://www.ncfhe.org.mt
Role of national body: NCFHE was officially launched on the 14th September, 2012 and is legislated by the revised Education Act which came into force on the 1st August 2012. Its mission statement is: "to foster the development and achievement of excellence in further and higher education in Malta through research, effective licensing, accreditation, quality assurance and recognition of qualifications established under the Malta Qualifications Framework."

Data for academic year: 2015–2016
Source: IAU from the website of the Ministry for Education and Employment and www.enic-naric.net, 2015. Bodies, 2017.

Institutions

IMO International Maritime Law Institute (IMLI)

P.O. Box 31
Msida 1000, MSD
Tel: +356 21319343, +356 21310816
Fax: +356 21343092

Website: http://www.imli.org
Director: David J. Attard

Course/Programme
International Maritime Law (International Law; Maritime Law)
History: Founded 1988.
Main language(s) of instruction: English
Degrees and diplomas: Also Advanced Diploma for professionals; specialised post-graduate course leading to the degree of Master of Laws (LL.M); degree of Magister Juris (M.Jur); Doctor of Philosophy (Ph.D) in International Maritime Law.
Student Services: Health Services, Canteen, Library, Residential Facilities
Last Update: 20-01-2015

University of Malta (UOM)

Msida MSD 2080
Tel: +356(21) 2340-2340
Fax: +356(21) 2340-2342
Website: http://www.um.edu.mt
Rector: Juanito Camilleri
Tel: +356(21) 333-907

Faculty
Arts (Archaeology; Art History; Arts and Humanities; Classical Languages; English; French; Geography; German; History; International Relations; Italian; Maltese; Oriental Studies; Philosophy; Sociology; Spanish; Translation and Interpretation); **Built Environment** (Architectural and Environmental Design; Architectural Restoration; Architecture; Civil Engineering; Construction Engineering; Heritage Preservation; Structural Architecture; Town Planning; Visual Arts); **Dental Surgery** (Dentistry; Surgery); **Economics, Management and Accountancy** (Accountancy; Banking; Economics; Finance; Management; Marketing; Public Administration; Social Policy; Social Work); **Education** (Art Education; Education; Educational Sciences; Foreign Languages Education; Mathematics Education; Primary Education; Psychology; Science Education; Technology Education); **Engineering** (Automation and Control Engineering; Electrical Engineering; Engineering; Industrial Engineering; Materials Engineering; Mechanical Engineering; Metallurgical Engineering; Power Engineering; Production Engineering); **Health Sciences** (Biomedicine; Food Science; Health Administration; Health Sciences; Midwifery; Nursing; Occupational Therapy; Physical Therapy; Podiatry; Radiology; Rehabilitation and Therapy); **Information and Communication Technology** (Artificial Intelligence; Computer Engineering; Computer Science; Information Technology;

Microelectronics; Nanotechnology; Telecommunications Engineering); **Laws** (Civil Law; Commercial Law; Communication Studies; Comparative Law; Criminal Law; Environmental Studies; European Union Law; International Law; Law; Media Studies; Public Law); **Media and Knowledge Sciences** (Archiving; Cognitive Sciences; Communication Studies; Information Management; Information Sciences; Library Science; Mass Communication; Media Studies); **Medicine and Surgery** (Anatomy; Biochemistry; Community Health; Gynaecology and Obstetrics; Medicine; Paediatrics; Pathology; Pharmacology; Pharmacy; Physiology; Psychiatry and Mental Health; Public Health; Surgery); **Science** (Biology; Chemistry; Materials Engineering; Operations Research; Physics; Statistics); **Social Wellbeing** (Criminology; Family Studies; Gender Studies; Gerontology; Psychology; Social Studies); **Theology** (Canon Law; Greek (Classical); Hebrew; History of Religion; Holy Writings; Pastoral Studies; Philosophy; Religious Practice; Theology)

Institute

Aerospace technologies (Aeronautical and Aerospace Engineering); **Anglo-Italian Studies** (Cultural Studies; English Studies; Italian; Literature); **Baroque Studies** (Architecture); **Confucius** (Asian Studies; Chinese); **Design and Development of Thinking** (*Edward de Bono*) (Cognitive Sciences); **Digital Games** (Computer Science); **Earth Systems** (Coastal Studies; Earth Sciences; Environmental Management; Food Science; Geography; Rural Studies); **European studies** (European Languages); **Islands and Small States** (Geography (Human); Island Studies); **Linguistics** (Bilingual and Bicultural Education; Linguistics); **Maltese Studies** (Maltese; Mediterranean Studies); **Mediterranean** (Anthropology; Dance; Geography; History; Mediterranean Studies; Music; Theatre); **Physical Education and Sport** (Physical Education; Sports); **Public Administration and Management** (Management; Public Administration); **Space sciences and astronomy** (Astronomy and Space Science); **Sustainable Development** (Development Studies); **Sustainable Energy** (Energy Engineering); **Tourism, Travel and Culture** (Cultural Studies; Tourism)

Academy

Diplomatic Studies (International Relations)

Centre

Biomedical Cybernetics (Biomedical Engineering); **Education Resilience and Socio-Emotional Health** (*European*) (Educational Sciences; Health Sciences); **Educational Research** (*Euro-Mediterranean*) (International and Comparative Education; Mediterranean Studies); **English Language Proficiency** (English; Modern Languages); **Entrepreneurship and Business incubation** (Business and Commerce; Management); **Environmental Education and research** (Environmental Studies); **Labour Studies** (Labour and Industrial Relations); **Liberal arts and sciences** (Arts and Humanities; Natural Sciences); **Literacy Education** (Literacy Education); **Molecular Medicine and Biobanking** (Biomedicine; Medicine)

Campus

Gozo (Arts and Humanities; Business and Commerce); **Valletta** (*Valletta - International Master's programme*)

Further information: Also Teaching Hospital at Guardamangia

History: Founded 1592 by the Jesuits as Collegium Melitense. Reconstituted by Grandmaster Pinto 1769.

Academic year: October to July (October-January; February-June)

Admission requirements: Matriculation Certificate, including 2 subjects taken at Advanced Level and 3 at Intermediate Level, together with Systems of Knowledge, or equivalent qualifications; passes in the Secondary Education Certificate at Grade 5 or better in Maltese, English Language and Mathematics. Enquiries to University Registrar or Director, International and EU Office.

Fees: All fees are available at the following link: http://www.um.edu.mt/finance/service/coursefees

Main language(s) of instruction: English, Maltese

Degrees and diplomas: Bachelor's Degree, Master's Degree, Doctorate (Accountancy; Agriculture; Art History; Biology; Communication Studies; Dentistry; Economics; Education; Engineering; English; Geography; Information Technology; Italian; Law; Maltese; Management; Medicine; Music; Pharmacy; Philosophy; Physiology; Sociology; Surgery; Theatre; Theology). Also Diplomas, 1-2 yrs (usually part-time evening courses); Honours Bachelor's degrees, 3-4 yrs; Higher Diplomas (3 yrs part-time evening); Full-time day Diploma courses in various branches of Health Sciences (3 yrs).

Student Services: Academic Counselling, Social Counselling, Sports Facilities, Health Services

Periodicals: International Journal of Emotional Education, Journal of Anglo-Italian Studies, Journal of Baroque Studies, Journal of Economic and Social Studies, Journal of Education, Journal of Maltese Studies, Journal of Mediterranean Studies, Journal of the Malta University History Society, Lehen il-Malti, Malta Medical Journal, Malta Review of Educational Research, Mediterranean Journal of Educational Studies, Mediterranean Journal of Human Rights, Melita Theologica, Register of Graduates, Symposia Melitensia

Publishing house: Malta University Press

Student Numbers 2013-2014	MALE	FEMALE	TOTAL
All (Foreign Included)	4734	6468	11202
Foreign only			600

Last Update: 19-01-2015

Mauritania

STRUCTURE OF HIGHER EDUCATION SYSTEM

Description

Public higher education is provided principally by the Université de Nouakchott Al Aasriya (formerly known as Université de Nouakchott) and follows the three-tier LMD system. There are several other higher education institutions, including some private higher education providers which were allowed in 2009, but which have still to be recognized by the Ministry of Higher Education and Scientific Research. Some institutions fall under the responsibility of other ministries, such as le Ministère des Affaires Islamiques et de l'Enseignement originel (Ministry of Islamic Affairs and Religious Education) and le Ministère de l'Emploi et de la Formation professionnelle (Ministry of Employment and Vocational Training).

Stages of studies

University level first stage

Licence
The first stage of higher education leads to the Licence after three years' university study. Institutions may offer Licences fondamentales (academically-oriented degrees) or Licences professionnelles (professionally-oriented degrees).

University level second stage

Master
The Master is conferred after two years' study beyond the Licence.

University level third stage

Doctorat
Doctoral degrees are conferred after three years' study and research; students must also write and defend a dissertation.

ADMISSION TO HIGHER EDUCATION

Admission to university-level studies

Name of Secondary school credential required: Baccalauréat

NATIONAL BODIES

Ministère de l'Enseignement Supérieur et de la Recherche Scientifique - MESRS (Ministry of Higher Education and Scientific Research)

Minister: Sidi Ould Salem
BP 3095, Avenue Jemal Abdel Nasser
Nouakchott
Tel: +222(45) 25 04 48, +222(45) 25 24 75
Fax: +222(45) 24 37 36
Website: http://www.mesrs.gov.mr

Data for academic year: 2016–2017
Source: IAU from MESRS website and institutional websites, and Fiche Curie (2016) 2017.

Public Institutions

Advanced Teacher Training College (ENS)

BP 990
Nouakchott
Tel: +222(525) 31-84
Fax: +222(525) 31-72
Website: http://www.ens.mr
Directeur: Mohamed Ould Siniya Ould Khabaz

Department/Division
Educational Sciences (Educational Sciences); **Exact Science** (Mathematics; Natural Sciences; Physics); **Human**

© International Association of Universities 2019
International Handbook of Universities 2019,
https://doi.org/10.1057/978-3-319-76971-4_121

Sciences (Civics; Geography; History; Philosophy); **Modern Languages** (Arabic; English; French; Modern Languages)
History: Founded 1970, acquired present status and title 2001.
Academic year: October to July
Admission requirements: School certificate for first year entry; Diploma of General University Studies (Second Year University Diploma) or Masters for Professor section depending on cycles. Assistant Inspector section is opened to primary school teacher with eight years of seniority. Inspector of the fundamental section is opened to primary school teacher with three year of seniority.
Main language(s) of instruction: Arabic, French
Degrees and diplomas: Licence, Master
Student Services: Academic Counselling, Cultural Activities, Sports Facilities, Language Laboratory, Health Services, Canteen
Periodicals: Ettarbia, Radisma
Last Update: 18-10-2017

Al Aasriya University of Nouakchott

BP 880
Nouakchott
Tel: +222-44-30-23-09
Website: http://www.una.mr
Président: Ahmedou Haouba

Faculty

Arts and Humanities (Arabic; Arts and Humanities; English; Geography; History; Linguistics; Native Language; Philosophy; Tourism; Translation and Interpretation); **Law and Economics** (Economics; Law; Management; Private Law; Public Law); **Medicine** (Medicine; Public Health); **Science and Technology** (Biology; Chemistry; Computer Science; Environmental Studies; Geology; Mathematics; Natural Sciences; Nutrition)

Institute

Professional Training (*Offers Licences professionnelles in areas deemed particularly important for the development of the country*) (Applied Mathematics; Industrial Management; Telecommunications Engineering; Transport Management)
History: Created 1981 as University of Nouakchott (founded in 1981) and acquired current title and status 2016 following merger with University of Science, Technology and Medicine (founded in 2012).
Main language(s) of instruction: French
Degrees and diplomas: Licence (Applied Mathematics; Applied Physics; Arts and Humanities; Biology; Business and Commerce; Chemistry; Computer Science; Economics;

Food Technology; Geology; Industrial Management; Information Technology; Management; Mathematics; Physics; Social Sciences; Telecommunications Engineering; Transport Management; Water Management), Master (Banking; Biology; Chemistry; Commercial Law; Computer Science; Environmental Studies; Finance; Geography (Human); Geology; Law; Literature; Mathematics; Medicine; Nutrition; Philosophy; Private Law; Public Health; Public Law; Sociology), Doctorat (Arabic; Biology; Chemistry; Economics; Geography; Geology; History; Law; Mathematics and Computer Science; Physics)
Last Update: 18-10-2017

National School of Administration, Journalism and Magistature (ENAJM)

Nouakchott
Tel: +222(226) 174-76
Website: http://enajm.mr
Directeur général: Mohamed Ould Abdekader Ould Alada

Department/Division

Administration and Management (Public Administration); **Diplomacy** (International Relations); **Finance** (Finance); **Journalism and Communication** (Communication Arts; Journalism); **Law** (Law)
History: Founded 1966 as Ecole Nationale d'Administration. Acquired present status and title 2010.
Degrees and diplomas: Master (Communication Arts; Finance; International Relations; Journalism; Law; Public Administration)
Last Update: 12-10-2017

Private Institutions

Lebanese International University of Mauritania (LIU- Mr)

Route Soukouk, Ilot F-Nord Ceinture Verte, Tevragh Zeina
Nouakchott
Tel: +222 45-24-15-64
Website: http://www.liu.mr
President: Abdul Rahim Mourad

Faculty

Arts and Sciences (Computer Engineering; Computer Science); **Business and Law** (Accountancy; Business Administration; Finance; Law; Management; Public Administration); **Education and Arts and Humanities** (Educational Sciences; English)

Further information: Also branches in Lebanon, Yemen and Senegal
History: Founded 2008.
Academic year: From October to July (October-January, February-May, June-July)
Admission requirements: Secondary School Certificate (Baccalauréat), entrance test
Main language(s) of instruction: Arabic, French, English
Degrees and diplomas: Licence (Business Administration; English; Information Sciences; Information Technology), Master (Accountancy; Business Administration; Computer Engineering; Computer Science; Educational Sciences; Finance; Law; Management; Public Administration)
Last Update: 14-01-2019

Sup' Management Mauritania

E-Nord Tevrag Zeina 586-587
Nouakchott
Tel: +222(524) 05-61
Fax: +222(524) 07-19
Website: http://www.supmgtmauritanie.org
President: Mohamed Radhy Ould Mohamed El Hacen

School

Diplomacy and Governance (Government; International Relations); **Engineering** (Computer Engineering; Computer Networks; Engineering; Information Technology; Telecommunications Engineering); **Management** (Business Administration; Engineering Management; Finance; Human Resources; International Business; Management); **Tourism** (Hotel Management; Tourism)
Further information: Also a branch in Nouadhibou
History: Sup' Management Mauritanie is being part of Université Intercontinentale Libre (UICL).
Admission requirements: Secondary School Certificate (Baccalauréat)
Degrees and diplomas: Licence (Finance; Information Technology; Management; Marketing; Tourism; Transport Management), Master (Business Administration; Computer Engineering; Computer Networks; Engineering Management; Finance; Human Resources; Information Technology; International Business; International Relations; Management; Telecommunications Engineering)
Last Update: 14-01-2019

Mauritius

STRUCTURE OF HIGHER EDUCATION SYSTEM

Description

The higher education system consists of universities, colleges and polytechnics operating in the public sector. There are several private organizations, overseas and regional institutions that deliver tertiary-level programmes. Most of these institutions are relatively small and are affiliated to an international institution in delivering tertiary-level courses using a mixed mode system, encompassing both distance learning and face-to-face tutorials.

Stages of studies

University level first stage
This stage consists of three- to four-year Bachelor (with Honours) degree programmes on a full-time basis.

University level second stage
The third level relates to Master's programmes which are offered either in the form of taught (e.g. MSc, MBA, etc) or research (i.e. M.Phil) programmes.

University level third stage
This stage normally relates to Doctor in Philosophy (PhD) programmes that are undertaken through research. PhD students are required to complete their research/studies within a maximum of five years' full-time or seven years' part-time studies.

ADMISSION TO HIGHER EDUCATION

Admission to university-level studies

Name of Secondary school credential required: Cambridge Higher School Certificate
For entry to: Undergraduate degrees
Minimum score/requirement: A pass in English Language or a pass in English Language and Credits in five other subjects or Credit in English Language and four other subjects.
Name of Secondary school credential required: General Certificate of Education Advanced Level

For entry to: Undergraduate degrees
Minimum score/requirement: Passes in three subjects at Advanced Level or at least two passes at Advanced level.
Alternatives to credentials: The French Baccalauréat; The IGCSE (International General Certificate of Secondary Education) and the International Baccalaureate awarded by the International Baccalaureate Organisation, Switzerland; Qualifications awarded by other universities and institutions which have been approved by the governing body as satisfying the minimum requirements for admission; or Relevant subjects/combinations of related subjects included in any qualifications as may be approved by the governing body as being equivalent or comparable to an 'O' level or 'A' level may be accepted in lieu of equivalence.

Foreign students admission

Definition of foreign student: Non-nationals of the Republic of Mauritius
Admission requirements: Higher degree students must hold a Bachelor's Degree (at least 2nd class Honours) or a first degree; for degree courses they must hold GCE 'O' level passes in five subjects, two of which must also be at 'A' level; for diploma courses they must hold five GCE 'O' level passes including English and Mathematics; for certificate courses they must generally hold a Cambridge SC with passes in five subjects, including English language.
Entry regulations: Foreign students must hold a visa (http://passport.gov.mu) and a residence permit and present financial guarantees.
Health requirements: As established by the Ministry of Health and Quality of Life (http://health.gov.mu).
Language Proficiency: Students must have a good command of English.

RECOGNITION OF STUDIES

Quality assurance system

The Mauritius Qualifications Authority (MQA) and the Tertiary Education Commission (TEC) are responsible for accreditation of institutions and programmes in respect of

© International Association of Universities 2019
International Handbook of Universities 2019,
https://doi.org/10.1057/978-3-319-76971-4_122

technical and vocational education and training and post-secondary education respectively.

Bodies dealing with recognition

Quality Assurance and Accreditation Division – Tertiary Education Commission
4th Floor, TEC Building
Reduit
Tel: +230 467 8800
Fax: +230 467 6579
Website: http://tec.intnet.mu

NATIONAL BODIES

Ministry of Education and Human Resources, Tertiary Education and Scientific Research

Minister: Leela Devi Dookun-Luchoomun
Senior Chief Executive: Ram Prakash Ramlugun
MITD House, Pont Fer
Phoenix
Tel: +230 601 5200
Fax: +230 698 9627
Website: http://ministry-education.govmu.org/English/Pages/default.aspx
Role of national body: To expand the tertiary education sector and to further increase access to tertiary education, and by developing research culture and setting up Science Parks to improve linkages between Universities and the world of work.

Quality Assurance and Accreditation Division – Tertiary Education Commission

Chair: Surendra Bissoondoyal
Executive Director: Chenicheri Sid Nair
4th Floor, TEC Building
Reduit
Tel: +230 467 8800
Fax: +230 467 6579
Website: http://tec.intnet.mu
Role of national body: The Tertiary Education Commission has as its mission to promote, plan, develop and coordinate post-secondary education in Mauritius and to implement an overarching regulatory framework to achieve high international quality. It also has the responsibility of allocating government funds to the Tertiary Education Institutions under its purview and to ensure accountability and optimum use of resources.

Careers Guidance Services

Ministry of Education and Human Resources, 2nd Floor, Social Security House, Old Moka Road
Rose Hill
Tel: +230 466 8104
Fax: +230 466 8073
Website: http://educare.intnet.mu

Study Mauritius

Level 1, Cyber Tower 1
Ebene
Tel: +230 454 7105
Fax: +230 454 7112
Role of national body: To promote information on programmes offered by public and private Tertiary Education Institutions operating in Mauritius and overseas. The office links up with local Tertiary Institutions, local recruiting agents and local embassies to coordinate information on available programmes and better guide students in their choice. It also provides a window for prospective international students wishing to study locally to secure information on tertiary education programmes available in tertiary institutions in Mauritius.

Data for academic year: 2016–2017
Source: IAU from Ministry of Education and Human Resources, Tertiary Education and Scientific Research (Tertiary Section) 2016. Bodies updated 2018.

Institutions

Mahatma Gandhi Institute (MGI)

Mahatma Gandhi Avenue
Moka
Tel: +230(403) 2000
Fax: +230(433) 2235
Website: http://www.mgirti.org
Director General: S.N. Gayan

School
Fine Arts (Art Education; Fine Arts); **Indian Studies** (Hindi; South and Southeast Asian Languages; Urdu); **Indological**

Studies (South Asian Studies); **Mauritian and Area Studies** (Chinese; Cultural Studies; Oriental Studies); **Performing Arts** (Dance; Music; Performing Arts)

History: Founded 1970.

Academic year: August to July

Main language(s) of instruction: English, French, Hindi, Urdu, Telegu, Marathi, Mandarin

Accrediting agency: Tertiary Education Commission

Degrees and diplomas: Diploma, Bachelor's Degree (Art Education; Dance; Fine Arts; Graphic Design; Hindi; Philosophy; Sanskrit; Singing; Southeast Asian Studies; Urdu), Master's Degree (Hindi; Musical Instruments; Performing Arts). Also Post Graduate Cerficate in Education: Hindi (PGCE); Islamic Studies (MA); Mauritian Studies (MA): 2 yrs Part-Time

Student Services: Cultural Activities, Language Laboratory

Periodicals: Journal of Mauritian Studies, Rimjhim, Vasant

Last Update: 12-04-2017

Mascareignes University (UdM)

Avenue de La Concorde Roche Brunes
Rose Hill
Tel: +230(466) 0444/0118
Fax: +230(466) 3774
Website: http://www.udm.ac.mu
Director-General: Radhakhrishna Somanah

Faculty

Business and Management (Accountancy; Finance; Human Resources; Management; Marketing; Public Relations; Retailing and Wholesaling); **Information and Communications Technology** (Computer Engineering; Information Technology; Multimedia; Software Engineering; Systems Analysis); **Sustainable Development and Engineering** (Automation and Control Engineering; Civil Engineering; Electrical Engineering; Electronic Engineering; Energy Engineering; Hotel Management; Industrial Engineering; Mechanical Engineering)

School

Geopolitics (*Stanley Campus*) (Political Sciences)

Institute

Research and Innnovation (*IRII*) (Energy Engineering; Environmental Studies; Political Sciences; Waste Management)

Further information: Also Pamplemousses and Stanley Campuses

History: Founded 1995 as Swami Dayanand Institute of Management. Acquired present title and status after merging with Institut Supérieur de Technologie, 2012.

Admission requirements: For Degree Courses: SC/GCE 'O' Level plus at least two principal subjects at HSG/GCE 'A' Level

Fees: National : Undergraduate: 45,000 per annum. PhD programmes: 60,000 (Mauritius Rupee), International : Undergraduate: 80,000 per annum (Mauritius Rupee)

Main language(s) of instruction: English

Accrediting agency: Tertiary Education Commission

Degrees and diplomas: Bachelor's Degree, Master's Degree (Computer Science; Human Resources; Industrial Engineering; Marketing)

Student Services: Sports Facilities, Canteen

Student Numbers 2015-2016	MALE	FEMALE	TOTAL
All (Foreign Included)			1100

Last Update: 25-10-2016

Mauritius Institute of Education (MIE)

Réduit, Moka
Tel: +230(401) 6555
Fax: +230(454) 1037
Website: http://www.mie.ac.mu
Director: Oomandra Nath Varma

School

Applied Sciences (Design; Home Economics; Physical Education; Preschool Education; Technology); **Arts and Humanities** (Business Education; English; French; Social Studies; Visual Arts); **Education** (Computer Education; Curriculum; Educational Administration; Multimedia; Special Education); **Science and Mathematics** (Mathematics Education; Natural Sciences)

History: Founded 1974.

Main language(s) of instruction: English, French

Accrediting agency: Tertiary Education Commission

Degrees and diplomas: Bachelor's Degree (Education), Master's Degree (Education), Doctor of Philosophy (Education). Also Postgraduate Certificate in Education, Advanced Certificate in Educational Administration

Student Services: Academic Counselling, Library

Last Update: 25-10-2016

Mauritius Institute of Health (MIH)

Powder Mill
Pamplemousses
Tel: +230(243) 3772
Fax: +230(243) 3270
Website: http://mih.govmu.org

Course/Programme

Health Science (Health Sciences; Medical Technology; Medicine; Nursing; Public Health)
History: Founded 2009.
Main language(s) of instruction: English
Accrediting agency: Tertiary Education Commission; Ministry of Health and Quality of Life
Degrees and diplomas: Postgraduate Programmes: Internal Medicine in collaborarion with University of Bordeaux
Student Services: Library
Last Update: 26-10-2016

Open University of Mauritius (OU)

Réduit, Moka
Tel: +230(403) 8200
Fax: +230(464) 8854
Website: http://www.open.ac.mu
Director-General: Kaviraj Sharma Sukon

Department/Division

Distance Education (Arts and Humanities; Business and Commerce; Computer Engineering; Management; Preschool Education; Teacher Trainers Education; Tourism; Transport Engineering); **Media** (Communication Studies; Media Studies; Multimedia)

Institute

Confucius (Chinese); **Language** (English; French; Modern Languages)
Further information: Forest-Side, Curepipe
History: The Open University of Mauritius (OU) has been established on 12 July 2012 according to the Open University of Mauritius ACT 2010. The Mauritius College of the Air, which was established in 1971, has integrated the Open University of Mauritius in July 2012. The Open University aims at delivering quality education to learners who are unable to be physically present on campus. With flexible study options, its prospective learners can study from home, work, or anywhere in the world, at a time that suits them and their lifestyle.
Academic year: From January to December
Fees: Degree programmes: 20,000 per semester. Postgraduate programmes: 25,000 per semester (Mauritius Rupee)
Main language(s) of instruction: English
Accrediting agency: Tertiary Education Commission
Degrees and diplomas: Bachelor's Degree (Banking; Business Administration; Communication Studies; Criminology; Economics; English; Finance; French; Graphic Design; Human Resources; Information Sciences; Information Technology; Journalism; Law; Library Science; Management; Marketing; Media Studies; Preschool Education; Primary

Education), Master's Degree (Business Administration; Education; Educational Administration; Finance; International and Comparative Education; Leadership; Nutrition; Public Administration; Public Health; Taxation), Doctor of Philosophy (Business Administration)
Student Services: Academic Counselling, Social Counselling, Careers Guidance, Sports Facilities, Language Laboratory, Foreign Studies Centre, Library

Academic Staff 2014-2015	MALE	FEMALE	TOTAL
FULL-TIME			16
STAFF WITH DOCTORATE			
FULL-TIME			1
Student Numbers 2014-2015			
All (Foreign Included)			3531

Last Update: 25-10-2016

University of Mauritius (UoM)

Réduit 80837, Moka
Tel: +230(454) 1041
Fax: +230(454) 9642
Website: http://www.uom.ac.mu
Vice-Chancellor: R. Mohee
Tel: +230(403) 7400, ext 7415

Faculty

Agriculture (Agricultural Engineering; Agricultural Management; Agriculture; Food Science); **Engineering** (Chemical Engineering; Civil Engineering; Computer Science; Electrical and Electronic Engineering; Engineering; Environmental Engineering; Industrial Engineering; Mechanical Engineering; Production Engineering; Textile Technology); **Law and Management** (Accountancy; Business Administration; Business and Commerce; Finance; International Business; Law; Management); **Ocean Studies** (Fishery; Marine Engineering; Marine Science and Oceanography); **Science** (Biology; Chemistry; Health Sciences; Mathematics; Medicine; Natural Sciences; Physics); **Social Studies and Humanities** (Arts and Humanities; Economics; English; French; History; Social Studies; Statistics)

Centre

Biomedical and Biomaterials Research (*CBBR*) (Biomedicine); **Information Technology and Systems** (Information Management; Information Technology; Systems Analysis); **Innovative Lifelong Learning** (*CILL*) (Computer Engineering; Educational Technology; Information Technology; Multimedia); **Professional Development and Lifelong Learning** (Computer Education; Information Technology; Library Science; Marine Transport; Nursing; Police Studies; Textile Technology)

History: Founded 1965.

Academic year: August to May (August-November; January-May)

Admission requirements: General Certificate of Education (GCE) with pass at Ordinary 'O' level or equivalent in English Language, and either passes in 5 other subjects with at least 2 passes at 'A' level or passes in 3 other subjects at 'A' level, or the French Baccalauréat, or the IGCSE and the International Baccalauréat

Fees: Mauritian secondary school leavers on full-time programmes, general fees, 14,400 per annum (no tuition fees). Mauritian students on part-time postgraduate programmes, general fees 16,000. Foreign students, general fees for undergraduate programmes, 15,200 and for postgraduate programmes: 16,800 per annum (Mauritius Rupee)

Main language(s) of instruction: English

Accrediting agency: Tertiary Education Commission

Degrees and diplomas: Diploma, Bachelor's Degree (Accountancy; Agriculture; Arts and Humanities; Banking; Business and Commerce; Chemical Engineering; Economics; Energy Engineering; English; Environmental Management; Finance; Food Science; Food Technology; French; Industrial Engineering; Insurance; International Relations; Law; Management; Marine Science and Oceanography; Mechanical Engineering; Medicine; Political Sciences; Psychology; Social Sciences; Social Work; Sociology; Surgery; Surveying and Mapping; Tourism; Town Planning; Translation and Interpretation), Master's Degree (Building Technologies; Business Administration; Cell Biology; Chemistry; Development Studies; Economics; Educational Technology; Electrical Engineering; Engineering Management; English; Environmental Management; Finance; French; History; Human Resources; Industrial Engineering; Insurance; International Business; Law; Marketing; Mathematics; Medicine; Microbiology; Molecular Biology; Public Health; Social Sciences; Software Engineering; Tourism; Transport Management), Master of Philosophy, Doctor of Philosophy. Also Certificates and Diplomas, 1-2 yrs. Also Master of Hindi, Marathi, Tamil, Telugu, Urdu in collaboration with Mahatma Gandhi Institute.

Student Services: Academic Counselling, Careers Guidance, Cultural Activities, Sports Facilities, Facilities for disabled people, Health Services, Canteen, Library

Periodicals: University of Mauritius Research Journal

Last Update: 25-10-2016

University of Technology, Mauritius (UTM)

La Tour Koenig Pointe aux Sables
Port Louis

Tel: +230(207) 5250
Fax: +230(234) 1660
Website: http://www.utm.ac.mu
Director-General: Sharmila Pamela Seetulsingh-Goorah

School

Business, Management and Finance (*SBMF*) (Business Administration; Economics; Finance; Management; Marketing; Public Administration); **Health Sciences** (Anaesthesiology; Dermatology; Gynaecology and Obstetrics; Health Sciences; Medicine; Orthopaedics; Paediatrics; Radiology; Surgery); **Innovative Technologies and Engineering** (*SITE*) (Applied Mathematics; Computer Engineering; Industrial Engineering; Software Engineering; Systems Analysis); **Sustainable Development and Tourism** (*SSDT*) (Environmental Studies; Leisure Studies; Tourism)

History: Founded 2000 following merger of Mauritius Institute of Public Administration and Management (MIPAM) and SITRAC.

Academic year: August to June

Admission requirements: 5 'O' level (pass) including English + 2 'A' level/'O' level in English (pass) + 3 'A' level/ French baccalaureat/IGCSE + International Baccalaureat

Fees: National : Undergraduate : 22,300 per semester; Postgraduate : 24,800 per semester. MPhil/PhD Degrees : 60,000 per annum MBA: 35,000 per semester (Mauritius Rupee), International : Undergraduate : 1,430 per semester; Postgraduate : 1,680 per semester; MPhil/PhD Degrees : 5,000 per annum; MBA: 2,500 per semester (US Dollar)

Main language(s) of instruction: English

Accrediting agency: Tertiary Education Commission

Degrees and diplomas: Bachelor's Degree (Accountancy; Banking; Business Administration; Business Computing; Commercial Law; Computer Engineering; Computer Networks; Computer Science; Design; Economics; Electronic Engineering; Finance; Graphic Design; Health Administration; Hotel and Restaurant; Human Resources; Information Technology; Insurance; Law; Management; Marketing; Mathematics; Medicine; Occupational Health; Public Administration; Safety Engineering; Software Engineering; Surgery; Telecommunications Engineering; Tourism; Transport Management), Master's Degree (Banking; Biology; Business Administration; Business and Commerce; Computer Engineering; Computer Networks; Computer Science; Data Processing; E- Business/Commerce; Educational Administration; Finance; Gender Studies; Graphic Design; Health Administration; Hotel Management; Human Resources; Industrial and Organizational Psychology; Information Technology; Insurance; International Business; Management; Marketing; Mathematics and Computer Science; Multimedia; Public Administration; Public Health; Public Relations; Retailing and Wholesaling; Software Engineering;

Statistics; Telecommunications Engineering; Tourism; Transport Management; Women's Studies). Also certificate in Industrial Relations (1 1/2 yrs); Post Graduate Diploma in Integrated Resort Management (1 yr part-time). Foundation Access Courses for Undergraduate Programmes (1 yr)

Student Services: Academic Counselling, Sports Facilities, Canteen, Library

Last Update: 25-10-2016